HARRAP'S

Spanish–English
Inglés–Español

MINI
Dictionary/Diccionario

saltar — to dive
un salto — a dive
carné de conducir — drivers liscense
  "   "   identidad — ID card

quejarse de — to complain
                          about
pan con mantequilla — bread and
                              butter
el fondo — bottom

HARRAP'S

Spanish–English
Inglés–Español

MINI
Dictionary/Diccionario

HARRAP

EDINBURGH NEW YORK

Distributed in the United States by
PRENTICE HALL
New York

First published in Great Britain 1992 by HARRAP BOOKS Ltd
43-45 Annandale Street, Edinburgh EH7 4AZ, Scotland
95 Madison Avenue, New York, NY10016, USA

This dictionary is a shortened version of *Harrap's Concise Spanish and English Dictionary*. The project management was carried out by LEXUS Ltd.

El presente diccionario es una versión abreviada del *Harrap's Concise Spanish and English Dictionary*. La dirección del proyecto corrió a cargo de LEXUS Ltd.

Editors/Redactores:

Joaquín Blasco   Fernando León Solís   Hugh O'Donnell

ISBN 0-245-60458-8

In the United States, ISBN 0-13-381005-4

Library of Congress Cataloging-in-Publication Data

Harrap's mini Spanish dictionary.

p.   cm.

ISBN 0-13-381005-4

1. Spanish Language — Dictionaries — English.
2. English Language — Dictionaries — Spanish.

PC4640.H34 1992   92-8271
463'.21—dc20   CIP

Printed in Great Britain by Clays Ltd, St Ives plc

Preface

This dictionary is a shortened version of *Harrap's Concise Spanish and English Dictionary*. The selection of headwords and phrases - over 57,000 in total - is aimed at providing a broad coverage of modern English and Spanish, including a considerable number of important Latin American and North American terms.

The new system for Spanish alphabetical order has been adopted. In this system 'ch' and 'll' are no longer considered as separate letters of the alphabet, but are each incorporated at their respective alphabetical positions under 'c' and 'l' - 'ñ', however, is treated as a separate letter.

Entries are divided into grammatical categories by Roman numerals (I, II etc) and into sense categories by Arabic numerals (1, 2 etc). A lozenge ◆ has been used i) to highlight adverbs which have been placed directly after their related adjective (for example: happily/happy) and which are not always therefore in strict alphabetical order and ii) to identify phrasal verbs (give up, come out, send back etc).

A major feature of this dictionary is the systematic use of signposting to guide users and to enable them to identify the translation they require quickly and accurately. There are two main types of signpost: **field labels** (of which a complete list is given on pages vii-x) identify the area of usage of a word, for example: *Ftb* is for football, *Comput* is for computers. **Indicators** show, for example, what might be the typical subject or object of a verb or what might be the typical noun used with a certain adjective. These help the user to identify the correct translation for a particular word by showing the context in which a certain translation is appropriate.

Gender markers for Spanish translations are not given where the presence of an adjective makes the gender of a noun self-evident. For example 'centro deportivo' has no gender marker whereas 'centro *m* comercial' does.

Spanish verbs with irregular conjugations are coded ([12], [24] etc). By looking at the information in the introductory section on pages xii-xxi it is possible to work out the form of an irregular Spanish verb in any required tense or person. A list of irregular English verbs is given on pages (ii)-(iv) of the English-Spanish section.

Full IPA (International Phonetic Alphabet) pronunciation is given for English headwords in the English-Spanish part of the dictionary with a guide to IPA on pages (v)-(vi) of the introduction. There is also an introduction to Spanish pronunciation on pages xxii-xxiii of the Spanish-English part of the dictionary.

Prólogo

El presente diccionario es una versión abreviada del *Harrap's Concise Spanish and English Dictionary*. La selección de las entradas y frases idiomáticas - más de 57000 en total - tiene como objetivo ofrecer una amplia cobertura del inglés y del español actuales, incluido un número importante de términos usados en Latinoamérica y Norteamérica.

Se ha adoptado la nueva ordenación alfabética del español. Según ésta, los dígrafos "ch" y "ll" no se consideran letras independientes, sino que ocupan el lugar que les corresponde alfabéticamente dentro de la "c" y "l", respectivamente. La "ñ", sin embargo, se considera letra independiente.

Las diferentes categorías gramaticales de una misma entrada se señalan mediante números romanos (I, II, etc), mientras que la numeración árabe (1, 2, etc) indica las diferentes categorías semánticas. Se utilizan los rombos ◆ para i) resaltar los adverbios colocados justo después del adjetivo del que derivan (por ejemplo: justo/justamente) que no siguen, por tanto, un riguroso orden alfabético y ii) para identificar los "phrasal verbs" (give up, come out, send back etc).

Una característica relevante de esta obra es el uso sistemático de señales indicadoras que orientan al usuario y le permiten identificar la traducción adecuada con rapidez y precisión. Hay dos tipos de señales indicadoras: las **abreviaturas de campo semántico** (de las que aparece una lista completa en las páginas vii-x) identifican el área de uso de una palabra, por ejemplo: *Ftb* es fútbol, *Inform* es informática. Los **indicadores** muestran, por ejemplo, un sujeto o un objeto típicos de un verbo, o un sustantivo que frecuentemente acompaña a determinado adjetivo. Estos ayudan al usuario a identificar la traducción correcta de una determinada palabra al mostrar el contexto adecuado para cada traducción.

Los indicadores de género de las traducciones españolas no aparecerán cuando la presencia de un adjetivo deje claro el género del sustantivo. Por ejemplo "centro deportivo" no lleva indicador de género, mientras que, por el contrario, sí aparece en "centro *m* comercial".

Los verbos españoles de conjugación irregular vienen seguidos de un número de referencia ([12], [24] etc). En la sección introductoria, en las páginas xii-xxi, viene dada la información necesaria para poder conjugar los verbos irregulares en español. Una lista de verbos irregulares del inglés aparece en las páginas (ii)-(iv) de la sección Inglés-Español.

Las entradas inglesas de la sección Inglés-Español del diccionario van acompañadas de una transcripción fonética basada en el Alfabeto Fonético Internacional (AFI). En la página (v)-(vi) de la introducción de la sección Inglés-Español aparece una guía explicativa de dicho alfabeto. También viene dada una guía introductoria de pronunciación española en las páginas xxii-xxiii de la sección Español-Inglés.

Abbreviations used in this dictionary
Abreviaturas usadas en este diccionario

abbreviation	*abbr, abr*	abreviatura
adjective	*adj*	adjetivo
adverb	*adv*	adverbio
agriculture	*Agr*	agricultura
chess	*Ajedrez*	
somebody, someone	*algn*	alguien
Latin American	*Am*	hispanoamericano
anatomy	*Anat*	anatomía
approximately	*approx, aprox*	aproximadamente
archaic	*arc, arch*	arcaico
architecture	*Archit*	arquitectura
slang	*arg*	argot
architecture	*Arquit*	arquitectura
article	*art*	artículo
art	*Art, Arte*	bellas artes
astronomy	*Astron*	astronomía
	Astronaut,	
space travel	*Astronáut*	astronáutica
Australian	*Austral*	australiano
motoring	*Aut*	automóviles
auxiliary	*aux*	auxiliar
aviation	*Av*	aviación
biology	*Biol*	biología
bowling	*Bolos*	
botany	*Bot*	botánica
	Bowling	bolos
boxing	*Box*	boxeo
Canary Islands	*Can*	Canarias
	Cards	naipes
chemistry	*Chem*	químico
	Chess	ajedrez
cycling	*Cicl*	ciclismo
cinema	*Cin*	cine
commerce	*Com*	comercio
comparative	*comp*	comparativo
computers	*Comput*	informática
conditional	*cond*	condicional
conjunction	*conj*	conjunción
building industry	*Constr*	construcción
sewing	*Cost*	costura
cookery	*Culin*	cocina
cycling	*Cycl*	ciclismo
definite	*def*	definido
defective	*defect*	defectivo
demonstrative	*dem*	demostrativo
sport	*Dep*	deporte
ecology	*Ecol*	ecología
economics	*Econ*	economía
education	*Educ*	educación
electricity	*Elec*	electricidad
entomology	*Ent*	entomología
especially	*esp*	especialmente
only in Spain	*Esp*	solo en España
etcetera	*etc*	etcétera

vii

euphemism	*euf, euph*	eufemismo
exclamatory	*exclam*	exclamativo
feminine	*f*	femenino
familiar	*fam*	familiar
pharmacy	*Farm*	farmacia
railways	*Ferroc*	ferrocarriles
figurative use	*fig*	uso figurado
finance	*Fin*	finanzas
physics	*Fís*	física
	Fishing	pesca
formal use	*fml*	uso formal
photography	*Fot*	fotografía
feminine plural	*fpl*	plural femenino
football	*Ftb*	fútbol
future	*fut*	futuro
British	*GB*	británico
geography	*Geog*	geografía
geology	*Geol*	geología
geometry	*Geom*	geometría
present participle	*ger*	gerundio
gymnastics	*Gimn, Gym*	gimnasia
history	*Hist*	historia
humorous	*hum*	humorístico
imperative	*imperat*	imperativo
imperfect	*imperf*	imperfecto
impersonal	*impers*	impersonal
printing	*Impr*	imprenta
industry	*Ind*	industria
indefinite	*indef*	indefinido
indeterminate	*indet*	indeterminado
indicative	*indic*	indicativo
infinitive	*infin*	infinitivo
computers	*Inform*	informática
insurance	*Ins*	seguros
interjection	*interj*	interjección
interrogative	*interr*	interrogativo
invariable	*inv*	invariable
ironic	*iron*	irónico
irregular	*irreg*	irregular
law	*Jur*	derecho
linguistics	*Ling*	lingüística
literary	*lit*	literario
literature	*Lit*	literatura
phrase	*loc*	locución
masculine	*m*	masculino
mathematics	*Mat, Math*	matemáticas
medicine	*Med*	medicina
meteorology	*Meteor*	meteorología
military	*Mil*	militar
mining	*Min*	minas
masculine plural	*mpl*	plural masculino
music	*Mus, Mús*	música
noun	*n*	nombre
cards	*Naipes*	
swimming	*Natación*	
nautical	*Naut, Náut*	náutica
negative	*neg*	negativo

neuter	*neut*	neutro
feminine noun	*nf*	nombre femenino
plural feminine noun	*nfpl*	nombre femenino plural
masculine noun	*nm*	nombre masculino
masculine and feminine noun	*nmf/nm,f*	nombre masculino y femenino
plural masculine noun	*nmpl*	nombre masculino plural
plural noun	*npl*	nombre plural
obsolete	*obs*	obsoleto
offensive	*ofens, offens*	ofensivo
optics	*Opt*	óptica
ornithology	*Orn*	ornitología
Parliament	*Parl*	parlamento
pejorative	*pej*	peyorativo
personal	*pers*	personal
fishing	*Pesca*	
petroleum industry	*Petrol, Petról*	industria petrolera
pejorative	*pey*	peyorativo
pharmacy	*Pharm*	farmacia
photography	*Phot*	fotografía
physics	*Phys*	física
plural	*pl*	plural
politics	*Pol*	política
possessive	*pos, poss*	posesivo
past participle	*pp*	participio pasado
prefix	*pref*	prefijo
press	*Prensa*	
preposition	*prep*	preposición
present	*pres*	presente
present participle	*pres p*	gerundio
	Press	prensa
preterite	*pret*	pretérito
printing	*Print*	imprenta
pronoun	*pron*	pronombre
psychology	*Psic, Psych*	psicología
past tense	*pt*	pretérito
chemistry	*Quím*	químico
radio	*Rad*	radio
railways	*Rail*	ferrocarriles
relative	*rel*	relativo
religion	*Rel*	religión
somebody, someone	*sb*	alguien
Scottish	*Scot*	escocés
insurance	*Seg*	seguros
sewing	*Sew*	costura
singular	*sing*	singular
slang	*sl*	argot
Spanish	*Span*	español
something	*sth*	algo
subjunctive	*subj*	subjuntivo
suffix	*suf, suff*	sufijo
superlative	*superl*	superlativo
	Swimming	natación
also	*tamb*	también
bullfighting	*Taur*	tauromaquia

ix

theatre	*Teat*	teatro
technical	*Téc, Tech*	técnica
telephones	*Tel*	teléfonos
telecommunications	*Telec*	telecomunicaciones
tennis	*Ten*	tenis
textiles	*Tex*	textiles
theatre	*Theat*	teatro
typography	*Tip*	tipografía
television	*TV*	televisión
typography	*Typ*	tipografía
university	*Univ*	universidad
United States	*US*	Estados Unidos
usually	*usu*	usualmente
verb	*v*	verbo
auxiliary verb	*v aux*	verbo auxiliar
veterinary medicine	*Vet*	veterinaria
intransitive verb	*vi*	verbo intransitivo
impersonal verb	*v impers*	verbo impersonal
reflexive verb	*vr*	verbo reflexivo
transitive verb	*vtr*	verbo transitivo
vulgar	*vulg*	vulgar
zoology	*Zool*	zoología
see	→	véase
cultural equivalent	≈	equivalencia cultural
registered trade mark	®	marca registrada

Spanish - English
Español - Inglés

SPANISH VERBS

Regular Spelling Changes

The rules of spelling in Spanish cause a number of verbs to have regular spelling changes. These are listed below.

Spanish verbs fall into three groups depending on whether their infinitive ends in **-ar**, **-er** or **-ir**. The stem of the verb is the part which is left when the **-ar**, **-er** or **-ir** is removed from the infinitive. For example, the stem of **tomar** is **tom**, the stem of **beber** is **beb**, and the stem of **salir** is **sal**.

In the lists given below, the following indicators are used:

> **(1)** = first person singular present indicative
> **(2)** = present subjunctive, all persons
> **(3)** = first person singular preterite

Verbs ending in -ar

Verbs with a stem ending in **c**, for example **buscar**

The **c** changes to **qu** in:

> **(2)** busque, busques, busque, busquemos, busquéis, busquen
> **(3)** busqué

Verbs with a stem ending in **g**, for example **cargar**

The **g** changes to **gu** in:

> **(2)** cargue, cargues, cargue, carguemos, carguéis, carguen
> **(3)** cargué

Verbs with a stem ending in **gu**, for example **averiguar**

The **gu** changes to **gü** in:

> **(2)** averigüe, averigües, averigüe, averigüemos, averigüéis, averigüen
> **(3)** averigüé

Verbs with a stem ending in **z**, for example **realizar**

The **z** changes to **c** in:

> **(2)** realice, realices, realice, realicemos, realicéis, realicen
> **(3)** realicé

Verbs ending in -er *or* -ir

Verbs with a stem ending in **c**, for example **esparcir**

The **c** changes to **z** in:

      (1) esparzo
      (2) esparza, esparzas, esparza, esparzamos, esparzáis, esparzan

Verbs with a stem ending in **g**, for example **coger**

The **g** changes to **j** in:

      (1) cojo
      (2) coja, cojas, coja, cojamos, cojáis, cojan

Verbs with a stem ending in **qu**, for example **delinquir**

The **qu** changes to **c** in:

      (1) delinco
      (2) delinca, delincas, delinca, delincamos, delincáis, delincan

Verbs with a stem ending in **gu**, for example **distinguir**

The **gu** changes to **g** in:

      (1) distingo
      (2) distinga, distingas, distinga, distingamos, distingáis, distingan

Models for regular conjugation

TOMAR to take

INDICATIVE

PRESENT	**FUTURE**	**CONDITIONAL**
1. tomo	tomaré	tomaría
2. tomas	tomarás	tomarías
3. toma	tomará	tomaría
1. tomamos	tomaremos	tomaríamos
2. tomáis	tomaréis	tomaríais
3. toman	tomarán	tomarían

IMPERFECT	**PRETERITE**	**PERFECT**
1. tomaba	tomé	he tomado
2. tomabas	tomaste	has tomado
3. tomaba	tomó	ha tomado
1. tomábamos	tomamos	hemos tomado
2. tomabais	tomasteis	habéis tomado
3. tomaban	tomaron	han tomado

FUTURE PERFECT	**CONDITIONAL PERFECT**	**PLUPERFECT**
1. habré tomado	habría tomado	había tomado
2. habrás tomado	habrías tomado	habías tomado
3. habrá tomado	habría tomado	había tomado
1. habremos tomado	habríamos tomado	habíamos tomado
2. habréis tomado	habríais tomado	habíais tomado
3. habrán tomado	habrían tomado	habían tomado

SUBJUNCTIVE

PRESENT	**IMPERFECT**	**PERFECT/PLUPERFECT**
1. tome	tom-ara/ase	haya/hubiera* tomado
2. tomes	tom-aras/ases	hayas/hubieras tomado
3. tome	tom-ara/ase	haya/hubiera tomado
1. tomemos	tom-áramos/ásemos	hayamos/hubiéramos tomado
2. toméis	tom-arais/aseis	hayáis/hubierais tomado
3. tomen	tom-aran/asen	hayan/hubieran tomado

IMPERATIVE	*INFINITIVE*	*PARTICIPLE*
(tú) toma	**PRESENT**	**PRESENT**
(Vd) tome	tomar	tomando
(nosotros) tomemos		
(vosotros) tomad	**PERFECT**	**PAST**
(Vds) tomen	haber tomado	tomado

* the alternative form 'hubiese' etc is also possible

COMER to eat

INDICATIVE

PRESENT	FUTURE	CONDITIONAL
1. como	comeré	comería
2. comes	comerás	comerías
3. come	comerá	comería
1. comemos	comeremos	comeríamos
2. coméis	comeréis	comeríais
3. comen	comerán	comerían

IMPERFECT	PRETERITE	PERFECT
1. comía	comí	he comido
2. comías	comiste	has comido
3. comía	comió	ha comido
1. comíamos	comimos	hemos comido
2. comíais	comisteis	habéis comido
3. comían	comieron	han comido

FUTURE PERFECT	CONDITIONAL PERFECT	PLUPERFECT
1. habré comido	habría comido	había comido
2. habrás comido	habrías comido	habías comido
3. habrá comido	habría comido	había comido
1. habremos comido	habríamos comido	habíamos comido
2. habréis comido	habríais comido	habíais comido
3. habrán comido	habrían comido	habían comido

SUBJUNCTIVE

PRESENT	IMPERFECT	PERFECT/PLUPERFECT
1. coma	com-iera/iese	haya/hubiera* comido
2. comas	com-ieras/ieses	hayas/hubieras comido
3. coma	com-iera/iese	haya/hubiera comido
1. comamos	com-iéramos/iésemos	hayamos/hubiéramos comido
2. comáis	com-ierais/ieseis	hayáis/hubierais comido
3. coman	com-ieran/iesen	hayan/hubieran comido

IMPERATIVE	INFINITIVE	PARTICIPLE
(tú) come	**PRESENT**	**PRESENT**
(Vd) coma	comer	comiendo
(nosotros) comamos		
(vosotros) comed	**PERFECT**	**PAST**
(Vds) coman	haber comido	comido

* the alternative form 'hubiese' etc is also possible

PARTIR to leave

INDICATIVE

PRESENT	FUTURE	CONDITIONAL
1. parto	partiré	partiría
2. partes	partirás	partirías
3. parte	partirá	partiría
1. partimos	partiremos	partiríamos
2. partís	partiréis	partiríais
3. parten	partirán	partirían

IMPERFECT	PRETERITE	PERFECT
1. partía	partí	he partido
2. partías	partiste	has partido
3. partía	partió	ha partido
1. partíamos	partimos	hemos partido
2. partíais	partisteis	habéis partido
3. partían	partieron	han partido

FUTURE PERFECT	CONDITIONAL PERFECT	PLUPERFECT
1. habré partido	habría partido	había partido
2. habrás partido	habrías partido	habías partido
3. habrá partido	habría partido	había partido
1. habremos partido	habríamos partido	habíamos partido
2. habréis partido	habríais partido	habíais partido
3. habrán partido	habrían partido	habían partido

SUBJUNCTIVE

PRESENT	IMPERFECT	PERFECT/PLUPERFECT
parta	parti-era/ese	haya/hubiera* partido
partas	parti-eras/eses	hayas/hubieras partido
parta	parti-era/ese	haya/hubiera partido
partamos	parti-éramos/ésemos	hayamos/hubiéramos partido
partáis	parti-erais/eseis	hayáis/hubierais partido
partan	parti-eran/esen	hayan/hubieran partido

IMPERATIVE	INFINITIVE	PARTICIPLE
	PRESENT	PRESENT
(tú) parte	partir	partiendo
(Vd) parta		
(nosotros) partamos		
(vosotros) partid	PERFECT	PAST
(Vds) partan	haber partido	partido

* the alternative form 'hubiese' etc is also possible

Models for irregular conjugation

[1] **pensar** *PRES* pienso, piensas, piensa, pensamos, pensáis, piensan; *PRES SUBJ* piense, pienses, piense, pensemos, penséis, piensen; *IMPERAT* piensa, piense, pensemos, pensad, piensen

[2] **contar** *PRES* cuento, cuentas, cuenta, contamos, contáis, cuentan; *PRES SUBJ* cuente, cuentes, cuente, contemos, contéis, cuenten; *IMPERAT* cuenta, cuente, contemos, contad, cuenten

[3] **perder** *PRES* pierdo, pierdes, pierde, perdemos, perdéis, pierden; *PRES SUBJ* pierda, pierdas, pierda, perdamos, perdáis, pierdan; *IMPERAT* pierde, pierda, perdamos, perded, pierdan

[4] **morder** *PRES* muerdo, muerdes, muerde, mordemos, mordéis, muerden; *PRES SUBJ* muerda, muerdas, muerda, mordamos, mordáis, muerdan; *IMPERAT* muerde, muerda, mordamos, morded, muerdan

[5] **sentir** *PRES* siento, sientes, siente, sentimos, sentís, sienten; *PRES SUBJ* sienta, sientas, sienta, sintamos, sintáis, sientan; *PRES P* sintiendo; *IMPERAT* siente, sienta, sintamos, sentid, sientan

[6] **vestir** *PRES* visto, vistes, viste, vestimos, vestís, visten; *PRES SUBJ* vista, vistas, vista, vistamos, vistáis, vistan; *PRES P* vistiendo; *IMPERAT* viste, vista, vistamos, vestid, vistan

[7] **dormir** *PRES* duermo, duermes, duerme, dormimos, dormís, duermen; *PRES SUBJ* duerma, duermas, duerma, durmamos, durmáis, duerman; *PRES P* durmiendo; *IMPERAT* duerme, duerma, durmamos, dormid, duerman

[8] **andar** *PRET* anduve, anduviste, anduvo, anduvimos, anduvisteis, anduvieron; *IMPERF SUBJ* anduviera/anduviese

[9] **caber** *PRES* quepo, cabes, cabe, cabemos, cabéis, caben; *PRES SUBJ* quepa, quepas, quepa, quepamos, quepáis, quepan; *FUT* cabré; *COND* cabría; *PRET* cupe, cupiste, cupo, cupimos, cupisteis, cupieron; *IMPERF SUBJ* cupiera/cupiese; *IMPERAT* cabe, quepa, quepamos, cabed, quepan

[10] **conducir** *PRES* conduzco, conduces, conduce, conducimos, conducís, conducen; *PRES SUBJ* conduzca, conduzcas, conduzca, conduzcamos, conduzcáis, conduzcan; *PRET* conduje, condujiste, condujo, condujimos, condujisteis, condujeron; *IMPERF SUBJ* condujera/condujese; *IMPERAT* conduce, conduzca, conduzcamos, conducid, conduzcan

[11] **dar** *PRES* doy, das, da, damos, dais, dan; *PRES SUBJ* dé, des, dé, demos, deis, den; *PRET* di, diste, dio, dimos, disteis, dieron; *IMPERF SUBJ* diera/diese; *IMPERAT* da, dé, demos, dad, den

[12] **decir** *PRES* digo, dices, dice, decimos, decís, dicen; *PRES SUBJ* diga, digas, diga, digamos, digáis, digan; *FUT* diré; *COND* diría; *PRET* dije, dijiste, dijo, dijimos, dijisteis, dijeron; *IMPERF SUBJ* dijera/dijese; *PRES P* diciendo; *PP* dicho; *IMPERAT* di, diga, digamos, decid, digan

[13] **ESTAR** to be

INDICATIVE

PRESENT	FUTURE	CONDITIONAL
1. estoy	estaré	estaría
2. estás	estarás	estarías
3. está	estará	estaría
1. estamos	estaremos	estaríamos
2. estáis	estaréis	estaríais
3. están	estarán	estarían

IMPERFECT	PRETERITE	PERFECT
1. estaba	estuve	he estado
2. estabas	estuviste	has estado
3. estaba	estuvo	ha estado
1. estábamos	estuvimos	hemos estado
2. estabais	estuvisteis	habéis estado
3. estaban	estuvieron	han estado

FUTURE PERFECT	CONDITIONAL PERFECT	PLUPERFECT
1. habré estado	habría estado	había estado
2. habrás estado	habrías estado	habías estado
3. habrá estado	habría estado	había estado
1. habremos estado	habríamos estado	habíamos estado
2. habréis estado	habríais estado	habíais estado
3. habrán estado	habrían estado	habían estado

SUBJUNCTIVE

PRESENT	IMPERFECT	PERFECT/PLUPERFECT
1. esté	estuv-iera/iese	haya/hubiera* estado
2. estés	estuv-ieras/ieses	hayas/hubieras estado
3. esté	estuv-iera/iese	haya/hubiera estado
1. estemos	estuv-iéramos/iésemos	hayamos/hubiéramos estado
2. estéis	estuv-ierais/ieseis	hayáis/hubierais estado
3. estén	estuv-ieran/iesen	hayan/hubieran estado

IMPERATIVE	INFINITIVE	PARTICIPLE
(tú) está	**PRESENT**	**PRESENT**
(Vd) esté	estar	estando
(nosotros) estemos		
(vosotros) estad	**PERFECT**	**PAST**
(Vds) estén	haber estado	estado

★ the alternative form 'hubiese' etc is also possible

xviii

INDICATIVE

PRESENT	FUTURE	CONDITIONAL
1. he	habré	habría
2. has	habrás	habrías
3. ha/hay*	habrá	habría
1. hemos	habremos	habríamos
2. habéis	habréis	habríais
3. han	habrán	habrían

IMPERFECT	PRETERITE	PERFECT
1. había	hube	
2. habías	hubiste	
3. había	hubo	ha habido*
1. habíamos	hubimos	
2. habíais	hubisteis	
3. habían	hubieron	

FUTURE PERFECT	CONDITIONAL PERFECT	PLUPERFECT
1.		
2.		
3. habrá habido*	habría habido*	había habido*
1.		
2.		
3.		

SUBJUNCTIVE

PRESENT	IMPERFECT	PERFECT/PLUPERFECT
1. haya	hub-iera/iese	
2. hayas	hub-ieras/ieses	
3. haya	hub-iera/iese	
1. hayamos	hub-iéramos/iésemos	haya/hubiera** habido*
2. hayáis	hub-ierais/ieseis	
3. hayan	hub-ieran/iesen	

INFINITIVE	PARTICIPLE
PRESENT	**PRESENT**
haber	habiendo
PERFECT	**PAST**
haber habido*	habido

* 'haber' is an auxiliary verb used with the participle of another verb to form compound tenses (eg he bebido - I have drunk). 'hay' means 'there is/are' and all third person singular forms in their respective tenses have this meaning. The forms highlighted with an asterisk are used only for this latter construction.

** the alternative form 'hubiese' is also possible

[15] **hacer** *PRES* hago, haces, hace, hacemos, hacéis, hacen; *PRES SUBJ* haga, hagas, haga, hagamos, hagáis, hagan; *FUT* haré; *COND* haría; *PRET* hice, hiciste, hizo, hicimos, hicisteis, hicieron; *IMPERF SUBJ* hiciera/hiciese; *PP* hecho; *IMPERAT* haz, haga, hagamos, haced, hagan

[16] **ir** *PRES* voy, vas, va, vamos, vais, van; *PRES SUBJ* vaya, vayas, vaya, vayamos, vayáis, vayan; *IMPERF* iba, ibas, iba, íbamos, ibais, iban; *PRET* fui, fuiste, fue, fuimos, fuisteis, fueron; *IMPERF SUBJ* fuera/fuese; *PRES P* yendo; *IMPERAT* ve, vaya, vamos, id, vayan

[17] **oír** *PRES* oigo, oyes, oye, oímos, oís, oyen; *PRES SUBJ* oiga, oigas, oiga, oigamos, oigáis, oigan; *PRET* oí, oíste, oyó, oímos, oísteis, oyeron; *IMPERF SUBJ* oyera/oyese; *PRES P* oyendo; *PP* oído; *IMPERAT* oye, oiga, oigamos, oíd, oigan

[18] **poder** *PRES* puedo, puedes, puede, podemos, podéis, pueden; *PRES SUBJ* pueda, puedas, pueda, podamos, podáis, puedan; *FUT* podré; *COND* podría; *PRET* pude, pudiste, pudo, pudimos, pudisteis, pudieron; *IMPERF SUBJ* pudiera/pudiese; *PRES P* pudiendo; *IMPERAT* puede, pueda, podamos, poded, puedan

[19] **poner** *PRES* pongo, pones, pone, ponemos, ponéis, ponen; *PRES SUBJ* ponga, pongas, ponga, pongamos, pongáis, pongan; *FUT* pondré; *COND* pondría; *PRET* puse, pusiste, puso, pusimos, pusisteis, pusieron; *IMPERF SUBJ* pusiera/pusiese; *PP* puesto; *IMPERAT* pon, ponga, pongamos, poned, pongan

[20] **querer** *PRES* quiero, quieres, quiere, queremos, queréis, quieren; *PRES SUBJ* quiera, quieras, quiera, queramos, queráis, quieran; *FUT* querré; *COND* querría; *PRET* quise, quisiste, quiso, quisimos, quisisteis, quisieron; *IMPERF SUBJ* quisiera/quisiese; *IMPERAT* quiere, quiera, queramos, quered, quieran

[21] **saber** *PRES* sé, sabes, sabe, sabemos, sabéis, saben; *PRES SUBJ* sepa, sepas, sepa, sepamos, sepáis, sepan; *FUT* sabré; *COND* sabría; *PRET* supe, supiste, supo, supimos, supisteis, supieron; *IMPERF SUBJ* supiera/supiese; *IMPERAT* sabe, sepa, sepamos, sabed, sepan

[22] **salir** *PRES* salgo, sales, sale, salimos, salís, salen; *PRES SUBJ* salga, salgas, salga, salgamos, salgáis, salgan; *FUT* saldré; *COND* saldría; *IMPERAT* sal, salga, salgamos, salid, salgan

[23] **ser** *PRES* soy, eres, es, somos, sois, son; *PRES SUBJ* sea, seas, sea, seamos, seáis, sean; *IMPERF* era, eras, era, éramos, erais, eran; *PRET* fui, fuiste, fue, fuimos, fuisteis, fueron; *IMPERF SUBJ* fuera/fuese; *IMPERAT* sé, sea, seamos, sed, sean

[24] **tener** *PRES* tengo, tienes, tiene, tenemos, tenéis, tienen; *PRES SUBJ* tenga, tengas, tenga, tengamos, tengáis, tengan; *FUT* tendré; *COND* tendría; *PRET* tuve, tuviste, tuvo, tuvimos, tuvisteis, tuvieron; *IMPERF SUBJ* tuviera/tuviese; *IMPERAT* ten, tenga, tengamos, tened, tengan

[25] **traer** *PRES* traigo, traes, trae, traemos, traéis, traen; *PRES SUBJ* traiga, traigas, traiga, traigamos, traigáis, traigan; *PRET* traje, trajiste, trajo, trajimos, trajisteis, trajeron; *IMPERF SUBJ* trajera/trajese; *IMPERAT* trae, traiga, traigamos, traed, traigan

[26] **valer** *PRES* valgo, vales, vale, valemos, valéis, valen; *PRES SUBJ* valga, valgas, valga, valgamos, valgáis, valgan; *FUT* valdré; *COND* valdría; *IMPERAT* vale, valga, valgamos, valed, valgan

[27] **venir** *PRES* vengo, vienes, viene, venimos, venís, vienen; *PRES SUBJ* venga, vengas, venga, vengamos, vengáis, vengan; *FUT* vendré; *COND* vendría; *PRET* vine, viniste, vino, vinimos, vinisteis, vinieron; *IMPERF SUBJ* viniera/viniese; *PRES P* viniendo; *IMPERAT* ven, venga, vengamos, venid, vengan

[28] **ver** *PRES* veo, ves, ve, vemos, veis, ven; *PRES SUBJ* vea, veas, vea, veamos, veáis, vean; *IMPERF* veía, veías, veía, veíamos, veíais, veían; *PRET* vi, viste, vio, vimos, visteis, vieron; *IMPERF SUBJ* viera/viese; *IMPERAT* ve, vea, veamos, ved, vean

[29] **desviar** *PRES* desvío, desvías, desvía, desviamos, desviáis, desvían; *PRES SUBJ* desvíe, desvíes, desvíe, desviemos, desviéis, desvíen; *IMPERAT* desvía, desvíe, desviemos, desviéis, desvíen

[30] **continuar** *PRES* continúo, continúas, continúa, continuamos, continuáis, continúan; *PRES SUBJ* continúe, continúes, continúe, continuemos, continuéis, continúen; *IMPERAT* continúa, continúe, continuemos, continuad, continúen

[31] **adquirir** *PRES* adquiero, adquieres, adquiere, adquirimos, adquirís, adquieren; *PRES SUBJ* adquiera, adquieras, adquiera, adquiramos, adquiráis, adquieran; *IMPERAT* adquiere, adquiera, adquiramos, adquirid, adquieran

[32] **jugar** *PRES* juego, juegas, juega, jugamos, jugáis, juegan; *PRES SUBJ* juegue, juegues, juegue, juguemos, juguéis, jueguen; *IMPERAT* juega, juegue, juguemos, jugad, jueguen

[33] **agradecer** *PRES* agradezco, agradeces, agradece, agradecemos, agradecéis, agradecen; *PRES SUBJ* agradezca, agradezcas, agradezca, agradezcamos, agradezcáis, agradezcan; *IMPERAT* agradece, agradezca, agradezcamos, agradeced, agradezcan

[34] **conocer** *PRES* conozco, conoces, conoce, conocemos, conocéis, conocen; *PRES SUBJ* conozca, conozcas, conozca, conozcamos, conozcáis, conozcan; *IMPERAT* conoce, conozca, conozcamos, conoced, conozcan

[35] **lucir** *PRES* luzco, luces, luce, lucimos, lucís, lucen; *PRES SUBJ* luzca, luzcas, luzca, luzcamos, luzcáis, luzcan; *IMPERAT* luce, luzca, luzcamos, lucid, luzcan

[36] **leer** *PRET* leí, leíste, leyó, leímos, leísteis, leyeron; *IMPERF SUBJ* leyera/leyese; *PRES P* leyendo; *PP* leído; *IMPERAT* lee, lea, leamos, leed, lean

[37] **huir** *PRES* huyo, huyes, huye, huimos, huís, huyen; *PRES SUBJ* huya, huyas, huya, huyamos, huyáis, huyan; *PRET* huí, huiste, huyó, huimos, huisteis, huyeron; *IMPERF SUBJ* huyera/huyese; *PRES P* huyendo; *PP* huido; *IMPERAT* huye, huya, huyamos, huid, huyan

[38] **roer** *PRES* roo/roigo/royo, roes, roe, roemos, roéis, roen; *PRES SUBJ* roa/roiga/roya, roas, roa, roamos, roáis, roan; *PRET* roí, roíste, royó, roímos, roísteis, royeron; *IMPERF SUBJ* royera/royese; *PRES P* royendo; *PP* roído; *IMPERAT* roe, roa, roamos, roed, roan

[39] **caer** *PRES* caigo, caes, cae, caemos, caéis, caen; *PRES SUBJ* caiga, caigas, caiga, caigamos, caigáis, caigan; *PRES P* cayendo; *PP* caído; *IMPERAT* cae, caiga, caigamos, caed, caigan

Guide to the Pronunciation of Spanish

The following table is based on IPA (the International Phonetic Alphabet) with certain modifications and attempts to give an approximate idea of the Spanish sound system as compared with the British English one.

Letter	Phonetic symbol	Examples	Approximate British English equivalent
Vowels:			
a	[a]	gato, amar, mesa	as in *father*, but shorter
e	[e]	estrella, vez, firme	as in *labour*
i	[i]	inicuo, iris	as in *see*, but shorter
o	[o]	bolo, cómodo, oso	between *lot* and *taught*
u	[u]	turuta, puro, tribu	as in *food*, but shorter, but u in -que- or -qui- and -gue- or -gui- is silent (unless -güe- or -güe-)
y	[i]	y	as in *see*, but shorter
Diphthongs:			
ai, ay	[ai]	baile, hay	as in *life*, *aisle*
au	[au]	fauna	as in *fowl*, *house*
ei, ey	[ei]	peine, ley	as in *hate*, *feign*
eu	[eu]	feudo	pronounce each vowel separately
oi, oy	[oi]	boina, hoy	as in *boy*
Semi-consonants:			
u	[w]	buey, cuando, fuiste	as in *wait*
i	[j]	viernes, vicio, ciudad, ciar	as in *yes*
y	[j]	yermo, ayer, rey	as in *yes*
Consonants:			
b	[b]	boda, burro, ambos	as in *be*
	[β]	haba, traba	a very light **b**
c	[k]	cabeza, cuco, acoso, frac	as in *car*, *keep*
	[θ]	cecina, cielo	as in *thing*, but in Andalusia and all of Latin America as **s** in *silly*
ch	[tʃ]	chepa, ocho	as in *chamber*
d	[d]	dedo, andar	as in *day*
	[ð]	dedo, ánade, abad	as in *this* (often omitted in spoken Spanish when at the end of a word)
f	[f]	fiesta, afición	as in *for*
g	[g]	gas, rango, gula	as in *get*
	[ɣ]	agua, agosto, lagar	a very light **g**
	[x]	genio, legión	similar to Scottish [x] in *loch*
h	-	hambre, ahíto	Spanish h is silent
j	[x]	jabón, ajo, carcaj	similar to Scottish [x] in *loch*
k	[k]	kilo, kimono	as in *car*, *keep*
l	[l]	labio, hábil, elegante	as in *law*
ll	[ʎ]	lluvia, calle	similar to the sound in *million*
m	[m]	mano, amigo, hambre	as in *man*
n	[n]	nata, ratón, antes, enemigo	as in *night*

xxii

ñ	[ɲ]	año, ñoño	similar to the sound in onion
p	[p]	pipa, pelo	as in point
q	[k]	quiosco, querer, alambique	as in car
r(r)	[r]	pero, correr, padre	always pronounced, rolled as in Scots
	[rr]	reír, honrado, perro	rr is a lengthened r sound
s	[s]	sauna, asado, cortés	similar to the s in hissing
t	[t]	teja, estén, atraco	as in time
v	[b]	verbena, vena	as in be
	[β]	ave, vivo	a very light b
w	[b]	wagón, waterpolo	as in be
x	[ks]	éxito, examen	as in exercise
	[s]	extensión	as in estate
z	[θ]	zorro, azul, caza, soez	as in thing, but in Andalusia and in all of Latin America as s in silly

Stress rules

If a word ends in a vowel, **-n** or **-s**, the stress should fall on the second last syllable, for example:

mano, examen, bocadillos

If a word has any other ending, the stress falls on the last syllable, for example:

hablar, Madrid, ayer

Exceptions to these rules carry a written accent on the stressed syllable, for example:

cómodo, legión, hábil

A

A, a |a| *nf (la letra)* A, a.

a *abr de área,* area.

a *prep* → **al. 1** *(dirección)* to; **ir a Colombia,** to go to Colombia; **llegar a Valencia,** to arrive in Valencia; **subir al tren,** to get on the train; **ir al cine,** to go to the cinema; **vete a casa,** go home. **2** *(lugar)* at, on; **a la derecha,** on the right; **a la entrada,** at the entrance; **a lo lejos,** in the distance; **a mi lado,** at *o* by my side, next to me; **al sol,** in the sun; **a la mesa,** at (the) table. **3** *(tiempo)* at; **a las doce,** at twelve o'clock; **a los sesenta años,** at the age of sixty; **a los tres meses/la media hora,** three months/half an hour later; **al final,** in the end; **al principio,** at first. **4** *(distancia)* away; **a cien kilómetros de aquí,** a hundred kilometres from here. **5** *(manera)* **a la inglesa,** (in the) English fashion *o* manner *o* style; **escrito a máquina,** typed, typewritten; **a mano,** by hand. **6** *(proporción)* **a 90 kilómetros por hora,** at 90 kilometres an hour; **a 300 pesetas el kilo,** three hundred pesetas a kilo; **tres veces a la semana,** three times a week. **7** *Dep* **ganar cuatro a dos,** to win four (to) two. **8** *(complemento indirecto)* to; *(procedencia)* from; **díselo a Javier,** tell Javier; **te lo di a ti,** I gave it to you; **comprarle algo a algn,** to buy sth from sb; *(para algn)* to buy sth for sb; *(complemento directo de persona)* **saludé a tu tía,** I said hello to your aunt. **9** *fam* **ir a por algn/algo,** to go and fetch sb/sth. **10** *(verbo + a + infin)* to; **aprender a nadar,** to learn (how) to swim; **fueron a ayudarle,** they went to help him. **11** *(nombre + a + infin)* **distancia a recorrer,** distance to be covered. **12** *a decir verdad,* to tell (you) the truth; **a no ser por ...,** if it were not for ...; **a no ser que,** unless; **a ver, let's see;** ¡**a comer!,** lunch/dinner *etc* is ready!; ¡**a dormir!,** bedtime!; ¿**a que no haces?,** *(desafío)* I bet you don't do it!

abad *nm* abbot.

abadía *nf* abbey.

abajeño,-a *nm,f Am* lowlander, coastal dweller.

abajo **I** *adv* **1** *(en una casa)* downstairs; **el piso de a.,** the flat downstairs. **2** *(dirección)* down, downwards; **ahí/aquí a.,** down there/here; **la parte de a.,** the bottom (part); **más a.,** further down; **hacia a.,** down, downwards; **calle a.,** down the street; **echar algo a.,** to knock sth down; **venirse a.,** *(edificio)* to fall down; *fig (proyecto)* to fall through. **II** *interj* ¡**a. la censura!,** down with censorship!

abalanzarse [4] *vr* **a. sobre/contra,** to

rush towards.

abalear *vtr Am* to shoot *o* fire at.

abalorio *nm* **1** *(cuenta)* glass bead. **2** *(baratija)* trinket.

abanderado,-a *nm,f* standard bearer.

abandonado,-a *adj* **1** abandoned; **tiene a su familia muy abandonada,** he takes absolutely no interest in his family. **2** *(desaseado)* untidy, unkempt.

abandonar **I** *vtr* **1** *(lugar)* to leave, quit; *(persona, cosa)* to abandon; *(proyecto, plan)* to give up. **2** *Dep (carrera)* to drop out of. **II abandonarse** *vr* to let oneself go.

abandono *nm* **1** *(acción)* abandoning, desertion. **2** *(de proyecto, idea)* giving up. **3** *(descuido)* neglect.

abanicarse *vr* to fan oneself.

abanico *nm* **1** fan. **2** *(gama)* range; **un amplio a. de posibilidades,** a wide range of possibilities.

abaratar **I** *vtr* to cut *o* reduce the price of. **II abaratarse** *vr (artículos)* to become cheaper, come down in price; *(precios)* to come down.

abarcar [1] *vtr* **1** to embrace. **2** *Am (acaparar)* to monopolize.

abarrotado,-a *adj* packed **(de,** with), crammed **(de,** with).

abarrotar *vtr* to pack, cram **(de,** with); **el público abarrotaba la sala,** the room was packed (with people).

abarrotes *nmpl Am* groceries.

abastecedor,-a *nm,f* supplier.

abastecer [33] **I** *vtr* to supply. **II abastecerse** *vr* **a. de,** to be supplied with.

abastecimiento *nm* supplying; **a. de agua,** water supply.

abasto *nm* **1** *fam* **no doy a.,** I can't cope, I can't keep up. **2** **mercado de abastos,** wholesale food market.

abatible *adj* folding, collapsible; **asiento a.,** reclining seat.

abatido,-a *adj* downcast.

abatir **I** *vtr* **1** *(derribar)* to knock down, pull down. **2** *(matar)* to kill; **a. a tiros,** to shoot down. **3** *(desanimar)* to depress, dishearten. **II abatirse** *vr (desanimarse)* to lose heart, become depressed.

abdicación *nf* abdication.

abdicar [1] *vtr & vi* to abdicate.

abdomen *nm* abdomen.

abdominales *nmpl* sit-ups.

abecedario *nm* alphabet.

abedul *nm* birch.

abeja *nf* bee; **a. reina,** queen bee.

abejorro *nm* bumblebee.

aberración *nf* aberration.

aberrante *adj* deviant.

abertura *nf (hueco)* opening, gap; *(grieta)*

crack, slit.

abertzale *adj* & *nm,f* Basque natidnalist.

abeto *nm Bot* fir (tree); **a. rojo,** spruce.

abierto,-a *adj* 1 open; *(grifo)* (turned) on; **a. de par en par,** wide open. 2 *(persona)* open-minded.

abigarrado,-a *adj* *(mezclado)* jumbled, mixed up.

abismal *adj* abysmal; *fig* **una diferencia a.,** a world of a difference.

abismo *nm* abyss; *fig* **al borde del a.,** on the brink of ruin; *fig* **entre ellos media un a.,** they are worlds apart.

ablandar I *vtr* to soften. II **ablandarse** *vr* 1 to soften, go soft o softer. 2 *fig (persona)* to mellow.

abnegación *nf* abnegation, self-denial.

abnegado,-a *adj* selfless, self-sacrificing.

abocado,-a *adj* **está a. al fracaso,** it is doomed to failure. 2 *(vino)* medium dry.

abochornar *vtr* to shame, embarrass.

abofetear *vtr* to slap.

abogacía *nf* legal profession.

abogado,-a *nm,f* lawyer, solicitor; *(en tribunal supremo)* barrister; **a. de oficio,** legal aid lawyer; **a. defensor,** counsel for the defense; **a. del diablo,** devil's advocate; **a. laboralista,** union lawyer.

abogar [7] *vtr* to plead; **a. a favor de,** to plead for, defend; **a. por algo,** to advocate o champion sth.

abolengo *nm* ancestry, lineage.

abolición *nf* abolition.

abolir *vtr defect* to abolish.

abolladura *nf* dent.

abollar *vtr* to dent.

abominable *adj* abominable.

abominar *vi* **a. (de),** to abominate, loathe.

abonado,-a I *nm,f* subscriber. II *adj Fin (pagado)* paid; **a. en cuenta,** credited.

abonar I *vtr* 1 *Agr* to fertilize. 2 *(pagar)* to pay (for). 3 *(subscribir)* to subscribe. II **abonarse** *vr* to subscribe (**a,** to).

abono *nm* 1 *Agr (producto)* fertilizer; *(estiércol)* manure. 2 *(pago)* payment. 3 *(a revista etc)* subscription; *(billete)* season ticket.

abordar *vtr (persona)* to approach; *(barco)* to board; **a. un asunto,** to tackle a subject.

aborigen *(pl aborígenes)* I *adj* native, indigenous; *esp Austral* aboriginal. II *nmf* native; *esp Austral* aborigine.

aborrecer |33| *vtr* to detest, loathe.

abortar I *vi (involuntariamente)* to miscarry, have a miscarriage; *(intencionadamente)* to abort, have an abortion. II *vtr* to abort.

abortista *nmf* abortionist.

aborto *nm* miscarriage; *(provocado)* abortion.

abotargado,-a *adj* swollen.

abotonar *vtr (ropa)* to button (up).

abovedado,-a *adj* vaulted, arched.

abracadabra *nm* abracadabra.

abrasador,-a *adj* scorching.

abrasar I *vtr* & *vi* to scorch. II **abrasarse** *vr* to burn.

abrazadera *nf* clamp.

abrazar |4| I *vtr* to embrace, hug; *fig (doctrina)* to embrace. II **abrazarse** *vr* **a. a algn,** to embrace sb; **se abrazaron,** they embraced each other.

abrazo *nm* embrace, hug; **un a., abrazos,** *(en carta)* best wishes.

abrecartas *nm inv* letter-opener, paperknife.

abrefácil *nm Com* **caja con a.,** easy-open carton.

abrelatas *nm inv* tin-opener, *US* can opener.

abreviar [12] I *vtr* to shorten; *(texto)* to abridge; *(palabra)* to abbreviate. II *vi* to be quick o brief; **para a.,** to cut a long story short.

abreviatura *nf* abbreviation.

abridor *nm (de latas, botellas)* opener.

abrigado,-a *adj* wrapped up; **ir muy a.,** to be well wrapped-up.

abrigar [7] *vtr* 1 to keep warm; **esta chaqueta abriga mucho,** this cardigan is very warm. 2 *(proteger)* to protect, shelter. 3 *(esperanza)* to cherish; *(duda)* to have, harbour, *US* harbor.

abrigo *nm* 1 *(prenda)* coat, overcoat; **ropa de a.,** warm clothes *pl.* 2 **al a. de,** protected o sheltered from.

abril *nm* April.

abrillantador *nm* polish.

abrillantar *vtr* to polish.

abrir[1] *nm* **en un a. y cerrar de ojos,** in the twinkling of an eye.

abrir[2] *(pp abierto)* I *vi* to open. II *vtr* 1 to open; *(cremallera)* to undo. 2 *(gas, grifo)* to turn on. 3 *Jur* **a. (un) expediente,** to start proceedings. III **abrirse** *vr* 1 to open; *fig* **a. paso,** to make one's way. 2 *arg* **¡me abro!,** I'm off!

abrochar *vtr,* **abrocharse** *vr* to do up; *(camisa)* to button (up); *(cinturón)* to fasten; *(zapatos)* to tie up; *(cremallera)* to do up.

abrumado,-a *adj* overwhelmed.

abrumador,-a *adj* overwhelming.

abrumar *vtr* to overwhelm, crush; **tantos problemas me abruman,** all these problems are getting on top of me.

abrupto,-a *adj* 1 *(terreno)* steep, abrupt. 2 *fig* abrupt, sudden.

absceso *nm* abscess.

absentismo *nm* absenteeism; **a. laboral,** absenteeism from work.

absolución *nf* 1 *Rel* absolution. 2 *Jur* acquittal.

absoluto,-a *adj* absolute; **en a.,** not at all, by no means. ◆**absolutamente** *adv* absolutely, completely; **a. nada,** nothing at all.

absolutorio,-a *adj Jur* **sentencia absolutoria,** verdict of not guilty.

absolver [4] (*pp* **absuelto**) *vtr* **1** *Rel* to absolve. **2** *Jur* to acquit.

absorbente *adj* **1** (*papel*) absorbent. **2** *fig* absorbing, engrossing.

absorber *vtr* to absorb.

absorción *nf* absorption.

absorto,-a *adj* absorbed, engrossed (**en**, in).

abstemio,-a **I** *adj* teetotal, abstemious. **II** *nm,f* teetotaller.

abstención *nf* abstention.

abstenerse [24] *vr* to abstain (**de**, from); (*privarse*) to refrain (**de**, from).

abstinencia *nf* abstinence; **síndrome de a.,** withdrawal symptoms *pl.*

abstracción *nf* abstraction.

abstracto,-a *adj* abstract.

abstraer [25] **I** *vtr* to abstract. **II** **abstraerse** *vr* to become lost in thought.

abstraído,-a *adj* (*ensimismado*) absorbed, engrossed (**en**, in); (*distraído*) absentminded.

absuelto,-a *pp* → **absolver.**

absurdo,-a **I** *adj* absurd. **II** *nm* absurdity, absurd thing.

abuchear *vt* to boo, jeer at.

abucheo *nm* booing, jeering.

abuela *nf* grandmother; *fam* ˈgrandma, granny; *fig* old woman.

abuelo *nm* **1** grandfather; *fam* grandad, grandpa; *fig* old man. **2** **abuelos,** grandparents.

abulense **I** *adj* of *o* from Avila. **II** *nmf* native *o* inhabitant of Avila.

abulia *nf* apathy, lack of willpower.

abultado,-a *adj* bulky, big.

abultar **I** *vi* to be bulky; **abulta mucho,** it takes up a lot of space. **II** *vtr* to exaggerate.

abundancia *nf* abundance, plenty; *fig* **nadar en la a.,** to be rolling in money.

abundante *adj* abundant, plentiful.

abundar *vi* to abound, be plentiful.

abur *interj fam* cheerio!, see you!

aburrido,-a *adj* **1 ser a.,** to be boring. **2 estar a.,** to be bored; (*harto*) to be tired (**de**, of).

aburrimiento *nm* boredom; **¡qué a.!,** how boring!, what a bore!

aburrir **I** *vtr* to bore. **II** **aburrirse** *vr* to get bored; **a. como una ostra,** to be bored stiff.

abusar *vi* **1** (*propasarse*) to go too far. **2 a. de,** (*situación, persona*) to take (unfair) advantage of; (*poder, amabilidad*) to abuse; **a. de la bebida/del tabaco,** to drink/smoke too much *o* to excess; *Jur* **a. de un niño/una mujer,** to abuse a child/woman.

abusivo,-a *adj* (*precio*) exorbitant.

abuso *nm* abuse.

abyecto,-a *adj* abject.

a. C. *abr de* **antes de Cristo,** before Christ, BC.

a/c *Com abr de* **a cuenta,** on account.

acá *adv* **1** (*lugar*) here, over here; **más a.,** nearer; **¡ven a.!,** come here! **2 de entonces a.,** since then.

acabado,-a **I** *adj* **1** (*terminado*) finished. **2** *fig* (*persona*) worn-out, spent. **II** *nm* finish.

acabar **I** *vtr* **1** to finish (off); (*completar*) to complete. **II** *vi* **1** to finish, end; **a. bien,** to have a happy ending; **a. con algo,** (*terminarlo*) to finish sth; (*romperlo*) to break sth. **2 a. de ...,** to have just ...; **acaba de entrar,** he has just come in; **no acaba de convencerme,** I'm not quite convinced. **3 acabaron casándose** *o* **por casarse,** they ended up getting married; **acabó en la cárcel,** he ended up in jail. **III acabarse** *vr* to finish, come to an end; **se nos acabó la gasolina,** we ran out of petrol; *fam* **¡se acabó!,** that's that!

acabóse *nm fam* **esto es el a.,** this is the end.

acacia *nf* acacia.

academia *nf* academy.

académico,-a *adj & nm,f* academic.

acaecer [33] *v impers* to happen, occur.

acallar *vtr* to silence.

acalorado,-a *adj* **1** hot. **2** *fig* (*excitado*) worked up, excited; (*debate etc*) heated, angry.

acalorarse **1** to get warm *o* hot. **2** *fig* to get excited *o* worked up.

acampada *nf* camping; **ir de a.,** to go camping; **zona de a.,** camp site.

acampanado,-a *adj* bell-shaped; (*prendas*) flared.

acampar *vi* to camp.

acantilado *nm* cliff.

acantonar *vtr* (*tropas*) to billet, quarter (**en**, in).

acaparar *vtr* **1** (*productos*) to hoard; (*el mercado*) to corner. **2** *fig* to monopolize.

acaramelado,-a *adj* **1** (*color*) caramel-coloured, *US* caramel-colored. **2** (*pareja*) lovey-dovey, starry-eyed.

acariciar [12] *vtr* to caress; (*pelo, animal*) to stroke; (*esperanza*) to cherish.

acarrear *vtr* **1** (*transportar*) to carry, transport. **2** *fig* (*conllevar*) to entail.

acaso *adv* perhaps, maybe; **¿a. no te lo dije?,** did I not tell you, by any chance?; **por si a.,** just in case; **si a. viene ...,** if he should come ....

acatamiento *nm* respect; (*de la ley*) observance.

acatar *vtr* to observe, comply with.

acatarrado,-a *adj* **estar a.,** to have a cold.

acatarrarse *vr* to catch a cold.

acaudalado,-a *adj* rich, wealthy.

acaudalar *vtr* to accumulate, amass.

acaudillar *vtr* to lead.

acceder *vi* **a.** **a,** *(consentir)* to accede to, consent to; *(tener acceso)* to gain admittance to; *Inform* to access.

accesible *adj* accessible; *(persona)* approachable.

acceso *nm* 1 *(entrada)* access, entry; *Inform* **a. al azar, a. directo,** random access; *Univ* **prueba de a.,** entrance examination. 2 *(carretera)* approach, access. 3 *Med & fig* fit.

accesorio,-a *adj & nm* accessory.

accidentado,-a I *adj* *(terreno)* uneven, hilly; *(viaje, vida)* eventful. II *nm,f* casualty, accident victim.

accidental *adj* accidental; **un encuentro a.,** a chance meeting.

accidente *nm* 1 accident; **por a.,** by chance; **a. laboral,** industrial accident. 2 *Geog* **accidentes geográficos,** geographical features.

acción *nf* 1 action; *(acto)* act; **poner en a.,** to put in action; **ponerse en a.,** to go into action; **campo de a.,** field of action; **película de a.,** adventure film. 2 *Fin* share.

accionar *vtr* to drive.

accionista *nmf* shareholder.

acebo *nm* *(hoja)* holly; *(árbol)* holly tree.

acechar *vtr* to lie in wait for; **un grave peligro nos acecha,** great danger awaits us.

acecho *nm* **estar al a. de,** *(esperar)* to lie in wait for.

acedía *nf* *(pez)* dab.

aceite *nm* oil; **a. de girasol/maíz/oliva,** sunflower/corn/olive oil.

aceitera *nf* 1 *Culin* oil bottle; **aceiteras,** oil and vinegar set *sing.* 2 *Aut* oil can.

aceitero,-a I *adj* oil. II *nm,f* oil merchant.

aceitoso,-a *adj* oily.

aceituna *nf* olive; **a. rellena,** stuffed olive.

aceitunado,-a *adj* olive, olive-coloured.

aceitunero,-a *nm,f* 1 *(recolector)* olive picker *o* harvester. 2 *(vendedor)* olive seller.

acelerado,-a *adj* accelerated, fast.

acelerador *nm* *Aut* accelerator.

acelerar *vtr* to accelerate.

acento *nm* 1 accent; *(de palabra)* stress. 2 *(énfasis)* stress, emphasis.

acentuar [30] I *vtr* 1 to stress. 2 *fig* to emphasize, stress. II **acentuarse** *vr fig* to become more pronounced *o* noticeable.

aceña *nf* watermill.

acepción *nf* meaning, sense.

aceptable *adj* acceptable.

aceptación *nf* 1 acceptance. 2 **tener poca a.,** to have little success, not to be popular.

aceptar *vtr* to accept.

acequia *nf* irrigation ditch *o* channel.

acera *nf* pavement, *US* sidewalk; *fam pey*

ser de la a. de enfrente, to be gay *o* queer.

acerado *nm* pavement.

acerbo,-a *adj* harsh, bitter.

acerca *adv* **a. de,** about.

acercamiento *nm* bringing together, coming together; *Pol* rapprochement.

acercar [1] I *vtr* to bring near *o* nearer, bring (over); *fig* to bring together; **¿te acerco a casa?,** can I give you a lift home? II **acercarse** *vr* 1 to approach (a, -). 2 *(ir)* to go; *(venir)* to come.

acerico *nm* pincushion.

acero *nm* steel; **a. inoxidable,** stainless steel.

acérrimo,-a *adj* *(partidario)* staunch; *(enemigo)* bitter.

acertado,-a *adj* 1 *(solución)* right, correct; *(decisión)* wise. 2 **no estuviste muy a. al decir eso,** it wasn't very wise of you to say that.

acertante *nmf* winner. II *adj* winning.

acertar [1] I *vtr* *(pregunta)* to get right; *(adivinar)* to guess correctly; **a. las quinielas,** to win the pools. II *vi* to be right; **acertó con la calle que buscaba,** she found the street she was looking for.

acertijo *nm* riddle.

acervo *nm* **a. cultural,** cultural tradition *o* heritage.

acetona *nf* acetone.

achacar [1] *vtr* *(atribuir)* to attribute.

achacoso,-a *adj* ailing, unwell.

achaque *nm* ailment, complaint.

achicar [1] I *vtr* 1 *(amilanar)* to intimidate. 2 *(encoger)* to reduce, make smaller. 3 *(barco)* to bale out. II **achicarse** *vr* 1 *(amilanarse)* to lose heart. 2 *(encogerse)* to get smaller.

achicharrar *vtr* to burn to a crisp.

achicoria *nf* chicory.

achinado,-a *adj* 1 *(ojos)* slanting. 2 *Am* with mestizo features.

acholado,-a *adj* *Am* half-caste.

achuchar *vtr* *(empujar)* to shove.

achuchón *nm* *(empujón)* push, shove.

aciago,-a *adj* ill-fated, fateful.

acicalado,-a *adj* well-dressed, smart.

acicalarse *vr* to dress up, smarten up.

acicate *nm fig* *(aliciente)* spur, incentive.

acidez *nf* *(de sabor)* sharpness, sourness; *Quím* acidity; *Med* **a. de estómago,** heartburn.

ácido,-a I *adj* *(sabor)* sharp, tart; *Quím* acidic; *fig* *(tono)* harsh. II *nm* *Quím* acid.

acierto *nm* *(buena decisión)* good choice *o* idea; **con gran a.,** very wisely.

aclamación *nf* acclamation, acclaim.

aclamar *vtr* to acclaim.

aclaración *nf* explanation.

aclarado *nm* rinsing, rinse.

aclarar I *vtr* 1 *(explicar)* to clarify, explain; *(color)* to lighten, make lighter. 2 *(enjuagar)* to rinse. II *v impers* *Meteor* clear (up). **III aclararse** *vr* 1 (*decidirse*) to make up one's mind; (*entender*) to understand. 2 *Meteor* to clear (up).

aclaratorio,-a *adj* explanatory.

aclimatación *nf* acclimatization, *US* acclimation.

aclimatar I *vtr* to acclimatize, *US* acclimate (**a**, to). **II aclimatarse** *vr fig* **a. a algo**, to get used to sth.

acné *nf* acne.

acobardar I *vtr* to frighten. **II acobardarse** *vr* to become frightened, lose one's nerve, shrink back (**ante**, from).

acodarse *vr* to lean (**en**, on).

acogedor,-a *adj* cosy, warm.

acoger [5] I *vtr* 1 (*recibir*) to receive; (*a invitado*) to welcome. 2 (*persona desvalida*) to take in. **II acogerse** *vr fig* **a. a**, to take refuge in; (*amnistía*) to avail oneself of; **a. a la ley**, to have recourse to the law.

acogida *nf* reception, welcome.

acojonado,-a *adj vulg* shit-scared.

acojonante *adj vulg* bloody great *o* terrific.

acojonarse *vr vulg* (*acobardarse*) to shit oneself, be shit-scared.

acolchar *vtr* (*rellenar*) to pad; (*prenda*) to quilt.

acometer *vtr* 1 (*emprender*) to undertake. 2 (*atacar*) to attack.

acometida *nf* (*ataque*) attack; (*de gas etc*) connection.

acomodado,-a *adj* well-off, well-to-do.

acomodador,-a *nm,f* (*hombre*) usher; (*mujer*) usherette.

acomodar I *vtr* 1 (*alojar*) to lodge, accommodate. 2 (*en cine etc*) to find a place for. **II acomodarse** *vr* 1 to make oneself comfortable. 2 (*adaptarse*) to adapt.

acomodaticio,-a *adj* 1 accommodating, easy-going. 2 *pey* pliable.

acompañado,-a *adj* (*rítmico*) rhythmic.

acompañado,-a *adj* estar **a.**, to have a complex (**por**, about).

acomplejar I *vtr* to give a complex. **II acomplejarse** *vr* **a. por**, to develop a complex about.

acondicionado,-a *adj* **aire a.**, air conditioning.

acondicionador *nm* conditioner.

acondicionar *vtr* to prepare, set up; (*mejorar*) to improve; (*cabello*) to condition.

acongojar *vtr* to distress.

aconsejable *adj* advisable.

aconsejar *vtr* to advise.

acontecer [33] *v impers* to happen, take place.

acontecimiento *nm* event.

acopio *nm* store, stock; **hacer a. de**, to store.

acoplar I *vtr* 1 to fit (together), join. 2 *Téc* to couple, connect. **II acoplarse** *vr* (*nave espacial*) to dock.

acorazado,-a I *adj* armoured, *US* armored, armour-plated, *US* armor-plated. **II** *nm* battleship.

acordado,-a *adj* agreed; **según lo a.**, as agreed.

acordar [2] I *vtr* to agree; (*decidir*) to decide. **II acordarse** *vr* to remember; **no me acuerdo (de Silvia)**, I can't remember (Silvia).

acorde I *adj* in agreement. **II** *nm* *Mús* chord.

acordeón *nm* accordion.

acordonado,-a *adj* cordoned off, sealed off.

acordonar *vtr* 1 (*zona*) to cordon off, seal off. 2 (*atar*) to lace up.

acorralar *vtr* to corner.

acortar *vtr* to shorten; **a. distancias**, to cut down the distance.

acosar *vtr* to harass; *fig* **a. a algn a preguntas**, to bombard sb with questions.

acoso *nm* harassment; **a. sexual**, sexual harassment.

acostar [2] I *vtr* to put to bed. **II acostarse** *vr* 1 to go to bed. 2 *fam* **a. con algn**, to sleep with sb, go to bed with sb.

acostumbrado,-a *adj* 1 usual, customary; **es lo a.**, it is the custom. 2 **a. al frío/calor**, used to the cold/heat.

acostumbrar I *vi* **a. a**, (*soler*) to be in the habit of. **II** *vtr* **a. a algn a algo**, (*habituar*) to get sb used to sth. **III acostumbrarse** *vr* (*habituarse*) to become accustomed (**a**, to); get used (**a**, to).

acotación *nf* 1 (*en escrito*) (marginal) note; *Teat* stage direction. 2 (*en mapa*) elevation mark.

acotar *vtr* 1 (*área*) to enclose; *fig* (*tema*) to delimit. 2 (*texto*) to annotate. 3 (*mapa*) to mark with elevations.

acotejar *vtr* *Am* to arrange.

ácrata *adj & nmf* anarchist.

acre[1] *adj* 1 (*sabor*) sour, bitter; (*olor*) acrid. 2 *fig* (*palabras*) bitter, harsh; (*crítica*) biting.

acre[2] *nm* (*medida*) acre.

acrecentar [1] *vtr* to increase.

acreditar *vtr* 1 to be a credit to. 2 (*probar*) to prove. 3 (*embajador*) to accredit. 4 *Fin* to credit.

acreditativo,-a *adj* which proves, which gives proof.

acreedor,-a *nm,f* *Com* creditor.

acribillar *vtr* to riddle, pepper; **a. a algn a balazos,** to riddle sb with bullets.

acrílico,-a *adj* acrylic.

acriollarse *vr Am* to adopt local customs.

acritud *nf* (*mordacidad*) acrimony.

acrobacia *nf* acrobatics *sing*.

acróbata *nmf* acrobat.

acta *nf* 1 (*de reunión*) minutes *pl*, record. 2 (*certificado*) certificate, official document; **a. notarial,** affidavit.

actitud *nf* attitude.

activar *vtr* 1 to activate. 2 (*avivar*) to liven up.

actividad *nf* activity.

activista *nmf* activist.

activo,-a I *adj* active; **en a.,** on active service. II *nm Fin* assets *pl*.

acto *nm* 1 act, action; **a. sexual,** sexual intercourse; **en el a.,** at once; **a. seguido,** immediately afterwards; **Mil en a. de servicio,** in action; **hacer a. de presencia,** to put in an appearance. 2 (*ceremonia*) ceremony. 3 *Teat* act.

actor *nm* actor.

actriz *nf* actress.

actuación *nf* 1 performance. 2 (*intervención*) intervention, action.

actual *adj* current, present; (*al día*) up-to-date; **un tema muy a.,** a very topical subject. ◆**actualmente** *adv* (*hoy en día*) nowadays, these days; (*ahora*) at the moment, at present.

actualidad *nf* 1 present time; **en la a.,** at present; **estar de a.,** to be fashionable; **temas de a.,** topical subjects. 2 (*hechos*) current affairs *pl*.

actualizar [4] *vtr* to update, bring up to date.

actuar [30] *vi* 1 to act; **a. como** *o* **de,** to act as. 2 *Cin Teat* to perform, act.

acuarela *nf* watercolour, *US* watercolor.

Acuario *nm* Aquarius.

acuario *nm* aquarium.

acuartelar *vtr* to confine to barracks.

acuático,-a *adj* aquatic; **esquí a.,** water skiing.

acuchillar *vtr* to knife, stab.

acuciante *adj* urgent, pressing.

acuciar [12] *vtr* to urge on.

acudir *vi* (*ir*) to go; (*venir*) to come, arrive; **nadie acudió en su ayuda,** nobody came to help him; **no sé dónde a.,** I don't know where to turn.

acueducto *nm* aqueduct.

acuerdo *nm* agreement; **¡de a.!,** all right!, O.K.!; **de a. con,** in accordance with; **de común a.,** by common consent; **estar de a. en algo,** to agree on sth; **ponerse de a.,** to agree; **a. marco,** framework agreement.

acumular I *vtr* to accumulate. II **acumularse** *vr* 1 to accumulate, build up. 2 (*gente*) to crowd.

acunar *vtr* to rock.

acuñar *vtr* (*moneda*) to mint; (*frase*) to coin.

acuoso,-a *adj* watery; (*jugoso*) juicy.

acupuntura *nf* acupuncture.

acurrucarse [1] *vr* to curl up, snuggle up.

acusación *nf* 1 accusation. 2 *Jur* charge.

acusado,-a I *nm,f* accused, defendant. II *adj* (*marcado*) marked, noticeable.

acusar I *vtr* 1 to accuse (**de,** of); *Jur* to charge (**de,** with). 2 (*golpe etc*) to feel; **su cara acusaba el cansancio,** his face showed his exhaustion. 3 *Com* **a. recibo,** to acknowledge receipt. II **acusarse** *vr* 1 (*acentuarse*) to become more pronounced. 2 *fig* (*notarse*) to show.

acuse *nm* **a. de recibo,** acknowledgment of receipt.

acústica *adj & nmf fam* telltale.

acústica *nf* acoustics *sing*.

acústico,-a *adj* acoustic.

adán *nm fam* untidy *o* slovenly person.

adaptable *adj* adaptable.

adaptación *nf* adaptation.

adaptador *nm* adapter.

adaptar I *vtr* 1 to adapt. 2 (*ajustar*) to adjust. II **adaptarse** *vr* to adapt oneself (**a,** to).

adecentar *vtr* to tidy (up), clean (up).

adecuado,-a *adj* appropriate, suitable.

adecuar [10] *vtr* to adapt.

adefesio *nm* (*persona*) freak; (*cosa*) monstrosity.

a. de J.C. *abr de* **antes de Jesucristo,** before Christ, BC.

adelantado,-a *adj* 1 advanced; (*desarrollado*) developed; (*precoz*) precocious. 2 (*reloj*) fast. 3 **pagar por a.,** to pay in advance.

adelantamiento *nm* overtaking; **hacer un a.,** to overtake.

adelantar I *vtr* 1 to move *o* bring forward; (*reloj*) to put forward; *fig* to advance. 2 *Aut* to overtake. 3 (*fecha*) to bring forward; *fig* **a. (los) acontecimientos,** to get ahead of oneself. II *vi* 1 to advance. 2 (*progresar*) to make progress. 3 (*reloj*) to be fast. III **adelantarse** *vr* 1 (*ir delante*) to go ahead. 2 (*reloj*) to gain, be fast. 3 **el verano se ha adelantado,** we are having an early summer.

adelante I *adv* forward; **más a.,** (*lugar*) further on; (*tiempo*) later; **seguir a.,** to keep going, carry on; **llevar a. un plan,** to carry out a plan. II *interj* **¡a!,** come in! to carry out a plan.

adelanto *nm* 1 advance; (*progreso*) progress. 2 **el reloj lleva diez minutos de a.,** the watch is ten minutes fast. 3 (*de dinero*) advance payment.

adelfa *nf* oleander, rosebay.

adelgazamiento *nm* slimming.

adelgazar [4] *vi* to slim, lose weight.

ademán *nm* 1 gesture. 2 **ademanes,** manners.

además *adv* moreover, furthermore; **a., no lo he visto nunca**, what's more, I've never seen him; **a. de él**, besides him.

adentrarse *vr* **a. en**, (*bosque*) to go deep into; (*asunto*) to study thoroughly.

adentro I *adv* (*dentro*) inside; then **a.**, out to sea; **tierra a.**, inland. **II** *nmpl* **decir algo para sus adentros**, to say sth to oneself.

adepto,-a *nm,f* follower, supporter.

aderezar [4] *vtr* (*comida*) to season; (*ensalada*) to dress.

aderezo *nm* (*de comida*) seasoning; (*de ensalada*) dressing.

adeudar I *vtr* to owe. **II adeudarse** *vr* to get into debt.

adherencia *nf* adherence; *Aut* roadholding.

adherir [5] **I** *vtr* to stick on. **II adherirse** *vr* **a. a**, to adhere to; (*partido*) to join.

adhesión *nf* adhesion; (*a partido*) joining; (*a teoría*) adherence.

adhesivo,-a *adj & nm* adhesive.

adicción *nf* addiction; **crear a.**, to be addictive.

adición *nf* addition.

adicional *adj* additional.

adicto,-a I *nm,f* addict. **II** *adj* addicted (**a**, to).

adiestrar *vtr* to train.

adinerado,-a I *adj* wealthy, rich. **II** *nm,f* rich person.

adiós (*pl* **adioses**) **I** *interj* goodbye; *fam* bye-bye; (*al cruzarse*) hello. **II** *nm* goodbye.

aditivo,-a *adj & nm* additive.

adivinanza *nf* riddle, puzzle.

adivinar *vtr* to guess; **a. el pensamiento de algn**, to read sb's mind.

adivino,-a *nm,f* fortune-teller.

adjetivo,-a nm I adjective. **II** *adj* adjectival.

adjudicación *nf* award; (*en subasta*) sale.

adjudicar [1] **I** *vtr* (*premio, contrato*) to award. **2** (*en subasta*) to sell. **II adjudicarse** *vr* to appropriate, take over.

adjuntar *vtr* to enclose.

adjunto,-a I *adj* **1** enclosed, attached. **2** *Educ* assistant. **II** *nm,f* *Educ* assistant teacher.

adm., admón. *abr de* **administración**, administration.

administración *nf* **1** (*gobierno*) administration, authorities *pl*; *Pol* **a. central**, central government; **a. pública**, civil service. **2** (*de empresa*) administration, management. **3** (*oficina*) (branch) office.

administrador,-a *nm,f* administrator. **I** *adj* administrating.

administrar I *vtr* **1** to administer. **2** (*dirigir*) to run, manage. **II administrarse** *vr* to manage one's own money.

administrativo,-a I *adj* administrative. **II** *nm,f* (*funcionario*) official.

admirable *adj* admirable.

admiración *nf* **1** admiration; **causar a.**, to impress. **2** *Ling* exclamation mark.

admirador,-a *nm,f* admirer.

admirar I *vtr* **1** to admire. **2** (*sorprender*) to amaze, astonish. **II admirarse** *vr* to be amazed, be astonished.

admisible *adj* admissible, acceptable.

admisión *nf* admission; '**reservado el derecho de a.**', 'the management reserves the right to refuse admission'.

admitir *vtr* **1** to admit, let in. **2** (*aceptar*) to accept; '**no se admiten cheques**', 'no cheques accepted'. **3** (*tolerar*) to allow. **4** (*reconocer*) to admit, acknowledge; **admito que mentí**, I admit that I lied.

admonición *nf* warning.

ADN *nm abr de ácido desoxirribonucleico*, desoxyribonucleic acid, DNA.

adobar *vtr Culin* to marinate.

adobe *nm* adobe.

adobo *nm* marinade.

adoctrinar *vtr* to indoctrinate.

adolecer [33] *vi* **a. de**, (*carecer de*) to lack; *fig fml* to suffer from.

adolescencia *nf* adolescence.

adolescente *adj & nmf* adolescent.

adónde *adv interr* where (to)?

adonde *adv* where.

adondequiera *adv* wherever.

adopción *nf* adoption.

adoptar *vtr* to adopt.

adoptivo,-a *adj* (*hijo*) adopted; (*padres*) adoptive; *fig* **país a.**, a country of adoption.

adoquín *nm* cobble, paving stone.

adorable *adj* adorable.

adorar *vtr* **1** *Rel* to worship. **2** *fig* to adore.

adormecer [33] **I** *vtr* to send to sleep, make sleepy. **II adormecerse** *vr* **1** (*dormirse*) to doze off. **2** (*brazo etc*) to go to sleep, go numb.

adormecido,-a *adj* sleepy, drowsy.

adormilarse *vr* to doze, drowse.

adornar *vtr* to adorn, decorate.

adorno *nm* decoration, adornment; **de a.**, decorative.

adosado,-a *adj* adjacent; (*casa*) semidetached.

adquirir [31] *vtr* to acquire; (*comprar*) to purchase.

adquisición *nf* acquisition; (*compra*) buy, purchase.

adquisitivo,-a *adj* **poder a.**, purchasing power.

adrede *adv* deliberately, on purpose.

adrenalina *nf* adrenalin.

adriático,-a *nm* **el (Mar) A.**, the Adriatic (Sea).

adscribir (*pp* **adscrito**) *vtr* **1** (*atribuir*) to ascribe to. **2** (*a un trabajo*) to appoint to. **II adscribirse** *vr* to affiliate (**a**, to).

adscrito,-a *pp de* **adscribir**.

aduana *nf* customs *pl*.

aduanero,-a I *adj* customs. II *nm,f* customs officer.

aducir [10] *vtr* to adduce, allege.

adueñarse *vr* a. de, to take over; (*pánico etc*) to take hold of.

aduje *pt indef* → **aducir**.

adulación *nf* adulation.

adular *vtr* to adulate.

adulterar *vtr* to adulterate.

adulterio *nm* adultery.

adúltero,-a I *adj* adulterous. II *nm,f* (*hombre*) adulterer; (*mujer*) adulteress.

adulto,-a *adj & nm,f* adult.

adusto,-a *adj* harsh, severe.

aduzco *indic pres* → **aducir**.

advenedizo,-a *adj & nm,f* upstart.

advenimiento *nm* advent, coming.

adverbio *nm* adverb.

adversario,-a I *nm,f* adversary, opponent. II *adj* opposing.

adversidad *nf* adversity; (*revés*) setback.

adverso,-a *adj* adverse.

advertencia *nf* warning.

advertido,-a *adj* warned; (*informado*) informed; estás o quedas a., you've been warned.

advertir [5] *vtr* 1 to warn; (*informar*) to inform, advise; *fam* te advierto que yo tampoco lo vi, mind you, I didn't see it either. 2 (*notar*) to realize, notice.

adviento *nm* Advent.

adyacente *adj* adjacent.

aéreo,-a *adj* 1 aerial. 2 *Av* air; tráfico a., air traffic; Com por vía aerea, by air.

aero- *pref* aero-.

aeróbic *nm* aerobics *sing*.

aerodinámico,-a *adj* aerodynamic; de línea aerodinámica, streamlined.

aeródromo *nm* aerodrome.

aeromodelismo *nm* aeroplane modelling o US modeling.

aeromoza *nf Am* air hostess.

aeronáutica *nf* aeronautics *sing*.

aeronáutico,-a *adj* la industria aeronáutica, the aeronautics industry.

aeronave *nf* airship.

aeroplano *nm* light aeroplane.

aeropuerto *nm* airport.

aerosol *nm* aerosol.

aerostático,-a *adj* globo a., hot-air balloon.

a/f *abr de* a favor, in favour o US favor.

afable *adj* affable.

afamado,-a *adj* famous, well-known.

afán *nm* (*pl* afanes) 1 (*esfuerzo*) effort. 2 (*celo*) zeal.

afanar I *vtr* (*robar*) to nick, pinch. II afanarse *vr* a. por conseguir algo, to do one's best to achieve sth.

afanoso,-a *adj* 1 (*persona*) keen, eager. 2 (*tarea*) hard, tough.

afección *nf* disease.

afectación *nf* affectation.

afectado,-a *adj* affected.

afectar *vtr* a. a, to affect; le afectó mucho, she was deeply affected; nos afecta a todos, it concerns all of us.

afecto *nm* affection; tomarle a. a algn, to become fond of sb.

afectuoso,-a *adj* affectionate.

afeitado *nm* shave.

afeitar *vtr*, afeitarse *vr* to shave.

afeminado,-a *adj* effeminate.

aferrado,-a *adj* a. a, clinging to.

aferrar I *vtr Náut* to anchor, moor. II aferrarse *vr* to clutch, cling; *fig* a. a una creencia, to cling to a belief.

Afganistán *n* Afghanistan.

afgano,-a *adj & nm,f* Afghan.

afianzamiento *nm* strengthening, reinforcement.

afianzar [4] I *vtr* to strengthen, reinforce. II afianzarse *vr* (*persona*) to become established.

afición *nf* 1 liking; tiene a. por la música, he is fond of music. 2 Dep la a., the fans *pl*.

aficionado,-a I *nm,f* 1 enthusiast; un a. a la música, a music lover. 2 (*no profesional*) amateur. I *adj* 1 keen, fond; ser a. a algo, to be fond of sth. 2 (*no profesional*) amateur.

aficionarse *vr* to become fond (a, of), take a liking (a, to).

afilado,-a *adj* sharp.

afilar *vtr* to sharpen.

afiliación *nf* affiliation.

afiliado,-a *nm,f* member.

afiliarse [12] *vtr* to become a member.

afín *adj* (*semejante*) kindred, similar; (*relacionado*) related.

afinar *vtr* 1 (*puntería*) to sharpen. 2 (*instrumento*) to tune.

afincarse [1] *vr* to settle down.

afinidad *nf* affinity.

afirmación *nf* affirmation; afirmaciones, (*declaracion*) statement.

afirmar 1 *vtr* (*aseverar*) to state, declare. 2 (*afianzar*) to strengthen, reinforce.

afirmativo,-a *adj* affirmative; en caso a. ..., if the answer is yes ...

aflicción *nf* affliction.

afligir [6] I *vtr* to afflict. II afligirse *vr* to grieve, be distressed.

aflojar I *vtr* to loosen. II *vi* (*viento etc*) to weaken, grow weak. III aflojarse *vr* to come o work loose; (*rueda*) to go down.

aflorar *vi* to come to the surface, appear.

afluencia *nf* inflow, influx; gran a. de público, great numbers of people.

afluente *nm* tributary.

afluir [37] *vi* to flow (a, into).

afónico,-a *adj* estar a., to have lost one's voice.

aforismo *nm* aphorism.

aforo *nm* (*capacidad*) seating capacity.

afortunado,-a *adj* fortunate; las Islas Afortunadas, the Canaries.

afrenta nf fml affront.

África n Africa.

africano,-a adj & nm,f African.

afrodisíaco,-a adj & nm aphrodisiac.

afrontar vtr to confront, face; **a. las consecuencias**, to face the consequences.

afuera I adv outside; **la parte de a.**, the outside; **más a.**, further out; **salir a.**, to come o go out. II nfpl **afueras**, outskirts.

agachar I vtr to lower. II **agacharse** vr to duck.

agalla nf 1 (de pez) gill. 2 **tiene agallas**, she's got guts.

agarraderas nfpl fam **tener buenas a.**, to be well connected.

agarrado,-a adj 1 fam stingy, tight. 2 **baile a.**, cheek-to-cheek dancing.

agarrar I vtr 1 to grasp, seize; **agárralo fuerte**, hold it tight. 2 Am to take. 3 fam (pillar) to catch; **a. una borrachera**, to get drunk o pissed. II **agarrarse** vr to hold on; **agarraos bien**, hold tight.

agarrotarse vr 1 (músculo) to stiffen. 2 (máquina) to seize up.

agasajar vtr to smother with attentions.

ágata nf agate.

agazaparse vr to crouch (down).

agencia nf agency; (sucursal) branch; **a. de viajes**, travel agency; **a. de seguros**, insurance agency; **a. inmobiliaria**, estate agency.

agenciarse |12| vr 1 to get oneself; **se agenció una moto**, he got himself a motorbike. 2 **agenciárselas**, to manage.

agenda nf diary.

agente nmf agent; **a. de policía**, (hombre) policeman; (mujer) policewoman; **a. de bolsa**, stockbroker; **a. de seguros**, insurance broker.

agigantado,-a adj **a pasos agigantados**, by leaps and bounds.

ágil adj agile.

agilidad nf agility.

agilización nf speeding up.

agilizar |4| vtr (trámites) to speed up.

agitación nf (intranquilidad) restlessness; (social, político) unrest.

agitado,-a adj (agitated); (persona) anxious; (mar) rough; **una vida muy agitada**, a very hectic life.

agitar I vtr (botella) to shake; (multitud) to agitate. II **agitarse** vr (persona) to become agitated; (mar) to become rough.

aglomeración nf agglomeration; (de gente) crowd.

aglomerar vtr, **aglomerarse** vr 1 (agruparse) to agglomerate, amass. 2 (gente) to crowd, form a crowd.

agnóstico,-a adj & nm,f agnostic.

agobiado,-a adj fig **a. de problemas**, snowed under with problems; fig **a. de trabajo**, up to one's eyes in work.

agobiante adj (trabajo) overwhelming; (lugar) claustrophobic; (calor) oppressive;

(persona) tiresome, tiring.

agobiar |12| I vtr to overwhelm. II **agobiarse** vr (con problemas) to be over-anxious; (por el calor) to suffocate.

agobio nm 1 (angustia) anxiety. 2 (sofoco) suffocation.

agolpamiento nm crowd, crush.

agolparse vr to crowd, throng.

agonía nf dying breath, last gasp.

agonizante adj dying.

agonizar |4| vi to be dying.

agosto nm August; fam **hacer su a.**, to make a packet.

agotado,-a adj 1 (cansado) exhausted, worn out. 2 Com sold out; (existencias) exhausted; (libro) out of print.

agotador,-a adj exhausting.

agotamiento nm exhaustion.

agotar I vtr (cansar) to exhaust, wear out. 2 (acabar) to exhaust, use up (completely). II **agotarse** vr 1 (acabarse) to run out, be used up; Com to be sold out. 2 (persona) to become exhausted o tired out.

agraciado,-a adj 1 (hermoso) pretty. 2 (ganador) winning; **ser a. con**, to win.

agradable adj pleasant.

agradar vi to please; **no me agrada**, I don't like it.

agradecer |33| vtr 1 (dar las gracias) to thank for; **les agradezco su atención**, (I) thank you for your attention; **te lo agradezco mucho**, thank you very much. 2 (estar agradecido) to be grateful to; **te agradecería que vinieras**, I'd be grateful if you'd come. 3 (uso impers) **siempre se agradece un descanso**, a rest is always welcome.

agradecido,-a adj grateful; **le estoy muy a.**, I am very grateful to you.

agradecimiento nm gratitude.

agrado nm pleasure; **no es de su a.**, it isn't to his liking.

agrandar I vtr to enlarge, make larger. II **agrandarse** vr to enlarge, become larger.

agrario,-a adj agrarian; **política agraria**, agricultural policy.

agravamiento nm aggravation.

agravante I adj Jur aggravating. II nm Jur aggravating circumstance.

agravar I vtr to aggravate. II **agravarse** vr to worsen, get worse.

agraviar |12| vtr to offend, insult.

agravio nm offense, insult.

agredir vtr defect to assault.

agregación nf aggregation.

agregado,-a I adj Educ **profesor a.**, (escuela) secondary school teacher; Univ assistant teacher. II nm,f Pol attaché.

agregar |7| I vtr 1 (añadir) to add. 2 (destinar) to appoint. II **agregarse** vr **a. a**, to join.

agresión nf aggression.

agresividad nf aggressiveness.

agresivo,-a adj aggressive.

agresor,-a I nm,f aggressor, attacker. II adj attacking.

agriarse vr to turn sour.

agrícola adj agricultural.

agricultor,-a nm,f farmer.

agricultura nf agriculture.

agridulce adj bittersweet.

agrietar I vtr to crack; (piel, labios) to chap. II **agrietarse** vr to crack; (piel) to get chapped.

agringarse [7] vr Am to behave like a gringo.

agrio,-a I adj sour. II nmpl **agrios**, citrus fruits.

agrónomo,-a nm,f (ingeniero a.), agronomist.

agropecuario,-a adj farming, agricultural.

agrupación nf association.

agrupar I vtr to group. II **agruparse** vr 1 (congregarse) to group together, form a group. 2 (asociarse) to associate.

agua nf water; **a. potable**, drinking water; **a. corriente/del grifo**, running/tap water; **a. dulce/salada**, fresh/salt water; **a. mineral sin/con gas**, still/fizzy or sparkling mineral water; **a. de colonia**, (eau de) cologne; fig **estar con el a. al cuello**, to be up to one's neck in it; **aguas jurisdiccionales**, territorial waters; **aguas residuales**, sewage sing.

aguacate nm (árbol) avocado; (fruto) avocado (pear).

aguacero nm shower, downpour.

aguado,-a adj watered down.

aguafiestas nmf inv spoilsport, wet blanket.

aguafuerte nm 1 Arte etching. 2 Quím nitric acid.

aguamarina nf aquamarine.

aguanieve nf sleet.

aguantar I vtr (soportar) to tolerate; **no lo aguanto más**, I can't stand it any longer. 2 (sostener) to support, hold; **aguanta esto**, hold this. 3 **aguanta la respiración**, hold your breath. II **aguantarse** vr 1 (contenerse) to keep back; (lágrimas) to hold back; **no pude aguantar la risa**, I couldn't help laughing. 2 (resignarse) to resign oneself.

aguante nm endurance; **tener mucho a.**, (ser paciente) to be very patient; (tener resistencia) to be strong, have a lot of stamina.

aguar [22] vtr to water down; fig **a. la fiesta a algn**, to spoil sb's fun.

aguardar I vtr to await. II vi to wait.

aguardiente nm liquor, brandy.

aguarrás nm turpentine.

aguatero,-a nm,f Am water carrier o seller.

agudeza nf 1 sharpness; (del dolor) acuteness. 2 fig (ingenio) witticism, witty say-

ing.

agudización nf 1 sharpening. 2 (empeoramiento) worsening.

agudizar |4| I vtr to intensify, make more acute. II **agudizarse** vr to intensify, become more acute.

agudo,-a adj (dolor) acute; (voz) high-pitched; (sonido) treble, high; fig (ingenioso) witty; fig (sentido) sharp, keen.

agüero nm omen.

aguijón nm sting; fig (estímulo) spur.

águila nf eagle; **á. real**, golden eagle.

aguileño,-a adj aquiline; **nariz aguileña**, aquiline nose.

aguinaldo nm Christmas box; **pedir el a.**, to go carol singing.

aguja nf 1 needle; (de reloj) hand; (de tocadiscos) stylus. 2 Arquit spire. 3 Ferroc point, US switch.

agujerear vtr to make holes in.

agujero nm 1 hole; **a. negro**, black hole. 2 Econ deficit, shortfall.

agujetas nfpl stiffness sing; **tener a.**, to be stiff.

agur interj fam bye!, see you!

aguzar |4| vtr (afilar) to sharpen. 2 fig **a. el oído**, to prick up one's ears; **a. la vista**, to look attentively; **aguzar el ingenio**, to sharpen one's wits.

ahí adv there; **a. está**, there he o she o it is; **ve por a.**, go that way; **está por a.**, it's over there; **setenta o por a.**, seventy or thereabouts; **de a.**, hence.

ahijado,-a nm,f godchild; (niño) godson; (niña) goddaughter; **ahijados**, godchildren.

ahínco nm eagerness; **con a.**, eagerly.

ahíto,-a adj (de comida) full, stuffed; (harto) fed up.

ahogado,-a I adj 1 (en líquido) drowned; **morir a.**, to drown. 2 (asfixiado) suffocated. II nm,f drowned person.

ahogar [7] vtr 1 (en líquido) to drown. 2 (asfixiar) to suffocate. II **ahogarse** vr 1 (en líquido) to drown, be drowned; fig **a. en un vaso de agua**, to make a mountain out of a molehill. 2 (asfixiarse) to suffocate. 3 (motor) to be flooded.

ahondar I vtr to deepen. II vi to go deep; fig **a. en un problema**, to go into a problem in depth.

ahora I adv 1 (en este momento) now; **a. mismo**, right now; **de a. en adelante**, from now on; **por a.**, for the time being. 2 **a. voy**, I'm coming; **a. vuelvo**, I'll be back in a minute. 3 **hasta a.**, (hasta el momento) until now, so far; (hasta luego) see you later. II conj **a. bien**, (sin embargo) however; (y bueno) well then.

ahorcado,-a I nm,f hanged person. II adj hanged.

ahorcar [1] I vtr to hang. II **ahorcarse** vr to hang oneself.

ahorita adv Am right now.

ahorrador,-a *adj* thrifty.

ahorrar I *vtr* to save. **II ahorrarse** *vr* **ahórrate los comentarios**, keep your comments to yourself.

ahorrativo,-a *adj* thrifty.

ahorro *nm* **1** saving; **a. energético**, energy saving. **2 ahorros**, savings; *Fin* **caja de a.**, savings bank.

ahuecar |1| *vtr* **1** to hollow out; *fam* **a. el ala**, to clear off, beat it. **2** (*voz*) to deepen.

ahuevado *adj Am* stupid.

ahumado,-a *adj* (*cristal, jamón*) smoked; (*bacon*) smoky; **salmón a.**, smoked salmon.

ahumar |16| *vtr* **1** to smoke. **II** *vi* (*echar humo*) to smoke, give off smoke.

ahuyentar *vtr* to scare away.

aindiado,-a *adj Am* Indian-like.

airado,-a *adj* angry.

airar |15| **1** *vtr* to anger. **II airarse** *vr* to get angry.

aire *nm* **1** air; **a. acondicionado**, air conditioning; **al a.**, (*hacia arriba*) into the air; (*al descubierto*) uncovered; **al a. libre**, in the open air; **en el a.**, (*pendiente*) in the air; *Rad* on the air; **hacerse a.**, to fan oneself; **saltar por los aires**, to blow up; **tomar el a.**, to get some fresh air; **necesito un cambio de aires**, I need a change of scene. **2** *Aut* choke. **3** (*viento*) wind; **hace a.**, it's windy. **4** (*aspecto*) air, appearance. **5 él va a su a.**, he goes his own sweet way. **6 darse aires**, to put on airs.

airear *vtr* (*ropa, lugar*) to air; *fig* (*asunto*) to publicize.

airoso,-a *adj* graceful, elegant; *fig* **salir a. de una situación**, to come out of a situation with flying colours.

aislacionismo *nm* isolationism.

aislado,-a *adj* **1** isolated. **2** *Téc* insulated.

aislamiento *nm* **1** isolation. **2** *Téc* insulation.

aislante I *adj* **cinta a.**, insulating tape. **II** *nm* insulator.

aislar |15| *vtr* **1** to isolate. **2** *Téc* to insulate.

ajar *vtr* to wear out.

ajedrez *nm* **1** (*juego*) chess. **2** (*piezas y tablero*) chess set.

ajeno,-a *adj* belonging to other people; **los bienes ajenos**, other peoples' goods; **por causas ajenas a nuestra voluntad**, for reasons beyond our control.

ajetreado,-a *adj* (very) busy, hectic.

ajetreo *nm* activity, hard work, bustle.

ajillo *nm Culin* **al a.**, fried with garlic.

ajo *nm* garlic; **cabeza/diente de a.**, head/clove of garlic; *fam* **estar en el a.**, to be in on it.

ajonjolí *nm* sesame.

ajorca *nf* bracelet; (*en el tobillo*) anklet.

ajuar *nm* (*de novia*) trousseau.

ajustado,-a *adj* tight.

ajustador,-a *nm,f* fitter.

ajustar *vtr* **1** to adjust. **2** (*apretar*) to tighten. **3** *Fin* (*cuenta*) to settle; *fig* **ajustarle las cuentas a algn**, to settle a score with sb.

ajuste *nm* **1** adjustment; *Téc* assembly; *TV* **carta de a.**, test card. **2** (*de precio*) fixing; (*de cuenta*) settlement; *fig* **a. de cuentas**, settling of scores.

ajusticiar |12| *vtr* to execute.

al (*contracción de a & el*) **1** → **a**. **2** (*al + infin*) **al salir**, on leaving; **está al caer**, it's about to happen; **al parecer**, apparently.

ala I *nf* **1** wing; *fig* **cortarle las alas a algn**, to clip sb's wings. **2** (*de sombrero*) brim. **II** *nmf Dep* winger.

alabanza *nf* praise.

alabar *vtr* to praise.

alabastro *nm* alabaster.

alacena *nf* (food) cupboard.

alacrán *nm* scorpion.

alambicado,-a *adj* intricate.

alambique *nm* still.

alambrada *nf*, **alambrado** *nm* wire fence.

alambrar *vtr* to fence with wire.

alambre *nm* wire; **a. de púas**, barbed wire.

alambrista *nmf* tightrope walker.

alameda *nf* **1** poplar grove. **2** (*paseo*) avenue, boulevard.

álamo *nm* poplar.

alano,-a *nm,f* (*perro*) **a.**, mastiff.

alarde *nm* (*ostentación*) bragging, boasting; **hacer a. de**, to show off.

alardear *vi* to brag, boast; **a. de rico** *o* **de riqueza**, to flaunt one's wealth.

alargadera *nf Elec* extension.

alargado,-a *adj* elongated.

alargar |7| **I** *vtr* **1** to lengthen; (*estirar*) to stretch; **ella alargó la mano para cogerlo**, she stretched out her hand to get it. **2** (*prolongar*) to prolong, extend. **3** (*dar*) to pass, hand over; **alárgame ese jersey**, can you pass me that jumper? **II alargarse** *vr* **1** to get longer. **2** (*prolongarse*) to go on. **3 ¿puedes a. a casa?**, can you give me a lift home?

alarido *nm* screech, shriek; **dar un a.**, to howl.

alarma *nf* alarm; **la a. saltó**, the alarm went off; **falsa a.**, false alarm; **señal de a.**, alarm (signal).

alarmado,-a *adj* alarmed.

alarmante *adj* alarming.

alarmar I *vtr* to alarm. **II alarmarse** *vr* to be alarmed.

alazán,-ana *adj & nm,f* (*caballo*) **a.**, chestnut.

alba *nf* dawn, daybreak.

albacea *nmf* (*hombre*) executor; (*mujer*) executrix.

albahaca *nf* basil.

albanés, -esa *adj & nm,f* Albanian.

Albania *n* Albania.

albañal *nm* sewer, drain.

albañil *nm* bricklayer.

albañilería *nf* bricklaying; **pared de a.**, (*obra*) brick wall.

albarán *nm* Com delivery note, despatch note.

albaricoque *nm* (*fruta*) apricot; (*árbol*) apricot tree.

albatros *nm inv* albatross.

albedrío *nm* will; **libre a.**, free will.

alberca *nf* (*small*) reservoir.

albergar [7] I *vtr* (*alojar*) to house, accommodate; *fig* (*sentimientos*) to cherish, harbour, US harbor. II **albergarse** *vtr* to stay.

albergue *nm* hostel; **a. juvenil**, youth hostel.

albino, -a *adj & nm,f* albino.

albóndiga *nf* meatball.

albores *nmpl* beginning *sing*; **en los a. de ...**, at the beginning of ...

albornoz *nm* bathrobe.

alborotado, -a *adj* 1 worked up, agitated. 2 (*desordenado*) untidy, messy. 3 (*mar*) rough; (*tiempo*) stormy.

alborotar I *vtr* 1 (*agitar*) to agitate, work up. 2 (*desordenar*) to make untidy, turn upside down. II *vi* to kick up a racket. III **alborotarse** *vr* 1 to get excited o worked up. 2 (*mar*) to get rough; (*tiempo*) to get stormy.

alboroto *nm* 1 (*jaleo*) din, racket. 2 (*desorden*) disturbance, uproar.

alborozo *nm* merriment, gaiety.

albufera *nf* lagoon.

álbum *nm* album.

alcachofa *nf* 1 Bot artichoke. 2 (*de tubo, regadera*) rose, sprinkler.

alcalde *nm* mayor.

alcaldesa *nf* mayoress.

alcaldía *nf* 1 (*cargo*) mayorship. 2 (*oficina*) mayor's office.

alcalino, -a *adj* alkaline.

alcance *nm* 1 reach; **al a. de cualquiera**, within everybody's reach; **dar a. a**, to catch up with; **fuera del a. de los niños**, out of the reach of children. 2 *fig* scope; (*de noticia*) importance.

alcancía *nf* money box; (*cerdito*) piggy bank.

alcanfor *nm* camphor.

alcantarilla *nf* sewer; (*boca*) drain.

alcantarillado *nm* sewer system.

alcanzar [4] I *vtr* 1 to reach; (*persona*) to catch up with; **la producción alcanza dos mil unidades**, production is up to two thousand units. 2 **alcánzame la sal**, (*pasar*) pass me the salt. 3 (*conseguir*) to attain, achieve. II *vi* (*ser suficiente*) to be sufficient; **con un kilo no alcanza para todos**, one kilo won't be enough for all of us.

alcaparra *nf* (*fruto*) caper; (*planta*) caper bush.

alcatraz *nm* Orn gannet.

alcazaba *nf* fortress, citadel.

alcázar *nm* 1 (*fortaleza*) fortress, citadel. 2 (*castillo*) castle, palace.

alcista I *adj* (*bolsa*) rising, bullish; **tendencia a.**, upward tendency. II *nmf* (*bolsa*) bull.

alcoba *nf* bedroom.

alcohol *nm* alcohol.

alcoholemia *nf* blood alcohol level; **prueba de a.**, breath test.

alcohólico, -a *adj & nm,f* alcoholic.

alcoholímetro *nm* Breathalyzer®.

alcoholismo *nm* alcoholism.

alcoholizado, -a *adj & nm,f* alcoholic.

alcornoque *nm* cork oak.

alcurnia *nf* lineage, ancestry; **de alta a.**, of noble lineage.

alcuzcuz *nm* couscous.

aldaba *nf* (*llamador*) door knocker.

aldabonazo *nm* 1 loud knock. 2 (*advertencia*) warning.

aldea *nf* village.

aldeano, -a I *adj* village. II *nm,f* villager.

aleación *nf* alloy.

aleatorio, -a *adj* random.

aleccionador, -a *adj* (*instructivo*) instructive; (*ejemplar*) exemplary.

aleccionar *vtr* (*instruir*) to teach, instruct; (*adiestrar*) to train.

aledaño, -a I *adj* adjoining, adjacent. II *nmpl* **aledaños**, outskirts.

alegar [7] *vtr* 1 (*aducir*) to claim; Jur to allege. 2 (*presentar*) to put forward.

alegato *nm* argument.

alegoría *nf* allegory.

alegrar I *vtr* 1 (*complacer*) to make happy o glad; **me alegra que se lo hayas dicho**, I am glad you told her. 2 *fig* (*avivar*) to enliven, brighten up. II **alegrarse** *vr* to be glad, be happy; **me alegro de verte**, I am pleased to see you; **me alegro por ti**, I am happy for you.

alegre *adj* 1 (*contento*) happy, glad. 2 (*color*) bright; (*música*) lively; (*lugar*) pleasant, cheerful. 3 *fig* (*borracho*) tipsy, merry.

alegría *nf* joy, happiness.

alejado, -a *adj* far away, remote.

alejar I *vtr* to move further away. II **alejarse** *vr* to go away, move away; **no te alejes de mí**, keep close to me.

aleluya *nm & f* hallelujah, alleluia.

alemán, -ana I *adj & nm,f* German. II *nm* (*idioma*) German.

Alemania *n* Germany; **A. del Este/Oeste**, East/West Germany; **A. Occidental/Oriental**, West/East Germany.

alentador, -a *adj* encouraging; **un panorama poco a.**, a rather bleak outlook.

alentar [1] *vtr fig* to encourage.

alergia *nf* allergy.

alérgico,-a *adj* allergic.

alero *nm* eaves *pl*.

alerón *nm Av* aileron.

alerta *nf & adj* alert; **estar en estado de a.**, to be (on the) alert.

alertar *vtr* to alert (**de**, to); **nos alertó del peligro**, he alerted us to the danger.

aleta *nf (de pez)* fin; *(de foca, de nadador)* flipper.

aletargado,-a *adj* lethargic.

aletargar [7] **I** *vtr* to make lethargic. **II aletargarse** *vr* to become lethargic.

aletear *vi* to flutter *o* flap its wings.

alevín *nm (pescado)* young fish; *fig (principiante)* beginner.

alevosía *nf (traición)* treachery; *(premeditación)* premeditation.

alevoso,-a *adj (persona)* treacherous; *(acto)* premeditated.

alfabético,-a *adj* alphabetic.

alfabetización *nf* teaching to read and write; **campaña de a.**, literacy campaign.

alfabeto *nm* alphabet.

alfalfa *nf* lucerne, alfalfa.

alfarería *nf* 1 *(arte)* pottery. 2 *(taller)* potter's workshop; *(tienda)* pottery shop.

alfarero,-a *nm,f* potter.

alféizar *nm* sill, windowsill.

alférez *nm* second lieutenant.

alfil *nm Ajedrez* bishop.

alfiler *nm* pin; *(broche)* pin, brooch; *(de corbata)* tiepin; *(para tender)* peg.

alfiletero *nm* pin box, pin case.

alfombra *nf* rug; *(moqueta)* carpet.

alfombrar *vtr* to carpet.

alfombrilla *nf* rug, mat.

alforja *nf (para caballos)* saddlebag; *(para hombro)* knapsack.

alga *nf* alga; *(marina)* seaweed.

algarabía *nf* hubbub, hullabaloo.

algarrobo *nm* carob tree.

algazara *nf* din, row.

álgebra *nf* algebra.

álgido,-a *adj* culminating, critical; **el punto a.**, the climax.

algo *pron indef* 1 *(afirmativo)* something; *(interrogativo)* anything; **a. así**, something like that; **¿a. más?**, anything else?; **por a. será**, there must be a reason for it; **fam a. es a.**, it's better than nothing. 2 *(cantidad indeterminada)* some; **¿queda a. de pastel?**, is there any cake left? **II** *adv (un poco)* quite, somewhat; **se siente a. mejor**, she's feeling a bit better.

algodón *nm* cotton; **a. (hidrófilo)**, cotton wool; **a. de azúcar**, candy floss.

algodonero,-a **I** *nm,f* cotton grower. **II** *adj* cotton.

alguacil *nm* bailiff.

alguien *pron indef (afirmativo)* somebody, someone; *(interrogativo)* anybody, anyone.

algún *adj (delante de nombres masculinos)*

→ **alguno,-a**.

alguno,-a I *adj* 1 *(delante de nombre)* *(afirmativo)* some; *(interrogativo)* any; **algunos días**, some days; **algunas veces**, some times; **alguna que otra vez**, now and then; **¿has tomado alguna medicina?**, have you taken any medicine?; **¿le has visto alguna vez?**, have you ever seen him? 2 *(después de nombre)* not at all; **no vino persona alguna**, nobody came. **II** *pron indef* 1 someone, somebody; **a. dirá que ...**, someone might say that ...; **a. que otro**, some. 2 **algunos,-as**, some (people).

alhaja *nf* jewel.

alhelí *nm (pl alhelíes)* wallflower, stock.

aliado,-a I *adj* allied. **II** *nm,f* **los Aliados**, the Allies.

alianza *nf* 1 *(pacto)* alliance. 2 *(anillo)* wedding ring.

aliarse [29] *vr* to become allies, form an alliance.

alias *adv & nm inv* alias.

alicaído,-a *adj* 1 *fig (débil)* weak, feeble. 2 *fig (deprimido)* down, depressed.

alicatar *vtr* to tile.

alicates *nmpl* pliers.

aliciente *nm* 1 *(atractivo)* lure, charm. 2 *(incentivo)* incentive.

alienación *nf* alienation.

alienado,-a *adj* insane, deranged.

alienar *vtr* to alienate.

alienígena *adj & nmf* alien.

aliento *nm* 1 breath; **sin a.**, breathless. 2 *(ánimo)* encouragement.

aligerar **I** *vtr (acelerar)* to speed up; **a. el paso**, to quicken one's pace. **II** *vi fam* **¡aligera!**, hurry up!

alijo *nm* haul; **un a. de drogas**, a consignment of drugs.

alimaña *nf* vermin.

alimentación *nf (comida)* food; *(acción)* feeding; *Téc* supply.

alimentar **I** *vtr* 1 *(dar alimento)* to feed; *(ser nutritivo)* to be nutritious. 2 *fig (sentimientos)* to nourish. 3 *Inform* to feed; *Téc* to supply. **II alimentarse** *vr* **a. con** *o* **de**, to live on.

alimentario,-a *adj* food.

alimenticio,-a *adj* nutritious; **productos alimenticios**, food products, foodstuffs; **valor a.**, nutritional value.

alimento *nm* 1 *(comida)* food. 2 *fig* **tiene poco a.**, it is not very nourishing.

alimón *adv* **al a.**, together.

alineación *nf* 1 alignment. 2 *Dep (equipo)* line-up.

alineado,-a *adj* aligned, lined-up; **países no alineados**, non-aligned countries.

alineamiento *nm* alignment.

alinear **I** *vtr* to align, line up. **II alinearse** *vr* to line up.

aliñar *vtr* to season, flavour, *US* flavor; *(ensalada)* to dress.

aliño *nm* seasoning, dressing.

alioli *nm* garlic mayonnaise.

alisar *vtr*, **alisarse** *vr* to smooth.

alistar I *vtr Mil* to recruit, enlist. II **alistarse** *vr Mil* to enlist, enrol, *US* enroll.

aliviar [12] I *vtr* (*dolor*) to soothe, relieve; (*carga*) to lighten, make lighter. II **aliviarse** *vr* (*dolor*) to diminish, get better.

alivio *nm* relief.

aljibe *nm* cistern, tank.

allá *adv* 1 (*lugar alejado*) there, over there; **a. abajo/arriba**, down/up there; **¡a. voy!**, here I go!; **más a.**, further on; **más a. de**, beyond; **el más a.**, the beyond. 2 (*tiempo*) **a. por los años veinte**, back in the twenties. 3 **a. tú**, that's your problem.

allanamiento *nm Jur* **a. de morada**, unlawful entry.

allanar *vtr* 1 (*terreno*) to level, flatten; *fig* (*camino*) to smooth. 2 *Jur* to break into.

allegado,-a I *adj* close. II *nm,f* close friend.

allende *adv fml* beyond; **a. los mares**, overseas.

allí *adv* there, over there; **a. abajo/arriba**, down/up there; **de a. para acá**, back and forth; **por a.**, (*movimiento*) that way; (*posición*) over there.

alma *nf* soul; **no había ni un a.**, there was not a soul.

almacén *nm* 1 (*local*) warehouse; (*habitación*) storeroom. 2 *Com* (*grandes*) **almacenes**, department store *sing*.

almacenaje *nm* storage, warehousing.

almacenamiento *nm* storage, warehousing; *Inform* storage.

almacenar *vtr* to store.

almacenista *nmf* (*vendedor*) wholesaler; (*propietario*) warehouse owner.

almanaque *nm* calendar.

almeja *nf* clam; *vulg* cunt.

almena *nf* merlon.

almendra *nf* almond; **a. garapiñada**, sugared almond.

almendro *nm* almond tree.

almiar *nm* haystack.

almíbar *nm* syrup.

almidón *nm* starch.

almidonar *vtr* to starch.

alminar *nm* minaret.

almirante *nm* admiral.

almizcle *nm* musk.

almohada *nf* pillow; *fam* **consultarlo con la a.**, to sleep on it.

almohadilla *nf* (*small*) cushion.

almohadón *nm* large pillow, cushion.

almorrana *nf fam* pile.

almorzar [2] I *vi* to have lunch. II *vtr* to have for lunch.

almuerzo *nm* lunch.

alocado,-a *adj* thoughtless, rash.

alocución *nf* speech, address.

alojamiento *nm* accommodation; **dar a.**, to accommodate.

alojar I *vtr* to accommodate. II **alojarse** *vr* to stay.

aló *interj Am Tel* hello.

alondra *nf* lark; **a. común**, skylark.

alpaca *nf* alpaca.

alpargata *nf* canvas sandal, espadrille.

Alpes *npl* **los A.**, the Alps.

alpinismo *nm* mountaineering, climbing.

alpinista *nmf* mountaineer, climber.

alpino,-a *adj* Alpine; **esquí a.**, downhill skiing.

alquilar *vtr* to hire; (*pisos, casas*) to rent; **'se alquila'**, 'to let'.

alquiler *nm* 1 (*de pisos, casas*) renting, letting; **a. de coches**, car hire; **de a.**, (*pisos, casas*) to let, rented; (*coche*) for hire; (*televisión*) for rent. 2 (*precio*) hire, rental; (*de pisos, casas*) rent.

alquimia *nf* alchemy.

alquitrán *nm* tar.

alrededor I *adv* (*lugar*) round, around; **mira a.**, look around; **a. de la mesa**, round the table; **a. de las dos**, around two o'clock; **a. de quince**, about fifteen; II *nmpl* **alrededores**, surrounding area *sing*; **en los alrededores de Murcia**, in the area round Murcia.

alta *nf* **dar de** o **el a.**, (*a un enfermo*) to discharge from hospital.

altanería *nf* arrogance.

altanero,-a *adj* arrogant.

altar *nm* altar.

altavoz *nm* loudspeaker.

alterable *adj* changeable.

alteración *nf* 1 (*cambio*) alteration. 2 (*alboroto*) quarrel, row; **a. del orden público**, disturbance of the peace. 3 (*excitación*) agitation.

alterar I *vtr* to alter, change; **a. el orden público**, to disturb the peace. II **alterarse** *vr* 1 (*cambiar*) to change. 2 (*inquietarse*) to be upset.

altercado *nm* quarrel, argument.

alternar I *vtr* to alternate. II *vi* (*relacionarse*) to meet people, socialize. III **alternarse** *vr* to alternate.

alternativa *nf* alternative.

alternativo,-a *adj* alternative.

alterno,-a *adj* alternate; **días alternos**, alternate days.

alteza *nf* Highness; **Su A. Real**, His o Her Royal Highness.

altibajos *nmpl fig* ups and downs.

altiplano *nm* high plateau.

altísimo,-a *nm* **el A.**, the Almighty.

altisonante *adj* grandiloquent.

altitud *nf* altitude.

altivez *nf* arrogance, haughtiness.

altivo,-a *adj* arrogant, haughty.

alto¹ *nm* 1 (*interrupción*) stop, break. 2 *Mil* halt; **dar el a.**, to order to halt; **un a. el fuego**, a cease-fire.

alto,-a² I *adj* 1 (*persona, árbol, edificio*) tall; (*montaña, techo, presión*) high; (*sonido*) loud; (*tono*) high-pitched; **los pisos altos**, the top floors; **en lo a.**, at the top; **alta sociedad**, high society; **clase alta**, upper class; **en voz alta**, aloud, in a loud voice; **a altas horas de la noche**, late at night. II *adv* 1 high, high up. 2 (*sonar, hablar etc*) loud, loudly; **pon la radio más alta**, turn the radio up; **¡habla más a.!**, speak up. III *nm* 1 (*altura*) height; **¿cuánto tiene de a.?**, how tall/high is it?; *fig* **por todo lo a.**, in a grand way. 2 (*elevación*) hill.
◆**altamente** *adv* highly, extremely.
altoparlante *nm Am* loudspeaker.
altozano *nm* hillock, hill.
altramuz *nm* lupin.
altruista I *adj* altruistic. II *nmf* altruist.
altura *nf* 1 height; **de diez metros de a.**, ten metres high. 2 (*nivel*) level; **a la misma a.**, on the same level; *Geog* on the same latitude; **a la a. del cine**, by the cinema; *fig* **estar a la a. de las circunstancias**, to meet the challenge; *fig* **no está a su a.**, he does not measure up to him; *fig* **a estas alturas**, at this stage. 3 *Rel* **alturas**, *arch* heaven *sing*.
alubia *nf* bean.
alucinación *nf* hallucination.
alucinado,-a I *adj arg* amazed.
alucinante *adj arg* brilliant, mind-blowing.
alucinar I *vtr* to hallucinate; *fig* (*encantar*) to fascinate. II *vi arg* to be amazed, be spaced out.
alucinógeno,-a I *adj* hallucinogenic. II *nm* hallucinogen.
alud *nm* avalanche.
aludido,-a *adj fig* **darse por a.**, to take it personally.
aludir *vi* to allude to, mention.
alumbrado,-a I *adj* lit. II *nm Elec* lighting; **a. público**, street lighting.
alumbrar I *vtr* (*iluminar*) to light, illuminate. II *vi* (*parir*) to give birth.
aluminio *nm* aluminium, *US* aluminum.
alumnado *nm* (*de colegio*) pupils *pl*; *Univ* student body.
alumno,-a *nm,f* 1 (*de colegio*) pupil; **a. externo**, day pupil; **a. interno**, boarder. 2 *Univ* student.
alusión *nf* allusion, mention.
aluvión *nm* downpour; *fig* **un a. de preguntas**, a barrage of questions.
alverja, alverjana *nf Am* pea.
alza *nf* 1 rise; **en a.**, rising; **jugar a al a.**, (*bolsa*) to bull the market. 2 *Mil* sight.
alzado,-a I *adj* raised, lifted; **votación a mano alzada**, vote by a show of hands. II *nm Arquit* elevation.
alzamiento *nm* (*rebelión*) uprising.
alzar [4] I *vtr* to raise, lift; **a. el vuelo**, to take off; **a. los ojos/la vista**, to look up;

álzate el cuello, turn your collar up. II **alzarse** *vr* 1 (*levantarse*) to get up, rise. 2 (*rebelarse*) to rise, rebel. 3 **a. con la victoria**, to win, be victorious.
ama *nf* (*señora*) lady of the house; (*dueña*) owner; **a. de casa**, housewife; **a. de llaves**, housekeeper.
amabilidad *nf* kindness; *fml* **tenga la a. de esperar**, would you be so kind as to wait?
amable *adj* kind, nice; *fml* **¿sería usted tan a. de ayudarme?**, would you be so kind as to help me?
a.m. *adv* a.m.
amado,-a I *adj* loved, beloved. II *nm,f* sweetheart.
amaestrar *vtr* to train; (*domar*) to tame.
amagar [7] *vtr* (*amenazar*) to threaten; **amaga tormenta**, a storm is threatening.
amago *nm* 1 (*indicio*) first sign; **a. de infarto**, onset of a heart attack. 2 (*intento*) attempt. 3 *fig* (*amenaza*) threat.
amainar *vi* (*viento etc*) to drop, die down.
amalgama *nf* amalgam.
amalgamar *vtr* to amalgamate.
amamantar *vtr* to breast-feed; *Zool* to suckle.
amancay *nm Am* amaryllis.
amancebarse *vr* to cohabit.
amanecer [33] I *v impers* to dawn; **¿a qué hora amanece?**, when does it get light?; **amaneció lluvioso**, it was rainy at daybreak. II *vi* **amanecimos en Finlandia**, we were in Finland at daybreak; **amaneció muy enfermo**, he woke up feeling very ill. III *nm* dawn, daybreak; **al a.**, at dawn.
amanerado,-a *adj* mannered, affected.
amansar *vtr* 1 to tame. 2 *fig* (*apaciguar*) to tame, calm.
amante *nmf* lover; **a. del arte**, art lover.
amañar *vtr* to fix, fiddle; (*elecciones*) to rig.
amapola *nf* poppy.
amar I *vtr* to love. II **amarse** *vr* to love each other.
amaraje *nm Av* landing at sea.
amargado,-a I *adj* (*rencoroso*) embittered, bitter; *fam* (*agobiado*) pissed off; **estoy a. con los exámenes**, I'm pissed off with the exams. II *nm,f* bitter person.
amargar [7] I *vtr* to make bitter; *fig* to embitter, sour. II **amargarse** *vr fig* to become embittered *o* bitter; **no te amargues por eso**, don't let that make you bitter.
amargo,-a *adj* bitter.
amargor *nm*, **amargura** *nf* bitterness.
amarillento,-a *adj* yellowish.
amarillo,-a *adj & nm* yellow; **prensa amarilla**, gutter press.
amarilloso,-a *adj Am* yellowish.
amarra *nf* mooring rope; **soltar amarras**, to cast off, let go.

amarradero nm mooring.

amarrar vtr Náut 1 to moor, tie up; (atar) to tie (up), bind.

amasar vtr 1 Culin to knead. 2 fig (fortuna) to amass.

amasijo nm fam hotchpotch, jumble.

amateur adj & nmf amateur.

amatista nf amethyst.

amazona nf 1 (jinete) horsewoman. 2 (en mitología) Amazon.

Amazonas n el A., the Amazon.

amazónico,-a adj Amazonian.

ambages nmpl hablar sin a., to go straight to the point.

ámbar nm amber.

Amberes n Antwerp.

ambición nf ambition.

ambicionar vtr to have as an ambition; **ambiciona ser presidente**, his ambition is to become president.

ambicioso,-a I adj ambitious. **II** nm,f ambitious person.

ambidextro,-a nm,f ambidextrous person.

ambientación nf Cin Teat setting.

ambientado,-a adj (bar etc) lively.

ambiental adj environmental.

ambientar I vtr 1 (bar etc) to liven up. 2 Cin Teat to set. **II ambientarse** vr (adaptarse) to get used to.

ambiente I nm environment; fig (medio) environment, milieu. **II** adj environmental; **temperatura a.**, room temperature.

ambigüedad nf ambiguity.

ambiguo,-a adj ambiguous.

ámbito nm field; **empresa de a. nacional**, nationwide company.

ambos,-as adj pl fml both; **por a. lados**, on both sides.

ambulancia nf ambulance.

ambulante adj travelling, US traveling, mobile; **biblioteca a.**, mobile library.

ambulatorio nm surgery, clinic.

amedrentar vtr to frighten, scare.

amén[1] nm amen.

amén[2] adv **a. de**, in addition to.

amenaza nf threat.

amenazador,-a, amenazante adj threatening, menacing.

amenazar [4] vtr to threaten; **a. de muerte a algn**, to threaten to kill sb.

amenizar [4] vtr to liven up.

ameno,-a adj entertaining.

América n America; **A. Central/del Norte/del Sur**, Central/North/South America.

americana nf (prenda) jacket.

americano,-a adj & nm,f American.

amerindio,-a adj & nm,f Amerindian, American Indian.

amerizar [4] vi → **amarar**.

ametralladora nf machine gun.

ametrallar vtr to machine-gun.

amianto nm asbestos sing.

amigable adj friendly.

amígdala nf tonsil.

amigdalitis nf tonsillitis.

amigo,-a I nm,f friend; **hacerse a. de**, to make friends with; **hacerse amigos**, to become friends; **son muy amigos**, they are very good friends. **II** adj (aficionado) fond (**de**, of).

amilanar I vtr to frighten, scare. **II amilanarse** vr to be frightened.

aminorar vtr to reduce; **a. el paso**, to slow down.

amistad nf 1 friendship. 2 **amistades**, friends.

amistoso,-a adj friendly.

amnesia nf amnesia.

amnistía nf amnesty.

amo nm 1 (dueño) owner. 2 (señor) master.

amodorrarse vr to become sleepy o drowsy.

amoldar I vtr to adapt, adjust. **II amoldarse** vr to adapt oneself.

amonestación nf 1 rebuke, reprimand; Dep warning. 2 Rel **amonestaciones**, banns.

amonestar vtr 1 (advertir) to rebuke, reprimand; Dep to warn. 2 Rel to publish the banns of.

amoníaco, amoniaco nm ammonia.

amontonar I vtr to pile up, heap up. **II amontonarse** vr to pile up, heap up; (gente) to crowd together.

amor nm love; **hacer el a.**, to make love; **a. propio**, self-esteem; **¡por el a. de Dios!**, for God's sake!

amoral adj amoral.

amoratado,-a adj (de frío) blue with cold; (de un golpe) black and blue.

amordazar [4] vtr (perro) to muzzle; (persona) to gag.

amorfo,-a adj amorphous.

amorío nm love affair, flirtation.

amoroso,-a adj loving, affectionate.

amortajar vtr to shroud, wrap in a shroud.

amortiguador nm Aut shock absorber.

amortiguar [22] vtr (golpe) to cushion; (ruido) to muffle; (luz) to subdue.

amortización nf payment.

amortizar [4] vtr to pay off.

amotinado,-a nm,f rioter; Mil mutineer.

amotinamiento nm riot, rioting; Mil mutiny.

amotinar I vtr to incite to riot; Mil to incite to mutiny. **II amotinarse** vr to rise up; Mil to mutiny.

amparar I vtr to protect. **II ampararse** vr to seek refuge.

amparo nm protection, shelter; **al a. de la ley**, under the protection of the law.

amperio nm ampère, amp.

ampliación nf enlargement; (de plazo, casa) extension.

ampliar [29] vtr to enlarge; (casa, plazo)

to extend.
amplificador *nm* amplifier.
amplificar [1] *vtr* to amplify.
amplio,-a *adj* large, roomy; *(ancho)* wide, broad; **en el sentido más a. de la palabra**, in the broadest sense of the word.
amplitud *nf* 1 spaciousness; **a. de miras**, broad-mindedness. 2 *(de espacio)* room, space. 3 *Fís* amplitude.
ampolla *nf* 1 *Med* blister; *fig* **levantar ampollas**, to raise people's hackles. 2 *(de medicina)* ampoule.
ampuloso,-a *adj* pompous, bombastic.
amputar *vtr Med* to amputate; *fig* to cut out.
amueblar *vtr* to furnish.
amuermar *vtr fam* 1 *(atontar)* to make feel dopey *o* groggy. 2 *(aburrir)* to bore.
amuleto *nm* amulet; **a. de la suerte**, lucky charm.
amurallar *vtr* to wall, fortify.
anacronismo *nm* anachronism.
ánade *nm* duck; **á. real**, mallard.
anales *nmpl* annals.
analfabetismo *nm* illiteracy.
analfabeto,-a *nm,f* illiterate.
analgésico,-a *adj & nm* analgesic.
análisis *nm inv* analysis; **a. de sangre**, blood test.
analista *nmf* analyst.
analizar [4] *vtr* to analyze.
analogía *nf* analogy.
analógico,-a *adj* analog.
análogo,-a *adj* analogous, similar.
ananá *nm (pl ananaes)*, **ananás** *nm (pl ananases)* pineapple.
anaquel *nm* shelf.
anaranjado,-a *adj & nm* orange.
anarquía *nf* anarchy.
anarquismo *nm* anarchism.
anarquista *adj & nmf* anarchist.
anatomía *nf* anatomy.
anatómico,-a *adj* anatomical.
anca *nf* haunch; **ancas de rana**, frogs' legs.
ancestral *adj* ancestral.
ancho,-a I *adj* wide, broad; **a lo a.**, breadthwise; **te está muy a.**, it's too big for you. II *nm* 1 *(anchura)* width, breadth; **dos metros de a.**, two metres wide; **¿qué a. tiene?**, how wide is it? 2 *Cost* width. III *nfpl fam* **a mis o tus anchas**, at ease, comfortable.
anchoa *nf* anchovy.
anchura *nf* width, breadth.
anciano,-a I *adj* very old. II *nm,f* old person; **los ancianos**, old people.
ancla *nf* anchor.
anclar *vtr & vi* to anchor.
andadas *nfpl* **volver a las a.**, to go back to one's old tricks.
andaderas *nfpl* baby-walker *sing*.
andadura *nf* walking.
Andalucía *n* Andalusia.

andaluz,-a *adj & nm,f* Andalusian.
andamiaje, andamio *nm* scaffolding.
andanza *nf* adventure, happening.
andar [8] I *vi* 1 to walk. 2 *(coche etc)* to move; **este coche anda despacio**, this car goes very slowly. 3 *(funcionar)* to work; **esto no anda**, this doesn't work. 4 *fam* **anda por los cuarenta**, he's about forty; **anda siempre diciendo que ...**, he's always saying that ...; **¿cómo andamos de tiempo?**, how are we off for time?; **tu bolso debe a. por ahí**, your bag must be over there somewhere. II *vtr (recorrer)* to walk.
andariego,-a *adj* fond of walking.
andén *nm* platform.
Andes *npl* Andes.
andinismo *nm Am* mountaineering.
andino,-a *adj & nm,f* Andean.
andrajo *nm* rag, tatter.
andrajoso,-a *adj* ragged, tattered.
androide *nm* android.
andurriales *nmpl fam* out-of-the way place *sing*.
anécdota *nf* anecdote.
anecdótico,-a *adj* anecdotal.
anegar *vtr*, **anegarse** *vr* [7] to flood.
anejo,-a I *adj* attached, joined (a, to). II *nm* appendix.
anemia *nf* anaemia, *US* anemia.
anestesia *nf* anaesthesia, *US* anesthesia.
anestésico,-a *adj & nm* anaesthetic, *US* anesthetic.
anexar *vtr* to annex.
anexión *nf* annexation.
anexionar *vtr* to annex.
anexo,-a I *adj* attached, joined (a, to). II *nm* appendix.
anfetamina *nf* amphetamine.
anfibio,-a I *adj* amphibious. II *nm* amphibian.
anfiteatro *nm* 1 amphitheatre, *US* amphitheater. 2 *Cin Teat* gallery.
anfitrión,-ona I *nm* host. II *nf* hostess.
ángel *nm* 1 angel; **á. de la guarda**, guardian angel. 2 *Am (micrófono)* hand microphone.
angelical, angélico,-a *adj* angelic.
angina *nf* angina; **tener anginas**, to have tonsilitis; *Med* **a. de pecho**, angina pectoris.
anglófono,-a I *adj* English speaking. II *nm,f* English speaker.
anglosajón,-ona *adj & nm,f* Anglo-Saxon.
angosto,-a *adj fml* narrow.
anguila *nf* eel; **a. de mar**, conger eel.
angula *nf* elver.
angular *adj* angular; *Fot* **(objetivo) gran a.**, wide-angle lens; **piedra a.**, cornerstone.
ángulo *nm* angle; *(rincón)* corner.

angustia nf anguish.

angustiar [12] vtr to distress.

angustioso,-a adj distressing.

anhelar vtr to long for, yearn for.

anhelo nm longing, yearning.

anhídrido nm a. **carbónico,** carbon dioxide.

anidar vi to nest.

anilla nf ring; **carpeta de anillas,** ring-binder.

anillo nm ring; a. **de boda,** wedding ring.

ánima nf soul.

animación nf (diversión) entertainment.

animado,-a adj (fiesta etc) lively.

animador,-a nm,f 1 entertainer; TV presenter; a. **cultural,** cultural organiser. 2 Dep cheerleader.

animadversión nf ill feeling, animosity.

animal I nm animal; fig (basto) brute; (necio) dunce. II adj animal.

animar I vtr 1 (alentar) to encourage. 2 (alegrar) (persona) to cheer up; (fiesta, bar) to liven up, brighten up. II **animarse** vr 1 (persona) to cheer up; (fiesta, reunión) to brighten up. 2 ¿te **animas a venir?,** do you fancy coming along?

anímico,-a adj **estado a.,** frame o state of mind.

ánimo nm 1 (espíritu) spirit; **estado de á.,** frame o state of mind. 2 **con á. de,** (intención) with the intention of. 3 (valor, coraje) courage; **dar ánimos a,** to encourage; ¡a.!, cheer up!.

animosidad nf animosity.

animoso,-a adj cheerful.

aniñado,-a adj childlike; pey childish.

aniquilación nf annihilation.

aniquilar vtr to annihilate.

anís nm 1 (bebida) anisette. 2 (grano) aniseed.

anisete nm anisette.

aniversario nm anniversary.

ano nm anus.

anoche adv last night; (por la tarde) yesterday evening; **antes de a.,** the night before last.

anochecer [33] I v impers to get dark; **cuando anochece,** at nightfall, at dusk. II vi to be somewhere at dusk; **anochecimos en Cuenca,** we were in Cuenca at dusk. III nm nightfall, dusk.

anodino,-a adj (insustancial) insubstantial; (soso) insipid, dull.

anomalía nf anomaly.

anómalo,-a adj anomalous.

anonadado,-a adj me **quedé/dejó a.,** I was astonished.

anonimato nm anonimity; **permanecer en el a.,** to remain anonymous o nameless.

anónimo,-a adj 1 (desconocido) anonymous. 2 Com **sociedad anónima,** public liability company, US corporation. II nm (carta) anonymous letter.

anorak nm (pl **anoraks**) anorak.

anorexia nf anorexia.

anormal I adj 1 abnormal. 2 (inhabitual) unusual; **una situación a.,** an irregular situation. 3 Med subnormal. II nmf Med subnormal person.

anotación nf 1 annotation. 2 (apunte) note.

anotar vtr 1 to annotate. 2 (apuntar) to take down, make a note of.

anquilosado,-a adj fig fossilized; a. **en el pasado,** locked in the past.

anquilosarse vr fig to stagnate.

ansia nf 1 (deseo) longing, yearning. 2 (ansiedad) anxiety. 3 Med sick feeling.

ansiar [29] vtr to long for, yearn for.

ansiedad nf anxiety; **con a.,** anxiously.

ansioso,-a adj (deseoso) eager (**por,** for). 2 (avaricioso) greedy.

antagónico,-a adj antagonistic.

antagonismo nm antagonism.

antagonista I adj antagonistic. II nmf antagonist.

antaño adv in the past, formerly.

antártico,-a I adj Antarctic. II nm **el A.,** the Antarctic.

Antártida n Antarctica.

ante¹ nm 1 Zool elk, moose. 2 (piel) suede.

ante² prep 1 before, in the presence of; Jur a. **notario,** in the presence of a notary; a. **todo,** most of all. 2 (en vista de) faced with, in view of; a. **la crisis energética,** faced with the energy crisis.

anteanoche adv the night before last.

anteayer adv the day before yesterday.

antecedente I adj previous. II nm antecedent. III nmpl **antecedentes,** (historial) record sing; Jur **antecedentes penales,** criminal record sing. 2 fig **poner en antecedentes,** to put in the picture.

anteceder vtr to precede, go before.

antecesor,-a nm,f (en un cargo) predecessor. 2 (antepasado) ancestor.

antedicho,-a adj abovementioned.

antelación nf notice; **con poca a.,** at short notice; **con un mes de a.,** a month beforehand, with a month's notice.

antemano adv **de a.,** beforehand, in advance.

antena nf 1 Rad TV aerial; a. **parabólica,** dish aerial; **en a.,** on the air. 2 Zool antenna, feeler.

anteojo nm 1 telescope. 2 **anteojos,** (binoculares) binoculars, field glasses; Am (gafas) glasses, spectacles.

antepasado,-a nm,f ancestor.

antepecho nm (de ventana) sill; (pretil) parapet, guardrail.

antepenúltimo,-a adj antepenultimate; **el capítulo a.,** the last chapter but two.

anteponer [19] (pp **antepuesto**) vtr fig to give preference to.

anteproyecto nm preliminary plan, draft;

Pol **a. de ley,** draft bill.
antepuesto,-a *pp* → **anteponer.**
antepuse *pt indef* → **anteponer.**
anterior *adj* 1 previous; **el día a.,** the day before. 2 *(delantero)* front; **parte a.,** front part. ◆**anteriormente** *adv* previously, before.
anterioridad *nf* **con a.,** before; **con a. a,** prior to, before.
antes *adv* 1 *(tiempo)* before; **a. de las tres,** before three o'clock; **mucho a.,** long before; **la noche a.,** the night before; **cuanto a.,** as soon as possible. 2 *(antaño)* in the past; **a. llovía más,** it used to rain more in the past. 3 *(lugar)* before; **a. del semáforo,** before the traffic lights. 4 **a. prefiero hacerlo yo,** I'd rather do it myself; **a. (bien),** on the contrary.
antesala *nf* antechamber, anteroom; *fig* **en la a. de,** on the eve of.
anti- *pref* anti-.
antiadherente *adj* nonstick.
antiaéreo,-a *adj* anti-aircraft.
antibiótico,-a *adj & nm* antibiotic.
anticaspa *adj* anti-dandruff.
anticiclón *nm* anticyclone, high pressure area.
anticipación *nf* bringing forward; **con a.,** in advance.
anticipado,-a *adj* brought forward; **elecciones anticipadas,** early elections; **gracias anticipadas,** thanks in advance; *Com* **por a.,** in advance. ◆**anticipadamente** *adv* in advance.
anticipar I *vtr (acontecimiento)* to bring forward; *(dinero)* to pay in advance; **no anticipemos acontecimientos,** we'll cross that bridge when we come to it. II **anticiparse** *vr* 1 *(adelantarse)* to beat to it; **iba a decírtelo, pero él se me anticipó,** I was going to tell you, but he beat me to it. 2 *(llegar pronto)* to arrive early; *fig* **a. a su tiempo,** to be ahead of one's time.
anticipo *nm (adelanto)* advance; **pedir un a.,** to ask for an advance on one's wages).
anticonceptivo,-a *adj & nm* contraceptive.
anticongelante *adj & nm (de radiador)* antifreeze; *(de parabrisas)* de-icer.
anticonstitucional *adj* unconstitutional.
anticuado,-a *adj* antiquated.
anticuario,-a *nm,f* antique dealer.
anticuerpo *nm* antibody.
antídoto *nm* antidote.
antier *adv* the day before yesterday.
antiestético,-a *adj* ugly, unsightly.
antifaz *nm* mask.
antigás *adj* careta/mascarilla a., gas mask.
antigualla *nf* old-fashioned thing.
antigüedad *nf* 1 *(período histórico)* antiquity; **en la a.,** in olden days, in for-

mer times. 2 *(en cargo)* seniority. 3 **tienda de antigüedades,** antique shop.
antiguo,-a *adj* 1 old, ancient. 2 *(pasado de moda)* old-fashioned. 3 *(en cargo)* senior. 4 *(anterior)* former.
antihigiénico,-a *adj* unhygienic, unhealthy.
antihistamínico,-a *adj & nm* antihistamine.
Antillas *npl* **las A.,** the West Indies, the Antilles.
antinatural *adj* unnatural, contrary to nature.
antiniebla *adj inv* **luces a.,** foglamps, *US* foglights.
antipatía *nf* antipathy, dislike; **tener a. a,** to dislike.
antipático,-a *adj* unpleasant; **Pedro me es a.,** I don't like Pedro.
antípodas *npl* **las A.,** the Antipodes.
antiquísimo,-a *(superl de antiguo) adj* very old, ancient.
antirrobo I *adj inv* antitheft; **alarma a.,** burglar alarm; *(para casa)* burglar alarm. II *nm (para coche) adj* car alarm; *(para casa)* burglar alarm.
antisemita I *adj* anti-Semitic. II *nmf* anti-Semite.
antiséptico,-a *adj & nm* antiseptic.
antítesis *nf inv* antithesis.
antojadizo,-a *adj* capricious, unpredictable.
antojarse *vr* 1 **cuando se me antoja,** when I feel like it; **se le antojó un helado,** he fancied an ice-cream. 2 *(suponer)* **se me antoja que no lo sabe,** I have the feeling that he doesn't know.
antojo *nm* 1 *(capricho)* whim, caprice; *(de embarazada)* craving; **a su a.,** in one's own way, as one pleases. 2 *(en la piel)* birthmark.
antología *nf* anthology.
antonomasia *nf* **por a.,** par excellence.
antorcha *nf* torch.
antro *nm* dump, hole; *fig* **a. de perdición,** den of vice.
antropología *nf* anthropology.
antropólogo,-a *nm,f* anthropologist.
anual *adj* annual; **ingresos anuales,** yearly income.
anualidad *nf* annual payment, annuity.
anuario *nm* yearbook.
anudar *vtr* 1 *(atar)* to knot, tie. 2 *fig (unir)* to join, bring together.
anulación *nf* cancellation; *(de matrimonio)* annulment; *(de ley)* repeal.
anular¹ *nm* ring finger.
anular² *vtr* 1 *Com (pedido)* to cancel; *Dep (gol)* to disallow; *(matrimonio)* to annul; *Jur (ley)* to repeal. 2 *Inform* to delete.
anunciador,-a *adj* **empresa anunciadora,** advertising company.
anunciante *nmf* advertiser.
anunciar |12| I *vtr* 1 *(producto etc)* to

advertise. 2 (avisar) to announce. II **anunciarse** vr to advertise oneself; **a. en un periódico**, to put an advert in a newspaper.

anuncio nm 1 (comercial) advertisement, advert, ad. 2 (aviso) announcement. 3 (cartel) notice, poster.

anzuelo nm (fish) hook.

añadidura nf addition; **por a.**, besides, on top of everything else.

añadir vtr to add (a, to).

añejo,-a adj 1 (vino, queso) mature. 2 (estropeado) stale.

añicos nmpl smithereens; **hacer a.**, to smash to smithereens.

añil I adj indigo, blue. II nm 1 Bot indigo plant. 2 (color) indigo.

año nm 1 year; **el a. pasado**, last year; **el a. que viene**, next year; **hace años**, a long time ago, years ago; **los años noventa**, the nineties; **todo el a.**, all the year (round); **a. luz**, light year. 2 ¿cuántos años tienes?, how old are you?; **tiene seis años**, he's six years old; **entrado en años**, getting on.

añoranza nf longing, yearning.

añorar vtr (pasado) to long for, yearn for; (país) to feel homesick for, miss.

apabullar vtr to bewilder.

apacentar |1| vtr to put out to pasture, graze.

apacible adj mild, calm.

apaciguar |22| I vtr (calmar) to pacify, appease. II **apaciguarse** vr (persona) to calm down; (tormenta) to abate.

apadrinar vtr 1 (bautizo) to act as godfather to; (en boda) to be best man for. 2 (artista) to sponsor.

apagado,-a adj 1 (luz, cigarro) out. 2 (color) dull; (voz) sad; (mirada) expressionless, lifeless; (carácter, persona) spiritless.

apagar |7| vtr (fuego) to put out; (luz, tele etc) to turn off, switch off; (color) to soften; (sed) to quench.

apagón nm power cut, blackout.

apaisado,-a adj 1 oblong. 2 (papel) landscape.

apalabrar vtr (concertar) to make a verbal agreement on.

apalancar |1| I vtr to lever up. II **apalancarse** vr arg to ensconce oneself, settle down.

apalear[1] vtr to beat, thrash.

apalear[2] vtr Agr (grano) to winnow.

apañar I vtr to mend, fix. II **apañarse** vr fam apañárselas; to manage.

apaño nm mend, repair.

aparador nm (mueble) sideboard; (de tienda) shop window.

aparato nm 1 (piece of) apparatus; (dispositivo) device; (instrumento) instrument; **a. de radio/televisión**, radio/television set; **a. digestivo**, digestive system; **a. eléctrico**, thunder and lightning. 2 Tel ¿quién

está al a.?, who's speaking? 3 (ostentación) display.

aparatoso,-a adj 1 (pomposo) ostentatious, showy. 2 (espectacular) spectacular. 3 (grande) bulky.

aparcamiento nm (en la calle) parking place; (parking) car park, US parking lot.

aparcar |1| vtr to park.

aparcería nf Agr sharecropping.

apareamiento nm 1 (de cosas) pairing off. 2 (de animales) mating.

aparear vtr, **aparearse** vr to mate.

aparecer [33] I vi 1 to appear; **no aparece en mi lista**, he is not on my list. 2 to turn up, show up; ¿apareció el dinero?, did the money turn up?; **no apareció nadie**, nobody turned up. II **aparecerse** vr to appear.

aparejado,-a adj llevar o traer a., to entail.

aparejador,-a nm,f quantity surveyor.

aparejar vtr 1 (caballo) to harness. 2 (emparejar) to pair off.

aparejo nm 1 (equipo) equipment. 2 (de caballo) harness.

aparentar I vtr 1 (fingir) to affect. 2 (tener aspecto) to look; **no aparenta esa edad**, she doesn't look that age. II vi to show off.

aparente adj 1 apparent; **sin motivo a.**, for no apparent reason. 2 fam (conveniente) suitable.

aparición nf 1 appearance. 2 (visión) apparition.

apariencia nf appearance; **en a.**, apparently; fig **guardar las apariencias**, to keep up appearances.

apartado,-a I adj (lugar) remote, isolated; **mantente a. de él**, keep away from him. II nm 1 (párrafo) section, paragraph. 2 **a. de correos**, Post Office Box.

apartamento nm (small) flat, apartment.

apartar I vtr (alejar) to move away, remove; **a. la mirada**, to look away. 2 (guardar) to put aside. II vi ¡aparta!, move out of the way! III **apartarse** vr (alejarse) to move over, move away; **apártate de en medio**, move out of the way.

aparte I adv 1 aside; **ponlo a.**, put it aside; **modestia/bromas a.**, modesty/joking apart. 2 **eso hay que pagarlo a.**, (separadamente) you have to pay for that separately. 3 **a. de eso**, (además) besides that; (excepto) apart from that. 4 **eso es caso a.**, that's completely different. II nm 1 Teat aside. 2 Ling **punto y a.**, full stop, new paragraph.

apasionado,-a I adj passionate; **a. de la música**, very fond of music. II nm,f enthusiast.

apasionante adj exciting.

apasionar vtr to excite, thrill; **le apasiona el jazz**, he is mad about jazz.

apatía *nf* apathy.

apático,-a I *adj* apathetic. **II** *nm,f* apathetic person.

apátrida I *adj* stateless. **II** *nmf* stateless person.

apdo. *abr de apartado*, Post Office Box, P.O.B.

apeadero *nm* halt.

apearse *vi* (*de un autobús, tren*) to get off, alight; (*de un coche*) to get out; **se apeó en Jerez**, he got off in Jerez.

apechugar [7] *vi* **a. con**, to shoulder.

apedrear *vtr* to throw stones at.

apegado,-a *adj* devoted, attached (**a**, to).

apegarse [7] *vr* to become devoted *o* attached (**a**, to).

apego *nm* love, affection; **tener a. a**, to be attached to.

apelación *nf* appeal; **interponer a.**, to lodge and appeal.

apelar *vi* **1** *Jur* to appeal. **2** (*recurrir*) to resort (**a**, to).

apellidarse *vr* to have as a surname, be called.

apellido *nm* surname; **a. de soltera**, maiden name.

apelmazado,-a *adj* stodgy.

apelotonar I *vtr* to pile up, put into a pile. **II apelotonarse** *vr* (*gente*) to crowd together.

apenar I *vtr* to grieve. **II apenarse** *vr* **1** to be grieved. **2** *Am* (*avergonzarse*) to be ashamed.

apenas *adv* **1** (*casi no*) hardly, scarcely; **a. come**, he hardly eats anything; **a. (si) hay nieve**, there is hardly any snow. **2** (*tan pronto como*) scarcely; **a. llegó, sonó el teléfono**, no sooner had he arrived than the phone rang.

apéndice *nm* appendix.

apendicitis *nf* appendicitis.

apercibir I *vtr* to warn. **II apercibirse** *vr* to notice (**de**, -).

aperitivo *nm* (*bebida*) apéritif; (*comida*) appetizer.

apero *nm* (*usu pl*) equipment, tools *pl*; **aperos de labranza**, farming implements.

apertura *nf* **1** (*comienzo*) opening. **2** *Pol* liberalization.

apestar I *vi* to stink (**a**, of). **II** *vtr* to infect with the plague.

apetecer [33]· *vi* to appeal to; **¿qué te apetece para cenar?**, what would you like for supper?; **¿te apetece ir al cine?**, do you fancy going to the cinema?

apetecible *adj* tempting, inviting.

apetito *nm* appetite; **tengo mucho a.**, I'm really hungry.

apetitoso,-a *adj* appetizing, tempting; (*comida*) delicious, tasty.

apiadarse *vr* to take pity (**de**, on).

ápice *nm* **1** (*punta*) apex. **2** *fig* **ni un á.**, not a bit.

apicultura *nf* beekeeping, apiculture.

apilar *vtr*, **apilarse** *vr* to pile up, heap up.

apiñarse *vr* to crowd together.

apio *nm* celery.

apisonadora *nf* roadroller, steamroller.

apisonar *vtr* to roll.

aplacar [1] I *vtr* to placate, calm. **II aplacarse** *vr* to calm down.

aplanar *vtr* to level.

aplastante *adj* crushing; *Pol* **victoria a.**, landslide victory.

aplastar *vtr* **1** to flatten, squash. **2** *fig* (*vencer*) to crush.

aplatanarse *vr fam* to become lethargic.

aplaudir *vtr* **1** to clap, applaud. **2** *fig* to applaud.

aplauso *nm* applause.

aplazamiento *nm* postponement, adjournment; (*de un pago*) deferment.

aplazar [4] *vtr* to postpone, adjourn; *Fin* (*pago*) to defer.

aplicación *nf* application.

aplicado,-a *adj* hard-working.

aplicar [1] I *vtr* to apply. **II aplicarse** *vr* **1** (*esforzarse*) to apply oneself, work hard. **2** (*norma, ley*) to apply, be applicable.

aplique *nm* wall light, wall lamp.

aplomo *nm* aplomb.

apocado,-a *adj* shy, timid.

apocamiento *nm* timidity, lack of self-confidence.

apocarse [1] *vr* to become frightened.

apodar *vtr* to nickname.

apoderado,-a *nm,f* **1** agent, representative. **2** (*de torero, deportista*) manager.

apoderarse *vr* to take possession (**de**, of), seize; *fig* **el miedo se apoderó de ella**, she was seized by fear.

apodo *nm* nickname.

apogeo *nm* height; **estar en pleno a.**, (*fama etc*) to be at its height.

apolillarse *vr* to get moth-eaten.

apolítico,-a *adj* apolitical.

apología *nf* apology, defence, *US* defense.

apoltronarse *vr fam* to vegetate.

apoplejía *nf* apoplexy.

apoquinar *vtr fam* to cough up, fork out.

aporrear *vtr* to beat, hit, thrash; (*puerta*) to bang; *fam* **a. el piano**, to bang (away) on the piano.

aportación *nf* contribution.

aportar I *vtr* to contribute. **II** *vi Náut* to reach port.

aposentarse *vr* to stay, lodge.

aposento *nm* room.

aposta *adv* on purpose, intentionally.

apostar¹ [2] I *vtr* to bet; **te apuesto una cena a que no viene**, I bet you a dinner that he won't come. **II** *vi* to bet (**por**, on); **a. a los caballos**, to bet on horses; **apuesto a que sí viene**, I bet she will come. **III apostarse** *vr* to bet; **me apuesto lo que quieras**, I bet you anything.

apostar² vtr (situar) to post, station.

apostilla nf note.

apóstol nm apostle.

apóstrofo nm apostrophe.

apostura nf good bearing.

apoteósico,-a adj enormous, tremendous.

apoyacabezas nm Aut headrest.

apoyar I vtr 1 to lean. 2 (causa) to support. **II apoyarse** vr 1 a. en, to lean on; apóyate en mi brazo, take my arm. 2 a. en, (opinión) to be based on, rest on.

apoyo nm support.

apreciable adj appreciable, noticeable.

apreciación nf appreciation.

apreciar [12] I vtr 1 to appreciate. 2 (percibir) to notice, see. **II apreciarse** vr to be noticeable.

aprecio nm regard, esteem; tener a. a algn, to be fond of sb.

aprehender vtr (alijo, botín) to apprehend, seize.

aprehensión nf seizure.

apremiante adj urgent, pressing.

apremiar [12] vtr to be urgent; el tiempo apremia, time is at a premium.

aprender vtr to learn; así aprenderás, that'll teach you.

aprendiz,-a nm,f apprentice, trainee.

aprendizaje nm 1 learning. 2 (instrucción) apprenticeship, traineeship.

aprensión nf apprehension.

aprensivo,-a adj apprehensive.

apresar vtr to seize, capture.

aprestar I vtr to prepare, get ready. **II aprestarse** vr to get ready.

apresurado,-a adj (persona) in a hurry; (cosa) hurried.

apresuramiento nm haste, hurry.

apresurar I vtr (paso etc) to speed up. **II apresurarse** vr to hurry up.

apretado,-a adj 1 (ropa, cordón) tight; íbamos todos apretados en el coche, we were all squashed together in the car. 2 (día, agenda) busy.

apretar [1] I vtr (botón) to press; (nudo, tornillo) to tighten; a. el gatillo, to pull the trigger; **me aprietan las botas**, these boots are too tight for me. **II** vi apretaba el calor, it was really hot. **III apretarse** vr to squeeze together, cram together; fig a. el cinturón, to tighten one's belt.

apretón nm squeeze; a. de manos, handshake.

apretujar I vtr to squeeze, crush. **II apretujarse** vr to squeeze together, cram together.

aprieto nm tight spot, fix, jam; poner a algn en un a., to put sb in an awkward position.

aprisa adv quickly.

aprisionar vtr (atrapar) to trap.

aprobación nf approval.

aprobado nm Educ pass.

aprobar [2] vtr 1 (autorizar) to approve. 2 (estar de acuerdo con) to approve of. 3 Educ to pass. 4 Pol (ley) to pass.

apropiado,-a adj suitable, appropriate.

apropiarse [12] vr to appropriate.

aprovechado,-a adj 1 mal a., (recurso, tiempo) wasted; bien a., put to good use. 2 (egoísta) well-planned. 3 pey (egoísta) self-seeking.

aprovechamiento nm use.

aprovechar I vtr to make good use of, make the most of; aprovechamos bien la tarde, we've done lots of things this afternoon. 2 (recursos etc) to take advantage of; a. la ocasión, to seize the opportunity. **II** vi ¡que aproveche!, enjoy your meal!, bon appétit!. **III aprovecharse** vr to use to one's advantage, take advantage; a. de algn, to take advantage of sb; a. de algo, to make the most of sth.

aprovisionar vtr to supply, provide; a. las tropas, to give supplies to the troops.

aproximación nf 1 approximation. 2 (en lotería) consolation prize.

aproximado,-a adj approximate; un cálculo a., a rough estimate. ◆**aproximadamente** approximately, roughly.

aproximar I vtr to bring o put nearer. **II aproximarse** vr to approach (a, -).

aproximativo,-a adj approximate, rough.

aptitud nf aptitude; prueba de a., aptitude test.

apto,-a adj 1 (apropiado) suitable, appropriate; Cin a. para todos los públicos, U-certificate film, US rated 'G'. 2 (capacitado) capable, able. 3 Educ passed.

apuesta nf bet, wager.

apuesto,-a adj good-looking; (hombre) handsome.

apuntador,-a nm,f Teat prompter.

apuntalar vtr to prop up, shore up, underpin.

apuntar I vtr 1 (con arma) to aim. 2 (señalar) to point out. 3 (anotar) to note down, make a note of. 4 (indicar) to indicate, suggest; todo parece a a ..., everything seems to point to .... **II** vi cuando apunta el día, when day breaks. **III apuntarse** vr 1 (en una lista) to put one's name down. 2 fam ¿te apuntas?, are you game?; me apunto, count me in.

apunte nm (usu pl) note; tomar apuntes, to take notes.

apuñalar vtr to stab.

apurado,-a adj 1 (necesitado) in need; a. de dinero, hard up for money; a. de tiempo, in a hurry. 2 (preocupado) worried; (avergonzado) embarrassed. 3 (situación) awkward, difficult. 4 (afeitado) close, fine; un a. (afeitado) close shave.

apurar I vtr 1 (terminar) to finish off, end. 2 (preocupar) to worry. **II apurarse** vr 1 *(preocuparse)* to worry, get worried; **no te apures,** don't worry. **2** *(darse prisa)* to rush, hurry, pester; **apúrate,** get a move on.

apuro *nm* **1** *(situación difícil)* tight spot, fix, jam; **estar en un a.,** to be in a tight spot. **2** *(escasez de dinero)* hardship; **pasar apuros,** to be hard up. **3** *(vergüenza)* embarrassment; **¡qué a.!,** how embarrassing!

aquejado,-a *adj* suffering *(de,* from).

aquel,-ella *adj dem* **1** that; **a. niño,** that boy. **2** **aquellos,-as,** those; **aquellas niñas,** those girls.

aquél,-élla *pron dem m,f* **1** that one; *(el anterior)* the former; **aquél/élla ... éste/ ésta,** the former ... the latter. **2** **todo a. que,** anyone who, whoever. **3** **aquéllos, -as,** those; *(los anteriores)* the former.

aquella *adj dem f* → **aquel.**

aquélla *pron dem f* → **aquél.**

aquello *pron dem neut* that, it.

aquellos,-as *adj dem pl* → **aquel,-ella.**

aquéllos,-as *pron dem m,fpl* → **aquél, -élla.**

aquí *adv* **1** *(lugar)* here; **a. arriba/fuera,** up/out here; **a. está,** here it is; **a. mismo,** right here; **de a. para allá,** up and down, to and fro; **hasta a.,** this far; **por a., por favor,** this way please; **está por a.,** it's around here somewhere. **2** *(tiempo)* **de a. en adelante,** from now on; **de aquí a junio,** between now and June; **hasta a.,** up till now.

aquietar *vtr* to pacify, calm down.

ara *nf fml* **en aras de,** for the sake of.

árabe **I** *adj* *(de Arabia)* Arab. **II** *nmf (persona)* Arab. **III** *nm (idioma)* Arabic.

Arabia *n* Arabia; **A. Saudita,** Saudi Arabia.

arado *nm* plough, *US* plow.

Aragón *n* Aragon.

aragonés,-esa *adj & nm,f* Aragonese.

arancel *nm* tariff, customs duty.

arancelario,-a *adj* tariff, duty; **derechos arancelarios,** duties; **barreras arancelarias,** customs barriers.

arandela *nf Téc* washer; *(anilla)* ring.

araña *nf* **1** spider. **2** *(lámpara)* chandelier.

arañar *vtr* to scratch.

arañazo *nm* scratch.

arar *vtr* to plough, *US* plow.

araucaria *nf* araucaria, monkey puzzle tree.

arbitraje *nm* **1** arbitration. **2** *Dep* refereeing; *Ten* umpiring.

arbitrar *vtr* **1** to arbitrate. **2** *Dep* to referee; *Ten* umpire.

arbitrariedad *nf* **1** arbitrariness. **2** *(acto)* arbitrary action.

arbitrario,-a *adj* arbitrary.

arbitrio *nm* *(voluntad)* will; *(juicio)* judgement.

árbitro,-a *nm,f* *Dep* referee; *(de tenis)*

umpire. 2 *(mediador)* arbitrator.

árbol *nm* **1** *Bot* tree. **2** *Téc* shaft. **3** *Náut* mast. **4** *(gráfico)* tree (diagram); **á. genealógico,** family o genealogical tree.

arbolado,-a **I** *adj* wooded. **II** *nm* woodland.

arboleda *nf* grove.

arbusto *nm* bush, shrub.

arca *nf* **1** chest. **2** *(para caudales)* strongbox, safe; **arcas públicas,** Treasury *sing.*

arcada *nf* **1** arcade; *(de puente)* arch. **2** *(náusea)* retching.

arcaico,-a *adj* archaic.

arcén *nm* verge; *(de autopista)* hard shoulder.

archi- *pref* super-.

archiconocido,-a *adj* extremely well-known.

archipiélago *nm* archipelago.

archivador *nm* filing cabinet.

archivar *vtr* **1** *(documento etc)* to file (away). **2** *(caso, asunto)* to shelve. **3** *Inform* to save.

archivo *nm* **1** file. **2** *(archivador)* filing cabinet. **3** **archivos,** archives.

arcilla *nf* clay.

arco *nm* **1** *Arquit* arch. **2** *Mat Elec* arc. **3** *(de violín)* bow. **4** *Dep* bow; **tiro con a.,** archery. **5** **a. iris,** rainbow.

arder *vi* to burn; *fam* **la conversación está que arde,** the conversation is really heating up; **Juan está que arde,** Juan is really fuming.

ardid *nm* scheme, plot.

ardiente *adj* **1** *(encendido)* burning; **capilla a.,** chapel of rest. **2** *fig (fervoroso)* eager.

ardilla *nf* squirrel.

ardor *nm* **1** heat; **Med a. de estómago,** heartburn. **2** *fig* ardour, *US* ardor, fervour, *US* fervor.

ardoroso,-a *adj fig* ardent, passionate.

arduo,-a *adj* arduous.

área *nf* **1** area; *Dep* penalty area. **2** *(medida)* are (100 square metres).

arena *nf* **1** sand; **playa de a.,** sandy beach. **2** *Taur* bullring.

arengar [7] *vtr* to harangue.

arenisca *nf* sandstone.

arenoso,-a *adj* sandy.

arenque *nm* herring; *Culin* **a. ahumado,** kipper.

arete *nm* earring.

argamasa *nf* mortar.

Argel *n* Algiers.

Argelia *n* Algeria.

argelino,-a *adj & nm,f* Algerian.

Argentina *n* Argentina.

argentino,-a *adj & nm,f* Argentinean, Argentine.

argolla *nf* **1** (large) ring. **2** *Am (alianza)* wedding ring.

argot *nm (popular)* slang; *(técnico)* jargon.

argucia *nf* ruse.

argüir [37] *vtr* **1** *(deducir)* to deduce, conclude. 2 (*argumentar*) to argue.

argumentación *nf* argument.

argumentar *vtr* → **argüir**.

argumento *nm* 1 *Lit Teat* (*trama*) plot. 2 (*razonamiento*) argument.

arguyo *indic pres* → **argüir**.

aridez *nf* aridity; *fig* dryness.

árido,-a *adj* arid; *fig* dry.

Aries *nm* Aries.

ariete *nm Mil* battering ram.

ario,-a *adj & nm,f* Aryan.

arisco,-a *adj* (*persona*) unfriendly, standoffish; (*animal*) unfriendly.

arista *nf* edge.

aristocracia *nf* aristocracy.

aristócrata *nmf* aristocrat.

aristocrático,-a *adj* aristocratic.

aritmética *nf* arithmetic.

arma *nf* weapon; **a. blanca**, knife; **a. de fuego**, firearm; **a. homicida**, murder weapon; **a. nuclear**, nuclear weapon; **a. de doble filo**, double-edged sword.

armada *nf* navy.

armado,-a *adj* armed; **ir a.**, to be armed; **lucha armada**, armed struggle.

armador,-a *nm,f* shipowner.

armadura *nf* 1 (*armazón*) frame. 2 *Hist* suit of armour *o US* armor.

armamentista *adj* arms; **la carrera a.**, the arms race.

armamento *nm* armaments *pl*; **a. nuclear**, nuclear weapons.

armar I *vtr* 1 (*tropa, soldado*) to arm. 2 (*piezas*) to fit *o* put together, assemble. 3 *fam* **armaron un escándalo**, they created a scandal. II **armarse** *vr* to arm oneself; *fig* **a. de paciencia**, to summon up one's patience; *fig* **a. de valor**, to pluck up courage; *fam* **se armó la gorda**, all hell broke loose.

armario *nm* (*para ropa*) wardrobe; (*de cocina*) cupboard; **a. empotrado**, built-in wardrobe *o* cupboard.

armatoste *nm* (*cosa*) monstrosity.

armazón *nm* frame; (*de madera*) timberwork; *Arquit* shell.

armería *nf* gunsmith's (shop).

armiño *nm* ermine.

armisticio *nm* armistice.

armonía *nf* harmony.

armonioso,-a *adj* harmonious.

armonizar [4] *vtr & vi* to harmonize.

aro *nm* hoop; (*servilletero*) serviette ring; *fam* **pasar por el a.**, to knuckle under.

aroma *nm* aroma; (*de vino*) bouquet.

aromático,-a *adj* aromatic.

arpa *nf* harp.

arpía *nf* (*en mitología*) harpy; *fig* harpy, old witch.

arpón *nm* harpoon.

arquear *vtr*, **arquearse** *vr* to bend, curve.

arqueología *nf* archaeology, *US* archeology.

arqueólogo,-a *nm,f* archaeologist, *US* archeologist.

arquero *nm,f* archer.

arquetipo *nm* archetype.

arquitecto,-a *nm,f* architect.

arquitectónico,-a *adj* architectural.

arquitectura *nf* architecture.

arrabales *nmpl* slums.

arrabalero,-a *adj pey* coarse.

arraigado,-a *adj* deeply rooted.

arraigar [7] *vi* to take root.

arraigo *nm fig* roots *pl*; **una tradición con mucho a.**, a deeply-rooted tradition.

arrancar [1] I *vtr* 1 (*planta*) to uproot, pull up; **a. de raíz**, to uproot. 2 (*extraer*) to pull *o* tear off *o* out; (*diente, pelo*) to pull out; *fig* (*confesión etc*) to extract; **arranca una hoja del cuaderno**, tear a page out of the notebook. 3 (*coche, motor*) to start. II *vi* 1 *Aut Téc* to start. 2 (*empezar*) to begin; **a. a llorar**, to burst out crying.

arranque *nm* 1 *Aut Téc* starting. 2 (*comienzo*) start. 3 *fam* (*arrebato*) outburst, fit.

arrasar I *vtr* to devastate, destroy. II *vi* (*en elecciones etc*) to win by a landslide.

arrastrado,-a *fam* I *adj* wretched. II *nm,f* bad egg.

arrastrar I *vtr* to pull (along), drag (along); **vas arrastrando el vestido**, your dress is trailing on the ground; **lo arrastró la corriente**, he was swept away by the current. II **arrastrarse** *vr* to drag oneself; *fig* (*humillarse*) to crawl.

arrastre *nm* 1 pulling, dragging; *fam* **para el a.**, (*persona*) on one's last legs; (*cosa*) done for. 2 (*pesca de a.*), trawling.

arrayán *nm* myrtle.

arre *interj* gee up!, giddy up!

arrear *fam vtr* 1 to spur on; (*caballos*) to urge on. 2 *fam* (*bofetada*) to give.

arrebatador,-a *adj fig* captivating, fascinating.

arrebatar I *vtr* (*coger*) to snatch, seize; *fig* (*cautivar*) to captivate, fascinate. II **arrebatarse** *vr* (*enfurecerse*) to become furious; (*exaltarse*) to get carried away.

arrebato *nm* outburst, fit.

arreciar [12] *vi* (*viento, tormenta*) to get worse.

arrecife *nm* reef.

arreglado,-a *adj* 1 (*reparado*) repaired, fixed. 2 (*solucionado*) settled. 3 (*habitación*) tidy, neat. 4 (*persona*) well-dressed, smart.

arreglar I *vtr* 1 to arrange; (*problema*) to sort out; (*habitación*) to tidy; (*papeles*) to put in order. 2 (*reparar*) to repair, fix. 3 (*vestir*) to get ready. II **arreglarse** *vr* 1 (*vestirse*) to get ready. 2 *fam* **arreglárselas**, to manage. 3 (*reconciliarse*) to make up.

arreglo *nm* 1 arrangement; (*acuerdo*) compromise. **2** (*reparación*) repair; **no tiene a.**, it is beyond repair; *fam* **¡no tienes a.!**, you're hopeless! **3** *fml* **con a. a**, in accordance with.

arrellanarse *vr* to sit back.

arremangarse [7] *vr* to roll one's sleeves *o* trousers up.

arremeter *vi* to attack.

arremolinarse *vr* to whirl about; *fig* (*gente*) to crowd together, cram together.

arrendamiento *nm* **1** (*alquiler*) renting. **2** (*precio*) rent.

arrendar [1] *vtr* (*piso*) to rent; (*dar en arriendo*) to let on lease; (*tomar en arriendo*) to take on lease.

arrendatario,-a *nm,f* leaseholder, lessee; (*inquilino*) tenant.

arreos *nmpl* **1** (*de caballería*) harness *sing*, trappings. **2** (*adornos*) adornments.

arrepentido,-a *adj* regretful.

arrepentimiento *nm* regret.

arrepentirse [5] *vr* **a. de**, to regret; *Rel* to repent.

arrestar *vtr* to arrest, detain; (*encarcelar*) to put in prison.

arresto *nm* arrest; *Jur* **a. domiciliario**, house arrest.

arriar [29] *vtr* (*bandera*) to strike; (*velas*) to lower.

arriba I *adv* up; (*encima*) on the top; **ahí a.**, up there; **de a. abajo**, from top to bottom; *fam* **mirar a algn de a. abajo**, to look sb up and down; **desde a.**, from above; **hacia a.**, upwards; **de un millón para a.**, from one million upwards; **más a.**, higher up, further up; **a. del todo**, right on *o* at the top; **la parte de a.**, the top (part); **vive a.**, he lives upstairs; **véase más a.**, see above. **II** *interj* get up! up you get!; **¡a. la República!**, long live the Republic!; **¡a. las manos!**, hands up! **III** *prep* **Am** on top of.

arribar *vi* to reach port, arrive.

arribeño,-a *Am* **I** *adj* highland. **II** *nm,f* highlander.

arribista *nmf* parvenu, social climber.

arriendo *nm* lease; (*de un piso*) renting; **dar en a.**, to let out on lease; **tomar en a.**, to take on lease.

arriesgado,-a *adj* **1** (*peligroso*) risky. **2** (*temerario*) fearless, daring.

arriesgar [7] **I** *vtr* to risk. **II arriesgarse** *vr* to risk; **se arriesga demasiado**, he's taking too many risks.

arrimar I *vtr* to move closer, bring near *o* nearer; *fam* **a. el hombro**, to lend a hand. **II arrimarse** *vr* to move *o* get close, come near *o* nearer.

arrinconar *vtr* **1** (*poner en un rincón*) to put in a corner. **2** (*abandonar*) to put away, lay aside. **3** (*acorralar*) to corner.

arrobo *nm* rapture, enthralment, *US* enthrallment.

arrocero,-a *adj* **la industria arrocera**, the

rice industry.

arrodillarse *vr* to kneel down.

arrogancia *nf* arrogance.

arrogante *adj* arrogant.

arrojadizo,-a *adj* **arma arrojadiza**, missile.

arrojado,-a *adj* (*osado*) bold, daring.

arrojar I *vtr* **1** (*tirar*) to throw, fling. **2** *Com* (*saldo*) to show. **II arrojarse** *vr* to throw oneself, fling oneself.

arrojo *nm* daring, courage.

arrollador,-a *adj fig* overwhelming; (*éxito*) resounding; (*personalidad*) captivating.

arrollar I *vtr* **1** (*atropellar*) to run over, knock down. **II** *vi Dep Pol* to win easily.

arropar I *vtr* to wrap up; (*en la cama*) to tuck in. **II arroparse** *vr* to wrap oneself up.

arrostrar *vtr* to face.

arroyo *nm* brook, stream.

arroz *nm* rice; **a. con leche**, rice pudding.

arruga *nf* (*en la piel*) wrinkle; (*en la ropa*) crease.

arrugar [7] **I** *vtr* (*piel*) to wrinkle; (*ropa*) to crease; (*papel*) to crumple (up). **II arrugarse** *vr* (*piel*) to wrinkle; (*ropa*) to crease.

arruinado,-a *adj* bankrupt, ruined.

arruinar I *vtr* to ruin. **II arruinarse** *vr* to be ruined.

arrullar I *vtr* (*bebé*) to lull. **II** *vi* (*paloma*) to coo.

arrullo *nm* **1** (*de paloma*) cooing. **2** (*nana*) lullaby.

arrumaco *nm fam* kissing and hugging; (*halago*) flattery.

arsenal *nm* arsenal.

arsénico *nm* arsenic.

arte *nm & f* **1** art; **bellas artes**, fine arts; *fam* **por amor al a.**, for the love of it. **2** (*habilidad*) skill.

artefacto *nm* device; **a. explosivo**, explosive device.

arteria *nf* artery; (*carretera*) highway.

artesanal *adj* handmade.

artesanía *nf* **1** (*cualidad*) craftsmanship. **2** (*objetos*) crafts *pl*, handicrafts *pl*.

artesano,-a I *nm,f* (*hombre*) craftsman; (*mujer*) craftswoman. **II** *adj* handmade.

ártico,-a *adj* arctic; **el océano á.**, the Arctic Ocean. **II** *nm* **el A.**, the Arctic.

articulación *nf* **1** *Anat* joint, articulation. **2** *Téc* joint.

articulado,-a *adj* (*tren etc*) articulated.

articular *vtr* to articulate.

artículo *nm* article; **a. de fondo**, leader (article).

artífice *nmf* author; *fig* **el a. del acuerdo**, the architect of the agreement.

artificial *adj* artificial; *Tex* man-made *o* synthetic.

artificio *nm* **1** artifice; **fuego de a.**, firework. **2** (*artimaña*) ruse.

artillería *nf* artillery; **a. antiaérea**, anti-aircraft guns *pl*.

artillero *nm* artilleryman.

artilugio *nm* gadget, device.

artimaña *nf* trick, ruse.

artista *nmf* artist; a. de cine, film star.

artístico,-a *adj* artistic.

artritis *nf* arthritis.

arveja *nf Am* pea.

arzobispo *nm* archbishop.

as *nm* ace.

asa *nf* handle.

asado-a I *adj Culin* roast; **pollo a.**, a. chicken; *fig* a. de calor, roasting, boiling hot. **II** *nm Culin* roast.

asaduras *nfpl* offal *sing*; (de ave) giblets.

asalariado,-a I *adj* salaried. **II** *nm,f* wage earner, salaried worker.

asaltador,-a *nm,f,* **asaltante** *nmf* attacker; (en un robo) robber.

asaltar *vtr* to assault, attack; (banco) to rob; *fig* to assail.

asalto *nm* 1 assault, attack; a. a un banco, bank robbery. 2 *Box* round.

asamblea *nf* meeting; a. general, general meeting.

asar I *vtr* to roast. **II asarse** *vr fig* to be roasting, be boiling hot.

ascendencia *nf* ancestry, ancestors *pl*; de a. escocesa, of Scottish descent.

ascender [3] **I** *vtr* (en un cargo) to promote. **II** *vi* 1 move upward; (temperatura) to rise; **la factura asciende a ...**, the bill adds up to ... 2 (al trono) to ascend. 3 (de categoría) to be promoted.

ascendiente *nmf* ancestor.

ascensión *nf* 1 climb. 2 (al trono) accession.

ascenso *nm* promotion; (subida) rise.

ascensor *nm* lift, *US* elevator.

asco *nm* disgust, repugnance; **me da a.**, it makes me (feel) sick; **¡qué a.!**, how disgusting o revolting!

ascua *nf* ember; *fig* en ascuas, on tenterhooks.

aseado,-a *adj* tidy, neat.

asear I *vtr* to clean, tidy up. **II asearse** *vr* to wash, get washed.

asediar [12] *vtr* to besiege.

asedio *nm* siege.

asegurado,-a *adj* insured. 2 (indudable) secure.

asegurador,-a I *adj* insurance. **II** *nm,f* insurer.

asegurar I *vtr* 1 to insure. 2 (garantizar) **me aseguró que ...**, he assured me that ...; a. el éxito de un proyecto, to ensure the success of a project. 3 (cuerda) to fasten. **II asegurarse** *vr* 1 to make sure; a. de que ..., to make sure that .... 2 *Seg* to insure onself.

asemejarse *vr* a. a, to look like.

asentado,-a *adj* (establecido) established, settled.

asentamiento *nm* settlement.

asentar [1] **I** *vtr* a. la cabeza, to settle down. **II asentarse** *vr* 1 (establecerse) to settle down, establish oneself. 2 (té, polvo) to settle.

asentimiento *nm* assent, consent.

asentir [5] *vi* to assent, agree; **a. con la cabeza**, to nod.

aseo *nm* 1 cleanliness, tidiness. 2 **aseos** o **(cuarto de) a.**, bathroom; (retrete) toilet.

asequible *adj* affordable; (comprensible) easy to understand; (alcanzable) attainable.

aserrín *nm* sawdust.

asesinar *vtr* to murder; (rey, ministro) to assassinate.

asesinato *nm* murder; (de rey, ministro) assassination.

asesino,-a I *adj* murderous. **II** *nm,f* killer; (hombre) murderer; (mujer) murderess; *Pol* assassin.

asesor,-a I *nm,f* adviser; **a. fiscal**, tax advisor. **II** *adj* advisory.

asesoramiento *nm* 1 (acción) advising. 2 (consejo) advice.

asesorar I *vtr* 1 to advise, give (profesional) advice to. 2 *Com* to act as consultant to. **II asesorarse** *vr* to consult.

asesoría *nf* consultant's office.

asestar *vtr* to deal; a. un golpe a algn, to deal sb a blow.

aseverar *vtr* to assert.

asfalto *nm* asphalt.

asfixia *nf* asphyxiation, suffocation.

asfixiante *adj* asphyxiating, suffocating; *fam* **hace un calor a.**, it's stifling.

asfixiar [12] *vtr,* **asfixiarse** *vr* to asphyxiate, suffocate.

así I *adv* 1 (de esta manera) like this o that, this way, thus; **ponlo a.**, put it this way; **a. de grande/alto**, this big/tall; **algo a.**, something like this o that; **¿no es a.?**, isn't that so o right?; **a. es la vida**, such is life; **a. a.**, so-so. 2 **a las seis o a.**, around six o'clock; **diez años o a.**, ten years more or less. 3 **a. como**, as well as. 4 **a. tenga que ...**, (aunque) even if I have to ... 5 **aun a.**, and despite that. 6 **a. pues**, so; **a. que ...**, so ... 7 **a. que llegues**, as soon as.

Asia *n* Asia; **A. Menor**, Asia Minor..

asiático,-a *adj & nm,f* Asian.

asidero *nm* (asa) handle; *fig* pretext, excuse.

asiduidad *nf* assiduity; **con a.**, frequently, regularly.

asiduo,-a I *adj* assiduous. **II** *nm,f* regular customer.

asiento *nm* 1 seat; **a. trasero/delantero**, front/back seat; **tome a.**, take a seat. 2 (poso) sediment. 3 *Fin* entry.

asignación *nf* 1 (de dinero) assignment, allocation. 2 (de puesto) appointment. 3 (paga) allowance.

asignar *vtr* 1 to assign, allocate. 2 (nombrar) to appoint.

asignatura nf subject; **a. pendiente,** failed subject.

asilado,-a nm,f refugee.

asilar vtr to grant o give political asylum to.

asilo nm asylum; **a. de ancianos,** old people's home; Pol **a. político,** political asylum.

asimilación nf assimilation.

asimilar vtr to assimilate.

asimismo adv also, as well.

asir [22] vtr to grasp, seize.

asistencia nf 1 (presencia) attendance; **falta de a.,** absence. 2 **a. médica/técnica,** medical/technical assistance. 3 (público) audience, public.

asistenta nf charlady, cleaning lady.

asistente I adj attending; **el público a.,** the audience. II nmf 1 (ayudante) assistant; **a. social,** social worker. 2 **los asistentes,** the public sing.

asistido,-a adj assisted. **a. por ordenador,** computer-assisted; Aut **dirección asistida,** power steering.

asistir I vtr to assist, help. II vi to attend **(a, -),** be present **(a, at).**

asma nf asthma.

asno nm donkey, ass.

asociación nf association.

asociado,-a I adj associated. III nm,f associate, partner.

asociar [12] I vtr to associate. II **asociarse** vr 1 to be associated. 2 Com to become partners.

asolar [2] vtr to devastate, destroy.

asomar I vtr to put out, stick out; **asomó la cabeza por la ventana,** he put his head out the window. II vi to appear. III **asomarse** vr 1 to lean out; **a. a la ventana,** to lean out of the window. 2 (entrar) to pop in; (salir) to pop out.

asombrar I vtr to amaze, astonish. II **asombrarse** vr to be astonished; **a. de algo,** to be amazed at sth.

asombro nm amazement, astonishment.

asombroso,-a adj amazing, astonishing.

asomo nm trace, hint.

asonada nf putsch.

asorocharse vr Am to suffer from altitude sickness.

aspa nf 1 (de molino) arm; (de ventilador) blade. 2 (cruz) cross.

aspaviento nm hacer aspavientos, to wave one's arms about.

aspecto nm 1 look, appearance. 2 (de un asunto) aspect.

aspereza nf roughness; fig limar asperezas, to smooth things over.

áspero,-a adj rough; fig (carácter) surly.

aspersión nf sprinkling.

aspersor nm sprinkler.

aspiración nf 1 inhalation, breathing in. 2 (pretensión) aspiration.

aspiradora nf vacuum cleaner.

aspirante nmf candidate, applicant.

aspirar I vtr 1 (respirar) to inhale, breathe in. 2 Téc (absorber) to suck in, draw in. II vi fig **a algo,** to aspire after sth.

aspirina nf aspirin.

asquear vtr to disgust.

asquerosidad nf filthy o revolting thing; **¡que a.!,** how revolting!

asqueroso,-a I adj (sucio) filthy; (desagradable) revolting, disgusting. II nm,f filthy o revolting person.

asta nf 1 (de bandera) staff, pole; **a media a.,** at half-mast. 2 Zool (cuerno) horn.

asterisco nm asterisk.

astilla nf splinter.

astillero nm shipyard.

astral adj astral; **carta a.,** birth chart.

astringente adj & nm astringent.

astro nm star.

astrología nf astrology.

astrólogo,-a nm,f astrologer.

astronauta nmf astronaut.

astronave nf spaceship.

astronomía nf astronomy.

astronómico,-a adj astronomical.

astrónomo,-a nm,f astronomer.

astucia nf shrewdness; (artimaña) ruse.

asturiano,-a adj & nm,f Asturian.

Asturias nf Asturias.

astuto,-a adj astute, shrewd.

asumir vtr to assume.

asunción nf assumption.

asunto nm 1 subject; **no es a. tuyo,** it's none of your business. 2 **Asuntos Exteriores,** Foreign Affairs.

asustar I vtr to frighten, scare. II **asustarse** vr to be frightened, be scared.

atacante nmf attacker, assailant.

atacar [1] vtr to attack, assault; fig me **ataca los nervios,** he gets on my nerves.

atado adj tied; (ocupado) tied up.

atadura nf fig hindrance.

atajar vi to take a shortcut (**por,** across o through).

atajo nm 1 shortcut. 2 (grupo) bunch.

atalaya nf watchtower.

atañer [38] v impers to concern, have to do with; **eso no te atañe,** that has nothing to do with you.

ataque nm 1 attack, assault; **a. aéreo,** air raid. 2 Med fit; **a. cardíaco** o al corazón, heart attack; **a. de nervios/tos,** fit of hysterics/coughing.

atar I vtr 1 to tie; fig **a. cabos,** to put two and two together; fam **loco de a.,** as mad as a hatter. 2 fig to tie down. II **atarse** vr fig to get tied up; **átate los zapatos,** do your shoes up.

atardecer [33] I v impers to get o grow dark. II nm evening, dusk.

atareado,-a adj busy.

atascado,-a adj stuck.

atascar [1] I vtr (bloquear) to block, obstruct. **II atascarse** vr **1** (bloquearse) to become obstructed, become blocked. **2** fig (estancarse) to get bogged down.

atasco nm traffic jam.

ataúd nm coffin.

ataviarse [29] vr to dress oneself up.

atavío nm dress, attire.

atemorizar [4] vtr to frighten, scare.

atemperar vtr to moderate, temper.

Atenas n Athens.

atención I nf attention; **llamar la a.,** to attract attention; **prestar/poner a.,** to pay attention (**a,** to). **II** interj attention!

atender [3] **I** vtr to attend to; (petición) to agree to. **II** vi (alumno) to pay attention (**a,** to).

atenerse [24] vr **1** (a reglas etc) to abide (**a,** by); **a. a las consecuencias,** to bear the consequences. **2** (remitirse) to go by; **me atengo a sus palabras,** I'm going by what he said; **no saber a qué a.,** not to know what to expect.

atentado nm attack; **a. terrorista,** terrorist attack.

atentar vi **a. a** o **contra,** to commit a crime against; **a. contra la vida de algn,** to make an attempt on sb's life.

atento,-a adj **1** attentive; **estar a. a,** to be mindful o aware of. **2** (amable) thoughtful, considerate; **atentos saludos de,** (en carta) yours faithfully. ◆**atentamente** adv **le saluda a.,** (en carta) yours sincerely o faithfully.

atenuante I adj attenuating. **II** nm Jur extenuating circumstance.

atenuar [30] vtr **1** to attenuate; Jur to extenuate. **2** (importancia) to lessen, diminish.

ateo,-a I adj atheistic. **II** nm,f atheist.

aterciopelado,-a adj velvety; (vino) smooth.

aterido,-a adj **a. de frío,** stiff with cold, numb.

aterrador,-a adj terrifying.

aterrar I vtr to terrify. **II aterrarse** vr to be terrified.

aterrizaje nm Av landing; **a. forzoso,** forced landing.

aterrizar [4] vi to land.

aterrorizar [4] **I** vtr to terrify; Mil Pol to terrorize. **II aterrorizarse** vr to be terrified.

atesorar vtr to accumulate; (dinero) to hoard.

atestado[1] nm Jur affidavit, statement; **atestados,** testimonials.

atestado,-a[2] adj packed, crammed; **estaba a. de gente,** it was full of people.

atestar[1] vtr Jur to testify.

atestar[2] [1] vtr (abarrotar) to pack, cram (**de,** with).

atestiguar [22] vtr **1** Jur to testify to. **2** fig to vouch for.

atiborrar vtr to pack (**de,** with). **II**

atiborrarse vr fam to stuff oneself (**de,** with).

ático nm attic.

atinado,-a adj (juicioso) sensible; (pertinente) pertinent.

atinar vi to get it right; **a. a hacer algo,** to succeed in doing sth; **a. al blanco,** to hit the target; **atinó con la solución,** he found the solution.

atingencia nf Am connection, relation.

atípico,-a adj atypical.

atisbar vtr to make out.

atisbo nm fig slight sign, inkling.

atizar [4] vtr **1** (fuego) to poke, stoke. **2** fig (rebelión) to stir up; (pasión) to rouse, excite.

atlántico,-a I adj Atlantic. **II** nm **el** (océano) **A.,** the Atlantic (Ocean).

atlas nm inv atlas.

atleta nmf athlete.

atlético,-a adj athletic.

atletismo nm athletics sing.

atmósfera nf atmosphere.

atmosférico,-a adj atmospheric.

atolladero nm fix, jam; **estar en un a.,** to be in a jam.

atolondrado,-a adj stunned, bewildered; (atontado) stupid.

atolondrar I vtr to confuse, bewilder. **II atolondrarse** vr to be confused, bewildered.

atómico,-a adj atomic.

átomo nm atom.

atónito,-a adj amazed, astonished.

atontado,-a adj **1** (tonto) silly, foolish. **2** (aturdido) bewildered, amazed.

atontar I vtr to confuse, bewilder. **II atontarse** vr to be o get confused, bewildered.

atorarse vr Am to get stuck.

atormentar I vtr to torment. **II atormentarse** vr to torment oneself, suffer agonies.

atornillar vtr to screw on.

atosigar [7] vtr to harass.

atracador,-a nm,f (de banco) (bank) robber; (en la calle) attacker, mugger.

atracar [1] **I** vtr to hold up; (persona) to rob. **II** vi Náut to come alongside, tie up. **III atracarse** vr (de comida) to stuff oneself (**de,** with), gorge oneself (**de,** on).

atracción nf attraction; **parque de atracciones,** funfair.

atraco nm hold-up, robbery; **a. a mano armada,** armed robbery.

atracón nm fam binge, blowout; **darse un a. de comer,** to make a pig of oneself.

atractivo,-a I adj attractive, appealing. **II** nm attraction, appeal.

atraer [25] vtr to attract.

atragantarse vr to choke (**con,** on), swallow the wrong way; fig **esa chica se me ha atragantado,** I can't stand that girl.

atraigo *indic pres* → **atraer**.

atraje *pt indef* → **atraer**.

atrancar [1] I *vtr* (*puerta*) to bolt. II **atrancarse** *vr* to get stuck; (*al hablar, leer*) to get bogged down.

atrapar *vtr* to catch.

atrás I *adv* 1 (*lugar*) at the back, behind; **hacia/para a.**, backwards; **puerta de a.**, back *o* rear door; *fig* **echarse a.**, to back out. 2 (*tiempo*) previously, in the past, ago; **un año a.**, a year ago; **venir de muy a.**, to go *o* date back a long time.

atrasado,-a *adj* late, slow; (*pago*) overdue; (*reloj*) slow; (*país*) backward; *Prensa* **número a.**, back number.

atrasar I *vtr* to put back. II *vi* (*reloj*) to be slow. III **atrasarse** *vr* 1 to remain *o* stay behind, lag behind. 2 (*tren*) to be late.

atraso *nm* 1 delay. 2 (*de país*) backwardness. 3 *Fin* **atrasos**, arrears.

atravesado,-a *adj* (*cruzado*) lying crosswise; (*persona*) difficult; **le tengo a.**, I can't stand him.

atravesar [1] I *vtr* 1 (*calle*) to cross. 2 (*muro*) to pierce, go through. 3 (*poner a través*) to lay across, put across, put crosswise. II **atravesarse** *vr* to get in the way; *fig* **se me ha atravesado Luis**, I can't stand Luis.

atrayente *adj* attractive.

atreverse *vr* to dare; **a. a hacer algo**, to dare to do sth.

atrevido,-a *adj* 1 (*osado*) daring, bold. 2 (*insolente*) insolent, impudent. 3 (*ropa etc*) daring, risqué.

atrevimiento *nm* 1 (*osadía*) daring, audacity. 2 (*insolencia*) insolence, impudence.

atribuir [37] I *vtr* to attribute, ascribe. II **atribuirse** *vr* to assume.

atribular *vtr* to afflict.

atributo *nm* attribute.

atril *nm* music stand.

atrochar *vi* to take a short cut.

atrocidad *nf* atrocity.

atrofia [12] *vtr*, **atrofiarse** *vr* to atrophy.

atropellado,-a *adj* hasty, impetuous.

atropellar *vtr* to knock down, run over.

atropello *nm* 1 *Aut* knocking down, running over. 2 (*abuso*) abuse.

atroz *adj* 1 (*bárbaro*) atrocious. 2 *fam* (*hambre, frío*) enormous, tremendous.

ATS *nmf abr de* **ayudante técnico sanitario**.

atta. *abr de* **atenta**.

atto. *abr de* **atento**.

atuendo *nm* dress, attire.

atún *nm* tuna, tunny.

aturdido,-a *adj* stunned, dazed.

aturdimiento *nm* confusion, bewilderment.

aturdir *vtr* 1 (*con un golpe*) to stun, daze. 2 (*confundir*) to bewilder, confuse.

aturrullar *vtr* to confuse, bewilder.

atuve *pt indef* → **atenerse**.

audacia *nf* audacity.

audaz *adj* audacious, bold.

audible *adj* audible.

audición *nf* 1 hearing. 2 *Teat* audition.

audiencia *nf* 1 (*público*) audience; *TV Rad* **horas de máxima a.**, prime time; **índice de a.**, viewing figures, ratings. 2 (*entrevista*) audience. 3 *Jur* high court.

audiovisual *adj* audio-visual.

auditivo,-a I *adj* auditory; **comprensión auditiva**, listening comprehension. II *nm* receiver.

auditor *nm Fin* auditor.

auditorio *nm* 1 (*público*) audience. 2 (*sala*) auditorium, hall.

auge *nm* peak; *Econ* boom; *fig* **estar en a.**, to be thriving *o* booming.

augurar *vtr* to augur.

augurio *nm* omen.

aula *nf* (*en colegio*) classroom; *Univ* lecture room; **a. magna**, amphitheatre.

aulaga *nf* gorse.

aullar [16] *vtr* to howl, yell.

aullido *nm* howl, yell.

aumentar I *vtr* to increase; (*precios*) to put up; (*producción*) to step up; *Fot* to enlarge; *Opt* to magnify. II *vi* (*precios*) to go up, rise; (*valor*) to appreciate. III **aumentarse** *vr* to increase, be on the increase.

aumento *nm* increase; *Opt* magnification; **a. de precios**, rise in prices; **ir en a.**, to be on the increase.

aun *adv* even; **a. así**, even so, even then; **a. más**, even more.

aún *adv* still; (*en negativas*) yet; **a. está aquí**, he's still here; **ella no ha venido a.**, she hasn't come yet.

aunar [16] *vtr* to unite, join.

aunque *conj* although, though; (*enfático*) even if, even though; **a. no vengas**, even if you don't come.

aúpa *interj* up!, get up!

aura *nf* aura.

aureola *nf* halo.

auricular *nm* 1 *Tel* receiver. 2 **auriculares**, earphones, headphones.

aurora *nf* daybreak, dawn.

auscultar *vtr* to sound (with a stethoscope).

ausencia *nf* absence.

ausentarse *vr* to leave.

ausente I *adj* absent. II *nmf* absentee.

austeridad *nf* austerity.

austero,-a *adj* austere.

austral I *adj* southern. II *nm Fin* standard monetary unit of Argentina.

Australia *n* Australia.

australiano,-a *adj & nm,f* Australian.

Austria *n* Austria.

austríaco,-a *adj & nm,f* Austrian.

autenticidad *nf* authenticity.

auténtico,-a *adj* authentic.

autentificar [1] *vtr* to authenticate.

autismo *nm* autism.
autista *adj* autistic.
auto[1] *nm* car.
auto[2] *nm* *Jur* decree, writ; **autos**, (*pleito*) papers, documents.
autoadhesivo,-a *adj* self-adhesive.
autobiografía *nf* autobiography.
autobiográfico,-a *adj* autobiographical.
autobombo *nm* *fam* self-praise, blowing one's own trumpet.
autobús *nm* bus.
autocar *nm* coach.
autocrítica *nf* self-criticism.
autóctono,-a *adj* indigenous, autochthonous.
autodefensa *nf* self-defence, *US* self-defense.
autodisciplina *nf* self-discipline.
autoescuela *nf* driving school, school of motoring.
autogobierno *nm* self-government.
autógrafo *nm* autograph.
autómata *nm* automaton.
automático,-a *adj* automatic.
automatización *nf* automation.
automatizar [4] *vtr* to automate.
automotor,-a I *adj* self-propelled. **II** *nm* *Ferroc* diesel train.
automóvil *nm* car.
automovilismo *nm* motoring.
automovilista *nmf* motorist.
automovilístico,-a *adj* car; **accidente a.**, car accident.
autonomía *nf* 1 autonomy. 2 (*región*) autonomous region.
autonómico,-a *adj* autonomous, self-governing; **elecciones autonómicas**, elections for the autonomous parliament; **televisión autonómica**, regional television.
autónomo,-a *adj* autonomous.
autopista *nf* motorway.
autopsia *nf* autopsy, post mortem.
autor,-a *nm,f* (*hombre*) author; (*mujer*) authoress; (*de crimen*) perpetrator.
autoridad *nf* authority.
autoritario,-a *adj* authoritarian.
autorizado,-a *adj* authoritative, official.
autorizar [4] *vtr* to authorize.
autorretrato *nm* self-portrait.
autoservicio *nm* self-service; (*supermercado*) supermarket.
autostop *nm* hitch-hiking; **hacer a.**, to hitch-hike.
autostopista *nmf* hitch-hiker.
autosuficiencia *nf* self-sufficiency.
autosuficiente *adj* self-sufficient.
auxiliar [14] **I** *adj* & *nmf* auxiliary, assistant. **II** *vtr* to help, assist.
auxilio *nm* help, assistance; **primeros auxilios**, first aid *sing*.
Av., Avda. *abr de* **Avenida**, Avenue, Ave.
aval *nm* *Com Fin* endorsement.
avalancha *nf* avalanche.

avalar *vtr* to guarantee, endorse.
avance *nm* 1 advance. 2 *Fin* advance payment. 3 *TV* **a. informativo**, headlines, *US* news brief.
avanzado,-a *adj* advanced; **de avanzada edad**, advanced in years.
avanzar [4] *vtr* to advance.
avaricia *nf* avarice.
avaricioso,-a *adj* greedy.
avaro,-a I *adj* avaricious, miserly. **II** *nm,f* miser.
avasallar *vtr* to subdue.
avatares *nmpl* quirks.
ave *nf* bird; **aves de corral**, poultry.
AVE *nf* *abr de* **Alta Velocidad Española**, High Speed Train.
avecinarse *vr* to approach, come near.
avellana *nf* hazelnut.
avellano *nm* hazelnut tree.
avena *nf* oats *pl*.
avendré *indic fut* → **avenir**.
avenencia *nf* compromise.
avengo *indic pres* → **avenir**.
avenida *nf* avenue.
avenido,-a *adj* **bien/mal avenidos**, on good/bad terms.
avenir [27] **I** *vtr* to reconcile. **II avenirse** *vr* to be on good terms; (*consentir*) to agree (**en**, to).
aventajado,-a *adj* (*destacado*) outstanding, exceptional; (*en cabeza*) in the lead.
aventajar *vtr* 1 to be ahead *o* in front (**a**, of). 2 (*superar*) to surpass, outdo.
aventar [1] *vtr* 1 *Agr* to winnow. 2 (*el fuego*) to blow (on), fan.
aventura *nf* 1 adventure. 2 (*amorosa*) (love) affair.
aventurado,-a *adj* risky.
aventurarse *vr* to venture.
aventurero,-a *adj* adventurous.
avergonzado,-a *adj* ashamed.
avergonzar [2] **I** *vtr* to shame. **II avergonzarse** *vr* to be ashamed (**de**, of).
avería *nf* breakdown.
averiado,-a *adj* out of order; (*coche*) broken down.
averiar [29] **I** *vtr* to break. **II averiarse** *vr* (*estropearse*) to malfunction, go wrong; (*coche*) to break down.
averiguación *nf* enquiry.
averiguar [22] *vtr* to ascertain.
aversión *nf* aversion.
avestruz *nm* ostrich.
aviación *nf* 1 aviation; **accidente de a.**, plane crash; **a. civil**, civil aviation. 2 *Mil* air force.
aviador,-a *nm,f* aviator, flier; *Mil* (*piloto*) air force pilot.
aviar [29] *vtr* (*preparar*) to prepare, get ready.
avícola *adj* poultry.
avicultura *nf* aviculture; (*de aves de corral*) poultry keeping.
avidez *nf* avidity, eagerness.

ávido,-a adj avid; **a. de,** eager for.

avinagrado,-a adj vinegary, sour; fig sour.

avinagrarse vr to turn sour; fig to become sour o bitter.

avión¹ nm aeroplane, US airplane, plane, aircraft; **viajar en a.,** to fly, go by plane; **por a.,** (en carta) airmail.

avión² nm Orn martin.

avioneta nf light aircraft o plane.

avíos nmpl Culin ingredients.

avisar vtr 1 (informar) to inform; **avísame cuando hayas acabado,** let me know when you finish. 2 (advertir) to warn; **ya te avisé,** I warned you. 3 (llamar) to call for; **a. a la policía,** to notify the police; **a. al médico,** to send for the doctor.

aviso nm 1 notice; (advertencia) warning; (nota) note; **hasta nuevo a.,** until further notice; **sin previo a.,** without notice. 2 **estar sobre a.,** to know what's going on, be in on it.

avispa nf wasp.

avispado,-a adj fam quick-witted.

avispero nm (nido) wasps' nest.

avistar vtr to see, sight.

avituallamiento nm provisioning.

avivar vtr (fuego) to stoke (up); (pasión) to intensify; (paso) to quicken.

avizor,-a adj **estar ojo a.,** to be on the alert o on the lookout.

axila nf armpit, axilla.

axioma nm axiom.

ay interj (dolor) ouch!

aya nf arc (niñera) nanny.

ayer I adv yesterday; **a. por la mañana/ por la tarde,** yesterday morning/ afternoon; **a. por la noche,** last night; **antes de a.,** the day before yesterday. II nm **el a.,** yesteryear.

ayuda nf help, assistance; **ir en a. de algn,** to come to sb's assistance.

ayudante nmf assistant; Med **a. técnico-sanitario,** nurse.

ayudar I vtr to help; **¿en qué puedo ayudarle?,** (how) can I help you? II ayu-

darse vr 1 (unos a otros) to help. 2 **a. de,** to use, make use of.

ayunar vi to fast.

ayunas nfpl **en a.,** without having eaten breakfast.

ayuno nm fasting; **guardar/hacer a.,** to fast.

ayuntamiento nm (institución) town council; (edificio) town hall.

azabache nm jet; **negro a.,** jet black.

azada nf hoe.

azafata nf 1 Av air hostess. 2 (de congresos) stewardess; (de concurso) hostess.

azafrán nm saffron.

azahar nm (del naranjo) orange blossom; (del limonero) lemon blossom.

azar nm chance; **por a.,** by chance; **al a.,** at random; **juegos de a.,** games of chance; **los azares de la vida,** the ups and downs of life.

azaroso,-a adj hazardous, dangerous.

azogue nm mercury, quicksilver.

azorado,-a adj embarrassed.

azorar I vtr to embarrass. II azorarse vr to be embarrassed.

Azores nfpl **las (Islas) A.,** the Azores.

azotar vtr to beat; (con látigo) to whip, flog; fig to scourge.

azote nm 1 (golpe) smacking; (latigazo) lash, stroke (of the whip). 2 fig scourge.

azotea nf flat roof.

azteca adj & nmf Aztec.

azúcar nm & f sugar; **a. blanco,** refined sugar; **a. moreno,** brown sugar.

azucarado,-a adj sweetened.

azucarero,-a I nm & f sugar bowl. II adj sugar.

azucena nf white lily.

azufre nm sulphur, US sulfur.

azul adj & nm blue; **a. celeste,** sky blue; **a. marino,** navy blue; **a. turquesa,** turquoise; **sangre a.,** blue blood.

azulado,-a adj bluish.

azulejo nm (glazed) tile.

azuzar [4] vtr **a. los perros a algn,** to set the dogs on sb.

B

B, b [be] nf (la letra) B, b.

baba nf dribble; fig **se le caía la b.,** he was delighted.

babear vi (niño) to dribble; (adulto, animal) to slobber.

babel nm & f bedlam.

babero nm bib.

Babia n fig **estar en B.,** to be daydreaming.

babor nm Náut port, port side.

babosa nf slug.

baboso,-a adj fam slimy; Am fool, idiot.

babucha nf slipper.

baca nf Aut roof rack.

bacalao nm (pez) cod.

bache nm 1 (en carretera) pot hole. 2 Av air pocket. 3 fig bad patch; **pasar un b.,** to go through a bad patch.

bachillerato nm = General Certificate of Secondary Education, US high school degree.

bacilo nm bacillus.

bacon nm bacon.

bacteria nf bacterium; **bacterias,** bacteria.

bacteriológico,-a adj bacteriological;

guerra bacteriológica, germ warfare.

báculo *nm* walking stick; *(de obispo)* crosier.

badén *nm Aut* bump.

bádminton *nm* badminton.

bafle *nm* loudspeaker.

bagaje *nm* baggage.

bagatela *nf (baratija)* knick-knack; *fig* trifle.

Bagdad *n* Baghdad.

Bahamas *npl* las **(Islas) B.,** the Bahamas.

bahía *nf* bay.

baila(d)or,-a *nm,f* flamenco dancer.

bailar [15] *vtr & vi* to dance; *fig* **b. al son que le tocan,** to toe the line; *fam* **¡que me quiten lo baila(d)o!,** but at least I had a good time!

bailarín,-ina *nm,f* dancer; *(clásico)* ballet dancer.

baile *nm* 1 *(danza)* dance. 2 *(fiesta popular)* dance; *(formal)* ball; **b. de disfraces,** fancy dress ball.

baja *nf* 1 drop, fall; *Fin* **jugar a la b.,** to bear. 2 *Mil* loss, casualty. 3 **dar de b. a algn,** *(despedir)* to lay sb off; **darse de b.,** *(por enfermedad)* to take sick leave; *(de un club)* to resign **(de,** from), drop out **(de,** of).

bajada *nf* 1 *(descenso)* descent. 2 *(cuesta)* slope. 3 **b. de bandera,** *(de taxi)* minimum fare.

bajamar *nf* low tide.

bajar I *vtr* 1 to come *o* go down; **b. la escalera,** to come *o* go downstairs. 2 *(descender)* to bring *o* take down; *(volumen)* to turn down; *(voz, telón)* to lower; *(precios etc)* to reduce, cut; *(persiana)* to let down; *(cabeza)* to bow *o* lower. II *vi* 1 to go *o* come down. 2 *(apearse)* to get off; *(de un coche)* to get out **(de,** of). 3 *(disminuir)* to fall, drop. III **bajarse** *vr* 1 to come *o* go down. 2 *(apearse)* to get off; *(de un coche)* to get out **(de,** of).

bajeza *nf* despicable action.

bajinis (por lo) *loc adv fam* on the sly.

bajío *nm* 1 sandbank. 2 *Am* lowland.

bajista I *adj Fin* bearish; **tendencia b.,** downward trend. II *nmf* 1 *Fin* bear. 2 *Mús* bass guitarist.

bajo,-a I *adj* 1 low; *(persona)* short; *(sonido)* faint, soft; **en voz baja,** in a low voice; **planta baja,** ground floor; **de baja calidad,** of poor quality; **la clase baja,** the lower class. 2 *fig (vil)* base, contemptible. II *nm* 1 *Mús* bass. 2 *(planta baja)* ground floor. III *adv* low; **hablar b.,** to speak quietly; *fig* **por lo b.,** on the sly. IV *prep* 1 *(lugar)* under, underneath; **b. tierra,** underground; **b. la lluvia,** in the rain. 2 *Pol Hist* under; **b. la República,** under the Republic. 3 **b. cero,** *(temperatura)* below zero. 4 *fur* under; **b. juramento,** under oath; **b. pena de muerte,**

on pain of death; **b. fianza,** on bail.

bajón *nm* 1 *(bajada)* sharp fall, decline. 2 *Com* slump. 3 *(de salud)* relapse, deterioration.

bajorrelieve *nm* bas-relief.

bajura *nf* **pesca de b.,** coastal fishing.

bala *nf* bullet; *fig* **como una b.,** like a shot.

balada *nf* ballad.

baladí *adj (pl baladíes)* trivial.

balance *nm* 1 *Fin* balance; *(declaración)* balance sheet; *fig* **hacer b. de una situación,** to take stock of a situation. 2 *(resultado)* outcome.

balancear I *vtr* to rock. II **balancearse** *vr (en mecedora)* to rock; *(en columpio)* to swing.

balanceo *nm* rocking, swinging.

balanza *nf* scales *pl*; *fig* **estar en la b.,** to be in the balance *o* in danger; **b. comercial,** balance of trade; **b. de pagos,** balance of payments.

balar *vi* to bleat.

balaustrada *nf* balustrade, railing.

balazo *nm* 1 *(disparo)* shot; **matar a algn de un b.,** to shoot sb dead. 2 *(herida)* bullet wound.

balboa *nf Fin* standard monetary unit of Panama.

balbucear *vi (adulto)* to stutter, stammer; *(niño)* to babble.

balbuceo *nm (de adulto)* stuttering, stammering; *(de niño)* babbling.

balbucir *vi defect* → **balbucear.**

Balcanes *npl* los **B.,** the Balkans.

balcón *nm* balcony.

baldado,-a *adj fam* shattered.

baldar *vtr* to cripple, maim.

balde[1] *nm* pail, bucket.

balde[2] *loc adv* 1 **de b.,** *(gratis)* free. 2 **en b.,** *(en vano)* in vain.

baldío,-a *adj (terreno)* uncultivated, waste; *(esfuerzo)* vain, useless.

baldosa *nf (ceramic)* floor tile; *(para pavimentar)* flagstone, paving stone.

balear I *adj* Balearic. II *nmf* native *o* inhabitant of the Balearic Islands.

Baleares *npl* las **(Islas) B.,** the Balearic Islands.

balido *nm* bleating, bleat.

balística *nf* ballistics *sing*.

balístico,-a *adj* ballistic.

baliza *nf* 1 *Náut* buoy. 2 *Av* beacon.

ballena *nf* whale.

ballet *nm* ballet.

balneario *nm* spa, health resort.

balompié *nm* football.

balón *nm* ball, football; *fig* **b. de oxígeno,** boost.

baloncesto *nm* basketball.

balonmano *nm* handball.

balonvolea *nm* volleyball.

balsa *nf* 1 *Náut* raft. 2 *fig* **como una b. de aceite,** very quiet.

bálsamo *nm* balsam, balm.

Báltico *nm* **el (Mar) B.**, the Baltic (Sea).

baluarte *nm fig* stronghold.

bambas® *nfpl* trainers.

bambolear *vi*, **bambolearse** *vr* to swing; *(persona, árbol)* to sway; *(mesa, silla)* to wobble.

bambú *(pl bambúes)* bamboo.

banal *adj* banal, trivial.

banalidad *nf* triviality, banality.

banana *nf* banana.

banano *nm (fruto)* banana; *(árbol)* banana tree.

banca *nf* 1 *(asiento)* bench. 2 *Com Fin* (the) banks; *(actividad)* banking. 3 *(en juegos)* bank.

bancario,-a *adj* banking.

bancarrota *nf Fin* bankruptcy; **estar en b.**, to be bankrupt.

banco *nm* 1 bench. 2 *Com Fin* bank. 3 **b. de arena**, sandbank. 4 *(de peces)* shoal, school. 5 *Geol* layer.

banda *nf* 1 *Mús* band. 2 *Cin* **b. sonora**, sound track. 3 *(de pájaros)* flock. 4 *(cinta)* sash. 5 *(lado)* side; *Ftb* **línea de b.**, touchline; **saque de b.**, throw-in.

bandada *nf* flock.

bandazo *nm* **dar bandazos**, to lurch.

bandeja *nf* tray; *fig* **servir algo a algn en b.**, to hand sth to sb on a plate.

bandera *nf* flag.

banderín *nm* pennant, small flag.

bandido *nm* bandit, outlaw.

bando¹ *nm* 1 *Jur (edicto)* edict, proclamation. 2 *bandos*, banns.

bando² *nm* faction, side; **pasarse al otro b.**, to go over to the other side, change allegiances.

bandolero *nm* bandit, outlaw.

banquero,-a *nm,f* banker.

banqueta *nf* stool.

banquete *nm* banquet, feast; **b. de bodas**, wedding reception.

banquillo *nm* 1 *Jur* dock. 2 *Dep* bench.

bañador *nm (de mujer)* bathing *o* swimming costume; *(de hombre)* swimming trunks *pl*.

bañar I *vtr* to bath. 2 *(cubrir)* to coat, cover; **b. en oro**, to goldplate. II **bañarse** *vr (en baño)* to have *o* take a bath; *(en mar, piscina)* to go for a swim.

bañera *nf* bath, bathtub.

bañista *nmf* bather, swimmer.

baño *nm* 1 bath; **tomar un b.**, to have *o* take a bath; *fig* **darse un b. de sol**, to sunbathe; **b. de sangre**, bloodbath. 2 *(de oro etc)* coat; *(de chocolate etc)* coating, covering. 3 *(cuarto de baño)* bathroom; *(lavabo)* toilet.

bar *nm* bar, pub.

barahúnda *nf* din, uproar.

baraja *nf* pack, deck.

barajar *vtr (cartas)* to shuffle; *fig (nombres, cifras)* to juggle with.

baranda, barandilla *nf (de escalera)* handrail, banister; *(de balcón)* handrail.

baratija *nf* trinket, knick-knack.

baratillo *nm* flea market.

barato,-a *adj* cheap. II *adv* cheaply.

baraúnda *nf* din, uproar.

barba *nf* 1 *Anat* chin. 2 *(pelo)* beard; *fig* **cien pesetas por b.**, a hundred pesetas a head.

barbacoa *nf* barbecue.

barbaridad *nf* 1 atrocity. 2 *(disparate)* piece of nonsense; **no digas barbaridades**, don't talk nonsense. 3 **una b.**, a lot; **costar una b.**, to cost a fortune.

barbarie *nf* savagery, cruelty.

bárbaro,-a I *adj* 1 *Hist* barbarian. 2 *(cruel)* barbaric, barbarous. 3 *fam (enorme)* massive. 4 *fam (estupendo)* tremendous, terrific. II *nm,f Hist* barbarian.

barbecho *nm* fallow land; **dejar en b.**, to leave fallow.

barbería *nf* barber's (shop).

barbero *nm* barber.

barbilla *nf* chin.

barbitúrico *nm* barbiturate.

barbudo,-a *adj* with a heavy beard.

barca *nf* small boat.

barcaza *nf* lighter.

barcelonés,-esa I *adj* of *o* from Barcelona. II *nm,f* native *o* inhabitant of Barcelona.

barco *nm* boat, ship; **b. de pasajeros**, liner; **b. de vapor**, steamer.

baremo *nm* scale.

barítono *nm* baritone.

barlovento *nm* windward.

barman *nm* barman.

barniz *nm* 1 *(en madera)* varnish; *(en cerámica)* glaze. 2 *fig* veneer.

barnizar [4] *vtr (madera)* to varnish; *(cerámica)* to glaze.

barómetro *nm* barometer.

barón *nm* baron.

baronesa *nf* baroness.

barquero,-a *nm,f (hombre)* boatman; *(mujer)* boatwoman.

barquillo *nm* wafer.

barra *nf* 1 bar; **b. de pan**, French loaf, baguette; **b. de labios**, lipstick. 2 *(mostrador)* bar. 3 *Gimn* **b. fija**, horizontal bar.

barraca *nf* 1 *(caseta)* shack, hut. 2 *(en Valencia y Murcia)* thatched farmhouse.

barracón *nm Mil* prefabricated hut.

barranco *nm (despeñadero)* cliff, precipice; *(torrentera)* gully, ravine.

barrena *nf* twist drill.

barrenar *vtr Téc* to drill.

barrendero,-a *nm,f* sweeper, street sweeper.

barreno *nm* 1 *(taladro)* large drill. 2 *Min* charge.

barreño *nm* tub.

barrer I *vtr* to sweep. II *vi (en elecciones)*

to win by landslide.

barrera I nf barrier.

barricada nf barricade.

barrida nf landslide victory.

barriga nf belly; fam tummy.

barrigón,-ona, **barrigudo,-a** adj potbellied.

barril nm barrel; **cerveza de b.,** draught beer.

barrillo nm pimple, spot.

barrio nm area, district; **del b.,** local; **el B. Gótico,** the Gothic Quarter; **b. chino,** red-light district; **barrios bajos,** slums.

barrizal nm mire, quagmire.

barro nm 1 (lodo) mud. 2 (arcilla) clay; **objetos de b.,** earthenware sing.

barroco,-a adj baroque.

barruntar vtr (sospechar) to suspect; (presentir) to have a feeling.

barrunto nm (presentimiento) feeling, presentiment; (sospecha) suspicion.

bártola (a la) loc adv fam **tenderse o tumbarse a la b.,** to laze around, idle away one's time.

bártulos nmpl fam things, bits and pieces.

barullo nm (alboroto) row, din; (confusión) confusion.

basar I vtr to base (**en,** on). II **basarse** vr (teoría, película) to be based (**en,** on); **¿en qué te basas para decir eso?,** what grounds do you have for saying that?

basca nf arg people, crowd.

báscula nf scales pl; (para camiones) weighbridge.

bascular vi to tilt.

base nf 1 base; **sueldo b.,** minimum wage; Inform **b. de datos,** data base. 2 (de argumento, teoría) basis; **en b. a,** on the basis of; **a b. de estudiar,** by studying; **a b. de productos naturales,** using natural products. 3 (de partido) grass roots; **miembro de b.,** rank and file member. 4 (nociones) grounding.

básico,-a adj basic.

basílica nf basilica.

básquet nm basketball.

bastante I adj 1 (suficiente) enough; **b. tiempo/comida,** enough time/food; **bastantes platos,** enough plates. 2 (abundante) quite a lot of; **hace b. calor/frío,** it's quite hot/cold; **bastantes amigos,** quite a lot of friends. II adv 1 (suficiente) enough; **con esto hay b.,** that is enough; **no soy lo b. rico (como) para ...,** I am not rich enough to .... 2 (considerablemente) fairly, quite; **me gusta b.,** I quite like it; **vamos b. al cine,** we go to the cinema quite o fairly often.

bastar I vi to be sufficient o enough, suffice; **basta con tres,** three will be enough; **¡basta de tonterías!,** enough of this nonsense!; **basta con tocarlo para que se abra,** you only have to touch it and it opens; **¡basta (ya)!,** that's

enough!, that will do! II **bastarse** vr **b. a sí mismo,** to be self-sufficient, rely only on oneself.

bastardilla nf Impr italics pl.

bastardo,-a adj & nm,f bastard.

bastidor nm 1 frame. 2 Teat **bastidores,** wings; fig **entre b.,** behind the scenes.

bastión nm bastion.

basto,-a adj (cosa) rough, coarse; (persona) coarse, uncouth.

bastos nm Naipes ≈ clubs.

bastón nm stick, walking stick.

basura nf rubbish, US trash, garbage.

basurero nm 1 (persona) dustman, refuse collector, US garbage collector. 2 (lugar) rubbish dump, US garbage dump.

bata nf (para casa) dressing gown; (de médico etc) white coat; (de científico) lab coat.

batacazo nm 1 crash, bang. 2 Am fluke, stroke of luck.

batalla nf battle; **librar b.,** to do o join battle; **b. campal,** pitched battle.

batallar vi to fight, quarrel.

batallón nm battalion.

batata nf sweet potato.

batatazo nm Am → batacazo.

batear I vi to bat. II vtr to hit.

batería I nf 1 battery. 2 Mús drums pl. 3 **b. de cocina,** pots and pans, set of pans. II nmf drummer.

batiburrillo nm jumble, mess.

batida nf 1 (de la policía) raid. 2 (en caza) beat.

batido,-a I adj 1 Culin whipped. 2 Dep **tierra batida,** clay. II nm milk shake.

batidora nf Culin beater, whisk.

batiente adj **reírse a mandíbula b.,** to laugh one's head off.

batín nm short dressing gown.

batir I vtr 1 to beat. 2 (huevo) to beat; (nata) to whip, whisk. 3 (récord) to break. 4 (en caza) to beat. II **batirse** vr to fight.

batuta nf Mús baton; fig **llevar la b.,** to be in charge.

baúl nm 1 trunk. 2 Am Aut boot, US trunk.

bautismo nm baptism, christening.

bautizar [4] vtr to baptize, christen; (vino) to water down.

bautizo nm baptism, christening.

Baviera nf Bavaria.

baya nf berry.

bayeta nf floorcloth.

bayo,-a adj whitish yellow.

bayoneta nf bayonet.

baza nf trick; fig **meter b.,** to butt in.

bazar nm bazaar.

bazo nm spleen.

bazofia nf pey rubbish.

beatería nf sanctimoniousness.

beato,-a adj (piadoso) devout; pey prudish, sanctimonious.

bebé *nm* baby; **b. probeta,** test-tube baby.

bebedero *nm* drinking trough, water trough.

bebedor,-a *nm,f* (hard *o* heavy) drinker.

beber *vtr & vi* to drink.

bebible *adj* drinkable.

bebida *nf* drink; **darse a la b.,** to take to drink.

bebido,-a *adj* drunk.

beca *nf* grant.

becar [1] *vtr* to award a grant to.

becario,-a *nm,f* grant holder.

becerro *nm* calf.

bechamel *nf* bechamel; **salsa b.,** bechamel sauce, white sauce.

becuadro *nm* Mús natural sign.

bedel *nm* beadle.

begonia *nf* begonia.

beige *adj & nm inv* beige.

béisbol *nm* baseball.

Belén *n* Bethlehem.

belén *nm* nativity scene, crib.

belga *adj & nmf* Belgian.

Bélgica *n* Belgium.

Belgrado *n* Belgrade.

Belice *n* Belize.

bélico,-a *adj* warlike, bellicose; *(preparativos etc)* war; **material b.,** armaments *pl*.

belicoso,-a *adj* warlike, bellicose; *(agresivo)* aggressive.

beligerancia *nf* belligerence.

beligerante *adj* belligerent; **los países beligerantes,** the countries at war.

bellaco,-a I *adj* wicked, roguish. II *nm,f* scoundrel, rogue.

belleza *nf* beauty.

bello,-a *adj* beautiful.

bellota *nf* Bot acorn; *fig* **animal de b.,** blockhead.

bemol I *adj* Mús flat. II *nm* **esto tiene bemoles,** this is a tough one.

bencina *nf Am* petrol.

bendecir [12] *vtr* to bless; **b. la mesa,** to say grace; **¡Dios la bendiga!,** God bless you!

bendición *nf* blessing.

bendito,-a I *adj* blessed; *(maldito)* damned. II *nm,f* *(bonachón)* good sort, kind soul; *(tontorrón)* simple soul.

beneficencia *nf* beneficence, charity.

beneficiado,-a *adj* favoured, *US* favored; **salir b. de algo,** to do well out of sth.

beneficiar [12] I *vtr* to benefit. II **beneficiarse** *vr* **b. de** *o* **con algo,** to profit from *o* by sth.

beneficiario,-a *nm,f* beneficiary; **margen b.,** profit margin.

beneficio *nm* 1 Com Fin profit. 2 *(bien)* benefit; **en b. propio,** in one's own interest; **un concierto a b. de ...,** a concert in aid of ....

beneficioso,-a *adj* beneficial.

benéfico,-a *adj* charitable.

benemérita *nf* **la B.,** the Spanish Civil Guard.

beneplácito *nm fml* approval, consent.

benevolencia *nf* benevolence.

benevolente, benévolo,-a *adj* benevolent.

bengala *nf* flare.

benigno,-a *adj (persona)* gentle, benign; *(clima)* mild; *(tumor)* benign.

benjamín,-ina *nm,f* youngest child.

beodo,-a *adj* drunk.

berberecho *nm* (common) cockle.

berbiquí *nm* Téc drill.

berenjena *nf* aubergine, *US* eggplant.

Berlín *n* Berlin.

berlina *nf (coche)* saloon; *(carruaje)* sedan.

berlinés,-esa I *adj* of *o* from Berlin. II *nm,f* Berliner.

bermejo,-a *adj* reddish.

bermellón *nm* vermilion.

Bermudas I *nfpl* **las (Islas) B.,** Bermuda *sing.* II *nmpl* **bermudas,** *(prenda)* Bermuda shorts.

Berna *n* Bern.

berrear *vi* to bellow, low.

berrido *nm* bellowing, lowing.

berrinche *nm fam* rage, tantrum.

berro *nm* cress, watercress.

berza *nf* cabbage.

besar I *vtr* to kiss. II **besarse** *vr* to kiss.

beso *nm* kiss.

best-seller *nm* best-seller.

bestia I *nf* beast, animal; **b. de carga,** beast of burden. II *nmf fam fig* brute, beast. III *adj fig* brutish, boorish; **a lo b.,** rudely.

bestial *adj* bestial; *fam (enorme)* huge, tremendous; *(extraordinario)* fantastic, terrific.

bestialidad *nf* 1 *fam (estupidez)* stupidity. 2 *(crueldad)* act of cruelty. 3 *fam* **una b. de,** tons of, stacks of.

besugo *nm* 1 *(pez)* sea bream. 2 *(persona)* idiot, half-wit.

besuquear *fam* I *vtr* to kiss, cover with kisses. II **besuquearse** *vr* to smooch.

betún *nm (para el calzado)* shoe polish; *Quím* bitumen.

biberón *nm* baby's bottle, feeding bottle.

Biblia *nf* Bible.

bíblico,-a *adj* biblical.

bibliografía *nf* bibliography.

biblioteca *nf* library; **b. ambulante,** mobile library.

bibliotecario,-a *nm,f* librarian.

BIC *nf abr de* **Brigada de Investigación Criminal,** ≈ Criminal Investigation Department, CID.

bicameral *adj* Pol bicameral, two-chamber.

bicarbonato *nm* bicarbonate; **b. sódico,** bicarbonate of soda.

bicentenario *nm* bicentenary, *US* bicentennial.

bíceps nm inv biceps.

bicha nf snake.

bicho nm 1 bug, insect; ¿qué b. te ha picado?, what's bugging you? 2 Taur bull. 3 fam todo b. viviente, every living soul; un b. raro, a weirdo, an oddball.

bici nf fam bike.

bicicleta nf bicycle; **montar en b.**, to ride a bicycle.

bicolor adj two-coloured; Pol **gobierno b.**, two-party government.

bidé nm bidet.

bidón nm drum.

biela nf Aut connecting rod.

bien[1] adv 1 (correctamente) well; **habla b. (el) inglés**, he speaks English well; **responder b.**, to answer correctly; **hiciste b. en decírmelo**, you were right to tell me; **las cosas le van b.**, things are going well for him; **¡b.!**, good!, great!; **¡muy b.!**, excellent, first class!; **¡qué b.!**, great!, fantastic! 2 (de salud) well; **sentirse/encontrarse/estar b.**, to feel well. 3 **vivir b.**, to be comfortably off; **¡está b.!**, **¡de acuerdo!** fine!, all right!; **¡ya está b.!**, that's (quite) enough!; **aquí se está muy b.**, it's really nice here; **esta falda te sienta b.**, this skirt suits you; fam **ese libro está muy b.**, that book is very good; fam **su novia está muy b.**, his girlfriend is very nice. 4 (intensificador) very, quite; **b. temprano**, very early, nice and early; **b. caliente**, pretty hot; **b. es verdad que ...**, it's quite clear that ... 5 **más b.**, rather, a little. 6 **b. podía haberme avisado**, she might have let me know. 7 (de buena gana) willingly, gladly; **b. me tomaría una cerveza**, I'd really love a beer.
II conj **ahora b.**, now, now then; **o b.**, or, or else; **b. ... o b. ...**, either ... or ...; **no b.**, as soon as; **no b. llegó ...**, no sooner had she arrived than ...; **si b.**, although, even if.
III adj **la gente b.**, the wealthy, the upper classes.

bien[2] nm 1 (bondad) good; **el b. y el mal**, good and evil; **un hombre/familia de b.**, a good man/family. 2 (bienestar) **por el b. de**, for the good of; **lo hace por tu b.**, he does it for your sake. 3 **bienes**, goods; **bienes de equipo**, capital goods; **bienes gananciales**, communal property; **bienes inmuebles**, real estate; **bienes de consumo**, consumer goods.

bienal nf biennial exhibition.

bienestar nm (personal) well-being, contentment; (comodidad) ease, comfort; **la sociedad del b.**, the affluent society.

bienhechor,-a nm,f (hombre) benefactor; (mujer) benefactress.

bienintencionado,-a adj well-meaning, well-intentioned.

bienio nm biennium, two-year period.

bienvenida nf welcome; **dar la b. a algn**, to welcome sb.

bienvenido,-a adj welcome.

bife nm steak.

bifocal adj bifocal; **gafas bifocales**, bifocals.

bifurcación nf bifurcation; (de la carretera) fork.

bifurcarse [1] vr to fork, branch off.

bigamia nf bigamy.

bígamo,-a I adj bigamous. II nm,f bigamist.

bigote nm (de persona) moustache, US mustache; (de animal) (usu pl) whiskers pl.

bilateral adj bilateral; **acuerdo b.**, bilateral agreement.

bilbaíno,-a I adj o of from Bilbao. II nm,f native o inhabitant of Bilbao.

bilingüe adj bilingual.

bilis nf bile.

billar nm 1 (juego) billiards sing; **b. americano**, pool; **b. ruso**, snooker. 2 (mesa) billiard table.

billete nm 1 ticket; **b. de ida y vuelta**, return (ticket), US round-trip ticket; **b. sencillo** o **de ida**, single (ticket). 2 (de banco) note, US bill; **un b. de mil pesetas**, a thousand peseta note.

billetera nf, **billetero** nm wallet, US billfold.

billón nm billion, US trillion.

bimensual adj twice-monthly, bimonthly.

bimotor I adj twin-engined. II nm twin-engined plane.

binario,-a adj binary.

bingo nm 1 (juego) bingo. 2 (sala) bingo hall.

binomio nm binomial.

biodegradable adj biodegradable.

biofísica nf biophysics.

biografía nf biography.

biográfico,-a adj biographical.

biógrafo,-a nm,f biographer.

biología nf biology.

biológico,-a adj biological.

biólogo,-a nm,f biologist.

biombo nm (folding) screen.

biomasa nf bio-mass.

biopsia nf biopsy.

bioquímica nf biochemistry.

bioquímico,-a I adj biochemical. II nm,f biochemist.

bióxido nm dioxide; **b. de carbono**, carbon dioxide.

bipartidismo nm two-party system.

biquini nm bikini.

birlar vtr fam to pinch, nick.

Birmania n Burma.

birmano,-a adj & nm,f Burmese.

birrete nm cap, beret; Rel biretta; Univ mortar-board.

birria nf fam rubbish.

bis I *nm* encore. II *adv* twice.

bisabuela *nf* great-grandmother.

bisabuelo *nm* great-grandfather; **bisabuelos**, great-grandparents.

bisagra *nf* hinge; **partido b.**, party holding the balance of power.

bisbisar, bisbisear *vtr* to whisper.

bisexual *adj & nmf* bisexual.

bisiesto *adj* año b., leap year.

bisnieto,-a *nm,f* (*niño*) great-grandson; (*niña*) great-granddaughter; **mis bisnietos**, my great-grandchildren.

bisonte *nm* bison, American buffalo.

bisoño,-a *adj* inexperienced.

bisté, bistec *nm* steak.

bisturí *nm* scalpel.

bisutería *nf* imitation jewellery *o* US jewelry.

bit *nm* Inform bit.

bíter *nm* bitters *pl*.

bizantino,-a *adj fig* **discusiones bizantinas**, hair-splitting arguments.

bizco,-a I *adj* cross-eyed. II *nm,f* cross-eyed person.

bizcocho *nm* sponge cake.

biznieto,-a *nm,f* → **bisnieto,-a**.

blanca *nf fam* **estar sin b.**, to be flat broke.

blanco,-a[1] I *adj* white; (*tez*) fair. II *nm,f* (*hombre*) white man; (*mujer*) white woman; **los blancos**, whites.

blanco[2] *nm* 1 (*color*) white. 2 (*hueco*) blank; **dejó la hoja en b.**, he left the page blank; **votos en b.**, blank votes; *fig* **pasar la noche en b.**, to have a sleepless night; **me quedé en b.**, my mind went blank. 3 (*diana*) target; **dar en el b.**, to hit the target; *fig* **ser el b. de todas las miradas**, to be the centre of attention.

blancura *nf* whiteness.

blandengue *adj pey* weak, soft.

blandir *vtr* to brandish.

blando,-a *adj* soft.

blanquear *vtr* 1 to whiten. 2 (*encalar*) to whitewash. 3 (*dinero*) to launder.

blanquecino,-a *adj* whitish.

blanqueo *nm* 1 whitening. 2 (*encalado*) whitewashing. 3 (*de dinero*) laundering.

blasfemar *vi* to blaspheme (**contra**, against).

blasfemia *nf* blasphemy.

blasón *nm* coat of arms.

bledo *nm fam* **me importa un b.**, I couldn't give a damn.

blindado,-a *adj* Mil armoured, US armored, armour-plated, US armor-plated; (*antibalas*) bullet-proof; **coche b.**, bullet-proof car; **puerta blindada**, reinforced door, security door.

blindaje *nm* armour, US armor; (*vehículo*) armour *o* US armor plating.

bloc *nm* pad; **b. de notas**, notepad.

bloque *nm* 1 block; **en b.**, en bloc; **b. de pisos**, (block of) flats. 2 Pol bloc; **el b.**

comunista, the Communist Bloc.

bloquear *vtr* 1 to block. 2 Mil to blockade.

bloqueo *nm* blockade; Dep block.

blues *nm* blues *pl*.

blusa *nf* blouse.

blusón *nm* loose blouse, smock.

boato *nm* show, ostentation.

bobada *nf* nonsense; **decir bobadas**, to talk nonsense.

bobalicón,-ona *fam* I *adj* simple, stupid. II *nm,f* simpleton, idiot.

bobería *nf* → **bobada**.

bobina *nf* 1 reel. 2 Elec coil.

bobo,-a I *adj* (*tonto*) stupid, silly; (*ingenuo*) naïve. II *nm,f* fool.

boca *nf* 1 mouth; **b. abajo**, face downward; **b. arriba**, face upward; *fig* **a pedir de b.**, in accordance with one's wishes; *fig* **andar de b. en b.**, to be the talk of the town; *fam* **¡cierra la b.!**, shut up!; *fam* **con la b. abierta**, open-mouthed; *fam* **se le hizo la b. agua**, his mouth watered; **el b. a b.**, kiss of life, mouth-to-mouth respiration. 2 **la b. del metro**, the entrance to the tube *o* underground station; **b. de riego**, hydrant.

bocacalle *nf* entrance to a street.

bocadillo *nm* 1 sandwich; **un b. de jamón/tortilla**, a ham/omelette sandwich. 2 (*de cómic*) balloon.

bocado *nm* 1 (*mordedura*) bite. 2 (*de caballo*) bit.

bocajarro **(a)** *loc adv* point-blank.

bocanada *nf* 1 (*de vino*) mouthful. 2 (*de humo*) puff; **una b. de viento**, a gust of wind.

bocata *nm* sandwich.

bocazas *nmf inv fam* bigmouth, blabbermouth.

boceto *nm* Arte sketch, outline; (*esquema*) outline, plan.

bochinche *nm fam* uproar; **armar un b.**, to kick up a row.

bochorno *nm* 1 (*tiempo*) sultry *o* close weather; (*calor sofocante*) stifling heat. 2 *fig* (*vergüenza*) shame, embarrassment.

bochornoso,-a *adj* 1 (*tiempo*) sultry, close, muggy; (*calor*) stifling. 2 *fig* (*vergonzoso*) shameful, embarrassing.

bocina *nf* horn; **tocar la b.**, to blow *o* sound one's horn.

bocinazo *nm* hoot, toot.

boda *nf* wedding, marriage; **bodas de plata**, silver wedding *sing*.

bodega *nf* 1 wine cellar; (*tienda*) wine shop. 2 Náut hold. 3 (*almacén*) warehouse. 4 Am grocery store, grocer's.

bodegón *nm* still-life.

bodrio *nm fam* rubbish, trash.

body *nm* bodystocking, leotard.

BOE *nm abr de* Boletín Oficial del Estado, Official Gazette.

bofetada *nf*, **bofetón** *nm* slap on the

face; **dar una b./un b. a algn**, to slap sb's face.

boga *nf fig* **estar en b.**, to be in vogue.

bogar [7] *vi* 1 (*remar*) to row. 2 (*navegar*) to sail.

bogavante *nm* lobster.

bogotano,-a I *adj* of *o* from Bogotá. II *n m,f* native of Bogotá.

bohío *nm Am* hut, cabin.

boicot *nm* (*pl* **boicots**) boycott.

boicotear *vtr* to boycott.

boicoteo *nm* boycott.

boina *nf* beret.

bol *nm* bowl.

bola *nf* 1 ball; (*canica*) marble; **b. de nieve**, snowball; **no dar pie con b.**, to be unable to do anything right. 2 *fam* (*mentira*) fib, lie; **meter bolas**, to tell fibs. 3 *Am* (*rumor*) rumour.

bolchevique *adj* & *nmf* Bolshevik.

bolear *vtr* to throw.

bolera *nf* bowling alley.

boletería *nf Am Dep Ferroc* ticket office; *GB* booking office; *Teat* ticket office, box office.

boletín *nm* bulletin; **B. Oficial del Estado**, Official Gazette.

boleto *nm* ticket.

boli *nm fam* ball-point pen, biro®.

boliche *nm* 1 (*juego*) bowling, skittles. 2 (*bola*) jack. 3 (*lugar*) bowling alley.

bólido *nm Aut* racing car.

bolígrafo *nm* ballpoint (pen), biro®.

bolívar *nm Fin* standard monetary unit of Venezuela.

Bolivia *n* Bolivia.

boliviano,-a I *adj* & *nm,f* Bolivian.

bollar *vtr* to dent.

bollo *nm* 1 *Culin* bun, bread roll. 2 (*abolladura*) dent.

bolo *nm* 1 skittle, ninepin. 2 **bolos**, (*juego*) skittles.

bolsa[1] *nf* bag; *Av* **b. de aire**, air pocket; **b. de deportes**, sports bag; **b. de la compra**, shopping bag; **b. de viaje**, travel bag.

bolsa[2] *nf Fin* Stock Exchange; **jugar a la b.**, to play the market.

bolsillo *nm* (*en prenda*) pocket; **de b.**, pocket, pocket-size; **libro de b.**, paperback; **lo pagó de su b.**, he paid for it out of his own pocket.

bolso *nm* handbag, bag, *US* purse.

bomba[1] *nf* pump; **b. de aire**, air pump; **b. de incendios**, fire engine.

bomba[2] *nf* bomb; **b. atómica/de hidrógeno/de neutrones**, atomic/hydrogen/neutron bomb; **b. de relojería**, time bomb; **b. fétida**, stink bomb; *fam* **noticia b.**, shattering piece of news; *fam* **pasarlo b.**, to have a whale of a time.

bombardear *vtr* to bomb, shell; **b. a algn a preguntas**, to bombard sb with questions.

bombardeo *nm* bombing, bombardment.

bombardero *nm Av* bomber.

bombazo *nm* bomb blast.

bombear *vtr* 1 (*agua etc*) to pump. 2 (*pelota*) to blow up.

bombeo *nm* (*de líquido*) pumping; **estación de b.**, pumping station.

bombero,-a *nm,f* (*hombre*) fireman; (*mujer*) firewoman; *US* (*ambos sexos*) firefighter; **cuerpo de bomberos**, fire brigade; **parque de bomberos**, fire station.

bombilla *nf* (light) bulb.

bombín *nm* bowler hat.

bombo *nm* 1 *Mús* bass drum; *fig* **a b. y platillo(s)**, with a great song and dance; *fam* **darse b.**, to blow one's own trumpet. 2 (*de sorteo*) lottery drum.

bombón *nm* chocolate.

bombona *nf* cylinder; **b. de butano**, butane gas cylinder.

bombonera *nf* chocolate box.

bonachón,-ona *adj* good-natured, easy-going.

bonaerense I *adj* of *o* from Buenos Aires. II *nmf* native *o* inhabitant of Buenos Aires.

bonanza *nf* 1 *Náut* (*tiempo*) fair weather; (*mar*) calm at sea. 2 *fig* (*prosperidad*) prosperity.

bondad *nf* goodness; *fml* **tenga la b. de esperar**, please be so kind as to wait.

bondadoso,-a *adj* kind, good-natured.

bonete *nm Rel* cap, biretta; *Univ* mortar-board.

boniato *nm* sweet potato.

bonificación *nf* bonus.

bonificar [1] *vtr Com* to give a bonus to.

bonito,-a[1] *adj* pretty, nice.

bonito[2] *nm* tuna.

bono *nm* (*vale*) voucher. 2 *Fin* bond, debenture; **bonos del tesoro** *o* **del Estado**, Treasury bonds.

bono-bus *nm* bus pass.

boom *nm* boom.

boomerang *nm* boomerang.

boquerón *nm* anchovy.

boquete *nm* hole.

boquiabierto,-a *adj* open-mouthed; **se quedó b.**, he was flabbergasted.

boquilla *nf* 1 (*de cigarro*) tip; (*de pipa*) mouthpiece; **decir algo de b.**, to pay lip service to sth. 2 *Mús* mouthpiece. 3 (*orificio*) opening.

borbotar, borbotear *vi* to bubble.

borbotón *nm* bubbling; *fig* **salir a borbotones**, to gush forth.

borda *nf Náut* gunwale; **arrojar** *o* **echar por la b.**, to throw overboard; **fuera b.**, (*motor*) outboard motor.

bordado,-a I *adj* embroidered; **el examen me salió b.**, I made a good job of that exam. II *nm* embroidery.

bordar *vtr* 1 to embroider. 2 *fig* to do excellently.

borde¹ *nm* (*de mesa, camino*) edge; *Cost* hem, edge; (*de vasija*) rim, brim; **al b. de**, on the brink of, on the verge of; **al b. del mar**, at the seaside.

borde² *fam* I *adj* stroppy. II *nmf* stroppy person.

bordear *vtr* to go round the edge of, skirt.

bordillo *nm* kerb, *US* curb.

bordo *nm* **a b.**, on board; **subir a b.** to go on board.

borla *nf* tassel.

borne *nm Elec* terminal.

borra *nf* 1 (*pelusa*) fluff. 2 (*poso*) sediment, dregs *pl*.

borrachera *nf* (*embriaguez*) drunkenness; (*curda*) binge; **coger** *o* **pillar una b.**, to get drunk.

borracho,-a *adj* 1 (*bebido*) drunk; **estar b.**, to be drunk. 2 (*bizcocho*) with rum. II *nm,f* drunkard, drunk.

borrador *nm* 1 (*escrito*) rough copy, *US* first draft. 2 (*croquis*) rough *o* preliminary sketch. 3 (*de pizarra*) duster.

borraja *nf* **quedar en agua de borrajas**, to come to nothing, fizzle *o* peter out.

borrar I *vtr* 1 (*con goma*) to erase, rub out; (*pizarra*) to clean. 2 *Inform* to delete. II **borrarse** *vr* (*de un club etc*) to drop out, withdraw.

borrasca *nf* area of low pressure.

borrascoso,-a *adj* stormy.

borrego,-a *nm,f* 1 yearling lamb. 2 *fam* (*persona*) sheep.

borrico *nm* ass, donkey; *fam fig* ass, dimwit.

borrón *nm* blot, smudge.

borroso,-a *adj* blurred; **veo b.**, I can't see clearly, everything's blurred.

bosque *nm* wood.

bosquejar *vtr* (*dibujo*) to sketch, outline; (*plan*) to draft, outline.

bosquejo *nm* (*de dibujo*) sketch, study; (*de plan*) draft, outline.

bostezar [4] *vi* to yawn.

bostezo *nm* yawn.

bota *nf* 1 boot; *fig* **ponerse las botas**, to make a killing. 2 (*de vino*) wineskin.

botana *nf Am* snack.

botánica *nf* botany.

botánico,-a I *adj* botanic; **jardín b.**, botanic gardens. II *nm,f* botanist.

botar I *vi* 1 (*saltar*) to jump. 2 (*pelota*) to bounce. II *vtr* 1 (*barco*) to launch. 2 (*pelota*) to bounce. 3 *Am* (*arrojar*) to throw *o* chuck out.

botarate *nmf* madcap, fool.

bote¹ *nm* 1 jump, bound; **dar botes**, to jump up and down; **de un b.**, with one leap. 2 (*de pelota*) bounce, rebound.

bote² *nm* (*lata*) can, tin; (*para propinas*) jar *o* box for tips; (*en lotería*) jackpot; *fam* **chupar del b.**, to scrounge.

bote³ *nm* (*lancha*) boat; **b. salvavidas**,

lifeboat.

bote *nm* **de b. en b.**, packed, full to bursting.

botella *nf* bottle.

botellín *nm* small bottle.

botepronto *nm fam* **a b.**, all of a sudden.

botica *nf* chemist's (shop), pharmacy, *US* drugstore; *fam* **hay de todo como en b.**, there's everything under the sun.

boticario,-a *nm,f* chemist, pharmacist, *US* druggist.

botijo *nm* earthenware pitcher (with spout and handle).

botín¹ *nm* (*de un robo*) loot, booty.

botín² *nm* (*calzado*) ankle boot.

botiquín *nm* 1 medicine chest *o* cabinet; (*portátil*) first aid kit. 2 (*enfermería*) first aid post.

botón *nm* button; **pulsar el b.**, to press the button; **b. de muestra**, sample.

botones *nm inv* (*en hotel*) bellboy, *US* bellhop; (*recadero*) messenger, errand boy.

boutique *nf* boutique.

bóveda *nf* vault.

bovino,-a *adj* bovine; **ganado b.**, cattle.

boxeador *nm* boxer.

boxear *vi* to box.

boxeo *nm* boxing.

boya *nf* 1 *Náut* buoy. 2 (*corcho*) float.

boyante *adj* buoyant.

boy-scout *nm* boy scout.

bozal *nm* muzzle.

bracero *nm* (*day*) labourer.

bragas *nfpl* panties *pl*, knickers *pl*.

bragueta *nf* (*de pantalón etc*) fly, flies *pl*.

braguetazo *nm vulg* **dar el b.**, to marry for money.

braille *nm* braille.

bramar *vi* to low, bellow.

bramido *nm* lowing, bellowing.

brandy *nm* brandy.

branquia *nf* gill.

brasa *nf* ember, red-hot coal; **chuletas a la b.**, barbecued chops.

brasero *nm* brazier.

Brasil *n* Brazil.

brasileño,-a, **brasilero,-a** *adj & nm,f* Brazilian.

bravata *nf* piece *o* act of bravado.

bravo,-a I *adj* 1 (*valiente*) brave, courageous. 2 (*feroz*) fierce, ferocious; **un toro b.**, a fighting bull. 3 (*mar*) rough, stormy. II *interj* **¡b.!**, well done!, bravo!

bravucón,-ona *adj nm,f* boaster, braggart.

bravura *nf* 1 (*de animal*) ferocity, fierceness. 2 (*de persona*) courage, bravery. 3 (*de toro*) fighting spirit.

braza *nf* 1 *Náut* fathom. 2 *Natación* breast stroke; **nadar a la b.**, to do the breast stroke.

brazada *nf Natación* stroke.

brazalete *nm* 1 (*insignia*) armband. 2 (*pulsera*) bracelet.

brazo nm arm; (de animal) foreleg; (de sillón, tocadiscos) arm; **en brazos**, in one's arms; **ir del b.**, to walk arm in arm; fig **con los brazos abiertos**, with open arms; fig **no dar su b. a torcer**, not to give in, stand firm; **b. de gitano**, type of Swiss roll containing cream.

brea nf tar, pitch.

brebaje nm concoction, brew.

brecha nf (en muro) opening, gap; Mil & fig breach; fig **estar siempre en la b.**, to be always in the thick of things.

brécol nm broccoli.

bregar [7] vi to fight.

Bretaña nf 1 Brittany. 2 **Gran B.**, Great Britain.

brete nm fig **poner a algn en un b.**, to put sb in a tight spot.

breva nf early fig; fam **de higos a brevas**, once in a blue moon; fam **¡no caerá esa b.!**, no such luck!

breve adj brief; **en b.**, **en breves momentos**, shortly, soon; **en breves palabras**, in short.

brevedad nf briefness; (concision) brevity; **con la mayor b. posible**, as soon as possible.

brezo nm heather.

bribón,-ona I adj roguish, dishonest. **II** nm,f rogue, rascal.

bricolaje nm do-it-yourself, DIY.

brida nf 1 (rienda) rein, bridle. 2 Téc flange.

bridge nm Naipes bridge.

brigada I nf 1 Mil brigade. 2 (de policías) squad; **b. antiterrorista**, anti-terrorist squad. **II** Mil sergeant major.

brigadier nm brigadier.

brillante I adj brilliant. **II** nm diamond.

brillantez nf brilliance.

brillantina nf brilliantine.

brillar vi (resplandecer) to shine; (ojos, joyas) to sparkle; (lentejuelas etc) to glitter; **b. por su ausencia**, to be conspicuous by one's absence.

brillo nm (resplandor) shine; (del sol, de la luna) brightness; (de lentejuelas etc) glittering; (del cabello, tela) sheen; (de color) brilliance; (de pantalla) brightness; (de zapatos) shine; **sacar b. a**, to shine, polish.

brincar [1] vi to skip.

brinco nm skip.

brindar I vi to drink a toast; **b. por algn/algo**, to drink to sb/sth. **II** vtr 1 (oportunidad) to offer, provide. 2 Taur to dedicate the bull (a, to). **III brindarse** vr to offer (a, to), volunteer (a, to).

brindis nm 1 toast. 2 Taur dedication (of the bull).

brío nm energy.

brioso,-a adj energetic, vigorous.

brisa nf breeze; **b. marina**, sea breeze.

británico,-a I adj British; **las Islas Británicas**, the British Isles. **II** nm,f Briton; **los británicos**, the British.

brizna nf (de hierba) blade; (de carne) string.

broca nf Téc bit.

brocha nf (para pintar) paintbrush; **b. de afeitar**, shaving brush.

broche nm 1 (joya) brooch; fig **poner el b. de oro**, to finish with a flourish. 2 (de vestido) fastener.

bróculi nm broccoli.

broma nf (chiste) joke; **bromas aparte**, joking apart; **en b.**, as a joke; **¡ni en b.!**, not on your life!; **b. pesada**, practical joke; **gastar una b.**, to play a joke.

bromear vi to joke.

bromista I adj fond of joking o playing jokes. **II** nmf joker, prankster.

bronca nf 1 (riña) quarrel, row. 2 **echar una b. a algn**, to bawl sb out.

bronce nm bronze.

bronceado,-a I adj suntanned, tanned. **II** nm suntan, tan.

bronceador,-a I adj **leche bronceadora**, suntan cream. **II** nm suntan cream o lotion.

broncearse vr to get a tan o a suntan.

bronco,-a adj rough, coarse.

bronquitis nf inv bronchitis.

brotar vi (planta) to sprout; (agua) to spring, gush; (lágrimas) to well up; (epidemia) to break out.

brote nm 1 Bot (renuevo) bud, shoot; (de agua) gushing. 2 (de epidemia, violencia) outbreak.

bruces (de) loc adv face downwards; **se cayó de b.**, he fell flat on his face.

bruja nf witch, sorceress.

brujería nf witchcraft, sorcery.

brújula nf compass.

bruma nf mist.

brumoso,-a adj misty.

bruñir vtr to polish.

brusco,-a adj 1 (persona) brusque, abrupt. 2 (repentino) sudden, sharp.

Bruselas n Brussels; **coles de B.**, Brussels sprouts.

brusquedad nf brusqueness, abruptness.

brutal adj brutal.

brutalidad nf brutality.

bruto,-a I adj 1 (necio) stupid, thick; (grosero) coarse, uncouth. 2 Fin gross; **peso b.**, gross weight. 3 **un diamante en b.**, an uncut diamond. **II** nm,f blockhead, brute.

búcaro nm earthenware jug.

bucear vi to swim under water.

buche nm maw; (de ave) craw; fam (estómago) belly, stomach.

bucle nm curl, ringlet.

budín nm pudding.

budismo nm Buddhism.

budista adj Buddhist.

buen adj (delante de un nombre masculino

singular) good; **¡b. viaje!**, have a good trip!; → **bueno,-a**.

buenaventura *nf* good fortune, good luck; **echar la b. a algn**, to tell sb's fortune.

bueno,-a I *adj* 1 good; **un alumno muy b.**, a very good pupil; **una buena película**, a good film; **lo b.**, the good thing. 2 (*amable*) (*con ser*) good, kind; **el b. de Carlos**, good old Carlos; **es muy buena persona**, he's a very kind soul. 3 (*sano*) (*con estar*) well, in good health. 4 (*tiempo*) good; **hoy hace buen tiempo**, it's fine today; **mañana hará b.**, it will be fine *o* a nice day tomorrow. 5 (*conveniente*) good; **no es b. comer tanto**, it's not good for you to eat so much; **sería b. que vinieras**, it would be a good idea if you came. 6 (*considerable*) considerable; **un buen número de**, a good number of; **una buena cantidad**, a considerable amount. 7 (*grande*) good, big; **un buen trozo de pastel**, a nice *o* good big piece of cake. 8 *fam* (*atractivo*) gorgeous, sexy; **Rosa está muy buena**, Rosa's a bit of all right!; **una tía buena**, a good-looking girl. 9 *irón* fine, real, proper; **¡en buen lío te has metido!**, that's a fine mess you've got yourself into! 10 **¡buenas!**, (*saludos*) hello!; **buenas tardes**, (*desde mediodía hasta las cinco*) good afternoon; (*desde las cinco*) good evening; **buenas noches**, (*al llegar*) good evening; (*al irse*) good night; **buenos días**, good morning. 11 (*locuciones*) **de buenas a primeras**, suddenly, all at once; **estar de buenas**, to be in a good mood; **los buenos tiempos**, the good old days; **por las buenas**, willingly; **por las buenas o por las malas**, willy-nilly; *irón* **¡buena la has hecho!**, that's done it!; **un susto de los buenos**, a real fright; *irón* **¡estaría b.!**, I should jolly well hope not!; *irón* **librarse de una buena**, to get off scot free. **II** *interj* **¡b.!**, (*vale*) all right, OK. ◆**buenamente** *adv* **haz lo que b. puedas**, just do what you can; **si b. puedes**, if you possibly can.

buey *nm* ox, bullock.

búfalo,-a *nm,f* buffalo.

bufanda *nf* scarf.

bufar *vi* 1 (*toro*) to snort; (*caballo*) to neigh. 2 (*persona*) to be fuming.

bufé *nm* buffet; **b. libre**, self-service buffet meal.

bufete *nm* (*despacho de abogado*) lawyer's office.

buffet *nm* (*pl* **buffets**) → **bufé**.

bufido *nm* (*de toro*) snort; (*de caballo*) neigh.

bufón,-ona *nm,f* clown, buffoon.

buhardilla *nf* attic, garret.

búho *nm* owl; **b. real**, eagle owl.

buhonero,-a *nm,f* pedlar, hawker.

buitre *nm* vulture.

bujía *nf* 1 *Aut* spark plug. 2 *Fís* candle-power.

bulbo *nm* bulb.

buldog *nm* bulldog.

bulevar *nm* boulevard.

Bulgaria *n* Bulgaria.

búlgaro,-a *adj* & *nm,f* Bulgarian.

bulla *nf* 1 (*muchedumbre*) crowd, mob. 2 (*ruido*) din; **armar b.**, to kick up a din.

bullicio *nm* din, hubbub.

bullir *vi* 1 (*hervir*) to boil, bubble (up). 2 **b. de gente**, to be teeming with people.

bulto *nm* 1 (*cosa indistinta*) shape, form. 2 (*maleta, caja*) piece of luggage. 3 *Med* lump. 4 **hacer mucho b.**, to be very bulky; *fam* **escurrir el b.**, to pass the buck.

bumerán, bumerang *nm* boomerang.

bungalow *nm* bungalow.

búnker *nm* bunker.

buñuelo *nm* doughnut.

BUP *nm abr de* **Bachillerato Unificado Polivalente**, ≈ GCSE studies.

buque *nm* ship; **b. de guerra**, warship; **b. de pasajeros**, liner, passenger ship; **b. insignia**, flagship.

burbuja *nf* bubble; **hacer burbujas**, to bubble, make bubbles.

burbujear *vi* to bubble.

burdel *nm* brothel.

Burdeos *n* Bordeaux.

burdo,-a *adj* coarse, rough.

burgalés,-a I *adj* of *o* from Burgos. **II** *nm,f* native *o* inhabitant of Burgos.

burgués,-a *adj* & *nm,f* bourgeois.

burguesía *nf* bourgeoisie.

burla *nf* gibe, jeer; **hacer b. de algo** *o* **algn**, to make fun of sth *o* sb; **hacer b. a algn**, to stick one's tongue out at sb.

burladero *nm* *Taur* refuge in bullring.

burlar **I** *vtr* 1 (*engañar*) to deceive. 2 (*eludir*) to dodge, evade. **II burlarse** *vr* to make fun (**de**, of), laugh (**de**, at).

burlón,-ona *adj* mocking.

buró *nm* 1 *Pol* executive committee. 2 (*escritorio*) bureau, desk.

burocracia *nf* bureaucracy.

burócrata *nmf* bureaucrat.

burocrático,-a *adj* bureaucratic.

burofax *nf* office automation.

burrada *nf* (*comentario*) stupid *o* foolish remark; (*hecho*) stupid *o* foolish act.

burro,-a I *nm,f* 1 donkey, ass; *fam fig* **bajarse del b.**, to climb *o* back down. 2 *fam* (*estúpido*) dimwit, blockhead. 3 **b. de carga**, dogsbody, drudge. **II** *adj* 1 *fam* (*necio*) stupid, dumb. 2 *fam* (*obstinado*) stubborn.

bursátil *adj* stock-market.

bus *nm* bus.

busca *nf* search; **ir en b. de**, to go in search of.

buscapersonas *nm* pager.

buscapleitos *nmf inv* troublemaker.
buscar |1| I *vtr* 1 to look *o* search for; **b. una palabra en el diccionario**, to look up a word in the dictionary. 2 **ir a b. algo**, to go and get sth, fetch sth; **fue a buscarme a la estación**, she picked me up at the station. II **buscarse** *vr fam* **b. la vida**, to try and earn one's living; *fam* **te la estás buscando**, you're asking for it; **se busca**, wanted.
búsqueda *nf* search, quest; *Inform* search.
busto *nm* bust.
butaca *nf* 1 *(sillón)* armchair, easy chair. 2 *Cin Teat* seat; **b. de platea** *o* **patio**, seat in the stalls.
butano *nm* butane; **(gas) b.**, butane gas.
butifarra *nf* sausage.
buzo *nm* diver.
buzón *nm* letter box, *US* mailbox; **echar una carta al b.**, to post a letter.
byte *nm Inform* byte.

C

C, c [θe] *nf (la letra)* C, c.
C 1 *abr de* Celsius, Celsius, C. 2 *abr de* centígrado, centigrade, C.
c/ 1 *abr de* calle, Street, St; Road, Rd. 2 *abr de* cargo, cargo, freight. 3 *abr de* cuenta, account, a/c.
C., Cª *abr de* compañía, Company, Co.
cabal I *adj* 1 *(exacto)* exact, precise. 2 *(honesto)* honest, upright. II *nmpl fam* **estar algn en sus cabales**, to be in full possession of one's faculties.
cábala *nf fig* **hacer cábalas sobre algo**, to speculate about sth.
cabalgadura *nf* mount.
cabalgar [7] *vtr & vi* to ride.
cabalgata *nf* cavalcade; **la c. de los Reyes Magos**, the procession of the Three Wise Men.
caballa *nf* mackerel.
caballar *adj* **ganado c.**, horses *pl*.
caballería *nf* 1 *(cabalgadura)* mount, steed. 2 *Mil* cavalry.
caballeriza *nf* stable.
caballero *nm* 1 gentleman; **¿qué desea, c.?**, can I help you, sir?; **ropa de c.**, menswear. 2 *Hist* knight. 3 **caballeros**, *(en letrero)* gents.
caballeroso,-a *adj* gentlemanly, chivalrous.
caballete *nm* 1 *(de pintor)* easel. 2 *Téc* trestle. 3 *(de nariz)* bridge.
caballito *nm* 1 **c. de mar**, sea-horse. 2 **caballitos**, merry-go-round *sing*, *US* carousel *sing*.
caballo *nm* 1 horse; **a c.**, on horseback; **montar a c.**, to ride; *fig* **a c. entre ...**, halfway between .... 2 *Téc* **c. de vapor**, horse power. 3 *Ajedrez* knight. 4 *Naipes* queen. 5 *arg (heroína)* horse, smack.
cabaña *nf* cabin.
cabaret *nm (pl* **cabarets)** cabaret.
cabecear I *vi* to nod. II *vtr Dep* to head.
cabecera *nf* 1 top, head. 2 *Tip* headline.
cabecilla *nmf* leader.
cabellera *nf* head of hair.
cabello *nm* 1 hair. 2 *Culin* **c. de ángel**, sweet made of gourd and syrup.
cabelludo,-a *adj* **cuero c.**, scalp.

caber [9] *vi* 1 to fit, be (able to be) contained; **cabe en el maletero**, it fits in the boot; **¿cabemos todos?**, is there room for all of us?; **en este coche/jarro caben ...**, this car/jug holds ...; **no cabe por la puerta**, it won't go through the door; **no c. en sí de gozo**, to be beside oneself with joy; **no me cabe en la cabeza**, I can't understand it; **no cabe duda**, there is no doubt; **cabe la posibilidad de que ...**, there is a possibility *o* chance that ...; **no está mal dentro de lo que cabe**, it isn't bad, under the circumstances. 2 **cabe señalar que ...**, we should point out that .... 3 *Mat* **doce entre cuatro caben a tres**, four into twelve goes three (times).
cabestrillo *nm* sling.
cabeza *nf* 1 head; **en c.**, in the lead; **por c.**, a head, per person; *fig* **a la c. de**, at the front *o* top of; *fig* **estar mal de la c.**, to be a mental case; **c. de turco**, scapegoat; **el o la c. de familia**, the head of the family. II *nm* **c. rapada**, skinhead.
cabezada *nf* 1 *(golpe)* butt, blow on the head. 2 *fam* **echar una c.**, to have a snooze; **dar cabezadas**, to nod.
cabezal *nm Téc* head; *(de tocadiscos)* pick-up.
cabezota *fam* I *adj* pigheaded. II *nmf* pigheaded person.
cabezudo *nm* carnival figure with a huge head.
cabida *nf* capacity; **dar c. a**, to leave room for.
cabildo *nm Rel* chapter.
cabina *nf* cabin; **c. telefónica**, telephone box, *US* telephone booth.
cabizbajo,-a *adj* crestfallen.
cable *nm* cable; *arg* **echarle un c. a algn**, to give sb a hand.
cabo *nm* 1 *(extremo)* end; **al c. de**, after; **de c. a rabo**, from start to finish. 2 *Mil* corporal; *(policía)* sergeant. 3 *Náut* rope, cable; *fig* **atar cabos**, to put two and two together; *fig* **no dejar ningún c. suelto**, to leave no loose ends. 4 *Geog* cape; **Ciudad del C.**, Cape Town; **C. Verde**, Cape

Verde.

cabra *nf* goat; *fam* **estar como una c.**, to be off one's head.

cabré *indic fut* → **caber**.

cabreado,-a *adj vulg* pissed-off.

cabrear I *vtr vulg* to make angry. II **cabrearse** *vr* to get worked up.

cabreo *nm vulg* anger.

cabrío,-a *adj* **macho c.**, billy goat; **ganado c.**, goats *pl*.

cabriola *nf* skip.

cabrito *nm Zool* kid.

cabrón,-ona *nm,f ofens* (*hombre*) bastard; (*woman*) bitch.

cabronada *nf vulg* dirty trick.

cabuya *nf Am* agave, pita.

caca *nf fam* poopoo.

cacahuete *nm* peanut.

cacao *nm* **1** *Bot* cacao. **2** (*polvo, bebida*) cocoa. **3** *fam* (*lío*) mess, cockup.

cacarear I *vi* (*gallina*) to cluck. II *vtr fig* to boast about.

cacareo *nm* **1** (*de gallina*) clucking. **2** *fig* boasting, bragging.

cacatúa *nf* cockatoo.

cacereño,-a I *adj* of *o* from Cáceres. II *nm,f* native *o* inhabitant of Cáceres.

cacería *nf* **1** (*actividad*) hunting, shooting. **2** (*partida*) hunt, shoot.

cacerola *nf* saucepan.

cacha *nf fam* (*muslo*) thigh; **estar cachas**, to be really muscular.

cachalote *nm* sperm whale.

cacharro *nm* **1** earthenware pot *o* jar. **2** *fam* (*cosa*) thing, piece of junk. **3** **cacharros**, (*de cocina*) pots and pans.

cachear *vtr* to frisk, search.

cachemir *nm*, **cachemira** *nf* cashmere.

cacheo *nm* frisk, frisking.

cachetada *nf Am* slap.

cachete *nm* **1** (*bofetada*) slap. **2** *Am* (*mejilla*) cheek.

cachimba *nf Am* pipe.

cachiporra *nf* club, truncheon.

cachivache *nm fam* thing, knick-knack.

cacho¹ *nm fam* (*pedazo*) bit, piece; *fig* **¡qué c. de animal!**, what a nasty piece of work!

cacho² *nm Am* (*cuerno*) horn.

cachondearse *vr fam* **c. de**, to take the mickey out of.

cachondeo *nm fam* laugh; **tomar algo a c.**, to take sth as a joke.

cachondo,-a *adj fam* **1** (*sexualmente*) randy. **2** (*divertido*) funny.

cachorro,-a *nm,f* (*de perro*) pup, puppy; (*de gato*) kitten; (*de otros animales*) cub, baby.

cacique *nm* (*jefe*) local boss.

caco *nm fam* thief.

cacofonía *nf* cacophony.

cacto *nm*, **cactus** *nm inv Bot* cactus *inv*.

cada *adj* (*de dos*) each; (*de varios*) each, every; **c. día**, every day; **c. dos días**

every second day; **c. vez más**, more and more; **¿c. cuánto?**, how often?; **c. dos por tres**, every other minute; **cuatro de c. diez**, four out of (every) ten; **¡tienes c. cosa!**, you come up with some fine ideas!

cadalso *nm* scaffold.

cadáver *nm* (*de persona*) corpse, (dead) body; (*de animal*) body, carcass; **ingresar c.**, to be dead on arrival.

cadena *nf* **1** chain; (*correa de perro*) lead, leash. **2** *TV* channel. **3** *Ind* line; **c. de montaje**, assembly line; **trabajo en c.**, assembly line work. **4** *Geog* **c. montañosa**, mountain range. **5** *Jur* **c. perpetua**, life imprisonment. **6** *Aut* **cadenas**, tyre *o* US tire chains.

cadencia *nf* rhythm; *Mús* cadenza.

cadera *nf* hip.

cadete *nm* cadet.

caducar [1] *vi* to expire.

caducidad *nf* expiry; **fecha de c.**, (*en alimentos*) ≈ sell-by date; (*en medicinas*) to be used before.

caduco,-a *adj* **1** *Bot* deciduous. **2** *pey* (*anticuado*) out-of-date.

caer [39] I *vi* **1** to fall; **dejar c.**, to drop; *fig* **está en c.**, (*llegar*) he'll arrive any minute now; (*ocurrir*) it's on the way. **2** (*fecha*) to be; **su cumpleaños cae en sábado**, his birthday falls on a Saturday. **3** (*entender*) to understand, see; **ya caigo**, I get it; **no caí**, I didn't twig. **4** (*hallarse*) to be; **cae por Granada**, it is somewhere near Granada. **5** **me cae bien/mal**, I like/don't like her. **6** **al c. el día**, in the evening; **al c. la noche**, at nightfall. II **caerse** *vr* to fall (down); **me caí de la moto**, I fell off the motorbike; **se le ha caído el pañuelo**, she dropped her handkerchief.

café *nm* **1** coffee; **c. solo/con leche**, black/white coffee. **2** (*cafetería*) café.

cafeína *nf* caffeine.

cafetal *nm* coffee plantation.

cafetera *nf* coffee-maker.

cafetería *nf* snack bar, coffee bar; *Ferroc* buffet car.

cafetero,-a *adj* **1** coffee. **2** *fam* **es muy c.**, (*persona*) he loves coffee.

cafre *nm,f* savage, beast.

cagado,-a *adj vulg* (*cobarde*) coward; **estar c. de miedo**, to be shit-scared.

cagar [7] *vulg* I *vi* **1** to (have a) shit. **2** (*estropear*) to ruin, spoil; **cagarla**, to cock it up. II **cagarse** *vr* to shit oneself; **c. de miedo**, to be shit-scared; **¡me cago en diez!**, damn it!

caída *nf* **1** fall; (*de pelo, diente*) loss. **2** (*de precios*) drop. **3** *Pol* downfall, collapse.

caído,-a I *adj* fallen. III *nmpl* **los caídos**, the fallen *pl*.

caigo *indic pres* → **caer**.

caimán *nm Zool* alligator.

Cairo *n* **El C.**, Cairo.

caja *nf* 1 box; **c. fuerte**, safe; *fam TV* **la c. tonta**, the idiot box. 2 *(de leche etc)* carton. 3 *(de embalaje)* crate, case; **una c. de cerveza**, a crate of beer. 4 *Fin (en tienda)* cash desk; *(en banco)* cashier's desk. 5 *Aut* **c. de cambios**, gearbox. 6 *Com* **c. de ahorros** *o* **de pensiones**, savings bank. 7 *(feretro)* coffin, *US* casket.

cajero,-a *nm,f* cashier; **c. automático**, cash point, dispenser.

cajetilla *nf* packet, *US* pack.

cajón *nm* 1 *(en un mueble)* drawer; *fig* **c. de sastre**, jumble; *fam* **de c.**, obvious, self-evident. 2 *(caja grande)* crate, chest.

cal¹ *nf* lime; *fig* **a c. y canto**, hermetically; *fam* **una de c. y otra de arena**, six of one and a half a dozen of the other.

cal² *abr de* **caloría(s)**, calorie(s), cal.

cala *nf* 1 *Geog* creek, cove. 2 *Náut* hold.

calabacín *nm* *Bot* 1 *(pequeño)* courgette, *US* zucchini. 2 *(grande)* marrow, *US* squash.

calabaza *nf* pumpkin, gourd.

calabobos *nm inv fam* drizzle.

calabozo *nm* 1 *(prisión)* jail, prison. 2 *(celda)* cell.

calada *nf* *fam (de cigarrillo)* drag, puff.

calado,-a I *adj* soaked. II *nm* *Náut* draught, *US* draft.

calamar *nm* squid *inv*; *Culin* **calamares a la romana**, squid fried in batter.

calambre *nm* 1 *Elec (descarga)* electric shock; **ese cable da c.**, that wire is live. 2 *(en músculo)* cramp.

calamidad *nf* calamity.

calaña *nf pey* kind, sort; **una persona de mala c.**, a bad sort.

calar I *vtr* 1 *(mojar)* to soak, drench. 2 *(agujerear)* to pierce, penetrate. 3 *fam (a alguien)* to rumble; **¡te hemos calado!**, we've got your number!. II *vi* 1 *(prenda)* to let in water. 2 *Náut* to draw. III **calarse** *vr* 1 *(prenda, techo)* to let in water; *(mojarse)* to get soaked. 2 *(el sombrero)* to pull down. 3 *Aut* to stall.

calavera I *nf* skull. II *nm* tearaway, madcap.

calcar [1] *vtr* 1 *(un dibujo)* to trace. 2 *fig (imitar)* to copy, imitate.

calceta *nf* 1 *(prenda)* stocking. 2 **hacer c.**, to knit.

calcetín *nm* sock.

calcinar *vtr* to burn.

calcio *nm* calcium.

calco *nm* tracing; **papel de c.**, carbon paper.

calcomanía *nf* transfer.

calculadora *nf* calculator.

calcular *vtr* 1 *Mat* to calculate. 2 *(evaluar)* to (make an) estimate. 3 *(suponer)* to figure, guess.

cálculo *nm* 1 calculation; **según mis cálculos**, by my reckoning. 2 *Med* gallstone. 3 *Mat* calculus.

caldear *vtr* to heat up.

caldera *nf* boiler.

caldereta *nf* stew.

calderilla *nf* small change.

caldo *nm* stock, broth; **c. de cultivo**, culture medium; *fig* breeding ground.

calé *adj* & *nm* gypsy.

calefacción *nf* heating; **c. central**, central heating.

calefactor *nm* heater.

caleidoscopio *nm* kaleidoscope.

calendario *nm* calendar.

calentador *nm* heater.

calentamiento *nm* *Dep* warm up.

calentar [1] I *vtr* 1 *(agua, horno)* to heat; *(comida, habitación)* to warm up; *fig* **no me calientes la cabeza**, don't bug me. 2 *fam (pegar)* to smack. 3 *fam (excitar)* to arouse (sexually), turn on. II **calentarse** *vr* 1 to get hot *o* warm, heat up. 2 *fig* se **calentaron los ánimos**, people became very excited.

calentón,-ona, **calentorro,-a** *adj fam* randy.

calentura *nf* fever, temperature.

calibrar *vtr* to gauge, bore.

calibre *nm* 1 *(de arma)* calibre. 2 *fig (importancia)* importance.

calidad *nf* 1 quality; **de primera c.**, first-class; **un vino de c.**, good-quality wine. 2 **en c. de**, as.

cálido,-a *adj* warm; **una cálida acogida**, a warm welcome.

calidoscopio *nm* → **caleidoscopio**.

caliente *adj* 1 hot. 2 *fig (debate)* heated; **en c.**, in the heat of the moment. 3 *fam (cachondo)* hot, randy.

calificación *nf* 1 qualification. 2 *Educ* mark.

calificar [1] *vtr* 1 to describe (de, as); **le calificó de inmoral**, he called him immoral. 2 *(examen)* to mark, grade.

calificativo *nm* epithet.

caligrafía *nf* calligraphy; *(modo de escribir)* handwriting.

calima *nf* haze, mist.

calimocho *nm* drink made with wine and Coca-Cola.

calina *nf* → **calima**.

cáliz *nm* chalice.

caliza *nf* limestone.

calizo,-a *adj* lime.

callado,-a *adj* quiet; **te lo tenías muy c.**, you were keeping that quiet.

callar I *vi* 1 *(dejar de hablar)* to stop talking; **¡calla!**, be quiet!, *fam* shut up! 2 *(no hablar)* to keep quiet, say nothing. II *vtr (noticia)* not to mention, keep to oneself. III **callarse** *vr* to stop talking, be quiet; **¡cállate!**, shut up!

calle *nf* 1 street, road; **c. de dirección única**, one-way street; **c. mayor**, high street, *US* main street; **el hombre de la c.**, the man in the street. 2 *Dep* lane.

calleja nf narrow street.

callejero,-a I nm (mapa) street directory. **II** adj street; **gato c.**, alley cat.

callejón nm back alley o street; **c. sin salida**, cul-de-sac, dead end.

callejuela nf narrow street, lane.

callista nmf chiropodist.

callo nm 1 Med callus, corn; fam **dar el c.**, to slog. 2 Culin **callos**, tripe sing.

calma nf 1 calm; jc.!, calm down!; **en c.**, calm; **tómatelo con c.**, take it easy. 2 Meteor calm weather; **c. chicha**, dead calm.

calmante nm painkiller.

calmar I vtr (persona) to calm (down); (dolor) to soothe, relieve. **II calmarse** vr 1 (persona) to calm down. 2 (dolor, viento) to ease off.

caló nm gypsy dialect.

calor nm 1 heat; **hace c.**, it's hot; **tengo c.**, I'm hot; **entrar en c.**, to warm up. 2 fig (afecto) warmth.

caloría nf calorie.

calumnia nf 1 calumny. 2 Jur slander.

calumniar [12] vtr 1 to calumniate. 2 Jur to slander.

caluroso,-a adj hot; (acogida etc) warm.

calva nf bald patch.

calvicie nf baldness.

calvinismo nm Calvinism.

calvo,-a I adj bald; **ni tanto ni tan c.**, neither one extreme nor the other. **II** nm bald man.

calza nf wedge.

calzada nf road, carriageway.

calzado nm shoes pl, footwear.

calzador nm shoehorn.

calzar [4] **I** vtr 1 (poner calzado) to put shoes on; **¿qué número calzas?**, what size do you take? 2 (mueble) to wedge. **II calzarse** vr **c. los zapatos**, to put on one's shoes.

calzones nmpl trousers.

calzonazos nm inv fam henpecked husband.

calzoncillos nmpl underpants, pants.

cama nf bed; **estar en** o **guardar c.**, to be confined to bed; **hacer la c.**, to make the bed; **irse a la c.**, to go to bed; **c. doble/sencilla**, double/single bed; **c. turca**, couch.

camada nf litter; (de pájaros) brood.

camafeo nm cameo.

camaleón nm chameleon.

cámara I nf 1 (aparato) camera; **a c. lenta**, in slow motion. 2 Pol Chamber, House; **C. Alta/Baja**, Lower/Upper House. 3 Aut inner tube. 4 (habitación) room, chamber; **c. de gas**, gas chamber; **c. frigorífica**, cold-storage room; **música de c.**, chamber music. **II** nmf (hombre) cameraman; (mujer) camerawoman.

camarada nmf comrade.

camaradería nf camaraderie.

camarera nf (de hotel) chambermaid.

camarero,-a nm,f 1 (de restaurante) (hombre) waiter; (mujer) waitress; (tras la barra) (hombre) barman; (mujer) barmaid. 2 (de avión) (hombre) steward; (mujer) stewardess.

camarilla nf clique.

camarón nm (common) prawn.

camarote nm cabin.

cambiante adj changing; (carácter) changeable.

cambiar [12] **I** vtr 1 to change; **c. algo de sitio**, to move sth. 2 (intercambiar) to swap, exchange. 3 (dinero) to change. **II** vi to change; **c. de casa**, to move (house); **c. de idea**, to change one's mind; **c. de trabajo**, to get another job; **c. de velocidad**, to change gear. **III cambiarse** vr 1 (de ropa) to change (clothes). 2 (de casa) to move (house).

cambiazo nm fam switch.

cambio nm 1 change; (de impresiones) exchange; **c. de planes**, change of plans; **un c. en la opinión pública**, a shift in public opinion; fig **a c. de**, in exchange for; **en c.**, on the other hand. 2 (dinero) change; **¿tienes c. de mil pesetas?**, have you got change for a thousand pesetas? 3 Fin (de divisas) exchange; (de acciones) price. 4 Aut gear change; **c. automático**, automatic transmission.

cambista nmf moneychanger.

Camboya nf Cambodia.

camelar vtr, **camelarse** vr fam 1 to cajole. 2 (galantear) to win over.

camelia nf camellia.

camello,-a I nm,f camel. **II** nm arg (traficante de drogas) (drug) pusher.

camelo nm fam 1 (engaño) hoax. 2 (trola) cock-and-bull story.

camerino nm dressing room.

Camerún n Cameroon.

camilla nf 1 stretcher. 2 **mesa c.**, small round table under which a heater is placed.

caminante nmf walker.

caminar I vi to walk. **II** vtr to cover, travel; **caminaron diez kilómetros**, they walked for ten kilometres.

caminata nf long walk.

camino nm 1 (ruta) route, way; **ir c. de**, to be going to; **ponerse en c.**, to set off; fig **ir por buen/mal c.**, to be on the right/wrong track; **abrirse c.**, to break through; **a medio c.**, half-way; **en el c.**, a o de c. a, on the way to; **estar en c.**, to be on the way; **nos coge** o **pilla de c.**, it is on the way. 2 (vía) path, track. 3 (modo) way.

camión nm 1 lorry, US truck; **c. cisterna**, tanker; **c. de la basura**, refuse lorry, US garbage truck; **c. frigorífico**, refrigerator lorry.

camionero,-a nm,f lorry o US truck

driver.

camioneta *nf* van.

camisa *nf* shirt; **en mangas de c.,** in one's shirtsleeves; *fig* **cambiar de c.,** to change sides; **c. de fuerza,** straightjacket.

camiseta *nf* 1 (*de uso interior*) vest, *US* undershirt. 2 (*de uso exterior*) T-shirt. 3 *Dep* shirt; **sudar la c.,** to run oneself into the ground.

camisón *nm* nightdress, *fam* nightie.

camomila *nf* camomile.

camorra *nf fam* trouble.

camorrista I *adj* quarrelsome, rowdy. II *nmf* troublemaker.

camote *nm Am* sweet potato.

campal *adj* **batalla c.,** pitched battle.

campamento *nm* camp.

campana *nf* bell; **pantalones de campana,** bell-bottom trousers.

campanada *nf* peal *o* ring of a bell.

campanario *nm* belfry, bell tower.

campanilla *nf* 1 small bell. 2 *Anat* uvula. 3 *Bot* bell flower.

campante *adj fam* **se quedó tan c.,** he didn't bat an eyelid.

campaña *nf* 1 campaign; **c. electoral,** election campaign; **c. publicitaria,** advertising campaign. 2 *Mil* expedition; **de c.,** field.

campar *vi* **c. por sus respetos,** to do as one pleases.

campechano,-a *adj* unpretentious.

campeón,-ona *nm,f* champion; **c. mundial,** world champion.

campeonato *nm* championship; **un tonto de c.,** an utter idiot.

campero,-a *adj* country, rural; (*botas*) **camperas,** leather boots.

campesino,-a *nm,f* (*hombre*) countryman; (*mujer*) countrywoman.

campestre *adj* rural.

camping *nm* campsite; **hacer** *o* **ir de c.,** to go camping.

campiña *nf* open country.

campista *nmf* camper.

campo *nm* 1 country, countryside; **a c. traviesa** *o* **través,** cross-country; **trabaja (en) el c.,** he works (on) the land; **trabajo de c.,** fieldwork. 2 (*parcela*) field. 3 *Fís Fot* field. 4 (*ámbito*) field; **c. de acción,** field of action; *Mil* **c. de batalla,** battlefield; **c. de concentración,** concentration camp; **c. de trabajo,** work camp. 5 *Dep* field; (*de fútbol*) pitch; (*de golf*) course.

camposanto *nm* cemetery.

camuflaje *nm* camouflage.

camuflar *vtr* to camouflage.

cana *nf* (*gris*) grey hair; (*blanco*) white hair; **tener canas,** to have grey hair; *fam* **echar una c. al aire,** to let one's hair down.

Canadá *n* Canada.

canadiense *adj & nmf* Canadian.

canal *nf* 1 (*artificial*) canal; (*natural*) channel; **C. de la Mancha,** English Channel. 2 *TV Elec Inform* channel.

canalizar [4] *vtr* to channel.

canalla *pey* I *nm* swine, rotter. II *nf* riffraff, mob.

canallesco,-a *adj pey* rotten, despicable.

canalón *nm* gutter.

canalones *nmpl* cannelloni.

canapé *nm* 1 *Culin* canapé. 2 (*sofá*) couch, sofa.

canario,-a I *adj & nm,f* Canarian; **Islas Canarias,** Canary Islands, Canaries. II *nm Orn* canary.

canasta *nf* basket.

canastilla *nf* small basket; (*de un bebé*) layette.

canasto *nm* big basket, hamper.

cancán *nm* frilly petticoat.

cancela *nf* wrought-iron gate.

cancelación *nf* cancellation.

cancelar *vtr* 1 (*acto etc*) to cancel. 2 (*deuda*) to pay off.

cáncer *nm* cancer; **c. de pulmón/mama,** lung/breast cancer.

cancerbero,-a *nm,f Ftb* goalkeeper.

cancerígeno,-a *adj* carcinogenic.

canceroso,-a *adj* cancerous.

cancha *nf* ground; *Ten* court.

canciller *nm* chancellor.

canción *nf* song.

candado *nm* padlock.

candela *nf* fire.

candelabro *nm* candelabrum.

candelero *nm* candlestick; *fig* **en el c.,** at the top.

candente *adj* red-hot; *fig* **tema c.,** topical issue.

candidato,-a *nm,f* candidate; (*a un puesto*) applicant.

candidatura *nf* 1 (*lista*) list of candidates. 2 **presentar su c.,** to submit one's application.

candidez *nf* candour, *US* candor.

cándido,-a *adj* candid.

candil *nm* oil lamp.

candilejas *nfpl Teat* footlights.

candor *nm* candour, *US* candor.

candoroso,-a *adj* innocent, pure.

canela *nf* cinnamon.

cangrejo *nm* (*de mar*) crab; (*de río*) freshwater crayfish.

canguro I *nm* kangaroo. II *nmf fam* baby-sitter.

caníbal *adj & nmf* cannibal.

canica *nf* marble.

canícula *nf* dog days, midsummer heat.

caniche *nm* poodle.

canijo,-a *adj fam* puny, weak.

canilla *nf Am* (*cobardía*) cowardice; (*miedo*) fear.

canillita *nm Am* newspaper boy.

canino,-a I *adj* canine; *fam* **tener un hambre canina,** to be starving. II *nm* *(colmillo)* canine.

canjear *vtr* to exchange.

cano,-a *adj (blanco)* white; *(gris)* grey.

canoa *nf* canoe.

canódromo *nm* dog *o* greyhound track.

canon *nm* **1** canon, norm. **2** *Mús Rel* canon. **3** *Com* royalty.

canónigo *nm* canon.

canonizar [4] *vtr* to canonize.

canoso,-a *adj (de pelo blanco)* white-haired; *(de pelo gris)* grey-haired; *(pelo)* white, grey.

cansado,-a *adj* **1** *(agotado)* tired, weary; estar c., to be tired. **2 ser c.,** *(pesado)* to be boring *o* tiresome.

cansancio *nm* tiredness, weariness; *fam* estoy muerto de c., I'm on my last legs.

cansar I *vtr* to tire. **II** *vi* to be tiring. **III cansarse** *vr* to get tired; se cansó de esperar, he got fed up (with) waiting.

Cantabria *n* Cantabria.

cantábrico,-a *adj* Cantabrian; **Mar C.,** Bay of Biscay.

cántabro,-a *adj & nm,f* Cantabrian.

cantante I *nmf* singer. **II** *adj* singing; llevar la voz c., to rule the roost.

cantaor,-a *nm,f* flamenco singer.

cantar¹ *vtr & vi* **1** *Mús* to sing; *fig* en menos que canta un gallo, in a flash. **2** *arg (confesar)* to sing, spill the beans. **3** *arg (oler mal)* to hum.

cantar² *nm* lit song; *fam* ¡eso es otro c.!, that's a totally different thing!

cantarín,-ina *adj (voz)* sing-song.

cántaro *nm* pitcher; *fig* llover a cántaros, to rain cats and dogs.

cante *nm* **1** *(canto)* singing; *Esp* c. hondo, c. jondo, flamenco. **2** *arg* dar el c., to attract attention.

cantera *nf* **1** *(de piedra)* quarry. **2** *fig Ftb* young players.

cantero *nm* stonemason.

cantidad I *nf* quantity; *(de dinero)* amount, sum; **en c.,** a lot; *(gente)* c. de gente, thousands of people. **II** *adv* *fam* a lot; **me gusta c.,** I love it.

cantimplora *nf* water bottle.

cantina *nf* canteen.

cantinero,-a *nm,f* bar attendant.

canto¹ *nm* **1** *(arte)* singing. **2** *(canción)* song.

canto² *nm (borde)* edge; **de c.,** on its side.

canto³ *nm (guijarro)* pebble, stone; c. rodado, *(grande)* boulder; *(pequeño)* pebble.

cantor,-a I *adj* singing; **pájaro c.,** songbird. **II** *nm,f* singer.

canturrear *vi* to hum, croon.

canutas *nfpl* *fam* pasarlas c., to have a hard time.

canuto *nm* **1** *(tubo)* tube. **2** *arg (porro)* joint.

caña *nf* **1** *(vaso)* glass; *(de cerveza)* glass of draught *o* US draft beer. **2** *Bot* reed; *(tallo)* cane, stem; **c. de azúcar,** sugar cane.

3 *(de pescar)* rod. **4** *fam* darle c. al coche, to go at full speed.

cañada *nf* gully, ravine.

cáñamo *nm* hemp.

cañería *nf* *(piece of)* piping; **cañerías,** plumbing.

cañí *adj & nmf (pl* cañís*) fam* gypsy.

caño *nm (tubo)* tube; *(tubería)* pipe.

cañón *nm* **1** cannon; *fig* estar siempre al pie del c., to be always ready for a fight. **2** *(de fusil)* barrel. **3** *Geog* canyon.

cañonazo *nm* gunshot.

caoba *nf* mahogany.

caos *nm* chaos.

caótico,-a *adj* chaotic.

cap. *abr de* capítulo, chapter, ch.

capa *nf* **1** *(prenda)* cloak, cape; **de c. caída,** low-spirited. **2** *(de pintura)* layer, coat; *Culin* coating. **3** *Geol* stratum, layer.

capacidad *nf* **1** *(cabida)* capacity. **2** *(aptitud)* capacity, ability.

capacitación *nf* qualification.

capacitar *vtr (autorizar)* to authorize.

capar *vtr* to castrate.

caparazón *nm* shell.

capataz *nm,f (hombre)* foreman; *(mujer)* forewoman.

capaz *adj* **1** capable, able; **ser c. de hacer algo,** *(tener la habilidad de)* to be able to do sth; *(atreverse a)* to dare to do sth; **si se entera es c. de despedirle,** if he finds out he could quite easily sack him. **2** *Am* es c. que, it is likely that.

capcioso,-a *adj* captious; **pregunta capciosa,** catch question.

capea *nf* amateur bullfight.

capear *vtr (dificultad etc)* to dodge, shirk; *fig* c. el temporal, to weather the storm.

capellán *nm* chaplain.

caperuza *nf* hood.

capicúa *adj* número c., reversible number; **palabra c.,** palindrome.

capilar *adj* hair; **loción c.,** hair lotion.

capilla *nf* chapel; **c. ardiente,** chapel of rest.

capirote *nm* *fam* tonto de c., silly idiot.

capital I *nf* capital. **II** *nm* *Fin* capital; c. activo *o* social, working *o* share capital. **III** *adj* capital, main; **de importancia c.,** of capital importance; **pena c.,** capital punishment.

capitalismo *nm* capitalism.

capitalista *adj & nmf* capitalist.

capitalizar [4] *vtr* to capitalize.

capitán,-ana *nm,f* captain; **c. general,** field marshal, US general of the army.

capitanear *vtr* **1** *Mil Náut* to captain, command. **2** *(dirigir)* to lead; *Dep* to captain.

capitulación *nf* agreement; *Mil* capitulation; **capitulaciones matrimoniales,** marriage settlement.

capítular *vi* **1** *Mil* to capitulate,

surrender. 2 *(convenir)* to reach an agreement.

capítulo *nm* 1 *(de libro)* chapter. 2 *fig* **dentro del c. de ...,** *(tema)* under the heading of ....

capó *nm Aut* bonnet, *US* hood.

capón *nm* rap on the head with the knuckles.

capota *nf Aut* folding hood *o* top.

capote *nm* 1 *Taur* cape. 2 *Mil* greatcoat.

capricho *nm* 1 *(antojo)* whim, caprice. 2 *Mús* caprice, capriccio.

caprichoso,-a *adj* whimsical.

Capricornio *nm* Capricorn.

cápsula *nf* capsule.

captar *vtr* 1 *(ondas)* to receive, pick up. 2 *(comprender)* to understand, grasp. 3 *(interés etc)* to attract.

captura *nf* capture.

capturar *vtr* *(criminal)* to capture; *(cazar, pescar)* to catch; *Mil* to seize.

capucha *nf* hood.

capuchino *nm (café)* capuccino.

capullo *nm* 1 *(de insecto)* cocoon. 2 *Bot* bud. 3 *vulg (prepucio)* foreskin. 4 *ofens (persona)* silly bugger.

caqui I *adj (color)* khaki. II *nm (fruto)* persimmon.

cara *nf* 1 face; **c. a c.,** face to face; **c. a la pared,** facing the wall; **poner mala c.,** to pull a long face; **tener buena/mala c.,** to look good/bad; *fig* **c. de circunstancias,** serious look; *fig* **dar la c.,** to face the consequences of one's acts); *fig* **dar la c. por algn,** to stand up for sb; *fig* **(de) c. a,** with a view to; *fig* **echarle a algn algo en c.,** to reproach sb for sth; *fig* **plantar c. a algn,** to face up to sb. 2 *(lado)* side; *(de moneda)* right side; **¿c. o cruz?,** heads or tails?; **echar algo a c. o cruz,** to toss (a coin) for sth. 3 *fam (desfachatez)* cheek, nerve; **¡qué c. (más dura) tienes!,** what a cheek you've got!; *fig* **¡qué c.!,** you're so cheeky!

carabela *nf* caravel.

carabina *nf* 1 *(arma)* carbine, rifle. 2 *(persona)* chaperon.

caracense I *adj* of *o* from Guadalajara. II *nmf* native *o* inhabitant of Guadalajara.

caracol *nm* 1 *(de tierra)* snail; *Am* shell. 2 *(rizo)* kiss-curl. II *interj* **¡caracoles!,** good heavens!

caracola *nf* conch.

carácter *nm (pl* **caracteres)** 1 *(temperamento)* character; **de mucho c.,** with a strong character; **tener buen/mal c.,** to be good-natured/bad-tempered. 2 *fig (índole)* nature; **con c. de invitado,** as a guest. 3 *Impr* character.

característica *nf* characteristic.

característico,-a *adj* characteristic.

caracterizar [4] *vtr* to characterize.

caradura *nmf fam* cheeky devil; **¡qué c. eres!,** you're so cheeky!

carajillo *nm fam* coffee with a dash of brandy.

carajo *interj vulg* shit!; **¡vete al c.!,** go to hell!

caramba *interj fam (sorpresa)* good grief!; *(enfado)* damn it!

carámbano *nm* icicle.

carambola *nf* cannon, *US* carom.

caramelo *nm* 1 *(dulce)* sweet, *US* candy. 2 *(azúcar quemado)* caramel; *Culin* **a punto de c.,** syrupy.

carantoña *nf* caress.

caraqueño,-a I *adj* of *o* from Caracas. II *nm,f* native *o* inhabitant of Caracas.

carátula *nf* 1 *(cubierta)* cover. 2 *(máscara)* mask.

caravana *nf* 1 *(vehículo)* caravan. 2 *(de tráfico)* tailback.

caray *interj* God!; good heavens!

carbón *nm* coal; **c. vegetal,** charcoal; **c. mineral,** coal.

carboncillo *nm* charcoal.

carbonero,-a *nm* coal merchant.

carbónico,-a *adj* carbonic; **agua carbónica,** mineral water.

carbonilla *nf* coal dust.

carbonizar [4] I *vtr* to carbonize, char; **morir carbonizado,** to be burnt to death. II **carbonizarse** *vr* to carbonize, char.

carbono *nm* carbon.

carburador *nm* carburettor, *US* carburetor.

carburante *nm* fuel.

carburar *vi fam (funcionar)* to work properly.

carca *adj & nmf fam* old fogey; *Pol* reactionary.

carcaj *nm* quiver.

carcajada *nf* guffaw.

carcamal *nm fam* old fogey.

cárcel *nf* prison, jail.

carcelario,-a *adj* prison, jail.

carcelero,-a *nm,f* jailer, warder, *US* warden.

carcoma *nf* woodworm.

carcomer I *vtr* to eat away. II **carcomerse** *vr* to be consumed *(de,* with).

cardar *vtr* 1 *(lana, algodón)* to card. 2 *(pelo)* to backcomb.

cardenal *nm* 1 *Rel* cardinal. 2 *Med* bruise.

cárdeno,-a *adj* purple.

cardíaco,-a, cardiaco,-a I *adj* cardiac, heart; **ataque c.,** heart attack. II *nm,f* person with a heart condition.

cardinal *adj* cardinal; **punto/número c.,** cardinal point/number.

cardiólogo,-a *nm,f* cardiologist.

cardo *nm (con espinas)* thistle.

carear *vtr* 1 *Jur* to bring two people face to face. 2 *(cotejar)* to compare.

carecer [33] *vi* **c. de,** to lack.

carencia *nf* lack *(de,* of).

carente *adj* lacking; **c. de interés,** lacking

interest.

careo nm Jur confrontation.

carestía nf 1 (falta) lack, shortage. 2 Fin high price o cost.

careta nf mask; c. antigás, gas mask.

carey nm tortoiseshell.

carezco indic pres → **carecer**.

carga nf 1 (acción) loading. 2 (cosa cargada) load; (de avión, barco) cargo, freight; fig c. afectiva, emotional content. 3 Fin (gasto) debit; c. fiscal, tax charge. 4 fig (obligación) burden. 5 Mil Elec charge.

cargado,-a adj 1 loaded. 2 (bebida) strong; un café c., a strong coffee. 3 (ambiente) heavy; atmósfera cargada, stuffy atmosphere. 4 fig burdened; c. de deudas, up to one's eyes in debt. 5 Elec charged.

cargamento nm 1 (carga) load. 2 (mercancías) cargo, freight.

cargante adj fam annoying.

cargar [7] I vtr 1 to load; (mechero, pluma) to fill; (batería) to charge; fig c. las culpas a algn, to put the blame on sb. 2 Com to charge; cárguelo a mi cuenta, charge it to my account; fam Educ me han cargado las matemáticas, I failed maths. II vi 1 c. con, (llevar) to carry; fig c. con la responsabilidad, to take the responsibility; fig c. con las consecuencias, to suffer the consequences. 2 Mil c. contra, (to charge). III cargarse vr 1 fam te la vas a c., you're asking for trouble and you're going to get it. 2 fam (estropear) to smash, ruin. 3 fam (matar) to kill, bump off.

cargo nm (puesto) post, position; alto c., (puesto) top job, high ranking position; (persona) top person. 2 estar al c. de, to be in charge of; correr a c. de, (gastos) to be met by; hacerse c. de, to take charge of; hazte c. de mi situación, please try to understand my situation; c. de conciencia, weight on one's conscience. 3 Fin charge, debit; con c. a mi cuenta, charged to my account. 4 Jur charge, accusation.

carguero nm 1 (avión) transport plane. 2 (barco) freighter.

cariarse vr to decay.

caribe nm (idioma) Carib; el (mar) C., the Caribbean Sea.

caricatura nf caricature.

caricaturizar [4] vtr to caricature.

caricia nf caress, stroke.

caridad nf charity.

caries nf inv decay, caries.

carilla nf page, side of a sheet of paper.

cariño nm 1 (amor) affection; coger/tener c. a algo/algn, to grow/to be fond of sth/sb; con c., (en carta) love. 2 (querido) darling. 3 (abrazo) cuddle.

cariñoso,-a adj loving, affectionate.

carisma nm charisma.

carismático,-a adj charismatic.

caritativo,-a adj charitable.

cariz nm look.

carmesí adj & nm crimson.

carmín nm (de color) c., carmine; c. (de labios), lipstick.

carnal adj 1 (de carne) carnal. 2 (pariente) first; primo c., first cousin.

carnaval nm carnival.

carne nf 1 flesh; fam ser de c. y hueso, to be only human; fig c. de cañón, cannon fodder; c. de gallina, goose-pimples; c. viva, raw flesh. 2 (alimento) meat; c. de cerdo/cordero/ternera/vaca, pork/lamb/veal/beef. 3 (de fruta) pulp.

carné, carnet nm (pl carnés) card; c. de conducir, driving licence; c. de identidad, identity card.

carnero nm ram; Culin mutton.

carnicería nf 1 butcher's (shop). 2 fig (masacre) slaughter.

carnicero,-a nm,f butcher.

cárnico,-a adj productos cárnicos, meat products.

carnívoro,-a adj carnivorous. II nm,f carnivore.

carnoso,-a adj fleshy.

caro,-a adj 1 expensive, dear. II adv salir c., to cost a lot; te costará c., (amenaza) you'll pay dearly for this.

carpa nf 1 (pez) carp. 2 (de circo) big top, marquee. 3 Am (de camping) tent.

carpeta nf folder.

carpetazo nm dar c. a un asunto, to shelve a matter.

Cárpatos npl Carpathians.

carpintería nf 1 (oficio) carpentry; c. metálica, metalwork. 2 (taller) carpenter's (shop).

carpintero,-a nm,f carpenter.

carraca nf rattle.

carraspear vi to clear one's throat.

carraspeo nm clearing of the throat.

carraspera nf hoarseness.

carrera nf 1 run; (de media) run, ladder; a la c., in a hurry. 2 (competición) race; c. contra reloj, race against the clock; c. de coches, rally, meeting; echar una c. a algn, to race sb; c. de armamentos, arms race. 3 (estudios) degree. 4 (profesión) career, profession.

carrerilla nf run; tomar c., to take a run; de c., parrot fashion.

carreta nf cart.

carrete nm (de hilo) reel; (de película) spool; (de cable) coil.

carretera nf road; c. comarcal/nacional, B/A road; c. de circunvalación, ring road; c. de acceso, access road; (en autopista) slip road.

carretilla nf wheelbarrow.

carricoche nm caravan.

carril nm 1 Ferroc rail. 2 Aut lane.

carrillo nm cheek; fam comer a dos carrillos, to devour, gobble up.

carro nm 1 *(carreta)* cart; *fam* ¡para el c.!, hold your horses! 2 *Mil* c. de combate, tank. 3 *(de máquina de escribir)* carriage. 4 *Am* car.

carrocería nf *Aut* bodywork.

carroña nf carrion.

carroza I nf 1 *(coche de caballos)* coach, carriage. 2 *(de carnaval)* float. II nmf *fam* old fogey.

carruaje nm carriage, coach.

carta nf 1 letter; c. certificada/urgente, registered/express letter. 2 *(menú)* menu; a la c., à la carte; c. de vinos, wine list. 3 *Naipes* card; echar las cartas a algn, to tell sb's fortune; *fig* poner las cartas sobre la mesa, to put o lay one's cards on the table, come clean. 4 *Geog* map, chart. 5 *fig* adquirir c. de naturaleza, to become widely accepted; tomar cartas en un asunto, to take part in an affair.

cartabón nm set square.

cartearse vr to correspond (con, with), exchange letters (con, with).

cartel nm poster; pegar/fijar carteles, to put o stick up bills.

cartel nm *Com* cartel.

cartelera nf *hoarding, US* billboard; *Prensa* c. de espectáculos, entertainments section o page.

cartera nf 1 *(de bolsillo)* wallet. 2 *(de mano)* handbag; *(para documentos etc)* briefcase; *(de colegial)* satchel, schoolbag. 3 *Pol (ministerio)* portfolio. 4 *Com* portfolio; c. de pedidos, order book. 5 *Am (bolso)* handbag, *US* purse.

carterista nmf pickpocket.

cartero,-a nm,f *(hombre)* postman; *(mujer)* postwoman.

cartilla nf 1 *(libreta)* book; c. de ahorros, savings book. 2 *(libro)* first reader; *fam* leerle la c. a algn, to tell sb off.

cartografía nf cartography.

cartón nm 1 *(material)* card, cardboard; c. piedra, papier mâché. 2 *(de cigarrillos)* carton.

cartucho nm 1 *(de balas)* cartridge. 2 *(de papel)* cone.

cartulina nf card.

casa nf 1 *(edificio)* house; c. de huéspedes, boarding house; c. de socorro, first aid post. 2 *(hogar)* home; vete a c., go home; en c. de Daniel, at Daniel's; de andar por c., everyday. 3 *(empresa)* company, firm; c. matriz/principal, head/central office.

casación nf *Jur* cassation, annulment.

casadero,-a adj of marrying age.

casado,-a I adj married. II nm,f married person; los recién casados, the newlyweds.

casamiento nm marriage; *(boda)* wedding.

casar[1] vtr to marry. II vi to match, go o

fit together. III casarse vr to marry, get married; c. por la iglesia/por lo civil, to get married in church/in a registry office.

casar[2] vtr to annul, quash.

cascabel nm bell.

cascada nf waterfall, cascade.

cascanueces nm inv nutcracker.

cascar[1] I vtr 1 to crack. 2 *fam* cascarla, to kick the bucket, snuff it. II vi *fam (charlar)* to chat away. III cascarse vr to crack.

cáscara nf shell; *(de fruta)* skin, peel; *(de grano)* husk.

cascarón nm eggshell.

cascarrabias nmf inv *fam* short-tempered person.

casco nm 1 *(para la cabeza)* helmet. 2 *(de caballo)* hoof. 3 *(envase)* empty bottle. 4 c. urbano, city centre. 5 *(de barco)* hull. 6 cascos, *(auriculares)* headphones.

cascote nm piece of rubble o debris.

caserío nm country house.

casero,-a I adj 1 *(hecho en casa)* homemade. 2 *(persona)* home-loving. II nm,f *(dueño) (hombre)* landlord; *(mujer)* landlady.

caseta nf hut, booth; *(de feria, exposición)* stand, stall.

casete I nm *(magnetófono)* cassette player o recorder. II nf *(cinta)* cassette (tape).

casi adv almost, nearly; c. mil personas, almost one thousand people; c. ni me acuerdo, I can hardly remember it; c. nunca, hardly ever; c. nadie, hardly anyone; c. me caigo, I almost fell.

casilla nf 1 *(de casillero)* pigeonhole. 2 *(recuadro)* box. 3 *Am* P.O. Box. 4 *fig* sacar a algn de sus casillas, to drive sb mad.

casillero nm pigeonholes pl.

casino nm casino.

caso nm case; el c. es que ..., the fact o thing is that ...; el c. Mattei, the Mattei affair; (en) c. contrario, otherwise; en c. de necesidad, if need be; en cualquier c., in any case; en el mejor/peor de los casos, at best/worst; en ese c., in such a case; en todo c., in any case; en un c. extremo, en último c., as a last resort; hacer c. a o de algn, to pay attention to sb; hacer c. omiso de, to take no notice of; no venir al c., to be beside the point; pongamos por c., let's say.

caspa nf dandruff.

casquete nm 1 *(de bala)* case, shell. 2 *Geog* c. polar, polar cap.

casquillo nm *(de bala)* case.

cassette nm & f — casete.

casta nf 1 *(linaje)* lineage, descent. 2 *(animales)* breed; de c., thoroughbred, purebred. 3 *(división social)* caste.

castaña nf chestnut; *fig* sacarle a algn las castañas del fuego, to save sb's bacon.

castañetear vi *(dientes)* to chatter.

castaño,-a I adj chestnut-brown; *(pelo,*

ojos) brown, dark. **II** *nm Bot* chestnut.

castañuela *nf* castanet.

castellano,-a I *adj* Castilian. **II** *nm,f* (*persona*) Castilian. **III** *nm* (*idioma*) Spanish, Castilian.

castidad *nf* chastity.

castigar [7] *vtr* 1 to punish. 2 (*dañar*) to harm, ruin. 3 *Jur Dep* to penalize.

castigo *nm* punishment; *Jur* penalty; *Dep* área de c., penalty area.

Castilla *n* Castile.

castillo *nm* castle.

castizo,-a *adj* pure, authentic.

casto,-a *adj* chaste.

castor *nm* beaver.

castrar *vtr* to castrate.

castrense *adj* military.

casual I *adj* accidental, chance. **II** *nm fam* chance. ◆**casualmente** *adv* by chance.

casualidad *nf* chance, coincidence; de o por c., by chance; dió la c. que ..., it so happened that ...; ¿tienes un lápiz, por c.?, do you happen to have a pencil?; ¡qué c.!, what a coincidence!

cata *nf* tasting.

cataclismo *nm* cataclysm.

catador,-a *nm,f* taster.

catalán,-ana I *adj & nm,f* Catalan. **II** *nm* (*idioma*) Catalan.

catalejo *nm* telescope.

catalepsia *nf* catalepsy.

catalizador *nm* catalyst; *Aut* catalytic converter.

catalizar [4] *vtr fig* to act as a catalyst for.

catalogar [7] *vtr* 1 to catalogue, *US* catalog. 2 (*clasificar*) to classify.

catálogo *nm* catalogue, *US* catalog.

Cataluña *n* Catalonia.

cataplasma *nf* 1 *Farm* cataplasm, poultice. 2 *fam* (*pelmazo*) bore.

catapulta *nf* catapult; *fig* springboard.

catapultar *vtr* to catapult.

catar *vtr* to taste.

catarata *nf* 1 waterfall. 2 *Med* cataract.

catarro *nm* (common) cold.

catastral *adj* valor c., rateable value.

catastro *nm* cadastre, cadaster.

catástrofe *nf* catastrophe.

catastrófico,-a *adj* catastrophic.

catear *vtr fam Educ* to fail, *US* flunk.

catecismo *nm* catechism.

cátedra *nf* (professorial) chair; **le han dado la c.**, they have appointed him professor.

catedral *nf* cathedral.

catedrático,-a *nm,f Educ* 1 *Univ* professor. 2 (*de instituto*) head of department.

categoría *nf* category; *fig* class; **de c.**, (*persona*) important; (*hotel etc*) quality.

categórico,-a *adj* categoric; **un no c.**, a flat refusal.

cateto *-a* *nm,f pey* yokel, bumpkin.

catolicismo *nm* Catholicism.

católico,-a *adj & nm,f* Catholic.

catorce *adj & nm inv* fourteen.

catre *nm fam* bed.

Cáucaso *n* Caucasus.

cauce *nm* 1 (*de un río*) bed. 2 *fig* (*canal*) channel; **cauces oficiales**, official channels.

caucho *nm* 1 rubber. 2 *Am* (*cubierta*) tyre, *US* tire.

caudal *nm* 1 (*de un río*) flow. 2 (*riqueza*) wealth, riches *pl*.

caudaloso,-a *adj* (*río*) plentiful.

caudillo *nm* leader, head.

causa *nf* 1 cause; **a o por c. de**, because of. 2 (*ideal*) cause. 3 *Jur* (*caso*) case; (*juicio*) trial.

causante I *adj* causal, causing. **II** *nm,f* **el c. del incendio**, the person who caused the fire.

causar *vtr* to cause, bring about; **me causa un gran placer**, it gives me great pleasure; **c. buena/mala impresión**, to make a good/bad impression.

cáustico,-a *adj* caustic.

cautela *nf* caution.

cautivar *vtr* 1 to capture, take prisoner. 2 *fig* (*fascinar*) to captivate.

cautiverio *nm*, **cautividad** *nf* captivity.

cautivo,-a *adj & nm,f* captive.

cauto,-a *adj* cautious, wary.

cava I *nf* (*bodega*) wine cellar. **II** *nm* (*vino espumoso*) cava, champagne.

cavar *vtr* to dig.

caverna *nf* cave; **hombre de las cavernas**, caveman.

cavernícola *nm,f* cave dweller.

caviar *nm* caviar.

cavidad *nf* cavity.

cavilar *vtr* to ponder.

cayado *nm* 1 (*de pastor*) crook. 2 (*de obispo*) crosier, crozier.

cayuco *nm Am* small flat-bottomed canoe.

caza I *nf* 1 hunting; **ir de c.**, to go hunting; **c. furtiva**, poaching. 2 (*animales*) game; **c. mayor/menor**, big/small game. 3 *fig* (*persecución*) hunt; **c. de brujas**, witch hunt. II *nm Av* fighter, fighter plane.

cazabombardero *nm Av* fighter bomber.

cazador,-a *nm,f* hunter; **c. furtivo**, poacher.

cazadora *nf* (waist-length) jacket.

cazar [4] *vtr* to hunt; *fam* **cazarlas al vuelo**, to be quick on the uptake.

cazatalentos *nmf inv* head-hunter.

cazo *nm* 1 (*cacerola*) saucepan. 2 (*cucharón*) ladle.

cazuela *nf* saucepan; (*guiso*) casserole, stew; **a la c.**, stewed.

c/c *abr de* **cuenta corriente**, current account, c/a.

CCOO *nfpl abr de* **Comisiones Obreras**.

CDS *nm Pol abr de* **Centro Democrático y Social**.

cebada *nf* barley.

cebar I *vtr* 1 (*animal*) to fatten; *fam* (*persona*) to feed up. 2 (*anzuelo*) to bait. II **cebarse** *vr* c. **con**, (*ensañarse*) to delight in tormenting.

cebo *nm* bait.

cebolla *nf* onion.

cebolleta *nf* 1 (*especie*) chives *pl.* 2 (*cebolla tierna*) spring onion.

cebra *nf* zebra; **paso de c.**, zebra crossing, *US* crosswalk.

cecear *vi* to lisp.

ceceo *nm* lisp.

cedazo *nm* sieve.

ceder I *vtr* to give, hand over; *Aut* **c. el paso**, to give way. II *vi* 1 (*cuerda, cable*) to give way. 2 (*lluvia, calor*) to diminish, slacken. 3 (*consentir*) to give in.

cedro *nm* cedar.

cédula *nf* 1 document, certificate; *Am* **c. de identidad**, identity card. 2 *Com* Fin bond, certificate, warrant.

C(E)E *nf abr de* Comunidad (Económica) Europea, European (Economic) Community, E(E)C.

cegador,-a *adj* blinding.

cegar [1] *vtr* 1 to blind. 2 (*puerta, ventana*) to wall up.

ceguera *nf* blindness.

CEI *abr de* Comunidad de Estados Independientes, Commonwealth of Independent States, CIS.

Ceilán *n* Ceylon.

ceja *nf* eyebrow.

cejar *vi* c. **en el empeño**, to give up.

celada *nf* trap, ambush.

celador,-a *nm,f* attendant; (*de una cárcel*) warder.

celda *nf* cell; **c. de castigo**, punishment cell.

celebración *nf* 1 (*festejo*) celebration. 2 (*de juicio etc*) holding.

celebrar I *vtr* 1 to celebrate; **celebro que todo saliera bien**, I'm glad everything went well. 2 (*reunión, juicio, elecciones*) to hold. 3 (*triunfo*) to laud. II **celebrarse** *vr* to take place, be held.

célebre *adj* famous, well-known.

celebridad *nf* 1 celebrity, fame. 2 (*persona*) celebrity.

celeste I *adj* 1 (*de cielo*) celestial. 2 (*color*) sky-blue. II *nm* sky blue.

celestial *adj* celestial, heavenly.

celibato *nm* celibacy.

célibe *adj & nmf* celibate.

celo *nm* 1 zeal. 2 **en c.**, (*macho*) in rut; (*hembra*) on *o* in heat. 3 **celos**, jealousy *sing*; **tener celos (de algn)**, to be jealous (of sb).

celo® *nm fam* sellotape®, *US* Scotch tape®.

celofán *nm* cellophane.

celosía *nf* lattice.

celoso,-a *adj* 1 jealous. 2 (*cumplidor*) con-

scientious.

celta I *adj* Celtic. II *nm,f* Celt. III *nm* (*idioma*) Celtic.

célula *nf* cell.

celular *adj* 1 cellular. 2 **coche c.**, Black Maria.

celulitis *nf inv* cellulitis.

celuloide *nm* celluloid.

celulosa *nf* cellulose.

cementerio *nm* cemetery, graveyard; **c. de coches**, scrapyard.

cemento *nm* cement; **c. armado**, reinforced cement.

cena *nf* evening meal; (*antes de acostarse*) supper; **la Última C.**, the Last Supper.

cenagal *nm* marsh, swamp.

cenar I *vi* to have supper *o* dinner. II *vtr* to have for supper *o* dinner.

cencerro *nm* cowbell.

cenefa *nf* (*de ropa*) edging, trimming; (*de suelo, techo*) ornamental border, frieze.

cenetista *adj* *o* related to the CNT (Confederación Nacional del Trabajo). II *nmf* member of the CNT.

cenicero *nm* ashtray.

cenit *nm* zenith.

ceniza *nf* ash.

cenizo *nm fam* (*gafe*) jinx.

censo *nm* census; **c. electoral**, electoral roll.

censor *nm* censor.

censura *nf* 1 censorship. 2 *Pol* **moción de c.**, vote of no confidence.

censurar *vtr* 1 (*libro, película*) to censor. 2 (*criticar*) to censure, criticize.

centavo *nm Am Fin* cent, centavo.

centella *nf* spark.

centellear *vi* to flash, sparkle.

centelleo *nm* flashing, sparkling.

centena *nf*, **centenar** *nm* hundred; **a centenares**, in hundreds.

centenario *nm* centenary, hundredth anniversary.

centeno *nm* rye.

centésimo,-a *adj & nm,f* hundredth.

centigrado,-a *adj* centigrade.

centilitro *nm* centilitre, *US* centiliter.

centímetro *nm* centimetre, *US* centimeter.

céntimo *nm* cent.

centinela *nm* sentry.

centollo *nm* spider crab.

centrado,-a *adj* 1 centred, *US* centered. 2 (*equilibrado*) balanced.

central I *adj* central. II *nf* 1 *Elec* **c. nuclear/térmica**, nuclear/coal-fired power station. 2 (*oficina principal*) head office.

centralismo *nm* centralism.

centralita *nf Tel* switchboard.

centralizar [4] *vtr* to centralize.

centrar I *vtr* 1 to centre, *US* center. 2 (*esfuerzos, atención*) to concentrate, centre, *US* center. II **centrarse** *vr* 1 to be centred *o US* centered *o* based. 2

(concentrarse) to concentrate (**en**, on).

céntrico,-a *adj* centrally situated; **zona céntrica,** centrally situated area.

centrifugar [7] *vtr* to centrifuge; *(ropa)* to spin-dry.

centrista *Pol* I *adj* centre, *US* center; **partido c.,** centre party. II *nmf* centrist.

centro *nm* 1 middle, centre, *US* center; **c. de la ciudad,** town *o* city centre. 2 *(establecimiento)* institution, centre, *US* center; **c. comercial,** shopping centre.

Centroamérica *n* Central America.

centroamericano,-a *adj & nm,f* Central American.

centrocampista *nmf Ftb* midfield player.

centuria *nf* century.

ceñido,-a *adj* tight-fitting, clinging.

ceñirse [6] *vr* 1 *(atenerse, limitarse)* to limit oneself, stick (**a**, to); **c. al tema,** to keep to the subject; **ciñéndonos a este caso en concreto,** coming down to this particular case. 2 *(prenda)* to cling (**a**, to).

ceño *nm* scowl, frown; **con el c. fruncido,** frowning.

CEOE *nf abr de* **Confederación Española de Organizaciones Empresariales,** ≈ Confederation of British Industry, CBI.

cepa *nf* 1 *(de vid)* vine. 2 *fig* **vasco de pura c.,** *(origen)* Basque through and through.

cepillar I *vtr* 1 to brush. 2 *(en carpintería)* to plane (down). 3 *fam (robar)* to pinch. II **cepillarse** *vr* 1 *(con cepillo)* to brush. 2 *fam (matar)* to do in. 3 *vulg* to lay.

cepillo *nm* brush; *(en carpintería)* plane; **c. de dientes,** toothbrush; **c. del pelo,** hairbrush.

cepo *nm* 1 *Caza* trap. 2 *Aut* clamp.

cera *nf* wax; *(de abeja)* beeswax.

cerámica *nf* ceramics *sing.*

cerca¹ *adv* 1 near, close; **ven más c.,** come closer; **ya estamos c.,** we are almost there. 2 **c. de,** *(al lado de)* near, close; **el colegio está c. de mi casa,** the school is near my house. 3 **c. de,** *(casi)* nearly, around; **c. de cien personas,** about one hundred people. 4 **de c.,** closely; **lo vi muy de c.,** I saw it close up.

cerca² *nf* fence, wall.

cercado *nm* 1 *(lugar cerrado)* enclosure. 2 *(valla)* fence, wall.

cercanía *nf* 1 proximity, nearness. 2 **cercanías,** outskirts, suburbs; **(tren de) c.,** suburban train.

cercano,-a *adj* nearby; **el C. Oriente,** the Near East.

cercar [1] *vtr* 1 *(tapiar)* to fence, enclose. 2 *(rodear)* to surround.

cercenar *vtr* to cut off, amputate.

cerciorar I *vtr* to assure. II **cerciorarse** *vr* to make sure.

cerco *nm* 1 circle, ring. 2 *Mil (sitio)* siege; **poner c. (a una ciudad),** to besiege (a town).

cerda *nf* 1 *Zool* sow. 2 *(pelo)* bristle; **cepillo de c.,** bristle brush.

Cerdeña *n* Sardinia.

cerdo *nm* 1 pig. 2 *(carne)* pork. 3 *fam* pey pig, arsehole.

cereal *nm* cereal.

cerebral *adj* 1 cerebral. 2 *(frío)* calculating.

cerebro *nm* brain; *fig (inteligencia)* brains *pl.*

ceremonia *nf* ceremony.

ceremonioso,-a *adj* ceremonious, formal; *pey* pompous, stiff.

cereza *nf* cherry.

cerezo *nm* cherry tree.

cerilla *nf* match.

cernerse [3] *fig* to loom (**sobre**, above).

cernícalo *nm* kestrel.

cernir [5] *vtr & vr* → **cerner.**

cero *nm* zero; *Dep* nil; *fig* **partir de c.,** to start from scratch; *fig* **ser un c. a la izquierda,** to be useless *o* a good-for-nothing.

cerrado,-a *adj* 1 closed, shut; **a puerta cerrada,** behind closed doors. 2 *(reservado)* reserved; *(intransigente)* uncompromising, unyielding; *fam (torpe)* thick; *(acento)* broad; *(curva)* tight, sharp. 3 *(barba)* bushy.

cerradura *nf* lock.

cerrajero,-a *nm,f* locksmith.

cerrar [1] I *vtr* to shut, close; *(grifo, gas)* to turn off; *(luz)* to turn off, switch off; *(cremallera)* to do up; *(negocio)* to close down; *(cuenta)* to close; *(carta)* to seal; *(puños)* to clench; **c. con llave,** to lock; **c. el paso a algn,** to block sb's way; *fam* **c. el pico,** to shut one's trap. II *vi* to close, shut. III **cerrarse** *vr* to close, shut; *fam* **c. en banda,** to stick to one's guns.

cerro *nm* hill; *fig* **irse por los cerros de Úbeda,** to beat around the bush.

cerrojo *nm* bolt; **echar el c. (de una puerta),** to bolt (a door).

certamen *nm* competition, contest.

certero,-a *adj* accurate.

certeza, certidumbre *nf* certainty; **saber (algo) con c.,** to be certain (of sth); **tener la c. de que ...,** to be sure o certain that ....

certificado,-a I *adj* 1 certified. 2 *(correo)* registered. II *nm* certificate.

certificar [1] *vtr* 1 to certify. 2 *(carta)* to register.

cervatillo *nm* fawn.

cervecería *nf* 1 *(bar)* pub, bar. 2 *(fábrica)* brewery.

cerveza *nf* beer; **c. de barril,** draught beer; **c. dorada o ligera,** lager; **c. negra,** stout.

cervical *adj* cervical.

cesar I *vi* to stop, cease (**de**, -); **sin c.,** incessantly. II *vtr (empleado)* to dismiss.

cesárea *nf* Caesarean (section), *US* Cesarcan (section).

cese nm 1 cessation, suspension. 2 (despido) dismissal.

CESID nm Mil abr de Centro Superior de Información de la Defensa.

césped nm lawn, grass.

cesta nf basket; **c. de Navidad**, Christmas hamper.

cesto nm basket.

cetáceo nm cetacean, whale.

cetrino,-a adj sallow.

cetro nm sceptre, US scepter.

Ceuta n Ceuta.

ceutí I adj of o from Ceuta. II nmf native o inhabitant of Ceuta.

chabacano,-a adj cheap.

chabola nf shack; **barrio de chabolas**, shanty town.

chacal nm jackal.

chacha nf maid.

cháchara nf fam small talk, chinwag; **estar de c.**, to have a yap.

chachi adj smashing.

chacinería nf pork bucher's shop.

chacra nf Am small farm o holding.

chafar vtr 1 fam (plan etc) to ruin, spoil. 2 (aplastar) to squash, flatten.

chal nm shawl.

chalado,-a adj fam crazy, nuts (por, about).

chalé nm (pl chalés) → chalet.

chaleco nm waistcoat, US vest; (de punto) sleeveless pullover; **c. antibalas**, bulletproof vest; **c. salvavidas**, life jacket.

chalet nm villa.

chalupa nf boat, launch.

chamarra nf sheepskin jacket.

chambelán nm chamberlain.

chambergo nm heavy coat.

chamizo nm thatched hut.

champán, champaña nm champagne.

champiñón nm mushroom.

champú nm shampoo.

chamuscar [1] vtr to singe, scorch.

chamusquina nf singeing, scorching; fam **esto me huele a c.**, there's something fishy going on here.

chancaca nf Am syrup cake.

chance nm Am opportunity.

chancear vi Am to joke, horse around.

chanchada nf Am fam dirty trick.

chancho,-a nm,f Am pig, hog.

chanchullo nm fam fiddle, wangle.

chancla nf flipflop.

chanclo nm (zueco) clog; (de goma) overshoe, galosh.

chándal nm track o jogging suit.

chantaje nm blackmail; **hacer c. a algn**, to blackmail sb.

chantajear vtr to blackmail.

chantajista nmf blackmailer.

chanza nf joke.

chapa nf 1 (de metal) sheet; (de madera) panel-board. 3 (tapón) bottle top, cap. 4 (de adorno) badge. 5 Am lock.

chapado,-a adj (metal) plated; **c. en oro**, gold-plated; fig **c. a la antigua**, old-fashioned.

chaparro nm Bot holm oak.

chaparrón nm downpour, heavy shower.

chapotear vi to splash about, paddle.

chapucero,-a adj (trabajo) slapdash, shoddy; (persona) bungling.

chapurrear vtr to speak badly o with difficulty; **sólo chapurrea el francés**, he spoke only a few words of French.

chapuza nf 1 (trabajo mal hecho) shoddy piece of work. 2 (trabajo ocasional) odd job.

chapuzón nm (baño corto) dip; **darse un c.**, to have a dip.

chaqué nm morning coat.

chaqueta nf jacket; Pol **cambiar de c.**, to change sides.

chaquetero,-a nm,f fam Pol turncoat.

chaquetilla nf short jacket.

charanga nf Mús brass band.

charca nf pond, pool.

charco nm puddle.

charcutería nf delicatessen.

charla nf (conversación) talk, chat; (conferencia) informal lecture o address.

charlar vi to talk, chat.

charlatán,-ana I adj (parlanchín) talkative; (chismoso) gossipy. II nm,f 1 (parlanchín) chatterbox; (chismoso) gossip; (bocazas) bigmouth. 2 (embaucador) trickster, charmer.

charol nm patent leather; **zapatos de c.**, patent leather shoes.

charqui nm Am (carne) dried beef, cured meat; (fruta) dried fruit.

chárter adj inv (vuelo) c., charter (flight).

chasca nf Am mop of hair, tangled hair.

chascar [1] vtr (lengua) to click; (dedos) to snap; (látigo) to crack.

chascarrillo nm shaggy dog story.

chasco nm fam disappointment; **llevarse un c.**, to be disappointed.

chasis nm inv chassis.

chasquear vtr (lengua) to click; (dedos) to snap; (látigo) to crack.

chasqui nm Am messenger, courier.

chasquido nm (de la lengua) click; (de los dedos) snap; (de látigo, madera) crack.

chatarra nf scrap (metal), scrap iron; fam junk.

chato,-a I adj 1 (nariz) snub; (persona) snub-nosed. 2 (objeto) flat, flattened. II nm (small) glass of wine.

chauvinista adj & nmf chauvinist.

chaval,-a nm,f fam (chico) boy, lad; (chica) girl.

checo,-a adj Czech.

checoslovaco,-a I adj Czechoslovakian, Czech. II nm,f (persona) Czechoslovakian, Czechoslovak, Czech.

Checoslovaquia n Czechoslovakia.

chelín *nm* shilling.

chepa *nf fam* hump.

cheque *nm* cheque, *US* check; **c. al portador**, cheque payable to bearer; **c. de viaje** *o* **(de) viajero**, traveller's cheque, *US* traveler's check.

chequeo *nm Med* checkup; *Aut* service.

chévere *adj Am fam* great, terrific, fantastic.

chic *adj inv* chic, elegant.

chicano,-a *adj & nm,f* chicano.

chicha¹ *nf Am* chicha, maize liquor.

chicha² *adj inv Náut* **calma c.**, dead calm.

chícharo *nm Am* pea.

chicharra *nf* cicada.

chichón *nm* bump, lump.

chichonera *nf* helmet.

chicle *nm* chewing gum.

chico,-a **I** *nm,f* (*muchacho*) boy, lad; (*muchacha*) girl. **II** *adj* small, little.

chicoria *nf* chicory.

chicote *nm Am* whip.

chiflado,-a *adj fam* mad, crazy (*por*, about).

chiflar *vtr* 1 (*silbar*) to hiss (at), boo (at). 2 *fam* **le chiflan las motos**, he's really into motorbikes.

chiflido *nm* whistle, whistling.

chiíta *adj & nmf* Shiite.

chile *nm* chili (pepper).

Chile *n* Chile.

chileno,-a *adj & nm,f* Chilean.

chillar *vi* (*persona*) to scream, shriek; (*ratón*) to squeak; (*frenos*) to screech, squeal; (*puerta*) to creak, squeak.

chillido *nm* (*de persona*) scream, shriek; (*de ratón*) squeak; (*de frenos*) screech, squeal; (*de puerta*) creaking, sweaking.

chillón,-ona *adj* 1 (*voz*) shrill, high-pitched; (*sonido*) harsh, strident. 2 (*color*) loud, gaudy.

chimenea *nf* 1 (*hogar abierto*) fireplace, hearth. 2 (*conducto*) chimney; (*de barco*) funnel, stack.

China *n* China.

china *nf* 1 pebble, small stone; *fam* **tocarle a uno la c.**, to get the short straw. 2 *arg* (*droga*) deal.

chinche I *nf* bug, bedbug; *fam* **caer como chinches**, to fall like flies. **II** *nm,f fam* nuisance, pest.

chincheta *nf* drawing pin, *US* thumbtack.

chinchín *interj* ¡c.!, cheers!, (to your good) health!

chinesco,-a *adj* **sombras chinescas**, shadow theatre *sing*.

chingana *nf Am* bar.

chingar [7] *vtr* 1 (*fastidiar*) to annoy. 2 *vulg* (*estropear*) to fuck up. 3 *vulg* (*joder*) to fuck, screw.

chino¹ *nm* (*piedrecita*) pebble, stone.

chino,-a² *adj* (*de la China*) Chinese; *fam* eso me suena a c., it's all Greek to me.

chip *nm* (*pl* **chips**) Inform chip.

chipirón *nm* baby squid.

Chipre *n* Cyprus.

chipriota *adj & nmf* Cypriot.

chiquillo,-a *nm,f* kid, youngster.

chiquito,-a *adj* tiny.

chirimiri *nm* drizzle, fine misty rain.

chirimoya *nf* custard apple.

chiringuito *nm* (*en playa etc*) refreshment stall; (*en carretera*) roadside snack bar.

chiripa *nf* fluke, lucky stroke; *fam* **fig de o por c.**, by a fluke, by chance; **cogió el tren por c.**, it was sheer luck that he caught the train.

chirla *nf* small clam.

chirona *nf arg* clink, nick.

chirriar [29] *vi* (*puerta etc*) to creak; (*frenos*) to screech, squeal.

chirrido *nm* (*de puerta etc*) crack, cracking; (*de frenos*) screech, squeal.

chisme *nm* 1 (*habladuría*) piece of gossip. 2 *fam* (*trasto*) knick-knack; (*cosa*) thing.

chismorrear *vi fam* to gossip.

chismorreo *nm fam* gossip, gossiping.

chismoso,-a I *adj* gossipy. II *nm,f* gossip.

chispa *nf* 1 spark; **echar chispas**, to fume. 2 *fam* (*un poco*) bit, tiny amount. 3 *fam* (*agudeza*) wit, sparkle; (*viveza*) liveliness.

chispear *vi* 1 to spark, throw out sparks. 2 (*lloviznar*) to spit.

chiste *nm* joke; **contar un c.**, to tell a joke; **c. verde**, blue joke, dirty joke.

chistera *nf* top hat.

chistoso,-a *adj* (*persona*) funny, witty; (*anécdota*) funny, amusing.

chivarse *vr fam* to tell tales.

chivatazo *nm fam* tip-off; **dar el c.**, to squeal.

chivato,-a *nm,f fam* (*delator*) squealer, grass; (*acusica*) telltale.

chivo,-a *nm,f Zool* kid, young goat; *fig* **c. expiatorio**, scapegoat.

chocante *adj* 1 (*persona*) off-putting. 2 (*sorprendente*) surprising, startling; (*raro*) strange.

chocar |1| I *vi* 1 (*topar*) to crash, collide; **c. con o contra**, to run into, collide with. 2 (*en discusión*) to clash. **II** *vtr* 1 to knock; (*la mano*) to shake; *fam* ¡chócala!, ¡choca esos cinco!, shake (on it)!, put it there! 2 (*sorprender*) to surprise.

chochear *vi* 1 to be senile *o* in one's dotage. 2 (*por cariño*) *fam* **c. con algn**, to dote on sb.

chocho,-a I *adj* (*senil*) senile; **viejo c.**, old dodderer. II *nm* 1 (*altramuz*) lupin. 2 *vulg* cunt.

chocolate *nm* 1 chocolate; **c. con leche**, milk chocolate. 2 *arg* (*droga*) dope.

chocolatina *nf* bar of chocolate, chocolate bar.

chófer *nm* (*pl* **chóferes**) *Am*, **chofer** *nm* (*pl* **choferes**) driver; (*particular*) chauffeur.

chollo nm fam (ganga) bargain, snip.

chomba nf Am jumper, pullover.

chonta nf Am palm tree.

chopo nm poplar.

choque nm 1 impact; (de coches etc) crash, collision; c. frontal, head-on collision; c. múltiple, pile-up. 2 fig (contienda) clash.

choricear, chorizar vtr fam to pinch.

chorizo 1 nm 1 chorizo, highly-seasoned pork sausage. 2 fam (ratero) thief, pickpocket.

chorlito nm Orn plover; fam fig cabeza de c., scatterbrain.

chorra I nmf vulg (tonto) idiot, fool. II nf fam (suerte) luck.

chorrada nf fam piece of nonsense.

chorrear vi to drip, trickle; fam c. de sudor, to pour with sweat; fam tengo el abrigo chorreando, my coat is dripping wet.

chorro nm 1 (de agua etc) spurt; (muy fino) trickle; salir a chorros, to gush forth. 2 Téc jet. 3 fig stream, flood.

chovinismo nm chauvinism.

chovinista I adj chauvinistic. II nmf chauvinist.

choza nf hut, shack.

christmas nm Christmas card.

chubasco nm heavy shower, downpour.

chubasquero nm raincoat.

chuchería nf fam sweet, US candy.

chufa nf groundnut.

chulear fam vi to strut around; c. de, to go on about.

chuleta nf 1 chop, cutlet; c. de cerdo, pork chop. 2 Educ fam crib (note), US trot.

chulo,-a fam I nmf show off. II nm (proxeneta) pimp. III adj (bonito) smashing.

chungo,-a adj fam dodgy.

chupa nf arg short jacket.

chupachup® nm lollipop.

chupado,-a adj 1 (flaco) skinny, thin. 2 fam está c., it's dead easy.

chupar I vtr 1 to suck. 2 (lamer) to lick. 3 (absorber) to soak up, absorb. II vi to suck. III chuparse vr 1 está para c. los dedos, it's really mouthwatering. 2 fam to put up with; nos chupamos toda la película, we sat through the whole film.

chupatintas nm inv pey penpusher.

chupete nm dummy, US pacifier.

chupi adj fam great, terrific, fantastic.

chupón nm 1 lollipop. 2 (desatrancador) plunger.

churrasco nm barbecued meat.

churrería nf fritter shop.

churrete nm dirty mark, grease spot.

churro nm 1 fritter, US cruller. 2 fam (chapuza) mess.

chusco nm chunk of stale bread; Mil fam ration bread.

chusma nf rabble, mob.

chutar I vi 1 Dep (a gol) to shoot. 2 fam ¡y vas que chutas!, and then you're well away! II chutarse vr arg (drogas) to shoot up.

chute nm 1 Dep shot. 2 arg (drogas) fix.

CI nm abr de coeficiente intelectual, intelligence quotient, IQ.

Cía., cía abr de compañía, Company, Co.

cianuro nm cyanide.

cibernética nf cybernetics sing.

cicatero,-a I adj stingy, mean. II nm,f miser.

cicatriz nf scar.

cicatrizar [4] vtr & vi Med to heal.

cíclico,-a adj cyclical.

ciclismo nm cycling.

ciclista I adj cycling. II nmf cyclist.

ciclo nm cycle; (de conferencias etc) course, series.

ciclocróss nm cyclo-cross.

ciclomotor nm moped.

ciclón nm cyclone.

ciego,-a I adj (persona) blind; fam (borracho) blind drunk; (de droga) stoned; a ciegas, blindly. II nm,f blind person; los ciegos, the blind pl.

cielo nm 1 sky. 2 Rel heaven; fig caído del c., (oportuno) heaven-sent; (inesperado) out of the blue; ¡c. santo!, good heavens! 3 Arquit c. raso, ceiling. 4 c. de la boca, roof of the mouth.

ciempiés nm inv centipede.

cien adj & nm inv hundred; c. libras, a o one hundred pounds; c. por c., one hundred per cent.

ciénaga nf marsh, bog.

ciencia nf 1 science; fig saber algo a c. cierta, to know something for certain; c. ficción, science fiction; c. infusa, intuition; ciencias ocultas, the occult sing. 2 (conocimiento) knowledge.

cieno nm mud, mire.

científico,-a I adj scientific. II nm,f scientist.

ciento adj hundred; c. tres, one hundred and three; por c., per cent.

cierne nm fig en ciernes, budding.

cierre nm 1 (acción) closing, shutting; (de fábrica) shutdown; TV close-down; c. patronal, lockout. 2 (de bolso) clasp; (de puerta) catch; (prenda) fastener; c. de seguridad, safety lock; c. centralizado, central locking.

cierto,-a I adj 1 (verdadero) true; (seguro) certain; estar en lo c., to be right; lo c. es que ..., the fact is that ...; por c., by the way. 2 (algún) certain; ciertas personas, certain o some people. II adv certainly.

ciervo,-a nm,f deer; (macho) stag; (hembra) doe, hind.

cifra nf 1 (número) figure, number. 2 (código) cipher, code.

cifrar vtr to express in figures.

cigala *nf* Norway lobster.

cigarra *nf* cicada.

cigarrillo *nm* cigarette.

cigarro *nm* 1 (*puro*) cigar. 2 (*cigarrillo*) cigarette.

cigüeña *nf* 1 *Orn* stork. 2 *Téc* crank. ·

cigüeñal *nm* crankshaft.

cilindrada *nf Aut* cylinder capacity.

cilíndrico,-a *adj* cylindrical.

cilindro *nm* cylinder.

cima *nf* summit.

cimbrearse *vt* to sway.

cimentar *vtr* to lay the foundations of; *fig* (*amistad*) to strengthen.

cimientos *nmpl* foundations; **echar o poner los c.,** to lay the foundations.

cinc *nm* zinc.

cincel *nm* chisel.

cincelar *vtr* to chisel.

cinco *adj & nm inf* five.

cincuenta *adj & nm inf* fifty.

cine *nm* 1 (*local*) cinema, *US* movie theater. 2 (*arte*) cinema; **c. mudo/sonoro,** silent/talking films *pl*.

cineasta *nmf* film director, film maker.

cinéfilo,-a *nm,f* film lover, *US* moviegoer.

cinematográfico,-a *adj* cinematographic; **la industria cinematográfica,** the film *o US* movie industry.

cíngaro,-a *adj & nm,f* gypsy.

cínico,-a I *adj* cynical. **II** *nm,f* cynic.

cinismo *nm* cynicism.

cinta *nf* 1 (*tira*) band, strip; (*para adornar*) ribbon; *Cost* braid, edging. 2 *Téc* Mús tape; **c. adhesiva/aislante,** adhesive/ insulating tape; **c. de vídeo,** video tape; **c. transportadora,** conveyor belt. 3 *Cin* film.

cinto *nm* belt.

cintura *nf* waist.

cinturón *nm* belt; *fig* **apretarse el c.,** to tighten one's belt; **c. de seguridad,** safety belt.

ciprés *nm* cypress.

circense *adj* circus.

circo *nm* circus.

circuito *nm* circuit.

circulación *nf* 1 circulation. 2 *Aut* (*tráfico*) traffic.

circular I *adj & nf* circular. **II** *vi* (*moverse*) to circulate; (*líquido*) to flow; (*tren*, *autobús*) to run; *fig* (*rumor*) to go round; **circule por la izquierda,** (*en letrero*) keep to the left.

circulatorio,-a *adj* circulatory; *Aut* **un caos c.,** traffic chaos.

círculo *nm* circle; *fig* **c. vicioso,** vicious circle.

circuncisión *nf* circumcision.

circundante *adj* surrounding.

circundar *vtr* to surround, encircle.

circunferencia *nf* circumference.

circunloquio *nm* circumlocution.

circunscribirse (*pp* *circunscrito*) *vr* to

confine *o* limit oneself (**a**, to).

circunscripción *nf* district; **c. electoral,** constituency.

circunscrito,-a *adj* circumscribed.

circunspecto,-a *adj* circumspect.

circunstancia *nf* circumstance; **en estas circunstancias ...,** under the circumstances ....

circunstancial *adj* circumstancial.

cirio *nm* wax candle.

cirrosis *nf* cirrhosis.

ciruela *nf* plum; **c. claudia,** greengage; **c. pasa,** prune.

ciruelo *nm* plum tree.

cirugía *nf* surgery; **c. estética *o* plástica,** plastic surgery.

cirujano,-a *nm,f* surgeon.

cisma *nm* 1 *Rel* schism. 2 *Pol* split.

cisne *nm* swan.

cisterna *nf* cistern, tank.

cistitis *nf inv* cystitis.

cita *nf* 1 appointment; **darse c.,** to come together. 2 (*amorosa*) date. 3 (*mención*) quotation.

citación *nf Jur* citation, summons *sing*.

citado,-a *adj* aforementioned.

citar I *vtr* 1 (*dar cita*) to arrange to meet, make an appointment with. 2 (*mencionar*) to quote. 3 *Jur* to summon. **II citarse** *vr* to arrange to meet, make a date (**con**, with).

cítrico,-a I *adj* citric, citrus. **II** *nmpl* **cítricos,** citrus fruits.

ciudad *nf* town; (*capital*) city.

ciudadanía *nf* citizenship.

ciudadano,-a I *nm,f* citizen; **c. de a pie,** the man in the street. **II** *adj* civic.

cívico,-a *adj* civic.

civil I *adj* 1 civil; **matrimonio c.,** civil marriage. 2 *Mil* civilian. **II** *nm* member of the Guardia Civil.

civilización *nf* civilization.

civilizado,-a *adj* civilized.

civilizar [4] *vtr* to civilize.

civismo *nm* civility.

cizaña *nf Bot* bearded darnel; *fig* **sembrar c.,** to sow discord.

cl *abr de* **centilitro(s),** centilitre(s), *US* centiliter(s), cl.

clamar *vtr* to cry out for, clamour *o US* clamor for.

clamor *nm* clamour, *US* clamor.

clamoroso,-a *adj* resounding.

clan *nm* clan.

clandestinidad *nf* **en la c.,** underground.

clandestino,-a *adj* clandestine, underground; **aborto c.,** backstreet abortion.

clara *nf* (*de huevo*) white.

claraboya *nf* skylight.

clarear *vi* 1 (*amanecer*) to dawn. 2 (*despejar*) to clear up. 3 (*transparentar*) to wear thin, become transparent.

clarete *adj & nm* claret.

claridad *nf* 1 (*luz*) light, brightness. 2

(inteligibilidad) clarity; **con c.**, clearly.
clarificador,-a *adj* clarifying.
clarificar [1] *vtr* to clarify.
clarín *nm* bugle.
clarinete *nm* clarinet.
clarividente I *adj* **1** far-sighted. **2** *(lúcido)* lucid. **II** *nmf (persona)* clairvoyant.
claro,-a I *adj* **1** clear; **dejar algo c.**, to make sth clear. **2** *(líquido, salsa)* thin. **3** *(color)* light. **II** *interj* of course!; **¡c. que no!**, of course not!; **¡c. que sí**, certainly!. **III** *nm* **1** *(espacio)* gap, space; *(en un bosque)* clearing. **2** *Meteor* bright spell. **IV** *adv* clearly.
clase *nf* **1** *(grupo)* class; **c. alta/media**, upper/middle class; **clases pasivas**, pensioners; **primera/segunda c.**, first/second class. **2** *(tipo)* kind, sort; **toda c. de ...**, all kinds of .... **3** *Educ (curso)* class; *(aula)* classroom; **c. particular**, private class o lesson. **4** *(estilo)* class; **tener c.**, to have class.
clásico,-a I *adj* classical; *(típico)* classic; *(en el vestir)* classic. **II** *nm* classic.
clasificación *nf* **1** classification; *Dep* league table. **2** *(para campeonato, concurso)* qualification.
clasificar [1] **I** *vtr* to classify, class. **II** **clasificarse** *vr Dep* to qualify.
claudicar [1] *vi* to give in.
claustro *nm* **1** *Arquit* cloister. **2** *(reunión)* staff meeting.
claustrofobia *nf* claustrophobia.
cláusula *nf* clause.
clausura *nf* **1** *(cierre)* closure; **ceremonia de c.**, closing ceremony. **2** *Rel* enclosure.
clausurar *vtr* to close.
clavar I *vtr* **1** to nail; *(clavo)* to bang o hammer in; *(estaca)* to drive in. **2** *fam (timar)* to sting o fleece. **II** **clavarse** *vr* **c. una astilla**, to get a splinter.
clave I *nf* **1** key; **la palabra c.**, the key word. **II** *nm* harpsichord.
clavel *nm* carnation.
clavícula *nf* collarbone.
clavija *nf Téc* jack.
clavo *nm* **1** nail; *fig* **dar en el c.**, to hit the nail on the head. **2** *Bot* clove.
claxon *nm (pl cláxones)* horn; **tocar el c.**, to sound the horn.
clemencia *nf* mercy, clemency.
clementina *nf* clementine.
cleptómano,-a *adj & nm,f* kleptomaniac.
clerical *adj* clerical.
clérigo *nm* priest.
clero *nm* clergy.
cliché *nm* **1** *fig (tópico)* cliché. **2** *Fot* negative. **3** *Impr* plate.
cliente *nmf* customer, client.
clientela *nf* clientele.
clima *nm* climate.
climatizado,-a *adj* air-conditioned.
climatizar [4] *vtr* to air-condition.
clímax *nm inv* climax.

clínica *nf* clinic.
clínico,-a *adj* clinical.
clip *nm* clip.
clítoris *nm inv* clitoris.
cloaca *nf* sewer, drain.
clorhídrico,-a *adj* hydrochloric.
cloro *nm* chlorine.
cloroformo *nm* chloroform.
cloruro *nm* chloride; **c. sódico**, sodium chloride.
club *nm (pl clubs o clubes)* club; **c. náutico**, yacht club.
cm *abr de* **centímetro(s)**, centimetre(s), *US* centimeter(s), cm.
CNT *nf abr de* **Confederación Nacional de Trabajadores.**
coacción *nf* coercion.
coaccionar *vtr* to coerce.
coactivo,-a *adj* coercive.
coadyuvar *vtr* to assist.
coagular *vtr & vi*, **coagularse** *vr* to coagulate; *(sangre)* to clot; *(leche)* to curdle.
coágulo *nm* coagulum, clot.
coalición *nf* coalition.
coartada *nf* alibi.
coartar *vtr* to restrict.
coba *nf fam* **dar c. a algn**, to soft-soap sb.
cobalto *nm* cobalt.
cobarde I *adj* cowardly. **II** *nmf* coward.
cobardía *nf* cowardice.
cobaya *nf* guinea pig.
cobertizo *nm* shed, shack.
cobertor *nm* bedspread.
cobertura *nf* cover; *(de noticia)* coverage.
cobija *nf Am* blanket.
cobijar I *vtr* to shelter. **II** **cobijarse** *vr* to take shelter.
cobijo *nm* shelter; *fig (protección)* protection.
cobra *nf* cobra.
cobrador,-a *nm,f* **1** *(de autobús)* *(hombre)* conductor; *(mujer)* conductress. **2** *(de luz, agua etc)* collector.
cobrar I *vtr* **1** *(dinero)* to charge; *(cheque)* to cash; *(salario)* to earn. **2** *fig (fuerza)* to gain, get; **c. ánimos**, to take courage o heart; **c. importancia**, to become important. **3** *vi fam* to catch it. **III** **cobrarse** *vr* **¿se cobra?**, *(al pagar)* take it out of this, please.
cobre *nm* **1** copper. **2** *Am (moneda)* copper cent.
cobrizo,-a *adj* copper, copper-coloured, *US* copper-colored.
cobro *nm (pago)* collecting; *(de cheque)* cashing; *Tel* **llamada a c. revertido**, reverse-charge, *US* collect call.
coca *nf* **1** *Bot* coca. **2** *arg (droga)* cocaine, coke.
cocaína *nf* cocaine.
cocainómano,-a *nm,f* cocaine addict.
cocción *nf* cooking; *(en agua)* boiling; *(en horno)* baking.
cocer [4] **I** *vtr* to cook; *(hervir)* to boil;

(hornear) to bake. II *vi (hervir)* to boil. III
cocerse *vr* 1 *(comida)* to cook; *(hervir)* to
boil; *(hornear)* to bake. 2 *(tramarse)* to be
going on.

cochambroso,-a *adj* squalid.

coche *nm* 1 car; **en c.**, by car; **c. de carreras**, racing car; **c. de bomberos**, fire
engine; **c. fúnebre**, hearse. 2 *Ferroc*
carriage, coach; **c. cama**, sleeping car,
US sleeper. 3 *(de caballos)* carriage,
coach.

cochecito *nm (de niño)* pram, *US* baby
carriage.

cochera *nf* 1 garage. 2 *(de autobuses)* depot.

cochinillo *nm* suckling pig.

cochino,-a I *nm,f (macho)* pig; *(hembra)*
sow. 2 *fam (persona)* filthy person, pig. II
adj (sucio) filthy, disgusting.

cocido *nm* stew.

cociente *nm* quotient.

cocina *nf* 1 kitchen. 2 *(aparato)* cooker,
US stove. 2 **c. eléctrica/de gas**, electric/
gas cooker. 3 *(arte)* cooking; **c. casera**,
home cooking; **c. española**, Spanish
cooking *o* cuisine.

cocinar *vtr & vi* to cook.

cocinero,-a *nm,f* cook.

cocktail *nm → c*óctel.

coco[1] *nm* coconut; *(cabeza)* nut; **co-
merle el c. a algn**, to brainwash sb; **comerse el c.**, to get obsessed.

coco[2] *nm fam (fantasma)* bogeyman.

cocodrilo *nm* crocodile.

cocotero *nm* coconut palm.

cóctel *nm* cocktail; **c. Molotov**, Molotov
cocktail.

coctelera *nf* cocktail shaker.

codazo *nm* 1 *(señal)* nudge with one's
elbow. 2 *(golpe)* blow with one's elbow.

codearse *vr* to rub shoulders *(con, with)*,
hobnob *(con, with)*.

codeína *nf* codeine.

codicia *nf* greed.

codiciar [12] *vtr* to covet.

codicioso,-a *adj* covetous, greedy.

codificar [1] *vtr (ley)* to codify; *(mensajes)*
to encode.

código *nm* code; **c. de circulación**, highway code.

codo *nm* elbow; *fig* **c. con c.**, side by
side; **fam hablar por los codos**, to talk
nonstop.

codorniz *nf* quail.

coeficiente *nm* 1 coefficient. 2 *(grado)*
rate; **c. intelectual**, intelligence quotient.

coercitivo,-a *adj* coercive.

coetáneo,-a *adj & nm,f* contemporary.

coexistencia *nf* coexistence.

coexistir *vi* to coexist.

cofia *nf* bonnet.

cofradía *nf (hermandad)* brotherhood;
(asociación) association.

cofre *nm (arca)* trunk, chest; *(para joyas)*

box, casket.

coger [5] I *vtr* 1 to take; *(del suelo)* to
pick (up); *(fruta, flores)* to pick; *(asir)* to
seize, take hold of; *(bus, tren)* to take,
catch; *(pelota, ladrón, resfriado)* to catch;
(entender) to grasp; *(costumbre)* to pick
up; *(velocidad, fuerza)* to gather; *(atropellar)* to run over, knock down. 2 *Am vulg*
to fuck. II *vi fam* **cogió y se fue**, he
upped and left. III **cogerse** *vr (agarrarse)*
to hold on.

cogida *nf* goring.

cogollo *nm (de lechuga)* heart.

cogotazo *nm* blow on the back of the
neck.

cogote *nm* nape *o* back of the neck.

cohabitación *nf* cohabitation.

cohabitar *vi* to live together, cohabit.

cohecho *nm Jur* bribery.

coherencia *nf* coherence.

coherente *adj* coherent.

cohesión *nf* cohesion.

cohete *nm* rocket; **c. espacial**, space
rocket.

cohibido,-a *adj* inhibited.

cohibir [21] I *vtr* to inhibit. II **cohibirse**
vr to feel inhibited.

COI *nm Dep abr de* **Comité Olímpico
Internacional**, International Olympic
Committee, IOC.

coincidencia *nf* coincidence.

coincidir *vi* 1 to coincide. 2 *(concordar)* to
agree; **todos coincidieron en señalar
que**, everyone agreed that. 3 *(encontrarse)*
to meet by chance.

coito *nm* coitus, intercourse.

cojear *vi (persona)* to limp, hobble; *(mueble)* to wobble.

cojera *nf* limp.

cojín *nm* cushion.

cojinete *nm Téc* bearing; **c. de agujas/
bolas**, needle/ball bearing.

cojo,-a I *adj (persona)* lame; *(mueble)* rickety. II *nm,f* lame person.

cojón *nm vulg* ball; **de cojones**, *(estupendo)* fucking brilliant *o* good; *(pésimo)*
fucking awful *o* bad.

cojonudo,-a *adj vulg* fucking great.

col *nf* cabbage; **c. de Bruselas**, Brussels
sprout.

cola[1] *nf* 1 *(de animal)* tail; *(de vestido)*
train; *(de pelo)* ponytail; **a la c.**, at the
back *o* rear; *fam* **traer c.**, to have consequences. 2 *(fila)* queue, line; **hacer
c.**, to queue (up), *US* stand in line.

cola[2] *nf (pegamento)* glue.

colaboración *nf* 1 collaboration. 2 *Prensa*
contribution.

colaboracionismo *nm Pol* collaboration.

colaborador,-a I *nm,f* 1 collaborator. 2
Prensa contributor. II *adj* collaborating.

colaborar *vi* to collaborate, cooperate.

colación *nf* **sacar** *o* **traer (algo) a c.**, to
bring (sth) up.

colada *nf* wash, laundry; **hacer la c.,** to do the washing *o* laundry.

colador *nm* colander, sieve; *(de té, café)* strainer.

colapsar I *vtr* to bring to a standstill. **II colapsarse** *vr* to come to a standstill.

colapso *nm* **1** *Med* collapse. **2** *Aut* **c. circulatorio,** traffic jam.

colar |2| **I** *vtr* **1** *(líquido)* to strain, filter. **2** *(por agujero)* to slip. **II** *vi fam* **esa mentira no cuela,** that lie won't wash. **III colarse** *vr* **1** to slip in; *(a fiesta)* to gatecrash; *(en una cola)* to jump the queue. **2** *fam (pasarse)* to go too far.

colateral *adj* collateral.

colcha *nf* bedspread.

colchón *nm* mattress.

colchoneta *nf* air bed.

colear *vi* **1** to wag its tail; *fam* **vivito y coleando,** alive and kicking. **2** *fam* **el asunto aún colea,** we haven't heard the last of it yet.

colección *nf* collection.

coleccionable *adj & nm* collectable.

coleccionar *vtr* to collect.

coleccionista *nmf* collector.

colecta *nf* collection.

colectividad *nf* community.

colectivo,-a I *adj* collective. **II** *nm* **1** *(asociación)* association. **2** *Am* long-distance taxi.

colega *nmf* **1** colleague. **2** *arg (amigo)* buddy, mate.

colegiado,-a *nm* *Dep* referee.

colegial I *adj (escolar)* school. **II** *nmf* *(alumno)* schoolboy; *(alumna)* schoolgirl; **los colegiales,** the schoolchildren.

colegio *nm* **1** *(escuela)* school; **c. privado,** *GB* public *o* independent school. **2** *(profesional)* association, college; **c. de abogados,** the Bar; *Pol* **c. electoral,** electoral college. **3** *Univ* **c. mayor** *o* **universitario,** hall of residence.

colegir |6| *vtr* to infer, deduce.

cólera[1] *nf* anger, rage.

cólera[2] *nm Med* cholera.

colérico,-a *adj* furious.

colesterol *nm* cholesterol.

coleta *nf* pigtail, ponytail; *fig* **cortarse la c.,** to retire.

coletazo *nm* **dar los últimos coletazos,** to be on one's last legs.

coletilla *nf* postscript.

colgado,-a *adj* **1** *arg* **dejar (a algn)** to leave (sb) in the lurch. **2** *arg* weird; *(drogado)* high.

colgante I *nm (joya)* pendant. **II** *adj* hanging.

colgar |2| **I** *vtr* **1** to hang (up); *(colada)* to hang (out). **2** *(ahorcar)* to hang. **II** *vi* **1** to hang *(de,* from); *fig* **c. de un hilo,** to hang by a thread. **2** *Tel* to hang up. **III colgarse** *vr (ahorcarse)* to hang oneself.

colibrí *nm* humming bird.

cólico *nm* colic.

coliflor *nf* cauliflower.

colijo *indic pres → **colegir.**

colilla *nf (cigarette)* end *o* butt.

colina *nf* hill.

colindante *adj* adjoining, adjacent.

colindar *vi* to be adjacent **(con,** to).

colirio *nm* eyedrops.

colisión *nf* collision, crash; *(de ideas)* clash.

colisionar *vi* to collide, crash.

colitis *nf* colitis.

collage *nm* collage.

collar *nm* **1** *(adorno)* necklace. **2** *(de perro)* collar.

colmado,-a *adj* full, filled; *(cucharada)* heaped.

colmar *vtr* **1** to fill (right up); *(vaso, copa)* to fill to the brim; *fig* to shower **(de,** with). **2** *(ambiciones)* to fulfil, satisfy.

colmena *nf* beehive.

colmillo *nm* eye *o* canine tooth; *Zool (de carnívoro)* fang; *(de jabalí, elefante)* tusk.

colmo *nm* height; **el c. de,** the height of; **¡eso es el c.!,** that's the last straw! **para c.,** to top it all.

colocación *nf* **1** *(acto)* positioning. **2** *(disposición)* lay-out. **3** *(empleo)* job, employment.

colocado,-a *adj* **1** *(empleado)* employed. **2** *arg (drogado)* high.

colocar |1| **I** *vtr* **1** to place, put. **2** *Fin (invertir)* to invest. **3** *(emplear)* to give work to. **4** *arg (drogar)* to stone. **II colocarse** *vr* **1** *(situarse)* to put oneself. **2** *(emplearse)* to take a job **(de,** as). **3** *arg (drogarse)* to get high.

colofón *nm* **1** *(apéndice)* colophon. **2** *fig* climax.

Colombia *n* Colombia.

colombiano,-a *adj y nm,f* Colombian.

colón *nm Fin* standard monetary unit of Costa Rica and El Salvador.

Colón *n* Columbus.

colonia[1] *nf* colony; *(campamento)* summer camp.

colonia[2] *nf (perfume)* cologne.

colonial *adj* colonial.

colonialismo *nm* colonialism.

colonización *nf* colonization.

colonizar |4| *vtr* to colonize.

coloquial *adj* colloquial.

coloquio *nm* discussion, colloquium.

color *nm* colour, *US* color; **Cin Fot en c.,** in colour; **de colores,** multicoloured; **persona de c.,** coloured person.

colorado,-a I *adj* red; **ponerse c.,** to blush. **II** *nm* red.

colorante *nm* colouring, *US* coloring.

colorear *vtr* to colour, *US* color.

colorete *nm* rouge.

colorido *nm* colour, *US* color.

colorín *nm* goldfinch.

colosal *adj* colossal.

columna *nf* column; *Anat* **c. vertebral**, vertebral column, spinal column.

columpiar |12| I *vtr* to swing. II **columpiarse** *vr* to swing.

columpio *nm* swing.

coma¹ *nf* 1 *Ling Mús* comma. 2 *Mat* point; **tres c. cinco**, three point five.

coma² *nm Med* coma.

comadre *nf* godmother.

comadreja *nf* weasel.

comadreo *nm* gossip, gossiping.

comadrona *nf* midwife.

comandancia *nf* command.

comandante *nm* 1 *Mil* commander, commanding officer. 2 *Av* captain.

comandar *vtr* to command.

comando *nm* 1 *Mil* commando. 2 *Inform* command.

comarca *nf* region.

comarcal *adj* regional.

comba *nf* 1 *(curvatura)* curve, bend. 2 *(cuerda)* skipping rope; **saltar a la c.**, to skip.

combar *vtr* to bend.

combate *nm* combat; *Box* fight; *Mil* battle; **fuera de c.**, out for the count; *(eliminado)* out of action.

combatiente I *adj* fighting. II *nmf* combatant.

combatir I *vtr* to combat. II *vi* to fight *(contra, against).

combativo,-a *adj* spirited, aggressive.

combinación *nf* 1 combination. 2 *(prenda)* slip.

combinado,-a I *adj* combined. III *nm* 1 *(cóctel)* cocktail. 2 *Dep* line-up.

combinar *vtr*, **combinarse** *vr* to combine.

combustible I *nm* fuel. II *adj* combustible.

combustión *nf* combustion.

comedia *nf* comedy.

comediante,-a *nm,f* *(hombre)* actor; *(mujer)* actress.

comedido,-a *adj* self-restrained, reserved.

comedor *nm* dining room.

comensal *nmf* companion at table.

comentar *vtr* **c. algo con algn**, to talk sth over with sb; **me han comentado que ...**, I've been told that ....

comentario *nm* 1 comment, remark; *(crítica)* commentary; **sin c.**, no comment. 2 **comentarios**, *(cotilleos)* gossip.

comentarista *nmf* commentator.

comenzar |1| *vtr & vi* to begin, start; **comenzó a llover**, it started raining *o* to rain; **comenzó diciendo que ...**, he started by saying that ....

comer I *vtr* 1 to eat. 2 *(en juegos)* to take, capture. II *vi* to eat; **dar de c. a algn**, to feed sb. III **comerse** *vr* 1 to eat. 2 *fig* *(saltarse)* to skip.

comercial *adj* commercial.

comercialización *nf* marketing.

comercializar |4| *vtr* to market.

comerciante *nmf* merchant.

comerciar |12| *vi* to trade; **comercia con oro**, he trades in gold.

comercio *nm* 1 commerce, trade; **c. exterior**, foreign trade. 2 *(tienda)* shop.

comestible I *adj* edible. II *nmpl* **comestibles**, food *sing*, foodstuff(s); **tienda de comestibles**, grocer's shop, *US* grocery store.

cometa I *nm Astron* comet. II *nf* *(juguete)* kite.

cometer *vtr* *(error, falta)* to make; *(delito, crimen)* to commit.

cometido *nm* 1 *(tarea)* task, assignment. 2 *(deber)* duty; **cumplir su c.**, to do one's duty.

comezón *nm* itch.

cómic *nm* comic.

comicios *nmpl* elections.

cómico,-a I *adj* 1 comical, funny. 2 *Teat* **actor c.**, comedian. II *nm,f* comic; *(hombre)* comedian; *(mujer)* comedienne.

comida *nf* 1 *(alimento)* food. 2 *(almuerzo, cena)* meal.

comidilla *nf fam* **la c. del pueblo**, the talk of the town.

comienzo *nm* beginning, start; **a comienzos de**, at the beginning of; **dar c.** **(a algo)**, to begin *o* start (sth).

comilón,-ona I *adj* greedy, gluttonous. II *nm,f* big eater, glutton.

comilona *nf fam* big meal, feast.

comillas *nfpl* inverted commas; **entre c.**, in inverted commas.

comino *nm* cumin, cummin; *fam* **me importa un c.**, I don't give a damn (about it).

comisaría *nf* police station.

comisario *nm* 1 *(de policía)* police inspector. 2 *(delegado)* commissioner.

comisión *nf* 1 *Com* *(retribución)* commission; **a o con c.**, on a commission basis. 2 *(comité)* committee.

comité *nm* committee.

comitiva *nf* suite, retinue.

como I *adv* 1 *(manera)* how; **me gusta c. cantas**, I like the way you sing; **dilo c. quieras**, say it however you like. 2 *(comparación)* as; **blanco c. la nieve**, as white as snow; **habla c. su padre**, he talks like his father. 3 *(según)* as; **c. decíamos ayer**, as we were saying yesterday. 4 *(en calidad de)* as; **c. presidente**, as president; **lo compré c. recuerdo**, I bought it as a souvenir. 5 *(aproximadamente)* about; **c. a la mitad de camino**, halfway; **c. unos diez**, about ten.

II *conj* 1 *+ subj*, *(si)* if; **c. no estudies vas a suspender**, if you don't study hard, you'll fail. 2 *(porque)* as, since; **c. no venías me marché**, as you didn't come I left. 3 **c. si**, as if; **c. si nada** *o* **tal cosa**, as if nothing had happened; *fam* **c.**

si lo viera, I can imagine perfectly well.

cómo I *adv* 1 ¿c.?, (¿*perdón?*) what? 2 (*interrogativo*) how; ¿c. estás?, how are you?; ¿c. lo sabes?, how do you know?; ¿c. es de grande/ancho?, how big/wide is it?; ¿a c. están los tomates?, how much are the tomatoes?; ¿c. es que no viniste a la fiesta?, (*por qué*) how come you didn't come to the party?; *fam* ¿c. es eso?, how come? 3 (*exclamativo*) how; ¡c. has crecido!, you've really grown a lot!; ¡c. no!, but of course!. II *nm* el c. y el porqué, the whys and wherefores.

cómoda *nf* chest of drawers.

comodidad *nf* 1 comfort. 2 (*conveniencia*) convenience.

comodín *nm Naipes* joker.

cómodo,-a *adj* 1 comfortable; ponerse c., to make oneself comfortable. 2 (*útil*) handy, convenient.

comoquiera *adv* 1 however, whatever way; c. que sea, one way or another. 2 c. que no estaba enterado, (*puesto que*) as he didn't know.

compacto,-a *adj* compact; disco c., compact disc.

compadecer [33] I *vtr* to feel sorry for, pity. II **compadecerse** *vr* to have *o* take pity (de, on).

compadre *nm* 1 (*padrino*) godfather. 2 *Am fam* (*amigo*) friend, mate.

compaginar *vtr* to combine.

compañerismo *nm* companionship, comradeship.

compañero,-a *nm,f* companion; c. de colegio, school friend; c. de piso, flatmate.

compañía *nf* company; hacer c. (a algn), to keep (sb) company; c. de seguros/de teatro, insurance/theatre company.

comparable *adj* comparable.

comparación *nf* comparison; en c., comparatively; en c. con, compared to; sin c., beyond compare.

comparar *vtr* to compare (con, with).

comparativo,-a *adj & nm* comparative.

comparecencia *nf* appearance.

comparecer [33] *vi Jur* to appear (ante, before).

comparsa *nf* band of revellers.

compartimento, compartimiento *nm* compartment; c. de primera/segunda clase, first-/second-class compartment.

compartir *vtr* to share.

compás *nm* 1 *Téc* (pair of) compasses. 2 *Náut* compass. 3 *Mús* (*división*) time; (*intervalo*) beat; (*ritmo*) rhythm; c. de espera, *Mús* bar rest; *fig* (*pausa*) delay; al c. de, in time to.

compasión *nf* compassion, pity; tener c. (de algn), to feel sorry (for sb).

compasivo,-a *adj* compassionate.

compatible *adj* compatible.

compatriota *nmf* compatriot; (*hombre*) fellow countryman; (*mujer*) fellow countrywoman.

compendiar [12] *vtr* to abridge, summarize.

compendio *nm* compendium.

compenetrarse *vr* to understand each other *o* one another.

compensación *nf* compensation.

compensar I *vtr* (*pérdida, error*) to make up for; (*indemnizar*) to compensate (for). II *vi* to be worthwhile; este trabajo no compensa, this job's not worth my time.

competencia *nf* 1 (*rivalidad, empresas rivales*) competition. 2 (*capacidad*) competence. 3 (*incumbencia*) field, province; no es de mi c., it's not up to me.

competente *adj* competent.

competición *nf* competition, contest.

competido,-a *adj* hard-fought.

competidor,-a I *nm,f Com Dep* competitor. 2 (*participante*) contestant. II *adj* competing.

competir [6] *vi* to compete (con, with *o* against; en, in; por, for).

competitividad *nf* competitiveness.

competitivo,-a *adj* competitive.

compilar *vtr* to compile.

compinche *nmf* 1 (*compañero*) chum, pal. 2 *pey* (*cómplice*) accomplice.

complacencia *nf* 1 (*satisfacción*) satisfaction. 2 (*indulgencia*) indulgence.

complacer [33] I *vtr* to please; *fml* me complace presentarles a ..., it gives me great pleasure to introduce to you .... II **complacerse** *vr* to delight (en, in), take pleasure (en, in).

complaciente *adj* obliging.

complejidad *nf* complexity.

complejo,-a *adj & nm* complex.

complementar I *vtr* to complement. II **complementarse** *vr* to complement (each other), be complementary to (each other).

complementario,-a *adj* complementary.

complemento *nm* complement; *Ling* object.

completar *vtr* to complete.

completo,-a *adj* 1 (*terminado*) complete; por c., completely. 2 (*lleno*) full; al c., full up, to capacity. ◆**completamente** *adv* completely.

complexión *nf* build; de c. fuerte, wellbuilt.

complicación *nf* complication.

complicado,-a *adj* 1 (*complejo*) complicated. 2 (*implicado*) involved.

complicar [1] I *vtr* 1 to complicate. 2 (*involucrar*) to involve (en, in). II **complicarse** *vr* to get complicated; c. la vida, to make life difficult for oneself.

cómplice *nmf* accomplice.

complot *nm* (*pl complots*) conspiracy, plot.

componente I *adj* component. II *nm* 1

(pieza) component; *(ingrediente)* ingredient. 2 *(persona)* member.

componer [19] *(pp* **compuesto)** I *vtr* 1 *(formar)* to compose, make up. 2 *Mús* Lit to compose. 3 *(reparar)* to mend, repair. II **componerse** *vr* 1 *(consistir)* to be made up **(de,** of), consist **(de,** of). 2 *(arreglarse)* to dress up. 3 *fam* **componérselas,** to manage.

comportamiento *nm* behaviour, *US* behavior.

comportar I *vtr* to entail, involve. II **comportarse** *vr* to behave; **c. mal,** to misbehave.

composición *nf* composition.

compositor,-a *nm,f* composer.

compostelano,-a *adj* from Santiago de Compostela.

compostura *nf* composure.

compota *nf* compote.

compra *nf (acción)* buying; *(cosa comprada)* purchase, buy; **ir de c.,** to go shopping.

comprador,-a *nm,f* purchaser, buyer.

comprar *vtr* 1 to buy. 2 *(sobornar)* to bribe, buy off.

compraventa *nf* buying and selling; **contrato de c.,** contract of sale.

comprender *vtr* 1 *(entender)* to understand; **se comprende,** it's understandable. 2 *(contener)* to comprise, include.

comprensible *adj* understandable.

comprensión *nf* understanding.

comprensivo,-a *adj* understanding.

compresa *nf* 1 *(para mujer)* sanitary towel. 2 *Med* compress.

comprimido,-a I *nm Farm* tablet. II *adj* compressed; **escopeta de aire c.,** air rifle.

comprimir *vtr* to compress.

comprobante *nm (de compra etc)* voucher, receipt.

comprobar [2] *vtr* to check.

comprometer I *vtr* 1 *(arriesgar)* to compromise, jeopardize. 2 *(obligar)* to compel, force. II **comprometerse** *vr* 1 **c. a hacer algo,** to undertake to do sth. 2 *(novios)* to become engaged.

comprometido,-a *adj* 1 *(situación)* difficult. 2 *(para casarse)* engaged.

compromiso *nm* 1 *(obligación)* obligation, commitment; **sin c.,** without obligation; **por c.,** out of a sense of duty. 2 **poner (a algn) en un c.,** to put (sb) in a difficult *o* embarrassing situation. 3 *(acuerdo)* agreement; *fml* **c. matrimonial,** engagement; **soltero y sin c.,** single and unattached.

compuesto,-a I *adj* 1 compound. 2 **c. de,** composed of. II *nm* compound.

compulsar *vtr* to make a certified true copy of.

compungido,-a *adj (arrepentido)* remorseful; *(triste)* sorrowful, sad.

compuse *pt indef →* **componer.**

computadora *nf* computer.

cómputo *nm* calculation.

comulgar [7] *vi* 1 to receive Holy Communion. 2 *fig* **no comulgo con sus ideas,** I don't share his ideas.

común I *adj* 1 common; **de c. acuerdo,** by common consent; **hacer algo en c.,** to do sth jointly; **poco c.,** unusual; **por lo c.,** generally. 2 *(compartido)* shared, communal; **amigos comunes,** mutual friends. II *nm GB Pol* **los Comunes,** the Commons.

comunal *adj* communal.

comunicación *nf* 1 communication; **ponerse en c. (con algn),** to get in touch (with sb). 2 *(comunicado)* communication; **c. oficial,** communiqué. 3 *Tel* connection; **se nos cortó la c.,** we were cut off. 4 *(unión)* link, connection.

comunicado,-a I *adj* **una zona bien comunicada,** a well-served zone; **dos ciudades bien comunicadas,** two towns with good connections (between them). II *nm* communiqué; **c. de prensa,** press release.

comunicar [1] I *vtr* 1 to communicate; **comuníquenoslo lo antes posible,** let us know as soon as possible. II *vi* 1 to communicate. 2 *Tel* to be engaged; **está comunicando,** it's engaged. III **comunicarse** *vr* to communicate.

comunicativo,-a *adj* communicative.

comunidad *nf* community; **C. Europea,** European Community; **C. de Estados Independientes,** Commonwealth of Independent States.

comunión *nf* communion.

comunismo *nm* communism.

comunista *adj & nmf* communist.

comunitario,-a *adj* 1 *o* relating to the community. 2 *(de CE)* *o* relating to the EC; **la política agraria comunitaria,** the common agricultural policy.

con *prep* 1 with; **córtalo c. las tijeras,** cut it with the scissors; **voy cómodo c. este jersey,** I'm comfortable in this sweater. 2 *(compañía)* with; **vine c. mi hermana,** I came with my sister. 3 **c. ese frío/niebla,** in that cold/fog; **estar c. (la) gripe,** to have the flu. 4 *(contenido)* with; **una bolsa c. dinero,** a bag full of money. 5 *(a)* to; **habló c. todos,** he spoke to everybody; **sé amable c. ella,** be nice to her. 6 *(con infinitivo)* **c. llamar será suficiente,** it will be enough just to phone; *(+ que + subjuntivo)* **bastará c. que lo esboces,** a general idea will do. 7 **c. tal (de) que ...,** provided that ...; **c. todo (y eso),** even so.

conato *nm* attempt; **c. de asesinato,** attempted murder.

concebible *adj* conceivable, imaginable.

concebir [6] I *vtr* 1 *(plan, hijo)* to conceive. 2 *(entender)* to understand. II *vi* *(mujer)* to become pregnant, conceive.

conceder *vtr* to grant; *(premio)* to award.

concejal,-a *nm,f* town councillor.

concejo *nm* council.

concentración *nf* concentration; *(de manifestantes)* gathering; *(de coches, motos)* rally; *(de equipo)* base.

concentrado *nm* concentrate.

concentrar I *vtr* to concentrate. II **concentrarse** *vr* 1 to concentrate (en, on). 2 *(reunirse)* to gather.

concepción *nf* conception.

concepto *nm* 1 *(idea)* concept; **tener buen/mal c. de**, to have a good/a bad opinion of; **bajo/por ningún c.**, under no circumstances. 2 **en c. de**, under the heading of. 3 *(en factura)* item.

concerniente *adj* concerning, regarding (a, -); *fml* **en lo c. a**, with regard to.

concernir [5] *v impers* 1 *(afectar)* to concern; **en lo que a mí concierne**, as far as I am concerned; **en lo que concierne a**, with regard/respect to. 2 *(corresponder)* to be up to.

concertación *nf* compromise.

concertar [1] I *vtr* 1 *(cita)* to arrange; *(precio)* to agree on; *(acuerdo)* to reach. 2 *(una acción etc)* to plan, co-ordinate. II *vi* to agree, tally.

concesión *nf* 1 concession. 2 *(de un premio, contrato)* awarding.

concesionario,-a *nm,f* dealer.

concha *nf* 1 *Zool (caparazón)* shell; *(carey)* tortoiseshell. 2 *Am vulg* cunt.

conchabarse *vr* to gang up.

conciencia *nf* 1 conscience; **tener la c. tranquila**, with a clear conscience. 2 *(conocimiento)* consciousness, awareness; **a c.**, conscientiously; **tener/tomar c. (de algo)**, to be/become aware (of sth).

concienciar [12] I *vtr* to make aware (de, of). II **concienciarse** *vr* to become aware (de, of).

concienzudo,-a *adj* conscientious.

concierto *nm* 1 *Mús* concert; *(composición)* concerto. 2 *(acuerdo)* agreement.

conciliar [12] *vtr* to reconcile; **c. el sueño**, to get to sleep.

concilio *nm* council.

conciso,-a *adj* concise.

conciudadano,-a *nm,f* fellow citizen.

concluir [37] *vtr* to conclude.

conclusión *nf* conclusion; **sacar una c.**, to draw a conclusion.

concluyente *adj* conclusive.

concomerse *vr* to be consumed; **c. de envidia**, to be green with envy.

concordar [2] I *vi* to agree; **esto no concuerda con lo que dijo ayer**, this doesn't fit in with what he said yesterday. II *vtr* to bring into agreement.

concordia *nf* concord.

concretar *vtr* *(precisar)* to specify, state explicitly; *(fecha, hora)* to fix.

concreto,-a *adj* 1 *(preciso, real)* concrete. 2 *(particular)* specific; **en c.**, specifically; **en el caso c. de ....**, in the specific case of ..... II *nm Am* concrete.
◆**concretamente** *adv* specifically.

concurrencia *nf* 1 *(de dos cosas)* concurrence. 2 *(público)* audience.

concurrido,-a *adj* crowded, busy.

concurrir *vi* 1 *(gente)* to converge (en, on), meet (en, in). 2 *(coincidir)* to concur, coincide. 3 *(participar)* to compete; *(en elecciones)* to be a candidate.

concursante *nm,f* 1 contestant, competitor. 2 *(para un empleo)* candidate.

concursar *vi* to compete, take part.

concurso *nm* 1 *(competición)* competition; *(de belleza etc)* contest; *TV* quiz show; **presentar (una obra) a c.**, to invite tenders (for a piece of work). 2 *fml (ayuda)* help.

condal *adj* of o relating to a count; **la Ciudad C.**, Barcelona.

conde *nm* count.

condecoración *nf* decoration.

condecorar *vtr* to decorate.

condena *nf* 1 *Jur* sentence. 2 *(desaprobación)* condemnation, disapproval.

condenado,-a I *adj* 1 *Jur* convicted; **c. a muerte**, condemned to death. 2 *Rel & fam* damned; **c. al fracaso**, doomed to failure. II *nm,f* 1 *Jur* convicted person; *(a muerte)* condemned person. 2 *Rel* damned.

condenar I *vtr* 1 *Jur* to convict, find guilty; **c. a algn a muerte**, to condemn sb to death. 2 *(desaprobar)* to condemn. II **condenarse** *vr Rel* to be damned.

condensado,-a *adj* condensed; **leche condensada**, condensed milk.

condensador *nm* condenser.

condensar *vtr*, **condensarse** *vr* to condense.

condesa *nf* countess.

condescender [3] *vi* 1 to condescend. 2 *(ceder)* to comply (with), consent (to).

condescendiente *adj* 1 *(displicente)* condescending. 2 *(complaciente)* complacent.

condición *nf* 1 condition; **en buenas/malas condiciones**, in good/bad condition; **condiciones de trabajo**, working conditions; **con la c. de que ....**, on the condition that ..... 2 *(manera de ser)* nature, character. 3 **en su c. de director**, *(calidad)* in his capacity as director.

condicional *adj* conditional.

condicionar *vtr* 1 to condition. 2 **una cosa condiciona la otra**, one thing determines the other.

condimentar *vtr* to season, flavour, *US* flavor.

condimento *nm* seasoning, flavouring, *US* flavoring.

condolerse [4] *vr* **c. de**, to sympathize with.

condón *nm* condom.

condonar *vtr (ofensa)* to condone; *(deuda)* to cancel.

cóndor *nm* condor.

conducir [10] I *vtr (coche)* to drive; *(electricidad)* to conduct. II *vi* 1 *Aut* to drive; **permiso de c.**, driving licence, *US* driver's license. 2 *(camino, actitud)* to lead; **eso no conduce a nada**, this leads nowhere.

conducta *nf* behaviour, *US* behavior, conduct; **mala c.**, misbehaviour, misconduct.

conducto *nm* 1 *(tubería)* pipe; *fig* **por conductos oficiales**, through official channels. 2 *Anat* duct, canal.

conductor,-a I *nm,f Aut* driver. II *nm Elec* conductor.

conectar *vtr* 1 to connect up. 2 *Elec* to plug in, switch on.

coneja *nf* doe rabbit.

conejillo *nm* **c. de Indias**, guinea pig.

conejo *nm* rabbit.

conexión *nf* connection.

confabularse *vr* to conspire, plot.

confección *nf* 1 *Cost* dressmaking, tailoring; **la i. de la c.**, the rag trade. 2 *(de un plan etc)* making, making up.

confeccionar *vtr* to make (up).

confederación *nf* confederation.

conferencia *nf* 1 lecture; **dar una c. (sobre algo)**, to give a lecture (on sth.) 2 **c. de prensa**, press conference. 3 *Tel* long-distance call.

conferenciante *nmf* lecturer.

conferir [5] *vtr fml (honor, privilegio)* to confer.

confesar [1] I *vtr* to confess, admit; *(crimen)* to own up to; *Rel (pecados)* to confess. II *vi Jur* to own up. III **confesarse** *vr* to confess; **c. culpable**, to admit one's guilt; *Rel* to go to confession.

confesión *nf* confession, admission; *Rel* confession.

confesionario *nm Rel* confessional.

confeti *nm (pl* **confetis)** confetti.

confiado,-a *adj* 1 *(seguro)* self-confident. 2 *(crédulo)* gullible, unsuspecting.

confianza *nf* 1 *(seguridad)* confidence; **tener c. en uno mismo**, to be self-confident. 2 **de c.**, reliable. 3 **tener c. con algn**, to be on intimate terms with sb; **con toda c.**, in all confidence; **tomarse (demasiadas) confianzas**, to take liberties.

confiar [29] I *vtr (entregar)* to entrust; *(información, secreto)* to confide. II *vi* **c. en**, to trust; **confío en ella**, I trust her; **no confíes en su ayuda**, don't count on his help. III **confiarse** *vr* to confide (**en** *o* **a**, in); **c. demasiado**, to be over-confident.

confidencia *nf* confidence.

confidencial *adj* confidential.

confidente,-a *nm,f* 1 *(hombre)* confidant; *(mujer)* confidante. 2 *(de la policía)* informer.

configuración *nf* configuration; *Inform* configuration.

configurar *vtr* to shape, form.

confín *nm* limit, boundary.

confinar *vtr Jur* to confine.

confirmación *nf* confirmation.

confirmar *vtr* to confirm; *prov* **la excepción confirma la regla**, the exception proves the rule.

confiscar [1] *vtr* to confiscate.

confite *nm* sweet, *US* candy.

confitería *nf* 1 confectioner's (shop), *US* candy store. 2 *Am* café.

confitura *nf* preserve, jam.

conflagración *nf fig* **c. mundial**, world war.

conflictividad *nf* **c. laboral**, industrial unrest.

conflictivo,-a *adj (asunto)* controversial; *(época)* unsettled; **niño c.**, problem child.

conflicto *nm* conflict; **c. laboral**, industrial dispute.

confluencia *nf* confluence.

confluir [37] *vi* to converge; *(caminos, ríos)* to meet, come together.

conformar I *vtr* to shape. II **conformarse** *vr* to resign oneself, be content.

conforme I *adj* 1 *(satisfecho)* satisfied; **c.**, agreed, all right; **no estoy c.**, I don't agree. 2 **c. a**, in accordance *o* keeping with. II *conj* 1 *(según, como)* as; **c. lo vi/lo oí**, as I saw/heard it. 2 *(a medida que)* as; **la policía los detenía c. iban saliendo**, the police were arresting them as they came out.

conformidad *nf* 1 approval, consent. 2 **en c.**, in conformity (**con**, with).

conformismo *nm* conformity.

conformista *adj & nmf* conformist.

confort *nm (pl* **conforts)** comfort; **'todo c.'**, 'all mod cons'.

confortable *adj* comfortable.

confortar *vtr* to comfort.

confraternizar [4] *vi* to fraternize.

confrontación *nf* 1 *(enfrentamiento)* confrontation. 2 *(comparación)* contrast.

confrontar *vtr* 1 to confront. 2 *(cotejar)* to compare, collate.

confundir *vtr* 1 to confuse (**con**, with); **c. a una persona con otra**, to mistake somebody for somebody else. 2 *(persona)* to mislead. 3 *(turbar)* to confound. II **confundirse** *vr* 1 *(equivocarse)* to be mistaken; *Tel* **se ha confundido**, you've got the wrong number. 2 *(mezclarse)* to mingle; **se confundió entre el gentío**, he disappeared into the crowd.

confusión *nf* confusion.

confuso,-a *adj* 1 confused; *(formas, recuerdo)* blurred, vague. 2 *(mezclado)* mixed up.

congelación nf 1 freezing. 2 Fin freeze. 3 Med frostbite.

congelado,-a I adj frozen; Med frostbitten. **II** nmpl **congelados,** frozen food sing.

congelador nm freezer.

congelar I vtr to freeze. **II congelarse** vr 1 to freeze; **fam me estoy congelando,** I'm freezing. 2 Med to get o become frostbitten.

congeniar [12] vi to get on (**con,** with).

congénito,-a adj congenital.

congestión nf congestion; Med **c. cerebral,** stroke.

congestionar vtr to congest.

conglomerado nm conglomerate.

conglomerar vtr, **conglomerarse** vr to conglomerate.

congoja nf sorrow, grief.

congraciarse [12] vr to ingratiate oneself (**con,** with).

congratular vtr fml to congratulate (**por,** on).

congregación nf congregation.

congregar [7] vtr, **congregarse** vr to congregate, assemble.

congresista nmf member of a congress.

congreso nm congress, conference; Pol **c. de los Diputados,** ≈ Parliament, US Congress.

congrio nm conger (eel).

congruente adj coherent, suitable.

conjetura nf conjecture; **por c.,** by guesswork.

conjeturar vtr to conjecture.

conjugación nf conjugation.

conjugar [7] vtr to conjugate; fig (planes, opiniones) to combine.

conjunción nf conjunction.

conjuntar vtr to co-ordinate.

conjuntivitis nf conjunctivitis.

conjunto,-a I nm 1 (grupo) collection, group. 2 (todo) whole; del o. overall; **en c.,** on the whole. 3 Mús (pop) group, band. 4 (prenda) outfit, ensemble. 5 Mat set. 6 Dep team. **II** adj joint.

conjurar I vtr 1 to exorcise; (peligro) to ward off. **II conjurarse** vr to conspire, plot.

conjuro nm 1 (exorcismo) exorcism. 2 (encantamiento) spell, incantation.

conllevar vtr to entail.

conmemoración nf commemoration.

conmemorar vtr to commemorate.

conmigo pron pers with me; **vino c., he** came with me; **él habló c.,** he talked to me.

conminar vtr to threaten, menace.

conmoción nf commotion, shock; **c. cerebral,** concussion.

conmocionar vtr to shock; Med to concuss.

conmovedor,-a adj touching; **una película conmovedora,** a moving film.

conmover [4] vtr to touch, move.

conmutador nm 1 Elec switch. 2 Am Tel switchboard.

conmutar vtr to exchange; Jur to commute; Elec to commutate.

connivencia nf connivance, collusion.

connotación nf connotation.

cono nm cone; C. Sur, South America.

conocedor,-a adj & nm,f expert; (de vino, arte etc) connoisseur.

conocer [34] **I** vtr 1 to know; **dar (algo/algn) a c.,** to make (sth/sb) known. 2 (a una persona) to meet. 2 (reconocer) to recognize; **te conocí por la voz,** I recognized you by your voice. **II conocerse** vr (dos personas) to know each other; (por primera vez) to meet.

conocido,-a I adj known; (famoso) well-known. **II** nm,f acquaintance.

conocimiento nm 1 knowledge; **con c. de causa,** with full knowledge of the facts. 2 (conciencia) consciousness; **perder/recobrar el c.,** to lose/regain consciousness. 3 **conocimientos,** knowledge.

conque conj so.

conquense I adj of o from Cuenca. **II** nmf native o inhabitant of Cuenca.

conquista nf conquest.

conquistador,-a nm,f conqueror.

conquistar vtr (país, ciudad) to conquer; fig (puesto, título) to win; (a una persona) to win over.

consabido,-a adj 1 (bien conocido) well-known. 2 (usual) familiar, usual.

consagración nf 1 Rel consecration. 2 (de un artista) recognition.

consagrar I vtr 1 Rel to consecrate. 2 (artista) to confirm. 3 (tiempo, vida) to devote. **II consagrarse** vr 1 (dedicarse) to devote oneself (**a,** to), dedicate oneself (**a,** to). 2 (lograr fama) to establish oneself.

consciente adj 1 conscious, aware; **ser c. de algo,** to be aware of sth. 2 Med conscious.

consecución nf 1 (de un objetivo) achievement. 2 (obtención) obtaining.

consecuencia nf 1 consequence; **a o como c. de,** as a consequence o result of; **en c.,** therefore; **tener o traer (malas) consecuencias,** to have (ill) effects; **sacar como o en c.,** to come to a conclusion. 2 (coherencia) consistency; **actuar en c.,** to be consistent.

consecuente adj consistent.

consecutivo,-a adj consecutive; **tres días consecutivos,** three days in a row.

conseguir [6] vtr 1 to get, obtain; (objetivo) to achieve. 2 **conseguí terminar,** I managed to finish.

consejero,-a nm,f 1 (asesor) adviser. 2 Pol councillor. 3 Com **c. delegado,** managing director.

consejo nm 1 (recomendación) advice; **un**

c., a piece of advice. 2 *(junta)* council; **c. de ministros**, cabinet; *(reunión)* cabinet meeting; **c. de administración**, board of directors; **c. de guerra**, court martial.

consenso nm consensus.

consensuar vtr to approve by consensus.

consentido,-a adj spoiled.

consentimiento nm consent.

consentir [5] I vtr 1 *(tolerar)* to allow, permit; **no consientas que haga eso**, don't allow him to do that. 2 *(mimar)* to spoil. II vi to consent; **c. en**, to agree to.

conserje nm commissionaire; *(en escuela etc)* janitor.

conserva nf tinned o canned food.

conservación nf 1 preservation. 2 *(mantenimiento)* maintenance, upkeep.

conservador,-a I adj & nm,f conservative; *Pol* Conservative. II nm *(de museo)* curator.

conservadurismo nm conservatism.

conservante nm preservative.

conservar I vtr to conserve, preserve; *(mantener)* to keep up, maintain; *(alimentos)* to preserve. II **conservarse** vr 1 *(tradición etc)* to survive. 2 **c. bien**, *(persona)* to age well.

conservatorio nm conservatory.

considerable adj considerable.

consideración nf 1 consideration; **tomar algo en c.**, to take sth into account. 2 *(respeto)* regard. 3 **de c.**, important, considerable; **herido de c.**, seriously injured.

considerado,-a adj 1 *(atento)* considerate, thoughtful. 2 **estar bien/mal c.**, to well/badly thought of.

considerar vtr to consider; **lo considero imposible**, I think it's impossible.

consigna nf 1 *(para maletas)* left-luggage office, *US* check-room. 2 *Mil* orders, instructions.

consignar vtr 1 *(puesto)* to allocate; *(cantidad)* to assign. 2 *(mercancía)* to ship, dispatch.

consigo[1] pron pers 1 *(tercera persona) (hombre)* with him; *(mujer)* with her; *(cosa, animal)* with it; *(plural)* with them; *(usted)* with you. 2 **hablar c. mismo**, to speak to oneself.

consigo[2] indic pres → **conseguir**.

consiguiente adj resulting, consequent; **por c.**, therefore, consequently.

consistencia nf 1 consistency. 2 *(de argumento)* soundness.

consistente adj 1 *(firme)* firm, solid. 2 *(teoría)* sound. 3 **c. en**, consisting of.

consistir vi to consist *(en, of)*; **el secreto consiste en tener paciencia**, the secret lies in being patient.

consistorial adj **casa c.**, town hall.

consola nf console table; *Inform* console.

consolación nf consolation; **premio de c.**, consolation prize.

consolador,-a I adj consoling, comfort-

ing. II nm dildo.

consolar [2] I vtr to console, comfort. II **consolarse** vr to console oneself, take comfort *(con, from)*.

consolidar vtr, **consolidarse** vr to consolidate.

consomé nm clear soup, consommé.

consonancia nf **en c. con**, in keeping with.

consonante adj & nf consonant.

consorcio nm consortium.

consorte I adj **príncipe c.**, prince consort. II nmf *(cónyuge)* partner, spouse.

conspicuo,-a adj prominent, outstanding.

conspiración nf conspiracy, plot.

conspirar vi to conspire, plot.

constancia nf 1 constancy, perseverance. 2 *(testimonio)* proof, evidence; **dejar c. de algo**, to put sth on record.

constante I adj constant; *(persona)* steadfast. II nf constant feature; *Mat* constant. ◆**constantemente** adv constantly.

constar vi 1 *(figurar)* to figure in, be included *(en)*; **c. en acta**, to be on record. 2 **me consta que ...**, I am absolutely certain that .... 3 **c. de**, to be made up of, consist of.

constatar vtr to state; *(comprobar)* to check.

constelación nf constellation.

consternación nf consternation.

consternar vtr to dismay.

constipado,-a I adj **estar c.**, to have a cold o a chill. II nm cold, chill.

constiparse vr to catch a cold o a chill.

constitución nf constitution.

constitucional adj constitutional.

constituir [37] I vtr 1 *(formar)* to constitute; **estar constituido por**, to consist of. 2 *(suponer)* to represent. 3 *(fundar)* to constitute, set up. II **constituirse** vr to set oneself up *(en, as)*.

constituyente adj & nmf constituent.

constreñir [6] vtr 1 *(forzar)* to compel, force. 2 *(oprimir)* to restrict. 3 *Med* to constrict.

construcción nf 1 construction; *(sector)* the building industry; **en c.**, under construction. 2 *(edificio)* building.

constructivo,-a adj constructive.

constructor,-a I nm,f builder. II adj **empresa constructora**, builders *pl*, construction company.

construir [37] vtr to construct, build.

consuelo nm consolation.

cónsul nmf consul.

consulado nm consulate.

consulta nf 1 consultation; **obra de c.**, reference book. 2 *Med* surgery; *(despacho)* consulting room; **horas de c.**, surgery hours.

consultar vtr to consult, seek advice *(con, from)*; *(libro)* to look up.

consultivo,-a adj consultative, advisory.

consultorio *nm* 1 *Med* medical center. 2 *Prensa* problem page, advice column.

consumado,-a *adj* 1 consummated; **hecho c.**, fait accompli, accomplished fact. 2 *fig (artista)* consummate.

consumar *vtr* to complete, carry out; *(crimen)* to commit.

consumición *nf* 1 consumption. 2 *(bebida)* drink.

consumidor,-a *nm,f* consumer. II *adj* consuming.

consumir *I vtr* to consume. II **consumirse** *vr (al hervir)* to boil away; *fig (persona)* to waste away.

consumismo *nm* consumerism.

consumo *nm* consumption; **bienes de c.**, consumer goods; **sociedad de c.**, consumer society.

contabilidad *nf Com* 1 *(profesión)* accountancy. 2 *(de empresa, sociedad)* accounting, book-keeping.

contabilizar [4] *vtr Com* to enter in the books; *Dep* to score.

contable *nmf* accountant.

contactar *vi* **c. con**, to contact, get in touch with.

contacto *nm* contact; *Aut* ignition; **perder el c.**, to lose touch; **ponerse en c.**, to get in touch.

contado,-a *I adj* few and far between; **contadas veces**, very seldom; **tiene los días contados**, his days are numbered. II *nm* **pagar al c.**, to pay cash.

contador *nm* meter; **c. de agua**, water meter.

contagiar [12] *I vtr Med* to pass on. II **contagiarse** *vr* 1 *(persona)* to get infected. 2 *(enfermedad)* to be contagious.

contagio *nm* contagion.

contagioso,-a *adj* contagious; *fam (risa)* infectious.

contaminación *nf* contamination; *(del aire)* pollution.

contaminar *vtr* to contaminate; *(aire, agua)* to pollute.

contante *adj* **dinero c. (y sonante)**, hard *o* ready cash.

contar [2] *I vtr* 1 *(sumar)* to count. 2 *(narrar)* to tell. II *vi* 1 to count. 2 **c. con**, *(confiar en)* to count on; *(tener)* to have. III **contarse** *vr* **fam ¿qué se cuentas?**, how's it going?

contemplación *nf* contemplation; *fam* **no andarse con contemplaciones**, to make no bones about it.

contemplar *vtr* to contemplate; *(considerar)* to consider; *(estipular)* to stipulate.

contemporáneo,-a *adj & nm,f* contemporary.

contención *nf* **muro de c.**, retaining wall; **c. salarial**, wage restraint.

contencioso,-a *I adj* contentious; *Jur* litigious. II *nm Jur* legal dispute.

contendiente *nmf* contender, contestant.

contenedor *nm* container.

contener [24] *I vtr* 1 to contain. 2 *(pasiones etc)* to restrain, hold back. II **contenerse** *vr* to control oneself, hold (oneself) back.

contenido *nm* content, contents *pl*.

contentar *I vtr* 1 *(satisfacer)* to please. 2 *(alegrar)* to cheer up. II **contentarse** *vr* 1 *(conformarse)* to make do (**con**, with), be satisfied (**con**, with). 2 *(alegrarse)* to cheer up.

contento,-a *adj* happy, pleased (**con**, with).

contestador *nm* **c. automático**, answering machine.

contestación *nf* answer; **dar c.**, to answer.

contestar *vtr* 1 to answer. 2 *fam (replicar)* to answer back.

contestatario,-a *adj* anti-establishment.

contexto *nm* context.

contienda *nf* struggle.

contigo *pron pers* with you.

contiguo,-a *adj* contiguous (**a**, to), adjoining.

continente *nm* 1 *Geog* continent. 2 *(compostura)* countenance.

contingencia *nf* limit, restriction.

contingente *nm* contingent.

continuación *nf* continuation; **a c.**, next.

continuar [30] *vtr & vi* to continue, carry on (with); **continúa en Francia**, he's still in France; **continuará**, to be continued.

continuidad *nf* continuity.

continuo,-a *adj* 1 continuous; *Aut* **línea continua**, solid white line. 2 *(reiterado)* continual, constant. II *nm* continuum.
◆**continuamente** *adv* continuously.

contonearse *vr* to swing one's hips.

contorno *nm* 1 outline. 2 **contornos**, surroundings *pl*, environment.

contorsión *nf* contortion.

contorsionarse *vr* to contort *o* twist oneself.

contra *I prep* against; **en c. de**, against. II *nm* **los pros y los contras**, the pros and cons.

contraataque *nm* counterattack.

contrabajo *nm* double bass.

contrabandista *nmf* smuggler; **c. de armas**, gunrunner.

contrabando *nm* smuggling; **c. de armas**, gunrunning; **pasar algo de c.**, to smuggle sth in.

contracción *nf* contraction.

contracepción *nf* contraception.

contrachapado *nm* plywood.

contracorriente *I nf* crosscurrent. II *adv* **ir (a) c.**, to go against the tide.

contradecir [12] *(pp* **contradicho**) *vtr* to contradict.

contradicción *nf* contradiction.

contradictorio,-a *adj* contradictory.

contraer [25] *I vtr* to contract; **c. matri-**

monio con algn, to marry sb. **II contraerse** *vr* to contract.

contraigo *indic pres* → **contraer**.

contraindicación *nf* contraindication.

contraje *pt indef* → **contraer**.

contraluz *nm* view against the light; **a c.**, against the light.

contramaestre *nm* foreman.

contramano (a) *loc adv* the wrong way *o* direction.

contrapartida *nf* **en c.**, in return.

contrapelo (a) *loc adv* the wrong way; *fig* against the grain.

contrapesar *vtr* **1** to counterbalance, counterpoise. **2** *fig* (*compensar*) to offset, balance.

contrapeso *nm* counterweight.

contraportada *nf* back page.

contraposición *nf* contrast.

contraproducente *adj* counterproductive.

contrapunto *nm* counterpoint.

contrariar [29] *vtr* **1** (*oponerse a*) to oppose, go against. **2** (*disgustar*) to upset.

contrariedad *nf* **1** (*contratiempo*) obstacle, setback. **2** (*disgusto*) annoyance.

contrario,-a **I** *adj* **1** opposite; **lo c. de**, the opposite of; **en el lado/sentido c.**, on the other side/in the other direction; **al c., por el c.**, on the contrary; **de lo c.**, otherwise; **todo lo c.**, quite the opposite. **2** (*perjudicial*) contrary (**a**, to). **II** *nm,f* opponent, rival. **III** *nf* **llevar la contraria**, to be contrary. ◆**contrariamente** *adv* **c. a ...**, contrary to ....

contrarrestar *vtr* to offset, counteract.

contrasentido *nm* contradiction.

contraseña *nf* password.

contrastar *vtr* to contrast (**con**, with).

contraste *nm* **1** contrast. **2** (*en oro, plata*) hallmark.

contrata *nf* contract.

contratar *vtr* to hire, engage.

contratiempo *nm* setback, hitch.

contratista *nmf* contractor.

contrato *nm* contract; **c. de trabajo**, work contract; **c. de alquiler**, lease, leasing agreement.

contravenir [27] *vtr* to contravene, infringe.

contraventana *nf* shutter.

contribución *nf* **1** contribution. **2** (*impuesto*) tax.

contribuir [37] **I** *vtr* to contribute (**a**, to). **II** *vi* **1** to contribute. **2** (*pagar impuestos*) to pay taxes.

contribuyente *nmf* taxpayer.

contrincante *nmf* rival, opponent.

control *nm* **1** control; **c. a distancia**, remote control. **2** (*inspección*) check; (*de policía etc*) checkpoint.

controlador,-a *nm,f* **c.** (**aéreo**), air traffic controller.

controlar I *vtr* to control. **2** (*comprobar*)

to check. **II controlarse** *vr* to control oneself.

controversia *nf* controversy.

controvertido,-a *adj* controversial.

contumaz *adj* obstinate.

contundente *adj* **1** (*arma*) blunt. **2** (*argumento*) forceful, convincing.

contusión *nf* contusion, bruise.

convalecencia *nf* convalescence.

convaleciente *adj & nmf* convalescent.

convalidar *vtr* to validate; (*documento*) to ratify.

convencer [2] *vtr* to convince; **c. a algn de algo**, to convince sb about sth.

convencimiento *nm* conviction; **tener la c. de que ...**, to be convinced that ....

convención *nf* convention.

convencional *adj* conventional.

convenido,-a *adj* agreed; **según lo c.**, as agreed.

conveniencia *nf* **1** (*provecho*) convenience. **2** **conveniencias sociales**, social proprieties.

conveniente *adj* (*oportuno*) convenient; (*aconsejable*) advisable; (*precio*) good, fair.

convenio *nm* agreement; **c. laboral**, agreement on salary and conditions.

convenir [27] *vtr & vi* **1** (*acordar*) to agree; **c. una fecha**, to agree on a date; **sueldo a c.**, salary negotiable; **c. en**, to agree on. **2** (*ser oportuno*) to suit, be good for; **conviene recordar que ...**, it's as well to remember that ....

convento *nm* (*de monjas*) convent; (*de monjes*) monastery.

convergente *adj* convergent.

converger [5] *vi* to converge.

conversación *nf* conversation.

conversar *vi* to converse, talk.

conversión *nf* conversion.

converso,-a *nm,f* convert.

convertible *adj* convertible.

convertir [5] **I** *vtr* to change, convert. **II convertirse** *vr* **1** **c. en**, to turn into, become. **2** *Rel* to be converted (**a**, to).

convexo,-a *adj* convex.

convicción *nf* conviction; **tengo la c. de que ...**, I am convinced that ...

convicto,-a *adj* convicted.

convidado,-a *adj & nm,f* guest.

convidar *vtr* to invite.

convincente *adj* convincing.

convite *nm* reception.

convivencia *nf* life together; *fig* coexistence.

convivir *vi* to live together; *fig* to coexist (**con**, with).

convocar [1] *vtr* to summon; (*reunión, elecciones*) to call.

convocatoria *nf* **1** (*a huelga etc*) call. **2** *Educ* diet.

convulsión *nf* *Med* convulsion; (*agitación social*) upheaval.

convulsivo,-a *adj* convulsive.

conyugal *adj* conjugal; **vida c.,** married life.

cónyuge *nmf* spouse; **cónyuges,** married couple *sing,* husband and wife.

coña *nf vulg* **estar de c.,** to be joking.

coñac *nm* brandy, cognac.

coñazo *nm vulg* pain, drag; **dar el c.,** to be a real pain.

coño I *nm vulg* cunt. II *interj vulg* for fuck's sake!

cooperación *nf* co-operation.

cooperador,-a *nm,f* collaborator, co-operator.

cooperar *vi* to co-operate (**a, en, in; con,** with).

cooperativa *nf* co-operative.

coordenada *nf* co-ordinate.

coordinación *nf* co-ordination.

coordinadora *nf* coordinating committee; **c. general,** joint committee.

coordinador,-a *nm,f* co-ordinator.

coordinar *vtr* to co-ordinate.

copa *nf* 1 glass; **tomar una c.,** to have a drink. 2 (*de árbol*) top. 3 *Dep* cup. 4 *Naipes* **copas,** hearts.

copar *vtr* to take up.

copartícipe *adj & nmf* (*socio*) partner; (*colaborador*) collaborator; (*copropietario*) joint owner, co-owner.

Copenhague *n* Copenhagen.

copia *nf* copy.

copiar [12] *vtr* to copy.

copiloto *nm Av* copilot; *Aut* co-driver.

copioso,-a *adj* abundant, copious.

copistería *nf* photocopying service.

copla *nf* verse, couplet.

copo *nm* flake; (*de nieve*) snowflake; **copos de maíz,** cornflakes.

coproducción *nf* co-production, joint production.

cópula *nf* 1 (*coito*) copulation, intercourse. 2 *Ling* conjunction.

copular *vi* to copulate (**con,** with).

COPYME *nm abr de* **Confederación de la Pequeña y Mediana Empresa.**

coquetear *vi* to flirt (**con,** with).

coqueta *nf* dressing table.

coqueto,-a I *adj* coquettish. II *nm,f* flirt.

coraje *nm* 1 (*valor*) courage. 2 (*ira*) anger, annoyance; **dar c. a algn,** to infuriate sb; **¡qué c.!,** how maddening!

coral¹ *nm Zool* coral.

coral² *nf Mús* choral, chorale.

Corán *nm* Koran.

coraza *nf* armour, *US* armor; *fig* protection.

corazón *nm* 1 heart; *fig* **de (todo) c.,** in all sincerity; **fig tener buen c.,** to be kind-hearted. 2 (*parte central*) heart; (*de fruta*) core. 3 *Naipes* **corazones,** hearts.

corazonada *nf* hunch, feeling.

corbata *nf* tie, *US* necktie; **con c.,** wearing a tie.

Córcega *n* Corsica.

corchete *nm* 1 *Impr* square bracket. 2 *Cost* hook and eye, snap fastener.

corcho *nm* cork; (*de pesca*) float.

cordel *nm* rope, cord.

cordero,-a *nm,f* lamb.

cordial *adj* cordial, warm.

cordialidad *nf* cordiality, warmth.

cordillera *nf* mountain chain *o* range.

córdoba *nm Fin* monetary unit of Nicaragua.

cordón *nm* string; (*de zapatos*) shoelace; *Anat* **c. umbilical,** umbilical cord; **c. policial,** police cordon.

cordura *nf* common sense.

Corea *n* Korea.

coreano,-a *adj & nm,f* Korean.

corear *vtr* 1 (*cantar a coro*) to sing in chorus. 2 (*aclamar*) to applaud.

coreografía *nf* choreography.

cornada *nf Taur* goring.

corneja *nf* crow.

córner *nm Ftb* corner (kick); **sacar un c.,** to take a corner.

corneta *nf* bugle; **c. de llaves,** cornet.

cornisa *nf* cornice.

cornudo,-a *nm ofens* cuckold.

coro *nm Mús* choir; *Teat* chorus; *fig* **a coro,** all together.

corona *nf* 1 crown. 2 (*de flores etc*) wreath, garland; **c. funeraria,** funeral wreath.

coronación *nf* 1 coronation. 2 *fig* (*culminación*) crowning point.

coronar *vtr* to crown.

coronel *nm* colonel.

coronilla *nf* crown of the head; *fam* **estar hasta la c.,** to be fed up (**de,** with).

corpiño *nm* bodice.

corporación *nf* corporation.

corporal *adj* corporal; **castigo c.,** corporal punishment; **olor c.,** body odour, BO.

corporativo,-a *adj* corporative.

corpulento,-a *adj* corpulent, stout.

corpus *nm* corpus.

corral *nm* farmyard, *US* corral; (*de casa*) courtyard.

correa *nf* 1 (*tira*) strap; (*de reloj*) watch-strap; (*de pantalón*) belt; (*de perro*) lead, *US* leash. 2 *Téc* belt.

corrección *nf* 1 (*rectificación*) correction. 2 (*urbanidad*) courtesy, politeness.

correcto,-a *adj* 1 (*sin errores*) correct. 2 (*educado*) polite, courteous (**con,** to); (*conducta*) proper.

corredera *nf* **puerta/ventana de c.,** sliding door/window.

corredizo,-a *adj* sliding; **nudo c.,** slipknot; **techo c.,** sunroof.

corredor,-a *nm,f* 1 *Dep* runner. 2 *Fin* **c. de bolsa,** stockbroker.

corregir [6] I *vtr* to correct. II **corregirse** *vr* to mend one's ways.

correo *nm* 1 post, *US* mail; **echar al c.,** to post; **por c.,** by post; **c. aéreo,** airmail; c. **certificado**, registered post; (tren) c., mail train. 2 correos, (edificio) post office sing.

correr I vi 1 to run; (coche) to go fast; (conductor) to drive fast; (viento) to blow; fig **no corras, habla más despacio**, don't rush, speak slower; c. **prisa**, to be urgent. 2 c. **con los gastos**, to foot the bill; **corre a mi cargo**, I'll take care of it. **II** vtr 1 (cortina) to draw; (cerrojo) to close; (aventura etc) to have; c. **el riesgo o peligro**, to run the risk. 2 (mover) to pull up, draw up. **III correrse** vr 1 (moverse) to move over. 2 fam **una juerga**, to go on a spree. 3 arg (tener orgasmo) to come.

correspondencia nf 1 correspondence. 2 Ferroc connection.

corresponder I vi 1 to correspond (a, to; con, with). 2 (incumbir) to concern, be incumbent upon; **esta tarea te corresponde a ti**, it's your job to do this. 3 (pertenecer) to belong; **me dieron lo que me correspondía**, they gave me my share. **II corresponderse** vr 1 (ajustarse) to correspond. 2 (dos cosas) to tally; **no se corresponde con la descripción**, it does not match the description. 3 (dos personas) to love each other.

correspondiente adj corresponding (a, to).

corresponsal nmf correspondent.

corrida nf c. (de toros), bullfight.

corrido,-a adj 1 (avergonzado) abashed. 2 **de c.**, without stopping.

corriente I adj 1 (común) common. 2 (agua) running. 3 (mes, año) current, present; **el diez del c.**, the tenth of this month. 4 Fin (cuenta) current. 5 **estar al c.**, to be up to date. **II** nf 1 current, stream; fig **ir o navegar contra la c.**, to go against the tide; fam **seguirle o llevarle la c. a algn**, to humour sb; Elec c. **eléctrica**, (electric) current. 2 (de aire) draught, US draft. 3 (tendencia) trend, current.

corrijo indic pres → **corregir**.

corrillo nm small group of people talking; fig clique.

corro nm 1 circle, ring. 2 (juego) ring-a-ring-a-roses.

corroborar vtr to corroborate.

corroer [38] vtr to corrode; fig **la envidia le corroe**, envy eats away at him.

corromper I vtr 1 (pudrir) to turn bad, rot. 2 (pervertir) to corrupt, pervert. **II corromperse** vr 1 (pudrirse) to go bad, rot. 2 (pervertirse) to become corrupted.

corrosivo,-a adj corrosive; fig (mordaz) caustic.

corrupción nf 1 (putrefacción) rot, decay. 2 fig corruption; Jur c. **de menores**, corruption of minors.

corrupto,-a adj corrupt.

corsé nm corset.

cortacésped nm & f lawnmower.

cortado,-a I adj 1 cut (up). 2 (leche) sour. 3 (labios) chapped. 4 fam (tímido) shy. **II** nm small coffee with a dash of milk.

cortafuego nm firebreak.

cortapisa nf fig restriction, limitation.

cortar I vtr 1 to cut; (carne) to carve; (árbol) to cut down; fam c. **por lo sano**, to take drastic measures; fam **cortó con su novio**, she split up with her boyfriend. 2 (piel) to chap, crack. 3 (luz, teléfono) to cut off. 4 (paso, carretera) to block. **II cortarse** vr 1 (herirse) to cut oneself. 2 c. **el pelo**, to have one's hair cut. 3 (leche etc) to curdle. 4 Tel **se cortó la comunicación**, we were cut off. 5 fam (aturdirse) to become all shy.

cortaúñas nm inv nail clippers pl.

corte[1] nm 1 cut; c. **de pelo**, haircut; TV c. **publicitario**, commercial break; c. **de mangas**, ≈ V-sign. 2 (sección) section; c. **transversal**, cross section. 3 fam rebuff; **dar un c. a algn**, to cut sb dead.

corte[2] nf 1 (real) court. 2 **Las Cortes**, (Spanish) Parliament sing.

cortejar vtr to court.

cortejo nm 1 (galanteo) courting. 2 (comitiva) entourage, retinue; c. **fúnebre**, funeral cortège.

cortés adj courteous, polite.

cortesía nf courtesy, politeness.

corteza nf (de árbol) bark; (de queso) rind; (de pan) crust.

cortijo nm Andalusian farm o farmhouse.

cortina nf curtain; c. **de humo**, smoke screen.

corto,-a I adj 1 (distancia, tiempo) short; fam c. **de luces**, dim-witted; c. **de vista**, short-sighted; Aut **luz corta**, dipped headlights pl. 2 fam **quedarse c.**, (calcular mal) to underestimate. 3 (apocado) timid, shy. **II** nm Cin short (film).

cortocircuito nm short circuit.

cortometraje nm short (film).

corvo,-a adj curved, bent.

cosa nf 1 thing; **no he visto c. igual**, I've never seen anything like it; **no ser gran c.**, not to be up to much. 2 (asunto) matter, business; **eso es c. tuya**, that's your business o affair; **eso es otra c.**, that's different. 3 **hace c. de una hora**, about an hour ago.

coscorrón nm knock o blow on the head.

cosecha nf 1 Agr harvest, crop. 2 (año del vino) vintage.

cosechadora nf combine harvester.

cosechar vtr to harvest, gather (in).

coser vtr 1 to sew; fam **es c. y cantar**, it's a piece of cake. 2 Med to stitch up.

cosmético,-a adj & nm cosmetic.

cósmico,-a adj cosmic.

cosmonauta nmf cosmonaut.

cosmopolita adj & nmf cosmopolitan.

cosmos *nm inv* cosmos.

coso *nm Taur* bullring.

cosquillas *nfpl* tickling *sing*; **hacer c. a algn**, to tickle sb; **tener c.**, to be ticklish.

cosquilleo *nm* tickling.

costa¹ *nf* coast; *(litoral)* coastline; *(playa)* beach, seaside; *US* shore.

costa² *nf* **a c. de**, at the expense of; **a toda c.**, at all costs, at any price; **vive a c. mía**, he lives off me.

costado *nm* side; **de c.**, sideways; **es catalana por los cuatro costados**, she's Catalan through and through.

costal *nm* sack.

costar [2] *vi* 1 to cost; **¿cuánto cuesta?**, how much is it?; **c. barato/caro**, to be cheap/expensive. 2 *fig* **te va a c. caro**, you'll pay dearly for this; **c. trabajo** *o* **mucho**, to be hard; **me cuesta hablar francés**, I find it difficult to speak French; **cueste lo que cueste**, at any cost.

costarricense, costarriqueño,-a *adj & nm,f* Costa Rican.

coste *nm* cost; **a precio de c.**, (at) cost price; **c. de la vida**, cost of living.

costear I *vtr* to afford, pay for; **c. los gastos**, to foot the bill. II **costearse** *vr* to pay for.

costero,-a *adj* coastal; **ciudad costera**, seaside town.

costilla *nf* 1 *Anat* rib. 2 *Culin* cutlet.

costo¹ *nm* cost.

costo² *nm arg (hachís)* dope, shit, stuff.

costoso,-a *adj* costly, expensive.

costra *nf* crust; *Med* scab.

costumbre *nf* 1 *(hábito)* habit; **como de c.**, as usual; **tengo la c. de levantarme temprano**, I usually get up early; **tenía la c. de ...**, he used to .... 2 *(tradición)* custom.

costura *nf* 1 sewing. 2 *(confección)* dressmaking; **alta c.**, haute couture. 3 *(línea de puntadas)* seam.

costurera *nf* seamstress.

costurero *nm* sewing basket.

cota *nf Geog* height above sea level; *fig* rating.

cotejar *vtr* to compare.

cotidiano,-a *adj* daily; **vida cotidiana**, everyday life.

cotilla *nmf fam* busybody, gossip.

cotillear *vi fam* to gossip (**de**, about).

cotilleo *nm fam* gossip.

cotización *nf* 1 *Fin* (market) price, quotation. 2 *(cuota)* membership fees *pl*, subscription.

cotizar [4] I *vtr Fin* to quote. II *vi* to pay national insurance. III **cotizarse** *vr Fin* **c. a**, to sell at.

coto *nm* 1 enclosure, reserve; **c. de caza**, game reserve. 2 **poner c. a**, to put a stop to.

cotorra *nf* parrot; *fig (persona)* chatterbox.

COU *nm Educ abr de* **Curso de Orientación Universitaria**, ≈ GCE A-level studies, sixth-form studies.

coyote *nm* coyote, prairie wolf.

coyuntura *nf* 1 *Anat* articulation, joint. 2 *fig (circunstancia)* juncture; **la c. económica**, the economic situation.

coz *nf* kick; **dar una c.**, to kick.

C.P. *abr de* **código postal**, postcode.

crac(k) *nm* 1 *Fin* crash. 2 *(droga)* crack.

cráneo *nm* cranium, skull.

cráter *nm* crater.

creación *nf* creation.

creador,-a *nm,f* creator.

crear *vtr* to create.

creatividad *nf* creativity.

creativo,-a *adj* creative.

crecer [33] *vi* 1 to grow; **c. en importancia**, to become more important. 2 *(al tricotar)* to increase.

creces *nfpl* **con c.**, fully, in full; **devolver con c.**, to return with interest.

crecido,-a *adj (persona)* grown-up.

creciente *adj* growing, increasing; **cuarto c.**, crescent.

crecimiento *nm* growth.

credencial *adj* credential; **(cartas) credenciales**, credentials.

credibilidad *nf* credibility.

crédito *nm* 1 *Com Fin* credit. 2 *(confianza)* belief; **dar c. a**, to believe.

credo *nm* creed.

crédulo,-a *adj* credulous, gullible.

creencia *nf* belief.

creer [36] I *vtr* 1 to believe. 2 *(pensar)* to think; **creo que no**, I don't think so; **creo que sí**, I think so; **ya lo creo**, I should think so. II *vi* to believe; **c. en**, to believe in. III **creerse** *vr* 1 to consider oneself to be; **¿qué te has creído?**, what *o* who do you think you are? 2 **no me lo creo**, I can't believe it.

creíble *adj* credible, believable.

creído,-a I *adj* arrogant, vain. II *nm,f* big head.

crema *nf* cream.

cremallera *nf* zip (fastener); *US* zipper.

crematorio,-a *nm (horno) c.*, crematorium.

cremoso,-a *adj* creamy.

crepe *nm* crêpe, pancake.

crepería *nf* creperie.

crepitar *vi* to crackle.

crepúsculo *nm* twilight.

crespo,-a *adj* frizzy.

crespón *nm* crepe.

cresta *nf* 1 crest; *(de gallo)* comb. 2 *(de punk)* mohican.

Creta *nf* Crete.

cretino,-a I *adj* stupid, cretinous. II *nm,f* cretin.

creyente *nmf* believer.

crezco *indic pres* → **crecer**.

cría *nf* 1 *(cachorro)* young. 2 *(crianza)*

breeding, raising.
criada *nf* maid.
criadero *nm* nursery.
criadilla *nf* Culin bull's testicle.
criado,-a I *adj* **mal c.**, spoilt. **II** *nm,f* servant.
crianza *nf* (*de animales*) breeding; *fig* **vinos de c.**, vintage wines.
criar [29] *vtr* **1** (*animales*) to breed, raise; (*niños*) to bring up, rear. **2** (*producir*) to have, grow.
criatura *nf* **1** (*living*) creature. **2** (*crío*) baby, child.
criba *nf* sieve.
cribar *vtr* to sieve, sift.
crimen *nm* (*pl* **crímenes**) murder.
criminal *adj & nm* criminal.
crin *nf*, **crines** *nfpl* mane *sing*.
crío,-a I *nm fam* kid. **II** *adj* babyish.
criollo,-a *adj & nm,f* Creole.
críquet *nm* cricket.
crisantemo *nm* chrysanthemum.
crisis *nf inv* **1** crisis. **2** (*ataque*) fit, attack; **c. nerviosa**, nervous breakdown.
crispación *nf* tension.
crispar *vtr* to make tense; *fig* **eso me crispa los nervios**, that sets my nerves on edge.
cristal *nm* **1** crystal; **c. de roca**, rock crystal. **2** (*vidrio*) glass; **c. de gafas**) lense; (*de ventana*) (window) pane.
cristalera *nf* window.
cristalería *nf* (*conjunto*) glassware; (*vasos*) glasses *pl*.
cristalino,-a *adj* crystal clear.
cristalizar [4] *vi* to crystallize.
cristiandad *nf* Christendom.
cristianismo *nm* Christianity.
cristiano,-a *adj & nm,f* Christian.
Cristo *nm* Christ.
criterio *nm* **1** (*pauta*) criterion. **2** (*opinión*) opinion. **3** (*discernimiento*) discretion; **lo dejo a tu c.**, I'll leave it up to you.
crítica *nf* **1** criticism. **2** Prensa review; **tener buena c.**, to get good reviews. **3** (*conjunto de críticos*) critics.
criticar [1] **I** *vtr* to criticize. **II** *vi* (*murmurar*) to gossip.
crítico,-a I *adj* critical. **II** *nm,f* critic.
oritición,-ona *nm,f fam* fault-finder.
croar *vi* to croak.
croché *nm* crochet.
croissant *nm* croissant.
crol *nm* Natación crawl.
cromo *nm* **1** (*metal*) chromium, chrome. **2** (*estampa*) picture card.
cromosoma *nm* chromosome.
crónica *nf* **1** account, chronicle. **2** Prensa feature, article.
crónico,-a *adj* chronic.
cronista *nmf* Prensa feature writer.
cronología *nf* chronology.
cronológico,-a *adj* chronological.
cronometrar *vtr* to time.

cronómetro *nm* stopwatch.
croqueta *nf* croquette.
croquis *nm inv* sketch.
cruce *nm* **1** crossing; (*de carreteras*) crossroads; (*de razas*) crossbreeding. **2** Tel crossed line.
crucero *nm* Náut cruise; (*barco*) cruiser.
crucial *adj* crucial.
crucificar [1] *vtr* to crucify.
crucifijo *nm* crucifix.
crucigrama *nm* crossword (puzzle).
crudeza *nf* crudeness, coarseness.
crudo,-a I *adj* **1** raw; (*comida*) underdone; *fam fig* **lo veo muy c.**, it doesn't look too good. **2** (*clima*) harsh. **3** (*color*) cream. **II** *nm* (*petróleo*) crude.
cruel *adj* cruel.
crueldad *nf* cruelty; *fig* (*del clima*) severity.
cruento,-a *adj* bloody.
crujido *nm* (*de puerta*) creak, creaking; (*de dientes*) grinding.
crujiente *adj* crunchy.
crujir *vi* (*madera*) to creak; (*comida*) to crunch; (*dientes*) to grind.
cruz *nf* **1** cross; **C. Roja**, Red Cross; **c. gamada**, swastika. **2** ¿**cara o c.?**, ≈ heads or tails?
cruzada *nf* crusade.
cruzado,-a I *adj* **1** crossed; **con los brazos cruzados**, arms folded. **2** Cost double-breasted. **3** (*atravesado*) lying across. **4** (*animal*) crossbred. **II** *nm* Hist crusader.
cruzar [4] **I** *vtr* **1** to cross. **2** (*palabras, miradas*) to exchange. **3** (*animal, planta*) to cross, crossbreed. **II** *vi* (*atravesar*) to cross. **III** **cruzarse** *vr* to cross; **c. con algn**, to pass sb.
cta. Com abr de **cuenta**, account, a/c.
cta. cte. Com abr de **cuenta corriente**, current account, c/a.
CTNE *nm* abr de **Compañía Telefónica Nacional de España**, ≈ British Telecom.
c/u abr de **cada uno**, each, ea.
cuaderno *nm* notebook.
cuadra *nf* **1** (*establo*) stable. **2** Am block (of houses).
cuadrado,-a I *adj* **1** Geom square. **2** (*complexión física*) broad, stocky. **3** *fig* (*mente*) rigid. **II** *nm* **1** Geom square. **2** Mat square; **elevar** (**un número**) **al c.**, to square (a number).
cuadrar I *vtr* Mat to square. **II** *vi* (*coincidir*) to square, agree (**con**, with); (*sumas, cifras*) to tally. **III** **cuadrarse** *vr* (*soldado*) to stand to attention.
cuadriculado,-a *adj* papel **c.**, square paper.
cuadrilátero,-a I *adj* quadrilateral. **II** *nm* Box ring.
cuadrilla *nf* (*equipo*) gang, team; Mil squad; Taur bullfighter's team.
cuadro *nm* **1** Geom square; **tela a cua-**

dros, checked cloth. 2 *Arte* painting,
picture. 3 *Teat* scene. 4 *Elec Téc* panel;
c. de mandos, control panel. 5 *(gráfico)*
chart, graph.
cuádruple *adj* quadruple, fourfold.
cuajada *nf* curd.
cuajar I *vtr (leche)* to curdle; *(sangre)* to
clot. II *vi* 1 *(nieve)* to lie. 2 *(moda)* to
catch on; *(plan, esfuerzo)* to get off the
ground.
cual I *pron rel (precedido de artículo)* 1 *(persona) (sujeto)* who; *(objeto)* whom. 2 *(cosa)*
which. II *pron* 1 **tal c.,** exactly as. 2 *arc
(comparativo)* such as, like.
cuál I *pron interr* which (one)?, what?; *¿c.
quieres?,* which one do you want? II *adj
interr* which. III *loc adv* **a c. más tonto,**
each more stupid than the other.
cualidad *nf* quality.
cualificado,-a *adj* qualified.
cualquier *adj indef* any; **c. cosa,** anything; **en c. momento,** at any moment *o*
time.
cualquiera *(pl* **cualesquiera)** I *adj indef* 1
(indefinido) any; **un profesor c.,** any
teacher. 2 *(corriente)* ordinary. II *pron
indef* 1 *(persona)* anybody; **c. te lo puede
decir,** anybody can tell you. 2 *(cosa, animal)* anyone. 3 **c. que sea,** whatever it is.
III *nmf fig pey* **ser un c.,** to be a nobody;
es una c., she's a tart.
cuando I *adv (de tiempo)* when; **c. más,**
at the most; **c. menos,** at least; **de c. en
c.,** de vez en c., from time to time. II
conj 1 *(temporal)* when; **c. quieras,** whenever you want; **c. vengas,** when you
come. 2 *(condicional)* (si) if. 3 *(concesiva)
(aunque)* **(aun)** c., even if. III *prep* during, at the time of; **c. la guerra,** during
the war; **c. niño,** as a child.
cuándo *adv interr* when?; *¿desde c.?,*
since when?; *¿para c. lo quieres?,* when
do you want it for?
cuantía *nf* quantity, amount.
cuantioso,-a *adj* substantial, considerable.
cuanto,-a I *adj* all; **gasta c. dinero gana,**
he spends all the money *o* as much as he
earns; **unas cuantas niñas,** a few girls. II
pron rel as much as; **coma c. quiera,** eat
as much as you want; **regala todo c. tiene,** he gives away everything he's got. III
pron indef pl **unos cuantos,** a few. IV *adv*
1 *(tiempo)* **c. antes,** as soon as possible;
en c., as soon as. 2 *(cantidad)* **c. más ...
más,** the more ... the more; **c. más lo
miro, más me gusta,** the more I look at
it the more I like it; **cuantas más personas (haya) mejor,** the more the merrier.
3 **en c. a,** with respect to, regarding; **en
c. a Juan,** as for Juan, as far as Juan is
concerned.
cuánto,-a I *adj & pron interr (sing)* how
much?; *(pl)* how many?; *¿cuántas ve*ces?, how many times?; *¿c. es?,* how
much is it? II *adv* how, how much;
¡cuánta gente hay!, what a lot of people
there are!
cuarenta *adj & nm inv* forty; *fam*
cantarle a algn las c., to give sb a piece
of one's mind.
cuarentena *nf Med* quarantine.
cuarentón,-ona *nm,f* forty-year old.
cuaresma *nf* Lent.
cuartear *vtr* to quarter.
cuartel *nm Mil* barracks *pl*; **c. general,**
headquarters; *fig* **no dar c.,** to give no
quarter.
cuartelada *nf,* **cuartelazo** *nm* putsch,
military uprising.
cuartelillo *nm Mil* post, station.
cuarteto *nm* quartet.
cuartilla *nf* sheet of paper.
cuarto,-a I *nm* 1 *(habitación)* room; **c. de
baño,** bathroom; **c. de estar,** living
room. 2 *(cuarta parte)* quarter; **c. de
hora,** quarter of an hour; *Dep* **cuartos de
final,** quarter finals. 3 *fam* **cuartos,** *(dinero)* dough, money. II *adj & nm,f* fourth.
cuarzo *nm* quartz.
cuatro I *adj & nm inv* four. II *nm fam* a
few; **cayeron c. gotas,** it rained a little
bit.
cuatrocientos,-as *adj & nm,f* four
hundred.
Cuba *n* Cuba.
cuba *nf* cask, barrel; *fam* **como una c.,**
(as) drunk as a lord.
cubalibre *nm* rum *o* gin and coke.
cubano,-a *adj & nm,f* Cuban.
cubata *nm fam* → **cubalibre.**
cubertería *nf* cutlery.
cúbico,-a *adj* cubic; *Mat* **raíz cúbica,**
cube root.
cubierta *nf* 1 cover. 2 *(de rueda)* tyre, *US*
tire. 3 *Náut* deck. 4 *(techo)* roof.
cubierto,-a I *adj* 1 covered; *(piscina)* indoors; *(cielo)* overcast. 2 *(trabajo, plaza)*
filled. II *nm* 1 *(en la mesa)* place setting.
2 **cubiertos,** cutlery *sing.*
cubil *nm* lair.
cubismo *nm* cubism.
cubito *nm* little cube; **c. de hielo,** ice
cube.
cubo *nm* 1 bucket; **c. de la basura,**
rubbish bin. 2 *Mat* cube. 3 *(de rueda)*
hub.
cubrecama *nm* bedspread.
cubrir *(pp* **cubierto)** I *vtr* to cover. II **cubrirse** *vr (cielo)* to become overcast.
cucaracha *nf* cockroach.
cuchara *nf* spoon.
cucharada *nf* spoonful; **c. rasa/colmada,**
level/heaped spoonful.
cucharilla *nf* teaspoon; **c. de café,** coffee
spoon.
cucharón *nm* ladle.
cuchichear *vi* to whisper.

cuchicheo *nm* whispering.
cuchilla *nf* blade; **c. de afeitar**, razor blade.
cuchillada *nf*, **cuchillazo** *nm* stab.
cuchillo *nm* knife.
cuchitril *nm fam* hovel, hole.
cuclillas *loc adv* **en c.**, crouching; **ponerse en c.**, to crouch down.
cuco,-a I *nm* cuckoo. II *adj fam (astuto)* shrewd, crafty.
cucurucho *nm 1 (para helado)* cornet. 2 *(de papel)* paper cone.
cuello *nm* 1 neck. 2 *(de camisa etc)* collar.
cuenca *nf* 1 *Geog* basin. 2 *(de los ojos)* socket.
cuenco *nm* earthenware bowl.
cuenta *nf* 1 *(factura)* bill. 2 *Fin (de banco)* account; **c. corriente**, current account. 3 *(cálculo)* count; **hacer cuentas**, to do sums; **c. atrás**, countdown. 4 *(de collar)* bead. 5 *(locuciones)* **caer en la c., darse c.**, to realize; **dar c.**, to report; **tener en c.**, to take into account; **traer c.**, to be worthwhile; **más sillas de la c.**, too many chairs; **en resumidas cuentas**, in short; **pedir cuentas**, to ask for an explanation; **trabajar por c. propia**, to be self-employed.
cuentagotas *nm inv* dropper.
cuentakilómetros *nm inv (distancia)* milometer; *(velocidad)* speedometer.
cuento *nm* 1 story; *Lit* short story; **contar un c.**, to tell a story; *fig* **eso no viene a c.**, that's beside the point; **c. chino**, tall story; **c. de hadas**, fairy story.
cuerda *nf* 1 *(cordel)* rope; *fig* **bajo c.**, dishonestly; **c. floja**, tightrope; **cuerdas vocales**, vocal chords. 2 *(de instrumento)* string. 3 *(del reloj)* spring; **dar c. al reloj**, to wind up a watch.
cuerdo,-a *adj* sane.
cuerno *nm* horn; *(de ciervo)* antler; *fam* **¡vete al c.!**, get lost!; *fam* **ponerle cuernos a algn**, to be unfaithful to sb.
cuero *nm* 1 leather; **chaqueta de c.**, leather jacket. 2 *c.* **cabelludo**, scalp; *fam* **en cueros (vivos)**, (stark) naked.
cuerpo *nm* 1 body; **de c. entero**, fulllength; *fig* **tomar c.**, to take shape. 2 *(cadáver)* corpse; **de c. presente**, lying in state. 3 *(parte)* section, part. 4 *(grupo)* corps, force; **c. de bomberos**, fire brigade; **c. diplomático**, diplomatic corps.
cuervo *nm* raven.
cuesta I *nf* slope; **c. abajo**, downhill; **c. arriba**, uphill. II *loc adv* **a cuestas**, on one's back *o* shoulders.
cuestión *nf* 1 *(asunto)* matter, question; **es c. de vida o muerte**, it's a matter of life or death; **en c. de unas horas**, in just a few hours. 2 *(pregunta)* question.
cuestionario *nm* questionnaire.
cueva *nf* cave.
cuezo *indic pres* → **cocer**.

cuidado,-a I *nm* 1 care; **con c.**, carefully; **tener c.**, to be careful; **estar al c. de, (cosa)** to be in charge of; *(persona)* to look after; **me trae sin c.**, I couldn't care less. 2 *Med* **cuidados intensivos**, intensive care *sing.* II *interj* **¡c.!**, look out!; **¡c. con lo que dices!**, watch what you say!; **¡c. con el escalón!**, mind the step!
cuidadoso,-a *adj* careful.
cuidar I *vtr* to care for, look after; **c. de que todo salga bien**, to make sure that everything goes alright; **c. los detalles**, to pay attention to details. II **cuidarse** *vr* **cuídate**, look after yourself.
culata *nf* 1 *(de arma)* butt. 2 *Aut* cylinder head.
culebra *nf* snake.
culebrilla *nf Med* ringworm.
culebrón *nm* soap opera.
culinario,-a *adj* culinary.
culminación *nf* culmination.
culminante *adj (punto)* highest; *(momento)* culminating.
culminar *vi* to culminate.
culo *nm* 1 *fam (trasero)* backside; *ofens* **¡vete a tomar por c.!**, fuck off! 2 *(de recipiente)* bottom.
culpa *nf* 1 blame; **echar la c. a algn**, to put the blame on sb; **fue c. mía**, it was my fault; **por tu c.**, because of you. 2 *(culpabilidad)* guilt.
culpabilidad *nf* guilt, culpability.
culpable I *nmf* offender, culprit. II *adj* guilty; *Jur* **declararse c.**, to plead guilty.
culpar *vtr* to blame; **c. a algn de un delito**, to accuse sb of an offence.
cultivado,-a *adj* 1 *Agr* cultivated. 2 *(con cultura)* cultured, refined.
cultivar *vtr* 1 to cultivate. 2 *Biol* to culture.
cultivo *nm* 1 cultivation; *(planta)* crop. 2 *Biol* culture.
culto,-a I *adj* educated; *(palabra)* learned. II *nm* cult; *Rel* worship.
cultura *nf* culture.
cultural *adj* cultural.
culturismo *nm* body building.
culturista *nmf* body builder.
cumbre *nf* 1 *(de montaña)* summit, top; *(conferencia)* **c.**, summit conference. 2 *fig (culminación)* pinnacle.
cumple *nm fam* birthday.
cumpleaños *nm inv* birthday; **¡feliz c.!**, happy birthday!
cumplido,-a I *adj* 1 completed; *(plazo)* expired; **misión cumplida**, mission accomplished. 2 *(cortés)* polite. II *nm* compliment.
cumplidor,-a *adj* reliable, dependable.
cumplimiento *nm* fulfilment, *US* fulfillment; **c. de la ley**, observance of the law.
cumplir I *vtr* 1 to carry out, fulfil, *US*

fulfill; (*deseo*) to fulfil; (*promesa*) to keep; (*sentencia*) to serve. **2 ayer cumplí veinte años,** I was twenty (years old) yesterday. **II** *vi* **1** (*plazo*) to expire, end. **2 c. con el deber,** to do one's duty. **III cumplirse** *vr* **1** (*deseo, sueño*) to be fulfilled, come true. **2** (*plazo*) to expire.

cúmulo *nm* pile, load.

cuna *nf* **1** cot. **2** *fig* (*origen*) cradle.

cundir *vi* **1 me cunde mucho el trabajo** *o* **el tiempo,** I seem to get a lot done. **2** (*extenderse*) to spread; **cundió el pánico,** panic spread; **cundió la voz de que ...,** rumour had it that ....

cuneta *nf* (*de la carretera*) gutter; **quedarse en la c.,** to be left behind.

cuña *nf* wedge; **c. publicitaria,** commercial break.

cuñado,-a *nm,f* (*hombre*) brother-in-law; (*mujer*) sister-in-law.

cuño *nm* **de nuevo c.,** newly-coined.

cuota *nf* **1** (*de club etc*) membership fees *pl*, dues *pl*. **2** (*porción*) quota, share. **3** *Am* **carretera de c.,** toll road.

cupe *pt indef* → **caber.**

cupiera *subj imperf* → **caber.**

cupo *nm* ceiling; *Mil* **excedente de c.,** exempt from military service.

cupón *nm* coupon, voucher.

cúpula *nf* dome, cupola; (*líderes*) leadership.

cura **I** *nm* *Rel* priest. **II** *nf* *Med* cure; *fig* **no tiene c.,** there's no remedy.

curación *nf* cure, treatment.

curandero,-a *nm,f* quack.

curar **I** *vtr* **1** (*sanar*) to cure; (*herida*) to dress; (*enfermedad*) to treat. **2** (*carne, pescado*) to cure. **II** *vi & vr* (*curar(se)* (*sanar*) to recover, get well; (*herida*) to heal up; **c. en salud,** to make sure.

curiosear *vi* to pry.

curiosidad *nf* curiosity; **tener c. de,** to be curious about.

curioso,-a **I** *adj* **1** (*indiscreto*) curious, in-

quisitive. **2** (*extraño*) strange, odd; **lo c. es que ...,** the strange thing is that .... **3** (*limpio*) neat, tidy. **II** *nm,f* **1** (*mirón*) onlooker. **2** *pey* (*chismoso*) nosey-parker, busybody.

currante *nmf arg* worker.

currar, currelar *vi arg* to graft, grind.

curriculum *nm* (*pl* **curricula**) **c. vitae,** curriculum vitae.

curro *nm arg* job, meal ticket.

cursar *vtr* (*estudiar*) to study; (*enviar*) to send.

cursi *adj pey* vulgar.

cursillo *nm* short course; **c. de reciclaje,** refresher course.

cursivo,-a *adj* **letra cursiva,** italics.

curso *nm* **1** (*año académico*) year; (*clase*) class. **2** *fig* **año** *o* **mes en c.,** current year *o* month; **en el c. de,** during. **3** (*de acontecimientos, río*) course. **4** *Fin* **moneda de c. legal,** legal tender.

cursor *nm* cursor.

curtido,-a *adj* **1** (*piel*) weatherbeaten; (*cuero*) tanned. **2** *fig* (*persona*) hardened.

curtir *vtr* **1** (*cuero*) to tan. **2** *fig* (*avezar*) to harden, toughen.

curva *nf* **1** curve. **2** (*en carretera*) bend; **c. cerrada,** sharp bend.

curvilíneo,-a *adj* curvaceous.

curvo,-a *adj* curved.

cuscús *nm* couscous.

cúspide *nf* summit, peak; *fig* peak.

custodia *nf* custody.

custodiar [12] *vtr* to watch over.

cutáneo,-a *adj* cutaneous, skin; *Med* **erupción cutánea,** rash.

cutícula *nf* cuticle.

cutis *nm* complexion.

cuyo,-a *pron rel & pos* (*de persona*) whose; (*de cosa*) of which; **en c. caso,** in which case.

cv *abr* **de caballos de vapor,** horse power, hp.

D

D, d |de| *nf* (*la letra*) D, d.

D. *abr* **de don,** Mister, Mr.

D.ª *abr* **de doña,** Mrs, Miss.

dactilar *adj* **huellas dactilares,** fingerprints.

dádiva *nf* (*regalo*) gift, present; (*donativo*) donation.

dadivoso,-a *adj* generous.

dado,-a¹ *adj* **1** given; **en un momento d.,** at a certain point. **2 ser d. a,** to be given to. **3 d. que,** since, given that.

dado² *nm* die, dice *pl*.

daga *nf* dagger.

dalia *nf* dahlia.

dálmata *nm* Dalmatian (dog).

daltónico,-a *adj* colour-blind *o* *US* color-blind.

dama *nf* **1** (*señora*) lady. **2** (*en damas*) king. **3 damas,** (*juego*) draughts, *US* checkers.

damasco *nm* damask.

damnificado,-a *nm,f* victim, injured person.

danés,-esa **I** *adj* Danish. **II** *nm,f* (*persona*) Dane. **III** *nm* **1** (*idioma*) Danish. **2 gran d.,** (*perro*) Great Dane.

Danubio *nm* **el D.,** the Danube.

danza *nf* dancing; (*baile*) dance.

danzar [4] *vi & vr* to dance.

dañar *vtr* (*cosa*) to damage; (*persona*) to

hurt, harm.

dañino,-a adj harmful, damaging (para, to).

daño nm (a cosa) damage; (a persona) (físico) hurt; (perjuicio) harm; **se hizo d.** en la pierna, he hurt his leg; **ƒur daños y perjuicios**, (legal) damages.

dar [11] I vtr 1 to give; (recado, recuerdos) to pass on, give; (noticia) to tell. 2 (mano de pintura, cera) to apply, put on. 3 (película) to show, screen; (fiesta) to throw, give. 4 (cosecha) to produce, yield; (fruto, flores) to bear; (beneficio, interés) to give, yield. 5 (bofetada etc) to deal; **d. a algn en la cabeza**, to hit sb on the head. 6 **dale la luz**, switch the light on; **d. la mano a algn**, to shake hands with sb; **d. los buenos días/las buenas noches a algn**, to say good morning/good evening to sb; **me da lo mismo, me da igual**, it's all the same to me; **¿qué más da?**, what difference does it make? **d.** (hora) to strike; **ya han dado las nueve**, it's gone nine (o'clock). **8 d. de comer a**, to feed. 9 **d. a conocer**, (noticia) to release; **d. a entender a algn que ...**, to give sb to understand that .... **10 d. por**, (considerar) to assume, consider; **lo dieron por muerto**, he was assumed dead, he was given up for dead; **d. por descontado/sabido**, to take for granted, to assume.

II vi 1 **me dio un ataque de tos/risa**, I had a coughing fit/an attack of the giggles. 2 **d. a**, (ventana, habitación) to look out onto, overlook; (puerta) to open onto, lead to. 3 **d. con**, (persona) to come across; **d. con la solución**, to hit upon the solution. 4 **d. de sí**, (ropa) to stretch, give. 5 **d. en**, to hit; **el sol me daba en los ojos**, the sun was (shining) in my eyes. 6 **d. para**, to be enough o sufficient for; **el presupuesto no da para más**, the budget will not stretch any further. 7 **le dio por nadar**, he took it into his head to go swimming. **8 d. que hablar**, to set people talking; **el suceso dio que pensar**, the incident gave people food for thought.

III **darse** vr 1 **se dio un caso extraño**, something strange happened. 2 (hallarse) to be found, exist. 3 **d. a**, to take to; **se dio a la bebida**, he took to drink. 4 **d. con o contra**, to bump o crash into. 5 **dárselas de**, to consider oneself. 6 **d. por satisfecho**, to feel satisfied; **d. por vencido**, to give in. 7 **se le da bien/mal el francés**, she's good/bad at French.

dardo nm dart.

dársena nf dock.

datar I vtr to date. II vi **d. de**, to date back to o from.

dátil nm date.

dato nm 1 piece of information; **datos personales**, personal details. 2 Inform da-

tos, data.

d.C. abr de después de Cristo, Anno Domini, AD.

dcha. abr de derecha, right.

de prep 1 (pertenencia) of; **el título de la novela**, the title of the novel; **el coche/hermano de Sofía**, Sofía's car/brother; **las bicicletas de los niños**, the boys' bicycles. 2 (procedencia) from; **de Madrid a Valencia**, from Madrid to Valencia; **soy de Palencia**, I'm from o I come from Palencia. 3 (descripción) of; **el niño de ojos azules**, the boy with blue eyes; **el señor de la chaqueta**, the man in the jacket; **el bobo del niño**, the silly boy; **un reloj de oro**, a gold watch; **un joven de veinte años**, a young man of twenty. 4 (contenido) of; **un saco de patatas**, a sack of potatoes. 5 **gafas de sol**, sunglasses; **goma de borrar**, rubber, US eraser. 6 (oficio) by, as; **es arquitecto de profesión**, he's an architect by profession; **trabaja de secretaria**, she's working as a secretary. 7 (acerca de about); **curso de informática**, computer course. 8 (tiempo) at; **a las tres de la tarde**, at three in the afternoon; **de día**, by day; **de noche**, at night; **de lunes a jueves**, from Monday to Thursday; **de pequeño**, as a child; **de año en año**, year in year out. 9 (precio) at; **patatas de treinta pesetas el kilo**, potatoes at thirty pesetas a kilo. 10 **una avenida de quince kilómetros**, an avenue fifteen kilometres long; **una botella de litro**, a litre bottle. 11 (con superlativo) in; **el más largo de España**, the longest in Spain. 12 (causa) with, because of; **llorar de alegría**, to cry with joy; **morir de hambre**, to die of hunger. 13 (condicional) **de haber llegado antes**, if he had arrived before; **de no ser así**, if that wasn't o weren't the case; **de ser cierto**, if it was o were true. 14 **lo mismo de siempre**, the usual thing. 15 **de cuatro en cuatro**, in fours, four at a time.

deambular vi to saunter, stroll.

debajo adv underneath, below; **el mío es el de d.**, mine is the one below; **está d. de la mesa**, it's under the table; **por d. de lo normal**, below normal; **salió por d. del coche**, he came out from under the car.

debate nm debate.

debatir I vtr to debate. II **debatirse** vr to struggle; **d. entre la vida y la muerte**, to fight for one's life.

debe nm Com debit, debit side.

deber¹ nm 1 duty; **cumplir con su d.**, to do one's duty. 2 Educ **deberes**, homework sing.

deber² I vtr (dinero, explicación) to owe. II vi 1 **debe (de) comer**, he must eat; **debe (de) irse ahora**, she has to leave now; **la factura debe pagarse mañana**, the bill

must be paid tomorrow; **el tren debe llegar a las dos**, the train is expected to
arrive at two. 2 (*consejo*) **deberías visitar
a tus padres**, you ought to visit your
parents; **debería haber ido ayer**, I
should have gone yesterday; **no debiste
hacerlo**, you shouldn't have done it. 3
(*suposición*) **deben de estar fuera**, they
must be out. III **deberse** *vr* d. a, to be
due to; **esto se debe a la falta de agua**,
this is due to lack of water.

debido,-a *adj* 1 due; **a su d. tiempo**, in
due course; **con el d. respeto**, with due
respect. 2 (*adecuado*) proper; **más de lo
d.**, too much; **tomaron las debidas pre-
cauciones**, they took the proper precautions; **como es d.**, properly. 3 d. a, because of, due to; **d. a que**, because of the
fact that.

debidamente *adv* duly, properly.

débil *adj* weak; (*luz*) dim; **punto d.**, weak
spot.

debilidad *nf* weakness; *fig* **tener d. por**,
(*persona*) to have a soft spot for; (*cosa*) to
have a weakness for.

debilitamiento *nm* weakening.

debilitar I *vtr* to weaken, debilitate. II
debilitarse *vr* to weaken, grow weak.

débito *nm* 1 (*deuda*) debt. 2 (*debe*) debit.

debut *nm* début, debut.

debutar *vi* to make one's début *o* debut.

década *nf* decade; **en la d. de los noventa**, during the nineties.

decadencia *nf* decadence.

decadente *adj & nmf* decadent.

decaer [39] *vi* to deteriorate.

decaído,-a *adj* down.

decaimiento *nm* 1 (*debilidad*) weakness. 2
(*desaliento*) low spirits *pl*.

decano,-a *nm,f* *Univ* dean.

decantarse *vr* to lean towards; **d. por**, to
come down on the side of.

decapitar *vtr* to behead, decapitate.

decena *nf* (about) ten; **una d. de veces**,
(about) ten times; **por decenas**, in tens.

decencia *nf* 1 (*decoro*) decency. 2 (*honradez*) honesty.

decenio *nm* decade.

decente *adj* decent; (*decoroso*) modest.

decepción *nf* disappointment.

decepcionante *adj* disappointing.

decepcionar *vtr* to disappoint.

decidido,-a *adj* determined, resolute.

decididamente *adv* 1 (*resueltamente*) resolutely. 2 (*definitivamente*) definitely.

decidir I *vtr & vi* to decide. II **decidirse**
vr to make up one's mind; **d. a hacer
algo**, to make up one's mind to do sth;
d. por algo, to decide on sth.

décima *nf* tenth.

decimal *adj & nm* decimal; **el sistema
métrico d.**, the decimal system.

décimo,-a I *adj & nm,f* tenth. II *nm* 1
(*parte*) tenth. 2 (*billete de lotería*) tenth

part of a lottery ticket.

decir¹ *nm* saying.

decir² [12] (*pp dicho*) I *vtr* 1 to say; **dice
que no quiere venir**, he says he doesn't
want to come. 2 **d. una mentira/la
verdad**, to tell a lie/the truth. 3 *Tel Esp*
dígame, hello. 4 **¿qué me dices del nuevo jefe?**, what do you think of the new
boss? 5 (*mostrar*) to tell, show; **su cara
dice que está mintiendo**, you can tell
from his face that he's lying. 6 (*sugerir*)
to mean; **esta película no me dice nada**,
this film doesn't appeal to me; **¿qué te
dice el cuadro?**, what does the picture
mean to you? 7 **querer d.**, to mean. 8
(*locuciones*) **es d.**, that is (to say); **por así
decirlo**, as it were, so to speak; **digamos**,
let's say; **digo yo**, in my opinion; **el qué
dirán**, what people say; **ni que d. tiene**,
needless to say; **¡no me digas!**, really!; **¡y
que lo digas!**, you bet!
II **decirse** *vr* **¿cómo se dice 'mesa' en
inglés?**, how do you say 'mesa' in English?; **se dice que ...**, they say that ...;
sé lo que me digo, I know what I am
saying.

decisión *nf* 1 decision; **tomar una d.**, to
take *o* make a decision. 2 (*resolución*) determination; **con d.**, decisively.

decisivo,-a *adj* decisive.

decisorio *adj* decision-making.

declamar *vtr & vi* to declaim, recite.

declaración *nf* 1 declaration; **d. de (la)
renta**, tax declaration *o* return. 2 (*afirmación*) statement; **hacer declaraciones**, to
comment. 3 *Jur* **prestar d.**, to give evidence.

declarante *nmf* *Jur* witness.

declarar I *vtr* 1 to declare; **d. la guerra a**,
to declare war on. 2 (*afirmar*) to state. 2
Jur **d. culpable/inocente a algn**, to find
sb guilty/not guilty. II *vi* 1 to declare. 2
Jur to testify. III **declararse** *vr* 1 **d. a
favor/en contra de**, to declare oneself in
favour of/against; **d. en huelga**, to go on
strike; **d. a algn** to declare one's love for
sb. 2 (*guerra, incendio*) to start, break
out. 3 *Jur* **d. culpable**, to plead guilty.

declinar *vi & vtr* to decline.

declive *nm* 1 (*del terreno*) incline, slope. 2
(*de imperio etc*) decline.

decolorante *nm* bleaching agent.

decolorar I *vtr* to fade; (*pelo*) to bleach.
II **decolorarse** *vr* to fade.

decomisar *vtr* to confiscate, seize.

decoración *nf* decoration.

decorado *nm* scenery, set.

decorador,-a *nm,f* 1 decorator. 2 *Teat* set
designer.

decorar *vtr* to decorate.

decorativo,-a *adj* decorative.

decoro *nm* 1 (*respeto*) dignity, decorum. 2
(*pudor*) modesty, decency.

decoroso,-a *adj* 1 (*correcto*) seemly, decorous. 2 *(decente)* decent, modest.

decrecer [33] *vi* to decrease, diminish.

decrépito,-a *adj* decrepit.

decretar *vtr* to decree.

decreto *nm* decree; **d.-ley,** decree.

dedal *nm* thimble.

dedicación *nf* dedication.

dedicar [1] I *vtr* to dedicate; *(tiempo, esfuerzos)* to devote (a, to). II **dedicarse** *vr* ¿a qué se dedica Vd.? what do you do for a living?; **los fines de semana ella se dedica a pescar,** at weekends she spends her time fishing.

dedicatoria *nf* dedication.

dedillo **nm saber algo al d.,** to have sth at one's fingertips, know sth very well.

dedo *nm (de la mano)* finger; *(del pie)* toe; **d. anular/corazón/índice/meñique,** ring/middle/index/little finger; **d. gordo,** thumb; **d. pulgar, d. hacer d.,** to hitchhike; *fig* **elegir a algn a d.,** to hand-pick sb.

deducción *nf* deduction.

deducible *adj Com* deductible.

deducir [10] I *vtr* 1 to deduce, infer. 2 *Com* to deduct. II **deducirse** *vr* **de aquí se deduce que ...,** from this it follows that ....

deductivo,-a *adj* deductive.

defecar [1] *vi* to defecate.

defecto *nm* defect, fault; **d. físico,** physical defect.

defectuoso,-a *adj* defective, faulty.

defender [3] I *vtr* to defend (contra, against; de, from); **d. del frío/viento,** to shelter from the cold/wind. II **defenderse** *vr* 1 to defend oneself. 2 *fam* **se defiende en francés,** he can get by in French.

defendido,-a *adj Jur* defendant.

defensa I *nf* defence, *US* defense; **en d. propia, en legítima d.,** in self-defence; **salir en d. de algn,** to come out in defence of sb. II *nm Dep* defender, back.

defensiva *nf* defensive; **estar/ponerse a la d.,** to be/go on the defensive.

defensivo,-a *adj* defensive.

defensor,-a *nm,f* defender; **abogado d.,** counsel for the defence; **el defensor del pueblo,** the ombudsman.

deferencia *nf* deference; **en *o* por d. a,** out of deference to.

deficiencia *nf* deficiency, shortcoming; **d. mental,** mental deficiency; **d. renal,** kidney failure.

deficiente I *adj* deficient. II *nmf* **d. mental,** mentally retarded person. III *nm Educ* fail.

déficit *nm (pl déficits)* deficit; *(carencia)* shortage.

deficitario,-a *adj* showing a deficit.

definición *nf* definition; **por d.,** by definition.

definido,-a *adj* clear; *Ling* definite.

definir *vtr* to define.

definitivo,-a *adj* definitive; **en definitiva,**

in short. ◆**definitivamente** *adv* 1 *(para siempre)* for good, once and for all. 2 *(con toda seguridad)* definitely.

deflación *nf Econ* deflation.

deflacionista *adj Econ* deflationary.

deformación *nf* deformation.

deformar I *vtr* to deform, put out of shape; *(cara)* to disfigure; *fig (la verdad, una imagen)* to distort. II **deformarse** *vr* to go out of shape, become distorted.

deforme *adj* deformed; *(objeto)* misshapen.

defraudación *nf* fraud; **d. fiscal,** tax evasion.

defraudar *vtr* 1 *(decepcionar)* to disappoint. 2 *(al fisco)* to defraud, cheat; **d. a Hacienda,** to evade taxes.

defunción *nf fml* decease, demise.

degeneración *nf* degeneration.

degenerado,-a *adj & nm,f* degenerate.

degenerar *vi* to degenerate.

degollar [2] *vtr* to behead.

degradación *nf* degradation.

degradante *adj* degrading.

degradar *vtr* to degrade.

degustación *nf* tasting.

degustar *vtr* to taste, sample.

dehesa *nf* pasture, meadow.

deificar [1] *vtr* to deify.

dejadez *nf* slovenliness.

dejado,-a *adj* 1 *(descuidado)* untidy, slovenly. 2 *(negligente)* negligent, careless. 3 *fam* **a la mano de Dios,** godforsaken.

dejar I *vtr* 1 to leave; **déjame en paz,** leave me alone; **d. dicho,** to leave word *o* a message. 2 *(prestar)* to lend. 3 *(abandonar)* to give up; **d. algo por imposible,** to give sth up; **dejé el tabaco y la bebida,** I gave up smoking and drinking. 4 *(permitir)* to let, allow; **d. caer,** to drop; **d. entrar/salir,** to let in/out. 5 *(omitir)* to leave out, omit. 6 *(ganancias)* to produce. 7 *(+ adj)* to make; **d. triste,** to make sad; **d. preocupado/sorprendido,** to worry/surprise. 8 *(posponer)* **dejaron el viaje para el verano,** they put the trip off until the summer.

II *v aux* **d. de + inf,** to stop, give up; **dejó de fumar el año pasado,** he gave up smoking last year; **no deja de llamarme,** she's always phoning me up.

III **dejarse** *vr* 1 **me he dejado las llaves dentro,** I've left the keys inside. 2 *(locuciones)* **d. barba,** to grow a beard; **d. caer,** to flop down; **d. llevar por,** to be influenced by.

del *(contracción de de + el)* → **de.**

delantal *nm* apron.

delante *adv* 1 in front; **la entrada de d.,** the front entrance. 2 **d. de,** in front of; *(en serie)* ahead of. 3 **por d.,** in front; **se lo lleva todo por d.,** he destroys everything in his path; **tiene toda la vida por**

d., he has his whole life ahead of him.

delantera nf 1 (ventaja) lead; **tomar la d.**, take the lead. 2 Ftb forward line, the forwards pl.

delantero,-a I adj front. II nm Ftb forward; **d. centro**, centre forward.

delatar vtr 1 to inform against. 2 fig to give away.

delator,-a nm,f informer.

delegación nf 1 (acto, delegados) delegation. 2 (oficina) local office, branch; **D. de Hacienda**, Tax Office.

delegado,-a nm,f 1 delegate; **d. de Hacienda**, chief tax inspector. 2 Com representative.

delegar [7] vtr to delegate (en, to).

deleitar I vtr to delight. II **deleitarse** vr to delight in, take delight in.

deleite nm delight.

deletrear vtr to spell (out).

deleznable adj brittle.

delfín nm dolphin.

delgadez nf slimness.

delgado,-a adj slim; (capa) fine.

deliberación nf deliberation.

deliberado,-a adj deliberate.

deliberar vi to deliberate (on), consider.

delicadeza nf 1 (finura) delicacy, daintiness. 2 (tacto) tactfulness; **falta de d.**, tactlessness.

delicado,-a adj 1 delicate. 2 (exigente) fussy, hard to please. 3 (sensible) hypersensitive.

delicia nf delight; **hacer las delicias de algn**, to delight sb.

delicioso,-a adj (comida) delicious; (agradable) delightful.

delictivo,-a adj criminal, punishable.

delimitar vtr to delimit.

delincuencia nf delinquency.

delincuente adj & nmf delinquent; **d. juvenil**, juvenile delinquent.

delineante nmf (hombre) draughtsman; (mujer) draughtswoman.

delinear vtr to delineate, outline.

delinquir [9] vi to break the law, commit an offence o US offense.

delirante adj delirious.

delirar vi to be delirious.

delirio nm delirium; **delirios de grandeza**, delusions of grandeur.

delito nm crime, offence, US offense.

delta nm delta; **ala d.**, hang-glider.

demacrado,-a adj emaciated.

demagogia nf demagogy.

demagogo,-a nm,f demagogue.

demanda nf 1 Jur lawsuit. 2 Com demand.

demandado,-a I nm,f defendant. II adj in demand.

demandante nmf claimant.

demandar vtr to sue.

demarcar [1] vtr to demarcate.

demás I adj **los/las d.**, the rest of; **la d.**

gente, the rest of the people. II pron **lo/los/las d.**, the rest; **por lo d.**, otherwise, apart from that; **y d.**, etcetera.

demasía nf **en d.**, excessively.

demasiado,-a I adj (singular) too much; (plural) too many; **hay demasiada comida**, there is too much food; **quieres demasiadas cosas**, you want too many things. II adv too (much); **es d. grande/caro**, it's too big/dear; **fumas/trabajas d.**, you smoke/work too much.

demencia nf dementia, insanity.

demente I adj insane, mad. II nmf mental patient.

democracia nf democracy.

demócrata I adj democratic. II nmf democrat.

democrático,-a adj democratic.

democratizar [4] vtr to democratize.

demografía nf demography.

demográfico,-a adj demographic; **crecimiento d.**, population growth.

demoledor,-a adj fig devastating.

demoler [4] vtr to demolish.

demonio nm devil, demon; fam **¿cómo/dónde demonios ...?**, how/where the hell ...?; fam **¡demonio(s)!**, hell!, damn!; fam **¡d. de niño!**, you little devil!

demora nf delay.

demorar I vtr to delay, hold up. II **demorarse** vr 1 (retrasarse) to be delayed, be held up. 2 (detenerse) to dally.

demostrable adj demonstrable.

demostración nf demonstration; **una d. de fuerza/afecto**, a show of strength.

demostrar [2] vtr 1 (mostrar) to show, demonstrate. 2 (evidenciar) to prove.

demudado,-a adj pale.

denegar [1] vtr to refuse; Jur **d. una demanda**, to dismiss a claim.

denigrante adj humiliating.

denigrar vtr to humiliate.

denominación nf denomination; **'d. de origen'**, (vinos) ≈ 'appellation d'origine'.

denominado,-a adj so-called.

denominador nm denominator.

denominar vtr to name, designate.

denotar vtr to denote.

densidad nf density; **d. de población**, population density.

denso,-a adj dense.

dentadura nf teeth, set of teeth; **d. postiza**, false teeth pl, dentures pl.

dental adj dental.

dentera nf **me da d.**, it sets my teeth on edge.

dentífrico,-a I adj **pasta/crema dentífrica**, toothpaste. II nm toothpaste.

dentista nmf dentist.

dentro adv 1 (en el interior) inside; **aquí d.**, in here; **por d.**, (on the) inside; **por d. está triste**, deep down (inside) he feels sad. 2 **d. de**, (lugar) inside. 3 **d. de poco**, shortly, soon; **d. de un mes**, in a month's time; **d. de lo que cabe**, all things considered.

denuncia nf 1 Jur report. 2 (crítica) denunciation.

denunciar [12] vtr 1 (delito) to report (a, to). 2 (criticar) to denounce.

deparar vtr to give; **no sabemos qué nos depara el destino**, we don't know what fate has in store for us.

departamento nm 1 department. 2 Ferroc compartment. 3 (territorial) province, district. 4 Am (piso) flat.

dependencia nf 1 dependence (de, on). 2 **dependencias**, premises.

depender vi to depend (de, on); (económicamente) to be dependent (de, on).

dependienta nf shop assistant.

dependiente I adj dependent (de, on). II nm shop assistant.

depilación nf depilation; **d. a la cera**, waxing.

depilar vtr to remove the hair from; (cejas) to pluck.

depilatorio,-a adj & nm depilatory; **crema depilatoria**, hair-remover, hair-removing cream.

deplorable adj deplorable.

deplorar vtr to deplore.

deponer [19] (pp depuesto) vtr 1 (destituir) to remove from office; (líder) to depose. 2 (actitud) to abandon.

deportado,-a nm,f deportee, deported person.

deportar vtr to deport.

deporte nm sport; **hacer d.**, to practise sports.

deportista I nmf (hombre) sportsman; (mujer) sportswoman. II adj sporty.

deportividad nf sportsmanship.

deportivo,-a I adj sports; **club/chaqueta d.**, sports club/jacket. II nm Aut sports car.

deposición nf removal from office; (de un líder) deposition.

depositar vtr 1 Fin to deposit. 2 (colocar) to place, put. II **depositarse** vr to settle.

depósito nm 1 Fin deposit; **en d.**, on deposit. 2 (de agua, gasolina) tank. 3 **d. de basuras**, rubbish tip o dump; **d. de cadáveres**, mortuary, US morgue.

depravación nf depravity.

depravar vtr to deprave.

depre nf fam downer, depression.

depreciación nf depreciation.

depreciar [12] I vtr to reduce the value of. II **depreciarse** vr to depreciate, lose value.

depredador,-a I adj predatory. II nm,f predator.

depresión nf depression; **d. nerviosa**, nervous breakdown.

depresivo,-a adj depressive.

deprimente adj depressing.

deprimido,-a adj depressed.

deprimir I vtr to depress. II **deprimirse** vr to get depressed.

deprisa adv quickly.

depuesto,-a pp → **deponer**.

depuración nf 1 (del agua) purification. 2 (purga) purge.

depurador,-a adj **planta depuradora**, purification plant.

depuradora nf purifier.

depurar vtr 1 (agua) to purify. 2 (partido) to purge. 3 (estilo) to refine.

derecha nf 1 (mano) right hand. 2 (lugar) right, right-hand side; **a la d.**, to o on the right, on the right-hand side. 3 Pol la **d.**, the right; **de derechas**, right-wing.

derechista nmf right-winger.

derecho,-a I adj 1 (de la derecha) right. 2 (recto) upright, straight. II nm 1 (privilegio) right; **derechos civiles/humanos**, civil/human rights; **tener d. a**, to be entitled to, have the right to; **estar en su d.**, to be within one's rights; **no hay d.**, it's not fair; **d. de admisión**, right to refuse admission. 2 Jur law; **d. penal/político**, criminal/constitutional law. 3 Com **derechos**, duties; **d. de autor**, royalties; **d. de matrícula**, enrolment fees. III adv **siga todo d.**, go straight ahead.

deriva nf drift; **ir a la d.**, to drift.

derivado nm (producto) derivative, by-product.

derivar I vtr 1 (conversación) to steer. II vi 1 to drift. 2 **d. de**, to derive from. III **derivarse** vr (proceder) to result o stem (de, from). 2 Ling to be derived (de, from).

dermatitis nf inv dermatitis.

dermatólogo,-a nm,f dermatologist.

derogar [7] vtr to repeal.

derramamiento nm spilling; **d. de sangre**, bloodshed.

derramar I vtr to spill; (lágrimas) to shed. II **derramarse** vr to spill.

derrame nm Med discharge; **d. cerebral**, brain haemorrhage.

derrapar vi to skid.

derredor nm **en d. de**, round, around.

derretir [6] vtr, **derretirse** vr to melt; (hielo, nieve) to thaw.

derribar vtr 1 (edificio) to pull down, knock down. 2 (avión) to shoot down. 3 (gobierno) to bring down.

derrocar [1] vtr to bring down; (violentamente) to overthrow.

derrochador,-a I adj wasteful. II nm,f wasteful person, squanderer.

derrochar vtr to waste, squander.

derroche nm 1 (de dinero, energía) waste, squandering. 2 (abundancia) profusion, abundance.

derrota nf 1 defeat. 2 Náut (ship's) course.

derrotar *vtr* to defeat, beat.

derrotero *nm* **1** *fig* path, course *o* plan of action. **2** *Náut* sailing directions *pl*.

derrotista *adj & nmf* defeatist.

derruido,-a *adj* in ruins.

derruir [37] *vtr* to demolish.

derrumbar **I** *vtr* (*edificio*) to knock down, pull down. **II derrumbarse** *vr* to collapse, fall down; (*techo*) to fall in, cave in.

desabastecido,-a *adj* **b. de**, out of.

desaborido,-a *adj* **1** (*comida*) tasteless. **2** *fig* (*persona*) dull. **II** *nm,f* dull person.

desabrido,-a *adj* **1** (*comida*) tasteless. **2** (*tiempo*) unpleasant. **3** *fig* (*tono*) harsh; (*persona*) moody, irritable.

desabrigado,-a *adj* ir/estar **d.**, to be lightly dressed.

desabrochar **I** *vtr* to undo. **II desabrocharse** *vr* **1 desabróchate la camisa**, undo your shirt. **2** (*prenda*) to come undone.

desacatar *vtr* to disobey.

desacato *nm* lack of respect, disrespect (**a**, for); *Jur* **d. al tribunal**, contempt of court.

desacertado,-a *adj* unwise.

desacierto *nm* mistake, error.

desaconsejar *vtr* to advise against.

desacorde *adj* **estar d. con**, to be in disagreement with.

desacreditar *vtr* **1** (*desprestigiar*) to discredit, bring into discredit. **2** (*criticar*) to disparage.

desactivador,-a *nm,f* bomb disposal expert.

desactivar *vtr* (*bomba*) to defuse.

desacuerdo *nm* disagreement.

desafiante *adj* defiant.

desafiar [29] *vtr* to challenge.

desafinado,-a *adj* out of tune.

desafinar **I** *vi* to sing out of tune; (*instrumento*) to play out of tune. **II** *vtr* to put out of tune. **III desafinarse** *vr* to go out of tune.

desafío *nm* challenge.

desaforado,-a *adj* wild.

desafortunado,-a *adj* unlucky, unfortunate.

desagradable *adj* unpleasant, disagreeable.

desagradar *vi* to displease.

desagradecido,-a **I** *adj* ungrateful. **II** *nm,f* ungrateful person.

desagrado *nm* displeasure.

desagraviar [12] *vtr* to make amends for.

desaguar [22] *vtr* to drain.

desagüe *nm* (*vaciado*) drain; (*cañería*) waste pipe, drainpipe.

desaguisado *nm* mess.

desahogado,-a *adj* **1** (*acomodado*) well-off, well-to-do. **2** (*espacioso*) spacious, roomy.

desahogarse [7] *vr* to let off steam; **se**

desahogó de su depresión, he got his depression out of his system.

desahogo *nm* **1** (*alivio*) relief. **2 vivir con d.**, to live comfortably.

desahuciado,-a *adj* **1** (*enfermo*) hopeless. **2** (*inquilino*) evicted.

desahuciar [12] *vtr* **1** (*desalojar*) to evict. **2** (*enfermo*) to deprive of all hope.

desahucio *nm* eviction.

desairado,-a *adj* **1** (*humillado*) spurned. **2** (*sin gracia*) awkward.

desairar *vtr* to slight, snub.

desaire *nm* slight, rebuff.

desajustar **I** *vtr* to upset. **II desajustarse** *vr* (*piezas*) to come apart.

desajuste *nm* upset; **d. económico**, economic imbalance; **un d. de horarios**, clashing timetables.

desalentador,-a *adj* discouraging, disheartening.

desalentar [1] **I** *vtr* to discourage, dishearten. **II desalentarse** *vr* to get discouraged, lose heart.

desaliento *nm* discouragement.

desaliñado,-a *adj* scruffy, untidy.

desaliño *nm* scruffiness, untidiness.

desalmado,-a *adj* cruel, heartless.

desalojamiento *nm* (*de inquilino*) eviction; (*de público*) removal; (*de lugar*) evacuation.

desalojar *vtr* **1** (*inquilino*) to evict; (*público*) to move on; (*lugar*) to evacuate. **2** (*abandonar*) to move out of, abandon.

desalojo *nm* → **desalojamiento**.

desamor *nm* lack of affection.

desamortizar [4] *vtr* to alienate, disentail.

desamparado,-a **I** *adj* (*persona*) helpless, unprotected; (*lugar*) abandoned, forsaken. **II** *nm,f* helpless *o* abandoned person.

desamparar *vtr* **1** to abandon, desert. **2** *Jur* to renounce, relinquish.

desamparo *nm* helplessness.

desamueblado,-a *adj* unfurnished.

desandar [8] *vtr* **d. lo andado**, to retrace one's steps.

desangrarse *vr* to lose (a lot of) blood.

desanimado,-a *adj* **1** (*persona*) disheartened, dejected. **2** (*fiesta etc*) dull, lifeless.

desanimar **I** *vtr* to discourage, dishearten. **II desanimarse** *vr* to lose heart, get discouraged.

desánimo *nm* discouragement, dejection.

desapacible *adj* unpleasant.

desaparecer [33] *vi* to disappear.

desaparecido,-a **I** *adj* missing. **II** *nm,f* missing person.

desaparición *nf* disappearance.

desapego *nm* indifference, lack of affection.

desapercibido,-a *adj* **1** (*inadvertido*) unnoticed; **pasar d.**, to go unnoticed. **2** (*desprevenido*) unprepared.

desaprensivo,-a I *adj* unscrupulous. II *nm,f* unscrupulous person.

desaprobar [2] *vtr* 1 (*no aprobar*) to disapprove of. 2 (*rechazar*) to reject.

desaprovechar *vtr* (*dinero, tiempo*) to waste; **d. una ocasión,** to fail to make the most of an opportunity.

desarmable *adj* that can be taken to pieces.

desarmar *vtr* 1 (*desmontar*) to dismantle, take to pieces. 2 *Mil* to disarm.

desarme *nm* disarmament; **d. nuclear,** nuclear disarmament.

desarraigado,-a *adj* rootless, without roots.

desarraigar [7] *vtr* to uproot.

desarraigo *nm* rootlessness.

desarreglado,-a *adj* 1 (*lugar*) untidy. 2 (*persona*) untidy, slovenly.

desarreglar *vtr* 1 (*desordenar*) to make untidy, mess up. 2 (*planes etc*) to spoil, upset.

desarreglo *nm* difference of opinion.

desarrollado,-a *adj* developed; **país d.,** developed country.

desarrollar I *vtr* to develop. II **desarrollarse** *vr* 1 (*persona, enfermedad*) to develop. 2 (*tener lugar*) to take place.

desarrollo *nm* development; **países en vías de d.,** developing countries.

desarticular *vtr* to dismantle; **d. un complot,** to foil a plot.

deseado,-a *adj* unkempt.

desasir [22] I *vtr* to release. II **desasirse** *vr* to get loose; **d. de,** to free *o* rid oneself of.

desasosegar [1] *vtr* to make restless *o* uneasy.

desasosiego *nm* restlessness, uneasiness.

desastrado,-a I *adj* untidy, scruffy. II *nm,f* scruffy person.

desastre *nm* disaster; **eres un d.,** you're just hopeless.

desastroso,-a *adj* disastrous.

desatar I *vtr* to untie, undo; (*provocar*) to unleash. II **desatarse** *vr* 1 (*zapato, cordón*) to come undone. 2 (*tormenta*) to break; (*pasión*) to run wild.

desatascar [1] *vtr* to unblock, clear.

desatender [3] *vtr* to neglect, not pay attention to.

desatento,-a *adj* inattentive; (*descortés*) impolite, discourteous.

desatinado,-a *adj* unwise.

desatino *nm* blunder.

desatornillar *vtr* to unscrew.

desatrancar [1] *vtr* to unblock; (*puerta*) to unbolt.

desautorizar [4] *vtr* 1 to disallow. 2 (*huelga etc*) to ban, forbid. 3 (*desmentir*) to deny.

desavenencia *nf* disagreement.

desaventajado,-a *adj* at a disadvantage.

desayunar I *vi* to have breakfast; *fml* to

breakfast. II *vtr* to have for breakfast.

desayuno *nm* breakfast.

desazón *nf* malaise.

desazonar *vtr* to cause malaise.

desbancar [1] *vtr* to oust.

desbandada *nf* scattering; **hubo una d. general,** everyone scattered.

desbandarse *vr* to scatter, disperse.

desbarajuste *nm* confusion, disorder.

desbaratar *vtr* to ruin, wreck; (*jersey*) to unravel.

desbloquear *vtr* 1 (*negociaciones*) to get going again. 2 (*créditos, precios*) to unfreeze.

desbocado,-a *adj* (*caballo*) runaway.

desbocarse *vr* (*caballo*) to bolt, run away.

desbordante *adj* overflowing, bursting.

desbordar I *vtr* to overflow; *fig* to overwhelm. II *vi* to overflow (**de,** with). II **desbordarse** *vr* to overflow, flood.

descabalgar [7] *vi* to dismount.

descabellado,-a *adj* crazy, wild.

descafeinado,-a *adj* 1 (*café*) decaffeinated. 2 *fig* watered-down, diluted.

descalabrar *vtr* 1 to wound in the head. 2 *fig* to damage, harm.

descalabro *nm* setback, misfortune.

descalificar [1] *vtr* to disqualify.

descalzarse [4] *vr* to take one's shoes off.

descalzo,-a *adj* barefoot.

descambiar [12] *vtr* to exchange.

descaminado,-a *adj fig* **ir d.,** to be on the wrong track.

descampado *nm* waste ground.

descansado,-a *adj* 1 (*persona*) rested. 2 (*vida, trabajo*) restful.

descansar *vi* 1 to rest, have a rest; (*corto tiempo*) to take a break. 2 *euf* **que en paz descanse,** may he *o* she rest in peace.

descansillo *nm* landing.

descanso *nm* 1 rest, break; **un día de d.,** a day off. 2 *Cin Teat* (*intervalo*) interval. *Dep* half-time, interval. 3 (*alivio*) relief. 4 (*rellano*) landing.

descapotable *adj & nm* convertible.

descarado,-a *adj* 1 (*insolente*) cheeky, insolent; (*desvergonzado*) shameless. 2 *fam* **d. que sí/no,** (*por supuesto*) of course/course not. II *nm,f* cheeky person.

descarga *nf* 1 unloading. 2 *Elec Mil* discharge.

descargar [7] I *vtr* 1 to unload. 2 *Elec* to discharge. 3 (*disparar*) to fire; (*golpe*) to deal. II *vi* (*tormenta*) to burst. III **descargarse** *vr* (*batería*) to go flat.

descargo *nm* *Jur* discharge; **testigo de d.,** witness for the defence.

descarnado,-a *adj* crude.

descaro *nm* cheek, nerve; **¡qué d.!,** what a cheek!

descarriar [29] I *vtr* to lead astray, put on the wrong road. II **descarriarse** *vr* to go astray, lose one's way.

descarrilar *vi* to go off the rails, be derailed.

descartar I *vtr* to rule out. II **descartarse** *vr Naipes* to discard, throw away.

descascarillarse *vr* to chip, peel.

descendencia *nf* descendants *pl*; **morir sin d.**, to die without issue.

descendente *adj* descending, downward.

descender [3] I *vi* 1 (*temperatura, nivel*) to fall, drop. 2 **d. de**, to descend from. II *vtr* to lower.

descendiente *nmf* descendant.

descenso *nm* 1 descent; (*de temperatura*) fall, drop. 2 *Dep* relegation.

descentrado,-a *adj* off-centre.

descentralizar [4] *vtr* to decentralize.

descifrar *vtr* to decipher; (*mensaje*) decode; (*misterio*) to solve; (*motivos, causas*) to figure out.

descojonarse *vr vulg* (*reírse*) to piss oneself laughing.

descolgar [2] I *vtr* (*el teléfono*) to pick up; (*cuadro, cortinas*) to take down. II **descolgarse** *vr* to let oneself down, slide down.

descolorido,-a *adj* faded.

descombros *nmpl* rubble, debris.

descompasado,-a *adj* inconsistent.

descomponer [19] (*pp* **descompuesto**) I *vtr* 1 to break down. 2 (*corromper*) to rot, decompose. II **descomponerse** *vi* (*corromperse*) to rot, decompose; (*ponerse nervioso*) to lose one's cool.

descomposición *nf* 1 (*de carne*) decomposition, rotting; (*de país*) disintegration. 2 *Quím* breakdown.

descompuesto,-a *adj* 1 (*podrido*) rotten, decomposed. 2 (*furioso*) furious.

descompuse *pt indef* → **descomponer**

descomunal *adj* huge, massive.

desconcertante *adj* disconcerting.

desconcertar [1] I *vtr* to disconcert. II **desconcertarse** *vr* to be bewildered, be puzzled.

desconchón *nm* bare patch.

desconcierto *nm* chaos, confusion.

desconectar *vtr* to disconnect.

desconexión *nf* disconnection.

desconfiado,-a *adj* distrustful, wary.

desconfianza *nf* distrust, mistrust.

desconfiar [29] *vi* to distrust (**de**, -), mistrust (**de**, -).

descongelar *vtr* (*nevera*) to defrost; (*créditos*) to unfreeze.

descongestionar *vtr* to clear.

desconocer [34] *vtr* not to know, be unaware of.

desconocido,-a I *adj* unknown; (*irreconocible*) unrecognizable. II *nm* **lo d.**, the unknown. III *nm,f* stranger.

desconsiderado,-a I *adj* inconsiderate, thoughtless. II *nm,f* inconsiderate *o* thoughtless person.

desconsolado,-a *adj* disconsolate, grief-stricken.

desconsuelo *nm* grief, sorrow.

descontado,-a *adj fam* **dar por d.**, to take for granted; **por d.**, needless to say, of course.

descontar [2] *vtr* 1 to deduct. 2 *Dep* (*tiempo*) to add on.

descontento,-a I *adj* unhappy. II *nm* dissatisfaction.

descontrol *nm fam* lack of control; **había un d. total**, it was absolute chaos.

descontrolarse *vr* to lose control.

desconvocar *vtr* to call off.

descorchar *vtr* to uncork.

descornarse [2] *vr fam* (*trabajar*) to slave (away).

descorrer *vtr* to draw back.

descortés *adj* impolite, discourteous.

descortesía *nf* discourtesy, impoliteness.

descoser *vtr* to unstitch, unpick.

descosido *nm* (*en camisa etc*) open seam; *fam* **como un d.**, like mad, wildly.

descoyuntar *vtr* to dislocate.

descrédito *nm* disrepute, discredit.

descremado,-a *adj* skimmed.

describir (*pp* **descrito**) *vtr* to describe.

descripción *nf* description.

descriptivo,-a *adj* descriptive.

descrito,-a *pp* → **describir**.

descuajaringar [7] *vtr fam* to pull *o* take to pieces.

descuartizar [4] *vtr* to cut up, cut into pieces.

descubierto,-a I *adj* open, uncovered; **a cielo d.**, in the open. II *nm* 1 *Fin* overdraft. 2 **al d.**, in the open; **poner al d.**, to uncover, bring out into the open.

descubridor,-a *nm,f* discoverer.

descubrimiento *nm* discovery.

descubrir (*pp* **descubierto**) *vtr* to discover; (*conspiración*) to uncover; (*placa*) to unveil.

descuento *nm* discount.

descuidado,-a *adj* 1 (*desaseado*) untidy, neglected. 2 (*negligente*) careless, negligent. 3 (*desprevenido*) off one's guard.

descuidar I *vtr* to neglect, overlook. II *vi* **descuida, voy yo**, don't worry, I'll go. III **descuidarse** *vr* (*despistarse*) to be careless; **como te descuides, llegarás tarde**, if you don't watch out, you'll be late.

descuido *nm* 1 oversight; mistake; **por d.**, inadvertently, by mistake. 2 (*negligencia*) negligence, carelessness.

desde *adv* 1 (*tiempo*) since; **d. ahora**, from now on; **d. el lunes/entonces**, since Monday/then; **espero a las media hora**, I've been waiting for half an hour; **no lo he visto d. hace un año**, I haven't seen him for a year; **¿d. cuándo?**, since when?; **d. siempre**, always. 2 (*lugar*) from; **d. aquí**, from here; **d. arriba/abajo**, from above/below. 3 **d. luego**, of course. 4 **d. que**, ever since; **d. que lo**

conozco, ever since I've known him.

desdecir [12] (pp **desdicho**) I vi not to live up (de, to). II **desdecirse** vr to go back on one's word.

desdén nm disdain.

desdentado,-a adj toothless.

desdeñar vtr to disdain.

desdeñoso,-a adj disdainful.

desdibujarse vr to become blurred o faint.

desdicha nf misfortune; **por d.**, unfortunately.

desdichado,-a I adj unfortunate. II nm,f poor devil, wretch.

desdigo indic pres → desdecir.

desdiré indic fut → desdecir.

desdoblar vtr to unfold.

deseable adj desirable.

desear vtr 1 to desire; **deja mucho que d.**, it leaves a lot to be desired. 2 (querer) to want; **¿qué desea?**, can I help you?; **estoy deseando que vengas**, I'm looking forward to your coming. 3 **te deseo buena suerte/feliz Navidad**, I wish you good luck/a merry Christmas.

desecar [1] vtr to dry up.

desechable adj disposable, throw-away.

desechar vtr 1 (tirar) to discard, throw out o away. 2 (oferta) to turn down, refuse; (idea, proyecto) to drop, discard.

desechos nmpl waste stuff.

desembalar vtr to unpack.

desembarcar [1] I vtr (mercancías) to unload; (personas) to disembark. II vi to disembark.

desembarco, desembarque nm (de mercancías) unloading; (de personas) disembarkation.

desembocadura nf mouth.

desembocar [1] vi (río) to flow (en, into); (calle, situación) to lead (en, to).

desembolsar vtr to pay out.

desembolso nm expenditure.

desembragar [7] vtr Aut to declutch.

desembrollar vtr fam 1 (aclarar) to clarify, clear up. 2 (desenredar) to disentangle.

desembuchar vtr fig to blurt out; fam **¡desembucha!**, out with it!

desempañar vtr to wipe the condensation from; Aut to demist.

desempaquetar vtr to unpack, unwrap.

desempatar vi Dep to break the deadlock.

desempate nm play-off; **partido de d.**, play-off, deciding match.

desempeñar vtr 1 (cargo) to hold, occupy; (función) to fulfil; (papel) to play. 2 (recuperar) to redeem.

desempleado,-a I adj unemployed, out of work. II nm,f unemployed person; **los desempleados**, the unemployed.

desempleo nm unemployment; **cobrar el d.**, to be on the dole.

desempolvar vtr 1 to dust. 2 fig (pasado) to revive.

desencadenar I vtr 1 to unchain. 2 (provocar) to unleash. II **desencadenarse** vr 1 (prisionero) to break loose; (viento, pasión) to rage. 2 (conflicto) to start, break out.

desencajar I vtr (pieza) to knock out; (hueso) to dislocate. II **desencajarse** vr 1 (pieza) to come out; (hueso) to become dislocated. 2 (cara) to become distorted.

desencaminado,-a adj → descaminado,-a.

desencanto nm disenchantment.

desenchufar vtr to unplug.

desenfadado,-a adj carefree, free and easy.

desenfado nm ease.

desenfocado,-a adj out of focus.

desenfoque nm incorrect focusing; fig (de asunto) wrong approach.

desenfrenado,-a adj frantic, uncontrolled; (vicio, pasión) unbridled.

desenfreno nm debauchery.

desenganchar vtr to unhook; (vagón) to uncouple.

desengañar I vtr d. a algn, to open sb's eyes. II **desengañarse** vr 1 to be disappointed. 2 fam **¡desengáñate!**, get real!

desengaño nm disappointment; **llevarse o sufrir un d. con algo**, to be disappointed in sth.

desengrasar vtr to degrease, remove the grease from.

desenlace nm 1 result, outcome; **un feliz d.**, a happy end. 2 Cin Teat ending, dénouement.

desenmarañar vtr (pelo) to untangle; (problema) to unravel; (asunto) to sort out.

desenmascarar vtr to unmask.

desenredar vtr to untangle, disentangle.

desenrollar vtr to unroll; (cable) to unwind.

desenroscar [1] vtr to unscrew.

desentenderse [3] vr se desentendió de mi problema, he didn't want to have anything to do with my problem.

desenterrar [1] vtr 1 (cadáver) to exhume, disinter; (tesoro etc) to dig up. 2 (recuerdo) to revive.

desentonar vi 1 Mús to sing out of tune, be out of tune. 2 (colores etc) not to match. 3 (persona, comentario) to be out of place.

desentrañar vtr (misterio) to unravel, get to the bottom of.

desentrenado,-a adj out of training o shape.

desentumecer [33] vtr to put the feeling back into.

desenvoltura nf ease.

desenvolver [4] (pp **desenvuelto**) I vtr to unwrap. II **desenvolverse** vr 1 (persona) to manage, cope. 2 (hecho) to develop.

desenvuelto,-a adj relaxed.

deseo nm wish; (sexual) desire; **formular un d.,** to make a wish.

deseoso,-a adj eager; **estar d. de,** be eager to.

desequilibrado,-a I adj unbalanced. **II** nm,f unbalanced person.

desequilibrar I vtr to unbalance, throw off balance. **II desequilibrarse** vr to become mentally disturbed.

desequilibrio nm imbalance; **d. mental,** mental disorder.

deserción nf desertion.

desertar vi to desert.

desértico,-a adj desert.

desertización nf desertification.

desertor,-a nm,f deserter.

desesperación nf (desesperanza) despair; (exasperación) desperation.

desesperado,-a adj **1** (sin esperanza) desperate, hopeless. **2** (exasperado) exasperated, infuriated.

desesperante adj exasperating.

desesperar I vtr to drive to despair; (exasperar) to exasperate. **II desesperarse** vr to despair.

desestabilizar [4] vtr to destabilize.

desestimar vtr to reject.

desfachatez nf cheek, nerve.

desfalco nm embezzlement, misappropriation.

desfallecer [33] vi **1** (debilitarse) to feel faint; (desmayarse) to faint. **2** (desanimarse) to lose heart.

desfasado,-a adj **1** outdated. **2** (persona) old-fashioned, behind the times. **3** Téc out of phase.

desfase nm gap; **d. horario,** time lag.

desfavorable adj unfavourable, US unfavorable.

desfigurar vtr (cara) to disfigure; (verdad) to distort.

desfiladero nm narrow pass.

desfilar vi **1** to march in single file. **2** Mil to march past, parade.

desfile nm Mil parade, march past; **d. de modas,** fashion show.

desfogar [7] I vtr to give vent to. **II desfogarse** vr to let off steam.

desgajar I vtr (arrancar) to rip o tear out; (rama) to tear off. **II desgajarse** vr to come off.

desgana nf **1** (inapetencia) lack of appetite. **2** (apatía) apathy, indifference; **con d.,** reluctantly, unwillingly.

desganado,-a adj **1 estar d.,** (inapetente) to have no appetite. **2** (apático) apathetic.

desgañitarse vr fam to shout oneself hoarse.

desgarbado,-a adj ungraceful, ungainly.

desgarrador,-a adj bloodcurdling.

desgarrar vtr to tear.

desgarrón nm big tear, rip.

desgastar I vtr to wear out. **II desgastarse** vr (consumirse) to wear out; (per-

sona) to wear oneself out.

desgaste nm wear; **d. del poder,** wear and tear of power.

desgracia nf **1** misfortune; **por d.,** unfortunately. **2** (deshonor) disgrace. **3 desgracias personales,** loss of life.

desgraciado,-a I adj **1** unfortunate; (infeliz) unhappy. **II** nm,f unfortunate person; **un pobre d.,** a poor devil. ◆**desgraciadamente** adv unfortunately.

desgravable adj tax-deductible.

desgravación nf deduction. **d. fiscal,** tax deduction.

desgravar vtr to deduct.

desguazar [4] vtr (un barco) to break up; Aut to scrap.

deshabitado,-a adj uninhabited, unoccupied.

deshabitar vtr to abandon, vacate.

deshacer [15] (pp deshecho) I vtr **1** (paquete) to undo; (maleta) to unpack. **2** (plan) to destroy, ruin. **3** (acuerdo) to break off. **4** (disolver) to dissolve; (derretir) to melt. **II deshacerse** vr **1** to come undone o untied. **2 d. de algn/algo,** to get rid of sb/sth. **3** (afligirse) to go to pieces; **d. en lágrimas,** to cry one's eyes out. **4** (disolverse) to dissolve; (derretirse) to melt. **5** (niebla) to fade away, disappear.

deshecho,-a adj **1** (cama) unmade; (maleta) unpacked; (paquete) unwrapped. **2** (roto) broken, smashed. **3** (disuelto) dissolved; (derretido) melted. **4** (abatido) devastated, shattered. **5** (cansado) exhausted, tired out.

desheredar vtr to disinherit.

deshidratar vtr to dehydrate.

deshielo nm thaw.

deshilachar vtr to fray.

deshilvanado,-a adj fig (inconexo) disjointed.

deshonesto,-a adj **1** dishonest. **2** (indecente) indecent, improper.

deshonor nm, **deshonra** nf dishonour, US dishonor.

deshonrar vtr **1** to dishonour, US dishonor. **2** (a la familia etc) to bring disgrace on.

deshora (a) loc adv at an inconvenient time; **comer a d.,** to eat at odd times.

deshuesar vtr (carne) to bone; (fruta) to stone.

deshumanizar [4] vtr to dehumanize.

desidia nf apathy.

desierto,-a I nm desert. **II** adj **1** (deshabitado) uninhabited. **2** (vacío) empty, deserted. **3** (premio) void.

designación nf designation.

designar vtr **1** to designate. **2** (fecha, lugar) to fix.

designio nm intention, plan.

desigual adj **1** uneven. **2** (lucha) unequal.

3 (*carácter*) changeable.

desigualdad *nf* 1 inequality. 2 (*del terreno*) unevenness.

desilusión *nf* disappointment, disillusionment.

desilusionar *vtr* to disappoint, disillusion.

desinfectante *adj & nm* disinfectant.

desinfectar *vtr* to disinfect.

desinflar I *vtr* to deflate; (*rueda*) to let down. II **desinflarse** *vr* to go flat.

desintegración *nf* disintegration.

desintegrar *vtr*, **desintegrarse** *vr* to disintegrate.

desinterés *nm* 1 (*indiferencia*) lack of interest, apathy. 2 (*generosidad*) unselfishness.

desinteresado,-a *adj* selfless, unselfish.

desintoxicar [1] I *vtr* to detoxicate; (*de alcohol*) to dry out. II **desintoxicarse** *vr* Med to detoxicate oneself; (*de alcohol*) to dry out.

desistir *vi* to desist.

deslavazado,-a *adj* disjointed.

desleal *adj* disloyal; (*competencia*) unfair.

deslealtad *nf* disloyalty.

deslenguado,-a *adj* (*insolente*) insolent, cheeky; (*grosero*) coarse, foul-mouthed.

desliar [29] *vtr* to unwrap.

desligar [7] I *vtr* 1 (*separar*) to separate. 2 (*desatar*) to untie, unfasten. II **desligarse** *vr* d. de, to disassociate oneself from.

desliz *nm* mistake, slip; **cometer** *o* **tener un d.**, to slip up.

deslizar [4] I *vtr* to slide. II **deslizarse** *vr* 1 (*patinar*) to slide. 2 (*fluir*) to flow.

deslucir [35] *vtr* 1 (*espectáculo*) to spoil. 2 (*metal*) to make dull.

deslumbrador,-a, **deslumbrante** *adj* dazzling; *fig* stunning.

deslumbrar *vtr* to dazzle.

desmadrarse *vr fam* to go wild.

desmadre *nm fam* hullabaloo.

desmandarse *vr* to get out of hand, run wild; (*caballo*) to bolt.

desmano (a) *loc adv* out of the way; **me coge a d.**, it is out of my way.

desmantelar *vtr* 1 to dismantle. 2 *Náut* to dismast, unrig.

desmaquillador,-a I *nm* make-up remover. II *adj* **leche desmaquilladora**, cleansing cream.

desmaquillarse *vr* to remove one's make-up.

desmarcarse [1] *vr Dep* to lose one's marker.

desmayado,-a *adj* unconscious; **caer d.**, to faint.

desmayarse *vr* to faint.

desmayo *nm* faint, fainting fit; **tener un d.**, to faint.

desmedido,-a *adj* disproportionate, out of all proportion; (*ambición*) unbounded.

desmejorar(se) *vi & vr* to deteriorate, go downhill.

desmelenarse *vr fam* to let one's hair down.

desmembración *nf*, **desmembramiento** *nm* dismemberment.

desmemoriado,-a *adj* forgetful, absent-minded.

desmentir [5] *vtr* to deny.

desmenuzar [4] *vtr* 1 (*deshacer*) to break into little pieces, crumble; (*carne*) to cut into little pieces. 2 (*asunto*) to examine in detail.

desmerecer [33] *vi* 1 to be unworthy (**de**, of). 2 (*deteriorarse*) to deteriorate.

desmesura *nf* excess.

desmesurado,-a *adj* excessive.

desmilitarizar [4] *vtr* to demilitarize.

desmontable *adj* that can be taken to pieces.

desmontar I *vtr* 1 (*desarmar*) to take to pieces, dismantle. 2 (*allanar*) to level. II *vi* to dismount (**de**, -), get off (**de**, -).

desmoralizar [4] *vtr* to demoralize.

desmoronarse *vr* to crumble, fall to pieces.

desnatado,-a *adj* (*leche*) skimmed.

desnivel *nm* (*en el terreno*) drop, difference in height.

desnivelar *vtr* to throw out of balance.

desnucarse [1] *vr* to break one's neck.

desnuclearizar *vtr* to denuclearize.

desnudar I *vtr* to undress. II **desnudarse** *vr* to get undressed.

desnudismo *nm* nudism.

desnudista *adj & nmf* nudist.

desnudo,-a I *adj* naked, nude. II *nm Arte* nude.

desnutrición *nf* malnutrition.

desnutrido,-a *adj* undernourished.

desobedecer [33] *vtr* to disobey.

desobediencia *nf* disobedience.

desobediente I *adj* disobedient. II *nmf* disobedient person.

desocupado,-a *adj* 1 (*vacío*) empty, vacant. 2 (*ocioso*) free, not busy. 3 (*sin empleo*) unemployed.

desocupar *vtr* to empty, vacate.

desodorante *adj & nm* deodorant.

desolación *nf* desolation.

desolar [2] *vtr* to devastate.

desollar [2] I *vtr* to skin. II **desollarse** *vr* to scrape; **me desollé el brazo**, I scraped my arm.

desorbitado,-a *adj* (*precio*) exhorbitant.

desorden *nm* untidiness, mess; **¡qué d.!**, what a mess!; **d. público**, civil disorder.

desordenado,-a *adj* messy, untidy.

desordenar *vtr* to make untidy, mess up.

desorganizar [4] *vtr* to disorganize, disrupt.

desorientación *nf* disorientation.

desorientar I *vtr* to disorientate. II **desorientarse** *vr* to lose one's sense of direction, lose one's bearings; *fig* to become disorientated.

despabilado,-a *adj* 1 (*sin sueño*) wide awake. 2 (*listo*) quick, smart.

despachar *vtr* 1 (*asunto*) to get through. 2 (*correo*) to send, dispatch. 3 (*en tienda*) to serve. 4 *fam* (*despedir*) to send packing, sack.

despacho *nm* 1 (*oficina*) office; (*en casa*) study. 2 (*venta*) sale. 3 (*comunicación*) dispatch.

despachurrar *vtr fam* to squash, flatten.

despacio *adv* 1 (*lentamente*) slowly. 2 (*en voz baja*) quietly.

despampanante *adj fam* stunning.

desparpajo *nm* self-assurance; **con d.**, in a carefree manner.

desparramar *vtr*, **desparramarse** *vr* to spread, scatter; (*líquido*) to spill.

despavorido,-a *adj* terrified.

despecho *nm* spite; **por d.**, out of spite.

despectivo,-a *adj* derogatory, disparaging.

despedazar [4] *vtr* to cut o tear to pieces.

despedida *nf* farewell, goodbye; **d. de soltera/soltero**, hen/stag party.

despedido,-a *adj* **salir d.**, to be off like a shot.

despedir [6] I *vtr* 1 (*empleado*) to sack, fire. 2 (*decir adiós*) to see off, say goodbye to. 3 (*olor, humo etc*) to give off. II **despedirse** *vr* 1 (*decir adiós*) to say goodbye (**de**, to). 2 *fig* to forget, give up; **ya puedes despedirte del coche**, you can say goodbye to the car.

despegado,-a *adj* 1 unstuck. 2 (*persona*) couldn't-care-less.

despegar [7] I *vtr* to take off, detach. II *vi* *Av* to take off. III **despegarse** *vr* to come unstuck.

despego *nm* detachment.

despegue *nm* takeoff.

despeinado,-a *adj* dishevelled, with untidy hair.

despejado,-a *adj* clear; (*cielo*) cloudless.

despejar I *vtr* to clear; (*misterio, dudas*) to clear up. II **despejarse** *vr* 1 (*cielo*) to clear. 2 (*persona*) to clear one's head.

despeje *nm* *Dep* clearance.

despellejar *vtr* to skin.

despelotarse *vr vulg* 1 (*desnudarse*) to strip. 2 **d. de risa**, to laugh one's head off.

despensa *nf* pantry, larder.

despeñadero *nm* cliff, precipice.

despeñarse *vr* to go over a cliff.

desperdiciar [12] *vtr* to waste; (*oportunidad*) to throw away.

desperdicio *nm* 1 (*acto*) waste. 2 **desperdicios**, (*basura*) rubbish sing; (*desechos*) scraps, leftovers.

desperdigar [7] *vtr*, **desperdigarse** *vr* to scatter, separate.

desperezarse [4] *vr* to stretch (oneself).

desperfecto *nm* 1 (*defecto*) flaw, imperfection. 2 (*daño*) damage.

despertador *nm* alarm clock; **reloj d.**, alarm watch.

despertar [1] I *vtr* to wake (up), awaken; *fig* (*sentimiento etc*) to arouse. II **despertarse** *vr* to wake (up).

despiadado,-a *adj* merciless.

despido *nm* dismissal, sacking.

despierto,-a *adj* 1 (*desvelado*) awake. 2 (*vivo*) quick, sharp.

despilfarrar *vtr* to waste, squander.

despilfarro *nm* wasting, squandering.

despintar *vi*, **despintarse** *vr* (*ropa*) to fade.

despistado,-a *adj* I 1 (*olvidadizo*) scatterbrained. 2 (*confuso*) confused. II *nm,f* scatterbrain.

despistar I *vtr* 1 (*hacer perder la pista a*) to lose, throw off one's scent. 2 *fig* to mislead. II **despistarse** *vr* 1 (*perderse*) to get lost. 2 (*distraerse*) to switch off.

despiste *nm* 1 (*cualidad*) absent-mindedness. 2 (*error*) slip-up.

desplazamiento *nm* (*viaje*) trip, journey; **dietas de d.**, travelling expenses.

desplazar [4] I *vtr* to displace. II **desplazarse** *vr* to travel.

desplegar [1] I *vtr* 1 to open (out), spread (out). 2 (*energías etc*) to use, deploy. II **desplegarse** *vr* 1 (*abrirse*) to open (out), spread (out). 2 *Mil* to deploy.

despliegue *nm* 1 *Mil* deployment. 2 (*de medios etc*) display.

desplomarse *vr* to collapse; (*precios*) to slump, fall sharply.

desplumar *vtr* to pluck.

despoblar [2] *vtr* to depopulate.

despojar *vtr* 1 to strip (**de**, of). 2 *fig* to divest, deprive (**de**, of).

despojo *nm* 1 stripping. 2 **despojos**, leftovers, scraps.

desposado,-a *adj fml* newly-wed.

desposar *vtr fml* to marry.

desposeer [36] *vtr* **d. de**, to dispossess of; (*autoridad*) to strip of.

desposeído *nm* **los desposeídos**, the have-nots.

déspota *nmf* despot.

despótico,-a *adj* despotic.

despotismo *nm* despotism.

despotricar [1] *vi* to rant and rave (**contra**, about).

despreciable *adj* despicable, contemptible; (*cantidad*) negligible.

despreciar [12] *vtr* 1 (*desdeñar*) to scorn, despise. 2 (*rechazar*) to reject, spurn.

desprecio *nm* 1 (*desdén*) scorn, disdain. 2 (*desaire*) slight, snub.

desprender I *vtr* 1 (*separar*) to remove, detach. 2 (*olor, humo etc*) to give off. II **desprenderse** *vr* 1 (*soltarse*) to come off o away. 2 **d. de**, to rid oneself (**de**, of), free oneself (**de**, from). 3 **de aquí se prende que ...**, it can be deduced from this that ....

desprendido,-a adj fig generous, un-selfish.

desprendimiento nm 1 loosening, detachment; **d. de tierras**, landslide. 2 fig (generosidad) generosity, unselfishness.

despreocupado,-a adj 1 (tranquilo) unconcerned. 2 (descuidado) careless; (estilo) casual.

despreocuparse vr 1 (tranquilizarse) to stop worrying. 2 (desentenderse) to be unconcerned, be indifferent (**de**, to).

desprestigiar [12] vtr to discredit, run down.

desprestigio nm discredit, loss of reputation; **campaña de d.**, smear campaign.

desprevenido,-a adj unprepared; **coger** o **pillar a algn d.**, to catch sb unawares.

desproporción nf disproportion, lack of proportion.

desproporcionado,-a adj disproportionate.

desprovisto,-a adj lacking (**de**, -), without (**de**, -), devoid (**de**, of).

después adv 1 afterwards, later; (entonces) then; (seguidamente) next; **una semana d.**, a week later; **poco d.**, soon after. 2 (lugar) next. 3 **d. de**, after; **d. de la guerra**, after the war; **mi calle está d. de la tuya**, my street is the one after yours; **d. de cenar**, after eating; **d. de todo**, after all. 4 **d. de que**, after; **d. de que viniera**, after he came.

despuntar I vtr to blunt, make blunt. II vi 1 (día) to dawn. 2 (destacar) to excel, stand out.

desquiciar [12] I vtr (persona) to unhinge. II **desquiciarse** vr (persona) to go crazy.

desquitarse vr to take revenge (**de**, for).

desquite nm revenge.

destacado,-a adj outstanding.

destacamento nm detachment.

destacar [1] I vtr fig to emphasize, stress. II **destacar(se)** vi & vr to stand out.

destajo nm piecework; **trabajar a d.**, to do piecework.

destapar I vtr to take the lid off; (botella) to open; fig (asunto) to uncover. II **destaparse** vr to get uncovered.

destartalado,-a adj rambling; (desvencijado) ramshackle.

destello nm flash, sparkle.

destemplado,-a adj 1 (voz, gesto) sharp, snappy; **con cajas destempladas**, rudely, brusquely. 2 (tiempo) unpleasant. 3 (enfermo) indisposed, out of sorts. 4 Mús out of tune, discordant.

desteñir [6] I vi & vtr to discolour, US discolor. II **desteñirse** vr to lose colour o US color, fade.

desternillarse vi **d. (de risa)**, to split one's sides laughing.

desterrar [1] vtr to exile.

destiempo (a) loc adv at the wrong time o moment.

destierro nm exile.

destilado,-a adj distilled; **agua destilada**, distilled water.

destilar vtr to distil.

destilería nf distillery.

destinado,-a adj destined; bound; fig **d. al fracaso**, doomed to failure.

destinar vtr 1 (dinero etc) to set aside, assign. 2 (empleado) to appoint.

destinatario,-a nm,f 1 (de carta) addressee. 2 (de mercancías) consignee.

destino nm 1 (rumbo) destination; **el avión con d. a Bilbao**, the plane to Bilbao. 2 (sino) fate, fortune. 3 (de empleo) post.

destitución nf dismissal from office.

destituir [37] vtr to dismiss o remove from office.

destornillador nm screwdriver.

destornillar vtr to unscrew.

destreza nf skill.

destrozado,-a adj 1 (roto) torn-up, smashed. 2 (cansado) worn-out, exhausted. 3 (abatido) shattered.

destrozar [4] vtr 1 (destruir) to destroy; (rasgar) to tear to shreds o pieces. 2 (afligir) to shatter; (vida, reputación) to ruin.

destrozo nm 1 destruction. 2 **destrozos**, damage sing.

destrucción nf destruction.

destructivo,-a adj destructive.

destructor,-a I adj destructive. II nm Náut destroyer.

destruir [37] vtr to destroy.

desusado,-a adj old-fashioned, outdated.

desuso nm disuse; **caer en d.**, to fall into disuse; **en d.**, obsolete, outdated.

desvalido,-a adj defenceless.

desvalijar vtr (robar) to clean out, rob; (casa, tienda) to burgle.

desvalorizar [4] vtr to devalue.

desván nm attic, loft.

desvanecerse [33] vr 1 (disiparse) to vanish, fade away. 2 (desmayarse) to faint.

desvariar [29] vi to talk nonsense.

desvarío nm 1 (delirio) raving, delirium. 2 (disparate) nonsense.

desvelado,-a adj awake, wide awake.

desvelar I vtr to keep awake. II **desvelarse** vr 1 (despabilarse) to stay awake. 2 (desvivirse) to devote oneself (**por**, to).

desvencijar I vtr to take apart. II **desvencijarse** vr to fall apart.

desventaja nf 1 disadvantage; **estar en d.**, to be at a disadvantage. 2 (inconveniente) drawback.

desventura nf misfortune, bad luck.

desvergonzado,-a I adj 1 (indecente) shameless. 2 (descarado) insolent. II nm,f 1 (sinvergüenza) shameless person. 2 (fresco) insolent o cheeky person.

desvergüenza nf 1 (indecencia) shamelessness. 2 (atrevimiento) insolence; **tuvo la d. de negarlo**, he had the cheek to deny it.

3 *(impertinencia)* insolent *o* rude remark.

desvestir [6] I *vtr* to undress. II **desvestirse** *vr* to undress, get undressed.

desviación *nf* deviation; *(de carretera)* diversion, detour; *Med* **d. de columna**, slipped disc.

desviar [29] I *vtr (río, carretera)* to divert; *(golpe, conversación)* to deflect; **d. la mirada**, to look away. II **desviarse** *vr* to go off course; *(coche)* to turn off; *fig* **d. del tema**, to digress.

desvincular I *vtr* to separate. II **desvincularse** *vr* to separate, cut oneself off.

desvío *nm* diversion, detour.

desvirgar [7] *vtr* to deflower.

desvirtuar [30] *vtr* to distort.

desvivirse *vr* to bend over backwards.

detallado,-a *adj* detailed, thorough.
◆**detalladamente** *adv* in (great) detail.

detallar *vtr* to give the details of.

detalle *nm* 1 detail; **entrar en detalles**, to go into details. 2 *(delicadeza)* nice thought, nicety; **¡qué d.!**, how nice!, how sweet! 3 *(toque decorativo)* touch, ornament.

detallista I *adj* perfectionist. II *nmf Com* retailer.

detectar *vtr* to detect.

detective *nmf* detective; **d. privado**, private detective *o* eye.

detector,-a *nm,f* detector; **d. de incendios**, fire detector.

detención *nf* 1 *Jur* detention, arrest. 2 **con d.**, thoroughly.

detener [24] I *vtr* 1 to stop, halt. 2 *Jur (arrestar)* to arrest, detain. II **detenerse** *vr* to stop.

detenido,-a I *adj* 1 *(parado)* standing still, stopped. 2 *(arrestado)* detained. 3 *(minucioso)* detailed, thorough. II *nm,f* detainee, person under arrest.
◆**detenidamente** *adv* carefully, thoroughly.

detenimiento *nm* **con d.**, carefully, thoroughly.

detentar *vtr* to hold.

detergente *adj & nm* detergent.

deteriorar I *vtr* to spoil, damage. II **deteriorarse** *vr* 1 *(estropearse)* to get damaged. 2 *(empeorar)* to get worse.

deterioro *nm* 1 *(empeoramiento)* deterioration, worsening. 2 *(daño)* damage; **ir en d. de**, to be to the detriment of.

determinación *nf* 1 determination; **con d.**, determinedly. 2 *(decisión)* decision.

determinado,-a *adj* 1 *(preciso)* definite, precise. 2 *(resuelto)* decisive, resolute. 3 *Ling* definite.

determinante *adj* decisive.

determinar I *vtr* 1 *(fecha etc)* to fix, set. 2 *(decidir)* to decide on. 3 *(condicionar)* to determine. 4 *(ocasionar)* to bring about. II **determinarse** *vr* to make up one's mind to.

detestable *adj* detestable, repulsive.

detestar *vtr* to detest, hate.

detonante *nm* detonator; *fig* trigger.

detonar *vtr* to detonate.

detractor,-a *nm,f* detractor.

detrás *adv* 1 behind, on *o* at the back (de, of). 2 **d. de**, behind.

detrimento *nm* detriment; **en d. de**, to the detriment of.

detuve *pt indef* → **detener**.

deuda *nf* debt; **estoy en d. contigo**, *(monetaria)* I am in debt to you; *(moral)* I am indebted to you; **d. del Estado**, public debt; **d. pública**, national debt.

deudor,-a I *adj* indebted. II *nm,f* debtor.

devaluación *nf* devaluation.

devaluar [30] *vtr* to devalue.

devanar I *vtr (hilo)* to wind; *(alambre)* to coil. II **devanarse** *vr fam* **d. los sesos**, to rack one's brains.

devaneo *nm* dabbling.

devastador,-a *adj* devastating.

devastar *vtr* to devastate, ravage.

devengar [7] *vtr Com* to earn, accrue.

devenir [27] *vi* to become.

devoción *nf* 1 *Rel* devoutness. 2 *(al trabajo etc)* devotion; *fam* **Juan no es santo de mi d.**, Juan isn't really my cup of tea.

devolución *nf* 1 giving back, return; *Com* refund, repayment. 2 *Jur* devolution.

devolver [4] I *vtr* 1 to give back, return; *(dinero)* to refund. II *vi* to vomit, throw *o* bring up. II **devolverse** *vr Am* to go *o* come back, return.

devorar *vtr* to devour.

devoto,-a I *adj* pious, devout. II *nm,f* 1 *Rel* pious person. 2 *(seguidor)* devotee.

devuelto,-a *pp de* → **devolver**.

DF *nm abr de* **Distrito Federal**, Federal District.

DGS *nf* 1 *abr de* **Dirección General de Seguridad**, government department responsible for National Security. 2 *abr de* **Dirección General de Sanidad**, government department responsible for Public Health.

DGT *nf abr de* **Dirección General de Tráfico**, government department responsible for Traffic.

di 1 *pt indef* → **dar**. 2 *imperat* → **decir**.

día *nm* day; **¿qué d. es hoy?**, what's the date today?; **d. a d.**, day by day; **de d.**, by day; **durante el d.**, during the daytime; **de un d. para otro**, overnight; **un d. sí y otro no**, every other day; **pan del d.**, fresh bread; **hoy (en) d.**, nowadays; **el d. de mañana**, in the future; **fig estar al d.**, to be up to date; *fig* **poner al d.**, to bring up to date; **d. festivo**, holiday; **d. laborable**, working day; **d. libre**, free day, day off; **es de d.**, it is daylight; **hace buen/mal d.**, it's a nice/bad day, the weather is nice/bad today.

diabetes *nf* diabetes.
diabético,-a *adj & nm,f* diabetic.
diablo *nm* devil; *fam* ¡al d. con ...!, to hell with ...!; *fam* vete al d., get lost; *fam* ¿qué/cómo diablos ...?, what/how the hell ...?
diablura *nf* mischief.
diácono *nm* deacon.
diadema *nf* tiara.
diáfano,-a *adj* clear.
diafragma *nm* diaphragm; *Fot* aperture; *Med* cap.
diagnosis *nf inv* diagnosis.
diagnosticar [1] *vt* to diagnose.
diagnóstico *nm* diagnosis.
diagonal *adj & nf* diagonal; **en d.,** diagonally.
diagrama *nm* diagram; *Inform* d. de flujo, flowchart.
dial *nm* dial.
dialecto *nm* dialect.
dialogar [7] *vi* to have a conversation; *(para negociar)* to talk.
diálogo *nm* dialogue.
diamante *nm* diamond.
diámetro *nm* diameter.
diana *nf* 1 *Mil* reveille. 2 *(blanco)* bull's eye.
diapositiva *nf* slide.
diario,-a I *nm* 1 *Prensa* (daily) newspaper. 2 *(memorias)* diary; *Náut* d. de a bordo, d. de navegación, logbook; **a d.,** daily, every day. ◆**diariamente** *adv* daily, every day.
diarrea *nf* diarrhoea, *US* diarrhea.
diatriba *nf* diatribe.
dibujante *nmf* 1 drawer. 2 *(de cómic)* cartoonist. 3 *Téc (hombre)* draughtsman, *US* draftsman; *(mujer)* draughtswoman, *US* draftswoman.
dibujar *vtr* to draw.
dibujo *nm* 1 drawing; **dibujos animados,** cartoons. 2 *(arte)* drawing; **d. artístico,** artistic drawing; **d. lineal,** draughtsmanship.
diccionario *nm* dictionary; **buscar/mirar una palabra en el d.,** to look up a word in the dictionary.
dicha *nf* happiness.
dicharachero,-a *adj* talkative and witty.
dicho,-a *adj* 1 said; **mejor d.,** or rather; **d. de otro modo,** to put it another way; **d. sea de paso,** let it be said in passing; **d. y hecho,** no sooner said than done. 2 **dicha persona,** *(mencionado)* the above mentioned person.
dichoso,-a *adj* 1 *(feliz)* happy. 2 *fam* damned; **¡este d. trabajo!,** this damned job!
diciembre *nm* December.
dictado *nm* dictation *fig* dictados, dictates.
dictador,-a *nm,f* dictator.
dictadura *nf* dictatorship.

dictáfono® *nm* Dictaphone®.
dictamen *nm (juicio)* ruling; *(informe)* report.
dictaminar *vi* to rule **(sobre,** on).
dictar *vtr* 1 to dictate. 2 *(ley)* to enact; *(sentencia)* to pass.
dictatorial *adj* dictatorial.
didáctico,-a *adj* didactic.
diecinueve *adj & nm inv* nineteen.
dieciocho *adj & nm inv* eighteen.
dieciséis *adj & nm inv* sixteen.
diecisiete *adj & nm inv* seventeen.
diente *nm* tooth; *Téc* cog; *(de ajo)* clove; **d. de leche,** milk tooth; **dientes postizos,** false teeth; *fig* **hablar entre dientes,** to mumble; *fig* **poner los dientes largos a algn,** to make sb green with envy.
diera *subj imperf → **dar.**
diéresis *nf inv* diaeresis.
diesel *adj & nm* diesel.
diestra *nf* right hand.
diestro,-a I *adj* 1 *(hábil)* skilful, *US* skillful, clever. 2 **a d. y siniestro,** right, left and centre. II *nm* *Taur* bullfighter, matador.
dieta *nf* 1 diet; **estar a d.,** to be on a diet. 2 **dietas,** expenses *o* subsistence allowance.
dietética *nf* dietetics *sing.*
dietista *nmf* dietician.
diez *adj & nm inv* ten.
difamación *nf* defamation, slander; *(escrita)* libel.
difamar *vtr* to defame, slander; *(por escrito)* to libel.
diferencia *nf* difference; **a d. de,** unlike.
diferencial I *adj* distinguishing. II *nm* differential.
diferenciar [12] I *vtr* to differentiate, distinguish **(entre,** between). II **diferenciarse** *vr* to differ **(de,** from), be different **(de,** from).
diferente I *adj* different **(de,** from, *US* than). II *adv* differently.
diferido,-a *adj* **TV en d.,** recorded.
difícil *adj* difficult, hard; **d. de creer/hacer,** difficult to believe/do; **es d. que venga,** it is unlikely that she'll come.
dificultad *nf (calidad); (aprieto)* trouble, problem.
dificultar *vtr* to make difficult.
dificultoso,-a *adj* difficult, hard.
difuminar *vtr* to blur.
difundir *vtr,* **difundirse** *vr* to spread.
difunto,-a I *adj* late, deceased. II *nm,f* deceased.
difusión *nf* 1 *(de noticia)* spreading; **tener gran d.,** to be widely broadcast. 2 *Rad TV* broadcasting.
difuso,-a *adj* diffuse.
digerir [5] *vtr* to digest; *fig* to assimilate.
digestión *nf* digestion; **corte de d.,** sudden indigestion.
digestivo,-a *adj* easy to digest.

digital adj digital; **huellas digitales,** fingerprints; **tocadiscos d.,** CD player.

digitalizar vtr digitize.

dígito nm digit.

dignarse vr to deign (**a,** to), condescend (**a,** to).

dignidad nf dignity.

digno,-a adj 1 (merecedor) worthy; **d. de admiración,** worthy of admiration; **d. de mención/verse,** worth mentioning/seeing. 2 (decoroso) decent, good.

digo indic pres → **decir.**

dije pt indef → **decir.**

dilación nf delay, hold-up; **sin d.,** without delay.

dilatado,-a adj 1 (agrandado) dilated. 2 (vasto) vast, extensive.

dilatar I vtr 1 (agrandar) to expand. 2 (pupila) to dilate. II **dilatarse** vr 1 (agrandarse) to expand. 2 (pupila) to dilate.

dilema nm dilemma.

diligencia nf 1 diligence; **con d.,** diligently. 2 **diligencias,** formalities.

diligente adj diligent.

dilucidar vtr to elucidate, clarify.

diluir [37] I vtr to dilute. II **diluirse** vr to dilute.

diluviar [12] v impers to pour with rain.

diluvio nm flood; **el D. (Universal),** the Flood.

diluyo indic pres → **diluir.**

dimensión nf 1 dimension, size; **de gran d.,** very large. 2 fig (importancia) importance.

diminutivo,-a adj & nm diminutive.

diminuto,-a adj minute, tiny.

dimisión nf resignation; **presentar la d.,** to hand in one's resignation.

dimitir vi to resign (**de,** from); **d. de un cargo,** to give in o tender one's resignation.

Dinamarca nf Denmark.

dinámica nf dynamics sing.

dinámico,-a adj dynamic.

dinamita nf dynamite.

dinamitar vtr to dynamite.

dinamo, dínamo nf dynamo.

dinar nm Fin dinar.

dinastía nf dynasty.

dineral nm fam fortune.

dinero nm money; **d. contante (y sonante),** cash; **d. efectivo** o **en metálico,** cash; **gente de d.,** wealthy people.

dinosaurio nm dinosaur.

diócesis nf inv diocese.

dios nm god; **¡D. mío!,** my God!; **¡por D.!,** for goodness sake!; **a la buena de D.,** any old how; **hacer algo como D. manda,** to do sth properly; **arg ni d.,** nobody; **arg todo d.,** everybody.

diosa nf goddess.

diploma nm diploma.

diplomacia nf diplomacy.

diplomarse vr to graduate.

diplomático,-a adj diplomatic; **cuerpo d.,** diplomatic corps. II nm,f diplomat.

diptongo nm diphthong.

diputación nf **d. provincial,** ≈ county council.

diputado,-a nm,f ≈ Member of Parliament, M.P.; US (hombre) Congressman; (mujer) Congresswoman; **Congreso de Diputados,** ≈ House of Commons, US Congress; **d. provincial,** ≈ county councillor.

dique nm dike.

diré fut → **decir.**

dirección nf 1 direction; **d. prohibida,** no entry; **calle de d. única,** one-way street. 2 (señas) address. 3 Cin Teat direction. 4 (destino) destination. 5 Aut Téc steering. 6 (dirigentes) management; (cargo) directorship; (de un partido) leadership; (de un colegio) headship.

directa nf Aut top gear.

directiva nf board of directors, management.

directivo,-a adj directive; **junta directiva,** board of directors.

directo,-a adj direct; TV Rad **en d.,** live. ◆**directamente** adv directly, straight away.

director,-a nm,f director; (de colegio) (hombre) headmaster; (mujer) headmistress; (de periódico) editor; **d. de cine,** (film) director; **d. de orquesta,** conductor; **d. gerente,** managing director.

directorio nm Inform directory.

directriz nf directive; Mat directrix.

dirigente I adj leading; **clase d.,** ruling class. II nm,f leader.

dirigir [6] I vtr to direct; (empresa) to manage; (negocio, colegio) to run; (orquesta) to conduct; (partido) to lead; (periódico) to edit; (coche, barco) to steer; **d. la palabra a algn,** to speak to sb. II **dirigirse** vr 1 **d. a** o **hacia,** to go to, make one's way towards. 2 (escribir) to write; **diríjase al apartado de correos 42,** write to P.O. Box 42. 3 (hablar) to speak.

discapacidad nf disability.

discernir [5] vtr to discern.

disciplina nf discipline.

disciplinado,-a adj disciplined.

discípulo,-a nm,f disciple.

disco nm 1 disc, US disk; **d. de freno,** brake disc. 2 Mús record; **d. compacto,** compact disc. 3 Inform disk; **d. duro** o **fijo/flexible,** hard/floppy disk. 4 Dep discus. 5 Tel dial.

discográfico,-a adj **casa/compañía discográfica,** record company.

disconforme adj **estar d. con,** to disagree with.

discontinuo,-a adj discontinuous; Aut **línea discontinua,** broken line.

discordante *adj* discordant; **ser la nota d.**, to be the odd man out.

discordia *nf* discord; **la manzana de la d.**, the bone of contention; **sembrar d.**, to sow discord.

discoteca *nf* 1 (*lugar*) discotheque. 2 (*colección*) record collection.

discreción *nf* 1 discretion. 2 **a d.**, at will.

discrecional *adj* optional; **servicio d.**, special service.

discrepancia *nf* (*desacuerdo*) disagreement; (*diferencia*) discrepancy.

discrepar *vi* (*disentir*) to disagree (**de**, with; **en**, on); (*diferenciarse*) to be different (**de**, from).

discreto,-a *adj* 1 discreet. 2 (*mediocre*) average.

discriminación *nf* discrimination.

discriminar *vtr* 1 to discriminate against. 2 *fml* (*diferenciar*) to discriminate between, distinguish.

disculpa *nf* excuse; **dar disculpas**, to make excuses; **pedir disculpas a algn**, to apologize to sb.

disculpar I *vtr* to excuse. II **disculparse** *vr* to apologize (**por**, for).

discurrir *vi* 1 (*reflexionar*) to think. 2 *fig* (*transcurrir*) to pass, go by. 3 *fml* (*río*) to wander.

discurso *nm* speech; **dar o pronunciar un d.**, to make a speech.

discusión *nf* argument.

discutir I *vi* to argue (**de**, about). II *vtr* to discuss, talk about.

disecar [1] *vtr* 1 (*animal*) to stuff. 2 (*planta*) to dry.

diseminar *vtr* to disseminate, spread.

disentir [5] *vi* to dissent, disagree (**de**, with).

diseñar *vtr* to design.

diseño *nm* design; **d. de interiores**, interior design.

disertar *vi* to expound (**sobre**, on, upon).

disfraz *nm* disguise; (*para fiesta*) fancy dress; **fiesta de disfraces**, fancy dress party.

disfrazar [4] I *vtr* to disguise. II **disfrazarse** *vr* to disguise oneself; **d. de pirata**, to dress up as a pirate.

disfrutar I *vi* 1 (*gozar*) to enjoy oneself. 2 (*poseer*) to enjoy (**de**, -). II *vtr* to enjoy.

disgregar [7] *vtr* 1 to disintegrate, break up. 2 (*dispersar*) to disperse.

disgustado,-a *adj* upset, displeased.

disgustar I *vtr* to upset. II **disgustarse** *vr* 1 (*molestarse*) to get upset, be annoyed. 2 (*dos amigos*) to quarrel.

disgusto *nm* 1 (*preocupación*) upset; **llevarse un d.**, to get upset; **dar un d. a algn**, to upset sb. 2 (*desgracia*) trouble; **a d.**, unwillingly; **sentirse o estar a d.**, to feel ill at ease. 3 (*desavenencia*) fall-out.

disidente *adj & nmf* dissident.

disimulado,-a *adj* 1 (*persona*) sly, crafty.

2 (*oculto*) hidden, concealed.

◆disimuladamente *adv* surreptitiously.

disimular *vtr* to conceal, hide.

disimulo *nm* pretence.

disipar I *vtr* (*niebla*) to drive away; (*temor*, *duda*) to dispel. II **disiparse** *vr* (*gaseosa*) to go flat; (*niebla*, *temor etc*) to disappear.

disketera *nf Inform* disk drive.

dislexia *nf* dyslexia.

dislocar [1] *vtr* to dislocate.

disminución *nf* decrease.

disminuir [37] I *vtr* to reduce. II *vi* to diminish.

disolución *nf* dissolution.

disolvente *adj & nm* solvent.

disolver [4] (*pp disuelto*) *vtr* to dissolve.

disparar I *vtr* (*pistola etc*) to fire; (*flecha*, *balón*) to shoot; **d. a algn**, to shoot at sb. II **dispararse** *vr* 1 (*arma*) to go off, fire. 2 (*precios*) to rocket.

disparatado,-a *adj* absurd.

disparate *nm* 1 (*dicho*) nonsense; **decir disparates**, to talk nonsense. 2 (*acto*) foolish act.

disparidad *nf* disparity.

disparo *nm* shot; *Dep* **d. a puerta**, shot.

dispensar *vtr* 1 (*disculpar*) to pardon, forgive. 2 (*eximir*) to exempt.

dispersar I *vtr* to disperse; (*esparcir*) to scatter. II **dispersarse** *vr* to disperse.

disperso,-a *adj* (*separado*) dispersed; (*esparcido*) scattered.

displicencia *nf* condescension.

displicente *adj* condescending.

disponer [19] (*pp dispuesto*) I *vtr* 1 (*arreglar*) to arrange, set out. 2 (*ordenar*) to order. II *vi* **d. de**, to have at one's disposal. III **disponerse** *vr* to prepare, get ready.

disponible *adj* available.

disposición *nf* 1 (*uso*) disposal; **a su d.**, at your disposal *o* service. 2 (*colocación*) arrangement, layout. 3 **no estar en d. de**, not to be prepared to. 4 (*orden*) order, law.

dispositivo *nm* device.

dispuesto,-a *adj* 1 (*ordenado*) arranged. 2 (*a punto*) ready. 3 (*decidido*) determined; **no estar a**, not to be prepared to. 4 **según lo d. por la ley**, in accordance with what the law stipulates.

disputa *nf* (*discusión*) argument; (*contienda*) contest.

disputar I *vtr* (*premio*) to compete for. 2 *Dep* (*partido*) to play. II **disputarse** *vr* (*premio*) to compete for.

disquete *nm Inform* diskette, floppy disk.

disquetera *nf Inform* disk drive.

distancia *nf* distance; **a d.**, from a distance.

distanciamiento *nm* distancing.

distanciar [12] I *vtr* to separate. II **distanciarse** *vr* to become separated; (*de*

otra persona) to distance oneself.
distante adj distant, far-off.
distar vi to be distant o away; fig to be far from; **dista mucho de ser perfecto**, it's far from (being) perfect.
distender [3] vtr fig to ease, relax.
distensión f Pol détente.
distinción nf distinction; **a d. de**, unlike; **sin d. de**, irrespective of.
distinguido,-a adj distinguished.
distinguir [8] I vtr 1 (diferenciar) to distinguish. 2 (reconocer) to recognize. 3 (honrar) to honour, US honor. II vi (diferenciar) to discriminate. III **distinguirse** vr to distinguish oneself.
distintivo,-a I adj distinctive, distinguishing. II nm distinctive sign o mark.
distinto,-a adj different.
distorsión nf 1 distortion. 2 Med sprain.
distracción nf 1 entertainment; (pasatiempo) pastime, hobby. 2 (descuido) distraction, absent-mindedness.
distraer [25] I vtr 1 (atención) to distract. 2 (divertir) to entertain, amuse. II **distraerse** vr 1 (divertirse) to amuse oneself. 2 (abstraerse) to let one's mind wander.
distraído,-a adj 1 (divertido) entertaining. 2 (abstraído) absent-minded.
distribución nf distribution. 2 (disposición) layout.
distribuidor,-a I adj distributing. II nm,f 1 distributor. 2 Com wholesaler.
distribuir [37] vtr to distribute; (trabajo) to share out.
distrito nm district; **d. postal**, postal district.
disturbio nm riot, disturbance.
disuadir vtr to dissuade.
disuasión nf dissuasion.
disuelto,-a pp → **disolver**.
DIU nm abr de **dispositivo intrauterino**, intrauterine device, IUD.
diurético,-a adj & nm diuretic.
diurno,-a adj daytime.
divagar [7] vi to digress, wander.
diván nm divan, couch.
divergencia nf divergence.
divergente adj diverging.
diversidad nf diversity.
diversificar [1] I vtr to diversify. II **diversificarse** vr to be diversified o varied; (empresa) to diversify.
diversión nf fun.
diverso,-a adj different; **diversos**, several, various.
divertido,-a adj amusing, funny.
divertir [5] I vtr to amuse, entertain. II **divertirse** vr to enjoy oneself, have a good time; **¡que te diviertas!**, enjoy yourself!, have fun!
dividendo nm dividend.
dividir vtr to divide (**en**, into); Mat 15 **dividido entre 3**, 15 divided by 3. II **dividirse** vr to divide, split up.

divinidad nf divinity.
divino,-a adj divine.
divisa nf 1 (emblema) symbol, emblem. 2 Com **divisas**, foreign currency sing.
divisar vtr to make out, discern.
división nf division.
divisorio,-a adj dividing.
divorciado,-a I adj divorced. II nm,f (hombre) divorcé; (mujer) divorcée.
divorciar [12] I vtr to divorce. II **divorciarse** vr to get divorced; **se divorció de él**, she divorced him, she got a divorce from him.
divorcio nm divorce.
divulgación nf disclosure.
divulgar [7] vtr to disclose; Rad TV to broadcast.
DNI nm abr de **Documento Nacional de Identidad**, Identity Card, ID card.
do nm Mús (de solfa) doh, do; (de escala diatónica) C; **do de pecho**, high C.
doberman nm Doberman (pinscher).
dobladillo nm hem.
doblaje nm Cin dubbing.
doblar [7] I vtr to double; **me dobla la edad**, he is twice as old as I am. 2 (plegar) to fold o turn up. 3 (torcer) to bend. 4 (la esquina) to go round. 5 (película) to dub. II vi 1 (girar) to turn; **d. a la derecha/izquierda**, to turn right/left. 2 (campanas) to toll. III **doblarse** o vr 1 (plegarse) to fold. 2 (torcerse) to bend.
doble I adj double; **arma de d. filo**, double-edged weapon. II nm 1 double; **gana el d. que tú**, she earns twice as much as you do. 2 Dep **dobles**, doubles.
doblegar [7] I vtr to bend. II **doblegarse** vr to give in.
doblez I nm (pliegue) fold. II nm & f fig two-facedness, hypocrisy.
doce adj & nm inv twelve.
docena nf dozen.
docencia nf teaching.
docente adj teaching; **centro d.**, educational centre.
dócil adj docile.
doctor,-a nm,f doctor.
doctorado nm Univ doctorate, PhD.
doctrina nf doctrine.
documentación nf documentation; (DNI, de conducir etc) papers pl.
documental adj & nm documentary.
documentar I vtr to document. II **documentarse** vr to research (**sobre**, -), get information (**sobre**, about o on).
documento nm document; **d. nacional de identidad**, identity card.
dogma nm dogma.
dogmático,-a adj & nm,f dogmatic.
dogo nm bulldog.
dólar nm dollar.
dolencia nf ailment.
doler [4] I vi 1 to hurt, ache; **me duele la cabeza**, I've got toothache/a headache;

me duele la mano, my hand is sore. II **dolerse** *vr* to be sorry *o* sad.

dolido,-a *adj* **estar d.,** to be hurt.

dolor *nm* 1 *Med* pain; **d. de cabeza,** headache; **d. de muelas,** toothache. 2 *(pena)* grief, sorrow.

dolorido,-a *adj* 1 *(dañado)* sore, aching. 2 *(apenado)* hurt.

doloroso,-a *adj* painful.

domar *vtr* to tame; *(caballo)* to break in.

domesticar [1] *vtr* to domesticate; *(animal)* to tame.

doméstico,-a *adj* domestic; **animal d.,** pet.

domiciliación *nf* payment by standing order.

domiciliar [12] *vtr* 1 to house. 2 *Fin* to pay by standing order.

domiciliario,-a *adj* **arresto d.,** house arrest.

domicilio *nm* home, residence; *(señas)* address; **sin d. fijo,** of no fixed abode; **d. fiscal,** registered office.

dominación *nf* domination.

dominante *adj* 1 dominant. 2 *(déspota)* domineering.

dominar I *vtr* 1 to dominate, rule. 2 *(situación)* to control; *(idioma)* to speak very well; *(asunto)* to master; *(paisaje etc)* to overlook. II *vi* 1 to dominate. 2 *(resaltar)* to stand out. III **dominarse** *vr* to control oneself.

domingo *nm inv* Sunday; **D. de Resurrección** *o* **Pascua,** Easter Sunday.

dominguero,-a *nm,f fam* *(excursionista)* weekend tripper; *(conductor)* weekend driver.

dominical I *adj* Sunday. II *nm* *(suplemento)* Sunday supplement.

dominicano,-a *adj & nm,f* Dominican; **República Dominicana,** Dominican Republic.

dominio *nm* 1 *(poder)* control; *(de un idioma)* command; **d. de sí mismo,** self-control. 2 *(ámbito)* scope, sphere; **ser del d. público,** to be public knowledge. 3 *(territorio)* dominion.

dominó, dómino *nm* dominoes *pl.*

don[1] *nm* 1 *(habilidad)* gift, talent; **tener el d. de,** to have a knack for; **tener d. de gentes,** to get on well with people. 2 *(regalo)* present, gift.

don[2] *nm* Señor D. José García, Mr José García; **D. Fulano de Tal,** Mr So-and-So; **d. nadie,** a nobody.

donaire *nm* grace, elegance.

donante *nmf* donor; *Med* **d. de sangre,** blood donor.

donar *vtr fml* to donate; *(sangre)* to give.

donativo *nm* donation.

doncella *nf arc* 1 *(joven)* maid, maiden. 2 *(criada)* maid, housemaid.

dónde *adv interr* where; **¿de d. eres?,** where are you from?; **¿por d. se va a la** playa?, which way is it to the beach?

donde *adv rel* where; **a** *o* **en d.,** where; **de** *o* **desde d.,** from where; **está d. lo dejaste,** it is where you left it; *fam* **está d. su tía,** he's at his aunt's.

dondequiera *adv* everywhere; **d. que vaya,** wherever I go.

donostiarra I *adj* of *o* from San Sebastián. II *nmf* native of San Sebastián.

doña *nf* (Señora) **D. Leonor Benítez,** Mrs Leonor Benítez.

dopaje *nm Dep* drug taking.

dopar I *vtr* *(caballo etc)* to dope. II **doparse** *vr* to take drugs.

doping *nm Dep* drug taking.

doquier, doquiera *adv lit* **por d.,** everywhere.

dorada *nf* *(pez)* gilthead bream.

dorado,-a I *adj* golden. II *nm Téc* gilding.

dorar *vtr* 1 to gild. 2 *Culin* to brown.

dormido,-a *adj* 1 asleep; **quedarse d.,** to fall asleep; *(no despertarse)* to oversleep, sleep in. 2 *(pierna, brazo)* numb.

dormilón,-ona I *adj fam* sleepyheaded. II *nm,f* sleepyhead.

dormir [7] I *vi* to sleep; **tener ganas de d.,** to feel sleepy; II *vtr* **d. la siesta,** to have an afternoon nap. III **dormirse** *vr* to fall asleep; **se me ha dormido el brazo,** my arm has gone to sleep.

dormitar *vi* to doze, snooze.

dormitorio *nm* 1 *(de una casa)* bedroom. 2 *(de colegio, residencia)* dormitory; **ciudad d.,** dormitory town.

dorsal I *adj* **espina d.,** spine. II *nm Dep* number.

dorso *nm* back; **instrucciones al d.,** instructions over; **véase al d.,** see overleaf.

dos *adj & nm inv* two; **los d.,** both; **nosotros/vosotros d.,** both of us/you; *fam* **cada d. por tres,** every other minute; *fam* **en un d. por tres,** in a flash.

doscientos,-as *adj & nm,f* two hundred.

dosel *nm* canopy.

dosificación *nf* dosage.

dosificar [1] *vtr* 1 to dose. 2 *(esfuerzos, energías)* to measure.

dosis *nf inv* dose.

dossier *nm* dossier.

dotación *nf* *(dinero)* grant; *(personal)* personnel, staff; *(de barco)* crew.

dotado,-a *adj* 1 *(persona)* gifted. 2 *(equipado)* equipped; **d. de,** provided with.

dotar *vtr* **d. de,** to provide with.

dote *nf* 1 *(de novia)* dowry. 2 **dotes,** *(talento)* gift, talent; *fam* **talent** *sing.*

doy *indic pres* → **dar.**

DP *nm abr de* **distrito postal,** postal district, PD.

dpt. *abr de* **departamento,** department, Dept.

Dr. *abr de* **doctor,** doctor, Dr.

Dra. *abr de* **doctora,** doctor, Dr.

dragar [7] *vtr* to dredge.

dragón *nm* dragon.

drama *nm* drama.

dramático,-a *adj* dramatic.

dramatismo *nm* drama.

dramaturgo,-a *nm,f* playwright, dramatist.

drástico,-a *adj* drastic.

drenar *vt* to drain.

driblar *vi* to dribble.

droga *nf* drug; **d. blanda/dura**, soft/hard drug.

drogadicto,-a *nm,f* drug addict.

drogar [7] **I** *vtr* to drug. **II drogarse** *vr* to drug oneself, take drugs.

droguería *nf* hardware and household goods shop.

dto. *abr de* **descuento**, discount.

dual *adj* dual.

dualidad *nf* duality.

dubitativo,-a *adj* doubtful.

Dublín *n* Dublin.

dublinés,-esa I *adj* of o from Dublin. **II** *nm,f* Dubliner.

ducha *nf* shower; **darse/tomar una d.**, to take/have a shower.

ducharse *vr* to shower, have o take a shower.

ducho,-a *adj* expert; **ser d. en**, to be well versed in.

duda *nf* doubt; **sin d.**, without a doubt; **no cabe d.**, (there is) no doubt; **poner algo en d.**, to question sth; **sacar a algn de dudas**, to dispel sb's doubts.

dudar I *vi* **1** to doubt. **2** (*vacilar*) to hesitate (**en**, to); **dudaba entre ir o quedarme**, I hesitated whether to go o to stay. **3 d. de algn**, (*desconfiar*) to suspect sb. **II** *vtr* to doubt.

dudoso,-a *adj* **1 ser d.**, (*incierto*) to be uncertain o doubtful. **2** (*vacilante*) (*indeciso*) to be undecide. **3** (*poco honrado*) dubious.

duelo¹ *nm* (*combate*) duel.

duelo² *nm* (*luto*) mourning.

duende *nm* **1** (*espíritu*) goblin, elf. **2** (*encanto*) magic, charm.

dueña *nf* owner; (*de pensión*) landlady.

dueño *nm* owner; (*de casa etc*) landlord; *fig* **ser d. de sí mismo**, to be self-possessed.

Duero *n* **el D.**, the Douro.

dulce I *adj* **1** (*sabor*) sweet. **2** (*carácter, voz*) gentle. **3** (*metal*) soft. **4 agua d.**, fresh water. **II** *nm* **1** Culin (*pastel*) cake. **2** (*caramelo*) sweet, US candy.

dulzura *nf* **1** sweetness. **2** *fig* gentleness, softness.

duna *nf* dune.

dúo *nm* duet.

duodécimo,-a *adj & nm,f* twelfth.

dúplex *nm* **1** (*piso*) duplex, duplex apartment. **2** *Telec* linkup.

duplicado,-a I *adj* **por d.**, in duplicate. **II** *nm* duplicate, copy.

duplicar [1] **I** *vtr* to duplicate; (*cifras*) to double. **II duplicarse** *vr* to double.

duplo,-a *adj & nm,f* double.

duque *nm* duke.

duquesa *nf* duchess.

duración *nf* duration, length; **disco de larga d.**, long-playing record.

duradero,-a *adj* durable, lasting.

durante *prep* during; **d. el día**, during the day; **d. todo el día**, all day long; **viví en La Coruña d. un año**, I lived in La Coruña for a year.

durar *vi* **1** to last. **2** (*ropa, calzado*) to wear well, last.

durazno *nm* (*fruto*) peach; (*árbol*) peach tree.

dureza *nf* **1** hardness; (*severidad*) harshness, severity. **2** (*callosidad*) corn.

duro,-a I *adj* **1** hard; *Dep* **juego d.**, rough play. **2** (*resistente*) tough; (*severo*) hard. **3** (*clima*) harsh. **4** *nm* (*moneda*) five-peseta coin. **III** *adv* hard; **trabajar d.**, to work hard.

E

E, e [e] *nf* (*la letra*) E, e.

E *abr de* **Este**, East, E.

e *conj* (*delante de palabras que empiecen por* **i** *o* **hi**) and; **verano e invierno**, summer and winter.

ebanista *nm* cabinet-maker.

ébano *nm* ebony.

ebrio,-a *adj* inebriated; **e. de dicha**, drunk with joy.

ebullición *nf* boiling; **punto de e.**, boiling point.

eccema *nm* eczema.

echar I *vtr* **1** (*lanzar*) to throw; *fig* **e. una mano**, to give a hand; *fig* **e. una mirada/ una ojeada**, to have a look/a quick look o glance. **2** (*carta*) to post; (*vino, agua*) to pour; **e. sal al estofado**, to put salt in the stew; **e. gasolina al coche**, to put petrol in the car. **3** (*expulsar*) to throw out; (*despedir*) to sack, fire. **4** (*humo, olor etc*) to give off. **5** *fam* (*película*) to show. **6 le echó 37 años**, he reckoned she was about 37. **7 e. de menos o en falta**, to miss. **8 e. abajo**, (*edificio*) to demolish. **II** *vi* (+ **a** + *infin*) (*empezar*) to begin to; **echó a correr**, he ran off. **III echarse** *vr* **1** (*tumbarse*) to lie down; (*lanzarse*) to throw oneself; *fig* **la noche se nos echó encima**, it was night before we knew it. **2 échate a un lado**, stand aside; *fig* e. atrás, to get cold feet. 3 *fam* e. novio/novia, to get a boyfriend/girlfriend. 4 (+ a + *infin*) (*empezar*) to begin to; e. a llorar, to burst into tears; e. a reír, to burst out laughing; e. a perder, (*comida*) to go bad.

ecléctico,-a *adj & nm,f* eclectic.

eclesiástico,-a I *adj* ecclesiastical. II *nm* clergyman.

eclipsar *vtr* to eclipse.

eclipse *nm* eclipse.

eco *nm* echo; *fig* hacerse e. de una noticia, to publish an item of news; tener e., to arouse interest.

ecografía *nf* scan.

ecología *nf* ecology.

ecológico,-a *adj* ecological.

ecologista I *adj* ecological; *Pol* partido e., ecology party. II *nmf* ecologist.

economía *nf* 1 economy; con e., economically. 2 (*ciencia*) economics.

económico,-a *adj* 1 economic. 2 (*barato*) economical, inexpensive. 3 (*persona*) thrifty.

economista *nmf* economist.

economizar [4] *vtr & vi* to economize.

ecosistema *nm* ecosystem.

ecuación *nf* equation.

Ecuador *n* Ecuador.

ecuador *nm Geog* equator.

ecualizador *nm* graphic equalizer.

ecuánime *adj* 1 (*temperamento*) equable, even-tempered. 2 (*juicio*) impartial.

ecuatorial *adj* equatorial; Guinea E., Ecuatorial Guinea.

ecuatoriano,-a *adj & nm,f* Ecuadorian.

ecuestre *adj* equestrian.

ecuménico,-a *adj* ecumenical.

eczema *nm* eczema.

edad *nf* age; ¿qué e. tienes?, how old are you?; la tercera e., senior citizens *pl*; E. Media, Middle Ages *pl*.

edición *nf* 1 (*publicación*) publication; (*de sellos*) issue. 2 (*conjunto de ejemplares*) edition.

edicto *nm* edict, proclamation.

edificante *adj* edifying.

edificar [1] *vtr* to build.

edificio *nm* building.

edil,-a *nm,f* town councillor.

Edimburgo *n* Edinburgh.

editar *vtr* 1 (*libro, periódico*) to publish; (*disco*) to release. 2 *Inform* to edit.

editor,-a I *adj* publishing. II *nm,f* publisher.

editorial I *adj* publishing. II *nf* publishers, publishing house. III *nm Prensa* editorial, leader article.

edredón *nm* continental quilt, duvet, *US* comforter.

educación *nf* 1 education. 2 (*formación*) upbringing. 3 buena/mala e., (*modales*) good/bad manners; falta de e., bad manners.

educado,-a *adj* polite.

educador,-a I *adj* educating. II *nm,f* educationalist.

educar [1] *vtr* (*hijos*) to raise; (*alumnos*) to educate; (*la voz*) to train.

educativo,-a *adj* educational; sistema e., education system.

edulcorante *nm* sweetener.

EE.UU. *abr de* Estados Unidos, United States of America, USA.

efectista *adj* spectacular.

efectividad *nf* effectiveness.

efectivo,-a I *adj* effective; hacer algo e., to carry sth out; *Fin* hacer e. un cheque, to cash a cheque. II *nm* 1 Fin en e., in cash. 2 efectivos, *Mil* forces. ◆efectivamente *adv* quite!, yes indeed!

efecto *nm* 1 (*resultado*) effect; efectos especiales/sonoros, special/sound effects; efectos personales, personal belongings *o* effects; a efectos de ..., for the purposes of ...; en e., quite!, yes indeed! 2 (*impresión*) impression; causar *o* hacer e., to make an impression. 3 *Dep* spin.

efectuar [30] *vtr* to carry out; (*viaje*) to make; (*pedido*) to place.

efeméride *nf* event.

efervescente *adj* effervescent; aspirina e., soluble aspirin.

eficacia *nf* (*de persona*) efficiency; (*de remedio etc*) effectiveness.

eficaz *adj* (*persona*) efficient; (*remedio, medida etc*) effective.

eficiencia *nf* efficiency.

eficiente *adj* efficient.

efigie *nf* effigy.

efímero,-a *adj* ephemeral.

efusivo,-a *adj* effusive.

EGB *nf Educ abr de* Enseñanza General Básica, ≈ Primary School Education.

Egeo *n* el (Mar) E., the Aegean Sea.

egipcio,-a *adj & nm,f* Egyptian.

Egipto *n* Egypt.

egocéntrico,-a *adj* egocentric, self-centred.

egoísmo *nm* egoism, selfishness.

egoísta I *adj* ego(t)istic, selfish. II *nmf* ego(t)ist, selfish person.

egregio,-a *adj* eminent, illustrious.

egresar *de Am* to leave school, *US* graduate.

Eire *n* Eire, Republic of Ireland.

ej. *abr de* ejemplo, example.

eje *nm* 1 Téc (*de rueda*) axle; (*de máquina*) shaft. 2 *Mat* axis. 3 *Hist* El E., the Axis.

ejecución *nf* 1 (*de orden*) carrying out. 2 (*ajusticiamiento*) execution. 3 *Mús* performance.

ejecutar *vtr* 1 (*orden*) to carry out. 2 (*ajusticiar*) to execute. 3 *Mús* to perform, play. 4 *Inform* to run.

ejecutiva *nf Pol* executive.

ejecutivo,-a I *adj* executive; *Pol* **el poder e.**, the government. II *nm* executive.

ejecutor,-a *nm,f* 1 *Jur* executor. 2 *(verdugo)* executioner.

ejemplar I *nm* 1 *(de libro)* copy; *(de revista, periódico)* number, issue. 2 *(especimen)* specimen. II *adj* exemplary, model.

ejemplificar [1] *vtr* to exemplify.

ejemplo *nm* example; **por e.**, for example; **dar e.**, to set an example.

ejercer [2] I *vtr* 1 *(profesión etc)* to practise. 2 *(influencia)* to exert. 3 **e. el derecho de/a ...**, to exercise one's right to .... II *vi* to practise *(de, as)*.

ejercicio *nm* 1 exercise; *(de profesión)* practice; **hacer e.**, to take *o* do exercise. 2 *Fin* tax year; **e. económico**, financial *o* fiscal year.

ejercitar *vtr* to practise.

ejército *nm* army.

el I *art def m* 1 the. 2 *(no se traduce)* **el Sr. García**, Mr. García; **el hambre/destino**, hunger/fate. 3 *(con partes del cuerpo, prendas de vestir)* **me he cortado el dedo**, I've cut my finger; **métetelo en el bolsillo**, put it in your pocket. 4 *(con días de la semana)* **el lunes**, on Monday. II *pron* 1 the one; **el de las once**, the eleven o'clock one; **el que tienes en la mano**, the one you've got in your hand; **el que quieras**, whichever one you want. 2 *(no se traduce)* **el de tu amigo**, your friend's.

él *pron pers* 1 *(sujeto)* *(persona)* he; *(animal, cosa)* it. 2 *(complemento)* *(persona)* him; *(animal, cosa)* it.

elaboración *nf* 1 *(de un producto)* manufacture, production. 2 *(de una idea)* working out, development.

elaborar *vtr* 1 *(producto)* to manufacture, produce. 2 *(teoría)* to develop.

elasticidad *nf* elasticity; *fig* flexibility.

elástico,-a *adj & nm* elastic.

elección *nf* choice; *Pol* election.

elector,-a *nm,f* elector.

electorado *nm* electorate *pl*.

electoral *adj* electoral; **campaña e.**, election campaign; **colegio e.**, polling station.

electoralismo *nm* electioneering.

electricidad *nf* electricity.

electricista *nmf* electrician.

eléctrico,-a *adj* electric.

electrificar [1] *vtr* to electrify.

electrizar [4] *vtr* to electrify.

electrochoque *nm* electric shock therapy.

electrocutar *vtr* to electrocute.

electrodo *nm* electrode.

electrodoméstico *nm* (domestic) electrical appliance.

electroimán *nm* electromagnet.

electromagnético,-a *adj* electromagnetic.

electrón *nm* electron.

electrónica *nf* electronics *sing*.

electrónico,-a *adj* electronic.

elefante *nm* elephant.

elegancia *nf* elegance.

elegante *adj* elegant.

elegía *nf* elegy.

elegir [6] *vtr* 1 to choose. 2 *Pol* to elect.

elemental *adj* 1 *(fundamental)* basic, fundamental. 2 *(simple)* elementary.

elemento *nm* 1 element. 2 *(componente)* component, part. 3 *(individuo)* type, individual. 4 **elementos**, elements; *(fundamentos)* rudiments.

elepé *nm* LP (record).

elevación *nf* elevation; **e. de precios**, rise in prices; **e. del terreno**, rise in the ground.

elevado,-a *adj* 1 high; *(edificio)* tall. 2 *(pensamiento etc)* lofty, noble.

elevalunas *nm inv Aut* **e. eléctrico**, electric windows.

elevar I *vtr* to raise. II **elevarse** *vr* 1 *(subir)* to rise; *(edificio)* to stand. 2 **e. a**, *(cantidad)* to amount *o* come to.

elijo *indic pres* → **elegir**.

eliminación *nf* elimination.

eliminar *vtr* to eliminate.

eliminatoria *nf* *Dep* heat, qualifying round.

eliminatorio,-a *adj* qualifying, eliminatory.

élite *nf* elite, élite.

elitista *adj* elitist.

elixir *nm* *(enjuage bucal)* mouthwash; *Lit* elixir.

ella *pron pers f* 1 *(sujeto)* she; *(animal, cosa)* it, she. 2 *(complemento)* her; *(animal, cosa)* it, her.

ellas *pron pers fpl* → **ellos**.

ello *pron pers neut* it; **por e.**, for that reason.

ellos *pron pers mpl* 1 *(sujeto)* they. 2 *(complemento)* them.

elocuencia *nf* eloquence.

elocuente *adj* eloquent; **los hechos son elocuentes**, the facts speak for themselves.

elogiar [12] *vtr* to praise.

elogio *nm* praise.

elote *nm* *Am* tender corncob.

El Salvador *n* El Salvador.

elucidar *vtr* to elucidate.

eludir *vtr* to avoid.

emanar *vi* to emanate; *fig* *(derivar)* to derive *o* come (**de**, from).

emancipar I *vtr* to emancipate. II **emanciparse** *vr* to become emancipated.

embadurnar *vtr* to daub, smear (**de**, with).

embajada *nf* embassy.

embajador,-a *nm,f* ambassador.

embalaje *nm* packing, packaging.

embalar *vtr* to pack.

embalarse *vr* to speed up; *fig* **no te embales**, hold your horses.

embalsamar *vtr* to embalm.

embalsar I *vtr* to dam; (*problema*) to contain. **II embalsarse** *vr* to form a pool.

embalse *nm* dam, reservoir.

embarazada I *adj* pregnant; **dejar e.**, to get pregnant. **II** *nf* pregnant woman, expectant mother.

embarazar [4] *vtr fig* to hinder.

embarazo *nm* **1** (*preñez*) pregnancy. **2** (*obstáculo*) obstacle. **3** (*turbación*) embarrassment.

embarazoso,-a *adj* awkward, embarrassing.

embarcación *nf* **1** (*nave*) boat, craft. **2** (*embarco*) embarkation.

embarcadero *nm* quay.

embarcar [1] **I** *vtr* to ship. **II** *vi* to embark, go on board. **III embarcarse** *vr* **1** *Naut* to go on board (**en**, -). **2 e. en un proyecto**, to embark on a project.

embarco *nm* embarkation.

embargar [7] *vtr* **1** *Jur* to seize, impound. **2** *fig* **le embarga la emoción**, he's overwhelmed with joy.

embargo *nm* **1** *Jur* seizure of property. **2** *Com Pol* embargo. **3 sin e.**, however, nevertheless.

embarque *nm* (*de persona*) boarding; (*de mercancías*) loading; **tarjeta de e.**, boarding card.

embarrancar(se) [1] *vi & vr Náut* to run aground.

embaucador,-a I *adj* deceitful. **II** *nm,f* swindler, cheat.

embaucar [1] *vtr* to swindle, cheat.

embeber I *vtr* to soak up. **II embeberse** *vr* to become absorbed *o* engrossed in.

embelesar *vtr* to fascinate.

embellecer [33] *vtr* to embellish.

embestida *nf* **1** onslaught. **2** *Taur* charge.

embestir [6] *vtr* **1** *Taur* to charge. **2** (*atacar*) to attack.

emblandecer [33] **I** *vtr* to soften. **II emblandecerse** *vr fig* to relent.

emblema *nm* emblem.

embobado,-a *adj* fascinated.

embobarse *vr* to be fascinated *o* besotted (**con, de**, by).

embolia *nf* embolism.

émbolo *nm* piston.

embolsar *vtr*, **embolsarse** *vr* to pocket.

emborrachar *vtr*, **emborracharse** *vr* to get drunk.

emboscada *nf* ambush; **tender una e.**, to lay an ambush.

embotar *vtr* to blunt; *fig* (*sentidos*) to dull; (*mente*) to befuddle.

embotellado *nm* bottling.

embotellamiento *nm* *Aut* traffic jam.

embotellar *vtr* **1** to bottle. **2** (*tráfico*) to block.

embragar [7] *vi Aut* to engage the clutch.

embrague *nm* clutch.

embravecerse [33] *vr* **1** (*enfadarse*) to become enraged. **2** (*mar*) to become rough.

embriagador,-a *adj* intoxicating.

embriagar [7] **I** *vtr* to intoxicate; *fig* to enrapture. **II embriagarse** *vr* to get drunk; *fig* to be enraptured.

embriaguez *nf* intoxication.

embridar *vtr* to bridle.

embrión *nm* embryo.

embrollar I *vtr* to confuse, muddle. **II embrollarse** *vr* to get muddled *o* confused.

embrollo *nm* **1** (*lío*) muddle, confusion. **2** (*aprieto*) fix, jam.

embrujado,-a *adj* (*persona*) bewitched; (*sitio*) haunted.

embrujo *nm* spell, charm; *fig* attraction, fascination.

embrutecer [33] *vtr* to stultify.

embuchar *vtr* to stuff.

embudo *nm* funnel.

embuste *nm* lie, trick.

embustero,-a *nm,f* cheater, liar.

embutido *nm* sausage.

embutir [3] *vtr* **1** (*carne*) to stuff. **2** (*meter*) to stuff *o* cram *o* squeeze (**en**, into). **3** (*incrustar*) to inlay.

emergencia *nf* emergency; **salida de e.**, emergency exit; **en caso de e.**, in an emergency.

emerger [5] *vi* to emerge.

emigración *nf* emigration; (*de pájaros*) migration.

emigrado,-a *nm,f* emigrant; *Pol* émigré.

emigrante *adj & nmf* emigrant.

emigrar *vi* to emigrate; (*pájaros*) to migrate.

eminencia *nf* eminence; (*genio*) genius.

eminente *adj* eminent.

emirato *nm* emirate.

emisario,-a *nm,f* emissary.

emisión *nf* **1** emission. **2** (*de bonos, sellos*) issue. **3** *Rad TV* broadcasting.

emisora *nf* radio *o* television station.

emitir *vtr* **1** to emit; (*luz, calor*) to give off. **2** (*opinión, juicio*) to express. **3** *Rad TV* to transmit. **4** (*bonos, sellos*) to issue.

emoción *nf* **1** emotion. **2** (*excitación*) excitement; **¡qué e.!**, how exciting!

emocionado,-a *adj* deeply moved *o* touched.

emocionante *adj* **1** (*conmovedor*) moving, touching. **2** (*excitante*) exciting, thrilling.

emocionar *vtr* **1** (*conmover*) to move, touch. **2** (*excitar*) to thrill. **II emocionarse** *vr* **1** (*conmoverse*) to be moved. **2** (*excitarse*) to get excited.

emotivo,-a *adj* emotional.

empacar [1] *vtr* **1** (*mercancías*) to pack. **2** *Am* to annoy.

empachar *vtr* to give indigestion to.

empacho *nm* (*de comida*) indigestion, upset stomach; *fig* surfeit.

empadronar *vtr*, **empadronarse** *vr* to register.

empalagar [7] *vi* to pall.
empalagoso,-a *adj* 1 *(dulce)* sickly sweet. 2 *fig (persona)* smarmy.
empalizada *nf* fence.
empalmar I *vtr* 1 *(unir)* to join; *(cuerdas, cables)* to splice. 2 *Ftb* to volley. II *vi* to converge; *Ferroc* to connect. III **empalmarse** *vr vulg* to get a hard-on.
empalme *nm* 1 connection. 2 *Ferroc* junction; *(en carretera)* intersection, T-junction.
empanada *nf* pie.
empanadilla *nf* pasty.
empanado,-a *adj (filete etc)* breaded, in breadcrumbs.
empantanarse *vr* 1 *(inundarse)* to become flooded. 2 *fig* to be bogged down.
empañar *vtr*, **empañarse** *vr (cristales)* to steam up.
empapado,-a *adj* soaked.
empapar I *vtr* 1 *(mojar)* to soak. 2 *(absorber)* to soak up. II **empaparse** *vr* 1 *(persona)* to get soaked. 3 *fam fig* to take in *(de, -)*.
empapelar *vtr* to wallpaper.
empaque *nm* bearing, presence.
empaquetar *vtr* to pack.
emparedado *nm* sandwich.
emparejar *vtr (cosas)* to match; *(personas)* to pair off.
emparentar *vtr (diente)* to fill.
empaste *nm (de diente)* filling.
empatado,-a *adj* drawn; **estar/ir empatados,** to be drawing.
empatar I *vi Dep* to tie, draw. II *vtr* 1 *Dep* **e. el partido,** to equalize. 2 *Am (unir)* to join.
empate *nm Dep* draw, tie.
empecinarse *vr* to dig one's heels in.
empedernido,-a *adj (fumador, bebedor)* hardened.
empedrado,-a I *adj* cobbled. III *nm* 1 *(adoquines)* cobblestones *pl.* 2 *(acción)* paving.
empeine *nm* instep.
empellón *nm* push, shove.
empeñar I *vtr* to pawn, *US* hock. II **empeñarse** *vr* 1 *(insistir)* to insist (en, on), be determined (en, to). 2 *(endeudarse)* to get into debt.
empeño *nm* 1 *(insistencia)* insistence; **poner e. en algo,** to put a lot of effort into sth. 2 *(deuda)* pledge; **casa de empeños,** pawnshop.
empeoramiento *nm* deterioration, worsening.
empeorar I *vi* to deteriorate, worsen. II *vtr* to make worse. III **empeorarse** *vr* to deteriorate, worsen.
empequeñecer [33] *vtr fig* to belittle.
emperador *nm* emperor.
emperatriz *nf* empress.
emperifollarse *vr fam* to get dolled up.
emperrarse *vr* to dig one's heels in, be-

come stubborn.
empezar [1] *vtr & vi (a hacer algo)* to begin; *(algo)* to start, commence.
empinado,-a *adj (cuesta)* steep.
empinar I *vtr* to raise; *fam* **e. el codo,** to drink. II **empinarse** *vr (persona)* to stand on tiptoe.
empírico,-a *adj* empirical.
emplasto *nm* poultice.
emplazamiento *nm* 1 *(colocación)* site, location. 2 *Jur* summons ring.
emplazar¹ [4] *vtr* to locate, situate.
emplazar² [4] *vtr* 1 *Jur* to summons. 2 *(a una reunión etc)* to call.
empleado,-a *nm,f* employee; *(de oficina, banco)* clerk; **empleada del hogar,** servant, maid.
emplear *vtr* 1 *(usar)* to use; *(contratar)* to employ. 2 *(dinero, tiempo)* to spend.
empleo *nm* 1 *(oficio)* job; *Pol* employment. 2 *(uso)* use; **modo de e.,** instructions for use.
emplomar *vtr Am (diente)* to fill.
empobrecer [33] I *vtr* to impoverish. II **empobrecerse** *vr* to become impoverished *o* poor.
empobrecimiento *nm* impoverishment.
empollar *vtr* 1 *(huevos)* to sit on. 2 *fam (estudiar)* to swot (up), *US* bone up on.
empollón,-ona *fam* I *adj* swotty. II *nm,f* swot.
empolvar I *vtr* to cover in dust. II **empolvarse** *vr (la cara)* to powder.
emponzoñar *vtr* to poison.
emporcar [1] *vtr* to foul, dirty.
emporio *nm* 1 *Com* emporium, trading *o* commercial centre. 2 *Am* department store.
emporrarse *vr arg* to get high.
empotrado,-a *adj* fitted.
emprendedor,-a *adj* enterprising.
emprender *vtr* to undertake; *fam* **emprenderla con algn,** to pick on sb.
empresa *nf* 1 *Com Ind* firm, company. 2 *Pol* **la libre e.,** free enterprise. 3 *(tarea)* undertaking.
empresariado *nm* employers *pl.*
empresarial *adj* 1 *(de empresa)* business; *(ciencias)* **empresariales,** business studies. 2 *(espíritu) entrepreneurial;* **organización e.,** employers' organization.
empresario,-a *nm,f* 1 *(hombre)* businessman; *(mujer)* businesswoman. 2 *(patrón)* employer.
empréstito *nm Fin* debenture loan.
empujar *vtr* to push, shove.
empuje *nm* push; *fig (brío)* verve, get-up-and-go.
empujón *nm* push, shove; **dar empujones,** to push and shove.
empuñadura *nf (de espada)* hilt.
empuñar *vtr* to grasp, seize.
emular *vtr* to emulate.
emulsión *nf* emulsion.

en prep 1 (posición) in, on, at; **en Madrid/ Bolivia,** in Madrid/Bolivia; **en la mesa,** on the table; **en el bolso,** in the bag; **en casa/el trabajo,** at home/work. 2 (movimiento) into; **entró en el cuarto,** he went into the room. 3 (tiempo) in, on, at; **en 1940,** in 1940; **en verano,** in summer; **Am en la mañana,** in the morning; **cae en martes,** it falls on a Tuesday; **en ese momento,** at that moment. 3 (transporte) by, in; **en coche/tren,** by car/train; **en avión,** by air. 4 (modo) in, in Spanish; **en broma,** jokingly; **en serio,** seriously. 5 (reducción, aumento) by; **los precios aumentaron en un diez por ciento,** the prices went up by ten percent. 6 (tema, materia) at, in; **bueno en deportes,** good at sports; **experto en política,** expert in politics. 7 (división, separación) in; **lo dividió en tres partes,** he divided it in three. 8 (con infinitivo) **fue rápido en responder,** he was quick to answer; **la conocí en el andar,** I recognized her by her walk; **ser sobrio en el vestir,** to dress simply.

enaguas nfpl underskirt sing, petticoat sing.

enajenación nf, **enajenamiento** nm alienation; **e. mental,** mental derangement, insanity.

enajenar I vtr 1 Jur to alienate. 2 (turbar) to drive insane. II **enajenarse** vr (enloquecer) to go insane.

enaltecer [33] vtr 1 (alabar) to praise, extol. 2 (ennoblecer) to do credit to.

enamorado,-a I adj in love. II nm,f person in love.

enamorar I vtr to win the heart of. II **enamorarse** vr to fall in love (de, with).

enano,-a adj & nm,f dwarf.

enardecer [33] I vtr (sentimientos) to rouse, stir up; (persona) to fill with enthusiasm. II **enardecerse** vr fig to become excited.

encabezamiento nm (de carta) heading; (de periódico) headline; (preámbulo) foreword, preamble.

encabezar [4] vtr 1 (carta, lista) to head; (periódico) to lead. 2 (rebelión, carrera, movimiento) to lead.

encabritarse vr 1 (caballo) to rear (up). 2 fig (persona) to get cross.

encadenar vtr to chain.

encajar I vtr 1 (ajustar) to insert; **e. la puerta,** to push the door to. 2 fam (asimilar) to take. 3 (comentario) to get in; **e. un golpe a algn,** to land sb a blow. II vi 1 (ajustarse) to fit. 2 fig **e. con,** to fit (in) with, square with.

encaje nm lace.

encalar vtr to whitewash.

encallar vi 1 Náut to run aground. 2 fig to flounder, fail.

encaminado,-a adj **estar bien/mal e.,** to

be on the right/wrong track.

encaminar I vtr to direct. II **encaminarse** vr to head (a, for; hacia, towards).

encandilar vtr to dazzle.

encantado,-a adj 1 (contento) delighted; **e. de conocerle,** pleased to meet you. 2 (embrujado) enchanted.

encantador,-a I adj charming, delightful. II nm,f magician.

encantamiento nm spell.

encantar vtr (hechizar) to bewitch, cast a spell on; fig **me encanta nadar,** I love swimming.

encanto nm 1 (atractivo) charm; **ser un e.,** to be charming. 2 (hechizo) spell.

encapricharse vr to set one's mind (con, on); (encariñarse) to take a fancy (con, to); (enamorarse) to get a crush (con, on).

encapuchado,-a adj hooded.

encaramarse vr to climb up.

encarar I vtr to face, confront. II **encararse** vr **e. con,** to face up to.

encarcelar vtr to imprison, jail.

encarecer [33] I vtr to put up the price of. II **encarecerse** vr to go up (in price).

encarecidamente adv earnestly, insistently; **le rogamos e. que ...,** we would earnestly request you to ....

encarecimiento nm increase o rise in price.

encargado,-a I nm,f Com (hombre) manager; (mujer) manager, manageress; (responsable) person in charge. II adj in charge.

encargar [7] I vtr 1 to put in charge of, entrust with. 2 Com (mercancías) to order, place an order for; (encuesta) to commission. II **encargarse** vr **e. de,** to see to, deal with.

encargo nm 1 Com order; **hecho de e.,** (a petición) made to order. 2 (recado) errand. 3 (tarea) job, assignment.

encariñarse vr to become fond (con, of), get attached (con, to).

encarnación nf incarnation, embodiment.

encarnado,-a adj (rojo) red.

encarnar vtr to personify, embody.

encarnizado,-a adj fierce.

encarrilar vtr (coche, tren) to put on the road or rails; fig to put on the right track.

encasillar vtr to pigeonhole.

encausar vtr to prosecute.

encauzar [4] vtr to channel.

encenagarse [7] vr to get covered in mud.

encendedor nm lighter.

encender [3] I vtr 1 (luz, radio, tele) to switch on, put on; (cigarro, vela, fuego) to light; (cerilla) to strike, light. 2 fig to inflame, stir up. II **encenderse** vr 1 (fuego) to catch; (luz) to go o come on. 2 (cara) to blush, go red.

encendido nm ignition.

encerado nm (pizarra) blackboard.

encerar vtr to wax, polish.

encerrar [1] I vtr to shut in; (con llave) to lock in. 2 fig (contener) to contain, include. II **encerrarse** vr to shut oneself up o in; (con llave) to lock oneself in.

encestar vi Dep to score (a basket).

enchaquetado,-a adj smartly dressed.

encharcar [1] I vtr to flood, swamp. II **encharcarse** vr to get flooded.

enchilada nf Culin stuffed corn pancake seasoned with chili.

enchironar vtr arg to put away.

enchufado,-a I adj fam estar e., to have good connections o contacts. III nm,f fam (favorito) pet.

enchufar vtr I Elec to plug in. 2 (unir) to join, connect. 3 fam (para un trabajo) to pull strings for.

enchufe nm I Elec (hembra) socket; (macho) plug. 2 fam contact.

enchufismo nm fam string-pulling.

encía nf gum.

enciclopedia nf encyclopaedia, encyclopedia.

encierro nm Pol (protesta) sit-in.

encima adv I on top; (arriba) above; (en el aire) overhead; déjalo e., put it on top; ¿llevas cambio e.?, do you have any change on you?; fig quitarse algo de e., to get rid of sth; ahí e., up there. 2 (además) besides. 3 e. de, (sobre) on; (en el aire) above; fig (además) besides; e. de la mesa, on the table. 4 por e., above; fig por e. de sus posibilidades, beyond his abilities; leer un libro por e., to skip through a book.

encimera nf (de cocina) worktop.

encina nf holm o evergreen oak, ilex.

encinta adj pregnant.

enclaustrarse vr to shut oneself up.

enclave nm enclave.

enclenque adj (débil) puny; (enfermizo) sickly.

encoger [5] I vi (contraerse) to contract; (prenda) to shrink. II vtr to contract; (prenda) to shrink. III **encogerse** vr (contraerse) to contract; (prenda) to shrink; e. de hombros, to shrug (one's shoulders).

encolar vtr (papel) to paste; (madera) to glue.

encolerizar [4] I vtr to infuriate, anger. II **encolerizarse** vr to become furious.

encomendar [1] I vtr to entrust with, put in charge of. II **encomendarse** vr to entrust oneself (a, to).

encomienda 1 nf assignment, mission. 2 (paquete postal) parcel.

encomio nm praise.

enconado,-a adj I (discusión) bitter, fierce. 2 Med inflamed, sore.

enconarse vr I (exasperarse) to get angry o irritated. 2 Med (herida) to become inflamed o sore.

encono nm spitefulness, ill feeling.

encontrado,-a adj (contrario) conflicting.

encontrar [2] I vtr I (hallar) to find; **no lo encuentro**, I can't find it; **lo encuentro muy agradable**, I find it very pleasant. 2 (dar con) to meet; (problema) to run into, come up against. II **encontrarse** vr I (persona) to meet. 2 (sentirse) to feel, be; **e. a gusto**, to feel comfortable. 3 (estar) to be.

encontronazo nm I (choque) collision, crash. 2 fig (de ideas etc) clash.

encorvar I vtr to bend. II **encorvarse** vr to stoop o bend (over).

encrespar I vtr (pelo) to curl. 2 (mar) to make choppy o rough. 3 fig (enfurecer) to infuriate. II **encresparse** vr I (mar) to get rough. 2 fig (enfurecerse) to get cross o irritated.

encrucijada nf crossroads.

encrudecer [33] vi, **encrudecerse** vr to get worse.

encuadernación nf I (oficio) bookbinding. 2 (cubierta) binding.

encuadernador,-a nm,f bookbinder.

encuadernar vtr to bind.

encuadrar vtr I (imagen etc) to frame. 2 fig (encajar) to fit, insert.

encuadre nm Cin TV framing.

encubierto,-a adj (secreto) hidden; (operación) covert.

encubridor,-a nm,f Jur accessory (after the fact), abettor.

encubrir vtr to conceal.

encuentro nm I encounter, meeting. 2 Dep meeting, match; **e. amistoso**, friendly match.

encuesta nf I (sondeo) (opinion) poll, survey. 2 (investigación) investigation, inquiry.

encuestado,-a nm,f pollster.

encuestador,-a nm,f pollster.

encuestar vtr to poll.

encumbrar I vtr to exalt. II **encumbrarse** vr to rise to a high (social) position.

ende (por) loc adv therefore.

endeble adj weak, feeble.

endeblez nf weakness, feebleness.

endémico,-a adj Med endemic; fig chronic.

endemoniado,-a adj I (poseso) possessed. 2 fig (travieso) mischievous.

enderezar [4] I vtr (poner derecho) to straighten out; (poner vertical) to set upright. II **enderezarse** vr to straighten up.

endeudarse vr to get o fall into debt.

endiablado,-a adj I (poseso) possessed. 2 (travieso) mischievous, devilish.

endibia nf endive.

endiosar vtr to deify.

endomingarse [7] vr fam to put on one's Sunday best.

endosar vtr I (cheque) to endorse. 2 fam (tarea) to lumber with.

endrina nf Bot sloe.

endrogarse [7] *vr Am* to take drugs, use drugs.

endulzar [4] *vtr* to sweeten.

endurecer [33] I *vtr* to harden. II **endurecerse** *vr* to harden, become hard.

enebro *nm* juniper.

enema *nm* enema.

enemigo,-a I *adj* enemy; **soy e. de la bebida**, I'm against drink. II *nm,f* enemy.

enemistad *nf* hostility, enmity.

enemistar I *vtr* to set at odds, cause a rift between. II **enemistarse** *vr* to become enemies; **e. con algn**, to fall out with sb.

energético,-a *adj* energy.

energía *nf* energy; **e. hidráulica/nuclear**, hydro-electric/nuclear power; **fig e. vital**, vitality.

enérgico,-a *adj* energetic; (*decisión*) firm; (*tono*) emphatic.

energúmeno,-a *nm,f fam* (*hombre*) madman; (*mujer*) mad woman; **ponerse como un e.**, to go up the wall.

enero *nm* January.

enervante *adj* enervating.

enervar *vtr fam* to enervate.

enésimo,-a *adj* 1 *Mat* nth. 2 *fam* umpteenth; **por enésima vez**, for the umpteenth time.

enfadado,-a *adj* angry, annoyed, *US* mad; **estamos enfadados**, we've fallen out with each other.

enfadar I *vtr* to make angry *o* annoyed. II **enfadarse** *vr* 1 to get angry (**con**, with). 2 (*dos personas*) to fall out.

enfado *nm* anger; (*desavenencia*) fall-out.

enfangarse [7] *vr* to get muddy; *fig* to get involved in (dirty business).

énfasis *nm inv* emphasis, stress; **poner e. en algo**, to lay stress on sth.

enfático,-a *adj* emphatic.

enfatizar [4] *vtr* to emphasize, stress.

enfermar *vi*, **enfermarse** *vr* to become *o* fall ill, be taken ill.

enfermedad *nf* illness; (*contagiosa*) disease.

enfermería *nf* infirmary.

enfermero,-a *nm,f* (*mujer*) nurse; (*hombre*) male nurse.

enfermizo,-a *adj* unhealthy, sickly.

enfermo,-a I *adj* ill; **caer e.**, to be taken ill; *fam* **esa gente me pone e.**, those people make me sick. II *nm,f* ill person; (*paciente*) patient.

enfervorizar [4] *vtr* to enthuse.

enfilar *vi* **e. hacia**, to make for.

enflaquecer [33] *vtr* (*adelgazar*) to make thin; (*debilitar*) to weaken.

enfocado,-a *adj Fot* **bien/mal enfocado**, in/out of focus.

enfocar [1] *vtr* 1 (*imagen*) to focus; (*persona*) to focus on. 2 (*tema*) to approach. 3 (*con linterna*) to shine a light on.

enfoque *nm* 1 focus; (*acción*) focusing. 2 (*de un tema*) approach.

enfrentamiento *nm* clash.

enfrentar I *vtr* 1 (*situación*, *peligro*) to confront. 2 (*enemistar*) to set at odds. II **enfrentarse** *vr* 1 **e. con** *o* **a**, to face up to, confront. 2 *Dep* (*rival*) to face (**a**, -), meet (**a**, -).

enfrente *adv* 1 opposite, facing; **la casa de e.**, the house opposite *o* across the road. 2 **e. de**, opposite *o* (across); **e. del colegio**, opposite the school.

enfriamiento *nm* 1 (*proceso*) cooling. 2 *Med* (*catarro*) cold, chill.

enfriar [29] I *vtr* to cool (down), chill. II *vi* to cool down. III **enfriarse** *vr* 1 to get *o* go cold. 2 (*resfriarse*) to get *o* catch a cold. 3 *fig* (*pasión*) to cool down.

enfurecer [33] I *vtr* to enrage, enfuriate. II **enfurecerse** *vr* to get furious, lose one's temper.

enfurruñarse *vr fam* to sulk.

engalanar I *vtr* to deck out, adorn. II **engalanarse** *vr* to dress up, get dressed up.

enganchado,-a *adj* **estar e. (a la droga)**, to be hooked (on drugs).

enganchar I *vtr* 1 to hook; *Ferroc* to couple. 2 *fam* (*pillar*) to nab. II **engancharse** *vr* to get caught *o* hooked; *arg* (*a la droga*) to get hooked.

enganche *nm* (*gancho*) hook; *Ferroc* coupling.

engañabobos *nm inv* (*persona*) con man, confidence trickster; (*truco*) con trick.

engañar I *vtr* to deceive, mislead; (*estafar*) to cheat, trick; (*mentir a*) to lie to; (*al marido*, *mujer*) to be unfaithful to. II **engañarse** *vr* to deceive oneself.

engañifa *nf fam* swindle.

engaño *nm* 1 deceit; (*estafa*) fraud, swindle; (*mentira*) lie. 2 (*error*) mistake, misunderstanding.

engañoso,-a *adj* (*palabras*) deceitful; (*apariencias*) deceptive; (*consejo*) misleading.

engarzar [4] *vtr* 1 (*unir*) to link. 2 (*engastar*) to mount, set.

engastar *vtr* to set, mount.

engatusar *vtr fam* to coax; **e. a algn para que haga algo**, to coax sb into doing sth.

engendrar *vtr* 1 *Biol* to engender. 2 *fig* to give rise to, cause.

engendro *nm* freak.

englobar *vtr* to include.

engomar *vtr* to gum, glue.

engordar I *vtr* to fatten (up), make fat. II *vi* 1 to put on weight, get fat; **he engordado tres kilos**, I've put on three kilos. 2 (*comida*, *bebida*) to be fattening.

engorro *nm fam* bother, nuisance.

engorroso,-a *adj fam* bothersome, tiresome.

engranaje *nm* 1 *Téc* gearing. 2 *fig* machinery.

engranar *vtr Téc* to engage.

engrandecer [33] *vtr* to exalt.

engrasar *vtr* 1 (*lubricar*) to lubricate, oil. 2 (*manchar*) to make greasy, stain with grease.

engrase *nm* lubrication.

engreído,-a *adj* vain, conceited.

engreírse [6] *vr* to become vain *o* conceited.

engrosar [2] *vtr* (*incrementar*) to enlarge; (*cantidad*) to increase, swell.

engrudo *nm* paste.

enguatar *vtr* to pad.

engullir *vtr* to gobble up.

enharinar *vtr* to cover with flour.

enhebrar *vtr* to thread.

enhorabuena *nf* congratulations *pl*; **dar la e. a algn**, to congratulate sb.

enigma *nm* enigma.

enigmático,-a *adj* enigmatic.

enjabonar *vtr* to soap.

enjalbegar [7] *vtr* to whitewash.

enjambre *nm* swarm.

enjaular *vtr* 1 (*animal*) to cage. 2 *fam* to put inside, put in jail.

enjuagar [7] *vtr* to rinse.

enjuague *nm* rinse; **e. bucal**, mouthwash.

enjugar [7] *vtr*, **enjugarse** *vr* 1 (*secar*) to mop up; (*lágrimas*) to wipe away. 2 (*deuda, déficit*) to clear, wipe out.

enjuiciamiento *nm* 1 (*opinión*) judgement. 2 *Jur* (*civil*) lawsuit; (*criminal*) trial, prosecution.

enjuiciar [12] *vtr* 1 (*juzgar*) to judge, examine. 2 *Jur* (*criminal*) to indict, prosecute.

enjundia *nf* *fig* (*sustancia*) substance; (*importancia*) importance.

enjuto,-a *adj* lean, skinny.

enlace *nm* 1 (*unión*) link, connection; **e. químico**, chemical bond. 2 *Ferroc* connection. 3 (*casamiento*) marriage. 4 (*persona*) liaison officer; **e. sindical**, shop steward, *US* union delegate.

enlatado,-a *adj* canned, tinned.

enlatar *vtr* to can, tin.

enlazar [4] *vtr & vi* to link, connect (**con**, with).

enlodar *vtr* 1 (*enfangar*) to muddy, cover with mud. 2 *fig* (*reputación*) to stain, besmirch.

enloquecedor,-a *adj* maddening.

enloquecer [33] I *vi* to go mad. II *vtr* 1 (*volver loco*) to drive mad. 2 *fam* **me enloquecen las motos**, I'm mad about motorbikes. II **enloquecerse** *vr* to go mad, go out of one's mind.

enlosar *vtr* to tile.

enlucir [35] *vtr* (*pared*) to plaster; (*plata, oro*) to polish.

enlutado,-a *adj* in mourning.

enmadrado,-a *adj* **estar e.**, to be tied to one's mother's apron strings.

enmarañar I *vtr* 1 (*pelo*) to tangle. 2 *fig* (*complicar*) to complicate, confuse. II

enmarañarse *vr* 1 (*pelo*) to get tangled. 2 *fig* (*situación*) to get confused, get into a mess *o* a muddle.

enmarcar [1] *vtr* to frame.

enmascarar I *vtr* 1 to mask. 2 (*problema, la verdad*) to mask, disguise. II **enmascararse** *vr* to put on a mask.

enmendar [1] I *vtr* (*corregir*) to correct, put right; *Jur* to amend. II **enmendarse** *vr* (*persona*) to reform, mend one's ways.

enmienda *nf* correction; *Jur Pol* amendment.

enmohecerse [33] *vr* (*metal*) to rust, get rusty; *Bot* to go mouldy *o US* moldy.

enmoquetar *vtr* to carpet.

enmudecer [33] *vi* (*callar*) to fall silent; *fig* to be dumbstruck.

ennegrecer [33] *vtr*, **ennegrecerse** *vr* to blacken, turn black.

ennoblecer *vtr* to ennoble.

enojado,-a *adj* angry, cross.

enojadizo,-a *adj* irritable, touchy.

enojar I *vtr* to anger, annoy. II **enojarse** *vr* to get angry, lose one's temper.

enojo *nm* anger, annoyance.

enorgullecer [33] I *vtr* to fill with pride. II **enorgullecerse** *vtr* to be *o* feel proud (**de**, of).

enorme *adj* enormous.

enormidad *nf* enormity; *fam* **una e.**, loads.

enraizado,-a *adj* rooted.

enraizar [24] *vi*, **enraizarse** *vr* (*persona*) to put down roots; (*planta, costumbre*) to take root.

enrarecerse [33] *vr* (*aire*) to become rarefied.

enredadera *nf* climbing plant, creeper.

enredar I *vtr* 1 (*pelo*) to entangle, tangle up. 2 *fig* (*asunto*) to confuse, complicate. 3 *fig* (*implicar*) to involve (**en**, in). 4 (*confundir*) to mix up. II **enredarse** *vr* 1 (*pelo*) to get entangled, get tangled (up) *o* in a tangle. 2 *fig* (*asunto*) to get complicated *o* confused. 3 *fig* (*involucrarse*) to get involved (**con**, with). 4 (*confundirse*) to get mixed up.

enredo *nm* 1 (*maraña*) tangle. 2 *fig* (*lío*) muddle, mess.

enrejado *nm* (*de ventana*) lattice.

enrevesado,-a *adj* complicated, difficult.

enriquecer [33] I *vtr* to make rich; *fig* to enrich. II **enriquecerse** *vr* to get *o* become rich, prosper; *fig* to become enriched.

enrocar [1] *vi* *Ajedrez* to castle.

enrojecer [33] I *vtr* to redden, turn red. II **enrojecer(se)** *vi & vr* (*ruborizarse*) to blush.

enrolarse *vr* to enrol, *US* enroll, sign on; *Mil* to enlist, join up.

enrollado,-a *adj* 1 rolled up. 2 (*persona*) great. 3 *fam* **estar e. con algn**, (*estar saliendo con*) to go out with sb.

enrollar I vtr to roll up; (cable) to coil; (hilo) to wind up. **II enrollarse** vr 1 fam (hablar) to chatter, go on and on. 2 fam **e. con algn**, (tener relaciones) to have an affair with sb.

enroque nm Ajedrez castling.

enroscar [1] I vtr 1 to coil (round), wind. 2 (tornillo, tapón) to screw in o on. **II enroscarse** vr to coil, wind.

ensaimada nf kind of spiral pastry from Majorca.

ensalada nf salad.

ensaladera nf salad bowl.

ensaladilla nf **e. rusa**, Russian salad.

ensalzar [4] vtr (enaltecer) to exalt; (elogiar) to praise, extol, US extoll.

ensamblador nm Inform assembler.

ensamblaje nm Téc assembly.

ensamblar vtr to assemble.

ensanchar I vtr to enlarge, widen; Cost to let out. **II ensancharse** vr to get wider.

ensanche nm enlargement, widening; (de ciudad) urban development.

ensangrentado,-a adj bloodstained, covered in blood.

ensangrentar [1] vtr to stain with blood, cover in blood.

ensañarse vr to be brutal (**con**, with); (cebarse) to delight in tormenting (**con**, -).

ensartar vtr 1 (perlas etc) to string together. 2 (mentiras etc) to reel off, rattle off.

ensayar vtr to test, try out; Teat to rehearse; Mús to practise.

ensayista nmf essayist.

ensayo nm 1 (prueba) test, trial. 2 Teat rehearsal; **e. general**, dress rehearsal. 3 (escrito) essay.

enseguida, en seguida adv (inmediatamente) at once, straight away; (poco después) in a minute, soon; **e. voy**, I'll be right there.

ensenada nf inlet, cove.

enseña nf ensign, standard.

enseñanza nf 1 (educación) education. 2 (de idioma etc) teaching. 3 **enseñanzas**, teachings.

enseñar vtr 1 to teach; **e. a algn a hacer algo**, to teach sb how to do sth. 2 (mostrar) to show; (señalar) to point out.

enseres nmpl (bártulos) belongings, goods; (de trabajo) tools.

ensillar vtr to saddle (up).

ensimismado,-a adj (en la lectura etc) engrossed; (abstraído) lost in thought.

ensimismarse vr (en la lectura etc) to become engrossed; (abstraerse) to be lost in thought.

ensombrecer [33] I vtr to cast a shadow over. **II ensombrecerse** vr to darken.

ensopar vtr Am to soak.

ensordecedor,-a adj deafening.

ensordecer [33] I vtr to deafen. II vi to go deaf.

ensortijado,-a adj curly.

ensuciar [12] I vtr 1 to get dirty. 2 fig (reputación) to harm, damage. **II ensuciarse** vr to get dirty.

ensueño nm dream; **una casa de e.**, a dream house.

entablado nm 1 (entarimado) planking, planks pl. 2 (suelo) wooden floor.

entablar vtr 1 (conversación) to open, begin; (amistad) to strike up; (negocios) to start. 2 Ajedrez to set up. 3 (pleito) to initiate.

entablillar vtr Med to splint.

entallado,-a adj (vestido) close-fitting; (camisa) fitted.

entallar I vtr to take in at the waist. II vi to fit at the waist.

entarimado nm parquet floor.

entarimar vtr to cover with parquet.

ente nm 1 (institución) organization, body; **e. público**, public service organization. 2 (ser) being.

entendederas nfpl fam brains; **ser duro de e.**, to be slow on the uptake.

entender [3] I vtr (comprender) to understand; **a mi e.**, to my way of thinking; **dar a algn a e. que ...**, to give sb to understand that .... **II** vi 1 (comprender) to understand. 2 **e. de**, (saber) to know about. **III entenderse** vr 1 (comprenderse) to be understood, be meant. 2 fam **e. (bien) con**, to get on (well) with.

entendido,-a I nm,f expert. II adj **tengo entendido que ...**, I understand that ....

entendimiento nm understanding.

enterado,-a adj knowledgeable, well-informed; **estar e.**, to be in the know; **estar e. de ...**, to be aware of .... II nm,f (listillo) know-all.

enterar I vtr to inform (**de**, about, of). **II enterarse** vr to find out; **me he enterado de que ...**, I understand ...; **ni me enteré**, I didn't even realize it.

entereza nf strength of character.

enternecedor,-a adj moving, touching.

enternecer [33] I vtr to move, touch. **II enternecerse** vr to be moved o touched.

entero,-a I adj 1 (completo) entire, whole; **por e.**, completely. 2 fig (íntegro) honest, upright. 3 fig (firme) strong. **II** nm 1 Mat whole number. 2 Fin point. ◆**enteramente** adv entirely, completely.

enterrador nm gravedigger.

enterramiento nm burial.

enterrar [1] vt to bury.

entidad nf organization, company, firm. **e. comercial**, company.

entierro nm 1 burial. 2 (ceremonia) funeral.

entomología nf entomology.

entonación nf intonation.

entonar I vtr 1 (canto) to sing. 2 Med to

tone up. **II** *vi* to be in harmony, be in tune (**con**, with).

entonces *adv* then; **por aquel e.**, at that time; **el e. ministro**, the then minister.

entornar *vtr* (*ojos etc*) to half-close; (*puerta*) to leave ajar.

entorno *nm* environment.

entorpecer [33] *vtr* (*obstaculizar*) to hinder, impede.

entrada *nf* 1 entrance. 2 (*billete*) ticket; (*recaudación*) takings *pl.* 3 **de e.**, for a start. 4 *Culin* entrée. 5 *Com* entry; (*pago inicial*) down payment, deposit; **e. de capital**, capital inflow. 6 *Com* **entradas**, (*ingresos*) receipts, takings. 7 (*en la frente*) receding hairline.

entrado,-a *adj* **e. en años**, advanced in years; **hasta bien entrada la noche**, well into the night.

entramado *nm* framework; (*de sistema etc*) network.

entramparse *vr fam* to get into debt.

entrante **I** *adj* coming; **el mes e.**, next month; **el ministro e.**, the incoming minister. **II** *Culin* starter.

entrañable *adj* 1 (*lugar*) intimate, close. 2 (*persona*) affectionate, warm-hearted.

entrañar *vtr* to entail.

entrañas *nfpl* bowels.

entrar **I** *vi* 1 to come in, go in, enter; *fig* **no me entran las matemáticas**, I can't get the hang of maths. 2 (*encajar*) to fit. 3 **el año que entra**, next year, the coming year. 4 (*venir*) to come over; **me entró dolor de cabeza**, I got a headache; **me entraron ganas de reír**, I felt like laughing. **II** *vtr* 1 to introduce. 2 *Inform* to enter.

entre *prep* 1 (*dos*) between. 2 (*más de dos*) among(st).

entreabierto,-a *adj* (*ojos etc*) half-open; (*puerta*) ajar.

entreacto *nm* interval, intermission.

entrecejo *nm* space between the eyebrows; **fruncir el e.**, to frown, knit one's brow.

entrecortado,-a *adj* (*voz*) faltering, hesitant.

entrecot *nm* fillet steak.

entrecruzar *vtr*, **entrecruzarse** [4] *vr* to entwine.

entredicho *nm* 1 *Jur* injunction. 2 **estar en e.**, to be suspect; **poner algo en e.**, to bring sth into question.

entrega *nf* 1 (*de productos*) delivery; (*de premios*) presentation. 2 (*fascículo*) part, instalment, *US* installment. 3 (*devoción*) selflessness.

entregar [7] **I** *vtr* to hand over; (*deberes etc*) to give in, hand in; *Com* to deliver. **II** **entregarse** *vr* 1 (*rendirse*) to give in, surrender. 2 **e. a**, to devote oneself to; *pey* to indulge in.

entreguismo *nm Pol* appeasement.

entrelazar [4] *vtr*, **entrelazarse** *vr* to entwine.

entremedias *adv* in between; (*mientras tanto*) meanwhile, in the meantime.

entremés *nm Culin* hors d'oeuvres.

entremeterse *vr* → **entrometerse**

entremezclarse *vr* to mix, mingle.

entrenador,-a *nm,f* trainer, coach.

entrenamiento *nm* training.

entrenar *vi*, **entrenarse** *vr* to train.

entrepierna *nf* crotch, crutch.

entresacar [1] *vtr* to pick out, select.

entresijos *nmpl* nooks and crannies.

entresuelo *nm* mezzanine.

entretanto **I** *adv* meanwhile. **II** *nm* **en el e.**, in the meantime.

entretejer *vtr* to interweave.

entretención *nf Am* amusement, entertainment.

entretener [24] **I** *vtr* 1 (*divertir*) to entertain, amuse. 2 (*retrasar*) to delay; (*detener*) to hold up, detain. **II** **entretenerse** *vr* 1 (*distraerse*) to amuse oneself, while away the time. 2 (*retrasarse*) to be delayed, be held up.

entretenido,-a *adj* enjoyable, entertaining.

entretenimiento *nm* entertainment, amusement.

entretiempo *adj* **ropa de e.**, lightweight clothing.

entrever [28] *vtr* to glimpse, catch sight of; *fig* **dejó e. que '...**, she hinted that ....

entrevista *nf* interview.

entrevistador,-a *nm,f* interviewer.

entrevistar **I** *vtr* to interview. **II** **entrevistarse** *vr* **e. con algn**, to have an interview with sb.

entristecer [33] **I** *vtr* to sadden, make sad. **II** **entristecerse** *vr* to be sad (**por**, about).

entrometerse *vr* to meddle, interfere (**en**, in).

entrometido,-a **I** *nm,f* meddler, busybody. **II** *adj* interfering.

entroncar *vi* to connect.

entumecer [33] **I** *vtr* to numb. **II** **entumecerse** *vr* to go numb.

entumecido,-a *adj* numb.

enturbiar [12] **I** *vtr* 1 (*agua*) to make cloudy. 2 *fig* (*asunto*) to cloud, obscure. **II** **enturbiarse** *vr* to become cloudy.

entusiasmar **I** *vtr* to fill with enthusiasm. **II** **entusiasmarse** *vr* to get excited *o* enthusiastic (**con**, about).

entusiasmo *nm* enthusiasm; **con e.**, enthusiastically.

entusiasta **I** *adj* enthusiastic, keen (**de**, on). **II** *nmf* enthusiast.

enumerar *vtr* to enumerate.

enunciado *nm* (*de teoría, problema*) wording.

envainar *vtr* to sheathe.

envanecer [33] **I** *vtr* to make proud *o*

vain. **II envanecerse** *vr* to become conceited *o* proud, give oneself airs.

envasado,-a I *nm* (*en botella*) bottling; (*en paquete*) packing; (*en lata*) canning. **II** *adj* **e. al vacío**, vacuum-packed.

envasar *vtr* (*embotellar*) to bottle; (*empaquetar*) to pack; (*enlatar*) to can, tin.

envase *nm* 1 (*acto*) packing; (*de botella*) bottling; (*de lata*) canning. 2 (*recipiente*) container. 3 (*botella vacía*) empty.

envejecer [33] **I** *vi* to grow old. **II** *vtr* to age.

envejecimiento *nm* ageing.

envenenar *vtr* to poison.

envergadura *nf* 1 (*importancia*) importance, scope; **de gran e.**, large-scale. 2 (*de pájaro, avión*) span, wingspan; *Náut* breadth (of sail).

envés *nm* other side.

envestidura *nf* investiture.

enviado *nm,f* envoy; *Prensa* **e. especial**, special correspondent.

enviar [29] *vtr* to send.

enviciarse [12] *vr* to become addicted (**con**, to).

envidia *nf* envy; **tener e. de algn**, to envy sb.

envidiable *adj* enviable.

envidiar [12] *vtr* to envy; **no tener nada que e.**, to be in no way inferior (**a**, to).

envidioso,-a *adj* envious.

envilecer [33] *vtr* to degrade, debase.

envío *nm* sending; (*remesa*) consignment; (*paquete*) parcel; **gastos de e.**, postage and packing; **e. contra reembolso**, cash on delivery.

enviudar *vi* (*hombre*) to become a widower, lose one's wife; (*mujer*) to become a widow, lose one's husband.

envoltorio *nm*, **envoltura** *nf* wrapper, wrapping.

envolver [4] (*pp* **envuelto**) **I** *vtr* 1 (*con papel*) to wrap. 2 (*cubrir*) to envelope. 3 (*en complot etc*) to involve (**en**, in). **II envolverse** *vr* 1 to wrap oneself up (**en**, in). 2 (*implicarse*) to become involved (**en**, in).

enyesar *vtr* to plaster; *Med* to put in plaster.

enzima *nf* enzyme.

épica *nf* epic poetry.

epicentro *nm* epicentre, *US* epicenter.

épico,-a *adj* epic.

epidemia *nf* epidemic.

epilepsia *nf* epilepsy.

epílogo *nm* epilogue, *US* epilog.

episcopal *adj* episcopal.

episodio *nm* episode.

epístola *nf* epistle.

epitafio *nm* epitaph.

epíteto *nm* epithet.

época *nf* time; *Hist* period, epoch; *Agr* season; **en esta é. del año**, at this time of the year; **hacer é.**, to be a landmark;

mueble de é., period furniture.

equidad *nf* equity.

equilátero *nm* equilateral.

equilibrar *vtr* to balance.

equilibrio *nm* balance.

equilibrismo *nm* balancing act.

equilibrista *nmf* 1 tightrope walker. 2 *Am Pol* opportunist.

equipaje *nm* luggage; **hacer el e.**, to pack, do the packing.

equipar *vtr* to equip, furnish (**con**, **de**, with).

equiparable *adj* comparable (**a**, to; **con**, with).

equiparar *vtr* to compare (**con**, with), liken (**con**, to).

equipo *nm* 1 (*de expertos, jugadores*) team. 2 (*aparatos*) equipment; **e. de alta fidelidad**, hi-fi stereo system. 3 (*ropas*) outfit.

equis *nf* name of the letter X in Spanish.

equitación *nf* horse *o US* horseback riding.

equitativo,-a *adj* equitable, fair.

equivalente *adj* equivalent.

equivaler [26] *vi* to be equivalent (**to**, a).

equivocación *nf* error, mistake.

equivocado,-a *adj* mistaken, wrong.

equivocar [1] **I** *vtr* to mix up. **II equivocarse** *vr* to make a mistake; *Tel* **se equivocó de número**, he dialled the wrong wrong; **se equivocó de fecha**, he got the wrong date.

equívoco,-a I *adj* equivocal, misleading. **II** *nm* misunderstanding.

era[1] *nf* (*época*) era, age.

era[2] *nf* *Agr* threshing floor.

era[3] *pt indef* → **ser**.

erario *nm* exchequer, treasury.

eras *pt indef* → **ser**.

erección *nf* erection.

erecto,-a *adj* upright; (*pene*) erect.

eres *indic pres* → **ser**.

erguir [5] **I** *vtr* to erect. **II erguirse** *vr* to straighten up, stand *o* sit up straight.

erial *nm* uncultivated land.

erigir [6] **I** *vtr* to erect. **II erigirse** *vr* **e. en algo**, to set oneself up in sth.

erizado,-a *adj* bristly, prickly.

erizarse [4] *vr* to bristle, stand on end.

erizo *nm* hedgehog; **e. de mar** *o* **marino**, sea urchin.

ermita *nf* hermitage, shrine.

ermitaño,-a *nm,f* hermit.

erosión *nf* erosion.

erosionar *vtr* to erode.

erótico,-a *adj* erotic.

erotismo *nm* eroticism.

erradicar [1] *vtr* to eradicate.

errante *adj* wandering.

errar [1] **I** *vtr* to miss, get wrong. **II** *vi* 1 (*vagar*) to wander, roam. 2 (*fallar*) to err.

errata *nf* erratum, misprint; **fe de erratas**, errata.

erre *nf* **e. que e.**, stubbornly, pigheadedly.

erróneo,-a adj erroneous, wrong.

error nm error, mistake; Inform bug; **por e.**, by mistake, in error; Impr **e. de imprenta**, misprint; **caer en un e.**, to make a mistake.

Ertzaintza nf Basque police force.

eructar vi to belch, burp.

eructo nm belch, burp.

erudición nf erudition.

erudito,-a I adj erudite, learned. II nm,f scholar.

erupción nf 1 (de volcán) eruption. 2 (en la piel) rash.

es indic pres → ser.

esa adj dem → ese.

ésa adj dem → ése.

esbelto,-a adj slender.

esbirro nm henchman.

esbozar [4] vi to sketch, outline.

esbozo nm sketch, outline, rough draft.

escabeche nm brine.

escabechina nf massacre.

escabroso,-a adj 1 (espinoso) tricky. 2 (indecente) crude.

escabullirse vr to slip away, scuttle o scurry off.

escacharrar vtr fam to break.

escafandra nf diving helmet or suit; **e. espacial**, spacesuit.

escala nf 1 scale; (de colores) range; **e. musical**, scale; **en gran e.**, on a large scale. 2 (parada) Náut port of call; Av stopover; **hacer e. en**, to call in at, stop over in. 3 (escalera) ladder, stepladder.

escalada nf 1 climb. 2 fig (de violencia) escalation; (de precios) rise.

escalador,-a nm,f climber, mountaineer.

escalafón nm (graduación) rank; (de salarios) salary o wage scale.

escalar vtr to climb, scale.

escaldar vtr to scald.

escalera nf 1 stair; **e. de incendios**, fire escape; **e. mecánica**, escalator; **e. de caracol**, spiral staircase. 2 (escala) ladder. 3 Naipes run.

escalerilla nf (de piscina) steps pl; Náut gangway; Av (boarding) ramp.

escalfar vtr to poach.

escalinata nf stoop.

escalofriante adj hair-raising, bloodcurdling.

escalofrío nm shiver; **me dió un e.**, it made me shiver.

escalón nm step; **e. lateral** (en letrero) ramp.

escalonar vtr to place at intervals, space out.

escalope nm escalope.

escalpelo nm scalpel.

escama nf Zool scale; (de jabón) flake.

escamarse vr to smell a rat, become suspicious.

escamotear vtr fam to diddle out of, do

out of.

escampar vi to stop raining, clear up.

escanciar [12] vtr (vino) to pour out, serve.

escandalizar [4] I vtr to scandalize, shock. II **escandalizarse** vr to be shocked (**de**, at, by).

escándalo nm 1 (alboroto) racket, din; **armar un e.**, to kick up a fuss. 2 (desvergüenza) scandal.

escandaloso,-a adj 1 (ruidoso) noisy, rowdy. 2 (ofensivo) scandalous.

Escandinavia n Scandinavia.

escandinavo,-a adj & nm,f Scandinavian.

escáner nm scanner.

escaño nm Parl seat.

escapada nf (de prisión) escape; Dep breakaway. 2 (viaje rápido) flying visit, quick trip.

escapar I vi to escape, run away. II **escaparse** vr 1 to escape, run away; **se me escapó de las manos**, it slipped out of my hands; **se me escapó el tren**, I missed the train. 2 (gas etc) to leak, escape.

escaparate nm shop window.

escapatoria nf escape; **no tener e.**, to have no way out.

escape nm 1 (de gas etc) leak, escape. 2 Téc exhaust; **tubo de e.**, exhaust (pipe). 3 (huida) escape; (escapatoria) way out.

escaquearse vr fam to shirk, skive off.

escarabajo nm beetle.

escaramuza nf Mil skirmish; fig (riña) squabble, brush.

escarbar vtr 1 (suelo) to scratch; (fuego) to poke. 2 fig to inquire into, investigate.⁴

escarceo nm attempt.

escarcha nf hoarfrost, frost.

escarchado,-a adj (fruta) crystallized, candied.

escardar vtr to hoe.

escardillo nm weeding hoe.

escarlata adj scarlet.

escarlatina nf scarlet fever.

escarmentar [1] vi to learn one's lesson.

escarmiento nm punishment, lesson.

escarnio nm derision, mockery.

escarola nf curly endive, US escarole.

escarpado,-a adj (paisaje) craggy; (pendiente) steep.

escasear vi to be scarce.

escasez nf scarcity.

escaso,-a adj scarce; (dinero) tight; (conocimientos) scant; **e. de dinero**, short of money.

escatimar vtr to skimp on; **no escatimó esfuerzos para ...**, he spared no efforts to ....

escayola nf 1 plaster of Paris, stucco. 2 Med plaster.

escayolar vtr Med to put in plaster.

escena nf 1 scene. 2 (escenario) stage; **poner en e.**, to stage.

escenario nm 1 Teat stage. 2 (entorno) scenario; (de crimen) scene; (de película) setting.

escénico,-a adj scenic.

escenografía nf Cin set design; Teat stage design.

escepticismo nm scepticism, US skepticism.

escéptico,-a adj & nm,f sceptic, US skeptic.

escindirse vr to split (off) (en, into).

escisión nf split.

esclarecer [33] vtr to shed light on.

esclavitud nf slavery.

esclavizar [4] vtr to enslave.

esclava nf bangle.

esclavo,-a adj & nm,f slave.

esclusa nf lock, sluicegate.

escoba nf brush, broom.

escocer [54] 1 vi to sting, smart. II **escocerse** vr (piel) to chafe.

escocés,-esa I adj Scottish, Scots; **falda escocesa**, kilt. II nm,f (hombre) Scotsman; (mujer) Scotswoman.

Escocia n Scotland.

escoger [5] vtr to choose.

escogido,-a adj chosen, selected; (producto) choice, select; Lit **obras escogidas**, selected works.

escolar I adj (curso, año) school. II nm,f (niño) schoolboy; (niña) schoolgirl.

escolaridad nf schooling.

escollo nm reef; fig pitfall.

escolta nf escort.

escoltar vtr to escort.

escombros nmpl rubbish sing, debris sing.

esconder I vtr to hide (de, from), conceal (de, from). II **esconderse** vr to hide (de, from).

escondidas adv a e., secretly.

escondite nm 1 (lugar) hiding place, hide-out. 2 (juego) hide-and-seek.

escondrijo nm hiding place, hide-out.

escopeta nf shotgun; e. de aire comprimido, air gun; e. de cañones recortados, sawn-off shotgun.

escopetazo nm gunshot.

escorbuto nm scurvy.

escoria nf 1 (de metal) slag. 2 fig pey scum, dregs pl.

Escorpio nm Scorpio.

escorpión nm scorpion.

escotado,-a adj low-cut.

escote nm low neckline.

escotilla nf hatch, hatchway.

escozor nm stinging, smarting.

escribano,-a nm,f Jur court clerk.

escribiente nmf clerk.

escribir (pp escrito) I vtr to write; e. a mano, to write in longhand; e. a máquina, to type. II **escribirse** vr 1 (dos personas) to write to each other, correspond. 2 se escribe con h, it is spelt with an h.

escrito,-a I adj written; e. a mano, handwritten, in longhand; por e., in writing. II nm writing.

escritor,-a nm,f writer.

escritorio nm (mueble) writing desk, bureau; (oficina) office.

escritura nf 1 Jur deed, document; e. de propiedad, title deed. 2 Rel Sagradas Escrituras, Holy Scriptures.

escrúpulo nm 1 scruple; una persona sin escrúpulos, an unscrupulous person. 2 (esmero) care. 3 me da e., (asco) it makes me feel squeamish.

escrupuloso,-a adj 1 (honesto) scrupulous. 2 (meticuloso) painstaking. 3 (delicado) squeamish.

escrutar vtr 1 to scrutinize. 2 (votos) to count.

escrutinio nm 1 scrutiny. 2 (de votos) count.

escuadra nf 1 (instrumento) square. 2 Mil squad; Naut squadron; Dep team; (de coches) fleet.

escuadrilla nf squadron.

escuadrón nm squadron.

escuálido,-a adj emaciated.

escucha nf listening; **escuchas telefónicas**, phone tapping sing; estar a la e., to be listening out (de, for).

escuchar I vtr to listen to; (oír) to hear. II vi to listen; (oír) to hear.

escudarse vr fig e. en algo, to hide behind sth.

escudería nf Aut racing team.

escudilla nf bowl.

escudo nm 1 (arma defensiva) shield. 2 (blasón) coat of arms.

escudriñar vtr to scrutinize.

escuela nf school; e. de Bellas Artes, Art School; e. de conducir/de idiomas, driving/language school.

escueto,-a adj plain, unadorned.

escuezo indic pres → escocer.

esculcar [1] vtr Am to search.

esculpir vtr to sculpt; (madera) to carve; (metal) to engrave.

escultor,-a nm,f (hombre) sculptor; (mujer) sculptress; (de madera) woodcarver; (de metales) engraver.

escultura nf sculpture.

escultural adj sculptural; (persona) statuesque.

escupidera nf 1 (recipiente) spittoon, US cuspidor. 2 (orinal) chamberpot.

escupir I vi to spit. II vtr to spit out.

escupitajo nm vulg spit.

escurreplatos nm inv dish rack.

escurridizo,-a adj 1 (resbaladizo) slippery. 2 fig (huidizo) elusive, slippery.

escurridor nm colander; (escurreplatos) dish rack.

escurrir I vtr (plato, vaso) to drain; (ropa) to wring out; e. el bulto, to wriggle out. II **escurrirse** vr (platos etc) to drip. 2

(escaparse) to run *o* slip away. **3** *(resbalarse)* to slip.

escúter *nm* (motor) scooter.

ese,-a *adj dem* 1 that. 2 esos,-as, those.

ése,-a *pron dem m,f* 1 that one. 2 esos,-as, those (ones); *fam* ¡ni por ésas!, no way!; *fam* ¡no me vengas con ésas!, come off it!

esencia *nf* essence.

esencial *adj* essential; **lo e.**, the main thing. ◆**esencialmente** *adv* essentially.

esfera *nf* 1 sphere; *fig* sphere, field. 2 *(de reloj de pulsera)* dial; *(de reloj de pared)* face.

esférico,-a I *adj* spherical. II *nm Ftb* ball.

esfinge *nf* sphinx.

esforzarse [2] *vr* to endeavour (por, to).

esfuerzo *nm* effort.

esfumarse *vr fam* to beat it.

esgrima *nf Dep* fencing.

esgrimir *vtr* to wield.

esguince *nm* sprain.

eslabón *nm* link.

eslavo,-a I *adj* Slav, Slavonic. II *nm,f (persona)* Slav. III *nm (idioma)* Slavonic.

eslip *nm (pl eslips)* men's briefs *pl*, underpants *pl*.

eslogan *nm (pl eslóganes)* slogan; **e. publicitario**, advertising slogan.

eslora *nf Náut* length.

esmaltar *vtr* to enamel.

esmalte *nm* enamel; *(de uñas)* nail polish *o* varnish.

esmerado,-a *adj* painstaking, careful.

esmeralda *nf* emerald.

esmerarse *vr* to be careful; *(esforzarse)* to go to great lengths.

esmero *nm* great care.

esmoquin *nm (pl esmóquines)* dinner jacket, *US* tuxedo.

esnifar *vtr arg (drogas)* to sniff.

esnob *(pl esnobs)* I *adj (persona)* snobbish; *(restaurante etc)* posh. II *nmf* snob.

esnobismo *nm* snobbery, snobbishness.

eso *pron dem neut* that; **¡e. es!**, that's it!; **por e.**, that's why; *fam* **a e. de las diez**, around ten; *fam* **e. de las Navidades sale muy caro**, this whole Christmas thing costs a fortune.

esófago *nm* oesophagus, *US* esophagus.

esos,-as *adj dem pl* → **ese,-a**.

ésos,-as *pron dem m,fpl* → **ése,-a**.

esotérico,-a *adj* esoteric.

espabilado,-a *adj* 1 *(despierto)* wide awake. 2 *(niño)* bright.

espabilar I *vtr* to wake up. II **espabilarse** *vr* to wake up, waken up.

espachurrar *vtr* to squash.

espacial *adj* spatial, spacial; **nave e.**, space ship.

espaciar [12] *vtr* to space out.

espacio *nm* 1 space; *(de tiempo)* length; **a doble e.**, double-spaced. 2 *Rad TV* programme, *US* program.

espacioso,-a *adj* spacious, roomy.

espada I *nf* 1 sword; **estar entre la e. y la pared**, to be between the devil and the deep blue sea; **pez e.**, swordfish. 2 *Naipes* spade. II *nm Taur* matador.

espadaña *nf* belfry.

espaguetis *nmpl* spaghetti *sing*.

espalda *nf* 1 *Anat* back; **espaldas**, back *sing*; **a espaldas de algn**, behind sb's back; **por la e.**, from behind; **volver la e. a algn**, to turn one's back on sb; *fam* **e. mojada**, *US* wetback. 2 *Natación* backstroke.

espaldar *nm (de silla)* back.

espaldilla *nf* shoulder blade.

espantapájaros *nm inv* scarecrow.

espantar I *vtr* 1 *(asustar)* to frighten, scare. 2 *(ahuyentar)* to frighten away. II **espantarse** *vr* to get *o* feel frightened (de, of), get *o* feel scared (de, of).

espanto *nm* fright; *fam* **de e.**, dreadful, shocking.

espantoso,-a *adj* dreadful.

España *n* Spain.

español,-a I *adj* Spanish. II *nm,f* Spaniard; **los españoles**, the Spanish. III *nm (idioma)* Spanish.

esparadrapo *nm* sticking plaster.

esparcimiento *nm (relajación)* relaxation.

esparcir [3] I *vtr (papeles, semillas)* to scatter; *fig (rumor)* to spread. II **esparcirse** *vr* 1 to be scattered. 2 *(relajarse)* to relax.

espárrago *nm* asparagus.

espartano,-a *adj fig* spartan.

espasmo *nm* spasm.

espástico,-a *adj* spastic.

espátula *nf Culin* spatula; *Art* palette knife; *Téc* stripping knife; *(de albañil)* trowel.

especia *nf* spice.

especial *adj* special; **en e.**, especially; **e. para ....**, suitable for .... ◆**especialmente** *adv (exclusivamente)* specially; *(muy)* especially.

especialidad *nf* speciality, *US* specialty; *Educ* main subject.

especialista *nmf* specialist.

especializarse [4] *vr* to specialize (en, in).

especie *nf* 1 *Biol* species *inv*. 2 *(clase)* kind; **una e. de salsa**, a kind of sauce. 3 *Com* **en e.**, in kind.

especificar [1] *vtr* to specify.

específico,-a *adj* specific; **peso e.**, specific gravity. ◆**específicamente** *adv* specifically.

espécimen *nm (pl especímenes)* specimen.

espectacular *adj* spectacular.

espectacularidad *nf* **de gran e.**, really spectacular.

espectáculo *nm* 1 *(escena)* spectacle,

sight; *fam* **dar un e.**, to make a spectacle of oneself. **2** *Teat Cin TV* show; **montar un e.**, to put on a show.

espectador,-a *nm,f* *Dep* spectator; *(de accidente)* onlooker; *Teat Cin* member of the audience; **los espectadores**, the audience *sing*; *TV* viewers.

espectro *nm* **1** *Fís* spectrum. **2** *(fantasma)* spectre, *US* specter. **3** *(gama)* range.

especulación *nf* speculation; **e. del suelo**, land speculation.

especulador,-a *nm,f* *Fin* speculator.

especular *vi* to speculate.

especulativo,-a *adj* speculative.

espejismo *nm* mirage.

espejo *nm* mirror; *Aut* **e. retrovisor**, rear-view mirror.

espeleología *nf* potholing, speleology.

espeluznante *adj* hair-raising, horrifying.

espera *nf* wait; **en e. de ...**, waiting for ...; **a la e. de**, expecting; **sala de e.**, waiting room.

esperanza *nf* hope; **tener la e. puesta en algo**, to have one's hopes pinned on sth; **e. de vida**, life expectancy; **en estado de buena e.**, expecting, pregnant.

esperanzador,-a *adj* encouraging.

esperanzar *vtr* to give hope to.

esperar I *vi* **1** *(aguardar)* to wait. **2** *(tener esperanza de)* to hope. **II** *vtr* **1** *(aguardar)* to wait for; **espero a mi hermano**, I'm waiting for my brother. **2** *(tener esperanza de)* to hope for; **espero que sí**, I hope so; **espero que vengas**, I hope you'll come. **3** *(estar a la espera de)* to expect; **te esperábamos ayer**, we were expecting you yesterday. **4** *fig (bebé)* to expect.

esperma 1 *nm* *Biol* sperm. **2** *Am (vela)* candle.

espermaticida *nm* spermicide.

espermatozoide *nm* spermatozoid.

esperpéntico,-a *adj fam* grotesque.

espesar I *vtr* to thicken. **II espesarse** *vr* to thicken, get thicker.

espeso,-a *adj (bosque, niebla)* dense; *(líquido)* thick; *(masa)* stiff.

espesor *nm* thickness; **tres metros de e.**, three metres thick.

espesura *nf* denseness.

espetar *vtr fig* to spit out.

espía *nmf* spy.

espiar [29] **I** *vi* to spy. **II** *vtr* to spy on.

espichar *vi vulg (morir)* to snuff it; **espicharla**, to kick the bucket.

espiga *nf* **1** *(de trigo)* ear. **2** *Téc* pin.

espigado,-a *adj* slender.

espina *nf* **1** *Bot* thorn. **2** *(de pescado)* bone. **3** *Anat* **e. dorsal**, spinal column, spine. **4** *fig* **ése me da mala e.**, there's something fishy about that one.

espinaca *nf* spinach.

espinal *adj* spinal; **médula e.**, spinal marrow.

espinazo *nm* spine, backbone.

espinilla *nf* **1** *Anat* shin. **2** *(en la piel)* spot.

espinillera *nf* *Dep* shin pad.

espino *nm* hawthorn; **alambre de e.**, barbed wire.

espionaje *nm* spying, espionage; **novela de e.**, spy story.

espiral *adj & nf* spiral.

espirar *vi* to breathe out, exhale.

espiritismo *nm* spiritualism.

espíritu *nm* **1** spirit; **e. deportivo**, sportsmanship. **2** *Rel (alma)* soul; **el E. Santo**, the Holy Ghost.

espiritual *adj* spiritual.

espléndido,-a *adj* **1** *(magnífico)* splendid. **2** *(generoso)* lavish, generous.

esplendor *nm* splendour, *US* splendor.

esplendoroso,-a *adj* magnificent.

espliego *nm* lavender.

espolear *vtr* to spur on.

espolio *nm* → **expolio**.

espolvorear *vtr* to sprinkle **(de**, with).

esponja *nf* sponge.

esponjoso,-a *adj* spongy; *(bizcocho)* light.

esponsales *nmpl* betrothal *sing*, engagement *sing*.

espontaneidad *nf* spontaneity; **con e.**, naturally.

espontáneo,-a I *adj* spontaneous. **II** *nm* *Taur* spectator who spontaneously joins in the bullfight.

esporádico,-a *adj* sporadic.

esposado,-a *adj* **1** *(recién casado)* newly married. **2** *(con esposas)* handcuffed.

esposar *vtr* to handcuff.

esposas *nfpl* handcuffs.

esposo,-a *nm,f* spouse; *(hombre)* husband; *(mujer)* wife.

esprint *nm* sprint.

esprintar *vi* to sprint.

espuela *nf* spur.

espuerta *nf* hod.

espuma *nf* foam; *(de olas)* surf; *(de cerveza)* froth, head; *(de jabón)* lather; **e. de afeitar**, shaving foam.

espumoso,-a *adj* frothy; *(vino)* sparkling.

esputo *nm* spit.

esquela *nf* notice, announcement; **e. mortuoria**, announcement of a death.

esquelético,-a *adj* **1** *Anat* skeletal. **2** *(flaco)* skinny.

esqueleto *nm* **1** skeleton. **2** *Constr* framework.

esquema *nm* diagram.

esquemático,-a *adj (escueto)* schematic; *(con diagramas)* diagrammatic.

esquí *nm* **1** *(objeto)* ski. **2** *(deporte)* skiing; **e. acuático**, water-skiing.

esquiador,-a *nm,f* skier.

esquiar [29] *vi* to ski.

esquilar *vtr* to shear.

esquimal *adj & nmf* Eskimo.

esquina *nf* corner; *Dep* **saque de e.**, corner kick.

esquinazo nm dar e. a algn, to give sb the slip.

esquirla nf splinter.

esquirol nm Ind blackleg, scab.

esquivar vtr (a una persona) to avoid; (un golpe) to dodge.

esquivo,-a adj cold, aloof.

esquizofrenia nf schizophrenia.

esquizofrénico,-a adj & nm,f schizophrenic.

esta adj dem → este,-a.

está indic pres → estar.

ésta pron dem f → éste.

estabilidad nf stability.

estabilizar [4] vtr to stabilize.

estable adj stable.

establecer [33] I vtr to establish; (fundar) to set up, found; (récord) to set. II **establecerse** vr to settle.

establecimiento nm establishment.

establo nm cow shed.

estaca nf stake, post; (de tienda de campaña) peg.

estacada nf fence; fig dejar a algn en la e., to leave sb in the lurch.

estacazo nm blow with a stick.

estación nf 1 station; e. de servicio, service station; e. de esquí, ski resort. 2 (del año) season.

estacional adj seasonal.

estacionamiento nm Aut (acción) parking; (lugar) car park, US parking lot.

estacionar vtr, **estacionarse** vr Aut to park.

estacionario,-a adj stationary.

estada nf, **estadía** nf Am stay.

estadio nm 1 Dep stadium. 2 (fase) stage, phase.

estadista nmf Pol (hombre) statesman; (mujer) stateswoman.

estadística nf statistics sing; una e., a statistic.

estado nm 1 Pol state. 2 (situación) state, condition; en buen e., in good condition; e. de salud, condition, state of health; e. de excepción, state of emergency; estar en e., to be pregnant; e. civil, marital status; Com e. de cuentas, statement of accounts. 3 Mil e. mayor, general staff. **Estados Unidos** npl the United States.

estadounidense I adj United States, American. II nmf United States citizen.

estafa nf swindle.

estafador,-a nm,f swindler.

estafar vtr to swindle.

estafeta nf e. de Correos, sub post office.

estalactita nf stalactite.

estalagmita nf stalagmite.

estallar vi 1 to burst; (bomba) to explode, go off; (guerra) to break out. 2 fig (de cólera etc) to explode; e. en sollozos, to burst into tears.

estallido nm explosion; (de guerra) out-

break.

estambre nm Bot stamen.

Estambul n Istanbul.

estamento nm Hist estate; fig (grupo) group.

estampa nf illustration.

estampado,-a I adj (tela) printed. II nm 1 (tela) print. 2 (proceso) printing.

estampar vtr 1 (tela) to print. 2 (dejar impreso) to imprint. 3 fig (bofetada, beso) to plant, place.

estampida nf 1 (estampido) bang. 2 (carrera rápida) stampede; de e., suddenly.

estampido nm bang.

estampilla nf Am (postage) stamp.

estancado,-a adj stagnant; fig static, at a standstill; quedarse e., to get stuck or bogged down.

estancar [1] I vtr 1 (agua) to hold back. 2 fig (asunto) to block; (negociaciones) to bring to a standstill. II **estancarse** vr 1 (agua) to stagnate; fig to get bogged down.

estancia nf 1 (permanencia) stay. 2 (habitación) room. 3 Am (hacienda) ranch, farm.

estanco,-a I adj tobacconist's. II adj watertight.

estándar (pl estándares) adj & nm standard.

estandarizar [4] vtr to standardize.

estandarte nm standard, banner.

estanque nm pool, pond.

estanquero,-a nm,f tobacconist.

estante nm shelf; (para libros) bookcase.

estantería nf shelves pl, shelving.

estaño nm tin.

estar [13] I vi 1 to be; está en la playa, he is at the beach; e. en casa, to be in, be at home; estamos en Caracas, we are in Caracas; ¿está tu madre?, is your mother in?; ¿cómo estás? how are you?; los precios están bajos, prices are low; el problema está en el dinero, the problem is money; e. en lo cierto, to be right; e. en todo, not to miss a trick. 2 (+ adj) to be; está cansado/enfermo, he's tired/ill; está vacío, it's empty. 3 (+ adv) to be; está bien/mal, it's all right/wrong; e. mal de dinero, he's short of money; estará enseguida, it'll be ready in a minute. 4 (+ ger) to be; está escribiendo, she is writing; estaba comiendo, he was eating. 5 (+ a + fecha) to be; ¿a cuántos estamos?, what's the date (today)?; estamos a 2 de Noviembre, it is the 2nd of November. 6 (+ precio) to be at; están a 100 pesetas el kilo, they're at 100 pesetas a kilo. 7 (locuciones) e. al caer, to be just round the corner; ¿estamos?, OK? 8 (+ de) e. de más, not to be needed; e. de paseo, to be out for a walk; e. de vacaciones/viaje to be (away) on holiday/a trip; estoy de jefe hoy, I'm the boss today. 9 (+ para) esta-

rá para las seis, it will be finished by six; **hoy no estoy para bromas,** I'm in no mood for jokes today; **el tren está para salir,** the train is just about to leave. 10 (+ por) **está por hacer,** it has still to be done; **eso está por ver,** it remains to be seen; **estoy por esperar,** (*a favor de*) I'm for waiting. 11 (+ con) to have; **e. con la gripe,** to have the flu, be down with flu; **estoy con Jaime,** (*de acuerdo con*) I agree with Jaime. 12 (+ sin) to have no; **e. sin luz/agua,** to have no light/water. 13 (+ que) **está que se duerme,** he is nearly asleep; *fam* **está que rabia,** he's hopping mad.
II **estarse** *vr* ¡estáte quieto!, keep still!, stop fidgeting!

estatal *adj* state; **enseñanza e.,** state education.
estático,-a *adj* static.
estatua *nf* statue.
estatura *nf* 1 height; **¿cuál es tu e.?,** how tall are you? 2 (*renombre*) stature.
estatus *nm* status; **e. quo,** status quo.
estatutario *adj* statutory.
estatuto *nm fur* statute; (*de ciudad*) by-law; (*de empresa etc*) rules.
este *adj* eastern; (*dirección*) easterly. II *nm* east; **al e. de,** to the east of.
esté *subj pres* → **estar.**
este,-a *dem* 1 this. 2 **estos,-as,** these.
éste,-a *pron dem m,f* 1 this one; **aquél ... é.,** the former ... the latter. 2 **éstos,-as,** these (ones); **aquéllos ... é.,** the former ... the latter.
estela *nf* (*de barco*) wake; (*de avión*) vapour trail; (*de cometa*) tail.
estelar *adj* 1 *Astron* stellar. 2 *fig Cin Teat* star.
estentóreo,-a *adj* stentorian, thundering.
estepa *nf* steppe.
estera *nf* rush mat.
estercolero *nm* dunghill; *fig* pigsty.
estéreo *nm & adj* stereo.
estereofónico,-a *adj* stereophonic, stereo.
estereotipar *vtr* to stereotype.
estereotipo *nm* stereotype.
estéril *adj* 1 sterile. 2 *fig* (*esfuerzo*) futile.
esterilidad *nf* 1 sterility. 2 *fig* futility, uselessness.
esterilizar [4] *vtr* to sterilize.
esterilla *nf* small mat.
esterlina *adj & nf* sterling; **libra e.,** pound (sterling).
esternón *nm* sternum, breastbone.
estero *nm Am* marsh, swamp.
estertor *nm* death rattle.
estética *nf* aesthetics, *US* esthetics *sing.*
esteticienne, esteticista *nf* beautician.
estético,-a *adj* aesthetic, *US* esthetic; **cirugía estética,** plastic surgery.
estibador *nm* docker, stevedore.
estiércol *nm* manure, dung.
estigma *nm* stigma; *Rel* stigmata.

estilarse *vr* to be in vogue, be fashionable.
estilete *nm* (*punzón*) stylus; (*puñal*) stiletto.
estilístico,-a *adj* stylistic.
estilizar [4] *vtr* to stylize.
estilo *nm* 1 style; (*modo*) manner, fashion; **algo por el e.,** something like that; **e. de vida,** way of life. 2 *Natación* stroke. 3 *Ling* **e. directo/indirecto,** direct/indirect speech.
estilográfica *nf* (*pluma*) e., fountain pen.
estima *nf* esteem, respect.
estimación *nf* 1 (*estima*) esteem, respect. 2 (*valoración*) evaluation; (*cálculo aproximado*) estimate.
estimado,-a *adj* esteemed, respected; **E. Señor,** (*en carta*) Dear Sir.
estimar *vtr* 1 (*apreciar*) to esteem. 2 (*considerar*) to consider, think; **lo estimo conveniente,** I think it appropriate. 3 (*valorar*) to value.
estimativo,-a *adj* approximate, estimated.
estimulante I *adj* stimulating. II *nm* stimulant.
estimular *vtr* 1 to stimulate. 2 *fig* to encourage.
estímulo *nm Biol Fís* stimulus; *fig* encouragement.
estío *nm* summer.
estipendio *nm* stipend, fee.
estipular *vtr* to stipulate.
estirado,-a *adj* stiff.
estirar I *vtr* to stretch; *fig* (*dinero*) to spin out; *fig* **e. la pata,** to kick the bucket. II **estirarse** *vr* to stretch.
estirón *nm* pull, jerk, tug; *fam* **dar o pegar un e.,** to shoot up *o* grow quickly.
estirpe *nf* stock, pedigree.
estival *adj* summer; **época e.,** summertime.
esto *pron dem neut* this, this thing, this matter; *fam* **e. de la fiesta,** this business about the party.
estocada *nf Taur* stab.
Estocolmo *n* Stockholm.
estofado *nm* stew.
estoico,-a I *adj* stoical. II *nm,f* stoic.
estómago *nm* stomach; **dolor de e.,** stomach ache.
estoque *nm Taur* sword.
estorbar I *vtr* (*dificultar*) to hinder, get in the way of. 2 (*molestar*) to disturb. II *vi* to be in the way.
estorbo *nm* 1 (*obstáculo*) obstruction, obstacle. 2 (*molestia*) nuisance.
estornino *nm* starling.
estornudar *vi* to sneeze.
estornudo *nm* sneeze.
estos,-as *adj dem* → **este,-a.**
éstos,-as *pron dem m,fpl* → **éste,-a.**
estoy *indic pres* → **estar.**
estrabismo *nm* squint.
estrado *nm* platform; *Mús* bandstand; *Jur*

stand.

estrafalario,-a *adj fam* outlandish.

estragos *nmpl* hacer **c. en,** to wreak havoc with o on.

estrambótico,-a *adj fam* outlandish, eccentric.

estrangulador,-a *nm,f* strangler.

estrangular *vtr* to strangle; *Med* to strangulate.

estraperlo *nm* black market; **tabaco de e.,** black market cigarettes.

Estrasburgo *n* Strasbourg.

estratagema *nf Mil* stratagem; *fam* trick, ruse.

estratega *nmf* strategist.

estrategia *nf* strategy.

estratégico,-a *adj* strategic.

estratificar [1] *vtr* to stratify.

estrato *nm* stratum.

estraza *nf* papel de e., brown paper.

estrechamiento *nm* 1 narrowing; 'e. de calzada', (en letrero) 'road narrows'. 2 (de amistad etc) tightening.

estrechar I *vtr* 1 to make narrow. 2 (mano) to shake; (lazos de amistad) to tighten; **me estrechó entre sus brazos,** he hugged me. II **estrecharse** *vr* to narrow, become narrower.

estrechez *nf* 1 narrowness; *fig* e. de miras, narrow-mindedness. 2 *fig* (dificultad económica) want, need; pasar estrecheces, to be hard up.

estrecho,-a I *adj* 1 narrow; (ropa, zapato) tight; (amistad, relación) close, intimate. 2 *fig* e. de miras, narrow-minded. II *nm Geog* strait, straits *pl.* ◆**estrechamente** *adv* (intimamente) closely, intimately; e. relacionados, closely related.

estregar *vtr* to scrub.

estrella *nf* star; e. de cine, film star; *Zool* e. de mar, starfish; e. fugaz, shooting star.

estrellado,-a *adj* 1 (en forma de estrella) star-shaped. 2 (cielo) starry. 3 (huevos) scrambled.

estrellar I *vtr fam* to smash. II **estrellarse** *vr Aut Av* (chocar) to crash (contra, into); (morir) to die in a car crash.

estrellato *nm* stardom.

estremecedor,-a *adj* bloodcurdling.

estremecer [33] *vtr,* **estremecerse** *vr* to shake.

estrenar *vtr* 1 to use for the first time; (ropa) to wear for the first time. 2 *Teat Cin* to premiere.

estreno *nm Teat* first performance; *Cin* premiere.

estreñido,-a *adj* constipated..

estreñimiento *nm* constipation.

estrépito *nm* din, racket.

estrepitoso,-a *adj* deafening; *fig (fracaso)* spectacular.

estrés *nm* stress.

estresante *adj* stressful.

estría *nf* 1 (en la piel) stretch mark. 2 *Arqui* flute, fluting.

estribar I *v.* e. en, to lie in, be based on.

estribillo *nm (en canción)* chorus; (en poema) refrain.

estribo *nm* 1 stirrup; *fig* perder los estribos, to lose one's temper, lose one's head. 2 *Arqui* buttress; (de puente) pier, support.

estribor *nm* starboard.

estricto,-a *adj* strict.

estridente *adj* strident.

estrofa *nf* verse.

estropajo *nm* scourer.

estropear I *vtr (máquina, cosecha)* to damage; *(fiesta, plan)* to spoil, ruin; *(pelo, manos)* to ruin. II **estropearse** *vr* to be ruined; (máquina) to break down.

estropicio *nm fam (destrozo)* damage; (ruido) crash, clatter.

estructura *nf* structure; (armazón) frame, framework.

estructurar *vtr* to structure.

estruendo *nm* roar.

estrujar I *vtr (limón etc)* to squeeze; (ropa) to wring; (apretar) to crush. II **estrujarse** *vr fam* e. los sesos o el cerebro, to rack one's brains.

estrujón *nm* tight squeeze, big hug.

estuche *nm* case; (para lápices) pencil case.

estuco *nm* stucco.

estudiante *nmf* student.

estudiantil *adj* student.

estudiar [12] *vtr & vi* to study.

estudio *nm* 1 study; (encuesta) survey; Com e. de mercado, market research. 2 (sala) studio; e. cinematográfico/de grabación, film/recording studios. 3 (apartamento) studio (flat). 4 estudios, studies.

estudioso,-a I *adj* studious. II *nm,f* specialist.

estufa *nf (calentador)* heater; (de leña) stove.

estupefaciente *nm* drug, narcotic.

estupefacto,-a *adj* astounded, flabbergasted.

estupendo,-a *adj* super, marvellous, *US* marvelous; ¡e.!, great! ◆**estupendamente** *adv* marvellously, *US* marvelously, wonderfully.

estupidez *nf* stupidity.

estúpido,-a I *adj* stupid. II *nm,f* berk, idiot.

estupor *nm* amazement, astonishment.

estupro *nm Jur* rape (of a minor).

estuve *pt indef* → estar.

esvástica *nf* swastika.

ETA *nf abr de* Euzkadi Ta Askatasuna *(Patria Vasca y Libertad),* ETA.

etapa *nf* stage; por etapas, in stages.

etarra *nmf* member of ETA.

etc. *abr de* etcétera, etcetera, etc.

etcétera *adv* etcetera.

éter nm ether.
etéreo,-a adj ethereal.
eternidad nf eternity; fam **una e.**, ages.
eterno,-a adj eternal.
ética nf ethic; (ciencia) ethics sing.
ético,-a adj ethical.
etílico,-a adj ethylic; **alcohol e.**, ethyl alcohol; **en estado e.**, intoxicated; **intoxicación etílica**, alcohol poisoning.
etimología nf etymology.
etimológico,-a adj etymological.
etíope, etiope adj & nmf Ethiopian.
Etiopía nf Ethiopia.
etiqueta nf I (de producto) label. 2 (ceremonia) etiquette; **de e.**, formal.
etiquetar vtr to label.
etnia nf ethnic group.
étnico,-a adj ethnic.
eucalipto nm eucalyptus.
eucaristía nf eucharist.
eufemismo nm euphemism.
euforia nf euphoria.
eufórico,-a adj euphoric.
eureka interj eureka!
eurocomunismo nm Eurocommunism.
eurodiputado,-a nm,f Euro MP.
euromisil nm Euromissile.
Europa nf Europe.
europeísmo nm Europeanism.
europeizar [26] vtr to europeanize.
europeo,-a adj & nm,f European.
euscalduna I adj Basque; (que habla vasco) Basque-speaking. II nmf Basque speaker.
euskera adj & nm Basque.
eutanasia nf euthanasia.
evacuación nf evacuation.
evacuar [10] vtr to evacuate.
evadir I vtr (respuesta, peligro, impuestos) to avoid; (responsabilidad) to shirk. II **evadirse** vr to escape.
evaluación nf evaluation; Educ assessment; **e. continua**, continuous assessment.
evaluar [30] vtr to evaluate, assess.
evangélico,-a adj evangelical.
evangelio nm gospel.
evangelista nm evangelist.
evaporación nf evaporation.
evaporar I vtr to evaporate. II **evaporarse** vr to evaporate; fig to vanish.
evasión nf (fuga) escape; fig evasion; **e. fiscal** o **de impuestos**, tax evasion.
evasiva nf evasive answer.
evasivo,-a adj evasive.
evento nm 1 (acontecimiento) event. 2 (incidente) contingency, unforeseen event.
eventual adj I (posible) possible; (gastos) incidental. 2 (trabajo, obrero) casual, temporary. ◆**eventualmente** adv by chance; **los problemas que e. surjan**, such problems as may arise.
eventualidad nf contingency.
evidencia nf obviousness; **poner a algn en e.**, to show sb up.
evidenciar [12] vtr to show, demonstrate.
evidente adj obvious. ◆**evidentemente** adv obviously.
evitar vtr to avoid; (prevenir) to prevent; (desastre) to avert.
evocador,-a adj evocative.
evocar [1] vtr (traer a la memoria) to evoke; (acordarse de) to recall.
evolución nf evolution; (desarrollo) development.
evolucionar vi to develop; Biol to evolve; **el enfermo evoluciona favorablemente**, the patient is improving.
ex pref former, ex-; **ex alumno**, former pupil, ex-student; **ex combatiente**, exserviceman, US veteran; **ex marido**, exhusband; fam **mi ex**, my ex.
exabrupto nm sharp comment.
exacerbar I vtr 1 (agravar) to exacerbate, aggravate. 2 (irritar) to exasperate, irritate. II **exacerbarse** vr (irritarse) to feel exasperated.
exactitud nf accuracy; **con e.**, precisely.
exacto,-a adj exact; **¡e.!**, precisely!; **para ser e.**, to be precise. ◆**exactamente** adv exactly, precisely.
exageración nf exaggeration.
exagerado,-a adj exaggerated; (excesivo) excessive.
exagerar I vtr to exaggerate. II vi to overdo it.
exaltado,-a adj I (persona) excitable, hotheaded. II nm,f fam fanatic.
exaltar I vtr 1 to praise, extol. II **exaltarse** vr (acalorarse) to get overexcited, get carried away.
examen nm examination, exam; **e. de conducir**, driving test; Med **e. médico**, checkup.
examinador,-a nm,f examiner.
examinar I vtr to examine. II **examinarse** vr to take o sit an examination.
exasperante adj exasperating.
exasperar I vtr to exasperate. II **exasperarse** vr to become exasperated.
Exc., Exca., Exc.ª abr de **Excelencia**, Excellency.
excavación nf excavation; (en arqueología) dig.
excavadora nf digger.
excavar vtr to excavate, dig.
excedencia nf leave (of absence).
excedente adj & nm excess, surplus.
exceder I vtr to exceed, surpass. II **excederse** vr to go too far.
excelencia nf I excellence; **por e.**, par excellence. 2 (título) **Su E.**, His o Her Excellency.
excelente adj excellent.
excelso,-a adj sublime, lofty.
excentricidad nf eccentricity.
excéntrico,-a adj eccentric.
excepción nf exception; **a e. de**, with the

exception of, except for; **de e.,** exceptional; *Pol* **estado de e.,** state of emergency.

excepcional *adj* exceptional.

excepto *adv* except (for), apart from.

exceptuar [30] *vtr* to except, exclude.

excesivo,-a *adj* excessive.

exceso *nm* excess; **en e.,** in excess, excessively; **e. de equipaje,** excess baggage; **e. de velocidad,** speeding.

excitable *adj* excitable.

excitación *nf* (*sentimiento*) excitement.

excitante I *adj* exciting; *Med* stimulating. II *nm* stimulant.

excitar I *vtr* to excite. II **excitarse** *vr* to get excited.

exclamación *nf* exclamation.

exclamar *vtr & vi* to exclaim, cry out.

excluir [37] *vtr* to exclude; (*rechazar*) to reject.

exclusión *nf* exclusion.

exclusiva *nf Prensa* exclusive; *Com* sole right.

exclusive *adv* (*en fechas*) exclusive.

exclusivo,-a *adj* exclusive.

Excma. *abr de* **Excelentísima,** Most Excellent.

Excmo. *abr de* **Excelentísimo,** Most Excellent.

excomulgar [7] *vtr Rel* to excommunicate.

excomunión *nf* excommunication.

excremento *nm* excrement.

exculpar *vtr* to exonerate.

excursión *nf* excursion.

excursionista *nmf* tripper; (*a pie*) hiker.

excusa *nf* (*pretexto*) excuse; (*disculpa*) apology.

excusado *nm* (*retrete*) toilet.

excusar I *vtr* 1 (*justificar*) to excuse. 2 (*eximir*) to exempt (**de,** from). II **excusarse** *vr* (*disculparse*) to apologize.

execrar *vtr* to execrate, abhor.

exención *nf* exemption; **e. de impuestos,** tax exemption.

exento,-a *adj* exempt, free (**de,** from).

exequias *nfpl* funeral rites.

exhalar *vtr* to exhale, breathe out; (*gas*) to give off, emit; (*suspiro*) to heave.

exhaustivo,-a *adj* exhaustive.

exhausto,-a *adj* exhausted.

exhibición *nf* exhibition.

exhibicionista *nmf* exhibitionist.

exhibir I *vtr* (*mostrar*) to exhibit, display. 2 (*lucir*) to show off. II **exhibirse** *vr* to show off, make an exhibition of oneself.

exhortar *vtr* to exhort.

exhumar *vtr* to exhume.

exigencia *nf* 1 demand. 2 (*requisito*) requirement.

exigente *adj* demanding, exacting.

exigir [6] *vtr* to demand.

exiguo,-a *adj* minute.

exilado,-a I *adj* exiled, in exile. II *nm,f* exile.

exilar I *vtr* to exile, send into exile. II **exilarse** *vr* to go into exile.

exiliado,-a *adj & nm,f* → **exilado,-a.**

exiliar [12] *vtr*, **exiliarse** *vr* → **exilar.**

exilio *nm* exile.

eximio,-a *adj* distinguished, eminent.

eximir *vtr* to exempt (**de,** from).

existencia *nf* 1 (*vida*) existence. 2 *Com* **existencias,** stock *sing*, stocks.

existente *adj* existing; *Com* in stock.

existir *vi* to exist, be (in existence).

éxito *nm* success; **con é.,** successfully; **tener é.,** to be successful.

exitoso,-a *adj* successful.

éxodo *nm* exodus.

exonerar *vtr* to exonerate.

exorbitante *adj* exorbitant, excessive.

exorcista *nmf* exorcist.

exorcizar [4] *vtr* to exorcize.

exótico,-a *adj* exotic.

expandir I *vtr* to expand. II **expandirse** (*gas etc*) to expand; (*noticia*) to spread.

expansión *nf* 1 expansion; (*de noticia*) spreading. 2 (*diversión*) relaxation, recreation.

expansionarse *vr fig* (*divertirse*) to relax, let one's hair down.

expatriado,-a *adj & nm,f* expatriate.

expatriar [19] I *vtr* to exile, banish. II **expatriarse** *vr* to leave one's country.

expectación *nf* excitement.

expectativa *nf* expectancy; **estar a la e. de,** to be on the lookout for.

expectorante *nm* expectorant.

expedición *nf* expedition.

expedientar *vtr* to place under enquiry.

expediente *nm* 1 (*informe*) dossier, record; (*ficha*) file; *Educ* **e. académico,** student's record; **abrirle a algn,** to place sb under enquiry. 2 *Jur* proceedings *pl*, action.

expedir [6] *vtr* 1 (*carta*) to send, dispatch. 2 (*pasaporte etc*) to issue.

expedito,-a *adj* free, clear.

expendedor,-a I *nm,f* seller. II *nm* **e. automático,** vending machine.

expendeduría *nf* tobacconist's.

expensas *nfpl* **a c. de,** at the expense of.

experiencia *nf* 1 experience; **por e.,** from experience. 2 (*experimento*) experiment.

experimentado,-a *adj* experienced.

experimental *adj* experimental.

experimentar I *vi* to experiment. II *vtr* to undergo; (*aumento*) to show; (*pérdida*) to suffer; (*sensación*) to experience, feel; *Med* **e. una mejoría,** to improve, make progress.

experimento *nm* experiment.

experto,-a *adj & nm,f* expert.

expiar [29] *vtr* to expiate, atone for.

expirar *vi* to expire.

explanada *nf* esplanade.

explayarse *vr* to talk at length (about).

explicación *nf* explanation.

explicar [1] I *vtr* to explain. II **explicarse** *vr* (*persona*) to explain (oneself); **no me lo explico,** I can't understand it.

explicativo,-a *adj* explanatory.

explícito,-a *adj* explicit.

exploración *nf* exploration; *Téc* scanning; *Med* probe; *Mil* reconnaissance.

explorador,-a *nm,f* 1 (*persona*) explorer. 2 *Med* probe; *Téc* scanner.

explorar *vtr* to explore; *Med* to probe; *Téc* to scan; *Mil* to reconnoitre.

explosión *nf* explosion, blast; **hacer e.,** to explode; **motor de e.,** internal combustion engine; **e. demográfica,** population explosion.

explosionar *vtr* & *vi* to explode, blow up.

explosivo,-a *adj* & *nm* explosive.

explotación *nf* 1 (*abuso*) exploitation. 2 (*uso*) exploitation, working; *Agr* cultivation (of land); (*granja*) farm.

explotador,-a *nm,f pey* exploiter.

explotar I *vi* (*bomba*) to explode, go off. II *vtr* 1 (*aprovechar*) to exploit; (*recursos*) to tap; (*tierra*) to cultivate. 2 (*abusar de*) to exploit.

expoliar [12] *vtr* to plunder, pillage.

exponente *nmf* exponent.

exponer [19] (*pp* **expuesto**) I *vtr* 1 (*mostrar*) to exhibit, display. 2 (*explicar*) to expound, put forward. 3 (*arriesgar*) to expose. II **exponerse** *vr* to expose oneself (a, to); **te expones a perder el trabajo,** you run the risk of losing your job.

exportación *nf* export.

exportador,-a I *adj* exporting. II *nm,f* exporter.

exportar *vtr* to export.

exposición *nf* 1 *Arte* exhibition; **e. universal,** world fair; **sala de exposiciones,** gallery. 2 (*de hechos, ideas*) exposé. 3 *Fot* exposure.

exprés *adj* express; (*olla*) **e.,** pressure cooker; (*café*) **e.,** espresso (coffee).

expresar I *vtr* to express; (*manifestar*) to state. II **expresarse** *vr* to express oneself.

expresión *nf* expression; **la mínima e.,** the bare minimum.

expresivo,-a *adj* expressive.

expreso,-a I *adj* express; **con el fin e. de,** with the express purpose of. II *nm Ferroc* express (train). III *adv* on purpose, deliberately. ◆**expresamente** *adv* specifically, expressly.

exprimidor *nm* squeezer, *US* juicer.

exprimir *vtr* (*limón*) to squeeze; (*zumo*) to squeeze out; *fig* (*persona*) to exploit, bleed dry.

expropiar [12] *vtr* to expropriate.

expuesto,-a *adj* 1 (*sin protección*) exposed; **estar e. a,** to be exposed to. 2 (*peligroso*) risky, dangerous. 3 (*exhibido*) on display,

on show.

expulsar *vtr* 1 to expel, throw out; *Dep* (*jugador*) to send off. 2 (*gas etc*) to belch out.

expulsión *nf* expulsion; *Dep* sending off.

expurgar [7] *vtr* to expurgate; *fig* to purge.

expuse *pt indef* → **exponer**.

exquisito,-a *adj* exquisite; (*comida*) delicious; (*gusto*) refined.

extasiado,-a *adj* ecstatic; **quedarse e.,** to go into ecstasies *o* raptures.

extasiarse [29] *vr* to go into ecstasies *o* raptures.

éxtasis *nm inv* ecstasy.

extender [3] I *vtr* 1 to extend; (*agrandar*) to enlarge. 2 (*mantel, mapa*) to spread (out), open (out); (*mano, brazo*) to stretch (out). 3 (*crema, mantequilla*) to spread. 3 (*cheque*) to make out; (*documento*) to draw up; (*certificado*) to issue. II **extenderse** *vr* 1 (*en el tiempo*) to extend, last. 2 (*en el espacio*) to spread out, stretch. 3 (*rumor, noticia*) to spread, extend. 4 *fig* (*hablar demasiado*) to go on.

extendido,-a *adj* 1 extended; (*mapa, plano*) spread out, open; (*mano, brazo*) outstretched. 2 (*costumbre, rumor*) widespread.

extensible *adj* extending.

extensión *nf* (*de libro etc*) length; (*de cuerpo*) size; (*de terreno*) area, expanse; (*edificio anexo*) extension; **en toda la e. de la palabra,** in every sense of the word; **por e.,** by extension.

extensivo,-a *adj* hacer **e.,** to extend; **ser e. a,** to cover.

extenso,-a *adj* (*terreno*) extensive; (*libro, película*) long.

extenuar [30] I *vtr* to exhaust. II **extenuarse** *vr* to exhaust oneself.

exterior I *adj* 1 (*de fuera*) outer; (*puerta*) outside. 2 (*política, deuda*) foreign; *Pol* **Ministerio de Asuntos Exteriores,** Ministry of Foreign Affairs, *GB* Foreign Office, *US* State Department. II *nm* 1 (*parte de fuera*) exterior, outside. 2 (*extranjero*) abroad. 3 **exteriores,** *Cin* location *sing*. ◆**exteriormente** *adv* outwardly.

exteriorizar [4] *vtr* to show.

exterminar *vtr* to exterminate.

exterminio *nm* extermination.

externo,-a I *adj* external; *Farm* **de uso e.,** for external use only. II *nm,f Educ* day pupil.

extinción *nf* extinction.

extinguir [8] I *vtr* (*fuego*) to extinguish, put out; (*raza*) to wipe out. II **extinguirse** *vr* (*fuego*) to go out; (*especie*) to become extinct, die out.

extinto,-a *adj* extinct.

extintor *nm* fire extinguisher.

extirpar *vtr* 1 *Med* to remove. 2 *fig* to

eradicate, stamp out.

extorsión *nf* extortion.

extorsionar *vtr* to extort.

extra¹ I *adj* 1 (*suplementario*) extra; **horas e.**, overtime; **paga e.**, bonus. 2 (*superior*) top quality. **II** *nm* extra. **III** *nm,f* Cin Teat extra.

extra² *pref* extra; **extramatrimonial**, extramarital.

extracción *nf* 1 extraction. 2 (*en lotería*) draw.

extracto *nm* 1 extract; **e. de fresa**, strawberry extract; **e. de regaliz**, liquorice; **Fin e. de cuenta**, statement of account. 2 (*resumen*) summary.

extractor *nm* extractor.

extradición *nf* extradition.

extraer [25] *vtr* to extract, take out.

extraescolar *adj* (*actividad etc*) extracurricular.

extrafino,-a *adj* superfine.

extralimitarse *vr* to overstep the mark.

extranjería *nf* ley de e., law on aliens.

extranjero,-a I *adj* foreign. **II** *nm,f* foreigner. **III** *nm* abroad; **en el e.**, abroad.

extrañar I *vtr* 1 (*sorprender*) to surprise; **no es de e.**, it's hardly surprising. 2 *Am* (*echar de menos*) to miss. **II extrañarse** *vr* **e. de**, to be surprised at.

extrañeza *nf* 1 (*sorpresa*) surprise, astonishment. 2 (*singularidad*) strangeness.

extraño,-a I *adj* strange; *Med* **cuerpo e.**, foreign body. **II** *nm,f* stranger.

extraoficial *adj* unofficial.

extraordinaria *nf* (*paga*) bonus.

extraordinario,-a *adj* extraordinary; *Prensa* **edición extraordinaria**, special edition.

extrarradio *nm* outskirts *pl*, suburbs *pl*.

extraterrestre *nmf* alien.

extravagancia *nf* extravagance.

extravagante *adj* odd, outlandish.

extravertido,-a *adj* → extrovertido,-a.

extraviado,-a *adj* lost, missing.

extraviar [29] **I** *vtr* to mislay, lose. **II extraviarse** *vr* to be missing, get mislaid.

extremado,-a *adj* extreme.
◆**extremadamente** *adv* extremely.

Extremadura *n* Estremadura.

extremar I *vtr* **e. la prudencia**, to be extremely careful. **II extremarse** *vr* to take great pains, do one's utmost.

extremaunción *nf* extreme unction.

extremeño,-a I *adj* of o from Estremadura. **II** *nm,f* native of Estremadura.

extremidad *nf* 1 (*extremo*) end, tip. 2 *Anat* (*miembro*) limb, extremity.

extremista *adj & nmf* extremist.

extremo,-a I *nm* (*de calle, cable*) end; (*máximo*) extreme; **en e.**, very much; **en último e.**, as a last resort. 2 *nm,f Dep* winger; **Ftb e. derecha/izquierda**, outside-right/left. **III** *adj* extreme; **E. Oriente**, Far East.

extrovertido,-a *adj & nm,f* extrovert.

exuberante *adj* exuberant; (*vegetación*) lush, abundant.

eyaculación *nf* ejaculation; **e. precoz**, premature ejaculation.

eyacular *vi* to ejaculate.

eyectable *adj* **asiento e.**, ejector seat.

F

F, f ['efe] *nf* (*la letra*) F, f.

F *abr de* Fahrenheit, Fahrenheit, F.

fa *nm* Mús F.

fabada *nf* stew of beans, pork sausage and bacon.

fábrica *nf* factory; **marca de f.**, trademark; **precio de f.**, factory o ex-works price.

fabricación *nf* manufacture; **de f. casera**, home-made; **de f. propia**, our own make; **f. en cadena**, mass production.

fabricante *nmf* manufacturer.

fabricar [1] *vtr* 1 *Ind* to manufacture. 2 *fig* (*mentiras etc*) to fabricate.

fabril *adj* manufacturing.

fábula *nf* fable.

fabuloso,-a *adj* fabulous.

faca *nf* large curved knife.

facción *nf* 1 *Pol* faction. 2 **facciones**, (*rasgos*) features.

faccioso,-a I *adj* seditious. **II** *nm,f* rebel.

faceta *nf* facet.

facha¹ *nf fam* appearance, look.

facha² *nmf pey* fascist.

fachada *nf* façade.

facial *adj* facial.

fácil *adj* 1 easy; **f. de comprender**, easy to understand. 2 (*probable*) likely, probable; **es f. que ...**, it's (quite) likely that ....
◆**fácilmente** *adv* easily.

facilidad *nf* 1 (*sencillez*) easiness. 2 (*soltura*) ease. 3 (*servicio*) facility; **dar facilidades**, to make things easy; *Com* **facilidades de pago**, easy terms. 4 **f. para los idiomas**, gift for languages.

facilitar *vtr* (*proporcionar*) to provide, supply (a, with).

facineroso,-a *adj* criminal.

facsímil, facsímile *nm* facsimile.

factible *adj* feasible.

fáctico,-a *adj* **poderes fácticos**, vested interests.

factor *nm* 1 factor. 2 *Ferroc* luggage clerk.

factoría *nf* (*fábrica*) factory.

factura *nf Com* invoice.

facturación *nf* 1 *Com* invoicing. 2 (*de

equipajes) (en aeropuerto) check-in; *(en estación)* registration.

facturar *vtr* 1 *Com* to invoice. 2 *(en aeropuerto)* to check in; *(en estación)* to register.

facultad *nf* faculty; **facultades mentales,** faculties.

facultativo,-a I *adj* optional. II *nm,f* doctor.

faena *nf* 1 *(tarea)* task. 2 *fam (mala pasada)* dirty trick. 3 *Taur* performance.

faenar *vi* to fish.

fagot *Mús* bassoon.

faisán *nm* pheasant.

faja *nf* 1 *(corsé)* girdle, corset. 2 *(banda)* sash. 3 *(de terreno)* strip.

fajo *nm (de ropa etc)* bundle; *(de billetes)* wad.

falacia *nf* fallacy.

falaz *adj* 1 *(erróneo)* fallacious. 2 *(engañoso)* deceitful.

falda *nf* 1 *(prenda)* skirt; **f. pantalón,** culottes *pl*. 2 *(de montaña)* slope, hillside. 3 *(de mesa)* cover. 4 *(regazo)* lap.

faldero,-a *adj* **perro f.,** lapdog.

falla¹ *nf Geol* fault.

falla² *nf Am (defecto)* defect, fault.

fallar¹ *vi Jur* to rule. II *vtr (premio)* to award.

fallar² *vi* to fail; **le falló la puntería,** he missed his aim; **tú no me falles,** don't let me down. II *vtr* to miss.

fallecer [33] *vi fml* to pass away, die.

fallecido,-a *adj* deceased.

fallecimiento *nm* demise.

fallido,-a *adj* unsuccessful, vain.

fallo¹ *nm* 1 *(error)* mistake; **f. humano,** human error. 2 *(del corazón, de los frenos)* failure.

fallo² *nm* 1 *Jur* judgement, sentence. 2 *(en concurso)* awarding.

falo *nm* phallus.

falsear *vtr* 1 *(informe etc)* to falsify; *(hechos, la verdad)* to distort. 2 *(moneda)* to forge.

falsedad *nf* 1 falseness, *(doblez)* hypocrisy. 2 *(mentira)* falsehood.

falsificar [1] *vtr* to falsify; *(cuadro, firma, moneda)* to forge.

falso,-a *adj* 1 false; **dar un paso en f.,** *(tropezar)* to trip, stumble; *fig* to make a blunder; **jurar en f.,** to commit perjury. 2 *(persona)* insincere.

falta *nf* 1 *(carencia)* lack; **por f. de,** for want *o* lack of; **sin f.,** without fail; **f. de educación,** bad manners. 2 *(escasez)* shortage. 3 *(ausencia)* absence; **echar algo/a algn en f.,** to miss sth/sb. 4 *(error)* mistake; *(defecto)* fault, defect; **f. de ortografía,** spelling mistake; **sacar faltas a algo/a algn,** to find fault with sth/sb. 5 *Jur* misdemeanour. 6 *Dep (fútbol)* foul; *(tenis)* fault. 7 **hacer f.,** to be necessary; **(nos) hace f. una escalera,** we need a

ladder; **harán f. dos personas para mover el piano,** it'll take two people to move the piano; **no hace f. que ...,** there is no need for ....

faltar *vi* 1 *(no estar)* to be missing; **¿quién falta?,** who is missing? 2 *(escasear)* to be lacking *o* needed; **le falta confianza en sí mismo,** he lacks confidence in himself; **¡lo que me faltaba!,** that's all I needed!; **¡no faltaría o faltaba más!,** *(por supuesto)* (but) of course! 3 *(quedar)* to be left; **¿cuántos kilómetros faltan para Managua?,** how many kilometres is it to Managua?; **ya falta poco para las vacaciones,** it won't be long now till the holidays; **faltó poco para que me cayera,** I very nearly fell. 4 **f. a la verdad,** not to tell the truth; **f. al deber,** to fail in one's duty; **f. a su palabra/promesa,** to break one's word/promise; **f. al respeto a algn,** to treat sb with disrespect.

falto,-a *adj* **f. de,** lacking in.

fama *nf* 1 fame, renown; **de f. mundial,** world-famous. 2 *(reputación)* reputation.

famélico,-a *adj* starving, famished.

familia *nf* family; **estar en f.,** to be among friends; **f. numerosa,** large family.

familiar I *adj* 1 *(de la familia)* family; **empresa f.,** family business. 2 *(conocido)* familiar. II *nmf* relation, relative.

familiaridad *nf* familiarity.

familiarizarse [4] *vr* to familiarize oneself (con, with).

famoso,-a I *adj* famous. II *nm* famous person.

fan *nmf* fan.

fanático,-a I *adj* fanatical. II *nm,f* fanatic.

fanatismo *nm* fanaticism.

fanfarrón,-ona I *adj* boastful. II *nm,f* show-off.

fanfarronear *vi fam (chulear)* to show off; *(bravear)* to brag, boast.

fango *nm* 1 *(barro)* mud. 2 *fig* degradation.

fantasear *vi* to daydream, dream.

fantasía *nf* fantasy; **joya de f.,** imitation jewellery.

fantasioso,-a *adj* imaginative.

fantasma *nm* 1 *(espectro)* ghost. 2 *fam (fanfarrón)* braggart, show-off.

fantasmal *adj* ghostly.

fantástico,-a *adj* fantastic.

fantoche *nm pey* nincompoop, ninny.

faraón *nm* Pharaoh.

fardar *vi arg* to show off.

fardo *nm* bundle.

farfullar *vtr* to jabber.

faringe *nf* pharynx.

faringitis *nf* pharyngitis.

fariseo,-a *nm,f (falso)* hypocrite.

farmacéutico,-a I *adj* pharmaceutical. II *nm,f* pharmacist.

farmacia *nf* 1 *(tienda)* chemist's (shop),

US pharmacy. 2 (*ciencia*) pharmacology.

fármaco *nm* medicine, medication.

faro *nm* 1 (*torre*) lighthouse. 2 (*de coche*) headlight, headlamp.

farol *nm* 1 lantern; (*en la calle*) streetlight, streetlamp. 2 *arg* (*fanfarronada*) bragging; **tirarse un f.**, to brag. 3 (*en naipes*) bluff.

farola *nf* streetlight, streetlamp.

farolear *vi arg* to brag.

farolillo *nm fig* **ser el f. rojo**, to bring up the rear.

farragoso,-a *adj* confused, rambling.

farruco,-a *adj fam* cocky.

farsa *nf* farce.

farsante *nmf* fake, impostor.

fascículo *nm Impr* instalment, *US* installment.

fascinador,-a, fascinante *adj* fascinating.

fascinar *vtr* to fascinate.

fascismo *nm* fascism.

fascista *adj & nmf* fascist.

fase *nf* 1 (*etapa*) phase, stage. 2 *Elec Fís* phase.

fastidiado,-a *adj fam* 1 (*roto*) broken. 2 (*enfermo*) sick; **tiene el estómago f.**, he's got a bad stomach.

fastidiar [12] I *vtr* 1 (*molestar*) to annoy, bother; (*dañar*) to hurt; *fam* **¡no fastidies!**, you're kidding! 2 *fam* (*estropear*) to damage, ruin; (*planes*) to spoil. II **fastidiarse** *vr* 1 (*aguantarse*) to put up with it, resign oneself; **que se fastidie**, that's his tough luck. 2 *fam* (*estropearse*) to get damaged, break down. 3 **me he fastidiado el tobillo**, I've hurt my ankle.

fastidio *nm* nuisance.

fastuoso,-a *adj* 1 (*acto*) splendid, lavish. 2 (*persona*) lavish, ostentatious.

fatal I *adj* 1 *fam* (*muy malo*) awful, dreadful. 2 (*mortal*) deadly, fatal. 3 (*inexorable*) fateful, inevitable. II *adv fam* awfully, terribly; **lo pasó f.**, he had a rotten time.

fatalidad *nf* 1 (*destino*) fate. 2 (*desgracia*) misfortune.

fatalista I *adj* fatalistic. II *nmf* fatalist.

fatiga *nf* 1 (*cansancio*) fatigue. 2 **fatigas**, (*dificultades*) troubles, difficulties.

fatigar [7] I *vtr* to tire, weary. II **fatigarse** *vr* to tire, become tired.

fatigoso,-a *adj* tiring, exhausting.

fatuo,-a *adj* 1 (*envanecido*) vain, conceited. 2 (*necio*) fatuous, foolish.

fauces *nfpl fig* jaws.

fauna *nf* fauna.

favor *nm* favour, *US* favor; **por f.**, please; **¿puedes hacerme un f.?**, can you do me a favour?; **estar a f. de**, to be in favour of; **haga el f. de sentarse**, please sit down.

favorable *adj* favourable, *US* favorable; **f. a**, in favour of.

favorecedor,-a *adj* flattering.

favorecer [33] *vtr* 1 to favour, *US* favor. 2 (*sentar bien*) to flatter.

favoritismo *nm* favouritism, *US* favoritism.

favorito,-a *adj & nm,f* favourite, *US* favorite.

faz *nf* (*pl* **faces**) *lit* (*cara*) face.

fe *nf* 1 faith; **de buena/mala fe**, with good/dishonest intentions. 2 (*certificado*) certificate; **fe de bautismo/matrimonio**, baptism/marriage certificate. 3 *Impr* **fe de erratas**, list of errata.

fealdad *nf* ugliness.

febrero *nm* February.

febril *adj* 1 *Med* feverish. 2 (*actividad*) hectic.

fecha *nf* 1 date; **f. límite** *o* **tope**, deadline; **f. de caducidad**, sell-by date; **hasta la f.**, so far; **en f. próxima**, at an early date. 2 **fechas**, (*época*) time *sing*; **el año pasado por estas fechas**, this time last year.

fechar *vtr* to date.

fechoría *nf* (*de niños*) mischief; *arc* misdeed.

fécula *nf* starch.

fecundación *nf* fertilization; **f. in vitro**, in vitro fertilization.

fecundar *vtr* to fertilize.

fecundo,-a *adj* fertile.

federación *nf* federation.

federal *adj & nmf* federal.

fehaciente *adj* 1 *fml* authentic, reliable. 2 *Jur* irrefutable; **documento** *o* **prueba f.**, irrefutable proof.

felicidad *nf* happiness; (*muchas*) **felicidades**, (*en cumpleaños*) many happy returns.

felicitación *nf* **tarjeta de f.** greetings card.

felicitar *vtr* to congratulate (*por*; on); **¡te felicito!**, congratulations!

feligrés,-a *nm,f* parishioner.

felino,-a *adj & nm* feline.

feliz *adj* (*contento*) happy; **¡felices Navidades!**, Happy *o* Merry Christmas! 2 (*decisión etc*) fortunate.

felonía *nf* treachery.

felpa *nf* 1 *Tex* plush; **oso** *o* **osito de f.**, teddy bear. 2 (*para el pelo*) hairband.

felpudo *nm* mat, doormat.

femenino,-a *adj* feminine; (*equipo, ropa*) women's; **sexo f.**, female sex.

feminismo *nm* feminism.

feminista *adj & nmf* feminist.

fémur *nm* femur.

fenecer [33] *vi euf* to pass away, die.

fenomenal I *adj* 1 phenomenal. 2 *fam* (*fantástico*) great, terrific. II *adv fam* wonderfully, marvellously; **lo pasamos f.**, we had a fantastic time.

fenómeno,-a I *nm* 1 phenomenon. 2 (*prodigio*) genius. 3 (*monstruo*) freak. II *adj fam* fantastic, terrific. III *interj* fantastic!, terrific!

feo,-a *adj* 1 ugly; (*asunto etc*) nasty. 2 *nm fam* **hacerle un f. a algn**, to offend sb.

féretro *nm* coffin.

feria nf fair; f. de muestras/del libro, trade/book fair.

feriado,-a adj día f., holiday.

ferial adj recinto f., (de exposiciones) exhibition centre; (de fiestas) fairground.

ferina adj tos f., whooping cough.

fermentar vi to ferment.

fermento nm ferment.

ferocidad nf ferocity, fierceness.

feroz adj fierce, ferocious; **el lobo f.**, the big bad wolf.

férreo,-a adj ferreous; fig iron.

ferretería nf ironmonger's (shop), hardware store.

ferrocarril nm railway, US railroad.

ferroviario,-a adj railway, rail.

ferry nm ferry.

fértil adj fertile.

fertilidad nf fertility.

fertilizante I adj fertilizing. II nm fertilizer.

fertilizar [4] vtr to fertilize.

ferviente adj fervent.

fervor nm fervour, US fervor.

fervoroso,-a adj fervent.

festejar vtr to celebrate.

festejos nmpl festivities.

festín nm feast, banquet.

festival nm festival.

festividad nf festivity.

festivo,-a I adj 1 (ambiente etc) festive. 2 día f., holiday. II nm holiday.

fetal adj foetal, US fetal.

fetiche nm fetish.

fétido,-a adj stinking, fetid.

feto nm foetus, US fetus.

feudalismo nm feudalism.

feudo nm fief; Pol stronghold.

FEVE nmpl abr de Ferrocarriles Españoles de Vía Estrecha.

FF.AA. nfpl abr de Fuerzas Armadas, Armed Forces.

FF.CC. nmpl abr de ferrocarriles, railways.

fiabilidad nf reliability, trustworthiness.

fiable adj reliable, trustworthy

fiador,-a nm,f guarantor; **salir o ser f. de algn**, (pagar fianza) to stand bail for sb; (avalar) to vouch for sb.

fiambre nm 1 Culin cold meat. 2 fam (cadáver) stiff, corpse.

fiambrera nf lunch box.

fianza nf (depósito) deposit; Jur bail; **en libertad bajo f.**, on bail.

fiar [29] I vtr 1 (avalar) to guarantee. 2 (vender sin cobrar) to sell on credit. II **fiarse** vr to trust (de, -).

fiasco nm fiasco.

fibra nf fibre, US fiber; (de madera) grain; f. de vidrio, fibreglass.

ficción nf fiction.

ficha nf 1 (tarjeta) filing card; f. técnica, specifications pl, technical data; (de créditos pl. 2 (en juegos) counter; (de ajedrez) piece, man; (de dominó) domino.

fichado,-a adj está f. por la policía, he has a police record.

fichaje nm Dep signing.

fichar I vtr 1 to put on file. 2 Dep to sign up. II vi 1 (en el trabajo) (al entrar) to clock in; (al salir) to clock out. 2 Dep to sign.

fichero nm card index.

ficticio,-a adj fictitious.

fidedigno,-a adj reliable, trustworthy; **fuentes fidedignas**, reliable sources.

fidelidad nf faithfulness; **alta f.**, high fidelity, hi-fi.

fideo nm noodle.

fiebre nf fever; **tener f.**, to have a temperature.

fiel I adj 1 (leal) faithful, loyal. 2 (exacto) accurate, exact. II nm 1 (de balanza) needle, pointer. 2 Rel **los fieles**, the congregation.

fieltro nm felt.

fiera nf 1 wild animal; **fam estaba hecho una f.**, he was hopping mad. 2 Taur bull.

fiero,-a adj (salvaje) wild; (feroz) fierce, ferocious.

fierro nm Am 1 (hierro) iron. 2 (navaja) knife.

fiesta nf 1 (entre amigos) party. 2 **día de f.**, holiday. 3 Rel feast; f. de guardar, holy day of obligation. 4 (festividad) celebration, festivity.

figura nf figure.

figurado,-a adj figurative; **en sentido f.**, figuratively.

figurar I vi (en lista) to figure. II **figurarse** vr 1 to imagine, suppose; **ya me lo figuraba**, I thought as much. 2 **¡figúrate!**, **¡figúrese!**, just imagine!

figurinista nmf Teat Cin costume designer.

fijador nm 1 (gomina) gel. 2 Fot fixative.

fijar I vtr to fix; **prohibido f. carteles**, (en letrero) post no bills. II **fijarse** vr 1 (darse cuenta) to notice. 2 (poner atención) to pay attention, watch.

fijo,-a adj 1 fixed; **sin domicilio f.**, of no fixed abode. 2 (trabajo) steady.
◆**fijamente** adv mirar f., to stare.

fila nf 1 file; **en f. india**, in single file; **poner en f.**, to line up. 2 (de cine, teatro) row. 3 Mil **filas**, ranks; **llamar a algn a f.**, to call sb up; **¡rompan f.!**, fall out!, dismiss!

filamento nm filament.

filantropía nf philanthropy.

filántropo,-a nm,f philanthropist.

filarmónico,-a adj philharmonic.

filatelia nf philately, stamp collecting.

filete nm (de carne, pescado) fillet.

filiación nf Pol affiliation.

filial I adj 1 (de hijos) filial. 2 Com subsidiary. II nf Com subsidiary.

filigrana nf 1 filigree. 2 fig **filigranas**, intricacy sing, intricate work sing.

Filipinas *npl* (las) F., (the) Philippines.

filipino,-a *adj & nm,f* Philippine, Filipino.

filmar *vtr* to film, shoot.

film(e) *nm* film.

fílmico,-a *adj* film.

filmoteca *nf* (*archivo*) film library.

filo *nm* (cutting) edge; **al f. de la medianoche**, on the stroke of midnight; *fig* **de doble f.**, double-edged.

filón *nm* 1 *Min* seam, vein. 2 *fig* (*buen negocio*) gold mine.

filoso,-a *adj Am* sharp-edged.

filosofal *adj* **piedra f.**, philosopher's stone.

filosofía *nf* philosophy; *fig* **con f.**, philosophically.

filosófico,-a *adj* philosophical.

filósofo,-a *nm,f* philosopher.

filtración *nf* filtration; (*de información*) leak.

filtrar I *vtr* 1 to filter. 2 (*información*) to leak. II **filtrarse** *vr* 1 (*líquido*) seep. 2 (*información*) to leak out.

filtro *nm* filter.

fin *nm* 1 (*final*) end; **dar** *o* **poner f. a**, to put an end to; **llegar** *o* **tocar a su f.**, to come to an end; **¡por** *o* **al f.!**, at last!; **f. de semana**, weekend; **al f. y al cabo**, when all's said and done; **noche de F. de Año**, New Year's Eve. 2 (*objetivo*) purpose, aim; **a f. de**, in order to, so as to; **a f. de que**, in order that, so that; **con el f. de**, with the intention of.

final I *adj* final. II *nm*; **al f.**, in the end; **f. de línea**, terminal; **f. feliz**, happy ending; **a finales de octubre**, at the end of October. III *nf* *Dep* final.
◆**finalmente** *adv* finally.

finalidad *nf* purpose, aim.

finalista I *nmf* finalist. II *adj* in the final.

finalizar [4] *vtr & vi* to end, finish.

financiación *nf* financing.

financiar [12] *vtr* to finance.

financiero,-a I *adj* financial. II *nm,f* financier.

financista *nmf Am* financier, financial expert.

finanzas *nfpl* finances.

finca *nf* (*inmueble*) property; (*de campo*) country house.

finés,-a *adj, nm,f → finlandés,-esa**.

fingido *nf adj* feigned, false; **nombre f.**, assumed name.

fingir [6] I *vtr* to feign. II **fingirse** *vr* to pretend to be.

finlandés,-a I *adj* Finnish. II *nm,f* (*persona*) Finn. III *nm* (*idioma*) Finnish.

Finlandia *n* Finland.

fino,-a I *adj* 1 (*hilo, capa*) fine. 2 (*flaco*) thin. 3 (*educado*) refined, polite. 4 (*oído*) sharp, acute; (*olfato*) keen. 5 (*humor, ironía*) subtle. II *nm* (*vino*) type of dry sherry.

finta *nf* (*en boxeo*) feint; (*en fútbol*) dummy.

finura *nf* 1 (*refinamiento*) refinement, politeness. 2 (*sutileza*) subtlety.

firma *nf* 1 signature. 2 (*empresa*) firm, company.

firmamento *nm* firmament.

firmante *adj & nmf* signatory; **el** *o* **la abajo f.**, the undersigned.

firmar *vtr* to sign.

firme I *adj* 1 firm; *fig* **mantenerse f.**, to hold one's ground; **tierra f.**, terra firma. 2 *Mil* ¡firmes!, attention!. II *nm* (*de carretera*) road surface. III *adv* hard.
◆**firmemente** *adv* firmly.

firmeza *nf* firmness.

fiscal I *adj* fiscal, tax. II *nmf Jur* public prosecutor, *US* district attorney.

fisco *nm* treasury, exchequer.

fisgar [7] *vi fam* to snoop, pry.

fisgón,-ona *nm,f* snooper.

fisgonear *vi* to snoop, pry.

física *nf* physics *sing*.

físico,-a I *adj* physical. II *nm,f* (*profesión*) physicist. III *nm* physique.

fisión *nf* fission.

fisioterapeuta *nmf* physiotherapist.

fisioterapia *nf Med* physiotherapy.

fisonomía *nf* physiognomy.

fisonomista *nmf fam* **ser buen/mal f.**, to be good/no good at remembering faces.

fisura *nf* fissure.

fláccido,-a *adj* flaccid, flabby.

flaco,-a *adj* 1 (*delgado*) skinny. 2 *fig* **punto f.**, weak spot.

flagelar *vtr* to flagellate.

flagelo *nm* (*látigo*) whip; *fig* scourge.

flagrante *adj* flagrant; **en f. delito**, red-handed.

flamante *adj* 1 **nuevecito**, (*nuevo*) brand-new. 2 (*vistoso*) splendid, brilliant.

flamenco,-a I *adj* 1 *Mús* flamenco. 2 (*de Flandes*) Flemish. II *nm* 1 *Mús* flamenco. 2 *Orn* flamingo. 3 (*idioma*) Flemish.

flan *nm* caramel custard.

flanco *nm* flank, side.

flanquear *vtr* to flank.

flaquear *vi* (*fuerzas, piernas*) to weaken, give way.

flaqueza *nf* weakness.

flash *nm Fot* flash.

flato *nm* wind, flatulence.

flatulencia *nf* flatulence.

flauta *nf* flute; **f. dulce**, recorder.

flautín *nm* (*instrumento*) piccolo.

flautista *nmf Mús* flautist, *US* flutist, flute player.

flecha *nf* arrow.

flechazo *nm fig* (*enamoramiento*) love at first sight.

fleco *nm* fringe.

flema *nf* phlegm.

flemático,-a *adj* phlegmatic.

flemón *nm* gumboil, abscess.

flequillo nm fringe, US bangs.

fletar vtr to charter.

flete nm 1 (alquiler) charter. 2 (carga) freight.

flexibilidad nf flexibility.

flexible adj flexible.

flexión nf 1 flexion. 2 Ling inflection. 3 Gimn **flexiones**, press-ups, US push-ups.

flexionar vtr to bend; (músculo) to flex.

flexo nm reading lamp.

flipante adj fam great, cool.

flipar vtr fam **le flipan las motos**, he's crazy about motorbikes.

flirtear vi to flirt.

flirteo nm flirting.

flojear vi (ventas etc) to fall off, go down; (piernas) to weaken, grow weak; (memoria) to fail.

flojera nf fam weakness, faintness.

flojo,-a I adj 1 (tornillo, cuerda etc) loose, slack. 2 (perezoso) lazy, idle; (exámen, trabajo, resultado) poor.

flor nf 1 flower; **en f.**, in blossom; fig **en la f. de la vida**, in the prime of life; fig **la f. y nata**, the cream (of society). 2 **a f. de piel**, skin-deep.

flora nf flora.

floreado,-a adj flowery.

florecer [33] vi 1 (plantas) to flower. 2 fig (negocio) to flourish, thrive.

floreciente adj fig flourishing, prosperous.

Florencia n Florence.

florero nm vase.

floricultura nf flower growing, floriculture.

florido,-a adj 1 (con flores) flowery. 2 (estilo) florid.

floripondio nm pey (adorno) heavy ornamentation.

florista nmf florist.

floristería nf florist's (shop).

flota nf fleet.

flotador nm 1 (de pesca) float. 2 (para nadar) rubber ring.

flotar vi to float.

flote nm floating; **a f.**, afloat; **sacar a f. un negocio**, to put a business on a sound footing.

flotilla nf flotilla.

fluctuación nf fluctuation.

fluctuar [30] vi to fluctuate.

fluidez nf fluency.

fluido,-a adj 1 fluid; (estilo etc) fluent. II nm fluid; **f. eléctrico**, current.

fluir [37] vi to flow.

flujo nm 1 flow. 2 rising tide; **f. y reflujo**, ebb and flow. 3 Fís flux. 4 Med discharge. 5 Inform stream.

flúor nm fluorine.

fluorescente adj fluorescent.

fluvial adj river.

FM nf abr de **Frecuencia Modulada**, frequency modulation, FM.

FMI nm abr de **Fondo Monetario Internacional**, International Monetary Fund, IMF.

fobia nf phobia (a, about).

foca nf seal.

foco nm 1 Elec spotlight, floodlight. 2 (de ideas, revolución etc) centre, US center, focal point. 2 Am (bombilla) (electric light) bulb; (de coche) (car) headlight; (farola) street light.

fofo,-a adj soft; (persona) flabby.

fogata nf bonfire.

fogón nm (de cocina) ring.

fogonazo nm flash.

fogosidad nf ardour, US ardor, fire.

fogoso,-a adj fiery, spirited.

fogueo nm **cartucho de f.**, blank cartridge.

folio nm sheet of paper.

folklore nm folklore.

folklórico,-a adj m. **folklórica**, folk music.

follaje nm foliage.

follar vulg I vi to fuck, screw. II vtr (suspender) to fail. III **follarse** vtr **f. a algn**, to fuck sb, screw sb.

folletín nm 1 (relato) newspaper serial. 2 fig melodrama.

folleto nm leaflet; (turístico) brochure.

follón nm fam 1 (alboroto) rumpus, shindy; **armar (un) f.**, to kick up a rumpus. 2 (enredo, confusión) mess, trouble; **meterse en un f.**, to get into a mess. 3 **un f. de**, (montón) a load of.

follonero,-a nm,f troublemaker.

fomentar vtr to promote.

fomento nm promotion.

fonda nf inn.

fondear vi to anchor.

fondista nmf Dep long-distance runner.

fondo¹ nm 1 (parte más baja) bottom; **a f.**, thoroughly; **al f. de la calle**, at the bottom of the street; **tocar f.**, Náut to touch bottom; fig to reach rock bottom; fig **en el f. es bueno**, deep down he's kind; **bajos fondos**, dregs of society; **doble f.**, false bottom. 2 (de habitación) back; (de pasillo) end. 3 (segundo término) background; **música de f.**, background music. 4 Prensa **artículo de f.**, leading article. 5 Dep **corredor de f.**, long-distance runner; **esquí de f.**, cross-country skiing.

fondo² Fin fund; **cheque sin fondos**, bad cheque; fam **f. común**, kitty.

fonendoscopio nm stethoscope.

fonética nf phonetics sing.

fonético,-a adj phonetic.

fontanería nf plumbing.

fontanero,-a nm,f plumber.

footing nm jogging; **hacer f.**, to go jogging.

forajido,-a nm,f outlaw.

foral adj **Comunidad F.**, Navarre.

foráneo,-a adj foreign.

forastero,-a nm,f outsider, stranger.

forcejar vi to wrestle, struggle.

forcejeo nm struggle.

fórceps nm inv forceps pl.

forense I adj forensic. II nmf (médico) f., forensic surgeon.

forestal adj forest; **repoblación** f., re-afforestation.

forjado,-a adj wrought.

forjar vtr (metal) to forge; fig to create, make.

forma nf 1 form, shape; **en f. de L**, L-shaped; **¿qué f. tiene?**, what shape is it? 2 (manera) way; **de esta f.**, in this way; **de f. que**, so that; **de todas formas**, anyway, in any case; **no hubo f. de convencerla**, there was no way we could convince her; **f. de pago**, method of payment. 3 Dep form; **estar en f.**, to be on form; **estar en baja f.**, to be off form. 4 Rel Sagrada F., Host. 5 formas, (modales) manners.

formación nf 1 formation. 2 (educación) upbringing. 3 (enseñanza) training; **f. profesional**, vocational training.

formal adj formal; (serio) serious, serious-minded; (fiable) reliable, dependable.

formalidad nf 1 formality. 2 (seriedad) seriousness. 3 (fiabilidad) reliability. 4 **formalidades**, (trámites) formalities.

formalizar [4] I vtr to formalize. II **formalizarse** vr to settle down.

formar I vtr 1 to form; **f. parte de algo**, to be a part of sth. 2 (educar) to bring up; (enseñar) to educate, train. II **formarse** vr 1 to be formed, form; **se formó un charco**, a puddle formed; **f. una impresión de algo**, to get an impression of sth. 2 (educarse) to be educated o trained.

formato nm format; (del papel) size.

formica® nf Formica®.

formidable adj 1 (estupendo) wonderful, terrific. 2 (espantoso) formidable.

fórmula nf formula; Aut f. uno, formula one.

formular vtr (quejas, peticiones) to make; (deseo) to express; (pregunta) to ask; (una teoría) to formulate.

formulario nm form.

fornicación nf fornication.

fornicar [1] vi to fornicate.

fornido,-a adj strapping, hefty.

foro nm 1 forum. 2 (mesa redonda) round table. 3 Teat back (of the stage). 4 Jur law court, court of justice.

forofo,-a nm,f fam fan, supporter.

forrado,-a adj lined; fam estar f., to be well-heeled, be well-off.

forraje nm fodder.

forrar I vtr (por dentro) to line; (por fuera) to cover. II **forrarse** vr fam (de dinero) to make a packet.

forro nm (por dentro) lining; (por fuera) cover, case.

fortalecer [33] vtr to fortify, strengthen.

fortaleza nf 1 strength; (de espíritu) fortitude. 2 Mil fortress, stronghold.

fortificante I adj fortifying. II nm tonic.

fortificar [1] vtr to fortify.

fortísimo,-a adj very strong.

fortuito,-a adj fortuitous.

fortuna nf 1 (destino) fortune, fate. 2 (suerte) luck; **por f.**, fortunately. 3 (capital) fortune.

forzado,-a adj forced; **a marchas forzadas**, at a brisk pace; **trabajos forzados**, hard labour sing.

forzar [2] vtr 1 (obligar) to force; **f. a algn a hacer algo**, to force sb to do sth. 2 (puerta, candado) to force, break open.

forzoso,-a adj obligatory, compulsory; Av **aterrizaje f.**, forced landing. ◆**forzosamente** adv necessarily.

fosa nf 1 (sepultura) grave. 2 (hoyo) pit. 3 Anat fosas nasales, nostrils.

fosforescente adj phosphorescent.

fósforo nm (cerilla) match.

fósil adj & nm fossil.

fosilizarse [4] vr to fossilize, become fossilized.

foso nm 1 (hoyo) pit. 2 (de fortificación) moat. 3 (en garaje) inspection pit.

foto nf fam photo; **sacar/echar una f.**, to take a photo.

fotocopia nf photocopy.

fotocopiadora nf photocopier.

fotocopiar [12] vtr to photocopy.

fotogénico,-a adj photogenic.

fotografía nf 1 photograph; **echar o hacer o sacar fotografías**, to take photographs. 2 (arte) photography.

fotografiar [29] vtr to photograph, take a photograph of.

fotográfico,-a adj photographic.

fotógrafo,-a nm,f photographer.

fotograma nm still, shot.

fotomatón nm automatic coin-operated photo machine.

fotómetro nm light meter, exposure meter.

FP nf Educ abr de **Formación Profesional**, vocational training.

frac nm (pl fracs o fraques) (prenda) dress coat, tails pl.

fracasado,-a I adj unsuccessful. II nm,f (persona) failure.

fracasar vi to fail.

fracaso nm failure.

fracción nf 1 fraction. 2 Pol faction.

fraccionar vtr, **fraccionarse** vr to break up, split up.

fraccionario,-a adj fractional; **moneda fraccionaria**, small change.

fractura nf fracture.

fracturar vtr, **fracturarse** vr to fracture, break.

fragancia nf fragrance.

fragata nf frigate.

frágil adj 1 (quebradizo) fragile. 2 (débil) frail.

fragmentar I vtr to fragment. II **fragmentarse** vr to break up.

fragmento nm fragment; (de novela etc) passage.

fragor nm din.

fragua nf forge.

fraguar [22] vtr 1 (metal) to forge. 2 (plan) to think up, fabricate; (conspiración) to hatch.

fraile nm friar, monk.

frailecillo nm puffin.

frambuesa nf raspberry.

francés, -a I adj French; Culin **tortilla francesa**, plain omelette. II nm,f (persona) Frenchman; (mujer) Frenchwoman. III nm (idioma) French.

Francfort, Francfurt n Frankfurt; Culin **salchicha estilo f.**, frankfurter.

Francia n France.

francmasón, -ona nm,f freemason.

franco, -a¹ adj 1 (persona) frank. 2 Com **f. a bordo**, free on board; **f. fábrica**, exworks; **puerto f.**, free port. ◆**francamente** adv frankly.

franco² nm Fin (moneda) franc.

francotirador, -a nm,f sniper.

franela nf flannel.

franja nf (de terreno) strip; (de bandera) stripe; Cost fringe, border.

franquear vtr 1 (atravesar) to cross; fig (dificultad, obstáculo) to overcome. 2 (carta) to frank. 3 (camino, paso) to free, clear.

franqueo nm postage.

franqueza nf frankness.

franquicia nf exemption; Com franchise.

franquismo nm Hist 1 (ideología) Francoism. 2 (régimen) the Franco regime.

franquista adj&nmf Francoist.

frasco nm small bottle, flask.

frase nf (oración) sentence; (expresión) phrase; **f. hecha**, set phrase o expression.

fraternidad nf brotherhood, fraternity.

fraternizar [4] vi to fraternize.

fraterno, -a adj fraternal, brotherly.

fraude nm fraud; **f. fiscal**, tax evasion.

fraudulento, -a adj fraudulent.

fray nm Rel brother.

frecuencia nf frequency; **con f.**, frequently, often.

frecuentar vtr to frequent.

frecuente adj frequent. ◆**frecuentemente** adv frequently, often.

fregadero nm (kitchen) sink.

fregado¹ nm 1 (lavado) washing. 2 fam (follón) racket.

fregado, -a² adj fam tiresome, annoying.

fregar [1] vtr 1 (lavar) to wash; (suelo) to mop. 2 Am vulg to annoy, irritate.

fregona nf mop.

fregón, -ona adj Am annoying.

freidora nf (deep) fryer.

freír [5] (pp **frito**) I vtr to fry. II **freírse** vr to fry; fig **f. de calor**, to be roasting.

frenar vtr to brake; fig (inflación etc) to slow down; (impulsos) to restrain.

frenazo nm sudden braking; **dar un f.**, to jam on the brakes.

frenesí nm frenzy.

frenético, -a adj frantic.

freno nm 1 brake; **pisar/soltar el f.**, to press/release the brake; **f. de disco/ tambor**, disc/drum brake; **f. de mano**, handbrake. 2 (de caballería) bit. 3 fig curb, check; **poner f. a algo**, to curb sth.

frente I nm 1 front; **al f. de**, at the head of; **chocar de f.**, to crash head on; **hacer f. a algo**, to face sth, stand up to sth. II nf Anat forehead; **f. a f.**, face to face. III adv **f. a**, in front of, opposite.

fresa nf 1 strawberry. 2 Téc milling cutter.

fresca nf fam cheeky remark.

fresco, -a I adj 1 (frío) cool. 2 (comida, fruta) fresh. 3 (reciente) fresh, new. 4 (descarado) cheeky, shameless; **se quedó tan f.**, he didn't bat an eyelid; **¡qué f.!**, what a nerve!. II nm 1 (frescor) fresh air, cool air; **al f.**, in the cool; **hace f.**, it's chilly. 2 Arte fresco.

frescor nm freshness.

frescura nf 1 freshness. 2 (desvergüenza) cheek, nerve.

fresno nm ash tree.

fresón nm (large) strawberry.

frialdad nf coldness.

fricción nf 1 friction. 2 (masaje) massage.

friega nf rub.

friegaplatos nm inv (persona) dishwasher.

frígido, -a adj frigid.

frigorífico, -a I nm refrigerator, fridge. II adj **cámara frigorífica**, coldstorage room.

frijol, frijol nm kidney bean.

frío, -a I adj 1 cold. 2 (indiferente) cold, cool, indifferent. 3 **su comentario me dejó f.**, I was stunned by her remark. II nm (cold); **hace f.**, it's cold. ◆**fríamente** adv coolly.

friolera nf fam **la f. de diez mil pesetas/ dos horas**, a mere ten thousand pesetas/ two hours.

friolero, -a adj sensitive to the cold.

fritanga nf 1 Am fried food. 2 Esp greasy food.

frito, -a I adj 1 Culin fried. 2 fam exasperated, fed up; **me tienes f.**, I'm sick to death of you. II nm fry, piece of fried food.

frívolo, -a adj frivolous.

frondoso, -a adj leafy, luxuriant.

frontera nf frontier.

fronterizo, -a adj frontier, border; **países fronterizos**, neighbouring countries.

frontón nm Dep pelota.

frotar I vtr to rub. II **frotarse** vr to rub; f. **las manos**, to rub one's hands together.

fructífero,-a adj (árbol) fruit-bearing; (esfuerzo) fruitful.

frugal adj frugal.

fruncir [3] vtr 1 Cost to gather. 2 (labios) to purse, pucker; f. **el ceño**, to frown, knit one's brow.

frustración nf frustration.

frustrado,-a adj frustrated; **intento f.**, unsuccessful attempt.

frustrante adj frustrating.

frustrar I vtr to frustrate; (defraudar) to disappoint. II **frustrarse** vr 1 (esperanza) to fail, go awry. 2 (persona) to be frustrated o disappointed.

fruta nf fruit; f. **del tiempo**, fresh fruit.

frutería nf fruit shop.

frutero,-a I nm,f fruiterer. II nm fruit dish o bowl.

frutilla nf Am (large) strawberry.

fruto nm fruit; **frutos secos**, nuts; **dar f.**, to bear fruit; fig (dar buen resultado) to be fruitful; **sacar f. de algo**, to profit from sth.

fu interj **ni fu ni fa**, so-so.

fucsia nf fuchsia.

fuego nm 1 fire; **fuegos artificiales**, fireworks. 2 (lumbre) light; **¿me da f., por favor?**, have you got a light, please? 3 Culin **a f. lento**, on a low flame; (al horno) in a slow oven.

fuel, fuel-oil nm diesel.

fuente nf 1 fountain. 2 (recipiente) dish, serving dish. 3 (de información) source.

fuera¹ adv 1 outside, out; **quédate f.**, stay outside; **sal f.**, go out; **desde f.**, from (the) outside; **por f.**, on the outside; **la puerta de f.**, the outer door. 2 f. **de**, out of; f. **de serie**, extraordinary; fig **estar f. de sí**, to be beside oneself. 3 Dep **el equipo de f.**, the away team; **jugar f.**, to play away; f. **de juego**, offside.

fuera² I subj imperf → **ir**. II subj imperf → **ser**.

fuero nm 1 Hist code of laws. 2 fig **en tu f. interno**, deep down, in your heart of hearts.

fuerte I adj 1 strong; (dolor) severe; (sonido) loud; (comida) heavy; **el plato f.**, the main course; fig the most important event. II nm 1 (fortaleza) fort. 2 (punto fuerte) forte, strong point. III adv **¡abrázame f.!**, hold me tight!; **comer f.**, to eat a lot; **¡habla más f.!**, speak up!; **¡pégale f.!**, hit him hard!

fuerza I nf 1 (fortaleza) strength; fig **a f. de**, by dint of. 2 (violencia) force; **a la f.**, (por obligación) of necessity; (con violencia) by force; **por f.**, of necessity; f. **mayor**, force majeure. 3 Fís force. 4 (cuerpo) force; **las fuerzas del orden**, the forces of law and order; **Fuerzas Aéreas**,

= GB Royal Air Force; **Fuerzas Armadas**, Armed Forces.

fuese I subj imperf → **ir**. II subj imperf → **ser**.

fuete nm Am whip.

fuga nf 1 (huida) escape; **darse a la f.**, to take flight. 2 (de gas etc) leak.

fugarse [7] vr to escape; f. **de casa**, to run away from home.

fugaz adj fleeting, brief.

fugitivo,-a nm,f fugitive.

fui I pt indef → **ir**. II pt indef → **ser**.

fulana nf pey whore, tart.

fulano,-a I nm,f so-and-so; (hombre) what's his name; (mujer) what's her name; **Doña Fulana de tal**, Mrs So-and-so. II nf fam pey tart, slag.

fular nm foulard, scarf.

fulgor nm lit brilliance, glow.

fullería nf cheating; **hacer fullerías**, to cheat.

fullero,-a I adj cheating. II nm,f cheat.

fulminante adj (cese) summary; (muerte, enfermedad) sudden; (mirada) withering.

fulminar vtr fig to strike dead; f. **a algn con la mirada**, to look daggers at sb.

fumada nf Am (calada) pull, drag.

fumado,-a adj arg (colocado) stoned.

fumador,-a nm,f smoker; **los no fumadores**, nonsmokers.

fumar I vtr & vi to smoke; **no f.**, (en letrero) no smoking. II **fumarse** vr to smoke; f. **un cigarro**, to smoke a cigarette.

fumigar [7] vtr to fumigate.

funámbulista nmf, **funámbulo,-a** nm,f tightrope walker.

función nf 1 function; **en f. de**, according to. 2 (cargo) duties pl; **entrar en funciones**, to take up one's duties; **presidente en funciones**, acting president. 3 Cin Teat performance.

funcionamiento nm operation; **poner/entrar en f.**, to put/come into operation.

funcionar vi to work; **no funciona**, (en letrero) out of order.

funcionario,-a nm,f civil servant; f. **público**, public official.

funda nf cover; (de gafas etc) case; (de espada) sheath; f. **de almohada**, pillowcase.

fundación nf foundation.

fundador,-a nm,f founder.

fundamental adj fundamental.

fundamentar vtr to base (en, on).

fundamento nm basis, grounds; **sin f.**, unfounded.

fundar I vtr 1 (empresa) to found. 2 (teoría) to base, found. II **fundarse** vr 1 (empresa) to be founded. 2 (teoría) to be based; (persona) to base oneself.

fundición nf 1 (de metales) smelting. 2 (fábrica) foundry.

fundir I vtr 1 to melt; (bombilla, plomos) to blow. 2 (unir) to unite, join. II

fundirse *vr* **1** (*derretirse*) to melt. **2** (*bombilla, plomos*) to blow. **3** (*unirse*) to merge.

fúnebre *adj* **1** (*mortuorio*) funeral; **coche f.**, hearse. **2** (*lúgubre*) mournful, lugubrious.

funeral *nm* funeral.

funeraria *nf* undertaker's, *US* funeral parlor.

funesto,-a *adj* ill-fated, fatal; (*consecuencias*) disastrous.

fungir *vi Am* to act (**de**, as).

funicular *nm* funicular (railway).

furcia *nf ofens* whore, tart.

furgón *nm Aut* van.

furgoneta *nf* van.

furia *nf* fury; **ponerse hecho una f.**, to become furious, fly into a rage.

furibundo,-a *adj* furious, enraged.

furioso,-a *adj* furious; **ponerse f.**, to get furious.

furor *nm* fury, rage; *fig* **hacer f.**, to be all the rage.

furtivo,-a *adj* furtive, stealthy; **caza/pesca furtiva,** poaching; **cazador/pescador f.,** poacher.

furúnculo *nm Med* boil.

fuselaje *nm* fuselage.

fusible *nm* fuse.

fusil *nm* gun, rifle.

fusilamiento *nm* shooting, execution.

fusilar *vtr* to shoot, execute.

fusión *nf* **1** (*de metales*) fusion; (*del hielo*) thawing, melting; **punto de f.**, melting point. **2** *Com* merger.

fusionar *vtr*, **fusionarse** *vr* **1** *Fis* to fuse. **2** *Com* to merge.

fútbol *nm* football, soccer.

futbolín *nm* table football.

futbolista *nmf* footballer, football *o* soccer player.

fútil *adj* futile, trivial.

futilidad *nf* futility, triviality.

futurista *adj* futuristic.

futuro,-a *adj* future. **II** *nm* future; **en un f. próximo**, in the near future.

G

G, g [xe] *nf* (*la letra*) G, g.

gabán *nm* overcoat.

gabardina *nf* (*prenda*) raincoat.

gabinete *nm* **1** (*despacho*) study; **g. de abogados,** lawyers' office. **2** *Pol* cabinet.

gaceta *nf* gazette.

gachas *nfpl* porridge *sing*.

gacho,-a *adj* **con la cabeza gacha**, hanging one's head.

gaditano,-a **I** *adj* of *o* from Cadiz. **II** *nm,f* inhabitant *o* native of Cadiz.

gafas *nfpl* glasses, spectacles; **g. de sol,** sunglasses.

gafar *vtr fam* to put a jinx on, bring bad luck to.

gafe *adj & nm fam* **ser g.**, to be a jinx.

gaita *nf* bagpipes *pl*.

gajes *nmpl fam irón* **g. del oficio**, occupational hazards.

gajo *nm* **1** (*de naranja, pomelo etc*) segment. **2** (*rama desprendida*) torn-off branch.

gala *nf* **1** (*vestido*) full dress; **de g.**, dressed up; (*ciudad*) decked out. **2** (*espectáculo*) gala; **hacer g. de**, to glory in. **3 galas**, finery *sing*.

galán *nm* **1** handsome young man; *hum* ladies' man. **2** *Teat* leading man.

galante *adj* gallant.

galantear *vtr* to court.

galanteo *nm* courtship.

galantería *nf* gallantry.

galápago *nm* turtle.

galardón *nm* prize.

galardonado,-a *nm,f* prizewinner.

galardonar *vtr* to award a prize to.

galaxia *nf* galaxy.

galeón *nm* galleon.

galeote *nm* galley slave.

galera *nf* **1** *Náut* galley. **2** (*carro*) covered wagon. **3** *Impr* galley proof.

galería *nf* **1** *Arquit* covered balcony. **2** (*museo*) art gallery. **3** *Teat* gallery, gods *pl*.

Gales *n* (**el país de**) G., Wales.

galés,-esa **I** *adj* Welsh. **II** *nm,f* (*hombre*) Welshman; (*mujer*) Welshwoman; **los galeses,** the Welsh. **III** *nm* (*idioma*) Welsh.

galgo *nm* greyhound.

Galicia *n* Galicia.

galimatías *nm inv fam* gibberish.

gallardo,-a *adj* **1** (*apuesto*) smart. **2** (*valeroso*) brave.

gallego,-a **I** *adj* **1** Galician. **2** *Am pey* Spanish. **II** *nm,f* **1** Galician, native of Galicia. **2** *Am pey* Spaniard. **III** *nm* (*idioma*) Galician.

galleta *nf* **1** *Culin* biscuit. **2** *fam* (*cachete*) slap.

gallina **I** *nf* hen. **II** *nmf fam* coward, chicken.

gallinero *nm* **1** hen run. **2** *Teat* **el g.**, the gods *pl*.

gallito *nm fam* (*peleón*) bully.

gallo *nm* **1** cock, rooster; *fam fig* **en menos que se canta de g.**, before you could say Jack Robinson. **2** *Mús fam* off-key note.

galón¹ *nm Mil* stripe.

galón² *nm* (*medida*) gallon; *GB* 4.55 litres, *US* 3.79 litres.

galopante *adj fig* (*inflación etc*) galloping.

galopar vi to gallop.

galope nm gallop; **a g. tendido**, flat out.

gama nf 1 range; Mús scale.

gamba nf prawn.

gamberrismo nm hooliganism.

gamberro,-a I nm,f hooligan. II adj uncouth.

gamo nm fallow deer.

gamuza nf 1 Zool chamois. 2 (trapo) chamois o shammy leather.

gana nf 1 (deseo) wish (de, for); **de buena g.**, willingly; **de mala g.**, reluctantly; **fam no me da la g.**, I don't feel like it. 2 **tener ganas de (hacer) algo**, to feel like (doing) sth; **quedarse con las ganas**, not to manage. 3 (apetito) appetite; **comer con ganas**, to eat heartily.

ganadería nf 1 (crianza) livestock farming. 2 (conjunto de ganado) livestock.

ganadero,-a nm,f livestock farmer.

ganado nm 1 livestock. 2 fam fig (gente) crowd.

ganador,-a I adj winning. II nm,f winner.

ganancia nf profit.

ganar I vtr 1 (sueldo) to earn. 2 (victoria) to win. 3 (aventajar) to beat. 4 (alcanzar) to reach. II **ganarse** vr 1 to earn; **g. el pan**, to earn one's daily bread. 2 (merecer) to deserve; **se lo ha ganado**, he deserves it.

ganchillo nm crochet work.

gancho nm 1 hook. 2 fam fig (gracia, atractivo) charm. 3 Am (horquilla) hairpin.

gandul,-a nm,f loafer.

ganga nf bargain.

gangoso,-a adj nasal.

gangrena nf gangrene.

gansada nf fam silly thing to say o do.

ganso,-a nm,f 1 goose; (macho) gander. 2 fam dolt. II adj fam ginormous; **pasta gansa**, bread, dough.

ganzúa nf picklock.

gañán nm (obrero) farmhand; fam (bribón) cheat.

garabatear vtr & vi to scribble.

garabato nm scrawl.

garaje nm garage.

garante nmf Fin guarantor.

garantía nf 1 guarantee. 2 Jur (fianza) bond, security.

garantizar [4] vtr to guarantee.

garbanzo nm chickpea.

garbeo nm arg (paseo) stroll; **darse un g.**, to go for a stroll.

garbo nm grace.

garfio nm hook, grappling iron.

gargajo nm spit.

garganta nf 1 throat. 2 (desfiladero) narrow pass.

gargantilla nf short necklace.

gárgaras nfpl 1 gargling sing; fam **¡vete a hacer g.!**, get lost! 2 Am (licor) gargling solution sing.

gárgola nf gargoyle.

garita nf (caseta) hut; Mil sentry box.

garito nm arg joint.

garra nf 1 Zool claw; (de ave) talon. 2 fig (fuerza) force; **tener g.**, to be compelling.

garrafa nf carafe.

garrafal adj monumental.

garrapata nf Ent tick.

garrote nm 1 (porra) club. 2 Jur garrotte.

garrucha nf pulley.

gárrulo,-a adj fig garrulous.

garza nf heron.

gas nm 1 gas; **g. ciudad**, town gas; **gases (nocivos)**, fumes; **g. de escape**, exhaust fumes. 2 (en bebida) fizz; **agua con g.**, fizzy water. 3 Med **gases**, flatulence sing.

gasa nf gauze.

gaseosa nf lemonade.

gasoducto nm gas pipeline.

gasoil, gasóleo nm diesel oil.

gasolina nf petrol, US gasoline.

gasolinera nf petrol o US gas station.

gastado,-a adj (zapatos etc) worn-out; fig (frase) hackneyed.

gastar I vtr 1 (consumir) (dinero, tiempo) to spend; (gasolina, electricidad) to consume. 2 fig (malgastar) to waste. 3 (ropa) to wear; **¿qué número gastas?**, what size do you take? 4 **g. una broma a algn**, to play a practical joke on sb. II **gastarse** vr 1 (zapatos etc) to wear out. 2 (gasolina etc) to run out.

gasto nm expenditure; **gastos**, expenses; **gastos de viaje**, travelling expenses.

gatas (a) loc adv on all fours.

gatear vi 1 to crawl. 2 (trepar) to climb.

gatillo nm (de armas) trigger; **apretar el g.**, to pull the trigger.

gato nm 1 cat. 2 Aut Téc jack.

gaveta nf 1 (cajón) drawer. 2 Am Aut (guantera) glove compartment.

gavilán nm Orn sparrowhawk.

gavilla nf (de ramillas etc) sheaf.

gaviota nf seagull.

gay adj inv & nm (pl gays) homosexual, gay.

gazapo nm 1 (error) misprint. 2 Zool young rabbit.

gaznate nm gullet.

gazpacho nm Culin gazpacho.

gel nm gel; **g. (de ducha)**, shower gel.

gelatina nf (ingrediente) gelatin; Culin jelly.

gema nf Min gem.

gemelo,-a I adj & nm,f (identical) twin. II nmpl **gemelos** 1 (de camisa) cufflinks. 2 (anteojos) binoculars.

gemido nm groan.

Géminis nm Gemini.

gemir [6] vi to groan.

generación nf generation.

general I adj general; **por lo o en g.**, in general, generally; II nm Mil Rel general.

♦**generalmente** adv generally.

Generalitat *nf* Catalan/Valencian/Balearic parliament.

generalización *nf* 1 generalization. 2 *(extensión)* spread.

generalizar [4] I *vtr* 1 to generalize. 2 *(extender)* to spread. II **generalizarse** *vr* to become widespread *o* common.

generar *vtr* to generate.

género *nm* 1 *(clase)* kind, sort. 2 *Arte Lit* genre. 3 *(mercancía)* article. 4 *Ling* gender. 5 *Biol* genus; **el g. humano**, mankind.

generosidad *nf* generosity.

generoso,-a *adj* 1 generous (**con, para**, to). 2 *(vino)* full-bodied.

Génesis *nm Rel* Genesis.

genética *nf* genetics *sing.*

genético,-a *adj* genetic.

genial *adj* brilliant; *fam* terrific.

genio *nm* 1 *(carácter)* temperament; *(mal carácter)* temper; **estar de mal g.**, to be in a bad mood. 2 *(facultad)* genius.

genocidio *nm* genocide.

Génova *n* Genoa.

gente *nf* 1 people *pl*. 2 *(familia)* folks *pl*. 3 Am respectable people.

gentil *adj* 1 *(amable)* kind. 2 *(pagano)* pagan.

gentileza *nf* kindness; *fml* **por g. de**, by courtesy of.

gentío *nm* crowd.

gentuza *nf pey* riffraff.

genuino,-a *adj* *(puro)* genuine; *(verdadero)* authentic.

geografía *nf* geography.

geología *nf* geology.

geometría *nf* geometry.

geranio *nm* geranium.

gerencia *nf* management.

gerente *nmf* manager.

germano,-a I *adj* German, Germanic. II *nm,f* German.

gérmen *nm* 1 *Biol* germ. 2 *fig (inicio)* germ; *(fuente)* origin.

germinar *vi* to germinate.

gerundio *nm* gerund.

gesta *nf arc* heroic exploit.

gestación *nf* gestation.

gestar *vtr* to gestate.

gesticular *vi* to gesticulate.

gestión *nf* 1 *(administración)* management. 2 **gestiones**, *(negociaciones)* negotiations; *(trámites)* formalities.

gestionar *vtr* to take steps to acquire *o* obtain; *(negociar)* to negotiate.

gesto *nm* 1 *(mueca)* face. 2 *(con las manos)* gesture.

gestor,-a *nm,f* ≈ solicitor.

giba *nf* hump.

gibar *vtr fam* to annoy.

Gibraltar *n* Gibraltar; **el peñón de G.**, the Rock of Gibraltar.

gibraltareño,-a I *adj* of *o* from Gibraltar. II *nm,f* Gibraltarian.

gigante,-a I *nm,f* giant. II *adj* giant, enormous.

gigantesco-a *adj* gigantic.

gigoló *nm* gigolo.

gili, gilí *nm arg ofens* → **gilipollas**.

gilipollas *nmf ofens* bloody fool *o* idiot.

gimnasia *nf* gymnastics *pl.*

gimnasio *nm* gymnasium.

gimotear *vi* to whine.

Ginebra *n* Geneva.

ginebra *nf (bebida)* gin.

ginecología *nf* gynaecology, *US* gynecology.

ginecólogo,-a *nm,f* gynaecologist, *US* gynecologist.

gira *nf Teat Mus* tour.

girar I *vi* 1 *(dar vueltas)* to spin. 2 **g. a la derecha/izquierda**, to turn right/left. 3 *Fin (expedir)* to draw. II *vtr Fin (dinero)* to send by giro.

girasol *nm* sunflower.

giratorio,-a *adj* revolving.

giro *nm* 1 *(vuelta)* turn. 2 *(de acontecimientos)* direction. 3 *(frase)* turn of phrase. 4 *Fin* draft; **g. telegráfico**, giro *o* money order; **g. postal**, postal *o* money order.

gitano,-a *adj* & *nm,f* gypsy, gipsy.

glacial *adj* icy.

glaciar *nm* glacier.

glándula *nf* gland.

glasear *vtr Culin* to glaze.

global *adj* comprehensive; **precio g.**, all-inclusive price. ◆**globalmente** *adv* as a whole.

globo *nm* 1 balloon. 2 *(esfera)* globe. 3 *(lámpara)* globe, glass lampshade.

glóbulo *nm* globule.

gloria *nf* 1 *(fama)* glory. 2 *Rel* heaven; *fam fig* **estar en la g.**, to be in seventh heaven. 3 *fam (delicia)* delight.

glorieta *nf* 1 *(plazoleta)* small square. 2 *(encrucijada de calles)* roundabout, *US* traffic circle. 3 *(en un jardín)* arbour, *US* arbor.

glorificar [1] *vtr* to glorify.

glorioso,-a *adj* glorious.

glosa *nf* 1 gloss. 2 *Lit (comentario)* notes *pl*, comment.

glosar *vtr* 1 *(explicar)* to gloss; *(texto)* to interpret. 2 *(comentar)* to comment on.

glosario *nm* glossary.

glotón,-ona I *adj* greedy. II *nm,f* glutton.

glotonería *nf* gluttony.

glucosa *nf Quím* glucose.

gobernación *nf* government; *Pol Hist* **Ministerio de la G.**, ≈ *GB* Home Office, *US* Department of the Interior.

gobernador,-a *nm,f* governor.

gobernante *adj* ruling.

gobernar [1] I *vtr* to govern; *(un país)* to rule. II *vi Náut* to steer.

gobierno *nm* 1 *Pol* government. 2 *(mando)* running. 3 *Náut* steering. 4 *Náut* *(timón)* rudder.

goce nm enjoyment.

gofio nm Am Can roasted maize meal.

gol nm goal.

goleada nf lots of goals; **ganar por g.**, to win by a barrowload.

golear vtr to hammer.

golf nm golf; **palo de g.**, golf club.

golfista nmf golfer.

golfo,-a¹ I nm,f good-for-nothing. II nf fam pey tart.

golfo² nm Geog gulf; **el g. Pérsico**, the Persian Gulf.

golondrina nf swallow.

golosina nf sweet, US candy.

goloso,-a adj sweet-toothed.

golpe nm 1 blow; *(llamada)* knock; *(puñetazo)* punch; **de g.**, all of a sudden; **g. de estado**, coup d'état; **g. de suerte**, stroke of luck; **no dar ni g.**, not to lift a finger. 2 Aut bump. 3 *(desgracia)* blow; **un duro g.**, a great blow. 4 *(de humor)* witticism.

golpear vtr to hit; *(con el puño)* to punch; *(puerta, cabeza)* to bang.

goma nf 1 rubber; **g. de pegar**, glue; **g. de borrar**, rubber, US eraser. 2 *(elástica)* rubber band. 3 arg *(preservativo)* condom.

gomaespuma nf foam rubber.

gomal nm Am Agr rubber plantation.

gomero nm Am 1 Bot gum tree. 2 *(recolector)* rubber collector.

gomina nf hair cream.

góndola nf gondola.

gordo,-a I adj 1 *(carnoso)* fat. 2 *(grueso)* thick. 3 *(importante)* big; **me cae g.**, I can't stand him; **de g.**, in a big way. II nm,f fat person; fam fatty. III nm el g., *(de lotería)* the jackpot.

gordura nf fatness.

gorgorito nm trill.

gorila nm 1 gorilla. 2 fig *(en discoteca etc)* bouncer.

gorjear I vi to chirp. II gorjearse vr Am **g. de algn**, to laugh at sb's expense.

gorjeo nm chirping.

gorra nf cap; *(con visera)* peaked cap; fam **de g.**, free.

gorrión nm sparrow.

gorro nm 1 cap. 2 fam **estar hasta el g.**, to be up to here *(de, with)*.

gorrón,-ona nm,f sponger.

gota nf 1 drop; *(de sudor)* bead; **g. a g.**, drop by drop; **ni g.**, not a bit. 2 Med gout.

gotear v impers to drip; **el techo gotea**, there's a leak in the ceiling.

gotera nf leak.

gótico,-a adj Gothic.

gozar [4] I vtr to enjoy. II vi *(disfrutar)* to enjoy *(de, -)*.

gozne nm hinge.

gozo nm pleasure.

grabación nf recording.

grabado,-a nm 1 *(arte)* engraving. 2 *(dibu-jo)* drawing.

grabadora nf tape recorder.

grabar vtr 1 *(sonidos, imágenes)* to record. 2 Inform to save. 3 Arte to engrave.

gracia nf 1 *(atractivo)* grace. 2 *(chiste)* joke; **hacer o tener g.**, to be funny. 3 *(indulto)* pardon.

gracias nfpl *(agradecimiento)* thanks; **g. a Dios**, thank God, thank goodness; **g. a**, thanks to; **muchas o muchísimas g.**, thank you very much.

gracioso,-a I adj 1 *(divertido)* funny. 2 *(garboso)* graceful. II nm,f Teat comic character.

grada nf 1 *(peldaño)* step. 2 gradas, flight sing of steps, US forecourt sing; *(en estadio)* terracing.

gradación nf gradation.

gradería nm tiers pl of seats; Dep terracing, US bleachers pl.

gradiente I nm gradient, US grade. II nf Am slope.

grado nm 1 degree. 2 Mil rank. 3 **de buen g.**, willingly, gladly.

graduable adj adjustable.

graduación nf 1 gradation. 2 Mil rank.

graduado,-a nmf graduate.

gradual adj gradual. ◆ **gradualmente** adv gradually.

graduar [30] I vtr 1 Educ Mil to confer a degree o a rank on. 2 *(regular)* to regulate. II graduarse vr 1 Educ Mil to graduate. 2 **g. la vista**, to have one's eyes tested.

gráfico,-a I adj graphic; **diseño g.**, graphic design. II nm,f graph.

grafista nmf graphic designer.

gragea nf Med pill.

grajo,-a I nm,f Orn rook. II nm Am body odour.

gral. abr de **General**, General, gen.

gramática nf grammar.

gramo nm gram, gramme.

gran adj → **grande**.

grana adj scarlet.

granada nf 1 *(fruto)* pomegranate. 2 Mil grenade.

granate I adj inv *(color)* maroon. II nm *(color)* maroon.

Gran Bretaña nf Great Britain.

grande adj *(before singular noun gran is used)* 1 *(tamaño)* big, large; fig *(persona)* great. 2 *(cantidad)* large; **vivir a lo g.**, to live in style; fig **pasarlo en g.**, to have a great time.

grandeza nf 1 *(importancia)* greatness. 2 *(grandiosidad)* grandeur; **delirios de g.**, delusions of grandeur.

grandioso,-a adj grandiose.

granel (a) loc adv *(sin medir exactamente)* loose.

granero nm Agr granary.

granito nm granite.

granizada nf, **granizado** nm iced drink.

granizar [4] *v impers* to hail.

granizo *nm* hail.

granja *nf* farm.

granjear(se) *vtr & vr* to gain.

granjero,-a *nm,f* farmer.

grano *nm* 1 grain; (*de café*) bean; **ir al g.**, to get to the point. 2 (*espinilla*) spot.

granuja *nm* 1 (*pilluelo*) ragamuffin. 2 (*estafador*) con-man.

grapa *nf* 1 staple. 2 *Constr* cramp.

grapadora *nf* stapler.

grapar *vtr* to staple.

grasa *nf* grease.

grasiento *adj* greasy.

graso,-a *adj* (*pelo*) greasy; (*materia*) fatty.

gratificar [1] *vtr* 1 (*satisfacer*) to gratify. 2 (*recompensar*) to reward.

gratinar *vtr* *Culin* to cook in a sauce until golden brown.

gratis *adv* *inv* free.

gratitud *nf* gratitude.

grato,-a *adj* pleasant.

gratuito,-a *adj* 1 (*de balde*) free (of charge). 2 (*arbitrario*) gratuitous.

grava *nf* (*guijas*) gravel; (*en carretera*) chippings.

gravamen *nm* *Jur* 1 (*carga*) burden. 2 (*impuesto*) tax.

gravar *vtr* *Jur* 1 (*cargar*) to burden. 2 (*impuestos*) to tax.

grave *adj* 1 (*importante*) serious. 2 (*muy enfermo*) seriously ill. 3 (*voz, nota*) low.

gravedad *nf* 1 (*seriedad, importancia*) seriousness. 2 *Fís* gravity.

gravilla *nf* chippings.

gravitar *vi* 1 *Fís* to gravitate. 2 **g. sobre**, to rest on.

gravoso,-a *adj* 1 (*costoso*) costly. 2 (*molesto*) burdensome.

graznar *vi* to squawk; (*de pato*) to quack; (*de cuervo*) to caw.

graznido *nm* (*un sonido*) squawk; (*varios*) squawking; (*de pato*) quack; (*de cuervo*) caw.

Grecia *n* Greece.

gregario,-a *adj* gregarious; **instinto g.**, herd instinct.

gremio *nm* 1 *Hist* guild. 2 (*profesión*) profession.

greña *nf* lock of entangled hair; *fam* **andar a la g.**, to squabble.

gres *nm* artículos de g., stoneware.

gresca *nf* 1 (*bulla*) racket. 2 (*riña*) row.

griego,-a *adj & nm,f* Greek.

grieta *nf* crack; (*en la piel*) chap.

grifo *nm* tap, *US* faucet.

grillete *nm* shackle.

grillo *nm* *Ent* cricket.

gringo,-a *pey* I *adj* foreign; *Am* yankee. II *nm,f* foreigner; *Am* yankee, gringo.

gripe *nf* flu.

gris *adj & nm* grey, *US* gray.

grisáceo,-a *adj* greyish.

gritar *vtr & vi* to shout.

grito *nm* shout; **a voz en g.**, at the top of one's voice.

grosella *nf* (*fruto*) redcurrant; **g. negra**, blackcurrant; **g. silvestre**, gooseberry.

grosería *nf* 1 (*ordinariez*) rude word o expression. 2 (*rusticidad*) rudeness.

grosero,-a *adj* 1 (*tosco*) coarse; (*maleducado*) rude.

grosor *nm* thickness.

grotesco,-a *adj* grotesque.

grúa *nf* 1 *Constr* crane. 2 *Aut* breakdown van, *US* tow truck.

grueso,-a I *adj* thick; (*persona*) stout. II *nm* (*parte principal*) bulk.

grulla *nf* *Orn* crane.

grumo *nm* lump; (*de leche*) curd.

gruñido *nm* grunt.

gruñir *vi* to grunt.

gruñón,-ona *adj* grumpy.

grupa *nf* hindquarters.

grupo *nm* 1 group. 2 *Téc* unit, set.

gruta *nf* cave.

guacamayo,-a *nm,f* *Orn* macaw.

guacamol, guacamole *nm* *Am* *Culin* guacamole, avocado sauce.

guachafita *nf* *Am* uproar.

guacho,-a *adj & nm,f* *Am* orphan.

guadaña *nf* scythe.

guagua[1] *nf* (*perro*) bow-wow. 2 *Can Cuba* bus.

guagua[2] *nf* *Am* baby.

guantazo *nm* slap.

guante *nm* glove.

guantera *nf* *Aut* glove compartment.

guapo,-a I *adj* 1 good-looking, *US* cute; (*mujer*) beautiful, pretty; (*hombre*) handsome. 2 *Am* (*matón*) bully.

guaraca *nf* *Am* sling.

guarango,-a *adj* *Am* rude.

guarda *nm,f* guard; **g. jurado**, security guard.

guardabarros *nm* *inv* *Aut* mudguard, *US* fender.

guardabosque *nmf* gamekeeper.

guardacoches *nmf* *inv* parking attendant.

guardacostas *nm* *inv* (*persona*) coastguard; (*embarcación*) coastguard vessel.

guardaespaldas *nmf* *inv* bodyguard.

guardameta *nmf* *Dep* goalkeeper.

guardapolvo *nm* overalls *pl*.

guardar I *vtr* 1 (*conservar*) to keep. 2 (*un secreto*) to keep; **g. silencio**, to remain silent; **g. cama**, to stay in bed. 3 (*poner en un sitio*) to put away. 4 (*reservar*) to keep. 5 *Inform* to save. II **guardarse** *vr* **g. de hacer algo**, (*abstenerse*) to be careful not to do sth; **guardársela a algn**, to have it in for sb.

guardarropa *nm* 1 (*cuarto*) cloakroom. 2 (*armario*) wardrobe.

guardería *nf* **g. infantil**, nursery (school).

guardia I *nf* 1 (*vigilancia*) watch. 2 **la G. Civil**, the civil guard. 3 (*turno de servicio*) duty; *Mil* guard duty; **de g.**, on duty;

farmacia de g., duty chemist. II *nmf* policeman; (*mujer*) policewoman.

guardián,-ana *nm,f* watchman.

guarecer [33] I *vtr* to shelter. II **guarecerse** *vr* to take shelter *o* refuge (**de,** from).

guarida *nf* (*de animal*) lair; (*refugio*) hide-out.

guarismo *nm* digit.

guarnecer [33] *vtr* 1 *Culin* to garnish. 2 (*dotar*) to provide (**de,** with). 3 *Mil* to garrison.

guarnición *nf* 1 *Culin* garnish. 2 *Mil* garrison.

guarro,-a *adj* filthy. II *nm,f* pig.

guasa *nf* mockery.

guasearse *vr fam* **g. de,** to make fun of.

guaso,-a *adj Am* peasant.

guasón,-ona I *adj* humorous. II *nm,f* joker.

guata *nf* 1 (*relleno*) padding. 2 *Am* (*barriga*) paunch.

guay *adj inv fam* brilliant, terrific.

guayabera *nf* short jacket.

guayabo,-a *nm,f Am fig* (*chica bonita*) pretty young girl; (*chico guapo*) good-looking boy.

guepardo *nm* cheetah.

guerra *nf* war; **en g.,** at war; **g. bacteriológica,** germ warfare; **g. civil/fría/ mundial/nuclear,** civil/cold/world/nuclear war; *fam* **dar g.,** to be a real nuisance.

guerrero,-a I *nm,f* warrior. II *adj* warlike.

guerrilla *nf* 1 (*partida armada*) guerrilla force *o* band. 2 (*lucha*) guerrilla warfare.

guía I *nmf* (*persona*) guide. II *nf* 1 (*norma*) guideline. 2 (*libro*) guide; (*lista*) directory; **g. de teléfonos,** telephone directory.

guiar [29] I *vtr* 1 (*indicar el camino*) to guide. 2 *Aut* to drive; *Náut* to steer; (*caballo, bici*) to ride. II **guiarse** *vr* to be guided, to go (**por,** by).

guija *nf* pebble.

guijarro *nm* pebble.

guinda *nf* (*fruto*) morello (cherry).

guindilla *nf* chilli.

guiñapo *nm* 1 (*andrajo*) rag. 2 *fig* (*persona*) wreck; **poner a algn como un g.,** to tear sb to pieces.

guiñar *vtr* to wink.

guiño *nm* wink.

guión *nm* 1 *Cin TV* script. 2 *Ling* hyphen, dash. 3 (*esquema*) sketch.

guionista *nmf* scriptwriter.

guiri *nmf arg* foreigner.

guirigay *nm* hubbub.

guirnalda *nf* garland.

guisa *nf* way, manner; **a g. de,** as, by way of.

guisado *nm Culin* stew.

guisante *nm* pea.

guisar *vtr* to cook.

guiso *nm* dish; (*guisado*) stew.

guita *nf* 1 (*cuerda*) rope. 2 *arg* dough.

guitarra I *nf* guitar. II *nmf* guitarist.

guitarrista *nmf* guitarist.

gula *nf* gluttony.

gusano *nm* worm; (*oruga*) caterpillar; **g. de seda,** silkworm.

gustar I *vtr* 1 **me gusta el vino,** I like wine; **me gustaban los caramelos,** I used to like sweets; **me gusta nadar,** I like swimming; **me gustaría ir,** I would like to go. 2 *fml* **¿gustas?,** would you like some?; **cuando gustes,** whenever you like. II *vi* **g. de,** to enjoy.

gusto *nm* (*sentido*) taste. 2 (*en fórmulas de cortesía*) pleasure; **con (mucho) g.,** with (great) pleasure; **tanto g.,** pleased to meet you. 3 **estar a g.,** to feel comfortable *o* at ease; **por g.,** for the sake of it; **ser de buen/mal g.,** to be in good/bad taste; **tener buen/mal g.,** to have good/bad taste; **tenemos el gusto de comunicarle que ...,** we are pleased to inform you that ....

gutural *adj* guttural.

H

H, h [atfe] *nf* (*la letra*) H,h; **bomba H,** H-bomb.

ha *indic pres* → haber.

haba *nf* broad bean.

Habana *nf* **La H.,** Havana.

habano *nm* Havana cigar.

haber [14] I *v aux* 1 (*en tiempos compuestos*) to have; **lo he visto,** I have seen it; **ya lo había hecho,** he had already done it. 2 **h. de** + *infin,* (*obligación*) to have to; **has de ser bueno,** you must be good.

II *v impers* (special form of present tense: **hay**) 1 (*existir, estar*) (singular used also with plural nouns) **hay,** there is *o* are; **había,** there was *o* were; **había un gato en** el tejado, there was a cat on the roof; **había muchos libros,** there were a lot of books; **hay 500 kilómetros entre Madrid y Granada,** it's 500 kilometers from Nadrid to Granada. 2 **h. que** + *infin,* it is necessary to; **hay que trabajar,** you've got to *o* you must work; **habrá que comprobarlo,** I/you/we *etc* will have to check it. 3 (*tener lugar*) **habrá una fiesta,** there will be a party; **hoy hay partido,** there's a match today; **los accidentes habidos en esta carretera,** the accidents which have happened on this road. 4 **había una vez ...,** once upon a time ...; **no hay de qué,** you're welcome, don't mention it; **¿qué hay?,** how are things?

III *nm* 1 *Fin* credit; **haberes**, assets. **2 en su h.**, in his possession.

habichuela *nf* kidney bean.

hábil *adj* 1 (*diestro*) skilful, *US* skillful. 2 (*astuto*) smart. **3 días hábiles**, working days.

habilidad *nf* 1 (*destreza*) skill. 2 (*astucia*) cleverness.

habilitar *vtr* 1 (*espacio*) to fit out. 2 (*persona*) to entitle. 3 *Fin* (*financiar*) to finance.

habitación *nf* (*cuarto*) room; (*dormitorio*) bedroom; **h. individual/doble**, single/ double room.

habitante *nmf* inhabitant.

habitar **I** *vtr* to live in, inhabit. **II** *vi* to live.

hábitat *nm* (*pl* **hábitats**) habitat.

hábito *nm* 1 (*costumbre*) habit. 2 *Rel* habit.

habitual *adj* usual, habitual; (*cliente, lector*) regular.

habituar [30] **I** *vtr* to accustom (a, to). **II habituarse** *vr* to get used (a, to), become accustomed (a, to).

habla *nf* 1 (*idioma*) language; **países de h. española**, Spanish-speaking countries. 2 (*facultad de hablar*) speech; **quedarse sin h.**, to be left speechless. 3 *Tel* **¡al h.!**, speaking!

hablado,-a *adj* spoken; **el inglés h.**, spoken English; **mal h.**, coarse, foul-mouthed.

hablador,-a *adj* (*parlanchín*) talkative; *pey* (*chismoso*) gossipy.

habladuría *nf* (*rumor*) rumour, *US* rumor; (*chisme*) piece of gossip.

hablante *nmf* speaker.

hablar **I** *vi* 1 to speak, talk; **h. con algn**, to speak to sb. 2 **¡ni h.!**, certainly not!; *fam* **¡quién fue a h.!**, look who's talking!. **II** *vtr* 1 (*idioma*) to speak; **habla alemán**, he speaks German. 2 (*tratar un asunto*) to talk over, discuss. **III hablarse** *vr* 1 to speak *o* talk to one another. 2 **'se habla español'**, (*en letrero*) 'Spanish spoken'.

habré *indic fut* → **haber**.

hacendoso,-a *adj* hardworking.

hacer [15] **I** *vtr* 1 (*crear, producir, fabricar*) to make; **h. una casa**, to build a house. 2 (*obrar, ejecutar*) to do; **eso no se hace**, it isn't done; **hazme un favor**, do me a favour; **¿qué haces?**, (*en este momento*) what are you doing? (*para vivir*) what do you do (for a living)?; **tengo mucho que h.**, I have a lot to do; **h. deporte**, to do sports; **h. una carrera/medicina**, to do a degree/medicine. 4 (*obligar*) to make; **hazle callar/trabajar**, make him shut up/work. 5 (*arreglar*) to make; **h. la cama**, to make the bed. 6 *Mat* (*sumar*) to make; **y con éste hacen cien**, and that makes a hundred. 7 (*dar aspecto*) to make look; **el negro le hace más delgado**, black makes

him look slimmer. 8 (*sustituyendo a otro verbo*) to do; **ya no puedo leer como solía hacerlo**, I can't read as well as I used to. 9 (*representar*) to play; **h. el bueno**, to play the (part of the) goody. 10 **¡bien hecho!**, well done!

II *vi* 1 (*actuar*) to play; **hizo de Desdémona**, she played Desdemona. 2 **h. por** *o* **para + infin**, to try to; **hice por venir**, I tried to come. 3 (*fingir*) to pretend; **h. como si**, to act as if. 4 (*convenir*) to be suitable; **a las ocho si te hace**, will eight o'clock be all right for you?

III *v impers* 1 **hace calor/frío**, it's hot/ cold. 2 (*tiempo transcurrido*) ago; **hace mucho (tiempo)**, a long time ago; **hace dos días que no le veo**, I haven't seen him for two days; **hace dos años que vivo en Glasgow**, I've been living in Glasgow for two years.

IV hacerse *vr* 1 (*volverse*) to become, grow; **h. viejo**, to grow old. 2 (*simular*) to pretend; **h. el dormido**, to pretend to be sleeping. 3 **h. con**, (*apropiarse*) to get hold of. 4 (*habituarse*) to get used (a, to); **enseguida me hago a todo**, I soon get used to anything.

hacha *nf* 1 (*herramienta*) axe, *US* ax. 2 *fam* **ser una h. en algo**, to be an ace *o* a wizard at sth.

hachís *nm* hashish.

hacia *prep* 1 (*dirección*) towards, to; **h. abajo**, down, downwards; **h. adelante**, forwards; **h. arriba**, up, upwards; **h. atrás**, back, backwards. 2 (*tiempo*) at about, at around; **h. las tres**, at about three o'clock.

hacienda *nf* 1 (*finca agrícola*) estate, *US* ranch. 2 *Fin* Treasury; **h. pública**, public funds *o* finances *pl*; **Ministerio de H.**, = Exchequer, Treasury.

hacinamiento *nm* 1 *Agr* stacking; *fig* (*montón*) piling. 2 (*de gente*) overcrowding.

hacinar **I** *vtr* *Agr* to stack; *fig* (*amontonar*) to pile up, heap up. **II hacinarse** *vr* (*gente*) to be packed (en, into).

hada *nf* fairy; **cuento de hadas**, fairy tale; **h. madrina**, fairy godmother.

hado *nm* destiny.

hago *indic pres* → **hacer**.

halagar [7] *vtr* to flatter.

halago *nm* flattery.

halagüeño,-a *adj* (*noticia, impresión*) promising.

halcón *nm* falcon; **h. peregrino**, peregrine (falcon).

hálito *nm* 1 (*aliento*) breath. 2 (*vapor*) vapour, *US* vapor.

hallar **I** *vtr* (*encontrar*) to find; (*averiguar*) to find out; (*descubrir*) to discover. **II hallarse** *vr* (*estar*) to be, find oneself; (*estar situado*) to be situated.

hallazgo *nm* 1 (*descubrimiento*) discovery.

2 (cosa encontrada) find.

hamaca nf hammock; (mecedora) rocking chair.

hambre nf (apetito) hunger; (inanición) starvation; (catástrofe) famine; **tener h.**, to be hungry.

hambriento,-a adj starving.

hamburguesa nf hamburger.

hampa nf underworld.

han indic pres → **haber**.

harapo nm rag; **hecho un h.**, in tatters.

haré indic fut → **hacer**.

harén nm (pl **harenes**) harem.

harina nf flour.

hartar I vtr 1 (cansar, fastidiar) to annoy. 2 (atiborrar) to satiate; **el dulce harta enseguida**, sweet things soon fill you up. II **hartarse** vr 1 (saciar el apetito) to eat one's fill. 2 (cansarse) to get fed up (**de**, with), grow tired (**de**, of).

harto,-a adj 1 (de comida) full. 2 (cansado) fed up; **¡me tienes h.!**, I'm fed up with you!; **estoy h. de trabajar**, I'm fed up working. ◆**harto** adv (muy) very.

hartura nf bellyful; **¡qué h.!**, what a drag!

has indic pres → **haber**.

hasta I prep 1 (lugar) up to, as far as, down to. 2 (tiempo) until, till, up to; **h. el domingo**, until Sunday; **h. el final**, right to the end; **h. la fecha**, up to now; **h. luego**, see you later. 3 (con cantidad) up to, as many as. 4 (incluso) even. II conj **h. que**, until.

hastiado,-a adj sick, tired (**de**, of).

hastiar [29] vtr to sicken.

hastío nm weariness.

hato nm bundle.

hay indic pres → **haber**.

Haya (La) nf The Hague.

haya¹ nf 1 Bot (árbol) beech. 2 (madera) beech (wood).

haya² subj pres → **haber**.

haz¹ nm 1 Agr sheaf. 2 (de luz) shaft.

haz² nf (de hoja) top side.

haz³ imperat → **hacer**.

hazaña nf deed, exploit.

hazmerreír nm laughing stock.

he¹ adv he ahí/aquí ..., there/here you have ....

he² indic pres → **haber**.

hebilla nf buckle.

hebra nf thread; (de carne) sinew; (de madera) grain; **pegar la h.**, to chat.

hebreo,-a I adj Hebrew. II nm,f Hebrew.

hecatombe nf disaster.

hechicería nf witchcraft.

hechicero,-a I adj bewitching. II nm,f (hombre) wizard, sorcerer; (mujer) witch, sorceress.

hechizar [4] vtr 1 (embrujar) to cast a spell on. 2 fig (fascinar) to bewitch, charm.

hechizo nm 1 (embrujo) spell. 2 fig (fascinación) fascination, charm.

hecho,-a I adj 1 made, done; **¡bien h.!**,

well done! 2 (carne) done. 3 (persona) mature. 4 (frase) set; (ropa) ready-made. II nm 1 (realidad) fact; **de h.**, in fact; **el h. es que ...**, the fact is that .... 2 (acto) act, deed. 3 (suceso) event, incident.

hechura nf (forma) shape; Cost cut.

hectárea nf hectare.

hectolitro nm hectolitre, US hectoliter.

heder [3] vi to stink, smell foul.

hediondo,-a adj foul-smelling.

hedor nm stink, stench.

hegemonía nf hegemony.

helada nf frost.

heladería nf ice-cream parlour.

helado,-a I nm ice cream. II adj 1 (muy frío) frozen, freezing cold; **estoy h. (de frío)**, I'm frozen. 2 fig **quedarse h.**, (atónito) to be flabbergasted.

helar [1] I vtr (congelar) to freeze. II v impers to freeze; **anoche heló**, there was a frost last night. III **helarse** vr (congelarse) to freeze.

helecho nm Bot fern.

hélice nf 1 Av Náut propeller. 2 Anat Arquit Mat helix.

helicóptero nm Av helicopter.

helipuerto nm Av heliport.

hematoma nm Med haematoma, US hematoma.

hembra nf 1 Bot Zool female. 2 (mujer) woman. 3 Téc female; (de tornillo) nut; (de enchufe) socket.

hemiciclo nm fam (Spanish) parliament.

hemisferio nm hemisphere.

hemorragia nf Med haemorrhage, US hemorrhage.

hemos indic pres → **haber**.

henchir [6] vtr to stuff.

hender [3] vtr (resquebrajar) to crack, split; fig (olas) to cut.

hendidura nf crack.

hendir [5] vtr → **hender**.

heno nm hay.

heráldica nf heraldry.

herbicida nm weedkiller, herbicide.

herbívoro,-a I adj herbivorous, grass-eating. II nm,f Zool herbivore.

herbolario nm herbalist's (shop).

herboso,-a adj grassy.

hercio nm Herz.

heredad nf 1 (finca) country estate. 2 (conjunto de bienes) private estate.

heredar vtr 1 Jur to inherit. 2 **ha heredado la sonrisa de su madre**, she's got her mother's smile.

heredero,-a nm,f (hombre) heir; (mujer) heiress; **príncipe h.**, crown prince.

hereditario,-a adj hereditary.

hereje nmf Rel heretic.

herejía nf Rel heresy.

herencia nf 1 Jur inheritance, legacy. 2 Biol heredity.

herida nf (lesión) injury; (corte) wound.

herido,-a n injured person; **no hubo heri-**

dos, there were no casualties.

herir [5] I vtr 1 *(físicamente) (lesionar)* to injure; *(cortar)* to wound. 2 *(emocionalmente)* to hurt, wound. 3 *(vista)* to offend. II **herirse** vr to injure o hurt oneself.

hermana 1 sister. 2 *Rel (monja)* sister (→ **hermano**).

hermanado,-a *adj* twinned; **ciudad hermanada**, twin town.

hermanar I vtr 1 *(personas)* to unite spiritually. 2 *(ciudades)* to twin. 3 *(unir)* to unite, combine. II **hermanarse** vr 1 *(ciudades)* to twin. 2 *(combinar)* to combine.

hermanastro,-a *nm,f (hombre)* stepbrother; *(mujer)* stepsister.

hermandad *nf 1 (grupo)* fraternity, brotherhood, sisterhood. 2 *(relación)* brotherhood, sisterhood.

hermano *nm* 1 brother; **h. político**, brother-in-law; **primo h.**, first cousin. 2 *Rel (fraile)* brother. 3 **hermanos**, brothers and sisters.

hermético,-a *adj (cierre)* hermetic, airtight. 2 *fig (abstruso)* secretive. ◆**herméticamente** *adv* **h. cerrado**, hermetically sealed.

hermetismo *nm* hermeticism; *fig* impenetrability.

hermoso,-a *adj* beautiful, lovely; *(grande)* fine.

hermosura *nf* beauty.

héroe *nm* hero.

heroico,-a *adj* heroic.

heroína 1 *(mujer)* heroine. 2 *(droga)* heroin.

heroinómano,-a *nm,f* heroin addict.

heroísmo *nm* heroism.

herrador *nm* blacksmith.

herradura *nf* horseshoe.

herramienta *nf Téc* tool; **caja de herramientas**, toolbox.

herrar [1] vtr 1 *(caballo)* to shoe. 2 *(ganado)* to brand.

herrería *nf* forge, smithy.

herrero *nm* blacksmith, smith.

herrumbre *nf* rust.

hervidero *nm fig (lugar)* hotbed.

hervir [5] I vtr *(hacer bullir)* to boil. II vi 1 *Culin* to boil; **romper a h.**, to come to the boil. 2 *(abundar)* to swarm, seethe (de, with).

heterodoxo,-a *adj* unorthodox.

heterogéneo,-a *adj* heterogeneous.

hez *nf 1 (usu pl) (poso)* sediment, dregs pl. 2 **heces**, faeces.

hiato *nm Ling* hiatus.

híbrido,-a *adj & nm,f* hybrid.

hice *pt indef* → **hacer**.

hiciste *pt indef* → **hacer**.

hidalgo *nm Hist* nobleman, gentleman.

hidalguía *nf* nobility; *fig* chivalry, gentlemanliness.

hidratación *nf 1 Quím* hydration. 2 *(de la*

piel) moisturizing.

hidratante *adj* moisturizing; **crema/leche h.**, moisturizing cream/lotion.

hidráulico,-a *adj* hydraulic; **energía hidráulica**, hydro-electric energy.

hidroavión *nm* seaplane, *US* hydroplane.

hidrocarburo *nm* hydrocarbon.

hidrófilo,-a *adj* absorbent; **algodón h.**, cotton wool.

hidrógeno *nm Quím* hydrogen.

hidroterapia *nf Med* hydrotherapy.

hiedra *nf* ivy.

hiel *nf 1 Anat* bile. 2 *fig* bitterness, gall.

hielo *nm* ice; *fig* **romper el h.**, to break the ice.

hiena *nf* hyena.

hierba *nf 1* grass; **mala h.**, *Bot* weed; *fig (persona)* bad lot; *fam* **hum ... y otras hierbas**, ... among others. 2 *Culin* herb; **h. luisa**, lemon verbena. 3 *sl (marihuana)* grass.

hierbabuena *nf* mint.

hierro *nm 1 (metal)* iron; **h. forjado**, wrought iron. 2 *(punta de arma)* head, point. 3 *(marca en el ganado)* brand.

hígado *nm 1 Anat* liver. 2 *euf* guts *pl*.

higiene *nf* hygiene.

higiénico,-a *adj* hygienic; **papel h.**, toilet paper.

higo *nm fam* fig **hecho un h.**, wizened, crumpled.

higuera *nf Bot* fig tree.

hija *nf* daughter (→ **hijo**).

hijastro,-a *nm,f (hombre)* stepson; *(mujer)* stepdaughter.

hijo *nm* 1 son, child; *pey* **h. de papá**, daddy's boy; *vulg ofens* **h. de puta**, bastard, son of a bitch. 2 **hijos**, children.

hijoputa *nm vulg ofens* bastard.

hilacha *nf*, **hilacho** *nm* loose o hanging thread.

hilandería *nf 1* mill; *(de algodón)* cotton mill.

hilandero,-a *nm,f* spinner.

hilar vtr & vi 1 to spin. 2 *fig (idea, plan)* to work out; **h. muy fino**, to split hairs.

hilaridad *nf* hilarity, mirth.

hilera *nf* line, row.

hilo *nm 1 Cost* thread; *(grueso)* yarn. 2 *fig (de historia, discurso)* thread; *(de pensamiento)* train; **perder el h.**, to lose the thread; **h. musical**, background music. 3 *Tex* linen.

hilvanar vtr 1 *Cost* to tack, baste. 2 *fig (ideas etc)* to outline.

himno *nm* hymn; **h. nacional**, national anthem.

hincapié *nm* **hacer h. en**, *(insistir)* to insist on; *(subrayar)* to emphasize, stress.

hincar [1] I vtr *(clavar)* to drive (in); **h. el diente a**, to sink one's teeth into. II **hincarse** vr **h. de rodillas**, to kneel (down).

hincha *fam 1 nmf Ftb* fan, supporter. II *nf*

(antipatía) grudge, dislike; **me tiene h.,** he's got it in for me.

hinchada *nf Ftb fam* fans *pl,* supporters *pl.*

hinchado,-a *adj* 1 inflated, blown up. 2 *Med (cara etc)* swollen, puffed up; *(estómago)* bloated. 3 *fig (estilo)* bombastic, pompous.

hinchar *vtr* 1 *(inflar)* to inflate, blow up. 2 *fig (exagerar)* to inflate, exaggerate. ∎ **hincharse** *vr* 1 *Med* to swell (up). 2 *fam* **me hinché de comida,** I stuffed myself; **me hinché de llorar,** I cried for all I was worth.

hinchazón *nf Med* swelling.

hindú *adj & nmf* Hindu.

hipermercado *nm* hypermarket.

hipertensión *nf* high blood pressure.

hípica *nf* (horse) riding.

hípico,-a *adj* horse; **club h.,** riding club.

hipnotizar [4] *vtr* to hypnotize.

hipo *nm* hiccups, hiccough; **me ha dado h.,** it's given me the hiccups.

hipocondríaco,-a *adj & nm,f* hypochondriac.

hipocresía *nf* hypocrisy.

hipócrita I *adj* hypocritical. II *nmf* hypocrite.

hipódromo *nm* racetrack, racecourse.

hipopótamo *nm* hippopotamus.

hipoteca *nf Fin* mortgage.

hipotecar [1] *vtr* 1 *Fin* to mortgage. 2 *fig* to jeopardize.

hipótesis *nf inv* hypothesis.

hipotético,-a *adj* hypothetical.

hiriente *adj* offensive, wounding; *(palabras)* cutting.

hirsuto,-a *adj* hirsute, hairy; *(cerdoso)* bristly.

hispánico,-a *adj* Hispanic, Spanish.

hispanidad *nf* el **Día de la H.,** Columbus Day (12 October).

hispano,-a I *adj (español)* Spanish; *(español y sudamericano)* Hispanic; *(sudamericano)* Spanish American. II *nm,f* Spanish American, *US* Hispanic.

Hispanoamérica *nf* Latin America.

hispanoamericano,-a *adj & nm,f* Latin American.

hispanohablante I *adj* Spanish-speaking. II *nmf* Spanish speaker.

histeria *nf* hysteria; **un ataque de h.,** hysterics *pl.*

histérico,-a I *adj* hysterical; *fam* **fig me pones h.,** you're driving me mad.

historia *nf* 1 history; **esto pasará a la h.,** this will go down in history. 2 *(narración)* story, tale; *fam* **¡déjate de historias!,** don't give me that!

historiador,-a *nm,f* historian.

historial *nm* 1 *Med* medical record, case history. 2 *(curriculum)* curriculum vitae. 3 *(antecedentes)* background.

historiar [29] *vtr* to recount.

histórico,-a *adj* 1 historical. 2 *(auténtico)* factual, true; **hechos históricos,** true facts. 3 *(de gran importancia)* historic, memorable.

historieta *nf* 1 *(cuento)* short story, tale. 2 *(tira cómica)* comic strip.

hito *nm* milestone; **mirar de h. en h.,** to stare at.

hizo *indic indef* → **hacer.**

hnos. *abr de* **Hermanos,** Brothers, Bros.

hocico *nm* 1 *(de animal)* snout. 2 *fam (de persona)* mug, snout; *fam* **meter los hocicos en algo,** to stick o poke one's nose into sth.

hogar *nm* 1 *(casa)* home. 2 *(de la chimenea)* hearth, fireplace. 3 *fig* **formar o crear un h.,** *(familia)* to start a family.

hogareño,-a *adj (vida)* home, family; *(persona)* home-loving, stay-at-home.

hoguera *nf* bonfire.

hoja *nf* 1 *Bot* leaf. 2 *(pétalo)* petal. 3 *(de papel)* sheet, leaf; **h. de cálculo,** spreadsheet. 4 *(de libro)* leaf, page. 5 *(de metal)* sheet. 6 *(de cuchillo, espada)* blade. 7 *(impreso)* hand-out, printed sheet. 8 *(de puerta o ventana)* leaf.

hojalata *nf* tin, tin plate.

hojaldre *nm Culin* puff pastry.

hojarasca *nf* fallen o dead leaves *pl.*

hojear *vtr* to leaf through, flick through.

hola *interj* hello!, hullo!, hi!

Holanda *nf* Holland.

holandés,-esa I *adj* Dutch. II *nm,f (hombre)* Dutchman; *(mujer)* Dutchwoman. III *nm (idioma)* Dutch.

holding *nm Fin* holding company.

holgado,-a *adj* 1 *(ropa)* loose, baggy. 2 *(económicamente)* comfortable. 3 *(espacio)* roomy; **andar h. de tiempo,** to have plenty of time.

holgar [2] *vi* 1 *(no trabajar)* to be idle. 2 *(sobrar)* **huelga decir que ...,** it goes without saying that ....

holgazán,-ana I *adj* lazy, idle. II *nm,f* lazybones *inv,* layabout.

holgura *nf* 1 *(ropa)* looseness. 2 *(espacio)* space, roominess; *Téc* play, give. 3 *(bienestar económico)* affluence, comfort; **vivir con h.,** to be comfortably off, be well-off.

hollar [2] *vtr fig* to walk on; **terrenos jamás hollados,** uncharted territory.

hollín *nm* soot.

hombre I *nm* 1 man; **de h. a h.,** man-to-man; **¡pobre h.!,** poor chap!; **ser muy h.,** to be every inch a man; **h. de estado,** statesman; **h. de negocios,** businessman. 2 *(especie)* mankind, man. II *interj* 1 *(saludo)* hey!, hey there!; **¡h., Juan!,** hey, Juan! 2 **¡sí h.!,** **¡h. claro!,** *(enfático)* sure!, you bet!; **¡anda, h.!,** *(incredulidad)* oh come on!

hombrera *nf* shoulder pad.

hombría *nf* manliness, virility.

hombro *nm* shoulder; **a hombros**, on one's shoulders; **encogerse de hombros**, to shrug one's shoulders; **mirar a algn por encima del h.**, to look down one's nose at sb.

hombruno,-a *adj* mannish, butch.

homenaje *nm* homage, tribute; **rendir h. a algn**, to pay homage *o* tribute to sb.

homenajear *vtr* to pay tribute to.

homicida I *nmf* (*hombre*) murderer; (*mujer*) murderess. **II** *adj* homicidal; **el arma h.**, the murder weapon.

homicidio *nm* homicide.

homogéneo,-a *adj* homogeneous, uniform.

homologable *adj* comparable (**con**, with).

homologar [7] *vtr* to give official approval *o* recognition to.

homólogo,-a I *adj* (*equiparable*) comparable. **II** *nm,f* (*persona con mismas condiciones*) counterpart.

homosexual *adj & nmf* homosexual.

homosexualidad *nf* homosexuality.

honda *nf* (*arma*) sling.

hondo,-a *adj* 1 (*profundo*) deep; **plato h.**, soup dish. 2 *fig* (*pesar*) profound, deep.

hondonada *nf Geog* hollow, depression.

hondura *nf* depth; *fig* **meterse en honduras**, (*profundizar*) to go into too much detail.

Honduras *n* Honduras.

hondureño,-a *adj & nm,f* Honduran.

honestidad *nf* 1 (*honradez*) honesty, uprightness. 2 (*decencia*) modesty.

honesto,-a *adj* 1 (*honrado*) honest, upright. 2 (*decente*) modest.

hongo *nm* 1 *Bot* fungus; **h. venenoso**, toadstool. 2 (*sombrero*) bowler, bowler *o* hat.

honor *nm* 1 (*virtud*) honour, *US* honor; **palabra de h.**, word of honour. 2 **en h. a la verdad ...**, to be fair ...; **es un h. para mí**, it's an honour for me. 3 **hacer h. a**, to live up to.

honorable *adj* honourable, *US* honorable; *Pol* **el h.**, head of the Catalan government.

honorario,-a I *adj* honorary. **II** *nmpl* **honorarios**, fees, fee *sing*.

honorífico,-a *adj* honorary.

honra *nf* 1 (*dignidad*) dignity, self-esteem. 2 (*fama*) reputation, good name. 3 (*honor*) honour, *US* honor; **me cabe la h. de ...**, I have the honour of ...; **¡a mucha h.!**, and proud of it!

honradez *nf* honesty, integrity.

honrado,-a *adj* 1 (*de fiar*) honest. 2 (*decente*) upright, respectable.

honrar *vtr* 1 (*respetar*) to honour, *US* honor. 2 (*enaltecer*) to be a credit to.

honrilla *nf* self-respect, pride.

honroso,-a *adj* (*loable*) honourable, *US* honorable.

hora *nf* 1 hour; **media h.**, half an hour; **a altas horas de la madrugada**, in the small hours; **dar la h.**, to strike the hour; (*trabajo*) **por horas**, (work) paid by the hour; **h. punta**, rush hour; **horas extra**, overtime (hours). 2 *fig* time; **¿qué h. es?**, what time is it?; **a su h.**, at the proper time; **a última h.**, at the last moment; **la h. de la verdad**, the moment of truth. 3 (*cita*) appointment; **pedir h.**, (*al médico etc*) to ask for an appointment.

horadar *vtr* (*perforar*) to drill *o* bore a hole in.

horario-a I *nm* timetable, *US* schedule. **II** *adj* time; **Rad señal horaria**, pips.

horca *nf* gallows *pl*.

horcajadas *nf* **a horcajadas**, astride.

horchata *nf Culin* sweet milky drink made from chufa nuts *o* almonds.

horda *nf* horde, mob.

horizonte *nm* horizon.

horma *nf* (*de zapato*) last.

hormiga *nf* ant.

hormigón *nm Constr* concrete; **h. armado**, reinforced concrete.

hormiguear *vi* to itch, tingle; **me hormigueaba la pierna**, I had pins and needles in my leg.

hormigueo *nm* 1 pins and needles *pl*, tingling *o* itching sensation. 2 *fig* anxiety.

hormiguero *nm* 1 anthill. 2 *fig* **ser un h.**, (*lugar*) to be swarming (with people).

hormona *nf* hormone.

hornada *nf* 1 (*pan*) batch. 2 *fig* set, bunch.

hornillo *nm* (*de cocinar*) stove; (*placa*) hotplate.

horno *nm* (*cocina*) oven; *Téc* furnace; (*para cerámica, ladrillos*) kiln; *Culin* **pescado al h.**, baked fish; *fam* **fig esta habitación es un h.**, this room is boiling hot.

Hornos *n* **Cabo de H.**, Cape Horn.

horóscopo *nm* horoscope.

horquilla *nf* 1 (*del pelo*) hair-grip, hairpin, *US* bobby pin. 2 (*estadística*) chart. 3 **h. de precios**, price range.

horrendo,-a *adj* horrifying, horrible.

hórreo *nm Agr* granary.

horrible *adj* horrible, dreadful, awful.

horripilante *adj* hair-raising, scary.

horror *nm* 1 horror, terror; **¡qué h.!**, how awful!; **tengo h. a las motos**, I hate motorbikes. 2 *fam fig* **me gusta horrores**, (*muchísimo*) I like it an awful lot.

horrorizar [4] *vtr* to horrify, terrify.

horroroso,-a *adj* 1 (*que da miedo*) horrifying, terrifying. 2 *fam* (*muy feo*) hideous, ghastly. 3 *fam* (*malísimo*) awful, dreadful.

hortaliza *nf* vegetable.

hortelano *nm,f* market gardener, *US* truck farmer.

hortensia *nf Bot* hydrangea.

hortera *nm arg* (*persona*) flashy; (*cosa*) tacky, kitsch.

horterada *nf arg* tacky thing *o* act.

hosco,-a *adj* **1** *(poco sociable)* surly, sullen. **2** *(tenebroso)* dark, gloomy. **3** *(difícil)* tough.

hospedaje *nm* lodgings *pl*, accommodation, *US* accommodations.

hospedar I *vtr* to put up, lodge. **II hospedarse** *vr* to stay **(en,** at).

hospicio *nm* orphanage.

hospital *nm* hospital.

hospitalario,-a *adj* **1** *(acogedor)* hospitable. **2** *Med* hospital; **instalaciones hospitalarias,** hospital facilities.

hospitalidad *nf* hospitality.

hospitalizar [4] *vtr* to take *o* send into hospital, hospitalize.

hostal *nm* guest house.

hostelería *nf (negocio)* catering business; *(estudios)* hotel management.

hostelero,-a *nm,f (hombre)* landlord; *(mujer)* landlady.

hostería *nf Am* inn, lodging house.

hostia I *nf* **1** *Rel* host. **2** *vulg (tortazo)* bash. **3 estar de mala h.,** to be in a foul mood; **ser la h.,** *(fantástico)* to be bloody amazing *o* fantastic; *(penoso)* to be bloody useless. **II** *interj* damn! bloody hell!

hostiar *vtr vulg* to bash, sock.

hostigar [7] *vtr* **1** to harass. **2** *(caballerías)* to whip.

hostil *adj* hostile.

hostilidad *nf* hostility.

hotel *nm* hotel.

hotelero,-a I *adj* hotel; **el sector h.,** the hotel sector. **II** *nm,f* hotel-keeper, hotelier.

hoy *adv* **1** *(día)* today. **2** *fig (presente)* now; **h. (en) día,** nowadays; **h. por h.,** at the present time.

hoya *nf Geog* dale, valley.

hoyo *nm* **1** *(agujero)* hole, pit. **2** *(sepultura)* grave. **3** *Golf* hole.

hoyuelo *nm* dimple.

hoz *nf Agr* sickle; **la h. y el martillo,** the hammer and sickle.

HR *nm abr de* **Hostal Residencia.**

hube *pt indef* → **haber.**

hubiera *subj imperf* → **haber.**

hucha *nf* piggy bank.

hueco,-a I *adj* **1** *(vacío)* empty, hollow. **2** *(sonido)* resonant. **II** *nm* **1** *(cavidad)* hollow, hole. **2** *(sitio no ocupado)* empty space. **3** *(rato libre)* free time.

huele *indic pres* → **oler.**

huelga *nf* strike; **estar en** *o* **de h.,** to be on strike; **h. de brazos caídos,** go-slow; **h. de celo,** work-to-rule.

huelguista *nmf* striker.

huella *nf* **1** *(del pie)* footprint; *(coche)* track; **h. dactilar,** fingerprint. **2** *fig (vestigio)* trace, sign; **dejar h.,** to leave one's mark.

huérfano,-a *nmf* orphan.

huero,-a *adj fig* empty.

huerta *nf Agr* **1** *(parcela)* market *o US* truck garden. **2** *(región)* irrigated area used for cultivation.

huerto *nm* *(de verduras)* vegetable garden, kitchen garden; *(de frutales)* orchard.

hueso *nm* **1** *Anat* bone; **estar en los huesos,** to be all skin and bone. **2** *(de fruto)* stone, *US* pit. **3** *fig (difícil)* hard work; *(profesor)* hard nut. **4** *Am (enchufe)* contact.

huésped,-a *nm,f (invitado)* guest; *(en hotel etc)* lodger, boarder; **casa de huéspedes,** guesthouse.

hueste *nf Mil* army, host.

huesudo,-a *adj* bony.

huevera *nf* **1** *(caja)* egg box. **2** *vulg (suspensorio)* jockstrap.

huevo *nm* **1** egg; **h. duro,** hard-boiled egg; **h. escalfado,** poached egg; **h. frito,** fried egg; **h. pasado por agua,** soft-boiled egg; **huevos revueltos,** scrambled eggs. **2** *vulg (usu pl)* balls *pl*; **hacer algo por huevos,** to do sth even if it kills you; **tener huevos,** to have guts.

huida *nf* flight, escape.

huidizo,-a *adj* elusive.

huir [37] *vi* to run away **(de,** from), flee; **h. de la cárcel,** to escape from prison; **h. de algn,** to avoid sb.

hule *nm* **1** *(tela impermeable)* oilcloth, oilskin. **2** *(de mesa)* tablecloth. **3** *Am* rubber.

hulla *nf Min* coal.

humanidad *nf* **1** *(género humano)* humanity, mankind. **2** *(cualidad)* humanity, humaneness. **3** *(bondad)* compassion, kindness.

humanitario,-a *adj* humanitarian.

humano,-a I *adj* **1** *(relativo al hombre)* human. **2** *(compasivo)* humane. **II** *nm* human *(being)*; **ser h.,** human being.

humear *vi (echar humo)* to smoke; *(arrojar vapor)* to steam, be steaming hot.

humedad *nf (atmosférica)* humidity; *(de lugar)* dampness; **a prueba de h.,** dampproof.

humedecer [33] **I** *vtr* to moisten, dampen. **II humedecerse** *vr* to become damp *o* wet *o* moist.

húmedo,-a *adj (casa, ropa)* damp; *(clima)* humid, damp, moist.

humildad *nf* humility; *(pobreza)* humbleness.

humilde *adj* humble, modest; *(pobre)* poor.

humillación *nf* humiliation.

humillante *adj* humiliating, humbling.

humillar I *vtr (rebajar)* to humiliate, humble. **II humillarse** *vr* **1 h. ante algn,** to humble oneself before sb.

humo *nm* **1** smoke; *(gas)* fumes *pl*; *(vapor)* vapour, *US* vapor, steam. **2 ¡qué humos tiene!,** she thinks a lot of herself.

humor *nm* **1** *(genio)* mood; **estar de buen**

o mal h., to be in a good o bad mood. 2 *(carácter)* temper; **es persona de mal h.,** he's bad tempered. 3 *(gracia)* humour, *US* humor; **sentido del h.,** sense of humour.

humorismo nm humour, *US* humor.

humorista nmf humorist; **h. gráfico,** cartoonist.

humorístico adj humorous; funny.

hundido,-a adj 1 *(barco)* sunken; *(ojos)* deep- set. 2 fig *(abatido)* down, demoralized.

hundimiento nm 1 *(de edificio)* collapse. 2 *(de barco)* sinking. 3 *(de tierra)* subsidence. 4 fig Fin crash, slump; *(ruina)* downfall.

hundir I vtr 1 *(barco)* to sink. 2 *(edificio)* to bring a knock down. 3 fig *(desmoralizar)* to demoralize. II **hundirse** vr 1 *(barco)* to sink. 2 *(edificio)* to collapse. 3 fig *(empresa)* to collapse, crash.

húngaro,-a I adj Hungarian. II nm,f *(persona)* Hungarian. III nm *(idioma)* Hungarian.

Hungría n Hungary.

huracán nm hurricane.

huraño,-a adj pey unsociable.

hurgar [7] I vi *(fisgar)* to poke one's nose in. II vtr *(fuego etc)* to poke, rake. III **hurgarse** vr **h. las narices,** to pick one's nose.

hurón,-ona I nm Zool ferret. II nm,f fam *(fisgón)* busybody, nosey-parker.

hurra nf Orn → **urraca.**

hurtadillas adv a h., stealthily, on the sly.

hurtar vtr to steal, pilfer.

hurto nm petty theft, pilfering.

husmear I vtr *(olfatear)* to sniff out, scent. II vi fig *(curiosear)* to snoop, pry.

huyo indic pres → **huir.**

I

I, i [i] nf *(la letra)* I, i; **i griega,** Y, y.

ib. abr de **ibídem,** ibidem, ibid., ib.

IB nm Educ abr de **Instituto de Bachillerato,** ≈ state secondary school.

ibérico,-a adj Iberian.

Iberoamérica n Latin America.

iberoamericano,-a adj & nm,f Latin American.

iceberg nm *(pl* **icebergs)** iceberg.

ICONA nm abr de **Instituto para la Conservación de la Naturaleza.**

icono nm icon; *Inform* icon.

iconoclasta I adj iconoclastic. II nmf iconoclast.

iconografía nf iconography.

icteria nf Med jaundice.

id. abr de **idem,** idem, id.

I+D abr de **Investigación más Desarrollo,** Research and Development, R&D.

ida nf billete de **i. y vuelta,** return ticket; **idas y venidas,** comings and goings.

idea nf 1 idea; **i. fija,** fixed idea. 2 *(noción)* idea; **hacerse a la i. de,** to get used to the idea of; fam **ni i.,** no idea, not a clue. 3 *(opinión)* opinion; **cambiar de i.,** to change one's mind. 4 *(intención)* intention; **a mala i.,** on purpose.

ideal adj & nm ideal.

idealismo nm idealism.

idealista I adj idealistic. II nmf idealist.

idealizar [4] vtr to idealize, glorify.

idear vtr 1 *(inventar)* to devise, invent. 2 *(concebir)* to think up, conceive.

ídem adv idem, ditto; fam **í. de i.,** exactly the same.

idéntico,-a adj identical.

identidad nf 1 identity; **carnet de i.,** identity card. 2 *(semejanza)* identity, sameness.

identificación nf identification.

identificar [1] I vtr to identify. II **identificarse** vr to identify oneself; fig **i. con,** to identify with.

ideología nf ideology.

ideológico,-a adj ideological.

idílico,-a adj idyllic.

idilio nm 1 Lit idyll. 2 fig *(romance)* romance, love affair.

idioma nm language.

idiomático,-a adj idiomatic.

idiosincrasia nf idiosyncrasy.

idiota I adj idiotic, stupid. II nmf idiot, fool.

idiotez nf idiocy, stupidity.

ido,-a adj 1 *(distraído)* absent-minded. 2 fam *(chiflado)* crazy, nuts.

idólatra I adj idolatrous. II nmf *(hombre)* idolater; *(mujer)* idolatress.

idolatrar vtr to worship; fig to idolize.

idolatría nf idolatry.

ídolo nm idol.

idóneo,-a adj suitable, fit.

iglesia nf 1 *(edificio)* church. 2 **la I.,** *(institución)* the Church.

ignominia nf ignominy.

ignominioso,-a adj ignominious, shameful.

ignorancia nf ignorance.

ignorante I adj 1 *(sin instrucción)* ignorant. 2 *(no informado)* ignorant, unaware *(de,* of). II nmf ignoramus.

ignorar I vtr 1 *(algo)* not to know. 2 *(a algn)* to ignore. II **ignorarse** vr to be unknown.

ignoto,-a adj unknown.

igual I adj 1 *(idéntico)* the same, alike;

son todos iguales, they're all the same; **es i.,** it doesn't matter; **i. que,** the same as. **2** (*equivalente*) equal; **a partes iguales,** fifty-fifty. **3** *Dep* (*empatados*) even; **treinta iguales,** thirty all. **4** *Mat* equal; **tres más tres i. a seis,** three plus three equals six. **5 al i. que,** just like. **6 por i.,** equally. **II** *nm* equal; **de i. a i.,** on an equal footing; **sin i.,** unique, unrivalled. **III** *adv* **1 lo haces i. que yo,** you do it the same way I do. **2** (*probablemente*) probably; **i. vengo,** I'll probably come. ◆**igualmente** *adv* equally; (*también*) also, likewise; *fam* **¡gracias! - ¡i.!,** thank you! - the same to you!

igualar I *vtr* **1** to make equal. **2** (*nivelar*) to level; **3** *Dep* **i. el partido,** to equalize, square the match. **II igualarse** *vr* **1** to be equal. **2 i. con algn,** to place oneself on an equal footing with sb.

igualdad *nf* **1** equality; **i. ante la ley,** equality before the law. **2** (*identidad*) sameness; **en i. de condiciones,** on equal terms.

igualitario,-a *adj* egalitarian.

ijada *nf,* **ijar** *nm* *Anat* flank.

ikastola *nf* Basque language school.

ikurriña *nf* Basque flag.

ilegal *adj* illegal. ◆**ilegalmente** *adv* illegally.

ilegalidad *nf* illegality.

ilegible *adj* illegible, unreadable.

ilegítimo,-a *adj* illegitimate.

ileso,-a *adj* unhurt, unharmed.

ilícito,-a *adj* illicit, unlawful.

ilimitado,-a *adj* unlimited, limitless.

Ilmo. *abr de* **Ilustrísimo,** His Excellence *o* Excellency.

ilógico,-a *adj* illogical.

iluminación *nf* (*alumbrado*) illumination, lighting.

iluminar *vtr* **1** to illuminate, light (up). **2** *fig* (*a persona*) to enlighten; (*tema*) to throw light upon.

ilusión *nf* **1** (*esperanza*) hope; (*esperanza vana*) illusion, delusion; **hacerse ilusiones,** to build up one's hopes. **2** (*sueño*) dream. **3** (*emoción*) excitement, thrill; **me hace i. verla,** I'm looking forward to seeing her; **¡qué i.!,** how exciting!

ilusionar I *vtr* **1** (*esperanzar*) to build up sb's hopes. **2** (*entusiasmar*) to excite, thrill. **II ilusionarse** *vr* **1** (*esperanzarse*) to build up one's hopes. **2** (*entusiasmarse*) to be excited *o* thrilled (**con,** about).

iluso,-a *adj* easily deceived, gullible.

ilusorio,-a *adj* illusory, unreal.

ilustración *nf* **1** (*grabado*) illustration, picture; (*ejemplo*) illustration. **2** (*erudición*) learning, erudition; *Hist* **la I.,** the Enlightenment.

ilustrado,-a *adj* **1** (*con dibujos, ejemplos*) illustrated. **2** (*erudito*) learned, erudite.

ilustrar I *vtr* **1** to illustrate. **2** (*aclarar*) to

explain, make clear. **II ilustrarse** *vr* to acquire knowledge (**sobre,** of), learn.

ilustrativo,-a *adj* illustrative.

ilustre *adj* illustrious, distinguished.

imagen *nf* **1** image; **ser la viva i. de algn,** to be the spitting image of sb; **tener buena i.,** to have a good image. **2** *Rel* image, statue. **3** *TV* picture.

imaginación *nf* imagination; **eso son imaginaciones tuyas,** you're imagining things.

imaginar I *vtr* to imagine. **II imaginarse** *vr* to imagine; **me imagino qué sí,** I suppose so.

imaginario,-a *adj* imaginary.

imaginativo,-a *adj* imaginative.

imán *nm* magnet.

imbatible *adj* unbeatable.

imbatido,-a *adj* unbeaten, undefeated.

imbécil I *adj* stupid, silly. **II** *nmf* idiot, imbecile.

imbecilidad *nf* stupidity, imbecility.

imborrable *adj* indelible.

imbuir [37] *vtr* *fml* to imbue.

imitación *nf* imitation.

imitar *vtr* to imitate; (*gestos*) to mimic; **este collar imita al oro,** this necklace is imitation gold.

impaciencia *nf* impatience.

impacientar I *vtr* **i. a algn,** to make sb lose patience, exasperate sb. **II impacientarse** *vr* to get *o* grow impatient (**por,** at).

impaciente *adj* (*deseoso*) impatient; (*intranquilo*) anxious.

impactar *vtr* to shock, stun.

impacto *nm* impact; *Mil* hit.

impactante *adj* **una noticia i.,** a sensational piece of news.

impar *adj* *Mat* odd; **número i.,** odd number.

imparable *adj* *Dep* unstoppable.

imparcial *adj* impartial, unbiased.

imparcialidad *nf* impartiality.

impartir *vtr* (*clases*) to give.

impasible *adj* impassive.

impávido,-a *adj* fearless.

impecable *adj* impeccable.

impedido,-a I *adj* disabled, handicapped. **II** *nm,f* disabled *o* handicapped person.

impedimento *nm* impediment; (*obstáculo*) hindrance, obstacle.

impedir [6] *vtr* (*obstaculizar*) to impede, hinder; (*imposibilitar*) to prevent, stop; **i. el paso,** to block the way.

impeler *vtr* *Téc* to drive, propel; *fig* to drive, impel.

impenetrable *adj* impenetrable.

impenitente *adj* *Rel* impenitent, unrepentant.

impensable *adj* unthinkable.

impepinable *adj* *fam* dead sure, certain.

imperante *adj* (*gobernante*) ruling; (*predominante*) prevailing.

imperar vi (gobernar) to rule; (predominar) to prevail.

imperativo,-a I adj imperative. **II** nm Ling imperative.

imperceptible adj imperceptible.

imperdible nm safety pin.

imperdonable adj unforgivable, inexcusable.

imperecedero,-a adj imperishable; fig enduring.

imperfección nf 1 imperfection. 2 (defecto) defect, fault.

imperfecto,-a adj 1 imperfect, fallible. 2 (defectuoso) defective, faulty. 3 Ling imperfect.

imperial adj imperial.

imperialismo nm imperialism.

impericia nf incompetence.

imperio nm empire; **el i. de la ley**, the rule of law.

imperioso,-a adj 1 (autoritario) imperious. 2 (ineludible) urgent, imperative; **una necesidad imperiosa**, a pressing need.

impermeable I adj impermeable, impervious; (ropa) waterproof. **II** nm raincoat, mac.

impersonal adj impersonal.

impertérrito,-a adj undaunted, fearless.

impertinencia nf impertinence.

impertinente I adj (insolente) impertinent; (inoportuno) irrelevant. **II** nmpl impertinentes, lorgnette sing.

imperturbable adj imperturbable, unruffled.

ímpetu nm 1 (impulso) impetus, momentum. 2 (violencia) violence. 3 (energía) energy.

impetuosidad nf 1 (violencia) violence. 2 (fogosidad) impetuosity, impulsiveness.

impetuoso,-a adj 1 (violento) violent. 2 (fogoso) impetuous, impulsive.

impío,-a adj ungodly, irreligious.

implacable adj relentless, implacable.

implantar vtr (costumbres) to implant, instil; (reformas) to introduce; Med to implant.

implicación nf (participación) involvement; (significado) implication.

implicar [1] vtr 1 (involucrar) to involve, implicate (en, in). 2 (conllevar) to imply.

implícito,-a adj implicit, implied.

implorar vtr to implore, beg.

impoluto,-a adj pure, spotless.

imponente adj 1 (impresionante) imposing, impressive. 2 (sobrecogedor) stunning. 2 fam (atractivo) terrific, tremendous, smashing.

imponer [19] (pp **impuesto**) I vtr 1 to impose. 2 (impresionar) to be impressive; (respeto) to inspire respect. 3 Fin to deposit. **II imponerse** vr 1 (infundir respeto) to command respect. 2 (prevalecer) to prevail. 3 (ser necesario) to be necessary.

imponible adj Fin taxable.

impopular adj unpopular, disliked.

importación nf (mercancía) import; (acción) importing; **artículos de i.**, imported goods.

importancia nf importance, significance; **dar i. a**, to attach importance to; **sin i.**, unimportant.

importante adj important, significant; **una suma i.**, a considerable sum.

importar¹ I vi 1 (atañer) **eso no te importa a ti**, that's none of your business. 2 (tener importancia) to be important; **no importa**, it doesn't matter; fam **me importa un bledo** o **un pito**, I couldn't care less. 3 (molestar) **¿te importaría repetirlo?**, would you mind repeating it?; **¿te importa si fumo?**, do you mind if I smoke? **II** vtr (valer) to amount to; **los libros importan dos mil pesetas**, the books come to two thousand pesetas.

importar² vtr to import.

importe nm Com Fin amount, total.

importunar vtr to bother, pester.

imposibilidad nf impossibility.

imposibilitar vtr 1 (impedir) to make impossible, prevent. 2 (incapacitar) to disable, cripple.

imposible adj impossible; **me es i. hacerlo**, I can't (possibly) do it.

imposición nf 1 (disciplina, condiciones) imposing. 2 Fin deposit; (impuesto) taxation.

impostor,-a nm,f (farsante) impostor.

impotencia nf powerlessness, helplessness; Med impotence.

impotente adj powerless, helpless; Med impotent.

impracticable adj 1 (inviable) impracticable, unviable. 2 (camino) impassable.

imprecar [1] vtr to imprecate, curse.

imprecisión nf imprecision, vagueness.

impreciso,-a adj imprecise, vague.

impregnar I vtr to impregnate (en, de, with). **II impregnarse** vr to become impregnated.

imprenta nf 1 (taller) printer's, print works. 2 (aparato) printing press. 3 **libertad de i.**, freedom of the press.

imprescindible adj essential, indispensable.

impresentable adj unpresentable.

impresión nf 1 fig (efecto) impression; **causar i.**, to make an impression. 2 fig (opinión) impression; **cambiar impresiones**, to exchange impressions. 3 Impr (acto) printing; (edición) edition. 4 (huella) impression, imprint.

impresionable adj impressionable.

impresionante adj impressive, striking; fam **un error i.**, (tremendo) a terrible mistake.

impresionar vtr 1 (causar admiración) to impress; (sorprender) to stun, shock. 2 Fot to expose.

impresionismo *nm Arte* impressionism.

impresionista *adj & nmf* impressionist.

impreso,-a I *adj* printed. II *nm* 1 (*papel, folleto*) printed matter. 2 (*formulario*) form; **i. de solicitud**, application form. 3 **impresos**, (*de correos*) printed matter *sing*.

impresora *nf Inform* printer; **i. láser**, laser printer.

imprevisible *adj* unforeseeable, unpredictable.

imprevisión *nf* lack of foresight.

imprevisto,-a I *adj* unforeseen, unexpected. II *nm* (*incidente*) unforeseen event.

imprimir *vtr* (*pp impreso*) 1 *Impr Inform* to print. 2 (*marcar*) to stamp.

improbable *adj* improbable, unlikely.

ímprobo,-a *adj* (*inmoral*) dishonest, corrupt.

improcedente *adj* 1 inappropriate, unsuitable. 2 *Jur* inadmissible.

improductivo,-a *adj* unproductive.

improperio *nm* insult, offensive remark.

impropio,-a *adj* (*inadecuado*) inappropriate, unsuitable; **i. de**, uncharacteristic of.

improvisación *nf* improvisation; *Mús* extemporization.

improvisado,-a *adj* (*espontáneo*) improvised, impromptu, ad lib; (*provisional*) makeshift; **discurso i.**, impromptu speech.

improvisar *vtr* to improvise; *Mús* to extemporize.

improviso *adj* **de i.**, unexpectedly, suddenly; *fam* **coger** o **pillar a algn de i.**, to catch sb unawares.

imprudencia *nf* imprudence, rashness; (*indiscreción*) indiscretion.

imprudente *adj* imprudent, unwise; (*indiscreto*) indiscreet.

impudicia *nf* (*falta de pudor*) immodesty; (*desvergüenza*) shamelessness.

impudor *nm* immodesty; (*desvergüenza*) shamelessness.

impuesto,-a I *nm Fin* tax; **i. sobre la renta**, income tax; **libre de impuestos**, tax-free; **i. sobre el valor añadido**, value added tax. II *adj* imposed.

impugnar *vtr* (*teoría*) to refute, disprove; (*decisión*) to challenge, contest.

impulsar *vtr* to impel, drive.

impulsivo,-a *adj* impulsive.

impulso *nm* impulse, thrust; *Dep* **tomar i.**, to take a run up.

impune *adj* unpunished.

◆**impunemente** *adv* with impunity.

impunidad *nf* impunity.

impureza *nf* impurity.

impuro,-a *adj* impure.

impuse *pt indef* → **imponer**.

imputar *vtr* to impute, attribute.

inabarcable *adj* unfathomable.

inabordable *adj* unapproachable, inaccessible.

inacabable *adj* interminable, endless.

inaccesible *adj* inaccessible.

inaceptable *adj* unacceptable.

inactividad *nf* inactivity; *Fin* lull, stagnation.

inactivo,-a *adj* inactive.

inadaptación *nf* maladjustment.

inadaptado,-a I *adj* maladjusted. II *nm,f* misfit.

inadecuado,-a *adj* unsuitable, inappropriate.

inadmisible *adj* inadmissible.

inadvertido,-a *adj* (*desapercibido*) unnoticed, unseen; **pasar i.**, to escape notice, pass unnoticed.

inagotable *adj* 1 (*recursos etc*) inexhaustible. 2 (*persona*) tireless, indefatigable.

inaguantable *adj* unbearable, intolerable.

inalámbrico,-a I *adj* cordless. II *nm* cordless telephone.

inalcanzable *adj* unattainable, unachievable.

inalterable *adj* 1 unalterable. 2 (*persona*) impassive, imperturbable.

inamovible *adj* immovable, fixed.

inanición *nf* starvation; *Med* inanition.

inanimado,-a *adj* inanimate.

inapreciable *adj* 1 (*valioso*) invaluable, inestimable. 2 (*insignificante*) insignificant, trivial.

inasequible *adj* 1 (*producto*) unaffordable. 2 (*meta*) unattainable, unachievable. 3 (*persona*) unapproachable, inaccessible. 4 (*cuestión*) incomprehensible.

inaudito,-a *adj* 1 (*sin precedente*) unprecedented. 2 *fig* (*escandaloso*) outrageous.

inauguración *nf* inauguration, opening.

inaugural *adj* inaugural, opening; **ceremonia i.**, inaugural ceremony.

inaugurar *vtr* to inaugurate, open.

inca *adj & nmf* Inca.

incalculable *adj* incalculable, indeterminate.

incandescente *adj* white hot, incandescent.

incansable *adj* tireless, indefatigable.

incapacidad *nf* 1 incapacity, inability; **i. física**, physical disability. 2 (*incompetencia*) incompetence, inefficiency.

incapacitado,-a *adj* (*imposibilitado*) incapacitated, disabled; (*desautorizado*) incapacitated.

incapacitar *vtr* 1 to incapacitate, disable. 2 (*inhabilitar*) to disqualify, make unfit (**para**, for).

incapaz *adj* 1 unable (**de**, to), incapable (**de**, of); **soy i. de continuar**, I can't go on. 2 *Jur* unfit.

incautación *nf Jur* seizure, confiscation.

incautarse *vr Jur* **i. de**, to seize, confiscate.

incauto,-a *adj* 1 (*imprudente*) incautious, unwary. 2 (*crédulo*) gullible.

incendiar [12] I *vtr* to set fire to, set alight. II **incendiarse** *vr* to catch fire.

incendiario,-a I *adj* incendiary; *fig (discurso etc)* inflammatory. II *nm,f (persona)* arsonist, fire-raiser.

incendio *nm* fire; **i. forestal,** forest fire.

incentivar *vtr* to give an incentive to.

incentivo *nm* incentive.

incertidumbre *nf* uncertainty, doubt.

incesante *adj* incessant, never-ending.

incesto *nm* incest.

incestuoso,-a *adj* incestuous.

incidencia *nf* 1 *(repercusión)* impact, effect; **la huelga tuvo escasa i.,** the strike had little effect. 2 *(hecho)* incident. 3 *Fís* incidence.

incidente *nm* incident.

incidir *vi* 1 *(incurrir)* to fall (**en,** into). 2 **i. en,** *(afectar)* to affect, influence.

incienso *nm* incense.

incierto,-a *adj (inseguro)* uncertain.

incineración *nf (de basuras)* incineration; *(de cadáveres)* cremation.

incinerar *vtr (basura)* to incinerate; *(cadáveres)* to cremate.

incipiente *adj* incipient, budding.

incisión *nf* incision, cut.

incisivo,-a I *adj (mordaz)* incisive, cutting; *(cortante)* sharp. II *nm* Anat incisor.

inciso *nm (paréntesis)* digression; **a modo de i.,** in passing, incidentally.

incitación *nf* incitement.

incitante *adj* 1 *(instigador)* inciting. 2 *(provocativo)* provocative.

incitar *vtr* to incite, urge.

incivil *adj* uncivil, rude.

inclemencia *nf* inclemency, harshness.

inclemente *adj* inclement, harsh.

inclinación *nf* 1 *(de terreno)* slope, incline; *(del cuerpo)* stoop. 2 *(reverencia)* bow. 3 *fig (tendencia)* tendency, inclination, penchant.

inclinado,-a *adj* inclined, slanting; *fig* **me siento i. a creerle,** I feel inclined to believe him.

inclinar I *vtr* 1 to incline, bend; *(cabeza)* to nod. 2 *fig (persuadir)* to persuade, induce. II **inclinarse** *vr* 1 to lean, slope, incline. 2 *(al saludar)* to bow; **i. ante,** to bow down to. 3 *fig (optar)* **i. a,** to be *o* feel inclined to; **me inclino por éste,** I'd rather have this one, I prefer this one.

incluido,-a *adj* 1 *(después del sustantivo)* included; *(antes del sustantivo)* including; **servicio no i.,** service not included; **I.V.A.,** including VAT; **todos pagan, incluidos los niños,** everyone has to pay, including children. 2 *(adjunto)* enclosed.

incluir [37] *vtr* 1 to include. 2 *(contener)* to contain, comprise. 3 *(adjuntar)* to enclose.

inclusión *nf* inclusion.

inclusive *adv* 1 *(incluido)* inclusive; de

martes a viernes i., from Tuesday to Friday inclusive; **hasta la lección ocho i.,** up to and including lesson eight. 2 *(incluso)* even.

incluso *adv* even; **i. mi madre,** even my mother.

incoar *vtr defect Jur* to initiate.

incógnita *nf* 1 *Mat* unknown quantity, unknown. 2 *(misterio)* mystery.

incógnito *nm* de i., incognito.

incoherencia *nf* incoherence.

incoherente *adj* incoherent.

incoloro,-a *adj* colourless.

incólume *adj fml* unharmed; **salir i.,** to escape unharmed.

incombustible *adj* incombustible, fireproof.

incomodar I *vtr* 1 *(causar molestia)* to inconvenience, put out. 2 *(fastidiar)* to bother, annoy. II **incomodarse** *vr* 1 *(tomarse molestias)* to put oneself out, go out of one's way. 2 *(disgustarse)* to get annoyed *o* angry.

incomodidad *nf (falta de comodidad)* discomfort; *(molestia)* inconvenience.

incómodo,-a *adj* uncomfortable; **sentirse i.,** to feel uncomfortable *o* awkward.

incompatibilidad *nf* incompatibility; *Jur* **i. de caracteres,** mutual incompatibility.

incompatible *adj* incompatible.

incompetencia *nf* incompetence.

incompetente *adj & nmf* incompetent.

incompleto,-a *adj* incomplete; *(inacabado)* unfinished.

incomprensible *adj* incomprehensible.

incomprensión *nf* lack of understanding, failure to understand; *(indiferencia)* lack of sympathy.

incomunicado,-a *adj (aislado)* isolated; **el pueblo se quedó i.,** the town was cut off. 2 *(en la cárcel)* in solitary confinement.

incomunicar [1] *vtr* 1 *(ciudad)* to isolate, cut off. 2 *(recluso)* to place in solitary confinement.

inconcebible *adj* inconceivable, unthinkable.

inconcluso,-a *adj* unfinished.

incondicional I *adj* unconditional; *(apoyo)* wholehearted; *(amigo)* faithful; *(partidario)* staunch. II *nm* diehard.

inconexo,-a *adj (incoherente)* incoherent, confused.

inconformismo *nm* nonconformism.

inconformista *adj & nmf* nonconformist.

inconfundible *adj* unmistakable, obvious.

incongruencia *nf* incongruity.

incongruente *adj* incongruous.

inconmensurable *adj* immeasurable, vast.

inconsciencia *nf Med* unconsciousness; *fig (irreflexión)* thoughtlessness; *(irresponsabilidad)* irresponsibility.

inconsciente I *adj* 1 *(con estar)* *(desmaya-*

do) unconscious. **2** (*con ser*) (*despreocupado*) unaware (**de**, of); *fig* (*irreflexivo*) thoughtless, irresponsible.
inconsecuente *adj* inconsistent.
inconsistente *adj* flimsy; (*argumento*) weak.
inconstancia *nf* inconstancy, fickleness.
inconstante *adj* inconstant, fickle.
incontable *adj* countless, innumerable.
incontenible *adj* uncontrollable, irrepressible.
incontestable *adj* indisputable, unquestionable.
incontinencia *nf* incontinence.
incontrolable *adj* uncontrollable.
incontrolado,-a I *adj* uncontrolled. **II** *nmf* troublemaker.
inconveniencia *nf* **1** inconvenience. **2** (*impiedad*) unsuitability.
inconveniente I *adj* **1** inconvenient. **2** (*inapropiado*) unsuitable. **II** *nm* **1** (*objeción*) objection; **poner inconvenientes**, to raise objections. **2** (*desventaja*) disadvantage, drawback; (*problema*) difficulty; **¿tienes i. en acompañarme?**, would you mind coming with me?
incordiar [12] *vtr fam* to bother, pester.
incordio *nm fam* nuisance, pain.
incorporación *nf* incorporation.
incorporar I *vtr* **1** to incorporate (**en**, into). **2** (*levantar*) to help to sit up. **II incorporarse** *vr* **1** i. **a**, (*sociedad*) to join; (*trabajo*) to start; **Mil** i. **a filas**, to join up. **2** (*en la cama*) to sit up.
incorrección *nf* **1** (*falta*) incorrectness, inaccuracy; (*gramatical*) mistake. **2** (*descortesía*) discourtesy, impropriety.
incorrecto,-a *adj* **1** (*equivocado*) incorrect, inaccurate. **2** (*grosero*) impolite, discourteous.
incorregible *adj* incorrigible.
incrédulo,-a I *adj* **1** incredulous, disbelieving. **2** *Rel* unbelieving. **II** *nm,f* **1** disbeliever. **2** *Rel* unbeliever.
increíble *adj* incredible, unbelievable.
incrementar I *vtr* to increase. **II incrementarse** *vr* to increase.
incremento *nm* (*aumento*) increase; (*crecimiento*) growth; **i. de la temperatura**, rise in temperature.
increpar *vtr fml* to rebuke, reprimand.
incruento,-a *adj* bloodless.
incrustar *vtr* **1** (*insertar*) to encrust o incrust. **2** (*embutir*) to inlay; **incrustado con perlas**, inlaid with pearls.
incubadora *nf* incubator.
incubar *vtr* to incubate.
incuestionable *adj* unquestionable, indisputable.
inculcar [1] *vtr* (*principios*, *ideas*) to instil (**en**, into).
inculpado,-a *nm,f* the accused.
inculpar *vtr* to accuse (**de**, of), blame (**de**, for); *Jur* to charge (**de**, with).

inculto,-a I *adj* (*ignorante*) uneducated, uncouth. **II** *nm,f* ignoramus.
incultura *nf* (*ignorancia*) ignorance, lack of culture.
incumbencia *nf* **no es de mi i.**, it doesn't come within my province, it isn't my concern.
incumbir *vi* be incumbent (**a**, upon); **esto no te incumbe**, this is none of your business.
incumplimiento *nm* (*de un deber*) nonfulfilment; (*de una orden*) failure to execute; **i. de contrato**, breach of contract.
incumplir *vtr* not to fulfil; (*deber*) fail to fulfil; (*promesa*, *contrato*) to break; (*orden*) to fail to carry out.
incurrir *vi* (*cometer*) to fall (**en**, into); **i. en delito**, to commit a crime; **i. en** (**un**) **error**, to fall into error.
incursión *nf* raid, incursion.
indagar [7] *vtr* to investigate, inquire into.
indebido,-a *adj* **1** (*desconsiderado*) improper, undue. **2** (*ilegal*) unlawful, illegal.
indecencia *nf* indecency, obscenity.
indecente *adj* **1** (*impúdico*) indecent. **2** (*impresentable*) dreadful.
indecible *adj* unspeakable; (*inefable*) indescribable; **sufrir lo i.**, to suffer agonies.
indecisión *nf* indecision, hesitation.
indeciso,-a *adj* **1** (*vacilante*) hesitant, irresolute. **2** (*resultados etc*) inconclusive.
indefenso,-a *adj* defenceless, helpless.
indefinido,-a *adj* **1** (*indeterminado*) indefinite; (*impreciso*) undefined, vague. **2** *Ling* indefinite. ◆**indefinidamente** *adv* indefinitely.
indeleble *adj* indelible.
indemne *adj* (*persona*) unharmed, unhurt; (*cosa*) undamaged.
indemnización *nf* **1** (*acto*) indemnification. **2** *Fin* (*compensación*) indemnity, compensation; **i. por despido**, redundancy payment.
indemnizar [4] *vtr* to indemnify, compensate (**de**, **por**, for).
independencia *nf* independence.
independiente *adj* (*libre*) independent; (*individualista*) self-reliant. ◆**independientemente** *adv* **1** independently (**de**, of). **2** (*aparte de*) regardless, irrespective (**de**, of).
independizar [4] **I** *vtr* to make independent, grant independence to. **II independizarse** *vr* to become independent.
indescifrable *adj* indecipherable.
indescriptible *adj* indescribable.
indeseable *adj & nmf* undesirable.
indeterminación *nf* indecision, irresolution.
indeterminado,-a *adj* **1** indefinite; (*impreciso*) vague. **2** (*persona*) irresolute. **3** *Ling* indefinite.
India *nf* (**la**) I., India.

Indias *nfpl* (las) I., the Indies; **las I. Orientales/Occidentales,** the East/West Indies.

indicación *nf* 1 (*señal*) indication, sign. 2 (*instrucción*) instruction, direction; **por i. de algn.,** at sb's suggestion.

indicado,-a *adj* right, suitable; **a la hora indicada,** at the specified time; **en el momento menos i.,** at the worst possible moment.

indicador,-a *nm* 1 indicator. 2 *Téc* gauge, dial, meter; *Aut* **i. del nivel de aceite,** (oil) dipstick; *Aut* **i. de velocidad,** speedometer.

indicar [1] *vtr* (*señalar*) to indicate, show, point out; **¿me podría i. el camino?,** could you show me the way?

indicativo,-a *adj* 1 indicative (**de,** of). 2 *Ling* (*modo*) i., indicative (mode).

índice *nm* 1 (*de libro*) index, table of contents. 2 (*relación*) rate. **í. de natalidad/mortalidad,** birth/death rate; *Fin* **í. de precios,** price index. 3 *Anat* (*dedo*) í., index finger, forefinger.

indicio *nm* 1 (*señal*) indication, sign, token (**de,** of). 2 *Jur* **indicios,** (*prueba*) evidence *sing*.

índico,-a *adj* Indian; **Océano I.,** Indian Ocean.

indiferencia *nf* indifference, apathy.

indiferente *adj* 1 (*no importante*) unimportant; **me es i.,** it makes no difference to me. 2 (*apático*) indifferent.

indígena I *adj* indigenous, native (**de,** to). II *nmf* native (**de,** of).

indigencia *nf fml* poverty, indigence.

indigente *fml adj* needy, poverty-stricken.

indigestarse *vr* 1 **se le indigestó la comida,** the meal gave her indigestion. 2 (*sufrir indigestión*) to get indigestion.

indigestión *nf* indigestion.

indigesto,-a *adj* (*comida*) indigestible, difficult to digest; **me siento i.,** I've got indigestion.

indignación *nf* indignation.

indignado,-a *adj* indignant (**por,** at, about).

indignante *adj* outrageous, infuriating.

indignar I *vtr* to infuriate, make angry. II **indignarse** *vr* to be o feel indignant (**por,** at, about).

indigno,-a *adj* 1 unworthy (**de,** of). 2 (*despreciable*) wretched, shameful.

indio,-a *adj* & *nm,f* Indian; **en fila india,** in single file; *fam* **hacer el i.,** to act the fool.

indirecta *nf fam* (*insinuación*) hint, insinuation; **tirar** o **lanzar una i.,** to drop a hint; **coger la i.,** to get the message.

indirecto,-a *adj* indirect; *Ling* **estilo i.,** indirect o reported speech.

indisciplinado,-a *adj* undisciplined, unruly.

indiscreción *nf* indiscretion; (*comentario*) tactless remark.

indiscreto,-a *adj* indiscreet, tactless.

indiscutible *adj* indisputable, unquestionable.

indispensable *adj* indispensable, essential.

indisponer [19] (*pp* **indispuesto**) I *vtr* to upset, make unwell. II **indisponerse** *vr* 1 to fall ill, become unwell. 2 *fig* **i. con algn,** to fall out with sb.

indispuesto,-a *adj* indisposed, unwell.

indispuse *pt indef* → **indisponer.**

indistinto,-a *adj* (*indiferente*) immaterial, inconsequential; **◆indistintamente** *adv* **pueden escribir en inglés o en español i.,** you can write in English or Spanish, it doesn't matter which.

individual I *adj* individual; **habitación i.,** single room. II *nmpl Dep* **individuales,** singles.

individualismo *nm* individualism.

individualista I *adj* individualistic. II *nmf* individualist.

individuo *nm* 1 individual. 2 (*tío*) bloke, guy.

índole *nf* 1 (*carácter*) character, nature. 2 (*clase, tipo*) kind, sort.

indolencia *nf* indolence, laziness.

indolente I *adj* indolent, lazy. II *nmf* idler.

indomable *adj* 1 (*animal*) untameable. 2 (*pueblo*) ungovernable, unruly; (*niño*) uncontrollable; (*pasión*) indomitable.

indómito,-a *adj* 1 (*no domado*) untamed; (*indomable*) untameable. 2 (*pueblo*) unruly; (*persona*) uncontrollable.

inducir [10] *vtr* 1 (*incitar, mover*) to lead, induce; **i. a error,** to lead into error, mislead. 2 *Elec* (*corriente*) to induce.

inductivo,-a *adj* inductive.

indudable *adj* indubitable, unquestionable; **es i. que,** there is no doubt that.

induje *pt indef* → **inducir.**

indulgencia *nf* indulgence, leniency.

indulgente *adj* indulgent (**con,** towards), lenient (**con,** with).

indultar *vtr Jur* to pardon.

indulto *nm Jur* pardon, amnesty.

indumentaria *nf* clothing, clothes *pl*.

industria *nf* industry.

industrial I *adj* industrial. II *nmf* industrialist.

industrialización *nf* industrialization.

industrializar [4] *vtr* to industrialize.

induzco *indic pres* → **inducir.**

INE *nm abr de* **Instituto Nacional de Estadística.**

inédito,-a *adj* 1 (*libro, texto*) unpublished. 2 (*nuevo*) completely new; (*desconocido*) unknown.

inefable *adj* ineffable, indescribable.

ineficacia *nf* (*ineptitud*) inefficiency; (*inutilidad*) ineffectiveness.

ineficaz adj (inepto) inefficient; (inefectivo) ineffective.

ineludible adj inescapable, unavoidable.

INEM nm abr de **Instituto Nacional de Empleo**.

ineptitud nf ineptitude, incompetence.

inepto,-a I adj inept, incompetent. II nm,f incompetent person.

inequívoco,-a adj unmistakable, unequivocal.

inercia nf 1 Fís inertia. 2 fig (pasividad) inertia, passivity; **hacer algo por i.**, to do sth out of habit.

inerte adj (inanimado) inert; (inmóvil) motionless.

inesperado,-a adj (fortuito) unexpected, unforeseen; (imprevisto) sudden.

inestabilidad nf instability.

inestable adj unstable, unsteady.

inestimable adj inestimable, invaluable.

inevitable adj inevitable, unavoidable.

inexistente adj non-existent.

inexorable adj inexorable.

inexperiencia nf lack of experience.

inexperto,-a adj (inexperto) inexpert; (sin experiencia) inexperienced.

inexplicable adj inexplicable.

inexpugnable adj Mil impregnable.

infalible adj infallible.

infamar vtr to defame, slander.

infame adj (vil) infamous, vile; (despreciable) dreadful, awful.

infamia nf disgrace, infamy.

infancia nf childhood, infancy.

infanta nf infanta, princess.

infante nm 1 infante, prince. 2 Mil infantryman.

infantería nf Mil infantry; **la i. de marina**, the marines.

infantil adj 1 literatura i., (para niños) children's literature. 2 (animado) childlike; pey childish, infantile.

infarto nm Med infarction, infarct; **i. (de miocardio)**, heart attack, coronary thrombosis; fam **de i.**, thrilling, stunning.

infatigable adj indefatigable, tireless.

infección nf infection.

infeccioso,-a adj infectious.

infectar I vtr to infect. II **infectarse** vr to become infected (de, with).

infeliz I adj unhappy; (desdichado) unfortunate. II nmf fam simpleton; **es un pobre i.**, he is a poor devil.

inferior I adj 1 (más bajo) lower. 2 (calidad) inferior; **de calidad i.**, of inferior quality. 3 (cantidad) lower, less; **i. a la media**, below average. II nmf (persona) subordinate, inferior.

inferioridad nf inferiority; **estar en i. de condiciones**, to be at a disadvantage; **complejo de i.**, inferiority complex.

inferir [5] vtr lit (deducir) to infer, deduce (de, from).

infernal adj infernal, hellish; fig **había un ruido i.**, there was a hell of a noise.

infestar vtr 1 infestado de, (parásitos) infested with; (plantas) overgrown with. 2 fig (llenar) to overrun, invade; **infestado de turistas**, swarming with tourists. 3 (infectar) to infect.

infidelidad nf infidelity, unfaithfulness.

infiel I adj (desleal) unfaithful. II nmf Rel infidel.

infierno nm 1 Rel hell. 2 fig (tormento) hell; **su vida es un i.**, his life is sheer hell. 3 (horno) inferno; **en verano esto es un i.**, in summer it's like an inferno here; fam **¡vete al i.!**, go to hell!, get lost!

infiltración nf (de agua) infiltration; (de noticia) leak.

infiltrado,-a nm,f infiltrator.

infiltrar I vtr to infiltrate; (noticia) to leak. II **infiltrarse** vr to infiltrate (en, into).

ínfimo,-a adj fml (mínimo) extremely low; **detalle í.**, smallest detail; **ínfima calidad**, very poor quality.

infinidad nf 1 infinity; 2 (sinfín) great number; **en i. de ocasiones**, on countless occasions.

infinitivo,-a adj & nm Ling infinitive.

infinito,-a I adj infinite, endless. II nm infinity. ◆**infinito** adv fam (muchísimo) infinitely, immensely.

inflación nf Econ inflation.

inflacionario,-a, inflacionista adj Econ inflationary.

inflamable adj flammable.

inflamación nf Med inflammation.

inflamar I vtr 1 Med to inflame. 2 (encender) to set on fire, ignite. II **inflamarse** vr 1 Med to become inflamed. 2 (incendiarse) to catch fire.

inflar I vtr 1 (hinchar) to inflate, blow up; Náut (vela) to swell. 2 fig (exagerar) to exaggerate. II **inflarse** vr 1 to inflate; Náut (vela) to swell. 2 fam **i. de**, to overdo; **se inflaron de macarrones**, they stuffed themselves with macaroni.

inflexible adj inflexible.

infligir [6] vtr to inflict.

influencia nf influence; **ejercer o tener i. sobre algn**, to have an influence on o upon sb; **tener influencias**, to be influential; **tráfico de influencias**, old boy network.

influenciar [12] vtr to influence.

influir [37] I vtr to influence. II vi 1 to have influence. 2 **i. en o sobre**, to influence, have an influence on.

influjo nm influence.

influyente adj influential.

información nf 1 information; **oficina de i.**, information bureau. 2 **una i.**, (noticia) a piece of news, news sing. 3 Tel directory enquiries pl. 4 (referencias) references pl.

informado,-a *adj* informed; **de fuentes bien informadas**, from well-informed sources.

informal *adj* 1 (*reunión, cena*) informal. 2 (*comportamiento*) casual. 3 (*persona*) unreliable, untrustworthy.

informalidad *nf* (*incumplimiento*) unreliability; (*desenfado*) informality.

informar I *vtr* to inform (de, of); (*dar informes*) to report. II **informarse** *vr* (*procurarse noticias*) to find out (de, about); (*enterarse*) to enquire (de, about).

informática *nf* information technology, IT; **ley de i.**, data protection act.

informático,-a I *adj* computer, computing. II *nm,f* (computer) technician.

informativo,-a I *adj* 1 *Rad TV* news; **boletín i.**, news (broadcast). 2 (*explicativo*) informative, explanatory. II *nm Rad TV* news bulletin.

informe *nm* 1 report. 2 *informes*, references; **pedir i. sobre algn**, to make enquiries about sb.

infracción *nf* (*de ley*) infringement, breach (de, of).

infractor,-a *nm,f* offender.

infraestructura *nf* infrastructure.

in fraganti *loc adv* in the act; **coger o pillar a algn in f.**, to catch sb red-handed.

infrahumano-o *adj* subhuman.

infranqueable *adj* impassable; *fig* insurmountable.

infrarrojo-a *adj* infra-red.

infrautilizar *vtr* to under-utilise.

infringir [6] *vtr* to infringe, contravene; **i. una ley**, to break a law.

infructuoso,-a *adj* fruitless, unsuccessful.

infundado,-a *adj* unfounded, groundless.

infundir *vtr* to infuse; *fig* to instil; **i. dudas**, to give rise to doubt; **i. respeto**, to command respect.

infusión *nf* infusion.

infuso,-a *adj fam irón* **ciencia infusa**, sheer genius.

ingeniar [12] I *vtr* to invent, devise. II **ingeniarse** *vr* **ingeniárselas para hacer algo**, to manage to do sth.

ingeniería *nf* engineering.

ingeniero,-a *nm,f* engineer; **i. agrónomo**, agricultural engineer; **i. de caminos**, civil engineer; **i. de minas/montes**, mining/forestry engineer; **i. de telecomunicaciones**, telecommunications engineer; **i. técnico**, technician.

ingenio *nm* 1 (*talento*) talent; (*inventiva*) inventiveness, creativeness; (*agudeza*) wit. 2 (*aparato*) device.

ingenioso,-a *adj* ingenious, clever; (*vivaz*) witty.

ingente *adj* huge, enormous.

ingenuidad *nf* ingenuousness, naïveté.

ingenuo,-a I *adj* ingenuous, naïve. II *nm,f* naïve person.

ingerir [5] *vtr* (*comida*) to ingest, consume; (*líquidos, alcohol*) to drink, consume.

Inglaterra *n* England.

ingle *nf Anat* groin.

inglés,-esa I *adj* English. II *nm,f* (*hombre*) Englishman; (*mujer*) Englishwoman; **los ingleses**, the English. III *nm* (*idioma*) English.

ingratitud *nf* ingratitude, ungratefulness.

ingrato,-a I *adj* 1 (*persona*) ungrateful. 2 (*noticia*) unpleasant. 3 (*trabajo*) thankless, unrewarding. 4 (*tierra*) unproductive. II *nm,f* ungrateful person.

ingrediente *nm* ingredient.

ingresar I *vtr* 1 *Fin* to deposit, pay in. 2 *Med* to admit; **la ingresaron en el hospital**, she was admitted to hospital. II *vi* 1 to enter; **i. en el ejército**, to enlist in the army, join the army; **i. en un club**, to join a club. 2 **i. cadáver**, to be dead on arrival.

ingreso *nm* 1 *Fin* deposit; **hacer un i. en una cuenta**, to pay money into an account. 2 (*entrada*) entry (en, into); (*admisión*) admission (en, to). 3 *ingresos*, (*sueldo, renta*) income *sing*; (*beneficios*) revenue *sing*.

inhábil *adj* 1 (*incapaz*) unfit; **i. para el trabajo**, unfit for work. 2 **día i.**, non-working day.

inhabilitación *nf* 1 *fml* (*incapacidad*) disablement. 2 *Jur* disqualification.

inhabilitar *vtr* 1 *fml* (*incapacitar*) to disable; **inhabilitado para el trabajo**, unfit for work. 2 *Jur* to disqualify.

inhabitable *adj* uninhabitable.

inhalación *nf* inhalation.

inhalador *nm Med* inhaler.

inhalar *vtr* to inhale.

inherente *adj* inherent (a, in).

inhibición *nf* inhibition.

inhibir I *vtr* to inhibit. II **inhibirse** *vr* 1 (*cohibirse*) to be o feel inhibited. 2 (*abstenerse*) to refrain (de, from).

inhóspito,-a *adj* inhospitable.

inhumación *nf* burial.

inhumano,-a *adj* inhumane; (*cruel*) inhuman.

inhumar *vtr* to bury.

INI *nm abr de* **Instituto Nacional de Industria**.

inicial *adj & nf* initial; **punto i.**, starting point.

iniciar [12] I *vtr* 1 (*empezar*) to begin, start; (*discusión*) to initiate; (*una cosa nueva*) to pioneer. 2 (*introducir*) to initiate. II **iniciarse** *vr* 1 **i. en algo**, (*aprender*) to start to study sth. 2 (*empezar*) to begin, start."

iniciativa *nf* initiative; **i. privada**, private enterprise; **por i. propia**, on one's own initiative.

inicio *nm* beginning, start; **a inicios de**, at the beginning of.

inimitable *adj* inimitable.
ininterrumpido,-a *adj* uninterrupted, continuous.
iniquidad *nf* iniquity.
injerencia *nf* interference, meddling (**en**, in).
injerirse *vr* to interfere, meddle (**en**, in).
injertar *vtr Agr Med* to graft.
injerto *nm* graft.
injuria *nf* (*insulto*) insult, affront; (*agravio*) outrage.
injuriar [12] *vtr* (*insultar*) to insult; (*ultrajar*) to outrage.
injusticia *nf* injustice, unfairness.
injustificado,-a *adj* unjustified.
injusto,-a *adj* unjust, unfair.
inmaculado,-a *adj* immaculate.
inmadurez *nf* immaturity.
inmaduro,-a *adj* immature.
inmediaciones *nfpl* neighbourhood *sing.*
inmediato,-a *adj* 1 (*en el tiempo*) immediate; **de i.**, at once. 2 (*en el espacio*) next (**a**, to), adjoining. ◆**inmediatamente** *adv* immediately, at once.
inmejorable *adj* (*trabajo*) excellent; (*precio*) unbeatable.
inmemorial *adj* immemorial; **desde tiempos inmemoriales**, since time immemorial.
inmensidad *nf* immensity, enormity.
inmenso,-a *adj* immense, vast.
inmerecido,-a *adj* undeserved, unmerited.
inmersión *nf* immersion; (*de submarino*) dive.
inmerso,-a *adj* immersed (**en**, in).
inmigración *nf* immigration.
inmigrante *adj & nm,f* immigrant.
inmigrar *vi* to immigrate.
inminente *adj* imminent, impending.
inmiscuirse [37] *vr* to interfere, meddle (**en**, in).
inmobiliaria *nf* estate agency, *US* real estate company.
inmobiliario,-a *adj* property, real-estate; **agente i.**, estate agent, *US* realtor.
inmolar *vtr fml* to immolate, sacrifice.
inmoral *adj* immoral.
inmoralidad *nf* immorality.
inmortal *adj & nmf* immortal.
inmortalidad *nf* immortality.
inmortalizar [4] *vtr* to immortalize.
inmóvil *adj* motionless, immobile.
inmovilista *adj* ultra-conservative.
inmovilizar [4] *vtr* I (*persona, cosa*) to immobilize. 2 *Fin* (*capital*) to immobilize, tie up.
inmueble I *adj* **bienes inmuebles**, real estate. II *nm* building.
inmundicia *nf* 1 (*suciedad*) dirt, filth; *fig* dirtiness. 2 (*basura*) rubbish, refuse.
inmundo,-a *adj* dirty, filthy; *fig* nasty.
inmune *adj* immune (**a**, to), exempt (**de**, from).

inmunidad *nf* immunity (**contra**, against); **i. diplomática/parlamentaria**, diplomatic/parliamentary immunity.
inmunizar [4] *vtr* to immunize (**contra**, against).
inmutarse *vr* to change countenance; **ni se inmutó**, he didn't turn a hair.
innato,-a *adj* innate, inborn.
innecesario,-a *adj* unnecessary.
innegable *adj* undeniable.
innovación *nf* innovation.
innovar *vtr & vi* to innovate.
innumerable *adj* innumerable, countless.
inocencia *nf* 1 innocence. 2 (*ingenuidad*) naïveté.
inocentada *nf fam* ≈ April Fool's joke; **hacer una i. a algn**, to play an April Fool's joke on sb.
inocente I *adj* innocent. II *nmf* innocent; **día de los Inocentes**, Holy Innocents' Day, 28th December, ≈ April Fools' Day.
inocuo,-a *adj* innocuous.
inodoro,-a I *adj* odourless. II *nm* toilet, lavatory.
inofensivo,-a *adj* harmless.
inolvidable *adj* unforgettable.
inoperante *adj* ineffective.
inopia *nf fig* **estar en la i.**, to be in the clouds, be miles away.
inopinado,-a *adj* unexpected.
inoportuno,-a *adj* inappropriate; **llegó en un momento muy i.**, he turned up at a very awkward moment.
inorgánico,-a *adj* inorganic.
inoxidable *adj* **acero i.**, stainless steel.
INP *nm abr de* **Instituto Nacional de Previsión**.
inquebrantable *adj fig* unshakeable; (*persona*) unyielding.
inquietante *adj* worrying.
inquietar I *vtr* to worry. II **inquietarse** *vr* to worry (**por**, about).
inquieto,-a *adj* 1 (*preocupado*) worried, (**por**, about). 2 (*intranquilo*) restless. 3 (*emprendedor*) eager.
inquietud *nf* 1 (*preocupación*) worry. 2 (*agitación*) restlessness. 3 (*anhelo*) eagerness.
inquilino,-a *nm,f* tenant.
inquirir [31] *vtr* to investigate.
inquisitivo,-a *adj* inquisitive.
inri *nm fam* insult; **para más o mayor i.**, to make matters worse.
insaciable *adj* insatiable.
insalubre *adj* unhealthy.
insano,-a *adj* 1 (*loco*) insane, mad. 2 (*insalubre*) unhealthy.
insatisfecho,-a *adj* dissatisfied.
inscribir (*pp* **inscrito**) I *vtr* 1 (*registrar*) to register; **i. a un niño en el registro civil**, to register a child's birth. 2 (*matricular*) to enrol, *US* enroll. 3 (*grabar*) to inscribe. II **inscribirse** *vr* 1 (*registrarse*) to

register; *(hacerse miembro)* to join. 2 *(matricularse)* to enrol, US enroll.
inscripción *nf* 1 *(matriculación)* enrolment, US enrollment, registration. 2 *(escrito etc)* inscription.
insecticida *nm* insecticide.
insecto *nm* insect.
inseguridad *nf* 1 *(falta de confianza)* insecurity. 2 *(duda)* uncertainty. 3 *(peligro)* lack of safety; **la i. ciudadana**, the breakdown of law and order.
inseguro,-a *adj* 1 *(poco confiado)* insecure. 2 *(dubitativo)* uncertain. 3 *(peligroso)* unsafe.
inseminar *vtr* to inseminate.
insensatez *nf* foolishness.
insensato,-a I *adj* foolish. II *nm,f* fool.
insensibilidad *nf* insensitivity.
insensible *adj* 1 *(indiferente)* insensitive (a, to), unfeeling. 2 *(imperceptible)* imperceptible. 3 *Med* numb.
inseparable *adj* inseparable.
insertar *vtr* to insert.
inservible *adj* useless.
insidia *nf* 1 *(trampa)* malicious ploy. 2 *(malicia)* maliciousness.
insidioso,-a *adj* insidious.
insigne *adj* distinguished.
insignia *nf* 1 *(emblema)* badge. 2 *(bandera)* flag.
insignificancia *nf* 1 *(intrascendencia)* insignificance. 2 *(nadería)* trifle.
insignificante *adj* insignificant.
insinuación *nf* insinuation.
insinuante *adj* insinuating; *(atrevido)* forward.
insinuar |30| I *vtr* to insinuate. II **insinuarse** *vr* i. **a algn**, to make advances to sb.
insípido,-a *adj* insipid; *fig* dull, flat.
insistencia *nf* insistence; **con i.**, insistently.
insistente *adj* insistent.
insistir *vi* to insist (en, on); **insistió en ese punto**, he stressed that point.
insociable *adj* unsociable.
insolación *nf Med* sunstroke; **coger una i.**, to get sunstroke.
insolencia *nf* insolence.
insolente *adj* insolent.
insolidaridad *nf* unsupportive stance.
insólito,-a *adj* *(poco usual)* unusual; *(extraño)* strange, odd.
insoluble *adj* insoluble.
insolvencia *nf Fin* insolvency.
insolvente *adj Fin* insolvent.
insomnio *nm* insomnia; **noche de i.**, sleepless night.
insondable *adj* unfathomable.
insonoro,-a *adj* soundproof.
insonorizar |4| *vtr* to soundproof.
insoportable *adj* unbearable.
insospechado,-a *adj* unsuspected.
insostenible *adj* untenable.

inspección *nf* inspection.
inspeccionar *vtr* to inspect.
inspector,-a *nm,f* inspector; **i. de Hacienda**, tax inspector.
inspiración *nf* 1 inspiration. 2 *(inhalación)* inhalation.
inspirado,-a *adj* inspired.
inspirar I *vtr* 1 to inspire. 2 *(inhalar)* to inhale, breathe in. II **inspirarse** *vr* i. **en**, to be inspired by.
instalación *nf* installation; **instalaciones deportivas**, sports facilities.
instalar I *vtr* 1 to instal, US install. 2 *(puesto, tienda)* to set up. II **instalarse** *vr (persona)* to settle (down).
instancia *nf* 1 *(solicitud)* request; **a instancia(s) de**, at the request of. 2 *(escrito)* application form. 3 *Jur* **tribunal de primera i.**, court of first instance. 4 **en primera i.**, first of all; **en última i.**, as a last resort.
instantánea *nf* snapshot.
instantáneo,-a *adj* instantaneous; **café i.**, instant coffee. ◆**instantáneamente** *adv* instantly.
instante *nm* instant, moment; **a cada i.**, constantly; **al i.**, immediately, right away; **por instantes**, with every second; **¡un i.!**, just a moment!
instar *vtr* to urge.
instauración *nf* founding.
instaurar *vtr* to found.
instigador,-a *nm,f* instigator.
instigar |7| *vtr* to instigate; **i. a la rebelión**, to incite a rebellion.
instintivo,-a *adj* instinctive.
instinto *nm* instinct; **por i.**, instinctively; **i. de conservación**, instinct of self-preservation.
institución *nf* institution.
instituir |37| *vtr* to institute.
instituto *nm* 1 institute. 2 *Educ* state secondary school, US high school.
institutriz *nf* governess.
instituyo *indic pres* → **instituir**.
instrucción *nf* 1 *(educación)* education. 2 *(usu pl)* *(indicación)* instruction; **instrucciones para el** *o* **de uso**, directions for use. 3 *Jur* preliminary investigation; **la i. del sumario**, proceedings *pl*; **juez de i.**, examining magistrate. 4 *Mil* drill.
instructivo,-a *adj* instructive.
instruido,-a *adj* educated, well-educated.
instruir |37| *vtr* 1 to instruct. 2 *(enseñar)* to educate. 3 *Mil* to drill. 4 *Jur* to investigate.
instrumental *adj* instrumental.
instrumento *nm* instrument.
insubordinación *nf* insubordination.
insubordinado-a *adj* insubordinate.
insubordinar *vtr (sublevarse)* to rebel (contra, against).
insuficiencia *nf* insufficiency.
insuficiente I *adj* insufficient. II *nm Educ*

(nota) fail.

insufrible *adj* insufferable.

insular I *adj* insular, island. **II** *nmf* islander.

insulso,-a *adj* insipid.

insultante *adj* insulting.

insultar *vtr* to insult.

insulto *nm* insult.

insumisión *nf* refusal to do military service.

insumiso,-a I *adj* unsubmissive. **II** *nm* person who refuses to do military service.

insuperable *adj* **1** *(inmejorable)* unsurpassable. **2** *(problema)* insurmountable.

insurgente *adj & nmf* insurgent.

insurrección *nf* insurrection.

intacto,-a *adj* intact.

intachable *adj* irreproachable; **conducta i.**, impeccable behaviour.

integral I *adj* integral; *Culin* **pan i.**, wholemeal bread; **arroz i.**, brown rice. **II** *nf* *Mat* integral.

integrante I *adj* integral; **ser parte i. de**, to be an integral part of. **II** *nmf* member.

integrar I *vtr (formar)* to compose, make up; **el equipo lo integran once jugadores**, there are eleven players in the team. **II integrarse** *vr* to integrate **(en, with)**.

integridad *nf* integrity.

íntegro,-a *adj* **1** *(entero)* whole, entire; *Cin Lit* **versión íntegra**, unabridged version. **2** *(honrado)* upright.

intelecto *nm* intellect.

intelectual *adj & nmf* intellectual.

inteligencia *nf* *(intelecto)* intelligence; **cociente de i.**, intelligence quotient, IQ.

inteligente *adj* intelligent.

inteligible *adj* intelligible.

intemperie *nf* bad weather; **a la i.**, in the open (air).

intempestivo,-a *adj* untimely.

intención *nf* intention; **con i.**, deliberately, on purpose; **con segunda/doble i.**, with an ulterior motive; **tener la i. de hacer algo**, to intend to do sth.

intencionado,-a *adj* deliberate.

intencional *adj* intentional.

◆**intencionadamente** *adv* on purpose.

intensidad *nf* intensity; *(del viento)* force.

intensificar [1] *vtr*, **intensificarse** *vr* to intensify; *(amistad)* to strengthen.

intensivo,-a *adj* intensive; *Agr* **cultivo i.**, intensive farming; *Educ* **curso i.**, crash course.

intenso,-a *adj* intense.

intentar *vtr* to try, attempt; *fam* **¡inténtalo!**, give it a go!.

intento *nm* attempt; **i. de suicidio**, attempted suicide.

intentona *nf* putsch.

inter- *pref* inter-.

intercalar *vtr* to insert.

intercambiar [12] *vtr* to exchange.

intercambio *nm* exchange; **i. comercial**,

trade.

interceder *vi* to intercede.

interceptar *vtr* **1** *(detener)* to intercept. **2** *(carretera)* to block; *(tráfico)* to hold up.

intercesión *nf* intercession.

intercontinental *adj* intercontinental.

interdicto *nm* prohibition.

interés *nm* **1** interest; **poner i. en**, to take an interest in; **tener i. en** *o* **por**, to be interested in. **2** *(provecho personal)* self-interest; **hacer algo (sólo) por i.**, to do sth out of self-interest; **intereses creados**, vested interests. **3** *Fin* interest; **con un i. del 11%**, at an interest of 11%; **tipos de i.**, interest rates.

interesado,-a I *adj* **1** interested **(en, in)**; **las partes interesadas**, the interested parties. **2** *(egoísta)* selfish. **II** *nm,f* interested person; **los interesados**, those interested *o* concerned.

interesante *adj* interesting.

interesar I *vtr (tener interés)* to interest; **la poesía no me interesa nada**, poetry doesn't interest me at all. **2** *(concernir)* to concern. **II** *vi (ser importante)* to be of interest, to be important; **interesaría llegar pronto**, it is important to get there early. **III interesarse** *vr* **i. por** *o* **en**, to be interested in; **se interesó por ti**, he asked about *o* after you.

interferencia *nf* interference; *Rad TV* jamming.

interferir [5] *vtr* **1** to interfere with; *(plan)* to upset. **2** *Rad TV* to jam.

interfono *nm* *Tel* intercom.

interinidad *nf* **1** *(temporalidad)* temporariness. **2** *(empleo)* temporary employment.

interino,-a I *adj (persona)* acting. **II** *nm,f (trabajador temporal)* temporary worker.

interior I *adj* **1** inner, inside, interior; **habitación i.**, inner room; **ropa i.**, underwear. **2** *Pol* domestic, internal. **3** *Geog* inland. **II** *nm* **1** inside, interior; *fig* **en su i. no estaba de acuerdo**, deep down she disagreed. **2** *Geog* interior; *Pol* **Ministerio del I.**, Home Office, *US* Department of the Interior.

interiorizar [4] *vtr* to internalize.

interjección *nf* *Ling* interjection.

interlocutor,-a *nm,f* speaker; *(negociador)* negotiator.

intermediario *nm* *Com* middleman.

intermedio,-a I *adj* intermediate. **II** *nm* *TV (intervalo)* break.

interminable *adj* endless.

intermitente I *adj* intermittent. **II** *nm* *Aut* indicator.

internacional *adj* international.

internado,-a I *nm,f* inmate. **II** *(colegio)* boarding school.

internar I *vtr (en hospital)* to confine. **II internarse** *vr* **1** *(penetrar)* to advance **(en, into)**. **2** *Dep* to break through.

interno,-a I *adj* **1** internal; **por vía**

interna, internally. 2 *Pol* domestic. II *nm,f (alumno)* boarder; *Med (enfermo)* patient; *(preso)* inmate.

interponer [19] *(pp* **interpuesto)** I *vtr* to insert; *Jur* i. **un recurso,** to give notice of appeal. II **interponerse** *vr* to intervene.

interpretación *nf* 1 interpretation. 2 *Mús Teat* performance.

interpretar *vtr* 1 to interpret. 2 *Teat (papel)* to play; *(obra)* to perform; *Mús (concierto)* to play, perform; *(canción)* to sing.

intérprete *nmf* 1 *(traductor)* interpreter. 2 *Teat* performer; *Mús (cantante)* singer; *(músico)* performer.

interpuse *pt indef* → **interponer.**

interrogación *nf* interrogation; *Ling* **(signo de) i.,** question o interrogation mark.

interrogante *nf fig* question mark.

interrogar [7] *vtr* to question; *(testigo etc)* to interrogate.

interrogatorio *nm* interrogation.

interrumpir *vtr* to interrupt; *(tráfico)* to block.

interrupción *nf* interruption; **i. del embarazo,** termination of pregnancy.

interruptor *nm Elec* switch.

intersección *nf* intersection.

interurbano,-a *adj* intercity; *Tel* **conferencia interurbana,** long-distance call.

intervalo *nm* interval; **habrá intervalos de lluvia,** there will be periods of rain.

intervención *nf* 1 *(participación)* intervention, participation **(en,** in); *(aportación)* contribution **(en,** to). 2 *Med* intervention.

intervenir [27] I *vi (mediar)* to intervene **(en,** in); *(participar)* to take part **(en,** in); *(contribuir)* to contribute **(en,** to). II *vtr* 1 *(confiscar)* to confiscate, seize. 2 *Tel (teléfono)* to tap. 3 *Med* to operate on.

interventor,-a *nm,f (supervisor)* inspector; *Fin* i. **(de cuentas),** auditor.

interviú *nf (pl* **interviús)** interview.

intestino,-a I *adj (luchas)* internal. II *nm Anat* intestine.

intimar *vi* to become close **(con,** to).

intimidad *nf (amistad)* intimacy; *(vida privada)* private life; *(privacidad)* privacy; **en la i.,** privately, in private.

intimidar *vtr* to intimidate.

íntimo,-a I *adj* 1 intimate. 2 *(vida)* private; **una boda íntima,** a quiet wedding. 3 *(amistad)* close. II *nm,f* close friend, intimate.

intolerable *adj* intolerable.

intolerancia *nf* intolerance.

intolerante I *adj* intolerant. II *nmf* intolerant person.

intoxicación *nf* poisoning; **i. alimentaria,** food poisoning.

intoxicar [1] *vtr* to poison.

intra- *pref* intra-.

intranquilidad *nf* worry.

intranquilizarse *vr* to get worried.

intranquilo,-a *adj (preocupado)* worried; *(agitado)* restless.

intransigente *adj* intransigent.

intransitable *adj* impassable.

intransitivo,-a *adj Ling* intransitive.

intratable *adj* 1 *(problema)* intractable. 2 *(persona)* unsociable.

intrépido,-a *adj* intrepid.

intriga *nf* intrigue; *Cin Teat* plot.

intrigante I *adj* 1 *(interesante)* intriguing, interesting. 2 *pey (maquinador)* scheming. II *nmf (persona)* schemer.

intrigar [7] I *vtr (interesar)* to intrigue, interest. II *vi (maquinar)* to plot.

intrincado,-a *adj* 1 *(cuestión, problema)* intricate. 2 *(bosque)* dense.

intrínseco,-a *adj* intrinsic.

introducción *nf* introduction.

introducir [10] I *vtr* 1 to introduce. 2 *(meter)* to insert, put in.

intromisión *nf (injerencia)* meddling; **perdón por la i.,** forgive the intrusion.

introspectivo,-a *adj* introspective.

introvertido,-a I *adj* introverted. II *nm,f* introvert.

intruso,-a I *adj* intrusive. II *nm,f* intruder; *Jur* trespasser.

intuición *nf* intuition.

intuir [37] *vtr* to know by intuition.

intuitivo,-a *adj* intuitive.

inundación *nf* flood.

inundar *vtr* to flood; *fig (de trabajo etc)* to swamp.

inusitado,-a *adj* unusual.

inútil I *adj* 1 useless; *(esfuerzo, intento)* vain, pointless. 2 *Mil* unfit (for service). II *nmf fam* good-for-nothing.

inutilidad *nf* uselessness.

inutilizar [4] *vtr* to make o render useless; *(máquina etc)* to put out of action.

invadir *vtr* to invade; *fig* **los estudiantes invadieron la calle,** students poured out onto the street.

invalidar *vtr* to invalidate.

invalidez *nf* 1 *Jur (nulidad)* invalidity. 2 *Med (minusvalía)* disability.

inválido,-a I *adj* 1 *Jur (nulo)* invalid. 2 *Med (minusválido)* disabled, handicapped. II *nm,f Med* disabled o handicapped person.

invariable *adj* invariable.

invasión *nf* invasion.

invasor,-a I *adj* invading. II *nm,f* invader.

invencible *adj* 1 *(enemigo)* invincible. 2 *(obstáculo)* insurmountable.

invención *nf (invento)* invention; *(mentira)* fabrication.

inventar *vtr* to invent; *(excusa, mentira)* to make up, concoct.

inventario *nm* inventory.

inventiva *nf* inventiveness; *(imaginación)* imagination.

invento *nm* invention.

inventor,-a *adj,f* inventor.

invernadero *nm* greenhouse; **efecto i.,** greenhouse effect.

invernal *adj* winter, wintry.

invernar [1] *vi* to hibernate.

inverosímil *adj* unlikely, improbable.

inversión *nf* 1 inversion. 2 *Fin* investment.

inverso,-a *adj* opposite; **en sentido i.,** in the opposite direction; **en orden i.,** in reverse order.

inversor,-a *nm,f* investor.

invertebrado,-a *adj & nm Zool* invertebrate.

invertido,-a I *adj* inverted, reversed. II *nm,f* homosexual.

invertir [5] *vtr* 1 (*orden*) to invert, reverse. 2 (*dinero*) to invest (**en,** in); (*tiempo*) to spend (**en,** on).

investidura *nf* investiture; *Pol* vote of confidence.

investigación *nf* 1 (*policial etc*) investigation. 2 (*científica*) research.

investigador,-a *nm,f* 1 (*detective*) investigator. 2 (*científico*) researcher, research worker.

investigar [7] *vtr* to research; (*indagar*) to investigate.

investir [6] *vtr* to invest.

invidente I *adj* unsighted. II *nmf* unsighted person.

invierno *nm* winter.

invisible *adj* invisible.

invitación *nf* invitation.

invitado,-a I *adj* invited; **artista i.,** guest artist. II *nm,f* guest.

invitar *vtr* to invite; **hoy invito yo,** it's on me today; **me invitó a una copa,** he treated me to a drink.

invocar [1] *vtr* to invoke.

involucrar I *vtr* to involve (**en,** in). II **involucrarse** *vr* to get involved (**en,** in).

involuntario,-a *adj* involuntary; (*impremeditado*) unintentional.

invulnerable *adj* invulnerable.

inyección *nf* injection; **poner una i.,** to give an injection.

inyectar *vtr* to inject (**en,** into); **i. algo a algn,** to inject sb with sth.

IPC *abr de* Índice de Precios al Consumo, Retail Price Index, RPI.

ir [16] I *vi* 1 to go; **¡vamos!,** let's go!; **voy a Lima,** I'm going to Lima; **¡ya voy!,** (I'm) coming! 2 (*río, camino*) to lead; **esta carretera va a la frontera,** this road leads to the border. 3 (*funcionar*) to work (properly); **el ascensor no va,** the lift is out of order. 4 (*desenvolverse*) **¿cómo le va el nuevo trabajo?,** how is he getting on in his new job?; **¿cómo te va?,** how are things?, how are you doing? 5 (*sentar bien*) to suit; **el verde te va mucho,** green really suits you. 6 (*combinar*) to

match; **el rojo no va con el verde,** red doesn't go with green. 7 (*vestir*) to wear; **ir con falda,** to wear a skirt; **ir de blanco/de uniforme,** to be dressed in white/in uniform. 8 *fam* (*importar, concernir*) to concern; **eso va por ti también,** and the same goes for you; **ni me va ni me viene,** I don't care one way or the other. 9 *fam* (*comportarse*) to act; **ir de guapo por la vida,** to be a flash Harry. 10 **va para abogado,** he's studying to be a lawyer. 11 (*ir + por*) **ir por la derecha,** to keep (to the right); (*ir a buscar*) **ve** (a) **por agua,** go and fetch some water; (*haber llegado*) **voy por la página noventa,** I've got as far as page ninety. 12 (*locuciones*) **a eso iba,** I was coming to that; **¡ahí va!,** catch!; **en lo que va de año,** so far this year; **ir a parar,** to end up; **¡qué va!,** of course not!, nothing of the sort!; **a lo suyo,** he looks after his own interests; **¡vamos a ver!,** let's see!; **¡vaya!,** fancy that; **¡vaya moto!,** what a bike!

II *v aux* 1 (*ir + gerundio*) **ir andando,** to go on foot; **va mejorando,** she's improving. 2 (*ir + pp*) **ya van rotos tres,** three (of them) have already been broken. 3 (*ir a + inf*) **iba a decir que,** I was going to say that; **va a llover,** it's going to rain; **vas a caerte,** you'll fall.

III **irse** *vr* 1 (*marcharse*) to go away, leave; **me voy,** I'm off; (*vámonos*) let's go!; **¡vete!,** go away!; **vete a casa,** go home. 2 (*líquido, gas*) (*escaparse*) to leak. 3 (*direcciones*) **¿por dónde se va a ...?** which is the way to ...? **por aquí se va al río,** this is the way to the river.

ira *nf* wrath, rage, anger.

iracundo,-a *adj* 1 (*irascible*) irascible. 2 (*enfadado*) irate, angry.

Irak *n* Irak.

Irán *n* Iran.

iraní *adj & nmf* (*pl iraníes*) Iranian.

Iraq *n →* Irak.

iraquí *adj & nmf* (*pl iraquíes*) Iraqi.

irascible *adj* irascible, irritable.

iris *nm inv Anat* iris; **arco i.,** rainbow.

Irlanda *n* Ireland; **I. del Norte,** Northern Ireland.

irlandés,-esa I *adj* Irish. II *nm,f* (*hombre*) Irishman; (*mujer*) Irishwoman; **los irlandeses,** the Irish. III *nm* (*idioma*) Irish.

ironía *nf* irony.

irónico,-a *adj* ironic.

IRPF *nm Econ abr de* impuesto sobre la renta de las personas físicas, income tax.

irracional *adj* irrational.

irradiar [12] *vtr* 1 (*emitir*) to radiate. 2 *Am fig* (*expulsar*) to expel.

irreal *adj* unreal.

irrealizable *adj* unattainable, unfeasible;

fig unreachable.

irreconocible *adj* unrecognizable.

irregular *adj* irregular.

irregularidad *nf* irregularity.

irremediable *adj* irremediable, incurable.

irremplazable *adj* irreplaceable.

irreparable *adj* irreparable.

irreprochable *adj* irreproachable, blameless.

irresistible *adj* 1 (*impulso, persona*) irresistible. 2 (*insoportable*) unbearable.

irresoluto,-a *adj* irresolute.

irresponsable *adj* irresponsible.

irreverente *adj* irreverent.

irrigación *nf* irrigation.

irrigar [7] *vtr* to irrigate, water.

irrisorio,-a *adj* derisory, ridiculous.

irritación *nf* irritation.

irritante *adj* irritating.

irritar I *vtr* 1 (*enfadar*) to irritate, exasperate. 2 *Med* to irritate. II **irritarse** *vr* 1 (*enfadarse*) to lose one's temper, get angry. 2 *Med* to become irritated.

irrompible *adj* unbreakable.

irrumpir *vi* to burst (**en**, into).

isla *nf* island, isle.

islam *nm* *Rel* Islam.

islámico,-a *adj* Islamic.

islandés,-esa I *adj* Icelandic. II *nm,f* (*per-*

sona) Icelander. III *nm* (*idioma*) Icelandic.

Islandia *n* Iceland.

isleño,-a I *adj* island. II *nm,f* islander.

islote *nm* small *o* rocky island.

ismo *nm* *fam* ism.

Israel *n* Israel.

israelí *adj* & *nmf* (*pl* **israelíes**) Israeli.

istmo *nm* *Geog* isthmus.

Italia *n* Italy.

italiano,-a I *adj* Italian. II *nm,f* (*persona*) Italian. III *nm* (*idioma*) Italian.

itinerante *adj* itinerant, itinerating.

itinerario *nm* itinerary, route.

IVA *nm* *Econ* *abr de* **impuesto sobre el valor añadido**, value-added tax, VAT.

izar [4] *vtr* to hoist, raise.

izqda., izqdª *abr de* **izquierda**, left.

izqdo., izqdº *abr de* **izquierdo**, left.

izquierda *nf* 1 left; **a la i.**, on the left; **girar a la i.**, to turn left. 2 (*mano*) left hand. 3 *Pol* **la i.**, the left; **de izquierdas**, left-wing.

izquierdista *Pol* I *adj* leftist, left-wing. II *nmf* leftist, left-winger.

izquierdo,-a *adj* 1 left; **brazo i.**, left arm. 2 (*zurdo*) left-handed.

izquierdoso,-a *adj* *fam* leftish.

J

J, j ['xota] *nf* (*la letra*) J,j.

jabalí *nm* (*pl* **jabalíes**) wild boar.

jabalina *nf* *Dep* javelin.

jabón *nm* soap; **j. de afeitar/tocador**, shaving/toilet soap.

jabonera *nf* soapdish.

jaca *nf* gelding.

jacaré *nm* *Am Zool* caiman.

jacinto *nm* *Bot* hyacinth.

jactancia *nf* boastfulness.

jactancioso,-a I *adj* boastful. II *nm,f* braggart.

jactarse *vr* to boast, brag (**de**, about).

jadeante *adj* panting, breathless.

jadear *vi* to pant, gasp.

jadeo *nm* panting, gasping.

jaez *nm* *pey* (*ralea*) kind, sort.

jalar I *vtr* *fam* (*comer*) to wolf down. II **jalarse** *vr* *fam* (*comerse*) to wolf down, scoff.

jalbegar [7] *vtr* to whitewash.

jalea *nf* jelly; **j. real**, royal jelly.

jalear *vtr* (*animar*) to cheer (on).

jaleo *nm* (*alboroto*) din, racket; (*riña*) row; (*confusión*) muddle; **armar j.**, to make a racket.

jalón¹ *nm* (*estaca*) stake; *fig* (*hito*) milestone.

jalón² *nm* 1 (*tirón*) pull, tug. 2 *Am Aut* lift.

jamaicano,-a *adj* & *nm,f* Jamaican.

jamar *vtr* *fam* to scoff, eat.

jamás *adv* 1 never; **j. he estado allí**, I have never been there. 2 ever; **el mejor libro que j. se ha escrito**, the best book ever written. 3 **nunca j.**, never again; **por siempre j.**, for ever (and ever).

jamba *nf* *Arquit* jamb.

jamón *nm* ham; **j. de York/serrano**, boiled/cured ham.

jamona *fam* *adj* buxom.

Japón *n* (**el**) J., Japan.

japonés,-esa I *adj* Japanese. II *nm,f* (*persona*) Japanese; **los japoneses**, the Japanese. III *nm* (*idioma*) Japanese.

japuta *nf* (*pez*) Ray's bream.

jaque *nm* *Ajedrez* check; **dar j. a**, to check; **j. mate**, checkmate; **j. al rey**, check; *fig* **estar en j.**, to be stymied.

jaqueca *nf* migraine.

jara *nf* *Bot* rockrose.

jarabe *nm* syrup; **j. para la tos**, cough mixture.

jarana *nf* *fam* 1 (*juerga*) wild party, spree; **ir de j.**, to go on a spree *o* a binge. 2 (*jaleo*) racket, din.

jaranero,-a I *adj* fun-loving, party-loving. II *nm,f* pleasure seeker, party-lover.

jardín *nm* garden; **j. botánico**, botanical garden; **j. de infancia**, nursery school, kindergarten.

jardinería *nf* gardening.

jardinero *nm* gardener.

jarra *nf* pitcher; **j. de cerveza**, beer mug; *fig* **de o en jarras**, arms akimbo, hands on hips.

jarro *nm* (*recipiente*) jug; (*contenido*) jugful; *fig* **echar un j. de agua fría a**, to pour cold water on.

jarrón *nm* vase; (*en arqueología*) urn.

jaspe *nm Min* jasper; **como el j.**, spotless, like a new pin.

Jauja *nf fig* promised land; **¡esto es J.!**, this is the life!

jaula *nf* (*para animales*) cage.

jauría *nf* pack of hounds.

jazmín *nm Bot* jasmine.

J.C. *abr de* **Jesucristo**, Jesus Christ, J.C.

jeep *nm Aut* jeep.

jefa *nf* female boss, manageress.

jefatura *nf* 1 (*cargo, dirección*) leadership. 2 (*sede*) central office; **j. de policía**, police headquarters.

jefe *nm* 1 head, chief, boss; *Com* manager; **j. de estación**, stationmaster; **j. de redacción**, editor-in-chief; **j. de ventas**, sales manager. 2 *Pol* leader; **J. de Estado**, Head of State. 3 *Mil* officer in command; **comandante en j.**, commander-in-chief.

Jehová *nm* Jehovah; **testigos de J.**, Jehovah's Witnesses.

jején *nm Am Ent* black fly.

jengibre *nm Bot* ginger.

jeque *nm* sheik, sheikh.

jerarquía *nf* 1 hierarchy. 2 (*categoría*) rank.

jerárquico,-a *adj* hierarchical.

jeremías *nmf inv* whiner, whinger.

jerez *nm* sherry.

jerga *nf* (*argot*) (*técnica*) jargon; (*vulgar*) slang; **la j. legal**, legal jargon.

jerigonza *nf* 1 (*extravagancia*) oddness. 2 (*galimatías*) gibberish.

jeringa *nf Med* syringe; *Aut* **j. de engrase**, grease gun.

jeringar [7] *vtr fam* 1 (*molestar*) to pester, annoy. 2 (*romper*) to break.

jeringuilla *nf* (*hypodermic*) syringe.

jeroglífico,-a I *adj* hieroglyphic. II *nm* 1 *Ling* hieroglyph, hieroglyphic. 2 (*juego*) rebus.

jersey *nm* (*pl* **jerseis**) sweater, pullover, jumper.

Jerusalén *n* Jerusalem.

Jesucristo *nm* Jesus Christ.

jesuita *adj & nmf* Jesuit.

Jesús I *nm* Jesus. II *interj* 1 (*expresa sorpresa*) good heavens! 2 (*al estornudar*) bless you!

jet *nf* jet set.

jeta *fam nf* 1 (*descaro*) cheek; **tener j.**, to be cheeky, have a nerve. 2 (*cara*) mug, face. 3 (*hocico*) snout.

jet-set *nf* jet set.

jíbaro,-a *nm,f Am* peasant.

jícara *nf* (*bol*) small cup; *Am* gourd.

jilguero,-a *nm,f Orn* goldfinch.

jilipollas *nmf inv fam ofens* → **gilipollas**.

jinete *nm* rider, horseman.

jiñar *vi vulg* to shit.

jirafa *nf* 1 giraffe. 2 (*de micrófono*) boom.

jirón *nm* (*trozo desgarrado*) shred, strip; (*pedazo suelto*) bit; *scrap*; **hecho jirones**, in shreds o tatters.

JJOO *nmpl abr de* **Juegos Olímpicos**, Olympic Games.

jocoso,-a *adj* funny, humorous.

joder *vulg ofens* I *interj* bloody hell!, shit! II *vtr* 1 (*fastidiar*) to piss off; **¡no me jodas!**, come on, don't give me that! 2 (*copular*) to fuck. 3 (*echar a perder*) to screw up; **¡la jodiste!**, you screwed it up! 4 (*romper*) to bugger. II **joderse** *vr* 1 (*aguantarse*) to put up with it; **¡hay que j.!**, you'll just have to grin and bear it. 2 (*echarse a perder*) to get screwed up; **¡se jodió el invento!**, that's really screwed things up. **¡que se joda!**, to hell with him! 3 (*romperse*) to break.

jodido,-a *adj vulg ofens* 1 (*maldito*) bloody, damned. 2 (*molesto*) annoying. 3 (*enfermo*) in a bad way; (*cansado*) knackered, exhausted. 4 (*estropeado, roto*) bust, kaput, buggered. 5 (*difícil*) shitty.

jodienda *nf vulg ofens* 1 (*coito*) fuck. 2 (*molestia*) pain in the arse.

jofaina *nf* washbasin.

jolgorio *nm fam* (*juerga*) binge; (*algazara*) fun.

jolín, jolines *interj fam* (*sorpresa*) gosh!, good grief!; (*enfado*) blast!, damn!

Jordania *n* Jordan.

jornada *nf* 1 (*laboral*) (*día de trabajo*) working day; **j. intensiva**, continuous working day; **j. partida**, working day with a lunch break; **trabajo de media j./j. completa**, part-time/full-time work. 2 *jornadas*, conference *sing*.

jornal *nm* (*paga*) day's wage; **trabajar a j.**, to be paid by the day.

jornalero,-a *nm,f* day labourer o *US* labborer.

joroba I *nf* (*jiba*) hump. II *interj* drat!

jorobado,-a I *adj* hunchbacked. II *nm,f* hunchback.

jorobar *fam* I *vtr* 1 (*fastidiar*) to annoy, bother; **me joroba**, it really gets up my nose; **¡no jorobes!**, (*incredulidad*) pull the other one! 2 (*estropear*) to ruin, wreck. II **jorobarse** *vr* 1 (*fastidiarse*) to grin and bear it. 2 (*estropearse*) to break.

jota¹ *nf* 1 name of the letter J in Spanish. 2 (*cantidad mínima*) jot, scrap; **ni j.**, not an iota; **no entiendo ni j.**, I don't understand a thing.

jota² *nf Mús* Spanish dance and music.

joven I *adj* young; **de aspecto j.**, young-looking. II *nmf* (*hombre*) youth, young man; (*mujer*) girl, young woman; **de j.**, as a young man *o* woman; **los jóvenes**, young people, youth.

jovial *adj* jovial, good-humoured.

joya *nf* jewel, piece of jewellery; **joyas de imitación**, imitation jewellery *sing*. 2 *fig* **ser una j.**, (*persona*) to be a real treasure *o* gem.

joyería *nf* (*tienda*) jewellery shop, jeweller's (shop).

joyero,-a I *nm,f* jeweller. II *nm* jewel case *o* box.

juanete *nm* (*en el pie*) bunion.

jubilación *nf* 1 (*acción*) retirement; **j. anticipada**, early retirement. 2 (*pensión*) pension.

jubilado,-a I *adj* retired. II *nm,f* retired person, pensioner; **los jubilados**, retired people.

jubilar I *vtr* (*retirar*) to retire, pension off; *fam* **j.** to get rid of, ditch. II **jubilarse** *vr* (*retirarse*) to retire, go into retirement.

júbilo *nm* jubilation, joy.

jubón *nm* doublet, jerkin.

judería *nf* (*barrio*) Jewish quarter.

judía *nf* bean; **j. verde**, French bean, green bean.

judicial *adj* judicial; **vía j.**, legal channels.

judío,-a I *adj* Jewish. II *nm,f* Jew.

judo *nm* *Dep* judo.

juego *nm* 1 game; **j. de azar**, game of chance; **j. de cartas**, card game; *fig* **j. de manos**, sleight of hand; *fig* **j. de palabras**, play on words, pun; *fig* **j. limpio/sucio**, fair/foul play; 2 *Dep* game; **Juegos Olímpicos**, Olympic Games; **terreno de j.**, *Ten* court; *Ftb* field; **fuera de j.**, offside. 3 (*apuestas*) gambling; *fig* **poner algo en j.**, to put sth at stake. 4 (*conjunto de piezas*) set; **j. de café/té**, coffee/tea service; *fig* **ir a j. con**, to match.

juerga *nf fam* binge, rave-up; **ir de j.**, to go on a binge.

juerguista I *adj* fun-loving. II *nmf* fun-loving person, raver.

jueves *nm inv* Thursday; **J. Santo**, Maundy Thursday.

juez *nmf* judge; **j. de instrucción**, examining magistrate; **j. de paz**, justice of the peace; *Dep* **j. de salida**, starter; **j. de línea**, linesman.

jugada *nf* 1 move; (*en billar*) shot. 2 *fam* dirty trick.

jugador,-a player; (*apostador*) gambler.

jugar [32] I *vi* 1 to play; **j. a(l) fútbol/tenis**, to play football/tennis; *fig* **j. sucio**, to play dirty. 2 **j. con**, (*no tomar en serio*) to toy with. II *vtr* 1 to play. 2 (*apostar*) to bet, stake. III **jugarse** *vr* 1 (*arriesgar*) to risk; *fam* **j. el pellejo**, to risk one's neck. 2 (*apostar*) to bet, stake.

jugarreta *nf fam* dirty trick.

jugo *nm* juice; *fig* **sacar el j. a**, (*aprove-*

char) to make the most of; (*explotar*) to squeeze dry.

jugoso,-a *adj* juicy; **un filete j.**, a juicy steak. 2 *fig* (*sustancioso*) substantial, meaty; **un tema j.**, a meaty topic.

juguete *nm* toy; **pistola de j.**, toy gun; *fig* **ser el j. de algn**, to be sb's plaything.

juguetear *vi* to play.

juguetón,-ona *adj* playful.

juicio *nm* 1 (*facultad mental*) judgement, discernment; (*opinión*) opinion, judgement; **a j. de**, in the opinion of; **a mi j.**, in my opinion. 2 (*sensatez*) reason, common sense; **en su sano j.**, in one's right mind; **perder el j.**, to go mad *o* insane. 3 *Jur* trial, lawsuit; **llevar a algn a j.**, to take legal action against sb, sue sb.

juicioso,-a *adj* judicious, wise.

julio *nm* July.

junco *nm* *Bot* rush.

jungla *nf* jungle.

junio *nm* June.

júnior *nm* *Dep* junior; **campeonato j. de golf**, junior golf championship.

junta *nf* 1 (*reunión*) meeting, assembly; *Pol* **j. de gobierno**, cabinet meeting. 2 (*dirección*) board, committee; **j. directiva**, board of directors. 3 *Mil* junta; **j. militar**, military junta. 4 (*parlamento regional*) regional parliament. 5 *Téc* joint.

juntar I *vtr* 1 (*unir*) to join, put together; (*piezas*) to assemble. 2 (*reunir*) (*sellos*) to collect; (*dinero*) to raise. II **juntarse** *vr* 1 (*unirse*) to join; (*ríos, caminos*) to meet; (*personas*) to gather. 2 (*amancebarse*) to live together.

junto,-a I *adj* together; **dos mesas juntas**, two tables side by side; **todos juntos**, all together. II **junto** *adv* **j. con**, together with; **j. a**, next to.

juntura *nf* 1 *Téc* joint, seam. 2 *Anat* joint.

jura *nf* (*acción*) oath; (*ceremonia*) swearing in; **j. de bandera**, oath of allegiance to the flag.

jurado *nm* 1 (*tribunal*) jury; (*en un concurso*) panel of judges, jury. 2 (*miembro del tribunal*) juror, member of the jury.

juramento *nm* 1 *Jur* oath; **bajo j.**, under oath. 2 (*blasfemia*) swearword, curse.

jurar I *vi* *Jur Rel* to swear, take an oath. II *vtr* to swear; **j. el cargo**, to take the oath of office; **j. por Dios**, to swear to God. III **jurarse** *vr fam* **jurársela(s) a algn**, to have it in for sb.

jurel *nm* (*pez*) scad, horse mackerel.

jurídico,-a *adj* legal.

jurisdicción *nf* jurisdiction.

jurisdiccional *adj* jurisdictional; **aguas jurisdiccionales**, territorial waters.

jurista *nmf* jurist, lawyer.

justicia *nf* justice; **tomarse la j. por su mano**, to take the law into one's own hands.

justiciero,-a *adj* severe.
justificable *adj* justifiable.
justificación *nf* justification.
justificado,-a *adj* justified, well-grounded.
justificante *nm* written proof; **j. de pago,** proof of payment.
justificar [1] I *vtr* to justify. II **justificarse** *vr* to clear oneself, justify oneself.
justo,-a I *adj* 1 just, fair, right; **un trato j.,** a fair deal. 2 (*apretado*) (*ropa*) tight; **estamos justos de tiempo,** we're pressed for time. 3 (*exacto*) right, accurate; **la palabra justa,** the right word. 4 (*preciso*) **llegamos en el momento j. en que salían,** we arrived just as they were leav-

ing. 5 **lo** j., just enough. II *nm,f* just *o* righteous person; **los justos,** the just, the righteous. III **justo** *adv* (*exactamente*) exactly, precisely; **j. al lado,** right beside. ♦**justamente** *adv* ¡j.!, precisely!; **j. detrás de,** right behind.
juvenil I *adj* (*aspecto*) youthful, young; **ropa j.,** young people's clothes; **delincuencia j.,** juvenile delinquency. II *nmf* **los juveniles,** the juveniles.
juventud *nf* 1 (*edad*) youth. 2 (*jóvenes*) young people.
juzgado *nm* court, tribunal; **j. de guardia,** police court.
juzgar [7] *vtr* to judge; **a j. por ...,** judging by ....

K

K, k [ka] *nf* (*la letra*) K, k.
ka *nf* name of the letter K in Spanish.
kárate *nm Dep* karate.
karateka *nmf Dep* person who does karate.
Kg, kg *abr de* **kilogramo(s),** kilograms, kilogrammes, kg.
kilo *nm* 1 (*medida*) kilo; *fam* **pesa un k.,** it weighs a ton. 2 *arg* (*millón*) a million pesetas.
kilogramo *nm* kilogram, kilogramme.
kilolitro *nm* kilolitre, *US* kiloliter.
kilometraje *nm* ≈ mileage.

kilométrico,-a *adj* kilometric, kilometrical; **billete k.,** multiple-journey ticket.
kilómetro *nm* kilometre, *US* kilometer.
kilovatio *nm* kilowatt; **k. hora,** kilowatt-hour.
kiosco *nm* → **quiosco.**
kiwi *nm* 1 *Orn* kiwi. 2 (*fruto*) kiwi (fruit), Chinese gooseberry.
Kleenex® *nm* Kleenex®, tissue.
Km, km *abr de* **kilómetro(s),** kilometre, kilometres, km, kms.
Kw, kw *abr de* **kilovatio(s),** kilowatt, kilowatts, kW, kw.

L

L, l ['ele] *nf* (*la letra*) L, l.
l *abr de* **litro(s),** litre, litres, *US* liter, liters, l.
la¹ *art def f* I the; **la mesa,** the table. II *pron dem* the one; **la del vestido azul,** the one in the blue dress; **la que vino ayer,** the one who came yesterday; → **el.**
la² *pron pers f* (*persona*) her; (*usted*) you; (*cosa*) it; **no la dejes abierta,** I'll invite her along; **ya la avisaremos, señora,** we'll let you know, madam; → **le.**
la³ *nm Mús* la, A.
laberinto *nm* labyrinth.
labia *nf fam* loquacity; *pey* glibness; **tener mucha l.,** to have the gift of the gab.
labio *nm* lip.
labor *nf* 1 job, task; **l. de equipo,** teamwork; (**de profesión**) **sus labores,** housewife. 2 *Agr* farmwork. 3 (*de costura*) needlework, sewing.
laborable *adj* 1 **día l.,** (*no festivo*) working day. 2 *Agr* arable.
laboral *adj* industrial; **accidente l.,** industrial accident; **conflictividad l.,** in-

dustrial unrest; **jornada l.,** working day; **Universidad L.,** technical training college.
laboratorio *nm* laboratory.
laborioso,-a *adj* 1 (*persona*) hardworking. 2 (*tarea*) laborious.
laborista *Pol* I *adj* Labour; **partido l.,** Labour Party. II *nmf* Labour (Party) member *o* supporter.
labrado,-a *adj Arte* carved.
labrador,-a *nm,f* (*granjero*) farmer; (*trabajador*) farm worker.
labranza *nf* farming.
labrar I *vtr* 1 *Agr* to till. 2 (*madera*) to carve; (*piedra*) to cut; (*metal*) to work. II **labrarse** *vr* **fig l. un porvenir,** to build a future for oneself.
laca *nf* 1 hair lacquer, hairspray; **l. de uñas,** nail polish *o* varnish. 2 *Arte* lacquer.
lacio,-a *adj* (*pelo*) lank, limp. 2 **qué l.!,** (*soso*) what a weed!
lacónico,-a *adj* laconic; (*conciso*) terse.
lacra *nf* evil, curse; **una l. social,** a scourge of society.

lacrar *vtr* to seal with wax.

lacre *nm* sealing wax.

lacrimógeno,-a *adj* **1** gas l., tear gas. **2** *fig* **una película lacrimógena**, a tear-jerker.

lactar *vi* to breastfeed.

lácteo,-a *adj* **productos lácteos**, milk *o* dairy products; *Astron* **Vía Láctea**, Milky Way.

ladear I *vtr* (*inclinar*) to tilt; (*cabeza*) to lean. **II ladearse** *vr* **1** (*inclinarse*) to lean, tilt. **2** (*desviarse*) to go off to one side.

ladera *nf* slope.

ladino,-a *adj* (*astuto*) cunning, crafty.

lado *nm* **1** side; **a un l.**, aside; **al l.**, close by, nearby; **al l. de**, next to, beside; **ponte de l.**, stand sideways. **2** (*en direcciones*) direction; **por todos lados**, on *o* from all sides. **3** *fig* **dar de l. a algn**, to cold-shoulder sb; **por otro l.**, (*además*) moreover; **por un l. ..., por otro l. ...**, on the one hand ..., on the other hand ....

ladrar *vi* to bark.

ladrillo *nm* **1** *Constr* brick. **2** *fam* (*pesado*) bore, drag.

ladrón,-ona *nm,f* thief, robber; **¡al l.!**, stop thief! **II** *nm Elec* multiple socket.

lagartija *nf* small lizard.

lagarto *nm* lizard.

lago *nm* lake.

lágrima *nf* **1** tear; **llorar a l. viva**, to cry one's eyes out. **2** (*en lámpara*) teardrop.

lagrimoso,-a *adj* tearful.

laguna *nf* **1** small lake. **2** *fig* (*hueco*) gap.

La Haya *n* The Hague.

laico,-a *adj* lay. **II** *nm,f* lay person; (*hombre*) layman; (*mujer*) laywoman.

lameculos *nmf inv ofens* bootlicker, arse-licker.

lamentable *adj* regrettable; (*infame*) lamentable.

lamentar I *vtr* to regret; **lo lamento**, I'm sorry. **II lamentarse** *vr* to complain.

lamento *nm* moan, wail.

lamer *vtr* to lick.

lámina *nf* **1** sheet, plate; **l. de acero**, steel sheet. **2** *Impr* plate.

laminado,-a I *adj* **1** laminated. **2** (*metales*) rolled; **acero l.**, rolled steel. **II** *nm* lamination.

laminar *vtr* (*metal*) to roll.

lámpara *nf* **1** lamp; **l. de pie**, standard lamp. **2** *Elec* (*bombilla*) bulb. **3** *Rad* valve.

lamparón *nm fam* oil *o* grease stain.

lana *nf* wool; **pura l. virgen**, pure new wool.

lanar *adj* **ganado l.**, sheep.

lance *nm lit* (*episodio*) incident.

lancha *nf* motorboat, launch; **l. motora**, speedboat; **l. neumática**, rubber dinghy; **l. salvavidas**, lifeboat.

langosta *nf* **1** lobster. **2** (*insecto*) locust.

langostino *nm* king prawn.

languidecer [33] *vi* to languish.

lánguido,-a *adj* languid; (*sin vigor*) listless.

lanudo,-a *adj* woolly, fleecy; (*peludo*) furry.

lanza *nf* spear, lance; **punta de l.**, spearhead; *fig* **romper una l. en favor de algn/de algo**, to defend sb/sth.

lanzadera *nf* shuttle; **l. espacial**, space shuttle.

lanzado,-a *adj fam* reckless; **ir l.**, to tear along.

lanzagranadas *nm inv Mil* grenade launcher.

lanzamiento *nm* **1** throwing, hurling. **2** *Dep* (*de disco, jabalina*) throw; (*de peso*) put. **3** *Mil* (*de cohete etc*) launching. **4** *Com* launch; **precio de l.**, launch price. **5** *Náut* launch.

lanzar [4] **I** *vtr* **1** (*arrojar*) to throw, fling. **2** *fig* (*grito*) to let out. **3** *Náut Com Mil* to launch. **II lanzarse** *vr* **1** (*arrojarse*) to throw *o* hurl oneself; **l. al suelo**, to throw oneself to the ground. **2** (*emprender*) to embark on; **l. a los negocios**, to go into business. **3** (*irse, largarse*) *fam* to scram.

lapa *nf* **1** *Zool* limpet. **2** *pey* **es una verdadera l.**, he/she sticks to you like glue.

lapicero *nm* pencil-case.

lápida *nf* headstone.

lapidario,-a *adj* lapidary.

lápiz *nm* pencil; **l. labial** *o* **de labios**, lipstick; **l. de ojos**, eyeliner.

lapso *nm* **1** (*periodo de tiempo*) period. **2** (*error*) lapse, slip.

lapsus *nm* slip; **l. linguae**, slip of the tongue.

largas *nfpl* **dar l. a un asunto**, to put a matter off.

largar [7] **I** *vtr* **1** *fam* (*golpe, discurso, dinero*) to give. **2** *Náut* **l. amarras**, to cast off. **II largarse** *vr fam* to clear off, split; **¡lárgate!**, beat it!

largo,-a I *adj* **1** (*espacio*) long; (*tiempo*) long, lengthy; **pasamos un mes l. allí**, we spent a good month there; **a lo l. de**, (*espacio*) along; (*tiempo*) through; **a la larga**, in the long run. **2** (*excesivo*) too long; **se hizo l. el día**, the day dragged on. **3 largos años**, many years. **II** *nm* **1** (*longitud*) length; **¿cuánto tiene de l.?**, how long is it? **2** *Mús* largo. **III** *largo adv* **l. y tendido**, at length; **¡l. (de aquí)!**, clear off!; **esto va para l.**, this is going to last a long time.

largometraje *nm* feature film, full-length film.

laringe *nf* larynx.

laringitis *nf* laryngitis.

las[1] *art def fpl* **1** the; **l. sillas**, the chairs; **lávate l. manos**, wash your hands; (*no se traduce*) **me gustan l. flores**, I like flowers. 2 **l. que**, *(personas)* the ones who, those who; *(objetos)* the ones that, those that; **toma l. que quieras**, take whichever ones you want; → **la y los**.

las² *pron pers fpl (ellas)* them; *(ustedes)* you; **l. llamaré mañana (a ustedes)**, I'll call you tomorrow; **no l. rompas**, don't break them; **Pepa piensa que l. mías**, Pepa thinks the way I do; → **los**.

lasaña *nf* lasagna, lasagne.

lascivo,-a *adj* lewd, lecherous.

láser *nm inv* laser; **impresora l.**, laser printer.

lástima *nf* pity; **¡qué l.!**, what a pity!, what a shame!; **es una l. que ...**, it's a pity (that) ...; **estar hecho una l.**, to be a sorry sight; **tener l. a algn**, to feel sorry for sb.

lastimar *vtr* to hurt, injure.

lastre *nm 1 (peso)* ballast. 2 *fig* dead weight.

lata¹ *nf 1 (envase)* tin, *US* can; **en l.**, tinned *o US* canned. 2 *(hojalata)* tin(plate); **hecho de l.**, made of tin.

lata² *nf fam* nuisance, drag; **dar la l.**, to be a nuisance *o* a pest.

latente *adj* latent.

lateral I *adj* side, lateral; **salió por la puerta l.**, he went out by the side door; **escalón l.**, *(en letrero)* ramp. II *nm* side passage; *Aut (carril)* **l.**, side lane.

latido *nm (del corazón)* beat.

latifundio *nm* large landed estate.

latigazo *nm 1* lash. 2 *arg (trago)* drink, swig.

látigo *nm* whip.

latín *nm* Latin.

latino,-a I *adj* Latin; **América Latina**, Latin America. II *nm,f* Latin American.

Latinoamérica *nf* Latin America.

latinoamericano,-a *adj & nm,f* Latin American.

latir *vi* to beat.

latitud *nf 1 Geog* latitude. 2 **latitudes**, region *sing*, area *sing*.

latón *nm* brass.

latoso,-a *adj fam* annoying.

laucha *nf Am* mouse.

laúd *nm* lute.

laurel *nm Bot* laurel, (sweet) bay; *Culin* bay leaf; *fig* **dormirse en los laureles**, to rest on one's laurels.

lava *nf* lava.

lavable *adj* washable.

lavabo *nm 1 (pila)* washbasin. 2 *(cuarto de aseo)* washroom. 3 *(retrete)* lavatory, toilet.

lavadero *nm (de coches)* carwash.

lavado *nm* wash, washing; *fig* **l. de cerebro**, brainwashing; **l. en seco**, dry-cleaning.

lavadora *nf* washing machine.

lavanda *nf* lavender.

lavandería *nf 1 (automática)* launderette,

US laundromat. 2 *(atendida por personal)* laundry.

lavaplatos *nm inv* dishwasher.

lavar *vtr* to wash; **l. en seco**, to dry-clean.

lavativa *nf* enema.

lavavajillas *nm inv* dishwasher.

laxante *adj & nm* laxative.

laxar *vtr (vientre)* to loosen.

laxitud *nf* laxity, laxness.

lazada *nf (nudo)* bow.

lazarillo *nm* **perro l.**, guide dog, *US* Seeing Eye dog.

lazo *nm 1 (adorno)* bow. 2 *(nudo)* knot; **l. corredizo**, slipknot. 3 *(para reses)* lasso. 4 *fig (usu pl) (vínculo)* tie, bond.

le I *pron pers mf (objeto indirecto) (a él)* (to *o* for) him; *(a ella)* (to *o* for) her; *(a cosa)* (to *o* for) it; *(a usted)* (to *o* for) you; **lávale la cara**, wash his face; **le compraré uno**, I'll buy one for her; **¿qué le pasa (a usted)?**, what's the matter with you? II *pron pers m (objeto directo) (él)* him; *(usted)* you; **no le oigo**, I can't hear him; **no quiero molestarle**, I don't wish to disturb you.

leal I *adj* loyal, faithful. II *nmf* loyalist.

lealtad *nf* loyalty, faithfulness.

lebrel *nm* greyhound.

lección *nf* lesson; *fig* **dar una l. a algn**, to teach sb a lesson; *fig* **te servirá de l.**, let that be a lesson to you.

leche *nf 1* milk; *Anat* **dientes de l.**, milk teeth; **l. descremada** *o* **desnatada**, skim *o* skimmed milk. 2 *fam* **mala l.**, badness. 3 **l.!**, damn! 4 *arg (golpe)* knock; **dar o pegar una l. a algn**, to clobber sb. 5 *vulg* semen.

lechera *nf 1 (vasija)* churn. 2 *arg* police car.

lechería *nf* dairy, creamery.

lechero,-a I *adj* milk, dairy; **central lechera**, dairy co-operative; **vaca lechera**, milk cow. II *nm* milkman.

lecho *nm Lit* bed; **l. del río**, river-bed; **l. mortuorio**, deathbed.

lechón *nm* sucking pig.

lechoso,-a *adj* milky.

lechuga *nf* lettuce.

lechuza *nf* owl.

lectivo,-a *adj* school; **horas lectivas**, teaching hours.

lector,-a I *nm,f 1 (persona)* reader. 2 *Univ* lector, (language) assistant. II *nm* **l. de microfichas**, *(aparato)* microfile reader.

lectura *nf* reading.

leer [36] *vtr* to read; **léenos el menú**, read out the menu for us; *fig* **l. entre líneas**, to read between the lines.

legado *nm (herencia)* legacy.

legajo *nm* bundle of papers.

legal *adj 1 Jur* legal, lawful; **requisitos legales**, legal formalities. 2 *fam (persona)* honest, trustworthy.

legalidad *nf* legality, lawfulness.

legalizar [4] vtr to legalize; (documento) to authenticate.

legaña nf sleep.

legar [7] vtr (propiedad etc) to bequeath; fig (tradiciones etc) to hand down, pass on.

legendario,-a adj legendary.

legión nf legion.

legionela nf legionnaire's disease.

legislación nf legislation.

legislar vi to legislate.

legislativo,-a adj legislative; **el poder l.**, parliament.

legislatura nf legislature.

legitimar vtr to legitimize; (legalizar) to legalize.

legitimidad nf Jur legitimacy; (licitud) justice.

legítimo,-a adj 1 Jur legitimate; **en legítima defensa**, in self-defence. 2 (auténtico) authentic, real; **oro l.**, pure gold.

lego,-a I adj Rel lay. II nm 1 layman; **ser l. en la materia**, to be a layman in the subject. 2 Rel lay brother.

legua nf (medida) league; fig **se nota a la l.**, it stands out a mile.

legumbres nfpl pulses.

lejanía nf distance.

lejano,-a adj distant, far-off; **parientes lejanos**, distant relatives; **el L. Oriente**, the Far East.

lejía nf bleach.

lejos adv far (away); **a lo l.**, in the distance; **de l.**, from a distance; fig **ir demasiado l.**, to go too far; fig **llegar l.**, to go a long way; fig **sin ir más l.**, to take an obvious example.

lelo,-a fam I adj stupid, silly. II nm,f ninny.

lema nm 1 (divisa) motto, slogan. 2 (contraseña) code name.

lencería nf 1 (prendas) lingerie. 2 (ropa blanca) linen (goods pl).

lendakari nm head of the Basque government.

lengua nf 1 tongue; fig **malas lenguas**, gossips; fam fig **irse de la l.**, to spill the beans; fam fig **tirarle a algn de la l.**, to try to draw sth out of sb. 2 Ling language; **l. materna**, native o mother tongue.

lenguado nm (pez) sole.

lenguaje nm language; Inform language; **l. corporal**, body language.

lengüeta nf 1 (de zapato) tongue. 2 Mús reed.

lente nmf lens; Opt **l. de contacto**, contact lenses.

lenteja nf lentil.

lentejuela nf sequin, spangle.

lentilla nf contact lens.

lentitud nf slowness; **con l.**, slowly.

lento,-a adj slow; **a fuego l.**, on a low heat.

leña nf 1 firewood; fig **echar l. al fuego**,

to add fuel to the fire. 2 fam (golpes) knocks pl.

leñazo nm arg (golpe) blow, smash.

leñe interj fam damn it!

leño nm 1 log. 2 fam (persona) blockhead, half-wit.

león nm lion.

leona nf lioness.

leonera nf lion's den; fig (habitación) den.

leopardo nm leopard.

leotardos nmpl thick tights.

lepra nf leprosy.

leproso,-a I adj leprous. II nm,f leper.

les I pron pers mfpl (objeto indirecto) (a ellos,-as) them; (a ustedes) you; **dales el dinero**, give them the money; **les he comprado un regalo**, I've bought you a present. II pron pers mpl (objeto directo) (ellos) them; (ustedes) you; **l. esperaré**, I shall wait for you; **no quiero molestarles**, I don't wish to disturb you.

lesbiana nf lesbian.

lesión nf 1 (corporal) injury. 2 Jur (perjuicio) damage.

lesionar vtr to injure.

leso,-a adj Jur **crimen de lesa humanidad**, crime against humanity.

letal adj lethal, deadly.

letanía nf litany.

letargo nm lethargy.

letón,-ona I adj Latvian. II nm,f Latvian. III nm (idioma) Latvian, Lettish.

Letonia n Latvia.

letra nf 1 letter; **l. de imprenta**, block capitals; **l. mayúscula** capital letter; **l. minúscula** small letter; **l. pequeña**, small print. 2 (escritura) (hand)writing. 3 Mús (texto) lyrics pl, words pl. 4 Fin **l. (de cambio)**, bill of exchange, draft. 5 Univ **letras**, arts.

letrado,-a nm,f lawyer.

letrero nm (aviso) notice, sign; (cartel) poster; **l. luminoso**, neon sign.

leucemia nf leukaemia, US leukemia.

levadizo,-a adj **puente l.**, drawbridge.

levadura nf yeast; **l. en polvo**, baking powder.

levantamiento nm 1 raising, lifting; Dep **l. de pesos**, weightlifting. 2 (insurrección) uprising, insurrection.

levantar I vtr 1 to raise, lift; (mano, voz) to raise; (edificio) to erect; fig (ánimos) to raise; **l. los ojos**, to look up. 2 (castigo) to suspend. II vr 1 (ponerse de pie) to stand up, rise. 2 (salir de la cama) to get up. 3 (concluir) to finish; **se levanta la sesión**, the meeting is closed. 4 Pol to rise, revolt; **l. en armas**, to rise up in arms. 5 (viento) to come up; (tormenta) to gather.

levante nm (el) **L.**, Levante, the regions of Valencia and Murcia. 2 (viento) east wind, Levanter.

levar vtr **l. ancla**, to weigh anchor.

leve *adj* (*ligero*) light; *fig* (*de poca importancia*) slight. ◆**levemente** *adv* slightly.

levedad *nf* (*ligereza*) lightness; *fig* slightness; *fig* (*de ánimo*) levity; **heridas de l.**, minor injuries.

levitar *vi* to levitate.

léxico Ling I *nm* (*diccionario*) lexicon; (*vocabulario*) vocabulary, word list. II *adj* lexical.

ley *nf* 1 law; *Parl* bill, act; **aprobar una l.**, to pass a bill. 2 **oro de l.**, pure gold; **plata de l.**, sterling silver.

leyenda *nf* 1 (*relato*) legend. 2 (*en un mapa*) legend; (*en una moneda*) inscription; (*bajo ilustración*) caption.

liar [29] *vtr* 1 (*envolver*) to wrap up; (*un cigarrillo*) to roll. 2 (*enredar*) to muddle up; (*confundir*) to confuse. II **liarse** *vr* 1 (*embarullarse*) to get muddled up. 2 *fam* (*salir con*) to get involved; (*besarse*) to neck. 3 **l. a bofetadas**, to come to blows.

libanés,-esa *adj & nm,f* Lebanese.

Líbano *n* **el L.**, the Lebanon.

libelo *nm* (*difamación*) lampoon, satire.

libélula *nf* dragonfly.

liberación *nf* (*de país*) liberation; (*de rehén*) release, freeing.

liberal I *adj* 1 liberal; (*carácter*) open-minded; *Pol* **Partido L.**, Liberal Party; **profesión l.**, profession. 2 (*generoso*) generous, liberal. II *nmf* liberal.

liberalizar [4] *vtr* to liberalize.

liberar *vtr* (*país*) to liberate; (*prisionero*) to free, release.

líbero *nm* *Ftb* sweeper.

libertad *nf* freedom, liberty; **en l.**, free; *Jur* (**en**) **l. bajo palabra/fianza**, (on) parole/bail; *Jur* (**en**) **l. condicional**, (on) parole; **l. de comercio**, free trade; **l. de expresión**, freedom of speech.

libertador,-a *nm,f* liberator.

libertar *vtr* to set free, release.

libertinaje *nm* licentiousness.

libertino,-a *adj & nm,f* libertine.

Libia *n* Libya.

libio,-a *adj & nm,f* Libyan.

libra *nf* (*moneda, peso*) pound; **l. esterlina**, pound sterling.

librador,-a *nm,f* *Fin* drawer.

librar I *vtr* 1 to free; *Jur* to free, release. 2 *Com* (*una letra*) to draw. 3 **l. batalla**, to do ◊ join battle. II **vi libro los martes**, (*no ir a trabajar*) I have Tuesdays off. III **librarse** *vr* to escape; **l. de algn**, to get rid of sb.

libre *adj* free; **entrada l.**, (*gratis*) admission free; (*sin restricción*) open to the public; **l. cambio**, free trade; **l. de impuestos**, tax-free.

librecambio, librecambismo *nm* free trade.

librería *nf* 1 (*tienda*) bookshop, *US* bookstore. 2 (*estante*) bookcase.

librero,-a *nm,f* bookseller.

libreta *nf* notebook; **l.** (**de ahorro**), savings book.

libro *nm* book; **l. de texto**, textbook; *Com* **l. de caja**, cashbook; *Fin* **l. mayor**, ledger.

licencia *nf* 1 (*permiso*) permission; (*documentos*) permit, licence, *US* license; **l. de armas/caza**, gun/hunting licence. 2 (*libertad abusiva*) licence, *US* license, licentiousness. 3 *Am Aut* driving licence, *US* driver's license.

licenciado,-a *nm,f* 1 *Univ* graduate; **l. en Ciencias**, Bachelor of Science. 2 *Am* lawyer.

licenciar [12] I *vtr* 1 *Mil* to discharge. 2 *Univ* to confer a degree on. II **licenciarse** *vr Univ* to graduate.

licenciatura *nf Univ* (*título*) (bachelor's) degree (course); (*carrera*) degree (course).

liceo *nm* 1 (*sociedad literaria*) literary society. 2 (*escuela*) secondary school.

licitar *vtr Com* (*pujar*) to bid for.

lícito,-a *adj* (*permisible*) allowed; *Jur* lawful.

licor *nm* liquor, spirits *pl*, *US* licor.

licuadora *nf* liquidizer.

licuar [10] *vtr* to liquidize.

lid *nf* (*combate*) contest.

líder *nmf* leader.

liderar *vtr* to lead, head.

liderato, liderazgo *nm* leadership; *Dep* top ◊ first position.

lidia *nf* (*de toros*) bullfighting.

lidiador *nm* bullfighter.

lidiar [12] I *vtr Taur* to fight. II *vi* to fight; **l. con**, to contend with, fight against.

liebre *nf* 1 hare. 2 *Dep* pacemaker.

liendre *nf* nit.

lienzo *nm* 1 *Tex* linen. 2 *Arte* canvas.

lifting *nm* facelift.

liga *nf* 1 *Dep Pol* league; **hacer buena l.**, to get on well together. 2 (*prenda*) garter.

ligamento *nm* ligament.

ligar [7] I *vtr* 1 to join; *fig* (*dos personas*) to unite. 2 *fam* (*coger*) to get. II *vi fam* (*seducir*) to get off with sb. III **ligarse** *vr* (*vincularse*) to become attached (**a**, to).

ligazón *nf* bond, tie.

ligereza *nf* 1 lightness; (*de tela, argumento*) flimsiness. 2 (*frivolidad*) flippancy; (*acto*) indiscretion; (*dicho*) indiscreet remark. 3 (*rapidez*) speed.

ligero,-a *adj* 1 (*peso*) light, lightweight; **l. de ropa**, lightly clad. 2 (*ágil*) light on one's feet; (*veloz*) swift, quick. 3 (*leve*) slight; **brisa/comida ligera**, light breeze/meal. 4 **a la ligera**, lightly. II *adv* **ligero** (*rápido*) fast, swiftly. ◆**ligeramente** *adv* 1 (*levemente*) lightly. 2 (*un poco*) slightly.

light *adj inv* (*tabaco*) mild; *fig* (*persona*) lightweight.

ligón,-ona *adj & nm,f fam* (hombre) ladies' man; **es muy ligona**, she's hot stuff.

ligue *nm* pick-up.

liguero,-a I *adj Dep* league; **partido l.**, league match. II *nm* suspenders *pl, US* garter belt.

lija *nf* sandpaper; **papel de l.**, sandpaper.

lijar *vtr* to sand *o* sandpaper (down).

lila[1] *adj inv & nf* lilac.

lila[2] *fam* I *adj* (tonto) dumb, stupid. II *nmf* (tonto) twit.

lima[1] *nf* (fruto) lime.

lima[2] *nf* (herramienta) file; **l. de uñas**, nailfile.

limar *vtr* to file; *fig* **l. asperezas**, to smooth things over.

limbo *nm* limbo.

limitación *nf* limitation; **l. de velocidad**, speed limit.

limitar I *vtr* to limit, restrict. II *vi* to border; **l. con**, to border on.

límite *nm* limit; *Geog Pol* boundary, border; **caso l.**, borderline case; **fecha l.**, deadline; **velocidad l.**, maximum speed.

limítrofe *adj* neighbouring, *US* neighboring.

limo *nm* slime.

limón *nm* lemon.

limonada *nf* lemonade.

limonada *nf* lemon squash.

limonero *nm* lemon tree.

limosna *nf* alms; **pedir l.**, to beg.

limpiabotas *nm inv* bootblack, shoeshine.

limpiacristales *nm inv* window cleaner.

limpiador,-a I *adj* cleansing. II *nm,f* (persona) cleaner. III *nm* (producto) cleaner.

limpiaparabrisas *nm inv* windscreen *o US* windshield wiper.

limpiar [12] *vtr* I to clean; (con un trapo) to wipe; (zapatos) to polish; *fig* to cleanse. 2 *fam* (hurtar) to pinch, nick.

limpieza *nf* (calidad) cleanliness; (acción) cleaning; *fig* (integridad) integrity; **con l.**, cleanly.

limpio,-a I *adj* (aseado) clean. 2 *Dep* **juego l.**, fair play. 3 *Fin* (neto) net; **beneficios en l.**, net profit. 4 *fam* **pasar algo a l.** to produce a fair copy of sth. II *adv fam* fairly; **jugar l.**, to play fair.

linaje *nm* lineage.

linaza *nf* **aceite de l.**, linseed oil.

lince *nm* lynx; **tiene ojos de l.**, he's eagle-eyed.

linchar *vtr* to lynch; *fam* (pegar) to beat up.

lindante *adj* bordering.

lindar *vi* **l. con**, to border on.

linde *nmf* boundary, limit.

lindero,-a I *adj* bordering, adjoining. II *nm* boundary.

lindo,-a I *adj* (bonito) pretty, lovely; **de lo l.**, a great deal. II *adv Am* (bien) nicely.

línea *nf* line; **l. aérea**, airline; **en líneas generales**, roughly speaking; *Inform* **fuera de l.**, off-line; **en l.**, on-line.

guardar la l., to watch one's figure.

lineal *adj* linear; **dibujo l.**, line drawing.

lingote *nm* ingot; (de oro, plata) bar.

lingüista *nmf* linguist.

lino *nm* 1 *Bot* flax. 2 *Tex* linen.

linterna *nf* torch.

lío *nm* 1 (paquete) bundle. 2 *fam* (embrollo) mess, muddle; **hacerse un l.**, to get mixed up; **meterse en líos**, to get into trouble; **armar un l.**, to kick up a fuss. 3 *fam* (relación amorosa) affair.

lioso,-a *adj fam* (asunto) confusing.

lipotimia *nf* fainting fit.

liquidación *nf* 1 *Com* (saldo) clearance sale. 2 *Fin* liquidation.

liquidar I *vtr Com* (deuda, cuenta) to settle; (mercancías) to sell off. II *vr* 1 *fam* (gastar) to spend. 2 *fam* **l. a algn**, (matar) to bump sb off.

liquidez *nf Fin* liquidity.

líquido,-a I *adj* 1 liquid. 2 *Fin* net. II *nm* 1 (fluido) liquid. 2 *Fin* liquid assets *pl*; **l. imponible**, taxable income.

lira *nf* (moneda) lira.

lírico,-a *adj* lyrical.

lirio *nm* iris.

lirismo *nm* lyricism.

lirón *nm* dormouse; *fig* **dormir como un l.**, to sleep like a log.

Lisboa *n* Lisbon.

lisiado,-a I *adj* crippled. II *nm,f* cripple.

lisiar [12] *vtr* to maim, cripple.

liso,-a *adj* 1 (superficie) smooth, even; *Dep* **los cien metros lisos**, the one hundred metres sprint. 2 (pelo, falda) straight. 3 (tela) self-coloured. 4 *Am* (desvergonzado) rude. II *adv* **lisa y llanamente**, purely and simply.

lisonjero,-a I *adj* flattering. II *nm,f* flatterer.

lista *nf* 1 (relación) list; **l. de espera**, waiting list; (en avión) standby; **pasar l.**, to call the register *o* the roll. 2 (franja) stripe; **de/a listas**, striped.

listado,-a I *adj* striped. II *nm* list; *Inform* listing.

listín *nm* **l. telefónico**, telephone directory.

listo,-a *adj* 1 **ser l.**, (inteligente) to be clever, smart. 2 **estar l.**, (a punto) to be ready.

listón *nm Dep* bar; *fig* **subir el l.**, to raise the requirements level.

litera *nf* (cama) bunk bed; (en tren) couchette.

literal *adj* literal.

literario,-a *adj* literary.

literato,-a *nm,f* writer, man *o* woman of letters.

literatura *nf* literature.

litigar [7] *vi Jur* to litigate.

litigio *nm Jur* lawsuit; *fig* dispute; **en l.**, in dispute.

litografía *nf* 1 (técnica) lithography. 2

(*imagen*) lithograph.

litoral I *nm* coast, seaboard. **II** *adj* coastal.

litro *nm* litre, *US* liter.

liturgia *nf* liturgy.

liviano,-a *adj* (*de poco peso*) lightweight.

lívido,-a *adj* livid.

liza *nf* contest.

llaga *nf* sore; (*herida*) wound.

llama *nf* flame; **en llamas,** in flames, ablaze.

llamada *nf* call; **l. interurbana,** long-distance call; **señal de l.,** ringing tone.

llamado,-a *adj* so-called.

llamamiento *nm* appeal.

llamar I *vtr* **1** to call; **l.** (*por teléfono*) to ring up, call. **2** (*atraer*) to draw, attract; **l. la atención,** to attract attention. **II** *vi* (*a la puerta*) to knock. **III llamarse** *vr* to be called; **¿cómo te llamas?,** what's your name?

llamarada *nf* blaze.

llamativo,-a *adj* **1** (*color, ropa*) loud, flashy. **2** (*persona*) striking.

llaneza *nf* (*sencillez*) simplicity.

llano,-a I *adj* **1** (*superficie*) flat, level. **2** (*claro*) clear. **3** (*sencillo*) simple; **el pueblo l.,** the common people. **II** *nm* plain.

llanta *nf* **1** (*de rueda*) wheel rim. **2** *Am* (*neumático*) tyre, *US* tire.

llanto *nm* crying, weeping.

llanura *nf* plain.

llave *nf* **1** key; **cerrar con l.,** to lock; **llaves en mano,** (*en anuncio*) available for immediate occupation; **Aut l. de contacto,** ignition key. **2** *Téc* spanner; **l. inglesa,** adjustable spanner. **3** (*interruptor*) switch; **l. de paso,** stopcock. **4** (*en lucha*) lock. **5** *Tip* brace.

llavero *nm* key ring.

llegada *nf* arrival; *Dep* finish.

llegar [7] **I** *vi* **1** to arrive; **l. a Madrid,** to arrive in Madrid. **2** (*ser bastante*) to be enough. **3** (*alcanzar*) to reach; **¿llegas al techo?,** can you reach the ceiling? **4** *fig* **l. a las manos,** to come to blows; **l. a presidente...,** to become president. **5 l. a +** *inf.,* to go so far as to. **6 l. a ser,** to become. **II llegarse** *vr* to stop by.

llenar I *vtr* **1** to fill; (*cubrir*) to cover. **2** (*satisfacer*) to satisfy. **II** *vi* (*comida*) to be filling. **III llenarse** *vr* to fill (up), become full.

lleno,-a I *adj* full (up); *fig* **de l.,** fully. **II** *nm Teat* full house.

llevadero,-a *adj* bearable, tolerable.

llevar I *vtr* **1** to take; (*hacia el oyente*) to bring; **¿adónde llevas eso?,** where are you taking that?; **te llevaré un regalo,** I'll bring you a present. **2** (*transportar*) to carry; **dejarse l.,** to get carried away. **3** (*prenda*) to wear; **llevaba falda,** she was wearing a skirt. **4** (*soportar*) to bear; **¿cómo lleva lo de su enfermedad?,** how's he bearing up? **5** (*tiempo*) **llevo dos**

años aquí, I've been here for two years; **esto lleva mucho tiempo,** this takes a long time. **6** (*negocio*) to be in charge of. **II** *v aux* **1 l. +** *gerundio,* to have been + present participle; **llevo dos años estudiando español,** I've been studying Spanish for two years. **2 l. +** *participio pasado,* to have + past participle; **llevaba escritas seis cartas,** I had written six letters. **III llevarse** *vr* **1** to take away; (*premio*) to win; (*recibir*) to get. **2** (*arrastrar*) to carry away. **3** (*estar de moda*) to be fashionable. **4 l. bien con algn,** to get on well with sb.

llorar *vi* to cry; *Lit* weep.

llorica *nmf fam* crybaby.

lloriquear *vi* to whimper, snivel.

llorón,-ona *adj* **un bebé l.,** a baby which cries a lot.

lloroso,-a *adj* tearful.

llover [4] *v impers* to rain.

llovizna *nf* drizzle.

lloviznar *v impers* to drizzle.

lluvia *nf* rain; **una l. de,** lots of; **l. radiactiva,** fallout; **l. ácida,** acid rain.

lluvioso,-a *adj* rainy.

lo¹ *art det neut* the; **lo mejor,** the best (part); **lo mismo,** the same thing; **lo mío,** mine; **lo tuyo,** yours.

lo² *pron pers m & neut* **1** (*cosa*) it; **debes hacerlo,** you must do it; **no lo creo,** I don't think so; (*no se traduce*) **no se lo dije,** I didn't tell her; → **l. 2 lo que ...,** what ...; **no sé lo que pasa,** I don't know what's going on. **3 lo cual ...,** which ... **4 lo de ...,** the business of ...; **cuéntame lo del juicio,** tell me about the trial.

loable *adj* praiseworthy, laudable.

loar *vtr* to praise.

lobo *nm* wolf; **como boca de l.,** pitch-dark; *fam* **¡menos lobos!,** pull the other one!

lóbrego,-a *adj* gloomy.

lóbulo *nm* lobe.

local I *adj* local. **II** *nm* (*recinto*) premises *pl,* site.

localidad *nf* **1** (*pueblo*) locality; (*en impreso*) place of residence. **2** *Cin Teat* (*asiento*) seat; (*entrada*) ticket.

localizar [4] *vtr* **1** (*encontrar*) to find. **2** (*fuego, dolor*) to localize.

loción *nf* lotion.

loco,-a I *adj* mad, crazy; **a lo l.,** crazily; **l. por,** crazy about; **volverse l.,** to go mad; *fam* **¡ni l.!,** I'd sooner die! **II** *nm,f* madman, madwoman; **hacerse el l.,** to act the fool.

locomotora *nf* locomotive.

locomotriz *adj* locomotive.

locuaz *adj* loquacious, talkative.

locución *nf* phrase.

locura *nf* (*enfermedad*) madness, insanity; **con l.,** madly; *fam* **esto es una l.,** this is crazy.

locutor,-a *nm,f TV Rad* presenter.

locutorio *nm* telephone booth.

lodo *nm* mud.

logaritmo *nm* logarithm.

lógica *nf* logic; **no tiene l.**, there's no logic to it.

lógico,-a *adj* logical; **era l. que ocurriera**, it was bound to happen.

logística *nf* logistics *sing o pl*.

logotipo *nm* logo.

lograr *vtr* 1 to get, obtain; *(premio)* to win; *(ambición)* to achieve. 2 **l. hacer algo**, to manage to do something.

logro *nm* achievement.

loma *nf* hillock, rise.

lombriz *nf* worm, earthworm.

lomo *nm* 1 back; **a lomo(s)**, on the back. 2 *Culin* loin. 3 *(de libro)* spine.

lona *nf* canvas.

loncha *nf* slice; **l. de bacon**, rasher.

lonchería *nf Am* snack bar.

londinense I *adj o* from London. II *nmf* native o inhabitant of London.

Londres *n* London.

longaniza *nf* spicy (pork) sausage.

longevo,-a *adj* long lived.

longitud *nf* 1 length; **dos metros de l.**, two metres long; **l. de onda**, wavelength; *Dep* **salto de l.**, long jump. 2 *Geog* longitude.

lonja¹ *nf (loncha)* slice; **l. de bacon**, rasher.

lonja² *nf* **l. de pescado**, fish market.

loquería *nf Am* mental asylum, mental hospital.

lord *nm (pl* **lores***)* lord; *GB Parl* **Cámara de los Lores**, House of Lords.

loro *nm* parrot.

los¹ I *art def mpl* the; **l. libros**, the books; **cierra l. ojos**, close your eyes; **l. García, los Garcías**; → **el, las y lo**. II *pron* 1 **l. que**, *(personas)* those who; *(cosas)* the ones (that); **toma l. que quieras**, take whichever ones you want; **esos son l. míos/tuyos**, these are mine/yours; → **les**.

los² *pron pers mpl* them; **¿l. has visto?**, have you seen them?

losa *nf (stone)* slab, flagstone.

lote *nm* 1 set. 2 *Com* lot. 3 *Inform* batch. 4 *fam* **darse el l.**, to pet.

lotería *nf* lottery; **me tocó la l.**, I won a prize in the lottery.

loto *nm* 1 *Bot* lotus. 2 *(lotería)* lottery.

loza *nf* 1 *(material)* earthenware. 2 *(de cocina)* crockery.

lozano,-a *adj* 1 *(persona)* healthy looking. 2 *(plantas)* lush, luxuriant.

Ltda. *abr de* **Limitada**, Limited, Ltd.

lubricante *nm* lubricant.

lubricar [1] *vtr* to lubricate.

lucero *nm* (bright) star.

lucidez *nf* lucidity.

lúcido,-a *adj* lucid, clear.

luciérnaga *nf* glow-worm.

lucir [35] I *vi* 1 *(brillar)* to shine. 2 *fam (compensar)* **no le luce lo que estudia**, his studies don't get him anywhere. II *vtr (ropas)* to sport; *(talento)* to display. III **lucirse** *vr* 1 *(hacer buen papel)* to do very well. 2 *(pavonearse)* to show off.

lucrativo,-a *adj* lucrative, profitable.

lucro *nm* profit; gain; **afán de l.**, greed for money.

lucha *nf* 1 fight, struggle; **l. de clases**, class struggle. 2 *Dep* wrestling; **l. libre**, free-style wrestling.

luchador,-a *nm,f* 1 fighter. 2 *Dep* wrestler.

luchar *vi* 1 to fight, struggle. 2 *Dep* to wrestle.

lúdico,-a *adj* relating to games, recreational.

luego I *adv* 1 *(después)* then, next, afterwards. 2 *(más tarde)* later (on); **¡hasta l.!**, so long!; *Am* l. de, after. 3 **desde l.**, of course. II *conj* therefore.

lugar *nm* 1 place; **en primer l.**, in the first place; **en l. de**, instead of; **sin l. a dudas**, without a doubt; **tener l.**, to take place. 2 **dar l. a**, to cause, give rise to.

lugareño,-a *adj & nm,f* local.

lugarteniente *nmf* lieutenant.

lúgubre *adj* gloomy, lugubrious.

lujo *nm* luxury; **productos de l.**, luxury products; **no puedo permitirme ese l.**, I can't afford that.

lujoso,-a *adj* luxurious.

lujuria *nf* lechery, lust.

lujurioso,-a *adj* lecherous, lustful.

lumbre *nf* fire.

lumbrera *nf* luminary.

luminoso,-a *adj* luminous; *fig* bright.

luna *nf* 1 moon; *fig* **estar en la l.**, to have one's head in the clouds; **l. creciente/llena**, crescent/full moon; *fig* **l. de miel**, honeymoon. 2 *(de escaparate)* pane; *(espejo)* mirror.

lunar *nm (redondel)* dot; *(en la piel)* mole, beauty spot; **vestido de lunares**, spotted dress.

lunar *adj* lunar.

lunático,-a *adj & nm,f* lunatic.

lunes *nm inv* Monday; **vendré el l.**, I'll come on Monday.

lupa *nf* magnifying glass.

luso,-a *adj & nm,f* Portuguese.

lustrar *vtr* to polish; *(zapatos)* to shine.

lustre *nm (brillo)* shine, lustre, *US* luster; *fig (esplendor)* splendour, *US* splendor, glory; **dar o sacar l. a algo**, to polish sth.

lustro *nm* five-year period.

lustroso,-a *adj* shiny, glossy.

luto *nm* mourning.

Luxemburgo *n* Luxembourg.

luz *nf* 1 light; **apagar la l.**, to put out the light; **a la l. de**, in the light of; **a todas luces**, obviously; *fig* **dar a l.**, *(parir)* to give birth to; *fig* **dar l. verde a,** to give the green light to. 2 *Aut* light; **luces de cruce,** dipped headlights; **luces de posición,** sidelights; **l. larga,** headlights *pl.* 3

luces, (*inteligencia*) intelligence *sing*; **corto de l.,** dim-witted. 4 traje de luces, bullfighter's costume.

luzco *indic pres* → lucir.

M

M, m ['eme] *nf* (*la letra*) M, m.

m 1 *abr de* metro(s), metre, metres, *US* meter, meters, m. 2 *abr de* minuto(s), minute, minutes, min. 3 *abr de* milla(s), mile, miles.

macabro,-a *adj* macabre.

macana *nf* 1 *Am* (*palo*) club. 2 (*trasto*) rubbish.

macanear *vtr Am* (*paparruchas*) to make up.

macanudo,-a *adj fam* great, terrific.

macarra *nm arg* yob.

macarrón *nm* 1 macaroon. 2 *Elec* sheath.

macarrones *nmpl* macaroni *sing*.

macedonia *nf* fruit salad.

macerar *vtr* to macerate.

maceta *nf* (*tiesto*) plant pot, flowerpot.

machacar [1] I *vtr* 1 to crush; *Dep* to smash. 2 *fam* (*estudiar con ahínco*) to swot up on, *US* grind away at. 3 *fam* (*insistir en*) to harp on about, go on about. II *vi* 1 *fam* (*insistir mucho*) to harp on, go on. 2 *fam* (*estudiar con ahínco*) to swot, cram, *US* grind. 3 (*en baloncesto*) to smash.

machacón,-ona *fam* I *adj* (*repetitivo*) repetitious; (*pesado*) boring, tiresome. II *nm,f* (*muy estudioso*) swot, *US* grind.

machamartillo (a) *loc adv* (*con firmeza*) firmly; (*con obstinación*) obstinately.

machete *nm* machete.

machismo *nm* machismo, male chauvinism.

machista *adj & nm* male chauvinist.

macho I *adj* 1 (*animal, planta*) male. 2 *fam* (*viril*) manly, virile, macho. II *nm* 1 (*animal, planta*) male. 2 *Téc* (*pieza*) male piece *o* part; (*de enchufe*) plug. 3 *fam* (*hombre viril*) macho, he-man, tough guy.

machote *nm Am* (*borrador*) rough draft.

macilento,-a *adj* gaunt.

macizo,-a *adj* 1 (*sólido*) solid; **de oro m.,** of solid gold. 2 (*robusto*) solid, robust; *fam* (*atractivo*) well built. II *nm* (*masa sólida*) mass.

macramé *nm* macramé.

macro- *pref* macro-.

macro *nf Inform* macro.

macroeconomía *nf* macroeconomics *sing*.

macuto *nm* (*moral*) knapsack, haversack.

madeja *nf* (*de lana, hilo*) hank, skein.

madera *nf* 1 wood; (*de construcción*) timber, *US* lumber; **de m.,** wood, wooden. 2 *fig* **tiene m. de líder,** he has all the makings of a leader.

madero *nm* 1 (*de construcción*) timber; (*le-*

ño) log. 2 *arg* (*policía*) cop; **los maderos,** the fuzz *pl*.

madrastra *nf* stepmother.

madre I *nf* 1 mother; **es m. de tres hijos,** she is a mother of three (children); **m. adoptiva,** adoptive mother; **m. alquilada,** surrogate mother; **m. de familia,** mother, housewife; **m. política,** mother-in-law; **m. soltera,** unmarried mother; *fig* **la m. patria,** one's motherland. 2 (*de río*) bed. II *interj* **¡m. de Dios!, ¡m. mía!,** good heavens!

madreperla *nf* (*nácar*) mother-of-pearl.

madreselva *nf* honeysuckle.

Madrid *n* Madrid.

madriguera *nf* burrow, hole.

madrileño,-a I *adj of o* from Madrid. II *nm,f* native *o* inhabitant of Madrid.

madrina *nf* 1 (*de bautizo*) godmother. 2 (*de boda*) ≈ bridesmaid. 3 *fig* (*protectora*) protectress.

madrugada *nf* 1 dawn; **de m.,** in the wee small hours. 2 early morning; **las tres de la m.,** three o'clock in the morning.

madrugador,-a I *adj* early rising. II *nm,f* early riser.

madrugar [7] *vi* to get up early.

madurar I *vtr fig* (*un plan*) to think out. II *vi* 1 (*persona*) to mature. 2 (*fruta*) to ripen.

madurez *nf* 1 maturity. 2 (*de la fruta*) ripeness.

maduro,-a *adj* 1 mature; **de edad madura,** middle-aged. 2 (*fruta*) ripe.

maestría *nf* mastery; **con m.,** masterfully.

maestro,-a I *nm,f* 1 *Educ* teacher; **m. de escuela,** schoolteacher. 2 (*especialista*) master; **m. de obras,** foreman. 3 *Mús* maestro. II *adj* obra maestra, masterpiece; **llave maestra,** master key.

mafia *nf* mafia.

mafioso,-a I *adj of o* relating to the mafia. II *nm,f* member of the mafia, mafioso.

magdalena *nf* bun, cake.

magia *nf* magic; **por arte de m.,** as if by magic.

mágico,-a *adj* 1 magic. 2 *fig* (*maravilloso*) magical, wonderful.

magisterio *nm* teaching.

magistrado,-a *nm,f* judge; *Am* primer m., prime minister.

magistral *adj* (*excelente*) masterly; **una jugada m.,** a master stroke.

magistratura *nf* magistracy.

magnánimo,-a *adj* magnanimous.

magnate *nm* magnate, tycoon.

magnesio *nm* magnesium.

magnético,-a *adj* magnetic.

magnetizar [4] *vtr* 1 (*imantar*) to magnetize. 2 *fig* (*hipnotizar*) to hypnotize.

magnetofón, magnetófono *nm* tape recorder.

magnetofónico,-a *adj* magnetic.

magnífico,-a *adj* magnificent, splendid.

magnitud *nf* magnitude, dimension; **de primera m.**, of the first order.

magno,-a *adj lit* great; **aula magna**, main amphitheatre.

mago,-a *nm,f* wizard, magician; **los tres Reyes Magos**, the Three Wise Men, the Three Kings.

magrear *vtr vulg* to grope.

magro,-a I *nm* (*de cerdo*) lean meat. II *adj* (*sin grasa*) lean.

magullar I *vtr* to bruise, damage. II **magullarse** *vr* to get bruised, get damaged.

mahometano,-a *adj & nm,f Rel* Mohammedan, Muslim.

mahonesa *nf* mayonnaise.

maillot *nm* (*malla*) leotard; *Dep* shirt.

maíz *nm* maize, *US* corn.

maizal *nm* field of maize *o US* corn.

majadería *nf* silly thing, absurdity.

majadero,-a *nm,f* fool, idiot.

majara, majareta *adj fam* loony, nutty.

majestad *nf* majesty.

majestuosidad *nf* majesty.

majestuoso,-a *adj* majestic, stately.

majo,-a *adj* (*bonito*) pretty, nice; *fam* (*simpático*) nice; **tiene un hijo muy m.**, she's got a lovely little boy; *fam* **ven aquí, m.**, come here, dear.

mal I *nm* 1 evil, wrong. 2 (*daño*) harm; **no le deseo ningún m.**, I don't wish him any harm. 3 (*enfermedad*) illness, disease. II *adj* bad; **un m. año**, a bad year; → **malo,-a**. III *adv* badly, wrong; **lo hizo muy m.**, he did it very badly; **menos m. que ...,** it's a good job (that) ...; **no está (nada) m.**, it is not bad (at all); **te oigo/ veo (muy) m.**, I can hardly hear/see you; **tomar a m.**, (*enfadarse*) to take badly.

malabar *adj* (*juegos*) malabares, juggling *sing*.

malabarista *nmf* juggler.

malapata *nf fam* (*mala suerte*) bad luck.

malaria *nf* malaria.

malcriado,-a I *adj* ill-mannered, ill-bred. II *nm,f* ill-mannered *o* uncivil person.

malcriar [29] *vtr* to spoil.

maldad *nf* 1 badness, evil. 2 (*acción perversa*) evil *o* wicked thing.

maldecir [12] I *vtr* to curse. II *vi* 1 (*blasfemar*) to curse. 2 (*criticar*) to speak ill (**de**, of).

maldición I *nf* curse. II *interj* damnation!

maldito,-a *adj* 1 *fam* (*molesto*) damned, bloody. 2 (*endemoniado*) damned, cursed;

¡maldita sea!, damn it!

maleante *adj & nmf* delinquent, criminal.

malear I *vtr fig* to corrupt, pervert. II **malearse** *vr* to go bad.

maleducado,-a I *adj* bad-mannered. II *nm,f* bad-mannered person.

maleficio *nm* (*hechizo*) curse, spell.

maléfico,-a *adj* evil, harmful.

malentendido *nm* misunderstanding.

malestar *nm* 1 (*molestia*) discomfort. 2 *fig* (*inquietud*) uneasiness; **tengo m.**, I feel uneasy.

maleta I *nf* suitcase, case; **hacer la m.**, to pack one's things *o* case. II *nm fam* (*persona*) bungler.

maletero *nm Aut* boot, *US* trunk.

maletín *nm* briefcase.

malévolo,-a *adj* malevolent.

maleza *nf* 1 (*arbustos*) thicket, undergrowth. 2 (*malas hierbas*) weeds *pl*.

malgastar *vtr & vt* to waste, squander.

malhablado,-a I *adj* foul-mouthed. II *nm,f* foulmouthed person.

malhechor,-a *nm,f* wrongdoer, criminal.

malhumor *nm* bad temper *o* mood; **de m.**, in a bad temper *o* mood.

malicia *nf* 1 (*mala intención*) malice, maliciousness. 2 (*astucia*) cunning, slyness. 3 (*maldad*) badness, evil.

malicioso,-a I *adj* malicious, spiteful. II *nm,f* malicious *o* spiteful person.

maligno,-a *adj* malignant.

malintencionado,-a I *adj* ill-intentioned. II *nm,f* ill-intentioned person.

malla *nf* 1 (*prenda*) leotard. 2 (*red*) mesh. 3 *Am* (*bañador*) swimsuit, swimming costume.

Mallorca *n* Majorca.

mallorquín,-ina *adj & nm,f* Majorcan.

malo,-a I *adj* → **mal**. 1 bad; **un año m.**, a bad year; **estar a malas**, to be on bad terms; **por las malas**, by force. 2 (*persona*) (*malvado*) wicked, bad; (*travieso*) naughty. 3 (*de poca calidad*) bad, poor; **una mala canción/comida**, a poor song/ meal. 4 (*perjudicial*) harmful; **el tabaco es m.**, tobacco is harmful. 5 **lo m. es que ...,** the problem is that .... 6 (*enfermo*) ill, sick. II *nm,f fam* **el m.**, the baddy *o* villain.

malograr I *vtr* to upset. II **malograrse** *vr* to fail, fall through.

maloliente *adj* foul-smelling.

malparado,-a *adj* **salir m.**, to end up in a sorry state.

malpensado,-a I *adj* nasty-minded. II *nm,f* nasty-minded person.

malsonante *adj* (*grosero*) rude, offensive; **palabras malsonantes**, foul language.

malta *nf* (*cebada*) malt.

maltratado,-a *adj* battered.

maltratar *vtr* to ill-treat, mistreat.

maltrecho,-a *adj* in a sorry state, wrecked.

malva I *adj inv* mauve. II *nm* (color) mauve. III *nf Bot* mallow.

malvado,-a I *adj* evil, wicked. II *nm,f* villain, evil person.

malvender *vtr* to sell at a loss.

malversar *vtr* to misappropriate, embezzle.

Malvinas *npl* las (Islas M.), the Falkland Islands.

malvivir *vi* to live very badly.

mamá *nf fam* mum, mummy.

mama *nf* 1 (de mujer) breast; (de animal) teat. 2 *fam* (mamá) mum, mummy.

mamada *nf* 1 (bebé) feed. 2 *vulg* (felatio) blow job.

mamadera *nf Am* feeding bottle.

mamar *vtr* (leche) to suck; *fig* (adquirir) to absorb.

mamarracho,-a *nm,f fam* (persona) ridiculous-looking person, mess, sight; (cosa) mess.

mameluco *nm fig* 1 fool, idiot, dim-wit. 2 *Am* boiler-suit.

mamífero,-a *nm,f* mammal.

mamón *nm vulg ofens* prick.

mampara *nf* screen.

mamporro *nm fam* wallop.

mampostería *nf* masonry.

mamut *nm* mammoth.

manada *nf* 1 *Zool* (de vacas, elefantes) herd; (de ovejas) flock; (de lobos, perros) pack; (de leones) pride. 2 *fam* (multitud) crowd, mob; **en manada(s)**, in crowds.

manager *nmf Dep Mús* manager.

manantial *nm* spring.

manar *vi* to flow, run (de, from). II *vtr* to run with, flow with; **la herida manaba sangre**, blood flowed from his wound.

manazas *nmf inv fam* ham-fisted person.

mancebo *nm* 1 (de farmacia) assistant. 2 *arc* (muchacho) young man.

Mancha (La) *n* La Mancha.

Mancha² *n* el Canal de la M., the English Channel.

mancha *nf* stain, spot; **m. solar**, sunspot; **m. de tinta/vino**, ink/wine stain.

manchado,-a *adj* dirty, stained; **leche manchada**, milky coffee.

manchar I *vtr* to stain, dirty; *fig* to stain, blemish. II **mancharse** *vr* to get dirty.

manchego,-a *adj* of o from La Mancha.

manco,-a *adj* 1 (de un brazo) one-armed; (sin brazos) armless. 2 (de una mano) one-handed; (sin manos) handless. II *nm,f* 1 (de brazos) one-armed o armless person. 2 (de manos) one-handed o handless person.

mancomunidad *nf* community, association.

mancornas *nfpl Am* cufflinks.

mandado *nm* (recado) order, errand; **hacer un m.**, to run an errand.

mandamás *nmf* (pl **mandamases**) *fam* bigwig, boss.

mandamiento *nm* 1 (orden) order, command. 2 **los Diez Mandamientos**, the Ten Commandments.

mandar *vtr* 1 to order; *fam* ¿**mande**?, pardon? 2 (grupo) to lead, be in charge o command of; *Mil* to command. 3 (enviar) to send; **m.** (**a**) **por**, to send for; **m. algo por correo**, to post sth, send sth by the post; **m. recuerdos**, to send regards.

mandarina *nf* mandarin (orange), tangerine.

mandatario,-a *nm,f Pol* president.

mandato *nm* 1 (orden) order, command. 2 *Jur* writ, warrant. 3 *Pol* (legislatura) mandate, term of office.

mandíbula *nf* jaw; *fam* **reír a m. batiente**, to laugh one's head off.

mandil *nm* apron.

mando *nm* 1 (autoridad) command, control. 2 **los altos mandos del ejército**, high-ranking army officers. 3 *Téc* (control) controls *pl*; *Aut* **cuadro o tablero de mandos**, dashboard; **m. a distancia**, remote control; **palanca de m.**, *Téc* control lever; (de avión, videojuego) joystick.

mandón,-ona I *adj fam* bossy, domineering. II *nm,f fam* bossy o domineering person. III *nm Am* (mine) foreman.

manecilla *nf* (de reloj) hand.

manejable *adj* manageable; (herramienta) easy-to-use; (coche) manoeuvrable, *US* maneuvrable.

manejar I *vtr* 1 (máquina) to handle, operate; *fig* (situación) to handle. 2 (negocio) to run, manage. 3 *fig* (a otra persona) to domineer, boss about. 4 (coche) to drive. II **manejarse** *vr* to manage.

manejo *nm* 1 (uso) handling, use; **de fácil m.**, easy-to-use. 2 *fig* (de un negocio) management; (de un coche) driving. 3 *fig* tricks *pl*.

manera *nf* 1 way, manner; **a mi/tu m.**, (in) my/your way; **de cualquier m.**, (mal) carelessly, any old how; (en cualquier caso) in any case; **de esta m.**, in this way; **de ninguna m.**, in no way, certainly not; **de todas maneras**, anyway, at any rate, in any case; **es mi m. de ser**, that's the way I am; **no hay m.**, it's impossible. 2 **de m. que**, so; **de tal m. que**, in such a way that. 3 **maneras**, manners; **de buenas maneras**, politely.

manga *nf* 1 sleeve; **de m. corta/larga**, short-/long-sleeved; **sin mangas**, sleeveless; *fig* **hacer un corte de mangas a algn**, ≈ to give sb the fingers; *fig* **m. por hombro**, messy and untidy; *fig* **sacarse algo de la m.**, to pull sth out of one's hat. 2 (de riego) hose. 3 (del mar) arm. 4 *Dep* leg, round; *Ten* set.

mangante *arg nmf* thief.

mangar [7] *vtr arg* to pinch, nick, swipe.

mango *nm* handle.

mangonear *vi* 1 *fam* (entrometerse) to

meddle. 2 *fam (dar órdenes)* to throw one's weight around.
manguera *nf* hose.
mangui *nmf arg* thief.
manguito *nm* 1 *(para las mangas)* oversleeve; *(para flotar)* armband. 2 *Téc* sleeve.
maní *nm (pl* manises) peanut.
manía *nf* 1 dislike, ill will; **me tiene m.,** he has it in for me. 2 *(costumbre)* habit; **tiene la m. de llegar tarde,** he's always arriving late. 3 *(afición exagerada)* craze; **la m. de las motos,** the motorbike craze. 4 *Med* mania.
maníaco,-a, maníaco,-a *adj & nm,f Psic* manic; *fam (obseso)* maniac.
maniatar *vtr* to tie the hands of.
maniático,-a I *adj* fussy. **II** *nm,f* fusspot.
manicomio *nm* mental hospital.
manicura *nf* manicure.
manido,-a *adj* 1 *(comida)* off. 2 *(asunto)* trite, hackneyed.
manifestación *nf* 1 demonstration. 2 *(expresión)* manifestation, expression.
manifestante *nmf* demonstrator.
manifestar [1] **I** *vtr* 1 *(declarar)* to state, declare. 2 *(mostrar)* to show, display. **II manifestarse** *vr* 1 *(por la calle)* to demonstrate. 2 *(declararse)* to declare oneself; **se manifestó contrario a ...,** he spoke out against ...
manifiesto,-a I *adj* clear, obvious; **poner de m.,** *(revelar)* to reveal, show; *(hacer patente)* to make clear. **II** *nm* manifesto.
manigua *nf Am Geog* scrubland.
manilla *nf* 1 *(de reloj)* hand. 2 *Am (palanca)* lever.
manillar *nm* handlebar.
maniobra *nf* manoeuvre, *US* maneuver.
maniobrar *vi* to manoeuvre, *US* maneuver.
manipulación *nf* manipulation.
manipular *vtr* to manipulate; *(máquina)* to handle.
maniquí *nm (muñeco)* dummy.
manitas *nmf inv fam* 1 **ser un m.,** to be handy, be very good with one's hands. 2 **hacer m.,** to hold hands.
manivela *nf Téc* crank.
manjar *nm* dish, food.
mano *nf* 1 hand; **a m.,** *(sin máquina)* by hand; *(asequible)* at hand; **escrito a m.,** hand-written; **hecho a m.,** hand-made; **a m. armada,** armed; **estrechar la m. a algn,** to shake hands with sb; **de seguida m.,** second-hand; **echar una m. a algn,** to give sb a hand; **¡manos a la obra!,** shoulders to the wheel!; **meter m.,** *(a un problema)* to tackle; *vulg* to touch up; **traerse algo entre manos,** to be up to sth; **equipaje de m.,** hand luggage. 2 *(lado)* side; **a m. derecha/izquierda,** on the right/left(-hand side). 3 **m. de pintura,** coat of paint. 4 **m. de**

obra, labour (force).
manojo *nm* bunch; **ser un m. de nervios,** to be a bundle of nerves.
manopla *nf* mitten.
manoseado,-a *adj (objeto)* worn(-out); *(tema)* hackneyed.
manosear *vtr* to touch repeatedly, finger; *fam* to paw.
manotazo *nm* cuff, slap.
mansalva (a) *loc adv (en gran cantidad)* galore.
mansedumbre *nf* 1 *(de persona)* meekness, gentleness. 2 *(de animal)* tameness, docility.
manso,-a *adj* 1 *(persona)* gentle, meek. 2 *(animal)* tame, docile.
manta I *nf* 1 blanket; **m. eléctrica,** electric blanket. 2 *(zurra)* beating, hiding. **II** *nmf fam* lazy person, idler.
manteca *nf* 1 *(de animal)* fat; **m. de cacao/cacahuete,** cocoa/peanut butter; **m. de cerdo,** lard.
mantecado *nm* shortcake.
mantel *nm* tablecloth.
mantener [24] **I** *vtr* 1 *(conservar)* to keep; **mantén el fuego encendido,** keep the fire burning; **m. la línea,** to keep in trim. 2 *(entrevista, reunión)* to have; **m. correspondencia con algn,** to correspond with sb. 3 *(ideas, opiniones)* to defend, maintain. 4 *(familia)* to support, feed. 5 *(peso)* to support, hold up. **II mantenerse** *vr* 1 *(sostenerse)* to stand. 2 **m. firme,** *(perseverar)* to hold one's ground. 3 *(sustentarse)* to live **(de,** on).
mantenimiento *nm* 1 *Téc* maintenance, upkeep; **servicio de m.,** maintenance service. 2 *(alimento)* sustenance, support. 3 **gimnasia y m.,** keep-fit.
mantequilla *nf* butter.
manto *nm* cloak.
mantón *nm* shawl.
mantuve *pt indef* → **mantener.**
manual I *adj* manual; **trabajo m.,** manual labour; *Educ* **trabajos manuales,** handicrafts. **II** *nm* manual, handbook.
manufactura *nf* 1 *(fabricación)* manufacture. 2 *(fábrica)* factory.
manufacturar *vtr* to manufacture.
manuscrito,-a *nm* manuscript.
manutención *nf* maintenance.
manzana *nf* 1 apple. 2 *(de edificios)* block.
manzanilla *nf* 1 *Bot* camomile. 2 *(infusión)* camomile tea. 3 *(vino)* manzanilla.
maña *nf* 1 *(astucia)* cunning. 2 *(habilidad)* skill.
mañana I *nf* morning; **a las dos de la m.,** at two in the morning; **de m.,** early in the morning; **por la m.,** in the morning. **II** *nm* tomorrow, the future. **III** *adv* tomorrow; **¡hasta m.!,** see you tomorrow! **m. por la m.,** tomorrow morning; **pasado m.,** the day after tomorrow.
mañoso,-a *adj* skilful, *US* skillful.

mapa nm map; **m. mudo**, blank map; *fam* **borrar del m.**, to wipe out.

maqueta nf 1 (*miniatura*) scale model, maquette. 2 *Mús* demo (tape).

maquiavélico,-a adj Machiavellian.

maquillaje nm make-up.

maquillar I vtr to make up. II **maquillarse** vr 1 (*ponerse maquillaje*) to put one's make-up on, make (oneself) up. 2 (*usar maquillaje*) to wear make-up.

máquina nf 1 machine; **escrito a m.**, typewritten; **hecho a m.**, machine-made; *fam* **a toda m.**, at full speed. **m. de afeitar** (*eléctrica*), (electric) razor *o* shaver; **m. de coser**, sewing machine; **m. de escribir**, typewriter; **m. fotográfica** *o* **de fotos**, camera; **m. tragaperras**, slot machine, one-armed bandit. 2 *fam* (*coche*) car.

maquinar vtr to machinate, plot.

maquinaria nf 1 machinery, machines *pl*. 2 (*de reloj etc*) (*mecanismo*) mechanism, works *pl*.

maquinilla nf **m. de afeitar**, safety razor.

maquinista nmf (*de tren*) engine driver.

mar I nm & f 1 sea; **en alta m.**, on the high seas; **m. adentro**, out to sea; **por m.**, by sea; **m. gruesa**, heavy sea; **m. picada**, rough sea. 2 *fam* **está la m. de guapa**, she's looking really beautiful; **llover a mares**, to rain cats and dogs. II nm sea. **M. del Norte**, North Sea; **M. Muerto/Negro**, Dead/Black Sea.

maraña nf tangle.

maratón nm marathon.

maratoniano,-a adj marathon.

maravilla nf marvel, wonder; **de m.**, wonderfully; **¡qué m. de película!**, what a wonderful film!; *fam* **a las mil maravillas**, marvellously.

maravillar I vtr to amaze, astonish. II **maravillarse** vr to marvel (**con**, at), wonder (**con**, at).

maravilloso,-a adj wonderful, marvellous, US marvelous.

marca nf 1 mark, sign. 2 *Com* brand, make; **ropa de m.**, brand-name clothes; **m. de fábrica**, trademark; **m. registrada**, registered trademark. 3 *Dep* (*récord*) record; **batir la m. mundial**, to break the world record.

marcador,-a nm 1 marker. 2 *Dep* (*tablero*) scoreboard; (*persona*) scorer.

marcaje nm *Dep* marking.

marcapasos nm inv *Med* pacemaker.

marcar [1] I vtr 1 to mark. 2 *Tel* to dial. 3 (*indicar*) to indicate, show; **el contador marca 1.327**, the meter reads 1,327. 4 *Dep* (*gol, puntos*) to score; (*a jugador*) to mark. 5 (*cabello*) to set. II **marcarse** vr *fam* **m. un farol**, to show off, boast.

marcha nf 1 march; **hacer algo sobre la m.**, to do sth as one goes along; **a marchas forzadas**, against the clock. 2 **estar**

en m., (*vehículo*) to be in motion; (*máquina*) to be working; (*proyecto etc*) to be under way; **poner en m.**, to start. 3 *Aut* gear; **m. atrás**, reverse (gear). 4 *Mús* march. 5 *fam* (*juerga*) **hay mucha m.**, there's lots going on; **ella tiene mucha m.**, she likes a good time.

marchar I vi 1 (*ir*) to go, walk; *fam* **¡marchando!**, on your way!; **¡una cerveza! -¡marchando!**, a beer, please! - coming right up! 2 (*aparato*) to go; **m. bien**, (*negocio*) to be going well. 3 *Mil* to march. II **marcharse** vr (*irse*) to leave, go away.

marchitar vtr, **marchitarse** vr to shrivel, wither.

marchito,-a adj shrivelled, US shriveled, withered.

marchoso,-a *fam* I adj (*persona*) fun-loving, wild. II nm,f raver, fun lover.

marcial adj martial; **artes marciales**, martial arts.

marcianitos nmpl (*juego*) space invaders.

marciano,-a adj *o* nm,f Martian.

marco nm 1 (*de cuadro etc*) frame. 2 *fig* (*ámbito*) framework; **acuerdo m.**, framework agreement. 3 *Fin* (*moneda*) mark.

marea nf 1 tide; **m. alta/baja**, high/low tide; **m. negra**, oil slick. 2 *fig* (*multitud*) crowd, mob.

mareado,-a adj 1 sick; (*en un avión*) airsick; (*en un coche*) carsick, travel-sick; (*en el mar*) seasick. 2 *euf* (*bebido*) tipsy. 3 (*aturdido*) dizzy.

marear I vtr 1 to make sick; (*en el mar*) to make seasick; (*en un avión*) to make airsick; (*en un coche*) to make carsick *o* travel-sick. 2 (*aturdir*) to make dizzy. 3 *fam* (*fastidiar*) to annoy, pester. 4 *Culin* to stir. II **marearse** vr 1 to get sick/seasick/airsick/carsick *o* travel-sick. 2 (*quedar aturdido*) to get dizzy. 3 *euf* (*emborracharse*) to get tipsy.

mareo nm 1 (*náusea*) sickness; (*en el mar*) seasickness; (*en un avión*) airsickness; (*en un coche*) carsickness, travel-sickness. 2 (*aturdimiento*) dizziness, lightheadedness.

marfil nm ivory.

margarina nf margarine.

margarita nf daisy.

margen nmf 1 border, edge; (*de río*) bank; *fig* **dejar algo/algo al m.**, to leave sth/sth out; *fig* **mantenerse al m.**, not to get involved; **al margen de**, leaving aside. 2 (*del papel*) margin. 3 *Com* **m. de beneficio**, profit margin.

marginación nf (*exclusión*) exclusion.

marginado,-a I adj excluded. II nm,f dropout.

marginal adj 1 marginal. 2 *Pol* fringe.

marginar vtr (*de un grupo, sociedad*) to leave out, exclude.

maría nf *arg* 1 (*droga*) marijuana, pot. 2 *Educ arg* (*asignatura fácil*) easy subject. 3

fam (ama de casa) housewife.
marica *nm vulg ofens* queer, poof.
maricón *nm vulg ofens* queer, poof.
marido *nm* husband.
mariguana, marihuana, marijuana *nf* marijuana.
marimacho *nm vulg* mannish woman, butch woman.
marimandón,-ona *nm,f fam* domineering person.
marimorena *nf fam* row, fuss; *fam* **armar(se) la m.**, to kick up a racket.
marina *nf* 1 *Náut* seamanship. 2 *Mil* navy; **m. de guerra**, navy; **m. mercante,** merchant navy. 3 *Geog (zona costera)* seacoast.
marinero,-a I *nm* sailor, seaman. II *adj* seafaring.
marino,-a *adj* marine; **brisa marina,** sea breeze. II *nm* sailor.
marioneta *nf* marionette, puppet.
mariposa *nf* 1 *Ent* butterfly. 2 *(lamparilla)* oil lamp. 3 *Natación* butterfly.
mariposear *vi fig* 1 *(flirtear)* to flirt. 2 *(ser inconstante)* to be fickle.
mariposón *nm* 1 *(galanteador)* flirt. 2 *ofens (marica)* queer, pansy, poof.
mariquita I *nf Ent* ladybird. II *nm fam ofens (marica)* queer, pansy, poof.
mariscal *nm Mil* marshal; **m. de campo,** field marshal.
marisco *nm* shellfish; **mariscos,** seafood.
marisma *nf* marsh.
marisquería *nf* seafood restaurant, shellfish bar.
marítimo,-a *adj* maritime, · sea; **ciudad marítima,** coastal town; **paseo m.,** promenade.
mármol *nm* marble.
marmóreo,-a *adj* marble.
maroma *nf* 1 *Náut* cable. 2 *(cuerda)* thick rope.
marqués *nm* marquis.
marquesa *nf* marchioness.
marquesina *nf* canopy; **m. (del autobús),** bus shelter.
marquetería *nf* marquetry, inlaid work.
marrano,-a I *adj (sucio)* filthy, dirty. II *nm,f* 1 *fam (persona)* dirty pig, slob. 2 *(animal)* pig.
marras (de) *loc adv* **el individuo de m.,** the man in question.
marrón I *adj (color)* brown. II *nm* 1 *(color)* brown. 2 *arg (condena)* sentence.
marroquí *adj & nmf* Moroccan.
marroquinería *nf* leather goods.
Marruecos *n* Morocco.
marrullero,-a I *adj* cajoling, wheedling. II *nm,f* cajoler, wheedler.
Marte *n* Mars.
martes *nm inv* Tuesday; **m. y trece,** ≈ Friday the thirteenth.
martillo *nm* hammer.
mártir *nmf* martyr.

martirio *nm* 1 martyrdom. 2 *fig (fastidio)* torment.
martirizar [4] *vtr* 1 to martyr. 2 *fig (fastidiar)* to torture, torment.
marxista *adj & nmf* Marxist.
marzo *nm* March.
mas *conj lit* but.
más I *adv* 1 *(adicional)* more; **no tengo m.,** I haven't got any more. 2 *(comparativo)* more; **es m. alta/inteligente que yo,** she's taller/more intelligent than me; **tengo más dinero que tú,** I've more money than you; **más gente de la que esperas,** more people than you're expecting; **m. de,** *(con numerales, cantidad)* more than, over. 3 *(superlativo)* most; **es el m. bonito/caro,** it's the prettiest/most expensive. 4 *exclam* so ..., what a ...; **¡qué casa m. bonita!,** what a lovely house! **¡está m. guapa!,** she looks so beautiful! 6 *(después de pron interr e indef)* else; **¿algo m.?,** anything else?; **no, nada m.,** no, nothing else; **¿quién m.?,** who else?; **nadie/alguien m.,** nobody/ somebody else. 7 **cada día** *o* **vez m.,** more and more; **estar de m.,** to be unnecessary; **traje uno de m.,** I brought a spare one; **es m.,** what's more, furthermore; **lo m. posible,** as much as possible; **m. bien,** rather; **m. o menos,** more or less; **m. aún,** even more; **¿qué m. da?,** what's the difference?; **todo lo m.,** at the most. 8 **por m. +** *(adj/adv +)* *que + subj,* however (much), no matter how (much); **por m. fuerte que sea,** however strong he may be; **por m. que grites no te oirá nadie,** no matter how much you shout nobody will hear you.
II *nm inv* **los/las m.,** the majority, most people; **sus m. y sus menos,** its pros and cons.
III *prep Mat* plus; **dos m. dos,** two plus *o* and two.
masa *nf* 1 *(de cosas)* bulk, volume; **m. salarial,** total wage bill. 2 *(gente)* mass; **en m.,** en masse; **medios de comunicación de masas,** mass media. 4 *Culin* dough. 3 *Constr* mortar.
masacrar *vtr* to massacre.
masacre *nf* massacre.
masaje *nm* massage; **dar masaje(s) (a),** to massage.
masajista *nmf (hombre)* masseur; *(mujer)* masseuse.
mascar [1] *vtr & vi* to chew, masticate.
máscara *nf* mask; **m. de gas,** gas mask; **traje de m.,** fancy dress.
mascarilla *nf* 1 mask; **m. de oxígeno,** oxygen mask. 2 *Med* face mask. 3 *(cosmética)* face pack.
mascota *nf* mascot.
masculino,-a *adj* 1 *Zool Bot* male. 2 *(de hombre)* male; manly; **una voz masculina,** a manly voice. 3 *(para hombre)*

men's; **ropa masculina,** men's clothes, menswear. **4** *Ling* masculine.

mascullar *vtr* to mumble.

masificación *nf* overcrowding.

masificado,-a *adj* overcrowded.

masilla *nf* putty.

masivo,-a *adj* massive.

masón *nm* freemason, mason.

masonería *nf* freemasonry, masonry.

masoquista I *adj* masochistic. **II** *nmf* masochist.

máster *nm* master's degree.

masticar [1] *vt* to chew.

mástil *nm* **1** (*asta*) mast, pole. **2** *Náut* mast. **3** (*de guitarra*) neck.

mastín *nm* mastiff.

masturbación *nf* masturbation.

masturbar *vtr,* **masturbarse** *vr* to masturbate.

mata *nf* **1** (*matorral*) bush, shrub; **m. de pelo,** head of hair. **2** (*ramita*) sprig.

matadero *nm* slaughterhouse, abattoir.

matador *nm* matador, bullfighter.

matadura *nf* sore.

matamoscas *nm inv* (*pala*) fly swat.

matanza *nf* slaughter.

matar *vtr* **1** to kill; *fam* **m. el hambre/el tiempo,** to kill one's hunger/the time; *fam* **que me maten si ...,** I'll be damned if .... **2** (*cigarro, bebida*) to finish off. **3** (*sello*) to frank.

matasellos *nm inv* postmark.

matasuegras *nm inv* party blower.

mate¹ *adj* (*sin brillo*) matt.

mate² *nm* *Ajedrez* mate; **jaque m.,** checkmate.

matemática *nf,* **matemáticas** *nfpl* mathematics *sing.*

matemático,-a I *adj* mathematical. **II** *nm,f* mathematician.

materia *nf* **1** matter; **m. prima,** raw material. **2** (*tema*) matter, question; **índice de materias,** table of contents. **3** *Educ* (*asignatura*) subject.

material I *adj* material, physical; **daños materiales,** damage to property. **II** *nm* **1** material; **m. escolar/de construcción,** teaching/building material *o* materials *pl.* **2** (*equipo*) equipment; **m. de oficina,** office equipment. **◆materialmente** *adv* physically.

materialista *adj & nmf* materialist.

maternal *adj* maternal, motherly.

maternidad *nf* maternity, motherhood.

materno,-a *adj* maternal; **abuelo m.,** maternal grandfather; **lengua materna,** native *o* mother tongue.

mates *nfpl fam* maths *sing,* *US* math *sing.*

matinal *adj* morning; **televisión m.,** breakfast television.

matiz *nm* **1** (*de color*) shade. **2** (*de palabra*) shade of meaning, nuance; **un m. irónico,** a touch of irony.

matización *nf* **hacer una m.,** to add a

rider.

matizar [1] *vtr* **1** *fig* (*precisar*) to be more precise *o* explicit about. **2** *Arte* to blend, harmonize. **3** *fig* (*palabras, discurso*) to tinge; (*voz*) to vary, modulate.

matón,-ona *nm,f fam* thug, bully.

matorral *nm* brushwood, thicket.

matraca *nf* (*ruido*) rattle; *fam* **dar la m. a algn,** to pester *o* bother sb.

matrero,-a *nm,f Am* (*bandolero*) bandit, brigand.

matriarcado *nm* matriarchy.

matrícula *nf* **1** registration; **derechos de m.,** registration fee; **m. de honor,** distinction; **plazo de m.,** registration period. **2** *Aut* (*número*) registration number; (*placa*) number *o* *US* license plate.

matriculación *nf* registration.

matricular *vtr,* **matricularse** *vr* to register.

matrimonial *adj* matrimonial; **agencia m.,** marriage bureau; **enlace m.,** wedding; **vida m.,** married life.

matrimonio *nm* **1** marriage; **m. civil/ religioso,** registry office/church wedding; **contraer m.,** to marry; **cama de m.,** double bed. **2** (*pareja casada*) married couple; **el m. y los niños,** the couple and their children; **el m. Romero,** Mr and Mrs Romero, the Romeros.

matriz *nf* **1** *Anat* womb, uterus. **2** *Mat* matrix. **3** (*de documento*) (*original*) original, master copy. **4** *Téc* mould, *US* mold. **5 casa m.,** parent company.

matrona *nf* midwife.

matutino,-a *adj* morning; **prensa matutina,** morning papers.

maullar [16] *vi* to miaow.

maullido *nm* miaowing, miaow.

maxilar *nm* jaw, jawbone.

máxima *nf* **1** *nf Meteor* maximum temperature. **2** (*aforismo*) maxim.

máxime *adv* especially, all the more so.

máximo,-a I *adj* maximum, highest; **la máxima puntuación,** the highest score. **II** *nm* maximum; **al m.,** to the utmost; **como m.,** (*como mucho*) at the most; (*lo más tarde*) at the latest.

mayo *nm* May.

mayonesa *nf* mayonnaise.

mayor I *adj* **1** (*comparativo*) (*tamaño*) larger, bigger (*que,* than); (*edad*) older, elder; **m. que yo,** older than me. **2** (*superlativo*) (*tamaño*) largest, biggest; (*edad*) oldest, eldest; **la m. parte,** the majority; **la m. parte de las veces,** most often. **3** (*adulto*) grown-up; **ser m. de edad,** to be of age. **4** (*maduro*) elderly, mature. **5** (*principal*) major, main; *Educ* **colegio m.,** hall of residence. **6** *Mús* major. **7** *Com* **al por m.,** wholesale; *fig* (*en abundancia*) by the score, galore. **II** *nm* **1** *Mil* major. **2 mayores,** (*adultos*) grown-ups, adults.

mayordomo *nm* butler.

mayoría *nf* majority; **en su m.**, in the main; **la m. de los niños**, most children; **m. absoluta/relativa**, absolute/relative majority; **m. de edad**, majority.

mayorista I *adj* wholesale. II *nmf* wholesaler; **precios de m.**, wholesale prices.

mayoritario,-a *adj* majority; **un gobierno m.**, a majority government.

mayúscula *nf* capital letter.

mayúsculo,-a *adj* 1 *Ling (letra)* capital. 2 *(error)* very big, enormous.

mazacote *nm* 1 *Culin* solid mass, stodge. 2 *(mezcla confusa)* hotch-potch.

mazapán *nm* marzipan.

mazmorra *nf* dungeon.

mazo *nm* mallet.

mazorca *nf Agr* cob.

me *pron* 1 *(objeto directo)* me; **no me mires**, don't look at me. 2 *(objeto indirecto)* me, to me, for me; **¿me das un caramelo?**, will you give me a sweet?; **me lo dio**, he gave it to me; **me es difícil hacerlo**, it is difficult for me to do it. 3 *(pron reflexivo)* myself; **me he cortado**, I've cut myself; **me voy/muero**, *(no se traduce)* I'm off/dying.

meada *nf vulg* piss; **echar una m.**, to have a piss.

meadero *nm vulg* bog.

meandro *nm* meander.

mear I *vi vulg* to have (a) piss. II **mearse** *vr* to wet oneself; *fig* **m. de risa**, to piss oneself (laughing).

MEC *nm abr de* Ministerio de Educación y Ciencia, Department of Education and Science.

mecachis *fam interj* darn it!, damn it!

mecánica *nf* 1 *(ciencia)* mechanics *sing*. 2 *(mecanismo)* mechanism, works *pl*.

mecánico,-a I *adj* mechanical. II *nm,f* mechanic.

mecanismo *nm* mechanism.

mecanizar [4] *vtr* to mechanize.

mecanografía *nf* typewriting, typing.

mecanografiar [29] *vtr* to type.

mecanógrafo,-a *nm,f* typist.

mecedora *nf* rocking chair.

mecenas *nmf inv* patron.

mecer [2] I *vtr* to rock. II **mecerse** *vr* to swing, rock.

mecha *nf* 1 *(de vela)* wick. 2 *Mil Min* fuse; *fam* **aguantar m.**, to grin and bear it. 3 *(de pelo)* streak; **hacerse mechas**, to have one's hair streaked.

mechar *vtr (carne)* to lard.

mechero,-a *nm* (cigarette) lighter.

mechón *nm* 1 *(de pelo)* lock. 2 *(de lana)* tuft.

medalla *nf* medal. II *nmf Dep (campeón)* medallist, *US* medalist.

medallón *nm* medallion.

media *nf* 1 stocking; *Am (calcetín)* sock. 2

(promedio) average; *Mat* mean; **m. aritmética/geométrica**, arithmetic/geometric mean. 3 **a medias**, *(incompleto)* unfinished; *(entre dos)* half and half; **ir a medias**, to go halves.

mediación *nf* mediation, intervention; **por m. de un amigo**, through a friend.

mediado,-a *adj* half-full, half-empty; **a mediados de mes/semana**, about the middle of the month/week.

mediador,-a *nm,f* mediator.

medialuna *nf* 1 *(símbolo musulmán)* crescent. 2 *Am Culin (pasta)* croissant.

mediano,-a *adj* 1 middling, average. 2 *(tamaño)* medium-sized.

medianoche *nf* midnight.

mediante *prep* by means of, with the help of, using; **Dios m.**, God willing.

mediar [12] *vi* 1 *(intervenir)* to mediate, intervene; **m. en favor de** *o* **por algn**, to intercede on behalf of sb. 2 *(tiempo)* to pass; **mediaron tres semanas**, three weeks passed.

mediático,-a *adj* media.

medicación *nf* medication, medical treatment.

medicamento *nm* medicine, medicament.

medicina *nf* medicine; **estudiante de m.**, medical student, medic.

médico,-a I *nm,f* doctor; **m. de cabecera**, family doctor, general practitioner, GP. II *adj* medical.

medida *nf* 1 measure; **a (la) m.**, *(ropa)* made-to-measure; **a m. que avanzaba**, as he advanced; **en gran m.**, to a great extent. 2 *(dimensión)* measurement. 3 *(disposición)* measure; **adoptar** *o* **tomar medidas**, to take steps; **m. represiva**, deterrent.

medieval *adj* medieval.

medievo *nm* Middle Ages *pl*.

medio,-a I *adj* 1 half; **a m. camino**, halfway; **m. kilo**, half a kilo; **una hora y media**, one and a half hours, an hour and a half. 2 *(intermedio)* middle; **a media mañana/tarde**, in the middle of the morning/afternoon; **clase media**, middle class; **punto m.**, middle ground. 3 *(normal)* average; **salario m.**, average wage. II *adv* half; **está m. muerta**, she is half dead. III *nm* 1 *(mitad)* half. 2 *(centro)* middle; **en m. (de)**, *(en el centro)* in the middle (of); *(entre dos)* in between. 3 **medios de transporte**, means of transport; **por m. de ...**, by means of ...; **medios económicos**, means; **medios de comunicación**, *(mass)* media. 4 **m. ambiente**, environment. 5 *Dep (jugador)* halfback.

medioambiental *adj* environmental.

medioambientalista *nmf* environmentalist.

mediocre *adj* mediocre.

mediocridad *nf* mediocrity.

mediodía *nm* 1 *(hora exacta)* midday,

noon. **2** *(período aproximado)* early afternoon, lunchtime. **3** *(sur)* south.

medir [6] **I** *vtr* **1** *(distancia, superficie, temperatura)* to measure. **2** *(moderar)* to weigh; **mide tus palabras**, weigh your words. **II** *vi* to measure, be; **¿cuánto mides?**, how tall are you?; **mide dos metros**, he is two metres tall; **mide dos metros de alto/ancho/largo**, it is two metres high/wide/long.

meditar *vtr & vi* to meditate, ponder; m. **sobre algo**, to ponder over sth.

mediterráneo,-a **I** *adj* Mediterranean. **II** *nm* **el M.**, the Mediterranean.

medrar *vi* to climb the social ladder.

medroso,-a *adj* **1** *(temeroso)* fearful, fainthearted. **2** *(que causa miedo)* frightening.

médula *nf* **1** marrow; **m. ósea**, bone marrow. **2** *fig (lo más profundo)* marrow, pith; **hasta la m.**, to the marrow.

medusa *nf* jellyfish.

megafonía *nf* public-address system, PA system.

megáfono *nm* megaphone.

megalito *nm* megalith.

megalómano,-a *adj* megalomaniac.

mejicano,-a *adj & nm,f* Mexican.

Méjico *n* Mexico; **ciudad de M.**, Mexico City; **Nuevo M.**, New Mexico.

mejilla *nf* cheek.

mejillón *nm* mussel.

mejor **I** *adj* **1** *(comparativo)* better *(que, than)*; **el m. de los dos**, the better of the two; **es m. no decírselo**, it's better not to tell her; **es m. que vayas**, you'd better go. **2** *(superlativo)* best; **el m. de los tres**, the best of the three; **tu m. amiga**, your best friend; **lo m.**, the best thing. **II** *adv* **1** *(comparativo)* better *(que, than)*; **cada vez m.**, better and better; **ella conduce m.**, she drives better; **ha dicho**, or rather; **¡mucho mejor!**, so much the better! **2** *(superlativo)* best; **es el que m. canta**, he is the one who sings the best; **a lo m.**, *(quizás)* perhaps; *(ojalá)* hopefully.

mejora *nf* improvement.

mejorar **I** *vtr* to improve; **m. la red vial**, to improve the road system; **m. una marca o un récord**, to break a record. **II** *vi* to improve, get better. **III** *mejorarse vr* to get better; **¡que te mejores!**, get well soon!

mejoría *nf* improvement.

melancolía *nf* melancholy.

melancólico,-a *adj* melancholic, melancholy.

melé *nf Dep* scrum.

melena *nf* (head of) hair; *(de león)* mane.

Melilla *n* Melilla.

melindroso,-a **I** *adj* affected, fussy, finicky. **II** *nm,f* affected o finicky person.

mella *nf* **1** *(hendedura)* nick, notch; *(en plato, taza etc)* chip. **2** *(en dentadura)* gap.

3 *fig* impression; **hacer m. en algn**, to make an impression on sb.

mellado,-a *adj* *(sin dientes)* gap-toothed.

mellizo,-a *adj & nm,f* twin.

melocotón *nm* peach.

melodía *nf* melody, tune.

melodrama *nm* melodrama.

melón *nm* **1** *(fruto)* melon. **2** *fam (tonto)* ninny. **3** *vulg* **melones**, *(tetas)* boobs.

melopea *nf fam* **coger** o **agarrar/llevar una m.**, to get/be drunk o pissed.

meloso,-a *adj* sweet, honeyed.

membrana *nf* membrane.

membrete *nm* letterhead.

membrillo *nm* **1** *Bot* quince; *(árbol)* quince tree; *(dulce)* quince preserve o jelly. **2** *fam (tonto)* dimwit.

memo,-a *fam* **I** *adj* silly, stupid. **II** *nm,f* nincompoop, ninny.

memorable *adj* memorable.

memorándum *nm (pl* **memorándums)** memorandum.

memoria *nf* **1** memory; **aprender/saber algo de m.**, to learn/know sth by heart; **irse de la m.**, to slip one's mind. **2** *(informe)* report, statement; **m. anual**, annual report. **3** *(recuerdo)* memory, recollection. **4** **memorias**, *(biografía)* memoirs.

memorístico *adj* acquired by memory.

memorizar [4] *vtr* to memorize.

menaje *nm* furniture and furnishing *pl*; **m. de cocina**, kitchen equipment o utensils.

mención *nf* mention; **m. honorífica**, honourable mention.

mencionar *vtr* to mention.

mendicidad *nf* begging.

mendigar [7] *vtr & vi* to beg.

mendigo,-a *nm,f* beggar.

mendrugo *nm* **1** crust o chunk (of stale bread). **2** *(tonto)* dimwit.

menear **I** *vtr* to shake, move; *(cola)* to wag, waggle; *fam (culo)* to wiggle. **II** **menearse** *vr* to move, shake; *fam* **una tormenta de no te menees**, a hell of a storm; *vulg* **meneársela**, to wank.

meneo *nm* shake; *(de cola)* wag, waggle; *(de culo)* wiggle.

menester *nm* **1** **es m.**, it is necessary. **2** **menesteres**, *(deberes)* jobs.

menestra *nf* vegetable stew.

mengano,-a *nm,f fam* so-and-so, what's-his o her-name.

menguante *adj* waning, on the wane; **cuarto m.**, last quarter.

menguar [22] **I** *vtr* **1** to diminish, reduce. **2** *(en labor de punto)* to decrease. **II** *vi* **1** to diminish, decrease. **2** *(la luna)* to wane.

meñique *adj & nm* **(dedo) m.**, little finger.

menopausia *nf Med* menopause.

menor **I** *adj* **1** *(comparativo)* *(de tamaño)*

smaller (que, than); (de edad) younger (que, than); **mal m.,** the lesser of two evils; **el m. de los dos,** the smaller of the two; **ser m. de edad,** to be a minor o under age. **2** (superlativo) (de tamaño) smallest; (de intensidad) least, slightest; **al m. ruido,** at the slightest noise; (de edad) youngest; **el m. de los tres,** the youngest of the three; **es la m.,** she's the youngest child. **3** *Mús* minor. **4** *Com* **al por m.,** retail. **II** *nmf* minor; *Jur* **tribunal de menores,** juvenile court.

menos I *adj* **1** (comparativo) (con singular) less; (con plural) fewer; **m. dinero/leche/tiempo que,** less money/milk/time than; **m. libros/pisos que,** fewer books/flats than; (con cláusula) **tiene m. años de lo que parece,** he's younger than he looks. **2** (superlativo) **fui el que perdí m. dinero,** I lost the least money. **II** *adv* **1** (con singular) less than; **m. de media hora,** less than a half hour; (con plural) fewer than, less than. **2** (superlativo) (con singular) least; (con plural) fewest; **el m. inteligente de la clase,** the least intelligent boy in the class; **ayer fue cuando vinieron m. personas,** yesterday was when the fewest people came; (con cantidad) the least. **III** (locuciones) **a m. que + subj,** unless; **al o por lo m.** at least; **echar a algn de m.,** to miss sb; **eso es lo de m.,** that's the least of it; **¡m. mal!,** just as well!; **nada m. que,** no less o no fewer than; **ni mucho m.,** far from it. **IV** *prep* **1** but, except; **todo m. eso,** anything but that. **2** *Mat* minus; **tres m. uno,** three minus one.

menoscabar *vtr* **1** (perjudicar) to damage. **2** *fig* (desacreditar) to discredit.

menoscabo *nm* harm, damage; **ir en m. de algo,** to be to the detriment of sth.

menospreciar [12] *vtr* to scorn, disdain.

menosprecio *nm* contempt, scorn, disdain.

mensáfono *nm* anaphone.

mensaje *nm* message.

mensajero,-a *nm,f* messenger, courier.

menstruación *nf* menstruation.

mensual *adj* monthly; **dos visitas mensuales,** two visits a month.

mensualidad *nf* (pago) monthly payment; (sueldo) monthly salary o wage.

menta *nf* **1** *Bot* mint. **2** (licor) crème de menthe.

mental *adj* mental.

mentalidad *nf* mentality; **de m. abierta/cerrada,** open-/narrow-minded.

mentalizar [4] **I** *vtr* (concienciar) to make aware. **II mentalizarse** *vr* **1** (concienciarse) to become aware. **2** (hacerse a la idea) to come to terms (a, with).

mentar [1] *vtr* to mention, name.

abierta/tolerante/cerrada, open/broad/closed mind.

mentecato,-a *nm,f* fool, idiot.

mentir [5] *vi* to lie, tell lies.

mentira *nf* lie; **aunque parezca m.,** strange as it may seem; **parece m.,** it is unbelievable.

mentiroso,-a I *adj* lying. **II** *nm,f* liar.

mentís *nm* denial.

mentón *nm Anat* chin.

menú *nm* menu.

menudillos *nmpl* giblets.

menudo,-a I *adj* minute, tiny; (irónico) tremendous; **la gente menuda,** the little ones *pl*; **¡m. lío/susto!,** what a mess/fright! **II** *adv* **a m.,** often.

meollo *nm* **1** *fig* (quid) essence. **2** (miga) crumb.

mercado *nm* market; **M. Común,** Common Market; **m. negro,** black market; **sacar algo al m.,** to put sth on the market.

mercadotecnia *nf* marketing.

mercancía *nf* commodity, goods *pl*.

mercante *adj* merchant; **barco/marina m.,** merchant ship/navy.

mercantil *adj* mercantile, commercial.

merced *nf fml* favour, *US* favor, grace; **a m. de,** at the mercy of.

mercenario,-a *adj* & *nm,f* mercenary.

mercería *nf* haberdasher's (shop), *US* notions store.

mercurio *nm* **1** *Quím* mercury, quicksilver. **2** *M.,* Mercury.

merecer [33] **I** *vtr* **1** to deserve. **2** (uso impers) **no merece la pena hacerlo,** it's not worth while doing it. **II merecerse** *vr* to deserve.

merecido,-a I *adj* deserved; **ella lo tiene m.,** (recompensa) she deserves it; (castigo) it serves her right. **II** *nm* just deserts *pl*.

merendar [1] **I** *vtr* to have as an afternoon snack, have for tea. **II** *vi* to have an afternoon snack, have tea.

merendero *nm* (establecimiento) tearoom, snack bar; (en el campo) picnic spot.

merengue *nm Culin* meringue.

merezco *indic pres* → **merecer.**

meridiano,-a *nm* meridian.

meridional I *adj* southern. **II** *nmf* southerner.

merienda *nf* afternoon snack, tea.

mérito *nm* merit, worth; **hacer méritos para algo,** to strive to deserve sth.

merluza *nf* (pez) hake.

merma *nf* decrease, reduction.

mermar I *vtr* to cause to decrease o diminish. **II** *vi* to decrease, diminish. **III mermarse** *vr* to decrease, diminish.

mermelada *nf* **1** jam; **m. de fresa,** strawberry jam. **2** (de agrios) marmalade; **m. de naranja,** orange marmalade.

mero,-a, *adj* mere, pure; **por el m. hecho de,** through the mere fact of.

merodear vi to prowl.

mes nm 1 month; **el m. pasado/que viene**, last/next month. 2 (cobro) monthly salary o wages pl; (pago) monthly payment. 3 fam (menstruación) period.

mesa nf 1 table; **poner/recoger la m.**, to set/clear the table; (de despacho etc) desk; **m. redonda**, round table. 2 (junta directiva) board, executive; **el presidente de la m.**, the chairman; **m. electoral**, electoral college.

meseta nf plateau, tableland, meseta; **la M.**, the plateau of Castile.

mesilla nf **m. de noche**, bedside table.

mesón nm old-style tavern.

mesonero,-a nm,f innkeeper.

mestizo,-a adj & nm,f half-breed, half-caste, mestizo.

mesura nf fml moderation, restraint.

meta nf 1 (objetivo) goal, aim, objective. 2 (de carrera) finish, finishing line. 3 Ftb (portería) goal.

metafísica nf metaphysics.

metáfora nf metaphor.

metal nm 1 metal; **metales preciosos**, precious metals. 2 (timbre de la voz) timbre. 3 Mús brass.

metálico,-a I adj metallic. II nm cash; **pagar en m.**, to pay (in) cash.

metalizado-a adj metallic.

metalúrgico,-a I adj metallurgical. II nm,f metallurgist.

metedura nf fam **m. de pata**, blunder.

meteorito nm meteorite.

meteorología nf meteorology.

meteorológico,-a adj meteorological; **parte m.**, weather report.

meter I vtr 1 (poner) to put (en, in); **fig m. las narices en algo**, to poke one's nose into sth. 2 (comprometer) to involve (en, in), to get mixed up (en, in). 3 fam fig (dar) to give; **m. un rollo**, to go on and on; **m. prisa a algn**, to hurry sb up. 4 (hacer) to make; **m. ruido**, to make a noise. II **meterse** vr 1 (entrar) to go o come in, get into. 2 (estar) to be; **¿dónde te habías metido?**, where have you been (all this time)? 3 (entrometerse) to meddle. 4 **m. con algn**, (en broma) to get at sb.

meticuloso,-a adj meticulous.

metido,-a adj fam **estar muy m. en algo**, to be deeply involved in sth; **m. en años**, getting on (in years).

metódico,-a adj methodical.

método nm 1 method. 2 Educ course.

metodología nf methodology.

metomentodo nmf inv fam busybody.

metralleta nf sub machine-gun.

métrico,-a adj metric; **sistema m.**, metric system.

metro nm 1 (medida) metre, US meter. 2 (tren) underground, tube, US subway.

metrópoli nf metropolis.

metropolitano,-a I adj metropolitan. II

nm fml underground, tube, US subway.

mexicano,-a adj & nm,f Mexican.

México nm Mexico.

mezcla nf 1 (acción) mixing, blending; Rad Cin mixing. 2 (producto) mixture, blend.

mezclar I vtr 1 (dos o más cosas) to mix, blend. 2 (desordenar) to mix up. 3 (involucrar) to involve, mix up. II **mezclarse** vr 1 (cosas) to get mixed up; (gente) to mix (con, with).

mezcolanza nf fml strange mixture, hotch-potch.

mezquino,-a adj 1 (persona) mean, stingy. 2 (sueldo) miserable.

mezquita nf mosque.

m/g abr de **miligramo**, milligramme, milligram, mg.

mi[1] adj my; **mi casa/trabajo**, my house/job; **mis cosas/libros**, my things/books.

mi[2] nm Mús E; **mi menor**, E minor.

mí pron pers me; **a mí me dio tres**, he gave me three; **compra otro para mí**, buy one for me too; **por mí mismo**, just by myself.

mía adj & pron pos f → **mío**.

miaja nf crumb; fig bit.

michelín nm fam spare tyre.

mico,-a nm 1 Zool long-tailed monkey. 2 fam (pequeñajo) little kid.

micra nf (medida) micron.

micro nm fam mike, microphone.

microbio nm microbe.

microbús nm minibus.

microchip nm (pl **microchips**) Inform microchip.

microficha nf microfiche.

micrófono nm microphone.

microonda nf un (**horno**) **microondas**, a microwave (oven).

microscopio nm microscope.

miedica nmf fam scaredy-cat.

miedo nm (pavor) fear; (temor) aprehension; **una película de m.**, a horror film; **tener m. de algo/algn**, to be afraid of sth/sb; fam **lo pasamos de m.**, we had a fantastic time; **un calor de m.**, sizzling heat.

miedoso,-a adj fearful.

miel nf honey; **luna de m.**, honeymoon.

miembro nm 1 (socio) member; **estado m.**, member state. 2 Anat limb; **m. viril**, penis.

mientras I conj 1 (al mismo tiempo que) while. 2 (durante el tiempo que) when, while; **m. vivi en Barcelona**, when I lived in Barcelona. 3 **m. que**, (por el contrario) whereas. 4 fam (cuanto más) **m. más/menos ...**, the more/less ... II adv **m. (tanto)**, meanwhile, in the meantime.

miércoles nm inv Wednesday; **M. de Ceniza**, Ash Wednesday.

mierda nf vulg 1 shit; **ese libro es una**

m., that book is crap; **¡vete a la m.!**, piss off! **2** fig (porquería) bender.

miga nf (de pan etc) crumb; fig **hacer buenas migas con algn**, to get on well with sb.

migaja nf **1** (de pan) crumb. **2** fig bit, scrap. **3 migajas**, (del pan) crumbs; fig leftovers.

migraña nf Med migraine.

mil adj & nm thousand; **m. pesetas**, a o one thousand pesetas.

milagro nm miracle.

milagroso,-a adj miraculous.

milano nm Orn kite; **m. real**, red kite.

milenario,-a I adj millenarian, millenial. **II** nm millenium.

milenio nm millennium.

milésimo,-a adj & nm,f thousandth.

mili nf fam military o national service; **hacer la m.**, to do one's military service.

milicia nf (ejército) militia; (servicio militar) military service.

milímetro nm millimetre, US millimeter.

militar I adj military. **II** nm military man, soldier. **III** vi Pol (en un partido) to be a member.

milla nf mile.

millar nm thousand.

millón nm million.

millonario,-a adj & nm,f millionaire.

mimar vtr to spoil, pamper.

mimbre nm wicker.

mimetismo nm mimicry.

mímica nf mimicry.

mimo nm **1** (delicadeza) care. **2** fig (zalamería) pampering. **3** Teat (actor) mime.

mina nf **1** mine; **ingeniero de minas**, mining engineer. **2** (explosivo) mine; **campo de minas**, minefield. **3** (de lápiz) lead; **lápiz de m.**, propelling pencil. **4** fig (ganga) gold mine.

minar vtr **1** Mil Min to mine. **2** fig (desgastar) to undermine.

mineral I adj mineral. **II** nm ore.

minería nf **1** Min mining. **2** Ind mining industry.

minero,-a I nm,f miner. **II** adj mining.

miniatura nf miniature.

minifalda nf miniskirt.

minifundio nm smallholding.

mínima nf minimum temperature.

minimizar vtr to minimize.

mínimo,-a I adj **1** (muy pequeño) minute, tiny. **2** Mat Téc minimum, lowest; **m. común múltiplo**, lowest common denominator. **II** nm minimum; **como m.**, at least; **ni lo más m.**, not in the least.

minipímer® nm o f liquidizer, blender.

ministerio nm **1** Pol ministry, US department. **2** Rel ministry.

ministro,-a nm,f **1** Pol minister; **primer m.**, Prime Minister. **2** Rel minister.

minoría nf minority; **m. de edad**,

minority.

minoritario,-a adj minority.

minucioso,-a adj **1** (persona) meticulous. **2** (informe, trabajo etc) minute, detailed.

minúsculo,-a adj miniscule, minute; **letra minúscula**, lower-case o small letter.

minusválido,-a I adj handicapped, disabled. **II** nm,f handicapped person, disabled person.

minuta nf **1** (cuenta) lawyer's bill. **2** (menú) menu.

minutero nm minute hand.

minuto nm minute.

mío,-a I adj pos of mine; **un amigo m.**, a friend of mine; **no es asunto m.**, it is none of my business. **II** pron pos mine; **ese libro es m.**, that book is mine; **lo m. es el tenis**, tennis is my strong point; fam **los míos**, my people o folks.

miope nmf myopic o short-sighted person.

miopía nf myopia, short-sightedness.

mira nf **1** Téc sight. **2** fig (objetivo) aim, target; **con miras a**, with a view to; **amplitud de miras**, broad-mindedness.

mirada nf look; **lanzar o echar una m.**, to glance at; **levantar la m.**, to raise one's eyes; **m. fija**, stare.

mirador nm **1** (lugar con vista) viewpoint. **2** (balcón) bay window, windowed balcony.

mirar vtr **1** to look at. **2** (observar) to watch. **3 m. por algn/algo**, (cuidar) to look after sb/sth. **4** (procurar) to see; **mira que no le pase nada**, see that nothing happens to him. **5** (dar a) to look, face; **la casa mira al sur**, the house faces south.

mirilla nf spyhole, peephole.

mirlo nm blackbird.

misa nf mass.

misántropo,-a I adj misanthropic. **II** nm,f misanthrope, misanthropist.

miserable I adj **1** (mezquino) (persona) despicable; (sueldo etc) miserable. **2** (pobre) wretched, poor; **una vida m.**, a wretched life. **II** nmf **1** (mezquino) miser. **2** (canalla) wretch.

miseria nf **1** (pobreza extrema) extreme poverty. **2** (insignificancia) pittance; **ganar una m.**, to earn next to nothing. **3** (tacañería) miserliness, meanness.

misericordia nf mercy, compassion.

mísero,-a adj miserable, wretched.

misil nm missile; **m. tierra-aire**, surface-to-air missile.

misión nf mission; **m. cumplida**, mission accomplished.

misionero,-a nm,f missionary.

mismísimo,-a adj superl fam **1** (preciso) very; **en el m. centro**, right in the centre. **2** (en persona) in person.

mismo,-a I adj **1** same. **2** (uso enfático) yo **m.**, I myself; **aquí m.**, right here. **II** pron same; **es el m. de ayer**, it's the same one

as yesterday; **estamos en las mismas,**
we're back to square one; **lo m.,** the
same (thing); **dar** o **ser lo m.,** to make
no difference; **por eso m.,** that is why;
por uno o **sí m.,** by oneself. III *adv* **1**
(por ejemplo) for instance; **que venga
algn, Juan m.,** ask one of them to come,
Juan, for instance. **2 así m.,** likewise.

misógino,-a I *adj* misogynous. **II** *nm,f*
misogynist.

miss *nf* beauty queen.

míster *nm* Ftb coach, trainer.

misterio *nm* mystery.

misterioso,-a *adj* mysterious.

MIT *nm abr de* **Ministerio de Información
y Turismo.**

mitad *nf* **1** half; **a m. de camino,** halfway there; **a m. de precio,** half price. **2**
(centro) middle; **en la m. del primer
acto,** half way through the first act; *fam*
eso me parte por la m., that really
screws things up for me.

mítico,-a *adj* mythical.

mitigar [7] *vtr fml* to mitigate, palliate;
(luz) to reduce.

mitin *nm* Pol meeting, rally.

mito *nm* myth.

mitología *nf* mythology.

mitote *nm Am (bulla)* uproar.

mixto *adj* mixed.

mobiliario *nm* furniture.

moca *nm* mocha, coffee.

mochila *nf* rucksack, backpack.

mochuelo *nm Zool* little owl.

moción *nf* motion; **m. de censura,** vote
of censure.

moco *nm* snot; **sonarse los mocos,** to
blow one's nose.

mocoso,-a *nm,f fam* brat.

moda *nf* **1** fashion; **a la m., de m.,** in
fashion; **pasado de m.,** old-fashioned. **2**
(furor pasajero) craze.

modales *nmpl* manners.

modalidad *nf* form, category; *Com* **m. de
pago,** method of payment; *Dep* **m. de-
portiva,** sport.

modelar *vtr* to model, shape.

modélico,-a *adj* model.

modelo I *adj inv & nm* model. **II** *nmf*
(fashion) model; **desfile de modelos,**
fashion show.

modem *nm Inform Tel* modem.

moderación *nf* moderation.

moderado,-a *adj* moderate; **un m. aumento de temperatura,** a mild increase
in temperature.

moderador,-a *nm,f* chairperson; *(hombre)*
chairman; *(mujer)* chairwoman.

moderar I *vtr* **1** to moderate; *(velocidad)*
to reduce. **2** *(debate)* to chair. **II moderarse** *vr* to be moderate.

modernizar [4] *vtr,* **modernizarse** *vr* to
modernize.

moderno,-a *adj* modern.

modestia *nf* modesty; **m. aparte,** without
wishing to be immodest.

modesto,-a *adj* modest.

módico,-a *adj* moderate; **una módica
suma,** a modest o small sum.

modificar [1] *vtr* to modify.

modismo *nm* idiom.

modisto,-a *nm,f* **1** *(diseñador)* fashion designer. **2** *(sastre)* (hombre) couturier; *(mujer)* couturière.

modo *nm* **1** *(manera)* way, manner; **m. de
empleo,** instructions for use; ≈ **manera.
2 modos,** manners. **3** *Ling* mood.

modorra *nf (somnolencia)* drowsiness.

modoso,-a *adj* **1** *(educado)* well-behaved.
2 *(recatado)* modest.

modulación *nf* modulation.

modular *vtr* to modulate.

módulo *nm* module.

mofa *nf* mockery; **en tono de m.,** in a gi-
bing tone.

mofarse *vr* to laugh *(de,* at), make fun
(de, of).

moflete *nm* chubby cheek.

mogollón *nm arg* **1 m. de,** loads of; **me
gusta un m.,** I like it loads. **2** *(confusión)*
commotion; *(ruido)* racket.

moho *nm* **1** *Bot* mould, *US* mold. **2** *(de
metales)* rust.

mohoso,-a *adj* **1** mouldy, *US* moldy. **2**
(oxidado) rusty.

mojado,-a *adj (empapado)* wet; *(húmedo)*
damp.

mojar I *vtr* **1** to wet; *(humedecer)* to damp;
m. pan en la leche, to dip o dunk bread
in one's milk. **2** *arg* **mojarla** to have it
off. **II mojarse** *vr* to get wet.

mojón *nm* **1 m. kilométrico,** ≈ milestone.
2 *arg (mierda)* shit.

moka *nm* mocha.

molar I *vi fam* **me mola cantidad,** I really
love it, it's brilliant. **II** *adj & nm Anat*
molar.

molde *nm* mould, *US* mold; **letras de
m.,** printed letters; **pan de m.,** ≈ sliced
bread.

moldeador *nm (del pelo)* wave.

moldear *vtr* to mould, *US* mold.

mole *nf* mass, bulk.

molécula *nf* molecule.

moler [4] *vtr* **1** *(triturar)* to grind. **2 m. a
algn a golpes,** to beat sb up.

molestar I *vtr* **1** *(incomodar)* to disturb,
bother. **2** *fml* to bother; **¿le molestaría
esperar fuera?,** would you mind waiting
outside? **3** *(causar malestar)* to hurt. **II
molestarse** *vr* **1** *(tomarse la molestia)* to
bother. **2** *(ofenderse)* to take offence o *US*
offense, get upset.

molestia *nf* **1** bother; **no es ninguna m.,**
it is no trouble at all; **perdone las molestias,** forgive the inconvenience. **2** *Med
(dolor)* trouble, slight pain.

molesto,-a *adj* **1** *(irritante)* annoying,

upsetting. 2 **estar m. con algn,** (*enfadado*) to be annoyed *o* upset with sb.

molinillo *nm* grinder.

molino *nm* mill; **m. de agua,** watermill; **m. de viento,** windmill.

mollera *nf fam* brains *pl*; **duro de m.,** (*tonto*) dense, thick; (*testarudo*) pigheaded.

molón,-ona *adj arg* flashy, showy.

momentáneo,-a *adj* momentary.

momento *nm* 1 (*instante*) moment; **al m.,** at once; **por momentos,** by the minute. 2 (*período*) time; **de m.,** for the time being; **en cualquier m.,** at any time.

momia *nf* mummy.

mona *nf fam* **coger una m.,** to get drunk; **dormir la m.,** to sleep it off.

monada *nf fam* **¡qué m.!,** how cute!

monaguillo *nm Rel* altar boy.

monarca *nm* monarch.

monarquía *nf* monarchy.

monasterio *nm Rel* monastery.

monda *nf* 1 (*piel*) peel, skin. 2 *fam* **ser la m.,** (*divertido*) to be a scream.

mondadientes *nm inv* toothpick.

mondar I *vtr* to peel. II **mondarse** *vr fam* **m. (de risa),** to laugh one's head off.

moneda *nf* 1 (*pieza*) coin; **m. suelta,** small change; **acuñar m.,** to mint money. 2 *Fin* currency.

monedero *nm* purse.

monería *nf* → **monada.**

monetario,-a *adj* monetary.

mongol I *adj* Mongolian. II *nmf* (*persona*) Mongolian. II *nm* (*idioma*) Mongolian.

mongólico,-a I *Med* 1 *adj* Down's syndrome. II *nm,f* **ser m.,** to have Down's syndrome.

monigote *nm* 1 *pey* (*persona*) wimp. 2 (*dibujo*) rough drawing *o* sketch (of a person).

monitor,-a *nm,f* monitor; (*profesor*) instructor.

monja *nf* nun.

monje *nm* monk.

mono,-a I *nm* 1 monkey. 2 (*prenda*) (de trabajo) boiler suit, overalls *pl*; (*de vestir*) catsuit. 3 *arg* (*droga*) cold turkey. II *adj fam* (*bonito*) pretty, cute.

monográfico,-a I *adj* monographic. II *nm* monograph.

monólogo *nm* monologue.

monopolio *nm* monopoly.

monopolizar [4] *vtr* to monopolize.

monótono,-a *adj* monotonous.

monserga *nf fam* drag.

monstruo *nm* 1 monster. 2 (*genio*) genius.

monstruoso,-a *adj* 1 (*repugnante*) monstrous. 2 (*enorme*) massive, huge.

monta *nf fig* **de poca m.,** of little importance.

montacargas *nm inv* service lift, *US* freight elevator.

montado,-a I *adj* (*nata*) whipped. II *nm*

sandwich.

montador,-a *nm,f* 1 (*operario*) fitter. 2 *Cin* TV film editor. 3 *Teat* producer.

montaje *nm* 1 *Téc* (*instalación*) fitting; (*ensamblaje*) assembling; **cadena de m.,** assembly line. 2 *Teat* staging. 4 *Fot* montage. 5 *fam* (*farsa*) farce.

montaña *nf* mountain; **m. rusa,** big dipper.

montañismo *nm* mountaineering.

montañoso,-a *adj* mountainous.

montante *nm* 1 *Fin* amount. 2 (*de puerta*) post.

montar I *vi* 1 (*subirse*) to get in; (*en bici, a caballo*) to ride. 2 *Fin* (*ascender*) m. a, to amount to, come to. II *vtr* 1 (*colocar*) to put on. 2 (*máquina etc*) to assemble, (*negocio*) to set up, start. 3 *Culin* to whip. 4 *Cin Fot* (*película*) to edit, mount; (*fotografía*) to mount. 5 *Teat* (*obra*) to stage, mount. 6 *Zool* (*cubrir*) to mount. III **montarse** *vr* 1 (*subirse*) to get on; (*en coche*) to get in (**en,** to). 2 (*armarse*) to break out. 3 *arg* **montárselo bien,** to have things (nicely) worked out *o* set up.

monte *nm* 1 (*montaña*) mountain; (*con nombre propio*) mount; **de m.,** wild. 2 **el m.,** (*zona*) the hills.

montés,-esa *adj* (*animal*) wild.

monto *nm* total.

montón *nm* heap, pile; **un m. de,** a load of; *arg* **me gusta un m.,** I really love it; *fam* **del m.,** run-of-the-mill, nothing special.

montura *nf* 1 (*cabalgadura*) mount. 2 (*de gafas*) frame.

monumento *nm* monument.

monzón *nm* monsoon.

moño *nm* (*de pelo*) bun.

MOPU *nm abr de* **Ministerio de Obras Públicas y Urbanismo,** ≈ Ministry of Public Works.

moquear *vi* to have a runny nose.

moqueta *nf* fitted carpet.

mora *nf* (*zarzamora*) blackberry.

morado,-a I *adj* black purple; *fam* **pasarlas moradas,** to have a tough time; **ponerse m.,** to stuff oneself. II *nm* purple.

moral I *adj* moral. II *nf* 1 (*ética*) morals *pl*. 2 (*ánimo*) morale, spirits *pl*; **levantar la m. a algn,** raise sb's spirits.

moraleja *nf* moral.

moralista I *adj* moralistic. II *nmf* moralist.

moratoria *nf* moratorium.

morbo *nm fam* (*interés malsano*) morbid curiosity.

morboso,-a *adj* (*malsano*) morbid.

morcilla *nf* black pudding; *fam* **que le den m.,** he can drop dead for all I care.

mordaz *adj* biting.

mordaza *nf* gag.

mordedura *nf* bite.

morder [4] *vtr* to bite; **me ha mordido,** it

has bitten me; *fig* m. el anzuelo, to take the bait.

mordida *nf Am (soborno)* bribe.

mordisco *nm* bite.

mordisquear *vtr* to nibble (at).

moreno,-a I *adj* 1 *(pelo)* dark-haired; *(piel)* dark-skinned. 2 *(bronceado)* tanned; **ponerse m.**, to get a suntan; **pan/azúcar m.**, brown bread/sugar. II *nm,f (persona) (de pelo)* dark-haired person; *(de piel)* dark-skinned person.

morera *nf Bot* white mulberry.

moretón *nm fam* bruise.

morfina *nf* morphine.

morfinómano,-a I *nm,f* morphine addict. II *adj* addicted to morphine.

morgue *nf* morgue.

moribundo,-a *adj & nm* moribund.

morir [7] 1 *vi* 1 to die; **m. de frío/hambre/cáncer**, to die of cold/hunger/cancer; **m. de amor o pena**, to die from a broken heart. II **morirse** *vr* to die; **m. de hambre**, to starve to death; *fig* to be starving; **m. de aburrimiento**, to be bored to death; **m. de ganas (de hacer algo)**, to be dying (to do sth); **m. de risa**, to die laughing.

mormón,-ona *adj & nm,f* Mormon.

moro,-a *adj, nm,f* 1 *Hist* Moor; *fam* **no hay moros en la costa**, the coast is clear. 2 *pey (musulmán)* Muslim; *(árabe)* Arab.

morocho,-a *adj Am (moreno)* swarthy.

moroso,-a *nm,f* bad debtor.

morral *nm* 1 *(para pienso)* nosebag. 2 *Mil* haversack; *(de cazador)* gamebag.

morralla *nf* 1 *(cosas sin valor)* rubbish, junk. 2 *(chusma)* scum.

morrear *vtr*, **morrearse** *vr vulg* to snog.

morreo *nm vulg* snog.

morro *nm* 1 *(de animal) (hocico)* snout. 2 *fam (de persona)* mouth, (thick) lips; **caerse de m.**, to fall flat on one's face; **por los morros**, without so much as a by your leave; *fam* **¡vaya m.!**, what a cheek! 3 *(de coche)* nose.

morrón *adj* **pimiento m.**, (fleshy) red pepper.

morsa *nf* walrus.

morse *nm* morse.

mortadela *nf* mortadella.

mortaja *nf* shroud.

mortal I *adj* 1 mortal. 2 *(mortífero)* fatal; **un accidente m.**, a fatal accident. II *nmf* mortal.

mortalidad *nf* mortality; **índice de m.**, death rate.

mortandad *nf* death toll.

mortecino,-a *adj* colourless, *US* colorless.

mortero *nm Culin Mil* mortar.

mortífero,-a *adj* deadly, lethal.

mortificar [1] *vtr* to mortify.

mortuorio,-a *adj* death; **lecho m.**, deathbed.

moruno,-a *adj* Moorish; *Culin* **pincho m.**, ≈ kebab.

mosaico *nm* mosaic.

mosca *nf* fly; **peso m.**, flyweight; *fam* **estar m.**, *(suspicaz)* to be suspicious; *(borracho)* to be pissed; *fam* **por si las moscas**, just in case; *fam* **¿qué m. te ha picado?**, what's biting you?

moscada *adj* **nuez m.**, nutmeg.

moscardón *nm* 1 *Ent* blowfly. 2 *fam (pesado)* pest.

moscovita *adj & nmf* Muscovite.

Moscú *n* Moscow.

mosquearse *vr fam* 1 *(enfadarse)* to get cross. 2 *(sospechar)* to smell a rat.

mosquetero *nm Hist* musketeer.

mosquitero *nm (red)* mosquito net.

mosquito *nm* mosquito.

mostaza *nf Bot Culin* mustard.

mosto *nm (bebida)* grape juice; *(del vino)* must.

mostrador *nm* 1 *(de tienda)* counter. 2 *(de bar)* bar.

mostrar I *vtr* to show; **muéstramelo**, show it to me. II **mostrarse** *vr* to be; **se mostró muy comprensiva**, she was very understanding.

mostrenco,-a I *nm,f* 1 *(ignorante)* blockhead. 2 *(gordo)* very fat person. II *adj (sin dueño)* ownerless; **bienes mostrencos**, ownerless property.

mota *nf* speck.

mote¹ *nm (apodo)* nickname; **poner m. a algn**, to give sb a nickname.

mote² *nm Am* boiled salted maize *o US* corn.

moteado,-a *adj* dotted.

motín *nm (amotinamiento)* mutiny; *(disturbio)* riot.

motivación *nf* motivation.

motivar *vtr* 1 *(causar)* to cause, give rise to. 2 *(inducir)* to motivate.

motivo *nm* 1 *(causa)* reason; *(usu pl)* grounds *pl*; **con este o tal m.**, for this reason; **con m. de**, on the occasion of; **sin m.**, for no reason at all; **bajo ningún m.**, under no circumstances. 2 *Art Mús* motif, leitmotif.

moto *nf Aut* motorbike.

motocicleta *nm* motorbike.

motociclismo *nm* motorcycling.

motociclista *nmf* motorcyclist.

motocross *nm* motocross.

motor,-a I *nm (grande)* engine; *(pequeño)* motor; **m. de reacción**, jet engine; **m. de explosión**, internal combustion engine; **m. eléctrico**, electric motor. II *adj Téc* motive.

motora *nf* motorboat.

motorista *nmf* motorcyclist.

motorizar [4] I *vtr* to motorize. II **motorizarse** *vr fam* to get oneself a car *o* motorbike.

motosierra *nf* power saw.

motriz *adj* fuerza m., motive power.

movedizo,-a *adj* arenas movedizas, quicksand *sing*.

mover [4] I *vtr* 1 to move; m. algo de su sitio, to move sth out of its place. 2 *(hacer funcionar)* to drive; el motor mueve el coche, the engine drives the car. II **moverse** *vr* 1 to move. 2 *fam (gestionar)* to do everything possible. 3 *(darse prisa)* to hurry up; ¡muévete!, get a move on!

movida *nf arg* hay mucha m., there's a lot going on.

movido,-a *adj* 1 Fot blurred. 2 *(ocupado)* busy.

móvil I *adj* mobile; TV Rad unidad m., outside broadcast unit. II *nm (de delito)* motive.

movilización *nf* mobilization.

movilizar [4] *vtr* to mobilize.

movimiento *nm* 1 movement; Fís Téc motion; (poner algo) en m., (to se⁹ sth) in motion; m. sísmico, earth tremor. 2 *(actividad)* activity. 3 Com Fin *(entradas y salidas)* operations. 4 Esp Hist el M., the Falangist Movement.

moviola *nf* Cin TV 1 *(cámara)* editing projector. 2 *(repetición)* action replay.

moza *nf* lass, young girl.

mozo *nm* 1 lad, boy. 2 *(de estación)* porter; *(de hotel)* bellboy, US bellhop. 3 Mil conscript.

mucamo,-a *nm,f Am* servant.

muchacha *nf* girl.

muchacho *nm* boy.

muchedumbre *nf (de gente)* crowd.

mucho,-a I *adj* 1 *sing (usu en frases afirmativas)* a lot of, lots of; *(usu en frases neg)* much; m. tiempo, a long time; tengo m. sueño/mucha sed, I am very sleepy/thirsty; hay m. tonto suelto, there are lots of idiots around; ¿bebes m. café? - no, no m., do you drink a lot of coffee? - no, not much. 2 *(demasiado)* m. coche para mí, this car is a bit too much for me. 3 muchos,-as, *(usu en frases afirmativas)* a lot of; *(usu en frases neg)* many; tiene m. años, he is very old. II *pron* 1 a lot, a great deal; ¿cuánta leche queda? - mucha, how much milk is there left? - a lot. 2 muchos,-as, a lot, lots, many; ¿cuántos libros tienes? - muchos, how many books have you got? - lots o a lot; muchos creemos que ..., many of us believe that ...

III *adv* 1 a lot, very much; lo siento m., I'm very sorry; como m., at the most; con m., by far; m. antes/después, long before/after; ¡ni m. menos!, no way!; por m. (que) + *subj*, however much. 2 *(tiempo)* hace m. que no viene por aquí, he has not been to see us for a long time. 3 *(a menudo)* vamos m. al cine, we go to the cinema quite often.

muda *nf (de ropa)* change of clothes.

mudanza *nf* move; estar de m., to be moving; camión de m., removal van.

mudar I *vtr* 1 *(ropa)* to change. 2 *(plumas, pelo)* to moult, US molt; *(piel)* to shed, slough. II **mudarse** *vr* m. de casa/ropa to move house/to change one's clothes.

mudo,-a I *adj* 1 *(que no habla)* dumb; cine m., silent films *pl*. 2 *fig (callado)* speechless. II *nm,f* mute.

mueble I *nm* piece of furniture; muebles, furniture *sing*; con/sin muebles, furnished/unfurnished; m. bar, cocktail cabinet. II *adj* movable.

mueca *nf* 1 *(de burla)* mocking face; hacer muecas, to pull faces. 2 *(de dolor, asco)* grimace.

muela *nf* 1 Anat molar; dolor de muelas, toothache; m. del juicio, wisdom tooth. 2 Téc *(de molino)* millstone.

muelle¹ *nm* spring.

muelle² *nm* Náut dock.

muermo *nm fam (tedio)* boredom; *(rollo)* drag.

muerte *nf* death; m. natural, natural death; dar m. a algn, to kill sb; odiar a algn a m., to loathe sb; fam de mala m., lousy, rotten; fam un susto de m., the fright of one's life.

muerto,-a I *adj* dead; caer m., to drop dead; m. de hambre, starving; m. de frío, frozen to death; m. de miedo, scared stiff; m. de risa, laughing one's head off; horas muertas, spare time; Aut (en) punto m., (in) neutral. II *nm,f* 1 *(difunto)* dead person; hacerse el m., to pretend to be dead; *fam* cargar con el m., to do the dirty work. 2 *(víctima)* fatality; hubo dos muertos, two (people) died.

muesca *nf* notch.

muestra *nf* 1 *(espécimen)* sample, specimen. 2 *(modelo a copiar)* model. 3 *(prueba, señal)* sign; dar muestras de, to show signs of; m. de cariño/respeto, token of affection/respect; una m. más de ..., yet another example of ...

muestral *adj* error m., margin of error.

muestreo *nm* sampling.

mugido *nm (de vaca)* moo; *(de toro)* bellow.

mugir [6] *vi (vaca)* to moo, low; *(toro)* to bellow.

mugre *nf* filth.

mugriento,-a *adj* filthy.

mujer *nf* 1 woman; dos mujeres, two women; m. de la limpieza, cleaner; m. de su casa, houseproud woman. 2 *(esposa)* wife; su futura m., his bride-to-be.

mujeriego I *adj* woman-chasing. II *nm* womanizer, woman chaser.

muleta *nf* 1 *(prótesis)* crutch. 2 Taur muleta.

muletilla *nf* pet word o phrase.

mullido,-a *adj* soft.

mulo *nm* mule.

multa *nf* fine; *Aut* ticket.

multar *vtr* to fine.

multi- *pref* multi-.

multicolor *adj* multicoloured, *US* multicolored.

multicopista *nf* duplicator.

multilateral *adj* multilateral.

multinacional *adj* & *nf* multinational.

múltiple *adj* 1 multiple; **accidente m.**, pile up. 2 **múltiples**, *(muchos)* many.

multiplicación *nf Mat* multiplication.

multiplicar [1] I *vtr* & *vi* to multiply *(por,* by). II **multiplicarse** *vr (reproducirse, aumentar)* to multiply.

múltiplo,-a *adj* & *nm* multiple.

multirriesgo *adj inv* **póliza m.**, multiple risk policy.

multitud *nf* 1 *(de personas)* crowd. 2 *(de cosas)* multitude.

mundano,-a *adj* mundane.

mundial I *adj* worldwide; **campeón m.**, world champion; **de fama m.**, world-famous. II *nm* world championship. ◆**mundialmente** *adv* **m. famoso**, world-famous, famous worldwide.

mundo *nm* world; **todo el m.**, everyone; **correr o ver m.**, to travel widely; **nada del otro m.**, nothing special; **el otro m.**, the hereafter.

muñeca *nf* 1 wrist. 2 *(juguete, muchacha)* doll.

muñeco *nm (juguete)* (little) boy doll; **m. de trapo**, rag doll; **m. de nieve**, snowman.

muñequera *nf* wristband.

munición *nf* ammunition.

municipal I *adj* municipal. II *nm (municipal)* policeman.

municipio *nm* 1 *(territorio)* municipality. 2 *(ayuntamiento)* town council.

muñón *nm Anat* stump.

muralla *nf* wall.

Murcia *n* Murcia.

murciélago *nm Zool* bat.

murmullo *nm* murmur.

murmuración *nf* gossip.

murmurar *vi* 1 *(criticar)* to gossip. 2 *(susurrar)* to whisper; *(refunfuñar)* to grumble. 3 *fig (río)* to murmur.

muro *nm* wall.

murrio,-a *adj fam* sad, blue.

musa *nf* muse.

musaraña *nf fam* **estar mirando a o pensando en las musarañas**, to be day-dreaming *o* in the clouds.

musculatura *nf* musculature; **desarrollar la m.**, to develop one's muscles.

músculo *nm* muscle.

musculoso,-a *adj* muscular.

museo *nm* museum; **m. de arte** *o* **pintura**, art gallery.

musgo *nm* moss.

música *nf* music; **m. clásica**, classical music; **m. de fondo**, background music.

musical I *adj* musical. II *nm* musical.

músico,-a I *adj* musical. II *nm,f* musician.

muslo *nm* thigh.

mustio,-a *adj* 1 *(plantas)* wilted, withered. 2 *(persona)* sad, gloomy.

musulmán,-ana *adj* & *nm,f* Muslim, Moslem.

mutación *nf Biol* mutation.

mutilación *nf* mutilation.

mutilado,-a *nm,f* disabled person; **m. de guerra**, disabled serviceman.

mutilar *vtr* to mutilate.

mutis *nm Teat* exit.

mutua *nf* mutual benefit society.

mutualidad *nf* 1 *(reciprocidad)* mutuality. 2 *(asociación)* mutual benefit society.

mutuo,-a *adj* mutual.

muy *adv* very; **m. bueno/malo**, very good/bad; **¡m. bien!**, very good!; **fam m. mucho**, very much; **M. señor mío**, Dear Sir; **m. de los andaluces**, typically Andalusian; **m. de mañana/noche**, very early/late.

N

N, n ['ene] *nf (la letra)* N, n.

N *abr de Norte*, North, N.

n/ *abr de nuestro,-a*, our.

nabo *nm* 1 *Bot* turnip. 2 *vulg (pene)* prick.

nácar *nm* mother-of-pearl.

nacer [33] *vi* 1 to be born; **al n.**, at birth; **nací en Montoro**, I was born in Montoro; *fam* **fig n. de pie**, to be born under a lucky star. 2 *(pájaro)* to hatch (out). 3 *(pelo)* to begin to grow. 4 *(río)* to rise.

nacido,-a *adj* born; **m. de padre español**, born of a Spanish father; **recién n.**, newborn; *fig* **mal n.**, despicable, mean.

naciente *adj (nuevo)* new, recent; *(sol)* rising.

nacimiento *nm* 1 birth; **sordo de n.**, deaf from birth; **lugar de n.**, birthplace, place of birth. 2 *fig (principio)* origin, beginning; *(de río)* source. 3 *(belén)* Nativity scene, crib.

nación *nf* nation; **las Naciones Unidas**, the United Nations.

nacional *adj* 1 national. 2 *(producto, mercado)* domestic; **vuelos nacionales**, domestic flights. II *nmf* national; *Hist* **los nacionales**, the Francoist forces.

nacionalidad *nf* nationality.

nacionalismo *nm* nationalism.

nacionalista *adj & nmf* nationalist.

nacionalizar [4] I *vtr 1 Econ (banca, industria)* to nationalize. 2 *(naturalizar)* to naturalize. II **nacionalizarse** *vr* to become naturalized; **n. español**, to take up Spanish citizenship.

nada I *pron 1 (como respuesta)* nothing; **qué quieres? - n.**, what do you want? - nothing. 2 *(con verbo)* not ... anything; *(enfático)* nothing; **no sé n.**, I don't know anything; **yo no digo n.**, I'm saying nothing. 3 *(con otro negativo)* anything; **no hace nunca n.**, he never does anything; **nadie sabía n.**, nobody knew anything. 4 *(en ciertas construcciones)* anything; **más que n.**, more than anything; **sin decir n.**, without saying anything; **casi n.**, hardly anything. 5 **gracias, - de n.**, thanks, - don't mention it; *fam* **para n.**, not at all; **casi n.**, almost nothing; **como si n.**, just like that; **un rasguño de n.**, an insignificant little scratch; **n. de eso**, nothing of the kind; **n. de**, nothing at all; **n. más verla**, as soon as he saw her. II *adv* not at all; **no me gusta n.**, I don't like it at all; **no lo encuentro n. interesante**, I don't find it remotely interesting. III *nf* nothingness; **salir de la n.**, to come out of nowhere.

nadar *vi 1 Dep* to swim; **n. a braza**, to do the breaststroke. 2 *(flotar)* to float.

nadador,-a *nm,f* swimmer.

nadie I *pron 1 (como respuesta)* no-one, nobody; **quién vino? - n.**, who came? - no-one. 2 *(con verbo)* not ... anyone, anybody; *(enfático)* no-one, nobody; **no conozco a n.**, I don't know anyone o anybody; **no vi a n.**, I saw no-one. 3 *(con otro negativo)* anyone, anybody; **nunca habla con n.**, he never speaks to anybody. 4 *(en ciertas construcciones)* anybody, anyone; **más que n.**, more than anyone; **sin decírselo a n.**, without telling anyone; **casi n.**, hardly anyone. II *nm* nobody; **ser un don n.**, to be a nobody.

nado (a) *loc adv* swimming; **cruzar** *o* **pasar a n.**, to swim across.

nafta *nf Am (gasolina)* petrol, *US* gasoline.

nailon *nm* nylon; **medias de n.**, nylons *pl*.

naipe *nm* playing card.

nalga *nf* buttock; **nalgas**, bottom *sing*, buttocks.

nana *nf* lullaby.

napalm *nm* napalm.

napias *nfpl fam* snout *sing*.

Nápoles *n* Naples.

napolitano,-a *adj & nm,f* Neapolitan.

naranja I *nf* orange; *fig* **mi media n.**, my better half. II *adj & nm (color)* orange.

naranjada *nf* orangeade.

naranjo *nm* orange tree.

narciso *nm 1 (blanco)* narcissus; *(amarillo)* daffodil. 2 *fig (hombre)* narcissist.

narcótico *nm* narcotic; *(droga)* drug.

narcotizar [4] *vtr (drogar)* to drug.

narcotraficante *nmf* drug trafficker.

narcotráfico *nm* drug trafficking.

nariz *nf 1* nose; *fam* **me da en la n. que ...**, I've got this feeling that .... 2 *fam* **narices**, nose *sing*; *fam* **en mis (propias) narices**, right under my very nose; *fam* **estar hasta las narices de**, to be totally fed up with; *fam* **meter las narices en algo**, to poke one's nose into sth; *fam* **por narices**, because I say so; *fam* **tocarle a algn las narices**, to get on sb's wick.

narración *nf* narration.

narrar *vtr* to narrate, tell.

narrativo,-a *adj & nf* narrative.

nata *nf 1* cream; **n. batida/montada**, whipped cream. 2 *(de leche hervida)* skin. 3 *fig* cream, best.

natación *nf Dep* swimming.

natal *adj* mi **país n.**, my native country; **su pueblo n.**, his home town.

natalicio *nm fml* birthday.

natalidad *nf* birth rate; **control de n.**, birth control.

natillas *nfpl Culin* custard *sing*.

natividad *nf* Nativity.

nativo,-a *adj & nm,f* native.

nato,-a *adj* born.

natura *nf lit* nature; **contra n.**, against nature.

natural I *adj* natural; *(fruta, flor)* fresh; **de tamaño n.**, life-size; **en estado n.**, in its natural state; *Jur* **hijo n.**, illegitimate child. II *nmf* native.

naturaleza *nf 1* nature; **en plena n.**, in the wild, in unspoilt countryside; *Arte* **n. muerta**, still life. 2 *(complexión)* physical constitution.

naturalidad *nf (sencillez)* naturalness; **con n.**, naturally, straightforwardly.

naturalismo *nm* naturalism.

naturalista I *adj* naturalistic. II *nmf* naturalist.

naturalización *nf* naturalization.

naturalizar [4] *vtr* to naturalize. II **naturalizarse** *vr* to become naturalized.

naturalmente *adv* naturally; **¡n.!**, of course!

naturismo *nm* naturism.

naturista *nmf* naturist.

naufragar [7] *vi (barco)* to sink, be wrecked; *(persona)* to be shipwrecked.

naufragio *nm Náut* shipwreck.

náufrago,-a *nm,f* shipwrecked person, castaway.

náusea *nf (usu pl)* nausea, sickness; **me da n.**, it makes me sick; **sentir náuseas**, to feel sick.

nauseabundo,-a *adj* nauseating, sickening.

náutico,-a *adj* nautical.

navaja *nf 1 (cuchillo)* penknife, pocketknife; **n. de afeitar**, razor. **2** *(molusco)* razor-shell.

navajada *nf*, **navajazo** *nm* stab, gash.

navajero,-a *nm fam* thug.

naval *adj* naval.

Navarra *n* Navarre.

navarro,-a I *adj* Navarrese, of o from Navarre. **II** *nm,f* native o inhabitant of Navarre.

nave *nf* **1** ship; **n. (espacial)**, spaceship, spacecraft. **2** *Ind* plant, building. **3** *(de iglesia)* nave; **n. lateral**, aisle.

navegable *adj* navigable.

navegación *nf* navigation; **n. costera**, coastal shipping.

navegar [7] *vi* **1** to navigate, sail. **2** *Av* to navigate, fly.

Navidad(es) *nf(pl)* Christmas; **árbol de Navidad**, Christmas tree; **Feliz Navidad/Felices Navidades**, Merry Christmas.

navideño,-a *adj* Christmas.

navío *nm* ship.

nazi *adj & nmf* Nazi.

nazismo *nm* Nazism.

n/c., n/cta. *abr* **de nuestra cuenta**, our account, our acct.

neblina *nf* mist, thin fog.

nebulosa *nf Astron* nebula.

nebuloso,-a *adj* **1** *Meteor* cloudy, hazy. **2** *fig* nebulous, vague.

necedad *nf* **1** *(estupidez)* stupidity, foolishness. **2** *(tontería)* stupid thing to say o to do.

necesario,-a *adj* necessary; **es n. hacerlo**, it has to be done; **es n. que vayas**, you must go; **no es n. que vayas**, there is no need for you to go; **si fuera n.**, if need be.

neceser *nm (de aseo)* toilet bag; *(de maquillaje)* make-up bag.

necesidad *nf* **1** necessity, need; **artículos de primera n.**, essentials; **por n.**, of necessity; **tener n. de**, to need. **2** *(pobreza)* poverty, hardship. **3** **hacer sus necesidades**, to relieve oneself.

necesitado,-a I *adj (pobre)* needy, poor; **n. de**, in need of. **II** *npl* **los necesitados**, the needy.

necesitar *vtr* to need; **'se necesita chico'**, *(en anuncios)* 'boy wanted'.

necio,-a I *adj* silly, stupid. **II** *nm,f* fool, idiot.

necrología *nf* obituary.

néctar *nm* nectar.

nectarina *nf* nectarine.

neerlandés,-esa I *adj* Dutch, of o from the Netherlands. **II** *nm,f (persona) (hombre)* Dutchman; *(mujer)* Dutchwoman; **los neerlandeses**, the Dutch. **III** *nm (idioma)* Dutch.

nefasto,-a *adj* **1** *(perjudicial)* harmful. **2** *(funesto)* unlucky, ill-fated. **3** *(inútil)* hopeless.

negación *nf* **1** negation. **2** *(negativa)* denial; *(rechazo)* refusal. **3** *Ling* negative.

negado,-a I *adj* ser **n. para algo**, to be hopeless o useless at sth. **II** *nm,f* no-hoper.

negar [1] **I** *vtr* **1** to deny; **negó haberlo robado**, he denied stealing it. **2** *(rechazar)* to refuse, deny; **le negaron la beca**, they refused him the grant. **II negarse** *vr* to refuse (a, to).

negativa *nf* denial.

negativo,-a *adj & nm* negative.

negligencia *nf* negligence.

negociación *nf* negotiation.

negociador,-a *adj* negotiating; **comité n.**, negotiating commitee.

negociante *nmf* dealer; *(hombre)* businessman; *(mujer)* businesswoman.

negociar [12] **I** *vtr Fin Pol* to negotiate. **II** *vi (comerciar)* to do business, deal.

negocio *nm Com Fin* business; *(transacción)* deal, transaction; *(asunto)* affair; **hombre de negocios**, businessman; **mujer de negocios**, businesswoman.

negra *nf* **1** *fig (mala suerte)* bad luck; **tener la n.**, to be very unlucky. **2** *Mús* crotchet, *US* quarter note.

negrilla, negrita *adj & nf Impr* bold (face).

negro,-a I *adj* **1** black; **estar n.**, *(bronceado)* to be suntanned. **2** *fig (suerte)* awful; *(desesperado)* desperate; *(furioso)* furious; **verlo todo n.**, to be very pessimistic; **vérselas negras para hacer algo**, to have a tough time doing sth. **II** *nm,f (hombre)* black; *(mujer)* black (woman). **III** *nm (color)* black.

nene *nm,f (niño)* baby boy; *(niña)* baby girl.

nenúfar *nm Bot* water lily.

neocelandés,-esa I *adj* of o from New Zealand. **II** *nm,f* New Zealander.

neoclásico,-a *adj Arte Lit* neoclassic, neoclassical.

neologismo *nm* neologism.

neón *nm* neon.

neoyorkino,-a I *adj* of o from New York. **II** *nm,f* New Yorker.

neozelandés,-esa *adj & nm,f →* **neocelandés,-esa**.

nepotismo *nm* nepotism.

Neptuno *n* Neptune.

nervio *nm* **1** *Anat Bot* nerve; *(de la carne)* sinew. **2** *fig (fuerza, vigor)* nerve, courage. **3** **nervios**, nerves; **ataque de n.**, a fit of hysterics; **ser un manojo de n.**, to be a bundle of nerves; **tener los nervios de acero**, to have nerves of steel.

nerviosismo *nm* nerves *pl*.

nervioso,-a *adj* **1** nervous; **poner n. a algn**, to get on sb's nerves. **2** *(inquieto)* fidgety.

neto,-a *adj* **1** *(peso, cantidad)* net. **2** *(nítido)* neat, clear.

neumático,-a I *adj* pneumatic. **II** *nm* tyre, *US* tire; **n. de recambio**, spare tyre.

neumonía *nf* pneumonia.

neurálgico,-a *adj* neuralgic; *fig* **punto n.**, nerve centre.

neurólogo,-a *nm,f* neurologist.

neurosis *nf* neurosis.

neurótico,-a *adj & nm,f* neurotic.

neutral *adj* neutral.

neutralidad *nf* neutrality.

neutralizar [4] *vtr* to neutralize.

neutro,-a *adj* **1** (*imparcial*) neutral. **2** *Ling* neuter.

neutrón *nm Fís* neutron; **bomba de neutrones**, neutron bomb.

nevada *nf* snowfall.

nevar [1] *v impers* to snow.

nevera *nf* **1** (*frigorífico*) refrigerator, *fam* fridge. **2** (*portátil*) cool box.

nexo *nm* connection, link.

ni *conj* **1** no ... ni, ni ... ni, neither ... nor, not ... or; **no tengo tiempo ni dinero**, I have got neither time nor money; **ni ha venido ni ha llamado**, he hasn't come or phoned; **no vengas ni hoy ni mañana**, don't come today or tomorrow. **2** (*ni siquiera*) not even; **ni por dinero**, not even for money; **ni se te ocurra**, don't even think about it; **¡ni hablar!**, no way!

Nicaragua *nf* Nicaragua.

nicaragüense, nicaragüeño,-a *adj & nm,f* Nicaraguan.

nicho *nm* niche.

nicotina *nf* nicotine.

nido *nm* nest.

niebla *nf* fog; **hay mucha n.**, it is very foggy.

nieto,-a *nm,f* (*niño*) grandson; (*niña*) granddaughter; **mis nietos**, my grandchildren.

nieve *nf* **1** *Meteor* snow; *Culin* **a punto de n.**, (beaten) stiff. **2** *arg* (*cocaína*) snow.

nigeriano,-a *adj & nm,f* Nigerian.

nigerino,-a *adj & nm,f* Nigerien.

Nilo *n* el N., the Nile.

nilón *nm Tex* nylon.

nimio,-a *adj* (*insignificante*) insignificant, petty.

ninfómana *nf* nymphomaniac.

ningún *adj* (*delante de nm sing*) → **ninguno,-a**.

ninguno,-a I *adj* **1** (*con verbo*) not ... any; **no leí ninguna revista**, I didn't read any magazines; **no tiene ninguna gracia**, it is not funny at all. **2** **en ninguna parte**, nowhere; **de ningún modo**, no way. **II** *pron* **1** (*persona*) nobody, no one; **n. lo vio**, no one saw it; **n. de los dos**, neither of the two; **n. de ellos**, none of them. **2** (*cosa*) not ... any of them; (*enfático*) none of them; **me gusta n.**, I don't like any of them; **no vi n.**, I saw none of them.

niña *nf* **1** girl; → **niño,-a**. **2** *Anat* pupil;

fig **es la n. de sus ojos**, she's the apple of his eye.

niñera *nf* nursemaid, nanny.

niñez *nf* infancy; (*a partir de los cuatro años*) childhood.

niño,-a *nm,f* **1** child; (*muchacho*) (small) boy; (*muchacha*) (little) girl; **de n.**, as a child; **n. prodigio**, child prodigy; *pey* **n. bien** *o* **de papá**, rich boy, rich kid; *pey* **n. bonito** *o* **mimado**, mummy's *o* daddy's boy. **2** (*bebé*) baby. **3 niños**, children; *fig* **juego de niños**, child's play.

nipón,-ona *adj & nm,f* Japanese; **los nipones**, the Japanese.

níquel *nm* nickel.

niqui *nm* T-shirt.

níspero *nm* (*fruto*) medlar; (*árbol*) medlar tree.

nítido,-a *adj* (*claro*) clear; (*imagen*) sharp.

nitrógeno *nm* nitrogen.

nitroglicerina *nf* nitroglycerine.

nivel *nm* **1** (*altura*) level; **a n. del mar**, at sea level. **2** (*categoría*) standard; **n. de vida**, standard of living. **3** (*instrumento*) level; **n. de aire**, spirit level. **4** *Ferroc* **paso a n.**, level crossing, *US* grade crossing.

nivelar *vtr* **1** to level out *o* off. **2** (*equilibrar*) to balance out.

n.º *abr de número*, number, n.

no I *adv* **1** (*como respuesta*) no; **¿te gusta? - no.**, do you like it? - no. **2** (*en otros contextos*) not. **n. vi a nadie**, I didn't see anyone; **aún no**, not yet; **ya no**, no longer, not any more. **no sin antes ...**, not without first ...; **¿por qué no?**, why not? **3 no fumar/aparcar**, (*en letrero*) no smoking/parking. **4 no sea que** + *subj*, in case. **5 es rubia, ¿no?**, she's blonde, isn't she? **6 llegaron anoche, ¿no?**, they arrived yesterday, didn't they? **6** (*como prefijo negativo*) non; **la no violencia**, non-violence. **II** *nm* no; **un no rotundo**, a definite no.

noble I *adj* noble. **II** *nmf* (*hombre*) nobleman; (*mujer*) noblewoman; **los nobles**, the nobility *sing*.

nobleza *nf* nobility.

noche *nf* evening; (*después de las diez*) night, night-time; **de n.**, **por la n.**, at night; **esta n.**, tonight; **mañana por la n.**, tomorrow night *o* evening; **buenas noches**, (*saludo*) good evening; (*despedida*) good night; **son las nueve de la noche**, it's nine p.m.

nochebuena *nf* Christmas Eve.

nochevieja *nf* New Year's Eve.

noción *nf* **1** notion, idea. **2 nociones**, smattering *sing*, basic knowledge *sing*; **n. de español**, a smattering of Spanish.

nocivo,-a *adj* noxious, harmful.

noctámbulo,-a *nm,f* sleepwalker; *fam* night-bird.

nocturno,-a *adj* **1** night; **vida nocturna**,

night life; **clases nocturnas,** evening classes. 2 *Bot* nocturnal.

nodriza *nf* 1 (*ama*) wet nurse. 2 **buque n.,** supply ship.

nogal *nm Bot* walnut (tree).

nómada I *adj* nomadic. II *nmf* nomad.

nombrado,-a *adj* (*célebre*) famous, well-known.

nombramiento *nm* appointment.

nombrar *vtr* 1 (*designar*) to name, appoint; **n. a algn director,** to appoint sb director. 2 (*mencionar*) to name, mention.

nombre *nm* 1 name; **n. de pila,** Christian name; **n. y apellidos,** full name; **a n. de,** addressed to; **en n. de,** on behalf of. 2 *Ling* noun; **n. propio,** proper noun.

nómina *nf* 1 (*de sueldo*) pay slip. 2 (*plantilla*) payroll.

nominar *vtr* to nominate.

nominativo,-a *adj* **cheque n. a,** cheque made out to.

non *nm* 1 *Mat* odd number; **pares y nones,** odds and evens. 2 *fam* **nones,** (*negación*) no; **decir (que) nones,** to refuse.

nono,-a *adj* → **noveno,-a.**

norcoreano,-a *adj & nm,f* North Korean.

nordeste *nm* → **noreste.**

nórdico,-a I *adj* 1 (*del norte*) northern. 2 (*escandinavo*) Nordic. II *nm,f* Nordic person.

noreste *nm* northeast.

noria *nf* 1 (*de feria*) big wheel. 2 (*para agua*) water-wheel.

norirlandés,-esa I *adj* Northern Irish. II *nm,f* (*persona*) (*hombre*) Northern Irishman; (*mujer*) Northern Irishwoman; **los norirlandeses,** the Northern Irish.

norma *nf* norm; **n. de seguridad,** safety standard.

normal *adj* normal, usual; **lo n.,** the normal thing, what usually happens.

normalidad *nf* normality; **volver a la n.,** to return to normal.

normalizar [4] I *vtr* to normalize, restore to normal. II **normalizarse** *vr* to return to normal.

normativa *nf* rules *pl*.

noroeste *nm* northwest.

norte *nm* 1 north; **al n. de,** to the north of. 2 *fig* aim, goal.

norteafricano,-a *adj & nm,f* North African.

Norteamérica *n* North America.

norteamericano,-a *adj & nm,f* (North) American.

norteño,-a I *adj* northern. II *nm,f* Northerner.

Noruega *n* Norway.

noruego,-a I *adj* Norwegian. II *nm,f* Norwegian. III *nm* (*idioma*) Norwegian.

nos I *pron pers* (*directo*) us; (*indirecto*) us; **n. ha visto,** he has seen us; **n. trajo un regalo,** he brought us a present; **n. lo dio,** he gave it to us. II *pron* (*reflexivo*)

ourselves; (*recíproco*) each other; **n. hemos divertido mucho,** we enjoyed ourselves a lot; **n. queremos mucho,** we love each other very much.

nosotros,-as *pron pers pl* 1 (*sujeto*) we; **n. lo vimos,** we saw it; **somos n.,** it is us. 2 (*complemento*) us; **con n.,** with us.

nostalgia *nf* nostalgia; (*morriña*) homesickness.

nostálgico,-a *adj* nostalgic; (*con morriña*) homesick.

nota *nf* 1 (*anotación*) note. 2 *Educ* mark, grade; **sacar buenas notas,** to get good marks. 3 *fig* (*detalle*) element, quality; **la n. dominante,** the prevailing quality. 4 *Mús* note; *fam* **dar la n.,** to make oneself noticed.

notable I *adj* (*apreciable*) noticeable; (*destacado*) outstanding, remarkable. II *nm* (*nota*) very good.

notar I *vtr* (*percibir*) to notice, note. II **notarse** *vr* 1 to be noticeable *o* evident, show; **no se nota,** it doesn't show; **se nota que ...,** one can see that ....

notaría *nf* (*despacho*) notary's office.

notarial *adj* notarial; **acta n.,** affidavit.

notario,-a *nm,f* notary (public), solicitor.

noticia *nf* news *sing*; **una n.,** a piece of news; **una buena n.,** good news; **no tengo n. de esto,** I don't know anything about it.

notificación *nf* notification; **sin n. previa,** without (previous) notice; *Jur* **n. judicial,** summons *sing*.

notificar [1] *vtr* to notify.

notorio,-a *adj* 1 (*evidente*) noticeable, evident. 2 (*famoso*) famous, well-known.

novatada *nf* (*broma*) rough joke, rag. 2 **pagar la n.,** to learn the hard way.

novato,-a I *adj* (*persona*) inexperienced; *fam* green. II *nm,f* 1 (*principiante*) novice, beginner. 2 *Univ* fresher.

novecientos,-as *adj & nm,f* nine hundred.

novedad *nf* 1 (*cosa nueva*) novelty; **últimas novedades,** latest arrivals. 2 (*cambio*) change, development. 3 (*cualidad*) newness.

novedoso,-a *adj* 1 (*nuevo*) new, full of novelties. 2 (*innovador*) innovative.

novel I *adj* new, inexperienced. II *nmf* beginner, novice.

novela *nf Lit* novel; **n. corta,** short story; **n. policíaca,** detective story.

novelero,-a *adj* 1 fond of new things. 2 (*fantasioso*) highly imaginative.

novelesco,-a *adj* 1 (*de novela*) novelistic, fictional. 2 (*extraordinario*) bizarre, fantastic.

novelista *nmf* novelist.

noveno,-a *adj & nm* ninth; **novena parte,** ninth.

noventa *adj & nm inv* ninety.

novia *nf* 1 (*amiga*) girlfriend. 2 (*prometida*)

fiancée. 3 (en boda) bride.

noviazgo nm engagement.

noviembre nm November.

novillada nf Taur bullfight with young bulls.

novillero,-a nm,f Taur apprentice matador.

novillo,-a nm,f 1 (toro) young bull; (vaca) young cow. 2 fam Educ hacer novillos, to play truant o US hooky.

novio nm 1 (amigo) boyfriend. 2 (prometido) fiancé. 3 (en boda) bridegroom; los novios, the bride and groom.

nubarrón nm storm cloud.

nube nf cloud; fig vivir en las nubes, to have one's head in the clouds; fig poner a algn por las nubes, to praise sb to the skies.

nublado,-a adj cloudy, overcast.

nublarse vr to become cloudy, cloud over; fig se le nubló la vista, his eyes clouded over.

nuboso,-a adj cloudy.

nuca nf nape, back of the neck.

nuclear adj nuclear; central n., nuclear power station.

núcleo nm nucleus; (parte central) core; n. urbano, city centre.

nudillo nm (usu pl) knuckle.

nudista adj & nmf nudist.

nudo nm 1 knot; hacer un n., to tie a knot; fig se me hizo un n. en la garganta, I got a lump in my throat. 2 (punto principal) crux, core. 3 (de comunicaciones) centre, US center.

nuera nf daughter-in-law.

nuestro,-a adj pos 1 our; nuestra familia, our family. 2 (después del sustantivo) of ours; un amigo n., a friend of ours. II pron pos ours; este libro es n., this book is ours.

nueve adj & nm inv nine.

nuevo,-a adj 1 new; fam ¿qué hay de n.?, what's new?; de n., again; N. York, New York; N. Zelanda, New Zealand. 2

(adicional) further. II nm,f newcomer; (principiante) beginner. ◆**nuevamente** adv again.

nuez nf 1 walnut; n. moscada, nutmeg. 2 Anat n. (de Adán), Adam's apple.

nulidad nf 1 (ineptitud) incompetence. 2 Jur nullity.

nulo,-a adj 1 (inepto) useless, totally incapable. 2 (sin valor) null and void, invalid; voto n., invalid vote. 3 crecimiento n., zero growth.

núm. abr de número, number, n.

numeral adj & nm numeral.

numerar vtr to number.

numerario,-a I adj profesor no n., teacher on a temporary contract. II nm 1 (miembro) full member. 2 (dinero) cash.

numérico,-a adj numerical.

número nm 1 number; n. de matrícula, registration number, US license number; n. de serie, serial number; fig sin n., countless. 2 Prensa number, issue; n. atrasado, back number. 3 (de zapatos) size. 4 (en espectáculo) sketch, act; fam montar un n., to make a scene.

numeroso,-a adj numerous.

nunca adv 1 (como respuesta) never; cuándo volverás? - n., when will you come back? - never. 2 (con verbo) never; (enfático) not ... ever; no he estado n. en España, I've never been to Spain; yo no haría n. eso, I wouldn't ever do that. 3 (en ciertas construcciones) ever; casi n., hardly ever; más que n., more than ever. 4 n. jamás, never ever; (futuro) never again.

nupcial adj wedding, nuptial; marcha n., wedding march.

nupcias nfpl fml wedding sing, nuptials; casarse en segundas n., to marry again.

nutrición nf nutrition.

nutrir vtr to nourish, feed. II nutrirse vr to feed (de, on).

nutritivo,-a adj nutritious, nourishing; valor n., nutritional value.

Ñ

Ñ, ñ ['eɲe] nf (la letra) Ñ, ñ.

ñam interj fam ¡ñ., ñ.!, yum-yum!, yummy!

ñame nm Am yarn.

ñapa nf Am bonus, little extra.

ñato,-a adj Am snub-nosed.

ñiquiñaque nm fam 1 (objeto) junk,

rubbish. 2 (persona) good-for-nothing.

ñoñería, ñoñez nf 1 (sosería) insipidness, bore. 2 (melindrería) fussiness.

ñoño,-a adj 1 (soso) insipid, dull. 2 (melindroso) fussy. II nm,f dull o spineless person.

ñu nm gnu.

O

O, o |o| *nf (la letra)* O, o.

o *conj* or; **jueves o viernes,** Thursday or Friday; **o ... o,** either ... or; **o sea,** that is (to say), in other words.

O. *abr de* Oeste, West, W.

oasis *nm inv* oasis.

obcecado,-a *adj fig* stubborn.

obcecar [1] I *vtr fig* to blind; **la ira lo obceca,** he is blinded by anger. II **obcecarse** *vr fig* to refuse to budge; *(obsesionarse)* to become obsessed.

obedecer [33] I *vtr* to obey. II **o. a,** *(provenir)* to be due to; **¿a qué obedece esa actitud?,** what's the reason behind this attitude?

obediencia *nf* obedience.

obediente *adj* obedient.

obertura *nf* overture.

obesidad *nf* obesity.

obeso,-a *adj* obese.

óbice *nm* obstacle; **eso no es ó. para que yo no ...,** it won't prevent me from ....

obispo *nm* bishop.

objeción *nf* objection; **poner una o.,** to raise an objection, object.

objetar I *vtr* to object to. II **no tengo nada que o.,** I've got no objections. II *vi* Mil to be a conscientious objector.

objetividad *nf* objectivity.

objetivo,-a I *nm* 1 *(fin, meta)* objective, aim. 2 Mil target. 3 Cin Fot lens; **o. zoom,** zoom lens. II *adj* objective.

objeto *nm* 1 object; **objetos perdidos,** lost property *sing*; **mujer o.,** sex object. 2 *(fin)* aim, purpose; **con o. de ...,** in order to ...; **tiene por o. ...,** it is designed to .... 3 Ling object.

objetor,-a I *nm,f* objector; **o. de conciencia,** conscientious objector. II *adj* objecting, dissenting.

obligación *nf* 1 *(deber)* obligation; **por o.,** out of a sense of duty; **tengo o. de ...,** I have to .... 2 Fin bond, debenture.

obligado,-a *adj* obliged; **verse o estar o. a,** to be obliged to.

obligar [7] *vtr* to compel, force.

obligatorio,-a *adj* compulsory, obligatory.

obra *nf* 1 *(trabajo)* (piece of) work; **por o. de,** thanks to. 2 Arte work; **o. maestra,** masterpiece. 3 *(acto)* deed. 4 Constr building site. 5 **obras,** *(arreglos)* repairs; **'carretera en o.',** 'roadworks'; **'cerrado por o.',** 'closed for repairs'.

obrar I *vi* 1 *(proceder)* to act, behave; **o. bien/mal,** to do the right/wrong thing. 2 *fml* **obra en nuestro poder ...,** we are in receipt of .... II *vtr (milagro)* to work.

obrero,-a I *nm,f* worker, labourer; *US* labourer. II *adj* working; **clase obrera,**

working class; **movimiento o.,** labour movement.

obscenidad *nf* obscenity.

obsceno,-a *adj* obscene.

obscurecer [33] I *vi impers* to get dark. II *vtr* to darken; *fig* obscurity. II **obscurecerse** *vr (nublarse)* to become cloudy.

obscuridad *nf* darkness; *fig* obscurity.

obscuro,-a *adj* 1 dark. 2 *fig (origen, idea)* obscure; *(futuro)* uncertain, gloomy; *(asunto)* shady; *(nublado)* overcast.

obsequiar [12] *vtr* to give away.

obsequio *nm* gift, present.

observación *nf* observation.

observador,-a I *nm,f* observer. II *adj* observant.

observancia *nf* observance.

observar *vtr* 1 *(mirar)* to observe, watch. 2 *(notar)* to notice. 3 *(cumplir)* to observe.

observatorio *nm* observatory.

obsesión *nf* obsession.

obsesionar I *vtr* to obsess; **estoy obsesionado con eso,** I can't get it out of my mind. II **obsesionarse** *vr* to get obsessed.

obsesivo,-a *adj* obsessive.

obseso,-a *nm,f* obsessed person; **un o. sexual,** a sex maniac.

obsoleto,-a *adj* obsolete.

obstaculizar [4] *vtr* to obstruct, get in the way of.

obstáculo *nm* obstacle.

obstante (no) *loc adv* nevertheless; *prep* notwithstanding.

obstetricia *nf* obstetrics *sing*.

obstinación *nf* obstinacy.

obstinado,-a *adj* obstinate.

obstinarse *vr* to persist (en, in).

obstrucción *nf* obstruction; Med blockage.

obstruir [37] I *vtr* 1 *(salida, paso)* to block, obstruct. 2 *(progreso)* to impede, block. II **obstruirse** *vr* to get blocked up.

obtención *nf* obtaining.

obtener [24] I *vtr (alcanzar)* to obtain, get. II **obtenerse** *vr* **o. de,** *(provenir)* to come from.

obturador *nm* Fot shutter.

obtuso,-a *adj* obtuse.

obús *nm* shell.

obviar [12] *vtr (problema)* to get round.

obvio,-a *adj* obvious.

oca *nf* goose.

ocasión *nf* 1 *(momento)* occasion; **con o. de ...,** on the occasion of ...; **en cierta o.,** once. 2 *(oportunidad)* opportunity, chance; **aprovechar la o.,** to make the most of an opportunity. 3 Com bargain; **de o.,** cheap; **precios de o.,** bargain prices.

ocasional *adj* 1 *(eventual)* occasional; **tra-**

bajo o., casual work; **de forma o.**, occasionally. 2 *(fortuito)* accidental, chance.
ocasionar *vtr* to cause, bring about.
ocaso *nm (anochecer)* sunset; *fig (declive)* fall, decline.
occidental *adj* western, occidental.
occidente *nm* west; **el O.**, the West.
OCDE *nf abr de* **Organización para la Cooperación y el Desarrollo Económico**, Organization for Economic Co-operation and Development, OECD.
Oceanía *nf* Oceania.
oceánico,-a *adj* oceanic.
océano *nm* ocean.
ochenta *adj & nm inv* eighty.
ocho *adj & nm inv* eight.
ochocientos,-as *adj & nm,f* eight hundred.
ocio *nm* leisure; **en mis ratos de o.**, in my spare o leisure time.
ocioso,-a *adj (inactivo)* idle. 2 *(inútil)* pointless.
ocre *nm* ochre, *US* ocher.
octavilla *nf (panfleto)* hand-out, leaflet.
octavo,-a *adj & nm,f* eighth.
octogenario,-a *adj & nm,f* octogenarian.
octogésimo,-a *adj & nm,f* eightieth.
octubre *nm* October.
ocular *adj* **testigo o.**, eye witness.
oculista *nmf* ophthalmologist.
ocultar I *vtr* to conceal, hide; **o. algo a algn**, to hide sth from sb. II **ocultarse** *vr* to hide.
oculto,-a *adj* concealed, hidden.
ocupación *nf* occupation.
ocupado,-a *adj (persona)* busy; *(asiento)* taken; *(aseos, teléfono)* engaged; *(puesto de trabajo)* filled.
ocupante *nmf (de casa)* occupant, occupier; *(ilegal)* squatter; *(de vehículo)* occupant.
ocupar I *vtr* 1 to occupy. 2 *(espacio, tiempo)* to take up; *(cargo)* to hold, fill. II **ocuparse** *vr* **o. de**, *(cuidar)* to look after; *(encargarse)* to see to.
ocurrencia *nf (agudeza)* witty remark, wisecrack; *(idea)* idea.
ocurrente *adj* witty.
ocurrir I *v impers* to happen, occur; **¿qué ocurre?**, what's going on?; **¿qué te ocurre?**, what's the matter with you? II **ocurrirse** *vr* **no se me ocurre nada**, I can't think of anything; **se me ocurre que ...**, it occurs to me that ....
odiar [12] *vtr* to detest, hate; **odio tener que ...**, I hate having to ....
odio *nm* hatred, loathing; **mirada de o.**, hateful look.
odioso,-a *adj* hateful.
odontología *nf* dentistry, odontology.
odontólogo,-a *nm,f* dental surgeon, odontologist.
odre *nm* wineskin.
OEA *nf abr de* **Organización de Estados**

Americanos, Organization of American States, OAS.
oeste *nm* west.
ofender I *vtr* to offend. II **ofenderse** *vr* to get offended *(con, por, by)*, take offence *o US* offense *(con, por, at)*.
ofensa *nf* offence, *US* offense.
ofensiva *nf* offensive.
ofensivo,-a *adj* offensive.
oferta *nf* offer; *Fin Ind* bid, tender, proposal; *Com* **de/en o.**, on (special) offer; **o. y demanda**, supply and demand.
ofertar *vtr* to offer.
off *adj* **voz en o.**, *Cin TV* voice-over; *Teat* voice offstage.
offset *nm Impr* offset.
oficial,-a I *adj* official. II *nm* 1 *Mil Náut* officer. 2 *(empleado)* clerk. 3 *(obrero)* skilled worker.
oficialía *nm Am (gobierno)* government.
oficina *nf* office; **o. de empleo**, job centre, *US* job office; **o. de turismo**, tourist office; **o. de correos**, post office; **horas/horario de o.**, business hours.
oficinista *nmf* office worker, clerk.
oficio *nm* 1 *(ocupación)* job, occupation; *(profesión)* trade; **ser del o.**, to be in the trade. 2 *(comunicación oficial)* official letter *o* note; **de o.**, ex-officio; **abogado de o.**, state-appointed lawyer. 3 *Rel* service.
oficioso,-a *adj (noticia, fuente)* unofficial.
ofimática *nf* office automation.
ofimático,-a *adj Inform* **paquete o.**, business package.
ofrecer [33] I *vtr* 1 to offer. 2 *(aspecto)* to present. II **ofrecerse** *vr* 1 *(prestarse)* to offer, volunteer. 2 *(situación)* to present itself. 3 *fml* **¿qué se le ofrece?**, what can I do for you?
ofrecimiento *nm* offering.
ofrendar *vtr Rel* to make offerings *o* an offering.
ofrezco *indic pres* → ofrecer.
oftalmología *nf* ophthalmology.
oftalmólogo,-a *nm,f* ophthalmologist.
ofuscación *nf*, **ofuscamiento** *nm* blinding, dazzling.
ofuscar [1] *vtr* 1 *fig (confundir)* to blind. 2 *(deslumbrar)* to dazzle.
oídas *(de) loc adv* by hearsay.
oído *nm* 1 *(sentido)* hearing. 2 *(órgano)* ear; **aprender de o.**, to learn by ear; *fig* **hacer oídos sordos**, to turn a deaf ear.
oír [17] *vtr* to hear; **¡oye!**, hey!; **¡oiga!**, excuse me!; *fam* **como lo oyes**, believe it or not.
OIT *nf abr de* **Organización Internacional del Trabajo**, International Labour Organization, ILO.
ojal *nm* buttonhole.
ojalá I *interj* let's hope so!, I hope so! II *conj (+ subj)* **¡o. sea cierto!**, I hope it's

true!

ojeada *nf* echar una o., to have a quick look.

ojeras *nfpl* rings o bags under the eyes.

ojeriza *nf* dislike.

ojo I *nm* 1 eye; **o. morado** black eye; **ojos saltones**, bulging eyes; *fig* **a ojos vista**, clearly, openly; *fig* **calcular a o.**, to guess; *fam* **no pegué o.**, I didn't sleep a wink. 2 *(de agua)* eye; *(de cerradura)* keyhole. 3 *(de un puente)* span. **II** *interj* careful!, look out!

ojota *nf Am* sandal.

okupa *nmf* squatter.

ola *nf* wave; **o. de calor**, heatwave.

ole, olé *interj* bravo!

oleada *nf* wave; *fig* **o. de turistas**, influx of tourists.

oleaje *nm* swell.

óleo *nm Arte* oil; **pintura** o **cuadro al ó.**, oil painting.

oleoducto *nm* pipeline.

oler [4] **I** *vtr* 1 *(percibir olor)* to smell. 2 *fig (adivinar)* to smell, feel. **II** *vi* 1 *(exhalar)* to smell; **o. a**, to smell of; **o. bien/mal**, to smell good/bad. 2 *fig (parecer)* to smack (a, of). **III olerse** *vr fig (adivinar)* to feel, sense; **me lo olía**, I thought as much.

olfatear *vtr* 1 *(oler)* to sniff. 2 *fig (indagar)* to pry into.

olfato *nm* sense of smell; *fig* good nose, instinct.

oligarquía *nf* oligarchy.

olimpiada *nf Dep* Olympiad, Olympic Games *pl*; **las olimpiadas**, the Olympic Games.

olímpico,-a *adj* Olympic; **Juegos Olímpicos**, Olympic Games.

olímpicamente *adv* paso o. de estudiar, I couldn't give a damn about studying.

oliva *nf* olive; **aceite de o.**, olive oil.

olivar *nm* olive grove.

olivo *nm* olive (tree).

olmo *nm* smooth-leaved elm.

olor *nm* smell; **o. corporal**, body odour.

oloroso,-a *adj* fragant, sweet-smelling.

OLP *nf abr de* **Organización para la Liberación de Palestina**, Palestine Liberation Organization, P.L.O.

olvidadizo,-a *adj* forgetful.

olvidar I *vtr* 1 to forget; *fam* ¡olvídame!, leave me alone! 2 olvidé el paraguas allí, I left my umbrella there. **II olvidarse** *vr* to forget; **se me ha olvidado hacerlo**, I forgot to do it.

olvido *nm* 1 *(desmemoria)* oblivion. 2 *(lapsus)* oversight.

olla *nf* saucepan, pot; **o. exprés** o a **presión**, pressure cooker.

ombligo *nm* navel.

ominoso,-a *adj* shameful.

omisión *nf* omission.

omiso,-a *adj* hacer caso o. de, to take no

notice of.

omitir *vtr* to omit, leave out.

omnipotente *adj* omnipotent, almighty.

omnipresente *adj* omnipresent.

omnisciente *adj* omniscient, all-knowing.

omnívoro,-a I *adj* omnivorous. **II** *nm,f* omnivore.

omóplato, omoplato *nm* shoulder blade.

OMS *nf abr de* **Organización Mundial de la Salud**, World Health Organization, WHO.

once I *adj inv* eleven. **II** *nm inv* eleven; *Ftb* eleven, team.

ONCE *nf abr de* **Organización Nacional de Ciegos Españoles**, ≈ Royal National Institute for the Blind, RNIB.

onda *nf* 1 *Fís* wave; *fam fig* **estar en la o.**, to be with it; **o. expansiva**, shock wave; *Rad* **o. larga/media/corta**, long/medium/short wave. 2 *(en el agua)* ripple. 3 *(de pelo)* wave.

ondear *vi* 1 *(bandera)* to flutter. 2 *(de agua)* to ripple.

ondulación *nf* undulation; *(de agua)* ripple.

ondulado,-a *adj* *(pelo)* wavy; *(paisaje)* rolling.

ondulante *adj* undulating.

ondular I *vtr* *(el pelo)* to wave. **II** *vi (moverse)* to undulate.

oneroso,-a *adj (impuesto)* heavy.

onomástica *nf* saint's day.

onomatopeya *nf* onomatopoeia.

ONU *nf abr de* **Organización de las Naciones Unidas**, United Nations (Organization), UN(O).

onubense I *adj* of o from Huelva. **II** *nmf* native o inhabitant of Huelva.

onza *nf (medida)* ounce.

OPA *abr de* **Oferta Pública de Adquisición**, takeover bid.

opaco,-a *adj* opaque.

ópalo *nm* opal.

opción *nf* 1 *(elección)* option, choice; *(alternativa)* alternative. 2 *(posibilidad)* opportunity, chance.

opcional *adj* optional.

open *nm Golf* open.

OPEP *nf abr de* **Organización de los Países Exportadores de Petróleo**, Organization of Petroleum Exporting Countries, OPEC.

ópera *nf Mús* opera.

operación *nf* 1 *Med* operation; **o. quirúrgica**, surgical operation. 2 *Fin* transaction, deal; **operaciones bursátiles**, stock exchange transactions. 3 *Mat* operation.

operador,-a *nm,f* 1 *(técnico)* operator. 2 *Cin (de cámara)* *(hombre)* cameraman; *(mujer)* camerawoman; *(del proyector)* projectionist. 3 *Tel* operator.

operante *adj* operative.

operar I *vtr* 1 *Med* to operate (a, on). 2 *(cambio etc)* to bring about. **II** *vi Fin* to deal, do business (**con**, with). **III ope-rarse** vr 1 *Med* to have an operation (**de**, for). 2 (*producirse*) to occur, come about.

operario,-a *nm,f* operator; (*obrero*) worker.

operativo,-a *adj* operative.

opereta *nf* operetta.

opinar *vi* 1 (*pensar*) to think. 2 (*declarar*) to give one's opinion, be of the opinion.

opinión *nf* 1 (*juicio*) opinion; **cambiar de o.**, to change one's mind.

opio *nm* opium.

oponente *nmf* opponent.

oponer [19] (*pp* **opuesto**) I vtr (*resistencia*) to offer. **II oponerse** vr (*estar en contra*) to be opposed, be against; **se opone a aceptarlo**, he refuses to accept it.

oporto *nm* (*vino*) port.

oportunidad *nf* opportunity, chance.

oportunista *adj & nmf* opportunist.

oportuno,-a *adj* 1 (*adecuado*) timely; **¡qué o.!**, what good timing! 2 (*conveniente*) appropriate; **si te parece o.**, if you think it appropriate.

oposición *nf* 1 opposition. 2 (*examen*) competitive examination.

opositar *vi* to sit a competitive examination.

opositor,-a *nm,f* 1 (*candidato*) candidate for a competitive examination. 2 *Am Pol* opponent.

opresión *nf* oppression; **o. en el pecho**, tightness of the chest.

opresivo,-a *adj* oppressive.

opresor,-a I *nm,f* oppressor. **II** *adj* oppressive, oppressing.

oprimir *vtr* 1 (*pulsar*) to press. 2 (*subyugar*) to oppress.

oprobio *nm* ignominy, opprobrium.

optar *vi* 1 (*elegir*) to choose (**entre**, between); **opté por ir yo mismo**, I decided to go myself. 2 (*aspirar*) to apply (**a**, for); **puede o. a medalla**, he's in with a chance of winning a medal.

optativo,-a *adj* optional.

óptica *nf* 1 (*tienda*) optician's (shop). 2 (*punto de vista*) angle.

óptico,-a I *adj* optical. **II** *nm,f* optician.

optimismo *nm* optimism.

optimista I *adj* optimistic. **II** *nmf* optimist.

óptimo,-a *adj* optimum, excellent.

opuesto,-a *adj* 1 (*contrario*) contrary; **en direcciones opuestas**, in opposite directions; **gustos opuestos**, conflicting tastes. 2 (*de enfrente*) opposite; **el extremo o.**, the other end.

opulencia *nf* opulence.

opulento,-a *adj* opulent.

opus *pt indef* → **oponer**.

oración *nf* 1 *Rel* prayer. 2 *Ling* clause, sentence.

oráculo *nm* oracle.

orador,-a *nm,f* speaker, orator.

oral *adj* oral; *Med* **por vía o.**, to be taken orally.

orangután *nm* orang-outang, orang-utan.

orar *vi Rel* to pray.

oratoria *nf* oratory.

órbita *nf* 1 orbit. 2 *Anat* eye socket.

orden I *nm* order; **o. público**, law and order; **por o. alfabético**, in alphabetical order; **de primer o.**, first-rate; **o. del día**, agenda; **del o. de**, approximately. **II** *nf* 1 (*mandato*) order; *Mil* **¡a la o.!**, sir! 2 *Jur* warrant, order; **o. de registro**, search warrant; **o. judicial**, court order.

ordenado,-a *adj* tidy.

ordenador,-a *nm* computer; **o. personal**, personal computer.

ordenamiento *nm* ordering.

ordenanza I *nm* (*empleado*) office boy. II *nf* regulations; **o. municipal**, by-laws.

ordenar I vtr 1 (*organizar*) to put in order; (*habitación*) to tidy up. 2 (*mandar*) to order. **II ordenarse** vr *Rel* to be ordained (**de**, as), take holy orders.

ordeñar *vtr* to milk.

ordinario,-a *adj* 1 (*corriente*) ordinary, common. 2 (*grosero*) vulgar, common.

orégano *nm* oregano, marjoram.

oreja *nf* ear; (*de sillón*) wing.

orejero,-a *adj Am* (*soplón*) grass.

orfanato *nm* orphanage.

orfebre *nm* (*del oro*) goldsmith; (*de la plata*) silversmith.

orfebrería *nf* gold o silver work.

orfelinato *nm* orphanage.

orgánico,-a *adj* organic.

organigrama *nm* organization chart; *Inform* flow chart.

organillo *nm* barrel organ.

organismo *nm* 1 (*ser vivo*) organism. 2 (*institución*) organization, body.

organista *nmf* organist.

organización *nf* organization.

organizado,-a *adj* organized; **viaje o.**, package tour.

organizador,-a I *adj* organizing. **II** *nm,f* organizer.

organizar [4] I vtr to organize. **II organizarse** vr *fig* (*armarse*) to happen.

órgano *nm* organ.

orgasmo *nm* orgasm.

orgía *nf* orgy.

orgullo *nm* 1 (*propia estima*) pride. 2 (*arrogancia*) arrogance.

orgulloso,-a *adj* 1 **estar o.**, (*satisfecho*) to be proud. 2 **ser o.**, (*arrogante*) to be arrogant, haughty.

orientación *nf* 1 (*dirección*) orientation, direction. 2 (*guía*) guidance; **curso de o.**, induction course.

oriental I *adj* eastern, oriental. **II** *nmf* Oriental.

orientar I vtr 1 (*enfocar*) to aim (**a**, at), intend (**a**, for); **orientado al consumo**, intended for consumption. 2 (*indicar camino*) to give directions to; *fig* (*aconsejar*) to

advise. **3** una casa orientada al sur, a house facing south. **4** (*esfuerzo*) to direct.
II orientarse *vr* (*encontrar el camino*) to get one's bearings, find one's way about.

oriente *nm* East, Orient; **el Extremo** *o* **Lejano/Medio/Próximo O.**, the Far/Middle/Near East.

orificio *nm* hole, opening; *Anat Téc* orifice; **o. de entrada**, inlet; **o. de salida**, outlet.

origen *nm* origin; **país de o.**, country of origin; **dar o. a**, to give rise to.

original *adj & nmf* original.

originalidad *nf* originality.

originar I *vtr* to cause, give rise to. **II originarse** *vr* to originate.

originario,-a *adj* native.
◆originariamente *adv* originally.

orilla *nf* (*borde*) edge; (*del río*) bank; (*del mar*) shore.

orillero,-a *adj Am* (*persona*) suburban.

orín¹ *nm* (*herrumbre*) rust.

orín² *nm* (*usu pl*) (*orina*) urine.

orina *nf* urine.

orinal *nm* chamberpot; *fam* potty.

orinar I *vi* to urinate. **II orinarse** *vr* to wet oneself.

oriundo,-a *adj* native of; **ser o. de**, to come from.

orla *nf Univ* graduation photograph.

ornamentar *vtr* to adorn, embellish.

ornamento *nm* ornament.

ornar *vt* to adorn, embellish.

ornato *nm* (*atavío*) finery; (*adorno*) decoration.

ornitología *nf* ornithology.

ornitólogo,-a *nm,f* ornithologist.

oro *nm* **1** gold; **de o.**, gold, golden; **o. de ley**, fine gold. **2** *Naipes* **oros**, (*baraja española*) ≈ diamonds.

orquesta *nf* orchestra; (*de verbena*) dance band.

orquestar *vtr* to orchestrate.

orquídea *nf* orchid.

ortiga *nf* (*stinging*) nettle.

ortodoxia *nf* orthodoxy.

ortodoxo,-a *adj & nm,f* orthodox.

ortografía *nf* orthography, spelling; **faltas de o.**, spelling mistakes.

ortográfico,-a *adj* orthografic, orthographical; **signos ortográficos**, punctuation *sing*.

ortopédico,-a *adj* orthopaedic, *US* orthopedic; **pierna ortopédica**, artificial leg.

oruga *nf* caterpillar.

orzuelo *nm Med* sty, stye.

os *pron pers pl* **1** (*complemento directo*) you; **os veo mañana**, I'll see you tomorrow. **2** (*complemento indirecto*) you, to you; **os daré el dinero**, I'll give you the money; **os escribiré**, I'll write to you. **3** (*con verbo reflexivo*) yourselves. **4** (*con verbo recíproco*) each other; **os queréis mucho**, you love each other very much.

osa *nf* **O. Mayor**, Great Bear, *US* Big Dipper; **O. Menor**, Little Bear, *US* Little Dipper.

osadía *nf* **1** (*audacia*) daring. **2** (*desvergüenza*) impudence.

osado,-a *adj* **1** (*audaz*) daring. **2** (*desvergonzado*) shameless.

osar *vi* to dare.

osario *nm* ossuary.

oscilación *nf* **1** oscillation. **2** (*de precios*) fluctuation.

oscilante *adj* **1** oscillating. **2** (*precios*) fluctuating.

oscilar *vi* **1** *Fís* to oscillate. **2** (*variar*) to vary, fluctuate.

oscuras (a) *loc adv* in the dark; **nos quedamos a o.**, we were left in darkness.

oscurecer [33] *vi impers & vtr & vr* → obscurecer.

oscuridad *nf* → obscuridad.

oscuro,-a *adj* → obscuro,-a.

óseo,-a *adj* osseous, bony; **tejido ó.**, bone tissue.

osito *nm fam* **o.** (de peluche), teddy bear.

ósmosis, osmosis *nf inv* osmosis.

oso *nm* bear; **o. polar**, polar bear; **o. hormiguero**, anteater; **o. marino**, fur seal; *fam fig* **hacer el o.**, to play the fool.

ostensible *adj* ostensible.

ostentación *nf* ostentation; **hacer o. de algo**, to show sth off.

ostentar *vt* **1** (*lucir*) to flaunt. **2** (*cargo*) to hold.

ostentoso,-a *adj* ostentatious.

osteópata *nmf* osteopath.

osteopatía *nf* osteopathy.

ostra *nf* oyster; *fig* **aburrirse como una o.**, to be bored stiff; *fam* **¡ostras!**, crikey!, *US* gee!

ostracismo *nm* ostracism.

OTAN *nf abr de* **Organización del Tratado del Atlántico Norte**, North Atlantic Treaty Organization, NATO.

otear *vtr* (*horizonte*) to scan, search.

OTI *nf abr de* **Organización de la Televisión Iberoamericana**.

otitis *nf inv* infection and inflammation of the ear, otitis.

otoñal *adj* autumnal, autumn, *US* fall.

otoño *nm* autumn, *US* fall.

otorgamiento *nm* (*concesión*) granting; (*de un premio*) award.

otorgar [7] *vtr* **1** (*premio*) to award (**a**, to); **o. un indulto**, to grant pardon. **2** (*permiso*) to grant (**a**, to).

otorrinolaringólogo,-a *nm,f* ear, nose and throat specialist.

otro,-a I *adj indef* **1** (*sin artículo*) another; (*pl*) other; **o. coche**, another car; **otras personas**, other people. **2** (*con artículo definido*) other; **el o. coche**, the other car. **3** **otra cosa**, something else; **otra vez**, again. **II** *pron indef* **1** (*sin artículo*) (*sing*) another (one); (*pl*) (*personas*)

others; (cosas) other ones; **dame o.,** give
me another (one); **no es mío, es de o.,**
it's not mine, it's somebody else's. **2** (con
artículo definido) (sing) the other (one);
(pl) (personas) the other ones; (cosas) the other
ones. **3 hacer o. tanto,** to do likewise.

ovación nf ovation.

ovacionar vtr to give an ovation to, applaud.

oval, ovalado,-a adj oval.

óvalo nm oval.

ovario nm ovary.

oveja nf **1** sheep; (hembra) ewe; fig **la o. negra,** the black sheep.

overol nm Am overalls pl.

ovillo nm ball (of wool); fig **hacerse un o.,** to curl up into a ball.

ovino,-a adj ovine; **ganado o.,** sheep pl.

OVNI nm abr de **objeto volador no identificado,** unidentified flying object,
UFO.

ovular I adj ovular. **II** vi to ovulate.

óvulo nm ovule.

oxidación nf (metal) rusting.

oxidado,-a adj (metal) rusty; fig **su inglés está un poco o.,** her English is a bit rusty.

oxidar I vtr Quím to oxidize; (metales) to rust. **II oxidarse** vr Quím to oxidize; (metales) to rust, go rusty.

óxido nm **1** oxide; **ó. de carbono,** carbon monoxide. **2** (orín) rust.

oxigenado,-a adj oxygenated; **agua oxigenada,** (hydrogen) peroxide.

oxígeno nm oxygen; **bomba de o.,** oxygen cylinder o tank.

oye indic pres & imperat → **oír.**

oyente nm **1** Rad listener. **2** Univ occasional student.

ozono nm ozone; **capa de o.,** ozone layer.

P

P, p [pe] nf (la letra) P, p.

pabellón nm **1 p. de deportes,** sports centre. **2** (en feria) stand. **3** (bloque) wing. **4** (bandera) flag.

pábulo nm fml fig fuel; **dar p. a,** to encourage.

pacer [33] vtr & vi to graze, pasture.

pachá nm fam fig **vivir como un p.,** to live like a king.

pachanguero,-a adj fam pey (música) catchy.

pachón,-ona nm,f (perro) pointer.

pachorra nf fam sluggishness; **tener p.,** to be phlegmatic.

paciencia nf patience; **armarse de p.,** to grin and bear it.

paciente adj & nmf patient.

pacificación nf pacification.

pacificador,-a I adj pacifying. **II** nm,f peacemaker.

pacificar [1] **I** vtr to pacify; fig (apaciguar) to appease, calm. **II pacificarse** vr to calm down.

pacífico,-a adj peaceful.

Pacífico nm **el (océano) P.,** the Pacific (Ocean).

pacifismo nm pacifism.

pacifista adj & nmf pacifist.

paco nm Am fam (policía) policeman.

pacotilla nf fam **de p.,** second-rate.

pactar vtr to agree.

pacto nm pact; **el P. de Varsovia,** the Warsaw Pact; **p. de caballeros,** gentlemen's agreement.

padecer [33] vtr & vi to suffer; **padece del corazón,** he suffers from heart trouble.

padecimiento nm suffering.

padrastro nm **1** stepfather. **2** (pellejo)
hangnail.

padrazo nm easy-going o indulgent father.

padre I nm **1** father; **p. de familia,** family man. **2 padres,** parents. **II** adj fam huge; **pegarse la vida p.,** to live like a king.

padrenuestro nm Lord's Prayer.

padrino nm **1** (de bautizo) godfather; (de boda) best man; (de niños) godparents. **2** (espónsor) sponsor.

padrón nm census.

paella nf paella (rice dish made with vegetables, meat and/or seafood).

paellera nf paella pan.

pág abr de **página,** page, p.

paga nf (salario) wage; (de niños) pocket money; **p. extra,** bonus.

pagadero,-a adj payable; Fin **cheque p. al portador,** cheque payable to bearer.

pagador,-a nm,f payer.

pagano,-a adj & nm,f pagan, heathen.

pagar [7] vtr **1** to pay; **p. en metálico** o **al contado,** to pay cash; **p. por,** (producto, mala acción) to pay for; fig **(ella) lo ha pagado caro,** she's paid dearly for it. **2** (recompensar) repay.

pagaré nm Fin promissory note, IOU; **p. del tesoro,** treasury note.

página nf page; **en la p. 3,** on page 3; fig **una p. importante de la historia,** an important chapter in history.

pago nm payment; **p. adelantado** o **anticipado,** advance payment; **p. contra reembolso,** cash on delivery; **p. inicial,** down payment.

paila nf Am (frying) pan.

paipái, paipay nm (pl **paipáis**) large palm fan.

país nm country, land; **vino del p.,** local wine; **P. Vasco,** Basque Country; **P. Va-**

lenciano, Valencia.

paisaje *nm* landscape, scenery.

paisano,-a I *adj* of the same country. II *nm,f (compatriota)* fellow countryman *o* countrywoman, compatriot; **en traje de p.**, in plain clothes.

Países Bajos *npl (los)* P. B., the Netherlands, the Low Countries.

paja *nf* 1 straw. 2 *fam fig (bazofia)* padding, waffle. 3 *vulg* **hacerse una p.**, to wank.

pajar *nm (almacén)* straw loft; *(en el exterior)* straw rick.

pajarita *nf* 1 bow tie. 2 *(de papel)* paper bird.

pájaro *nm* 1 bird; **Madrid a vista de p.**, a bird's-eye view of Madrid; **p. carpintero**, woodpecker. 2 *fam* **tener pájaros**, to have daft ideas.

Pakistán *n* Pakistan.

pakistaní *adj & nmf* Pakistani.

pala *nf* 1 shovel; *(de jardinero)* spade; *(de cocina)* slice. 2 *Dep (de ping-pong, frontón* bat; *(de remo)* blade.

palabra *nf* 1 word; **de p.**, by word of mouth; **dirigir la p. a algn**, to address sb; **juego de palabras**, pun. 2 *(promesa)* word; **p. de honor**, word of honour. 3 *(turno para hablar)* right to speak; **tener la p.**, to have the floor.

palabrería *nf* palaver.

palabrota *nf* swearword.

palacio *nm (grande)* palace; *(pequeño)* mansion; **P. de Justicia**, Law Courts.

paladar *nm* 1 palate. 2 *(sabor)* taste.

paladear *vtr* to savour, *US* savor, relish.

palanca *nf* 1 lever. 2 *(manecilla)* handle, stick; *Aut* **p. de cambio**, gearstick, *US* gearshift; **p. de mando**, control lever. 3 *Dep (trampolín)* diving board.

palangana *nf* washbasin.

palco *nm* box.

paleolítico *adj* palaeolithic, paleolithic.

paleontología *nf* palaeontology, paleontology.

Palestina *n* Palestine.

palestino,-a *adj & nm,f* Palestinian.

palestra *nf* arena; *fig* **salir *o* saltar a la p.**, to enter the fray, take the field.

paleta *nf* 1 *(espátula)* slice. 2 *(de pintor)* palette; *(de albañil)* trowel. 3 *Dep (de cricket, pingpong)* bat.

paletilla *nf* 1 shoulder blade. 2 *Culin* shoulder.

paleto,-a I *adj fam pey* unsophisticated, boorish. II *nm,f fam pey* country bumpkin, yokel.

paliar [12] *vtr* to alleviate, palliate.

paliativo,-a *adj & nm* palliative.

palidecer [33] *vi* 1 *(persona)* to turn pale. 2 *fig (disminuir)* to diminish, be on the wane.

palidez *nf* paleness, pallor.

pálido,-a *adj* pale.

palillero *nm* toothpick case.

palillo *nm* 1 *(mondadientes)* toothpick; **palillos chinos**, chopsticks. 2 *Mús* drumstick.

palio *nm* 1 canopy. 2 *Rel* pallium.

palique *nm fam* chat, small talk.

paliza *nf* 1 *(zurra)* thrashing, beating; **darle a algn una p.**, to beat sb up. 2 *(derrota)* beating. 3 *fam (pesadez)* bore, pain (in the neck).

palma *nf* 1 *Anat* palm. 2 *Bot* palm tree. 3 **hacer palmas**, to applaud.

palmada *nf* 1 *(golpe)* slap. 2 **palmadas**, applause, clapping.

palmar *vtr fam* **palmarla**, to snuff it, kick the bucket.

palmarés *nm* 1 *(historial)* service record. 2 *(vencedores)* list of winners.

palmatoria *nf* candlestick.

palmera *nf* palm tree.

palmo *nm (medida)* span; *fig* **p. a p.**, inch by inch.

palo *nm* 1 stick; *(vara)* rod; *(de escoba)* broomstick; *fig* **a p. seco**, on its own. 2 *(golpe)* blow; *fig* **dar un p. a algn**, to let sb down. 3 *Dep*, wooden. 4 *Dep (de portería)* woodwork. 5 *Golf* club. 6 *Naipes* suit.

paloma *nf* pigeon; *Lit* dove; **p. mensajera**, homing *o* carrier pigeon.

palomar *nm* pigeon house, dovecote.

palomilla *nf* 1 grain moth. 2 *(tuerca)* wing *o* butterfly nut.

palomitas (de maíz) *nfpl* popcorn *sing*.

palpable *adj* palpable.

palpar *vtr* to touch, feel; *Med* to palpate.

palpitación *nf* palpitation, throbbing.

palpitante *adj* palpitating, throbbing; *(asunto)* burning.

palpitar *vi* to palpitate, throb.

palúdico,-a *adj* malarial.

paludismo *nm* malaria.

palurdo,-a *adj* uncouth, boorish.

pamela *nf* broad-brimmed hat.

pampa *nf* pampa, pampas *pl*.

pamplina *nf fam* nonsense.

pan *nm* bread; **p. de molde**, loaf of bread; **p. integral**, wholemeal *o* wholewheat bread; **p. rallado**, breadcrumbs *pl*; *fam fig* **más bueno que el p.**, as good as gold; *fam fig* **es p. comido**, it's a piece of cake.

pana *nf* corduroy.

panacea *nf* panacea.

panadería *nf* baker's (shop), bakery.

panadero,-a *nm,f* baker.

panal *nm* honeycomb.

Panamá *n* Panama.

panamá *nm (sombrero)* Panama hat.

panameño,-a *adj & nm,f* Panamanian.

pancarta *nf* placard; *(en manifestación)* banner.

páncreas *nm inv* pancreas.

panda¹ *nm* panda.

panda² *nf* gang.

pandereta nf tambourine.

pandilla nf fam gang.

panecillo nm bread roll.

panel nm panel.

panera nf breadbasket.

pánfilo,-a adj fam (bobo) silly, stupid; (crédulo) gullible.

panfleto nm lampoon, political pamphlet.

pánico nm panic; **sembrar el p.,** to cause panic.

panocha nf Bot corncob; (de trigo etc) ear.

panoli nmf fam idiot.

panorama nm (vista) panorama, view; fig panorama.

panorámico,-a adj panoramic.

pantaletas nfpl Am panties.

pantalón nm (usu pl) trousers pl; **p. vaquero,** jeans pl.

pantalla nf 1 Cin TV Inform screen. 2 (de lámpara) shade. 3 fig **servir de p.,** to act as a decoy.

pantano nm Geog 1 (natural) marsh, bog. 2 (artificial) reservoir.

panteón nm pantheon, mausoleum; **p. familiar,** family vault.

pantera nf panther.

pantomima nf Teat pantomime, mime; pey (farsa) farce.

pantorrilla nf Anat calf.

pantufla nf slipper.

panty nm (pair of) tights pl.

panza nf fam belly, paunch.

panzada nf fam bellyful.

panzudo,-a o **panzón,-ona,** adj potbellied, paunchy.

pañal nm nappy, US diaper; fig **estar en pañales,** to be in one's infancy.

paño nm 1 cloth material; (de lana) woollen o US woollen cloth; (para polvo) duster, rag; (de cocina) dishcloth; fig **paños calientes,** half measures. 2 **paños,** (ropa) clothes; **en p. menores,** in one's underclothes.

pañoleta nf 1 shawl. 2 Taur bullfighter's tie.

pañuelo nm handkerchief; (pañoleta) shawl.

papa nf potato; fam **no saber ni p. (de algo),** not to have the faintest idea (about sth).

Papa nm el P., the Pope.

papá nm fam dad, daddy.

papada nf double chin.

papagayo nm parrot.

papamoscas nm inv flycatcher.

papanatas nmf inv sucker, twit.

paparrucha(da) nf (piece o) of nonsense.

papaya nf papaya o papaw fruit.

papear vi arg to eat.

papel nm 1 paper; (hoja) piece o sheet of paper; **papeles,** (documentos) documents, identification papers; **p. higiénico,** toilet paper; **p. carbón,** carbon paper; **p. de carta,** writing paper, stationery; **p. de**

alumimio/de estraza, aluminium foil/ brown paper; **p. de fumar,** cigarette paper; **p. de lija,** sandpaper; Fin **p. moneda,** paper money, banknotes pl; **p. pintado,** wallpaper; **p. secante,** blotting paper. 2 Cin Teat role, part.

papeleo nm fam paperwork.

papelera nf (en despacho) wastepaper basket; (en calle) litter bin.

papelería nf (tienda) stationer's.

papeleta nf 1 (de rifa) ticket; (de votación) ballot paper; (de resultados) report. 2 fam (dificultad) tricky problem, difficult job.

papeo nm arg grub.

paperas nfpl Med mumps.

papilla nf pap, mush; (de niños) baby food.

papista nmf papist.

Papúa Nueva Guinea n Papua New Guinea.

paquete nm 1 (de cigarrillos etc) packet; (postal) parcel, package. 2 (conjunto) set, package; Fin **p. de acciones,** share package. 3 Inform software package. 4 arg (castigo) punishment. 5 arg (pene) prick.

Paquistán n Pakistan.

paquistaní adj o nmf Pakistani.

par I adj Mat even. II nm 1 (pareja) pair; (dos) couple. 2 Mat even number; **pares y nones,** odds and evens. 3 (noble) peer. 4 (locuciones) **a la p.,** (a la vez) at the same time; **de p. en p.,** wide open; fig **sin p.,** matchless.

para prep 1 for; **bueno p. la salud,** good for your health; **¿p. qué?,** what for?; **p. ser inglés habla muy bien español,** for an Englishman he speaks very good Spanish. 2 (finalidad) to, in order to; **p. terminar antes,** in o in order to finish earlier; **p. que lo disfrutes,** for you to enjoy. 3 (tiempo) by; **p. entonces,** by then. 4 (a punto de) **está p. salir,** it's about to leave. 5 (locuciones) **decir p. sí,** to say to oneself; **ir p. viejo,** to be getting old; **no es p. tanto,** it's not as bad as all that; **p. mí,** in my opinion.

parábola nf 1 Geom parabola. 2 Rel parable.

parabólico,-a adj parabolic; TV **antena parabólica,** satellite dish.

parabrisas nm inv Aut windscreen, US windshield.

paraca nm fam para(chutist).

paracaídas nm inv parachute.

paracaidista nmf Dep parachutist; Mil paratrooper.

parachoques nm inv bumper, US fender.

parada nf 1 (lugar) stop; **p. de autobús,** bus stop; **p. de taxis,** taxi stand o rank. 2 Ftb save, stop.

paradero nm 1 (lugar) whereabouts pl. 2 Am (apeadero) stop.

parado,-a I adj 1 stopped, stationary; (quieto) still; (fábrica) at a standstill; fig

salir bien/mal p., to come off well/badly. **2** (desempleado) unemployed, out of work. **3** fig (lento) slow. **4** Am (de pie) standing. **II** nm,f unemployed person.

paradoja nf paradox.

paradójico,-a adj paradoxical.

parador nm roadside inn; **p. nacional** o **de turismo**,state-run hotel.

parafernalia nf paraphernalia pl.

parafrasear vtr to paraphrase.

paráfrasis nf inv paraphrase.

paraguas nm inv umbrella.

Paraguay n Paraguay.

paragüero nm umbrella stand.

paraíso nm **1** paradise; **p. terrenal**, heaven on earth; Fin **p. fiscal**, tax haven. **2** Teat gods pl, gallery.

paraje nm spot, place.

paralelo,-a adj & nm parallel.

parálisis nf inv paralysis; **p. infantil**, poliomyelitis.

paralítico,-a adj & nm,f paralytic.

paralización nf **1** Med paralysis. **2** (detención) halting, stopping.

paralizar [1] **I** vtr to paralyse; (circulación) to stop. **II paralizarse** vr fig to come to a standstill.

parámetro nm parameter.

paramilitar adj paramilitary.

páramo nm bleak plain o plateau, moor.

parangón nm fml comparison; **sin p.**, incomparable.

paranoia nf paranoia.

paranoico,-a adj & nm,f paranoiac, paranoid.

parapeto nm **1** parapet. **2** (de defensa) barricade.

parapléjico,-a adj & nm,f paraplegic.

parar **I** vtr **1** to stop. **2** Dep to save. **II** vi **1** to stop; **p. de hacer algo**, to stop doing sth; **sin p.**, nonstop, without stopping; fam **no p.**, to be always on the go. **2** (alojarse) to stay. **3** (acabar) **fue a p. a la cárcel**, he ended up in jail. **III pararse** vtr **1** to stop; **p. a pensar**, to stop to think. **2** Am (ponerse en pie) to stand up.

pararrayos nm inv lightning conductor, US lightning rod.

parásito,-a adj nm parasite.

parasol nm sunshade, parasol.

parcela nf plot.

parche nm **1** patch. **2** (emplasto) plaster. **3** pey (chapuza) botched up o slapdash job.

parchís nm ludo.

parcial **I** adj **1** (partidario) biased. **2** (no completo) partial; **a tiempo p.**, part-time. **II** adj & nm (examen) p., class examination.

parcialmente adv partially, partly.

parco,-a adj (moderado) sparing; (frugal) scant.

pardillo,-a **I** nm,f pey yokel, bumpkin. **II** nm Orn linnet.

pardo,-a adj (marrón) brown; (gris) dark grey.

parecer¹ nm **1** (opinión) opinion. **2** (aspecto) appearance.

parecer² [33] **I** vi **1** to seem, look (like); **parece difícil**, it seems o looks difficult; **parecía (de) cera**, it looked like wax; (uso impers) **parece que no arranca**, it looks as if it won't start; **como te parezca**, whatever you like; **¿te parece?**, is that okay with you?; **parece que sí/no**, I think/don't think so; **¿qué te parece?**, what do you think of it? **II parecerse 1** vr to be alike; **no se parecen**, they're not alike. **2 p**. **a**, to look like, resemble; **se parecen a su madre**, they look like their mother.

parecido,-a adj **1** alike, similar. **2 bien p.**, good-looking. **II** nm likeness, resemblance; **tener p. con algn**, to bear a resemblance to sb.

pared nf wall.

paredón nm **1** thick wall. **2** fam **le llevaron al p.**, he was shot by firing squad.

pareja nf **1** pair; **por parejas**, in pairs. **2** (hombre y mujer) couple; (hijo e hija) boy and girl; **hacen buena p.**, they make a nice couple, they're well matched. **3** (en naipes) pair; **doble p.**, two pairs. **4** (de baile, juego) partner.

parejo,-a adj **1** (parecido) similar, alike. **2 ir parejos**, to be neck and neck.

parentela nf fam relations pl, relatives pl.

parentesco nm relationship, kinship.

paréntesis nm inv **1** parenthesis, bracket; **entre p.**, in parentheses o brackets. **2** (descanso) break, interruption; (digresión) digression.

parezco indic pres → parecer.

paria nmf pariah.

parida nf fam silly thing.

pariente nmf relative, relation.

parir vtr & vi to give birth (to).

París n Paris.

parking nm car park, US parking lot.

parlamentario,-a I adj parliamentary. **II** nm,f member of parliament, MP, US congressman.

parlamento nm parliament.

parlanchín,-ina adj fam talkative, chatty.

parné nm arg dough, cash.

paro nm **1** (huelga) strike, stoppage. **2** (desempleo) unemployment; **estar en p.**, to be unemployed; **cobrar el p.**, to be on the dole.

parodia nf parody.

parodiar [12] vtr to parody.

parpadear vi (ojos) to blink; (luz) to flicker.

parpadeo nm (de ojos) blinking; fig (de luz) flickering.

párpado nm eyelid.

parque nm **1** park; **p. de atracciones**, funfair; **p. zoológico**, zoo; **p. nacional**/**natural**, national park/nature reserve. **2**

(de niños) playpen. **3 p. móvil,** total number of cars.

parqué nm parquet.

parquear vtr Am to park.

parquet nm → **parqué.**

parquímetro nm Aut parking meter.

parra nf grapevine.

párrafo nm paragraph.

parranda nf fam spree.

parricidio nm parricide.

parrilla nf 1 Culin grill; **pescado a la p.,** grilled fish. 2 Téc grate. 3 Aut Dep starting grid.

párroco nm parish priest.

parroquia nf parish; *(iglesia)* parish church.

parroquiano,-a nm,f *(regular)* customer.

parsimonia nf phlegm, calmness.

parte I nf 1 *(sección)* part. 2 *(en una repartición)* share. 3 *(lugar)* place, spot; **en o por todas partes,** everywhere; **se fue por otra p.,** he went another way. 4 *Jur* party. 5 *(bando)* side; **estoy de tu p.** I'm on your side. 6 *euf* **partes,** *(genitales)* private parts. 7 *(locuciones)* **por mi p.,** as far as I am concerned; **de p. de ...,** on behalf of ...; *Tel* **¿de p. de quién?,** who's calling?; **en gran p.,** to a large extent; **en p.,** partly; **la mayor p.,** the majority; **por otra p.,** on the other hand; **tomar p. en,** to take part in. **II** nm *(informe)* report.

partición nf *(reparto)* division, sharing out; *(de herencia)* partition; *(de territorio)* partition.

participación nf 1 participation. 2 Fin *(acción)* share, US stock; **p. en los beneficios,** profit-sharing. 3 *(en lotería)* part of a lottery ticket. 4 *(notificación)* notice, notification.

participante I adj participating. **II** nmf participant.

participar I vi 1 to take part, participate *(en,* in*)*. 2 Fin to have shares in. 3 fig **p. de,** to share. **II** vtr *(notificar)* to notify.

partícipe nmf 1 participant; **hacer p. de algo,** *(notificar)* to inform about sth. 2 Com Fin partner.

participio nm Ling participle.

partícula nf particle.

particular I adj 1 *(concreto)* particular. 2 *(privado)* private, personal. 3 *(raro)* peculiar. **II** nmf *(individuo)* private individual. **III** nm *(asunto)* subject, matter.

particularidad nf special feature.

partida nf 1 *(salida)* departure. 2 Com *(remesa)* batch, consignment. 3 *(juego)* game. 4 Fin *(entrada)* item. 5 Jur *(certificado)* certificate; **p. de nacimiento,** birth certificate.

partidario,-a I adj ser/no ser **p. de algo,** to be for/against sth. **II** nm,f supporter, follower; **es p. del aborto,** he is in favour of abortion.

partidista adj biased, partisan.

partido,-a nm 1 Pol party. 2 Dep match, game; **p. amistoso,** friendly game; **p. de vuelta,** return match. 3 *(provecho)* advantage; **sacar p. de,** to profit from. 4 Jur *(distrito)* district. 5 **tomar p. por,** to side with. 6 **ser un buen p.,** to be a good catch.

partir I vtr to break; *(dividir)* to split, divide; *(cortar)* to cut; **p. a algn por la mitad,** to mess things up for sb. **II** vi 1 *(marcharse)* to leave, set out o off. 2 **a p. de,** from. **III** partirse vr to split *(up)*, break *(up)*; fam **p. de risa,** to split one's sides laughing.

partisano,-a nm,f partisan.

partitura nf Mús score.

parto nm childbirth, labour, US labor; **estar de p.,** to be in labour.

parvulario nm nursery school, kindergarten.

párvulo,-a nm,f infant.

pasa nf raisin; **p. de Corinto,** currant.

pasable adj passable, tolerable.

pasada nf 1 **de p.,** in passing. 2 *(jugarreta)* dirty trick. 3 fam **eso es una p.,** it's too much!

pasadizo nm corridor, passage.

pasado,-a I adj 1 *(último)* last; **el año/lunes p.,** last year/Monday. 2 *(anticuado)* dated, old-fashioned; **p.** *(de moda)*, out of date o fashion. 3 *(alimento)* bad. 4 Culin *(cocido)* **lo quiero muy p.,** I want it well done. 5 **p. mañana,** the day after tomorrow. **II** nm past.

pasador nm 1 *(prenda)* pin, clasp; *(para el pelo)* (hair) slide, hairpin. 2 *(pestillo)* bolt, fastener.

pasaje nm 1 passage. 2 *(calle)* alley. 3 *(pasajeros)* passengers pl. 4 *(billete)* ticket.

pasajero,-a I adj passing, temporary; **aventura pasajera,** fling. **II** nm,f passenger.

pasamanos nm inv *(barra)* handrail; *(de escalera)* banister, bannister.

pasamontañas nm inv balaclava.

pasaporte nm passport.

pasapurés nm inv Culin potato masher.

pasar I vtr 1 to pass, give; *(objeto)* to pass, give; *(mensaje)* to give; *(página)* to turn; *(trasladar)* to move; **p. algo a limpio,** to make a clean copy of sth. 2 *(tiempo)* to spend, pass; **p. el rato,** to kill time. 3 *(padecer)* to suffer, endure; **p. hambre,** to go hungry. 4 *(río, calle)* to cross; *(barrera)* to pass through o over; *(límite)* to go beyond. 5 *(perdonar)* to forgive, tolerate; **p. algo** *(por alto)*, to overlook sth. 6 *(introducir)* to insert, put through. 7 *(examen)* to pass. 8 Cin to run, show.

II vi 1 to pass; **¿ha pasado el autobús?,** has the bus gone by?; **ha pasado un hombre,** a man has gone past; **p. de largo,** to go by (without stopping); **el tren pasa por Burgos,** the train goes via

Burgos; **pasa por casa mañana**, come round to my house tomorrow. **2 p. a**, *(continuar)* to go on to; **p. a ser**, to become. **3** *(entrar)* to come in. **4** *(tiempo)* to pass, go by. **5 p. sin**, to do without; *fam* **paso de ti**, I couldn't care less about you; *fam* **yo paso**, count me out.

III *v impers* *(suceder)* to happen; **¿qué pasa aquí?**, what's going on here?; **¿qué te pasa?**, what's the matter?; **fam ¿qué pasa?**, *(saludo)* how are you?; **pase lo que pase**, whatever happens, come what may.

IV pasarse *vr* **1 se me pasó la ocasión**, I missed my chance; **se le pasó llamarme**, he forgot to phone me. **2** *(gastar tiempo)* to spend *o* pass time; **pasárselo bien/mal**, to have a good/bad time. **3** *(comida)* to go off. **4** *fam (excederse)* to go too far; **no te pases**, don't overdo it. **5 pásate por mi casa**, call round to my place.

pasarela *nf (puente)* footbridge; *(de barco)* gangway; *(de moda)* catwalk.

pasatiempo *nm* pastime, hobby.

pascua *nf* **1** Easter. **2 pascuas**, *(Navidad)* Christmas *sing*; **¡felices Pascuas!**, Merry Christmas!

pase *nm* **1** pass, permit. **2** *Cin* showing.

pasear I *vi* to go for a walk, take a walk. **II** *vt* **1** *(persona)* to take for a walk; *(perro)* to walk. **2** *fig (exhibir)* to show off. **III pasearse** *vr* to go for a walk.

paseíllo *nm Taur* opening parade.

paseo *nm* **1** walk; *(en bicicleta, caballo)* ride; *(en coche)* drive; **dar un p.**, to go for a walk *o* a ride. **2** *(avenida)* avenue.

pasillo *nm* corridor; *Av* **p. aéreo**, air corridor.

pasión *nf* passion.

pasional *adj* passionate; **crimen p.**, crime of passion.

pasividad *nf* passivity, passiveness.

pasivo,-a I *adj* passive; *(inactivo)* inactive.
II *nm Com* liabilities *pl*.

pasmado,-a *adj (asombrado)* astounded, amazed; *(atontado)* flabbergasted; **dejar p.**, to astonish; **quedarse p.**, to be amazed.

pasmo *nm* astonishment, amazement.

paso,-a¹ *adj* **ciruela pasa**, prune; **uva pasa**, raisin.

paso² *nm* **1** step; *(modo de andar)* gait; *(ruido al andar)* footstep; *Mil* **llevar el p.**, to keep in step; *fig* **a dos pasos**, a short distance away; *fig* **seguir los pasos de algn**, to follow in sb's footsteps. **2** *(camino)* passage, way; **abrirse p.**, to force one's way through; *Aut* **'ceda el p.'**, 'give way'; **'prohibido el p.'**, 'no entry'; **a nivel**, level *o* *US* grade crossing; **p. de cebra**, zebra crossing; **p. de peatones**, pedestrian crossing, *US* crosswalk; **p. elevado**, flyover, *US* overpass; **p. subterráneo**, *(para peatones)* subway; *(para co-*

ches) underpass. **3** *(acción)* passage, passing; **a su p. por la ciudad**, when he was in town; **el p. del tiempo**, the passage of time; **estar de p.**, to be just passing through. **4 p. de montaña**, mountain pass.

pasodoble *nm* paso doble.

pasota *nmf fam* waster.

pasta *nf* **1** paste; **p. de dientes** *o* **dentífrica**, toothpaste. **2** *(de pan, pasteles)* dough; *(italiana)* pasta. **3** *(galleta)* biscuit. **4** *fam (dinero)* dough, bread.

pastar *vtr & vi* to graze, pasture.

pastel *nm* **1** cake; *(de carne, fruta)* pie. **2** *Arte* pastel. **3 fam descubrir el p.**, to spill the beans.

pastelería *nf* **1** *(tienda)* confectioner's (shop). **2** *(dulces)* confectionery.

pastelero,-a *nm,f* pastrycook, confectioner.

pastiche *nm* **1** pastiche. **2** *fam (chapuza)* botch(-up).

pastilla *nf* **1** tablet, pill; **pastillas para la tos**, cough drops. **2** *(de jabón)* bar. **3** *fam* **a toda p.**, at full speed.

pastizal *nm* grazing land, pasture.

pasto *nm* **1** *(hierba)* grass. **2** *(alimento)* fodder; **ser p. de**, to fall prey to.

pastor,-a I *nm,f* shepherd; *(mujer)* shepherdess; **perro p.**, sheepdog; **p. alemán**, Alsatian. **II** *nm Rel* pastor, minister.

pastoreo *nm* shepherding.

pastoso,-a *adj* pasty; *(lengua)* furry.

pata *nf* leg; *fig* **patas arriba**, upside down; **estirar la p.**, to kick the bucket; **mala p.**, bad luck; **meter la p.**, to put one's foot in it; **p. de gallo**, crow's foot.

patada *nf (puntapié)* kick, stamp.

patalear *vi* to stamp one's feet (with rage).

pataleo *nm* kicking; *(de rabia)* stamping.

patán *nm* bumpkin, yokel.

patata *nf* potato; **patatas fritas**, chips, *US* French fries; *(de bolsa)* crisps, *US* potato chips.

patatús *nm inv fam* dizzy spell, queer turn.

paté *nm* pâté.

patear I *vtr (pelota)* to kick; *(pisotear)* to stamp on. **II** *vi (patalear)* to stamp (one's foot with rage).

patentar *vtr* to patent.

patente I *nf (autorización)* licence, *US* license; *(de invención)* patent. **II** *adj (evidente)* patent, obvious.

pateo *nm* stamping; *(abucheo)* boo(ing), jeer(ing).

paternal *adj* paternal, fatherly.

paternalista *adj* paternalistic.

paternidad *nf* paternity, fatherhood.

paterno,-a *adj* paternal.

patético,-a *adj* moving.

patíbulo *nm* scaffold, gallows *pl*.

patidifuso,-a *adj fam* dumbfounded, flabbergasted.

patilla *nf* 1 *(de gafas)* leg. 2 **patillas**, *(pelo)* sideboards, *US* sideburns.

patín *nm* 1 skate; *(patinete)* scooter; **p. de ruedas/de hielo**, roller/ice skate. 2 *Náut* pedal boat.

patinaje *nm* skating; **p. artístico**, figure skating; **p. sobre hielo/ruedas**, ice-roller skating.

patinar *vi* 1 to skate; *(sobre ruedas)* to roller-skate; *(sobre hielo)* to ice-skate. 2 *(deslizarse)* to slide; *(resbalar)* to slip; *(vehículo)* to skid. 3 *fam (equivocarse)* to put one's foot in it, slip up.

patinazo *nm* 1 skid. 2 *fam (equivocación)* blunder, boob.

patinete *nm* scooter.

patio *nm* 1 *(de una casa)* yard, patio; *(de recreo)* playground. 2 *Teat Cin* **p. de butacas**, stalls.

pato *nm* duck; *fam* **pagar el p.**, to carry the can.

patochada *nf* blunder, boob.

patógeno,-a *adj* pathogenic.

patología *nf* pathology.

patológico,-a *adj* pathological.

patoso,-a *adj* clumsy, awkward.

patraña *nf* nonsense.

patria *nf* fatherland, native country; **madre p.**, motherland; **p. chica**, one's home town o region.

patriarca *nm* patriarch.

patrimonio *nm (bienes)* wealth; *(herencia)* inheritance.

patriota *nmf* patriot.

patriótico,-a *adj* patriotic.

patriotismo *nm* patriotism.

patrocinador,-a I *adj* sponsoring. II *nm,f* sponsor.

patrocinar *vtr* to sponsor.

patrocinio *nm* sponsorship, patronage.

patrón,-ona I *nm,f (jefe)* boss. 2 *(de pensión) (hombre)* landlord; *(mujer)* landlady. 3 *Rel* patron saint. II *nm* 1 pattern. 2 *(medida)* standard.

patronal I *adj* employers'; **cierre p.**, lockout; **clase p.**, managerial class. II *nf (dirección)* management.

patronato, patronazgo *nm* 1 *(institución benéfica)* foundation. 2 *(protección)* patronage.

patrono,-a *nm,f* 1 boss; *(empresario)* employer. 2 *Rel* patron saint.

patrulla *nf* 1 patrol; **estar de p.**, to be on patrol; **coche p.**, patrol car. 2 *(grupo)* group, band; **p. de rescate**, rescue party; **p. ciudadana**, vigilante group.

patrullar I *vtr* to patrol. II *vi* to be on patrol.

paulatino,-a *adj* gradual.

paupérrimo,-a *(adj superl de* **pobre)** extremely poor, poverty-stricken.

pausa *nf* pause, break; *Mús* rest.

pausado,-a *adj* unhurried, calm.

pauta *nf* guidelines *pl.*

pava *nf fam* **pelar la p.**, to chat.

pavesa *nf* ash.

pavimentar *vtr* to pave.

pavimento *nm (de calle)* paving; *(de habitación)* flooring.

pavo *nm* 1 turkey; *fam* **no ser moco de p.**, to be nothing to scoff at. 2 *fam (tonto)* twit; *fam* **estar en la edad del p.**, to be growing up.

pavonearse *vr fam* to show off, strut.

pavoneo *nm fam* showing off, strutting.

pavor *nm* terror, dread.

payaso *nm* clown; **hacer el p.**, to act the clown.

payés,-a *nm,f* Catalan o Balearic peasant.

payo,-a *nm,f* non-Gipsy person.

paz *nf* peace; *(sosiego)* peacefulness; *fam* **¡déjame en p.!**, leave me alone!, **hacer las paces**, to make (it) up.

pazguato,-a *adj* 1 *(estúpido)* silly, stupid. 2 *(mojigato)* prudish.

PCE *nm Pol abr de* **Partido Comunista de España**, Spanish Communist party.

pe *nf (am* **de pe a pa**, from A to Z.

peaje *nf* toll; **autopista de p.**, toll motorway, *US* turnpike.

peatón *nm* pedestrian.

peca *nf* freckle.

pecado *nm Rel* sin; **p. capital** o **mortal**, deadly sin.

pecador,-a *nm,f* sinner.

pecaminoso,-a *adj* sinful.

pecar [1] *vi* to sin; *fig* **p. por defecto**, to fall short of the mark.

pecera *nf* fishbowl, fishtank.

pecho *nm* chest; *(de mujer)* breast, bust; *(de animal)* breast; **dar el p. (a un bebé)**, to breast-feed (a baby); *fig* **tomar(se) (algo) a p.**, to take (sth) to heart.

pechuga *nf* 1 *(de ave)* breast. 2 *fam pey (de mujer)* boob.

pectoral *adj* pectoral, chest.

peculiar *adj (raro)* peculiar; *(característico)* characteristic.

peculiaridad *nf* peculiarity.

pedagogía *nf* pedagogy.

pedagógico,-a *adj* pedagogical.

pedal *nm* pedal.

pedalear *vi* to pedal.

pedante I *adj* pedantic. II *nmf* pedant.

pedantería *nf* pedantry.

pedazo *nm* piece, bit; **a pedazos**, in pieces; **caerse a pedazos**, to fall apart o to pieces; **hacer pedazos**, to break o tear to pieces, smash (up); *fam* **¡qué p. de coche!**, what a terrific car!

pederasta *nm* pederast.

pedernal *nm* flint.

pedestal *nm* pedestal.

pediatra *nmf* paediatrician, *US* pediatrician.

pediatría *nf* paediatrics *sing*, *US* pediatrics *sing.*

pedicuro,-a *nm,f* chiropodist.

pedido *nm* **1** *Com* order; **hacer un p. a**, to place an order with. **2** *(petición)* request.

pedigrí *nm* pedigree.

pedir [6] *vtr* **1** to ask (for); **p. algo a algn**, to ask sb for sth; **te pido que te quedes**, I'm asking you to stay; **p. prestado**, to borrow; *fig* **p. cuentas**, to ask for an explanation. **2** *Com & (en bar etc)* to order. **3** *(mendigar)* to beg.

pedo *nm vulg* **1** fart; **tirarse un p.**, to fart. **2** *(borrachera)* bender.

pedrada *nf (golpe)* blow from a stone; *(lanzamiento)* throw of a stone.

pedrea *nf (en lotería)* small prizes *pl.*

pedregoso,-a *adj* stony, rocky.

pedrería *nf* precious stones *pl*, gems *pl.*

pedrisco *nm* hailstorm.

pega *nf* **1** *fam (objeción)* objection; **poner pegas**, to find fault. **2 de p.**, *(falso)* sham.

pegadizo,-a *adj* catchy.

pegado,-a *adj* **1** *(adherido)* stuck. **2** *(quemado)* burnt.

pegajoso,-a *adj (pegadizo)* sticky; *fig (persona)* tiresome, hard to get rid of.

pegamento *nm* glue.

pegar [7] **I** *vtr* **1** *(adherir)* to stick; *(con pegamento)* to glue; *(coser)* to sew on; *fam* **no pegó ojo**, he didn't sleep a wink; **p. fuego a**, to set fire to. **2** *(golpear)* to hit. **3 p. un grito**, to shout; **p. un salto**, to jump. **4** *fam (contagiar)* to give; **me ha pegado sus manías**, I've caught his bad habits. **5** *(arrimar)* to put against; **lean against. II** *vi* **1** *(adherirse)* to stick. **2** *(armonizar)* to match, go; **el azul no pega con el verde**, blue and green don't go together *o* don't match; *fig* **ella no pegaría aquí**, she wouldn't fit in here. **3** *(sol)* to beat down. **III pegarse** *vr* **1** *(adherirse)* to stick; *(pelearse)* to fight. **2** *fam (darse)* to have, get; **p. un tiro**, to shoot oneself. **3** *(comida)* to get burnt; **se me ha pegado el sol**, I've got a touch of the sun. **4** *fam* **pegársela a algn**, to trick *o* deceive sb. **5** *(arrimarse)* to get close. **6** *fam fig* to stick. **7** *Med (enfermedad)* to be catching *o* contagious; *fig (melodía)* to be catchy.

pegatina *nf* sticker.

peinado,-a *nm* hairstyle, *fam* hairdo.

peinar I *vtr* **1** *(pelo)* to comb. **2** *(registrar)* to comb. **II peinarse** *vr* to comb one's hair.

peine *nm* comb.

peineta *nf* ornamental comb.

pela *nf fam* peseta.

pelado,-a I *adj* **1** *(cabeza)* shorn; *(piel, fruta)* peeled; *(terreno)* bare. **2** *fam* **saqué un cinco p.**, *(en escuela)* I just scraped a pass; **a grito p.**, shouting and bawling. **3** *fam (arruinado)* broke, penniless. **4** *(des-*

vergonzado) impudent, insolent. **II** *nm fam* haircut.

peladura *nf* peeling.

pelagatos *nmf inv fam* poor devil, nobody.

pelaje *nm* **1** fur, hair. **2** *pey (apariencia)* looks *pl*, appearance.

pelambrera *nf fam* mop (of hair), long *o* thick hair.

pelapatatas *nm inv* potato peeler.

pelar I *vtr (cortar el pelo a)* to cut the hair of; *(fruta, patata)* to peel; *fam* **hace un frío que pela**, it's brass monkey weather. **II** *vi (despellejar)* to peel. **II pelarse** *vr* **1** *(cortarse el pelo)* to get one's hair cut. **2** *fam* **pelárselas**, to do sth fast.

peldaño *nm* step; *(de escalera de mano)* rung.

pelea *nf* fight; *(riña)* row, quarrel; **buscar p.**, to look for trouble.

peleado,-a *adj* **estar p. (con algn)**, not to be on speaking terms (with sb).

pelear I *vi* to fight; *(reñir)* to quarrel. **II pelearse** *vr* **1** to fight; *(reñir)* to quarrel. **2** *(enemistarse)* to fall out.

pelele *nm (muñeco)* straw puppet; *fig* puppet.

peleón,-ona *adj* **1** quarrelsome, aggressive. **2** *(vino)* cheap.

peletería *nf* furrier's; *(tienda)* fur shop.

peletero,-a *nm,f* furrier.

peliagudo,-a *adj* difficult, tricky.

pelícano *nm* pelican.

película *nf* **1** *Cin* film, picture, *US* movie; **p. de miedo** *o* **terror**, horror film; **p. del Oeste**, Western; *fam* **de p.**, fabulous. **2** *Fot* film.

peligrar *vi* to be in danger, be threatened; **hacer p.**, to endanger, jeopardize.

peligro *nm* danger; *(riesgo)* risk; **con p. de ...**, at the risk of ...; **correr (el) p. de ...**, to run the risk of ...; **poner en p.**, to endanger.

peligroso,-a *adj* dangerous, risky.

pelirrojo,-a I *adj* red-haired; *(anaranjado)* ginger-haired. **II** *nm,f* redhead.

pellejo *nm* **1** *(piel)* skin. **2** *(odre)* wineskin. **3** *fam* **arriesgar** *o* **jugarse el p.**, to risk one's neck.

pelliza *nf* fur jacket.

pellizcar [1] *vtr* to pinch, nip.

pellizco *nm* pinch, nip.

pelma *nmf*, **pelmazo,-a** *nm,f (persona)* bore, drag.

pelo *nm* **1** hair; **cortarse el p.**, *(uno mismo)* to cut one's hair; *(en la peluquería)* to have one's hair cut; *fig* **no tiene ni un p. de tonto**, he's no fool; **fig no tener pelos en la lengua**, to be very outspoken; *fig* **tomar el p. a algn**, to pull sb's leg, take the mickey out of sb; *fam* **con pelos y señales**, in full detail; **fam por los pelos**, by the skin of one's teeth; *fam* **me puso el p. de punta**, it gave me the

creeps. 2 *(de animal)* fur, coat, hair. 3
Tex (de una tela) nap, pile. 4 *(cerda)*
bristle.

pelón,-ona *adj (sin pelo)* bald.

pelota I *nf* 1 ball; *fam* devolver la p., to
give tit for tat. 2 *Dep* pelota. 3 *fam (cabeza)* nut. 4 hacer la p. a algn, to toady to
sb, butter sb up. 5 *vulg* pelotas, *(testícu-
los)* balls; en p., starkers. II *nmf fam (pelotillero)* crawler.

pelotari *nm* pelota player.

pelotear *vi Dep* to kick a ball around;
Ten to knock up.

peloteo *nm Ten* knock-up.

pelotilla *nf fam* hacer la p. (a algn), to
fawn on (sb).

pelotillero,-a *nm,f fam* crawler.

pelotón *nm* 1 *Mil* squad. 2 *fam (grupo)*
small crowd, bunch; *(en ciclismo)* pack. 3
(amasijo) bundle.

pelotudo,-a *adj Am* slack, sloppy.

peluca *nf* wig.

peluche *nf* osito de p., teddy bear.

peludo,-a *adj* hairy, furry.

peluquería *nf* hairdresser's (shop).

peluquero,-a *nm,f* hairdresser.

peluquín *nm* toupee.

pelusa *nf*, **pelusilla** *nf* 1 fluff; *(de planta)*
down. 2 *fam* jealousy (among children).

pelvis *nf inv* pelvis.

pena *nf* 1 *(tristeza)* grief, sorrow; *fig* me
da p. de ella, I feel sorry for her; ¡qué
p.!, what a pity! 2 *(dificultad)* hardships
pl, trouble; no merece o vale la p. 2 *(risk),
it's not worth while (going); a duras penas, with great difficulty. 3 *(castigo)* punishment, penalty; p. de muerte o capital, death penalty.

penacho *nm* 1 *(de ave)* crest, tuft. 2 *Mil*
(de plumas) plume.

penal I *adj* penal; *Jur* código p., penal
code. II *nm* prison, jail.

penalidad *nf (usu pl)* hardships *pl*,
troubles *pl*.

penalización *nf* penalization; *Dep* penalty.

penalizar [4] *vtr* to penalize.

penalti *nm (pl* **penaltis)** *Dep* penalty; *fam*
casarse de p., to have a shotgun
wedding.

penar I *vtr* to punish. II *vi* to be in torment, suffer.

pendejo *nm Am (tonto)* jerk, dummy.

pendenciero,-a *adj* quarrelsome, argumentative.

pendiente I *adj* 1 *(por resolver)* pending;
Educ asignatura p., failed subject; *Com*
p. de pago, unpaid. 2 estar p. de, *(esperar)* to be waiting for; *(vigilar)* to be on
the lookout for. 3 *(colgante)* hanging *(de,
from)*. II *nm (joya)* earring. III *nf (cuesta)
(de tejado)* pitch.

pendón *nm* 1 *(bandera)* banner. 2 *pey
(mujer)* slut, whore; *(hombre)* playboy.

péndulo *nm* pendulum.

pene *nm* penis.

penetración *nf* penetration; *(perspicacia)*
insight, perception.

penetrante *adj* penetrating; *(frío, voz, mirada)* piercing; *fig (inteligencia)* sharp,
acute.

penetrar I *vtr* to penetrate; p. un misterio, to get to the bottom of a mystery. II
vi (entrar) to go o get (en, in).

penicilina *nf* penicillin.

península *nf* peninsula.

penique *nm* penny, *pl* pence.

penitencia *nf* penance.

penitenciaria *nf* prison.

penitenciario,-a *adj* penitentiary, prison.

penoso,-a *adj* 1 *(lamentable)* sorry, distressing. 2 *(laborioso)* laborious, difficult.

pensado,-a *adj* 1 thought out; bien p., ...
on reflection, ...; en el momento menos
p., when least expected; mal p., twisted;
tener algo p., to have sth planned, have
sth in mind; tengo p. ir, I intend to go.
2 *(concebido)* designed.

pensamiento *nm* 1 thought. 2 *(máxima)*
saying, motto. 3 *Bot* pansy.

pensar [1] I *vi* to think (en, of, about;
sobre, about, over); *fig* sin p., *(con precipitación)* without thinking; *(involuntariamente)* involuntarily. II *vtr* 1 to think (de,
of); *(considerar)* to think over o about;
piénsalo bien, think it over; *fam* ¡ni
pensarlo!, not on your life! 2 *(proponerse)*
to intend; pienso quedarme, I plan to
stay. 3 *(concebir)* to make; p. un plan, to
make a plan; p. una solución, to find a
solution.

pensativo,-a *adj* pensive, thoughtful.

pensión *nf 1 (residencia)* boarding house;
(hotel) guesthouse; media p., half board;
p. completa, full board. 2 *(paga)* pension, allowance; p. vitalicia, life annuity.

pensionista *nmf* pensioner.

pentágono *nm* pentagon.

pentagrama *nm* staff, stave.

penúltimo,-a *adj & nm,f* next to the last,
penultimate.

penumbra *nf* penumbra, half-light.

penuria *nf* scarcity, shortage.

peña *nf* 1 rock, crag. 2 *(de amigos)* club. 3
fam (gente) people.

peñasco *nm* rock, crag.

peñón *nm* rock; el P. de Gibraltar, the
Rock of Gibraltar.

peón *nm* 1 unskilled labourer o US laborer; p. agrícola, farmhand. 2 *Ajedrez*
pawn.

peonada *nf* day's work.

peonza *nf (spinning)* top.

peor I *adj* 1 *(comparativo)* worse. 2 *(superlativo)* worst; en el p. de los casos, if
the worst comes to the worst; lo p. es
que, the worst of it is that. II *adv* 1
(comparativo) worse; ¡p. para mí o ti!, too

bad! 2 *(superlativo)* worst.

pepinillo nm gherkin.

pepino nm cucumber; *fam* **me importa un p.**, I don't give a hoot.

pepita nf *(de fruta)* pip, seed; *(de metal)* nugget.

pepitoria nf fricassee; **pollo en p.**, fricassee of chicken.

peque nm *fam (niño)* kid.

pequeño,-a I adj small, little; *(bajo)* short. **II** nm,f child; **de p.**, as a child.

Pequín n Peking.

pera nf **I** *Bot* pear; **p. de agua**, juicy pear. **2** *vulg (pene)* prick.

peral nm pear tree.

percance nm mishap, setback.

percatarse vr **p. de**, to realise.

percepción nf perception.

perceptible adj **1** perceptible. **2** *Fin* receivable, payable.

percha nf *(colgador)* (coat) hanger; *(de gallina)* perch.

perchero nm clothes rack.

percibir vtr **1** *(notar)* to perceive, notice. **2** *(cobrar)* to receive.

percusión nf percussion.

perdedor,-a I adj losing. **II** nm,f loser.

perder [3] I vtr **1** to lose. **2** *(tren, autobús)* to miss; *(tiempo)* to waste; *(oportunidad)* to miss. **3** *(pervertir)* to be the ruin o downfall of. **II** vi to lose; **echar (algo) a p.**, to spoil (sth); **echarse a p.**, to be spoilt; **salir perdiendo**, to come off worst. **III perderse** vr **1** *(extraviarse)* *(persona)* to get lost; **se me ha perdido la llave**, I've lost my key; **no te lo pierdas**, don't miss it. **2** *(pervertirse)* to go to rack and ruin.

perdición nf undoing, downfall.

pérdida nf **1** loss; **no tiene p.**, you can't miss it. **2** *(de tiempo, esfuerzos)* waste. **3** *Mil* **pérdidas**, losses.

perdido,-a adj **1** *(extraviado)* lost. **2** *fam (sucio)* filthy. **3** *fam* **loco p.**, mad as a hatter. **4** **estar p. por algn**, *(enamorado)* to be crazy about sb. **5** *(acabado)* finished; **¡estoy p.!**, I'm a goner!

perdigón nm pellet.

perdiguero,-a adj partridge-hunting; **perro p.**, setter.

perdiz nf partridge.

perdón nm pardon, forgiveness; **¡p.!**, sorry!; **pedir p.**, to apologize.

perdonar vtr **1** *(remitir)* to forgive. **2** **perdone!**, sorry!; **perdone que le moleste**, sorry for bothering you. **3** *(eximir)* to pardon; **perdonar la vida a algn**, to spare sb's life; **p. una deuda**, to write off a debt.

perdurable adj **1** *(eterno)* everlasting. **2** *(duradero)* durable, long-lasting.

perdurar vi **1** *(durar)* to endure, last. **2** *(persistir)* to persist, continue to exist.

perecedero,-a adj perishable; **artículos perecederos**, perishables.

perecer [33] vi to perish, die.

peregrinación nf, **peregrinaje** nm pilgrimage.

peregrino,-a I nm,f pilgrim. **II** adj **ideas peregrinas**, crazy ideas.

perejil nm parsley.

perenne adj perennial, everlasting.

perentorio,-a adj peremptory, urgent.

pereza nf laziness, idleness.

perezoso,-a adj *(vago)* lazy, idle.

perfección nf perfection; **a la p.**, to perfection.

perfeccionamiento nm **1** *(acción)* perfecting. **2** *(mejora)* improvement.

perfeccionar vtr **1** to perfect; *(mejorar)* improve, make better.

perfeccionista adj & nmf perfectionist.

perfecto,-a adj perfect.

◆**perfectamente** adv perfectly; **¡p.!**, *(de acuerdo)* agreed!; all right!

perfidia nf perfidy, treachery.

perfil nm **1** profile; *(contorno)* outline, contour; **de p.**, in profile. **2** *Geom* cross section.

perfilar I vtr *(dar forma)* to shape, outline. **II perfilarse** vr *(tomar forma)* to take shape.

perforación nf, **perforado** nm perforation; *Min* drilling, boring; *Inform (de tarjetas)* punching.

perforadora nf punch; *Min* drill; *Inform* **p. de teclado**, keypunch.

perforar vtr to perforate; *Min* to drill, bore; *Inform* to punch.

perfumar I vtr & vi to perfume. **II perfumarse** vr to put on perfume.

perfume nm perfume, scent.

pergamino nm parchment.

pericia nf expertise, skill.

periferia nf periphery; *(alrededores)* outskirts *pl*.

periférico,-a adj & nm peripheral.

perifrasis nf inv periphrasis, long-winded explanation.

perilla nf *(barba)* goatee; *fam* **de perilla(s)**, *(oportuno)* at the right moment; *(útil)* very handy.

perímetro nm perimeter.

periódico,-a I nm newspaper. **II** adj periodic; *Quím* **tabla periódica**, periodic table.

periodismo nm journalism.

periodista nmf journalist, reporter.

periodo, **período** nm period.

peripecia nf sudden change, vicissitude.

periplo nm voyage, tour.

periquete nm *fam* **en un p.**, in a jiffy.

periquito nm budgerigar, *fam* budgie.

periscopio nm periscope.

peritaje nm *(estudios)* technical studies *pl*.

perito,-a nm,f technician; expert; **p. industrial/agrónomo**, ≈ industrial/agricultural expert.

peritonitis nf peritonitis.

perjudicar [1] vtr to harm, injure; (intereses) to prejudice.

perjudicial adj prejudicial, harmful.

perjuicio nm harm, damage; **en p. de**, to the detriment of; **sin p. de**, without prejudice to.

perjurar vi to commit perjury.

perjurio nm perjury.

perla nf pearl; fig (persona) gem, jewel; fam **me viene de perlas**, it's just the ticket.

permanecer [33] vi to remain, stay.

permanencia nf 1 (inmutabilidad) permanence. 2 (estancia) stay.

permanente I adj permanent. II nf (de pelo) permanent wave, perm; **hacerse la p.**, to have one's hair permed.

permisivo,-a adj permissive.

permiso nm 1 (autorización) permission. 2 (licencia) licence, US license permit; **p. de conducir**, driving licence, US driver's license; **p. de residencia/trabajo**, residence/work permit. 3 Mil leave; **estar de p.**, to be on leave.

permitir I vtr to permit, allow; **¿me permite?**, may I? II **permitirse** vr 1 to permit o allow oneself; **me permito recordarle que**, let me remind you that. 2 'no se permite fumar', 'no smoking'.

permutar vtr to exchange.

pernicioso,-a adj pernicious.

pernil nm (de pantalón) leg; (jamón) leg of pork.

pernocta nf Mil (pase de) p., overnight pass.

pero I conj but; **p., ¿qué pasa aquí?**, now, what's going on here? II nm objection.

perogrullada nf truism, platitude.

perol nm large saucepan, pot.

perorata nf boring speech.

perpendicular adj & nf perpendicular.

perpetrar vtr to perpetrate, commit.

perpetuar [30] vtr to perpetuate.

perpetuo,-a adj perpetual, everlasting; Jur **cadena perpetua**, life imprisonment.

perplejidad nf perplexity, bewilderment.

perplejo,-a adj perplexed, bewildered.

perra nf 1 bitch. 2 fam (moneda) penny; **estar sin una p.**, to be broke.

perrera nf kennel, kennels pl.

perrería nf fam dirty trick.

perro,-a I nm dog; fam **un día de perros**, a lousy day; fam **vida de perros**, dog's life; Culin **p. caliente**, hot dog. II adj fam (vago) lazy.

persecución nf 1 pursuit. 2 Pol (represión) persecution.

perseguir [6] vtr 1 to pursue, chase; (correr tras) to run after, follow. 2 (reprimir) to persecute.

perseverante adj persevering.

perseverar vi 1 to persevere, persist. 2

(durar) to last.

persiana nf blinds pl.

pérsico,-a adj Persian; **golfo P.**, Persian Gulf.

persignarse vr to cross oneself.

persistencia nf persistence.

persistente adj persistent.

persistir vi to persist.

persona nf person; **algunas personas**, some people; fam **p. mayor**, grown-up.

personaje nm 1 Cin Lit Teat character. 2 (celebridad) celebrity, important person.

personal I adj personal, private. II nm 1 (plantilla) staff, personnel. 2 fam (gente) people.

personalidad nf personality.

personarse vr to present oneself, appear in person.

personificar [1] vtr to personify.

perspectiva nf 1 perspective. 2 (futuro) prospect.

perspicacia nf insight, perspicacity.

perspicaz adj sharp, perspicacious.

persuadir vtr to persuade; **estar persuadido de que**, to be convinced that.

persuasión nf persuasion.

persuasivo,-a adj persuasive, convincing.

pertenecer [33] vi to belong (a, to).

perteneciente adj belonging.

pertenencia nf 1 possessions pl, property. 2 (a un partido etc) affiliation, membership.

pértiga nf pole; Dep **salto con p.**, pole vault.

pertinaz adj 1 persistent. 2 (obstinado) obstinate, stubborn.

pertinente adj 1 pertinent, relevant. 2 (apropiado) appropriate.

perturbación nf disturbance; **p. del orden público**, breach of the peace; Med **p. mental**, mental disorder.

perturbado,-a adj (mentally) deranged o unbalanced.

perturbador,-a I adj disturbing. II nm,f unruly person.

perturbar vtr (el orden) to disturb.

Perú (el) n Peru.

peruano,-a adj & nm,f Peruvian.

perversión nf perversion.

perverso,-a adj perverse, evil.

pervertir [5] vtr to pervert, corrupt.

pervivir vi to survive.

pesa nf weight; **levantamiento de pesas**, weightlifting.

pesadez nf 1 heaviness; (de estómago) fullness. 2 fam (fastidio) drag, nuisance.

pesadilla nf nightmare; **de p.**, nightmarish.

pesado,-a I adj 1 heavy. 2 (aburrido) tedious, dull; **¡qué p.!**, what a drag!. II nm,f bore.

pesadumbre nf grief, affliction.

pésame nm condolence, sympathy; **dar el p.**, to offer one's condolences; **mi más**

sentido p., my deepest sympathy.

pesar I *vtr* to weigh; *fig (entristecer)* to grieve. **II** *vi* 1 to weigh; ¿cuánto pesas?, how much do you weigh? 2 *(ser pesado)* to be heavy. 3 *fig (tener importancia)* este factor pesa mucho, this is a very important factor. **III** *nm* 1 *(pena)* sorrow, grief. 2 *(arrepentimiento)* regret; **a su p.**, to his regret. 3 **a p. de**, in spite of.

pesaroso,-a *adj* 1 *(triste)* sorrowful, sad. 2 *(arrepentido)* regretful, sorry.

pesca *nf* fishing; *fam* **y toda la p.**, and all that.

pescadería *nf* fish shop, fishmonger's (shop).

pescadero,-a *nm,f* fishmonger.

pescadilla *nf* young hake.

pescado *nm* fish.

pescador,-a *nm* 1 *(hombre)* fisherman; *(mujer)* fisherwoman.

pescante *nm* 1 *(de carruaje)* coachman's seat. 2 *Constr* jib, boom. 3 *Náut* davit.

pescar [1] **I** *vi* to fish. **II** *vtr* 1 to fish. 2 *fam (coger)* to catch.

pescozada *nf*, **pescozón** *nm* slap on the neck *o* head.

pescuezo *nm fam* neck.

pese a (que) *loc adv* in spite of (the fact that).

pesebre *nm* manger, stall.

peseta *nf* peseta; *fam* **hacer la p. a algn**, to give sb the fingers.

pesetero,-a *nm,f* skinflint.

pesimismo *nm* pessimism.

pesimista I *adj* pessimistic. **II** *nmf* pessimist.

pésimo,-a *adj* very bad, awful, terrible.

peso *nm* 1 weight; **al p.**, by weight; **p. bruto/neto**, gross/net weight; *fig* **me quité un p. de encima**, it took a load off my mind; *Box* **p. mosca/pesado**, flyweight/ heavyweight. 2 *(importancia)* importance; **de p.**, *(persona)* influential; *(razón)* convincing.

pespunte *nm* backstitch.

pesquero,-a I *adj* fishing. **II** *nm* fishing boat.

pesquisa *nf* inquiry.

pestaña *nf* 1 eyelash, lash. 2 *Téc* flange; *(de neumático)* rim.

pestañear *vi* to blink; **sin p.**, without batting an eyelid.

peste *nf* 1 *(hedor)* stench, stink. 2 *Med* plague; *Hist* **la p. negra**, the Black Death. 3 **decir** *o* **echar pestes**, to curse.

pesticida *nm* pesticide.

pestilencia *nf* stench, stink.

pestilente *adj* stinking, foul.

pestillo *nm* bolt, latch.

petaca *nf* 1 *(para cigarrillos)* cigarette case; *(para bebidas)* flask. 2 *Am (maleta)* suitcase.

petaco *nm (de juego)* flipper; **máquina de petacos**, pinball machine.

pétalo *nm* petal.

petardo *nm* 1 firecracker, firework; *Mil* petard. 2 *fam (persona aburrida)* bore. 3 *(droga)* joint.

petate *nm Mil* luggage.

petición *nf* request; *Jur* petition, plea.

peto *nm* pantalón de p., dungarees *pl*.

petrificar [1] *vtr*, **petrificarse** *vr* to petrify.

petróleo *nm* petroleum, oil.

petrolero *nm* oil tanker.

petulante *adj* arrogant, vain.

petunia *nf* petunia.

peyorativo,-a *adj* pejorative, derogatory.

pez[1] *nm* fish; **ella está como p. en el agua**, she's in her element; **p. gordo**, big shot.

pez[2] *nf* pitch, tar.

pezón *nm* nipple.

pezuña *nf* hoof.

piadoso,-a *adj* 1 *(devoto)* pious. 2 *(compasivo)* compassionate; **mentira piadosa**, white lie.

pianista *nmf* pianist, piano player.

piano *nm* piano.

piar [29] *vi* to chirp, tweet.

piara *nf* herd of pigs.

PIB *nm Fin abr de producto interior bruto*, gross domestic product, GDP.

pibe,-a *nm,f Am (niño)* kid.

picadero *nm* riding school.

picadillo *nm (de carne)* minced meat; *(de verduras)* vegetable salad.

picado,-a I *adj* 1 *(carne)* minced. 2 *(fruta)* bad; *(diente)* decayed. 3 *(mar)* choppy. 4 *fam (enfadado)* narked. 5 **estar p. con**, *(en competición)* to be at loggerheads with. **II** *Av* dive; **caer en p.**, to plummet.

picador *nm Taur* mounted bullfighter, picador.

picadora *nf* mincer.

picadura *nf* 1 *(mordedura)* bite; *(de avispa, abeja)* sting. 2 *(en fruta)* spot; *Med (de viruela)* pockmark; *(en diente)* decay, caries sing; *(en metalurgia)* pitting.

picajoso,-a I *adj* touchy. **II** *nm,f* touchy person.

picante *adj* 1 *Culin* hot, spicy. 2 *fig (chiste etc)* risqué, spicy.

picapica *nm* polvos p., itching powder sing.

picaporte *nm (aldaba)* door knocker; *(pomo)* door handle.

picar [1] **I** *vtr* 1 *(de insecto, serpiente)* to bite; *(de avispas, abejas)* to sting; *(barba)* to prick. 2 *(comer) (aves)* to peck (at); *(persona)* to nibble, pick at. 3 *Pesca* to bite. 4 *(perforar)* to prick, puncture. 5 *Culin (carne)* to mince. 6 *(incitar)* to incite, goad; **p. la curiosidad (de algn)**, to arouse (sb's) curiosity. **II** *vi* 1 *(escocer)* to itch; *(herida)* to smart; *(el sol)* to burn. 2 *Culin* to be hot. 3 *Pesca* to bite. 4 *fig (dejarse engañar)* to swallow it. **III picarse** *vr*

1 (*hacerse rivales*) to be at loggerheads. **2** (*fruta*) to spot, rot; (*ropa*) to become moth-eaten; (*dientes*) to decay. **3** (*enfadarse*) to get cross. **4** (*drogadicto*) to shoot up.

picardía *nf* **1** (*astucia*) craftiness. **2** (*palabrota*) swear word. **3** (*prenda*) baby-doll pyjamas.

pícaro,-a I *adj* **1** (*travieso*) naughty, mischievous; (*astuto*) sly, crafty. **2** (*procaz*) risqué. II *nm,f* rascal, rogue.

picatoste *nm* crouton.

pichi *nm* pinafore dress.

pichón *nm* young pigeon; **tiro al** *o* **de p.,** pigeon shooting.

pico *nm* **1** (*de ave*) beak, bill; *fam* (*boca*) mouth; **tener un p. de oro,** to have the gift of the gab. **2** (*punta*) corner. **3** *Geog* peak. **4** (*herramienta*) pick, pickaxe, *US* pickax. **5** (*cantidad*) odd amount; **cincuenta y p.,** fifty odd; **las dos y p.,** just after two. **6** (*drogas*) fix.

picoleto *nm fam* civil guard.

picor *nm* itch, tingling.

picotazo *nm* peck.

picotear *vtr & vi* **1** (*pájaro*) to peck. **2** (*comer*) to nibble.

pictórico,-a *adj* pictorial.

pídola *nf* leapfrog.

pie *nm* **1** foot; **pies,** feet; **a p.,** on foot; **de p.,** standing up; **de pies a cabeza,** from head to foot; **en p.,** standing; **el acuerdo sigue en p.,** the agreement still stands; **hacer p.,** to touch the bottom; **perder p.,** to get out of one's depth; *fig* **a p.** *o* **pies juntillas,** blindly; *fig* **al p. de la letra,** to the letter, word for word; *fig* **con buen/mal p.,** on the right/wrong footing; *fig* **con pies de plomo,** gingerly, cautiously; *fig* **dar p. a,** to give cause for. **2** (*de instrumento*) stand; (*de copa*) stem. **3** foot; (*de una ilustración*) caption; **p. de página,** foot of the page. **4** (*medida*) foot. **5** *Teat* cue. **6** *Lit* foot.

piedad *nf* **1** devoutness, piety. **2** (*compasión*) compassion, pity.

piedra *nf* stone; (*de mechero*) flint; **poner la primera p.,** to lay the foundation stone; *fam* **fig me dejó** *o* **me quedé de p.,** I was flabbergasted.

piel *nf* **1** skin; **p. de gallina,** goose pimples *pl.* **2** (*de fruta, de patata*) skin, peel. **3** (*cuero*) leather; (*con pelo*) fur.

pienso *nm* fodder, feed; **piensos compuestos,** mixed feed *sing.*

pierna *nf* leg.

pieza *nf* **1** piece, part; **p. de recambio,** spare part; *fig* **me dejó** *o* **me quedé de una p.,** I was speechless *o* dumbfounded *o* flabbergasted. **2** (*habitación*) room. **3** *Teat* play.

pigmento *nm* pigment.

pigmeo,-a I *adj* pigmy; *fig* pygmean. II *nm,f* Pygmy, Pigmy; *fig* pygmy, pigmy.

pijama *nm* pyjamas *pl.*

pijo,-a I *adj* posh; **un barrio p.,** a posh area. II *nm,f* (*chico*) poor little rich boy; (*chica*) poor little rich girl. III *nm* (*pene*) willy.

pila *nf* **1** *Elec* battery. **2** (*montón*) pile, heap; *fig* (*muchos*) piles *pl,* heaps *pl,* loads *pl.* **3** (*lavadero*) basin. **4** *fig* **nombre de p.,** Christian name.

pilar *nm* **1** *Arquit* pillar. **2** (*fuente*) waterhole.

píldora *nf* pill; **p. abortiva,** morning-after pill; *fig* **dorar la p. a algn,** to butter sb up.

pileta *nf* **1** (*pila*) sink. **2** *Am* (*piscina*) swimming pool.

pilila *nf fam* willy.

pillaje *nm* looting, pillage.

pillar I *vtr* **1** (*robar*) to plunder, loot. **2** (*coger*) to catch; (*alcanzar*) to catch up with; **lo pilló un coche,** he was run over by a car. **3** *fam* to be; **me pilla un poco lejos,** it's a bit far for *o* from me. II **pillarse** *vtr* to catch; **p. un dedo/una mano,** to catch one's finger/hand.

pillo,-a I *adj* **1** (*travieso*) naughty. **2** (*astuto*) sly, cunning. II *nm,f* rogue.

pilotar *vtr* *Av* to pilot, fly; *Aut* to drive; *Náut* to pilot, steer.

piloto *nm* **1** *Av Náut* pilot; *Aut* driver; **piso p.,** show flat; **programa p.,** pilot programme. **2** (*luz*) pilot lamp, light.

piltrafa *nf fam* **1** weakling; **estar hecho una p.,** to be on one's last legs. **2** (*desecho*) scraps.

pimentón *nm* paprika, red pepper.

pimienta *nf* pepper.

pimiento *nm* (*fruto*) pepper; (*planta*) pimiento; **p. morrón,** sweet pepper; *fam* **me importa un p.,** I don't give a damn, I couldn't care less.

pimpollo *nm* **1** *Bot* shoot. **2** *fam* (*hombre*) handsome young man; (*mujer*) elegant young woman.

pinacoteca *nf* art gallery.

pináculo *nm* pinnacle.

pinar *nm* pine grove, pine wood.

pincel *nm* brush, paintbrush.

pincelada *nf* brushstroke, stroke of a brush.

pinchadiscos *nmf inv fam* disc jockey, DJ.

pinchar I *vtr* **1** (*punzar*) to jag; (*balón, globo*) to burst; (*rueda*) to puncture. **2** *fam* (*incitar*) to prod; (*molestar*) to get at, nag. **3** *Med* to inject, give an injection to. **4** *Tel* to bug. II *vi* **1** *Aut* to get a puncture. **2** *fam* **ni pincha ni corta,** he cuts no ice.

pinchazo *nm* **1** (*punzadura*) prick; *Aut* puncture, blowout. **2** (*de dolor*) sudden *o* sharp pain.

pinche *nm* **1 p. de cocina,** kitchen assistant. **2** *Am* (*bribón*) rogue.

pinchito *nm* (*de carne*) type of kebab.

pincho nm 1 (púa) barb. 2 p. moruno, shish kebab; **p. de tortilla**, small portion of omelette.

ping-pong® nm table tennis, ping-pong.

pingüe adj abundant, plentiful; **pingües beneficios**, fat profits.

pingüino nm penguin.

pino nm pine; fig **hacer el p.**, to do a handstand; fam **en el quinto p.**, in the back of beyond.

pinole nm Am maize drink.

pinta¹ nf 1 (aspecto) look; **tiene p. de ser interesante**, it looks interesting. 2 (mota) dot; (lunar) spot. 3 (medida) pint. II nmf fam shameless person.

pintada nf graffiti.

pintado,-a adj 'recién p.', 'wet paint'; fam fig **nos viene que ni p.**, it is just the ticket; fam fig **te está que ni p.**, it suits you to a tee.

pintar I vtr 1 (dar color) to paint. 2 (dibujar) to draw, sketch. II vi (importar) to count; fig **yo aquí no pinto nada**, I am out of place here. III **pintarse** vr 1 (maquillarse) to put make-up on. 2 fam **pintárselas**, to manage.

pintor,-a nm,f painter.

pintoresco,-a adj 1 (lugar) picturesque. 2 (raro) eccentric, bizarre.

pintura nf 1 painting; **p. rupestre**, cave painting; fam fig **no la puedo ver ni en p.**, I can't stand the sight of her. 2 (materia) paint.

pinza nf 1 (para depilar) tweezers pl; (para tender) clothes peg; (de animal) pincer, nipper; Téc tongs pl.

piña nf 1 (de pino) pine cone; (ananás) pineapple. 2 fig (grupo) clan, clique. 3 fam (golpe) thump.

piñón nm 1 pine seed o nut. 2 Téc pinion.

pío¹ nm fam **no dijo ni p.**, there wasn't a cheep out of him.

pío,-a² adj pious.

piojo nm louse.

pionero,-a nm,f pioneer.

pipa¹ nf 1 (de fumar) pipe; **fumar en p.**, to smoke a pipe. 2 (de fruta) pip; (de girasol) sunflower seed.

pipí nm fam pee, wee-wee; **hacer p.**, to pee, wee-wee.

pique nm 1 (rivalidad) resentment. 2 (rivalidad) needle. 3 **a p. de**, on the point of. 4 **irse a p.**, Náut to sink; (un plan) to fall through; (un negocio) to go bust.

piqueta nf pickaxe, US pickax.

piquete nm 1 (de huelga) picket. 2 Mil **p. de ejecución**, firing squad.

pira nf pyre.

pirado,-a adj arg crazy.

piragua nf canoe.

piragüismo nm canoeing.

piragüista nmf canoeist.

pirámide nf pyramid.

piraña nf piranha.

pirarse, pirárselas vr arg to clear off, hop it.

pirata adj & nmf pirate.

piratear vtr fig to pirate.

Pirineo(s) nmpl Pyrenees.

pirita nf pyrite.

pirómano,-a nm,f Med pyromaniac; Jur arsonist.

piropo nm **echar un p.**, to pay a compliment.

pirueta nf pirouette; fig Pol **hacer una p.**, to do a U-turn.

pirulí nm lollipop; TV television tower.

pis nm fam wee-wee, pee; **hacer p.**, to wee-wee, have a pee.

pisada nf 1 step, footstep; (huella) footprint.

pisapapeles nm inv paperweight.

pisar vtr to tread on, step on.

piscifactoría nf fish farm.

piscina nf swimming pool.

piscolabis nm inv fam snack.

piso nm 1 flat, apartment; Pol **p. franco**, safe house. 2 (planta) floor; (de carretera) surface.

pisotear vtr (aplastar) to stamp on; (pisar) to trample on.

pisotón nm **me dio un p.**, he stood on my foot.

pista nf 1 track; **p. de baile**, dance floor; Dep **p. de esquí**, ski run o slope; Dep **p. de patinaje**, ice rink; Dep **p. de tenis**, tennis court; **p. de aterrizaje**, landing strip; **p. de despegue**, runway. 2 (rastro) trail, track. 3 **dame una p.**, give me a clue.

pistacho nm pistachio nut.

pisto nm Culin ≈ ratatouille.

pistola nf 1 gun, pistol. 2 (para pintar) spray gun.

pistolero nm gunman, gangster.

pistón nm 1 Téc (émbolo) piston. 2 (de arma) cartridge cap. 3 Mús key.

pita nf agave.

pitada nf booing, hissing.

pitar I vtr 1 (silbato) to blow. 2 Dep **el árbitro pitó un penalti**, the referee awarded a penalty. II vi 1 to whistle. 2 Aut to toot one's horn. 3 Dep to referee. 4 fam **salir pitando**, to fly off.

pitido nm whistle.

pitillera nf cigarette case.

pitillo nm cigarette, fag.

pito nm 1 whistle; Aut horn; fam **me importa un p.**, I don't give a hoot. 2 fam (cigarrillo) fag. 3 fam (pene) prick, willie.

pitón nm 1 (serpiente) python. 2 (de toro) horn.

pitorreo nm fam scoffing, teasing; **hacer algo de p.**, to do sth for a laugh.

pivot, pivote nmf pivot.

pizarra nf 1 (encerado) blackboard. 2 Min slate.

pizca *nf* little bit, tiny piece; **ni p.**, not a bit; **una p. de sal**, a pinch of salt.

placa *nf* 1 plate. 2 (*conmemorativa*) plaque.

placaje *nm Dep* tackle.

placentero,-a *adj* pleasant, agreeable.

placer *nm* pleasure; **ha sido un p.** (*conocerle*), it's been a pleasure (meeting you); *fml* **tengo el p. de**, it gives me great pleasure to; **un viaje de p.**, a holiday trip.

placer [33] *vtr* to please.

placidez *nf* placidity.

plácido,-a *adj* placid, easy-going.

plaga *nf* 1 plague. 2 *Agr* pest, blight.

plagar [7] *vtr* to cover, fill.

plagiar [12] *vtr* 1 (*copiar*) to plagiarize. 2 *Am* (*secuestrar*) to kidnap.

plagiario,-a *nm,f Am* (*secuestrador*) kidnapper.

plagio *nm* plagiarism.

plan *nm* 1 (*proyecto*) plan. 2 (*programa*) scheme, programme; *Educ* **p. de estudios**, syllabus; **estar a p.**, to be on a diet. 3 *fam* **en p. de broma**, for a laugh; **si te pones en ese p.**, if you're going to be like that (about it); **en p. barato**, cheaply. 4 *fam* (*cita*) date.

plana *nf* 1 page; **a toda p.**, full page; **primera p.**, front page. 2 *Mil* **p. mayor**, staff.

plancha *nf* 1 iron; (*de metal*) plate. 2 *Culin* hotplate; **sardinas a la p.**, grilled sardines. 3 *Impr* plate.

planchado *nm* ironing.

planchar *vtr* to iron.

planchazo *nm fam* blunder, boob.

planeador *nm* glider.

planear *vtr* to plan. II *vi* to glide.

planeta *nm* planet.

planetario,-a I *adj* planetary. II *nm* planetarium.

planicie *nf* plain.

planificación *nf* planning; **p. familiar**, family planning.

planificar [1] *vtr* to plan.

planilla *nf Am* application form.

plano,-a I *nm* 1 (*de ciudad*) map; *Arquit* plan, draft. 2 *Cin* shot; **un primer p.**, a close-up; *fig* **estar en primer/segundo p.**, to be in the limelight/in the background. 3 *Mat* plane. II *adj* flat, even.

planta *nf* 1 plant. 2 (*del pie*) sole. 3 (*piso*) floor, storey; **p. baja**, ground floor.

plantación *nf* 1 plantation. 2 (*acción*) planting.

plantado,-a *fam* **dejar a algn p.**, to stand sb up.

plantar I *vtr* 1 (*árboles, campo*) to plant. 2 (*poner*) to put, place; **p. cara a algn**, to stand up to sb. 3 *fam* **p. a algn en la calle**, to throw sb out; **le ha plantado su novia**, his girlfriend has ditched him. II **plantarse** *vr* 1 to stand. 2 (*llegar*) to

arrive; **en cinco minutos se plantó aquí**, he got here in five minutes flat.

planteamiento *nm* (*enfoque*) approach.

plantear I *vtr* 1 (*problema*) to pose, raise. 2 (*planear*) to plan. 3 (*proponer*) to put forward. 4 (*exponer*) to present. II **plantearse** *vtr* & *vr* 1 (*considerar*) to consider. 2 (*problema*) to arise.

plantel *nm fig* cadre, clique.

plantilla *nf* 1 (*personal*) staff, personnel. 2 (*de zapato*) insole. 3 (*patrón*) model, pattern.

plantón *nm fam* **dar un p. a algn**, to stand sb up.

plañir *vi* to mourn.

plasmar I *vtr* 1 (*reproducir*) to capture. 2 (*expresar*) to express. II **plasmarse** *vr* **p. en**, to take the shape of.

plasta *nmf fam* bore.

plástico,-a I *adj* plastic. II *nm* 1 plastic. 2 (*disco*) record.

plastificar [1] *vtr* to coat o cover with plastic.

plastilina *nf* Plasticine®.

plata *nf* 1 silver; (*objetos de plata*) silverware; *fam* **hablar en p.**, to lay (it) on the line; **p. de ley**, sterling silver. 2 *Am* money.

plataforma *nm* platform.

plátano *nm* 1 (*fruta*) banana. 2 (*árbol*) plane tree; **falso p.**, sycamore.

platea *nf Cin Teat* stalls *pl*, *US* ground floor.

platear *vtr* to silver-plate.

platense I *adj* of o from the River Plate. II *nmf* native o inhabitant of the River Plate.

plática *nf* chat, talk.

platicar [1] *vi* to chat, talk.

platillo *nm* 1 saucer; **p. volante**, flying saucer. 2 *Mús* cymbal.

platina *nf* (*de tocadiscos*) deck; **doble p.**, double deck.

platino *nm* 1 platinum. 2 *Aut* **platinos**, contact breaker *sing*, points.

plato *nm* 1 plate, dish. 2 (*parte de una comida*) course; **de primer p.**, for starters; **p. fuerte**, main course; **p. combinado**, one-course meal. 3 (*guiso*) dish. 4 (*de balanza*) pan, tray. 5 (*de tocadiscos*) turntable.

plató *nm Cin* TV (film) set.

plausible *adj* 1 (*admisible*) plausible, acceptable. 2 (*loable*) commendable.

playa *nf* 1 beach; (*costa*) seaside. 2 *Am* **p. de estacionamiento**, car park, *US* parking lot.

playera *nf* 1 (*zapatilla*) sandshoe, *US* sneaker. 2 *Am* (*camiseta*) teeshirt.

plaza *nf* 1 square. 2 (*mercado*) market, marketplace. 3 *Aut* seat. 4 (*laboral*) post, position. 5 **p. de toros**, bullring.

plazo *nm* 1 (*periodo*) time, period; (*término*) deadline; **a corto/largo p.**, in the short term/in the long run; **el p. termina el viernes**, Friday is the deadline. 2 *Fin* **comprar a plazos**, to buy on hire purchase, *US* buy on an installment plan; **en seis plazos**, in six instalments.

pleamar *nf* high tide.

plebe *nf* masses *pl*, plebs *pl*.

plebeyo,-a I *adj* plebeian. II *nm,f* plebeian, pleb.

plebiscito *nm* plebiscite.

plegable *adj* folding, collapsible.

plegar [1] I *vtr* to fold. II **plegarse** *vr* to give way, bow.

plegaria *nf* prayer.

pleitear *vi* to conduct a lawsuit, plead.

pleito *nm fur* lawsuit, litigation; **poner un p. (a algn)**, to sue (sb).

plenilunio *nm* full moon.

plenitud *nf* plenitude, fullness; **en la p. de la vida**, in the prime of life.

pleno,-a I *adj* full; **en plena noche**, in the middle of the night; **los empleados en p.**, the entire staff. II *nm* plenary meeting.

pletórico,-a *adj* abundant.

plexiglás® *nm* (*plástico*) Perspex®, *US* Plexiglass®.

pliego *nm* 1 (*hoja*) sheet *o* piece of paper; **p. de condiciones**, bidding specifications. 2 (*carta*) sealed letter.

pliegue *nm* 1 fold. 2 (*de vestido*) pleat.

plinto *nm* (*Gimn*) horse.

plisar *vtr* to pleat.

plomero,-a I *nm Am* plumber.

plomizo,-a *adj* lead, leaden; (*color*) lead-colored, *US* lead-colored.

plomo *nm* 1 (*en metalurgia*) lead. 2 *Elec* (*fusible*) fuse. 3 (*bala*) slug, pellet.

pluma *nf* 1 feather. 2 (*de escribir*) fountain pen.

plumaje *nm* plumage.

plumazo *nm* **de un p.**, at a stroke.

plumero *nm* 1 (*para el polvo*) feather duster. 2 *fam* **se te ve el p.**, I can see through you.

plumier *nm* pencil box.

plural *adj & nm* plural.

pluralismo *nm* pluralism.

pluriempleo *nm* moonlighting.

plus *nm* bonus, bonus payment.

plusmarca *nf* record.

plusmarquista *nmf* record breaker.

plusvalía *nf* capital gain.

población *nf* 1 (*ciudad*) town; (*pueblo*) village. 2 (*habitantes*) population.

poblado,-a I *adj* populated; **fig p. de**, full of. 2 (*barba*) bushy, thick.

poblador,-a *nm,f* settler.

poblar [2] *vtr* 1 (*con gente*) to settle, people; (*con plantas*) to plant. 2 (*vivir*) to inhabit.

pobre I *adj* poor; **¡p.!**, poor thing!; **un hombre p.**, a poor man; **un p. hombre**, a poor devil. II *nmf* poor person; **los po-**

bres, the poor.

pobreza *nf* poverty; *fig* (*de medios, recursos*) lack.

pocilga *nf* pigsty.

pocillo *nm Am* cup.

pócima, poción *nf* potion; *pey* concoction, brew.

poco,-a I *nm* 1 **un p.**, (*con adj o adv*) a little; **un p. tarde/frío**, a little late/cold. 2 **un p.**, (*con sustantivo*) a little; **un p. de azúcar**, a little sugar. II *adj* 1 not much, little; **p. sitio/tiempo**, not much *o* little space/time; **poca cosa**, not much. 2 **pocos,-as**, not many, few; **pocas personas**, not many *o* few people. 3 **unos-as pocos-as**, a few. III *pron* 1 not much; **queda**, there isn't much left. 2 **pocos,-as**, (*cosas*) few, not many; **tengo muy pocos**, I have very few, I don't have very many. 3 **pocos,-as**, (*personas*) few people, not many people; **vinieron pocos**, few people came, not many people came. IV *adv* 1 (*con verbo*) not (very) much, little; **ella come p.**, she doesn't eat much, she eats little. 2 (*con adj*) not very; **es p. probable**, it's not very likely. V (*locuciones*) **a p. de**, shortly *o* a little after; **dentro de p.**, soon; **p. a p.**, little by little, gradually; **p. antes/después**, shortly *o* a little before/afterwards; **por p.**, almost.

pocho,-a *adj* 1 (*fruta*) bad, overripe. 2 *fig* (*persona*) (*débil*) off-colour, *US* off-color; (*triste*) depressed, down.

podar *vtr* to prune.

poder¹ *nm* power; *Econ* **p. adquisitivo**, purchasing power.

poder² [18] I *vtr* 1 (*capacidad*) to be able to; **no puede hablar**, she can't speak; **no podré llamarte**, I won't be able to phone; **no puedo más**, I can't take anymore; **guapa a más no p.**, unbelievably pretty. 2 (*permiso*) may, might; **¿puedo pasar?**, can *o* may I come in?; **¿se puede (entrar)?**, may I (come in)?; **aquí no se puede fumar**, you can't smoke here. 3 (*uso impers*) (*posibilidad*) may, might; **puede que no lo sepan**, they may *o* might not know; **no puede ser**, that's impossible; **puede (ser)** (*que sí*), maybe, perhaps. 4 (*deber*) **podrías haberme advertido**, you might have warned me. II *vi* 1 to cope (*con*, with); **no puede con tanto trabajo**, he can't cope with so much work. 2 (*batir*) to be stronger than; **les puede a todos**, he can take on anybody.

poderoso,-a *adj* powerful.

podio, pódium *nm Dep* podium.

podré *indic fut → poder.*

podrido,-a *adj* 1 (*putrefacto*) rotten, putrid. 2 (*corrupto*) corrupt; *fam* **p. de dinero**, stinking rich.

podrir *vtr defect → pudrir.*

poema nm poem.

poesía nf 1 (género) poetry. 2 (poema) poem.

poeta nmf poet.

poético,-a adj poetic.

póker nm poker.

polaco,-a I adj Polish. II nm,f Pole. III nm (idioma) Polish.

polaridad nf polarity.

polarizar [4] vtr 1 Fís to polarize. 2 fig (ánimo, atención) to concentrate.

polea nf pulley.

polémica nf controversy.

polémico,-a adj controversial.

polemizar [4] vi to argue, debate.

polen nm pollen.

poli- pref poly-.

poli I fam 1 nmf cop. II nf la p., the fuzz pl.

policía I nf police (force). II nmf (hombre) policeman; (mujer) policewoman.

policíaco,-a, policiaco,-a, policial adj police; novela/película policíaca, detective story/film.

polideportivo nm sports centre o US center o complex.

poliéster nm polyester.

polietileno nm polythene, US polyethylene.

polifacético,-a adj versatile, many-sided; es un hombre muy p., he's a man of many talents.

poligamia nf polygamy.

poliglota adj & nm,f polyglot.

polígono nm polygon; p. industrial, industrial estate.

polilla nf moth.

poliomielitis nf polio, poliomyelitis.

politécnico,-a adj & nm polytechnic.

política nf 1 politics sing. 2 (estrategia) policy.

político,-a I adj 1 political. 2 (pariente) in-law; hermano p., brother-in-law; su familia política, her in-laws. II nm,f politician.

póliza nf 1 (sello) stamp. 2 p. de seguros, insurance policy.

polizón nm stowaway.

polo nm 1 Elec Geog pole; P. Norte/Sur, North/South Pole. 2 (helado) ice lolly, US Popsicle®. 2 (prenda) sports shirt, polo neck (sweater). 3 Dep polo.

Polonia nf Poland.

polución nf pollution.

poltrona nf easy chair.

polvareda nf cloud of dust.

polvera nf powder compact.

polvo nm 1 dust; limpiar o quitar el p., to dust; en p., powdered; polvo(s) de talco, talcum powder. 2 fam estar hecho p., (cansado) to be knackered; (deprimido) to be depressed. 3 vulg echar un p., to have a screw.

pólvora nf gunpowder.

polvoriento,-a adj dusty.

polvorín nm gunpowder arsenal; fig powder keg.

polvorón nm sweet pastry.

polla nf 1 vulg (pene) prick. 2 Orn p. de agua, moorhen.

pollo nm 1 chicken. 2 fam (joven) lad.

pomada nf ointment.

pomelo nm (fruto) grapefruit; (árbol) grapefruit tree.

pómez adj inv piedra p., pumice (stone).

pomo nm (de puerta) knob.

pompa nf 1 bubble. 2 (ostentación) pomp.

pompis nm inv fam bottom.

pomposo,-a adj pompous.

pómulo nm cheekbone.

ponche nm punch.

poncho nm poncho.

ponderar vtr 1 (asunto) to weigh up o consider. 2 (alabar) to praise.

pondré indic fut → poner.

ponencia nf paper.

poner [19] (pp puesto) I vtr 1 to put; (mesa, huevo) to lay; (gesto) to make; (multa) to impose; (telegrama) to send; (negocio) to set up. 2 (tele, radio etc) to turn o switch on. 3 (+ adj) to make; p. triste a algn, to make sb sad; p. colorado a algn, to make sb blush. 4 ¿qué llevaba puesto?, what was he wearing? 5 (decir) ¿qué pone aquí?, what does it say here? 6 (suponer) to suppose; pongamos que Ana no viene, supposing Ana doesn't turn up. 7 TV Cin to put on, show; ¿qué ponen en la tele?, what's on the telly? 8 Tel ponme con Manuel, put me through to Manuel. 9 (nombrar) le pondremos de nombre) Pilar, we are going to call her Pilar.

II ponerse vr 1 to put oneself; ponte en mi lugar, put yourself in my place; ponte más cerca, come closer. 2 (vestirse) to put on; ella se puso el jersey, she put her jumper on. 3 (+ adj) to become; p. furioso/malo, to become furious/ill. 4 (sol) to set. 5 Tel p. al teléfono, to answer the phone. 6 p. a, to start to; p. a trabajar, to get down to work.

poney nm pony.

pongo indic pres → poner.

poniente nm 1 (occidente) West. 2 (viento) westerly (wind).

pontífice nm Pontiff; el Sumo P., His Holiness the Pope.

ponzoña nf 1 venom, poison. 2 tener p., (tristeza) to be down in the dumps.

ponzoñoso,-a adj 1 venomous, poisonous. 2 (triste) down in the dumps.

popa nf stern; fig ir viento en p., to go full speed ahead.

populacho nm pey plebs pl, masses pl.

popular adj 1 folk; arte/música p., folk art/music. 2 (medida) popular. 3 (actor) well-known.

popularidad *nf* popularity.

popularizar [4] *vtr* to popularize.

populoso,-a *adj* densely populated.

popurri *nm* *Mús* medley.

póquer *nm* poker.

por *prep* 1 (*agente*) by; **pintado p. Picasso**, painted by Picasso. 2 **p. qué**, why. 3 (*causa*) because of; **p. sus ideas**, because of her ideas; **p. necesidad/amor**, out of need/love; **suspendió p. no estudiar**, he failed because he didn't study. 4 (*tiempo*) **p. la mañana/noche**, in the morning/at night; **p. ahora**, for the time being; **p. entonces**, at that time. 5 (*en favor de*) for; **lo hago p. mi hermano**, I'm doing it for my brother('s sake). 6 (*lugar*) **pasamos p. Córdoba**, we went through Córdoba; **p. ahí**, over there; **p. dónde vamos?**, which way are we taking?; **p. la calle**, in the street; **mirar p. la ventana**, to look out the window; **entrar p. la ventana**, to get in through the window. 7 (*medio*) by; **p. avión/correo**, by plane/post. 8 (*a cambio de*) for; **cambiar algo p. otra cosa**, to exchange sth for sth else. 9 (*distributivo*) **p. cabeza**, per person; **p. hora/mes**, per hour/month. 10 *Mat* **dos p. tres**, six, two times three is six; **un diez p. ciento**, ten per cent. 11 (*con infinitivo*) in order to, so as to; **hablar p. hablar**, to talk for the sake of it. 12 (*locuciones*) **p. así decirlo**, so to speak; **p. más/muy ... que sea**, no matter how ... he *o* she is; **p. mí**, as far as I'm concerned.

porcelana *nf* porcelain.

porcentaje *nm* percentage.

porcino,-a *adj* **ganado p.**, pigs.

porción *nf* portion, part.

porche *nm* porch.

pordiosero,-a *nm,f* tramp.

porfía *nf* (*obstinación*) obstinacy, stubbornness.

porfolio *nm* portfolio.

pormenor *nm* detail; **venta al p.**, retail.

porno *adj inv fam* porn.

pornografía *nf* pornography.

pornográfico,-a *adj* pornographic.

poro *nm* pore.

poroso,-a *adj* porous.

porque *conj* 1 (*causal*) because; **¡p. no!**, just because. 2 (*final*) (+ *subj*) so that, in order that.

porqué *nm* reason.

porquería *nf* 1 (*suciedad*) dirt, filth. 2 (*birria*) rubbish. 3 *fam* (*chuchería*) rubbish, *US* junk food.

porra *nf* 1 (*de policía*) truncheon, baton. 2 *fam* (*locuciones*) **¡una p.!**, rubbish!; **¡vete a la p.!**, get lost!

porrazo *nm* thump.

porro *nm arg* joint.

porrón *nm* glass bottle with a spout coming out of its base, used for drinking wine.

porta(a)viones *nm inv* aircraft carrier.

portada *nf* 1 (*de libro etc*) cover; (*de periódico*) front page; (*de disco*) sleeve. 2 (*fachada*) front, facade.

portador,-a *nm,f Com* bearer; *Med* carrier.

portaequipajes *nm inv* 1 *Aut* (*maletero*) boot, *US* trunk; (*baca*) roof rack. 2 (*carrito*) luggage trolley.

portafolios *nm inv* briefcase.

portal *nm* 1 (*zaguán*) porch, entrance hall. 2 (*puerta de la calle*) main door. 3 **p. de Belén**, Nativity scene.

portamaletas *nm inv* → **portaequipajes**.

portaminas *nm inv* propelling pencil.

portamonedas *nm inv* purse.

portarse *vr* to behave; **p. mal**, to misbehave.

portátil *adj* portable.

portavoz *nmf* spokesperson; (*hombre*) spokesman; (*mujer*) spokeswoman.

portazo *nm* slam of a door; **dar un p.**, to slam the door.

porte *nm* 1 (*aspecto*) bearing. 2 (*transporte*) carriage.

portento *nm* 1 (*cosa*) wonder, marvel. 2 (*persona*) genius.

portentoso,-a *adj* extraordinary, prodigious.

porteño,-a I *adj* of *o* from Buenos Aires. II *nm,f* native *o* inhabitant of Buenos Aires.

portería *nf* 1 porter's lodge. 2 *Dep* goal.

portero,-a *nm,f* 1 (*de vivienda*) porter, caretaker; (*de edificio público*) doorman; **p. automático**, entryphone. 2 *Dep* goalkeeper.

pórtico *nm* 1 (*portal*) portico, porch. 2 (*con arcadas*) arcade.

portorriqueño,-a *adj & nm,f* Puerto Rican.

portuario,-a *adj* harbour, *US* harbor, port.

Portugal *n* Portugal.

portugués,-a I *adj* Portuguese. II *nm* (*idioma*) Portuguese.

porvenir *nm* future; **sin p.**, with no prospects.

pos- *pref* post-.

pos *adv en* **p. de**, after.

posada *nf* inn.

posaderas *nfpl fam* buttocks.

posadero,-a *nm,f* innkeeper.

posar I *vi* (*para retrato etc*) to pose. II *vtr* to put *o* lay down. III **posarse** *vr* to settle, alight.

posdata *nf* postscript.

pose *nf* 1 (*postura*) pose. 2 (*afectación*) posing.

poseedor,-a *nm,f* possessor.

poseer [36] *vtr* to possess, own.

poseído,-a *adj* possessed.

posesión *nf* possession; **estar en p. de**, to

have; **tomar p.**, (de un cargo) to take up (a post).

posesivo,-a adj possessive.

poseso,-a adj & nm,f possessed.

posguerra nf postwar period.

posibilidad nf possibility; (oportunidad) chance.

posibilitar vtr to make possible.

posible I adj possible; **de ser p.**, if possible; **en (la medida de) lo p.**, as far as possible; **haré todo lo p.**, I'll do everything I can; **lo antes p.**, as soon as possible; **es p. que venga**, he might come. **II** nmpl **posibles**, means.

posición nf position.

positivo,-a adj positive.

posmoderno,-a adj postmodern.

poso nm dregs pl, sediment.

posponer [19] vtr 1 (aplazar) to postpone, put off. 2 (relegar) to put in second place o behind, relegate.

post- pref post-.

posta nf a p., on purpose.

postal I adj postal. **II** nf postcard.

poste nm pole; **Dep** (de portería) post.

póster nm poster.

postergar [7] vtr 1 (relegar) to relegate. 2 (retrasar) to delay; (aplazar) to postpone.

posteridad nf posterity; **pasar a la p.**, to go down in history.

posterior adj 1 (lugar) posterior, rear. 2 (tiempo) later (a, than), subsequent (a, to). ◆**posteriormente** adv subsequently, later.

posterioridad nf posteriority; **con p.**, later.

postgraduado,-a adj & nm,f postgraduate.

postigo nm (de puerta) wicket; (de ventana) shutter.

postín nm fam boasting, showing-off; **darse p.**, to show off, swank; **de p.**, posh, swanky.

postizo,-a I adj false, artificial; **dentadura postiza**, false teeth, dentures. **II** nm hairpiece.

postor nm bidder.

postrarse vr to prostrate oneself, kneel down.

postre nm dessert, sweet.

postrero,-a adj (delante de nm sing, postrer) last.

postrimería nf (usu pl) last part o period.

postular vtr to collect.

póstumo,-a adj posthumous.

postura nf 1 position, posture. 2 fig (actitud) attitude.

pos(t)venta adj **servicio p.**, after-sales service.

potable adj drinkable; **agua p./no p.**, drinking water/not drinking water.

potaje nm hotpot, stew.

pote nm pot; (jarra) jug.

potencia nf power; **en p.**, potential.

potencial I adj potential. **II** nm 1 potential; **p. eléctrico**, voltage; **p. humano**, manpower. 2 Ling conditional (tense).

potenciar [12] vtr to promote, strengthen.

potente adj powerful, strong.

potestad nf power, authority.

potingue nm fam pey (bebida) concoction. 2 (maquillaje) make-up, face cream o lotion.

potra nf fam luck.

potro nm Zool colt; (de gimnasia) horse.

poyo nm stone bench.

pozo nm well; Min shaft, pit.

PP nm Pol abr de **Partido Popular**.

práctica nf 1 practice; **en la p.**, in practice. 2 (formación) placement; **período de prácticas**, practical training period.

practicante I adj Rel practising, US practicing. **II** nmf Med medical assistant.

practicar [1] **I** vtr to practise, US practice; (operación) to carry out. **II** vi to practise, US practice.

práctico,-a adj practical; (útil) handy, useful.

pradera nf meadow.

prado nm meadow, field.

Praga n Prague.

pragmático,-a I adj pragmatic. **II** nm,f pragmatist.

pre- pref pre-.

preámbulo nm 1 (introducción) preamble. 2 (rodeo) circumlocution.

preaviso nm previous warning, notice.

precalentamiento nm warm-up.

precalentar [1] vtr to preheat.

precario,-a adj precarious.

precaución nf 1 (cautela) caution; **con p.**, cautiously. 2 (medida) precaution.

precaver I vtr to guard against. **II** precaverse vr to take precautions (de, contra, against).

precavido,-a adj cautious, prudent.

precedencia nf precedence, priority.

precedente I adj preceding. **II** nmf predecessor. **III** nm precedent; **sin p.**, unprecedented.

preceder vtr to precede.

precepto nm precept.

preciarse [12] vr to fancy oneself (de, as).

precintar vtr to seal.

precinto nm seal.

precio nm price; **p. de coste**, cost price; **a cualquier p.**, at any price.

preciosidad nf 1 (hermosura) (cosa) lovely thing; (persona) darling. 2 fml (cualidad) preciousness.

precioso,-a adj 1 (hermoso) lovely, beautiful. 2 (valioso) precious, valuable.

precipicio nm precipice.

precipitación nf 1 (prisa) haste. 2 (lluvia) rainfall.

precipitado,-a adj (apresurado) hasty, hurried; (irreflexivo) rash.

precipitar I *vtr* **1** *(acelerar)* to hurry, rush. **2** *(arrojar)* to throw, hurl down. **II precipitarse** *vr* **1** *(persona)* to hurl oneself; *(acontecimientos)* to gather speed. **2** *(actuar irreflexivamente)* to hurry, rush.

precisar I *vtr* **1** *(determinar)* to determine, give full details of; *(especificar)* to specify. **2** *(necesitar)* to require, need.

precisión *nm* **1** *(exactitud)* precision, accuracy; **con p.**, precisely, accurately. **2** *(aclaración)* clarification.

preciso,-a *adj* **1** *(necesario)* necessary, essential. **2** *(exacto)* accurate, exact; **en este p. momento,** at this very moment. **3** *(claro)* concise, clear. ◆**precisamente** *adv* *(con precisión)* precisely; *(exactamente)* exactly; **p. por eso,** for that very reason.

preconizar [4] *vtr* to advocate.

precoz *adj* **1** *(persona)* precocious. **2** *(fruta)* early.

precursor,-a *nm,f* precursor.

predecesor,-a *nm,f* predecessor.

predecir [12] *(pp* predicho*)* *vtr* to foretell, predict.

predestinado,-a *adj* predestined.

predeterminar *vtr* to predetermine.

predicador,-a *nm,f* preacher.

predicado *nm* predicate.

predicar [1] *vtr* to preach.

predicción *nf* prediction, forecast.

predice *indic pres* → **predecir.**

predije *pt indef* → **predecir.**

predilección *nf* predilection.

predilecto,-a *adj* favourite, US favorite, preferred.

predisponer [19] *(pp* predispuesto*)* *vtr* to predispose.

predisposición *nf* predisposition.

predominante *adj* predominant.

predominar *vi* to predominate.

predominio *nm* predominance.

preescolar *adj* preschool; **en p.,** in the nursery school.

prefabricado,-a *adj* prefabricated.

prefacio *nm* preface.

preferencia *nf* preference.

preferente *adj* preferable, preferential.

preferible *adj* preferable; **es p. que no vengas,** you'd better not come.

preferido,-a *nm,f* favourite, US favorite.

preferir [5] *vtr* to prefer.

prefijo *nm* **1** *Tel* code, US area code. **2** *Ling* prefix.

pregonar *vtr* *(anunciar)* to announce publicly; *fig* *(divulgar)* to reveal, disclose.

pregunta *nf* question; **hacer una p.** to ask a question.

preguntar I *vtr* to ask; **p. algo a algn** to ask sb sth; **p. por algn,** to ask after *o* about sb. **II preguntarse** *vr* to wonder; **me preguntó si ...,** I wonder whether ....

preguntón,-ona *nm,f fam* busybody.

prehistoria *nf* prehistory.

prehistórico,-a *adj* prehistoric.

prejuicio *nm* prejudice; **tener prejuicios,** to be prejudiced, be biased.

preliminar *adj & nm* preliminary.

preludio *nm* prelude.

prematrimonial *adj* premarital.

prematuro,-a *adj* premature.

premeditación *nf* premeditation; **con p.,** deliberately.

premeditado,-a *adj* premeditated, deliberate.

premiado,-a *adj* prize-winning.

premiar [12] *vtr* **1** to award a prize (a, to). **2** *(recompesar)* to reward.

premio *nm* prize, award; *(recompensa)* reward.

premisa *nf* premise.

premonición *nf* premonition.

premura *nf* *(urgencia)* urgency; **p. de tiempo,** haste.

prenatal *adj* antenatal, prenatal.

prenda *nf* **1** *(prenda)* garment. **2** *(garantía)* token, pledge.

prendar I *vtr* to captivate, delight. **II prendarse** *vr* *(enamorarse)* to fall in love (de, with).

prendedor *nm* brooch, pin.

prender I *vtr* **1** *(sujetar)* to fasten, attach; *(con alfileres)* to pin. **2 p. fuego a,** to set fire to. **3** *(arrestar)* to arrest. **II** *vi* *(fuego)* to catch; *(madera)* to catch fire; *(planta)* to take root. **III prenderse** *vr* to catch fire.

prensa *nf* press; *fig* **tener buena/mala p.,** to have a good/bad press.

prensar *vtr* to press.

preñado,-a *adj* **1** pregnant. **2** *fig* *(lleno)* pregnant (de, with), full (de, of).

preñar *vtr* *(mujer)* to make pregnant; *(animal)* to impregnate.

preocupación *nf* worry, concern.

preocupado,-a *adj* worried, concerned.

preocupar I *vtr* to worry; **me preocupa que llegue tan tarde,** I'm worried about him arriving so late. **II preocuparse** *vr* to worry, get worried (por, about); **no te preocupes,** don't worry; **p. de algn/algo,** to look after sb/sth or to see sth.

preparación *nf* preparation; *(formación)* training.

preparado,-a I *adj* **1** *(dispuesto)* ready, prepared; **comidas preparadas,** ready-cooked meals. **2** *(capacitado)* trained, qualified. **II** *nm Farm* preparation.

preparador,-a *nm,f* coach, trainer.

preparar I *vtr* **1** to prepare, get ready; **p. un examen,** to prepare for an exam. **2** *Dep* *(entrenar)* to train, coach. **II prepararse** *vr* **1** to prepare oneself, get ready. **2** *Dep* *(entrenarse)* to train.

preparativo *nm* preparation.

preparatorio,-a *adj* preparatory.

preponderante *adj* preponderant.

preposición *nf Ling* preposition.

prepotente *adj* domineering; *(arrogante)*

overbearing.

prerrogativa nf prerogative.

presa nf 1 prey; fig **ser p. de**, to be a victim of; **p. del pánico**, panic-stricken. 2 (embalse) dam.

presagiar [12] vtr to predict, foretell.

presagio nm 1 (señal) omen; **buen/mal p.**, good/bad omen. 2 (premonición) premonition.

presbiteriano,-a adj & nm,f Presbyterian.

presbítero nm priest.

prescindir vi **p. de**, to do without.

prescribir (pp **prescrito**) vtr to prescribe.

prescripción nf prescription; **p. facultativa**, medical prescription.

presencia nf presence; **hacer acto de p.**, to put in an appearance; **p. de ánimo**, presence of mind.

presencial adj **testigo p.**, eyewitness.

presenciar [12] vtr (ver) to witness.

presentable adj presentable; **no estoy p.**, I'm not dressed for the occasion.

presentación nf presentation; (aspecto) appearance; (de personas) introduction.

presentador,-a nm,f Rad TV presenter, host, hostess.

presentar I vtr 1 to present; (mostrar) to show, display; (ofrecer) to offer. 2 (una persona a otra) to introduce; **le presento al doctor Ruiz**, may I introduce you to Dr Ruiz. II **presentarse** vr 1 (comparecer) to present oneself; (inesperadamente) to turn o come up. 2 (ocasión, oportunidad) to present itself, arise. 3 (candidato) to stand; **p. a unas elecciones**, to stand for election, US run for office; **p. a un examen**, to sit an examination. 4 (darse a conocer) to introduce oneself (a, to).

presente I adj present; **la p. (carta)**, this letter; **hacer p.**, to declare, state; **tener p.**, (tener en cuenta) to bear in mind; (recordar) to remember. II nm present.

presentimiento nm presentiment, premonition; **tengo el p. de que ...**, I have the feeling that ....

presentir [5] vtr to have a presentiment o premonition of; **presiento que lloverá**, I've got the feeling that it's going to rain.

preservación nf preservation, protection.

preservar vtr to preserve, protect (**de**, from; **contra**, against).

preservativo,-a nm sheath, condom.

presidencia nf 1 Pol presidency. 2 (de una reunión) (hombre) chairmanship; (mujer) chairwomanship.

presidencial adj presidential.

presidente,-a nm,f 1 Pol president; **p. del gobierno**, Prime Minister, Premier. 2 (de una reunión) chairperson.

presidiario,-a nm,f prisoner, convict.

presidio nm prison, penitentiary.

presidir vtr 1 Pol to rule, head. 2 (reunión) to chair, preside over.

presión nf pressure; **a o bajo p.**, under

pressure; **grupo de p.**, pressure group, lobby; **p. arterial o sanguínea**, blood pressure; **p. atmosférica**, atmospheric pressure.

presionar vtr to press; fig to pressurize, put pressure on.

preso,-a I adj imprisoned. II nm,f prisoner.

prestación nf 1 service. 2 **prestaciones**, (de coche etc) performance.

prestado,-a adj **dejar p.**, to lend; **pedir p.**, to borrow; **vivir de p.**, to scrounge.

prestamista nm,f moneylender.

préstamo nm loan.

prestar I vtr to lend, loan; **¿me prestas tu pluma?**, can I borrow your pen? 2 (atención) to pay; (ayuda) to give; (servicio) to do. II **prestarse** vr 1 (ofrecerse) to offer oneself (**a**, to). 2 **p. a**, (dar motivo) to cause; **se presta a (crear) malentendidos**, it makes for misunderstandings.

presteza nf promptness; **con p.**, promptly.

prestidigitador,-a nm,f conjuror, magician.

prestigiar [12] vtr to give prestige to.

prestigio nm prestige.

prestigioso,-a adj prestigious.

presto,-a adj fml 1 (dispuesto) ready, prepared. 2 (rápido) swift, prompt.

presumible adj probable, likely.

presumido,-a I adj vain, conceited. II nm,f vain person.

presumir I vtr (suponer) to presume, suppose. II vi 1 (ser vanidoso) to show off. 2 **presume de guapo**, he thinks he's good-looking.

presunción nf 1 (suposición) presumption, supposition. 2 (vanidad) vanity, conceit.

presunto,-a adj supposed; Jur alleged.

presuntuoso,-a adj 1 (vanidoso) vain, conceited. 2 (pretencioso) pretentious, showy.

presuponer [19] (pp **presupuesto**) vtr to presuppose.

presupuestar vtr to budget for; (importe) to estimate for.

presupuestario,-a adj budgetary.

presupuesto,-a nm 1 Fin budget; (cálculo) estimate. 2 (supuesto) supposition, assumption.

presuroso,-a adj (rápido) quick; (con prisa) in a hurry.

pretencioso,-a adj pretentious.

pretender vtr 1 (intentar) to try; **¿qué pretendes insinuar?**, what are you getting at? 2 (afirmar) to claim. 3 (aspirar a) to try for. 4 (cortejar) to court, woo.

pretendiente nm,f 1 (al trono) pretender. 2 (a un cargo) applicant, candidate. 3 (amante) suitor.

pretensión nf 1 (aspiración) aim, aspiration. 2 (presunción) pretentiousness.

pretérito,-a I adj past, former. II nm Ling

preterite, simple past tense.

pretextar *vtr* to plead, allege.

pretexto *nm* pretext, excuse.

pretil *nm* parapet.

prevalecer [33] *vi* to prevail.

prevaler [26] *vi* → **prevalecer**.

prevención *nf* 1 (*precaución*) prevention; **en p. de**, as a prevention against. 2 (*medida*) precaution.

prevenir [27] *vtr* 1 (*preparar*) to prepare, get ready. 2 (*prever*) to prevent, forestall; (*evitar*) to avoid; **para p. la gripe**, to prevent flu; *prov* **más vale p. que curar**, prevention is better than cure. 3 (*advertir*) to warn.

preventivo,-a *adj* preventive; (*medidas*) precautionary; *Jur* **detención** *o* **prisión preventiva**, remand in custody.

prever [28] (*pp* **previsto**) *vtr* 1 (*prevenir*) to foresee, forecast. 2 (*preparar de antemano*) to cater for.

previo,-a *adj* previous, prior; **p. pago de su importe**, only on payment; **sin p. aviso**, without prior notice.

previsible *adj* predictable.

previsión *nf* 1 (*predicción*) forecast; **p. del tiempo**, weather forecast. 2 (*precaución*) precaution; **en p. de**, as a precaution against.

previsor,-a *adj* careful, far-sighted.

previsto,-a *adj* foreseen, forecast; **según lo p.**, as expected.

prima *nf* 1 (*gratificación*) bonus; **p. de seguro**, insurance premium. 2 (*persona*) → **primo,-a**.

primacía *nf* primacy.

primar 1 *vi* to have priority, prevail. II *vtr* to give a bonus to.

primario,-a *adj* primary.

primavera *nf* spring.

primer *adj* (*delante de nm*) → **primero,-a**.

primera *nf* 1 (*en tren*) first class. 2 *Aut* (*marcha*) first gear. 3 **a la p.**, at the first attempt; *fam* **de p.**, great, first class.

primero,-a I *adj* first; **a primera hora de la mañana**, first thing in the morning; **primera página/plana**, front page; **de primera necesidad**, basic. II *nm,f* first; **a primero(s) de mes**, at the beginning of the month. III *adv* 1 first. 2 (*más bien*) rather, sooner; → **primera**.

primicia *nf* novelty; **p. informativa**, scoop; **p. mundial**, world premiere.

primitivo,-a *adj* 1 primitive. 2 (*tosco*) coarse, rough.

primo,-a I *nm,f* 1 cousin; **p. hermano**, first cousin. 2 *fam* (*tonto*) fool, drip, dunce. II *adj* **materia prima**, raw material. 2 (*número*) prime.

primogénito,-a *adj & nm,f* first-born.

primor *nm* 1 (*delicadeza*) delicacy. 2 (*belleza*) beauty.

primordial *adj* essential, fundamental.

primoroso,-a *adj* delicate, exquisite.

princesa *nf* princess.

principado *nm* principality.

principal *adj* main, principal; **lo p. es que ...**, the main thing is that ...; **puerta p.**, front door.

príncipe *nm* prince.

principiante I *adj* novice. II *nmf* beginner, novice.

principio [7] I *nm* 1 beginning, start; **a principio(s) de**, at the beginning of; **al p., en un p.**, at first, in the beginning. 2 (*fundamento*) principle; **en p.**, in principle. 3 **principios**, rudiments, basics.

pringar [7] I *vtr* (*ensuciar*) to make greasy *o* dirty. II *vi arg* (*trabajar*) to work hard. III **pringarse** *vr* 1 (*ensuciarse*) to get greasy *o* dirty. 2 *fam* (*meterse de lleno*) to get involved.

pringoso,-a *adj* (*grasiento*) greasy; (*sucio*) dirty.

pringue *nm* (*grasa*) grease.

prior,-a *nm,f* (*hombre*) prior; (*mujer*) prioress.

priori (a) *adv* a priori.

prioridad *nf* priority.

prioritario,-a *adj* priority.

prisa *nf* 1 (*rapidez*) hurry; **date p.**, hurry up; **tener p.**, to be in a hurry; **de/a p.**, in a hurry. 2 **correr p.**, to be urgent; **me corre mucha p.**, I need it right away.

prisión *nf* prison, jail.

prisionero,-a *nm,f* prisoner.

prisma *nm* prism.

prismáticos *nmpl* binoculars, field glasses.

priva *nf arg* booze.

privación *nf* deprivation.

privado,-a *adj* private.

privar I *vtr* (*despojar*) to deprive (**de**, of). II *vi* 1 *arg* (*gustar*) to like; (*estar de moda*) to be fashionable *o* popular. 2 *fam* (*beber*) to booze. III **privarse** *vr* (*abstenerse*) to deprive oneself (**de**, of), go without.

privativo,-a *adj* exclusive (**de**, of).

privilegiado,-a I *adj* privileged. II *nm,f* privileged person.

privilegio *nm* privilege.

pro I *nm* advantage; **los pros y los contras**, the pros and cons; **en p. de**, in favour of. II *prep* in favour *o* US favor of; **campaña p. desarme**, campaign for disarmament, disarmament campaign.

pro- *pref* pro-.

proa *nf* prow, bows *pl*.

probabilidad *nf* probability, likelihood; **tiene pocas probabilidades**, he stands little chance.

probable *adj* probable, likely; **es p. que llueva**, it'll probably rain.

probador *nm* fitting room.

probar [2] I *vtr* 1 (*comida, bebida*) to try. 2 (*comprobar*) to test, check. 3 (*intentar*) to try. 4 (*demostrar*) to prove, show. II *vi* to try; **p. a**, to attempt *o* try to. III **pro-**

barse *vr (ropa)* to try on.
probeta *nf* test tube; **niño p.**, test-tube baby.
problema *nm* problem.
problemático,-a *adj* problematic.
procedencia *nf* origin, source.
procedente *adj* 1 *(originario)* coming (**de**, from). 2 *(adecuado)* appropriate; *Jur* proper.
proceder I *vi* 1 **p. de**, *(provenir)* to come from. 2 *(actuar)* to act. 3 *(ser oportuno)* to be advisable *o* appropriate; *Jur* **la protesta no procede**, objection overruled. 4 **p. a**, *(continuar)* to go on to. II *nm (comportamiento)* behaviour, *US* behavior.
procedimiento *nm* 1 *(método)* procedure. 2 *Jur (trámites)* proceedings *pl*.
procesado,-a I *nm,f* accused. II *nm Inform* processing.
procesador *nm* processor; **p. de textos**, word processor.
procesamiento *nm* 1 *Jur* prosecution. 2 *Inform* **p. de datos/textos**, data/word processing.
procesar *vtr* 1 *Jur* to prosecute. 2 *(elaborar, transformar)* to process; *Inform* to process.
procesión *nf* procession.
proceso *nm* 1 process; *Inform* **p. de datos**, data processing. 2 *Jur* trial.
proclamación *nf* proclamation.
proclamar *vtr* to proclaim.
proclive *adj* prone, inclined.
procreación *nf* procreation.
procrear *vtr* to procreate.
procurador,-a *nm,f Jur* attorney.
procurar *vtr* 1 *(intentar)* to try, attempt; **procura que no te vean**, make sure they don't see you. 2 *(proporcionar)* to manage *o* to get.
prodigar [7] *fml* I *vtr (dar generosamente)* to lavish. II **prodigarse** *vr* **p. en**, to be lavish in.
prodigio *nm* prodigy, miracle; **hacer prodigios**, to work wonders; **niño p.**, child prodigy.
prodigioso,-a *adj (sobrenatural)* prodigious; *(maravilloso)* wonderful, marvellous, *US* marvelous.
pródigo,-a *adj* generous, lavish; **ella es pródiga en regalos**, she's very generous with presents.
producción *nf (acción)* production; *(producto)* product; *Cin* production; **p. en cadena/serie**, assembly-line/mass production.
producir [10] I *vtr* 1 to produce; *(fruto, cosecha)* to yield, bear; *(ganancias)* to yield. 2 *fig (originar)* to cause, bring about. II **producirse** *vr* to take place, happen.
productividad *nf* productivity.
productivo,-a *adj* productive; *(beneficioso)* profitable.

producto *nm* product; *Agr (producción)* produce.
productor,-a I *adj* producing. II *nm,f* producer.
proeza *nf* heroic deed, exploit.
profanación *nf* desecration, profanation.
profanar *vtr* to desecrate, profane.
profano,-a I *adj* profane, secular. II *nm,f (hombre)* layman; *(mujer)* laywoman.
profecía *nf* prophecy.
proferir [5] *vtr* to utter; **p. insultos**, to hurl insults.
profesar *vtr* to profess.
profesión *nf* profession; **de p.**, by profession.
profesional *adj & nmf* professional.
profeso *adv* **ex p.**, intentionally.
profesor,-a *nm,f* teacher; *Univ* lecturer.
profesorado *nm (profesión)* teaching; *(grupo de profesores)* staff.
profeta *nm* prophet.
profetizar [4] *vtr* to prophesy, foretell.
profiláctico,-a I *adj* prophylactic. II *nm* condom, *US* prophylactic.
prófugo,-a I *adj & nm,f* fugitive. II *nm Mil* deserter.
profundidad *nf* depth; **un metro de p.**, one metre deep *o* in depth; *fig (de ideas etc)* profundity, depth.
profundizar [4] *vtr & vi (cavar)* to deepen; *fig (examinar)* to study in depth.
profundo,-a *adj* deep; *fig (idea, sentimiento)* profound.
profusión *nf* profusion.
progenitor,-a *nm,f (antepasado)* ancestor, progenitor; **progenitores**, *(padres)* parents.
programa *nm* programme, *US* program; *Inform* program; *Educ* syllabus.
programación *nf Rad TV* programme planning.
programador,-a *nm,f Inform* programmer.
programar *vtr* to programme, *US* program; *Inform* to program.
progre *adj & nmf fam* trendy, lefty.
progresar *vi* to progress, make progress.
progresista *adj & nmf* progressive.
progresivo,-a *adj* progressive.
progreso *nm* progress; **hace grandes progresos**, he's making great progress.
prohibición *nf* prohibition, ban.
prohibido,-a *adj* forbidden, prohibited; **'prohibida la entrada'**, 'no admittance'; **p. aparcar/fumar**, no parking/smoking.
prohibir [21] *vtr* to forbid, prohibit; **'se prohíbe pasar'**, 'no admittance *o* entry'.
prohibitivo,-a, **prohibitorio,-a** *adj* prohibitive.
prójimo,-a *nm,f* one's fellow man, one's neighbour *o US* neighbor.
proletariado *nm* proletariat.
proletario,-a *adj & nm,f* proletarian.
proliferar *vi* to proliferate.

prolífico,-a adj prolific.

prolijo,-a adj verbose, long-winded.

prólogo nm prologue, US prolog.

prolongación nf prolonging, extension, prolongation.

prolongado,-a adj long.

prolongar [7] I vtr (alargar) to prolong, extend. II **prolongarse** vr (continuar) to carry on.

promedio nm average; **como p.**, on average.

promesa nf promise; fig **la joven p. de la música**, the promising young musician.

prometedor,-a adj promising.

prometer I vtr to promise; **te lo prometo**, I promise. II vi to be promising. III **prometerse** vr (pareja) to get engaged.

prometido,-a I adj promised. II nm,f (hombre) fiancé; (mujer) fiancée.

prominente adj (elevado) protruding, projecting; (importante) prominent.

prosmicuo,-a adj promiscuous.

promoción nf promotion; Educ **p. universitaria**, class o year.

promocionar vtr (cosas) to promote; (personas) to give promotion to.

promotor,-a I adj promoting. II nm,f promoter.

promover [4] vtr 1 (cosas, personas) to promote; (juicio, querella) to initiate. 2 (causar) to cause, give rise to.

promulgar [7] vtr to promulgate.

pronombre nm pronoun.

pronosticar [1] vtr to predict, forecast; Med to make a prognosis of.

pronóstico nm (del tiempo) forecast; Med prognosis.

pronto,-a I adj quick, prompt; fml (dispuesto) prepared. II nm (impulso) sudden impulse. III adv 1 (deprisa) quickly, rapidly; **al p.**, at first; **de p.**, suddenly; **por de o lo p.**, (para empezar) to start with. 2 (temprano) soon, early; **hasta p.**, see you soon!

pronunciación nf pronunciation.

pronunciamiento nm 1 Mil uprising, insurrection. 2 Jur pronouncement.

pronunciar [12] I vtr to pronounce; (discurso) to deliver. II **pronunciarse** vr 1 (opinar) to declare oneself. 2 (sublevarse) to rise up.

propagación nf propagation, spreading.

propagador,-a nm,f propagator.

propaganda nf (política) propaganda; (comercial) advertising, publicity.

propagar [7] I vtr to propagate, spread. II **propagarse** vr to spread.

propano nm propane.

propasarse vr to go too far.

propensión nf tendency, inclination.

propenso,-a adj 1 (inclinado) prone, inclined. 2 Med susceptible.

propiciar [12] vtr 1 (causar) to cause. 2 Am (patrocinar) to sponsor.

propicio,-a adj propitious, suitable; **ser p. a**, to be inclined to.

propiedad nf 1 (posesión) ownership; (cosa poseída) property. 2 (cualidad) property, quality; fig **con p.**, properly, appropriately.

propietario,-a nm,f owner.

propina nf tip; **dar p. (a algn)**, to tip (sb).

propinar vtr to give.

propio,-a adj 1 (de uno) own; **en su propia casa**, in his own house. 2 (correcto) suitable, appropriate; **juegos propios para su edad**, games suitable for their age. 3 (característico) typical, peculiar. 4 (mismo) (hombre) himself; (mujer) herself; (animal, cosa) itself; **el p. autor**, the author himself. 5 **propios,-as**, themselves; **los propios inquilinos**, the tenants themselves. 6 Ling proper. ♦**propiamente** adv **p. dicho**, strictly speaking.

proponer [19] (pp **propuesto**) I vtr to propose, suggest. II **proponerse** vr to intend.

proporción nf 1 proportion; **en p. con**, in proportion to. 2 **proporciones**, (tamaño) size sing.

proporcionado,-a adj (mesurado) proportionate, in proportion.

proporcional adj proportional.

proporcionar vtr (dar) to give; to supply o provide.

proposición nf 1 (propuesta) proposal. 2 (oración) clause.

propósito nm 1 (intención) intention. 2 **a p.**, (por cierto) by the way; (adrede) on purpose, intentionally; **a p. de viajes ...**, speaking of travelling.

propuesta nf suggestion, proposal.

propuesto,-a pp → **proponer**.

propugnar vtr to advocate.

propulsar vtr (vehículo) to drive; fig (idea) to promote.

propulsión nf propulsion.

propulsor,-a I adj, nm,f (persona) promoter.

propuse pt indef → **proponer**.

prórroga nf 1 (prolongación) extension; Dep extra time, US overtime. 2 (aplazamiento) postponement; Mil deferment.

prorrogar [7] vtr 1 (prolongar) to extend. 2 (aplazar) to postpone; Mil to defer.

prorrumpir vi to burst (en, into).

prosa nf prose.

proscrito,-a I adj (persona) exiled, banished; (cosa) banned. II nm,f exile, outlaw.

proseguir [6] vtr & vi to carry on, continue.

prospección nf 1 Min prospect. 2 Com survey.

prospecto nm leaflet, prospectus.

prosperar vi (negocio, país) to prosper, thrive; (propuesta) to be accepted.

prosperidad *nf* prosperity.

próspero,-a *adj* prosperous, thriving; **p. año nuevo**, Happy New Year.

prostíbulo *nm* brothel.

prostitución *nf* prostitution.

prostituir [37] **I** *vtr* to prostitute. **II prostituirse** *vr* to prostitute oneself.

prostituta *nf* prostitute.

protagonista *nmf* **1** main character, leading role; **¿quién es el p.?**, who plays the lead? **2** *fig* (*centro*) centre *o* US center of attraction.

protagonizar [4] *vtr* to play the lead in, star in.

protección *nf* protection.

proteccionismo *nm* protectionism.

protector,-a I *adj* protecting, protective. **II** *nm,f* protector.

proteger [5] *vtr* to protect, defend.

protegido,-a *nm,f* (*hombre*) protégé; (*mujer*) protégée.

proteína *nf* protein.

prótesis *nf inv* prosthesis.

protesta *nf* protest; *Jur* objection.

protestante *adj & nmf Rel* Protestant.

protestar *vi* **1** to protest; *Jur* to object. **2** *fam* (*quejarse*) to complain.

protestón,-ona *nm,f* moaner, grumbler.

protocolo *nm* protocol.

protón *nm* proton.

prototipo *nm* prototype.

protuberancia *nf* protuberance.

protuberante *adj* protuberant, bulging.

prov. *abr de* **provincia**, province, prov.

provecho *nm* profit, benefit; **¡buen p.!**, enjoy your meal!; **sacar p. de algo**, to benefit from sth.

provechoso,-a *adj* beneficial.

proveedor,-a *nm,f* supplier, purveyor.

proveer [36] (*pp* **provisto**) *vtr* to supply, provide.

proveniente *adj* (*procedente*) coming; (*resultante*) arising, resulting.

provenir [27] *vi* **p. de**, to come from.

proverbio *nm* proverb.

providencia *nf* providence.

provincia *nf* province.

provincial *adj* provincial.

provinciano,-a *adj & nm,f pey* provincial.

provisión *nf* provision.

provisional *adj* provisional.

provisto,-a *adj* **p. de**, equipped with.

provocación *nf* provocation.

provocado,-a *adj* provoked, caused; **incendio p.**, arson.

provocador,-a I *nm,f* instigator, agent provocateur. **II** *adj* provocative.

provocar [1] *vtr* **1** (*causar*) to cause; **p. un incendio**, to start a fire. **2** (*instigar*) to provoke. **3** *Am* **si no le provoca**, if he doesn't feel like it.

provocativo,-a *adj* provocative.

proxeneta *nmf* procurer, pimp.

proximidad *nf* proximity, closeness; **en las proximidades de**, close to, in the vicinity of.

próximo,-a *adj* **1** (*cercano*) near, close. **2** (*siguiente*) next. ◆**próximamente** *adv* (*pronto*) soon; *Cin Teat* 'coming soon'.

proyección *nf* **1** projection. **2** *Cin* showing.

proyectar *vtr* **1** (*luz*) to project. **2** (*planear*) to plan. **3** *Cin* to show.

proyectil *nm* projectile.

proyecto *nm* (*plan*) project, plan; **tener algo en p.**, to be planning sth; **p. de ley**, bill.

proyector *nm Cin* projector.

prudencia *nf* prudence, discretion; (*moderación*) care.

prudente *adj* prudent, sensible; (*conductor*) careful; **a una hora p.**, at a reasonable time.

prueba *nf* **1** proof; **en p. de**, as a sign of. **2** (*examen etc*) test; **a p.**, on trial; **a p. de agua/balas**, waterproof/bullet-proof; **haz la p.**, try it. **3** *Dep* event.

pseudo *adj* pseud, pseudo.

psicoanálisis *nm inv* psychoanalysis.

psicodélico,-a *adj* psychedelic.

psicología *nf* psychology.

psicológico,-a *adj* psychological.

psicólogo,-a *nm,f* psychologist.

psicópata *nmf* psychopath.

psicosis *nf inv* psychosis.

psicotécnico,-a *adj* psychometric.

psicoterapia *nf* psychotherapy.

psique *nf* psyche.

psiquiatra *nmf* psychiatrist.

psiquiatría *nf* psychiatry.

psiquiátrico,-a I *adj* psychiatric; **hospital p.**, psychiatric hospital. **II** *nm* psychiatric hospital.

psíquico,-a *adj* psychic.

PSOE *nm Pol abr de* **Partido Socialista Obrero Español**, Socialist Workers' Party.

pta(s). *abr de* peseta(s), peseta(s).

pts *abr de* pesetas.

púa *nf* **1** (*de planta*) thorn; (*de animal*) quill, spine; (*de peine*) tooth; **alambre de púas**, barbed wire. **2** *Mús* plectrum.

pub *nm* (*pl* **pubs**, **pubes**) pub.

pubertad *nf* puberty.

publicación *nf* publication.

publicar [1] *vtr* **1** (*libro etc*) to publish. **2** (*secreto*) to publicize.

publicidad *nf* **1** *Com* advertising. **2** (*conocimiento público*) publicity.

publicitario,-a *adj* advertising.

público,-a I *adj* public. **II** *nm* public; *Teat* audience; *Dep* spectators *pl*.

pucherazo *nm* rigging of an election.

puchero *nm* **1** (*olla*) cooking pot; (*cocido*) stew. **2** **hacer pucheros**, to pout.

pucho *nm Am* dog-end.

pude *pt indef* → **poder**.

pudendo,-a *adj* **partes pudendas**, private

parts.

púdico,-a *adj* modest.

pudiente *adj* rich, wealthy.

pudor *nm* modesty.

pudoroso,-a *adj* modest.

pudrir *vtr* defect, **pudrirse** *vr* to rot, decay.

pueblerino,-a *adj* pey *(provinciano)* countrified, provincial.

pueblo *nm* 1 village; *(small)* town. 2 *(gente)* people; **el p. español,** the Spanish people.

puente *nm* 1 bridge; *Av* **p. aéreo,** *(civil)* air shuttle service; *Mil* airlift; **p. colgante,** suspension bridge; **p. levadizo,** drawbridge. 2 *(entre dos fiestas)* long weekend.

puerco,-a I *adj* filthy. II *nm,f* pig; **p. espín,** porcupine.

puericultura *nf* paediatrics *sing,* US pediatrics *sing.*

pueril *adj* childish, puerile.

puerro *nm* leek.

puerta *nf* door; *(verja, en aeropuerto)* gate; *Dep* goal; **p. corredera/giratoria,** sliding/revolving door; *fig* **a las puertas, en puertas,** imminent; *fig* **a p. cerrada,** behind closed doors.

puerto *nm* 1 *(de mar)* port, harbour, US harbor; **p. deportivo,** marina. 2 *(de montaña)* (mountain) pass.

Puerto Rico *n* Puerto Rico.

puertorriqueño,-a *adj & nm,f* Puerto Rican.

pues *conj* 1 *(puesto que)* as, since. 2 *(por lo tanto)* therefore. 3 *(entonces)* so. 4 *(para reforzar)* **¡p. claro que sí!,** but of course!; **p. como iba diciendo,** well, as I was saying; **¡p. mejor!,** so much the better!; **¡p. no!,** certainly not! 5 *(como pregunta)* **¿p.?,** why?

puesta *nf* 1 **p. de sol,** sunset. 2 *fig* **p. a punto,** tuning, adjusting; *fig* **p. al día,** updating; *Teat* **p. en escena,** staging; **p. en marcha,** starting-up, start-up; → **puesto,-a.**

puestero,-a *nm,f Am* stallholder.

puesto,-a I *conj* **p. que,** since, as. II *nm* 1 *(lugar)* place; *(asiento)* seat. 2 *(empleo)* position, post, job; **p. de trabajo,** job, post. 3 *(tienda)* stall. 4 *Mil* post. III *adj* 1 *(colocado)* set, put. 2 **llevar p.,** *(ropa)* to have on; *fam* **ir muy p.,** to be all dressed up. 3 *fam (borracho)* drunk. 4 *fam* **estar p. en una materia,** to be well up in a subject.

púgil *nm* boxer.

pugilato *nm* boxing.

pugna *nf* battle, fight.

pugnar *vi* to fight, struggle *(por,* for).

puja *nf (acción)* bidding; *(cantidad)* bid.

pujante *adj* thriving, prosperous.

pujanza *nf* strength, vigour, US vigor.

pujar *vtr* 1 *(pugnar)* to struggle. 2 *(en una subasta)* to bid higher.

pulcro,-a *adj* (extremely) neat.

pulga *nf* flea; *fam* **tener malas pulgas,** to be nasty, have a nasty streak.

pulgada *nf* inch.

pulgar *nm* thumb.

pulimentar *vtr* to polish.

pulir *vtr* 1 *(metal, madera)* to polish. 2 *(mejorar)* to polish up.

pulmón *nm* lung.

pulmonía *nf* pneumonia.

pulpa *nf* pulp.

pulpería *nf Am* store.

púlpito *nm* pulpit.

pulpo *nm* octopus.

pulsación *nf* pulsation; *(en mecanografía)* stroke, tap; **pulsaciones por minuto,** ≈ keystrokes per minute.

pulsar *vtr (timbre, botón)* to press; *(tecla)* to hit, strike.

pulsera *nf (aro)* bracelet; *(de reloj)* watch-strap; **reloj de p.,** wristwatch.

pulso *nm* 1 pulse; *fig* **tomar el p. a la opinión pública,** to sound out opinion. 2 *(mano firme)* steady hand; **a p.,** freehand; **ganarse algo a p.,** to deserve sth. 3 *fig* trial of strength; **echarse un p.,** to arm-wrestle.

pulverizador,-a *nm* spray, atomizer.

pulverizar |4| *vtr (sólidos)* to pulverize; *(líquidos)* to spray; *(un récord)* to smash.

pulla *nf* dig.

puma *nm* puma.

puna *nf Am* 1 high moor. 2 *(mal)* mountain *o* altitude sickness.

pundonor *nm* self-respect, self-esteem.

punta *nf* 1 *(extremo)* tip; *(extremo afilado)* point; *(de cabello)* end; **sacar p. a un lápiz,** to sharpen a pencil; **tecnología p.,** state-of-the-art technology; **me pone los nervios de p.,** he makes me very nervous. 2 *(período)* peak; **hora p.,** rush hour. 3 *(pequeña cantidad)* bit; **una p. de sal,** a pinch of salt. 4 *(clavo)* nail.

puntal *nm* prop; *(travesaño)* beam; *fig (soporte)* pillar, support.

puntapié *nm* kick.

puntear *vtr* 1 *(dibujar)* to dot. 2 *Mús (guitarra)* to pluck.

punteo *nm* plucking.

puntería *nf* aim; **tener buena/mala p.,** to be a good/bad shot.

puntero,-a *adj* leading.

puntiagudo,-a *adj* pointed, sharp.

puntilla *nf* 1 *(encaje)* lace. 2 **dar la p.,** *Taur* to finish (the bull) off; *fig (liquidar)* to finish off. 3 **de puntillas,** on tiptoe.

puntilloso,-a *adj* touchy.

punto *nm* 1 point; **a p.,** ready; *Culin* **en su p.,** just right; **a p. de,** on the point of; **hasta cierto p.,** to a certain *o* some extent; **p. muerto,** *Aut* neutral; *fig (impasse)* deadlock; **p. de vista,** point of view. 2 *(marca)* dot; **línea de puntos,** dotted line. 3 *(lugar)* place, point. 4 **p. y seguido,**

full stop; **p. y coma,** semicolon; **dos puntos,** colon; **p. y aparte,** full stop, new paragraph. **5** (tiempo) **en p.,** sharp, on the dot. **6** Dep (tanto) point. **7** Cost Med stitch; **hacer p.,** to knit.

puntuable adj Dep **una prueba p. para,** a race counting towards.

puntuación nf **1** Ling punctuation. **2** Dep score. **3** Educ mark.

puntual I adj **1** punctual. **2** (exacto) accurate, precise. **3** (caso) specific. II adv punctually.

puntualidad nf punctuality.

puntualizar [4] vtr **1** to make it clear.

puntuar [30] I vtr **1** (al escribir) to punctuate. **2** Educ (calificar) to mark. II vi Dep **1** (marcar) to score. **2** (ser puntuable) to count.

punzada nf (de dolor) sudden sharp pain.

punzante adj (objeto) sharp; (dolor) acute, piercing.

punzar [4] vtr Téc to punch.

puñado nm handful; fam **a puñados,** by the score, galore.

puñal nm dagger.

puñalada nf stab; fig **p. trapera,** stab in the back.

puñeta nf fam **hacer la p. a algn,** to pester sb, annoy sb; **¡puñetas!,** damn!; **¡vete a hacer puñetas!,** go to hell!

puñetazo nm punch.

puño nm **1** fist. **2** (de camisa etc) cuff. **3** (de herramienta) handle.

pupa nf **1** (herida) cold sore. **2** fam (daño) pain.

pupila nf pupil.

pupilo,-a nm,f pupil.

pupitre nm desk.

purasangre adj & nm thoroughbred.

puré nm purée; **p. de patata,** mashed potatoes; **p. de verduras,** thick vegetable soup.

pureta nmf old fogey.

pureza nf **1** purity. **2** (castidad) chastity.

purga nf Med purgative; fig purge.

purgante adj & nm purgative.

purgar [7] vtr Med & fig to purge.

purgatorio nm purgatory.

purificación nf purification.

purificar [1] vtr to purify.

purista nmf purist.

puritano,-a I adj puritanical. II nm,f puritan, Puritan.

puro,-a I adj **1** (sin mezclas) pure; **aire p.,** fresh air; **la pura verdad,** the plain truth; Pol **p. y duro,** hardline. **2** (mero) sheer, mere; **por pura curiosidad,** out of sheer curiosity. **3** (casto) chaste, pure. II nm (cigarro) cigar.

púrpura adj inv purple.

purpúreo,-a adj purple.

pus nm pus.

puse pt indef → **poner.**

pusilánime adj faint-hearted.

pústula nf sore, pustule.

puta nf ofens whore; **de p. madre,** great, terrific; **de p. pena,** bloody awful; **no tengo ni p. idea,** I haven't (got) a bloody clue; **pasarlas putas,** to go through hell, have a rotten time.

putada nf vulg dirty trick.

putear vtr to fuck o piss around.

puticlub nm brothel.

puto,-a I adj ofens bloody. II nm male prostitute, stud.

putrefacto,-a, pútrido,-a adj putrefied, rotten.

puzzle nm jigsaw puzzle.

P.V.P. nm abr de precio de venta al público, recommended retail price, RRP.

Pza., Plza. abr de plaza, square, Sq.

Q

Q, q [ku] nf (la letra) Q, q.

que[1] pron rel **1** (sujeto) (persona) who; (cosa) that, which; **el hombre q. vino,** the man who came; **la bomba q. estalló,** the bomb that o which went off. **2** (complemento) (persona) no se traduce o that o who o that whom; (cosa) no se traduce o that o which; **la chica q. conocí,** the girl (that o who o whom) I met; **el coche q. compré,** the car (that o which) I bought. **3** lo q., what; **lo q. más me gusta,** what I like best. **4** (con infinitivo) no se traduce; **hay mucho q. hacer,** there's a lot to do.

que[2] conj **1** no se traduce o that; **dijo que llamaría,** he said (that) he would call; **quiero q. vengas,** I want you to come. **2** (consecutivo) no se traduce o that; (en comparativas) than; **habla tan bajo q. no**

se le oye, he speaks so quietly (that) he can't be heard; **más alto q. yo,** taller than me. **3** (causal) no se traduce date deprisa q. no tenemos mucho tiempo, hurry up, we haven't got much time. **4** (enfático) no se traduce **¡q. no!,** no!; **¡q. te calles!,** I said be quiet! **5** (deseo, mandato) (+ subj) no se traduce **¡q. te diviertas!,** enjoy yourself! **6** (final) so that; **ven q. te dé un beso,** come and let me give you a kiss. **7** (disyuntivo) whether; **me da igual que suba o no,** I couldn't care whether he comes up or not. **8** (locuciones) **¿a q. no...?,** I bet you can't ...!; **q. yo sepa,** as far as I know; **yo q. tú,** if I were you.

qué I pron interr **1** what; **¿q. quieres?,** what do you want?; fam **¡y q.!,** so what? **2** (exclamativo) (+ adj) how; **¡q. bonito!,**

how pretty! **3** (+ *n*) what a; ¡q. lástima!, what a pity! **4** *fam* ¡q. de ...!, what a lot of ...!. **II** *adj interr* which; ¿q. libro quieres?, which book do you want?

quebrada *nf Am* stream.

quebradero,-a *adj* q. de cabeza, headache.

quebradizo,-a *adj* (*débil*) fragile; (*cabello, hielo*) brittle.

quebrado,-a *nm Mat* fraction.

quebradura *nf* **1** (*grieta*) crack. **2** *Med* hernia, rupture.

quebrantamiento *nm* (*de una ley*) violation, infringement.

quebrantar **I** *vtr* (*promesa, ley*) to break. **II quebrantarse** *vr* to break down.

quebrar [1] **I** *vtr* (*romper*) to break. **II** *vi* *Fin* to go bankrupt. **III quebrarse** *vr* to break; *Med* to rupture oneself.

queda *nf* toque de q., curfew.

quedar **I** *vi* **1** (*restar*) to be left, remain; **quedan dos**, there are two left. **2** (*en un lugar*) to arrange to meet; **quedamos en el bar**, I'll meet you in the bar. **3** me **queda corta**, (*ropa*) it is too short for me; **quedaría muy bien allí**, (*objeto*) it would look very nice there. **4** (*acordar*) to agree (en, to); **¿en qué quedamos?**, so what's it to be? **5** (*estar situado*) to be; **¿dónde queda la estación?**, where's the station? **6** (*terminar*) to end; **¿en qué quedó la película?**, how did the film end? **7** (*locuciones*) **q. en ridículo**, to make a fool of oneself; **q. bien/mal**, to make a good/bad impression. **II quedarse** *vr* **1** (*permanecer*) to stay; **se quedó en casa**, she stayed home; **q. sin dinero/pan**, to run out of money/bread; **q. con hambre**, to still be hungry. **2 q.** (**con**), (*retener*) to keep; **quédese** (**con**) **el cambio**, keep the change. **3** *fam* **q. con algn**, to make a fool of sb.

quedo *adv* softly, quietly.

quehacer *nm* task, chore.

queja *nf* complaint; (*de dolor*) groan, moan.

quejarse *vr* to complain (de, about).

quejica *fam* **I** *adj* grumpy. **II** *nmf* moaner.

quejido *nm* groan, cry.

quemado,-a *adj* **1** burnt, burned; (*del sol*) sunburnt. **2** *fig* (*agotado*) burnt-out.

quemador *nm* (*de cocina etc*) burner.

quemadura *nf* burn.

quemar **I** *vtr* to burn; *fig* (*agotar*) to burn out. **II** *vi* to be burning hot; **este café quema**, this coffee's boiling hot. **III quemarse** *vr fig* to burn oneself out.

quemarropa *loc adv* a q., point-blank.

quemazón *nf* smarting.

quepo *indic pres* → **caber**.

querella *nf fur* lawsuit.

querer [20] **I** *vtr* **1** (*amar*) to love. **2** (*desear*) to want; **¿cuánto quiere por la casa?**, how much does he want for the

house?; **sin q.**, without meaning to; **queriendo**, on purpose; **¡por lo que más quieras!**, for heaven's sake!; **¿quiere pasarme el pan?**, would you pass me the bread? **3 q. decir**, to mean. **4 no quiso darme permiso**, he refused me permission. **II quererse** *vr* to love each other. **III** *nm* love, affection.

querido,-a **I** *adj* dear, beloved; **q. amigo**, (*en carta*) dear friend. **II** *nm,f* (*amante*) lover; (*mujer*) mistress.

queroseno *nm* kerosene, kerosine.

querré *indic fut* → **querer**.

queso *nm* cheese; **q. rallado**, grated cheese; **q. de cerdo**, brawn, *US* headcheese.

quetzal *nm* (*moneda*) standard monetary unit of Guatemala.

quicio *nm* **1** (*de puerta*) doorpost. **2** *fig* **fuera de q.**, beside oneself; **sacar de q.**, (*a algn*) to infuriate; (*algo*) to take too far.

quid *nm* crux; **has dado en el q.**, you've hit the nail on the head.

quiebra *nf Fin* (*bancarrota*) bankruptcy; (*crack*) crash.

quiebro *nm* (*con el cuerpo*) dodge; *Ftb* dribbling.

quien *pron rel* **1** (*con prep*) *no se traduce o* *fml* whom; **el hombre con q. vino**, the man she came with; *fml* the man with whom she came. **2** (*indefinido*) whoever, anyone who; **q. quiera venir que venga**, whoever wants to can come; **hay q. dice lo contrario**, some people say the opposite; *fig* **q. más q. menos**, everybody.

quién *pron interr* **1** (*sujeto*) who?; **¿q. es?**, who is it? **2** (*complemento*) who?; *fml* whom; **¿para q. es?**, who is it for?; **¿de q. es esa bici?**, whose bike is that?

quienquiera *pron indef* (*pl* **quienesquiera**) whoever.

quieto,-a *adj* still; (*mar*) calm; **¡estáte q.!**, keep still!, don't move!

quietud *nf* stillness; (*calma*) calm.

quijada *nf* jawbone.

quilate *nm* carat.

quilo *nm* → **kilo**.

quilla *nf* keel.

quimera *nf fig* fantasy, pipe dream.

química *nf* chemistry.

químico,-a **I** *adj* chemical. **II** *nm,f* chemist.

quimioterapia *nf* chemotherapy.

quimono *nm* kimono.

quincalla *nf* metal pots and pans *pl*, tinware.

quince *adj & nm inv* fifteen.

quinceañero,-a *adj & nm,f* fifteen-year-old.

quincena *nf* fortnight, two weeks.

quincenal *adj* fortnightly.

quiniela *nf* football pools *pl*.

quinientos,-as *adj & nm,f* five

hundred.

quinina *nf* quinine.

quinqué *nm* oil lamp.

quinquenal *adj* quinquennial, five-year.

quinqui *nm fam* delinquent, petty criminal.

quinta *nf* 1 (*casa*) country house. 2 *Mil* conscription, *US* draft.

quintaesencia *nf* quintessence.

quintal *nm* (*medida*) 46 kg; q. métrico, ≈ 100 kg.

quinteto *nm* quintet.

quinto,-a I *adj & nm,f* fifth. II *nm Mil* conscript, recruit.

quiosco *nm* kiosk; q. de periódicos, newspaper stand.

quirófano *nm* operating theatre.

quiromancia *nf* palmistry.

quirúrgico,-a *adj* surgical.

quise *indic fut* → **querer**.

quisque, quisqui *pron fam* todo *o* cada q., everyone, everybody.

quisquilloso,-a I *adj* fussy, finicky. II *nm,f* fusspot.

quiste *nm* cyst.

quitaesmalte(s) *nm inv* nail varnish *o* polish remover.

quitamanchas *nm inv* stain remover.

quitanieves *nm* (*máquina*) q., snow-plough, *US* snowplow.

quitar I *vtr* 1 to remove; (*ropa*) to take off; (*la mesa*) to clear; (*mancha*) to remove; (*dolor*) to relieve; (*hipo*) to stop; (*sed*) quench; (*hambre*) to take away. 2 (*apartar*) to take away, take off; *fig* q. importancia a algo, to play sth down; *fig* q. las ganas a algn, to put sb off. 3 (*robar*) to steal, take; *fig* (*tiempo*) to take up; (*sitio*) to take. 4 (*descontar*) to take off. 5 *fam* (*apagar*) to turn off. 6 eso no quita para que ..., that's no reason not to be .... 7 ¡quita!, go away!. II **quitarse** *vr* 1 (*apartarse*) to move away. 2 (*mancha*) to come out; (*dolor*) to go away; se me han quitado las ganas, I don't feel like it any more. 3 (*ropa, gafas*) to take off. 4 q. de beber/fumar, to give up drinking/smoking. 5 q. a algn de encima, to get rid of sb.

quizá(s) *adv* perhaps, maybe.

R

R, r ['erre] *nf* (*la letra*) R, r.

rábano *nm* radish; *fam* me importa un r., I couldn't care less.

rabia *nf* 1 *fig* (*ira*) fury, rage; ¡qué r.!, how annoying!; me da r., it gets up my nose; me tiene r., he's got it in for me. 2 *Med* rabies *sing*.

rabiar [12] *vi* 1 *fig* (*sufrir*) to be in great pain. 2 *fig* (*enfadar*) to rage; hacer r. a algn, to make sb see red. 3 *Med* to have rabies.

rabieta *nf fam* tantrum; coger una r., to throw a tantrum.

rabillo *nm* (*del ojo*) corner.

rabino *nm* rabbi.

rabioso,-a *adj* 1 *Med* rabid; perro r., rabid dog. 2 *fig* (*enfadado*) furious. 3 de rabiosa actualidad, up-to-the-minute.

rabo *nm* tail; (*de fruta etc*) stalk.

racanear *vi fam* (*ser tacaño*) to be stingy.

rácano,-a *adj fam* 1 (*tacaño*) stingy, mean. 2 *pey* (*novato*) fresher.

racha *nf* (*de viento*) gust, squall; *fam* (*período*) spell, patch; a rachas, in fits and starts.

racial *adj* racial; discriminación r., racial discrimination; disturbios raciales, race riots.

racimo *nm* bunch, cluster.

raciocinio *nm* reason.

ración *nf* portion.

racional *adj* rational.

racionalizar [4] *vtr* to rationalize.

racionamiento *nm* rationing; cartilla de r., ration book.

racionar *vtr* (*limitar*) to ration; (*repartir*) to ration out.

racismo *nm* racism.

racista *adj & nmf* racist.

radar *nm* (*pl* radares) *Téc* radar.

radiación *nf* radiation.

radiactividad *nf* radioactivity.

radiactivo,-a *adj* radioactive.

radiador *nm* radiator.

radiante *adj* radiant (de, with).

radiar [12] *vtr* to broadcast, transmit.

radical *adj* radical.

radicalizar [4] *vtr*, **radicalizarse** *vr* (*conflicto*) to intensify; (*postura*) to harden.

radicar [1] *vi* (*estar*) to be (situated) (en, in), to be rooted (en, in).

radio I *nf* radio, wireless; (*aparato*) radio (set). II *nm* 1 radius; r. de acción, field of action, scope.*2 (de rueda*) spoke.

radioactividad *nf* radioactivity.

radioactivo,-a *adj* radioactive.

radioaficionado,-a *nm,f* radio ham.

radiocasete *nm* (*pl* radiocasetes) radio cassette.

radioescucha *nmf* listener.

radiografía *nf* (*imagen*) X-ray.

radioyente *nmf* listener.

ráfaga *nf* (*de viento*) gust, squall; (*de disparos*) burst.

raido,-a *adj* 1 (*gastado*) worn. 2 *fam* (*desvergonzado*) insolent.

raigambre *nf* roots *pl*.

rail *nm* rail.

raíz nf (pl **raíces**) root; **r. cuadrada**, square root; fig **a r. de**, as a result of.

raja nf (corte) cut, slit; (hendidura) crack, split.

rajar I vtr (hender) to crack, split; arg (acuchillar) to cut up. II vi fam to backbite. III **rajarse** vr 1 (partirse) to crack, split. 2 fam (echarse atrás) to back out. 3 Am (acobardarse) to chicken out.

rajatabla (a) loc adv strictly.

ralea nf pey type, sort.

ralentí nm neutral; **estar al r.**, to be ticking over.

ralentizar vtr to slow down.

rallado,-a adj **queso r.**, grated cheese; **pan r.**, breadcrumbs.

rallador nm grater.

ralladura nf gratings pl.

rallar vtr to grate.

ralo,-a adj sparse, thin.

rama nf branch; fam **andarse o irse por las ramas**, to beat about the bush.

ramaje nm branches pl.

ramalazo nm fam (toque) touch.

rambla nf (avenida) boulevard, avenue.

ramera nf prostitute, whore.

ramificación nf ramification.

ramificarse [1] vr to ramify, branch (out).

ramillete nm (de flores) posy.

ramo nm 1 (de flores) bunch, bouquet. 2 (sector) branch.

rampa nf ramp; **r. de lanzamiento**, launch pad.

ramplón,-ona adj coarse, vulgar.

rana nf frog; fam **salir r.**, to be a disappointment.

ranchero,-a nm,f (granjero) rancher, farmer.

rancho nm 1 (granja) ranch. 2 Mil (comida) mess.

rancio,-a adj 1 (comida) stale. 2 (antiguo) ancient.

rango nm rank; (jerarquía elevada) high social standing.

ranura nf slot.

rapar vtr (afeitar) to shave; (pelo) to crop.

rapaz I adj predatory; **ave r.**, bird of prey. II nm,f youngster; (muchacho) lad; (muchacha) lass.

rape nm 1 (pez) angler fish. 2 fam **cortado al r.**, close-cropped.

rapidez nf speed, rapidity.

rápido,-a I adj quick, fast, rapid. II adv quickly. III nm 1 (tren) fast train. 2 **rápidos**, (de un río) rapids.

rapiña nf robbery, theft; **ave de r.**, bird of prey.

raptar vtr to kidnap, abduct.

rapto nm 1 (secuestro) kidnapping, abduction. 2 fig (arrebato) outburst, fit.

raqueta nf 1 (de tenis) racket; (de pingpong) bat, US paddle. 2 (de nieve) snowshoe.

raquítico,-a adj fam (escaso) small,

meagre, US meager; (delgado) emaciated.

raquitismo nm rickets pl.

rareza nf 1 rarity, rareness. 2 (extravagancia) eccentricity.

raro,-a adj 1 rare; **rara vez**, seldom. 2 (extraño) odd, strange.

ras nm level; **a r. de**, (on a) level with; **a r. de tierra**, at ground level.

rasante I nf Aut cambio de **r.**, brow of a hill. II adj (vuelo) low.

rasar vtr (nivelar) to level.

rasca nf fam (frío) cold.

rascacielos nm inv skyscraper.

rascar [1] I vtr (con las uñas) to scratch; (guitarra) to strum. II vi to chafe.

rasero nm fig **medir con el mismo r.**, to treat impartially.

rasgado,-a adj (ojos) slit, almond-shaped.

rasgar [7] vtr to tear, rip.

rasgo nm (característica) characteristic, feature; (de la cara) feature; fig **a grandes rasgos**, broadly speaking.

rasgón nm tear, rip.

rasguñar vtr to scratch, scrape.

rasguño nm scratch, scrape.

rasilla nf (ladrillo) tile.

raso,-a I adj (llano) flat, level; (vuelo) low; (cielo) clear, cloudless; **soldado r.**, private. II nm satin.

raspa nf (de pescado) bone, backbone.

raspador nm scraper.

raspadura nf (ralladura) scraping, scrapings pl.

raspar I vtr (limar) to scrape (off). II vi (ropa etc) to chafe.

rasposo,-a adj rough, sharp.

rastra nf Agr harrow; **a la r.**, **a rastras**, dragging; fig (de mal grado) grudgingly.

rastreador nm tracker.

rastrear vtr (zona) to comb.

rastreo nm search.

rastrero,-a adj creeping; fig (despreciable) vile, base.

rastrillo nm 1 rake. 2 fam (mercadillo) flea market.

rastro nm 1 trace, sign; (en el suelo) track, trail. 2 **el R.**, the Madrid flea market.

rastrojo nm stubble.

rasurar vtr, **rasurarse** vr to shave.

rata I nf rat. II nm fam (tacaño) mean o stingy person.

ratero,-a nm,f pickpocket.

raticida nm rat poison.

ratificar [1] vtr to ratify.

rato nm 1 (momento) while, time; **a ratos**, at times; **al poco r.**, shortly after; **hay para r.**, it'll take a while; **pasar un buen/mal r.**, to have a good/bad time; **ratos libres**, free time sing. 2 fam **un r.**, (mucho) very, a lot.

ratón nm mouse; Inform mouse.

ratonera nf mousetrap.

raudal nm torrent, flood; fig **a raudales**, in abundance.

raya nf 1 (*línea*) line; (*del pantalón*) crease; (*del pelo*) parting; **camisa a rayas**, striped shirt. 2 *fig* **tener a r.**, to keep at bay; **pasarse de la r.**, to go over the score. 3 (*de droga*) fix, dose.

rayano,-a adj bordering (**en**, on).

rayar I *vtr* (*arañar*) to scratch. II *vi* **r. en/con**, to border on.

rayo nm 1 ray, beam. 2 (*relámpago*) (flash of) lightning; **¡mal r. la parta!**, to hell with her!

rayón nm rayon.

rayuela nf *Am* hopscotch.

raza nf 1 (*humana*) race. 2 (*de animal*) breed.

razón nf 1 (*facultad*) reason; **uso de r.**, power of reasoning. 2 (*motivo*) reason; **r. de más para**, all the more reason to. 3 (*justicia*) rightness, justice; **dar la r. a algn**, to say that sb is right; **tienes r.**, you're right. 4 (*proporción*) ratio, rate; **a r. de**, at the rate of. 5 **'r. aquí'**, 'enquire within', 'apply within'.

razonable adj reasonable.

razonado,-a adj reasoned, well-reasoned.

razonamiento nm reasoning.

razonar I *vtr* (*argumentar*) to reason out. II *vi* (*discurrir*) to reason.

RDA nf *Hist abr de* **República Democrática Alemana** *o de* **Alemania, GDR**.

re- pref re-.

reacción nf reaction; **avión de r.**, jet (plane); **r. en cadena**, chain reaction.

reaccionar *vi* to react.

reaccionario,-a adj & nm,f reactionary.

reacio,-a adj reluctant, unwilling.

reactor nm reactor; (*avión*) jet (plane).

readaptación nf rehabilitation; **r. profesional**, industrial retraining.

reafirmar *vtr* to reaffirm, reassert.

reagrupar *vtr*, **reagruparse** *vr* to regroup.

reajuste nm readjustment; **r. ministerial**, cabinet reshuffle.

real[1] adj (*efectivo*, *verdadero*) real; **en la vida r.**, in real life. ◆**realmente** adv really; (*en realidad*) actually, in fact.

real[2] adj (*regio*) royal.

realce nm (*relieve*) relief; *fig* (*esplendor*) splendour, *US* splendor.

realeza nf royalty.

realidad nf reality; **en r.**, in fact, actually; **la r. es que ...**, the fact of the matter is that ....

realismo nm realism.

realista I adj realistic. II nmf realist.

realizable adj feasible.

realización nf (*ejecución*) carrying out; *Cin TV* production.

realizador,-a nm,f *Cin TV* producer.

realizar [4] I *vtr* 1 (*hacer*) to carry out; (*ambición*) to achieve fulfil, *US* fulfill. 2 *Cin TV* to produce. 3 *Fin* to realize. II **realizarse** *vr* (*persona*) to fulfil *o US*

fulfill oneself; (*sueño*) to come true.

realzar [4] *vtr* (*recalcar*) to highlight; *fig* (*belleza*, *importancia*) to enhance, heighten.

reanimación nf revival.

reanimar *vtr*, **reanimarse** *vr* to revive.

reanudación nf renewal, resumption, re-establishment; **r. de las clases**, return to school.

reanudar I *vtr* to renew, resume; **r. el paso** *o* **la marcha**, to set off again; **r. las clases**, to go back to school. II **reanudarse** *vr* to start again, resume.

reaparición nf reappearance, recurrence; (*de artista etc*) comeback.

reapertura nf reopening.

rearme nm rearmament.

reaseguro nm reinsurance.

reavivar *vtr* to revive.

rebaja nf (*descuento*) reduction, discount; **rebajas**, sales; **precio de r.**, sale price.

rebajar I *vtr* 1 (*precio*) to cut, reduce; (*cantidad*) to take off. 2 (*color*) to tone down, soften; (*intensidad*) to diminish. 3 (*trabajador*) to excuse, exempt (**de**, from). 4 (*humillar*) to humiliate. II **rebajarse** *vr* (*humillarse*) to humble oneself.

rebanada nf slice.

rebanar *vtr* to slice, cut into slices.

rebañar *vtr* (*plato etc*) to finish off.

rebaño nm (*de ovejas*) flock; (*de otros animales*) herd.

rebasar *vtr* 1 (*exceder*) to exceed, go beyond. 2 *Aut* to overtake.

rebatir *vtr* to refute.

rebeca nf cardigan.

rebelarse *vr* to rebel, revolt.

rebelde I nmf rebel. II adj rebellious; *fig* **una tos r.**, a persistent cough.

rebeldía nf 1 rebelliousness. 2 *Jur* default.

rebelión nf rebellion, revolt.

rebenque nm *Am* whip.

reblandecer [33] *vtr* to soften.

rebobinar *vtr* to rewind.

rebosante adj overflowing (**de**, with), brimming (**de**, with).

rebosar I *vtr* to overflow, brim over; *fig* **r. de**, to be overflowing *o* brimming with. II *vtr* (*irradiar*) to radiate.

rebotar *vi* (*pelota*) to bounce, rebound; (*bala*) to ricochet.

rebote nm (*de pelota*) bounce, rebound; (*de bala*) ricochet; **de r.**, on the rebound.

rebozar [4] *vtr* to coat in breadcrumbs *o* batter.

rebullir *vi*, **rebullirse** *vr* to stir.

rebuscado,-a adj recherché.

rebuznar *vi* to bray.

recabar *vtr* (*información*) to obtain, manage to get.

recado nm (*mandado*) errand; (*mensaje*) message; **dejar un r.**, to leave a message.

recaer [39] *vi* 1 *Med* to relapse. 2 (*culpa*,

responsabilidad) to fall (**sobre**, on).

recaída *nf* relapse.

recalcar [1] *vtr* to stress, emphasize.

recalcitrante *adj* recalcitrant.

recalentar [1] *vtr* (*comida*) to reheat, warm up; (*calentar demasiado*) to overheat.

recámara *nf* 1 (*de rueda*) tube. 2 *Am* (*habitación*) dressing room.

recambiar [12] *vtr* to change (over).

recambio *nm* 1 (*repuesto*) spare (part); **rueda de r.**, spare wheel. 2 (*de pluma etc*) refill.

recapacitar *vi* to think over.

recargable *adj* (*pluma*) refillable; (*mechero*) rechargeable.

recargado,-a *adj* overloaded; *fig* (*estilo*) overelaborate, affected.

recargar [7] *vtr* 1 *Elec* to recharge. 2 (*sobrecargar*) to overload; (*adornar mucho*) to overelaborate. 3 *Fin* to increase.

recargo *nm* extra charge, surcharge.

recatado,-a *adj* (*prudente*) prudent, cautious; (*modesto*) modest, decent.

recato *nm* (*cautela*) caution, prudence; (*pudor*) modesty.

recaudación *nf* (*cobro*) collection; (*cantidad recaudada*) takings *pl*; *Dep* gate.

recaudador,-a *nm,f* tax collector.

recaudar *vtr* to collect.

recaudo *nm* **estar a buen r.**, to be in safe-keeping.

recelar *vtr* **r. de**, to distrust.

recelo *nm* suspicion, distrust.

receloso,-a *adj* suspicious, distrustful.

recepción *nf* reception; (*en hotel*) reception (desk).

recepcionista *nmf* receptionist.

receptivo,-a *adj* receptive.

receptor,-a I *nm,f* (*persona*) recipient. II *nm Rad TV* receiver.

recesión *nf* recession.

receta *nf* recipe; *Med* prescription.

recetar *vtr Med* to prescribe.

rechace *nm Dep* rebound.

rechazar [4] *vtr* to reject, turn down; *Mil* to repel, drive back.

rechazo *nm* rejection.

rechiflar *vtr* 1 (*silbar*) to hiss, boo. 2 (*mofarse*) to mock, jeer at.

rechinar *vi* (*madera*) to creak; (*metal*) to squeak, screech; (*dientes*) to chatter.

rechistar *vi* **sin r.**, that's final.

rechoncho,-a *adj fam* chubby, tubby.

rechupete (de) *loc fam* **me sé el tema de r.**, I know the subject inside out; **la comida estaba de r.**, the food was mouthwateringly good.

recibidor *nm* entrance hall.

recibimiento *nm* reception, welcome.

recibir I *vtr* to receive; (*en casa*) to welcome; (*en la estación*) to meet. II **recibirse** *vr Am* **r. de**, to qualify as.

recibo *nm* 1 (*factura*) invoice, bill;

(*resguardo*) receipt; **r. de la luz**, electricity bill. 2 **acusar r. de**, to acknowledge receipt of.

reciclado,-a I *adj* recycled. II *nm* (*reciclaje*) recycling.

reciclaje *nm* (*de residuos*) recycling; *fig* (*renovación*) retraining; **curso de r.**, refresher course.

reciclar *vtr* (*residuos*) to recycle; *fig* (*profesores etc*) to retrain.

recién *adv* 1 (*recientemente*) (*antes de pp*) recently, newly; **café r. hecho**, freshly-made coffee; **r. casados**, newlyweds; **r. nacido**, newborn baby. 2 *Am* (*hace poco*) recently. ◆**recientemente** *adv* recently, lately.

reciente *adj* recent.

recinto *nm* (*cercado*) enclosure; **r. comercial**, shopping precinct.

recio,-a *adj* (*robusto*) strong, sturdy; (*grueso*) thick; (*voz*) loud. II *adv* hard.

recipiente *nm* receptacle, container.

recíproco,-a *adj* reciprocal.

recital *nm Mús* recital; *Lit* reading.

recitar *vtr* to recite.

reclamación *nf* 1 (*demanda*) claim, demand. 2 (*queja*) complaint.

reclamar I *vtr* to claim, demand. II *vi* 1 to protest (**contra**, against). 2 *Jur* to appeal.

reclamo *nm* 1 (*publicitario*) appeal. 2 (*en caza*) decoy bird, lure; *fig* inducement.

reclinar *vtr* to lean (**sobre**, on). II **reclinarse** *vr* to lean back, recline.

recluir [37] *vtr* to shut away, lock away; (*encarcelar*) to imprison, intern.

reclusión *nf* seclusion; (*encarcelamiento*) imprisonment, internment.

recluso,-a *nm,f* prisoner, inmate.

recluta *nm,f* recruit.

reclutamiento *nm* (*voluntario*) recruitment; (*obligatorio*) conscription.

recobrar I *vtr* to recover, retrieve; (*conocimiento*) to regain; **r. el aliento**, to get one's breath back. II **recobrarse** *vr* to recover, recuperate.

recochineo *nm fam* mockery.

recodo *nm* (*de río*) twist, turn; (*de camino*) bend.

recogedor *nm* dustpan.

recoger [5] I *vtr* 1 (*del suelo etc*) to pick up. 2 (*datos etc*) to gather, collect. 3 (*ordenar, limpiar*) to clean; **r. la mesa**, to clear the table. 4 (*ir a buscar*) to pick up, fetch. 5 (*cosecha*) to gather, pick. II **recogerse** *vr* 1 (*irse a casa*) to go home. 2 (*pelo*) to lift up.

recogida *nf* collection; *Agr* (*cosecha*) harvest, harvesting.

recolección *nf Agr* harvest, harvesting; (*recogida*) collection, gathering.

recomendable *adj* recommendable.

recomendación *nf* recommendation, reference.

recomendar [1] *vtr* to recommend.

recompensa *nf* reward.

recompensar *vtr* to reward.

recomponer [19] (*pp recompuesto*) *vtr* to repair, mend.

reconciliación *nf* reconciliation.

reconciliar [12] **I** *vtr* to reconcile. **II -conciliarse** *vr* to be reconciled.

recóndito,-a *adj* hidden, secret.

reconfortante *adj* comforting.

reconfortar *vtr* to comfort.

reconocer [34] *vtr* **1** to recognize. **2** (*admitir*) to recognize, admit. **3** *Med* (*paciente*) to examine.

reconocimiento *nm* **1** recognition. **2** *Med* examination, checkup.

reconquista *nf* reconquest.

reconstituyente *nm* tonic.

reconstruir [37] *vtr* to reconstruct.

reconversión *nf* reconversion; **r. industrial**, industrial redeployment.

reconvertir [5] *vtr* to reconvert; *Ind* to modernize.

recopilación *nf* **1** (*resumen*) summary, resumé. **2** (*compendio*) compilation, collection.

recopilar *vtr* to compile, collect.

récord *nm* record.

recordar [2] **I** *vtr* **1** (*rememorar*) to remember. **2 r. algo a algn**, to remind sb of sth. **II** *vi* to remember.

recordatorio *nm* (*aviso*) reminder; (*de defunción*) notice of death.

recordman *nmf* record holder.

recorrer *vtr* (*distancia*) to cover, travel; (*país*) to tour, travel through *o* round; (*ciudad*) to visit, walk round.

recorrido *nm* (*distancia*) distance travelled; (*trayecto*) trip, journey; (*itinerario*) itinerary, route.

recortable *adj & nm* cutout.

recortar *vtr* to cut out.

recorte *nm* (*acción, de periódico*) cutting; (*de pelo*) trim, cut; *fig* (*de salarios etc*) cut.

recostado,-a *adj* reclining, leaning.

recostar [2] **I** *vtr* to lean. **II recostarse** *vr* (*tumbarse*) to lie down.

recoveco *nm* (*curva*) turn, bend; (*rincón*) nook, corner.

recreación *nf* recreation.

recrear **I** *vtr* **1** (*divertir*) to amuse, entertain. **2** (*crear de nuevo*) to recreate. **II recrearse** *vr* to amuse oneself, enjoy oneself; **r. con**, to take pleasure *o* delight in.

recreativo,-a *adj* recreational.

recreo *nm* **1** (*diversión*) recreation. **2** (*en el colegio*) break, recreation.

recriminar *vtr* to recriminate; (*reprochar*) to reproach.

recrudecer(se) [33] *vtr & vr* to worsen.

recrudecimiento *nm* worsening.

recta *nf Geom* straight line; (*de carretera*) straight stretch; *Dep* **la r. final**, the home straight.

rectangular *adj* rectangular.

rectángulo *nm* rectangle.

rectificación *nf* rectification; (*corrección*) correction.

rectificar [1] *vtr* to rectify; (*corregir*) to correct, remedy.

rectilíneo,-a *adj* straight.

rectitud *nf* straightness; *fig* uprightness, rectitude.

recto,-a I *adj* **1** (*derecho*) straight. **2** (*honesto*) upright, honest. **3** *Geom* right. **II** *nm Anat* rectum. **III** *adv* straight (on).

rector,-a I *adj* (*principio*) guiding, ruling. **II** *nm,f* rector.

recua *nf fig* string, series.

recuadro *nm Prensa* box.

recuento *nm* **1** count; **hacer (el) r. de**, to count.

recuerdo *nm* **1** (*memoria*) memory. **2** (*regalo etc*) souvenir. **3 recuerdos**, regards.

recuperación *nf* recovery; (*examen*) resit.

recuperar I *vtr* (*salud*) to recover; (*conocimiento*) to regain; (*tiempo, clases*) to make up. **II recuperarse** *vr* to recover.

recurrir *vi* **1** *Jur* to appeal. **2 r. a**, (*a algn*) to turn to; (*a algo*) to make use of, resort to.

recurso *nm* **1** resource; **recursos naturales**, natural resources; **como último r.**, as a last resort. **2** *Jur* appeal.

recusar *vtr* to challenge, object to.

red *nf* net; (*sistema*) network; *Com* (*cadena*) chain of supermarkets; *fig* (*trampa*) trap.

redacción *nf* (*escrito*) composition, essay; (*acción*) writing; *Prensa* editing; (*redactores*) editorial staff.

redactar *vtr* to draft; *Prensa* to edit.

redactor,-a *nm,f Prensa* editor.

redada *nf* **r. policial**, (*en un solo sitio*) raid; (*en varios lugares a la vez*) round-up.

redentor,-a *nm,f* redeemer.

redicho,-a *adj fam* affected, pretentious.

redil *nm* fold, sheepfold.

redimir *vtr* to redeem.

rédito *nm* yield, interest.

redivivo *adj* revived.

redoblar I *vtr* to redouble. **II** *vi* (*tambor*) to roll.

redoble *nm* roll; (*de campanas*) peal.

redomado,-a *adj* utter, out-and-out.

redonda *nf* **a la r.**, around.

redondear *vtr* (*objeto*) to round, make round; (*cantidad*) to round up.

redondel *nm fam* (*círculo*) circle, ring; *Taur* ring, arena.

redondo,-a *adj* **1** round; *fig* **caer r.**, to collapse. **2** (*rotundo*) categorical; (*perfecto*) perfect.

reducción *nf* reduction.

reducido,-a *adj* (*disminuido*) reduced, decreased; (*pequeño*) limited, small.

reducir [10] **I** *vtr* (*disminuir*) to reduce. **II**

reducirse *vr* **1** *(disminuirse)* to be reduced, diminish. **2** *(limitarse)* to confine oneself.

redundancia *nf* redundancy, superfluousness; **valga la r.,** if I might say so again.

redundante *adj* redundant.

redundar *vi* **r. en,** *(resultar)* to result in, lead to.

reduplicar [1] *vtr* to redouble.

reembolsar *vtr* to reimburse; *(deuda)* to repay; *(importe)* to refund.

reembolso *nm* reimbursement; *(de deuda)* repayment; *(devolución)* refund; **contra r.,** cash on delivery.

reemplazar [4] *vtr* to replace *(con,* with).

reemplazo *nm* replacement; *Mil* call-up.

reestructuración *nf* restructuring.

reestructurar *vtr* to restructure.

ref. *abr de* **referencia,** reference, ref.

refaccionar *vtr Am* to repair, do up.

refectorio *nm* refectory, canteen.

referencia *nf* reference; **con r. a,** with reference to.

referéndum *nm (pl* **referéndums)** referendum.

referente *adj* **r. a,** concerning, regarding.

referir [5] **I** *vtr* to tell, relate. **II referirse** *vr (aludir)* to refer *(a,* to); **¿a qué te refieres?,** what do you mean?

refilón (de) *loc adv (de pasada)* briefly.

refinado,-a *adj* refined.

refinamiento *nm* refinement.

refinar *vtr* to refine.

refinería *nf* refinery.

reflector,-a I *adj* reflecting. **II** *nm Elec* spotlight, searchlight.

reflejar I *vtr* to reflect. **II reflejarse** *vr* to be reflected *(en,* in).

reflejo,-a I *nm* **1** *(imagen)* reflection. **2** *(destello)* gleam, glint. **3** *Anat* reflex. **4 reflejos,** *(en el cabello)* streaks, highlights. **II** *adj (movimiento)* reflex.

reflexión *nf* reflection.

reflexionar *vi* to reflect *(sobre,* on), think *(sobre,* about).

reflexivo,-a *adj* **1** *(persona)* thoughtful. **2** *Ling* reflexive.

reflujo *nm* ebb (tide).

reforma *nf* **1** reform; **r. fiscal,** tax reform. **2** *(reparación)* repair.

reformador,-a *nm,f* reformer.

reformar I *vtr* to reform; *(edificio)* to renovate. **II reformarse** *vr* to reform.

reformatorio *nm* reformatory, reform school.

reforzar [2] *vtr* to reinforce, strengthen.

refractario,-a *adj* **1** *Téc* heat-resistant. **2** *(persona)* unwilling, reluctant.

refrán *nm* proverb, saying.

refregar [1] *vtr* to rub vigorously; *fig* **no me lo refriegues,** don't rub it in.

refrenar I *vtr (contener)* to restrain, curb. **II refrenarse** *vr* to restrain oneself.

refrendar *vtr (firmar)* to endorse, countersign; *(aprobar)* to approve.

refrescante *adj* refreshing.

refrescar [1] **I** *vtr* to refresh. **II** *vi* **1** *(tiempo)* to turn cool. **2** *(bebida)* to be refreshing. **III refrescarse** *vr* to cool down.

refresco *nm* soft drink, refreshments *pl.*

refriega *nf (lucha)* scuffle, brawl; *(escaramuza)* skirmish.

refrigeración *nf (enfriamiento)* refrigeration; *(aire acondicionado)* air conditioning.

refrigerado,-a *adj* air-conditioned.

refrigerador *nm* refrigerator, fridge.

refrigerar *vtr* to refrigerate; *(habitación)* to air-condition.

refrigerio *nm* snack, refreshments *pl.*

refuerzo *nm* reinforcement, strengthening.

refugiado,-a *adj & nm,f* refugee.

refugiarse [12] *vr* to shelter, take refuge.

refugio *nm* refuge.

refulgente *adj* radiant, brilliant.

refulgir [6] *vi (brillar)* to shine; *(resplandecer)* to glitter, sparkle.

refunfuñar *vi* to grumble, moan.

refutar *vtr* to refute.

regadera *nf* watering can; *fam* **estar como una r.,** to be as mad as a hatter.

regadío *nm (tierra)* irrigated land.

regalado,-a *adj* **1** *(gratis)* free; *(muy barato)* dirt cheap. **2 una vida regalada,** an easy life.

regalar *vtr* **1** *(dar)* to give (as a present); *(en ofertas etc)* to give away. **2 r. el oído a algn,** to flatter sb.

regaliz *nm* liquorice, *US* licorice.

regalo *nm* **1** gift, present; **de r.,** as a present. **2** *(comodidad)* pleasure, comfort.

regañadientes (a) *loc adv* reluctantly, unwillingly.

regañar I *vtr fam* to scold, tell off. **II** *vi* to nag.

regañina *nf* scolding, telling-off.

regañón,-ona *nm,f fam* nag.

regar [1] *vtr* to water.

regata *nf* boat race.

regatear I *vi* **1** to haggle, bargain. **2** *Dep* to dribble. **II** *vtr* **no r. esfuerzos,** to spare no effort.

regateo *nm* **1** *(de precios)* haggling. **2** *Dep* dribbling.

regazo *nm* lap.

regeneración *nf* regeneration.

regenerar *vtr* to regenerate.

regentar *vtr* to rule, govern; *(cargo)* to hold.

regente I *nmf Pol* regent. **II** *nm (director)* manager.

régimen *nm (pl* **regímenes) 1** *Pol* regime. **2** *Med* diet; **estar a r.,** to be on a diet.

regimiento *nm* regiment.

regio,-a *adj* **1** *(real)* royal, regal. **2** *(suntuoso)* sumptuous, luxurious; *Am (magnífico)* splendid, majestic.

región *nf* region.

regional adj regional.
regionalista adj & nmf regionalist.
regir [6] I vtr to govern. II vi to be in force. III regirse vr to be guided, go (por, by).
registrado,-a adj marca registrada, registered trademark.
registrador,-a nf caja registradora, cash register.
registrar I vtr 1 (examinar) to inspect; (cachear) to frisk. 2 (inscribir) to register. 3 (grabar) to record. II registrarse vr 1 (inscribirse) to register, enrol. 2 (detectarse) to be recorded.
registro nm 1 inspection. 2 (inscripción) registration, recording; (oficina) registry office. 3 Mús register.
regla nf 1 (norma) rule; en r., in order; por r. general, as a (general) rule; r. de oro, golden rule. 2 (instrumento) ruler. 3 Mat rule. 4 Med (periodo) period.
reglamentación nf 1 (acción) regulation. 2 (reglamento) regulations pl, rules pl.
reglamentar vtr to regulate.
reglamentario,-a adj statutory; Mil arma reglamentaria, regulation gun.
reglamento nm regulations pl, rules pl.
reglar vtr to regulate.
regocijar I vtr to delight, amuse. II regocijarse vr to be delighted, rejoice.
regocijo nm (placer) delight, joy; (alborozo) rejoicing, merriment.
regodearse vr fam to delight (con, in).
regodeo nm fam delight.
regordete,-a adj fam plump, chubby.
regresar vi to return.
regresión nf regression; (decaimiento) deterioration, decline.
regreso nm return.
reguero nm (corriente) trickle; (de humo) trail.
regulable adj adjustable.
regular I vtr 1 to regulate, control. 2 (ajustar) to adjust. II adj 1 regular; por lo r., as a rule; vuelo r., scheduled flight. 2 fam (mediano) average, so-so. III adv so-so.
regularidad nf regularity; con r., regularly.
regularizar [4] vtr to regularize.
regusto nm aftertaste.
rehabilitar vtr to rehabilitate; (edificio) to convert.
rehacer [15] (pp rehecho) I vtr to redo. II rehacerse vr (recuperarse) to recover, recuperate.
rehén nm hostage.
rehogar [7] vtr to brown.
rehuir [37] vtr to shun, avoid.
rehusar [18] vtr to refuse.
reina nf queen.
reinado nm reign.
reinante adj (que reina) reigning, ruling; (prevaleciente) prevailing.

reinar vi to reign.
reincidente nmf Jur recidivist.
reincidir vi to relapse, fall back (en, into).
reincorporarse vr r. al trabajo, to return to work.
reino nm kingdom; el R. Unido, the United Kingdom.
reinserción nf reintegration.
reinsertar(se) & vr to reintegrate.
reintegrar vtr 1 (trabajador) to reinstate. 2 (dinero) to reimburse, refund.
reintegro nm (en lotería) winning of one's stake.
reír [6] I vi to laugh. II reírse vr 1 to laugh. 2 (mofarse) to laugh (de, at), make fun (de, of).
reiterar vtr to reiterate, repeat.
reivindicación nf claim, demand.
reivindicar [1] vtr to claim, demand; el atentado fue reivindicado por los terroristas, the terrorists claimed responsibility for the attack.
reivindicativo,-a adj protest.
reja nf 1 (de ventana) grill, grating; fam estar entre rejas, to be behind bars. 2 Agr ploughshare, US plowshare.
rejilla nf (de ventana, ventilador, radiador) grill; (de horno) gridiron; (para equipaje) luggage rack.
rejoneador,-a nm,f Taur bullfighter on horseback.
rejonear vtr Taur to fight on horseback.
rejuvenecer [33] vtr to rejuvenate.
relación nf 1 relationship; (conexión) connection, link; con o en r. a, with regard to; relaciones públicas, public relations. 2 (lista) list. 3 (relato) account. 4 Mat Téc ratio.
relacionado,-a adj related (con, to), connected (con, with).
relacionar I vtr to relate (con, to), connect (con, with). II relacionarse vr 1 to be related to, be connected. 2 (alternar) to mix, get acquainted.
relajación nf relaxation.
relajante adj relaxing.
relajar I vtr to relax. II relajarse vr to relax; (moral) to deteriorate.
relamerse vr to lick one's lips.
relamido,-a adj (afectado) affected; (pulcro) prim and proper.
relámpago nm flash of lightning; fig pasó como un r., he flashed past; fig visita r., flying visit.
relampaguear vi impers to flash.
relanzar vtr to relaunch.
relatar vtr to narrate, relate.
relatividad nf relativity.
relativo,-a adj relative (a, to); en lo r. a, with regard to, concerning.
relato nm (cuento) tale, story.
relax nm fam relaxation.
relegar [7] vtr to relegate.
relente nm dew.

relevante adj important.

relevancia nf importance.

relevar I vtr to relieve, take over from; **fue relevado del cargo**, he was relieved of his duties. II **relevarse** vr (turnarse) to relieve one another.

relevo nm relief; Dep relay.

relieve nm Arte relief; fig **poner de r.**, to emphasize.

religión nf religion.

religioso,-a I adj religious. II nm,f (hombre) monk; (mujer) nun.

relinchar vi to neigh, whinny.

relincho nm neigh, whinny.

reliquia nf relic.

rellamada nf Tel redial.

rellano nm landing.

rellenar vtr 1 (impreso etc) to fill in. 2 (un ave) to stuff; (un pastel) to fill.

relleno,-a I nm (de aves) stuffing; (de pasteles) filling. II adj stuffed.

reloj nm clock; (de pulsera) watch; **r. de arena**, hourglass; **r. de sol**, sundial; **r. despertador**, alarm clock.

relojería nf (tienda) watchmaker's, clockmaker's; **bomba de r.**, time bomb.

relojero,-a nm,f watchmaker, clockmaker.

reluciente adj shining, gleaming.

relucir [35] vi (brillar) to shine, gleam; **sacar a r. un tema**, to bring up a subject.

relumbrar vi to shine, gleam.

reluzco indic pres → **relucir**.

remachar vtr to drive home, hammer home.

remache nm rivet.

remanente nm (restos) remainder; (extra) surplus.

remangar(se) [7] vtr & vr (mangas, pantalones) to roll up; (camisa) to tuck up.

remanso nm pool; (lugar tranquilo) quiet place.

remar vi to row.

remarcar [1] vtr to stress, underline.

rematadamente adv **r. loco**, as mad as a hatter.

rematar vtr 1 to finish off, put the finishing touches to. 2 Com to sell off cheaply. 3 Dep to shoot.

remate nm 1 (final) end, finish; **para r.**, to crown it all. 2 Dep shot at goal. 3 **de r.**, utter, utterly.

rembolsar vtr → **reembolsar**.

rembolso nm → **reembolso**.

remedar vtr to imitate, copy.

remediar [12] vtr I to remedy; (enmendar) to repair, make good. 2 (evitar) to avoid, prevent; **no pude remediarlo**, I couldn't help it.

remedio nm (cura) remedy, cure; (solución) solution; **¡qué r.!**, what else can I do!; **no hay más r.**, there's no choice; **sin r.**, without fail; fam **¡no tienes r.!**, you're hopeless!

remedo nm (imitación) imitation, copy; (parodia) parody.

rememorar vtr to remember, recall.

remendar [1] vtr (ropa) to patch.

remero,-a nm,f rower.

remesa nf (de mercancías) consignment, shipment; (de dinero) remittance.

remiendo nm (parche) patch.

remilgado,-a adj (afectado) affected; (melindroso) fussy, finicky; (gazmoño) prudish.

remilgo nm affectation; (gazmoñería) prudishness.

reminiscencia nf reminiscence.

remiso,-a adj reluctant.

remite nm (en carta) sender's name and address.

remitente nmf sender.

remitir I vtr 1 (enviar) to send. 2 (referir) to refer. II vi (fiebre, temporal) to subside. III **remitirse** vr **si nos remitimos a los hechos**, if we look at the facts; **remítase a la página diez**, see page ten.

remo nm oar; (deporte) rowing.

remodelación nf (modificación) reshaping; (reorganización) reorganization; Pol **r. ministerial** o **del gobierno**, cabinet reshuffle.

remodelar vtr to reshape; (reorganizar) to reorganize.

remojar vtr to soak (en, in).

remojo nm **dejar** o **poner en r.**, to soak, leave to soak.

remojón nm fam **darse un r.**, to go for a dip.

remolacha nf beetroot.

remolcador nm 1 Náut tug, tugboat. 2 Aut breakdown truck, US tow truck.

remolcar [1] vtr to tow.

remolino nm (de agua) whirlpool, eddy; (de aire) whirlwind.

remolón,-a adj **hacerse el r.**, to shirk, slack.

remolonear vi to shirk, slack.

remolque nm (acción) towing; (vehículo) trailer; fig **ir a r. de algn**, to trundle along behind sb.

remontar I vtr 1 (subir) to go up. 2 (superar) to overcome. II **remontarse** vr 1 (pájaros, aviones) to soar. 2 (datar) to go back, date back (a, to).

remorder [4] vtr to trouble; **me remuerde la conciencia por ...**, I've got a bad conscience about ....

remordimiento nm remorse.

remoto,-a adj remote, faraway; **no tengo la más remota idea**, I haven't got the faintest idea.

remover [4] vtr 1 (trasladar) to move over. 2 (tierra) to turn over; (líquido) to shake up; (comida etc) to stir; (asunto) to stir up.

remozar [4] vtr to modernize.

remplazar [4] vtr → **reemplazar**.

remplazo *nm* → **reemplazo**.

remuneración *nf* remuneration.

remunerar *vtr* to remunerate.

renacer [33] *vi* to be reborn; *fig* (*revivir*) to revive, come back to life.

renacentista *adj* Renaissance.

renacimiento *nm* el R., the Renaissance.

renacuajo *nm* tadpole; *fam* (*niño pequeño*) shrimp.

renal *adj* kidney; **insuficiencia r.**, kidney failure.

rencilla *nf* quarrel.

rencor *nm* rancour, *US* rancor; (*resentimiento*) resentment; **guardar r. a algn**, to have a grudge against sb.

rencoroso,-a *adj* (*hostil*) rancorous; (*resentido*) resentful.

rendición *nf* surrender.

rendido,-a *adj* (*muy cansado*) exhausted, worn out.

rendija *nf* crack, split.

rendimiento *nm* (*producción*) yield, output; (*de máquina, motor*) efficiency, performance.

rendir [6] I *vtr* 1 (*fruto, beneficios*) to yield, produce. 2 (*cansar*) to exhaust, wear out. 3 **r. culto a**, to worship; **r. homenaje a**, to pay homage to. II *vi* (*dar beneficios*) to pay, be profitable. III **rendirse** *vr* 1 to surrender, give in; **¡me rindo!**, I give up! 2 (*cansarse*) to wear oneself out.

renegado,-a *adj & nmf* renegade.

renegar [1] *vtr* **r. de**, to renounce, disown.

renegrido,-a *adj* blackened.

RENFE *abr de* Red Nacional de los Ferrocarriles Españoles.

renglón *nm* line; **a r. seguido**, immediately afterwards.

reno *nm* reindeer.

renombrado,-a *adj* renowned, famous.

renombre *nm* renown, fame.

renovable *adj* renewable.

renovación *nf* (*de contrato, pasaporte*) renewal; (*de una casa*) renovation.

renovar [2] *vtr* to renew; (*edificio*) to renovate.

renta *nf* 1 *Fin* (*ingresos*) income; (*beneficio*) interest, return; **r. per cápita**, per capita income; **r. fija**, fixed interest security. 2 (*alquiler*) rent.

rentable *adj* profitable.

rentar *vtr* to produce, yield.

renuncia *nf* 1 renunciation. 2 (*dimisión*) resignation.

renunciar [12] *vi* 1 **r. a**, to renounce, give up; (*no aceptar*) to decline. 2 (*dimitir*) to resign.

reñido,-a *adj* (*disputado*) tough, hard-fought.

reñir [6] I *vtr* (*regañar*) to scold, tell off. II *vi* (*discutir*) to quarrel, argue; (*pelear*) to fight; **r. con algn**, to fall out with sb.

reo *nmf* (*acusado*) defendant, accused; (*culpable*) culprit.

reojo (de) *loc adv* **mirar algo de r.**, to look at sth out of the corner of one's eye.

reparación *nf* repair; (*compensación*) reparation, amends *pl*.

reparar I *vtr* to repair; (*ofensa, injuria*) to make amends for; (*daño*) to make good. II *vi* **r. en**, (*darse cuenta de*) to notice; (*reflexionar sobre*) to think about.

reparo *nm* **no tener reparos en**, not to hesitate to; **me da r.**, I feel embarrassed.

repartidor,-a *nmf* distributor.

repartir *vtr* 1 (*dividir*) to distribute, share out. 2 (*regalo, premio*) to give out, hand out; (*correo*) to deliver; *Naipes* to deal.

reparto *nm* 1 distribution, sharing out. 2 (*distribución*) handing out; (*de mercancías*) delivery. 3 *Cin Teat* cast.

repasar *vtr* 1 to revise, go over. 2 (*ropa*) to mend.

repaso *nm* revision.

repatear *vtr fam* to annoy, turn off.

repatriar [14] *vtr* to repatriate.

repecho *nm* short steep slope.

repelente *adj* repulsive, repellent; *fam* **niño r.**, little know-all.

repeler *vtr* (*rechazar*) to repel, repulse; (*repugnar*) to disgust.

repente *nm fam* (*arrebato*) fit, outburst; **de r.**, suddenly, all of a sudden.

repentino,-a *adj* sudden.

repercusión *nf* repercussion.

repercutir *vi* 1 (*sonido*) to resound, reverberate; (*objeto*) to rebound. 2 *fig* **r. en**, to have repercussions on, affect.

repertorio *nm* repertoire, repertory.

repesca *nf fam* second chance; (*examen*) resit.

repetición *nf* repetition; **r. de la jugada**, action replay.

repetido,-a *adj* **repetidas veces**, repeatedly.

repetidor,-a I *adj* repeating. II *nm,f fam Educ* student who is repeating a year.

repetir [6] I *vtr* 1 to repeat. 2 (*plato*) to have a second helping. II *vi Educ* to repeat a year. III **repetirse** *vr* 1 (*persona*) to repeat oneself. 2 (*hecho*) to recur. 3 **el pepino se repite**, cucumber repeats (on me/you/him etc).

repicar [1] *vtr* (*las campanas*) to peal, ring out.

repipi *adj fam* **niño r.**, little know-all.

repique *nm* (*de campanas*) peal, ringing.

repiquetear *vtr & vi* (*campanas*) to ring; (*tambor*) to beat.

repisa *nf* shelf, ledge.

replantear *vtr*, **replantearse** *vr* to reconsider, rethink.

replegarse [1] *vr* to fall back, retreat.

repleto,-a *adj* full (up), jam-packed; **r. de**, packed with, crammed with.

réplica *nf* 1 answer, reply. 2 (*copia*) réplica.

replicar [1] I *vtr* to answer back. II *vi* 1 to reply, retort. 2 (*objetar*) to argue. 3 *Jur* to answer.

repliegue *nm Mil* withdrawal, retreat.

repoblación *nf* repopulation; **r. forestal**, reafforestation.

repoblar [2] *vtr* to repopulate; (*bosque*) to reafforest.

repollo *nm* cabbage.

reponer [19] I *vtr* 1 to put back, replace. 2 *Teat* (*obra*) to put on again; *Cin* (*película*) to rerun; *TV* (*programa*) to repeat. II **reponerse** *vr* **r. de**, to recover from, get over.

reportaje *nm Prensa Rad* report; (*noticias*) article, news item.

reportar *vtr* (*beneficios etc*) to bring.

reportero,-a *nm,f* reporter.

reposar I *vtr* to rest (**en**, on). II *vi* (*descansar*) to rest, take a rest; (*té*) to infuse; (*comida*) to stand.

reposición *nf TV* repeat; *Cin* rerun, reshowing.

reposo *nm* rest; **en r.**, at rest.

repostar *vtr* (*provisiones*) to stock up with; *Aut* (*gasolina*) to fill up.

repostería *nf* confectionery; (*tienda*) confectioner's (shop).

repostero,-a *nm,f* confectioner.

reprender *vtr* to reprimand, scold.

represalia *nf* (*usu pl*) reprisals *pl*, retaliation.

representación *nf* 1 representation. 2 *Teat* performance.

representante *nmf* representative.

representar *vtr* 1 to represent. 2 (*significar*) to mean, represent. 3 *Teat* (*obra*) to perform.

representativo,-a *adj* representative.

represión *nf* repression.

represivo,-a *adj* repressive.

reprimenda *nf* reprimand.

reprimir *vtr* to repress.

reprobar [2] *vtr* (*cosa*) to condemn; (*a persona*) to reproach, reprove.

réprobo,-a *adj & nm,f* reprobate.

reprochable *adj* reproachable.

reprochar *vtr* to reproach; **r. algo a algn**, to reproach sb for sth.

reproche *nm* reproach.

reproducción *nf* reproduction.

reproducir [10] I *vtr* to reproduce. II **reproducirse** *vr* 1 to reproduce, breed. 2 (*repetirse*) to recur, happen again.

reproductor,-a *adj* reproductive.

reptar *vi* to slither.

reptil *nm* reptile.

república *nf* republic.

republicano,-a *adj & nm,f* republican.

repudiar [12] *vtr* to repudiate.

repuesto *nm* (*recambio*) spare part, spare; *Aut* **rueda de r.**, spare wheel.

repugnancia *nf* loathing, disgust.

repugnante *adj* disgusting, revolting.

repugnar *vtr* to disgust, revolt.

repujar *vtr* to emboss.

repulsa *nf* rebuff.

repulsión *nf* repulsion, repugnance.

repulsivo,-a *adj* repulsive, revolting.

repuse *pt indef* → **reponer**.

reputación *nf* reputation.

reputar *vtr* to consider, deem.

requemar *vtr* to scorch.

requerimiento *nm* 1 (*súplica*) request. 2 *Jur* (*aviso*) summons *pl*.

requerir [5] *vtr* 1 to require. 2 (*solicitar*) to request. 3 *Jur* (*avisar*) to summon.

requesón *nm* cottage cheese.

requete- *pref fam* really, very, incredibly; **requetebueno**, brilliant.

réquiem *nm* (*pl* **réquiems**) requiem.

requisa *nf* 1 (*inspección*) inspection. 2 *Mil* requisition.

requisar *vtr* to requisition.

requisito *nm* requirement, requisite.

res *nf* animal.

resabiado,-a *adj pey* pedantic.

resabio *nm* 1 (*mal sabor*) unpleasant o bad aftertaste. 2 (*vicio*) bad habit.

resaca *nf* 1 hangover. 2 *Náut* undertow, undercurrent.

resaltar *vi* 1 (*sobresalir*) to project, jut out. 2 *fig* to stand out.

resarcir [3] *vtr* to compensate.

resbaladizo,-a *adj* slippery.

resbalar(se) *vi & vr* to slip; *Aut* to skid.

resbalón *nm* slip.

rescatar (*persona*) to rescue; (*objeto*) to recover.

rescate *nm* 1 (*salvamento*) rescue; (*recuperación*) recovery. 2 (*suma*) ransom.

rescindir *vtr* to rescind, annul; (*contrato*) to cancel.

rescisión *nf* rescission, annulment.

rescoldo *nm* 1 embers *pl*. 2 *fig* (*recelo*) lingering doubt.

resecarse [1] *vr* to dry up, become parched.

reseco,-a *adj* very dry, parched.

resentido,-a *adj* resentful.

resentimiento *nm* resentment.

resentirse [5] *vr* 1 **r. de**, to suffer from, feel the effects of. 2 (*ofenderse*) to feel offended; **r. por algo**, to take offence at sth, feel bitter about sth.

reseña *nf* review; *Prensa* write-up.

reserva I *nf* 1 (*de entradas etc*) reservation, booking. 2 (*provisión*) reserve, stock; **un vino de r.**, a vintage wine. 3 *Mil* reserve, reserves *pl*. 4 (*duda*) reservation. II *nmf Dep* reserve, substitute.

reservado,-a I *adj* (*persona*) reserved, quiet. II *nm* private room.

reservar [5] *vtr* 1 (*billetes etc*) to reserve, book. 2 (*dinero, tiempo etc*) to keep, save. II **reservarse** *vr* 1 to save oneself (*para*, for). 2 (*sentimientos*) to keep to oneself. 3 **r. el derecho de**, to reserve the right to.

resfriado,-a I nm (catarro) cold; **coger un r.,** to catch (a) cold. **II** adj estar **r.,** to have a cold.

resfriarse vr to catch (a) cold.

resguardar vtr (proteger) to protect, shelter (de, from).

resguardo nm **1** (recibo) receipt. **2** (protección) protection, shelter.

residencia nf residence; **r. de ancianos,** old people's home.

residencial adj residential.

residente adj & nmf resident.

residir vi to reside, live (en, in); fig to lie (en, in).

residuo nm **1** residue. **2 residuos,** waste sing.

resignación nf resignation.

resignado,-a adj resigned.

resignarse vr to resign oneself (a, to).

resina nf resin.

resistencia nf **1** resistance. **2** (aguante) endurance, stamina. **3** Elec element.

resistente adj **1** resistant (a, to). **2** (fuerte) tough, hardy.

resistir I vi **1** to resist. **2** (aguantar) to hold (out). **II** vtr (situación, presión) to put up with; (tentación) to resist. **III resistirse** vr to resist; (oponerse) to offer resistance; (negarse) to refuse.

resolución nf **1** (solución) solution. **2** (decisión) resolution.

resolver [4] (pp **resuelto**) **I** vtr (problema) to solve; (asunto) to settle. **II** vi (decidir) to resolve, decide. **III resolverse** vr **1** (solucionarse) to be solved. **2** (decidirse) to resolve, make up one's mind (a, to).

resollar [7] vi to breathe heavily; (con silbido) to wheeze.

resonancia nf **1** (sonora) resonance. **2** (repercusión) repercussions pl.

resonar [6] vi to resound; (tener eco) to echo.

resoplar vi (respirar) to breathe heavily; (de cansancio) to puff and pant; (de enfado) to huff and puff.

resoplido nm (silbido) wheezing; (de cansancio) panting; (de enfado) snort.

resorte nm **1** (muelle) spring. **2** fig means pl.

respaldar vtr to support, back (up).

respaldo nm (de silla etc) back; fig (apoyo) support, backing.

respectar vtr to concern, regard; **por lo que a mí respecta,** as far as I'm concerned.

respectivo,-a adj respective; **en lo r. a,** with regard to, regarding.

respecto nm **al r., a este r.,** in this respect; **con r. a, r. a, r. de,** with regard to; **r. a mí,** as for me, as far as I am concerned.

respetable I adj respectable. **II** nm fam **el r.,** the audience.

respetar vtr to respect; **hacerse r. de to-**

dos, to command everyone's respect.

respeto nm **1** respect; **por r.,** out of consideration. **2** (recelo) fear.

respetuoso,-a adj respectful.

respingar [7] vi to shy.

respingo nm start, jump.

respingón,-ona adj (nariz) snub, upturned.

respiración nf (acción) breathing, respiration; (aliento) breath; **r. artificial,** artificial resuscitation.

respirar vi to breathe; **¡por fin respiro!,** well, that's a relief!

respiratorio,-a adj respiratory.

respiro nm **1** breathing. **2** (descanso) breather, break.

resplandecer [33] vi to shine.

resplandeciente adj (brillante) shining; (esplendoroso) resplendent, radiant.

resplandor nm (brillo) brightness; (muy intenso) brilliance; (de fuego) glow, blaze.

responder I vtr to answer. **II** vi **1** (una carta) to reply. **2** (reaccionar) to respond. **3** (protestar) to answer back. **4 r. de algn,** to be responsible for sb; **r. por algn,** to vouch for sb.

respondón,-ona adj fam argumentative, cheeky.

responsabilidad nf responsibility.

responsabilizar [4] **I** vtr to make o hold responsible (de, for). **II responsabilizarse** vr to assume o claim responsibility (de, for).

responsable I adj responsible. **II** nmf **el/ la r.,** (encargado) the person in charge; (de robo etc) the perpetrator.

respuesta nf answer, reply; (reacción) response.

resquebrajarse vr to crack.

resquemor nm resentment, ill feeling.

resquicio nm crack, chink.

resta nf subtraction.

restablecer [33] **I** vtr to re-establish; (el orden) to restore. **II restablecerse** vr Med to recover.

restablecimiento nm **1** re-establishment; (del orden etc) restoration. **2** Med recovery.

restante adj remaining; **lo r.,** the rest, the remainder.

restar I vtr **1** Mat to subtract, take away. **2 r. importancia a algo,** to play sth down. **II** vi (quedar) to be left, remain.

restauración nf restoration.

restaurador,-a nm **1** nm,f restorer. **II** adj restoring.

restaurante nm restaurant.

restaurar vtr to restore.

restitución nf restitution.

restituir [37] vtr (restablecer) to restore; (devolver) to return, give back.

resto nm **1** rest, remainder; Mat remainder. **2 restos,** remains; (de comida) leftovers.

restregar [1] *vtr* to rub hard, scrub.
restricción *nf* restriction.
restrictivo,-a *adj* restrictive.
restringir [6] *vtr* to restrict, limit.
resucitar *vtr & vi* to resuscitate.
resuelto,-a *adj (decidido)* resolute, determined.
resuello *nm* breath, gasp.
resultas *nfpl* **a r. de,** as a result of.
resultado *nm* result; *(consecuencia)* outcome; **dar buen r.,** to work, give results.
resultante *adj* resulting.
resultar *vi* **1** *(ser)* to turn o work out; **así resulta más barato,** it works out cheaper this way; **me resultó fácil,** it turned out to be easy for me. **2** *(ocurrir)* **resulta que ...,** the thing is ...; **y ahora resulta que no puede venir,** and now it turns out that she can't come. **3** *(tener éxito)* to be successful; **la fiesta no resultó,** the party wasn't a success.
resumen *nm* summary; **en r.,** in short, to sum up.
resumir **I** *vtr* to sum up; *(recapitular)* to summarize. **II resumirse** *vr (reducirse)* to be reduced to.
resurgir [6] *vi* to reappear.
resurrección *nf* resurrection.
retablo *nm* altarpiece.
retaguardia *nf* rearguard.
retahíla *nf* series *sing*, string.
retal *nm (pedazo)* scrap.
retar *vtr* to challenge.
retardarse *vr* to be delayed.
retardo *nm* delay.
retazo *nm (pedazo)* scrap; *(fragmento)* fragment, piece.
rete- *pref fam Am* very.
retención *nf* retention; *Fin* withholding; **r. de tráfico,** (traffic) hold-up, traffic jam.
retener [24] *vtr* **1** *(detener)* to retain. **2** *Fin (descontar)* to deduct. **3** *(detener)* to detain.
reticencia *nf* reticence, reserve.
reticente *adj* reticent, reserved.
retina *nf* retina.
retintín *nm (tono irónico)* innuendo, sarcastic tone.
retirada *nf* retreat, withdrawal.
retirado,-a **I** *adj* **1** *(alejado)* remote. **2** *(jubilado)* retired. **II** *nm,f* retired person, *US* retiree.
retirar **I** *vtr* to take away, remove; *(dinero)* to withdraw; *(ofensa)* to take back. **II retirarse** *vr* **1** *(apartarse)* to withdraw, draw back; *(irse)* to retire. **2** *(jubilarse)* to retire. **3** *Mil* to retreat, withdraw.
retiro *nm* **1** *(jubilación)* retirement; *(pensión)* pension. **2** *(lugar tranquilo)* retreat. **3** *Rel* retreat.
reto *nm* challenge.
retocar [1] *vtr* to touch up.
retoño *nm (rebrote)* shoot, sprout; *fig (ni-*

ño) kid.
retoque *nm* retouching, touching up; **los últimos retoques,** the finishing touches.
retorcer [4] **I** *vtr (cuerda, hilo)* to twist; *(ropa)* to wring (out). **II retorcerse** *vr* to twist, become twisted; **r. de dolor,** to writhe in pain.
retorcido,-a *adj fig* twisted.
retórica *nf* rhetoric.
retórico,-a *adj* rhetorical.
retornable *adj* returnable; **'envase no r.',** 'nondeposit bottle'.
retornar **I** *vtr* to return, give back. **II** *vi* to return, come back, go back.
retorno *nm* return.
retortijón *nm (dolor)* stomach cramp.
retozar [4] *vi* to frolic, romp.
retracción *nf* retraction.
retractar **I** *vtr* to retract. **II retractarse** *vr* to retract, take back *(de, -).*
retraerse *vr (retirarse)* to withdraw; *(por miedo)* to shy away.
retraído,-a *adj* shy, reserved.
retraimiento *nm (timidez)* shyness.
retransmisión *nf* broadcast, transmission.
retransmitir *vtr* to broadcast.
retrasado,-a **I** *adj* **1** *(tren)* late; *(reloj)* slow; **voy r.,** I'm behind schedule. **2** *(país)* backward, underdeveloped. **3** *(mental)* retarded, backward. **II** *nm,f* **r. (mental),** mentally retarded person.
retrasar **I** *vtr* **1** *(retardar)* to slow down. **2** *(atrasar)* to delay, postpone. **3** *(reloj)* to put back. **II retrasarse** *vr* to be late, be delayed; *(reloj)* to be slow.
retraso *nm* delay; **con r.,** late; **una hora de r.,** an hour behind schedule; **r. mental,** mental deficiency.
retratar **I** *vtr (pintar)* to paint a portrait of; *Fot* to take a photograph of; *fig (describir)* to describe, depict. **II retratarse** *vr* *Fot* to have one's photograph taken.
retrato *nm (pintura)* portrait; *Fot* photograph; **r. robot,** identikit picture, photofit picture; **ser el vivo r. de,** to be the spitting image of.
retreta *nf* retreat.
retrete *nm* lavatory, toilet.
retribución *nf (pago)* pay, payment; *(recompensa)* reward.
retribuir *vtr (pagar)* to pay; *(recompensar)* to reward.
retro *adj inv fam (retrógrado)* reactionary; *(antiguo)* old-fashioned.
retroactivo,-a *adj* retroactive; **con efecto r.,** retrospectively.
retroceder *vi* to move back, back away.
retroceso *nm* **1** *(movimiento)* backward movement. **2** *Med* deterioration, worsening. **3** *Econ* recession.
retrógrado,-a *adj & nm,f (reaccionario)* reactionary.
retropropulsión *nf Av* jet propulsion.
retrospectivo,-a *adj & nf* retrospective.

retrovisor nm Aut rear-view mirror.

retumbar vi (resonar) to resound, echo; (tronar) to thunder, boom.

retuve pt indef → retener.

reúma, reumatismo nm rheumatism.

reumático,-a adj & nm,f rheumatic.

reunión nf meeting; (reencuentro) reunion.

reunir [1] I vtr to gather together; (dinero) to raise; (cualidades) to have, possess; (requisitos) to fulfil. II **reunirse** vr to meet, gather; r. con algn, to meet sb.

revalidar vtr to ratify, confirm; Dep (título) to retain.

revalorizar [4] vtr, **revalorizarse** vr (moneda) to revalue.

revancha nf revenge; Dep return match.

revanchista adj vengeful, vindictive.

revelación nf revelation.

revelado nm Fot developing.

revelar vtr 1 to reveal, disclose. 2 Fot (película) to develop.

revender vtr (entradas) to tout.

reventa nf (de entradas) touting.

reventado,-a adj fam (cansado) knackered.

reventar [1] I vtr 1 to burst. 2 (romper) to break, smash. 3 (fastidiar) to annoy, bother. II vi (estallar) to burst; **r. de ganas de hacer algo**, to be dying to do sth; **está que revienta**, he's bursting at the seams. III **reventarse** vr (estallar) to burst, explode.

reventón nm (de neumático) blowout, puncture, flat tyre o US tire.

reverberación nf reverberation.

reverberar vi to reverberate.

reverencia nf 1 (respeto) reverence. 2 (inclinación) (de hombre) bow; (de mujer) curtsy.

reverenciar [12] vtr to revere, venerate.

reverendo,-a adj & nm,f reverend.

reversible adj reversible.

reverso nm reverse, back.

revertido,-a adj **llamada a cobro r.**, reverse-charge call, US collect call.

revertir [5] vi to result (en, in).

revés nm 1 (reverso) reverse; **al o del r.**, (al contrario) the other way round; (la parte interior en el exterior) inside out; (boca abajo) upside down; (la parte de detrás delante) back to front; **al r. de lo que dicen**, contrary to what they say. 2 (bofetada) slap; Ten backhand (stroke). 3 fig (contrariedad) setback, reverse; **los reveses de la vida**, life's misfortunes; **reveses de fortuna**, setbacks, blows of fate.

revestimiento nm Téc covering, coating.

revestir [6] vtr 1 (recubrir) to cover (de, with), coat (de, with), line (de, with). 2 fig **la herida no reviste importancia**, the wound is not serious.

revisar vtr to check; (coche) to service.

revisión nf checking; (de coche) service, overhaul; **r. médica**, checkup.

revisor,-a nm,f ticket inspector.

revista nf 1 magazine. 2 **pasar r. a**, to inspect, review. 3 Teat revue.

revitalizar [4] vtr to revitalize.

revivir vi & vtr to revive.

revocar [1] vtr to revoke, repeal.

revolcar [2] I vtr fam (oponente) to floor, crush. II **revolcarse** vr to roll about.

revolcón nm fall, tumble; vulg (sexual) romp.

revolotear vi to fly about, flutter about.

revoltijo, revoltillo nm mess, jumble.

revoltoso,-a adj (travieso) mischievous, naughty.

revolución nf revolution.

revolucionar vtr to revolutionize.

revolucionario,-a adj & nm,f revolutionary.

revolver [4] (pp **revuelto**) I vtr (desordenar) to mess up, disturb; **me revuelve el estómago**, it turns my stomach. II **revolverse** vr 1 (agitarse) to roll. 2 fig **r. contra algn**, to turn against sb. 3 (el tiempo) to turn stormy; (el mar) to become rough.

revólver nm (pl **revólveres**) revolver.

revuelo nm fig stir, commotion.

revuelta nf 1 (insurrección) revolt. 2 (curva) bend, turn.

revuelto,-a adj 1 (desordenado) jumbled, in a mess. 2 (tiempo) stormy, unsettled; (mar) rough. 3 (agitado) excited.

revulsivo,-a adj & nm revulsive.

rey nm king; Rel (**el día de) Reyes**, (the) Epiphany, 6 January.

reyerta nf quarrel, dispute.

rezagado,-a nm,f straggler, latecomer.

rezagarse vr to lag o fall behind.

rezar [4] I vi 1 (orar) to pray. 2 (decir) to say, read. II vtr (oración) to say.

rezo nm prayer.

rezumar vtr to ooze; fig to exude.

RFA nf Hist abr de **República Federal de Alemania**, Federal Republic of Germany, FRG.

ría nf estuary.

riada nf flood.

ribera nf (de río) bank; (zona) riverside, waterfront.

ribete nm edging, border.

ribetear vtr to edge, border.

rico,-a I adj 1 **ser r.**, (adinerado) to be rich, wealthy; (abundante) to be rich; (bonito) to be lovely o adorable; (fértil) to be rich o fertile. 2 **estar r.**, (delicioso) to be delicious. II nm,f rich person. ◆**ricamente** adv fam **tan r.**, very well.

rictus nm inv grin.

ridiculez nf ridiculous thing; (cualidad) ridiculousness.

ridiculizar [4] vtr to ridicule.

ridículo,-a I adj ridiculous. II nm ridicule; **hacer el r.**, quedar en r., to make a fool of oneself; **poner a algn en r.**, to make a fool of sb.

riego nm watering, irrigation; **r. sanguíneo**, blood circulation.

riel nm rail.

rienda nf rein; fig **dar r. suelta a**, to give free rein to; fig **llevar las riendas**, to hold the reins, be in control.

riesgo nm risk; **correr el r. de**, to run the risk of; **seguro a todo r.**, fully-comprehensive insurance.

rifa nf raffle.

rifar vtr to raffle (off).

rifle nm rifle.

rigidez nf rigidity, stiffness; fig (severidad) strictness, inflexibility.

rígido,-a adj rigid, stiff; fig (severo) strict, inflexible.

rigor nm rigour, US rigor; (severidad) severity; **con r.**, rigorously; **de r.**, indispensable.

riguroso,-a adj rigorous; (severo) severe, strict. ◆**rigurosamente** adv rigorously; (meticulosamente) meticulously; (severamente) severely; **r. cierto**, absolutely true.

rijo indic pres → **regir**.

rima nf rhyme.

rimar vtr & vi to rhyme (**con**, with).

rimbombante adj (lenguaje) pompous, pretentious.

rímel nm mascara.

Rin n **el R.**, the Rhine.

rincón nm corner; fam (lugar remoto) nook.

rinoceronte nm rhinoceros.

riña nf (pelea) fight; (discusión) row, quarrel.

riñón nm kidney; fam **costar un r.**, to cost an arm and a leg; Med **r. artificial**, kidney machine.

río nm river; **r. abajo**, downstream; **r. arriba**, upstream.

Rioja n Rioja.

rioplatense adj from o of Buenos Aires.

ripio nm (palabras de relleno) waffle; fam **no perder r.**, not to miss a trick.

riqueza nf 1 wealth. 2 (cualidad) wealthiness.

risa nf laugh; (carcajadas) laughter; **es** (cosa) **de r.**, it's laughable; **me da r.**, it makes me laugh; **tomarse algo a r.**, to laugh sth off; fig **morirse** o **mondarse de r.**, to die o fall about laughing; fam **mi hermano es una r.**, my brother is a laugh; fam fig **tener algo muerto de r.**, to leave sth lying around.

risco nm crag, cliff.

risible adj laughable.

risilla, risita nf giggle, titter; (risa falsa) false laugh.

risotada nf guffaw.

ristra nf string.

ristre nm **en r.**, at the ready.

risueño,-a adj smiling.

rítmico,-a adj rhythmic; **gimnasia rítmica**, eurhythmics sing, US eurythmics sing.

ritmo nm 1 rhythm. 2 (paso) rate; **llevar un buen r. de trabajo**, to work at a good pace.

rito nm 1 rite. 2 (ritual) ritual.

ritual adj & nm ritual.

rival adj & nmf rival.

rivalidad nf rivalry.

rivalizar [4] vi to rival (**en**, in).

rizado,-a adj 1 (pelo) curly. 2 (mar) choppy.

rizar [4] I vtr (pelo) to curl; (tela, papel) to crease; **r. el rizo**, fig to make things even more complicated. II **rizarse** vr (pelo) to curl, go curly.

rizo nm 1 (de pelo) curl. 2 (en el agua) ripple.

RNE nf abr de **Radio Nacional de España**.

róbalo nm (pez) bass.

robar vtr 1 (objeto) to steal; (banco, persona) to rob; (casa) to burgle; fig **en aquel supermercado te roban**, they really rip you off in that supermarket. 2 Naipes to draw.

roble nm oak (tree).

robledal, robledo nm oak grove o wood.

robo nm robbery, theft; (en casa) burglary; fam (timo) rip-off.

robot nm (pl **robots**) robot; **r. de cocina**, food processor.

robótica nf robotics sing.

robustecer [33] vtr to strengthen.

robusto,-a adj robust, sturdy.

roca nf rock.

rocalla nf pebbles pl, stone chippings pl.

rocambolesco,-a adj incredible, farfetched.

roce nm 1 (fricción) rubbing; (en la piel) chafing. 2 (marca) (en la pared etc) scuff mark; (en la piel) chafing mark, graze. 3 (contacto ligero) brush, light touch. 4 fam (trato entre personas) contact. 5 fam (discusión) brush.

rociar [29] vtr (salpicar) to spray, sprinkle.

rocín nm nag, hack.

rocío nm dew.

Rocosas npl **las R.**, the Rockies.

rocoso,-a adj rocky, stony.

rodaballo nm (pez) turbot.

rodado,-a adj 1 (piedra) smooth, rounded; **canto r.**, boulder. 2 **tráfico r.**, road traffic, vehicular traffic.

rodaja nf slice; **en rodajas**, sliced.

rodaje nm 1 (filmación) filming, shooting. 2 Aut running in.

Ródano n **el R.**, the Rhone.

rodante adj rolling.

rodar [2] I vtr (película etc) to film, shoot. II vi to roll, turn.

rodear I vtr to surround, encircle. II **rodearse** vr to surround oneself (**de**, with).

rodeo nm 1 (desvío) detour. 2 (al hablar)

evasiveness; **andarse con rodeos**, to beat about the bush; **no andarse con rodeos**, to get straight to the point. **3** *Am* rodeo.
rodilla *nf* knee; **de rodillas**, *(arrodillado)* kneeling; **hincarse/ponerse de rodillas**, to kneel down, go down on one's knees.
rodillera *nf (de pantalón)* knee patch; *Dep* knee pad.
rodillo *nm* roller; **r. de cocina**, rolling pin.
rododendro *nm* rhododendron.
roedor,-a *nm* rodent.
roer [38] *vtr (hueso)* to gnaw; *(galleta)* to nibble at; *fig (conciencia)* to gnaw at, nag at; *fig* **un hueso duro de r.**, a hard nut to crack.
rogar [2] *vtr (pedir)* to request, ask; *(implorar)* to beg; **hacerse de r.**, to play hard to get; **'se ruega silencio'**, 'silence please'; **rogamos disculpen la molestia**, please forgive the inconvenience.
roído,-a *adj* gnawed, eaten away.
rojizo,-a *adj* reddish.
rojo,-a I *adj* **1** red; **Fin estar en números rojos**, to be in the red. **2** *Pol (comunista)* red. **II** *nm (color)* red; **al r. vivo**, *(caliente)* red-hot; *fig (tenso)* very tense. **III** *nm,f Pol (comunista)* red.
rol *nm* role; **juego de r.**, role play.
rollizo,-a *adj* chubby, plump.
rollo *nm* **1** *(de papel etc)* roll. **2** *fam (pesadez)* drag, bore; **es el mismo de siempre**, it's the same old story; **un r. de libro**, a boring book. **3** *fam (amorío)* affair.
Roma *n* Rome.
romana *nf* calamares a la r., squid in batter.
romance *nm* **1** *(aventura amorosa)* romance. **2** *(idioma)* Romance; *fig* **hablar en r.**, to speak plainly. **3** *Lit* narrative poem, ballad.
románico,-a *adj & nf* Romanesque.
romanticismo *nm* romanticism.
romántico,-a *adj & nm,f* romantic.
rombo *nm* rhombus.
romería *nf Rel* pilgrimage.
romero *nm Bot* rosemary.
romo,-a *adj* **1** blunt. **2** *(nariz)* snub.
rompecabezas *nm inv (juego)* (jigsaw) puzzle; *fig (problema)* riddle, puzzle.
rompeolas *nm inv* breakwater, jetty.
romper *(pp* roto) I *vtr* **1** to break; *(papel, tela)* to tear; *(vajilla, cristal)* to smash, shatter. **2** *(relaciones)* to break off. **II** *vi* **1** *(olas, día)* to break. **2** *(acabar)* to break *(con*, with); **rompió con su novio**, she broke it off with her boyfriend. **3 r. a llorar**, to burst out crying; **r. en llanto**, to burst into tears. **III romperse** *vr* to break; *(papel, tela)* to tear; **se rompió por la mitad**, it broke o split in half; *fig* **r. la cabeza**, to rack one's brains.
ron *nm* rum.
roncar [1] *vi* to snore.

roncha *nf (en la piel)* swelling, lump.
ronco,-a *adj* hoarse; **quedarse r.**, to lose one's voice.
ronda *nf* **1** round; *(patrulla)* patrol. **2** *(carretera)* ring road; *(paseo)* avenue. **3 pagar una r.**, to pay for a round of drinks.
rondar I *vtr* **1** *(vigilar)* to patrol, do the rounds of. **2** *pey (merodear)* to prowl around, hang about. **3** *(estar cerca de)* to be about o approximately; **ronda los cuarenta**, she is about forty. **II** *vi* **1** *(vigilar)* to patrol. **2** *(merodear)* to prowl around, roam around.
ronquera *nf* hoarseness.
ronquido *nm* snore.
ronronear *vi* to purr.
ronroneo *nm* purring.
roña *nf* **1** *(mugre)* filth, dirt. **2** *Vet (sarna)* mange.
roñica *fam* **I** *adj* mean, stingy. **II** *nmf* scrooge, miser.
roñoso,-a *adj* **1** *(mugriento)* filthy, dirty. **2** *Vet (sarnoso)* mangy. **3** *fam (tacaño)* mean, stingy.
ropa *nf* clothes *pl*, clothing; *fig* **a quema r.**, point-blank; **r. blanca**, *(household)* linen; **r. interior**, underwear.
ropaje *nm* clothes.
ropero *nm (armario)* r., wardrobe, *US* (clothes) closet.
roque *nm* **1** *(en ajedrez)* rook. **2** *fam* **quedarse r.**, to fall fast asleep.
rosa I *adj nf (color)* pink; **novela r.**, romantic novel. **II** *nf Bot* rose; *(en la piel)* birthmark; **r. de los vientos**, compass (rose). **III** *nm (color)* pink.
rosáceo,-a *adj* rose-coloured, rosy.
rosado,-a I *adj (color)* pink, rosy; *(vino)* rosé. **II** *nm (vino)* rosé.
rosal *nm* rosebush.
rosaleda *nf* rose garden.
rosario *nm Rel* rosary; *(sarta)* string, series *sing*.
rosbif *nm* roast beef.
rosca *nf* **1** *(de tornillo)* thread; **tapón de r.**, screw top; *fig* **pasarse de r.**, to go too far. **2** *(espiral)* spiral, coil.
rosco *nm (pastel)* ring-shaped roll o pastry; *arg* **no comerse un r.**, not to get one's oats.
rosetón *nm* rose window.
rosquilla *nf* ring-shaped pastry; *fam fig* **venderse como rosquillas**, to sell like hot cakes.
rostro *nm* face; *fam* **tener mucho r.**, to have a lot of nerve; *fam* **¡vaya r.!**, what cheek!
rotación *nf* rotation.
rotativo,-a I *adj* rotary, revolving. **II** *nm* newspaper.
roto,-a I *adj* broken; *(papel)* torn; *(ropa)* in tatters, tattered. **II** *nm (agujero)* hole, tear.
rótula *nf* **1** *Anat* kneecap. **2** *Téc* ball-and-

socket joint.

rotulador *nm* felt-tip pen.

rotular *vtr* to letter, label.

rótulo *nm* (*letrero*) sign, notice; (*titular*) title, heading.

rotundo,-a *adj* categorical; **éxito r.**, resounding success; **un no rotundo**, a flat refusal.

rotura *nf* (*ruptura*) breaking; *Med* fracture.

roturar *vtr* to plough, *US* plow.

roulotte *nf* caravan.

rozadura *nf* scratch, abrasion.

rozamiento *nm* rubbing, friction.

rozar [4] **I** *vtr* to touch, rub against, brush against. **II** *vi* to rub. **III** **rozarse** *vr* to rub, brush (**con**, against).

Rte. *abr de* **remite, remitente**, sender.

RTVE *nf abr de* **Radio Televisión Española.**

rubéola *nf* German measles *pl*, rubella.

rubí *nm* (*pl* **rubíes**) ruby.

rubicundo,-a *adj* rosy, reddish.

rubio,-a I *adj* (*pelo, persona*) fair, blond; **r. de bote**, peroxide blonde; **tabaco r.**, Virginia tobacco. **II** *nm,f* blond.

rublo *nm* rouble.

rubor *nm* blush, flush.

ruborizarse [4] *vr* to blush, go red.

ruboroso,-a *adj* blushing, bashful.

rúbrica *nf* **1** (*de firma*) flourish added to a signature. **2** (*título*) title, heading.

rubricar [1] *vtr* **1** (*firmar*) to sign with a flourish. **2** (*respaldar*) to endorse, ratify.

rudeza *nf* roughness, coarseness.

rudimentario,-a *adj* rudimentary.

rudimento *nm* rudiment.

rudo,-a *adj* rough, coarse.

rueda *nf* **1** wheel; *Aut* **r. de recambio**, spare wheel; *Aut* **r. delantera/trasera**, front/rear wheel; **r. de prensa**, press conference; *fam* **ir sobre ruedas**, to go very smoothly. **2** (*rodaja*) round slice.

ruedo *nm* **1** *Taur* bullring, arena. **2** (*de falda*) hem.

ruego *nm* request.

rufián *nm* villain, scoundrel.

---

rugby *nm* rugby.

rugido *nm* (*de animal*) roar; (*del viento*) howl; (*de tripas*) rumbling *sing*.

rugir [6] *vi* to roar; (*viento*) to howl.

rugoso,-a *adj* rough.

ruibarbo *nm* rhubarb.

ruido *nm* noise; (*sonido*) sound; (*jaleo*) din, row; *fig* stir, commotion; **hacer r.**, to make a noise.

ruidoso,-a *adj* noisy, loud.

ruin *adj* **1** (*vil*) vile, despicable. **2** (*tacaño*) mean, stingy.

ruina *nf* ruin; (*derrumbamiento*) collapse; (*de persona*) downfall.

ruindad *nf* vileness, meanness; (*acto*) mean act, low trick.

ruinoso,-a *adj* dilapidated, tumbledown.

ruiseñor *nm* nightingale.

ruleta *nf* roulette.

rulo *nm* **1** (*para el pelo*) curler, roller. **2** *Culin* rolling pin.

rulot(a) *nf* (*pl* **rulots**) caravan.

Rumanía *n* Rumania, Roumania.

rumba *nf* rhumba, rumba.

rumbo *nm* direction, course; (**con**) **r. a**, bound for, heading for.

rumiante *nm* ruminant.

rumiar [12] **I** *vtr* **1** (*mascar*) to chew. **2** *fig* (*pensar*) to ruminate, reflect on, chew over. **II** *vi* to ruminate, chew the cud.

rumor *nm* **1** rumour, *US* rumor. **2** (*murmullo*) murmur.

rumorearse *v impers* to be rumoured, *US* be rumored.

runrún, runruneo *nm* buzz, noise.

rupestre *adj* **pintura r.**, cave painting.

ruptura *nf* breaking; (*de relaciones*) breaking-off.

rural *adj* rural, country.

Rusia *n* Russia.

ruso,-a *adj & nm,f* Russian.

rústico,-a *adj* rustic, rural.

ruta *nf* route, road.

rutilar *vi* to sparkle.

rutina *nf* routine; **por r.**, as a matter of course.

rutinario,-a *adj* routine.

S

S, s ['ese] *nf* (*la letra*) S,s.

S *abr de* **Sur**, South, S.

S. *abr de* **San** *o* **Santo**, Saint, St.

s. *abr de* **siglo**, century, c.

S.A. *abr de* **Sociedad Anónima**, PLC, plc.

sábado *nm* Saturday.

sabana *nf* savannah.

sábana *nf* sheet; *fam* **se me pegaron las sábanas**, I overslept.

sabandija *nf* (*insecto*) creepy-crawly; (*persona*) creep.

sabañón *nm* chilblain.

---

sabático,-a *adj* sabbatical.

sabelotodo *nmf inv* know-all.

saber¹ *nm* knowledge.

saber² [21] **I** *vtr* **1** to know; **hacer s.**, to inform; **para que lo sepas**, for your information; **que yo sepa**, as far as I know; **vete tú a s.**, goodness knows; **¡y yo qué sé!**, how should I know!; **fig a s.**, namely. **2** (*tener habilidad*) to be able to; **¿sabes cocinar?**, can you cook?; **¿sabes hablar inglés?**, can you speak English? **3** (*enterarse*) to learn, find out; **lo supe**

ayer, I found this out yesterday. II *vi* 1
(*tener sabor a*) to taste (a, of); **sabe a fre-**
sa, it tastes of strawberries; *fig* **me sabe**
mal, I feel guilty o bad about that. 2 *Am*
(*soler*) to be accustomed to.
sabido,-a *adj* known; **como es s.**, as
everyone knows.
sabiduría *nf* wisdom.
sabiendas (a) *loc adv* **lo hizo a s.**, he did
it in the full knowledge of what he was
doing; **a s. de que ...**, knowing full well
that ....
sabihondo,-a *fam* *nm,f* (*sabelotodo*)
know-all; (*pedante*) pedant.
sabio,-a I *adj* (*prudente*) wise. II *nm,f*
scholar.
sabiondo,-a *adj fam* → **sabihondo,-a**.
sable *nm* sabre, *US* saber.
sabor *nm* (*gusto*) taste, flavour, *US* flavor;
con s. a limón, lemon-flavoured; **sin s.**,
tasteless; **me deja mal s. de boca**, it
leaves a bad taste in my mouth.
saborear *vtr* (*degustar*) to taste; *fig* (*apre-*
ciar) to savour, *US* savor.
sabotaje *nm* sabotage.
saboteador,-a *nm,f* saboteur.
sabotear *vtr* to sabotage.
sabré *indic fut* → **saber**.
sabroso,-a *adj* 1 tasty; (*delicioso*) delicious. 2 (*agradable*) delightful.
sabueso *nm* bloodhound.
sacacorchos *nm inv* corkscrew.
sacamuelas *nm inv fam* dentist.
sacapuntas *nm inv* pencil sharpener.
sacar [1] *vtr* 1 to take out; (*con más*
fuerza) to pull out; **s. dinero del banco**,
to withdraw money from the bank; **s. la**
lengua, to stick one's tongue out; *fig* **s.**
faltas a algo, to find fault with sth; *fig* **s.**
adelante, to help to get on; **s. provecho**
de algo, to benefit from sth; **s. algo en**
claro o **en limpio**, to make sense of sth.
2 (*obtener*) to get; (*dinero*) to get, make;
(*conclusiones*) to draw, reach; (*entrada*) to
get, buy. 3 (*producto*) to bring out; (*nueva*
moda) to bring in; (*libro, disco*) to bring
out. 4 (*fotografía*) to take; (*fotocopia*) to
make. 5 *Ten* to serve; *Ftb* to kick off.
sacarina *nf* saccharin.
sacerdotal *adj* priestly.
sacerdote *nm* priest; **sumo s.**, high
priest.
saciar [12] *vtr* to satiate; (*sed*) to quench;
(*deseos, hambre*) to satisfy; (*ambiciones*) to
fulfil, *US* fulfill.
saciedad *nf* satiety; **repetir algo hasta la**
s., to repeat sth ad nauseam.
saco *nm* 1 sack; **s. de dormir**, sleeping
bag. 2 *Mil* **entrar a s. en una ciudad**, to
pillage a town. 3 *Am* (*chaqueta*) jacket.
sacralizar [4] *vtr* to consecrate.
sacramento *nm* sacrament.
sacrificar [1] I *vtr* to sacrifice. II **sa-**
crificarse *vr* to make a sacrifice o sa-

crifices.
sacrificio *nm* sacrifice.
sacrilegio *nm* sacrilege.
sacrílego,-a *adj* sacrilegious.
sacristán *nm* verger, sexton.
sacristía *nf* vestry, sacristy.
sacro,-a *adj* sacred.
sacudida *nf* 1 shake; (*espasmo*) jolt, jerk;
s. eléctrica, electric shock. 2 (*de terremo-*
to) tremor.
sacudir *vtr* 1 (*agitar*) to shake; (*alfombra,*
sábana) to shake out; (*arena, polvo*) to
shake off. 2 (*golpear*) to beat. 3 (*conmo-*
ver) to shock, stun.
sádico,-a I *adj* sadistic. II *nm,f* sadist.
sadismo *nm* sadism.
sadomasoquista I *adj* sadomasochistic.
II *nmf* sadomasochist.
saeta *nf* 1 (*dardo*) dart. 2 (*canción*)
popular religious song.
safari *nm* (*cacería*) safari; (*parque*) safari
park.
sagacidad *nf* *fml* (*listeza*) cleverness;
(*astucia*) astuteness, shrewdness.
sagaz *adj* (*listo*) clever; (*astuto*) astute,
shrewd.
Sagitario *nm* Sagittarius.
sagrado,-a *adj* sacred.
sagrario *nm* tabernacle.
Sáhara *n* Sahara.
saharaui *adj & nmf* Saharan.
sahariana *nf* safari jacket.
sainete *nm* *Teat* comic sketch, one-act
farce.
sajón,-ona *adj & nm,f* Saxon.
sal *nf* 1 salt; **s. fina**, table salt; **s. gema**,
salt crystals; **s. gorda**, cooking salt. 2 *fig*
(*gracia*) wit.
sal *imperat* → **salir**.
sala *nf* room; (*en un hospital*) ward; *Jur*
courtroom. **s. de estar**, lounge, living
room; **s. de espera**, waiting room; **s. de**
exposiciones, exhibition hall; **s. de**
fiestas, nightclub, discotheque; **s. de**
lectura, reading room.
salado,-a *adj* 1 (*con sal*) salted; (*con exceso*
de sal) salty; **agua salada**, salt water. 2
fig (*encantador*) charming. 3 *Am* (*infortu-*
nado) unlucky.
salamandra *nf* salamander.
salamanquesa *nf* gecko.
salame, salami *nm* salami.
salar *vtr* to salt, add salt to.
salarial *adj* salary, wage.
salario *nm* salary, wages *pl*; **s. mínimo**,
minimum wage.
salazón *nm* salted meat o fish.
salchicha *nf* sausage.
salchichón *nm* (salami-type) sausage.
saldar *vtr* 1 *Fin* (*cuenta*) to settle; (*deuda*)
to pay off. 2 *Com* (*vender barato*) to sell
off. 3 *fig* (*diferencias*) to settle, resolve.
saldo *nm* 1 **saldos**, sales; **a precio de s.**,
at bargain prices. 2 *Fin* balance. 3 (*de*

una deuda) liquidation, settlement. **4** *(resto de mercancía)* remainder, leftover.

saldré *indic fut* → **salir**.

saledizo,-a *adj* projecting.

salero *nm* **1** *(recipiente)* saltcellar. **2** *fig (gracia)* charm.

salgo *indic pres* → **salir**.

salida *nf* **1** *(partida)* departure; *(puerta etc)* exit, way out; **callejón sin s.,** dead end; **s. de emergencia,** emergency exit. **2** *Dep* start; **línea de s.,** starting line; **s. nula,** false start. **3** **te vi a la s. del cine,** I saw you leaving the cinema. **4** *(de un astro)* rising; **s. del sol,** sunrise. **5** *(profesional)* opening; *Com* outlet. **6** *(recurso)* solution, way out; **no tengo otra s.,** I have no other option. **7** *fam (ocurrencia)* witty remark, witticism. **8** *Inform* output.

salido,-a *adj* **1** prominent, projecting. **2** *vulg (persona)* horny.

saliente *nm* **1** projecting, prominent; *fig* outstanding. **2** *(cesante)* outgoing.

salina *nf* salt mine.

salino,-a *adj* saline.

salir [22] **I** *vi* **1** *(de un sitio)* to go out, leave; *(venir de dentro)* to come out; **salió de la habitación,** she left the room; **s. de la carretera,** to turn off the road. **2** *(tren etc)* to depart. **3** *(novios)* to go out *(con,* with.) **4** *(aparecer)* to appear; *(revista, disco)* to come out; *(ley)* to come in; *(trabajo, vacante)* to come up. **5** *(resultar)* to turn out, turn out to be; **el pequeño les ha salido muy listo,** their son has turned out to be very clever; **¿cómo te salió el examen?,** how did your exam go?; **s. ganando,** to come out ahead or on top; **salió presidente,** he was elected president. **6** **s. a,** *(precio)* to come to, work out at; **s. barato/caro,** to work out cheap/expensive. **7** **ha salido al abuelo,** she takes after her grandfather. **8** *(problema)* to work out; **esta cuenta no me sale,** I can't work this sum out. **8** **¡con qué cosas sales!,** the things you come out with! **II salirse** *vr* **1** *(líquido, gas)* to leak (out); *fig* **s. de lo normal,** to be out of the ordinary; **se salió de la carretera,** he went off the road. **2** *fam* **s. con la suya,** to get one's own way.

saliva *nf* saliva.

salivar *vi* to salivate.

salivazo *nm* spit.

salmantino,-a **I** *adj* of o from Salamanca. **II** *nm,f* native o inhabitant of Salamanca.

salmo *nm* psalm.

salmón **I** *nm (pescado)* salmon. **II** *adj inv (color)* salmon pink, salmon.

salmonete *nm (pescado)* red mullet.

salmorejo *nm (salsa)* sauce made from vinegar, water, pepper and salt.

salmuera *nf* brine.

salobre *adj (agua)* brackish; *(gusto)* salty, briny.

salón *nm* **1** *(en una casa)* lounge, sitting room. **2 s. de actos,** assembly hall; **s. de baile,** dance hall. **3 s. de belleza,** beauty salon; **s. de té,** tearoom, teashop. **4 s. del automóvil,** motor show.

salpicadura *nf* splashing.

salpicar [1] *vtr* **1** *(rociar)* to splash; **me salpicó el abrigo de barro,** he splashed mud on my coat. **2** *fig (esparcir)* to sprinkle.

salpicón *nm* **1** splash. **2** *Culin* cocktail.

salpimentar [1] *vtr* to season.

salpullido *nm* rash.

salsa *nf* **1** sauce; *(de carne)* gravy; *fig* **en su (propia) s.,** in one's element. **2** *Mús Dep* jumper.

saltador,-a *nm,f Dep* jumper.

saltamontes *nm inv* grasshopper.

saltar **I** *vtr* **1** *(obstáculo, valla)* to jump (over). **II** *vi* **1** to jump; *fig* **s. a la vista,** to be obvious. **2** *(cristal etc)* to break, shatter; *(plomos)* to go, blow. **3** *(desprenderse)* to come off. **4** *(encolerizarse)* to explode, blow up; **por menos de nada salta,** the smallest thing makes him explode. **III saltarse** *vr* **1** *(omitir)* to skip, miss out; **s. el semáforo/turno,** to jump the lights/the queue. **2** *(botón)* to come off; **se me saltaron las lágrimas,** tears came to my eyes.

salteado,-a *adj* **1** *(espaciado)* spaced out. **2** *Culin* sauté, sautéed.

saltear *vtr Culin* to sauté.

saltimbanqui *nmf* acrobat, tumbler.

salto *nm* **1** *(acción)* jump, leap; *fig (paso adelante)* leap forward; **a saltos,** in leaps and bounds; **dar** o **pegar un s.,** to jump, leap; **de un s.,** in a flash; *fig* **a s. de mata,** every now and then; **s. de agua,** waterfall; **s. de cama,** negligée. **2** *Dep* jump; **s. de altura,** high jump; **s. de longitud,** long jump; **s. mortal,** somersault.

saltón,-ona *adj* prominent; **ojos saltones,** bulging eyes.

salubre *adj* salubrious.

salubridad *nf* healthiness; **por razones de s.,** for health reasons.

salud *nf* health; **beber a la s. de algn,** to drink to sb's health; *fam* **¡s.!,** cheers!

saludable *adj* **1** *(sano)* healthy, wholesome. **2** *fig (beneficioso)* good, beneficial.

saludar *vtr* **1** *(decir hola a)* to say hello to, to greet; **saluda de mi parte a,** give my regards to; **le saluda atentamente,** *(en una carta)* yours faithfully. **2** *Mil* to salute.

saludo *nm* **1** greeting; **un s. de,** best wishes from. **2** *Mil* salute.

salva *nf Mil* volley.

salvación *nf* salvation.

salvado *nm* bran. *#*

salvador,-a **I** *nm,f (salvador)* saviour; *(rescatador)* rescuer. **II** *nm* **El S.,** El Salvador.

salvadoreño,-a *adj* & *nm,f* Salvadoran,

Salvadorian.

salvaguarda *nf* → **salvaguardia**.

salvaguardar *vtr* to safeguard (de, from), protect (de, from).

salvajada *nf* brutal act.

salvaje *adj* 1 *Bot* wild, uncultivated; *Zool* wild; (*pueblo, tribu*) savage, uncivilized. 2 *fam* (*violento*) savage, wild.

salvajismo *nm* savagery.

salvamento, salvamiento *nm* rescue.

salvar I *vtr* 1 to save, rescue (de, from). 2 (*obstáculo*) to clear; (*dificultad*) to get round, overcome. 3 (*exceptuar*) to exclude, except; **salvando ciertos errores**, except for a few mistakes. II **salvarse** *vr* 1 (*sobrevivir*) to survive, come out alive; *fam* (*escaparse*) to escape (de, from); **¡sálvese quien pueda!**, every man for himself!; *fam* **s. por los pelos**, to have a narrow escape. 2 *Rel* to be saved, save one's soul.

salvavidas *nm inv* life belt.

salvedad *nf* 1 (*excepción*) exception. 2 (*reserva*) proviso.

salvia *nf Bot* sage.

salvo,-a I *adj* unharmed, safe; **a s.**, safe. II *adv* (*exceptuando*) except (for); **s. que**, unless.

salvoconducto *nm* safe-conduct.

san *adj* saint; → **santo,-a**.

sanar I *vtr* (*curar*) to cure, heal. II *vi* 1 (*persona*) to recover, get better. 2 (*herida*) to heal.

sanatorio *nm* sanatorium.

sanción *nf* 1 sanction. 2 (*aprobación*) sanction, approval. 3 *Jur* penalty.

sancionar *vtr* 1 (*castigar*) to penalize. 2 (*aprobar*) to sanction.

sancochar *vtr* to parboil; *Am* to boil meat in water and salt.

sandalia *nf* sandal.

sándalo *nm* sandalwood.

sandez *nf* piece of nonsense.

sandía *nf* watermelon.

sandwich *nm* sandwich.

sandwichera *nf* toasted sandwich maker.

saneamiento *nm* (*de terreno*) drainage, draining; (*de una empresa*) reorganisation.

sanear *vtr* (*terrenos*) to drain; (*empresa*) to reorganise.

sangrar I *vtr* 1 to bleed. 2 *fam* (*sacar dinero*) to bleed dry. II *vi* to bleed.

sangre *nf* blood; **donar s.**, to give blood; **s. fría**, sang-froid; **a s. fría**, in cold blood.

sangría *nf* 1 *Med* bleeding, bloodletting; *fig* drain. 2 (*timo*) rip-off. 3 (*bebida*) sangría.

sangriento,-a *adj* (*guerra etc*) bloody.

sanguijuela *nf* leech, bloodsucker.

sanguinario,-a *adj* bloodthirsty.

sanguíneo,-a *adj* blood; **grupo s.**, blood group.

sanidad *nf* health; **Ministerio de S.**,

Department of Health.

sanitario,-a I *adj* health. II *nm* toilet.

sano,-a *adj* 1 (*bien de salud*) healthy; **s. y salvo**, safe and sound. 2 (*comida*) healthy, wholesome. 3 **en su s. juicio**, in one's right mind.

santiamén *nm fam* **en un s.**, in a flash, in no time at all.

santidad *nf* saintliness, holiness.

santificar *vtr* to sanctify.

santiguarse [22] *vr* to cross oneself.

santo,-a I *adj* 1 holy, sacred. 2 (*bueno*) saintly; **un s. varón**, a saint. II *nm,f* 1 saint; *fam* **¡por todos los santos!**, for heaven's sake!; *fig* **se me fue el s. al cielo**, I clean forgot. 2 (*día onomástico*) saint's day; *fig* **¿a s. de qué?**, why on earth?

santuario *nm* sanctuary, shrine.

saña *nf* fury; **con s.**, furiously.

sapo *nm* toad; *fam* **echar sapos y culebras**, to rant and rave.

saque *nm* 1 *Ftb* **s. inicial**, kick-off; **s. de banda**, throw-in; **s. de esquina**, corner kick. 2 *Ten* service.

saquear *vtr* (*ciudad*) to sack, plunder; (*casas, tiendas*) to loot.

saqueo *nm* (*de ciudades*) sacking, plundering; (*de casa, tienda*) looting.

S.A.R. *abr de* **Su Alteza Real**, His o Her Royal Highness, H.R.H.

sarampión *nm* measles *pl*.

sarao *nm* knees-up.

sarcasmo *nm* sarcasm.

sarcástico,-a *adj* sarcastic.

sarcófago *nm* sarcophagus.

sardana *nf* sardana (Catalan dance and music).

sardina *nf* sardine.

sardónico,-a *adj* sardonic.

sargento *nm* sergeant.

sarmiento *nm* vine shoot.

sarna *nf Med* scabies *sing*; *Zool* mange.

sarpullido *nm* rash.

sarracina *nf* massacre.

sarro *nm* (*sedimento*) deposit; (*en los dientes*) tartar; (*en la lengua*) fur.

sarta *nf* string.

sartén *nf* frying pan, *US* skillet; *fig* **tener la s. por el mango**, to have the upper hand.

sastre *nm* tailor.

Satanás *nm* Satan.

satánico,-a *adj* satanic.

satélite *nm* satellite; *fig* **país s.**, satellite state; **televisión vía s.**, satellite TV.

satén *nm* satin.

satinar *vtr* to gloss, make glossy.

sátira *nf* satire.

satírico,-a *adj* satirical.

satirizar [4] *vtr* to satirize.

satisfacción *nf* satisfaction; **s. de un deseo**, fulfilment of a desire.

satisfacer [15] (*pp* **satisfecho**) *vtr* 1 (*de*-

seos, necesidades) to satisfy. **2** (*requisitos*) to meet, satisfy. **3** (*deuda*) to pay.

satisfactorio,-a *adj* satisfactory.

satisfecho,-a *adj* satisfied; **me doy por s.**, that's good enough for me; **s. de sí mismo**, self-satisfied, smug.

saturar *vtr* to saturate.

Saturno *nm* Saturn.

sauce *nm* willow; **s. llorón**, weeping willow.

saudí, saudita *adj & nmf* Saudi; **Arabia Saudita**, Saudi Arabia.

sauna *nf* sauna.

savia *nf* sap.

saxo *nm* Mús fam sax.

saxofón *nm* saxophone.

saxofonista *nmf* saxophonist.

sayo *nm* cassock, smock.

sazonar *vtr* to season, flavour, US flavor.

s/c. *abr de* su cuenta, your account.

Sdad. *abr de* sociedad, Society, Soc.

se¹ *pron* **1** (*reflexivo*) (*objeto directo*) (*a él mismo*) himself; (*animal*) itself; (*a ella misma*) herself; (*animal*) itself; (*a usted mismo*) yourself; (*a ellos mismos*) themselves; (*a ustedes mismos*) yourselves. **2** (*objeto indirecto*) (*a él mismo*) (to o for) himself; (*animal*) (to o for) itself; (*a ella misma*) (to o for) herself; (*animal*) (to o for) itself; (*a usted mismo*) (to o for) yourself; (*a ellos mismos*) (to o for) themselves; (*a ustedes mismos*) (to o for) yourselves; **se compró un nuevo coche**, he bought himself a new car; **todos los días se lava el pelo**, she washes her hair every day. **3** (*recíproco*) one another, each other. **4** (*voz pasiva*) **el vino se guarda en cubas**, wine is kept in casks. **5** (*impersonal*) **nunca se sabe**, you never know; **se habla inglés**, English spoken; **se dice que ...**, it is said that ....

se² *pron* pers (*a él*) (to o for) him; (*a ella*) (to o for) her; (*a usted o ustedes*) (to o for) you; (*a ellos*) (to o for) them; **se lo diré en cuanto les vea**, I'll tell them as soon as I see them; **¿se lo explico?**, shall I explain it to you?; **¿se lo has dado ya?**, have you given it to him yet?

se¹ *indic pres* → saber.

se² *imperat* → ser.

S.E. *abr de* Su Excelencia, His o Her Excellency, HE.

sea *subj pres* → ser.

sebo *nm* (*grasa*) fat.

secado *nm* drying.

secador,-a *nm* dryer, drier; **s. de pelo**, hairdryer. **II** *nf* tumble dryer.

secano *nm* dry land.

secante *adj* papel s., blotting paper.

secar |11| **I** *vtr* to dry. **II secarse** *vr* **1** to dry; sécate, dry yourself; **s. las manos**, to dry one's hands. **2** (*marchitarse*) to dry up, wither.

sección *nf* section.

seco,-a *adj* **1** dry; **frutos secos**, dried fruit; **limpieza en s.**, dry-cleaning; *fig* **a palo s.**, on its own; *fig* **a secas**, just, only. **2** (*tono*) curt, sharp; (*golpe, ruido*) sharp; *fig* **frenar en s.**, to pull up sharply; *fig* **parar en s.**, to stop dead. **3** (*delgado*) skinny.

secreción *nf* secretion.

secretaría *nf* (*oficina*) secretary's office; **S. de Estado**, State Department.

secretariado *nm* **1** (*oficina*) secretariat. **2** Educ secretarial course.

secretario,-a *nm,f* secretary.

secreto,-a I *adj* secret; **en s.**, in secret, secretly. **II** *nm* secret; **guardar un s.**, to keep a secret; **con mucho s.**, in great secrecy.

secta *nf* sect.

sectario,-a *adj* sectarian.

sector *nm* **1** sector. **2** (*zona*) area; **un s. de la ciudad**, an area of the city.

sectorial *adj* sectoral.

secuela *nf* consequence.

secuencia *nf* sequence.

secuestrador,-a *nm,f* **1** (*de persona*) kidnapper; (*de un avión*) hijacker. **2** Jur sequestrator.

secuestrar *vtr* **1** (*persona*) to kidnap; (*aviones*) to hijack. **2** Jur to confiscate.

secuestro *nm* **1** (*de persona*) kidnapping; (*de un avión*) highjacking. **2** Jur confiscation.

secular *adj* **1** Rel secular, lay. **2** (*antiquísimo*) ancient, age-old.

secundar *vtr* to back.

secundario,-a *adj* secondary.

secuoya *nf* Bot redwood, sequoia; **s. gigante**, giant sequoia.

sed *nf* thirst; **tener s.**, to be thirsty.

seda *nf* silk.

sedal *nm* fishing line.

sedante *adj & nm* sedative.

sede *nf* **1** headquarters, head office; (*de gobierno*) seat. **2** **la Santa S.**, the Holy See.

sedentario,-a *adj* sedentary.

sedición *nf* sedition.

sedicioso,-a I *adj* rebellious. **II** rebel.

sediento,-a *adj* thirsty; *fig* **s. de poder**, hungry for power.

sedimentarse *vr* to settle.

sedimentario,-a *adj* sedimentary.

sedimento *nm* sediment, deposit.

sedoso,-a *adj* silky, silken.

seducción *nf* seduction.

seducir |10| *vtr* to seduce; (*persuadir*) to tempt.

seductor,-a I *adj* seductive; (*persuasivo*) tempting. **II** *nm,f* seducer.

segadora *nf* (*máquina*) reaper, harvester.

segar |1| *vtr* to reap, cut.

seglar I *adj* secular, lay. **II** *nmf* lay person; (*hombre*) layman; (*mujer*) laywoman.

segmento *nm* segment.
segregación *nf* 1 (*separación*) segregation. 2 (*secreción*) secretion.
segregar [7] *vtr* 1 (*separar*) to segregate. 2 (*secretar*) to secrete.
seguida *nf* en s., immediately, straight away.
seguido,-a *adj* 1 (*continuo*) continuous. 2 (*consecutivo*) consecutive, successive; **tres veces seguidas**, on three consecutive occasions; **tres lunes seguidos**, three Mondays in a row.
seguido *adv* straight; **todo s.**, straight on, straight ahead.
seguidor,-a *nm,f* follower.
seguimiento *nm* 1 pursuit. 2 *Prensa* indepth coverage. 3 **estación de s.** (*espacial*), tracking station.
seguir [6] *vtr* 1 to follow. 2 (*camino*) to continue. 3 (*perseguir*) to chase. II *vi* 1 to follow. 2 s. + *ger*, (*continuar*) to continue, go on, keep on; **siguió hablando**, he continued o went on o kept on speaking. 3 s. + *adj/pp*, to continue to be, be still; **sigo resfriado**, I've still got the cold; **sigue con vida**, he's still alive. III **seguirse** *vtr* to follow, ensue.
según I *prep* 1 according to; **s. la Biblia**, according to the Bible. 2 (*en función de*) depending on; **varía s. el tiempo (que haga)**, it varies depending on the weather. II *adv* 1 depending on; **s. están las cosas**, depending on how things stand; **¿vendrás mañana? - s.**, will you come tomorrow? - it depends. 2 (*tal como*) just as; **estaba s. lo dejé**, it was just as I had left it. 3 (*a medida que*) as; **s. iba leyendo ...**, as I read on ....
segundero *nm* second hand.
segundo,-a[1] I *adj* second; *fig* **decir algo con segundas (intenciones)**, to say sth with a double meaning. II *nm,f* (*de una serie*) second (one).
segundo[2] *nm* (*tiempo*) second; **sesenta segundos**, sixty seconds.
seguramente *adv* 1 (*seguro*) surely. 2 (*probablemente*) most probably; **s. no lloverá**, it isn't likely to rain.
seguridad *nf* 1 security; **cerradura de s.**, security lock. 2 (*física*) safety; **s. en carretera**, road safety; **para mayor s.**, to be on the safe side. 3 (*confianza*) confidence; **s. en sí mismo**, self-confidence. 4 (*certeza*) sureness; **con toda s.**, most probably; **tener la s. de que ...**, to be certain that .... 5 **S. Social**, ≈ Social Security, *GB* National Health Service. 6 (*fiabilidad*) reliability.
seguro,-a I *adj* 1 (*cierto*) sure; **estoy s. de que ...**, I am sure that ...; **dar algo por s.**, to take sth for granted. 2 (*libre de peligro*) safe; **fig ir sobre s.**, to play safe. 3 (*protegido*) secure. 4 (*fiable*) reliable. **s. está segura de ella misma**, she has self-

confidence. 6 (*firme*) steady, firm. II *nm* 1 *Seg* insurance; **s. a todo riesgo**, fully comprehensive insurance; **s. contra terceros**, third party insurance; **s. de vida**, life insurance. 2 (*dispositivo*) safety catch o device. III *adv* for sure, definitely.
seis *adj & nm* inv six.
seiscientos,-as *adj & nm,f* six hundred.
seísmo *nm* (*terremoto*) earthquake; (*temblor de tierra*) earth tremor.
selección *nf* 1 selection. 2 *Dep* team.
seleccionador,-a *nm,f* 1 selector. 2 *Dep* manager.
seleccionar *vtr* to select.
selectividad *nf* selectivity; *Univ* (*prueba de*) s., entrance examination.
selectivo,-a *adj* selective.
selecto,-a *adj* select; **ambiente s.**, exclusive atmosphere.
self-service *nm* self-service cafeteria.
selva *nf* jungle.
sellar *vtr* (*documento*) to seal; (*carta*) to stamp.
sello *nm* 1 (*de correos*) stamp; (*para documentos*) seal. 2 (*precinto*) seal.
semáforo *nm* traffic lights *pl*.
semana *nf* week; **entre s.**, during the week; **S. Santa**, Holy Week.
semanal *adj & nm* weekly.
semanario *nm* weekly magazine.
semblante *nf lit* (*cara*) face; *fig* (*aspecto*) look.
sembrado *nm* sown field.
sembrar [26] *vtr* 1 *Agr* to sow. 2 *fig* **s. el pánico**, to spread panic.
semejante I *adj* 1 (*parecido*) similar; **nunca he visto nada s.**, I've never seen anything like it. 2 *pey* (*comparativo*) such; **s. desvergüenza**, such insolence. II *nm* (*prójimo*) fellow being.
semejanza *nf* similarity, likeness.
semen *nm* semen.
semental *nm* stud.
semestral *adj* half-yearly.
semestre *nm* six-month period, semester.
semicírculo *nm* semicircle.
semifinal *nf* semifinal.
semifinalista *nmf* semifinalist.
semilla *nf* seed.
semillero *nm* seedbed.
seminario *nm* 1 *Educ* seminar. 2 *Rel* seminary.
sémola *nf* semolina.
Sena *n* el S., the Seine.
senado *nm* senate.
senador,-a *nm,f* senator.
sencillez *nf* simplicity.
sencillo,-a *adj* 1 (*fácil*) simple, easy. 2 (*natural*) natural, unaffected. 3 (*billete*) single. 4 (*sin adornos*) simple, plain.
senda *nf*, **sendero** *nm* path.
sendos,-as *adj pl* one each; **con sendas carteras**, each carrying a briefcase.

senil *adj* senile.

seno *nm* **1** (*pecho*) breast. **2** *fig* bosom, heart; **en el s. de**, within. **3** *Mat* sine.

sensación *nf* **1** sensation, feeling; **tengo la s. de que ...**, I have a feeling that .... **2** (*impresión*) sensation; **causar s.**, to cause a sensation.

sensacional *adj* sensational.

sensacionalista *adj* sensationalist; **prensa s.**, gutter press.

sensato,-a *adj* sensible.

sensibilizar [4] *vtr* to make aware; **s. a la opinión pública**, to increase public awareness.

sensible *adj* **1** sensitive. **2** (*perceptible*) perceptible. ◆**sensiblemente** *adv* noticeably, considerably.

sensiblero,-a *adj* over-sentimental, mawkish.

sensitivo,-a *adj* sense; **órgano s.**, sense organ.

sensorial, sensorio,-a *adj* sensory.

sensual *adj* sensual.

sensualidad *nf* sensuality.

sentada *nf* **1** sitting. **2** *fam* (*protesta*) sit-in (demonstration).

sentado,-a *adj* (*establecido*) established, settled; **dar algo por s.**, to take sth for granted; **dejar s. que ...**, to make it clear that ....

sentar [1] **I** *vtr* **1** to sit. **2** (*establecer*) to establish; **s. las bases**, to lay the foundations. **II** *vi* **1** (*color, ropa etc*) to suit; **el pelo corto le sienta mal**, short hair doesn't suit you. **2** **s. bien/mal a**, (*comida*) to agree/disagree with; **la sopa te sentará bien**, the soup will do you good. **3** **le sentó mal la broma**, she didn't like the joke. **III sentarse** *vr* to sit, sit down.

sentencia *nf* **1** sentence; **visto para s.**, ready for judgement. **2** (*aforismo*) maxim, saying.

sentenciar [12] *vtr* *Jur* to sentence (a, to).

sentido,-a **I** *nm* **1** sense; **los cinco sentidos**, the five senses; **s. común**, common sense; **s. del humor**, sense of humour. **2** (*significado*) meaning; **doble s.**, double meaning; **no tiene s.**, it doesn't make sense. **3** (*dirección*) direction; **de s. único**, one-way. **4** (*conciencia*) consciousness; **perder el s.**, to faint. **II** *adj* (*hondo*) deeply felt; *fml* **mi más s. pésame**, my deepest sympathy.

sentimental I *adj* sentimental; **vida s.**, love life. **II** *nmf* sentimental person.

sentimiento *nm* **1** feeling. **2** (*pesar*) sorrow, grief; *fml* **le acompaño en el s.**, my deepest sympathy.

sentir[1] *nm* **1** (*sentimiento*) feeling. **2** (*opinión*) opinion, view.

sentir[2] [5] **I** *vtr* **1** to feel; **s. hambre/calor**, to feel hungry/hot. **2** (*lamentar*) to regret, be sorry about; **lo siento** (*mu-*

cho), I'm (very) sorry; **siento molestarle**, I'm sorry to bother you. **II sentirse** *vr* to feel; **me siento mal**, I feel ill; **s. con ánimos de hacer algo**, to feel like doing sth.

senyera *nf* Catalan flag.

seña *nf* **1** mark. **2** (*gesto*) sign; **hacer señas a algn**, to signal to sb. **3** (*indicio*) sign. **3 señas**, (*dirección*) address *sing*.

señal *nf* **1** (*indicio*) sign, indication; **en s. de**, as a sign of, as a token of. **2** (*placa*) sign; **s. de tráfico**, road sign. **3** (*gesto etc*) signal, sign. **4** (*marca*) mark; (*vestigio*) trace. **5** *Tel* tone; **s. de llamada**, dialling *o US* dial tone. **6** *Com* deposit.

señalado,-a *adj* (*importante*) important; **un día s.**, a red-letter day.

señalar *vtr* **1** (*indicar*) to mark, indicate; **s. con el dedo**, to point at. **2** (*resaltar*) to point out. **3** (*precio, fecha*) to fix, arrange.

señor *nm* **1** (*hombre*) man; (*caballero*) gentleman. **2** *Rel* **El S.**, the Lord. **3** (*con apellido*) Mr; (*tratamiento de respeto*) sir; **el Sr. Gutiérrez**, Mr Gutiérrez; **muy s. mío**, (*en carta*) Dear Sir. **4** (*con título*) (*no se traduce*) **el s. ministro**, the Minister.

señora *nf* **1** (*mujer*) woman; *fml* lady; **¡señoras y señores!**, ladies and gentlemen! **2** *Rel* **Nuestra S.**, Our Lady. **3** (*con apellido*) Mrs; (*tratamiento de respeto*) madam; **la Sra. Salinas**, Mrs Salinas; **muy s. mía**, (*en carta*) Dear Madam. **4** (*con título*) (*no se traduce*) **la s. ministra**, the Minister. **5** (*esposa*) wife.

señoría *nf* **1** *Jur* (*hombre*) lordship; (*mujer*) ladyship. **2** *Pol* **sus señorías**, the honourable gentlemen.

señorita *nf* **1** (*joven*) young woman; *fml* young lady. **2** (*tratamiento de respeto*) Miss; **S. Padilla**, Miss Padilla. **3** *Educ* **la s.**, the teacher, Miss.

señuelo *nm* (*en caza*) decoy.

sepa *subj pres* → **saber**.

separación *nf* **1** separation. **2** *Jur* **s. conyugal**, legal separation. **2** (*espacio*) space, gap.

separado,-a *adj* **1** separate; **por s.**, separately, individually. **2** (*divorciado*) separated.

separar I *vtr* **1** to separate. **2** (*desunir*) to detach, remove. **3** (*dividir*) to divide, separate. **4** (*apartar*) to move away. **II separarse** *vr* **1** to separate, part company. **2** (*matrimonio*) to separate. **3** (*apartarse*) to move away (**de**, from).

separata *nf* offprint.

separatismo *nm* separatism.

separatista *adj & nmf* separatist.

sepia **I** *nf* (*pez*) cuttlefish. **II** *adj & nm* (*color*) sepia.

septentrional *adj* northern.

septiembre *nm* September; **el 5 de s.**, the 5th of September; **en s.**, in September.

séptimo,-a *adj & nm,f* seventh; **la** *o* **una séptima parte**, a seventh.

sepulcral *adj* (*silencio*) deathly.

sepulcro *nm* tomb.

sepultura *nf* grave.

sepulturero,-a *nm,f* gravedigger.

sequía *nf* drought.

séquito *nm* entourage, retinue.

SER *nf Rad TV abr de* Sociedad Española de Radiodifusión.

ser¹ *nm* being; **s. humano**, human being; **s. vivo**, living being.

ser² [23] *vi* 1 (+ *adj*) to be; **es alto y rubio**, he is tall and fair; **el edificio es gris**, the building is grey. 2 (+ *profesión*) to be a(n); **Rafael es músico**, Rafael is a musician. 3 **s. de**, (*procedencia*) to be *o* come from; **¿de dónde eres?**, where are you from?, where do you come from? 4 **s. de**, (+ *material*) to be made of. 5 **s. de**, (+ *poseedor*) to belong to; **el perro es de Miguel**, the dog belongs to Miguel; **¿de quién es este abrigo?**, whose coat is this? 6 **s. para**, (*finalidad*) to be for; **esta agua es para lavar**, this water is for washing. 7 (+ *día, hora*) to be; **hoy es dos de noviembre**, today is the second of November; **son las cinco de la tarde**, it's five o'clock. 8 (+ *cantidad*) **¿cuántos estaremos en la fiesta?** how many of us will there be at the party? 9 (*costar*) to be, cost; **¿cuánto es?**, how much is it? 10 (*tener lugar*) to be; **el estreno será mañana**, tomorrow is the opening night. 11 **¿qué es de Gonzalo?**, what has become of Gonzalo? 12 (*auxiliar en pasiva*) to be; **fue asesinado**, he was murdered. 13 (*locuciones*) **¿cómo es eso?**, **¿cómo puede s.?**, how can that be?; **es más**, furthermore; **es que ...**, it's just that ...; **como sea**, anyhow; **lo que sea**, whatever; **o sea**, that is (to say); **por si fuera poco**, to top it all; **sea como sea**, in any case, be that as it may; **a no s. que**, unless; **de no s. por ...**, had it not been for ...; **eso era de esperar**, it was to be expected.

serenarse *vr* to calm down.

serenidad *nf* serenity.

sereno¹ *nm* (*vigilante*) night watchman.

sereno,-a² *adj* 1 calm. 2 *fam* **estar s.**, (*sobrio*) to be sober.

serial *nm Rad TV* serial.

serie *nf* 1 series *sing*; **fabricación en s.**, mass production; **lleva ABS de s.**, it has ABS fitted as standard; **fuera de s.**, out of the ordinary. 2 *Rad TV* series *sing*.

seriedad *nf* 1 seriousness. 2 (*formalidad*) reliability, dependability; **falta de s.**, irresponsibility.

serio,-a *adj* 1 (*severo*) serious; **en s.**, seriously. 2 (*formal*) reliable, responsible.

sermón *nm* sermon.

sermonear *vi & vtr fam* to lecture.

seropositivo,-a *adj* HIV-positive.

serpentear *vi* (*zigzaguear*) to wind one's way, meander.

serpentina *nf* (*de papel*) streamer.

serpiente *nf* snake; **s. de cascabel**, rattlesnake; **s. pitón**, python.

serranía *nf* mountainous area *o* country.

serrar [1] *vtr* to saw.

serrín *nm* sawdust.

serrucho *nm* handsaw.

servicial *adj* helpful, obliging.

servicio *nm* 1 service; **s. a domicilio**, delivery service. 2 *Mil* service; **s. militar**, military service; **estar de s.**, to be on duty. 3 **servicios**, (*retrete*) toilet *sing*, *US* rest room *sing*.

servidor,-a *nm,f* servant; *fam* **un s.**, yours truly.

servil *adj* servile.

servilleta *nf* serviette, napkin.

servilletero *nm* serviette ring, napkin ring.

servio,-a *adj & nm,f* Serbian.

servir [6] I *vtr* to serve; **¿en qué puedo servirle?**, what can I do for you?, may I help you?; **¿te sirvo una copa?**, will I pour you a drink? II *vi* 1 to serve. 2 (*valer*) to be useful, be suitable; **no sirve de nada llorar**, it's no use crying; **ya no sirve**, it's no use; **¿para qué sirve esto?**, what is this (used) for? 3 **s. de**, to serve as, act as. III **servirse** *vr* 1 (*comida etc*) to help oneself. 2 *fml* **sírvase comunicarnos su decisión**, please inform us of your decision.

sésamo *nm* sesame.

sesenta *adj & nm inv* sixty.

sesgar [7] *vtr* 1 (*cortar*) to cut diagonally. 2 (*torcer*) to slant.

sesgo *nm fig* slant, turn; **tomar un s. favorable**, to take a turn for the better.

sesión *nf* 1 (*reunión*) meeting, session; *Jur* session, sitting. 2 *Cin* showing.

seso *nm* brain.

set *nm Ten* set.

seta *nf* (*comestible*) mushroom; **s. venenosa**, toadstool.

setecientos,-as *adj & nm inv* seven hundred.

setenta *adj & nm inv* seventy.

setiembre *nm* September.

seto *nm* hedge.

seudónimo *nm* pseudonym; (*de escritores*) pen name.

severidad *nf* severity.

severo,-a *adj* severe.

Sevilla *n* Seville.

sexismo *nm* sexism.

sexista *adj* sexist.

sexo *nm* 1 sex. 2 (*órgano*) genitals *pl*.

sexólogo,-a *nm,f* sexologist.

sexto,-a *adj & nm* sixth.

sexual *adj* sexual; **vida s.**, sex life.

sexualidad *nf* sexuality.

sexy *adj* sexy.

s/f. *abr de* su favor, your favour o US favor.

shock *nm* shock.

show *nm* show.

si¹ *conj* 1 (*condicional*) if; **como si**, as if; **si no**, if not; **si quieres**, if you like, if you wish. 2 (*pregunta indirecta*) whether, if; **me preguntó si me gustaba**, he asked me if I liked it; **no sé si ir o no**, (*disyuntivo*) I don't know whether to go or not. 3 (*sorpresa*) **¡si está llorando!**, but she's crying!

si² *nm* (*pl* **sis**) *Mús* B: (*en solfeo*) ti.

sí¹ *pron pers* 1 (*singular*) (*él*) himself; (*ella*) herself; (*cosa*) itself; (*plural*) themselves; **de por sí, en sí**, in itself; **hablaban entre sí**, they were talking among themselves o to each other; **por sí mismo**, by himself. 2 (*uno mismo*) oneself; **decir para sí**, to say to oneself.

sí² *adv* 1 yes; **dije que sí**, I said yes, I accepted, I agreed; **porque sí**, just because; **¡que sí!**, yes, I tell you!; **un día sí y otro no**, every other day. 2 (*uso enfático*) (*no se traduce*) **sí que me gusta**, of course I like it; **¡eso sí que no!**, certainly not!. II *nm* (*pl* **síes**) yes; **los síes**, (*en parlamento*) the ayes.

siamés,-esa *nm,f* Siamese twin.

sibarita *nmf* sybarite.

sicario *nm* hired gunman; *fam* hitman.

Sicilia *nf* Sicily.

sico- → psico-.

sicómoro *nm* sycamore.

SIDA *nm* *abr de* síndrome de inmunodeficiencia adquirida, acquired immune deficiency syndrome, AIDS.

sidecar *nm* sidecar.

siderurgia *nf* iron and steel industry.

siderúrgico,-a *adj* iron and steel; **la industria siderúrgica**, the iron and steel industry.

sidra *nf* cider.

siempre *adv* always; **s. pasa lo mismo**, it's always the same; **como s.**, as usual; **a la hora de s.**, at the usual time; **eso es así desde s.**, it has always been like that; **para s.**, for ever; **s. que**, (*cada vez que*) whenever; (*a condición de que*) provided, as long as; **s. y cuando**, provided, as long as.

sien *nf* temple.

sierra *nf* 1 saw; **s. mecánica**, power saw. 2 *Geog* mountain range, sierra.

siervo,-a *nm,f* slave.

siesta *nf* siesta, nap; **dormir la s.**, to have a siesta o an afternoon nap.

siete *adj & nm* seven.

sietemesino,-a *nm,f* seven-month baby, premature baby.

sífilis *nf inv* syphilis.

sifón *nm* siphon; **whisky con s.**, whisky and soda.

sig. *abr de* siguiente, following.

sigilo *nm* secrecy; **entrar con mucho s.**, to tiptoe in.

sigiloso,-a *adj* secretive.

◆**sigilosamente** *adv* (*secretamente*) secretly; **entró s. en la habitación**, she crept o slipped into the room.

sigla *nf* acronym.

siglo *nm* century; **el s. veintiuno**, the twenty-first century; *fam* **hace siglos que no le veo**, I haven't seen him for ages.

signatario,-a *adj & nm,f* signatory.

significación *nf* 1 (*sentido*) meaning. 2 (*importancia*) significance.

significado *nm* meaning.

significar [1] *vtr* to mean.

significativo,-a *adj* significant; (*expresivo*) meaningful.

signo *nm* 1 sign; **s. del zodíaco**, zodiac sign. 2 *Ling* mark; **s. de interrogación**, question mark.

sigo *indic pres* → seguir.

siguiente *adj* following, next; **¡el s.!**, next, please!; **al día s.**, the following day.

sílaba *nf* syllable.

silbar *vi* to whistle; (*abuchear*) to hiss, boo.

silbato *nm* whistle.

silbido *nm* whistle, whistling; (*agudo*) hiss.

silenciador *nm* (*de arma*) silencer; (*de coche, moto*) silencer, US muffler.

silenciar [12] *vtr* 1 (*un sonido*) to muffle. 2 (*noticia*) to hush up.

silencio *nm* silence; **imponer s. a algn**, to make sb be quiet.

silencioso,-a *adj* (*persona*) quiet; (*motor etc*) silent.

silicio *nm* silicon.

silicona *nf* silicone.

silla *nf* 1 chair; **s. de ruedas**, wheelchair; **s. giratoria**, swivel chair. 2 (*de montura*) saddle.

sillín *nm* saddle.

sillón *nm* armchair.

silo *nm* silo.

silueta *nf* silhouette; (*de cuerpo*) figure.

silvestre *adj* wild.

simbólico,-a *adj* symbolic; **precio s.**, token price.

simbolizar [4] *vtr* to symbolize.

símbolo *nm* symbol.

simetría *nf* symmetry.

simétrico,-a *adj* symmetrical.

simiente *nf* seed.

simil *nm* simile.

similar *adj* similar.

similitud *nf* similarity.

simio *nm* monkey.

simpatía *nf* liking, affection; **le tengo mucha s.**, I am very fond of him.

simpático,-a *adj* (*amable*) nice, likeable; **me cae s.**, I like him.

simpatizante *nmf* sympathizer.

simpatizar [4] *vi* 1 to sympathise (con, with). 2 (*llevarse bien*) to hit it off (con, with).

simple I *adj* 1 simple. 2 (*fácil*) simple, easy. 3 (*mero*) mere. 4 (*persona*) simple, simple-minded. **II** *nm* (*persona*) simpleton.

simpleza *nf* simple-mindedness; (*tontería*) nonsense.

simplificar [1] *vtr* to simplify.

simposio *nm* symposium.

simulacro *nm* sham, pretence; **un s. de ataque**, a mock attack.

simular *vtr* to simulate.

simultanear *vtr* to combine; **simultanea el trabajo y los estudios**, he's working and studying at the same time.

simultáneo,-a *adj* simultaneous.

sin *prep* 1 without; **s. dinero/ti**, without money/you; **estamos s. pan**, we're out of bread; **s. hacer nada**, without doing anything; **cerveza s. alcohol**, alcohol-free beer; **s. más ni más**, without further ado. 2 (+ *inf*) **está s. secar**, it hasn't been dried.

sinagoga *nf* synagogue.

sincerarse *vr* to open one's heart (con, to).

sinceridad *nf* sincerity; **con toda s.**, in all sincerity.

sincero,-a *adj* sincere.

sincronizar [4] *vtr* to synchronize.

sindical *adj* trade union, union.

sindicalista *nmf* trade unionist.

sindicato *nm* union, trade union.

síndrome *nm* syndrome.

sinfín *nm* endless number; **un s. de**, lots of.

sinfonía *nf* symphony.

single *nm* single, 7-inch.

singular I *adj* 1 singular. 2 (*excepcional*) exceptional, unique. 3 (*raro*) peculiar, odd. **II** *nm* *Ling* singular; **en s.**, in the singular.

siniestrado,-a *adj* stricken.

siniestro,-a I *adj* sinister, ominous. **II** *nm* disaster, catastrophe.

sino¹ *nm* *fml* fate, destiny.

sino² *conj* 1 but; **no fui a Madrid, s. a Barcelona**, I didn't go to Madrid but to Barcelona. 2 (*excepto*) **nadie s. él**, no-one but him; **no quiero s. que me oigan**, I only want them to listen (to me).

sinónimo,-a I *adj* synonymous. **II** *nm* synonym.

sinóptico,-a *adj* **cuadro s.**, diagram, chart.

sinsabor *nm* (*usu pl*) trouble, worry.

sintético,-a *adj* synthetic.

sintetizador *nm* synthesizer.

sintetizar [4] *vtr* to synthesize.

síntoma *nm* symptom.

sintonía *nf* 1 *Elec Rad* tuning. 2 *Mús Rad* (*de programa*) signature tune. 3 *fig* harmony.

sintonizador *nm* *Rad* tuning knob.

sintonizar [4] *vtr* 1 *Rad* to tune in. 2 (*simpatizar*) to be in tune (con, with).

sinuoso,-a *adj* (*camino*) winding.

sinvergüenza I *adj* (*desvergonzado*) shameless; (*descarado*) cheeky. **II** *nmf* (*desvergonzado*) rogue; (*caradura*) cheeky devil.

sionismo *nm* Zionism.

siquiera I *adv* (*por lo menos*) at least; **ni s.**, not even. **II** *conj* *fml* (*aunque*) although, even though.

sirena *nf* 1 siren, mermaid. 2 (*señal acústica*) siren.

Siria *n* Syria.

sirimiri *nm* fine drizzle.

sirio,-a *adj & nm,f* Syrian.

sirviente,-a *nm,f* servant.

sisar *vtr* (*hurtar*) to pilfer, filch.

sisear *vi* to hiss.

sísmico,-a *adj* seismic.

sismógrafo *nm* seismograph.

sistema *nm* system; **por s.**, as a rule; **s. nervioso**, nervous system; **s. montañoso**, mountain chain.

sistemático,-a *adj* systematic.

sitiar [12] *vtr* to besiege.

sitio¹ *nm* 1 (*lugar*) place; **en cualquier s.**, anywhere; **en todos los sitios**, everywhere; *fig* **quedarse en el s.**, to die. 2 (*espacio*) room; **hacer s.**, to make room.

sitio² *nm* siege; **estado de s.**, state of emergency.

sito,-a *adj* *fml* situated, located.

situación *nf* 1 situation; **su s. económica es buena**, his financial position is good. 2 (*ubicación*) situation, location.

situado,-a *adj* situated; *fig* **estar bien s.**, to have a good position.

situar [30] 1 *vtr* to locate. II **situarse** *vr* to be situated *o* located.

sketch *nm* *Cin Teat* sketch.

s/l *abr de* **su letra** (**de crédito**).

S.L. *abr de* **Sociedad Limitada**, limited company, Ltd.

slip *nm* underpants *pl*.

slogan *nm* slogan.

S.M. *abr de* **Su Majestad**, (*rey*) His Majesty; (*reina*) Her Majesty.

smoking *nm* dinner jacket, *US* tuxedo.

s/n. *abr de* **sin número**.

snob *adj & nmf* → **esnob**.

snobismo *nm* → **esnobismo**.

so¹ *prep* (*bajo*) under; **so pena de**, under penalty of.

so² *nm* *fam* **¡so imbécil!**, you damned idiot!

sobaco *nm* armpit.

sobar *vtr* 1 *fam* (*dormir*) to sleep. 2 *vulg* (*manosear*) to fondle, paw.

soberanía *nf* sovereignty.

soberano,-a I *adj* 1 sovereign. 2 *fam* huge, great. **II** *nm,f* (*monarca*) sovereign.

soberbia *nf* pride.

soberbio,-a *adj* 1 proud. 2 *(magnífico)* splendid, magnificent.

sobón,-ona *nmf fam* **ser un s.**, to be fresh *o* all hands.

sobornar *vtr* to bribe.

soborno *nm (acción)* bribery; *(dinero etc)* bribe.

sobra *nf* 1 **de s.**, *(no necesario)* superfluous; **tener de s.**, to have plenty; **estar de s.**, not to be needed; **saber algo de s.**, to know sth only too well. 2 **sobras**, *(restos)* leftovers.

sobrado,-a *adj (que sobra)* abundant, more than enough; **sobradas veces**, repeatedly; **andar s. de tiempo/dinero**, to have plenty of time/money.
◆**sobradamente** *adv* only too well.

sobrante I *adj* remaining, spare. II *nm* surplus, excess.

sobrar *vi* 1 to be more than enough, *(sing)* be too much, *(pl)* be too many; **sobran tres sillas**, there are three chairs too many; **sobran comentarios**, I've nothing further to add; **fam tú sobras aquí**, you are not wanted here. 2 *(quedar)* to be left over; **ha sobrado carne**, there's still some meat left.

sobrasada *nf* sausage spread.

sobre¹ *nm* 1 *(para carta)* envelope. 2 *(de sopa etc)* packet.

sobre² *prep* 1 *(encima de)* on, upon, on top of. 2 *(por encima de)* over, above. 3 *(acerca de)* about, on. 4 *(aproximadamente)* about; **vendré s. las ocho**, I'll come at about eight o'clock. 5 **s. todo**, especially, above all.

sobre- *pref* super-, over-.

sobrealimentado,-a *adj* overfed.

sobrecarga *nf* overload.

sobrecargar [7] *vtr* to overload.

sobrecogedor,-a *adj* dramatic, awesome.

sobrecoger [5] *vtr (conmover)* to shock.

sobredosis *nf inv* overdose.

sobreentenderse *vr* **se sobreentiende**, that goes without saying.

sobrehumano,-a *adj* superhuman.

sobregiro *nm* overdraft.

sobreimpresión *nf* Fot Cin superimposing.

sobrellevar *vtr* to endure, bear.

sobremesa¹ *nf* afternoon.

sobremesa² *nf* **ordenador de s.**, desktop computer.

sobrenatural *adj* supernatural.

sobrenombre *nm* nickname.

sobrepasar I *vtr* to exceed, surpass; *(rival)* to beat. II **sobrepasarse** *vr* to go too far.

sobrepeso *nm (de carga)* overload, excess weight; *(de persona)* excess weight.

sobreponerse *vr* 1 **s. a**, *(superar)* to overcome. 2 **s. al dolor**, to overcome pain. 2 *(animarse)* to pull oneself together.

sobreproducción *nf* overproduction.

sobresaliente I *nm (nota)* A. II *adj (que destaca)* outstanding, excellent.

sobresalir [22] *vi* stick out, protrude; *fig (destacar)* to stand out, excel.

sobresaltar I *vtr* to startle. II **sobresaltarse** *vr* to be startled, start.

sobresalto *nm (movimiento)* start; *(susto)* fright.

sobreseer [36] *vtr Jur* to stay; **s. una causa**, to stay proceedings.

sobretodo *nm (abrigo)* overcoat; *(guardapolvo)* overalls *pl*.

sobrevalorar *vtr* to overestimate.

sobrevenir [27] *vi* to happen unexpectedly.

sobreviviente I *adj* surviving. II *nmf* survivor.

sobrevivir *vi* to survive.

sobrevolar [2] *vtr* to fly over.

sobriedad *nf* sobriety; *(en la bebida)* soberness.

sobrina *nf* niece.

sobrino *nm* nephew.

sobrio,-a *adj* sober.

socarrón,-ona *nm,f* 1 *(sarcástico)* sarcastic. 2 *(astuto)* sly, cunning.

socavar *vtr fig* to undermine.

socavón *nm (bache)* pothole.

sociable *adj* sociable, friendly.

social *adj* social.

socialdemócrata I *adj* social democratic. II *nmf* social democrat.

socialismo *nm* socialism.

socialista *adj & nmf* socialist.

socializar [4] *vtr* to socialize.

sociedad *nf* 1 society; **s. de consumo**, consumer society. 2 *(asociación)* association, society. 3 Com company; **s. anónima**, public liability company; **s. limitada**, limited company.

socio,-a *nm,f* 1 *(miembro)* member; **hacerse s. de un club**, to become a member of a club, join a club. 2 Com *(asociado)* partner.

sociología *nf* sociology.

sociológico,-a *adj* sociological.

sociólogo,-a *nm,f* sociologist.

socorrer *vtr* to help, assist.

socorrido,-a *adj* handy, useful.

socorrista *nmf* life-saver, lifeguard.

socorro *nm* help, assistance; **¡s.!**, help!; **puesto de s.**, first-aid post.

soda *nf* soda water.

soez *adj* vulgar, crude.

sofá *nm (pl* **sofás***)* sofa, settee; **s. cama**, sofa bed, studio couch.

Sofía *n* Sophia.

sofisticado,-a *adj* sophisticated.

sofocado,-a *adj* suffocated.

sofocante *adj* suffocating, stifling; **hacía un calor s.**, it was unbearably hot.

sofocar [1] I *vtr (ahogar)* to suffocate, smother. 2 *(incendio)* to extinguish, put out. II **sofocarse** *vr* 1 *(ahogarse)* to suffocate, stifle. 2 *fam* (*irritarse*) to get upset.

sofoco *nm fig* (*vergüenza*) embarrassment; **le dio un s.**, (*disgusto*) it gave her quite a turn.

sofocón *nm fam* shock; **llevarse un s.**, to get upset.

sofreír [6] *vtr* to fry lightly, brown.

sofrito *nm* fried tomato and onion sauce.

software *nm* software.

soga *nf* rope; *fig* **estar con la s. al cuello**, to be in dire straits.

soja *nf* soya bean, US soybean.

sojuzgar [7] *vtr* to subjugate.

sol[1] *nm* 1 sun. 2 (*luz*) sunlight; (*luz y calor*) sunshine; **hace s.**, it's sunny, the sun is shining; **tomar el s.**, to sunbathe; **al o bajo el s.**, in the sun; **de s. a s.**, from sunrise to sunset. 3 *Fin* standard monetary unit of Perú.

sol[2] *nm Mús* G; (*solfeo*) so.

solamente *adv* only; **no s.**, not only; **s. con mirarte lo sé**, I know just by looking at you; **s. que ...**, except that ....

solapa *nf* (*de chaqueta*) lapel; (*de sobre, bolsillo, libro*) flap.

solapado,-a *adj* (*persona*) sly. ◆ **solapadamente** *adv* stealthily, in an underhand way.

solapamiento *nm* overlap.

solapar I *vtr fig* to conceal, cover up. II *vi* to overlap.

solar[1] *adj* solar; **luz s.**, sunlight.

solar[2] *nm* (*terreno*) plot; (*en obras*) building site.

solario, solárium *nm* sunbed.

solaz *nm fml* (*descanso*) rest, relaxation; (*esparcimiento*) recreation, entertainment.

solazarse [4] *vr* (*relajar*) to relax; (*divertir*) to entertain oneself, amuse oneself.

soldado *nm* soldier; **s. raso**, private.

soldador,-a I *nm,f* welder. II *nm* soldering iron.

soldar [2] *vtr* (*cable*) to solder; (*chapa*) to weld.

soleado,-a *adj* sunny.

soledad *nf* (*estado*) solitude; (*sentimiento*) loneliness.

solemne *adj* 1 (*majestuoso*) solemn. 2 *pey* downright.

solemnidad *nf* solemnity.

soler [4] *vi defect* 1 (*en presente*) to be in the habit of; **solemos ir en coche**, we usually go by car; **sueles equivocarte**, you are usually wrong. 2 (*en pasado*) to use to; **solía pasear por aquí**, he used to walk round here.

solera *nf fig* tradition; **de s.**, old-established; **vino de s.**, vintage wine.

solfa *nf* 1 *Mús* solfa; *fam* **poner en s.**, to ridicule. 2 *fam* (*paliza*) thrashing, beating.

solicitar *vtr* (*información etc*) to request, ask for; (*trabajo*) to apply for.

solícito,-a *adj* obliging, attentive.

solicitud *nf* (*petición*) request; (*de trabajo*) application.

solidaridad *nf* solidarity.

solidario,-a *adj* 1 supportive; **una sociedad solidaria**, a caring society. 2 *Jur* jointly responsible.

solidarizarse *vr* to show one's solidarity (**con**, with).

solidez *nf* solidity, strength.

sólido,-a *adj* solid, strong.

soliloquio *nm* soliloquy.

solista *nmf* soloist.

solitario,-a I *adj* 1 (*que está solo*) solitary, lone; (*que se siente solo*) lonely. II *nm* 1 (*diamante*) solitaire. 2 *Naipes* solitaire, patience.

soliviantar *vtr* (*irritar*) to irritate.

sollozar [4] *vi* to sob.

sollozo *nm* sob.

solo,-a I *adj* 1 only, single; **ni un s. día**, not a single day; **una sola vez**, only once, just once. 2 (*solitario*) lonely. 3 **hablar s.**, to talk to oneself; **se enciende s.**, it switches itself on automatically; **a solas**, alone, by oneself. II *nm Mús* solo.

sólo *adv* only; **tan s.**, only; **no s. ... sino** (**también**), not only ... but (also); **con s.**, (**tan**) s., just by.

solomillo *nm* sirloin.

soltar [2] I *vtr* 1 (*desasir*) to let go of; **¡suéltame!**, let me go! 2 (*prisionero*) to release. 3 (*humo, olor*) to give off. 4 (*bofetada*) to deal; (*carcajada*) to let out; **me soltó un rollo**, he bored me to tears. II **soltarse** *vr* 1 (*desatarse*) to come loose. 2 (*perro etc*) to get loose, break loose. 3 (*desprenderse*) to come off.

soltero,-a I *adj* single, unmarried. II *nm* (*hombre*) bachelor, single man. III *nf* (*mujer*) single woman, spinster.

solterón,-ona *pey* I *nm* (*hombre*) old bachelor. II *nf* (*mujer*) old maid.

soltura *nf* (*agilidad*) agility; (*seguridad*) confidence, assurance; **habla italiano con s.**, he speaks Italian fluently.

soluble *adj* soluble; **café s.**, instant coffee.

solución *nf* solution.

solucionar *vtr* to solve; (*arreglar*) to settle.

solvencia *nf* 1 *Fin* solvency. 2 (*fiabilidad*) reliability; **fuentes de toda s.**, completely reliable sources.

solventar *vtr* (*problema*) to solve, resolve; (*deuda, asunto*) to settle.

solvente *adj* 1 *Fin* solvent. 2 (*fiable*) reliable.

sombra *nf* 1 shade. 2 (*silueta proyectada*) shadow; **s. de ojos**, eyeshadow; **sin s. de duda**, beyond a shadow of doubt. 3 **tener buena s.**, (*tener suerte*) to be lucky.

sombrero *nm* hat; **s. de copa**, top hat; **s. hongo**, bowler hat.

sombrilla *nf* parasol, sunshade.

sombrío,-a *adj* (*oscuro*) dark; (*tenebroso*)

sombre, gloomy; *fig (persona)* gloomy, sullen.

somero,-a *adj* superficial, shallow.

someter I *vtr* 1 to subject; **s. a prueba**, to put to the test; **s. algo a votación**, to put sth to the vote. 2 *(rebeldes)* to subdue, put down. II **someterse** *vr* 1 *(subordinarse)* to submit. 2 *(rendirse)* to surrender, yield. 3 **s. a un tratamiento**, to undergo treatment.

somier *nm (pl* **somieres)** spring mattress.

somnífero *nm* sleeping pill.

somnolencia *adj* sleepy, drowsy.

son *nm* sound; **al s. del tambor**, to the sound of the drum; **venir en s. de paz**, to come in peace.

sonado,-a *adj* 1 much talked of. 2 *(trastocado)* mad, crazy.

sonajero *nm* baby's rattle.

sonámbulo,-a *nm,f* somnambulist, sleepwalker.

sonar [2] I *vi* 1 to sound; **s. a**, to sound like; **suena bien**, it sounds good. 2 *(timbre, teléfono)* to ring; **sonaron las cinco**, the clock struck five. 3 **tu nombre/cara me suena**, your name/face rings a bell. II **sonarse** *vr* **s. (la nariz)**, to blow one's nose.

sonda *nf* Med sound, probe. 2 **s. espacial**, space probe.

sondear *vtr* 1 *(opinión)* to test, sound out. 2 Med to sound, probe. 3 *Náut* to sound.

sondeo *nm* 1 *(encuesta)* poll. 2 Med sounding, probing. 3 *Náut* sounding.

soneto *nm* Lit sonnet.

sonido *nm* sound.

sonoro,-a *adj* Cin sound; **banda sonora**, soundtrack. 2 *(resonante)* loud, resounding. 3 Ling voiced.

sonreír [6] *vi*, **sonreírse** *vr* to smile; **me sonrió**, he smiled to me.

sonriente *adj* smiling.

sonrisa *nf* smile.

sonrojarse *vr* to blush.

sonrojo *nm* blush.

sonsacar [1] *vtr* to wheedle; *(secreto)* to worm out.

soñador,-a *nm,f* dreamer.

soñar [2] *vtr & vi* 1 to dream; **s. con**, to dream of *o* about; *fig* **¡ni soñarlo!**, not on your life! 2 *(fantasear)* to daydream, dream.

soñoliento,-a *adj* sleepy, drowsy.

sopa *nf* soup; **s. juliana**, spring vegetable soup; *fig* **quedar hecho una s.**, to get soaked to the skin.

sopera *nf* soup tureen.

sopero,-a *adj* **cucharada sopera**, soup spoon.

sopesar *vtr* to try the weight of; *fig* to weigh up.

sopetón *nm fam* slap; **de s.**, all of a sudden.

soplado *nm* glass-blowing.

soplar I *vi (viento)* to blow. II *vtr* 1 *(polvo etc)* to blow away; *(para enfriar)* to blow on. 2 *(para apagar)* to blow out. 3 *(para inflar)* to blow up. 4 *(en examen etc)* to whisper *o* tell the answer.

soplete *nm* blowlamp, blowtorch.

soplido *nm* blow, puff.

soplillo *nm* fan; *fam* **orejas de s.**, cauliflower ears.

soplo *nm* 1 *(acción)* blow, puff; *(de viento)* gust. 2 Med murmur.

soplón,-ona *nm,f fam (niño)* telltale, sneak; *(delator)* informer, squealer.

soporífero,-a *adj* 1 *(que adormece)* soporific, sleep-inducing. 2 *(aburrido)* boring, dull.

soportable *adj* bearable.

soportal *nm* porch; **soportales**, arcade *sing*.

soportar *vtr* 1 *(peso)* to support, bear. 2 *fig (calor, ruido)* to bear, endure; *(situación)* to put up with, to bear; **no te soporto**, I can't stand you.

soporte *nm* support; **s. publicitario**, advertising medium.

soprano *nmf* soprano.

sorber *vtr* 1 *(beber)* to sip. 2 *(absorber)* to soak up, absorb.

sorbete *nm* sorbet, sherbet.

sorbo *nm* sip; *(trago)* gulp; **de un s.**, in one gulp.

sordera *nf* deafness.

sórdido,-a *adj* squalid, sordid.

sordo,-a I *adj* 1 *(persona)* deaf; **s. como una tapia**, stone-deaf. 2 *(golpe, ruido, dolor)* dull. II *nm,f* deaf person; **los sordos**, the deaf *pl*; *fam fig* **hacerse el s.**, to turn a deaf ear.

sordomudez *nf* deaf-muteness.

sordomudo,-a I *adj* deaf and dumb, deaf-mute. II *nm,f* deaf and dumb person, deaf-mute.

sorprendente *adj* surprising.

sorprender *vtr* 1 *(extrañar)* to surprise. 2 *(coger desprevenido)* to catch unawares, take by surprise.

sorpresa *nf* surprise; **coger de *o* por s.**, to take by surprise.

sorpresivo,-a *adj* Am unexpected, surprising.

sortear *vtr* 1 to draw *o* cast lots for; *(rifar)* to raffle (off). 2 *(evitar)* to avoid, get round.

sorteo *nm* draw; *(rifa)* raffle.

sortija *nf* ring.

sortilegio *nm* spell.

S.O.S. *nm* SOS.

sosa *nf* soda; **s. cáustica**, caustic soda.

sosegado,-a *adj (tranquilo)* calm, quiet; *(pacífico)* peaceful.

sosegar [1] I *vtr* to calm, quieten. II **sosegarse** *vr* to calm down.

sosiego *nm (calma)* calmness; *(paz)* peace, tranquility.

soslayo (al, de) *loc adv* mirar de s., to look sideways (at).

soso,-a *adj* lacking in salt; *fig (persona)* insipid, dull.

sospecha *nf* suspicion.

sospechar I *vi (desconfiar)* to suspect; **s. de algn**, to suspect sb. **II** *vtr (pensar)* to suspect.

sospechoso,-a I *adj* suspicious; **s. de**, suspected of. **II** *nm,f* suspect.

sostén *nm* 1 *(apoyo)* support. 2 *(sustento)* sustenance. 3 *(prenda)* bra, brassière.

sostener [24] **I** *vtr* 1 *(sujetar)* to support, hold up. 2 *(con la mano)* to hold. 3 *fig (teoría etc)* to defend, uphold; **s. que ...**, to maintain that .... 4 *(conversación)* to hold, sustain. 5 *(familia)* to support. **II sostenerse** *vr* 1 *(mantenerse)* to support oneself. 2 *(permanecer)* to stay, remain.

sostenido,-a *adj (continuado)* sustained. 2 *Mús* sharp.

sostuve *pt indef →* sostener.

sota *nf Naipes* jack, knave.

sotana *nf* cassock, soutane.

sótano *nm* basement, cellar.

soto *nm* grove.

soviético,-a *adj & nm,f* Soviet; *Hist* la Unión Soviética, the Soviet Union.

soy *indic pres →* ser.

S.P. *abr de* Servicio Público.

sport (de) *loc adj* casual, sports; **chaqueta s.**, sports jacket.

spot *nm (pl spots)* TV commercial, advert, ad.

spray *nm (pl sprays)* spray.

sprint *nm* sprint.

Sr. *abr de* Señor, Mister, Mr.

Sra. *abr de* Señora, Mrs.

S.R.C., s.r.c. *abr de* se ruega contestación, please reply, R.S.V.P.

Srta. *abr de* Señorita, Miss.

SS *nf abr de* Seguridad Social, ≈ National Health Service, NHS.

SS.AA. *abr de* Sus Altezas, Their Royal Highnesses.

Sta., sta. *abr de* Santa, Saint, St.

stand *nm Com* stand.

standard *adj & nm* standard.

status *nm inv* status.

Sto., sto. *abr de* Santo, Saint, St.

su *adj pos (de él)* his; *(de ella)* her; *(de usted, ustedes)* your; *(de animales o cosas)* its; *(impersonal)* one's; *(de ellos)* their; **su coche**, his o her o your o their car; **su pata**, its leg; **sus libros**, his o her o your o their books; **sus patas**, its legs.

suave *adj* 1 smooth; *(luz, voz etc)* soft. 2 *Meteor (templado)* mild.

suavidad *nf* 1 smoothness; *(dulzura)* softness. 2 *Meteor* mildness.

suavizante *nm (para el pelo)* (hair) conditioner; *(para la ropa)* fabric softener.

suavizar [4] **I** *vtr* to smooth (out). **II suavizarse** *vr (temperatura)* to get milder;

(persona) to calm down.

subacuático,-a *adj* underwater.

subalimentado,-a *adj* undernourished, underfed.

subalterno,-a *adj & nm,f* subordinate, subaltern.

subarrendar [1] *vtr Com* to sublet, sublease.

subasta *nf* auction.

subastar *vtr* to auction (off), sell at auction.

subcampeón *nm Dep* runner-up.

subconsciente *adj & nm* subconscious.

subdesarrollado,-a *adj* underdeveloped.

subdesarrollo *nm* underdevelopment.

subdirector,-a *nm,f* assistant director o manager.

súbdito,-a *nm,f* subject, citizen; **s. francés**, French citizen.

subdividir *vtr* to subdivide.

subestimar *vtr* to underestimate.

subida *nf* 1 *(de temperatura)* rise; *(de precios, salarios)* rise, increase. 2 *(ascenso)* ascent, climb. 3 *(pendiente)* slope, hill. 4 *fam (drogas)* high.

subido,-a *adj* **s. de tono**, daring, risqué.

subir I *vtr* 1 to go up. 2 *(llevar arriba)* to take up, bring up. 3 *(cabeza, mano)* to lift, raise. 4 *(precio, salario)* to raise, put up. 5 *(volumen)* to turn up; *(voz)* to raise. **II** *vi* 1 *(ir arriba)* to go up, come up. 2 **s. a**, *(un coche)* to get into; *(un autobús)* to get on; *(un barco, avión, tren)* to board, get on. 3 *(aumentar)* to rise, go up. **III subirse** *vr* 1 to climb up; *fig* el vino se le subió a la cabeza, the wine went to his head. 2 **s. a**, *(un coche)* to get into; *(un autobús, avión, tren)* to get on, board; *(caballo, bici)* to get on. 3 *(cremallera)* to do up; *(mangas)* to roll up.

súbito,-a *adj* sudden. ◆**súbitamente** *adv* suddenly.

subjetivo,-a *adj* subjective.

sublevación *nf* rising, rebellion.

sublevar I *vtr fig (indignar)* to infuriate, enrage. **II sublevarse** *vr* to rebel, revolt.

sublime *adj* sublime.

submarinismo *nm* skin-diving.

submarino,-a I *adj* submarine, underwater. **II** *nm* submarine.

subnormal I *adj* mentally handicapped. **II** *nmf* mentally handicapped person.

suboficial *nm* 1 *Mil* noncommissioned officer. 2 *Náut* petty officer.

subordinado,-a *adj & nm,f* subordinate.

subordinar *vtr* to subordinate.

subproducto *nm* by-product.

subrayar *vtr* to underline; *fig (recalcar)* to emphasize, stress.

subrepticio,-a *adj* surreptitious.

subrutina *nf* subroutine.

subsanar *vtr (error)* to rectify, put right; *(daño)* to make up for.

subscribir *(pp subscrito) vtr →* suscribir.

subscripción *nf* subscription.
subscrito,-a *o* **suscrito,-a** → **suscrito,-a.**
subsecretario,-a *nm,f* undersecretary.
subsidiario,-a *adj* subsidiary.
subsidio *nm* allowance, benefit; **s. de desempleo,** unemployment benefit.
subsistencia *nf* subsistence.
subsistir *vi* to subsist, remain; *(vivir)* to live on, survive.
subsuelo *nm* subsoil.
subterráneo,-a **I** *adj* underground. **II** *nm (túnel)* tunnel, underground passage.
subtítulo *nm* subtitle.
suburbano,-a *adj* suburban.
suburbio *nm (barrio pobre)* slums *pl*; *(barrio periférico)* suburb.
subvención *nf* subsidy.
subvencionar *vtr* to subsidize.
subversión *nf* subversion.
subversivo,-a *adj* subversive.
subyacente *adj* underlying.
subyugar [7] *vtr* to subjugate.
succionar *vtr* to suck (in).
sucedáneo,-a *adj* & *nm* substitute.
suceder **I** *vi* **1** *(ocurrir) (uso impers)* to happen, occur; **¿qué sucede?,** what's going on?, what's the matter? **2** *(seguir)* to follow, succeed. **II sucederse** *vr* to follow one another, come after the other.
sucesión *nf* **1** *(serie)* series *sing*, succession. **2** *(al trono)* succession. **3** *(descendencia)* issue, heirs *pl*.
sucesivo,-a *adj* following, successive; **en lo s.,** from now on. ◆**sucesivamente** *adv* y **así s.,** and so on.
suceso *nm (hecho)* event, occurrence; *(incidente)* incident; *Prensa* **sección de sucesos,** accident and crime reports.
sucesor,-a *nm,f* successor.
suciedad *nf* **1** dirt. **2** *(calidad)* dirtiness.
sucinto,-a *adj* concise, succinct.
sucio,-a **I** *adj* dirty; **en s.,** in rough; *fig* **juego s.,** foul play; *fig* **negocio s.,** shady business. **II** *adv* **jugar s.,** to play dirty.
sucre *nm Fin* standard monetary unit of Ecuador.
suculento,-a *adj* succulent, juicy.
sucumbir *vi* to succumb, yield.
sucursal *nf Com Fin* branch, branch office.
sudaca *nmf pey* South American.
sudadera *nf* sweatshirt.
Sudáfrica *n* South Africa.
sudafricano,-a *adj* & *nm,f* South African.
Sudamérica *n* South America.
sudamericano,-a *adj* & *nm,f* South American.
sudar *vtr* & *vi* to sweat; *fam fig* **s. la gota gorda,** to sweat blood.
sudeste *nm* southeast.
sudoeste *nm* southwest.
sudor *nm* sweat; *fig* **con el s. de mi frente,** by the sweat of my brow.
sudoroso,-a *adj* sweaty.

Suecia *n* Sweden.
sueco,-a **I** *adj* Swedish. **II** *nm,f (persona)* Swede. **III** *nm (idioma)* Swedish.
suegra *nf* mother-in-law.
suegro *nm* father-in-law; **mis suegros,** my in-laws.
suela *nf (de zapato)* sole.
sueldo *nm* salary, wages *pl*.
suelo *nm* **1** *(superficie)* ground; *(de interior)* floor; *fig* **estar por los suelos,** *(precios)* to be rock-bottom. **2** *(territorio)* soil, land. **3** *(campo, terreno)* land; **s. cultivable,** arable land. **4** *(de carretera)* surface.
suelto,-a **I** *adj* **1** *(no sujeto) (desatado)* undone. **2** *fig* **dinero s.,** loose change; **hojas sueltas,** loose sheets (of paper); **se venden sueltos,** they are sold singly *o* separately *o* loose. **3** *(en libertad)* free; *(huido)* at large. **4** *(vestido, camisa)* loose, loose-fitting. **II** *nm (dinero)* (loose) change.
sueño *nm* **1** sleep; *(ganas de dormir)* sleepiness; **tener s.,** to feel *o* be sleepy. **2** *(cosa soñada)* dream.
suero *nm Med* serum; *(de la leche)* whey.
suerte *nf* **1** *(fortuna)* luck; **por s.,** fortunately; **probar s.,** to try one's luck; **tener s.,** to be lucky; **¡que tengas s.!,** good luck! **2** **echar algo a suertes,** to draw lots for sth. **3** *(destino)* fate, destiny. **4** *fml (género)* kind, sort, type.
suéter *nm* sweater.
suficiencia *nf* **1** *(engreimiento)* smugness, complacency. **2** *Educ* **prueba de s.,** final exam.
suficiente **I** *adj (bastante)* sufficient, enough. **II** *nm Educ* pass. ◆ **suficientemente** *adv* sufficiently; **no es lo s. rico como para ...** he isn't rich enough to ...
sufijo *nm* suffix.
sufragar [7] **I** *vtr (gastos)* to pay, defray. **II** *vi Am* to vote (**por,** for).
sufragio *nm Pol* suffrage; *(voto)* vote.
sufrido,-a *adj (persona)* long-suffering.
sufrimiento *nm* suffering.
sufrir **I** *vi* **1** to suffer; **s. del corazón,** to have a heart condition. **II** *vtr* **1** *(accidente)* to have; *(operación)* to undergo; *(dificultades, cambios)* to experience; **s. dolores de cabeza,** to suffer from headaches. **2** *(aguantar)* to bear, put up with.
sugerencia *nf* suggestion.
sugerente *adj* suggestive.
sugerir [5] *vtr* to suggest.
sugestión *nf* suggestion.
sugestionar *vtr* to influence, persuade.
sugestivo,-a *adj* suggestive; *(atractivo)* alluring.
suicida **I** *nmf (persona)* suicide. **II** *adj* suicidal.
suicidarse *vr* to commit suicide, kill oneself.
suicidio *nm* suicide.
suite *nf* suite.

Suiza n Switzerland.
suizo,-a I adj Swiss. II nm,f (persona) Swiss. III nm Culin eclair.
sujetador nm (prenda) bra, brassière.
sujetar I vtr 1 (agarrar) to hold. 2 (fijar) to hold down, hold in place. 3 fig (someter) to restrain. II **sujetarse** vr (agarrarse) to hold on.
sujeto,-a I nm subject; (individuo) fellow, individual. II adj (atado) fastened, secure; **s. a,** (sometido) subject to, liable to.
sulfato nm sulphate.
sulfurar I vtr fam (exasperar) to exasperate, infuriate. II **sulfurarse** vr fam to lose one's temper, blow one's top.
sultán nm sultan.
suma nf 1 (cantidad) sum, amount. 2 Mat sum, addition; **s. total,** sum total. 3 **en s.,** in short.
sumamente adv extremely, highly.
sumar I vtr Mat to add, add up. II **sumarse** vr **s. a,** (huelga) to join; (proyecto) to support.
sumario,-a I adj summary, brief; Jur **juicio s.,** summary proceedings pl. II nm Jur summary.
sumarísimo,-a adj Jur swift, expeditious.
sumergible adj & nm submersible.
sumergir [6] I vtr to submerge; submerse; (hundir) to sink, plunge. II **sumergirse** vr to submerge, go underwater; (hundirse) to sink.
sumidero nm drain, sewer.
suministrar vtr to supply, provide; **s. algo a algn,** to supply sb with sth.
suministro nm supply.
sumir vtr (hundir) to sink; plunge; fig to plunge.
sumiso,-a adj submissive, obedient.
sumo,-a adj (supremo) supreme; **con s. cuidado,** with extreme care; **a lo s.,** at (the) most.
suntuoso,-a adj sumptuous, magnificent.
supe pt indef → **saber**.
supeditar vtr to subject (a, to).
super- pref super-.
súper fam I adj super, great. II nm 1 (supermercado) supermarket. 2 (gasolina) 4 star.
superado,-a adj outdated, obsolete.
superar I vtr 1 (obstáculo etc) to overcome, surmount; (prueba) pass. 2 (aventajar) to surpass, excel. II **superarse** vr to improve o better oneself.
superávit nm surplus.
superdotado,-a I adj exceptionally gifted. II nm,f genius.
superficial adj superficial.
superficialidad nf superficiality.
superficie nf surface; (área) area; Com **grandes superficies,** hypermarkets.
superfluo,-a adj superfluous.
superhombre nm superman.
superior I adj 1 (posición) top, upper. 2

(cantidad) greater, higher, larger (a, than). 3 (calidad) superior; **calidad s.,** top quality. 4 Educ higher. II nm (jefe) superior.
superioridad nf superiority.
supermán nm (pl supermanes) superman.
supermercado nm supermarket.
superpoblación nf overpopulation.
superponer [19] vtr to superimpose.
superpotencia nf superpower.
superproducción nf 1 Ind overproduction. 2 Cin mammoth production.
supersónico,-a adj supersonic.
superstición nf superstition.
supersticioso,-a adj superstitious.
supervisar vtr to supervise.
supervisor,-a nm,f supervisor.
supervivencia nf survival.
supino,-a adj 1 (boca arriba) supine, face up. 2 fig (absoluto) total absolute.
súpito,-a adj Am sudden.
suplantar vtr to supplant, take the place of.
suplementario,-a adj supplementary, additional.
suplemento nm supplement; **sin s.,** without extra charge.
suplente adj & nmf (sustituto) substitute, deputy; Dep substitute.
supletorio,-a adj supplementary, additional; **cama supletoria,** extra bed; **teléfono s.,** extension.
súplica nf entreaty, plea.
suplicar [1] vtr to beseech, beg.
suplicio nm (tortura) torture; fig (tormento) torment.
suplir vtr 1 (reemplazar) to replace, substitute. 2 (compensar) to make up for.
suponer [19] (pp **supuesto**) vtr 1 (significar) to mean. 2 (implicar) to entail. 3 (representar) to account for. 4 (pensar) to suppose; **supongo que sí,** I suppose so; **supongamos que ...,** let's assume that .... 5 (adivinar) to guess; **(me) lo suponía,** I guessed as much.
suposición nf supposition.
supositorio nm suppository.
supremacía nf supremacy.
supremo,-a adj supreme.
supresión nf (de una ley etc) abolition; (de restricciones) lifting; (de una palabra) deletion; (de una rebelión) suppression; (omisión) omission.
suprimir vtr 1 (ley, impuesto) to abolish; (restricción) to lift; (palabra) to delete, take o leave out; (rebelión) to suppress. 2 (omitir) to omit.
supuesto,-a I adj 1 (asumido) supposed, assumed; **¡por s.!,** of course!; **dar algo por s.,** to take sth for granted. 2 (presunto) alleged. II nm assumption; **en el s. de que,** on the assumption that.
supurar vtr to suppurate, fester.
supuse pt indef → **saber**.

sur nm south.

Suramérica nf South America.

suramericano,-a adj & nm,f South American.

surcar [1] vtr Agr to plough; fig (olas) to cut through.

surco nm Agr furrow; (en un disco) groove.

sureño,-a I adj southern. II nm,f southerner.

sureste adj & nm → **sudeste**.

surf(ing) nm Dep surfing.

surfista nmf surfer.

surgir [6] vi (aparecer) to arise, emerge, appear; (problema, dificultad) to crop up.

suroeste adj & nm → **sudoeste**.

surrealista adj & nmf surrealist.

surtido,-a I adj 1 (variado) assorted. 2 **bien s.**, well stocked. II nm selection, assortment.

surtidor nm spout; **s. de gasolina**, petrol o US gas pump.

surtir vtr 1 to supply, provide. 2 **s. efecto**, to have the desired effect.

susceptible adj susceptible; (quisquilloso) oversensitive, touchy.

suscitar vtr (provocar) to cause, provoke; (rebelión) to stir up, arouse; (interés etc) to arouse.

suscribir (pp **suscrito**) I vtr 1 to subscribe to, endorse. 2 fml (firmar) to sign. II **suscribirse** vr to subscribe (a, to).

suscripción nf subscription.

susodicho,-a adj above-mentioned, aforesaid.

suspender I vtr 1 (ley) to suspend; (reunión) to adjourn. 2 (examen) to fail; **me han suspendido**, I've failed (the exam). 3 (colgar) to hang, suspend. II vi Educ **he suspendido**, I've failed.

suspense nm suspense; **novela/película de s.**, thriller.

suspensión nf 1 hanging (up), suspension. 2 Aut suspension. 3 Fin Jur **s. de pagos**, suspension of payments.

suspensivo,-a adj **puntos suspensivos**,

suspension points.

suspenso nm 1 Educ fail. 2 **en s.**, (asunto, trabajo) pending; **estar en s.**, to be pending.

suspicacia nf suspiciousness.

suspicaz adj suspicious; (desconfiado) distrustful.

suspirar vi to sigh.

suspiro nm sigh.

sustancia nf substance.

sustancial adj 1 substantial. 2 (fundamental) essential, fundamental.

sustantivo,-a I adj substantive. II nm Ling noun.

sustentar vtr 1 (peso) to support. 2 (familia) to maintain, support. 3 (teoría) to support, defend.

sustento nm 1 (alimento) sustenance, food. 2 (apoyo) support.

sustitución nf substitution, replacement.

sustituir [37] vtr to substitute, replace.

sustituto,-a nm,f substitute, stand-in.

susto nm fright, scare; **llevarse o darse un s.**, to get a fright.

sustraer [25] vtr 1 Mat to subtract. 2 (robar) to steal, remove.

sustrato nm substratum.

susurrar vtr to whisper.

susurro nm whisper.

sutil adj 1 (diferencia, pregunta) subtle. 2 (delgado) thin, fine. 3 (aroma) delicate.

sutileza nf 1 (dicho) subtlety. 2 (finura) fineness.

suyo,-a adj & pron pos (de él) his; (de ella) hers; (de usted, ustedes) yours; (de animal o cosa) its; (de ellos, ellas) theirs; **los zapatos no son suyos**, the shoes aren't hers; **varios amigos suyos**, several friends of his o hers o yours o theirs; fam **es muy s.**, he's very aloof; fam **hacer de las suyas**, to be up to one's tricks; fam **ir (cada uno) a lo s.**, to mind one's own business; fam **salirse con la suya**, to get one's way.

svástica nf swastika.

T

T, t [te] nf (la letra) T, t.

t abr de **tonelada(s)**, ton, tons.

tabacalero,-a I nm,f (vendedor) tobacco trader. II nf **La Tabacalera**, Spanish state tobacco monopoly.

tabaco nm 1 (planta, hoja) tobacco; **t. rubio**, Virginia tobacco. 2 (cigarrillos) cigarettes pl.

tábano nm horsefly.

tabaquismo nm nicotine poisoning.

tabarra nf fam nuisance, bore; **dar la t.**, to go on and on.

tabasco nm tabasco sauce.

taberna nf pub, bar; (antiguamente)

tavern.

tabernero,-a nm,f publican; (hombre) landlord; (mujer) landlady.

tabique nm 1 (pared) partition (wall). 2 Anat **t. nasal**, nasal wall.

tabla nf 1 board; Dep **t. de surf**, surfboard; Dep **t. de windsurf**, sailboard. 2 (de vestido) pleat. 3 Mat table. 4 Ajedrez **tablas**, stalemate sing, draw sing; **quedar en t.**, (juego) to end in a draw. 5 Taur **tablas**, fence sing. 6 Teat **las tablas**, the stage sing; fig **tener (muchas) t.**, to be an old hand.

tablado nm 1 (plataforma) wooden platform. 2 *Teat* stage.

tablao *nm fam* flamenco bar *o* show.

tablero *nm* 1 (*tablón*) panel, board; **t. de mandos**, (*de coche*) dash(board). 2 (*en juegos*) board; **t. de ajedrez**, chessboard.

tableta *nf* (*de chocolate*) bar.

tablón *nm* plank; (*en construcción*) beam; **t. de anuncios**, notice *o US* bulletin board.

tabú *adj & nm* (*pl* **tabúes**) taboo.

tabular *vtr* to tabulate.

taburete *nm* stool.

tacaño,-a I *adj* mean, stingy. II *nm,f* miser.

tacatá, tacataca *nm* baby-walker.

tacha *nf* (*defecto*) flaw, defect; **sin t.**, flawless, without blemish.

tachar *vtr* 1 to cross out. 2 *fig* **t. de**, to accuse of.

tacho *nm Am* bucket.

tachón *nm* (*borrón*) crossing out.

tachuela *nf* tack, stud.

tácito,-a *adj* tacit.

taciturno,-a *adj* 1 (*callado*) taciturn. 2 (*triste*) sullen.

taco *nm* 1 (*plug*) plug; (*de billetes*) wad; *Culin* (*de jamón, queso*) cube, piece; (*de bota de fútbol*) stud; (*en billar*) cue. 2 *Culin* taco, rolled-up tortilla pancake. 3 *fam* (*palabrota*) swearword. 4 *fam* (*lío*) mess, muddle; **armarse** *o* **hacerse un t.**, to get all mixed up. 5 **me gusta un t.**, I like it a lot. 6 *fam* **tacos**, (*años*) years.

tacón *nm* heel; **zapatos de t.**, high-heeled shoes.

taconeo *nm* (*pisada*) heel tapping; (*golpe*) stamping with the heels.

táctica *nf* tactics *pl*.

táctil *adj* tactile; **pantalla t.**, touch screen.

táctico,-a *adj* tactical.

tacto *nm* 1 (*sentido*) touch. 2 *fig* (*delicadeza*) tact; **tener t.**, to be tactful.

taekwondo *nm* tae kwon do.

tafetán *nm* taffeta.

tahúr *nm* cardsharp.

Tailandia *n* Thailand.

tailandés,-esa I *adj* Thai. II *nm,f* (*persona*) Thai; **los tailandeses**, the Thai *o* Thais. III *nm* (*idioma*) Thai.

taimado,-a *adj* sly, crafty.

tajada *nf* 1 slice; *fig* **sacar** *o* **llevarse t.**, to take one's share. 2 *fam* (*borrachera*) drunkenness.

tajante *adj* incisive.

Tajo *n* el T., the Tagus.

tal I *adj* 1 (*semejante*) such; (*más sustantivo singular contable*) such a; **en tales condiciones**, in such conditions; **nunca dije t. cosa**, I never said such a thing. 2 (*indeterminado*) such and such; **t. día y a t. hora**, such and such a day and at such and such a time. 3 (*persona*) person called ...; **te llamó una t. Amelia**, someone called Amelia phoned you. 4 (*locuciones*)

t. vez, perhaps, maybe; **como si t. cosa**, as if nothing had happened. II *adv* 1 (*así*) just; **t. cual**, just as it is; **t. (y) como**, just as. 2 **¿qué t.?**, how are things?; **¿qué t. ese vino?**, how do you find this wine? III *conj* así; **con t.** (**de) que** + *subj*, so long as; provided. IV *pron* (*cosa*) something; (*persona*) someone, somebody; **t. para cual**, two of a kind; **y t. y cual**, and so on.

tala *nf* tree felling.

taladradora *nf* drill.

taladrar *vtr* to drill; (*pared*) to bore through; (*papeles*) to punch.

taladro *nm* (*herramienta*) drill. 2 (*agujero*) hole.

talante *nm* 1 (*carácter*) disposition. 2 (*voluntad*) **de buen t.**, willingly; **de mal t.**, unwillingly, reluctantly.

talar *vtr* (*árboles*) to fell, cut down.

talco *nm* talc; **polvos de t.**, talcum powder.

talega *nf* bag, sack.

talego *nm* 1 long bag, long sack. 2 *arg* (*cárcel*) clink, hole. 3 *arg* (*mil pesetas*) one thousand peseta note.

talento *nm* talent.

Talgo *nm* fast passenger train.

talismán *nm* talisman, lucky charm.

talla *nf* 1 (*de prenda*) size; **¿qué t. usas?**, what size are you? 2 (*estatura*) height; *fig* stature; *fig* **dar la t.**, to make the grade. 3 (*escultura*) carving, sculpture. 4 (*tallado*) cutting, carving.

tallado,-a *nm* (*de madera*) carving; (*de piedras preciosas*) cutting; (*de metales*) engraving.

tallar *vtr* 1 (*madera, piedra*) to carve, shape; (*piedras preciosas*) to cut; (*metales*) to engrave. 2 (*medir*) to measure the height of.

tallarines *nmpl* tagliatelle *sing*.

talle *nm* 1 (*cintura*) waist. 2 (*cuerpo*) (*de hombre*) build, physique; (*de mujer*) figure, shape.

taller *nm* 1 (*obrador*) workshop; *Aut* **t. de reparaciones**, garage. 2 *Ind* factory, mill.

tallo *nm* stem, stalk.

talón *nm* 1 (*del pie*) heel. 2 (*cheque*) cheque, *US* check.

talonario *nm* (*de cheques*) cheque *o US* check book; (*de billetes*) book of tickets.

tamaño *nm* size; **de gran t.**, large; **del t. de**, as large as, as big as.

tamaño,-a *adj* such a big, so big a.

tamarindo *nm* tamarind.

tambalearse *vr* (*persona*) to stagger; (*mesa*) to wobble; *fig* to teeter.

tambero *nm Am* (*mesonero*) innkeeper, landlord.

también *adv* (*igualmente*) too, also, as well; **tú t. puedes venir**, you can come too; **¿lo harás?**, **yo t.**, are you going to do it?, so am I.

tambor nm 1 (Mús, de lavadora, de freno) drum. 2 Anat eardrum.

Támesis n el T., the Thames.

tamiz nm sieve.

tamizar [1] vtr to sieve.

tampoco adv 1 (en afirmativas) nor, neither; Juan no vendrá y María t., Juan won't come and neither will Maria; no lo sé, - yo t., I don't know, - neither do I. 2 (en negativas) either, not ... either; la Bolsa no sube, pero t. baja, the stock market isn't going up, but it's not going down either.

tampón nm tampon.

tan adv 1 such; (más sustantivo singular contable) such a; es t. listo, he's such a clever fellow; no me gusta t. dulce, I don't like it so sweet; ¡qué gente t. agradable!, such nice people!; ¡qué vestido t. bonito!, what a beautiful dress! 2 (comparativo) t. ... como, as ... as; t. alto como tú, as tall as you (are). 3 (consecutivo) so ... (that); iba t. deprisa que no lo vi, he was going so fast that I couldn't see him. 4 t. siquiera, at least; t. sólo, only.

tanda nf (conjunto) batch, lot; (serie) series sing; por tandas, in groups.

tándem nm tandem.

tanga nm tanga.

tangente nf tangent; fig salirse o escaparse por la t., to go off at a tangent.

Tánger n Tangier.

tangible adj tangible.

tango nm tango.

tanque nm tank.

tantear vtr 1 fig t. a algn, to sound sb out; t. el terreno, to see how the land lies. 2 (calcular) to estimate, guess. II vi Dep (to keep) score.

tanteo nm 1 (cálculo) estimate, guess. 2 Dep score.

tanto,-a I nm 1 (punto) point. 2 (cantidad imprecisa) so much, a certain amount; t. por ciento, percentage. 3 un t., a bit; la casa es un t. pequeña, the house is rather o somewhat small. 4 estar al t., (informado) to be informed; (pendiente) to be on the lookout.
II adj 1 (+ singular) so much; (+ plural) so many; no le des t. dinero, don't give him so much money; ¡ha pasado t. tiempo!, it's been so long!; no comas tantas manzanas, don't eat so many apples. 2 cincuenta y tantas personas, fifty odd people; en el año sesenta y tantos, in nineteen sixty something. 3 t. como, as much as; tantos,-as como, as many as.
III pron 1 (+ singular) so much; otro t., as much again, the same again; no es o hay para t., it's not that bad. 2 (+ plural) so many; otros tantos, as many again; uno de tantos, run-of-the-mill; fam a las tantas, very late, at an un-

earthly hour.
IV adv 1 (cantidad) so much; t. mejor/peor, so much the better/worse; t. más cuanto que, all the more so because. 2 (tiempo) so long. 3 (frecuencia) so often. 4 t. ... como, both ... and; t. tú como yo, both you and I; t. si vienes como si no, whether you come or not. 5 (locuciones) por lo t., therefore; ¡y t.!, oh yes!, and how!

tañer [38] vtr to play.

tapa nf 1 (cubierta) lid; (de botella) cap, top; (de libro) cover; (de zapato) heelplate; Aut (de cilindro) head. 2 (aperitivo) appetizer.

tapadera nf (tapa) cover, lid; fig cover, front.

tapadillo nm hacer algo de t., to do sth secretly.

tapar I vtr 1 to cover; (botella etc) to put the lid o top on; (con ropas o mantas) to wrap up. 2 (ocultar) to hide; (vista) to block. 3 (encubrir) to cover up for sb. II **taparse** vr (cubrirse) to cover oneself; (abrigarse) to wrap up.

taparrabos nm inv loincloth.

tapete nm (table) cover; fig poner algo sobre el t., to table sth.

tapia nf garden wall.

tapiar [12] vtr 1 (área) to wall off. 2 (puerta, ventana etc) to wall, close up.

tapicería nf 1 tapestry; (de muebles, coche) upholstery. 2 (tienda) upholsterer's shop o workshop.

tapioca nf tapioca.

tapiz nm tapestry.

tapizar [4] vtr to upholster.

tapón nm 1 (de lavabo etc) stopper, plug; (de botella) cap, cork; t. de rosca, screw-on cap. 2 (de oídos) earplug. 3 (en baloncesto) block. 4 Aut traffic jam.

taponar I vtr 1 (tubería, hueco) to plug. 2 Med (herida) to tampon. II **taponarse** vr se me han taponado los oídos, my ears are blocked up.

taquigrafía nf shorthand.

taquígrafo,-a nm,f shorthand writer.

taquilla nf 1 ticket office, booking office; Cin Teat box-office; un éxito de t., a box-office success. 2 (recaudación) takings pl. 3 (armario) locker.

taquillero,-a I adj popular; película taquillera, box office hit. II nm,f booking o ticket clerk.

tara nf 1 (peso) tare. 2 (defecto) defect, fault.

tarántula nf tarantula.

tararear vtr to hum.

tardanza nf delay.

tardar I vtr to take time; ¿cuánto va a t.?, how long will it take?; tardé dos horas en venir, it took me two hours to get here. II vi (demorar) to take long; si tarda mucho me voy, if it takes much longer, I'm going; **no tardes**, don't be long; **a más t.**, at the latest. **III tardarse** *vr* ¿cuánto se tarda en llegar?, how long does it take to get there?

tarde I *nf* **1** *(hasta las cinco)* afternoon. **2** *(después de las cinco)* evening. **3 la t.- noche**, late evening. **II** *adv* **1** late; **siento llegar t.**, sorry I'm late. **2** *(locuciones)* **de t. en t.**, very rarely, not very often; **(más) t. o (más) temprano**, sooner or later.

tardío,-a *adj* late, belated.

tardo,-a *adj* slow.

tarea *nf* **1** job, task; **tareas**, *(de ama de casa)* housework *sing*; *(de estudiante)* homework *sing*.

tarifa *nf* **1** *(precio)* tariff, rate; *(en transportes)* fare. **2** *(lista de precios)* price list.

tarima *nf* platform, dais.

tarjeta *nf* card; **t. postal**, postcard; **t. de crédito**, credit card; **t. de visita**, visiting o US calling card; *Inform* **t. perforada**, punch o punched card.

tarraconense I *adj* of o from Tarragona. II *nmf* native o inhabitant of Tarragona.

tarro *nm* **1** *(vasija)* jar, pot, tub. **2** *fam (cabeza)* bonce. **3** *Am (lata)* tin, can.

tarta *nf* tart, pie.

tartamudear *vi* to stutter, stammer.

tartamudo,-a I *adj* stuttering, stammering. II *nm,f* stutterer, stammerer.

tartana *nf* *fam (coche viejo)* banger, heap.

tártaro,-a *adj* **salsa tártara**, tartar sauce.

tartera *nf* **1** *(fiambrera)* lunch box. **2** *(cazuela)* baking tin.

tarugo *nm* **1** *(de madera)* lump of wood. **2** *fam (persona)* blockhead.

tarumba *adj fam* crazy, mad; **estar t.**, to be bonkers.

tasa *nf* **1** *(precio)* fee; **tasas académicas**, course fees. **2** *(impuesto)* tax. **3** *(índice)* rate; **t. de natalidad/mortalidad**, birth/ death rate. **4** *(valoración)* valuation, appraisal.

tasación *nf* valuation.

tasador,-a *nm,f* valuer.

tasar *vtr* **1** *(valorar)* to value; **t. una casa en diez millones de pesetas**, to value a house at ten million pesetas. **2** *(poner precio)* to set o fix the price of.

tasca *nf fam* bar, pub.

tata *nf fam* nanny.

tatarabuelo,-a *nm,f (hombre)* great-great-grandfather; *(mujer)* great-great-grandmother; **tatarabuelos**, great-great-grandparents.

tataranieto,-a *nm,f (hombre)* great-great-grandson; *(mujer)* great-great-granddaughter; **tataranietos**, great-great-grandchildren.

tatuaje *nm* tattoo.

tatuar [10] *vtr* to tattoo.

taurino,-a *adj* of o relating to bullfighting.

Tauro *nm* Taurus.

tauromaquia *nf* tauromachy, (art of) bullfighting.

TAV *abr de* **Tren de Alta Velocidad**.

taxativo,-a *adj* categorical.

taxi *nm* taxi.

taxímetro *nm* taximeter, clock.

taxista *nmf* taxi driver.

taza *nf* **1** cup; **una t. de café**, *(recipiente)* coffee cup; *(contenido)* a cup of coffee. **2** *(de retrete)* bowl.

tazón *nm* bowl.

te *pron pers* **1** *(complemento directo)* you; *(complemento indirecto)* (to o for) you; **no quiero verte**, I don't want to see you; **te compraré uno**, I'll buy one for you; **te lo buy you one; te lo dije**, I told you so. **2** *(reflexivo)* yourself; **lávate**, wash yourself; *(sin traducción)* **bébetelo todo**, drink it up; **no te vayas**, don't go.

té *nm (pl tés)* tea; **t. con limón**, lemon tea.

tea *nf* torch.

teatral *adj* **grupo t.**, theatre company; **obra t.**, play. **2** *fig (teatrero)* theatrical.

teatrero,-a *adj* theatrical.

teatro *nm* **1** theatre, *US* theater; **obra de t.**, play; **autor de t.**, playwright. **2** *Lit* drama.

tebeo *nm* children's comic.

techar *vtr* to roof.

techo *nm* **1** *(de habitación)* ceiling; *(tejado)* roof; *Aut* **t. corredizo**, sun roof.

tecla *nf* key; *fig* **dar en la t.**, to get it right.

teclado *nm* keyboard; *Inform* **t. expandido**, expanded keyboard.

teclear I *vtr* to key in. II *vi* to drum with one's fingers.

técnica *nf* **1** *(tecnología)* technology. **2** *(método)* technique. **3** *(habilidad)* skill.

técnico,-a I *adj* technical. II *nm,f* technician, technical expert.

tecnicolor *nm* Technicolor.

tecno- *pref* techno-.

tecnócrata *nmf* technocrat.

tecnología *nf* technology.

tecnológico,-a *adj* technological.

tedio *nm* tedium, boredom.

tedioso,-a *adj* tedious, boring.

teja *nf Constr* tile; *fam fig* **a toca t.**, on the nail.

tejado *nm* roof.

tejanos *nmpl* jeans.

tejemaneje *nm fam* **1** *(actividad)* bustle, fuss. **2** *(maquinación)* intrigue, scheming.

tejer *vtr (en el telar)* to weave; *(hacer punto)* to knit; *(telaraña)* to spin; *fig (plan)* to plot, to scheme.

tejido *nm* **1** fabric; **t. de punto**, knitted fabric. **2** *Anat* tissue.

tejo *nm fam* **tirar los tejos a algn**, to make a play for sb.

tejón *nm* badger.

tel. *abr de* **teléfono**, telephone, tel.

tela *nf* **1** *Tex* material, fabric, cloth; *(de la*

leche) skin; t. de araña, cobweb; t. metálica, gauze. 2 *fam* (*dinero*) dough. 3 *Arte* canvass. 4 *fig* poner en t. de juicio, to question; *fig* tiene mucha t., it's not an easy thing.

telar *nm Tex* loom.

telaraña *nf* cobweb, spider's web.

tele *nf fam* telly, TV.

telearrastre *nm* ski lift.

telecabina *nm* cable car.

telecomunicaciones *nfpl* telecommunications.

telediario *nm TV* television news bulletin.

teledirigido,-a *adj* remote-controlled.

telefax *nm* telefax, fax.

teleférico *nm* cable car *o* railway.

telefilm, telefilme *nm* TV film.

telefonazo *nm* dar un t. (a algn), to give (sb) a ring.

telefonear *vt & vi* to telephone, phone.

telefónica *nf* Compañía T., ≈ British Telecom.

telefónico,-a *adj* telephone; llamada telefónica, telephone call.

telefonista *nmf* (telephone) operator.

teléfono *nm* telephone, phone; t. portátil, portable telephone; t. móvil, car phone; está hablando por t., she's on the phone; te llamó por t., she phoned you.

telegrafiar [29] *vtr* to telegraph, wire.

telegráfico,-a *adj* telegraphic; giro t., giro, money order.

telégrafo *nm* 1 telegraph. 2 telégrafos, post office *sing*.

telegrama *nm* telegram, cable.

teleimpresor *nm*, teleimpresora *nf* teleprinter.

telele *nm fam* darle a uno un t., to have a fit.

telemando *nm* remote control (unit).

telenovela *nf* television serial.

teleobjetivo *nm* telephoto lens *sing*.

telepático,-a *adj* telepathic.

telescopio *nm* telescope.

teleserie *nf* television series.

telesilla *nm* chair lift.

telespectador,-a *nm,f* TV viewer.

telesquí *nm* ski lift.

teletexto *nm* teletext.

teletipo *nm* teleprinter.

televidente *nm,f* TV viewer.

televisar *vtr* to televise.

televisión *nf* 1 (*sistema*) television. 2 *fam* (*aparato*) television set; t. en color/en blanco y negro, colour/black and white television; ver la t., to watch television.

televisivo,-a *adj* television; espacio t., television programme.

televisor *nm* television set.

télex *nm inv* telex.

telón *nm Teat* curtain; *Pol Hist* t. de acero, iron curtain; t. de fondo, *Teat* backdrop; *fig* background.

telonero,-a *adj* (*grupo*) t., support band.

tema *nm* 1 (*asunto*) topic, subject; (*de examen*) subject; temas de actualidad, current affairs. 2 *Mús* theme.

temario *nm* (*de examen*) programme.

temática *nf* subject matter.

temático,-a *adj* thematic.

temblar [1] *vi* (*de frío*) to shiver; (*de miedo*) to tremble (de, with); (*voz*) to quiver; (*pulso*) to shake.

tembleque *nm fam* shaking fit.

temblón,-ona *adj* trembling, shaky.

temblor *nm* tremor, shudder; t. de tierra, earth tremor.

tembloroso,-a, tembloso,-a *adj* shaking; (*voz*) quivering, (*de frío*) shivering; (*de miedo*) trembling; manos temblorosas, shaky hands.

temer I *vtr* to fear, be afraid; temo que esté muerto, I fear he's dead; teme que no podrá recibirte, I'm afraid (that) he won't be able to see you. II *vi* to be afraid. III temerse *vr* to fear, be afraid; ¡me lo temía!, I was afraid this would happen!

temerario,-a *adj* reckless, rash.

temeridad *nf* 1 (*actitud*) temerity, rashness. 2 (*acto temerario*) reckless act.

temeroso,-a *adj* fearful, timid. (*temible*) frightful.

temible *adj* fearful, frightful.

temor *nm* 1 fear. 2 (*recelo*) worry, apprehension.

témpano *nm* ice floe.

temperamental *adj* temperamental.

temperamento *nm* temperament; tener t., to have a strong character.

temperatura *nf* temperature.

tempestad *nf* storm; *fig* turmoil, uproar.

tempestuoso,-a *adj* stormy, tempestuous.

templado,-a *adj* 1 (*agua*) lukewarm; (*clima*) mild, temperate. 2 *Mús* (*afinado*) tuned.

templanza *nf* moderation, restraint.

templar *vtr* 1 to moderate. 2 (*algo frío*) to warm up; (*algo caliente*) to cool down. 3 *Mús* (*instrumento*) to tune. 4 *Téc* (*metal*) to temper.

temple *nm* 1 (*fortaleza*) boldness, courage. 2 *Arte* tempera.

templete *nm* bandstand.

templo *nm* temple.

temporada *nf* 1 season; t. alta, high *o* peak season; t. baja, low *o* off season. 2 (*período*) period, time; por temporadas, on and off.

temporal I *adj* temporary, provisional. II *nm* storm.

temporero,-a *nm,f* seasonal *o* temporary worker.

temprano,-a *adj* 1 (*persona*) early-rising. 2 (*cosecha*) early.

temprano,-a *adj & adv* early.

tenacidad *nf* 1 (*perseverancia*) tenacity,

perseverance. **2** (de metal) tensile strength.

tenacillas nfpl (para pelo) curling tongs.

tenaz adj tenacious.

tenaza nf, **tenazas** nfpl (herramienta) pliers, pincers; (para el fuego) tongs.

tendedero nm clothesline, drying place.

tendencia nf tendency.

tendencioso,-a adj tendentious, biased.

tender [3] I vtr **1** (mantel etc) to spread out; (para secar) to hang out. **2** (red) to cast; (puente) to build; (vía, cable) to lay; (trampa) to lay, set. **3** (mano) to stretch o hold out. **4** (tumbar) to lay. II vi to tend (a, to), have a tendency (a, to). III **tenderse** vr to lie down, stretch out.

tenderete nm (puesto) market stall.

tendero,-a nm,f shopkeeper.

tendido,-a nm **1** (de vía, cable) laying; (de puente) construction; t. eléctrico, electrical installation. **2** Taur (asientos) front tiers pl of seats, US bleachers pl.

tendón nm tendon, sinew.

tenebroso,-a adj (sombrío) dark, gloomy; (siniestro) sinister, shady.

tenedor,-a nm fork.

teneduría nf t. de libros, book-keeping.

tenencia nf Jur ilícita de armas, illegal possession of arms.

tener [24] I vtr **1** to have, have got; **tenemos un examen**, we've got o we have an exam; **va a t. un niño**, she's going to have a baby, she's expecting; **¡ahí (lo) tienes!**, here you are! **2** (poseer) to own, possess. **3** (sostener) to hold; **tenme el bolso un momento**, hold my bag a minute; **ten, es para ti**, take this o here you are, it's for you. **4** t. calor/frío, to be hot/cold; **t. cariño a algn**, to be fond of sb; **t. miedo**, to be frightened. **5** (edad) to be; **tiene dieciocho (años)**, he's eighteen (years old). **6** (medida) **la casa tiene cien metros cuadrados**, the house is 100 square metres. **7** (contener) to hold, contain. **8** (mantener) to keep; **me tuvo despierto toda la noche**, he kept me up all night. **9** t. por, (considerar) to consider, think; **me tienen por estúpido**, they think I'm a fool; **ten por seguro que lloverá**, you can be sure it'll rain. **10** t. que, to have (got) to; **tengo que irme**, I must leave; **tienes/tendrías que verlo**, you must/should see it.

II **tenerse** vr **1** t. **en pie**, to stand (up). **2** t. **por**, (considerarse) to think o consider oneself; **se tiene por muy inteligente**, he thinks he's very intelligent.

tenga subj pres → tener.

tengo indic pres → tener.

teniente nm **1** Mil lieutenant. **2** t. (de) alcalde, deputy mayor.

tenis nm tennis.

tenista nmf tennis player.

tenor¹ nm Mús tenor.

tenor² nm a t. de, according to.

tensar vtr (cable etc) to tighten; (arco) to draw.

tensión nf **1** tension; **en t.**, tense. **2** Elec tension, voltage. **3** Med t. arterial, blood pressure; t. nerviosa, nervous strain. **4** Téc stress.

tenso,-a adj **1** (cuerda, cable) tense, taut. **2** (persona) tense; (relaciones) strained.

tentación nf temptation.

tentáculo nm tentacle.

tentador,-a adj tempting.

tentar [1] vtr **1** (palpar) to feel, touch. **2** (incitar) to tempt.

tentativa nf attempt; Jur t. de asesinato, attempted murder.

tentempié nm fam (pl **tentempiés**) **1** (comida) snack, bite. **2** (juguete) tumbler.

tenue adj (luz, sonido) subdued, faint. **2** (delgado) thin, light.

teñir [6] I vtr **1** (pelo etc) to dye. **2** fig to tinge with. II **teñirse** vr **t. el pelo**, to dye one's hair.

teología nf theology.

teorema nm theorem.

teoría nf theory; **en t.**, theoretically.

teórico,-a adj theoretical.

teorizar [4] vi to theorize (sobre, on).

tequila nm tequila.

terapeuta nmf therapist.

terapia nf therapy.

tercer adj third; **el t. mundo**, the third world.

tercermundista adj third-world.

tercero,-a I adj third. II nm,f **1** (de una serie) third. **2** **a la tercera va la vencida**, third time lucky. III nm (mediador) mediator; Jur third party.

terceto nm Mús trio.

terciar [12] I vi **1** (mediar) to mediate, arbitrate. **2** (participar) to take part, participate. II **terciarse** vr **si se tercia**, should the occasion arise.

terciario,-a adj tertiary.

tercio nm **1** (parte) (one) third. **2** (de cerveza) medium-size bottle of beer. **3** Taur stage, part of a bullfight.

terciopelo nm velvet.

terco,-a adj stubborn, obstinate.

tergiversar vtr (verdad) to distort; (palabras) to twist.

termal adj thermal.

termas nfpl (baños) spa sing, hot baths o springs pl.

térmico,-a adj thermal; **central térmica**, coal-fired power station.

terminación nf completion.

terminal I adj terminal. II nf **1** (de aeropuerto) terminal; (de autobuses) terminus. **2** Elec Inform terminal.

terminante adj **1** (categórico) categorical, final. **2** (dato, resultado) conclusive.

◆**terminantemente** adv categorically; t. prohibido, strictly forbidden.

terminar I *vtr* (*acabar*) to finish, complete; (*completamente*) to finish off. II *vi* 1 (*acabarse*) to finish, end; **termina en seis, it ends with a six; no termina de convencerse,** he still isn't quite convinced. 2 (*ir a parar*) to end up (en, in); **terminó por comprarlo,** he ended up buying it. 3 **t. con,** (*eliminar*) to put an end to. III **terminarse** *vr* 1 to finish, end, be over. 2 (*vino, dinero etc*) to run out.

término *nm* 1 (*final*) end, finish. 2 (*palabra*) term, word; **en otros términos,** in other words; **en términos generales,** generally speaking. 3 **t. municipal,** district. 4 **por t. medio,** on average. 5 *fig* **en último t.,** as a last resort.

terminología *nf* terminology.

termo *nm* thermos (flask), flask.

termodinámico,-a *adj* thermodynamic.

termómetro *nm* thermometer.

termonuclear *adj* thermonuclear.

termostato *nm* thermostat.

ternera *nf* calf; (*carne*) veal.

ternero *nm* calf.

ternura *nf* tenderness.

terquedad *nf* stubbornness, obstinacy.

terracota *nf* terracotta.

Terranova *nf* Newfoundland.

terraplén *nm* embankment.

terráqueo,-a *adj* **globo t.,** (*tierra*) (the) earth; (*esfera*) globe.

terrateniente *nmf* landowner.

terremoto *nm* earthquake.

terrenal *adj* **un paraíso t.,** a heaven on earth.

terreno *nm* 1 (*tierra*) (piece of) land, ground; *Geol* terrain; (*campo*) field; **ganar/perder t.,** to gain/lose ground. 2 *Dep* field, ground. 3 *fig* field, sphere.

terrestre *adj* 1 (*de la tierra*) terrestrial, earthly. 2 (*por tierra*) by land; **por vía t.,** by land.

terrible *adj* terrible, awful.

terrícola *nmf* (*en ciencia ficción*) earthling.

terrier *nm* terrier.

territorio *nm* territory.

terrón *nm* (*de azúcar*) lump; (*de tierra*) clod.

terror *nm* terror; *Cin* horror.

terrorífico,-a *adj* terrifying, frightening.

terrorismo *nm* terrorism.

terrorista *adj & nmf* terrorist.

terroso,-a *adj* (*color*) earth-coloured, *US* earth-colored.

terruño *nm* (*terreno*) piece of land; (*patria chica*) homeland, native land.

terso,-a *adj* smooth.

tersura *nf* smoothness.

tertulia *nf* get-together; **t. literaria,** literary gathering.

tesina *nf* first degree dissertation.

tesis *nf inv* thesis; (*opinión*) view, theory.

tesón *nm* tenacity, firmness.

tesorero,-a *nm,f* treasurer.

tesoro *nm* 1 treasure. 2 (*erario*) exchequer; **T. Público,** Treasury.

test *nm* test.

testaferro *nm* front man.

testamentario,-a *Jur* I *adj* testamentary. II *nm,f* executor.

testamento *nm* 1 *Jur* will; **hacer o otorgar t.,** to make o draw up one's will. 2 *Rel* Testament.

testar *vi* to make o draw up one's will.

testarudo,-a *adj* stubborn, obstinate.

testículo *nm* testicle.

testificar [1] *vtr* to testify.

testigo I *nmf* witness; *Jur* **t. de cargo/descargo,** witness for the prosecution/defence; *Jur* **t. ocular/presencial,** eyewitness; *Rel* **Testigos de Jehová,** Jehovah's Witnesses. II *nm* *Dep* baton.

testimoniar [12] *vtr* 1 (*dar testimonio*) to testify to, attest to. 2 (*mostrar*) to show.

testimonio *nm* *Jur* testimony; (*prueba*) evidence, proof.

teta *nf fam* 1 tit, boob; **niño de t.,** breastfeeding baby. 2 (*de vaca*) udder.

tétano *nm* tetanus.

tetera *nf* teapot.

tetilla *nf* 1 *Anat* man's nipple. 2 (*de biberón*) (rubber) teat.

tetina *nf* (rubber) teat.

tétrico,-a *adj* gloomy, dull.

textil *adj & nm* textile.

texto *nm* text; **libro de t.,** textbook.

textual *adj* textual; (*exacto*) literal; **en palabras textuales,** literally.

textura *nf* *Tex* texture; (*en minerales*) structure.

tez *nf* complexion.

ti *pron pers* you; **es para ti,** it's for you; **hazlo por ti,** do it for your own sake; **piensas demasiado en ti mismo,** you think too much about yourself.

tía *nf* 1 (*pariente*) aunt. 2 *arg* (*mujer*) girl, woman.

tibieza *nf* tepidity; *fig* lack of enthusiasm.

tibio,-a *adj* tepid, lukewarm; *fam* **ponerse t. de cerveza,** to get drunk.

tiburón *nm* shark.

tic *nm* (*pl* **tiques**) tic, twitch; **t. nervioso,** nervous tic o twitch.

ticket *nm* (*pl* **tickets**) (*billete*) ticket; (*recibo*) receipt.

tictac *nm* tick-tock, ticking.

tiempo *nm* 1 time; **a t.,** in time; **a su** (**debido**) **t.,** in due course; **a un t., al mismo t.,** at the same time; **al poco t.,** soon afterwards; **antes de t.,** (too) early o soon; **con el t.,** in the course of time, with time; **con t.,** in advance; **¿cuánto t.?,** how long?; **¿cuánto t. hace?,** how long ago?; **demasiado t.,** too long; **estar a t. de,** to still have time to; **hacer t.,** to kill time; **¿nos da t. de llegar?,** have we got (enough) time to get there?; **t. libre,** free time; *fig* **dar t. al t.,** to let matters take their course. 2 (*meteorológico*) weather; ¿**qué t. hace?**, what's the weather like?; **hace buen/mal t.**, the weather is good/bad. 3 (*edad*) age; ¿**cuánto o qué t. tiene tu niño?**, how old is your baby o child? 4 *Mús* movement. 5 *Dep* half. 6 *Ling* tense.

tienda *nf* 1 shop, *US* store; **ir de tiendas**, to go shopping. 2 **t. (de campaña)**, tent.

tienta *nf* **a tientas**, by touch; **andar a tientas**, to feel one's way; **buscar (algo) a tientas**, to grope (for sth).

tiento *nm* tact; **con t.**, tactfully.

tierno,-a *adj* (*blando*) tender, soft. 2 (*reciente*) fresh.

tierra *nf* 1 (*planeta*) earth. 2 *Agr* land, soil. 3 (*continente*) land; **tocar t.**, to land. 4 (*país*) country; **t. de nadie**, no-man's-land. 5 (*suelo*) ground; *fig* **echar o tirar por t.**, to spoil. 6 *Elec* earth, *US* ground.

tierral *nm* *Am* cloud of dust.

tieso,-a *adj* (*rígido*) stiff, rigid; (*erguido*) upright, erect.

tiesto *nm* flowerpot.

tifoidea *nf* (*fiebre*) **t.**, typhoid (fever).

tifón *nm* typhoon.

tifus *nm inv* typhus (fever).

tigre *nm* tiger; *Am* jaguar.

tijeras *nfpl* (pair of) scissors *pl*.

tijereta *nf* 1 (*insecto*) earwig. 2 *Dep* scissors *pl*.

tila *nf* (*flor*) lime o linden blossom; (*infusión*) lime o linden blossom tea.

tildar *vtr* to call, brand; **me tildó de ladrón**, he called me a thief.

tilde *nm & f* written accent.

tilín *nm* (*sonido*) ting-a-ling; *fig* José le hace t., she fancies José.

tilo *nm* lime tree.

timar *vtr* to swindle; **me han timado**, they did me.

timbal *nm* kettledrum.

timbrar *vtr* (*carta*) to stamp; (*documento*) to seal.

timbre *nm* 1 (*de la puerta*) bell. 2 (*sello*) stamp, seal; *Fin* impuesto del t. revenue stamp. 3 *Mús* (*sonido*) timbre.

timidez *nf* shyness, timidity.

tímido,-a *adj* shy, timid; *fig* (*mejoría*) light; (*intento*) cautious.

timo *nm* swindle, fiddle; **es un t.**, it's a rip-off.

timón *nm* 1 *Náut Av* rudder; **golpe de t.**, U-turn. 2 *Am Aut* steering wheel.

timonel *nm* helmsman.

tímpano *nm Anat* eardrum.

tinaja *nf* large earthenware jar.

tinerfeño,-a I *adj* of o from to Tenerife. II *nm,f* native o inhabitant of Tenerife.

tinglado *nm* 1 (*intriga*) intrigue. 2 (*cobertizo*) shed.

tinieblas *nfpl* darkness *sing*.

tino *nm* 1 (*puntería*) (good) aim; **tener buen t.**, to be a good shot. 2 (*tacto*)

(common) sense, good judgement.

tinta *nf* 1 ink; **t. china**, Indian ink; **t. simpática**, invisible ink. 2 *fig* **medias tintas**, ambiguities, half measures.

tintar *vtr* to dye.

tinte *nm* 1 dye. 2 *fig* (*matiz*) shade, overtone.

tintero *nm* inkpot, inkwell; *fig* **se quedó en el t.**, it wasn't said.

tintinear *vi* (*vidrio*) to clink; (*campana*) to jingle, tinkle.

tintineo *nm* (*de vidrio*) clinking; (*de campana*) jingling.

tinto,-a *adj* (*vino*) red. II *nm* (*vino*) red wine.

tintorería *nf* dry-cleaner's.

tintura *nf* 1 (*colorante*) dye. 2 *Quím* tincture; **t. de yodo**, iodine.

tío *nm* 1 (*pariente*) uncle; **mis tíos**, my uncle and aunt. 2 *fam* fellow, bloke, *US* guy.

tiovivo *nm* roundabout, merry-go-round.

tipazo *nm fam* good figure.

típico,-a *adj* 1 typical; **eso es t. de Antonio**, that's just like Antonio. 2 (*baile, traje*) traditional.

tipificar [1] *vtr* 1 (*normalizar*) to standardize. 2 (*caracterizar*) to typify.

tipismo *nm* local colour.

tipo *nm* 1 (*clase*) type, kind. 2 *fam* (*persona*) guy, fellow, bloke, *US* guy; **t. raro**, weirdo. 3 *Anat* (*de hombre*) build, physique; (*de mujer*) figure; *fig* **jugarse el t.**, to risk one's neck; **aguantar el t.**, to keep one's cool o head. 4 *Fin* rate; **t. bancario o de descuento**, bank rate; **t. de cambio/interés**, rate of exchange/interest. 5 **el político t. de la izquierda**, the typical left-wing politician.

tipografía *nf* typography.

tipográfico,-a *adj* typographic; **error t.**, printing error.

tipógrafo,-a *nm,f* typographer.

tiquismiquis *fam* I *nmf inv* fusspot. II *nmpl* 1 (*escrúpulos*) silly scruples. 2 (*rencillas*) bickering sing.

tira *nf* 1 (*banda, cinta*) strip. 2 (*de dibujos*) comic strip. 3 *fam* la t. de gente, a lot o loads of people. 4 **t. y afloja**, tug of war.

tirabuzón *nm* ringlet.

tirachinas *nm inv* catapult, *US* slingshot.

tirada *nf* (*impresión*) printing; (*edición*) edition.

tirado,-a *adj fam* 1 (*precio*) dirt cheap. 2 (*examen*) dead easy. 3 *fam* dejar t. (a algn), to let (sb) down.

tirador *nm* 1 (*persona*) marksman. 2 (*pomo*) knob, handle; (*cordón*) bell pull. 3 (*tirachinas*) catapult, *US* slingshot.

tiralíneas *nm inv* tracer, drawing o ruling pen.

tiranía *nf* tyranny.

tiránico,-a *adj* tyrannical.

tiranizar [4] *vtr* to tyrannize.

tirano,-a nm,f tyrant.

tirante I adj (cable etc) tight, taut; (situación, relación) tense. **II** nm **1** (de vestido etc) strap; **tirantes**, braces, US suspenders. **2** Téc brace, stay.

tirar I vtr **1** (echar) to throw, fling. **2** (dejar caer) to drop. **3** (desechar) to throw away; fig (dinero) to squander. **4** (derribar) to knock down; **t. la puerta (abajo)**, to smash the door in. **5** (foto) to take. **6** Impr to print. **II** vi **1** (beso) to blow. **2** t. de, (cuerda, puerta) to pull. **2** (chimenea, estufa) to draw. **3** (funcionar) to work, run. **4** ir tirando, to get by. **5 t. a**, to tend towards; **tira a rojo**, it's reddish. **6 tira a la izquierda**, turn left; ¡**venga, tira ya!**, come on, get going! **7** (disparar) to shoot, fire; Ftb **t. a puerta**, to shoot at goal. **III tirarse** vr **1** (lanzarse) to throw o hurl oneself; **t. de cabeza al agua**, to dive into the water. **2** (tumbarse) to lie down. **3** fam (tiempo) to spend; **me tiré una hora esperando**, I waited (for) a good hour. **4** vulg **t. a algn**, to lay sb.

tirita® nf Elastoplast®, Band-aid®, plaster.

tiritar vi to shiver, to shake.

tiro nm **1** (lanzamiento) throw. **2** (disparo, ruido) shot; Ftb **t. a gol**, shot at goal; **t. al blanco**, target shooting; **t. al plato**, clay pigeon shooting; **t. con arco**, archery. **3** (de vestido) shoulder width. **4** (de chimenea) draught, US draft; **animal de t.**, draught animal.

tirón nm pull, tug; (del bolso) snatch; fam **de un t.**, in one go.

tirotear vtr to shoot, snipe.

tiroteo nm shooting, firing to and fro.

tirria nf fam dislike; **le tengo t.**, I dislike him, I can't stand him.

tísico,-a adj tubercular, consumptive.

tisis nf inv tuberculosis, consumption.

tisú nm tissue, paper hankie.

títere nm (marioneta) puppet; **no dejar t. con cabeza**, to spare no-one.

titilar vi (luz) to flicker; (estrella) to twinkle.

titiritero,-a nm,f **1** puppeteer. **2** (acróbata) travelling acrobat.

titubeante adj (indeciso) hesitant; (al hablar) stammering.

titubear vi **1** (dudar) to hesitate, waver. **2** (al hablar) to stammer.

titubeo nm **1** (duda) hesitation. **2** (al hablar) stammering.

titulación nf qualifications pl.

titulado,-a adj (licenciado) graduate; (diplomado) qualified.

titular¹ I nmf (persona) holder. **II** Prensa headline. **III** adj appointed, official.

titular² **I** vtr (poner título) to call. **II** titularse vr **1** (película etc) to be called; ¿cómo se titula?, what is it called? **2** Educ to graduate (en, in).

titulariedad nf Educ tenure.

titulitis nf obsession with qualifications.

II nm certificate.

título nm **1** title. **2** Educ degree; (diploma) diploma. **3** Prensa (titular) headline. **4 a t. de ejemplo**, by way of example.

tiza nf chalk; **una t.**, a piece of chalk.

tiznada nf Am hijo de la **t.**, son of a bitch.

tiznar vtr to blacken (with soot).

tizne nm soot.

tizón nm half-burnt stick, brand.

toalla nf towel; **tirar la t.**, to throw in the towel.

toallero nm towel rack o rail.

tobera nf nozzle.

tobillo nm ankle.

tobogán nm slide, chute.

toca nf (sombrero) headdress; (de monja) wimple.

tocadiscos nm inv record player; **t. digital o compacto**, CD player.

tocado¹ nm **1** (peinado) coiffure, hairdo. **2** (prenda) headdress.

tocado,-a² adj fam crazy, touched.

tocador nm **1** (mueble) dressing table. **2** (habitación) dressing room; **t. de señoras**, powder room.

tocante a loc adv **en lo t. a ...**, with reference to ...

tocar [1] **I** vtr **1** to touch; fam fig toca madera, touch wood. **2** (instrumento, canción) to play; (timbre, campana) to ring; (puerta) to knock; (bocina) to blow. **3** (tema, asunto) to touch on. **4** (afectar) to concern; por lo que a mí me toca, as far as I am concerned. **II** vi **1 a quién le toca?**, (en juegos) whose turn is it? **2 me tocó el gordo**, (en rifa) I won the jackpot. **3 t. con**, to be next to; fig **t. a su fin**, to be coming to an end. **III tocarse** vr (una cosa con otra) to touch each other; ¿os tocáis algo?, (ser parientes) are you related?

tocarse vr (cubrirse) to cover one's head.

tocata I nf Mús toccata. **II** nm fam record player.

tocateja (a) loc adv **pagar a t.**, to pay on the nail.

tocayo,-a nm,f namesake.

tocho nm fam (libro) (grande) tome.

tocino nm lard; **t. ahumado**, smoked bacon; **t. de cielo**, sweet made with egg yolk.

tocólogo,-a nm tocologist, obstetrician.

tocuyo nm Am coarse cotton cloth.

todavía adv **1** (aún) still; (en negativas) yet; **t. la quiere**, he still loves her; **t. no, not yet**; **no mires t.**, don't look yet. **2** (para reforzar) even, still; **t. más/menos**, even more/less.

todo,-a I adj **1** all; **t. el pan**, all the bread; **t. el mundo**, (absolutely) everybody; **t. el día**, all day, the whole o en-

tire day; *fam* t. quisqui, every Tom, Dick and Harry. **2** (*cada*) every; **t. ciudadano de más de dieciocho años**, every citizen over eighteen years of age. **3** (*entero*) complete, thorough; **es toda una mujer**, she is every inch a woman. **4 todos,-as**, all; (*con expresiones de tiempo*) every; **t. los niños**, all the children; **t. los martes**, every Tuesday.
II *nm* (*totalidad*) whole.
III *pron* **1** (*sin excluir nada*) all, everything; **ante t.**, first of all; **con t.**, in spite of everything; **del t.**, completely; **después de t.**, after all; **eso es t.**, that's all, that's it; **estar en t.**, to be really with it; **hay de t.**, there are all sorts; **lo sé t.**, I know all about it; **t. lo contrario**, quite the contrary *o* opposite; **t. lo más**, at the most. **2** (*cualquiera*) anybody; **t. aquél** *o* **el que quiera**, anybody who wants (to). **3 todos,-as**, (*cada uno*) all; **t. aprobamos**, we all passed; **t. fueron**, they all went.
IV *adv* completely, totally; **volvió t. sucio**, he was all dirty when he got back.
todopoderoso,-a *adj* all-powerful, almighty.
todoterreno *nm* all-terrain vehicle.
toga *nf* **1** gown, robe. **2** *Hist* toga.
Tokio *n* Tokyo.
toldo *nm* **1** (*cubierta*) awning. **2** *Am* (*cabaña*) tent, teepee.
tolerancia *nf* tolerance.
tolerante *adj* tolerant.
tolerar *vtr* to tolerate; (*situación*) to stand; (*gente*) to put up with.
toma *nf* **1** (*acción*) taking; *Elec* t. de corriente, plug, socket. **2** *Med* dose. **3** *Mil* capture. **4** *Cin* take, shot. **5** t. de posesión, swearing-in. **6** *fam* **t. y daca**, give and take.
tomado,-a *adj* **1** (*voz*) hoarse. **2** *Am* (*borracho*) drunk. **3 tenerla tomada con algn**, to have it in for sb.
tomadura *nf fam* t. de pelo, leg-pull; (*timo*) rip-off.
tomar **I** *vtr* **1** (*coger*) to take; (*autobús, tren*) to catch; (*decisión*) to make, take; **toma**, here (you are); **t. el sol**, to sunbathe; *Av* **t. tierra**, to land; *fam* **tomarla con algn**, to have it in for sb. **2** (*comer, beber*) to have. **3 t. algo a mal**, to take sth badly; **t. en serio/broma**, to take seriously/as a joke. **4** (*confundir*) to take (por, for). **5** *Mil* to take. **II tomarse** *vr* **1** (*comer*) to eat; (*beber*) to drink. **2** *fam* **no te lo tomes así**, don't take it like that.
tomate *nm* tomato; **salsa de t.**, (*de lata*) tomato sauce; (*de botella*) ketchup.
tomavistas *nm inv* cine *o* US movie camera.
tómbola *nf* tombola.
tomillo *nm* thyme.
tomo *nm* volume; *fam* **de t. y lomo**, utter, out-and-out.

ton *nm* sin t. ni son, without rhyme or reason.
tonada *nf* **1** *Mús* tune, song. **2** *Am* (*acento*) accent.
tonalidad *nf* tonality.
tonel *nm* barrel, cask.
tonelada *nf* ton; **t. métrica**, tonne.
tonelaje *nm* tonnage.
tonelero,-a *nm,f* cooper.
tongo *nm* fix.
tónico,-a **I** *nm* *Med* tonic; (*cosméticos*) skin tonic. **II** *nf* **1** (*tendencia*) tendency, trend; **tónica general**, overall trend. **2** (*bebida*) tonic (water). **3** *Mús* tonic. **III** *adj* **1** *Ling* tonic, stressed. **2** *Mús* *Med* tonic.
tonificante *adj* invigorating.
tonificar [1] *vtr* to tone up, invigorate.
tono *nm* tone; **a t. con**, in tune *o* harmony with; **subir de t.** *o* **el t.**, to speak louder; **un t. alto/bajo**, a high/low pitch; *fig* **darse t.**, to put on airs; *fig* **fuera de t.**, inappropriate, out of place; **dar el t.**, to set the tone.
tontear *vi* **1** to act the clown, fool about. **2** (*galantear*) to flirt.
tontería *nf* **1** stupidity, silliness. **2** (*dicho, hecho*) silly *o* stupid thing. **3** (*insignificancia*) trifle.
tonto,-a **I** *adj* silly, dumb. **II** *nm,f* fool, idiot; **t. de remate** *o* **de capirote**, prize idiot.
topacio *nm* topaz.
toparse *vr* **t. con**, to bump into; (*dificultades*) to run up against, encounter; **t. con algo**, to come across sth.
tope **I** *nm* **1** (*límite*) limit, end; *fam* **a t.**, (*al máximo*) flat out; *fig* **estar hasta los topes**, to be full up; **fecha t.**, deadline. **2** *Téc* stop, check. **3** *Ferroc* buffer. **II** *adv fam* incredibly; **t. difícil**, really difficult.
tópico,-a **I** *nm* commonplace, cliché. **II** *adj* *Med* *Farm* for external use.
topo *nm* mole.
topografía *nf* topography.
topónimo *nm* place name.
toque *nm* **1** touch; *fam* **dar un t. a algn**, (*avisar*) to let sb know; (*advertir*) to warn sb. **2** (*de campanas*) peal; *fig* warning; **t. de queda**, curfew.
toquetear *vtr* to fiddle with, finger.
toquilla *nf* (knitted) shawl.
tórax *nm* thorax.
torbellino *nm* **1** (*de viento*) whirlwind. **2** *fig* (*confusión*) whirl, turmoil.
torcedura *nf* (*acción*) twist, twisting; *Med* sprain.
torcer [4] **I** *vtr* **1** (*metal*) to bend; (*cuerda, hilo*) to twist; *Med* to sprain; *fig* (*esquina*) to turn. **2** (*inclinar*) to slant. **II** *vi* to turn (left *o* right). **III torcerse** *vr* **1** (*doblarse*) to twist, bend. **2** **me se torció el tobillo**, I sprained my ankle. **3** (*plan*) to fall through. **4** (*desviarse*) to go off to the side.

torcido,-a adj twisted; (ladeado) slanted, lopsided; (corbata) crooked.

tordo,-a I adj dapple-grey. **II** nm Orn thrush.

torear I vtr to fight; fam **t. a algn,** to tease o confuse sb; fam **t. un asunto,** to tackle a matter skilfully. **II** vi to fight.

toreo nm bullfighting.

torero,-a nm,f bullfighter.

tormenta nf storm.

tormento nm (tortura) torture; (padecimiento) torment.

tormentoso,-a adj stormy.

tornado nm tornado.

tornar fml **I** vtr (convertir) to transform, to turn (en, into). **II** vi (regresar) to return, go back; **t. en sí,** to regain consciousness. **III tornarse** vr to become, turn.

tornasolado,-a adj iridescent.

torneo nm 1 Dep tournament. 2 Hist tourney, joust.

tornillo nm screw.

torniquete nm 1 turnstile. 2 Med tourniquet.

torno nm 1 Téc lathe; (de alfarero) wheel. 2 **en t. a,** (alrededor de) around; (acerca de) about.

toro nm bull; **¿te gustan los toros?,** do you like bullfighting?

toronja nf grapefruit.

torpe adj 1 (sin habilidad) clumsy. 2 (tonto) dim, thick. 3 (movimiento) slow, awkward.

torpedear vtr to torpedo.

torpedo nm torpedo.

torpeza nf 1 (física) clumsiness; (mental) dimness, stupidity. 2 (lentitud) slowness, heaviness. 3 (error) blunder.

torre nf 1 tower. 2 Mil Náut turret. 3 Ajedrez rook, castle.

torrefacto,-a adj roasted; **café t.,** high roast coffee.

torrencial adj torrential.

torrente nm 1 (de agua) torrent. 2 fig **t. de voz,** strong o powerful voice.

torrezno nm rasher of fried bacon.

tórrido,-a adj torrid.

torrija nf French toast.

torsión nf 1 (torcedura) twist, twisting. 2 Téc torsion.

torso nm 1 Anat torso. 2 Arte bust.

torta nf 1 Culin cake; 2 fam (golpe) slap, punch.

tortazo nm fam 1 (bofetada) slap, punch. 2 (golpe) whack, thump.

tortícolis nf inv crick in the neck.

tortilla nf 1 (egg) omelette, US omelet; **t. francesa/española,** (plain)/potato omelette. 2 Am tortilla.

tortillera nf vulg dyke, lesbian.

tórtola nf dove.

tortuga nf (de tierra) tortoise, US turtle; (de mar) turtle.

tortuoso,-a adj tortuous.

tortura nf torture.

torturar vtr to torture.

tos nf cough; **t. ferina,** whooping cough.

tosco,-a adj (basto) rustic, rough; (persona) uncouth.

toser vi to cough.

tosquedad nf roughness.

tostada nf (slice of) toast.

tostado,-a adj 1 (pan) toasted. 2 (moreno) tanned, brown.

tostador nm toaster.

tostar [2] vtr (pan) to toast; (café) to roast; (carne, pescado) to brown; fig (la piel) to tan.

tostón nm 1 Culin (pan frito) crouton. 2 fam (tabarra) bore, drag.

total I adj (completo) total. **II** nm 1 (todo) whole; **en t.,** in all. 2 Mat total. **III** adv so, in short; **¿t. para qué?,** what's the point anyhow?; fam **t. que ...,** so ...; **t., tampoco te hará caso,** he won't listen to you, anyway.

totalidad nf whole, totality; **la t. de,** all of; **en su t.,** as a whole.

totalitario,-a adj totalitarian.

totalizar [4] vtr to total. **II** vi to amount to.

tóxico,-a I adj toxic, poisonous. **II** nm poison.

toxicología nf toxicology.

toxicólogo,-a nm,f toxicologist.

toxicomanía nf drug addiction.

toxicómano,-a Med **I** adj addicted to drugs. **II** nm drug addict.

tozudo,-a adj obstinate, stubborn.

traba nf 1 (de rueda) chock; (enlace) bond, tie. 2 fig (obstáculo) hindrance, obstacle.

trabajador,-a I nm,f worker, labourer, US laborer. **II** adj hard-working.

trabajar I vi to work; **trabaja mucho,** he works hard; **t. de camarera,** to work as a waitress. **II** vtr 1 to work (on); (la tierra) to till. 2 (asignatura etc) to work on. 3 fam (convencer) to (try to) persuade.

trabajo nm 1 (ocupación) work; **t. a destajo,** piecework; **t. eventual,** casual labour; **trabajos manuales,** arts and crafts. 2 (empleo) employment, job. 3 (tarea) task, job. 4 Educ (redacción) report, paper. 5 (esfuerzo) effort; **cuesta t. creerlo,** it's hard to believe.

trabajoadicto nm,f workaholic.

trabajoso,-a adj (laborioso) hard, laborious; (difícil) difficult.

trabalenguas nm inv tongue twister.

trabar I vtr 1 (sujetar) to lock, fasten; (un plan) to obstruct. 2 (conversación, amistad) to start, to strike up. 3 Culin to thicken. **II trabarse** vr 1 (cuerdas) to get tangled up. 2 fig **se le trabó la lengua,** he got tongue-tied.

trabazón nf (de ideas) link.

trabilla nf (de pantalón) belt loop.

trabuco nm blunderbuss.

tracción *nf* traction; *Aut* **t. delantera/ trasera**, front-/rear-wheel drive; *Aut* **t. en las cuatro ruedas**, four-wheel drive.

tractor *nm* tractor.

tradición *nf* tradition.

tradicional *adj* traditional.

traducción *nf* translation; **t. directa/ inversa**, translation from/into a foreign language.

traducir [10] I *vtr* to translate (**a**, into). II **traducirse** *vr fig* to result (**en**, in).

traductor,-a *nm,f* translator.

traer [25] I *vtr* 1 to bring; **trae**, give it to me. 2 (*llevar puesto*) to wear. 3 (*llevar consigo*) to carry. 4 (*problemas*) to cause; **traerá como consecuencia ...**, it will result in .... II **traerse** *vr* (*llevar consigo*) to bring along; *fig* **¿qué se trae entre manos?**, what is he up to?

traficante *nmf* (*de drogas etc*) trafficker, pusher.

traficar [1] *vi* (*ilegalmente*) to traffic (**con**, in).

tráfico *nm* 1 *Aut* traffic; **t. rodado**, road traffic. 2 *Com* traffic, trade; **t. de drogas**, drug traffic.

tragaluz *nm* skylight.

tragaperras *nf inv* (**máquina**) **t.**, slot machine.

tragar [7] I *vtr* 1 (*ingerir*) to swallow. 2 *fam* (*engullir*) to gobble up, tuck away. 3 *fig* (*a una persona*) to stand, stomach. 4 *fig* (*creer*) to believe, swallow. II **tragarse** *vr* 1 (*ingerir*) to swallow. 2 *fig* (*creer*) to believe, swallow.

tragedia *nf* tragedy.

trágico,-a *adj* tragic.

trago *nm* 1 (*bebida*) swig; **de un t.**, in one go. 2 **pasar un mal t.**, to have a bad time of it.

tragón,-ona *nm,f* glutton, big eater.

traición *nf* treason, betrayal; **a t.**, treacherously; **alta t.**, high treason.

traicionar *vtr* to betray; (*delatar*) to give away, betray.

traicionero,-a *adj* treacherous.

traidor,-a I *adj* treacherous. II *nm,f* traitor.

traigo *indic pres* → **traer.**

tráiler *nm* (*pl* **tráilers**) 1 *Cin* trailer, *US* preview. 2 *Aut* articulated lorry, *US* trailer truck.

traje¹ *nm* 1 (*de hombre*) suit; **t. de baño**, bathing suit *o* costume, swimsuit; **t. de paisano**, civilian clothes *o* dress; **t. de luces**, bullfighter's costume. 2 (*de mujer*) dress; **t. de chaqueta**, two-piece suit; **t. de novia**, wedding dress.

traje² *pt indef* → **traer.**

trajeado,-a *adj fam* sharp, dapper.

trajearse *vr* to dress up.

trajín *nm fam* comings and goings *pl*, hustle and bustle.

trajinar *vi* to run *o* bustle about.

trama *nf* 1 *Tex* weft, woof. 2 *Lit* plot.

tramar *vtr* to plot, cook up; **¿qué tramas?**, what are you up to?

tramitar *vtr* 1 (*gestionar*) to take the necessary (legal) steps to obtain. 2 *fml* (*despachar*) to convey, transmit. 3 *Com Jur Fin* to carry out, to process.

trámite *nm* (*paso*) step; (*formalidad*) formality; *Com Jur Fin* procedures *pl*, proceeding.

tramo *nm* (*de carretera*) section, stretch; (*de escalera*) flight.

tramoya *nf* (*maquinaria*) stage machinery; (*trama*) plot, scheme.

trampa *nf* 1 (*de caza*) trap, snare. 2 (*puerta*) trap door. 3 (*engaño*) fiddle; **hacer trampa(s)**, to cheat. 4 (*truco*) trick.

trampilla *nf* trap door, hatch.

trampolín *nm* 1 *Natación* diving board. 2 *Esquí* ski jump.

tramposo,-a I *adj* deceitful. II *nm,f* cheat; *Naipes* cardsharp.

tranca *nf* 1 (*garrote*) cudgel; *fam* **a trancas y barrancas**, with great difficulty. 2 (*en puerta, ventana*) bar.

trance *nm* 1 (*coyuntura*) (critical) moment; **estar en t. de ...**, to be on the point of ... 2 (*éxtasis*) trance.

tranquilidad *nf* calmness, tranquillity, *US* tranquility; **con t.**, calmly; **pídemelo con toda t.**, don't hesitate to ask me.

tranquilizante *nm* tranquillizer, *US* tranquilizer.

tranquilizar [4] I *vtr* to calm down; **lo dijo para tranquilizarme**, he said it to reassure me. II **tranquilizarse** *vr* (*calmarse*) to calm down.

tranquilo,-a *adj* 1 (*persona, lugar*) calm; (*agua*) still; (*conciencia*) clear; *fam* **tú t.**, don't you worry. 2 (*despreocupado*) placid, easy-going.

tranquillo *nm fig* knack; **coger el t. a algo**, to get the knack of sth.

transacción *nf* transaction, deal.

transatlántico,-a I *nm Náut* (ocean) liner. II *adj* transatlantic.

transbordador *nm* (car) ferry; **t. espacial**, space shuttle.

transbordar I *vtr* to transfer; *Náut* (*mercancías*) to transship. II *vi Ferroc* to change trains, *US* transfer.

transbordo *nm* 1 *Ferroc* change, *US* transfer; **hacer t.**, to change *o* transfer. 2 *Náut* transshipment.

transcurrir *vi* 1 (*tiempo*) to pass, to go by. 2 (*acontecer*) to take place.

transcurso *nm* course *o* passing (of time); **en el t. de**, in the course of, during.

transeúnte *nm,f* 1 (*peatón*) passer-by. 2 (*residente temporal*) temporary resident, *US* transient.

transferencia *nf* transference; *Fin* transfer; **t. bancaria**, banker's order.

transferible *adj* transferable.

transferir [5] *vtr* to transfer.

transformación *nf* transformation.

transformador *nm Elec* transformer.

transformar I *vtr* to transform, change. II **transformarse** *vr* to change, to turn (en, into); (*algo plegable*) to convert.

tránsfuga *nmf* 1 *Mil* deserter. 2 *Pol* turncoat.

transfusión *nf* transfusion.

transgredir *vtr* defect to transgress, break.

transgresor,-a *nm,f* transgressor, lawbreaker.

transición *nf* transition.

transido,-a *adj fml* **t. de angustia**, overcome by anxiety; **t. de dolor**, racked with pain.

transigente *adj* tolerant.

transigir [6] *vi* to compromise.

transistor *nm* transistor.

transitable *adj* passable.

transitado,-a *adj* (*carretera*) busy.

transitar *vi* to pass.

transitivo,-a *adj* transitive.

tránsito *nm* 1 *Aut* traffic. 2 (*movimiento*) movement, passage; **pasajeros en t.**, passengers in transit.

transitorio,-a *adj* transitory.

translucir [35] *vtr* → **traslucir**.

transmisión *nf* 1 transmission. 2 *Téc* drive; **t. delantera/trasera**, front-/rear-wheel drive. 3 *Rad TV* transmission, broadcast.

transmisor *nm* transmitter.

transmitir *vtr* 1 to transmit, pass on. 2 *Rad TV* to transmit, broadcast. 3 *Jur* to transfer, hand down.

transparencia *nf* 1 transparency; *Pol* openness. 2 *Fot* slide.

transparentarse *vr* to be transparent; **esta tela se transparenta**, this is seethrough material; **se le transparentaban las bragas**, you could see her underpants.

transparente I *adj* transparent; *Pol* open. II *nm* 1 (*visillo*) net curtain. 2 (*pantalla*) shade, blind.

transpiración *nf* perspiration.

transpirar *vi* to perspire.

transplante *nm* transplant; *Med* **t. de corazón/córnea**, heart/eye transplant.

transponer [19] I *vtr* (*mudar de sitio*) to transpose, move about. II **transponerse** *vr* (*desmayarse*) to faint.

transportar *vtr* to transport; (*pasajeros*) to carry; (*mercancías*) to ship.

transporte *nm* 1 transport. 2 *Com* freight; **t. de mercancías**, freight transport; **t. marítimo**, shipment.

transportista *nmf* carrier.

transvase *nm* 1 (*de líquidos*) decanting. 2 (*de ríos*) transfer.

transversal *adj* transverse, cross.

tranvía *nm* tram, tramcar, *US* streetcar.

trapecio *nm* trapeze.

trapecista *nmf* trapeze artiste.

trapero,-a I *nm* rag-and-bone man, *US* junkman. II *adj* **puñalada trapera**, stab in the back.

trapichear *vi* to be up to something.

trapicheo *nm* jiggery-pokery.

trapo *nm* 1 (*viejo*, *roto*) rag. 2 (*bayeta*) cloth; **t. de cocina**, dishcloth; **t. del polvo**, duster; *fam* **poner a (algn) como un t. (sucio)**, to tear sb apart.

tráquea *nf* trachea, windpipe.

traqueteo *nm* rattle, clatter.

tras *prep* 1 (*después de*) after; **uno t. otro**, one after the other. 2 (*detrás*) behind; **sentados uno t. oto**, sitting one behind the other. 3 **andar/ir t.**, to be after; **la policía iba t. ella**, the police were after her.

trasatlántico,-a *adj* & *nm* → **transatlántico,-a**.

trasbordador *nm* → **transbordador**.

trasbordar *vtr* & *vi* → **transbordar**.

trasbordo *nm* → **transbordo**.

trascendencia *nf* 1 (*importancia*) importance, significance. 2 (*en filosofía*) transcendence.

trascendental, trascendente *adj* 1 significant, far-reaching. 2 (*en filosofía*) transcendental.

trascender [33] *vtr vi* 1 (*noticia*) to become known, leak out. 2 (*tener consecuencias*) to have far-reaching consequences. 3 **t. de**, to go beyond.

trascribir *vtr* → **transcribir**.

trascripción *nf* → **transcripción**.

trascurrir *vi* → **transcurrir**.

trascurso *nm* → **transcurso**.

trasero,-a I *adj* back, rear; **en la parte trasera**, at the back. II *nm euf* bottom, bum.

trasferencia *nf* → **transferencia**.

trasferible *adj* → **transferible**.

trasferir [5] *vtr* → **transferir**.

trasfondo *nm* background.

trasformación *nf* → **transformación**.

trasformador *adj* & *nm* → **transformador**.

trasformar *vtr* → **transformar**.

trásfuga *nmf* → **tránsfuga**.

trasfusión *nf* → **transfusión**.

trasgredir *vtr* → **transgredir**.

trasgresión *nf* → **transgresión**.

trasgresor,-a *nm,f* → **transgresor,-a**.

trashumancia *nf* seasonal movement of livestock.

trasiego *nm* comings and goings *pl*, hustle and bustle.

trasladar I *vtr* (*cosa*) to move; (*persona*) to move, transfer. II **trasladarse** *vr* to go, move.

traslado *nm* (*de casa*) move, removal; (*de personal*) transfer; *Educ* **t. de expediente**, transfer of student record.

traslucirse *vr* to show (through).

trasluz *nm* mirar algo al t., to hold sth against the light.

trasmano *nm* a t., out of reach; (me) coge a t., it's out of my way.

trasmisión *nf* → transmisión.

trasmisor,-a *adj & nm* → transmisor,-a.

trasmitir *vtr* → transmitir.

trasnochado,-a *adj (desfasado)* old, hackneyed.

trasnochador,-a I *adj* given to staying up late. II *nm,f* night bird, nighthawk.

trasnochar *vi* to stay up (very) late.

traspapelarse *vr* to get mislaid o misplaced.

trasparencia *nf* → transparencia.

trasparentar *vtr* → transparentar.

trasparente *adj & nm* → transparente.

traspasar *vtr* 1 *(atravesar)* to go through; *(río)* to cross. 2 *(negocio, local)* to transfer; 'se traspasa', 'for sale'. 3 *fig (exceder)* to exceed, go beyond.

traspaso *nm* 1 *(de propiedad etc)* transfer. 2 Com *(venta)* sale.

traspié *nm (pl traspiés)* stumble, trip; dar un t., to trip; *fig* to slip up.

traspiración *nf* → transpiración.

traspirar *vi* → transpirar.

trasplantar *vtr* → transplantar.

trasplante *nm* → transplante.

trasponer [19] *vtr* → transponer.

trasportador,a *adj & nm* → transportador,-a.

trasportar *vtr* → transportar.

trasporte *nm* → transporte.

traspuesto,-a *adj* quedarse t., to faint.

trasquilar *vtr (oveja)* to shear; *(pelo)* to crop.

trastabillar *vi (tambalearse)* to stagger, totter.

trastada *nf fam* hacer trastadas, to be up to mischief.

trastazo *nm fam* wallop, thump.

traste[1] *nm* Mús fret.

traste[2] *nm* 1 *(trasto)* piece of junk. 2 *fig* dar al t. (con un plan), to spoil (a plan); irse al t., to fall through.

trastear *vi (revolver)* to rummage about.

trastero *nm (cuarto)* t., junk room.

trastienda *nf* back shop.

trasto *nm (objeto cualquiera)* thing; *(cosa inservible)* piece of junk.

trastocar [2] *vtr* → trastornar.

trastornado,-a *adj (loco)* mad, unhinged.

trastornar I *vtr (planes)* to disrupt. 2 *fig (persona)* to unhinge. II **trastornarse** *vr (enloquecer)* to go out of one's mind, go mad.

trastorno *nm (molestia)* trouble, inconvenience; t. mental, mental disorder o disturbance.

trasvasar *vtr* → transvasar.

trasvase *nm* → transvase.

trasverso,-a *adj* → transverso,-a.

trata *nf* slave trade o traffic; t. de blancas, white slave trade.

tratable *adj* easy to get along with, congenial.

tratado *nm* 1 *(pacto)* treaty. 2 *(estudio)* treatise.

tratamiento *nm* 1 treatment. 2 Téc processing, treatment. 3 *Inform* processing.

tratar I *vtr* 1 *(atender)* to treat; t. bien/mal, to treat well/badly. 2 Med to treat. 3 *(asunto)* to discuss. 4 *Inform Téc* to process. 5 me trata de tú, he addresses me as 'tu'. II *vi* 1 t. de, *(intentar)* to try. 2 t. de o sobre o acerca, to be about; ¿de qué trata?, what is it about? 3 t. con, *(tener tratos)* to deal with; *(negociar)* to negotiate with; *(relacionarse)* to move among. 4 Com t. en, to deal in. III **tratarse** *vr* 1 *(relacionarse)* to be on speaking terms. 2 se trata de, *(es cuestión de)* it's a question of; se trata de un caso excepcional, it's an exceptional case.

trato *nm* 1 *(de personas)* manner; *(contacto)* contact; malos tratos, ill-treatment sing. 2 *(acuerdo)* agreement; ¡t. hecho!, it's a deal! 3 Com deal.

trauma *nm* trauma.

traumático,-a *adj* traumatic.

traumatizar *vtr* Med to traumatize; *fam* to shock.

través I *prep* 1 a t. de, *(superficie)* across, over; *(agujero etc)* through; a t. del río, across the river; a t. del agujero, through the hole. 2 *fig* a t. de, through; a t. del periódico, through the newspaper. II *adv* de t., *(transversalmente)* crosswise; *(de lado)* sideways. III *nm (pl traveses) fig (desgracia)* misfortune.

travesaño *nm* Ftb crossbar.

travesía *nf (viaje)* crossing.

travestí, travestí *nmf* transvestite.

travesura *nf* mischief, childish prank.

travieso,-a *adj* mischievous.

trayecto *nm* 1 *(distancia)* distance; *(recorrido)* route; *(trecho)* stretch. 2 *(viaje)* journey.

trayectoria *nf* 1 *(de proyectil, geométrica)* trajectory. 2 *fig (orientación)* line, course.

traza *nf* 1 *(apariencia)* looks *pl*, appearance; no lleva trazas de curarse, it doesn't look as if he's going to get better. 2 *Arquit* plan, design.

trazado *nm* 1 *(plano)* layout, plan. 2 *(de carretera, ferrocarril)* route.

trazar [4] *vtr (línea)* to draw; *(plano)* to design; *fig (plan)* to draw up the broad lines of.

trazo *nm* 1 *(línea)* line. 2 *(de letra)* stroke.

trébol *nm* 1 trefoil. 2 *Naipes* club.

trece *inv* I *adj* thirteen. II *nm* thirteen; *fig* estar o mantenerse o seguir en sus t., to stick to one's guns.

trecho *nm* 1 *(distancia)* distance, way; *(tramo)* stretch; de t. en t., from time to time.

tregua nf Mil truce; fig respite.

treinta adj & nm inv thirty.

treintena nf una t. de, (about) thirty.

treintavo,-a adj & nm thirtieth.

tremendista adj over the top.

tremendo,-a adj 1 (terrible) terrible, dreadful. 2 (muy grande) enormous; fig tremendous.

trementina nf turpentine.

trémulo,-a adj lit (vacilante) quivering, tremulous; (luz) flickering.

tren nm 1 train. 2 Av t. de aterrizaje, undercarriage; t. de lavado, car wash. 3 t. de vida, life style.

trenca nf duffle coat.

trenza nf (de pelo) plait, US braid.

trepador,-a adj climbing.

trepar vtr & vi to climb.

trepidante adj vibrating, shaking; fig lleva un ritmo de vida t., he leads a hectic o frantic life.

trepidar vi to vibrate, shake.

tres I adj inv (cardinal) three; (ordinal) third; fam de t. al cuarto, cheap, of little value. II nm (pl treses) three; t. en raya, noughts and crosses, US tick-tack-toe.

trescientos,-as adj & nm,f three hundred.

tresillo nm 1 (mueble) (three-piece) suite. 2 Mús triplet.

treta nf trick, ruse.

triángulo nm triangle; fig t. amoroso, eternal triangle.

tribal adj tribal.

tribu nf tribe.

tribuna nf 1 (plataforma) rostrum, dais; t. de (la) prensa, press box. 2 Dep stand.

tribunal nm 1 Jur court; t. de apelación, court of appeal; T. Supremo, High Court, US Supreme Court; t. (tutelar) de menores, juvenile court. 2 (de examen) board of examiners.

tributar vtr to pay.

tributario,-a adj sistema t., tax system.

tributo nm 1 Com tax. 2 pagar t. a, (homenaje) to pay tribute to.

triciclo nm tricycle.

tricornio nm three-cornered hat.

tridimensional adj three-dimensional.

trienio nm three year period.

trifásico,-a I adj Elec three-phase. II nm adapter.

trigésimo,-a adj & nm,f thirtieth; t. primero, thirty-first.

trigo nm wheat.

trilogía nf trilogy.

trilla nf threshing.

trillado,-a adj fig well-worn.

trilladora nf threshing machine; t. segadora, combine harvester.

trillar vtr to thresh.

trimestral adj quarterly, three-monthly.

trimestre nm quarter; Educ term.

trinar vi 1 to warble. 2 fam to rage, fume;

Santiago está que trina, Santiago is really fuming.

trincar¹ [1] vtr fam (capturar) to catch.

trincar² vtr fam to drink.

trinchar vtr (carne) to carve, slice (up).

trinchera nf trench.

trineo nm sledge, sleigh.

trinidad nf la Santísima T., the Holy Trinity.

trino nm 1 warble, trill. 2 Mús trill.

trío nm trio.

tripa nf 1 (intestino) gut, intestine; fam tummy; dolor de t., stomach ache. 2 tripas, innards.

triple adj & nm triple.

triplicado,-a adj triplicate; por t., in triplicate.

triplicar [1] vtr to triple, treble.

trípode nm tripod.

tríptico nm 1 (cuadro) triptych. 2 (folleto) leaflet.

tripulación nf crew.

tripulante nmf crew member.

tripular vtr to man.

trip(y) nm arg (droga) trip.

triquiñuela nf fam trick, dodge.

tris nm estar en un t. de, to be on the verge of.

triste adj 1 (persona, situación) sad. 2 (lugar) gloomy.

tristeza nf sadness.

triturar vtr (machacar) to grind (up).

triunfador,-a I adj winning. II nm,f winner.

triunfal adj triumphant.

triunfar vtr to triumph.

triunfo nm 1 (victoria) triumph, victory; Dep win. 2 (éxito) success.

trivial adj trivial.

trivialidad nf triviality.

trivializar vtr to trivialize, minimize.

triza nf bit, fragment; hacer trizas, to tear to shreds.

trocar [2] vtr to barter.

trocear vtr to cut up (into bits o pieces).

trochemoche (a) loc adv fam haphazardly.

trofeo nm trophy.

trola nf fam fib.

trolebús nm trolley bus.

tromba nf t. de agua, violent downpour.

trombón nm trombone.

trombosis nf inv thrombosis.

trompa nf 1 Mús horn. 2 (de elefante) trunk. 3 Anat tube. 4 fam estar t., to be sloshed o plastered.

trompazo nm fam bump; darse o pegarse un t., to have a bump.

trompeta nf trumpet.

trompetista nmf trumpet player, trumpeter.

trompicón nm trip, stumble; hacer algo a trompicones, to do sth in fits and starts.

trompo nm spinning top.

tronar [2] I vi to thunder. II vtr Am to shoot.

tronchar I vtr (rama, tronco) to cut down, fell; fig (esperanzas etc) to destroy. II **troncharse** vr **t. de risa**, to split one's sides with laughter.

troncho nm stem, stalk.

tronco nm 1 Anat trunk, torso. 2 Bot (de árbol) trunk; (leño) log; fam fig **dormir como un t.**, to sleep like a log.

tronera nf 1 (de billar) pocket. 2 (ventana) small window; (de fortificación) loophole; Náut porthole.

trono nm throne.

tropa nf 1 squad. 2 **tropas**, troops pl.

tropel nm throng, mob; **en t.**, in a mad rush.

tropezar [1] vi 1 to trip, stumble (con, on). 2 **t. con algo**, to come across sth; **t. con algn/dificultades**, to run into sb/difficulties.

tropezón nm 1 (traspié) trip, stumble; **dar un t.**, to trip. 2 (error) slip-up, faux pas. 3 (de comida) chunk of meat.

tropical adj tropical.

trópico nm tropic.

tropiezo I nm 1 (obstáculo) trip. 2 fig (error) blunder, faux pas. II indic pres → tropezar.

trotamundos nmf inv globe-trotter.

trotar vi to trot.

trote nm 1 trot; **al t.**, at a trot. 2 fam **ya no está para esos trotes**, he cannot keep up the pace any more.

trovador nm troubadour.

trozo nm piece.

trucar [1] vtr to doctor, alter.

truco nm 1 (ardid) trick; **aquí hay t.**, there's something fishy going on here. 2 **coger el t. (a algo)**, to get the knack o hang (of sth).

truculento,-a adj cruel.

trucha nf trout.

trueno nm thunder; **un t.**, a thunderclap.

trueque nm barter.

trufa nf truffle.

truhán,-ana nm,f rogue, crook.

truncar [1] vtr to truncate; (fig vida etc) to cut short; fig (esperanzas) to shatter.

trust nm (pl **trusts**) trust, cartel.

tu adj pos your; **tu libro**, your book; **tus libros**, your books.

tú pron you; **de tú a tú**, on equal terms.

tuba nf tuba.

tubérculo nm 1 Bot tuber. 2 Med tubercle.

tuberculosis nf inv tuberculosis.

tubería nf 1 (de agua) piping, pipes pl. 2 (de gas) pipeline.

tubo nm 1 tube; **t. de ensayo**, test tube. 2 (tubería) pipe; Aut **t. de escape**, exhaust (pipe).

tucán nm toucan.

tuerca nf nut.

tuerto,-a I adj one-eyed, blind in one eye. II nm,f one-eyed person.

tuerzo indic pres → **torcer**.

tuétano nm marrow; **hasta el t.**, to one's fingertips.

tufo nm foul odour o US odor o smell.

tugurio nm hovel.

tul nm tulle.

tulipa nf small tulip.

tulipán nm tulip.

tullido,-a adj crippled, disabled.

tullir vtr to cripple.

tumba nf grave, tomb.

tumbar I vtr to knock down o over. II **tumbarse** vr (acostarse) to lie down, to stretch out.

tumbo nm **dar tumbos**, to reel.

tumbona nf easy chair; (de lona) deck chair.

tumor nm tumour, US tumor.

tumulto nm tumult, commotion.

tumultuoso,-a adj tumultuous, riotous.

tuna nf student folkloric music group.

tunante nm,f adj rogue, crook.

túnel nm tunnel; **el t. del Canal de la Mancha**, the Channel Tunnel.

Túnez n 1 (país) Tunisia. 2 (ciudad) Tunis.

túnica nf tunic.

tuno,-a nm,f (bribón) rogue, crook. II nm member of a tuna.

tuntún (al) nm haphazardly, any old how.

tupé nm (pl **tupés**) (flequillo) quiff.

tupido,-a adj thick, dense.

turba¹ nf (combustible) peat.

turba² nf (muchedumbre) mob, crowd.

turbado,-a adj 1 (alterado) disturbed. 2 (preocupado) worried, anxious. 3 (desconcertado) confused.

turbante nm turban.

turbar I vtr 1 (alterar) to unsettle. 2 (preocupar) to upset o worry. 3 (desconcertar) to baffle, put off. II **turbarse** vr 1 (preocuparse) to be o become upset. 2 (desconcertarse) to be o become confused o baffled.

turbina nf turbine.

turbio,-a adj (agua) cloudy; pey (negocio etc) shady, dubious.

turborreactor nm turbojet (engine).

turbulencia nf turbulence.

turbulento,-a adj turbulent.

turco,-a I adj Turkish. II nm,f (persona) Turk; fig **cabeza de t.**, scapegoat. III nm (idioma) Turkish.

turismo nm 1 tourism; **ir de t.**, to go touring. 2 Aut car.

turista nmf tourist.

turístico,-a adj tourist; **de interés t.**, of interest to tourists.

turnarse vtr to take turns.

turno nm 1 (en juegos etc) turn, go. 2 (de trabajo) shift; **estar de t.**, to be on duty;

t. de día/noche, day/night shift.

turquesa *adj* & *nf* turquoise.

Turquía *n* Turkey.

turrón *nm* nougat.

tute *nm fam* darse un t. de algo, to go to town doing sth.

tutear I *vtr* to address as tú. II **tutearse** *vr* to address (each other *o* one another) as tú.

tutela *nf* 1 *Jur* guardianship, tutelage. 2 *fig* (protección) protection, guidance.

tutelar *vtr* to guard.

tuteo *nm* use of the tú form of address.

tutor *nm* 1 *Jur* guardian. 2 *Educ* tutor.

tuve *pt indef* → **tener**.

tuyo,-a I *adj pos* (con personas) of yours; (con objetos) one of your; ¿es amigo t.?, is he a friend of yours?; unas amigas tuyas, some friends of yours; un libro t., one of your books. II *pron pos* yours; éste es t., this one is yours; *fam* los tuyos, (familiares) your family.

TV *abr de* televisión, television, TV.

TVE *nf abr de* Televisión Española.

U

U, u [u] *nf* (la letra) U, u.

u *conj* (delante de palabras que empiecen por o *b* ho) or; siete u ocho, seven or eight; ayer u hoy, yesterday or today.

ubicación *nf* location, position.

ubicar [1] I *vtr Am* (situar) to locate, situate. II **ubicarse** *vr* to be situated *o* located.

ubicuo,-a *adj* ubiquitous.

ubre *nf* udder.

Ucrania *n* Ukraine.

ucraniano,-a *adj* & *nm,f* Ukrainian.

Ud. *abr de* usted, you.

Uds. *abr de* ustedes, you.

ufanarse *vr* to boast (de, of).

ufano,-a *adj* conceited.

UGT *nf abr de* Unión General de Trabajadores.

ugetista *adj* relating to the UGT.

ujier *nm* usher.

úlcera *nf* ulcer.

ulcerar *vtr*, **ulcerarse** *vr* to ulcerate.

ulterior *adj* (siguiente) subsequent.

ultimar *vtr* 1 (terminar) to finalize. 2 *Am* (matar) to kill, finish off.

ultimátum *nm* (pl **ultimátums**) ultimatum.

último,-a *adj* 1 last; el u. día, the last day; llegar el ú., to arrive last; por ú., finally; a últimos de mes, at the end of the month; en las últimas, on one's last legs. 2 (más reciente) latest; últimas noticias, latest news; *fam* a la última, up to the minute. 3 (más alto) top; el ú. piso, the top flat. 4 (más bajo) lowest; el u. de la lista, the lowest in the list. 5 (más lejano) back, last; la última fila, the back row. 6 (definitivo) final. ◆**últimamente** *adv* lately, recently.

ultra *nmf* extreme right-winger; los ultras, the extreme right *sing*.

ultra- *pref* ultra-.

ultraderecha *nf Pol* extreme right.

ultraderechista *Pol* I *adj* extreme rightwing. II *nmf* extreme right-winger.

ultraizquierda *nf* extreme left.

ultrajar *vtr* to outrage, offend.

ultraje *nm* outrage, offence.

ultramar *nm* overseas (countries), abroad; del *o* en u., overseas.

ultramarinos *nm* groceries; tienda de u., greengrocer.

ultranza (a) *loc adv* 1 (a todo trance) at all costs, at any price; defender algo a u., to defend sth to the death. 2 (acérrimo) out-and-out, extreme.

ultrasónico,-a *adj* ultrasonic.

ultratumba *nf* afterlife.

ultravioleta *adj inv* ultraviolet.

ulular *vi* (viento) to howl; (búho) to hoot.

umbral *nm* threshold.

umbrío,-a, umbroso,-a *adj* shady.

un,-a I *art indef* 1 a; (antes de vocal) an; un coche, a car; un huevo, an egg; una flor, a flower. 2 unos,-as, some; unas flores, some flowers. II *adj* (delante de nom sing) one; un chico y dos chicas, one boy and two girls; → *tamb* **uno,-a** I.

unánime *adj* unanimous.

unanimidad *nf* unanimity; por u., unanimously.

unción *nf* unction.

undécimo,-a *adj* eleventh.

UNED *nf abr de* Universidad Nacional de Educación a Distancia, ≈ Open University, OU.

ungir [6] *vtr Rel* to anoint.

ungüento *nm* ointment.

único,-a *adj* 1 (solo) only; es el ú. que tengo, it's the only one I've got; hijo ú., only child; lo ú. que quiero, the only thing I want; el Mercado Ú., the Single Market; el Acta Única, the Single European Act. 2 (extraordinario) unique. ◆**únicamente** *adv* only, solely.

unidad *nf* 1 unit. 2 (cohesión) unity.

unido,-a *adj* united; están muy unidos, they are very attached to one another; una familia muy unida, a very close family.

unifamiliar *adj* vivienda u., detached house.

unificación *nf* unification.

unificar [1] *vtr* to unify.

uniformar vtr 1 (igualar) to make uniform, standardize. 2 (poner un uniforme a) to put into uniform, give a uniform to.

uniforme I nm (prenda) uniform. II adj 1 (igual) uniform. 2 (superficie) even.

uniformidad nf 1 (igualdad) uniformity. 2 (de superficie) evenness.

unilateral adj unilateral.

unión nf union.

Unión Soviética n Soviet Union.

unir I vtr (juntar) to unite, join (together); **esta carretera une las dos comarcas**, this road links both districts. II **unirse** vr (juntarse) to unite, join.

unisex adj inv unisex.

unísono,-a adj; **al u.**, in unison.

unitario,-a adj unitary; **precio u.**, unit price.

universal adj universal; **historia u.**, world history.

universidad nf university; **u. a distancia**, ≈ Open University; **u. laboral**, technical college.

universitario,-a I adj university. II nm,f university student.

universo nm universe.

uno,-a I nm inv one; **el u.**, (number) one; **el u. de mayo**, the first of May. II nf (hora) **es la una**, it's one o'clock. III adj **unos,-as**, some; **unas cajas**, some boxes; **habrá unos o unas veinte**, there must be around twenty. IV pron 1 one; **u.** (de ellos), **una** (de ellas), one of them; **unos cuantos**, a few; **se miraron el u. al otro**, they looked at each other; **de u. en u.**, one by one; **un trás otro**, one after the other; **una de dos**, one of the two. 2 (persona) someone, somebody; **u. que pasaba por allí**, some passer-by; **vive con u.**, she's living with some man. **unos ... otros**, some people ... others. 3 (impers) you, one; **u. tiene que ...**, you have to ....

untar vtr to grease, smear; (mantequilla) to spread.

untura nf ointment.

uña nf 1 nail; **morderse o comerse las uñas** to bite one's fingernails; **fig ser u. y carne**, to be hand in glove. 2 Zool (garra) claw; (pezuña) hoof.

uperizado,-a adj **leche uperizada**, UHT milk.

Urales nmpl **los U.**, the Urals.

uranio nm uranium.

Urano nm Uranus.

urbanidad nf urbanity, politeness.

urbanismo nm town planning.

urbanístico,-a adj town-planning.

urbanización nf 1 (barrio) housing development o estate. 2 (proceso) urbanization.

urbanizar vtr to build up.

urbano,-a adj urban, city; **guardia u.**, (traffic) policeman.

urbe nf large city.

urdimbre nf 1 Tex warp. 2 (trama) intrigue.

urdir vtr 1 Tex to warp. 2 (tramar) to plot, scheme.

urgencia nf 1 urgency. 2 (emergencia) emergency.

urgente adj urgent; **correo u.**, express mail.

urgir [6] vi to be urgent o pressing; **me urge (tenerlo)**, I need it urgently.

urinario nm urinal.

urna nf 1 Pol ballot box. 2 (vasija) urn.

urólogo,-a nm,f Med urologist.

urraca nf magpie.

URSS nf Hist abr de **Unión de Repúblicas Socialistas Soviéticas**, Union of Socialist Soviet Republics, USSR.

urticaria nf Med hives.

Uruguay n (el) U., Uruguay.

uruguayo,-a adj & nm,f Uruguayan.

usado,-a adj (ropa) second-hand, used.

usanza nf lit **a la antigua u.**, in the old style.

usar I vtr 1 to use. 2 (prenda) to wear. II **usarse** vr to be used o in fashion.

usina nf Am (central eléctrica) power station.

USO nf abr de **Unión Sindical Obrera**.

uso nm 1 use; Farm **u. externo/tópico**, external/local application. 2 (de poder, privilegio) exercise. 3 (de prenda) wearing; **haga u. del casco**, wear a helmet. 4 (costumbre) usage, custom; **al u.**, conventional.

usted, pl **ustedes** pron pers fml you; **¿quién es u.?, ¿quiénes son ustedes?**, who are you?

usual adj usual, common.

usuario,-a nm,f user.

usura nf usury.

usurero,-a nm,f usurer.

usurpar vtr to usurp.

utensilio nm utensil; (herramienta) tool.

útero nm uterus, womb.

útil I adj useful; (día) working. II nm (herramienta) tool, instrument.

utilidad nf usefulness, utility; (beneficio) profit.

utilitario,-a I nm (coche) utility vehicle. II adj utilitarian.

utilización nf use, utilization.

utilizar [4] vtr to use, utilize.

utopía nf utopia.

utópico,-a adj & nm,f utopian.

uva nf grape; **u. blanca**, green grape.

UVI nf abr de **unidad de vigilancia intensiva**, intensive care unit, ICU.

úvula nf uvula.

V

V, v ['uβε] *nf (la letra)* V, v.

V *Elec abr de* **voltio(s)**, volt, volts, V.

vaca *nf* 1 cow. 2 *(carne)* beef.

vacaciones *nfpl* holidays *pl*, *US* vacation; *(viaje)* holiday; **durante las v.**, during the holidays; **estar/irse de v.**, to be/go on holiday.

vacante I *adj* vacant. II *nf* vacancy.

vaciar [29] I *vtr* 1 *(recipiente)* to empty; *(contenido)* to empty out. 2 *(terreno)* to hollow out. 3 *Arte* to cast, mould, *US* mold. II **vaciarse** *vr* to empty.

vacilación *nf* hesitation.

vacilante *adj* 1 *(persona)* hesitant, irresolute. 2 *(voz)* hesitant, faltering. 3 *(luz)* flickering.

vacilar *vi* 1 *(dudar)* to hesitate; **sin v.**, without hesitation. 2 *(voz)* to falter. 3 *(luz)* to flicker. 4 *fam (jactarse)* to show off.

vacío,-a I *adj* 1 empty; *(hueco)* hollow. 2 *(sin ocupar)* vacant, unoccupied. II *nm* 1 emptiness, void. 2 *(hueco)* gap; *(espacio)* *(empty)* space. 3 *Fís* vacuum; **envasado al v.**, vacuum-packed.

vacuna *nf* vaccine; *Vet* cowpox.

vacunación *nf* vaccination.

vacunar I *vtr* to vaccinate (**contra**, against); *fig* to inure. II **vacunarse** *vr* to get oneself vaccinated.

vacuno,-a *adj* bovine; **ganado v.**, cattle.

vacuo,-a *adj* vacuous, empty.

vadear *vtr (río)* to ford; *fig (dificultad)* to overcome.

vado *nm* 1 *(de un río)* ford. 2 *Aut* **'v. permanente'**, 'keep clear'.

vagabundear *vi* to wander, roam.

vagabundo,-a I *adj (errante)* wandering; *pey* vagrant; **perro v.**, stray dog. II *nm,f* wanderer; *(sin casa)* tramp, *US* hobo; *pey* vagrant, tramp.

vagancia *nf* idleness, laziness.

vagar [7] *vi* to wander about, roam about.

vagido *nm* cry of a newborn baby.

vagina *nf* vagina.

vago,-a I *adj* 1 *(perezoso)* lazy. 2 *(indefinido)* vague. II *nm,f* 1 *(holgazán)* layabout. 2 *fur* vagrant.

vagón *nm (para pasajeros)* carriage, coach, *US* car; *(para mercancías)* truck, wagon, *US* freight car, *US* boxcar.

vaguedad *nf* vagueness.

vaho *nm (de aliento)* breath; *(vapor)* vapour, *US* vapor.

vaina I *nf* 1 *(de espada)* sheath, scabbard. 2 *Bot* pod. 3 *Am fam (molestia)* bother, nuisance. II *nmf (persona)* dimwit.

vainilla *nf* vanilla.

vaivén *nm* 1 *(oscilación)* swinging, to-and-fro movement. 2 *(de gente)* coming and go-

ing, bustle; *fig* **vaivenes**, ups and downs.

vajilla *nf* crockery, dishes *pl*; **una v.**, a set of dishes, a dinner service.

valdré *indic fut* → **valer**.

vale¹ *interj* all right, O.K.

vale² *nm* 1 *(comprobante)* voucher. 2 *(pagaré)* promissory note, IOU (I owe you).

valedero,-a *adj* valid.

valedor,-a *nm,f* protector.

valenciano,-a *adj* Valencian; **Comunidad Valenciana**, Valencia.

valentía *nf* courage, bravery.

valentón,-ona *pey* I *adj* bragging, boastful. II *nm,f* braggart.

valer [26] I *vtr* 1 to be worth; **no vale nada**, it is worthless; **vale una fortuna**, it is worth a fortune; **no vale la pena** (ir), it's not worth while (going). 2 *(costar)* to cost; **¿cuánto vale?**, how much is it? 3 *(proporcionar)* to earn. II *vi* 1 *(servir)* to be useful, be of use. 2 *(ser válido)* to be valid, count; **no vale hacer trampa**, cheating isn't on. 3 **más vale**, it is better; **más vale que te vayas ya**, you had better leave now. III **valerse** *vr* to use, make use (**de**, of); **v. por sí mismo**, to be able to manage on one's own.

valeroso,-a *adj* brave, courageous.

valgo *indic pres* → **valer**.

valía *nf* value, worth.

validez *nf* validity.

válido,-a *adj* valid.

valiente *adj* 1 *(valeroso)* brave, courageous. 2 *irón* ¡v. **amigo eres tú!**, a fine friend you are!

valija *nf (de correos)* mailbag; **v. diplomática**, diplomatic bag.

valioso,-a *adj* valuable.

valor *nm* 1 *(valía)* value, worth; *(precio)* price; **objetos de v.**, valuables; **sin v.**, worthless; **v. alimenticio**, food value. 2 *(valentía)* courage. 3 *Fin* **valores**, securities, bonds.

valoración *nf* valuation.

valorar *vtr* to value, calculate the value of.

valorización *nf* 1 *(tasación)* valuation. 2 *(revalorización)* appreciation.

valorizar [4] *vtr* 1 *(tasar)* to value. 2 *(revalorizar)* to raise the value of.

vals *nm* waltz; **bailar el v.**, to waltz.

válvula *nf* valve; **v. de seguridad**, safety valve.

valla *nf* 1 *(cerca)* fence; *(muro)* wall; **v. publicitaria**, hoarding, *US* billboard. 2 *Dep* hurdle; **las 100 metros vallas**, the 100 metres hurdle race.

vallado *nm* fence.

vallar *vtr* to fence (in).

valle *nm* valley.

vallisoletano,-a I *adj* of *o* from Valladolid. **II** *nm,f* native *o* inhabitant of Valladolid.

vampiro *nm* vampire.

vanagloriarse [12] *vr* to boast (**de**, of).

vandalismo *nm* vandalism.

vándalo,-a *nm,f* vandal.

vanguardia *nf* 1 avant-garde, vanguard; *fig* **ir a la v.**, to be at the forefront of. 2 *Mil* vanguard, van.

vanguardista I *adj* avant-garde. **II** *nm,f* avant-gardist.

vanidad *nf* vanity.

vanidoso,-a *adj* vain, conceited.

vano,-a *adj* 1 (*vanidoso*) vain, conceited. 2 (*esfuerzo, esperanza*) vain, futile; **en v.**, in vain.

vapor *nm* 1 (*de agua hirviendo*) steam; *Culin* **al v.**, steamed. 2 (*gas*) vapour, *US* vapor; **v. de agua**, water vapour.

vaporizador *nm* vaporizer, spray.

vaporizar [4] **I** *vtr* to vaporize. **II vaporizarse** *vr* to vaporize, become vaporized, evaporate.

vaporoso,-a *adj* vaporous.

vapulear *vtr* (*físicamente*) to shake; (*con palabras*) to slate.

vaqueriza *nf* cowshed.

vaquero,-a I *nm* cowherd, *US* cowboy. **II** *adj* **pantalón v.**, jeans *pl*, pair *sing* of jeans. **III** *nmpl* **vaqueros**, (*prenda*) jeans, pair *sing* of jeans.

vara *nf* pole, rod.

varar I *vtr* to beach, dock. **II** *vi* to run aground.

variable *adj & nf* variable.

variación *nf* variation.

variado,-a *adj* varied; **galletas variadas**, assorted biscuits.

variante *nf* variant; *Aut* detour.

variar [29] **I** *vtr* to vary, change. **II** *vi* to vary, change; *irón* **para v.**, as usual, just for a change.

varice, várice *nf* → varix.

varicela *nf* chickenpox.

variedad *nf* 1 variety. 2 *Teat* **variedades**, variety show *sing*.

varilla *nf* (*vara*) rod, stick; (*de abanico, paraguas*) rib.

varios,-as *adj* several.

variopinto,-a *adj* diverse, assorted; **un público o.**, a varied audience.

varita *nf* **v. mágica**, magic wand.

variz *nm* varicose vein.

varón *nm* (*hombre*) man; (*chico*) boy; **hijo v.**, male child; **sexo v.**, male sex.

varonil *adj* manly, virile.

Varsovia *n* Warsaw.

vas *indic pres* → ir.

vasallo,-a *nm,f Hist* vassal.

vasco,-a *adj* Basque; **el País V.**, the Basque Country.

vascuence *nm* (*idioma*) Basque.

vasectomía *nf* vasectomy.

vaselina *nf* vaseline®.

vasija *nf* pot.

vaso *nm* 1 (*para beber*) glass. 2 (*florero*) vase. 3 *Anat* vessel.

vástago *nm* 1 *Bot* shoot. 2 *fig* (*hijo*) offspring. 3 *Téc* rod, stem.

vasto,-a *adj* vast.

Vaticano *nm* **el V.**, Vatican.

vaticinar *vtr* to prophesy, predict.

vaticinio *nm* prophesy, prediction.

vatio *nm* watt.

vaya I *interj* **¡v. lío!**, what a mess!

vaya² *subj pres* → ir.

Vd. Vds. *abr de* usted, ustedes, you.

ve I *imperat* → ir. **II** *indic pres* → ver.

vecinal *adj* local.

vecindad *nf*, **vecindario** *nm* 1 (*área*) neighbourhood, *US* neighborhood, vicinity. 2 (*vecinos*) community, residents *pl*.

vecino,-a I *nm,f* (*persona*) neighbour, *US* neighbor; **el v. de al lado**, the next-door neighbour. 2 (*residente*) resident. **II** *adj* neighbouring, *US* neighboring, nearby.

veda *nf* (*de caza*) close season, *US* closed season; **levantar la v.**, to open the season.

vedado *adj* **coto v. de caza**, private hunting ground.

vedar *vtr* to forbid, prohibit.

vega *nf* fertile plain *o* lowland.

vegetación *nf* 1 *Bot* vegetation. 2 *Med* **vegetaciones**, adenoids.

vegetal *nm* vegetable.

vegetar *vi fig* to vegetate.

vegetariano,-a *adj & nm,f* vegetarian.

vehemencia *nf* vehemence.

vehemente *adj* vehement.

vehículo *nm* vehicle.

veinte *adj & nm inv* twenty.

veintena *nf* (*veinte*) twenty; **una v. de**, about twenty.

vejación *nf* humiliation.

vejar *vtr* to humiliate.

vejatorio,-a *adj* humiliating.

vejez *nf* old age.

vejiga *nf* bladder.

vela¹ *nf* 1 candle. 2 *fam* **quedarse a dos velas**, to be in the dark. 3 **pasar la noche en v.**, to have a sleepless night.

vela² *nf Náut* sail.

velada *nf* evening (party).

velado,-a *adj* 1 (*oculto*) veiled, hidden. 2 *Fot* blurred.

velador *nm* 1 (*mesa*) table. 2 *Am* (*mesilla de noche*) bedside table.

velar¹ *vi* 1 **v. por**, to watch over. 2 (*hacer guardia*) to keep watch.

velar² *Fot* **I** *vtr* to blur. **II velarse** *vr* to become blurred.

velatorio *nm* vigil, wake.

veleidad *nf* fickleness.

veleidoso,-a *adj* fickle.

velero *nm* sailing boat *o* ship.

veleta I *nf* weather vane, weathercock. **II**

nmf fam fickle *o* changeable person.

velo *nm* veil.

velocidad *nf* 1 *(rapidez)* speed; *(de proyectil etc)* velocity; Aut v. **máxima**, speed limit; Inform v. **de transmisión**, bit rate; Inform v. **operativa**, operating speed. 2 Aut *(marcha)* gear.

velocímetro *nm* speedometer.

velocista *nmf* sprinter.

velódromo *nm* cycle track, US velodrome.

veloz I *adj* swift, rapid. II *adv* quickly, fast.

vello *nm* hair.

vellón *nm* fleece.

velloso,-a, velludo,-a *adj* downy.

vena *nf* vein.

venado *nm* deer, stag; Culin venison.

vencedor,-a I *nm,f* winner. II *adj* winning.

vencejo *nm* Orn swift.

vencer [2] I *vtr* 1 *(al enemigo)* to defeat; *(al contrincante)* to beat. 2 *(dificultad)* to overcome, surmount. II *vi* 1 *(pago, deuda)* to fall due, be payable. 2 *(plazo)* to expire. III *vencerse vr (torcerse)* to warp.

vencido,-a *adj* 1 Mil *(derrotado)* defeated; Dep beaten; *fig* **darse por v.**, to give up, accept defeat. 2 *(pago, deuda)* due, payable. 3 *(plazo)* expired. 4 *fam* **a la tercera va la vencida**, third time lucky.

vencimiento *nm* 1 Com maturity. 2 *(de un plazo)* expiry.

venda *nf* bandage.

vendaje *nm* dressing.

vendar *vtr* to bandage; *fig* **v. los ojos a algn**, to blindfold sb.

vendaval *nm* gale.

vendedor,-a *nm,f* seller; *(hombre)* salesman; *(mujer)* saleswoman.

vender I *vtr* to sell; **v. a plazos/al contado**, to sell on credit/for cash; **v. al por mayor/menor**, to (sell) wholesale/retail. II **venderse** *vr* 1 to sell; **este disco se vende bien**, this record is selling well; **for sale**. 2 *(claudicar)* to sell out.

vendimia *nf* grape harvest.

vendré *indic fut* → **venir**.

Venecia *nf* Venice.

veneno *nm* poison; *(de serpiente)* venom.

venenoso,-a *adj* poisonous.

venerable *adj* venerable.

veneración *nf* veneration.

venerar *vtr* to venerate, revere.

venéreo,-a *adj* venereal.

venero *nm* spring.

venezolano,-a *adj & nm,f* Venezuelan.

Venezuela *nf* Venezuela.

venga *subj pres* → **venir**.

venganza *nf* vengeance, revenge.

vengar [7] I *vtr* to avenge. II **vengarse** *vr* to avenge oneself; **v. de algn**, to take revenge on sb.

vengativo,-a *adj* vengeful, vindictive.

vengo *indic pres* → **venir**.

venia *nf* 1 *fml (permiso)* permission. 2 *(perdón)* pardon.

venial *adj* venial.

venida *nf* coming, arrival.

venidero,-a *adj* future, coming.

venir [27] I *vi* 1 to come; *fig* **v. a menos**, to come down in the world; *fig* **v. al mundo**, to be born; **el año que viene**, next year; *fig* **v. a la memoria**, to remember; *fam* **¡venga ya!, (vamos)** come on!; *(expresa incredulidad)* come off it! 2 **v. grande/pequeño**, *(ropa)* to be too big/small; **v. mal/bien**, to be inconvenient/convenient; **el metro me viene muy bien**, I find the underground very handy. 3 *(en pasivas)* **esto vino provocado por ...**, this was brought about by .... 4 **esto viene ocurriendo desde hace mucho tiempo**, this has been going on for a long time now. II **venirse** *vr* **v. abajo**, to collapse.

venta *nf* 1 sale; **en v.**, for sale; **a la v.**, on sale; **v. a plazos/al contado**, credit/cash sale; **v. al por mayor/al por menor**, wholesale/retail. 2 *(posada)* country inn.

ventaja *nf* advantage; **llevar v. a**, to have the advantage over; **le sacó dos metros de v. a**, he beat him by two metres.

ventajoso,-a *adj* advantageous.

ventana *nf* 1 window. 2 *(de la nariz)* nostril.

ventanal *nm* large window.

ventanilla *nf* 1 window. 2 *(de la nariz)* nostril.

ventanuco *nm* small window.

ventilación *nf* ventilation; **sin v.**, unventilated.

ventilador *nm* ventilator; *(de coche)* fan.

ventilar I *vtr* 1 *(habitación)* to ventilate, air. 2 *fig (opinión)* to air. II **ventilarse** *vr* *fam (terminar)* to finish off.

ventisca *nf* blizzard; *(de nieve)* snowstorm.

ventosa *nf* sucker; Med cupping glass.

ventosear *vi* to break wind.

ventoso,-a *adj* windy.

ventrílocuo,-a *nm,f* ventriloquist.

ventura *nf* 1 *(felicidad)* happiness. 2 *(suerte)* luck; *(casualidad)* chance.

venturoso,-a *adj* lucky, fortunate.

Venus *nm* Venus.

veo-veo *nm* *fam* **el (juego del) v.-v.**, I-spy.

ver[1] *nm* de buen **v.**, good-looking.

ver[2] [28] I *vtr* 1 to see; *(televisión)* to watch; **a v.**, let me see, let's see; **a v. si escribes**, I hope you'll write; **(ya) veremos**, we'll see; *fam* **había un jaleo que no veas**, you should have seen the fuss that was made; **no veo por qué**, I can't see why; **a mi modo de v.**, as I see it. 2 **no tener nada que v. con**, to have nothing to do with. II **verse** *vr* 1 *(imagen etc)* to be seen. 2 *(encontrarse con algn)* to meet, see each other; ¡nos vemos!, see you later! **3 no se pueden ni v.**, (*soportarse*) they can't stand (the sight of) each other. **4** *Am* **te ves divina**, you look divine.

vera *nf* edge, border; **a la v. de**, beside, next to.

veracidad *nf* veracity, truthfulness.

veraneante *nmf* holidaymaker, *US* (summer) vacationist.

veranear *vi* to spend one's summer holiday.

veraneo *nm* summer holiday.

veraniego,-a *adj* summer.

verano *nm* summer.

veras *nfpl* **de v.**, really, seriously.

veraz *adj* veracious, truthful.

verbal *adj* verbal.

verbena *nf* street party.

verbo *nm* verb.

verborrea *nf fam* verbosity, verbal diarrhoea.

verdad *nf* **1** truth; **es v.**, it is true; **a decir v.**, to tell the truth; **de v!**, really, truly; **un amigo de v.**, a real friend. **2** (*en frase afirmativa*) **está muy bien**, ¿(*no es*) **v.?**, it is very good, isn't it?; (*en frase negativa*) **no te gusta**, ¿v.?, you don't like it, do you?

verdadero,-a *adj* true, real. ◆**verdaderamente** *adv* truly, really.

verde I *adj* **1** green. **2** (*fruta*) unripe. **3** *fam* (*chiste, película*) blue; **viejo v.**, dirty old man. **4** *fam* **fig poner v. a algn**, to call sb every name under the sun. II *nm* **1** (*color*) green. **2** *Pol* **los verdes**, the Greens.

verdear *vi* to turn green.

verdor *nm* (*color*) greenness; (*de plantas*) verdure.

verdoso,-a *adj* greenish.

verdugo,-a I *nm* executioner. II *nmf fig* tyrant.

verdulería *nf* greengrocer's (shop).

verdulero,-a *nm,f* greengrocer.

verdura *nf* vegetables *pl*, greens *pl*.

vereda *nf* **1** (*camino*) path, lane. **2** *Am* (*acera*) pavement, *US* sidewalk.

veredicto *nm* verdict.

verga *nf* penis.

vergonzoso,-a *adj* **1** (*penoso*) shameful, disgraceful. **2** (*tímido*) timid, bashful.

vergüenza *nf* **1** shame; ¿no te da v.?, aren't you ashamed?, have you no shame?; **es una v.**, it's a disgrace. **2** (*timidez*) shyness, bashfulness; **tener v.**, to be shy; **me da v.**, I'm too embarrassed.

vericueto *nm* winding path; *fig* **los vericuetos**, the ins and outs.

verídico,-a *adj* truthful, true.

verificar [1] I *vtr* (*comprobar*) to check. II **verificarse** *vr* to take place, occur.

vermut, vermú *nm* (*pl* **vermús**) vermouth.

verosímil *adj* probable, likely; (*creíble*) credible.

verruga *nf* wart.

versado,-a *adj* well-versed (**en**, in).

versar *vi* **v. sobre**, to be about, deal with.

versátil *adj* **1** versatile. **2** (*voluble*) changeable, inconstant.

versatilidad *nf* **1** versatility. **2** (*volubilidad*) changeableness, inconstancy.

versículo *nm* verse.

versión *nf* version; **película en v. original**, film in the original language.

verso *nm* **1** (*poesía*) verse. **2** (*línea*) line.

vértebra *nf* vertebra.

vertebrado,-a *adj & nm* vertebrate.

vertedero *nm* (*de basura*) rubbish dump, tip.

verter [3] I *vtr* **1** to pour (out). **2** (*basura*) to dump. II *vi* (*río*) to flow, run (**a**, into).

vertical *adj* vertical.

vértice *nm* vertex.

vertiente *nf* **1** (*de una montaña, un tejado*) slope; *fig* aspect. **2** *Am* (*manantial*) spring.

vertiginoso,-a *adj* dizzy, giddy; *fig* (*velocidad*) breakneck.

vértigo *nm* vertigo; **me da v.**, it makes me dizzy.

vesícula *nf* vesicle; **v. biliar**, gall bladder.

vespa® *nf* (motor) scooter.

vespertino,-a I *adj* evening. II *nm Prensa* evening newspaper.

vespino *nm* moped.

vestíbulo *nm* (*de casa*) hall; (*de edificio público*) foyer.

vestido,-a I *nm* (*ropa*) clothes *pl*; (*de mujer*) dress. II *adj* dressed; **policía v. de paisano**, plain clothes policeman.

vestidura *nf* clothing, clothes *pl*.

vestigio *nm* vestige, trace.

vestimenta *nf* clothes *pl*, garments *pl*.

vestir [6] I *vtr* **1** (*a alguien*) to dress. **2** (*llevar puesto*) to wear. II *vi* **1** to dress; **ropa de (mucho) v.**, formal dress. **2** *fam* **la seda viste mucho**, silk always looks very elegant. III **vestirse** *vr* **1** to get dressed. **2 v. de**, to wear, dress in; (*disfrazarse*) to disguise oneself as, to dress up as.

vestuario *nm* **1** (*conjunto de vestidos*) clothes *pl*, wardrobe; *Teat* wardrobe, costumes *pl*. **2** (*camerino*) dressing room. **3** *Dep* changing room sing.

veta *nf Min* vein, seam; (*de carne*) streak.

vetar *vtr* to veto.

veterano,-a *adj & nm,f* veteran.

veterinario,-a I *nm,f* veterinary surgeon, vet, *US* veterinarian. II *nf* veterinary medicine o science.

veto *nm* veto; **derecho a v.**, power o right of veto.

vetusto,-a *adj fml* ancient.

vez *nf* 1 time; **una v.**, once; **dos veces**, twice; **cinco veces**, five times; **a o alguna nas veces**, sometimes; **cada v.**, each *o* every time; **cada v. más**, more and more; **de v. en cuando**, now and again, every now and then; **¿le has visto alguna v.?**, have you ever seen him?; **otra v.**, again; **a la v.**, at the same time; **tal v.**, perhaps, maybe; **de una v.**, in one go; **de una v. para siempre**, once and for all; **en v. de**, instead of; **érase o había una v.**, (*en cuentos etc*) once upon a time. 2 (*turno*) turn. 3 **hacer las veces de**, to do duty as.

v.g(r). *abr de* verbigracia, for example, eg.

vía I *nf* 1 *Ferroc* track, line. 2 (*camino*) road; **v. pública**, public thoroughfare; **V. Láctea**, Milky Way. 3 *Anat* passage, tract; **Farm (por) v. oral**, to be taken orally. 4 *fig* por v. **oficial**, through official channels; **por v. aérea/marítima**, by air/sea. 5 **en vías de**, in the process of; **países en vías de desarrollo**, developing countries. **II** *prep* (*a través de*) via, through; **v. París**, via Paris; **transmisión v. satélite**, satellite transmission.

viable *adj* viable.

viaducto *nm* viaduct.

viajante *nmf* commercial traveller, travelling salesman *o* saleswoman.

viajar *vi* to travel.

viaje *nm* (*recorrido*) journey, trip; (*largo, en barco*) voyage; **¡buen v.!**, bon voyage!, have a good trip!; **estar de v.**, to be away (on a trip); **irse o marcharse de v.**, to go on a journey *o* trip; **v. de negocios**, business trip; **v. de novios**, honeymoon.

viajero,-a I *nm,f* 1 traveller. 2 (*en transporte público*) passenger. **II** *adj* **cheque v.**, travellers cheque.

viandante *nmf* passer-by.

viario,-a *adj* road, highway; **red viaria**, road network.

víbora *nf* viper.

vibración *nf* vibration.

vibrador *nm* vibrator.

vibrar *vtr & vi* to vibrate.

vicario,-a *nm,f* vicar.

vicepresidente,-a *nm,f* 1 *Pol* vice president. 2 (*de compañía, comité*) vice chairperson; (*hombre*) vice-chairman; (*mujer*) vice-chairwoman.

vicesecretario,-a *nm,f* assistant secretary.

viceversa *adv* vice versa.

viciado,-a *adj* 1 (*corrompido*) corrupt. 2 (*aire*) foul.

viciar [12] **I** *vtr* 1 (*corromper*) to corrupt. 2 (*estropear*) to waste. **II viciarse** *vr* 1 (*deformarse*) to go out of shape. 2 (*corromperse*) to become corrupted.

vicio *nm* 1 vice. 2 (*mala costumbre*) bad habit. 3 *fam* (*destreza*) skill.

vicioso,-a I *adj* 1 (*persona*) depraved,

perverted. 2 **círculo v.**, vicious circle. **II** *nm,f* depraved person; *fam* **v. del trabajo**, workaholic.

vicisitud *nf* (*usu pl*) vicissitude.

víctima *nf* victim.

victoria *nf* victory.

victorioso,-a *adj* victorious.

vicuña *nf* vicuna.

vid *nf* vine, grapevine.

vida *nf* life; (*periodo*) lifetime; **de toda la v.**, life-long; **en mi v.**, never in my life; **de por v.**, for life; **ganarse la v.**, to earn one's living; **¿qué es de tu v.?**, how's life?; **estar con/sin v.**, to be alive/dead.

vidente *nmf* clairvoyant.

vídeo *nm* video; **grabar en v.**, to video tape.

videoclub *nm* video club.

videocámara *nf* video camera.

videoconferencia *nf* videoconferencing; (*sesión*) videoconference.

videojuego *nm* video game.

vidriera *nf* 1 stained-glass window. 2 *Am* (*escaparate*) shop window.

vidrio *nm* glass.

viejo,-a I *adj* old; **hacerse v.**, to grow old; **un v. amigo**, an old friend. **II** *nm,f* (*hombre, padre*) old man; (*mujer, madre*) old woman; **los viejos**, old people; *fam* **mis viejos**, my parents.

Viena *n* Vienna.

vienés,-esa *adj & nm,f* Viennese.

viento *nm* wind; **hace o sopla mucho v.**, it is very windy; *fam* **vete a tomar v.**, get lost.

vientre *nm* 1 belly; **hacer de v.**, to have a bowel movement. 2 (*útero*) womb.

viernes *nm inv* Friday; **V. Santo**, Good Friday.

Vietnam *nm* Vietnam.

vietnamita *adj & nmf* Vietnamese.

viga *nf* (*de madera*) beam; (*de hierro*) girder.

vigencia *nf* validity; **entrar en v.**, to come into force *o* effect.

vigente *adj* in force.

vigésimo,-a *adj & nm,f* twentieth.

vigía I *nf* watchtower, lookout post. **II** *nmf* lookout; (*hombre*) watchman; (*mujer*) watchwoman.

vigilancia *nf* vigilance, watchfulness; *Med* **unidad de v. intensiva**, intensive care unit.

vigilante *nmf* watchman; (*de banco*) guard.

vigilar I *vtr* to watch; (*un lugar*) to guard; **vigila que no entren**, make sure they don't get in. **II** *vi* (*gen*) to keep watch.

vigilia *nf* 1 vigil. 2 (*víspera*) eve. 3 *Rel* (*abstinencia*) abstinence.

vigor *nm* 1 vigour, *US* vigor; (*fuerza*) strength. 2 **en v.**, in force.

vigoroso,-a *adj* vigorous.

VIH *abr de* Virus de Inmunodeficiencia Humana, Human Immunodeficiency

Virus, HIV.

vikingo nm Viking.

vil adj fml vile, base.

vileza nf 1 vileness, baseness. 2 (acto) vile act, despicable deed.

vilipendiar [12] vtr fml to vilify, revile.

vilo (en) loc adv (persona) on tenterhooks; (cosa) up in the air.

villa nf 1 (población) town. 2 (casa) villa, country house.

villancico nm (Christmas) carol.

vinagre nm vinegar.

vinagrera nf vinagreras, oil and vinegar cruets, cruet (stand) sing.

vinagreta nf vinaigrette sauce.

vinajeras nfpl cruets.

vincha nf Am headband.

vinculante adj binding.

vincular vtr to link, bind; (relacionar) to relate, connect.

vínculo nm link.

vine pt indef → **venir**.

vinícola adj wine-producing.

vinicultor,-a nm,f wine producer.

vinicultura nf wine production o growing.

vinilo nm vinyl.

vino nm wine; **tomar un v.**, to have a glass of wine; **v. blanco/tinto/dulce/seco**, white/red/sweet/dry wine; **v. rosado**, rosé.

viña nf vineyard.

viñedo nm vineyard.

viñeta nf illustration.

viola nf viola.

violación nf 1 (de una persona) rape. 2 (de ley, derecho) violation, infringement.

violador,-a n rapist.

violar vtr 1 (persona) to rape. 2 (ley, derecho) to violate, infringe.

violencia nf 1 violence; **la no v.**, non-violence. 2 (incomodidad) embarrassment.

violentar vtr 1 (forzar) to force, break open; (sitio) to break into, enter by force. 2 (enojar) to infuriate.

violento,-a adj 1 violent. 2 (situación) embarrassing, awkward. 3 **sentirse v.**, (incómodo) to feel embarrassed o awkward.

violeta adj & nm & nf violet.

violín nm violin; fam fiddle.

violinista nmf violinist.

violón nm double bass.

violoncelista, violonchelista nmf cellist.

violoncelo, violonchelo nm violoncello, cello.

viraje nm 1 turn. 2 fig about-face, U-turn.

virar vi 1 (girar) to turn round. 2 fig to change.

virgen I adj 1 (persona, selva) virgin. 2 (aceite, lana) pure; (cinta) blank. II nf virgin; fam **ser un o una viva la v.**, to be a devil-may-care person.

virginidad nf virginity.

virgo nm hymen.

Virgo nm Virgo.

virguería nf arg gem, marvel; **hacer virguerías**, to work wonders, be a dab hand.

virguero,-a adj arg smart, great; **esta camisa es muy virguera**, that shirt is the business.

vírico,-a adj viral.

viril adj virile, manly; **miembro v.**, penis.

virilidad nf virility.

virtual adj virtual.

virtud nf 1 virtue; fig **en v. de**, by virtue of. 2 (propiedad) property, quality.

virtuoso,-a I adj virtuous. II nm,f 1 virtuous person. 2 (músico) virtuoso.

viruela nf smallpox; **viruelas**, pockmarks pl.

virulé (a la) loc adv fam 1 (torcido) crooked, twisted. 2 **un ojo a la v.**, a black eye.

virulencia nf virulence.

virulento,-a adj virulent.

virus nm inv virus.

visa nf Am visa.

visado nm visa.

víscera nf 1 internal organ. 2 **vísceras**, viscera, entrails.

visceral adj 1 Anat visceral. 2 fig profound, deep-rooted.

viscoso,-a adj viscous.

visera nf (de gorra) peak; (de casco) visor.

visibilidad nf visibility; **curva con mala v.**, blind corner.

visible adj visible; (evidente) evident.

visillo nm small lace o net curtain.

visión nf 1 vision. 2 (vista) sight; fig **v. de conjunto**, overall view; **con v. de futuro**, forward-looking. 3 (aparición) vision.

visionario,-a nm,f visionary; (iluso) person who imagines things.

visita nf 1 (acción) visit; **hacer una v.**, to pay a visit; **estar de v.**, to be visiting. 2 (invitado) visitor, guest.

visitador,-a nm,f Farm pharmaceutical salesman o saleswoman.

visitante I nmf visitor. II adj (equipo) away.

visitar vtr to visit.

vislumbrar vtr to glimpse.

viso nm 1 (reflejo) sheen. 2 fig **tener visos de**, to seem, appear.

visón nm mink.

visor nm Fot viewfinder.

víspera nf (día anterior) day before; (de festivo) eve; **en vísperas de**, in the period leading up to.

vista nf 1 sight; **a la v.**, visible; **a primera o simple v.**, at first sight, on the face of it; **con vistas a**, with a view to; **en v. de**, in view of, considering; **corto de v.**, short-sighted; **conocer a algn de v.**, to know sb by sight; **perder de v. a**, to lose sight of; **quítalo de mi v.**, take it away;

vistazo *fig* tener mucha v. para, to have a good eye for; *fig* volver la v. atrás, to look back; *fam* ¡hasta la v.!, goodbye!, see you!; *fam* hacer la v. gorda, to turn a blind eye. 2 *(panorama)* view; con vista(s) al mar, overlooking the sea. 3 *Jur* trial, hearing.

vistazo *nm* glance; echar un v. a algo, *(ojear)* to have a (quick) look at sth; *(tener cuidado de)* to keep an eye on sth.

visto,-a I *adj* 1 está v. que ..., it is obvious that ...; por lo v., evidently, apparently; v. que, in view of the fact that, seeing o given that. 2 estar bien v., to be well looked upon, to be considered acceptable; estar mal v., to be frowned upon. 3 estar muy v., to be old hat. II *nm* v. bueno, approval, O.K.

vistoso,-a *adj* eye-catching.

visual *adj* visual; campo v., field of vision.

visualizar [4] *vtr* to visualize; *(película)* to view.

vital *adj* 1 vital. 2 *(persona)* full of vitality.

vitalicio,-a *adj* life, for life; pensión/cargo v., life pension/permanent post.

vitalidad *nf* vitality.

vitamina *nf* vitamin.

vitamínico,-a *adj* vitamin; complejo v., multivitamins.

viticultura *nf* wine growing.

viticultor,-a *nmf* wine grower.

vitorear *vtr* to cheer.

vítreo,-a *adj* vitreous.

vitrina *nf (aparador)* glass o display cabinet; *(de exposición)* glass case, showcase; *Am (escaparate)* shop window.

vituallas *nfpl* provisions.

vituperar *vtr* to condemn.

vituperio *nm* condemnation.

viudo,-a *nm,f (hombre)* widower; *(mujer)* widow.

viva *interj* ¡v.!, hurrah!

vivacidad *nf* vivacity.

vivaracho,-a *adj fam* lively, sprightly.

vivaz *adj* 1 lively, vivacious. 2 *(perspicaz)* sharp, quick-witted.

vivencias *nfpl* personal experience.

víveres *nmpl* provisions, supplies.

vivero *nm (de plantas)* nursery; *(de peces)* fish farm o hatchery; *fig* breeding ground, hotbed.

viveza *nf* 1 liveliness, vivacity; *(en los ojos)* sparkle. 2 *(agudeza)* sharpness, quick-wittedness.

vividor,-a *nm,f pey* sponger, scrounger.

vivienda *nf* 1 housing. 2 *(casa)* house; *(piso)* flat.

vivir I *vi* to live; vive de sus ahorros, she lives off her savings; viven de la pesca, they make their living by fishing. II *vtr* to live through. III *nm* life.

vivito,-a *adj fam* v. y coleando, alive and kicking.

vivo,-a I *adj* 1 alive; de viva voz, verbally, by word of mouth; en v., *(programa)* live; *fam* es el v. retrato o la viva imagen de, she is the spitting image of. 2 al rojo v., red-hot. 3 *(vivaz)* lively, vivacious. 4 *(listo)* sharp, clever. 5 *(color)* vivid, bright. 6 *(descripción)* lively, graphic. II *nm* los vivos, the living.

Vizcaya *n* el golfo de V., the Bay of Biscay.

VºBº *abr de* visto bueno.

vocablo *nm* word, term.

vocabulario *nm* vocabulary.

vocación *nf* vocation, calling; con v. europea, with leanings towards Europe.

vocacional *adj* vocational.

vocal I *nf Ling* vowel. II *nmf* member.

vocalista *nmf Mús* vocalist, singer.

vocalizar [4] *vtr & vi* to vocalize.

voceador,-a *nm,f Am* vendor.

vocerío *nm* shouting.

vocero,-a *nm,f Am* spokesperson; *(hombre)* spokesman; *(mujer)* spokeswoman.

vociferante *adj* vociferous.

vociferar *vtr & vi* to vociferate.

vodka *nm* vodka.

vol. *abr de* volumen, volume, vol.

volado,-a *adj fam* estar v., to have a screw loose.

volador,-a *adj* flying.

volandas (en) *loc adv (por el aire)* in the air, flying through the air.

volante I *nm* 1 *Aut* steering wheel; ir al v., to be driving; un as del v., a motor-racing champion. 2 *Cost* frill, ruffle. 3 *Med* note. II *adj* flying; platillo v., flying saucer.

volantín *nm Am (cometa)* small kite.

volar [2] I *vi* 1 to fly; *fig* lo hizo volando, he did it in a flash. 2 *fam (desaparecer)* to disappear, vanish. II *vtr (edificios)* to blow up; *(caja fuerte)* to blow open; *Min* to blast. III *volarse* *vr (papel etc)* to be blown away.

volátil *adj* volatile.

volatinero,-a *nm,f* acrobat.

volcán *nm* volcano.

volcánico,-a *adj* volcanic.

volcar [2] I *vtr* 1 *(cubo etc)* to knock over; *(barco, bote)* to capsize. 2 *(vaciar)* to empty out. 3 *(tiempo)* to invest. II *vi (coche)* to turn over; *(barco)* to capsize. III **volcarse** *vr* 1 *(vaso, jarra)* to fall over, tip over; *(coche)* to turn over; *(barco)* to capsize. 2 *fig* v. con, to do one's utmost for.

voleibol *nm* volleyball.

voleo *nm fig* a(l) v., at random, haphazardly.

voltaje *nm* voltage.

voltear I *vtr* to turn upside down. II *vi* to turn over, roll over.

voltereta *nf* somersault.

voltio *nm* volt.

voluble *adj* fickle, changeable.

volumen *nm* volume.

voluminoso,-a *adj* voluminous; *(enorme)* massive, bulky.

voluntad *nf* will; **fuerza de v.,** willpower; **tiene mucha v.,** he is very strong-willed; **a v.,** at will.

voluntario,-a I *adj* voluntary; **ofrecerse v.,** to volunteer. **II** *nm,f* volunteer.

voluntarioso,-a *adj* willing.

voluptuoso,-a *adj* voluptuous.

volver [4] *(pp vuelto)* **I** *vi* **1** to return; *(venir)* to come back; *(ir)* to go back; **v. en sí,** to come round, recover consciousness. **2 v. a hacer algo,** to do sth again. **II** *vtr* **1** *(convertir)* to turn, make; **me vas a v. loco,** you are driving me mad. **2** *(dar vuelta a)* to turn; *(boca abajo)* to turn upside down; *(de fuera adentro)* to turn inside out; *(de atrás adelante)* to turn back to front; *(dar la vuelta a)* to turn over; **volverle la espalda a algn,** to turn one's back on sb; *fig* **v. la vista atrás,** to look back; *fig* **v. la esquina,** to turn the corner. **III volverse** *vr* **1** to turn. **2** *(regresar)* *(venir)* to come back; *(ir)* to go back. **3** *(convertirse)* to become; **v. loco -a,** to go mad.

vomitar I *vi* to vomit, be sick; **tengo ganas de v.,** I feel sick, I want to be sick. **II** *vtr* to vomit, bring up.

vómito *nm* *(lo vomitado)* vomit; *(acción)* vomiting.

vomitona *nf fam* vomit.

voracidad *nf* voracity, voraciousness.

vorágine *nf* whirlpool; *fig* maelstrom.

voraz *adj* voracious; *fig* raging, fierce.

vórtice *nm* vortex.

vos *pron pers* **1** *arc (usted)* ye, you. **2** *Am (tú)* you.

vosotros,-as *pron pers pl* **1** *(sujeto)* you. **2** *(con prep)* you; **entre v.,** among yourselves; **sin vosotras,** without you.

votación *nf* **1** *(voto)* vote, ballot. **2** *(acción)* voting.

votante *nmf* voter.

votar *vi* to vote; **v. a algn,** to vote (for) sb.

voto *nm* **1** vote; **tener v.,** to have the right to vote; **v. secreto,** secret ballot. **2** *Rel* vow.

vox *nf* **esto es v. populi,** this is common knowledge.

voy *indic pres* → **ir.**

voz *nf* **1** voice; **en v. alta,** aloud; **en v. baja,** in a low voice; **a media v.,** in a low voice, softly; **de viva v.,** verbally. **2** *(grito)* shout; **a voces,** shouting; **dar voces,** to shout; *fig* **estar pidiendo algo a voces,** to be crying out for sth; *fig* **secreto a voces,** open secret; **a v. en grito,** at the top of one's voice. **3 no tener ni v. ni voto,** to have no say in the matter; *fig* **llevar la v. cantante,** to rule the roost. **4** *Gram* **v. pasiva,** passive voice.

vudú *nm* voodoo.

vuelco *nm* upset, tumble; **dar un v.,** *(coche)* to overturn; *fig* **me dio un v. el corazón,** my heart missed a beat.

vuelo *nm* **1** flight; **v. chárter/regular,** charter/scheduled flight; **v. sin motor,** gliding; *fig* **cazarlas** *o* **cogerlas al v.,** to be quick on the uptake. **2** *Cost* **una falda de v.,** a full skirt.

vuelta *nf* **1** *(regreso)* return; *(viaje)* return journey; **a v. de correo,** by return post; **estar de v.,** to be back; *Dep* **partido de v.,** return match. **2** *(giro)* turn; *(en carreras)* lap; *Dep* *(ciclista)* tour; **dar media v.,** to turn round; *fig* **la cabeza me da vueltas,** my head is spinning; *fig* **no le des más vueltas,** stop worrying about it; **v. de campana,** somersault. **3** *(dinero)* change. **4 dar una v.,** *(a pie)* to go for a walk *o* stroll; *(en coche)* to go for a drive *o* a spin (in the car). **5** *fig* **no tiene v. de hoja,** there's no doubt about it.

vuelto,-a I *adj* jersey de cuello v., roll-neck sweater. **II** *nm Am* change.

vuestro,-a I *adj pos (antes del sustantivo)* your; *(después del sustantivo)* of yours; **v. libro,** your book; **un amigo v.,** a friend of yours. **II** *pron pos* yours; **éstos son los vuestros,** these are yours; **lo v.,** what is yours, what belongs to you.

vulgar *adj* **1** vulgar. **2 el término v.,** the everyday term. ◆**vulgarmente** *adv* **v. llamado,** commonly known as.

vulgaridad *nf* vulgarity.

vulgarizar [4] *vtr* *(popularizar)* to popularize.

vulgo *nm* **el v.,** the common people *pl*; *pey* the masses.

vulnerable *adj* vulnerable.

vulnerar *vtr* *(ley, acuerdo)* to violate.

vulva *nf* vulva.

W

W, w [uβe'ðoβle] *nf (la letra)* W, w.

W *abr de vatio(s),* Watt, Watts, W.

walkie-talkie *nm* walkie-talkie.

walkman® *nm* walkman®.

wáter *nm (pl wáteres) fam* toilet.

waterpolo *nm* water polo.

whisky *nm (escocés)* whisky; *(irlandés, US)* whiskey.

windsurf, windsurfing *nm* windsurfing.

windsurfista *nmf* windsurfer.

X

X, x ['ekis] *nf (la letra)* X, x.
xenofobia *nf* xenophobia.
xenófobo,-a I *adj* xenophobic. II *nm,f* xe-
nophobe.
xerografía *nf* xerography.
xilófono *nm* xylophone.

Y

Y, y [i'γri'eγa] *nf (la letra)* Y, y.
y *conj* 1 and; **una chica alta y morena,** a
tall, dark-haired girl; **son las tres y
cuarto,** it's a quarter past three. 2 *¿y
qué?,* so what?; *¿y si no llega a tiempo?,*
what if he doesn't arrive in time?; *¿y tú?,*
what about you?; *¿y eso?,* how come?; *¡y
eso que,* although, even though; *¡y
tanto!,* you bet!, and how!; → **e.**
ya I *adv* 1 already; **yo lo sabía,** I already
knew; **ya en la Edad Media,** as far back
as the Middle Ages. 2 *(ahora mismo)* now;
es preciso actuar ya, it is vital that we
act now; *¡hazlo ya!,* do it at once!; **ya
mismo,** right away. 3 *(en el futuro)* **ya hablaremos luego,** we'll talk about it later;
ya nos veremos, see you!; **ya verás,**
you'll see. 4 **ya no,** no longer; **ya no viene por aquí,** he doesn't come round here
any more. 5 *(refuerza el verbo)* **ya era
hora,** about time too; **ya lo creo,** of
course, I should think so; *¡ya voy!,* coming!; *¡ya está!,* that's it!. II *conj* **ya que,**
since.
yacaré *nm Am* alligator, cayman.
yacer [33] *vi* to lie, be lying.
yacimiento *nm* bed, deposit; **yacimientos
petrolíferos,** oilfields.
yaguar *nm* jaguar.
yanqui *pey* I *adj* Yankee. II *nmf* Yankee,
Yank.
yarará *nm Am* large poisonous snake.
yaraví *nm Am* Quechuan song.
yarda *nf* yard.
yate *nm* yacht.
yaya *nf Am Bot* lancewood; *fam (abuela)*
granny.
yedra *nf* → **hiedra.**
yegua *nf* mare.
yema *nf* 1 *(de huevo)* yolk. 2 *Bot* bud. 3

y. del dedo, fingertip. 4 *Culin* sweet
made from sugar and egg yolk.
Yemen *n* Yemen.
yen *nm (moneda)* yen.
yendo *ger* → **ir.**
yerba *nf* 1 → **hierba.** 2 *Am* maté.
yerbatero,-a *Am* I *nm,f (curandero)* witch
doctor who uses herbs. II *adj* maté.
yermo,-a *adj* 1 *(baldío)* barren, uncultivated. 2 *(despoblado)* deserted, uninhabited.
yerno *nm* son-in-law.
yerro *indic pres* → **errar.**
yeso *nm* 1 *Geol* gypsum. 2 *Constr* plaster.
Yibuti *n* Djibouti.
yiu-yitsu *nm* jujitsu.
yo *pron pers* I; **entre tú y yo,** between you
and me; *¿quién es? - soy yo,* who is it? -
it's me; **yo no,** not me; **yo que tú,** if I
were you; **yo mismo,** I myself.
yodo *nm* iodine.
yoga *nm* yoga.
yogur *nm* yogurt, yoghurt.
yogurtera *nf* yoghurt maker.
yonqui *nm arg* junkie, drug addict.
yoyo, yoyó *nm* yo-yo.
yuca *nf* yucca.
Yucatán *n* Yucatan.
yudo *nm* judo.
yudoka *nmf* judoka.
yugo *nm* yoke.
Yugoslavia *n* Yugoslavia.
yugoslavo,-a, yugoeslavo,-a *adj & nm,f*
Yugoslav, Yugoslavian.
yugular *nf* jugular.
yunque *nm* anvil.
yunta *nf* yoke *o* team of oxen.
yuxtaponer [19] *(pp yuxtapuesto) vtr* to
juxtapose.
yuxtaposición *nf* juxtaposition.

Z

Z, z ['θeta] *nf (la letra)* Z, z.
zafarse *vr (librarse)* to get away **(de,**
from), escape **(de,** from).
zafio,-a *adj* uncouth.
zafiro *nm* sapphire.
zaga *nf* **a la z.,** behind, at the rear.
zaguán *nm* hall, hallway.

zaherir [5] *vtr* to hurt.
zahúrda *nf* pigsty.
zaino,-a *adj (caballo)* chestnut; *(toro)*
black.
Zaire *n* Zaire.
zalamería *nf* flattery.
zalamero,-a I *nm,f* flatterer, fawner. II

adj flattering, fawning.
zamarra *nf (prenda)* sheepskin jacket.
Zambia *n* Zambia.
zambo,-a I *adj* **1** *(patizambo)* knock-kneed. **2** *Am (persona)* half Indian and half Negro. **II** *nm,f Am (persona)* person who is half Indian and half Negro.
zambomba *nf* kind of primitive drum.
zambullida *nf* plunge.
zambullirse *vr* to plunge.
zamparse *vr fam* to gobble down.
zanahoria *nf* carrot.
zancada *nf* stride.
zancadilla *nf* **ponerle la z. a algn**, to trip sb up.
zanco *nm* stilt.
zancudo,-a I *adj* **1** long-legged. **2** *Orn* wading; **ave zancuda**, wading bird, wader. **II** *nm Am* mosquito.
zángano,-a I *nm (insecto)* drone. **II** *nm,f fam (persona)* idler, lazybones *inv.*
zanja *nf* ditch, trench.
zanjar *vtr (asunto)* to settle.
zapallo *nm Am* pumpkin, calabash.
zapata *nf* **1** *(cuña)* wedge. **2** *Téc* shoe.
zapatear *vi* to tap one's feet.
zapatería *nf* shoe shop.
zapatero,-a *nm,f (vendedor)* shoe dealer; *(fabricante)* shoemaker, cobbler.
zapatilla *nf* slipper; **zapatillas de deporte**, trainers.
zapato *nm* shoe; **zapatos de tacón**, high-heeled shoes.
zar *nm* czar, tsar.
Zaragoza *n* Saragossa.
zaragozano,-a I *adj* of *o* from Saragossa. **II** *nm,f* native *o* inhabitant of Saragossa.
zarandear *vtr* to shake.
zarandeo *nm* shaking.
zarcillo *nm* **1** *(pendiente)* earring. **2** *Bot* tendril.
zarina *nf* czarina, tsarina.
zarpa *nf* claw.
zarpar *vi* to weigh anchor, set sail.
zarpazo *nm* clawing; **dar** *o* **pegar un z. a**, to claw.
zarza *nf* bramble, blackberry bush.
zarzal *nm* bramble patch.

zarzamora *nf (zarza)* blackberry bush; *(fruto)* blackberry.
zarzuela *nf* **1** Spanish operetta. **2 la Z.**, royal residence in Madrid. **3** *Culin* fish stew.
zenit *nm* zenith.
zigzag *nm (pl* **zigzags** *o* **zigzagues)** zigzag.
zigzaguear *vi* to zigzag.
Zimbabwe *n* Zimbabwe.
zinc *nm* zinc.
zócalo *nm* **1** *(de pared)* skirting board. **2** *(pedestal)* plinth.
zodiaco, zodíaco *nm* zodiac; **signo del z.**, sign of the zodiac.
zona *nf* zone; *(región)* region; **z. verde**, park.
zoo *nm* zoo.
zoología *nf* zoology.
zoológico,-a I *adj* zoological; **parque z.**, zoo. **II** *nm* zoo.
zoom *nm Cin Fot* zoom.
zopenco,-a *nm,f fam* dope, half-wit.
zopilote *nm Am* buzzard.
zoquete *nmf fam* blockhead.
zorra *nf* **1** vixen. **2** *fam* slut.
zorro,-a I *nm* fox. **II** *adj fam* **1** *(astuto)* cunning, sly. **2** *vulg* **no tener ni zorra** *(idea)*, not to have the slightest idea.
zorzal *nm Orn* thrush.
zozobrar *vi* to be in danger of going under.
zueco *nm* clog.
zumbado,-a *adj fam* crazy, mad.
zumbar I *vi* to buzz, hum; **me zumban los oídos**, my ears are buzzing; *fam* **salir zumbando**, to zoom off. **II** *vtr fam* to thrash.
zumbido *nm* buzzing, humming.
zumo *nm* juice.
zurcir [3] *vtr Cost* to darn; *fam* **¡que te zurzan!**, go to hell!
zurda *nf (mano)* left hand.
zurdo,-a I *nm,f (persona)* left-handed person. **II** *adj* left-handed.
zurrar *vtr (pegar)* to beat, flog.
zutano,-a *nm,f fam* so-and-so; *(hombre)* what's-his-name; *(mujer)* what's-her-name.

English - Spanish
Inglés - Español

TABLA DE VERBOS IRREGULARES INGLESES

American forms have been indicated by *. Unusual, archaic or literary forms are given in brackets.

infinitive	past tense	past participle
abide	abided, (abode)	abided
arise	arose	arisen
be	was, were	been
awake	awoke, awaked	awoken, (awaked)
bear	bore	borne
beat	beat	beaten
become	became	become
befall	befell	befallen
begin	began	begun
behold	beheld	beheld
bend	bent	bent
beseech	besought	besought
bet	bet, betted	bet, betted
bid (offer)	bid	bid
bid (command)	bade	bidden
bind	bound	bound
bite	bit	bitten
bleed	bled	bled
blow	blew	blown
break	broke	broken
breed	bred	bred
bring	brought	brought
broadcast	broadcast	broadcast
build	built	built
burn	burnt, burned	burnt, burned
burst	burst	burst
buy	bought	bought
cast	cast	cast
catch	caught	caught
choose	chose	chosen
cling	clung	clung
clothe	clothed, (clad)	clothed, (clad)
come	came	come
cost	cost	cost
creep	crept	crept
crow	crowed, (crew)	crowed
cut	cut	cut
deal	dealt	dealt
dig	dug	dug
dive	dived, dove*	dived
do	did	done
draw	drew	drawn
dream	dreamt, dreamed	dreamt, dreamed
drink	drank	drunk
drive	drove	driven
dwell	dwelt, dwelled	dwelt, dwelled
eat	ate	eaten
fall	fell	fallen
feed	fed	fed
feel	felt	felt
fight	fought	fought
find	found	found

fit	fit*, fitted	fit*, fitted
flee	fled	fled
fling	flung	flung
fly	flew	flown
forbid	forbad(e)	forbidden
forget	forgot	forgotten
forgive	forgave	forgiven
forsake	forsook	forsaken
freeze	froze	frozen
get	got	got, gotten*
give	gave	given
go	went	gone
grind	ground	ground
grow	grew	grown
hang	hung, hanged	hung, hanged
have	had	had
hear	heard	heard
hide	hid	hidden
hit	hit	hit
hold	held	held
hurt	hurt	hurt
keep	kept	kept
kneel	knelt, kneeled	knelt, kneeled
know	knew	known
lay	laid	laid
lead	led	led
lean	leant, leaned	leant, leaned
leap	leapt, leaped	leapt, leaped
learn	learnt, learned	learnt, learned
leave	left	left
lend	lent	lent
let	let	let
lie	lay	lain
light	lit, lighted	lit, lighted
lose	lost	lost
make	made	made
mean	meant	meant
meet	met	met
mow	mowed	mown, mowed
pay	paid	paid
plead	pled*, pleaded	pled*, pleaded
put	put	put
quit	quit, (quitted)	quit, (quitted)
read	read [red]	read [red]
rend	rent	rent
rid	rid	rid
ride	rode	ridden
ring	rang	rung
rise	rose	risen
run	ran	run
saw	sawed	sawn, sawed
say	said	said
see	saw	seen
seek	sought	sought
sell	sold	sold
send	sent	sent
set	set	set
sew	sewed	sewn, sewed

(iii)

shake	shook	shaken
shear	sheared	shorn, sheared
shed	shed	shed
shine	shone	shone
shoe	shod, shoed	shod, shoed
shoot	shot	shot
show	showed	shown, showed
shrink	shrank, shrunk	shrunk
shut	shut	shut
sing	sang	sung
sink	sank	sunk
sit	sat	sat
slay	slew	slain
sleep	slept	slept
slide	slid	slid
sling	slung	slung
slink	slunk	slunk
slit	slit	slit
smell	smelt, smelled	smelt, smelled
sneak	snuck*, sneaked	snuck*, sneaked
sow	sowed	sown, sowed
speak	spoke	spoken
speed	sped, speeded	sped, speeded
spell	spelt, spelled	spelt, spelled
spend	spent	spent
spill	spilt, spilled	spilt, spilled
spin	spun	spun
spit	spat, spit*	spat, spit*
split	split	split
spoil	spoilt, spoiled	spoilt, spoiled
spread	spread	spread
spring	sprang	sprung
stand	stood	stood
steal	stole	stolen
stick	stuck	stuck
sting	stung	stung
stink	stank	stunk
strew	strewed	strewn, strewed
stride	strode	stridden
strike	struck	struck
string	strung	strung
strive	strove	striven
swear	swore	sworn
sweat	sweat*, sweated	sweat*, sweated
sweep	swept	swept
swell	swelled	swollen, swelled
swim	swam	swum
swing	swung	swung
take	took	taken
teach	taught	taught
tear	tore	torn
tell	told	told
think	thought	thought
thrive	thrived, (throve)	thrived, (thriven)
throw	threw	thrown
thrust	thrust	thrust
tread	trod	trodden
understand	understood	understood

undertake	undertook	undertaken
wake	woke	woken
wear	wore	worn
weave	wove	woven
weep	wept	wept
wet	wet, wetted	wet, wetted
win	won	won
wind	wound	wound
wring	wrung	wrung
write	wrote	written

Fonética Inglesa

En este diccionario la transcripción fonética de las palabras inglesas se basa en e
sistema de la Asociación Fonética Internacional (AFI) con algunas modificacione
Cada entrada viene seguida de su correspondiente transcripción fonética entr
corchetes ([ ]). El acento primario se indica mediante un ' delante de la sílab
acentuada.

Las consonantes

[p]	*p*en
[b]	*b*ill
[t]	*t*en*t*
[d]	*d*esk
[k]	*c*ar
[g]	*g*oal
[tʃ]	tea*ch*er
[dʒ]	a*g*e
[f]	*f*ish
[v]	ha*v*e
[θ]	me*th*od
[ð]	mo*th*er
[s]	i*c*y
[z]	ea*s*y
[ʃ]	*sh*oe
[ʒ]	mea*s*ure
[h]	*h*at
[m]	*m*ilk
[n]	*n*ame
[ŋ]	si*ng*
[l]	*l*ight
[r]	*r*ead
[j]	*y*oghurt
[w]	*w*atch
[x]	lo*ch* (como en legión)
[ʳ]	se llama *'linking' r* y se encuentra únicamente a final de palabra. Se pronuncia sólo cuando la palabra siguiente empieza por una vocal: mother ['mʌðəʳ]

Las vocales y los diptongos

[iː]	sh*ee*p
[ɪ]	sh*i*p, hous*e*s
[e]	b*e*d
[æ]	c*a*t
[ɑː]	*fa*ther
[ɒ]	d*o*g
[ɔː]	h*or*se
[ʊ]	w*o*man
[uː]	bl*ue*
[ʌ]	c*u*p
[ɜː]	*ear*th
[ə]	*a*bout
[ə]	opcional. En algunos casos se pronuncia y en otros se omite: trifle ['traɪfəl]
[eɪ]	t*a*ble
[əʊ]	g*o*
[aɪ]	t*i*me
[aʊ]	h*ou*se
[ɔɪ]	b*oy*
[ɪə]	f*ie*rce
[eə]	c*are*
[ʊə]	d*u*ring

(vi)

A

A, a [eɪ] n 1 (the letter) A, a f. 2 Mus la m.

a [eɪ, unstressed ə] indef art (before vowel or silent h **an**) 1 un, una; **a** man/**a woman**, un hombre/una mujer; **he has a big nose**, tiene la nariz grande. 2 (omitted in Span) half a litre/an hour, medio litro/media hora; **a hundred/thousand people**, cien/mil personas; **let's have a drink**, vamos a beber algo; **he's a teacher**, es profesor; **what a pity**, qué pena. 3 (each) 60 pence a kilo, 60 peniques el kilo; **to eat grapes two at a time**, comer las uvas de dos en dos; **three times a week**, tres veces a la semana. 4 (a certain) un a una tal; **a Mr Rees phoned**, llamó un tal Sr. Rees.

AA [eɪ'eɪ] 1 abbr of **Alcoholics Anonymous**, Alcohólicos Anónimos, AA. 2 abbr of **Automobile Association**, ≈ Automóvil Club m, AC.

AAA [eɪeɪ'eɪ] 1 GB abbr of **Amateur Athletic Association**, Asociación Atlética Amateur, AAA. 2 US abbr of **Automobile Association of America**, ≈ Automóvil Club m, AC.

aback [ə'bæk] adv **to be taken a.**, quedarse de una pieza (by, por).

abandon [ə'bændən] I n desenfreno m; **with reckless a.**, desenfrenadamente. II vtr (child) abandonar; (job) dejar; (project) renunciar a.

abase [ə'beɪs] vtr **to a. oneself**, humillarse.

abashed [ə'bæʃt] adj desconcertado,-a.

abate [ə'beɪt] vi (anger) apaciguarse; (storm) amainar.

abattoir ['æbətwɑːr] n matadero m.

abbey ['æbɪ] n abadía f.

abbot ['æbət] n abad m.

abbreviate [ə'briːvɪeɪt] vtr abreviar.

abbreviation [əbriːvɪ'eɪʃən] n abreviatura f.

abdicate ['æbdɪkeɪt] vtr & vi abdicar.

abdication [æbdɪ'keɪʃən] n abdicación f.

abdomen ['æbdəmən] n abdomen m.

abduct [æb'dʌkt] vtr raptar, secuestrar.

aberration [æbə'reɪʃən] n aberración f.

abet [ə'bet] vtr **to aid and a. a sb**, ser cómplice de algn.

abeyance [ə'beɪəns] n **to be in a.**, estar en desuso.

abhor [əb'hɔːr] vtr aborrecer.

abhorrent [əb'hɒrənt] adj aborrecible.

abide [ə'baɪd] vtr aguantar; **I can't a. it**, no lo aguanto. **◆abide by** vtr (promise) cumplir con; (rules) atenerse a.

ability [ə'bɪlɪtɪ] n (capability) capacidad f, aptitud f; (talent) talento m.

abject ['æbdʒekt] adj (state) miserable; (apology) rastrero,-a.

ablaze [ə'bleɪz] adj & adv en llamas, ardiendo.

able ['eɪbl] adj (capable) capaz; **will you be a. to come on Tuesday?**, ¿podrás venir el martes?

able-bodied [eɪbl'bɒdɪd] adj sano,-a; **a.-b. seaman**, marinero m de primera.

abnormal [æb'nɔːməl] adj anormal. **◆abnormally** adv anormalmente; (large) extraordinariamente.

aboard [ə'bɔːd] I adv a bordo; **to go a.**, (ship) embarcarse; (train) subir. II prep a bordo de.

abode [ə'bəʊd] n Jur **of no fixed a.**, sin domicilio fijo.

abolish [ə'bɒlɪʃ] vtr abolir.

abolition [æbə'lɪʃən] n abolición f.

abominable [ə'bɒmɪnəbəl] adj abominable; (dreadful) terrible.

aborigine [æbə'rɪdʒɪnɪ] n aborigen mf australiano,-a.

abort [ə'bɔːt] I vtr Med hacer abortar; fig (plan etc) archivar. II vi Med abortar.

abortion [ə'bɔːʃən] n Med aborto m; **a. law**, ley f del aborto; **to have an a.**, abortar.

abortive [ə'bɔːtɪv] adj (plan) fracasado,-a; (attempt) frustrado,-a.

abound [ə'baʊnd] vi **to a. in** or **with**, abundar en.

about [ə'baʊt] adv & prep 1 (concerning) acerca de, sobre; **a programme a. Paris**, un programa sobre París; **to be worried a. sth**, estar preocupado,-a por algo; **to speak a. sth**, hablar de algo; **what's it all a.?**, (what's happening?) ¿qué pasa?; (story etc) ¿de qué se trata?; **fam how a. a game of tennis?**, ¿qué te parece un partido de tenis? 2 (around) por todas partes; **don't leave things lying a.**, no dejes las cosas por medio; **there's nobody a.**, no hay nadie; **to look a.**, mirar alrededor; **to rush a.**, correr de un lado para otro; **we went for a walk a. the town**, dimos una vuelta por el pueblo. 3 (approximately) más o menos; **it's a. 3 o'clock**, son más o menos las 3; **it's a. time you got up**, ya es hora de que te levantes; **it's just a. finished**, está casi terminado; **she's a. 40**, tiene unos 40 años. 4 **it's a. to start**, está a punto de empezar; **not to be a. to do sth**, no estar dispuesto,-a a hacer algo.

about-turn [əbaʊt'tɜːn, US **about-face**] n media vuelta f; **to do an a.-t.**, dar media vuelta; fig cambiar de idea por completo.

about-face [əbaʊt'feɪs] n media vuelta f; **to do an a.-t.**, dar media vuelta; fig cambiar de idea por completo.

above [ə'bʌv] adv & prep 1 (higher than) encima de, sobre, arriba; **100 metres a. sea level**, 100 metros sobre el nivel del mar; **it's a. the door**, está encima de la puerta; **the flat** a., el piso de arriba. **2** (*greater than*) superior (a); **amounts a. £10**, cantidades superiores a las 10 libras; *fig* **a policy imposed from a.**, una política impuesta desde arriba. **3** a. **all**, sobre todo; **he's not a. stealing**, no es capaz incluso de robar. **4** (*in book etc*) más arriba.

above-board [ə'bʌvbɔːd] *adj* (*scheme*) legítimo,-a.

above-mentioned [ə'bʌvmenʃənd] *adj* susodicho,-a.

abrasive [ə'breɪsɪv] I *adj* (*substance*) abrasivo,-a; *fig* (*voice, wit etc*) cáustico,-a. II *n* abrasivo *m*.

abreast [ə'brest] *adv* **to walk 3 a.**, ir de 3 en fondo; *fig* **to keep a. of things**, mantenerse al día.

abridged [ə'brɪdʒd] *adj* (*book*) abreviado,-a.

abroad [ə'brɔːd] *adv* **to be a.**, estar en el extranjero; **to go a.**, irse al extranjero.

abrupt [ə'brʌpt] *adj* (*manner*) brusco,-a; (*tone*) áspero,-a; (*change*) súbito,-a.
◆**abruptly** *adv* (*act*) bruscamente; (*speak*) con aspereza; (*change*) repentinamente.

abscess ['æbses] *n* absceso *m*; (*on gum*) flemón *m*.

abscond [əb'skɒnd] *vi* huir.

absence ['æbsəns] *n* (*of person*) ausencia *f*; (*of thing*) falta *f*.

absent ['æbsənt] *adj* ausente; *fig* **an a. look**, una mirada distraída. ◆**absently** *adv* distraídamente.

absentee [æbsən'tiː] *n* ausente *mf*.

absenteeism [æbsən'tiːɪzəm] *n* absentismo *m*.

absent-minded [æbsənt'maɪndɪd] *adj* distraído,-a.

absolute ['æbsəluːt] *adj* absoluto,-a; (*failure*) total; (*truth*) puro,-a; **it's an a. disgrace**, es una auténtica vergüenza.
◆**absolutely** I *adv* (*completely*) completamente; **a. wrong**, totalmente equivocado,-a; **a. not**, en absoluto; **you're a. right**, tienes toda la razón. II *interj* a.!, ¡desde luego!

absolve [əb'zɒlv] *vtr* absolver (**from**, de).

absorb [əb'zɔːb] *vtr* (*liquid*) absorber; (*sound, blow*) amortiguar; *fig* **to be absorbed in sth**, estar absorto,-a en algo.

absorbing [əb'zɔːbɪŋ] *adj* (*book, work*) absorbente.

abstain [əb'steɪn] *vi* abstenerse (**from**, de).

abstemious [əb'stiːmɪəs] *adj* abstemio,-a.

abstention [əb'stenʃən] *n* abstención *f*.

abstinence ['æbstɪnəns] *n* abstinencia *f*.

abstract ['æbstrækt] I *adj* abstracto,-a. II *n* (*of thesis etc*) resumen *m*.

abstruse [əb'struːs] *adj* abstruso,-a.

absurd [əb'sɜːd] *adj* absurdo,-a.

abundance [ə'bʌndəns] *n* abundancia *f*.

abundant [ə'bʌndənt] *adj* abundante.

rico,-a (**in**, en).

abuse [ə'bjuːs] I *n* **1** (*ill-treatment*) malos tratos; (*misuse*) abuso *m*. **2** (*insults*) injurias *fpl*. II [ə'bjuːz] *vtr* **1** (*ill-treat*) maltratar; (*misuse*) abusar de. **2** (*insult*) injuriar.

abusive [ə'bjuːsɪv] *adj* (*insulting*) insultante.

abysmal [ə'bɪzməl] *adj* (*conditions*) extremo,-a; *fam* (*very bad*) fatal, pésimo,-a.

abyss [ə'bɪs] *n* abismo *m*; *fig* extremo *m*.

AC ['eɪsiː] *abbr of* **alternating current**, corriente alterna, CA.

academic [ækə'demɪk] I *adj* académico, -a; (*career*) universitario,-a; (*discussion*) teórico,-a; **a. year**, año *m* escolar. II *n* académico,-a *m*,*f*.

academy [ə'kædəmɪ] *n* (*society*) academia *f*; *Educ* instituto *m* de enseñanza media; **a. of music**, conservatorio *m*.

accede [æk'siːd] *vi* acceder (**to**, a).

accelerate [æk'seləreɪt] I *vtr* (*engine*) acelerar; (*step*) aligerar. II *vi* (*car, engine*) acelerar.

acceleration [ækselə'reɪʃən] *n* aceleración *f*.

accelerator [æk'seləreɪtə] *n* acelerador *m*.

accent ['æksənt] *n* acento *m*.

accentuate [æk'sentjʊeɪt] *vtr* subrayar.

accept [ək'sept] *vtr & vi* aceptar; (*theory*) admitir; **do you a. that ...?**, ¿estás de acuerdo en que ...?

acceptable [ək'septəbəl] *adj* (*satisfactory*) aceptable; (*tolerable*) admisible.

acceptance [ək'septəns] *n* (*act of accepting*) aceptación *f*; (*good reception*) aprobación *f*.

access ['ækses] *n* acceso *m*; **a. road**, carretera *f* de acceso; **to have a. to sth**, tener libre acceso a algo.

accessible [æk'sesəbəl] *adj* (*place, position*) accesible; (*person*) asequible.

accession [æk'seʃən] *n* subida *f* (al trono).

accessory [ək'sesərɪ] *n* **1** *Jur* cómplice *mf*. **2** **accessories**, accesorios *mpl*; (*for outfit*) complementos *mpl*.

accident ['æksɪdənt] *n* accidente *m*; (*coincidence*) casualidad *f*; **it was an a. on my part**, lo hice sin querer; **car a.**, accidente *m* de carretera; **by a.**, por casualidad.

accidental [æksɪ'dentəl] *adj* fortuito,-a; (*unintended*) imprevisto,-a.
◆**accidentally** *adv* (*by chance*) por casualidad; **he did it a.**, lo hizo sin querer.

accident-prone ['æksɪdəntprəʊn] *adj* propenso,-a a los accidentes.

acclaim [ə'kleɪm] I *n* aclamación *f*. II *vtr* aclamar.

acclimatize [ə'klaɪmətaɪz] *vtr* aclimatar.

acclimatized [ə'klaɪmətaɪzd] *adj* aclimatado,-a; **to become a.**, aclimatarse.

accolade [ˈækəleɪd] n elogio m.

accommodate [əˈkɒmədeɪt] vtr 1 (guests) alojar. 2 to a. sb's wishes, complacer a algn.

accommodating [əˈkɒmədeɪtɪŋ] adj (obliging) complaciente; (understanding) comprensivo,-a.

accommodation [əkɒməˈdeɪʃən] n (US also accommodations) (lodgings) alojamiento m.

accompany [əˈkʌmpəni] vtr acompañar.

accomplice [əˈkʌmplɪs] n cómplice mf.

accomplish [əˈkʌmplɪʃ] vtr (aim) conseguir; (task, mission) llevar a cabo.

accomplished [əˈkʌmplɪʃt] adj dotado,-a, experto,-a.

accomplishment [əˈkʌmplɪʃmənt] n 1 (of task) realización f; (of duty) cumplimiento m. 2 accomplishments, (talents) dotes fpl.

accord [əˈkɔːd] I n (agreement) acuerdo m; of her or his own a., espontáneamente. II vtr (honour etc) conceder.

accordance [əˈkɔːdəns] n in a. with, de acuerdo con.

according [əˈkɔːdɪŋ] prep a. to, según; everything went a. to plan, todo salió conforme a los planes.

accordingly [əˈkɔːdɪŋli] adv 1 to act a., (appropriately) obrar según y conforme. 2 (therefore) así pues.

accordion [əˈkɔːdɪən] n acordeón m.

account [əˈkaʊnt] n 1 (report) informe m; by all accounts, al decir de todos. 2 I was fearful on her a., sufría por ella; it's of no a., no tiene importancia; on a. of, a causa de; on no a., bajo ningún concepto; to take a. of, to take into a., tener en cuenta. 3 Com cuenta f; to keep the accounts, llevar las cuentas; accounts department, servicio m de contabilidad; to open/close an a., abrir/cancelar una cuenta; current a., cuenta corriente; a. number, número m de cuenta. ◆**account for** vtr (explain) explicar.

accountable [əˈkaʊntəbəl] adj to be a. to sb for sth, ser responsable ante algn de algo.

accountancy [əˈkaʊntənsi] n contabilidad f.

accountant [əˈkaʊntənt] n contable mf.

accredited [əˈkredɪtɪd] adj acreditado,-a.

accrue [əˈkruː] vi (interest) acumularse.

accumulate [əˈkjuːmjʊleɪt] I vtr acumular; (fortune) amasar. II vi acumularse.

accuracy [ˈækjʊrəsi] n (of number etc) exactitud f; (of shot, criticism) certeza f.

accurate [ˈækjʊrɪt] adj (number) exacto,-a; (shot, criticism) certero,-a; (answer) correcto,-a; (observation) acertado,-a; (instrument) de precisión; (translation) fiel.

accusation [ækjʊˈzeɪʃən] n acusación f.

accuse [əˈkjuːz] vtr acusar.

accused [əˈkjuːzd] n the a., el/la acusado,-a.

accustom [əˈkʌstəm] vtr acostumbrar; to be accustomed to doing sth, estar acostumbrado,-a a hacer algo.

ace [eɪs] n 1 Cards & fig as m. 2 Ten as m.

acetate [ˈæsɪteɪt] n acetato m.

acetone [ˈæsɪtəʊn] n acetona f.

ache [eɪk] I n dolor m; aches and pains, achaques mpl. II vi doler; my back aches, me duele la espalda.

achieve [əˈtʃiːv] vtr (attain) conseguir, alcanzar; (accomplish) llevar a cabo, realizar.

achievement [əˈtʃiːvmənt] n (attainment) logro m; (completion) realización f; (feat) hazaña f.

acid [ˈæsɪd] I adj ácido,-a; (taste) agrio,-a; (remark) mordaz; a. rain, lluvia ácida; fig a. test, prueba decisiva. II n ácido m.

acknowledge [əkˈnɒlɪdʒ] vtr 1 (recognize) reconocer; (claim, defeat) admitir; (present) agradecer; (letter) acusar recibo de. 2 (greet) saludar.

acknowledgement [əkˈnɒlɪdʒmənt] n 1 (recognition) reconocimiento m; (of letter) acuse m de recibo. 2 acknowledgements, (in preface) menciones fpl.

acne [ˈækni] n acné m.

acorn [ˈeɪkɔːn] n bellota f.

acoustic [əˈkuːstɪk] I adj acústico,-a. II npl acoustics, acústica f sing.

acquaint [əˈkweɪnt] vtr to a. sb with the facts, informar a algn de los detalles; to be acquainted with the procedure, estar al corriente de como se procede; to be acquainted with sb, conocer a algn.

acquaintance [əˈkweɪntəns] n 1 conocimiento m; to make sb's a., conocer a algn. 2 (person) conocido,-a m,f.

acquiesce [ækwɪˈes] vi consentir (in, en).

acquiescent [ækwɪˈesənt] adj conforme.

acquire [əˈkwaɪər] vtr adquirir.

acquisition [ækwɪˈzɪʃən] n adquisición f.

acquisitive [əˈkwɪzɪtɪv] adj codicioso,-a.

acquit [əˈkwɪt] vtr 1 Jur to a. sb of sth, absolver a algn de algo. 2 to a. oneself well, defenderse bien.

acquittal [əˈkwɪtəl] n absolución f.

acre [ˈeɪkər] n acre m (aprox 40,47 áreas).

acrid [ˈækrɪd] adj (smell, taste) acre.

acrimonious [ækrɪˈməʊnɪəs] adj (remark) cáustico,-a; (dispute) enconado,-a.

acrobat [ˈækrəbæt] n acróbata mf.

across [əˈkrɒs] I adv a. way, the river is 30 metres a., el río mide 30 metros de ancho; to go a., atravesar; to run a., atravesar corriendo. II prep 1 a través de; they live a. the road, viven enfrente; to go a. the street, cruzar la calle. 2 (at the other side of) al otro lado de.

acrylic [əˈkrɪlɪk] adj acrílico,-a.

act [ækt] I n 1 (action) acto m, acción f; a.

of God, caso *m* de fuerza mayor. 2 *Parl* ley *f*, decreto *m*. 3 *Theat* acto *m*; (turn in show) número *m*. II *vtr Theat* (part) interpretar; (character) representar; fig to a. the fool, hacer el tonto. III *vi* 1 *Theat* hacer teatro; *Cin* hacer cine; fig (pretend) fingir. 2 (behave) comportarse. 3 (take action) actuar, obrar; to a. on sb's advice, seguir el consejo de algn. 4 (work) funcionar; (drug etc) actuar; to a. as a deterrent, servir de disuasivo. 5 to a. as director, hacer de director. ◆act out *vtr* exteriorizar. ◆act up *vi fam* (machine) funcionar mal; (child) dar guerra.

acting ['æktɪŋ] I *adj* interino,-a. II *n* (profession) teatro *m*; he's done some a., ha hecho algo de teatro.

action ['ækʃən] *n* 1 (deed) acción *f*; *Mil* acción de combate; to be out of a., (person) estar fuera de servicio; (machine) estar estropeado,-a; to take a., tomar medidas. 2 *Jur* demanda *f*. 3 *TV* a. replay, repetición *f*.

activate ['æktɪveɪt] *vtr* activar.

active ['æktɪv] *adj* activo,-a; (energetic) vigoroso,-a; (interest) vivo,-a; *Ling* a. voice, voz activa.

activist ['æktɪvɪst] *n* activista *mf*.

activity [æk'tɪvɪtɪ] *n* (of person) actividad *f*; (on street etc) bullicio *m*.

actor ['æktər] *n* actor *m*.

actress ['æktrɪs] *n* actriz *f*.

actual ['æktʃʊəl] *adj* real, verdadero,-a.

actually ['æktʃʊəlɪ] *adv* (really) en efecto, realmente; (even) incluso, hasta; (in fact) de hecho.

acumen ['ækjʊmən] *n* perspicacia *f*.

acupuncture ['ækjʊpʌŋktʃər] *n* acupuntura *f*.

acute [ə'kjuːt] *adj* agudo,-a; (pain) intenso,-a; (hearing) muy fino,-a; (shortage) grave; (mind) perspicaz.

ad [æd] *n fam* anuncio *m*.

AD [eɪ'diː] *abbr of* Anno Domini, después de Cristo, d.C.

adamant ['ædəmənt] *adj* firme, inflexible.

adapt [ə'dæpt] I *vtr* adaptar (to, a); to a. oneself to sth, adaptarse a algo. II *vi* adaptarse.

adaptable [ə'dæptəbəl] *adj* (instrument) ajustable; he's very a., se amolda fácilmente a las circunstancias.

adaptation [ædəp'teɪʃən] *n* adaptación *f*.

adapter, adaptor [ə'dæptər] *n Elec* ladrón *m*.

add [æd] I *vtr* (numbers) sumar; (one thing to another) añadir. II *vi* (count) sumar. ◆add to *vtr* aumentar. ◆add up I *vtr* sumar. II *vi* (numbers) sumar; fig it doesn't a. up, no tiene sentido; it doesn't a. up to much, no es gran cosa.

added ['ædɪd] *adj* adicional.

adder ['ædər] *n* víbora *f*.

addict ['ædɪkt] *n* adicto,-a *m,f*; *fam* television a., teleadicto,-a *m,f*.

addicted [ə'dɪktɪd] *adj* adicto,-a; to become a. to sth, enviciarse con algo.

addiction [ə'dɪkʃən] *n* (to gambling etc) vicio *m*; (to drugs) adicción *f*.

addictive [ə'dɪktɪv] *adj* que crea adicción.

addition [ə'dɪʃən] *n Math* adición *f*; (increase) aumento *m*; an a. to the family, un nuevo miembro de la familia; in a. to, además de.

additional [ə'dɪʃənəl] *adj* adicional.

additive ['ædɪtɪv] *n* aditivo *m*.

address [ə'dres] I *n* 1 (on letter) dirección *f*, señas *fpl*. 2 (speech) discurso *m*. II *vtr* 1 (letter) dirigir. 2 (speak to) dirigirse (to, a); to a. the floor, tomar la palabra. 3 (use form of address to) tratar de.

adenoids ['ædɪnɔɪdz] *npl* vegetaciones *fpl* (adenoides).

adept [ə'dept] I *adj* experto,-a, (at, en). II *n* experto,-a.

adequate ['ædɪkwɪt] *adj* (enough) suficiente; (satisfactory) adecuado,-a.

adhere [əd'hɪər] *vi* (stick) pegarse (to, a). ◆adhere to *vtr* (policy) adherirse a; (contract) cumplir con.

adherent [əd'hɪərənt] *n* partidario,-a *m,f*.

adhesive [əd'hiːsɪv] I *adj* adhesivo,-a; (sticky) pegajoso,-a; a. tape, cinta adhesiva. II *n* adhesivo *m*.

ad hoc [æd'hɒk] *adj* (remark) improvisado,-a; an ad h. committee, un comité especial.

ad infinitum [ædɪnfɪ'naɪtəm] *adv* hasta el infinito.

adjacent [ə'dʒeɪsənt] *adj* (building) contiguo,-a; (land) colindante; a. to, contiguo,-a a.

adjective ['ædʒɪktɪv] *n* adjetivo *m*.

adjoining [ə'dʒɔɪnɪŋ] *adj* contiguo,-a; (land) colindante; the a. room, la habitación de al lado.

adjourn [ə'dʒɜːn] I *vtr* (postpone) aplazar; (court) levantar. II *vi* aplazarse (until, hasta).

adjudicate [ə'dʒuːdɪkeɪt] *vtr* juzgar.

adjudicator [ə'dʒuːdɪkeɪtər] *n* juez,-a *m,f*.

adjust [ə'dʒʌst] I *vtr* (machine etc) ajustar; fig (methods) variar. II *vi* (person) adaptarse (to, a).

adjustable [ə'dʒʌstəbəl] *adj* ajustable.

adjustment [ə'dʒʌstmənt] *n* 1 (to machine etc) ajuste *m*; (by person) adaptación *f*. 2 (change) modificación *f*.

ad lib [æd'lɪb] I *adv* (speak) sin preparación; (continue) a voluntad. II *vi* (speech) improvisado,-a. III **ad-lib** *vi* improvisar.

administer [əd'mɪnɪstər] *vtr* (country) gobernar; (justice) administrar.

administration [ədmɪnɪ'streɪʃən] *n* (of country) gobierno *m*; (of justice) administración *f*; (governing body) dirección *f*.

administrative [əd'mɪnɪstrɪtɪv] *adj*

administrativo,-a.

admirable [ˈædmərəbəl] *adj* admirable.

admiral [ˈædmərəl] *n* almirante *m*.

admiration [ædməˈreɪʃən] *n* admiración *f*.

admire [ədˈmaɪər] *vtr* admirar.

admirer [ədˈmaɪərər] *n* admirador,-a *m,f*.

admissible [ədˈmɪsəbəl] *adj* admisible.

admission [ədˈmɪʃən] *n* 1 (to school etc) ingreso *m*; (price) entrada *f*. 2 (of fact) reconocimiento *m*; (confession) confesión *f*.

admit [ədˈmɪt] *vtr* 1 (person) dejar entrar; **to be admitted to hospital**, ser ingresado,-a en el hospital. 2 (acknowledge) reconocer; (crime, guilt) confesar.

admittance [ədˈmɪtəns] *n* (entry) entrada *f*.

admittedly [ədˈmɪtɪdlɪ] *adv* la verdad es que ....

admonish [ədˈmɒnɪʃ] *vtr* amonestar.

ad nauseam [ædˈnɔːzɪæm] *adv* hasta la saciedad.

ado [əˈduː] *n* **without further a.**, sin más.

adolescence [ædəˈlesəns] *n* adolescencia *f*.

adolescent [ædəˈlesənt] *n* adolescente *mf*.

adopt [əˈdɒpt] *vtr* adoptar; (suggestion) aceptar.

adopted [əˈdɒptɪd] *adj* **a. child**, hijo,-a *m,f* adoptivo,-a.

adoption [əˈdɒpʃən] *n* adopción *f*; **country of a.**, país adoptivo.

adore [əˈdɔːr] *vtr* adorar.

adorn [əˈdɔːn] *vtr* adornar.

adornment [əˈdɔːnmənt] *n* adorno *m*.

adrenalin [əˈdrenəlɪn] *n* adrenalina *f*.

Adriatic [eɪdrɪˈætɪk] *adj* **the A.** (Sea), el (Mar) Adriático.

adrift [əˈdrɪft] *adv* **to come a.**, (boat) irse a la deriva; (rope) soltarse; fig **to go a.**, (plans) ir a la deriva.

adult [ˈædʌlt] **I** *adj* (person) adulto,-a, mayor; (film, education) para adultos. **II** *n* adulto,-a *m,f*.

adulterate [əˈdʌltəreɪt] *vtr* adulterar.

adulterer [əˈdʌltərər] *n* adúltero *m*.

adulteress [əˈdʌltrɪs] *n* adúltera *f*.

adultery [əˈdʌltərɪ] *n* adulterio *m*.

advance [ədˈvɑːns] **I** *n* 1 (movement) avance *m*; fig (progress) progreso *m*; **to have sth ready in a.**, tener algo preparado de antemano; **to make advances**, (to a person) insinuarse (**to**, a). 2 (loan) anticipo *m*. **II** *adj* (before time) adelantado,-a; (time, date) adelantar. **III** *vtr* 1 (troops) avanzar; (time, date) adelantar. 2 (idea) proponer; (opinion) dar. 3 Fin (sum of money) anticipar. **IV** *vi* (move forward) avanzar, adelantarse; (make progress) hacer progresos; (gain promotion) ascender.

advanced [ədˈvɑːnst] *adj* (developed)

avanzado,-a; (student) adelantado,-a; (course) superior; Educ **A. level**, examen *m* superior de segunda enseñanza, ≈ COU *m*.

advancement [ədˈvɑːnsmənt] *n* (progress) adelanto *m*; (promotion) ascenso *m*.

advantage [ədˈvɑːntɪdʒ] *n* ventaja *f*; Ten **a. Velasco**, ventaja para Velasco; **to take a. of sb/sth**, abusar de algn/aprovechar algo.

advantageous [ædvənˈteɪdʒəs] *adj* ventajoso,-a.

advent [ˈædvent] *n* (arrival) llegada *f*; (of Christ) advenimiento *m*; A., Adviento *m*.

adventure [ədˈventʃər] *n* aventura *f*.

adventurous [ədˈventʃərəs] *adj* aventurero,-a.

adverb [ˈædvɜːb] *n* adverbio *m*.

adversary [ˈædvəsərɪ] *n* adversario,-a *m,f*.

adverse [ˈædvɜːs] *adj* (effect) desfavorable; (conditions) adverso,-a; (winds) contrario,-a.

adversity [ədˈvɜːsɪtɪ] *n* adversidad *f*.

advert [ˈædvɜːt] *n* fam anuncio *m*.

advertise [ˈædvətaɪz] **I** *vtr* anunciar. **II** *vi* hacer publicidad; (in newspaper) poner un anuncio; **to a. for sth/sb**, buscar algo/a algn mediante un anuncio.

advertisement [ədˈvɜːtɪsmənt] *n* anuncio *m*; **advertisements**, publicidad *f sing*.

advertiser [ˈædvətaɪzər] *n* anunciante *mf*.

advertising [ˈædvətaɪzɪŋ] **I** *n* publicidad *f*, propaganda *f*; (in newspaper) anuncios *mpl*. **II** *adj* publicitario,-a; **a. agency**, agencia *f* de publicidad.

advice [ədˈvaɪs] *n* consejos *mpl*; **a piece of a.**, un consejo; **to take legal a. on a matter**, consultar el caso con un abogado; **to take sb's a.**, seguir los consejos de algn.

advisable [ədˈvaɪzəbəl] *adj* aconsejable.

advise [ədˈvaɪz] *vtr* aconsejar; (on business etc) asesorar; **I a. you to do it**, te aconsejo que lo hagas.

adviser [ədˈvaɪzər] *n* consejero,-a *m,f*; (in business etc) asesor,-a *m,f*.

advisory [ədˈvaɪzərɪ] *adj* asesor,-a.

advocate [ˈædvəkɪt] **I** *n* Scot Jur abogado,-a *m,f*; (supporter) defensor,-a *m,f*. **II** [ˈædvəkeɪt] *vtr* (reform) abogar por; (plan) apoyar.

aerial [ˈeərɪəl] **I** *adj* aéreo,-a. **II** *n* antena *f*.

aerobics [eəˈrəubɪks] *n* aerobic *m*.

aerodrome [ˈeərədrəum] *n* GB aeródromo *m*.

aerodynamics [eərəudaɪˈnæmɪks] *n* aerodinámica *f*.

aeroplane [ˈeərəpleɪn] *n* avión *m*.

aerosol [ˈeərəsɒl] *n* aerosol *m*.

aerospace [ˈeərəspeɪs] *adj* aeroespacial.

aesthetic [iːsˈθetɪk] *adj* estético,-a.

afar [əˈfɑːr] *adv* lejos; **from a.**, desde lejos.

affair [əˈfeər] n (matter) asunto m; (event) acontecimiento m; **that's my a.**, eso es asunto mío; **business affairs**, negocios mpl; **foreign affairs**, asuntos exteriores; **love a.**, aventura f amorosa.

affect [əˈfekt] vtr (person, health) afectar; (prices, future) influir en; (touch emotionally) conmover.

affected [əˈfektɪd] adj 1 (unnatural) afectado,-a. 2 (influenced) influido,-a. 3 (touched emotionally) conmovido,-a. 4 (pretended) fingido,-a.

affection [əˈfekʃən] n afecto m, cariño m.

affectionate [əˈfekʃənɪt] adj cariñoso,-a.

affidavit [æfɪˈdeɪvɪt] n declaración escrita y jurada.

affiliated [əˈfɪlɪeɪtɪd] adj afiliado,-a; **to be** or **become a.**, afiliarse (to, with, a).

affinity [əˈfɪnɪtɪ] n afinidad f; (liking) simpatía f.

affirm [əˈfɜːm] vtr afirmar, sostener.

affirmation [æfəˈmeɪʃən] n afirmación f.

affirmative [əˈfɜːmətɪv] I adj afirmativo,-a. II **he answered in the a.**, contestó que sí.

affix [əˈfɪks] vtr (stamp) pegar.

afflict [əˈflɪkt] vtr afligir.

affluence [ˈæfluəns] n opulencia f.

affluent [ˈæfluənt] adj (society) opulento, -a; (person) rico,-a.

afford [əˈfɔːd] vtr 1 (be able to buy) permitirse el lujo de; **I can't a. a new car**, no puedo pagar un coche nuevo. 2 (be able to do) permitirse; **you can't a. to miss the opportunity**, no puedes perderte la ocasión.

affront [əˈfrʌnt] I n afrenta f. II vtr afrentar.

afield [əˈfiːld] adv far a., muy lejos.

afloat [əˈfləʊt] adv to keep a., mantenerse a flote.

afoot [əˈfʊt] adv there's a plan a., hay un proyecto en marcha; **there's something strange a.**, se está tramando algo.

aforementioned [əˈfɔːmenʃənd], **aforesaid** [əˈfɔːsed] adj susodicho,-a.

afraid [əˈfreɪd] adj 1 to be a., tener miedo (of sb, a algn; of sth, de algo); **I'm a. of it**, me da miedo. 2 **I'm a. not**, me temo que no; **I'm a. so**, me temo que sí; **I'm a. you're wrong**, me temo que estás equivocado,-a.

afresh [əˈfreʃ] adv de nuevo.

Africa [ˈæfrɪkə] n África.

African [ˈæfrɪkən] adj & n africano,-a (m,f).

Afro [ˈæfrəʊ] n & adj fam (hairstyle) afro (m).

aft [ɑːft] adv en popa; **to go a.**, ir en popa.

after [ˈɑːftər] I adv después; **soon a.**, poco después; **the day a.**, el día siguiente. II prep 1 (later) después de; US **it's ten a. five**, son las cinco y diez; **soon

a. arriving**, al poco rato de llegar; **the day a. tomorrow**, pasado mañana. 2 (behind) detrás de, tras; **a. you!**, ¡pase usted!; **they went in one a. the other**, entraron uno tras otro; **the police are a. them**, la policía anda tras ellos. 3 (about) por; **they asked a. you**, preguntaron por ti; **what's he a.?**, ¿qué pretende? 4 **he takes a. his uncle**, se parece a su tío; **she was named a. her grandmother**, le llamaron como su abuela. III conj después (de) que; **a. it happened**, después de que ocurriera.

after-effect [ˈɑːftərɪfekt] n efecto m secundario.

afterlife [ˈɑːftəlaɪf] n vida f después de la muerte.

aftermath [ˈɑːftəmæθ] n secuelas fpl.

afternoon [ɑːftəˈnuːn] n tarde f; **good a.!**, ¡buenas tardes!; **in the a.**, por la tarde.

afters [ˈɑːftəz] npl fam postre m.

after-sales service [ɑːftəseɪlzˈsɜːvɪs] n Com servicio m posventa.

aftershave (lotion) [ˈɑːftəʃeɪv(ˈləʊʃən)] n loción f para después del afeitado.

afterthought [ˈɑːftəθɔːt] n ocurrencia f tardía.

afterwards [ˈɑːftəwədz] adv después, más tarde.

again [əˈgen] adv 1 otra vez, de nuevo; **I tried a. and a.**, lo intenté una y otra vez; **to do sth a.**, volver a hacer algo; **never a.!**, ¡nunca más!; **now and a.**, de vez en cuando; **once a.**, otra vez. 2 (besides) además; **then a.**, por otra parte.

against [əˈgenst] prep 1 (touching) contra. 2 (opposing) contra, en contra (de); **a. the grain**, a contrapelo; **it's a. the law**, es ilegal. 3 **as a.**, en contraste con, comparado con.

age [eɪdʒ] I n 1 edad f; **she's 18 years of a.**, tiene 18 años; **to be under a.**, ser menor de edad; **to come of a.**, llegar a la mayoría de edad; **a. limit**, límite m de edad; **old a.**, vejez f. 2 (period) época f; **the Iron A.**, la Edad de Hierro. 3 fam (long time) eternidad f; **it's ages since I last saw her**, hace siglos que no la veo. II vtr & vi envejecer.

aged¹ [eɪdʒd] adj de or a la edad de.

aged² [ˈeɪdʒɪd] npl **the a.**, los ancianos.

agency [ˈeɪdʒənsɪ] n 1 Com agencia f. 2 **by the a. of**, por medio de.

agenda [əˈdʒendə] n orden m del día.

agent [ˈeɪdʒənt] n agente mf; (representative) representante mf.

aggravate [ˈægrəveɪt] vtr (worsen) agravar; (annoy) molestar.

aggregate [ˈægrɪgɪt] n conjunto m; **on a.**, en conjunto.

aggression [əˈgreʃən] n agresión f.

aggressive [əˈgresɪv] adj (violent) agresivo,-a, violento,-a; (dynamic) dinámico,-a.

aggrieved [ə'gri:vd] *adj* apenado,-a.

aghast [ə'gɑːst] *adj* espantado,-a.

agile ['ædʒail] *adj* ágil.

agitate ['ædʒiteit] I *vtr* (shake) agitar; *fig* (worry) perturbar. II *vi Pol* to a. **against sth**, hacer campaña en contra de algo.

agitator ['ædʒiteitə'] *n Pol* agitador,-a *m,f.*

AGM [eidʒi:'em] *abbr of* **annual general meeting**, junta *f* general anual.

ago [ə'gəu] *adv* **a long time a.**, hace mucho tiempo; **as long as 1910**, ya en 1910; **a week a.**, hace una semana; **how long a.?**, ¿hace cuánto tiempo?

agog [ə'gɒg] *adj* ansioso,-a.

agonizing ['ægənaiziŋ] *adj* (pain) atroz; (decision) desesperante.

agony ['ægəni] *n* dolor *m* muy fuerte; (anguish) angustia *f*; **he was in a. with his back**, tenía un dolor insoportable de espalda.

agree [ə'gri:] I *vi* 1 (be in agreement) estar de acuerdo; (reach agreement) ponerse de acuerdo; (consent) consentir; **to a. to do sth**, consentir en hacer algo; **to a. with sb**, estar de acuerdo con algn. 2 (harmonize) (things) concordar; (people) congeniar; **onions don't a. with me**, la cebolla no me sienta bien. II *vtr* acordar.

agreeable [ə'gri:əbl] *adj* (pleasant) agradable; (person) simpático,-a; (in agreement) de acuerdo.

agreement [ə'gri:mənt] *n* (arrangement) acuerdo *m*; *Com* contrato *m*; **to reach an a.**, llegar a un acuerdo.

agricultural [ægri'kʌltʃərəl] *adj* agrícola; (college) de agricultura.

agriculture ['ægrikʌltʃə'] *n* agricultura *f.*

aground [ə'graund] *adv* **to run a.**, encallar, varar.

ahead [ə'hed] *adv* delante; (early) antes; **go a.!**, ¡adelante!; **to be a.**, llevar la ventaja; **to go a.**, ir adelante; *fig* **to go a. with sth**, llevar algo adelante; (start) comenzar algo; **to get a.**, triunfar; **to look a.**, pensar en el futuro.

aid [eid] I *n* ayuda *f*; (rescue) auxilio *m*; **in a. of**, a beneficio de; **to come to the a. of sb**, acudir en ayuda de algn. II *vtr* ayudar; **to a. and abet sb**, ser cómplice de algn.

aide [eid] *n* ayudante *mf.*

Aids [eidz] *n* (abbr of **Acquired Immune Deficiency Syndrome**), SIDA *m* (Síndrome *m* de Inmunodeficiencia Adquirida).

ailing ['eiliŋ] *adj* achacoso,-a.

ailment ['eilmənt] *n* enfermedad *f* (leve), achaque *m.*

aim [eim] I *n* (with weapon) puntería *f*; (target) propósito *m.* II *vtr* (gun) apuntar (at, a, hacia); (attack, action) dirigir (at, a, hacia). ◆**aim at** *vtr* (target) tirar para;

to a. at doing sth, tener pensado hacer algo. ◆**aim to** *vtr* **to a. to do sth**, tener la intención de hacer algo.

aimless ['eimlis] *adj* sin objeto, sin propósito. ◆**aimlessly** *adv* (wander) sin rumbo fijo.

air [eə'] I *n* 1 aire *m*; **to travel by a.**, viajar en avión; **to throw sth up in the a.**, lanzar algo al aire; *fig* **it's still in the a.**, todavía queda por resolver; **a. base**, base aérea; **a. bed**, colchón *m* hinchable; **a. conditioning**, aire acondicionado; **A. Force**, Fuerzas Aéreas; **a. freshener**, ambientador *m*; **a. gun**, pistola *f* de aire comprimido; **a. hostess**, azafata *f*; **a. letter**, carta aérea; **a. pocket**, bache *m*; **a. pressure**, presión atmosférica; **a. raid**, ataque aéreo; **a. terminal**, terminal aérea; **a. traffic control**, control *m* de tráfico aéreo; **a. traffic controller**, controlador,-a *m,f* aéreo. -a 2 *Rad TV* **to be on the a.**, (programme) estar emitiendo; (person) estar transmitiendo. 3 (appearance) aspecto *m.* II *vtr* (bed, clothes) airear; (room) ventilar; *fig* (grievance) airear; (knowledge) hacer alarde de.

airborne ['eəbɔːn] *adj* (aircraft) en vuelo; (troops) aerotransportado,-a.

air-conditioned ['eəkɒndiʃənd] *adj* climatizado,-a.

aircraft ['eəkrɑːft] *n inv* avión *m*; **a. carrier**, portaaviones *m inv.*

airfield ['eəfiːld] *n* campo *m* de aviación.

airlift ['eəlift] *n* puente aéreo.

airline ['eəlain] *n* línea aérea.

airlock ['eəlɒk] *n* (in pipe) bolsa *f* de aire; (in spacecraft) esclusa *f* de aire.

airmail ['eəmeil] *n* correo *m* aéreo; **by a.**, por avión.

airplane ['eəplein] *n US* avión *m.*

airport ['eəpɔːt] *n* aeropuerto *m.*

airsick ['eəsik] *adj* **to be a.**, marearse en avión.

airstrip ['eəstrip] *n* pista *f* de aterrizaje.

airtight ['eətait] *adj* hermético,-a.

airy ['eəri] *adj* (airier, airiest) (well-ventilated) bien ventilado,-a; (vague, carefree) ligero,-a.

aisle [ail] *n* (in church) nave *f*; (in theatre) pasillo *m.*

ajar [ə'dʒɑː'] *adj & adv* entreabierto,-a.

akin [ə'kin] *adj* semejante.

alacrity [ə'lækriti] *n* with a., con presteza.

alarm [ə'lɑːm] I *n* 1 alarma *f*; **a. clock**, despertador *m.* 2 (fear) inquietud *f*; **to cause a.**, provocar temor. II *vtr* alarmar.

alas [ə'læs] *interj* ¡ay!, ¡ay de mí!

albatross ['ælbətrɒs] *n* albatros *m.*

albeit [ɔːl'biːit] *conj* aunque, no obstante.

album ['ælbəm] *n* álbum *m.*

alcohol ['ælkəhɒl] *n* alcohol *m.*

alcoholic [ælkə'hɒlik] *adj & n* alcohólico,-a (m,f).

alcove ['ælkəʊv] *n* hueco *m*.

ale [eɪl] *n* cerveza *f*; **brown/pale a.**, cerveza negra/rubia.

alert [ə'lɜːt] **I** *adj* alerta; *(lively)* despabilado,-a. **II** *n* alerta *m*; **to be on the a.**, estar alerta. **III** *vtr* **to a. sb to sth**, avisar a algn de algo.

A-level ['eɪlevəl] *n GB Educ abbr of Advanced level*, ≈ Curso *m* de Orientación Universitaria, COU *f*.

algae ['ældʒiː] *npl* algas *fpl*.

algebra ['ældʒɪbrə] *n* álgebra *f*.

Algeria [æl'dʒɪərɪə] *n* Argelia.

Algerian [æl'dʒɪərɪən] *adj & n* argelino,-a (*m,f*).

Algiers [æl'dʒɪəz] *n* Argel.

alias ['eɪlɪəs] **I** *n* alias *m*. **II** *adv* alias.

alibi ['ælɪbaɪ] *n* coartada *f*.

alien ['eɪlɪən] **I** *adj (foreign)* extranjero,-a; *(from space)* extraterrestre. **a. to**, ajeno a. **II** *n (foreigner)* extranjero,-a *m,f*; *(from space)* extraterrestre *mf*.

alienate ['eɪlɪəneɪt] *vtr* **1 to a. sb**, ofender a algn; **to a. oneself from sb**, alejarse de algn. **2** *Jur* enajenar.

alight[1] [ə'laɪt] *adj (on fire)* ardiendo,-a.

alight[2] [ə'laɪt] *vi (get off)* apearse (**from**, de).

align [ə'laɪn] *vtr (alinear)*.

alike [ə'laɪk] **I** *adj (similar)* parecidos,-as; *(the same)* iguales. **II** *adv (in the same way)* de la misma manera, igualmente; **dressed a.**, vestidos,-as iguales.

alimony ['ælɪmənɪ] *n Jur* pensión alimenticia.

alive [ə'laɪv] *adj* vivo,-a; *fig (teeming)* lleno,-a **with**, de; **to be a.**, estar vivo, -a.

alkaline ['ælkəlaɪn] *adj* alcalino,-a.

all [ɔːl] **I** *adj* todo,-a, todos,-as; **a. year**, *(durante)* todo el año; **a. kinds of things**, todo tipo de cosas; **a. hours**, a todas horas; **a. times**, siempre; **she works a. the time**, siempre está trabajando; **all six of us were there**, los seis estábamos allí. **II** *pron* todo,-a, todos,-as; **after a.**, al fin y al cabo; **a. of his work**, toda su obra; **a. of us**, todos,-as nosotros,-as; **a. who saw it**, todos los que lo vieron; **a. you can do is wait**, lo único que puedes hacer es esperar; **I don't like it at a.**, no me gusta en absoluto; **is that a.?**, ¿eso es todo?; **most of or above a.**, sobre todo; **once and for a.**, de una vez por todas; **thanks - not at a.**, gracias - de nada; **in a.**, en conjunto; **that's a.**, ya está; **the score was one a.**, empataron a uno. **III** *adv* **a. by myself**, completamente solo,-a; **a. at once**, *(suddenly)* de repente; *(altogether)* de una vez; **a. the better**, tanto mejor; **a. the same**, de todos modos; **he knew a. along**, lo sabía desde el principio; **if it's the same to you**, si no te importa; **it's a. but impossible**, es

casi imposible; **I'm not a. that tired**, no estoy tan cansado,-a como eso.

IV *n* **to give one's a.**, darse por completo.

Allah ['ælə] *n* Alá *m*.

allay [ə'leɪ] *vtr (fears, doubts)* apaciguar.

allegation [ælɪ'geɪʃən] *n* alegato *m*.

allege [ə'ledʒ] *vtr* sostener, pretender (**that**, que).

allegedly [ə'ledʒɪdlɪ] *adv* supuestamente.

allegiance [ə'liːdʒəns] *n* lealtad *f*.

allergic [ə'lɜːdʒɪk] *adj* alérgico,-a (**to**, a).

allergy ['ælədʒɪ] *n* alergia *f*.

alleviate [ə'liːvɪeɪt] *vtr (pain)* aliviar.

alley ['ælɪ] *n* callejón *m*.

alliance [ə'laɪəns] *n* alianza *f*.

allied ['ælaɪd] *adj* aliado,-a.

alligator ['ælɪgeɪtər] *n* caimán *m*.

all-in ['ɔːlɪn] *adj (price)* todo incluido; *Sport* **a.-in wrestling**, lucha *f* libre.

alliteration [əlɪtə'reɪʃən] *n* aliteración *f*.

all-night ['ɔːlnaɪt] *adj (café etc)* abierto,-a toda la noche; *(vigil)* que dura toda la noche.

allocate ['æləkeɪt] *vtr* destinar (**to**, para).

allocation [ælə'keɪʃən] *n* **1** *(distribution)* asignación *f*. **2** *(amount allocated)* cuota *f*.

allot [ə'lɒt] *vtr* asignar.

allotment [ə'lɒtmənt] *n* **1** *(distribution)* asignación *f*. **2** *(land)* parcela *f*.

all-out ['ɔːlaʊt] **I** *adj (effort)* supremo,-a; *(attack)* concentrado,-a. **II all out** *adv* **to go a. o. to do sth**, emplearse a fondo para hacer algo.

allow [ə'laʊ] *vtr* **1** *(permit)* permitir; *(a request)* acceder a; **to a. sb to do sth**, permitir que algn haga algo. **2** *(allot)* dejar; *(money)* destinar. ◆ **allow for** *vtr* tener en cuenta.

allowance [ə'laʊəns] *n (payment)* pensión *f*, subvención *f*; *(discount)* descuento *m*; **to make allowances for sb/sth**, disculpar a algn/tener algo en cuenta; **tax a.**, desgravación *f* fiscal; **travel a.**, dietas *fpl* de viaje.

alloy ['ælɔɪ] *n* aleación *f*.

all right [ɔːl'raɪt] **I** *adj (okay)* bien; **thank you very much - that's a. r.**, muchas gracias - de nada. **II** *adv* **1** *(well)* bien. **2** *(definitely)* sin duda. **3** *(okay)* de acuerdo, vale.

all-round [ɔːl'raʊnd] *adj (athlete etc)* completo,-a.

all-terrain [ɔːltə'reɪn] *adj* **a.-t. vehicle**, todoterreno *m*.

all-time ['ɔːltaɪm] *adj* **an a.-t. low**, una baja sin antecedente; **the a.-t. greats**, los grandes de siempre.

allude [ə'luːd] *vi* **to a. to**, aludir a.

alluring [ə'ljʊərɪŋ] *adj* atractivo,-a.

allusion [ə'luːʒən] *n* alusión *f*.

ally ['ælaɪ] **I** *n* aliado,-a *m,f*. **II** *vtr* **to a. oneself to/with sb**, aliarse a/con algn.

almighty [ɔːl'maɪtɪ] **I** *adj (all-powerful)*

todopoderoso,-a. **II** *n* the A., El Todopoderoso.

almond ['ɑ:mənd] *n* almendra *f*.

almost ['ɔ:lməust] *adv* casi.

alms [ɑ:mz] *npl* limosna *f sing*.

aloft [ə'lɒft] *adv* arriba.

alone [ə'ləun] **I** *adj* solo,-a; **can I speak to you a.?**, ¿puedo hablar contigo a solas?; **let a.**, ni mucho menos; **leave it a.!**, ¡no lo toques!; **leave me a.**, déjame en paz; **to be a.**, estar solo,-a. **II** *adv* solamente, sólo.

along [ə'lɒŋ] **I** *adv* come a.!, ¡anda, ven!; **he'll be a. in 10 minutes**, llegará dentro de 10 minutos; **a. with**, junto con. **II** *prep* (*the length of*) a lo largo de; **to walk a. the street**, andar por la calle; **it's just a. the street**, está un poco más abajo.

alongside [ə'lɒŋsaɪd] **I** *adv* Naut de costado. **II** *prep* al lado de.

aloof [ə'lu:f] **I** *adj* (*person*) distante. **II** *adv* **to keep oneself a.**, mantenerse a distancia (**from**, de).

aloud [ə'laud] *adv* en voz alta.

alphabet ['ælfəbet] *n* alfabeto *m*.

alphabetical [ælfə'betɪkəl] *adj* alfabético,-a. ◆**alphabetically** *adv* por orden alfabético.

alpine ['ælpaɪn] *adj* alpino,-a.

Alps [ælps] *npl* the A., los Alpes.

already [ɔ:l'redɪ] *adv* ya.

alright [ɔ:l'raɪt] *adj & adv →* **all right**.

Alsatian [æl'seɪʃən] *n* pastor *m* alemán.

also ['ɔ:lsəu] *adv* también, además.

also-ran ['ɔ:lsəuræn] *n fam* (*person*) segundón,-ona *m,f*.

altar ['ɔ:ltə'] *n* altar *m*.

alter ['ɔ:ltə'] **I** *vtr* (*plan*) cambiar, retocar; (*project*) modificar; (*clothing*) arreglar; (*timetable*) revisar. **II** *vi* cambiar, cambiarse.

alteration [ɔ:ltə'reɪʃən] *n* (*to plan*) cambio *m*; (*to project*) modificación *f*; (*to clothing*) arreglo *m*; (*to timetable*) revisión *f*; **alterations**, (*to building*) reformas *fpl*.

alternate [ɔ:l'tɜ:nɪt] **I** *adj* alterno,-a; **on a. days**, cada dos días. **II** [ɔ:l'tɜ:neɪt] *vi* alternar. ◆**alternately** *adv* a. hot and cold, ahora caliente, ahora frío.

alternative [ɔ:l'tɜ:nətɪv] **I** *adj* alternativo,-a. **II** *n* alternativa *f*; **I have no a. but to accept**, no tengo más remedio que aceptar. ◆**alternatively** *adv* o bien; **a. you could walk**, o bien podrías ir andando.

alternator ['ɔ:ltəneɪtə'] *n* Aut alternador *m*.

although [ɔ:l'ðəu] *conj* aunque.

altitude ['æltɪtju:d] *n* altitud *f*.

alto ['æltəu] *adj & n* (*male singer, instrument*) alto (*m*); (*female singer*) contralto (*f*).

altogether [ɔ:ltə'geðə'] *adv* (*in total*) en conjunto, en total; (*completely*) completamente, del todo.

altruism ['æltru:ɪzəm] *n* altruismo *m*.

aluminium [ælju'mɪnɪəm], US **aluminum** [ə'lu:mɪnəm] *n* aluminio *m*.

always ['ɔ:lweɪz] *adv* siempre.

AM [eɪ'em] Rad *abbr of* **amplitude modulation, AM**.

am [æm] *1st person sing pres →* **be**.

a.m. [eɪ'em] *abbr of* **ante meridiem**, de la mañana.

amalgamate [ə'mælgəmeɪt] **I** *vtr* (*metals*) amalgamar. **II** *vi* (*metals*) amalgamarse; (*companies*) fusionarse.

amalgamation [əmælgə'meɪʃən] *n* fusión *f*.

amass [ə'mæs] *vtr* (*money*) amontonar; (*information*) acumular.

amateur ['æmətə'] **I** *n* amateur *mf*, aficionado,-a *m,f*. **II** *adj* aficionado,-a; (*work etc*) *pej* chapucero,-a.

amateurish ['æmətərɪʃ] *adj* chapucero,-a.

amaze [ə'meɪz] *vtr* asombrar, pasmar; **to be amazed at sth**, quedarse pasmado,-a de algo.

amazement [ə'meɪzmənt] *n* asombro *m*, sorpresa *f*.

amazing [ə'meɪzɪŋ] *adj* asombroso,-a, increíble.

ambassador [æm'bæsədə'] *n* embajador,-a *m,f*.

amber ['æmbə'] **I** *n* ámbar *m*. **II** *adj* ambarino,-a; (*traffic light*) amarillo,-a.

ambiguity [æmbɪ'gju:ɪtɪ] *n* ambigüedad *f*.

ambiguous [æm'bɪgjuəs] *adj* ambiguo,-a.

ambition [æm'bɪʃən] *n* ambición *f*.

ambitious [æm'bɪʃəs] *adj* ambicioso,-a.

ambivalent [æm'bɪvələnt] *adj* ambivalente.

amble ['æmbəl] *vi* deambular.

ambulance ['æmbjuləns] *n* ambulancia *f*; **a. man**, ambulanciero *m*.

ambush ['æmbuʃ] **I** *n* emboscada *f*. **II** *vtr* tender una emboscada a; *fig* atacar por sorpresa.

amen [ɑ:'men] *interj* amén.

amenable [ə'mi:nəbəl] *adj* I'd be quite **a. to doing that**, no me importaría nada hacer eso; **a. to reason**, razonable.

amend [ə'mend] *vtr* (*law*) enmendar; (*error*) subsanar.

amendment [ə'mendmənt] *n* enmienda *f*.

amends [ə'mendz] *npl* **to make a. to sb for sth**, compensar a algn por algo.

amenities [ə'mi:nɪtɪz] *npl* comodidades *fpl*.

America [ə'merɪkə] *n* (*continent*) América *f*; (*USA*) (los) Estados *mpl* Unidos; **South A.**, América del Sur, Sudamérica *f*.

American [ə'merɪkən] *adj & n* americano,-a (*m,f*); (*of USA*) norteamericano,-a (*m,f*), estadounidense (*mf*).

amiable ['eɪmɪəbəl] *adj* amable, afable.

amicable ['æmɪkəbəl] *adj* amistoso,-a.

amid(st) [ə'mɪd(st)] *prep* entre, en medio de.

amiss [ə'mɪs] *adj & adv* mal; **there's sth a.**, algo anda mal; **to take sth a.**, tomar algo a mal.

ammonia [ə'məʊnɪə] *n* amoníaco *m*.

ammunition [æmjʊ'nɪʃən] *n* municiones *fpl*.

amnesia [æm'niːʒə] *n* amnesia *f*.

amnesty ['æmnəstɪ] *n* amnistía *f*.

amok [ə'mɒk] *adv fig* **to run a.**, (*child*) desmadrarse; (*mob*) dispararse.

among(st) [ə'mʌŋ(st)] *prep* entre.

amoral [eɪ'mɒrəl] *adj* amoral.

amorous ['æmərəs] *adj* cariñoso,-a.

amorphous [ə'mɔːfəs] *adj* amorfo,-a.

amount [ə'maʊnt] *n* cantidad *f*; (*of money*) suma *f*; (*of bill*) importe *m*. ◆**amount to** *vtr* ascender a; *fig* equivaler a.

amp [æmp], **ampère** ['æmpeər] *n* amperio *m*.

amphetamine [æm'fetəmiːn] *n* anfetamina *f*.

amphibian [æm'fɪbɪən] *adj & n* anfibio,-a (*m*).

amphibious [æm'fɪbɪəs] *adj* anfibio,-a.

amphitheatre ['æmfɪθɪətər] *n* anfiteatro *m*.

ample ['æmpəl] *adj* (*enough*) bastante; (*more than enough*) abundante; (*large*) amplio,-a.

amplifier ['æmplɪfaɪər] *n* amplificador *m*.

amputate ['æmpjʊteɪt] *vtr* amputar.

amuck [ə'mʌk] *adv* → **amok**.

amuse [ə'mjuːz] *vtr* divertir, entretener.

amusement [ə'mjuːzmənt] *n* (*enjoyment*) diversión *f*; (*laughter*) risa *f*; (*pastime*) pasatiempo *m*; **a. arcade**, salón *m* de juegos; **a. park**, parque *m* de atracciones.

amusing [ə'mjuːzɪŋ] *adj* divertido,-a.

an [æn, *unstressed* ən] *indef art* → **a**.

anabolic steroid [ænəbɒlɪk'stɪːrɔɪd] *n* esteroide *m* anabolizante.

anaemia [ə'niːmɪə] *n* anemia *f*.

anaemic [ə'niːmɪk] *adj* anémico,-a; *fig* (*weak*) débil.

anaesthesia [ænɪs'θiːtɪk] *n* anestesia *f*.

anaesthetist [ə'niːsθətɪst] *n* anestesista *mf*.

analog(ue) ['ænəlɒg] *n* análogo *m*; **a. computer**, ordenador analógico; **a. watch**, reloj *m* de agujas.

analogy [ə'nælədʒɪ] *n* analogía *f*.

analyse ['ænəlaɪz] *vtr* analizar.

analysis [ə'næləsɪs] *n* (*pl* **analyses** [ə'næləsiːz]) análisis *m inv*.

analyst ['ænəlɪst] *n* analista *mf*; (*psychoanalyst*) psicoanalista *mf*.

analyze ['ænəlaɪz] *vtr US* → **analyse**.

analytic(al) [ænə'lɪtɪk(əl)] *adj* analítico,-a.

anarchist ['ænəkɪst] *n* anarquista *mf*.

anarchy ['ænəkɪ] *n* anarquía *f*.

anathema [ə'næθəmə] *n* **the very idea was a. to him**, le repugnaba sólo de pensarlo.

anatomy [ə'nætəmɪ] *n* anatomía *f*.

ancestor ['ænsestər] *n* antepasado *m*.

anchor ['æŋkər] **I** *n Naut* ancla *f*; *fig* áncora *f*; **to drop a.**, echar el ancla; **to weigh a.**, zarpar. **II** *vtr Naut* anclar; *fig* (*fix securely*) sujetar. **III** *vi* anclar.

anchovy ['ænʧəvɪ] *n* anchoa *f*.

ancient ['eɪnʃənt] *adj* antiguo,-a.

ancillary [æn'sɪlərɪ] *adj & n* auxiliar (*mf*).

and [ænd, *unstressed* ənd, ən] *conj* y; (*before* i-, hi-) e; **a hundred a. one**, ciento uno; **a. so on** etcétera; **Bill a. Pat**, Bill y Pat; **Chinese a. Indian**, chino e indio; **come a. see us**, ven a vernos; **four a. a half**, cuatro y medio; **she cried a. cried**, no paró de llorar; **try a. help me**, trata de ayudarme; **wait a. see**, espera a ver; **worse a. worse**, cada vez peor.

Andalusia [ændə'luːzɪə] *n* Andalucía.

Andalusian [ændə'luːzɪən] *adj* andaluz, -a.

Andes ['ændiːz] *npl* **the A.**, los Andes.

Andorra [æn'dɔːrə] *n* Andorra.

anecdote ['ænɪkdəʊt] *n* anécdota *f*.

anemia [ə'niːmɪə] *n US* → **anaemia**.

anesthetic [ænɪs'θetɪk] *n US* → **anaesthetic**.

angel ['eɪndʒəl] *n* ángel *m*.

anger ['æŋgər] **I** *n* cólera *f*. **II** *vtr* enojar.

angina [æn'dʒaɪnə] *n* angina *f* (de pecho).

angle ['æŋgəl] *n* ángulo *m*; *fig* punto *m* de vista.

angler ['æŋglər] *n* pescador,-a *m,f* de caña.

Anglican ['æŋglɪkən] *adj & n* anglicano,-a (*m,f*).

Anglo-Saxon [æŋgləʊ'sæksən] *adj & n* anglosajón,-ona (*m,f*).

Angola [æŋ'gəʊlə] *n* Angola.

angry ['æŋgrɪ] *adj* (*angrier*, *angriest*) (*person etc*) enfadado,-a; (*voice*) airado,-a; **to get a. with sb about sth**, enfadarse con algn por algo. ◆**angrily** *adv* furiosamente.

anguish ['æŋgwɪʃ] *n* angustia *f*.

angular ['æŋgjʊlər] *adj* (*shape*) angular; (*face*) anguloso,-a.

animal ['ænɪməl] **I** *adj* animal. **II** *n* animal *m*; *fig* bestia *f*.

animate ['ænɪmɪt] **I** *adj* vivo,-a. **II** ['ænɪmeɪt] *vtr* animar; *fig* estimular.

animated ['ænɪmeɪtɪd] *adj* (*lively*) animado,-a.

animosity [ænɪ'mɒsɪtɪ] *n* animosidad *f*.

aniseed ['ænɪsiːd] *n* anís *m*.

ankle ['æŋkəl] *n* tobillo *m*; **a. boots**, botines *mpl*; **a. socks**, calcetines cortos.

annex [æ'neks] *vtr* (*territory*) anexionar.

annexe, *US* **annex** ['æneks] *n* (*building*) (*edificio m*) anexo *m*.

annihilate [ə'naɪəleɪt] *vtr* aniquilar.

anniversary [ænɪˈvɜːsərɪ] n aniversario m; **wedding a.,** aniversario de bodas.

announce [əˈnaʊns] vtr anunciar; *(news)* comunicar; *(fact)* hacer saber.

announcement [əˈnaʊnsmənt] n anuncio m; *(news)* comunicación f; *(statement)* declaración f.

announcer [əˈnaʊnsər] n TV Rad locutor,-a m,f.

annoy [əˈnɔɪ] vtr molestar, fastidiar; **to get annoyed,** enfadarse, molestarse.

annoyance [əˈnɔɪəns] n *(feeling)* enojo m; *(thing)* molestia f, fastidio m.

annoying [əˈnɔɪɪŋ] adj molesto,-a, fastidioso,-a.

annual [ˈænjʊəl] I adj anual. II n *(book)* anuario m; *(plant)* anual m. ◆**annually** adv anualmente.

annul [əˈnʌl] vtr anular.

annulment [əˈnʌlmənt] n anulación f.

anomaly [əˈnɒmɪlɪ] n anomalía f.

anonymity [ænəˈnɪmɪtɪ] n anonimato m.

anonymous [əˈnɒnɪməs] adj anónimo,-a.

anorak [ˈænəræk] n anorak m.

anorexia [ænəˈreksɪə] n anorexia f.

another [əˈnʌðər] I adj otro,-a; **a. one,** otro,-a; **without a. word,** sin más. II pron otro,-a; **have a.,** toma otro,-a; **to love one a.,** quererse el uno al otro.

ansaphone [ˈɑːnsəfəʊn] n mensáfono m.

answer [ˈɑːnsər] I n *(to letter etc)* contestación f; *(to question)* respuesta f; *(to problem)* solución f; **in a. to your letter,** contestando a su carta; **there's no a.,** *(on telephone)* no contestan; *(at door)* no abren. II vtr contestar a; *(problem)* resolver; *(door)* abrir; *(phone)* contestar. III vi contestar, responder. ◆**answer back** vi replicar; **don't a. back!,** ¡no seas respondón! ◆**answer for** vtr responder de; **he's got a lot to a. for,** es responsable de muchas cosas. ◆**answer to** vtr *(name)* responder a; *(description)* corresponder a.

answerable [ˈɑːnsərəbəl] adj **to be a. to sb for sth,** ser responsable ante algn de algo.

answering machine [ˈɑːnsərɪŋməʃiːn] n contestador automático.

ant [ænt] n hormiga f; **a. hill,** hormiguero m.

antagonism [ænˈtægənɪzəm] n antagonismo m *(between,* entre), hostilidad f *(towards,* hacia).

antagonize [ænˈtægənaɪz] vtr enemistar, malquistar.

Antarctic [ænˈtɑːktɪk] I adj antártico,-a; **A. Ocean,** océano Antártico. II n **the A.,** La Antártica.

Antarctica [ænˈtɑːktɪkə] n Antártida f.

antecedent [æntɪˈsiːdənt] n antecedente m.

antelope [ˈæntɪləʊp] n antílope m.

antenatal [æntɪˈneɪtəl] adj antenatal; *(clinic)* prenatal.

antenna [ænˈtenə] n 1 *(pl antennae* [ænˈteniː]) *(of animal, insect)* antena f. 2 *(pl antennas)* TV Rad antena f.

anthem [ˈænθəm] n motete m; **national a.,** himno m nacional.

anthology [ænˈθɒlədʒɪ] n antología f.

anthracite [ˈænθrəsaɪt] n antracita f.

anthropology [ænθrəˈpɒlədʒɪ] n antropología f.

anti-aircraft [æntɪˈeəkrɑːft] adj antiaéreo,-a.

antibiotic [æntɪbaɪˈɒtɪk] n antibiótico m.

antibody [ˈæntɪbɒdɪ] n anticuerpo m.

anticipate [ænˈtɪsɪpeɪt] vtr 1 *(expect)* esperar. 2 *(predict)* prever; *(get ahead of)* anticiparse a, adelantarse a.

anticipation [æntɪsɪˈpeɪʃən] n *(expectation)* esperanza f; *(expectancy)* ilusión f.

anticlimax [æntɪˈklaɪmæks] n *(disappointment)* decepción f.

anticlockwise [æntɪˈklɒkwaɪz] adv en sentido contrario a las agujas del reloj.

antics [ˈæntɪks] npl payasadas fpl; *(naughtiness)* travesuras fpl.

anticyclone [æntɪˈsaɪkləʊn] n anticiclón m.

antidote [ˈæntɪdəʊt] n antídoto m.

antifreeze [ˈæntɪfriːz] n anticongelante m.

antihistamine [æntɪˈhɪstəmɪn] n antihistamínico m.

antinuclear [æntɪˈnjuːklɪər] adj antinuclear.

antipathy [ænˈtɪpəθɪ] n antipatía f *(to,* a).

antiquated [ˈæntɪkweɪtɪd] adj anticuado,-a.

antique [ænˈtiːk] I adj antiguo,-a. II n antigüedad f; **a. dealer,** anticuario,-a m,f; **a. shop,** tienda f de antigüedades.

antiquity [ænˈtɪkwɪtɪ] n antigüedad f.

anti-Semitism [æntɪˈsemɪtɪzəm] n antisemitismo m.

antiseptic [æntɪˈseptɪk] adj & n antiséptico,-a f.

antisocial [æntɪˈsəʊʃəl] adj *(delinquent)* antisocial; *(unsociable)* insociable.

antithesis [ænˈtɪθɪsɪs] n antítesis f.

antler [ˈæntlər] n cuerna f; **antlers,** cornamenta f.

Antwerp [ˈæntwɜːp] n Amberes.

anus [ˈeɪnəs] n ano m.

anvil [ˈænvɪl] n yunque m.

anxiety [æŋˈzaɪɪtɪ] n *(concern)* inquietud f; *(worry)* preocupación f; *(fear)* angustia f; *(eagerness)* ansia f.

anxious [ˈæŋkʃəs] adj *(concerned)* inquieto,-a; *(worried)* preocupado,-a; *(fearful)* angustiado,-a; *(eager)* ansioso,-a; **to be a. about sth,** estar preocupado,-a por algo.

any [ˈenɪ] I adj *(in questions, conditionals)* algún,-una; *(in negative clauses)* ningún, -una; *(no matter which)* cualquier,-a; *(every)* todo,-a; **a. doctor will say the**

same, cualquier médico te dirá lo mismo; **are there a.** seats left?, ¿quedan plazas?; **at a. moment,** en cualquier momento; **have you a. apples?,** ¿tienes manzanas?; **have you a. money?,** ¿tienes (algo de) dinero?; **I don't have a. time,** no tengo tiempo; **in a. case,** de todas formas.

II *pron (in questions)* alguno,-a; *(in negative clauses)* ninguno,-a; *(no matter which)* cualquiera; **do they have a.?,** ¿tienen alguno?; **I don't want a.,** no quiero ninguno,-a; **I need some paper, have you a.?,** necesito papel, ¿tienes?; **you can have a. (one),** coge el *or* la que quieras.

III *adv* **is there a. more?,** ¿hay más?; **I used to like it but not a. more/longer,** antes me gustaba pero ya no; **is he a. better?,** ¿está mejor?

anybody ['enɪbɒdɪ] *pron (in questions, conditionals)* alguien, alguno,-a; *(in negative clauses)* nadie, ninguno,-a; *(no matter who)* cualquiera; **a. but me,** cualquiera menos yo; **bring a. you like,** trae a quien quieras; **do you see a. over there?,** ¿ves a alguien allí?; **I can't find a.,** no encuentro a nadie.

anyhow ['enɪhaʊ] *adv* 1 *(in spite of that)* en todo caso, de todas formas; *(changing the subject)* bueno, pues. 2 *(carelessly)* desordenadamente, de cualquier modo *or* forma.

anyone ['enɪwʌn] *pron* → **anybody.**

anything ['enɪθɪŋ] I *pron (in questions, conditionals)* algo, alguna cosa; *(in negative clauses)* nada; *(no matter what)* cualquier cosa; **a. but that,** cualquier cosa menos eso; **a. else?,** ¿algo más?; **can I do a. for you?,** ¿puedo ayudarte en algo?; **hardly a.,** casi nada; **if a., I'd buy the big one,** de comprar uno compraría el grande; **to run/work like a.,** correr/trabajar a más no poder. II *adv* **is this a. like what you wanted?,** ¿viene a ser éste lo que querías?

anyway ['enɪweɪ] *adv* → **anyhow.**

anywhere ['enɪweər] *adv* 1 *(in questions, conditionals)* (*situation)* en alguna parte; *(movement)* a alguna parte; **could it be a. else?,** ¿podría estar en otro sitio? 2 *(in negative clauses)* (*situation)* en ninguna parte; *(movement)* a ninguna parte; *(no matter where)* dondequiera, en cualquier parte; **go a. you like,** ve a donde quieras; **we aren't a. near finished,** no hemos terminado ni mucho menos.

apart [ə'pɑːt] *adv* 1 aparte; **to fall a.,** deshacerse; **to take sth a.,** desmontar algo. 2 *(distant)* alejado,-a; *(separate)* separado,-a; **to be poles a.,** ser polos opuestos; **you can't tell the twins a.,** no se puede distinguir los mellizos el uno del otro. 3 **a. from,** aparte de.

apartheid [ə'pɑːtheɪt] *n* apartheid *m.*

apartment [ə'pɑːtmənt] *n (large room)* salón *m; US (flat)* piso *m,* apartamento *m;* **a. block,** bloque *m* de pisos.

apathetic [æpə'θetɪk] *adj* apático,-a.

apathy ['æpəθɪ] *n* apatía *f.*

ape [eɪp] I *n* mono *m.* II *vtr* imitar, copiar.

apéritif [ə'perɪtiːf] *n* aperitivo *m.*

aperture ['æpətʃər] *n (hole, crack)* resquicio *m,* rendija *f; Phot* abertura *f.*

apex ['eɪpeks] *n (of triangle)* vértice *m; fig* cumbre *f.*

aphrodisiac [æfrə'dɪzɪæk] *n* afrodisíaco *m.*

apiece [ə'piːs] *adv* cada uno,-a.

aplomb [ə'plɒm] *n* aplomo *m.*

apocalypse [ə'pɒkəlɪps] *n* apocalipsis *m inv.*

apolitical [eɪpə'lɪtɪkəl] *adj* apolítico,-a.

apologetic [əpɒlə'dʒetɪk] *adj (remorseful)* de disculpa; **he was very a.,** pidió mil perdones. ◆**apologetically** *adv* disculpándose, pidiendo perdón.

apologize [ə'pɒlədʒaɪz] *vi (say sorry)* disculparse; **they apologized to us for the delay,** se disculparon con nosotros por el retraso.

apology [ə'pɒlədʒɪ] *n* disculpa *f,* excusa *f; fam* **what an a. for a meal!,** ¡vaya birria de comida!

apoplectic [æpə'plektɪk] *adj Med* apoplético,-a; *fam* **to be a. with rage,** estar furioso,-a.

apostle [ə'pɒsəl] *n* apóstol *m.*

apostrophe [ə'pɒstrəfɪ] *n* apóstrofo *m.*

appal, *US* **appall** [ə'pɔːl] *vtr* horrorizar; **to be appalled by sth,** quedar horrorizado,-a por algo.

appalling [ə'pɔːlɪŋ] *adj (horrifying)* horroroso,-a; *fam (very bad)* pésimo,-a, fatal.

apparatus [æpə'reɪtəs] *n* aparato *m; (equipment)* equipo *m.*

apparent [ə'pærənt] *adj (obvious)* evidente; *(seeming)* aparente; **to become a.,** ponerse de manifiesto. ◆**apparently** *adv (seemingly)* por lo visto.

apparition [æpə'rɪʃən] *n* aparición *f.*

appeal [ə'piːl] I *n* 1 *(request)* solicitud *f; (plea)* súplica *f.* 2 *(attraction)* atractivo *m; (interest)* interés *m.* 3 *Jur* apelación *f.* II *vi* 1 *(plead)* rogar, suplicar (**to,** a); **to a. for help,** solicitar ayuda. 2 *(attract)* atraer; *(interest)* interesar; **it doesn't a. to me,** no me dice nada. 3 *Jur* apelar.

appealing [ə'piːlɪŋ] *adj (moving)* conmovedor,-a; *(attractive)* atractivo,-a; *(tempting)* atrayente.

appear [ə'pɪər] *vi* 1 *(become visible)* aparecer; *(publicly)* presentarse; *(on stage)* actuar; **to a. before a court,** comparecer ante un tribunal; **to a. on television,** salir en la televisión. 2 *(seem)* parecer; **he**

appears relaxed, parece relajado; **so it appears**, según parece.

appearance [ə'pɪərəns] n 1 (becoming visible) aparición f; (publicly) presentación f; (on stage) actuación f; (before court) comparecencia f; (of book etc) publicación f; **to put in an a.**, hacer acto de presencia. 2 (look) apariencia f, aspecto m; **to all appearances**, al parecer.

appease [ə'piːz] vtr apaciguar; (curiosity) satisfacer.

appeasement [ə'piːzmənt] n Pol entreguismo m.

appendicitis [əpendɪ'saɪtɪs] n appendicitis f.

appendix [ə'pendɪks] n (pl **appendices** [ə'pendɪsiːz]) apéndice m.

appetite ['æpɪtaɪt] n apetito m; fig deseo m.

appetizer ['æpɪtaɪzə*] n (drink) aperitivo m; (snack) tapa f, pincho m.

applaud [ə'plɔːd] vtr & vi aplaudir.

applause [ə'plɔːz] n aplausos mpl.

apple ['æpəl] n manzana f; **a. tree**, manzano m.

appliance [ə'plaɪəns] n dispositivo m.

applicable [ə'plɪkəbəl] adj aplicable.

applicant ['æplɪkənt] n (for post) candidato,-a m,f; (to court, for tickets) solicitante mf.

application [æplɪ'keɪʃən] n 1 (of cream) aplicación f. 2 (for post etc) solicitud f; **a. form**, solicitud f; **job a.**, solicitud de empleo. 3 (effort) aplicación f; **she lacks a.**, no se aplica.

applied [ə'plaɪd] adj aplicado,-a.

apply [ə'plaɪ] I vtr aplicar; (brake) echar; (law) recurrir a; (force) usar; **to a. oneself to**, dedicarse a. II vi 1 (refer) aplicarse (to, a). 2 (for job) presentar una solicitud; (for information, to court) presentar una petición. ◆**apply for** vtr (post, information) solicitar; (tickets) pedir.

appoint [ə'pɔɪnt] vtr (person) nombrar; (time, place etc) fijar, señalar.

appointment [ə'pɔɪntmənt] n 1 (to post) nombramiento m; (post) cargo m. 2 (meeting) cita f; **to make an a. with**, citarse con; (at doctor's) pedir hora a.

apportion [ə'pɔːʃən] vtr fig (blame) echar.

appraisal [ə'preɪzəl] n evaluación f.

appreciable [ə'priːʃəbəl] adj (difference) apreciable; (sum) importante.

appreciate [ə'priːʃɪeɪt] I vtr 1 (be thankful for) agradecer. 2 (understand) entender. 3 (value) apreciar, valorar. II vi (increase in value) apreciarse.

appreciation [əpriːʃɪ'eɪʃən] n 1 (of help, advice) agradecimiento m; (of difficulty) comprensión f; (of wine etc) aprecio m; (appraisal) evaluación f. 2 (increase in value) apreciación f.

appreciative [ə'priːʃɪətɪv] adj (thankful) agradecido,-a; (responsive) apreciativo,-a.

apprehend [æprɪ'hend] vtr (arrest) detener.

apprehension [æprɪ'henʃən] n 1 (arrest) detención f. 2 (fear) aprensión f.

apprehensive [æprɪ'hensɪv] adj (fearful) aprensivo,-a.

apprentice [ə'prentɪs] n aprendiz,-a m,f.

apprenticeship [ə'prentɪsʃɪp] n aprendizaje m.

approach [ə'prəʊtʃ] I n 1 (coming near) acercamiento m; (to town) acceso m; **a. road**, vía f de acceso. 2 (to problem) enfoque m. II vtr (come near to) acercarse a; (be similar to) aproximarse a; fig (problem) abordar; (person) dirigirse a. **to a. sb about sth**, dirigirse a algn a propósito de algo. III vi acercarse.

approachable [ə'prəʊtʃəbəl] adj (person) accesible.

appropriate¹ [ə'prəʊprɪɪt] adj (suitable) apropiado,-a, adecuado,-a; (convenient) oportuno,-a.

appropriate² [ə'prəʊprɪeɪt] vtr (allocate) asignar; (steal) apropiarse de.

approval [ə'pruːvəl] n aprobación f, visto m bueno; **Com to get sth on a.**, adquirir algo sin compromiso de compra.

approve [ə'pruːv] vtr 1 aprobar; **approved school**, reformatorio m. ◆**approve of** vtr aprobar.

approving [ə'pruːvɪŋ] adj (look etc) aprobatorio,-a.

approx [ə'prɒks] abbr of **approximately**, aprox.

approximate [ə'prɒksɪmɪt] I adj aproximado,-a. II [ə'prɒksɪmeɪt] vtr aproximarse a. ◆**approximately** adv aproximadamente.

apricot ['eɪprɪkɒt] n albaricoque m.

April ['eɪprəl] n abril m; **A. Fools' Day**, día m uno de abril, ≈ día de los Inocentes (28 de diciembre).

apron ['eɪprən] n delantal m; (for workman) mandil m.

apt [æpt] adj 1 (suitable) apropiado,-a; (remark) acertado,-a, oportuno,-a; (name) justo,-a; (description) exacto,-a. 2 **to be a. to do sth**, ser propenso,-a a hacer algo. ◆**aptly** adv acertadamente.

aptitude ['æptɪtjuːd] n capacidad f; **a. test**, prueba f de aptitud.

aqualung ['ækwəlʌŋ] n botella f de oxígeno.

aquamarine [ækwəmə'riːn] I n Min aguamarina f. II adj de color de aguamarina.

aquarium [ə'kweərɪəm] n acuario m.

Aquarius [ə'kweərɪəs] n Acuario m.

aquatic [ə'kwætɪk] adj acuático,-a.

aqueduct ['ækwɪdʌkt] n acueducto m.

Arab ['ærəb] adj & n árabe (mf).

Arabian [ə'reɪbɪən] adj árabe.

Arabic ['ærəbɪk] I adj árabe, arábigo,-a; **A. numerals**, numeración arábiga. II n (language) árabe m.

arable ['ærəbəl] adj cultivable.

Aragon ['ærəgən] n Aragón.

arbitrary ['ɑːbɪtrərɪ] adj arbitrario,-a.

arbitrate ['ɑːbɪtreɪt] vtr & vi arbitrar.

arbitration [ɑːbɪ'treɪʃən] n arbitraje m.

arc [ɑːk] n arco m; a. **lamp**, arco voltaico.

arcade [ɑː'keɪd] n arcada f; (passageway) pasaje m; **shopping a.**, galerías fpl (comerciales).

arch [ɑːtʃ] I n 1 Archit arco m; (vault) bóveda f. 2 Anat empeine m. II vtr (back) arquear.

archaeologist [ɑːkɪ'ɒlədʒɪst] n arqueólogo,-a m,f.

archaeology [ɑːkɪ'ɒlədʒɪ] n arqueología f.

archaic [ɑː'keɪɪk] adj arcaico,-a.

archbishop [ɑːtʃ'bɪʃəp] n arzobispo m.

arched [ɑːtʃt] adj arqueado,-a.

archeology [ɑːkɪ'ɒlədʒɪ] n US → **archaeology**.

archer ['ɑːtʃəʳ] n arquero,-a m,f.

archery ['ɑːtʃərɪ] n tiro m con arco.

archetypal [ɑːkɪ'taɪpəl] adj arquetípico,-a.

archipelago [ɑːkɪ'pelɪgəʊ] n archipiélago m.

architect ['ɑːkɪtekt] n arquitecto,-a m,f.

architectural [ɑːkɪ'tektʃərəl] adj arquitectónico,-a.

architecture ['ɑːkɪtektʃəʳ] n arquitectura f.

archives ['ɑːkaɪvz] npl archivos mpl.

archway ['ɑːtʃweɪ] n (arch) arco m; (vault) bóveda f; (in church) atrio m; (passage) pasaje m.

arctic ['ɑːktɪk] I adj ártico,-a; **A. Circle**, círculo m polar Ártico. II n the A., el Ártico.

ardent ['ɑːdənt] adj (supporter etc) apasionado,-a; (desire) ardiente.

ardour, US **ardor** ['ɑːdəʳ] n pasión f, ardor m.

arduous ['ɑːdjʊəs] adj arduo,-a, penoso,-a.

are [ɑːʳ] 2nd person sing pres, 1st, 2nd, 3rd person pl pres → **be**.

area ['eərɪə] n (surface) área f, superficie f; (space) extensión f; (region) región f; (of town) zona f; fig (field) campo m; US Tel **a. code**, prefijo m local.

arena [ə'riːnə] n (stadium) estadio m; (bullring) plaza f; (circus) pista f; fig (stage) campo m de batalla.

Argentina [ɑːdʒən'tiːnə] n Argentina f.

Argentinian [ɑːdʒən'tɪnɪən] adj & n argentino,-a (m,f).

arguable [ɑːgjʊəbəl] adj discutible.
◆**arguably** adv it's a. the best, hay quienes dicen que es el mejor.

argue ['ɑːgjuː] I vtr (reason) discutir; (point of view) mantener. II vi (quarrel) discutir; (reason) argumentar, razonar; to **a. for**, abogar por; to **a. against sth**, po-

nerse en contra de algo.

argument ['ɑːgjʊmənt] n (reason) argumento m (for, a favor de; against, en contra de); (quarrel) discusión f, disputa f; for the **sake of a.**, por decir algo.

argumentative [ɑːgjʊ'mentətɪv] adj she's very a., le gusta discutir por todo.

aria ['ɑːrɪə] n aria f.

arid ['ærɪd] adj árido,-a.

Aries ['eəriːz] n Aries m.

arise [ə'raɪz] vi (pt arose; pp arisen [ə'rɪzən]) (get up) levantarse; (happen) surgir; should the occasion a., si se presenta la ocasión.

aristocracy [ærɪ'stɒkrəsɪ] n aristocracia f.

aristocrat ['ærɪstəkræt] n aristócrata mf.

arithmetic [ə'rɪθmətɪk] n aritmética f.

ark [ɑːk] n arca f; **Noah's A.**, el arca de Noé.

arm [ɑːm] I n 1 brazo m; (of garment) manga f; to **walk a. in a.**, ir cogidos,-as del brazo. 2 Mil **arms**, armas fpl; **arms race**, carrera armamentística; **coat of arms**, escudo m. II vtr armar; to **a. one-self against sth**, armarse contra algo.

armaments ['ɑːməmənts] npl armamentos mpl.

armchair ['ɑːmtʃeəʳ] n sillón m.

armed ['ɑːmd] adj armado,-a; **a. forces**, fuerzas armadas; **a. robbery**, robo m a mano armada.

armistice ['ɑːmɪstɪs] n armisticio m.

armour, US **armor** ['ɑːməʳ] n (on vehicle) blindaje m; (suit of) a., armadura f.

armoured car, US **armored car** [ə'mɑːd'kɑːʳ] n coche m blindado.

armour-plated ['ɑːməpleɪtɪd] adj acorazado,-a.

armoury, US **armory** ['ɑːmərɪ] n arsenal m.

armpit ['ɑːmpɪt] n axila f, sobaco m.

army ['ɑːmɪ] n ejército m.

aroma [ə'rəʊmə] n aroma m.

arose [ə'rəʊz] pt → **arise**.

around [ə'raʊnd] I adv alrededor; all a., por todos los lados; are the children a.?, ¿están los niños por aquí?; he looked a., miró (a su) alrededor. II prep 1 alrededor de; a. the corner, a la vuelta de la esquina; a. here, por aquí. 2 (approximately) aproximadamente.

arouse [ə'raʊz] vtr despertar; (sexually) excitar.

arrange [ə'reɪndʒ] I vtr 1 (order) ordenar; (hair, flowers) arreglar; Mus adaptar. 2 (plan) organizar; (agree on) quedar en; to **a. a time**, fijar una hora; **arranged marriage**, boda arreglada. II vi I shall a. for him to be there, lo arreglaré para que pueda asistir.

arrangement [ə'reɪndʒmənt] n 1 (display) colocación f; Mus adaptación f. 2 (agreement) acuerdo m. 3 **arrangements**, (plans) planes mpl; (preparations) preparativos *mpl.*

array [əˈreɪ] *n* colección *f*; **a great. of goods,** un gran surtido de productos.

arrears [əˈrɪəz] *npl* atrasos *mpl*; **to be in a. with the rent,** estar atrasado,-a con el alquiler; **to be paid in a.,** cobrar con retraso.

arrest [əˈrest] I *n* detención *f*; **to be under a.,** estar detenido,-a. II *vtr* (*criminal*) detener; *fig* (*progress*) frenar.

arresting [əˈrestɪŋ] *adj* llamativo,-a.

arrival [əˈraɪvəl] *n* llegada *f*; **a new a.,** un,-a recién llegado,-a.

arrive [əˈraɪv] *vi* llegar (**at, in, a**).

arrogance [ˈærəgəns] *n* arrogancia *f*.

arrogant [ˈærəgənt] *adj* arrogante.

arrow [ˈærəʊ] *n* flecha *f*.

arse [ɑːs] *n* *vulg* culo *m*.

arsenal [ˈɑːsənəl] *n* arsenal *m*.

arsenic [ˈɑːsənɪk] *n* arsénico *m*.

arson [ˈɑːsən] *n* incendio *m* provocado.

art [ɑːt] *n* 1 arte *m*; (*drawing*) dibujo *m*; **the arts,** las bellas artes; **arts and crafts,** artes *fpl* y oficios *mpl*; **a. gallery,** galería *f* de arte. 2 **arts,** (*branch of knowledge*) letras *fpl*.

artefact [ˈɑːtɪfækt] *n* artefacto *m*; (*in archaelogy*) objeto *m* de arte.

artery [ˈɑːtəri] *n* arteria *f*.

artful [ˈɑːtfʊl] *adj* (*cunning*) ladino,-a.

arthritis [ɑːˈθraɪtɪs] *n* artritis *f*.

artichoke [ˈɑːtɪtʃəʊk] *n* alcachofa *f*.

article [ˈɑːtɪkəl] *n* 1 artículo *m*; *Press* artículo; **a. of clothing,** prenda *f* de vestir. 2 *Jur* **articles,** contrato *m sing* de aprendizaje.

articulate¹ [ɑːˈtɪkjʊlɪt] *adj* (*speech*) claro,-a; (*person*) que se expresa bien.

articulate² [ɑːˈtɪkjʊlɪt] *vtr & vi* articular; (*words*) pronunciar; **articulated lorry,** camión articulado.

artificial [ɑːtɪˈfɪʃəl] *adj* artificial; (*limb*) postizo,-a; **a. intelligence,** inteligencia *f* artificial.

artillery [ɑːˈtɪləri] *n* artillería *f*.

artisan [ˈɑːtɪzæn] *n* artesano,-a *m,f*.

artist [ˈɑːtɪst] *n* artista *mf*; (*painter*) pintor,-a *m,f*.

artistic [ɑːˈtɪstɪk] *adj* artístico,-a.

artistry [ˈɑːtɪstrɪ] *n* arte *m*, talento artístico.

as [æz, *unstressed* əz] I *adv & conj* 1 (*comparison*) **as ... as ...,** tan ... como ...; **as far as,** hasta; *fig* **as far as I'm concerned,** por lo que a mí respecta; **as many as,** tantos,-as como; **as much as,** tanto,-a como; **as tall as me,** tan alto,-a como yo; **as opposed to,** a diferencia de; **as little as £5,** tan sólos cinco libras ; **as soon as they arrive,** en cuanto lleguen; **I'll stay as long as I can,** quedaré todo el tiempo que pueda; **just as big,** igual de grande; **three times as fast,** tres veces más rápido; **the same as,** igual que. 2

(*manner*) como; **as a rule,** por regla general; **as you know,** como ya sabéis; **as you like,** como quieras; **do as I say,** haz lo que yo te digo; **he's working as a doctor,** está trabajando de médico; **I thought as much,** ya me lo suponía; **it serves as a table,** sirve de mesa; **leave it as it is,** déjalo tal como está; **he was dressed as a pirate,** iba vestido de pirata. 3 (*while, when*) mientras (que); **as a child,** de niño,-a; **as I was eating,** mientras comía; **as we were leaving we saw Pat,** al salir vimos a Pat. 4 (*though*) aunque; **be that as it may,** por mucho que así sea; **young as he is,** aunque es joven. 5 (*because*) como, ya que. 6 (*and so*) igual que; **as do I,** igual que yo; **as well,** también. 7 (*purpose*) para; so as **to do sth,** para hacer algo. 8 **as for my brother,** en cuanto a mi hermano. 9 **as from, as of,** a partir de. 10 **to act as if,** actuar como si + *subj*; **it looks as if the concert is off,** parece ser que no habrá concierto. 11 **it's late enough as it is,** ya es muy tarde; **as it were,** por así decirlo. 12 **as long as,** (*only if*) siempre que, con tal de que. 13 **as regards,** en cuanto a, por lo que se refiere a; **as usual,** como siempre; **as yet,** aún, todavía.
II *rel pron* such as, tal(es) como.

asbestos [æzˈbestəs] *n* amianto *m*, asbesto *m*.

ascend [əˈsend] *vi* subir, ascender.

ascendancy [əˈsendənsi] *n* dominio *m*, influencia *f*.

ascendant [əˈsendənt] *n* **to be in the a.,** estar en auge.

ascent [əˈsent] *n* subida *f*.

ascertain [æsəˈteɪn] *vtr* averiguar, enterarse de.

ascribe [əˈskraɪb] *vtr* **a. sth to,** imputar algo a.

aseptic [əˈseptɪk] *adj* aséptico,-a.

ash¹ [æʃ] *n Bot* fresno *m*.

ash² [æʃ] *n* ceniza *f*; **a. bin,** *US* **a. can,** cubo *m* de la basura; *Rel* **A. Wednesday,** miércoles *m inv* de ceniza.

ashamed [əˈʃeɪmd] *adj* avergonzado,-a; **you ought to be a. of yourself!,** ¡te debería dar vergüenza!

ashen [ˈæʃən] *adj* (*face*) pálido,-a.

ashore [əˈʃɔːr] *adv* (*position*) en tierra; **to go a.,** desembarcar; **to swim a.,** nadar hacia tierra.

ashtray [ˈæʃtreɪ] *n* cenicero *m*.

Asia [ˈeɪʒə] *n* Asia; **A. Minor,** Asia Menor.

Asian [ˈeɪʒən] *adj & n* asiático,-a (*m,f*).

aside [əˈsaɪd] I *adv* al lado, aparte; **to cast a.,** echar a un lado; **to stand a.,** apartarse. II *prep* **a. from,** (*apart from*) aparte de; (*as well as*) además de. III *n Theat* aparte *m*.

ask [ɑːsk] I *vtr* 1 preguntar; **to a. sb a**

question, hacer una pregunta a algn. **2** (*request*) pedir, solicitar; **she asked me to post it**, me pidió que le echara al buzón. **3** (*invite*) invitar. ◆**ask after** *vtr* to a. **after sb**, preguntar por algn. ◆**ask for** *vtr* (*help*) pedir, solicitar; (*person*) preguntar por. ◆**ask out** *vtr* to a. **sb out**, invitar a algn a salir.

askance [əˈskæns] *adv* to look a. at sb, mirar a algn con recelo.

askew [əˈskjuː] I *adj* ladeado,-a. II *adv* de lado.

asleep [əˈsliːp] *adj* (*person*) dormido,-a; (*limb*) adormecido,-a; **to fall a.**, quedarse dormido,-a.

asparagus [əˈspærəgəs] *n inv* espárragos *mpl*.

aspect [ˈæspekt] *n* **1** (*of question*) aspecto *m*. **2** (*of building*) orientación *f*.

aspersions [əˈspɜːʃənz] *npl* **to cast a. on sb**, difamar a algn.

asphalt [ˈæsfælt] *n* asfalto *m*.

asphyxiation [æsfiksiˈeɪʃən] *n* asfixia *f*.

aspiration [æspəˈreɪʃən] *n* aspiración *f*.

aspire [əˈspaɪər] *vi* to a. to, aspirar a.

aspirin® [ˈæsprin] *n* aspirina® *f*.

ass¹ [æs] *n* Zool asno,-a *m,f*, burro,-a *m,f*; *fam fig* burro,-a.

ass² [æs] *n* US *vulg* culo *m*.

assailant [əˈseɪlənt] *n* agresor,-a *m,f*, atacante *mf*.

assassin [əˈsæsin] *n* asesino,-a *m,f*.

assassinate [əˈsæsineɪt] *vtr* asesinar.

assassination [əsæsiˈneɪʃən] *n* asesinato *m*.

assault [əˈsɔːlt] I *n* Mil ataque *m* (**on**, a); *Jur* agresión *f*. II *vtr* Mil asaltar, atacar; *Jur* agredir; (*sexually*) violar.

assemble [əˈsembl] I *vtr* (*people*) reunir, juntar; (*furniture*) montar. II *vi* (*people*) reunirse, juntarse.

assembly [əˈsembli] *n* reunión *f*, asamblea *f*; *Tech* montaje *m*; *Ind* a. line, cadena *f* de montaje; *Educ* morning a., servicio *m* matinal.

assent [əˈsent] I *n* (*agreement*) asentimiento *m*; (*consent*) consentimiento *m*; (*approval*) aprobación *f*. II *vi* asentir, consentir (**to**, en).

assert [əˈsɜːt] *vtr* afirmar; **to a. oneself**, imponerse; **to a. one's rights**, hacer valer sus derechos.

assertive [əˈsɜːtiv] *adj* enérgico,-a.

assess [əˈses] *vtr* (*estimate value*) valorar; (*damages, price*) calcular; (*tax*) gravar; *fig* (*effect*) evaluar.

assessment [əˈsesmənt] *n* (*of value*) valoración *f*; (*of damages etc*) cálculo *m*; (*of taxes*) gravamen *m*; *fig* juicio *m*.

assessor [əˈsesər] *n* asesor,-a *m,f*.

asset [ˈæset] *n* **1** ventaja *f*; **to be an a.**, (*person*) ser de gran valor. **2** *Fin* **assets**, bienes *mpl*; **fixed assets**, bienes raíces.

assiduous [əˈsidjuəs] *adj* asiduo,-a.

assign [əˈsain] *vtr* (*task*) asignar; (*property etc*) ceder; **to a. sb to a job**, designar a algn para un trabajo.

assignment [əˈsainmənt] *n* (*allocation*) asignación *f*; (*task*) tarea *f*; (*mission*) misión *f*; (*appointment*) cita *f*.

assimilate [əˈsimileit] *vtr* asimilar.

assist [əˈsist] *vtr & vi* ayudar.

assistance [əˈsistəns] *n* ayuda *f*, auxilio *m*.

assistant [əˈsistənt] *n* ayudante *mf*; a. manager, subdirector,-a *m,f*; shop a., dependiente,-a *m,f*; (*language*) a., lector,-a *m,f*.

associate¹ [əˈsəuʃieit] I *vtr* (*ideas*) relacionar; (*companies*) asociar; **to be associated with sth**, estar relacionado,-a con algo. II *vi* to a. with, tratar con.

associate² [əˈsəuʃiit] I *adj* asociado,-a. II *n* (*colleague*) colega *mf*; (*partner*) socio,-a *m,f*; (*accomplice*) cómplice *mf*.

association [əsəusiˈeiʃən] *n* asociación *f*; (*company*) sociedad *f*.

assorted [əˈsɔːtid] *adj* surtido,-a, variado,-a.

assortment [əˈsɔːtmənt] *n* surtido *m*, variedad *f*.

assume [əˈsjuːm] I *vtr* (*power*) asumir; (*attitude, name*) adoptar; **an assumed name**, un nombre falso. II *vi* (*suppose*) suponer.

assumption [əˈsʌmpʃən] *n* **1** (*of power*) toma *f*; **a. of office**, toma de posesión. **2** (*supposition*) suposición *f*.

assurance [əˈʃuərəns] *n* **1** (*guarantee*) garantía *f*. **2** (*confidence*) confianza *f*. **3** (*insurance*) seguro *m*.

assure [əˈʃuər] *vtr* asegurar.

asterisk [ˈæstərisk] *n* asterisco *m*.

astern [əˈstɜːn] *adv* a popa.

asthma [ˈæsmə] *n* asma *f*.

astonish [əˈstɒniʃ] *vtr* asombrar, pasmar; **I was astonished**, me quedé pasmado,-a.

astonishing [əˈstɒniʃiŋ] *adj* asombroso,-a, pasmoso,-a.

astonishment [əˈstɒniʃmənt] *n* asombro *m*; **to my a.**, para gran sorpresa mía.

astound [əˈstaund] *vtr* asombrar, pasmar.

astray [əˈstrei] *adv* to go a., extraviarse; (*fig*) equivocarse; **to lead sb a.**, llevar a algn por mal camino.

astride [əˈstraid] *prep* a horcajadas sobre.

astrology [əˈstrɒlədʒi] *n* astrología *f*.

astronaut [ˈæstrənɔːt] *n* astronauta *mf*.

astronomer [əˈstrɒnəmər] *n* astrónomo,-a *m,f*.

astronomical [æstrəˈnɒmikəl] *adj* astronómico,-a.

astronomy [əˈstrɒnəmi] *n* astronomía *f*.

Asturias [æˈstuəriəs] *n* Asturias *f*.

astute [əˈstjuːt] *adj* astuto,-a.

asylum [əˈsailəm] *n* **1** (*protection*) asilo *m*; **to seek political a.**, pedir asilo político.

2 mental a., manicomio m.

at [æt] *prep* **1** *(position)* a, en; **at school/work**, en el colegio/trabajo; **at the window**, a la ventana; **at the top**, en lo alto. **2** *(direction)* a; **to be angry at sb/sth**, enfadarse con algn/por algo; **to laugh at sb**, reírse de algn; **to look at sth/sb**, mirar algo/a algn; **to shout at sb**, gritarle a algn. **3** *(time)* a; **at Easter/Christmas**, en Semana Santa/Navidad; **at six o'clock**, a las seis; **at first**, al principio; **at last**, por fin; **at once**, enseguida; **at that time**, entonces; **at the moment**, ahora. **4** *(manner)* a, en; **at best/worst**, en el mejor/peor de los casos; **at hand**, a mano; **at least**, por lo menos; **not at all**, en absoluto; *(don't mention it)* de nada. **5** *(rate)* a; **they retail at 100 pesetas each**, se venden a 100 pesetas la unidad; **two at a time**, de dos en dos.

ate [et, eɪt] *pt* → **eat**.

atheist ['eɪθɪɪst] *n* ateo,-a *m,f*.

Athens ['æθɪnz] *n* Atenas.

athlete ['æθliːt] *n* atleta *mf*.

athletic [æθ'letɪk] **I** *adj* atlético,-a, *(sporty)* deportista. **II** *npl* **athletics** atletismo *m sing*.

Atlantic [ət'læntɪk] *adj* the A. (Ocean), el (océano) Atlántico.

atlas ['ætləs] *n* atlas *m*.

atmosphere ['ætməsfɪər] *n* atmósfera *f*; *fig (ambience)* ambiente *m*.

atmospheric [ætməs'ferɪk] *adj* atmosférico,-a.

atom ['ætəm] *n* átomo *m*; **a. bomb**, bomba atómica.

atomic [ə'tɒmɪk] *adj* atómico,-a.

atone [ə'təʊn] *vi* **to a. for**, expiar.

atrocious [ə'trəʊʃəs] *adj* atroz.

attach [ə'tætʃ] *vtr (stick)* pegar; *(fasten)* sujetar; *(document)* adjuntar; **to a. importance to sth**, dar importancia a algo; *fig* **to be attached to**, *(be fond of)* tener cariño a.

attaché [ə'tæʃeɪ] *n* agregado,-a *m,f*; **a. case**, maletín *m*.

attachment [ə'tætʃmənt] *n* **1** *Tech* accesorio *m*; *(action)* acoplamiento *m*. **2** *(fondness)* apego *m* (**to**, por).

attack [ə'tæk] **I** *n* **1** *(assault)* ataque *m*, asalto *m*; **an a. on sb's life**, un atentado contra la vida de algn. **2** *Med* ataque *m*. **II** *vtr (assault)* atacar, asaltar; *fig (problem)* abordar; *(job)* emprender; *fig (criticize)* atacar.

attacker [ə'tækər] *n* asaltante *mf*, agresor,-a *m,f*.

attain [ə'teɪn] *vtr (aim)* lograr; *(rank, age)* llegar a.

attainment [ə'teɪnmənt] *n* *(achievement)* logro *m*; *(skill)* talento *m*.

attempt [ə'tempt] **I** *n* intento *m*, tentativa *f*; **at the second a.**, a la segunda; **an a. on sb's life**, un atentado contra la vida

de algn. **II** *vtr* intentar; **to a. to do sth**, tratar de *or* intentar hacer algo; *Jur* **attempted murder/rape**, intento *m* de asesinato/violación.

attend [ə'tend] **I** *vtr (be present at)* asistir a; *(care for, wait on)* atender. **II** *vi (be present)* asistir; *(pay attention)* prestar atención. ◆**attend to** *vtr (business)* ocuparse de; *(in shop)* atender a.

attendance [ə'tendəns] *n* asistencia *f*.

attendant [ə'tendənt] *n (in cinema etc)* acomodador,-a *m,f*; *(in museum)* guía *mf*; *(in car park)* vigilante,-a *m,f*.

attention [ə'tenʃən] *n* **1** atención *f*; **for the a. of Miss Jones**, a la atención de la Srta. Jones; **pay a.!**, ¡atiende!; **to pay a. to sb/sth**, prestar atención a algn/algo. **2** *Mil* **a.!**, ¡firmes!; **to stand to a.**, estar firmes.

attentive [ə'tentɪv] *adj (listener)* atento,-a; *(helpful)* solícito,-a.

attest [ə'test] *vi* **to a. to**, dar testimonio a.

attic ['ætɪk] *n* ático *m*.

attire [ə'taɪər] *n* *fml* traje *m*.

attitude ['ætɪtjuːd] *n* actitud *f*; *(position of body)* postura *f*; **an a. of mind**, un estado de ánimo.

attorney [ə'tɜːnɪ] *n* **1** *US (lawyer)* abogado,-a *m,f*; **A. General**, ≈ Ministro,-a *m,f* de Justicia; **district a.**, fiscal *mf*. **2** *Jur* **power of a.**, poderes *mpl*.

attract [ə'trækt] *vtr* atraer; **to a. attention**, llamar la atención; **to a. a waiter's attention**, llamar a un camarero.

attraction [ə'trækʃən] *n* **1** *(power)* atracción *f*. **2** *(attractive thing)* atractivo *m*; *(charm)* encanto *m*; *(incentive)* aliciente *m*; **the main a.**, el número fuerte.

attractive [ə'træktɪv] *adj* atractivo,-a; *(good-looking)* guapo,-a; *(idea, proposition)* atrayente.

attribute¹ ['ætrɪbjuːt] *n (quality)* atributo *m*.

attribute² [ə'trɪbjuːt] *vtr* atribuir.

attrition [ə'trɪʃən] *n* **war of a.**, guerra *f* de desgaste.

aubergine ['əʊbəʒiːn] *n* berenjena *f*.

auburn ['ɔːbən] *adj* castaño rojizo *inv*.

auction ['ɔːkʃən] **I** *n* subasta *f*. **II** *vtr* subastar.

auctioneer [ɔːkʃə'nɪər] *n* subastador,-a *m,f*.

audacious [ɔː'deɪʃəs] *adj (daring)* audaz; *(bold)* atrevido,-a; *(impudent)* descarado,-a.

audible ['ɔːdɪbl] *adj* audible.

audience ['ɔːdɪəns] *n* **1** *(spectators)* público *m*; *(at concert, conference)* auditorio *m*; *(television)* telespectadores *mpl*. **2** *(meeting)* audiencia *f*.

audio-visual [ɔːdɪəʊ'vɪʒʊəl] *adj* audiovisual; **a.-v. aids**, apoyo *m* audiovisual.

audit ['ɔːdɪt] **I** *n* revisión *f* de cuentas. **II**

vtr revisar, intervenir.

audition [ɔːˈdɪʃən] I *n* prueba *f*. II *vtr* **to a. sb for a part**, probar a algn para un papel.

auditor [ˈɔːdɪtər] *n* revisor,-a *m,f*, de cuentas.

auditorium [ɔːdɪˈtɔːrɪəm] *n* auditorio *m*.

augment [ɔːɡˈment] *vtr* aumentar.

augur [ˈɔːɡər] *vi* **to a. well**, ser de buen agüero.

August [ˈɔːɡəst] *n* agosto *m*.

aunt [ɑːnt] *n* (*also fam* **auntie, aunty** [ˈɑːntɪ]) tía *f*.

au pair [əʊˈpeər] *n* **au p. (girl)**, au pair *f*.

aura [ˈɔːrə] *n* aura *f*; *Rel* aureola *f*.

aural [ˈɔːrəl] *adj* auditivo,-a, del oído.

auspices [ˈɔːspɪsɪz] *npl* **under the a. of**, bajo los auspicios de.

auspicious [ɔːˈspɪʃəs] *adj* de buen augurio.

austere [ɒˈstɪər] *adj* austero,-a.

austerity [ɒˈsterɪtɪ] *n* austeridad *f*.

Australia [ɒˈstreɪlɪə] *n* Australia *f*.

Australian [ɒˈstreɪlɪən] *adj & n* australiano,-a (*m,f*).

Austria [ˈɒstrɪə] *n* Austria *f*.

Austrian [ˈɒstrɪən] *adj & n* austríaco,-a (*m,f*).

authentic [ɔːˈθentɪk] *adj* auténtico,-a.

author [ˈɔːθər] *n* autor,-a *m,f*.

authoritarian [ɔːθɒrɪˈteərɪən] *adj* autoritario,-a.

authoritative [ɔːˈθɒrɪtətɪv] *adj* (*reliable*) autorizado,-a; (*authoritarian*) autoritario,-a.

authority [ɔːˈθɒrɪtɪ] *n* autoridad *f*; **local a.**, ayuntamiento *m*.

authorize [ˈɔːθəraɪz] *vtr* autorizar; (*payment etc*) aprobar; **to a. sb to do sth**, autorizar a algn a hacer algo.

auto [ˈɔːtəʊ] *n* US coche *m*, *Am* carro *m*.

autobiography [ɔːtəʊbaɪˈɒɡrəfɪ] *n* autobiografía *f*.

autograph [ˈɔːtəɡrɑːf] I *n* autógrafo *m*. II *vtr* (*sign*) firmar; (*book, photo*) dedicar.

automatic [ɔːtəˈmætɪk] I *adj* automático,-a. II *n* (*car*) coche automático; (*gun*) pistola automática. ◆**automatically** *adv* automáticamente.

automation [ɔːtəˈmeɪʃən] *n* automatización *f*; *office a.*, ofimática *f*.

automaton [ɔːˈtɒmətɒn] *n* (*pl* **automata** [ɔːˈtɒmətə]) autómata *m*.

automobile [ˈɔːtəməbiːl] *n* US coche *m*, automóvil *m*, *Am* carro *m*.

autonomous [ɔːˈtɒnəməs] *adj* autónomo,-a.

autonomy [ɔːˈtɒnəmɪ] *n* autonomía *f*.

autopsy [ˈɔːtɒpsɪ] *n* autopsia *f*.

autumn [ˈɔːtəm] *n* otoño *m*.

auxiliary [ɔːɡˈzɪlɪərɪ] *adj* auxiliar.

Av., av. *abbr of* **Avenue**, avenida *f*, Av., Avda.

avail [əˈveɪl] I *n* **to no a.**, en vano. II *vtr*

to a. oneself of sth, aprovecharse de algo.

available [əˈveɪləbəl] *adj* (*thing*) disponible; (*person*) libre.

avalanche [ˈævəlɑːnʃ] *n* avalancha *f*.

avarice [ˈævərɪs] *n* avaricia *f*.

Ave *abbr of* **Avenue**, Avenida *f*, Av., Avda.

avenge [əˈvendʒ] *vtr* vengar.

avenue [ˈævɪnjuː] *n* avenida *f*; *fig* vía *f*.

average [ˈævərɪdʒ] I *n* promedio *m*, media *f*; **on a.**, por término medio. II *adj* medio,-a; (*condition*) regular. III *vtr* sacar la media de; **he averages 8 hours' work a day**, trabaja una media de 8 horas al día. ◆**average out at** *vtr* salir a una media de.

averse [əˈvɜːs] *adj* **to be a. to sth**, ser reacio,-a a algo.

aversion [əˈvɜːʃən] *n* (*feeling*) aversión *f*; (*thing*) bestia negra.

avert [əˈvɜːt] *vtr* (*eyes, thoughts*) apartar (**from**, de); (*accident*) impedir; (*danger*) evitar.

avid [ˈævɪd] *adj* (*reader*) voraz. ◆**avidly** *adv* vorazmente.

avocado [ævəˈkɑːdəʊ] *n* (*also* **avocado pear**) aguacate *m*.

avoid [əˈvɔɪd] *vtr* evitar; (*question*) eludir.

avoidable [əˈvɔɪdəbəl] *adj* evitable.

await [əˈweɪt] *vtr* esperar, aguardar.

awake [əˈweɪk] I *adj* despierto,-a; **to be a.**, estar despierto,-a. II *vtr* (*pt* **awoke**, **awaked**; *pp* **awoken, awaked**) despertar.

awaken [əˈweɪkən] *vtr & vi* (*pt* **awakened**; *pp* **awoken**) → **awake** II.

awakening [əˈweɪkənɪŋ] *n* despertar *m*.

award [əˈwɔːd] I *n* (*prize*) premio *m*; (*medal*) condecoración *f*; *Jur* indemnización *f*; (*grant*) beca *f*. II *vtr* (*prize*) conceder, otorgar; (*medal*) dar; (*damages*) adjudicar.

aware [əˈweər] *adj* (*informed*) enterado,-a; **not that I'm a. of**, que yo sepa no; **to be a. of sth**, ser consciente de algo; **to become a. of sth**, darse cuenta de algo.

awareness [əˈweənɪs] *n* conciencia *f* (**of**, de).

awash [əˈwɒʃ] *adj* inundado,-a (**with**, de).

away [əˈweɪ] *adv* far a., lejos; go a.!, ¡lárgate!; **it's 3 miles a.**, está a 3 millas (de distancia); **keep a. from the fire!**, ¡no te acerques al fuego!; **right a.**, en seguida; **to be a.**, (*absent*) estar ausente; (*out*) estar fuera; **to die a.**, desvanecerse; **to give sth a.**, regalar algo; (*secret*) revelar algo; **to go a.**, irse; *Sport* **to play a.**, jugar fuera; **to turn a.**, volver la cara; **to work a.**, trabajar.

awe [ɔː] *n* (*fear*) temor *m*; (*amazement*) asombro *m*; **he was in a. of his father**, le intimidaba su padre.

awe-inspiring [ˈɔːɪnspaɪərɪŋ] *adj* impresionante, imponente.

awesome [ˈɔːsəm] *adj* impresionante.

awful ['ɔ:ful] adj fam espantoso,-a; **an a. lot of work**, muchísimo trabajo.
◆**awfully** adv fam terriblemente.

awkward ['ɔ:kwəd] adj (clumsy) torpe; (difficult) pesado,-a; (object) incómodo,-a; (moment) inoportuno,-a; (situation) embarazoso,-a; (problem) difícil.

awning ['ɔ:nɪŋ] n (on ship) toldo m; (on shop) marquesina f.

awoke [ə'wəʊk] pt → awake.
awoken [ə'wəʊkən] pp → awake.

axe, US **ax** [æks] I n hacha f. II vtr fig (jobs) eliminar; (costs) reducir; (plan) cancelar; (person) despedir.

axis ['æksɪs] n (pl axes ['æksi:z]) eje m.

axle ['æksəl] n eje m; Tech árbol m.

ayatollah [aɪə'tɒlə] n ayatolá m.

Aztec ['æztek] adj & n azteca (mf).

B

B, b [bi:] n 1 (the letter) B, b f; Aut **B road**, carretera secundaria. 2 Mus si m; **B flat**, si m bemol.

BA [bi:'eɪ] abbr of **Bachelor of Arts**, Licenciado en Filosofía y Letras.

babble ['bæbəl] vi (baby) balbucear; (brook) murmurar.

babe [beɪb] n 1 (baby) bebé m. 2 US fam **hi, b.!**, ¡hola, guapa!

baboon [bə'bu:n] n zambo m.

baby ['beɪbɪ] n 1 bebé m; (young child) niño,-a m,f; **b. buggy**, US b. carriage, cochecito m de niño; **b. face**, cara f de niño. 2 (animal) cría f. 3 fam (darling) querido,-a m,f.

baby-sit ['beɪbɪsɪt] vi hacer de canguro.

baby-sitter ['beɪbɪsɪtər] n canguro mf.

baby-walker ['beɪbɪwɔ:kər] n tacataca m.

bachelor ['bætʃələr] n 1 soltero m. 2 Univ licenciado,-a m,f; **B. of Arts/Science**, licenciado,-a m,f en Filosofía y Letras/Ciencias.

back [bæk] I n 1 (of person) espalda f; (of animal) lomo m; **b. to front**, al revés; fig **to get sb's b. up**, poner negro a algn; fig **to have one's b. to the wall**, estar en un aprieto. 2 (of book) lomo m; (of chair) respaldo m; (of coin) reverso m; (of hand) dorso m; (of house, car) parte f de atrás; fig **he knows Leeds like the b. of his hand**, se conoce Leeds como la palma de la mano. 3 (of stage, cupboard) fondo m; fam **at the b. of beyond**, en el quinto pino. 4 Ftb defensa mf.

II adj 1 trasero,-a, de atrás; **b. door**, puerta f de atrás; **b. seat**, asiento m de detrás; fig **to take a b. seat**, pasar a segundo plano; Aut **b. wheel**, rueda trasera. 2 **b. rent**, alquiler atrasado; **b. pay**, atrasos mpl; Press **b. number**, número m atrasado.

III adv 1 (to the rear) atrás; (towards the rear) hacia atrás; **b. and forth**, de acá para allá. 2 **some years b.**, hace unos años.

IV vtr 1 (support) apoyar, respaldar. 2 Fin financiar. 3 (bet on) apostar por. 4 (car etc) dar marcha atrás a.

V vi 1 (move backwards) retroceder. 2 (car etc) dar marcha atrás.

◆**back away** vi retirarse. ◆**back down** vi echarse atrás. ◆**back off** vi desistir. ◆**back out** vi (withdraw) retractarse, volverse atrás. ◆**back up** I vtr apoyar. II vi Aut ir marcha atrás.

backache ['bækeɪk] n dolor m de espalda.

backbencher ['bækbentʃər] n diputado,-a m,f que no es ministro.

backbiting ['bækbaɪtɪŋ] n murmuración f.

backbone ['bækbəʊn] n Anat columna f.

backcloth ['bækklɒθ] n telón m de fondo.

backdate [bæk'deɪt] vtr antedatar.

backdated [bæk'deɪtɪd] adj con efecto retroactivo.

backdrop ['bækdrɒp] n telón m de fondo.

backer ['bækər] n 1 Fin promotor,-a m,f. 2 Pol partidario, -a m,f. 3 (person who bets) apostante m.

backfire [bæk'faɪər] vi 1 Aut petardear. 2 fig **our plan backfired**, nos salió el tiro por la culata.

background ['bækgraʊnd] n 1 fondo m; **to stay in the b.**, quedarse en segundo plano; **b. music**, música de fondo. 2 (origin) origen m; (past) pasado m; (education) formación f. 3 (circumstances) antecedentes mpl. 4 (atmosphere) ambiente m.

backhand ['bækhænd] n Sport revés m.

backhanded [bæk'hændɪd] adj equívoco,-a, ambiguo,-a.

backhander ['bækhændər] n sl (bribe) soborno m.

backing ['bækɪŋ] n 1 (support) apoyo m; Com Fin respaldo financiero. 2 Mus acompañamiento m.

backlash ['bæklæʃ] n reacción violenta y repentina.

backlog ['bæklɒg] n **to have a b. of work**, tener un montón de trabajo atrasado.

backpack ['bækpæk] n mochila f.

backpedal ['bækpedəl] vi fam dar marcha atrás.

backside [bæk'saɪd] n fam trasero m, culo m.

backstage [bæk'steɪdʒ] adv entre bastidores.

backstroke ['bækstrəʊk] n espalda f.

backtrack ['bæktræk] vi fig volverse atrás.

backup ['bækʌp] n apoyo m, respaldo m; *Comput* b. (**file**), fichero m de *apoyo*.

backward ['bækwəd] I adj 1 (*movement*) hacia atrás. 2 (*country*) subdesarrollado, -a; (*child*) retrasado,-a. II adv esp US hacia atrás.

backwards ['bækwədz] adv hacia atrás; **to walk b.**, andar de espaldas.

backyard [bæk'jɑːd] n patio trasero; US jardín trasero.

bacon ['beɪkən] n tocino m, beicon m.

bacteria [bæk'tɪərɪə] npl bacterias fpl.

bad [bæd] I adj (**worse, worst**) 1 (*poor*) malo,-a; **to go from b. to worse**, ir de mal en peor. 2 (*decayed*) podrido,-a; **to go b.**, echarse a perder. 3 **that's too b.**, ¡qué pena! 4 (*wicked*) malo,-a; **to use b. language**, ser mal hablado,-a. 5 (*accident*) grave; (*headache*) fuerte. 6 (*ill*) enfermo, -a. 7 **b. debt**, deuda f incobrable. II n lo malo. ◆**badly** adv 1 mal; **he did b. in the exam**, le salió mal el examen; **to be b. off**, andar mal de dinero. 2 (*seriously*) gravemente. 3 (*very much*) mucho; **to miss sb b.**, echar mucho de menos a algn; **we need it b.**, nos hace mucha falta.

bade [beɪd] pt → **bid**.

badge [bædʒ] n insignia f; (*metal disc*) chapa f.

badger ['bædʒər] I n tejón m. II vtr acosar.

badminton ['bædmɪntən] n bádminton m.

bad-tempered [bæd'tempəd] adj **to be b.-t.**, (*temperament*) tener mal genio; (*temporarily*) estar de mal humor.

baffle ['bæfəl] I vtr desconcertar. II n *Tech* pantalla acústica.

baffling ['bæflɪŋ] adj incomprensible, enigmático,-a.

bag [bæg] I n 1 (*large*) bolsa f; (*handbag*) bolso m; *fam* **bags of**, montones de; **travel b.**, bolsa de viaje. 2 (*hunting*) caza f; *fam* **it's in the b.**, es cosa hecha. 3 *pej* **old b.**, (*woman*) bruja f. 4 **bags**, (*under eyes*) ojeras fpl. II vtr 1 (*put into sacks*) meter en sacos. 2 fam coger.

baggage ['bægɪdʒ] n 1 equipaje m. 2 *Mil* bagaje m.

baggy ['bægɪ] adj (**baggier, baggiest**) holgado,-a; **b. trousers**, pantalones anchos.

bagpipes ['bægpaɪps] npl gaita f sing.

Bahamas [bə'hɑːməz] npl **the B.**, las Bahamas.

bail[1] [beɪl] n *Jur* fianza f; **on b.**, bajo fianza; **to stand b. for sb**, salir fiador por algn. ◆**bail out** vtr fig (*person*) sacar de un apuro.

bail[2] [beɪl] vi *Naut* to b., achicar.

bailiff ['beɪlɪf] n 1 *Jur* alguacil m. 2 (*steward*) administrador m.

bait [beɪt] I n cebo m; **to rise to the b.**,

tragar el anzuelo, picar. II vtr 1 *Fishing* cebar. 2 (*torment*) hostigar.

baize [beɪz] n bayeta f; **green b.**, tapete m verde.

bake [beɪk] I vtr 1 cocer al horno. 2 (*harden*) endurecer. II vi fam hacer mucho calor.

baked [beɪkt] adj al horno; **b. potato**, patata f al horno.

baker ['beɪkər] n panadero,-a m,f.

bakery ['beɪkərɪ] n panadería f.

baking ['beɪkɪŋ] n cocción f; **b. dish**, fuente f para horno; **b. powder**, levadura f en polvo; **b. tin**, molde m.

balaclava [bælə'klɑːvə] n pasamontañas m inv.

balance ['bæləns] I n 1 (*scales*) balanza f; *fig* **to hang in the b.**, estar en juego. 2 (*equilibrium*) equilibrio m; *Pol* **b. of power**, equilibrio de fuerzas. 3 *Fin* saldo m; **b. of payments**, balanza f de pagos; **b. sheet**, balance m; **credit b.**, saldo acreedor. 4 (*remainder*) resto m. II vtr 1 poner en equilibrio (**on**, en). 2 (*budget*) equilibrar; **to b. the books**, hacer el balance. 3 (*weigh up*) sopesar. III vi guardar el equilibrio. ◆**balance out** vi (*figures*) corresponderse.

balanced ['bælənst] adj equilibrado,-a.

balcony ['bælkənɪ] n balcón m; *Theat* anfiteatro m.

bald [bɔːld] adj 1 (*person*) calvo,-a. 2 (*tyre*) desgastado,-a. 3 (*style*) escueto,-a.

baldness ['bɔːldnɪs] n 1 (*of person*) calvicie f. 2 (*of tyre*) desgaste m. 3 (*of style*) sencillez f.

bale[1] [beɪl] I n fardo m. II vtr embalar.

bale[2] [beɪl] vtr → **bail**[2]. ◆**bale out** I vi *Av* saltar en paracaídas de un avión. II vtr fig (*person*) sacar de apuros.

Balearic [bælɪ'ærɪk] adj **the B. Islands**, las Islas Baleares.

baleful ['beɪlful] adj funesto,-a, siniestro,-a.

Balkan ['bɔːlkən] adj **the Balkans**, los Balcanes.

ball[1] [bɔːl] n 1 (*in cricket, tennis etc*) pelota f; *Ftb* balón m; (*in billiards, golf etc*) bola f; *fig* **the b. is in your court**, ahora te toca a ti; *fig* **to play b. with sb**, cooperar con algn; *fam* **to be on the b.**, ser un espabilado; *Tech* **b. bearing**, rodamiento m de bolas. 2 (*of paper*) bola f; (*of wool*) ovillo m. 3 US béisbol m; *fig* **it's a whole new b. game**, es otra historia. 4 *vulg offens* **balls**, cojones mpl.

ball[2] [bɔːl] n baile m.

ballad ['bæləd] n balada f.

ballast ['bæləst] n *Naut* lastre m.

ballerina [bælə'riːnə] n bailarina f.

ballet ['bæleɪ] n ballet m; **b. dancer**, bailarín,-ina m,f.

ballistic [bə'lɪstɪk] adj balístico,-a.

ballistics [bə'lɪstɪks] n balística f.

balloon [bə'lu:n] **I** n **1** globo m. **2** (in cartoon) bocadillo m. **II** vi hincharse; fig aumentar rápidamente.

ballot ['bælət] **I** n votación f; **b. box**, urna f; **b. paper**, papeleta f. **II** vtr someter a votación.

ballpoint (pen) ['bɔ:lpɔɪnt ('pen)] n bolígrafo m.

ballroom ['bɔ:lru:m] n salón m de baile.

ballyhoo [bælɪ'hu:] n fam (fuss) jaleo m.

balm [bɑ:m] n bálsamo m.

balmy ['bɑ:mɪ] adj (balmier, balmiest) (weather) suave.

Baltic ['bɔ:ltɪk] adj báltico,-a; **the B. (Sea)**, el (Mar) Báltico.

balustrade [bæləstreɪd] n barandilla f.

bamboo [bæm'bu:] n bambú m.

bamboozle [bæm'bu:zəl] vtr fam **1** (puzzle) dejar perplejo. **2** (trick) engañar, embaucar.

ban [bæn] **I** n prohibición f. **II** vtr **1** (prohibit) prohibir. **2** (exclude) excluir.

banal [bə'nɑ:l] adj banal, trivial.

banana [bə'nɑ:nə] n plátano m, Am banana f; fam **to go bananas**, volverse loco,-a.

band [bænd] **I** n **1** (strip) tira f; (ribbon) cinta f. **2** (stripe) raya f. **3** Rad banda f. **4** (group) grupo m; (of youths) pandilla f; (of thieves) banda f. **II** vi **to b. together**, unirse, juntarse.

bandage ['bændɪdʒ] **I** n venda f. **II** vtr vendar.

Band-Aid® ['bændeɪd] n US tirita® f.

B & B [bi:ən'bi:] n abbr of bed and breakfast.

bandit ['bændɪt] n bandido m.

bandstand ['bændstænd] n quiosco m de música.

bandwagon ['bændwægən] n fig **to jump on the b.**, subirse al tren.

bandy ['bændɪ] **I** vtr (words, ideas) intercambiar. **II** adj (bandier, bandiest) torcido,-a hacia fuera. ◆**bandy about** vtr (ideas) propagar, difundir.

bandy-legged ['bændɪleg(ɪ)d] adj patizambo,-a.

bang [bæŋ] **I** n **1** (blow) golpe m. **2** (noise) ruido m; (explosion) estallido m; (of gun) estampido m; **to shut the door with a b.**, dar un portazo. **II** vtr golpear; **to b. sth shut**, cerrar algo de golpe. **III** vi golpear; **to b. shut**, cerrarse de golpe. **IV** interj (blow) ¡zas!; **b., b.!**, (of gun) ¡pum, pum! **V** adv fam justo.

banger ['bæŋər] n **1** (firework) petardo m. **2** fam (sausage) salchicha f. **3** fam old b., (car) tartana f.

bangle ['bæŋgəl] n brazalete m.

banish ['bænɪʃ] vtr desterrar.

banister ['bænɪstər] n pasamanos m inv.

bank¹ [bæŋk] **I** n **1** Com Fin banco m; **b. account**, cuenta bancaria; **b. card**, tarjeta bancaria; **b. clerk**, empleado, -a m,f de

banca; **b. draft**, letra bancaria; **b. holiday**, fiesta f nacional; **b. statement**, extracto m de cuenta. **2** (in gambling) banca f. **3** (store) banco m. **II** vtr Com Fin depositar, ingresar. **III** vi Com Fin **to b. with**, tener una cuenta en. ◆**bank on** vtr contar con.

bank² [bæŋk] **I** n **1** (mound) loma f; (embankment) terraplén m. **2** (of river) ribera f; (edge) orilla f. **II** vtr & vi Av ladearse.

bankbook ['bæŋkbʊk] n libreta f de ahorros.

banker ['bæŋkər] n banquero,-a m,f.

banking ['bæŋkɪŋ] n banca f.

banknote ['bæŋknəʊt] n billete m de banco.

bankrupt ['bæŋkrʌpt] **I** adj en quiebra; **to go b.**, quebrar. **II** vtr llevar a la bancarrota.

bankruptcy ['bæŋkrʌptsɪ] n quiebra f, bancarrota f.

banner ['bænər] n (in demonstration) pancarta f; (flag) bandera f.

banns [bænz] npl amonestaciones fpl.

banquet ['bæŋkwɪt] n banquete m.

banter ['bæntər] **I** n bromas fpl. **II** vi bromear.

bap [bæp] n bollo m, panecillo m.

baptism ['bæptɪzəm] n bautismo m.

baptize [bæp'taɪz] vtr bautizar.

bar [bɑ:r] **I** n **1** (of gold) barra f; (of chocolate) tableta f; (of soap) pastilla f; Com **b. code**, código m de barras. **2** (of cage) barrote m; fam **to be behind bars**, estar en la cárcel. **3** (obstacle) obstáculo m. **4** Jur (dock) banquillo m; (court) tribunal m. **5** Jur **the B.**, (profession) abogacía f; (body of lawyers) colegio m de abogados. **6** (pub) bar m; (counter) barra f. **7** Mus compás m. **II** vtr **1** (door) atrancar; (road) cortar. **2** (exclude) excluir (from, de). **3** (prohibit) prohibir. **III** prep salvo; **b. none**, sin excepción.

barbarian [bɑ:'beərɪən] adj & n bárbaro,-a (m,f).

barbaric [bɑ:'bærɪk] adj bárbaro,-a.

barbecue ['bɑ:bɪkju:] **I** n barbacoa f. **II** vtr asar a la parrilla.

barbed [bɑ:bd] adj **1 b. wire**, alambre m de púas. **2** fig (remark) mordaz.

barber ['bɑ:bər] n barbero m,f; **b.'s (shop)**, barbería f.

barbiturate [bɑ:'bɪtjʊrɪt] n barbitúrico m.

bare [beər] **I** adj **1** (naked) desnudo,-a; (head) descubierto,-a; (foot) descalzo,-a; (room) sin muebles; **to lay b.**, poner al descubierto; **with his b. hands**, sólo con las manos. **2** (basic) mero,-a; **the b. minimum**, lo mínimo. **II** vtr desnudar; (uncover) descubrir.

bareback(ed) ['beəbæk(t)] adj & adv **to ride b.**, montar un caballo a pelo.

barefaced ['beəfeɪst] adj desvergonzado,-a,

-a.

barefoot ['beəfut] *adj & adv* descalzo,-a.

barely ['beəlɪ] *adv* apenas.

bargain ['bɑːgɪn] **I** *n* 1 *(agreement)* pacto *m*; *(deal)* negocio *m*; **into the b.**, por añadidura, además; **to drive a hard b.**, imponer condiciones duras; **to strike a b.**, cerrar un trato. 2 *(cheap purchase)* ganga *f*; **b. price**, precio *m* de oferta. **II** *vi* 1 negociar. 2 *(haggle)* regatear. ◆**bargain for** *vtr* esperar, contar con.

barge [bɑːdʒ] **I** *n* gabarra *f*. **II** *vtr* **fam to b. into**, *(room)* irrumpir en; *(person)* tropezar con. ◆**barge in** *vi* 1 *(go in)* entrar sin permiso. 2 *(interfere)* entrometerse.

baritone ['bærɪtəʊn] *adj & n* barítono *(m)*.

bark¹ [bɑːk] **I** *n* ladrido *m*. **II** *vi (dog)* ladrar.

bark² [bɑːk] *n Bot* corteza *f*.

barley ['bɑːlɪ] *n* cebada *f*; **b. sugar**, azúcar *m* cande.

barmaid ['bɑːmeɪd] *n* camarera *f*.

barman ['bɑːmən] *n* camarero *m*, barman *m*.

barn [bɑːn] *n* granero *m*; **b. dance**, baile *m* popular.

barnacle ['bɑːnəkəl] *n* percebe *m*.

barometer [bə'rɒmɪtər] *n* barómetro *m*.

baron ['bærən] *n* barón *m*.

baroness ['bærənɪs] *n* baronesa *f*.

baroque [bə'rɒk] *adj* barroco,-a.

barrack ['bærək] *vtr* abuchear.

barracks ['bærəks] *n Mil* cuartel *m sing*.

barrage ['bærɑːʒ] *n* 1 *(dam)* presa *f*. 2 *Mil* barrera *f* de fuego. 3 *fig (of questions)* lluvia *f*.

barrel ['bærəl] *n* 1 *(of wine)* tonel *m*; *(of beer, oil)* barril *m*. 2 *(of firearm)* cañón *m*.

barren ['bærən] *adj* estéril; *(land)* yermo,-a.

barricade [bærɪ'keɪd] **I** *n* barricada *f*. **II** *vtr* levantar barricadas; **to b. oneself in**, parapetarse.

barrier ['bærɪər] *n* barrera *f*.

barrister ['bærɪstər] *n GB* abogado,-a *m,f* (capacitado,-a para ejercer ante tribunales superiores).

barrow ['bærəʊ] *n* carretilla *f*.

bartender ['bɑːtendər] *n US* camarero *m*, barman *m*.

barter ['bɑːtər] *vtr* trocar (**for**, por).

base [beɪs] **I** *n* 1 base *f*; *(foot)* pie *m*; *(of column)* base *f*. **air/naval b.**, base *f* aérea/naval. **II** *vtr* 1 basar, fundar (**on, en**). 2 *(troops)* estacionar. **III** *adj* 1 *(despicable)* bajo,-a, despreciable. 2 *(metals)* común.

baseball ['beɪsbɔːl] *n* béisbol *m*.

baseline ['beɪslaɪn] *n Ten* línea *f* de saque.

basement ['beɪsmənt] *n* sótano *m*.

bash [bæʃ] **I** *n (heavy blow)* golpetazo *m*;

(dent) bollo *m*; *fam (attempt)* intento *m*. **II** *vtr* golpear.

bashful ['bæʃfʊl] *adj* tímido,-a.

basic ['beɪsɪk] **I** *adj* básico,-a; **b. pay**, sueldo *m* base. **II** *npl* **basics**, lo fundamental. ◆**basically** *adv* fundamentalmente.

basil ['bæzɪl] *n* albahaca *f*.

basin ['beɪsən] *n* 1 *(washbowl)* palangana *f*; *(for washing up)* barreño *m*; *(in bathroom)* lavabo *m*; *(dish)* cuenco *m*. 2 *(of river)* cuenca *f*.

basis ['beɪsɪs] *n (pl bases* ['beɪsiːz]) base *f*; **on the b. of**, en base a.

bask [bɑːsk] *vi* tostarse; **to b. in the sun**, tomar el sol.

basket ['bɑːskɪt] *n* cesta *f*, cesto *m*.

basketball ['bɑːskɪtbɔːl] *n* baloncesto *m*.

Basque [bæsk, bɑːsk] *adj* vasco,-a; **B. Country**, País Vasco, Euskadi; **B. flag**, ikurriña *f*; **B. nationalist**, abertzale *mf*. **II** *n* 1 *(person)* vasco,-a *m,f*. 2 *(language)* vasco *m*, euskera *m*.

bass¹ [bæs] *n inv (seawater)* lubina *f*; *(freshwater)* perca *f*.

bass² [beɪs] **I** *n* 1 *(singer)* bajo *m*. 2 *(notes)* graves *mpl*; **b. drum**, bombo *m*; **b. guitar**, bajo *m*. **II** *adj* bajo,-a.

bassoon [bə'suːn] *n* fagot *m*.

bastard ['bɑːstəd, 'bæstəd] **I** *n* 1 bastardo,-a *m,f*. 2 *offens* cabrón *m*, hijo *m* de puta; **poor b.!**, ¡el pobre! **II** *adj* bastardo,-a.

baste [beɪst] *vtr Culin* untar.

bastion ['bæstɪən] *n* baluarte *m*, bastión *m*.

bat¹ [bæt] *n (in cricket, baseball)* bate *m*; *(in table tennis)* pala *f*; *fig* **to do sth off one's own b.**, hacer algo por cuenta propia. **II** *vi (in cricket, baseball)* batear.

bat² [bæt] *n Zool* murciélago *m*.

bat³ [bæt] *vtr fam* **without batting an eyelid**, sin pestañear.

batch [bætʃ] *n (of bread)* hornada *f*; *(of goods)* lote *m*; *Comput* **b. processing**, procesamiento *m* por lotes.

bated ['beɪtɪd] *adj* **with b. breath**, sin respirar.

bath [bɑːθ] *n* 1 baño *m*; **to have a b.**, bañarse; **b. towel**, toalla *f* de baño. 2 *(tub)* bañera *f*. **3 baths**, piscina *f* municipal. **II** *vtr* bañar.

bathe [beɪð] **I** *vi* bañarse. **II** *vtr* 1 *(wound)* lavar. **2 he was bathed in sweat**, *(covered)* estaba empapado de sudor.

bather ['beɪðər] *n* bañista *mf*.

bathing ['beɪðɪŋ] *n* baño *m*; **b. cap**, gorro *m* de baño; **b. costume**, traje *m* de baño; **b. trunks**, bañador *m* de hombre.

bathrobe ['bɑːθrəʊb] *n* albornoz *m*.

bathroom ['bɑːθruːm] *n* cuarto *m* de baño.

bathtub ['bɑːθtʌb] *n* bañera *f*.

baton ['bætən, 'bætɒn] *n* 1 *Mus* batuta *f*.

2 (*truncheon*) porra *f*. 3 *Sport* testigo *m*.

battalion [bə'tæljən] *n* batallón *m*.

batter¹ ['bætə'] *vtr* aporrear, apalear.

batter² ['bætə'] *n* (*in cricket, baseball*) bateador-a, *m,f*.

batter³ ['bætə'] *n Culin* pasta *f* (para rebozar); **fish in b.**, pescado rebozado. II *vtr* rebozar.

battered ['bætəd] *adj* (*car*) abollado,-a; (*person*) maltratado,-a.

battering ['bætərɪŋ] *n* paliza *f*; **to take a b.**, recibir una paliza; *Mil* **b. ram**, ariete *m*.

battery ['bætərɪ] *n* 1 (*for torch, radio*) pila *f*; *Aut* batería *f*. 2 *Jur* **assault and b.**, lesiones *fpl*.

battle ['bætəl] I *n* batalla *f*; *fig* lucha *f*; **to do b.**, librar batalla; *fig* **b. cry**, lema *m*. II *vi* luchar.

battlefield ['bætəlfiːld] *n* campo *m* de batalla.

battleship ['bætəlʃɪp] *n* acorazado *m*.

bauble ['bɔːbəl] *n* chuchería *f*.

bawdy ['bɔːdɪ] *adj* (*joke etc*) verde.

bawl [bɔːl] *vi* gritar, chillar.

bay¹ [beɪ] *n Geog* bahía *f*; (*large*) golfo *m*; **B. of Biscay**, golfo de Vizcaya; **B. of Bengal**, golfo de Bengala.

bay² [beɪ] *n* 1 (*recess*) hueco *m*; **b. window**, ventana salediza. 2 (*in factory*) nave *f*; **cargo b.**, bodega *f* de carga.

bay³ [beɪ] *n* 1 laurel *m*.

bay⁴ [beɪ] I *vi* (*dog*) aullar. II *n* ladrido *m*; *fig* **at b.**, acorralado,-a; *fig* **to keep sb at b.**, mantener a algn a raya.

bayonet ['beɪənɪt] *n* bayoneta *f*.

bazaar [bə'zɑː'] *n* 1 (*market*) bazar *m*. 2 (*Church*) **b.**, (*charity sale*) rastrillo benéfico.

BBC [biːbiː'siː] *abbr of* **British Broadcasting Corporation**, Compañía británica de radiofusión, BBC *f*.

BC [biː'siː] *abbr of* **before Christ**, a.d.C.

be [biː], *unstressed* bɪ] I *vi* (*pres* 1st *person sing* **am**; 3rd *person sing* **is**; 2nd *person sing & all persons pl* **are**; *pt* 1st *& 3rd persons sing* **was**; 2nd *person sing & all persons pl* **were**; *pp* **been**) 1 ser; **he is very tall**, es muy alto; **Madrid is the capital**, Madrid es la capital; **sugar is sweet**, el azúcar es dulce. 2 (*nationality, occupation*) ser; **he's Italian**, es italiano. 3 (*origin, ownership*) ser; **the car is Domingo's**, el coche es de Domingo; **this painting is by Goya**, este cuadro es de Goya. 4 (*price*) costar; (*total*) ser; **a return ticket is £24**, un billete de ida y vuelta cuesta £24; **how much is a kilo of cod?**, ¿a cuánto está el kilo de bacalao?; **how much is it?**, ¿cuánto es? 5 (*temporary state*) estar; **how are you? - I'm very well**, ¿cómo estás? - estoy muy bien; **this soup is cold**, esta sopa está fría; **to be cold/afraid/hungry**, tener frío/miedo/hambre; **to be lucky**, tener

suerte. 6 (*location*) estar; **Aberdeen is in Scotland**, Aberdeen está en Escocia; **Birmingham is two hundred miles from London**, Birmingham está a doscientas millas de Londres. 7 (*age*) tener; **she is thirty (years old)**, tiene treinta años.

II *v aux* 1 (*with pres p*) estar; **he is writing a letter**, está escribiendo una carta; **she was singing**, estaba cantando; **they are leaving next week**, se van la semana que viene; **we have been waiting for a long time**, hace mucho que estamos esperando; **he is coming**, (*emphatic*) es seguro que viene. 2 (*passive*) ser; **he was murdered**, fue asesinado; **she is allowed to smoke**, se le permite fumar. 3 (*obligation*) **I am to see him this afternoon**, debo verle esta tarde; **you are not to smoke here**, no se puede fumar aquí.

III *v impers* 1 (*with there*) haber; **there is, there are**, hay; **there was, there were**, había; **there will be**, habrá; **there would be**, habría; **there have been a lot of complaints**, ha habido muchas quejas; **there were ten of us**, éramos diez. 2 (*with it*) it's late, es tarde; it is said that, se dice que; **who is it?** - it's me, ¿quién es? - soy yo; **what is it?**, ¿qué pasa? 3 (*weather*) it's foggy, hay niebla; it's cold/hot, hace frío/calor. 4 (*time*) ser; it's one o'clock, es la una; it's four o'clock, son las cuatro. 5 (*date*) it's the 11th/Tuesday today, hoy es 11/martes. 6 (*tag questions*) ¿verdad?; ¿no?; it's lovely, isn't it?, es bonito, ¿no?; **you're happy, aren't you?**, estás contento, ¿verdad? **he's not very clever, is he?**, no es muy listo, ¿verdad? 7 (*unreal conditions*) **if I was/were you** ..., yo en tu lugar ...; **if you were a millionaire** ..., si fueras millonario .... 8 *pres & past perfect* (*visit, go*) estar, ir; **I've been to Paris**, he estado en París.

beach [biːtʃ] I *n* playa *f*. II *vtr* varar.

beacon ['biːkən] *n* 1 *Av Naut* baliza *f*. 2 (*lighthouse*) faro *m*.

bead [biːd] *n* 1 (*of necklace etc*) cuenta *f*; **glass b.**, abalorio *m*. 2 (*of liquid*) gota *f*.

beady ['biːdɪ] *adj* (**beadier, beadiest**) (*eyes*) pequeños y brillantes.

beagle ['biːgəl] *n* beagle *m*.

beak [biːk] *n* 1 (*of bird*) pico *m*. 2 *fam* (*nose*) nariz ganchuda.

beaker ['biːkə'] *n* (*tumbler*) taza alta, jarra *f*.

beam [biːm] I *n* 1 *Archit* viga *f*. 2 (*of light*) rayo *m*; *Phys* haz *m*. 3 *Gymn* barra fija. 4 (*smile*) sonrisa *f* radiante. II *vi* 1 (*sun*) brillar. 2 (*smile*) sonreír. III *vtr* 1 (*broadcast*) difundir, emitir. 2 (*transmit*) transmitir.

beaming ['biːmɪŋ] *adj* (*smiling*) radiante.

bean [biːn] *n* alubia *f*, judía *f*, frijol *m*; *fam* **to spill the beans**, descubrir el pastel; **baked beans**, alubias cocidas en salsa de tomate; **broad b.**, haba *f*; **butter b.**, judía; **coffee b.**, grano *m* de café; **green/runner b.**, judía verde; **haricot b.**, alubia; **kidney b.**, frijol.

beansprout ['bi:nspraʊt] *n* brote *m* de soja.

bear¹ [beəʳ] (*pt* bore; *pp* borne) I *vtr* 1 (*carry*) llevar. 2 (*support*) sostener. 3 (*endure*) soportar, aguantar; **I can't b. him**, no lo soporto. 4 (*fruit*) dar; *Fin* (*interest*) devengar. 5 (*resemblance to*) b. a resemblance to, parecerse a. 6 to b. a grudge against sb, guardar rencor a algn; to b. in mind, tener presente. 7 to b. witness, atestiguar. 8 (*pp* born passive only, not followed by by) (*give birth to*) dar a luz; **he was born in Wakefield**, nació en Wakefield. II *vi* (*turn*) girar, torcer; **to b. left**, girar a la izquierda. ◆**bear down** *vi* (*approach*) correr (**on**, sobre). ◆**bear out** *vtr* (*confirm*) confirmar. ◆**bear with** *vtr* tener paciencia con.

bear² [beəʳ] *n* 1 bestia *f*; **b. cub**, osezno *m*; *Astr* **Great B.**, Osa *f* Mayor; **Little B.**, Osa Menor. 2 *Fin* bajista *mf*.

beard [bɪəd] *n* barba *f*.

bearer ['beərəʳ] *n* portador,-a *m/s*; (*of passport, office*) titular *mf*.

bearing ['beərɪŋ] *n* 1 (*posture*) porte *m*. 2 (*relevance*) relación *f*; **to have a b. on**, estar relacionado,-a con. 3 *Tech* cojinete *m*. 4 *Naut* **bearings**, posición *f*, orientación *f*; **to get one's bearings**, orientarse; **to lose one's bearings**, desorientarse.

beast [bi:st] *n* 1 bestia *f*; **b. of burden**, bestia de carga. 2 *fig* bestia *f*, bruto *m*. 3 **beasts**, (*cattle*) reses *fpl*.

beastly ['bi:stlɪ] *adj* (*beastlier, beastliest*) *fam* asqueroso,-a.

beat [bi:t] I *vtr* (*pt* beat; *pp* beaten ['bi:tən]) 1 (*hit*) pegar, golpear; (*clothes*) sacudir; (*drum*) tocar; **off the beaten track**, en un lugar muy apartado; **sl b. it!**, ¡lárgate! 2 *Culin* batir. 3 (*defeat*) batir, vencer; **we b. them 5-2**, les ganamos 5 a 2. 4 to b. a retreat, batirse en retirada. 5 *Mus* (*time*) marcar. 6 to b. the traffic, evitar los embotellamientos de tráfico. 7 *sl* (*puzzle*) extrañar; **it beats me**, no lo entiendo. II *vi* 1 (*heart*) latir. 2 (*strike*) dar golpes; *fig* **to b. about the bush**, andarse por las ramas. III *n* 1 (*of heart*) latido *m*. 2 *Mus* ritmo *m*, compás *m*. 3 (*of policeman*) ronda *f*. IV *adj fam* (*exhausted*) agotado,-a. ◆**beat down** *vi* (*sun*) apretar. ◆**beat off** *vtr* rechazar. ◆**beat up** *vtr fam* dar una paliza a.

beating ['bi:tɪŋ] *n* 1 (*thrashing*) paliza *f*. 2 (*defeat*) derrota *f*. 3 (*of drum*) toque *m*. 4 (*of heart*) latido *m*.

beautician [bju:'tɪʃən] *n* esteticista *mf*.

beautiful ['bju:tɪfʊl] *adj* hermoso,-a,

bello,-a; (*delicious*) delicioso,-a; **b. people**, gente *f* guapa.

beauty [bju:tɪ] *n* belleza *f*, hermosura *f*; **b. contest**, concurso *m* de belleza; **b. queen**, miss *f*; **b. salon**, salón *m* de belleza; **b. spot**, (*on face*) lunar *m*; (*place*) lugar pintoresco.

beaver ['bi:vəʳ] I *n* castor *m*. II *vi* **to b. away at sth**, meterse de lleno en algo.

became [bɪ'keɪm] *pt* → **become**.

because [bɪ'kɒz] I *conj* porque. II *prep* **b. of**, a causa de, debido a.

beckon ['bekən] *vtr & vi* llamar (con la mano); **to b. to sb**, llamar a algn con señas.

becoming [bɪ'kʌmɪŋ] *adj* 1 (*dress*) favorecedor,-a. 2 (*behaviour*) conveniente, apropiado,-a.

bed [bed] *n* 1 cama *f*; **to get out of b.**, levantarse de la cama; **to go to b.**, acostarse; **to make the b.**, hacer la cama; *GB* **b. and breakfast**, (*service*) cama y desayuno *m*; (*sign*) 'pensión'; **b. linen**, ropa *f* de cama. 2 (*of river*) lecho *m*; (*of sea*) fondo *m*. 3 *Geol* capa *f*. 4 (*flower*) **b.**, arriate *m*.

bedbug ['bedbʌg] *n* chinche *mf*.

bedclothes ['bedkləʊðz] *npl*, **bedding** ['bedɪŋ] *n* ropa *f* de cama.

bedlam ['bedləm] *n* algarabía *f*, alboroto *m*.

bedraggled [bɪ'drægəld] *adj* (*wet*) mojado,-a; (*dirty*) ensuciado,-a.

bedridden ['bedrɪdən] *adj* postrado,-a en cama.

bedroom ['bedru:m] *n* dormitorio *m*.

bedside ['bedsaɪd] *n* **at sb's b.**, junto a la cama de algn; **b. table**, mesilla *f* de noche.

bedsit ['bedsɪt] *n fam*, **bedsitter** ['bed'sɪtəʳ] *n* estudio *m*.

bedspread ['bedspred] *n* colcha *f*.

bedtime ['bedtaɪm] *n* hora *f* de acostarse.

bee [bi:] *n* abeja *f*.

beech [bi:tʃ] *n* haya *f*.

beef [bi:f] *n* carne *f* de vaca, *Am* carne de res; **roast b.**, rosbif *m*. ◆**beef up** *vtr fam* reforzar.

beefburger ['bi:fbɜ:gəʳ] *n* hamburguesa *f*.

beefsteak ['bi:fsteɪk] *n* bistec *m*.

beehive ['bi:haɪv] *n* colmena *f*.

beeline ['bi:laɪn] *n fam* **to make a b. for sth**, ir directo hacia algo.

been [bi:n, bɪn] *pp* → **be**.

beep [bi:p] *n* (*of apparatus*) pitido *m*; (*of horn*) pito *m*.

beer [bɪəʳ] *n* cerveza *f*; **a glass of b.**, una caña.

beet [bi:t] *n* remolacha *f*; *US* **red b.**, remolacha.

beetle ['bi:təl] *n* escarabajo *m*.

beetroot ['bi:tru:t] *n* remolacha *f*.

befit [bɪ'fɪt] *vtr* convenir a, corresponder a.

efore [bɪˈfɔːr] I *conj* 1 (*earlier than*) antes de que (+ *subj*), antes de (+ *infin*); **b. she goes**, antes de que se vaya; **b. leaving**, antes de salir. 2 (*rather than*) antes que (+ *infin*). II *prep* 1 (*place*) delante de; (*in the presence of*) ante. 2 (*order, time*) antes de; **b. Christ**, antes de Cristo; **b. long**, dentro de poco; **b. 1950**, antes de 1950; **I saw it b. you**, lo vi antes que tú. III *adv* 1 (*time*) antes; **I have met him b.**, ya lo conozco; **not long b.**, poco antes; **the night b.**, la noche anterior. 2 (*place*) delante, por delante.

eforehand [bɪˈfɔːhænd] *adv* 1 (*earlier*) antes. 2 (*in advance*) de antemano, con anticipación.

efriend [bɪˈfrend] *vtr* trabar amistad con.

eg [beg] I *vtr* 1 (*money etc*) pedir. 2 (*beseech*) rogar, suplicar; **I b. your pardon!**, ¡perdone usted!; **I b. your pardon?**, ¿cómo ha dicho usted? II *vi* 1 (*solicit*) mendigar; (*dog*) pedir; **to b. for money**, pedir limosna. 2 **to b. for help/mercy**, (*beseech*) implorar ayuda/compasión.

egan [bɪˈgæn] *pt* → **begin**.

eggar [ˈbegər] *n* 1 mendigo,-a *m,f*. 2 *fam* euph (*chap*) tío *m*.

egin [bɪˈgɪn] *vtr* & *vi* (*pt* began; *pp* begun) empezar, comenzar; **to b. again**, volver a empezar; **to b. at the beginning**, empezar por el principio; **to b. doing** or **to do sth**, empezar a hacer algo; **to b. with ...**, (*initially*) para empezar ....

eginner [bɪˈgɪnər] *n* principiante *m*.

eginning [bɪˈgɪnɪŋ] *n* 1 principio *m*, comienzo *m*; **at the b. of May**, a principios de mayo; **from the b.**, desde el principio; **in the b.**, al principio. 2 (*origin*) origen *m*.

egonia [bɪˈgəʊnjə] *n* begonia *f*.

egrudge [bɪˈgrʌdʒ] *vtr* dar de mala gana; (*envy*) envidiar.

eguile [bɪˈgaɪl] *vtr* (*charm*) seducir.

egun [bɪˈgʌn] *pp* → **begin**.

ehalf [bɪˈhɑːf] *n* **on b. of**, US **in b. of**, en nombre de, de parte de; **don't worry on my b.**, no te preocupes por mí.

ehave [bɪˈheɪv] *vi* 1 (*person*) portarse, comportarse; **b. yourself!**, ¡pórtate bien!; **to b. well/badly**, portarse bien/mal. 2 (*machine*) funcionar.

ehaviour, US **behavior** [bɪˈheɪvjər] *n* 1 (*of person*) comportamiento *m*, conducta *f*. 2 (*of machine*) funcionamiento *m*.

ehead [bɪˈhed] *vtr* decapitar.

eheld [bɪˈheld] *pt* & *pp* → **behold**.

ehind [bɪˈhaɪnd] I *prep* 1 detrás de; **b. sb's back**, a espaldas de algn; **b. the scenes**, entre bastidores; **to be b. sb**, apoyar a algn; **what motive was there b. the crime?**, ¿cuál fue el móvil del crimen? 2 **b. the times**, (*less advanced than*) anticuado,-a. II *adv* 1 (*in the rear*) detrás,

atrás; **I've left my umbrella b.**, se me ha olvidado el paraguas. 2 **to be b. with one's payments**, (*late*) estar atrasado,-a en los pagos. III *n fam* trasero *m*.

behold [bɪˈhəʊld] *vtr* (*pt* & *pp* beheld) *arch* contemplar.

beige [beɪʒ] *adj* & *n* beige (*m*).

being [ˈbiːɪŋ] *n* 1 ser *m*. 2 (*existence*) existencia *f*; **to come into b.**, nacer.

belated [bɪˈleɪtɪd] *adj* tardío,-a.

belch [beltʃ] I *vi* (*person*) eructar. II *vtr* (*smoke, flames*) vomitar, arrojar. III *n* eructo *m*.

beleaguered [bɪˈliːgəd] *adj* asediado,-a.

belfry [ˈbelfrɪ] *n* campanario *m*.

Belgian [ˈbeldʒən] *adj* & *n* belga (*mf*).

Belgium [ˈbeldʒəm] *n* Bélgica *f*.

Belgrade [belˈgreɪd] *n* Belgrado.

belie [bɪˈlaɪ] *vtr* desmentir.

belief [bɪˈliːf] *n* 1 creencia *f*; **beyond b.**, increíble. 2 (*opinion*) opinión *f*. 3 (*faith*) fe *f*. 4 (*confidence*) confianza *f* (**in**, en).

believe [bɪˈliːv] I *vi* 1 (*have faith*) creer. 2 **to b. in**, (*be in favour of*) ser partidario,-a de. 3 (*think*) creer; **I b. so**, creo que sí. II *vtr* creer.

believer [bɪˈliːvər] *n* 1 *Rel* creyente *mf*. 2 partidario,-a *m,f* (**in**, de).

belittle [bɪˈlɪtl] *vtr* (*person*) menospreciar; (*problem*) minimizar.

bell [bel] *n* (*of church*) campana *f*; (*small*) campanilla *f*; (*of school, door, bicycle etc*) timbre *m*; (*on cat*) cascabel *m*; (*on cow*) cencerro *m*; *fig* **that rings a b.**, eso me suena; **b. jar**, campana; **b. tower**, campanario *m*.

bell-bottoms [ˈbelbotəmz] *npl* pantalones *mpl* de campana.

belligerent [bɪˈlɪdʒərənt] *adj* agresivo,-a.

bellow [ˈbeləʊ] *vi* (*bull*) bramar; (*person*) rugir.

bellows [ˈbeləʊz] *npl* (*pair of*) fuelle *m sing*.

belly [ˈbelɪ] *n* 1 (*of person*) barriga *f*, *fam* flop, panzazo *m*. 2 (*of animal*) panza *f*.

bellyache [ˈbelɪeɪk] *n fam* dolor *m* de vientre.

belong [bɪˈlɒŋ] *vi* 1 pertenecer (**to**, a). 2 (*be a member*) ser socio,-a (**to**, de); *Pol* **to b. to a party**, ser miembro de un partido. 3 (*have a proper place*) corresponder; **this chair belongs here**, esta silla va aquí.

belongings [bɪˈlɒŋɪŋz] *npl* efectos *mpl* personales.

beloved [bɪˈlʌvɪd, bɪˈlʌvd] I *adj* amado,-a, querido,-a. II *n* amado,-a *m,f*.

below [bɪˈləʊ] I *prep* debajo de; **b. average**, por debajo de la media; **ten degrees b. zero**, diez grados bajo cero. II *adv* abajo; **above and b.**, arriba y abajo; **see b.**, véase más abajo.

belt [belt] I *n* 1 cinturón *m*; **blow below the b.**, golpe *m* bajo. 2 *Tech* correa *f*, cinta f. 3 (area) zona f. II vtr sl pegar una paliza a. ◆belt along vi fam ir a todo gas. ◆belt out vtr fam (song) cantar a voz en grito. ◆belt up vi fam callarse.

bemused [bɪ'mjuːzd] adj perplejo,-a.

bench [bentʃ] n 1 (seat) banco m. 2 Parl escaño m. 3 *Jur* the b., (judges) la magistratura. 4 Sport banquillo m. 5 b. mark, Geol cota f de referencia; fig punto m de referencia.

bend [bend] I vtr (pt & pp bent) doblar; (back) encorvar; (head) inclinar; fam to b. the rules, hacer una excepción. II vi 1 doblarse; (road) torcerse. 2 to b. (over), inclinarse; fam he bends over backwards to please her, hace lo imposible por complacerla. III n 1 (in river, road) curva f; (in pipe) recodo m; GB sl round the b., loco,-a perdido,-a. ◆bend down vi inclinarse.

beneath [bɪ'niːθ] I prep (below) bajo, debajo de; fig it's b. him, es indigno de él. II adv debajo.

benefactor ['benɪfæktər] n bienhechor,-a m,f.

beneficial [benɪ'fɪʃəl] adj 1 (doing good) benéfico,-a. 2 (advantageous) beneficioso,-a.

beneficiary [benɪ'fɪʃərɪ] n beneficiario,-a m,f.

benefit ['benɪfɪt] I vtr beneficiar. II vi sacar provecho (from or by, de). III n 1 (advantage) beneficio m, provecho m; for the b. of, en beneficio de; I did it for your b., lo hice por tu bien. 2 (allowance) subsidio m; unemployment b., subsidio de desempleo. 3 (event) función f benéfica.

benevolent [bɪ'nevələnt] adj benévolo,-a.

Bengal [beŋ'gɔːl] n Bengala.

benign [bɪ'naɪn] adj benigno,-a.

bent [bent] I adj 1 (curved) curvado,-a. 2 to be b. on doing sth, (determined) estar empeñado,-a en hacer algo. 3 sl (corrupt) deshonesto,-a. 4 sl (homosexual) gay. II n (inclination) inclinación f (towards, hacia).

benzine ['benziːn] n Chem bencina f.

bequeath [bɪ'kwiːð] vtr Jur legar.

bequest [bɪ'kwest] n Jur legado m.

bereaved [bɪ'riːvd] npl the b., los familiares del/de un difunto.

bereavement [bɪ'riːvmənt] n (mourning) duelo m.

bereft [bɪ'reft] adj b. of, privado,-a de.

beret ['bereɪ] n boina f.

Berlin [bɜː'lɪn] n Berlín.

Bermuda [bə'mjuːdə] n las (Islas) Bermudas; **B. shorts**, bermudas fpl.

Bern [bɜːn] n Berna.

berry ['berɪ] n baya f.

berserk [bə'sɜːk, bə'zɜːk] adj to go b., volverse loco,-a.

berth [bɜːθ] Naut I n 1 (mooring) amarra-

dero m; fig to give sb a wide b., evitar a algn. 2 (bed) litera f. II vi atracar.

beseech [bɪ'siːtʃ] vtr suplicar, implorar.

beset [bɪ'set] vtr (pt & pp beset) acosar; it is b. with dangers, está plagado de peligros.

beside [bɪ'saɪd] prep 1 (next to) al lado de, junto a. 2 (compared with) comparado con. 3 he was b. himself with joy, estaba loco de alegría; that's b. the point, eso no viene al caso; to be b. oneself, estar fuera de sí.

besides [bɪ'saɪdz] I prep 1 (in addition to) además de. 2 (except) excepto, menos; no one b. me, nadie más que yo. II adv además.

besiege [bɪ'siːdʒ] vtr (city) sitiar; fig asediar.

besought [bɪ'sɔːt] pt & pp → beseech.

best [best] I adj (superl of good) mejor; man, ≈ padrino m de boda; her b. friend, su mejor amiga; the b. thing would be to phone them, lo mejor sería llamarles; we had to wait the b. part of a year, tuvimos que esperar casi un año; with b. wishes from Mary, (in letter) con mis mejores deseos, Mary. II adv (superl of well) mejor; as b. I can, lo mejor que pueda; I like this one b., éste es el que más me gusta; the world's b. dressed man, el hombre mejor vestido del mundo. III n lo mejor; all the b.!, que te vaya bien!; at b., a lo más; to be at one's b., estar en plena forma; to do one's b., hacer todo lo posible; to make the b. of sth, sacar el mejor partido de algo; to the b. of my knowledge, que yo sepa.

bestiality [bestɪ'ælɪtɪ] n bestialidad f.

bestow [bɪ'stəʊ] vtr (favour etc) conceder; (honours, power) otorgar (on, a); (title etc) conferir (on, a).

best-seller [best'selər] n best-seller m.

best-selling ['bestselɪŋ] adj a b.-s. author, un autor de superventas.

bet [bet] I n apuesta f. II vtr (pt & pp bet or betted) apostar. III vi apostar (on, por); fam you b.!, ¡y tanto!

Bethlehem ['beθlɪhem] n Belén.

betray [bɪ'treɪ] vtr 1 traicionar. 2 (be unfaithful to) engañar. 3 (reveal) revelar.

betrayal [bɪ'treɪəl] n traición f.

better ['betər] I adj 1 (comp of good) mejor; that's b.!, ¡así está mejor!; the weather is b. than last week, hace mejor tiempo que la semana pasada; to be no b. than, ..., no ser más que ...; to get b., mejorar. 2 (healthier) mejor (de salud). 3 b. off, (better) mejor; (richer) más rico,-a; you'd be b. off going home, lo mejor es que te vayas a casa. 4 the b. part of the day, la mayor parte del día. II adv (comp of well) 1 mejor; all the b., so much the b., tanto mejor; b. and b., cada vez mejor; *prov* b. late than never, más vale tarde que nunca. **2 we had b.** leave, más vale que nos vayamos. **3 to think b.** of, (*plan*) cambiar de. III *n* mejor; a **change for the b.,** una mejora; **to get the b.** of sb, vencer a algn. IV *vtr* 1 (*improve*) mejorar. 2 (*surpass*) superar.

betting ['betɪŋ] *n* apuestas *fpl*; GB **b. shop,** quiosco *m* de apuestas.

between [bɪ'twiːn] I *prep* entre; b. **you and me,** entre nosotros; **closed b. 1 and 2,** cerrado de 1 a 2. II *adv* in b., (*position*) en medio; (*time*) entretanto, mientras (tanto).

beverage ['bevərɪdʒ] *n* bebida *f*.

bevy ['bevɪ] *n* bandada *f*.

beware [bɪ'weər] *vi* tener cuidado (of, con); **b.!,** ¡cuidado!; '**b. of the dog**,' (*sign*) 'cuidado con el perro!'

bewildered [bɪ'wɪldəd] *adj* desconcertado,-a.

bewilderment [bɪ'wɪldəmənt] *n* desconcierto *m*.

bewitching [bɪ'wɪtʃɪŋ] *adj* fascinador,- a.

beyond [bɪ'jɒnd] I *prep* más allá de; **b. belief,** increíble; **b. doubt,** sin lugar a dudas; **it is b. me why ...,** no comprendo por qué ...; **it's b. a joke,** eso ya no tiene gracia; **she is b.** caring, ya no le importa; **this task is b. me,** no puedo con esta tarea. II *adv* más allá, más lejos.

bias ['baɪəs] *n* (*tendency*) tendencia *f* (to- wards, hacia); (*prejudice*) prejuicio *m*.

bias(s)ed ['baɪəst] *adj* parcial; **to be b. against sth/sb,** tener prejuicio en contra de algo/algn.

bib [bɪb] *n* (*for baby*) babero *m*; (*of apron*) peto *m*.

Bible ['baɪbəl] *n* Biblia *f*; *sl* **B. basher, B. thumper,** evangelista *mf*.

bibliography [bɪblɪ'ɒgrəfɪ] *n* bibliografía *f*.

bicarbonate [baɪ'kɑːbənɪt] *n* bicarbonato *m*; **b. of soda,** bicarbonato sódico.

biceps ['baɪseps] *n* bíceps *m*.

bicker ['bɪkər] *vi* reñir.

bicycle ['baɪsɪkəl] *n* bicicleta *f*; **b. pump,** bomba *f* (de aire); **to go by b.,** ir en bicicleta.

bid [bɪd] I *vtr* (*pt* bid *or* bade; *pp* bid *or* bidden ['bɪdən]) 1 (*say*) decir; **to b. sb farewell,** despedirse de algn. 2 (*command*) mandar, ordenar; **she bade him be quiet,** le mandó que se callase. 3 (*invite*) invitar; **he bade me sit down,** me invitó a sentarme. 4 (*at auction*) (*pt & pp* bid) pujar. II *vi* (*at auction*) pujar (for, por). III *n* 1 (*offer*) oferta *f*. 2 (*at auction*) puja *f*. 3 (*attempt*) intento *m*, tentativa *f*.

bidder ['bɪdər] *n* the highest b., el mejor postor.

bidding ['bɪdɪŋ] *n* 1 (*at auction*) puja *f*. 2 (*order*) orden *f*; **to do sb's b.,** cumplir la orden de algn.

bide [baɪd] *vtr* (*pt* bided *or* bode; *pp* bided) esperar; **to b. one's time,** esperar el momento oportuno.

bidet ['biːdeɪ] *n* bidé *m*.

bifocal [baɪ'fəʊkəl] I *adj* bifocal. II *npl* **bifocals** lentes *fpl* bifocales.

big [bɪg] I *adj* (bigger, biggest) grande (gran *before sing noun*); **a b. clock,** un reloj grande; **a b. surprise,** una gran sorpresa; **my b. brother,** mi hermano mayor; *fam iron* **b. deal!,** ¿y qué?; *fam* **b. business,** los grandes negocios; **b. dipper,** montaña rusa; *Astron US* **B. Dipper,** Osa *f* Mayor; **b. toe,** dedo gordo del pie; *fam* **b. gun, b. shot,** pez gordo; *fam* **to make the b. time,** tener éxito; *fam* **b. top,** carpa *f*. II *adv* 1 (*on a grand scale*) a lo grande. 2 (*well*) de manera excepcional.

bigamy ['bɪgəmɪ] *n* bigamia *f*.

bighead ['bɪghed] *n fam* creído,-a *m,f*, engreído,-a *m,f*.

bigheaded [bɪg'hedɪd] *adj* creído,-a, engreído,-a.

bigot ['bɪgət] *n* intolerante *mf*.

bigoted ['bɪgətɪd] *adj* intolerante.

bigotry ['bɪgətrɪ] *n* intolerancia *f*.

bigwig ['bɪgwɪg] *n fam* pez gordo.

bike [baɪk] *n fam* (*abbr of* bicycle *or* motorbike) *n* (*bicycle*) bici *f*; (*motorcycle*) moto *f*; *sl* **on your b.!,** ¡vete de aquí!

bikini [bɪ'kiːnɪ] *n* bikini *m*.

bilateral [baɪ'lætərəl] *adj* bilateral.

bile [baɪl] *n* bilis *f*.

bilingual [baɪ'lɪŋgwəl] *adj* bilingüe.

bill¹ [bɪl] I *n* 1 (*for gas etc*) factura *f*, recibo *m*. 2 *esp GB* (*in restaurant*) cuenta *f*. 3 *Parl* proyecto *m* de ley. 4 *US* (*banknote*) billete *m* de banco. 5 (*poster*) cartel *m*; **on the b.,** en cartel; '**post no bills**,' 'prohibido fijar carteles'; *Theat* **to top the b.,** encabezar el reparto; **b. of exchange,** letra *f* de cambio; *Pol* **B. of Rights,** declaración *f* de derechos. II *vtr* 1 (*send bill to*) facturar. 2 *Theat* programar.

bill² [bɪl] *n* (*of bird*) pico *m*.

Bill [bɪl] *n* dimin of **William**; GB *sl* **the Old B.,** la poli.

billboard ['bɪlbɔːd] *n US* (*hoarding*) cartelera *f*.

billet ['bɪlɪt] I *n* alojamiento *m*. II *vtr* alojar.

billfold ['bɪlfəʊld] *n US* cartera *f*, billetero *m*.

billiards ['bɪljədz] *n* billar *m*.

billion ['bɪljən] *n US* mil millones *mpl*; GB (*former use*) billón *m*.

billionaire [bɪljə'neər] *n* multimillonario,-a *m,f*.

billow ['bɪləʊ] I *n* (*of water*) ola *f*; (*of smoke*) nube *f*. II *vi* (*sea*) ondear; (*sail*) hincharse.

billy goat ['bɪlɪgəʊt] *n* macho cabrío.

bin [bɪn] *n* (*for storage*) cajón *m*; **bread b.,** panera *f*; (*rubbish*) **b.,** cubo *m* de la basura.

binary ['bamərɪ] *adj* b. number, número binario.

bind [baınd] *vtr* (*pt & pp* **bound**) 1 (*tie up*) atar. 2 *Med* (*bandage*) vendar. 3 (*book*) encuadernar. 4 (*require*) obligar. 5 (*join etc*) unir. ◆**bind over** *vtr Jur* obligar legalmente.

binder ['bamdər] *n* (*file*) carpeta *f*.

binding ['baındıŋ] *adj* (*promise*) comprometedor,-a; (*contract*) vinculante.

binge [bındʒ] *n fam* borrachera *f*; **to go on a b.,** irse de juerga.

bingo ['bıŋgəʊ] *n* bingo *m*.

binoculars [bɪ'nɒkjʊləz] *npl* prismáticos *mpl*, gemelos *mpl*.

biochemistry [baɪəʊ'kemɪstrɪ] *n* bioquímica *f*.

biodegradable [baɪəʊdɪ'greɪdəbəl] *adj* biodegradable.

biography [baɪ'ɒgrəfɪ] *n* biografía *f*.

biological [baɪə'lɒdʒɪkəl] *adj* biológico, -a; b. warfare, guerra biológica.

biologist [baɪ'ɒlədʒɪst] *n* biólogo,-a *m,f*.

biology [baɪ'ɒlədʒɪ] *n* biología *f*.

biorhythm ['baɪəʊrɪðəm] *n* biorritmo *m*.

biosphere ['baɪəsfɪər] *n* biosfera *f*.

birch [bɜːtʃ] I *n* 1 *Bot* abedul *m*. 2 (*rod*) vara *f* (de abedul). II *vtr* azotar.

bird [bɜːd] *n* 1 pájaro *m*, ave *f*; *fig* **to kill two birds with one stone**, matar dos pájaros de un tiro; **they're birds of a feather**, son tal para cual; b. **of prey**, ave de rapiña. 2 *GB sl* (*girl*) tía *f*, chica *f*.

birdcage ['bɜːdkeɪdʒ] *n* jaula *f*.

birdie ['bɜːdɪ] *n Golf* birdie *m*.

bird's-eye view [bɜːdzaɪ'vjuː] *n* vista *f* de pájaro.

bird-watcher ['bɜːdwɒtʃər] *n* ornitólogo,-a *m,f*.

Biro® ['baɪrəʊ] *n fam* boli *m*.

birth [bɜːθ] *n* 1 nacimiento *m*; (*childbirth*) parto *m*; **by b.,** de nacimiento; **to give b. to a child,** dar a luz a un niño; b. **certificate,** partida *f* de nacimiento; b. **control,** (*family planning*) control *m* de la natalidad; (*contraception*) métodos anticonceptivos; b. **rate,** índice *m* de natalidad. 2 of noble b., (*parentage*) de noble linaje.

birthday ['bɜːθdeɪ] *n* cumpleaños *m inv*.

birthmark ['bɜːθmɑːk] *n* antojo *m*.

birthplace ['bɜːθpleɪs] *n* lugar *m* de nacimiento.

Biscay ['bɪskeɪ] *n* Vizcaya; **the Bay of B.,** el golfo de Vizcaya.

biscuit ['bɪskɪt] *n* galleta *f*; (*muffin*) bollo *m*, bizcocho *m*; *fam* **that really takes the b.!,** ¡eso ya es el colmo!

bisect [baɪ'sekt] *vtr* bisegmentar; *Geom* bisecar.

bisexual [baɪ'seksjʊəl] *adj* bisexual.

bishop ['bɪʃəp] *n* 1 *Rel* obispo *m*. 2 *Chess* alfil *m*.

bison ['baɪsən] *n inv* bisonte *m*.

bit¹ [bɪt] *n* 1 (*small piece*) trozo *m*, pedazo *m*; **to smash sth to bits,** hacer añicos algo; *fig* **thrilled to bits,** muy emocionado,-a; *fig* **to do one's b.,** poner de su parte. 2 (*small quantity*) poco *m*; a b. **of sugar,** un poco de azúcar; a b. **of advice,** un consejo; a b. **of news,** una noticia; **bits and pieces,** trastos *mpl*; *fig* **b. by b.,** poco a poco. 3 a b., (*slightly*) un poco; a b. **longer,** un ratito más; a b. **worried,** un poco preocupado. 4 (*coin*) moneda *f*.

bit² [bɪt] *n* (*of tool*) broca *f*.

bit³ [bɪt] *n Comput* bit *m*.

bit⁴ [bɪt] *pt* → **bite**.

bitch [bɪtʃ] I *n* 1 *Zool* (*female*) hembra *f*; (*dog*) perra *f*. 2 *fam* (*spiteful woman*) bruja *f*. II *vi fam* **to b. (about),** (*criticize*) criticar.

bitchy ['bɪtʃɪ] *adj fam* (*spiteful*) maldiciente; (*malicious*) malicioso,-a; (*malevolent*) malintencionado,-a.

bite [baɪt] I *n* 1 (*act*) mordisco *m*. 2 (*wound*) mordedura *f*; (*insect*) b., picadura *f*. 3 (*mouthful*) bocado *m*. 4 *fam* (*snack*) bocado *m*. II *vtr* (*pt* **bit**; *pp* **bitten**) morder; (*insect*) picar; **to b. one's nails,** morderse las uñas; *fig* **to b. the dust,** (*suffer defeat*) morder el polvo; (*die*) palmarla; *fam* **to b. sb's head off,** echarle una bronca a algn. III *vi* 1 morder; (*insect*) picar. 2 *fig* (*take effect*) surtir efecto. 3 *Fishing* picar.

biting ['baɪtɪŋ] *adj* (*wind*) cortante; *fig* (*criticism*) mordaz.

bitten ['bɪtən] *pp* → **bite**.

bitter ['bɪtər] I *adj* 1 amargo,-a. 2 (*weather*) glacial; (*wind*) cortante. 3 (*person*) amargado,-a. 4 (*struggle*) enconado,-a; (*hatred*) implacable. II *n* 1 (*beer*) cerveza amarga. 2 **bitters,** biter *m*. ◆**bitterly** *adv* **she was b. disappointed,** sufrió una terrible decepción.

bitterness ['bɪtənɪs] *n* 1 amargura *f*. 2 (*of weather*) crudeza *f*. 3 (*of person*) rencor *m*.

bittersweet ['bɪtəswiːt] *adj* agridulce.

bitumen ['bɪtjʊmɪn] *n* betún *m*.

bizarre [bɪ'zɑːr] *adj* (*odd*) extraño,-a; (*eccentric*) estrafalario,-a.

blab [blæb] *vi fam* parlotear; (*let out a secret*) chivarse.

black [blæk] I *adj* 1 (*colour*) negro,-a; a b. **and white television,** un televisor en blanco y negro; *fig* b. **and blue,** amoratado,-a; **to put sth down in b. and white,** poner algo por escrito; *Av* b. **box,** caja negra; b. **coffee,** café solo; b. **eye,** ojo morado; b. **hole,** agujero negro; b. **humour,** humor negro; b. **magic,** magia negra; b. **market,** mercado negro; b. **pudding,** morcilla *f*; B. **Sea,** Mar Negro; *Aut* b. **spot,** punto negro; *GB* **the B. Country,** la región de los Midlands; *fig*

sheep, oveja negra. 2 (*gloomy*) negro,-a; *fig* **a b. day**, un día aciago. II n 1 (*colour*) negro m. 2 (*person*) negro,-a m,f. III vtr 1 (*make black*) ennegrecer. 2 (*polish*) lustrar. 3 (*boycott*) boicotear. ◆**black out I** vtr 1 (*extinguish lights in*) apagar las luces de. 2 (*censor*) censurar. II vi (*faint*) desmayarse.

blackberry ['blækbəri] n zarzamora f.

blackbird ['blækbɜːd] n mirlo m.

blackboard ['blækbɔːd] n pizarra f, encerado m.

blackcurrant [blæk'kʌrənt] n grosella negra.

blacken ['blækən] vtr 1 (*make black*) ennegrecer. 2 (*defame*) manchar.

blackhead ['blækhed] n espinilla f.

blackjack ['blækdʒæk] n Cards veintiuna f.

blackleg ['blækleg] n esquirol m.

blacklist ['blæklɪst] n lista negra.

blackmail ['blækmeɪl] I n chantaje m. II vtr chantajear.

blackout ['blækaʊt] n 1 (*of lights*) apagón m. 2 Rad TV censura f. 3 (*fainting*) pérdida f de conocimiento.

blacksmith ['blæksmɪθ] n herrero m.

bladder ['blædər] n vejiga f; **gall b.**, vesícula f biliar.

blade [bleɪd] n 1 (*of grass*) brizna f. 2 (*of knife etc*) hoja f. 3 (*of propeller, oar*) pala f.

blame [bleɪm] I n culpa f; **to take the b. for sth**, asumir la responsabilidad de algo. II vtr echar la culpa a; **he is to b.**, él tiene la culpa.

blameless ['bleɪmlɪs] adj (*person*) inocente; (*conduct*) intachable.

blancmange [blə'mɒnʒ] n tipo de budín m dulce.

bland [blænd] adj (*climate*) suave; (*food*) soso,-a.

blank [blæŋk] I adj 1 (*without writing*) en blanco; Fin **b. cheque**, cheque m en blanco. 2 (*empty*) vacío,-a; **a. b. look**, una mirada inexpresiva. 3 **a b. refusal**, (*absolute*) una negativa rotunda. II n 1 (*space*) espacio m en blanco; **to draw a b.**, no tener éxito. 2 Mil cartucho m de fogueo. 3 US (*form*) impreso m.

blanket ['blæŋkɪt] I n manta f; fig capa f. II adj general.

blare [bleər] vi resonar. ◆**blare out** vtr pregonar.

blasé ['blɑːzeɪ] adj de vuelta (de todo).

blasphemous ['blæsfɪməs] adj blasfemo,-a.

blasphemy ['blæsfɪmɪ] n blasfemia f.

blast [blɑːst] I n 1 (*of wind*) ráfaga f. 2 (*of horn etc*) toque m; **at full b.**, a toda marcha. 3 (*explosion*) explosión f; **b. furnace**, alto horno. 4 (*shock wave*) onda f de choque. II vtr 1 (*blow up*) volar; fam **b. (it)!**, ¡maldito sea! 2 fig (*destroy*) arruinar. 3 fig

(*criticize*) criticar.

blasted ['blɑːstɪd] adj maldito,-a.

blast-off ['blɑːstɒf] n despegue m.

blatant ['bleɪtənt] adj (*very obvious*) evidente; (*shameless*) descarado,-a; **a b. lie**, una mentira patente.

blaze¹ [bleɪz] I n 1 (*burst of flame*) llamarada f. 2 (*fierce fire*) incendio m. 3 (*of sun*) resplandor m. 4 fig (*of anger*) arranque m. II vi 1 (*fire*) arder. 2 (*sun etc*) brillar.

blaze² [bleɪz] vtr **to b. a trail**, abrir un camino.

blazer ['bleɪzər] n chaqueta f sport.

bleach [bliːtʃ] I n (*household*) lejía f. II vtr 1 (*whiten*) blanquear; (*fade*) descolorir. 2 (*hair*) decolorar.

bleachers ['bliːtʃəz] npl US Sport (*seats*) gradas fpl.

bleak [bliːk] adj 1 (*countryside*) desolado, -a. 2 (*weather*) desapacible. 3 (*future*) poco prometedor,-a.

bleary ['blɪərɪ] adj (**blearier, bleariest**) (*eyes*) (*due to tears*) lloroso,-a; (*due to tiredness*) cansado,-a.

bleary-eyed ['blɪərɪaɪd] adj con los ojos llorosos or cansados.

bleat [bliːt] I n balido m. II vi (*animal*) balar.

bled [bled] pt & pp → **bleed**.

bleed [bliːd] I vi (pt & pp **bled**) sangrar. II vtr Med **to b. sb dry**, sacarle a algn hasta el último céntimo.

bleeding ['bliːdɪŋ] I n (*loss of blood*) pérdida f de sangre. II n 1 Med sangrante. 2 sl offens puñetero,-a.

bleep [bliːp] I n bip m, pitido m. II vi pitar.

bleeper ['bliːpər] n fam busca m, buscapersonas m inv.

blemish ['blemɪʃ] n (*flaw*) defecto m; (*on fruit*) maca f; fig mancha f; fig **without b.**, sin tacha.

blend [blend] I n mezcla f. II vtr (*mix*) mezclar; (*colours*) armonizar. III vi (*mix*) mezclarse; (*colours*) armonizar.

blender ['blendər] n licuadora f.

bless [bles] vtr (pt & pp **blessed** or **blest**) 1 bendecir; fam **b. you!**, (*after a sneeze*) ¡Jesús! 2 **blessed with good eyesight**, dotado,-a de buena vista.

blessing ['blesɪŋ] n bendición f; (*advantage*) ventaja f; **a mixed b.**, una ventaja relativa.

blew [bluː] pt → **blow**.

blight [blaɪt] I n plaga f. II vtr fig (*spoil*) arruinar; (*frustrate*) frustrar.

blimey ['blaɪmɪ] interj fam ¡caramba!, ¡caray!

blind [blaɪnd] I adj ciego,-a; **a b. man**, un ciego; **a b. woman**, una ciega; fig **b. faith**, fe ciega; fig **to turn a b. eye**, hacer la vista gorda; **b. alley**, callejón m sin salida; Aut **b. corner**, curva f sin visibilidad; **b. spot**, ángulo muerto; fam **b.**

date, cita *f* a ciegas. **II** *adv* a ciegas; *fam* **to get b. drunk**, agarrar una curda. **III** *n* 1 (*on window*) persiana *f*. 2 *pl* the b., los ciegos. **IV** *vtr* 1 cegar, dejar ciego; fig **blinded by ambition**, cegado por la ambición. 2 (*dazzle*) deslumbrar.

blinders ['blaindəz] *npl US* anteojeras *fpl*.

blindfold ['blaindfəuld] **I** *n* venda *f*. **II** *vtr* vendar los ojos a.

blinding ['blaindiŋ] *adj* cegador,-a, deslumbrante.

blindly ['blaindli] *adv* a ciegas, ciegamente.

blindness ['blaindnis] *n* ceguera *f*.

blink [bliŋk] *vi* (*eyes*) pestañear; (*lights*) parpadear.

blinkered ['bliŋkəd] *adj* fig de miras estrechas.

blinkers ['bliŋkəz] *npl* (*on horse*) anteojeras *fpl*.

bliss [blis] *n* felicidad *f*; **it was b.!**, ¡fue maravilloso!

blissful ['blisful] *adj* (*happy*) feliz; (*marvellous*) maravilloso,-a.

blister ['blistə'] **I** *n* (*on skin*) ampolla *f*; (*on paint*) burbuja *f*. **II** *vi* ampollarse.

blithe [blaið] *adj* alegre. ◆**blithely** *adv* alegremente.

blitz [blits] **I** *n* bombardeo aéreo. **II** *vtr* bombardear.

blizzard ['blizəd] *n* ventisca *f*.

bloated ['bləutid] *adj* hinchado,-a.

blob [blɒb] *n* (*drop*) gota *f*; (*spot*) mancha *f*.

bloc [blɒk] *n Pol* bloque *m*.

block [blɒk] **I** *n* 1 bloque *m*; (*of wood*) taco *m*; **in b. capitals**, en mayúsculas. 2 **a b. of flats**, un bloque de pisos. 3 (*group of buildings*) manzana *f*. 4 (*obstruction*) bloqueo *m*. 5 Fin **a b. of shares**, un paquete de acciones. 6 *fam* (*head*) coco *m*. **II** *vtr* 1 (*obstruct*) obstruir; *Aut* 'road blocked', 'carretera cortada'; **to b. the way**, cerrar el paso. 2 Sport (*player*) obstaculizar. 3 Fin Parl bloquear. ◆**block up** *vtr* bloquear, obstruir; **to get blocked up**, (*pipe*) obstruirse.

blockade [blɒ'keid] *n* bloqueo *m*.

blockage ['blɒkidʒ] *n* bloqueo *m*, obstrucción *f*; (*traffic jam*) atasco *m*.

blockbuster ['blɒkbʌstə'] *n fam* exitazo *m*; *Cin TV* gran éxito *m* de taquilla; (*book*) éxito de ventas.

bloke [bləuk] *n fam* tío *m*, tipo *m*.

blond [blɒnd] *adj & n* rubio (*m*).

blonde [blɒnd] *adj & n* rubia (*m*).

blood [blʌd] *n* 1 sangre *f*; **b. bank**, banco *m* de sangre; **b. cell**, glóbulo *m* de sangre; **b. donor**, donante *mf* de sangre; **b. group**, grupo sanguíneo; **b. pressure**, tensión *f* arterial; **b. test**, análisis *m* de sangre; **b. transfusion**, transfusión *f* de sangre; **b. vessel**, vaso sanguíneo; **blue b.**, sangre

azul; **high/low b. pressure**, hipertensión *f*/hipotensión *f*. 2 (*race*) sangre *f*, raza *f*.

bloodbath ['blʌdbɑːθ] *n* fig baño *m* de sangre.

bloodhound ['blʌdhaund] *n* sabueso *m*.

bloodshed ['blʌdʃed] *n* derramamiento *m* de sangre.

bloodshot ['blʌdʃɒt] *adj* inyectado,-a de sangre.

bloodstream ['blʌdstriːm] *n* corriente *f* sanguínea.

bloodthirsty ['blʌdθɜːsti] *adj* sanguinario,-a.

bloody ['blʌdi] **I** *adj* (**bloodier, bloodiest**) 1 (*battle*) sangriento,-a. 2 (*bloodstained*) manchado,-a de sangre. 3 *sl* (*damned*) condenado,-a, puñetero,-a. **II** *adv sl* **it's b. difficult**, ¡joder, qué difícil!; **not b. likely!**, ¡ni de coña!

bloody-minded ['blʌdi'maindid] *adj fam* terco,-a.

bloom [bluːm] **I** *n* 1 (*flower*) flor *f*; **in full b.**, en flor. 2 (*on fruit*) vello *m*. **II** *vi* (*blossom*) florecer.

blooming ['bluːmiŋ] *adj* 1 (*blossoming*) floreciente. 2 *fam euph* (*damned*) maldito,-a, condenado,-a.

blossom ['blɒsəm] **I** *n* (*flower*) flor *f*. **II** *vi* florecer; fig **to b. out**, alcanzar la plenitud.

blot [blɒt] **I** *n* (*of ink*) borrón *m*; fig mancha *f*. **II** *vtr* 1 (*with ink*) emborronar. 2 (*dry*) secar. **III** *vi* (*ink*) correrse. ◆**blot out** *vtr* (*memories*) borrar; (*view*) ocultar.

blotchy ['blɒtʃi] *adj* (*skin etc*) enrojecido,-a; (*paint etc*) cubierto,-a de manchas.

blotting-paper ['blɒtiŋpeipə'] *n* papel *m* secante.

blouse [blauz] *n* blusa *f*.

blow¹ [bləu] *n* golpe *m*; **to come to blows**, llegar a las manos; **it came as a terrible b.**, fue un duro golpe.

blow² [bləu] **I** *vi* (*pt* **blew**, *pp* **blown**) 1 (*wind*) soplar; **to b. shut**, cerrarse de golpe. 2 (*fuse*) fundirse. 3 (*tyre*) reventar. **II** *vtr* 1 (*kiss*) mandar. 2 (*trumpet etc*) tocar; fig **to b. one's own trumpet**, darse bombo. 3 (*one's nose*) sonarse. 4 (*fuse*) fundir. 5 *fam* (*waste*) despilfarrar. 6 *fam* (*chances*) dar al traste con. 7 (*explode*) volar; fig **to b. sb's cover**, descubrir la tapadera de algn; *fam* **to b. one's top**, salirse de sus casillas. ◆**blow away** *vtr* ◆**blow down** *vtr* derribar. ◆**blow off** *vtr* (*by wind*) llevarse. ◆**blow** *vi* (*hat*) salir volando. ◆**blow out** *vtr* apagar. **II** *vi* apagarse. ◆**blow over** *vi* (*storm*) calmarse; (*scandal*) olvidarse. ◆**blow up** *vtr* 1 (*building*) volar. 2 (*inflate*) inflar. 3 Phot ampliar. **II** *vi* (*explode*) explotar.

blowlamp ['bləulæmp] *n* soplete *m*.

blown [bləun] *pp* → **blow**.

blowout ['bləʊaʊt] *n Aut* reventón *m*; *sl* comilona *f*.

blowtorch ['bləʊtɔːtʃ] *n US* soplete *m*.

blow-up ['bləʊʌp] *n Phot* ampliación *f*.

blubber ['blʌbə'] **I** *n* grasa *f* de ballena. **II** *vi* llorar a moco tendido.

bludgeon ['blʌdʒən] *vtr* aporrear; *fig* **to b. sb into doing sth**, forzar a algn a hacer algo.

blue [bluː] **I** *adj* **1** (*colour*) azul; *fig* **once in a b. moon**, de higos a brevas; *fam* **to scream b. murder**, gritar como un loco; **b. jeans**, vaqueros *mpl*, tejanos *mpl*. **2** (*sad*) triste; **to feel b.**, sentirse deprimido. **3** (*obscene*) verde; **b. joke**, chiste *m* verde. **II** *n* **1** (*colour*) azul *m*; *fam* **the boys in b.**, los maderos. **2 out of the b.**, (*suddenly*) de repente; (*unexpectedly*) como llovido del cielo.

bluebell ['bluːbel] *n* campanilla *f*.

blueberry ['bluːbəri] *n* arándano *m*.

bluebottle ['bluːbɒtəl] *n* moscarda *f*, mosca *f* azul.

blue-collar ['bluːkɒlə'] *adj* **b.-c. worker**, obrero, -a *m,f*.

blueprint ['bluːprint] *n* anteproyecto *m*.

blues [bluːz] *npl* **1** *Mus* **the b.**, el blues. **2** *fam* (*sadness*) tristeza *f*, melancolía *f*; **to have the b.**, sentirse deprimido.

bluetit ['bluːtɪt] *n* herrerillo *m* común.

bluff [blʌf] **I** *n* (*trick*) farol *m*; **to call sb's b.**, hacer que algn ponga sus cartas encima de la mesa. **II** *adj* (*abrupt*) brusco,-a; (*forthright*) francote,-a. **III** *vi* tirarse un farol; **to b. one's way through sth**, hacer colar algo.

blunder ['blʌndə'] **I** *n* metedura *f* de pata; *fam* patinazo *m*. **II** *vi* meter la pata, pegar un planchazo.

blunt [blʌnt] **I** *adj* **1** (*knife*) desafilado,-a; (*pencil*) despuntado,-a; **b. instrument**, instrumento *m* contundente. **2** (*frank*) directo,-a, francote,-a; (*statement*) tajante. **II** *vtr* (*pencil*) despuntar; (*knife*) desafilar.
◆**bluntly** *adv* francamente.

blur [blɜː'] **I** *n* aspecto borroso. **II** *vtr* (*windows*) empañar; (*shape*) desdibujar; (*memory*) enturbiar.

blurb [blɜːb] *n* (*in book*) resumen *m*.

blurred [blɜːd] *adj* borroso,-a.

blurt [blɜːt] *vtr* **to b. out**, dejar escapar.

blush [blʌʃ] **I** *n* rubor *m*. **II** *vi* ruborizarse.

blusher ['blʌʃə'] *n* colorete *m*.

blustery ['blʌstəri] *adj* borrascoso,-a.

boar [bɔː'] *n* verraco *m*; **wild b.**, jabalí *m*.

board [bɔːd] **I** *n* **1** (*plank*) tabla *f*. **2** (*work surface*) mesa *f*; (*blackboard*) pizarra *f*; (*for games*) tablero *m*. **3** (*meals provided*) pensión *f*; **full b.**, pensión completa; **b. and lodging**, casa *f* y comida. **4** (*committee*) junta *f*, consejo *m*; **b. of directors**, consejo de administración; **b. room**, sala *f* del consejo. **5** *Naut* **on b.**, a bordo. **6** *fig* **above b.**,

en regla; **across-the-b.**, general; **to let sth go by the b.**, abandonar algo. **II** *vtr* (*ship, plane etc*) embarcarse en, subir a. **III** *vi* **1** (*lodge*) alojarse. **2** (*at school*) estar interno,-a. ◆**board up** *vtr* tapar.

boarder ['bɔːdə'] *n* **1** (*in boarding house*) huésped *mf*. **2** (*at school*) interno,-a *m,f*.

boarding ['bɔːdɪŋ] *n* **1** (*embarkation*) embarque *m*; **b. card**, **b. pass**, tarjeta *f* de embarque. **2** (*lodging*) alojamiento *m*, pensión *f*; **b. house**, pensión *f*; **b. school**, internado *m*.

boast [bəʊst] **I** *n* jactancia *f*, alarde *m*. **II** *vi* jactarse, alardear (**about**, de); **III** *vtr* presumir de, alardear de; **the town boasts an Olympic swimming pool**, la ciudad disfruta de una piscina olímpica.

boat [bəʊt] *n* (*small*) barca *f*, bote *m*; (*launch*) lancha *f*; (*large*) buque *m*; *fig* **we're all in the same b.**, todos estamos en el mismo barco; **fishing b.**, barco de pesca.

boater ['bəʊtə'] *n* canotié *m*, canotier *m*.

boatswain ['bəʊsən] *n* contramaestre *m*.

boatyard ['bəʊtjɑːd] *n* astillero *m*.

bob [bɒb] **I** *n* **1** (*haircut*) pelo *m* a lo chico. **2** *fam inv* (*shilling*) chelín *m*. **II** *vi* **to b. up and down**, subir y bajar.

bobbin ['bɒbɪn] *n* (*of sewing machine*) canilla *f*; (*for lace-making*) bolillo *m*.

bobby ['bɒbɪ] *n fam* (*policeman*) poli *m*.

bobsleigh ['bɒbsleɪ] *n* bobsleigh *m*.

bode[1] [bəʊd] *pt* → **bide**.

bode[2] [bəʊd] *vtr* & *vi* presagiar; **to b. well/ill**, ser de buen/mal agüero.

bodice ['bɒdɪs] *n* **1** (*sleeveless undergarment*) corpiño *m*. **2** (*of dress*) cuerpo *m*.

bodily ['bɒdɪlɪ] **I** *adj* físico,-a; **b. harm**, daños *mpl* corporales. **II** *adv* **to carry sb b.**, llevar a algn en brazos.

body ['bɒdɪ] *n* **1** cuerpo *m*; **b. language**, expresión *f* corporal; **b. odour**, olor *m* corporal. **2** (*corpse*) cadáver *m*. **3** (*main part*) parte *f* principal. **4** *Aut* carrocería *f*; *Naut* casco *m*. **5** (*organization*) organismo *m*; (*profession*) cuerpo *m*; **the b. politic**, el estado. **6** (*group of people*) conjunto *m*, grupo *m*.

body-blow ['bɒdɪbləʊ] *n fig* duro golpe *m*.

body-builder ['bɒdɪbɪldə'] *n* culturista *mf*.

body-building ['bɒdɪbɪldɪŋ] *n* culturismo *m*.

bodyguard ['bɒdɪgɑːd] *n* guardaespaldas *mf inv*.

bodywork ['bɒdɪwɜːk] *n Aut* carrocería *f*.

Boer ['bəʊə'] *adj* **the B. War**, la guerra del Transvaal.

bog [bɒg] *n* **1** ciénaga *f*. **2** *sl* (*lavatory*) meódromo *m*. ◆**bog down** *vtr* **to get bogged down**, atascarse.

bogey ['bəʊgɪ] *n* **1** (*spectre*) espectro *m*, fantasma *m*. **2** (*bugbear*) pesadilla *f*. **3**

Golf bogey m. **4** *sl* (*mucus*) moco m.

boggle ['bɒgəl] vi *fam* the mind boggles, ¡es alucinante!

bogus ['bəʊgəs] adj falso,-a; b. company, compañía fantasma.

boil¹ [bɔɪl] I n to come to the b., empezar a hervir. II *vtr* (*water*) hervir; (*food*) cocer; (*egg*) cocer, pasar por agua. III *vi* hervir; *fig* to b. with rage, estar furioso. ◆**boil down** vi reducirse (to, a). ◆**boil over** vi (*milk*) salirse.

boil² [bɔɪl] n *Med* furúnculo m.

boiled [bɔɪld] adj b. egg, huevo cocido or pasado por agua.

boiler ['bɔɪləʳ] n caldera f; b. suit, mono m.

boiling ['bɔɪlɪŋ] adj b. water, agua hirviendo; it's b. hot, (*food*) quema; (*weather*) hace un calor agobiante; b. point, punto m de ebullición.

boisterous ['bɔɪstərəs] adj 1 (*person, party*) bullicioso,-a. 2 (*weather*) borrascoso,-a.

bold [bəʊld] adj 1 (*brave*) valiente. 2 (*daring*) audaz. 3 (*features*) marcado,-a; *Typ* b. type, negrita f. 4 (*impudent*) descarado,-a.

Bolivia [bə'lɪvɪə] n Bolivia.

Bolivian [bə'lɪvɪən] adj & n boliviano,-a (m,f).

bollard ['bɒlɑːd] n *Aut* baliza f.

bollocks ['bɒləks] npl vulg cojones mpl; b.!, (*disagreement*) ¡y un huevo!

Bolshevik ['bɒlʃəvɪk] adj & n bolchevique (mf).

bolster ['bəʊlstəʳ] I n (*pillow*) cabezal m, travesaño m. II *vtr* (*strengthen*) reforzar; (*support*) apoyar.

bolt [bəʊlt] I n 1 (*on door*) cerrojo m; (*small*) pestillo m. 2 *Tech* perno m, tornillo m. 3 (*of lightning*) rayo m. 4 (*crossbow*) flecha f. II *vtr* 1 (*lock*) cerrar con cerrojo. 2 *Tech* sujetar con pernos. 3 *fam* (*food*) engullir. III *vi* (*person*) largarse; (*horse*) desbocarse. IV *adv* b. upright, derecho.

bomb [bɒm] I n bomba f; *GB sl* to cost a b., costar un ojo de la cara; b. disposal squad, brigada f de artificieros; b. scare, amenaza f de bomba; car b., coche-bomba m; letter b., carta-bomba f. II *vtr* (*city etc*) bombardear; (*by terrorists*) volar. III *vi fam* to b. (along), (*car*) ir a toda pastilla.

bombard [bɒm'bɑːd] *vtr* bombardear.

bombardment [bɒm'bɑːdmənt] n bombardeo m.

bombastic [bɒm'bæstɪk] adj rimbombante.

bomber ['bɒməʳ] n 1 *Av* bombardero m; b. jacket, cazadora f. 2 *terrorist* mf que coloca bombas.

bombshell ['bɒmʃel] n 1 *Mil* obús m. 2 *fig* (*surprise*) bomba f. 3 *fam* a blonde b., una rubia explosiva.

bona fide [bəʊnə'faɪdɪ] adj 1 (*genuine*) auténtico,-a. 2 (*in good faith*) bienintencionado,-a.

bond [bɒnd] I n 1 (*link*) lazo m, vínculo m. 2 *Fin* bono m. 3 *Jur* (*bail*) fianza f. 4 (*binding agreement*) acuerdo m. 5 (*warehouse*) depósito m; in b., en depósito. 6 *US* (*guarantee*) garantía f. 7 bonds, (*shackles*) cadenas fpl. II *vtr* 1 (*join*) pegar. 2 (*merchandise*) poner en depósito.

bondage ['bɒndɪdʒ] n esclavitud f.

bone [bəʊn] I n hueso m; (*in fish*) espina f; *fig* b. of contention, manzana f de la discordia; *fig* to make no bones about sth, no andarse con rodeos en un asunto; b. china, porcelana fina. 2 bones, (*remains*) restos mpl; the bare bones, lo esencial. II *vtr* (*meat*) deshuesar; (*fish*) quitar las espinas a. ◆**bone up on** *vtr fam* empollar.

bone-dry [bəʊn'draɪ] adj completamente seco,-a.

bone-idle [bəʊn'aɪdl] adj gandul,-a.

bonfire ['bɒnfaɪəʳ] n hoguera f, fogata f; B. Night, noche f del cinco de noviembre.

bonkers ['bɒŋkəz] adj *GB sl* chalado,-a.

bonnet ['bɒnɪt] n 1 (*child's*) gorra f. 2 *Aut* capó m.

bonus ['bəʊnəs] n 1 (*on wages*) prima f. 2 *Fin* (*on shares*) dividendo m extraordinario. 3 *GB Ins* beneficio m.

bony ['bəʊnɪ] adj (bonier, boniest) (*person*) huesudo,-a; (*fish*) lleno,-a de espinas.

boo [buː] I interj ¡bu!. II n abucheo m. III *vtr* abuchear.

boob [buːb] n *GB sl* 1 (*silly mistake*) patinazo m. 2 boobs, (*breasts*) tetas fpl.

booby ['buːbɪ] n b. prize, premio m de consolación; b. trap, trampa f; *Mil* trampa explosiva.

boogie ['buːgɪ] vi *fam* bailar.

book [bʊk] I n 1 libro m; *fig* in my b., según mi punto de vista; *fig* by the b., según las reglas; b. end, sujetalibros m inv; *GB* b. token, vale m para comprar libros; savings b., libreta f de ahorros. 2 (*of stamps*) carpeta f; (*of matches*) cajetilla f. 3 *Com* books, cuentas fpl; to keep the books, llevar las cuentas. II *vtr* 1 (*reserve*) reservar; (*return flight*) cerrar. 2 (*engage*) contratar. 3 (*by police*) poner una multa a. 4 *Ftb* amonestar. ◆**book into** *vtr* (*hotel*) reservar una habitación en. ◆**book out** vi (*of hotel*) marcharse. ◆**book up** *vtr* booked up, completo.

booking ['bʊkɪŋ] n *esp GB* (*reservation*) reserva f; b. office, taquilla f.

bookmaker ['bʊkmeɪkəʳ] n corredor,-a m,f de apuestas.

bookseller ['bʊkseləʳ] n librero,-a m,f.

bookshelf ['bʊkʃelf] n bookshelves, estantería f sing.

bookshop ['bukʃɒp] n librería f.

bookstall ['bukstɔ:l] n quiosco m.

bookstore ['bukstɔ:r] n US librería f.

bookworm ['bukwɜ:m] n fam ratón m de biblioteca.

boom¹ [bu:m] I n 1 (noise) estampido m, trueno m. 2 (sudden prosperity) boom m, auge m. II vi 1 (thunder) retumbar; (cannon) tronar. 2 (prosper) estar en auge.

boom² [bu:m] n (of microphone) jirafa f.

boomerang ['bu:məræŋ] n bumerang m, bumerán m.

booming ['bu:mɪŋ] adj 1 (voice, thunder) que retumba. 2 (prosperous) en auge.

boon [bu:n] n (blessing) bendición f.

boost [bu:st] I n estímulo m, empuje m. II vtr 1 (increase) aumentar. 2 to b. sb's confidence, subirle la moral a algn. 3 (tourism, exports) fomentar. 4 (voltage) elevar.

booster ['bu:stər] n 1 Elec elevador m de voltaje. 2 Rad TV (amplifier) amplificador m. 3 Med b. (shot), revacunación f.

boot¹ [bu:t] I n 1 bota f; (short) botín m; fig he's too big for his boots, es muy creído; fam to put the b. in, pisotear; fam she got the b., la echaron del trabajo; b. polish, betún m. 2 GB Aut maletero m. II vtr fam 1 Ftb (ball) chutar. 2 to b. (out), echar a patadas.

boot² [bu:t] n to b., además.

bootblack ['bu:tblæk] n esp US limpiabotas mf inv.

booth [bu:ð, bu:θ] n 1 (in language lab etc) cabina f; telephone b., cabina telefónica. 2 (at fair) puesto m.

bootleg ['bu:tleg] adj de contrabando.

bootlegger ['bu:tlegər] n contrabandista m.

booty ['bu:tɪ] n botín m.

booze [bu:z] fam I n priva f. II vi privar.

bop [bɒp] I n 1 Mus be-bop m. 2 fam (dance) baile m. II vi fam (dance) bailar.

Bordeaux [bɔ:'dəu] n 1 (city) Burdeos. 2 (wine) burdeos m.

border ['bɔ:dər] I n 1 borde m, margen m. 2 Sew ribete m. 3 (frontier) frontera f; b. town, pueblo fronterizo. 4 (flower bed) arriate m. III vtr Sew ribetear. ◆**border on** vtr 1 Geog lindar con. 2 fig rayar en.

borderline ['bɔ:dəlaɪn] I n 1 (border) frontera f. 2 (dividing line) línea divisoria. II adj 1 (on the border) fronterizo,-a. 2 fig (case etc) dudoso,-a.

bore¹ [bɔ:r] I vtr Tech taladrar, perforar. II n 1 Tech (hole) taladro m. 2 (of gun) calibre m.

bore² [bɔ:r] I vtr aburrir. II n (person) pesado,-a m,f, pelma mf; (thing) lata f, rollo m; what a b.!, ¡qué rollo!

bore³ [bɔ:r] pt → **bear¹**.

bored [bɔ:d] adj aburrido,-a; to be b. stiff or to tears, estar aburrido,-a como una ostra.

boredom ['bɔ:dəm] n aburrimiento m.

boring ['bɔ:rɪŋ] adj (uninteresting) aburrido,-a; (tedious) pesado,-a, latoso,-a.

born [bɔ:n] I pp → **bear¹**; to be b., nacer; I wasn't b. yesterday, no nací ayer. II adj (having natural ability) nato,-a; b. poet, poeta nato.

born-again ['bɔ:nəgen] adj Rel converso,-a.

borne [bɔ:n] pp → **bear¹**.

borough ['bʌrə] n 1 (town) ciudad f; US (municipality) municipio m. 2 esp GB (constituency) distrito m electoral.

borrow ['bɒrəu] I vtr 1 pedir or tomar prestado; can I b. your pen?, ¿me dejas tu bolígrafo? 2 (ideas etc) apropiarse. II vi pedir or tomar prestado.

borstal ['bɔ:stəl] n GB fam reformatorio m.

bosom ['buzəm] n 1 (breast) pecho m; (breasts) pechos mpl; b. friend, amigo,-a m,f del alma. 2 fig seno m.

boss [bɒs] I n 1 (head) jefe,-a m,f; (factory owner etc) patrón,-ona m,f. 2 esp US Pol jefe m; pej cacique m. II vtr to b. sb about or around, mandar sobre algn.

bossy ['bɒsɪ] adj (bossier, bossiest) fam mandón,-ona.

bosun ['bəusən] n contramaestre m.

botanic(al) [bə'tænɪk(əl)] adj botánico,-a; b. garden, jardín botánico.

botany ['bɒtənɪ] n botánica f.

botch [bɒtʃ] I vtr chapucear; a botched job, una chapuza f. II n chapuza f.

both [bəuθ] I adj ambos,-as, los dos, las dos; b. men are teachers, ambos son profesores; hold it with b. hands, sujétalo con las dos manos. II pron b. (of them), ambos,-as, los dos, las dos; b. of you, vosotros dos. III conj a la vez; b. England and Spain are in Europe, tanto Inglaterra como España están en Europa.

bother ['bɒðər] I vtr 1 (disturb) molestar; (be a nuisance to) dar la lata a. 2 (worry) preocupar; I can't be bothered, no tengo ganas. II vi molestarse; don't b. about me, no te preocupes por mí; he didn't b. shaving, no se molestó en afeitarse. III n 1 (disturbance) molestia f; (nuisance) lata f. 2 (trouble) problemas mpl. IV interj ¡GB maldito sea!

bothersome ['bɒðəsəm] adj molesto,-a.

bottle ['bɒtəl] I n 1 botella f; (of perfume, ink) frasco m; fam to hit the b., darle a la bebida; baby's b., biberón m; b. opener, abrebotellas m inv. 2 GB sl to have a lot of b., (nerve) tener muchas agallas. II vtr (wine) embotellar; (fruit) enfrascar. ◆**bottle out** vi GB sl encogerse. ◆**bottle up** vtr reprimir.

bottle-bank ['bɒtəlbæŋk] n contenedor m de vidrio.

bottled ['bɒtəld] adj (beer, wine) en botella, embotellado,-a; (fruit) envasado,-a.

bottle-green ['bɒtlgriːn] *adj* verde botella.

bottleneck ['bɒtlnek] *n* Aut embotellamiento *m*, atasco *m*.

bottom ['bɒtəm] I *adj* 1 *(lowest)* más bajo,-a; *(drawer, shelf)* de abajo; Aut **b. gear**, primera *f*. 2 *(last)* último,-a; **b. line**, Fin saldo *m* final; *fig* resultado *m* final. II *n* 1 parte *f* inferior; *(of sea, garden, street, box)* fondo *m*; *(of bottle)* culo *m*; *(of page, hill)* pie *m*; Educ **to be (at) the b. of the class**, ser el último *or* la última de la clase; **to touch b.**, tocar fondo; *fam* **bottoms up!**, ¡salud! 2 **to get to the b. of a matter**, llegar al meollo de una cuestión; *fig* ¿quién está detrás de todo esto? 3 *(buttocks)* trasero *m*. ◆**bottom out** *vi* Fin tocar fondo.

bottomless ['bɒtəmlɪs] *adj* *(pit)* sin fondo; *(mystery)* insondable.

boudoir ['buːdwɑːr] *n* tocador *m*.

bough [baʊ] *n* rama *f*.

bought [bɔːt] *pt & pp* → **buy**.

bouillon ['buːjɒn] *n* caldo *m*.

boulder ['bəʊldər] *n* canto rodado.

boulevard ['buːlvɑːr] *n* bulevar *m*.

bounce [baʊns] I *vi* 1 *(ball)* rebotar. 2 *(jump)* saltar. 3 *sl* *(cheque)* ser rechazado (por el banco). II *vtr* *(ball)* botar. III *n* 1 *(of ball)* bote *m*. 2 *(jump)* salto *m*. 3 *(energy)* vitalidad *f*. ◆**bounce back** *vi* *(recover health)* recuperarse, recobrarse.

bouncer ['baʊnsər] *n* *sl* gorila *m*.

bound¹ [baʊnd] *adj* 1 *(tied up)* atado,-a. 2 *(obliged)* encuadernado,-a. 3 *(obliged)* obligado,-a. **b. (up)**, *(linked)* vinculado,-a *(with, a)*. 5 **it's b. to happen**, sucederá con toda seguridad; **it was b. to fail**, estaba destinado al fracaso.

bound² [baʊnd] I *vi* saltar. II *n* salto *m*.

bound³ [baʊnd] *adj* **b. for**, con destino a, rumbo a; **to be b. for**, dirigirse a.

boundary ['baʊndərɪ] *n* límite *m*.

boundless ['baʊndlɪs] *adj* ilimitado,-a, sin límites.

bounds [baʊndz] *npl* **beyond the b. of reality**, más allá de la realidad; **her ambition knows no b.**, su ambición no conoce límites; **the river is out of b.**, está prohibido bajar al río.

bounty ['baʊntɪ] *n* prima *f*, gratificación *f*.

bouquet [buːˈkeɪ, bəʊˈkeɪ] *n* 1 *(of flowers)* ramillete *m*. 2 [buːˈkeɪ] *(of wine)* aroma *m*, buqué *m*.

bourbon ['bɜːbən] *n* bourbon *m*.

bourgeois ['bʊəʒwɑː] *adj & n* burgués, -esa *(m,f)*.

bourgeoisie [bʊəʒwɑːˈziː] *n* burguesía *f*.

bout [baʊt] *n* 1 *(of work)* turno *m*; *(of illness)* ataque *m*. 2 Box combate *m*.

boutique [buːˈtiːk] *n* boutique *f*, tienda *f*.

bow¹ [baʊ] I *vi* 1 hacer una reverencia. 2

(give in) ceder. II *n* *(with head, body)* reverencia *f*. ◆**bow out** *vi* retirarse *(of, de)*.

bow² [bəʊ] I *n* Sport & Mus arco *m*; *fig* **to have more than one string to one's b.**, ser una persona de recursos. 2 *(knot)* lazo *m*; **b. tie**, pajarita *f*.

bow³ [baʊ] *n* esp Naut proa *f*.

bowel ['baʊəl] *n* 1 intestino *m*. 2 **bowels**, entrañas *fpl*.

bowl¹ [bəʊl] *n* 1 *(dish)* cuenco *m*; *(for soup)* tazón *m*; *(for washing hands)* palangana *f*; *(for washing clothes, dishes)* barreño *m*; *(of toilet)* taza *f*. 2 Geol cuenca *f*.

bowl² [bəʊl] *n* bola *f*. II *vtr* *(in cricket)* lanzar. III *vi* 1 *(play bowls)* jugar a los bolos. 2 *(in cricket)* lanzar la pelota. ◆**bowl along** *vi* *fam* *(car)* ir volando. ◆**bowl out** *vtr* *(in cricket)* eliminar. ◆**bowl over** *vtr* 1 *(knock down)* derribar. 2 *fig* *(astonish)* desconcertar.

bow-legged ['bəʊleg(ɪ)d] *adj* patizambo,-a.

bowler¹ ['bəʊlər] *n* *(in cricket)* lanzador,-a *m,f*.

bowler² ['bəʊlər] *n* *(hat)* bombín *m*.

bowling ['bəʊlɪŋ] *n* *(game)* bolos *mpl*; **b. alley**, bolera *f*; **b. green**, campo *m* de bolos.

bowls [bəʊlz] *npl* Sport bolos *mpl*.

box¹ [bɒks] *n* 1 caja *f*; *(large)* cajón *m*; *(of matches)* cajetilla *f*; **jewellery b.**, joyero *m*; Theat **b. office**, taquilla *f*; **b. office success**, éxito taquillero. 2 Press recuadro *m*. 3 *fur* *(witness)* **b.**, barra *f* de los testigos. 4 Theat palco *m*. 5 GB *fam* *(television)* caja tonta. II *vtr* *(pack)* embalar.

box² [bɒks] *n* Sport I *vi* boxear. II *vtr* *(hit)* pegar; **to b. sb's ears**, dar un cachete a algn.

boxer ['bɒksər] *n* 1 Box boxeador *m*. 2 *(dog)* bóxer *m*.

boxing ['bɒksɪŋ] *n* boxeo *m*; **b. ring**, cuadrilátero *m*.

Boxing Day ['bɒksɪŋdeɪ] *n* GB el día de San Esteban (26 de diciembre).

boxroom ['bɒksruːm] *n* trastero *m*.

boy [bɔɪ] *n* 1 *(child)* niño *m*, chico *m*; *(youth)* joven *m*; *fam* **oh b.!**, ¡vaya! 2 *(son)* hijo *m*.

boycott ['bɔɪkɒt] I *n* boicot *m*. II *vtr* boicotear.

boyfriend ['bɔɪfrend] *n* novio *m*; *(live-in)* compañero *m*.

boyhood ['bɔɪhʊd] *n* niñez *f*, juventud *f*.

boyish ['bɔɪɪʃ] *adj* juvenil, de muchacho.

bra [brɑː] *n* *abbr* de **brassiere**.

brace [breɪs] *n* 1 *(clamp)* abrazadera *f*; *(of drill)* berbiquí *m*; *(for teeth)* aparato *m*. 2 *(of wood)* puntal *m*. 3 *(pair)* par *m*. 4 GB **braces**, tirantes *mpl*. II *vtr* 1 *(wall)* apuntalar. 2 *(strengthen)* reforzar. 3 **to b. oneself**, prepararse (for, para). ◆**brace**

up *vi* cobrar ánimo.

bracelet [ˈbreɪslɪt] *n* pulsera *f*.

bracing [ˈbreɪsɪŋ] *adj* (*wind*) fresco,-a; (*stimulating*) tonificante.

bracken [ˈbrækən] *n* helecho *m*.

bracket [ˈbrækɪt] **I** *n* **1** *Typ* (*round*) paréntesis *m*; (*square*) corchete *m*; (*curly*) llave *f*; **in brackets**, entre paréntesis. **2** (*support*) soporte *m*; (*for lamp*) brazo *m*; (*shelf*) repisa *f*. **3** (*for tax*) sector *m*. **II** *vtr* **1** *Ling* (*phrase etc*) poner entre paréntesis. **2** (*group together*) agrupar, juntar.

brag [bræg] *vi* jactarse (**about**, de).

braggart [ˈbrægət] *n* fanfarrón,-ona *m,f*.

braid [breɪd] **I** *vtr* trenzar. **II** *n* **1** *Sew* galón *m*. **2** *esp US* (*plait*) trenza *f*.

Braille [breɪl] *n* Braille *m*.

brain [breɪn] *n* **1** cerebro *m*; **she's got cars on the b.**, está obsesionada por los coches; *fig* **b. drain**, fuga *f* de cerebros; **b. wave**, idea *f* genial. **2** *fam* **brains**, inteligencia *f*; **to have brains**, ser inteligente; **b. trust**, grupo *m* de expertos. **3** *Culin* **brains**, sesos *mpl*.

brainchild [ˈbreɪntʃaɪld] *n* invento *m*, idea *f* genial.

brainpower [ˈbreɪnpaʊəʳ] *n* capacidad *f* intelectual.

brainstorm [ˈbreɪnstɔːm] *n* **1** (*outburst*) arranque *m*. **2** (*brain wave*) genialidad *f*, lluvia *f* de ideas.

brainwash [ˈbreɪnwɒʃ] *vtr* lavar el cerebro a.

brainy [ˈbreɪnɪ] *adj* (*brainier, brainiest*) *fam* listo,-a.

braise [breɪz] *vtr* cocer a fuego lento.

brake [breɪk] **I** *n* *Aut* (*also pl*) freno *m*; **b. drum**, tambor *m* del freno; **b. fluid**, líquido *m* de frenos; **b. light**, luz *f* de freno. **II** *vi* frenar, echar el freno.

bramble [ˈbræmbəl] *n* zarza *f*, zarzamora *f*.

bran [bræn] *n* salvado *m*.

branch [brɑːntʃ] **I** *n* (*of tree*) rama *f*; (*of road*) bifurcación *f*; (*of science etc*) ramo *m*; *Com* **b.** (*office*), sucursal *f*. **II** *vi* (*road*) bifurcarse. ◆**branch off** *vi* desviarse. ◆**branch out** *vi* diversificarse.

brand [brænd] **I** *n* **1** *Com* marca *f*; **b. name**, marca de fábrica. **2** (*type*) clase *f*. **3** (*on cattle*) hierro *m*. **II** *vtr* **1** (*animal*) marcar con hierro candente. **2** (*label*) tildar.

brandish [ˈbrændɪʃ] *vtr* blandir.

brand-new [ˈbrændˈnjuː] *adj* flamante.

brandy [ˈbrændɪ] *n* coñac *m*, brandy *m*.

brash [bræʃ] *adj* **1** (*impudent*) descarado,-a. **2** (*reckless*) temerario,-a. **3** (*loud, showy*) chillón,-ona.

brass [brɑːs] *n* **1** latón *m*; *sl* (*money*) pasta *f*; **b.** instrumentos *mpl* de metal; **b. band**, banda *f* de metal.

brassiere [ˈbræzɪəʳ] *n* sostén *m*, sujetador

m.

brat [bræt] *n* *fam* mocoso,-a *m,f*.

bravado [brəˈvɑːdəʊ] *n* bravuconería *f*.

brave [breɪv] **I** *adj* valiente, valeroso,-a. **II** *n* *US* (*Indian*) b., guerrero *m* indio. **III** *vtr* **1** (*face*) hacer frente a. **2** (*defy*) desafiar. ◆**bravely** *adv* valientemente.

bravery [ˈbreɪvərɪ] *n* valentía *f*, valor *m*.

bravo [brɑːˈvəʊ] *interj* ¡bravo!

brawl [brɔːl] **I** *n* reyerta *f*. **II** *vi* pelearse.

brawn [brɔːn] *n* **1** (*strength*) fuerza física. **2** *Culin GB* carne *f* de cerdo adobada.

bray [breɪ] **I** *n* (*of donkey*) rebuzno *m*. **II** *vi* rebuznar.

brazen [ˈbreɪzən] *adj* descarado,-a.

brazil [brəˈzɪl] *n* **b. nut**, nuez *f* del Brasil.

Brazil [brəˈzɪl] *n* (el) Brasil.

Brazilian [brəˈzɪlɪən] *adj* & *n* brasileño,-a (*m,f*).

breach [briːtʃ] **I** *n* **1** (*in wall*) brecha *f*. **2** (*violation*) incumplimiento *m*; **b. of confidence**, abuso *m* de confianza; **b. of contract**, incumplimiento de contrato; **b. of the law**, violación *f* de la ley; **b. of the peace**, alteración *f* del orden público. **3** (*in relations*) ruptura *f*. **II** *vtr* violar.

bread [bred] *n* **1** pan *m*; **b. and butter**, pan con mantequilla; *fig* our daily b., el pan nuestro de cada día. **2** *sl* (*money*) pasta *f*, plata *f*.

breadboard [ˈbredbɔːd] *n* tabla *f* (para cortar el pan).

breadcrumb [ˈbredkrʌm] *n* miga *f* de pan; **breadcrumbs**, pan *m sing* rallado.

breadline [ˈbredlaɪn] *n* *fam* miseria *f*; **to be on the b.**, vivir en la miseria.

breadth [bredθ] *n* **1** (*width*) anchura *f*; **it is two metres in b.**, tiene dos metros de ancho. **2** (*extent*) amplitud *f*.

breadwinner [ˈbredwɪnəʳ] *n* cabeza *mf* de familia.

break [breɪk] **I** *vtr* (*pt* **broke**; *pp* **broken**) **1** romper; **to b. a leg**, romperse la pierna; **to b. a record**, batir un récord; **to b. even**, no tener ni ganancias ni pérdidas; *fig* **to b. one's back**, matarse a trabajar; *fig* **to b. sb's heart**, partirle el corazón a algn; *fig* **to b. the ice**, romper el hielo. **2** (*fail to keep*) faltar a; **to b. a contract**, romper un contrato; **to b. the law**, violar la ley. **3** (*destroy*) destrozar; *Fin* arruinar. **4** (*interrupt*) interrumpir. **5** (*code*) descifrar. **6** (*fall*) amortiguar. **7** **she broke the news to him**, le comunicó la noticia.

II *vi* **1** romperse; (*clouds*) dispersarse; (*waves*) romper. **2** (*storm*) estallar. **3** (*voice*) cambiar. **4** (*health*) resentirse. **5** **when day breaks**, al rayar el alba. **6** (*story*) divulgarse.

III *n* **1** (*fracture*) rotura *f*; (*crack*) grieta *f*; (*opening*) abertura *f*. **2** (*in relationship*) ruptura *f*. **3** (*pause*) pausa *f*, descanso *m*; (*at school*) recreo *m*; **to take a b.**, descansar un rato; (*holiday*) tomar unos días libres; **without a b.**, sin parar. 4 *fam* (*chance*) oportunidad *f*; **a lucky b.**, un golpe de suerte.

◆**break away** *vi* 1 (*become separate*) desprenderse (**from**, de). 2 (*escape*) escaparse. ◆**break down** I *vtr* 1 (*door*) derribar. 2 (*resistance*) acabar con. 3 (*costs*) desglosar. II *vi* 1 *Aut* tener una avería. 2 (*resistance*) ceder. 3 (*health*) debilitarse. 4 (*weep*) ponerse a llorar. ◆**break in** I *vtr* acostumbrar; **to b. in a pair of shoes**, cogerle la forma a los zapatos. II *vi* (*burglar*) entrar por la fuerza. ◆**break into** *vtr* 1 (*burgle*) (*house*) allanar; (*safe*) forzar. 2 **to b. into song**, empezar a cantar. ◆**break off** I *vtr* partir. II *vi* 1 (*become detached*) desprenderse. 2 (*talks*) interrumpirse. 3 (*stop*) pararse. ◆**break out** *vi* 1 (*prisoners*) escaparse. 2 (*war etc*) estallar; **to b. out in a rash**, salirle a uno una erupción. ◆**break through** I *vtr* 1 (*crowd*) abrirse paso por; (*cordon*) romper. 2 (*clouds*) atravesar. II *vi* 1 (*crowd*) abrirse paso. 2 (*sun*) salir. ◆**break up** I *vtr* 1 (*object*) romper; (*car*) desguazar; (*crowd*) disolver. II *vi* 1 (*object*) romperse. 2 (*crowd*) disolverse; (*meeting*) levantarse. 3 (*relationship*) fracasar; (*couple*) separarse. 4 *Educ* terminar. ◆**break with** *vtr* (*past*) romper con.

breakable ['breɪkəbəl] *adj* frágil.

breakage ['breɪkɪdʒ] *n* (*breaking*) rotura *f*.

breakaway ['breɪkəweɪ] *adj* disidente.

breakdown ['breɪkdaʊn] *n* 1 *Aut* avería *f*; **b. truck**, grúa *f*. 2 (*nervous*) **b.**, crisis *f* nerviosa. 3 (*in communications*) ruptura *f*. 4 (*analysis*) análisis *m*; *Fin* desglose *m*.

breaker ['breɪkər] *n* 1 (*wave*) ola *f* grande. 2 *Tech* trituradora *f*. 3 (*switch*) interruptor automático.

breakfast ['brekfəst] I *n* desayuno *m*; **to have b.**, desayunar. II *vi* desayunar.

break-in ['breɪkɪn] *n* robo *m* (con allanamiento de morada).

breaking ['breɪkɪŋ] *n* 1 rotura *f*; **b. point**, punto *m* de ruptura. 2 *Jur* **b. and entering**, allanamiento *m* de morada.

breakthrough ['breɪkθruː] *n* paso *m* adelante, avance *m*.

breakwater ['breɪkwɔːtər] *n* rompeolas *m* inv.

breast [brest] *n* (*chest*) pecho *m*; (*of woman*) pecho, seno *m*; (*of chicken etc*) pechuga *f*; *fig* **to make a clean b. of it**, dar la cara.

breast-feed ['brestfiːd] *vtr* dar el pecho a, amamantar a.

breaststroke ['breststrəʊk] *n* braza *f*.

breath [breθ] *n* 1 aliento *m*; (*breathing*) respiración *f*; **in the same b.**, al mismo tiempo; **out of b.**, sin aliento; **to catch one's b.**, recobrar el aliento; **to draw b.**,

respirar; **under one's b.**, en voz baja; *fig* **to take sb's b. away**, dejar pasmado a algn; *Aut* **b. test**, alcoholemia *f*. 2 **to go out for a b. of fresh air**, salir a tomar el aire.

Breathalyzer® ['breθəlaɪzər] *n GB* alcoholímetro *m*.

breathe [briːð] I *vtr* respirar; **to b. a sigh of relief**, dar un suspiro de alivio. II *vi* respirar; **to b. in**, aspirar; **to b. out**, espirar; **to b. heavily**, resoplar.

breather ['briːðər] *n fam* (*rest*) descanso *m*.

breathing ['briːðɪŋ] *n* respiración *f*; **b. space**, pausa *f*, respiro *m*.

breathless ['breθlɪs] *adj* sin aliento, jadeante.

breathtaking ['breθteɪkɪŋ] *adj* impresionante.

breeches ['brɪtʃɪz, 'briːtʃɪz] *npl* bombachos *mpl*; **knee b.**, **riding b.**, pantalones *mpl* de montar.

breed [briːd] I *n* (*of animal*) raza *f*; *fig* (*class*) clase *f*. II *vtr* (*pt & pp bred*) (*animals*) criar; *fig* (*ideas*) engendrar. III *vi* (*animals*) reproducirse.

breeder ['briːdər] *n* 1-(*person*) criador,-a *m,f*. 2 (*fast*) **b. reactor**, reactor *m* generador.

breeding ['briːdɪŋ] *n* 1 (*of animals*) cría *f*; *fig* **b. ground**, caldo *m* de cultivo. 2 (*of person*) educación *f*.

breeze [briːz] I *n* brisa *f*; *Constr* **b. block**, bloque *m* de cemento. II *vi* **to b. in/out**, entrar/salir despreocupadamente.

breezy ['briːzɪ] *adj* (*breezier*, *breeziest*) 1 (*weather*) ventoso,-a. 2 (*person*) despreocupado,-a.

brevity ['brevɪtɪ] *n* brevedad *f*.

brew [bruː] I *vtr* (*beer*) elaborar; (*hot drink*) preparar. II *vi* (*tea*) reposar; *fig* **a storm is brewing**, se prepara una tormenta; *fam* **something's brewing**, algo se está cociendo. III *n* (*of tea*) infusión *f*; *fam* (*of beer*) birra *f*. 2 (*magic potion*) brebaje *m*.

brewer ['bruːər] *n* cervecero,-a *m,f*.

brewery ['bruərɪ] *n* cervecería *f*.

brewing ['bruːɪŋ] I *adj* cervecero,-a. II *n* (*of beer*) elaboración *f* de la cerveza.

briar ['braɪər] *n* brezo *m*.

bribe [braɪb] I *vtr* sobornar. II *n* soborno *m*.

bribery ['braɪbərɪ] *n* soborno *m*.

bric-a-brac ['brɪkəbræk] *n* baratijas *fpl*.

brick [brɪk] *n* ladrillo *m*; *fam* (*reliable person*) persona *f* de confianza.

bricklayer ['brɪkleɪər] *n* albañil *m*.

brickwork ['brɪkwɜːk] *n* ladrillos *mpl*.

bridal ['braɪdəl] *adj* nupcial.

bride [braɪd] *n* novia *f*; **the b. and groom**, los novios.

bridegroom ['braɪdgruːm] *n* novio *m*.

bridesmaid ['braɪdzmeɪd] *n* dama *f* de

honor.

bridge¹ [brɪdʒ] **I** n puente m; (of nose) caballete m; (of ship) puente de mando. **II** vtr 1 (river) tender un puente sobre. 2 (gap) llenar; Fin bridging loan, crédito m a corto plazo.

bridge² [brɪdʒ] n Cards bridge m.

bridle [ˈbraɪdəl] **I** n brida f; (bit) freno m; **b. path**, camino m de herradura. **II** vtr (horse) embridar.

brief [briːf] **I** adj 1 (short) breve. 2 (concise) conciso,-a. **II** n 1 (report) informe m; **in b.**, en resumen. 2 Jur expediente m. 3 Mil instrucciones fpl. 4 **briefs**, (for men) calzoncillos mpl; (for women) bragas fpl. **III** vtr 1 (inform) informar. 2 (instruct) dar instrucciones a. ◆**briefly** adv brevemente; **as b. as possible**, con la mayor brevedad (posible).

briefcase [ˈbriːfkeɪs] n cartera f, portafolios mpl.

briefing [ˈbriːfɪŋ] n (meeting) reunión informativa.

brigade [brɪˈɡeɪd] n brigada f.

brigadier [brɪɡəˈdɪəʳ] n general m de brigada.

bright [braɪt] adj 1 (light, sun, eyes) brillante; (colour) vivo,-a; (day) claro,-a. 2 (cheerful) alegre; **to look on the b. side**, mirar el lado bueno. 3 (clever) listo,-a, espabilado,-a. 4 (promising) prometedor, -a. ◆**brightly** adv.

brighten [ˈbraɪtən] vi (prospects) mejorarse; (face) iluminarse. ◆**brighten up I** vtr (room etc) alegrar. **II** vi (weather) despejarse; (person) animarse.

brightness [ˈbraɪtnɪs] n 1 (of sun) resplandor m; (of day) claridad f; (of colour) viveza f. 2 (cleverness) inteligencia f.

brilliance [ˈbrɪljəns] n 1 (of light) brillo m; (of colour) viveza f. 2 (of person) brillantez f.

brilliant [ˈbrɪljənt] **I** adj brillante; (idea) genial; fam (very good) estupendo,-a. **II** n brillante m.

brim [brɪm] **I** n borde m; (of hat) ala f; **full to the b.**, lleno hasta el borde. **II** vi rebosar (with, de). ◆**brim over** rebosar.

brine [braɪn] n salmuera f.

bring [brɪŋ] vtr (pt & pp brought) 1 (carry sth to sb, take sth or sb with you) traer; **could you b. that book?**, ¿podrías traerme el libro? 2 (take to a different position) llevar; **the war brought hunger to many homes**, la guerra llevó el hambre a muchos hogares. 3 (cause) provocar; **he brought it upon himself**, se lo buscó. 4 (persuade) convencer; **how did they b. themselves to do it?**, ¿cómo llegaron a hacerlo? 5 (lead) llevar. **6 to b. an action against**, acusar. ◆**bring about** vtr provocar. ◆**bring along** vtr traer. ◆**bring back** vtr 1 (re-

turn) devolver. 2 (reintroduce) volver a introducir. 3 (make one remember) traerle a la memoria. ◆**bring down** vtr 1 (from upstairs) bajar. 2 (government) derribar; **Theat to b. the house down**, echar el teatro abajo con los aplausos. 3 (reduce) rebajar. ◆**bring forward** vtr 1 (meeting etc) adelantar. 2 (present) presentar. 3 Fin **brought forward**, suma y sigue. ◆**bring in** vtr 1 (yield) dar. 2 (person etc) hacer entrar. 3 (law etc) introducir; (fashion) lanzar. ◆**bring off** vtr lograr, conseguir. ◆**bring on** vtr provocar. ◆**bring out** vtr 1 (publish) publicar. 2 (reveal) recalcar; **he brings out the worst in me**, despierta lo peor que hay en mí. ◆**bring round** vtr 1 (revive) hacer volver en sí. 2 (persuade) convencer. ◆**bring to** vtr reanimar. ◆**bring up** vtr 1 (educate) criar, educar. 2 (subject) plantear. 3 (vomit) devolver.

brink [brɪŋk] n (edge) borde m; fig **on the b. of ruin**, al borde de la ruina; **on the b. of tears**, a punto de llorar.

brisk [brɪsk] adj enérgico,-a; (pace) rápido,-a; (trade) activo,-a; (weather) fresco,-a.

bristle [ˈbrɪsəl] **I** n cerda f. **II** vi 1 erizarse. 2 (show anger) enfurecer (at, con). ◆**bristle with** vtr (be full of) estar lleno,-a de.

Brit [brɪt] n fam británico,-a m,f.

Britain [ˈbrɪtən] n (Great) **B.**, Gran Bretaña.

British [ˈbrɪtɪʃ] **I** adj británico,-a; **the B. Isles**, las Islas Británicas. **II** npl **the B.**, los británicos.

brittle [ˈbrɪtəl] adj quebradizo,-a, frágil.

broach [brəʊtʃ] vtr (subject) abordar.

broad [brɔːd] **I** adj 1 (wide) ancho,-a; (large) extenso,-a. 2 **a b. hint**, (clear) una indirecta clara. 3 (daylight) pleno,-a. 4 (not detailed) general. 5 (accent) marcado,-a, cerrado,-a. **II** n US sl (woman) tía f. ◆**broadly** adv en términos generales.

broadcast [ˈbrɔːdkɑːst] Rad TV **I** n emisión f. **II** vtr (pt & pp broadcast) emitir, transmitir.

broadcaster [ˈbrɔːdkɑːstəʳ] n locutor,-a m,f.

broadcasting [ˈbrɔːdkɑːstɪŋ] n Rad radiodifusión f; TV transmisión f; Rad **b. station**, emisora f.

broaden [ˈbrɔːdən] vtr ensanchar.

broad-minded [brɔːdˈmaɪndɪd] adj liberal, tolerante.

broadsheet [ˈbrɔːdʃiːt] n folleto m.

broccoli [ˈbrɒkəlɪ] n brócol m.

brochure [ˈbrəʊʃəʳ, ˈbrəʊʃʊəʳ] n folleto m.

broil [brɔɪl] vtr US asar a la parrilla.

broke [brəʊk] adj fam **to be (flat) b.**, estar sin blanca.

broken ['brəʊkən] adj 1 roto,-a; (machinery) averiado,-a; (leg) fracturado,-a. 2 (home) deshecho,-a; (person) destrozado,-a; (ground) accidentado,-a; **to speak b. English**, chapurrear el inglés.

broken-hearted [brəʊkən'hɑːtɪd] adj fig con el corazón destrozado.

broker ['brəʊkəʳ] n corredor m, agente mf de Bolsa.

brolly ['brɒlɪ] n fam paraguas m inv.

bronchitis [brɒŋ'kaɪtɪs] n bronquitis f.

bronze [brɒnz] I n bronce m. II adj (material) de bronce; (colour) bronceado,-a.

bronzed [brɒnzd] adj (suntanned) bronceado,-a.

brooch [brəʊtʃ] n broche m.

brood [bruːd] I n (birds) cría f; hum (children) prole m. II vi (hen) empollar; fig (ponder) rumiar; fig **to b. over a problem**, darle vueltas a un problema.

broody ['bruːdɪ] adj 1 fam (woman) con ganas de tener hijos. 2 (pensive) pensativo,-a 3 (moody) melancólico,-a.

brook¹ [brʊk] n arroyo m.

brook² [brʊk] vtr (usu in negative) soportar, aguantar.

broom [bruːm] n 1 escoba f. 2 Bot retama f.

broomstick ['bruːmstɪk] n palo m de escoba.

Bros Com abbr of **Brothers**, Hermanos mpl, Hnos.

broth [brɒθ] n caldo m.

brothel ['brɒθəl] n burdel m.

brother ['brʌðəʳ] n hermano m; **brothers and sisters**, hermanos.

brotherhood ['brʌðəhʊd] n hermandad f.

brother-in-law ['brʌðərɪnlɔː] n cuñado m.

brotherly ['brʌðəlɪ] adj fraternal.

brought [brɔːt] pt & pp → **bring**.

brow [braʊ] n 1 (forehead) frente f. 2 (eyebrow) ceja f. 3 (of hill) cima f.

brown [braʊn] I adj 1 marrón,-a; (hair, eyes) castaño,-a; **b. bread**, pan m integral; **b. paper**, papel m de estraza; **b. sugar**, azúcar moreno. 2 (tanned) moreno,-a. II n marrón m. III vtr Culin dorar; (tan) broncear.

Brownie ['braʊnɪ] n niña exploradora.

brownish ['braʊnɪʃ] adj pardusco,-a.

browse [braʊz] I vi (person in shop) mirar; (through book) hojear. II n **to have a b.**, dar un vistazo (**in**, a).

bruise [bruːz] I n morado m, cardenal m. II vtr (body) contusionar; (fruit) estropear. III vi (body) magullarse; (fruit) estropearse.

brunch [brʌntʃ] n combinación f de desayuno y almuerzo.

brunette [bruː'net] adj & n morena (f).

brunt [brʌnt] n lo peor; **to bear the b.**, llevar el peso.

brush¹ [brʌʃ] I n 1 (for hair, teeth) cepillo

m; Art pincel m; (for house-painting) brocha f. 2 (with the law) roce m. II vtr 1 cepillar; **to b. one's hair**, cepillarse el pelo; **to b. one's teeth**, cepillarse los dientes. 2 (touch lightly) rozar. III vi **to b. against**, rozar al pasar. ◆**brush aside** vtr dejar de lado. ◆**brush off** vtr ignorar. ◆**brush up** vtr repasar.

brush² [brʌʃ] n (undergrowth) broza f, maleza f.

brushwood ['brʌʃwʊd] n maleza f.

brusque [bruːsk, brʊsk] adj brusco,-a; (words) áspero,-a.

Brussels ['brʌsəlz] n Bruselas.

brutal ['bruːtəl] adj brutal, cruel.

brute [bruːt] I adj bruto,-a; **b. force**, fuerza bruta. II n (animal) bruto m; (person) bestia f.

BSc [biːes'siː] abbr of **Bachelor of Science**.

bubble ['bʌbəl] I n burbuja f; **b. bath**, espuma f de baño; **b. gum**, chicle m; **soap b.**, pompa f de jabón. II vi burbujear; Culin borbotear.

bubbly ['bʌblɪ] I adj (bubblier, bubbliest) efervescente. II n fam champán m, cava m.

buck¹ [bʌk] n 1 Zool macho m; (male deer) ciervo m; (male goat) macho cabrío; fam **to pass the b. to sb**, echarle el muerto a algn. II vi (horse) corcovear. ◆**buck up** I vtr fam **b. your ideas up!**, ¡espabílate! II vi (cheer up) animarse.

buck² [bʌk] n US fam dólar m.

bucket ['bʌkɪt] I n cubo m; fam **it rained buckets**, llovía a cántaros. II vi fam (rain) llover a cántaros.

buckle ['bʌkəl] I n hebilla f. II vtr abrochar con hebilla. III vi 1 (wall, metal) combarse. 2 (knees) doblarse.

bud [bʌd] I n (shoot) brote m; (flower) capullo m. II vi (tree) brotar; fig florecer.

Buddhism ['bʊdɪzəm] n budismo m.

budding ['bʌdɪŋ] adj en ciernes.

buddy ['bʌdɪ] n US fam amigote m, compinche m.

budge [bʌdʒ] vi 1 (move) moverse. 2 (yield) ceder.

budgerigar ['bʌdʒərɪgɑːʳ] n periquito m.

budget ['bʌdʒɪt] I n presupuesto m; Pol **the B.**, los presupuestos del Estado. II vi hacer un presupuesto (**for**, para).

budgie ['bʌdʒɪ] n fam → **budgerigar**.

buff¹ [bʌf] I adj & n (colour) color (m) de ante. II vtr dar brillo a.

buff² [bʌf] n fam (enthusiast) aficionado,-a m,f.

buffalo ['bʌfələʊ] n (pl **buffaloes** or **buffalo**) búfalo m.

buffer ['bʌfəʳ] I n 1 (device) amortiguador m; Rail tope m; **b. zone**, zona f de seguridad. 2 Comput memoria intermedia. II vtr amortiguar.

buffet¹ ['bʊfeɪ] n 1 (snack bar) bar m; (at

railway station) cantina f; *Rail* b. car, coche m restaurante. 2 (*self-service meal*) bufet m libre. 3 (*item of furniture*) aparador m.

buffet² ['bʌfɪt] vtr golpear.

buffoon [bə'fuːn] n bufón m, payaso m.

bug [bʌg] I n 1 (*insect*) bicho m. 2 fam (*microbe*) microbio m; **the flu b.**, el virus de la gripe. 3 (*hidden microphone*) micrófono oculto. 4 *Comput* error m. II vtr fam 1 **to b. a room**, ocultar micrófonos en una habitación; **to b. a phone**, pinchar un teléfono. 2 (*annoy*) fastidiar, molestar.

bugger ['bʌgəʳ] I n 1 sodomita m. 2 sl offens (*person*) gilipollas mf inv; (*thing*) coñazo m; **poor b.!**, ¡el pobre! II interj sl offens **¡joder!**. III vtr sodomizar. ◆**bugger about** *vulg* I vi hacer chorradas. II vtr **they easily buggered him about**, se les hicieron pasar canutas. ◆**bugger off** vi sl offens pirarse; **b. off!**, ¡vete a la mierda! ◆**bugger up** vtr sl *vulg* jorobar.

buggy ['bʌgɪ] n (*baby's pushchair*) cochecito m de niño.

bugle ['bjuːgəl] n bugle m.

build [bɪld] I vtr (pt & pp **built**) construir. II n (*physique*) tipo m; físico m. ◆**build up** vtr (*accumulate*) acumular; **to b. up a reputation**, labrarse una buena reputación.

builder ['bɪldəʳ] n constructor,-a m,f; (*contractor*) contratista mf.

building ['bɪldɪŋ] n edificio m, construcción f; b. **site**, obra f; b. **society**, sociedad f hipotecaria.

build-up ['bɪldʌp] n 1 (*accumulation*) aumento m; (*of gas*) acumulación f. 2 (*publicity*) propaganda f.

built [bɪlt] pt & pp → **build**.

built-in ['bɪlt'ɪn] adj 1 (*cupboard*) empotrado,-a. 2 (*incorporated*) incorporado,-a.

built-up ['bɪlt'ʌp] adj urbanizado,-a.

bulb [bʌlb] n 1 *Bot* bulbo m. 2 (*lightbulb*) bombilla f.

Bulgaria [bʌl'geərɪə] n Bulgaria.

Bulgarian [bʌl'geərɪən] I adj búlgaro,-a. II n 1 (*person*) búlgaro,-a m,f. 2 (*language*) búlgaro m.

bulge [bʌldʒ] I n protuberancia f; (*in pocket*) bulto m. II vi (*swell*) hincharse; (*be full*) estar repleto,-a.

bulk [bʌlk] n 1 (*mass*) masa f, volumen m; *Com* **in b.**, a granel; **to buy in b.**, comprar algo al por mayor. 2 (*greater part*) mayor parte f.

bulky ['bʌlkɪ] adj (bulkier, bulkiest) 1 (*large*) voluminoso,-a. 2 **this crate is rather b.**, esta caja es un armatoste.

bull [bul] n 1 toro m; fig **to take the b. by the horns**, coger al toro por los cuernos. 2 *Fin* alcista mf.

bulldog ['buldɒg] n buldog m.

bulldoze ['buldəʊz] vtr (*land*) nivelar; (*building*) derribar.

bulldozer ['buldəʊzəʳ] n bulldozer m.

bullet ['bulɪt] n bala f; b. **wound**, balazo m.

bulletin ['bulɪtɪn] n boletín m; *Rad TV* **news b.**, boletín de noticias.

bullet-proof ['bulɪtpruːf] adj a prueba de balas; b.-p. **vest**, chaleco m antibalas.

bullfight ['bulfaɪt] n corrida f de toros.

bullfighter ['bulfaɪtəʳ] n torero,-a m,f.

bullfighting ['bulfaɪtɪŋ] n los toros mpl; (*art*) tauromaquia f.

bullion ['buljən] n (*gold, silver*) lingote m.

bullish ['bulɪʃ] adj *Fin* (*market*) en alza.

bullock ['bulək] n buey m.

bullring ['bulrɪŋ] n plaza f de toros.

bull's-eye ['bulzaɪ] n (*of target*) blanco m.

bully ['bulɪ] I n matón m. II vtr (*terrorize*) intimidar; (*bulldoze*) tiranizar. III interj iron **b. for you!**, ¡bravo!

bulwark ['bulwək] n baluarte m.

bum¹ [bʌm] n fam (*bottom*) culo m.

bum² [bʌm] fam I n 1 *US* (*tramp*) vagabundo m. 2 (*idler*) holgazán,-ana m,f. II vi gorronear. ◆**bum around** vi fam vaguear.

bumblebee ['bʌmblbiː] n abejorro m.

bumbling ['bʌmblɪŋ] adj torpe.

bump [bʌmp] I n 1 (*swelling*) chichón m; (*lump*) abolladura f; (*on road*) bache m. 2 (*blow*) choque m, golpe m. 3 (*jolt*) sacudida f. II vtr golpear; **to b. one's head**, darse un golpe en la cabeza. III vi chocar (**into**, contra). ◆**bump into** vtr (*meet*) tropezar con. ◆**bump off** vtr sl liquidar.

bumper ['bʌmpəʳ] I adj abundante; b. **edition**, edición f especial. II n *Aut* parachoques m inv.

bumptious ['bʌmpʃəs] adj presuntuoso,-a, engreído,-a.

bumpy ['bʌmpɪ] adj (bumpier, bumpiest) con muchos baches.

bun [bʌn] n 1 (*bread*) panecillo m; (*sweet*) bollo m; fig *vulg* **she's got a b. in the oven**, está preñada. 2 (*of hair*) moño m.

bunch [bʌntʃ] I n (*of keys*) manojo m; (*of flowers*) ramo m; (*of grapes*) racimo m; (*of people*) grupo m; (*gang*) pandilla f. II vi **to b. together**, juntarse, agruparse.

bundle ['bʌndəl] I n (*of clothes*) bulto m, fardo m; (*of papers*) fajo m; (*of wood*) haz m. II vtr 1 (*make a bundle of*) liar, atar. 2 (*push*) empujar.

bung [bʌŋ] I n tapón m. II vtr fam 1 (*throw*) arrojar. 2 (*put*) meter. ◆**bung up** vtr fam atascar.

bungalow ['bʌŋgələʊ] n chalé m, bungalow m.

bungle ['bʌŋgəl] vtr chapucear.

bunion ['bʌnjən] n juanete m.

bunk [bʌŋk] n (*bed*) litera f.

bunker ['bʌŋkə'] n 1 (coal) carbonera. 2 Mil búnker m. 3 Golf bunker m.

bunny ['bʌnɪ] n fam (baby talk) b. (rabbit), conejito m.

bunting ['bʌntɪŋ] n (material) lanilla f; (flags) banderines mpl; Naut empavesada f.

buoy [bɔɪ] I n boya f. II vtr mantener a flote (up, a). ◆**buoy up** vtr fig alentar, animar.

buoyancy ['bɔɪənsɪ] n 1 (of object) flotabilidad f. 2 Fin tendencia f alcista. 3 (optimism) optimismo m.

buoyant ['bɔɪənt] adj 1 (object) flotante. 2 Fin con tendencia alcista. 3 (optimistic) optimista.

burble ['bɜːbəl] vi 1 (stream) murmurar; (baby) balbucear. 2 (talk quickly) farfullar.

burden ['bɜːdən] I n carga f; fig to be a b. to sb, ser una carga para algn. II vtr cargar (with, con).

bureau ['bjʊərəʊ] n (pl bureaux) 1 (desk) escritorio m. 2 (office) agencia f, oficina f. 3 US (chest of drawers) cómoda f. 4 US Pol ministerio m del Estado.

bureaucracy [bjʊə'rɒkrəsɪ] n burocracia f.

bureaucrat ['bjʊərəkræt] n burócrata mf.

bureaucratic [bjʊərə'krætɪk] adj burocrático,-a.

burgeon ['bɜːdʒən] vi florecer.

burger ['bɜːgə'] n fam abbr of hamburger.

burglar ['bɜːglə'] n ladrón,-ona m,f; b. alarm, alarma f antirrobo.

burglary ['bɜːglərɪ] n robo m con allanamiento de morada.

burial ['berɪəl] n entierro m.

burly ['bɜːlɪ] adj (burlier, burliest) fornido,-a, fuerte.

Burma ['bɜːmə] n Birmania.

Burmese [bɜː'miːz] I adj birmano,-a. II n 1 (person) birmano,-a m,f. 2 (language) birmano m.

burn [bɜːn] I n quemadura f. II vtr (pt & pp burnt or burned) quemar. III vi 1 (fire) arder; (building, food) quemarse. 2 (lamp) estar encendido,-a. 3 (sore) escocer. ◆**burn down** I vtr incendiar. II vi incendiarse. ◆**burn out** vi (people) quemarse. ◆**burn up** vtr (energy, calories) quemar.

burner ['bɜːnə'] n quemador m.

burning ['bɜːnɪŋ] adj 1 (on fire) incendiado,-a; (hot) abrasador,-a. 2 (passionate) ardiente. 3 a b. question, una cuestión candente.

burnt [bɜːnt] adj quemado,-a; b. almonds, almendras tostadas.

burp [bɜːp] I n eructo m. II vi eructar.

burrow ['bʌrəʊ] I n madriguera f; (for rabbits) conejera f. II vi 1 hacer una madriguera. 2 (search) hurgar.

bursar ['bɜːsə'] n tesorero,-a m,f.

bursary ['bɜːsərɪ] n beca f.

burst [bɜːst] I n 1 (explosion) estallido m; (of tyre) reventón m. 2 (of applause) arranque m; (rage) arrebato m; b. of gunfire, ráfaga f de tiros; b. of laughter, carcajada fpl. II vtr (pt & pp burst) (balloon) reventar; fig the river b. its banks, el río se salió de madre. III vi 1 reventarse; (shell) estallar. 2 (enter suddenly) irrumpir (into, en). ◆**burst into** vi to b. into laughter/tears, echarse a reír/llorar. ◆**burst open** vi abrirse violentamente. ◆**burst out** vi to b. out laughing, echarse a reír.

bursting ['bɜːstɪŋ] adj the bar was b. with people, el bar estaba atestado de gente; fam to be b. to do sth, reventar por hacer algo.

bury ['berɪ] vtr 1 enterrar; to be buried in thought, estar absorto en pensamientos. 2 (hide) ocultar.

bus [bʌs] n (pl buses, US busses) autobús m; b. conductor, revisor m; b. driver, conductor,-a m,f; b. stop, parada f de autobús.

bush [bʊʃ] n 1 (shrub) arbusto m. 2 Austral the b., el monte; fam b. telegraph, radio f macuto.

bushy ['bʊʃɪ] adj espeso,-a, tupido,-a.

business ['bɪznɪs] n 1 (commerce) negocios mpl; how's b.?, ¿cómo andan los negocios?; to be away on b., estar en viaje de negocios; b. deal, negocio m; b. hours, horas fpl de oficina; b. trip, viaje m de negocios. 2 (firm) empresa f. 3 (matter) asunto m; I mean b., estoy hablando en serio; it's no b. of mine, no es asunto mío; to make it one's b. to ..., encargarse de ...; to get down to b., ir al grano; to go about one's b., ocuparse de sus asuntos.

businesslike ['bɪznɪslaɪk] adj (practical) eficiente; (methodical) metódico,-a; (serious) serio,-a.

businessman ['bɪznɪsmən] n hombre m de negocios.

businesswoman ['bɪznɪswʊmən] n mujer f de negocios.

busker ['bʌskə'] n fam músico,-a m,f callejero,-a.

bust¹ [bʌst] n 1 (of woman) pecho m. 2 Art busto m.

bust² [bʌst] I vtr 1 fam estropear. 2 sl (person) trincar; (place) hacer una redada. II adj fam 1 (damaged) estropeado,-a. 2 to go b., (bankrupt) quebrar.

bustle ['bʌsəl] I n (activity, noise) bullicio m. II vi to b. about, ir y venir.

bustling ['bʌslɪŋ] adj bullicioso,-a.

bust-up ['bʌstʌp] n fam riña f, pelea f.

busy ['bɪzɪ] I adj 1 ocupado,-a, atareado,-a; (life) ajetreado,-a; (street) concurrido,-a. 2 esp US Tel ocupado,-a.

b. signal, señal f de comunicando. ‖ *vtr* **to b. oneself doing sth,** ocuparse haciendo algo.

busybody ['bızıbɒdı] *n* entrometido,-a *m,f.*

but [bʌt] I *conj* 1 pero; **b. yet,** a pesar de todo. 2 *(after negative)* sino; **not two b. three,** no dos sino tres; **she's not Spanish b. Portuguese,** no es española sino portuguesa. ‖ *adv* **had we b. known,** de haberlo sabido; **we can b. try,** al menos podemos intentarlo; **for her we would have drowned,** si no hubiera sido por ella, nos habríamos ahogado. ‖ III *prep* salvo, menos; **everyone b. her,** todos menos ella; **he's anything b. handsome,** es todo menos guapo. IV *npl* **ifs and buts,** pegas *fpl.*

butane ['bjuːteɪn] *n* butano *m*; **b. gas,** gas butano.

butcher ['bʊtʃər] I *n* carnicero,-a *m,f*; **b.'s (shop),** carnicería *f.* ‖ *vtr (animals)* matar; *(people)* masacrar.

butler ['bʌtlər] *n* mayordomo *m.*

butt¹ [bʌt] *n* 1 *(end)* extremo *m*; *(of rifle)* culata *f*; *(of cigarette)* colilla *f.* 2 **he was the b. of all the jokes,** era el blanco de todas las bromas. 3 *US fam (bottom)* culo *m.*

butt² [bʌt] I *n (with head)* cabezazo *m.* ‖ *vtr* 1 *(strike with head)* dar un cabezazo a. 2 **to b. your way through,** *(shove)* abrirte paso. ◆**butt in** *vi* entrar en la conversación.

butt³ [bʌt] *n (barrel)* tonel *m.*

butter ['bʌtər] I *n* mantequilla *f*; **b. dish,** mantequera *f.* ‖ *vtr* untar con mantequilla.

buttercup ['bʌtəkʌp] *n* ranúnculo *m*, botón *m* de oro.

butterfingers ['bʌtəfɪŋgəz] *n fam* manazas *mf inv.*

butterfly ['bʌtəflaɪ] *n* mariposa *f.*

buttock ['bʌtək] *n* nalga *f*; **buttocks,** nalgas *fpl.*

button ['bʌtən] I *n* botón *m.* ‖ *vtr* **to b. (up),** abrochar(se), abotonar(se).

buttonhole ['bʌtənhəʊl] *n* ojal *m.*

buttress ['bʌtrɪs] I *n* 1 contrafuerte *m.* 2 *(support)* apoyo *m.* ‖ *vtr* apuntalar; *fig* reforzar, apoyar.

buxom ['bʌksəm] *adj (woman)* pechugona.

buy [baɪ] I *n* compra *f*; **a good b.,** una ganga. ‖ *vtr (pt & pp bought)* 1 comprar; **she bought that car from a neighbour,** compró ese coche a un vecino. 2 *sl (believe)* tragar. ◆**buy off** *vtr* sobornar. ◆**buy out** *vtr* adquirir la parte de. ◆**buy up** *vtr* comprar en grandes cantidades.

buyer ['baɪər] *n* comprador,-a *m,f.*

buzz [bʌz] I *n* 1 *(of bee)* zumbido *m*; *(of conversation)* rumor *m.* 2 *fam (telephone call)* telefonazo *m.* ‖ *vi* zumbar.

buzzer ['bʌzər] *n* timbre *m.*

by [baɪ] I *prep* 1 *(indicating agent)* por; **composed by Bach,** compuesto,-a por Bach; **a film by Almodóvar,** una película de Almodóvar. 2 *(via)* por; **he left by the back door,** salió por la puerta trasera. 3 *(manner)* por; **by train,** en coche/tren; **by credit card,** con tarjeta de crédito; **by chance,** por casualidad; **by oneself,** solo,-a; **made by hand,** hecho a mano; **you can obtain a ticket by filling in the coupon,** puede conseguir una entrada llenando el cupón. 4 *(amount)* por; **little by little,** poco a poco; **they are sold by the dozen,** se venden por docenas; **to be paid by the hour,** cobrar por horas. 5 **by far,** con mucho; **he won by a foot,** ganó por un pie. 6 *(beside)* al lado de, junto a; **side by side,** juntos. 7 **to walk by a building,** *(pass)* pasar por delante de un edificio. 8 *(time)* para; **by now,** ya; **by then,** para entonces; **we have to be there by nine,** tenemos que estar allí para las nueve; **by the time we arrive,** (para) cuando lleguemos; **by this time next year,** el año que viene por estas fechas. 9 *(during)* de; **by day/night,** de día/noche. 10 *(in an oath)* por; **by God!,** ¡por Dios! 11 *Math* por. 12 *(according to)* según; **is that O.K by you?,** ¿te viene bien? 13 **he had two children by his first wife,** tuvo dos hijos con su primera esposa. 14 *(phrases)* **bit by bit,** poco a poco; **day by day,** día a día; **what do you mean by that?,** ¿qué quieres decir con eso?; **by the way,** a propósito. ‖ II *adv* 1 **to go by,** *(past)* pasar; **he just walked by,** pasó de largo. 2 **by and by,** con el tiempo; **by and large,** en conjunto.

bye [baɪ] *n* 1 *fam* ¡hasta luego! 2 **by the b.** por cierto.

bye-bye ['baɪbaɪ] *n fam* ¡adiós!, ¡hasta luego!

by-election ['baɪɪlekʃən] *n* elección *f* parcial.

bygone ['baɪgɒn] I *adj* pasado,-a. II *npl* **let bygones be bygones,** lo pasado pasado está.

by-law ['baɪlɔː] *n* ley *f* municipal.

bypass ['baɪpɑːs] I *n* 1 *(road)* carretera *f* de circunvalación. 2 *Med* **b. surgery,** cirugía *f* de by-pass. II *vtr* evitar.

by-product ['baɪprɒdʌkt] *n Chem Ind* derivado *m*, subproducto *m*; *fig* consecuencia *f.*

by-road ['baɪrəʊd] *n* carretera secundaria.

bystander ['baɪstændər] *n* testigo *mf.*

byte [baɪt] *n Comput* byte *m*, octeto *m.*

byword ['baɪwɜːd] *n* **it became a b. for modernity,** se convirtió en sinónimo de modernidad.

C

C, c [siː] n **1** (the letter) C, c f. **2** Mus do m.

C 1 abbr of **Celsius**. C. **2** abbr of **Centigrade**, C.

cab [kæb] n US taxi m; **c. driver**, taxista mf.

cabaret ['kæbəreɪ] n cabaret m.

cabbage ['kæbɪdʒ] n col f, berza f; **red c.**, (col) lombarda f.

cabin ['kæbɪn] n **1** (hut) choza f, cabaña f. **2** Naut camarote m. **3** (of lorry, plane) cabina f.

cabinet ['kæbɪnɪt] n **1** (item of furniture) armario m; (glassfronted) vitrina f; **c. maker**, ebanista mf. **2** Pol gabinete m, consejo m de ministros.

cable ['keɪbəl] I n cable m; **c. car**, teleférico m; **c. TV**, televisión f por cable. II vtr & vi cablegrafiar, telegrafiar.

cache [kæʃ] n alijo m.

cackle ['kækəl] vi cacarear.

cactus ['kæktəs] n (pl **cacti** ['kæktaɪ]) cactus m.

CAD [kæd] abbr of **computer-aided or -assisted design or draughting**, diseño m con ayuda de ordenador.

cad [kæd] n GB fam canalla m.

caddie ['kædɪ] n Golf cadi m.

cadet [kə'det] n Mil cadete m.

cadge [kædʒ] fam vtr & vi gorronear.

Caesarean [siː'zeərɪən] n Med **she had a c.**, le hicieron una cesárea; **C. section**, operación f cesárea.

café ['kæfeɪ] n, **cafeteria** [kæfɪ'tɪərɪə] n cafetería f.

caffeine ['kæfiːn] n cafeína f.

cage [keɪdʒ] I n jaula f. II vtr enjaular.

cagey ['keɪdʒɪ] adj (**cagier**, **cagiest**) fam reservado,-a.

cagoule [kə'guːl] n (garment) canguro m.

Cairo ['kaɪrəʊ] n (el) Cairo.

cajole [kə'dʒəʊl] vtr engatusar.

cake [keɪk] n **1** pastel m, tarta f; fam fig **it's a piece of c.**, está chupado; **birthday c.**, pastel de cumpleaños; **c. shop**, pastelería f. **2** (of soap) pastilla f. II vi (mud) endurecerse. II vtr **caked with ...**, cubierto,-a de ....

calamity [kə'læmɪtɪ] n calamidad f.

calcium ['kælsɪəm] n calcio m.

calculate ['kælkjʊleɪt] vtr calcular.

calculated ['kælkjʊleɪtɪd] adj intencionado,-a.

calculating ['kælkjʊleɪtɪŋ] adj **1 c. machine**, calculadora f. **2** pej (person) calculador,-a.

calculation [kælkjʊ'leɪʃən] n cálculo m.

calculator ['kælkjʊleɪtə'] n calculadora f.

calendar ['kælɪndə'] n calendario m; **c. year**, año m civil.

calf¹ [kɑːf] n (pl **calves** [kɑːvz]) (of cattle) becerro,-a m,f, ternero,-a m,f; (of other animals) cría f.

calf² [kɑːf] n (pl **calves** [kɑːvz]) Anat pantorrilla f.

calfskin ['kɑːfskɪn] n piel f de becerro.

caliber ['kælɪbə'], **calibre** ['kælɪbə'] n calibre m.

call [kɔːl] I vtr **1** llamar; **to c. sb names**, poner verde a algn; **what's he called?**, ¿cómo se llama? **2** (meeting etc) convocar; **to c. sth to mind**, traer algo a la memoria.
II vi **1** llamar; Tel **who's calling?**, ¿de parte de quién? **2 to c. at sb's (house)**, pasar por casa de algn; **to c. for sth/sb**, pasar a recoger algo/a algn. **3** (trains) parar. **4 to c. for**, (require) exigir; **that wasn't called for**, eso no estaba justificado.
III n **1** llamada f, grito m. **2** (visit) visita f; **to pay a c. on sb**, visitar a algn. **3** Tel (phone) llamada f, cabina telefónica. **4** Med **to be on c.**, estar de guardia. **5** **there's no c. for you to worry**, no hay motivo para que te preocupes.
◆**call away** vtr **to be called away on business**, tener que ausentarse por motivos de trabajo. ◆**call back** vi (phone again) llamar otra vez; (visit again) volver. ◆**call in** I vtr (doctor) llamar. II vi **1 I'll c. in tomorrow**, (visit) mañana me paso. **2** Naut hacer escala (at, en). ◆**call off** vtr suspender. ◆**call on** vtr **1** visitar. **2 to c. on sb for support**, recurrir a algn en busca de apoyo. ◆**call out** I vtr **1** (shout) gritar. **2** (doctor) hacer venir; (workers) convocar a la huelga. II vi gritar. ◆**call up** vtr **1** Tel llamar (por teléfono). **2** Mil llamar a filas, reclutar.

caller ['kɔːlə'] n visita mf; Tel persona f que llama.

calling ['kɔːlɪŋ] n esp Rel llamada f, vocación f.

callous ['kæləs] adj insensible, duro,-a.

call-up ['kɔːlʌp] n llamamiento m a filas.

calm [kɑːm] I adj **1** (weather, sea) en calma. **2** (relaxed) tranquilo,-a; **keep c.!**, ¡tranquilo,-a!. II n **1** (of weather, sea) calma f. **2** (tranquility) tranquilidad f. III vtr calmar, tranquilizar. IV vi **to c. (down)**, calmarse, tranquilizarse.

Calor Gas® ['kæləgæs] n (gas m) butano m.

calorie, calory ['kælərɪ] n caloría f.

calve [kɑːv] vi (cow) parir (un becerro).

calves [kɑːvz] npl → **calf¹**, **calf²**.

Cambodia [kæm'bəʊdɪə] n Camboya.

came [keɪm] pt → **come**.

camel ['kæməl] n camello,-a m,f.

cameo ['kæmɪəʊ] n camafeo m.

camera ['kæmərə] n 1 cámara f or máquina f fotográfica. C*in* TV cámara. 2 *Jur* in c., a puerta cerrada.

cameraman ['kæmərəmən] n cámara mf.

Cameroon [kæmə'ru:n] n Camerún m.

camomile ['kæməmaɪl] n camomila f. c. tea, (infusión f de) manzanilla f.

camouflage ['kæməflɑ:ʒ] I n camuflaje m. II vtr camuflar.

camp¹ [kæmp] I n campamento m; c. bed, cama f plegable; c. site, camping m. II vi to go camping, ir de camping.

camp² [kæmp] adj fam afeminado,-a; *(affected)* amanerado,-a.

campaign [kæm'peɪn] I n campaña f. II vi to c. for sb/sth, hacer una campaña a favor de algn/de algo.

campaigner [kæm'peɪnər] n defensor,-a m,f (for, de).

camper ['kæmpər] n 1 *(person)* campista mf. 2 US *(vehicle)* caravana f.

camping ['kæmpɪŋ] n c. ground, c. site, camping m.

campus ['kæmpəs] n campus m, ciudad f universitaria.

can¹ [kæn] v aux *(pt could)* 1 *(be able to)* poder; **he could have come**, podría haber venido; **I'll show you as soon as I** c., te llamaré en cuanto pueda; **she can't do it**, no puede hacerlo; **I cannot understand why**, *(fml & emphatic)* no entiendo por qué. 2 *(know how to)* saber; c. you ski?, ¿sabes esquiar?; **I can't speak English**, no sé hablar inglés. 3 *(be permitted to)* poder; **he can't go out tonight**, no le dejan salir esta noche. 4 *(be possible)* poder; **she could have forgotten**, puede (ser) que lo haya olvidado; **they can't be very poor**, no deben ser muy pobres; **what c. it be?**, ¿qué será?

can² [kæn] I n 1 *(of oil)* bidón m. 2 US *(tin)* lata f, bote m. II vtr 1 *(fish, fruit)* envasar, enlatar. 2 US fam desestimar.

Canada ['kænədə] n Canadá.

Canadian [kə'neɪdɪən] adj & n canadiense *(mf)*.

canal [kə'næl] n canal m.

canary [kə'neərɪ] n canario m.

Canary Islands [kə'neərɪaɪləndz] npl (Islas fpl) Canarias fpl.

cancel ['kænsəl] vtr *(train, contract)* cancelar; Com anular; *(permission)* retirar; *(decree)* revocar.

cancellation [kænsɪ'leɪʃən] n cancelación f; Com anulación f.

cancer ['kænsər] n 1 Med cáncer m; **breast c.**, cáncer de mama; c. research, cancerología f. 2 C., *(in astrology)* Cáncer m.

candelabra [kændɪ'lɑ:brə] n candelabro m.

candid ['kændɪd] adj franco,-a, sincero,-a.

candidate ['kændɪdeɪt, 'kændɪdɪt] n candidato,-a m,f; *(in exam)* opositor,-a m,f.

candle ['kændəl] n vela f; *(in church)* cirio m.

candlelight ['kændəlaɪt] n luz f de vela; by c., a la luz de las velas.

candlestick ['kændəlstɪk] n candelero m, palmatoria f; *(in church)* cirial m.

candour, US **candor** ['kændər] n franqueza f.

candy ['kændɪ] n US caramelo m.

candyfloss ['kændɪflɒs] n GB algodón m dulce.

cane [keɪn] I n 1 Bot caña f; c. sugar, azúcar m de caña. 2 *(wicker)* mimbre m. 3 *(walking stick)* bastón m; *(for punishment)* palmeta f. II vtr castigar con la palmeta.

canine ['keɪnaɪn] adj Zool canino,-a; c. tooth, colmillo m.

canister ['kænɪstər] n bote m.

canned [kænd] adj enlatado,-a; c. foods, conservas fpl.

cannibal ['kænɪbəl] adj & n caníbal *(mf)*.

cannon ['kænən] I n *(pl cannons or cannon)* cañón m; fig c. fodder, carne f de cañón. II vi chocar (into, contra).

cannonball ['kænənbɔ:l] n bala f de cañón.

cannot ['kænɒt, kæ'nɒt] v aux → can¹.

canoe [kə'nu:] n canoa f; Sport piragua f.

canon ['kænən] n Rel canon m.

canopy ['kænəpɪ] n 1 *(on throne)* dosel m. 2 *(awning)* toldo m.

can't [kɑ:nt] v aux → can¹.

Cantabria n Cantabria f.

cantankerous [kæn'tæŋkərəs] adj intratable.

canteen [kæn'ti:n] n 1 *(restaurant)* cantina f. 2 *(set of cutlery)* juego m de cubiertos. 3 *(flask)* cantimplora f.

canter ['kæntər] I n medio galope. II vi ir a medio galope.

canvas ['kænvəs] n 1 Tex lona f. 2 *(painting)* lienzo m.

canvass ['kænvəs] vi 1 Pol hacer propaganda electoral. 2 Com hacer promoción, buscar clientes.

canvasser ['kænvəsər] n Pol persona f que hace propaganda electoral de puerta en puerta.

canyon ['kænjən] n cañón m; **the Grand** C., el Gran Cañón.

cap [kæp] I n 1 gorro m; *(soldier's)* gorra f. 2 GB Sport to win a c. for England, ser seleccionado,-a para el equipo de Inglaterra. 3 *(of pen)* capuchón m; *(of bottle)* chapa f. II vtr 1 *(bottle)* poner la chapa a; fig to c. it all, para colmo. 2 GB Sport seleccionar.

capability [keɪpə'bɪlɪtɪ] n habilidad f.

capable ['keɪpəbəl] adj 1 *(skilful)* hábil. 2 *(able)* capaz (of, de).

capacity [kə'pæsɪtɪ] n 1 capacidad f. 2

(*position*) puesto *m*; **in her c. as manageress**, en calidad de gerente.

cape[1] [keɪp] *n* (*garment*) capa *f*.

cape[2] [keɪp] *n* *Geog* cabo *m*, promontorio *m*; **C. Horn**, Cabo de Hornos; **C. Town**, Ciudad del Cabo; **C. Verde**, Cabo Verde.

caper ['keɪpər] *n* (*prank*) travesura *f*.

capital ['kæpɪtəl] **I** *n* **1** (*town*) capital *f*. **2** *Fin* capital *m*; **c. expenditure**, inversión *f* de capital. **3** (*letter*) mayúscula *f*. **II** *adj* **1** (*city*) capital. **2** **c. punishment**, pena *f* capital. **3** (*primary*) primordial. **4** **c. letter**, mayúscula *f*.

capitalism ['kæpɪtəlɪzəm] *n* capitalismo *m*.

capitalist ['kæpɪtəlɪst] *adj & n* capitalista (*mf*).

capitalize ['kæpɪtəlaɪz] *vi Fin* capitalizar; *fig* **to c. on sth**, sacar provecho *or* beneficio de algo.

capitulate [kə'pɪtjʊleɪt] *vi* capitular.

Capricorn ['kæprɪkɔːn] *n* Capricornio *m*.

capsicum ['kæpsɪkəm] *n* pimiento *m*.

capsize [kæp'saɪz] **I** *vtr* hacer zozobrar. **II** *vi* zozobrar.

capsule ['kæpsjuːl] *n* cápsula *f*.

captain ['kæptɪn] **I** *n* capitán *m*. **II** *vtr* capitanear.

caption ['kæpʃən] *n* (*under picture*) leyenda *f*; *Cin* subtítulo *m*.

captivating ['kæptɪveɪtɪŋ] *adj* seductor, -a.

captive ['kæptɪv] **I** *n* cautivo,-a *m,f*. **II** *adj* cautivo,-a.

captivity [kæp'tɪvɪtɪ] *n* cautiverio *m*.

capture ['kæptʃər] **I** *vtr* **1** capturar, apresar; *Mil* (*town*) tomar. **2** (*market*) acaparar. **3** *fig* (*mood*) captar. **II** *n* (*of fugitive*) captura *f*; (*of town*) toma *f*.

car [kɑːr] *n* **1** coche *m*, *Am* carro *m*; **c. ferry**, transbordador *m* para coches; *GB* **c. park**, parking *m* or aparcamiento *m*; **c. wash**, túnel *m* de lavado. **2** *GB Rail* coche *m*.

carafe [kə'ræf, kə'rɑːf] *n* garrafa *f*.

caramel ['kærəmel] *n* azúcar *m* quemado; (*sweet*) caramelo *m*.

carat, US karat ['kærət] *n* kilate *m*.

caravan ['kærəvæn] *n* **1** (*vehicle*) remolque *m*, caravana *f*. **2** (*in the desert*) caravana *f*.

carbohydrate [kɑːbəʊ'haɪdreɪt] *n* hidrato *m* de carbono, carbohidrato *m*.

carbon ['kɑːbən] *n* carbono *m*; **c. copy**, copia *f* al papel carbón; *fig* copia exacta; **c. dioxide**, dióxido *m* de carbono; **c. paper**, papel *m* de carbón.

carburettor [kɑːbjʊ'retər], **US carburetor** [kɑːbjʊretər] *n* carburador *m*.

carcass ['kɑːkəs] *n* res *f* muerta.

card [kɑːd] *n* **1** tarjeta *f*; (*of cardboard*) cartulina *f*; **birthday/visiting c.**, tarjeta de cumpleaños/de visita. **2** (*in file*) ficha *f*; (*identity*) carnet *m*; **c. index**, fichero *m*. **3** **pack of cards**, baraja *f*, cartas *fpl*; (*play-*

ing) c., naipe *m*, carta *f*; *fig* **on the cards**, previsto.

cardboard ['kɑːdbɔːd] *n* cartón *m*; **c. box**, caja *f* de cartón; **c. cutout**, recortable *m*.

cardiac ['kɑːdɪæk] *adj* cardíaco,-a; **c. arrest**, paro cardíaco.

cardigan ['kɑːdɪgən] *n* rebeca *f*.

cardinal ['kɑːdɪnəl] **I** *n* *Rel* cardenal *m*. **II** *adj* cardinal; **c. numbers**, números *mpl* cardinales.

care [keər] **I** *vi* (*be concerned*) preocuparse (**about**, por); **I don't c.**, no me importa; **fam for all I c.**, me trae sin cuidado; **fam he couldn't c. less**, le importa un bledo. **II** *n* **1** (*attention*, *protection*) cuidado *m*, atención *f*; **c. of...**, (*on letter*) 'al cuidado de...'; **medical c.**, asistencia *f* médica; **to take c. of**, cuidar; (*business*) ocuparse de. **2** (*carefulness*) cuidado *m*; **take c.**, (*be careful*) ten cuidado; (*as farewell*) ¡cuídate! **3** (*worry*) preocupación *f*. ◆**care for** *vtr* **1** (*look after*) cuidar. **2** (*like*) gustar, interesar; **would you c. for a coffee?**, ¿te apetece un café?

career [kə'rɪər] **I** *n* carrera *f*. **II** *vi* correr a toda velocidad.

carefree ['keəfriː] *adj* despreocupado,-a.

careful ['keəfʊl] *adj* cuidadoso,-a; (*cautious*) prudente; **be c.!**, ¡ojo!; **to be c.**, tener cuidado. ◆**carefully** *adv* (*painstakingly*) cuidadosamente; (*cautiously*) con cuidado.

careless ['keəlɪs] *adj* descuidado,-a; (*about clothes*) desaliñado,-a; (*driving*) negligente; **a c. mistake**, un descuido. ◆**carelessly** *adv* descuidadamente, a la ligera.

carelessness ['keəlɪsnɪs] *n* descuido *m*.

caress [kə'res] **I** *n* caricia *f*. **II** *vtr* acariciar.

caretaker ['keəteɪkər] *n* (*in school etc*) bedel *mf*; (*in block of flats*) portero,-a *m,f*.

cargo ['kɑːgəʊ] *n* (*pl* **cargoes** *or* **cargos**) carga *f*, cargamento *m*; *Naut* **c. boat**, buque *m* de carga, carguero *m*.

Caribbean [kærɪ'bɪən, *US* kə'rɪbɪən] *adj* caribe, caribeño,-a; **the C. (Sea)**, el (Mar) Caribe.

caricature ['kærɪkətjʊər] *n* caricatura *f*.

caring ['keərɪŋ] *adj* solidario,-a.

carnage ['kɑːnɪdʒ] *n* *fig* carnicería *f*.

carnal ['kɑːnəl] *adj* carnal.

carnation [kɑː'neɪʃən] *n* clavel *m*.

carnival ['kɑːnɪvəl] *n* carnaval *m*.

carnivorous [kɑː'nɪvərəs] *adj* carnívoro, -a.

carol ['kærəl] *n* villancico *m*.

carp[1] [kɑːp] *n* (*fish*) carpa *f*.

carp[2] [kɑːp] *vi* refunfuñar.

carpenter ['kɑːpɪntər] *n* carpintero,-a *m,f*.

carpentry ['kɑːpɪntrɪ] *n* carpintería *f*.

carpet ['kɑːpɪt] **I** *n* moqueta *f*. **II** *vtr* *fig* **carpeted with**, cubierto,-a de.

carriage [ˈkærɪdʒ] *n* 1 (*horse-drawn*) carruaje *m*; *Rail* vagón *m*, coche *m*; (*of goods*) porte *m*, transporte *m*.

carriageway [ˈkærɪdʒweɪ] *n* GB carril *m*, autovía *f*; **dual c.**, autovía.

carrier [ˈkærɪər] *n* 1 (*company*) transportista *mf*; GB **c. bag**, bolsa *f* de plástico; **c. pigeon**, paloma mensajera. 2 *Med* portador,-a *m,f*.

carrot [ˈkærət] *n* zanahoria *f*.

carry [ˈkærɪ] **I** *vtr* 1 llevar; (*goods*) transportar. 2 (*stock*) tener; (*responsibility, penalty*) conllevar, implicar. 3 **the motion was carried**, se aprobó la moción. 4 (*disease*) ser portador,-a de. **II** *vi* (*sound*) oírse. ◆**carry away** *vtr* llevarse; **to get carried away**, entusiasmarse. ◆**carry forward** *vtr* Fin carried forward, suma y sigue. ◆**carry off** *vtr* (*prize*) llevarse; **fam to c. it off**, salir airoso,-a. ◆**carry on I** *vtr* continuar; (*conversation*) mantener. **II** *vi* 1 continuar, seguir adelante; **c. on!**, ¡adelante! 2 *fam* (*make a fuss*) hacer una escena; **don't c. on about it**, ¡no te enrolles! 3 *fam* **to c. on with sb**, estar liado,-a con algn. ◆**carry out** *vtr* (*plan*) llevar a cabo, realizar; (*test*) verificar.

carrycot [ˈkærɪkɒt] *n* cuna *f* portátil.

carsick [ˈkɑːsɪk] *adj* mareado,-a (en el coche).

cart [kɑːt] **I** *n* (*horse-drawn*) carro *m*; (*handcart*) carretilla *f*. **II** *vtr* carretear.

cartel [kɑːˈtel] *n* cártel *m*.

carton [ˈkɑːtən] *n* (*of cream etc*) caja *f*.

cartoon [kɑːˈtuːn] *n* (*strip*) tira cómica, historieta *f*; *Art* cartón *m*; (*animated*) dibujos *mpl* animados.

cartoonist [kɑːˈtuːnɪst] *n* caricaturista *mf*.

cartridge [ˈkɑːtrɪdʒ] *n* 1 cartucho *m*. 2 (*for pen*) recambio *m*; **c. paper**, papel guarro.

carve [kɑːv] *vtr* 1 (*wood*) tallar; (*stone, metal*) cincelar, esculpir. 2 (*meat*) trinchar.

cascade [kæsˈkeɪd] *n* cascada *f*.

case¹ [keɪs] *n* 1 caso *m*; **a c. in point**, un buen ejemplo; **in any c.**, en cualquier caso, de todas formas; **in c. of doubt**, en caso de duda; **just in c.**, por si acaso. 2 *Med* caso *m*; **c. history**, historial clínico. 3 *Jur* causa *f*.

case² [keɪs] **I** *n* 1 (*suitcase*) maleta *f*; (*small*) estuche *m*; (*soft*) funda *f*. 2 **a c. of wine**, una caja de botellas de vino. 3 *Typ* **lower c.**, minúscula *f*; **upper c.**, mayúscula *f*.

cash [kæʃ] **I** *n* dinero efectivo; **to pay c.**, pagar al contado o en efectivo; **c. desk**, caja *f*; **c. on delivery**, pago contra reembolso; **c. dispenser**, cajero automático; **c. register**, caja registradora. **II** *vtr* (*cheque*) cobrar. ◆**cash in I** *vi fam* fig to **in on sth**, sacar provecho de algo. **II** *vtr* hacer efectivo,-a.

cash-and-carry [kæʃənˈkærɪ] *adj & adv* de venta al por mayor y pago al contado.

cashew [ˈkæʃuː] *n* c. (**nut**), anacardo *m*.

cashier [kæˈʃɪər] *n* cajero,-a *m,f*.

cashmere [ˈkæʃmɪər] *n* cachemira *f*.

casino [kəˈsiːnəʊ] *n* casino *m*.

cask [kɑːsk] *n* tonel *m*, barril *m*.

casket [ˈkɑːskɪt] *n* (*box*) cofre *m*; (*coffin*) ataúd *m*.

casserole [ˈkæsərəʊl] *n* 1 (*container*) cacerola *f*. 2 *Culin* guisado *m*.

cassette [kæˈset] *n* cassette *f*; **c. recorder**, cassette *m*.

cast [kɑːst] **I** *vtr* (*pt & pp* **cast**) 1 (*net, fishing line*) echar, arrojar; (*light*) proyectar; (*glance*) lanzar; (*anchor*) echar; (*vote*) emitir; (*skin*) mudar. 2 *fig* **to c. doubts on sth**, poner algo en duda; **to c. suspicion on sb**, levantar sospechas sobre algn. 3 (*metal*) moldear; **c. iron**, hierro fundido. 4 *Theat* (*play*) hacer el reparto de. **II** *n* 1 (*mould*) molde *m*; (*product*) pieza *f*. 2 *Med* (*plaster*) c., escayola *f*. 3 *Theat* reparto *m*. ◆**cast off** *vi Naut* soltar (las) amarras.

castanets [kæstəˈnets] *npl* castañuelas *fpl*.

castaway [ˈkɑːstəweɪ] *n* náufrago,-a *m,f*.

caste [kɑːst] *n* casta *f*.

caster [ˈkɑːstər] *n* **c. sugar**, azúcar molido muy fino.

Castile [kæˈstiːl] *n* Castilla *f*.

Castilian [kæˈstɪljən] **I** *adj* castellano,-a. **II** *n* C. (**Spanish**), (*language*) castellano *m*.

casting [ˈkɑːstɪŋ] *n* **c. vote**, voto *m* de calidad.

cast-iron [ˈkɑːstaɪən] *adj* de hierro fundido.

castle [ˈkɑːsəl] **I** *n* 1 castillo *m*. 2 *Chess* torre *f*. **II** *vi Chess* enrocar.

castor¹ [ˈkɑːstər] *n* **c. oil**, aceite *m* de ricino.

castor² [ˈkɑːstər] *n* (*on furniture*) ruedecilla *f*.

castrate [kæˈstreɪt] *vtr* castrar.

casual [ˈkæʒjʊəl] *adj* 1 (*meeting etc*) fortuito,-a. 2 (*worker*) eventual. 3 (*clothes*) (de) sport. 4 (*visit*) de paso. 5 (*person, attitude*) despreocupado,-a, informal.

casualty [ˈkæʒjʊəltɪ] *n* 1 *Mil* baja *f*; **casualties**, pérdidas *fpl*. 2 (*injured*) herido,-a *m,f*.

cat [kæt] *n* gato,-a *m,f*; *fig* **to let the c. out of the bag**, descubrir el pastel.

Catalan [ˈkætələn] **I** *adj* catalán,-ana; C. **flag**, senyera *f*. **II** *n* 1 (*person*) catalán,-ana *m,f*. 2 (*language*) catalán *m*.

catalogue, US **catalog** [ˈkætəlɒg] **I** *n* catálogo *m*. **II** *vtr* catalogar.

Catalonia [kætəˈləʊnɪə] *n* Cataluña *f*.

catalyst [ˈkætəlɪst] *n* catalizador *m*.

catapult [ˈkætəpʌlt] *n* tirachinas *m inv*.

catarrh [kəˈtɑːr] *n* catarro *m*.

catastrophe [kəˈtæstrəfɪ] *n* catástrofe *f*.

catastrophic [kætəˈstrɒfɪk] *adj*

catastrófico,-a.

catch [kætʃ] I vtr (pt & pp **caught**) 1 (ball, thief) coger; (fish) pescar; (mouse etc) atrapar; (train, bus) coger, Am agarrar; to c. a cold, coger un resfriado; to c. fire, (log) prenderse; (building) incendiarse; to c. hold of, agarrar; to c. sb's eye, captar la atención de algn; to c. sight of, entrever. 2 (surprise) pillar, sorprender. 3 (hear) entender. 4 to c. one's breath, (hold) sostener la respiración; (recover) recuperar el aliento. II vi (become popular) enganancharse (on, en); (fire) encenderse. III n 1 (of ball) parada f; (of fish) presa f. 2 (on door) pestillo m. 3 (drawback) pega f; c. question, pregunta f con pega. 4 c. phrase, slogan m. ◆**catch on** vi fam 1 (become popular) ganar popularidad. 2 (understand) caer en la cuenta. ◆**catch out** vtr fam to c. sb out, pillar a algn cometiendo una falta. ◆**catch up** vi 1 to c. up with sb, (reach) alcanzar a algn. 2 (with news) ponerse al corriente (on, de); to c. up on sleep, recuperar el sueño perdido; to c. up with work, ponerse al día de trabajo.

catching ['kætʃɪŋ] adj (disease) contagioso,-a.

catchment ['kætʃmənt] n c. area, zona f de captación.

catchword ['kætʃwɜːd] n lema m.

catchy ['kætʃɪ] adj (catchier, catchiest) fam (tune) pegadizo,-a.

categoric(al) [kætɪ'gɒrɪk(ə)l] adj categórico,-a.

categorize ['kætɪgəraɪz] vtr clasificar.

category ['kætɪgərɪ] n categoría f.

cater ['keɪtər] vi 1 to c. for, (wedding etc) proveer comida para. 2 to c. for, (taste) atender a.

caterer ['keɪtərər] n proveedor,-a m,f.

catering ['keɪtərɪŋ] n abastecimiento m (de comidas por encargo).

caterpillar ['kætəpɪlər] n 1 oruga f. 2 c. (tractor), tractor m de oruga.

cathedral [kə'θiːdrəl] n catedral f.

Catholic ['kæθəlɪk] adj & n católico,-a (m,f).

catholic ['kæθəlɪk] adj católico,-a.

Catholicism [kə'θɒlɪsɪzəm] n catolicismo m.

Catseye® ['kætsaɪ] n GB catafaro m.

cattle ['kætəl] npl ganado m (vacuno).

catty ['kætɪ] adj (cattier, cattiest) fam (remark) malintencionado,-a; (person) malicioso,-a.

catwalk ['kætwɔːk] n pasarela f.

Caucasian [kɔː'keɪzɪən] adj & n caucásico,-a (m,f), blanco,-a (m,f).

caucus ['kɔːkəs] n comité m central, ejecutiva f.

caught [kɔːt] pt & pp → **catch**.

cauliflower ['kɒlɪflaʊər] n coliflor f.

cause [kɔːz] I n 1 (origin) causa f. 2

(reason) motivo m. 3 for a good c., por una buena causa. II vtr causar; to c. sb to do sth, hacer que algn haga algo.

caustic ['kɔːstɪk] adj cáustico,-a; fig mordaz.

caution ['kɔːʃən] I n 1 (care) cautela f, prudencia f. 2 (warning) aviso m, advertencia f. 3 GB Jur reprensión f. II vtr advertir, amonestar.

cautious ['kɔːʃəs] adj cauteloso,-a, prudente.

cavalcade [kævəl'keɪd] n cabalgata f.

cavalier [kævə'lɪər] I adj arrogante. II n caballero m.

cavalry ['kævəlrɪ] n caballería f.

cave [keɪv] n cueva f. ◆**cave in** vi (roof etc) derrumbarse, hundirse.

caveman ['keɪvmæn] n hombre m de las cavernas.

cavern ['kævən] n caverna f.

caviar(e) ['kævɪɑːr] n caviar m.

cavity ['kævɪtɪ] n 1 (hole) cavidad f. 2 (in tooth) caries f inv.

cavort [kə'vɔːt] vi retozar, brincar.

CB [siː'biː] abbr Citizens' Band, banda ciudadana, CB.

CBI [siːbiː'aɪ] GB abbr of **Confederation of British Industry**, ≈ CEOE f.

cc [siː'siː] abbr of cubic centimetre(s), cc.

CD [siː'diː] abbr of compact disc, CD m; **CD player**, tocadiscos m digital o compacto.

cease [siːs] I vtr cesar; to c. doing or to do sth, dejar de hacer algo. II vi terminar.

cease-fire [siːs'faɪər] n alto m el fuego.

ceaseless ['siːslɪs] adj incesante.

cedar ['siːdər] n cedro m.

cede [siːd] vtr ceder.

ceiling ['siːlɪŋ] n techo m.

celebrate ['selɪbreɪt] I vtr (occasion) celebrar. II vi divertirse.

celebrated ['selɪbreɪtɪd] adj célebre.

celebration [selɪ'breɪʃən] n 1 celebración f. 2 celebrations, festividades fpl.

celebrity [sɪ'lebrɪtɪ] n celebridad f.

celery ['selərɪ] n apio m.

celibate ['selɪbɪt] adj & n célibe (mf).

cell [sel] n 1 (in prison) celda f. 2 Biol Pol célula f. 3 Elec pila f.

cellar ['selər] n sótano m; (for wine) bodega f.

cello ['tʃeləʊ] n violoncelo m.

cellophane ['seləfeɪn] n celofán m.

celluloid ['seljʊlɔɪd] n celuloide m.

cellulose ['seljʊləʊs] n celulosa f.

Celsius ['selsɪəs] adj Celsio.

Celt [selt, kelt] n celta mf.

Celtic ['keltɪk, 'seltɪk] I n (language) celta m. II adj celta.

cement [sɪ'ment] I n cemento m; c. mixer, hormigonera f. II vtr Constr unir con cemento; fig (friendship) cimentar.

cemetery ['semɪtrɪ] n cementerio m.

censor ['sensər] **I** n censor,-a m,f. **II** vtr censurar.

censorship ['sensəʃip] n censura f.

censure ['senʃər] **I** n censura f. **II** vtr censurar.

census ['sensəs] n censo m.

cent [sent] n **1** centavo m, céntimo m. **2** per c., por ciento.

centenary [sen'ti:nəri] n centenario m.

center ['sentər] n & vtr US → **centre**.

centigrade ['sentigreid] adj centígrado, -a.

centilitre, US **centiliter** ['sentili:tər] n centilitro m.

centimetre, US **centimeter** ['sentimi:tər] n centímetro m.

centipede ['sentipi:d] n ciempiés m inv.

central ['sentrəl] adj central; c. heating, calefacción f central; **C. America**, Centroamérica; **C. American**, centroamericano,-a m,f. ◆**centrally** adv c. heated, con calefacción central; c. situated, céntrico,-a.

centralize ['sentrəlaiz] vtr centralizar.

centre ['sentər] **I** n centro m; town c., centro de la ciudad; Ftb c. forward, delantero centro; Ftb c. half, medio centro; Pol c. party, partido m centrista; sports c., centro deportivo. **II** vtr (attention etc) centrar (on, en).

century ['sentʃəri] n siglo m; the nineteenth c., el siglo diecinueve.

ceramic [si'ræmik] **I** n cerámica f. **II** adj de cerámica.

ceramics [si'ræmiks] n sing cerámica f.

cereal ['siəriəl] n cereal m.

cerebral ['seribrəl, si'ri:brəl] adj cerebral; c. palsy, parálisis f cerebral.

ceremony ['seriməni] n ceremonia f.

certain ['sɜ:tən] **I** adj **1** (sure) seguro,-a; to be c., estar seguro,-a; to make c. of sth, asegurarse de algo. **2** to a c. extent, hasta cierto punto. **3** (not known) cierto, -a; a c. Miss Ward, una tal señorita Ward. **4** (true) cierto,-a. **II** adv for c., a ciencia cierta. ◆**certainly** adv desde luego; c. not, de ninguna manera.

certainty ['sɜ:tənti] n certeza f; (assurance) seguridad f.

certificate [sə'tifikit] n certificado m; Educ diploma m.

certified ['sɜ:tifaid] adj certificado,-a; (copy) compulsado,-a.

certify ['sɜ:tifai] vtr certificar.

cervical ['sɜ:vikəl, sə'vaikəl] adj c. cancer, cáncer m del útero; c. smear, frotis m cervical.

cervix ['sɜ:viks] n **1** (uterus) cuello m del útero. **2** (neck) cerviz f, cuello m.

cessation [se'seiʃən] n cese m.

cesspit ['sespit] n pozo negro.

Ceuta n Ceuta.

Ceylon [si'lɒn] n Ceilán.

cf abbr of confer, (compare) compárese, cfr.

chafe [tʃeif] **I** vtr (make sore) rozar. **II** vi (skin) irritarse; (item of clothing) rozar.

chaffinch ['tʃæfintʃ] n pinzón m vulgar.

chagrin ['ʃægrin] n disgusto m, desilusión f.

chain [tʃein] **I** n cadena f; fig (of events) serie f; c. of mountains, cordillera f; c. reaction, reacción f en cadena; c. saw, sierra mecánica. **II** vtr to c. (up), encadenar.

chain-smoke ['tʃeinsməuk] vi fumar un pitillo tras otro.

chair [tʃeər] **I** n **1** silla f; (with arms) sillón m; c. lift, telesilla m. **2** (position) presidencia f; Univ cátedra f. **II** vtr presidir.

chairman ['tʃeəmən] n presidente m.

chairperson ['tʃeəpɜ:sən] n presidente,-a m,f.

chalet ['ʃælei] n chalet m, chalé m.

chalk [tʃɔ:k] **I** n (for writing) tiza f. **II** ◆**chalk up** vtr fam (victory etc) apuntarse.

challenge ['tʃælindʒ] **I** n **1** reto m, desafiar; to c. sb to do sth, retar a algn a que haga algo. **2** (authority etc) poner a prueba; (statement) poner en duda. **3** Mil dar el alto a. **II** n **1** reto m, desafío m. **2** Mil quién vive m.

challenging ['tʃælindʒiŋ] adj (idea) desafiante; (task) que presenta un desafío.

chamber ['tʃeimbər] n **1** (hall) cámara f. C. of Commerce, Cámara de Comercio. **2** Mus c. music, música f de cámara. **3** GB Jur chambers, gabinete m sing.

chambermaid ['tʃeimbəmeid] n camarera f.

chameleon [kə'mi:liən] n camaleón m.

champagne [ʃæm'pein] n (French) champán m; (from Catalonia) cava m.

champion ['tʃæmpiən] n campeón,-ona m,f; fig c. of human rights, defensor,-a de los derechos humanos.

championship ['tʃæmpiənʃip] n campeonato m.

chance [tʃɑ:ns] **I** n **1** (fortune) casualidad f, azar m; by c., por casualidad; to take a c., arriesgarse; c. meeting, encuentro m casual. **2** (likelihood) posibilidad f; (the) chances are that ..., lo más posible es que .... **3** (opportunity) oportunidad f. **II** vtr to c. upon, encontrar por casualidad. **III** vtr arriesgar.

chancellor ['tʃɑ:nsələr] n **1** (head of state, in embassy) canciller m. **2** GB Univ rector,-a m,f. **3** GB C. of the Exchequer, ministro,-a m,f de Hacienda.

chandelier [ʃændi'liər] n araña f (de luces).

change [tʃeindʒ] **I** vtr cambiar; to c. gear, cambiar de marcha; to c. one's mind/the subject, cambiar de opinión/de tema; to c. trains, hacer trasbordo; to get changed, cambiarse de ropa; fig to c.

hands, cambiar de dueño,-a. II *vi* cambiar, cambiarse; to c. for the better/**worse**, mejorar/empeorar; to c. into, convertirse en. III *n* 1 cambio *m*. 2 (money) cambio *m*; (after purchase) vuelta *f*; **small c.**, suelto *m*. ◆**change over** *vi* cambiarse.

changeable ['tʃeɪndʒəbəl] *adj* (weather) variable; (person) inconstante.

changeover ['tʃeɪndʒəʊvəʳ] *n* conversión *f*.

changing ['tʃeɪndʒɪŋ] I *n* 1 c. **room**, vestuario *m*. 2 Mil relevo *m* (de la guardia). II *adj* cambiante.

channel ['tʃænəl] I *n* 1 Geog canal *m*; (of river) cauce *m*; the C. Islands, las Islas Anglonormandas; the **English** C., el Canal de la Mancha. 2 (administrative) vía *f*. 3 TV Rad canal *m*, cadena *f*. II *vtr* fig (ideas etc) canalizar, encauzar.

chant [tʃɑ:nt] I *n* Rel cántico *m*; (of demonstrators) slogan *m*. II *vtr & vi* Rel cantar; (demonstrators) corear.

chaos ['keɪɒs] *n* caos *m*.

chaotic [keɪ'ɒtɪk] *adj* caótico,-a.

chap [tʃæp] *n fam* chico *m*, tío *m*.

chapel ['tʃæpəl] *n* capilla *f*.

chaperon(e) ['ʃæpərəʊn] *n* carabina *f*.

chaplain ['tʃæplɪn] *n* capellán *m*.

chapter ['tʃæptəʳ] *n* 1 capítulo *m*. 2 Rel cabildo *m*.

char [tʃɑ:ʳ] *vtr* chamuscar, carbonizar.

character ['kærɪktəʳ] *n* 1 carácter *m*. 2 *fam* (person) tipo *m*. 3 Theat personaje *m*.

characteristic [kærɪktə'rɪstɪk] I *n* característica *f*. II *adj* característico,-a.

characterize ['kærɪktəraɪz] *vtr* caracterizar.

charcoal ['tʃɑ:kəʊl] *n* Min carbón *m* vegetal; Art c. **drawing**, carboncillo *m*; grey, gris marengo *or* oscuro.

charge [tʃɑ:dʒ] I *vtr* 1 cobrar; c. it to my **account**, cárguelo en mi cuenta. 2 to **sb with a crime**, acusar a algn de un crimen. 3 Mil cargar contra. 4 Elec cargar. II *vi* Elec Mil cargar; to c. **about**, andar a lo loco. III *n* 1 (cost) precio *m*; bank **charges**, comisión *f*; free of c., gratis; **service c.**, servicio *m*; c. **account**, cuenta *f* corriente. 2 to be in c. of, estar a cargo de; to **take** c. of, hacerse cargo de. 3 Jur cargo *m*, acusación *f*. 4 (explosive) carga explosiva. 5 Elec carga *f*.

charged [tʃɑ:dʒd] *adj fig* emotivo,-a.

charismatic ['kærɪz'mætɪk] *adj* carismático,-a.

charitable ['tʃærɪtəbəl] *adj* (person) caritativo,-a; (organization) benéfico,-a.

charity ['tʃærɪtɪ] *n* caridad *f*; (organization) institución benéfica.

charlady ['tʃɑ:leɪdɪ] *n* GB mujer *f* de la limpieza.

charlatan ['ʃɑ:lətən] *n* (doctor) curandero,-a *m,f*.

charm [tʃɑ:m] I *n* 1 (quality) encanto *m*. 2 (spell) hechizo *m*; **lucky** c., amuleto *m*. II *vtr* encantar.

charming ['tʃɑ:mɪŋ] *adj* encantador,-a.

chart [tʃɑ:t] I *n* 1 (giving information) tabla *f*; (graph) gráfico *m*. 2 (map) carta *f* de navegación. 3 Mus **the charts**, la lista de éxitos. II *vtr* Av Naut (on map) trazar.

charter ['tʃɑ:təʳ] I *n* 1 (of institution) estatutos *mpl*; (of rights) carta *f*. 2 c. **flight**, vuelo *m* chárter. II *vtr* (plane, boat) fletar.

chartered accountant ['tʃɑ:tədə'kaʊntənt] *n* GB contable *mf* diplomado,-a.

charwoman ['tʃɑ:wʊmən] *n* GB → **charlady**.

chase [tʃeɪs] *vtr* perseguir; (hunt) cazar. II *n* persecución *f*; (hunt) caza *f*.

chasm ['kæzəm] *n* Geog sima *f*; *fig* abismo *m*.

chassis ['ʃæsɪ] *n* chasis *m inv*.

chastise [tʃæs'taɪz] *vtr* castigar.

chastity ['tʃæstɪtɪ] *n* castidad *f*.

chat [tʃæt] I *n* charla *f*; GB c. **show**, coloquio *m*. II *vi* charlar. ◆**chat up** *vtr fam* (intentar) ligar con algn.

chatter ['tʃætəʳ] I *vi* (person) parlotear; (bird) piar; (teeth) castañetear. II *n* (of person) parloteo *m*; (of birds) gorjeo *m*; (of teeth) castañeteo *m*.

chatterbox ['tʃætəbɒks] *n fam* parlanchín,-ina *m,f*.

chatty ['tʃætɪ] *adj* (chattier, chattiest) hablador,-a.

chauffeur ['ʃəʊfəʳ, ʃəʊ'fɜ:ʳ] *n* chófer *mf*.

chauvinism ['ʃəʊvɪnɪzəm] *n* chovinismo *m*; **male** c., machismo *m*.

chauvinist ['ʃəʊvɪnɪst] *adj & n* chovinista (*mf*); **male** c., machista *m,f*.

cheap [tʃi:p] I *adj* barato,-a; (fare) económico,-a; (joke) de mal gusto; (contemptible) bajo,-a; **male** dirt c., tirado,-a. II *n* GB *fam* **on the** c., en plan barato. III *adv* barato. ◆**cheaply** *adv* barato, en plan económico.

cheapen ['tʃi:pən] *vtr fig* degradar.

cheat [tʃi:t] I *vtr* engañar; to c. **sb out of sth**, estafar algo a algn. II *vi* 1 (at games) hacer trampa; (in exam etc) copiar(se). 2 *fam* (husband, wife) poner cuernos (on, a). III *n* (trickster) tramposo,-a.

check [tʃek] I *vtr* 1 repasar; (facts) comprobar; (tickets) controlar; (tyres, oil) revisar. 2 (impulse) refrenar; (growth) retardar. 3 (stop) detener. 4 Chess dar jaque a. II *vi* comprobar. III *n* 1 (of documents etc) revisión *f*; (of facts) comprobación *f*. 2 Chess jaque *m*. 3 (pattern) cuadro *m*. 4 **to keep in** c., (feelings) contener; (enemy) mantener a raya. 5 US → **cheque**. ◆**check in** *vi* (at airport) facturar; (at hotel) registrarse (at, en). ◆**check out** I *vi* (of ho-

tel) dejar el hotel. **II** *vtr (facts)* verificar. **◆check up** *vi* to c. **up on sb,** hacer averiguaciones sobre algn; **to c. up on sth,** comprobar algo.

checked ['tʃekt] *adj* a cuadros.

checker ['tʃekər] *n US (cashier)* cajero,-a *m,f*.

checkered ['tʃekəd] *adj US* → **chequered.**

checkers ['tʃekəz] *n US (game)* damas *fpl.*

check-in ['tʃekɪn] *n* **c.-in desk,** *(at airport)* mostrador *m* de facturación.

checkmate ['tʃekmeɪt] **I** *n Chess* jaque mate *m*. **II** *vtr Chess* dar (jaque) mate a; *fig* poner en un callejón sin salida.

checkout ['tʃekaʊt] *n (counter)* caja *f.*

checkpoint ['tʃekpɔɪnt] *n* control *m.*

checkup ['tʃekʌp] *n Med* chequeo *m*, examen médico.

cheek [tʃiːk] *n* **1** mejilla *f*. **2** *fam (nerve)* cara *f*; **what c.!,** ¡vaya jeta!

cheekbone ['tʃiːkbəʊn] *n* pómulo *m.*

cheeky ['tʃiːkɪ] *adj* **(cheekier, cheekiest)** *fam* fresco,-a, descarado,-a.

cheep [tʃiːp] **I** *n (of bird)* pío *m*, piar. **II** *vi* piar.

cheer [tʃɪər] **I** *vi* aplaudir, aclamar. **II** *vtr* **1** *(applaud)* vitorear, aclamar. **2** *(make hopeful)* animar. **III** *n* viva *m*; cheers, aplausos *mpl*; **cheers!,** *(thank you)* gracias; *(before drinking)* ¡salud! **◆cheer up I** *vi* animarse. **II** *vtr* to c. **sb up,** alegrar *or* animar a algn.

cheerful ['tʃɪəfʊl] *adj* alegre.

cheerio [tʃɪərɪ'əʊ] *interj GB fam* ¡hasta luego!

cheese [tʃiːz] *n* queso *m.*

cheesecake ['tʃiːzkeɪk] *n* tarta *f* de queso.

cheetah ['tʃiːtə] *n* guepardo *m.*

chef [ʃef] *n* chef *m.*

chemical ['kemɪkəl] **I** *n* sustancia química, producto químico. **II** *adj* químico,-a.

chemist ['kemɪst] *n* **1** químico,-a *m,f*. **2** *GB* **c.'s (shop),** farmacia *f*; **dispensing** c., farmacéutico,-a *m,f.*

chemistry ['kemɪstrɪ] *n* química *f.*

cheque [tʃek] *n* cheque *m*; **to pay by c.,** pagar con (un) cheque; **c. book,** talonario *m* (de cheques); **c. card,** tarjeta *f* de identificación bancaria.

chequered ['tʃekəd] *adj* a cuadros; *fig* a **c. career,** una carrera con altibajos.

cherish ['tʃerɪʃ] *vtr* **1** *(person)* tenerle mucho cariño a. **2** *fig (hopes etc)* abrigar.

cherry ['tʃerɪ] *n* cereza *f.*

chess [tʃes] *n* ajedrez *m.*

chessboard ['tʃesbɔːd] *n* tablero *m* de ajedrez.

chesspiece ['tʃespiːs] *n* pieza *f* de ajedrez.

chest [tʃest] *n* **1** *Anat* pecho *m*. **2** *(for linen)* arca *f*; *(for valuables)* cofre *m*; **c. of**

drawers, cómoda *f.*

chestnut ['tʃesnʌt] *n (tree, colour)* castaño *m*; *(nut)* castaña *f.*

chew [tʃuː] *vtr* masticar, mascar.

chewing gum ['tʃuːɪŋɡʌm] *n* chicle *m.*

chic [ʃiːk] *adj* elegante.

chick [tʃɪk] *n* pollito *m.*

chicken ['tʃɪkɪn] **I** *n* **1** pollo *m*. **2** *sl (coward)* gallina *f*. **II** *vi fam* to c. **out,** rajarse (por miedo).

chickenpox ['tʃɪkɪnpɒks] *n* varicela *f.*

chickpea ['tʃɪkpiː] *n* garbanzo *m.*

chicory ['tʃɪkərɪ] *n* achicoria *f.*

chief [tʃiːf] **I** *n* jefe *m*. **II** *adj* principal. **◆chiefly** *adv (above all)* sobre todo; *(mainly)* principalmente.

chiffon [ʃɪ'fɒn, 'ʃɪfɒn] *n* gasa *f.*

chilblain ['tʃɪlbleɪn] *n* sabañón *m.*

child [tʃaɪld] *n (pl* **children)** niño,-a *m,f*; *(son)* hijo *m*; *(daughter)* hija *f*; c. **minder,** persona *f* que cuida niños en su propia casa.

childbirth ['tʃaɪldbɜːθ] *n* parto *m.*

childhood ['tʃaɪldhʊd] *n* infancia *f*, niñez *f.*

childish ['tʃaɪldɪʃ] *adj* pueril, aniñado.

childlike ['tʃaɪldlaɪk] *adj* infantil.

children ['tʃɪldrən] *npl* → **child.**

Chile ['tʃɪlɪ] *n* Chile.

Chilean ['tʃɪlɪən] *adj & n* chileno,-a *(m,f).*

chill [tʃɪl] **I** *n* **1** *Med* resfriado *m*. **2** *(coldness)* fresco *m*. **II** *adj* frío,-a. **III** *vtr (meat)* refrigerar; *(wine)* enfriar.

chill(i) ['tʃɪlɪ] *n* chile *m.*

chilly ['tʃɪlɪ] *adj* **(chillier, chilliest)** frío, -a.

chime [tʃaɪm] **I** *n (peal)* campanada *f*. **II** *vtr* to c. **five o'clock,** *(of clock)* dar las cinco. **III** *vi* sonar. **◆chime in** *vi fam* intervenir.

chimney ['tʃɪmnɪ] *n* chimenea *f*; **c. sweep,** deshollinador *m.*

chimpanzee [tʃɪmpæn'ziː] *n* chimpancé *m.*

chin [tʃɪn] *n* barbilla *f*, mentón *m*; **double c.,** papada *f.*

china ['tʃaɪnə] *n* loza *f.*

China ['tʃaɪnə] *n* China.

Chinese [tʃaɪ'niːz] **I** *adj* chino,-a. **II** *n* **1** *(person)* chino,-a *m,f*. **2** *(language)* chino *m.*

chink¹ [tʃɪŋk] *n (opening)* resquicio *m*; *(crack)* grieta *f.*

chink² [tʃɪŋk] **I** *vi* tintinear. **II** *n* tintineo *m.*

chip [tʃɪp] **I** *n* **1** *(of wood)* astilla *f*; *(of stone)* lasca *f*; *(in cup)* mella *f*. **2** *GB Culin* chips, patatas fritas. **3** *Comput* chip *m*. **4** *(in gambling)* ficha *f*. **II** *vtr (wood)* astillar; *(stone)* resquebrajar; *(china, glass)* mellar. **III** *vi (wood)* astillarse; *(china, glass)* mellarse; *(paint)* desconcharse. **◆chip in** *vi fam* **1** meterse. **2** *(with money)* poner algo (de dinero).

chiropodist [kɪ'rɒpədɪst] *n* pedicuro,-a *m,f*.

chirp [tʃɜːp] *vi* (*birds*) gorjear.

chisel ['tʃɪzəl] *n* cincel *m*.

chit [tʃɪt] *n* nota *f*; (*small invoice*) vale *m*.

chitchat ['tʃɪttʃæt] *n fam* palique *m*.

chivalry ['ʃɪvəlrɪ] *n* caballerosidad *f*.

chives [tʃaɪvz] *npl* cebolleta *f sing*.

chlorine ['klɔːriːn] *n* cloro *m*.

chock-a-block [tʃɒkə'blɒk], **chock-full** [tʃɒk'ful] *adj fam* (lleno,-a) hasta los topes.

chocolate ['tʃɒkəlɪt] I *n* chocolate *m*; **chocolates**, bombones *mpl*. II *adj* de chocolate.

choice [tʃɔɪs] I *n* elección *f*; a wide c., un gran surtido; **by c.**, por gusto. II *adj* selecto,-a.

choir ['kwaɪər] *n* coro *m*, coral *f*.

choirboy ['kwaɪəbɔɪ] *n* niño *m* de coro.

choke [tʃəʊk] I *vtr* 1 (*person*) ahogar. 2 (*obstruct*) obstruir. II *vi* ahogarse; **to c. on food**, atragantarse con la comida. III *n Aut* estárter *m*. ◆**choke back** *vtr* (*emotions*) tragarse.

cholera ['kɒlərə] *n* cólera *m*.

cholesterol [kə'lestərɒl] *n* colesterol *m*.

choose [tʃuːz] I *vtr* (*pt chose; pp chosen*) escoger, elegir; (*decide on*) optar por. II *vi* escoger, elegir.

choos(e)y ['tʃuːzɪ] *adj* (**choosier, choosiest**) *fam* exigente.

chop [tʃɒp] I *vtr* 1 (*wood*) cortar; (*tree*) talar. 2 *Culin* cortar a pedacitos. II *n* 1 (*blow*) tajo *m*; (*with axe*) hachazo *m*. 2 *Culin* chuleta *f*.

chopper ['tʃɒpər] *n fam* helicóptero *m*.

choppy ['tʃɒpɪ] *adj* (**choppier, choppiest**) (*sea*) picado,-a.

chopsticks ['tʃɒpstɪks] *npl* palillos *mpl*.

chord [kɔːd] *n Mus* acorde *m*; **fig it strikes a c.**, (me) suena.

chore [tʃɔːr] *n* quehacer *m*, tarea *f*.

chortle ['tʃɔːtəl] *vi* reír con ganas.

chorus ['kɔːrəs] *n Mus Theat* coro *m*; (*in a song*) estribillo *m*; **c. girl**, corista *f*.

chose [tʃəʊz] *pt* → **choose**.

chosen ['tʃəʊzən] *pp* → **choose**.

Christ [kraɪst] *n* Cristo *m*, Jesucristo *m*.

christen ['krɪsən] *vtr* bautizar.

christening ['krɪsənɪŋ] *n* bautizo *m*.

Christian ['krɪstʃən] I *adj* cristiano,-a; **c. name**, nombre *m* de pila. II *n* cristiano,-a *m,f*.

Christianity [krɪstɪ'ænɪtɪ] *n* cristianismo *m*.

Christmas ['krɪsməs] *n* Navidad *f*; **merry C.**, feliz Navidad; **C. card**, tarjeta *f* de Navidad; **C. carol**, villancico *m*; **C. Day**, día *m* de Navidad; **C. Eve**, Nochebuena *f*.

chrome [krəʊm] *n* cromo *m*.

chromium ['krəʊmɪəm] *n* cromo *m*; **c. plating**, cromado *m*.

chromosome ['krəʊməsəʊm] *n* cromosoma *m*.

chronic ['krɒnɪk] *adj* crónico,-a.

chronicle ['krɒnɪkəl] I *n* crónica *f*. II *vtr* hacer la crónica de.

chronological [krɒnə'lɒdʒɪkəl] *adj* cronológico,-a.

chrysanthemum [krɪ'sænθəməm] *n* crisantemo *m*.

chubby ['tʃʌbɪ] *adj* (**chubbier, chubbiest**) rellenito,-a.

chuck [tʃʌk] *vtr fam* tirar; **to c. one's job in** *or* **up**, dejar el trabajo; **to c. sb out**, echar a algn; **to c. sth away** *or* **out**, tirar algo.

chuckle ['tʃʌkəl] I *vi* reír entre dientes. II *n* sonrisa *f*.

chug [tʃʌg] *vi* traquetear.

chum [tʃʌm] *n* compinche *mf*, compañero,-a *m,f*.

chunk [tʃʌŋk] *n fam* cacho *m*, pedazo *m*.

church [tʃɜːtʃ] *n* iglesia *f*; **to go to c.**, ir a misa; **C. of England**, Iglesia Anglicana.

churchyard ['tʃɜːtʃjɑːd] *n* cementerio *m*, campo santo.

churlish ['tʃɜːlɪʃ] *adj* grosero,-a.

churn [tʃɜːn] I *n* (*for butter*) mantequera *f*; **GB** (*for milk*) lechera *f*. II *vtr* (*butter*) hacer. III *vi* revolverse, agitarse. ◆**churn out** *vtr fam* producir en serie.

chute [ʃuːt] *n* (*channel*) conducto *m*; (*slide*) tobogán *m*.

chutney ['tʃʌtnɪ] *n* conserva *f* (de frutas) picante.

CIA [siːaɪ'eɪ] *US abbr of* **Central Intelligence Agency**, Agencia *f* Central de Información, CIA *f*.

CID [siːaɪ'diː] *GB abbr of* **Criminal Investigation Department**, ≈ Brigada *f* de Investigación Criminal, BIC.

cider ['saɪdər] *n* sidra *f*.

cigar [sɪ'gɑːr] *n* puro *m*.

cigarette [sɪgə'ret] *n* cigarrillo *m*; **c. case**, pitillera *f*; **c. end**, colilla *f*; **c. holder**, boquilla *f*; **c. lighter**, mechero *m*.

Cinderella [sɪndə'relə] *n* Cenicienta *f*.

cine camera ['sɪnɪkæmərə] *n GB* cámara cinematográfica.

cinema ['sɪnɪmə] *n* cine *m*.

cinnamon ['sɪnəmən] *n* canela *f*.

cipher ['saɪfər] *n* (*numeral*) cifra *f*.

circle ['sɜːkəl] I *n* 1 círculo *m*; (*of people*) corro *m*; **in business circles**, en el mundo de los negocios. 2 *Theat* anfiteatro *m*. II *vtr* (*surround*) rodear; (*move round*) dar la vuelta a. III *vi* dar vueltas.

circular ['sɜːkjʊlər] *adj* & *n* circular (*f*).

circulate ['sɜːkjʊleɪt] I *vtr* (*news*) hacer circular. II *vi* circular.

circulation [sɜːkjʊ'leɪʃən] *n* 1 (*of blood*)

circulación f. 2 (of newspaper) tirada f.

circumcise ['sɜːkəmsaɪz] vtr circuncidar.

circumference [sə'kʌmfərəns] n circunferencia f.

circumspect ['sɜːkəmspekt] adj prudente.

circumstance ['sɜːkəmstəns] n (usu pl) circunstancia f; **under no circumstances**, en ningún caso; **economic circumstances**, situación económica.

circumvent [sɜːkəm'vent] vtr fig burlar.

circus ['sɜːkəs] n circo m.

cirrhosis [sɪ'rəʊsɪs] n cirrosis f.

CIS [siːaɪ'es] n abbr of **Commonwealth of Independent States**, CEI.

cistern ['sɪstən] n cisterna f.

cite [saɪt] vtr (quote) citar.

citizen ['sɪtɪzən] n ciudadano,-a m,f.

citizenship ['sɪtɪzənʃɪp] n ciudadanía f.

citr(o)us ['sɪtrəs] adj c. fruit, agrios mpl.

city ['sɪtɪ] n 1 ciudad f. 2 Fin the C., el centro financiero de Londres.

civic ['sɪvɪk] adj cívico,-a; **c. centre**, centro cívico; **c. duties**, obligaciones cívicas.

civil ['sɪvəl] adj 1 civil; **c. defence**, defensa f civil; **c. rights**, derechos mpl civiles; **c. servant**, funcionario,-a m,f; Pol **c. service**, administración pública. 2 (polite) cortés, educado,-a.

civilian [sɪ'vɪljən] adj & n civil (mf); **c. clothing** traje m de paisano.

civilization [sɪvɪlaɪ'zeɪʃən] n civilización f.

civilized ['sɪvɪlaɪzd] adj civilizado,-a.

clad [klæd] adj lit vestido,-a.

claim [kleɪm] I vtr 1 (benefits, rights) reclamar; Jur (compensation) exigir. 2 (assert) afirmar. II n 1 (demand) reclamación f; Jur demanda f; **to put in a c.**, reclamar una indemnización. 2 (right) derecho m. 3 (assertion) pretensión f.

claimant ['kleɪmənt] n Jur demandante mf.

clairvoyant [kleə'vɔɪənt] n clarividente mf.

clam [klæm] n almeja f. ◆**clam up** vi fam callarse.

clamber ['klæmbər] vi trepar (over, por).

clammy ['klæmɪ] adj (clammier, clammiest) (weather) bochornoso,-a; (hand) pegajoso,-a.

clamor ['klæmər] n US → clamour.

clamour ['klæmər] I n clamor m. II vi clamar; **to c. for**, pedir a gritos.

clamp [klæmp] I n 1 (for carpentry) tornillo m de banco; Tech abrazadera f; wheel **c.**, cepo m. II vtr sujetar con abrazaderas. ◆**clamp down** vtr aumentar los esfuerzos contra.

clan [klæn] n clan m.

clandestine [klæn'destɪn] adj clandestino,-a.

clang [klæŋ] I vi sonar. II n sonido metálico.

clap [klæp] I vi aplaudir. II n 1 palmada f. 2 **a c. of thunder**, un trueno.

clapping ['klæpɪŋ] n aplausos mpl.

claret ['klærət] n GB (wine) clarete m; (colour) burdeos m.

clarify ['klærɪfaɪ] vtr aclarar.

clarinet [klærɪ'net] n clarinete m.

clarity ['klærɪtɪ] n claridad f.

clash [klæʃ] I vi 1 (cymbals) sonar; (swords) chocar; fig (disagree) estar en desacuerdo. 2 (colours) desentonar. 3 (dates) coincidir. II n 1 (sound) sonido m. 2 (fight) choque m; fig (conflict) conflicto m.

clasp [klɑːsp] I n 1 (on belt) cierre m; (on necklace) broche m. 2 (grasp) apretón m; **c. knife**, navaja f. II vtr (object) agarrar; **to c. hands**, juntar las manos.

class [klɑːs] I n 1 clase f; **working c.**, lucha f de clases; Educ **c. of '84**, promoción f de 1984; Rail **second c. ticket**, billete m de segunda (clase). II vtr clasificar.

classic ['klæsɪk] I adj clásico,-a. II n 1 (author) autor clásico; (work) obra clásica. 2 **the classics**, (literature) las obras clásicas; (languages) clásicas fpl.

classical ['klæsɪkəl] adj clásico,-a.

classified ['klæsɪfaɪd] adj (information) secreto,-a; **c. advertisements**, anuncios mpl por palabras.

classify ['klæsɪfaɪ] vtr clasificar.

classless ['klɑːslɪs] adj sin clases.

classmate ['klɑːsmeɪt] n compañero,-a m,f de clase.

classroom ['klɑːsruːm] n aula f, clase f.

clatter ['klætər] I vi hacer ruido; (things falling) hacer estrépito. II n ruido m, estrépito m.

clause [klɔːz] n 1 Jur cláusula f. 2 Ling oración f.

claw [klɔː] I n (of bird, lion) garra f; (of cat) uña f; (of crab) pinza f. II vtr agarrar, arañar; (tear) desgarrar. ◆**claw at** vtr agarrar, arañar.

clay [kleɪ] n arcilla f; **c. pigeon shooting**, tiro m al plato.

clean [kliːn] I adj 1 limpio,-a. 2 (unmarked, pure) sin defecto; **a c. copy**, una copia en limpio; **to have a c. record**, no tener antecedentes (penales). 3 (not obscene) decente. 4 fig **to make a c. sweep of it**, arrasar. II adv 1 **to play c.**, jugar limpio; fam **to come c.**, confesarlo todo. 2 fam por completo; **it went c. through the middle**, pasó justo por el medio. III vtr (room) limpiar; **to c. one's teeth**, lavarse los dientes. ◆**clean out** vtr (room) limpiar a fondo. ◆**clean up** vtr & vi limpiar.

clean-cut ['kliːnkʌt] adj (person) limpio,-a, pulcro,-a.

cleaner ['kliːnər] n limpiador,-a m,f.

cleaning ['kliːnɪŋ] n limpieza f.

cleanliness ['klenlɪnɪs] n limpieza f.

cleanse [klenz] *vtr* limpiar.

cleansing [ˈklenzɪŋ] *n* **c. lotion**, leche limpiadora.

clear [klɪər] **I** *adj* **1** claro,-a; *(road, day)* despejado,-a; *(obvious)* claro,-a; **to make sth c.**, aclarar algo. **3** *(majority)* absoluto; *(profit)* neto; **three c. days**, tres días completos. **4** *(free)* libre. **II** *adv* **1** *fig* **loud and c.**, claramente. **2 stand c.!**, ¡apártese!; **to stay c. of**, evitar. **III** *vtr* **1** *(room)* vaciar; *Com* liquidar; **to c. one's throat**, aclararse la garganta; **to c. the table**, quitar la mesa. **2** *(authorize)* autorizar. **3** *(hurdle)* salvar. **4** **to c. sb of a charge**, exculpar a algn de un delito. **IV** *vi* *(sky)* despejarse. ◆**clear away** *vtr* quitar. ◆**clear off** *vi fam* largarse; **c. off!**, ¡largo! ◆**clear out** *vtr* *(room)* limpiar a fondo; *(cupboard)* vaciar. ◆**clear up I** *vtr* **1** *(tidy)* recoger; *(arrange)* ordenar. **2** *(mystery)* aclarar; *(misunderstanding)* aclarar. **II** *vi* *(weather)* despejarse; *(problem)* desaparecer. ◆**clearly** *adv* **1** claramente. **2** *(at start of sentence)* evidentemente.

clearance [ˈklɪərəns] *n* **1** *(of area)* despeje *m*; *Com* **c. sale**, liquidación *f* (de existencias). **2** *(space)* espacio *m* libre. **3** *(authorization)* autorización *f*.

clear-cut [klɪəˈkʌt] *adj* claro,-a.

clearing [ˈklɪərɪŋ] *n* **1** *(in wood)* claro *m*. **2** *(of rubbish)* limpieza *f*. **3** *(of cheque)* compensación *f*.

clearway [ˈklɪəweɪ] *n* *GB* carretera *f* donde está prohibido parar.

cleaver [ˈkliːvər] *n* cuchillo *m* de carnicero.

clef [klef] *n* clave *f*; **bass/treble c.**, clave de fa/de sol.

cleft [kleft] *n* hendidura *f*, grieta *f*.

clementine [ˈkleməntaɪn] *n* clementina *f*.

clench [klentʃ] *vtr* *(teeth, fist)* apretar.

clergy [ˈklɜːdʒɪ] *n* clero *m*.

clergyman [ˈklɜːdʒɪmən] *n* clérigo *m*.

clerical [ˈklerɪkəl] *adj* **1** *Rel* clerical. **2** *(staff, work)* de oficina.

clerk [klɑːk, *US* klɜːrk] *n* **1** *(office worker)* oficinista *mf*; *(civil servant)* funcionario,-a *m,f*. **2** *US Com* dependiente,-a *m,f*, vendedor,-a *m,f*.

clever [ˈklevər] *adj* **1** *(person)* inteligente, listo,-a; **to be c. at sth**, tener aptitud para algo; *fam* **c. Dick**, sabiondo,-a *m,f*. **2** *(argument)* ingenioso,-a.

cliché [ˈkliːʃeɪ] *n* cliché *m*.

click [klɪk] **I** *n* *(sound)* clic *m*. **II** *vtr* *(tongue)* chasquear. **III** *vi* **it didn't c.**, (*I didn't realise*) no me di cuenta.

client [ˈklaɪənt] *n* cliente *m*.

clientele [kliːɒnˈtel] *n* clientela *f*.

cliff [klɪf] *n* acantilado *m*.

climate [ˈklaɪmɪt] *n* clima *m*.

climax [ˈklaɪmæks] *n* **1** *(peak)* clímax *m*, punto *m* culminante. **2** *(sexual)* orgasmo *m*.

climb [klaɪm] **I** *vtr* *(ladder)* subir a; *(mountain)* escalar; *(tree)* trepar a. **II** *vi* *(plants)* trepar; *Av* subir; *fig (socially)* ascender. **III** *n* subida *f*, ascensión *f*. ◆**climb down** *vi* bajar; *fig* volverse atrás.

climber [ˈklaɪmər] *n* alpinista *mf*, *Am* andinista *mf*.

climbing [ˈklaɪmɪŋ] *n Sport* montañismo *m*, alpinismo *m*, *Am* andinismo *m*.

clinch [klɪntʃ] **I** *vtr* resolver; *(deal)* cerrar. **II** *n* sl* abrazo apasionado.

cling [klɪŋ] *vi* *(pt & pp* **clung**) *(hang on)* agarrarse; *(clothes)* ajustarse; *(smell)* pegarse; **to c. together**, unirse.

clinic [ˈklɪnɪk] *n (in state hospital)* ambulatorio *m*; *(specialized)* clínica *f*.

clinical [ˈklɪnɪkəl] *adj* **1** *Med* clínico,-a. **2** *(detached)* frío,-a.

clink [klɪŋk] **I** *vi* tintinear. **II** *n* tintineo *m*.

clip¹ [klɪp] **I** *vtr* *(cut)* cortar; *(ticket)* picar. **II** *n* **1** *(of film)* extracto *m*. **2** *(with scissors)* tijeretada *f*.

clip² [klɪp] **I** *n* *(for hair)* pasador *m*; *(for paper)* clip *m*, sujetapapeles *m inv*; *(brooch)* clip. **II** *vtr* sujetar.

clippers [ˈklɪpəz] *npl* *(for hair)* maquinilla *f* para rapar; *(for nails)* cortaúñas *m inv*; *(for hedge)* tijeras *fpl* de podar.

clipping [ˈklɪpɪŋ] *n* recorte *m*.

clique [kliːk, klɪk] *n* pej camarilla *f*.

cloak [kləʊk] **I** *n* *(garment)* capa *f*. **II** *vtr* encubrir.

cloakroom [ˈkləʊkruːm] *n* guardarropa *m*; *euph (toilets)* servicios *mpl*.

clock [klɒk] **I** *n* reloj *m*. **II** *vtr* *(race)* cronometrar. ◆**clock in, clock on** *vi* fichar. ◆**clock off, clock out** *vi* fichar a la salida. ◆**clock up** *vtr* *(mileage)* hacer.

clockwise [ˈklɒkwaɪz] *adj & adv* en el sentido de las agujas del reloj.

clockwork [ˈklɒkwɜːk] *n* mecanismo *m*; **c. toy**, juguete *m* de cuerda.

clog [klɒg] **I** *vtr* obstruir; *(pipe)* atascar; **to get clogged up**, atascarse. **II** *n* *(footwear)* zueco *m*.

cloister [ˈklɔɪstər] *n* claustro *m*.

close¹ [kləʊs] **I** *adj* **1** *(in space, time)* cercano,-a; *(print, weave)* compacto,-a; *(encounter)* cara a cara; *(contact)* directo, -a; **c. to**, cerca de; **c. together**, juntos; *fig* **we had a c. shave**, nos libramos por los pelos. **2** *(relationship)* estrecho,-a; *(friend)* íntimo,-a. **3** *(inspection)* detallado,-a; *(watch)* atento,-a. **4** *(contest)* reñido,-a; **a c. resemblance**, un gran parecido. **5** *(air)* cargado,-a; *(weather)* bochornoso,-a. **6** *(secretive)* reservado,-a. **7 c. season**, *(in hunting)* veda *f*. **II** *adv* cerca; **they live c. by** or **c. at hand**, viven cerca; **to stand c. together**, estar apretados,-as. ◆**closely** *adv* **1** *(tightly)* estrechamente; *(c.*

contested, muy reñido,-a; **they are c. re-**
lated, *(people)* son parientes próximos. 2
(attentively) con atención; **to follow**
(events) c., seguir de cerca (los acontecimientos).

close² [kləʊz] I *vtr* 1 cerrar; **closing**
time, hora *f* de cierre. 2 *(end)* concluir,
terminar; *(meeting)* levantar. II *vi* 1 *(shut)*
cerrar, cerrarse. 2 *(end)* concluirse, terminarse. III *n* fin *m*, final *m*. ◆**close**
down *vi (business)* cerrar para siempre;
Rad TV cerrar. ◆**close in** *vi* to c. in
on sb, rodear a algn.

closed [kləʊzd] *adj* cerrado,-a; *Ind* c.
shop, empresa *f* que emplea solamente a
miembros de un sindicato.

close-knit [kləʊs'nɪt] *adj* fig unido,-a.

closet ['klɒzɪt] *n US* armario *m*.

close-up ['kləʊsʌp] *n* primer plano *m*.

closure ['kləʊʒər] *n* cierre *m*.

clot [klɒt] I *n* 1 *(of blood)* coágulo *m*; *Med*
c. on the brain, embolia *f* cerebral. 2 *GB*
fam tonto,-a *m,f*. II *vi* coagularse.

cloth [klɒθ] *n* tela *f*, paño *m*; *(rag)* trapo
m; *(tablecloth)* mantel *m*.

clothe [kləʊð] *vtr (pt & pp clothed or
clad)* vestir **(in,** with, de); fig revestir, cubrir **(in,** with, de).

clothes [kləʊðz] *npl* ropa *f sing,* vestidos
mpl, c. **brush,** cepillo *m* de la ropa; c.
hanger, percha *f*; c. **horse,** tendedero *m*
plegable; c. **line,** tendedero *m*; c. **peg,**
pinza *f*.

clothing ['kləʊðɪŋ] *n* ropa *f*.

cloud [klaʊd] I *n* nube *f*. II *vtr* nublar; fig
to c. the issue, complicar el asunto. III
vi to c. over, nublarse.

cloudy ['klaʊdɪ] *adj (cloudier, cloudiest)*
1 *(sky)* nublado,-a. 2 *(liquid)* turbio,-a.

clout [klaʊt] *fam* I *n* 1 *(blow)* tortazo *m*. 2
(influence) influencia *f*. II *vtr* dar un tortazo a.

clove¹ [kləʊv] *n (spice)* clavo *m*.

clove² [kləʊv] *n (of garlic)* diente *m*.

clover ['kləʊvər] *n* trébol *m*.

clown [klaʊn] I *n* payaso *m*. II *vi* to c.
(about or around), hacer el payaso.

cloying ['klɔɪɪŋ] *adj* empalagoso,-a.

club [klʌb] I *n* 1 *(society)* club *m*; sports
c., club deportivo. 2 *(heavy stick)* garrote
m, porra *f*; *Golf* palo *m*. 3 *Cards* trébol
m. 4 *Culin* c. **sandwich,** sandwich *m* doble. II *vtr* aporrear. III *vi* to c. **together,**
pagar entre varios.

clubhouse ['klʌbhaʊs] *n* sede *f* de un
club.

cluck [klʌk] I *n* cloqueo *m*. II *vi* cloquear.

clue [kluː] *n (sign)* indicio *m*; *(to mystery)*
pista *f*; *(in crossword)* clave *f*; *fam* I
haven't a c., no tengo ni idea.

clump [klʌmp] *n (of trees)* grupo *m*; *(of
plants)* mata *f*.

clumsy ['klʌmzɪ] *adj (clumsier, clums-
iest)* desmañado,-a, torpe; *(awkward)*

tosco,-a.

clung [klʌŋ] *pt & pp* ⟶ **cling.**

cluster ['klʌstər] I *n* grupo *m*; *(of grapes)*
racimo *m*. II *vi* agruparse.

clutch [klʌtʃ] I *vtr* agarrar. II *vi* fig to c.
at straws, aferrarse a cualquier cosa. III
n 1 *Aut* embrague *m*. 2 fig **to fall into**
sb's clutches, caer en las garras de algn.

clutter ['klʌtər] *vtr* to c. **(up),** llenar,
atestar.

cm *abbr of centimetre(s),* centímetro(s),
cm.

CND [siːen'diː] *GB abbr of* Campaign for
Nuclear Disarmament, campaña *f* para
el desarme nuclear.

Co 1 *Com abbr of* Company, C., Cª, Cía.
2 *abbr of* County.

c/o [siː'əʊ] *abbr of care of,* en casa de, c/
o

coach [kəʊtʃ] I *n* 1 *(carriage)* carruaje *m*; c. **tour,** excursión *f* en
autocar. 2 *Rail* coche *m*, vagón *m*. 3
Sport entrenador,-a *m,f*. II *vtr Sport* entrenar; *Educ* dar clases particulares a.

coagulate [kəʊ'æɡjʊleɪt] *vi* coagularse.

coal [kəʊl] *n* carbón *m*, hulla *f*; c. **bunk-**
er, carbonera *f*; c. **merchant,** carbonero
m; c. **mine,** mina *f* de carbón.

coalfield ['kəʊlfiːld] *n* yacimiento *m* de
carbón.

coalition [kəʊə'lɪʃən] *n* coalición *f*.

coarse [kɔːs] *adj (material)* basto,-a; *(skin)*
áspero,-a; *(language)* grosero,-a,
ordinario,-a.

coast [kəʊst] I *n* costa *f*, litoral *m*; *fam* fig
the c. is clear, no hay moros en la costa.
II *vi Aut* ir en punto muerto.

coastal ['kəʊstəl] *adj* costero,-a.

coaster ['kəʊstər] *n (mat)* salvamanteles *m*
inv.

coastguard ['kəʊstɡɑːd] *n* guardacostas *m*
inv.

coastline ['kəʊstlaɪn] *n* litoral *m*, costa *f*.

coat [kəʊt] I *n* 1 *(overcoat)* abrigo *m*;
(short) chaquetón *m*; c. **hanger,** percha *f*.
2 *(of animal)* pelo *m*. 3 *(of paint)* mano *f*,
capa *f*. 4 c. **of arms,** escudo *m* de armas.
II *vtr* cubrir **(with,** de); *(with liquid)* bañar **(with,** en).

coating ['kəʊtɪŋ] *n* capa *f*, baño *m*.

coax [kəʊks] *vtr* engatusar.

cob [kɒb] *n* mazorca *f*.

cobble ['kɒbəl] *n* adoquín *m*.

cobbler ['kɒblər] *n* zapatero *m*.

cobweb ['kɒbweb] *n* telaraña *f*.

cocaine [kə'keɪn] *n* cocaína *f*.

cock [kɒk] I *n* 1 *Orn* gallo *m*; *(male bird)*
macho *m*. 2 *(on gun)* percutor *m*. 3 *sl vulg*
(penis) polla *f*. II *vtr* 1 *(gun)* amartillar;
(ears) erguir. ◆**cock up** *vtr GB sl* chapucear.

cocker ['kɒkər] *n* c. **spaniel,** cocker *m*.

cockerel ['kɒkərəl] *n* gallo *m* joven.

cockeyed ['kɒkaɪd] *adj fam (lopsided)*

torcido,-a; *(scheme)* disparatado,-a.
cockle ['kɒkəl] *n* berberecho *m*.
cockney ['kɒknɪ] **I** *adj* del East End
londinense. **II** *n* persona *f* del East End
londinense.
cockpit ['kɒkpɪt] *n* cabina *f* del piloto.
cockroach ['kɒkrəʊtʃ] *n* cucaracha *f*.
cocktail ['kɒkteɪl] *n* cóctel *m*; **c. lounge**,
bar *m*; **c. party**, cóctel *m*; **prawn c.**, cóctel
de gambas; **Molotov c.**, cóctel Molotov.
cocky ['kɒkɪ] *adj* (**cockier**, **cockiest**) *fam*
creído,-a.
cocoa ['kəʊkəʊ] *n* cacao *m*.
coconut ['kəʊkənʌt] *n* coco *m*.
cocoon [kə'kuːn] *n* capullo *m*.
COD [siːəʊ'diː] *GB abbr of* **cash on delivery**, CAE.
cod [kɒd] *n* bacalao *m*; **c. liver oil**, aceite
m de hígado de bacalao.
code [kəʊd] **I** *n* código *m*; *(symbol)* clave
f; *Tel* prefijo *m*. **II** *vtr (message)* cifrar,
poner en clave.
co-ed [kəʊ'ed] *fam* **I** *adj* mixto,-a. **II** *n*
colegio mixto.
coerce [kəʊ'ɜːs] *vtr* coaccionar.
coercion [kəʊ'ɜːʃən] *n* coacción *f*.
coexist [kəʊɪg'zɪst] *vi* coexistir.
coffee ['kɒfɪ] *n* café *m*; **c. bar/shop**, cafetería *f*; **c. break**, descanso *m*; **c. table**,
mesita *f* de café.
coffeepot ['kɒfɪpɒt] *n* cafetera *f*.
coffer ['kɒfər] *n* arca *f*.
coffin ['kɒfɪn] *n* ataúd *m*.
cog [kɒg] *n* diente *m*.
cognac ['kɒnjæk] *n* coñac *m*.
coherent [kəʊ'hɪərənt] *adj* coherente.
coil [kɔɪl] **I** *vtr to* **c.** (**up**), enrollar. **II** *vi*
enroscarse. **III** *n* 1 *(loop)* vuelta *f*; *(of
rope)* rollo *m*; *(of hair)* rizo *m*. 2 *(contraceptive)* espiral *f*. 3 *Elec* carrete *m*, bobina *f*.
coin [kɔɪn] **I** *n* moneda *f*. **II** *vtr* 1 *(money)*
acuñar. 2 *fig to* **c. a phrase**, por así decirlo.
coinage ['kɔɪnɪdʒ] *n* moneda *f*, sistema *m*
monetario.
coincide [kəʊɪn'saɪd] *vi* coincidir (**with**,
con).
coincidence [kəʊ'ɪnsɪdəns] *n* coincidencia
f.
coincidental [kəʊɪnsɪ'dentəl] *adj* casual.
◆**coincidentally** *adv* por casualidad *or*
coincidencia.
Coke® [kəʊk] *n (abbr of* Coca-Cola®) *fam*
coca-cola *f*.
coke [kəʊk] *n (coal)* coque *m*.
colander ['kɒləndər] *n* colador *m*.
cold [kəʊld] **I** *adj* frío,-a; **I'm c.**, tengo
frío; **it's c.**, *(weather)* hace frío; *(thing)*
está frío,-a; *fig to* **get c. feet** *(about
doing sth)*, entrarle miedo a algn (de hacer algo); **c. cream**, crema *f* hidratante;
fig it **leaves me c.**, no me dice nada; **c.
war**, guerra fría. **II** *n* 1 frío *m*. 2 *Med* res-

friado *m*; *to* **catch a c.**, resfriarse, acatarrarse; *to* **have a c.**, estar resfriado,-a; **c.
sore**, herpes *m* (en el labio).
cold-blooded [kəʊld'blʌdɪd] *adj* 1 *(animal)* de sangre fría. 2 *fig (person)* frío,-a;
(crime) a sangre fría.
coleslaw ['kəʊlslɔː] *n* ensalada *f* de col.
collaborate [kə'læbəreɪt] *vi* colaborar
(**with**, con).
collaborator [kə'læbəreɪtər] *n Pol* colabo-
racionista *mf*.
collapse [kə'læps] **I** *vi (break down)* derrumbarse; *(cave in)* hundirse; *fig (prices)*
caer en picado; *Med* sufrir un colapso. **II**
vtr (table) plegar. **III** *n (breaking down)*
derrumbamiento *m*; *(caving in)* hundimiento *m*; *Med* colapso *m*.
collapsible [kə'læpsəbəl] *adj* plegable.
collar ['kɒlər] **I** *n (of garment)* cuello *m*;
(for dog) collar *m*. **II** *vtr fam* pescar, agarrar.
collarbone ['kɒləbəʊn] *n* clavícula *f*.
collateral [kə'lætərəl] **I** *n Fin* garantía
subsidiaria. **II** *adj* colateral.
colleague ['kɒliːg] *n* colega *mf*.
collect [kə'lekt] **I** *vtr* 1 *(gather)* recoger. 2
(stamps etc) coleccionar. 3 *(taxes)* recaudar. **II** *vi* 1 *(people)* reunirse. 2 *(for charity)* hacer una colecta (**for**, para). **III** *adv
US Tel to* **call c.**, llamar a cobro revertido.
collection [kə'lekʃən] *n* 1 *(of mail)* recogida *f*; *(of money)* colecta *f*. 2 *(of stamps)*
colección *f*. 3 *(of taxes)* recaudación *f*. 4
(of people) grupo *m*.
collective [kə'lektɪv] **I** *adj* colectivo,-a; **c.
bargaining**, negociación colectiva. **II** *n*
colectivo *m*.
collector [kə'lektər] *n* 1 *(of stamps)* coleccionista *mf*. 2 **tax c.**, recaudador,-a
m,f de impuestos.
college ['kɒlɪdʒ] *n* colegio *m*; *(of university)* colegio mayor.
collide [kə'laɪd] *vi* chocar, colisionar.
collie ['kɒlɪ] *n* perro *m* pastor escocés.
colliery ['kɒljərɪ] *n GB* mina *f* de carbón.
collision [kə'lɪʒən] *n* choque *m*.
colloquial [kə'ləʊkwɪəl] *adj* coloquial.
collusion [kə'luːʒən] *n* conspiración *f*.
cologne [kə'ləʊn] *n* (agua *f* de) colonia *f*.
Colombia [kə'lɒmbɪə] *n* Colombia.
Colombian [kə'lɒmbɪən] *adj* & *n*
colombiano,-a (*m,f*).
colon[1] ['kəʊlən] *n Typ* dos puntos *mpl*.
colon[2] ['kəʊlən] *n Anat* colon *m*.
colonel ['kɜːnəl] *n* coronel *m*.
colonial [kə'ləʊnɪəl] *adj* colonial.
colonize ['kɒlənaɪz] *vtr* colonizar.
colony ['kɒlənɪ] *n* colonia *f*.
color ['kʌlər] *n* & *vtr* & *vi US* → **colour**.
colossal [kə'lɒsəl] *adj* colosal.
colour ['kʌlər] **I** *n* 1 color *m*; **what c. is
it?**, ¿de qué color es?; **c. film/television**,
película *f*/televisión *f* en color; **c.**

scheme, combinación f de colores. 2 *(race)* color m; **c. bar,** discriminación f racial. 3 **colours,** *GB Sport* colores mpl; *Mil (flag)* bandera f *sing.* II *vtr* colorear. III *vi* **c. (up),** ruborizarse.

colour-blind ['kʌləblaınd] *adj* daltónico, -a.

Coloured ['kʌləd] *adj* de color.

coloured ['kʌləd] *adj (photograph)* en color.

colourful ['kʌləful] *adj* 1 con muchos colores; *fig* lleno/-a de color; *(person)* pintoresco,-a.

colouring ['kʌlərıŋ] *n (colour)* colorido m.

colourless ['kʌləlıs] *adj* incoloro,-a; *fig* soso,-a.

colt [kəult] *n* potro m.

column ['kɒləm] *n* columna f.

columnist ['kɒləmnıst] *n* columnista mf.

coma ['kəumə] *n* coma m; **to go into a c.,** entrar en coma.

comb [kəum] I *n* peine m. II *vtr* 1 peinar; **to c. one's hair,** peinarse.

combat ['kɒmbæt] I *n* combate m. II *vtr (enemy, disease)* combatir. III *vi* combatir *(against,* contra).

combination [kɒmbı'neıʃən] *n* combinación f.

combine [kəm'baın] I *vtr* combinar. II *vi* combinarse; *(companies)* asociarse. II ['kɒmbaın] *n* 1 *Com* asociación f. 2 **c. harvester,** cosechadora f.

combustion [kəm'bʌstʃən] *n* combustión f.

come [kʌm] *vi (pt* **came;** *pp* **come)** 1 venir; *(arrive)* llegar; **coming!,** ¡voy!; **to go,** ir y venir; *fig* **in years to c.,** en el futuro. 2 **to c. apart/undone,** desatarse/ soltarse. 3 *(happen)* suceder; **that's what comes of being too impatient,** es lo que pasa por ser demasiado impaciente; *fam* **how c.?,** ¿y eso? 4 **I came to believe that ...,** llegué a creer que .... 5 *fig* **c. what may,** pase lo que pase. 6 *sl (have orgasm)* correrse.

◆**come about** *vi* ocurrir, suceder.
◆**come across** I *vtr (thing)* encontrar por casualidad; **to c. across sb,** tropezar con algn. II *vi fig* **to c. across well,** causar buena impresión.
◆**come along** *vi* 1 *(arrive)* venir; **c. along!,** ¡venga! 2 *(make progress)* progresar.
◆**come away** *vi (leave)* salir; *(part)* desprenderse *(from,* de).
◆**come back** *vtr (return)* volver.
◆**come before** *vtr* 1 preceder a. 2 *(court)* comparecer ante.
◆**come by** *vtr* adquirir.
◆**come down** *vi (lower)* bajar; *(rain)* caer; *(building)* ser derribado,-a; **to c. down with the flu,** coger la gripe.
◆**come forward** *vi (advance)* avanzar; *(volunteer)* ofrecerse.
◆**come in** *vi* 1 *(enter)* entrar; **c. in!,** ¡pase! 2 *(arrive) (train)* llegar; *(tide)* subir; **to c. in where do I c. in?,** ¿yo qué pinto? 3 **to c. in handy,** venir

bien. 4 **to c. in for,** ser objeto de.
◆**come into** *vtr* 1 *(enter)* entrar en. 2 *(inherit)* heredar.
◆**come off** I *vtr (fall from)* caerse de; *fam* **c. off it!,** ¡venga ya!. II *vi* 1 *(fall)* caerse; *(stain)* quitarse; *(button)* caerse de. 2 *fam (take place)* tener lugar; *(succeed)* salir bien; **to c. off badly,** salir mal.
◆**come on** *vi* 1 **c. on!,** *(hurry)* ¡venga! 2 *(make progress)* progresar. 3 *(rain, illness)* comenzar.
◆**come out** *vi* 1 salir *(of,* de); *(book)* aparecer; *(product)* estrenarse; *(facts)* revelarse; 2 *(stain)* quitarse; *(colour)* desteñir. 3 **to c. out against/in favour of sth,** declararse en contra/a favor de algo; *GB Ind* **to c. out (on strike),** declararse en huelga. 4 *(turn out)* salir.
◆**come over** I *vi* venir. II *vtr* 1 *(hill)* aparecer en lo alto de. 2 *fam* **what's c. over you?,** ¿qué te pasa?
◆**come round** I *vtr (corner)* dar la vuelta a. II *vi* 1 *(visit)* venir. 2 *(regain consciousness)* volver en sí. 3 **to c. round to sb's way of thinking,** dejarse convencer por algn.
◆**come through** I *vtr* 1 *(cross)* cruzar. 2 *(illness)* recuperarse de; *(accident)* sobrevivir. II *vi (message)* llegar.
◆**come to** I *vi (regain consciousness)* volver en sí. II *vtr* 1 **to c. to one's senses,** *fig* recobrar la razón. 2 *(amount to)* costar. 3 *(arrive at)* llegar a; **to c. to an end,** terminar; *fam* **c. to that,** a propósito.
◆**come under** *vtr fig* **to c. under fire from sb,** ser criticado,-a por algn.
◆**come up** *vi* 1 *(rise)* subir; *(approach)* acercarse *(to,* a). 2 *(difficulty, question)* surgir; **to c. up with a solution,** encontrar una solución; **c. up against problems,** encontrarse con problemas. 3 *(sun)* salir. 4 **to c. up to,** igualar; **to c. up to sb's expectations,** satisfacer a algn. 5 *fam* **three chips, coming up!,** ¡van tres de patatas fritas!
◆**come upon** *vtr* → **come across.**

comeback ['kʌmbæk] *n fam* 1 *(of person)* reaparición f y vuelta a c., reaparecer. 2 *(answer)* réplica f.

comedian [kə'mi:dıən] *n* cómico m.

comedienne [kəmi:dı'en] *n* cómica f.

comedown ['kʌmdaun] *n fam* desilusión f, revés m.

comedy ['kɒmıdı] *n* comedia f.

comet ['kɒmıt] *n* cometa m.

comeuppance [kʌm'ʌpəns] *n fam* **to get one's c.,** llevarse su merecido.

comfort ['kʌmfət] I *n* comodidad f; *US* **c. station,** servicios mpl. 2 *(consolation)* consuelo m; **to take c. in or from sth,** consolarse con algo. II *vtr* consolar.

comfortable ['kʌmfətəbəl] *adj (chair, person, margin)* cómodo,-a; *(temperature)* agradable.
◆**comfortably** *adv* con facilidad; **to be c. off,** vivir cómodamente.

comforter ['kʌmfətə'] *n* 1 *GB (scarf)* bufanda *f.* 2 *(for baby)* chupete *m.* 3 *US* edredón *m.*

comforting ['kʌmfətɪŋ] *adj* consolador,-a.

comic ['kɒmɪk] I *adj* cómico,-a; c. **strip**, tira cómica, historieta *f.* II *n* 1 *(person)* cómico,-a *m,f.* 2 *Press* tebeo *m,* comic *m.*

coming ['kʌmɪŋ] I *adj (year)* próximo,-a; *(generation)* futuro,-a. II *n* venida *f,* llegada *f;* **comings and goings,** idas y venidas; *fig* c. **and going,** ajetreo *m.*

comma ['kɒmə] *n* coma *f.*

command [kə'mɑːnd] I *vtr* 1 mandar. 2 *(respect)* infundir; *(sympathy)* merecer; *(money etc)* disponer de. II *n* 1 *(order)* orden *f; (authority)* mando *m;* to be at sb's c., estar a las órdenes de algn. 2 *(of language)* dominio *m.* 3 *(disposal)* disposición *f.*

commandeer [kɒmən'dɪə] *vtr* requisar.

commander [kə'mɑːndə] *n* comandante *m.*

commanding [kə'mɑːndɪŋ] *adj* dominante; *Mil* c. **officer,** comandante *m.*

commandment [kə'mɑːndmənt] *n* mandamiento *m.*

commando [kə'mɑːndəʊ] *n* comando *m.*

commemorate [kə'meməreɪt] *vtr* conmemorar.

commence [kə'mens] *vtr & vi fml* comenzar.

commend [kə'mend] *vtr* 1 *(praise)* alabar, elogiar. 2 *(entrust)* encomendar. 3 *(recommend)* recomendar.

commensurate [kə'menʃərɪt] *adj* proporcional; c. **to** *or* **with,** en proporción con.

comment ['kɒment] I *n* comentario *m;* **no c.,** sin comentario. II *vi* hacer comentarios.

commentary ['kɒmentərɪ] *n* comentario *m.*

commentator ['kɒmenteɪtə] *n* comentarista *mf.*

commerce ['kɒmɜːs] *n* comercio *m.*

commercial [kə'mɜːʃəl] I *adj* comercial; *TV* c. **break,** corte publicitario. II *n TV* anuncio *m.*

commiserate [kə'mɪzəreɪt] *vi* compadecerse (with, de).

commission [kə'mɪʃən] I *n* 1 *Mil* despacho *m* (de oficial); **out of c.,** fuera de servicio. 2 *(of enquiry)* comisión *f; (job)* encargo *m.* 3 *(payment)* comisión *f.* II *vtr* 1 *Mil* nombrar. 2 *(order)* encargar. 3 *Naut* poner en servicio.

commissionaire [kəmɪʃə'neə] *n GB* portero *m.*

commissioner [kə'mɪʃənə] *n (official)* comisario *m;* c. **of police,** comisario de policía.

commit [kə'mɪt] *vtr* 1 *(crime)* cometer; **to c. suicide,** suicidarse. 2 **to c. oneself (to do sth),** comprometerse (a hacer algo). 3

to c. sth to sb's care, confiar algo a algn.

commitment [kə'mɪtmənt] *n* compromiso *m.*

committee [kə'mɪtɪ] *n* comisión *f,* comité *m.*

commode [kə'məʊd] *n (chair)* silla *f* con orinal; *(chest of drawers)* cómoda *f.*

commodity [kə'mɒdɪtɪ] *n* artículo *m.*

common ['kɒmən] I *adj* 1 común; **that's c. knowledge,** eso lo sabe todo el mundo; c. **law,** derecho consuetudinario; **C. Market,** Mercado *m* Común; *GB* c. **room,** sala *f* de profesores *or* de estudiantes. 2 *(ordinary)* corriente. 3 *(vulgar)* ordinario,-a, maleducado,-a. II *n (land)* campo *m or* terreno *m* comunal.

commonplace ['kɒmənpleɪs] *adj* corriente.

Commons ['kɒmənz] *npl GB* **the (House of) C.,** (la Cámara de) los Comunes.

Commonwealth ['kɒmənwelθ] *n GB* **the C.,** la Commonwealth; **C. of Independent States,** Comunidad *f* de Estados Independientes.

commotion [kə'məʊʃən] *n* alboroto *m.*

commune[1] [kə'mjuːn] *vi (converse)* conversar íntimamente; *(with nature)* estar en comunión (with, con).

commune[2] ['kɒmjuːn] *n* comuna *f.*

communicate [kə'mjuːnɪkeɪt] I *vi* comunicarse (with, con). II *vtr* comunicar.

communication [kəmjuːnɪ'keɪʃən] *n* 1 comunicación *f.* 2 *GB Rail* c. **cord,** timbre *m* de alarma.

communion [kə'mjuːnjən] *n* comunión *f;* **to take c.,** comulgar.

communiqué [kə'mjuːnɪkeɪ] *n* comunicado *m* oficial.

communism ['kɒmjʊnɪzəm] *n* comunismo *m.*

communist ['kɒmjʊnɪst] *adj & n* comunista *(mf).*

community [kə'mjuːnɪtɪ] *n* comunidad *f; (people)* colectividad *f;* c. **centre,** centro *m* social.

commute [kə'mjuːt] I *vi* viajar diariamente al lugar de trabajo. II *vtr Jur* conmutar.

commuter [kə'mjuːtə] *n* persona *f* que viaja diariamente al lugar de trabajo.

compact[1] [kəm'pækt] I *adj* compacto,-a; *(style)* conciso,-a; c. **disc,** disco compacto. II ['kɒmpækt] *n (for powder)* polvera *f.*

compact[2] ['kɒmpækt] *n Pol* pacto *m.*

companion [kəm'pænjən] *n* compañero, -a *m,f.*

companionship [kəm'pænjənʃɪp] *n* compañerismo *m.*

company ['kʌmpənɪ] *n* 1 compañía *f;* **to keep sb c.,** hacer compañía a algn. 2 *Com* empresa *f,* compañía *f.*

comparable ['kɒmpərəbəl] *adj* comparable **(to, with,** con).

comparative [kəm'pærətɪv] **I** *adj* comparativo,-a; *(relative)* relativo,-a. **II** *n Ling* comparativo *m.* ◆**comparatively** *adv* relativamente.

compare [kəm'peəʳ] **I** *vtr* comparar **(to, with,** con); **(as) compared with,** en comparación con. **II** *vi* compararse.

comparison [kəm'pærɪsən] *n* comparación *f;* **by c.,** en comparación; **there's no c.,** no se puede comparar.

compartment [kəm'pɑːtmənt] *n (section)* compartimiento *m; Rail* departamento *m.*

compass ['kʌmpəs] *n* **1** brújula. *f.* **2** **(pair of) compasses,** compás *m.* **3** *fig (range)* límites *mpl.*

compassion [kəm'pæʃən] *n* compasión *f.*

compassionate [kəm'pæʃənət] *adj* compasivo,-a.

compatible [kəm'pætəbəl] *adj* compatible.

compel [kəm'pel] *vtr* **1** *(oblige)* obligar; **to c. sb to do sth,** obligar a algn a hacer algo. **2** *(admiration)* despertar.

compelling [kəm'pelɪŋ] *adj* irresistible.

compensate ['kɒmpenseɪt] **I** *vtr* compensar; **to c. sb for sth,** indemnizar a algn de algo. **II** *vi* compensar.

compensation [kɒmpen'seɪʃən] *n* compensación *f; (for loss)* indemnización *f.*

compere ['kɒmpeəʳ] *GB n* animador,-a *m,f.*

compete [kəm'piːt] *vi* competir.

competence ['kɒmpɪtəns] *n* **1** *(ability)* aptitud *f.* **2** *(of court etc)* competencia *f.*

competent ['kɒmpɪtənt] *adj* competente.

competition [kɒmpɪ'tɪʃən] *n* **1** *(contest)* concurso *m.* **2** *Com* competencia *f.*

competitive [kəm'petɪtɪv] *adj* competitivo,-a.

competitor [kəm'petɪtəʳ] *n* competidor,-a *m,f.*

compilation [kɒmpɪ'leɪʃən] *n* recopilación *f.*

compile [kəm'paɪl] *vtr* compilar, recopilar.

complacency [kəm'pleɪsənsɪ] *n* complacencia *f.*

complacent [kəm'pleɪsənt] *adj* autocomplaciente.

complain [kəm'pleɪn] *vi* quejarse **(of, about,** de).

complaint [kəm'pleɪnt] *n* **1** queja *f; Com* reclamación *f.* **2** *Jur* demanda *f.* **3** *Med* enfermedad *f.*

complement ['kɒmplɪmənt] **I** *n* **1** complemento *m.* **2** *Naut* dotación *f.* **II** *vtr* complementar.

complementary [kɒmplɪ'mentərɪ] *adj* complementario,-a.

complete [kəm'pliːt] **I** *adj* **1** *(entire)* completo,-a. **2** *(absolute)* total. **II** *vtr* completar; **to c. a form,** rellenar un formulario. ◆**completely** *adv* completamente,

por completo.

completion [kəm'pliːʃən] *n* terminación *f;* **near c.,** casi terminado,-a; **on c.,** en cuanto se termine.

complex ['kɒmpleks] **I** *adj* complejo,-a. **II** *n* complejo *m;* **inferiority c.,** complejo de inferioridad.

complexion [kəm'plekʃən] *n* tez *f; fig* aspecto *m.*

compliance [kəm'plaɪəns] *n* conformidad *f;* **in c. with,** de acuerdo con.

complicate ['kɒmplɪkeɪt] *vtr* complicar.

complicated ['kɒmplɪkeɪtɪd] *adj* complicado,-a.

complication [kɒmplɪ'keɪʃən] *n* complicación *f.*

complicity [kəm'plɪsɪtɪ] *n* complicidad *f.*

compliment ['kɒmplɪmənt] **I** *n* **1** cumplido *m;* **to pay sb a c.,** hacerle un cumplido a algn. **2** **compliments,** saludos *mpl.* **II** ['kɒmplɪment] *vtr* felicitar; **to c. sb on sth,** felicitar a algn por algo.

complimentary [kɒmplɪ'mentərɪ] *adj* **1** *(praising)* elogioso,-a. **2** *(free)* gratis.

comply [kəm'plaɪ] *vi* obedecer; **to c. with,** *(order)* cumplir con; *(request)* acceder a.

component [kəm'pəʊnənt] **I** *n* componente *m.* **II** *adj* componente; **c. part,** parte *f.*

compose [kəm'pəʊz] *vtr & vi* componer; **to be composed of,** componerse de. **2 to c. oneself,** calmarse.

composed [kəm'pəʊzd] *adj (calm)* sereno,-a.

composer [kəm'pəʊzəʳ] *n* compositor,-a *m,f.*

composite ['kɒmpəzɪt] *adj* compuesto,-a.

composition [kɒmpə'zɪʃən] *n* composición *f; (essay)* redacción *f.*

compost ['kɒmpɒst] *n* abono *m.*

composure [kəm'pəʊʒəʳ] *n* calma *f,* serenidad *f.*

compound¹ ['kɒmpaʊnd] **I** *n* compuesto *m.* **II** ['kɒmpaʊnd] *vtr (problem)* agravar. **III** ['kɒmpaʊnd] *adj* compuesto,-a; *(fracture)* complicado.

compound² ['kɒmpaʊnd] *n (enclosure)* recinto *m.*

comprehend [kɒmprɪ'hend] *vtr* comprender.

comprehensible [kɒmprɪ'hensəbəl] *adj* comprensible.

comprehension [kɒmprɪ'henʃən] *n* comprensión *f.*

comprehensive [kɒmprɪ'hensɪv] **I** *adj* **1** *(knowledge)* amplio,-a; *(study)* detallado, -a. **2** *Ins* a todo riesgo. **3** *GB* **c. school,** ≈ instituto *m* de segunda enseñanza.

compress [kəm'pres] **I** *vtr* comprimir. **II** ['kɒmpres] *n* compresa *f.*

comprise [kəm'praɪz] *vtr* comprender; *(consist of)* constar de.

compromise ['kɒmprəmaɪz] **I** *n* término

medio; **to reach a c.,** llegar a un acuerdo. **II** vi (two people) llegar a un acuerdo; (individual) transigir. **III** vtr (person) comprometer.

compulsion [kəm'pʌlʃən] n obligación f.

compulsive [kəm'pʌlsɪv] adj compulsivo,-a.

compulsory [kəm'pʌlsəri] adj obligatorio,-a.

computer [kəm'pjuːtəʳ] n ordenador m, computadora f; **c. programmer,** programador,-a m,f de ordenadores; **c. science,** informática f; **personal c.,** ordenador personal.

computerize [kəm'pjuːtəraɪz] vtr informatizar.

computing [kəm'pjuːtɪŋ] n informática f.

comrade ['kɒmreɪd] n 1 (companion) compañero,-a m,f. 2 Pol camarada mf.

comradeship ['kɒmreɪdʃɪp] n camaradería f.

con [kɒn] sl I vtr estafar, timar. II n estafa f, camelo m; **c. man,** estafador m.

concave ['kɒnkeɪv] adj cóncavo,-a.

conceal [kən'siːl] vtr ocultar; (emotions) disimular.

concede [kən'siːd] vtr conceder.

conceit [kən'siːt] n presunción f, vanidad f.

conceited [kən'siːtɪd] adj presuntuoso,-a.

conceivable [kən'siːvəbəl] adj concebible.

conceive [kən'siːv] vtr & vi concebir.

concentrate ['kɒnsəntreɪt] I vtr concentrar. II vi **to c. on sth,** concentrarse en algo.

concentration [kɒnsən'treɪʃən] n concentración f; **c. camp,** campo m de concentración.

concept ['kɒnsept] n concepto m.

conception [kən'sepʃən] n Med concepción f; (understanding) concepto m, idea f.

concern [kən'sɜːn] I vtr 1 concernir, afectar; **as far as I'm concerned,** por lo que a mí se refiere. 2 (worry) preocupar. II n 1 **it's no c. of mine,** no es asunto mío. 2 (worry) preocupación f. 3 Com negocio m.

concerned [kən'sɜːnd] adj 1 (affected) afectado,-a. 2 (worried) preocupado,-a (about, por).

concerning [kən'sɜːnɪŋ] prep con respecto a, en cuanto a.

concert ['kɒnsət, 'kɒnsɜːt] n Mus concierto m; **c. hall,** sala f de conciertos.

concerted [kən'sɜːtɪd] adj concertado,-a.

concertina [kɒnsə'tiːnə] n concertina f.

concerto [kən'tʃeətəʊ] n concierto m.

concession [kən'seʃən] n 1 concesión f; **tax c.,** privilegio m fiscal. 2 Com reducción f.

concise [kən'saɪs] adj conciso,-a.

conclude [kən'kluːd] vtr & vi concluir.

conclusion [kən'kluːʒən] n conclusión f; **to reach a c.,** llegar a una conclusión.

conclusive [kən'kluːsɪv] adj concluyente.

concoct [kən'kɒkt] vtr (dish) confeccionar; fig (plan) fraguar; (excuse) inventar.

concoction [kən'kɒkʃən] n (mixture) mezcolanza f; pej (brew) brebaje m.

concourse ['kɒŋkɔːs] n explanada f.

concrete ['kɒnkriːt] I n hormigón m; **c. mixer,** hormigonera f. II adj 1 (definite) concreto,-a. 2 (made of concrete) de hormigón.

concur [kən'kɜːʳ] vi 1 **to c. with,** (agree) estar de acuerdo con. 2 (coincide) coincidir.

concurrent [kən'kʌrənt] adj simultáneo,-a.

concussion [kən'kʌʃən] n conmoción f cerebral.

condemn [kən'dem] vtr condenar.

condemnation [kɒndem'neɪʃən] n condena f.

condensation [kɒnden'seɪʃən] n condensación f.

condense [kən'dens] I vtr condensar. II vi condensarse.

condensed [kən'denst] adj **c. milk,** leche condensada.

condescending [kɒndɪ'sendɪŋ] adj condescendiente.

condition [kən'dɪʃən] I n condición f; **to be in good c.,** estar en buen estado; **on c. that ...,** a condición de que ...; **on one c.,** con una condición; **heart c.,** enfermedad cardíaca; **conditions,** (circumstances) circunstancias fpl. II vtr condicionar.

conditional [kən'dɪʃənəl] adj condicional.

conditioner [kən'dɪʃənəʳ] n acondicionador m.

condolences [kən'dəʊlənsɪz] npl pésame m sing; **please accept my c.,** le acompaño en el sentimiento.

condom ['kɒndəm] n preservativo m.

condone [kən'dəʊn] vtr perdonar, consentir.

condor ['kɒndɔːʳ] n cóndor m.

conducive [kən'djuːsɪv] adj conducente.

conduct ['kɒndʌkt] n 1 (behaviour) conducta f, comportamiento m. II [kən'dʌkt] vtr (lead) guiar; (business, orchestra) dirigir; **conducted tour,** visita acompañada; **to c. oneself,** comportarse. III vi Mus dirigir.

conductor [kən'dʌktəʳ] n 1 (on bus) cobrador m. 2 US Rail revisor,-a m,f. 3 Mus director,-a m,f. 4 Phys conductor m.

conductress [kən'dʌktrɪs] n (on bus) cobradora f.

cone [kəʊn] n 1 cono m; **ice-cream c.,** cucurucho m. 2 Bot piña f.

confectioner [kən'fekʃənəʳ] n confitero,-a m,f; **c.'s (shop),** confitería f.

confectionery [kən'fekʃənərɪ] n dulces

mpl.
confederate [kən'fedərɪt] **I** adj confederado,-a. **II** n confederado,-a m/f; Jur cómplice mf.
confer [kən'fɜːr] **I** vtr to c. a title on sb, conferir un título a algn. **II** vi consultar.
conference ['kɒnfərəns] n conferencia f.
confess [kən'fes] **I** vi confesar; Rel confesarse. **II** vtr confesar.
confession [kən'feʃən] n confesión f.
confessional [kən'feʃənəl] n confesionario m.
confetti [kən'fetɪ] n confeti m.
confide [kən'faɪd] vi to c. in sb, confiar en algn.
confidence ['kɒnfɪdəns] n **1** confianza f; vote of c./no c., voto m de confianza/de censura; c. trick, camelo m. **2** (secret) confidencia f; **in c.**, en confianza.
confident ['kɒnfɪdənt] adj seguro,-a.
confidential [kɒnfɪ'denʃəl] adj (secret) confidencial; (entrusted) de confianza.
confine [kən'faɪn] vtr encerrar; fig limitar.
confinement [kən'faɪnmənt] n **1** (prison) prisión f; **to be in solitary c.**, estar incomunicado,-a. **2** Med parto m.
confirm [kən'fɜːm] vtr confirmar.
confirmation [kɒnfə'meɪʃən] n confirmación f.
confirmed [kən'fɜːmd] adj empedernido,-a.
confiscate ['kɒnfɪskeɪt] vtr confiscar.
conflict ['kɒnflɪkt] **I** n conflicto m. **II** [kən'flɪkt] vi chocar (with, con).
conflicting [kən'flɪktɪŋ] adj contradictorio,-a.
conform [kən'fɔːm] vi conformarse; **to c. to or with**, (customs) amoldarse a; (rules) someterse a.
confound [kən'faʊnd] vtr confundir, desconcertar.
confront [kən'frʌnt] vtr hacer frente a.
confrontation [kɒnfrʌn'teɪʃən] n confrontación f.
confuse [kən'fjuːz] vtr (person) despistar; (thing) confundir (with, con); **to get confused**, confundirse.
confused [kən'fjuːzd] adj (person) confundido,-a; (mind, ideas) confuso,-a.
confusing [kən'fjuːzɪŋ] adj confuso,-a.
confusion [kən'fjuːʒən] n confusión f.
congeal [kən'dʒiːl] vi coagularse.
congenial [kən'dʒiːnjəl] adj agradable.
congenital [kən'dʒenɪtəl] adj congénito, -a.
congested [kən'dʒestɪd] adj **1** (street) repleto,-a de gente; (city) superpoblado, -a. **2** Med congestionado,-a.
congestion [kən'dʒestʃən] n congestión f.
conglomeration [kənɡlɒmə'reɪʃən] n conglomeración f.
congratulate [kən'ɡrætjʊleɪt] vtr felicitar.
congratulations [kənɡrætjʊ'leɪʃənz] npl

felicitaciones fpl; **c.!**, ¡enhorabuena!
congregate ['kɒnɡrɪgeɪt] vi congregarse.
congregation [kɒnɡrɪ'geɪʃən] n (group) congregación f; Rel fieles mpl.
congress ['kɒnɡres] n congreso m.
Congressman ['kɒnɡresmən] n congresista m.
conifer ['kɒnɪfər] n conífera f.
conjecture [kən'dʒektʃər] **I** n conjetura f. **II** vtr conjeturar. **III** vi hacer conjeturas.
conjugal ['kɒndʒʊɡəl] adj conyugal.
conjugate ['kɒndʒʊɡeɪt] vtr conjugar.
conjunction [kən'dʒʌŋkʃən] n conjunción f; fig **in c. with**, conjuntamente con.
conjunctivitis [kəndʒʌŋktɪ'vaɪtɪs] n conjuntivitis f.
conjure ['kʌndʒər] **I** vtr to c. (up), (magician) hacer aparecer; (memories) evocar. **II** vi hacer juegos de manos.
conjurer ['kʌndʒərər] n prestidigitador,-a m/f.
conker ['kɒŋkər] n fam castaña f.
connect [kə'nekt] **I** vtr (join) juntar, unir; (wires) empalmar; fig **to be connected by marriage**, estar emparentado,-a por matrimonio. **2** (instal) instalar; Elec conectar. **3** Tel (person) poner. **4** fig (associate) asociar. **II** vi unirse; (rooms) comunicarse; (train, flight) enlazar or empalmar (with, con).
connected [kə'nektɪd] adj unido,-a; (events) relacionado,-a; fig **to be well c.**, (person) fam tener enchufe.
connection [kə'nekʃən] n **1** (joint) juntura f, unión f; Elec conexión f; Tel instalación f. **2** Rail correspondencia f. **3** fig (of ideas) relación f; **in c. with**, (regarding) con respecto a. **4** (person) contacto m.
connive [kə'naɪv] vi to c. at, hacer la vista gorda con.
connoisseur [kɒnɪ'sɜːr] n conocedor,-a m/f.
connotation [kɒnə'teɪʃən] n connotación f.
conquer ['kɒŋkər] vtr (enemy, bad habit) vencer; (country) conquistar.
conqueror ['kɒŋkərər] n conquistador m.
conquest ['kɒŋkwest] n conquista f.
conscience ['kɒnʃəns] n conciencia f; **to have a clear c.**, tener la conciencia tranquila; **to have a guilty c.**, sentirse culpable.
conscientious [kɒnʃɪ'enʃəs] adj concienzudo,-a; **c. objector**, objetor,-a m,f de conciencia.
conscious ['kɒnʃəs] adj (aware) consciente; (choice etc) deliberado,-a.
consciousness ['kɒnʃəsnɪs] n Med conocimiento m; (awareness) conciencia f.
conscript ['kɒnskrɪpt] n recluta m.
conscription [kən'skrɪpʃən] n servicio m militar obligatorio.
consecrate ['kɒnsɪkreɪt] vtr consagrar.

consecutive [kən'sekjʊtɪv] adj consecutivo,-a.

consensus [kən'sensəs] n consenso m.

consent [kən'sent] I n consentimiento m; by common c., de común acuerdo. II vi consentir (to, en).

consequence ['kɒnsɪkwəns] n consecuencia f.

consequent ['kɒnsɪkwənt] adj consiguiente. ◆**consequently** adv por consiguiente.

conservation [kɒnsə'veɪʃən] n conservación f.

conservative [kən'sɜːvətɪv] I adj cauteloso,-a. II adj & n Pol C., conservador,-a (m,f).

conservatory [kən'sɜːvətrɪ] n 1 (greenhouse) invernadero m. 2 Mus conservatorio m.

conserve [kən'sɜːv] I vtr conservar. II ['kɒnsɜːv] n conserva f.

consider [kən'sɪdər] vtr 1 (ponder on, regard) considerar; to c. doing sth, pensar hacer algo. 2 (keep in mind) tener en cuenta.

considerable [kən'sɪdərəbəl] adj considerable. ◆**considerably** adv bastante.

considerate [kən'sɪdərɪt] adj considerado,-a.

consideration [kənsɪdə'reɪʃən] n consideración f; without due c., sin reflexión.

considering [kən'sɪdərɪŋ] prep teniendo en cuenta.

consign [kən'saɪn] vtr Com consignar; fig entregar.

consignment [kən'saɪnmənt] n envío m.

consist [kən'sɪst] vi to c. of, consistir en.

consistency [kən'sɪstənsɪ] n 1 (of actions) consecuencia f. 2 (of mixture) consistencia f.

consistent [kən'sɪstənt] adj consecuente; c. with, de acuerdo con.

consolation [kɒnsə'leɪʃən] n consuelo m; c. prize, premio m de consolación.

console¹ [kən'səʊl] vtr consolar.

console² ['kɒnsəʊl] n consola f.

consolidate [kən'sɒlɪdeɪt] I vtr consolidar. II vi consolidarse.

consonant ['kɒnsənənt] n consonante f.

consortium [kən'sɔːtɪəm] n consorcio m.

conspicuous [kən'spɪkjʊəs] adj (striking) llamativo,-a; (easily seen) visible; (mistake) evidente.

conspiracy [kən'spɪrəsɪ] n conjura f.

conspire [kən'spaɪər] vi conspirar.

constable ['kʌnstəbəl] n policía m, guardia m; chief c., jefe m de policía.

constabulary [kən'stæbjʊlərɪ] n GB comisaría f.

constant ['kɒnstənt] I adj constante; (continuous) incesante; (loyal) fiel, leal. II n constante f.

constellation [kɒnstɪ'leɪʃən] n constelación f.

consternation [kɒnstə'neɪʃən] n consternación f.

constipated ['kɒnstɪpeɪtɪd] adj to be c., estar estreñido,-a.

constipation [kɒnstɪ'peɪʃən] n estreñimiento m.

constituency [kən'stɪtjʊənsɪ] n circunscripción f electoral.

constituent [kən'stɪtjʊənt] I adj (component) constituyente. II n 1 (part) componente m. 2 Pol votante m.

constitute ['kɒnstɪtjuːt] vtr constituir.

constitution [kɒnstɪ'tjuːʃən] n constitución f.

constitutional [kɒnstɪ'tjuːʃənəl] adj constitucional.

constrained [kən'streɪnd] adj to feel c. to do sth, sentirse obligado,-a a hacer algo.

constraint [kən'streɪnt] n coacción f; to feel c. in sb's presence, sentirse cohibido,-a ante algn.

construct [kən'strʌkt] vtr construir.

construction [kən'strʌkʃən] n construcción f.

constructive [kən'strʌktɪv] adj constructivo,-a.

construe [kən'struː] vtr interpretar.

consul ['kɒnsəl] n cónsul mf.

consulate ['kɒnsjʊlɪt] n consulado m.

consult [kən'sʌlt] vtr & vi consultar (about, sobre).

consultant [kən'sʌltənt] n Med especialista mf; Com Ind asesor,-a m,f.

consultation [kɒnsəl'teɪʃən] n consulta f.

consulting [kən'sʌltɪŋ] adj c. room, consulta f.

consume [kən'sjuːm] vtr consumir.

consumer [kən'sjuːmər] n consumidor,-a m,f; c. goods, bienes mpl de consumo.

consummate ['kɒnsəmeɪt] I vtr consumar. II ['kɒnsəmɪt] adj consumado,-a.

consumption [kən'sʌmpʃən] n 1 (of food) consumo m; fit for c., apto,-a para el consumo. 2 Med tisis f.

cont. abbr of **continued**, sigue.

contact ['kɒntækt] I n contacto m; c. lenses, lentes fpl de contacto. II vtr ponerse en contacto con.

contagious [kən'teɪdʒəs] adj contagioso,-a.

contain [kən'teɪn] vtr contener; to c. oneself, contenerse.

container [kən'teɪnər] n 1 (box, package) recipiente m; (bottle) envase m. 2 Naut contenedor m.

contaminate [kən'tæmɪneɪt] vtr contaminar.

contamination [kəntæmɪ'neɪʃən] n contaminación f.

contd. abbr of **continued**, sigue.

contemplate ['kɒntempleɪt] vtr 1 (consider) considerar, pensar en. 2 (look at) contemplar.

contemporary [kən'tempərərı] *adj & n* contemporáneo,-a *(m,f)*.

contempt [kən'tempt] *n* desprecio *m*; **to hold in t.**, despreciar; **c. of court**, desacato *m* a los tribunales.

contemptible [kən'temptəbəl] *adj* despreciable.

contemptuous [kən'temptjʊəs] *adj* despectivo,-a.

contend [kən'tend] **I** *vi* competir; *fig* **there are many problems to c. with**, se han planteado muchos problemas. **II** *vtr* afirmar.

contender [kən'tendər] *n* contendiente *mf*.

content¹ ['kɒntent] *n* contenido *m*; **table of contents**, índice *m* de materias.

content² [kən'tent] **I** *adj* contento,-a. **II** *vtr* contentar. **III** *n* contento *m*; **to one's heart's c.**, todo lo que uno quiera.

contented [kən'tentɪd] *adj* contento,-a, satisfecho,-a.

contention [kən'tenʃən] *n* **1** *(dispute)* controversia *f*. **2** *(point)* punto *m* de vista.

contentment [kən'tentmənt] *n* contento *m*.

contest ['kɒntest] **I** *n* concurso *m*; *Sport* prueba *f*. **II** [kən'test] *vtr* **1** *(matter)* rebatir; *(verdict)* impugnar; *fig (will)* disputar. **2** *Pol (seat)* luchar por.

contestant [kən'testant] *n* concursante *mf*.

context ['kɒntekst] *n* contexto *m*.

continent ['kɒntɪnənt] *n* continente *m*; **(on the C.)**, (en) Europa.

continental [kɒntɪ'nentəl] *adj* **1** continental; **c. shelf**, plataforma *m* continental. **2** *GB* **C.**, europeo,-a; **c. quilt**, edredón *m* de pluma.

contingency [kən'tɪndʒənsɪ] *n* contingencia *f*; **c. plans**, planes *mpl* para casos de emergencia.

contingent [kən'tɪndʒənt] *adj & n* contingente *m*,-).

continual [kən'tɪnjʊəl] *adj* continuo,-a, constante.

continuation [kəntɪnjʊ'eɪʃən] *n* *(sequel etc)* continuación *f*; *(extension)* prolongación *f*.

continue [kən'tɪnjuː] *vtr & vi* continuar, seguir; **to c. to do sth**, seguir *or* continuar haciendo algo.

continuous [kən'tɪnjʊəs] *adj* continuo,-a.

contort [kən'tɔːt] *vtr* retorcer.

contortion [kən'tɔːʃən] *n* contorsión *f*.

contour ['kɒntʊər] *n* contorno *m*; **c. line**, línea *f* de nivel.

contraband ['kɒntrəbænd] *n* contrabando *m*.

contraception [kɒntrə'sepʃən] *n* anticoncepción *f*.

contraceptive [kɒntrə'septɪv] *adj & n* anticonceptivo *(m,f)*.

contract [kən'trækt] **I** *vi Phys* contraerse.

II *vtr* **1** contraer. **2 to c. to do sth**, *(make agreement)* comprometerse por contrato a hacer algo. **III** ['kɒntrækt] *n* contrato *m*; **to enter into a c.**, hacer un contrato.

contraction [kən'trækʃən] *n* contracción *f*.

contractor [kən'træktər] *n* contratista *mf*.

contradict [kɒntrə'dɪkt] *vtr* contradecir.

contradiction [kɒntrə'dɪkʃən] *n* contradicción *f*; **it's a c. in terms**, no tiene lógica.

contradictory [kɒntrə'dɪktərɪ] *adj* contradictorio,-a.

contraption [kən'træpʃən] *n fam* cacharro *m*.

contrary ['kɒntrərɪ] **I** *adj* **1** contrario,-a. **2** [kən'treərɪ] terco,-a. **II** *n* **on the c.**, todo lo contrario; **unless I tell you to the c.**, a menos que te diga lo contrario. **III** *adv* **c. to**, en contra de.

contrast [kən'trɑːst] **I** *vi* contrastar. **II** ['kɒntrɑːst] *n* contraste *m*.

contrasting [kən'trɑːstɪŋ] *adj* opuesto,-a.

contravene [kɒntrə'viːn] *vtr* contravenir.

contribute [kən'trɪbjuːt] **I** *vtr (money)* contribuir con; *(ideas, information)* aportar. **II** *vi* **1** contribuir; *(in discussion)* participar. **2** *Press* colaborar (**to**, en).

contribution [kɒntrɪ'bjuːʃən] *n* **1** *(of money)* contribución *f*; *(of ideas etc)* aportación *f*. **2** *Press* colaboración *f*.

contributor [kən'trɪbjʊtər] *n* *(to newspaper)* colaborador,-a *m,f*.

contrive [kən'traɪv] *vtr* inventar, idear; **to c. to do sth**, buscar la forma de hacer algo.

contrived [kən'traɪvd] *adj* artificial, forzado,-a.

control [kən'trəʊl] **I** *vtr* controlar; *(person, animal)* dominar; *(vehicle)* manejar; **to c. one's temper**, controlarse. **II** *n* **1** *(power)* control *m*, dominio *m*; *(authority)* autoridad *f*; **out of c.**, fuera de control; **to be in c.**, estar al mando; **to be under c.**, *(situation)* estar bajo control; **to go out of c.**, descontrolarse; **to lose c.**, perder los estribos. **2** *Aut Av (device)* mando *m*; *Rad TV* botón *m* de control; **c. panel**, tablero *m* de instrumentos; **c. room**, sala *f* de control; *Av* **c. tower**, torre *f* de control.

controversial [kɒntrə'vɜːʃəl] *adj* controvertido,-a, polémico,-a.

controversy ['kɒntrəvɜːsɪ, kən'trɒvəsɪ] *n* polémica *f*.

conurbation [kɒnɜː'beɪʃən] *n* conurbación *f*.

convalesce [kɒnvə'les] *vi* convalecer.

convalescence [kɒnvə'lesəns] *n* convalecencia *f*.

convalescent [kɒnvə'lesənt] *adj* convaleciente; **c. home**, clínica *f* de reposo.

convene [kən'viːn] **I** *vtr* convocar. **II** *vi* reunirse.

convenience [kən'viːnɪəns] *n* conveniencia f, comodidad f; **all modern conveniences**, todas las comodidades; **at your c.**, cuando le convenga; **c. food**, comida precocinada; *GB euph* **public conveniences**, aseos públicos.

convenient [kən'viːnɪənt] *adj (time, arrangement)* conveniente, oportuno,-a; *(place)* bien situado,-a.

convent ['kɒnvənt] *n* convento *m.*

convention [kən'venʃən] *n* convención *f.*

conventional [kən'venʃənəl] *adj* clásico,-a; *(behaviour)* convencional.

converge [kən'vɜːdʒ] *vi* convergir.

conversant [kən'vɜːsənt] *adj fml* **to be c. with a subject**, ser versado,-a en una materia.

conversation [kɒnvə'seɪʃən] *n* conversación *f.*

conversational [kɒnvə'seɪʃənəl] *adj* coloquial.

converse¹ [kən'vɜːs] *vi* conversar.

converse² ['kɒnvɜːs] *n* **the c.**, lo opuesto. ◆**conversely** *adv* a la inversa.

conversion [kən'vɜːʃən] *n Math Rel* conversión *f* **(to, a; into, en).**

convert [kən'vɜːt] **I** *vtr* convertir. **II** ['kɒnvɜːt] *n* converso,-a *m,f.*

convertible [kən'vɜːtəbəl] **I** *adj* convertible. **II** *n Aut* descapotable *m.*

convex ['kɒnveks, kɒn'veks] *adj* convexo,-a.

convey [kən'veɪ] *vtr* 1 *(carry)* transportar. 2 *(sound)* transmitir; *(idea)* comunicar.

conveyor [kən'veɪəʳ] *n* **c. belt**, cinta transportadora.

convict [kən'vɪkt] **I** *vtr* declarar culpable a, condenar. **II** ['kɒnvɪkt] *n* presidiario,-a *m,f.*

conviction [kən'vɪkʃən] *n* 1 *(belief)* creencia *f*, convicción *f.* 2 *Jur* condena *f.*

convince [kən'vɪns] *vtr* convencer.

convincing [kən'vɪnsɪŋ] *adj* convincente.

convoluted ['kɒnvəluːtɪd] *adj* intrincado,-a.

convoy ['kɒnvɔɪ] *n* convoy *m.*

convulse [kən'vʌls] *vtr* convulsionar; *fam* **to be convulsed with laughter**, troncharse de risa.

convulsion [kən'vʌlʃən] *n* convulsión *f.*

coo [kuː] *vi (pigeon)* arrullar.

cook [kʊk] **I** *vtr* cocinar, guisar; *(dinner)* preparar; *sl* **to c. the books**, falsificar las cuentas. **II** *vi (person)* cocinar, guisar; *(food)* cocerse. **III** *n* cocinero,-a *m,f.*

cookbook ['kʊkbʊk] *n US* libro de cocina.

cooker ['kʊkəʳ] *n* cocina *f.*

cookery ['kʊkərɪ] *n* cocina *f*; **c. book**, libro *m* de cocina.

cookie ['kʊkɪ] *n US* galleta *f.*

cooking ['kʊkɪŋ] *n* cocina *f.*

cool [kuːl] **I** *adj* 1 fresco,-a; **it's c.**, *(weather)* hace fresquito. 2 *fig (calm)* tranquilo,-a; *(reserved)* frío,-a. **II** *n* 1

(coolness) fresco *m.* 2 *sl* **to lose one's c.**, perder la calma. **III** *vtr (air)* refrescar; *(drink)* enfriar. **IV** *adv fam* **to play it c.**, hacer como si nada. ◆**cool down, cool off** *vi fig* calmarse; *(feelings)* enfriarse.

coolness ['kuːlnɪs] *n* 1 *fig (calmness)* calma *f*; *(composure)* aplomo *m.* 2 *fam (nerve, cheek)* frescura *f.*

coop [kuːp] **I** *n* gallinero *m.* **II** *vtr* **to c. (up)**, encerrar.

co-operate [kəʊ'ɒpəreɪt] *vi* cooperar.

co-operation [kəʊpə'reɪʃən] *n* cooperación *f.*

co-operative [kəʊ'ɒpərətɪv] **I** *adj (helpful)* cooperador,-a. **II** *n* cooperativa *f.*

co-ordinate [kəʊ'ɔːdɪneɪt] **I** *vtr* coordinar. **II** [kəʊ'ɔːdɪnɪt] *n* 1 *Math* coordenada *f.* 2 **co-ordinates**, *(clothes)* conjunto *m sing.*

co-ordination [kəʊɔːdɪ'neɪʃən] *n* coordinación *f.*

cop [kɒp] *sl* **I** *n (policeman)* poli *m.* **II** *vtr* **you'll c. it**, te vas a ganar una buena. ◆**cop out** *vi* rajarse.

cope [kəʊp] *vi* arreglárselas; **to c. with**, *(person, work)* poder con; *(problem)* hacer frente a.

Copenhagen [kəʊpən'heɪgən] *n* Copenhague.

copious ['kəʊpɪəs] *adj* copioso,-a, abundante.

copper¹ ['kɒpəʳ] **I** *n Min* cobre *m.* **II** *adj (colour)* cobrizo,-a.

copper² ['kɒpəʳ] *n sl* poli *mf.*

coppice ['kɒpɪs], **copse** [kɒps] *n* arboleda *f*, bosquecillo *m.*

copulate ['kɒpjʊleɪt] *vi* copular.

copy ['kɒpɪ] **I** *n* 1 copia *f.* 2 *(of book)* ejemplar *m.* 3 *Print* manuscrito *m.* 4 *Press fam* asunto *m.* **II** *vtr & vi* copiar.

copycat ['kɒpɪkæt] *n fam* copión,-ona *m,f.*

copyright ['kɒpɪraɪt] *n* derechos *mpl* de autor.

coral ['kɒrəl] *n* coral *m*; **c. reef**, arrecife *m* de coral.

cord [kɔːd] *n* 1 *(string)* cuerda *f*; *Elec* cordón *m.* 2 *Tex (corduroy)* pana *f*; **cords**, pantalones *mpl* de pana.

cordial ['kɔːdɪəl] **I** *adj* cordial. **II** *n* licor *m.*

cordon ['kɔːdən] **I** *n* cordón *m.* **II** *vtr* **to c. off a street**, acordonar una calle.

corduroy ['kɔːdərɔɪ] *n* pana *f.*

core [kɔːʳ] *n* 1 *(of fruit)* corazón *m*; *Elec* núcleo *m*; *fig* **hard c.**, los incondicionales. **II** *vtr* quitarle el corazón a.

coriander [kɒrɪ'ændəʳ] *n* culantro *m.*

cork [kɔːk] *n* corcho *m*; **c. oak**, alcornoque *m.*

corkscrew ['kɔːkskruː] *n* sacacorchos *m inv.*

corn¹ [kɔːn] *n* cereal *m*; *(grain)* granos *mpl*; *(maize)* maíz *m*; **c. on the cob**, mazorca f de maíz.

corn² [kɔːn] n Med callo m.

cornea [ˈkɔːnɪə] n córnea f.

corner [ˈkɔːnəʳ] I n 1 (of street) esquina f; (bend in road) curva f; **round the c.,** a la vuelta de la esquina; *Ftb* **c. kick,** córner m; **c. shop,** tienda pequeña de barrio. 2 (of room) rincón m. II vtr 1 (enemy) arrinconar. 2 Com acaparar. III vi Aut tomar una curva.

cornerstone [ˈkɔːnəstəʊn] n piedra f angular.

cornet [ˈkɔːnɪt] n 1 Mus corneta f. 2 GB (for ice cream) cucurucho m.

cornflakes [ˈkɔːnfleɪks] npl copos mpl de maíz, cornflakes mpl.

cornflour [ˈkɔːnflaʊəʳ] n harina f de maíz, cornflour.

cornstarch [ˈkɔːnstɑːtʃ] n US → cornflour.

Cornwall [ˈkɔːnwəl] n Cornualles.

corny [ˈkɔːnɪ] adj (cornier, corniest) fam gastado,-a.

corollary [kəˈrɒlərɪ] n corolario m.

coronary [ˈkɒrənərɪ] adj coronario,-a; **c. thrombosis,** trombosis coronaria.

coronation [kɒrəˈneɪʃən] n coronación f.

coroner [ˈkɒrənəʳ] n juez mf de instrucción.

corporal¹ [ˈkɔːpərəl] adj corporal; **c. punishment,** castigo m corporal.

corporal² [ˈkɔːpərəl] n Mil cabo m.

corporate [ˈkɔːpərɪt] adj corporativo,-a.

corporation [kɔːpəˈreɪʃən] n 1 (business) sociedad anónima. 2 (of city) ayuntamiento m.

corps [kɔː] n (pl corps [kɔːz]) cuerpo m.

corpse [kɔːps] n cadáver m.

corpulent [ˈkɔːpjʊlənt] adj corpulento,-a.

corpuscle [ˈkɔːpʌsəl] n corpúsculo m.

corral [kəˈrɑːl] n US corral m.

correct [kəˈrekt] I vtr 1 (mistake) corregir. 2 (child) reprender. II adj correcto,-a, exacto,-a; (behaviour) formal.

correction [kəˈrekʃən] n corrección f.

correlation [kɒrəˈleɪʃən] n correlación f.

correspond [kɒrɪˈspɒnd] vi 1 corresponder; **to c. to,** equivaler a. 2 (by letter) escribirse.

correspondence [kɒrɪˈspɒndəns] n correspondencia f; **c. course,** curso m por correspondencia.

correspondent [kɒrɪˈspɒndənt] n Press corresponsal mf; **special c.,** enviado,-a m,f especial.

corridor [ˈkɒrɪdɔː] n pasillo m.

corroborate [kəˈrɒbəreɪt] vtr corroborar.

corrode [kəˈrəʊd] I vtr corroer. II vi corroerse.

corrosion [kəˈrəʊʒən] n corrosión f.

corrugated [ˈkɒrʊgeɪtɪd] adj **c. iron,** hierro ondulado.

corrupt [kəˈrʌpt] I adj (person) corrompido,-a, corrupto,-a; (actions) deshonesto,-a. II vtr & vi corromper.

corruption [kəˈrʌpʃən] n corrupción f.

corset [ˈkɔːsɪt] n (garment) faja f.

Corsica [ˈkɔːsɪkə] n Córcega.

cortège [kɔːˈteɪʒ] n cortejo m, comitiva f.

cosh [kɒʃ] n GB porra f.

cosmetic [kɒzˈmetɪk] I n cosmético m. II adj cosmético,-a; **c. surgery,** cirugía plástica.

cosmic [ˈkɒzmɪk] adj cósmico,-a.

cosmonaut [ˈkɒzmənɔːt] n cosmonauta mf.

cosmopolitan [kɒzməˈpɒlɪtən] adj cosmopolita.

cosset [ˈkɒsɪt] vtr mimar.

cost [kɒst] I n (price) precio m, coste m; **c. of living,** coste m de la vida; **to count the c.,** considerar las desventajas; **at all costs,** a toda costa. II vtr & vi (pt & pp cost) costar, valer; **how much does it c.?,** ¿cuánto cuesta?; **whatever it costs,** cueste lo que cueste. III vtr (pt & pp costed) Com Ind calcular el coste de.

co-star [ˈkəʊstɑːʳ] n Cin Theat coprotagonista mf.

Costa Rica [kɒstəˈriːkə] n Costa Rica.

Costa Rican [kɒstəˈriːkən] adj & n costarricense (mf).

cost-effective [kɒstɪˈfektɪv] adj rentable.

costly [ˈkɒstlɪ] adj (costlier, costliest) costoso,-a.

costume [ˈkɒstjuːm] n traje m; **swimming c.,** bañador m; **c. jewellery,** bisutería f.

cosy [ˈkəʊzɪ] adj (cosier, cosiest) (atmosphere) acogedor,-a; (bed) calentito,-a; **it's c. in here,** aquí se está bien.

cot [kɒt] n cuna f.

cottage [ˈkɒtɪdʒ] n casa f de campo; **c. cheese,** requesón m; **c. industry,** industria casera; GB **c. pie,** pastel m de carne picada con puré de patatas.

cotton [ˈkɒtən] n 1 Bot algodonero m; Tex algodón m; **c. wool,** algodón hidrófilo. 2 (thread) hilo m. ◆**cotton on** vi fam **to c. on to sth,** caer en la cuenta de algo.

couch [kaʊtʃ] n sofá m; (in surgery) camilla f.

couchette [kuːˈʃet] n Rail litera f.

cough [kɒf] I vi toser. II n tos f; **c. drop,** pastilla f para la tos; **c. mixture,** jarabe m para la tos. ◆**cough up** vtr fam **to c. up the money,** soltar la pasta.

could [kʊd] v aux → **can¹.**

council [ˈkaʊnsəl] n (body) consejo m; GB **c. house,** vivienda f de protección oficial; **town c.,** consejo m municipal, ayuntamiento m.

councillor, US **councilor** [ˈkaʊnsələʳ] n concejal m.

counsel [ˈkaʊnsəl] n 1 (advice) consejo m. 2 Jur abogado,-a m,f. II vtr aconsejar.

counsellor, US **counselor** [ˈkaʊnsələʳ] n 1 (adviser) asesor,-a m,f. 2 US Jur abogado,-a m,f.

count¹ [kaʊnt] I *vtr* 1 contar. 2 *fig* to c. oneself lucky, considerarse afortunado, -a. II *vi* contar; **that doesn't c.,** eso no vale; **to c. to ten,** contar hasta diez. III *n* 1 cuenta *f;* (*total*) recuento *m.* 2 *Jur* cargo *m.* ◆**count on** *vtr* contar con.

count² [kaʊnt] *n* (*nobleman*) conde *m.*

countdown ['kaʊntdaʊn] *n* cuenta *f* atrás.

countenance ['kaʊntɪnəns] I *n* semblante *m,* rostro *m.* II *vtr* aprobar.

counter¹ ['kaʊntə'] *n* 1 (*in shop*) mostrador *m;* (*in bank*) ventanilla *f.* 2 (*in board games*) ficha *f.*

counter² ['kaʊntə'] *n* contador *m.*

counter³ ['kaʊntə'] I *adv* c. to, en contra de. II *vtr* (*attack*) contestar a; (*trend*) contrarrestar. III *vi* (*attack*) contestar.

counteract [kaʊntə'ækt] *vtr* contrarrestar.

counterattack ['kaʊntərətæk] *n* contraataque *m.*

counterfeit ['kaʊntəfɪt] I *adj* falsificado, -a; c. coin, moneda falsa. II *n* falsificación *f.* III *vtr* falsificar.

counterfoil ['kaʊntəfɔɪl] *n* GB (*of cheque*) matriz *f.*

countermand [kaʊntə'mɑːnd] *vtr* (*command*) revocar; Com (*order*) anular.

counterpart ['kaʊntəpɑːt] *n* homólogo,-a *m,f.*

counterproductive [kaʊntəprə'dʌktɪv] *adj* contraproducente.

countersign ['kaʊntəsaɪn] *vtr* refrendar.

countess ['kaʊntɪs] *n* condesa *f.*

countless ['kaʊntlɪs] *adj* innumerable, incontable.

country ['kʌntrɪ] *n* 1 (*state*) país *m;* **native c.,** patria *f.* 2 (*rural area*) campo *m;* c. **dancing,** baile *m* popular.

countryman ['kʌntrɪmən] *n* 1 (*rural*) hombre *m* del campo. 2 (*compatriot*) compatriota *m.*

countryside ['kʌntrɪsaɪd] *n* (*area*) campo *m;* (*scenery*) paisaje *m.*

county ['kaʊntɪ] *n* condado *m.*

coup [kuː] *n* golpe *m;* c. **d'état,** golpe de estado.

couple ['kʌpəl] I *n* 1 (*of people*) pareja *f;* **a married c.,** un matrimonio. 2 (*of things*) par *m; fam* a c. of times, un par de veces. II *vtr* (*wagons*) enganchar.

coupling ['kʌplɪŋ] *n* Rail enganche *m.*

coupon ['kuːpɒn] *n* 1 cupón *m.* 2 GB Ftb quiniela *f.*

courage ['kʌrɪdʒ] *n* coraje *m,* valentía *f.*

courageous [kə'reɪdʒəs] *adj* valeroso,-a, valiente.

courgette [kʊə'ʒet] *n* calabacín *m.*

courier ['kʊərɪə'] *n* 1 (*messenger*) mensajero,-a *m.f.* 2 (*guide*) guía *mf* turístico,-a.

course [kɔːs] *n* 1 (*of river*) curso *m; Naut Av* rumbo *m.* 2 *fig* desarrollo *m;* **in the c.**

of construction, en vías de construcción; **in the c. of time,** con el tiempo. 3 (*series*) ciclo *m;* a c. **of treatment,** un tratamiento. 4 *Educ* curso *m; Univ* asignatura *f.* 5 (*for golf*) campo *m.* 6 *Culin* plato *m.* 7 of c., claro, por supuesto; **of c. not!,** ¡claro que no!.

court [kɔːt] I *n* 1 *Jur* tribunal *m;* c. **martial,** consejo *m* de guerra; c. **order,** orden *f* judicial. 2 (*royal*) corte *f.* 3 *Sport* pista *f,* cancha *f.* II *vtr* (*woman*) hacer la corte a; *fig* to c. **danger,** buscar el peligro; *fig* to c. **disaster,** exponerse al desastre. III *vi* (*couple*) tener relaciones.

courteous ['kɜːtɪəs] *adj* cortés.

courtesy ['kɜːtɪsɪ] *n* 1 cortesía *f,* educación *f.* 2 **by c. of,** por cortesía de.

courthouse ['kɔːthaʊs] *n* palacio *m* de justicia.

courtier ['kɔːtɪə'] *n* cortesano,-a *m,f.*

court-martial ['kɔːtmɑːʃəl] *vtr* someter a consejo de guerra.

courtroom ['kɔːtruːm] *n* sala *f* de justicia.

courtyard ['kɔːtjɑːd] *n* patio *m.*

cousin ['kʌzən] *n* primo,-a *m,f;* **first c.,** primo,-a hermano,-a.

cove [kəʊv] *n* cala *f,* ensenada *f.*

covenant ['kʌvənənt] *n* convenio *m,* pacto *m.*

cover ['kʌvə'] I *vtr* 1 cubrir (**with,** de); (*furniture*) revestir (**with,** de); (*with lid*) tapar. 2 (*hide*) disimular. 3 (*protect*) abrigar. 4 (*distance*) recorrer. 5 *Journ* investigar. 6 (*deal with*) abarcar. 7 (*include*) incluir. 8 *Sport* marcar. II *vi* to c. **for sb,** sustituir a algn. III *n* 1 cubierta *f;* (*lid*) tapa *f;* (*on bed*) manta *f;* (*of chair etc*) funda *f.* 2 (*of book*) tapa *f;* (*of magazine*) portada *f;* c. **girl,** modelo *f* de revista. 3 (*in restaurant*) cubierto *m.* 4 **under separate c.,** por separado. 5 *In full* c., cobertura completa; GB c. **note,** seguro *m* provisional. 6 (*protection*) abrigo *m;* **to take c.,** abrigarse; **under c.,** al abrigo; (*indoors*) bajo techo. ◆**cover up** I *vtr* cubrir. 2 (*crime*) encubrir. II *vi* 1 (*person*) abrigarse. 2 to c. **up for sb,** encubrir a algn.

coverage ['kʌvərɪdʒ] *n* cobertura *f.*

coveralls ['kʌvərɔːlz] *npl* US mono *m sing.*

covering ['kʌvərɪŋ] I *n* cubierta *f,* envoltura *f.* II *adj* (*letter*) explicatorio,-a.

covert ['kʌvət] *adj* disimulado,-a, secreto,-a.

cover-up ['kʌvərʌp] *n* encubrimiento *m.*

covet ['kʌvɪt] *vtr* codiciar.

cow¹ [kaʊ] *n* vaca *f; pej* (*woman*) arpía *f,* bruja *f.*

cow² [kaʊ] *vtr* intimidar.

coward ['kaʊəd] *n* cobarde *mf.*

cowardice ['kaʊədɪs] *n* cobardía *f.*

cowardly ['kauədlɪ] *adj* cobarde.

cowboy ['kaubɔɪ] *n* vaquero *m*.

cower ['kauə'] *vi (with fear)* encogerse.

cox [kɒks] *n* timonel *m*.

coy [kɔɪ] *adj (shy)* tímido,-a; *(demure)* coquetón,-ona.

cozy ['kəuzɪ] *adj US → cosy.*

crab [kræb] *n* 1 cangrejo *m*. 2 c. apple, manzana *f* silvestre.

crack [kræk] I *vtr* 1 *(cup)* partir; *(bone)* fracturar; *(nut)* cascar; *(safe)* forzar. 2 *(whip)* hacer restallar. 3 *fig (problem)* dar con la solución de; *(joke)* contar. II *vi* 1 *(glass)* partirse; *(wall)* agrietarse. 2 *(whip)* restallar. 3 *fam* to get cracking on sth, ponerse a hacer algo. III *n* 1 *(in cup)* raja *f*; *(in wall, ground)* grieta *f*; *(of whip)* restallido *m*; *(of gun)* detonación *f*. 2 *fam (blow)* golpetazo *m*. 4 *fam* to have a c. at sth, *(attempt)* intentar hacer algo. 5 *sl (wisecrack)* réplica aguda. 6 *sl (drug)* crack *m*. IV *adj sl* de primera. ◆**crack down on** *vtr* atajar con mano dura. ◆**crack up** *vi fam fig (go mad)* desquiciarse; *(with laughter)* partirse de risa.

cracker ['krækə'] *n* 1 *(biscuit)* galleta salada. 2 *(firework)* petardo *m*.

crackle ['krækəl] *vi* crujir; *(fire)* crepitar.

cradle ['kreɪdəl] *n (baby's)* cuna *f*.

craft [krɑːft] *n* 1 *(occupation)* oficio *m*; *(art)* arte *m*; *(skill)* destreza *f*. 2 *(cunning)* maña *f*. 3 *Naut* embarcación *f*.

craftsman ['krɑːftsmən] *n* artesano *m*.

craftsmanship ['krɑːftsmənʃɪp] *n* arte *f*.

crafty ['krɑːftɪ] *adj (craftier, craftiest)* astuto,-a.

crag [kræg] *n* peña *f*, peñasco *m*.

cram [kræm] I *vtr* atiborrar; *(packed with*, atestado,-a, de. II *vi* Educ empollar.

cramp¹ [kræmp] *n* Med calambre *m*; cramps, retortijones *mpl*.

cramp² [kræmp] *vtr (development etc)* poner trabas a.

cramped [kræmpt] *adj* atestado,-a; *(writing)* apretado,-a.

cranberry ['krænbərɪ] *n* arándano *m*.

crane [kreɪn] I *n* 1 Zool grulla *f* común. 2 *(device)* grúa *f*. II *vtr* estirar.

crank [kræŋk] *n* 1 Tech manivela *f*. 2 *fam (eccentric)* tío raro.

crankshaft ['kræŋkʃɑːft] *n* árbol *m* del cigüeñal.

cranny ['krænɪ] *n fig* in every nook and c., en todos los rincones.

crap [kræp] *n fam* mierda *f*.

crash [kræʃ] I *vtr* to c. one's car, tener un accidente con el coche. II *vi* 1 *(car, plane)* estrellarse; *(collide)* chocar; to c. into, estrellarse contra. 2 Com quebrar. III *n* 1 *(noise)* estrépito *m*. 2 *(collision)* choque *m*; car/plane c., accidente *m* de coche/avión; *fig* c. course, curso intensivo; c. helmet, casco *m* protector. 3 Com

quiebra *f*.

crash-land [kræʃ'lænd] *vi* hacer un aterrizaje forzoso.

crass [kræs] *adj (person)* grosero,-a; *(error)* garrafal.

crate [kreɪt] *n* caja *f*, cajón *m* (para embalaje).

crater ['kreɪtə'] *n* cráter *m*.

cravat [krə'væt] *n* pañuelo *m* (de hombre).

crave [kreɪv] *vi* to c. for sth, ansiar algo.

craving ['kreɪvɪŋ] *n* ansia *f*; *(in pregnancy)* antojo *m*.

crawfish ['krɔːfɪʃ] *n* langosta *f*.

crawl [krɔːl] I *vi (baby)* gatear; *(vehicle)* avanzar lentamente; *fig* to c. to sb, arrastrarse a los pies de algn. II *n (swimming)* crol *m*.

crayfish ['kreɪfɪʃ] *n* cangrejo *m* de río.

crayon ['kreɪɒn] *n* cera *f*.

craze [kreɪz] *n* manía *f*; *(fashion)* moda *f*; it's the latest c., es el último grito.

crazy ['kreɪzɪ] *adj (crazier, craziest)* fam loco,-a, chalado,-a; *GB* c. paving, pavimento *m* en mosaico.

creak [kriːk] *vi (floor)* crujir; *(hinge)* chirriar.

cream [kriːm] *n* 1 *(of milk)* nata *f*; c. coloured, color crema; *fig* the c., la flor y nata; c. cheese, queso *m* crema. 2 *(cosmetic)* crema *f*. II *vtr* 1 *(milk)* desnatar. 2 Culin batir; creamed potatoes, puré *m* de patatas.

creamy ['kriːmɪ] *adj (creamier, creamiest)* cremoso,-a.

crease [kriːs] I *n (wrinkle)* arruga *f*; *(fold)* pliegue *m*; *(on trousers)* raya *f*. II *vtr (clothes)* arrugar. III *vi* arrugarse.

create [kriː'eɪt] *vtr* crear.

creation [kriː'eɪʃən] *n* creación *f*.

creative [kriː'eɪtɪv] *adj (person)* creativo,-a.

creativity [kriːeɪ'tɪvɪtɪ] *n* creatividad *f*.

creator [kriː'eɪtə'] *n* creador,-a *m,f*.

creature ['kriːtʃə'] *n (animal)* criatura *f*.

crèche [kreʃ, kreɪʃ] *n* guardería *f*.

credence ['kriːdəns] *n* to give c. to, dar crédito a.

credentials [krɪ'denʃəlz] *npl* credenciales *fpl*.

credible ['kredɪbəl] *adj* creíble.

credit ['kredɪt] I *n* 1 Com crédito *m*; on c., a crédito; c. card, tarjeta *f* de crédito. 2 to give c. to sb for sth, reconocer algo a algn. 3 *(benefit)* honor *m*; to be to c., hacer honor a. 4 Cin TV credits, créditos *mpl*. II *vtr* 1 Com abonar. 2 *(believe)* creer. 3 *fig* atribuir; he is credited with having ..., se le atribuye haber ....

creditor ['kredɪtə'] *n* acreedor,-a *m,f*.

creed [kriːd] *n* credo *m*.

creek [kriːk] *n* 1 GB cala *f*. 2 US Austral riachuelo *m*.

creep [kriːp] I *vi (pt & pp crept)* andar silenciosamente; (insect) arrastrarse; (plant) trepar; to c. up on sb, sorprender a algn. II n fam (person) pelotillero,-a m,f.

creeper ['kri:pər] n Bot trepadora f.

creepy ['kri:pi] adj (creepier, creepiest) fam espeluznante.

cremate [krə'meit] vtr incinerar.

crematorium [kremə'tɔ:riəm] n crematorio m.

crepe [kreip] n 1 Tex crepé m. 2 c. paper, papel m crespón.

crept [krept] pt & pp → creep.

crescendo [kri'ʃendəʊ] n crescendo m.

crescent ['kresənt] I n (shape) medialuna f; GB (street) calle f en medialuna. II adj creciente.

cress [kres] n berro m.

crest [krest] n 1 (of cock, wave) cresta f; (on helmet) penacho m; (of hill) cima f. 2 (heraldic) blasón m.

crestfallen ['krestfɔːlən] adj abatido,-a.

Crete [kri:t] n Creta.

cretin ['kretin] n cretino,-a m,f.

crevasse [kri'væs] n grieta f, fisura f.

crevice ['krevis] n grieta f, hendedura f.

crew [kru:] n Av Naut tripulación f. ◆c. cut, corte m al rape; c.-neck sweater, jersey m con cuello redondo.

crib [krib] n (manger) pesebre m; (for baby) cuna f. II vtr fam 1 (copy) copiar. 2 (steal) quitar.

crick [krik] n fam a c. in the neck, una tortícolis.

cricket¹ ['krikit] n Ent grillo m.

cricket² ['krikit] n Sport criquet m.

crime [kraim] n delincuencia f; (offence) delito m.

criminal ['kriminəl] adj & n criminal (mf); c. law, derecho m penal; c. record, antecedentes mpl penales.

crimson ['krimzən] adj & n carmesí (m).

cringe [krindʒ] vi abatirse, encogerse.

crinkle ['krinkəl] vtr fruncir, arrugar.

cripple ['kripəl] I n lisiado,-a m,f, mutilado,-a m,f. II vtr mutilar, dejar cojo,-a; fig paralizar.

crisis ['kraisis] n (pl crises ['kraisi:z]) crisis f inv.

crisp [krisp] I adj crujiente; (lettuce) fresco,-a; (banknote) nuevo,-a; (weather) frío,-a y seco,-a; fig (style) directo,-a. II n GB (potato) c., patata frita.

crisscross ['kriskrɒs] n líneas fpl entrecruzadas.

criterion [krai'tiəriən] n (pl criteria [krai'tiəriə]) criterio m.

critic ['kritik] n Art Theat crítico,-a m,f.

critical ['kritikəl] adj crítico,-a. ◆critically adv críticamente; c. ill, gravemente enfermo,-a.

criticism ['kritisizəm] n crítica f.

criticize ['kritisaiz] vtr criticar.

croak [krəʊk] vi (frog) croar; (raven) graznar; (person) hablar con voz ronca.

crochet ['krəʊʃei] n ganchillo m.

crockery ['krɒkəri] n loza f.

crocodile ['krɒkədail] n cocodrilo m.

crocus ['krəʊkəs] n azafrán m.

crony ['krəʊni] n compinche mf.

crook [krʊk] n 1 (of shepherd) cayado m. 2 fam caco m. II vtr (arm) doblar.

crooked ['krʊkid] adj 1 (stick, picture) torcido,-a; (path) tortuoso,-a. 2 fam (dishonest) deshonesto,-a.

crop [krɒp] I n 1 cultivo m; (harvest) cosecha f; (of hair) mata f. 2 (whip) fusta f. II vtr (hair) rapar; (grass) cortar. ◆crop up vi form surgir, presentarse.

croquet ['krəʊkei] n croquet m.

cross [krɒs] I n 1 cruz f. 2 (breeds) cruce m. 3 c. section, sección f transversal. II vtr 1 cruzar. 2 Rel to c. oneself, hacer la señal de la cruz; fam c. my heart!, ¡te lo juro! 3 (thwart) contrariar. III vi cruzar; (roads) cruzarse; to c. over, cruzar. IV adj 1 fig they are at c. purposes, hay un malentendido entre ellos. 2 (angry) enfadado,-a. ◆cross off, cross out vtr tachar, rayar.

crossbar ['krɒsbɑ:] n travesaño m.

cross-country ['krɒskʌntri] I n c.-c. race, cros m. II ['krɒs'kʌntri] adv campo través.

cross-examine ['krɒsig'zæmin] vtr interrogar.

cross-eyed ['krɒsaid] adj bizco,-a.

crossfire ['krɒsfaiər] n fuego cruzado.

crossing ['krɒsiŋ] n cruce m; pedestrian c., paso m de peatones; sea c., travesía f.

cross-legged ['krɒs'legid] adj con las piernas cruzadas.

cross-reference ['krɒs'refərəns] n remisión f.

crossroads ['krɒsrəʊdz] n cruce m; fig encrucijada f.

crosswind ['krɒswind] n viento m lateral.

crossword ['krɒswɜ:d] n (puzzle), crucigrama m.

crotch [krɒtʃ] n entrepierna f.

crotchet ['krɒtʃit] n Mus negra f.

crotchety ['krɒtʃiti] adj fam gruñón,-ona.

crouch [kraʊtʃ] vi to c. (down), agacharse.

crow¹ [krəʊ] n cuervo m; fig as the c. flies, en línea recta; c.'s-feet, patas fpl de gallo.

crow² [krəʊ] vi (cock) cantar; fig to c. over sth, jactarse de algo. 2 (baby) balbucir. II n (of cock) canto m.

crowbar ['krəʊbɑ:] n palanca f.

crowd [kraʊd] I n muchedumbre f; the c., el populacho; fam (gang) pandilla f. II vtr (streets) llenar. III vi apiñarse; to c. in/out, entrar/salir en tropel.

crowded ['kraʊdid] adj atestado,-a, lleno,-a.

crown [kraʊn] I n 1 corona f; (garland) guirnalda f; the c. jewels, las joyas de la corona; *GB Jur* c. **court**, tribunal *m* superior; **C. Prince**, príncipe heredero. 2 *Anat* coronilla *f*; *(of hat, tree)* copa *f*. II *vtr* coronar; *fam fig* to c. it all, y para más inri.

crucial ['kru:ʃəl] *adj* decisivo,-a.

crucifix ['kru:sɪfɪks] *n* crucifijo *m*.

crucifixion [kru:sɪ'fɪkʃən] *n* crucifixión *f*.

crucify ['kru:sɪfaɪ] *vtr* crucificar.

crude [kru:d] *adj* 1 *(manners, style)* tosco,-a, grosero,-a; *(tool)* primitivo,-a. 2 c. oil, crudo *m*.

cruel [kruəl] *adj* cruel (to, con).

cruelty ['kru:ltɪ] *n* crueldad *f* (to, hacia).

cruet ['kru:ɪt] *n* c. set, vinagreras *fpl*.

cruise [kru:z] I *vi* 1 *Naut* hacer un crucero. 2 *Aut* viajar a velocidad constante; *Av* viajar a velocidad de crucero. II *n* 1 *Naut* crucero *m*. 2 c. missile, misil teledirigido.

cruiser ['kru:zə'] *n* (barco *m*) crucero *m*.

crumb [krʌm] *n* miga *f*, migaja *f*.

crumble ['krʌmbəl] I *vtr* desmigar. II *vi* *(wall)* desmoronarse; *fig (hopes)* desvanecerse.

crumbly ['krʌmblɪ] *adj* (**crumblier, crumbliest**) que se desmigaja.

crumpet ['krʌmpɪt] *n GB* clase *f* de crepe grueso que se puede tostar.

crumple ['krʌmpəl] *vtr* arrugar.

crunch [krʌntʃ] I *vtr (food)* ronchar; *(with feet)* hacer crujir. II *n fam* when it comes to the c., a la hora de la verdad.

crunchy ['krʌntʃɪ] *adj* (**crunchier, crunchiest**) crujiente.

crusade [kru:'seɪd] *n* cruzada *f*.

crush [krʌʃ] I *vtr* aplastar; *(wrinkle)* arrugar; *(grind)* moler; *(squeeze)* exprimir. II *n* 1 *(of people)* gentío *m*. 2 orange c., naranjada *f*.

crushing ['krʌʃɪŋ] *adj fig (defeat, reply)* aplastante.

crust [krʌst] *n* corteza *f*.

crutch [krʌtʃ] *n Med* muleta *f*; *fig* apoyo *m*.

crux [krʌks] *n* the c. of the matter, el quid de la cuestión.

cry [kraɪ] I *vi (pt & pp cried)* 1 gritar. 2 *(weep)* llorar. II *vtr* gritar; *fig* to c. wolf, dar una falsa alarma. III *n* 1 grito *m*. 2 *(weep)* llanto *m*. ◆**cry off** *vi* fam negarse. ◆**cry out** *vi* gritar; to c. out for sth, pedir algo a gritos.

crying ['kraɪɪŋ] *adj* it's a c. shame, es una vergüenza.

cryptic ['krɪptɪk] *adj* enigmático,-a.

crystal ['krɪstəl] *n* cristal *m*.

crystal-clear [krɪstəl'klɪə'] *adj* claro,-a como el agua.

crystallize ['krɪstəlaɪz] I *vtr* cristalizar. II *vi* cristalizarse.

cub [kʌb] *n* 1 *(animal)* cachorro *m*. 2 *(junior scout)* niño *m* explorador.

Cuba ['kju:bə] *n* Cuba.

Cuban ['kju:bən] *adj & n* cubano,-a *(m,f)*.

cubbyhole ['kʌbɪhəʊl] *n* cuchitril *m*.

cube [kju:b] I *n* cubo *m*; *(of sugar)* terrón *m*; c. **root**, raíz cúbica. II *vtr Math* elevar al cubo.

cubic ['kju:bɪk] *adj* cúbico,-a.

cubicle ['kju:bɪkəl] *n* cubículo *m*; *(at swimming pool)* caseta *f*.

cuckoo ['kuku:] I *n* cuco *m*; c. **clock**, reloj *m* de cuco. II *adj fam* lelo,-a.

cucumber ['kju:kʌmbə'] *n* pepino *m*.

cuddle ['kʌdəl] I *vtr* abrazar. II *vi* abrazarse.

cuddly ['kʌdlɪ] *adj* c. **toy**, muñeco *m* de peluche.

cue[1] [kju:] *n Theat* pie *m*.

cue[2] [kju:] *n (in billiards)* taco *m*; c. **ball**, bola blanca.

cuff[1] [kʌf] *n (of sleeve)* puño *m*; *US (of trousers)* dobladillo *m*; *fig* to do sth off the c., improvisar algo.

cuff[2] [kʌf] I *vtr* abofetear. II *n* bofetada *f*.

cufflinks ['kʌflɪŋks] *npl* gemelos *mpl*.

cul-de-sac ['kʌldəsæk] *n* callejón *m* sin salida.

cull [kʌl] *vtr* 1 *(choose)* escoger. 2 *(animals)* eliminar.

culminate ['kʌlmɪneɪt] *vi* to c. **in**, terminar en.

culmination [kʌlmɪ'neɪʃən] *n* culminación *f*, punto *m* culminante.

culottes [kju:'lɒts] *npl* falda-pantalón *f sing*.

culprit ['kʌlprɪt] *n* culpable *mf*.

cult [kʌlt] *n* culto *m*; c. **figure**, ídolo *m*.

cultivate ['kʌltɪveɪt] *vtr* cultivar.

cultivated ['kʌltɪveɪtɪd] *adj (person)* culto,-a.

cultivation [kʌltɪ'veɪʃən] *n* cultivo *m* (de la tierra).

cultural ['kʌltʃərəl] *adj* cultural.

culture ['kʌltʃə'] *n* cultura *f*.

cultured ['kʌltʃəd] *adj* → **cultivated**.

cumbersome ['kʌmbəsəm] *adj (awkward)* incómodo,-a; *(bulky)* voluminoso,-a.

cum(m)in ['kʌmɪn] *n* comino *m*.

cumulative ['kju:mjʊlətɪv] *adj* acumulativo,-a.

cunning ['kʌnɪŋ] I *adj* astuto,-a. II *n* astucia *f*.

cup [kʌp] *n* taza *f*; *Sport* copa *f*; **C. Final**, final *f* de copa; c. **tie**, partido *m* de copa. II *vtr (hands)* ahuecar.

cupboard ['kʌbəd] *n* armario *m*; *(on wall)* alacena *f*.

curate ['kjʊərɪt] *n* cura *m* coadjutor.

curator [kjʊə'reɪtə'] *n* conservador,-a *m,f*.

curb [kɜ:b] I *n (kerb)* bordillo *m*. II *vtr (horse)* refrenar; *fig (public spending)* contener.

curd [kɜ:d] *n* cuajada *f*.

curdle ['kɜ:dəl] *vi* cuajarse.

cure [kjʊəʳ] I *vtr* curar. II *n* (*remedy*) cura *f*, remedio *m*.

curfew [ˈkɜːfjuː] *n* toque *m* de queda.

curiosity [kjʊərɪˈɒsɪtɪ] *n* curiosidad *f*.

curious [ˈkjʊərɪəs] *adj* 1 (*inquisitive*) curioso,-a. 2 (*odd*) extraño,-a.

curl [kɜːl] I *vtr* (*hair*) rizar; (*lip*) fruncir. II *vi* rizarse. III *n* (*of hair*) rizo *m*; (*of smoke*) espiral *f*. ◆**curl up** *vi* enroscarse.

curly [ˈkɜːlɪ] *adj* (**curlier, curliest**) rizado,-a.

currant [ˈkʌrənt] *n* pasa *f* (de Corinto).

currency [ˈkʌrənsɪ] *n* 1 moneda *f*, divisa *f*. 2 **to gain c.**, cobrar fuerza.

current [ˈkʌrənt] I *adj* 1 (*opinion*) general; (*word*) en uso; (*year*) en curso; **c. account**, cuenta *f* corriente; **c. affairs**, actualidad *f sing* (política); Fin **c. assets**, activo *m sing* disponible. 2 **the c. issue**, (*of magazine, newspaper*) el último número. II *n* corriente *f*. ◆**currently** *adv* actualmente.

curriculum [kəˈrɪkjʊləm] *n* (*pl* **curricula** [kəˈrɪkjʊlə]) plan *m* de estudios; **c. vitae**, curriculum *m* (vitae).

curry[1] [ˈkʌrɪ] *n* curry *m*; **chicken c.**, pollo *m* al curry.

curry[2] [ˈkʌrɪ] *vtr* **to c. favour with**, congraciarse con.

curse [kɜːs] I *n* maldición *f*; (*oath*) palabrota *f*; *fig* azote *m*. II *vtr* maldecir. III *vi* blasfemar.

cursor [ˈkɜːsəʳ] *n* cursor *m*.

cursory [ˈkɜːsərɪ] *adj* rápido,-a.

curt [kɜːt] *adj* brusco,-a, seco,-a.

curtail [kɜːˈteɪl] *vtr* (*expenses*) reducir; (*text*) acortar.

curtain [ˈkɜːtən] *n* cortina *f*; *Theat* telón *m*; *fig* velo *m*.

curts(e)y [ˈkɜːtsɪ] I *n* reverencia *f*. II *vi* hacer una reverencia (**to**, a).

curve [kɜːv] I *n* curva *f*. II *vtr* encorvar. III *vi* torcerse, describir una curva.

cushion [ˈkʊʃən] I *n* cojín *m*; (*large*) almohadón *m*; (*of billiard table*) banda *f*. II *vtr fig* amortiguar; (*person*) proteger.

cushy [ˈkʊʃɪ] *adj* (**cushier, cushiest**) *fam* cómodo,-a.

custard [ˈkʌstəd] *n* natillas *fpl*; **c. powder**, polvos *mpl* para natillas.

custodian [kʌsˈtəʊdɪən] *n* conserje *mf*, guarda *mf*.

custody [ˈkʌstədɪ] *n* custodia *f*; **to take into c.**, detener.

custom [ˈkʌstəm] *n* 1 (*habit*) costumbre *f*. 2 Com clientela *f*.

customary [ˈkʌstəmərɪ] *adj* habitual.

customer [ˈkʌstəməʳ] *n* cliente *mf*.

customize [ˈkʌstəmaɪz] *vtr* hacer por encargo.

custom-made [kʌstəmˈmeɪd] *adj* hecho,-a a la medida.

customs [ˈkʌstəmz] *n sing or pl* aduana *f*;

c. duty, derechos *mpl* de aduana; **c. officer**, **agente** *mf* de aduana.

cut [kʌt] I *vtr* (*pt & pp cut*) 1 cortar; (*stone*) tallar; (*record*) grabar; **he's cutting a tooth**, le está saliendo un diente; **to c. one's finger**, cortarse el dedo; *fig* **to c. a long story short**, en resumidas cuentas; *fig* **to c. corners**, recortar presupuestos. 2 (*reduce*) reducir. 3 (*divide up*) dividir (*into*, en).

II *n* 1 corte *m*; (*in skin*) cortadura *f*; (*wound*) herida *f*; (*with knife*) cuchillada *f*. 2 (*of meat*) clase *f* de carne. 3 (*reduction*) reducción *f*. 4 *fig* **to be a c. above sb**, estar por encima de algn.

III *adj* cortado,-a; (*price*) reducido,-a; *fig* **c. and dried**, convenido,-a de antemano; **c. glass**, cristal tallado.

IV *vi* 1 cortar; *fam fig* **to c. loose**, romper con todo. 2 Cin **c. !**, ¡corten! ◆**cut back** *vtr* (*expenses*) reducir; (*production*) disminuir. ◆**cut down** *vtr* (*tree*) talar; **to c. down on**, reducir. ◆**cut in** *vi* (*driver*) adelantar bruscamente. ◆**cut off** *vtr* (*water etc*) cortar; (*place*) aislar; (*heir*) excluir; *Tel* **I've been c. off**, me han cortado (la comunicación). ◆**cut out** I *vtr* 1 (*from newspaper*) recortar; (*person*) **to be c. out for sth**, estar hecho,-a para algo. 2 (*delete*) suprimir. II *vi* (*engine*) calarse. ◆**cut up** *vtr* cortar en pedazos.

cutback [ˈkʌtbæk] *n* reducción *f* (**in**, de).

cute [kjuːt] *adj* mono,-a, lindo,-a; *US fam pej* listillo,-a.

cuticle [ˈkjuːtɪkəl] *n* cutícula *f*.

cutlery [ˈkʌtlərɪ] *n* cubiertos *mpl*.

cutlet [ˈkʌtlɪt] *n* chuleta *f*.

cut-price [kʌtˈpraɪs] *adj* (*article*) a precio rebajado.

cutthroat [ˈkʌtθrəʊt] I *n* asesino,-a *m,f*, matón *m*. II *adj* (*cruel*) cruel; (*competition*) feroz.

cutting [ˈkʌtɪŋ] I *n* (*from newspaper*) recorte *m*; *Rail* tajo *m*. II *adj* cortante; (*remark*) mordaz.

CV, cv [siːˈviː] *abbr* of **curriculum vitae**.

cwt. *abbr* of **hundredweight**, quintal *m*.

cyanide [ˈsaɪənaɪd] *n* cianuro *m*.

cycle [ˈsaɪkəl] I *n* 1 ciclo *m*. 2 (*bicycle*) bicicleta *f*; (*motorcycle*) moto *f*. II *vi* ir en bicicleta.

cycling [ˈsaɪklɪŋ] *n* ciclismo *m*.

cyclist [ˈsaɪklɪst] *n* ciclista *mf*.

cyclone [ˈsaɪkləʊn] *n* ciclón *m*.

cygnet [ˈsɪgnɪt] *n* pollo *m* de cisne.

cylinder [ˈsɪlɪndəʳ] *n* 1 cilindro *m*. 2 (*for gas*) bombona *f*.

cymbal [ˈsɪmbəl] *n* címbalo *m*, platillo *m*.

cynic [ˈsɪnɪk] *n* cínico,-a *m,f*.

cynical [ˈsɪnɪkəl] *adj* cínico,-a.

cynicism [ˈsɪnɪsɪzəm] *n* cinismo *m*.

cypress [ˈsaɪprəs] *n* ciprés *m*.

Cypriot ['sɪprɪət] *adj & n* chipriota (*mf*).

Cyprus ['saɪprəs] *n* Chipre.

cyst [sɪst] *n* quiste *m*.

cystitis [sɪ'staɪtɪs] *n* cistitis *f*.

czar [zɑː] *n* zar *m*.

Czech [tʃek] I *adj* checo,-a. II *n* 1 (*person*) checo,-a *m,f*. 2 (*language*) checo *m*.

Czechoslovakia [tʃekəʊsləʊ'vækɪə] *n* Checoslovaquia.

D

D, d [diː] *n* 1 (*the letter*) D, d *f*. 2 *Mus* re *m*.

D.A. [diː'eɪ] *US abbr of* **District Attorney**.

dab [dæb] I *n* (*small quantity*) toque *m*. II *vtr* 1 (*apply*) aplicar. 2 (*touch lightly*) tocar ligeramente.

dabble ['dæbəl] *vi* to d. in politics, meterse en política.

dachshund ['dækshʊnd] *n* perro *m* salchicha.

dad [dæd], **daddy** ['dædɪ] *n fam* papá *m*, papi *m*.

daddy-longlegs [dædɪ'lɒŋlegz] *n inv GB fam* típula *f*.

daffodil ['dæfədɪl] *n* narciso *m*.

daft [dɑːft] *adj GB fam* chalado,-a; (*idea*) tonto,-a.

dagger ['dægə] *n* puñal *m*, daga *f*.

dahlia ['deɪljə] *n* dalia *f*.

daily ['deɪlɪ] I *adj* diario,-a, cotidiano,-a. II *adv* diariamente; **three times d.**, tres veces al día. III *n* 1 (*newspaper*) diario *m*. 2 *GB fam* (*cleaning lady*) asistenta *f*.

dainty ['deɪntɪ] *adj* (*daintier, daintiest*) (*flower*) delicado,-a; (*child*) precioso,-a; (*food*) exquisito,-a.

dairy ['deərɪ] *n* (*on farm*) vaquería *f*; (*shop*) lechería *f*; **d. farming**, industria lechera; **d. produce**, productos lácteos.

dais ['deɪɪs] *n* (*in hall*) tarima *f*; (*in ceremony*) estrado *m*.

daisy ['deɪzɪ] *n* margarita *f*.

daisywheel ['deɪzɪwiːl] *n* (*printer*) margarita *f*.

dale [deɪl] *n* valle *m*, hondonada *f*.

Dalmatian [dæl'meɪʃən] *n* (*perro m*) dálmata *m*.

dam [dæm] I *n* (*barrier*) dique *m*; (*lake*) presa *f*. II *vtr* (*water*) represar. ◆**dam up** *vtr fig* (*emotion*) contener.

damage ['dæmɪdʒ] I *n* 1 daño *m*; (*to health, reputation*) perjuicio *m*; (*to relationship*) deterioro *m*. 2 *Jur* **damages**, daños *mpl* y perjuicios *mpl*. II *vtr* (*harm*) dañar, hacer daño a; (*spoil*) estropear; (*undermine*) perjudicar.

damaging ['dæmɪdʒɪŋ] *adj* perjudicial.

damn [dæm] I *vtr* condenar. II *interj fam* d. (it)!, ¡maldito,-a sea!; **well, I'll be damned!**, ¡vaya por Dios!. III *n* *fam* I don't give a d., me importa un bledo. IV *adj fam* maldito,-a. V *adv fam* muy, sumamente.

damned [dæmd] I *adj* → **damn** IV. II *adv* → **damn** V.

damnedest ['dæmdɪst] *n fam* **to do one's d. to ...**, hacer todo lo posible para ....

damning ['dæmɪŋ] *adj* (*evidence*) irrefutable; (*criticism*) mordaz.

damp [dæmp] I *adj* húmedo,-a; (*wet*) mojado,-a. II *n* humedad *f*. III *vtr* 1 (*for ironing*) humedecer. 2 **to d. (down)**, (*fire*) sofocar; *fig* (*violence*) frenar.

dampen ['dæmpən] *vtr* humedecer; *fig* frenar.

damper ['dæmpə] *n fig* **to put a d. on sth**, poner freno a algo.

damsel ['dæmzəl] *n lit* doncella *f*.

damson ['dæmzən] *n* ciruela damascena.

dance [dɑːns] I *n* baile *m*; (*classical, tribal*) danza *f*; **d. band**, orquesta *f* de baile; **d. floor**, pista *f* de baile; **d. hall**, salón *m* de baile. II *vi & vtr* bailar.

dancer ['dɑːnsə] *n* (*by profession*) bailarín,-ina *m,f*.

dandelion ['dændɪlaɪən] *n* diente *m* de león.

dandruff ['dændrəf] *n* caspa *f*.

Dane [deɪn] *n* danés,-esa *m,f*.

danger ['deɪndʒə] *n* 1 (*risk*) riesgo *m*; (*of war etc*) amenaza *f*. 2 (*peril*) peligro *m*; **'d.'**, 'peligro'; **out of d.**, fuera de peligro.

dangerous ['deɪndʒərəs] *adj* peligroso,-a; (*risky*) arriesgado,-a; (*harmful*) nocivo,-a; (*illness*) grave. ◆**dangerously** *adv* peligrosamente.

dangle ['dæŋgəl] I *vi* (*hang*) colgar; (*swing*) balancearse. II *vtr* (*legs*) colgar; (*bait*) dejar colgado,-a; (*swing*) balancear en el aire.

Danish ['deɪnɪʃ] I *adj* danés,-esa; **D. pastry**, pastel *m* de hojaldre. II *n* (*language*) danés *m*.

dapper ['dæpə] *adj* pulcro,-a.

dappled ['dæpld] *adj* (*shade*) moteado,-a.

dare [deə] I *vi* atreverse, osar; **he doesn't d. be late**, no se atreve a llegar tarde; **how d. you!**, ¡cómo te atreves?; *esp GB* I d. say, quizás; *iron* ya (lo creo). II *vtr* (*challenge*) desafiar. III *n* desafío *m*.

daredevil ['deədevəl] *adj & n* atrevido,-a (*m,f*), temerario,-a (*m,f*).

daring ['deərɪŋ] I *adj* 1 (*bold*) audaz, osado,-a. 2 (*clothes*) atrevido,-a. II *n* atrevimiento *m*, osadía *f*.

dark [dɑːk] I *adj* 1 (*room, colour*) oscuro,-a; (*hair, complexion*) moreno,-a; (*eyes, fu-*

ture) negro,-a. 2 fig (gloomy) triste. 3 fig
to be a d. horse, ser una incógnita; (discreet) ser una caja de sorpresas. 4 fig
(sinister) siniestro,-a. II n 1 (darkness)
oscuridad f, tinieblas fpl; **after d.,** después del anochecer. 2 fig **to be in the d.**
(about), estar a oscuras (sobre).

darken ['dɑːkən] I vtr (sky) oscurecer;
(colour) hacer más oscuro,-a. II vi oscure-
cerse; (sky) nublarse; fig (face) ensombrecerse.

darkness ['dɑːknɪs] n oscuridad f, tinieblas fpl.

darkroom ['dɑːkruːm] n cuarto oscuro.

darling ['dɑːlɪŋ] adj & n querido,-a (m,f).

darn [dɑːn] I vtr zurcir. II n zurcido m.

dart [dɑːt] I n 1 (missile) dardo m. 2
darts, sing dardos mpl. II n 1 (fly about) revolotear; **to d. in/out,** entrar/salir corriendo.

dartboard ['dɑːtbɔːd] n diana f.

dash [dæʃ] I n 1 (rush) carrera f. 2 esp US
(race) sprint m. 3 (small amount) poquito
m; (of salt) pizca f; (of liquid) gota f. 4
Typ (hyphen) guión largo; (hyphen) guión. 5 (vitality) brío m. II n 1 vtr 1 (throw) arrojar. 2
(smash) estrellar; fig **to d. sb's hopes,**
desvanecer las esperanzas de algn. III vi
(rush) correr; **to d. around,** correr de un
lado a otro; **to d. out,** salir corriendo;
fam **I must d.!,** ¡me voy pitando!
◆**dash off** vi salir corriendo.

dashboard ['dæʃbɔːd] n Aut salpicadero
m.

dashing ['dæʃɪŋ] adj (appearance)
garboso,-a.

data ['deɪtə, 'dɑːtə] npl datos mpl; **d.
bank** o **base,** banco m de datos; **d. processing,** (act) proceso m de datos;
(science) informática f; **d. protection act,**
ley f de informática.

date¹ [deɪt] I n 1 fecha f; **what's the d.
today?** ¿qué día es hoy?; **out of d.,**
(ideas) anticuado,-a; (expression)
desusado,-a; (invalid) caducado,-a; **to d.,**
hasta la fecha; **to be up to d.,** estar al
día; **d. of birth,** fecha de nacimiento. 2
(social event) compromiso m; fam (with
girl, boy) cita f. 3 US fam (person dated)
ligue m. II vtr (ruins) datar. III vi (ideas)
quedar anticuado,-a. ◆**d. back to,** date
from vtr remontar a, datar de.

date² [deɪt] n (fruit) dátil m; **d. palm,** datilera f.

dated ['deɪtɪd] adj (idea) anticuado,-a;
(fashion) pasado,-a de moda; (expression)
desusado,-a.

daub [dɔːb] vtr embadurnar; (with oil,
grease) untar.

daughter ['dɔːtər] n hija f.

daughter-in-law ['dɔːtərɪnlɔː] n nuera f,
hija política.

daunting ['dɔːntɪŋ] adj desalentador,-a.

dawdle ['dɔːdəl] vi fam (walk slowly)

andar despacio; (waste time) perder el
tiempo.

dawn [dɔːn] I n alba f, amanecer m. II vi
1 (day) amanecer. 2 fig (age, hope) comenzar. 3 fig **suddenly it dawned on him
that ...,** de repente cayó en la cuenta de
que ....

day [deɪ] n 1 día m. 2 **d. in, d. out,** día tras
día; **d. by d.,** diariamente; **good d.!,**
¡buenos días!; **once a d.,** una vez al día;
one of these days, un día de éstos; **(on)
the next** o **following d.,** el o al día siguiente; **the d. after tomorrow,** pasado
mañana; **the d. before yesterday,** anteayer; **the other d.,** el otro día; fig **to live
from d. to d.,** vivir al día; fig **to win the
d.,** llevarse la palma; fam **to call it a d.,**
(finish) dar por acabado un trabajo; (give
up) darse por vencido,-a; fam **to make
sb's d.,** alegrarle a algn el día; GB Rail **d.
return (ticket),** billete m de ida y
vuelta para el mismo día; **d. trip,**
excursión f de un día. 2 (daylight) día m;
by d., de día; **d. and night,** de día y de
noche; GB **d. shift,** turno m de día. 3
(period of work) jornada f; **an eight-hour
d.,** una jornada de ocho horas; **paid by
the d.,** pagado,-a a jornal; **d. off,** día de
fiesta; **I'll take a d. off tomorrow,** mañana me tomaré el día libre. 4 (era) época f;
in those days, en aquellos tiempos; **these
days, in this d. and age,** hoy (en) día.

daybreak ['deɪbreɪk] n amanecer m.

daydream ['deɪdriːm] I n ensueño m;
(vain hope) fantasía f. II vi soñar
despierto,-a; (hope vainly) hacerse ilusiones.

daylight ['deɪlaɪt] n luz f del día; **in
broad d.,** en pleno día; **to scare the (living) daylights out of sb,** pegarle a algn
un susto de muerte.

daytime ['deɪtaɪm] n día m; **in the d.,** de
día.

day-to-day ['deɪtədeɪ] adj cotidiano,-a,
diario,-a.

daze [deɪz] n aturdimiento m; **in a d.,**
aturdido,-a.

dazed [deɪzd] adj aturdido,-a, atontado,-
a.

dazzle ['dæzəl] vtr deslumbrar.

D-day ['diːdeɪ] n día m D.

deacon ['diːkən] n diácono m.

dead [ded] I adj 1 muerto,-a; **he was shot
d.,** le mataron a tiros; **to be d.,** estar
muerto,-a; fam fig **over my d. body!,** ¡sobre mi cadáver!; **d. man,** muerto m. 2
(machine) averiado,-a; (phone) cortado,-a.
3 (numb) entumecido,-a; (limb)
adormecido,-a; **my leg's gone d.,** se me
ha dormido la pierna. 4 (silence, scenery)
total; **d. end,** callejón m sin salida; Sport
d. heat, empate m; fam **d. loss,** inútil m,
birria f. 5 (exactly) justo; **d. on
time,** a la hora en punto. 2 **to stop d.,**

pararse en seco. 3 (very) muy; fam **d. beat,** d. tired, rendido,-a; fam **it's d. easy!**, ¡está chupado,-a!; Aut **'d. slow'**, 'al paso'; fam **you're d. right,** tienes toda la razón. III n **the d.,** (pl) los muertos. 2 **at d. of night,** a altas horas de la noche.

deaden ['dedən] vtr (impact, noise) amortiguar; fig (pain, feeling) calmar, aliviar.

deadline ['dedlaɪn] n (date) fecha f tope; (time) hora f tope; **we have to meet the d.,** tenemos que hacerlo dentro del plazo.

deadlock ['dedlɒk] n punto muerto.

deadly ['dedlɪ] I adj (deadlier, deadliest) mortal; (weapon) mortífero,-a; (aim) certero,-a. II adv (extremely) terriblemente, sumamente.

deadpan ['dedpæn] adj fam (face) sin expresión; (humour) guasón,-ona.

deaf [def] I adj sordo,-a; fig **to turn a d. ear,** hacerse el sordo; **d. mute,** sordomudo,-a m.f. II npl **the d.,** los sordos; **the d. and dumb,** los sordomudos.

deafen ['defən] vtr ensordecer.

deafening ['defənɪŋ] adj ensordecedor,-a.

deafness ['defnɪs] n sordera f.

deal [diːl] I n 1 Com Pol trato m, pacto m; business d., negocio m, transacción f; **to do a d. with sb,** (transaction) cerrar un trato con algn; (agreement) pactar algo con algn; fam **it's a d.!,** ¡trato hecho! 2 (amount) cantidad f; **a good d. of** criticism, muchas críticas; **a good d. slower,** mucho más despacio. 3 Cards reparto m. II vtr (pt & pp dealt) 1 Cards dar (to, a). 2 **to d. sb a blow,** asestarle un golpe a algn. ◆**deal in** vtr (goods) comerciar en, tratar en; (drugs) traficar con. ◆**deal out** vtr repartir. ◆**deal with** vtr (firm, person) tratar con; (subject, problem) abordar, ocuparse de; (in book etc) tratar de.

dealer ['diːlər] n 1 Com (in goods) comerciante mf; (in drugs) traficante mf. 2 Cards repartidor,-a m.f.

dealings ['diːlɪŋz] npl 1 (relations) trato n sing. 2 Com negocios mpl.

dealt [delt] pt & pp → **deal.**

dean [diːn] n 1 Rel deán m. 2 Univ decano m.

dear [dɪər] I adj 1 (loved) querido,-a; **to hold sth/sb d.,** apreciar mucho algo/a algn. 2 (in letter) Querido,-a; fam **D. Andrew,** Querido Andrew; fml **D. Madam,** Estimada señora; fml **D. Sir(s),** Muy señor(es) mío(s). 3 **it is very d. to me,** (precious) le tengo un gran cariño. 4 GB (expensive) caro,-a. II n querido,-a m.f.; **my d.,** mi vida. III interj oh **d.!,** **d. me!,** (surprise) ¡caramba!; (disappointment) ¡qué pena! ◆**dearly** adv muchísimo; fig **he paid d. for his mistake,** su error le costó

caro.

dearth [dɜːθ] n fml escasez f.

death [deθ] n 1 muerte f; fml fallecimiento m; **to put sb to d.,** dar muerte a algn; fam **to be bored to d.,** aburrirse como una ostra; fam **to be scared to d.,** estar muerto,-a de miedo; fam fig **to be sick to d. of,** estar hasta la coronilla de; **d. certificate,** certificado m de defunción; **d. penalty, d. sentence,** pena f de muerte; **d. rate,** índice m de mortalidad; **d. squad,** escuadrón m de la muerte. 2 fig (end) fin m.

deathbed ['deθbed] n **to be on one's d.,** estar en el lecho de muerte.

deathly ['deθlɪ] adj (deathlier, deathliest) (silence) sepulcral; **d. pale,** pálido,-a como un muerto.

debacle [deɪˈbɑːkəl] n debacle f.

debar [dɪˈbɑːr] vtr fml excluir, prohibir.

debase [dɪˈbeɪs] vtr fig envilecer; **to d. oneself,** humillarse.

debate [dɪˈbeɪt] I n debate m; **a heated d.,** una discusión acalorada. II vtr 1 (discuss) discutir. 2 (wonder about) dar vueltas a. III vi discutir.

debat(e)able [dɪˈbeɪtəbəl] adj discutible.

debauchery [dɪˈbɔːtʃərɪ] n libertinaje m.

debilitating [dɪˈbɪlɪteɪtɪŋ] adj debilitante; (heat, climate) agotador,-a.

debit ['debɪt] I n débito m; **d. balance,** saldo negativo. II vtr **d. Mr Jones with £20,** cargar la suma de veinte libras en la cuenta del Sr. Jones.

debris ['debriː, 'deɪbriː] n sing escombros mpl.

debt [det] n deuda f; **to be deeply in d.,** estar cargado,-a de deudas; fig **to be in sb's d.,** estar en deuda con algn.

debtor ['detər] n deudor,-a m.f.

debug [diːˈbʌg] vtr Comput eliminar fallos de.

debunk [diːˈbʌŋk] vtr fam desacreditar, desprestigiar.

debut ['deɪbjuː, 'deɪbjuː] n debut m; **to make one's d.,** debutar.

debutante ['debjuːtɑːnt] n debutante f.

decade ['dekeɪd, 'dekeɪd] n decenio m, década f.

decadence ['dekədəns] n decadencia f.

decadent ['dekədənt] adj decadente.

decaffeinated [diːˈkæfɪneɪtɪd] adj descafeinado,-a.

decanter [dɪˈkæntər] n jarra f, jarro m.

decapitate [dɪˈkæpɪteɪt] vtr decapitar.

decay [dɪˈkeɪ] I n (of food, body) descomposición f; (of teeth) caries f inv; (of buildings) desmoronamiento m; fig decadencia f. II vi descomponerse; (teeth) cariarse; (building) deteriorarse; fig corromperse.

deceased [dɪˈsiːst] fml adj difunto,-a, fallecido,-a.

deceit [dɪˈsiːt] n 1 (dishonesty) falta f de

honradez, falsedad f. 2 (trick) engaño m, mentira f.

deceitful [dɪ'siːtful] adj falso,-a.

deceive [dɪ'siːv] vtr (mislead) engañar; (lie to) mentir.

December [dɪ'sembər] n diciembre m.

decency ['diːsənsɪ] n decencia f; (modesty) pudor m; (morality) moralidad f.

decent ['diːsənt] adj decente; (person) honrado,-a; fam (kind) simpático,-a.

decentralize [diː'sentrəlaɪz] vtr descentralizar.

deception [dɪ'sepʃən] n engaño m.

deceptive [dɪ'septɪv] adj engañoso,-a. ◆**deceptively** adv it looks d. simple, parece engañosamente sencillo,-a.

decibel ['desɪbel] n decibelio m.

decide [dɪ'saɪd] I vtr 1 to d. to do sth, decidir hacer algo. 2 (matter, question) resolver, determinar. 3 vi (reach decision) decidirse; to d. against sth, decidirse en contra de algo. ◆**decide on** vtr (choose) optar por.

decided [dɪ'saɪdɪd] adj 1 (noticeable) marcado,-a. 2 (resolute) decidido,-a; (views) categórico,-a. ◆**decidedly** adv fml 1 (clearly) indudablemente. 2 (resolutely) decididamente.

deciding [dɪ'saɪdɪŋ] adj decisivo,-a.

deciduous [dɪ'sɪdjuːəs] adj de hoja caduca.

decimal ['desɪməl] I adj decimal, d. point, coma f (de fracción decimal). II n decimal m.

decimate ['desɪmeɪt] vtr diezmar.

decipher [dɪ'saɪfər] vtr descifrar.

decision [dɪ'sɪʒən] n 1 decisión f; Jur fallo m; to come to a d., llegar a una decisión; to make a d., tomar una decisión. 2 (resolution) resolución f.

decisive [dɪ'saɪsɪv] adj 1 (resolute) decidido,-a, resuelto,-a. 2 (conclusive) decisivo,-a.

deck [dek] I n 1 (of ship) cubierta f; on/ below d., en/bajo cubierta. 2 (of bus) piso m; top d., piso de arriba. 3 esp US (of cards) baraja f. 4 (of record player) plato m. II vtr to d. out, adornar.

declaration [deklə'reɪʃən] n declaración f.

declare [dɪ'kleər] vtr declarar; (winner, innocence) proclamar; (decision) manifestar.

declared [dɪ'kleəd] adj (opponent) declarado,-a; (intention) manifiesto,-a.

decline [dɪ'klaɪn] I n 1 (decrease) disminución f. 2 (deterioration) deterioro m; (of health) empeoramiento m; to fall into d., empezar a decaer. II vi 1 (decrease) disminuir; (amount) bajar; (business) decaer. 2 (deteriorate) deteriorarse; (health) empeorar. 3 (refuse) negarse. III vtr 1 (refuse) rechazar. 2 Ling declinar.

declutch [dɪ'klʌtʃ] vi soltar el embrague.

decode [diː'kəud] vtr descifrar.

decompose [diːkəm'pəuz] vi descomponerse.

décor ['deɪkɔːr] n decoración f; Theat decorado m.

decorate ['dekəreɪt] vtr 1 (adorn) decorar, adornar (with, con). 2 (paint) pintar; (wallpaper) empapelar. 3 (honour) condecorar.

decoration [dekə'reɪʃən] n 1 (decor) decoración f; Christmas decorations, adornos navideños. 2 (medal) condecoración f.

decorative ['dekərətɪv] adj decorativo,-a.

decorator ['dekəreɪtər] n decorador,-a m,f; (painter) pintor,-a m,f; (paperhanger) empapelador,-a m,f.

decorum [dɪ'kɔːrəm] n decoro m.

decoy ['diːkɔɪ] n fig señuelo m.

decrease [dɪ'kriːs] I n disminución f; (in speed, size, price) reducción f. II [dɪ'kriːs] vi disminuir; (strength) menguar; (price, temperature) bajar; (speed, size) reducir. III vtr disminuir, reducir; (price, temperature) bajar.

decree [dɪ'kriː] I n 1 Pol Rel decreto m. 2 esp US Jur sentencia f; d. absolute, sentencia definitiva de divorcio; d. nisi, sentencia provisional de divorcio. II vtr Pol Rel pronunciar.

decrepit [dɪ'krepɪt] adj decrépito,-a.

dedicate ['dedɪkeɪt] vtr consagrar, dedicar.

dedicated ['dedɪkeɪtɪd] adj ardiente; d. to, entregado,-a a.

dedication [dedɪ'keɪʃən] n (act) dedicación f; (commitment) entrega f; (in book) dedicatoria f.

deduce [dɪ'djuːs] vtr deducir (from, de).

deduct [dɪ'dʌkt] vtr descontar (from, de).

deduction [dɪ'dʌkʃən] n 1 (conclusion) conclusión f. 2 (subtraction) descuento m.

deed [diːd] n 1 (act) acto m. 2 (feat) hazaña f. 2 Jur escritura f; title deeds, título m sing de propiedad.

deem [diːm] vtr fml estimar.

deep [diːp] I adj 1 profundo,-a; (breath, sigh) hondo,-a; it's ten metres d., tiene diez metros de profundidad. 2 (voice) grave; (shame) grande; (interest) vivo,-a. 3 (colour) oscuro,-a. 4 (serious) grave. II adv to dig d., cavar hondo; to be d. in thought, estar absorto,-a; to look d. into sb's eyes, penetrar a algn con la mirada; fig nine d., de nueve en fondo. ◆**deeply** adv profundamente; (breathe) hondo; to be d. in debt, estar cargado,-a de deudas.

deepen [diː'pən] I vtr (well) profundizar, ahondar; fig (knowledge) aumentar. II vi (river etc) hacerse más hondo o profundo; fig (knowledge) aumentar; (colour, emotion) intensificarse; (sound, voice) hacerse más grave.

deep-freeze [di:p'fri:z] **I** n congelador m. **II** vtr congelar.

deep-fry [di:p'frai] vtr freír en mucho aceite.

deep-rooted [di:p'ru:tid] adj fig arraigado,-a.

deep-seated [di:p'si:tid] adj fig arraigado,-a.

deep-set [di:p'set] adj (eyes) hundido,-a.

deer [diə] n inv ciervo m.

deface [di'feis] vtr (book, poster) garabatear.

de facto [dei'fæktəu] adj & adv fml de hecho.

defamation [defə'meiʃən] n difamación f.

default [di'fɔ:lt] **I** vi 1 (not act) faltar a sus compromisos. 2 Jur estar en rebeldía. 3 (not pay) suspender pagos. **II** n 1 (failure to act) omisión f. 2 (failure to pay) incumplimiento m de pago. 3 Jur rebeldía f; **in d. of**, a falta de; **to win by d.**, ganar por incomparecencia del adversario.

defaulter [di'fɔ:ltə] n (on loan) moroso,-a mf; Jur Mil rebelde mf.

defeat [di'fi:t] **I** vtr 1 derrotar, vencer; (motion) rechazar. 2 fig frustrar. **II** n 1 (of army, team) derrota f; (of motion) rechazo m. 2 fig fracaso m.

defeatist [di'fi:tist] adj & n derrotista (mf).

defect ['di:fekt] **I** n defecto m; (flaw) desperfecto m. **II** [di'fekt] vi desertar (from, de); (from country) huir.

defective [di'fektiv] adj (faulty) defectuoso,-a; (flawed) con desperfectos; (lacking) incompleto,-a.

defector [di'fektə] n Pol tránsfuga mf, tránsfuga mf.

defence [di'fens] n 1 defensa f; **the Ministry of D.**, el Ministerio de Defensa; **to come to sb's d.**, salir en defensa de algn. 2 usu sing Jur defensa f. 3 Sport GB [di'fens], US ['di:fens] **the d.**, la defensa.

defenceless [di'fenslis] adj indefenso,-a.

defend [di'fend] vtr defender.

defendant [di'fendənt] n Jur acusado,-a m,f.

defender [di'fendə] n defensor,-a m,f; Sport defensa mf.

defending [di'fendiŋ] adj Sport defensor,-a; **d. champion**, campeón,-ona m,f titular.

defense [di'fens, 'di:fens] n US → **defence**.

defensive [di'fensiv] **I** adj defensivo,-a. **II** n **to be on the d.**, estar a la defensiva.

defer¹ [di'fɜ:] vtr aplazar, retrasar.

defer² [di'fɜ:] vi to d. to, someterse a.

deference ['defərəns] n fml deferencia f, respeto m; **out of** or **in d. to**, por respeto or por deferencia a.

defiance [di'faiəns] n 1 (challenge) desafío m; **in d. of**, a despecho de. 2 (resistance) resistencia f.

defiant [di'faiənt] adj (challenging) desafiante; (bold) insolente.

deficiency [di'fiʃənsi] n 1 (lack) falta f, carencia f. 2 (shortcoming) defecto m.

deficient [di'fiʃənt] adj deficiente; **to be d. in sth**, carecer de algo.

deficit ['defisit] n déficit m.

defile [di'fail] vtr fml 1 (mind) corromper; (honour) manchar; (woman) deshonrar. 2 (desecrate) profanar.

define [di'fain] vtr definir; (duties, powers) delimitar.

definite ['definit] adj 1 (clear) claro,-a; (progress) notable. 2 (date, place) determinado,-a. 3 (sure) seguro,-a; **are you sure?** ¿es seguro? ◆**definitely I** adv sin duda; **he was d. drunk**, no cabe duda de que estaba borracho. **II** interj ¡desde luego!

definition [defi'niʃən] n definición f; **by d.**, por definición.

definitive [di'finitiv] adj definitivo,-a.

deflate [di'fleit] vtr 1 (tyre etc) desinflar. 2 fig rebajar; **to d. sb**, hacer bajar los humos a algn. 3 **to d. the economy**, tomar medidas deflacionistas.

deflationary [di'fleiʃənəri] adj Econ deflacionista.

deflect [di'flekt] vtr desviar.

deflection [di'flekʃən] n desviación f.

deforestation [di:foris'teiʃən] n deforestación f.

deformed [di'fɔ:md] adj deforme.

deformity [di'fɔ:miti] n deformidad f.

defraud [di'frɔ:d] vtr estafar.

defrost [di:'frɒst] vtr 1 (freezer, food) descongelar. 2 US (windscreen) desempañar.

deft [deft] adj hábil, diestro,-a.

defunct [di'fʌŋkt] adj (person) difunto,-a; (thing) en desuso.

defuse [di:'fju:z] vtr (bomb) desactivar; fig **to d. a situation**, reducir la tensión de una situación.

defy [di'fai] vtr 1 (person) desafiar; (law, order) contravenir. 2 (challenge) retar, desafiar.

degenerate [di'dʒenəreit] **I** vi degenerar (into, en). **II** [di'dʒenərit] adj & n degenerado,-a (m,f).

degrading [di'greidiŋ] adj degradante.

degree [di'gri:] n 1 grado m; **to some d.**, hasta cierto punto. 2 (stage) etapa f; **by degrees**, poco a poco. 3 (qualification) título m; (doctorate) doctorado m; **to have a d. in science**, ser licenciado en ciencias.

dehydrated [di:hai'dreitid] adj (person) deshidratado,-a; (vegetables) seco,-a.

de-ice [di:'ais] vtr quitar el hielo a, deshelar.

de-icer [di:'aisə] n anticongelante m.

deign [dein] vi dignarse.

deity ['deiiti] n deidad f.

dejected |dɪ'dʒektɪd| *adj* desalentado,-a, abatido,-a.

delay |dɪ'leɪ| **I** *vtr* **1** (*flight, train*) retrasar; (*person*) entretener; **delayed action,** acción retardada. **2** (*postpone*) aplazar. **II** *vi* don't d., no lo deje para más tarde. **III** *n* retraso *m*.

delectable |dɪ'lektəbəl| *adj* delicioso,-a.

delegate |'delɪgɪt| **I** *n* delegado,-a *m,f*. **II** |'delɪgeɪt| *vtr* delegar (to, en); to d. sb to do sth, encargar a algn que haga algo.

delegation |delɪ'geɪʃən| *n* delegación *f*.

delete |dɪ'liːt| *vtr* tachar, suprimir.

deliberate |dɪ'lɪbərɪt| **I** *adj* (*intentional*) deliberado,-a, intencionado,-a; (*studied*) premeditado,-a; (*careful*) prudente; (*unhurried*) pausado,-a. **II** |dɪ'lɪbəreɪt| *vtr* deliberar. **III** *vi* deliberar (on, about, sobre). ◆**deliberately** *adv* (*intentionally*) a propósito, (*unhurriedly*) pausadamente.

deliberation |dɪlɪbə'reɪʃən| *n* **1** *esp pl* (*consideration*) deliberación *f*. **2** (*care*) cuidado *m*; (*unhurriedness*) pausa *f*.

delicacy |'delɪkəsɪ| *n* **1** delicadeza *f*. **2** (*food*) manjar *m* (exquisito).

delicate |'delɪkɪt| *adj* delicado,-a; (*handiwork*) fino,-a; (*instrument*) sensible; (*flavour*) sutil.

delicious |dɪ'lɪʃəs| *adj* delicioso,-a.

delight |dɪ'laɪt| **I** *n* **1** (*pleasure*) placer *m*; **he took d. in it,** le encantó. **2** (*source of pleasure*) encanto *m*, delicia *f*. **II** *vtr* encantar.

delighted |dɪ'laɪtɪd| *adj* (*smile*) de alegría; **I'm d. to see you,** me alegro mucho de verte.

delightful |dɪ'laɪtfʊl| *adj* encantador,-a; (*view, person*) muy agradable; (*meal, weather*) delicioso,-a.

delinquency |dɪ'lɪŋkwənsɪ| *n* delincuencia *f*; **juvenile d.,** delincuencia juvenil.

delinquent |dɪ'lɪŋkwənt| *adj & n* delincuente (*mf*).

delirious |dɪ'lɪrɪəs| *adj* delirante.

deliver |dɪ'lɪvər| *vtr* **1** (*goods*) repartir, entregar; (*message*) dar; (*order*) despachar; **fig to d. the goods,** cumplir con la obligación. **2** (*blow*) asestar; (*speech, verdict*) pronunciar. **3** *Med* ayudar en el nacimiento de. **4** *fml* (*rescue*) liberar.

delivery |dɪ'lɪvərɪ| *n* **1** (*of goods*) reparto *m*, entrega *f*; **to take d. of an order,** recibir un pedido; **d. note,** albarán *m* de entrega; *GB* **d. van,** furgoneta *f* de reparto. **2** (*of speech*) declamación *f*. **3** (*of baby*) parto *m*.

delta |'deltə| *n* *Geog* delta *m*.

delude |dɪ'luːd| *vtr* engañar; **don't d. yourself,** no te hagas ilusiones.

deluge |'deljuːdʒ| **I** *n* (*flood*) inundación *f*; (*rain*) diluvio *m*; *fig* (*of letters etc*) avalancha *f*. **II** *vtr fml* inundar.

delusion |dɪ'luːʒən| *n* **1** (*state, act*) enga-

ño *m*. **2** (*false belief*) ilusión *f* (vana); **delusions of grandeur,** delirios *mpl* de grandeza.

de luxe |də'lʌks, də'lʊks| *adj* de lujo *inv*.

delve |delv| *vi* **to d. into,** (*pocket*) hurgar en; (*subject*) profundizar en.

demand |dɪ'mɑːnd| **I** *n* **1** solicitud *f*; (*for pay rise, rights*) reclamación *f*; (*need*) necesidad *f*; **on d.,** a petición. **2** (*claim*) exigencia *f*; **to be in d.,** ser solicitado,-a. **3** *Econ* demanda *f*. **II** *vtr* **1** exigir; (*rights*) reclamar; **to d. that ...,** insistir en que ... (+ *subj*). **2** (*need*) requerir.

demanding |dɪ'mɑːndɪŋ| *adj* **1** (*person*) exigente. **2** (*job*) agotador,-a.

demean |dɪ'miːn| *vtr fml* **to d. oneself,** rebajarse.

demeaning |dɪ'miːnɪŋ| *adj fml* humillante.

demeanour, *US* **demeanor** |dɪ'miːnər| *n fml* **1** (*behaviour*) comportamiento *m*, conducta *f*. **2** (*bearing*) porte *m*.

demented |dɪ'mentɪd| *adj Med* demente; *· fam* loco,-a.

demise |dɪ'maɪz| *n* (*death*) *fml* fallecimiento *m*; *fig* (*of institution*) desaparición *f*; (*of ambition etc*) fracaso *m*.

demist |diː'mɪst| *vtr Aut* desempañar.

demo |'deməʊ| *n fam* manifestación *f*; **d. tape,** maqueta *f*.

demobilize |diː'məʊbɪlaɪz| *vtr* desmovilizar.

democracy |dɪ'mɒkrəsɪ| *n* democracia *f*.

democrat |'deməkræt| *n* demócrata *mf*; *Pol* **Christian D.,** democratacristiano,-a *m,f*; **Social D.,** socialdemócrata *mf*.

democratic |demə'krætɪk| *adj* democrático,-a; *US Pol* **D. party,** partido *m* demócrata.

demographic |demə'græfɪk| *adj* demográfico,-a.

demolish |dɪ'mɒlɪʃ| *vtr* (*building*) derribar, demoler; *fig* (*theory, proposal*) echar por tierra.

demolition |demə'lɪʃən| *n* demolición *f*.

demon |'diːmən| *n* demonio *m*.

demonstrate |'demənstreɪt| **I** *vtr* demostrar. **II** *vi Pol* manifestarse.

demonstration |demən'streɪʃən| *n* **1** (*proof*) demostración *f*, prueba *f*. **2** (*explanation*) explicación *f*. **3** *Pol* manifestación *f*.

demonstrative |dɪ'mɒnstrətɪv| *adj* expresivo.

demonstrator |'demənstreɪtər| *n* manifestante *mf*.

demoralize |dɪ'mɒrəlaɪz| *vtr* desmoralizar.

demoralizing |dɪ'mɒrəlaɪzɪŋ| *adj* desmoralizador,-a, desmoralizante.

demote |dɪ'məʊt| *vtr* rebajar de graduación a.

demure |dɪ'mjʊər| *adj* (*person*) recatado, -a.

den [den] n 1 (of animal) guarida f. 2 fam (study) estudio m.

denial [dɪ'naɪəl] n 1 (of charge) desmentido m. 2 (of rights) denegación f; (of request) negativa f.

denim ['denɪm] n 1 dril m; **d. skirt**, falda tejana; **denims**, tejanos mpl, vaqueros mpl.

Denmark ['denmɑːk] n Dinamarca.

denomination [dɪnɒmɪ'neɪʃən] n 1 Rel confesión f. 2 Fin (of coins) valor m.

denominator [dɪ'nɒmɪneɪtər] n denominador m.

denote [dɪ'nəʊt] vtr (show) indicar; (mean) significar.

denounce [dɪ'naʊns] vtr denunciar; (criticize) censurar.

dense [dens] adj 1 denso,-a; (crowd) numeroso,-a. 2 fam (stupid) torpe. ◆**densely** adv densamente.

density ['densɪtɪ] n densidad f.

dent [dent] I n abolladura f. II vtr (car) abollar.

dental ['dentəl] adj dental; **d. floss**, hilo m dental; **d. surgeon**, odontólogo,-a m,f; **d. surgery**, (place) clínica f dental; (treatment) cirugía f dental.

dentist ['dentɪst] n dentista mf.

dentistry ['dentɪstrɪ] n odontología f.

denture ['dentʃər] n (usu pl) dentadura postiza.

denunciation [dɪnʌnsɪ'eɪʃən] n denuncia f, condena f.

deny [dɪ'naɪ] vtr 1 (repudiate) negar; (rumour, report) desmentir; (charge) rechazar. 2 (refuse) negar.

deodorant [diː'əʊdərənt] n desodorante m.

depart [dɪ'pɑːt] vi marcharse, irse; fig (from subject) desviarse (**from**, de).

department [dɪ'pɑːtmənt] n sección f; (in university) departamento m; (in government) ministerio m; **d. store**, grandes almacenes mpl.

departure [dɪ'pɑːtʃər] n partida f, Av Rail salida f; Av **d. lounge**, sala f de embarque.

depend [dɪ'pend] I vi (rely) fiarse (**on**, **upon**, de). II v impers (be determined by) depender (**on**, **upon**, de); **it depends on the weather**, según el tiempo que haga; **that depends**, según.

dependable [dɪ'pendəbəl] adj (person) responsable, fiable; (income) seguro,-a; (machine) fiable.

dependant, US **dependent** [dɪ'pendənt] n dependiente mf.

dependence [dɪ'pendəns] n dependencia f.

dependent [dɪ'pendənt] I adj dependiente; **to be d. on sth**, depender de algo. II n US → **dependant**.

depict [dɪ'pɪkt] vtr Art representar; fig describir.

deplete [dɪ'pliːt] vtr reducir.

deplorable [dɪ'plɔːrəbəl] adj lamentable.

deplore [dɪ'plɔːr] vtr deplorar.

deploy [dɪ'plɔɪ] vtr Mil desplegar; fig utilizar.

depopulate [diː'pɒpjʊleɪt] vtr despoblar.

deport [dɪ'pɔːt] vtr expulsar (**from**, de; **to**, a).

deportation [diːpɔː'teɪʃən] n expulsión f.

deportment [dɪ'pɔːtmənt] n fml porte m.

depose [dɪ'pəʊz] vtr deponer.

deposit [dɪ'pɒzɪt] I n 1 sedimento m, Min yacimiento m; (in wine) poso m. 2 (in bank) depósito m; **d. account**, cuenta f de ahorros. 3 Com (on purchase) señal f; (on rented car, flat) depósito m; (on house) entrada f. II vtr depositar; (into account) ingresar.

deposition [depə'zɪʃən] n 1 (of leader) destitución f. 2 Jur (of witness) declaración f.

depositor [dɪ'pɒzɪtər] n depositante mf.

depot ['depəʊ] n almacén m; Mil depósito m; (bus garage) garaje m (de autobuses).

depraved [dɪ'preɪvd] adj (person) depravado,-a.

deprecate ['deprɪkeɪt] vtr desaprobar, censurar.

depreciate [dɪ'priːʃɪeɪt] vi depreciarse.

depreciation [dɪpriːʃɪ'eɪʃən] n depreciación f.

depress [dɪ'pres] vtr 1 (person) deprimir. 2 Econ (profits) reducir; (trade) dificultar. 3 fml (switch, lever etc) presionar; (clutch, piano pedal) pisar.

depressed [dɪ'prest] adj 1 (person) deprimido,-a; **to get d.**, deprimirse. 2 (market) en crisis. 3 (surface) hundido,-a.

depressing [dɪ'presɪŋ] adj deprimente.

depression [dɪ'preʃən] n depresión f.

deprivation [deprɪ'veɪʃən] n (hardship) privación f; (loss) pérdida f.

deprive [dɪ'praɪv] vtr privar (**of**, de).

deprived [dɪ'praɪvd] adj necesitado,-a.

Dept abbr of **Department**, dpt, dpto; (in store) sección f.

depth [depθ] n 1 profundidad f. 2 fig (of emotion) intensidad f; (of thought) complejidad f; **to be in the depths of despair**, estar completamente desesperado,-a; **in d.**, a fondo.

deputation [depjʊ'teɪʃən] n delegación f.

deputy ['depjʊtɪ] n 1 (substitute) suplente mf; **d. chairman**, vicepresidente m; **d. head**, subdirector,-a m,f. 2 Pol diputado,-a m,f.

derail [dɪ'reɪl] vtr hacer descarrilar.

deranged [dɪ'reɪndʒd] adj trastornado,-a.

derby ['dɜːbɪ] n 1 Sport prueba f. 2 ['dɜːrbɪ] US sombrero hongo.

derelict ['derɪlɪkt] adj abandonado,-a, en ruinas.

deride [dɪ'raɪd] vtr ridiculizar, burlarse de.

derisive [dɪ'raɪsɪv] adj burlón,-ona.

derisory [dɪ'raɪsərɪ] adj irrisorio,-a.

derivative [dɪ'rɪvətɪv] I adj (art, writing) sin originalidad. II n (of word, substance) derivado m.

derive [dɪ'raɪv] I vtr sacar. II vi (word) derivarse (from, de); (skill) provenir (from, de).

derogatory [dɪ'rɒɡətɔːrɪ] adj (remark, article) despectivo,-a; (meaning) peyorativo,-a.

derrick ['derɪk] n Petrol torre f de perforación.

descend [dɪ'send] I vi I descender; to d. from, (be related to) descender de. II vtr (stairs) bajar.

descendant [dɪ'sendənt] n descendiente mf.

descent [dɪ'sent] n 1 descenso m. 2 fig (into madness, poverty) caída f. 3 (slope) declive m. 4 (ancestry) ascendencia f.

describe [dɪ'skraɪb] vtr 1 describir. 2 (circle) trazar.

description [dɪ'skrɪpʃən] n 1 descripción f; to defy d., superar la descripción. 2 (type) clase f.

desecrate ['desɪkreɪt] vtr profanar.

desert¹ ['dezət] n desierto m.

desert² [dɪ'zɜːt] I vtr (place, family) abandonar. II vi Mil desertar (from, de).

deserter [dɪ'zɜːtər] n desertor,-a m,f.

desertion [dɪ'zɜːʃən] n abandono m; Pol defección f; Mil deserción f.

deserts [dɪ'zɜːts] npl to get one's just d., llevarse su merecido.

deserve [dɪ'zɜːv] vtr (rest, punishment) merecer; (prize, praise) ser digno,-a de.

deservedly [dɪ'zɜːvɪdlɪ] adv con (toda) razón.

deserving [dɪ'zɜːvɪŋ] adj (person) de valía; (cause) meritorio,-a.

design [dɪ'zaɪn] I n 1 diseño m 2 (drawing, blueprint) plano m. 3 (layout) disposición f. 4 (pattern) dibujo m. 5 fig (scheme) intención f; by d., a propósito; fam to have designs on, tener puestas las miras en. II vtr diseñar.

designate ['dezɪɡneɪt] I vtr 1 (appoint) designar, nombrar. 2 fml (boundary) señalar. II ['dezɪɡnɪt] adj designado,-a.

designer [dɪ'zaɪnər] n Art diseñador,-a m,f; d. jeans, pantalones mpl de marca.

desirable [dɪ'zaɪərəbəl] adj deseable; (asset, offer) atractivo,-a.

desire [dɪ'zaɪər] I n deseo m; I haven't the slightest d. to go, no me apetece nada ir. II vtr desear.

desist [dɪ'zɪst] vi fml desistir (from, de).

desk [desk] n (in school) pupitre m; (in office) escritorio m; US d. clerk, recepcionista mf; d. job, trabajo m de oficina; news d., redacción f; reception d., recepción f.

desktop ['desktɒp] n d. computer, orde-

nador m de sobremesa; **d. publishing**, autoedición f.

desolate ['desəlɪt] adj 1 (uninhabited) desierto,-a; (barren) yermo,-a. 2 (person) desconsolado,-a.

desolation [desə'leɪʃən] n 1 (of place) desolación f; (by destruction) asolamiento m. 2 (of person) desconsuelo m.

despair [dɪ'speər] I n desesperación f; to drive sb to d., desesperar a algn. II vi desesperar(se) (of, de).

despairing [dɪ'speərɪŋ] adj desesperado,-a.

despatch [dɪ'spætʃ] n & vtr → dispatch.

desperate ['despərɪt] adj 1 desesperado,-a; (struggle) encarnizado,-a. 2 (need) apremiante. ◆**desperately** adv (recklessly) desesperadamente; (struggle) encarnizadamente; (ill) gravemente; (in love) locamente; (difficult) sumamente.

desperation [despə'reɪʃən] n desesperación f; in d., a la desesperada.

despicable [dɪ'spɪkəbəl] adj despreciable; (behaviour) indigno,-a.

despise [dɪ'spaɪz] vtr despreciar, menospreciar.

despite [dɪ'spaɪt] prep fml a pesar de.

despondent [dɪ'spɒndənt] adj abatido,-a.

despot ['despɒt] n déspota mf.

dessert [dɪ'zɜːt] n postre m; **d. wine**, vino m dulce.

dessertspoon [dɪ'zɜːtspuːn] n 1 cuchara f de postre. 2 **d.(ful)**, (measure) cucharada f de postre.

destination [destɪ'neɪʃən] n destino m.

destined ['destɪnd] adj 1 d. to fail, condenado,-a al fracaso. 2 (bound) con destino (for, a).

destiny ['destɪnɪ] n destino m.

destitute ['destɪtjuːt] adj indigente.

destroy [dɪ'strɔɪ] vtr destruir; (vehicle, old furniture) destrozar.

destroyer [dɪ'strɔɪər] n Naut destructor m.

destruction [dɪ'strʌkʃən] n destrucción f; fig ruina f.

destructive [dɪ'strʌktɪv] adj (gale etc) destructor,-a; (tendency, criticism) destructivo,-a.

detach [dɪ'tætʃ] vtr (remove) separar.

detachable [dɪ'tætʃəbəl] adj separable (from, de).

detached [dɪ'tætʃt] adj 1 (separated) separado,-a; **d. house**, casa f independiente. 2 (impartial) objetivo,-a.

detachment [dɪ'tætʃmənt] n 1 (impartiality) objetividad f; (aloofness) despego m. 2 Mil destacamento m.

detail [dɪ'teɪl] I n 1 detalle m, pormenor m; **without going into detail(s)**, sin entrar en detalles; **details**, (information) información f sing. 2 Mil destacamento m. II vtr 1 (list) detallar, enumerar. 2 Mil (appoint) destacar.

detailed ['diːteɪld] adj detallado,-a,

minucioso,-a.

detain [dɪ'teɪn] *vtr* & *Jur* detener. 2 (*delay*) retener.

detainee [dɪteɪ'niː] *n Pol* preso,-a *m,f*.

detect [dɪ'tekt] *vtr* 1 (*error, movement*) advertir; (*difference*) notar; (*smell, sound*) percibir. 2 (*discover*) descubrir; (*enemy ship*) detectar; (*position*) localizar.

detection [dɪ'tekʃən] *n* 1 descubrimiento *m*; (*of smell, sound*) percepción *f*. 2 (*discovery*) (*of enemy ship*) detección *f*.

detective [dɪ'tektɪv] *n* detective *mf*; d. story, novela policíaca.

detector [dɪ'tektər] *n* aparato *m* detector.

detention [dɪ'tenʃən] *n* (*of suspect etc*) detención *f*, arresto *m*; *Educ* to get d., quedarse castigado,-a.

deter [dɪ'tɜːr] *vtr* (*dissuade*) disuadir (**from**, de); (*stop*) impedir.

detergent [dɪ'tɜːdʒənt] *n* detergente *m*.

deteriorate [dɪ'tɪərɪəreɪt] *vi* deteriorarse.

deterioration [dɪtɪərɪə'reɪʃən] *n* empeoramiento *m*; (*of substance, friendship*) deterioro *m*.

determination [dɪtɜːmɪ'neɪʃən] *n* (*resolution*) resolución *f*.

determine [dɪ'tɜːmɪn] *vtr* determinar.

determined [dɪ'tɜːmɪnd] *adj* (*person*) decidido,-a; (*effort*) enérgico,-a.

deterrent [dɪ'terənt] **I** *adj* disuasivo,-a. **II** *n* fuerza disuasoria.

detest [dɪ'test] *vtr* detestar, odiar.

detonate ['detəneɪt] *vtr* & *vi* detonar.

detonation [detə'neɪʃən] *n* detonación *f*.

detour ['diːtuər] *n* desvío *m*.

detract [dɪ'trækt] *vi* quitar mérito (**from**, a).

detractor [dɪ'træktər] *n* detractor,-a *m,f*.

detriment ['detrɪmənt] *n* perjuicio *m* (**to**, de).

detrimental [detrɪ'mentəl] *adj* perjudicial (**to**, para).

deuce [djuːs] *n Ten* cuarenta iguales *mpl*.

devaluation [diːvæljuː'eɪʃən] *n* devaluación *f*.

devastate ['devəsteɪt] *vtr* (*city, area*) asolar; *fig* (*person*) desolar.

devastating ['devəsteɪtɪŋ] *adj* (*fire*) devastador,-a; (*wind, flood*) arrollador,-a.

devastation [devə'steɪʃən] *n* asolación *f*.

develop [dɪ'veləp] **I** *vtr* 1 desarrollar; (*trade*) fomentar; (*skill*) perfeccionar; (*plan*) elaborar; (*habit*) contraer; (*interest*) mostrar. 2 (*natural resources*) aprovechar, *Constr* (*site*) urbanizar. 3 *Phot* revelar. **II** *vi* 1 (*body, industry*) desarrollarse; (*system*) perfeccionarse; (*interest*) crecer. 2 (*appear*) crearse; (*evolve*) evolucionar.

developer [dɪ'veləpər] *n* (*property*) *m*, inmobiliaria *f*.

development [dɪ'veləpmənt] *n* 1 desarrollo *m*; (*of trade*) fomento *m*; (*of skill*) perfección *f*; (*of character*) formación *f*. 2 (*advance*) avance *m*. 3 **there are no new**

developments, no hay ninguna novedad. 4 (*exploitation*) explotación *f*. 5 *Constr* urbanización *f*.

deviate ['diːvɪeɪt] *vi* desviarse (**from**, de).

deviation [diːvɪ'eɪʃən] *n* (*from norm, route*) desviación *f* (**from**, de); (*from truth*) alejamiento *m*.

device [dɪ'vaɪs] *n* 1 aparato *m*; (*mechanism*) mecanismo *m*. 2 (*trick, scheme*) ardid *m*.

devil ['devəl] *n* diablo *m*, demonio *m*; **d.'s advocate**, abogado,-a *m,f* del diablo; **fam where the d. did you put it?**, ¿dónde demonios lo pusiste?; **you lucky d.!**, ¡vaya suerte que tienes!

devious ['diːvɪəs] *adj* 1 (*winding*) tortuoso,-a. 2 *esp pej* (*person*) taimado,-a.

devise [dɪ'vaɪz] *vtr* idear, concebir.

devoid [dɪ'vɔɪd] *adj* desprovisto,-a (**of**, de).

devolution [diːvə'luːʃən] *n Pol* transmisión *f* de poderes a las regiones.

devote [dɪ'vəut] *vtr* dedicar; **she devoted her life to helping the poor**, consagró su vida a la ayuda de los pobres.

devoted [dɪ'vəutɪd] *adj* fiel, leal (**to**, a).

devotee [devə'tiː] *n* (*of religion*) devoto,-a *m,f*; (*of theatre, sport*) aficionado,-a *m,f*; *Pol* partidario,-a *m,f*.

devotion [dɪ'vəuʃən] *n* devoción *f*; (*to cause*) dedicación *f*.

devour [dɪ'vauər] *vtr* devorar.

devout [dɪ'vaut] *adj* devoto,-a.

dew [djuː] *n* rocío *m*.

dexterity [deks'terɪtɪ] *n* destreza *f*.

dext(e)rous ['dekstrəs] *adj* diestro,-a.

diabetes [daɪə'biːtiːz, daɪə'biːtis] *n* diabetes *f*.

diabetic [daɪə'betik] *adj* & *n* diabético,-a (*m,f*).

diabolical [daɪə'bɒlɪkəl] *adj* 1 (*evil*) diabólico,-a. 2 *fam* (*unbearable*) espantoso,-a.

diagnose ['daɪəgnəuz] *vtr* diagnosticar.

diagnosis [daɪəg'nəusɪs] *n* (*pl* **diagnoses** [daɪəg'nəusiːz]) diagnóstico *m*.

diagonal [daɪ'ægənəl] *adj* & *n* diagonal (*f*). ◆ **diagonally** *adv* en diagonal, diagonalmente.

diagram ['daɪəgræm] *n* diagrama *m*; (*of process, system*) esquema *m*; (*of workings*) gráfico *m*.

dial ['daɪəl, daɪl] **I** *n* (*of clock*) esfera *f*; (*of radio*) cuadrante *m*; (*of telephone*) disco *m*; (*of machine*) botón *m* selector. **II** *vi* & *vtr Tel* marcar; **dialling code**, prefijo *m*; **dialling tone**, señal *f* de marcar.

dialect ['daɪəlekt] *n* dialecto *m*.

dialogue, US **dialog** ['daɪəlɒg] *n* diálogo *m*.

diameter [daɪ'æmɪtər] *n* diámetro *m*.

diametrically [daɪə'metrɪkəlɪ] *adv* diametralmente.

diamond ['daɪəmənd] *n* 1 diamante *m*. 2

(shape) rombo m.

diaper ['daɪəpər] n US pañal m.

diaphragm ['daɪəfræm] n diafragma m.

diarrhoea, US **diarrhea** [daɪə'rɪə] n diarrea f.

diary ['daɪərɪ] n 1 diario m; **to keep a d.**, llevar un diario. 2 GB *(for appointments)* agenda f.

dice [daɪs] I npl dados mpl. II vtr Culin cortar en rodajas.

dichotomy [daɪ'kɒtəmɪ] n dicotomía f.

dictate [dɪk'teɪt] n *(letter, order)* dictar. II vi **to d. to sb**, dar órdenes a algn. III ['dɪkteɪt] n fig **the dictates of conscience**, los dictados de la conciencia.

dictation [dɪk'teɪʃən] n dictado m.

dictator [dɪk'teɪtər] n dictador,-a m,f.

dictatorship [dɪk'teɪtəʃɪp] n dictadura f.

diction ['dɪkʃən] n dicción f.

dictionary ['dɪkʃənərɪ] n diccionario m.

did [dɪd] pt → do.

die [daɪ] vi 1 morir, morirse; fam fig **to be dying for sth/to do sth**, morirse por algo/de ganas de hacer algo. 2 fig *(flame)* extinguirse; fig **to d. hard**, *(habit)* tardar en desaparecer. 3 *(engine)* calarse; *(battery)* agotarse. ◆**die away** vi desvanecerse. ◆**die down** vi *(wind)* amainar; *(noise, excitement)* disminuir. ◆**die off** vi morir uno por uno. ◆**die out** vi extinguirse.

die-hard ['daɪhɑːd] n reaccionario,-a m,f.

diesel ['diːzəl] n 1 *(oil)* gasoil m; **d. engine**, motor m diesel. 2 fam *(vehicle)* vehículo m diesel.

diet ['daɪət] I n *(normal food)* dieta f; *(selected food)* régimen m; **to be on a d.**, estar a régimen. II vi estar a régimen.

dietician [daɪə'tɪʃən] n especialista mf en dietética.

differ ['dɪfər] vi *(be unlike)* ser distinto,-a; *(disagree)* discrepar.

difference ['dɪfərəns] n 1 *(dissimilarity)* diferencia f; **it makes no d. (to me)**, *(me)* da igual; **what d. does it make?**, ¿qué más da? 2 *(disagreement)* desacuerdo m.

different ['dɪfərənt] adj diferente, distinto,-a; **you look d.**, pareces otro,-a. ◆**differently** adv de otra manera.

differentiate [dɪfə'renʃɪeɪt] I vtr distinguir, diferenciar *(from, de)*. II vi distinguir *(between, entre)*.

difficult ['dɪfɪkəlt] adj difícil.

difficulty ['dɪfɪkəltɪ] n dificultad f; *(problem)* problema m; **to be in difficulties**, estar en un apuro.

diffident ['dɪfɪdənt] adj tímido,-a.

diffuse [dɪ'fjuːs] I adj *(light)* difuso,-a; fig vago,-a. II [dɪ'fjuːz] vtr difundir; *(heat)* desprender.

dig [dɪg] I n 1 *(poke)* codazo m. 2 fam *(gibe)* pulla f. 3 *(archeological)* excavación

f. 3 GB **digs**, *(lodgings)* alojamiento m sing; *(room)* habitación f sing alquilada. II vtr *(pt & pp* **dug**) 1 *(earth)* cavar; *(tunnel)* excavar. 2 fam fig **to d. one's heels in**, mantenerse en sus trece. III vi *(person)* cavar; *(animal)* escarbar; *(excavate)* excavar. ◆**dig out** vtr fig *(old suit)* sacar; *(information)* descubrir. ◆**dig up** vtr *(weeds)* arrancar; *(buried object)* desenterrar; *(road)* levantar; fig sacar a relucir.

digest [daɪ'dʒest] I n *(summary)* resumen m. II [dɪ'dʒest] vtr *(food)* digerir; fig *(facts)* asimilar.

digestion [dɪ'dʒestʃən] n digestión f.

digestive [dɪ'dʒestɪv] adj digestivo,-a; GB **d. biscuit**, galleta f integral.

digger ['dɪgər] n excavadora f.

digit ['dɪdʒɪt] n 1 Math dígito m. 2 fml Anat dedo m.

digital ['dɪdʒɪtəl] adj digital.

dignified ['dɪgnɪfaɪd] adj *(manner)* solemne, serio,-a; *(appearance)* majestuoso,-a.

dignitary ['dɪgnɪtərɪ] n dignatario m.

dignity ['dɪgnɪtɪ] n dignidad f.

digress [daɪ'gres] vi apartarse del tema.

dike [daɪk] n US → **dyke**.

dilapidated [dɪ'læpɪdeɪtɪd] adj en mal estado.

dilemma [dɪ'lemə, daɪ'lemə] n dilema m.

diligent ['dɪlɪdʒənt] adj *(worker)* diligente; *(inquiries, search)* esmerado,-a.

dilute [daɪ'luːt] I vtr diluir; *(wine, milk)* aguar; fig *(effect, influence)* atenuar. II vi diluirse.

dim [dɪm] I adj *(dimmer, dimmest)* 1 *(light)* débil, tenue; *(room)* oscuro,-a; *(outline)* borroso,-a; *(eyesight)* defectuoso,-a; fig *(memory)* vago,-a; fig *(future)* sombrío,-a. 2 fam *(stupid)* torpe. II vtr *(light)* bajar. III vi *(light)* bajarse; *(joy)* extinguirse. ◆**dimly** adv vagamente.

dime [daɪm] n US moneda f de diez centavos.

dimension [daɪ'menʃən] n dimensión f.

diminish [dɪ'mɪnɪʃ] vtr & vi disminuir.

diminutive [dɪ'mɪnjutɪv] I adj diminuto,-a. II n Ling diminutivo m.

dimmer ['dɪmər] n **d.** *(switch)*, regulador m de voltaje.

dimple ['dɪmpəl] n hoyuelo m.

din [dɪn] n *(of crowd)* alboroto m; *(of machinery)* estruendo m.

dine [daɪn] vi fml cenar; **to d. out**, cenar fuera.

diner ['daɪnər] n 1 *(person)* comensal mf. 2 US *(restaurant)* restaurante barato.

dinghy ['dɪŋgɪ] n bote m; *(rubber)* **d.**, bote neumático.

dingy ['dɪndʒɪ] adj *(dingier, dingiest)* 1 *(dark)* oscuro,-a. 2 *(dirty)* sucio,-a; *(colour)* desteñido,-a.

dining car [ˈdaɪnɪŋkɑːʳ] n vagón m restaurante.

dining room [ˈdaɪnɪŋruːm] n comedor m.

dinner [ˈdɪnəʳ] n (at midday) comida f; (in evening) cena f; **d. jacket**, smoking m; **d. service**, vajilla f; **d. table**, mesa f de comedor.

dinosaur [ˈdaɪnəsɔːʳ] n dinosaurio m.

dint [dɪnt] n **by d. of**, a fuerza de.

diocese [ˈdaɪəsɪs] n diócesis f inv.

dioxide [daɪˈɒksaɪd] n bióxido m.

dip [dɪp] **I** n **1** fam (bathe) chapuzón m. **2** (of road) pendiente f; (in ground) depresión f. **3** Culin salsa f. **II** vtr **1** bañar; (spoon, hand) meter. **2** GB Aut to **d. one's lights**, poner luces de cruce. **III** vi (road) bajar. ◆**dip into** vtr **1** (savings) echar mano de. **2** (book) hojear.

diphthong [ˈdɪfθɒŋ] n diptongo m.

diploma [dɪˈpləʊmə] n diploma m.

diplomacy [dɪˈpləʊməsɪ] n diplomacia f.

diplomat [ˈdɪpləmæt] n diplomático,-a m,f.

diplomatic [dɪpləˈmætɪk] adj diplomático,-a.

dipstick [ˈdɪpstɪk] n indicador m de nivel del aceite.

dire [daɪəʳ] adj (urgent) extremo,-a; (serious) grave.

direct [dɪˈrekt, ˈdaɪrekt] **I** adj (direct),-a; **d. current**, corriente continua. **2** the **d. opposite**, todo lo contrario. **II** adv directamente. **III** vtr **1** dirigir; **can you d. me to a bank?**, ¿me puede indicar dónde hay un banco? **2** fml (order) mandar.

direction [dɪˈrekʃən, daɪˈrekʃən] n **1** dirección f; **sense of d.**, sentido m de la orientación. **2** directions, (to place) señas fpl; **d. for use**, modo m de empleo. **3** Theat puesta f en escena.

directive [dɪˈrektɪv, daɪˈrektɪv] n directiva f.

directly [dɪˈrektlɪ, daɪˈrektlɪ] **I** adv **1** (above etc) exactamente, justo. **2** (speak) francamente. **3** (descend) directamente. **4** (come) en seguida. **II** conj fam en cuanto.

director [dɪˈrektəʳ, daɪˈrektəʳ] n director,-a m,f.

directory [dɪˈrektərɪ, daɪˈrektərɪ] n Tel guía telefónica; **d. enquiries**, (servicio m de) información f.

dirt [dɜːt] n suciedad f.

dirt-cheap [dɜːtˈtʃiːp] adv & adj fam tirado,-a.

dirty [ˈdɜːtɪ] **I** adj (dirtier, dirtiest) **1** sucio,-a. **2** to **give sb a d. look**, fulminar a algn con la mirada. **3** (joke) verde; (mind) pervertido,-a; **d. word**, palabrota f; **d. old man**, viejo m verde. **II** vtr ensuciar.

disability [dɪsəˈbɪlɪtɪ] n incapacidad f, discapacidad f; **d. pension**, pensión f por invalidez.

disabled [dɪˈseɪbəld] **I** adj minusválido,-a. **II** npl the **d.**, los minusválidos.

disadvantage [dɪsədˈvɑːntɪdʒ] n desventaja f; (obstacle) inconveniente m.

disaffection [dɪsəˈfekʃən] n descontento m.

disagree [dɪsəˈgriː] vi (differ) no estar de acuerdo (with, con); to **d. on** or **over** sth, reñir por algo. **2** (not admit) discrepar (with, de, con). **3** garlic disagrees with me, el ajo no me sienta bien.

disagreeable [dɪsəˈgrɪəbəl] adj desagradable.

disagreement [dɪsəˈgriːmənt] n **1** desacuerdo m; (argument) riña f. **2** (non-correspondence) discrepancia f.

disallow [dɪsəˈlaʊ] vtr (goal) anular; (objection) rechazar.

disappear [dɪsəˈpɪəʳ] vi desaparecer.

disappearance [dɪsəˈpɪərəns] n desaparición f.

disappoint [dɪsəˈpɔɪnt] vtr (person) decepcionar, defraudar; (hope, ambition) frustrar.

disappointed [dɪsəˈpɔɪntɪd] adj decepcionado,-a.

disappointing [dɪsəˈpɔɪntɪŋ] adj decepcionante.

disappointment [dɪsəˈpɔɪntmənt] n decepción f.

disapproval [dɪsəˈpruːvəl] n desaprobación f.

disapprove [dɪsəˈpruːv] vi to **d. of**, desaprobar.

disarm [dɪsˈɑːm] **I** vtr desarmar. **II** vi desarmarse.

disarmament [dɪsˈɑːməmənt] n desarme m.

disarray [dɪsəˈreɪ] n fml in **d.**, (room, papers) en desorden; (hair) desarreglado,-a; (thoughts) confuso,-a.

disaster [dɪˈzɑːstəʳ] n desastre m.

disastrous [dɪˈzɑːstrəs] adj desastroso,-a.

disband [dɪsˈbænd] **I** vtr disolver. **II** vi disolverse.

disbelief [dɪsbɪˈliːf] n incredulidad f.

disc [dɪsk] n disco m; Comput disquete m; **d. jockey**, disc-jockey mf, pinchadiscos mf inv.

discard [dɪsˈkɑːd] vtr (old things) deshacerse de; (plan) descartar.

discern [dɪˈsɜːn] vtr (shape, difference) percibir; (truth) darse cuenta de.

discerning [dɪˈsɜːnɪŋ] adj (person) perspicaz; (taste) refinado,-a.

discharge [dɪsˈtʃɑːdʒ] fml **I** vtr **1** (smoke) emitir; (liquid) echar; (cargo) descargar. **2** (prisoner) soltar; (patient) dar de alta a; (soldier) licenciar; (employee) despedir. **3** (debt) saldar. **4** (fulfil) cumplir. **II** [ˈdɪstʃɑːdʒ] n **1** (of current, load) descarga f; (of gases) escape m. **2** (of prisoner) liberación f; (of patient) alta f; (of soldier) licencia f. **3** (of debt) descargo m. **4** (of duty) cumplimiento m.

disciple [dɪˈsaɪpəl] n discípulo,-a m,f.

discipline [ˈdɪsɪplɪn] I n disciplina f. II vtr (child) castigar; (worker) sancionar; (official) expedientar.

disclaim [dɪsˈkleɪm] vtr fml negar tener.

disclose [dɪsˈkləʊz] vtr revelar.

disclosure [dɪsˈkləʊʒəʳ] n revelación f.

disco [ˈdɪskəʊ] n (abbr of discotheque) fam disco f.

discolour, US **discolor** [dɪsˈkʌləʳ] vtr descolorir.

discomfort [dɪsˈkʌmfət] n 1 (lack of comfort) incomodidad f. 2 (pain) malestar m. 3 (unease) inquietud f.

disconcert [dɪskənˈsɜːt] vtr desconcertar.

disconcerting [dɪskənˈsɜːtɪŋ] adj desconcertante.

disconnect [dɪskəˈnekt] vtr desconectar (from, de); (gas, electricity) cortar.

disconnected [dɪskəˈnektɪd] adj inconexo,-a.

disconsolate [dɪsˈkɒnsəlɪt] adj desconsolado,-a.

discontent [dɪskənˈtent] n descontento m.

discontented [dɪskənˈtentɪd] adj descontento,-a.

discontinue [dɪskənˈtɪnjuː] vtr fml abandonar; (work) interrumpir.

discord [ˈdɪskɔːd] n 1 fml discordia f. 2 Mus disonancia f.

discordant [dɪsˈkɔːdənt] adj discordante.

discotheque [ˈdɪskətek] n discoteca f.

discount [ˈdɪskaʊnt] I n descuento m. II [dɪsˈkaʊnt] vtr 1 (price) rebajar. 2 (view, suggestion) descartar.

discourage [dɪsˈkʌrɪdʒ] vtr (dishearten) desanimar; (advances) rechazar.

discouraging [dɪsˈkʌrɪdʒɪŋ] adj desalentador,-a.

discover [dɪsˈkʌvəʳ] vtr descubrir; (missing person, object) encontrar.

discovery [dɪsˈkʌvərɪ] n descubrimiento m.

discredit [dɪsˈkredɪt] I n descrédito m. II vtr (person, régime) desacreditar; (theory) poner en duda.

discreet [dɪsˈkriːt] adj discreto,-a; (distance, silence) prudente; (hat, house) modesto,-a.

discrepancy [dɪsˈkrepənsɪ] n diferencia f.

discretion [dɪsˈkreʃən] n discreción f; (prudence) prudencia f; at the d. of ..., a juicio de ....

discriminate [dɪsˈkrɪmɪneɪt] vi discriminar (between, entre); to d. against sth/sb, discriminar algo/a algn.

discriminating [dɪsˈkrɪmɪneɪtɪŋ] adj (person) entendido,-a; (taste) refinado,-a.

discrimination [dɪskrɪmɪˈneɪʃən] n 1 (bias) discriminación f. 2 (distinction) diferenciación f.

discuss [dɪsˈkʌs] vtr discutir; (in writing) tratar de.

discussion [dɪsˈkʌʃən] n discusión f.

disdain [dɪsˈdeɪn] fml I n desdén m. II vtr desdeñar.

disdainful [dɪsˈdeɪnfʊl] adj fml desdeñoso,-a.

disease [dɪˈziːz] n enfermedad f; fig mal m.

disembark [dɪsɪmˈbɑːk] vtr & vi desembarcar.

disenchanted [dɪsɪnˈtʃɑːntɪd] adj desencantado,-a, desilusionado,-a.

disengage [dɪsɪnˈgeɪdʒ] vtr soltar; Aut to d. the clutch, soltar el embrague, desembragar.

disentangle [dɪsɪnˈtæŋgəl] vtr desenredar.

disfigure [dɪsˈfɪgəʳ] vtr desfigurar.

disgrace [dɪsˈgreɪs] I n 1 desgracia f; to be in d., estar desacreditado,-a; to fall into d., caer en desgracia. 2 (shame) vergüenza f, escándalo m. II vtr deshonrar, desacreditar.

disgraceful [dɪsˈgreɪsfʊl] adj vergonzoso,-a.

disgruntled [dɪsˈgrʌntəld] adj contrariado,-a, disgustado,-a.

disguise [dɪsˈgaɪz] I n disfraz m; in d., disfrazado,-a. II vtr 1 (person) disfrazar (as, de). 2 (feelings) disimular.

disgust [dɪsˈgʌst] I n 1 (loathing) repugnancia f, asco m. 2 (strong disapproval) indignación f. II vtr 1 (revolt) repugnar, dar asco a. 2 (offend) indignar.

disgusting [dɪsˈgʌstɪŋ] adj asqueroso,-a, repugnante; (behaviour, state of affairs) intolerable.

dish [dɪʃ] n (for serving) fuente f; (course) plato m; to wash or do the dishes, fregar los platos. ◆**dish out** vtr fam (food) servir; (books, advice) repartir; to d. it out (to sb), (criticize) criticar (a algn). ◆**dish up** vtr (meal) servir.

dishcloth [ˈdɪʃklɒθ] n trapo m de fregar.

dishearten [dɪsˈhɑːtən] vtr desanimar.

dishevelled, US **disheveled** [dɪˈʃevəld] adj (hair) despeinado,-a; (appearance) desaliñado,-a.

dishonest [dɪsˈɒnɪst] adj (person) poco honrado,-a; (means) fraudulento,-a.

dishonesty [dɪsˈɒnɪstɪ] n (of person) falta f de honradez.

dishonour, US **dishonor** [dɪsˈɒnəʳ] I n fml deshonra f. II vtr (name) deshonrar.

dishonourable [dɪsˈɒnərəbl] adj deshonroso,-a.

dishtowel [ˈdɪʃtaʊəl] n US trapo m de cocina.

dishwasher [ˈdɪʃwɒʃəʳ] n lavaplatos m inv; (person) lavaplatos mf inv.

disillusion [dɪsɪˈluːʒən] vtr desilusionar.

disincentive [dɪsɪnˈsentɪv] n freno m.

disinfect [dɪsɪnˈfekt] vtr desinfectar.

disinfectant [dɪsɪnˈfektənt] n desinfectante m.

disinherit [dɪsɪnˈherɪt] vtr desheredar.

disintegrate [dɪs'ɪntɪɡreɪt] *vi* desintegrarse.

disintegration [dɪsɪntɪ'ɡreɪʃən] *n* desintegración *f*.

disinterested [dɪs'ɪntrɪstɪd] *adj* desinteresado,-a.

disjointed [dɪs'dʒɔɪntɪd] *adj* inconexo,-a.

disk [dɪsk] *n US* disco *m*; *Comput* disquete *m*; **d. drive**, disquetera *f*, disketera *f*.

diskette [dɪs'ket] *n Comput* disquete *m*.

dislike [dɪs'laɪk] I *n* antipatía *f*, aversión *f* (**for**, **of**, a, hacia). II *vtr* tener antipatía *or* aversión a *or* hacia.

dislocate ['dɪsləkeɪt] *vtr* (*joint*) dislocar.

dislodge [dɪs'lɒdʒ] *vtr* sacar.

disloyal [dɪs'lɔɪəl] *adj* desleal.

dismal ['dɪzməl] *adj* 1 (*prospect*) sombrío,-a; (*place*, *weather*) deprimente; (*person*) triste. 2 (*failure*) lamentable.

dismantle [dɪs'mæntəl] *vtr* desmontar.

dismay [dɪs'meɪ] I *n* consternación *f*. II *vtr* consternar.

dismiss [dɪs'mɪs] *vtr* 1 (*idea*) descartar. 2 (*employee*) despedir; (*official*) destituir. 3 **to d. sb**, (*from room*, *presence*) dar permiso a algn para retirarse. 4 (*reject*) rechazar; *Jur* desestimar; (*case*) sobreseer.

dismissal [dɪs'mɪsəl] *n* 1 (*of employee*) despido *m*; (*of official*) destitución *f*. 2 (*of claim*) rechazo *m*; *Jur* desestimación *f*.

dismount [dɪs'maʊnt] *vi fml* apearse (**from**, de).

disobedience [dɪsə'biːdɪəns] *n* desobediencia *f*.

disobedient [dɪsə'biːdɪənt] *adj* desobediente.

disobey [dɪsə'beɪ] *vtr & vi* desobedecer; (*law*) violar.

disorder [dɪs'ɔːdər] *n* 1 (*untidiness*) desorden *m*. 2 (*riot*) disturbio *m*. 3 (*of organ*, *mind*) trastorno *m*; (*of speech*) defecto *m*.

disorderly [dɪs'ɔːdəlɪ] *adj* 1 (*untidy*) desordenado,-a. 2 (*meeting*) alborotado,-a; (*conduct*) escandaloso,-a.

disorganized [dɪs'ɔːɡənaɪzd] *adj* desorganizado,-a.

disorient [dɪs'ɔːrɪənt], **disorientate** [dɪs'ɔːrɪənteɪt] *vtr* desorientar.

disown [dɪs'əʊn] *vtr* desconocer.

disparaging [dɪs'pærɪdʒɪŋ] *adj* despectivo,-a.

disparity [dɪs'pærɪtɪ] *n fml* disparidad *f*.

dispassionate [dɪs'pæʃənɪt] *adj* desapasionado,-a.

dispatch [dɪs'pætʃ] I *n* 1 (*official message*) despacho *m*; (*journalist's report*) reportaje *m*; (*military message*) parte *m*. 2 (*of mail*) envío *m*; (*of goods*) consignación *f*. II *vtr* 1 (*mail*) enviar; (*goods*) expedir. 2 *fam* (*food*) zamparse; (*job*) despachar.

dispel [dɪs'pel] *vtr* disipar.

dispensary [dɪs'pensərɪ] *n* dispensario *m*.

dispense [dɪs'pens] *vtr* (*supplies*) repartir;

(*justice*) administrar. ◆**dispense with** *vtr* (*do without*) prescindir de.

dispenser [dɪs'pensər] *n* máquina expendedora; **cash d.**, cajero automático; **soap d.**, dosificador *m* de jabón.

dispensing chemist [dɪspensɪŋ'kemɪst] *n GB* farmacéutico,-a *m,f*.

dispersal [dɪs'pɜːsəl] *n* dispersión *f*.

disperse [dɪs'pɜːs] I *vtr* dispersar. II *vi* dispersarse; (*fog*) disiparse.

dispirited [dɪs'pɪrɪtɪd] *adj* abatido,-a.

displace [dɪs'pleɪs] *vtr* 1 desplazar; **displaced person**, desterrado,-a *m,f*. 2 (*supplant*) sustituir.

display [dɪs'pleɪ] I *n* (*exhibition*) exposición *f*; *Comput* visualización *f*. 2 (*of feelings*, *skills*) demostración *f*; (*of force*) despliegue *m*; **d. window**, escaparate *m*; **military d.**, desfile *m* militar. II *vtr* 1 mostrar; (*goods*) exponer; *Comput* visualizar. 2 (*feelings*) manifestar.

displease [dɪs'pliːz] *vtr* disgustar; (*offend*) ofender.

displeasure [dɪs'pleʒər] *n* disgusto *m*.

disposable [dɪs'pəʊzəbəl] *adj* (*throwaway*) desechable. 2 (*available*) disponible.

disposal [dɪs'pəʊzəl] *n* 1 (*removal*) eliminación *f*. 2 (*availability*) disponibilidad *f*; **at my d.**, a mi disposición. 3 *fml* (*arrangement*) disposición *f*. 4 (*sale*) venta *f*; (*of property*) traspaso *m*.

dispose [dɪs'pəʊz] I *vi* **to d. of**, (*remove*) eliminar; (*rubbish*) tirar; (*unwanted object*) deshacerse de; (*matter*) resolver; (*sell*) vender; (*property*) traspasar. II *vtr fml* (*arrange*) disponer.

disposed [dɪs'pəʊzd] *adj* (*inclined*) dispuesto,-a.

disposition [dɪspə'zɪʃən] *n* 1 (*temperament*) genio *m*. 2 *fml* (*arrangement*) disposición *f*.

disproportionate [dɪsprə'pɔːʃənɪt] *adj* desproporcionado,-a (**to**, a).

disprove [dɪs'pruːv] *vtr* refutar.

dispute [dɪs'pjuːt] I *n* (*disagreement*) discusión *f*; (*quarrel*) disputa *f*; **industrial d.**, conflicto *m* laboral. II [dɪs'pjuːt] *vtr* (*claim*) refutar; (*territory*) disputar; (*matter*) discutir. III *vi* discutir (**about**, **over**, de, sobre).

disqualify [dɪs'kwɒlɪfaɪ] *vtr* 1 *Sport* descalificar. 2 (*make ineligible*) incapacitar.

disquiet [dɪs'kwaɪət] *n* preocupación *f*, inquietud *f*.

disregard [dɪsrɪ'ɡɑːd] I *n* indiferencia *f*; (*for safety*) despreocupación *f*. II *vtr* descuidar; (*ignore*) ignorar.

disrepair [dɪsrɪ'peər] *n* mal estado *m*; **in** (**a state of**) **d.**, en mal estado; **to fall into d.**, deteriorarse.

disreputable [dɪs'repjʊtəbəl] *adj* (*person*, *area*) de mala fama; (*behaviour*) vergonzoso,-a.

disrepute |dɪsrɪ'pjuːt| n mala fama f, oprobio m.

disrespectful |dɪsrɪ'spektful| adj irrespetuoso,-a.

disrupt |dɪs'rʌpt| vtr (meeting, traffic) interrumpir; (schedule etc) desbaratar.

disruption |dɪs'rʌpʃən| n (of meeting, traffic) interrupción f; (of schedule etc) desbaratamiento m.

dissatisfaction |dɪssætɪs'fækʃən| n descontento m, insatisfacción f.

dissatisfied |dɪ'sætɪsfaɪd| adj descontento,-a.

dissect |dɪ'sekt, daɪ'sekt| vtr disecar.

disseminate |dɪ'semɪneɪt| vtr fml diseminar, difundir.

dissent |dɪ'sent| I n disentimiento m. II vi disentir.

dissertation |dɪsə'teɪʃən| n disertación f; Univ tesina f (on, sobre).

disservice |dɪs'sɜːvɪs| n perjuicio m; to do sth/sb a d., perjudicar algo/a algn.

dissident |'dɪsɪdənt| adj & n disidente (mf).

dissimilar |dɪ'sɪmɪlər| adj distinto,-a.

dissipate |'dɪsɪpeɪt| I vtr 1 disipar. 2 (waste) derrochar. II vi disiparse.

dissociate |dɪ'səʊʃɪeɪt| vtr to d. oneself, distanciarse.

dissolute |'dɪsəluːt| adj disoluto,-a.

dissolution |dɪsə'luːʃən| n disolución f; (of agreement) rescisión f.

dissolve |dɪ'zɒlv| I vtr disolver. II vi disolverse.

dissuade |dɪ'sweɪd| vtr disuadir (from, de).

distance |'dɪstəns| I n distancia f; in the d., a lo lejos; fam to stay the d., completar la prueba. II vtr distanciarse.

distant |'dɪstənt| adj 1 (place, time) lejano,-a; (look) distraído,-a. 2 (aloof) distante, frío,-a.

distaste |dɪs'teɪst| n aversión f.

distasteful |dɪs'teɪstful| adj desagradable.

distend |dɪ'stend| fml I vtr dilatar. II vi dilatarse.

distil, US distill |dɪs'tɪl| vtr destilar.

distillery |dɪs'tɪlərɪ| n destilería f.

distinct |dɪ'stɪŋkt| adj 1 (different) diferente; as d. from, a diferencia de. 2 (smell, change) marcado,-a; (idea, intention) claro,-a.

distinction |dɪ'stɪŋkʃən| n 1 (difference) diferencia f. 2 (excellence) distinción f. 3 Educ sobresaliente m.

distinctive |dɪ'stɪŋktɪv| adj distintivo,-a.

distinguish |dɪ'stɪŋgwɪʃ| vtr distinguir.

distinguished |dɪ'stɪŋgwɪʃt| adj distinguido,-a.

distinguishing |dɪ'stɪŋgwɪʃɪŋ| adj distintivo,-a, característico,-a.

distort |dɪ'stɔːt| vtr (misrepresent) deformar; (words) tergiversar.

distortion |dɪ'stɔːʃən| n deformación f;

(of sound, image) distorsión f.

distract |dɪs'trækt| vtr distraer.

distracted |dɪ'stræktɪd| adj distraído,-a.

distraction |dɪ'strækʃən| n (interruption) distracción f; (confusion) confusión f; to drive sb to d., sacar a algn de quicio.

distraught |dɪ'strɔːt| adj (anguished) afligido,-a.

distress |dɪ'stres| I n (mental) angustia f; (physical) dolor m; d. signal, señal f de socorro. II vtr (upset) apenar.

distressing |dɪ'stresɪŋ| adj penoso,-a.

distribute |dɪ'strɪbjuːt| vtr distribuir, repartir.

distribution |dɪstrɪ'bjuːʃən| n distribución f.

distributor |dɪ'strɪbjʊtər| n 1 Com distribuidor,-a m,f. 2 Aut delco m.

district |'dɪstrɪkt| n (of country) región f; (of town) barrio m; US d. attorney, fiscal m; d. council, corporación f local; d. nurse, practicante mf.

distrust |dɪs'trʌst| I n recelo m. II vtr desconfiar de.

disturb |dɪ'stɜːb| vtr 1 (inconvenience) molestar. 2 (silence) romper; (sleep) interrumpir. 3 (worry) perturbar. 4 (papers) desordenar.

disturbance |dɪ'stɜːbəns| n 1 (of routine) alteración f. 2 (commotion) disturbio m, alboroto m.

disturbed |dɪ'stɜːbd| adj (mentally) inestable.

disturbing |dɪ'stɜːbɪŋ| adj inquietante.

disuse |dɪs'juːs| n desuso m.

disused |dɪs'juːzd| adj abandonado,-a.

ditch |dɪtʃ| I n zanja f; (at roadside) cuneta f; (for irrigation) acequia f. II vtr fam (plan, friend) abandonar.

dither |'dɪðər| vi GB fam vacilar, titubear.

ditto |'dɪtəʊ| n ídem, lo mismo.

dive |daɪv| I n 1 (into water) salto m de cabeza; (of submarine) inmersión f; (of plane) picado m; Sport salto m. 2 fam (bar) antro m. II vi tirarse de cabeza; (submarine) sumergirse; (plane) bajar en picado; Sport saltar. 3 he dived for the phone, se precipitó hacia el teléfono.

diver |'daɪvər| n (person) buceador,-a m,f; (professional) buzo m; Sport saltador,-a m,f .

diverge |daɪ'vɜːdʒ| vi divergir.

diverse |daɪ'vɜːs| adj (varied) diverso,-a, variado,-a; (different) distinto,-a, diferente.

diversion |daɪ'vɜːʃən| n 1 (distraction) distracción f. 2 GB (detour) desvío m.

divert |daɪ'vɜːt| vtr desviar.

divide |dɪ'vaɪd| I vtr dividir. II vi (road, stream) bifurcarse. III n división f, diferencia f.

dividend |'dɪvɪdend| n Com dividendo m;

fig beneficio *m.*
divine [dɪ'vaɪn] *adj* divino,-a.
diving board ['daɪvɪŋbɔːd] *n* trampolín *m.*
divinity [dɪ'vɪnɪtɪ] *n* 1 divinidad *f.* 2 (*subject*) teología *f.*
division [dɪ'vɪʒən] *n* 1 división *f.* 2 (*sharing*) reparto *m.* 3 (*of organization*) sección *f.*
divorce [dɪ'vɔːs] *n* 1 divorcio *m.* II *vtr* she **divorced him,** se divorció de él. III *vi* divorciarse.
divorcé [dɪ'vɔːseɪ], **divorcée** [dɪvɔː'siː] *n* divorciado,-a *m,f.*
divulge [daɪ'vʌldʒ] *vtr fml* divulgar, revelar.
DIY [diːaɪ'waɪ] *n GB abbr of* do-it-yourself, bricolaje *m.*
dizziness ['dɪzɪnɪs] *n* vértigo *m.*
dizzy ['dɪzɪ] *adj* (**dizzier,** **dizziest**) 1 (*person*) (*unwell*) mareado,-a. 2 (*height, pace*) vertiginoso,-a.
DJ ['diːdʒeɪ] *n fam abbr of* disc jockey.
DNA [diːen'eɪ] *n abbr of* deoxyribonucleic acid, ácido *m* desoxirribonucleico, ADN *m.*
do [duː, *unstressed* dʊ, də] I *v aux* (*3rd person sing pres* **does**; *pt* **did**; *pp* **done**) 1 (*in negatives and questions*) (*not translated in Span*) **do you want some coffee?** ¿quieres café?; **do you drive?** ¿tienes carnet de conducir?; **don't you want to come?** ¿no quieres venir?; **he doesn't smoke,** no fuma. 2 (*emphatic*) (*not translated in Span*) **do come with us!,** ¡ánimo, vente con nosotros!; **I do like your bag,** me encanta tu bolso. 3 (*substituting main verb*) (*in sentence*) (*not translated in Span*) **I don't believe him** — **neither do I,** no le creo - yo tampoco; **I'll go if you do,** si vas tú, voy yo; **I think it's dear, but he doesn't,** a mí me parece caro pero a él no; **who went?** - **I did,** ¿quién asistió? - yo. 4 (*in question tags*) **he refused,** **didn't he?,** dijo que no, ¿verdad?; **I don't like it, do you?** a mí no me gusta, ¿y a ti?
II *vtr* 1 hacer; (*task*) realizar; (*duty*) cumplir con; **to do one's best,** hacer todo lo posible; **to do sth again,** volver a hacer algo; **to do sth for sb,** hacer algo por algn; **to do the cooking/cleaning,** cocinar/limpiar; **to do the dishes,** lavar los platos; **what can I do for you?,** ¿en qué puedo servirle?; **what do you do (for a living)?,** ¿a qué te dedicas?; **what's to be done?,** ¿qué se puede hacer?; **he's done it!,** ¡lo ha conseguido! 2 **do you do sportswear?,** (*make, offer*) ¿(aquí) tienen ropa de deporte? 3 (*distance*) recorrer; (*speed*) **we were doing eighty,** íbamos a ochenta; **this car can do a hundred and twenty,** este coche puede alcanzar los ciento veinte.

III *vi* 1 (*act*) hacer; **do as I tell you,** haz lo que te digo; **you did right,** hiciste bien. 2 **he did badly in the exams,** los exámenes le salieron mal; **how are you doing?,** ¿qué tal?; **how do you do?,** (*greeting*) ¿cómo está usted?; (*answer*) mucho gusto; **to do well,** (*person*) tener éxito; (*business*) ir bien. 3 **five pounds will do,** (*suffice*) con cinco libras será suficiente; **that will do!,** ¡basta ya! 4 **this cushion will do as a pillow,** (*be suitable*) este cojín servirá de almohada; **this won't do,** esto no puede ser.
IV *n fam* 1 *GB* (*party*) fiesta *f;* (*event*) ceremonia *f.* 2 **do's and don'ts,** reglas *fpl* de conducta.
◆**do away with** *vtr* 1 (*abolish*) abolir; (*discard*) deshacerse de. 2 (*kill*) asesinar. ◆**do down** *vtr fam* (*humiliate*) hacer quedar mal. ◆**do for** *vtr fam* (*destroy, ruin*) arruinar; *fig* **I'm done for if I don't finish this,** estoy perdido,-a si no acabo esto. ◆**do in** *vtr sl* 1 (*kill*) cargarse. 2 **I'm done in,** (*exhausted*) estoy hecho,-a polvo. ◆**do over** *vtr fam* 1 *US* (*repeat*) repetir. 2 *GB* (*thrash*) dar una paliza a. ◆**do up** *vtr* 1 (*wrap*) envolver. 2 (*belt etc*) abrochar; (*laces*) atar. 3 (*dress up*) arreglar. 4 (*redecorate*) renovar. ◆**do with** *vtr* 1 **I could do with a rest,** (*need*) un descanso no me vendría nada mal. 2 **to have** *or* **be to do with,** (*concern*) tener que ver con. ◆**do without** *vtr* pasar sin, prescindir de.
docile ['dəʊsaɪl] *adj* dócil; (*animal*) manso,-a.
dock¹ [dɒk] I *n Naut* the docks, el muelle. II *vi* 1 (*ship*) atracar. 2 (*spacecraft*) acoplarse.
dock² [dɒk] *vtr* (*money*) descontar.
dock³ [dɒk] *n Jur* banquillo *m* (de los acusados).
docker ['dɒkər] *n* estibador *m.*
dockland ['dɒklænd] *n* zona *f* del puerto.
dockyard ['dɒkjɑːd] *n* astillero *m.*
doctor ['dɒktər] I *n* 1 *Med* médico,-a *m,f.* 2 *Univ* doctor,-a *m,f;* **D. of Law,** doctor en derecho. II *vtr pej* (*figures*) falsificar; (*text*) arreglar; (*drink etc*) adulterar.
doctorate ['dɒktərɪt] *n* doctorado *m.*
doctrine ['dɒktrɪn] *n* doctrina *f.*
document ['dɒkjʊmənt] I *n* documento *m;* **documents,** documentación *f.* II *vtr* documentar.
documentary [dɒkjʊ'mentərɪ] *adj* & *n* documental (*m*).
dodge [dɒdʒ] I *vtr* 1 (*blow*) esquivar; (*pursuer*) despistar; *fig* eludir. 2 *fam* **to d. one's taxes,** engañar a Hacienda. II *vi* (*move aside*) echarse a un lado. III *n* 1 (*movement*) regate *m.* 2 *fam* (*trick*) truco *m.*
dodgem® ['dɒdʒəm] *n fam* **d.** (**car**), coche *m* de choque.

dodgy ['dɒdʒɪ] adj (**dodgier, dodgiest**) GB fam (risky) arriesgado,-a; (tricky) difícil; (dishonest, not working properly) chungo,-a.

doe [dəʊ] n inv (of deer) gama f; (of rabbit) coneja f.

does [dʌz] 3rd person sing pres → **do**.

doesn't ['dʌzənt] = **does not**.

dog [dɒg] I n 1 perro,-a m,f; fam fig a d.'s life, una vida de perros; d. collar, (of dog) collar m de perro; Rel fam alzacuello m. 2 (male canine) macho m; (fox) zorro m; (wolf) lobo m. 3 fam dirty d., canalla m. 4 US fam (disappointment) desastre m. II vtr acosar; **to d. sb's footsteps**, seguir los pasos de algn; fig **dogged by bad luck**, perseguido,-a por la mala suerte.

dog-eared ['dɒgɪəd] adj (book) con los bordes de las páginas doblados; (shabby) sobado,-a.

dogged ['dɒgɪd] adj obstinado,-a, tenaz.

doghouse ['dɒghaʊs] n US fam perrera f; fig **to be in the d.**, estar castigado,-a.

dogma ['dɒgmə] n dogma m.

dogmatic [dɒg'mætɪk] adj dogmático,-a.

dogsbody ['dɒgzbɒdɪ] n GB fam (drudge) burro m de carga.

doh [dəʊ] n Mus do m.

doing ['duːɪŋ] n 1 (action) obra f; it was none of my d., yo no tuve nada que ver; fig it took some d., costó trabajo hacerlo. 2 **doings**, (activities) actividades fpl.

do-it-yourself [duːɪtjə'self] n bricolaje m.

doldrums ['dɒldrəmz] npl fam fig **to be in the d.**, (person) estar abatido,-a; (trade) estar estancado,-a.

dole [dəʊl] I n GB fam the d., el paro; **to be or go on the d.**, estar en el paro; fig **d. queue**, los parados. II vtr **to d. (out)**, repartir.

doleful ['dəʊlfʊl] adj triste, afligido,-a.

doll [dɒl] I n 1 (toy) muñeca f. 2 US fam (girl) muñeca f. II vtr fam **to d. oneself up**, ponerse guapa.

dollar ['dɒlə'] n dólar m.

dolphin ['dɒlfɪn] n delfín m.

domain [də'meɪn] n 1 (sphere) campo m, esfera f; that's not my d., no es de mi competencia. 2 (territory) dominio m.

dome [dəʊm] n (roof) cúpula f; (ceiling) bóveda f.

domestic [də'mestɪk] adj 1 (appliance, pet) doméstico,-a; **d. science**, economía doméstica. 2 (home-loving) casero,-a. 3 (flight, news) nacional; (trade, policy) interior.

domesticate [də'mestɪkeɪt] vtr (make home-loving) volver hogareño,-a or casero,-a.

domicile ['dɒmɪsaɪl] n domicilio m.

dominant ['dɒmɪnənt] adj dominante.

dominate ['dɒmɪneɪt] vtr & vi dominar.

domineering [dɒmɪ'nɪərɪŋ] adj domi-

nante.

Dominican [də'mɪnɪkən] adj & n (of Dominica) dominicano,-a (m,f); **D. Republic**, República Dominicana.

dominion [də'mɪnjən] n dominio m.

domino ['dɒmɪnəʊ] n (pl **dominoes**) (piece) ficha f de dominó; **dominoes**, (game) dominó m sing.

don [dɒn] n GB Univ catedrático,-a m,f.

donate [dəʊ'neɪt] vtr donar.

donation [dəʊ'neɪʃən] n donativo m.

done [dʌn] adj 1 (finished) terminado,-a; it's over and d. with, se acabó. 2 fam (tired) rendido,-a. 3 (meat) hecho,-a; (vegetables) cocido,-a.

donkey ['dɒŋkɪ] n burro,-a m,f.

donor ['dəʊnə'] n donante m.

don't [dəʊnt] = **do not**.

doodle ['duːdəl] vi fam (write) garabatear; (draw) hacer dibujos.

doom [duːm] I n (fate) destino m (funesto); (ruin) perdición f; (death) muerte f. II vtr usu pass (destine) destinar; **doomed to failure**, condenado,-a al fracaso.

doomsday ['duːmzdeɪ] n día m del juicio final.

door [dɔː'] n puerta f; **front/back d.**, puerta principal/trasera; fig **behind closed doors**, a puerta cerrada; d. handle, manilla f (de la puerta); **d. knocker**, picaporte m; **next d. (to)**, (en) la casa de al lado (de).

doorbell ['dɔːbel] n timbre m (de la puerta).

doorknob ['dɔːnɒb] n pomo m.

doorman ['dɔːmən] n portero m.

doormat ['dɔːmæt] n felpudo m, esterilla f; fam fig (person) trapo m.

doorstep ['dɔːstep] n peldaño m; fig **on one's d.**, a la vuelta de la esquina.

door-to-door [dɔːtə'dɔː'] adj a domicilio.

doorway ['dɔːweɪ] n portal m, entrada f.

dope [dəʊp] I n 1 sl (drug) chocolate m. 2 fam (person) imbécil mf. II vtr (food, drink) adulterar con drogas; Sport dopar.

dop(e)y ['dəʊpɪ] adj (**dopier, dopiest**) fam 1 (sleepy) medio dormido,-a; (fuddled) atontado,-a. 2 sl (silly) torpe.

dormant ['dɔːmənt] adj inactivo,-a; fig (rivalry) latente.

dormitory ['dɔːmɪtərɪ] n 1 (in school) dormitorio m. 2 US (in university) colegio m mayor.

dosage ['dəʊsɪdʒ] n fml (amount) dosis f inv.

dose [dəʊs] I n dosis f inv. II vtr (patient) medicar.

doss [dɒs] vi GB sl sobar.

dosshouse ['dɒshaʊs] n GB sl pensión f de mala muerte.

dossier ['dɒsɪeɪ] n expediente m.

dot [dɒt] I n punto m; **on the d.**, en punto. II vtr 1 fam **to d. one's i's and**

cross one's t's, poner los puntos sobre las íes. 2 (scatter) esparcir, salpicar.

dote [dəʊt] vi to d. on sb, chochear con algn.

double ['dʌbəl] I adj doble; **it's the d. price,** cuesta dos veces más; **d. bass,** contrabajo m; **d. bed,** cama f de matrimonio; **d. bill,** programa m doble; GB **d. cream,** nata f para montar; **d. glazing,** ventana f doble. II adv doble; **folded d.,** doblado,-a por la mitad. III n 1 vivo retrato m; Cin Theat doble m. 2 to earn d., ganar el doble; **fam at or on the d.,** corriendo. 3 Ten **doubles,** (partido m singde) dobles mpl. IV vtr doblar; fig (efforts) redoblar. V vi 1 (increase) doblarse. 2 to **d. as,** (serve) hacer las veces de.
◆**double back** vi to d. back on one's tracks, volver sobre sus pasos.
◆**double up** I vtr (bend) doblar. II vi 1 (bend) doblarse. 2 (share room) compartir la habitación (with, con).

double-barrelled ['dʌbəlbærəld] adj 1 (gun) de dos cañones. 2 GB (surname) compuesto,-a.

double-breasted ['dʌbəlbrestid] adj cruzado,-a.

double-check [dʌbəl'tʃek] vtr & vi repasar dos veces.

double-cross [dʌbəl'krɒs] fam I vtr engañar, traicionar. II n engaño m, traición f.

double-decker [dʌbəl'dekər] n GB **d.-d.** (bus), autobús m de dos pisos.

double-edged [dʌbəl'edʒd] adj de doble filo.

doubt [daʊt] I n 1 duda f; **beyond (all) d.,** sin duda alguna; **no d.,** sin duda; **there's no d. about it,** no cabe la menor duda; **to be in d. about sth,** dudar algo; **to be open to d.,** (fact) ser dudoso,-a; (outcome) ser incierto,-a. II vtr 1 (distrust) desconfiar de. 2 (not be sure of) dudar; **I d. if or whether he'll come,** dudo que venga.

doubtful ['daʊtfʊl] adj 1 (future) dudoso,-a, (look) dubitativo,-a; **I'm a bit d. about it,** no me convence del todo; **it's d. whether ...,** no se sabe seguro si .... 2 (questionable) sospechoso,-a.

doubtless ['daʊtlɪs] adv sin duda, seguramente.

dough [dəʊ] n 1 (for bread) masa f; (for pastries) pasta f. 2 sl (money) pasta f.

doughnut ['dəʊnʌt] n rosquilla f, dónut® m.

douse [daʊs] vtr 1 (extinguish) apagar. 1 (soak) mojar.

dove [dʌv] n paloma f.

dovetail ['dʌvteɪl] vtr fig (plans) sincronizar.

dowdy ['daʊdɪ] adj (dowdier, dowdiest) poco elegante.

down¹ ['daʊn] I prep 1 (to or at a lower level) -a. the river, río abajo; **to go d. the road,** bajar la calle. 2 (along) por. II adv

1 (to lower level) (hacia) abajo; (to floor) al suelo; (to ground) a tierra; **to fall d.,** caerse; **to go d.,** (price, person) bajar; (sun) ponerse. 2 (at lower level) abajo; **d. there,** allí abajo; **face d.,** boca abajo; fig **to be d. with a cold,** estar resfriado,-a; fam fig **to feel d.,** estar deprimido,-a; fam fig **d. under,** Australia f, Nueva Zelanda f. 3 **I'm d. to my last stamp,** no me queda más que un solo sello; **sales are d. by five percent,** las ventas han bajado en cinco por ciento. 4 **to take sth d.,** (in writing) apuntar algo. 5 **d. through the ages,** a través de los siglos. III adj (payment) al contado; (on property) de entrada. IV vtr fam (drink) tomarse de un trago; (food) zamparse. V n **ups and downs,** altibajos mpl. VI interj **d. with taxes!,** ¡abajo los impuestos!

down² [daʊn] n 1 (on bird) plumón m. 2 (on cheek, peach) pelusa f; (on body) vello m.

down-and-out ['daʊnənaʊt] I adj en las últimas. II n vagabundo,-a m,f.

downbeat ['daʊnbiːt] adj fam (gloomy) deprimido,-a.

downcast ['daʊnkɑːst] adj abatido,-a.

downfall ['daʊnfɔːl] n 1 (of régime) caída f; (of person) perdición f.

downgrade [daʊnˈgreɪd] vtr degradar.

downhearted [daʊnˈhɑːtɪd] adj desalentado,-a.

downhill [daʊnˈhɪl] I adj (skiing) de descenso; fam **after his first exam, the rest were all d.,** después del primer examen, los demás le fueron sobre ruedas. II adv **to go d.,** ir cuesta abajo; fig (standards) deteriorarse.

down-market [daʊnˈmɑːkɪt] I adj barato,-a. II adv **to move d.,** (of company) producir artículos más asequibles.

downpour ['daʊnpɔːr] n chaparrón m.

downright ['daʊnraɪt] adj (blunt) tajante; (categorical) categórico,-a; **it's a d. lie,** es una mentira y gorda. II adv (totally) completamente.

downstairs [daʊnˈsteəz] I adv abajo; (to ground floor) a la planta baja; **to go d.,** bajar la escalera. II adj (on ground floor) de la planta baja.

downstream [daʊnˈstriːm] adv río abajo.

down-to-earth [daʊntʊˈɜːθ] adj realista.

downtown [daʊnˈtaʊn] adv US en el centro (de la ciudad).

downturn ['daʊntɜːn] n baja f.

downward ['daʊnwəd] adj (slope) descendente; (look) hacia abajo; Fin (tendency) a la baja.

downward(s) ['daʊnwəd(z)] adv hacia abajo.

dowry ['daʊərɪ] n dote f.

doz abbr of **dozen,** docena f, doc.

doze [dəʊz] I vi dormitar. II n cabezada f; **to have a d.,** echar una cabezada.

◆**doze off** vi quedarse dormido,-a.

dozen ['dʌzən] n docena f; **half a d./a d. eggs**, media docena/una docena de huevos; **fam dozens of**, un montón de.

Dr abbr of **Doctor**, Doctor,-a m,f, Dra.

drab [dræb] adj (drabber, drabbest) 1 (ugly) feo,-a; (dreary) monótono,-a. 2 (colour) pardo,-a.

draft [drɑːft] n 1 borrador m. 2 (bill of exchange) giro m. 3 US servicio militar obligatorio. 4 US → **draught**. II vtr 1 hacer un borrador de. 2 US Mil reclutar.

draftsman ['drɑːftsmən] n US → **draughtsman**.

drag [dræg] I vtr 1 (pull) arrastrar; **fig to d. one's heels** (over sth), dar largas (a algo). 2 (lake) rastrear. II vi 1 (trail) arrastrarse. 2 (person) rezagarse. III n 1 Tech resistencia f (aerodinámica). 2 fam (nuisance) lata f. 3 fam (on cigarette) calada f. 4 sl **to be in d.**, ir vestido de mujer. ◆**drag off** vtr llevarse arrastrando. ◆**drag on** vi (of war, strike) hacerse interminable. ◆**drag out** vtr (speech etc) alargar.

dragon ['drægən] n dragón m.

dragonfly ['drægənflai] n libélula f.

drain [drein] I n 1 (for water) desagüe m; (for sewage) alcantarilla f. 2 (grating) sumidero m. 3 fig the boys are a d. on her strength, los niños la dejan agotada. II vtr 1 (marsh etc) avenar; (reservoir) desecar. 2 (crockery) escurrir. 3 (empty) (glass) apurar; fig (capital etc) agotar. III vi 1 (crockery) escurrirse. **2 to d. (away)**, (liquid) irse.

drainage ['dreinidʒ] n (of marsh) drenaje m; (of reservoir, building) desagüe m; (of town) alcantarillado m.

drainpipe ['dreinpaip] n tubo m de desagüe.

dram [dræm] n fam trago m (de whisky).

drama ['drɑːmə] n 1 (play) obra f de teatro; fig drama. 2 Lit (subject) teatro m.

dramatic [drə'mætik] adj 1 (change) impresionante; (moment) emocionante. 2 Theat dramático,-a, teatral.

dramatist ['dræmətist] n dramaturgo,-a m,f.

dramatization [dræmətai'zeiʃən] n adaptación f teatral.

dramatize ['dræmətaiz] vtr 1 (adapt) hacer una adaptación teatral de. 2 (exaggerate) dramatizar.

drank [dræŋk] pt → **drink**.

drape [dreip] I vtr 1 **to d. sth over sth**, colgar algo sobre algo; **draped with**, cubierto,-a de. II n 1 (of fabric) caída f. 2 US cortina f.

draper ['dreipər] n GB pañero,-a m,f.

drastic ['dræstik] adj 1 (measures) drástico,-a, severo,-a. 2 (change) radical.

draught [drɑːft] I n 1 (of cold air) co-

rriente f (de aire). 2 (of liquid) trago m. 3 **d. (beer)**, cerveza f de barril. 4 GB **draughts**, (game) damas fpl. 5 Naut calado m. II adj (animal) de tiro.

draughtboard ['drɑːftbɔːd] n GB tablero m de damas.

draughtsman ['drɑːftsmən] n delineante mf.

draw [drɔː] I vtr (pt drew; pp drawn) 1 (picture) dibujar; (line) trazar. 2 (pull) tirar de; (train, carriage) arrastrar; (curtains) (open) descorrer; (close) correr; (blinds) bajar. 3 (remove) sacar; (salary) cobrar; (cheque) librar. 4 (attract) atraer; (attention) llamar. 5 fig (strength) sacar. **6 to d. breath**, respirar. **7 to d. lots**, echar a suertes. **8** (comparison) hacer; (conclusion) sacar. II vi 1 (sketch) dibujar. 2 (move) **the train drew into/out of the station**, el tren entró en/salió de la estación; **to d. apart (from)**, separarse (de); **to d. to an end**, acabarse. 3 Sport **they drew two all**, empataron a dos. III n 1 (raffle) sorteo m. 2 Sport empate m. 3 fig (attraction) atracción f. ◆**draw in** vi (days) acortarse. ◆**draw on** vtr (savings) recurrir a; (experience) aprovecharse de. ◆**draw out** vtr 1 (make long) alargar. 2 (encourage to speak) desatar la lengua a. 3 (from pocket, drawer etc) sacar. ◆**draw up** vtr (contract) preparar; (plan) esbozar.

drawback ['drɔːbæk] n desventaja f, inconveniente m.

drawbridge ['drɔːbridʒ] n puente levadizo.

drawer ['drɔːər] n cajón m.

drawing ['drɔːiŋ] n dibujo m; **fam fig to go back to the d. board**, volver a empezar; **GB d. pin**, chincheta f; **fml d. room**, sala f de estar.

drawl [drɔːl] I vi hablar arrastrando las palabras. II n voz cansina; US a Southern d., un acento sureño.

drawn [drɔːn] adj (tired) ojeroso,-a.

dread [dred] I vtr temer a, tener pavor a. II n temor m.

dreadful ['dredful] adj 1 (shocking) espantoso,-a. 2 fam (awful) fatal; **how d.!**, ¡qué horror! ◆**dreadfully** adv fam (horribly) terriblemente; (very) muy, sumamente.

dream [driːm] I n 1 sueño m. 2 (daydream) ensueño m. 3 fam (marvel) maravilla f. II vtr (pt & pp dreamed or dreamt) soñar. III vi soñar (of, about, con).

dreamer ['driːmər] n soñador,-a f.

dreamy ['driːmi] adj (dreamier, dreamiest) (absent-minded) distraído,-a; (wonderful) de ensueño.

dreary ['driəri] adj (drearier, dreariest) 1 (gloomy) triste. 2 fam (boring) aburrido,-a, pesado,-a.

dredge [dredʒ] vtr & vi dragar, rastrear. ◆**dredge up** vtr 1 (body) sacar del agua. **2** *fam fig* sacar a relucir.

dregs [dregz] *npl* poso *m sing*.

drench [drentʃ] *vtr* empapar.

dress [dres] **I** *n* **1** (*frock*) vestido *m*. **2** (*clothing*) ropa *f*; **d. rehearsal**, ensayo *m* general; **d. shirt**, camisa *f* de etiqueta. **II** *vtr* **1** (*person*) vestir; **he was dressed in a grey suit**, llevaba (puesto) un traje gris. **2** (*salad*) aliñar. **3** (*wound*) vendar. **III** *vi* vestirse. ◆**dress up I** *vi* **1** (*in disguise*) disfrazarse (**as**, de). **2** (*in best clothes*) vestirse elegante. **II** *vtr fig* disfrazar.

dresser [dresə^r] *n* **1** *GB* (*in kitchen*) aparador *m*. **2** *US* (*in bedroom*) tocador *m*. **3** *Theat* ayudante *mf* de camerino.

dressing [dresɪŋ] *n* **1** (*bandage*) vendaje *m*. **2** (*salad*) **d.**, aliño *m*. **3 d. gown**, bata *f*; **d. room**, *Theat* camerino *m*; *Sport* vestuario *m*; **d. table**, tocador *m*.

dressmaker [dresmeɪkə^r] *n* modista *mf*.

dressy [dresɪ] *adj* (**dressier, dressiest**) vistoso,-a.

drew [dru:] *pt* → **draw**.

dribble [drɪbəl] **I** *vi* **1** (*baby*) babear. **2** (*liquid*) gotear. **II** *vtr Sport* (*ball*) driblar. **III** *n* (*saliva*) saliva *f*; (*of water, blood*) gotas *fpl*.

dried [draɪd] *adj* (*fruit*) seco,-a; (*milk*) en polvo.

drier [draɪə^r] *n* → **dryer**.

drift [drɪft] **I** *vi* **1** (*boat*) ir a la deriva; *fig* (*person*) ir sin rumbo; **they drifted away**, se marcharon poco a poco. **2** (*snow*) amontonarse. **II** *n* **1** (*flow*) flujo *m*. **2** (*of snow*) ventisquero *m*; (*of sand*) montón *m*. **3** *fig* (*meaning*) idea *f*.

driftwood [drɪftwʊd] *n* madera *f* flotante.

drill [drɪl] **I** *n* **1** (*handtool*) taladro *m*; *Min* barrena *f*; **dentist's d.**, fresa *f*; **pneumatic d.**, martillo neumático. **2** *esp Mil* instrucción *f*. **II** *vtr* **1** (*wood etc*) taladrar. **2** (*soldiers, children*) instruir. **III** *vi* (*by hand*) taladrar; (*for oil, coal*) perforar, sondar.

drink [drɪŋk] **I** *vtr* (*pt* **drank**; *pp* **drunk**) beber. **II** *vi* beber; **to have sth to d.**, tomarse algo; **to d. to sth/sb**, brindar por algo/algn. **III** *n* bebida *f*; (*alcoholic*) copa *f*.

drinker [drɪŋkə^r] *n* bebedor,-a *m,f*.

drinking [drɪŋkɪŋ] *n* **d. water**, agua *f* potable.

drip [drɪp] **I** *n* **1** goteo *m*. **2** *Med* gota a gota *m inv*. **3** *fam* (*person*) necio,-a *m,f*. **II** *vi* gotear; **he was dripping with sweat**, el sudor le caía a gotas.

drip-dry [drɪpdraɪ] *adj* que no necesita planchado.

dripping [drɪpɪŋ] *n Culin* pringue *f*.

drive [draɪv] **I** *vtr* (*pt* **drove**; *pp* **driven**) **1** (*vehicle*) conducir, *Am* manejar; (*person*) llevar. **2** (*power*) impulsar. **3** (*enemy*) acosar; (*ball*) mandar. **4** (*stake*) hincar; (*nail*)

clavar. **5** (*compel*) forzar, obligar; **to d. sb mad**, volver loco,-a a algn. **6 to d.** (**off**), rechazar. **II** *vi* conducir, *Am* manejar. **III** *n* **1** (*trip*) paseo *m* en coche; **to go for a d.**, dar una vuelta en coche. **2** (*to house*) camino *m* de entrada. **2** (*transmission*) transmisión *f*; *Aut* tracción *f*; *Aut* **left-hand d.**, conducción *f* por la izquierda. **4** *Golf* golpe *m* inicial. **5** (*campaign*) campaña *f*. **6** (*need*) necesidad *f*; (*energy*) energía *f*, vigor *m*, instinto *m* sexual.

drive-in [draɪvɪn] *n US* (*cinema*) autocine *m*.

driven [drɪvən] *pp* → **drive**.

driver [draɪvə^r] *n* (*of car, bus*) conductor,-a *m,f*; (*of train*) maquinista *mf*; (*of racing car*) piloto *mf*; *US* **d.'s license**, carnet *m* de conducir.

driveway [draɪvweɪ] *n* (*to house*) camino *m* de entrada.

driving [draɪvɪŋ] **I** *n* **d. licence**, carnet *m* de conducir; **d. school**, autoescuela *f*; **d. test**, examen *m* de conducir. **II** *adj* **1** (*rain*) intenso,-a. **2 d. force**, fuerza *f* motriz.

drizzle [drɪzəl] **I** *n* llovizna *f*. **II** *vi* lloviznar.

droll [drəʊl] *adj* gracioso,-a.

dromedary [dromədərɪ] *n* dromedario *m*.

drone [drəʊn] *vi* (*bee etc*) zumbar.

droop [dru:p] *vi* (*flower*) marchitarse; (*eyelids*) caerse.

drop [drop] **I** *n* **1** (*of liquid*) gota *f*; **eye drops**, colirio *m sing*. **2** (*sweet*) pastilla *f*. **3** (*descent*) desnivel *m*. **4** (*in price*) bajada *f*; (*in temperature*) descenso *m*. **II** *vtr* **1** (*let fall*) dejar caer; (*lower*) bajar; (*reduce*) disminuir; **to d. a hint**, soltar una indirecta. **2** (*abandon*) (*subject, charge etc*) abandonar, dejar; *Sport* **he was dropped from the team**, lo echaron del equipo. **3** (*omit*) (*spoken syllable*) comerse. **III** *vi* **1** (*object*) caerse; (*person*) tirarse; (*voice, price, temperature*) bajar; (*wind*) amainar; (*speed*) disminuir. ◆**drop by, drop in, drop round** *vi fam* (*visit*) pasarse (at, por). ◆**drop off I** *vi fam* (*fall asleep*) quedarse dormido,-a. **II** *vtr* (*deliver*) dejar. ◆**drop out** *vi* (*from college*) dejar los estudios; (*from society*) marginarse; (*from competition*) retirarse.

dropout [dropaʊt] *n fam pej* automarginado,-a *m,f*.

dropper [dropə^r] *n* cuentagotas *m inv*.

droppings [dropɪŋz] *npl* excrementos *mpl*.

drought [draʊt] *n* sequía *f*.

drove [drəʊv] *n* (*of cattle*) manada *f*.

drown [draʊn] **I** *vtr* **1** ahogar. **2** (*place*) inundar. **II** *vi* ahogarse; **he** (**was**) **drowned**, murió ahogado.

drowsy ['draʊzɪ] *adj* (**drowsier, drowsiest**) soñoliento,-a; **to feel d.**, tener sueño.

drudgery ['drʌdʒərɪ] *n* trabajo duro y pesado.

drug [drʌg] **I** *n* 1 (*medicine*) medicamento *m*. 2 (*narcotic*) droga *f*, estupefaciente *m*; **to be on drugs**, drogarse; **d. addict**, drogadicto,-a *m,f*; **d. addiction**, drogadicción *f*; **d. squad**, brigada *f* antidroga. **II** *vtr* (*person*) drogar; (*food, drink*) adulterar con drogas.

druggist ['drʌgɪst] *n* US farmacéutico,-a *m,f*.

drugstore ['drʌgstɔːr] *n* US establecimiento *m* donde se compran medicamentos, periódicos etc.

drum [drʌm] **I** *n* 1 tambor *m*; **to play the drums**, tocar la batería. 2 (*container*) bidón *m*. **II** *vi* *fig* (*with fingers*) tabalear. **III** *vtr fig* **to d. sth into sb**, enseñar algo a algn a machamartillo. ◆**drum up** *vtr fam* solicitar.

drummer ['drʌmər] *n* (*in band*) tambor *m*; (*in pop group*) batería *mf*.

drumstick ['drʌmstɪk] *n* Mus baqueta *f*, *fam* palillo *m*.

drunk [drʌŋk] **I** *adj* borracho,-a; **to get d.**, emborracharse. **II** *n* borracho,-a *m,f*.

drunkard ['drʌŋkəd] *n* borracho,-a *m,f*.

dry [draɪ] **I** *adj* (**drier, driest** *or* **dryer, dryest**) 1 seco,-a. 2 (*wit*) socarrón,-ona. **II** *vtr* (*pt & pp* **dried**) secar. **II** *vi* **to d. (off)**, secarse.

dry-clean ['draɪkliːn] *vtr* limpiar *or* lavar en seco.

dryer ['draɪər] *n* secadora *f*.

dub¹ [dʌb] *vtr* (*subtitle*) doblar (**into**, a).

dub² [dʌb] *vtr* 1 (*give nickname to*) apodar. 2 (*knight*) armar.

dubious ['djuːbɪəs] *adj* 1 (*morals etc*) dudoso,-a; (*compliment*) equívoco,-a. 2 (*doubting*) indeciso,-a.

Dublin ['dʌblɪn] *n* Dublín *m*.

duchess ['dʌtʃɪs] *n* duquesa *f*.

duck¹ [dʌk] *n* pato *m*; *Culin* pato *m*.

duck² [dʌk] **I** *vtr* 1 (*submerge*) dar una ahogadilla a. 2 (*evade*) esquivar. **II** *vi* 1 (*evade blow*) esquivar. 2 *fam* **to d. (out)**, rajarse.

duckling ['dʌklɪŋ] *n* patito *m*.

duct [dʌkt] *n* 1 (*for fuel etc*) conducto *m*; *Anat* canal *m*.

dud [dʌd] *fam* **I** *adj* 1 (*useless*) inútil; (*defective*) estropeado,-a. 2 (*banknote*) falso,-a; (*cheque*) sin fondos. **II** *n* 1 (*useless thing*) engañifa *f*; (*person*) desastre *m*.

due [djuː] **I** *adj* 1 (*expected*) esperado,-a; **the train is d.** (*to arrive*) **at ten**, el tren debe llegar a las diez. 2 *fml* (*proper*) debido,-a; **in d. course**, a su debido tiempo. 3 (*owing*) pagadero,-a; **how much are you d.?**, ¿cuánto te deben? 4 **to be d. to**, (*caused by*) deberse a;

d. to, (*because of*) debido de. **II** *adv* (*north etc*) derecho hacia. **III** *n* 1 **to give sb their d.**, dar a algn su merecido. 2 **dues**, (*fee*) cuota *f sing*.

duel ['djuːəl] *n* duelo *m*.

duet [djuː'et] *n* dúo *m*.

duffel ['dʌfəl] *n* **d. bag**, petate *m*; **d. coat**, trenca *f*.

dug [dʌg] *pt & pp* → **dig**.

duke [djuːk] *n* duque *m*.

dull [dʌl] **I** *adj* 1 (*boring*) pesado,-a; (*place*) sin interés. 2 (*light*) apagado,-a; (*weather*) gris. 3 (*sound, ache*) sordo,-a. 4 *fig* (*slow-witted*) torpe. **II** *vtr* 1 (*pain*) aliviar. 2 *fig* (*faculty*) embotar.

duly ['djuːlɪ] *adv fml* (*properly*) debidamente; (*as expected*) como era de esperar; (*in due course*) a su debido tiempo.

dumb [dʌm] *adj* 1 Med mudo,-a. 2 *fam* (*stupid*) tonto,-a. **II** *npl* **the d.**, los mudos.

dumbbell ['dʌmbel] *n* Sport pesa *f*.

dumbfounded [dʌm'faʊndɪd], **dumbstruck** ['dʌmstrʌk] *adj* pasmado,-a.

dummy ['dʌmɪ] *n* 1 (*sham*) imitación *f*. 2 (*in shop window*) maniquí *m*; (*of ventriloquist*) muñeco *m*. 3 GB (*for baby*) chupete *m*.

dump [dʌmp] **I** *n* 1 (*tip*) vertedero *m*; (*for old cars*) cementerio *m* (de coches). 2 *fam pej* (*place*) estercolero *m*; (*town*) poblacho *m*; (*dwelling*) tugurio *m*. 3 Mil depósito *m*. **II** *vtr* 1 (*rubbish*) verter; (*truck contents*) descargar. 2 (*person*) dejar; Com inundar el mercado con. 3 Comput (*transfer*) copiar de memoria interna.

dumping ['dʌmpɪŋ] *n* vertido *m*.

dumpling ['dʌmplɪŋ] *n* Culin bola *f* de masa hervida.

dumpy ['dʌmpɪ] *adj* (**dumpier, dumpiest**) *fam* rechoncho,-a.

dunce [dʌns] *n fam* tonto,-a *m,f*.

dune [djuːn] *n* (**sand**) **d.**, duna *f*.

dung [dʌŋ] *n* estiércol *m*.

dungarees [dʌŋgə'riːz] *npl* mono *m sing*.

dungeon ['dʌndʒən] *n* calabozo *m*, mazmorra *f*.

duo ['djuːəʊ] *n* Mus dúo *m*; fam pareja *f*.

dupe [djuːp] **I** *vtr* engañar. **II** *n* ingenuo,-a *m,f*.

duplex ['djuːpleks] *n* US (*house*) casa adosada; US **d. apartment**, dúplex *m inv*.

duplicate ['djuːplɪkeɪt] **I** *vtr* 1 (*copy*) duplicar; (*film, tape*) reproducir. 2 (*repeat*) repetir. 3 ['djuːplɪkɪt] *n* duplicado *m*; **in d.**, por duplicado.

durable ['djʊərəbəl] *adj* duradero,-a.

duration [djʊ'reɪʃən] *n fml* duración *f*.

duress [djʊ'res] *n fml* coacción *f*.

during ['djʊərɪŋ] *prep* durante.

dusk [dʌsk] *n fml* crepúsculo *m*; **at d.**, al anochecer.

dust [dʌst] **I** *n* polvo *m*; **d. cloud**, polvareda *f*; **d. jacket**, sobrecubierta *f*. **II** *vtr* 1 *(furniture)* quitar el polvo a. **2** *(cake)* espolvorear.

dustbin ['dʌstbɪn] *n GB* cubo *m* de la basura.

duster ['dʌstər] *n (for housework)* trapo *m or* paño *m* (del polvo); **feather d.**, plumero *m*.

dustman ['dʌstmən] *n GB* basurero *m*.

dustpan ['dʌstpæn] *n* recogedor *m*.

dusty ['dʌstɪ] *adj (dustier, dustiest)* polvoriento,-a.

Dutch [dʌtʃ] **I** *adj (dustier, dustiest)* holandés,-esa; *fig* **D. cap**, diafragma *m*. **II** *n* **1** *pl* the D., los holandeses. **2** *(language)* holandés *m*; **it's double D. to me**, me suena a chino. **III** *adv fig* **to go D. (with sb)**, pagar cada uno lo suyo.

Dutchman ['dʌtʃmən] *n* holandés *m*.

Dutchwoman ['dʌtʃwumən] *n* holandesa *f*.

duty ['dju:tɪ] *n* **1** deber *m*; **to do one's d.**, cumplir con su deber. **2** *(task)* función *f*. **3** **to be on d.**, estar de servicio; *Med Mil* estar de guardia; **d. chemist**, farmacia *f* de guardia. **4** *(tax)* impuesto *m*; **customs d.**, derechos *mpl* de aduana.

duty-free ['dju:tɪfri:] **I** *adj* libre de impuestos. **II** *adv* sin pagar impuestos. **III** *n* duty-free *m*.

duvet ['du:veɪ] *n* edredón *m*.

dwarf [dwɔːf] **I** *n (pl* **dwarves** [dwɔːvz]*) (person)* enano,-a *m.f*. **II** *vtr* hacer parecer pequeño,-a a.

dwell [dwel] *vi (pt & pp* **dwelt**) *fml* morar. ◆**dwell on** *vtr* hablar extensamente de; **let's not d. on it**, olvidémoslo.

dwelling ['dwelɪŋ] *n fml & hum* morada *f*, vivienda *f*.

dwindle ['dwɪndəl] *vi* menguar, disminuir.

dye [daɪ] **I** *n* tinte *m*. **II** *vtr (pres p* **dyeing**; *pt & pp* **dyed**) teñir; **to d. one's hair black**, teñirse el pelo de negro.

dying ['daɪɪŋ] *adj (person)* moribundo,-a *m.f*, agonizante *mf*; *fig (custom)* en vías de desaparición.

dyke [daɪk] *n* **1** *(bank)* dique *m*; *(causeway)* terraplén *m*. **2** *offens sl* tortillera *f*.

dynamic [daɪ'næmɪk] *adj* dinámico,-a.

dynamics [daɪ'næmɪks] *n* dinámica *f*.

dynamism ['daɪnəmɪzəm] *n fig* dinamismo *m*.

dynamite ['daɪnəmaɪt] *n* dinamita *f*.

dynamo ['daɪnəməʊ] *n* dínamo *f*.

dynasty ['dɪnəstɪ] *n* dinastía *f*.

dysentery ['dɪsəntrɪ] *n* disentería *f*.

dyslexia [dɪs'leksɪə] *n* dislexia *f*.

E

E, e [iː] *n* **1** *(the letter)* E, e *f*. **2** *Mus* mi *m*.

E *abbr of* **East**, Este, E.

each [iːtʃ] **I** *adj* cada; **e. day/month**, todos los días/meses; **e. person**, cada cual; **e. time I see him**, cada vez que lo veo. **II** *pron* **1** cada uno,-a; **two pounds e.**, dos libras cada uno; **we bought one e.**, nos compramos uno cada uno. **2 e. other**, el uno al otro; **they hate e. other**, se odian.

eager ['iːgər] *adj (anxious)* impaciente; *(desirous)* deseoso,-a; **e. to begin**, impaciente por empezar; **to be e. for success**, codiciar el éxito. ◆**eagerly** *adv (anxiously)* con impaciencia; *(keenly)* con ilusión.

eagle ['iːgəl] *n* águila *f*.

ear [ɪər] *n* **1** oreja *f*; *(sense of hearing)* oído *m*. **2** *(of corn etc)* espiga *f*.

earache ['ɪəreɪk] *n* dolor *m* de oídos.

eardrum ['ɪədrʌm] *n* tímpano *m*.

earl [ɜːl] *n* conde *m*.

earlobe ['ɪələʊb] *n* lóbulo *m*.

early ['ɜːlɪ] *(earlier, earliest)* **I** *adj* **1** *(before the usual time)* temprano,-a; **to have an e. night**, acostarse pronto; **you're e.!**, ¡qué pronto has venido! **2** *(at first stage, period)* at an **e. age**, siendo joven; **e. on**, al principio; **e. work**, obra de juventud; **in her e. forties**, a los cuarenta y pocos;

it's still e. days, aún es pronto. **3** *(in the near future)* **e. reply**, una respuesta pronta; **at the earliest**, cuanto antes. **II** *adv (before the expected time)* temprano, pronto; **earlier on**, antes; **five minutes e.**, con cinco minutos de adelanto; **to leave e.**, irse pronto. **2** *(near the beginning)* as **e. as 1914**, ya en 1914; **as e. as possible**, tan pronto como sea posible; **to book e.**, reservar con tiempo; **in e. July**, a principios de julio.

earmark ['ɪəmɑːk] *vtr* destinar *(for*, para, a).

earn [ɜːn] *vtr* **1** *(money)* ganar; **to e. one's living**, ganarse la vida. **2** *(reputation)* ganarse. **3 to e. interest**, cobrar interés *or* intereses.

earnest ['ɜːnɪst] **I** *adj* serio,-a, formal. **II** *n* **in e.**, de veras, en serio.

earnings ['ɜːnɪŋz] *npl* ingresos *mpl*.

earring ['ɪərɪŋ] *n* pendiente *m*.

earshot ['ɪəʃɒt] *n* **out of e.**, fuera del alcance del oído; **within e.**, al alcance del oído.

earth [ɜːθ] **I** *n* **1** tierra *f*; *fig* **to be down to e.**, ser práctico; *fam* **where/why on e. ...?**, ¿pero dónde/por qué demonios ...? **2** *Elec* toma *f* de tierra. **II** *vtr Elec* conectar a tierra.

earthenware ['ɜːðənweər] **I** *n* loza *f*. **II**

adj de barro.
earthquake ['ɜːθkweɪk] *n* terremoto *m*.
earthshattering ['ɜːθʃætərɪŋ] *adj* trascendental; e. **news**, noticia bomba.
earthworm ['ɜːθwɜːm] *n* lombriz *f* de tierra.
earthy ['ɜːθɪ] *adj* (*earthier*, *earthiest*) 1 (*taste*) terroso,-a. 2 (*bawdy*) tosco,-a.
earwig ['ɪəwɪg] *n* tijereta *f*.
ease [iːz] I *n* 1 (*freedom from discomfort*) tranquilidad *f*; *Mil* posición *f* de descanso; **at e.**, relajado,-a. 2 (*lack of difficulty*) facilidad *f*. 3 (*affluence*) comodidad *f*. 4 **e. of manner**, naturalidad *f*. II *vtr* 1 (*pain*) aliviar. 2 (*move gently*) deslizar con cuidado. ◆**ease off, ease up** *vi* 1 (*decrease*) disminuir. 2 (*slow down*) ir más despacio.
easel ['iːzəl] *n* caballete *m*.
east [iːst] I *n* este *m*; **the Middle E.**, el Oriente Medio. II *adj* del este, oriental; **E. Germany**, Alemania Oriental. III *adv* al *o* hacia el este.
Easter ['iːstər] *n* Semana Santa, Pascua *f*; **E. egg**, huevo *m* de Pascua; **E. Sunday**, Domingo *m* de Resurrección.
easterly ['iːstəlɪ] *adj* (*from the east*) del este; (*to the east*) hacia el este.
eastern ['iːstən] *adj* oriental, del este.
eastward(s) ['iːstwəd(z)] *adv* hacia el este.
easy ['iːzɪ] (*easier, easiest*) I *adj* 1 (*simple*) fácil, sencillo,-a. 2 (*unworried, comfortable*) cómodo,-a, tranquilo,-a; *fam* **I'm e.!**, me da lo mismo; **e. chair**, butacón *m*. II *adv* **go e. on the wine**, no te pases con el vino; *fam* **to take things e.**, tomarse las cosas con calma; *fam* **take it e.!**, ¡tranquilo! ◆**easily** fácilmente; **e. the best**, con mucho el mejor.
easy-going [iːzɪ'gəʊɪŋ] *adj* (*calm*) tranquilo,-a; (*lax*) despreocupado,-a; (*undemanding*) poco exigente.
eat [iːt] (*pt* **ate** [et, eɪt], *pp* **eaten**) *vtr* comer. ◆**eat away** *vtr* desgastar; (*metal*) corroer. ◆**eat into** *vtr* 1 (*wood*) roer. 2 *fig* (*savings*) consumir. ◆**eat out** *vi* comer fuera. ◆**eat up** *vtr* 1 (*meal*) terminar. 2 *fig* (*petrol*) consumir; (*miles*) recorrer rápidamente.
eatable ['iːtəbəl] *adj* comestible.
eaten ['iːtən] *pp* → **eat**.
eau de Cologne [əʊdəkə'ləʊn] *n* colonia *f*.
eaves [iːvz] *npl* alero *m sing*.
eavesdrop ['iːvzdrɒp] *vi* escuchar disimuladamente.
ebb [eb] I *n* reflujo *m*; **e. and flow**, flujo y reflujo; *fig* **to be at a low e.**, estar decaído. II *vi* 1 (*tide*) bajar; **to e. and flow**, subir y bajar. 2 *fig* **to e. away**, decaer.
ebony ['ebənɪ] I *n* ébano *m*. II *adj* de ébano.
eccentric [ɪk'sentrɪk] *adj & nm,f*

excéntrico,-a.
ecclesiastic [ɪkliːzɪ'æstɪk] *adj & nm,f* eclesiástico,-a.
echelon ['eʃəlɒn] *n* escalafón *m*.
echo ['ekəʊ] I *n* (*pl* **echoes**) eco *m*. II *vtr* (*repeat*) repetir. III *vi* resonar, hacer eco.
eclectic [ɪ'klektɪk] *adj* ecléctico,-a.
eclipse [ɪ'klɪps] I *n* eclipse *m*. II *vtr* eclipsar.
ecological [iːkə'lɒdʒɪkəl] *adj* ecológico,-a.
ecology [ɪ'kɒlədʒɪ] *n* ecología *f*.
economic [iːkə'nɒmɪk] *adj* económico,-a; (*profitable*) rentable.
economical [iːkə'nɒmɪkəl] *adj* económico,-a.
economics [iːkə'nɒmɪks] *n sing* (*science*) economía *f*; *Educ* (ciencias *fpl*) económicas *fpl*.
economist [ɪ'kɒnəmɪst] *n* economista *mf*.
economize [ɪ'kɒnəmaɪz] *vi* economizar.
economy [ɪ'kɒnəmɪ] *n* 1 *Pol* **the e.**, la economía. 2 (*saving*) ahorro *m*; **e. class**, clase *f* turista.
ecosystem ['iːkəʊsɪstəm] *n* ecosistema *m*.
ecstasy ['ekstəsɪ] *n* éxtasis *m*.
ecstatic [ek'stætɪk] *adj* extático,-a.
Ecuador ['ekwədɔːr] *n* Ecuador.
eczema ['eksɪmə] *n* eczema *m*.
eddy [edɪ] I *n* remolino *m*. II *vi* arremolinarse.
edge [edʒ] I *n* borde *m*; (*of knife*) filo *m*; (*of coin*) canto *m*; (*of water*) orilla *f*; **on the e. of town**, en las afueras de la ciudad; **to have the e. on sb**, llevar ventaja a algn; *fig* **to be on the e.**, tener los nervios de punta. II *vtr Sew* ribetear. III *vi* **to e. closer**, acercarse lentamente; **to e. forward**, avanzar poco a poco.
edgeways ['edʒweɪz] *adv* de lado; *fig* **I couldn't get a word in e.**, no pude decir ni pío.
edging ['edʒɪŋ] *n* borde *m*; *Sew* ribete *m*.
edgy ['edʒɪ] *adj* (*edgier, edgiest*) nervioso,-a.
edible ['edɪbəl] *adj* comestible.
edict ['iːdɪkt] *Hist n* edicto *m*; *Jur* decreto *m*.
Edinburgh ['edɪnbrə] *n* Edimburgo.
edit ['edɪt] *vtr* 1 (*prepare for printing*) preparar para la imprenta. 2 (*rewrite*) corregir; **to e. sth out**, suprimir algo. 3 *Press* ser redactor,-a de. 4 *Cin Rad TV* montar; (*cut*) cortar.
edition [ɪ'dɪʃən] *n* edición *f*.
editor ['edɪtər] *n* (*of book*) editor,-a *m,f*; *Press* redactor, -a *m,f*; *Cin TV* montador,-a *m,f*.
editorial [edɪ'tɔːrɪəl] I *adj* editorial; **e. staff**, redacción *f*. II *n* editorial *m*.
educate ['edjʊkeɪt] *vtr* educar.
educated ['edjʊkeɪtɪd] *adj* culto,-a.
education [edjʊ'keɪʃən] *n* 1 (*schooling*) enseñanza *f*; **adult e.**, educación *f* de

adultos; **Ministry of E.**, Ministerio *m* de Educación. 2 *(training)* formación *f.* 3 *(studies)* estudios *mpl.* 4 *(culture)* cultura *f.*

educational [edjʊˈkeɪʃənəl] *adj* educativo,-a, educacional.

eel [iːl] *n* anguila *f.*

eerie [ˈɪərɪ] *adj (eerier, eeriest)* siniestro,-a.

efface [ɪˈfeɪs] *vtr* borrar.

effect [ɪˈfekt] I *n* 1 efecto *m*; **in e.**, efectivamente; **to come into e.**, entrar en vigor; **to have an e. on**, afectar a; **to no e.**, sin resultado alguno; **to take e.**, *(drug)* surtir efecto; *(law)* entrar en vigor. 2 *(impression)* impresión *f.* 3 **effects,** *(possessions)* efectos *mpl.* II *vtr fml* provocar.

effective [ɪˈfektɪv] *adj* 1 *(successful)* eficaz. 2 *(real)* efectivo,-a. 3 *(impressive)* impresionante. ◆**effectively** *adv* 1 *(successfully)* eficazmente. 2 *(in fact)* en efecto.

effeminate [ɪˈfemɪnɪt] *adj* afeminado,-a.

effervescent [efəˈvesənt] *adj* efervescente.

efficiency [ɪˈfɪʃənsɪ] *n (of person)* eficacia *f*; *(of machine)* rendimiento *m.*

efficient [ɪˈfɪʃənt] *adj* eficaz, eficiente; *(machine)* de buen rendimiento.

effigy [ˈefɪdʒɪ] *n* efigie *f.*

effluent [ˈefluənt] *n* vertidos *mpl.*

effort [ˈefət] *n* 1 esfuerzo *m*; **to make an e.**, hacer un esfuerzo, esforzarse. 2 *(attempt)* intento *m.*

effortless [ˈefətlɪs] *adj* sin esfuerzo.

effrontery [ɪˈfrʌntərɪ] *n* desfachatez *f.*

effusive [ɪˈfjuːsɪv] *adj* efusivo,-a.

eg [ˈiːˈdʒiː] *abbr of exempli gratia, (p. ej).*

egalitarian [ɪgælɪˈteərɪən] *adj* igualitario,-a.

egg [eg] I *n* huevo *m*; *fam fig* **to put all one's eggs in one basket**, jugárselo todo a una carta; **e. cup**, huevera *f*; **e. timer**, reloj *m* de arena; **e. white**, clara *f* de huevo. II *vtr* **to e. sb on (to do sth)**, empujar a algn (a hacer algo).

eggplant [ˈegplɑːnt] *n US* berenjena *f.*

eggshell [ˈegʃel] *n* cáscara *f* de huevo.

ego [ˈiːgəʊ, ˈegəʊ] *n* 1 ego *m*; **e. trip**, autobombo *m.* 2 *fam* amor propio.

egocentric(al) [iːgəʊˈsentrɪk(ə)l] *adj* egocéntrico,-a.

egoism [ˈiːgəʊɪzəm] *n* egoísmo *m.*

egoist [ˈiːgəʊɪst] *n* egoísta *mf.*

egotistic(al) [iːgəʊˈtɪstɪk(ə)l] *adj* egotista.

Egypt [ˈiːdʒɪpt] *n* Egipto.

Egyptian [ɪˈdʒɪpʃən] *adj & n* egipcio,-a *(m,f).*

eiderdown [ˈaɪdədaʊn] *n* edredón *m.*

eight [eɪt] *adj & n* ocho *(m) inv.*

eighteen [eɪˈtiːn] *adj & n* dieciocho *(m) inv.*

eighteenth [eɪˈtiːnθ] I *adj & n* decimoctavo *(m,f).* II *n (fraction)* decimoctavo *m.*

eighth [eɪtθ] I *adj & n* octavo,-a *(m,f).* II *n (fraction)* octavo *m.*

eighty [ˈeɪtɪ] *adj & n* ochenta *(m) inv.*

Eire [ˈeərə] *n* Eire.

either [ˈaɪðəʳ, ˈiːðəʳ] I *pron* 1 *(affirmative)* cualquiera; **e. of them**, cualquiera de los dos; **e. of us**, cualquiera de nosotros dos. 2 *(negative)* ninguno, ninguna, ni el uno ni el otro, ni la una ni la otra; **I don't want e. of them**, no quiero ninguno de los dos. II *adj (both)* cada, los dos, las dos; **on e. side**, en ambos lados; **in e. case**, en cualquiera de los dos casos. III *conj* o; **e. ... or ...**, o ... o ...; **e. Friday or Saturday**, o (bien) el viernes o el sábado. IV *adv (after negative)* tampoco; **I don't want to do it e.**, yo tampoco quiero hacerlo.

ejaculate [ɪˈdʒækjʊleɪt] *vi (man)* eyacular.

eject [ɪˈdʒekt] I *vtr* expulsar. II *vi Av* eyectarse.

eke [iːk] *vtr* **e. out a living**, ganarse la vida a duras penas.

elaborate [ɪˈlæbəreɪt] I *vtr* 1 *(devise)* elaborar. 2 *(explain)* explicar detalladamente. II *vi* explicarse; **to e. on sth**, explicar algo con más detalles. III [ɪˈlæbərɪt] *adj* 1 *(complicated)* complicado,-a. 2 *(detailed)* detallado,-a; *(style)* esmerado,-a.

elapse [ɪˈlæps] *vi* transcurrir, pasar.

elastic [ɪˈlæstɪk] I *adj* elástico,-a; *fig* flexible; **e. band**, goma elástica. II *n* elástico *m.*

Elastoplast® [ɪˈlɑːstəplɑːst] *n* tirita *f.*

elated [ɪˈleɪtɪd] *adj* eufórico,-a.

elation [ɪˈleɪʃən] *n* regocijo *m.*

elbow [ˈelbəʊ] I *n* 1 codo *m*; *fig* **e. room**, espacio *m.* 2 *(bend)* recodo *m.* II *vtr* **to e. sb**, dar un codazo a algn.

elder[1] [ˈeldəʳ] I *adj* mayor. II *n* **the elders**, los ancianos.

elder[2] [ˈeldəʳ] *n Bot* saúco *m.*

elderly [ˈeldəlɪ] I *adj* anciano,-a. II *npl* **the e.**, los ancianos.

eldest [ˈeldɪst] I *adj* mayor. II *n* el or la mayor.

elect [ɪˈlekt] I *n* 1 *Pol* elegir. 2 **to e. to do sth**, *(choose)* decidir hacer algo. II *adj* **the president e.**, el presidente electo.

election [ɪˈlekʃən] I *n* elección *f*; **general e.**, elecciones *fpl* generales. II *adj* electoral.

electioneering [ɪlekʃəˈnɪərɪŋ] *n* electoralismo *m.*

elector [ɪˈlektəʳ] *n* elector,-a *m,f.*

electoral [ɪˈlektərəl] *adj* electoral.

electorate [ɪˈlektərɪt] *n* electorado *m.*

electric [ɪˈlektrɪk] *adj* 1 eléctrico,-a; **e. blanket**, manta eléctrica; **e. chair**, silla eléctrica; **e. shock**, electrochoque *m.* 2 *fig* electrizante.

electrical [ɪ'lektrɪkəl] *adj* eléctrico,-a.

electrician [ɪlek'trɪʃən] *n* electricista *mf*.

electricity [ɪlek'trɪsɪtɪ] *n* electricidad *f*; e. bill, recibo *m* de la luz.

electrify [ɪ'lektrɪfaɪ] *vtr* 1 (*railway line*) electrificar. 2 *fig* (*excite*) electrizar.

electrocute [ɪ'lektrəkjuːt] *vtr* electrocutar.

electron [ɪ'lektrɒn] *n* electrón *m*.

electronic [ɪlek'trɒnɪk] *adj* electrónico,-a.

electronics [ɪlek'trɒnɪks] *n* 1 (*science*) electrónica *f*. 2 (*of machine*) componentes *mpl* electrónicos.

elegant ['elɪgənt] *adj* elegante.

element ['elɪmənt] *n* 1 elemento *m*. 2 (*part*) parte *f*. 3 (*electrical*) resistencia *f*. 4 *fam fig* to be in one's e., estar en su salsa.

elementary [elɪ'mentərɪ] *adj* (*basic*) elemental; (*not developed*) rudimentario,-a; (*easy*) fácil; e. school, escuela primaria.

elephant ['elɪfənt] *n* elefante *m*.

elevate ['elɪveɪt] *vtr* elevar; (*in rank*) ascender.

elevation [elɪ'veɪʃən] *n* 1 elevación *f*. 2 *Archit* alzado *m*. 3 (*above sea level*) altitud *f*.

elevator ['elɪveɪtər] *n US* ascensor *m*.

eleven [ɪ'levən] *adj & once* (*m*) *inv*.

elevenses [ɪ'levənzɪz] *npl fam* bocadillo *m* de las once.

eleventh [ɪ'levənθ] I *adj & n,f* undécimo,-a. II *n* (*fraction*) undécimo *m*.

elicit [ɪ'lɪsɪt] *vtr* obtener.

eligible ['elɪdʒəbl] *adj* apto,-a; he isn't e. to vote, no tiene derecho al voto.

eliminate [ɪ'lɪmɪneɪt] *vtr* eliminar.

elite [eɪ'liːt] *n* élite *f*.

elitist [ɪ'liːtɪst] *adj* elitista.

elm [elm] *n* olmo *m*.

elocution [elə'kjuːʃən] *n* elocución *f*.

elongate [iː'lɒŋgeɪt] *vtr* alargar.

elope [ɪ'ləup] *vi* fugarse para casarse.

eloquent ['eləkwənt] *adj* elocuente.

else [els] *adv* 1 anyone e., alguien más; anything e.?, ¿algo más? everything e., todo lo demás; no-one e., nadie más; someone e., otro,-a; something e., otra cosa, algo más; somewhere e., en otra parte; what e.?, ¿qué más?; where e.?, ¿en qué otro sitio? 2 or e., (*otherwise*) si no.

elsewhere [els'weər] *adv* en otra parte.

elucidate [ɪ'luːsɪdeɪt] *vtr* aclarar.

elude [ɪ'luːd] *vtr* 1 (*escape*) eludir; his name eludes me, no consigo acordarme de su nombre. 2 (*avoid*) esquivar.

elusive [ɪ'luːsɪv] *adj* esquivo,-a; (*evasive*) evasivo,-a.

emaciated [ɪ'meɪsɪeɪtɪd] *adj* demacrado,-a.

emanate ['eməneɪt] *vi* provenir (from, de).

emancipate [ɪ'mænsɪpeɪt] *vtr* emancipar.

emancipation [ɪmænsɪ'peɪʃən] *n* emancipación *f*.

embankment [ɪm'bæŋkmənt] *n* 1 (*made of earth*) terraplén *m*. 2 (*of river*) dique *m*.

embargo [em'bɑːgəu], *n* (*pl* embargoes) embargo *m*.

embark [em'bɑːk] I *vtr* (*merchandize*) embarcar. II *vi* embarcar, embarcarse; *fig* to e. upon, emprender; (*sth difficult*) embarcarse en.

embarkation [embɑː'keɪʃən] *n* embarque *m*.

embarrass [ɪm'bærəs] *vtr* avergonzar.

embarrassed [ɪm'bærəst] *adj* avergonzado,-a.

embarrassing [ɪm'bærəsɪŋ] *adj* embarazoso,-a.

embarrassment [ɪm'bærəsmənt] *n* vergüenza *f*.

embassy ['embəsɪ] *n* embajada *f*.

embed [ɪm'bed] *vtr* (*jewels*) incrustar; *fig* grabar.

embellish [ɪm'belɪʃ] *vtr* embellecer; (*story*) exagerar.

ember ['embər] *n* ascua *f*, rescoldo *m*.

embezzle [ɪm'bezəl] *vtr* desfalcar, malversar.

embezzlement [ɪm'bezəlmənt] *n* malversación *f*.

embitter [ɪm'bɪtər] *vtr* amargar.

embittered [ɪm'bɪtəd] *adj* amargado,-a, resentido,-a.

emblem ['embləm] *n* emblema *m*.

embody [ɪm'bɒdɪ] *vtr* 1 (*include*) abarcar. 2 (*personify*) encarnar.

embossed [ɪm'bɒst] *adj* en relieve.

embrace [ɪm'breɪs] I *vtr* 1 abrazar. 2 (*accept*) adoptar. 3 (*include*) abarcar. II *vi* abrazarse. III *n* abrazo *m*.

embroider [ɪm'brɔɪdər] *vtr* 1 *Sew* bordar. 2 *fig* (*story, truth*) adornar, embellecer.

embroidery [ɪm'brɔɪdərɪ] *n* bordado *m*.

embryo ['embrɪəu] *n* embrión *m*.

emerald ['emərəld] *n* esmeralda *f*.

emerge [ɪ'mɜːdʒ] *vi* salir; (*problem*) surgir; it emerged that ..., resultó que ....

emergence [ɪ'mɜːdʒəns] *n* aparición *f*.

emergency [ɪ'mɜːdʒənsɪ] *n* emergencia *f*; *Med* urgencia *f*; in an e., en caso de emergencia; e. exit, salida *f* de emergencia; e. landing, aterrizaje forzoso; e. measures, medidas *fpl* de urgencia; *Aut* e. stop, frenazo *m* en seco; *Pol* state of e., estado *m* de excepción.

emery ['emərɪ] *n* e. board, lima *f* de uñas.

emigrant ['emɪgrənt] *n* emigrante *mf*.

emigrate ['emɪgreɪt] *vi* emigrar.

emigration [emɪ'greɪʃən] *n* emigración *f*.

eminent ['emɪnənt] *adj* eminente.

emission [ɪ'mɪʃən] *n* emisión *f*.

emit [ɪ'mɪt] *vtr* (*signals*) emitir; (*smells*) despedir; (*sound*) producir.

emotion [ɪˈməʊʃən] *n* emoción *f*.

emotional [ɪˈməʊʃənəl] *adj* 1 emocional. 2 *(moving)* conmovedor,-a.

emotive [ɪˈməʊtɪv] *adj* emotivo,-a.

emperor [ˈempərə^r] *n* emperador *m*.

emphasis [ˈemfəsɪs] *n (pl* **emphases** [ˈemfəsiːz]) énfasis *m;* **to place e. on sth,** hacer hincapié en algo.

emphasize [ˈemfəsaɪz] *vtr* subrayar, hacer hincapié en; *(insist)* insistir; *(highlight)* hacer resaltar.

emphatic [emˈfætɪk] *adj (forceful)* enfático,-a; *(convinced)* categórico,-a. ◆**emphatically** *adv* categóricamente.

empire [ˈempaɪə^r] *n* imperio *m*.

employ [ɪmˈplɔɪ] *vtr* emplear; *(time)* ocupar.

employee [emˈplɔɪiː, emplɔɪˈiː] *n* empleado,-a *m, f*.

employer [ɪmˈplɔɪə^r] *n* patrón,-ona *m, f*.

employment [ɪmˈplɔɪmənt] *n* empleo *m;* **e. agency,** agencia *f* de colocaciones; **full e.,** pleno empleo.

empower [ɪmˈpaʊə^r] *vtr* autorizar.

empress [ˈemprɪs] *n* emperatriz *f*.

emptiness [ˈemptɪnɪs] *n* vacío *m*.

empty [ˈemptɪ] **I** *adj (emptier, emptiest)* vacío,-a; **an e. house,** una casa deshabitada; **e. promises,** promesas *fpl* vanas. **II** *vtr* vaciar. **III** *vi* 1 vaciarse. 2 *(river)* desembocar (**into,** en). **IV** *npl* **empties,** envases vacíos.

empty-handed [emptɪˈhændɪd] *adj* con las manos vacías.

emulate [ˈemjʊleɪt] *vtr* emular.

emulsion [ɪˈmʌlʃən] *n* emulsión *f;* **e. paint,** pintura *f* mate.

enable [ɪˈneɪbəl] *vtr* permitir.

enact [ɪˈnækt] *vtr (play)* representar; *(law)* promulgar.

enamel [ɪˈnæməl] *n* esmalte *m*.

enamoured, *US* **enamored** [ɪˈnæməd] *adj* enamorado,-a; **to be e. of** *or* **by sth,** encantarle algo a algn.

encase [ɪnˈkeɪs] *vtr* encased in, revestido de.

enchant [ɪnˈtʃɑːnt] *vtr* encantar.

enchanting [ɪnˈtʃɑːntɪŋ] *adj* encantador,-a.

encircle [ɪnˈsɜːkəl] *vtr* rodear.

enclave [ˈenkleɪv] *n* enclave *m*.

enclose [ɪnˈkləʊz] *vtr* 1 *(surround)* rodear. 2 *(fence in)* cercar. 3 *(in envelope)* adjuntar; **please find enclosed,** le enviamos adjunto.

enclosure [ɪnˈkləʊʒə^r] *n* 1 *(fenced area)* cercado *m*. 2 *(in envelope)* documento adjunto. 3 *(of racecourse)* recinto *m*.

encompass [ɪnˈkʌmpəs] *vtr* abarcar.

encore [ˈɒŋkɔː^r] **I** *interj* ¡otra!, ¡bis! **II** *n* repetición *f*, bis *m*.

encounter [ɪnˈkaʊntə^r] **I** *n (meeting)* encuentro *m*. **II** *vtr* encontrar, encontrarse con; *(problems)* tropezar con.

encourage [ɪnˈkʌrɪdʒ] *vtr* 1 *(person)* animar. 2 *(tourism, trade)* fomentar.

encouragement [ɪnˈkʌrɪdʒmənt] *n* estímulo *m*.

encroach [ɪnˈkrəʊtʃ] *vi* **to e. on,** *(territory)* invadir; *(rights)* usurpar; *(time, freedom)* quitar.

encrusted [ɪnˈkrʌstɪd] *adj* incrustado,-a (**with,** de).

encumber [ɪnˈkʌmbə^r] *vtr* estorbar; *(with debts)* gravar.

encyclop(a)edia [ensaɪkləʊˈpiːdɪə] *n* enciclopedia *f*.

end [end] **I** *n* 1 *(of stick)* punta *f; (of street)* final *m; (of table)* extremo *m; fig* **to make ends meet,** llegar a final de mes; *fig* **it makes my hair stand on e.,** me pone el pelo de punta. 2 *(conclusion)* fin *m,* final *m;* **in the e.,** al final; **for hours on e.,** hora tras hora; **no e. of,** un sinfín de; **to bring an e. to sth,** poner fin a algo; **to put an e. to,** acabar con. 3 *(aim)* objetivo *m,* fin *m;* **to no e.,** en vano. **II** *vtr* acabar, terminar. **III** *vi* acabarse, terminarse. ◆**end up** *vi* terminar; **it ended up in the dustbin,** fue a parar al cubo de la basura; **to e. up doing sth,** terminar por hacer algo.

endanger [ɪnˈdeɪndʒə^r] *vtr* poner en peligro.

endangered [ɪnˈdeɪndʒəd] *adj* en peligro.

endearing [ɪnˈdɪərɪŋ] *adj* simpático,-a.

endeavour, *US* **endeavor** [ɪnˈdevə^r] **I** *n* esfuerzo *m*. **II** *vtr* intentar, procurar.

ending [ˈendɪŋ] *n* final *m*.

endive [ˈendaɪv] *n Bot* 1 endibia *f.* 2 *US* escarola *f*.

endless [ˈendlɪs] *adj* interminable.

endorse [ɪnˈdɔːs] *vtr* 1 *Fin* endosar. 2 *(approve)* aprobar; *(support)* apoyar.

endorsement [ɪnˈdɔːsmənt] *n* 1 *Fin* endoso *m.* 2 *Aut* nota *f* de sanción. 3 *(approval)* aprobación *f*.

endow [ɪnˈdaʊ] *vtr* dotar; **to be endowed with,** estar dotado,-a de.

endurance [ɪnˈdjʊərəns] *n* resistencia *f*.

endure [ɪnˈdjʊə^r] **I** *vtr (bear)* aguantar, soportar. **II** *vi* perdurar.

enemy [ˈenəmɪ] *adj & n* enemigo,-a *m, f*).

energetic [enəˈdʒetɪk] *adj* enérgico,-a.

energy [ˈenədʒɪ] *n* energía *f*.

enforce [ɪnˈfɔːs] *vtr (law)* hacer cumplir.

enforcement [ɪnˈfɔːsmənt] *n* aplicación *f*.

engage [ɪnˈɡeɪdʒ] *vtr* 1 *(hire)* contratar. 2 *(attention)* llamar. 3 *(in conversation)* entablar. 4 *Tech* engranar; *Aut* **to e. the clutch,** pisar el embrague.

engaged [ɪnˈɡeɪdʒd] *adj* 1 *(betrothed)* prometido,-a; **to get e.,** prometerse. 2 *(busy)* ocupado,-a; *Tel* **it's e.,** está comunicando.

engagement [ɪnˈɡeɪdʒmənt] *n* 1 *(betrothal)* petición *f* de mano; *(period)* noviazgo *m*; e. ring, anillo *m* de compromiso. 2 (*appointment*) cita *f*. 3 *Mil* combate *m*.

engaging [ɪnˈgeɪdʒɪŋ] *adj* simpático,-a, agradable.

engender [ɪnˈdʒendər] *vtr* engendrar.

engine [ˈendʒɪn] *n* motor *m*; *Rail* locomotora *f*; e. room, sala *f* de máquinas; e. driver, maquinista *mf*.

engineer [endʒɪˈnɪər] I *n* 1 ingeniero,-a *m, f*; civil e., ingeniero de caminos. 2 *US Rail* maquinista *mf*. II *vtr fig* (*contrive*) maquinar.

engineering [endʒɪˈnɪərɪŋ] *n* ingeniería *f*; electrical e., electrotecnia *f*; civil e., ingeniería civil.

England [ˈɪŋglənd] *n* Inglaterra *f*.

English [ˈɪŋglɪʃ] I *adj* inglés,-esa. II *n* 1 (*language*) inglés *m*. 2 *pl* the E., los ingleses.

Englishman [ˈɪŋglɪʃmən] *n* inglés *m*.

English-speaking [ˈɪŋglɪʃspiːkɪŋ] *adj* de habla inglesa.

Englishwoman [ˈɪŋglɪʃwumən] *n* inglesa *f*.

engraving [ɪnˈgreɪvɪŋ] *n* grabado *m*.

engrossed [ɪnˈgrəʊst] *adj* absorto,-a (**in**, en).

engulf [ɪnˈgʌlf] *vtr* tragarse.

enhance [ɪnˈhɑːns] *vtr* (*beauty*) realzar; (*power, chances*) aumentar.

enigma [ɪˈnɪgmə] *n* enigma *m*.

enjoy [ɪnˈdʒɔɪ] I *vtr* 1 disfrutar de; to e. oneself, pasarlo bien. 2 (*benefit from*) gozar de.

enjoyable [ɪnˈdʒɔɪəbəl] *adj* agradable; (*amusing*) divertido,-a.

enjoyment [ɪnˈdʒɔɪmənt] *n* placer *m*, gusto *m*.

enlarge [ɪnˈlɑːdʒ] I *vtr* extender, ampliar; *Phot* ampliar. II *vi* to e. upon a subject, extenderse sobre un tema.

enlargement [ɪnˈlɑːdʒmənt] *n Phot* ampliación *f*.

enlighten [ɪnˈlaɪtən] *vtr* iluminar.

enlightened [ɪnˈlaɪtənd] *adj* 1 (*learned*) culto,-a; (*informed*) bien informado,-a. 2 *Hist* ilustrado,-a.

enlightenment [ɪnˈlaɪtənmənt] *n* the Age of E., el Siglo de las Luces.

enlist [ɪnˈlɪst] I *vtr Mil* reclutar; to e. sb's help, conseguir ayuda de algn. II *vi Mil* alistarse.

enmity [ˈenmɪtɪ] *n* enemistad *f*, hostilidad *f*.

enormous [ɪˈnɔːməs] *adj* enorme.
◆**enormously** *adv* enormemente; I e. enjoyed myself ..., lo pasé genial.

enough [ɪˈnʌf] I *adj* bastante, suficiente; e. books, bastantes libros; e. money, bastante dinero; have we got e. petrol?, ¿tenemos suficiente gasolina? II *adv* bastante; oddly e. ..., lo curioso es que ...; sure e., en efecto. III *n* lo bastante,

lo suficiente; e. to live on, lo suficiente para vivir; it isn't e., no basta; more than e., más que suficiente; fam e. is e., ya está!; fam I've had e.!, estoy harto!

enquire [ɪnˈkwaɪər] *vi* preguntar.

enquiry [ɪnˈkwaɪərɪ] *n* 1 (*question*) pregunta *f*; to make an e., preguntar; enquiries, información *f*. 2 (*investigation*) investigación *f*.

enrage [ɪnˈreɪdʒ] *vtr* enfurecer.

enrich [ɪnˈrɪtʃ] *vtr* enriquecer.

enrol, *US* **enroll** [ɪnˈrəʊl] I *vtr* matricular. II *vi* matricularse, inscribirse.

enrolment [ɪnˈrəʊlmənt] *n* matrícula *f*.

en route [ɒnˈruːt] *adv* en or por el camino.

ensign [ˈensaɪn] *n* (*flag*) bandera *f*; *Naut* pabellón *m*.

enslave [ɪnˈsleɪv] *vtr* esclavizar.

ensue [ɪnˈsjuː] *vi* 1 (*follow*) seguir. 2 (*result*) resultar (**from**, de).

ensure [ɪnˈʃʊər] *vtr* asegurar.

entail [ɪnˈteɪl] *vtr* (*involve*) suponer.

entangle [ɪnˈtæŋgəl] *vtr* enredar.

enter [ˈentər] I *vtr* 1 (*go into*) entrar en; *fig* (*join*) ingresar en. 2 (*write down*) apuntar, anotar. 3 to e. one's name for a course, (*register*) matricularse en un curso. 4 *Comput* dar entrada a. II *vi* entrar.
◆**enter into** *vtr* 1 (*agreement*) firmar; (*negotiations*) iniciar; (*bargain*) cerrar. 2 (*relations*) establecer; (*conversation*) entablar.

enterprise [ˈentəpraɪz] *n* empresa *f*; free e., libre empresa; private e., iniciativa privada; (*as a whole*) el sector privado; public e., el sector público.

enterprising [ˈentəpraɪzɪŋ] *adj* emprendedor,-a.

entertain [entəˈteɪn] I *vtr* 1 (*amuse*) divertir. 2 (*consider*) considerar; to e. an idea, abrigar una idea. II *vi* tener invitados.

entertainer [entəˈteɪnər] *n* artista *mf*.

entertaining [entəˈteɪnɪŋ] *adj* divertido,-a.

entertainment [entəˈteɪnmənt] *n* 1 diversión *f*. 2 *Theat* espectáculo *m*.

enthralling [ɪnˈθrɔːlɪŋ] *adj* fascinante.

enthuse [ɪnˈθjuːz] *vi* entusiasmarse (**over**, por).

enthusiasm [ɪnˈθjuːzɪæzəm] *n* entusiasmo *m*.

enthusiast [ɪnˈθjuːzɪæst] *n* entusiasta *mf*.

enthusiastic [ɪnθjuːzɪˈæstɪk] *adj* entusiasta; (*praise*) caluroso,-a; to be e. about sth, entusiasmarse por algo.

entice [ɪnˈtaɪs] *vtr* seducir, atraer.

enticing [ɪnˈtaɪsɪŋ] *adj* atractivo,-a, tentador,-a.

entire [ɪnˈtaɪər] *adj* entero,-a, todo,-a.
◆**entirely** *adv* 1 (*completely*) totalmente. 2 (*solely*) exclusivamente.

entirety [ɪnˈtaɪərɪtɪ] *n* in its e., en su totalidad.

entitle [ɪn'taɪtl] *vtr* 1 dar derecho a; **to be entitled to,** tener derecho a. 2 (*book etc*) titular.

entity ['entɪtɪ] *n* entidad *f*.

entourage [ɒntʊ'rɑːʒ] *n* séquito *m*.

entrails ['entreɪlz] *npl* tripas *fpl*; *fig* entrañas *fpl*.

entrance[1] ['entrəns] *n* 1 entrada *f*; **e. fee,** (*to museum etc*) entrada; (*to organization*) cuota *f*. 2 (*admission*) ingreso *m*; **e. examination,** examen *m* de ingreso.

entrance[2] [ɪn'trɑːns] *vtr* encantar.

entrant ['entrənt] *n* (*in competition*) participante *mf*; (*applicant*) aspirante *mf*.

entreat [ɪn'triːt] *vtr fml* suplicar, rogar.

entrenched [ɪn'trentʃt] *adj* firmemente enraizado,-a.

entrepreneur [ɒntrəprə'nɜːr] *n* empresario,-a *mf*.

entrust [ɪn'trʌst] *vtr* encargar (**with**, de); **to e. sth to sb,** dejar algo al cuidado de algn.

entry ['entrɪ] *n* 1 (*entrance*) entrada *f*; **no e.,** dirección prohibida. 2 (*in competition*) participante *mf*.

enumerate [ɪ'njuːməreɪt] *vtr* enumerar.

enunciate [ɪ'nʌnsɪeɪt] *vtr* (*words*) articular; (*ideas*) formular.

envelop [ɪn'veləp] *vtr* envolver.

envelope ['envələʊp] *n* sobre *m*.

envious ['envɪəs] *adj* envidioso,-a; **to feel e.,** tener envidia.

environment [ɪn'vaɪərənmənt] *n* medio *m* ambiente.

environmental [ɪnvaɪərən'mentəl] *adj* medioambiental.

envisage [ɪn'vɪzɪdʒ] *vtr* (*imagine*) imaginarse; (*foresee*) prever.

envoy ['envɔɪ] *n* enviado,-a *m,f*.

envy ['envɪ] I *n* envidia *f*. II *vtr* envidiar, tener envidia de.

enzyme ['enzaɪm] *n* enzima *m*.

ephemeral [ɪ'femərəl] *adj* efímero,-a.

epic ['epɪk] I *n* epopeya *f*. II *adj* épico,-a.

epidemic [epɪ'demɪk] *n* epidemia *f*; *fig* (*of crime etc*) ola *f*.

epilepsy ['epɪlepsɪ] *n* epilepsia *f*.

epilogue, US **epilog** ['epɪlɒg] *n* epílogo *m*.

episode ['epɪsəʊd] *n* episodio *m*.

epistle [ɪ'pɪsəl] *n* epístola *f*.

epitaph ['epɪtɑːf] *n* epitafio *m*.

epitome [ɪ'pɪtəmɪ] *n fml* personificación *f*.

epitomize [ɪ'pɪtəmaɪz] *vtr fml* personificar.

epoch ['iːpɒk] *n* época *f*.

equable ['ekwəbəl] *adj* 1 (*person*) ecuánime. 2 (*climate*) uniforme.

equal ['iːkwəl] I *adj* igual; **to be e. to the occasion,** estar a la altura de las circunstancias; **e. pay,** igualdad *f* de salarios. II *n* igual *mf*; **to treat sb as an e.,**

tratar a algn de igual a igual. III *vtr* 1 *Math* equivaler. 2 (*match*) igualar.

◆equally *adv* igualmente; **e. pretty,** igual de bonito; **to share sth e.,** dividir algo en partes iguales.

· **equality** [iː'kwɒlɪtɪ] *n* igualdad *f*.

equalize ['iːkwəlaɪz] I *vi* Ftb empatar. II *vtr* igualar.

equalizer ['iːkwəlaɪzər] *n* Ftb gol *m* del empate; (*of sound*) ecualizador *m*.

equanimity [ekwə'nɪmɪtɪ] *n* ecuanimidad *f*.

equate [ɪ'kweɪt] *vtr* equiparar, comparar (**to, a**, con).

equation [ɪ'kweɪʒən, ɪ'kweɪʃən] *n Math* ecuación *f*.

equator [ɪ'kweɪtər] *n* ecuador *m*.

equatorial [ekwə'tɔːrɪəl] *adj* ecuatorial.

equestrian [ɪ'kwestrɪən] *adj* ecuestre.

equilibrium [iːkwɪ'lɪbrɪəm] *n* equilibrio *m*.

equinox ['iːkwɪnɒks] *n* equinoccio *m*.

equip [ɪ'kwɪp] *vtr* (*with tools, machines*) equipar; (*with food*) proveer.

equipment [ɪ'kwɪpmənt] *n* (*materials*) equipo *m*; **office e.,** material *m* de oficina.

equipped [ɪ'kwɪpt] *adj* (*with tools, machines*) equipado,-a; (*with skills*) dotado,-a.

equitable ['ekwɪtəbəl] *adj* equitativo,-a.

equities ['ekwɪtɪz] *npl* acciones ordinarias.

equivalent [ɪ'kwɪvələnt] *adj & n* equivalente (*m*); **to be e. to,** equivaler a, ser equivalente a.

equivocal [ɪ'kwɪvəkəl] *adj* equívoco,-a.

era ['ɪərə] *n* era *f*.

eradicate [ɪ'rædɪkeɪt] *vtr* erradicar.

erase [ɪ'reɪz] *vtr* borrar.

eraser [ɪ'reɪzər] *n* goma *f* de borrar.

erect [ɪ'rekt] I *adj* 1 (*upright*) erguido,-a. 2 (*penis*) erecto,-a. II *vtr* (*monument*) levantar, erigir.

erection [ɪ'rekʃən] *n* 1 (*of building*) construcción *f*. 2 (*penis*) erección *f*.

ermine ['ɜːmɪn] *n* armiño *m*.

erode [ɪ'rəʊd] *vtr* 1 (*rock, soil*) erosionar. 2 (*metal*) corroer, desgastar; *fig* (*power, confidence*) hacer perder.

erosion [ɪ'rəʊʒən] *n Geol* erosión *f*.

erotic [ɪ'rɒtɪk] *adj* erótico,-a.

err [ɜːr] *vi* errar; **to e. on the side of ...,** pecar por exceso de ....

errand ['erənd] *n* recado *m*; **e. boy,** recadero *m*.

erratic [ɪ'rætɪk] *adj* (*performance, behaviour*) irregular; (*weather*) muy variable; (*person*) caprichoso,-a.

erroneous [ɪ'rəʊnɪəs] *adj* erróneo,-a.

error ['erər] *n* error *m*.

erupt [ɪ'rʌpt] *vi* 1 (*volcano*) entrar en erupción; (*violence*) estallar. 2 **his skin erupted in a rash,** le salió una erupción.

eruption [ɪ'rʌpʃən] n erupción f.

escalate ['eskəleɪt] vi (war) intensificarse; (prices) aumentar; (change) convertirse (into, en).

escalation [eskə'leɪʃən] n (of war) intensificación f, escalada f; (of prices) subida f.

escalator ['eskəleɪtə] n escalera mecánica.

escalope ['eskəlɒp] n escalope m.

escapade ['eskəpeɪd] n aventura f.

escape [ɪs'keɪp] I n huida f, fuga f; (of gas) escape m; **e. route**, vía f de escape. II vi escaparse. II vtr 1 (avoid) evitar, huir de; **to e. punishment**, librarse del castigo. 2 fig **his name escapes me**, no recuerdo su nombre.

escapism [ɪs'keɪpɪzəm] n evasión f.

escort ['eskɔːt] I n 1 (companion) acompañante mf. 2 Mil escolta f. II ['eskɔːt] vtr 1 (accompany) acompañar. 2 (protect) escoltar.

Eskimo ['eskɪməʊ] adj & n esquimal (mf).

esoteric [esəʊ'terɪk] adj esotérico,-a.

especial [ɪ'speʃəl] adj especial. ◆**especially** adv especialmente, sobre todo.

espionage ['espɪənɑːʒ] n espionaje m.

esplanade [esplə'neɪd] n paseo marítimo.

espouse [ɪ'spaʊz] vtr fml (cause) abrazar, adoptar.

espresso [e'spresəʊ] n e. (coffee), café m exprés.

esquire [ɪ'skwaɪə] n GB señor m; **Timothy Whiteman E.**, Sr. Don Timothy Whiteman.

essay ['eseɪ] n Educ redacción f.

essence ['esəns] n esencia f; **in e.**, esencialmente.

essential [ɪ'senʃəl] I adj esencial, imprescindible. II n necesidad básica; **the essentials**, lo fundamental. ◆**essentially** adv esencialmente.

establish [ɪ'stæblɪʃ] vtr 1 (found) establecer; (business) montar. 2 Jur **to e. a fact**, probar un hecho; **to e. the truth**, demostrar la verdad.

established [ɪ'stæblɪʃt] adj (person) establecido,-a; (fact) conocido,-a.

establishment [ɪ'stæblɪʃmənt] n establecimiento m; **the E.**, el sistema.

estate [ɪ'steɪt] n 1 (land) finca f; GB **e. agent**, agente mf inmobiliario,-a; GB **e. car**, coche m modelo familiar. 2 (housing) **e.**, zona urbanizada. 3 (property) bienes mpl. 4 (inheritance) herencia f.

esteem [ɪ'stiːm] I n **to hold sb in great e.**, apreciar mucho a algn. II vtr estimar.

esthetic [es'θetɪk] adj US estético,-a.

estimate ['estɪmeɪt] I n (calculation) cálculo m; (likely cost of work) presupuesto m; **rough e.**, cálculo aproximado. II ['estɪmeɪt] vtr calcular; fig pensar, creer.

estimation [estɪ'meɪʃən] n 1 (opinion) juicio m, opinión f. 2 (esteem) estima f.

estrange [ɪ'streɪndʒ] vtr **to become estranged**, alejarse (from, de).

Estremadura [estremə'dʊrə] n Extremadura.

estuary ['estjʊərɪ] n estuario m.

etching ['etʃɪŋ] n aguafuerte m.

eternal [ɪ'tɜːnəl] adj eterno,-a, incesante; **e. triangle**, triángulo amoroso.

eternity [ɪ'tɜːnɪtɪ] n eternidad f.

ether ['iːθə] n éter m.

ethereal [ɪ'θɪərɪəl] adj etéreo,-a.

ethical ['eθɪkəl] adj ético,-a.

ethics ['eθɪks] n ética f.

Ethiopia [iːθɪ'əʊpɪə] n Etiopía.

ethnic ['eθnɪk] adj étnico,-a.

ethos ['iːθɒs] n carácter distintivo.

etiquette ['etɪket] n protocolo m, etiqueta f.

etymology [etɪ'mɒlədʒɪ] n etimología f.

eucalyptus [juːkə'lɪptəs] n eucalipto m.

euphemism ['juːfɪmɪzəm] n eufemismo m.

euphoria [juː'fɔːrɪə] n euforia f.

Eurocheque ['jʊərəʊtʃek] n eurocheque m.

Eurocrat ['jʊərəʊkræt] n eurócrata mf.

Euro-MP ['jʊərəʊempiː] n eurodiputado, -a m,f.

Europe ['jʊərəp] n Europa.

European [jʊərə'pɪən] adj & n europeo,-a (m,f); **E. Economic Community**, Comunidad Económica Europea.

euthanasia [juːθə'neɪzɪə] n eutanasia f.

evacuate [ɪ'vækjʊeɪt] vtr evacuar.

evacuation [ɪvækjʊ'eɪʃən] n evacuación f.

evade [ɪ'veɪd] vtr evadir.

evaluate [ɪ'væljʊeɪt] vtr evaluar.

evaluation [ɪvælju'eɪʃən] n evaluación f.

evangelical [iːvæn'dʒelɪkəl] adj evangélico,-a.

evangelist [ɪ'vændʒɪlɪst] n evangelista m.

evaporate [ɪ'væpəreɪt] I vtr evaporar; **evaporated milk**, leche condensada sin endulzar. II vi evaporarse; fig desvanecerse.

evasion [ɪ'veɪʒən] n 1 evasión f. 2 (evasive answer) evasiva f.

evasive [ɪ'veɪsɪv] adj evasivo,-a.

eve [iːv] n víspera f; **on the e. of**, en vísperas de.

even ['iːvən] I adj 1 (smooth) liso,-a; (level) llano,-a. 2 (regular) uniforme. 3 (equally balanced) igual; Sport **to be e.**, ir empatados,-as; **to get e. with sb.**, desquitarse con algn. 4 (number) par. 5 (at the same level) **to a nivel**. 6 (quantity) exacto,-a. II adv 1 incluso, hasta, aun; **e. now**, incluso ahora; **e. so**, aun así; **e. the children knew**, hasta los niños lo sabían. 2 (negative) ni siquiera; **she can't e. write her name**, ni siquiera sabe escribir su nombre; **without e. speaking**, sin hablar siquiera. **3** (before comparative) aun, todavía; **e. worse,** aun peor. **4 e. as,** mientras; **e. if,** incluso si; **e. though,** aunque. **III** vtr igualar.

evening ['i:vnɪŋ] n **1** (early) tarde f; (late) noche f; **in the e.,** por la tarde; **tomorrow e.,** mañana por la tarde; **e. class,** clase nocturna; **e. dress,** (man) traje m de etiqueta; (woman) traje m de noche; **e. paper,** periódico vespertino. **2** (greeting) **good e.!,** (early) ¡buenas tardes!; (late) ¡buenas noches!

event [ɪ'vent] n **1** (happening) suceso m, acontecimiento m. **2** (case) caso m; **at all events,** en todo caso; **in the e. of fire,** en caso de incendio. **3** Sport prueba f.

eventful [ɪ'ventful] adj **an e. day,** (busy) un día agitado; (memorable) un día memorable.

eventual [ɪ'ventʃuəl] adj (ultimate) final; (resulting) consiguiente. ◆**eventually** adv finalmente.

eventuality [ɪventʃu'ælɪtɪ] n eventualidad f.

ever ['evər] adv **1** nunca, jamás; **stronger than e.,** más fuerte que nunca. **2** (interrogative) alguna vez; **have you e. been there?,** ¿has estado allí alguna vez? **3** (always) siempre; **for e.,** para siempre; **for e. and e.,** para siempre jamás. **4** (emphasis) **how e. did you manage it?,** ¿cómo diablos lo conseguiste?; **why e. not?,** ¿por qué no?; **fam e. so, e. such,** muy; **thank you e. so much,** muchísimas gracias.

evergreen ['evəgri:n] **I** adj de hoja perenne. **II** n árbol m or planta f de hoja perenne.

everlasting [evə'lɑ:stɪŋ] adj eterno,-a.

evermore [evə'mɔ:r] adv **for e.,** para siempre jamás.

every ['evrɪ] adj **1** (each) cada; **e. now and then,** de vez en cuando; **e. day,** todos los días; **e. other day,** cada dos días; **e. one of you,** todos,-as vosotros,-as; **e. citizen,** todo ciudadano. **2 you had e. right to be angry,** tenías toda la razón para estar enfadado.

everybody ['evrɪbɒdɪ] pron todo el mundo, todos,-as.

everyday ['evrɪdeɪ] adj diario,-a, de todos los días; **an e. occurrence,** un suceso cotidiano.

everyone ['evrɪwʌn] pron todo el mundo, todos,-as.

everything ['evrɪθɪŋ] pron todo; **he eats e.,** come de todo; **she means e. to me,** ella es todo para mí.

everywhere ['evrɪweər] adv en todas partes, por todas partes.

evict [ɪ'vɪkt] vtr desahuciar.

evidence ['evɪdəns] **I** n **1** (proof) evidencia f. **2** Jur testimonio m; **to give e.,** prestar declaración. **3** (sign) indicio m, se-

ñal f; **to be in e.,** dejarse notar.

evident ['evɪdənt] adj evidente, manifiesto,-a. ◆**evidently** adv evidentemente, al parecer.

evil ['i:vəl] **I** adj (wicked) malo,-a, malvado,-a; (harmful) nocivo,-a; (unfortunate) aciago,-a. **II** n mal m.

evocative [ɪ'vɒkətɪv] adj evocador,-a.

evoke [ɪ'vəʊk] vtr evocar.

evolution [i:və'lu:ʃən] n evolución f; Biol desarrollo m.

evolve [ɪ'vɒlv] **I** vi (species) evolucionar; (ideas) desarrollarse. **II** vtr desarrollar.

ewe [ju:] n oveja f.

ex [eks] n **her e.,** su ex marido; **his e.,** su ex mujer.

ex- [eks] pref ex, antiguo,-a; **ex-minister,** ex ministro m.

exacerbate [ɪg'zæsəbeɪt] vtr exacerbar.

exact [ɪg'zækt] **I** adj (accurate) exacto,-a; (definition) preciso,-a; **this e. spot,** ese mismo lugar. **II** vtr exigir. ◆**exactly** adv exactamente; precisamente; **e.!,** ¡exacto!

exacting [ɪg'zæktɪŋ] adj exigente.

exaggerate [ɪg'zædʒəreɪt] vi & vtr exagerar.

exaggeration [ɪgzædʒə'reɪʃən] n exageración f.

exalt [ɪg'zɔ:lt] vtr fml exaltar.

exam [ɪg'zæm] n fam examen m.

examination [ɪgzæmɪ'neɪʃən] n **1** Educ examen m; **to sit an e.,** hacer un examen. **2** Med reconocimiento m. **3** Jur interrogatorio m.

examine [ɪg'zæmɪn] vtr Educ examinar; (customs) registrar; Med hacer un reconocimiento médico a; Jur interrogar.

examiner [ɪg'zæmɪnər] n examinador,-a m,f.

example [ɪg'zɑ:mpəl] n ejemplo m; (specimen) ejemplar m; **for e.,** por ejemplo.

exasperate [ɪg'zɑ:spəreɪt] vtr exasperar.

exasperation [ɪgzɑ:spə'reɪʃən] n exasperación f.

excavate ['ekskəveɪt] vtr excavar.

excavation [ekskə'veɪʃən] n excavación f.

exceed [ek'si:d] vtr exceder, sobrepasar. ◆**exceedingly** adv extremadamente, sumamente.

excel [ɪk'sel] **I** vi sobresalir. **II** vtr superar.

excellency ['eksələnsɪ] n **His E.,** Su Excelencia.

excellent ['eksələnt] adj excelente.

except [ɪk'sept] **I** prep excepto, salvo; **e. for the little ones,** excepto los pequeños; **e. that ...,** salvo que .... **II** vtr exceptuar.

exception [ɪk'sepʃən] n **1** excepción f; **with the e. of,** a excepción de; **without e.,** sin excepción. **2** (objection) objeción f; **to take e. to sth,** ofenderse por algo.

exceptional [ɪk'sepʃənəl] adj excepcional.

excerpt [ek'sɜːpt] n extracto m.

excess [ɪk'ses] I n exceso m. II adj ['ekses] excedente; **e. baggage,** exceso m de equipaje; **e. fare,** suplemento m.

excessive [ɪk'sesɪv] adj excesivo,-a. ◆**excessively** adv excesivamente, en exceso.

exchange [ɪks'tʃeɪndʒ] I n 1 cambio m; **e. of ideas,** intercambio m de ideas; **in e. for,** a cambio de. 2 Fin **e. rate,** tipo m de cambio. 3 (telephone) m, central telefónica. II vtr intercambiar; **to e. blows,** golpearse. 2 (prisoners) canjear.

exchequer [ɪks'tʃekər] n GB **the E.,** Hacienda f; **Chancellor of the E.,** Ministro m de Hacienda.

excise [ɪk'saɪz] n impuesto m sobre el consumo; **e. duty,** derechos mpl de aduana.

excitable [ɪk'saɪtəbəl] adj excitable.

excite [ɪk'saɪt] vtr (stimulate) excitar; (move) emocionar; (enthuse) entusiasmar; (arouse) provocar.

excitement [ɪk'saɪtmənt] n (stimulation) excitación f; (emotion) emoción f; (commotion) agitación f.

exciting [ɪk'saɪtɪŋ] adj apasionante, emocionante.

exclaim [ɪk'skleɪm] I vi exclamar. II vtr gritar.

exclamation [eksklə'meɪʃən] n exclamación f; **e. mark,** US **e. point,** signo m de admiración.

exclude [ɪk'skluːd] vtr excluir; (from club) no admitir.

excluding [ɪk'skluːdɪŋ] prep excepto.

exclusion [ɪk'skluːʒən] n exclusión f.

exclusive [ɪk'skluːsɪv] I adj exclusivo,-a; (neighbourhood) selecto,-a; (club) cerrado, -a. II n Press exclusiva f. ◆**exclusively** adv exclusivamente.

excommunicate [ekskə'mjuːnɪkeɪt] vtr excomulgar.

excrement ['ekskrɪmənt] n excremento m.

excruciating [ɪk'skruːʃɪeɪtɪŋ] adj insoportable. ◆**excruciatingly** adv horriblemente.

excursion [ɪk'skɜːʃən] n excursión f.

excusable [ɪk'skjuːzəbəl] adj perdonable.

excuse [ɪk'skjuːz] I vtr 1 perdonar, disculpar; **e. me!,** con permiso; **may I be excused for a moment?,** ¿puedo salir un momento? 2 (exempt) dispensar. 3 (justify) justificar. II [ɪk'skjuːs] n excusa f; **to e.,** dar excusas.

ex-directory [eksdɪ'rektərɪ] adj Tel que no se encuentra en la guía telefónica.

execute ['eksɪkjuːt] vtr 1 (order) cumplir; (task) realizar. 2 Jur cumplir. 3 (dog) ejecutar.

execution [eksɪ'kjuːʃən] n 1 (of order) cumplimiento m; (of task) realización f. 2 Jur cumplimiento m. 3 (of person) ejecución f.

executioner [eksɪ'kjuːʃənər] n verdugo m.

executive [ɪg'zekjutɪv] I adj ejecutivo,-a. II n ejecutivo,-a m,f.

executor [ɪg'zekjutər] n albacea m.

exemplary [ɪg'zemplərɪ] adj ejemplar.

exemplify [ɪg'zemplɪfaɪ] vtr ejemplificar.

exempt [ɪg'zempt] I vtr eximir (from, de). II adj exento,-a; **e. from tax,** libre de impuesto.

exemption [ɪg'zempʃən] n exención f.

exercise ['eksəsaɪz] I n ejercicio m; **e. book,** cuaderno m. II vtr 1 (rights, duties) ejercer. 2 (dog) sacar de paseo. III vi hacer ejercicio.

exert [ɪg'zɜːt] vtr (influence) ejercer; **to e. oneself,** esforzarse.

exertion [ɪg'zɜːʃən] n esfuerzo m.

exhale [eks'heɪl] I vtr (breathe) exhalar. II vi espirar.

exhaust [ɪg'zɔːst] I vtr agotar. II n (gas) gases mpl de combustión; **e. pipe,** tubo m de escape.

exhausted [ɪg'zɔːstɪd] adj agotado,-a.

exhaustion [ɪg'zɔːstʃən] n agotamiento m.

exhaustive [ɪg'zɔːstɪv] adj exhaustivo,-a.

exhibit [ɪg'zɪbɪt] I n Art objeto expuesto; Jur prueba f instrumental. II vtr Art exponer; (surprise etc) mostrar.

exhibition [eksɪ'bɪʃən] n exposición f.

exhibitionist [eksɪ'bɪʃənɪst] adj & n exhibicionista (mf).

exhilarating [ɪg'zɪləreɪtɪŋ] adj estimulante.

exhilaration [ɪgzɪlə'reɪʃən] n regocijo m.

exhume [eks'hjuːm] vtr exhumar.

exile ['eksaɪl] I n 1 (banishment) exilio m. 2 (person) exiliado,-a m,f. II vtr exiliar.

exist [ɪg'zɪst] vi existir; (have little money) malvivir.

existence [ɪg'zɪstəns] n existencia f.

existing [ɪg'zɪstɪŋ] adj existente, actual.

exit ['eksɪt] I n 1 salida f. 2 Theat mutis m. II vi Theat hacer mutis.

exodus ['eksədəs] n éxodo m.

exonerate [ɪg'zɒnəreɪt] vtr fml exonerar (from, de).

exorbitant [ɪg'zɔːbɪtənt] adj exorbitante, desorbitado,-a.

exotic [ɪg'zɒtɪk] adj exótico,-a.

expand [ɪk'spænd] I vtr (enlarge) ampliar; (gas, metal) dilatar. II vi (grow) ampliarse; (metal) dilatarse; (become more friendly) abrirse. ◆**expand on** vtr ampliar.

expanse [ɪk'spæns] n extensión f.

expansion [ɪk'spænʃən] n (in size) expansión f; (of gas, metal) dilatación f.

expatriate [eks'pætrɪɪt] I adj & n expatriado,-a (m,f). II [eks'pætrɪeɪt] vtr expatriar.

expect [ɪk'spekt] I *vtr* 1 (*anticipate*) esperar; **I half-expected that to happen,** suponía que iba a ocurrir. 2 (*demand*) contar con. 3 (*suppose*) suponer. II *vi fam* **to be expecting,** estar embarazada.

expectancy [ɪk'spektənsɪ] *n* expectación *f*.

expectant [ɪk'spektənt] *adj* ilusionado,-a; **e. mother,** mujer embarazada.

expectation [ekspek'teɪʃən] *n* esperanza *f*; **contrary to e.,** contrariamente a lo que se esperaba.

expedient [ɪk'spiːdɪənt] I *adj* conveniente, oportuno,-a. II *n* expediente *m*, recurso *m*.

expedition [ekspɪ'dɪʃən] *n* expedición *f*.

expel [ɪk'spel] *vtr* expulsar.

expend [ɪk'spend] *vtr* gastar.

expendable [ɪk'spendəbəl] *adj* prescindible.

expenditure [ɪk'spendɪtʃər] *n* desembolso *m*.

expense [ɪk'spens] *n* gasto *m*; **all expenses paid,** con todos los gastos pagados; **to spare no e.,** no escatimar gastos; **fig at the e. of,** a costa de; **e. account,** cuenta *f* de gastos de representación.

expensive [ɪk'spensɪv] *adj* caro,-a, costoso,-a.

experience [ɪk'spɪərɪəns] I *n* experiencia *f*. II *vtr* (*sensation*) experimentar; (*difficulty, loss*) sufrir.

experienced [ɪk'spɪərɪənst] *adj* experimentado,-a.

experiment [ɪk'sperɪmənt] I *n* experimento *m*. II *vi* experimentar, hacer experimentos (**on, with,** con).

experimental [ɪksperɪ'mentəl] *adj* experimental.

expert ['ekspɔːt] I *adj* experto,-a. II *n* experto,-a *m,f*, especialista *mf*.

expertise [ekspɔː'tiːz] *n* pericia *f*.

expire [ɪk'spaɪər] *vi* 1 (*die*) expirar; (*mandate*) terminar. 2 *Com Ins* vencer; (*ticket*) caducar.

expiry [ɪk'spaɪərɪ] *n* vencimiento *m*; **e. date,** fecha *f* de caducidad.

explain [ɪk'spleɪn] I *vtr* explicar; (*clarify*) aclarar; **to e. oneself,** justificarse. II *vi* explicarse.

explanation [eksplə'neɪʃən] *n* explicación *f*; (*clarification*) aclaración *f*.

explanatory [ɪk'splænətərɪ] *adj* explicativo,-a, aclaratorio,-a.

explicit [ɪk'splɪsɪt] *adj* explícito,-a.

explode [ɪk'spləʊd] I *vtr* 1 (*bomb*) hacer explotar. 2 *fig* (*theory*) echar por tierra. II *vi* 1 (*bomb*) estallar, explotar; *fig* **to e. with** *or* **in anger,** montar en cólera.

exploit ['eksplɔɪt] I *n* proeza *f*, hazaña *f*. II [ɪk'splɔɪt] *vtr* explotar.

exploitation [eksplɔɪ'teɪʃən] *n* explotación *f*.

exploratory [ek'splɒrətərɪ] *adj*

exploratorio,-a.

explore [ɪk'splɔːr] *vtr* explorar.

explorer [ɪk'splɔːrər] *n* explorador,-a *m,f*.

explosion [ɪk'spləʊʒən] *n* explosión *f*.

explosive [ɪk'spləʊsɪv] I *adj* explosivo,-a; **e. issue,** asunto delicado. II *n* explosivo *m*.

exponent [ɪk'spəʊnənt] *n* exponente *m*; (*supporter*) defensor,-a *m,f*.

export [ɪk'spɔːt] I *vtr* exportar. II ['ekspɔːt] *n* 1 (*trade*) exportación *f*. 2 (*commodity*) artículo *m* de exportación.

exporter [eks'pɔːtər] *n* exportador,-a *m,f*.

expose [ɪk'spəʊz] *vtr* (*uncover*) exponer; (*secret*) revelar; (*plot*) descubrir; **to e. oneself,** exhibirse desnudo.

exposed [ɪk'spəʊzd] *adj* expuesto,-a.

exposure [ɪk'spəʊʒər] *n* 1 (*to light, cold, heat*) exposición *f*; **to die of e.,** morir de frío. 2 *Phot* fotografía *f*; **e. meter,** fotómetro *m*. 3 (*of criminal*) descubrimiento *m*.

expound [ɪk'spaʊnd] *vtr* exponer.

express [ɪk'spres] I *adj* 1 (*explicit*) expreso,-a. 2 *GB* (*letter*) urgente; **e. train,** expreso *m*. II *n Rail* expreso *m*. III *vtr* expresar. IV *adv* **send it e.,** mándalo urgente. ◆**expressly** *adv fml* expresamente.

expression [ɪk'spreʃən] *n* expresión *f*.

expulsion [ɪk'spʌlʃən] *n* expulsión *f*.

exquisite [ɪk'skwɪzɪt] *adj* exquisito,-a.

extend [ɪk'stend] I *vtr* 1 (*enlarge*) ampliar; (*lengthen*) alargar; (*increase*) aumentar; *fig* **the prohibition was extended to cover cigarettes,** extendieron la prohibición a los cigarrillos. 2 (*give*) rendir, dar; **to e. a welcome to sb,** recibir a algn. 3 (*prolong*) prolongar. II *vi* 1 (*stretch*) extenderse. 2 (*last*) prolongarse.

extension [ɪk'stenʃən] *n* 1 extensión *f*; (*of time*) prórroga *f*. 2 *Constr* anexo *m*.

extensive [ɪk'stensɪv] *adj* extenso,-a.

extent [ɪk'stent] *n* 1 (*area*) extensión *f*. 2 **to some e.,** hasta cierto punto; **to a large e.,** en gran parte; **to a lesser e.,** en menor grado; **to such an e.,** hasta tal punto.

extenuating [ɪk'stenjʊeɪtɪŋ] *adj* atenuante.

exterior [ɪk'stɪərɪər] I *adj* exterior, externo,-a. II *n* exterior *m*.

exterminate [ɪk'stɜːmɪneɪt] *vtr* exterminar.

extermination [ɪkstɜːmɪ'neɪʃən] *n* exterminación *f*, exterminio *m*.

external [ɪk'stɜːnəl] *adj* externo,-a, exterior.

extinct [ɪk'stɪŋkt] *adj* extinguido,-a.

extinction [ɪk'stɪŋkʃən] *n* extinción *f*.

extinguish [ɪk'stɪŋgwɪʃ] *vtr* extinguir, apagar.

extinguisher [ɪk'stɪŋgwɪʃər] *n* extintor *m*.

extol, *US* **extoll** [ɪk'stəʊl] *vtr* ensalzar,

alabar.
extort [ɪk'stɔːt] *vtr* arrancar; *(money)* sacar.
extortion [ɪk'stɔːʃən] *n* extorsión *f*.
extortionate [ɪk'stɔːʃənɪt] *adj* desorbitado,-a.
extra ['ekstrə] I *adj* extra; *(spare)* de sobra. II *adv* extra; **e. fine**, extra fino. III *n* *(additional charge)* suplemento *m*; *Cin* extra *mf*; *(newspaper)* edición *f* especial.
extract ['ekstrækt] I *n* extracto *m*. II [ɪk'strækt] *vtr* (*tooth, information*) extraer; (*confession*) arrancar.
extraction [ɪk'strækʃən] *n* extracción *f*.
extracurricular [ekstrəkə'rɪkjʊlə^r] *adj* extracurricular.
extradite ['ekstrədaɪt] *vtr* extraditar.
extramarital [ekstrə'mærɪtəl] *adj* extramatrimonial.
extramural [ekstrə'mjʊərəl] *adj* **e. course**, curso *m* para estudiantes libres.
extraordinary [ɪk'strɔːdənərɪ] *adj* (*amazing*) extraordinario,-a; (*behaviour etc*) extraño,-a.
extravagance [ɪk'strævɪgəns] *n* (*with money*) derroche *m*; (*of behaviour*) extravagancia *f*.
extravagant [ɪk'strævɪgənt] *adj* (*wasteful*) derrochador,-a; (*excessive*) exagerado,-a; (*luxurious*) lujoso,-a.
extreme [ɪk'striːm] I *adj* extremo,-a; **an e. case**, un caso excepcional; **to hold e. views**, tener opiniones radicales. II *n* extremo *m*; **in the e.**, en sumo grado. ◆**extremely** *adv* extremadamente; **I'm e. sorry**, lo siento de veras.
extremist [ɪk'striːmɪst] *n* extremista *mf*.
extremity [ɪk'stremɪtɪ] *n* extremidad *f*.
extricate ['ekstrɪkeɪt] *vtr* sacar; **to e. one-**

self, lograr salir (**from**, de).
extrovert ['ekstrəvɜːt] *adj* & *n* extrovertido,-a (*m,f*).
exuberant [ɪg'zjuːbərənt] *adj* exuberante.
exude [ɪg'zjuːd] *vtr* & *vi* (*moisture, sap*) exudar; *fig* rebosar.
exultant [ɪg'zʌltənt] *adj* jubiloso,-a.
eye [aɪ] I *n* ojo *m*; *fig* **I couldn't believe my eyes**, no podía creerlo; *fig* **in the eyes of**, según; *fig* **not to take one's eyes off sb/sth**, no quitar la vista de encima a algn/algo; *fig* **to catch sb's e.**, llamar la atención a algn; *fig* **to have an e. for**, tener buen ojo para; *fig* **to make eyes at sb**, echar miraditas a algn; *fig* **to see e. to e. with sb**, estar de acuerdo con algn; *fig* **to turn a blind e.**, hacer la vista gorda (**to**, a); *fig* **with an e. to**, con miras a; **to keep an e. on sb/sth**, vigilar a algn/algo; **to keep an e. out for**, estar pendiente de; **black e.**, ojo morado. II *vtr* observar.
eyeball ['aɪbɔːl] *n* globo *m* ocular.
eyebrow ['aɪbraʊ] *n* ceja *f*.
eyecatching ['aɪkætʃɪŋ] *adj* llamativo,-a.
eyelash ['aɪlæʃ] *n* pestaña *f*.
eyelid ['aɪlɪd] *n* párpado *m*.
eyeliner ['aɪlaɪnə^r] *n* lápiz *m* de ojos.
eye-opener ['aɪəʊpənə^r] *n* revelación *f*, gran sorpresa *f*.
eyeshadow ['aɪʃædəʊ] *n* sombra *f* de ojos.
eyesight ['aɪsaɪt] *n* vista *f*.
eyesore ['aɪsɔː^r] *n* monstruosidad *f*.
eyestrain ['aɪstreɪn] *n* vista cansada.
eyewash ['aɪwɒʃ] *n* colirio *m*; *fig* **it's all e.**, eso son disparates.
eyewitness ['aɪwɪtnɪs] *n* testigo *mf* ocular.

F

F, f [ef] *n* 1 (*the letter*) F, f *f*. 2 *Mus* fa *m*.
F [ef] *abbr of* **Fahrenheit**, Fahrenheit, F.
fable ['feɪbəl] *n* fábula *f*.
fabric ['fæbrɪk] *n* 1 *Tex* tela *f*, tejido *m*. 2 *Constr* estructura *f*.
fabricate ['fæbrɪkeɪt] *vtr* fabricar.
fabrication [fæbrɪ'keɪʃən] *n* *fig* fabricación *f*.
fabulous ['fæbjʊləs] *adj* fabuloso,-a.
façade *n* [fə'sɑːd, fæ'sɑːd] *n* fachada *f*.
face [feɪs] I *n* 1 cara *f*, rostro *m*; **f. to f.**, cara a cara; **I told him to his f.**, se lo dije en la cara; **he slammed the door in my f.**, me dió con la puerta en las narices; **to look sb in the f.**, mirarle a algn a la cara; **f. cloth**, paño *m*; **f. cream**, crema *f* facial; **f. pack**, mascarilla *f* facial. 2 (*expression*) cara *f*, expresión *f*; **to pull a long f.**, poner cara larga; **to pull faces**, hacer muecas. 3 (*surface*) superficie *f*; (*of*

card, coin) cara *f*; (*of watch*) esfera *f*; **f. down/up**, boca abajo/arriba; *fig* **in the f. of danger**, ante el peligro; **f. value**, valor *m* nominal; **to take sth at f. value**, entender algo sólo en su sentido literal. 4 (*appearance*) aspecto *m*; **on the f. of it**, a primera vista; **to lose f.**, desprestigiarse; **to save f.**, salvar las apariencias.
II *vtr* 1 (*look onto*) dar a; **(be opposite)** estar enfrente de. 2 **to f. the wall/window**, *(of person)* estar de cara a la pared/ventana. 3 (*problem*) hacer frente a; **let's f. it**, hay que reconocerlo; **to f. up to**, hacer cara a. 4 (*tolerate*) soportar, aguantar.
III *vi* **to f. on to**, dar a; **to f. towards**, mirar hacia; **f. this way**, vuélvase de este lado.
facelift ['feɪslɪft] *n* *Med* lifting *m*; *fig* renovación *f*.

facet ['fæsɪt] n faceta f.

facetious [fə'si:ʃəs] adj bromista.

facial ['feɪʃəl] adj facial.

facile ['fæsaɪl] adj superficial.

facilitate [fə'sɪlɪteɪt] vtr facilitar.

facility [fə'sɪlɪtɪ] n 1 (ease) facilidad f. 2 **facilities**, (means) facilidades fpl; **credit f.**, facilidades de crédito. 3 **facilities**, (rooms, equipment) instalaciones fpl; **cooking f.**, derecho m a cocina.

facing ['feɪsɪŋ] adj de enfrente.

facsimile [fæk'sɪmɪlɪ] n 1 (copy) facsímil m. 2 (message) telefax m. 3 (machine) facsímil m.

fact [fækt] n hecho m; **as a matter of f.**, de hecho; **the f. that he confessed**, el hecho de que confesara; **in f.**, en realidad.

fact-finding ['fæktfaɪndɪŋ] adj investigador,-a.

faction ['fækʃən] n (group) facción f.

factor ['fæktər] n factor m.

factory ['fæktərɪ] n fábrica f.

factual ['fæktʃʊəl] adj **a f. error**, un error de hecho.

faculty ['fækəltɪ] n 1 facultad f. 2 US Univ profesorado m, cuerpo m docente.

fad [fæd] n fam (craze) moda pasajera; (whim) capricho m.

fade [feɪd] vi (colour) destreñirse; (flower) marchitarse; (light) apagarse. ◆**fade away** vi desvanecerse. ◆**fade in, fade out** vtr Cin TV fundir.

faded ['feɪdɪd] adj (colour) destreñido,-a; (flower) marchito,-a.

fag [fæg] n sl 1 GB fam (cigarette) pitillo m. 2 US sl (homosexual) marica m.

fail [feɪl] I n 1 Educ suspenso m. **without f.**, sin falta. II vtr 1 **don't f. me**, no me falles; **words f. me**, no encuentro palabras. 2 (exam) suspender. 3 (to be unable) no lograr; **he failed to score**, no logró marcar. 4 (neglect) dejar de; **don't f. to come**, no deje de venir. 5 (of health) deteriorarse. III vi 1 (show, film) fracasar; (brakes) fallar. 2 (business) quebrar; Educ suspender.

failing ['feɪlɪŋ] I n 1 (shortcoming) defecto m. 2 (weakness) punto m débil. II prep a falta de.

failure ['feɪljər] n 1 fracaso m. 2 Com calibra f. 3 Educ suspenso m. 4 (person) fracasado,-a m,f. 5 (breakdown) avería f; **brake f.**, fallo m de los frenos; **power f.**, apagón m; Med **heart f.**, paro cardíaco. 6 **her f. to answer**, (neglect) el hecho de que no contestara.

faint [feɪnt] I adj 1 (sound) débil; (colour) pálido,-a; (outline) borroso,-a; (recollection) vago,-a; **I haven't the faintest idea**, no tengo la más mínima idea. 2 (giddy) mareado,-a. II n desmayo m. III vi desmayarse.

faint-hearted [feɪnt'hɑːtɪd] adj temeroso,-a.

fair¹ [feər] I adj 1 (impartial) imparcial; (just) justo,-a; **it's not f.**, no hay derecho; **fam f. enough!**, ¡vale! 2 (hair) rubio,-a. 3 (weather) bueno,-a. 4 (beautiful) bello,-a. 5 **a f. number**, un buen número; **he has a f. chance**, tiene bastantes probabilidades. II adv **to play f.**, jugar limpio. ◆**fairly** adv 1 (justly) justamente. 2 (moderately) bastante.

fair² [feər] n 1 feria f; **trade f.**, feria de muestras.

fairground ['feəgraʊnd] n real m de la feria.

fairness ['feənɪs] n justicia f, equidad f; **in all f.**, para ser justo,-a.

fairy ['feərɪ] n 1 hada f; **f. godmother**, hada madrina; **f. tale**, cuento m de hadas. 2 sl offens marica m.

fait accompli [feɪtə'kɒmpliː] n fml hecho consumado.

faith [feɪθ] n 1 Rel fe f. 2 (trust) confianza f; **in good f.**, de buena fe.

faithful ['feɪθfʊl] I adj fiel. II npl **the f.**, los fieles. ◆**faithfully** adv fielmente; **yours f.**, (in letter) le saluda atentamente.

fake [feɪk] I adj falso,-a. II n 1 (object) falsificación f. 2 (person) impostor,-a m,f. III vtr 1 (forge) falsificar. 2 (feign) fingir. IV vi (pretend) fingir.

falcon ['fɔːlkən] n halcón m.

Falklands ['fɔːlkləndz] npl **the F.**, las (Islas) Malvinas.

fall [fɔːl] I n 1 caída f. 2 (of rock) desprendimiento m; **f. of snow**, nevada f. 3 (decrease) baja f. 4 US otoño m. 5 (usu pl) cascada f; **Niagara Falls**, las cataratas del Niágara. II vi (pt fell; pp fallen) 1 caer, caerse; **they f. into two categories**, se dividen en dos categorías; fig **night was falling**, anochecía; fig **to f. into line**, aceptar las reglas; fig **to f. short**, no alcanzar (of, -). 2 (in battle) caer. 3 (temperature, prices) bajar. 4 **to f. asleep**, dormirse; **to f. ill**, caer enfermo,-a; **to f. in love**, enamorarse. ◆**fall back** vi replegarse. ◆**fall back on** vtr echar mano a, recurrir a. ◆**fall behind** vi (in race) quedarse atrás; **to f. behind with one's work**, retrasarse en el trabajo. ◆**fall down** vi 1 (picture etc) caerse. 2 (building) derrumbarse. 3 (argument) fallar. ◆**fall for** vtr 1 (person) enamorarse de. 2 (trick) dejarse engañar por. ◆**fall in** vi 1 (roof) desplomarse. 2 Mil formar filas. ◆**fall off** vi 1 (drop off) caerse. II vtr **to f. off sth**, caerse de algo. 2 (part) desprenderse. 2 (diminish) disminuir. ◆**fall out** vi 1 (hair) caerse. 2 Mil romper filas. 3 (quarrel) reñir. ◆**fall over** vi caerse. ◆**fall through** vi (plan) fracasar.

fallacy ['fæləsɪ] n falacia f.

fallen ['fɔːlən] pp → **fall**.

fallible ['fælɪbəl] *adj* falible.

fall-out ['fɔːlaut] *n* (**radioactive**) f., lluvia radioactiva; f. **shelter**, refugio antiatómico.

fallow ['fæləu] *adj* Agr en barbecho.

false [fɔːls] *adj* falso,-a; f. **step**, paso *m* en falso; f. **start**, salida nula; f. **teeth**, dentadura postiza; f. **alarm**, falsa alarma.

falsehood ['fɔːlshud] *n* falsedad *f*.

falsify ['fɔːlsɪfaɪ] *vt* (**records, accounts**) falsificar; (**story**) falsear.

falter ['fɔːltər] *vi* vacilar; (**voice**) fallar.

faltering ['fɔːltərɪŋ] *adj* vacilante.

fame [feɪm] *n* fama *f*.

familiar [fə'mɪlɪər] *adj* 1 (**common**) familiar, conocido,-a; **his face is f.**, su cara me suena. 2 (**aware, knowledgeable**) enterado,-a, al corriente (**with, de**); 3 **to be on f. terms with sb**, (**know well**) tener confianza con algn.

familiarity [fəmɪlɪ'ærɪtɪ] *n* 1 (**awareness, knowledge**) familiaridad (**with, con**). 2 (**intimacy**) confianza *f*.

familiarize [fə'mɪljəraɪz] *vtr* 1 (**become acquainted**) familiarizarse (**with, con**). 2 (**make understandable**) popularizar.

family ['fæmɪlɪ] *n* familia *f*; f. **allowance**, subsidio *m* familiar; f. **doctor**, médico *m* de cabecera; f. **man**, hombre hogareño; f. **planning**, planificación *f* familiar; f. **tree**, árbol genealógico.

famine ['fæmɪn] *n* hambre *f*, escasez *f* de alimentos.

famished ['fæmɪʃt] *adj fam* muerto,-a de hambre.

famous ['feɪməs] *adj* célebre, famoso,-a (**for, por**). ◆**famously** *adv fam* estupendamente.

fan [fæn] I *n* 1 abanico *m*; *Elec* ventilador *m*. 2 (**person**) aficionado-a *m,f*; (**of pop star etc**) fan *m,f*; f. **club**, club *m* de fans; **football** f., hincha *mf*. II *vtr* 1 abanicar. 2 (**fire, passions**) avivar. ◆**fan out** *vi* (**troops**) desplegarse en abanico.

fanatic [fə'nætɪk] *adj* & *n* fanático,-a (*m,f*).

fanatical [fə'nætɪkəl] *adj* fanático,-a.

fanciful ['fænsɪful] *adj* 1 (**person**) caprichoso,-a. 2 (**idea**) fantástico,-a.

fancy ['fænsɪ] I *adj* (**fancier, fanciest**) de fantasía; f. **dress**, disfraz *m*; f. **dress ball**, baile *m* de disfraces; f. **prices**, precios *mpl* exorbitantes. II *n* 1 (**imagination**) fantasía *f*. 2 (**whim**) capricho *m*, antojo *m*; **to take a f. to sth**, cogerle cariño a algn; **to take a f. to sth**, encapricharse con algo; **what takes your f.?**, ¿qué se le antoja? III *vtr* 1 (**imagine**) imaginar(se); *fam* f. **that!**, ¡fíjate!; *fam* f. **seeing you here!**, ¡qué casualidad verte por aquí! 2 (**like, want**) apetecer; **do you f. a drink?**, ¿te apetece una copa? *fam* I f. **her**, ella me gusta; *fam* **to f. oneself**, ser creído,-a *or* presumido,-a.

fanfare ['fænfeər] *n* fanfarria *f*.

fang [fæŋ] *n* colmillo *m*.

fantasize ['fæntəsaɪz] *vi* fantasear.

fantastic [fæn'tæstɪk] *adj* fantástico,-a.

fantasy ['fæntəsɪ] *n* fantasía *f*.

far [fɑːr] (**farther or further, farthest or furthest**) I *adj* 1 (**distant**) lejano,-a; the F. **East**, el Lejano Oriente. 2 **at the f. end**, en el otro extremo. 3 **the f. left**, la extrema izquierda. II *adv* 1 (**distant**) lejos; f. **and wide**, por todas partes; f. **off**, a lo lejos; **farther back**, más atrás; **farther north**, más al norte; **how f. is it to Cardiff?**, ¿cuánto hay de aquí a Cardiff?; *fig* **as f. as I can**, en lo que puedo; **as f. as I know**, que yo sepa; **as f. as possible**, en lo posible; *fig* f. **from complaining, he seemed pleased**, lejos de quejarse, parecía contento; *fig* **he went so f. as to swear**, llegó a jurar; *fig* **I'm f. from satisfied**, no estoy satisfecho,-a en mucho menos; *fig* **in so f. as ...**, en la medida en que ...; *fam* **to go too f.**, pasarse de la raya. 2 (**in time**) **as f. back as the fifties**, ya en los años cincuenta; f. **into the night**, hasta muy entrada la noche; **so f.**, hasta ahora. 3 (**much**) mucho; **by f.**, con mucho; f. **cleverer**, mucho más listo,-a; f. **too much**, demasiado; **you're not f. wrong**, casi aciertas.

faraway ['fɑːrəweɪ] *adj* lejano,-a, remoto,-a.

farce [fɑːs] *n* farsa *f*.

farcical ['fɑːsɪkəl] *adj* absurdo,-a.

fare [feər] I *n* 1 (**ticket price**) tarifa *f*, precio *m* del billete; (**for boat**) pasaje *m*; **half f.**, media tarifa. 2 (**passenger**) pasajero,-a *m,f*. 3 (**food**) comida *f*. II *vi* **how did you f.?**, ¿qué tal te fue?

farewell [feə'wel] I *interj arch* ¡adiós! II *n* despedida *f*.

far-fetched [fɑː'fetʃt] *adj* rebuscado,-a.

farm [fɑːm] I *n* granja *f*, Am hacienda *f*. II *vtr* cultivar, labrar. ◆**farm out** *vtr* encargar fuera.

farmer ['fɑːmər] *n* granjero,-a *m,f*, Am hacendado,-a *m,f*.

farmhand ['fɑːmhænd] *n* peón *m*, labriego,-a *m,f*.

farmhouse ['fɑːmhaus] *n* granja *f*, Am hacienda *f*.

farming ['fɑːmɪŋ] I *n* 1 (**agriculture**) agricultura *f*. 2 (**of land**) cultivo *m*, labranza *f*. II *adj* agrícola.

farmyard ['fɑːmjɑːd] *n* corral *m*.

far-reaching [fɑː'riːtʃɪŋ] *adj* de gran alcance.

far-sighted [fɑː'saɪtɪd] *adj* 1 (**person**) con visión de futuro. 2 (**plan**) con miras al futuro.

fart [fɑːt] *vulg* I *n* pedo *m*. II *vi* echarse un pedo.

farther ['fɑːðər] *adj* & *adv comp* → **far**.

farthest ['fɑːðɪst] *adj* & *adv superl* → **far**.

fascinate ['fæsɪneɪt] *vtr* fascinar.

fascinating ['fæsɪneɪtɪŋ] *adj* fascinante.

fascination [fæsɪ'neɪʃən] *n* fascinación *f*.

fascism ['fæʃɪzəm] *n* fascismo *m*.

fascist ['fæʃɪst] *adj & n* fascista (*mf*).

fashion ['fæʃən] **I** *n* 1 (*manner*) manera *f*, modo *m*; **after a f.**, más o menos. 2 (*latest style*) moda *f*; **to go/be out of f.**, pasar/no estar de moda; **f. designer**, diseñador,-a *m,f* de moda; **f. parade**, desfile *m* de modelos. **II** *vtr* (*metal*) labrar; (*clay*) formar.

fashionable ['fæʃənəbəl] *adj* 1 de moda. 2 (*area, hotel*) elegante.

fast[1] [fɑːst] **I** *adj* 1 (*quick*) rápido,-a. 2 **hard and f. rules**, reglas estrictas. 3 (*clock*) adelantado,-a. **II** *adv* 1 rápidamente, deprisa; **how f.?**, ¿a qué velocidad? 2 (*securely*) firmemente; **f. asleep**, profundamente dormido,-a.

fast[2] [fɑːst] **I** *n* ayuno *m*. **II** *vi* ayunar.

fasten ['fɑːsən] **I** *vtr* 1 (*attach*) sujetar; (*fix*) fijar. 2 (*belt*) abrochar; (*bag*) asegurar; (*shoe laces*) atar. **II** *vi* (*dress*) abrocharse.

fastener ['fɑːsənər] *n* cierre *m*.

fastidious [fæ'stɪdɪəs] *adj* quisquilloso,-a.

fat [fæt] **I** *adj* (*fatter, fattest*) 1 gordo,-a. 2 (*book, file*) grueso,-a. 3 (*meat*) que tiene mucha grasa. **II** *n* grasa *f*; **cooking f.**, manteca *f* de cerdo.

fatal ['feɪtəl] *adj* 1 (*accident, illness*) mortal. 2 (*ill-fated*) fatal, funesto,-a. 3 (*fateful*) fatídico,-a. ◆**fatally** *adv* **f. wounded**, mortalmente herido,-a.

fatalistic [feɪtə'lɪstɪk] *adj* fatalista.

fatality [fə'tælɪtɪ] *n* víctima *f* mortal.

fate [feɪt] *n* destino *m*, suerte *f*.

fateful ['feɪtfʊl] *adj* fatídico,-a, aciago,-a.

father ['fɑːðər] *n* 1 padre *m*; **my f. and mother**, mis padres; **F. Christmas**, Papá *m* Noel. 2 *Rel* padre *m*.

father-in-law ['fɑːðərɪnlɔː] *n* suegro *m*.

fatherland ['fɑːðəlænd] *n* patria *f*.

fatherly ['fɑːðəlɪ] *adj* paternal.

fathom ['fæðəm] **I** *n* Naut braza *f*. **II** *vtr* comprender. ◆**fathom out** *vtr* comprobar; **I can't f. it out**, no me lo explico.

fatigue [fə'tiːg] *n* 1 (*tiredness*) fatiga *f*. 2 *Mil* faena *f*; **f. dress**, traje *m* de faena.

fatten ['fætən] *vtr* engordar.

fattening ['fætənɪŋ] *adj* que engorda.

fatty ['fætɪ] *adj* 1 (*food*) graso,-a; *Anat* (*tissue*) adiposo,-a. **II** *n* *fam* (*person*) gordinflón,-ona *m,f*.

fatuous ['fætjʊəs] *adj* necio,-a.

faucet ['fɔːsɪt] *n* US grifo *m*.

fault [fɔːlt] **I** *n* 1 (*defect*) defecto *m*. 2 (*in merchandise*) desperfecto *m*; **to find f. with**, poner reparos a. 3 (*blame*) culpa *f*; **to be at f.**, tener la culpa *f*. 4 (*mistake*) error *m*. 5 *Geol* falla *f*. 6 *Ten* falta *f*. **II** *vtr* criticar.

faultless ['fɔːltlɪs] *adj* intachable.

faulty ['fɔːltɪ] *adj* defectuoso,-a.

fauna ['fɔːnə] *n* fauna *f*.

faux pas [fəʊ'pɑː] *n inv fml* (*mistake*) paso *m* en falso; (*blunder*) metedura *f* de pata.

favour, US favor ['feɪvər] **I** *n* 1 favor *m*; **in f. of**, a favor de; **to be in f. with sb**, gozar del favor de algn; **to ask sb a f.**, pedirle un favor a algn. 2 1-0 in our f., (*advantage*)1-0 a favor nuestro. **II** *vtr* 1 (*person*) favorecer a. 2 (*approve*) estar a favor de.

favourable ['feɪvərəbəl] *adj* favorable.

favourite ['feɪvərɪt] *adj & n* favorito,-a, *m,f*.

favouritism ['feɪvərɪtɪzəm] *n* favoritismo *m*.

fawn[1] [fɔːn] **I** *adj* (de) color café claro. **II** *n* 1 *Zool* cervato *m*. 2 color *m* café claro.

fawn[2] [fɔːn] *vi* adular (**on**, a).

fax [fæks] **I** *n* (*machine, message*) fax *m*. **II** *vtr* mandar por fax.

fear [fɪər] **I** *n* miedo *m*, temor *m*; **for f. of**, por temor a; **fam no f.!**, ¡ni pensarlo!. **II** *vtr* temer; **I f. it's too late**, me temo que ya es tarde. **III** *vi* temer (**for**, por).

fearful ['fɪəfʊl] *adj* 1 (*person*) temeroso,-a. 2 (*frightening*) espantoso,-a.

fearless ['fɪəlɪs] *adj* intrépido,-a.

feasible ['fiːzəbəl] *adj* (*practicable*) factible; (*possible*) viable.

feasibility [fiːzə'bɪlɪtɪ] *n* viabilidad *f*.

feast [fiːst] *n* 1 banquete *m*; *fam* comilona *f*. 2 *Rel* **f. day**, fiesta *f* de guardar.

feat [fiːt] *n* hazaña *f*.

feather ['feðər] *n* pluma *f*; **f. duster**, plumero *m*. **II** *vtr fam* **to f. one's nest**, hacer su agosto.

feature ['fiːtʃər] **I** *n* 1 (*of face*) rasgo *m*, facción *f*. 2 (*characteristic*) característica *f*. 3 **f. film**, largometraje *m*. 4 *Press* crónica *f* especial. **II** *vtr* 1 poner de relieve. 2 *Cin* tener como protagonista a. **III** *vi* figurar.

February ['februərɪ] *n* febrero *m*.

fed [fed] *adj fam* **f. up**, harto,-a (**with**, de).

federal ['fedərəl] *adj* federal.

federation [fedə'reɪʃən] *n* federación *f*.

fee [fiː] *n* 1 (*of lawyer, doctor*) honorarios *mpl*; *Ftb* **transfer f.**, prima *f* de traslado; *Univ* **tuition fees**, derechos *mpl* de matrícula.

feeble ['fiːbəl] *adj* débil.

feed [fiːd] **I** *vtr* (*pt* & *pp* **fed**) 1 (*give food to*) dar de comer a; *fig* (*fire*) alimentar; **to f. a baby**, (*breast-feed*) amamantar a un bebé; (*with bottle*) dar el biberón a un bebé. 2 *Elec* alimentar. 3 (*insert*) introducir. **II** *vi* comer (**on**, -); (*cows, sheep*) pacer. **III** *n* 1 (*food*) comida *f*; **cattle f.**, pienso *m*. 2 *Tech* alimentación *f*. ◆**feed up** *vtr* cebar.

feedback ['fiːdbæk] *n* 1 *Tech* feedback *m*. 2 *fig* reacción *f*.

feeder ['fiːdər] *n* *Tech* alimentador *m*.

feeding ['fi:dɪŋ] *n* f. bottle, biberón *m*.

feel [fi:l] I *vi* (*pt* & *pp* felt) 1 (*emotion, sensation*) sentir; **how do you f.?**, ¿qué tal te encuentras?; **I f. bad about it**, me da pena; **I f. (sorry) for him**, le compadezco; **to f. happy/uncomfortable**, sentirse feliz/incómodo; **to f. cold/sleepy**, tener frío/sueño; **⬧m to f. up to sth**, sentirse con ánimos para hacer algo. 2 (*seem*) **your hand feels cold**, tienes la mano fría; **it feels like summer**, parece verano. 3 (*opinion*) opinar; **I f. sure that ...**, estoy seguro,-a de que ... 4 **I f. like an ice cream**, me apetece un helado; **to f. like doing sth**, tener ganas de hacer algo. II *vtr* 1 (*touch*) tocar. 2 **she feels a failure**, se siente inútil. 3 (*notice, be aware of*) notar. III *n* 1 (*touch*) tacto *m*; *fig* **to get the f. for sth**, cogerle el truco a algo. 2 (*atmosphere*) ambiente *m*. **◆feel for** *vtr* 1 (*search for*) buscar. 2 (*have sympathy for*) compadecer.

feeler ['fi:lər] *n* Ent antena *f*; *fig* **to put one's feelers out**, tantear el terreno.

feeling ['fi:lɪŋ] I *n* 1 (*emotion*) sentimiento *m*; ill f., rencor *m*. 2 (*compassion*) compasión *f*. 3 **I had the f. that ...**, (*impression*) tuve la impresión de que ... 4 (*sensitivity*) sensibilidad *f*. 5 (*opinion*) opinión *f*; **to express one's feelings**, expresar sus opiniones. II *adj* sensible, compasivo,-a.

feet [fi:t] *npl* → **foot**.

feign [feɪn] *vtr* fingir.

feint [feɪnt] *Sport* I *n* finta *f*. II *vi* fintar.

fell¹ [fel] *pt* → **fall**.

fell² [fel] *vtr* (*trees*) talar; *fig* (*enemy*) derribar.

fellow ['feləʊ] *n* 1 (*companion*) compañero,-a *m,f*; (*citizen, conciudadano,-a*) *m,f*; **f. countryman/ countrywoman**, compatriota *mf*; f. men, prójimos *mpl*; **f. passenger/student**, compañero,-a *m,f*, de viaje/estudios. 2 *fam* (*chap*) tipo *m*, tío *m*. 3 (*of society*) socio,-a *m,f*.

fellowship ['feləʊʃɪp] *n* 1 (*comradeship*) camaradería *f*. 2 *Univ* beca *f* de investigación.

felony ['felənɪ] *n* crimen *m*, delito *m* mayor.

felt¹ [felt] *pt* & *pp* → **feel**.

felt² [felt] *n* Tex fieltro *m*.

felt-tip(ped) ['felttɪp(t)] *adj* f.-t. pen, rotulador *m*.

female ['fi:meɪl] I *adj* 1 Zool hembra. 2 femenino,-a. II *n* 1 Zool hembra *f*. 2 (*woman*) mujer *f*; (*girl*) chica *f*.

feminine ['femɪnɪn] *adj* femenino,-a.

feminism ['femɪnɪzəm] *n* feminismo *m*.

feminist ['femɪnɪst] *adj* & *n* feminista (*mf*).

fence [fens] I *n* cerca *f*, valla *f*; *fig* **to sit on the f.**, ver los toros desde la barrera. II *vi* Sport practicar la esgrima. **◆fence**

in *vtr* meter en un cercado.

fencing ['fensɪŋ] *n* Sport esgrima *f*.

fend [fend] *vi* **to f. for oneself**, valerse por sí mismo. **◆fend off** *vtr* (*blow*) parar; (*question*) rehuir; (*attack*) rechazar.

fender ['fendər] *n* 1 (*fireplace*) pantalla *f*. 2 US Aut parachoques *m inv*. 3 Naut defensa *f*.

ferment ['fɜ:mənt] I *n* *fig* **in a state of f.**, agitado,-a. II ['fə'ment] *vtr* & *vi* fermentar.

fern [fɜ:n] *n* helecho *m*.

ferocious [fə'rəʊʃəs] *adj* feroz.

ferocity [fə'rɒsɪtɪ] *n* ferocidad *f*.

ferret ['ferɪt] I *n* hurón *m*. II *vi* huronear, husmear. **◆ferret out** *vtr* descubrir.

ferry ['ferɪ] I *n* 1 (*small*) barca *f* de pasaje. 2 (*large, for cars*) transbordador *m*, ferry *m*. II *vtr* transportar.

fertile ['fɜ:taɪl] *adj* fértil.

fertility [fə'tɪlɪtɪ] *n* (*of soil*) fertilidad *f*.

fertilize ['fɜ:tɪlaɪz] *vtr* 1 (*soil*) abonar. 2 (*egg*) fecundar.

fertilizer ['fɜ:tɪlaɪzər] *n* abono *m*.

fervent ['fɜ:vənt] *adj* ferviente.

fervour, US **fervor** ['fɜ:vər] *n* fervor *m*.

fester ['festər] *vi* supurar.

festival ['festɪvəl] *n* (*event*) festival *m*; (*celebration*) fiesta *f*.

festive ['festɪv] *adj* festivo,-a; **the f. season**, las fiestas de Navidad.

festivity [fes'tɪvɪtɪ] *n* **the festivities**, las fiestas.

festoon [fe'stu:n] *vtr* adornar.

fetch [fetʃ] I *vtr* 1 (*go for*) ir a buscar. 2 (*bring*) traer. 3 **how much did it f.?**, (*sell for*) ¿por cuánto se vendió?

fetching ['fetʃɪŋ] *adj* atractivo,-a.

fete [feɪt] I *n* fiesta *f*. II *vtr* festejar.

fetish ['fetɪʃ, 'fi:tɪʃ] *n* fetiche *m*.

fetus ['fi:təs] *n* US → **foetus**.

feud [fju:d] I *n* enemistad duradera. II *vi* pelear.

feudal ['fju:dəl] *adj* feudal.

fever ['fi:vər] *n* fiebre *f*.

feverish ['fi:vərɪʃ] *adj* febril.

few [fju:] I *adj* 1 (*not many*) pocos,-as; **as f. as**, solamente. 2 (*some*) algunos,-as, unos,-as cuantos,-as; **a f. books**, unos *or* algunos libros; **she has fewer books than I thought**, tiene menos libros de lo que pensaba; **for the past f. years**, durante estos últimos años; **in the next f. days**, dentro de unos días; **quite a f.**, bastantes. II *pron* 1 (*not many*) pocos,-as; **there are too f.**, no hay suficientes; **the fewer the better**, cuantos menos mejor. 2 **a f.**, (*some*) algunos,-as, unos,-as cuantos,-as; **the chosen f.**, los elegidos; **who has the fewest?**, ¿quién tiene menos?

fiancé [fɪ'ɒnseɪ] *n* prometido *m*.

fiancée [fɪ'ɒnseɪ] *n* prometida *f*.

fiasco [fɪ'æskəʊ] *n* fiasco *m*.

fib [fɪb] *fam* I *n* trola *f*. II *vi* contar trolas.

fibre, US **fiber** ['faɪbə'] *n* fibra *f*.

fibreglass, US **fiberglass** ['faɪbəglɑːs] *n* fibra *f* de vidrio.

fickle ['fɪkəl] *adj* inconstante, voluble.

fiction ['fɪkʃən] *n* ficción *f*.

fictional ['fɪkʃənəl] *adj* *Lit* novelesco,-a. 2 (imaginative) ficticio,-a.

fictitious [fɪk'tɪʃəs] *adj* ficticio,-a.

fiddle ['fɪdəl] *fam* I *n* 1 *Mus* violín *m*. 2 (shady deal) trampa *f*. II *vtr* estafar; (accounts) falsificar. III *vi* juguetear (with, con). ◆**fiddle about** *vi* perder tiempo.

fiddly ['fɪdlɪ] *adj fam* laborioso,-a.

fidelity [fɪ'delɪtɪ] *n* fidelidad *f*.

fidget ['fɪdʒɪt] *vi* 1 moverse; **stop fidgeting!**, ¡estáte quieto! 2 jugar (with, con).

field [fiːld] I *n* 1 campo *m*; **f. glasses**, gemelos *mpl*; **f. marshal**, mariscal *m* de campo. 2 *Geol Min* yacimiento *m*. 3 **f. trip**, viaje *m* de estudios; **f. work**, trabajo *m* de campo. II *vtr* *Sport* 1 (ball) parar y devolver. 2 (team) presentar.

fiend [fiːnd] *n* demonio *m*; *fam* (fanatic) fanático,-a *m,f*.

fiendish ['fiːndɪʃ] *adj fam* diabólico,-a.

fierce [fɪəs] *adj* (animal) feroz; (argument) acalorado,-a; (heat, competition) intenso, -a; (wind) violento,-a.

fiery ['faɪərɪ] *adj* (temper) fogoso,-a; (speech) acalorado,-a; (colour) encendido,-a.

fifteen [fɪf'tiːn] *adj & n* quince (*m*) inv.

fifteenth [fɪf'tiːnθ] I *adj & n* decimoquinto,-a (*m,f*). II *n* (fraction) quinzavo *m*.

fifth [fɪfθ] I *adj & n* quinto,-a (*m,f*). II *n* (fraction) quinto *m*.

fifty ['fɪftɪ] I *adj* cincuenta inv; *fam* **a f.-f. chance**, una probabilidad del cincuenta por ciento; **fam to go f.-f.**, ir a medias. II *n* cincuenta *m* inv.

fig[1] [fɪg] *n* (fruit) higo *m*.

fig[2] [fɪg] *abbr of* figure, fig.

fight [faɪt] I *vtr* (*pt* & *pp* **fought**) 1 pelear(se) con, luchar con; (of boxer) enfrentarse a, luchar con; *fig* (corruption) combatir (against, contra). 2 (battle) librar; (war) hacer. 3 (decision) recurrir contra. II *vi* 1 pelear(se), luchar; (quarrel) reñir; **to f. over sth**, disputarse la posesión de algo. 2 *fig* (struggle) luchar (for/against, por/contra). III *n* 1 pelea *f*, lucha *f*; *Box* combate *m*. 2 (quarrel) riña *f*. 3 *fig* (struggle) lucha *f*. 4 (spirit) combatividad *f*. ◆**fight back** I *vtr* (tears) contener. II *vi* contraatacar. ◆**fight off** *vtr* 1 (attack) rechazar. 2 (illness) cortar. ◆**fight out** *vtr* discutir.

fighter ['faɪtə'] *n* 1 (person) combatiente *mf*; *Box* púgil *m*. 2 *fig* luchador,-a *m,f*; (plane), (avión *m* de) caza *m*; **f. bomber**, cazabombardero *m*.

fighting ['faɪtɪŋ] I *adj* **he's got a f.**

chance, tiene verdaderas posibilidades. II *n* lucha *f*.

figment ['fɪgmənt] *n* **it's a f. of your imagination**, es un producto de tu imaginación.

figurative ['fɪgərətɪv] *adj* figurado,-a.

figure ['fɪgə', US 'fɪgjər] I *n* 1 (form, outline) forma *f*, silueta *f*. 2 (shape, statue, character) figura *f*; **she has a good f.**, tiene buen tipo. 3 (in book) dibujo *m*. 4 **f. of speech**, figura retórica. 5 *Math* cifra *f*. II *vtr* US *fam* imaginarse. III *vi* 1 (appear) figurar. 2 US *fam* **that figures**, eso tiene sentido. ◆**figure out** *vtr* fam comprender; **I can't f. it out**, no me lo explico.

figurehead ['fɪgəhed] *n* *fig* figura decorativa.

filament ['fɪləmənt] *n* filamento *m*.

filch [fɪltʃ] *vtr* *sl* mangar, birlar.

file [faɪl] I *n* 1 (tool) lima *f*. 2 (folder) carpeta *f*. 3 (archive, of computer) archivo *m*; **on f.**, archivado,-a. 4 (line) fila *m*; **in single f.**, en fila india. II *vtr* 1 (smooth) limar. 2 (put away) archivar. III *vi* **to f. past**, desfilar.

filing ['faɪlɪŋ] *n* clasificación *f*; **f. cabinet**, archivador *m*; (for cards) fichero *m*.

Filipino [fɪlɪ'piːnəʊ] *n* filipino,-a *m,f*.

fill [fɪl] I *vtr* 1 (space, time) llenar (with, de). 2 (post, requirements) cubrir. 3 *Culin* rellenar. II *vi* llenarse (with, de). III *n* **to eat one's f.**, comer hasta hartarse. ◆**fill in** I *vtr* 1 (space, form) rellenar. 2 (inform) *fam* poner al corriente (on, de). 3 (time) pasar. II *vi* **to f. in for sb**, sustituir a algn. ◆**fill out** I *vtr* US (form) llenar. II *vi* engordar. ◆**fill up** I *vtr* llenar hasta arriba; *Aut* **fam f. her up!**, ¡llénelo!. II *vi* llenarse.

fillet ['fɪlɪt] *n* filete *m*; **f. steak**, filete.

filling ['fɪlɪŋ] I *adj* que llena mucho. II *n* (stuffing) relleno *m*. 2 (in tooth) empaste *m*. 3 *GB* **f. station**, gasolinera *f*.

filip ['fɪlɪp] *n* fam estímulo *m*.

film [fɪlm] I *n* 1 *Cin*, *Phot* película *f*; **f. star**, estrella *f* de cine. 2 (layer) capa *f*. II *vtr* *Cin* filmar. III *vi* *Cin* rodar.

film-strip ['fɪlmstrɪp] *n* cortometraje *m*.

filter ['fɪltə'] I *n* filtro *m*; *Aut* **f. lane**, carril *m* de acceso. II *vtr* filtrar. III *vi* *Aut* **to f. to the right**, girar a la derecha. ◆**filter through** *vi* *fig* filtrarse (to, a).

filth [fɪlθ] *n* (dirt) porquería *f*; *fig* porquerías *fpl*.

filthy ['fɪlθɪ] *adj* (filthier, filthiest) 1 (dirty) asqueroso,-a. 2 (obscene) obsceno, -a.

fin [fɪn] *n* *Zool Av* aleta *f*.

final ['faɪnəl] I *adj* 1 (last) último,-a, final. 2 (definitive) definitivo,-a. II *n* 1 *Sport* final *f*. 2 *Univ* **finals**, exámenes *mpl* de fin de carrera. ◆**finally** adv (lastly) por último;~(at last) por fin.

finale [fɪ'nɑːlɪ] n final m.

finalist ['faɪnəlɪst] n finalista mf.

finalize ['faɪnəlaɪz] vtr ultimar; (date) fijar.

finance ['faɪnæns, fɪ'næns] I n 1 finanzas fpl. 2 **finances**, fondos mpl. II vtr financiar.

financial [faɪ'nænʃəl, fɪ'nænʃəl] adj financiero,-a; **f. crisis**, crisis económica; **f. year**, año económico.

financier [faɪ'nænsɪəʳ, fɪ'nænsɪəʳ] n financiero,-a m,f.

finch [fɪntʃ] n pinzón m.

find [faɪnd] I vtr (pt & pp found) 1 (locate) encontrar. 2 (think) encontrar. 3 **this found its way into my bag**, esto vino a parar a mi bolso. 4 (discover) descubrir; **it has been found that …**, se ha comprobado que … 5 Jur **to f. sb guilty/not guilty**, declarar culpable/inocente a algn. 6 **I can't f. the courage to tell him**, no tengo valor para decírselo; **I found it impossible to get away**, me resultó imposible irme. II n hallazgo m. ◆**find out** I vtr 1 (enquire) averiguar. 2 (discover) descubrir. II vi 1 **to f. out about sth**, informarse sobre algo. 2 (discover) enterarse.

findings ['faɪndɪŋz] npl conclusiones fpl.

fine¹ [faɪn] I n multa f. II vtr multar.

fine² [faɪn] I adj 1 (delicate etc) fino,-a. 2 (subtle) sutil. 3 (excellent) excelente. 4 (weather) bueno; **it was f.**, hacía buen tiempo. 5 **the f. arts**, las bellas artes. 6 (all right) bien. II adv fam muy bien. III interj ¡vale! ◆**finely** adv 1 finamente; **f. chopped**, picado fino. 2 **f. tuned**, a punto.

finery ['faɪnərɪ] n galas fpl.

finesse [fɪ'nes] n (delicacy) finura f; (cunning) astucia f; (tact) sutileza f.

finger ['fɪŋgəʳ] I n dedo m (de la mano); fam **to keep one's fingers crossed**, esperar que todo salga bien; fam **you've put your f. on it**, has dado en el clavo; **middle f.**, dedo corazón. II vtr tocar; pej manosear.

fingernail ['fɪŋgəneɪl] n uña f.

fingerprint ['fɪŋgəprɪnt] n huella f dactilar.

fingertip ['fɪŋgətɪp] n punta f or yema f del dedo.

finicky ['fɪnɪkɪ] adj (person) quisquilloso, -a.

finish ['fɪnɪʃ] I n 1 fin m; (of race) llegada f. 2 (surface) acabado m. II vtr 1 (complete) acabar, terminar; **to f. doing sth**, terminar de hacer algo. 2 (use up) agotar. III vi acabar, terminar; **to f. second**, quedar el segundo. ◆**finish off** vtr 1 (complete) terminar completamente. 2 (kill) fam rematar. ◆**finish up** I vtr aca-

bar, agotar. II vi **to f. up in jail**, ir a parar a la carcel.

finished ['fɪnɪʃt] adj 1 (product) acabado, -a. 2 fam (exhausted) rendido,-a.

finishing ['fɪnɪʃɪŋ] adj **to put the f. touch(es) to sth**, darle los últimos toques a algo; **f. line**, (línea f de) meta f; **f. school**, escuela privada de modales para señoritas.

finite ['faɪnaɪt] adj finito,-a; (verb) conjugable.

Finland ['fɪnlənd] n Finlandia f.

Finn [fɪn] n finlandés,-esa m,f.

Finnish ['fɪnɪʃ] I adj finlandés,-esa. II n (language) finlandés m.

fir [fɜːʳ] n abeto m.

fire [faɪəʳ] I n 1 fuego m. 2 (accident) incendio m; **to be on f.**, estar en llamas; **to catch f.**, incendiarse; **f. alarm**, alarma f de incendios; **f. brigade**, (cuerpo m de) bomberos mpl; **f. engine**, coche m de bomberos; **f. escape**, escalera f de incendios; **f. exit**, salida f de emergencia; **f. extinguisher**, extintor m; **f. fighting**, extinción f de incendios; **f. station**, parque m de bomberos. 3 (heater) estufa f. 4 Mil fuego m; **to open f.**, abrir fuego; fig **to come under f.**, ser el blanco de las críticas. II vtr 1 (gun) disparar (at, a); (rocket) lanzar; fig **to f. questions at sb**, bombardear a algn a preguntas. 2 fam (dismiss) despedir. III vi (shoot) disparar (at, sobre).

firearm ['faɪərɑːm] n arma f de fuego.

fire-fighter ['faɪəfaɪtəʳ] n US bombero m.

fireman ['faɪəmən] n bombero m.

fireplace ['faɪəpleɪs] n chimenea f; (hearth) hogar m.

fireside ['faɪəsaɪd] n hogar m; **by the f.**, al calor de la lumbre.

firewood ['faɪəwʊd] n leña f.

fireworks ['faɪəwɜːks] npl fuegos mpl artificiales.

firing ['faɪərɪŋ] n Mil tiroteo m; **f. line**, línea f de fuego; **f. squad**, pelotón m de fusilamiento.

firm [fɜːm] I adj firme; **to be f. with sb**, (strict) tratar a algn con firmeza. II n Com empresa f, firma f. ◆**firmly** adv firmemente.

firmness ['fɜːmnɪs] n firmeza f.

first [fɜːst] I adj primero,-a; (before masculine singular noun) primer; **Charles the F.**, Carlos Primero; **for the f. time**, por primera vez; **in the f. place**, en primer lugar; **f. floor**, primer piso m, US planta baja; **f. name**, nombre m de pila. II adv (before anything else) primero; **f. and foremost**, ante todo; **f. of all**, en primer lugar. III n 1 **the f.**, el primero, la primera; **the f. of April**, el uno or el primero de abril; **f. aid**, primeros auxilios; **f. aid box**, botiquín m. 2 **at f.**, al principio; **from the (very) f.**, desde el principio. 3

Aut primera *f.* **4** *Univ* **to get a f.**, sacar un sobresaliente. ◆**firstly** *adv* en primer lugar.

first-class ['fɜːstklɑːs] **I** *adj* de primera clase. **II first class** *adv* **to travel f. c.**, viajar en primera.

first-hand ['fɜːsthænd] *adv & adj* de primera mano.

first-rate ['fɜːstreɪt] *adj* de primera.

fiscal ['fɪskəl] *adj* fiscal.

fish [fɪʃ] **I** *n* (*pl* **fish**) **1** pez *m*; (*food*) pescadería *f.* **2** *Culin* pescado *m*; **f. shop**, pescadería *f.* **2** *Culin* pescado *m*; **f. and chips**, pescado frito con patatas fritas; *US* **f. stick**, palito *m* de pescado. **II** *vi* pescar; *fig* **to f. in one's pocket for sth**, buscar algo en el bolsillo.

fishbone ['fɪʃbəʊn] *n* espina *f*, raspa *f.*

fisherman ['fɪʃəmən] *n* pescador *m.*

fishfinger [fɪʃ'fɪŋgəʳ] *n* palito *m* de pescado.

fishing ['fɪʃɪŋ] *n* pesca *f*; **to go f.**, ir de pesca; **f. net**, red *f* de pesca; **f. rod**, caña *f* de pescar; **f. tackle**, aparejo *m* de pescar.

fishmonger ['fɪʃmʌŋgəʳ] *n* *GB* pescadero,-a *m,f*; **fishmonger's (shop)**, pescadería *f.*

fishy ['fɪʃɪ] *adj* (**fishier, fishiest**) de pescado; *fam fig* **there's something f. going on**, aquí hay gato encerrado.

fist [fɪst] *n* puño *m.*

fit¹ [fɪt] **I** *vtr* **1** ir bien a; **that suit doesn't f. you**, ese traje no te entalla. **2** *Sew* probar. **3** **the key doesn't f. the lock**, la llave no es de esta cerradura. **4** (*install*) colocar; **a car fitted with a radio**, un coche provisto de radio. **5** *fig* **she doesn't f. the description**, no responde a la descripción. **II** *vi* **1** (*be of right size*) caber. **2** (*facts etc*) cuadrar. **III** *adj* **1** (*suitable*) apto,-a, adecuado,-a (*for*, para); **are you f. to drive?**, ¿estás en condiciones de conducir? **2** (*healthy*) en (plena) forma; **to keep f.**, mantenerse en forma. **IV** *n* ajuste *m*; *Sew* corte *m*; **to be a good f.**, encajar bien. ◆**fit in I** *vi* **1** he didn't **f. in with my colleagues**, no encajó con sus compañeros de trabajo. **II** *vtr* (*find time for*) encontrar un hueco para. ◆**fit out** *vtr* equipar.

fit² [fɪt] *n* **1** *Med* ataque *m.* **2** *fig* arrebato *m*; **f. of anger**, arranque *m* de cólera; *fig* **by fits and starts**, a trompicones.

fitful ['fɪtfʊl] *adj* discontinuo,-a.

fitness ['fɪtnɪs] *n* **1** (*aptitude*) aptitud *f*, capacidad *f.* **2** (*health*) (buen) estado físico.

fitted ['fɪtɪd] *adj* empotrado,-a; **f. carpet**, moqueta *f*; **f. cupboard**, armario empotrado.

fitter ['fɪtəʳ] *n* ajustador,-a *m,f.*

fitting ['fɪtɪŋ] **I** *adj* apropiado,-a. **II** *n* **1** (*of dress*) prueba *f*; **f. room**, probador *m.* **2** (*usu pl*) accesorio *m*; **light fittings**, apli-

ques eléctricos.

five [faɪv] *adj & n* cinco (*m*) *inv.*

fiver ['faɪvəʳ] *n* *fam* billete *m* de cinco libras or dólares.

fix [fɪks] **I** *n* **1** *fam* **to be in a f.**, estar en un apuro. **2** (*drugs*) sl chute *m.* **II** *vtr* **1** (*fasten*) fijar, asegurar. **2** (*date, price*) fijar; (*limit*) señalar. **3** **he'll f. it with the boss**, (*arrange*) se las arreglará con el jefe. **4** (*repair*) arreglar. **5** *US* (*food, drink*) preparar. ◆**fix up** *vtr* (*arrange*) arreglar; **to f. sb up with sth**, proveer a algn de algo.

fixation [fɪk'seɪʃən] *n* idea fija.

fixed [fɪkst] *adj* **1** fijo,-a. **2** *fam* (*match etc*) amañado,-a.

fixture ['fɪkstʃəʳ] *n* **1** *Sport* encuentro *m.* **2** **fixtures**, (*in building*) accesorios *mpl.*

fizz [fɪz] *vi* **1** burbujear. **2** hacer burbujear. ◆**fizzle out** ['fɪzləʊt] *vi* quedar en nada.

fizzy ['fɪzɪ] *adj* (**fizzier, fizziest**) (*water*) con gas.

flabbergasted ['flæbəgɑːstɪd] *adj* pasmado,-a.

flabby ['flæbɪ] *adj* (**flabbier, flabbiest**) fofo,-a.

flag [flæg] **I** *n* bandera *f*; *Naut* pabellón *m.* **II** *vtr fig* **to f. down a car**, hacer señales a un coche para que pare. **III** *vi* (*interest*) decaer; (*conversation*) languidecer.

flagpole ['flægpəʊl] *n* asta *f* de bandera.

flagrant ['fleɪɡrənt] *adj* flagrante.

flagship ['flægʃɪp] *n* buque insignia *m.*

flagstone ['flæɡstəʊn] *n* losa *f.*

flair [fleəʳ] *n* facilidad *f.*

flak [flæk] *n* **1** *Mil* fuego antiaéreo. **2** *fam* críticas *fpl.*

flake [fleɪk] **I** *n* (*of snow*) copo *m*; (*of skin, soap*) escama *f*; (*of paint*) desconchón *m.* **II** *vi* (*skin*) descamarse; (*paint*) desconcharse.

flamboyant [flæm'bɔɪənt] *adj* extravagante.

flame [fleɪm] *n* llama *f*; **to go up in flames**, incendiarse.

flameproof ['fleɪmpruːf] *adj* ininflamable.

flamingo [flə'mɪŋɡəʊ] *n* flamenco *m.*

flammable ['flæməbəl] *adj* inflamable.

flan [flæn] *n* tarta rellena; **fruit f.**, tarta de fruta.

flank [flæŋk] **I** *n* **1** (*of animal*) ijada *f.* **2** *Mil* flanco *m.* **II** *vtr* flanquear.

flannel ['flænəl] *n* **1** *Tex* franela *f.* **2** *GB* (*face cloth*) toallita *f.*

flap [flæp] **I** *vtr* (*wings, arms*) batir. **II** *vi* (*wings, arms*) aletear; (*flag*) ondear. **III** *n* **1** (*of envelope, pocket*) solapa *f*; (*of tent*) faldón *m.* **2** (*of wing*) aletazo *m.* **3** *fam* **to get into a f.**, ponerse nervioso,-a.

flare [fleəʳ] **I** *n* **1** (*flame*) llamarada *f.* **2** *Mil Naut* bengala *f.* **II** *vi* **to f. (up)**, (*fire*) llamear; *fig* (*person*) encolerizarse; (*trouble*) estallar.

flared [fleəd] *adj* (*trousers etc*)

acampanado,-a.

flash [flæʃ] **I** n 1 (of light) destello m; (of lightning) relámpago m; fig **in a f.**, en un santiamén; fig **a f. in the pan**, un éxito fugaz. 2 **news f.**, noticia f de última hora. 3 Phot flash m. **II** adj sl chulo,-a. **III** vtr 1 (torch) dirigir. 2 Rad TV transmitir. 3 **he flashed his card**, enseñó rápidamente su carnet. **IV** vi 1 (light) destellar. 2 **a car flashed past**, un coche pasó como un rayo.

flashback ['flæʃbæk] n flashback m.

flashcube ['flæʃkjuːb] n cubo m flash.

flashlight ['flæʃlaɪt] n US linterna f.

flashy ['flæʃɪ] adj (flashier, flashiest) fam chillón,-a.

flask [flɑːsk, flæsk] n frasco m; (**thermos**) f., termo m.

flat [flæt] **I** adj (flatter, flattest) 1 (surface) llano,-a. 2 (beer) sin gas. 3 (battery) descargado,-a; (tyre) desinflado,-a. 4 (rate) fijo,-a. 5 (categorical) rotundo,-a. 6 (dull) soso,-a. 7 Mus **B f.**, si m bemol. **II** adv 1 **to fall f. on one's face**, caerse de bruces. 2 **in ten seconds f.**, en diez segundos justos. 3 fam **to go f. out**, ir a todo gas. **III** n 1 (appartment) piso m. 2 US Aut pinchazo m. 3 **mud flats**, marismas fpl. ◆**flatly** adv rotundamente.

flatmate ['flætmeɪt] n GB compañero,-a m,f de piso.

flatten ['flætən] vtr 1 (make level) allanar. 2 (crush) aplastar.

flatter ['flætə'] vtr 1 adular, halagar. 2 (clothes, portrait) favorecer. 3 **to f. one-self**, hacerse ilusiones.

flattering ['flætərɪŋ] adj 1 (words) halagador,-a. 2 (dress, portrait) favorecedor,-a.

flattery ['flætərɪ] n adulación f, halago m.

flaunt [flɔːnt] vtr hacer alarde de.

flavour, US **flavor** ['fleɪvə'] **I** n sabor m. **II** vtr Culin sazonar (**with**, con).

flavoured, US **flavored** ['fleɪvəd] adj strawberry f., con sabor a fresa.

flavouring, US **flavoring** ['fleɪvərɪŋ] n condimento m; **artificial f.**, aroma m artificial.

flaw [flɔː] n (failing) defecto m; (fault) desperfecto m.

flawless ['flɔːlɪs] adj perfecto,-a.

flax [flæks] n lino m.

flaxen ['flæksən] adj (hair) rubio pajizo.

flea [fliː] n pulga f; **f. market**, rastro m.

fleck [flek] n (speck) mota f, punto m.

fledg(e)ling ['fledʒlɪŋ] adj fig novato,-a.

flee [fliː] **I** vtr (pt & pp **fled**) huir de. **II** vi huir (**from**, de).

fleece [fliːs] **I** n 1 (sheep's coat) lana f. 2 (sheared) vellón m. **II** vtr fam (cheat) sangrar.

fleet [fliːt] n flota f.

fleeting ['fliːtɪŋ] adj fugaz.

Flemish ['flemɪʃ] **I** adj flamenco,-a. **II** n (language) flamenco m.

flesh [fleʃ] n 1 carne f; fig **in the f.**, en persona; fig **to be of f. and blood**, ser de carne y hueso; **f. wound**, herida f superficial. 2 (of fruit) pulpa f.

flew [fluː] pt → **fly**.

flex [fleks] **I** n GB Elec cable m. **II** vtr (muscles) flexionar.

flexible ['fleksɪbəl] adj flexible.

flexibility [fleksɪ'bɪlɪtɪ] n flexibilidad f.

flick [flik] **I** n movimiento rápido; (of finger) capirotazo m. **II** vtr (with finger) dar un capirotazo a. ◆**flick through** vtr (book) hojear.

flicker ['flikə'] **I** n 1 parpadeo m; (of light) titileo m. 2 fig **a f. of hope**, un destello de esperanza. **II** vi (eyes) parpadear; (flame) vacilar.

flier ['flaɪə'] n aviador,-a m,f.

flight [flaɪt] n 1 vuelo m; **f. path**, trayectoria f de vuelo; **f. recorder**, registrador m de vuelo. 2 (of ball) trayectoria f. 3 (escape) huida f, fuga f; **to take f.**, darse a la fuga. 4 (of stairs) tramo m.

flight-deck ['flaɪtdek] n (cockpit) cabina f del piloto.

flimsy ['flimzɪ] adj (flimsier, flimsiest) (cloth) ligero,-a; (paper) fino,-a; (structure) poco sólido,-a; (excuse) poco convincente.

flinch [flintʃ] vi (wince) estremecerse.

fling [flɪŋ] **I** vtr (pt & pp **flung**) arrojar. **II** n fam **to have a f.**, echar una cana al aire.

flint [flint] n 1 (stone) pedernal m. 2 (in lighter) piedra f de mechero.

flip [flɪp] **I** n (flick) capirotazo m. **II** vtr (toss) tirar (al aire); **to f. a coin**, echar a cara o cruz.

flip-flop ['flipflop] n 1 Compu báscula f biestable. 2 (footwear) chancleta f.

flippant ['flipənt] adj frívolo,-a.

flipper ['flipə'] n aleta f.

flirt [flɜːt] **I** n coqueto,-a m,f. **II** vi flirtear, coquetear; **to f. with death**, jugar con la muerte.

flirtation [flɜː'teɪʃən] n flirteo m, coqueteo m.

flit [flit] vi revolotear.

float [fləut] **I** n 1 (angling) flotador m. 2 (money) cambio m. 3 (in procession) carroza f. **II** vtr 1 poner a flote. 2 (shares) emitir; (currency, business) hacer flotar. **III** vi flotar.

floating ['fləutɪŋ] adj flotante; (voter) indeciso,-a.

flock [flok] **I** n Zool rebaño m; Orn bandada f; Rel grey f; (crowd) multitud f. **II** vi acudir en masa.

flog [flog] vtr azotar; fam fig **flogged to death**, (idea) trillado. 2 sl (sell) vender.

flood [flʌd] **I** n inundación f; (of river) riada f; fig torrente m. **II** vtr inundar. **III** vi (river) desbordarse; fig **to f. in**, entrar a raudales.

flooding |'flʌdɪŋ| n inundaciones fpl.

floodlight |'flʌdlaɪt| n foco m.

floor |flɔːr| I n 1 (of room) suelo m; **dance f.**, pista f de baile. 2 (of ocean, forest) fondo m. 3 (storey) piso m; **first f.**, GB primer piso m, US planta baja; **GB ground f.**, planta baja. II vtr fig dejar perplejo,-a.

floorboard |'flɔːbɔːd| n tabla f (del suelo).

flop |flɒp| I n fam fracaso m. II vi 1 to **f. down on the bed**, tumbarse en la cama. 2 fam fracasar.

floppy |'flɒpɪ| adj (floppier, floppiest) flojo,-a; Comput f. disk, disco m flexible.

flora |'flɔːrə| n flora f.

florid |'flɒrɪd| adj (style) florido,-a.

florist |'flɒrɪst| n florista mf; **f.'s**, floristería f.

flounce¹ |flaʊns| vi to **f. in/out**, entrar/salir airadamente.

flounce² |flaʊns| n Sew volante m.

flounder¹ |'flaʊndər| n (fish) platija f.

flounder² |'flaʊndər| vi 1 (struggle) forcejear; fig enredarse. 2 (be at a loss) no saber que decir or hacer.

flour |'flaʊər| n harina f.

flourish |'flʌrɪʃ| I n 1 (gesture) ademán m (teatral). 2 (under signature) rúbrica f. II vtr (brandish) agitar. III vi (thrive) florecer; (plant) crecer.

flourishing |'flʌrɪʃɪŋ| adj floreciente.

flout |flaʊt| vtr fur desacatar.

flow |fləʊ| I n (of river) corriente f; (of traffic) circulación f; (of capital) movimiento m; (of people, goods) afluencia f; **f. chart**, diagrama m de flujo; Comput organigrama m. II vi (blood, river) fluir; (sea) subir; (traffic) circular.

flower |'flaʊər| I n flor f; **f. bed**, arriate m. II vi florecer.

flowerpot |'flaʊəpɒt| n maceta f.

flowery |'flaʊrɪ| adj fig florido,-a.

flowing |'fləʊɪŋ| adj (hair) suelto,-a; (dress) de mucho vuelo; (style) fluido,-a; (shape, movement) natural.

flown |fləʊn| pp → **fly**.

flu |fluː| n (abbr of **influenza**) gripe f.

fluctuate |'flʌktjʊeɪt| vi fluctuar.

fluctuation |flʌktjʊ'eɪʃən| n fluctuación f.

flue |fluː| n conducto m de humos; (chimney) cañón m.

fluent |'fluːənt| adj 1 he speaks f. German, habla el alemán con soltura. 2 (eloquent) fluido,-a.

fluff |flʌf| I n (down) pelusa f II vtr to **f. sth**, hacer algo mal.

fluffy |'flʌfɪ| adj (fluffier, fluffiest) (pillow) mullido,-a; (toy) de peluche; (cake) esponjoso,-a.

fluid |'fluːɪd| I adj (movement) natural; (style, prose) fluido,-a; (situation) incierto,-a. II n fluido m, líquido m.

fluke |fluːk| n fam chiripa f; **by a f.**, por chiripa.

flummox |'flʌməks| vtr fam desconcertar.

flung |flʌŋ| pt & pp → **fling.**

fluorescent |flʊə'resənt| adj fluorescente.

fluoride |'flʊəraɪd| n fluoruro m.

flurry |'flʌrɪ| n 1 (of wind) ráfaga f; (of snow) nevasca f. 2 fig (bustle) agitación f.

flush |flʌʃ| I adj f. with, a ras de. II n (blush) rubor m. III vtr to **f. the lavatory**, tirar de la cadena. IV vi 1 the **loo won't f.**, la cisterna del wáter no funciona. 2 (blush) ruborizarse.

flushed |flʌʃt| adj (cheeks) rojo,-a, encendido,-a; fig f. **with success**, emocionado,-a ante su éxito.

fluster |'flʌstər| vtr to get flustered, ponerse nervioso,-a.

flute |fluːt| n flauta f.

flutter |'flʌtər| I vi (leaves, birds) revolotear; (flag) ondear. II n fam (bet, gambling) apuesta pequeña.

flux |flʌks| n (flow) flujo m; (instability) inestabilidad f; fig to **be in a state of f.**, estar cambiando constantemente.

fly¹ |flaɪ| I vtr (pt flew; pp flown) 1 Av pilotar. 2 (merchandize, troops) transportar. 3 (distance) recorrer. 4 (kite) hacer volar. II vi 1 (bird, plane) volar. 2 (go by plane) ir en avión. 3 (flag) ondear. 4 to **f. into a rage**, montar en cólera. 5 the train **flew past**, el tren pasó volando. 6 fam to **go flying**, (fall) caerse. III n flies, bragueta f sing.

fly² |flaɪ| n (insect) mosca f; **f. spray**, spray m matamoscas.

flying |'flaɪɪŋ| adj volador,-a; (rapid) rápido,-a; a **f. visit**, una visita relámpago; fig to **come out of an affair with f. colours**, salir airoso,-a de un asunto; fig to **get off to a f. start**, empezar con buen pie; **f. picket**, piquete m (informativo); **f. saucer**, platillo m volante. II n 1 (action) vuelo m. 2 (aviation) aviación f.

flyleaf |'flaɪliːf| n (of book) guarda f.

flyover |'flaɪəʊvər| n paso elevado.

flypast |'flaɪpɑːst| n GB Av desfile aéreo.

flyweight |'flaɪweɪt| n Box peso m mosca.

foal |fəʊl| n potro,-a m,f.

foam |fəʊm| I n espuma f; **f. bath**, espuma de baño; **f. rubber**, goma espuma. II vi hacer espuma.

fob |fɒb| vtr fam to **f. sb off with excuses**, darle largas a algn. ◆**fob off** vtr fam **he fobbed off his old radio on a stranger**, le colocó su radio vieja a un desconocido.

focus |'fəʊkəs| I vtr centrarse (on, en). II vi enfocar; to **f. on sth**, Phot enfocar algo; fig centrarse en algo; **f.** (pl focuses) foco m; to **be in f./out of f.**, estar enfocado,-a/desenfocado,-a.

fodder |'fɒdər| n pienso m.

foe |fəʊ| n fml enemigo,-a m,f.

foetus |'fiːtəs| n feto m.

fog [fɒg] n niebla f; (at sea) bruma f.

fogey ['fəugi] n fam old f., cascarrabias mf inv.

foggy ['fɒgi] adj (foggier, foggiest) it is f., hay niebla; fam I haven't the foggiest (idea), no tengo la más mínima idea.

foghorn ['fɒghɔːn] n sirena f (de niebla).

foglamp ['fɒglæmp], US **foglight** ['fɒglait] n faro m antiniebla.

foil [fɔil] n 1 **aluminium f.**, papel m de aluminio. 2 (in fencing) florete m. II vtr (plot) desbaratar.

fold [fəuld] I n (crease) pliegue m. II vtr plegar, doblar; to f. one's arms, cruzar los brazos. III vi to f. (up), (chair etc) plegarse; Com quebrar.

folder ['fəuldər] n carpeta f.

folding ['fəuldiŋ] adj (chair etc) plegable.

foliage ['fəulidʒ] n follaje m.

folk [fəuk] I n pl (people) gente f. 2 fam **folks**, (family) padres mpl; one's f., la familia. II adj popular; f. music, música f folk; f. song, canción f popular.

folklore ['fəuklɔːr] n folklore m.

follow ['fɒləu] I vtr seguir; (pursue) perseguir; (understand) comprender; (way of life) llevar. II vi 1 (come after) seguir; as **follows**, como sigue. 2 (result) resultar; that doesn't f., eso no es lógico. 3 (understand) entender. ◆**follow through, follow up** vtr (idea) llevar a cabo; (clue) investigar.

follower ['fɒləuər] n seguidor,-a m,f.

following ['fɒləuiŋ] I adj siguiente. II n seguidores mpl.

folly ['fɒli] n locura f, desatino m.

fond [fɒnd] adj (loving) cariñoso,-a; to be f. of sb, tenerle mucho cariño a algn; to be f. of doing sth, ser aficionado,-a a hacer algo.

fondness ['fɒndnis] n (love) cariño m (for, a); (liking) afición f (for, a).

fondle ['fɒndl] vtr acariciar.

font [fɒnt] n Rel pila f.

food [fuːd] n comida f; f. chain, cadena trófica; f. **poisoning**, intoxicación alimenticia.

foodstuffs ['fuːdstʌfs] npl productos alimenticios.

fool [fuːl] I n 1 tonto,-a m,f, imbécil mf; to make a f. of sb, poner a algn en ridículo; to play the f., hacer el tonto. 2 Culin = mousse f de fruta. II vtr (deceive) engañar. III vi (joke) bromear; to f. about or around, hacer el tonto.

foolhardy ['fuːlhɑːdi] adj (foolhardier, foolhardiest) temerario,-a; (person) intrépido,-a.

foolish ['fuːliʃ] adj estúpido,-a.

foolproof ['fuːlpruːf] adj infalible.

foot [fut] n (pl **feet** [fiːt]) pie m; Zool pata f; on f., a pie, andando; fig to find one's feet, acostumbrarse; fam fig to put one's f. down, (control) imponerse; (in car) pisar a fondo; fam fig to put one's f. in it, meter la pata; fam fig to put one's feet up, descansar. II vtr to f. the bill, (pay) pagar la cuenta.

footage ['futidʒ] n Cin metraje m.

football ['futbɔːl] n 1 (soccer) fútbol m; bar f., futbolín m; f. **ground**, campo m de fútbol; f. **match**, partido m de fútbol; f. **pools**, quinielas fpl. 2 (ball) balón m.

footballer ['futbɔːlər] n futbolista mf.

footbridge ['futbridʒ] n puente m para peatones.

foothills ['futhilz] npl estribaciones fpl.

foothold ['futhəuld] n fig to gain a f., afianzarse en una posición.

footing ['futiŋ] n to lose one's f., perder el equilibrio; on a friendly f., en plan amistoso; on an equal f., en pie de igualdad.

footlights ['futlaits] npl candilejas fpl.

footman ['futmən] n lacayo m.

footnote ['futnəut] n nota f a pie de página.

footpath ['futpɑːθ] n (track) sendero m.

footprint ['futprint] n pisada f.

footsore ['futsɔːr] adj con los pies doloridos.

footstep ['futstep] n paso m.

footwear ['futweər] n calzado m.

for [fɔːr] I prep 1 (intended) para; **curtains f. the bedroom**, cortinas para el dormitorio; f. **sale**, en venta; it's time f. bed, es hora de acostarse. 2 (representing) por; a **cheque f. ten pounds**, un cheque de diez libras; J f. John, J de Juan; what's the Spanish f. 'rivet'?, ¿cómo se dice 'rivet' en español? 3 (purpose) para; it's good f. the digestion, es bueno para la digestión; what's this f.?, ¿para qué sirve esto? 4 (because of) por; **famous f. its cuisine**, famoso,-a por su cocina; to jump f. joy, saltar de alegría. 5 (on behalf of) por; the **campaign f. peace**, la campaña por la paz; will you do it f. me?, ¿lo harás por mí? 6 (during) por, durante; I lent it to her f. a year, se lo presté por un año; I shall stay f. two weeks, me quedaré dos semanas; I was ill f. a month, estuve enfermo,-a durante un mes; I've been here f. three months, hace tres meses que estoy aquí. 7 (distance) I walked f. ten kilometres, caminé diez kilómetros. 8 (at a point in time) para; I can do it f. next Monday, puedo hacerlo para el lunes que viene; f. the last time, por última vez. 9 (destination) para; I got the car f. five hundred pounds, conseguí el coche por quinientas libras. 11 (in favour of) a favor de; are you f. or against?, ¿estás a favor o en contra?; to vote f. sb, votar a algn. 12 (to obtain) para; to run f. the bus, correr para coger el autobús; to send sb f. water, mandar a algn a por agua. 13

(with respect to) en cuanto a; **as f. him**, en cuanto a él; **f. all I care**, por mí; **f. all I know**, que yo sepa; **f. one thing**, para empezar. **14** (despite) a pesar de; **f. all that**, aún así; **he's tall f. his age**, está muy alto para su edad. **15** (instead of) por; **can you go f. me?**, puede ir por mí? **16** (towards) hacia, por; **affection f. sb**, cariño hacia algn; **his love f. you**, su amor por ti. **17** (as) por; **to leave sb f. dead**, dar a algn por muerto,-a; **what do you use f. fuel?**, ¿qué utilizan como combustible? **18** (in exchange) por; **to exchange one thing f. another**, cambiar una cosa por otra; **how much did you sell it f.?**, ¿por cuánto lo vendiste? **19** (+ object + infin) **there's no reason f. us to quarrel**, no hay motivo para que riñamos; **it's time f. you to go**, es hora de que os marchéis; **it's easy f. him to say that**, le es fácil decir eso.
II conj (since, as) ya que, puesto que.

forage ['fɒrɪdʒ] **I** n forraje m. **II** vi hurgar.

foray ['fɒreɪ] n incursión f.

forbearance [fɔː'beərəns] n paciencia f.

forbid [fə'bɪd] vtr (pt forbade, pp forbidden) ['fə'bɪdn]) prohibir; **to f. sb to do sth**, prohibirle a algn hacer algo.

forbidding [fə'bɪdɪŋ] adj (stern) severo,-a; (bleak) inhóspito,-a.

force [fɔːs] **I** n **1** fuerza f.; **by f.**, por la fuerza; **to come into f.**, entrar en vigor. **2** Mil cuerpo m; **the (armed) forces**, las fuerzas armadas; **the police f.**, la policía. **II** vtr forzar; **to f. sb to do sth**, forzar a algn a hacer algo.

forced [fɔːst] adj forzado,-a; **f. landing**, aterrizaje forzoso.

force-feed ['fɔːsfiːd] vtr alimentar a la fuerza.

forceful ['fɔːsfʊl] adj **1** (person) enérgico, -a. **2** (argument) convincente.

forcible ['fɔːsəbəl] adj **f. entry**, allanamiento m de morada. ◆**forcibly** adv a or por la fuerza.

forceps ['fɔːseps] npl fórceps m sing.

ford [fɔːd] **I** n vado m. **II** vtr vadear.

fore [fɔː] fig **to come to the f.**, empezar a destacar.

forearm ['fɔːrɑːm] n antebrazo m.

foreboding [fɔː'bəʊdɪŋ] n presentimiento m.

forecast ['fɔːkɑːst] **I** n pronóstico m. **II** vtr (pt & pp forecast or forecasted) pronosticar.

forecourt ['fɔːkɔːt] n (of garage) área f de servicio.

forefathers ['fɔːfɑːðəz] npl antepasados mpl.

forefinger ['fɔːfɪŋgə] n índice m.

forefront ['fɔːfrʌnt] n **in the f.**, a la vanguardia.

forego [fɔː'gəʊ] vtr fml (pt forewent; pp foregone) sacrificar.

foregone ['fɔːgɒn] adj **a f. conclusion**, un resultado inevitable.

foreground ['fɔːgraʊnd] n primer plano m.

forehead ['fɒrɪd, 'fɔːhed] n frente f.

foreign ['fɒrɪn] adj extranjero,-a; (trade, policy) exterior; **f. exchange**, divisas fpl; **the F. Office**, el Ministerio de Asuntos Exteriores; **f. body**, cuerpo extraño.

foreigner ['fɒrɪnə] n extranjero,-a m,f.

foreman ['fɔːmən] n **1** Ind capataz m. **2** Jur presidente m del jurado.

foremost ['fɔːməʊst] adj principal; **first and f.**, ante todo.

forename ['fɔːneɪm] n nombre m de pila.

forensic [fə'rensɪk] adj forense.

forerunner ['fɔːrʌnə] n precursor,-a m,f.

foresee [fɔː'siː] vtr (pt foresaw pp foreseen) prever.

foreseeable [fɔː'siːəbəl] adj previsible; **in the f. future**, en un futuro próximo.

foreshadow [fɔː'ʃædəʊ] vtr presagiar.

foresight ['fɔːsaɪt] n previsión f.

forest ['fɒrɪst] n bosque m.

forestall [fɔː'stɔːl] vtr (plan) anticiparse; (danger) prevenir.

forestry ['fɒrɪstrɪ] n silvicultura f.

foretaste ['fɔːteɪst] n anticipo m (of, de).

foretell [fɔː'tel] vtr (pt & pp foretold) presagiar.

forever [fə'revə] adv **1** (eternally) siempre. **2** (for good) para siempre. **3** fam (ages) siglos mpl.

foreword ['fɔːwɜːd] n prefacio m.

forfeit ['fɔːfɪt] **I** n (penalty) pena f; (in games) prenda f. **II** vtr perder.

forgave [fə'geɪv] pt → **forgive**.

forge [fɔːdʒ] **I** n **1** (furnace) fragua f. **2** (blacksmith's) herrería f. **II** vtr **1** (counterfeit) falsificar. **2** (metal) forjar. **III** vi **to f. ahead**, hacer grandes progresos.

forger ['fɔːdʒə] n falsificador,-a m,f.

forgery ['fɔːdʒərɪ] n falsificación f.

forget [fə'get] **I** vtr (pt forgot; pp forgotten) olvidar, olvidarse de; **I forgot to close the window**, se me olvidó cerrar or me olvidé de cerrar la ventana; **I've forgotten my key**, he olvidado la llave. **II** vi olvidarse.

forgetful [fə'getful] adj olvidadizo,-a.

forget-me-not [fə'getmɪnɒt] n nomeolvides f inv.

forgive [fə'gɪv] vtr (pt forgave pp forgiven [fə'gɪvn]) perdonar; **to f. sb for sth**, perdonarle algo a algn.

forgiveness [fə'gɪvnɪs] n perdón m.

forgo [fɔː'gəʊ] vtr → **forgo**.

forgot [fə'gɒt] pt, **forgotten** [fə'gɒtən] pp → **forget**.

fork [fɔːk] n **1** Agr horca f. **2** (cutlery) tenedor m. **3** (in road) bifurcación f. **II** vi (roads) bifurcarse. ◆**fork out** vtr fam (money) soltar.

fork-lift truck [fɔːklɪf'trʌk] n carretilla f

elevadora de horquilla.

forlorn [fə'lɔːn] *adj* *(forsaken)* abandonado,-a; *(desolate)* triste; *(without hope)* desesperado,-a.

form [fɔːm] **I** *n* **1** *(shape)* forma *f.* **2** *(type)* clase *f.* **3 for f.'s sake**, para guardar las formas. **4** *(document)* formulario *m.* **5 on top/off f.**, en/en plena/en baja forma. **6** *Educ* clase *f.* **the first f.**, el primer curso. **II** *vtr* formar; **to f. an impression**, formarse una impresión. **III** *vi* formarse.

formal ['fɔːməl] *adj* **1** *(official)* oficial; **a f. application**, una solicitud en forma. **2** *(party, dress)* de etiqueta. **3** *(ordered)* formal. **4** *(person)* formalista. ◆**formally** *adv* oficialmente.

formality [fɔː'mælɪtɪ] *n* formalidad *f.*

format ['fɔːmæt] **I** *n* formato *m.* **II** *vtr* *Comput* formatear.

formation [fɔː'meɪʃən] *n* formación *f.*

formative ['fɔːmətɪv] *adj* formativo,-a.

former ['fɔːmər] *adj* **1** *(time)* anterior. **2** *(one-time)* antiguo,-a; *(person)* ex; **the f. champion**, el excampeón. **3** *(first)* aquél, aquélla; **Peter and Lisa came, the f. wearing a hat**, vinieron Peter y Lisa, aquél llevaba sombrero. ◆**formerly** *adv* antiguamente.

formidable ['fɔːmɪdəbəl] *adj* *(prodigious)* formidable; *(daunting)* terrible.

formula ['fɔːmjʊlə] *n* fórmula *f.*

forsake [fə'seɪk] *vtr* *(pt forsook* [fɔː'sʊk] *pp forsaken* [fɔː'seɪkən]) *Lit* **1** *(abandon, desert)* abandonar. **2** *(give up)* renunciar a.

fort [fɔːt] *n* fortaleza *f.*

forte ['fɔːteɪ] *n* fuerte *m.*

forth [fɔːθ] *adv fml* **and so f.**, y así sucesivamente; **to go back and f.**, ir de acá para allá.

forthcoming [fɔːθ'kʌmɪŋ] *adj* **1** *(event)* próximo,-a. **2 no money was f.**, no hubo oferta de dinero. **3** *(communicative)* comunicativo,-a.

forthright ['fɔːθraɪt] *adj* franco,-a.

fortify ['fɔːtɪfaɪ] *vtr* fortificar.

fortitude ['fɔːtɪtjuːd] *n* fortaleza *f*, fuerza *f.*

fortnight ['fɔːtnaɪt] *n GB* quincena *f.*

fortnightly ['fɔːtnaɪtlɪ] *GB* **I** *adj* quincenal. **II** *adv* cada quince días.

fortress ['fɔːtrɪs] *n* fortaleza *f.*

fortunate ['fɔːtʃənɪt] *adj* afortunado,-a; **it was f. that he came**, fue una suerte que viniera. ◆**fortunately** *adv* afortunadamente.

fortune ['fɔːtʃən] *n* **1** *(luck, fate)* suerte *f*; **to tell sb's f.**, echar la buenaventura a algn. **2** *(money)* fortuna *f.*

fortune-teller ['fɔːtʃəntelər] *n* adivino,-a *m,f.*

forty ['fɔːtɪ] *adj & n* cuarenta *(m)* inv.

forum ['fɔːrəm] *n* foro *m.*

forward ['fɔːwəd] **I** *adv* **1** *(also forwards)* *(direction and movement)* hacia adelante. **2**

fig **to come f.**, ofrecerse. **3 from this day f.**, de ahora en adelante. **II** *adj* **1** *(movement)* hacia adelante; *(position)* delantero,-a. **2** *(person)* fresco,-a. **III** *n Sport* delantero,-a *m.f.* **IV** *vtr* **1** *(send on)* remitir. **2** *fml* *(send goods)* expedir. **3** *fml* *(further)* fomentar.

forwent [fɔː'went] *pt* → **forego.**

fossil ['fɒsɪl] *n* fósil *m*; **f. fuel**, combustible *m* fósil.

foster ['fɒstər] **I** *vtr* **1** *(child)* criar. **2** *fml* *(hopes)* abrigar; *(relations)* fomentar. **II** *adj* **f. child**, hijo,-a adoptivo,-a; **f. father**, padre adoptivo; **f. mother**, madre adoptiva; **f. parents**, padres adoptivos.

fought [fɔːt] *pt & pp* → **fight.**

foul [faʊl] **I** *adj* **1** *(smell)* fétido,-a; *(taste)* asqueroso,-a. **2** *(deed)* atroz; *(weather)* de perros. **3** *(language)* grosero,-a. **4** **to fall f. of**, tener problemas con; *Sport* **f. play**, juego sucio; *Jur* **f. play is suspected**, se sospecha que se haya cometido un acto criminal. **II** *n Sport* falta *f.* **III** *vtr* **1** *(dirty)* ensuciar; *(air)* contaminar. **2** *Sport* cometer una falta contra.

found¹ [faʊnd] *pt & pp* → **find.**

found² [faʊnd] *vtr* *(establish)* fundar.

foundation [faʊn'deɪʃən] *n* **1** *(establishment)* fundación *f.* **2** *(basis)* fundamento *m.* **3 f.** *(cream)*, maquillaje *m* de fondo. **II** *Constr* **foundations**, cimientos *mpl.*

founder¹ ['faʊndər] *n* fundador,-a *m.f.*

founder² ['faʊndər] *vi* **1** *fml* *(sink)* hundirse. **2** *fig* *(plan, hopes)* fracasar.

foundry ['faʊndrɪ] *n* fundición *f.*

fountain ['faʊntɪn] *n* *(structure)* fuente *f*; *(jet)* surtidor *m*; **f. pen**, pluma estilográfica.

four [fɔːr] *adj & n* cuatro *(m)* inv; **on all fours**, a gatas.

four-door ['fɔːdɔːr] *adj* *Aut* de cuatro puertas.

four-poster [fɔː'pəʊstər] *n* **f.-p. (bed)**, cama *f* con dosel.

foursome ['fɔːsəm] *n* grupo *m* de cuatro personas.

fourteen [fɔː'tiːn] *adj & n* catorce *(m)* inv.

fourteenth [fɔː'tiːnθ] **I** *adj & n* decimocuarto,-a *(m,f).* **II** *n* *(fraction)* catorceavo *m.*

fourth [fɔːθ] **I** *adj & n* cuarto,-a *(m,f).* **II** *n* **1** *(fraction)* cuarto *m.* **2** *Aut* cuarta *f* *(velocidad).*

fowl [faʊl] *n* aves *fpl* de corral.

fox [fɒks] **I** *n* zorro,-a *m.f.* **II** *vtr* **1** *(perplex)* dejar perplejo,-a. **2** *(deceive)* engañar.

foyer ['fɔɪeɪ, 'fɔɪə] *n* vestíbulo *m.*

fracas ['frækɑː] *n* gresca *f*, reyerta *f.*

fraction ['frækʃən] *n* fracción *f.*

fracture ['fræktʃər] **I** *n* fractura *f.* **II** *vtr* fracturar.

fragile ['frædʒaɪl] *adj* frágil.

fragment ['frægmənt] n fragmento m.

fragrance ['freigrəns] n fragancia f, perfume m.

fragrant ['freigrənt] adj fragante, aromático,-a.

frail [freil] adj frágil, delicado,-a.

frame [freim] I n 1 (of window, door, picture) marco m; (of machine) armazón m; (of bicycle) cuadro m; (of spectacles) montura f; fig f. of mind, estado m de ánimo. 2 Cin TV fotograma m. II vtr 1 (picture) enmarcar. 2 (question) formular. 3 fam (innocent person) incriminar.

framework ['freimwɜːk] n fig within the f. of ..., dentro del marco de ...

franc [fræŋk] n franco m.

France [frɑːns] n Francia.

franchise ['fræntʃaiz] n 1 Pol derecho m al voto. 2 Com concesión f, licencia f.

frank [fræŋk] I adj franco,-a. II vtr (mail) franquear. ◆**frankly** adv francamente.

frankness ['fræŋknis] n franqueza f.

frantic ['fræntik] adj (anxious) desesperado,-a; (hectic) frenético,-a.

fraternal [frə'tɜːnəl] adj fraterno,-a.

fraternity [frə'tɜːniti] n (society) asociación f; Rel cofradía f; US Univ club m de estudiantes.

fraud [frɔːd] n 1 fraude m. 2 (person) impostor,-a m,f.

fraught [frɔːt] adj 1 (full) cargado,-a (with, de). 2 (tense) nervioso,-a.

fray[1] [frei] vi 1 (cloth) deshilacharse. 2 (nerves) crisparse; his temper frequently frayed, se irritaba a menudo.

fray[2] [frei] n combate m.

freak [friːk] I n 1 (monster) monstruo m. 2 fam (eccentric) estrafalario,-a m,f. 3 fam (fan) fanático,-a m,f. II adj 1 (unexpected) inesperado,-a. 2 (unusual) insólito,-a.

freckle ['frekəl] n peca f.

free [friː] I adj 1 libre; to set sb f., poner en libertad a algn; f. kick, tiro m libre; f. speech, libertad f de expresión; f. will, libre albedrío m; f. trade, libre cambio m; f. time, tiempo m libre. 2 f. (of charge), (gratis) gratuito,-a; f. gift, obsequio m. 3 (generous) generoso,-a. II adv 1 (for) f., gratis. 2 (loose) suelto,-a. III vtr 1 (liberate) poner en libertad. 2 (let loose, work loose) soltar. 3 (untie) desatar. 4 (exempt) eximir (from, de). ◆**freely** adv 1 libremente. 2 (openly) abiertamente.

freedom ['friːdəm] n 1 (liberty) libertad f; f. of the press, libertad de prensa. 2 (exemption) exención f.

free-for-all ['friːfərɔːl] n pelea f.

freehold ['friːhəʊld] adj en propiedad absoluta.

freelance ['friːlɑːns] adj independiente.

freemason ['friːmeisən] n francmasón, -ona m,f.

free-range ['friːreindʒ] adj GB de granja.

free-style ['friːstail] n Swimming estilo m

libre.

freeway ['friːwei] n US autopista f.

freewheel [friː'wiːl] vi ir en punto muerto.

freeze [friːz] I vtr (pt froze; pp frozen) congelar. II n Meteor helada f; price f., congelación f de precios; TV Cin f. frame, imagen congelada. III vi (liquid) helarse; (food) congelarse.

freeze-dried ['friːzdraid] adj liofilizado,-a.

freezer ['friːzə] n congelador m.

freezing ['friːziŋ] adj 1 glacial. 2 f. point, punto m de congelación; above/below f. point, sobre/bajo cero.

freight [freit] n 1 (transport) transporte m. 2 (goods, price) flete m; f. train, tren m de mercancías.

French [frentʃ] I adj francés,-esa; f. bean, judía f verde; F. dressing, vinagreta f; US F. fries, patatas fpl fritas; F. window, puerta f vidriera. II n 1 (language) francés m. 2 pl the F., los franceses.

Frenchman ['frentʃmən] n francés m.

Frenchwoman ['frentʃwumən] n francesa f.

frenetic [fri'netik] adj frenético,-a.

frenzy ['frenzi] n frenesí m.

frequency ['friːkwənsi] n frecuencia f.

frequent ['friːkwənt] adj frecuente. II [fri'kwent] vtr frecuentar. ◆**frequently** adv frecuentemente, a menudo.

fresh [freʃ] adj 1 fresco,-a; f. water, agua f dulce; f. bread, pan del día. 2 (new) nuevo,-a; open a f. packet, abrir otro paquete. 3 (air) puro,-a; in the f. air, al aire libre. ◆**freshly** adv recién, recientemente.

freshen ['freʃən] vi (wind) refrescar. ◆**freshen up** vi asearse.

fresher ['freʃə], **freshman** ['freʃmən] n Univ estudiante mf de primer año, novato,-a m,f.

freshness ['freʃnis] n frescura f.

freshwater ['freʃwɔːtə] adj de agua dulce.

fret [fret] vi preocuparse (about, por).

FRG [efɑː'dʒiː] n Hist abbr of Federal Republic of Germany, República Federal de Alemania, RFA.

friar ['fraiə] n fraile m.

friction ['frikʃən] n fricción f.

Friday ['fraidi] n viernes m.

fridge [fridʒ] n fam nevera f, frigorífico m.

friend [frend] n amigo,-a m,f; a f. of mine, un,-a amigo,-a mío,-a; to make friends with sb, hacerse amigo,-a de algn; to make friends again, hacer las paces.

friendliness ['frendlinis] n amabilidad f, simpatía f.

friendly ['frendli] adj (friendlier, friendliest) (person) simpático,-a; (at-

mosphere) acogedor,-a; f. **advice**, consejo *m* de amigo; f. **nation**, nación amiga.

friendship ['frendʃɪp] *n* amistad *f*.

frieze [friːz] *n* friso *m*.

frigate ['frɪgɪt] *n* fragata *f*.

fright [fraɪt] *n* (*fear*) miedo *m*; **to take f.**, asustarse. 2 (*shock*) susto *m*; **to get a f.**, pegarse un susto.

frighten ['fraɪtən] *vtr* asustar. ◆**frighten away, frighten off** *vtr* ahuyentar.

frightened ['fraɪtənd] *adj* asustado,-a; **to be f. of sb**, tenerle miedo a algn.

frightening ['fraɪtənɪŋ] *adj* espantoso,-a.

frightful ['fraɪtfʊl] *adj* espantoso,-a, horroroso,-a. ◆**frightfully** *adv* tremendamente, terriblemente.

frigid ['frɪdʒɪd] *adj* frígido,-a.

frill [frɪl] *n* (*on dress*) volante *m*; *fig* **frills**, (*decorations*) adornos *mpl*.

fringe [frɪndʒ] *n* 1 (*of hair*) flequillo *m*. 2 (*edge*) borde *m*; *fig* **on the f. of society**, al margen de la sociedad; **f. theatre**, teatro *m* experimental; **f. benefits**, extras *mpl*.

Frisbee® ['frɪzbɪ] *n* platillo *m*.

frisk [frɪsk] *vtr fam* (*search*) registrar.

frisky ['frɪskɪ] *adj* (*friskier, friskiest*) 1 (*children, animals*) juguetón,-a. 2 (*adult*) vivo,-a.

fritter ['frɪtər] *n* buñuelo *m*. ◆**fritter away** *vtr* malgastar.

frivolous ['frɪvələs] *adj* frívolo,-a.

frizzy ['frɪzɪ] *adj* (*frizzier, frizziest*) crespo,-a.

frock [frɒk] *n* vestido *m*; **f. coat**, levita *f*.

frog [frɒg] *n* rana *f*; **frogs' legs**, ancas *fpl* de rana; *fig* **to have a f. in one's throat**, tener carraspera.

frogman ['frɒgmæn] *n* hombre *m* rana.

frolic ['frɒlɪk] *vi* retozar, juguetear.

from [frɒm, *unstressed* frəm] *prep* 1 (*time*) desde, a partir de; **f. now on**, a partir de ahora; **f. Monday to Friday**, de lunes a viernes; **f. the eighth to the seventeenth**, desde el ocho hasta el diecisiete; **f. time to time**, de vez en cuando. 2 (*price, number*) desde, de; **dresses f. five pounds**, vestidos desde cinco libras; **a number f. one to ten**, un número del uno a diez. 3 (*origin*) de; **a letter f. her father**, una carta de su padre; **f. English into Spanish**, del inglés al español; **he's f. Malaga**, es de Málaga; **the train f. Bilbao**, el tren procedente de Bilbao; **to go f. door to door**, ir de puerta en puerta; **her eyes were red f. crying**, tenía los ojos rojos de llorar. 4 (*distance*) de; **the town is four miles f. the coast**, el pueblo está a cuatro millas de la costa. 5 (*out of*) de; **bread is made f. flour**, el pan se hace con harina. 6 (*remove, subtract*) a; **he took the book f. the child**, le quitó el libro al niño; **take three f. five**, resta tres a cinco. 7 (*according to*) según,

por; **f. what the author said**, según lo que dijo el autor; **speaking f. my own experience**, hablando por experiencia propia. 8 (*position*) desde, de; **f. here**, desde aquí. 9 **can you tell margarine f. butter?**, ¿puedes distinguir entre la margarina y la mantequilla?

front [frʌnt] **I** *n* 1 parte delantera; **in f.** (**of**), delante (de). 2 (*of building*) fachada *f*. 3 *Mil Pol Meteor* frente *m*. 4 (*seaside*) paseo marítimo. 5 *fig* **she put on a brave f.**, hizo de tripas corazón. **II** *adj* delantero,-a, de delante; *Parl* **f. bench**, primera fila de escaños donde se sientan los ministros del Gobierno y de la Oposición; **f. door**, puerta *f* principal; **f. room**, salón *m*; **f. seat**, asiento *m* de delante.

frontier ['frʌntɪər] *n* frontera *f*.

front-page ['frʌntpeɪdʒ] *adj* de primera página.

frost [frɒst] **I** *n* 1 (*covering*) escarcha *f*. 2 (*freezing*) helada *f*. **II** *vt US Culin* recubrir con azúcar glas. ◆**frost over** *vi* escarchar.

frostbite ['frɒstbaɪt] *n* congelación *f*.

frosted ['frɒstɪd] *adj* 1 (*glass*) esmerilado,-a. 2 *US Culin* recubierto,-a de azúcar glas.

frosty ['frɒstɪ] *adj* (*frostier, frostiest*) 1 **it will be a f. night tonight**, esta noche habrá helada. 2 *fig* glacial.

froth [frɒθ] **I** *n* espuma *f*; (*from mouth*) espumarajos *mpl*. **II** *vi* espumar.

frothy ['frɒθɪ] *adj* (*frothier, frothiest*) espumoso,-a.

frown [fraʊn] *vi* fruncir el ceño. ◆**frown upon** *vtr* desaprobar.

froze [frəʊz] *pt* → **freeze**.

frozen ['frəʊzən] *adj* (*liquid, feet etc*) helado,-a; (*food*) congelado,-a.

frugal ['fruːgəl] *adj* frugal.

fruit [fruːt] *n* 1 *Bot* fruto *m*. 2 (*apple, orange etc*) fruta *f*; **f. cake**, pastel *m* con fruto seco; **f. machine**, máquina *f* tragaperras; **f. salad**, macedonia *f* de frutas. 3 *fruits*, (*rewards*) frutos *mpl*.

fruitful ['fruːtfʊl] *adj fig* provechoso,-a.

fruition [fruːˈɪʃən] *n fml* **to come to f.**, realizarse.

frustrate [frʌˈstreɪt] *vtr* frustrar.

frustrated [frʌˈstreɪtɪd] *adj* frustrado,-a.

frustration [frʌˈstreɪʃən] *n* frustración *f*.

fry¹ [fraɪ] **I** *vtr* (*pt & pp fried*) freír. **II** *vi fig* asarse.

fry² [fraɪ] *npl* **small f.**, gente *f* de poca monta.

frying pan ['fraɪɪŋpæn], *US* **fry-pan** ['fraɪpæn] *n* sartén *f*.

ft *abbr of foot*, pie *m*; *abbr of feet*, pies *mpl*.

fuck [fʌk] *vulg offens vtr & vi* joder; (it)!, ¡joder! ◆**fuck off** *vi* **f. off!**, ¡vete a la mierda! ◆**fuck up** *vtr* joder.

fucking ['fʌkɪŋ] *vulg* **I** *adj* **f. idiot!**, ¡gilipollas!; **where are my f. keys?**, ¿dónde coño están las llaves? **II** *adv* **a f. good film**, una película de puta madre.

fuddy-duddy ['fʌdɪdʌdɪ] *n* persona chapada a la antigua.

fudge [fʌdʒ] **I** *n Culin* dulce *m* hecho con azúcar, leche y mantequilla. **II** *vtr* (*figures*) amañar.

fuel ['fjʊəl] **I** *n* **1** combustible *m*; (*for engines*) carburante *m*; **f. tank**, depósito *m* de combustible. **II** *vtr fig* (*ambition*) estimular; (*difficult situation*) empeorar.

fugitive ['fjuːdʒɪtɪv] *n fml* fugitivo,-a *m,f.*

fulfil, US **fulfill** [fʊl'fɪl] *vtr* **1** (*task, ambition*) realizar; (*promise*) cumplir; (*role*) desempeñar. **2** (*wishes*) satisfacer.

fulfilment, US **fulfillment** [fʊl'fɪlmənt] *n* **1** (*of ambition*) realización *f.* **2** (*of duty, promise*) cumplimiento *m.*

full [fʊl] **I** *adj* **1** lleno,-a; **f. of**, lleno,-a de; **I'm f. (up)**, no puedo más. **2** (*complete*) completo,-a; **at f. speed**, a toda velocidad; **f. text**, texto íntegro; *fam* **in f. swing**, en plena marcha; **f. board**, pensión completa; **f. employment**, pleno empleo *m*; **f. house**, lleno total; **f. moon**, luna llena; **f. stop**, punto *m*. **II** *n* **in f.**, en su totalidad; **name in f.**, nombre y apellidos completos. **III** *adv* **f. well**, perfectamente. ◆**fully** *adv* completamente.

full-blown ['fʊlbləʊn] *adj* auténtico,-a.

fullness ['fʊlnɪs] *n* **in the f. of time**, con el tiempo.

full-scale ['fʊlskeɪl] *adj* **1** (*model*) de tamaño natural. **2** **f.-s. search**, registro *m* a fondo; **f.-s. war**, guerra generalizada *or* total.

full-time ['fʊltaɪm] **I** *adj* de jornada completa. **II** *adv* **to work f. t.**, trabajar a tiempo completo.

fully-fledged ['fʊlɪfledʒd] *adj* hecho,-a y derecho,-a.

fulsome ['fʊlsəm] *adj* excesivo,-a, exagerado,-a.

fumble ['fʌmbəl] *vi* hurgar; **to f. for sth**, buscar algo a tientas; **to f. with sth**, manejar algo con torpeza.

fume [fjuːm] **I** *n* (*usu pl*) humo *m*. **II** *vi* echar humo.

fun [fʌn] **I** *n* **1** (*amusement*) diversión *f*; **in** *or* **for f.**, en broma; **to have f.**, divertirse, pasarlo bien; **to make f. of sb**, reírse de algn. **II** *adj* divertido,-a.

function ['fʌŋkʃən] **I** *n* **1** función *f.* **2** (*ceremony*) acto *m*; (*party*) recepción *f.* **II** *vi* funcionar.

functional ['fʌŋkʃənəl] *adj* funcional.

fund [fʌnd] **I** *n* **1** *Com* fondo *m*. **2 funds**, fondos *mpl*. **II** *vtr* (*finance*) patrocinar.

fundamental [fʌndə'mentəl] **I** *adj* fundamental. **II** *npl* **fundamentals**, los fundamentos *mpl*.

funeral ['fjuːnərəl] *n* funeral *m*; **f. march**, marcha *f* fúnebre; *US* **f. parlor**, funeraria

f; **f. service**, misa *f* de cuerpo presente.

funfair ['fʌnfeər] *n GB* parque *m* de atracciones.

fungus ['fʌŋɡəs] *n* (*pl* **fungi** ['fʌŋɡaɪ]) **1** *Bot* hongo *m*. **2** *Med* fungo *m*.

funnel ['fʌnəl] **I** *n* **1** (*for liquids*) embudo *m*. **2** *Naut* chimenea *f*. **II** *vtr fig* (*funds, energy*) encauzar.

funny ['fʌnɪ] *adj* (**funnier, funniest**) **1** (*peculiar*) raro,-a, extraño,-a; **that's f.!**, ¡qué raro! **2** (*amusing*) divertido,-a, gracioso, -a; **I found it very f.**, me hizo mucha gracia. **3** *fam* (*ill*) mal. **4** *fam* (*dishonest*) dudoso,-a. ◆**funnily** *adv fam* **f. enough**, aunque parezca extraño.

fur [fɜːr] *n* **1** (*of living animal*) pelo *m*. **2** (*of dead animal*) piel *f*. **3** (*in kettle, on tongue*) sarro *m*. **II** *adj* de piel; **f. coat**, abrigo *m* de pieles.

furious ['fjʊərɪəs] *adj* **1** (*angry*) furioso,-a. **2** (*vigorous*) violento,-a.

furlong ['fɜːlɒŋ] *n* (*measurement*) = *aprox* 201 metros.

furnace ['fɜːnɪs] *n* horno *m*.

furnish ['fɜːnɪʃ] *vtr* **1** (*house*) amueblar. **2** *fml* (*food*) suministrar; (*details*) facilitar.

furnishings ['fɜːnɪʃɪŋz] *npl* muebles *mpl.* **2** (*fittings*) accesorios *mpl.*

furniture ['fɜːnɪtʃər] *n* muebles *mpl*; **a piece of f.**, un mueble.

furrow ['fʌrəʊ] *n Agr* surco *m*; (*on forehead*) arruga *f*.

furry ['fɜːrɪ] *adj* (**furrier, furriest**) **1** (*hairy*) peludo,-a. **2** (*tongue, kettle*) sarroso,-a.

further ['fɜːðər] **I** *adj* → **far. 1** (*new*) nuevo,-a; **until f. notice**, hasta nuevo aviso. **2** (*additional*) otro,-a, adicional. **3** (*later*) posterior; **f. education**, estudios *mpl* superiores. **II** *adv* **1** (*more*) más; **f. back**, más atrás; **f. along**, más adelante; **she heard nothing f.**, no volvió a saber nada más. **2** *fml* **f. to your letter of the 9th**, con referencia a su carta del 9 del corriente. **3** *fml* (*besides*) además. **III** *vtr* (*cause*) fomentar.

furthermore ['fɜːðəmɔːr] *adv fml* además.

furthest ['fɜːðɪst] *adj* → **far**; más lejano, -a.

furtive ['fɜːtɪv] *adj* furtivo,-a.

fury ['fjʊərɪ] *n* furia *f*, furor *m*.

fuse [fjuːz] **I** *n* **1** *Elec* fusible *m*; **f. box**, caja *f* de fusibles. **2** (*of bomb*) mecha *f*. **II** *vi* **1** *Elec* **the lights fused**, se fundieron los plomos. **2** *fig* (*merge*) fusionarse. **3** (*melt*) fundirse. **III** *vtr* **1** *Elec* fundir los plomos de. **2** *fig* (*merge*) fusionar. **3** (*melt*) fundir.

fuselage ['fjuːzɪlɑːʒ] *n* fuselaje *m*.

fuss [fʌs] **I** *n* (*commotion*) jaleo *m*; **to kick up a f.**, armar un escándalo; **stop making a f.**, (*complaining*) deja ya de quejarte; **to make a f. of**, (*pay attention to*) mimar a. **II** *vi* preocuparse (**about**, por).

fussy ['fʌsɪ] *adj* (*fussier, fussiest*) exigente; (*nitpicking*) quisquilloso,-a.
futile ['fju:taɪl] *adj* inútil, vano,-a.
futility [fju:'tɪlɪtɪ] *n* inutilidad *f*.
future ['fju:tʃər] I *n* futuro *m*, porvenir *m*;

in the near f., en un futuro próximo; in f., de aquí en adelante. II *adj* futuro,-a.
futuristic [fju:tʃə'rɪstɪk] *adj* futurista.
fuzzy ['fʌzɪ] *adj* (*fuzzier, fuzziest*) 1 (*hair*) muy rizado,-a. 2 (*blurred*) borroso,-a.

G

G, g [dʒi:] *n* 1 (*the letter*) G, g *f*. 2 *Mus* G, sol *m*.
g [dʒi:] *abbr of* **gram**(s), **gramme**(s), g.
gabble ['gæbəl] I *n* chapurreo *m*. II *vi* hablar atropelladamente.
gable ['geɪbəl] *n* aguilón *m*.
gadget ['gædʒɪt] *n* artilugio *m*, aparato *m*.
Gaelic ['geɪlɪk] I *adj* gaélico,-a. II *n* (*language*) gaélico *m*.
gaffe [gæf] *n* metedura *f* de pata, plancha *f*; **to make a g.,** meter la pata, patinar.
gag [gæg] I *n* 1 mordaza *f*. 2 *fam* (*joke*) chiste *m*. II *vtr* amordazar.
gage [geɪdʒ] *n & vtr US* → **gauge**.
gaiety ['geɪətɪ] *n* regocijo *m*.
gaily ['geɪlɪ] *adv* alegremente.
gain [geɪn] I *n* ganancia *f*, beneficio *m*; (*increase*) aumento *m*. II *vtr* ganar; *fig* **to g. ground**, ganar terreno; **to g. speed,** ganar velocidad, acelerar; **to g. weight,** aumentar de peso.
gait [geɪt] *n* (*manera f de*) andar *m*.
gal (*pl* **gal** *or* **gals**) *abbr of* **gallon**.
gala ['gɑːlə, 'geɪlə] *n* gala *f*, fiesta *f*.
galaxy ['gæləksɪ] *n* galaxia *f*.
gale [geɪl] *n* vendaval *m*.
Galicia [gə'lɪʃə] *n* Galicia *f*.
Galician [gə'lɪʃɪən, gə'lɪʃən] I *adj* gallego,-a. II *n* 1 (*person*) gallego,-a *m,f*. 2 (*language*) gallego *m*.
gall [gɔːl] I *n fam* descaro *m*. II *vtr* molestar, irritar.
gallant ['gælənt] *adj* (*brave*) valiente; (*also* [gə'lænt]) (*chivalrous*) galante.
gallantry ['gæləntrɪ] *n* (*bravery*) gallardía *f*; (*politeness*) galantería *f*.
galleon ['gælɪən] *n* galeón *m*.
gallery ['gælərɪ] *n* 1 galería *f*. 2 *Theat* gallinero *m*. 3 (*court*) tribuna *f*.
galley ['gælɪ] *n* 1 (*ship*) galera *f*; **g. slave,** galeote *m*. 2 (*kitchen*) cocina *f*.
Gallicism ['gælɪsɪzəm] *n* galicismo *m*.
gallivant ['gælɪvænt] *vi fam* callejear.
gallon ['gælən] *n* galón *m* (≈ 4,55 litros; *US* 3,79 litros).
gallop ['gæləp] I *n* galope *m*. II *vi* galopar.
gallows ['gæləʊz] *npl* horca *f sing*, patíbulo *m sing*.
gallstone ['gɔːlstəʊn] *n* cálculo *m* biliar.
galore [gə'lɔːr] *adv fam* en cantidad, en abundancia.
galvanize ['gælvənaɪz] *vtr* (*metal*) galvanizar; *fig* **to g. sb into action,** galvanizar a

algn.
galvanized ['gælvənaɪzd] *adj* galvanizado,-a.
gambit ['gæmbɪt] *n* Chess gambito *m*; *fig* táctica *f*.
gamble ['gæmbəl] I *n* (*risk*) riesgo *m*; (*risky undertaking*) empresa arriesgada; (*bet*) apuesta *f*. II *vi* (*bet*) jugar; (*take a risk*) arriesgarse.
gambler ['gæmblər] *n* jugador,-a *m,f*.
gambling ['gæmblɪŋ] *n* juego *m*.
gambol ['gæmbəl] *vi* brincar.
game [geɪm] I *n* 1 juego *m*; **g. of chance,** juego de azar. 2 (*match*) partido *m*; (*of bridge*) partida *f*. 3 **games,** Sport juegos *mpl*; *GB Educ* educación física. 4 (*hunting*) caza *f*; *fig* presa *f*; **g. reserve,** coto *m* de caza. II *adj* **g. for anything,** dispuesto,-a a todo. ◆**gamely** *adv* resueltamente.
gamekeeper ['geɪmkiːpər] *n* guardabosque *mf*.
gammon ['gæmən] *n GB* jamón ahumado *or* curado.
gamut ['gæmət] *n* gama *f*; **to run the g. of ...,** experimentar todas las posibilidades de ....
gang [gæŋ] *n* (*of criminals*) banda *f*; (*of youths*) pandilla *f*; (*of workers*) cuadrilla *f*. ◆**gang up** *vi fam* confabularse (**on,** contra).
gangplank ['gæŋplæŋk] *n* plancha *f*.
gangrene ['gæŋgriːn] *n* gangrena *f*.
gangster ['gæŋstər] *n* gángster *m*.
gangway ['gæŋweɪ] *n Naut* pasarela *f*; *Theat* pasillo *m*.
gantry ['gæntrɪ] *n* puente *m* transversal.
gaol [dʒeɪl] *n & vtr GB* → **jail**.
gap [gæp] *n* 1 abertura *f*, hueco *m*; (*blank space*) blanco *m*; (*in traffic*) claro *m*; **to bridge a g.,** rellenar un hueco. 2 (*in time*) intervalo *m*; (*emptiness*) vacío *m*. 3 (*gulf*) diferencia *f*. 4 (*deficiency*) laguna *f*.
gape [geɪp] *vi* (*person*) quedarse boquiabierto,-a, mirar boquiabierto,-a; (*thing*) estar abierto,-a.
gaping ['geɪpɪŋ] *adj fig* profundo,-a.
garage ['gærɑːʒ, 'gærɪdʒ] *n* garaje *m*; (*for repairs*) taller mecánico; (*filling station*) gasolinera *f*.
garbage ['gɑːbɪdʒ] *n US* basura *f*; *fig* tonterías *fpl*; **g. can,** cubo *m* de la basura; **g. truck,** camión *m* de la basura.
garbled ['gɑːbəld] *adj* embrollado,-a; **g.**

account, relato confuso.

garden ['gɑːdən] n jardín m; **g. centre**, centro m de jardinería; **g. party**, recepción f al aire libre.

gardener ['gɑːdənəʳ] n jardinero,-a f.

gardening ['gɑːdənɪŋ] n jardinería f; **his mother does the g.**, su madre es la que cuida el jardín.

gardenia [gɑːˈdiːnɪə] n gardenia f.

gargle ['gɑːgəl] vi hacer gárgaras.

gargoyle ['gɑːgɔɪl] n gárgola f.

garish ['geərɪʃ] adj chillón,-ona.

garland ['gɑːlənd] n guirnalda f.

garlic ['gɑːlɪk] n ajo m.

garment ['gɑːmənt] n prenda f.

garnish ['gɑːnɪʃ] vtr aderezar.

garrison ['gærɪsən] n guarnición f.

garrulous ['gærʊləs] adj locuaz.

garter ['gɑːtəʳ] n liga f.

gas [gæs] I n 1 gas m; **g. chamber**, cámara f de gas; **g. cooker**, cocina f de gas; **g. fire**, estufa f de gas; **g. mask**, careta f antigás; **g. ring**, hornillo m de gas; 2 US gasolina f; **g. station**, gasolinera f. II vtr (asphyxiate) asfixiar con gas. III vi fam (talk) charlotear.

gash [gæʃ] I n herida profunda. II vtr hacer un corte en; **he gashed his forehead**, se hizo una herida en la frente.

gasket ['gæskɪt] n junta f.

gasoline ['gæsəliːn] n US gasolina f.

gasp [gɑːsp] I n (cry) grito sordo; (breath) bocanada f; fig **to be at one's last g.**, estar en las últimas. II vi (in surprise) quedar boquiabierto,-a; (breathe) jadear.

gassy ['gæsɪ] adj (gassier, gassiest) gaseoso,-a.

gastric ['gæstrɪk] adj gástrico,-a.

gastronomic [gæstrəˈnɒmɪk] adj gastronómico,-a.

gate [geɪt] n 1 puerta f. 2 (at football ground) entrada f; **g. (money)**, taquilla f. 3 (attendance) entrada f.

gateau ['gætəʊ] n pastel m con nata.

gatecrash ['geɪtkræʃ] I vtr colarse en. II vi colarse.

gateway ['geɪtweɪ] n puerta f; fig pasaporte m.

gather ['gæðəʳ] I vtr 1 (collect) juntar; (pick) coger; (pick up) recoger. 2 (bring together) reunir. 3 (harvest) cosechar. 4 **to g. speed**, ir ganando velocidad; **to g. strength**, cobrar fuerzas. 5 (understand) suponer; **I g. that ...**, tengo entendido que .... 6 Sew fruncir. II vi 1 (come together) reunirse. 2 (form) formarse. ◆**gather round** vi agruparse.

gathering ['gæðərɪŋ] I adj creciente. II n reunión f.

gauche [gəʊʃ] adj (clumsy) torpe; (tactless) sin tacto.

gaudy ['gɔːdɪ] adj (gaudier, gaudiest) chillón,-ona.

gauge [geɪdʒ] n 1 medida f estándar; (of gun, wire) calibre m. 2 Rail ancho m de vía. 3 (calibrator) indicador m. II vtr 1 (measure) medir, calibrar. 2 fig (judge) juzgar.

gaunt [gɔːnt] adj (lean) demacrado,-a; (desolate) lúgubre.

gauntlet ['gɔːntlɪt] n guantelete m; fig **to run the g. of ...**, estar sometido,-a a ...; fig **to throw down the g.**, arrojar el guante.

gauze [gɔːz] n gasa f.

gave [geɪv] pt → **give**.

gawky ['gɔːkɪ] adj (gawkier, gawkiest) desgarbado,-a.

gay [geɪ] adj 1 (homosexual) gay. 2 (happy) alegre.

gaze [geɪz] I n mirada fija. II vi mirar fijamente.

gazelle [gəˈzel] n gacela f.

gazette [gəˈzet] n gaceta f; US periódico m.

gazump [gəˈzʌmp] vtr GB fam romper un compromiso de venta para vender a un precio más alto.

GB [dʒiːˈbiː] abbr of **Great Britain**.

GCE [dʒiːsiːˈiː] abbr of **General Certificate of Education (A-Level)**, ≈ COU m.

GCSE [dʒiːsiːesˈiː] abbr of **General Certificate of Secondary Education**, ≈ BUP m.

GDP [dʒiːdiːˈpiː] abbr of **gross domestic product**, producto m interior bruto, PIB m.

GDR [dʒiːdiːˈɑːʳ] n Hist abbr of **German Democratic Republic**, RDA.

gear [gɪəʳ] I n 1 (equipment) equipo m. 2 fam (belongings) bártulos mpl. 3 fam (clothing) ropa f. 4 Tech engranaje m. 5 Aut velocidad f, marcha f; **first g.**, primera f (velocidad f); **g. lever**, palanca f de cambio. II vtr ajustar, adaptar.

gearbox ['gɪəbɒks] n caja f de cambios.

gearstick ['gɪəstɪk], US **gearshift** ['gɪəʃɪft] n palanca f de cambio.

geese [giːs] npl → **goose**.

gel [dʒel] I n gel m; (for hair) gomina f. II vi fig (ideas etc) cuajar. III vtr (hair) engominar.

gelatin ['dʒelətɪn] n gelatina f.

gelignite ['dʒelɪgnaɪt] n gelignita f.

gem [dʒem] n piedra preciosa; fig (person) joya f.

Gemini ['dʒemɪnaɪ] n Géminis m sing.

gen [dʒen] n fam **to get the g. on sth**, informarse sobre algo.

gender ['dʒendəʳ] n género m.

gene [dʒiːn] n gene m, gen m.

general ['dʒenərəl] I adj general; **g. knowledge**, conocimientos generales; **in g.**, en general; **the g. public**, el público; **g. practitioner (GP)**, médico m de cabecera. II n Mil general m. ◆**generally** adv generalmente, en general.

generalization [dʒenərəlaɪ'zeɪʃən] n generalización f.

generalize ['dʒenərəlaɪz] vtr & vi generalizar.

generate ['dʒenəreɪt] vtr generar.

generation [dʒenə'reɪʃən] n generación f; g. **gap**, abismo m or conflicto m generacional.

generator ['dʒenəreɪtə'] n generador m.

generosity [dʒenə'rɒsɪtɪ] n generosidad f.

generous ['dʒenərəs] adj generoso,-a; (plentiful) copioso,-a.

genetic [dʒɪ'netɪk] adj genético,-a; g. **engineering**, ingeniería genética.

genetics [dʒɪ'netɪks] n genética f.

Geneva [dʒɪ'niːvə] n Ginebra.

genial ['dʒiːnɪəl, 'dʒiːnjəl] adj cordial.

genie ['dʒiːnɪ] n duende m, genio m.

genitals ['dʒenɪtəlz] npl órganos mpl genitales.

genius ['dʒiːnjəs, 'dʒiːnɪəs] n 1 (person) genio m. 2 (gift) don m.

genre ['ʒɒnrə] n género m.

gent [dʒent] n 1 (abbr of **gentleman**) fam señor m, caballero m; **the gents**, los servicios (de caballeros).

genteel [dʒen'tiːl] adj fino,-a, distinguido,-a.

gentle ['dʒentəl] adj dulce, tierno,-a; (breeze) suave. ◆**gently** con cuidado.

gentleman ['dʒentəlmən] n caballero m; g.'s **agreement**, pacto m de caballeros.

gentry ['dʒentrɪ] n pequeña nobleza, alta burguesía.

genuine ['dʒenjuɪn] adj auténtico,-a, genuino,-a; (sincere) sincero,-a. ◆**genuinely** adv auténticamente.

geographic(al) [dʒɪə'græfɪk(əl)] adj geográfico,-a.

geography [dʒɪ'ɒgrəfɪ, 'dʒɒgrəfɪ] n geografía f.

geologic(al) [dʒɪə'lɒdʒɪk(əl)] adj geológico,-a.

geology [dʒɪ'ɒlədʒɪ] n geología f.

geometric(al) [dʒɪə'metrɪk(əl)] adj geométrico,-a.

geometry [dʒɪ'ɒmɪtrɪ] n geometría f.

geopolitical [dʒɪːəʊpə'lɪtɪkəl] adj geopolítico,-a.

geranium [dʒɪ'reɪnɪəm] n geranio m.

geriatric [dʒerɪ'ætrɪk] adj geriátrico,-a.

germ [dʒɜːm] n 1 Biol & fig germen m. 2 Med microbio m.

German ['dʒɜːmən] I adj alemán,-ana; G. **measles**, rubeola f. II n 1 alemán,-ana m,f. 2 (language) alemán m.

Germany ['dʒɜːmənɪ] n Alemania.

germinate ['dʒɜːmɪneɪt] vi germinar.

gestation [dʒe'steɪʃən] n gestación f.

gesticulate [dʒe'stɪkjuleɪt] vi gesticular.

gesture ['dʒestʃə'] I n gesto m, ademán m; it's an empty g., es pura formalidad. II vi gesticular, hacer gestos.

get [get] I vtr (pt & pp **got**, pp US also

gotten) 1 (obtain) obtener, conseguir; to g. one's own way, salirse con la suya. 2 (earn) ganar. 3 (fetch) (something) traer; (somebody) ir a por; g. me the police!, ¡llama a la policía!; Tel g. me Mr Brown, póngame con el Sr. Brown. 4 (receive) recibir; fam he got the sack, lo despidieron. 5 (bus, train, thief etc) Span coger; Am agarrar. 6 (prepare) preparar; can I g. you something to eat?, ¿quieres comer algo? 7 (ask) pedir; g. him to call me, dile que me llame. 8 to g. sb to agree to sth, conseguir que algn acepte algo. 9 when did you g. the house painted? ¿cuándo os pintaron la casa?; to get one's hair cut, cortarse el pelo. 10 they got him in the chest, le dieron en el pecho. 11 have got, have got to → have. 12 fam (understand) entender. 13 (record) (in writing) apuntar; (on tape) grabar.

II vi 1 (become) ponerse; to g. dark, anochecer; to g. dressed, vestirse; to g. drunk, emborracharse; to g. late, hacerse tarde; to g. married, casarse; to g. used to doing sth, acostumbrarse a hacer algo; to get paid, cobrar. 2 fig we are not getting anywhere, así no vamos a ninguna parte. 3 (arrive) llegar. 4 to g. to, (come to) llegar a; to g. to know sb, llegar a conocer a algn.
◆**get about** vi (person) salir; (news) difundirse. ◆**get across** vtr (idea etc) hacer comprender. ◆**get ahead** vi progresar. ◆**get along** vi 1 (leave) marcharse. 2 (manage) arreglárselas. 3 (two people) llevarse bien. ◆**get around** vi (person) salir; (travel) viajar; (news) difundirse. ◆**get at** vtr 1 (reach) alcanzar. 2 (ascertain) descubrir. 3 (insinuate) insinuar; what are you getting at?, ¿a dónde quieres llegar? 4 (criticize) criticar. ◆**get away** vi escaparse. ◆**get away with** vtr salir impune de. ◆**get back** I vi 1 (return) regresar, volver. 2 g. back!, (move backwards) ¡atrás!. II vtr (recover) recuperar; fam to g. one's own back on sb, vengarse de algn. ◆**get by** vi 1 (manage) arreglárselas; she can g. by in French, sabe defenderse en francés. 2 (pass) pasar. ◆**get down** I vtr (depress) deprimir. II vi (descend) bajar. ◆**get down to** vi ponerse a; to g. down to the facts, al grano. ◆**get in** vi 1 (arrive) llegar. 2 Pol ser elegido,-a. II vtr 1 (buy) comprar. 2 (collect) recoger; fam he couldn't g. a word in edgeways, no pudo decir ni pío. ◆**get into** vtr fig to g. into bad habits, adquirir malas costumbres; g. into trouble, meterse en un lío. ◆**get off** I vtr 1 (bus etc) bajarse de. 2 (remove) quitarse. II vi 1 bajarse; fam g. off!, ¡fuera! 2 to g. off to a good start, (begin) empezar bien. 3 (escape) escaparse; to g. off lightly, salir

bien librado,-a. **get off with** vtr fam ligar. **get on I** vtr (board) subir. **II** vi 1 (board) subirse. 2 (make progress) hacer progresos; **how are you getting on?**, ¿cómo te van las cosas? 3 **to g. on (well with sb)**, llevarse bien (con algn). 4 (continue) seguir; **to g. on with one's work**, seguir trabajando. 5 **it's getting on for eleven**, son casi las once; **time's getting on**, se está haciendo tarde. **get on to** vtr 1 (find a person) localizar; (find out) descubrir. 2 (continue) pasar a. **get out** I vtr (object) sacar. II vi 1 (room etc) salir (of, de); (train) bajar (of, de). 2 (escape) escaparse (of, de); **to g. out of an obligation**, librarse de un compromiso. 3 (news) difundirse; (secret) hacerse público. **get over** vtr 1 (illness) recuperarse; **I can't g. over him**, no le puedo olvidar. 2 (difficulty) vencer. 3 (convey) hacer comprender. **get round** vtr 1 (problem) salvar; (difficulty) vencer. 2 (rule) soslayar. 3 (win over) persuadir. **get round to** vi if I g. round to it, si tengo tiempo. **get through** I vi 1 (message) llegar. 2 Educ aprobar. 3 Tel **to g. through to sb**, conseguir comunicar con algn. II vtr 1 **to g. through a lot of work**, trabajar mucho. 2 (consume) consumir. 3 Educ aprobar. **get together** I vi (people) juntarse, reunirse. II vtr (people) juntar, reunir. **get up** I vi (rise) levantarse. II vtr (wake) despertar. 2 (disguise) **to oneself up as ...**, disfrazarse de .... **get up to** vi hacer; **to g. up to mischief**, hacer de las suyas.

getaway ['getəweɪ] n fuga f; **to make one's g.**, fugarse.

get-together ['getəgeðər] n reunión f.

geyser ['giːzə, US 'gaɪzər] n 1 Geog géiser m. 2 (water heater) calentador m de agua.

ghastly ['gɑːstlɪ] adj (ghastlier, ghastliest) horrible, espantoso,-a.

gherkin ['gɜːkɪn] n pepinillo m.

ghetto ['getəʊ] n gueto m.

ghost [gəʊst] n fantasma m; **g. story**, cuento m de fantasmas; **g. town**, pueblo m fantasma.

ghost-writer ['gəʊstraɪtər] n negro,-a, m,f.

ghoulish ['guːlɪʃ] adj macabro,-a.

giant ['dʒaɪənt] adj & n gigante m.

gibberish ['dʒɪbərɪʃ] n galimatías m inv.

gibe [dʒaɪb] I n mofa f. II vi mofarse (at, de).

giblets ['dʒɪblɪts] npl menudillos mpl.

Gibraltar [dʒɪ'brɔːltər] n Gibraltar m.

Gibraltarian [dʒɪbrɔːl'teərɪən] adj & n gibraltareño,-a (m,f).

giddiness ['gɪdɪnɪs] n mareo m; (vertigo) vértigo m.

giddy ['gɪdɪ] adj (giddier, giddiest) mareado,-a; **it makes me g.**, me da vértigo.

go; **to feel g.**, sentirse mareado,-a.

gift [gɪft] n 1 regalo m; Com obsequio m; **g. token**, vale m. 2 (talent) don m; **to have a g. for music**, estar muy dotado,-a para la música.

gifted ['gɪftɪd] adj dotado,-a.

gig [gɪg] n sl Mus actuación f.

gigantic [dʒaɪ'gæntɪk] adj gigantesco,-a.

giggle ['gɪgəl] I n 1 risita f. 2 (lark) broma f, diversión f. II vi reírse tontamente.

gild [gɪld] vtr dorar.

gill¹ [dʒɪl] n (measurement) medida f de líquidos (= 0,142 litro).

gill² [gɪl] n (of fish) branquia f, agalla f.

gilt [gɪlt] I adj dorado,-a. II n (colour) dorado m.

gilt-edged ['gɪltedʒd] adj **g.-e. securities**, valores mpl de máxima garantía.

gimmick ['gɪmɪk] n truco m; (in advertising) reclamo m.

gin [dʒɪn] n ginebra f; **g. and tonic**, gin tonic m.

ginger ['dʒɪndʒər] I n jengibre m; **g. ale**, ginger ale m. II adj 1 de jengibre. 2 (hair) pelirrojo,-a.

gingerbread ['dʒɪndʒəbred] n pan m de jengibre.

gingerly ['dʒɪndʒəlɪ] adv cautelosamente.

gipsy ['dʒɪpsɪ] adj & n gitano,-a (m,f).

giraffe [dʒɪ'rɑːf] n jirafa f.

girder ['gɜːdər] n viga f.

girdle ['gɜːdəl] n faja f.

girl [gɜːl] n 1 chica f, joven f; (child) niña f; **g. guide**, US **g. scout**, exploradora f. 2 (daughter) hija f. 3 (sweetheart) novia f.

girlfriend ['gɜːlfrend] n 1 (lover) novia f. 2 (female friend) amiga f.

girlhood ['gɜːlhʊd] n niñez f.

girlish ['gɜːlɪʃ] adj 1 de niña. 2 (effeminate) afeminado,-a.

giro ['dʒaɪrəʊ] n GB giro m (postal); (cheque) cheque m de giros postales.

gist [dʒɪst] n esencia f, lo esencial; **did you get the g. of what he was saying?**, ¿cogiste la idea de lo que decía?

give [gɪv] I n (elasticity) elasticidad f. II vtr (pt gave; pp given) 1 dar; **to g. sth to sb**, dar algo a algn. II **to g. a start**, pegar un salto; **to g. sb a present**, regalar algo a algn. 2 (provide) suministrar; **to g. sb sth to eat**, dar de comer a algn. 3 (pay) pagar. 4 (concert) dar; (speech) pronunciar. 5 (dedicate) dedicar. 6 (grant) otorgar; **to g. sb one's attention**, prestar atención a algn. 7 **to g. sb to understand that ...**, dar a entender a algn que .... 8 (yield) ceder; **to g. way**, Aut ceder el paso; fig ceder; (of legs) flaquear. III vi 1 **to g. as good as one gets**, devolver golpe por golpe. 2 (yield) ceder; (fabric) dar de sí.

give away vtr 1 repartir; (present) regalar. 2 (disclose) revelar; **to g. the game away**, descubrir el pastel. 3 (betray) trai-

cionar. ◆**give back** vtr devolver.
◆**give in** I vi 1 (*admit defeat*) darse por vencido,-a; (*surrender*) rendirse. 2 **to g. in to**, ceder ante. II vtr (*hand in*) entregar.
◆**give off** vtr (*smell etc*) despedir.
◆**give out** vtr distribuir, repartir.
◆**give over** vtr (*hand over*) entregar; (*devote*) dedicar. II vi (*stop*) ¡basta ya! ◆**give up** vtr 1 (*idea*) abandonar; **to g. up smoking**, dejar de fumar. 2 (*betray*) traicionar. 3 (*hand over*) entregar; **to g. oneself up**, entregarse. II vi (*admit defeat*) darse por vencido,-a, rendirse.
◆**give up on** vtr darse por vencido con.
given ['gɪvən] I adj 1 (*particular*) dado,-a; **at a g. time**, en un momento dado. 2 **g. to**, dado,-a. II conj 1 (*considering*) dado,-a. 2 (*if*) si.
glacial ['gleɪsɪəl] adj 1 Geol glaciar. 2 (*icy*) glacial; fig **g. look**, mirada f glacial.
glacier ['glæsɪə] n glaciar m.
glad [glæd] adj (**gladder**, **gladdest**) contento,-a; (*happy*) alegre; **he'll be only too g. to help you**, tendrá mucho gusto en ayudarle; **to be g.**, alegrarse.
◆**gladly** adv con mucho gusto.
gladiator ['glædɪeɪtə] n Hist gladiador m.
glamor ['glæmə] n US → **glamour**.
glamorous ['glæmərəs] adj atractivo,-a, encantador,-a.
glamour ['glæmə] n atractivo m; (*charm*) encanto m; **a g. girl**, una belleza.
glance [glɑːns] I n mirada f, vistazo m; **at a g.**, de un vistazo; **at first g.**, a primera vista. II vi echar una mirada (**at**, a).
◆**glance off** vtr (*ball etc*) rebotar de.
glancing ['glɑːnsɪŋ] adj (*blow*) oblicuo,-a.
gland [glænd] n glándula f.
glandular ['glændjʊlə] adj glandular; **g. fever**, mononucleosis infecciosa.
glare [gleə] I n (*light*) luz f deslumbrante; (*dazzle*) deslumbramiento m; (*look*) mirada f feroz. II vi (*dazzle*) deslumbrar; (*look*) lanzar una mirada furiosa (**at**, a).
glaring ['gleərɪŋ] adj (*light*) deslumbrante; (*colour*) chillón,-ona; (*obvious*) evidente.
glass [glɑːs] n 1 (*material*) vidrio m; **pane of g.**, cristal m. 2 (*drinking vessel*) vaso m; **wine g.**, copa f (para vino). 3 **glasses**, gafas fpl; **to wear g.**, llevar gafas.
glasshouse ['glɑːshaʊs] n invernadero m.
glassware ['glɑːsweə] n cristalería f.
glassy ['glɑːsɪ] adj (**glassier**, **glassiest**) (*water*) cristalino,-a; (*eyes*) vidrioso,-a.
glaze [gleɪz] I n (*varnish*) barniz m; (*for pottery*) vidriado m. II vtr 1 (*windows*) acristalar; 2 (*varnish*) barnizar; (*ceramics*) vidriar. 3 Culin glasear.
glazed [gleɪzd] adj (*eyes*) de mirada ausente.
glazier ['gleɪzɪə] n vidriero,-a m,f.
gleam [gliːm] I n 1 destello m. 2 fig (*glimmer*) rayo m. II vi brillar, relucir.
gleaming ['gliːmɪŋ] adj brillante, relu-

ciente.
glean [gliːn] vtr fig recoger, cosechar.
glee [gliː] n gozo m.
gleeful ['gliːfʊl] adj gozoso,-a.
glen [glen] n cañada f.
glib [glɪb] adj (**glibber**, **glibbest**) pej de mucha labia.
glide [glaɪd] vi 1 (*slip, slide*) deslizarse. 2 Av planear.
glider ['glaɪdə] n planeador m.
gliding ['glaɪdɪŋ] n vuelo m sin motor.
glimmer ['glɪmə] n 1 (*light*) luz f tenue. 2 fig (*trace*) destello m.
glimpse [glɪmps] I n atisbo m. II vtr atisbar.
glint [glɪnt] I n destello m, centelleo m; **he had a g. in his eye**, le brillaban los ojos. II vi destellar, centellear.
glisten ['glɪsən] vi relucir, brillar.
glitter ['glɪtə] I n brillo m. II vi relucir.
gloat [gləʊt] vi jactarse; **to g. over another's misfortune**, recrearse con la desgracia de otro.
global ['gləʊbəl] adj 1 (*of the world*) mundial. 2 (*overall*) global.
globe [gləʊb] n globo m, esfera f.
gloom [gluːm] n (*obscurity*) penumbra f; (*melancholy*) melancolía f; (*despair*) desolación f.
gloomy ['gluːmɪ] adj (**gloomier**, **gloomiest**) (*dark*) oscuro,-a; (*weather*) gris; (*dismal*) deprimente; (*despairing*) pesimista; (*sad*) triste.
glorify ['glɔːrɪfaɪ] vtr glorificar.
glorious ['glɔːrɪəs] adj (*momentous*) glorioso,-a; (*splendid*) magnífico,-a, espléndido,-a.
glory ['glɔːrɪ] n gloria f; fig (*splendour*) esplendor m; fig (*triumph*) triunfo m.
gloss [glɒs] I n 1 (*explanation*) glosa f. 2 (*sheen*) brillo m; **g.** (**paint**), pintura f brillante. II vi glosar. ◆**gloss over** vtr fig encubrir.
glossary ['glɒsərɪ] n glosario m.
glossy ['glɒsɪ] adj (**glossier**, **glossiest**) lustroso,-a; **g. magazine**, revista f de lujo.
glove [glʌv] n guante m; Aut **g. compartment**, guantera f.
glow [gləʊ] I n (*of fire*) incandescencia f; (*of sun*) arrebol m; (*heat*) calor m; (*light*) luz f; (*in cheeks*) rubor m. II vi brillar; (*fire*) arder; fig rebosar de.
glower ['glaʊə] vi poner cara de enfadado,-a.
glowing ['gləʊɪŋ] adj 1 (*fire*) incandescente; (*colour*) vivo,-a; (*light*) brillante. 2 (*cheeks*) encendido,-a. 3 fig (*report*) entusiasta.
glucose ['gluːkəʊz] n glucosa f.
glue [gluː] I n pegamento m, cola f. II vtr pegar (**to**, a).
glum [glʌm] adj (**glummer**, **glummest**)

alicaído,-a.

glut |glʌt| n superabundancia f, exceso m.

glutton |'glʌtən| n glotón,-ona m,f; fam fig a g. for punishment, masoquista m,f.

GMT |dʒi:em'ti:| abbr of **Greenwich Mean Time**, Hora media de Greenwich, GMT.

gnarled |nɑːld| adj nudoso,-a.

gnash |næʃ| vtr rechinar.

gnat |næt| n mosquito m.

gnaw |nɔː| vtr & vi (chew) roer.

GNP |dʒi:en'pi:| abbr of **gross national product**, producto nacional bruto, PNB m.

gnome |nəʊm| n gnomo m.

go |gəʊ| I vi (3rd person sing pres goes; pt went; pp gone) 1 ir; to go by air/on foot, ir en coche/a pie; to go for a walk, (ir a) dar un paseo; to g. on a journey, ir de viaje; to go shopping, ir de compras; fig to go too far, pasarse (de la raya). 2 (depart) irse, marcharse; (bus) salir. 3 (disappear) desaparecer. 4 (function) funcionar; fig to get things going, poner las cosas en marcha. 5 (sell) venderse; shoes going cheap, zapatos a precios de rebaja. 6 (become) quedarse, volverse; to go blind, quedarse ciego,-a; to go mad, volverse loco,-a. 7 (progress) ir, marchar; everything went well, todo salió bien; how's it going?, qué tal (te van las cosas)? 8 to be going to, (in the future) ir a; (on the point of) estar a punto de. 9 (fit) caber. 10 (be kept) guardarse. 11 (be available) quedar; I'll take whatever's going, me conformo con lo que hay. 12 (be acceptable) valer; anything goes, todo vale. 13 (break) romperse; (yield) ceder. 14 how does that song go?, ¿cómo es aquella canción? 15 (time) pasar; there are only two weeks to go, sólo quedan dos semanas. 16 (be inherited) pasar (to, a). 17 (say) decir; as the saying goes, según el dicho. 18 to let sth go, soltar algo.
II vtr 1 (travel) hacer, recorrer. 2 to go it alone, apañárselas solo.
III n 1 (energy) energía f, dinamismo m. 2 (try) intento m; to have a go at sth, probar suerte con algo. 3 (turn) turno m; it's your go, te toca a ti. 4 to make a go of sth, tener éxito en algo. 5 I knew from the word go, lo sabía desde el principio. 6 to have a go at sb, criticar a algn.
◆**go about** I vtr 1 (task) emprender; how do you go about it?, ¿cómo hay que hacerlo? 2 to go about one's business, ocuparse de sus asuntos. II vi (rumour) correr. ◆**go after** vtr (pursue) andar tras. ◆**go against** vtr (oppose) ir en contra de; (verdict) ser desfavorable a. ◆**go ahead** vi 1 (proceed) proceder. 2 we'll go on ahead, iremos delante. ◆**go along** I vtr (street) pasar por. II vi

(progress) progresar. ◆**go along with** vtr 1 (agree with) estar de acuerdo con. 2 (accompany) acompañar. ◆**go around** vi 1 (rumour) correr. 2 there's enough to go around, hay para todos. ◆**go away** vi marcharse. ◆**go back** vi 1 (return) volver, regresar. 2 fig to go back to, (date from) datar de. ◆**go back** on vtr to go back on one's word, faltar a su palabra. ◆**go back to** vtr volver a. ◆**go by** vi pasar; as time goes by, con el tiempo. ◆**go down** vi 1 (descend) bajar; (sun) ponerse; (ship) hundirse. 2 (diminish) disminuir; (temperature) bajar. 3 (be received) ser acogido,-a. ◆**go down with** vtr (contract) coger. ◆**go for** vtr 1 (attack) lanzarse sobre; fam fig go for it!, ¡a por ello! 2 (fetch) ir por. 3 fam (like) gustar. ◆**go in** vi entrar. ◆**go in for** vtr (exam) presentarse a; (hobby) dedicarse a. ◆**go into** vtr 1 (enter) entrar en; to go into journalism, dedicarse al periodismo. 2 (study) examinar; (matter) investigar. 3 (energy, money) invertir en. ◆**go off** I vi 1 (leave) irse, marcharse. 2 (bomb) explotar; (gun) dispararse; (alarm) sonar. 3 (food) pasarse. 4 (event) resultar. II vtr fam to go off sth, perder el gusto o el interés por algo. ◆**go on** vi 1 (continue) seguir, continuar; to go on talking, seguir hablando; fam to go on and on about sth, no parar de hablar sobre algo; (complain) quejarse constantemente de algo. 2 (happen) pasar, ocurrir. 3 (time) transcurrir, pasar. 4 (light) encenderse. ◆**go out** vi 1 (leave) salir; to go out for a meal, comer o cenar fuera. 2 (boy and girl) salir juntos. 3 (fire, light) apagarse. 4 (tide) bajar. 5 TV Rad transmitirse. 6 to go (all) out, ir a por todas. 7 (in competition) perder la eliminatoria. ◆**go over** vtr (revise) repasar. ◆**go over to** vtr 1 acercarse a. 2 to go over to the enemy, pasarse al enemigo. 2 (switch to) pasar a. ◆**go round** vi 1 (revolve) dar vueltas. 2 to go round to sb's house, pasar por casa de algn. ◆**go through** I vi (bill) ser aprobado,-a. II vtr 1 (examine) examinar; (search) registrar. 2 (rehearse) ensayar. 3 (spend) gastar. 4 (list etc) explicar. 5 (endure) sufrir. ◆**go through** with vtr llevar a cabo. ◆**go under** vi 1 (ship) hundirse. 2 (business) fracasar. ◆**go up** vi 1 (price etc) subir. 2 to go up to sb, acercarse a algn. 3 (in a lift) subir. 4 to go up in flames, quemarse. 5 Sport (be promoted) subir. ◆**go with** vtr 1 (accompany) acompañar. 2 (colours) hacer juego con. ◆**go without** I vtr 1 (do without) pasarse sin, prescindir de. 2 fam that goes without saying, eso es evidente. II vi (not have) aguantarse sin nada.

goad |gəʊd| vtr aguijonear.

go-ahead |'gəʊəhed| fam n to give sb the

go-a., dar luz verde a algn.

goal [gǝʊl] n 1 Sport gol m; **g. kick**, saque m de puerta; **(g.) post**, poste m; **g. scorer**, goleador,-a m,f. 2 (aim, objective) meta f, objetivo m.

goalkeeper [ˈgǝʊlkiːpǝʳ] n portero,-a m,f.

goat [gǝʊt] n (female) cabra f; (male) macho cabrío.

gob [gɒb] n GB sl boca f.

gobble [ˈgɒbl] vtr engullir.

go-between [ˈgǝʊbɪtwiːn] n intermediario,-a m,f.

goblet [ˈgɒblɪt] n copa f.

god [gɒd] n dios m; **for G.'s sake!**, ¡por Dios!; **G.**, Dios; **(my) G.!**, ¡Dios mío!; **G. forbid**, ¡Dios no lo quiera!; **G. only knows**, sabe Dios.

godchild [ˈgɒdtʃaɪld] n ahijado,-a.

goddaughter [ˈgɒdɔːtǝʳ] n ahijada f.

goddess [ˈgɒdɪs] n diosa f.

godfather [ˈgɒdfɑːðǝʳ] n padrino m.

godforsaken [ˈgɒdfǝseɪkǝn] adj (place) remoto,-a.

godmother [ˈgɒdmʌðǝʳ] n madrina f.

godparents [ˈgɒdpeǝrǝnts] npl padrinos mpl.

godsend [ˈgɒdsend] n regalo inesperado.

godson [ˈgɒdsʌn] n ahijado m.

goggles [ˈgɒglz] npl gafas protectoras.

going [ˈgǝʊɪŋ] I adj 1 (price) corriente; **the g. rate**, el precio medio. 2 **a g. concern**, un negocio que marcha bien. 3 **to get** or **be g.**, marcharse. 4 **to keep g.**, resistir. II n 1 **that was good g.!**, ¡qué rápido! 2 fig **we got out while the g. is good**, retirarse antes que sea demasiado tarde.

goings-on [gǝʊɪŋzˈɒn] npl fam tejemanejes mpl.

go-kart [ˈgǝʊkɑːt] n Sport kart m.

gold [gǝʊld] I n oro m; **g. leaf**, pan m de oro; **g. medal**, medalla f de oro; **g. mine**, mina f de oro. II adj de oro; (colour) oro, dorado,-a.

golden [ˈgǝʊldǝn] adj de oro; (colour) dorado,-a; fig **a g. opportunity**, una excelente oportunidad; Orn **g. eagle**, águila f real; fig **g. handshake**, indemnización f por despido; **g. wedding**, bodas fpl de oro.

goldfish [ˈgǝʊldfɪʃ] n pez m de colores.

gold-plated [gǝʊldˈpleɪtɪd] adj chapado, -a en oro.

goldsmith [ˈgǝʊldsmɪθ] n orfebre m.

golf [gɒlf] n golf m; **g. ball**, pelota f de golf; **g. club**, (stick) palo m de golf; (place) club m de golf; **g. course**, campo m de golf.

golfer [ˈgɒlfǝʳ] n golfista mf.

golly [ˈgɒlɪ] interj ¡vaya!.

gone [gɒn] adj desaparecido,-a.

gong [gɒŋ] n gong m.

good [gʊd] I adj (better, best) 1 (before noun) bueno,-a; (after noun) bueno,-a; a g.

book, un buen libro; **g. afternoon**, **g. evening**, buenas tardes; **g. morning**, buenos días; **g. night**, buenas noches; it looks g., tiene buena pinta; **to be as g. as new**, como nuevo,-a; **to feel g.**, sentirse bien; **to have a g. time**, pasarlo bien; **to smell g.**, oler bien; **G. Friday**, Viernes m Santo. 2 (kind) amable; (generous) generoso,-a. 3 (healthy) sano,-a. 4 (morally correct) correcto,-a; **be g.!**, ¡pórtate bien! 5 **he's g. at languages**, tiene facilidad para los idiomas. 6 (attractive) bonito,-a; **red looks g. on you**, el rojo te favorece mucho; **g. looks**, atractivo m sing, belleza f sing. 7 **it's as g. as an offer**, equivale a una oferta; **it's as g. a way as any**, es una manera como otra cualquiera. 8 (at least) como mínimo. 9 (sufficient) bastante. 10 **to make g.**, (injustice) reparar; (loss) compensar; (succeed in life) triunfar. 11 (reliable) de confianza. 12 (propitious) propicio,-a. 13 **she comes from a g. family**, es de buena familia. 14 (character) agradable; **he's in a g. mood**, está de buen humor.
II n 1 bien m; **good and evil**, el bien y el mal; **to do g.**, hacer el bien. 2 (advantage) bien m, provecho m; **for your own g.**, para tu propio bien; **it's no g. waiting**, no sirve de nada esperar; **it'll do you g.**, te hará bien. 3 **goods**, (possessions) bienes mpl. 4 Com **goods**, artículos mpl, géneros mpl; **g. train**, tren m de mercancías.
III adv **she's gone for g.**, se ha ido para siempre.
IV interj **g.!**, ¡muy bien!

goodbye [gʊdˈbaɪ] I interj ¡adiós!. II n adiós m, despedida f; **to say g. to sb**, despedirse de algn.

good-for-nothing [ˈgʊdfǝnʌθɪŋ] adj & n inútil (mf).

good-hearted [gʊdˈhɑːtɪd] adj de buen corazón.

good-looking [gʊdˈlʊkɪŋ] adj guapo,-a.

good-natured [gʊdˈneɪtʃǝd] adj amable, bondadoso,-a.

goodness [ˈgʊdnɪs] n bondad f; **my g.!**, ¡Dios mío!; **thank g.!**, ¡gracias a Dios!; **for g. sake!**, ¡por Dios!

good-tempered [gʊdˈtempǝd] adj apacible.

goodwill [gʊdˈwɪl] n 1 buena voluntad f. 2 Com (reputation) buen nombre m.

goose [guːs] n (pl geese [giːs]) ganso m, oca f.

gooseberry [ˈgʊzbǝrɪ, ˈguːsbǝrɪ] n uva espina, grosella espinosa; fam **to play g.**, hacer de carabina.

gooseflesh [ˈguːsfleʃ] n, **goosepimples** [ˈguːspɪmpǝlz] npl carne f de gallina.

goose-step [ˈguːsstep] vi ir a paso de oca.

gore¹ [gɔːʳ] n sangre derramada.

gore² [gɔːr] *vtr* *Taur* cornear, dar cornadas a.

gorge [gɔːdʒ] **I** *n* desfiladero *m*. **II** *vtr & vi* to g. (oneself), atiborrarse (on, de).

gorgeous ['gɔːdʒəs] *adj* magnífico,-a, estupendo,-a; (*person*) atractivo,-a, guapo,-a.

gorilla [gə'rɪlə] *n* gorila *m*.

gorse [gɔːs] *n* aulaga *f*.

gory ['gɔːrɪ] *adj* (**gorier, goriest**) sangriento,-a.

gosh [gɒʃ] *interj fam* ¡cielos!, ¡caray!

go-slow ['gəʊ'sləʊ] *n* huelga *f* de celo.

gospel ['gɒspəl] *n* the G., el Evangelio; *fam* it's the g. truth, es la pura verdad.

gossip ['gɒsɪp] **I** *n* **1** (*rumour*) cotilleo *m*; **g. column**, ecos *mpl* de sociedad. **2** (*person*) chismoso,-a *m,f*; cotilla *m,f*. **II** *vi* (*natter*) cotillear, chismorrear.

got [gɒt] *pt & pp* → get.

Gothic ['gɒθɪk] *adj* gótico,-a.

gotten ['gɒtən] *pp US* → get.

gourmet ['gʊəmeɪ] *n* gourmet *mf*.

gout [gaʊt] *n* gota *f*.

govern ['gʌvən] *vtr* **1** gobernar. **2** (*determine*) determinar.

governess ['gʌvənɪs] *n* institutriz *f*.

governing ['gʌvənɪŋ] *adj* gobernante; **g. body**, consejo *m* de administración.

government ['gʌvənmənt] *n* gobierno *m*.

governmental [gʌvən'mentəl] *adj* gubernamental.

governor ['gʌvənər] *n* (*ruler*) gobernador,-a *m,f*; (*of prison*) director,-a *m,f*; (*of school*) administrador,-a *m,f*.

gown [gaʊn] *n* (*dress*) vestido largo; *Jur Univ* toga *f*.

GP [dʒiː'piː] *abbr of* general practitioner.

GPO [dʒiːpiː'əʊ] *GB abbr of* General Post Office.

grab [græb] **I** *n* agarrón *m*; *fam* to be up for grabs, estar disponible. **II** *vtr* **1** agarrar; to g. hold of sb, agarrarse a algn. **2** *fig* e. a bottle of wine, pillate una botella de vino. **3** *fig* how does that g. you?, ¿qué te parece?

grace [greɪs] **I** *n* **1** gracia *f*; *fig* to fall from g., caer en desgracia. **2** to say g., bendecir la mesa. **3** to do sth with good g., hacer algo de buena gana. **4** five days' g., (*reprieve*) un plazo de cinco días. **5** (*elegance*) elegancia *f*. **6** Your G., (Su) Excelencia. **II** *vtr* **1** (*adorn*) adornar. **2** (*honour*) honrar.

graceful ['greɪsful] *adj* elegante; (*movement*) garboso,-a. ◆**gracefully** *adv* **1** (*beautifully*) con gracia, con elegancia. **2** (*accept*) con cortesía.

gracious ['greɪʃəs] *adj* **1** (*elegant*) elegante. **2** (*courteous*) cortés. **3** (*kind*) amable. **II** *interj* good g. (me)!, goodness g.!, ¡santo cielo!

grade [greɪd] **I** *n* **1** (*quality*) grado *m*; (*rank*) categoría *f*; *Mil* rango *m*. **2** *Educ*

(*mark*) nota *f*. **3** *US Educ* (*class*) clase *f*; *US* **g. school**, escuela *f* primaria. **4** (*level*) nivel *m*; to make the g., llegar al nivel deseado. **5** *US* (*slope*) pendiente *f*. **6** *US* **g. crossing**, paso *m* a nivel. **II** *vtr* clasificar.

gradient ['greɪdɪənt] *n* (*graph*) declive *m*; (*hill*) cuesta *f*.

gradual ['grædjʊəl] *adj* gradual, progresivo,-a. ◆**gradually** *adv* poco a poco.

graduate ['grædjʊɪt] **I** *n* *Educ* titulado,-a *m,f*; *Univ* licenciado,-a *m,f*; *US* **g. school**, escuela *f* para graduados. **II** *vi* ['grædjʊeɪt] **1** *Educ* sacarse el título; *Univ* licenciarse (in, en). **2** to g. to, pasar a.

graduation [grædjʊ'eɪʃən] *n* graduación *f*; *Univ* **g. ceremony**, ceremonia *f* de entrega de los títulos.

graffiti [grə'fiːtɪ] *npl* grafiti *mpl*.

graft [grɑːft] **I** *n* **1** *Med* injerto *m*. **2** *fam* (*work*) trabajo *m*. **3** *US* (*bribery*) soborno *m*. **II** *vtr Med* injertar (on to, en). **III** *vi* *fam* trabajar duro.

grain [greɪn] *n* **1** (*cereals*) cereales *mpl*. **2** (*particle*) grano *m*; *fig* there's not a g. of truth in it, no tiene ni pizca de verdad. **3** (*in wood*) fibra *f*, (*in stone*) veta *f*; (*in leather*) flor *f*; *fig* to go against the g., ir a contrapelo.

gram [græm] *n* gramo *m*.

grammar ['græmər] *n* gramática *f*; (*book*) libro *m* de gramática; **g. school**, instituto estatal de segunda enseñanza al que se ingresa por examen selectivo.

grammatical [grə'mætɪkəl] *adj* gramatical.

gramme [græm] *n* gramo *m*.

gramophone ['græməfəʊn] *n* gramófono *m*.

granary ['grænərɪ] *n* granero *m*.

grand [grænd] **I** *adj* **1** grande; (*before sing noun*) gran; **g. piano**, piano *m* de cola; **G. Prix**, Gran Premio *m*. **2** (*splendid*) grandioso,-a, magnífico,-a; (*impressive*) impresionante. **3** **g. total**, total *m*. **4** *fam* (*wonderful*) estupendo,-a. **II** *n sl* mil libras *fpl*, *US* mil dólares *mpl*.

grandchild ['græntʃaɪld] *n* nieto,-a *m,f*.

granddad ['grændæd] *n fam* abuelo *m*.

granddaughter ['grændɔːtər] *n* nieta *f*.

grandeur ['grændʒər] *n* grandeza *f*, grandiosidad *f*.

grandfather ['grænfɑːðər] *n* abuelo *m*; **g. clock**, reloj *m* de caja.

grandiose ['grændɪəʊs] *adj* grandioso,-a.

grandma ['grænmɑː] *n fam* abuelita *f*.

grandmother ['grænmʌðər] *n* abuela *f*.

grandpa ['grænpɑː] *n fam* abuelito *m*.

grandparents ['grænpeərənts] *npl* abuelos *mpl*.

grandson ['grænsʌn] *n* nieto *m*.

grandstand ['grænstænd] *n* tribuna *f*.

granite ['grænɪt] *n* granito *m.*

granny ['grænɪ] *n fam* abuelita *f.*

grant [grɑːnt] I *vtr* 1 (*allow*) conceder, otorgar. 2 (*admit*) admitir; to take sb for granted, no apreciar a algn en lo que vale; to take sth for granted, dar algo por sentado. II *n Educ* beca *f;* (*subsidy*) subvención *f.*

granulated ['grænjʊleɪtɪd] *adj* granulado,-a.

granule ['grænjuːl] *n* gránulo *m.*

grape [greɪp] *n* uva *f;* **g. juice,** mosto *m.*

grapefruit ['greɪpfruːt] *n* pomelo *m.*

grapevine ['greɪpvaɪn] *n Bot* vid *f;* (*against wall*) parra *f; fam* **I heard it on** or **through the g.,** me enteré por ahí.

graph [grɑːf, græf] *n* gráfica *f.*

graphic ['græfɪk] *adj* gráfico,-a; **g. arts,** artes *fpl* gráficas; **g. designer,** grafista *mf.*

graphics ['græfɪks] *n* 1 (*study*) grafismo *m.* 2 *pl Comput* gráficas *fpl.*

grapple ['græpəl] *n* 1 (*struggle*) luchar cuerpo a cuerpo (**with,** con); *fig* to g. **with a problem,** intentar resolver un problema. II *n* (*hook*) garfio *m.*

grasp [grɑːsp] I *vtr* 1 agarrar. 2 (*understand*) comprender. II *n* 1 (*grip*) agarrón *m.* 2 (*understanding*) comprensión *f;* **within sb's g.,** al alcance de algn.

grasping ['grɑːspɪŋ] *adj* avaro,-a.

grass [grɑːs] I *n* 1 hierba *f;* (*lawn*) césped *m;* (*pasture*) pasto *m;* **'keep off the g.,'** 'prohibido pisar el césped'; **g. court,** pista *f* de hierba; **g. roots,** base *f;* **g. snake,** culebra *f.* 2 *sl* (*drug*) hierba *f.* II *vi GB sl* chivarse (**on,** a). ◆**grass over** *vi* cubrirse de hierba.

grasshopper ['grɑːshɒpə'] *n* saltamontes *m inv.*

grassland ['grɑːslænd] *n* pradera *f.*

grass-roots ['grɑːsruːts] *adj* de base; **at g.-r. level,** a nivel popular.

grassy ['grɑːsɪ] *adj* (*grassier, grassiest*) cubierto,-a de hierba.

grate¹ [greɪt] I *vtr Culin* rallar. II *vi* chirriar.

grate² [greɪt] *n* 1 (*in fireplace*) rejilla *f.* 2 (*fireplace*) chimenea *f.* 3 *Constr* rejilla *f,* reja *f.*

grateful ['greɪtfʊl] *adj* agradecido,-a; **to be g. for,** agradecer.

grater ['greɪtə'] *n Culin* rallador *m.*

gratification [grætɪfɪ'keɪʃən] *n* (*pleasure*) placer *m,* satisfacción *f.*

gratify ['grætɪfaɪ] *vtr* 1 (*please*) complacer. 2 (*yield to*) sucumbir a.

gratifying ['grætɪfaɪɪŋ] *adj* grato,-a.

grating¹ ['greɪtɪŋ] *n* rejilla *f,* reja *f.*

grating² ['greɪtɪŋ] *adj* chirriante; (*tone*) áspero,-a.

gratis ['greɪtɪs, 'grætɪs] *adv* gratis.

gratitude ['grætɪtjuːd] *n* agradecimiento *m.*

gratuitous [grə'tjuːɪtəs] *adj* gratuito,-a.

gratuity [grə'tjuːɪtɪ] *n* gratificación *f.*

grave¹ [greɪv] *n* sepultura *f,* tumba *f.*

grave² [greɪv] *adj* (*look etc*) serio,-a; (*situation*) grave.

gravel ['grævəl] *n* grava *f,* gravilla *f.*

gravestone ['greɪvstəʊn] *n* lápida *f* sepulcral.

graveyard ['greɪvjɑːd] *n* cementerio *m.*

gravity ['grævɪtɪ] *n* gravedad *f.*

gravy ['greɪvɪ] *n* salsa *f,* jugo *m* (de la carne).

gray [greɪ] *adj & n US* → **grey.**

graze¹ [greɪz] *vi* pacer, pastar.

graze² [greɪz] I *vtr* (*scratch*) rasguñar; (*brush against*) rozar. II *n* rasguño *m.*

grease [griːs, griːz] I *n* grasa *f.* II *vtr* engrasar.

greaseproof ['griːspruːf] *adj* **g. paper,** papel graso.

greasy ['griːsɪ] *adj* (*greasier, greasiest*) 1 (*oily*) grasiento,-a; (*hair, food*) graso,-a. 2 (*slippery*) resbaladizo,-a. 3 *fam* (*ingratiating*) pelotillero,-a.

great [greɪt] I *adj* 1 grande; (*before sing noun*) gran; (*pain, heat*) fuerte; **a g. many,** muchos,-as; **G. Britain,** Gran Bretaña. 2 *fam* (*excellent*) estupendo,-a, magnífico,-a; **to have a g. time,** pasarlo en grande. II *adv fam* muy bien, estupendamente. ◆**greatly** *adv* muy, mucho.

great-aunt [greɪt'ɑːnt] *n* tía abuela.

great-grandchild [greɪt'grænʧaɪld] *n* bisnieto,-a *mf.*

great-grandfather [greɪt'grænfɑːðə'] *n* bisabuelo *m.*

great-grandmother [greɪt'grænmʌðə'] *n* bisabuela *f.*

greatness ['greɪtnɪs] *n* grandeza *f.*

great-uncle [greɪt'ʌŋkəl] *n* tío abuelo.

Greece [griːs] *n* Grecia.

greed [griːd], **greediness** ['griːdɪnɪs] *n* (*for food*) gula *f;* (*for money*) codicia *f,* avaricia *f.*

greedy ['griːdɪ] *adj* (*greedier, greediest*) (*for food*) glotón,-ona; (*for money*) codicioso,-a (**for,** de).

Greek [griːk] I *adj* griego,-a. II *n* 1 (*person*) griego,-a *m,f.* 2 (*language*) griego *m.*

green [griːn] I *n* 1 (*colour*) verde *m.* 2 *Golf* campo *m;* **village g.,** plaza *f* (del pueblo). 3 **greens,** verdura *f sing,* verduras *fpl.* II *adj* 1 verde; **g. bean,** judía *f* verde; **g. belt,** zona *f* verde; **g. pepper,** pimiento *m* verde; **she was g. with envy,** se la comía la envidia. 2 (*inexperienced*) verde, novato,-a; (*gullible*) crédulo,-a. 3 *Pol* **G. Party,** Partido *m* Verde.

greenery ['griːnərɪ] *n* follaje *m.*

greenfly ['griːnflaɪ] *n* pulgón *m.*

greengage ['griːngeɪdʒ] *n* ciruela claudia.

greengrocer ['griːngrəʊsə'] *n GB* verdulero,-a *m,f.*

greenhouse ['gri:nhaus] n invernadero m; **g. effect**, efecto invernadero.

greenish ['gri:nɪʃ] adj verdoso,-a.

Greenland ['gri:nlənd] n Groenlandia.

greet [gri:t] vtr (wave at) saludar; (receive) recibir; (welcome) dar la bienvenida a.

greeting ['gri:tɪŋ] n 1 saludo m; **greetings card**, tarjeta f de felicitación. 2 (reception) recibimiento m; (welcome) bienvenida f.

gregarious [grɪ'geərɪəs] adj gregario,-a, sociable.

Grenada [gre'neɪdə] n Granada.

grenade [grɪ'neɪd] n granada f.

grew [gru:] pt → **grow**.

grey [greɪ] **I** adj (colour) gris; (hair) cano,-a; (sky) nublado,-a. **II** n 1 (colour) gris m. 2 (horse) caballo tordo.

grey-haired ['greɪheəd] adj canoso,-a.

greyhound ['greɪhaund] n galgo m.

greyish ['greɪɪʃ] adj grisáceo,-a.

grid [grɪd] n 1 (on map) cuadrícula f. 2 (of electricity etc) red f nacional. 3 → **gridiron**.

gridiron ['grɪdaɪən] n Culin parrilla f.

grief [gri:f] n dolor m, pena f; fam **to come to g.**, (car, driver) sufrir un accidente; (plans) irse al traste.

grievance ['gri:vəns] n (wrong) agravio m; (resentment) queja f.

grieve [gri:v] **I** vtr apenar, dar pena a. **II** vi apenarse, afligirse; **to g. for sb**, llorar la muerte de algn.

grievous ['gri:vəs] adj (offence) grave; **bodily harm**, lesiones fpl corporales graves.

grill [grɪl] **I** vtr 1 Culin asar a la parrilla. 2 fam (interrogate) interrogar duramente. **II** n parrilla f; (dish) parrillada f.

grill(e) [grɪl] n (grating) reja f.

grim [grɪm] adj (**grimmer**, **grimmest**) 1 (sinister) macabro,-a; (landscape) lúgubre; (smile) sardónico,-a. 2 (manner) severo,-a; (person) ceñudo,-a. 3 (resolute) inexorable. 4 fam (unpleasant) desagradable; **to g. reality**, la dura realidad.

grimace [grɪ'meɪs] **I** n mueca f. **II** vi hacer una mueca.

grimy ['graɪmɪ] adj (**grimier**, **grimiest**) mugriento,-a.

grin [grɪn] **I** vi sonreír abiertamente. **II** n sonrisa abierta f.

grind [graɪnd] **I** vtr (pt & pp **ground**) (mill) moler; (crush) triturar; (sharpen) afilar; **to g. one's teeth**, hacer rechinar los dientes. **II** vi rechinar; fig **to g. to a halt**, (vehicle) pararse lentamente; (production etc) pararse poco a poco. **III** n fam **the daily g.**, la rutina cotidiana; **what a g.!**, ¡qué rollo! ◆**grind down** vtr fig **to g. down the opposition**, acabar con la oposición.

grip [grɪp] **I** n 1 (hold) agarrón m; (handshake) apretón m; (of tyre) adherencia f;

get a g. on yourself!, ¡tranquilízate!; **to get to grips with a problem**, superar un problema. 2 (handle) asidero m. 3 (travel bag) maletín m. 4 (hairgrip) pasador m. **II** vtr 1 agarrar, asir; (hand) apretar. 2 fig (of film, story) captar la atención de; **to be gripped by fear**, ser presa del miedo.

gripe [graɪp] **I** vi fam (complain) quejarse. **II** n 1 Med (pain) retortijón m. 2 fam (complaint) queja f.

gripping ['grɪpɪŋ] adj (film, story) apasionante.

grisly ['grɪzlɪ] adj (**grislier**, **grisliest**) espeluznante.

gristle ['grɪsəl] n cartílago m, ternilla f.

grit [grɪt] **I** n 1 (gravel) grava f. 2 fam (courage) valor m. **II** vtr fig **to g. one's teeth**, apretar los dientes.

gritty ['grɪtɪ] adj (**grittier**, **grittiest**) valiente.

grizzly ['grɪzlɪ] adj **g. bear**, oso pardo.

groan [grəun] **I** n 1 (of pain) gemido m. 2 fam (of disapproval) gruñido m. **II** vi 1 (in pain) gemir. 2 fam (complain) quejarse (about, de).

grocer ['grəusə'] n tendero,-a m,f.

groceries ['grəusərɪz] npl comestibles mpl.

grocery ['grəusərɪ] n (shop) tienda f de ultramarinos; US **g. store**, supermercado m.

groggy ['grɒgɪ] adj (**groggier**, **groggiest**) fam Box grogui; fig (unsteady) atontado, -a; (weak) débil.

groin [grɔɪn] n 1 Anat ingle f. 2 US → **groyne**.

groom [gru:m] **I** n 1 mozo m de cuadra. 2 (bridegroom) novio m. **II** vtr (horse) almohazar; (clothes, appearance) cuidar.

groove [gru:v] n (furrow etc) ranura f; (of record) surco m.

grope [grəup] vi 1 (search about) andar a tientas; **to g. for sth**, buscar algo a tientas. 2 sl (fondle) meter mano.

gross [grəus] **I** adj 1 grosero,-a; (joke) verde. 2 (fat) obeso,-a. 3 (flagrant) flagrante; (ignorance) craso,-a. 4 Com Econ bruto,-a; **g. national product**, producto nacional bruto. **II** vtr Com recaudar (en bruto). ◆**grossly** adv enormemente.

grotesque [grəu'tesk] adj grotesco,-a.

grotto ['grɒtəu] n gruta f.

ground¹ [graund] **I** n 1 suelo m, tierra f; **at g. level**, al nivel del suelo; **to get off the g.**, despegar; Av **g. control**, control m de tierra; **g. floor**, planta baja; Av **g. staff**, personal m de tierra; **g. swell**, marejada f. 2 (terrain) terreno m; **to gain/lose g.**, ganar/perder terreno; fig **to stand one's g.**, mantenerse firme; **football g.**, campo m de fútbol. 3 US Elec tierra f. 4 **grounds**, (gardens) jardines mpl. 5 **grounds**, (reason) motivo m sing. 6 **grounds**, (sediment) poso m sing. **II** vtr 1 Av obligar a quedarse en tierra; Naut varar. 2 *US Elec* conectar con tierra.

ground² ['graʊnd] *adj (coffee)* molido,-a;
US (meat) picado,-a.

grounding ['graʊndɪŋ] *n* base *f*; **to have
a good g. in,** tener buenos conocimientos
de.

groundless ['graʊndlɪs] *adj* infundado,-a.

groundsheet ['graʊndʃiːt] *n* tela *f*
impermeable.

groundsman ['graʊndzmən] *n* encargado
m de campo.

groundwork ['graʊndwɜːk] *n* trabajo preparatorio.

group [gruːp] I *n* grupo *m*, conjunto *m*. II
vtr agrupar, juntar (**into,** en). III *vi* to g.
(**together**), agruparse, juntarse.

grouse¹ [graʊs] *n Orn* urogallo *m*.

grouse² [graʊs] *fam* I *vi* quejarse (**about,**
de). II *n* queja *f*.

grove [graʊv] *n* arboleda *f*.

grovel ['grɒvəl] *vi* humillarse (**to,** ante);
(*crawl*) arrastrarse (**to,** ante).

grow [graʊ] I *vtr* (*pt* grew; *pp* grown)
(*cultivate*) cultivar; to g. a beard, dejarse
(crecer) la barba. II *vi* crecer; (*increase*)
aumentar. 2 (*become*) hacerse, volverse;
to g. accustomed to, acostumbrarse a; to
g. dark, oscurecer; to g. old, envejecer.
◆**grow out of** *vtr* I he's grown out of
his shirt, se le ha quedado pequeña la camisa. 2 *fig* (*phase etc*) superar. ◆**grow
up** *vi* crecer, hacerse mayor.

grower ['graʊə'] *n* cultivador,-a *m,f*.

growing ['graʊɪŋ] *adj* (*child*) que crece;
(*problem etc*) creciente; he's a g. boy,
está dando el estirón.

growl [graʊl] I *vi* gruñir. II *n* gruñido *m*.

grown [graʊn] *adj* crecido,-a, adulto,-a.

grown-up ['graʊnʌp] *adj & n* adulto,-a
(*m,f*); the g.-ups, los mayores.

growth [graʊθ] *n* 1 crecimiento *m*; (*increase*) aumento *m*; (*development*) desarrollo *m*. 2 *Med* bulto *m*.

groyne [grɔɪn] *n* espigón *m*.

grub [grʌb] *n* 1 (*larva*) gusano *m*. 2 *sl
(food)* papeo *m*.

grubby ['grʌbɪ] *adj (grubbier, grubbiest)*
sucio,-a.

grudge [grʌdʒ] I *n* rencor *m*; to bear sb a
g., guardar rencor a algn. II *vtr* (*give unwillingly*) dar a regañadientes; he grudges
me my success, me envidia el éxito.

grudgingly ['grʌdʒɪŋlɪ] *adv* a regañadientes.

gruelling, *US* **grueling** ['gruːəlɪŋ] *adj*
penoso,-a.

gruesome ['gruːsəm] *adj* espantoso,-a,
horrible.

gruff [grʌf] *adj* (*manner*) brusco,-a; (*voice*)
áspero,-a.

grumble ['grʌmbəl] I *vi* refunfuñar. II *n*
queja *f*.

grumpy ['grʌmpɪ] *adj* (*grumpier,
grumpiest*) gruñón,-ona.

grunt [grʌnt] I *vi* gruñir. II *n* gruñido *m*.

guarantee [gærən'tiː] I *n* garantía *f*;
(*certificate*) certificado *m* de garantía. II
vtr garantizar; (*assure*) asegurar.

guard [gɑːd] I *vtr* 1 (*protect*) defender,
proteger; (*keep watch over*) vigilar. 2 (*control*) guardar. II *vi* protegerse (**against,**
de, contra). III *n* 1 to be on one's g.,
estar en guardia; to catch sb off his g.,
coger desprevenido a algn. 2 (*sentry*)
guardia *m/f*; g. of honour, guardia de honor; to stand g., montar la guardia; the g.
dog, perro *m* guardián. 3 *GB Rail* jefe *m*
de tren; g.'s van, furgón *m* de cola. 4 (*on
machine*) dispositivo *m* de seguridad; fire
g., pantalla *f*.

guarded ['gɑːdɪd] *adj* cauteloso,-a,
precavido,-a.

guardhouse ['gɑːdhaʊs] *n Mil* 1 (*headquarters*) cuerpo *m* de guardia. 2 (*prison*)
prisión *f* militar.

guardian ['gɑːdɪən] *n* 1 guardián,-ana
m,f; g. angel, ángel *m* de la guarda. 2 *Jur
(of minor)* tutor,-a *m,f*.

Guatemala [gwɑːtə'mɑːlə] *n* Guatemala *f*.

Guatemalan [gwɑːtə'mɑːlən] *adj & n*
guatemalteco,-a (*m,f*).

guava ['gwɑːvə] *n Bot* guayaba *f*; g. tree,
guayabo *m*.

guer(r)illa [gə'rɪlə] *n* guerrillero,-a *m,f*; g.
warfare, guerra *f* de guerrillas.

guess [ges] I *vtr & vi* 1 adivinar; I
guessed as much, me lo imaginaba; to
g. right/wrong, acertar/no acertar. 2 *US
fam* pensar, suponer; I g. so, supongo
que sí. II *n* conjetura *f*, cálculo (*calcule*
m; at a rough g., a ojo de buen cubero;
to have or make a g., intentar adivinar.

guesswork ['geswɜːk] *n* conjetura *f*.

guest [gest] *n* (*at home*) invitado,-a *m,f*;
(*in hotel*) cliente,-a *m,f*, huésped,-a *m,f*;
g. artist, artista *mf* invitado,-a; g. room,
cuarto *m* de los invitados.

guesthouse ['gesthaʊs] *n* casa *f* de
huéspedes.

guffaw [gə'fɔː] *vi* reírse a carcajadas.

guidance ['gaɪdəns] *n* orientación *f*,
consejos *mpl*; for your g., a título de
información.

guide [gaɪd] I *vtr* guiar, dirigir. II *n*
(*person*) guía *mf*; *GB* girl g., exploradora
f; g. dog, perro lazarillo. 2 (*guidebook*)
guía *f*.

guidebook ['gaɪdbʊk] *n* guía *f*.

guided ['gaɪdɪd] *adj* dirigido,-a; g. tour,
visita con guía; g. missile, misil teledirigido.

guideline ['gaɪdlaɪn] *n* pauta *f*.

guild [gɪld] *n* gremio *m*.

guile [gaɪl] *n* astucia *f*.

guillotine ['gɪlətiːn] *n* guillotina *f*.

guilt [gɪlt] *n* 1 culpa *f*. 2 *Jur* culpabilidad
f.

guilty ['gɪltɪ] *adj* (*guiltier, guiltiest*)

culpable (**of, de**); **to have a g. con-science**, remorderle a uno la conciencia.
guinea¹ ['gɪnɪ] n g. **pig**, conejillo m de Indias, cobayo m; fig to act as a g. **pig**, servir de conejillo de Indias.
guinea² ['gɪnɪ] n (coin) guinea f (approx 21 chelines).
guise [gaɪz] n **under the g. of**, so pretexto de.
guitar [gɪ'tɑːr] n guitarra f.
guitarist [gɪ'tɑːrɪst] n guitarrista mf.
gulf [gʌlf] n 1 golfo m; G. **of Mexico**, Golfo de Méjico; G. **Stream**, corriente f del Golfo de Méjico. 2 fig abismo m.
gull [gʌl] n gaviota f.
gull(e)y ['gʌlɪ] n barranco m, hondonada f.
gullible ['gʌləbəl] adj crédulo,-a.
gulp [gʌlp] I n trago m. II vtr tragar; **to g. sth down**, (drink) tomarse algo de un trago; (food) engullir algo. III vi 1 (swallow air) tragar aire. 2 fig (with fear) tragar saliva.
gum¹ [gʌm] I n goma f. II vtr pegar con goma.
gum² [gʌm] n Anat encía f.
gumboots ['gʌmbuːts] npl botas fpl de agua.
gun [gʌn] n arma f de fuego; (handgun) pistola f, revólver m; (rifle) fusil m, escopeta f; (cannon) cañón m; fam **the big guns**, los peces gordos. ◆**gun down** vtr matar a tiros.
gunboat ['gʌnbəʊt] n cañonero m.
gunfire ['gʌnfaɪər] n tiros mpl.
gunman ['gʌnmən] n pistolero m, gángster m.
gunpoint ['gʌnpɔɪnt] n **at g.**, a punta de pistola.
gunpowder ['gʌnpaʊdər] n pólvora f.

gunrunner ['gʌnrʌnər] n traficante mf de armas.
gunshot ['gʌnʃɒt] n disparo m, tiro m.
gunsmith ['gʌnsmɪθ] n armero m.
gurgle ['gɜːgəl] vi (baby) gorjear; (liquid) gorgotear; (stream) murmurar.
guru ['guruː, 'guːruː] n gurú m.
gush [gʌʃ] I vi 1 brotar. 2 fig **to g. over sb**, enjabonar a algn. II n (of water) cho-rro m; (of words) torrente m.
gushing ['gʌʃɪŋ] adj fig (person) efusivo, -a.
gusset ['gʌsɪt] n escudete m.
gust [gʌst] n (of wind) ráfaga f, racha f.
gusto ['gʌstəʊ] n entusiasmo m.
gut [gʌt] I n 1 Anat intestino m. 2 (catgut) cuerda f de tripa. 3 **guts**, (en-trails) tripas fpl; sl **to have g.**, tener aga-llas. II vtr 1 (fish) destripar. 2 (destroy) destruir por dentro. III adj fam **g. reac-tion**, reacción f visceral.
gutter ['gʌtər] n (in street) arroyo m; (on roof) canalón m; fig **g. press**, prensa ama-rilla.
guttural ['gʌtərəl] adj gutural.
guy¹ [gaɪ] n fam tipo m, tío m.
guy² [gaɪ] n (rope) viento m, cuerda f.
guzzle ['gʌzəl] vtr & vi fam (food etc) zamparse; (car) tragar mucho.
gym [dʒɪm] fam 1 (gymnasium) gimnasio m. 2 (gymnastics) gimnasia f; **g. shoes**, zapatillas fpl de deporte.
gymnasium [dʒɪm'neɪzɪəm] n gimnasio m.
gymnast ['dʒɪmnæst] n gimnasta mf.
gymnastics [dʒɪm'næstɪks] n gimnasia f.
gynaecologist, US **gynecologist** [gaɪnɪ'kɒlədʒɪst] n ginecólogo,-a m,f.
gypsy ['dʒɪpsɪ] adj & n gitano,-a (m,f).
gyrate [dʒəˈreɪt] vi girar.

H

H, h [eɪtʃ] n (the letter) H, h f.
haberdashery [hæbə'dæʃərɪ] n 1 GB artí-culos mpl de mercería. 2 US ropa mascu-lina.
habit ['hæbɪt] n 1 costumbre f. 2 (gar-ment) hábito m.
habitable ['hæbɪtəbəl] adj habitable.
habitat ['hæbɪtæt] n hábitat m.
habitual [hə'bɪtjʊəl] adj habitual; (drink-er, liar) empedernido,-a. ◆**habitually** adv por costumbre.
hack¹ [hæk] I n (cut) corte m; (with an axe) hachazo m. II vtr (with knife, axe) cortar; (kick) dar un puntapié a.
hack² [hæk] n fam (writer) escritorzuelo,-a m,f; (journalist) gacetillero,-a m,f.
hackneyed ['hæknɪd] adj trillado,-a.
hacksaw ['hæksɔː] n sierra f para meta-

les.
had [hæd] pt & pp → **have**.
haddock ['hædək] n abadejo m.
haemophilia [hiːməʊ'fɪlɪə] n hemofilia f.
haemophiliac [hiːməʊ'fɪlɪæk] adj & n hemofílico,-a (m,f).
haemorrhage ['hemərɪdʒ] n hemorragia f.
haemorrhoids ['hemərɔɪdz] npl hemo-rroides fpl.
hag [hæg] n pej bruja f, arpía f.
haggard ['hægəd] adj ojeroso,-a.
haggle ['hægəl] vi regatear.
Hague [heɪg] n **The H.**, La Haya.
hail¹ [heɪl] I n granizo m; fig **a h. of** **bullets/insults**, una lluvia de balas/ insultos. II vi granizar.
hail² [heɪl] I vtr 1 (taxi etc) parar. 2 (ac-claim) aclamar. II vi **to h. from**, (origi-

nate) ser nativo,-a de.

hailstone ['heɪlstəʊn] n granizo m.

hailstorm ['heɪlstɔːm] n granizada f.

hair [heəʳ] n (*strand*) pelo m, cabello m; (*mass*) pelo m, cabellos mpl; (*on arm, leg*) vello m; **to have long h.**, tener el pelo largo.

hairbrush ['heəbrʌʃ] n cepillo m (para el pelo).

haircut ['heəkʌt] n corte m de pelo; **to have a h.**, cortarse el pelo.

hairdo ['heəduː] n fam peinado m.

hairdresser ['heədresəʳ] n peluquero,-a m,f; **h.'s** (**shop**), peluquería f.

hairdryer, hairdrier ['heədraɪəʳ] n secador m (de pelo).

hair-grip ['heəgrɪp] n horquilla f, pasador m.

hairline ['heəlaɪn] I *adj* muy fino,-a. II n nacimiento m del pelo; **receding h.**, entradas fpl.

hairnet ['heənet] n redecilla f.

hairpiece ['heəpiːs] n postizo m.

hairpin ['heəpɪn] n horquilla f; **h. bend**, curva muy cerrada.

hair-raising ['heəreɪzɪŋ] *adj* espeluznante.

hair-remover ['heərɪmuːvəʳ] n depilatorio m.

hairspray ['heəspreɪ] n laca f (para el pelo).

hairstyle ['heəstaɪl] n peinado m, corte m de pelo.

hairy ['heərɪ] *adj* (**hairier, hairiest**) 1 (*with- hair*) peludo,-a. 2 *fig* (*frightening*) enervante, espantoso,-a.

hake [heɪk] n merluza f; (*young*) pescadilla f.

half [hɑːf] I n (*pl* **halves**) mitad f; *Sport* (*period*) tiempo m; **he's four and a h.**, tiene cuatro años y medio; **to cut in h.**, cortar por la mitad. II *adj* medio,-a; **h. a dozen/an hour**, media docena/hora; **h. board**, media pensión; **h. fare**, media tarifa; **h. term**, medio trimestre; **h. year**, semestre m. III *adv* medio, a medias; **h. asleep**, medio dormido,-a.

half-caste ['hɑːfkɑːst] *adj & n* mestizo,-a (m,f).

half-day [hɑːf'deɪ] n media jornada.

half-hearted [hɑːf'hɑːtɪd] *adj* poco entusiasta.

half-hour [hɑːf'aʊəʳ] n media hora.

half-life ['hɑːflaɪf] n media vida.

half-mast [hɑːf'mɑːst] n **at h.**, a media asta.

half-price [hɑːf'praɪs] *adv* a mitad de precio.

half-time [hɑːf'taɪm] n descanso m.

half-way [hɑːf'weɪ] *adj* intermedio,-a. II **halfway** [hɑːf'weɪ] *adv* a medio camino, a mitad de camino.

half-yearly [hɑːf'jɪəlɪ] *adj* semestral.

halibut ['hælɪbət] n mero m.

hall [hɔːl] n 1 (*lobby*) vestíbulo m. 2

(*building*) sala f; *Univ* **h. of residence**, colegio m mayor.

hallmark ['hɔːlmɑːk] n 1 (*on gold, silver*) contraste m. 2 *fig* sello m.

hallo [hə'ləʊ] *interj* ¡hola!

hallowed ['hæləʊd] *adj* santificado,-a.

Hallowe')en [hæləʊ'iːn] n víspera f de Todos los Santos.

hallucinate [hə'luːsɪneɪt] vi alucinar.

hallucination [həluːsɪ'neɪʃən] n alucinación f.

hallucinogenic [həluːsɪnəʊ'dʒenɪk] *adj* alucinógeno,-a.

hallway ['hɔːlweɪ] n vestíbulo m.

halo ['heɪləʊ] n 1 *Rel* aureola f. 2 *Astron* halo m.

halt [hɔːlt] I n (*stop*) alto m, parada f; **to call a h. to sth**, poner fin a algo. II *vtr* parar. III vi pararse.

halting ['hɔːltɪŋ] *adj* vacilante.

halve [hɑːv] *vtr* 1 partir por la mitad; (*reduce by half*) reducir a la mitad. 2 (*share*) compartir.

halves [hɑːvz] *pl* → **half**.

ham [hæm] n jamón m; **boiled h.**, jamón de York; **Parma** *or* **cured h.**, jamón serrano.

hamburger ['hæmbɜːgəʳ] n hamburguesa f.

hamlet ['hæmlɪt] n aldea f.

hammer ['hæməʳ] I n 1 martillo m; **the h. and sickle**, la hoz y el martillo. 2 (*of gun*) percursor m. 3 *Sport* lanzamiento m de martillo. II *vtr* 1 martillar; (*nail*) clavar; *fig* **to h. home**, insistir sobre. 2 *fam* (*defeat*) dar una paliza a. III vi martillar, dar golpes.

hammering ['hæmərɪŋ] n *fam* paliza f.

hammock ['hæmək] n hamaca f; *Naut* coy m.

hamper[1] ['hæmpəʳ] n cesta f.

hamper[2] ['hæmpəʳ] *vtr* estorbar, dificultar.

hamster ['hæmstəʳ] n hámster m.

hamstring ['hæmstrɪŋ] n tendón m de la corva.

hand [hænd] I n 1 mano f; **by h.**, a mano; (*close*) **at h.**, a mano; **hands up!**, ¡manos arriba!; **on the one/other h.**, por una/ otra parte; *fig* **to get out of h.**, descontrolarse; *fig* **to be on h.**, estar a mano; *fig* **to have a h. in**, intervenir en; *fig* **to have time in h.**, sobrarle a uno tiempo; *fig* **to wash one's hands of sth**, lavarse las manos de algo; *fig* **to give sb a h.**, echarle una mano a algn; **h. grenade**, granada f de mano. 2 (*worker*) trabajador,-a m,f; *Naut* tripulante m. 3 (*of clock*) aguja f. 4 **to give sb a big h.**, (*applause*) dedicar a algn una gran ovación. 5 (*handwriting*) letra f.

II *vtr* (*give*) dar, entregar; *fig* **I have to h. it to you**, tengo que reconocerlo.

◆**hand back** *vtr* devolver. ◆**hand**

down *vtr* dejar en herencia. ◆**hand in** *vtr* (*homework*) entregar; (*resignation*) presentar. ◆**hand out** *vtr* repartir. ◆**hand over** *vtr* entregar. ◆**hand round** *vtr* repartir.

handbag ['hændbæg] *n* bolso *m*.

handball ['hændbɔ:l] *n* Sport balonmano *m*.

handbook ['hændbʊk] *n* manual *m*.

handbrake ['hændbreɪk] *n* freno *m* de mano.

handcuff ['hændkʌf] I *vtr* esposar. II *npl* **handcuffs**, esposas *fpl*.

handful ['hændfʊl] *n* puñado *m*.

handicap ['hændɪkæp] *n* 1 Med minusvalía *f*. 2 (Sport) hándicap *m*, desventaja *f*. II *vtr* impedir.

handicapped ['hændɪkæpt] *adj* 1 (*physically*) minusválido,-a; (*mentally*) retrasado,-a. 2 Sport en desventaja. 3 *fig* desfavorecido,-a.

handicraft ['hændɪkrɑ:ft] *n* artesanía *f*.

handiwork ['hændɪwɜ:k] *n* (*work*) obra *f*; (*craft*) artesanía *f*.

handkerchief ['hæŋkətʃi:f] *n* pañuelo *m*.

handle ['hændəl] I *n* (*of knife*) mango *m*; (*of cup*) asa *f*; (*of door*) pomo *m*; (*of lever*) palanca *f*; (*of drawer*) tirador *m*. II *vtr* 1 manejar; '**h. with care**', 'frágil'. 2 (*problem*) encargarse de; (*people*) tratar; *fam* (*put up with*) soportar. III *vi* (*car*) comportarse.

handlebar ['hændəlbɑ:r] *n* manillar *m*.

handmade ['hænd'meɪd] *adj* hecho,-a a mano.

hand-out ['hændaʊt] *n* 1 (*leaflet*) folleto *m*; Press nota *f* de prensa. 2 (*charity*) limosna *f*.

hand-picked [hænd'pɪkt] *adj* selecto,-a.

handrail ['hændreɪl] *n* pasamanos *m* sing inv.

handshake ['hændʃeɪk] *n* apretón *m* de manos.

handsome ['hænsəm] *adj* 1 (*person*) guapo,-a. 2 (*substantial*) considerable.

handwriting ['hændraɪtɪŋ] *n* letra *f*.

handy ['hændɪ] *adj* (**handier**, **handiest**) 1 (*useful*) útil, práctico,-a; (*nearby*) a mano. 2 (*dextrous*) diestro,-a.

hang [hæŋ] I *vtr* (*pt & pp* **hung**) 1 colgar. 2 (*head*) bajar. 3 (*pt & pp* **hanged**) ahorcar. II *vi* 1 colgar (from, de); (*in air*) flotar. 2 (*criminal*) ser ahorcado,-a; to **h. oneself**, ahorcarse. ◆**hang about**, **hang round** *vi* *fam* 1 perder el tiempo. 2 *fam* (*wait*) esperar. ◆**hang around** *vi* *fam* 1 esperar. 2 *fam* frecuentar; **where does he h. around?**, ¿a qué lugares suele ir? ◆**hang on** *vi* 1 agarrarse. 2 (*wait*) esperar. ◆**hang out** I *vtr* (*washing*) tender. II *vi* *fam* (*frequent*) frecuentar. ◆**hang together** *vi* (*ideas*) ser coherente. ◆**hang up** *vtr* (*picture*, *telephone*) colgar.

hangar ['hæŋər] *n* hangar *m*.

hanger ['hæŋər] *n* percha *f*.

hang-glider ['hæŋglaɪdər] *n* ala delta.

hang-gliding ['hæŋglaɪdɪŋ] *n* vuelo *m* libre.

hangman ['hæŋmən] *n* verdugo *m*.

hangover ['hæŋəʊvər] *n* resaca *f*.

hang-up ['hæŋʌp] *n* *fam* (*complex*) complejo *m*.

hanker ['hæŋkər] *vi* to **h. after** sth, anhelar algo.

hankie, **hanky** ['hæŋkɪ] *n* *fam* pañuelo *m*.

haphazard [hæp'hæzəd] *adj* caótico,-a, desordenado,-a.

happen ['hæpən] *vi* suceder, ocurrir; **it so happens that**, lo que pasa es que; **if you h. to see my friend**, si por casualidad ves a mi amigo.

happening ['hæpənɪŋ] *n* acontecimiento *m*.

happiness ['hæpɪnɪs] *n* felicidad *f*.

happy ['hæpɪ] *adj* (**happier**, **happiest**) (*cheerful*) feliz, contento,-a; (*fortunate*) afortunado,-a; **h. birthday!**, ¡feliz cumpleaños! ◆**happily** *adv* (*with pleasure*) felizmente; (*fortunately*) afortunadamente.

happy-go-lucky [hæpɪgəʊˈlʌkɪ] *adj* despreocupado,-a; **a h.-go-l. fellow**, un viva la virgen.

harangue [hə'ræŋ] I *vtr* arengar. II *n* arenga *f*.

harass ['hærəs] *vtr* acosar.

harassment ['hærəsmənt, hə'ræsmənt] *n* hostigamiento *m*, acoso *m*.

harbour, US **harbor** ['hɑ:bər] I *n* puerto *m*. II *vtr* 1 (*criminal*) encubrir. 2 (*doubts*) abrigar.

hard [hɑ:d] I *adj* 1 duro,-a; (*solid*) sólido,-a; **h. court**, pista *f* (de tenis) rápida; Comput **h. disk**, disco duro; **h. shoulder**, arcén *m*. 2 (*difficult*) difícil; **h. of hearing**, duro,-a de oído; *fam* to **be h. up**, estar sin blanca. 3 (*harsh*) severo,-a; (*strict*) estricto,-a; to **take a h. line**, tomar medidas severas; **h. drugs**, droga dura; Pol **h. left**, extrema izquierda; **h. porn**, pornografía dura; **h. sell**, promoción *f* de venta agresiva. 4 **a h. drinker**, un bebedor inveterado; **h. worker**, un trabajador concienzudo. 5 **h. luck!**, ¡mala suerte! 6 **h. evidence**, pruebas definitivas; Comput **h. cash**, dinero en metálico; **h. currency**, divisa *f* fuerte. II *adv* 1 (*hit*) fuerte. 2 (*work*) mucho, concienzudamente; *fig* to **be h. on sb's heels**, pisar los talones a algn. 3 to **be h. done by**, ser tratado,-a injustamente.

hardback ['hɑ:dbæk] *n* edición *f* de tapas duras.

hard-boiled ['hɑ:dbɔɪld] *adj* duro,-a.

hard-core ['hɑ:dkɔ:r] *adj* irreductible.

harden ['hɑ:dən] I *vtr* endurecer. II *vi* endurecerse.

hardened ['hɑ:dənd] *adj* *fig* habitual.

hard-headed ['hɑːd'hedɪd] *adj* realista.

hard-hearted ['hɑːd'hɑːtɪd] *adj* insensible.

hardliner ['hɑːd'laɪnər] *n* duro,-a, *m,f*.

hardly ['hɑːdlɪ] *adv* apenas; h. anyone/ever, casi nadie/nunca; he had h. begun when ...., apenas había comenzado cuando ...; I can h. believe it, apenas lo puedo creer.

hardship ['hɑːdʃɪp] *n* privación *f*, apuro *m*.

hardware ['hɑːdweər] *n* 1 (goods) ferretería *f*; h. shop, ferretería. 2 Comput hardware *m*.

hardwearing [hɑːd'weərɪŋ] *adj* duradero,-a.

hardworking ['hɑːd'wɜːkɪŋ] *adj* muy trabajador,-a.

hardy ['hɑːdɪ] *adj* (hardier, hardiest) (person) robusto,-a, fuerte; (plant) resistente.

hare [heər] I *n* liebre *f*. II *vi* correr muy de prisa.

haricot ['hærɪkəʊ] *n* h. (bean), alubia *f*.

harm [hɑːm] I *n* daño *m*, perjuicio *m*; to be out of h.'s way, estar a salvo. II *vtr* hacer daño a, perjudicar.

harmful ['hɑːmfʊl] *adj* perjudicial (to, para).

harmless ['hɑːmlɪs] *adj* inofensivo,-a.

harmonica [hɑː'mɒnɪkə] *n* armónica *f*.

harmonize ['hɑːmənaɪz] *vtr & vi* armonizar.

harmony ['hɑːmənɪ] *n* armonía *f*.

harness ['hɑːnɪs] I *n* (for horse) arreos mpl. II *vtr* 1 (horse) enjaezar. 2 fig (resources etc) aprovechar.

harp [hɑːp] *n* arpa *f*. ◆**harp on** *vi fam* hablar sin parar.

harpoon [hɑː'puːn] I *n* arpón *m*. II *vtr* arponear.

harrowing ['hærəʊɪŋ] *adj* angustioso,-a.

harsh [hɑːʃ] *adj* severo,-a; (voice) áspero,-a; (sound) discordante.

harvest ['hɑːvɪst] I *n* cosecha *f*; (of grapes) vendimia *f*. II *vtr* cosechar, recoger.

harvester ['hɑːvɪstər] *n* 1 (person) segador,-a *m,f*. 2 (machine) cosechadora *f*.

has [hæz] 3rd person sing pres → **have**.

hash¹ [hæʃ] *n* Culin sofrito *m* de carne; fam fig to make a h. of sth, estropear algo.

hash² [hæʃ] *n sl* hachís *m*.

hashish ['hæʃɪʃ] *n* hachís *m*.

hassle ['hæsəl] fam I *n* 1 (nuisance) rollo *m*. 2 (wrangle) bronca *f*. II *vtr* fastidiar.

haste [heɪst] *n fml* prisa *f*; to make h., darse prisa.

hasten ['heɪsən] *vi* apresurarse.

hasty ['heɪstɪ] *adj* (hastier, hastiest) apresurado,-a; (rash) precipitado,-a. ◆**hastily** *adv* (quickly) de prisa.

hat [hæt] *n* sombrero *m*.

hatch¹ [hætʃ] *n* escotilla *f*; serving h.,

hatch² [hætʃ] *vtr* 1 (eggs) empollar. 2 fig (plan) tramar. ◆**hatch out** *vi* salirse del huevo.

hatchback ['hætʃbæk] *n* coche *m* de 3 or 5 puertas.

hatchet ['hætʃɪt] *n* hacha *f*; fam h. man, matón *m*.

hate [heɪt] I *n* odio *m*. II *vtr* odiar.

hateful ['heɪtfʊl] *adj* odioso,-a.

hatred ['heɪtrɪd] *n* odio *m*.

haughty ['hɔːtɪ] *adj* (haughtier, haughtiest) altanero,-a, arrogante.

haul [hɔːl] I *n* 1 (journey) trayecto *m*. 2 Fishing redada *f*. 3 (loot) botín *m*. II *vtr* 1 tirar; (drag) arrastrar. 2 (transport) acarrear. ◆**haul up** *vtr fam* (to court) llevar.

haulage ['hɔːlɪdʒ] *n* transporte *m*.

haulier ['hɔːljər] *n* transportista *mf*.

haunch [hɔːntʃ] *n* cadera *f*; Culin pernil *m*.

haunt [hɔːnt] I *n* guarida *f*. II *vtr* 1 (of ghost) aparecerse en. 2 fig atormentar. 3 (frequent) frecuentar.

haunted ['hɔːntɪd] *adj* encantado,-a, embrujado,-a.

Havana [hə'vænə] *n* La Habana; H. cigar, habano *m*.

have [hæv] I *vtr* (3rd person sing pres has) (pt & pp had) 1 (possess) tener; have you got a car?, ¿tienes coche? 2 (get, experience, suffer) tener; to h. a holiday, tomarse unas vacaciones. 3 (partake of) tomar; to h. a cigarette, fumarse un cigarrillo; to h. breakfast/lunch/tea/dinner, desayunar/comer/merendar/cenar. 4 to h. a bath/shave, bañarse/afeitarse; to h. a nap, echar la siesta. 5 to h. to, (obligation) tener que, deber. 6 (make happen) hacer que; I'll h. someone come round, haré que venga alguien. 7 (receive) recibir; to h. people round, invitar a gente. 8 can I h. your pen a moment?, (borrow) ¿me dejas tu bolígrafo un momento? 9 (party, meeting) hacer, celebrar. 10 to h. a baby, tener un niño. 11 we won't h. it, (allow) no lo consentiremos. 12 (hold) tener; fig to h. sth against sb, tener algo en contra de algn. 13 legend has it that ..., según la leyenda .... 14 (deceive) engañar. 15 you'd better stay, más vale que te quedes.

II *v aux* 1 (compound) haber; I had been waiting for half an hour, hacía media hora que esperaba; he hasn't eaten yet, no ha comido aún; she had broken the window, había roto el cristal; we h. lived here for ten years, hace diez años que vivimos aquí; so I h.!, (emphatic) ¡ay, sí!, es verdad; yes I h.!, que sí! 2 (tag questions) you haven't seen my book, h. you?, no has visto mis gafas, ¿verdad?; he's been to France, hasn't he?, ha estado en Francia, ¿verdad? o ¿no? 3 (have

+ *just*) acabar de.
◆**have on** *vtr* 1 (*wear*) vestir. 2 *fam* to h. sb on, tomarle el pelo a algn. ◆**have out** *vtr fam* to h. it out with sb, ajustar cuentas con algn. ◆**have over** *vtr* (*invite*) recibir.

haven ['heɪvn] *n* puerto *m*; *fig* refugio *m*.

haversack ['hævəsæk] *n* mochila *f*.

havoc ['hævək] *n* to play h. with, hacer estragos en.

hawk [hɔːk] *n Orn Pol* halcón *m*.

hawker ['hɔːkə'] *n* vendedor,-a *m,f* ambulante.

hawthorn ['hɔːθɔːn] *n* espino *m* albar.

hay [heɪ] *n* heno *m*; h. fever, fiebre *f* del heno.

haystack ['heɪstæk] *n* almiar *m*.

haywire ['heɪwaɪə'] *adj fam* en desorden; to go h., (*machine etc*) estropearse; (*person*) volverse loco,-a.

hazard ['hæzəd] I *n* peligro *m*, riesgo *m*; *Golf* obstáculo *m*. II *vtr fml* arriesgar; to h. a guess, intentar adivinar.

hazardous ['hæzədəs] *adj* arriesgado,-a, peligroso,-a.

haze [heɪz] *n* (*mist*) neblina *f*, *fig* (*blur*) confusión *f*.

hazel ['heɪzəl] *adj* (de color) avellana.

hazelnut ['heɪzəlnʌt] *n* avellana *f*.

hazy ['heɪzɪ] *adj* (*hazier, haziest*) nebuloso,-a.

he [hiː] *pers pron* él; he did it, ha sido él; he who, el que.

head [hed] I *n* 1 cabeza *f*; (*mind*) mente *f*; *fig* three pounds a h., tres libras por cabeza; *fig* to be h. over heels in love, estar locamente enamorado,-a; *fig* to keep one's h., mantener la calma; *fig* to lose one's h., perder la cabeza; success went to his h., se le subió el éxito a cabeza; h. start, ventaja *f*. 2 (*of nail*) cabeza *f*; (*of beer*) espuma *f*; (*of tape recorder*) cabezal *m*; (*of steam*) presión *f*; to come to a h., llegar a un momento decisivo. 3 (*boss*) cabeza *m* (*of company*) director,-a *m,f*; h. teacher, director,-a *m,f*. 4 (*of coin*) cara *f*; heads or tails, cara o cruz. II *adj* principal; h. office, oficina *f* central. III *vtr* 1 (*list etc*) encabezar. 2 *Ftb* cabecear. ◆**head for** *vtr* dirigirse hacia. ◆**head off** I *vi* irse. II *vtr* (*avert*) evitar.

headache ['hedeɪk] *n* dolor *m* de cabeza; *fig* quebradero *m* de cabeza.

header ['hedə'] *n Ftb* cabezazo *m*.

head-first [hed'fɜːst] *adv* de cabeza.

head-hunter ['hedhʌntə'] *n fig* cazatalentos *m inv*.

heading ['hedɪŋ] *n* título *m*; (*of letter*) membrete *m*.

headlamp ['hedlæmp] *n* faro *m*.

headland ['hedlənd] *n* punta *f*, cabo *m*.

headlight ['hedlaɪt] *n* faro *m*.

headline ['hedlaɪn] *n* titular *m*.

headlong ['hedlɒŋ] *adj & adv* de cabeza;

to rush h. into sth, lanzarse a hacer algo sin pensar.

headmaster [hed'mɑːstə'] *n* director *m*.

headmistress [hed'mɪstrɪs] *n* directora *f*.

head-on ['hedɒn] *adj* a h.-on collision, un choque frontal.

headphones ['hedfəʊnz] *npl* auriculares *mpl*.

headquarters [hedkwɔːtəz] *npl* 1 oficina *f* central, sede *f*. 2 *Mil* cuartel *m* general.

headrest ['hedrest] *n Aut* apoyacabezas *m*.

headroom ['hedruːm] *n* altura *f* libre.

headscarf ['hedskɑːf] *n* pañuelo *m*.

headstrong ['hedstrɒŋ] *adj* testarudo,-a.

headway ['hedweɪ] *n* to make h., avanzar, progresar.

headwind ['hedwɪnd] *n* viento *m* de proa.

heady ['hedɪ] *adj* (*headier, headiest*) embriagador,-a.

heal [hiːl] I *vi* cicatrizar. II *vtr* (*illness*) curar.

health [helθ] *n* salud *f*; *fig* prosperidad *f*; to be in good/bad h., estar bien/mal de salud; your good h.!, ¡salud!; h. foods, alimentos *mpl* naturales; h. food shop, tienda *f* de alimentos naturales; h. service, ≈ Insalud *m*.

healthy ['helθɪ] *adj* (*healthier, healthiest*) sano,-a; (*good for health*) saludable; (*thriving*) próspero,-a.

heap [hiːp] I *n* montón *m*. II *vtr* amontonar; *fig* (*praises*) colmar de; a heaped spoonful, una cucharada colmada.

hear [hɪə'] I *vtr* (*pt & pp* heard [hɜːd]) 1 oír. 2 (*listen to*) escuchar. 3 I won't h. of it!, ¡ni hablar! 4 (*find out*) enterarse. 5 *Jur* ver; (*evidence*) oír. II *vi* to h. from sb, tener noticias de algn.

hearing ['hɪərɪŋ] *n* 1 oído *m*; h. aid, audífono *m*. 2 *Jur* audiencia *f*; *fig* to give sb a fair h., escuchar a algn.

hearsay ['hɪəseɪ] *n* rumores *mpl*.

hearse [hɜːs] *n* coche *m* fúnebre.

heart [hɑːt] *n* 1 corazón *m*; h. attack, infarto *m* de miocardio; h. transplant, trasplante *m* de corazón; a broken h., un corazón roto; at h., en el fondo; to take sth to h., tomarse algo a pecho; to have a good h., (*be kind*) tener buen corazón. 2 (*courage*) valor *m*; his h. wasn't in it, no ponía interés en ello; to lose h.; desanimarse. 3 (*core*) meollo *m*; (*of lettuce*) cogollo *m*.

heartbeat ['hɑːtbiːt] *n* latido *m* del corazón.

heart-breaking ['hɑːtbreɪkɪŋ] *adj* desgarrador,-a.

heart-broken ['hɑːtbrəʊkən] *adj* hundido,-a; he's h.-b., tiene el corazón destrozado

heartburn ['hɑːtbɜːn] *n* acedía *f*.

heartening ['hɑːtənɪŋ] *adj* alentador,-a.

heartfelt ['hɑːtfelt] *adj* sincero,-a.

hearth [hɑːθ] *n* 1 (*fireplace*) chimenea *f.* 2 *fml* (*home*) hogar *m.*

heartless ['hɑːtlɪs] *adj* cruel, insensible.

heart-throb ['hɑːtθrɒb] *n* ídolo *m.*

hearty ['hɑːtɪ] *adj* (**heartier, heartiest**) (*person*) francote; (*meal*) abundante; (*welcome*) cordial; **to have a h. appetite**, ser de buen comer.

heat [hiːt] **I** *n* 1 calor *m.* 2 *Sport* eliminatoria *f.* 3 *Zool* **on h.**, en celo. **II** *vtr* calentar. ◆**heat up** *vi* 1 (*warm up*) calentarse. 2 (*increase excitement*) acalorarse.

heated ['hiːtɪd] *adj fig* (*argument*) acalorado,-a.

heater ['hiːtə'] *n* calentador *m.*

heath [hiːθ] *n* (*land*) brezal *m.*

heathen ['hiːðən] *adj & n* pagano,-a (*m,f*).

heather ['heðə'] *n* brezo *m.*

heating ['hiːtɪŋ] *n* calefacción *f.*

heatwave ['hiːtweɪv] *n* ola *f* de calor.

heave [hiːv] **I** *n* (*pull*) tirón *m*; (*push*) empujón *m.* **II** *vtr* 1 (*lift*) levantar; (*haul*) tirar; (*push*) empujar. 2 (*throw*) arrojar. **III** *vi* subir y bajar.

heaven ['hevən] **I** *n* 1 cielo *m*; **for heaven's sake!**, ¡por Dios!; **h. on earth**, un paraíso en la tierra. 2 **heavens**, cielo *m sing.* **II** *interj* **good heavens!**, ¡por Dios!

heavenly ['hevənlɪ] *adj* celestial.

heavy ['hevɪ] **I** *adj* (**heavier, heaviest**) pesado,-a; (*rain, meal*) fuerte; (*traffic*) denso,-a; (*loss*) grande; **h. going**, duro,-a, is it h.?, ¿pesa mucho?; **a h. drinker/smoker**, un,-a bebedor,-a/fumador,-a empedernido,-a; *Mus* **h. metal**, heavy metal *m.* **II** *n sl* gorila *m.* ◆**heavily** *adv* **it rained h.**, llovió mucho; **to sleep h.**, dormir profundamente.

heavyweight ['hevɪweɪt] *n Box* peso pesado.

Hebrew ['hiːbruː] **I** *adj* hebreo,-a *m,f.* **II** *n* (*language*) hebreo *m.*

Hebrides ['hebrɪdiːz] *npl* **the H.**, las (Islas) Hébridas.

heckle ['hekəl] *vtr* interrumpir.

heckler ['heklə'] *n* altercador,-a *m,f.*

hectare ['hektɑːr] *n* hectárea *f.*

hectic ['hektɪk] *adj* agitado,-a.

hedge [hedʒ] **I** *n* seto *m.* **II** *vtr* cercar con un seto; *fig* **to h. one's bets**, cubrirse.

hedgehog ['hedʒhɒg] *n* erizo *m.*

hedgerow ['hedʒrəu] *n* seto vivo.

heed [hiːd] *n* **to take h. of**, hacer caso de.

heedless ['hiːdlɪs] *adj* desatento,-a.

heel [hiːl] *n* talón *m*; (*of shoe*) tacón *m*; (*of palm*) pulpejo *m*; *fig* **to be on sb's heels**, pisarle los talones a algn; **high heels**, zapatos *mpl* de tacón alto.

heeled [hiːld] *adj fam fig* **well-h.**, adinerado,-a.

hefty ['heftɪ] *adj* (**heftier, heftiest**) (*person*) fornido,-a; (*package*) pesado,-a. 2 (*large*) grande.

height [haɪt] *n* 1 altura *f*; (*of person*) estatura *f*; *Av* **to gain/lose h.**, subir/bajar; **what h. are you?**, ¿cuánto mides?; *fig* **the h. of ignorance**, el colmo de la ignorancia. 2 *Geog* cumbre *f.*

heighten ['haɪtən] *vtr* (*intensify*) realzar; (*increase*) aumentar.

heir [eə'] *n* heredero *m.*

heiress ['eərɪs] *n* heredera *f.*

heirloom ['eəluːm] *n* reliquia *f* or joya *f* de familia.

held [held] *pt & pp →* **hold**.

helicopter ['helɪkɒptə'] *n* helicóptero *m.*

helium ['hiːlɪəm] *n* helio *m.*

hell [hel] *n* infierno *m*; *fam* **what the h. are you doing?**, ¿qué diablos estás haciendo?; *offens* **go to h.!**, ¡vete a hacer puñetas!; *fam* **a h. of a party**, una fiesta estupenda; *fam* **she's had a h. of a day**, ha tenido un día fatal.

hellish ['helɪʃ] *adj fam* infernal.

hello [hə'ləu, 'heləu] *interj* ¡hola!; *Tel* ¡diga!; (*showing surprise*) ¡hala!

helm [helm] *n* timón *m*; **to be at the h.**, llevar el timón.

helmet ['helmɪt] *n* casco *m.*

help [help] **I** *n* 1 ayuda *f*; **h.!**, ¡socorro! 2 (*daily*) *ns*, asistenta *f.* **II** *vtr* 1 ayudar; **can I h. you?**, (*in shop*) ¿qué desea? 2 (*alleviate*) aliviar. 3 **h. yourself!**, (*to food etc*) ¡sírvete! 4 (*avoid*) evitar; **I can't h. it**, no lo puedo remediar. ◆**help out** *vtr* **to h. sb out**, echarle una mano a algn.

helper ['helpə'] *n* ayudante,-a *m,f.*

helpful ['helpful] *adj* (*person*) amable; (*thing*) útil.

helping ['helpɪŋ] *n* ración *f*; **who wants a second h.?**, ¿quién quiere repetir?

helpless ['helplɪs] *adj* (*defenceless*) desamparado,-a; (*powerless*) incapaz. ◆**helplessly** *adv* inútilmente, en vano.

helter-skelter [heltə'skeltə'] **I** *n* tobogán *m.* **II** *adj* atropellado,-a. **III** *adv* atropelladamente.

hem [hem] **I** *n Sew* dobladillo *m.* **II** *vtr Sew* hacer un dobladillo a. ◆**hem in** *vtr* cercar, rodear.

hemisphere ['hemɪsfɪə'] *n* hemisferio *m.*

hemophilia [hiːməu'fɪlɪə] *n US →* **haemophilia**.

hemorrhage ['hemərɪdʒ] *n US →* **haemorrhage**.

hen [hen] *n* gallina *f*; *fam* **h. party**, reunión *f* de mujeres.

hence [hens] *adv fml* 1 **six months h.**, (*from now*) de aquí a seis meses. 2 (*consequently*) por lo tanto.

henceforth [hens'fɔːθ] *adv fml* de ahora en adelante.

henchman ['hentʃmən] *n pej* secuaz *m.*

henna ['henə] *n Bot* alheña *f*; (*dye*) henna *f.*

henpecked ['henpekt] *adj fam* **a h. husband**, un calzonazos.

hepatitis [hepə'taɪtɪs] n hepatitis f.

her [hɜːr, unstressed hə] I poss adj (one thing) su; (more than one) sus; (to distinguish) de ella; **are they h. books or his?**, ¿los libros son de ella o de él?; **she has cut h. finger**, se ha cortado el dedo. II object pron 1 (direct object) la; **I saw h. recently**, la vi hace poco. 2 (indirect object) le; (with other third person pronouns) se; **he gave h. money**, le dio dinero; **they handed it to h.**, se lo entregaron. 3 (after prep) ella; **for h.**, para ella. 4 (as subject) fam ella; **look, it's h.!**, ¡mira, es ella!

herald ['herəld] I n heraldo m. II vtr anunciar.

heraldry ['herəldrɪ] n heráldica f.

herb [hɜːb] n hierba f; **h. tea**, infusión f.

herbal ['hɜːbəl] adj herbario,-a; **h. remedies**, curas fpl de hierbas.

herd [hɜːd] n (of cattle) manada f; (of goats) rebaño m; fig (large group) multitud f.

here [hɪər] I adv aquí; **come h.**, ven aquí; **h.!**, ¡presente!; **h. goes!**, ¡vamos a ver!; **here's to success!**, ¡brindemos por el éxito!; **h. you are!**, ¡toma!. II interj **look h., you can't do that!**, ¡oiga, que no se permite hacer eso!

hereafter [hɪər'ɑːftər] fml I adv de ahora en adelante. II n the h., la otra vida, el más allá.

hereby [hɪə'baɪ] adv fml por la presente.

hereditary [hɪ'redɪtərɪ] adj hereditario,-a.

heresy ['herəsɪ] n herejía f.

heretic ['herətɪk] n hereje mf.

heritage ['herɪtɪdʒ] n patrimonio m; Jur herencia f.

hermetically [hɜː'metɪklɪ] adv **h. sealed**, herméticamente cerrado.

hermit ['hɜːmɪt] n ermitaño,-a m,f.

hermitage ['hɜːmɪtɪdʒ] n ermita f.

hernia ['hɜːnɪə] n hernia f.

hero ['hɪərəʊ] n (pl heroes) héroe m; (in novel) protagonista m; **h. worship**, idolatría f.

heroic [hɪ'rəʊɪk] adj heroico,-a.

heroin ['herəʊɪn] n heroína f.

heroine ['herəʊɪn] n heroína f; (in novel) protagonista f.

heron ['herən] n garza f.

herring ['herɪŋ] n arenque m.

hers [hɜːz] poss pron 1 (attribute) (one thing) suyo,-a; (more than one) suyos,-as; (to distinguish) de ella; **they are h. not his**, son de ella, no de él. 2 (noun reference) (one thing) el suyo, la suya; (more than one) los suyos, las suyas; **my car is blue and h. is red**, mi coche es azul y el suyo es rojo.

herself [hɜː'self] pers pron 1 (reflexive) se; **she dressed h.**, se vistió. 2 (alone) ella misma; **she was by h.**, estaba sola. 3 (emphatic) **she told me so h.**, eso dijo ella.

hesitant ['hezɪtənt] adj vacilante.

hesitate ['hezɪteɪt] vi vacilar.

hesitation [hezɪ'teɪʃən] n indecisión f.

heterogeneous [hetərəʊ'dʒiːnɪəs] adj heterogéneo,-a.

heterosexual [hetərəʊ'seksjʊəl] adj & n heterosexual (mf).

hey [heɪ] interj ¡oye!, ¡oiga!

heyday ['heɪdeɪ] n auge m, apogeo m.

HGV [eɪtʃdʒiː'viː] GB abbr of heavy goods vehicle, vehículo m de carga pesada.

hi [haɪ] interj fam ¡hola!

hiatus [haɪ'eɪtəs] n fml laguna f.

hibernate ['haɪbəneɪt] vi hibernar.

hibernation [haɪbə'neɪʃən] n hibernación f.

hibiscus [haɪ'bɪskəs] n hibisco m.

hiccough ['hɪkʌp] n & vi → hiccup.

hiccup ['hɪkʌp] n hipo m; fam (minor problem) problemilla m; **to have hiccups**, tener hipo.

hide¹ [haɪd] I vtr (pt hid [hɪd] pp hidden ['hɪdən]) (conceal) esconder; (obscure) ocultar. II vi esconderse, ocultarse. III n puesto m.

hide² [haɪd] n (of animal) piel f.

hide-and-seek [haɪdən'siːk] n escondite m.

hideous ['hɪdɪəs] adj (horrific) horroroso,-a; (extremely ugly) espantoso, -a.

hide-out ['haɪdaʊt] n escondrijo m, guarida f.

hiding¹ ['haɪdɪŋ] n **to go into h.**, esconderse.

hiding² ['haɪdɪŋ] n fam paliza f.

hierarchy ['haɪərɑːkɪ] n jerarquía f.

hi-fi ['haɪfaɪ] n hifi m; **hi-fi equipment**, equipo m de alta fidelidad.

high [haɪ] I adj 1 alto,-a; **how h. is that wall?**, ¿qué altura tiene esa pared?; **it's three feet h.**, tiene tres pies de alto; **h. chair**, silla alta para niños; **h. jump**, salto m de altura. 2 (elevated) elevado,-a; **h. blood pressure**, tensión alta; **h. prices**, precios elevados; **to be in h. spirits**, estar de buen humor. 3 (important) importante; **h. wind**, viento m fuerte; **to have a h. opinion of sb**, tener muy buena opinión de algn; **H. Court**, Tribunal Supremo; **h. fidelity**, alta fidelidad f; **h. road**, carretera f principal; **h. school**, instituto m de enseñanza media; **the H. Street**, la Calle Mayor. 4 sl (drugged) colocado,-a. II adv alto; **to fly h.**, volar a gran altura. III n (high point) punto máximo.

highbrow ['haɪbraʊ] adj & n intelectual (mf).

high-class ['haɪklɑːs] adj de alta categoría.

higher ['haɪər] adj superior; **h. education**, enseñanza f superior.

high-flier, high-flyer [hai'flaiər] n fig persona dotada y ambiciosa.

high-handed [hai'hændid] adj despótico,-a.

high-heeled [hai'hi:ld] adj de tacón alto.

highlands ['hailəndz] npl tierras altas.

highlight ['hailait] I n 1 (in hair) reflejo m. 2 (of event) atracción f principal. II vtr 1 hacer resaltar. 2 (a text) marcar con un rotulador fosforescente.

highly ['haili] adv (very) sumamente; to speak h. of sb, hablar muy bien de algn.

highly-strung [haili'strʌŋ] adj muy nervioso,-a.

Highness ['hainis] n alteza mf; Your H., Su Alteza.

high-pitched ['haipitʃt] adj estridente.

high-powered ['haipauəd] adj (person) dinámico,-a.

high-ranking [hai'ræŋkiŋ] adj h. official, alto funcionario.

high-rise ['hairaiz] adj h.-r. building, rascacielos m inv.

high-speed ['haispi:d] adj & adv h.-s. lens, objetivo ultrarrápido; h.-s. train, tren m de alta velocidad.

highway ['haiwei] n 1 US carretera f, autopista f; GB H. Code, código m de la circulación.

highwayman ['haiweimən] n salteador m de caminos.

hijack ['haidʒæk] I vtr secuestrar. II n secuestro m.

hijacker ['haidʒækər] n secuestrador,-a m,f; (of planes) pirata mf del aire.

hike [haik] I n 1 (walk) excursión f. 2 price h., aumento m de precio. II vi de excursión.

hiker ['haikər] n excursionista mf.

hilarious [hi'leəriəs] adj graciosísimo,-a.

hill [hil] n colina f; (slope) cuesta f.

hillside ['hilsaid] n ladera f.

hilltop ['hiltop] n cima f de una colina.

hilly ['hili] adj (hillier, hilliest) accidentado,-a.

hit [hit] I n 1 (blow) golpe m; direct h., impacto directo; fam h. list, lista negra; fam h. man, asesino m a sueldo. 2 (success) éxito m; h. parade, lista f de éxitos. II vtr (pt & pp hit) 1 (strike) golpear, pegar; he was h. in the leg, le dieron en la pierna; the car h. the kerb, el coche chocó contra el bordillo; fam fig to h. the roof, poner el grito en el cielo. 2 (affect) afectar. 3 to h. the headlines, ser noticia. ◆**hit back** vi (reply to criticism) replicar. ◆**hit on, hit upon** vtr dar con; we h. on the idea of ..., se nos ocurrió la idea de .... ◆**hit out** vi to h. out at sb, atacar a algn.

hit-and-run [hitən'rʌn] h.-and-r. driver, conductor que atropella a algn y no para.

h. sb from doing sth, impedir a algn hacer algo.

hindrance ['hindrəns] n estorbo m.

hindsight ['haindsait] n retrospectiva f.

Hindu [hin'du:, 'hindu:] adj & n hindú (mf).

Hinduism ['hindu:izəm] n hinduismo m.

hinge [hindʒ] I n bisagra f; fig eje m. II vtr engoznar. ◆**hinge on** vtr depender de.

hint [hint] I n 1 indirecta f; to take the h., coger la indirecta. 2 (clue) pista f. 3 (trace) pizca f. 4 (advice) consejo m. II vi 1 lanzar indirectas. 2 (imply) insinuar algo.

hip¹ [hip] n cadera f; h. flask, petaca f.

hip² [hip] adj & n fam hippy (mf).

hippie ['hipi] adj & n fam hippy (mf).

hippopotamus [hipə'potəməs] n hipopótamo m.

hire ['haiər] I n alquiler m; bicycles for h., se alquilan bicicletas; taxi for h., taxi m libre; h. purchase, compra f a plazos. II vtr 1 (rent) alquilar. 2 (employ) contratar. ◆**hire out** vtr (car) alquilar; (people) contratar.

his [hiz] I poss adj (one thing) su; (more than one) sus; (to distinguish) de él; he washed h. face, se lavó la cara; is it h. dog or hers?, ¿el perro es de él o de ella? II poss pron 1 (attribute) (one thing) suyo, -a; (more than one) suyos,-as; (to distinguish) de él. 2 (noun reference) (one thing) el suyo, la suya; (more than one) los suyos, las suyas; my car is blue and h. is red, mi coche es azul y el suyo es rojo.

Hispanic [hi'spænik] I adj hispánico,-a. II n US hispano,-a m,f, latino,-a m,f.

hiss [his] I n siseo m; Theat silbido m. II vtr & vi silbar.

historian [hi'stɔ:riən] n historiador,-a m,f.

historic [hi'storik] adj histórico,-a.

historical [hi'storikəl] adj histórico,-a; h. novel, novela histórica.

history ['histəri] n historia f.

hitch [hɪtʃ] **I** n dificultad f. **II** vtr (fasten) atar. **III** vi fam (hitch-hike) hacer autostop. ◆**hitch up** vtr remangarse.

hitch-hike ['hɪtʃhaɪk] vi hacer autostop or dedo.

hitch-hiker ['hɪtʃhaɪkə'] n autostopista mf.

hitherto [hɪðə'tu:] adv fml hasta la fecha.

HIV [eɪtʃaɪ'vi:] abbr of **human immuno-deficiency virus**, virus m de inmunodeficiencia humano, VIH; **to be diagnosed HIV positive/negative**, dar seropositivo,-a/seronegativo,-a en la prueba del SIDA.

hive [haɪv] n colmena f; fig lugar muy activo.

HM abbr of **His** or **Her Majesty**, Su Majestad mf, SM.

hoard [hɔ:d] **I** n (provisions) reserva fpl; (money etc) tesoro m. **II** vtr (objects) acumular; (money) atesorar.

hoarding ['hɔ:dɪŋ] n (billboard) valla publicitaria; (temporary fence) valla.

hoarfrost ['hɔ:frɒst] n escarcha f.

hoarse [hɔ:s] adj ronco,-a; **to be h.**, tener la voz ronca.

hoax [həʊks] n (joke) broma pesada; (trick) engaño m.

hob [hɒb] n (of cooker) encimera f.

hobble ['hɒbl] vi cojear.

hobby ['hɒbɪ] n pasatiempo m, afición f.

hobbyhorse ['hɒbɪhɔ:s] n (toy) caballito m de juguete; fig (fixed idea) idea fija, manía f.

hobo ['həʊbəʊ] n US vagabundo,-a m,f.

hockey ['hɒkɪ] n hockey m.

hog [hɒg] **I** n cerdo m, puerco m; fam **to go the whole h.**, liarse la manta a la cabeza. **II** vtr fam acaparar.

hoist [hɔɪst] **I** n (crane) grúa f; (lift) montacargas m inv. **II** vtr levantar, subir; **to h. the flag**, izar la bandera.

hold [həʊld] **I** vtr (pt & pp **held**) **1** (keep in hand) aguantar, tener (en la mano); (grip) agarrar; (support) (weight) soportar; (opinion) sostener; **to h. sb**, abrazar a algn; **to h. sb's hand**, cogerle la mano a algn; fig **she can h. her own in French**, se defiende en francés. **2** (contain) dar cabida a; **the jug holds a litre**, en la jarra cabe un litro. **3** (meeting) celebrar; (conversation) mantener. **4** (reserve) guardar. **5** **to h. office**, ocupar un puesto. **6** (consider) considerar. **7** **he was held for two hours at the police station**, estuvo detenido durante dos horas en la comisaría; **to h. one's breath**, contener la respiración; **to h. sb hostage**, retener a algn como rehén. **8** Tel **to h. the line**, no colgar.

II vi **1** (rope) aguantar. **2** fig (offer) ser válido,-a.

III n **1 to get h. of**, (grip) coger, agarrar; fig localizar; **can you get h. of a newspa-**

per?, ¿puedes conseguir un periódico? **2** (control) control m. **3** Naut bodega f. **4** (in wrestling) llave f.
◆**hold back I** vtr (crowd) contener; (feelings) reprimir; (truth) ocultar; **I don't want to h. you back**, (delay) no quiero entretenerte. **II** vi (hesitate) vacilar. ◆**hold down** vtr **1** (control) dominar. **2** fam (job) desempeñar. ◆**hold off** vtr mantener a distancia. ◆**hold on** vi **1** (keep a firm grasp) agarrarse bien. **2** (wait) esperar; Tel **h. on!**, ¡no cuelgue! ◆**hold out I** vtr (hand) tender. **II** vi **1** (last) (things) durar; (person) resistir. **2** **to h. out for**, insistir en. ◆**hold up** vtr **1** (rob) (train) asaltar; (bank) atracar. **2** (delay) retrasar; **we were held up for half an hour**, sufrimos media hora de retraso. **3** (raise) levantar. **4** (support) apuntalar.

holdall ['həʊldɔ:l] n GB bolsa f de viaje.

holder ['həʊldə'] n **1** (receptacle) recipiente m. **2** (owner) poseedor,-a mf; (bearer) portador,-a m,f; (of passport) titular mf; **record h.**, plusmarquista mf.

holding ['həʊldɪŋ] n **1** (property) propiedad f. **2** Fin valor m en cartera; **h. company**, holding m.

hold-up ['həʊldʌp] n **1** (robbery) atraco m. **2** (delay) retraso m; (in traffic) atasco m.

hole [həʊl] n **1** agujero m; (large) hoyo m; (in the road) bache m. **2** Golf hoyo m. **3** sl (of place) antro m.

holiday ['hɒlɪdeɪ] **I** n (one day) día m de fiesta; GB (several days) vacaciones fpl; **to be/go on h.**, estar/ir de vacaciones; **h. resort**, lugar turístico. **II** vi GB pasar las vacaciones; (in summer) veranear.

holiday-maker ['hɒlɪdeɪmeɪkə'] n GB turista mf; (in summer) veraneante mf.

holiness ['həʊlɪnɪs] n santidad f.

Holland ['hɒlənd] n Holanda.

hollow ['hɒləʊ] **I** adj **1** hueco,-a. **2** (cheeks, eyes) hundido,-a. **3** fig (insincere) falso,-a; (empty) vacío,-a. **II** n hueco m; Geog hondonada f. **III** vtr **to h. (out)**, hacer un hueco en.

holly ['hɒlɪ] n acebo m.

holocaust ['hɒləkɔ:st] n holocausto m.

holster ['həʊlstə'] n pistolera f.

holy ['həʊlɪ] adj sagrado,-a, santo,-a; (blessed) bendito,-a; **H. Ghost**, Espíritu Santo; **H. Land**, Tierra Santa; **H. See**, Santa Sede.

homage ['hɒmɪdʒ] n homenaje m; **to pay h. to sb**, rendir homenaje a algn.

home [həʊm] **I** n **1** casa f, hogar m; **at h.**, en casa; fig **make yourself at h.!**, ¡estás en tu casa!; fig **to feel at h.**, estar a gusto. **2** (institution) asilo m; **old people's h.**, asilo de ancianos. **3** (country) patria f. **4** Sport **to play at h.**, jugar en casa; US **h. base**, (in baseball) base f del bateador; **h. run**, carrera completa. **II** adj **1** (domestic) del hogar; GB **h. help**, asistenta f. **2**

Pol interior; **h. affairs,** asuntos *mpl* interiores; *GB* **H. Office,** Ministerio *m* del Interior; *GB* **H. Secretary,** Ministro *m,f* del Interior. 3 *(native)* natal. III *adv* en casa; **to go h.,** irse a casa; **to leave h.,** irse de casa.

homeland ['həʊmlænd] *n* patria *f; (birthplace)* tierra *f* natal.

homeless ['həʊmlɪs] I *adj* sin techo. II *npl* **the h.,** los sin techo.

homely ['həʊmlɪ] *adj* **(homelier, homeliest)** 1 *GB (person)* casero,-a; *(atmosphere)* familiar. 2 *US (unattractive)* sin atractivo.

home-made ['həʊmmeɪd] *adj* casero,-a.

homeopathy [həʊmɪ'ɒpəθɪ] *n US* → **homoeopathy.**

homesick ['həʊmsɪk] *adj* **to be h.,** tener morriña.

homeward(s) ['həʊmwəd(z)] *adv* hacia casa.

homework ['həʊmwɜːk] *n* deberes *mpl.*

homicide ['hɒmɪsaɪd] *n* homicidio *m.*

homing ['həʊmɪŋ] *adj* 1 **h. device,** cabeza buscadora. 2 **h. pigeon,** paloma mensajera.

homoeopathy [həʊmɪ'ɒpəθɪ] *n* homeopatía *f.*

homogeneous [hɒmə'dʒiːnɪəs] *adj* homogéneo,-a.

homosexual [həʊməʊ'seksjʊəl] *adj & n* homosexual *(mf).*

Honduran [hɒn'djʊərən] *adj & n* hondureño,-a *(m,f).*

Honduras [hɒn'djʊərəs] *n* Honduras *f.*

honest ['ɒnɪst] *adj* honrado,-a; *(sincere)* sincero,-a, franco,-a; *(fair)* justo,-a; **the h. truth,** la pura verdad; ◆**honestly** *adv* honradamente; *(question)* ¿de verdad?; *(exclamation)* ¡hay que ver!; **h., it doesn't matter,** de verdad, no tiene importancia.

honesty ['ɒnɪstɪ] *n* honradez *f.*

honey ['hʌnɪ] *n* miel *f; US fam (endearment)* cariño *m.*

honeycomb ['hʌnɪkəʊm] *n* panal *m.*

honeymoon ['hʌnɪmuːn] *n* luna *f* de miel.

honeysuckle ['hʌnɪsʌkəl] *n* madreselva *f.*

honk [hɒŋk] *vi Aut* tocar la bocina.

honor ['ɒnər] *n & vtr US* → **honour.**

honorary ['ɒnərərɪ] *adj (member)* honorario,-a; *(duties)* honorífico,-a.

honour ['ɒnər] I *n* honor *m.* 2 *US fur* **Her H., His H., Your H.,** Su Señoría *f.* 3 *Mil* **honours,** honores *mpl.* 4 **Honours degree,** licenciatura *f* superior. II *vtr* 1 *(respect)* honrar. 2 *(obligation)* cumplir con.

honourable ['ɒnərəbəl] *adj (person)* honrado,-a; *(action)* honroso,-a.

hood [hʊd] *n* 1 *(of garment)* capucha *f.* 2 *(of car)* capota *f; US (bonnet)* capó *m.*

hoodlum ['huːdləm] *n* matón *m.*

hoodwink ['hʊdwɪŋk] *vtr* engañar.

hoof [huːf] *n (pl* **hoofs** *or* **hooves** [huːvz]*) (of horse)* casco *m; (of cow, sheep)* pezuña *f.*

hook [hʊk] I *n* 1 gancho *m; Fishing* anzuelo *m; Sew* **hooks and eyes,** corchetes *mpl;* **to take the phone off the h.,** descolgar el teléfono. 2 *Box* gancho *m.* II *vtr* 1 enganchar. 2 *Box* hacer un gancho a. ◆**hook up** *vtr & vi Rad TV Comput* conectar (with, con).

hooked [hʊkt] *adj* 1 *(nose)* aguileño,-a. 2 *sl (addicted)* enganchado,-a (on, a); **to get h.,** engancharse.

hook-up ['hʊkʌp] *n* 1 *Comput* conexión *f.* 2 *Rad TV* emisión *f* múltiple.

hooligan ['huːlɪɡən] *n sl* gamberro,-a *m,f.*

hoop [huːp] *n* aro *m; (of barrel)* fleje *m.*

hooray [huː'reɪ] *interj* ¡hurra!

hoot [huːt] I *n* 1 ululato *m; fam* **hoots of laughter,** carcajadas *fpl; fam* **I don't care a h.,** me importa un pepino. 2 *(of car horn)* bocinazo *m.* II *vi* 1 *(owl)* ulular. 2 *(car)* dar un bocinazo; *(train)* silbar; *(siren)* pitar.

hooter ['huːtər] *n esp GB (of car)* bocina *f; (siren)* sirena *f.*

Hoover® ['huːvər] *GB* I *n* aspiradora *f.* II *vtr* **to h.,** pasar la aspiradora por.

hop¹ [hɒp] I *vi* saltar; **to h. on one leg,** andar a la pata coja. II *n (small jump)* brinco *m.*

hop² [hɒp] *n Bot* lúpulo *m.*

hope [həʊp] I *n* esperanza *f; (false)* ilusión *f;* **to have little h. of doing sth,** tener pocas posibilidades de hacer algo. II *vtr & vi* esperar; **I h. so/not,** espero que sí/no; **we h. you're well,** esperamos que estés bien.

hopeful ['həʊpfʊl] *adj (confident)* optimista; *(promising)* prometedor,-a. ◆**hopefully** *adv (confidently)* con optimismo. **2 h. the weather will be fine,** *(it is hoped)* esperemos que haga buen tiempo.

hopeless ['həʊplɪs] *adj* desesperado,-a; *fam* **to be h. at sports,** ser negado,-a para los deportes. ◆**hopelessly** *adv* desesperadamente; **h. lost,** completamente perdido,-a.

horde [hɔːd] *n* multitud *f.*

horizon [hə'raɪzən] *n* horizonte *m.*

horizontal [hɒrɪ'zɒntəl] *adj* horizontal.

hormone ['hɔːməʊn] *n* hormona *f.*

horn [hɔːn] *n* 1 cuerno *m.* 2 *Mus fam* trompeta *f;* **French h.,** trompa *f; hunting h.,** cuerno *m* de caza. 3 *Aut* bocina *f.*

hornet ['hɔːnɪt] *n* avispón *m.*

horny ['hɔːnɪ] *adj* **(hornier, horniest)** 1 *(hands)* calloso,-a. 2 *sl (sexually aroused)* caliente, cachondo,-a.

horoscope ['hɒrəskəʊp] *n* horóscopo *m.*

horrendous [hɒ'rendəs] *adj* horrendo,-a.

horrible ['hɒrəbəl] *adj* horrible.

horrid ['hɒrɪd] *adj* horrible.

horrific [hə'rɪfɪk] *adj* horrendo,-a.

horrify ['hɒrɪfaɪ] *vtr* horrorizar.

horror ['hɒrəʳ] *n* horror *m*; *fam* a little h., un diablillo; **h. film**, película *f* de miedo *or* de terror.

hors d'oeuvre [ɔː'dɜːvr] *n* entremés *m*.

horse [hɔːs] *n* 1 caballo *m*; **h. race**, carrera *f* de caballos. 2 *Gymn* potro *m*. 3 *Tech* caballete *m*. 4 **h. chestnut**, (tree) castaño *m* de Indias.

horseback ['hɔːsbæk] *n* **on h.**, a caballo.

horseman ['hɔːsmən] *n* jinete *m*.

horseplay ['hɔːspleɪ] *n* payasadas *fpl*.

horsepower ['hɔːspaʊəʳ] *n* caballo *m* (de vapor).

horseradish ['hɔːsrædɪʃ] *n* rábano rusticano.

horseshoe ['hɔːsʃuː] *n* herradura *f*.

horsewoman ['hɔːswʊmən] *n* amazona *f*.

horticulture ['hɔːtɪkʌltʃəʳ] *n* horticultura *f*.

hose [həʊz] *n* (pipe) manguera *f*.

hosiery ['həʊzɪərɪ] *n* medias *fpl* y calcetines *mpl*.

hospice ['hɒspɪs] *n* residencia *f* para enfermos terminales.

hospitable ['hɒspɪtəbəl, hɒ'spɪtəbəl] *adj* hospitalario,-a; **h. atmosphere**, ambiente acogedor.

hospital ['hɒspɪtəl] *n* hospital *m*.

hospitality [hɒspɪ'tælɪtɪ] *n* hospitalidad *f*.

host¹ [həʊst] *n* 1 (at home) anfitrión *m*. 2 *Theat TV* presentador *m*. 3 *Biol* huésped *m*. II *vtr Theat TV* presentar.

host² [həʊst] *n* (large number) montón *m*.

Host [həʊst] *n Rel* hostia *f*.

hostage ['hɒstɪdʒ] *n* rehén *m*.

hostel ['hɒstəl] *n* hostal *m*.

hostess ['həʊstɪs] *n* 1 (at home etc) anfitriona *f*. 2 *Theat TV* presentadora *f*. 3 (air) h., azafata *f*.

hostile ['hɒstaɪl] *adj* hostil.

hostility [hɒ'stɪlɪtɪ] *n* hostilidad *f*.

hot [hɒt] *adj* (hotter, hottest) 1 caliente; *fig* **h. line**, teléfono rojo; **h. spot**, (nightclub) club nocturno. 2 (weather) caluroso,-a; **it's very h.**, hace mucho calor; **to feel h.**, tener calor. 3 (spicy) picante; **h. dog**, perrito *m* caliente. 4 (temper) fuerte. 5 *fam* (fresh) de última hora. 6 *fam* (good) bueno,-a; **it's not so h.**, no es nada del otro mundo. 7 (popular) popular. 8 (dangerous) peligroso,-a; *fig* **to get oneself into h. water**, meterse en un lío; *fam* **h. seat**, primera fila. ◆**hot up** *vi fam* **things are hotting up**, la cosa se está poniendo al rojo vivo.

hotbed ['hɒtbed] *n fig* hervidero *m*.

hotel [həʊ'tel] *n* hotel *m*.

hotelier [həʊ'teljeɪ] *n* hotelero,-a *m.f*.

hot-headed [hɒt'hedɪd] *adj* impetuoso,-a.

hothouse ['hɒthaʊs] *n* invernadero *f*.

hotplate ['hɒtpleɪt] *n* (cooker) placa *f* de cocina; (to keep food warm) calientaplatos *m inv*.

hotshot ['hɒtʃɒt] *n fam* as *m*.

hot-water ['hɒtwɔːtəʳ] *adj* **h.-w. bottle**, bolsa *f* de agua caliente.

hound [haʊnd] *n* perro *m* de caza. II *vtr* acosar.

hour ['aʊəʳ] *n* hora *f*; **60 miles an h.**, 60 millas por hora; **by the h.**, por horas; **h. hand**, manecilla *f*.

hourly ['aʊəlɪ] I *adj* cada hora. II *adv* por horas.

house [haʊs] I *n* 1 casa *f*; **at my h.**, en mi casa; *fig* **on the h.**, cortesía de la casa; **h. arrest**, arresto domiciliario; **h. plant**, planta *f* de interior. 2 *Pol* **H. of Commons**, Cámara *f* de los Comunes; **H. of Lords**, Cámara de los Lores; *US* **H. of Representatives**, Cámara de Representantes; **Houses of Parliament**, Parlamento *m*. 3 (company) empresa *f*; **publishing h.**, editorial *f*. 4 *Theat* sala *f*. II [haʊz] *vtr* alojar; (store) guardar.

houseboat ['haʊsbəʊt] *n* casa *f* flotante.

housebreaking ['haʊsbreɪkɪŋ] *n* allanamiento *m* de morada.

housecoat ['haʊskəʊt] *n* bata *f*.

household ['haʊshəʊld] *n* hogar *m*; **h. products**, productos domésticos.

housekeeper ['haʊskiːpəʳ] *n* ama *f* de llaves.

housekeeping ['haʊskiːpɪŋ] *n* administración doméstica; **h. money**, dinero *m* para los gastos domésticos.

house-train ['haʊstreɪn] *vtr* (pet) educar.

house-warming ['haʊswɔːmɪŋ] *n* **h.-w. (party)**, fiesta *f* que se da al estrenar casa.

housewife ['haʊswaɪf] *n* ama *f* de casa.

housework ['haʊswɜːk] *n* trabajo *m* doméstico.

housing ['haʊzɪŋ] *n* vivienda *f*; **h. estate**, urbanización *f*.

hovel ['hʌvəl, 'hɒvəl] *n* casucha *f*.

hover ['hɒvəʳ] *vi* (bird) cernerse; (aircraft) permanecer inmóvil (en el aire).

hovercraft ['hɒvəkrɑːft] *n* aerodeslizador *m*.

how [haʊ] *adv* 1 (direct question) ¿cómo?; **h. are you?**, ¿cómo estás?; *fam* **h. come?**, ¿por qué? 2 (indirect question) cómo; **I don't know h. to tell you**, no sé cómo decírtelo. 3 (very) qué; **h. funny!**, ¡qué divertido! 4 **h. about going to the cinema?**, (suggestion) ¿te apetece ir al cine?; **h. about a stroll?**, ¿qué te parece un paseo? 5 (quantity) cuánto; **h. old is she?**, ¿cuántos años tiene?; **h. tall are you?**, ¿cuánto mides? 6 **h. many?**, ¿cuántos,-as?; **h. much?**, ¿cuánto,-a?; **I don't know h. many people there were**, no sé cuánta gente había.

however [haʊ'evəʳ] *adv* 1 (nevertheless) no obstante, sin embargo. 2 (with adjective)

h. difficult it may be, por difícil que sea; **h. much,** por mucho que (+ subj).

howl [haʊl] I n aullido m. II vi aullar.

howler ['haʊlə*] n fam despiste m.

HP, hp [eɪtʃ'pi:] 1 GB abbr of hire purchase. 2 abbr of horsepower, cv mpl.

HQ [eɪtʃ'kju:] Mil abbr of headquarters.

hub [hʌb] n Aut cubo m; fig eje m.

hubbub ['hʌbʌb] n alboroto m.

hubcap ['hʌbkæp] n Aut tapacubos m inv.

huddle ['hʌdəl] I n grupo m. II vi to h. (up or together), acurrucarse.

hue[1] [hju:] n (colour) tinte m; (shade) matiz m.

hue[2] [hju:] n h. and cry, fuerte protesta f.

huff [hʌf] n to be in a h., estar de mala uva.

hug [hʌg] I vtr abrazar. II n abrazo m.

huge [hju:dʒ] adj enorme. ◆**hugely** adv enormemente.

hulk [hʌlk] n 1 Naut casco m. 2 (thing, person) armatoste m.

hull [hʌl] n Naut casco m.

hullaba(l)oo [hʌləbə'lu:] n fam follón m.

hullo [hʌ'ləʊ] interj GB ¡hola!

hum [hʌm] I vtr (tune) tararear. II vi (bees, engine) zumbar; (sing) tararear. III n (of bees) zumbido m.

human ['hju:mən] I adj humano,-a; h. race, raza humana; h. being, ser humano. II n ser humano.

humane [hju:'meɪn] adj humano,-a.

humanitarian [hju:mænɪ'teərɪən] adj humanitario,-a.

humanity [hju:'mænɪtɪ] n 1 humanidad f. 2 Univ the humanities, las humanidades.

humble ['hʌmbəl] I adj humilde. II vtr humillar.

humbug ['hʌmbʌg] n 1 fam tonterías fpl. 2 GB (mint) h., caramelo m de menta.

humdrum ['hʌmdrʌm] adj monótono,-a, aburrido,-a.

humid ['hju:mɪd] adj húmedo,-a.

humidity [hju:'mɪdɪtɪ] n humedad f.

humiliate [hju:'mɪlɪeɪt] vtr humillar.

humiliation [hju:mɪlɪ'eɪʃən] n humillación f.

humility [hju:'mɪlɪtɪ] n humildad f.

humor ['hju:mərəs] n US → humour.

humorous ['hju:mərəs] adj (writer) humorístico,-a; (person, story) gracioso,-a, divertido,-a.

humour ['hju:mə*] I n humor m. II vtr seguir la corriente a.

hump [hʌmp] I n 1 (on back) joroba f. 2 (small hill) montículo m. II vtr GB sl cargar (a la espalda).

humus ['hju:məs] n mantillo m, humus m.

hunch [hʌntʃ] n fam corazonada f.

hunchback ['hʌntʃbæk] n jorobado,-a m,f.

hundred ['hʌndrəd] I n cien m, ciento m;

(rough number) centenar m; **a h. and twenty-five,** ciento veinticinco; **five h.,** quinientos. II adj cien; **a h. people,** cien personas; **a h. per cent,** cien por cien; **two h. chairs,** doscientas sillas.

hundredth ['hʌndrədθ] adj & n centésimo,-a (m).

hundredweight ['hʌndrədweɪt] n ciento doce libras fpl (≈ quintal m).

hung [hʌŋ] adj 1 fam h. over, con resaca. 2 fam h. up, acomplejado,-a.

Hungarian [hʌŋ'geərɪən] adj & n húngaro,-a (m,f).

Hungary ['hʌŋgərɪ] n Hungría.

hunger ['hʌŋgə*] I n hambre f; h. strike, huelga f de hambre. II vi fig tener hambre (for, de).

hungry ['hʌŋgrɪ] adj (hungrier, hungriest) hambriento,-a; to be h., tener hambre; to go h., pasar hambre.

hunk [hʌŋk] n 1 (piece) buen pedazo m. 2 sl (man) machote m.

hunt [hʌnt] I vtr cazar. II vi (for game) cazar; (search) buscar. III n caza f, (search) búsqueda f. ◆**hunt down** vtr perseguir.

hunter ['hʌntə*] n cazador,-a m,f.

hunting ['hʌntɪŋ] n caza f; (expedition) cacería f.

hurdle ['hɜ:dəl] n Sport valla f; fig obstáculo m.

hurl [hɜ:l] vtr arrojar, lanzar.

hurrah [hʊ'rɑ:], **hurray** [hʊ'reɪ] interj ¡hurra!; h. for John!, ¡viva John!

hurricane ['hʌrɪkən, 'hʌrɪkeɪn] n huracán m.

hurried ['hʌrɪd] adj apresurado,-a; (action etc) hecho,-a de prisa. ◆**hurriedly** adv deprisa, apresuradamente.

hurry ['hʌrɪ] I vi darse prisa a. II vtr meter prisa a. III n to be in a h., tener prisa.

hurt [hɜ:t] I vtr (pt & pp hurt) hacer daño a; (wound) herir; (feelings) ofender. II vi doler; **my arm hurts,** me duele el brazo; fam **it doesn't h. to go out once in a while,** no viene mal salir de vez en cuando. III adj (physically) herido,-a; (mentally) dolido,-a.

hurtful ['hɜ:tfʊl] adj hiriente.

hurtle ['hɜ:təl] vi lanzarse; to h. down, desplomarse.

husband ['hʌzbənd] n marido m, esposo m.

hush [hʌʃ] I vtr callar; to h. sth up, echar tierra a un asunto. II n silencio m. III interj ¡silencio!

hush-hush [hʌʃ'hʌʃ] adj fam confidencial.

husky[1] ['hʌskɪ] adj (huskier, huskiest) ronco,-a.

husky[2] ['hʌskɪ] n (dog) perro m esquimal.

hustings ['hʌstɪŋz] npl Pol 1 (platform) tribuna f sing electoral. 2 (election) elecciones fpl.

hustle ['hʌsəl] I *vtr* 1 (*jostle*) empujar. 2 *fam* meter prisa a. II *n* bullicio *m*; **h. and bustle,** ajetreo *m*.

hut [hʌt] *n* cabaña *f*; (*shed*) cobertizo *m*; *Mil* barraca *f*.

hutch [hʌtʃ] *n* jaula *f*; **rabbit h.,** conejera *f*.

hyacinth ['haɪəsɪnθ] *n* jacinto *m*.

hybrid ['haɪbrɪd] *adj & n* híbrido,-a (*m,f*).

hydrant ['haɪdrənt] *n* **fire h.,** boca *f* de incendio.

hydraulic [haɪ'drɔlɪk] *adj* hidráulico,-a.

hydrocarbon [haɪdrəʊ'kɑːbən] *n* hidrocarburo *m*.

hydrochloric [haɪdrəʊ'klɒrɪk] *adj* **h. acid,** ácido clorhídrico.

hydroelectric [haɪdrəʊ'lektrɪk] *adj* hidroeléctrico,-a.

hydrofoil ['haɪdrəfɔɪl] *n* hidroala *f*.

hydrogen ['haɪdrɪdʒən] *n* hidrógeno *m*.

hyena [haɪ'iːnə] *n* hiena *f*.

hygiene ['haɪdʒiːn] *n* higiene *f*.

hygienic [haɪ'dʒiːnɪk] *adj* higiénico,-a.

hymn [hɪm] *n* himno *m*; **h. book,** cantoral *m*.

hype [haɪp] *n fam* campaña publicitaria, movida *f*.

hyper- ['haɪpə] *pref* hiper-; **hyperactive,** hiperactivo,-a.

hypermarket ['haɪpəmɑːkɪt] *n GB* hipermercado *m*.

hypersensitive [haɪpə'sensɪtɪv] *adj* hipersensible.

hyphen ['haɪfən] *n* guión *m*.

hypnosis [hɪp'nəʊsɪs] *n* hipnosis *f*.

hypnotist ['hɪpnətɪst] *n* hipnotizador,-a *m,f*.

hypnotize ['hɪpnətaɪz] *vtr* hipnotizar.

hypochondriac [haɪpə'kɒndrɪæk] *adj & n* hipocondríaco,-a (*m,f*).

hypocrisy [hɪ'pɒkrəsɪ] *n* hipocresía *f*.

hypocrite ['hɪpəkrɪt] *n* hipócrita *mf*.

hypocritical [hɪpə'krɪtɪkəl] *adj* hipócrita.

hypodermic [haɪpə'dɜːmɪk] *adj Med* hipodérmico,-a; **h. needle,** aguja hipodérmica.

hypothesis [haɪ'pɒθɪsɪs] *n* (*pl* **hypotheses** [haɪ'pɒθɪsiːz]) hipótesis *f*.

hypothetic(al) [haɪpə'θetɪk(əl)] *adj* hipotético,-a.

hysteria [hɪ'stɪərɪə] *n* histeria *f*.

hysterical [hɪ'sterɪkəl] *adj* histérico,-a.

hysterics [hɪ'sterɪks] *n or npl* 1 ataque *m* de histeria. 2 *fam* (*of laughter*) ataque *m* de risa.

I

I, i [aɪ] *n* (*the letter*) I, i *f*.

I [aɪ] *pers pron* yo; **I know her,** (yo) la conozco.

ICBM [aɪsiːbiː'em] *abbr of* **intercontinental ballistic missile,** MBI *m*.

ice [aɪs] I *n* hielo *m*; **i. axe,** pico *m* (de alpinista); **i. cream,** helado *m*; **i. cube,** cubito *m* de hielo; **i. hockey,** hockey *m* sobre hielo; **i. lolly,** polo *m*; **i. rink,** pista *f* de patinaje; **i. skate,** patín *m* de cuchilla. II *vtr* (*cake*) alcorzar. ◆**ice over, ice up** *vi* (*pond etc*) helarse; (*windscreen, plane wings*) cubrirse de hielo.

iceberg ['aɪsbɜːg] *n* iceberg *m*.

icebox ['aɪsbɒks] *n* 1 (*compartment of fridge*) congelador *m*. 2 *US* (*fridge*) nevera *f*, frigorífico *m*.

icecap ['aɪskæp] *n* casquete *m* glaciar.

Iceland ['aɪslənd] *n* Islandia.

ice-skating ['aɪsskeɪtɪŋ] *n* patinaje *m* sobre hielo.

icicle ['aɪsɪkəl] *n* carámbano *m*.

icing ['aɪsɪŋ] *n* alcorza *f*; **i. sugar,** azúcar *m* glas.

icon ['aɪkɒn] *n* icono *m*.

icy ['aɪsɪ] *adj* (*icier, iciest*) (*road etc*) helado,-a; *fig* (*smile*) glacial.

ID [aɪ'diː] *US abbr of* **identification, identity; ID card,** documento *m* nacional de identidad, DNI *m*.

I'd [aɪd] = **I would; I had.**

idea [aɪ'dɪə] *n* 1 idea *f*. 2 (*aim*) intención *f*. 3 (*impression*) impresión *f*.

ideal [aɪ'dɪəl] *adj & n* ideal (*m*). ◆**ideally** *adv* 1 (*perfectly*) perfectamente. 2 (*in the best conditions*) de ser posible.

idealist [aɪ'dɪəlɪst] *n* idealista *mf*.

idealistic [aɪdɪə'lɪstɪk] *adj* idealista.

idealize [aɪ'dɪəlaɪz] *vtr* idealizar.

identical [aɪ'dentɪkəl] *adj* idéntico,-a.

identification [aɪdentɪfɪ'keɪʃən] *n* 1 identificación *f*. 2 (*papers*) documentación *f*.

identify [aɪ'dentɪfaɪ] I *vtr* (*body*) identificar; (*cause*) descubrir. II *vi* identificarse (**with,** con).

Identikit® [aɪ'dentɪkɪt] *n* **I. picture,** retrato *m* robot.

identity [aɪ'dentɪtɪ] *n* identidad *f*; **i. card,** carné *m* de identidad; **proof of i.,** prueba *f* de identidad.

ideological [aɪdɪə'lɒdʒɪkəl] *adj* ideológico,-a.

ideology [aɪdɪ'ɒlədʒɪ] *n* ideología *f*.

idiom ['ɪdɪəm] *n* modismo *m*; *fig* (*style*) lenguaje *m*.

idiomatic [ɪdɪə'mætɪk] *adj* idiomático,-a.

idiosyncrasy [ɪdɪəʊ'sɪŋkrəsɪ] *n* idiosincrasia *f*.

idiot ['ɪdɪət] *n* idiota *mf*, tonto,-a *m,f*.

idiotic [ɪdɪ'ɒtɪk] *adj* (*behaviour*) idiota,

tonto,-a; (joke, plan) estúpido,-a.

idle ['aɪdl] **I** adj holgazán,-ana; (not working) (person) desempleado,-a; (machinery) parado,-a; (gossip) frívolo,-a; (threat) vano,-a. **II** vi (engine) funcionar en vacío. ◆**idle away** vtr (time) desperdiciar.

idleness ['aɪdlnɪs] n (laziness) holgazanería f; (unemployment) desempleo m; (stoppage) paro m.

idol ['aɪdl] n ídolo m.

idolize ['aɪdəlaɪz] vtr idolatrar.

idyllic [ɪ'dɪlɪk] adj idílico,-a.

i.e. abbr of **id est** (that is to say), esto es, a saber, i.e.

if [ɪf] **I** conj 1 si; if at all, si acaso; **rarely**, **if ever**, raras veces; **if I were rich**, si fuera rico,-a; **if necessary**, (en) caso de que sea necesario; **if not**, si no; **if so**, de ser así; **if I were you**, yo en tu lugar. 3 (whenever) si; **if you need help, ask**, siempre que necesites ayuda, pídela. **3** (although) aunque, si bien. **4** (exclamation) **if only I'd known!**, ¡de haberlo sabido!; **if only you were here!**, ¡ojalá estuviera aquí!. **II** n **ifs and buts**, pegas fpl.

igloo ['ɪgluː] n iglú m.

ignite [ɪg'naɪt] **I** vtr encender. **II** vi encenderse.

ignition [ɪg'nɪʃən] n ignición f; Aut encendido m; **i. key**, llave f de contacto.

ignorance ['ɪgnərəns] n ignorancia f.

ignorant ['ɪgnərənt] adj ignorante (of, de); **to be i. of the facts**, ignorar or desconocer los hechos.

ignore [ɪg'nɔːr] vtr (warning, remark) no hacer caso de; (behaviour, fact) pasar por alto.

ill [ɪl] **I** adj 1 enfermo,-a; **to be taken i.**, caer enfermo,-a; **to feel i.**, encontrarse mal. 2 (bad) malo,-a; **i. feeling**, resentimiento m; **i. will**, mala voluntad. **II** n mal m. **III** adv difícilmente.

I'll [aɪl] = **I shall; I will**.

ill-advised [ɪləd'vaɪzd] adj (person) imprudente; (act) desatinado,-a; **you'd be i.-a. to go**, harías mal en ir.

ill-disposed [ɪldɪ'spəʊzd] adj poco dispuesto,-a.

illegal [ɪ'liːgəl] adj ilegal.

illegible [ɪ'ledʒɪbəl] adj ilegible.

illegitimate [ɪlɪ'dʒɪtɪmɪt] adj ilegítimo,-a.

ill-fated [ɪl'feɪtɪd] adj abocado,-a al fracaso.

ill-founded [ɪl'faʊndɪd] adj infundado,-a.

illicit [ɪ'lɪsɪt] adj ilícito,-a.

illiteracy [ɪ'lɪtərəsɪ] n analfabetismo m.

illiterate [ɪ'lɪtərɪt] adj (person) analfabeto,-a; fam (uneducated) inculto,-a.

illness ['ɪlnɪs] n enfermedad f.

illogical [ɪ'lɒdʒɪkəl] adj ilógico,-a.

ill-treat [ɪl'triːt] vtr maltratar.

illuminate [ɪ'luːmɪneɪt] vtr 1 (light up) iluminar, alumbrar; fig (clarify) aclarar. 2 (manuscript) iluminar.

illuminating [ɪ'luːmɪneɪtɪŋ] adj (experience, book) instructivo,-a; (remark) revelador,-a.

illumination [ɪluːmɪ'neɪʃən] n 1 iluminación f; fig (clarification) aclaración f. 2 GB **illuminations**, iluminación f sing.

illusion [ɪ'luːʒən] n ilusión f; **to be under the i. that ...**, engañarse pensando que ...

illusory [ɪ'luːsərɪ] adj ilusorio,-a.

illustrate ['ɪləstreɪt] vtr ilustrar.

illustration [ɪlə'streɪʃən] n ilustración f; (example) ejemplo m.

illustrious [ɪ'lʌstrɪəs] adj ilustre.

I'm [aɪm] = **I am**.

image ['ɪmɪdʒ] n imagen f.

imagery ['ɪmɪdʒərɪ] n Lit imágenes fpl.

imaginary [ɪ'mædʒɪnərɪ] adj imaginario,-a.

imagination [ɪmædʒɪ'neɪʃən] n imaginación f; (inventiveness) inventiva f.

imaginative [ɪ'mædʒɪnətɪv] adj imaginativo,-a.

imagine [ɪ'mædʒɪn] vtr (visualize) imaginar; (think) suponer, imaginarse; **just i.!**, ¡imagínate!

imbalance [ɪm'bæləns] n desequilibrio m.

imbecile ['ɪmbɪsiːl] n imbécil mf.

imitate ['ɪmɪteɪt] vtr imitar.

imitation [ɪmɪ'teɪʃən] **I** n imitación f, copia f; pej remedo m. **II** adj de imitación.

immaculate [ɪ'mækjʊlɪt] adj (clean) inmaculado,-a; (tidy) perfectamente ordenado,-a; (clothes) impecable; (work) perfecto,-a; **the I. Conception**, la Inmaculada Concepción.

immaterial [ɪmə'tɪərɪəl] adj irrelevante; **it's i. to me whether ...**, me trae sin cuidado si ....

immature [ɪmə'tjʊər] adj inmaduro,-a.

immediate [ɪ'miːdɪət] adj 1 inmediato,-a; (urgent) urgente. 2 (close) cercano,-a; (danger) inminente. 3 (cause) primero,-a. ◆**immediately I** adv 1 inmediatamente. 2 (directly) directamente. **II** conj en cuanto.

immense [ɪ'mens] adj inmenso,-a, enorme. ◆**immensely** adv (rich) enormemente; (interesting, difficult) sumamente.

immerse [ɪ'mɜːs] vtr sumergir (in, en); fig **to be immersed in sth**, estar absorto,-a en algo.

immersion [ɪ'mɜːʃən] n inmersión f; GB **i. heater**, calentador m de inmersión; **i. course**, cursillo intensivo.

immigrant ['ɪmɪgrənt] adj & n inmigrante (mf).

immigration [ɪmɪ'greɪʃən] n inmigración f.

imminent ['ɪmɪnənt] adj inminente.

immobile [ɪ'məʊbaɪl] adj inmóvil.

immobilize [ɪ'məʊbɪlaɪz] vtr inmovilizar.

immodest [ɪˈmɒdɪst] *adj* indecente.

immoral [ɪˈmɒrəl] *adj* inmoral.

immortal [ɪˈmɔːtəl] *adj* inmortal.

immortality [ɪmɔːˈtælɪtɪ] *n* inmortalidad *f.*

immortalize [ɪˈmɔːtəlaɪz] *vtr* inmortalizar.

immune [ɪˈmjuːn] *adj* inmune; *(exempt)* exento,-a.

immunity [ɪˈmjuːnɪtɪ] *n* inmunidad *f.*

immunize [ˈɪmjʊnaɪz] *vtr* inmunizar *(against,* contra).

impact [ˈɪmpækt] *n* impacto *m*; *(crash)* choque *m.*

impair [ɪmˈpeər] *vtr* perjudicar; *(sight etc)* dañar.

impart [ɪmˈpɑːt] *vtr fml (news)* comunicar; *(knowledge)* transmitir.

impartial [ɪmˈpɑːʃəl] *adj* imparcial.

impassable [ɪmˈpɑːsəbəl] *adj (road, ground)* intransitable; *(barrier)* infranqueable.

impasse [æmˈpɑːs] *n* punto muerto.

impassive [ɪmˈpæsɪv] *adj* impasible.

impatience [ɪmˈpeɪʃəns] *n* impaciencia *f.*

impatient [ɪmˈpeɪʃənt] *adj* impaciente; *(fretful)* irritable; **to get i.,** perder la paciencia.

impeccable [ɪmˈpekəbəl] *adj* impecable.

impede [ɪmˈpiːd] *vtr (prevent)* impedir; *(hinder)* estorbar; *(obstruct)* poner trabas a.

impediment [ɪmˈpedɪmənt] *n* impedimento *m*; *(obstacle)* estorbo *m*; **speech i.,** defecto *m* del habla.

impending [ɪmˈpendɪŋ] *adj fml* inminente.

impenetrable [ɪmˈpenɪtrəbəl] *adj* impenetrable; *fig (mystery, thoughts)* insondable.

imperative [ɪmˈperətɪv] I *adj fml* imperativo,-a; *(tone)* imperioso,-a; *(urgent)* urgente. II *n* Ling imperativo *m.*

imperceptible [ɪmpəˈseptəbəl] *adj* imperceptible.

imperfect [ɪmˈpɜːfɪkt] I *adj* imperfecto, -a; *(goods)* defectuoso,-a. II *n* Ling imperfecto *m.*

imperfection [ɪmpəˈfekʃən] *n* defecto *m.*

imperial [ɪmˈpɪərɪəl] *adj* 1 imperial. 2 *(measure)* **i. gallon,** galón británico *(approx* 4,543 litres).

imperialism [ɪmˈpɪərɪəlɪzəm] *n* imperialismo *m.*

imperialist [ɪmˈpɪərɪəlɪst] *adj & n* imperialista *(mf).*

imperious [ɪmˈpɪərɪəs] *adj* imperioso,-a.

impersonal [ɪmˈpɜːsənəl] *adj* impersonal.

impersonate [ɪmˈpɜːsəneɪt] *vtr* hacerse pasar por; *(famous people)* imitar.

impersonation [ɪmpɜːsəˈneɪʃən] *n* imitación *f.*

impertinent [ɪmˈpɜːtɪnənt] *adj* impertinente.

impervious [ɪmˈpɜːvɪəs] *adj (rock)* impermeable; *fig* **to be i. to reason,** no atender a razones.

impetuous [ɪmˈpetjʊəs] *adj* impetuoso,-a.

impetus [ˈɪmpɪtəs] *n* ímpetu *m*; *fig* impulso *m.*

impinge [ɪmˈpɪndʒ] *vi fml* afectar *(on,* a).

implant [ɪmˈplɑːnt] Med I *vtr* implantar. II [ˈɪmplɑːnt] *n* implantación *f.*

implement [ˈɪmplɪmənt] I *n (tool)* herramienta *f*; *(instrument)* instrumento *m*; **farm implements,** aperos *mpl* de labranza. II [ˈɪmplɪment] *vtr (decision, plan)* llevar a cabo; *(law, policy)* aplicar.

implicate [ˈɪmplɪkeɪt] *vtr* implicar *(in,* en).

implication [ɪmplɪˈkeɪʃən] *n* implicación *f*; *(consequence)* consecuencia *f.*

implicit [ɪmˈplɪsɪt] *adj (implied)* implícito,-a; *(trust)* absoluto,-a; *(faith)* incondicional.

implore [ɪmˈplɔːr] *vtr* implorar, suplicar.

imply [ɪmˈplaɪ] *vtr* 1 *(involve)* implicar. 2 *(hint)* dar a entender; *(mean)* significar.

impolite [ɪmpəˈlaɪt] *adj* maleducado,-a.

import [ɪmˈpɔːt] I *n* 1 Com *(usu pl)* importación *f*; **i. duty,** derechos *mpl* de importación. 2 *fml (meaning)* sentido *m.* II [ɪmˈpɔːt] *vtr Com* importar.

importance [ɪmˈpɔːtəns] *n* importancia *f*; *(standing)* envergadura *f*; **of little i.,** de poca monta.

important [ɪmˈpɔːtənt] *adj* importante; **it's not i.,** no importa.

importer [ɪmˈpɔːtər] *n* Com importador,-a *m,f.*

impose [ɪmˈpəʊz] I *vtr* imponer *(on, upon,* a). II *vi* **to i. on** or **upon,** *(take advantage of)* abusar de.

imposing [ɪmˈpəʊzɪŋ] *adj* imponente, impresionante.

imposition [ɪmpəˈzɪʃən] *n (of tax etc)* imposición *f*; *(unfair demand)* abuso *m*; **would it be an i. if ...?,** ¿le molestaría si ...?

impossibility [ɪmpɒsəˈbɪlɪtɪ] *n* imposibilidad *f.*

impossible [ɪmˈpɒsəbəl] I *adj* imposible; *(person)* insoportable. II *n* **to do the i.,** hacer lo imposible. ◆**impossibly** *adv* de manera insoportable; **i. difficult,** de una dificultad insuperable.

impostor [ɪmˈpɒstər] *n* impostor,-a *m,f.*

impotent [ˈɪmpətənt] *adj* impotente.

impound [ɪmˈpaʊnd] *vtr* incautarse de.

impoverished [ɪmˈpɒvərɪʃt] *adj (person, country)* empobrecido,-a; *(soil)* agotado,-a.

impracticable [ɪmˈpræktɪkəbəl] *adj* impracticable, irrealizable.

impractical [ɪmˈpræktɪkəl] *adj (person)* poco práctico,-a; *(project, solution etc)* poco viable.

imprecise [ɪmprɪˈsaɪs] *adj* impreciso,-a.

impregnable [ɪmˈpregnəbəl] *adj*

inexpugnable.

impregnate [ˈɪmpregneɪt] *vtr* **1** (*soak*) impregnar (**with**, de). **2** *fml* (*fertilize*) fecundar.

impress [ɪmˈpres] *vtr* **1** impresionar; **to i. sb favourably/unfavourably**, dar a algn buena/mala impresión. **2** (*mark*) imprimir (**on**, en); (*pattern*) estampar (**on**, en); *fig* **to i. sth on sb**, convencer a algn de la importancia de algo.

impression [ɪmˈpreʃən] *n* **1** impresión *f*; **to be under the i. that ...**, tener la presión de que ...; **to give the i. of ...**, dar la impresión de ...; **2** (*imprint*) marca *f*; (*in snow*) huella *f*. **3** (*imitation*) imitación *f*. **4** *Print* (*number of copies*) edición *f*.

impressionist [ɪmˈpreʃənɪst] *adj & n* impresionista (*mf*).

impressive [ɪmˈpresɪv] *adj* impresionante.

imprint [ˈɪmprɪnt] **I** *vtr* (*mark*) dejar huella (**on**, en). **II** [ˈɪmprɪnt] *n* **1** (*mark*) marca *f*; (*left by foot etc*) huella *f*. **2** (*publisher's name*) pie *m* de imprenta.

imprison [ɪmˈprɪzən] *vtr* encarcelar.

imprisonment [ɪmˈprɪzənmənt] *n* encarcelamiento *m*.

improbable [ɪmˈprobəbl] *adj* (*event*) improbable; (*story*) inverosímil.

impromptu [ɪmˈprɒmptju:] **I** *adj* (*speech*) improvisado,-a; (*visit*) imprevisto,-a. **II** *adv* de improviso.

improper [ɪmˈprɒpə] *adj* **1** impropio,-a; (*method*) inadecuado,-a. **2** (*indecent*) indecente; (*behaviour*) deshonesto,-a. **3** (*wrong*) incorrecto,-a.

improve [ɪmˈpru:v] **I** *vtr* mejorar; (*knowledge*) perfeccionar; (*mind*) cultivar; (*increase*) aumentar. **II** *vi* mejorarse; (*increase*) aumentar. ◆**improve on** *vtr* superar; (*offer*, *bid*) sobrepujar.

improvement [ɪmˈpru:vmənt] *n* mejora *f*; (*in skill*) perfeccionamiento *m*; (*increase*) aumento *m*.

improvise [ˈɪmprəvaɪz] *vtr & vi* improvisar.

imprudent [ɪmˈpru:dənt] *adj* imprudente.

impudence [ˈɪmpjʊdəns] *n* insolencia *f*.

impudent [ˈɪmpjʊdənt] *adj* insolente.

impulse [ˈɪmpʌls] *n* impulso *m*; **to act on (an) i.**, dejarse llevar por un impulso.

impulsive [ɪmˈpʌlsɪv] *adj* irreflexivo,-a.

impunity [ɪmˈpju:nɪtɪ] *n* impunidad *f*.

impure [ɪmˈpjʊə] *adj* **1** (*act*) impuro,-a; (*thought*) impúdico,-a. **2** (*air*) contaminado,-a.

impurity [ɪmˈpjʊərɪtɪ] *n* **1** (*of act*) deshonestidad *f*. **2** (*usu pl*) (*in air, substance*) impureza *f*.

in [ɪn] **I** *prep* **1** (*place*) en; (*within*) dentro de; **in bed**, en la cama; **in England/ Brazil/China**, en Inglaterra/Brasil/China; **in prison**, en la cárcel; **in the distance**, a

lo lejos. **2** (*motion*) en; **I threw it in the fire**, lo eché al fuego; **she arrived in Paris**, llegó a París. **3** (*time*) (*during*) en, durante; **I haven't seen her in years**, hace años que no la veo; **in May/1945**, en mayo/1945; **in spring**, en primavera; **in the daytime**, durante el día; **in the morning**, por la mañana; **at ten in the morning**, a las diez de la mañana. **4** (*time*) (*within*) dentro de; **I arrived in time**, llegué a tiempo. **5** (*time*) (*after*) al cabo de. **6** (*manner*) en; **in alphabetical order**, en orden alfabético; **in a loud/ quiet voice**, en voz alta/baja; **in fashion**, de moda; **in French**, en francés; **in an odd way**, de una manera rara; **in writing**, por escrito; **write in pencil**, escribe con lápiz. **7** (*wearing*) en; **dressed in blue**, vestido,-a de azul; **in uniform**, de uniforme. **8** (*weather etc*) a, en; **in the rain**, bajo la lluvia; **in the sun**, al sol; **in darkness**, en la oscuridad; **in daylight**, a la luz del día; **in the shade**, a la sombra. **9** (*state*, *emotion*) en; **carved in wood**, tallado,-a en madera; **in bloom/danger/ public/silence**, en flor/peligro/público/ silencio; **in love**, enamorado,-a; **in tears**, llorando. **10** (*ratio*, *numbers*) de; **cut in half**, cortado,-a por la mitad; **in threes**, de tres en tres; **one in six**, uno de cada seis; **two metres in length**, dos metros de largo. **11** (*profession*) en; **to be in insurance**, trabajar en seguros. **12** (*person*) en; **he has it in him to succeed**, es capaz de ganar. **13** (*after superlative*) de; **the smallest car in the world**, el coche más pequeño del mundo. **14** (*before present participle*) **in behaving this way**, con su comportamiento; **in so doing**, con ello. **15** (*phrases*) **in all**, en total; **in itself/ himself/herself**, en sí; **in that ...**, dado que ....
II *adv* **in here/there**, aquí/allí dentro; **let's go in**, vamos adentro; **to be in**, (*at home*) estar (en casa); (*at work*) estar; (*tide*) estar alta; *fam* (*in fashion*) estar de moda; **the bus is in**, el autobús ha llegado; **to invite sb in**, invitar a algn a entrar; *fam* **to be in on sth**, estar enterado,-a de algo; *fam* **we're in for a storm**, vamos a tener tormenta.
III *adj fam* **1** (*fashionable*) (*place*) de moda; (*clothes*) del último grito. **2** **an in joke**, una broma privada.
IV *n fam* **ins and outs**, detalles *mpl*.

inability [ɪnəˈbɪlɪtɪ] *n* incapacidad *f*.

inaccessible [ɪnækˈsesəbl] *adj* inaccesible.

inaccurate [ɪnˈækjʊrɪt] *adj* inexacto,-a; (*statement*) erróneo,-a; (*figures*, *total*) incorrecto,-a.

inactivity [ɪnækˈtɪvɪtɪ] *n* inactividad *f*.

inadequate [ɪnˈædɪkwɪt] *adj* **1** (*lacking*) insuficiente. **2** (*not capable*) incapaz; (*un-

suitable) inadecuado,-a. **3** (*defective*) defectuoso,-a.

inadvertent [ɪnəd'vɜːtənt] *adj* involuntario,-a. ◆**inadvertently** *adv* involuntariamente.

inadvisable [ɪnəd'vaɪzəbl] *adj* imprudente.

inane [ɪ'neɪn] *adj* necio,-a, fatuo,-a.

inanimate [ɪn'ænɪmɪt] *adj* inanimado,-a.

inappropriate [ɪnə'prəuprɪɪt] *adj* inoportuno,-a; (*behaviour*) poco apropiado,-a.

inarticulate [ɪnɑː'tɪkjulɪt] *adj* (*cry, sound*) inarticulado,-a; (*words*) mal pronunciado,-a.

inasmuch as [ɪnəz'mʌtʃəz] *conj fml* **1** (*since*) puesto que, ya que. **2** (*in so far as*) en la medida en que.

inattentive [ɪnə'tentɪv] *adj* desatento,-a.

inaudible [ɪn'ɔːdəbl] *adj* inaudible.

inaugural [ɪn'ɔːgjurəl] *adj* inaugural.

inaugurate [ɪn'ɔːgjureɪt] *vtr* (*building*) inaugurar; (*president*) investir.

inauguration [ɪnɔːgju'reɪʃən] *n* (*of building*) inauguración *f*; (*of president*) investidura *f*.

inauspicious [ɪnɔː'spɪʃəs] *adj* (*start*) poco prometedor,-a; (*circumstances*) desfavorable.

inborn [ɪn'bɔːn] *adj* innato,-a.

inbred [ɪn'bred] *adj* **1** (*quality*) innato,-a. **2** (*family*) endogámico,-a.

Inc, inc *US Com abbr of* Incorporated, ≈ S.A.

incalculable [ɪn'kælkjuləbəl] *adj* incalculable.

incapable [ɪn'keɪpəbəl] *adj* incapaz.

incapacitate [ɪnkə'pæsɪteɪt] *vtr fml* incapacitar.

incapacity [ɪnkə'pæsɪtɪ] *n* incapacidad *f*.

incarcerate [ɪn'kɑːsəreɪt] *vtr fml* encarcelar.

incarnation [ɪnkɑː'neɪʃən] *n* encarnación *f*.

incendiary [ɪn'sendɪərɪ] **I** *adj* incendiario,-a. **II** *n* bomba incendiaria.

incense[1] ['ɪnsens] *n* incienso *m*.

incense[2] [ɪn'sens] *vtr* enfurecer, sacar de quicio.

incentive [ɪn'sentɪv] *n* incentivo *m*.

incessant [ɪn'sesənt] *adj* incesante; (*demands*) constante. ◆**incessantly** *adv* sin cesar.

incest ['ɪnsest] *n* incesto *m*.

inch [ɪntʃ] *n* pulgada *f* (*approx* 2,54 cm); *fig* **i. by i.**, poco a poco; *fig* **she wouldn't give an i.**, no quería ceder ni un ápice. ◆**inch forward** *vtr & vi* avanzar poco a poco.

incidence ['ɪnsɪdəns] *n* frecuencia *f*.

incident ['ɪnsɪdənt] *n* incidente *m*.

incidental [ɪnsɪ'dentəl] *adj* (*accessory*) incidental, accesorio,-a; (*risk*) inherente (**to, a**); **i. music**, música *f* de fondo.

◆**incidentally** *adv* a propósito.

incinerator [ɪn'sɪnəreɪtə[r]] *n* incinerador *m*.

incipient [ɪn'sɪpɪənt] *adj fml* incipiente.

incision [ɪn'sɪʒən] *n* incisión *f*.

incisive [ɪn'saɪsɪv] *adj* (*comment*) incisivo,-a; (*reply*) tajante; (*mind*) penetrante.

incite [ɪn'saɪt] *vtr* incitar; **to i. sb to do sth**, incitar a algn a hacer algo.

inclination [ɪnklɪ'neɪʃən] *n* inclinación *f*; **my i. is to stay**, yo prefiero quedarme.

incline [ɪn'klaɪn] **I** *vtr* **1** **I'm inclined to believe him**, me inclino a creerlo; (*if you feel so inclined*) si quieres; **she's inclined to be aggressive**, tiende a ser agresiva. **2** (*head etc*) inclinar. **II** *vi* (*slope*) inclinarse. **III** [ɪn'klaɪn, 'ɪnklaɪn] *n* (*slope*) pendiente *f*; **steep i.**, cuesta empinada.

include [ɪn'kluːd] *vtr* incluir (**in, en**); (*in price*) comprender (**in, en**); (*in list*) figurar (**in, en**).

including [ɪn'kluːdɪŋ] *prep* incluso, inclusive.

inclusion [ɪn'kluːʒən] *n* inclusión *f*.

inclusive [ɪn'kluːsɪv] *adj* inclusivo,-a; **pages six to ten i.**, de la página seis a la diez, ambas inclusive; **the rent is i. of bills**, el alquiler incluye las facturas.

incognito [ɪnkɒg'niːtəu] *adv* de incógnito.

incoherent [ɪnkəu'hɪərənt] *adj* incoherente.

income ['ɪnkʌm] *n* ingresos *mpl*; (*from investment*) réditos *mpl*; **i. tax**, impuesto *m* sobre la renta; **i. tax return**, declaración *f* de la renta.

incoming ['ɪnkʌmɪŋ] *adj* (*flight, train*) de llegada; (*tide*) ascendente; (*mail, message, call*) recibido,-a.

incomparable [ɪn'kɒmpərəbəl] *adj* incomparable, sin par.

incompatible [ɪnkəm'pætəbəl] *adj* incompatible (**with, con**).

incompetence [ɪn'kɒmpɪtəns] *n* incompetencia *f*.

incompetent [ɪn'kɒmpɪtənt] *adj* incompetente.

incomplete [ɪnkəm'pliːt] *adj* incompleto,-a.

incomprehensible [ɪnkɒmprɪ'hensəbəl] *adj* incomprensible.

inconceivable [ɪnkən'siːvəbəl] *adj* inconcebible.

inconclusive [ɪnkən'kluːsɪv] *adj* (*vote*) no decisivo,-a; (*proof*) no concluyente.

incongruous [ɪn'kɒŋgruəs] *adj* incongruente.

inconsiderate [ɪnkən'sɪdərɪt] *adj* desconsiderado,-a; **how i. of you!**, ¡qué falta de consideración por tu parte!

inconsistency [ɪnkən'sɪstənsɪ] *n* inconsecuencia *f*; (*contradiction*) contradicción *f*.

inconsistent [ɪnkən'sɪstənt] adj inconsecuente; (contradictory) contradictorio,-a; **your evidence is i. with the facts**, su testimonio no concuerda con los hechos.

inconspicuous [ɪnkən'spɪkjuəs] adj que pasa desapercibido,-a; (discrete) discreto,-a.

incontrovertible [ɪnkɒntrə'vɜːtəbəl] adj fml incontrovertible.

inconvenience [ɪnkən'viːnɪəns] **I** n inconveniente f; (annoyance) molestia f. **II** vtr (annoy) molestar; (cause difficulty to) incomodar.

inconvenient [ɪnkən'viːnɪənt] adj molesto,-a; (time) inoportuno,-a; (design) poco práctico,-a.

incorporate [ɪn'kɔːpəreɪt] vtr incorporar (in, into, a); (include) incluir; (contain) contener.

incorporated [ɪn'kɔːpəreɪtɪd] adj US Com i. company, sociedad anónima.

incorrect [ɪnkə'rekt] adj incorrecto,-a.

incorrigible [ɪn'kɒrɪdʒəbəl] adj incorregible.

increase ['ɪnkriːs] **I** n aumento m; (in number) incremento m; (in price etc) subida f. **II** [ɪn'kriːs] vtr aumentar; (price etc) subir. **III** vi aumentar.

increasing [ɪn'kriːsɪŋ] adj creciente.
◆**increasingly** adv cada vez más.

incredible [ɪn'kredəbəl] adj increíble.

incredulous [ɪn'kredjʊləs] adj incrédulo,-a.

increment ['ɪnkrɪmənt] n incremento m.

incriminate [ɪn'krɪmɪneɪt] vtr incriminar.

incriminating [ɪn'krɪmɪneɪtɪŋ] adj incriminatorio,-a.

incubation [ɪnkjʊ'beɪʃən] n incubación f.

incubator ['ɪnkjʊbeɪtə'] n incubadora f.

incumbent [ɪn'kʌmbənt] **I** n titular mf. **II** adj fml to be i. on sb to do sth, ser la obligación de algn hacer algo.

incur [ɪn'kɜː'] vtr (blame) incurrir en; (risk) correr; (debt) contraer; (loss) sufrir.

incurable [ɪn'kjʊərəbəl] adj incurable.

indebted [ɪn'detɪd] adj endeudado,-a; fig (grateful) agradecido,-a; fig to be i. to sb, estar en deuda con algn.

indecent [ɪn'diːsənt] adj indecente; i. assault, atentado m contra el pudor; i. exposure, exhibicionismo m.

indecision [ɪndɪ'sɪʒən] n indecisión f.

indecisive [ɪndɪ'saɪsɪv] adj (person) indeciso,-a; (evidence) poco concluyente; (victory) no decisivo,-a.

indeed [ɪn'diːd] adv 1 fml (in fact) efectivamente, en realidad. 2 **I'm very sorry i.**, lo siento de veras; **it's very hard i.**, es verdaderamente difícil; **thank you very much i.**, muchísimas gracias.

indefinite [ɪn'defɪnɪt] adj indefinido,-a.

indelible [ɪn'deləbəl] adj indeleble.

indemnify [ɪn'demnɪfaɪ] vtr indemnizar (for, por).

indemnity [ɪn'demnɪtɪ] n 1 (insurance) indemnidad f. 2 (compensation) indemnización f.

indentation [ɪnden'teɪʃən] n 1 Typ sangría f. 2 (of edge) muesca f; (of surface) depresión f.

independence [ɪndɪ'pendəns] n independencia f; US **I. Day**, día m de la Independencia (4 julio).

independent [ɪndɪ'pendənt] adj independiente; GB i. school, colegio m no subvencionado por el estado; to become i., independizarse.

in-depth ['ɪndepθ] adj minucioso,-a, exhaustivo,-a.

indestructible [ɪndɪ'strʌktəbəl] adj indestructible.

indeterminate [ɪndɪ'tɜːmɪnɪt] adj indeterminado,-a.

index ['ɪndeks] **I** n (pl indexes or indices) 1 (in book) índice m; (in library) catálogo m; i. card, ficha f. 2 Math exponente m; Econ índice m. 3 i. finger, dedo m índice. **II** vtr catalogar.

index-linked ['ɪndekslɪŋkt] adj sujeto,-a al aumento de la inflación.

India ['ɪndɪə] n (la) India.

Indian ['ɪndɪən] adj & n (of America) indio,-a (m,f); (of India) hindú (m,f); **I. Ocean**, Océano Indico; **I. Summer**, veranillo m de San Martín.

indicate ['ɪndɪkeɪt] **I** vtr indicar. **II** vi Aut poner el intermitente.

indication [ɪndɪ'keɪʃən] n indicio m.

indicative [ɪn'dɪkətɪv] **I** adj indicativo,-a. **II** n Ling indicativo m.

indicator ['ɪndɪkeɪtə'] n indicador m; Aut intermitente m.

indices ['ɪndɪsiːz] npl → index.

indict [ɪn'daɪt] vtr acusar (for, de).

indictment [ɪn'daɪtmənt] n Jur acusación f; fig a damning i. of his books, una crítica feroz de sus libros.

indifference [ɪn'dɪfərəns] n indiferencia f.

indifferent [ɪn'dɪfərənt] adj 1 (uninterested) indiferente. 2 (mediocre) regular.

indigenous [ɪn'dɪdʒɪnəs] adj indígena.

indigestion [ɪndɪ'dʒestʃən] n indigestión f; **to suffer from i.**, tener un empacho.

indignant [ɪn'dɪgnənt] adj indignado,-a; (look) de indignación; **to get i. about sth**, indignarse por algo.

indignity [ɪn'dɪgnɪtɪ] n indignidad f.

indigo ['ɪndɪgəʊ] **I** n añil m. **II** adj (de color) añil.

indirect [ɪndɪ'rekt, ɪndaɪ'rekt] adj indirecto,-a.

indiscreet [ɪndɪ'skriːt] adj indiscreto,-a.

indiscretion [ɪndɪ'skreʃən] n indiscreción f.

indiscriminate [ɪndɪ'skrɪmɪnɪt] adj (punishment, shooting) indiscriminado,-a; (praise, reading) sin criterio.

indispensable [ɪndɪ'spensəbəl] adj

indispensable, imprescindible.

indisposed [ɪndɪ'spəʊzd] *adj fml* indispuesto,-a.

indisputable [ɪndɪ'spju:təbəl] *adj* indiscutible, incontestable.

indistinct [ɪndɪ'stɪŋkt] *adj* indistinto,-a; *(memory)* confuso,-a, vago,-a; *(shape etc)* borroso,-a.

indistinguishable [ɪndɪ'stɪŋgwɪʃəbəl] *adj* indistinguible.

individual [ɪndɪ'vɪdjʊəl] **I** *adj* 1 *(separate)* individual; *(for one)* particular; *(personal)* personal. 2 *(characteristic)* particular; *(original)* original. **II** *n (person)* individuo *m*; private i., particular *m*.

individualist [ɪndɪ'vɪdjʊəlɪst] *n* individualista *mf*.

indoctrinate [ɪn'dɒktrɪneɪt] *vtr* adoctrinar.

indoctrination [ɪndɒktrɪ'neɪʃən] *n* adoctrinamiento *m*.

indolent ['ɪndələnt] *adj fml* indolente.

Indonesia [ɪndəʊ'niːzɪə] *n* Indonesia.

Indonesian [ɪndəʊ'niːzɪən] **I** *adj* indonesio,-a. **II** *n* 1 *(person)* indonesio,-a *m,f*. 2 *(language)* indonesio *m*.

indoor ['ɪndɔːr] *adj (plant)* de interior; i. football, fútbol *m* sala; i. pool, piscina cubierta.

indoors [ɪn'dɔːz] *adv (inside)* dentro (de casa); *(at home)* en casa; let's go i., vamos adentro.

induce [ɪn'djuːs] *vtr* 1 *(persuade)* inducir, persuadir. 2 *(cause)* producir; *Med (labour)* provocar.

inducement [ɪn'djuːsmənt] *n* incentivo *m*, aliciente *m*.

induction [ɪn'dʌkʃən] *n* 1 *Med (of labour)* provocación *f*. 2 *Elec* inducción *f*. 3 *Educ* introducción *f*.

indulge [ɪn'dʌldʒ] **I** *vtr* 1 *(child)* consentir; *(person)* complacer; to i. oneself, darse gusto. 2 *(whim)* ceder a, satisfacer. **II** *vi* darse el gusto (in, de).

indulgence [ɪn'dʌldʒəns] *n* 1 *(of child)* mimo *m*; *(of attitude)* indulgencia *f*. 2 *(of whim)* satisfacción *f*.

indulgent [ɪn'dʌldʒənt] *adj* indulgente.

industrial [ɪn'dʌstrɪəl] *adj* industrial; *(accident)* laboral; *(disease)* profesional; *GB* to take i. action, declararse en huelga; *GB* i. dispute, conflicto *m* laboral; i. estate, polígono *m* industrial; i. relations, relaciones *fpl* laborales.

industrialist [ɪn'dʌstrɪəlɪst] *n* industrial *mf*.

industrialize [ɪn'dʌstrɪəlaɪz] *vtr* industrializar; to become industrialized, industrializarse.

industrious [ɪn'dʌstrɪəs] *adj* trabajador, -a.

industry ['ɪndəstrɪ] *n* 1 industria *f*. 2 *(diligence)* aplicación *f*.

inebriated [ɪn'iːbrɪeɪtɪd] *adj* embriagado,-a.

inedible [ɪn'edəbəl] *adj* incomible.

ineffective [ɪnɪ'fektɪv] *adj* ineficaz.

ineffectual [ɪnɪ'fektʃʊəl] *adj (aim, protest)* ineficaz; *(person)* incompetente.

inefficiency [ɪnɪ'fɪʃənsɪ] *n* ineficacia *f*; *(of person)* incompetencia *f*.

inefficient [ɪnɪ'fɪʃənt] *adj* ineficaz; *(person)* inepto,-a.

ineligible [ɪn'elɪdʒəbəl] *adj* no apto (for, para).

inept [ɪn'ept] *adj (person)* inepto,-a; *(remark)* estúpido,-a.

inequality [ɪnɪ'kwɒlɪtɪ] *n* desigualdad *f*.

inert [ɪn'ɜːt] *adj* inerte.

inertia [ɪn'ɜːʃə] *n* inercia *f*.

inescapable [ɪnɪ'skeɪpəbəl] *adj* ineludible.

inevitability [ɪnevɪtə'bɪlɪtɪ] *n* inevitabilidad *f*.

inevitable [ɪn'evɪtəbəl] *adj* inevitable.

inexcusable [ɪnɪk'skju:zəbəl] *adj* inexcusable, imperdonable.

inexhaustible [ɪnɪg'zɔːstəbəl] *adj* inagotable.

inexorable [ɪn'eksərəbəl] *adj fml* inexorable.

inexpensive [ɪnɪk'spensɪv] *adj* económico,-a.

inexperience [ɪnɪk'spɪərɪəns] *n* inexperiencia *f*.

inexperienced [ɪnɪk'spɪərɪənst] *adj* inexperto,-a.

inexplicable [ɪnɪk'splɪkəbəl] *adj* inexplicable.

infallible [ɪn'fæləbəl] *adj* infalible.

infamous ['ɪnfəməs] *adj* infame.

infancy ['ɪnfənsɪ] *n* infancia *f*.

infant ['ɪnfənt] *n* niño,-a *m,f*; *GB* i. school, parvulario *m*.

infantile ['ɪnfəntaɪl] *adj* infantil.

infantry ['ɪnfəntrɪ] *n* infantería *f*.

infatuated [ɪn'fætjʊeɪtɪd] *adj* encaprichado,-a.

infatuation [ɪnfætjʊ'eɪʃən] *n* encaprichamiento *m*.

infect [ɪn'fekt] *vtr (cut)* infectar; *(water)* contaminar; *(person)* contagiar.

infection [ɪn'fekʃən] *n (of cut)* infección *f*; *(of water)* contaminación *f*; *(with illness)* contagio *m*.

infectious [ɪn'fekʃəs] *adj (disease)* infeccioso,-a; *fig* contagioso,-a.

infer [ɪn'fɜːr] *vtr* inferir (from, de).

inference ['ɪnfərəns] *n* inferencia *f*.

inferior [ɪn'fɪərɪər] **I** *adj* inferior (to, a). **II** *n pej* inferior *mf*.

inferiority [ɪnfɪərɪ'ɒrɪtɪ] *n* inferioridad *f*.

inferno [ɪn'fɜːnəʊ] *n lit* infierno *m*; *fig* the house was a raging i., la casa ardía en llamas.

infertile [ɪn'fɜːtaɪl] *adj* estéril.

infertility [ɪnfə'tɪlɪtɪ] *n* esterilidad *f*.

infest [ɪn'fest] *vtr* infestar, plagar (with,

de).

infighting ['ɪnfaɪtɪŋ] *n fig* luchas *fpl* internas.

infiltrate ['ɪnfɪltreɪt] *vtr* infiltrarse (**into**, en).

infinite ['ɪnfɪnɪt] *adj* infinito,-a.

infinitive [ɪn'fɪnɪtɪv] *n* infinitivo *m*.

infinity [ɪn'fɪnɪtɪ] *n* infinidad *f*; *Math* infinito *m*.

infirm [ɪn'fɜːm] I *adj* (*ailing*) enfermizo,-a; (*weak*) débil. II *npl* the i., los inválidos.

infirmary [ɪn'fɜːmərɪ] *n* hospital *m*.

infirmity [ɪn'fɜːmɪtɪ] *n fml* (*ailment*) enfermedad *f*; (*weakness*) debilidad *f*.

inflame [ɪn'fleɪm] *vtr* (*passion*) encender; (*curiosity*) avivar; (*crowd*) excitar; **to be inflamed with rage**, rabiar.

inflamed [ɪn'fleɪmd] *adj* inflamado,-a; **to become i.**, inflamarse.

inflammable [ɪn'flæməbəl] *adj* (*material*) inflamable; *fig* (*situation*) explosivo,-a.

inflammation [ɪnflə'meɪʃən] *n* inflamación *f*.

inflatable [ɪn'fleɪtəbəl] *adj* inflable.

inflate [ɪn'fleɪt] I *vtr* inflar. II *vi* inflarse.

inflated [ɪn'fleɪtɪd] *adj* 1 *fig* (*prices*) inflacionista. 2 *pej* (*view*, *idea*) exagerado,-a.

inflation [ɪn'fleɪʃən] *n* inflación *f*.

inflexible [ɪn'fleksəbəl] *adj* inflexible.

inflict [ɪn'flɪkt] *vtr* (*blow*) asestar (**on**, a); (*damage*) causar (**on**, a); (*defeat*) infligir (**on**, a).

in-flight ['ɪnflaɪt] *adj* durante el vuelo.

influence ['ɪnflʊəns] I *n* influencia *f*; **to be under the i.**, llevar una copa de más. II *vtr* influir en.

influential [ɪnflʊ'enʃəl] *adj* influyente.

influenza [ɪnflʊ'enzə] *n* gripe *f*.

influx ['ɪnflʌks] *n* afluencia *f*.

inform [ɪn'fɔːm] I *vtr* informar (**of**, **about**, de, sobre); (*police*) avisar (**of**, **about**, de). II *vi* **to i. against** or **on**, denunciar.

informal [ɪn'fɔːməl] *adj* 1 (*occasion*, *behaviour*) informal; (*language*, *treatment*) familiar. 2 (*unofficial*) no oficial.

informality [ɪnfɔː'mælɪtɪ] *n* (*of occasion*, *behaviour*) sencillez *f*; (*of treatment*) familiaridad *f*.

informant [ɪn'fɔːmənt] *n* informante *mf*.

information [ɪnfə'meɪʃən] *n* información *f*; (*details*) detalles *mpl*; (*facts*) datos *mpl* (*knowledge*) conocimientos *mpl*; (*news*) noticias *fpl*; **a piece of i.**, un dato; **i. bureau**, centro *m* de información; **i. technology**, informática *f*.

informative [ɪn'fɔːmətɪv] *adj* informativo,-a.

informed [ɪn'fɔːmd] *adj* enterado,-a; **keep me i.**, téngame al corriente.

informer [ɪn'fɔːmər] *n* delator,-a *m,f*; (*to the police*) soplón,-ona *m,f*.

infrared [ɪnfrə'red] *adj* infrarrojo,-a.

infrastructure ['ɪnfrəstrʌktʃər] *n* infraes-

tructura *f*.

infringe [ɪn'frɪndʒ] I *vtr* (*law*, *rule*) infringir; (*copyright*) no respetar. II *vi* **to i. on** or **upon**, (*rights*) violar; (*privacy*) invadir.

infringement [ɪn'frɪndʒmənt] *n* (*of law*, *rule*) infracción *f*; (*of rights*) violación *f*.

infuriate [ɪn'fjʊərɪeɪt] *vtr* poner furioso, -a.

infuriating [ɪn'fjʊərɪeɪtɪŋ] *adj* exasperante.

infusion [ɪn'fjuːʒən] *n* infusión *f*.

ingenious [ɪn'dʒiːnɪəs] *adj* ingenioso,-a.

ingenuity [ɪndʒɪ'njuːɪtɪ] *n* ingenio *m*.

ingenuous [ɪn'dʒenjʊəs] *adj* ingenuo,-a.

ingot ['ɪŋgət] *n* lingote *m*.

ingrained [ɪn'greɪnd] *adj fig* arraigado,-a.

ingratiate [ɪn'greɪʃɪeɪt] *vtr pej* **to i. one-self with sb**, congraciarse con.

ingratiating [ɪn'greɪʃɪeɪtɪŋ] *adj* zalamero,-a.

ingratitude [ɪn'grætɪtjuːd] *n* ingratitud *f*.

ingredient [ɪn'griːdɪənt] *n* ingrediente *m*.

inhabit [ɪn'hæbɪt] *vtr* vivir en, ocupar.

inhabitant [ɪn'hæbɪtənt] *n* habitante *mf*.

inhale [ɪn'heɪl] I *vtr* (*gas*) inhalar; (*air*) aspirar. II *vi* aspirar; (*smoker*) tragar el humo.

inherent [ɪn'hɪərənt] *adj* inherente.

inherit [ɪn'herɪt] *vtr* heredar (**from**, de).

inheritance [ɪn'herɪtəns] *n* herencia *f*.

inhibit [ɪn'hɪbɪt] *vtr* (*freedom*) limitar; (*person*) cohibir; **to i. sb from doing sth**, impedir a algn hacer algo.

inhibited [ɪn'hɪbɪtɪd] *adj* cohibido,-a.

inhibition [ɪnhɪ'bɪʃən] *n* cohibición *f*.

inhospitable [ɪnhɒ'spɪtəbəl] *adj* inhospitalario,-a; (*climate*, *place*) inhóspito,-a.

inhuman [ɪn'hjuːmən] *adj* inhumano,-a.

iniquity [ɪ'nɪkwɪtɪ] *n fml* iniquidad *f*.

initial [ɪ'nɪʃəl] I *adj* inicial, primero,-a. II *n* 1 inicial *f*. 2 **initials**, (*of name*) iniciales *fpl*; (*of abbreviation*) siglas *fpl*. III *vtr* firmar con las iniciales. ◆**initially** *adv* al principio.

initiate [ɪ'nɪʃɪeɪt] *vtr* 1 iniciar; (*reform*) promover; (*lawsuit*) entablar. 2 (*into society*) admitir (**into**, en); (*into knowledge*) iniciar (**into**, en).

initiation [ɪnɪʃɪ'eɪʃən] *n* 1 (*start*) principio *m*. 2 (*admission*) iniciación *f*.

initiative [ɪ'nɪʃətɪv] *n* iniciativa *f*.

inject [ɪn'dʒekt] *vtr* 1 (*drug etc*) inyectar. 2 *fig* (*capital*) invertir; (*life*, *hope*) infundir.

injection [ɪn'dʒekʃən] *n* 1 inyección *f*. 2 *fig* (*of capital*) inversión *f*.

injunction [ɪn'dʒʌŋkʃən] *n* interdicto *m*.

injure ['ɪndʒər] *vtr* herir; **to i. oneself**, hacerse daño; *fig* (*health*, *reputation*) perjudicar.

injured ['ɪndʒəd] I *adj* herido,-a; *fig* (*look*, *tone*) ofendido,-a. II *npl* the i., los heridos.

injury ['ɪndʒərɪ] n (hurt) herida f; fig (harm) daño m; Sport i. time, (tiempo m de) descuento m.

injustice [ɪn'dʒʌstɪs] n injusticia f.

ink [ɪŋk] n tinta f; **invisible i.**, tinta simpática.

inkling ['ɪŋklɪŋ] n (idea) idea f; (suspicion) sospecha f; (sign) señal f.

inkwell ['ɪŋkwel] n tintero m.

inlaid [ɪn'leɪd] adj (wood) taraceado,-a; (ivory, gems) incrustado,-a.

inland ['ɪnlənd] I adj (del) interior; GB I. Revenue, Hacienda f. II [ɪn'lænd] adv (travel) tierra adentro.

in-laws ['ɪnlɔːz] npl fam familia f sing política.

inlet ['ɪnlet] n 1 (in coastline) ensenada f, cala f. 2 (in pipe, machine) entrada f, admisión f.

inmate ['ɪnmeɪt] n (of prison) preso,-a m,f; (of hospital) enfermo,-a m,f; (of asylum, camp) internado,-a m,f.

inn [ɪn] n (with lodging) posada f, mesón m.

innate [ɪ'neɪt] adj innato,-a.

inner ['ɪnə] adj 1 (region) interior; (structure) interno,-a; i. city, zona urbana desfavorecida; i. tube, cámara f de aire. 2 fig (thoughts) íntimo,-a; (peace etc) interior.

innermost ['ɪnəməʊst] adj (room) más interior; fig (thoughts) más íntimo,-a.

innings ['ɪnɪŋz] n (in cricket) entrada f, turno m.

innocence ['ɪnəsəns] n inocencia f.

innocent ['ɪnəsənt] adj & n inocente (mf).

innocuous [ɪ'nɒkjʊəs] adj inocuo,-a.

innovation [ɪnə'veɪʃən] n novedad f.

innuendo [ɪnjʊ'endəʊ] n indirecta f.

inoculate [ɪ'nɒkjʊleɪt] vtr inocular.

inoculation [ɪnɒkjʊ'leɪʃən] n inoculación f.

inoffensive [ɪnə'fensɪv] adj inofensivo,-a.

inopportune [ɪn'ɒpətjuːn, ɪnɒpə'tjuːn] adj inoportuno,-a.

inordinate [ɪ'nɔːdɪnɪt] adj desmesurado,-a.

inpatient ['ɪnpeɪʃənt] n interno,-a m,f.

input ['ɪnpʊt] n (of resources) inversión f; (of power) entrada f; Comput (of data) input m, entrada f.

inquest ['ɪnkwest] n investigación f judicial.

inquire [ɪn'kwaɪə] I vtr preguntar; (find out) averiguar. II vi preguntar (about, por); (find out) informarse (about, de).
◆**inquire after** vtr preguntar por.
◆**inquire into** vtr investigar, indagar.

inquiry [ɪn'kwaɪərɪ] n 1 pregunta f; 'inquiries', 'información'. 2 (investigation) investigación f.

inquisitive [ɪn'kwɪzɪtɪv] adj (curious) curioso,-a; (questioning) preguntón,-ona.

inroads ['ɪnrəʊdz] npl the firm is making i. into the market, la empresa está ganando terreno en el mercado; to make i. into one's capital, reducir su capital.

insane [ɪn'seɪn] adj loco,-a; (act) insensato,-a; fig to drive sb i., volver loco,-a a algn.

insanity [ɪn'sænɪtɪ] n demencia f, locura f.

insatiable [ɪn'seɪʃəbəl] adj insaciable.

inscribe [ɪn'skraɪb] vtr fml inscribir; (book) dedicar.

inscription [ɪn'skrɪpʃən] n (on stone, coin) inscripción f; (in book, on photo) dedicatoria f.

inscrutable [ɪn'skruːtəbəl] adj inescrutable, insondable.

insect ['ɪnsekt] n insecto m; i. bite, picadura f.

insecticide [ɪn'sektɪsaɪd] n insecticida m.

insecure [ɪnsɪ'kjʊə] adj inseguro,-a.

insecurity [ɪnsɪ'kjʊərɪtɪ] n inseguridad f.

insemination [ɪnsemɪ'neɪʃən] n inseminación f.

insensible [ɪn'sensəbəl] adj fml inconsciente.

insensitive [ɪn'sensɪtɪv] adj insensible.

inseparable [ɪn'sepərəbəl] adj inseparable.

insert ['ɪnsɜːt] I n encarte m. II [ɪn'sɜːt] vtr introducir.

insertion [ɪn'sɜːʃən] n introducción f; (of clause, text) inserción f.

inshore [ɪn'ʃɔː] I adj (fishing) de bajura. II [ɪn'ʃɔː] adv cerca de la costa.

inside [ɪn'saɪd] I n 1 interior m; on the i., por dentro; to turn sth i. out, volver algo al revés. 2 fam insides, tripas fpl. II ['ɪnsaɪd] adj interior; (part) interno,-a; i. lane, carril m interior. III [ɪn'saɪd] adv (be) dentro, adentro; (run etc) (hacia) adentro; to come i., entrar; GB fam he spent a year i., pasó un año en chirona. IV prep 1 (place) dentro de. 2 fam i. (of), (time) en menos de.

insider [ɪn'saɪdə] n i. dealing, uso indebido de información privilegiada y confidencial para operaciones comerciales.

insidious [ɪn'sɪdɪəs] adj insidioso,-a.

insight ['ɪnsaɪt] n perspicacia f.

insignia [ɪn'sɪgnɪə] n inv insignia f.

insignificant [ɪnsɪg'nɪfɪkənt] adj insignificante.

insincere [ɪnsɪn'sɪə] adj poco sincero,-a.

insinuate [ɪn'sɪnjʊeɪt] vtr insinuar.

insipid [ɪn'sɪpɪd] adj soso,-a, insulso,-a.

insist [ɪn'sɪst] I vi insistir (on, en); (argue) obstinarse (on, en). II vtr to i. that ..., insistir en que ....

insistence [ɪn'sɪstəns] n insistencia f.

insistent [ɪn'sɪstənt] adj insistente.

in so far as [ɪnsəʊ'fɑːrəz] adv en tanto que.

insole ['ɪnsəʊl] n (of shoe) plantilla f.

insolent ['ɪnsələnt] adj insolente.

insoluble [ɪn'sɒljʊbəl] adj insoluble.

insomnia [ɪn'sɒmnɪə] n insomnio m.

insomniac [ɪn'sɒmnɪæk] n insomne mf.

inspect [ɪn'spekt] vtr inspeccionar, examinar; (troops) pasar revista a.

inspection [ɪn'spekʃən] n inspección f; (of troops) revista f.

inspector [ɪn'spektər] n inspector,-a m,f; (on bus, train) revisor,-a m,f.

inspiration [ɪnspɪ'reɪʃən] n inspiración f; to get i. from sb/sth, inspirarse en algn/algo.

inspire [ɪn'spaɪər] vtr 1 inspirar; to i. respect in sb, infundir respeto a algn. 2 to i. sb to do sth, animar a algn a hacer algo.

inspired [ɪn'spaɪəd] adj inspirado,-a.

instability [ɪnstə'bɪlɪtɪ] n inestabilidad f.

install, US **instal** [ɪn'stɔːl] vtr instalar.

installation [ɪnstə'leɪʃən] n instalación f.

instalment, US **installment** [ɪn'stɔːlmənt] n 1 (of payment) plazo m; to pay by instalments, pagar a plazos; US i. plan, venta f or compra f a plazos. 2 (of novel, programme) entrega f; (of journal) fascículo m.

instance ['ɪnstəns] n ejemplo m, caso m; for i., por ejemplo; in the first i., en primer lugar.

instant ['ɪnstənt] I n (moment) instante m, momento m; in an i., en un instante. II adj inmediato,-a; (coffee, meal) instantáneo,-a. ◆**instantly** adv inmediatamente.

instead [ɪn'sted] I adv en cambio. II prep i. of, en vez de, en lugar de.

instep ['ɪnstep] n empeine m.

instigation [ɪnstɪ'geɪʃən] n instigación f.

instil, US **instill** [ɪn'stɪl] vtr (idea, habit) inculcar (in, a, en); (courage, respect) infundir (in, a).

instinct ['ɪnstɪŋkt] n instinto m.

instinctive [ɪn'stɪŋktɪv] adj instintivo,-a.

institute ['ɪnstɪtjuːt] I n instituto m; (centre) centro m; (professional body) colegio m. II vtr fml (system) establecer. 2 (start) iniciar; (proceedings) entablar.

institution [ɪnstɪ'tjuːʃən] n 1 institución f. 2 (home) asilo m; (asylum) manicomio m.

instruct [ɪn'strʌkt] vtr instruir; (order) mandar; I am instructed to say that ..., me han encargado decir que ....

instruction [ɪn'strʌkʃən] n 1 instrucción f. 2 instructions, instrucciones fpl; 'instructions for use', 'modo de empleo'.

instructive [ɪn'strʌktɪv] adj instructivo,-a.

instructor [ɪn'strʌktər] n instructor,-a m,f; (of driving) profesor,-a m,f.

instrument ['ɪnstrəmənt] n instrumento m; i. panel, tablero m de mandos.

instrumental [ɪnstrə'mentəl] adj 1 Mus instrumental. 2 to be i. in sth, contribuir decisivamente a algo.

insubordinate [ɪnsə'bɔːdɪnɪt] adj insubordinado,-a.

insubstantial [ɪnsəb'stænʃəl] adj insubstancial; (structure) poco sólido,-a.

insufferable [ɪn'sʌfərəbəl] adj insoportable.

insufficient [ɪnsə'fɪʃənt] adj insuficiente.

insular ['ɪnsjʊlər] adj 1 Geog insular. 2 fig pej estrecho,-a de miras.

insulate ['ɪnsjʊleɪt] vtr aislar (against, from, de).

insulating tape ['ɪnsjʊleɪtɪŋteɪp] n cinta f aislante.

insulation [ɪnsjʊ'leɪʃən] n aislamiento m.

insulin ['ɪnsjʊlɪn] n insulina f.

insult ['ɪnsʌlt] I n (words) insulto m; (action) afrenta f, ofensa f. II [ɪn'sʌlt] vtr insultar, ofender.

insulting [ɪn'sʌltɪŋ] adj insultante, ofensivo,-a.

insuperable [ɪn'suːpərəbəl] adj insuperable.

insurance [ɪn'ʃʊərəns] n seguro m; fire i., seguro contra incendios; i. broker, agente mf de seguros; i. company, compañía f de seguros; i. policy, póliza f (de seguros); private health i., seguro médico privado.

insure [ɪn'ʃʊər] vtr asegurar (against, contra).

insurgent [ɪn'sɜːdʒənt] adj & n insurrecto,-a, (m,f).

insurmountable [ɪnsə'maʊntəbəl] adj (problem etc) insuperable; (barrier) infranqueable.

intact [ɪn'tækt] adj intacto,-a.

intake ['ɪnteɪk] n 1 (of air, water) entrada f; (of electricity etc) toma f. 2 (of food, calories) consumo m. 3 (of students, recruits) número m de admitidos.

integral ['ɪntɪgrəl] adj 1 (intrinsic) integrante. 2 (whole) íntegro,-a. 3 Math integral. II n Math integral f.

integrate ['ɪntɪgreɪt] I vtr integrar. II vi integrarse.

integration [ɪntɪ'greɪʃən] n integración f.

integrity [ɪn'tegrɪtɪ] n integridad f, honradez f.

intellect ['ɪntɪlekt] n intelecto m.

intellectual [ɪntɪ'lektʃʊəl] adj & n intelectual (mf).

intelligence [ɪn'telɪdʒəns] n 1 inteligencia f. 2 (information) información f.

intelligent [ɪn'telɪdʒənt] adj inteligente.

intelligentsia [ɪntelɪ'dʒentsɪə] n intelectualidad f.

intelligible [ɪn'telɪdʒəbəl] adj inteligible.

intend [ɪn'tend] vtr 1 (mean) tener la intención de. 2 to i. sth for sb, destinar algo a algn.

intended [ɪn'tendɪd] adj (planned) previsto,-a.

intense [ɪn'tens] *adj* intenso,-a; *(person)* muy serio,-a. ◆**intensely** *adv (extremely)* enormemente, sumamente.

intensify [ɪn'tensɪfaɪ] *vtr (search)* intensificar; *(effort)* redoblar; *(production, pollution)* aumentar.

intensity [ɪn'tensɪtɪ] *n* intensidad *f*.

intensive [ɪn'tensɪv] *adj* intensivo,-a; *Med* **i. care unit,** unidad *f* de vigilancia intensiva.

intent [ɪn'tent] **I** *adj (absorbed)* absorto,-a; *(gaze etc)* atento,-a; **to be i.** on doing sth, estar resuelto,-a a hacer algo. **II** *n fml* intención *f*, propósito *m*; **to all intents and purposes,** a todos los efectos.

intention [ɪn'tenʃən] *n* intención *f*.

intentional [ɪn'tenʃənəl] *adj* deliberado, -a. ◆**intentionally** *adv* a propósito.

interact [ɪntər'ækt] *vi (people)* interrelacionarse.

interaction [ɪntər'ækʃən] *n* interacción *f*.

interactive [ɪntər'æktɪv] *adj* interactivo, -a.

intercede [ɪntə'siːd] *vi* interceder (with, ante).

intercept [ɪntə'sept] *vtr* interceptar.

interchange ['ɪntətʃeɪndʒ] **I** *n* **1** *(exchange)* intercambio *m*. **2** *(on motorway)* cruce *m*. **II** [ɪntə'tʃeɪndʒ] *vtr* intercambiar (with, con).

interchangeable [ɪntə'tʃeɪndʒəbəl] *adj* intercambiable.

intercity [ɪntə'sɪtɪ] *adj Rail* de largo recorrido.

intercom ['ɪntəkɒm] *n* portero automático.

intercontinental [ɪntəkɒntɪ'nentəl] *adj* **i. ballistic missile,** misil balístico intercontinental.

intercourse ['ɪntəkɔːs] *n* **1** *(dealings)* trato *m*. **2** *(sexual)* relaciones *fpl* sexuales.

interest ['ɪntrɪst] **I** *n* **1** interés *m*. **2** *(advantage)* provecho *m*; **in the i. of,** en pro de. **3** *Com (share)* participación *f*. **4** *Fin* interés *m*; **i. rate,** tipo *m* de interés. **II** *vtr* interesar; **he's interested in politics,** le interesa la política.

interesting ['ɪntrɪstɪŋ] *adj* interesante.

interface ['ɪntəfeɪs] *n* interface *f*.

interfere [ɪntə'fɪə'] *vi* **1** *(meddle)* entrometerse (in, en); to i. with, *(hinder)* dificultar; *(spoil)* estropear; *(prevent)* impedir. **2** *Rad TV* interferir (with, con).

interference [ɪntə'fɪərəns] *n* *(meddling)* intromisión *f*; *(hindrance)* estorbo *m*; *Rad TV* interferencia *f*.

interim ['ɪntərɪm] **I** *n fml* **in the i.,** en el ínterin. **II** *adj* interino,-a, provisional.

interior [ɪn'tɪərɪə'] **I** *adj* interior. **II** *n* interior *m*; **i. design,** diseño *m* de interiores.

interlock [ɪntə'lɒk] *vi* encajarse; *(fingers)* entrelazarse; *(cogs)* engranarse.

interloper ['ɪntələupə'] *n* intruso *m,f*.

interlude ['ɪntəluːd] *n (break)* intervalo *m*; *Cin Theat* intermedio *m*; *Mus* interludio *m*.

intermediary [ɪntə'miːdɪərɪ] *n* intermediario,-a *m,f*.

intermediate [ɪntə'miːdɪɪt] *adj* intermedio,-a.

interminable [ɪn'tɜːmɪnəbəl] *adj* interminable.

intermission [ɪntə'mɪʃən] *n* *Cin Theat* intermedio *m*.

intermittent [ɪntə'mɪtənt] *adj* intermitente.

intern [ɪn'tɜːn] **I** *vtr* internar. **II** ['ɪntɜːn] *n US Med* interno,-a *m,f*.

internal [ɪn'tɜːnəl] *adj* interior; *(dispute, injury)* interno,-a; *US* **I. Revenue,** ≈ Hacienda *f*. ◆**internally** *adv* interiormente; **'not to be taken i.',** 'uso externo'.

international [ɪntə'næʃənəl] **I** *adj* internacional. **II** *n Sport (player)* internacional *m,f*; *(match)* partido *m* internacional.

interplay ['ɪntəpleɪ] *n* interacción *f*.

interpret [ɪn'tɜːprɪt] **I** *vtr* interpretar. **II** *vi* actuar de intérprete.

interpretation [ɪntɜːprɪ'teɪʃən] *n* interpretación *f*.

interpreter [ɪn'tɜːprɪtə'] *n* intérprete *mf*.

interrelated [ɪntərɪ'leɪtɪd] *adj* estrechamente relacionado,-a.

interrogate [ɪn'terəgeɪt] *vtr* interrogar.

interrogation [ɪntərə'geɪʃən] *n* interrogatorio *m*.

interrogative [ɪntə'rɒgətɪv] *Ling* **I** *adj* interrogativo,-a. **II** *n (word)* palabra interrogativa.

interrupt [ɪntə'rʌpt] *vtr & vi* interrumpir.

interruption [ɪntə'rʌpʃən] *n* interrupción *f*.

intersect [ɪntə'sekt] **I** *vtr* cruzar. **II** *vi* cruzarse.

intersection [ɪntə'sekʃən] *n* **1** *(crossroads)* cruce *m*. **2** *(of two lines)* intersección *f*.

intersperse [ɪntə'spɜːs] *vtr* esparcir.

intertwine [ɪntə'twaɪn] **I** *vtr* entrelazar (with, con). **II** *vi* entrelazarse (with, con).

interval ['ɪntəvəl] *n* **1** *(of time, space)* intervalo *m*; **at intervals,** *(time, space)* a intervalos; *(time)* de vez en cuando. **2** *GB Cin Theat* intermedio *m*.

intervene [ɪntə'viːn] *vi* **1** *(person)* intervenir (in, en). **2** *(event)* sobrevenir. **3** *(time)* transcurrir.

intervention [ɪntə'venʃən] *n* intervención *f*.

interview ['ɪntəvjuː] **I** *n* entrevista *f*; **to give an i.,** conceder una entrevista. **II** *vtr* entrevistar.

interviewer ['ɪntəvjuːə'] *n* entrevistador,-a *m,f*.

intestine [ɪn'testɪn] *n (usu pl)* intestino *m*; **large/small i.,** intestino grueso/delgado.

intimacy ['ɪntɪməsɪ] *n (closeness)* intimi-

dad f; euph (sex) relación íntima; **intimacies**, intimidades fpl.

intimate¹ ['ɪntɪmɪt] adj íntimo,-a; (knowledge) profundo,-a.

intimate² ['ɪntɪmeɪt] vtr fml dar a entender.

intimidate [ɪn'tɪmɪdeɪt] vtr intimidar.

intimidating [ɪn'tɪmɪdeɪtɪŋ] adj atemorizante.

into ['ɪntu:, unstressed 'ɪntə] prep 1 (motion) en, a, con; **he fell i. the water**, se cayó al agua; **I bumped i. a friend**, me topé con un amigo; **to get i. a car**, subir a un coche; **to go i. a house**, entrar en una casa. 2 (state) en, a; **he grew i. a man**, se hizo un hombre; **to burst i. tears**, echarse a llorar; **to change pounds i. pesetas**, cambiar libras en or por pesetas; **to translate sth i. French**, traducir algo al francés. 3 **to work i. the night**, trabajar hasta muy avanzada la noche. 4 **to divide sth i. three**, dividir algo en tres. 5 fam **to be i. sth**, ser aficionado,-a a algo.

intolerable [ɪn'tɒlərəbəl] adj intolerable.

intolerant [ɪn'tɒlərənt] adj intolerante.

intonation [ɪntəʊ'neɪʃən] n entonación f.

intoxicated [ɪn'tɒksɪkeɪtɪd] adj borracho,-a.

intoxicating [ɪn'tɒksɪkeɪtɪŋ] adj embriagador,-a; **i. liquor**, bebida alcohólica.

intoxication [ɪntɒksɪ'keɪʃən] n embriaguez f.

intractable [ɪn'træktəbəl] adj fml (person) intratable; (problem) insoluble.

intransigent [ɪn'trænsɪdʒənt] adj fml intransigente, intolerante.

intransitive [ɪn'trænsɪtɪv] adj intransitivo,-a.

intravenous [ɪntrə'vi:nəs] adj intravenoso,-a.

in-tray ['ɪntreɪ] n bandeja f de asuntos pendientes.

intrepid [ɪn'trepɪd] adj intrépido,-a, audaz.

intricate ['ɪntrɪkɪt] adj intrincado,-a.

intrigue [ɪn'tri:g, 'ɪntrɪg] I n intriga f. II [ɪn'tri:g] vtr intrigar. III vi intrigar, conspirar.

intriguing [ɪn'tri:gɪŋ] adj intrigante.

intrinsic [ɪn'trɪnsɪk] adj fml intrínseco,-a.

introduce [ɪntrə'dju:s] vtr 1 (person, programme) presentar (to, a). 2 (bring in) introducir (into, to, en); Com lanzar (into, to, a); (topic) proponer.

introduction [ɪntrə'dʌkʃən] n 1 (of person, programme) presentación f; (in book) introducción f. 2 (bringing in) introducción f; Com (of product) lanzamiento m.

introductory [ɪntrə'dʌktərɪ] adj introductorio,-a; (remarks) preliminar; Com de lanzamiento.

introspective [ɪntrə'spektɪv] adj introspectivo,-a.

introvert ['ɪntrəvɜːt] n introvertido,-a m,f.

intrude [ɪn'tru:d] vi entrometerse (into, on, en); (disturb) molestar.

intruder [ɪn'tru:dər] n intruso,-a m,f.

intrusion [ɪn'tru:ʒən] n incursión f.

intuition [ɪntjʊ'ɪʃən] n intuición f.

inundate [ɪn'ʌndeɪt] vtr inundar (with, de).

invade [ɪn'veɪd] vtr invadir.

invader [ɪn'veɪdər] n invasor,-a m,f.

invalid¹ [ɪn'vælɪd] n (disabled person) minusválido,-a m,f; (sick person) enfermo,-a m,f.

invalid² [ɪn'vælɪd] adj inválido,-a, nulo,-a.

invalidate [ɪn'vælɪdeɪt] vtr invalidar.

invaluable [ɪn'væljʊəbəl] adj inestimable.

invariable [ɪn'veərɪəbəl] adj invariable.

invasion [ɪn'veɪʒən] n invasión f.

invent [ɪn'vent] vtr inventar.

invention [ɪn'venʃən] n (of machine) invento m; (creativity) inventiva f; (lie) mentira f.

inventive [ɪn'ventɪv] adj inventivo,-a.

inventor [ɪn'ventər] n inventor,-a m,f.

inventory ['ɪnvəntərɪ] n inventario m.

invert [ɪn'vɜːt] vtr invertir.

invertebrate [ɪn'vɜːtɪbrɪt] I adj invertebrado,-a. II n invertebrado m.

inverted [ɪn'vɜːtɪd] adj (in) **i. commas**, (entre) comillas fpl.

invest [ɪn'vest] I vtr invertir (in, en); **to i. sb with sth**, conferir algo a algn. II vi invertir (in, en).

investigate [ɪn'vestɪgeɪt] vtr (crime, subject) investigar; (cause, possibility) estudiar.

investigation [ɪnvestɪ'geɪʃən] n (of crime) investigación f; (of cause) examen m.

investigator [ɪn'vestɪgeɪtər] n investigador,-a m,f; private i., detective privado.

investment [ɪn'vestmənt] n inversión f.

investor [ɪn'vestər] n inversor,-a m,f.

inveterate [ɪn'vetərɪt] adj empedernido,-a.

invidious [ɪn'vɪdɪəs] adj (task) ingrato,-a; (comparison) injusto,-a.

invigilator [ɪn'vɪdʒɪleɪtər] n GB vigilante m,f.

invigorating [ɪn'vɪgəreɪtɪŋ] adj vigorizante.

invincible [ɪn'vɪnsəbəl] adj invencible.

invisible [ɪn'vɪzəbəl] adj invisible.

invitation [ɪnvɪ'teɪʃən] n invitación f.

invite [ɪn'vaɪt] vtr 1 invitar (to, a). 2 (comments etc) solicitar; (criticism) provocar; **to i. trouble**, buscarse problemas.

inviting [ɪn'vaɪtɪŋ] adj (attractive) atractivo,-a; (food) apetitoso,-a.

invoice ['ɪnvɔɪs] I n factura f. II vtr facturar.

invoke [ɪn'vəʊk] *vtr fml* invocar.

involuntary [ɪn'vɒləntərɪ] *adj* involuntario,-a.

involve [ɪn'vɒlv] *vtr* 1 (*concern*) implicar (in, en); **the issues involved,** las cuestiones en juego; **to be involved in an accident,** sufrir un accidente. 2 (*entail*) suponer, implicar; (*trouble, risk*) acarrear.

involved [ɪn'vɒlvd] *adj* (*complicated*) complicado,-a; *fam* (*romantically attached*) enredado,-a, liado,-a.

involvement [ɪn'vɒlvmənt] *n* (*participation*) participación *f*; (*in crime*) implicación *f*.

inward ['ɪnwəd] **I** *adj* interior. **II** *adv* → **inwards.** ◆**inwardly** *adv* interiormente, por dentro.

inwards ['ɪnwədz] *adv* hacia dentro.

iodine ['aɪədi:n] *n* yodo *m*.

iota [aɪ'əʊtə] *n* pizca *f*, ápice *m*.

IOU [aɪəʊ'ju:] *abbr of* **I owe you,** pagaré *m*.

IQ [aɪ'kju:] *abbr of* **intelligence quotient,** coeficiente *m* intelectual, CI *m*.

IRA [aɪɑ:r'eɪ] *abbr of* **Irish Republican Army,** Ejército *m* Republicano irlandés, IRA *m*.

Iran [ɪ'rɑ:n] *n* Irán.

Iranian [ɪ'reɪnɪən] *adj & n* iraní (*mf*).

Iraq [ɪ'rɑ:k] *n* Irak.

Iraqi [ɪ'rɑ:kɪ] *adj & n* iraquí (*mf*).

irascible [ɪ'ræsɪbəl] *adj fml* irascible.

irate [aɪ'reɪt] *adj* airado,-a, furioso,-a.

Ireland ['aɪələnd] *n* Irlanda; **Republic of I.,** República de Irlanda.

iris ['aɪərɪs] *n* 1 *Anat* iris *m inv.* 2 *Bot* lirio *m.*

Irish ['aɪrɪʃ] **I** *adj* irlandés,-esa; **I. coffee,** café *m* irlandés; **I. Sea,** Mar *m* de Irlanda. **II** *n* 1 (*language*) irlandés *m.* 2 *pl* **the I.,** los irlandeses.

Irishman ['aɪrɪʃmən] *n* irlandés *m.*

Irishwoman ['aɪrɪʃwʊmən] *n* irlandesa *f.*

irksome ['ɜːksəm] *adj* fastidioso,-a.

iron ['aɪən] **I** *n* 1 hierro *m*; **the i. and steel industry,** la industria siderúrgica; **I. Curtain,** Telón *m* de Acero; **i. ore,** mineral *m* de hierro. 2 (*for clothes*) plancha *f.* 3 (*for golf*) hierro *m.* 4 **irons,** (*chains*) grillos *mpl.* **II** *vtr* (*clothes*) planchar. ◆**iron out** *vtr* 1 (*crease*) planchar. 2 *fam fig* (*problem*) resolver.

ironic(al) [aɪ'rɒnɪk(əl)] *adj* irónico,-a.

ironing ['aɪənɪŋ] *n* 1 to do the i., planchar; **i. board,** mesa *f* de la plancha. 2 (*clothes to be ironed*) ropa *f* para planchar; (*clothes ironed*) ropa planchada.

ironmonger ['aɪənmʌŋgər] *n GB* ferretero,-a *m,f*; **i.'s (shop),** ferretería *f.*

irony ['aɪrənɪ] *n* ironía *f.*

irrational [ɪ'ræʃənəl] *adj* irracional.

irreconcilable [ɪrekən'saɪləbəl] irreconciliable.

irrefutable [ɪrɪ'fju:təbəl] *adj fml* irrefutable.

irregular [ɪ'regjʊlər] *adj* 1 irregular. 2 (*abnormal*) anormal. 2 (*uneven*) desigual.

irrelevant [ɪ'reləvənt] *adj* no pertinente.

irreparable [ɪ'repərəbəl] *adj* irreparable.

irreplaceable [ɪrɪ'pleɪsəbəl] *adj* irremplazable.

irrepressible [ɪrɪ'presəbəl] *adj* incontenible.

irresistible [ɪrɪ'zɪstəbəl] *adj* irresistible.

irresolute [ɪ'rezəlu:t] *adj fml* indeciso,-a.

irrespective [ɪrɪ'spektɪv] *adj* **i. of,** sin tener en cuenta.

irresponsible [ɪrɪ'spɒnsəbəl] *adj* irresponsable.

irreverent [ɪ'revərənt] *adj* irreverente.

irrevocable [ɪ'revəkəbəl] *adj* irrevocable.

irrigate ['ɪrɪgeɪt] *vtr* regar.

irrigation [ɪrɪ'geɪʃən] *n* riego *m*; **i. channel,** acequia *f*; **i. system,** sistema *m* de regadío.

irritable ['ɪrɪtəbəl] *adj* irritable.

irritate ['ɪrɪteɪt] *vtr* (*annoy*) fastidiar; *Med* irritar.

irritating ['ɪrɪteɪtɪŋ] *adj* irritante.

irritation [ɪrɪ'teɪʃən] *n* 1 (*annoyance*) fastidio *m*; (*ill humour*) mal humor *m*. 2 *Med* irritación *f*.

is [ɪz] *3rd person sing pres* → **be.**

Islam ['ɪzlɑːm] *n* Islam *m*.

Islamic [ɪz'læmɪk] *adj* islámico,-a.

island ['aɪlənd] *n* isla *f*; (*traffic*) isleta *f*.

islander ['aɪləndər] *n* isleño,-a *m,f*.

isle [aɪl] *n* isla *f*.

isn't ['ɪzənt] = **is not.**

isolate ['aɪsəleɪt] *vtr* aislar (**from,** de).

isolated ['aɪsəleɪtɪd] *adj* aislado,-a.

isolation [aɪsə'leɪʃən] *n* aislamiento *m*.

Israel ['ɪzreɪəl] *n* Israel *m*.

Israeli [ɪz'reɪlɪ] **I** *adj* israelí. **II** *n* israelí *mf*.

issue ['ɪʃju:] **I** *n* 1 (*matter*) cuestión *f*; **to take i. with sb (over sth),** manifestar su desacuerdo con algn (en algo). 2 (*of banknotes etc*) emisión *f*; (*of passport*) expedición *f*. 3 (*of journal etc*) ejemplar *m*. 4 (*of supplies*) reparto *m*. 5 *fml* (*outcome*) resultado *m*. 6 *Jur* (*offspring*) descendencia *f*. **II** *vtr* 1 (*book*) publicar; (*banknotes etc*) emitir; (*passport*) expedir. 2 (*supplies*) repartir. 3 (*order, instructions*) dar; (*warrant*) dictar. **III** *vi fml* (*blood*) brotar (**from,** de); (*smoke*) salir (**from,** de).

isthmus ['ɪsməs] *n* istmo *m*.

it [ɪt] *pers pron* 1 (*subject*) él, ella, ello (*often omitted*) **it's here,** está aquí. 2 (*direct object*) lo, la; **I don't believe it,** no me lo creo; **I liked the house and bought it,** me gustó la casa y la compré. 3 (*indirect object*) le; **give it a kick,** dale una patada. 4 (*after prep*) él, ella, ello; **I saw the beach and ran towards it,** vi la playa y fui corriendo hacia ella; **we'll talk about**

it later, ya hablaremos de ello. 5 (abstract) ello; **let's get down to it**, ¡vamos a ello! 6 (impersonal) **it's late**, es tarde; **it's me**, soy yo; **it's raining**, está lloviendo; **it's said that ...**, se dice que ...; **it's two miles to town**, hay dos millas de aquí al pueblo; **that's it!**, (agreeing) ¡precisamente!; (finishing) ¡se acabó!; **this is it!**, ¡ha llegado la hora!; **who is it?**, ¿quién es?

Italian [ı'tæljən] I adj italiano,-a. II n 1 (person) italiano,-a m,f. 2 (language) italiano m.

italic [ı'tælɪk] n cursiva f.

Italy [ˈɪtəlɪ] n Italia.

itch [ɪtʃ] I n picor m; fig al n i. to travel, unas ganas locas de viajar. II vi 1 (skin) picar. 2 fig anhelar; fam to be itching to do sth, tener muchas ganas de hacer algo.

itchy [ˈɪtʃɪ] adj (itchier, itchiest) que pica.

item [ˈaɪtəm] n 1 (in list) artículo m; (in collection) pieza f; **i. of clothing**, prenda f de vestir. 2 (on agenda) asunto m; (in show) número m; **news i.**, noticia f.

itemize [ˈaɪtəmaɪz] vtr detallar.

itinerant [ı'tınərənt] adj fml itinerante.

itinerary [aı'tınərərı] n itinerario m.

it'll [ˈɪtəl] = it will.

its [ɪts] poss adj (one thing) su; (more than one) sus.

itself [ɪt'self] pers pron 1 (reflexive) se; **the cat scratched i.**, el gato se arañó. 2 (emphatic) él o ella o ello mismo,-a; (after prep) sí (mismo,-a); **in i.**, en sí.

ITV [aɪtiː'viː] GB abbr of Independent Television, Televisión f independiente, ITV f.

IUD [aɪjuː'diː] abbr of intrauterine (contraceptive) device, dispositivo intrauterino, DIU m.

ivory [ˈaɪvərɪ] n marfil m.

ivy [ˈaɪvɪ] n hiedra f.

J

J, j [dʒeɪ] n (the letter) J, j f.

jab [dʒæb] I n pinchazo m; (poke) golpe seco. II vtr pinchar; (with fist) dar un puñetazo a.

jabber [ˈdʒæbə'] fam vi (chatter) charlotear; (speak quickly) hablar atropelladamente.

jack [dʒæk] n 1 Aut gato m. 2 Cards sota f. 3 (bowls) boliche m. ◆**jack in** vtr GB fam dejar. ◆**jack up** vtr Aut levantar (con el gato); fig (prices) aumentar.

jackal [ˈdʒækɔːl] n chacal m.

jackdaw [ˈdʒækdɔː] n Orn grajilla f.

jacket [ˈdʒækɪt] n 1 chaqueta f; (of suit) americana f; (bomber jacket) cazadora f. 2 (of book) sobrecubierta f; US (of record) funda f. 3 **j. potatoes**, patatas fpl al horno.

jack-knife [ˈdʒæknaɪf] I n navaja f. II vi colear.

jack-of-all-trades [dʒækəv'ɔːltreɪdz] n persona f mañosa or de muchos oficios.

jackpot [ˈdʒækpɒt] n (premio m) gordo m.

Jacuzzi [dʒə'kuːzɪ] n jacuzzi m.

jade [dʒeɪd] n jade m.

jaded [ˈdʒeɪdɪd] adj (tired) agotado,-a; (palate) hastiado,-a.

jagged [ˈdʒægɪd] adj dentado,-a.

jaguar [ˈdʒægjʊə'] n jaguar m.

jail [dʒeɪl] I n cárcel f, prisión f. II vtr encarcelar.

jailbreak [ˈdʒeɪlbreɪk] n fuga f, evasión f.

jailer [ˈdʒeɪlə'] n carcelero,-a m,f.

jam¹ [dʒæm] n Culin mermelada f.

jam² [dʒæm] I n 1 (blockage) atasco m; fam (fix) apuro m. 2 Mus improvisación f. II vtr (cram) meter a la fuerza. 2 (block)

atascar; Rad interferir. III vi (door) atrancarse; (brakes) agarrotarse.

Jamaica [dʒə'meɪkə] n Jamaica.

jam-packed [dʒæm'pækt] adj fam (with people) atestado,-a; (with things) atiborrado,-a.

jangle [ˈdʒæŋgəl] vi tintinear.

janitor [ˈdʒænɪtə'] n portero m, conserje m.

January [ˈdʒænjʊərɪ] n enero m.

Japan [dʒə'pæn] n (el) Japón.

Japanese [dʒæpə'niːz] I adj japonés,-esa. II n (person) japonés,-esa m,f; (language) japonés m.

jar¹ [dʒɑː'] n (glass) tarro m; (earthenware) tinaja f; (jug) jarra f; GB fam to have a j., tomar una copa.

jar² [dʒɑː'] vi (sounds) chirriar; (appearance) chocar; (colours) desentonar; fig **to j. on one's nerves**, ponerle a uno los nervios de punta.

jargon [ˈdʒɑːgən] n jerga f, argot m.

jasmin(e) [ˈdʒæzmɪn] n jazmín m.

jaundice [ˈdʒɔːndɪs] n ictericia f.

jaundiced [ˈdʒɔːndɪst] adj Med ictérico, -a; fig (bitter) amargado,-a.

jaunt [dʒɔːnt] n (walk) paseo m; (trip) excursión f.

jaunty [ˈdʒɔːntɪ] adj (jauntier, jauntiest) (sprightly) garboso,-a; (lively) vivaz.

javelin [ˈdʒævəlɪn] n jabalina f.

jaw [dʒɔː] I n mandíbula f. II vi fam estar de palique.

jay [dʒeɪ] n Orn arrendajo m (común).

jaywalker [ˈdʒeɪwɔːkə'] n peatón m imprudente.

jazz [dʒæz] n jazz m. ◆**jazz up** alegrar; (*premises*) arreglar.

jazzy ['dʒæzɪ] *adj* (**jazzier, jazziest**) *fam* (*showy*) llamativo,-a; (*brightly coloured*) de colores chillones.

jealous ['dʒeləs] *adj* celoso,-a; (*envious*) envidioso,-a; **to b. of ...**, tener celos de ...

jealousy ['dʒeləsɪ] *n* celos *mpl*; (*envy*) envidia *f*.

jeans [dʒiːnz] *npl* vaqueros *mpl*, tejanos *mpl*.

jeep [dʒiːp] *n* jeep *m*, todo terreno *m inv*.

jeer [dʒɪəʳ] I *n* (*boo*) abucheo *m*; (*mocking*) mofa *f*. II *vi* (*boo*) abuchear; (*mock*) burlarse.

jeering ['dʒɪərɪŋ] *adj* burlón,-ona.

Jehovah [dʒɪ'həʊvə] *n* J.'s Witness, testigo *mf* de Jehová.

jelly ['dʒelɪ] *n* gelatina *f*.

jellyfish ['dʒelɪfɪʃ] *n* medusa *f*.

jeopardize ['dʒepədaɪz] *vtr* poner en peligro; (*agreement etc*) comprometer.

jeopardy ['dʒepədɪ] *n* riesgo *m*, peligro *m*.

jerk [dʒɜːk] I *n* 1 (*jolt*) sacudida *f*; (*pull*) tirón *m*. 2 *pej* (*idiot*) imbécil *mf*. II *vtr* (*shake*) sacudir; (*pull*) dar un tirón a. III *vi* (*move suddenly*) dar una sacudida; **the car jerked forward**, el coche avanzaba a tirones.

jerkin ['dʒɜːkɪn] *n* chaleco *m*.

jersey ['dʒɜːzɪ] *n* jersey *m*, suéter *m*.

jest [dʒest] I *n* broma *f*. II *vi* bromear.

Jesuit ['dʒezjʊɪt] *adj & n* jesuita (*m*).

Jesus ['dʒiːzəs] *n* Jesús *m*; **J. Christ**, Jesucristo *m*.

jet[1] [dʒet] I *n* 1 (*stream of water*) chorro *m*. 2 (*spout*) surtidor *m*. 3 *Av* reactor *m*; **j. engine**, reactor *m*; **j. lag**, cansancio debido al desfase horario. II *vi fam* volar.

jet[2] [dʒet] *n* **j. black**, negro,-a como el azabache.

jet-set ['dʒetset] *n* **the j.-s.**, la alta sociedad, la jet.

jettison ['dʒetɪsən] *vtr* echar al mar; *fig* deshacerse de; (*project etc*) abandonar.

jetty ['dʒetɪ] *n* muelle *m*, malecón *m*.

Jew [dʒuː] *n* judío,-a *mf*.

jewel ['dʒuːəl] *n* joya *f*; (*stone*) piedra preciosa; (*in watch*) rubí *m*; *fig* (*person*) joya *f*.

jeweller, jeweler ['dʒuːələʳ] *n* joyero,-a *m,f*; **j.'s (shop)**, joyería *f*.

jewellery, jewelry ['dʒuːəlrɪ] *n* joyas *fpl*, alhajas *fpl*.

Jewess ['dʒuːɪs] *n* judía *f*.

Jewish ['dʒuːɪʃ] *adj* judío,-a.

jibe [dʒaɪb] *n & vi* = **gibe**.

jiffy ['dʒɪfɪ] *n fam* momento *m*; **in a j.**, en un santiamén; **just a j.!**, ¡un momento!

jig [dʒɪg] *n Mus* giga *f*.

jigsaw ['dʒɪgsɔː] *n* (*puzzle*) rompecabezas *m inv*.

jilt [dʒɪlt] *vtr fam* dejar plantado,-a.

jingle ['dʒɪŋgəl] I *n Rad TV* canción *f*

que acompaña un anuncio. II *vi* tintinear.

jingoistic [dʒɪŋgəʊ'ɪstɪk] *adj* patriotero, -a.

jinx [dʒɪŋks] I *n* (*person*) gafe *mf*. II *vtr* gafar.

jitters ['dʒɪtəz] *npl fam* **to get the j.**, tener canguelo.

jive [dʒaɪv] I *n* swing *m*. II *vi* bailar el swing.

job [dʒɒb] *n* 1 trabajo *m*; (*task*) tarea *f*; **to give sth up as a bad j.**, darse por vencido,-a; *fam* **just the j.!**, ¡me viene de perlas! 2 (*occupation*) (puesto *m* de) trabajo *m*, empleo *m*; (*trade*) oficio *m*; *GB fam* **jobs for the boys**, enchufismo *m*; **j. centre**, oficina *f* de empleo; **j. hunting**, búsqueda *f* de empleo; **j. sharing**, trabajo compartido a tiempo parcial. 3 *fam* **we had a j. to ...**, nos costó (trabajo) .... 4 (*duty*) deber *m*. 5 *fam* **it's a good j. that ...**, menos mal que ....

jobless ['dʒɒblɪs] *adj* parado,-a.

jockey ['dʒɒkɪ] I *n* jinete *m*, jockey *m*. II *vi* **to j. for position**, luchar para conseguir una posición aventajada.

jocular ['dʒɒkjʊləʳ] *adj* jocoso,-a.

jog [dʒɒg] I *n* trote *m*. II *vtr* empujar; *fig* (*memory*) refrescar. III *vi Sport* hacer footing; *fig* **to j. along**, (*progress slowly*) avanzar poco a poco; (*manage*) ir tirando.

jogging ['dʒɒgɪŋ] *n* footing *m*.

join [dʒɔɪn] I *vtr* 1 juntar; **to j. forces with sb**, unir fuerzas con algn. 2 (*road*) empalmar con; (*river*) desembocar en. 3 (*meet*) reunirse con. 4 (*group*) unirse a; (*institution*) entrar; (*army*) alistarse a. 5 (*party*) afiliarse a; (*club*) hacerse socio,-a de. II *vi* 1 unirse. 2 (*roads*) empalmar; (*rivers*) confluir. 3 (*become a member of political party*) afiliarse; (*become member of club*) hacerse socio,-a. III *n* juntura *f*. ◆**join in** I *vi* participar, tomar parte; (*debate*) intervenir. II *vtr* participar en, tomar parte en. ◆**join up** I *vi* *Mil* alistarse. II *vi* (*of roads*) unirse; *Mil* alistarse.

joiner ['dʒɔɪnəʳ] *n GB* carpintero,-a *m,f*.

joinery ['dʒɔɪnərɪ] *n* carpintería *f*.

joint [dʒɔɪnt] *n* 1 juntura *f*, unión *f*; *Tech Anat* articulación *f*; **out of j.**, dislocado,-a. 2 *Culin* corte *m* de carne para asar; (*once roasted*) asado *m*. 3 *sl* (*nightclub etc*) garito *m*. 4 *sl* (*drug*) porro *m*. II *adj* colectivo,-a; (*bank*) **account**, cuenta conjunta; **j. venture**, empresa conjunta. ◆**jointly** *adv* conjuntamente, en común.

joist [dʒɔɪst] *n* vigueta *f*.

joke [dʒəʊk] I *n* chiste *m*; (*prank*) broma *f*; **to play a j. on sb**, gastarle una broma a algn; **to tell a j.**, contar un chiste; *fam* (*person, thing*) hazmerreír *m*, payaso,-a *m,f*. II *vi* estar de broma; **you must be joking!**, ¡no hablarás en serio!

joker ['dʒəʊkə'] n 1 bromista mf. 2 Cards comodín m.

jolly ['dʒɒlɪ] I adj (jollier, jolliest) alegre. II adv fam (very) muy; **she played j. well**, jugó muy bien.

jolt [dʒəʊlt] I n 1 sacudida f; (pull) tirón m. 2 fig (fright) susto m. II vi moverse a sacudidas. III vtr sacudir.

Jordan ['dʒɔːdən] n 1 (river) Jordán m. 2 (country) Jordania.

joss-stick ['dʒɒstɪk] n varita f de incienso.

jostle ['dʒɒsəl] I vi dar empujones. II vtr dar empujones a.

jot [dʒɒt] n jota f, pizca f; **not a j.**, ni jota. ◆**jot down** vtr apuntar.

jotter ['dʒɒtə'] n GB bloc m.

journal ['dʒɜːnəl] n 1 revista f. 2 (diary) diario m. 3 (newspaper) periódico m.

journalism ['dʒɜːnəlɪzəm] n periodismo m.

journalist ['dʒɜːnəlɪst] n periodista mf.

journey ['dʒɜːnɪ] I n viaje m; (distance) trayecto m. II vi fml viajar.

jovial ['dʒəʊvɪəl] adj jovial.

jowl [dʒaʊl] n quijada f.

joy [dʒɔɪ] n alegría f; (pleasure) placer m.

joyful ['dʒɔɪfʊl] adj alegre, contento,-a.

joyous ['dʒɔɪəs] adj lit alegre.

joyride ['dʒɔɪraɪd] n fam paseo m en un coche robado.

joystick ['dʒɔɪstɪk] n Av palanca f de mando; (of video game) joystick m.

JP [dʒeɪ'piː] abbr of Justice of the Peace.

Jr abbr of junior.

jubilant ['dʒuːbɪlənt] adj jubiloso,-a.

jubilation [dʒuːbɪ'leɪʃən] n júbilo m.

jubilee ['dʒuːbɪliː] n festejos mpl; **golden j.**, quincuagésimo aniversario.

judge [dʒʌdʒ] I n juez mf, jueza f; (in competition) jurado m. II vtr 1 Jur juzgar. 2 (estimate) considerar. 3 (competition) actuar de juez de. 4 (assess) juzgar. III vi juzgar; **judging from what you say**, a juzgar por lo que dices.

judg(e)ment ['dʒʌdʒmənt] n 1 Jur sentencia f, fallo m; **to pass j.**, dictar sentencia. 2 (opinion) juicio m; **to pass j.**, opinar (**on**, sobre); **to reserve j.**, no opinar (**on**, sobre). 3 (ability) buen juicio m. 4 (trial) juicio m.

judicial [dʒuː'dɪʃəl] adj judicial.

judiciary [dʒuː'dɪʃɪərɪ] n magistratura f.

judicious [dʒuː'dɪʃəs] adj fml juicioso,-a.

judo ['dʒuːdəʊ] n judo m.

jug [dʒʌg] n GB jarra f; **milk j.**, jarra de leche.

juggernaut ['dʒʌgənɔːt] n GB camión pesado.

juggle ['dʒʌgəl] vi (perform) hacer juegos malabares (**with**, con); fig (responsibilities) ajustar.

juggler ['dʒʌglə'] n malabarista mf.

juice [dʒuːs] n jugo m; (of citrus fruits)

zumo m.

juicy ['dʒuːsɪ] adj (juicier, juiciest) 1 jugoso,-a. 2 fam fig picante.

jukebox ['dʒuːkbɒks] n rocola f.

July [dʒuː'laɪ, dʒə'laɪ] n julio m.

jumble ['dʒʌmbəl] I n revoltijo m; **j. sale**, mercadillo m de caridad. II vtr revolver.

jumbo ['dʒʌmbəʊ] *j.* (jet), jumbo m.

jump [dʒʌmp] I n salto m; (sudden increase) subida repentina; **j. leads**, cables mpl de emergencia; **j. suit**, mono m. II vi 1 saltar, dar un salto; fig **to j. to conclusions**, sacar conclusiones precipitadas. 2 fig (start) sobresaltarse. 3 (increase) aumentar de golpe. III vtr saltar; fam fig **to j. the gun**, precipitarse; GB **to j. the queue**, colarse; **to j. the lights**, saltarse el semáforo. ◆**jump at** vtr aceptar sin pensarlo.

jumper ['dʒʌmpə'] n 1 GB (sweater) jersey m. 2 US (dress) pichi m, falda f con peto. 3 US Aut **j. cables**, cables mpl de emergencia.

jumpy ['dʒʌmpɪ] adj (jumpier, jumpiest) fam nervioso,-a.

junction ['dʒʌŋkʃən] n (of roads) cruce m; Rail Elec empalme m.

juncture ['dʒʌŋktʃə'] n fml **at this j.**, en esta coyuntura.

June [dʒuːn] n junio m.

jungle ['dʒʌŋgəl] n jungla f, selva f; fig laberinto m; **the concrete j.**, la jungla de asfalto.

junior ['dʒuːnjə'] I adj 1 (son of) hijo; **David Hughes j.**, David Hughes hijo. 2 **j. school**, escuela f de EGB (Enseñanza General Básica); **j. team**, equipo m juvenil. 3 (lower in rank) subalterno,-a. II n 1 (person of lower rank) subalterno,-a m,f. 2 (younger person) menor mf.

junk [dʒʌŋk] n 1 fam trastos mpl; **j. food**, comida basura; **j. mail**, propaganda f (por correo); **j. shop**, tienda f de segunda mano. 2 (boat) junco m.

junkie ['dʒʌŋkɪ] n sl yonqui mf.

junta ['dʒʌntə, 'dʒʊntə, US 'hʊntə] n junta f militar.

jurisdiction [dʒʊərɪs'dɪkʃən] n fml jurisdicción f.

juror ['dʒʊərə'] n jurado,-a m,f.

jury ['dʒʊərɪ] n jurado m.

just [dʒʌst] I adj (fair) justo,-a; fml (well-founded) justificado,-a. II adv 1 **he had j. arrived**, acababa de llegar. 2 (at this very moment) ahora mismo, en este momento; **he was j. leaving when Rosa arrived**, estaba a punto de salir cuando llegó Rosa; **I'm j. coming!**, ¡ya voy!; **j. as ..., cuando ...**, justo al...; **j. as I thought**, me lo figuraba. 3 (only) solamente; **j. in case**, por si acaso; **j. a minute!**, ¡un momento! 4 (barely) por poco; **I only j. caught the bus**, cogí el autobús por los pelos; **j. about**, casi; **j. enough**, justo lo suficiente. **5** (*emphatic*) it's j. **fantastic!**, ¡es sencillamente fantástico!; **you'll j. have to wait,** tendrás que esperar. **6** (*exactly*) exactamente, justo; **¡precisamente!** **7** (*equally*) j. **as fast as,** tan rápido como.

justice ['dʒʌstɪs] *n* **1** justicia *f*; **he was brought to j.,** lo llevaron ante los tribunales; **you didn't do yourself j.,** no diste lo mejor de ti. **2** *US* (*judge*) juez *mf*; *GB* **J. of the Peace,** juez de paz.

justifiable ['dʒʌstɪfaɪəbəl] *adj* justificable.

justification [dʒʌstɪfɪ'keɪʃən] *n* justifica-

ción *f*.

justified ['dʒʌstɪfaɪd] *adj* **to be j. in doing sth,** tener razón en hacer algo.

justify ['dʒʌstɪfaɪ] *vtr* justificar.

jut [dʒʌt] *vi* sobresalir; **to j. out over,** proyectarse sobre.

juvenile ['dʒuːvənaɪl] **I** *adj* **1** juvenil; **j. court,** tribunal *m* de menores; **j. delinquent,** delincuente *mf* juvenil. **2** (*immature*) infantil. **II** *n* menor *mf*, joven *mf*.

juxtapose [dʒʌkstə'pəuz] *vtr* yuxtaponer.

K

K, k [keɪ] *n* (*the letter*) K, k *f*.

kaleidoscope [kə'laɪdəskəup] *n* caleidoscopio *m*.

Kampuchea [kæmpu'tʃɪə] *n* Kampuchea.

kangaroo [kæŋgə'ruː] *n* canguro *m*.

karat ['kærət] *n US* quilate *m*.

karate [kə'rɑːtɪ] *n* kárate *m*.

kebab [kə'bæb] *n* *Culin* pincho moruno, brocheta *f*.

keel [kiːl] *n* quilla *f*; *fig* **to be on an even k.,** estar en calma. ◆**keel over** *vi* *fam* desmayarse.

keen [kiːn] *adj* **1** (*eager*) entusiasta. **2** (*intense*) profundo,-a. **3** (*mind, senses*) agudo,-a; (*look*) penetrante; (*blade*) afilado,-a; (*competition*) fuerte.

keep [kiːp] **I** *n* **1** **to earn one's k.,** ganarse el pan. **2** (*tower*) torreón *m*. **3** *fam* **for keeps,** para siempre.

II *vtr* (*pt* & *pp* **kept**) **1** guardar; **to k. one's room tidy,** mantener su cuarto limpio; **to k. sb informed,** tener a algn al corriente; **to k. sth in mind,** tener en cuenta. **2** (*not give back*) quedarse con. **3** (*detain*) detener; **to k. sb waiting,** hacer esperar a algn. **4** (*maintain*) mantener; (*animals*) criar. **5** (*the law*) observar; (*a promise*) cumplir. **6** (*a secret*) guardar. **7** (*diary, accounts*) llevar. **8** (*prevent*) **to k. sb from doing sth,** impedir a algn hacer algo. **9** (*own, manage*) tener; (*shop, hotel*) llevar. **10** (*stock*) tener.

III *vi* **1** (*remain*) seguir; **k. still!,** ¡estate quieto,-a!; **to k. fit,** mantenerse en forma; **to k. going,** seguir adelante; **to k. in touch,** no perder el contacto. **2** (*do frequently*) no dejar de; **she keeps forgetting her keys,** siempre se olvida las llaves. **3** (*food*) conservar.

◆**keep at** *vi* perseverar en. ◆**keep away** **I** *vtr* mantener a distancia. **II** *vi* mantenerse a distancia. ◆**keep back** *vtr* (*information*) ocultar, callar; (*money etc*) retener. ◆**keep down** *vtr* **to k. prices down,** mantener los precios bajos. ◆**keep off** *vtr* **k. off the grass,** prohibi-

do pisar la hierba. ◆**keep on** *vtr* **1** (*clothes, etc*) no quitarse; **to k. an eye on sth/sb,** vigilar algo/a algn. **2** (*continue to employ*) no despedir a. **II** *vi* (*continue to do*) seguir. ◆**keep out** *vtr* no dejar pasar. **II** *vi* no entrar; **k. out!,** ¡prohibida la entrada! ◆**keep to** *vtr* (*subject*) limitarse a; **to k. to one's room,** quedarse en el cuarto; **k. to the point!,** ¡cíñete a la cuestión!; **to k. to the left,** circular por la izquierda. ◆**keep up** *vtr* **1** mantener; **to k. up appearances,** guardar las apariencias. **2** **k. it up!,** ¡sigue así! **3** (*prevent from sleeping*) mantener despierto,-a. ◆**keep up with** *vtr* **to k. up with the times,** estar al día.

keeper ['kiːpər] *n* (*in zoo*) guarda *mf*; (*in record office*) archivero,-a *m,f*; (*in museum*) conservador,-a *m,f*.

keeping ['kiːpɪŋ] *n* **1** (*care*) cuidado *m*. **2 in k. with,** en armonía con; **out of k. with,** en desacuerdo con.

keepsake ['kiːpseɪk] *n* recuerdo *m*.

keg [keg] *n* barril *m*.

kennel ['kenəl] *n* caseta *f* para perros; **kennels,** hotel *m sing* de perros.

Kenya ['kenjə, 'kiːnjə] *n* Kenia.

Kenyan ['kenjən, 'kiːnjən] *adj* & *n* keniano,-a (*m,f*).

kept [kept] *pt* & *pp* → **keep**.

kerb [kɜːb] *n* bordillo *m*.

kernel ['kɜːnəl] *n* (*of fruit, nut*) pepita *f*; (*of wheat*) grano *m*; *fig* meollo *m*.

kerosene, kerosine ['kerəsiːn] *n US* queroseno *m*.

ketchup ['ketʃəp] *n* ketchup *m*, salsa *f* de tomate.

kettle ['ketəl] *n* hervidor *m*; **that's a different k. of fish,** eso es harina de otro costal.

key [kiː] **I** *n* **1** (*for lock*) llave *f*; **k. ring,** llavero *m*. **2** (*to code*) clave *f*. **3** (*of piano, typewriter*) tecla *f*. **4** *Mus* tono *m*. **II** *adj* clave. **III** *vtr* *Comput* teclear. ◆**key in** *vtr* *Comput* introducir.

keyboard ['kiːbɔːd] *n* teclado *m*.

keyed up [ki:d'ʌp] *adj* nervioso,-a.

keyhole ['ki:həʊl] *n* ojo *m* de la cerradura.

keynote ['ki:nəʊt] *n* Mus tónica *f*; *fig* nota *f* dominante.

kg *abbr of* **kilogram(s)**, kilogramo(s) *m* (*pl*), kg.

khaki ['ka:kı] *adj & n* caqui (*m*).

kick [kık] I *n* 1 (*from person*) patada *f*, puntapié *m*; (*from horse etc*) coz *f*; (*from gun*) culatazo *m*. 2 *fam* I get a k. out of it, eso me encanta; to do sth for kicks, hacer algo por gusto. II *vi* (*animal*) cocear; (*person*) dar patadas; (*gun*) dar un culatazo. III *vtr* dar un puntapié a. ◆**kick off** *vi fam* empezar; *Ftb* sacar. ◆**kick out** *vtr* echar a patadas. ◆**kick up** *vtr fam* (*fuss*) armar.

kick-off ['kıkɒf] *n* Ftb saque *m* inicial.

kid¹ [kıd] *n* 1 *Zool* cabrito *m*; *fig* to handle sb with k. gloves, tratar a algn con guante blanco. 2 *fam* niño,-a *m,f*, chiquillo,-a *m,f*; the kids, los críos.

kid² [kıd] I *vi fam* tomar el pelo; no kidding!, ¡va en serio! II *vtr* tomar el pelo a; to k. oneself, (*fool*) hacerse ilusiones.

kidnap ['kıdnæp] *vtr* secuestrar.

kidnapper ['kıdnæpər] *n* secuestrador,-a *m,f*.

kidnapping ['kıdnæpıŋ] *n* secuestro *m*.

kidney ['kıdnı] *n* riñón *m*.

kill [kıl] *vtr* matar; *fig* to k. time, pasar el rato; *fam* my feet are killing me, ¡cómo me duelen los pies! ◆**kill off** *vtr* exterminar.

killer ['kılər] *n* asesino,-a *m,f*; k. whale, orca *f*.

killing ['kılıŋ] *n* asesinato *m*; *fig* to make a k., forrarse de dinero.

killjoy ['kıldʒɔı] *n* aguafiestas *mf inv*.

kiln [kıln] *n* horno *m*.

kilo ['ki:ləʊ] *n* kilo *m*.

kilogram(me) ['kıləʊgræm] *n* kilogramo *m*.

kilometre, US **kilometer** [kı'lɒmıtər] *n* kilómetro *m*.

kilowatt ['kıləʊwɒt] *n* kilovatio *m*.

kilt [kılt] *n* falda escocesa, kilt *m*.

kin [kın] *n* familiares *mpl*, parientes *mpl*.

kind¹ [kaınd] I *n* tipo *m*, clase *f*; they are two of a k., son tal para cual; in k., (*payment*) en especie; (*treatment*) con la misma moneda. II *adv* fam k. of, en cierta manera.

kind² [kaınd] *adj* amable, simpático,-a; *fml* would you be so k. as to ...?, ¿me haría usted el favor de ...?

kindergarten ['kındəga:tən] *n* jardín *m* de infancia.

kind-hearted [kaınd'ha:tıd] *adj* bondadoso,-a.

kindle ['kındəl] *vtr* encender.

kindly ['kaındlı] I *adj* (**kindlier, kindliest**)

amable, bondadoso,-a. II *adv* fml (*please*) por favor; k. remit a cheque, sírvase enviar cheque; to look k. on, aprobar.

kindness ['kaındnıs] *n* bondad *f*, amabilidad *f*.

kindred ['kındrıd] *adj* k. spirits, almas gemelas.

kinetic [kı'netık] *adj* cinético,-a.

king [kıŋ] *n* rey *m*; (*draughts*) dama *f*.

kingdom ['kıŋdəm] *n* reino *m*.

kingfisher ['kıŋfıʃər] *n* Orn martín *m* pescador.

king-size ['kıŋsaız] *adj* extralargo,-a.

kink [kıŋk] *n* (*in rope*) coca *f*; (*in hair*) rizo *m*.

kinky ['kıŋkı] *adj* (**kinkier, kinkiest**) fam raro,-a; (*sexually*) pervertido,-a.

kiosk ['ki:ɒsk] *n* quiosco *m*.

kiss [kıs] I *n* beso *m*. II *vtr* besar. III *vi* besarse.

kit [kıt] *n* 1 (*gear*) equipo *m*; *Mil* avíos *mpl*. 2 (*clothing*) ropa *f*. 3 (*toy model*) maqueta *f*. ◆**kit out** *vtr* equipar.

kitchen ['kıtʃın] *n* cocina *f*; k. sink, fregadero *m*.

kite [kaıt] *n* 1 (*toy*) cometa *f*. 2 Orn milano *m*.

kitten ['kıtən] *n* gatito,-a *m,f*.

kitty ['kıtı] *n* (*money*) fondo *m* común; Cards bote *m*.

kiwi ['ki:wi:] *n* Bot Orn kiwi *m*.

km (*pl km or* kms) *abbr of* kilometre(s), km.

knack [næk] *n* to get the k. of doing sth, cogerle el truquillo a algo.

knapsack ['næpsæk] *n* mochila *f*.

knead [ni:d] *vtr* dar masaje a; (*bread etc*) amasar.

knee [ni:] I *n* rodilla *f*. II *vtr* dar un rodillazo a.

kneecap ['ni:kæp] I *n* rótula *f*. II *vtr* romper la rótula a.

kneel [ni:l] *vi* (*pt & pp* knelt) to k. (down), arrodillarse.

knell [nel] *n* lit toque *m* de difuntos.

knelt [nelt] *pt & pp* → **kneel**.

knew [nju:] *pt* → **know**.

knickers ['nıkəz] *npl* bragas *fpl*.

knife [naıf] I *n* (*pl* knives [naıvz]) cuchillo *m*. II *vtr* apuñalar, dar una puñalada a.

knight [naıt] I *n* Hist caballero *m*; Chess caballo *m*. II *vtr* armar caballero.

knighthood ['naıthʊd] *n* (*rank*) título *m* de caballero.

knit [nıt] I *vtr* (*pt & pp* knit) 1 tejer. 2 (*join*) juntar (**together**, -); *fig* to k. one's brow, fruncir el ceño. II *vi* 1 tejer, hacer punto. 2 (*bone*) soldarse.

knitting ['nıtıŋ] *n* punto *m*; k. machine, máquina *f* de tejer; k. needle, aguja *f* de tejer.

knit-wear ['nıtweər] *n* géneros *mpl* de punto.

knob [nɒb] *n* 1 (*of stick*) puño *m*; (*of*

drawer) tirador *m*; *(button)* botón *m*. **2** *(small portion)* trozo *m*.

knock [nɒk] **I** *n* golpe *m*; *fig* revés *m*. **II** *vtr* **1** golpear. **2** *fam (criticize)* criticar. **III** *vi* chocar *(against, into,* contra); *(at door)* llamar *(at,* a). ◆**knock down** *vtr* **1** *(demolish)* derribar. **2** *Aut* atropellar. **3** *(price)* rebajar. ◆**knock off** *vtr* **1** tirar. **2** *fam (steal)* birlar. **3** *sl (kill)* liquidar. *vi fam* **they k. off at five,** se piran a las cinco. ◆**knock out** *vtr* **1** *(make unconscious)* dejar sin conocimiento; *Box* poner fuera de combate, derrotar por K.O. **2** *(surprise)* dejar pasmado,-a. ◆**knock over** *vtr (cup)* volcar; *(with car)* atropellar.

knocker ['nɒkər] *n (on door)* aldaba *f*.

knock-kneed [nɒk'niːd] *adj* patizambo,-a.

knockout ['nɒkaʊt] *n* **1** *Box* K.O. *m*, knock-out *m*. **2** *fam* maravilla *f*.

knot [nɒt] **I** *n* nudo *m*; *(group)* grupo *m*. **II** *vtr* anudar.

knotty ['nɒtɪ] *adj (knottier, knottiest)* nudoso,-a; *fig* **a k. problem,** un problema espinoso.

know [nəʊ] *vtr & vi (pt knew; pp known)* **1** saber; **as far as I k.,** que yo sepa; **she knows how to ski,** sabe esquiar; **to get to k. sth,** enterarse de algo; **to let sb k.,**

avisar al algn. **2** *(be acquainted with)* conocer; **we got to k. each other at the party,** nos conocimos en la fiesta.

know-all ['nəʊɔːl] *n fam* sabelotodo *mf*.

know-how ['nəʊhaʊw] *n fam* conocimiento práctico.

knowing ['nəʊɪŋ] *adj (deliberate)* deliberado,-a; *(shrewd)* una sonrisa de complicidad. ◆**knowingly** *adv (shrewd)* a sabiendas; *(deliberately)* deliberadamente.

knowledge ['nɒlɪdʒ] *n* **1** conocimiento *m*; **without my k.,** sin saberlo yo. **2** *(learning)* conocimientos *mpl*.

knowledgeable ['nɒlɪdʒəbəl] *adj* erudito,-a; **k. about,** muy entendido,-a en.

known [nəʊn] *adj* conocido,-a.

knuckle ['nʌkəl] *n Anat* nudillo *m*; *Culin* hueso *m*. ◆**knuckle down** *vi fam* ponerse a trabajar en serio.

KO [keɪˈəʊ] *fam abbr of* **knockout,** K.O. *m*.

Koran [kɔːˈrɑːn] *n* Corán *m*.

Korea [kəˈrɪə] *n* Corea.

Korean [kəˈrɪən] *adj & n* coreano,-a *(m,f)*.

Kurd [kɜːd] *n* curdo,-a *m,f*.

Kuwait [kʊˈweɪt] *n* Kuwait.

L

L, l [el] *n (the letter)* L, l *f*.

lab [læb] *n fam abbr of* **laboratory.**

label ['leɪbəl] **I** *n* etiqueta *f*; **record l.,** ≈ casa discográfica. **II** *vtr* poner etiqueta a.

laboratory [ləˈbɒrətərɪ, *US* ˈlæbrətɔːrɪ] *n* laboratorio *m*.

laborious [ləˈbɔːrɪəs] *adj* penoso,-a.

labour ['leɪbər] **I** *n* **1** *(work)* trabajo *m*; *(task)* tarea *f*. **2** *(workforce)* mano *f* de obra. **3 labours,** esfuerzos *mpl*. **4** *L.* **(Party),** el Partido Laborista. **5** *(childbirth)* parto *m*; **to be in l.,** estar de parto. **II** *adj* laboral. **III** *vi* **1** *(work)* trabajar *(duro)*. **2** *(move with difficulty)* avanzar penosamente. **IV** *vtr (stress, linger on)* machacar; *(a point)* insistir en.

laboured ['leɪbəd] *adj (breathing)* fatigoso,-a; *(style)* forzado,-a.

labourer ['leɪbərər] *n* peón *m*; **farm l.,** peón *m* agrícola.

labour-saving ['leɪbəseɪvɪŋ] *adj* **l.-s. devices,** electrodomésticos *mpl*.

labyrinth ['læbərɪnθ] *n* laberinto *m*.

lace [leɪs] **I** *n* **1** *(fabric)* encaje *m*. **2** **laces,** cordones *mpl*. **II** *vtr* **1** *(shoes)* atarse los cordones. **2** *(spirits to)* echar licor *(with,* a). ◆**lace up** *vtr* atar con cordones.

lacerate ['læsəreɪt] *vtr* lacerar.

lack [læk] **I** *n* falta *f*, escasez *f*; **for l. of,** por falta de. **II** *vtr* carecer de. **III** *vi* carecer *(in,* de).

lackadaisical [lækəˈdeɪzɪkəl] *adj (lazy)* perezoso,-a; *(indifferent)* indiferente.

lacklustre, *US* **lackluster** ['læklʌstər] *adj (eyes)* apagado,-a; *(performance)* anodino,-a.

laconic [ləˈkɒnɪk] *adj* lacónico,-a.

lacquer ['lækər] **I** *n* laca *f*. **II** *vtr (hair)* poner laca en.

lad [læd] *n fam* chaval *m*, muchacho *m*; *fam* **the lads,** los amigotes; *(stable)* l., mozo *m* de cuadra.

ladder ['lædər] **I** *n* **1** escalera *f* (de mano); *(in stocking)* carrera *f*. **2** *(in stocking)* carrera *f*. **II** *vtr* **I've laddered my stocking,** me he hecho una carrera en las medias.

laden ['leɪdən] *adj* cargado,-a *(with,* de).

ladle ['leɪdəl] *n* cucharón *n*.

lady ['leɪdɪ] *n* señora *f*; *Pol* **First L.,** primera dama; *(WC)* **'Ladies',** 'Señoras'; **ladies and gentlemen!** ¡señoras y señores!; **L. Brown,** Lady Brown.

ladybird ['leɪdɪbɜːd], *US Canada* **ladybug** ['leɪdɪbʌg] *n* mariquita *f*.

lady-in-waiting [leɪdɪnˈweɪtɪŋ] *n* dama *f* de honor.

ladylike ['leɪdɪlaɪk] *adj* elegante.

ladyship ['leɪdɪʃɪp] *n* **Her L., Your L.,**

su señoría.

lag ['læg] **I** n time l., demora f. **II** vi to l. (behind), quedarse atrás, retrasarse. **III** vtr Tech revestir.

lager ['lɑːgər] n cerveza rubia.

lagoon [lə'guːn] n laguna f.

laid [leɪd] pt & pp **lay**.

laid-back [leɪd'bæk] adj fam tranquilo,-a.

lain [leɪn] pp of **lie**.

lair [leər] n guarida f.

lake [leɪk] n lago m.

lamb [læm] n cordero m; l. chop, chuleta f de cordero; l.'s wool, lana f de cordero.

lame [leɪm] adj cojo,-a. 2 fig (excuse) poco convincente; (argument) flojo,-a.

lament [lə'ment] **I** n Mus elegía f. **II** vtr (death) llorar, lamentar. **III** vi llorar (for, a), lamentarse (over, de).

lamentable ['læmɪntəbəl] adj lamentable.

laminated ['læmɪneɪtɪd] adj (metal) laminado,-a; (glass) inastillable; (paper) plastificado,-a.

lamp [læmp] n lámpara f; Aut faro m.

lampoon [læm'puːn] **I** n sátira f. **II** vtr satirizar.

lamp-post ['læmppəʊst] n farola f.

lampshade ['læmpʃeɪd] n pantalla f.

lance [lɑːns] **I** n lanza f; GB Mil l. corporal, cabo interino; Med lanceta f. **II** vtr Med abrir con lanceta.

land [lænd] **I** n tierra f; (soil) suelo m; by l., por tierra; farm l., tierras fpl de cultivo. 2 (country) país m. 3 (property) tierras fpl; (estate) finca f; piece of l., terreno m. **II** vtr 1 (plane) hacer aterrizar. 2 (disembark) desembarcar. 3 Fishing pescar. 4 fam (obtain) conseguir; (contract) ganar. 5 fam **she got landed with the responsibility**, tuvo que cargar con la responsabilidad. 6 fam (blow) asestar. **III** vi 1 (plane) aterrizar. 2 (disembark) desembarcar. 3 (after falling) caer (on, sobre). ◆**land up** vi fam ir a parar.

landing ['lændɪŋ] n 1 (of staircase) rellano m. 2 (of plane) aterrizaje m; l. strip, pista f de aterrizaje. 3 (of passengers) desembarco m; l. stage, desembarcadero m.

landlady ['lændleɪdɪ] n (of flat) dueña f, propietaria f; (of boarding house) patrona f; (of pub) dueña.

landlord ['lændlɔːd] n (of flat) dueño m, propietario m; (of pub) patrón m, dueño.

landmark ['lændmɑːk] n 1 señal f, marca f; (well-known place) lugar muy conocido. 2 fig hito m.

landowner ['lændəʊnər] n terrateniente mf.

landscape ['lændskeɪp] **I** n paisaje m. **II** vtr ajardinar.

landslide ['lændslaɪd] n desprendimiento m de tierras; l. victory, victoria arrolladora.

lane [leɪn] n (in country) camino m; (in town) callejón m; (of motorway) carril m; Sport calle f; Naut ruta f.

language ['læŋgwɪdʒ] n 1 lenguaje m; bad l., palabrotas fpl. 2 (of a country) idioma m, lengua f; l. laboratory, laboratorio m de idiomas.

languid ['læŋgwɪd] adj lánguido,-a.

languish ['læŋgwɪʃ] vi languidecer; (project, plan etc) quedar abandonado,-a; (in prison) pudrirse.

lank [læŋk] adj (hair) lacio,-a.

lanky ['læŋkɪ] adj (lankier, lankiest) larguirucho,-a.

lantern ['læntən] n farol m.

lap¹ [læp] n Anat regazo m.

lap² [læp] n 1 (circuit) vuelta f; fig etapa f. **II** vtr (overtake) doblar.

lap³ [læp] **I** vtr (pt & pp **lapped**) (cat) beber a lengüetadas. **II** vi (waves) lamer, besar. ◆**lap up** vtr 1 (cat) beber a lengüetadas. 2 fig (wallow in) disfrutar con; (flattery) recibir con estusiasmo. 3 fig (believe) tragar.

lapel [lə'pel] n solapa f.

Lapland ['læplænd] n Laponia f.

lapse [læps] **I** n 1 (of time) lapso m. 2 (error) error m, desliz m; (of memory) fallo m. **II** vi 1 (time) pasar, transcurrir. 2 (expire) caducar. 3 (err) cometer un error; (fall back) caer (into, en). 4 Rel perder la fe.

larceny ['lɑːsənɪ] n GB latrocinio m; US hurto m.

larch [lɑːtʃ] n alerce m.

lard [lɑːd] n manteca f de cerdo.

larder ['lɑːdər] n despensa f.

large [lɑːdʒ] **I** adj grande; (amount) importante; (extensive) amplio,-a; by and l., por lo general. **II** n to be at l., andar suelto,-a; the public at l., el público en general. ◆**largely** adv (mainly) en gran parte; (chiefly) principalmente.

large-scale ['lɑːdʒskeɪl] adj (project, problem etc) de gran envergadura; (map) a gran escala.

lark¹ [lɑːk] n Orn alondra f.

lark² [lɑːk] n fam (joke) broma f; **what a l.!**, ¡qué risa! ◆**lark about, lark around** vi fam hacer el tonto.

larva ['lɑːvə] n larva f.

laryngitis [lærɪn'dʒaɪtɪs] n laringitis f.

larynx ['lærɪŋks] n Anat laringe f.

laser ['leɪzər] n láser m; l. printer, impresora f láser.

lash [læʃ] **I** n 1 (eyelash) pestaña f. 2 (blow with whip) latigazo m. **II** vtr 1 (beat) azotar. 2 (rain) caer con fuerza. 3 (tie) atar. ◆**lash out** vi 1 (with fists) repartir golpes a diestro y siniestro; (verbally) criticar (at, a). 2 fam (spend money) tirar la casa por la ventana.

lass [læs] n fam chavala f, muchacha f.

lasso [læ'suː] **I** n lazo m. **II** vtr coger con el lazo.

last [lɑːst] I adj (final) último,-a, final; fam the l. straw, el colmo. 2 (most recent) último,-a. 3 (past) pasado,-a; (previous) anterior; l. but one, penúltimo,-a; l. month, el mes pasado; l. night, anoche; the night before l., anteanoche. II adv l when I l. saw her, la última vez que la vi. 2 (at the end) en último lugar; (in race etc) último; at (long) l., por fin; l. but not least, el último en orden pero no en importancia. III n el último, la última. IV vi 1 (time) durar; (hold out) aguantar. 2 (be enough for) llegar, alcanzar. ◆lastly adv por último, finalmente.

last-ditch ['lɑːstdɪtʃ] adj (effort, attempt) último,-a y desesperado,-a.

lasting ['lɑːstɪŋ] adj duradero,-a.

last-minute ['lɑːstmɪnɪt] adj de última hora.

latch [lætʃ] n picaporte m, pestillo m.

late [leɪt] I adj 1 (not on time) tardío,-a; (hour) avanzado,-a; to be five minutes l., llegar con cinco minutos de retraso. 2 (far on in time) in l. autumn, a finales del otoño; in the l. afternoon, a última hora de la tarde; she's in her l. twenties, ronda los treinta. 3 (dead) difunto,-a. II adv (not on time) tarde; to arrive l., llegar tarde. 2 (far on in time) tarde; l. at night, a altas horas de la noche; l. in life, a una edad avanzada. 3 as l. as 1950, todavía en 1950; of l., últimamente. ◆lately adv últimamente, recientemente.

latecomer ['leɪtkʌmə'] n tardón,-ona m,f.

latent ['leɪtənt] adj latente. 2 (hidden) oculto,-a.

later ['leɪtə'] I adj (comp of late) 1 (subsequent) más tarde; in her l. novels, en sus novelas posteriores. 2 (more recent) más reciente. II adv (comp of late) más tarde, después; l. on, más adelante, más tarde.

lateral ['lætərəl] adj lateral.

latest ['leɪtɪst] I adj (superl of late) (most recent) último,-a, más reciente. II n l. lo último; have you heard the l.?, ¿te enteraste de lo último?; Friday at the l., el viernes a más tardar.

lathe [leɪð] n Tech torno m.

lather ['lɑːðə'] I n (of soap) espuma f; (horse's sweat) sudor m. II vtr (with soap) enjabonar.

Latin ['lætɪn] I adj & n latino,-a (m,f); L. America, América Latina, Latinoamérica f; L. American, latinoamericano,-a (m,f). II (language) latín m.

latitude ['lætɪtjuːd] n latitud f.

latrine [lə'triːn] n letrina f.

latter ['lætə'] adj 1 (last) último,-a. 2 (second of two) segundo,-a. II pron éste,-a; the former ... the l., aquél ... éste, aquél ... ésta.

lattice ['lætɪs] n enrejado m, rejilla f.

laudable ['lɔːdəbəl] adj loable.

laugh [lɑːf] I n risa f; (guffaw) carcajada f; for a l., para divertirse. II vi reír, reírse. ◆laugh at vi to l. at sb/sth, reírse de algn/algo. ◆laugh about vi to l. about sb/sth, reírse de algn/algo. ◆laugh off vtr tomar a risa.

laughable ['lɑːfəbəl] adj (situation, suggestion) ridículo,-a; (amount, offer) irrisorio,-a.

laughing-stock ['lɑːfɪŋstɒk] n hazmerreír m inv.

laughter ['lɑːftə'] n risa f.

launch [lɔːntʃ] I n (vessel) lancha f. 2 → launching. II vtr 1 (attack, rocket, new product) lanzar. 2 (ship) botar. 3 (film, play) estrenar. 4 (company) fundar. 5 fig (scheme) iniciar.

launching ['lɔːntʃɪŋ] n 1 (of rocket, new product) lanzamiento m. 2 (of ship) botadura f. 3 (of film, play) estreno m. 4 (of new company) fundación f.

launchpad ['lɔːntʃpæd] n plataforma f de lanzamiento.

launder ['lɔːndə'] vtr lavar y planchar; fig (money) blanquear.

launderette ['lɔːndə'ret], US **Laundromat**® ['lɔːndrəmæt] n lavandería automática.

laundry ['lɔːndrɪ] n 1 (place) lavandería f. 2 (dirty clothes) ropa sucia; to do the l., lavar la ropa.

laurel ['lɒrəl] n laurel m; fam fig to rest on one's laurels, dormirse en los laureles.

lava ['lɑːvə] n lava f.

lavatory ['lævətrɪ] n 1 excusado m, retrete m. 2 (room) baño m; public l., servicios mpl, aseos mpl.

lavender ['lævəndə'] n lavanda f.

lavish ['lævɪʃ] I adj 1 (generous) pródigo,-a. 2 (abundant) abundante. 3 (luxurious) lujoso,-a. II vtr (praise) colmar de (on, a); (care, attention) prodigarse en (on, con).

law [lɔː] n 1 ley f; by l., según la ley; l. and order, el orden público; to lay down the l., dictar la ley. 2 (as subject) derecho m; l. court, tribunal m de justicia. 3 fam the l., los maderos.

law-abiding ['lɔːəbaɪdɪŋ] adj respetuoso,-a de la ley.

lawful ['lɔːfʊl] adj legal; (permitted by law) lícito,-a; (legitimate) legítimo,-a.

lawn [lɔːn] n césped m; l. tennis, tenis m sobre hierba.

lawnmower ['lɔːnməʊə'] n cortacésped m.

lawsuit ['lɔːsjuːt] n pleito m.

lawyer ['lɔːjə'] n abogado,-a m,f; l.'s office, bufete m de abogados.

lax [læks] adj (not strict) relajado,-a; (not demanding) poco exigente; (careless) descuidado,-a.

laxative ['læksətɪv] adj & n laxante (m).

laxity ['læksɪtɪ] n relajamiento m; (careless-

ness). descuido *m*; (*negligence*) negligencia *f*.

lay¹ [leɪ] *adj* 1 *Rel* laico,-a. 2 (*non-specialist*) lego,-a.

lay² [leɪ] *vtr* (*pt & pp* **laid**) 1 (*place*) poner, colocar; (*cable, trap*) tender; (*foundations*) echar. 2 (*fire*) preparar; (*table*) poner. 3 (*lever*) dejar. 4 (*eggs*) poner. 5 *vulg* follar. 6 (*set down*) asentar; (*blame*) echar. ◆**lay aside** *vtr* dejar a un lado. ◆**lay by** *vtr* (*save*) guardar; (*money*) ahorrar. ◆**lay down** *vtr* (*put down*) poner; (*let go*) dejar; **to l. down one's arms**, rendir las armas. 2 (*plan*) formular. 3 (*establish*) fijar, imponer; (*principles*) sentar. ◆**lay into** *vtr fam* (*physically*) dar una paliza a; (*verbally*) arremeter contra. ◆**lay off** I *vtr* 1 (*dismiss*) despedir. 2 *fam* dejar en paz. II *vi* **l. off!**, ¡para ya! ◆**lay on** *vtr* 1 (*provide*) proveer de; (*food*) preparar. 2 (*spread*) aplicar; *fam* **to l. it on** (**thick**), cargar las tintas. ◆**lay out** *vtr* 1 (*open out*) extender. 2 (*arrange*) disponer. 3 (*ideas*) exponer. 4 (*plan*) trazar. 5 *fam* (*spend*) gastar. 6 *fam* (*knock out*) derribar. ◆**lay up** *vtr* 1 (*store*) guardar. 2 (*accumulate*) almacenar. 3 *fam* **to be laid up**, tener que guardar cama.

lay³ [leɪ] *pt* of **lie².**

layabout ['leɪəbaʊt] *n fam* vago,-a *m,f*.

lay-by ['leɪbaɪ] *n* área *f* de descanso.

layer ['leɪə'] *n* capa *f*.

layman ['leɪmən] *n* lego,-a *m,f*.

layout ['leɪaʊt] *n* (*arrangement*) disposición *f*; (*presentation*) presentación *f*; *Typ* composición *f*; (*plan*) diseño *m*, trazado *m*.

laze [leɪz] *vi* holgazanear, gandulear.

laziness ['leɪzɪnɪs] *n* pereza *f*, holgazanería *f*.

lazy ['leɪzɪ] *adj* (**lazier, laziest**) perezoso, -a, holgazán,-ana; **at a l. pace**, a paso lento.

lb *abbr of* **pound**, libra *f*.

lead¹ [led] *n* 1 (*metal*) plomo *m*. 2 (*in pencil*) mina *f*.

lead² [liːd] I *n* 1 (*front position*) delantera *f*; (*advantage*) ventaja *f*; **to take the l.**, (*in race*) tomar la delantera; (*score*) adelantarse. 2 (*clue*) pista *f*. 3 *Theat* primer papel *m*; **l. singer**, cantante *mf* principal. 4 (*leash*) correa *f*. 5 *Elec* cable *m*. II *vtr* (*pt & pp* **led**) 1 (*conduct*) llevar, conducir. 2 (*be the leader of*) dirigir, encabezar. 3 (*influence*) llevar a; **this leads me to believe that**, esto me lleva a creer que; **she's easily led**, se deja llevar fácilmente. 4 (*life*) llevar. III *vi* 1 (*road*) llevar, conducir (**to**, a). 2 (*go first*) ir delante; (*in race*) llevar la delantera. 3 **to l. to**, llevar a. ◆**lead away** *vtr* llevar. ◆**lead on** I *vi* (*go ahead*) ir adelante. II *vtr* (*deceive*) engañar, timar. ◆**lead up to** *vtr* llevar a.

leaden ['ledən] *adj* (*sky*) plomizo,-a; (*food*) pesado,-a.

leader ['liːdə'] *n* 1 jefe,-a *m,f*, líder *mf*; (*in race*) líder. 2 *Press* editorial *m*, artículo *m* de fondo.

leadership ['liːdəʃɪp] *n* 1 (*command*) dirección *f*, mando *m*; *Pol* liderazgo *m*. 2 (*leaders*) dirigentes *mpl*, cúpula *f*.

lead-free ['ledfriː] *adj* sin plomo.

leading ['liːdɪŋ] *adj* 1 (*main*) principal. 2 (*outstanding*) destacado,-a.

leaf [liːf] *n* (*pl* **leaves** [liːvz]) hoja *f*; **to turn over a new l.**, hacer borrón y cuenta nueva. ◆**leaf through** *vtr* hojear.

leaflet ['liːflɪt] *n* folleto *m*.

league [liːg] *n* 1 (*alliance*) alianza *f*; (*association*) sociedad *f*; *fam* **to be in l. with sb**, estar conchabado,-a con algn. 2 *Sport* liga *f*.

leak [liːk] I *n* 1 (*hole*) agujero *m*; (*in roof*) gotera *f*. 2 (*of gas, liquid*) fuga *f*, escape *m*; (*of information*) filtración *f*. II *vi* 1 (*container*) tener un agujero; (*pipe*) tener un escape; (*roof*) gotear; (*boat*) hacer agua. 2 (*gas, liquid*) escaparse; (*information*) filtrarse; (*news*) trascender. III *vtr* (*information*) filtrar (**to**, a).

leaky ['liːkɪ] *adj* (**leakier, leakiest**) (*container*) agujereado,-a; (*roof*) que tiene goteras; (*ship*) que hace agua.

lean¹ [liːn] *adj* (*meat*) magro,-a; (*person*) flaco,-a; (*harvest*) escaso,-a.

lean² [liːn] I *vi* (*pt & pp* **leaned** *or* **leant**) 1 inclinarse. 2 **to l. on/against**, apoyarse en/contra; *fig* **to l. on sb**, (*pressurize*) presionar a algn; (*depend*) depender de algn. II *vtr* apoyar (**on**, en). ◆**lean back** *vi* reclinarse. ◆**lean forward** *vi* inclinarse hacia delante. ◆**lean out** *vi* asomarse. ◆**lean over** *vi* inclinarse.

leaning ['liːnɪŋ] *adj* inclinado,-a. II *n fig* (*tendency*) inclinación *f*, tendencia *f*.

leant [lent] *pt & pp* → **lean².**

lean-to ['liːntuː] *n* (*hut*) cobertizo *m*.

leap [liːp] I *n* (*jump*) salto *m*; *fig* paso *m*; **l. year**, año bisiesto. II *vi* (*pt & pp* **leaped** *or* **leapt**) saltar; *fig* **my heart leapt**, se me corazón dio un vuelco. ◆**leap at** *vtr fig* (*chance*) no dejar escapar.

leapfrog ['liːpfrɒg] *n* pídola *f*.

leapt [lept] *pt & pp* → **leap.**

learn [lɜːn] I *vtr* (*pt & pp* **learned** *or* **learnt**) 1 aprender; **to l. (how) to ski**, aprender a esquiar. 2 **to l. that**, enterarse de que. II *vi* 1 aprender. 2 **to l. about** *o* **of**, (*find out*) enterarse de.

learned ['lɜːnɪd] *adj* erudito,-a.

learner ['lɜːnə'] *n* (*beginner*) principiante *mf*; **l. driver**, aprendiz,-a *m,f* de conductor.

learning ['lɜːnɪŋ] *n* (*knowledge*) conocimientos *mpl*; (*erudition*) saber *m*.

learnt [lɜːnt] *pt & pp* → **learn.**

lease [li:s] **I** *n* contrato *m* de arrendamiento; *fig* **to give sb a new l. of life**, dar nueva vida a algn. **II** *vtr* arrendar.

leasehold [li:shəuld] **I** *n* derechos *mpl* de arrendamiento. **II** *adj* (*property*) arrendado,-a.

leash [li:ʃ] *n* correa *f*.

least [li:st] (*superl* of *little*) **I** *adj* menor, mínimo,-a; **he has the l. time**, él es quien menos tiempo tiene. **II** *adv* menos; **l. of all him**, él menos que nadie. **III** *n* lo menos; **at l.**, por lo menos, al menos; **not in the l.!**, ¡en absoluto!; **to say the l.**, por no decir más.

leather [leðər] **I** *n* piel *f*, cuero *m*. **II** *adj* de piel.

leave[1] [li:v] *vtr* (*pt & pp* **left**) **1** dejar; (*go away from*) abandonar; (*go out of*) salir de. **2 l. him alone!** ¡déjale en paz!; *fam* **l. it to me**, yo me encargo. **3** (*bequeath*) legar. **4** (*forget*) dejarse, olvidarse. **5 I have two biscuits left**, me quedan dos galletas. **6 to be left over**, sobrar. **II** *vi* (*go away*) irse, marcharse; (*go out*) salir; **the train leaves in five minutes**, el tren sale dentro de cinco minutos. ◆**leave behind** *vtr* **1** dejar atrás. (*forget*) olvidarse. ◆**leave on** *vtr* **1** (*clothes*) dejar puesto,-a. **2** (*lights, radio*) dejar encendido,-a. ◆**leave out** *vtr* (*omit*) omitir; *fig* **to feel left out**, sentirse excluido,-a.

leave[2] [li:v] *n* **1** (*permission*) permiso *m*. **2** (*time off*) vacaciones *fpl*; **Mil** on **l.**, de permiso; **l. of absence**, excedencia *f*. **3 to take one's l.** of sb, despedirse de algn.

leaves [li:vz] *npl* → **leaf**.

Lebanon [lebənən] *n* (**the**) **L.**, (el) Líbano.

lecherous [letʃərəs] *adj* lascivo,-a.

lecture [lektʃər] **I** *n* **1** (*address*) *Univ* clase *f*; **to give a l.**, dar una conferencia (**on**, sobre); **l. hall, l. room, l. theatre**, sala *f* de conferencias; *Univ* aula *f*. **2** (*rebuke*) sermón *m*. **II** *vi* dar una conferencia; *Univ* dar clases. **III** *vtr* (*reproach*) sermonear.

lecturer [lektʃərər] *n* conferenciante *mf*; *Univ* profesor,-a *m,f*.

led [led] *pt & pp* → **lead**[2].

ledge [ledʒ] *n* **1** (*shelf*) repisa *f*; (*of window*) alféizar *m*. **2** (*on mountain*) saliente *m*.

ledger [ledʒər] *n* libro *m* mayor.

lee [li:] *n* **1** *Naut* sotavento *m*. **2** *fig* abrigo *m*.

leech [li:tʃ] *n* sanguijuela *f*.

leek [li:k] *n* puerro *m*.

leer [liər] *vi* mirar con lascivia.

leeway [li:weɪ] *n* libertad *f*; **this gives me a certain amount of l.**, esto me da cierto margen de libertad.

left[1] [left] **I** *adj* izquierdo,-a; *Pol* **l. wing**,

izquierda *f*. **II** *adv* a la izquierda. **III** *n* **1** izquierda *f*; **on the l.**, a mano izquierda. **2** *Pol* **to be on the l.**, ser de izquierdas.

left[2] [left] *pt & pp* → **leave**[1].

left-hand [lefthænd] *adj* **l.-h. drive**, con el volante a la izquierda; **on the l.-h. side**, a mano izquierda.

left-handed [lefthændid] *adj* zurdo,-a.

left-luggage [leftlʌgɪdʒ] *n* GB **l.-l. office**, consigna *f*.

leftovers [leftəuvəz] *npl* sobras *fpl*.

left-wing [leftwɪŋ] *adj* de izquierdas, izquierdista.

leg [leg] *n* **1** (*of person*) pierna *f*; (*of animal, table*) pata *f*; **Culin** (*of lamb*) pierna; (*of trousers*) pernera *f*. **2** (*stage*) etapa *f*.

legacy [legəsɪ] *n* herencia *f*, legado *m*.

legal [li:gəl] *adj* **1** legal; (*permitted by law*) lícito,-a. **2 l. tender**, moneda *f* de curso legal. **2** (*relating to the law*) jurídico,-a; **l. aid**, asesoramiento jurídico gratuito; **l. dispute**, contencioso *m*; US **l. holiday**, fiesta *f* nacional. ◆**legally** *adv* legalmente.

legalize [li:gəlaɪz] *vtr* legalizar.

legend [ledʒənd] *n* leyenda *f*.

legendary [ledʒəndərɪ] *adj* legendario,-a.

leggings [legɪŋz] *npl* polainas *fpl*.

legible [ledʒəbəl] *adj* legible.

legion [li:dʒən] *n* legión *f*.

legislation [ledʒɪsleɪʃən] *n* legislación *f*.

legislative [ledʒɪslətɪv] *adj* legislativo,-a.

legislator [ledʒɪsleɪtər] *n* legislador,-a *m,f*.

legislature [ledʒɪsleɪtʃər] *n* asamblea legislativa.

legitimate [lɪdʒɪtɪmɪt] *adj* legítimo,-a.

legroom [legruːm] *n* espacio *m* para las piernas.

leisure [leʒər, US li:ʒər] *n* ocio *m*, tiempo *m* libre; **at l.**, con calma; **do it at your l.**, hazlo cuando tengas tiempo; **l. activities**, pasatiempos *mpl*; **l. centre**, centro recreativo.

leisurely [leʒəlɪ, US li:ʒəlɪ] *adj* (*unhurried*) tranquilo,-a; (*slow*) lento,-a.

lemon [lemən] *n* limón *m*; **l. curd**, crema *f* de limón; **l. juice**, zumo de limón; **l. tea**, té *m* con limón.

lemonade [leməneɪd] *n* limonada *f*.

lend [lend] *vtr* (*pt & pp* **lent**) prestar; **to l. oneself or itself to sth**, prestarse a or para algo.

lending [lendɪŋ] *n* **l. library**, biblioteca pública.

length [leŋkθ, leŋθ] *n* **1** longitud *f*, largo *m*; **it is five metres in l.**, tiene cinco metros de largo. **2** (*duration*) duración *f*. **3** (*of string*) trozo *m*; (*of cloth*) retal *m*. **4** (*of swimming pool*) largo *m*; *fig* **to go to any lengths to achieve sth**, hacer lo que sea para conseguir algo. **5 at l.**, (*finally*) finalmente; (*in depth*) a fondo.

lengthen [leŋkθən, leŋθən] **I** *vtr* alargar;

(lifetime) prolongar. **II** *vi* alargarse; *(lifetime)* prolongarse.

lengthways ['leŋθweɪz] *adv* a lo largo.

lengthy ['leŋkθɪ, 'leŋθɪ] *adj* (*lengthier, lengthiest*) largo,-a; *(film, illness)* de larga duración; *(meeting, discussion)* prolongado,-a.

lenient ['liːnɪənt] *adj* indulgente.

lens [lenz] *n* *(of eye)* cristalino *m*; *(of spectacles)* lente *f*; Phot objetivo *m*.

Lent [lent] *n* Cuaresma *f*.

lent [lent] *pt & pp* → **lend**.

lentil ['lentɪl] *n* lenteja *f*.

Leo ['liːəʊ] *n* Leo *m*.

leopard ['lepəd] *n* leopardo *m*.

leotard ['liːətɑːd] *n* leotardo *m*.

leper ['lepə'] *n* leproso,-a *m,f*.

leprosy ['leprəsɪ] *n* lepra *f*.

lesbian ['lezbɪən] *adj & n* lesbiana (*f*).

less [les] **I** *adj* (*comp of little*) menos. **II** *pron* menos; the l. said about it, the better, cuanto menos se hable de eso mejor. **III** *adv* menos; l. and l., cada vez menos; still l., menos aún. **IV** *prep* menos; a year l. two days, un año menos dos días.

lessen ['lesən] *vtr & vi* disminuir.

lesser ['lesə'] *adj* menor; to a l. extent, en menor grado.

lesson ['lesən] *n* 1 clase *f*; *(in book)* lección *f*; Spanish lessons, clases de español. 2 Rel lectura *f*.

lest [lest] *conj fml* 1 para (que) no; l. we forget, para que no lo olvidemos. 2 *(for fear that)* por miedo a que.

let [let] **I** *vtr* (*pt & pp* let) 1 dejar, permitir; to l. go of sth, soltar algo; to l. sb know, avisar a algn; fig to l. oneself go, dejarse ir. 2 *(rent out)* alquilar; 'to l.', se alquila'. 3 l. alone, ni mucho menos. **II** *v aux* 1 him wait, que espere; l. me go!, ¡suéltame!; l.'s go!, ¡vamos!, ¡vámonos! l.'s see, a ver. ◆**let down** *vtr* 1 *(lower)* bajar; *(lengthen)* alargar; fam fig to l. one's hair down, desmelenarse. 2 *(deflate)* desinflar. 3 *(fail)* fallar, defraudar. ◆**let in** *vtr* 1 *(admit)* dejar entrar. 2 to l. oneself in for, meterse en. ◆**let off** *vtr* 1 *(bomb)* hacer explotar; *(fireworks)* hacer estallar. 2 *(liquid, air)* soltar. 3 fam to l. sb off, *(pardon)* perdonar. ◆**let on** *vi* fam don't l. on, *(reveal information)* no se lo digas. ◆**let out** *vtr* 1 *(release)* soltar; *(news)* divulgar; *(secret)* revelar. 2 *(air, water)* dejar salir. 3 *(cry)* soltar. 4 Sew ensanchar. ◆**let up** *vi* cesar, parar.

letdown ['letdaʊn] *n* decepción *f*.

lethal ['liːθəl] *adj* letal.

lethargic [lɪ'θɑːdʒɪk] *adj* aletargado,-a.

letter ['letə'] *n* 1 *(of alphabet)* letra *f*; fig to the l., al pie de la letra. 2 *(written message)* carta *f*; GB l. box, buzón *m*; Com l. of credit, carta de crédito.

letterhead ['letəhed] *n* membrete *m*.

lettering ['letərɪŋ] *n* rótulo *m*.

lettuce ['letɪs] *n* lechuga *f*.

let-up ['letʌp] *n* fam descanso *m*, respiro *m*.

leukaemia, US **leukemia** [luː'kiːmɪə] *n* leucemia *f*.

level ['levəl] **I** *adj* 1 *(flat)* llano,-a; *(even)* nivelado,-a; *(equal)* igual, parejo,-a; a spoonful of, una cucharada rasa de; to be l. with, estar a nivel de; GB l. crossing, paso *m* a nivel. 2 *(steady)* estable; *(tone)* uniforme. **II** *vtr* 1 nivelar, allanar. 2 *(building)* arrasar. 3 *(stare, criticism)* dirigir. **III** *n* nivel *m*; to be on a l. with, estar al mismo nivel que; fam to be on the l., *(be honest)* ser de fiar; *(be truthful)* decir la verdad. ◆**level off, level out** *vi* estabilizarse. ◆**level with** *vtr* fam ser franco,-a con.

level-headed [levəl'hedɪd] *adj* sensato,-a.

lever ['liːvə'] **I** *n* palanca *f*. **II** *vtr* apalancar; to l. sth out, sacar algo con palanca.

leverage ['liːvərɪdʒ] *n* fig influencia *f*.

levy ['levɪ] **I** *vtr* *(tax)* recaudar; *(fine)* imponer. **II** *n* *(of tax)* recaudación *f*; *(of fine)* imposición *f*.

- **lewd** [luːd] *adj* *(person)* lascivo,-a; *(story)* obsceno,-a.

liability [laɪə'bɪlɪtɪ] *n* 1 Jur responsabilidad *f*. 2 *(handicap)* estorbo *m*. 3 Fin liabilities, pasivo *m sing*.

liable ['laɪəbəl] *adj* 1 Jur responsable; *(susceptible)* sujeto,-a; to be l. for, ser responsable de. 2 to be l. to do sth, ser propenso,-a a hacer algo; it's l. to happen, es muy probable que (así) suceda.

liaise [lɪ'eɪz] *vi* comunicarse (with, con).

liaison [lɪ'eɪzɒn] *n* 1 enlace *m*; l. officer, oficial *m* de enlace. 2 *(love affair)* amorío *m*.

liar ['laɪə'] *n* mentiroso,-a *m,f*, embustero,-a *m,f*.

libel ['laɪbəl] **I** *n* libelo *m*. **II** *vtr* difamar, calumniar.

liberal ['lɪbərəl] **I** *adj* 1 liberal; L. Party, Partido *m* Liberal. 2 *(abundant)* abundante. **II** *n* Pol L., liberal *mf*.

liberate ['lɪbəreɪt] *vtr* liberar; *(prisoner etc)* poner en libertad; **liberated woman**, mujer liberada.

liberation [lɪbə'reɪʃən] *n* liberación *f*.

liberty ['lɪbətɪ] *n* libertad *f*; to be at l. to say sth, ser libre de decir algo; to take liberties, tomarse libertades.

Libra ['liːbrə] *n* Libra *f*.

librarian [laɪ'breərɪən] *n* bibliotecario,-a *m,f*.

library ['laɪbrərɪ] *n* biblioteca *f*.

Libya ['lɪbɪə] *n* Libia.

Libyan ['lɪbɪən] *adj & n* libio,-a (*m,f*).

lice [laɪs] *npl* → **louse**.

licence ['laɪsəns] *n* 1 *(permit)* licencia *f*, permiso *m*; Aut l. number, matrícula *f*. 2

(freedom) libertad *f*; *(excessive freedom)* libertinaje *m*.

license ['laɪsəns] **I** *vtr* dar licencia a, autorizar. **II** *n US* → **licence**.

licensed ['laɪsənst] *adj* autorizado,-a; **l. premises**, local autorizado para la venta de bebidas alcohólicas.

licentious [laɪ'senfəs] *adj* licencioso,-a.

lichen ['laɪkən, 'lɪtfən] *n* liquen *m*.

lick [lɪk] **I** *vtr* lamer; **to l. one's lips**, relamerse. **II** *n* lamedura *f*; *fam* **a l. of paint**, una mano de pintura.

licorice ['lɪkərɪs, 'lɪkərɪf] *n US* → **liquorice**.

lid [lɪd] *n* **1** *(cover)* tapa *f*. **2** *(of eye)* párpado *m*.

lie¹ [laɪ] **I** *vi* mentir. **II** *n* mentira *f*.

lie² [laɪ] **I** *vi* (*pt* **lay**; *pp* **lain**) **1** *(act)* echarse, acostarse; *(state)* estar echado,-a, estar acostado,-a; *(be buried)* yacer. **2** *(be situated)* encontrarse, hallarse; **the valley lay before us**, el valle se extendía ante nosotros. **3** *(remain)* quedarse. **II** *n* *(position)* situación *f*; *(direction)* orientación *f*. ◆**lie about, lie around** *vi* *(person)* estar tumbado,-a; *(things)* estar tirado,-a. ◆**lie down** *vi* acostarse, echarse.

lie-in ['laɪɪn] *n fam* **to have a l.-in**, levantarse tarde.

lieu [ljuː, luː] *n* **in l. of**, en lugar de.

lieutenant [lef'tenənt, *US* luː'tenənt] *n* **1** *Mil* teniente *m*. **2** *(non-military)* lugarteniente *m*.

life [laɪf] *n* (*pl* **lives** [laɪvz]) **1** vida *f*; **to come to l.**, cobrar vida; **to take one's own l.**, suicidarse; *fam* **how's l.?**, ¿qué tal?; **l. belt**, cinturón *m* salvavidas; **l. imprisonment**, cadena perpetua; **l. insurance**, seguro *m* de vida; **l. jacket**, chaleco *m* salvavidas; **l. style**, estilo *m* de vida; **l. story**, biografía *f*. **2** *(liveliness)* vitalidad *f*; *fam* **fig to be the l. (and soul) of the party**, ser el alma de la fiesta.

lifeboat ['laɪfbəʊt] *n* *(on ship)* bote *m* salvavidas; *(on shore)* lancha *f* de socorro.

lifeguard ['laɪfgɑːd] *n* socorrista *mf*.

lifeless ['laɪflɪs] *adj* sin vida.

lifelike ['laɪflaɪk] *adj* natural; *(portrait)* fiel.

lifeline ['laɪflaɪn] *n fig* cordón *m* umbilical.

lifelong ['laɪflɒŋ] *adj* de toda la vida.

life-size(d) ['laɪfsaɪz(d)] *adj* (de) tamaño natural.

lifetime ['laɪftaɪm] *n* vida *f*; **in his l.**, durante su vida; **it's the chance of a l.**, es una ocasión única.

lift [lɪft] **I** *vtr* **1** levantar; *(head etc)* alzar; *(pick up)* coger. **2** *(troops)* transportar. **3** *fam* *(steal)* birlar; *(plagiarize)* plagiar. **II** *vi* *(clouds, mist)* disiparse. **III** *n* **1** *GB* *(elevator)* ascensor *m*. **2** **to give sb a l.**, llevar a algn en coche. **3** *fig* *(boost)* estímulo *m*. ◆**lift up** *vtr* levantar, alzar.

lift-off ['lɪftɒf] *n* despegue *m*.

light¹ [laɪt] **I** *n* **1** luz *f*; *fig* **in the l. of**, en vista de; *fig* **to bring sth to l.**, sacar algo a la luz; *fig* **to come to l.**, salir a la luz; **l. bulb**, bombilla *f*; **l. meter**, fotómetro *m*; **l. pen**, lápiz óptico; **l. year**, año *m* luz. **2** *(lamp)* luz *f*, lámpara *f*; *(traffic light)* semáforo *m*; *(headlight)* faro *m*. **3** *(flame)* lumbre *f*; **to set l. to sth**, prender fuego a algo; *fam* **have you got a l.?**, ¿tiene fuego? **II** *vtr* (*pt & pp* **lighted** *or* **lit**) **1** *(illuminate)* iluminar, alumbrar. **2** *(ignite)* encender. **III** *adj* claro,-a; *(hair)* rubio,-a. ◆**light up I** *vtr* iluminar, alumbrar. **II** *vi* **1** iluminarse. **2** *fam* encender un cigarrillo.

light² [laɪt] **I** *adj* ligero,-a; *(rain)* fino,-a; *(breeze)* suave; *fig* *(sentence etc)* leve; *fig* **to make l. of sth**, dar poca importancia a algo. **II** *adv* **to travel l.**, ir ligero,-a de equipaje. ◆**lightly** *adv* **1** ligeramente. **2** **to get off l.**, salir casi indemne.

lighten¹ ['laɪtən] *vtr* **1** *(colour)* aclarar. **2** *(illuminate)* iluminar. **II** *vi* aclararse.

lighten² ['laɪtən] *vtr* **1** *(weight)* aligerar. **2** *fig* *(mitigate)* aliviar; *(heart)* alegrar.

lighter¹ ['laɪtər] *n* *(cigarette)* l., encendedor *m*, mechero *m*.

light-headed [laɪt'hedɪd] *adj* **1** *(dizzy)* mareado,-a. **2** *(frivolous)* frívolo,-a.

light-hearted [laɪt'hɑːtɪd] *adj* alegre.

lighthouse ['laɪthaʊs] *n* faro *m*.

lighting ['laɪtɪŋ] *n* **1** *(act)* iluminación *f*. **2** *(system)* alumbrado *m*.

lightness¹ ['laɪtnɪs] *n* luminosidad *f*, claridad *f*.

lightness² ['laɪtnɪs] *n* *(of weight)* ligereza *f*.

lightning ['laɪtnɪŋ] *n* *(flash)* relámpago *m*; *(stroke)* rayo *m*; **l. conductor**, **l. rod**, pararrayos *m inv*; **l. strike**, huelga *f* relámpago.

lightweight ['laɪtweɪt] *adj* *(suit etc)* ligero,-a; *Box* de peso ligero; *fig* *(person)* light.

like¹ [laɪk] **I** *adj* **1** parecido,-a, semejante. **2** *(equal)* igual. **II** *adv* **1** **as l. as not**, a lo mejor. **III** *prep* **1** *(similar to)* como, parecido,-a a; *(the same as)* igual que; **it's not l. her to do that**, no es propio de ella hacer eso; **I've never seen anything l. it**, nunca he visto cosa igual; **l. that**, así; **people l. that**, ese tipo de gente; **what's he l.?**, ¿cómo es?; *fam* **that's more l. it!**, ¡así se hace! **2** **to feel l.**, *(want)* tener ganas de; **I feel l. a change**, me apetece un cambio. **IV** *n* **brushes, combs and the l.**, cepillos, peines y cosas por el estilo.

like² [laɪk] *vtr* **1** **do you l. chocolate?**, ¿te gusta el chocolate?; **he likes dancing**, le gusta bailar; **she likes children**, le gustan los niños. **2** *(want)* querer; **whether you l. it or not**, quieras o no (quieras); **would** you l. a drink?, ¿te apetece tomar algo? **II** *vi* querer, gustar; **as you l.**, como quieras; **whenever you l.**, cuando quieras. **III** *n* gusto *m*.

likeable ['laɪkəbəl] *adj* simpático,-a.

likelihood ['laɪklɪhʊd] *n* probabilidad *f*.

likely ['laɪklɪ] **I** *adj* (**likelier**, **likeliest**) probable; **he's l. to cause trouble**, es probable que cause problemas; **where are you l. to be this afternoon?**, ¿dónde piensas estar esta tarde? **II** *adv* probablemente; **not l.!**, ¡ni hablar!

likeness ['laɪknɪs] *n* 1 semejanza *f*, parecido *m*. 2 (*portrait*) retrato *m*.

likewise ['laɪkwaɪz] *adv* 1 (*also*) también, asimismo. 2 (*the same*) lo mismo, igual.

liking ['laɪkɪŋ] *n* (*for thing*) afición *f*; (*for person*) simpatía *f*; (*for friend*) cariño *m*; **to take a l. to sth**, cogerle el gusto a algo; **to take a l. to sb**, coger cariño a algn.

lilac ['laɪlək] **I** *n* 1 *Bot* lila *f*. 2 (*colour*) lila *m*. **II** *adj* lila, de color lila.

lilt [lɪlt] *n* melodía *f*.

lily ['lɪlɪ] *n* lirio *m*, azucena *f*; **l. of the valley**, lirio de los valles.

limb [lɪm] *n* miembro *m*; **to be out on a l.**, (*in danger*) estar en peligro; *GB* (*isolated*) estar aislado,-a.

limber up ['lɪmbər] *vi Sport* entrar en calor; *fig* prepararse (**for**, para).

limbo ['lɪmbəʊ] *n* limbo *m*; *fig* olvido *m*; **to be in l.**, caer en el olvido.

lime¹ [laɪm] *n Chem* cal *f*.

lime² [laɪm] *n* (*fruit*) lima *f*; (*tree*) limero *m*.

limelight ['laɪmlaɪt] *n fig* **to be in the l.**, estar en el candelero.

limerick ['lɪmərɪk] *n* quintilla humorística.

limestone ['laɪmstəʊn] *n* piedra caliza.

limit ['lɪmɪt] **I** *n* límite *m*; (*maximum*) máximo *m*; (*minimum*) mínimo *m*. **II** *vtr* (*restrict*) limitar.

limitation [lɪmɪ'teɪʃən] *n* limitación *f*.

limited ['lɪmɪtɪd] *adj* limitado,-a; **l. edition**, edición limitada; *GB* **l.** (**liability**) **company**, sociedad anónima.

limitless ['lɪmɪtlɪs] *adj* ilimitado,-a.

limousine ['lɪməziːn, lɪmə'ziːn] *n* limusina *f*.

limp¹ [lɪmp] **I** *vi* cojear. **II** *n* cojera *f*.

limp² [lɪmp] *adj* 1 (*floppy*) flojo,-a. 2 (*weak*) débil.

limpet ['lɪmpɪt] *n* lapa *f*.

linchpin ['lɪntʃpɪn] *n Tech* pezonera *f*; *fig* eje *m*.

line¹ [laɪn] *n* 1 línea *f*; (*straight*) raya *f*; **to be on the right lines**, ir por buen camino; *US* **State l.**, límite *m* de un Estado. 2 (*of writing*) renglón *m*; (*of poetry*) verso *m*; *Theat* **to learn one's lines**, aprenderse el papel. 3 (*row*) fila *f*; (*of trees*) hilera *f*; *US* (*queue*) cola *f*; *Mil* **l. of fire**, línea *f*

de fuego; *Mil* **to be in the front l.**, estar en primera línea; *fig* **to be in l.**, coincidir (**with**, con); *fam* **to bring sb into l.**, pararle los pies a algn; *fam* **to step out of l.**, salirse de las reglas; *fig* **sth along these lines**, algo por el estilo. 4 (*rope*) cuerda *f*; (*wire*) cable *m*; *fishing* **l.**, sedal *m*. 5 *Tel* línea *f*; **hold the l.!**, ¡no cuelgue! 6 *GB Rail* vía *f*. 7 (*range of goods*) surtido *m*; **a new l.**, una nueva línea. 8 (*of descent*) linaje *m*.

line² [laɪn] **I** *vtr* (*pipe etc*) revestir; *Sew* forrar; *fam* **to l. one's pockets**, forrarse. ◆**line up** **I** *vtr* 1 (*arrange in rows*) poner en fila. 2 **he has something lined up for this evening**, tiene algo organizado para esta noche. **II** *vi* (*people*) ponerse en fila; (*troops*) formar; (*in queue*) hacer cola.

linear ['lɪnɪər] *adj* lineal.

lined [laɪnd] *adj* 1 (*paper*) rayado,-a; (*face*) arrugado,-a. 2 (*garment*) forrado,-a.

linen ['lɪnɪn] *n* 1 (*cloth*) lino *m*. 2 (*clothes*) ropa *f*; (*sheets etc*) ropa blanca.

liner ['laɪnər] *n* transatlántico *m*.

linesman ['laɪnzmən] *n Sport* juez *m* de línea.

line-up ['laɪnʌp] *n Sport* alineación *f*.

linger ['lɪŋɡər] *vi* tardar; (*dawdle*) rezagarse; (*smell, doubt*) persistir; *fig* (*memory*) perdurar.

lingerie ['lænʒəriː] *n fml* ropa *f* interior (de mujer).

lingering ['lɪŋɡərɪŋ] *adj* (*doubt*) persistente; (*look*) fijo,-a.

lingo ['lɪŋɡəʊ] *n* (*pl* **lingoes**) *fam* 1 (*language*) lengua *f*, idioma *m*. 2 (*jargon*) jerga *f*.

linguist ['lɪŋɡwɪst] *n* lingüista *mf*; **he's a good l.**, se le dan bien los idiomas.

linguistic [lɪŋ'ɡwɪstɪk] *adj* lingüístico,-a.

linguistics [lɪŋ'ɡwɪstɪks] *n* lingüística *f*.

lining ['laɪnɪŋ] *n* forro *m*.

link [lɪŋk] **I** *n* 1 (*of chain*) eslabón *m*. 2 (*connection*) conexión *f*; *fig* vínculo *m*; rail **l.**, enlace ferroviario. 3 **links**, campo *m* *sing* de golf. **II** *vtr* unir. ◆**link up** *vi* unirse; (*meet*) encontrarse; (*spaceships*) acoplarse.

link-up ['lɪŋkʌp] *n Tel* TV conexión *f*; (*meeting*) encuentro *m*; (*of spaceships*) acoplamiento *m*.

lino ['laɪnəʊ] *n fam* linóleo *m*.

linoleum [lɪ'nəʊlɪəm] *n* linóleo *m*, linóleum *m*.

lion ['laɪən] *n* león *m*.

lioness ['laɪənɪs] *n* leona *f*.

lip [lɪp] *n* 1 labio *m*. 2 (*of jug*) pico *m*.

lip-read ['lɪprɪːd] *vtr & vi* leer en los labios.

lip-service ['lɪpsɜːvɪs] *n* palabrería *f*.

lipstick ['lɪpstɪk] *n* lápiz *m* de labios.

liqueur [lɪ'kjʊər] *n* licor *m*.

liquid ['lɪkwɪd] *adj & n* líquido,-a (*m*).

liquidate ['lɪkwɪdeɪt] *vtr* liquidar.

liquidation [lɪkwɪ'deɪʃən] n liquidación f; **to go into l.**, entrar en liquidación.

liquidize ['lɪkwɪdaɪz] vtr licuar.

liquidizer ['lɪkwɪdaɪzə'] n licuadora f.

liquor ['lɪkə'] n US alcohol m, bebidas alcohólicas.

liquorice ['lɪkərɪs, 'lɪkərɪʃ] n regaliz m.

Lisbon ['lɪzbən] n Lisboa.

lisp [lɪsp] I n ceceo m. II vi cecear.

list¹ [lɪst] I n lista f; (catalogue) catálogo m. II vtr (make a list of) hacer una lista de; (put on a list) poner en una lista; **it is not listed**, no figura en la lista.

list² [lɪst] Naut I n escora f. II vi escorar.

listen ['lɪsən] vi escuchar; (pay attention) prestar atención. ◆**listen out for** vtr estar atento,-a.

listener ['lɪsənə'] n oyente mf.

listless ['lɪstlɪs] adj apático,-a.

lit [lɪt] pt & pp → **light¹**.

liter ['liːtə'] n US → litre.

literacy ['lɪtərəsɪ] n alfabetización f.

literal ['lɪtərəl] adj literal. ◆**literally** adv literalmente.

literary ['lɪtərərɪ] adj literario,-a.

literate ['lɪtərɪt] adj alfabetizado,-a.

literature ['lɪtərɪtʃə'] n 1 literatura f. 2 fam (documentation) folleto informativo.

lithe [laɪð] adj fml ágil.

Lithuania [lɪθjʊ'eɪnɪə] n Lituania.

Lithuanian [lɪθjʊ'eɪnɪən] I adj lituano,-a. II n (person) lituano,-a m,f; (language) lituano m.

litigation [lɪtɪ'geɪʃən] n litigio m.

litmus ['lɪtməs] n fig l. **test**, prueba f contundente.

litre ['liːtə'] n litro m.

litter ['lɪtə'] I n 1 (rubbish) basura f; (papers) papeles mpl; l. **bin**, papelera f. 2 (offspring) camada f. 3 arch (stretcher) camilla f. II vtr ensuciar.

littered ['lɪtəd] adj cubierto,-a (with, de).

little ['lɪtəl] I adj 1 pequeño,-a; a l. **dog**, un perrito; a l. **house**, una casita; l. **finger**, dedo m meñique. 2 (not much) poco,-a; a l. **cheese**, un poco de queso. II pron poco m; **save me a l.**, guárdame un poco. III adv poco; l. **by l.**, poco a poco; **as l. as possible**, lo menos posible; **they were a l. surprised**, se quedaron algo sorprendidos.

live¹ [lɪv] I vi vivir; **long l. the King!**, ¡viva el Rey! II vtr vivir; **to l. an interesting life**, vivir una vida interesante. ◆**live down** vtr conseguir que se olvide. ◆**live for** vtr vivir para. ◆**live off** vtr vivir de. ◆**live on I** vtr (food, money) vivir de. II vi (memory) persistir. ◆**live through** vi vivir (durante). ◆**live together** vi vivir juntos. ◆**live it up** vi, pegarse la gran vida. ◆**live up to** vtr (promises) cumplir con; **it didn't l. up to expectations**, no fue lo

que se esperaba. ◆**live with** vtr 1 vivir con. 2 fig (accept) aceptar.

live² [laɪv] adj 1 (living) vivo,-a. 2 TV Rad en directo, en vivo. 3 (ammunition) real; (bomb) sin explotar; fam **he's a real l. wire!**, ¡éste no para nunca!

livelihood ['laɪvlɪhʊd] n sustento m.

lively ['laɪvlɪ] adj (**livelier**, **liveliest**) (person) vivo,-a; (place) animado,-a; fig (interest) entusiástico,-a.

liven ['laɪvən] vtr **to l. (up)**, animar.

liver ['lɪvə'] n hígado m.

livery ['lɪvərɪ] n librea f.

livestock ['laɪvstɒk] n ganado m.

livid ['lɪvɪd] adj lívido,-a; fam (angry) furioso,-a.

living ['lɪvɪŋ] I adj vivo,-a. II n vida f; l. **conditions**, condiciones fpl de vida; l. **expenses**, dietas fpl; **to earn** or **make one's l.**, ganarse la vida; l. **room**, sala f de estar; l. **standards**, nivel m de vida; l. **wage**, sueldo mínimo.

lizard ['lɪzəd] n (large) lagarto m; (small) lagartija f.

llama ['lɑːmə] n llama f.

load [ləʊd] I n (cargo) carga f; (weight) peso m; Elec Tech carga; fam **loads (of)**, montones de; fam **that's a l. of rubbish!**, ¡no son más que tonterías!. II vtr cargar. ◆**load up** vi & vtr cargar.

loaded ['ləʊdɪd] adj cargado,-a (with, de); fig a l. **question**, una pregunta intencionada. 2 fam **to be l.**, (rich) estar forrado,-a. 3 (dice) trucado,-a.

loading ['ləʊdɪŋ] n carga f; l. **bay**, carga zona.

loaf¹ [ləʊf] n (pl **loaves**) pan m; (French stick) barra f de pan; (sliced) pan de molde.

loaf² [ləʊf] vi **to l.** (about or around), holgazanear.

loan [ləʊn] I n préstamo m; Fin empréstito m; **on l.**, prestado,-a; (footballer) cedido,-a. II vtr prestar.

loath [ləʊθ] adj **to be l. to do sth**, ser reacio,-a a hacer algo.

loathe [ləʊð] vtr aborrecer, odiar.

loathing ['ləʊðɪŋ] n aborrecimiento m, odio m.

loathsome ['ləʊðsəm] adj odioso,-a, repugnante.

loaves [ləʊvz] npl → **loaf**.

lob [lɒb] n Ten hacer un lob.

lobby ['lɒbɪ] I n 1 (hall) vestíbulo m. 2 (pressure group) grupo m de presión, lobby m. II vtr presionar. III vi ejercer presiones.

lobe [ləʊb] n lóbulo m.

lobster ['lɒbstə'] n langosta f.

local ['ləʊkəl] I adj local; (person) del pueblo; Med l. **anaesthetic**, anestesia f local; Tel l. **call**, llamada urbana; l. **government**, gobierno m municipal. II n fam 1

the locals, los vecinos. **2** *GB* (*pub*) bar m del barrio. ◆**locally** *adv* en or de la localidad.

locality [ləʊˈkælɪtɪ] *n* localidad *f*.

locate [ləʊˈkeɪt] *vtr* (*situate*) situar, ubicar; (*find*) localizar.

location [ləʊˈkeɪʃən] *n* **1** lugar m, situación *f*. **2** *Cin* **1. shots**, exteriores *mpl*; **they're on l. in Australia,** están rodando en Australia.

loch [lɒx, lɒk] *n Scot* lago m.

lock¹ [lɒk] **I** *n* **1** (*on door etc*) cerradura *f*; (*bolt*) cerrojo m; (*padlock*) candado m. **2** (*on canal*) esclusa *f*. **II** *vtr* cerrar con llave or cerrojo or candado. **III** *vi* (*door etc*) cerrarse; (*wheels*) trabarse. ◆**lock up** *vtr* (*house*) cerrar; (*jail*) meter en la cárcel.

lock² [lɒk] *n lit* (*of hair*) mechón m.

locker [ˈlɒkəʳ] *n* (*cupboard*) armario ropero; **l. room,** vestuario m con armarios roperos.

locket [ˈlɒkɪt] *n* medallón m.

lockout [ˈlɒkaʊt] *n* cierre m patronal.

locksmith [ˈlɒksmɪθ] *n* cerrajero m.

lockup [ˈlɒkʌp] *n* (*garage*) garaje alejado de la casa; *US* (*prison*) cárcel *f*.

locomotive [ləʊkəˈməʊtɪv] *n* locomotora *f*.

locust [ˈləʊkəst] *n* langosta *f*.

lodge [lɒdʒ] **I** *n* **1** (*gamekeeper's*) casa *f* del guarda; (*porter's*) portería *f*; (*hunter's*) refugio m. **2** (*masonic*) logia *f*. **3** (*beaver's den*) madriguera *f*. **II** *vtr* **1** (*accommodate*) alojar. **2** (*complaint*) presentar. **III** *vi* **1** (*live*) alojarse. **2** (*get stuck*) meterse (**in,** en).

lodger [ˈlɒdʒəʳ] *n* huésped,-a *m,f*.

lodging [ˈlɒdʒɪŋ] *n* alojamiento m; **l. house,** casa *f* de huéspedes.

loft [lɒft] *n* desván m.

lofty [ˈlɒftɪ] *adj* (*loftier, loftiest*) *lit* (*high*) alto,-a; *pej* (*haughty*) altivo,-a.

log [lɒg] **I** *n* **1** tronco m; (*for fuel*) leño m; **l. cabin,** cabaña *f* de troncos. **2** *Naut* diario m de a bordo. **II** *vtr* (*record*) registrar. ◆**log in, log on** *vi Comput* entrar (en sistema). ◆**log out, log off** *vi Comput* salir (del sistema).

logarithm [ˈlɒgərɪðəm] *n* logaritmo m.

log-book [ˈlɒgbʊk] *n Naut* diario m de a bordo; *Av* diario de vuelo; *Aut* documentación *f* (del coche).

loggerheads [ˈlɒgəhedz] *npl* **to be at l. with sb,** estar a mal con algn.

logic [ˈlɒdʒɪk] *n* lógica *f*.

logical [ˈlɒdʒɪkəl] *adj* lógico,-a.

logistics [ləˈdʒɪstɪks] *npl* logística *f*.

logo [ˈləʊgəʊ] *n* logotipo m.

loin [lɔɪn] *n* (*of animal*) ijada *f*; *Culin* (*of pork*) lomo m; (*of beef*) solomillo m.

loiter [ˈlɔɪtəʳ] *vi* (*hang about*) holgazanear; (*lag behind*) rezagarse; (*prowl*) merodear.

loll [lɒl] *vi* (*tongue, head*) colgar. ◆**loll about, loll around** *vi* repantigarse.

lollipop [ˈlɒlɪpɒp] *n* piruli m, chupachup® m; (*ice* (*d*)) polo m; *GB fam* **l. lady** or **man,** guardia *mf* (que para el tráfico para que crucen los colegiales).

lolly [ˈlɒlɪ] *n fam* **1** (*sweet*) piruli m, chupachup® m; (*ice* (*d*)) polo m. **2** *fam* (*money*) pasta *f*.

London [ˈlʌndən] *n* Londres.

Londoner [ˈlʌndənəʳ] *n* londinense *mf*.

lone [ləʊn] *adj* (*solitary*) solitario,-a; (*single*) solo,-a.

loneliness [ˈləʊnlɪnɪs] *n* soledad *f*.

lonely [ˈləʊnlɪ] *adj* (*lonelier, loneliest*) solo,-a, solitario,-a.

long¹ [lɒŋ] **I** *adj* **1** (*size*) largo,-a; **how l. is the table?,** ¿cuánto tiene de largo la mesa?; **it's three metres l.,** tiene tres metros de largo; **l. jump,** salto m de longitud. **2** (*time*) mucho,-a; **at l. last,** por fin; **how l. is the film?,** ¿cuánto tiempo dura la película? **II** *adv* mucho, mucho tiempo; **all day l.,** todo el día; **as l. as the exhibition lasts,** mientras dure la exposición; **as l. as** or **so l. as you don't mind,** con tal de que no te importe; **before l.,** dentro de poco; **how l. have you been here?,** ¿cuánto tiempo llevas aquí?

long² [lɒŋ] *vi* añorar; **to l. for,** anhelar.

long-distance [lɒŋdɪstəns] *adj* de larga distancia; **l.-d. call,** conferencia interurbana; **l.-d. runner,** corredor,-a *m,f* de fondo.

longhand [ˈlɒŋhænd] *n* escritura *f* a mano.

longing [ˈlɒŋɪŋ] *n* (*desire*) anhelo m; (*nostalgia*) nostalgia *f*.

longitude [ˈlɒndʒɪtjuːd] *n* longitud *f*.

long-playing [ˈlɒŋpleɪɪŋ] *adj* de larga duración; **l.-p. record,** elepé m.

long-range [ˈlɒŋreɪndʒ] *adj* (*missile etc*) de largo alcance; (*weather forecast*) de largo plazo.

long-sighted [ˈlɒŋsaɪtɪd] *adj* **1** *Med* présbita. **2** *fig* previsor,-a.

long-standing [ˈlɒŋstændɪŋ] *adj* antiguo,-a, de mucho tiempo.

long-suffering [ˈlɒŋsʌfrɪŋ] *adj* sufrido,-a.

long-term [ˈlɒŋtɜːm] *adj* a largo plazo.

long-winded [ˈlɒŋwɪndɪd] *adj* prolijo,-a.

loo [luː] *n GB fam* wáter m.

look [lʊk] **I** *n* **1** (*glance*) mirada *f*; **to take a l. at,** (*peep*) echar un vistazo a; (*examine*) examinar. **2** (*appearance*) aspecto m, apariencia *f*; **I don't like the l. of it,** me da mala espina. **3** (*fashion*) moda *f*. **4** (*good*) **looks,** belleza *f*. **II** *vi* **1** mirar. **2** (*seem*) parecer; **he looks well,** tiene buena cara; **it looks delicious,** tiene un aspecto buenísimo; **she looks like her father,** (*resembles*) se parece a su padre. **III** *vtr* mirar.

◆**look after** *vtr* cuidar a, ocuparse de.

◆**look at** vtr mirar; fig whichever way you l. at it, desde cualquier punto de vista. ◆**look away** vi apartar la mirada. ◆**look back** vi 1 mirar hacia atrás; fig since then he has never looked back, desde entonces ha ido prosperando. 2 (remember) recordar. ◆**look down** vi fig lo l. down on sth/sb, despreciar algo/a algn. ◆**look for** vtr buscar. ◆**look forward to** vtr esperar con ansia; I l. forward to hearing from you, (in letter) espero noticias suyas. ◆**look into** vtr examinar, investigar. ◆**look on** I vtr (consider) considerar. II vi quedarse mirando. ◆**look onto** vtr ◆**look out** vi 1 the bedroom looks out onto the garden, el dormitorio da al jardín. 2 I. out!, ¡cuidado!, ¡ojo! ◆**look over** vtr (examine) revisar; (place) inspeccionar. ◆**look round** I vi mirar alrededor; (turn head) volver la cabeza. II vtr (house, shop) ver. ◆**look through** vtr 1 (window) mirar por. 2 (leaf through) hojear; (examine) revisar; (check) registrar. ◆**look to** vtr 1 (take care of) velar por. 2 (turn to) recurrir a. ◆**look up** I vi 1 (glance upwards) alzar la vista. 2 fam (improve) mejorar. II vtr 1 (look for) buscar. 2 (visit) ir a visitar. ◆**look upon** vtr considerar. ◆**look up to** vtr (person) respetar.

lookout ['lukaut] n (person) centinela mf; (place) mirador m; **to be on the l. for**, estar al acecho de; fam that's his l.!, ¡eso es asunto suyo!

loom¹ [lu:m] n telar m.

loom² [lu:m] vi alzarse; fig (threaten) amenazar.

loony ['lu:nɪ] adj (**loonier, looniest**) fam loco,-a.

loop [lu:p] I n 1 lazo m. 2 Comput bucle m. II vtr 1 encordar. 2 Av to l. the loop, rizar el rizo.

loophole ['lu:phəul] n fig escapatoria f.

loose [lu:s] adj 1 (not secure) flojo,-a; (papers, hair, clothes) suelto,-a; (knot) desatado,-a; (baggy) holgado,-a; **to set sb l.**, soltar a algn; **to come l.**, (a knot) no saber qué hacer. 2 (not packaged) a granel; l. tobacco, tabaco m en hebras; l. change, suelto m. 3 (not exact) vago,-a; (translation) libre. 4 (lax) relajado,-a; a l. woman, una mujer fácil. ◆**loosely** adv 1 (approximately) aproximadamente. 2 (vaguely) vagamente.

loosen ['lu:sən] I vtr aflojar; (belt) desabrochar; fig (restrictions) flexibilizar. II vi (slacken) aflojarse.

loot [lu:t] I n botín m. II vtr saquear.

lop [lɒp] vtr podar. ◆**lop off** vtr cortar.

lope [ləup] vi andar a zancadas.

lopsided [lɒp'saɪdɪd] adj ladeado,-a.

lord [lɔ:d] n 1 señor m; (British peer) lord m; **the House of Lords**, la Cámara de los Lores; **the L. Mayor**, el señor alcalde. 2

Rel **the L.**, El Señor; **good L.!**, ¡Dios mío!; **the L.'s Prayer**, el Padrenuestro. 3 (judge) señoría mf.

lordship ['lɔ:dʃɪp] n GB **His L.**, **Your L.**, su señoría.

lorry ['lɒrɪ] n GB camión m; **l. driver**, camionero,-a mf.; l. load, carga f.

lose [lu:z] I vtr (pt & pp lost) perder; to l. time, (of clock) atrasarse. II vi perder; to l. to sb, perder contra algn; to l. out, salir perdiendo.

loser ['lu:zər] n perdedor,-a m,f.

loss [lɒs] n pérdida f; **to make a l.**, perder; fig **to be at a l. for words**, quedarse de una pieza; **to be at a l. what to do**, no saber qué hacer.

lost [lɒst] adj 1 perdido,-a; **to get l.**, perderse; fam **get l.!**, ¡vete a la porra!; **l. property office**, US **l. and found department**, oficina f de objetos perdidos. 2 (disoriented) desorientado,-a; (distracted) distraído,-a; l. in thought, ensimismado,-a.

lot [lɒt] n 1 (fate) suerte f. **2 to cast lots for sth**, echar algo a suertes. 3 US (plot of land) parcela f. 4 (in an auction) lote m. 5 (everything) todo m; he ate the l., se lo comió todo. **6 a l. of**, (much) mucho, -a; (many) muchos,-as; **he feels a l. better**, se encuentra mucho mejor; **she reads a l.**, lee mucho; fam **lots of**, montones de, cantidad de.

lotion ['ləuʃən] n loción f.

lottery ['lɒtərɪ] n lotería f; **l. ticket**, ≈ décimo m de lotería.

loud [laud] I adj 1 (voice) alto,-a; (noise) fuerte; (laugh) estrepitoso,-a; (applause) clamoroso,-a; (protests, party) ruidoso,-a. 2 (flashy) chillón,-ona. 3 (vulgar) hortera. II adv **to read/think out l.**, leer/pensar en voz alta.

loud-hailer [laud'heɪlər] n megáfono m.

loudspeaker [laud'spi:kər] n altavoz m.

lounge [laundʒ] I n GB salón m, sala f de estar. II vi hacer el vago.

louse [laus] n (pl lice [laɪs]) piojo m.

lousy ['lauzɪ] adj (lousier, lousiest) fam fatal; a l. trick, una cochinada.

lout [laut] n gamberro m.

lovable ['lʌvəbl] adj adorable.

love [lʌv] I n 1 amor m (for, por); (passion) pasión f (for, por); **to be in l. with sb**, estar enamorado,-a de algn; **to fall in l.**, enamorarse; **to make l.**, hacer el amor; (with) l. (from) Mary, (in letter) un abrazo, Mary; l. affair, amorío m; l. letter/story, carta f/historia f de amor; l. life, vida f sentimental. 2 (person) amor m, cariño m; fam chato,-a m,f; my l., mi amor. 3 Ten forty l., cuarenta a cero. II vtr (person) querer a, amar a; he loves cooking/football, le encanta cocinar/el fútbol.

lovely ['lʌvlɪ] adj (**lovelier, loveliest**)

(charming) encantador,-a; *(beautiful)* hermoso,-a, precioso,-a; *(delicious)* riquísimo,-a.

lover ['lʌvəʳ] *n* **1** *(sexual partner)* amante *mf*. **2** *(enthusiast)* aficionado,-a *m,f*, amigo,-a *m,f*.

loving ['lʌvɪŋ] *adj* cariñoso,-a.

low¹ [ləʊ] **I** *adj* **1** bajo,-a; *(neckline)* escotado,-a; **the L. Countries**, los Países Bajos. **2** *(in quantity)* bajo,-a. **3** *(poor)* pobre. **4** *(battery)* gastado,-a; **l. frequency**, baja frecuencia. **5 to feel l.**, sentirse deprimido,-a. **6** *(reprehensible)* malo,-a. **II** *adv* bajo. **III** *n* **1** *Meteor* área *f* de baja presión. **2** *(low point)* punto más bajo; **to reach an all-time l.**, tocar fondo.

low² [ləʊ] *vi (cow)* mugir.

lowdown ['ləʊdaʊn] *n fam* pormenores *mpl*.

lower ['ləʊəʳ] **I** *adj (comp of low)* inferior; *Typ* **l. case**, minúscula *f*; **l. class**, clase baja. **II** *adv comp → low.* **III** *vtr* bajar; *(flag)* arriar; *(reduce)* reducir; *(price)* rebajar.

lower-class ['ləʊəklɑːs] *adj* de clase baja.

lowest ['ləʊɪst] **I** *adj (superl of low)* más bajo,-a; *(price, speed)* mínimo,-a. **II** *n* **at the l.**, como mínimo.

low-key [ləʊ'kiː] *adj* sin ceremonia.

lowlands ['ləʊləndz] *npl* tierras bajas.

lowly ['ləʊlɪ] *adj (lowlier, lowliest)* humilde.

low-necked [ləʊ'nekt] *adj* escotado,-a.

loyal ['lɔɪəl] *adj* leal, fiel.

loyalty ['lɔɪəltɪ] *n* lealtad *f*, fidelidad *f*.

lozenge ['lɒzɪndʒ] *n* pastilla *f*.

LP [el'piː] *abbr of* **long-playing record**, LP *m*.

L-plate ['elpleɪt] *n GB* (placa *f* de) la ele.

LSD [eles'diː] *abbr of* **lysergic acid diethylamide**, dietilamida *f* del ácido lisérgico, LSD *m*.

Ltd *GB Com abbr of* **Limited (Liability)**, Sociedad Anónima, S.A..

lubricant ['luːbrɪkənt] *n* lubricante *m*.

lubricate ['luːbrɪkeɪt] *vtr* lubricar; *(engine)* engrasar.

lubrication [luːbrɪ'keɪʃən] *n* engrase *m*.

lucid ['luːsɪd] *adj* lúcido,-a.

luck [lʌk] *n* suerte *f*; **bad l.!**, ¡mala suerte!; **good l.!**, ¡(buena) suerte!; **to be in l.**, estar de suerte; **to be out of l.**, no tener suerte; *fig* **to push one's l.**, tentar la suerte; *fig* **to try one's l.**, probar fortuna.

lucky ['lʌkɪ] *adj (luckier, luckiest)* *(person)* afortunado,-a; *(day)* de suerte; *(move)* oportuno,-a; *(charm)* de la suerte; **a l. break**, una oportunidad. ◆**luckily** *adv* por suerte, afortunadamente.

lucrative ['luːkrətɪv] *adj* lucrativo,-a.

ludicrous ['luːdɪkrəs] *adj* absurdo,-a, ridículo,-a.

lug [lʌg] *vtr fam* arrastrar.

luggage ['lʌgɪdʒ] *n* equipaje *m*; **l. rack**, *Aut* baca *f*; *Rail* portaequipajes *m inv*.

lukewarm ['luːkwɔːm] *adj (water etc)* tibio,-a; *fig (reception etc)* poco entusiasta.

lull [lʌl] **I** *n (in storm)* calma chicha; *(in fighting)* tregua *f*. **II** *vtr (cause to sleep)* adormecer; **to l. sb into a false sense of security**, infundir una falsa seguridad a algn.

lullaby ['lʌləbaɪ] *n* canción *f* de cuna, nana *f*.

lumbago [lʌm'beɪgəʊ] *n* lumbago *m*.

lumber ['lʌmbəʳ] **I** *n* **1** *GB (junk)* trastos viejos. **2** *US (timber)* maderos *mpl*. **II** *vtr fam* cargar (**with**, de).

lumberjack ['lʌmbədʒæk] *n* leñador *m*.

luminous ['luːmɪnəs] *adj* luminoso,-a.

lump [lʌmp] **I** *n (of coal etc)* trozo *m*; *(of sugar, earth)* terrón *m*; *(in sauce)* grumo *m*; *(swelling)* bulto *m*; *fam fig (in throat)* nudo *m*; **l. sum**, cantidad *f* global. **II** *vtr fam (endure)* aguantar. ◆**lump together** *vtr* apelotonar.

lumpy ['lʌmpɪ] *adj (lumpier, lumpiest)* *(bed)* lleno,-a de bultos; *(sauce)* grumoso,-a.

lunacy ['luːnəsɪ] *n* locura *f*.

lunar ['luːnəʳ] *adj* lunar.

lunatic ['luːnətɪk] *adj & n* loco,-a *(m,f)*; **l. asylum**, manicomio *m*.

lunch [lʌntʃ] **I** *n* comida *f*, almuerzo *m*; **l. hour**, hora *f* de comer. **II** *vi* comer, almorzar.

luncheon ['lʌntʃən] *n arch fml* almuerzo *m*; **l. voucher**, vale *m* de comida; *(pork)* **l. meat**, carne *f* de cerdo troceada, chopped *m*.

lunchtime ['lʌntʃtaɪm] *n* hora *f* de comer.

lung [lʌŋ] *n* pulmón *m*.

lunge [lʌndʒ] **I** *n* arremetida *f*. **II** *vi (also* **l. forward**) arremeter; **to l. (out) at sb**, arremeter contra algn.

lurch [lɜːtʃ] **I** *n* **1** *(of vehicle)* sacudida *f*; *(of person)* tambaleo *m*. **2** *fam* **to leave sb in the l.**, dejar a algn en la cuneta. **II** *vi (vehicle)* dar sacudidas; *(person)* tambalearse.

lure [lʊəʳ] **I** *n (decoy)* señuelo *m*; *(bait)* cebo *m*; *fig (charm)* aliciente *m*. **II** *vtr* atraer con engaños.

lurid ['lʊərɪd] *adj* **1** *(gruesome)* espeluznante; *(sensational)* sensacionalista. **2** *(gaudy)* chillón,-ona.

lurk [lɜːk] *vi (lie in wait)* estar al acecho; *(hide)* esconderse.

luscious ['lʌʃəs] *adj (food)* delicioso,-a.

lush [lʌʃ] *adj (vegetation)* exuberante.

lust [lʌst] **I** *n (sexual desire)* lujuria *f*; *(craving)* ansia *f*; *(greed)* codicia *f*. **II** *vi* **to l. after sth/sb**, codiciar algo/desear a algn.

luster ['lʌstəʳ] *n US* → **lustre**.

lustre ['lʌstəʳ] *n* lustre *m*.

lusty ['lʌstɪ] *adj* **(lustier, lustiest)** robusto,-a.

lute [luːt] *n* laúd *m*.

Luxembourg ['lʌksəmbɜːg] *n* Luxemburgo.

luxuriant [lʌg'zjʊərɪənt] *adj (plants)* exuberante; *(hair etc)* abundante.

luxurious [lʌg'zjʊərɪəs] *adj* lujoso,-a.

luxury ['lʌkʃərɪ] *n* lujo *m*; **l. flat,** piso *m* de lujo.

lychee ['laɪtʃiː] *n* lichi *m*.

lying ['laɪɪŋ] **I** *adj* mentiroso,-a. **II** *n* mentiras *fpl*.

lynch [lɪntʃ] *vtr* linchar.

lyre [laɪər] *n* Mus lira *f*.

lyric ['lɪrɪk] *adj* lírico,-a. **II** *n* **1** *(poem)* poema *m* lírico. **2 lyrics,** *(words of song)* letra *f sing*.

lyrical ['lɪrɪkəl] *adj* lírico,-a.

M

M, m [em] *n (the letter)* M, m *f*.

m 1 *abbr of* **metre(s),** m. **2** *abbr of* **million(s),** m.

macabre [mə'kɑːbrə] *adj* macabro,-a.

mac(c)aroni [mækə'rəʊnɪ] *n* macarrones *mpl*.

mace¹ [meɪs] *n (club, ceremonial staff)* maza *f*.

mace² [meɪs] *n (spice)* macis *f inv*.

machine [mə'ʃiːn] **I** *n* máquina *f*; **m. gun,** ametralladora *f*; **m. language,** lenguaje *m* máquina. **II** *vtr* trabajar a máquina.

machine-gun [mə'ʃiːngʌn] *vtr* ametrallar.

machine-readable [məʃiːn'riːdəbəl] *adj* Comput para ser leído,-a por ordenador.

machinery [mə'ʃiːnərɪ] *n (machines)* maquinaria *f*; *(workings of machine)* mecanismo *m*; *fig* the bureaucratic m., la maquinaria burocrática.

mac [mæk] *n GB fam abbr of* **mackintosh**.

mackerel ['mækrəl] *n (pl mackerel)* caballa *f*.

mac(k)intosh ['mækɪntɒʃ] *n* impermeable *m*.

macroeconomics [mækrəʊiːkə'nɒmɪks] *n* macroeconomía *f*.

mad [mæd] *adj* **(madder, maddest)** **1** loco,-a; *(animal)* furioso,-a; *(dog)* rabioso,-a; **to be m.,** estar loco,-a; **to drive sb m.,** volver loco,-a a algn; **to go m.,** volverse loco,-a; **you must be m.!,** ¿estás loco? **2** *(idea, plan)* disparatado,-a. **3** *fam* **to be m. about sth/sb,** estar loco, -a por algo/algn. **4** *fam* **to be m. at sb,** estar enfadado,-a con algn. **5** *(gallop, race etc)* desenfrenado,-a. ◆**madly** *adv fam (extremely)* terriblemente; **to be m. in love with sb,** estar locamente enamorado,-a de algn.

madam ['mædəm] *n* **1** señora *f*; **Dear M.,** *(in letter)* Muy señora mía, Estimada señora. **2** *(brothelkeeper)* madam *f*.

madden ['mædən] *vtr* volver loco,-a.

maddening ['mædənɪŋ] *adv* exasperante.

made [meɪd] *pt & pp* → **make**.

Madeira [mə'dɪərə] *n* **1** *(island)* Madeira *f*. **2** *(wine)* madeira *m*; **M. cake,** bizcocho

m.

made-to-measure [meɪdtə'meʒər] *adj* hecho,-a a (la) medida.

made-up ['meɪdʌp] *adj* **1** *(face, person)* maquillado,-a; *(eyes, lips)* pintado,-a. **2** *(story, excuse)* inventado,-a.

madman ['mædmən] *n* loco *m*.

madness ['mædnɪs] *n* locura *f*.

Madrid [mə'drɪd] *n* Madrid *m*.

Mafia ['mæfɪə] *n* mafia *f*.

magazine [mægə'ziːn] *n* **1** *(periodical)* revista *f*. **2** *(in rifle)* recámara *f*. **3** *Mil (storehouse)* almacén *m*; *(for explosives)* polvorín *m*.

maggot ['mægət] *n* larva *f*, gusano *m*.

magic ['mædʒɪk] **I** *n* magia *f*. **II** *adj* **1** mágico,-a; **m. wand,** varita mágica. **2** *fam (wonderful)* estupendo,-a.

magical ['mædʒɪkəl] *adj* mágico,-a.

magician [mə'dʒɪʃən] *n* **1** *(wizard)* mago,-a *m,f*. **2** *(conjuror)* prestidigitador,-a *m,f*.

magistrate ['mædʒɪstreɪt] *n* juez *mf* de paz; **magistrates' court,** juzgado *m* de paz.

magnanimous [mæg'nænɪməs] *adj* magnánimo,-a.

magnet ['mægnɪt] *n* imán *m*.

magnetic [mæg'netɪk] *adj* magnético,-a; *fig (personality)* carismático,-a; **m. tape,** cinta magnetofónica.

magnetism ['mægnɪtɪzəm] *n* magnetismo *m*.

magnificence [mæg'nɪfɪsəns] *n* magnificencia *f*.

magnificent [mæg'nɪfɪsənt] *adj* magnífico,-a.

magnify ['mægnɪfaɪ] *vtr* **1** *(enlarge)* aumentar. **2** *fig (exaggerate)* exagerar.

magnifying glass ['mægnɪfaɪɪŋglɑːs] *n* lupa *f*.

magnitude ['mægnɪtjuːd] *n* magnitud *f*.

magpie ['mægpaɪ] *n* urraca *f*.

mahogany [mə'hɒgənɪ] *n* **1** caoba *f*. **II** *adj* de caoba.

maid [meɪd] *n* **1** criada *f*, Am mucama *f*. **2** *pej* old m., solterona *f*.

maiden ['meɪdən] **I** *n* *lit* doncella *f*. **II** *adj* **1** *(unmarried)* soltera; **m. aunt,** tía soltera;

m. name, apellido m de soltera. 2 (voyage, flight) inaugural.

mail [meɪl] I n correo m; **by m.**, por correo; **m. order**, venta f por correo; **m. train**, (tren m) correo. II vtr (post) echar al buzón; (send) enviar por correo.

mailbox ['meɪlbɒks] n US buzón m.

mailing list ['meɪlɪŋlɪst] n lista f de direcciones.

mailman ['meɪlmæn] n US cartero m.

maim [meɪm] vtr lisiar.

main [meɪn] I adj (problem, door etc) principal; (square, mast, sail) mayor; (office) central; **the m. thing is to keep calm**, lo esencial es mantener la calma; **Culin m. course**, plato m principal; **m. road**, carretera f principal. II n 1 (pipe, wire) conducto m principal; **the mains**, (water or gas system) la cañería maestra; Elec la red eléctrica; **a radio that works on battery or mains**, una radio que funciona con pilas o con corriente. 2 in **the m.**, por regla general. II **mainly** adv principalmente, sobre todo; (for the most part) en su mayoría.

mainframe ['meɪnfreɪm] n m. computer, unidad f, central f.

mainland ['meɪnlænd] n continente m.

mainstay ['meɪnsteɪ] n fig sustento m, sostén m.

mainstream ['meɪnstriːm] n corriente f principal.

maintain [meɪnˈteɪn] vtr mantener; (conversation) sostener; (silence, appearances) guardar; (road, machine) conservar en buen estado.

maintenance ['meɪntənəns] n 1 mantenimiento m. 2 (divorce allowance) pensión f.

maisonette [meɪzəˈnet] n dúplex m.

maize [meɪz] n maíz m.

majestic [məˈdʒestɪk] adj majestuoso,-a.

majesty ['mædʒɪstɪ] n majestad f.

major ['meɪdʒər] I adj 1 principal, mayor; (contribution, operation) importante. 2 Mus mayor. II n 1 Mil comandante m. 2 US Univ especialidad f. III vi US Univ **to m. in**, especializarse en.

Majorca [məˈjɔːkə] n Mallorca.

Majorcan [məˈjɔːkən] adj & n mallorquín,-ina (m,f).

majority [məˈdʒɒrɪtɪ] n mayoría f; **to be in the m.**, ser (la) mayoría.

make [meɪk] (pt & pp made) I vtr 1 hacer; (manufacture) fabricar; (create) crear; (clothes, curtains) confeccionar; (meal) preparar; (payment) efectuar; (speech) pronunciar; (decision) tomar; (mistake) cometer; **to be made of**, ser de; **to m. a noise**, hacer ruido. 2 (render) poner, volver; (convert) convertir (into, en); (appoint) nombrar; **he made it clear that ...**, dejó claro que .... 3 (force, compel) obligar; (cause) causar; **to m. do with sth**, arreglárselas con algo. 4 (earn) ga-

nar; **to m. a living**, ganarse la vida; **to m. a name for oneself**, hacerse famoso, -a; fig **to m. the best of sth**, sacar partido de algo. 5 7 and 5 m. 12, 7 y 5 son 12. 6 (calculate, reckon) calcular; **what time do you m. it?**, ¿qué hora tienes? 7 (think) opinar; **I don't know what to m. of it**, no sé qué pensar de eso; **it doesn't m. sense**, no tiene sentido. 8 (achieve) alcanzar, conseguir. 9 **it will m. or break her**, será su consagración o su ruina. 10 **to m. a fresh start**, volver a empezar.
II vi 1 hacer; **to m. sure of sth**, asegurarse de algo. 2 **she made as if to leave**, hizo como si quisiera marcharse.
III n 1 (brand) marca f. 2 fam **to be on the m.**, andar tras el dinero.

◆**make for** vtr 1 (move towards) dirigirse hacia; (attack) atacar a. 2 **this makes for less work**, esto ahorra trabajo.

◆**make out** I vtr 1 (list, receipt) hacer; (cheque) extender; (perceive) distinguir; (writing) descifrar. 3 (understand) entender. 4 (claim) pretender. 5 **to m. out a case for doing sth**, exponer los argumentos para hacer algo. II vi **how did you m. out?**, ¿qué tal te fue?

◆**make up** I vtr 1 (parcel, list) hacer; (prescription) preparar; (assemble) montar. 2 (story) inventar. 3 (apply cosmetics to) maquillar; (one's face) maquillarse. 4 (loss) compensar; (lost time) recuperar. 5 (constitute) componer. 6 **to m. it up with sb**, hacer las paces (con algn). 7 **to m. up one's mind**, decidirse. II vi maquillarse. ◆**make up to** vi **to m. up to sb**, congraciarse con algn. 2 **to m. it up to sb for sth**, compensar a algn por algo.

make-believe ['meɪkbɪliːv] n (fantasy) fantasía f; (pretence) fingimiento m; **to live in a world of m.-b.**, vivir en un mundo de ensueño.

maker ['meɪkər] n fabricante mf.

makeshift ['meɪkʃɪft] adj (improvised) improvisado,-a; (temporary) provisional.

make-up ['meɪkʌp] n 1 (cosmetics) maquillaje m; **m.-up remover**, desmaquillador m. 2 (composition) composición f; (character) carácter m.

making ['meɪkɪŋ] n 1 (manufacture) fabricación f; (preparation) preparación f. 2 **he has the makings of a politician**, tiene madera de político.

malaise [mæˈleɪz] n malestar m.

malaria [məˈleərɪə] n malaria f.

Malay [məˈleɪ] I adj malayo,-a. II n 1 (person) malayo,-a m,f. 2 (language) malayo m.

Malaysia [məˈleɪzɪə] n Malasia.

male [meɪl] I adj (animal, plant) macho; (person) varón; (sex) masculino; pej **m. chauvinism**, machismo m. II n (person) varón m; (animal, plant) macho m.

malevolent [məˈlevələnt] adj malévolo,-

-a.

malfunction [mæl'fʌŋkʃən] I n mal funcionamiento m. II vi funcionar mal.

malice ['mælɪs] n malicia f; Jur **with m. aforethought**, con premeditación.

malicious [mə'lɪʃəs] adj malévolo,-a.

malign [mə'laɪn] I adj maligno,-a; (influence) perjudicial. II vtr calumniar, difamar.

malignant [mə'lɪgnənt] adj 1 (person) malvado,-a. 2 Med maligno,-a.

mall [mɔːl, mæl] n US centro m comercial.

malleable ['mælɪəbəl] adj maleable.

mallet ['mælɪt] n mazo m.

malnutrition [mælnju:'trɪʃən] n desnutrición f.

malpractice [mæl'præktɪs] n procedimiento m ilegal; Med negligencia f.

malt [mɔːlt] n malta f.

Malta ['mɔːltə] n Malta.

mammal ['mæməl] n mamífero m.

mammary ['mæmərɪ] adj **m. gland**, mama f.

mammoth ['mæməθ] I n Zool mamut m. II adj gigantesco,-a.

man [mæn] I n (pl men) 1 hombre m; old m., viejo m; young m., joven m; fig he's a m. of his word, es hombre de palabra; fig the m. in the street, el hombre de la calle; m. Friday, factótum m; fam dirty old m., viejo verde. 2 (humanity) el hombre; (human being) el humano. 3 (husband) marido m; (partner) pareja f. 4 our m. in Madrid, nuestro hombre en Madrid. 5 Chess pieza f. II vtr (boat, plane) tripular; (post) servir; **manned flight**, vuelo tripulado.

manage ['mænɪdʒ] I vtr 1 (company, household) llevar; (money, affairs, person) manejar. 2 (succeed) conseguir; **to m. to do sth**, lograr hacer algo. II vi (cope physically) poder; (esp financially) arreglárselas; **we're managing**, vamos tirando.

manageable ['mænɪdʒəbəl] adj manejable.

management ['mænɪdʒmənt] n dirección f.

manager ['mænɪdʒər] n 1 (of company, bank) director,-a m,f; (head of department) jefe,-a m,f. 2 (of pop group etc) mánager m. 3 Sport entrenador m.

manageress [mænɪdʒə'res] n (of shop, restaurant) encargada f; (of company) directora f.

managerial [mænɪ'dʒɪərɪəl] adj directivo,-a.

managing ['mænɪdʒɪŋ] adj directivo,-a; **m. director**, director,-a m,f, gerente.

mandarin ['mændərɪn] n **m.** (orange), mandarina f.

mandate ['mændeɪt] n mandato m.

mandatory ['mændətərɪ] adj fml obligatorio,-a.

mane [meɪn] n (of horse) crin f; (of lion) melena f.

maneuver [mə'nuːvər] n & vtr US → **manoeuvre**.

manfully ['mænfʊlɪ] adv valientemente.

manger ['meɪndʒər] n pesebre m.

mangle¹ ['mæŋgəl] n (for wringing) rodillo m.

mangle² ['mæŋgəl] vtr (crush) aplastar; (destroy by cutting) despedazar.

mango ['mæŋgəʊ] n (pl **mangoes**) mango m.

mangy ['meɪndʒɪ] adj (mangier, mangiest) (animal) sarnoso,-a; fam (carpet) raído,-a.

manhandle ['mænhændəl] vtr maltratar.

manhole ['mænhəʊl] n boca f de acceso.

manhood ['mænhʊd] n 1 (age) mayoría f de edad; **to reach m.**, llegar a la edad viril. 2 (manly qualities) virilidad f.

mania ['meɪnɪə] n manía f.

maniac ['meɪnɪæk] n maníaco,-a m,f; fam loco,-a m,f.

manic ['mænɪk] adj maníaco,-a.

manic-depressive [mænɪkdɪ'presɪv] adj & n maníaco,-a (m,f) depresivo,-a.

manicure ['mænɪkjʊər] I n manicura f. II vtr **to m. one's nails**, hacerse la manicura.

manifest ['mænɪfest] fml I adj manifiesto,-a. II vtr manifestar.

manifesto [mænɪ'festəʊ] n programa m electoral.

manifold ['mænɪfəʊld] adj fml (many) múltiples; (varied) diversos,-as.

manipulate [mə'nɪpjʊleɪt] vtr 1 manipular. 2 fig (accounts etc) falsificar.

mankind [mæn'kaɪnd] n la humanidad, el género humano.

manly ['mænlɪ] adj (manlier, manliest) varonil, viril.

man-made ['mænmeɪd] adj (lake) artificial; (fibres, fabric) sintético,-a.

manner ['mænər] n 1 (way, method) manera f, modo m; **in this m.**, de esta manera. 2 (way of behaving) forma f de ser. 3 fml (type, class) clase f. 4 (good) **manners**, buenos modales; **bad manners**, falta f sing de educación.

mannerism ['mænərɪzəm] n (gesture) gesto m; (affectation) amaneramiento m.

manoeuvre [mə'nuːvər] I n maniobra f. II vtr maniobrar; (person) manejar. III vi maniobrar.

manor ['mænər] n **m. house**, casa solariega.

manpower ['mænpaʊər] n mano f de obra.

mansion ['mænʃən] n casa f grande; (in country) casa solariega.

manslaughter ['mænslɔːtər] n homicidio involuntario.

mantelpiece ['mæntelpiːs] n (shelf) repisa f de chimenea; (fireplace) chimenea f.

mantle ['mæntəl] *n fig (of snow)* manto *m*, capa *f*.

manual ['mænjuəl] *adj & n* manual (*m*).

manufacture [mænju'fæktʃər] I *vtr* fabricar. II *n* fabricación *f*.

manufacturer [mænju'fæktʃərər] *n* fabricante *mf*.

manure [mə'njuər] *n* abono *m*, estiércol *m*.

manuscript ['mænjuskript] *n* manuscrito *m*.

many ['meni] I *adj (more, most)* mucho,-a, muchos,-as; **a great m.**, muchísimos,-as; **as m. ... as ...**, tantos -as ... como ...; **how m. days?**, ¿cuántos días?; **m. a time**, muchas veces; **so m. flowers!**, ¡cuántas flores!; **too m.**, demasiados,-as. II *pron* muchos,-as.

map [mæp] I *n (of country)* mapa *m*; *(of town, bus route)* plano *m*. II *vtr* trazar un mapa de. ◆**map out** *vtr (route)* planear.

maple ['meipəl] *n* arce *m*.

mar [mɑːr] *vtr* estropear; **to m. sb's enjoyment**, aguarle la fiesta a algn.

marathon ['mærəθən] *n* maratón *m*.

marble ['mɑːbəl] I *n* 1 *(stone)* mármol *m*. 2 *(glass ball)* canica *f*. II *adj* de mármol.

March [mɑːtʃ] *n* marzo *m*.

march [mɑːtʃ] I *n* 1 *Mil* marcha *f*; *fig* **to steal a m. on sb**, tomar la delantera a algn. 2 *(demonstration)* manifestación *f*. II *vi* 1 marchar. 2 *(demonstrate)* manifestarse. III *vtr Mil* hacer marchar.

march past ['mɑːtʃpɑːst] *n* desfile *m*.

mare [meər] *n* yegua *f*.

margarine [mɑːdʒə'riːn] *n* margarina *f*.

margin ['mɑːdʒin] *n* margen *m*; *fig* **to win by a narrow m.**, ganar por escaso margen; **m. of error**, *(in statistics)* error muestral.

marginal ['mɑːdʒinəl] *adj* marginal; *Pol* **m. seat**, escaño *m* pendiente. ◆**marginally** *adv* ligeramente.

marigold ['mærigəuld] *n* caléndula *f*.

marijuana, marihuana [mæri'hwɑːnə] *n* marihuana *f*, mariguana *f*.

marinate ['mærineit] *vtr* adobar.

marine [mə'riːn] I *adj* marino,-a. II *n* soldado *m* de infantería de marina; *GB* **the Marines**, *US* **the M. Corps**, la infantería de marina.

marital ['mæritəl] *adj* matrimonial; **m. status**, estado *m* civil.

maritime ['mæritaim] *adj* marítimo,-a.

marjoram ['mɑːdʒərəm] *n* mejorana *f*.

mark[1] [mɑːk] *n* 1 *(left by blow etc)* señal *f*; *(stain)* mancha *f*; *fig* **to make one's m.**, distinguirse. 2 *(sign, token)* señal *f*; *(indication)* indicio *m*. 3 *(in exam etc)* nota *f*; **to get high marks**, sacar buenas notas. 4 *fig* **to hit the m.**, dar en el clavo; *fig* **to be wide of the m.**, estar lejos de la verdad. II *vtr* 1 *(stain)* manchar. 2 *(with*

tick, cross) señalar. 3 *(exam)* corregir; *(student)* dar notas a. 4 **'10% off marked price'**, 'descuento del 10% sobre el precio indicado'. 5 **m. my words**, fíjate en lo que te digo. 6 *Sport* marcar. 7 **to m. time**, *Mil* marcar el paso; *fig* hacer tiempo. ◆**mark out** *vtr* 1 *(area)* delimitar. 2 **to m. sb out for**, destinar a algn a.

mark[2] [mɑːk] *n (unit of currency)* marco *m*.

marked [mɑːkt] *adj (noticeable)* marcado,-a, acusado,-a.

marker ['mɑːkər] *n* 1 *(bookmark)* registro *m*. 2 *Sport* marcador,-a *m,f*. 3 *(pen)* rotulador *m* fluorescente.

market ['mɑːkit] I *n* 1 mercado *m*; **m. garden**, *(small)* huerto *m*; *(large)* huerta *f*; **on the m.**, en venta; **m. forces**, tendencias *fpl* del mercado; **m. price**, precio *m* de mercado; **m. research**, estudio *m* de mercado. II *vtr (sell)* poner en venta; *(promote)* promocionar.

marketable ['mɑːkitəbəl] *adj* comerciable.

marketing ['mɑːkitiŋ] *n* marketing *m*, mercadotecnia *f*.

marketplace ['mɑːkitpleis] *n* mercado *m*.

marksman ['mɑːksmən] *n* tirador *m*.

marmalade ['mɑːməleid] *n* mermelada *f* (de cítricos).

maroon [mə'ruːn] *adj (de color)* granate.

marooned [mə'ruːnd] *adj* bloqueado,-a.

marquee [mɑː'kiː] *n* carpa *f*, entoldado *m*.

marquess, marquis ['mɑːkwis] *n* marqués *m*.

marriage ['mæridʒ] *n (state)* matrimonio *m*; *(wedding)* boda *f*; **m. bureau**, agencia *f* matrimonial; **m. certificate**, certificado *f* de matrimonio.

married ['mærid] *adj* casado,-a; **m. life**, vida *f* conyugal.

marrow ['mærəu] *n* 1 *(bone)* m., médula *f*. 2 *Bot* calabacín *m*.

marry ['mæri] *vtr (take in marriage)* casarse con; *(give in marriage)* casar (**to**, con); *(unite in marriage)* casar; **to get married**, casarse.

Mars [mɑːz] *n* Marte *m*.

marsh [mɑːʃ] *n* pantano *m*; **salt m.**, marisma *f*.

marshal ['mɑːʃəl] I *n* 1 *Mil* mariscal *m*. 2 *GB (at sports event etc)* oficial *mf*. 3 *US (sheriff)* alguacil *m*. 4 *US (of police or fire department)* jefe *m*. II *vtr* 1 *Mil* formar. 2 *(facts etc)* ordenar.

marshy ['mɑːʃi] *adj (marshier, marshiest)* pantanoso,-a.

martial ['mɑːʃəl] *adj* marcial; **m. arts**, artes *fpl* marciales; **m. law**, ley *f* marcial.

martyr ['mɑːtər] I *n* mártir *mf*. II *vtr* martirizar.

martyrdom ['mɑːtədəm] *n* martirio *m*.

marvel ['mɑːvəl] I *n* maravilla *f*. II *vi* to

m. at, maravillarse de.

marvellous, *US* **marvelous** ['mɑːvələs] *adj* maravilloso,-a.

Marxism ['mɑːksɪzəm] *n* marxismo *m*.

Marxist ['mɑːksɪst] *adj & n* marxista (*mf*).

marzipan ['mɑːzɪpæn] *n* mazapán *m*.

mascara [mæ'skɑːrə] *n* rímel *m*.

mascot ['mæskət] *n* mascota *f*.

masculine ['mæskjʊlɪn] *adj* masculino,-a; (*woman*) hombruna.

mash [mæʃ] I *n* (*for animals*) afrecho *m*. II *vtr* to m. (up), machacar; **mashed potatoes**, puré *m* de patatas.

mask [mɑːsk] I *n* máscara *f*; (*of doctor, dentist etc*) mascarilla *f*. II *vtr* enmascarar; *fig* (*conceal*) ocultar (**from**, de).

masochist ['mæsəkɪst] *adj & n* masoquista (*mf*).

mason ['meɪsən] *n* 1 (*builder*) albañil *m*. 2 (*freemason*) masón *m*, francmasón *m*.

masonic [mə'sɒnɪk] *adj* masónico,-a.

masonry ['meɪsənrɪ] *n* (*stonework*) albañilería *f*.

masquerade [mæskə'reɪd] I *n* (*pretence*) farsa *f*. II *vi* to m. as, hacerse pasar por.

mass¹ [mæs] *n Rel* misa *f*; **to say m.**, decir misa.

mass² [mæs] I *n* 1 masa *f*. 2 (*large quantity*) montón *m*; (*of people*) multitud *f*. 3 **the masses**, las masas. II *adj* masivo,-a; **m. media**, medios *mpl* de comunicación (de masas); **m. production**, fabricación *f* en serie. III *vi* (*people*) congregarse; *Mil* concentrarse.

massacre ['mæsəkər] I *n* masacre *f*. II *vtr* masacrar.

massage ['mæsɑːʒ, mæ'sɑːdʒ] I *n* masaje *m*. II *vtr* 1 dar masajes a. 2 *fig* (*figures*) amañar.

masseur [mæ'sɜːr] *n* masajista *m*.

masseuse [mæ'sɜːz] *n* masajista *f*.

massive ['mæsɪv] *adj* enorme; (*heart attack*) grave.

mast [mɑːst] *n* 1 *Naut* mástil *m*. 2 *Rad TV* torre *f*.

master ['mɑːstər] I *n* 1 (*of dog, servant*) amo *m*; (*of household*) señor *m*. 2 *GB* (*teacher*) profesor *m*. 3 *Univ* **m.'s degree**, ≈ máster *m*. 4 (*expert*) maestro *m*. 5 (*boy*) **M. James Brown**, el señor James Brown. II *adj* 1 **m. copy**, original *m*; **m. key**, llave *f* maestra. 2 (*expert*) maestro,-a. III *vtr* 1 (*person, situation*) dominar. 2 (*subject, skill*) llegar a dominar.

masterful ['mɑːstəfʊl] *adj* autoritario,-a; (*imperious*) imperioso,-a; (*personality*) dominante.

masterly ['mɑːstəlɪ] *adj* magistral.

mastermind ['mɑːstəmaɪnd] I *n* (*person*) cerebro *m*. II *vtr* ser el cerebro de.

masterpiece ['mɑːstəpiːs] *n* obra *f* maestra.

masturbate ['mæstəbeɪt] *vi* masturbarse.

mat¹ [mæt] *n* (*rug*) alfombrilla *f*; (*door-mat*) felpudo *m*; (*rush mat*) estera *f*; *Sport* colchoneta *f*.

mat² [mæt] *adj* mate.

match¹ [mætʃ] *n* cerilla *f*, fósforo *m*.

match² [mætʃ] I *n* 1 *Sport* partido *m*; *Box* combate *m*. 2 *fig* **to meet one's m.**, (*equal*) encontrar uno la horma de su zapato. II *vtr* 1 (*equal, be the equal of*) igualar. 2 (*be in harmony with*) armonizar; **they are well matched**, (*teams*) van iguales; (*couple*) hacen buena pareja. 3 (*colours, clothes*) hacer juego con; (*pair of socks, gloves*) ser el compañero de. III *vi* (*harmonize*) hacer juego.

matchbox ['mætʃbɒks] *n* caja *f* de cerillas.

matching ['mætʃɪŋ] *adj* que hace juego.

mate [meɪt] I *n* 1 (*at school, work*) compañero,-a *m,f*, colega *mf*; *GB* (*friend*) amigo,-a *m,f*. 2 *Zool* (*male*) macho *m*; (*female*) hembra *f*. 3 (*assistant*) ayudante *mf*. 4 *Naut* **first/second m.**, primer/segundo oficial. II *vtr Zool* aparear. III *vi Zool* aparearse.

material [mə'tɪərɪəl] I *n* 1 (*substance*) materia *f*. 2 (*cloth*) tejido *m*, tela *f*. 3 (*information*) material *m*. 4 **materials**, (*ingredients, equipment*) materiales *mpl*. II *adj* 1 substancial. 2 (*not spiritual*) material.

materialistic [mətɪərɪə'lɪstɪk] *adj* materialista.

materialize [mə'tɪərɪəlaɪz] *vi* 1 (*hopes*) realizarse; (*plan, idea*) concretarse. 2 (*show up*) presentarse.

maternal [mə'tɜːnəl] *adj* maternal; (*uncle etc*) materno,-a.

maternity [mə'tɜːnɪtɪ] *n* maternidad *f*; **m. dress**, vestido *m* premamá; **m. hospital**, maternidad.

math [mæθ] *n US* → **maths**.

mathematical [mæθə'mætɪkəl] *adj* matemático,-a.

mathematician [mæθəmə'tɪʃən] *n* matemático,-a *m,f*.

mathematics [mæθə'mætɪks] *n* matemáticas *fpl*.

maths [mæθs] *n fam* matemáticas *fpl*.

matinée ['mætɪneɪ] *n Cin* sesión *f* de tarde; *Theat* función *f* de tarde.

mating ['meɪtɪŋ] *n* apareamiento *m*; **m. call**, reclamo *m*; **m. season**, época *f* de celo.

matriculation [mətrɪkjʊ'leɪʃən] *n Univ* matriculación *f*.

matrimonial [mætrɪ'məʊnɪəl] *adj* matrimonial.

matrimony ['mætrɪmənɪ] *n* matrimonio *m*; (*married life*) vida *f* conyugal.

matrix ['meɪtrɪks] *n* (*pl* **matrices** ['meɪtrɪsiːz]) matriz *f*.

matron ['meɪtrən] *n* (*in hospital*) enfermera *f* jefe.

matronly ['meɪtrənlɪ] adj madura y recia.

matt [mæt] adj mate.

matted ['mætɪd] adj enmarañado,-a.

matter ['mætər] n 1 (affair, question) asunto m; as a m. of course, por rutina; as a m. of fact, en realidad; that's another m., eso es otra cosa. 2 (problem) what's the m.?, ¿qué pasa? 3 no m. what he does, haga lo que haga; no m. when, no importa cuando; no m. where you go, dondequiera que vayas; no m. how clever he is, por muy inteligente que sea; no m. how, como sea. 4 (substance) materia f, sustancia f. 5 (content) contenido m; (subject) tema m. 6 Med (pus) pus m. II vi importar; it doesn't m., no importa, da igual.

matter-of-fact ['mætərəvfækt] adj (person) práctico,-a; (account) realista; (style) prosaico,-a.

mattress ['mætrɪs] n colchón f.

mature [mə'tʃʊər] I adj maduro,-a; Fin vencido,-a. II vi madurar; Fin vencer. III vtr madurar.

maturity [mə'tʃʊərɪtɪ] n madurez f.

maul [mɔːl] vtr 1 (wound) agredir. 2 (handle roughly) maltratar. 3 (touch in unpleasant way) sobar.

mauve [məʊv] adj & n malva (m).

max [mæks] abbr of **maximum**, máximo m, max.

maxim ['mæksɪm] n máxima f.

maximize ['mæksɪmaɪz] vtr maximizar.

maximum ['mæksɪməm] I n (pl maxima ['mæksɪmə]) máximo m. II adj máximo,-a.

may [meɪ] v aux (pt might) 1 (possibility, probability) poder, ser posible; be that as it m., sea como sea; come what m., pase lo que pase; he m. or might come, puede que venga; you m. or might as well stay, más vale que te quedes. 2 (permission) poder; m. I?, ¿me permite?; you m. smoke, pueden fumar. 3 (wish) ojalá (+ subj); m. you always be happy!, ¡ojalá seas siempre feliz!

May [meɪ] n mayo m; **M. Day**, el Primero or el Uno de Mayo.

maybe ['meɪbiː] adv quizá(s), tal vez.

mayhem ['meɪhem] n 1 (disturbance) alboroto m; (havoc) estragos mpl.

mayonnaise [meɪə'neɪz] n mayonesa f, mahonesa f.

mayor [meər] n (man) alcalde m; (woman) alcaldesa f.

mayoress ['meərɪs] n alcaldesa f.

maze [meɪz] n laberinto m.

MD [em'diː] 1 abbr of **Doctor of Medicine**, Dr. en Medicina. 2 fam abbr of **Managing Director**.

me [miː] pron 1 (as object) me; he gave it to me, me lo dio; listen to me, escúchame; she knows me, me conoce. 2 (after prep) mí; it's for me, es para mí; with

me, conmigo. 3 (emphatic) yo; it's me, soy yo; what about me?, ¿y yo, qué?

meadow ['medəʊ] n prado m, pradera f.

meagre, *US* **meager** ['miːgər] adj exiguo,-a.

meal[1] [miːl] n (flour) harina f.

meal[2] [miːl] n (food) comida f.

mealtime ['miːltaɪm] n hora f de comer.

mean[1] [miːn] vtr (pt & pp meant) 1 (signify) significar, querer decir; what do you m. by that?, ¿qué quieres decir con eso? 2 (intend) pensar, tener la intención de; I m. it, (te) lo digo en serio; she was meant to arrive on the 7th, tenía que or debía llegar el día 7; they m. well, tienen buenas intenciones; she didn't m. to do it, lo hizo sin querer. 3 (entail) suponer. 4 (refer to) referirse a. 5 (destine) destinar (for, a, para).

mean[2] [miːn] adj (meaner, meanest) 1 (miserly) tacaño,-a. 2 (unkind) malo,-a; (petty) mezquino,-a; *US* (bad-tempered) malhumorado,-a; to be m. to sb, tratar mal a algn. 3 (inferior) mediocre; (origins) humilde. 4 it was no m. feat, fue toda una hazaña.

mean[3] [miːn] I adj (average) medio,-a. II n (average) promedio m; Math media f.

meander [mɪ'ændər] vi (river) serpentear; (person) vagar; fig (digress) divagar.

meaning ['miːnɪŋ] n sentido m, significado m.

meaningful ['miːnɪŋfʊl] adj significativo,-a.

meaningless ['miːnɪŋlɪs] adj sin sentido.

meanness ['miːnnɪs] n 1 (miserliness) tacañería f. 2 (nastiness) maldad f.

means [miːnz] n 1 sing or pl (method) medio m, manera f; by m. of, por medio de, mediante. 2 pl (resources, wealth) medios mpl (de vida), recursos mpl (económicos); to live beyond one's m., vivir por encima de sus posibilidades. 3 by all m.!, ¡por supuesto!; by no m., de ninguna manera.

meant [ment] pt & pp → **mean**[1].

meantime ['miːntaɪm] I adv mientras tanto. II n in the m., mientras tanto.

meanwhile ['miːnwaɪl] adv mientras tanto.

measles ['miːzəlz] n sarampión m.

measure ['meʒər] I n 1 (action, step) medida f. 2 (ruler) regla f. 3 in some m., hasta cierto punto. 4 Mus compás m. II vtr (object, area) medir; (person) tomar las medidas de. ◆**measure up** vi to m. (up) (to sth), estar a la altura de (algo).

measurement ['meʒəmənt] n medida f.

meat [miːt] n carne f; Culin m. pie, empanada f de carne.

meatball ['miːtbɔːl] n albóndiga f.

meaty ['miːtɪ] adj (meatier, meatiest) 1 carnoso,-a. 2 fig (story) jugoso,-a.

Mecca ['mekə] n la Meca.

mechanic [mɪ'kænɪk] n (person) mecánico,-a m,f.

mechanical [mɪ'kænɪkəl] adj mecánico,-a.

mechanics [mɪ'kænɪks] n 1 sing (science) mecánica f. 2 pl (technical aspects) mecanismo m sing.

mechanism ['mekənɪzəm] n mecanismo m.

medal ['medəl] n medalla f.

medallion [mɪ'dæljən] n medallón m.

medallist, US **medalist** ['medəlɪst] n medalla f.

meddle ['medəl] vi entrometerse (in, en); **to m. with sth**, manosear algo.

media ['miːdɪə] npl medios mpl de comunicación; **m. coverage**, cobertura periodística.

median ['miːdɪən] I adj mediano,-a. II n Geom mediana f; Math valor mediano.

mediate ['miːdɪeɪt] vi mediar.

mediator ['miːdɪeɪtə] n mediador,-a m,f.

medical ['medɪkəl] I adj (treatment) médico,-a; (book) de medicina. II n fam reconocimiento médico.

medicated ['medɪkeɪtɪd] adj medicinal.

medicine ['medsɪn, 'medɪsɪn] n (science) medicina f; (drugs etc) medicamento m.

medieval [medɪ'iːvəl] adj medieval.

mediocre [miːdɪ'əʊkə] adj mediocre.

meditate ['medɪteɪt] vi meditar (on, sobre).

meditation [medɪ'teɪʃən] n meditación f.

Mediterranean [medɪtə'reɪnɪən] I adj mediterráneo,-a. II n the M., el Mediterráneo.

medium ['miːdɪəm] I adj (average) mediano,-a; Rad **m. wave**, onda media. II n 1 (pl media) (means) medio m. 2 (pl mediums) (spiritualist) médium mf.

medley ['medlɪ] n (mixture) mezcla f; Mus popurrí m.

meek [miːk] adj manso,-a, sumiso,-a; (humble) humilde.

meet [miːt] I vtr (pt & pp met) 1 (by chance) encontrar, encontrarse con; (by arrangement) reunirse con; (in formal meeting) entrevistarse con. 2 (get to know) conocer; **I'd like you to m. my mother**, quiero presentarle a mi madre; **the first time I met him**, cuando lo conocí; **pleased to m. you!**, ¡mucho gusto! 3 (await arrival of) esperar; (collect) ir a buscar. 4 (danger) encontrar; (opponent) enfrentarse con. 5 (satisfy) satisfacer; (obligations) cumplir con; (expenses) hacer frente a. II vi (by chance) encontrarse; (by arrangement) reunirse; (get to know each other) conocerse; Sport enfrentarse; (join) unirse; (rivers) confluir; **their eyes met**, cruzaron las miradas. III n (hunting) partida f de caza. ◆**meet with** vtr (difficulty) trope-

zar con; (loss) sufrir; (success) tener; esp US (person) reunirse con.

meeting ['miːtɪŋ] n (chance encounter) encuentro m; (by arrangement) cita f; (formal) entrevista f; (of committee etc) reunión f; (of assembly) sesión f; (of shareholders) junta f; (rally) mitin m; Sport encuentro m; (of rivers) confluencia f.

megabyte ['megəbaɪt] n Comput megabyte m.

megaphone ['megəfəʊn] n megáfono m.

melancholy ['melənkəlɪ] I n melancolía f. II adj melancólico,-a.

Melilla [me'liːjə] n Melilla f.

mellow ['meləʊ] I adj maduro,-a; (wine) añejo,-a; (colour, voice) suave; (person) apacible. II vi (fruit) madurar; (colour, voice) suavizarse.

melodramatic [melədrə'mætɪk] adj melodramático,-a.

melody ['melədɪ] n melodía f.

melon ['melən] n melón m.

melt [melt] I vtr (metal) fundir; fig (sb's heart) ablandar. II vi (snow) derretirse; (metal) fundirse; fig ablandarse. ◆**melt away** vi (snow) derretirse; fig (money) desaparecer; fig (confidence) desvanecerse. ◆**melt down** vtr (metal) fundir.

melting ['meltɪŋ] n fundición f; **m. point**, punto m de fusión; **m. pot**, crisol m.

member ['membə] n miembro mf; (of a society) socio,-a m,f; (of party, union) afiliado,-a m,f; **M. of Parliament**, diputado,-a m,f.

membership ['membəʃɪp] n (state) calidad f de socio; (entry) ingreso m; Pol afiliación f; (number of members) número m de socios; **m. card**, carnet m de socio.

memento [mə'mentəʊ] n recuerdo m.

memo ['meməʊ] n (official note) memorándum m; (personal note) nota f, apunte m.

memoirs ['memwɑːz] npl memorias fpl.

memorable ['memərəbəl] adj memorable.

memorandum [memə'rændəm] n (pl memoranda) (official note) memorándum m; (personal note) nota f, apunte m.

memorial [mɪ'mɔːrɪəl] I adj (plaque etc) conmemorativo,-a. II n monumento conmemorativo.

memorize ['meməraɪz] vtr memorizar, aprender de memoria.

memory ['memərɪ] n memoria f; (recollection) recuerdo m.

men [men] npl → **man**.

menace ['menɪs] I n (threat) amenaza f; (danger) peligro m; fam (person) pesado,-a m,f. II vtr amenazar.

menacing ['menɪsɪŋ] adj amenazador,-a.

menagerie [mɪ'nædʒərɪ] n casa f de fieras.

mend [mend] I vtr reparar, arreglar; (clothes) remendar; (socks etc) zurcir. II vi *(ill person)* reponerse. III n *(patch)* remiendo m; *(darn)* zurcido m; *fig* to be on the m., ir mejorando.

mending ['mendɪŋ] n *(repair)* reparación f; *(darning)* zurcido m; *(clothes for mending)* ropa f para remendar.

menial ['miːnɪəl] adj *(task)* servil, bajo,-a.

menopause ['menəpɔːz] n menopausia f.

menstrual ['menstrʊəl] adj menstrual.

menstruation [menstrʊ'eɪʃən] n menstruación f.

mental ['mentəl] adj 1 mental; **m. home, m. hospital,** hospital psiquiátrico; **m. illness,** enfermedad f mental. 2 fam *(crazy)* chalado,-a. ◆**mentally** adv **m.** ill, enfermo,-a mental; **to be m. handicapped,** ser un,-a disminuido,-a psíquico,-a.

mentality [men'tælɪtɪ] n mentalidad f.

mention ['menʃən] I n mención f. II vtr mencionar; **don't m. it!,** ¡de nada!

mentor ['mentɔːr] n mentor m.

menu ['menjuː] n 1 *(card)* carta f; *(fixed meal)* menú m; **today's m.,** menú del día. 2 *Comput* menú m.

MEP [emiː'piː] abbr of **Member of the European Parliament,** eurodiputado,-a mf.

mercenary ['mɜːsɪnərɪ] adj & n mercenario,-a *(m,f)*.

merchandise ['mɜːtʃəndaɪz] n mercancías fpl, géneros mpl.

merchant ['mɜːtʃənt] n Com Fin comerciante mf; *(retailer)* detallista mf; **m. bank,** banco m comercial; **m. navy,** marina f mercante.

merciful ['mɜːsɪfʊl] adj clemente, compasivo,-a *(towards,* con).

merciless ['mɜːsɪlɪs] adj despiadado,-a.

mercury ['mɜːkjʊrɪ] n mercurio m.

Mercury ['mɜːkjʊrɪ] n Mercurio m.

mercy ['mɜːsɪ] n misericordia f, compasión f; **at the m. of,** a la merced de; **to have m. on,** tener compasión de.

mere [mɪər] adj mero,-a, simple. ◆**merely** adv simplemente.

merge [mɜːdʒ] I vtr *(blend)* unir *(with,* con); Com fusionar. II vi unirse; *(roads)* empalmar; Com fusionarse.

merger ['mɜːdʒər] n Com fusión f.

meringue [mə'ræŋ] n merengue m.

merit ['merɪt] I n *(of person)* mérito m; *(of plan etc)* ventaja f. II vtr merecer.

mermaid ['mɜːmeɪd] n sirena f.

merry ['merɪ] adj *(merrier, merriest)* alegre; fam *(tipsy)* achispado,-a; **m. Christmas!,** ¡felices Navidades!

merry-go-round ['merɪgəʊraʊnd] n tiovivo m.

mesh [meʃ] I n Tex malla f; Tech engranaje m; fig red f. II vtr Tech engranar.

mesmerize ['mezməraɪz] vtr hipnotizar.

mess [mes] I n 1 *(confusion)* confusión f; *(disorder)* desorden m; **to be in a m.,** *(of* room etc) estar desordenado,-a. 2 *(in life, affairs)* lío m; **to get into a m.,** meterse en un lío. 3 *(dirt)* suciedad f. 4 Mil *(food)* rancho m. 5 Mil *(room)* comedor m. ◆**mess about, mess around** fam I vtr fastidiar. II vi *(act the fool)* hacer el primo; *(idle)* gandulear; *(kill time)* pasar el rato. ◆**mess about with** vtr fam *(fiddle with)* manosear; **to m. about with sb,** tener un lío con algn. ◆**mess up** vtr fam *(make untidy)* desordenar; *(dirty)* ensuciar; *(spoil)* estropear.

message ['mesɪdʒ] n *(communication)* recado m; *(of story etc)* mensaje m; fam **to get the m.,** comprender.

messenger ['mesɪndʒər] n mensajero,-a m,f.

Messrs ['mesəz] Com abbr of pl of **Mr,** Sres.

messy ['mesɪ] adj *(messier, messiest)* *(untidy)* desordenado,-a; *(confused)* enredado,-a; *(dirty)* sucio,-a.

met [met] pt & pp → **meet.**

metabolism [me'tæbəlɪzəm] n metabolismo m.

metal ['metəl] I n metal m. II adj metálico,-a.

metallic [mɪ'tælɪk] adj metálico,-a; **m. blue,** azul metalizado.

metallurgy [me'tælədʒɪ] n metalurgia f.

metalwork ['metəlwɜːk] n *(craft)* metalistería f; *(objects)* objetos mpl de metal.

metaphor ['metəfər, 'metəfɔːr] n metáfora f.

mete [miːt] vtr **to m. out,** imponer.

meteor ['miːtɪər] n bólido m.

meteoric [miːtɪ'ɒrɪk] adj meteórico,-a.

meteorite ['miːtɪəraɪt] n meteorito m.

meteorology [miːtɪə'rɒlədʒɪ] n meteorología f.

meter[1] ['miːtər] n contador m.

meter[2] ['miːtər] n US → **metre.**

method ['meθəd] n método m.

methodical [mɪ'θɒdɪkəl] adj metódico,-a.

Methodist ['meθədɪst] adj & n metodista *(mf)*.

meths [meθs] n fam abbr of **methylated spirits.**

methylated spirits [meθɪleɪtɪd'spɪrɪts] n alcohol metilado or desnaturalizado.

meticulous [mə'tɪkjʊləs] adj meticuloso,-a.

metre ['miːtər] n metro m.

metric ['metrɪk] adj métrico,-a.

metropolis [mɪ'trɒpəlɪs] n metrópoli f.

metropolitan [metrə'pɒlɪtən] adj metropolitano,-a.

mettle ['metəl] n valor m.

mew [mjuː] vi *(cat)* maullar.

mews [mjuːz] n *(street)* callejuela f; **m. flat,** apartamento m de lujo en unas caballerizas reconvertidas.

Mexican ['meksɪkən] adj & n mejicano,-a *(m,f)*, mexicano,-a *(m,f)*.

Mexico [ˈmeksɪkəʊ] n Méjico, México.

miaow [miːˈaʊ] I vi maullar. II n maullido m.

mice [maɪs] npl → **mouse**.

mickey [ˈmɪkɪ] n fam to take the m. (out of sb), tomar el pelo (a algn).

microbe [ˈmaɪkrəʊb] n microbio m.

microchip [ˈmaɪkrəʊtʃɪp] n microplaqueta f, microchip m.

microcomputer [maɪkrəʊkəmˈpjuːtər] n microordenador m.

microcosm [ˈmaɪkrəʊkɒzəm] n microcosmo m.

microfilm [ˈmaɪkrəʊfɪlm] n microfilm m.

microphone [ˈmaɪkrəfəʊn] n micrófono m.

microprocessor [maɪkrəʊˈprəʊsesər] n microprocesador m.

microscope [ˈmaɪkrəskəʊp] n microscopio m.

microwave [ˈmaɪkrəʊweɪv] n microonda f; m. (oven), (horno m) microondas m inv.

mid [mɪd] adj (in) m. afternoon, a media tarde; (in) m. April, a mediados de abril; to be in one's m. thirties, tener unos treinta y cinco años.

midair [mɪdˈeər] I n (collision, explosion) en el aire. II n fig to leave sth in m., dejar algo en el aire.

midday [mɪdˈdeɪ] I n mediodía m. II adj de mediodía.

middle [ˈmɪdəl] I adj de en medio; m. age, mediana edad f; the M. Ages, la Edad Media; the m. class, la clase media. II n 1 centro m, medio m; in the m. of, en medio de; in the m. of winter, en pleno invierno; fam in the m. of nowhere, en el quinto pino. 2 (waist) cintura f.

middle-aged [mɪdəlˈeɪdʒd] adj de mediana edad.

middle-class [mɪdəlˈklɑːs] adj de clase media.

middleman [ˈmɪdəlmæn] n intermediario m.

middleweight [ˈmɪdəlweɪt] n peso medio.

middling [ˈmɪdlɪŋ] adj mediano,-a.

midfielder [mɪdˈfiːldər] n Sport centrocampista m.

midge [mɪdʒ] n mosca enana.

midget [ˈmɪdʒɪt] n enano,-a m,f.

Midlands [ˈmɪdləndz] npl the M., la región central de Inglaterra.

midnight [ˈmɪdnaɪt] n medianoche f.

midst [mɪdst] prep in the m. of, en medio de.

midsummer [mɪdˈsʌmər] n pleno verano; M.'s Day, Día m de San Juan (24 de junio).

midway [mɪdˈweɪ] adv a medio camino.

midweek [mɪdˈwiːk] I adv entre semana. II adj de entre semana.

midwife [ˈmɪdwaɪf] n comadrona f, partera f.

midwifery [ˈmɪdwɪfərɪ] n obstetricia f.

midwinter [mɪdˈwɪntər] n pleno invierno m.

might¹ [maɪt] v aux → **may**.

might² [maɪt] n fml fuerza f, poder m.

mighty [ˈmaɪtɪ] I adj (mightier, mightiest) (strong) fuerte; (powerful) poderoso, -a; (great) enorme.

migraine [ˈmiːgreɪn, ˈmaɪgreɪn] n jaqueca f.

migrant [ˈmaɪgrənt] I adj migratorio,-a. II n (person) emigrante mf; (bird) ave migratoria.

migrate [maɪˈgreɪt] vi emigrar.

migration [maɪˈgreɪʃən] n migración f.

mike [maɪk] n fam (abbr of **microphone**) micro m.

mild [maɪld] adj (person, character) apacible; (climate) templado,-a; (punishment) leve; (tobacco, taste) suave. ◆**mildly** adv (softly, gently) suavemente; (slightly) ligeramente; and that's putting it m., y esto es decir poco.

mildew [ˈmɪldjuː] n moho m; (on plants) añublo m.

mildness [ˈmaɪldnəs] n (of character) apacibilidad f; (of climate, taste) suavidad f; (of punishment) levedad f.

mile [maɪl] n milla f; fam miles better, muchísimo mejor.

mileage [ˈmaɪlɪdʒ] n kilometraje m.

milestone [ˈmaɪlstəʊn] n hito m.

milieu [ˈmiːljɜː] n medio m ambiente.

militant [ˈmɪlɪtənt] adj & n militante (mf).

military [ˈmɪlɪtərɪ] adj militar; to do one's m. service, hacer el servicio militar.

militia [mɪˈlɪʃə] n milicia f.

milk [mɪlk] I n leche f; m. chocolate, chocolate m con leche; m. shake, batido m. II vtr 1 (cow, goat) ordeñar. 2 they milked him of all his money, le sangraron hasta la última peseta.

milkman [ˈmɪlkmən] n lechero m.

milky [ˈmɪlkɪ] adj (milkier, milkiest) lechoso,-a; (colour) pálido,-a; M. Way, Vía Láctea.

mill [mɪl] I n (grinder) molino m; (for coffee) molinillo m; (factory) fábrica f; cotton m., hilandería f. II vtr moler. ◆**mill about, mill around** vi arremolinarse.

millennium [mɪˈlenɪəm] n (pl millenniums or millenia [mɪˈlenɪə]) milenio m.

miller [ˈmɪlər] n molinero,-a m,f.

millet [ˈmɪlɪt] n mijo m.

milligram(me) [ˈmɪlɪgræm] n miligramo m.

millilitre, US **milliliter** [ˈmɪlɪliːtər] n mililitro m.

millimetre, US **millimeter** [ˈmɪlɪmiːtər]

n milímetro *m*.

milliner ['mɪlɪnər] *n* sombrerero,-a *m,f*.

millinery ['mɪlɪnərɪ] *n* sombreros *mpl* de señora.

million ['mɪljən] *n* millón *m*.

millionaire [mɪljə'neər] *n* millonario,-a *m,f*.

millstone ['mɪlstəʊn] *n* muela *f*; *fig* carga *f*.

mime [maɪm] I *n* (*art*) mímica *f*; (*play*) pantomima *f*. II *vtr* representar con gestos.

mimic ['mɪmɪk] I *adj* & *n* mímico,-a (*m,f*). II *vtr* imitar.

mimicry ['mɪmɪkrɪ] *n* imitación *f*.

minaret [mɪnə'ret] *n* alminar *m*, minarete *m*.

mince [mɪns] I *n* GB (*meat*) carne picada; **m. pie**, pastel *m* de picadillo de fruta. II *vtr fig*; **he doesn't m. his words**, no tiene pelos en la lengua. III *vi* (*walk*) **to m.** (**along**), andar con pasos menuditos.

mincemeat ['mɪnsmiːt] *n* (*dried fruit*) conserva *f* de picadillo de fruta; (*meat*) carne picada.

mincer ['mɪnsər] *n* picadora *f* de carne.

mind [maɪnd] I *n* 1 (*intellect*) mente *f*; (*brain*) cabeza *f*; **what kind of car do you have in m.?**, ¿en qué clase de coche estás pensando?; **to lose one's m.**, perder el juicio; **it slipped my m.**, lo olvidé por completo; **to call sth to m.**, recordar algo. 2 (*opinion*) **to be in two minds about sth**, estar indeciso,-a; **to my m.**, a mi parecer. II *vtr* 1 (*child*) cuidar; (*house*) vigilar; (*be careful of*) tener cuidado con; **m. the step!**, ¡ojo con el escalón!; **m. your own business!**, ¡no te metas donde no te llaman! 2 (*object to*) tener inconveniente en; **I wouldn't m. a cup of coffee**, me vendría bien un café; **never m.**, no importa. III *vi* 1 **m. you, he is fifty**, ten en cuenta que tiene cincuenta años. 2 (*object*) importar; **do you m. if I open the window?**, ¿le importa que abra la ventana?

minder ['maɪndər] *n fam* (*bodyguard*) guardaespaldas *m inv*; (*for child*) niñera *f*; (*babysitter*) canguro *mf*.

mindful ['maɪndfʊl] *adj* consciente.

mindless ['maɪndlɪs] *adj* (*task*) de autómata; (*violence*) injustificable.

mine¹ [maɪn] *poss pron* (el) mío, (la) mía, (los) míos, (las) mías, lo mío; **a friend of m.**, un amigo mío; **these gloves are m.**, estos guantes son míos; **which is m.?**, ¿cuál es el mío?

mine² [maɪn] I *n* mina *f*; *fig* **a m. of information**, un pozo de información. II *vtr* (*coal etc*) extraer; *Mil* minar.

minefield ['maɪnfiːld] *n* campo *m* de minas.

miner ['maɪnər] *n* minero,-a *m,f*.

mineral ['mɪnərəl] I *adj* mineral; **m.**

water, agua *f* mineral. II *n* mineral *m*.

minesweeper ['maɪnswiːpər] *n* dragaminas *m inv*.

mingle ['mɪŋgəl] *vi* mezclarse.

miniature [mɪnɪtʃər] I *n* miniatura *f*. II *adj* (*railway*) en miniatura; (*camera, garden*) diminuto,-a.

minibus ['mɪnɪbʌs] *n* microbús *m*.

minim ['mɪnɪm] *n Mus* blanca *f*.

minimal ['mɪnɪməl] *adj* mínimo,-a.

minimum ['mɪnɪməm] I *adj* mínimo,-a; **m. wage**, salario mínimo. II *n* mínimo *m*.

mining ['maɪnɪŋ] I *n* minería *f*, explotación *f* de minas; *Mil Naut* minado *m*. II *adj* minero,-a.

miniskirt ['mɪnɪskɜːt] *n* minifalda *f*.

minister ['mɪnɪstər] I *n* ministro,-a *m,f*; *Rel* pastor,-a *m,f*. II *vi* **to m. to sb**, atender a algn.

ministerial [mɪnɪ'stɪərɪəl] *adj Pol* ministerial.

ministry ['mɪnɪstrɪ] *n Pol* ministerio *m*; *Rel* sacerdocio *m*.

mink [mɪŋk] *n* visón *m*; **m. coat**, abrigo *m* de visón.

minnow ['mɪnəʊ] *n* piscardo *m*.

minor ['maɪnər] I *adj* (*lesser*) menor; (*unimportant*) sin importancia; (*role*) secundario,-a; *Mus* menor. II *n Jur* menor *mf* de edad.

Minorca [mɪ'nɔːkə] *n* Menorca *f*.

minority [maɪ'nɒrɪtɪ] *n* minoría *f*; **to be in the m.**, ser (la) minoría; *Pol* **m. party**, partido minoritario.

mint¹ [mɪnt] *n Fin* **the M.**, la Casa de la Moneda; **in m. condition**, en perfecto estado. II *vtr* (*coin, words*) acuñar.

mint² [mɪnt] *n Bot* menta *f*; (*sweet*) pastilla *f* de menta.

minus ['maɪnəs] I *prep* 5 **m. 3**, 5 menos 3; **m. 10 degrees**, 10 grados bajo cero. II *adj* negativo,-a. III *n* **m.** (**sign**), signo *m* (de) menos.

minute¹ ['mɪnɪt] *n* 1 minuto *m*; **at the last m.**, a última hora; **just a m.**, (espera) un momento; **this very m.**, ahora mismo. 2 **minutes**, (*notes*) acta *f*.

minute² [maɪ'njuːt] *adj* (*tiny*) diminuto, -a; (*examination*) minucioso,-a.

miracle ['mɪrəkəl] *n* milagro *m*.

miraculous [mɪ'rækjʊləs] *adj* milagroso, -a.

mirage ['mɪrɑːʒ] *n* espejismo *m*.

mire [maɪər] *n* fango *m*, lodo *m*; (*muddy place*) lodazal *m*.

mirror ['mɪrər] I *n* espejo *m*; *fig* reflejo *m*; **rear-view m.**, retrovisor *m*; **m. image**, réplica *f*. II *vtr* reflejar.

mirth [mɜːθ] *n* alegría *f*; (*laughter*) risas *fpl*.

misadventure [mɪsəd'ventʃər] *n* desgracia *f*; **death by m.**, muerte *f* accidental.

misanthropist [mɪ'zænθrəpɪst] *n* misántropo,-a *m,f*.

misapprehension [ˌmisæpriˈhenʃən] n malentendido m.

misbehave [misbiˈheiv] vi portarse mal.

miscalculate [misˈkælkjuleit] vtr & vi calcular mal.

miscarriage [misˈkæridʒ] n Med aborto m (espontáneo); **m. of justice**, error m judicial.

miscellaneous [misiˈleiniəs] adj variado,-a; **m. expenses**, gastos diversos.

mischief [ˈmistʃif] n (naughtiness) travesura f; fml (evil) malicia f; fam (harm) daño m; **to get up to m.**, hacer travesuras.

mischievous [ˈmistʃivəs] adj (naughty) travieso,-a; (playful) juguetón,-ona f; fml (wicked) malicioso,-a.

misconception [miskənˈsepʃən] n concepto erróneo.

misconduct [misˈkɒndʌkt] n mala conducta; **professional m.**, error m profesional.

misconstrue [miskənˈstruː] vtr interpretar mal.

miscount [misˈkaunt] vtr (votes etc) contar mal.

misdeed [misˈdiːd] n fechoría f.

misdemeanour, US **misdemeanor** [misdiˈmiːnər] n (misdeed) fechoría f; Jur delito m menor.

miser [ˈmaizər] n avaro,-a m,f.

miserable [ˈmizərəbəl] adj (sad) triste; (unfortunate) desgraciado,-a; (wretched) miserable.

miserly [ˈmaizəli] adj avaro,-a, tacaño,-a.

misery [ˈmizəri] n (sadness) tristeza f; (wretchedness) desgracia f; (suffering) sufrimiento m; (poverty) miseria f; fam (person) aguafiestas mf.

misfire [misˈfaiər] vi (engine, plan etc) fallar.

misfit [ˈmisfit] n (person) inadaptado,-a m,f.

misfortune [misˈfɔːtʃən] n desgracia f.

misgiving [misˈgiviŋ] n (doubt) recelo m; (fear) temor m.

misguided [misˈgaidid] adj equivocado,-a.

mishandle [misˈhændl] vtr llevar or manejar mal.

mishap [ˈmishæp] n contratiempo m.

misinform [misinˈfɔːm] vtr informar mal.

misinterpret [misinˈtɜːprit] vtr interpretar mal.

misjudge [misˈdʒʌdʒ] vtr juzgar mal.

mislay [misˈlei] vtr extraviar.

mislead [misˈliːd] vtr despistar; (deliberately) engañar.

misleading [misˈliːdiŋ] adj (erroneous) erróneo,-a; (deliberately) engañoso,-a.

mismanagement [misˈmænidʒmənt] n mala administración f.

misnomer [misˈnəumər] n nombre equivocado.

misogynist [miˈsɒdʒinist] n misógino,-a

m,f.

misplace [misˈpleis] vtr (trust) encauzar mal; (book, spectacles etc) extraviar.

misprint [ˈmisprint] n errata f, error m de imprenta.

misrepresent [misrepriˈzent] vtr (facts) desvirtuar; (words) tergiversar.

miss¹ [mis] n señorita f.

miss² [mis] I n (throw etc) fallo m; fam **to give sth a m.**, pasar de algo. II vtr 1 (when throwing) fallar; (when shooting) errar. 2 (train etc) perder; (opportunity) dejar pasar; **you have missed the point**, no has captado la idea; fig **to m. the boat**, perder el tren. 3 (omit) saltarse. 4 **I m. you**, te echo de menos. III vi (when throwing) fallar; (when shooting) errar; **is anything missing?**, ¿falta algo? ◆**miss out I** vtr (omit) saltarse; (on purpose) pasar por alto. II vtr **to m. out on**, perderse.

misshapen [misˈʃeipən] adj deforme.

missile [ˈmisail] US [ˈmisəl] n Mil misil m; (object thrown) proyectil m.

missing [ˈmisiŋ] adj (object) perdido,-a; (person) desaparecido,-a; (from meeting etc) ausente; **m. person**, desaparecido,-a m,f; **three cups are m.**, faltan tres tazas.

mission [ˈmiʃən] n misión f.

missionary [ˈmiʃənəri] n misionero,-a m,f.

misspent [ˈmisspent] adj (youth) malgastado,-a.

mist [mist] I n neblina f; (thick) niebla f; (at sea) bruma f. II vi **to m. over or up**, (countryside) cubrirse de neblina; (window etc) empañarse.

mistake [misˈteik] I n error m; **by m.**, por equivocación; **I hurt him by m.**, le golpeé sin querer; **to make a m.**, equivocarse, cometer un error. II vtr (pt mistook; pp mistaken) (meaning) malentender; **to m. Jack for Bill**, confundir a Jack con Bill.

mistaken [misˈteikən] adj equivocado,-a, erróneo,-a; **you are m.**, estás equivocado,-a.

mister [ˈmistər] n señor m.

mistletoe [ˈmisəltəu] n muérdago m.

mistook [misˈtuk] pt → **mistake**.

mistreat [misˈtriːt] vtr tratar mal.

mistress [ˈmistris] n (of house) señora f, ama f; (lover) amante f; Educ (primary school) maestra f; (secondary school) profesora f.

mistrust [misˈtrʌst] I n recelo m. II vtr desconfiar de.

misty [ˈmisti] adj (mistier, mistiest) (day) de niebla; (window etc) empañado,-a.

misunderstand [misʌndəˈstænd] vtr & vi malentender.

misunderstanding [misʌndəˈstændiŋ] n malentendido m; (disagreement) desavenencia f.

misuse [mɪs'juːs] **I** n mal uso m; (of funds) malversación f; (of power) abuso m. **II** [mɪs'juːz] vtr emplear mal; (funds) malversar; (power) abusar de.

miter ['maɪtər] n US → **mitre**.

mitigate ['mɪtɪgeɪt] vtr atenuar.

mitigating ['mɪtɪgeɪtɪŋ] adj m. circumstances, circunstancias fpl atenuantes.

mitre ['maɪtər] n mitra f.

mitten ['mɪtən] n manopla f; (fingerless) mitón m.

mix [mɪks]. **I** n mezcla f. **II** vtr mezclar. **III** vi (blend) mezclarse (with, con); (go well together) ir bien juntos. ◆**mix up** vtr (confuse) confundir (with, con); (papers) revolver; **to be mixed up in sth**, estar involucrado,-a en algo.

mixed [mɪkst] adj (assorted) surtido,-a; (varied) variado,-a; (school) mixto,-a; (feelings) contradictorio,-a.

mixed-up [mɪkst'ʌp] adj (objects, papers etc) revuelto,-a; (person) confuso,-a.

mixer ['mɪksər] n **1** Culin batidora f. **2** **to be a good m.**, (person) tener don de gentes.

mixture ['mɪkstʃər] n mezcla f.

mix-up ['mɪksʌp] n fam confusión f, lío m.

mm abbr of **millimetre(s)**, mm.

moan [məʊn] **I** n (groan) gemido m, quejido m. **II** vi (groan) gemir; (complain) quejarse (about, de).

moat [məʊt] n foso m.

mob [mɒb] **I** n multitud f; (riff-raff) gentuza f; **the m.**, el populacho. **II** vtr acosar.

mobile ['məʊbaɪl, US 'məʊbəl] **I** adj móvil; **m. home**, caravana f. **II** n (hanging ornament) móvil m.

mobility [məʊ'bɪlɪtɪ] n movilidad f.

mobilize ['məʊbɪlaɪz] vtr movilizar.

mock [mɒk] **I** adj (sympathy etc) fingido, -a; (objects) de imitación. **II** vtr hacer burla f of) burlarse de. **III** vi burlarse (at, de).

mockery ['mɒkərɪ] n burla f.

mode [məʊd] n (manner) modo m, estilo m; (fashion) moda f.

model ['mɒdəl] **I** n modelo m; (fashion model) modelo mf; (scale) m., maqueta f. **II** adj (railway) en miniatura; (pupil) ejemplar; (school) modelo. **III** vtr (clay etc) modelar; (clothes) presentar. **IV** vi (make models) modelar; (work as model) trabajar de modelo.

modem ['məʊdem] n Comput modem m.

moderate¹ ['mɒdərɪt] **I** adj moderado,-a; (reasonable) razonable; (average) regular; (ability) mediocre. **II** n Pol moderado,-a m,f. ◆**moderately** adv medianamente.

moderate² ['mɒdəreɪt] **I** vtr moderar. **II** vi moderarse; (wind) calmarse; (in debate) arbitrar.

moderation [mɒdə'reɪʃən] n moderación f; **in m.**, con moderación.

modern ['mɒdən] adj moderno,-a; (history) contemporáneo,-a; **m. languages**, lenguas modernas.

modernize ['mɒdənaɪz] vtr modernizar.

modest ['mɒdɪst] adj modesto,-a; (chaste) púdico,-a; (price) módico,-a; (success) discreto,-a.

modesty ['mɒdɪstɪ] n (humility) modestia f; (chastity) pudor m.

modification [mɒdɪfɪ'keɪʃən] n modificación f.

modify ['mɒdɪfaɪ] vtr modificar.

module ['mɒdjuːl] n módulo m.

mogul ['məʊgəl] n magnate m.

mohair ['məʊheər] **I** n mohair m. **II** adj de mohair.

moist [mɔɪst] adj húmedo,-a.

moisten ['mɔɪsən] vtr humedecer.

moisture ['mɔɪstʃər] n humedad f.

moisturizer ['mɔɪstʃəraɪzər] n crema f or leche f hidratante.

molar ['məʊlər] n muela f.

molasses [mə'læsɪz] n melaza f.

mold [məʊld] n US → **mould**.

mole¹ [məʊl] n (beauty spot) lunar m.

mole² [məʊl] n (animal) topo m.

molecule ['mɒlɪkjuːl] n molécula f.

molest [mə'lest] vtr importunar; (sexually assault) acosar (sexualmente).

mollycoddle ['mɒlɪkɒdəl] vtr fam mimar, consentir.

molt [məʊlt] vi US → **moult**.

molten ['məʊltən] adj fundido,-a; (lava) líquido,-a.

mom [mɒm] n US fam mamá f.

moment ['məʊmənt] n momento m; **at the m.**, en este momento; **for the m.**, de momento; **in a m.**, dentro de un momento; **at any m.**, de un momento a otro.

momentary ['məʊməntərɪ] adj momentáneo,-a. ◆**momentarily** adv momentáneamente; US (soon) dentro de poco.

momentous [məʊ'mentəs] adj trascendental.

momentum [məʊ'mentəm] n Phys momento m; (speed) velocidad f; fig **to gather m.**, cobrar velocidad.

mommy ['mɒmɪ] n US fam mamá f.

Monaco ['mɒnəkəʊ] n Mónaco.

monarch ['mɒnək] n monarca m.

monarchy ['mɒnəkɪ] n monarquía f.

monastery ['mɒnəstərɪ] n monasterio m.

Monday ['mʌndɪ] n lunes m.

monetarism ['mʌnɪtərɪzəm] n monetarismo m.

monetary ['mʌnɪtərɪ] adj monetario,-a.

money ['mʌnɪ] n dinero m; (currency) moneda f; **to make m.**, ganar dinero; **to put m. on**, apostar por.

moneylender ['mʌnɪlendər] n prestamista mf.

money-spinner ['mʌnɪspɪnər] n fam negocio m rentable.

Mongolia [mɒŋˈgəʊlɪə] n Mongolia.

mongolism [ˈmɒŋgəlɪzəm] n mongolismo m.

mongrel [ˈmʌŋgrəl] n perro mestizo.

monitor [ˈmɒnɪtər] I n (screen) monitor m; Educ delegado,-a m,f. II vtr (check) controlar; (progress, events) seguir de cerca.

monk [mʌŋk] n monje m.

monkey [ˈmʌŋkɪ] n mono m; m. nut, cacahuete m; m. wrench, llave inglesa.

monochrome [ˈmɒnəkrəʊm] adj monocromo,-a; (television, photo) en blanco y negro.

monocle [ˈmɒnəkəl] n monóculo m.

monologue [ˈmɒnəlɒg], US **monolog** [ˈmɒnəlɒg] n monólogo m.

monopolize [məˈnɒpəlaɪz] vtr Fin monopolizar; (attention etc) acaparar.

monopoly [məˈnɒpəlɪ] n monopolio m.

monotone [ˈmɒnətəʊn] n in a m., con una voz monótona.

monotonous [məˈnɒtənəs] adj monótono,-a.

monotony [məˈnɒtənɪ] n monotonía f.

monsoon [mɒnˈsuːn] n monzón m.

monster [ˈmɒnstər] n monstruo m.

monstrosity [mɒnˈstrɒsɪtɪ] n monstruosidad f.

monstrous [ˈmɒnstrəs] adj (huge) enorme; (hideous) monstruoso,-a; (outrageous) escandaloso,-a.

montage [mɒnˈtɑːʒ] n montaje m.

month [mʌnθ] n mes m.

monthly [ˈmʌnθlɪ] I adj mensual; m. instalment, mensualidad f. II n (periodical) revista f mensual. III adv mensualmente, cada mes.

monument [ˈmɒnjʊmənt] n monumento m.

monumental [mɒnjʊˈmentəl] adj monumental; fam (huge) enorme.

moo [muː] I n mugido m. II vi mugir.

mood [muːd] n humor m; to be in a good/bad m., estar de buen/mal humor; to be in the m. for (doing) sth, estar de humor para (hacer) algo.

moody [ˈmuːdɪ] adj (moodier, moodiest) (changeable) de humor variable; (badtempered) malhumorado,-a.

moon [muːn] n luna f; fam over the m., en el séptimo cielo.

moonlight [ˈmuːnlaɪt] n luz f de la luna.

moonlighting [ˈmuːnlaɪtɪŋ] n fam pluriempleo m.

moonlit [ˈmuːnlɪt] adj (night) de luna.

moor[1] [mʊər] n (heath) páramo m.

moor[2] [mʊər, mɔːr] vtr Naut amarrar.

Moor [mʊər] n moro,-a m,f.

Moorish [ˈmʊərɪʃ] adj moro,-a.

moorland [ˈmʊələnd] n páramo m.

moose [muːs] n inv alce m.

moot [muːt] adj it's a m. point, es discutible.

mop [mɒp] I n (for floor) fregona f; fam m. of hair, melena f. II vtr fregar. ◆**mop up** vtr (liquids) enjugar; (enemy forces) acabar con.

mope [məʊp] vi estar alicaído,-a. ◆**mope about, mope around** vi andar abatido,-a.

moped [ˈməʊped] n ciclomotor m, vespa f.

moral [ˈmɒrəl] I adj moral. II n moraleja f; **morals**, moral f sing, moralidad f sing.

morale [məˈrɑːl] n moral f, estado m de ánimo.

morality [məˈrælɪtɪ] n moralidad f.

morass [məˈræs] n pantano m; fig lío m.

morbid [ˈmɔːbɪd] adj Med mórbido,-a; (mind) morboso,-a.

more [mɔːr] I adj más; and what is m., y lo que es más; is there any m. tea?, ¿queda más té?; I've no m. money, no me queda más dinero; m. tourists, más turistas. II pron más; how many m.?, ¿cuántos más?; I need some m., necesito más; it's m. than enough, es más que suficiente; many/much m., muchos,-as/ mucho más; m. than a hundred, más de cien; the m. he has, the m. he wants, cuanto más tiene más quiere. III adv más; I won't do it any m., ya no lo volveré a hacer; she doesn't live here any m., ya no vive aquí; m. and m. difficult, cada vez más difícil; m. or less, más o menos; once m., una vez más.

moreover [mɔːˈrəʊvər] adv además.

morgue [mɔːg] n depósito m de cadáveres.

morning [ˈmɔːnɪŋ] n mañana f; (before dawn) madrugada f; in the m., por la mañana; on Monday mornings, los lunes por la mañana; tomorrow m., mañana por la mañana. II adj matutino,-a.

Moroccan [məˈrɒkən] adj & n marroquí (mf).

Morocco [məˈrɒkəʊ] n Marruecos m.

moron [ˈmɔːrɒn] n fam imbécil mf.

morose [məˈrəʊs] adj malhumorado,-a, hosco,-a.

morphine [ˈmɔːfiːn] n morfina f.

Morse [mɔːs] n M. (code), (alfabeto m) Morse m.

morsel [ˈmɔːsəl] n (of food) bocado m; fig trozo m.

mortal [ˈmɔːtəl] I adj mortal. II n mortal mf. ◆**mortally** adv mortalmente; m. wounded, herido,-a de muerte.

mortality [mɔːˈtælɪtɪ] n mortalidad f.

mortar [ˈmɔːtər] n mortero m.

mortgage [ˈmɔːgɪdʒ] I n hipoteca f. II vtr hipotecar.

mortify [ˈmɔːtɪfaɪ] vtr mortificar; fam I was mortified, me sentí avergonzado,-a.

mortuary [ˈmɔːtʃʊərɪ] n depósito m de cadáveres.

mosaic [məˈzeɪɪk] n mosaico m.

Moscow ['mɒskəʊ, US 'mɑːskəʊ] n Moscú.

Moslem ['mɒzləm] adj & n musulmán, -ana (m,f).

mosque [mɒsk] n mezquita f.

mosquito [mɒs'kiːtəʊ] n (pl **mosquitoes**) mosquito m; **m. net**, mosquitero m.

moss [mɒs] n musgo m.

most [məʊst] I adj (superl of **much**, **many**) I (greatest in quantity etc) más; **this house suffered (the) m. damage**, esta casa fue la más afectada; **who made (the) m. mistakes?**, ¿quién cometió más errores? 2 (the majority of) la mayoría de, la mayor parte de; **for the m. part**, por lo general; **m. of the time**, la mayor parte del tiempo; **m. people**, la mayoría de la gente. II pron (greatest part) la mayor parte; (greatest number) lo máximo, lo más; (the majority of people) la mayoría; **at the (very) m.**, como máximo; **to make the m. of sth**, aprovechar algo al máximo. III adv (superl of **much**) I más; **the m. intelligent student**, el estudiante más inteligente; **what I like m.**, lo que más me gusta. 2 (very) muy; **m. likely**, muy probablemente; **m. of all**, sobre todo. ◆**mostly** adv (chiefly) en su mayor parte; (generally) generalmente; (usually) normalmente.

MOT [eməʊ'tiː] GB abbr of Ministry of Transport; **MOT test**, inspección técnica de vehículos, ITV.

motel [məʊ'tel] n motel m.

moth [mɒθ] n mariposa nocturna; **clothes m.**, polilla f.

mother ['mʌðər] I n madre f; **unmarried m.**, madre soltera; **M.'s Day**, Día m de la Madre; **m. tongue**, lengua materna. II vtr cuidar maternalmente.

motherhood ['mʌðəhʊd] n maternidad f.

mother-in-law ['mʌðərɪnlɔː] n suegra f.

motherly ['mʌðəlɪ] adj maternal.

mother-of-pearl [mʌðərəv'pɜːl] n madreperla f, nácar m.

mother-to-be [mʌðətə'biː] n futura madre.

motif [məʊ'tiːf] n Art Mus motivo m; (embroidered etc) adorno m; fig (main subject) tema m.

motion ['məʊʃən] I n (movement) movimiento m; (gesture) además m; (proposal) moción f. II vtr & vi hacer señas; **to m. (to) sb to do sth**, hacer señas a algn para que haga algo.

motionless ['məʊʃənlɪs] adj inmóvil.

motivate ['məʊtɪveɪt] vtr motivar.

motivation [məʊtɪ'veɪʃən] n motivación f.

motive ['məʊtɪv] I adj (force) motriz. II n (reason) motivo m; Jur móvil m; **with the best of motives**, con la mejor intención.

motley ['mɒtlɪ] adj (**motlier**, **motliest**)

(multicoloured) abigarrado,-a; (varied) variado,-a.

motor ['məʊtər] n (engine) motor m; fam (car) máquina f; **m. racing**, carreras fpl de coches.

motorbike ['məʊtəbaɪk] n fam motocicleta f, moto f.

motorboat ['məʊtəbəʊt] n (lancha) motora f.

motorcar ['məʊtəkɑːr] n coche m, automóvil m.

motorcycle ['məʊtəsaɪkəl] n motocicleta f.

motorcyclist ['məʊtəsaɪklɪst] n motociclista mf.

motoring ['məʊtərɪŋ] n automovilismo m.

motorist ['məʊtərɪst] n automovilista mf.

motorway ['məʊtəweɪ] n GB autopista f.

mottled ['mɒtəld] adj (skin, animal) con manchas; (surface) moteado,-a.

motto ['mɒtəʊ] n lema m.

mould¹, US **mold** [məʊld] n (fungus) moho m.

mould², US **mold** [məʊld] I n molde m. II vtr moldear; (clay) modelar.

moulder, US **molder** ['məʊldər] vi **to m. (away)**, desmoronarse.

moulding, US **molding** ['məʊldɪŋ] n moldura f.

mouldy, US **moldy** ['məʊldɪ] adj (**mouldier**, **mouldiest**) mohoso,-a; **to go m.**, enmohecerse.

moult [məʊlt] vi mudar.

mound [maʊnd] n montón m; (small hill) montículo m.

mount¹ [maʊnt] n monte m; **M. Everest**, (Monte) Everest m.

mount² [maʊnt] I n (horse) montura f; (support) soporte m, base f; (for photograph) marco m; (for jewel) engaste m. II vtr (horse) subirse or montar a; (campaign) organizar; (photograph) enmarcar; (jewel) engastar. III vi (go up) subir; (get on horse, bike) montar; (increase) subir. ◆**mount up** vi (accumulate) acumularse.

mountain ['maʊntɪn] I n montaña f; fig (pile) montón m. II adj de montaña, montañés,-esa; **m. bike**, bicicleta f de montaña; **m. range**, sierra f, cordillera f.

mountaineer [maʊntɪ'nɪər] n alpinista mf, Am andinista mf.

mountaineering [maʊntɪ'nɪərɪŋ] n alpinismo m, Am andinismo m.

mountainous ['maʊntɪnəs] adj montañoso,-a.

mourn [mɔːn] vtr & vi **to m. (for) sb**, llorar la muerte de algn.

mourner ['mɔːnər] n doliente mf.

mournful ['mɔːnfʊl] adj triste; (voice) lúgubre.

mourning ['mɔːnɪŋ] n luto m; **in m.**, de luto.

mouse [maʊs] n (pl **mice**) also Comput ratón m.

mousetrap ['maʊstræp] n ratonera f.

mousse [muːs] n Culin mousse f; (for hair) (styling) m., espuma f (moldeadora).

moustache [məˈstɑːʃ] n bigote(s) m(pl).

mousy ['maʊsɪ] adj (mousier, mousiest) (colour) pardusco,-a; (hair) castaño claro; (shy) tímido,-a.

mouth [maʊθ] I n (pl mouths [maʊðz]) 1 boca f; fam down in the m., deprimido, -a. 2 (of cave etc) entrada f; (of river) desembocadura f. II vtr [maʊð] pronunciar; (insults) proferir.

mouthful ['maʊθfʊl] n (of food) bocado m; (of drink) sorbo m; to be a bit of a m., ser difícil de pronunciar.

mouth organ ['maʊθɔːɡən] n armónica f.

mouthpiece ['maʊθpiːs] n Mus boquilla f; (of telephone) micrófono m; fig (spokesman) portavoz m.

mouthwash ['maʊθwɒʃ] n elixir m, enjuague m bucal.

mouthwatering ['maʊθwɔːtərɪŋ] adj muy apetitoso,-a, que le hace a uno la boca agua.

movable ['muːvəbəl] adj movible, móvil.

move [muːv] I n 1 (movement) movimiento m; to be on the m., estar en marcha; we must make a m., debemos irnos ya; fam get a m. on!, ¡date prisa! 2 (in game) jugada f; (turn) turno m. 3 (course of action) medida f; to make the first m., dar el primer paso. 4 (to new home) mudanza f; (to new job) traslado m.
II vtr 1 mover; (furniture etc) cambiar de sitio; (transfer) trasladar; to m. house, mudarse (de casa). 2 (in game) mover. 3 (motivate) inducir; (persuade) persuadir; I won't be moved, no me harán cambiar de parecer. 4 (affect emotionally) conmover. 5 (resolution etc) proponer.
III vi 1 (change position) moverse, desplazarse; (change house) mudarse (de casa); (change post) trasladarse; to m. out of the way!, ¡quítate de en medio! 2 (train etc) estar en marcha; to start moving, ponerse en marcha. 3 (travel) ir. 4 (leave) irse, marcharse. 5 (in game) hacer una jugada. 6 (take action) tomar medidas.
◆**move about, move around** I vtr cambiar de sitio. II vi (be restless) ir y venir; (travel) viajar de un lugar a otro.
◆**move along** I vtr (move forward) hacer avanzar; (keep moving) hacer circular. II vi (move forward) avanzar; (keep moving) circular; fam along!, (to person on bench) ¡haz sitio! ◆**move away** I vtr alejar, apartar (from, de). II vi (move aside) apartarse; (leave) irse; (change house) mudarse (de casa).
◆**move back** I vtr (to original place) volver. II vi (withdraw) retirarse; (to original place) volver. ◆**move forward** I

vtr avanzar; (clock) adelantar. II vi avanzar, adelantarse. ◆**move in** vi (into new home) instalarse. ◆**move off** vi (go away) irse, marcharse; (train) salir.
◆**move on** vi (keep moving) circular; (go forward) avanzar; (time) transcurrir.
◆**move out** vi (leave) irse, marcharse; (leave house) mudarse. ◆**move over** vi correrse. ◆**move up** vi (go up) subir; fig (be promoted) ser ascendido,-a, ascender; (move along) correrse, hacer sitio.

movement ['muːvmənt] n 1 movimiento m; (gesture) gesto m, ademán m. 2 (of goods) transporte m; (of employees) traslado m. 3 (trend) corriente f. 4 (of machine) mecanismo m. 5 (of goods, capital) circulación f.

movie ['muːvɪ] n US película f; to go to the movies, ir al cine; fig m. star, estrella f de cine.

moving ['muːvɪŋ] adj (that moves) móvil; (car etc) en marcha; fig (touching) conmovedor,-a.

mow [məʊ] vtr (pt mowed; pp mown or mowed) (lawn) cortar; (corn, wheat) segar; fig to m. down, segar.

mower ['məʊə] n cortacésped m & f.

MP [emˈpiː] abbr of Member of Parliament.

mph [empiːˈeɪtʃ] abbr of miles per hour, millas fpl por hora.

MPhil [emˈfɪl] abbr of Master of Philosophy.

Mr ['mɪstə] abbr of mister, señor m, Sr.

Mrs ['mɪsɪz] abbr of señora f, Sra.

Ms [məz] abbr of señora f, Sra, señorita f, Srta.

MSc [emesˈsiː] abbr of Master of Science.

much [mʌtʃ] I adj mucho,-a; as m. ... as, tanto,-a ... como; how m. chocolate?, ¿cuánto chocolate?; m. admiration, mucha admiración; so m., tanto,-a. II adv mucho; as m. as, tanto como; as m. as possible, todo lo posible; how m.?, ¿cuánto?; how m. is it?, ¿cuánto es?; ¿cuánto vale?; m. better, mucho mejor; m. more, mucho más; so m. the better, ¡tanto mejor!; thank you very m., muchísimas gracias; they are m. the same, son más o menos iguales; too m., demasiado; without so m. as, sin siquiera. III pron mucho; I thought as m., lo suponía; m. of the town was destroyed, gran parte de la ciudad quedó destruida; m. remains to be done, queda mucho por hacer.

muck [mʌk] n (dirt) suciedad f; (mud) lodo m; fig porquería f. ◆**muck about, muck around** fam I vi (idle) perder el tiempo; (play the fool) hacer el tonto. II vtr to m. sb about, fastidiar a algn.
◆**muck up** vtr (dirty) ensuciar; fig (spoil) echar a perder.

mucky ['mʌki] adj (muckier, muckiest) sucio,-a.

mucus ['mju:kəs] n moco m, mucosidad f.

mud [mʌd] n lodo m, barro m; (thick) fango m; to sling m. at sb, poner a algn por los suelos; m. flat, marisma f.

muddle ['mʌdəl] I n desorden m; fig (mix-up) embrollo m, lío m; to get into a m., hacerse un lío. II vtr to m. (up), confundir. ◆muddle through vi arreglárselas, ingeniárselas.

muddy ['mʌdi] adj (muddier, muddiest) (lane) fangoso,-a; (hands) cubierto,-a de lodo; (liquid) turbio,-a.

mudguard ['mʌdgɑːd] n guardabarros m inv.

muff¹ [mʌf] n manguito m; ear muffs, orejeras fpl.

muff² [mʌf] vtr fam pifiar; to m. it (up), estropearlo.

muffin ['mʌfin] n panecillo m.

muffle ['mʌfəl] vtr (sound) amortiguar; to m. (up), (person) abrigar.

muffler ['mʌflər] n US Aut silenciador m.

mug¹ [mʌg] n (large cup) tazón m; (beer tankard) jarra f.

mug² [mʌg] I n fam (fool) tonto,-a m,f; (face) jeta f. II vtr atracar, asaltar.

mugging ['mʌgɪŋ] n asalto m.

muggy ['mʌgi] adj (muggier, muggiest) bochornoso,-a.

mule [mju:l] n mulo,-a m,f.

mull [mʌl] vtr mulled wine, vino m caliente con especias. ◆mull over vtr to m. over sth, reflexionar sobre algo.

multicoloured, US multicolored ['mʌltɪkʌləd] adj multicolor.

multinational [mʌltɪ'næʃənəl] adj & nf multinacional.

multiple ['mʌltɪpəl] I adj múltiple; m. sclerosis, esclerosis f múltiple. II n múltiplo m.

multiplication [mʌltɪplɪ'keɪʃən] n multiplicación f; m. sign, signo m de multiplicar.

multiply ['mʌltɪplaɪ] I vtr multiplicar (by, por). II vi multiplicarse.

multipurpose [mʌltɪ'pɜːpəs] adj multiuso inv.

multistorey [mʌltɪ'stɔːri] adj (building) de varios pisos; m. car park, parking m de varias plantas.

multitude ['mʌltɪtjuːd] n multitud f, muchedumbre f.

mum¹ [mʌm] n fam mamá f.

mum² [mʌm] adj to keep m., no decir ni pío.

mumble ['mʌmbəl] I vi hablar entre dientes. II vtr decir entre dientes.

mummy¹ ['mʌmi] n fam (mother) mamá f, mami f.

mummy² ['mʌmi] n (body) momia f.

mumps [mʌmps] n paperas fpl.

munch [mʌntʃ] vtr & vi mascar.

mundane [mʌn'deɪn] adj pej (ordinary) banal; (job, life) rutinario,-a.

municipal [mjuː'nɪsɪpəl] adj municipal.

municipality [mjuːnɪsɪ'pælɪti] n municipio m.

mural ['mjʊərəl] adj & nm mural.

Murcia [mɜː'siːə] n Murcia.

murder ['mɜːdər] I n asesinato m, homicidio m. II vtr asesinar.

murderer ['mɜːdərər] n asesino m.

murderess ['mɜːdərɪs] n asesina f.

murderous ['mɜːdərəs] adj homicida.

murky ['mɜːki] adj (murkier, murkiest) oscuro,-a; (water) turbio,-a.

murmur ['mɜːmər] I n murmullo m; (of traffic) ruido m; (complaint) queja f. II vtr & vi murmurar.

muscle ['mʌsəl] I n músculo m. II vi fam to m. in on sth, entrometerse en asuntos ajenos.

muscular ['mʌskjʊlər] adj (pain, tissue) muscular; (person) musculoso,-a.

muse [mjuːz] vi to m. on or about sth, meditar algo.

Muse [mjuːz] n (in mythology) musa f.

museum [mjuː'zɪəm] n museo m.

mushroom ['mʌʃruːm] I n seta f, hongo m; Culin champiñón m. II vi fig crecer de la noche a la mañana.

music ['mjuːzɪk] n música f; m. hall, teatro m de variedades.

musical ['mjuːzɪkəl] I adj musical; to be m., estar dotado,-a para la música. II n musical m.

musician [mjuː'zɪʃən] n músico,-a m,f.

Muslim ['mʊzlɪm] adj & n musulmán, -ana (m,f).

muslin ['mʌzlɪn] n muselina f.

mussel ['mʌsəl] n mejillón m.

must [mʌst] I v aux 1 (obligation) deber, tener que; you m. arrive on time, tienes que or debes llegar a la hora: 2 (probability) deber de; he m. be ill, debe de estar enfermo. II n fam necesidad f.

mustard ['mʌstəd] n mostaza f.

muster ['mʌstər] I vtr fig to m. (up) courage, cobrar fuerzas. II vi reunirse, juntarse.

mustn't ['mʌsənt] = must not.

musty ['mʌsti] adj (mustier, mustiest) que huele a cerrado or a humedad.

mute [mjuːt] I adj mudo,-a. II n (person) mudo,-a m,f; Mús sordina f.

muted ['mjuːtɪd] adj (sound) sordo,-a; (colour) suave.

mutilate ['mjuːtɪleɪt] vtr mutilar.

mutiny ['mjuːtɪni] I n motín m. II vi amotinarse.

mutter ['mʌtər] I n (mumble) murmullo m. II vtr murmurar, decir entre dientes. III vi (angrily) refunfuñar.

mutton ['mʌtən] n (carne f de) cordero m.

mutual ['mju:tʃuəl] *adj* mutuo,-a; *(shared)* común.

muzzle ['mʌzəl] **I** *n (snout)* hocico *m*; *(for dog)* bozal *m*; *(of gun)* boca *f*. **II** *vtr (dog)* abozalar; *fig* amordazar.

my [maɪ] *poss adj* mi; **my cousins**, mis primos; **my father**, mi padre; **one of my friends**, un amigo mío; **I washed my hair**, me lavé el pelo; **I twisted my ankle**, me torcí el tobillo.

myriad ['mɪrɪəd] *n lit* miríada *f*.

myself [maɪ'self] *pers pron* 1 *(emphatic)* yo mismo,-a; **my husband and m.**, mi marido y yo. 2 *(reflexive)* me; **I hurt m.**, me hice daño. 3 *(after prep)* mí (mismo,-a).

mysterious [mɪs'tɪərɪəs] *adj* misterioso,-a.

mystery ['mɪstərɪ] *n* misterio *m*.

mystical ['mɪstɪkəl] *adj* místico,-a.

mystify ['mɪstɪfaɪ] *vtr* dejar perplejo,-a.

mystique [mɪs'ti:k] *n* mística *f*.

myth [mɪθ] *n* mito *m*; **it's a complete m.**, es pura fantasía.

mythology [mɪ'θɒlədʒɪ] *n* mitología *f*.

N

N, n [en] *n (the letter)* N, n *f*.

N *abbr of* **North**, Norte, N.

nab [næb] *vtr fam* pillar.

nag [næg] **I** *vtr* dar la tabarra a; **to n. sb to do sth**, dar la tabarra a algn para que haga algo. **II** *vi* quejarse.

nagging ['nægɪŋ] *adj (persistent)* continuo,-a.

nail [neɪl] **I** *n* 1 *(of finger, toe)* uña *f*; **n. clippers**, cortaúñas *m inv*; **n. polish**, **n. varnish**, esmalte *m or* laca *f* de uñas. 2 *(metal)* clavo *m*; *fig* **to hit the n. on the head**, dar en el clavo. **II** *vtr* 1 clavar. 2 *fam (catch, trap)* pillar, coger.

nailbrush ['neɪlbrʌʃ] *n* cepillo *m* de uñas.

nailfile ['neɪlfaɪl] *n* lima *f* de uñas.

nail-scissors ['neɪlsɪzəz] *npl* tijeras *fpl* de uñas.

naïve [naɪ'i:v] *adj* ingenuo,-a.

naked ['neɪkɪd] *adj* desnudo,-a; *(flame)* sin protección; **the n. truth**, la pura verdad.

name [neɪm] **I** *n* 1 nombre *m*; *(surname)* apellido *m*; **what's your n.?**, ¿cómo te llamas?; **to call sb names**, poner verde a algn. 2 *(reputation)* reputación *f*; **to have a bad/good n.**, tener mala/buena reputación; **to make a n. for oneself**, hacerse famoso,-a. **II** *vtr* 1 llamar. 2 *(appoint)* nombrar. 3 *(refer to)* mencionar.

nameless ['neɪmlɪs] *adj* anónimo,-a; **to remain n.**, permanecer en el anonimato.

namely ['neɪmlɪ] *adv* a saber.

namesake ['neɪmseɪk] *n* tocayo,-a *m,f*.

nanny ['nænɪ] *n* niñera *f*.

nap [næp] **I** *n (sleep)* siesta *f*; **to have a n.**, echar la *or* una siesta. **II** *vi fig* **to catch sb napping**, coger a algn desprevenido.

napalm ['neɪpɑ:m] *n* napalm *m*.

nape [neɪp] *n* nuca *f*, cogote *m*.

napkin ['næpkɪn] *n* **(table) n.**, servilleta *f*.

Naples ['neɪpəlz] *n* Nápoles *f*.

nappy ['næpɪ] *n GB* pañal *m*.

narcissus [nɑ:'sɪsəs] *n Bot* narciso *m*.

narcotic [nɑ:'kɒtɪk] **I** *adj* narcótico,-a. **II** *n (usu pl)* narcótico *m*, estupefaciente *m*.

narrate [nə'reɪt] *vtr* narrar, relatar.

narration [nə'reɪʃən] *n* narración *f*, relato *m*.

narrative ['nærətɪv] **I** *n Lit* narrativa *f*; *(story)* narración *f*. **II** *adj* narrativo,-a.

narrator [nə'reɪtə] *n* narrador,-a *m,f*.

narrow ['nærəʊ] **I** *adj* 1 *(passage, road etc)* estrecho,-a, angosto,-a. 2 *(restricted)* reducido,-a; *(sense)* estricto,-a; **to have a n. escape**, librarse por los pelos. **II** *vi* estrecharse. ◆**narrowly** *adv* 1 *(closely)* de cerca. 2 *(by a small margin)* por poco. ◆**narrow down I** *vtr* reducir, limitar. **II** *vi* **n. down to**, reducirse a.

narrow-minded [nærəʊ'maɪndɪd] *adj* de miras estrechas.

nasal ['neɪzəl] *adj* nasal; *(voice)* gangoso,-a.

nastiness ['nɑ:stɪnɪs] *n* 1 *(unpleasantness)* carácter *m* desagradable. 2 *(maliciousness)* mala intención.

nasty ['nɑ:stɪ] *adj (nastier, nastiest)* 1 *(person)* desagradable; **a n. business**, un asunto feo; **a n. trick**, una mala jugada *or* pasada; **cheap and n.**, hortera; **to turn n.**, *(of weather, situation)* ponerse feo. 2 *(unfriendly)* antipático,-a; *(malicious)* mal intencionado,-a; *fam* **he's a n. piece of work**, es un asco de tío. 3 *(dirty)* sucio,-a, asqueroso,-a. 4 *(illness, accident)* grave.

nation ['neɪʃən] *n* nación *f*.

national ['næʃənəl] **I** *adj* nacional; **n. anthem**, himno *m* nacional; **n. insurance**, seguridad *f* social; *GB Mil* **n. service**, servicio *m* militar. **II** *n* súbdito,-a *m,f*.

nationalism ['næʃnəlɪzəm] *n* nacionalismo *m*.

nationalist ['næʃnəlɪst] *adj & n* nacionalista *(mf)*.

nationality [næʃə'nælɪtɪ] *n* nacionalidad *f*.

nationalization [næʃnəlaɪ'zeɪʃən] *n* nacionalización *f*.

nationalize ['næʃnəlaɪz] *vtr* nacionalizar.

nationwide ['neɪʃənwaɪd] *adj* de ámbito nacional.

native ['neɪtɪv] I *adj* 1 (*place*) natal; n. land, patria *f*; **n. language**, lengua materna. 2 (*innate*) innato,-a. 3 (*plant, animal*) originario,-a (*to*, de). II *n* nativo,-a *m,f*, natural *mf*; (*original inhabitant*) indígena *mf*.

NATO, Nato ['neɪtəʊ] *abbr of* **North Atlantic Treaty Organization**, Organización *f* del Tratado del Atlántico Norte, OTAN *f*.

natter ['nætə*r*] *fam* I *vi* charlar. II *n* charla *f*.

natural ['nætʃərəl] I *adj* 1 natural. 2 (*normal*) normal; **it's only n. that ...,** es lógico que .... 3 (*born*) nato,-a. II *n* 1 **she's a n. for the job**, es la persona ideal para el trabajo. 2 *Mus* becuadro *m*. ◆**naturally** *adv* 1 (*of course*) naturalmente. 2 (*by nature*) por naturaleza. 3 (*in a relaxed manner*) con naturalidad.

naturalize ['nætʃərəlaɪz] *vtr* **to become naturalized,** naturalizarse.

nature ['neɪtʃə*r*] *n* 1 naturaleza *f*. 2 (*character*) naturaleza *f*, carácter *m*; **by n.,** por naturaleza; **human n.,** la naturaleza humana. 3 (*sort, kind*) índole *f*, clase *f*.

naught [nɔːt] *n arch* nada *f*; **to come to n.,** fracasar.

naughty ['nɔːtɪ] *adj* (**naughtier, naughtiest**) 1 (*child*) travieso,-a. 2 (*joke, story*) atrevido,-a, picante. ◆**naughtily** *adv* **to behave n.,** portarse mal.

nausea ['nɔːzɪə] *n Med* (*sickness*) náusea *f*.

nauseate ['nɔːzɪeɪt] *vtr* (*disgust*) dar asco a.

nauseating ['nɔːzɪeɪtɪŋ] *adj* nauseabundo,-a.

nautical ['nɔːtɪkəl] *adj* náutico,-a; **n. mile,** milla marítima.

naval ['neɪvəl] *adj* naval; **n. officer,** oficial *mf* de marina; **n. power,** potencia marítima *or* naval.

Navarre [nə'vɑː*r*] *n* Navarra.

nave [neɪv] *n Arch* nave *f*.

navel ['neɪvəl] *n Anat* ombligo *m*.

navigate ['nævɪgeɪt] I *vtr* (*river*) navegar por; *Naut* (*ship*) gobernar. II *vi* navegar; (*in driving*) indicar la dirección.

navigation [nævɪ'geɪʃən] *n Naut* navegación *f*.

navigator ['nævɪgeɪtə*r*] *n* 1 *Naut* navegante *mf*, oficial *mf* de derrota. 2 *Aut Av* copiloto *mf*.

navvy ['nævɪ] *n GB fam* peón *m*.

navy ['neɪvɪ] *n* marina *f*; **n. blue,** azul marino.

Nazi ['nɑːtsɪ] *adj & n* nazi (*mf*).

Nazism ['nɑːtsɪzəm] *n* nazismo *m*.

NB, nb [en'biː] *abbr of* **nota bene** (note well), N.B.

neap [niːp] *n* **n. (tide),** marea muerta.

near [nɪə*r*] I *adj* (*in space*) cercano,-a; (*in time*) próximo,-a; **in the n. future,** en un

futuro próximo; **it was a n. thing,** poco faltó. II *adv* (*in space*) cerca; **n. and far,** por todas partes; **that's n. enough,** (ya) vale, está bien. III *prep* cerca de; **n. the end of the film,** hacia el final de la película. IV *vtr* acercarse a. ◆**nearly** *adv* casi; **very n.,** casi, casi; **we haven't n. enough,** no alcanza ni con mucho.

nearby [nɪə'baɪ] I *adj* cercano,-a. II *adv* cerca.

nearside ['nɪəsaɪd] *n Aut* (*with left-hand drive*) lado izquierdo; (*with right-hand drive*) lado derecho.

near-sighted [nɪə'saɪtɪd] *adj* miope.

neat [niːt] *adj* 1 (*room, habits etc*) ordenado,-a; (*handwriting*) claro,-a; (*appearance*) pulcro,-a. 2 (*idea*) ingenioso,-a. 3 (*whisky etc*) solo,-a. 4 *US fam* (*fine*) chulísimo,-a. ◆**neatly** *adv* 1 (*carefully*) cuidadosamente. 2 (*cleverly*) hábilmente.

necessary ['nesɪsərɪ] I *adj* 1 (*essential*) necesario,-a; **to do what is n.,** hacer lo que haga falta; **if n.,** si es preciso. 2 (*unavoidable*) inevitable. II *n* lo necesario. ◆**necessarily** [nesɪ'serəlɪ] *adv* necesariamente, por fuerza.

necessitate [nɪ'sesɪteɪt] *vtr* necesitar, exigir.

necessity [nɪ'sesɪtɪ] *n* 1 necesidad *f*; **out of n.,** por necesidad. 2 (*article*) requisito *m* indispensable; **necessities,** artículos *mpl* de primera necesidad.

neck [nek] I *n* 1 cuello *m*; (*of animal*) pescuezo *m*; **to be n. and n.,** ir parejos; **to be up to one's n. in debt,** estar hasta el cuello de deudas; **to risk one's n.,** jugarse el tipo; **to stick one's n. out,** arriesgarse; **to win/lose by a n.,** (*in horse racing*) ganar/perder por una cabeza; **low n.,** escote bajo. II *vi fam* magrearse.

necklace ['neklɪs] *n* collar *m*.

neckline ['neklaɪn] *n* (*of dress*) escote *m*.

necktie ['nektaɪ] *n* corbata *f*.

nectar ['nektə*r*] *n* néctar *m*.

nectarine ['nektəriːn] *n* nectarina *f*.

née [neɪ] *adj* **n. Brown,** de soltera Brown.

need [niːd] I *n* 1 necesidad *f*; **if n. be,** si fuera necesario; **there's no n. for you to do that,** no hace falta que hagas eso. 2 (*poverty*) indigencia *f*; **to be in n.,** estar necesitado; **to help a friend in n.,** sacar a un amigo de un apuro. II *vtr* 1 necesitar; **I n. to see him,** tengo que verle; *iron* **that's all I n.,** sólo me faltaba eso. 2 (*action, solution etc*) requerir, exigir. III *aux v* tener que, deber; **n. he go?,** ¿tiene que ir?; **you needn't wait,** no hace falta que esperes.

needle ['niːdəl] I *n* 1 (*for sewing, knitting*) aguja *f*. 2 *Bot* hoja *f*. 3 *GB fam* **to get the n.,** picarse. II *vtr fam* pinchar.

needless ['niːdlɪs] *adj* innecesario,-a; **n. to say,** huelga decir. ◆**needlessly** *adv*

innecesariamente.
needlework ['ni:dəlwɜːk] *n (sewing)* costura *f*; *(embroidery)* bordado *m*.
needy ['ni:dɪ] *adj (needier, neediest)* necesitado,-a.
negate [nɪ'geɪt] *vtr* 1 *(deny)* negar. 2 *(nullify)* anular.
negative ['negətɪv] I *adj* negativo,-a. II *n* 1 *Ling* negación *f*. 2 *Phot* negativo *m*.
neglect [nɪ'glekt] I *vtr* 1 *(child, duty etc)* descuidar, desatender. 2 **to n. to do sth,** *(omit to do)* no hacer algo. II *n* dejadez *f*; **n. of duty,** incumplimiento *m* del deber.
neglectful [nɪ'glektful] *adj* descuidado,-a, negligente.
negligée ['neglɪʒeɪ] *n* salto *m* de cama.
negligence ['neglɪdʒəns] *n* negligencia *f*, descuido *m*.
negligent ['neglɪdʒənt] *adj* negligente, descuidado,-a.
negligible ['neglɪdʒɪbəl] *adj* insignificante.
negotiate [nɪ'gəʊʃɪeɪt] I *vtr* 1 *(contract)* negociar. 2 *fig (obstacle)* salvar, franquear. II *vi* negociar.
negotiation [nɪgəʊʃɪ'eɪʃən] *n* negociación *f*.
negro ['ni:grəʊ] *n (pl negroes)* negro,-a *m,f*.
neigh [neɪ] I *n* relincho *m*. II *vi* relinchar.
neighbour, *US* **neighbor** ['neɪbəʳ] *n* vecino,-a *m,f*; *Rel* prójimo *m*.
neighbourhood, *US* **neighborhood** ['neɪbəhud] *n (district)* vecindad *f*, barrio *m*; *(people)* vecindario *m*.
neighbouring, *US* **neighboring** ['neɪbərɪŋ] *adj* vecino,-a.
neither ['naɪðəʳ, 'niːðəʳ] I *adj & pron* ninguno de los dos, ninguna de las dos. II *adv & conj* 1 ni; **n. ... nor,** ni ... ni; *fig* **it's n. here nor there,** no viene al caso. 2 tampoco; **she was not there and n. was her sister,** ella no estaba, ni su hermana tampoco.
neon ['ni:ɒn] *n* neón *m*; **n. light,** luz *f* de neón.
nephew ['nevju:, 'nefju:] *n* sobrino *m*.
nerve [nɜːv] *n* 1 *Anat* nervio *m*; **to get on sb's nerves,** poner los nervios de punta a algn; **n. gas,** gas nervioso *m*. 2 *(courage)* valor *m*. 3 *fam (cheek)* cara *f*, descaro *m*; **what a n.!,** ¡qué cara!
nerve-racking ['nɜːvrækɪŋ] *adj* crispante, exasperante.
nervous ['nɜːvəs] *adj* 1 nervioso,-a; **n. breakdown,** depresión nerviosa. 2 *(afraid)* miedoso,-a. 3 *(timid)* tímido,-a.
nest [nest] I *n* **Orn** nido *m*; *(hen's)* nidal *m*; *(animal's)* madriguera *f*; **n. egg,** ahorros *mpl*. II *vi (birds)* anidar.
nestle ['nesəl] I *vtr* recostar. II *vi (settle comfortably)* acomodarse.
net¹ [net] *n* red *f*; *GB* **n. curtains,** visillos *mpl*.

net² [net] I *adj* neto,-a; **n. weight,** peso neto. II *vtr (earn)* ganar neto.
netball ['netbɔːl] *n Sport* baloncesto femenino.
Netherlands ['neðələndz] *npl* **the N.,** los Países Bajos.
netting ['netɪŋ] *n* redes *fpl*, malla *f*.
nettle ['netəl] I *n Bot* ortiga *f*. II *vtr fam* irritar.
network ['netwɜːk] *n* red *f*.
neurosis [nju'rəʊsɪs] *n* neurosis *f*.
neurotic [nju'rɒtɪk] *adj & n* neurótico,-a *(m,f)*.
neuter ['nju:təʳ] I *adj* neutro,-a. II *n Ling* neutro *m*. III *vtr (geld)* castrar.
neutral ['nju:trəl] I *adj* neutro,-a; *Pol* **to remain n.,** permanecer neutral. II *n Aut* punto muerto.
neutrality [nju:'trælɪtɪ] *n* neutralidad *f*.
neutralize ['nju:trəlaɪz] *vtr* neutralizar.
neutron ['nju:trɒn] *n Phys* neutrón *m*; **n. bomb,** bomba *f* de neutrones.
never ['nevəʳ] *adv* nunca, jamás; **he n. complains,** nunca se queja, no se queja nunca; **n. again,** nunca (ja)más; **n. in all my life,** jamás en la vida; *fam* **n. mind,** da igual, no importa; *fam* **well, I n. (did)!,** ¡no me digas!
never-ending [nevər'endɪŋ] *adj* sin fin, interminable.
nevertheless [nevəðə'les] *adv* sin embargo, no obstante.
new [nju:] *adj* nuevo,-a; **as good as n.,** como nuevo; **n. baby,** recién nacido *m*; **n. moon,** luna nueva; **N. Year,** Año nuevo; **N. Year's Eve,** Nochevieja *f*; **N. York,** Nueva York; **N. Zealand,** Nueva Zelanda. ◆**newly** *adv* recién, recientemente.
newborn ['nju:bɔːn] *adj* recién nacido,-a.
newcomer ['nju:kʌməʳ] *n* recién llegado,-a *m,f*; *(to job etc)* nuevo,-a *m,f*.
newfangled ['nju:fæŋgəld] *adj* novedoso,-a.
newlywed ['nju:lɪwed] *n* recién casado,-a *m,f*.
news [nju:z] *n* noticias *fpl*; **a piece of n.,** una noticia; *fam* **it's n. to me,** ahora me entero; **n. agency,** agencia *f* de información; **n. bulletin,** boletín informativo; **n. clipping,** recorte *m* de periódico.
newsagent ['nju:zeɪdʒənt] *n* vendedor,-a *m,f* de periódicos.
newsflash ['nju:zflæʃ] *n* noticia *f* de última hora.
newsletter ['nju:zletəʳ] *n* hoja informativa.
newspaper ['nju:zpeɪpəʳ] *n* periódico *m*, diario *m*.
newsprint ['nju:zprɪnt] *n* papel *m* de periódico.
newsreader ['nju:zri:dəʳ] *n TV Rad* presentador,-a *m,f* de los informativos.
newsreel ['nju:zri:l] *n* noticiario *m*.

news-stand ['njuːstænd] n quiosco m de periódicos.

newt [njuːt] n Zool tritón m.

next [nekst] I adj 1 (in place) de al lado. 2 (in time) próximo,-a; **the n. day**, el día siguiente; **the n. Friday**, el viernes que viene; **the week after n.**, dentro de dos semanas. 3 (in order) siguiente, próximo,-a; **n. of kin**, pariente m más cercano. II adv 1 después, luego; **what shall we do n.?**, ¿qué hacemos ahora? 2 (next time) la próxima vez. III prep **n. to**, al lado de, junto a; **n. to nothing**, casi nada.

next door [neks'dɔːr] adj & adv de al lado; **our n.-d. neighbour**, el vecino o la vecina de al lado.

NHS [eneɪtʃ'es] GB abbr of National Health Service, ≈ Seguridad f Social, SS f.

nib [nɪb] n plumilla f.

nibble ['nɪbəl] vtr & vi mordisquear.

nice [naɪs] adj 1 (person) simpático,-a; (thing) agradable; **n. and cool**, fresquito,-a; **to smell/taste n.**, oler/saber bien. 2 (nice-looking) bonito,-a. 3 iron menudo,-a; **a n. mess you've made!**, ¡menudo lío has hecho! 4 fml (subtle) sutil. ◆**nicely** adv muy bien.

niche [niːtʃ] n 1 hornacina f, nicho m. 2 fig hueco m.

nick [nɪk] I n 1 (notch) muesca f; (cut) herida pequeña; fam **in the n. of time**, en el momento preciso. 2 GB sl **the n.**, (prison) chirona f. II vtr GB sl 1 (steal) birlar. 2 (arrest) pillar.

nickel ['nɪkəl] n 1 níquel m; **n. silver**, alpaca f. 2 US moneda f de cinco centavos.

nickname ['nɪkneɪm] I n apodo m. II vtr apodar.

nicotine ['nɪkətiːn] n nicotina f.

niece [niːs] n sobrina f.

nifty ['nɪftɪ] adj (niftier, niftiest) 1 (quick) rápido,-a; (agile) ágil. 2 (ingenious) ingenioso,-a.

Nigeria [naɪ'dʒɪərɪə] n Nigeria.

nigger ['nɪgər] n offens negro,-a m,f.

niggling ['nɪgəlɪŋ] adj (trifling) insignificante; (irritating) molesto,-a.

night [naɪt] n noche f; **at n.**, de noche; **at twelve o'clock at n.**, a las doce de la noche; **last n.**, anoche; **to have a n. out**, salir por la noche; **n. life**, vida nocturna; fam **n. owl**, trasnochador,-a m,f; **n. school**, escuela nocturna; **n. shift**, turno m de noche.

nightclub ['naɪtklʌb] n sala f de fiestas; (disco) discoteca f.

nightdress ['naɪtdres] n camisón m.

nightfall ['naɪtfɔːl] n anochecer m.

nightgown ['naɪtgaʊn] n camisón m.

nightingale ['naɪtɪŋgeɪl] n ruiseñor m.

nightly ['naɪtlɪ] I adj de cada noche. II

adv todas las noches.

nightmare ['naɪtmeər] n pesadilla f.

nightshade ['naɪtʃeɪd] n Bot **deadly n.**, belladona f.

night-time ['naɪttaɪm] n noche f; **at n.**, por la noche.

nil [nɪl] n nada f; Sport cero m; **two n.**, dos a cero.

Nile [naɪl] n **the N.**, el Nilo.

nimble ['nɪmbəl] adj ágil, rápido,-a.

nine [naɪn] adj & n nueve (m) inv; fam **dressed up to the nines**, de punta en blanco.

nineteen [naɪn'tiːn] adj & n diecinueve (m) inv.

nineteenth [naɪn'tiːnθ] adj decimonoveno,-a.

ninety ['naɪntɪ] adj & n noventa (m) inv.

ninth [naɪnθ] I adj & n noveno,-a (m,f). II n (fraction) noveno m.

nip [nɪp] I vtr 1 (pinch) pellizcar. 2 (bite) morder; **to n. sth in the bud**, cortar algo de raíz. II n 1 (pinch) pellizco m. 2 (bite) mordisco m.

nipple ['nɪpəl] n Anat (female) pezón m; (male) tetilla f.

nippy ['nɪpɪ] adj (nippier, nippiest) fam 1 GB (quick) rápido,-a. 2 (cold) fresquito,-a.

nit [nɪt] n liendre f.

nitrogen ['naɪtrədʒən] n Chem nitrógeno m.

nitroglycerin(e) [naɪtrəʊ'glɪsəriːn] n Chem nitroglicerina f.

nitty-gritty [nɪtɪ'grɪtɪ] n fam **to get down to the n.g.**, ir al grano.

nitwit ['nɪtwɪt] n fam imbécil mf.

no [nəʊ] I adv no; **come here! - no!**, ¡ven aquí! - ¡no!; **no longer**, ya no; **no less than**, no menos de. II adj ninguno,-a; **she has no children**, no tiene hijos; **I have no idea**, no tengo (ni) idea; **it's no good or use**, no vale la pena; Aut **'no parking'**, 'prohibido aparcar'; **no sensible person**, ninguna persona razonable; fam **no way!**, ¡ni hablar! III n no m; **she won't take no for an answer**, no se dará por vencida; **to say no**, decir que no.

no. (pl nos.) abbr of **number**, número m, nº, núm.

nobility [nəʊ'bɪlɪtɪ] n nobleza f.

noble ['nəʊbəl] adj noble.

nobleman ['nəʊbəlmən] n noble m.

noblewoman ['nəʊbəlwʊmən] n noble f.

nobody ['nəʊbədɪ] I pron nadie; **there was n. there**, no había nadie; **n. else**, nadie más. II n nadie m; **he's a n.**, es un don nadie.

nocturnal [nɒk'tɜːnəl] adj nocturno,-a.

nod [nɒd] I n (of greeting) saludo m con la cabeza; (of agreement) señal f de asentimiento. II vi (greet) saludar con la cabeza; (agree) asentir con la cabeza. III vtr **to n. one's head**, inclinar la cabeza. ◆**nod**

off *vi* dormirse.

no-go ['nəʊ'gəʊ] *adj* **no-go area,** zona prohibida.

noise [nɔɪz] *n* ruido *m*; **to make a n.,** hacer ruido.

noiseless ['nɔɪzləs] *adj* silencioso,-a, sin ruido.

noisy ['nɔɪzɪ] *adj* (**noisier, noisiest**) ruidoso,-a.

nomad ['nəʊmæd] *n* nómada *mf*.

no-man's-land ['nəʊmænzlænd] *n* tierra *f* de nadie.

nominal ['nɒmɪnəl] *adj* nominal; (*payment, rent*) simbólico,-a.

nominate ['nɒmɪneɪt] *vtr* **1** (*propose*) designar, proponer. **2** (*appoint*) nombrar.

nomination [nɒmɪ'neɪʃən] *n* **1** (*proposal*) propuesta *f*. **2** (*appointment*) nombramiento *m*.

nominative ['nɒmɪnətɪv] *n* nominativo *m*.

nominee [nɒmɪ'niː] *n* persona propuesta.

non- [nɒn] *pref* no.

non-aggression [nɒnə'greʃən] *n* Pol no agresión *f*; **n.-a. pact,** pacto *m* de no agresión.

non-alcoholic [nɒnælkə'hɒlɪk] *adj* sin alcohol.

non-aligned [nɒnə'laɪnd] *adj* Pol no alineado,-a.

nonchalant ['nɒnʃələnt] *adj* (*indifferent*) indiferente; (*calm*) imperturbable, impasible.

noncommittal ['nɒnkəmɪtəl] *adj* (*person*) evasivo,-a; (*answer*) que no compromete (a nada).

nonconformist [nɒnkən'fɔːmɪst] *n* inconformista *mf*.

nondescript ['nɒndɪskrɪpt] *adj* indescriptible; (*uninteresting*) soso,-a.

none [nʌn] **I** *pron* ninguno,-a; **I know n. of them,** no conozco a ninguno de ellos; **n. at all,** nada en absoluto; **n. other than ...,** nada menos que .... **II** *adv* de ningún modo; **she's n. the worse for it,** no se ha visto afectada *or* perjudicada por ello; **n. too soon,** a buena hora.

nonentity [nɒ'nentɪtɪ] *n* (*person*) cero *m* a la izquierda.

nonetheless [nʌnðə'les] *adv* no obstante, sin embargo.

nonevent [nɒnɪ'vent] *n* fracaso *m*.

nonexistent [nɒnɪg'zɪstənt] *adj* inexistente.

nonfiction [nɒn'fɪkʃən] *n* literatura *f* no novelesca.

no-nonsense [nəʊ'nɒnsens] *adj* (*person*) recto,-a, serio,-a.

nonplussed [nɒn'plʌst] *adj* perplejo,-a.

non-profit(-making) [nɒn'prɒfɪt(meɪkɪŋ)] *adj* sin fin lucrativo.

nonreturnable [nɒnrɪ'tɜːnəbəl] *adj* no retornable.

nonsense ['nɒnsens] *n* tonterías *fpl*, disparates *mpl*; **that's n.,** eso es absurdo.

nonsmoker [nɒn'sməʊkə'] *n* no fumador,-a *m,f*, persona *f* que no fuma.

nonstarter [nɒn'stɑːtə'] *n* *fig* **to be a n.,** (*person*) estar destinado a fracasar; (*plan*) ser irrealizable.

nonstick [nɒn'stɪk] *adj* antiadherente.

nonstop [nɒn'stɒp] **I** *adj* sin parar; (*train*) directo,-a. **II** *adv* sin parar.

noodles ['nuːdəlz] *npl* Culin fideos *mpl*.

nook [nʊk] *n* recoveco *m*, rincón *m*.

noon [nuːn] *n* mediodía *m*; **at n.,** a mediodía.

no-one ['nəʊwʌn] *pron* nadie; **n. came,** no vino nadie.

noose [nuːs] *n* lazo *m*; (*hangman's*) soga *f*.

nor [nɔː'] *conj* ni, ni tampoco; **neither ... n.** ..., ni; **neither you n. I,** ni tú ni yo; **n. do I,** (ni) yo tampoco.

norm [nɔːm] *n* norma *f*.

normal ['nɔːməl] *adj* normal.

normality [nɔː'mælɪtɪ] *n* normalidad *f*.

normally ['nɔːməlɪ] *adv* normalmente.

Normandy ['nɔːməndɪ] *n* Normandía.

north [nɔːθ] **I** *n* norte *m*; **the N.,** el norte; **N. America,** América del Norte; **N. América;** **N. Pole,** Polo *m* Norte; **N. Sea,** Mar *m* del Norte. **II** *adv* hacia el norte, al norte. **III** *adj* del norte; **n. wind,** viento *m* del norte.

northeast [nɔːθ'iːst] *n* nor(d)este *m*.

northerly ['nɔːðəlɪ] *adj* norte, del norte.

northern ['nɔːðən] *adj* del norte, septentrional; **n. hemisphere,** hemisferio *m* norte; **N. Ireland,** Irlanda del Norte.

northerner ['nɔːðənə'] *n* norteño,-a *mf*.

northward ['nɔːθwəd] *adj* & *adv* hacia el norte.

northwest [nɔːθ'west] *n* noroeste *m*.

Norway ['nɔːweɪ] *n* Noruega.

Norwegian [nɔː'wiːdʒən] **I** *adj* noruego, -a. **II** *n* **1** (*person*) noruego,-a *m,f*. **2** (*language*) noruego *m*.

nose [nəʊz] *n* **1** nariz *f*; *fig* (**right**) **under sb's n.,** delante de las propias narices de algn; *GB fam* **to get up sb's n.,** hincharle a algn las narices. **2** (*sense of smell*) olfato *m*. **3** (*of car, plane*) morro *m*.
◆**nose about, nose around** *vi* curiosear.

nosebleed ['nəʊzbliːd] *n* hemorragia *f* nasal.

nosedive ['nəʊzdaɪv] *Av* **I** *n* picado *m*. **II** *vi* descender en picado.

nostalgia [nɒ'stældʒə] *n* nostalgia *f*.

nostalgic [nɒ'stældʒɪk] *adj* nostálgico,-a.

nostril ['nɒstrɪl] *n* Anat orificio *m* nasal.

nosy ['nəʊzɪ] *adj* (**nosier, nosiest**) *fam* entrometido,-a.

not [nɒt] *adv* no; **he's n. in today,** hoy no está; **I'm n. sorry to leave,** no siento nada irme; **n. at all,** en absoluto; **thank you - n. at all,** gracias - no hay de qué; **n. one (of them)** thanked me, nadie me dio las gracias; **n. that I don't want to**

come, no es que no quiera ir; **n. too well**, bastante mal; **n. without reason**, no sin razón; **fam n. likely!**, ¡ni hablar!

notable ['nəʊtəbəl] *adj* notable.
▶ **notably** *adv* notablemente.

notary ['nəʊtəri] *n* notario *m*.

notch [nɒtʃ] *n* muesca *f*; (*cut*) corte *m*.
▶ **notch up** *vtr fig* to n. up a victory, apuntarse una victoria.

note [nəʊt] I *n* 1 *Mus* nota *f*; *fig* to strike the right n., acertar. 2 (*on paper*) nota *f*. 3 to take n. of, (*notice*) prestar atención a. 4 *Fin* billete *m* (de banco). 5 notes, apuntes *mpl*; **to take n.**, tomar apuntes. II *vtr* 1 (*write down*) apuntar, anotar. 2 (*notice*) notar, fijarse en.

notebook ['nəʊtbʊk] *n* cuaderno *m*, libreta *f*.

noted ['nəʊtɪd] *adj* notable, célebre.

notepad ['nəʊtpæd] *n* bloc *m* de notas.

notepaper ['nəʊtpeɪpə'] *n* papel *m* de carta.

noteworthy ['nəʊtwɜːðɪ] *adj* digno,-a de mención.

nothing ['nʌθɪŋ] I *n* nada; **I saw n.**, no vi nada; **for n.**, (*free of charge*) gratis; **it's n.**, no es nada; **it's n. to do with you**, no tiene nada que ver contigo; **n. else**, nada más; **there's n. in it**, no es cierto; *fam* **n. much**, poca cosa; *fam* **there's n. to it**, es facilísimo. II *adv* **she looks n. like her sister**, no se parece en nada a su hermana.

notice ['nəʊtɪs] I *n* 1 (*warning*) aviso *m*; **he gave a month's n.**, presentó la dimisión con un mes de antelación; **at short n.**, con poca antelación; **until further n.**, hasta nuevo aviso; **without n.**, sin previo aviso. 2 (*attention*) atención *f*; **to take no n. of sth**, no hacer caso de algo; **to take n. of sth**, prestar atención a algo; **it escaped my n.**, se me escapó; **to come to one's n.**, llegar al conocimiento de uno. 3 (*in newspaper etc*) anuncio *m*. 4 (*sign*) letrero *m*, aviso *m*. II *vtr* darse cuenta de, notar.

noticeable ['nəʊtɪsəbəl] *adj* que se nota, evidente.

noticeboard ['nəʊtɪsbɔːd] *n* tablón *m* de anuncios.

notification [nəʊtɪfɪ'keɪʃən] *n* aviso *m*.

notify ['nəʊtɪfaɪ] *vtr* avisar.

notion ['nəʊʃən] *n* 1 idea *f*, concepto *m*. 2 (*whim*) capricho *m*. 3 *US Sew* **notions**, artículos *mpl* de mercería.

notorious [nəʊ'tɔːrɪəs] *adj* muy conocido,-a.

notwithstanding [nɒtwɪθ'stændɪŋ] I *prep* a pesar de. II *adv* sin embargo, no obstante.

nougat ['nuːgɑː] *n* turrón blando.

nought [nɔːt] *n* cero *m*.

noun [naʊn] *n* nombre *m*, sustantivo *m*.

nourish ['nʌrɪʃ] *vtr* nutrir; *fig* (*hopes*) abrigar.

nourishing ['nʌrɪʃɪŋ] *adj* nutritivo,-a.

nourishment ['nʌrɪʃmənt] *n* alimentación *f*, nutrición *f*.

novel¹ ['nɒvəl] *n* novela *f*.

novel² ['nɒvəl] *adj* original, novedoso,-a.

novelist ['nɒvəlɪst] *n* novelista *mf*.

novelty ['nɒvəltɪ] *n* novedad *f*.

November [nəʊ'vembə'] *n* noviembre *m*.

novice ['nɒvɪs] *n* 1 (*beginner*) novato,-a *m,f*, principiante *mf*. 2 *Rel* novicio,-a *m,f*.

now [naʊ] I *adv* 1 (*at this moment*) ahora; **just n.**, **right n.**, ahora mismo; **from n. on**, de ahora en adelante; **n. and then**, **n. and again**, de vez en cuando. 2 (*for events in past*) entonces. 3 (*not related to time*) **n.**, ¡vamos!; **n.!**, ¡ya está bien! II *conj* **n. (that)**, ahora que, ya que. III *n* **until n.**, hasta ahora; **he'll be home by n.**, ya habrá llegado a casa.

nowadays ['naʊədeɪz] *adv* hoy (en) día, actualmente.

nowhere ['nəʊweə'] *adv* en ninguna parte; **that will get you n.**, eso no te servirá de nada; **it's n. near ready**, no está preparado, ni mucho menos.

noxious ['nɒkʃəs] *adv* nocivo,-a.

nozzle ['nɒzəl] *n* boca *f*, boquilla *f*.

nuance [njuː'ɑːns] *n* matiz *m*.

nub [nʌb] *n* **the n. of the matter**, el quid de la cuestión.

nuclear ['njuːklɪə'] *adj* nuclear; **n. arms**, armas *fpl* nucleares; **n. disarmament**, desarme *m* nuclear; **n. power**, energía *f* nuclear; **n. power station**, central *f* nuclear.

nucleus ['njuːklɪəs] *n* núcleo *m*.

nude [njuːd] I *adj* desnudo,-a. II *n Art Phot* desnudo *m*; **in the n.**, al desnudo.

nudge [nʌdʒ] I *vtr* dar un codazo a. II *n* codazo *m*.

nudist ['njuːdɪst] *adj & n* nudista (*mf*).

nudity ['njuːdɪtɪ] *n* desnudez *f*.

nugget ['nʌgɪt] *n Min* pepita *f*; **gold n.**, pepita de oro.

nuisance ['njuːsəns] *n* 1 molestia *f*, pesadez *f*; **what a n.!**, ¡qué lata! 2 (*person*) pesado,-a *m,f*.

nuke [njuːk] *sl* I *n* (*bomb*) bomba *f* nuclear or atómica. II *vtr* atacar con armas nucleares.

null [nʌl] *adj* nulo,-a; **n. and void**, nulo y sin valor.

nullify ['nʌlɪfaɪ] *vtr* (*pt & pp* **nullified**) anular.

numb [nʌm] I *adj* (*without feeling*) entumecido,-a; *fig* paralizado,-a; **n. with fear**, paralizado de miedo. II *vtr* (*with cold*) entumecer (de frío); (*with anaesthetic*) adormecer.

number ['nʌmbə'] I *n* 1 número *m*; *Tel*

have you got my n.?, ¿tienes mi (número de) teléfono?; *fam* **to look after n. one**, barrer para adentro. 2 *(quantity)* **a n.** of people, varias personas. II *vtr* 1 *(put a number on)* numerar. 2 *(count)* contar; **his days are numbered**, tiene los días contados.

numberplate ['nʌmbəpleɪt] *n* GB Aut matrícula *f*.

numeral ['njuːmərəl] *n* número *m*, cifra *f*.

numerate ['njuːmərət] *adj* **to be n.**, tener un conocimiento básico de matemáticas.

numerical [njuː'merɪkəl] *adj* numérico,-a.
◆**numerically** *adv* numéricamente.

numerous ['njuːmərəs] *adj* numeroso,-a.

numismatics [njuːmɪz'mætɪks] *n* numismática *f*.

nun [nʌn] *n* monja *f*.

nuptial ['nʌpʃəl] *adj* nupcial.

nurse [nɜːs] I *n* enfermera *f*; *(male)* enfermero *m*; **children's n.**, niñera *f*. II *vtr* 1 *(look after)* cuidar, atender. 2 *(baby)* acunar. 3 *(suckle)* amamantar. 4 *fig (grudge etc)* guardar.

nursery ['nɜːsərɪ] *n* 1 *(institution)* guardería *f*; **n. school**, jardín *m* de infancia. 2 *(in house)* cuarto *m* de los niños; **n.**

rhyme, poema *m* infantil. 3 *(garden centre)* vivero *m*.

nursing ['nɜːsɪŋ] *n* **n. home**, clínica *f*.

nurture ['nɜːtʃər] *vtr (animal)* alimentar; *(feelings)* abrigar.

nut [nʌt] *n* 1 *(fruit)* fruto seco; *fig* **a tough n. to crack**, un hueso duro de roer. 2 *sl (head)* coco *m*. 3 *sl (mad person)* loco,-a m,f. 4 *Tech* tuerca *f*.

nutcracker ['nʌtkrækər] *n* cascanueces *m inv*.

nutmeg ['nʌtmeg] *n* nuez moscada.

nutrition [njuː'trɪʃən] *n* nutrición *f*.

nutritious [njuː'trɪʃəs] *adj* nutritivo,-a, alimenticio,-a.

nuts [nʌts] *adj fam* **to go n.**, volverse loco; **he's n. about motorbikes**, las motos le chiflan.

nutshell ['nʌtʃel] *n* cáscara *f*; *fig* **in a n.**, en pocas palabras.

nylon ['naɪlɒn] I *n* 1 nilón *m*, nailon *m*. 2 **nylons**, medias *fpl* de nilón. II *adj* de nilón.

nymph [nɪmf] *n* ninfa *f*.

nymphomaniac [nɪmfə'meɪnɪæk] *n* ninfómana *f*.

O

O, o [əʊ] *n* 1 *(the letter)* O, o *f*. 2 *Math Tel* cero *m*.

oak [əʊk] *n* roble *m*.

OAP [əʊeɪ'piː] GB *fam abbr of* **old-age pensioner**.

oar [ɔːr] *n* remo *m*.

oarsman ['ɔːzmən] *n* remero *m*.

oasis [əʊ'eɪsɪs] *n (pl* **oases** [əʊ'eɪsiːz]) oasis *m inv*.

oat [əʊt] *n* avena *f*; **rolled oats**, copos *mpl* de avena.

oath [əʊθ] *n (pl* **oaths** [əʊðz]) 1 *Jur* juramento *m*; **to take an o.**, prestar juramento; *fam* **on my o.**, palabra de honor. 2 *(swearword)* palabrota *f*.

oatmeal ['əʊtmiːl] *n* harina *f* de avena.

obedience [ə'biːdɪəns] *n* obediencia *f*.

obedient [ə'biːdɪənt] *adj* obediente.

obese [əʊ'biːs] *adj* obeso,-a.

obey [ə'beɪ] *vtr* obedecer; *(law)* cumplir con.

obituary [ə'bɪtjʊərɪ] *n* necrología *f*.

object¹ ['ɒbdʒɪkt] *n* 1 *(thing)* objeto *m*. 2 *(aim, purpose)* fin *m*, objetivo *m*. 3 **the o. of criticism**, el blanco de las críticas. 4 *(obstacle)* inconveniente *m*. 5 *Ling* complemento *m*.

object² [əb'dʒekt] *vi* oponerse (to, a); **do you o. to my smoking?**, ¿le molesta que fume?

objection [əb'dʒekʃən] *n* 1 objeción *f*. 2 *(drawback)* inconveniente *m*; **provided**

there's no o., si no hay inconveniente.

objectionable [əb'dʒekʃənəbəl] *adj (unacceptable)* inaceptable; *(unpleasant)* ofensivo,-a.

objective [əb'dʒektɪv] I *adj* objetivo,-a. II *n* objetivo *m*.

objector [əb'dʒektər] *n* objetor,-a m,f.

obligation [ɒblɪ'geɪʃən] *n* obligación *f*; **to be under an o. to sb**, estarle muy agradecido,-a a algn.

obligatory [ə'blɪgətərɪ] *adj* obligatorio,-a.

oblige [ə'blaɪdʒ] *vtr* 1 *(compel)* obligar; **I'm obliged to do it**, me veo obligado,-a a hacerlo. 2 *(do a favour for)* hacer un favor a. 3 **to be obliged**, *(grateful)* estar agradecido,-a.

obliging [ə'blaɪdʒɪŋ] *adj* solícito,-a.

oblique [ə'bliːk] *adj* oblicuo,-a, inclinado,-a; *fig* **an o. reference**, una alusión indirecta.

obliterate [ə'blɪtəreɪt] *vtr* 1 *(memory)* borrar. 2 *(species, race)* eliminar; *(village)* arrasar.

oblivion [ə'blɪvɪən] *n* olvido *m*; **to sink into o.**, caer en el olvido.

oblivious [ə'blɪvɪəs] *adj* inconsciente.

oblong ['ɒblɒŋ] I *adj* oblongo,-a. II *n* rectángulo *m*.

obnoxious [əb'nɒkʃəs] *adj* repugnante.

oboe ['əʊbəʊ] *n* oboe *m*.

obscene [əb'siːn] *adj* obsceno,-a.

obscure [əb'skjʊər] I *adj* 1 oscuro,-a,

(vague) vago,-a. 2 *(author, poet etc)* desconocido,-a. II *vtr (truth)* ocultar.

obsequious |əb'si:kwɪəs| *adj* servil.

observance |əb'zɜ:vəns| *n* 1 observancia *f*. 2 *Rel* observances, prácticas religiosas.

observant |əb'zɜ:vənt| *adj* observador,-a.

observation |ɒbzə'veɪʃən| *n* observación *f*; *(surveillance)* vigilancia *f*.

observatory |əb'zɜ:vətərɪ| *n* observatorio *m*.

observe |əb'zɜ:v| *vtr* 1 observar; *(in surveillance)* vigilar. 2 *(remark)* advertir. 3 *(obey)* respetar.

observer |əb'zɜ:və°| *n* observador,-a *m,f*.

obsess |əb'ses| *vtr* obsesionar; to **be obsessed**, estar obsesionado,-a **(with**, **by**, **con)**.

obsession |əb'seʃən| *n* obsesión *f*.

obsessive |əb'sesɪv| *adj* obsesivo,-a.

obsolete |'ɒbsəli:t, ɒbsə'li:t| *adj* obsoleto,-a.

obstacle |'ɒbstəkəl| *n* obstáculo *m*; *fig* impedimento *m*; **o. race**, cárrera *f* de obstáculos.

obstinate |'ɒbstɪnɪt| *adj* 1 *(person)* obstinado,-a, terco,-a. 2 *(pain)* persistente.

obstruct |əb'strʌkt| *vtr* 1 obstruir; *(pipe etc)* atascar; *(view)* tapar. 2 *(hinder)* estorbar; *(progress)* dificultar.

obstruction |əb'strʌkʃən| *n* 1 obstrucción *f*. 2 *(hindrance)* obstáculo *m*.

obtain |əb'teɪn| *vtr* obtener, conseguir.

obtainable |əb'teɪnəbəl| *adj* obtenible.

obtrusive |əb'tru:sɪv| *adj* 1 *(interfering)* entrometido,-a. 2 *(noticeable)* llamativo, -a.

obtuse |əb'tju:s| *adj* obtuso,-a.

obviate |'ɒbvɪeɪt| *vtr fml* obviar.

obvious |'ɒbvɪəs| *adj* obvio,-a, evidente.
   ◆**obviously** *adv* evidentemente; o.!, ¡claro!, ¡por supuesto!

occasion |ə'keɪʒən| I *n* 1 ocasión *f*; on o., de vez en cuando; **on the o. of**, con motivo de. 2 *(event)* acontecimiento *m*. 3 *(cause)* motivo *m*. II *vtr fml* ocasionar.

occasional |ə'keɪʒənəl| *adj* 1 esporádico,-a, eventual. ◆**occasionally** *adv* de vez en cuando.

occupant |'ɒkjʊpənt| *n* ocupante *mf*; *(tenant)* inquilino,-a *m,f*.

occupation |ɒkjʊ'peɪʃən| *n* 1 *(job, profession)* profesión *f*, ocupación *f*. 2 *(pastime)* pasatiempo *m*. 3 *(of building, house, country)* ocupación *f*.

occupational |ɒkjʊ'peɪʃənəl| *adj* profesional, laboral; **o. hazards**, gajes *mpl* del oficio.

occupied |'ɒkjʊpaɪd| *adj* ocupado,-a.

occupier |'ɒkjʊpaɪə°| *n GB* ocupante *mf*; *(tenant)* inquilino,-a *m,f*.

occupy |'ɒkjʊpaɪ| *vtr* 1 *(live in)* ocupar, habitar. 2 *(time)* pasar; **to o. one's time**

in doing sth, dedicar su tiempo a hacer algo. 3 *(building, factory etc in protest)* tomar posesión de.

occur |ə'kɜ:°| *vi* 1 *(event)* suceder, acaecer; *(change)* producirse. 2 *(be found)* encontrarse. 3 **it occurred to me that ...**, se me ocurrió que ....

occurrence |ə'kʌrəns| *n* acontecimiento *m*.

ocean |'əʊʃən| *n* océano *m*.

ocean-going |'əʊʃəngəʊɪŋ| *adj* de alta mar.

ochre, *US* **ocher** |'əʊkə°| I *n* ocre *m*; red o., almagre *m*; yellow o., ocre amarillo. II *adj* (de color) ocre.

o'clock |ə'klɒk| *adv* (it's) one o'c., (es) la una; (it's) two o'c., (son) las dos.

octave |'ɒktɪv| *n* octava *f*.

October |ɒk'təʊbə°| *n* octubre *m*.

octogenarian |ɒktəʊdʒɪ'neərɪən| *adj & n* octogenario,-a *m,f*.

octopus |'ɒktəpəs| *n* pulpo *m*.

odd |ɒd| I *adj* 1 *(strange)* raro,-a, extraño,-a. 2 *(occasional)* esporádico,-a; at o. times, de vez en cuando; the o. customer, algún que otro cliente; o. job, trabajillo *m*. 3 an o. number, *(not even)* un impar. 4 *(unpaired)* desparejado,-a; an o. sock, un calcetín suelto; *fig* to be the o. man out, estar de más. II *adv* y pico; twenty o. people, veinte y pico *or* y tantas personas. ◆**oddly** *adv* extrañamente; o. enough, por extraño que parezca.

oddity |'ɒdɪtɪ| *n* 1 *(thing)* curiosidad *f*; *(person)* estrafalario,-a *m,f*. 2 *(quality)* rareza *f*.

odds |ɒdz| *npl* 1 *(chances)* probabilidades *fpl*; he's fighting against the o., lleva las de perder; the o. are that ..., lo más probable es que ... (+ subj). 2 *(in betting)* puntos *mpl* de ventaja; the o. are five to one, las apuestas están cinco a uno. 3 *GB* it makes no o., da lo mismo; *fig* at o. with sb, reñido,-a con algn. 4 o. and ends, *(small things)* cositas *fpl*; *(trinkets)* chucherías *fpl*.

odds-on |'ɒdzɒn| *adj* seguro,-a; **o.-on favourite**, *(horse)* caballo favorito.

ode |əʊd| *n* oda *f*.

odious |'əʊdɪəs| *adj* repugnante.

odour, *US* **odor** |'əʊdə°| *n* olor *m*; *(fragrance)* perfume *m*.

OECD |əʊi:si:'di:| *abbr of* **Organization for Economic Co-operation and Development**, = Organización *f* para la Cooperación y el Desarrollo Económico, OCDE *f*.

of |ɒv, *unstressed* əv| *prep* 1 *(belonging to, part of)* de; a friend of mine, un amigo mío; the end of the novel, el final de la novela. 2 *(containing)* de; a bottle of wine, una botella de vino. 3 *(origin)* de; of good family, de buena familia. 4 *(by)* de, por; **beloved of all**, amado,-a por todos. 5 *(quantity)* de; **there are four of us**, somos cuatro; **two of them**, dos de ellos. 6 *(from)* de; **free of**, libre de; **south of**, al sur de. 7 *(material)* de; **a dress (made) of silk**, un vestido de seda. 8 *(apposition)* de; **the city of Lisbon**, la ciudad de Lisboa. 9 *(characteristic)* de; **that's typical of her**, es muy propio de ella; **that's very kind of you**, es usted muy amable. 10 *(with adj)* de; **hard of hearing**, duro,-a de oído. 11 *(after superlative)* de; **the thing she wanted most of all**, lo que más quería. 12 *(cause)* por, de; **because of**, a causa de; **of necessity**, por necesidad. 13 *(concerning, about)* de, sobre; **to dream of sth/sb**, soñar con algo/algn; **to think of sb**, pensar en algn. 14 *(with dates)* de; **the seventh of November**, el siete de noviembre.

off [ɒf] I *prep* 1 *(movement)* de; **she fell o. her horse**, se cayó del caballo. 2 *(removal)* de; **I'll take sth o. the price for you**, se lo rebajaré un poco. 3 *(distance, situation)* de; **a few kilometres o. the coast**, a unos kilómetros de la costa; **a house o. the road**, una casa apartada de la carretera. 4 **the ship went o. course**, el barco se desvió; **to be o. form**, no estar en forma. 5 **I'm o. wine**, he perdido el gusto al vino.
II *adv* 1 **he turned o. the radio**, apagó la radio. 2 *(absent)* fuera; **I have a day o.**, tengo un día libre; **to be o. sick**, estar de baja por enfermedad. 3 *(completely)* completamente; **this will kill o. any germs**, esto rematará cualquier germen. 4 **his arrival is three days o.**, faltan tres días para su llegada; **six miles o.**, a seis millas. 5 **I'm o. to London**, me voy a Londres; **she ran o.**, se fue corriendo. 6 **ten per cent o.**, un descuento del diez por ciento; **to take one's shoes o.**, quitarse los zapatos. 7 **o. and on**, de vez en cuando.
III *adj* 1 *(gas etc)* apagado,-a; *(water)* cortado,-a. 2 *(cancelled)* cancelado,-a. 3 *(low)* bajo,-a; *(unsatisfactory)* malo,-a; **on the o. chance**, por si acaso; **the o. season**, la temporada baja. 4 **you're better o. like that**, así estás mejor. 5 *(gone bad)* *(meat, fish)* malo,-a, pasado,-a; *(milk)* agrio,-a.

offal [ˈɒfəl] *n (of chicken etc)* menudillos *mpl*, *(of cattle, pigs)* asaduras *fpl*.

off-colour, *US* **off-color** [ˈɒfkʌlər] *adj* 1 *GB (ill)* indispuesto,-a. 2 *(joke, story)* indecente.

offence [əˈfens] *n* 1 *Jur* delito *m*. 2 *(insult)* ofensa *f*; **to give o.**, ofender; **to take o. at sth**, ofenderse por algo. 3 *Mil (attack)* ofensiva *f*.

offend [əˈfend] *vtr* ofender.

offender [əˈfendər] *n (criminal)* delincuente *mf*.

offense [əˈfens] *n US* → **offence**.

offensive [əˈfensɪv] I *adj* 1 *(insulting)* ofensivo,-a. 2 *(repulsive)* repugnante. II *n Mil* ofensiva *f*; **to be on the o.**, estar a la ofensiva.

offer [ˈɒfər] I *vtr* 1 ofrecer; **to o. to do a job**, ofrecerse para hacer un trabajo. 2 *(propose)* proponer. II *n* 1 oferta *f*; *(proposal)* propuesta *f*; **o. of marriage**, proposición *f* de matrimonio. 2 *Com* **on o.**, de oferta.

offering [ˈɒfərɪŋ] *n* 1 ofrecimiento *m*. 2 *Rel* ofrenda *f*.

offhand [ɒfˈhænd] I *adj (abrupt)* brusco, -a; *(inconsiderate)* descortés. II *adv* I **don't know o.**, así sin pensarlo, no lo sé.

office [ˈɒfɪs] *n* 1 *(room)* despacho *m*; *(building)* oficina *f*; **o. hours**, horas *fpl* de oficina. 2 *GB Pol* ministerio *m*. 3 *US (federal agency)* agencia *f* gubernamental. 4 *(position)* cargo *m*; **to hold o.**, ocupar un cargo. 5 *Pol* **to be in o.**, estar en el poder.

officer [ˈɒfɪsər] *n* 1 *Mil* oficial *mf*. 2 *(police)* o., agente *mf* de policía. 3 *(government official)* funcionario,-a *m,f*. 4 *(of company, society)* director,-a *m,f*.

official [əˈfɪʃəl] I *adj* oficial. II *n* funcionario,-a *m,f*.

officiate [əˈfɪʃɪeɪt] *vi* 1 ejercer; **to o. as**, ejercer de. 2 *Rel* oficiar.

officious [əˈfɪʃəs] *adj pej* entrometido,-a.

off-line [ˈɒflaɪn] *adj Comput* desconectado,-a.

off-licence [ˈɒflaɪsəns] *n GB* tienda *f* de bebidas alcohólicas.

off-peak [ɒfˈpiːk] *adj (flight)* de temporada baja; *(rate)* de fuera de las horas punta.

off-putting [ˈɒfpʊtɪŋ] *adj GB fam* desconcertante.

offset [ɒfˈset] *vtr (pt & pp offset)* *(balance out)* compensar.

offshoot [ˈɒfʃuːt] *n* 1 *Bot* renuevo *m*. 2 *fig (of organization)* ramificación *f*.

offshore [ɒfˈʃɔːr] *adj* 1 *(breeze etc)* terral. 2 *(oil rig)* costa afuera. 3 *(overseas)* en el extranjero; **o. investment**, inversión *f* en el extranjero.

offside [ɒfˈsaɪd] I *adv Ftb* fuera de juego. II *n Aut (with left-hand drive)* lado derecho; *(with right-hand drive)* lado izquierdo.

offspring [ˈɒfsprɪŋ] *n inv (child)* vástago *m*; *(children)* progenitura *f*.

offstage [ɒfˈsteɪdʒ] *adj & adv* entre bastidores.

often [ˈɒfən, ˈɒftən] *adv* a menudo, con frecuencia; **every so o.**, de vez en cuando.

ogle [ˈəʊgəl] *vtr & vi* **to o. (at) sb**, comerse a algn con los ojos.

oh [əʊ] *interj* ¡oh!, ¡ay!; **oh, my God!**,

¡Dios mío!

oil [ɔɪl] I *n* aceite *m*; **o. lamp,** lámpara *f* de aceite, quinqué *m*; **o. slick,** mancha *f* de aceite; **olive o.,** aceite de oliva. 2 *Petrol* petróleo *m*; **o. rig,** plataforma petrolera; **o. tanker,** petrolero *m*. 3 *(painting)* pintura *f* al óleo; **o. colour, o. paint,** óleo *m*. II *vtr* engrasar.

oilcan [ˈɔɪlkæn] *n* aceitera *f*.

oilfield [ˈɔɪlfiːld] *n* yacimiento petrolífero.

oilskin [ˈɔɪlskɪn] *n* 1 hule *m*. 2 **oilskins,** chubasquero *m sing,* impermeable *m sing* de hule.

oily [ˈɔɪlɪ] *adj* (**oilier, oiliest**) aceitoso,-a, grasiento,-a; *(hair, skin)* graso,-a.

ointment [ˈɔɪntmənt] *n* ungüento *m,* pomada *f.*

O.K., okay [əʊˈkeɪ] *fam* I *interj* ¡vale!, ¡de acuerdo!. II *adj* bien; is it **O.K.** if ...?, ¿está bien si ...? III *vtr* dar el visto bueno a.

old [əʊld] I *adj* 1 viejo,-a; **an o. man,** un anciano; **o. age,** vejez *f*; **o.-age pensioner,** pensionista *mf*; *GB* **o. boy,** antiguo alumno; **o. hand,** veterano,-a *m,f*; **good o. John!,** ¡el bueno de John! 2 **how o. are you?,** ¿cuántos años tienes?; **she's five years o.,** tiene cinco años. 3 *(previous)* antiguo,-a. II *n* of o., de antaño.

old-fashioned [əʊldˈfæʃənd] *(outdated)* a la antigua; *(unfashionable)* anticuado,-a, pasado,-a de moda.

olive [ˈɒlɪv] *n* 1 *(tree)* olivo *m*; **o. grove,** olivar *m*. 2 *(fruit)* aceituna *f*, oliva *f*. 3 *(wood)* olivo *m*. 4 **o. (green),** *(colour)* verde *m* oliva.

Olympic [əˈlɪmpɪk] I *adj* olímpico,-a; **O. Games,** Juegos Olímpicos. II *npl* **the Olympics,** las Olimpíadas.

omelette, *US* **omelet** [ˈɒmlɪt] *n* tortilla *f*; **Spanish o.,** tortilla española *or* de patatas.

omen [ˈəʊmen] *n* presagio *m.*

ominous [ˈɒmɪnəs] *adj* de mal agüero.

omission [əʊˈmɪʃən] *n* omisión *f*; *fig* olvido *m.*

omit [əʊˈmɪt] *vtr* omitir; *(accidentally)* pasar por alto; *(forget)* olvidarse (**to,** de).

omnipotent [ɒmˈnɪpətənt] I *adj* omnipotente. II *n* the **O.,** el Todopoderoso.

on [ɒn] I *prep* 1 *(location)* sobre, encima de, en; **I hit him on the head,** le di un golpe en la cabeza; **it's on the desk,** está encima de *or* sobre el escritorio; **hanging on the wall,** colgado de la pared; **on page four,** en la página cuatro; **have you got any money on you?,** ¿llevas dinero?; **the drinks are on me/the house,** invito yo/invita la casa. 2 *(alongside)* en; **a town on the coast,** un pueblo en la costa. 3 *(direction)* en, a; **on the right,** a la derecha; **on the way,** en el camino. 4 *(time)* **on April 3rd,** el tres de abril; **on a sunny day,** un día de sol; **on Monday,** el lunes;

on Mondays, los lunes; **on that occasion,** en aquella ocasión; **on the following day,** al día siguiente; **on time,** a tiempo. 5 **en; on TV/the radio,** en la tele/radio; **to play sth on the piano,** tocar algo al piano; **on the phone,** al teléfono. 6 *(at the time of)* a; **on his arrival,** a su llegada; **on second thoughts,** pensándolo bien; **on learning of this,** al conocer esto. 7 **she lives on bread,** vive de pan; **to depend on,** depender de. 8 *(transport)* en, a; **on foot,** a pie; **on the train/plane/bus,** en el tren/avión/autobús; *(travel by)* en tren/avión/autobús. 9 *(state, process)* en; **on holiday,** de vacaciones; **she is here on business,** está aquí de negocios. 10 *(regarding)* sobre; **a lecture on numismatics,** una conferencia sobre numismática; **they congratulated him on his success,** le felicitaron por su éxito. 11 **on condition that,** *(subject to)* bajo la condición de que. 12 *(against)* contra; **an attack on,** un ataque contra. 13 **he's on the Times,** *(working for)* trabaja para el Times.

II *adv* 1 *(covering)* encima, puesto; **she had a coat on,** llevaba puesto un abrigo. 2 *fam* **have you anything on tonight?,** ¿tienes algún plan para esta noche? 3 **and so on,** y así sucesivamente; **go on!,** ¡sigue!; **he talks on and on,** habla sin parar; **to work on,** seguir trabajando. 4 **from that day on,** a partir de aquel día; **later on,** más tarde.

III *adj fam* 1 **to be on,** *(TV, radio, light)* estar encendido,-a; *(engine)* estar en marcha; *(film, play)* en cartelera; **that film was on last week,** pusieron esa película la semana pasada. 2 **Theat TV you're on!,** ¡a escena! 3 *(definitely planned)* previsto,-a; **that isn't on, eso no vale.

once [wʌns] I *adv* 1 *(one time)* una vez; **o. a week,** una vez por semana; **o. in a while,** de vez en cuando; **o. more,** una vez más; **o. or twice,** un par de veces; *fig* **o. and for all,** de una vez por todas. 2 *(formerly)* en otro tiempo; **o. upon a time)** there was, érase una vez. 3 at **o.,** en seguida, inmediatamente; **don't all speak at o.,** no habléis todos a la vez. II *conj* una vez que (+ *subj*), en cuanto (+ *subj*).

oncoming [ˈɒnkʌmɪŋ] *adj* *(car, traffic)* que viene en dirección contraria.

one [wʌn] I *adj* 1 un, uno; **for o. thing,** primero; **o. o. person who knows,** tú eres el único que lo sabe; **the o. and only,** el único, la única; **o. and the same,** el mismo, la misma. 2 *(indefinite)* un, una; **he'll come back o. day,** un día volverá.

II *dem pron* **any o.,** cualquiera; **that o.,** ése, ésa; **this o.,** éste, ésta; *(distant)* aquél, aquélla; **the blue ones,** los azules, las azules; **the o. on the table,** el *or* la que está encima de la mesa; **the ones that, the ones who,** los *or* las que.

III *indef pron* **1** uno,-a *m,f;* **I, for o., am against it,** yo, por lo menos, estoy en contra; **I'm not o. to complain,** no soy de los que se quejan; **o. at a time,** de uno en uno; **o. by o.,** uno tras otro; *fig* **o. and all,** todo el mundo. **2** *(indefinite person)* uno,-a *m,f;* **o. has to fight,** hay que luchar; **o. hopes that will never happen,** esperemos que no ocurra; **to break o.'s leg/arm,** romperse la pierna/el brazo. **3 o. another,** el uno al otro; **they love o. another,** se aman.

IV *n (digit)* uno *m;* **o. hundred/thousand,** cien/mil.

one-armed [ˈwʌnɑːmd] *adj fig* **o.-a. bandit,** máquina *f* tragaperras.

one-man [ˈwʌnmæn] *adj* **a o.-m. show,** un espectáculo con un solo artista.

one-man band [wʌnmænˈbænd] *n* hombre *m* orquesta *(inv).*

one-off [ˈwʌnɒf] *adj GB fam* único,-a, fuera de serie.

oneself [wʌnˈself] *pron* **1** *(reflexive)* uno,-a mismo,-a *m,f,* sí mismo,-a *m,f;* **to talk to o.,** hablar para sí. **2** *(alone)* uno,-a mismo,-a *m,f;* **by o.,** solo,-a. **3** *(one's usual self)* el *or* la de siempre.

one-sided [wʌnˈsaɪdɪd] *adj (bargain)* desigual; *(judgement)* parcial; *(decision)* unilateral.

one-to-one [ˈwʌntəwʌn] *adj* **o.-to-o. tuition,** clase *f* individual.

one-way [ˈwʌnweɪ] *adj* **1** *(ticket)* de ida. **2** *(street)* de dirección única.

ongoing [ˈɒnɡəʊɪŋ] *adj* **1** *(in progress)* en curso, actual. **2** *(developing)* en desarrollo.

onion [ˈʌnjən] *n* cebolla *f.*

on-line [ˈɒnlaɪn] *adj Comput* conectado,-a.

onlooker [ˈɒnlʊkər] *n* espectador,-a *m,f.*

only [ˈəʊnlɪ] **I** *adj* único,-a; **o. son,** hijo único. **II** *adv* **1** solamente, sólo; **'staff o.,'** 'reservado al personal'. **2** *(not earlier than)* apenas; **he has o. just left,** acaba de marcharse hace un momento; **o. yesterday,** ayer mismo. **3** *o.* **too glad!,** ¡con mucho gusto! **III** *conj* pero.

onset [ˈɒnset] *n (start)* comienzo *m.*

onslaught [ˈɒnslɔːt] *n* embestida *f.*

onto [ˈɒntʊ, *unstressed* ˈɒntə] *prep* → **on.**

onus [ˈəʊnəs] *n* responsabilidad *f.*

onward [ˈɒnwəd] *adj* hacia adelante.

onward(s) [ˈɒnwəd(z)] *adv* a partir de, en adelante; **from this time o.,** de ahora en adelante.

ooze [uːz] **I** *vi* rezumar. **II** *vtr* rebosar.

opaque [əʊˈpeɪk] *adj* opaco,-a.

OPEC [ˈəʊpek] *abbr of* Organization of Petroleum Exporting Countries, Organización *f* de los Países Exportadores de

Petróleo, OPEP *f.*

open [ˈəʊpən] **I** *adj* **1** abierto,-a; **half o.,** entreabierto; **wide o.,** abierto de par en par; **in the o. air,** al aire libre; **to be o. with sb,** ser sincero,-a con algn; *fig* **with o. arms,** con los brazos abiertos; **to keep an o. mind,** no tener prejuicios; **I am o. to suggestions,** acepto cualquier sugerencia; **o. to criticism,** susceptible a la crítica; **o. admiration,** franca admiración; *US* **o. house,** fiesta *f* de inauguración de residencia; **an o. question,** una cuestión sin resolver; **o. season,** *(in hunting)* temporada *f* de caza; *Av Rail* **o. ticket,** billete abierto; *GB* **O. University,** Universidad *f* a Distancia; **o. verdict,** veredicto inconcluso. **2** *(car etc)* descubierto,-a. **3** *(opposition)* manifiesto,-a.

II *vt* **1** abrir; **to o. fire,** abrir fuego; **to o. one's heart to sb,** sincerarse con algn. **2** *(exhibition etc)* inaugurar; *(negotiations, conversation)* entablar.

III *vi* **1** abrir, abrirse; **to o. onto,** *(of door, window)* dar a. **2** *(start)* empezar; *Theat Cin* estrenarse.

IV *n* **1** abrir; **in the o. air,** al aire libre; *fig* **to bring into the o.,** hacer público. **2** *Sport* open *m.*

◆**open out I** *vtr* abrir, desplegar. **II** *vi (flowers)* abrirse; *(view)* extenderse.

◆**open up I** *vtr (market etc)* abrir; *(possibilities)* crear. **II** *vi* **1** abrirse; *fam* **o. up!,** ¡abre la puerta! **2** *(start)* empezar.

◆**openly** *adv* abiertamente.

opener [ˈəʊpənər] *n* **tin o.,** *US* **can o.,** abrelatas *m inv.*

opening [ˈəʊpənɪŋ] *n* **1** *(act)* apertura *f;* **o. night,** noche *f* de estreno; *GB* **o. time,** hora *f* de apertura de los bares. **2** *(beginning)* comienzo *m.* **3** *(aperture)* abertura *f;* *(gap)* brecha *f.* **4** *Com* oportunidad *f.* **5** *(vacancy)* vacante *f.*

open-minded [əʊpənˈmaɪndɪd] *adj* sin prejuicios.

openness [ˈəʊpənnɪs] *n* franqueza *f.*

open-plan [ˈəʊpənplæn] *adj (office)* abierto,-a.

opera [ˈɒpərə] *n* ópera *f;* **o. house,** ópera, teatro *m* de la ópera.

operate [ˈɒpəreɪt] **I** *vi* **1** *(function)* funcionar. **2** *Med* operar; **to o. on sb for appendicitis,** operar a algn de apendicitis. **II** *vtr* **1** *(control)* manejar. **2** *(business)* dirigir.

operatic [ɒpəˈrætɪk] *adj* de ópera.

operating [ˈɒpəreɪtɪŋ] *n* **1** **o. costs,** gastos *mpl* de funcionamiento. **2** *Med* **o. table,** mesa *f* de operaciones; **o. theatre,** *US* **o. theater,** quirófano *m.*

operation [ɒpəˈreɪʃən] *n* **1** *(of machine)* funcionamiento *m;* *(by person)* manejo *m.* **2** *Mil* maniobra *f.* **3** *Med* operación *f,* intervención *f* quirúrgica; **to undergo an o. for,** ser operado,-a de.

operational [ɒpəˈreɪʃənəl] adj 1 (ready for use) operativo,-a. 2 Mil operacional.

operative [ˈɒpərətɪv] adj 1 Jur (in force) vigente; **to become o.**, entrar en vigor. 2 (significant) clave, significativo,-a; **the o. word**, la palabra clave.

operator [ˈɒpəreɪtəʳ] n 1 Ind operario,-a m,f. 2 Tel operador,-a m,f. 3 (dealer) negociante m,f, agente m,f; **tour o.**, agente de viajes.

opinion [əˈpɪnjən] n opinión f; **in my o.**, en mi opinión, a mi juicio; **it's a matter of o.**, es cuestión de opiniones; **to have a high o. of sb**, tener buen concepto de algn; **o. poll**, encuesta f, sondeo m.

opinionated [əˈpɪnjəneɪtɪd] adj dogmático,-a.

opium [ˈəupɪəm] n opio m.

opponent [əˈpəunənt] n adversario,-a m,f.

opportune [ˈɒpətjuːn] adj oportuno,-a.

opportunist [ɒpəˈtjuːnɪst] adj & n oportunista (mf).

opportunity [ɒpəˈtjuːnɪtɪ] n 1 oportunidad f, ocasión f. 2 (prospect) perspectiva f.

oppose [əˈpəuz] vtr oponerse a.

opposed [əˈpəuzd] adj opuesto,-a; **to be o. to sth**, estar en contra de algo; **as o. to**, comparado,-a con.

opposing [əˈpəuzɪŋ] adj adversario,-a.

opposite [ˈɒpəzɪt, ˈɒpəsɪt] I adj 1 (facing) de enfrente; (page) contiguo,-a. 2 (contrary) opuesto,-a, contrario,-a; **in the o. direction**, en dirección contraria. II n lo contrario m; **quite the o.!**, ¡al contrario! III prep enfrente de, frente a. IV adv enfrente.

opposition [ɒpəˈzɪʃən] n 1 oposición f; **in o. to**, en contra de. 2 Pol the o., la oposición.

oppress [əˈpres] vtr oprimir.

oppression [əˈpreʃən] n opresión f.

oppressive [əˈpresɪv] adj opresivo,-a; (atmosphere) agobiante; (heat) sofocante.

opt [ɒpt] vi optar; **to o. for**, optar por; **to o. to do sth**, optar por hacer algo. ◆**opt out** vi retirarse; **to o. out of doing sth**, decidir no hacer algo.

optical [ˈɒptɪkəl] adj óptico,-a.

optician [ɒpˈtɪʃən] n óptico,-a m,f.

optics [ˈɒptɪks] n óptica f.

optimist [ˈɒptɪmɪst] n optimista m,f.

optimistic [ɒptɪˈmɪstɪk] adj optimista. ◆**optimistically** adv con optimismo.

optimum [ˈɒptɪməm] I n grado óptimo. II adj óptimo,-a.

option [ˈɒpʃən] n opción f; **I have no o.**, no tengo más remedio; **to keep one's options open**, no comprometerse; **with the o. of**, con opción a.

optional [ˈɒpʃənəl] adj optativo,-a, facultativo,-a; Educ **o. subject**, (asignatura f) optativa f.

opulence [ˈɒpjuləns] n opulencia f.

or [ɔːʳ, unstressed əʳ] conj 1 o; (before a word beginning with o or ho) u; (else, si no, o bien; **whether you like it or not**, tanto si te gusta como si no; **either a bun or a piece of cake**, (o) una magdalena o un trozo de pastel. 2 (with negative) ni; **he can't read or write**, no sabe leer ni escribir; → **nor**.

oral [ˈɔːrəl] I adj oral. II n examen m oral. ◆**orally** adv **to be taken o.**, por vía oral.

orange [ˈɒrɪndʒ] I n naranja f; **o. juice**, zumo m de naranja. II adj de color naranja.

orator [ˈɒrətəʳ] n orador,-a m,f.

oratory [ˈɒrətərɪ] n oratoria f.

orbit [ˈɔːbɪt] I n Astron órbita f. II vtr girar alrededor de. III vi girar.

orchard [ˈɔːtʃəd] n huerto m.

orchestra [ˈɔːkɪstrə] n orquesta f.

orchestral [ɔːˈkestrəl] adj orquestal.

orchid [ˈɔːkɪd] n orquídea f.

ordain [ɔːˈdeɪn] vtr 1 Rel ordenar; **to be ordained**, ordenarse. 2 (decree) decretar.

ordeal [ɔːˈdiːl] n mala experiencia.

order [ˈɔːdəʳ] I n 1 (sequence) orden m; in alphabetical o., por orden alfabético; **to put in o.**, ordenar. 2 (condition) estado m; **is your passport in o.?**, ¿tienes el pasaporte en regla?; **'out of o.'**, averiado,-a. 3 (peace) orden m; **to restore o.**, reestablecer el orden público. 4 (command) orden f. 5 Com pedido m, encargo m; **to be on o.**, estar pedido; **to o.**, a la medida; **o. form**, hoja f de pedido. 6 Rel orden f. 7 **of the highest o.**, (quality) de primera calidad. 8 (kind) índole f, tipo m; Biol orden m. 9 **in the o. of**, del orden de. 10 **in o. that**, para que (+ subj), a fin de que (+ subj); **in o. to** (+ infin), para, a fin de (+ infin). II vtr 1 (command) ordenar, mandar; **to o. sb to do sth**, mandar a algn hacer algo. 2 Com pedir, encargar; **to o. a dish**, pedir un plato.

orderly [ˈɔːdəlɪ] I adj (tidy etc) ordenado,-a. II n 1 Med enfermero m. 2 Mil ordenanza m.

ordinary [ˈɔːdənrɪ] I adj usual, normal; (average) corriente, común; **the o. citizen**, el ciudadano de a pie. II n **the o.**, lo corriente, lo normal; **out of the o.**, fuera de lo común.

ordnance [ˈɔːdnəns] n GB **O. Survey**, servicio m oficial de topografía y cartografía.

ore [ɔːʳ] n mineral m.

organ [ˈɔːgən] n Mus Anat etc órgano m.

organic [ɔːˈgænɪk] adj orgánico,-a.

organism [ˈɔːgənɪzəm] n organismo m.

organization [ɔːgənaɪˈzeɪʃən] n organización f.

organize [ˈɔːgənaɪz] vtr organizar.

organizer [ˈɔːgənaɪzəʳ] n organizador,-a

m, f.

orgasm ['ɔːgæzəm] *n* orgasmo *m.*

orgy ['ɔːdʒɪ] *n* orgía *f.*

Orient ['ɔːrɪənt] *n* the O., el Oriente.

Oriental [ɔːrɪ'entəl] *adj & n* oriental *(mf).*

origin ['ɒrɪdʒɪn] *n* origen *m;* **country of** o., país *m* natal *or* de origen.

original [ə'rɪdʒɪnəl] I *adj* 1 original; *(first)* primero,-a. 2 *(imaginative)* original. II *n* original *m.* ◆**originally** *adv* 1 *(at first)* en un principio. 2 *(with imagination)* con originalidad.

originality [ərɪdʒɪ'nælɪtɪ] *n* originalidad *f.*

originate [ə'rɪdʒɪneɪt] I *vtr* originar. II *vi* to o. from *or* in, tener su origen en.

Orkneys ['ɔːknɪz] *npl* (Islas) Órcadas.

ornament ['ɔːnəmənt] *n* ornamento *m,* adorno *m.*

ornamental [ɔːnə'mentəl] *adj* decorativo,-a.

ornate [ɔː'neɪt] *adj* vistoso,-a.

ornithology [ɔːnɪ'θɒlədʒɪ] *n* ornitología *f.*

orphan ['ɔːfən] I *n* huérfano,-a, *m,f.* II *vtr* she was orphaned, quedó huérfana.

orphanage ['ɔːfənɪdʒ] *n* orfanato *m.*

orthodox ['ɔːθədɒks] *adj* ortodoxo,-a.

orthodoxy ['ɔːθədɒksɪ] *n* ortodoxia *f.*

orthopaedic, *US* **orthopedic** [ɔːθəʊ'piːdɪk] *adj* ortopédico,-a.

oscillate ['ɒsɪleɪt] *vi* oscilar.

ostensible [ɒ'stensɪbəl] *adj* 1 *(apparent)* ostensible. 2 *(pretended)* aparente.

ostentatious [ɒsten'teɪʃəs] *adj* ostentoso,-a.

osteopath ['ɒstɪəpæθ] *n* osteópata *mf.*

ostracize ['ɒstrəsaɪz] *vtr (from society)* condenar al ostracismo; *(from group)* aislar, excluir.

ostrich ['ɒstrɪtʃ] *n* avestruz *f.*

other ['ʌðər] I *adj* 1 otro,-a; every o. day, cada dos días; on the o. hand, por otra parte; o. people have seen it, otros lo han visto; the o. four, los otros cuatro; the o. one, el otro, la otra; the o. thing, lo otro. 2 he must be somewhere or o., debe de estar en alguna parte. II *pron* otro,-a *m,f;* many others, otros muchos; the others, los otros, los demás; we see each o. quite often, nos vemos con bastante frecuencia.

otherwise ['ʌðəwaɪz] I *adv* 1 *(if not)* si no. 2 *(differently)* de otra manera. 3 *(in other respects)* por lo demás. II *adj* distinto,-a.

otter ['ɒtər] *n* nutria *f.*

ought [ɔːt] *v aux* 1 *(obligation)* deber; I thought I o. to tell you, creí que debía decírtelo; she o. to do it, debería hacerlo. 2 *(vague desirability)* tener que, deber; you o. to see the exhibition, deberías ver la exposición. 3 *(expectation)* he o. to pass the exam, seguramente aprobará el examen; that o. to do, con eso bastará.

ounce [aʊns] *n* onza *f.*

our [aʊər] *poss adj* nuestro,-a.

ours [aʊəz] *poss pron* 1 (el) nuestro, (la) nuestra. 2 of o., nuestro,-a; a friend of o., un amigo nuestro.

ourselves [aʊə'selvz] *pers pron pl* 1 *(reflexive)* nos. 2 *(emphatic)* nosotros mismos, nosotras mismas. 3 by o., a solas.

oust [aʊst] *vtr* 1 *(from a post)* desbancar. 2 *(from property etc)* desalojar.

out [aʊt] I *adv* 1 *(outside, away)* fuera; to. there, ahí fuera; to go o., salir. 2 I told him straight o., se lo dije muy claramente; o. loud, en voz alta. 3 hear me o., escúchame hasta el final. 4 o. of, *(place)* fuera de; move o. of the way!, ¡quítate de en medio!; o. of danger, fuera de peligro; to go o. of the room, salir de la habitación; o. of control, fuera de control; o. of date, *(expired)* caducado,-a; *(old-fashioned)* pasado,-a, de moda. 5 o. of, *(cause, motive)* por. 6 o. of, *(made from)* de. 7 o. of, *(short of, without)* sin; I'm o. of money, se me ha acabado el dinero; o. of breath, sin aliento. 8 o. of, *(among)* entre; forty o. of fifty, cuarenta de cada cincuenta; *(in exam etc)* cuarenta sobre cincuenta.

II *adj* 1 the sun is o., ha salido el sol. 2 *(unfashionable)* pasado,-a, de moda. 3 *(fire)* apagado,-a. 4 *(not working)* estropeado,-a. 5 she's o., *(not in)* ha salido, no está. 6 to be o. for sth/to do sth, buscar algo. 7 the book is just o., el libro acaba de salir. 8 *(inaccurate)* equivocado,-a; to be o. in one's calculations, equivocarse en los cálculos. 9 before the week is o., antes de que acabe la semana.

III *prep (out of)* por; he jumped o. the window, saltó por la ventana.

out-and-out ['aʊtənaʊt] *adj* redomado,-a.

outboard ['aʊtbɔːd] *adj* o. motor, fuera-borda *m.*

outbreak ['aʊtbreɪk] *n (of war)* comienzo *m;* *(of spots)* erupción *f;* *(of disease)* brote *m;* *(of violence)* ola *f;* *(of anger)* arrebato *m;* at the o. of war, cuando estalló la guerra.

outbuilding ['aʊtbɪldɪŋ] *n* dependencia *f.*

outburst ['aʊtbɜːst] *n (of anger)* arrebato *m;* *(of generosity)* arranque *m.*

outcast ['aʊtkɑːst] *n* marginado,-a *m,f.*

outcome ['aʊtkʌm] *n* resultado *m.*

outcrop ['aʊtkrɒp] *n Geol* afloramiento *m.*

outcry ['aʊtkraɪ] *n* there was an o., hubo fuertes protestas.

outdated [aʊt'deɪtɪd] *adj* anticuado,-a, obsoleto,-a.

outdo [aʊt'duː] *vtr* to o. sb, superar a algn.

outdoor ['aʊtdɔːr] *adj* 1 al aire libre. 2 *(clothes)* de calle.

outdoors [aʊt'dɔːz] *adv* fuera, al aire libre.

outer ['autər] *adj* exterior, externo,-a.

outfit ['autfɪt] *n* **1** (*kit, equipment*) equipo *m*. **2** (*set of clothes*) conjunto *m*. **3** *fam* (*group*) grupo *m*.

outgoing '['autɡəʊɪŋ] I *adj* **1** (*departing*) saliente. **2** (*sociable*) extrovertido,-a. II *npl* **outgoings**, gastos *mpl*.

outgrow [aut'ɡrəʊ] *vtr* **he's outgrowing all his clothes**, toda la ropa se le está quedando pequeña; **she'll o. it**, se le pasará con la edad.

outhouse ['authaus] *n* → **outbuilding**.

outing ['autɪŋ] *n* excursión *f*.

outlandish [aut'lændɪʃ] *adj* estrafalario, -a.

outlast [aut'lɑːst] *vtr* durar más que.

outlaw ['autlɔː] I *n* proscrito,-a *m,f*. II *vtr* prohibir.

outlet ['autlet, 'autlɪt] *n* **1** (*opening*) salida *f*. **2** (*for emotions*) válvula *f* de escape. **3** *Com* mercado *m*. **4** (*for water*) desagüe *m*.

outline ['autlaɪn] I *n* **1** (*draft*) bosquejo *m*. **2** (*outer line*) contorno *m*; (*silhouette*) perfil *m*. II *vtr* **1** (*draw lines of*) perfilar. **2** (*summarize*) resumir. **3** (*describe roughly*) trazar las líneas generales de.

outlive [aut'lɪv] *vtr* sobrevivir a.

outlook ['autlʊk] *n* **1** (*point of view*) punto *m* de vista. **2** (*prospect*) perspectiva *f*; *Meteor* previsión *f*.

outlying ['autlaɪɪŋ] *adj* (*remote*) aislado,-a.

outmoded [aut'məʊdɪd] *adj* anticuado,-a.

outnumber [aut'nʌmbər] *vtr* exceder en número.

out-of-the-way [autʌvðə'weɪ] *adj* **1** (*distant*) apartado,-a, aislado,-a. **2** (*uncommon*) poco corriente.

outpatient ['autpeɪʃənt] *n* paciente externo,-a; **outpatients' department**, departamento *m* de consulta externa.

outpost ['autpəʊst] *n* avanzada *f*.

output ['autput] *n* **1** (*production*) producción *f*; (*of machine*) rendimiento *m*. **2** *Elec* potencia *f*. **3** *Comput* salida *f*.

outrage ['autreɪdʒ] I *n* ultraje *m*; **it's an o.!**, ¡es un escándalo!. II *vtr* **to be outraged by sth**, indignarse por algo.

outrageous [aut'reɪdʒəs] *adj* (*behaviour*) escandaloso,-a; (*clothes*) extravagante; (*price*) exhorbitante.

outright ['autraɪt] I *adj* (*absolute*) absoluto,-a. II [aut'raɪt] *adv* **1** (*completely*) por completo. **2** (*directly*) directamente, sin reserva. **3** (*immediately*) en el acto.

outset ['autset] *n* comienzo *m*, principio *m*.

outside [aut'saɪd] I *prep* **1** fuera de. **2** (*beyond*) más allá de. **3** (*other than*) aparte de. II ['autsaɪd] *adj* **1** (*exterior*) exterior, externo,-a. **2** (*remote*) remoto,-a. III [aut'saɪd] *adv* fuera, afuera. IV *n* exterior *m*; **on the o.**, por fuera; *fam* **at the o.**,

como mucho.

outsider [aut'saɪdər] *n* **1** (*stranger*) extraño,-a *m,f*, forastero,-a *m,f*. **2** *Pol* candidato,-a *m,f* con pocas posibilidades de ganar.

outsize(d) [aut'saɪz(d)] *adj* (*clothes*) de talla muy grande.

outskirts [aut'skɜːts] *npl* afueras *fpl*.

outspoken [aut'spəʊkən] *adj* directo,-a, abierto,-a.

outstanding [aut'stændɪŋ] *adj* **1** (*exceptional*) destacado,-a. **2** (*unpaid, unresolved*) pendiente.

outstretched [aut'stretʃt] *adj* extendido,-a.

outward ['autwəd] *adj* **1** (*external*) exterior. **2** **the o. journey**, el viaje de ida. ◆**outwardly** *adv* aparentemente.

outward(s) ['autwəd(z)] *adv* hacia (a)fuera.

outweigh [aut'weɪ] *vtr* **1** (*prevail over*) prevalecer sobre. **2** (*weigh more than*) pesar más que.

oval ['əʊvəl] I *adj* oval, ovalado,-a. II *n* óvalo *m*.

ovary ['əʊvərɪ] *n* ovario *m*.

ovation [əʊ'veɪʃən] *n* ovación *f*.

oven ['ʌvən] *n* horno *m*.

ovenproof ['ʌvənpruːf] *adj* refractario,-a.

over ['əʊvər] I *prep* **1** (*above*) encima de. **2** (*on top of*) sobre, encima de. **3** (*across*) al otro lado de; **the bridge o. the river**, el puente que cruza el río. **4** (*during*) durante. **5** (*throughout*) por. **6 all o.**, por todo,-a; **famous all o. the world**, famoso en el mundo entero. **7** (*by the agency of*) por; **o. the phone**, por teléfono. **8** (*more than*) más de; **men o. twenty-five**, hombres mayores de veinticinco años; **o. and above**, además de. **9** (*recovered from*) recuperado,-a de. II *adv* **1 o. there**, allá; **why don't you come o. tomorrow?**, ¿por qué no vienes a casa mañana? **2** (*throughout*) por; **all o.**, por todas partes. **3** (*more*) más. **4** (*again*) otra vez; **o. and o.** (**again**), una y otra vez; **twice o.**, dos veces seguidas. **5** (*in excess*) de más. III *adj* (*finished*) acabado,-a; **it's (all) o.**, se acabó; **the danger is o.**, ha pasado el peligro.

overall ['əʊvərɔːl] I *adj* total, global. II [əʊvər'ɔːl] *adv* (*on the whole*) por lo general, en conjunto. III ['əʊvərɔːl] *n* **1** *GB* guardapolvo *m*. **2 overalls**, mono *m sing*.

overawe [əʊvər'ɔː] *vtr* **to be overawed**, sobrecogerse.

overbearing [əʊvə'beərɪŋ] *adj* (*domineering*) dominante; (*important*) significativo, -a.

overboard ['əʊvəbɔːd] *adv* por la borda; **man o.!**, ¡hombre al agua!; *fam* **to go o.**, pasarse.

overcast ['əʊvəkɑːst] *adj* nublado,-a.

overcharge [əʊvə'tʃɑːdʒ] *vtr* **1** (*charge too much*) cobrar demasiado. **2** (*overload*) sobrecargar.

overcoat ['əʊvəkəʊt] *n* abrigo *m*.

overcome [əʊvə'kʌm] *vtr* **1** (*conquer*) vencer; **o. by grief**, deshecho por el dolor. **2** (*obstacle*) superar.

overconfident [əʊvə'kɒnfɪdənt] *adj* presumido,-a, creído,-a.

overcrowded [əʊvə'kraʊdɪd] *adj* (*room*) atestado,-a (**de** de gente); (*country*) superpoblado,-a.

overcrowding [əʊvə'kraʊdɪŋ] *n* (*of prisons etc*) hacinamiento *m*; (*of country*) superpoblación *f*.

overdo [əʊvə'duː] *vtr* **1** (*carry too far*) exagerar; **don't o. it**, no te pases. **2** *Culin* cocer *or* asar demasiado.

overdose ['əʊvədəʊs] *n* sobredosis *f*.

overdraft ['əʊvədrɑːft] *n* giro *m* en descubierto; (*amount*) saldo *m* deudor.

overdraw [əʊvə'drɔː] *vtr* **to be overdrawn**, tener la cuenta en descubierto.

overdue [əʊvə'djuː] *adj* (*rent, train etc*) atrasado,-a; (*reform*) largamente esperado,-a.

overestimate [əʊvə'estɪmeɪt] *vtr* sobreestimar.

overflow [əʊvə'fləʊ] **I** *vi* (*river*) desbordarse; (*cup etc*) derramarse. **II** ['əʊvəfləʊ] *n* (*of river etc*) desbordamiento *m*; **o. pipe**, cañería *f* de desagüe.

overgrown [əʊvə'grəʊn] *adj* **1** (*with grass*) cubierto,-a (de hierba). **2** (*in size*) demasiado grande.

overhaul [əʊvə'hɔːl] **I** *vtr* revisar. **II** ['əʊvəhɔːl] *n* revisión *f* y reparación *f*.

overhead ['əʊvəhed] **I** *adj* (por) encima de la cabeza; **o. cable**, cable aéreo. **II** [əʊvə'hed] *adv* arriba, por encima de la cabeza.

overheads ['əʊvəhedz] *npl* gastos *mpl* generales.

overhear [əʊvə'hɪər] *vtr* oír por casualidad.

overheat [əʊvə'hiːt] *vi* recalentarse.

overjoyed [əʊvə'dʒɔɪd] *adj* rebosante de alegría.

overlap [əʊvə'læp] *vi* superponerse; *fig* **our plans o.**, nuestros planes coinciden parcialmente.

overleaf [əʊvə'liːf] *adv* al dorso.

overload [əʊvə'ləʊd] **I** *vtr* sobrecargar. **II** *n* sobrecarga *f*.

overlook [əʊvə'lʊk] *vtr* **1** (*fail to notice*) saltarse. **2** (*ignore*) no hacer caso de; **we'll o. it this time**, esta vez haremos la vista gorda. **3** (*have a view of*) dar a, tener vista a.

overnight [əʊvə'naɪt] **I** *adv* **1** (*during the night*) por la noche; **we stayed there o.**, pasamos la noche allí. **2** (*suddenly*) de la noche a la mañana. **II** ['əʊvənaɪt] *adj* (*sudden*) repentino,-a.

overpay [əʊvə'peɪ] *vtr* pagar demasiado.

overpower [əʊvə'paʊər] *vtr* **1** (*subdue*) dominar. **2** (*affect strongly*) abrumar.

overrate [əʊvə'reɪt] *vtr* sobreestimar, supervalorar.

override [əʊvə'raɪd] *vtr* **1** (*disregard*) hacer caso omiso de. **2** (*annul, cancel out*) anular. **3** (*be more important than*) contar más que.

overriding [əʊvə'raɪdɪŋ] *adj* principal; (*importance*) primordial; (*need*) imperioso,-a.

overrule [əʊvə'ruːl] *vtr* invalidar; *Jur* denegar.

overrun [əʊvə'rʌn] *vtr* **1** (*country*) invadir. **2** (*allotted time*) excederse de.

overseas [əʊvə'siːz] **I** *adv* en ultramar; **to live o.**, vivir en el extranjero. **II** ['əʊvəsiːz] *adj* de ultramar; (*person*) extranjero,-a; (*trade*) exterior.

oversee [əʊvə'siː] *vtr* supervisar.

overseer ['əʊvəsiːər] *n* supervisor,-a *m,f*; (*foreman*) capataz *m*.

overshadow [əʊvə'ʃædəʊ] *vtr* *fig* eclipsar.

overshoot [əʊvə'ʃuːt] *vtr* **to o. a turning**, pasarse un cruce; *fig* **to o. the mark**, pasarse de la raya.

oversight ['əʊvəsaɪt] *n* descuido *m*.

oversleep [əʊvə'sliːp] *vi* quedarse dormido,-a.

overspill ['əʊvəspɪl] *n* exceso *m* de población.

overstate [əʊvə'steɪt] *vtr* exagerar.

overstep [əʊvə'step] *vtr* *fig* **to o. the mark**, pasarse de la raya.

overt [əʊ'vɜːt, əʊ'vɜːt] *adj* patente.

overtake [əʊvə'teɪk] *vtr* **1** *GB Aut* adelantar. **2** (*surpass*) superar a. **3** (*of night*) sorprender.

overthrow [əʊvə'θrəʊ] *vtr* (*government*) derribar.

overtime [əʊvə'taɪm] *n* horas *fpl* extra.

overtone ['əʊvətəʊn] *n* matiz *m*.

overture ['əʊvətjʊər] *n* **1** *Mus* obertura *f*; *fig* (*introduction*) introducción *f*. **2** (*proposal*) propuesta *f*.

overturn [əʊvə'tɜːn] *vtr & vi* volcar.

overweight [əʊvə'weɪt] *adj* demasiado pesado,-a.

overwhelm [əʊvə'welm] *vtr* **1** (*defeat*) aplastar; (*overpower*) abrumar; **I'm overwhelmed**, estoy abrumado. **2** (*with letters, work etc*) inundar.

overwhelming [əʊvə'welmɪŋ] *adj* (*defeat*) aplastante; (*desire etc*) irresistible.

overwork [əʊvə'wɜːk] **I** *vi* trabajar demasiado. **II** *vtr* (*person*) forzar; (*excuse etc*) abusar de.

overwrought [əʊvə'rɔːt] *adj* **1** (*tense*) muy nervioso,-a. **2** *lit* (*too elaborate*) forzado,-a.

owe [əʊ] *vtr* deber.

owing ['əʊɪŋ] *adj* **o. to**, debido a, a causa

de.
owl [aʊl] *n* lechuza *f*, búho *m*.
own [əʊn] **I** *adj* propio,-a; **it's his o. fault**, es culpa suya. **II** *pron* **1** my o., your o., his o. etc, lo mío, lo tuyo, lo suyo, etc; *fig* **to come into one's o.**, realizarse; *fam* **to get one's o. back**, tomarse la revancha. **2** on one's o., (*without help*) uno,-a mismo,-a; (*alone*) solo,-a. **III** *vtr* poseer, ser dueño,-a de. ◆**own up** *vtr* to o. **up (to)**, confesar.
owner [ˈəʊnər] *n* propietario,-a *m,f*,

dueño,-a *m,f*.
ownership [ˈəʊnəʃɪp] *n* propiedad *f*, posesión *f*.
ox [ɒks] *n* (*pl* **oxen**) buey *m*.
oxide [ˈɒksaɪd] *n* *Chem* óxido *m*.
oxtail [ˈɒksteɪl] *n* rabo *m* de buey.
oxygen [ˈɒksɪdʒən] *n* oxígeno *m*; o. **mask**, máscara *f* de oxígeno.
oyster [ˈɔɪstər] *n* ostra *f*.
ozone [ˈəʊzəʊn] *n* ozono *m*; o. **layer**, capa *f* de ozono.

P

P, p [piː] *n* (*the letter*) P, p *f*.
p 1 (*pl* **pp**) *abbr of* **page**, pág., p. **2** [piː] *GB* *fam* *abbr of* **penny, pence**, penique(s) *m(pl)*.
PA [piːˈeɪ] *fam* **1** *abbr of* **personal assistant**, ayudante *mf* personal. **2** *abbr of* **public-address (system)**.
pa *abbr of* **per annum** (per year), al año.
pace [peɪs] **I** *n* (*step*) paso *m*; (*speed*) ritmo *m*; **to keep p. with**, seguir a; *fig* avanzar al mismo ritmo que; **to set the p.**, marcar el paso a; *fig* marcar la pauta. **II** *vi* **to p. up and down**, ir de un lado a otro.
pacemaker [ˈpeɪsmeɪkər] *n* *Sport* liebre *f*; *Med* marcapasos *m inv*.
Pacific [pəˈsɪfɪk] *adj* **the P. (Ocean)**, (el océano) Pacífico.
pacifist [ˈpæsɪfɪst] *adj & n* pacifista (*mf*).
pacify [ˈpæsɪfaɪ] *vtr* (*person*) calmar; (*country*) pacificar.
pack¹ [pæk] **I** *n* (*parcel*) paquete *m*; (*bundle*) bulto *m*; *US* (*of cigarettes*) paquete *m*; *GB* (*of cards*) baraja *f*; (*of hounds*) jauría *f*. **II** *vtr* **1** (*goods*) embalar, envasar; (*in suitcase*) meter; **to p. one's bags**, hacer las maletas; *fig* marcharse. **2** (*fill*) atestar. **3** (*press down*) (*snow*) apretar. **III** *vi* **1** hacer las maletas; *fam* **to send sb packing**, mandar a paseo a algn. **2** (*of people*) apiñarse (**into**, en). ◆**pack in** *vtr* *GB* *fam* (*give up*) dejar. ◆**pack off** *vtr* *fam* mandar. ◆**pack up** *fam* **I** *vtr* (*give up*) dejar. **II** *vi* (*stop working*) terminar; (*machine etc*) estropearse.
pack² [pæk] *vtr* (*meeting*) llenar de partidarios.
package [ˈpækɪdʒ] **I** *n* **1** (*parcel*) paquete *m*; (*bundle*) bulto *m*; **p. tour**, viaje *m* todo incluido. **2** (*of proposals etc*) paquete *m*; (*agreement*) acuerdo *m*; **p. deal**, convenio *m* general. **II** *vtr* (*goods*) envasar, embalar.
packet [ˈpækɪt] *n* paquete *m*; *fam* (*fortune*) dineral *m*.
packing [ˈpækɪŋ] *n* embalaje *m*; **p. case**, caja *f* de embalar; **to do one's p.**, hacer

las maletas.
pact [pækt] *n* pacto *m*.
pad¹ [pæd] **I** *n* **1** almohadilla *f*; (*of paper*) bloc *m*, taco *m*. **2** **launch p.**, plataforma *f* de lanzamiento. **3** *fam* (*flat*) piso *m*. **II** *vtr* (*chair*) acolchar. ◆**pad out** *vtr* *fig* meter paja en.
pad² [pæd] *vi* **to p. about** or **around**, andar silenciosamente.
padding [ˈpædɪŋ] *n* (*material*) relleno *m*; *fig* (*in speech etc*) paja *f*.
paddle¹ [ˈpædəl] **I** *n* (*oar*) pala *f*; **p. boat** or **steamer**, vapor *m* de ruedas. **II** *vtr* (*boat*) remar con pala en. **III** *vi* (*in boat*) remar con pala.
paddle² [ˈpædəl] *vi* chapotear.
paddling pool [ˈpædlɪŋpuːl] *n* piscina *f* para niños.
paddock [ˈpædək] *n* potrero *m*; (*in race course*) paddock *m*.
paddy [ˈpædɪ] *n* arrozal *m*.
padlock [ˈpædlɒk] **I** *n* candado *m*. **II** *vtr* cerrar con candado.
paediatrician [piːdɪəˈtrɪʃən] *n* pediatra *mf*.
pagan [ˈpeɪɡən] *adj & n* pagano,-a (*m,f*).
page¹ [peɪdʒ] *n* página *f*.
page² [peɪdʒ] **I** *n* (*servant*) paje *m*; (*of knight*) escudero *m*; (*at club*) botones *m inv*. **II** *vtr* (*call*) llamar por altavoz.
pageant [ˈpædʒənt] *n* (*show*) espectáculo *m*; (*procession*) desfile *m*; (*on horses*) cabalgata *f*.
pageantry [ˈpædʒəntrɪ] *n* pompa *f*, boato *m*.
paid [peɪd] *adj* pagado,-a; *fig* **to put p. to sth**, acabar con algo.
pail [peɪl] *n* cubo *m*; (*child's*) cubito *m*.
pain [peɪn] **I** *n* **1** dolor *m*; (*grief*) sufrimiento *m*; *fam* **he's a p. (in the neck)**, es un pelmazo; **on p. of death**, so pena de muerte. **2** **to take pains over sth**, esmerarse en algo. **II** *vtr* (*grieve*) dar pena a.
pained [peɪnd] *adj* de reproche.
painful [ˈpeɪnfʊl] *adj* doloroso,-a; *fam* (*very bad*) malísimo,-a. ◆**painfully** *adv* **1** p. **shy**, lastimosamente tímido,-a. **2**

fam terriblemente.

painkiller ['peɪnkɪləʳ] *n* analgésico *m*.

painless ['peɪnlɪs] *adj* sin dolor; *fig* sin dificultades.

painstaking ['peɪnzteɪkɪŋ] *adj* (*person*) concienzudo,-a; (*care*, *research*) esmerado,-a.

paint [peɪnt] **I** *n* pintura *f*. **II** *vtr* pintar; **to p. sth white**, pintar algo de blanco. **III** *vi* pintar.

paintbrush ['peɪntbrʌʃ] *n* Art pincel *m*; (*for walls*) brocha *f*.

painter ['peɪntəʳ] *n* pintor,-a *m,f*.

painting ['peɪntɪŋ] *n* cuadro *m*; (*activity*) pintura *f*.

paintwork ['peɪntwɜːk] *n* pintura *f*.

pair [peəʳ] *n* (*of gloves*, *shoes*) par *m*; (*of people*, *cards*) pareja *f*; **a p. of scissors**, unas tijeras; **a p. of trousers**, un pantalón, unos pantalones.

pajamas [pəˈdʒæməz] *npl US* → **pyjamas**.

Pakistan [pɑːkɪˈstɑːn] *n* Paquistán.

Pakistani [pɑːkɪˈstɑːnɪ] *adj* & *n* paquistaní (*mf*).

pal [pæl] *n fam* amigo,-a *m,f*, colega *mf*.

palace ['pælɪs] *n* palacio *m*.

palatable ['pælətəbəl] *adj* (*tasty*) sabroso,-a; *fig* aceptable.

palate ['pælɪt] *n* paladar *m*.

palatial [pəˈleɪʃəl] *adj* magnífico,-a, suntuoso,-a.

palaver [pəˈlɑːvəʳ] *n fam* lío *m*, follón *m*.

pale¹ [peɪl] **I** *adj* (*skin*) pálido,-a; (*colour*) claro,-a; (*light*) tenue; **to turn p.**, palidecer. **II** *vi* palidecer.

pale² [peɪl] *n fig* **to be beyond the p.**, ser inaceptable.

Palestine ['pælɪstaɪn] *n* Palestina.

Palestinian [pælɪˈstɪnɪən] *adj* & *n* palestino,-a (*m,f*).

palette ['pælɪt] *n* paleta *f*; **p. knife**, espátula *f*.

paling ['peɪlɪŋ] *n* valla *f*.

palisade [pælɪˈseɪd] *n* palizada *f*, estacada *f*.

pall¹ [pɔːl] *n fig* manto *m*; (*of smoke*) cortina *f*.

pall² [pɔːl] *vi* aburrir; **it never palls**, nunca cansa.

pallet ['pælɪt] *n* plataforma *f* de carga.

pallid ['pælɪd] *adj* pálido,-a.

pallor ['pæləʳ] *n* palidez *f*.

palm¹ [pɑːm] *n* (*tree*) palmera *f*; (*leaf*) palma *f*; **date p.**, palma datilera; **P. Sunday**, domingo *m* de Ramos.

palm² [pɑːm] *n Anat* palma *f*. ◆**palm off** *vtr* **to p. sth off on sb**, colocar *o* endosar algo a algn.

palmistry ['pɑːmɪstrɪ] *n* quiromancia *f*.

palpable ['pælpəbəl] *adj* palpable.

palpitate ['pælpɪteɪt] *vi* palpitar.

palpitation [pælpɪˈteɪʃən] *n* palpitación *f*.

paltry ['pɔːltrɪ] *adj* (*paltrier*, *paltriest*)

insignificante.

pamper ['pæmpəʳ] *vtr* mimar, consentir.

pamphlet ['pæmflɪt] *n* folleto *m*.

pan¹ [pæn] **I** *n* **1** (*saucepan*) cazuela *f*, cacerola *f*. **2** (*of scales*) platillo *m*. **3** (*of lavatory*) taza *f*. **II** *vtr fam* (*criinse*) dejar por los suelos.

pan² [pæn] *vi Cin* tomar vistas panorámicas.

panacea [pænəˈsɪə] *n* panacea *f*.

panache [pəˈnæʃ] *n* garbo *m*, salero *m*.

Panama ['pænəmɑː] *n* Panamá; **P. Canal**, Canal *m* de Panamá.

pancake ['pænkeɪk] *n* crepe *f*.

panda ['pændə] *n* panda *m*; *GB* **p. car**, coche *m* patrulla.

pandemonium [pændɪˈməʊnɪəm] *n* alboroto *m*.

pander ['pændəʳ] *vi* **to p. to**, (*person*) complacer a; (*wishes*) acceder a.

pane [peɪn] *n* cristal *m*, vidrio *m*.

panel ['pænəl] *n* **1** (*of wall*) panel *m*; (*flat surface*) tabla *f*; (*of instruments*) tablero *m*; (*of ceiling*) artesón *m*. **2** (*jury*) jurado *m*; *Rad TV* concursantes *mpl*.

panelling, *US* **paneling** ['pænəlɪŋ] *n* paneles *mpl*.

pang [pæŋ] *n* (*of pain*, *hunger*) punzada *f*; (*of childbirth*) dolores *mpl*; *fig* (*of conscience*) remordimiento *m*.

panic ['pænɪk] **I** *n* pánico *m*; **to get into a p.**, ponerse histérico,-a. **II** *vi* aterrarse.

panicky ['pænɪkɪ] *adj* asustadizo,-a.

panic-stricken ['pænɪkstrɪkən] *adj* aterrado,-a.

panorama [pænəˈrɑːmə] *n* panorama *m*.

pansy ['pænzɪ] *n Bot* pensamiento *m*; *fam pej* mariquita *m*.

pant [pænt] **I** *n* jadeo *m*. **II** *vi* jadear.

panther ['pænθəʳ] *n* pantera *f*.

panties ['pæntɪz] *npl* bragas *fpl*.

pantomime ['pæntəmaɪm] *n Theat* (*play*) función *f* musical navideña; (*mime*) pantomima *f*.

pantry ['pæntrɪ] *n* despensa *f*.

pants [pænts] *npl* (*underpants*) (*ladies'*) bragas *fpl*; (*men's*) calzoncillos *mpl*; *US* (*trousers*) pantalones *mpl*, pantalón *m*.

papal ['peɪpəl] *adj* papal.

paper ['peɪpəʳ] **I** *n* **1** papel *m*; *fig* **on p.**, en teoría; **p. money**, papel moneda; **writing p.**, papel de escribir. **2** (*exam*) examen *m*; (*essay*) trabajo *m* (escrito). **3** *Pol* libro *m*. **4** (*newspaper*) periódico *m*; **the papers**, la prensa. **5 papers**, (*documents*) documentos *mpl*. **II** *vtr* empapelar.

paperback ['peɪpəbæk] *n* libro *m* en rústica.

paperclip ['peɪpəklɪp] *n* clip *m*, sujetapapeles *m inv*.

paperweight ['peɪpəweɪt] *n* pisapapeles *m inv*.

paperwork ['peɪpəwɜːk] *n* papeleo *m*.

papier-mâché [pæpjeɪˈmæʃeɪ] *n* cartón *m*

piedra.

paprika ['pæprɪkə] *n* pimentón molido.

par [pɑːɾ] *n (parity)* igualdad *f*; *Golf* par *m*; *fig* **it's p. for the course,** es lo normal en estos casos; *fig* **to feel below p.,** estar en baja forma.

parable ['pærəbəl] *n* parábola *f*.

parachute ['pærəʃuːt] **I** *n* paracaídas *m inv*. **II** *vi* **to p. (down),** saltar or lanzarse en paracaídas.

parade [pə'reɪd] **I** *n* desfile *m*; *Mil* **to be on p.,** pasar revista. **II** *vtr Mil* hacer desfilar; *fig (flaunt)* hacer alarde de. **III** *vi (troops)* pasar revista; *(procession)* desfilar.

paradise ['pærədaɪs] *n* paraíso *m*.

paradox ['pærədɒks] *n* paradoja *f*.

paradoxical [pærə'dɒksɪkəl] *adj* paradójico,-a.

paraffin ['pærəfɪn] *n* parafina *f*; **liquid p.,** aceite *m* de parafina; **p. lamp,** lámpara *f* de petróleo.

paragon ['pærəgən] *n* modelo *m*.

paragraph ['pærəgrɑːf] *n* párrafo *m*.

Paraguay ['pærəgwaɪ] *n* Paraguay *m*.

Paraguayan [pærə'gwaɪən] *adj & n* paraguayo,-a *(m,f)*.

parallel ['pærəlel] **I** *adj* paralelo,-a **(to, with,** a); *fig* comparable **(to, with,** a). **II** *n Geog* paralelo *m*; *Geom* paralela *f*; *fig* paralelo. **III** *vtr fig* ser paralelo,-a a.

paralysis [pə'rælɪsɪs] *n* parálisis *f*.

paralyse, *US* **paralyze** ['pærəlaɪz] *vtr* paralizar.

parameter [pə'ræmɪtəɾ] *n* parámetro *m*.

paramilitary [pærə'mɪlɪtəɾɪ] *adj* paramilitar.

paramount ['pærəmaʊnt] *adj* **of p. importance,** de suma importancia.

paranoid ['pærənɔɪd] *adj & n* paranoico,-a *(m,f)*.

paraphernalia [pærəfə'neɪlɪə] *n* parafernalia *f*.

paraphrase ['pærəfreɪz] *vtr* parafrasear.

parasite ['pærəsaɪt] *n* parásito *m*.

parasol ['pærəsɒl] *n* sombrilla *f*.

paratrooper ['pærətruːpəɾ] *n* paracaidista *mf*.

parcel ['pɑːsəl] **I** *n* paquete *m*; **p. bomb,** paquete bomba. **II** *vtr* **to p. up,** envolver, empaquetar.

parched [pɑːtʃt] *adj (land)* reseco,-a; *(lips, mouth)* seco,-a; *fig* **to be p.,** estar muerto,-a de sed.

parchment ['pɑːtʃmənt] *n* pergamino *m*.

pardon ['pɑːdən] **I** *n* perdón *m*; *Jur* indulto *m*; **I beg your p.,** (Usted) perdone; **(I beg your p.)?,** ¿cómo (dice)? **II** *vtr* perdonar; *Jur* indultar; **p. me!,** ¡Usted perdone!

parent ['peərənt] *n* **parents,** padres *mpl*.

parental [pə'rentəl] *adj* paternal; **p. guidance,** consejos *mpl* paternales.

parenthesis [pə'renθɪsɪs] *n (pl* **parentheses** [pə'renθɪsiːz]) paréntesis *m inv*; **in**

p., entre paréntesis.

pariah [pə'raɪə] *n* paria *mf*.

Paris ['pærɪs] *n* París.

parish ['pærɪʃ] *n* parroquia *f*.

Parisian [pə'rɪzɪən] *adj & n* parisino,-a *(m,f)*.

parity ['pærɪtɪ] *n* igualdad *f*; *(of shares)* paridad *f*.

park [pɑːk] **I** *n* parque *m*. **II** *vtr (car)* aparcar, *Am* parquear.

parking ['pɑːkɪŋ] *n* aparcamiento *m*, estacionamiento *m*; **'no p.',** 'prohibido aparcar'; *US* **p. lot,** aparcamiento; **p. meter,** parquímetro *m*; **p. space,** aparcamiento.

parliament ['pɑːləmənt] *n* parlamento *m*.

parliamentary [pɑːlə'mentərɪ] *adj* parlamentario,-a.

parlour, *US* **parlor** ['pɑːləɾ] *n* salón *m*.

parochial [pə'rəʊkɪəl] *adj* parroquial; *pej (narrow-minded)* de miras estrechas.

parody ['pærədɪ] *n* parodia *f*.

parole [pə'rəʊl] *n Jur* libertad *f* condicional; **on p.,** en libertad bajo palabra.

parquet ['pɑːkeɪ] *n* **p. floor,** suelo *m* de parqué.

parrot ['pærət] *n* loro *m*, papagayo *m*.

parry ['pærɪ] *vtr* parar.

parsimonious [pɑːsɪ'məʊnɪəs] *adj* tacaño,-a.

parsley ['pɑːslɪ] *n* perejil *m*.

parsnip ['pɑːsnɪp] *n* chirivía *f*.

parson ['pɑːsən] *n* cura *m*.

part [pɑːt] **I** *n* **1** parte *f*; *(piece)* trozo *m*; *(episode)* capítulo *m*; *Tech* pieza *f*; **for the most p.,** en la mayor parte. **2** *Cin Theat* papel *m*; **to play a p. in sth,** desempeñar un papel en algo; **to take p. in sth,** participar en algo. **3** *(place)* lugar *m*; **in these parts,** por estos lugares. **4 for my p.,** por mi parte; **to take sb's p.,** tomar partido por algn; **to take sth in good p.,** tomarse bien algo. **II** *adj (partial)* parcial; **in p. exchange,** como parte del pago. **III** *adv (partly)* en parte. **IV** *vtr (separate)* separar; **to p. company with sb,** separarse de algn; **to p. one's hair,** hacerse la raya (en el pelo). **V** *vi* separarse; *(say goodbye)* despedirse. ◆**part with** *vtr* separarse de. ◆**partly** *adv* en parte.

partial ['pɑːʃəl] *adj* parcial; **to be p. to sth,** ser aficionado,-a a algo.

participant [pɑː'tɪsɪpənt] *n* participante *mf*; *(in competition)* concursante *mf*.

participate [pɑː'tɪsɪpeɪt] *vi* participar **(in,** en).

participation [pɑːtɪsɪ'peɪʃən] *n* participación *f*.

participle ['pɑːtɪsɪpəl] *n* participio *m*.

particle ['pɑːtɪkəl] *n* partícula *f*.

particular [pə'tɪkjʊləɾ] **I** *adj* **1** *(special)* particular, especial; **in this p. case,** en este caso concreto; **that p. person,** esa persona en particular. **2** *(fussy)* exigente.

II *npl* particulars, pormenores *mpl*; to take down sb's particulars, anotar los datos personales de algn. ◆**particularly** *adv* particularmente, en particular.

parting ['pɑːtɪŋ] I *n* (*separation*) separación *f*; (*farewell*) despedida *f*; (*in hair*) raya *f*. II *adj* de despedida.

partisan [pɑːtɪ'zæn, 'pɑːtɪzæn] I *n* Mil guerrillero,-a *m,f*; (*supporter*) partidario,-a *m,f*. II *adj* (*supporter*) a ultranza; (*of party*) partidista.

partition [pɑː'tɪʃən] I *n* (*wall*) tabique *m*; (*of country*) partición *f*. II *vtr* dividir.

partner ['pɑːtnəʳ] I *n* compañero,-a *m,f*; (*in dancing, tennis*) pareja *f*; (*husband*) marido *m*; (*wife*) mujer *f*; Com socio,-a *m,f*. II *vtr* acompañar.

partnership ['pɑːtnəʃɪp] *n* (*relationship*) vida *f* en común; Com sociedad *f*.

partridge ['pɑːtrɪdʒ] *n* perdiz pardilla.

part-time [pɑːt'taɪm] I *adj* (*work etc*) de tiempo parcial. II *adv* a tiempo parcial.

party ['pɑːtɪ] I *n* 1 (*celebration*) fiesta *f*. 2 (*group*) grupo *m*. 3 Pol partido *m*; p. **political broadcast**, espacio *m* electoral. 4 Jur parte *f*. II *adj* de fiesta; Tel p. **line**, línea compartida.

pass [pɑːs] I *n* 1 (*of mountain*) desfiladero *m*. 2 (*permit*) permiso *m*; bus p., abono *m* de autobús. 3 Sport pase *m*. 4 *fam* to **make a p. at sb**, intentar ligar con algn. II *vtr* 1 pasar; (*overtake*) adelantar. 2 (*exam, law*) aprobar; Jur to p. **sentence**, dictar sentencia.

III *vi* 1 pasar; (*procession*) desfilar; (*car*) adelantar; (*people*) cruzarse; Sport hacer un pase; **we passed on the stairs**, nos cruzamos en la escalera. 2 (*pain*) remitir; (*opportunity*) perderse; (*time*) pasar. 3 (*happen*) ocurrir, pasar. 4 (*in exam*) aprobar.

◆**pass away** *vi euph* pasar a mejor vida. ◆**pass by** I *vtr* pasar de largo. II *vi* pasar cerca (de). ◆**pass for** *vtr* pasar por. ◆**pass off** I *vtr* hacer pasar; to p. **oneself off as sth**, hacerse pasar por algo. II *vi* (*happen*) transcurrir. ◆**pass on** I *vtr* (*hand on*) transmitir. II *vi euph* pasar a mejor vida. ◆**pass out** *vi* (*faint*) desmayarse; Mil graduarse. ◆**pass over** *vtr* 1 (*aircraft*) volar por. 2 pasar por alto. ◆**pass up** *vtr fam* (*opportunity*) renunciar; (*offer*) rechazar.

passable ['pɑːsəbəl] *adj* (*road*) transitable; (*acceptable*) pasable.

passage ['pæsɪdʒ] *n* 1 (*alleyway*) callejón *m*; (*hallway*) pasillo *m*. 2 (*movement*) tránsito *m*; Naut travesía *f*; Mus Lit pasaje *m*.

passageway ['pæsɪdʒweɪ] *n* (*interior*) pasillo *m*; (*exterior*) pasaje *m*.

passbook ['pɑːsbʊk] *n* libreta *f* de banco.

passenger ['pæsɪndʒəʳ] *n* pasajero,-a *m,f*.

passer-by [pɑːsə'baɪ] *n* transeúnte *mf*.

passing ['pɑːsɪŋ] I *n* 1 (*of time*) transcurso *m*; in p., de pasada. 2 (*of law*) aprobación *f*. II *adj* que pasa; (*glance*) rápido,-a; (*thought*) pasajero,-a.

passion ['pæʃən] *n* pasión *f*; p. **fruit**, granadilla *f*.

passionate ['pæʃənɪt] *adj* apasionado,-a.

passive ['pæsɪv] *adj* pasivo,-a.

Passover ['pɑːsəʊvəʳ] *n* Pascua *f* de los judíos.

passport ['pɑːspɔːt] *n* pasaporte *m*.

password ['pɑːswɜːd] *n* contraseña *f*.

past [pɑːst] I *n* pasado *m*; in the p., en el pasado; **to have a p.**, tener antecedentes. II *adj* pasado,-a; (*former*) anterior; **in the p. weeks**, en las últimas semanas. III *adv* por delante; to p., pasar corriendo. IV *prep* (*beyond*) más allá de; (*more than*) más de; **he's p. forty**, pasa de los cuarenta (años); **it's five p. ten**, son las diez y cinco; **to be p. it**, estar muy carroza.

pasta ['pæstə] *n* pasta *f*, pastas *fpl*.

paste [peɪst] I *n* pasta *f*; (*glue*) engrudo *m*. II *vtr* (*stick*) pegar; (*put paste on*) engomar.

pastel ['pæstəl] *adj & n* pastel.

pasteurized ['pæstʃəraɪzd] *adj* pasteurizado,-a.

pastille ['pæstɪl] *n* pastilla *f*.

pastime ['pɑːstaɪm] *n* pasatiempo *m*.

pastor ['pɑːstəʳ] *n* pastor *m*.

pastoral ['pɑːstərəl] *adj* pastoral.

pastry ['peɪstrɪ] *n* (*dough*) pasta *f*; (*cake*) pastel *m*.

pasture ['pɑːstʃəʳ] *n* pasto *m*.

pasty[1] ['pæstɪ] *n* Culin empanada *f*, pastel *m* de carne.

pasty[2] ['peɪstɪ] *adj* (*pastier, pastiest*) (*complexion*) pálido,-a.

pat [pæt] I *n* (*caress*) caricia *f*; (*tap*) palmada *f*; *fig* **to give sb a p. on the back**, felicitar a algn. II *vtr* acariciar; to p. **sb on the back**, dar a algn una palmadita en la espalda.

patch [pætʃ] I *n* (*of material*) parche *m*; (*of land*) terreno *m*; (*of colour*) mancha *f*; *fig* **to go through a bad p.**, pasar por una mala racha. ◆**patch up** *vtr* (*garment*) poner un parche en; to p. **things up**, (*after argument*) limar asperezas.

patchwork ['pætʃwɜːk] I *n* labor *f* de retales. II *adj* (*quilt etc*) hecho,-a con retales distintos.

patchy ['pætʃɪ] *adj* (*patchier, patchiest*) (*colour, performance*) desigual; (*knowledge*) incompleto,-a.

pâté ['pæteɪ] *n* paté *m*.

patent[1] ['peɪtənt] I *n* Com patente *f*. II *adj* (*obvious*) patente, evidente; p. **medicine**, específico *m*. III *vtr* Com patentar. ◆**patently** *adv* it's p. obvious, está clarísimo.

patent[2] ['peɪtənt] *n* p. (**leather**), charol

m.

paternal [pəˈtɜːnəl] *adj* paternal; *(grandmother etc)* paterno,-a.

paternity [pəˈtɜːnɪti] *n* paternidad *f*.

path [pɑːθ] *n* camino *m*, sendero *m*; *(route)* ruta *f*; *(of missile)* trayectoria *f*.

pathetic [pəˈθetɪk] *adj (pitiful)* patético, -a; *fam (hopeless)* malísimo,-a; **she was a p. sight,** daba lástima verla.

pathological [pæθəˈlɒdʒɪkəl] *adj* patológico,-a.

pathologist [pəˈθɒlədʒɪst] *n* patólogo,-a *m,f*.

pathology [pəˈθɒlədʒi] *n* patología *f*.

pathos [ˈpeɪθɒs] *n* patetismo *m*.

pathway [ˈpɑːθweɪ] *n* camino *m*, sendero *m*.

patience [ˈpeɪʃəns] *n* 1 paciencia *f*; **to lose one's p. with sb,** perder la paciencia con algn. 2 *GB Cards* solitario *m*.

patient [ˈpeɪʃənt] I *adj* paciente; **to be p. with sb,** tener paciencia con algn. II *n Med* paciente *mf*.

patio [ˈpætiəʊ] *n* patio *m*.

patriotic [pætrɪˈɒtɪk] *adj (person)* patriota, *(speech, act)* patriótico,-a.

patrol [pəˈtrəʊl] I *n* patrulla *f*; **p. car,** coche *m* patrulla. II *vtr* patrullar por.

patrolman [pəˈtrəʊlmən] *n US* policía *m*.

patron [ˈpeɪtrən] *n* 1 *(of charity)* patrocinador,-a *m,f*; *(of arts)* mecenas *m inv*; **p. saint,** (santo,-a *m,f*) patrón,-ona *m,f*. 2 *(customer)* cliente,-a *m,f* habitual.

patronize [ˈpætrənaɪz] *vtr* 1 *(arts)* fomentar; *(shop)* ser cliente,-a *m,f* habitual de; *(club etc)* frecuentar. 2 *pej (person)* tratar con condescendencia.

patronizing [ˈpætrənaɪzɪŋ] *adj pej* condescendiente.

patter¹ [ˈpætər] I *n (of rain)* repiqueteo *m*; *(of feet)* pasito *m*. II *vi (rain)* repiquetear; *(feet)* hacer ruido sordo.

patter² [ˈpætər] *n fam* labia *f*; *(of salesman)* discursillo preparado.

pattern [ˈpætən] *n Sew* patrón *m*; *(design)* dibujo *m*; *(on material)* estampado *m*; *fig (of behaviour)* modelo *m*.

paunch [pɔːntʃ] *n* panza *f*.

pauper [ˈpɔːpər] *n* pobre *mf*.

pause [pɔːz] I *n* pausa *f*; *(silence)* silencio *m*. II *vi* hacer una pausa; *(be silent)* callarse.

pave [peɪv] *vtr* pavimentar; *(with stones)* empedrar; *fig* **to p. the way for sb/sth,** preparar el terreno para algn/algo.

pavement [ˈpeɪvmənt] *n* acera *f*; *US (road surface)* calzada *f*, pavimento *m*.

pavilion [pəˈvɪljən] *n* pabellón *m*; *GB Sport (changing rooms)* vestuarios *mpl*.

paving [ˈpeɪvɪŋ] *n* *(on road)* pavimento *m*; *(on floor)* enlosado *m*; *(with stones)* empedrado *m*; **p. stone,** losa *f*.

paw [pɔː] I *n (foot)* pata *f*; *(of cat)* garra *f*; *(of lion)* zarpa *f*. II *vtr (of lion)* dar zarpa-

zos a; *pej (of person)* manosear, sobar.

pawn¹ [pɔːn] *n Chess* peón *m*; *fig* **to be sb's p.,** ser el juguete de algn.

pawn² [pɔːn] *vtr* empeñar.

pawnbroker [ˈpɔːnbrəʊkər] *n* prestamista *mf*.

pawnshop [ˈpɔːnʃɒp] *n* casa *f* de empeños.

pay [peɪ] I *n (wages)* paga *f*, sueldo *m*; **p. packet,** sobre *m* de la paga; **p. rise,** aumento *m* del sueldo; **p. slip,** nómina *f*. II *vtr (pt & pp paid)* 1 pagar; **to be or get paid,** cobrar. 2 *(attention)* prestar; *(homage)* rendir; *(visit)* hacer; **to p. sb a compliment,** halagar a algn. 3 *(be profitable for)* compensar. III *vi* 1 pagar; **to p. for sth,** pagar (por) algo. 2 *(be profitable)* ser rentable. ◆**pay back** *vtr* reembolsar; *fig* **to p. sb back,** vengarse de algn. ◆**pay in** *vtr (money)* ingresar. ◆**pay off** I *vtr (debt)* liquidar; *(mortgage)* cancelar. II *vi (be successful)* dar resultado. ◆**pay out** *vtr (spend)* gastar (**on,** en). ◆**pay up** *vi* pagar.

payable [ˈpeɪəbəl] *adj* pagadero,-a.

payday [ˈpeɪdeɪ] *n* día *m* de pago.

payee [peɪˈiː] *n* portador,-a *m,f*.

payment [ˈpeɪmənt] *n* pago *m*; *(of cheque)* cobro *m*; **advance p.,** anticipo *m*; **down p.,** entrada *f*; **monthly p.,** mensualidad *f*.

payoff [ˈpeɪɒf] *n (reward)* recompensa *f*; *fam (bribe)* soborno *m*.

payroll [ˈpeɪrəʊl] *n* nómina *f*.

pc *abbr of* per cent, p.c.; *abbr of* **personal computer,** PC.

PE [piːˈiː] *abbr of* **physical education.**

pea [piː] *n* guisante *m*.

peace [piːs] *n* paz *f*; *(calm)* tranquilidad *f*; **at or in p.,** en paz; **p. and quiet,** tranquilidad; **to make p.,** hacer las paces; *(of countries)* firmar la paz.

peaceable [ˈpiːsəbəl] *adj* pacífico,-a.

peaceful [ˈpiːsfʊl] *adj (demonstration)* pacífico,-a; *(place)* tranquilo,-a.

peace-keeping [ˈpiːskiːpɪŋ] *adj* pacificador,-a; **p.-k. forces,** fuerzas *fpl* de pacificación.

peach [piːtʃ] *n* melocotón *m*.

peacock [ˈpiːkɒk] *n* pavo *m* real.

peak [piːk] *n (of cap)* visera *f*; *(of mountain)* pico *m*; *(summit)* cima *f*; *fig* cumbre *f*; **p. hours,** horas *fpl* punta; **p. period,** horas de mayor consumo; **p. season,** temporada alta.

peal [piːl] *n (of bells)* repique *m*; **p. of thunder,** trueno *m*; **peals of laughter,** carcajadas *fpl*.

peanut [ˈpiːnʌt] *n* cacahuete *m*; **p. butter,** mantequilla *f* or manteca *f* de cacahuete.

pear [peər] *n* pera *f*.

pearl [pɜːl] *n* perla *f*.

peasant [ˈpezənt] *adj & n* campesino,-a *(m,f)*.

peat [piːt] *n* turba *f*; **p. bog,** turbera *f*.

pebble ['pebəl] n guijarro m; (small) china f.

pecan [pɪ'kæn] n (nut) pacana f.

peck [pek] I n (of bird) picotazo m; fam (kiss) besito m. II vtr (bird) picotear; fam (kiss) dar un besito a. III vi to p. at one's food, picar la comida.

pecking order ['pekɪŋɔːdə] n fig jerarquía f.

peckish ['pekɪʃ] adj fam to feel p., empezar a tener hambre.

peculiar [pɪ'kjuːlɪə] adj (odd) extraño,-a; (particular) característico,-a.

peculiarity [pɪkjuːlɪ'ærɪtɪ] n (oddity) rareza f; (characteristic) característica f, peculiaridad f.

pedal ['pedəl] I n pedal m. II vi pedalear.

pedantic [pɪ'dæntɪk] adj pedante.

peddle ['pedəl] vtr & vi Com vender de puerta en puerta; to p. drugs, traficar con drogas.

peddler ['pedlə] n (of drugs) traficante mf; US → pedlar.

pedestal ['pedɪstəl] n pedestal m; fig to put sb on a p., poner a algn sobre un pedestal.

pedestrian [pɪ'destrɪən] I n peatón,-ona m,f; p. crossing, paso m de peatones. II adj pej prosaico,-a.

pediatrician [piːdɪə'trɪʃən] n US → paediatrician.

pedigree ['pedɪgriː] I n linaje m; (family tree) árbol genealógico; (of animal) pedigrí m. II adj (animal) de raza.

pedlar ['pedlə] n vendedor,-a m,f ambulante.

pée [piː] fam I n p vis m. II vi hacer pis.

peek [piːk] I n ojeada f. II vi to p. at sth, mirar algo a hurtadillas.

peel [piːl] I n piel f; (of orange, lemon) cáscara f. II vtr (fruit) pelar. III vi (paint) desconcharse; (wallpaper) despegarse; (skin) pelarse.

peeler ['piːlə] n potato p., pelapatatas m inv.

peelings ['piːlɪŋz] npl peladuras fpl, mondaduras fpl.

peep¹ [piːp] n (sound) pío m.

peep² [piːp] I n (glance) ojeada f; (furtive look) mirada furtiva. II vi to p. at sth, echar una ojeada a algo; to p. out from behind sth, dejarse ver detrás de algo.

peephole ['piːphəʊl] n mirilla f.

peer¹ [pɪə] n (noble) par m; (equal) igual mf; p. group, grupo parejo.

peer² [pɪə] vi mirar detenidamente; (shortsightedly) mirar con ojos de miope.

peerage ['pɪərɪdʒ] n título m de nobleza.

peeved [piːvd] adj fam fastidiado,-a, de mal humor.

peevish ['piːvɪʃ] adj malhumorado,-a.

peg [peg] I n clavija f; (for coat, hat) percha f. II vtr (clothes) tender; (prices) fijar.

pejorative [pɪ'dʒɒrətɪv] adj peyorativo,-a.

Pekinese [piːkə'niːz] adj & n pequinés, -esa (m,f).

Peking [piː'kɪŋ] n Pekín.

pelican ['pelɪkən] n pelícano m; GB p. crossing, paso m de peatones.

pellet ['pelɪt] n bolita f; (for gun) perdigón m.

pelt¹ [pelt] n (skin) pellejo m.

pelt² [pelt] I vtr to p. sb with sth, tirar algo a algn. II vi fam 1 it's pelting (down), (raining) llueve a cántaros. 2 to p. along, (rush) correr a toda prisa.

pelvis ['pelvɪs] n pelvis f.

pen¹ [pen] I n pluma f. II vtr escribir.

pen² [pen] I n (enclosure) corral m; (for sheep) redil m; (for children) corralito m. II vtr to p. in, acorralar.

penal ['piːnəl] adj penal.

penalize ['piːnəlaɪz] vtr castigar; Sport penalizar.

penalty ['penltɪ] n (punishment) pena f; Sport castigo; Ftb penalti m; to pay the p. for sth, cargar con las consecuencias de algo; p. area, área f de castigo.

penance ['penəns] n penitencia f.

pence [pens] npl → penny.

pencil ['pensəl] n lápiz m; p. case, estuche m de lápices; p. sharpener, sacapuntas m inv.

pendant ['pendənt] n colgante m.

pending ['pendɪŋ] I adj pendiente. II prep (while) mientras; p. a decision, (until) hasta que se tome una decisión.

pendulum ['pendjʊləm] n péndulo m.

penetrate ['penɪtreɪt] I vtr penetrar; fig adentrarse en. II vi atravesar; (get inside) penetrar.

penetrating ['penɪtreɪtɪŋ] adj (look) penetrante; (mind) perspicaz; (sound) agudo, -a.

penfriend ['penfrend] n amigo,-a m,f por carta.

penguin ['peŋgwɪn] n pingüino m.

penicillin [penɪ'sɪlɪn] n penicilina f.

peninsula [pɪ'nɪnsjʊlə] n península f.

penis ['piːnɪs] n pene m.

penitent ['penɪtənt] adj Rel penitente; (repentant) arrepentido,-a.

penitentiary [penɪ'tenʃərɪ] n US cárcel f, penal m.

penknife ['pennaɪf] n navaja f, cortaplumas m inv.

penniless ['penɪlɪs] adj sin dinero.

penny ['penɪ] n (pl pennies, pence [pens]) penique m.

penpal ['penpæl] n US → penfriend.

pension ['penʃən] n pensión f; retirement p., jubilación f.

pensioner ['penʃənə] n jubilado,-a m,f.

pensive ['pensɪv] adj pensativo,-a.

pentagon ['pentəgən] n US Pol the P., el Pentágono.

Pentecost ['pentɪkɒst] n Pentecostés m.

penthouse ['penthaʊs] *n* ático *m*.
pent-up ['pentʌp] *adj* reprimido,-a.
penultimate [pɪ'nʌltɪmət] *adj* penúltimo,-a.
people ['piːpəl] *npl* 1 gente *f sing*; *(individuals)* personas *fpl*; **many p.**, mucha gente; **old p.'s home**, asilo *m* de ancianos; **p. say that ...**, se dice que ...; **some p.**, algunas personas. 2 *(citizens)* ciudadanos *mpl*; *(inhabitants)* habitantes *mpl*; **the p.**, el pueblo. 3 *(nation)* pueblo *m*, nación *f*.
pep [pep] *n fam* ánimo *m*, energía *f*; **p. talk**, discurso *m* enardecedor. ◆**pep up** *vtr fam* animar.
pepper ['pepər] I *n (spice)* pimienta *f*; *(fruit)* pimiento *m*; **black p.**, pimienta negra; **p. pot**, pimentero *m*; **red/green p.**, pimiento rojo/verde; **p. mill**, molinillo *m* de pimienta. II *vtr fig* **peppered with**, salpicado,-a de.
peppermint ['pepəmint] *n* menta *f*; *(sweet)* pastilla *f* de menta.
per [pɜːr] *prep* por; **5 times p. week**, 5 veces a la semana; **p. cent**, por ciento; **p. day/annum**, al *or* por día/año; **p. capita**, per cápita.
perceive [pə'siːv] *vtr (see)* percibir.
percentage [pə'sentɪdʒ] *n* porcentaje *m*.
perceptible [pə'septəbəl] *adj (visible)* perceptible; *(sound)* audible; *(improvement)* sensible.
perception [pə'sepʃən] *n* percepción *f*.
perceptive [pə'septɪv] *adj* perspicaz.
perch¹ [pɜːtʃ] *n (fish)* perca *f*.
perch² [pɜːtʃ] I *n (for bird)* percha *f*. II *vi (bird)* posarse **(on, en)**.
percolate ['pɜːkəleɪt] I *vtr* filtrar; **percolated coffee**, café *m* filtro. II *vi* filtrarse.
percolator ['pɜːkəleɪtər] *n* cafetera *f* de filtro.
percussion [pə'kʌʃən] *n* percusión *f*.
perennial [pə'renɪəl] *adj Bot* perenne.
perfect ['pɜːfɪkt] I *adj* perfecto,-a; **he's a p. stranger to us**, nos es totalmente desconocido; **p. tense**, tiempo perfecto. II [pə'fekt] *vtr* perfeccionar. ◆**perfectly** *adv* perfectamente; *(absolutely)* completamente.
perfection [pə'fekʃən] *n* perfección *f*.
perforate ['pɜːfəreɪt] *vtr* perforar.
perforation [pɜːfə'reɪʃən] *n* perforación *f*; *(on stamps etc)* perforado *m*.
perform [pə'fɔːm] I *vtr (task)* ejecutar, realizar; *(piece of music)* interpretar; *Theat* representar. II *vi (machine)* funcionar; *Mus* interpretar; *Theat* actuar.
performance [pə'fɔːməns] *n (of task)* ejecución *f*, realización *f*; *Mus* interpretación *f*; *Theat* representación *f*; *Sport* actuación *f*; *(of machine etc)* rendimiento *m*.
performer [pə'fɔːmər] *n Mus* intérprete *mf*; *Theat* actor *m*, actriz *f*.

perfume ['pɜːfjuːm] *n* perfume *m*.
perfunctory [pə'fʌŋktərɪ] *adj* superficial.
perhaps [pə'hæps, præps] *adv* tal vez, quizá(s).
peril ['perɪl] *n (risk)* riesgo *m*; *(danger)* peligro *m*.
perilous ['perɪləs] *adj (risky)* arriesgado, -a; *(dangerous)* peligroso,-a. ◆**perilously** *adv* peligrosamente.
perimeter [pə'rɪmɪtər] *n* perímetro *m*.
period ['pɪərɪəd] I *n* 1 período *m*; *(stage)* etapa *f*. 2 *Educ* clase *f*. 3 *(full stop)* punto *m*. 4 *(menstruation)* regla *f*. II *adj (dress, furniture)* de época.
periodic [pɪərɪ'ɒdɪk] *adj* periódico,-a. ◆**periodically** *adv* de vez en cuando.
periodical [pɪərɪ'ɒdɪkəl] I *adj* periódico, -a. II *n* revista *f*.
peripheral [pə'rɪfərəl] I *adj* periférico,-a. II *n Comput* unidad periférica.
perish ['perɪʃ] *vi* perecer; *(material)* echarse a perder.
perishable ['perɪʃəbəl] *adj* perecedero,-a.
perjury ['pɜːdʒərɪ] *n* perjurio *m*.
perk [pɜːk] *n fam* extra *m*. ◆**perk up** *vi (person)* animarse; *(after illness)* reponerse.
perky ['pɜːkɪ] *adj (perkier, perkiest)* animado,-a, alegre.
perm [pɜːm] I *n* permanente *f*. II *vtr* **to have one's hair permed**, hacerse la permanente.
permanent ['pɜːmənənt] *adj* permanente; *(address, job)* fijo,-a.
permeate ['pɜːmɪeɪt] *vtr & vi* penetrar; *fig* extenderse por.
permissible [pə'mɪsəbəl] *adj* admisible.
permission [pə'mɪʃən] *n* permiso *m*.
permissive [pə'mɪsɪv] *adj* permisivo,-a.
permit ['pɜːmɪt] I *n* permiso *m*; *Com* licencia *f*. II [pə'mɪt] *vtr* **to p. sb to do sth**, permitir a algn hacer algo.
pernicious [pə'nɪʃəs] *adj* pernicioso,-a.
perpendicular [pɜːpən'dɪkjʊlər] I *adj* perpendicular; *(cliff)* vertical. II *n* perpendicular *f*.
perpetrate ['pɜːpɪtreɪt] *vtr* cometer.
perpetual [pə'petʃʊəl] *adj (noise)* continuo,-a; *(arguing)* interminable; *(snow)* perpetuo,-a.
perplex [pə'pleks] *vtr* dejar perplejo,-a.
perplexing [pə'pleksɪŋ] *adj* desconcertante.
persecute ['pɜːsɪkjuːt] *vtr* perseguir; *(harass)* acosar.
persecution [pɜːsɪ'kjuːʃən] *n* persecución *f*; *(harassment)* acoso *m*.
perseverance [pɜːsɪ'vɪərəns] *n* perseverancia *f*.
persevere [pɜːsɪ'vɪər] *vi* perseverar.
Persian ['pɜːʃən] *adj* persa *m*; **P. Gulf**, golfo Pérsico.
persist [pə'sɪst] *vi* empeñarse **(in, en)**.
persistence [pə'sɪstəns] *n* empeño *m*.

persistent [pəˈsɪstənt] *adj* (*person*) perseverante; (*smell etc*) persistente; (*continual*) constante.

person [ˈpɜːsən] *n* (*pl* **people** [ˈpiːpəl]) persona *f*; (*individual*) individuo *m*; **in p.**, en persona.

personable [ˈpɜːsənəbəl] *adj* (*handsome*) bien parecido,-a; (*pleasant*) amable.

personal [ˈpɜːsənəl] I *adj* (*private*) personal; (*friend*) íntimo,-a. **p. computer**, ordenador *m* personal; **p. column**, anuncios *mpl* personales; **p. pronoun**, pronombre *m* personal. 2 (*in person*) en persona; **he will make a p. appearance**, estará aquí en persona. 3 *pej* (*comment etc*) indiscreto,-a. ◆**personally** *adv* (*for my part*) personalmente; (*in person*) en persona.

personality [pɜːsəˈnælɪtɪ] *n* personalidad *f*.

personify [pɜːˈsɒnɪfaɪ] *vtr* personificar, encarnar.

personnel [pɜːsəˈnel] *n* personal *m*.

perspective [pəˈspektɪv] *n* perspectiva *f*.

Perspex® [ˈpɜːspeks] *n* plexiglás® *m*.

perspiration [pɜːspɪˈreɪʃən] *n* transpiración *f*.

perspire [pəˈspaɪəʳ] *vi* transpirar.

persuade [pəˈsweɪd] *vtr* persuadir; **to p. sb to do sth**, persuadir a algn para que haga algo.

persuasion [pəˈsweɪʒən] *n* persuasión *f*; (*opinion*, *belief*) credo *m*.

persuasive [pəˈsweɪsɪv] *adj* persuasivo,-a.

pert [pɜːt] *adj* pizpireta, coqueto,-a.

pertain [pəˈteɪn] *vi* estar relacionado,-a (**to**, con).

pertinent [ˈpɜːtɪnənt] *adj* (*relevant*) pertinente; **p. to**, relacionado,-a con, a propósito de.

perturbing [pəˈtɜːbɪŋ] *adj* inquietante.

Peru [pəˈruː] *n* Perú.

peruse [pəˈruːz] *vtr* *fml* leer.

Peruvian [pəˈruːvɪən] *adj* & *n* peruano,-a (*m,f*).

pervade [pɜːˈveɪd] *vtr* (*of smell*) penetrar. (*of light*) difundirse por; *fig* (*of influence*) extenderse por.

pervasive [pɜːˈveɪsɪv] *adj* (*smell*) penetrante; (*influence*) extendido,-a.

perverse [pɜːˈvɜːs] *adj* (*wicked*) perverso,-a; (*contrary*) contrario,-a a todo.

perversion [pɜːˈvɜːʃən] *n* *Med Psych* perversión *f*; (*of justice*, *truth*) desvirtuación *f*.

pervert [ˈpɜːvɜːt] I *n* *Med* pervertido,-a *m,f* (*sexual*). II [pəˈvɜːt] *vtr* pervertir; (*justice*, *truth*) desvirtuar.

pessimist [ˈpesɪmɪst] *n* pesimista *mf*.

pessimistic [pesɪˈmɪstɪk] *adj* pesimista.

pest [pest] *n* 1 *Zool* animal nocivo; *fam* planta nociva. 2 *fam* (*person*) pelma *mf*; (*thing*) lata *f*.

pester [ˈpestəʳ] *vtr* molestar, fastidiar.

pet [pet] I *n* 1 animal doméstico. 2 (*favourite*) preferido,-a *m,f*; *fam* cariño *m*. II *adj* (*favourite*) preferido,-a. III *vtr* acariciar. IV *vi* (*sexually*) besuquearse.

petal [ˈpetəl] *n* pétalo *m*.

peter [ˈpiːtəʳ] *vi* **to p. out**, agotarse.

petite [pəˈtiːt] *adj* menuda, chiquita.

petition [pɪˈtɪʃən] *n* petición *f*.

petrify [ˈpetrɪfaɪ] *vtr* *lit* petrificar; *fig* **they were petrified**, se quedaron de piedra.

petrol [ˈpetrəl] *n* gasolina *f*; **p. can**, bidón de gasolina; **p. pump**, surtidor *m* de gasolina; **p. station**, gasolinera *f*; **p. tank**, depósito *m* de gasolina.

petroleum [pəˈtrəʊlɪəm] *n* petróleo *m*.

petticoat [ˈpetɪkəʊt] *n* enaguas *fpl*.

petty [ˈpetɪ] *adj* (*pettier*, *pettiest*) (*trivial*) insignificante; (*small-minded*) mezquino,-a; **p. cash**, dinero *m* para gastos pequeños; *Naut* **p. officer**, sargento *m* de marina.

petulant [ˈpetjʊlənt] *adj* malhumorado,-a.

pew [pjuː] *n* banco *m* de iglesia; *fam* **take a p.!**, ¡siéntate!

pewter [ˈpjuːtəʳ] *n* peltre *m*.

phantom [ˈfæntəm] *adj* & *n* fantasma (*m*).

pharmaceutical [fɑːməˈsjuːtɪkəl] *adj* farmacéutico,-a.

pharmacist [ˈfɑːməsɪst] *n* farmacéutico,-a *m,f*.

pharmacy [ˈfɑːməsɪ] *n* farmacia *f*.

phase [feɪz] I *n* fase *f*. II *vtr* **to p. sth in/out**, introducir/retirar algo progresivamente.

PhD [piːeɪtʃˈdiː] *abbr* **of Doctor of Philosophy**, Doctor,-a *m,f* en Filosofía.

pheasant [ˈfezənt] *n* faisán *m* (*vulgar*).

phenomenal [fɪˈnɒmɪnəl] *adj* fenomenal.

phenomenon [fɪˈnɒmɪnən] *n* (*pl* **phenomena** [fɪˈnɒmɪnə]) fenómeno *m*.

phial [ˈfaɪəl] *n* frasco *m*.

philanthropist [fɪˈlænθrəpɪst] *n* filántropo,-a *m,f*.

philately [fɪˈlætəlɪ] *n* filatelia *f*.

Philippines [ˈfɪlɪpiːnz] *n* **the P.**, las (Islas) Filipinas.

philosopher [fɪˈlɒsəfəʳ] *n* filósofo,-a *m,f*.

philosophical [fɪləˈsɒfɪkəl] *adj* filosófico,-a.

philosophy [fɪˈlɒsəfɪ] *n* filosofía *f*.

phlegm [flem] *n* flema *f*.

phlegmatic [flegˈmætɪk] *adj* flemático,-a.

phobia [ˈfəʊbɪə] *n* fobia *f*.

phone [fəʊn] *n* → **telephone**.

phone-in [ˈfəʊnɪn] *n* *fam* programa *m* de radio o televisión con línea telefónica abierta.

phonetic [fəˈnetɪk] *adj* fonético,-a. II *n* **phonetics**, fonética *f* *sing*.

phoney [ˈfəʊnɪ] *adj* (*phonier*, *phoniest*) (*thing*) falso,-a; (*person*) farsante. II *n* (*person*) farsante *mf*.

phonograph [ˈfəʊnəgrɑːf] *n* *US* tocadiscos m inv.

phosphate ['fɒsfeɪt] n fosfato m.

photo ['fəʊtəʊ] n (abbr of **photograph**) foto f.

photocopier ['fəʊtəʊkɒpɪər] n fotocopiadora f.

photocopy ['fəʊtəʊkɒpɪ] I n fotocopia f. II vtr fotocopiar.

photogenic [fəʊtəʊ'dʒenɪk] adj fotogénico,-a.

photograph ['fəʊtəɡræf, 'fəʊtəɡrɑːf] I n fotografía f; black and white/colour p., fotografía en blanco y negro/en color. II vtr fotografiar.

photographer [fə'tɒɡrəfər] n fotógrafo,-a m,f.

photography [fə'tɒɡrəfɪ] n fotografía f.

phrase [freɪz] I n frase f; **p. book,** libro m de frases. II vtr expresar.

physical ['fɪzɪkəl] adj físico,-a; **p. education,** educación física. **◆physically** adv físicamente; **p. handicapped,** minusválido,-a; **to be p. fit,** estar en forma.

physician [fɪ'zɪʃən] n médico,-a m,f.

physicist ['fɪzɪsɪst] n físico,-a m,f.

physics ['fɪzɪks] n física f.

physiological [fɪzɪə'lɒdʒɪkəl] adj fisiológico,-a.

physiotherapist [fɪzɪəʊ'θerəpɪst] n fisioterapeuta mf.

physique [fɪ'ziːk] n físico m.

pianist ['pɪənɪst] n pianista mf.

piano [pɪ'ænəʊ] n piano m.

piccolo ['pɪkələʊ] n flautín m.

pick [pɪk] I n 1 (tool) pico m, piqueta f. 2 **take your p.,** (choice) elige el que quieras. II vtr 1 (choose) escoger; (team) seleccionar. 2 (flowers, fruit) coger, recoger. 3 (scratch) hurgar; **to p. one's nose,** hurgarse la nariz; **to p. one's teeth,** mondarse los dientes. 4 **to p. sb's pocket,** robar algo del bolsillo de algn. 5 (lock) forzar. III vi **to p. at one's food,** comer sin ganas. **◆pick off** vtr 1 (remove) quitar. 2 (shoot) matar uno a uno. **◆pick on** vtr (persecute) meterse con. **◆pick out** vtr (choose) elegir; (distinguish) distinguir; (identify) identificar. **◆pick up** I vtr 1 (object on floor) recoger; (telephone) descolgar; **to p. oneself up,** levantarse; fig reponerse. 2 (collect) recoger; (shopping, person) buscar; **to p. up speed,** ganar velocidad. 3 (acquire) conseguir; (learn) aprender. II vi (improve) mejorarse, ir -mejorando; (prices) subir.

pickaxe, US **pickax** ['pɪkæks] n piqueta f.

picket ['pɪkɪt] I n piquete m; **p. line,** piquete m. II vtr piquetear. III vi hacer piquete.

pickle ['pɪkəl] I n 1 Culin salsa f picante. 2 fam (mess) lío m, apuro m. II vtr Culin

conservar en adobo or escabeche; **pickled onions,** cebollas fpl en vinagre.

pickpocket ['pɪkpɒkɪt] n carterista mf.

pick-up ['pɪkʌp] n **p.-up (arm),** (on record player) brazo m; **p.-up (truck),** furgoneta f.

picnic ['pɪknɪk] I n comida f de campo, picnic m. II vi hacer una comida de campo.

pictorial [pɪk'tɔːrɪəl] adj ilustrado,-a.

picture ['pɪktʃər] I n 1 (painting) cuadro m; (drawing) dibujo m; (portrait) retrato m; (photo) foto f; (illustration) ilustración f; **p. book,** libro ilustrado; **p. postcard,** tarjeta f postal. 2 TV imagen m; Cin película f; **to go to the pictures,** ir al cine. II vtr (imagine) imaginarse.

picturesque [pɪktʃə'resk] adj pintoresco, -ca.

pie [paɪ] n (of fruit) tarta f, pastel m; (of meat etc) pastel, empanada f; (pasty) empanadilla f.

piece [piːs] n 1 (of food) pedazo m, trozo m; (of paper) trozo; (part) pieza f; **a p. of advice,** un consejo; **a p. of furniture,** un mueble; **a p. of land,** una parcela; **a p. of news,** una noticia; **to break sth into pieces,** hacer algo pedazos; fig **to go to pieces,** perder el control (de sí mismo). 2 Lit Mus obra f, pieza f. 3 (coin) moneda f. 4 (in chess) pieza f; (in draughts) ficha f. **◆piece together** vtr (facts) reconstruir; (jigsaw) hacer.

piecemeal ['piːsmiːl] adv (by degrees) poco a poco, a etapas; (unsystematically) desordenadamente.

piecework ['piːswɜːk] n trabajo m a destajo; **to be on p.,** trabajar a destajo.

pier [pɪər] n embarcadero m, muelle m; (promenade) paseo m de madera que entra en el mar.

pierce [pɪəs] vtr perforar; (penetrate) penetrar en.

piercing ['pɪəsɪŋ] adj (sound etc) penetrante.

piety ['paɪɪtɪ] n piedad f.

pig [pɪɡ] n cerdo m; fam (person) cochino m; (glutton) tragón,-ona m,f; sl offens (policeman) madero m.

pigeon ['pɪdʒɪn] n paloma f; Culin Sport pichón m.

pigeonhole ['pɪdʒɪnhəʊl] n casilla f.

piggy ['pɪɡɪ] n **p. bank,** hucha f en forma de cerdito.

pigheaded [pɪɡ'hedɪd] adj terco,-a, cabezota.

piglet ['pɪɡlɪt] n cerdito m, lechón m.

pigment ['pɪɡmənt] n pigmento m.

pigskin ['pɪɡskɪn] n piel f de cerdo.

pigsty ['pɪɡstaɪ] n pocilga f.

pigtail ['pɪɡteɪl] n trenza f; (bullfighter's) coleta f.

pike [paɪk] n (fish) lucio m.

pilchard ['pɪltʃəd] n sardina f.

pile¹ [paɪl] **I** n montón m. **II** vtr amontonar. **III** vi to p. into, apiñarse en, p. on/off a bus, subir a/bajar de un autobús en tropel. ◆**pile up** I vtr (things) amontonar; (riches, debts) acumular. **II** vi amontonarse.

pile² [paɪl] n (on carpet) pelo m; **thick p.**, pelo largo.

piles [paɪlz] npl Med almorranas fpl, hemorroides fpl.

pile-up ['paɪlʌp] n Aut choque m en cadena.

pilfer ['pɪlfər] vtr & vi hurtar.

pilgrim ['pɪlgrɪm] n peregrino,-a m,f.

pilgrimage ['pɪlgrɪmɪdʒ] n peregrinación f.

pill [pɪl] n píldora f, pastilla f; to be on the p., estar tomando la píldora (anticonceptiva).

pillage ['pɪlɪdʒ] vtr & vi pillar, saquear.

pillar ['pɪlər] n pilar m, columna f; GB p. box, buzón m.

pillion ['pɪljən] n asiento trasero (de una moto).

pillow ['pɪləʊ] n almohada f.

pillowcase ['pɪləʊkeɪs] n funda f de almohada.

pilot ['paɪlət] **I** n piloto m. **II** adj (trial) piloto inv; **p. light**, piloto m; **p. scheme**, proyecto piloto. **III** vtr pilotar.

pimp [pɪmp] n chulo m.

pimple ['pɪmpəl] n grano m, espinilla f.

pin [pɪn] **I** n alfiler m; Tech clavija f; (wooden) espiga f; (in plug) polo m; Bowling bolo m; US (brooch) broche m; **pins and needles**, hormigueo m. **II** vtr (on board) clavar con chinchetas; (garment etc) sujetar con alfileres; to p. sb against a wall, tener a algn contra una pared; fig to p. one's hopes on sth, poner sus esperanzas en algo; fam to p. a crime on sb, endosar un delito a algn. ◆**pin down** vtr fig to p. sb down, hacer que algn se comprometa.

pinafore ['pɪnəfɔːr] n (apron) delantal m; **p. dress**, pichi m.

pinball ['pɪnbɔːl] n flipper m, máquina f de petacos.

pincers ['pɪnsəz] npl (on crab) pinzas fpl; (tool) tenazas fpl.

pinch [pɪntʃ] **I** n (nip) pellizco m; fig at a p., en caso de apuro; **a p. of salt**, una pizca de sal. **II** vtr pellizcar; fam (steal) birlar. **III** vi (shoes) apretar.

pincushion ['pɪnkʊʃən] n acerico m.

pine¹ [paɪn] n (tree) pino m; **p. cone**, piña f.

pine² [paɪn] vi to p. (away), consumirse, morirse de pena; to p. for sth/sb, añorar algo/a algn.

pineapple ['paɪnæpəl] n piña f.

ping [pɪŋ] n sonido metálico; (of bullet) silbido m.

ping-pong ['pɪŋpɒŋ] n ping-pong m.

pink [pɪŋk] **I** n (colour) rosa m; Bot clavel m. **II** adj (colour) rosa inv; Pol fam rojillo,-a.

pinnacle ['pɪnəkəl] n (of building) pináculo m; (of mountain) cima f, pico m; fig (of success) cumbre f.

pinpoint ['pɪnpɔɪnt] vtr señalar.

pinstripe ['pɪnstraɪp] adj a rayas.

pint [paɪnt] n pinta f; GB fam **a p. (of beer)**, una pinta (de cerveza).

pioneer [paɪə'nɪər] **I** n (settler) pionero,-a m,f; (forerunner) precursor,-a m,f. **II** vtr ser pionero,-a en.

pious ['paɪəs] adj piadoso,-a, devoto,-a; pej beato,-a.

pip¹ [pɪp] n (seed) pepita f.

pip² [pɪp] n (sound) señal f (corta); (on dice) punto m.

pipe [paɪp] **I** n 1 conducto m, tubería f; (of organ) caramillo m; fam **the pipes**, (bagpipes) la gaita. 2 (for smoking) pipa f; **p. cleaner**, limpiapipas m inv; fig **p. dream**, sueño m imposible. **II** vtr (water) llevar por tubería; (oil) transportar por oleoducto; **piped music**, hilo m musical. ◆**pipe down** vi fam callarse. ◆**pipe up** vi fam hacerse oír.

pipeline ['paɪplaɪn] n tubería f, cañería f; (for gas) gasoducto m; (for oil) oleoducto m.

piper ['paɪpər] n gaitero,-a m,f.

piping ['paɪpɪŋ] **I** n (for water, gas etc) tubería f, cañería f. **II** adj **p. hot**, bien caliente.

piquant ['piːkənt] adj picante; fig intrigante.

pique [piːk] **I** n enojo m. **II** vtr herir.

pirate ['paɪrɪt] n pirata m; **p. edition**, edición pirata; **p. radio**, emisora pirata; **p. ship**, barco m pirata.

pirouette [pɪruˈet] **I** n pirueta f. **II** vi hacer piruetas.

Pisces ['paɪsiːz] n Piscis m.

piss [pɪs] sl **I** vi mear. **II** n meada f.

pissed [pɪst] adj GB sl (drunk) borracho,-a.

pistachio [pɪsˈtɑːʃɪəʊ] n (nut) pistacho m.

pistol ['pɪstəl] n pistola f.

piston ['pɪstən] n pistón m.

pit [pɪt] **I** n hoyo m; (large) hoya f; (coal mine) mina f de carbón; Theat platea f; (in motor racing) foso m, box m. **II** vtr to p. one's wits against sb, medirse con algn.

pitch¹ [pɪtʃ] **I** vtr 1 Mus (sound) entonar. 2 (throw) lanzar, arrojar. 3 (tent) armar. **II** vi (ship) cabecear; to p. forward, caerse hacia adelante. **III** n 1 Mus (of sound) tono m 2 Sport campo m, cancha f. 3 (in market etc) puesto m. 4 (throw) lanzamiento m.

pitch² [pɪtʃ] n (tar) brea f, pez f.

pitch-black [pɪtʃˈblæk], **pitch-dark** [pɪtʃˈdɑːk] adj negro,-a como la boca del lobo.

pitched [pɪtʃt] *adj* p. **battle**, batalla *f* campal.

pitcher [ˈpɪtʃər] *n* (*container*) cántaro *m*, jarro *m*.

pitchfork [ˈpɪtʃfɔːk] *n* horca *f*.

piteous [ˈpɪtiəs] *adj* lastimoso,-a.

pitfall [ˈpɪtfɔːl] *n* dificultad *f*, obstáculo *m*.

pith [pɪθ] *n* (*of orange*) piel blanca; *fig* meollo *m*.

pithy [ˈpɪθɪ] *adj* (**pithier, pithiest**) *fig* contundente.

pitiful [ˈpɪtifʊl] *adj* (*producing pity*) lastimoso,-a, (*terrible*) lamentable.

pitiless [ˈpɪtiləs] *adj* despiadado,-a, implacable.

pittance [ˈpɪtəns] *n* miseria *f*.

pity [ˈpɪtɪ] **I** *n* 1 (*compassion*) compasión *f*, piedad *f*; to take p. on sb, compadecerse de algn. 2 (*shame*) lástima *f*, pena *f*; what a p.!, ¡qué pena!, ¡qué lástima! **II** *vtr* compadecerse de; **I p. them**, me dan pena.

pivot [ˈpɪvət] **I** *n* pivote *m*. **II** *vi* girar sobre su eje.

pizza [ˈpiːtsə] *n* pizza *f*; **p. parlour**, pizzería *f*.

placard [ˈplækɑːd] *n* pancarta *f*.

placate [pləˈkeɪt] *vtr* aplacar, apaciguar.

place [pleɪs] **I** *n* 1 sitio *m*, lugar *m*; to be in/out of p., estar en/fuera de su sitio; to take p., tener lugar. 2 (*seat*) sitio *m*; (*on bus*) asiento *m*; (*at university*) plaza *m*; to change places with sb, intercambiar el sitio con algn; to feel out of p., encontrarse fuera de lugar; to take sb's p., sustituir a algn. 3 (*position on scale*) posición *f*; (*social position*) rango *m*; in the first p., en primer lugar; to take first p., ganar el primer lugar. 4 (*house*) casa *f*, (*building*) lugar *m*; we're going to his p., vamos a su casa. **II** *vtr* 1 poner, colocar; to p. a bet, hacer una apuesta; to p. an order with sb, hacer un pedido a algn. 2 (*face, person*) recordar; (*in job*) colocar en un empleo.

placid [ˈplæsɪd] *adj* apacible.

plagiarize [ˈpleɪdʒəraɪz] *vtr* plagiar.

plague [pleɪɡ] **I** *n* (*of insects*) plaga *f*; *Med* peste *f*. **II** *vtr* to p. sb with requests, acosar a algn a peticiones.

plaice [pleɪs] *n inv* (*fish*) platija *f*.

plaid [plæd, pleɪd] *n* (*cloth*) tejido *m* escocés.

plain [pleɪn] **I** *adj* 1 (*clear*) claro,- a, evidente; *fig* **he likes p. speaking**, le gusta hablar con franqueza. 2 (*simple*) sencillo,-a; (*chocolate*) amargo,-a; (*flour*) sin levadura; *in* p. **clothes**, vestido,-a de paisano; the p. **truth**, la verdad lisa y llana. 3 (*unattractive*) poco atractivo,-a. **II** *n Geog* llanura *f*, llano *m*. ◆**plainly** *adv* claramente, (*simply*) sencillamente.

speak p., hablar con franqueza.

plaintiff [ˈpleɪntɪf] *n* demandante *mf*.

plaintive [ˈpleɪntɪv] *adj* lastimero,-a.

plait [plæt] **I** *n* trenza *f*. **II** *vtr* trenzar.

plan [plæn] **I** *n* (*scheme*) plan *m*, proyecto *m*; (*drawing*) plano *m*. **II** *vtr* 1 (*for future*) planear, proyectar; (*economy*) planificar. 2 (*intend*) pensar, tener la intención de; **it wasn't planned**, no estaba previsto. **III** *vi* hacer planes; to p. on doing sth, tener la intención de hacer algo.

plane¹ [pleɪn] *n* 1 *Math* plano *m*; *fig* nivel *m*. 2 *Av fam* avión *m*. **III** *adj Geom* plano,-a **III** *vi* (*glide*) planear.

plane² [pleɪn] *n* (*tool*) cepillo *m*. **II** *vtr* cepillar.

plane³ [pleɪn] *n Bot* p. (**tree**), plátano *m*.

planet [ˈplænɪt] *n* planeta *m*.

plank [plæŋk] *n* tabla *f*, tablón *m*.

planner [ˈplænər] *n* planificador,-a *m,f*.

planning [ˈplænɪŋ] *n* planificación *f*; **family p.**, planificación familiar; **p. permission**, permiso *m* de obras.

plant¹ [plɑːnt] **I** *n* planta *f*. **II** *vtr* (*flowers*) plantar; (*seeds*) sembrar; (*bomb*) colocar.

plant² [plɑːnt] *n* (*factory*) planta *f*, fábrica *f*; (*machinery*) maquinaria *f*.

plantation [plænˈteɪʃən] *n* plantación *f*.

plaque [plæk] *n* placa *f*; (*on teeth*) sarro *m*.

plaster [ˈplɑːstər] **I** *n Constr* yeso *m*; *Med* escayola *f*, *GB* **sticking p.**, esparadrapo *m*, tirita *f*; **p. of Paris**, yeso mate. **II** *vtr Constr* enyesar; *fig* (*cover*) cubrir de.

plastered [ˈplɑːstəd] *adj sl* borracho,-a, trompa.

plasterer [ˈplɑːstərər] *n* yesero,-a *m,f*.

plastic [ˈplæstɪk, ˈplɑːstɪk] **I** *n* plástico *m*. **II** *adj* (*cup, bag*) de plástico; **p. surgery**, cirugía plástica.

Plasticine® [ˈplæstɪsiːn] *n* plastilina *f*.

plate [pleɪt] **I** *n* 1 plato *m*. 2 (*sheet*) placa *f*; **gold p.**, chapa *f* de oro; **p. glass**, vidrio cilindrado. 3 *Print* grabado *m*, lámina *f*. **II** *vtr* chapar.

plateau [ˈplætəʊ] *n* meseta *f*.

platform [ˈplætfɔːm] *n* 1 plataforma *f*; (*stage*) estrado *m*; (*at meeting*) tribuna *f*. 2 *Rail* andén *m*; **p. ticket**, billete *m* de andén. 3 *Pol* (*programme*) programa *m*.

platinum [ˈplætɪnəm] *n* platino *m*.

platitude [ˈplætɪtjuːd] *n* lugar *m* común, tópico *m*.

platoon [pləˈtuːn] *n Mil* pelotón *m*.

platter [ˈplætər] *n* fuente *f*.

plausible [ˈplɔːzəbəl] *adj* plausible.

play [pleɪ] *vtr* 1 (*game*) jugar a. 2 *Sport* (*position*) jugar de; (*team*) jugar contra; to **p. a shot**, (*in golf, tennis*) golpear. 3 (*instrument, tune*) tocar; to **p. a record**, poner un disco. 4 *Theat* (*part*) hacer (el papel de); (*play*) representar; *fig* to **p.** a **part in sth**, participar en algo; *fig* to **p.**

the fool, hacer el tonto. II vi 1 (children) jugar (with, con); (animals) juguetear. 2 Sport jugar; to p. fair, jugar limpio; fig to p. for time, tratar de ganar tiempo. 3 (joke) bromear. 4 Mus tocar; (instrument) sonar. III n 1 Theat obra f de teatro. 2 Sport juego m; fair/foul p., juego limpio/sucio. 3 Tech & fig (movement) juego m; fig to bring sth into p., poner algo en juego; at p., en juego. 4 (of words, un juego de palabras. ◆play around vi (waste time) gandulear; (be unfaithful) tener líos. ◆play down vtr minimizar, quitar importancia a. ◆play on vtr (take advantage of) aprovecharse de; (nerves etc) exacerbar. ◆play up I vtr (annoy) dar la lata, fastidiar. II vi (child etc) dar guerra.
playboy ['pleɪbɔɪ] n playboy m.
player ['pleɪər] n Sport jugador,-a m,f; Mus músico,-a m,f; Theat (man) actor m; (woman) actriz f.
playful ['pleɪful] adj juguetón,-ona.
playground ['pleɪɡraund] n patio m de recreo.
playgroup ['pleɪɡruːp] n jardín m de infancia.
playing ['pleɪɪŋ] n juego m; p. card, carta f, naipe m; p. field, campo m de deportes.
playmate ['pleɪmeɪt] n compañero,-a m,f de juego.
play-off ['pleɪɒf] n Sport partido m de desempate.
playpen ['pleɪpen] n corralito m or parque m (de niños).
playschool ['pleɪskuːl] n jardín m de infancia.
plaything ['pleɪθɪŋ] n juguete m.
playwright ['pleɪraɪt] n dramaturgo,-a m,f.
PLC, plc [piːel'siː] GB abbr of Public Limited Company, Sociedad f Anónima, S.A.
plea [pliː] n 1 (request) petición f, súplica f; (excuse) pretexto m, disculpa f. 2 Jur alegato m.
plead [pliːd] I vtr 1 Jur fig to p. sb's cause, defender la causa de algn. 2 to p. ignorance, (give as excuse) alegar ignorancia. II vi 1 (beg) rogar, suplicar; to p. with sb to do sth, suplicar a algn que haga algo. 2 Jur to p. guilty/not guilty, declararse culpable/inocente.
pleasant ['plezənt] adj agradable.
pleasantry ['plezəntrɪ] n cumplido m.
please [pliːz] I vtr (give pleasure to) agradar, complacer; (satisfy) satisfacer; fam p. yourself, como quieras. II vi complacer; (give satisfaction) satisfacer; easy/hard to p., poco/muy exigente. III adv por favor; may I? - p. do, ¿me permite? - desde luego; 'p. do not smoke', 'se ruega no fumar'; yes, p., sí, por favor.
pleased [pliːzd] adj (happy) contento,-a;

(satisfied) satisfecho,-a; p. to meet you!, ¡encantado,-a!, ¡mucho gusto!; to be p. about sth, alegrarse de algo.
pleasing ['pliːzɪŋ] adj (pleasant) agradable, grato,-a; (satisfactory) satisfactorio,-a.
pleasure ['pleʒər] n placer m; it's a p. to talk to him, da gusto hablar con él; to take great p. in doing sth, disfrutar mucho haciendo algo; with p., con mucho gusto.
pleat [pliːt] I n pliegue m. II vtr hacer pliegues en.
pledge [pledʒ] I n promesa f; (token of love etc) señal f; (guarantee) prenda f. II vtr (promise) prometer; (pawn) empeñar.
plentiful ['plentɪful] adj abundante.
plenty ['plentɪ] n abundancia f; p. of potatoes, muchas patatas; p. of time, tiempo de sobra; we've got p., tenemos de sobra.
pliable ['plaɪəbəl] adj flexible.
pliers ['plaɪəz] npl alicates mpl, tenazas fpl.
plight [plaɪt] n situación f grave.
plimsolls ['plɪmsəlz] npl GB zapatos mpl de tenis.
plinth [plɪnθ] n plinto m.
plod [plɒd] vi andar con paso pesado; fig to p. on, perseverar; fig to p. through a report, estudiar laboriosamente un informe.
plodder ['plɒdər] n trabajador,-a m,f or estudiante mf tenaz.
plonk¹ [plɒŋk] vtr fam dejar caer.
plonk² [plɒŋk] n GB fam (wine) vinazo m.
plot¹ [plɒt] n 1 (conspiracy) complot m. 2 Theat Lit (story) argumento m, trama f. II vtr 1 (course, route) trazar. 2 (scheme) fraguar. III vi conspirar, tramar.
plot² [plɒt] n Agr terreno m; (for building) solar m; vegetable p., campo m de hortalizas.
plough [plau] I n arado m. II vtr arar. III vi fig the car ploughed through the fencing, el coche atravesó la valla; to p. into sth, chocar contra algo; fig to p. through a book, leer un libro con dificultad. ◆plough back vtr (profits) reinvertir.
plow [plau] n US → **plough**.
ploy [plɔɪ] n estratagema f.
pluck [plʌk] I vtr 1 arrancar (out of, de). 2 (flowers) coger. 3 (chicken) desplumar. 4 (guitar) puntear. II n (courage) valor m, ánimo m. ◆pluck up vtr to p. up courage, armarse de valor.
plucky ['plʌkɪ] adj (pluckier, pluckiest) valiente.
plug [plʌɡ] I n 1 (in bath etc) tapón m. 2 Elec enchufe m, clavija f; 2/3 pin p., clavija bipolar/tripolar. II vtr 1 (hole) tapar. 2 fam (publicize) dar publicidad a; (idea etc) hacer hincapié en. ◆plug in vtr &

vi enchufar.

plum [plʌm] *n (fruit)* ciruela *f; fig* a p. job, un chollo.

plumage ['pluːmɪdʒ] *n* plumaje *m*.

plumb [plʌm] *n* plomo *m*; **p. line**, plomada *f*. II *adj* vertical. III *adv* US **p. in the middle**, justo en medio. IV *vtr* **to p. the depths**, tocar fondo.

plumber ['plʌmər] *n* fontanero,-a *m,f*.

plumbing ['plʌmɪŋ] *n (occupation)* fontanería *f; (system)* tuberías *fpl*, cañerías *fpl*.

plume [pluːm] *n* penacho *m*.

plummet ['plʌmɪt] *vi 1 (bird, plane)* caer en picado; *fig (prices)* bajar vertiginosamente; *(morale)* caer a plomo.

plump¹ [plʌmp] *adj (person)* relleno,-a; *(baby)* rechoncho,-a.

plump² [plʌmp] *vi* **to p. for sth**, optar por algo. ◆**plump down** *vtr* dejar caer. ◆**plump up** *vtr (cushions)* ahuecar.

plunder ['plʌndər] I *vtr* saquear. II *n (action)* saqueo *m*, pillaje *m*; *(loot)* botín *m*.

plunge [plʌndʒ] I *vtr (immerse)* sumergir; *(thrust)* arrojar. II *vi (dive)* lanzarse, zambullirse; *fig (fall)* caer, hundirse; *(prices)* desplomarse. III *n (dive)* zambullida *f; fig (fall)* desplome *m*; **to take the p.**, dar el paso decisivo.

plunger ['plʌndʒər] *n Tech* émbolo *m; (for pipes)* desatascador *m*.

pluperfect [pluː'pɜːfɪkt] *n* pluscuamperfecto *m*.

plural ['plʊərəl] *adj & n* plural *(m)*.

plus [plʌs] I *prep* más; **three p. four makes seven**, tres más cuatro hacen siete. II *n Math* signo *m* más; *fig (advantage)* ventaja *f*.

plush [plʌʃ] I *n* felpa *f*. II *adj fam* lujoso,-a.

plutonium [pluː'təʊnɪəm] *n* plutonio *m*.

ply [plaɪ] I *vtr* **to p. one's trade**, ejercer su oficio; **to p. sb with drinks**, no parar de ofrecer copas a algn. II *vi (ship)* ir y venir; **to p. for hire**, ir en busca de clientes.

plywood ['plaɪwʊd] *n* madera contrachapada.

p.m. [piː'em] *abbr of* **post meridiem** *(after noon)*, después del mediodía; **at 2 p.m.**, a las dos de la tarde.

PM [piː'em] *GB fam abbr of* **Prime Minister**.

PMT [piːem'tiː] *fam abbr of* **premenstrual tension**.

pneumatic [njuː'mætɪk] *adj* neumático,-a.

pneumonia [njuː'məʊnɪə] *n* pulmonía *f*.

PO ['piː'əʊ] *abbr of* **Post Office**.

poach¹ [pəʊtʃ] *vtr* 1 **to p. fish/game**, pescar/cazar furtivamente. 2 *fig fam (steal)* birlar.

poach² [pəʊtʃ] *vtr Culin (egg)* escalfar; *(fish)* hervir.

poacher ['pəʊtʃər] *n* pescador/cazador furtivo.

pocket ['pɒkɪt] I *n* 1 bolsillo *m; fig* **to be £10 in/out of p.**, salir ganando/perdiendo 10 libras; **p. money**, dinero *m* de bolsillo. 2 *(of air)* bolsa *f*. 3 *(of resistance)* foco *m*. II *vtr (money)* embolsar.

pocketbook ['pɒkɪtbʊk] *n US* bolso *m*.

pocketknife ['pɒkɪtnaɪf] *n* navaja *f*.

pod [pɒd] *n* vaina *f*.

podgy ['pɒdʒɪ] *adj (podgier, podgiest)* gordinflón,-ona, regordete.

podium ['pəʊdɪəm] *n* podio *m*.

poem ['pəʊɪm] *n* poema *m*.

poet ['pəʊɪt] *n* poeta *mf*.

poetic [pəʊ'etɪk] *adj* poético,-a.

poetry ['pəʊɪtrɪ] *n* poesía *f*.

poignant ['pɔɪnjənt] *adj* conmovedor,-a.

point [pɔɪnt] I *n* 1 *(sharp end)* punta *f*. 2 *(place)* punto *m; fig* **p. of no return**, punto sin retorno. 3 *(quality)* good/bad p., cualidad buena/mala; **weak/strong p.**, punto débil/fuerte. 4 *(moment)* at that p., en aquel momento; **from that p. onwards**, desde entonces; **to be on the p. of doing sth**, estar a punto de hacer algo. 5 *(score)* punto *m*, tanto *m*; **to win on points**, ganar por puntos; **match p.**, *(in tennis)* pelota *f* de match. 6 *(in argument)* punto *m*; **to make one's p.**, insistir en el argumento; **to take your p.**, entiendo lo que quieres decir. 7 *(purpose)* propósito *m*; **I don't see the p.**, no veo el sentido; **that isn't the p.**, no es el caso; **there's no p. in going**, no merece la pena ir; **to come to the p.**, llegar al meollo de la cuestión. 8 *(on scale)* punto *m; (in share index)* entero *m*; **six p. three**, seis coma tres; **it's up to a p.**, hasta cierto punto. 9 *Geog* punta *f*. 10 *power* p., toma *f* de corriente. 11 **points**, *Aut* platinos *mpl; Rail* agujas *fpl*. II *vtr (way etc)* señalar, indicar; **to p. a gun at sb**, apuntar a algn con una pistola. III *vi* señalar, indicar; **to p. at sth/sb**, señalar algo/a algn con el dedo. ◆**point out** *vtr* indicar, señalar; *(mention)* hacer resaltar.

point-blank [pɔɪnt'blæŋk] I *adj* a quemarropa; *(refusal)* rotundo,-a. II *adv (shoot)* a quemarropa; *(refuse)* rotundamente.

pointed ['pɔɪntɪd] *adj (sharp)* puntiagudo,-a; *fig (comment)* intencionado,-a; *(cutting)* mordaz. ◆**pointedly** *adv fig (significantly)* con intención; *(cuttingly)* con mordacidad.

pointer ['pɔɪntər] *n* 1 *(indicator)* indicador *m*, aguja *f; (for map)* puntero *m*. 2 *(dog)* perro *m* de muestra.

pointless ['pɔɪntlɪs] *adj* sin sentido.

poise [pɔɪz] I *n (bearing)* porte *m; (self-assurance)* aplomo *m*. II *vtr fig* **to be poised to do sth**, estar listo,-a para hacer algo.

poison ['pɔɪzən] I *n* veneno *m*. II *vtr* envenenar.

poisoning ['pɔɪzəŋɪŋ] n envenenamiento m; (by food etc) intoxicación f.

poisonous ['pɔɪzənəs] adj (plant, snake) venenoso,-a; (gas) tóxico,-a; fig (rumour) pernicioso,-a.

poke [pəʊk] vtr (with finger or stick) dar con la punta del dedo or del bastón a; to p. one's head out, asomar la cabeza; to p. the fire, atizar el fuego. ◆**poke about, poke around** vi fisgonear, hurgar en. ◆**poke out** vtr (eye) sacar.

poker¹ ['pəʊkər] n (for fire) atizador m.

poker² ['pəʊkər] n Cards póquer m.

poker-faced ['pəʊkəfeɪst] adj fam de cara impasible.

poky ['pəʊkɪ] adj (pokier, pokiest) US fam pej minúsculo,-a; a p. little room, un cuartucho.

Poland ['pəʊlənd] n Polonia.

polar ['pəʊlər] adj polar; p. bear, oso m polar.

Pole [pəʊl] n polaco,-a m,f.

pole¹ [pəʊl] n palo m; p. vault, salto m con pértiga.

pole² [pəʊl] n Geog polo m; fig to be poles apart, ser polos opuestos.

police [pə'liːs] I npl policía f sing; p. car, coche m patrulla; p. constable, policía m; p. force, cuerpo m de policía; p. record, antecedentes mpl penales; p. state, estado m policial; p. station, comisaría f. II vtr vigilar.

policeman [pə'liːsmən] n policía m.

policewoman [pə'liːswʊmən] n (mujer f) policía f.

policy ['pɒlɪsɪ] n Pol política f; (of company) norma f, principio m; Ins póliza f (de seguros).

polio ['pəʊlɪəʊ] n poliomielitis f.

polish ['pɒlɪʃ] I vtr pulir; (furniture) encerar; (shoes) limpiar; (silver) sacar brillo a. II n 1 (for furniture) cera f; (for shoes) betún m; (for nails) esmalte m. 2 (shine) brillo m; fig (refinement) refinamiento m. ◆**polish off** vtr fam (work) despachar; (food) zamparse. ◆**polish up** vtr fig perfeccionar.

Polish ['pəʊlɪʃ] I adj polaco,-a. II n 1 the P., pl los polacos. 2 (language) polaco m.

polished ['pɒlɪʃt] adj fig (manners) refinado,-a; (style) pulido,-a; (performance) impecable.

polite [pə'laɪt] adj educado,-a.

politeness [pə'laɪtnɪs] n educación f.

politic ['pɒlɪtɪk] adj prudente.

political [pə'lɪtɪkəl] adj político,-a.

politician [pɒlɪ'tɪʃən] n político,-a m,f.

politics ['pɒlɪtɪks] n sing política f.

polka ['pɒlkə] n (dance) polca f; p. dot, lunar m.

poll [pəʊl] n 1 votación f; the polls, las elecciones; to go to the polls, acudir a las urnas. 2 (survey) encuesta f; GB p. tax, contribución urbana. II vtr (votes)

obtener.

pollen ['pɒlən] n polen m.

polling ['pəʊlɪŋ] n votación f; p. booth, cabina f electoral; p. station, colegio m electoral.

pollute [pə'luːt] vtr contaminar.

pollution [pə'luːʃən] n contaminación f, polución f; environmental p., contaminación ambiental.

polo ['pəʊləʊ] n Sport polo m; p. neck (sweater), jersey m de cuello vuelto.

polyester [pɒlɪ'estər] n poliéster m.

polymer ['pɒlɪmər] n Chem polímero m.

Polynesia [pɒlɪ'niːzɪə] n Polinesia.

polystyrene [pɒlɪ'staɪriːn] n poliestireno m.

polytechnic [pɒlɪ'teknɪk] n escuela politécnica, politécnico m.

polythene ['pɒlɪθiːn] n polietileno m.

pomegranate ['pɒmɪgrænɪt] n granada f.

pomp [pɒmp] n pompa f.

pompom ['pɒmpɒm], **pompon** ['pɒmpɒn] n borla f, pompón m.

pompous ['pɒmpəs] adj (person) presumido,-a; (speech) rimbombante.

pond [pɒnd] n estanque m.

ponder ['pɒndər] I vtr considerar. II vi to p. over sth, meditar sobre algo.

ponderous ['pɒndərəs] adj pesado,-a.

pong [pɒŋ] n GB fam hedor m.

pontoon¹ [pɒn'tuːn] n Constr pontón m.

pontoon² [pɒn'tuːn] n Cards veintiuna f.

pony ['pəʊnɪ] n poney m.

ponytail ['pəʊnɪteɪl] n cola f de caballo.

poodle ['puːdəl] n caniche m.

poof [pʊf] n GB sl offens marica m.

pool¹ [puːl] n (of water, oil etc) charco m; (pond) estanque m; (in river) pozo m; swimming p., piscina f.

pool² [puːl] n 1 (common fund) fondo m común. 2 typing p., servicio m de mecanografía. 3 US (snooker) billar americano. 4 GB football pools, quinielas fpl. II vtr (funds) reunir; (ideas, resources) juntar.

poor [pʊər, pɔːr] I adj pobre; (quality) malo,-a; fam you p. thing!, ¡pobrecito! II pl npl the p., los pobres.

poorly ['pʊəlɪ, 'pɔːlɪ] I adv (badly) mal. II adj (poorlier, poorliest) (ill) mal, malo,-a.

pop [pɒp] I vtr (burst) hacer reventar; (cork) hacer saltar; vi (burst) reventar; (cork) saltar; fam I'm just popping over to Ian's, voy un momento a casa de Ian. III n 1 (noise) pequeña explosión. 2 fam (drink) gaseosa f. 3 fam (father) papá m. 4 Mus fam música f pop; p. singer, cantante mf pop. ◆**pop in** vi fam entrar un momento, pasar.

popcorn ['pɒpkɔːn] n palomitas fpl.

Pope [pəʊp] n the P., el Papa.

poplar ['pɒplər] n álamo m.

poppy ['pɒpɪ] n amapola f.

populace ['pɒpjʊləs] n (people) pueblo m.

popular ['popjulər] *adj* popular; *(fashionable)* de moda; *(common)* corriente.

popularity [popju'læriti] *n* popularidad *f*.

popularize ['popjularaiz] *vtr* popularizar.

populate ['popjuleit] *vtr* poblar.

population [popju'leifən] *n* población *f*; **the p. explosion**, la explosión demográfica.

porcelain ['pɔːslin] *n* porcelana *f*.

porch [pɔːtʃ] *n* (*of church*) pórtico *m*; (*of house*) porche *m*, entrada *f*; *US* (*veranda*) terraza *f*.

porcupine ['pɔːkjupain] *n* puerco *m* espín.

pore¹ [pɔː] *vi* **to p. over sth**, leer or estudiar algo detenidamente.

pore² [pɔː] *n Anat* poro *m*.

pork [pɔːk] *n* carne *f* de cerdo.

pornography [pɔː'nɒgrəfi] *n* pornografía *f*.

porous ['pɔːrəs] *adj* poroso,-a.

porpoise ['pɔːpəs] *n* marsopa *f*.

porridge ['pɒridʒ] *n* gachas *fpl* de avena.

port¹ [pɔːt] *n* (*harbour*) puerto *m*; **p. of call**, puerto de escala.

port² [pɔːt] *n Naut Av* (*larboard*) babor *m*.

port³ [pɔːt] *n* (*wine*) vino *m* de Oporto, oporto *m*.

portable ['pɔːtəbəl] *adj* portátil.

portent ['pɔːtent] *n fml* augurio *m*, presagio *m*.

porter ['pɔːtər] *n* (*in hotel etc*) portero,-a *m,f*; *Rail* mozo *m* de estación; *US* mozo de los coches-cama.

portfolio [pɔːt'fəuliəu] *n* (*file*) carpeta *f*; (*of artist, politician*) cartera *f*.

porthole ['pɔːthəul] *n* portilla *f*.

portion ['pɔːʃən] *n* (*part, piece*) parte *f*, porción *f*; (*of food*) ración *f*. ◆**portion out** *vtr* repartir.

portly ['pɔːtli] *adj* (*portlier, portliest*) corpulento,-a.

portrait ['pɔːtrit, 'pɔːtreit] *n* retrato *m*.

portray [pɔː'trei] *vtr* (*paint portrait of*) retratar; (*describe*) describir; *Theat* representar.

Portugal ['pɔːtjugəl] *n* Portugal.

Portuguese ['pɔːtju'giːz] I *adj* portugués,-esa. II *n* (*person*) portugués, -esa *m,f*; (*language*) portugués *m*.

pose [pəuz] I *vtr* (*problem*) plantear; (*threat*) representar. II *vi* (*for painting*) posar; *pej* (*behave affectedly*) hacer pose; **to p. as**, hacerse pasar por. III *n* (*stance*) postura *f*; *pej* (*affectation*) pose *f*.

posh [pɒʃ] *GB fam* I *adj* elegante, de lujo; (*person*) presumido,-a; (*accent*) de clase alta.

position [pə'ziʃən] I *n* 1 posición *f*; (*location*) situación *f*; (*rank*) rango *m*; **to be in a p. to do sth**, estar en condiciones de hacer algo. 2 (*opinion*) postura *f*. 3 (*job*) puesto *m*. II *vtr* colocar.

positive ['pɒzitiv] *adj* positivo,-a; (*sign*) favorable; (*proof*) incontrovertible; (*sure*) seguro,-a; *fam* (*absolute*) auténtico,-a.

possess [pə'zes] *vtr* poseer; (*of fear*) apoderarse de.

possessed [pə'zest] *adj* poseído,-a.

possession [pə'zeʃən] *n* posesión *f*; **possessions**, bienes *mpl*.

possessive [pə'zesiv] *adj* posesivo,-a.

possibility [pɒsi'biliti] *n* posibilidad *f*; **possibilities**, (*potential*) potencial *m sing*.

possible ['pɒsibəl] *adj* posible; **as much as p.**, todo lo posible; **as often as p.**, cuanto más mejor; **as soon as p.**, cuanto antes. ◆**possibly** *adv* posiblemente; (*perhaps*) tal vez, quizás; **I can't p. come**, no puedo venir de ninguna manera.

post¹ [pəust] I *n* (*of wood*) poste *m*. II *vtr* (*fix*) fijar.

post² [pəust] I *n* (*job*) puesto *m*; *US* **trading p.**, factoría *f*. II *vtr* enviar.

post³ [pəust] *GB* I *n* (*mail*) correo *m*; **by p.**, por correo; **p. office**, oficina *f* de correos; **P. Office Box**, apartado *m* de correos. II *vtr* (*letter*) echar al correo; **to p. sth to sb**, mandar algo por correo a algn.

postage ['pəustidʒ] *n* franqueo *m*.

postal ['pəustəl] *adj* postal, de correos; **p. order**, giro *m* postal; **p. vote**, voto *m* por correo.

postbox ['pəustbɒks] *n GB* buzón *m*.

postcard ['pəustkɑːd] *n* (tarjeta *f*) postal *f*.

postcode ['pəustkəud] *n GB* código *m* postal.

postdate [pəust'deit] *vtr* poner fecha adelantada a.

poster ['pəustər] *n* póster *m*; (*advertising*) cartel *m*.

posterior [pɒ'stiəriər] I *n hum* trasero *m*, pompis *m*. II *adj* posterior.

posterity [pɒ'steriti] *n* posteridad *f*.

postgraduate [pəust'grædjuit] I *n* posgraduado,-a *m,f*. II *adj* de posgraduado.

posthumous ['pɒstjuməs] *adj* póstumo, -a.

postman ['pəustmən] *n GB* cartero *m*.

postmark ['pəustmɑːk] *n* matasellos *m inv*.

postmaster ['pəustmɑːstər] *n* administrador *m* de correos; **p. general**, director *m* general de correos.

postmortem ['pəust'mɔːtəm] *n* autopsia *f*.

postpone [pəust'pəun, pə'spəun] *vtr* aplazar.

postscript ['pəusskript] *n* posdata *f*.

posture ['pɒstʃər] I *n* postura *f*; (*affected*) pose *f*. II *vi* adoptar una pose.

postwar ['pəustwɔːr] *adj* de la posguerra.

posy ['pəuzi] *n* ramillete *m*.

pot [pɒt] I *n* (*container*) tarro *m*, pote *m*; (*for cooking*) olla *f*; (*for flowers*) maceta *f*;

fam to go to p., irse al traste; **p. shot**, tiro *m* al azar. II *vtr* (*plant*) poner en una maceta.

potassium [pə'tæsɪəm] *n* potasio *m*.

potato [pə'teɪtəʊ] *n* (*pl* **potatoes**) patata *f*.

potent ['pəʊtənt] *adj* potente.

potential [pə'tenʃəl] I *adj* potencial, posible. II *n* potencial *m*. ◆**potentially** *adv* en potencia.

pothole ['pɒthəʊl] *n* Geol cueva *f*; (*in road*) bache *m*.

potholing ['pɒthəʊlɪŋ] *n* GB espeleología *f*.

potion ['pəʊʃən] *n* poción *f*, pócima *f*.

potluck ['pɒt'lʌk] *n fam* **to take p.**, conformarse con lo que haya.

potted ['pɒtɪd] *adj* (*food*) en conserva; (*plant*) en maceta o tiesto.

potter¹ ['pɒtə'] *n* alfarero, -a *m,f*.

potter² ['pɒtə'] *vi* GB **to p. about or around**, entretenerse.

pottery ['pɒtərɪ] *n* (*craft, place*) alfarería *f*; (*objects*) cerámica *f*.

potty¹ ['pɒtɪ] *adj* (**pottier, pottiest**) GB *fam* chiflado,-a.

potty² ['pɒtɪ] *n fam* orinal *m*.

pouch [paʊtʃ] *n* 1 bolsa pequeña; (*for ammunition*) morral *m*; (*for tobacco*) petaca *f*. 2 Zool bolsa *f* abdominal.

poultry ['pəʊltrɪ] *n* (*live*) aves *fpl* de corral; (*food*) pollos *mpl*.

pounce [paʊns] *vi* **to p. on**, abalanzarse encima de.

pound¹ [paʊnd] I *vtr* (*strike*) aporrear. II *vi* (*heart*) palpitar; (*walk heavily*) andar con paso pesado.

pound² [paʊnd] *n* (*money, weight*) libra *f*.

pound³ [paʊnd] *n* (*for dogs*) perrera *f*; (*for cars*) depósito *m* de coches.

pour [pɔːr] I *vtr* echar, verter; **to p. sb a drink**, servirle una copa a algn. II *vi* correr, fluir; **it's pouring with rain**, está lloviendo a cántaros. ◆**pour out** *vtr* echar, verter; *fig* **to p. one's heart out to sb**, desahogarse con algn.

pouring ['pɔːrɪŋ] *adj* (*rain*) torrencial.

pout [paʊt] I *vi* hacer pucheros. II *n* puchero *m*.

poverty ['pɒvətɪ] *n* pobreza *f*.

poverty-stricken ['pɒvətɪstrɪkən] *adj* necesitado,-a; **to be p.-s.**, vivir en la miseria.

powder ['paʊdə'] I *n* polvo *m*; **p. compact**, polvera *f*; **p. keg**, polvorín *m*; **p. puff**, borla *f*; **p. room**, servicios *mpl* de señoras. II *vtr* **to p. one's nose**, ponerse polvos en la cara; *euph* ir a los servicios or al tocador.

powdered ['paʊdəd] *adj* (*milk*) en polvo.

power ['paʊə'] *n* 1 fuerza *f*; (*energy*) energía *f*; Elec **to cut off the p.**, cortar la corriente; **p. point**, enchufe *m*; **p. station**, central eléctrica. 2 (*ability*) poder

m. 3 (*authority*) poder *m*; (*nation*) potencia *f*; (*influence*) influencia *f*; **to be in p.**, estar en el poder; *Pol* **to come into p.**, subir al poder; **the p. of veto**, el derecho de veto. 4 *Tech* potencia *f*; (*output*) rendimiento *m*, impulsar.

powerboat ['paʊəbəʊt] *n* lancha *f* (motora).

powerful ['paʊəfʊl] *adj* (*strong*) fuerte; (*influential*) poderoso,-a; (*remedy*) eficaz; (*engine, machine*) potente; (*emotion*) fuerte; (*speech*) conmovedor,-a.

powerless ['paʊəlɪs] *adj* impotente, ineficaz.

pp *abbr of* **pages**, *n* pp., págs.

PR [piː'ɑːr] *abbr of* **public relations**.

practicable ['præktɪkəbəl] *adj* factible.

practical ['præktɪkəl] *adj* práctico,-a; (*useful*) útil; (*sensible*) adecuado,-a. ◆**practically** *adv* (*almost*) casi.

practicality [præktɪ'kælɪtɪ] *n* (*of suggestion, plan*) factibilidad *f*; **practicalities**, detalles prácticos.

practice ['præktɪs] I *n* 1 (*habit*) costumbre *f*. 2 (*exercise*) práctica *f*; Sport entrenamiento *m*; Mus ensayo *m*; **to be out of p.**, no estar en forma. 3 (*way of doing sth*) práctica *f*; **in p.**, en la práctica; **to put sth into p.**, poner algo en práctica. 4 (*of profession*) ejercicio *m*. 5 (*place*) (*of doctors*) consultorio *m*; (*of lawyers*) bufete *m*. 6 (*clients*) (*of doctors*) pacientes *mpl*; (*of lawyers*) clientela *f*. II *vtr & vi* US = **practise**.

practise ['præktɪs] I *vtr* practicar; (*method*) seguir; (*principle*) poner en práctica; Mus ensayar; (*profession*) ejercer. II *vi* practicar; Sport entrenar; Mus ensayar; (*doctor*) practicar; (*lawyer*) ejercer.

practising, US **practicing** ['præktɪsɪŋ] *adj* (*doctor etc*) en ejercicio; (*Christian etc*) practicante.

practitioner [præk'tɪʃənə'] *n* GB Med **general p.**, médico,-a *m,f* de cabecera; **medical p.**, médico,-a *m,f*.

pragmatic [præg'mætɪk] *adj* pragmático,-a.

prairie ['preərɪ] *n* pradera *f*; US llanura *f*.

praise [preɪz] I *n* alabanza *f*. II *vtr* alabar, elogiar.

praiseworthy ['preɪzwɜːðɪ] *adj* loable.

pram [præm] *n* GB cochecito *m* de niño.

prance [prɑːns] *vi* (*horse*) encabritarse; **to p. about**, (*person*) pegar brincos.

prank [præŋk] *n* broma *f*; (*of child*) travesura *f*.

prawn [prɔːn] *n* gamba *f*.

pray [preɪ] *vi* rezar, orar.

prayer [preə'] *n* rezo *m*, oración *f*; (*entreaty*) súplica *f*; **p. book**, misal *m*.

preach [priːtʃ] *vi* predicar.

preacher ['priːtʃə'] *n* predicador,-a *m,f*.

precarious [prɪ'keərɪəs] *adj* precario,-a.

precaution [prɪ'kɔ:ʃən] *n* precaución *f*.

precede [prɪ'si:d] *vtr* preceder.

precedence ['presɪdəns] *n* preferencia *f*, prioridad *f*; **to take p. over sth/sb**, tener prioridad sobre algo/algn.

precedent ['presɪdənt] *n* precedente *m*.

preceding [prɪ'si:dɪŋ] *adj* precedente.

precinct ['pri:sɪŋkt] *n* recinto *m*; *US (district)* distrito *m*; **pedestrian/shopping p.**, zona *f* peatonal/comercial.

precious ['preʃəs] I *adj* precioso,-a; **p. stones**, piedras preciosas. II *adv fam* **p. little/few**, muy poco/pocos.

precipice ['presɪpɪs] *n* precipicio *m*.

precipitate [prɪ'sɪpɪteɪt] I *vtr* precipitar; *fig* arrojar. II *adj* precipitado,-a.

precise [prɪ'saɪs] *adj* preciso,-a, exacto,-a; *(meticulous)* meticuloso,-a. ◆**precisely** *adv (exactly)* precisamente, exactamente; **p.!**, ¡eso es!, ¡exacto!

precision [prɪ'sɪʒən] *n* precisión *f*.

preclude [prɪ'klu:d] *vtr* excluir; *(misunderstanding)* evitar.

precocious [prɪ'kəʊʃəs] *adj* precoz.

preconceived [pri:kən'si:vd] *adj* preconcebido,-a.

precondition [pri:kən'dɪʃən] *n* condición previa.

precursor [prɪ'kɜ:sər] *n* precursor,-a *m,f*.

predator ['predətər] *n* depredador *m*.

predecessor ['pri:dɪsesər] *n* antecesor,-a *m,f*.

predetermine [pri:dɪ'tɜ:mɪn] *vtr* predeterminar.

predicament [prɪ'dɪkəmənt] *n* apuro *m*, aprieto *m*.

predict [prɪ'dɪkt] *vtr* predecir, pronosticar.

predictable [prɪ'dɪktəbəl] *adj* previsible.

prediction [prɪ'dɪkʃən] *n* pronóstico *m*.

predispose [pri:dɪ'spəʊz] *vtr* **to be predisposed to doing sth**, estar predispuesto,-a a hacer algo.

predominant [prɪ'dɒmɪnənt] *adj* predominante. ◆**predominantly** *adv* en su mayoría.

predominate [prɪ'dɒmɪneɪt] *vi* predominar.

pre-empt [prɪ'empt] *vtr* adelantarse a.

preen [pri:n] *vtr* **to p. oneself**, *(of bird)* arreglarse las plumas; *fig (of person)* pavonearse.

prefab ['pri:fæb] *n GB fam (house)* casa prefabricada.

prefabricated [pri:'fæbrɪkeɪtɪd] *adj* prefabricado,-a.

preface ['prefɪs] I *n* prefacio *m*. II *vtr* prologar.

prefect ['pri:fekt] *n GB Educ* monitor,-a *m,f*.

prefer [prɪ'fɜ:r] *vtr* preferir; **I p. coffee to tea**, prefiero el café al té.

preferable ['prefərəbəl] *adj* preferible

(to, a). ◆**preferably** *adv* preferentemente.

preference ['prefərəns] *n* preferencia *f*; *(priority)* prioridad *f*; **to give p. to sth**, dar prioridad a algo.

preferential [prefə'renʃəl] *adj* preferente.

prefix ['pri:fɪks] *n* prefijo *m*.

pregnancy ['pregnənsɪ] *n* embarazo *m*.

pregnant ['pregnənt] *adj (woman)* embarazada; *(animal)* preñada; *fig* **a p. pause**, una pausa cargada de significado.

prehistoric(al) [pri:hɪ'stɒrɪk(əl)] *adj* prehistórico,-a.

prejudice ['predʒʊdɪs] I *n (bias)* prejuicio *m*; *(harm)* perjuicio *m*. II *vtr (bias)* predisponer; *(harm)* perjudicar.

prejudiced ['predʒʊdɪst] *adj* parcial; **to be p. against/in favour of**, estar predispuesto,-a en contra/a favor de.

preliminary [prɪ'lɪmɪnərɪ] I *adj* preliminar; *Sport (round)* eliminatorio,-a. II *n* **preliminaries**, preliminares *mpl*.

prelude ['prelju:d] *n* preludio *m*.

premarital [pri:'mærɪtəl] *adj* prematrimonial.

premature [premə'tjʊər, 'prematjʊər] *adj* prematuro,-a. ◆**prematurely** *adv* antes de tiempo.

premeditate [prɪ'medɪteɪt] *vtr (crime)* premeditar.

premenstrual [pri:'menstrʊəl] *adj* **p. tension**, tensión *f* premenstrual.

premier ['premjər] I *n Pol* primer,-a ministro,-a *m,f*. II *adj* primer, primero,-a.

premiere ['premɪeər] *n Cin* estreno *m*.

premise ['premɪs] *n* premisa *f*.

premises ['premɪsɪz] *npl* local *m sing*; **on the p.**, en el local.

premium ['pri:mɪəm] *n Com Fin Ind* prima *f*; **to be at a p.**, tener sobreprecio; *fig* estar muy solicitado,-a; *GB* **p. bonds**, bonos cotizados sobre la par.

premonition [premə'nɪʃən] *n* presentimiento *m*.

preoccupied [prɪ'ɒkjʊpaɪd] *adj* preocupado,-a; **to be p. with sth**, preocuparse por algo.

prep [prep] **1** *fam abbr of* **preparation**, deberes *mpl*. **2** *abbr of* **preparatory school**.

prepaid [pri:'peɪd] *adj* con el porte pagado.

preparation [prepə'reɪʃən] *n* preparación *f*; *(plan)* preparativo *m*; *GB Educ (homework)* deberes *mpl*.

preparatory [prɪ'pærətərɪ] *adj* preparatorio,-a, preliminar; **p. school**, escuela primaria privada.

prepare [prɪ'peər] I *vtr* preparar; **to p. to do sth**, prepararse para hacer algo. II *vi* prepararse *(for, para)*.

prepared [prɪ'peəd] *adj (ready)* preparado,-a; **to be p. to do sth**, *(willing)* estar dispuesto,-a a hacer algo.

preponderance [prɪ'pɒndərəns] *n* pre-ponderancia *f*.

preposition [prepə'zɪʃən] *n* preposición *f*.

preposterous [prɪ'pɒstərəs] *adj* absurdo,-a, ridículo,-a.

prerequisite [priː'rekwɪzɪt] *n* condición *f* previa.

prerogative [prɪ'rɒgətɪv] *n* prerrogativa *f*.

preschool [priː'skuːl] *adj* preescolar.

prescribe [prɪ'skraɪb] *vtr* 1 (*set down*) prescribir; *Med* recetar; *fig* (*recommend*) recomendar.

prescription [prɪ'skrɪpʃən] *n Med* receta *f*.

presence ['prezəns] *n* presencia *f*; (*attendance*) asistencia *f*; *fig* p. of mind, presencia de ánimo.

present¹ ['prezənt] **I** *adj* 1 (*in attendance*) presente; *Ling* p. tense, (tiempo *m*) presente *m*; to be p. at estar presente en. 2 (*current*) actual. **II** *n* (*time*) presente *m*, actualidad *f*; at p., actualmente; for the p., de momento; up to the p., hasta ahora. ◆**presently** *adv* (*soon*) dentro de poco; *US* (*now*) ahora.

present² [prɪ'zent] **I** *vtr* 1 (*give as gift*) regalar; (*medals, prizes etc*) entregar; to p. sb with sth, obsequiar a algn con algo. 2 (*report etc*) presentar; (*opportunity*) ofrecer; (*problems*) plantear. 3 (*introduce*) (*person, programme*) presentar. **II** ['prezənt] *n* (*gift*) regalo *m*; (*formal*) obsequio *m*.

presentable [prɪ'zentəbəl] *adj* presentable; to make oneself p., arreglarse.

presentation [prezən'teɪʃən] *n* 1 presentación *f*; p. ceremony, ceremonia *f* de entrega. 2 *Rad TV* representación *f*.

present-day ['prezəntdeɪ] *adj* actual, de hoy en día.

presenter [prɪ'zentə] *n Rad* locutor,-a *m,f*; *TV* presentador,-a *m,f*.

preservation [prezə'veɪʃən] *n* conservación *f*.

preservative [prɪ'zɜːvətɪv] *n* conservante *m*.

preserve [prɪ'zɜːv] **I** *vtr* 1 (*keep*) mantener. 2 *Culin* conservar. **II** *n* 1 (*hunting*) coto *m*. 2 *Culin* conserva *f*.

preside [prɪ'zaɪd] *vi* presidir.

president ['prezɪdənt] *n Pol* presidente,-a *m,f*; *US Com* director,-a *m,f*, gerente *mf*.

presidential [prezɪ'denʃəl] *adj* presidencial.

press [pres] **I** *vtr* 1 apretar; (*button*) pulsar; (*grapes*) pisar; (*trousers etc*) planchar. 2 (*urge*) presionar; to p. sb to do sth, acosar a algn para que haga algo. **II** *vi* 1 (*push*) apretar; to p. against sb/sth, apretarse contra algn/algo; to p. (down) on sth, hacer presión sobre algo. 2 (*urge*) apremiar; time presses, el tiempo apre-

mia. **III** *n* 1 p. stud, botón *m* de presión. 2 (*machine*) prensa *f*; to go to p., entrar en prensa. 3 *Press* prensa *f*; the p., la prensa; to get a good/bad p., tener buena/mala prensa; p. agency, agencia *f* de prensa; p. conference, rueda *f* de prensa; p. cutting, recorte *m* de prensa. ◆**press on** *vi* seguir adelante.

pressed [prest] *adj* to be (hard) p. for, andar escaso,-a de; I'd be hard p. to do it, me costaría mucho hacerlo.

pressing ['presɪŋ] *adj* apremiante, urgente.

pressure ['preʃə] *n Med Meteor* high/low p., altas/bajas presiones; p. cooker, olla *f* a presión; p. gauge, manómetro *m*; *fig* to bring p. (to bear) on sb, ejercer presión sobre algn.

pressurize ['preʃəraɪz] *vtr fig* presionar; pressurized cabin, cabina presurizada.

prestige [pre'stiːʒ] *n* prestigio *m*.

presumably [prɪ'zjuːməblɪ] *adv* es de suponer que.

presume [prɪ'zjuːm] **I** *vtr* suponer, presumir. **II** *vi* (*suppose*) suponer; we p. so/not, suponemos que sí/no.

presumption [prɪ'zʌmpʃən] *n* 1 (*supposition*) suposición *f*. 2 (*boldness*) osadía *f*; (*conceit*) presunción *f*.

presumptuous [prɪ'zʌmptjʊəs] *adj* presuntuoso,-a.

presuppose [priːsə'pəʊz] *vtr* presuponer.

pretence, *US* **pretense** [prɪ'tens] *n* 1 (*deception*) fingimiento *f*; false pretences, estafa *f* sing; under the p. of, so pretexto de. 2 (*claim*) pretensión *f*.

pretend [prɪ'tend] **I** *vtr* (*feign*) fingir, aparentar; (*claim*) pretender. **II** *vi* (*feign*) fingir.

pretense [prɪ'tens] *n US* → pretence.

pretention [prɪ'tenʃən] *n* pretensión *f*.

pretentious [prɪ'tenʃəs] *adj* presuntuoso,-a, pretencioso,-a.

pretext ['priːtekst] *n* pretexto *m*; on the p. of, so pretexto de.

pretty ['prɪtɪ] **I** *adj* (**prettier, prettiest**) bonito,-a, guapo,-a. **II** *adv fam* bastante; p. much the same, más o menos lo mismo.

prevail [prɪ'veɪl] *vi* 1 predominar. 2 (*win through*) prevalecer. 3 to p. upon *or* on sb to do sth, (*persuade*) persuadir o convencer a algn para que haga algo.

prevailing [prɪ'veɪlɪŋ] *adj* (*wind*) predominante; (*opinion*) general; (*condition, fashion*) actual.

prevalent ['prevələnt] *adj* predominante; (*illness*) extendido,-a.

prevaricate [prɪ'værɪkeɪt] *vi* andar con ambages.

prevent [prɪ'vent] *vtr* impedir; (*accident*) evitar; (*illness*) prevenir; to p. sb from doing sth, impedir a algn hacer algo; to p. sth from happening, evitar que pase

algo.
prevention |prɪ'venʃən| n prevención f.
preventive |prɪ'ventɪv| adj preventivo,-a.
preview |'priːvjuː| n (of film etc) preestreno m.
previous |'priːvɪəs| I adj anterior, previo,-a; **p. conviction**, antecedente m penal. II adv **p. to going**, antes de ir. ◆**previously** adv anteriormente, previamente.
prewar |'priːwɔːr| adj de antes de la guerra.
prey |preɪ| I n presa f; fig víctima f. II vi **to p. on**, alimentarse de.
price |praɪs| I n precio m; **what p. is that coat?**, ¿cuánto cuesta el abrigo?; **p. list**, lista f de precios; **p. tag**, etiqueta f. II vtr (put price on) poner un precio a; (value) valorar.
priceless |'praɪslɪs| adj que no tiene precio.
prick |prɪk| I vtr picar; **top. one's finger**, pincharse el dedo; **to p. up one's ears**, aguzar el oído. II n 1 (with pin) pinchazo m. 2 sl (penis) polla f. 3 sl offens (person) gilipollas mf inv.
prickle |'prɪkəl| I n espina f; (spike) pincho m; (sensation) picor m. II vtr & vi pinchar, picar.
prickly |'prɪklɪ| adj (pricklier, prickliest) espinoso,-a; fig (touchy) enojadizo,-a; **p. heat**, sarpullido m por causa del calor; **p. pear**, higo chumbo.
pride |praɪd| I n orgullo m; (arrogance) soberbia f; **to take p. in sth**, enorgullecerse de algo. II vtr **to p. oneself on**, enorgullecerse de.
priest |priːst| n sacerdote m, cura m.
priestess |'priːstɪs| n sacerdotisa f.
priesthood |'priːsthʊd| n (clergy) clero m; (office) sacerdocio m.
prig |prɪg| n gazmoño,-a m,f, mojigato,-a m,f.
prim |prɪm| adj (primmer, primmest) **p. (and proper)**, remilgado,-a.
prim(a)eval |praɪ'miːvəl| adj primitivo,-a.
primary |'praɪmərɪ| I adj fundamental, principal; **of p. importance**, primordial; **p. colour**, color primario; **p. education/school**, enseñanza/escuela primaria. II n US Pol (elección f) primaria f. ◆**primarily** adv ante todo.
primate¹ |'praɪmeɪt| n Rel primado m.
primate² |'praɪmeɪt| n Zool primate m.
prime |praɪm| I adj 1 principal; (major) primordial; **P. Minister**, primer,-a ministro,-a m,f. 2 (first-rate) de primera; **p. number**, número primo. II n **the p. of life** en la flor de la vida. III vtr (pump, engine) cebar; (surface) imprimar; fig (prepare) preparar.
primer¹ |'praɪmər| n (textbook) cartilla f.
primer² |'praɪmər| n (paint) imprimación f.

primitive |'prɪmɪtɪv| adj primitivo,-a; (method, tool) rudimentario,-a.
primrose |'prɪmrəʊz| n primavera f.
Primus® |'praɪməs| n hornillo m de camping.
prince |prɪns| n príncipe m; **P. Charming**, Príncipe Azul.
princess |prɪn'ses| n princesa f.
principal |'prɪnsɪpəl| I adj principal. II n Educ director,-a m,f; Theat (in play) protagonista mf principal.
principle |'prɪnsɪpəl| n principio m; **in p.**, en principio; **on p.**, por principio.
print |prɪnt| I vtr 1 (impress); (publish) publicar; fig grabar; **printed matter**, impresos mpl. 2 (write) escribir con letra de imprenta. II n 1 (of hand, foot) huella f; **Print** letra f; **out of p.**, agotado,-a. 2 Tex estampado m; **p. skirt**, falda estampada. 3 Art grabado m; Phot copia f. ◆**print out** vtr Comput imprimir.
printer |'prɪntər| n (person) impresor,-a m,f; (machine) impresora f.
printing |'prɪntɪŋ| n (industry) imprenta f; (process) impresión f; (print run) tirada f; **p. press**, prensa f.
print-out |'prɪntaʊt| n Comput impresión f; (copy) copia impresa.
prior |'praɪər| adj previo,-a, anterior; **p. to leaving**, antes de salir.
priority |praɪ'ɒrɪtɪ| n prioridad f.
prise |praɪz| vtr **to p. sth open/off**, abrir algo con palanca.
prism |'prɪzəm| n prisma f.
prison |'prɪzən| n cárcel f, prisión f.
prisoner |'prɪzənər| n preso,-a m,f; **to hold sb p.**, detener a algn; **p. of war**, prisionero,-a m,f de guerra.
privacy |'praɪvəsɪ, 'prɪvəsɪ| n intimidad f.
private |'praɪvɪt| I adj privado,-a; (secretary) particular; (matter) personal; (letter) confidencial; **one's p. life**, la vida privada de uno; **'P.'**, (notice) (on road) 'carretera privada'; (on gate) 'propiedad privada'; (on envelope) 'confidencial'; **p. detective**, fam **p. eye**, detective mf privado,-a; **p. school**, escuela privada. II n Mil soldado raso. ◆**privately** adv en privado; (personally) personalmente.
privet |'prɪvɪt| n alheña f.
privilege |'prɪvɪlɪdʒ| n privilegio m.
privileged |'prɪvɪlɪdʒd| adj privilegiado,-a.
privy |'prɪvɪ| I adj GB **P. Council**, Consejo Privado; **to be p. to sth**, estar enterado,-a de algo. II n (lavatory) retrete m.
prize |praɪz| I n premio m. II adj (first-class) de primera (categoría or clase). III vtr (value) apreciar, valorar.
prize-giving |'praɪzgɪvɪŋ| n distribución f de premios.
prizewinner |'praɪzwɪnər| n premiado,-a m,f.

pro¹ [prəʊ] *n* pro *m*; **the pros and cons of an issue,** los pros y los contras de una cuestión.

pro² [prəʊ] *n* (abbr of **professional**) *fam* profesional *mf.*

pro-3 [prəʊ] *pref* (in favour of) pro-.

probability [prɒbə'bɪlɪtɪ] *n* probabilidad *f.*

probable ['prɒbəbəl] *adj* probable.
◆**probably** *adv* probablemente.

probation [prə'beɪʃən] *n* Jur **to be on p.,** estar en libertad condicional; **to be on two months' p.,** (at work) trabajar dos meses de prueba.

probe [prəʊb] **I** *n* Med Astronaut sonda *f*; (investigation) sondeo *m*. **II** *vtr* Med sondar; (investigate) investigar. ◆**probe into** *vtr* investigar.

problem ['prɒbləm] *n* problema *m.*

problematic(al) [prɒblə'mætɪk(əl)] *adj* problemático,-a; **it's p.,** tiene sus problemas.

procedure [prə'siːdʒər] *n* procedimiento *m*; (legal, business) gestión *f*, trámite *m.*

proceed [prə'siːd] *vi* seguir, proceder; **to p. to do sth,** ponerse a hacer algo; **to p. to the next matter,** pasar a la siguiente cuestión.

proceedings [prə'siːdɪŋz] *npl* (of meeting) actas *fpl*; (measures) medidas *fpl*; Jur proceso *m sing.*

proceeds ['prəʊsiːdz] *npl* ganancias *fpl.*

process ['prəʊses] **I** *n* proceso *m*; (method) método *m*, sistema *m*; **in the p. of,** en vías de. **II** *vtr* (information) tramitar; (food) tratar; Comput procesar.

processing ['prəʊsesɪŋ] *n* (of information) evaluación *f*; Comput tratamiento *m.*

procession [prə'seʃən] *n* desfile *m*; Rel procesión *f.*

proclaim [prə'kleɪm] *vtr* proclamar, declarar.

proclamation [prɒklə'meɪʃən] *n* proclamación *f.*

procrastinate [prəʊ'kræstɪneɪt] *vi* dejar las cosas para después.

procure [prə'kjʊər] *vtr* conseguir, procurarse.

prod [prɒd] *vtr* (with stick etc) golpear; (push) empujar.

prodigal ['prɒdɪgəl] *adj* pródigo,-a.

prodigious [prə'dɪdʒəs] *adj* prodigioso,-a.

prodigy ['prɒdɪdʒɪ] *n* prodigio *m.*

produce [prə'djuːs] **I** *vtr* 1 producir; Ind fabricar. 2 Theat dirigir; Rad TV realizar; Cin producir. 3 (give birth to) dar a luz a. 4 (document) enseñar; (bring out) sacar. **II** ['prɒdjuːs] *n* productos *mpl*; **p. of Spain,** producto *m* de España.

producer [prə'djuːsər] *n* 1 productor,-a *m,f*; Ind fabricante *mf*. 2 Theat director, -a *m,f* de escena; Rad TV realizador,-a *m,f*; Cin productor,-a *m,f.*

product ['prɒdʌkt] *n* producto *m.*

production [prə'dʌkʃən] *n* 1 producción *f*; Ind fabricación *f*. 2 Theat representación *f*; Rad TV realización *f*; Cin producción *f*; **p. line,** cadena *f* de montaje.

productive [prə'dʌktɪv] *adj* productivo, -a.

productivity [prɒdʌk'tɪvɪtɪ] *n* productividad *f.*

profane [prə'feɪn] *adj* (secular) profano,-a; (language) blasfemo,-a.

profess [prə'fes] *vtr* (faith) profesar; (opinion) expresar; (claim) pretender.

profession [prə'feʃən] *n* profesión *f.*

professional [prə'feʃənəl] **I** *adj* profesional; (soldier) de profesión; (polished) de gran calidad. **II** *n* profesional *mf.*

professor [prə'fesər] *n* catedrático,-a *m,f.*

proficiency [prə'fɪʃənsɪ] *n* (in language) capacidad *f*; (in skill) pericia *f.*

proficient [prə'fɪʃənt] *adj* (in language) experto,-a; (in skill) hábil.

profile ['prəʊfaɪl] *n* perfil *m*; **in p.,** de perfil.

profit ['prɒfɪt] **I** *n* 1 beneficio *m*, ganancia *f*; **to make a p. on,** sacar beneficios de. 2 *fml* (benefit) provecho *m*. **II** *vi* fig sacar provecho; **to p. from,** aprovecharse de.

profitability [prɒfɪtə'bɪlɪtɪ] *n* rentabilidad *f.*

profitable ['prɒfɪtəbəl] *adj* Com rentable; fig (worthwhile) provechoso,-a.

profiteer [prɒfɪ'tɪər] **I** *n* especulador,-a *m,f*. **II** *vi* obtener beneficios excesivos.

profound [prə'faʊnd] *adj* profundo,-a.

profuse [prə'fjuːs] *adj* profuso,-a, abundante. ◆**profusely** *adv* con profusión; **to sweat p.,** sudar mucho.

profusion [prə'fjuːʒən] *n* profusión *f*, abundancia *f.*

prognosis [prɒg'nəʊsɪs] *n* Med pronóstico *m*; fig (prediction) augurio *m.*

program ['prəʊgræm] Comput **I** *n* programa *m*. **II** *vi* & *vtr* programar.

programme, US **program** ['prəʊgræm] **I** *n* programa *m*; (plan) plan *m*. **II** *vtr* 1 (plan) planear, planificar. 2 (computer) programar.

programmer, US **programer** ['prəʊgræmər] *n* programador,-a *m,f.*

progress ['prəʊgres] **I** *n* progreso *m*; (development) desarrollo *m*; Med mejora *f*; **to make p.,** hacer progresos; **in p.,** en curso. **II** [prəʊ'gres] *vi* avanzar; (develop) desarrollar; (improve) hacer progresos; Med mejorar.

progressive [prə'gresɪv] *adj* (increasing) progresivo,-a; Pol progresista. ◆**progressively** *adv* progresivamente.

prohibit [prə'hɪbɪt] *vtr* prohibir; **to p. sb from doing sth,** prohibir a algn hacer algo.

prohibitive [prə'hɪbɪtɪv] *adj* prohibitivo, -a.

project ['prɒdʒekt] **I** *n* proyecto *m*; (plan)

plan *m; Educ* trabajo *m.* II [prə'dʒekt] *vtr* proyectar, planear. III *vi* (*stick out*) sobresalir.

projectile [prə'dʒektaɪl] *n fml* (*overhang*) proyectil *m.*

projection [prə'dʒekʃən] *n* 1 (*overhang*) saliente *m.* 2 *Cin* proyección *f.* 3 (*forecast*) proyección *f.*

projector [prə'dʒektər] *n Cin* proyector *m.*

proletariat [prəʊlɪ'eərɪət] *n* proletariado *m.*

prolific [prə'lɪfɪk] *adj* prolífico,-a.

prologue ['prəʊlɒg] *n* prólogo *m.*

prolong [prə'lɒŋ] *vtr* prolongar.

prom [prɒm] *n* (*abbr of promenade*) *GB fam* (*seafront*) paseo marítimo; (*concert*) concierto sinfónico en que parte del público está de pie.

promenade [prɒmə'nɑːd] I *n* (*at seaside*) paseo marítimo. II *vi* pasearse.

prominence ['prɒmɪnəns] *n* prominencia *f;* *fig* (*importance*) importancia *f.*

prominent ['prɒmɪnənt] *adj* (*standing out*) saliente; *fig* (*important*) importante; (*famous*) eminente.

promiscuous [prə'mɪskjʊəs] *adj* promiscuo,-a.

promise ['prɒmɪs] I *n* promesa *f;* **to show p.**, ser prometedor,-a. II *vtr & vi* prometer.

promising ['prɒmɪsɪŋ] *adj* prometedor,-a.

promontory ['prɒməntərɪ] *n* promontorio *m.*

promote [prə'məʊt] *vtr* ascender; (*product*) promocionar; (*ideas*) fomentar; *Ftb* **they've been promoted**, han subido.

promoter [prə'məʊtər] *n* promotor,-a *m,f.*

promotion [prə'məʊʃən] *n* (*in rank*) promoción *f*, ascenso *m;* (*of product*) promoción *f;* (*of arts etc*) fomento *m.*

prompt [prɒmpt] I *adj* (*quick*) rápido,-a; (*punctual*) puntual. II *adv* **at 2 o'clock p.**, a las 2 en punto. III *vtr* 1 (*motivate*) incitar; **to p. sb to do sth**, instar a algn a hacer algo. 2 (*actor*) apuntar. ◆**promptly** *adv* (*quickly*) rápidamente; (*punctually*) puntualmente.

prone [prəʊn] *adj* 1 **to be p. to do sth**, ser propenso,-a a hacer algo. 2 *fml* (*face down*) prono,-a.

prong [prɒŋ] *n* punta *f*, diente *m.*

pronoun ['prəʊnaʊn] *n* pronombre *m.*

pronounce [prə'naʊns] I *vtr* pronunciar; *fml* (*declare*) declarar. II *vi fml* **to p. on sth**, opinar sobre algo.

pronounced [prə'naʊnst] *adj* pronunciado,-a.

pronouncement [prə'naʊnsmənt] *n fml* declaración *f.*

pronunciation [prənʌnsɪ'eɪʃən] *n* pronunciación *f.*

proof [pruːf] I *n* prueba *f.* II *adj* 1 (*secure*) a prueba de. 2 **this rum is 70% p.**, este ron tiene 70 grados. III *vtr* impermeabilizar.

prop[1] [prɒp] I *n* (*support*) puntal *m;* *fig* sostén *m.* II *vtr* (*support*) apoyar; *fig* sostener. ◆**prop up** *vtr* apoyar.

prop[2] [prɒp] *n Theat fam* accesorio *m.*

propaganda [prɒpə'gændə] *n* propaganda *f.*

propel [prə'pel] *vtr* propulsar.

propeller [prə'pelər] *n* hélice *f.*

propelling pencil [prəpelɪŋ'pensəl] *n* portaminas *m inv.*

propensity [prə'pensɪtɪ] *n fml* propensión *f.*

proper ['prɒpər] *adj* 1 adecuado,-a, correcto,-a; **the p. time**, el momento oportuno. 2 (*real*) real, auténtico,-a; (*actual, exact*) propiamente dicho,-a. 3 (*characteristic*) propio,-a; *Ling* **p. noun**, nombre propio. ◆**properly** *adv* (*suitably, correctly, decently*) correctamente; **it wasn't p. closed**, no estaba bien cerrado,-a; **she refused, quite p.**, se negó, y con razón.

property ['prɒpətɪ] *n* 1 (*quality*) propiedad *f.* 2 (*possession*) propiedad *f*, posesión *f;* **personal p.**, bienes *mpl;* **public p.**, dominio público. 3 (*estate*) finca *f.*

prophecy ['prɒfɪsɪ] *n* profecía *f.*

prophesy ['prɒfɪsaɪ] *vtr* (*predict*) predecir; *Rel* profetizar.

prophet ['prɒfɪt] *n* profeta *mf.*

proportion [prə'pɔːʃən] *n* proporción *f;* (*part, quantity*) parte *f;* **in p. to** or **with**, en proporción a.

proportional [prə'pɔːʃənəl] *adj* proporcional (**to**, a); *Pol* **p. representation**, representación *f* proporcional.

proportionate [prə'pɔːʃənɪt] *adj* proporcional.

proposal [prə'pəʊzəl] *n* propuesta *f;* (*suggestion*) sugerencia *f;* **p. of marriage**, propuesta de matrimonio.

propose [prə'pəʊz] I *vtr* proponer; (*suggest*) sugerir; *fml* (*intend*) tener la intención de. II *vi* declararse.

proposition [prɒpə'zɪʃən] *n* propuesta *f;* *Math* proposición *f.*

proprietor [prə'praɪətər] *n* propietario,-a *m,f.*

propriety [prə'praɪətɪ] *n* (*decency*) decoro *m.*

propulsion [prə'pʌlʃən] *n* propulsión *f.*

prosaic [prə'zeɪɪk] *adj* prosaico,-a.

prose [prəʊz] *n Lit* prosa *f;* *Educ* texto *m* para traducir.

prosecute ['prɒsɪkjuːt] *vtr* procesar.

prosecution [prɒsɪ'kjuːʃən] *n* (*action*) proceso *m*, juicio *m;* **the p.**, la acusación.

prosecutor ['prɒsɪkjuːtər] *n* acusador,-a *m,f.*

prospect ['prɒspekt] I *n* (*outlook*) perspectiva *f;* (*hope*) esperanza *f;* **the job has**

prospects, es un trabajo con porvenir. II [prə'spekt] *vtr* explorar. III *vi* to p. for gold/oil, buscar oro/petróleo.

prospective [prə'spektɪv] *adj (future)* futuro,-a; *(possible)* eventual, probable.

prospector [prə'spektər] *n* gold p., buscador,-a *m,f* del oro.

prospectus [prə'spektəs] *n* prospecto m.

prosper ['prɒspər] *vi* prosperar.

prosperity [prɒ'sperɪtɪ] *n* prosperidad f.

prosperous ['prɒspərəs] *adj* próspero,-a.

prostitute ['prɒstɪtjuːt] *n* prostituta f.

prostitution [prɒstɪ'tjuːʃn] *n* prostitución f.

prostrate ['prɒstreɪt] *adj (face down)* boca abajo; p. with grief, deshecho de dolor.

protagonist [prə'tægənɪst] *n* protagonista mf.

protect [prə'tekt] *vtr* proteger; *(interests etc)* salvaguardar; **to p. sb from sth,** proteger a algn de algo.

protection [prə'tekʃən] *n* protección f.

protective [prə'tektɪv] *adj* protector,-a.

protégé(e) ['prɒtəʒeɪ] *n* protegido,-a m,f.

protein ['prəʊtiːn] *n* proteína f.

protest ['prəʊtest] I *n* protesta f; *(complaint)* queja f. II [prə'test] *vtr* protestar de. III *vi GB* protestar.

Protestant ['prɒtɪstənt] *adj & n* protestante (mf).

protester [prə'testər] *n* manifestante mf.

protocol ['prəʊtəkɒl] *n* protocolo m.

prototype ['prəʊtətaɪp] *n* prototipo m.

protracted [prə'træktɪd] *adj* prolongado,-a.

protrude [prə'truːd] *vi fml* sobresalir.

protuberance [prə'tjuːbərəns] *n fml* protuberancia f.

proud [praʊd] *adj* orgulloso,-a; *(arrogant)* soberbio,-a.

prove [pruːv] I *vtr* I probar, demostrar; Math comprobar; **to p. oneself,** dar pruebas de valor. 2 it proved to be disastrous, *(turned out)* resultó ser desastroso,-a.

proverb ['prɒvɜːb] *n* refrán m, proverbio m.

provide [prə'vaɪd] I *vtr* proporcionar, *(supplies)* suministrar, proveer. II *vi* proveer; **to p. for sb,** mantener a algn.

provided [prə'vaɪdɪd] *conj* p. (that), con tal de que.

providing [prə'vaɪdɪŋ] *conj* → provided.

province ['prɒvɪns] *n* provincia f; *fig (field of knowledge)* campo m.

provincial [prə'vɪnʃəl] I *adj* provincial; *pej* provinciano,-a. II *n pej (person)* provinciano,-a m,f.

provision [prə'vɪʒən] *n* provisión f; *(supply)* suministro m; **provisions,** *(food)* provisiones fpl, víveres mpl.

provisional [prə'vɪʒənəl] *adj* provisional.

proviso [prə'vaɪzəʊ] *n* with the p. that, a

condición de que.

provocation [prɒvə'keɪʃən] *n* provocación f.

provocative [prə'vɒkətɪv] *adj* provocador,-a; *(flirtatious)* provocativo,-a.

provoke [prə'vəʊk] *vtr* provocar.

prow [praʊ] *n* proa f.

prowess ['praʊɪs] *n* destreza f.

prowl [praʊl] I *n* merodeo m; **to be on the p.,** merodear, rondar. II *vi* merodear; *fam* **to p. about** *or* **around,** rondar.

prowler ['praʊlər] *n fam* merodeador m.

proximity [prɒk'sɪmɪtɪ] *n* proximidad f; **in p. to,** in the p. of, cerca de.

proxy ['prɒksɪ] *n Jur (power)* poderes mpl; *(person)* apoderado,-a m,f; **by p.,** por poderes.

prudence ['pruːdəns] *n* prudencia f.

prudent ['pruːdənt] *adj* prudente.

prudish ['pruːdɪʃ] *adj* remilgado,-a.

prune[1] [pruːn] *n* ciruela pasa.

prune[2] [pruːn] *vtr (roses etc)* podar; *fig* acortar.

pry [praɪ] *vi* curiosear, husmear; **to p. into sb's affairs,** meterse en asuntos ajenos.

PS, ps [piː'es] *abbr of (postscript),* P.S., P.D.

psalm [sɑːm] *n* salmo m.

pseudo- ['sjuːdəʊ] *pref* pseudo-, seudo-.

pseudonym ['sjuːdənɪm] *n* (p)seudónimo m.

psyche ['saɪkɪ] *n* psique f.

psychiatric [saɪkɪ'ætrɪk] *adj* psiquiátrico,-a.

psychiatrist [saɪ'kaɪətrɪst] *n* psiquiatra mf.

psychiatry [saɪ'kaɪətrɪ] *n* psiquiatría f.

psychic ['saɪkɪk] I *adj* psíquico,-a. II *n* médium mf.

psychoanalysis [saɪkəʊə'nælɪsɪs] *n* psicoanálisis f.

psychoanalyst [saɪkəʊ'ænəlɪst] *n* psicoanalista mf.

psychological [saɪkə'lɒdʒɪkəl] *adj* psicológico,-a.

psychologist [saɪ'kɒlədʒɪst] *n* psicólogo,-a m,f.

psychology [saɪ'kɒlədʒɪ] *n* psicología f.

psychopath ['saɪkəʊpæθ] *n* psicópata mf.

PTO, pto [piːtiː'əʊ] *abbr of* please turn over, sigue.

pub [pʌb] *n GB fam* bar m, pub m.

puberty ['pjuːbətɪ] *n* pubertad f.

pubic ['pjuːbɪk] *adj* púbico,-a.

public ['pʌblɪk] I *adj* público,-a; **to make sth p.,** hacer público algo; p. company, empresa pública; p. convenience, servicios mpl, aseos mpl; p. holiday, fiesta f nacional; p. house, pub m, taberna f; p. opinion, opinión pública; p. relations, relaciones públicas; GB p. school, colegio privado; p. transport, transporte público. II *n* the p., el público; **in p.,** en público.

public-address system [pʌblɪkə'dres sɪstəm] n megafonía f.

publican [pʌblɪkan] n tabernero,-a m,f.

publication [pʌblɪ'keɪʃən] n publicación f.

publicity [pʌ'blɪsɪt] n publicidad f.

publicize [pʌblɪsaɪz] vtr (make public) hacer público,-a; (advertise) hacer publicidad a.

public-spirited [pʌblɪk'spɪrɪtɪd] adj de espíritu cívico.

publish [pʌblɪʃ] vtr publicar, editar.

publisher [pʌblɪʃə] n (person) editor,-a m,f; (firm) (casa f) editorial f.

publishing [pʌblɪʃɪŋ] n (business) industria f editorial; **p. company** or **house**, casa f editorial.

pucker [pʌkə] vtr (lips, brow) fruncir, arrugar.

pudding [pudɪŋ] n Culin pudín m; (dessert) postre m; **Christmas p.**, pudín a base de frutos secos típico de Navidad; **p. basin**, cuenco m; **steamed p.**, budín m.

puddle [pʌdəl] n charco m.

puff [pʌf] I n (of wind) racha f; (of smoke) bocanada f; **p. pastry**, pasta f de hojaldre. II vi (person) jadear, resoplar; (train) echar humo; **to p. on one's pipe**, chupar la pipa. III vtr (cigarette) dar una calada a. ◆**puff up** vi hincharse.

puffy [pʌfɪ] adj (puffier, puffiest) hinchado,-a.

pugnacious [pʌg'neɪʃəs] adj belicoso,-a.

pull [pul] I n **1 to give sth a p.**, (tug) dar un tirón a algo. **2** (of engine) tracción f; fig (attraction) atracción f; (influence) enchufe m. II vtr **1** (tug) dar un tirón a; **to p. a muscle**, sufrir un tirón en un músculo; **to p. the trigger**, apretar el gatillo; **to p. to pieces**, hacer pedazos; **to p.** poner algo por los suelos; fig **to p. sb's leg**, tomar el pelo a algn. **2** (draw) tirar, arrastrar; fig **to p. one's weight**, hacer su parte del trabajo. **3** (draw out) sacar. **4** fam (people) atraer. III vi (drag) tirar; **to p. alongside sb**, acercarse a algn. ◆**pull apart** vtr desmontar; fig (criticize) poner por los suelos. ◆**pull down** vtr (building) derribar. ◆**pull in I** vtr (crowds) atraer. II vi (train) entrar en la estación; (stop) parar. ◆**pull off I** vtr fam (carry out) llevar a cabo. II vi (vehicle) arrancar. ◆**pull out I** vtr (withdraw) retirar. II vi Aut **to p. out to overtake**, salir para adelantar. ◆**pull over** vi hacerse a un lado. ◆**pull through** vi reponerse, restablecerse. ◆**pull together** vtr **to p. oneself together**, calmarse. ◆**pull up I** vtr **1** (uproot) desarraigar; fig **to p. up one's socks**, subirse los calcetines; fig espabilarse. **2** (chair) acercar. II vi (stop) pararse.

pulley [pulɪ] n polea f.

pullover [pʊləʊvə] n jersey m.

pulp [pʌlp] I n (of paper, wood) pasta f; (of fruit) pulpa f; fam fig (book etc) basura f. II vtr reducir a pulpa.

pulpit [pʊlpɪt] n púlpito m.

pulsate [pʌl'seɪt] vi vibrar, palpitar.

pulse¹ [pʌls] n Anat pulso m.

pulse² [pʌls] n Bot Culin legumbre f.

pumice (stone) [pʌmɪs(stəʊn)] n piedra f pómez.

pummel [pʌməl] vtr aporrear.

pump¹ [pʌmp] I n bomba f. II vtr bombear; **to p. sth in/out**, meter/sacar algo con una bomba; fam fig **to p. sb for information**, sonsacar información a algn. ◆**pump out** vtr (empty) vaciar. ◆**pump up** vtr (tyre) inflar.

pump² [pʌmp] n (shoe) zapatilla f.

pumpkin [pʌmpkɪn] n calabaza f.

pun [pʌn] n juego m de palabras.

punch¹ [pʌntʃ] I n (for making holes) perforadora f; (for tickets) taladradora f; (in leather etc) punzón m. II vtr (make hole in) perforar; (in ticket) picar; (in leather) punzar.

punch² [pʌntʃ] I n (blow) puñetazo m; (in boxing) pegada f; fig **it lacks p.**, le falta fuerza; **p. line**, remate m (de un chiste). II vtr (with fist) dar un puñetazo a.

punch³ [pʌntʃ] n (drink) ponche m.

punch-up [pʌntʃʌp] n fam pelea f.

punctual [pʌŋktjʊəl] adj puntual.

punctuate [pʌŋktjʊeɪt] vtr puntuar; fig salpicar.

punctuation [pʌŋktjʊ'eɪʃən] n puntuación f.

puncture [pʌŋktʃə] I n pinchazo m. II vtr (tyre) pinchar.

pundit [pʌndɪt] n fam experto,-a m,f.

pungent [pʌndʒənt] adj (smell) acre; (taste) fuerte.

punish [pʌnɪʃ] vtr castigar.

punishable [pʌnɪʃəbəl] adj castigable, punible.

punishment [pʌnɪʃmənt] n castigo m.

punk [pʌŋk] n fam **1** punk mf; **p. music**, música f punk. **2** US mamón m.

punt [pʌnt] I n (boat) batea f. II vi ir en batea.

punter [pʌntə] n GB (gambler) jugador,-a m,f; (customer) cliente,-a m,f.

puny [pju:nɪ] adj (punier, puniest) enclenque, endeble.

pup [pʌp] n cachorro,-a m,f.

pupil¹ [pju:pɪl] n Educ alumno,-a m,f.

pupil² [pju:pɪl] n Anat pupila f.

puppet [pʌpɪt] n títere m.

puppy [pʌpɪ] n cachorro,-a m,f, perrito m.

purchase [pɜːtʃɪs] I n compra f. II vtr comprar; **purchasing power**, poder adquisitivo.

purchaser ['pɜːtʃɪsər] n comprador,-a m,f.

pure [pjuər] adj puro,-a. ◆**purely** adv simplemente.

purée ['pjuəreɪ] n puré m.

purge [pɜːdʒ] I n purga f. II vtr purgar.

purify ['pjuərɪfaɪ] vtr purificar.

purl [pɜːl] vtr (in knitting) hacer punto del revés.

purple ['pɜːpəl] adj morado,-a, purpúreo,-a; **to go p. (in the face)**, ponerse morado,-a.

purport [pɜːˈpɔːt] vi fml pretender; **to p. to be sth**, pretender ser algo.

purpose ['pɜːpəs] n 1 propósito m, intención f; **on p.**, a propósito. 2 (use) utilidad f.

purposeful ['pɜːpəsful] adj (resolute) decidido,-a, resoluto,-a.

purr [pɜːr] vi (cat) ronronear; (engine) zumbar.

purse [pɜːs] I n GB monedero m; US (bag) bolso m; (prize money) premio m en metálico f. II vtr **to p. one's lips**, apretarse los labios.

purser ['pɜːsər] n contador,-a m,f.

pursue [pəˈsjuː] vtr (criminal) perseguir; (person) seguir; (pleasure) buscar; (career) ejercer.

pursuer [pəˈsjuːər] n fml perseguidor,-a m,f.

pursuit [pəˈsjuːt] n (of criminal) persecución f; (of animal) caza f; (of pleasure) búsqueda f; (pastime) pasatiempo m.

purveyor [pəˈveɪər] n fml proveedor,-a m,f.

pus [pʌs] n pus m.

push [puʃ] I n empujón m; fig (drive) brío m, dinamismo m. II vtr 1 empujar; (button) pulsar, apretar; **to p. one's finger into a hole**, meter el dedo en un agujero. 2 fig (pressurize) instar; (harass) acosar; fam **to be (hard) pushed for time**, andar justo,-a de tiempo. 3 fam (product) promover; **to p. drugs**, pasar droga. III vi empujar. ◆**push aside** vtr (object) apartar. ◆**push in** vi colarse. ◆**push off** vi (in boat) desatracar; fam **p. off!**, ¡lárgate! ◆**push on** vi (continue) seguir adelante. ◆**push through** vtr abrirse paso entre.

pushchair ['puʃtʃeər] n GB sillita f (de ruedas).

pusher ['puʃər] n sl (of drugs) camello m.

pushover ['puʃəuvər] n fam **it's a p.**, está chupado; **she's a p.**, es un ligue fácil.

push-up ['puʃʌp] n Gymn flexión f (de brazos).

pushy ['puʃɪ] adj (pushier, pushiest) fam agresivo,-a.

puss [pus], **pussy** ['pusɪ] n fam minino m.

put [put] I vtr (pt & pp **put**) 1 poner; (place) colocar; (insert) meter; to

bed, acostar a; **to p. a picture up on the wall**, colgar un cuadro en la pared; **to p. a stop to sth**, poner término a algo; fig **to p. one's foot in it**, meter la pata. 2 (present) presentar, exponer; **to p. a question to sb**, hacer una pregunta a algn. 3 (express) expresar, decir; **to p. it mildly**, y me quedo corto; **to p. sth simply**, explicar algo de manera sencilla. 4 (estimate) calcular. 5 (money) ingresar; (invest) invertir. II vi Naut **to p. to sea**, zarpar.

III adv **to stay p.**, quedarse quieto,-a. ◆**put about** vtr (rumour) hacer correr. ◆**put across** vtr (idea etc) comunicar. ◆**put aside** vtr (money) ahorrar; (time) reservar. ◆**put away** vtr (tidy away) recoger; fam (eat) zamparse; (save money) ahorrar. ◆**put back** vtr (postpone) aplazar; **to p. the clock back**, retrasar la hora. ◆**put by** vtr (money) ahorrar. ◆**put down** vtr (set down) dejar; (suppress) sofocar; (humiliate) humillar; (criticize) criticar; (animal) provocar la muerte de; (write down) apuntar. ◆**put down to** vtr achacar a. ◆**put forward** vtr (theory) exponer; (proposal) hacer; **to p. one's name forward for sth**, presentarse como candidato,-a para algo. ◆**put in** I vtr (install) instalar; (complaint, request) presentar; (time) pasar. II vi Naut hacer escala (at, en). ◆**put off** vtr (postpone) aplazar; **to p. sb off (doing) sth**, disuadir a algn de (hacer) algo. ◆**put on** vtr (clothes) poner, ponerse; (show) montar; (concert) dar; (switch on) (radio) poner; (light) encender; (water, gas) abrir; **to p. on weight**, aumentar de peso; **to p. on the brakes**, frenar; fig **to p. on a straight face**, poner cara de serio,-a. ◆**put out** vtr (light, fire) apagar; (place outside) sacar; (extend) (arm) extender; (tongue) sacar; (hand) tender; (spread) (rumour) hacer correr; (annoy) molestar; (inconvenience) incordiar; (anger) **to be p. out by sth**, enojarse por algo. ◆**put through** vtr Tel **p. me through to Pat, please**, póngame con Pat, por favor. ◆**put together** vtr (join) unir, reunir; (assemble) armar, montar. ◆**put up** vtr (raise) levantar, subir; (picture) colocar; (curtains) colgar; (building) construir; (tent) armar; (prices) subir, aumentar; (accommodate) alojar, hospedar; **to p. up a fight**, ofrecer resistencia. ◆**put up to** vtr **to p. sb up to sth**, incitar a algn a hacer algo. ◆**put up with** vtr aguantar, soportar.

putrid ['pjuːtrɪd] adj fml putrefacto,-a.

putt [pʌt] I n tiro m al hoyo. II vtr & vi tirar al hoyo.

putting ['pʌtɪŋ] n **p. green**, minigolf m.

putty ['pʌtɪ] n masilla f.

puzzle ['pʌzəl] I n rompecabezas m inv;

(*crossword*) crucigrama *m*; *fig* (*mystery*) misterio *m*. **II** *vtr* dejar perplejo,-a; **to be puzzled about sth**, no entender algo.
◆**puzzle over** *vtr* **to p. over sth**, dar vueltas a algo (en la cabeza).

puzzling ['pʌzəlɪŋ] *adj* extraño,-a, curioso,-a.

pygmy ['pɪgmɪ] *n* pigmeo,-a *m,f*; *fig* enano,-a *m,f*.

pyjamas [pə'dʒɑːməz] *npl* pijama *m sing*.

pylon ['paɪlən] *n* torre *f* (de conducción eléctrica).

pyramid ['pɪrəmɪd] *n* pirámide *f*.

Pyrenees [pɪrə'niːz] *npl* the P., los Pirineos.

Pyrex® ['paɪreks] *n* pírex® *m*.

python ['paɪθən] *n* pitón *m*.

Q

Q, q [kjuː] *n* (*the letter*) Q, q *f*.

quack [kwæk] **I** *n* **1** (*of duck*) graznido *m*. **2** *fam* (*doctor*) curandero,-a *m,f*. **II** *vi* graznar.

quad [kwɒd] *n fam* **1** *GB* (*of school, university*) patio *m* interior. **2** (*quadruplet*) cuatrillizo,-a *m,f*.

quadrangle ['kwɒdræŋgəl] *n* **1** *Geom* cuadrángulo *m*. **2** (*courtyard*) patio *m* interior.

quadruple ['kwɒdrupəl, kwɒ'druːpəl] **I** *n* cuádruplo *m*. **II** *adj* cuádruple. **III** *vtr* cuadruplicar. **IV** *vi* cuadruplicarse.

quadruplet ['kwɒdruplɪt, kwɒ'druːplɪt] *n* cuatrillizo,-a *m,f*.

quagmire ['kwægmaɪəʳ, 'kwɒgmaɪəʳ] *n* (*land*) cenagal *m*.

quail¹ [kweɪl] *n Orn* codorniz *f*.

quail² [kweɪl] *vi fig* encogerse.

quaint [kweɪnt] *adj* (*picturesque*) pintoresco,-a; (*original*) singular.

quake [kweɪk] **I** *vi* temblar. **II** *n fam* temblor *m* de tierra.

Quaker ['kweɪkəʳ] *n* cuáquero,-a *m,f*.

qualification [kwɒlɪfɪ'keɪʃən] *n* **1** (*ability*) aptitud *f*. **2** (*requirement*) requisito *m*. **3** (*diploma etc*) título *m*. **4** (*reservation*) reserva *f*.

qualified ['kwɒlɪfaɪd] *adj* **1** capacitado,-a; **q. teacher**, profesor titulado. **2** *ap-proval*, (*modified*) aprobación condicional.

qualify ['kwɒlɪfaɪ] **I** *vtr* **1** (*entitle*) capacitar. **2** (*modify*) modificar; (*statement*) matizar; *Ling* calificar. **II** *vi* **1** **to q. as**, (*doctor etc*) sacar el título de; **when did you q.?**, ¿cuándo terminaste la carrera? **2** (*in competition*) quedar clasificado,-a.

qualifying ['kwɒlɪfaɪɪŋ] *adj* (*round, exam*) eliminatorio,-a.

quality ['kwɒlɪtɪ] *n* **1** (*excellence*) calidad *f*; **q. control**, control *m* de calidad; **q. newspapers**, prensa *f* no sensacionalista. **2** (*attribute*) cualidad *f*.

qualm [kwɑːm] *n* **1** (*scruple*) escrúpulo *m*. **2** (*doubt*) duda *f*.

quandary ['kwɒndərɪ, 'kwɒndrɪ] *n* **to be in a q.**, estar en un dilema.

quango ['kwæŋgəʊ] *n* organización semi-autónoma paralela.

quantity ['kwɒntɪtɪ] *n* cantidad *f*.

quarantine ['kwɒrəntiːn] *n* cuarentena *f*.

quarrel ['kwɒrəl] **I** *n* (*argument*) riña *f*, pelea *f*; (*disagreement*) desacuerdo *m*. **II** *vi* (*argue*) pelearse, reñir; **to q. with sth**, discrepar de algo.

quarrelsome ['kwɒrəlsəm] *adj* camorrista.

quarry¹ ['kwɒrɪ] *Min* **I** *n* cantera *f*. **II** *vtr* extraer.

quarry² ['kwɒrɪ] *n* presa *f*.

quart [kwɔːt] *n* (*measurement*) cuarto *m* de galón (*GB approx* 1,13 litros; *US approx* 0,94 litros).

quarter ['kwɔːtəʳ] **I** *n* **1** cuarto *m*, cuarta parte *f*; **a q. of an hour**, un cuarto de hora; **a q. of a cake**, la cuarta parte de un pastel. **2** **it's a q. to three**, *US* it's a q. of three, son las tres menos cuarto. **3** (*three months*) trimestre *m*. **4** *GB* (*weight*) cuarto *m* de libra. **5** *US* (*coin*) cuarto *m* (de dólar). **6** (*district*) barrio *m*. **7** **there was criticism from all quarters**, (*areas, people*) todos lo criticaron. **8** (*of moon*) cuarto *m*. **9** **quarters**, (*lodgings*) alojamiento *m sing*; *Mil* **officers' q.**, residencia *f sing* de oficiales; **at close quarters**, muy cerca. **II** *vtr* **1** (*cut into quarters*) dividir en cuartos. **2** (*accommodate*) alojar.

quarterfinal ['kwɔːtəfaɪnəl] *n Sport* cuarto *m* de final.

quarterly ['kwɔːtəlɪ] **I** *adj* trimestral. **II** *n* publicación *f* trimestral. **III** *adv* trimestralmente.

quartermaster ['kwɔːtəmɑːstəʳ] *n* **1** *Mil* oficial *m* de intendencia. **2** *Naut* cabo *m* de la Marina.

quartet(te) [kwɔː'tet] *n* cuarteto *m*.

quartz [kwɔːts] *n* cuarzo *m*; **q. watch**, reloj *m* de cuarzo.

quash [kwɒʃ] *vtr Jur* anular; (*uprising*) aplastar.

quasi ['kwɑːzɪ, 'kweɪzaɪ, 'kweɪsaɪ] *pref* cuasi.

quaver ['kweɪvəʳ] **I** *n* **1** *Mus* corchea *f*. **2** (*in voice*) temblor *m*. **II** *vi* (*voice*) temblar.

quay(side) ['kiː(saɪd)] *n* muelle *m*.

queasy ['kwiːzɪ] *adj* (*queasier, queasiest*)

to feel q., *(ill)* tener náuseas.
queen [kwi:n] *n* **1** reina *f*. **2** *offens* loca *f*, marica *m*.
queer [kwɪəʳ] **I** *adj* **1** *(strange)* extraño,-a, raro,-a. **2** *fam (mad)* loco,-a. **3** *fam (unwell)* mareado,-a. **4** *offens* maricón. **II** *n sl offens* marica *m*, maricón *m*.
quell [kwel] *vtr* reprimir.
quench [kwentʃ] *vtr* apagar.
querulous [ˈkwerʊləs, ˈkwerjʊləs] *adj fml* quejumbroso,-a.
query [ˈkwɪərɪ] **I** *n (question)* pregunta *f*. **II** *vtr (ask questions about)* preguntar acerca de; *(have doubts about)* poner en duda.
quest [kwest] *n lit* búsqueda *f*, busca *f*.
question [ˈkwestʃən] **I** *n* **1** *(interrogative)* pregunta *f*; **to ask sb a q.,** hacer una pregunta a algn; **he did it without q.,** lo hizo sin rechistar; **q. mark,** signo *m* de interrogación; *fig* interrogante *m*. **2** *(problem, issue)* asunto *m*, cuestión *f*; **it's a q. of two hours,** es cuestión de dos horas. **3** *(doubt)* duda *f*; **beyond q.,** fuera de duda; **in q.,** en duda; **to call sth into q.,** poner algo en duda. **4** **out of the q.,** imposible; **that's out of the q.,** ¡ni hablar! **5** *Educ* problema *m*. **II** *vtr (ask questions of)* hacer preguntas a; *(interrogate)* interrogar; *(query)* poner en duda.
questionable [ˈkwestʃənəbəl] *adj (doubtful)* dudoso,-a; *(debatable)* discutible.
questionnaire [kwestʃəˈneəʳ] *n* cuestionario *m*.
queue [kjuː] *GB* **I** *n* cola *f*. **II** *vi* **to q. (up),** hacer cola.
quibble [ˈkwɪbəl] **I** *n* pega *f*. **II** *vi* poner pegas **(with,** a); *fam* buscarle tres pies al gato.
quick [kwɪk] *adj* **1** *(fast)* rápido,-a; **a q. look,** un vistazo; **a q. snack,** un bocado; **be q.!,** ¡date prisa! **2** *(clever)* espabilado,-a; *(wit)* agudo,-a. **3** **she has a q. temper,** se fada con nada. ◆**quickly** *adv* rápidamente, de prisa.
quicken [ˈkwɪkən] **I** *vtr* acelerar; **to q. one's pace,** acelerar el paso. **II** *vi (speed up)* acelerarse.
quickness [ˈkwɪknɪs] *n* **1** *(speed)* rapidez *f*. **2** *(of wit)* agudeza *f*, viveza *f*.
quicksand [ˈkwɪksænd] *n* arenas movedizas.
quicksilver [ˈkwɪksɪlvəʳ] *n* mercurio *m*.
quick-witted [kwɪkˈwɪtɪd] *adj* agudo,-a.
quid [kwɪd] *n GB sl* libra *f* (esterlina).
quiet [ˈkwaɪət] **I** *n* **1** *(silence)* silencio *m*. **2** *(calm)* tranquilidad *f*. **II** *adj* **1** *(silent)* silencioso,-a; *(street)* tranquilo,-a; **a q. voice,** una voz suave; **keep q.!** *(silence)* **2** *(calm)* tranquilo,-a. **3** *Com Fin* **business is q. today,** hoy hay poco negocio. **4** *(person)* reservado,-a. **5** *(secret)* confidencial. **6** *(not showy) (clothes)*

sobrio,-a; *(colours)* apagado,-a. **7** *(ceremony, dinner)* íntimo,-a. **II** *adv US* calmar. **III** *vi US* calmarse. ◆**quietly** *adv* **1** *(silently)* silenciosamente; **he spoke q.,** habló en voz baja. **2** *(calmly)* tranquilamente. **3** *(discreetly)* discretamente.
quieten [ˈkwaɪətən] **I** *vtr (silence)* callar; *(calm)* calmar. **II** *vi (silence)* callarse; *(calm)* calmarse. ◆**quieten down** *GB* **I** *vtr* calmar. **II** *vi* calmarse.
quietness [ˈkwaɪətnɪs] *n* **1** *(silence)* silencio *m*. **2** *(calm)* tranquilidad *f*.
quill [kwɪl] *n (feather, pen)* pluma *f*; *(of porcupine)* púa *f*.
quilt [kwɪlt] **I** *n* edredón *m*. **II** *vtr* acolchar.
quin [kwɪn] *n* quintillizo,-a *m,f*.
quinine [ˈkwɪniːn, *US* ˈkwaɪnaɪn] *n* quinina *f*.
quintessential [kwɪntɪˈsenʃəl] *adj* fundamental.
quintet(te) [kwɪnˈtet] *n* quinteto *m*.
quintuple [ˈkwɪntjʊpəl, kwɪnˈtjuːpəl] *adj* quíntuplo,-a. **II** *n* quíntuplo *m*. **III** *vtr* quintuplicar.
quintuplet [ˈkwɪntjʊplɪt, kwɪnˈtjuːplɪt] *n* quintillizo,-a *m,f*.
quip [kwɪp] **I** *n* salida *f*; *(joke)* chiste *m*. **II** *vi* bromear.
quirk [kwɜːk] *n* **1** *(peculiarity)* manía *f*. **2** *(of fate)* arbitrariedad *f*.
quit [kwɪt] **I** *vtr (pt & pp* **quitted** *or esp US* **quit)** **1**-*(leave)* dejar, abandonar. **2** **making that noise!,** ¡deja de hacer ese ruido!. **II** *vi* **1** *(go)* irse; *(give up)* dimitir. **2** *(cease)* dejar de hacer algo. **III** *adj* **let's call it quits,** dejémoslo estar.
quite [kwaɪt] *adv* **1** *(entirely)* totalmente; **she's q. right,** tiene toda la razón. **2** *(rather)* bastante; **q. a few,** bastantes; **q. a while,** un buen rato; **q. often,** con bastante frecuencia; **that's q. enough!,** ¡ya está bien! **3** **he's q. a character,** es un tipo original; **to be q. sth,** ser increíble. **4** *(exactly)* exactamente; **q. (so)!,** ¡exacto!
quiver¹ [ˈkwɪvəʳ] *vi* temblar.
quiver² [ˈkwɪvəʳ] *n (for arrows)* aljaba *f*, carcaj *m*.
quiz [kwɪz] **I** *n Rad TV* **q. show,** concurso *m*. **II** *vtr* hacer preguntas a.
quizzical [ˈkwɪzɪkəl] *adj* **1** *(bemused)* burlón,-ona. **2** *(enquiring)* curioso,-a.
quota [ˈkwəʊtə] *n* **1** *(proportional share)* cuota *f*, parte *f*. **2** *(prescribed amount, number)* cupo *m*.
quotation [kwəʊˈteɪʃən] *n* **1** *Lit* cita *f*; **q. marks,** comillas *fpl*. **2** *Fin* cotización *f*.
quote [kwəʊt] **I** *vtr* **1** *(cite)* citar. **2** *Com* **to q. a price,** dar un presupuesto. **3** *Fin* cotizar. **II** *n* **1** *Lit* cita *f*. **2** *Com* presupuesto *m*.
quotient [ˈkwəʊʃənt] *n* cociente *m*.

R

R, r [aːr] n (the letter) R, r f.

rabbi ['ræbaɪ] n rabí m, rabino m.

rabbit ['ræbɪt] I n conejo, -a m,f; r. hutch, conejera f. II vi fam to r. (on), enrollarse.

rabble ['ræbəl] n pej the r., el populacho.

rabies ['reɪbiːz] n rabia f.

RAC [aːreɪ'siː] GB abbr of **Royal Automobile Club**, ≈ Real Automóvil Club m de España, RACE.

race¹ [reɪs] I n 1 Sport carrera f. 2 GB **the races**, las carreras (de caballos). II vtr 1 I'll r. you!, ¡te echo una carrera! 2 (car, horse) hacer correr. 3 (engine) acelerar. III vi (go quickly) correr; (pulse) acelerarse.

race² [reɪs] n (people) raza f.

racecourse ['reɪskɔːs] n GB hipódromo m.

racehorse ['reɪshɔːs] n caballo m de carreras.

racer ['reɪsər] n Sport 1 (person) corredor, -a m,f. 2 (bicycle) bicicleta f de carreras; (car) coche m de carreras.

racetrack ['reɪstræk] n (for cars, people, bikes) pista f; US (for horses) hipódromo m.

racial ['reɪʃəl] adj racial.

racing ['reɪsɪŋ] I n carreras fpl. II adj de carreras; r. car/bike, coche m/moto f de carreras.

racism ['reɪsɪzəm] n racismo m.

racist ['reɪsɪst] adj & n racista (mf).

rack [ræk] I n 1 (shelf) estante m; (for clothes) percha f; (luggage) r., portaequipajes m inv; roof r., baca f. 2 (for torture) potro m. II vtr lit (torment) atormentar; fam fig to r. one's brains, devanarse los sesos.

racket¹ ['rækɪt] n 1 (din) ruido m, jaleo m. 2 (swindle) timo m; (shady business) chanchullo m.

racket² ['rækɪt] n → **racket**.

racquet ['rækɪt] n Sport raqueta f.

racy ['reɪsɪ] adj (racier, raciest) (lively) vivo, -a; (risqué) atrevido, -a.

radar ['reɪdɑːr] n radar m.

radiance ['reɪdɪəns] n resplandor m.

radiant ['reɪdɪənt] adj radiante, resplandeciente.

radiate ['reɪdɪeɪt] vtr irradiar; fig she radiated happiness, rebosaba de alegría.

radiation [reɪdɪ'eɪʃən] n radiación f.

radiator ['reɪdɪeɪtər] n radiador m.

radical ['rædɪkəl] adj radical.

radio ['reɪdɪəʊ] n radio f; on the r., en or por la radio; r. station, emisora f de (radio).

radioactive [reɪdɪəʊ'æktɪv] adj radiactivo, -a.

radio-controlled [reɪdɪəʊkən'trəʊld] adj teledirigido, -a.

radiography [reɪdɪ'ɒgrəfɪ] n radiografía f.

radiology [reɪdɪ'ɒlədʒɪ] n radiología f.

radiotherapy [reɪdɪəʊ'θerəpɪ] n radioterapia f.

radish ['rædɪʃ] n rábano m.

radius ['reɪdɪəs] n radio m; within a r. of, en un radio de.

RAF [aːreɪ'ef] GB abbr of **Royal Air Force**, fuerzas aéreas británicas.

raffle ['ræfəl] I n rifa f. II vtr rifar.

raft [rɑːft] n balsa f.

rafter ['rɑːftər] n viga f de madera.

rag¹ [ræg] I n 1 (torn piece) harapo m; r. doll, muñeca f de trapo. 2 (for cleaning) trapo m. 3 fam rags, (clothes) trapos mpl. 4 Press pej periodicucho m.

rag² [ræg] I n GB Univ función benéfica. II vtr gastar bromas a.

rag-and-bone [rægən'bəʊn] adj GB r.-and-b. man, trapero m.

rage [reɪdʒ] I n 1 (fury) cólera f. 2 fam it's all the r., hace furor. II vi 1 (person) rabiar, estar furioso, -a. 2 fig (storm, sea) rugir; (wind) bramar.

ragged ['rægɪd] adj 1 (clothes) hecho,-a jirones. 2 (person) harapiento, -a. 3 (edge) mellado, -a. 4 fig (uneven) desigual.

raging ['reɪdʒɪŋ] adj 1 (angry) furioso, -a. 2 fig (sea) embravecido, -a. 3 (intense) feroz; (storm) violento, -a.

raid [reɪd] I n Mil incursión f; (by police) redada f; (robbery etc) atraco m. II vtr Mil hacer una incursión en; (police) hacer una redada en; (rob) asaltar; fam to r. the larder, vaciar la despensa.

raider ['reɪdər] n (invader) invasor, -a m,f.

rail [reɪl] n 1 barra f. 2 (railing) barandilla f. 3 Rail carril m; by r., (send sth) por ferrocarril; (travel) en tren.

railcard ['reɪlkɑːd] n GB abono m.

railing ['reɪlɪŋ] n (usu pl) verja f.

railroad ['reɪlrəʊd] n US ferrocarril m.

railway ['reɪlweɪ] n GB ferrocarril m; r. line, r. track, vía férrea; r. station, estación f de ferrocarril.

railwayman ['reɪlweɪmən] n GB ferroviario m.

rain [reɪn] I n lluvia f; in the r., bajo la lluvia. II vi llover; it's raining, llueve.

rainbow ['reɪnbəʊ] n arco m iris.

raincoat ['reɪnkəʊt] n impermeable m.

raindrop ['reɪndrɒp] n gota f de lluvia.

rainfall ['reɪnfɔːl] n (falling of rain) precipitación f; (amount) pluviosidad f.

rainforest ['reɪnfɒrɪst] n selva f tropical.

rainy ['reɪnɪ] adj (rainier, rainiest) lluvioso, -a.

raise [reɪz] I n US aumento m (de

sueldo). **II** *vtr* **1** levantar; *(glass)* brindar; *(voice)* subir; *(building)* erigir. **2** *(prices)* aumentar. **3** *(money, help)* reunir. **4** *(issue)* plantear. **5** *(crops, children)* criar. **6** *Rad* comunicar con. **7** *(standards)* mejorar. **8** *(laugh)* provocar.

raisin ['reɪzɪn] *n* pasa *f*.

rake¹ [reɪk] **I** *n* *(garden tool)* rastrillo *m*; *(for fire)* hurgón *m*. **II** *vtr* *(leaves)* rastrillar; *(fire)* hurgar; *(with machine gun)* barrer.

rake² [reɪk] *n* *(dissolute man)* calavera *m*, libertino *m*.

rally ['rælɪ] **I** *n* **1** *(gathering)* reunión *f*; *Pol* mitin *m*. **2** *Aut* rallye *m*. **3** *Ten* jugada *f*. **II** *vtr* *(support)* reunir. **III** *vi* recuperarse.
◆**rally round** *vi* formar una piña.

RAM *Comput abbr of* **random access memory**, RAM.

ram [ræm] **I** *n* **1** *Zool* carnero *m*. **2** *Tech* maza *f*. **II** *vtr* **1** *(drive into place)* hincar; *(cram)* embutir; *fam* to r. **sth home**, hacer algo patente. **2** *(crash into)* chocar con.

ramble ['ræmbəl] **I** *n* *(walk)* caminata *f*. **II** *vi* **1** *(walk)* hacer una excursión a pie. **2** *fig (digress)* divagar.

rambler ['ræmblər] *n* **1** *(person)* excursionista *mf*. **2** *Bot* rosal *m* trepador.

rambling ['ræmblɪŋ] *adj* **1** *(incoherent)* incoherente. **2** *(house)* laberíntico,-a. **3** *Bot* trepador,-a.

ramp [ræmp] *n* **1** rampa *f*. **2** *Av (movable stairway)* escalerilla *f*.

rampage [ræm'peɪdʒ] **I** *n* to **be on the r.**, desmandarse. **II** *vi* to **r. about**, comportarse como un loco.

rampant ['ræmpənt] *adj* incontrolado,-a; **corruption is r.**, la corrupción está muy extendida.

rampart ['ræmpɑːt] *n* muralla *f*.

ramshackle ['ræmʃækəl] *adj* destartalado,-a.

ran [ræn] *pt* → **run**.

ranch [rɑːntʃ] *n US* rancho *m*, hacienda *f*.

rancher ['rɑːntʃər] *n US* ranchero,-a *m,f*.

rancid ['rænsɪd] *adj* rancio,-a.

rancour, *US* **rancor** ['ræŋkər] *n fml* rencor *m*.

R&D [ɑːrən'diː] *n abbr of* **Research and Development**, I+D.

random ['rændəm] **I** *n* **at r.**, al azar. **II** *adj* fortuito,-a; **r. selection**, selección hecha al azar.

randy ['rændɪ] *adj (randier, randiest) GB fam* cachondo,-a, caliente.

rang [ræŋ] *pt* → **ring**.

range [reɪndʒ] **I** *n* **1** *(of mountains)* cordillera *f*, sierra *f*. **2** *US (open land)* pradera *f*. **3** *(choice)* surtido *m*; *(of products)* gama *f*. **4** *Mus* registro *m*. **5** *firing r.*, campo *m* de tiro. **6** *(of missile)* alcance *m*; **at close r.**, de cerca; **long-/short-r. missiles**, misiles *mpl* de largo/corto alcance. **7** **r. of vision**, campo *m* de visión. **8** *Culin* coci-

na *f* de carbón. **II** *vi (extend)* extenderse *(to, hasta)*; **prices r. from five to twenty pounds**, los precios oscilan entre cinco y veinte libras. **III** *vtr lit (wander)* vagar por.

ranger ['reɪndʒər] *n* **1** *(forest)* r., guardabosques *mf inv*. **2** *US (mounted policeman)* policía *m* montada.

rank¹ [ræŋk] *n* **1** *Mil (row)* fila *f*; **the ranks**, los soldados rasos; **the r. and file**, la base. **2** *(position in army)* graduación *f*; *(in society)* rango *m*. **3** *(taxi)* r., parada *f* de taxis. **II** *vtr (classify)* clasificar. **III** *vi (figure)* figurar; **to r. above/below sb**, figurar por encima/debajo de algn; **to r. with**, estar al mismo nivel que.

rank² [ræŋk] *adj fml* **1** *(vegetation)* exuberante. **2** *(foul-smelling)* fétido,-a. **3** *(thorough)* total, absoluto,-a.

ransack ['rænsæk] *vtr (plunder)* saquear; *(rummage in)* registrar.

ransom ['rænsəm] *n* rescate *m*; **to hold sb to r.**, pedir rescate por algn; *fig* poner a algn entre la espada y la pared.

rant [rænt] *vi* vociferar; *fam* **to r. and rave**, pegar gritos.

rap [ræp] *n* **1** *(blow)* golpe *m* seco; *(on door)* golpecito *m*. **2** *Mus* rap *m*. **II** *vtr & vi (knock)* golpear.

rape¹ [reɪp] *Jur* **I** *n* violación *f*. **II** *vtr* violar.

rape² [reɪp] *n Bot* colza *f*.

rapeseed ['reɪpsiːd] *n* r. oil, aceite *m* de colza.

rapid ['ræpɪd] **I** *adj* rápido,-a. **II** *npl* **rapids**, *(in river)* rápidos *mpl*.

rapidity [rə'pɪdɪtɪ] *n* rapidez *f*.

rapist ['reɪpɪst] *n* violador,-a *m,f*.

rapport [ræ'pɔːr] *n* compenetración *f*.

rapture ['ræptʃər] *n* éxtasis *m*.

rapturous ['ræptʃərəs] *adj* muy entusiasta.

rare¹ [reər] *adj* raro,-a, poco común.
◆**rarely** *adv* raras veces.

rare² [reər] *adj (steak)* poco hecho,-a.

rarefied ['reərɪfaɪd] *adj* enrarecido,-a.

raring ['reərɪŋ] *adj fam* **to be r. to do sth**, morirse de ganas de hacer algo.

rarity ['reərɪtɪ] *n* rareza *f*.

rascal ['rɑːskəl] *n* granuja *mf*.

rash¹ [ræʃ] *n* **1** *Med* erupción *f*, sarpullido *m*. **2** *fig (of robberies etc)* racha *f*.

rash² [ræʃ] *adj (reckless)* impetuoso,-a; *(words, actions)* precipitado,-a, imprudente.

rasher ['ræʃər] *n* loncha *f*.

rasping ['rɑːspɪŋ] *adj* áspero,-a.

raspberry ['rɑːzbərɪ] *n* frambuesa *f*.

rat [ræt] *n* **1** rata *f*; **r. poison**, raticida *m*.

rate [reɪt] **I** *n* **1** *(ratio)* índice *m*, tasa *f*; **at any r.**, *(at least)* al menos; *(anyway)* en cualquier caso. **2** *(cost)* precio *m*; *Fin (of interest, exchange)* tipo *m*. **3** **at the r. of**, *(speed)* a la velocidad de; *(quantity)* a ra-

zón de. **4 first r.,** de primera categoría. **5
GB rates,** impuestos *mpl* municipales. II
vtr **1** *(estimate)* estimar. **2** *(evaluate)* tasar.
3 *(consider)* considerar.

rateable ['reɪtəbəl] *adj* GB **r. value,** valor
m catastral.

ratepayer ['reɪtpeɪə'] *n* GB contribuyente
mf.

rather ['rɑːðə'] *adv* **1** *(quite)* más bien,
bastante; *(very much so)* muy. **2** *(more
accurately)* mejor dicho; **r. than,** *(instead
of)* en vez de; *(more than)* más que. **3** **she
would r. stay here,** *(prefer to)* prefiere
quedarse aquí.

ratify ['rætɪfaɪ] *vtr* ratificar.

rating ['reɪtɪŋ] *n* **1** *(valuation)* tasación *f*;
(score) valoración *f*. **2** TV **(programme)
ratings,** índice *m* sing de audiencia. **3**
Naut marinero *m* sin graduación.

ratio ['reɪʃɪəʊ] *n* razón *f*; **in the r. of,** a
razón de.

ration ['ræʃən] I *n* **1** *(allowance)* ración *f*.
2 rations, víveres *mpl*. II *vtr* racionar.

rational ['ræʃənəl] *adj* racional.

rationale [ræʃə'nɑːl] *n* base *f*.

rationalize ['ræʃənəlaɪz] *vtr* racionalizar.

rattle ['rætəl] I *n* **1** *(of train, cart)* traqueteo *m*; *(of metal)* repiqueteo *m*; *(of glass)*
tintineo *m*. **2** *(toy)* sonajero *m*; *(instrument)* carraca *f*. II *vtr* **1** *(keys etc)* hacer
sonar. **2** *fam (unsettle)* poner nervioso,-a.
III *vi* sonar; *(metal)* repiquetear; *(glass)*
tintinear.

rattlesnake ['rætəlsneɪk] *n* serpiente *f* de
cascabel.

raucous ['rɔːkəs] *adj* estridente.

ravage ['rævɪdʒ] I *n* (*usu pl*) estragos
mpl. II *vtr* asolar, devastar.

rave [reɪv] I *vi* **1** *(be delirious)* delirar. **2**
(be angry) enfurecerse (**at,** con). **3** *fam
(show enthusiasm)* entusiasmarse (**about,**
por). II *n fam* **r. review,** crítica *f* muy favorable.

raven ['reɪvən] *n* cuervo *m*.

ravenous ['rævənəs] *adj* **I'm r.,** tengo un
hambre que no veo.

ravine [rə'viːn] *n* barranco *m*.

raving ['reɪvɪŋ] *n fam* **r. mad,** loco,-a de
atar.

ravishing ['rævɪʃɪŋ] *adj (person)*
encantador,-a.

raw [rɔː] I *adj* **1** *(uncooked)* crudo,-a. **2**
(not processed) bruto,-a; *(alcohol)* puro,-a;
r. material, materia prima. **3** *(emotion)*
instintivo,-a. **4** *(weather)* crudo,-a. **5 r.
deal,** trato injusto. **6** *(wound)* abierto,-a;
r. flesh, carne viva. **7** US *(inexperienced)*
novato,-a. **8** *(frank)* franco,-a.

ray[1] [reɪ] *n* rayo *m*; *fig* **r. of hope,** rayo
de esperanza.

ray[2] [reɪ] *n (fish)* raya *f*.

rayon ['reɪɒn] *n* rayón *m*.

raze [reɪz] *vtr* arrasar.

razor ['reɪzə'] *n (for shaving)* maquinilla *f*

de afeitar; **r. blade,** hoja *f* de afeitar.

Rd *abbr of* Road, calle *f*, C.

re [riː] *prep* respecto a, con referencia a.

reach [riːtʃ] I *vtr* **1** *(arrive at)* llegar a. **2**
(contact) localizar. II *vi* alcanzar; **to r. for
sth,** intentar coger algo; **to r. out,**
extender la mano. III *n* **1** *(range)* alcance
m; **out of r.,** fuera del alcance; **within r.,**
al alcance. **2** *Box* extensión *f* del brazo. **3
reaches,** *(on a river)* recta *f* sing.

react [rɪ'ækt] *vi* reaccionar.

reaction [rɪ'ækʃən] *n* reacción *f*.

reactor [rɪ'æktə'] *n* reactor *m*.

read [riːd] I *vtr (pt & pp* **read** [red]**) 1**
leer. **2** *(decipher)* descifrar. **3** *(understand)*
entender; *(interpret)* interpretar. II *Univ*
estudiar. II *vi* **1** *(dial)* marcar. **2** *(signpost,
text)* decir. ◆**read out** *vtr* leer en voz
alta.

readable ['riːdəbəl] *adj* **1** *(interesting)* interesante. **2** *(legible)* legible.

reader ['riːdə'] *n* **1** lector,-a *m,f*. **2** *(book)*
libro *m* de lectura. **3** GB *Univ* profesor,-a
adjunto,-a.

readership ['riːdəʃɪp] *n* *Press* lectores
mpl.

readiness ['redɪnɪs] *n* **1** *(preparedness)*
preparación *f*. **2** *(willingness)* buena disposición.

reading ['riːdɪŋ] *n* **1** lectura *f*. **2** *fig* interpretación *f*. **3** *(of laws, bill)* presentación
f.

readjust [riːə'dʒʌst] I *vtr* reajustar. II *vi*
(adapt oneself) adaptarse.

ready ['redɪ] *adj* **1** *(prepared)* listo,-a,
preparado,-a; **r., steady, go!,** ¡prepara-
dos, listos, ya! **2 r. to,** *(about to)* a punto
de. **3** *(to hand)* a mano; **r. cash,** dinero *m*
en efectivo. **4** *(willing)* dispuesto,-a. ◆**readily** *adv* **1** *(easily)* fácilmente; **r.
available,** disponible en el acto. **2** *(will-
ingly)* de buena gana.

ready-cooked [redɪ'kʊkt] *adj*
precocinado,-a.

ready-made [redɪ'meɪd] *adj*
confeccionado,-a; *(food)* preparado,-a.

real [rɪəl] *adj* **1** real, verdadero,-a; *fam for
r.,* de veras. **2** *(genuine)* auténtico,-a; **r.
leather,** piel legítima. **3** US *Com* **r.
estate,** bienes *mpl* inmuebles; **r. estate
agent,** agente inmobiliario. ◆**really** *adv*
verdaderamente, realmente; Y **r.?,** ¿de
verdad?; ¡no lo sé de verdad!; **r.?,** ¿de veras?

realism ['rɪəlɪzəm] *n* realismo *m*.

realistic ['rɪəlɪstɪk] *adj* realista.

reality [rɪ'ælɪtɪ] *n* realidad *f*; **in r.,** en realidad.

realize ['rɪəlaɪz] *vtr* **1** *(become aware of)*
darse cuenta de. **2** *(assets, plan)* realizar.

realization [rɪəlaɪ'zeɪʃən] *n* **1** *(understanding)* comprensión *f*. **2** *(of plan, assets)* realización *f*.

realm [relm] *n* *(kingdom)* reino *m*; *fig
(field)* terreno *m*.

ream [ri:m] n (of paper) resma f.

reap [ri:p] vtr Agr cosechar; fig to r. the benefits, llevarse los beneficios.

reappear [ri:ə'pɪər] vi reaparecer.

reappraisal [ri:ə'preɪzəl] n revaluación f.

rear¹ [rɪər] I n 1 (back part) parte f de atrás. 2 fam (buttocks) trasero m. II adj trasero,-a; r. entrance, puerta f de atrás.

rear² [rɪər] I vtr 1 (breed, raise) criar. 2 (lift up) levantar. II vi to r. up, (horse) encabritarse.

rearguard ['rɪəgɑ:d] n retaguardia f.

rearmament [ri:'ɑ:məmənt] n rearme m.

rearrange [ri:ə'reɪndʒ] vtr 1 (furniture) colocar de otra manera. 2 (appointment) fijar otra fecha para.

rear-view ['rɪəvju:] adj r.-v. mirror, (espejo m) retrovisor m.

reason ['ri:zən] I n 1 motivo m, razón f; for no r., sin razón; for some r., por algún motivo. 2 (good sense) razón f; it stands to r., es lógico; to listen to r., atender a razones. II vi 1 to r. with sb, convencer a algn. 2 (argue, work out) razonar.

reasonable ['ri:zənəbəl] adj 1 (fair) razonable. 2 (sensible) sensato,-a. 3 (average) regular. ◆**reasonably** adv (fairly) bastante.

reasoning ['ri:zənɪŋ] n razonamiento m.

reassurance [ri:ə'ʃʊərəns] n consuelo m.

reassure [ri:ə'ʃʊər] vtr 1 (comfort) tranquilizar. 2 (restore confidence) dar confianza a.

reassuring [ri:ə'ʃʊərɪŋ] adj consolador,-a.

rebate ['ri:beɪt] n devolución f; tax r., devolución fiscal.

rebel ['rebəl] I adj & n rebelde (mf). II [rɪ'bel] vi rebelarse, sublevarse (against, contra).

rebellion [rɪ'beljən] n rebelión f.

rebellious [rɪ'beljəs] adj rebelde.

rebound [rɪ'baʊnd] I n (of ball) rebote m; fig on the r., de rebote. II [rɪ'baʊnd] vi (ball) rebotar.

rebuff [rɪ'bʌf] I n desaire m. II vtr desairar.

rebuild [ri:'bɪld] vtr reconstruir.

rebuke [rɪ'bju:k] I n reproche m. II vtr reprochar.

rebut [rɪ'bʌt] vtr refutar.

recalcitrant [rɪ'kælsɪtrənt] adj fml recalcitrante.

recall [rɪ'kɔ:l] vtr 1 (soldiers, products) hacer volver; (ambassador) retirar. 2 (remember) recordar.

recant [rɪ'kænt] vi fml retractarse.

recap [rɪ'kæp] I vtr & vi resumir; to r., en resumen. II ['ri:kæp] n recapitulación f.

recapitulate [ri:kə'pɪtjʊleɪt] vtr & vi fml recapitular.

recapture [ri:'kæptʃər] vtr fig recuperar.

recd Com abbr of received, recibido,

-a.

recede [rɪ'si:d] vi retroceder; (fade) desvanecerse.

receipt [rɪ'si:t] n 1 (act) recepción f; to acknowledge r. of sth, acusar recibo de algo. 2 Com (paper) recibo m. 3 receipts, (takings) recaudación f sing.

receive [rɪ'si:v] vtr 1 recibir. 2 Jur (stolen goods) ocultar. 3 (welcome) acoger. 4 TV Rad captar.

receiver [rɪ'si:vər] n 1 (person) receptor,-a m,f. 2 Jur (of stolen goods) perista mf. 3 GB Jur official r., síndico m. 4 Tel auricular m. 5 Rad receptor m.

recent ['ri:sənt] adj reciente; in r. years, en los últimos años. ◆**recently** adv hace poco, recientemente.

receptacle [rɪ'septəkəl] n receptáculo m.

reception [rɪ'sepʃən] n 1 (welcome) acogida f. 2 (party) recepción f; wedding r., banquete m de bodas. 3 r. (desk), recepción f. 4 Rad TV recepción f.

receptionist [rɪ'sepʃənɪst] n recepcionista mf.

recess ['ri:ses, rɪ'ses] n 1 (in a wall) hueco m. 2 (secret place) escondrijo m. 3 US Educ recreo m; Parl período m de vacaciones.

recession [rɪ'seʃən] n recesión f.

recharge [ri:'tʃɑ:dʒ] vtr (battery) recargar.

rechargeable [ri:'tʃɑ:dʒəbəl] adj recargable.

recipe ['resɪpɪ] n Culin receta f; fig fórmula f.

recipient [rɪ'sɪpɪənt] n receptor,-a m,f; (of letter) destinatario,-a m,f.

reciprocate [rɪ'sɪprəkeɪt] I vtr (favour etc) devolver. II vi hacer lo mismo.

recital [rɪ'saɪtəl] n recital m.

recite [rɪ'saɪt] vtr & vi recitar.

reckless ['reklɪs] adj (unwise) imprudente; (fearless) temerario,-a.

reckon ['rekən] vtr & vi 1 (calculate) calcular; (count) contar. 2 fam (think) creer; (consider) considerar. ◆**reckon on** vtr contar con.

reckoner ['rekənər] n ready r., tabla f de cálculo.

reckoning ['rekənɪŋ] n cálculo m; by my r. ..., según mis cálculos ...; fig day of r., día m del juicio final.

reclaim [rɪ'kleɪm] vtr 1 (recover) recuperar; (demand back) reclamar. 2 (marshland etc) convertir.

recline [rɪ'klaɪn] vi recostarse, reclinarse.

reclining [rɪ'klaɪnɪŋ] adj recostado,-a; r. seat, asiento m abatible.

recluse [rɪ'klu:s] n recluso,-a m,f.

recognition [rekəg'nɪʃən] n reconocimiento m; (appreciation) apreciación f; changed beyond all r., irreconocible.

recognizable [rekəg'naɪzəbəl] adj reconocible.

recognize ['rekəgnaɪz] vtr reconocer.

recoil [rɪ'kɔɪl] **I** n (of gun) culatazo m; (of spring) aflojamiento m. **II** [rɪ'kɔɪl] vi 1 (gun) dar un culatazo; (spring) aflojarse. 2 (in fear) espantarse.

recollect [rekə'lekt] vtr recordar.

recollection [rekə'lekʃən] n recuerdo m.

recommend [rekə'mend] vtr recomendar.

recommendation [rekəmen'deɪʃən] n recomendación f.

recompense ['rekəmpens] **I** n recompensa f; Jur indemnización f. **II** vtr recompensar; Jur indemnizar.

reconcile ['rekənsaɪl] vtr (two people) reconciliar; (two ideas) conciliar; **to r. oneself to**, resignarse a.

recondition [ri:kən'dɪʃən] vtr (engine) revisar.

reconnaissance [rɪ'kɒnɪsəns] n Mil reconocimiento m.

reconnoitre, US **reconnoiter** [rekə'nɔɪtər] vtr Mil reconocer.

reconsider [ri:kən'sɪdər] vtr reconsiderar.

reconstruct [ri:kən'strʌkt] vtr reconstruir.

reconstruction [ri:kən'strʌkʃən] n reconstrucción f.

record ['rekɔːd] **I** n 1 (account) relación f; (of meeting) actas fpl; **off the r.**, confidencialmente. 2 (document) documento m; **r. of attendance**, registro m de asistencia; **public records**, archivos mpl. 3 Med historial médico. 4 Mus disco m; **r. player**, tocadiscos m inv. 5 Sport récord m. **II** [rɪ'kɔːd] vtr 1 (relate) hacer constar; (note down) apuntar. 2 (record, voice) grabar. 3 (of thermometer etc) marcar.

recorded [rɪ'kɔːdɪd] adj **r. delivery**, correo certificado; **r. message**, mensaje grabado.

recorder [rɪ'kɔːdər] n 1 (person) registrador,-a m,f; Jur magistrado,-a. 2 Mus flauta f.

recording [rɪ'kɔːdɪŋ] n (registering) registro m; (recorded music, message etc) grabación f.

recount [rɪ'kaʊnt] vtr (tell) contar.

re-count [ri:'kaʊnt] **I** vi Pol hacer un recuento. **II** ['ri:kaʊnt] n Pol recuento m.

recoup [rɪ'kuːp] vtr (losses etc) recuperar.

recourse [rɪ'kɔːs] n **to have r. to**, recurrir a.

recover [rɪ'kʌvər] **I** vtr (items, lost time) recuperar; (consciousness) recobrar. **II** vi (from illness etc) reponerse.

recovery [rɪ'kʌvərɪ] n 1 (retrieval) recuperación f. 2 (from illness) restablecimiento m.

recreation [rekrɪ'eɪʃən] n 1 diversión f, Educ (playtime) recreo m; **r. ground**, terreno m de juegos.

recreational [rekrɪ'eɪʃənəl] adj recreativo,-a.

recrimination [rɪkrɪmɪ'neɪʃən] n repro-

che m.

recruit [rɪ'kruːt] **I** n recluta m. **II** vtr (soldiers) reclutar; (workers) contratar.

recruitment [rɪ'kruːtmənt] n (of soldiers) reclutamiento m; (of employees) contratación f.

rectangle ['rektæŋgəl] n rectángulo m.

rectangular [rek'tæŋgjʊlər] adj rectangular.

rectify ['rektɪfaɪ] vtr rectificar.

rector ['rektər] n 1 Rel párroco m. 2 Scot Educ director,-a m,f.

recuperate [rɪ'kuːpəreɪt] vi reponerse.

recur [rɪ'kɜːr] vi repetirse.

recurrence [rɪ'kʌrəns] n repetición f, reaparición f.

recurrent [rɪ'kʌrənt] adj constante; Med recurrente.

recycle [riː'saɪkəl] vtr reciclar.

recycling [riː'saɪklɪŋ] n reciclaje m.

red [red] **I** adj (redder, reddest) rojo,-a; **r. light**, semáforo m en rojo; **r. wine**, vino tinto; **to go r.**, ponerse colorado,-a; **to have r. hair**, ser pelirrojo,-a; fig **r. herring**, truco m para despistar; fam **to roll out the r. carpet for sb**, recibir a algn con todos los honores; **R. Cross**, Cruz Roja; **R. Indian**, piel roja m,f; **R. Riding Hood**, Caperucita Roja; **R. Sea**, Mar Rojo; **r. tape**, papeleo m. **II** n 1 (colour) rojo m; Fin **to be in the r.**, estar en números rojos.

redcurrant ['redkʌrənt] n grosella roja.

redden ['redən] vi 1 (blush) enrojecerse, ponerse colorado,-a. **II** vtr (make red) teñir de rojo.

reddish ['redɪʃ] adj rojizo,-a.

redeem [rɪ'diːm] vtr 1 (regain) recobrar; (from pawn) desempeñar; (voucher) canjear. 2 (debt) amortizar. 3 (film, novel etc) salvar. 4 Rel redimir; fig **to r. oneself**, redimirse.

redeeming [rɪ'diːmɪŋ] adj compensatorio,-a; **his only r. feature**, lo único que le salva.

redemption [rɪ'dempʃən] n fml 1 (of debt) amortización f. 2 Rel redención f; **beyond r.**, sin remedio.

redeploy [riːdɪ'plɔɪ] vtr transferir.

red-handed [red'hændɪd] adj **to catch sb r.-h.**, coger a algn con las manos en la masa.

redhead ['redhed] n pelirrojo,-a m,f.

red-hot [red'hɒt] adj 1 candente; **r.-h. news**, noticia(s) f(pl) de última hora. 2 fam (passionate) ardiente.

redial [riː'daɪəl] n Tel (facility) rellamada f.

redirect [riːdɪ'rekt] vtr 1 (funds) redistribuir. 2 (letter) remitir a la nueva dirección.

red-light [red'laɪt] adj fam **r.-l. district**, barrio chino.

redouble [riː'dʌbəl] vtr redoblar.

redress [rɪ'dres] *fml* **I** *n* reparación *f*. **II** *vtr* reparar.

redskin ['redskɪn] *n offens* piel roja *mf*.

reduce [rɪ'djuːs] *vtr* **1** reducir. **2** (*in rank*) degradar. **3** *Culin* (*sauce*) espesar. **4** *Med* recomponer.

reduction [rɪ'dʌkʃən] *n* reducción *f*; *Com* (*in purchase price*) descuento *m*, rebaja *f*.

redundancy [rɪ'dʌndənsɪ] *n* despido *m*.

redundant [rɪ'dʌndənt] *adj* **1** (*superfluous*) redundante. **2** *Ind* to be made r., perder el empleo; **to make sb r.**, despedir a algn.

reed [riːd] *n* **1** *Bot* caña *f*. **2** *Mus* caramillo *m*.

reef [riːf] *n* arrecife *m*.

reek [riːk] **I** *n* tufo *m*. **II** *vi* apestar.

reel [riːl] **I** *n* **1** (*spool*) bobina *f*, carrete *m*. **2** *Scot Mus* danza *f* tradicional. **II** *vi* (*stagger*) tambalearse.

re-elect [riːɪ'lekt] *vtr* reelegir.

ref [ref] *n* **1** *Sport fam abbr of* referee. **2** *Com abbr of* reference, ref.

refectory [rɪ'fektərɪ] *n* refectorio *m*.

refer [rɪ'fɜː] **I** *vtr* mandar, enviar; **to r. a matter to a tribunal**, remitir un asunto a un tribunal. **II** *vi* **1** (*allude*) referirse, aludir (**to**, a). **2** (*consult*) consultar (**to**, -).

referee [refə'riː] **I** *n* **1** *Sport* árbitro,-a *m,f*. **2** (*for job application*) garante *mf*. **II** *vtr Sport* arbitrar.

reference ['refərəns] *n* **1** referencia *f*; **with r. to**, referente a, con referencia a; **r. book**, libro *m* de consulta; **r. library**, biblioteca *f* de consulta. **2** (*character report*) informe *m*, referencia *f*.

referendum [refə'rendəm] *n* referéndum *m*.

refill ['riːfɪl] **I** *n* **1** (*replacement*) recambio *m*, carga *f*. **2** *fam* (*drink*) otra copa. **II** [riː'fɪl] *vtr* rellenar.

refine [rɪ'faɪn] *vtr* refinar.

refined [rɪ'faɪnd] *adj* refinado,-a.

refinement [rɪ'faɪnmənt] *n* refinamiento *m*.

refinery [rɪ'faɪnərɪ] *n* refinería *f*.

reflect [rɪ'flekt] **I** *vtr* (*light, attitude*) reflejar. **II** *vi* (*think*) reflexionar; **to r. on sth**, meditar sobre algo.

reflection [rɪ'flekʃən] *n* **1** (*indication, mirror image*) reflejo *m*. **2** (*thought*) reflexión *f*; **on r.**, pensándolo bien. **3** (*criticism*) crítica *f*.

reflector [rɪ'flektə] *n* **1** *Astron* reflector *m*. **2** (*of vehicle*) catafaro *m*.

reflex ['riːfleks] *n* reflejo *m*.

reflexive [rɪ'fleksɪv] *adj* reflexivo,-a.

reform [rɪ'fɔːm] **I** *n* reforma *f*. **II** *vtr* reformar.

reformation [refə'meɪʃən] *n* reforma *f*.

reformatory [rɪ'fɔːmətərɪ] *n* reformatorio *m*.

reformer [rɪ'fɔːmə] *n* reformador,-a *m,f*.

refrain [rɪ'freɪn] **I** *n* *Mus* estribillo *m*; *fig*

lema *m*. **II** *vi* abstenerse (**from**, de).

refresh [rɪ'freʃ] *vtr* refrescar.

refresher [rɪ'freʃə] *n* **r. course**, cursillo *m* de reciclaje.

refreshing [rɪ'freʃɪŋ] *adj* refrescante; **a r. change**, un cambio muy agradable.

refreshment [rɪ'freʃmənt] *n* refresco *m*.

refrigerator [rɪ'frɪdʒəreɪtə] *n* nevera *f*, frigorífico *m*.

refuel [riː'fjuːəl] *vi* repostar combustible.

refuge ['refjuːdʒ] *n* refugio *m*, cobijo *m*; **to take r.**, refugiarse.

refugee [refjuˈdʒiː] *n* refugiado,-a *m,f*.

refund ['riːfʌnd] **I** *n* reembolso *m*. **II** [rɪ'fʌnd] *vtr* reembolsar, devolver.

refurbish [riː'fɜːbɪʃ] *vtr* redecorar.

refusal [rɪ'fjuːzəl] *n* negativa *f*; **to have first r. on sth**, tener la primera opción en algo.

refuse¹ [rɪ'fjuːz] **I** *vtr* rechazar; **to r. sb sth**, negar algo a algn. **II** *vi* negarse.

refuse² ['refjuːs] *n* basura *f*; **r. collector**, basurero *m*.

refute [rɪ'fjuːt] *vtr* refutar, rebatir.

regain [rɪ'geɪn] *vtr* recuperar; (*consciousness*) recobrar.

regal ['riːgəl] *adj* regio,-a.

regard [rɪ'gɑːd] **I** *n* **1** (*concern*) consideración *f*, respeto *m*; **with r. to**, respecto a. **2** (*esteem*) estima *f*. **3** **regards**, (*good wishes*) recuerdos *mpl*; **give him my regards**, dale recuerdos de mi parte. **II** *vtr* **1** (*consider*) considerar. **2** **as regards**, (*regarding*) respecto a.

regarding [rɪ'gɑːdɪŋ] *prep* respecto a.

regardless [rɪ'gɑːdlɪs] **I** *prep* a pesar de; **r. of the outcome**, pase lo que pase. **II** *adv* a toda costa.

regime [reɪ'ʒiːm] *n* régimen *m*.

regiment ['redʒɪmənt] **I** *n* regimiento *m*. **II** *vtr* regimentar.

regimental [redʒɪ'mentəl] *adj* del regimiento.

region ['riːdʒən] *n* **1** región *f*. **2** **in the r. of**, aproximadamente.

regional ['riːdʒənəl] *adj* regional.

regionalism ['riːdʒənəlɪzəm] *n* regionalismo *m*.

register ['redʒɪstə] **I** *n* registro *m*. **II** *vtr* **1** (*record*) registrar. **2** (*letter*) certificar. **3** (*show*) mostrar; **his face registered fear**, en su rostro se reflejaba el miedo. **III** *vi* **1** (*for course*) inscribirse; *Univ* matricularse.

registered ['redʒɪstəd] *adj* certificado,-a; **r. letter**, carta certificada; **r. trademark**, marca registrada.

registrar [redʒɪ'strɑː, 'redʒɪstrɑː] *n* **1** (*record keeper*) registrador,-a *m,f*. **2** *GB Med* interno,-a *m,f*. **3** *Univ* secretario,-a *m,f* general.

registration [redʒɪ'streɪʃən] *n* inscripción *f*; *Univ* matrícula *f*; *GB Aut* **r. number**, matrícula *f*.

registry ['redʒɪstrɪ] *n* registro *m*; **to get**

married in a r. office, casarse por lo civil; **r. office**, registro civil.

regret [rɪ'gret] **I** n (remorse) remordimiento m; (sadness) pesar m; **regrets**, (excuses) excusas fpl; **to have no regrets**, no arrepentirse de nada. **II** vtr arrepentirse de, lamentar.

regretful [rɪ'gretful] adj arrepentido,-a.

regrettable [rɪ'gretəbəl] adj lamentable.

regroup [ri:'gru:p] **I** vtr reagrupar. **II** vi reagruparse.

regular ['regjʊlər] **I** adj 1 regular. 2 (usual) normal. 3 (staff) permanente. 4 (frequent) 5 r. **army**, tropas fpl regulares. **II** n 1 (customer) cliente mf habitual. 2 Mil militar m de carrera. ◆**regularly** adv con regularidad.

regularity [regjʊ'lærɪtɪ] n regularidad f.

regulate ['regjʊleɪt] vtr regular.

regulation [regjʊ'leɪʃən] **I** n 1 (control) regulación f. 2 (rule) regla f. **II** adj reglamentario,-a.

rehabilitation [ri:əbɪlɪ'teɪʃən] n rehabilitación f; **r. centre**, centro m de reinserción.

rehearsal [rɪ'hɜːsəl] n ensayo m.

rehearse [rɪ'hɜːs] vtr & vi ensayar.

reign [reɪn] **I** n reinado m. **II** vi reinar.

reigning ['reɪnɪŋ] adj r. **champion**, campeón m actual.

reimburse [ri:ɪm'bɜːs] vtr reembolsar.

rein [reɪn] n 1 (for horse) rienda f; fig **he gave free r. to his emotions**, dio rienda suelta a sus emociones.

reindeer ['reɪndɪər] n reno m.

reinforce [ri:ɪn'fɔːs] vtr (strengthen) reforzar; (support) apoyar; **reinforced concrete**, hormigón armado.

reinforcement [ri:ɪn'fɔːsmənt] n 1 refuerzo m; Constr armazón m. 2 Mil **reinforcements**, refuerzos mpl.

reinstate [ri:ɪn'steɪt] vtr (to job) reincorporar.

reiterate [ri:'ɪtəreɪt] vtr & vi reiterar.

reject [rɪ'dʒekt] **I** n 1 desecho m. 2 Com **rejects**, artículos defectuosos. **II** [rɪ'dʒekt] vtr rechazar.

rejection [rɪ'dʒekʃən] n rechazo m.

rejoice [rɪ'dʒɔɪs] vi regocijarse (at, over, de).

rejuvenate [rɪ'dʒuːvɪneɪt] vtr rejuvenecer; fig revitalizar.

relapse [rɪ'læps] **I** n 1 Med recaída f; **to have a r.**, sufrir una recaída. 2 (into crime, alcoholism) reincidencia f. **II** vi recaer.

relate [rɪ'leɪt] **I** vtr 1 (connect) relacionar. 2 (tell) relatar. **II** vi relacionarse.

related [rɪ'leɪtɪd] adj (linked) relacionado,-a (to, con). 2 **to be r.** to sb, ser pariente de algn.

relation [rɪ'leɪʃən] n 1 (link) relación f; **in** or **with r. to**, respecto a; **it bears no r. to what we said**, no tiene nada que ver con

lo que dijimos. 2 (member of family) pariente,-a m,f.

relationship [rɪ'leɪʃənʃɪp] n 1 (link) relación f. 2 (between people) relaciones fpl; **to have a good/bad r. with sb**, llevarse bien/mal con algn.

relative ['relətɪv] **I** n pariente mf. **II** adj relativo,-a. ◆**relatively** adv relativamente.

relax [rɪ'læks] **I** vtr (muscles, rules) relajar. **II** vi relajarse.

relaxation [ri:læk'seɪʃən] n 1 (rest) descanso m, relajación f. 2 (of rules) relajación f. 3 (pastime) distracción f.

relaxed [rɪ'lækst] adj relajado,-a; (peaceful) tranquilo,-a.

relaxing [rɪ'læksɪŋ] adj relajante.

relay ['ri:leɪ] **I** n 1 relevo m; r. **(race)**, carrera f de relevos. 2 Rad TV retransmisión f. **II** [rɪ'leɪ] vtr 1 (pass on) difundir. 2 Rad TV retransmitir.

release [rɪ'liːs] **I** n 1 (of prisoner) liberación f, puesta f en libertad; (of gas) escape m. 2 Com (record) disco m. 5 Cin estreno m. 4 (record) disco m. 5 Press comunicado m. **II** vtr 1 (let go) soltar; (prisoner) poner en libertad; (gas) despedir. 2 Com poner en venta. 3 Cin estrenar. 4 (record) editar. 5 (publish) publicar.

relegate ['relɪgeɪt] vtr 1 relegar. 2 Ftb **to be relegated**, bajar a una división inferior.

relent [rɪ'lent] vi ceder; (storm) aplacarse.

relentless [rɪ'lentlɪs] adj implacable.

relevant ['reləvənt] adj pertinente (to, a); **it is not r.**, no viene al caso.

reliable [rɪ'laɪəbəl] adj (person) de fiar; **a r. car**, un coche seguro; **a r. source**, una fuente fidedigna. ◆**reliably** adv **to be r. informed that**, saber de buena tinta que.

reliability [rɪlaɪə'bɪlɪtɪ] n 1 (of person) formalidad f. 2 (of car, machine) fiabilidad f.

reliant [rɪ'laɪənt] adj **to be r. on**, depender de.

relic ['relɪk] n 1 Rel reliquia f. 2 (reminder of past) vestigio m. 3 **relics**, (human remains) restos mpl mortales.

relief [rɪ'liːf] n 1 alivio m. 2 (help) auxilio m, ayuda f. 3 Art Geog relieve m.

relieve [rɪ'liːv] vtr 1 aliviar; (monotony) romper. 2 (take over from) relevar. 3 euph **to r. oneself**, hacer sus necesidades. 4 **to r. sb of sth**, coger algo a algn.

relieved [rɪ'liːvd] adj aliviado,-a, tranquilizado,-a.

religion [rɪ'lɪdʒən] n religión f.

religious [rɪ'lɪdʒəs] adj religioso,-a.

relinquish [rɪ'lɪŋkwɪʃ] vtr renunciar a; **to r. one's hold on sth**, soltar algo.

relish ['relɪʃ] **I** n 1 (enjoyment) deleite m. 2 Culin condimento m. **II** vtr agradar.

relocate [ri:ləʊ'keɪt] vtr trasladar.

reluctance [rɪ'lʌktəns] *n* desgana *f*.

reluctant [rɪ'lʌktənt] *adj* reacio,-a; **to be r. to do sth**, estar poco dispuesto,-a a hacer algo. ◆**reluctantly** *adv* de mala gana, a regañadientes.

rely [rɪ'laɪ] *vi* contar (**on**, con), confiar (**on**, en).

remain [rɪ'meɪn] I *vi* 1 (*stay*) permanecer, quedarse. 2 (*be left*) quedar; **it remains to be seen**, está por ver. II *npl* **remains**, restos *mpl*.

remainder [rɪ'meɪndər] *n* resto *m*.

remaining [rɪ'meɪnɪŋ] *adj* restante.

remand [rɪ'mɑːnd] *Jur* I *vtr* remitir; **remanded in custody**, en prevención; **r. in detención** *f*; **on r.**, detenido,-a.

remark [rɪ'mɑːk] I *n* comentario *m*. II *vtr* comentar.

remarkable [rɪ'mɑːkəbəl] *adj* extraordinario,-a; (*strange*) curioso,-a.

remedial [rɪ'miːdɪəl] *adj* reparador,-a; **r. classes**, clases *fpl* para niños atrasados en los estudios.

remedy ['remɪdɪ] I *n* remedio *m*. II *vtr* remediar.

remember [rɪ'membər] I *vtr* 1 acordarse de, recordar. 2 **r. me to your mother**, dale recuerdos a tu madre. II *vi* acordarse, recordar; **I don't r.**, no me acuerdo.

remembrance [rɪ'membrəns] *n* **in r. of**, en recuerdo de; **R. Day**, día *m* en que se conmemora el armisticio de 1918.

remind [rɪ'maɪnd] *vtr* recordar; **r. me to do it**, recuérdame que lo haga; **she reminds me of your sister**, me recuerda a tu hermana; **that reminds me**, ahora que me acuerdo.

reminder [rɪ'maɪndər] *n* recordatorio *m*, aviso *m*.

reminisce [remɪ'nɪs] *vi* rememorar.

reminiscent [remɪ'nɪsənt] *adj* *fml* nostálgico,-a; **to be r. of**, recordar.

remiss [rɪ'mɪs] *adj* (*negligent*) descuidado,-a.

remission [rɪ'mɪʃən] *n* 1 *Med* remisión *f*. 2 *Jur* perdón *m*.

remit [rɪ'mɪt] *vtr* 1 (*send*) remitir. 2 *Jur* referir a otro tribunal.

remittance [rɪ'mɪtəns] *n* 1 (*sending*) envío *m*. 2 (*payment*) giro *m*, pago *m*.

remnant ['remnənt] *n* resto *m*; **remnants**, (*of cloth*) retales *mpl*.

remorse [rɪ'mɔːs] *n* remordimiento *m*.

remorseful [rɪ'mɔːsful] *adj* lleno,-a de remordimiento.

remorseless [rɪ'mɔːsləs] *adj* despiadado,-a.

remote [rɪ'məʊt] *adj* 1 (*far away*) remoto,-a; **r. control**, mando *m* a distancia. 2 (*isolated*) aislado,-a. 3 **r. person**, persona reservada. 4 (*possibility*) remoto,-a; **I haven't the remotest idea**, no tengo la más mínima idea. ◆**remotely** *adv* 1 (*vaguely*) vagamente. 2 (*distantly*) en lugar aislado.

remote-controlled [rɪ'məʊtkən'trəʊld] *adj* teledirigido,-a.

remould, US **remold** ['riːməʊld] *n* *Aut* neumático recauchutado.

removable [rɪ'muːvəbəl] *adj* (*detachable*) que se puede quitar.

removal [rɪ'muːvəl] *n* 1 (*moving house*) mudanza *f*; **r. van**, camión *m* de mudanzas. 2 (*of stain etc*) eliminación *f*.

remove [rɪ'muːv] *vtr* 1 (*move*) quitar; **to r. one's make-up**, desmaquillarse; **to r. one's name from a list**, tachar su nombre de una lista. 2 (*from office*) despedir.

removed [rɪ'muːvd] *adj* **far r. from**, muy diferente de.

remover [rɪ'muːvər] *n* **make-up r.**, desmaquillador *m*; **nail varnish r.**, quitaesmalte *m*; **stain r.**, quitamanchas *m inv*.

remuneration [rɪmjuːnə'reɪʃən] *n* *fml* remuneración *f*.

renaissance [rə'neɪsəns] *n* renacimiento *m*; **the R.**, el Renacimiento. II *adj* renacentista.

rend [rend] *vtr* (*pt & pp* **rent**) *fml* rasgar.

render ['rendər] *vtr* *fml* 1 (*give*) dar. 2 (*make*) hacer. 3 *Com* presentar. 4 (*translate*) traducir.

rendering ['rendərɪŋ] *n* 1 (*of song, piece of music*) interpretación *f*. 2 (*translation*) traducción *f*.

rendezvous ['rɒndɪvuː] I *n* 1 (*meeting*) cita *f*. 2 (*place*) lugar *m* de reunión. II *vi* reunirse.

renegade ['renɪgeɪd] *n* renegado,-a *m,f*.

renew [rɪ'njuː] *vtr* (*contract etc*) renovar; (*talks etc*) reanudar; **with renewed vigour**, con renovadas fuerzas.

renewal [rɪ'njuːəl] *n* (*of contract etc*) renovación *f*; (*of talks etc*) reanudación *f*.

renounce [rɪ'naʊns] *vtr* *fml* renunciar.

renovate ['renəveɪt] *vtr* renovar, hacer reformas en.

renown [rɪ'naʊn] *n* renombre *m*.

renowned [rɪ'naʊnd] *adj* renombrado,-a.

rent [rent] I *n* 1 (*for building, car, TV*) alquiler *m*. 2 (*for land*) arriendo *m*. II *vtr* 1 (*building, car, TV*) alquilar. 2 (*land*) arrendar.

rental ['rentəl] *n* (*of house etc*) alquiler *m*.

renunciation [rɪnʌnsɪ'eɪʃən] *n* *fml* renuncia *f*.

reorganize [riː'ɔːgənaɪz] *vtr* reorganizar.

rep [rep] *fam* I *Com* representante *mf*. 2 *Theat* teatro *m* de repertorio.

repair [rɪ'peər] I *n* reparación *f*, arreglo *m*; **in good/bad r.**, en buen/mal estado. II *vtr* 1 arreglar; (*car*) reparar; (*clothes*) remendar. 2 (*make amends for*) reparar.

repartee [repɑː'tiː] *n* réplica aguda.

repatriate [riː'pætrɪeɪt] *vtr* repatriar.

repay [riː'peɪ] *vtr* (*pt & pp* **repaid**) devolver; **to r. a debt,** liquidar una deuda; **to r. a kindness,** devolver un favor.

repayment [rɪ'peɪmənt] *n* pago *m*.

repeal [rɪ'piːl] *Jur* I *n* revocación *f*. II *vtr* revocar.

repeat [rɪ'piːt] I *vtr* repetir; **to r. oneself,** repetirse. II *n* (*repetition*) repetición *f*; *TV* reposición *f*.

repeated [rɪ'piːtɪd] *adj* repetido,-a. ◆**repeatedly** *adv* repetidas veces.

repel [rɪ'pel] *vtr* 1 (*fight off*) repeler. 2 (*disgust*) repugnar.

repellent [rɪ'pelənt] I *adj* repelente. II *n* (*insect*) r., loción *f* or spray *m* antiinsectos; **water-r.,** impermeable *m*.

repent [rɪ'pent] *vtr & vi* arrepentirse (de).

repentance [rɪ'pentəns] *n* arrepentimiento *m*.

repercussion [riːpə'kʌʃən] *n* (*usu pl*) repercusión *f*.

repertoire ['repətwɑː] *n* repertorio *m*.

repertory ['repətərɪ] *n Theat* teatro *m* de repertorio.

repetition [repɪ'tɪʃən] *n* repetición *f*.

repetitive [rɪ'petɪtɪv] *adj* repetitivo,-a.

replace [rɪ'pleɪs] *vtr* 1 (*put back*) volver a poner en su sitio. 2 (*substitute for*) sustituir, reemplazar.

replacement [rɪ'pleɪsmənt] *n* 1 (*returning*) reemplazo *m*. 2 (*person*) sustituto,-a *m,f*. 3 (*part*) pieza *f* de recambio.

replay ['riːpleɪ] *n* repetición *f*.

replenish [rɪ'plenɪʃ] *vtr* 1 (*fill up*) rellenar. 2 **to r. stocks,** reponer las existencias.

replete [rɪ'pliːt] *adj fml* repleto,-a.

replica ['replɪkə] *n* réplica *f*.

reply [rɪ'plaɪ] I *n* respuesta *f*, contestación *f*. II *vi* responder, contestar.

report [rɪ'pɔːt] I *n* 1 informe *m*; **medical r.,** parte médico; *GB* **school r.,** informe escolar. 2 (*piece of news*) noticia *f*. 3 *Press Rad TV* reportaje *m*. 4 (*rumour*) rumor *m*. 5 *fml* (*of gun*) estampido *m*. II *vtr* 1 **it is reported that ...,** se dice que .... 2 (*tell authorities about*) denunciar. 3 *Press* hacer un reportaje sobre. III *vi* (*of committee member etc*) hacer un informe. 2 *Press* hacer un reportaje. 3 (*for duty etc*) presentarse; *Mil* **to r. sick,** coger la baja por enfermedad.

reported [rɪ'pɔːtɪd] *adj* **r. speech,** estilo indirecto. ◆**reportedly** *adv fml* según se dice.

reporter [rɪ'pɔːtə] *n* periodista *mf*.

repose [rɪ'pəʊz] *fml* I *n* reposo *m*. II *vi* reposar.

repossess [riːpə'zes] *vtr* volver a tomar posesión.

reprehensible [reprɪ'hensəbəl] *adj* reprensible, censurable.

represent [reprɪ'zent] *vtr* representar.

representation [reprɪzen'teɪʃən] *n* 1 representación *f*. 2 *fml* **representations,**

queja *f sing*.

representative [reprɪ'zentətɪv] I *adj* representativo,-a. II *n* 1 representante *mf*. 2 *US Pol* diputado,-a *m,f*; **House of Representatives,** Cámara *f* de Representantes.

repress [rɪ'pres] *vtr* reprimir, contener.

repression [rɪ'preʃən] *n* represión *f*.

repressive [rɪ'presɪv] *adj* represivo,-a.

reprieve [rɪ'priːv] I *n* 1 *Jur* indulto *m*. 2 *fig* alivio *m*. II *vtr* 1 *Jur* indultar. 2 (*give temporary relief to*) aliviar temporalmente.

reprimand ['reprɪmɑːnd] I *n* reprimenda *f*. II *vtr* reprender.

reprisal [rɪ'praɪzəl] *n* represalia *f*.

reproach [rɪ'prəʊtʃ] I *n* reproche *m*; **beyond r.,** intachable. II *vtr* reprochar.

reproachful [rɪ'prəʊtʃfʊl] *adj* reprobador,-a.

reproduce [riːprə'djuːs] I *vtr* reproducir. II *vi* reproducirse.

reproduction [riːprə'dʌkʃən] *n* reproducción *f*.

reproof [rɪ'pruːf] *n fml* reprobación *f*, censura *f*.

reprove [rɪ'pruːv] *vtr fml* reprobar, censurar.

reptile ['reptaɪl] *n* reptil *m*.

republic [rɪ'pʌblɪk] *n* república *f*.

republican [rɪ'pʌblɪkən] *adj & n* republicano,-a *(m,f)*; *US Pol* **R. Party,** Partido Republicano.

repudiate [rɪ'pjuːdɪeɪt] *vtr fml* 1 (*reject*) rechazar. 2 (*not acknowledge*) negarse a reconocer.

repugnant [rɪ'pʌgnənt] *adj* repugnante.

repulse [rɪ'pʌls] *vtr* rechazar.

repulsive [rɪ'pʌlsɪv] *adj* repulsivo,-a.

reputable ['repjʊtəbəl] *adj* (*company etc*) acreditado,-a; (*person, products*) de toda confianza.

reputation [repjʊ'teɪʃən] *n* reputación *f*.

repute [rɪ'pjuːt] *n fml* reputación *f*.

reputed [rɪ'pjuːtɪd] *adj* supuesto,-a; **to be r. to be,** ser considerado,-a como. ◆**reputedly** *adv* según se dice.

request [rɪ'kwest] I *n* petición *f*, solicitud *f*; **available on r.,** disponible a petición de los interesados; *GB* **r. stop,** (*for bus*) parada *f* discrecional. II *vtr* pedir, solicitar.

require [rɪ'kwaɪə] *vtr* 1 (*need*) necesitar, requerir. 2 (*demand*) exigir.

requirement [rɪ'kwaɪəmənt] *n* 1 (*need*) necesidad *f*. 2 (*demand*) requisito *m*.

requisite ['rekwɪzɪt] *fml* I *adj* requerido,-a. II *n* requisito *m*.

requisition [rekwɪ'zɪʃən] I *n* requisición *f*. II *vtr* requisar.

rescind [rɪ'sɪnd] *vtr fml* (*contract*) rescindir; (*law*) abrogar.

rescue ['reskjuː] I *n* rescate *m*; **r. team,** equipo *m* de rescate. II *vtr* rescatar.

rescuer ['reskjʊə] *n* rescatador,-a *m,f*.

research [rɪ'sɜːtʃ] I n investigación f; **R. and Development**, Investigación más Desarrollo. II vtr & vi investigar.

researcher [rɪ'sɜːtʃər] n investigador,-a m,f.

resemblance [rɪ'zembləns] n semejanza f.

resemble [rɪ'zembəl] vtr parecerse a.

resent [rɪ'zent] vtr ofenderse por.

resentful [rɪ'zentful] adj ofendido,-a.

resentment [rɪ'zentmənt] n resentimiento m.

reservation [rezə'veɪʃən] n reserva f.

reserve [rɪ'zɜːv] I n 1 reserva f; **to keep sth in r.**, guardar algo de reserva. 2 Sport suplente m. 3 Mil reserves, reservas fpl. II vtr reservar.

reserved [rɪ'zɜːvd] adj reservado,-a.

reservoir [rezəvwɑː] n embalse m, pantano m; fig reserva f.

reshape [riː'ʃeɪp] vtr rehacer; fig reorganizar.

reshuffle [riː'ʃʌfəl] n Pol remodelación f.

reside [rɪ'zaɪd] vi fml residir.

residence [rezɪdəns] n fml (home) residencia f; (address) domicilio m; (period of time) permanencia f.

resident [rezɪdənt] adj & n residente (mf); **to be r. in**, estar domiciliado,-a en.

residential [rezɪ'denʃəl] adj residencial.

residue [rezɪdjuː] n residuo m.

resign [rɪ'zaɪn] I vtr 1 (give up) dimitir. 2 **to r. oneself to sth**, resignarse a algo. II vi (from job) dimitir.

resignation [rezɪg'neɪʃən] n 1 (from a job) dimisión f. 2 (acceptance) resignación f.

resigned [rɪ'zaɪnd] adj resignado,-a.

resilience [rɪ'zɪliəns] n resistencia f.

resilient [rɪ'zɪliənt] adj (strong) resistente.

resin [rezɪn] n resina f.

resist [rɪ'zɪst] vtr 1 (not yield to) resistir. 2 (oppose) oponerse a.

resistance [rɪ'zɪstəns] n resistencia f.

resit [riː'sɪt] vtr (exam) volver a presentarse a.

resolute [rezəluːt] adj resuelto,-a, decidido,-a.

resolution [rezə'luːʃən] n resolución f.

resolve [rɪ'zɒlv] I n resolución f. II vtr resolver; **to r. to do**, resolverse a hacer. III vi resolverse.

resonant [rezənənt] adj resonante.

resort [rɪ'zɔːt] I n 1 (place) lugar m de vacaciones; **tourist r.**, centro turístico. 2 (recourse) recurso m; **as a last r.**, como último recurso. II vi recurrir (**to**, a).

resound [rɪ'zaʊnd] vi resonar; fig tener resonancia.

resounding [rɪ'zaʊndɪŋ] adj **a r. failure**, un fracaso total; **a r. success**, un éxito rotundo.

resource [rɪ'sɔːs] n recurso m.

resourceful [rɪ'sɔːsful] adj ingenioso,-a.

respect [rɪ'spekt] I n 1 (deference) respeto m; **to pay one's respects to sb**, presentar sus respetos a algn. 2 (relation, reference) respecto m; **in that r.**, a ese respecto; **with r. to**, con referencia a. II vtr respetar.

respectable [rɪ'spektəbəl] adj respetable; (clothes) decente.

respectful [rɪ'spektful] adj respetuoso,-a.

respective [rɪ'spektɪv] adj respectivo,-a. ◆**respectively** adv respectivamente.

respite [respaɪt] n fml respiro m.

resplendent [rɪ'splendənt] adj resplandeciente.

respond [rɪ'spɒnd] vi responder.

response [rɪ'spɒns] n 1 (reply) respuesta f. 2 (reaction) reacción f.

responsibility [rɪspɒnsə'bɪlɪtɪ] n responsabilidad f.

responsible [rɪ'spɒnsəbəl] adj responsable (**for**, de); **to be r. to sb**, tener que dar cuentas a algn.

responsive [rɪ'spɒnsɪv] adj sensible.

rest¹ [rest] I n 1 (break) descanso m; **r. cure**, cura f de reposo; US **r. room**, aseos mpl. 2 (peace) tranquilidad f; **at r.**, (object) inmóbil. 3 (support) apoyo m. 4 Mus pausa f. II vtr 1 descansar. 2 (lean) apoyar; **to r. a ladder against a wall**, apoyar una escalera contra una pared. III vi 1 descansar. 2 (be calm) quedarse tranquilo,-a. 3 **it doesn't r. with me**, no depende de mí; **we'll let the matter r.**, dejémoslo estar.

rest² [rest] n **the r.**, (remainder) el resto, lo demás; **the r. of the day**, el resto del día; **the r. of the girls**, las demás chicas; **the r. of us**, los demás.

restaurant [restərɒnt] n restaurante m; Rail **r. car**, coche m restaurante.

restful [restful] adj relajante.

restitution [restɪ'tjuːʃən] n fml restitución f; **to make r.**, restituir.

restive [restɪv] adj inquieto,-a, nervioso,-a.

restless [restlɪs] adj agitado,-a, inquieto,-a.

restoration [restə'reɪʃən] n 1 (giving back) devolución f. 2 GB Hist **the R.**, la Restauración. 3 (of building, piece of furniture) restauración f.

restore [rɪ'stɔː] vtr 1 (give back) devolver. 2 (re-establish) restablecer. 3 (building etc) restaurar.

restrain [rɪ'streɪn] vtr contener; **to r. one's anger**, reprimir la cólera; **to r. oneself**, contenerse.

restrained [rɪ'streɪnd] adj (person) moderado,-a; (emotion) contenido,-a.

restraint [rɪ'streɪnt] n 1 (restriction) restricción f; (hindrance) traba f. 2 (moderation) moderación f.

restrict [rɪ'strɪkt] vtr restringir, limitar.

restriction [rɪ'strɪkʃən] n restricción f, limitación f.

restrictive [rɪ'strɪktɪv] adj restrictivo,-a.

result [rɪ'zʌlt] **I** n **1** resultado m. **2** (consequence) consecuencia f; **as a r. of**, como consecuencia de. **II** vi **1** resultar; **to r. from**, resultar de. **2** to r. in, causar.

resume [rɪ'zjuːm] **I** vtr (journey, work, conversation) reanudar; (control) reasumir. **II** vi recomenzar.

résumé ['rezjʊmeɪ] n resumen m.

resumption [rɪ'zʌmpʃən] n (of journey, work, conversation) reanudación f.

resurface [ri:'sɜːfɪs] **I** vtr (road) rehacer el firme en. **II** vi fig resurgir.

resurgence [rɪ'sɜːdʒəns] n resurgimiento m.

resurrection [rezə'rekʃən] n resurrección f.

resuscitate [rɪ'sʌsɪteɪt] vtr Med reanimar.

retail ['riːteɪl] **I** n venta f al por menor; r. **outlet**, punto m de venta; r. **price**, precio m de venta al público; **R. Price Index**, Indice m de Precios al Consumo. **II** vtr vender al por menor. **III** vi venderse al por menor. **IV** adv al por menor.

retailer ['riːteɪlə'] n detallista mf.

retain [rɪ'teɪn] vtr **1** (heat) conservar; (personal effects) guardar. **2** (water) retener. **3** (facts, information) recordar. **4** to r. **the services of a lawyer**, contratar a un abogado.

retainer [rɪ'teɪnə'] n **1** (payment) anticipo m sobre los honorarios. **2** (servant) criado,-a m,f.

retaliate [rɪ'tælɪeɪt] vi tomar represalias (against, contra).

retaliation [rɪtælɪ'eɪʃən] n represalias fpl; **in r.**, en represalia.

retarded [rɪ'tɑːdɪd] adj retrasado,-a.

retch [retʃ] vi tener náuseas.

retentive [rɪ'tentɪv] adj retentivo,-a.

rethink [riː'θɪŋk] n fam **to have a r. about sth**, volver a reflexionar sobre algo.

reticent ['retɪsənt] adj reticente.

retina ['retɪnə] n retina f.

retinue ['retɪnjuː] n séquito m.

retire [rɪ'taɪə'] **I** vtr jubilar. **II** vi **1** (stop working) jubilarse. **2** (from race) retirarse; **to r. for the night**, irse a la cama, acostarse.

retired [rɪ'taɪəd] adj jubilado,-a.

retirement [rɪ'taɪəmənt] n jubilación f.

retiring [rɪ'taɪərɪŋ] adj **1** (reserved) reservado,-a. **2** (official) saliente.

retort [rɪ'tɔːt] **I** n réplica f. **II** vi replicar.

retrace [rɪ'treɪs] vtr (recall) reconstruir; **to r. one's steps**, volver sobre sus pasos.

retract [rɪ'trækt] **I** vtr **1** (claws) retraer; (landing gear) replegar. **2** (statement) retirar. **II** vi **1** (claws) retraerse; (landing gear) replegarse. **2** fml retractarse.

retread ['riːtred] n Aut neumático recauchutado.

retreat [rɪ'triːt] **I** n **1** Mil retirada f. **2** (shelter) refugio m. **3** Rel retiro m. **II** vi retirarse (from, de).

retribution [retrɪ'bjuːʃən] n merecido m.

retrieval [rɪ'triːvəl] n recuperación f; Comput information r. system, sistema m de recuperación de datos.

retrieve [rɪ'triːv] vtr **1** (recover) recuperar; (of dog) cobrar; Comput recoger. **2** (rescue) salvar. **3** Ten devolver.

retriever [rɪ'triːvə'] n perro m cazador.

retrograde ['retrəʊgreɪd] adj retrógrado,-a.

retrospect ['retrəʊspekt] n **in r.**, retrospectivamente.

retrospective [retrəʊ'spektɪv] **I** adj retrospectivo,-a. **II** n Art (exposición f) retrospectiva f.

return [rɪ'tɜːn] **I** n **1** (of person) regreso m, vuelta f; **by r. of post**, a vuelta de correo; **in r. for**, a cambio de; **many happy returns!**, ¡felicidades!; r. **match**, partido m de vuelta; r. **ticket**, billete m de ida y vuelta. **2** (of sth borrowed, stolen) devolución f. **3** (profit) beneficio m, ganancia f. **4** (interest) interés m. **II** vtr **1** (give back) devolver; 'r. **to sender**', 'devuélvase al remitente'; **to r. a favour/sb's love**, corresponder a un favor/al amor de algn. **2** Pol reelegir. **3** Jur (verdict) pronunciar. **III** vi **1** (come or go back) volver, regresar. **2** (reappear) reaparecer.

returnable [rɪ'tɜːnəbəl] adj (bottle) retornable.

reunion [riː'juːnjən] n reunión f.

reunite [riːjuː'naɪt] vtr **to be reunited with**, (after separation) reunirse con.

rev [rev] fam **I** n Aut revolución f. **II** vi **to r. (up)**, acelerar el motor.

revamp [riː'væmp] vtr modernizar, renovar.

reveal [rɪ'viːl] vtr (make known) revelar; (show) dejar ver.

revealing [rɪ'viːlɪŋ] adj revelador,-a.

reveille [rɪ'vælɪ] n diana f.

revel ['revəl] vi disfrutar (in, con); **to r. in doing sth**, gozar muchísimo haciendo algo.

revelation [revə'leɪʃən] n revelación f.

revelry ['revəlrɪ] n jarana f, juerga f.

revenge [rɪ'vendʒ] n venganza f; **to take r. on sb for sth**, vengarse de algo en algn.

revenue ['revɪnjuː] n renta f.

reverberate [rɪ'vɜːbəreɪt] vi **1** (sound) reverberar. **2** (ideas, news) resonar.

reverberation [rɪvɜːbə'reɪʃən] n resonancia f.

revere [rɪ'vɪə'] vtr reverenciar.

reverence ['revərəns] n reverencia f.

reverend ['revərənd] Rel **I** adj reverendo,-a; **R. Mother**, reverenda madre. **II** n (Protestant) pastor m; (Catholic) padre m.

reverie ['revərɪ] n ensueño m.

reversal [rɪ'vɜːsəl] n 1 (of order) inversión f. 2 (of attitude, policy) cambio m total. 3 Jur revocación f.

reverse [rɪ'vɜːs] I adj inverso,-a. II n 1 quite the r., todo lo contrario. 2 (other side) (of cloth) revés m; (of coin) cruz f; (of page) dorso m. 3 Aut r. gear, marcha f atrás. III vtr 1 (order) invertir. 2 (turn round) volver del revés. 3 (change) cambiar totalmente. 4 Jur revocar. 5 GB Tel to r. the charges, poner una conferencia a cobro revertido. IV vi Aut dar marcha atrás.

revert [rɪ'vɜːt] vi volver (to, a).

review [rɪ'vjuː] I n 1 (examination) examen m. 2 Mil revista f. 3 Press crítica f, reseña f. 4 (magazine) revista f. II vtr 1 (examine) examinar. 2 Mil to r. the troops, pasar revista a las tropas. 3 (book etc) hacer una crítica de.

reviewer [rɪ'vjuːər] n crítico,-a m,f.

revile [rɪ'vaɪl] vtr fml injuriar.

revise [rɪ'vaɪz] vtr 1 (look over) revisar; (at school) repasar. 2 (change) modificar. 3 (proofs) corregir.

revision [rɪ'vɪʒən] n 1 revisión f; (at school) repaso m. 2 (change) modificación f. 3. (of proofs) corrección f.

revitalize [riː'vaɪtəlaɪz] vtr revivificar.

revival [rɪ'vaɪvəl] n 1 (of interest) renacimiento m; (of the economy) reactivación f; (of a country) resurgimiento m. 2 Theat reestreno m. 3 Med reanimación f.

revive [rɪ'vaɪv] I vtr 1 (interest) renovar; (a law) restablecer; (the economy) reactivar; (hopes) despertar. 2 Theat reestrenar. 3 Med reanimar. II vi 1 (interest, hopes) renacer. 2 Med volver en sí.

revoke [rɪ'vəʊk] vtr revocar; (permission) suspender.

revolt [rɪ'vəʊlt] I n rebelión f, sublevación f. II vi rebelarse, sublevarse. III vtr repugnar, dar asco a.

revolting [rɪ'vəʊltɪŋ] adj repugnante.

revolution [revə'luːʃən] n revolución f.

revolutionary [revə'luːʃənərɪ] adj & n revolucionario,-a (m,f).

revolve [rɪ'vɒlv] I vi girar; fig to r. around, girar en torno a. II vtr hacer girar.

revolver [rɪ'vɒlvər] n revólver m.

revolving [rɪ'vɒlvɪŋ] adj giratorio,-a.

revue [rɪ'vjuː] n revista f.

revulsion [rɪ'vʌlʃən] n repulsión f.

reward [rɪ'wɔːd] I n recompensa f. II vtr recompensar.

rewarding [rɪ'wɔːdɪŋ] adj provechoso,-a.

rewire [riː'waɪər] vtr Elec to r. a house, poner nueva instalación eléctrica a una casa.

reword [riː'wɜːd] vtr expresar con otras palabras.

rewrite [riː'raɪt] vtr (pt **rewrote** [riː'rəʊt] pp **rewritten** [riː'rɪtən]) escribir de nue-

vo.

rhapsody ['ræpsədɪ] n Mus rapsodia f.

rhetoric ['retərɪk] n retórica f.

rhetorical [rɪ'tɒrɪkəl] adj retórico,-a.

rheumatism ['ruːmətɪzəm] n reuma m.

rheumatoid ['ruːmətɔɪd] adj r. arthritis, reuma m articular.

Rhine [raɪn] n the R., el Rin.

rhinoceros [raɪ'nɒsərəs] n rinoceronte m.

rhododendron [rəʊdə'dendrən] n rododendro m.

Rhone [rəʊn] n the R., el Ródano.

rhubarb ['ruːbɑːb] n ruibarbo m.

rhyme [raɪm] I n rima f; (poem) poema m. II vi rimar.

rhythm ['rɪðəm] n ritmo m.

rib¹ [rɪb] n 1 Anat costilla f; r. cage, caja torácica. 2 Knit canalé m. 3 (of umbrella) varilla f. 4 Bot (of leaf) nervio m.

rib² [rɪb] vtr fam burlarse de.

ribald ['rɪbəld] adj (humour) verde.

ribbon ['rɪbən] n cinta f; (in hair etc) lazo m; torn to ribbons, hecho,-a jirones.

rice [raɪs] n arroz m; **brown r.**, arroz integral; r. paper, papel de arroz; r. pudding, arroz con leche.

rich [rɪtʃ] I adj (person, food) rico,-a; (soil) fértil; (voice) sonoro,-a; (colour) vivo,-a. II npl the r., los ricos. ◆**richly** adv ricamente; r. deserved, bien merecido,-a.

riches ['rɪtʃɪz] npl riquezas fpl.

richness ['rɪtʃnɪs] n riqueza f; (of soil) fertilidad f; (of voice) sonoridad f; (of colour) viveza f.

rickets ['rɪkɪts] n Med raquitismo m.

rickety ['rɪkɪtɪ] adj (chair etc) cojo,-a; (car) desvencijado,-a.

ricochet ['rɪkəʃeɪ, 'rɪkəʃet] I n rebote m. II vi rebotar.

rid [rɪd] vtr (pt & pp **rid**) librar; to get r. of sth, deshacerse de algo; to r. oneself of, librarse de.

riddance ['rɪdəns] n fam good r.!, ¡ya era hora!

ridden ['rɪdən] pp → ride.

riddle¹ ['rɪdəl] n 1 (puzzle) acertijo m, adivinanza f. 2 (mystery) enigma m.

riddle² ['rɪdəl] vtr (with bullets) acribillar.

ride [raɪd] I n paseo m, vuelta f; a short bus r., un corto trayecto en autobús; fam to take sb for a r., tomar el pelo a algn; horse r., paseo a caballo. II vtr (pt rode; pp ridden) (bicycle, horse) montar en; can you r. a bike?, ¿sabes montar en bici? III vi 1 (on horse) montar a caballo. 2 (travel) (in bus, train etc) viajar. 3 Naut to r. at anchor, estar anclado,-a. ◆**ride out** vtr sobrevivir; to r. out the storm, capear el temporal.

rider ['raɪdər] n (of horse) (man) jinete m, (woman) amazona f; (of bicycle) ciclista mf; (of motorbike) motociclista mf.

ridge [rɪdʒ] n (of crest of a hill) cresta f; (hillock) loma f; (of roof) caballete m; Meteor

ridicule [ˈrɪdɪkjuːl] **I** n burla f. **II** vtr burlarse de.

ridiculous [rɪˈdɪkjʊləs] adj ridículo,-a.

riding [ˈraɪdɪŋ] n equitación f; r. breeches, pantalones mpl de montar; r. school, escuela hípica.

rife [raɪf] adj abundante; rumour is r. that ..., corre la voz de que ...; to be r. with, abundar en.

riffraff [ˈrɪfræf] n fam chusma f, gentuza f.

rifle¹ [ˈraɪfəl] n fusil m, rifle m; r. range, campo m de tiro.

rifle² [ˈraɪfəl] vtr desvalijar.

rift [rɪft] n **1** Geol falla f. **2** fig (in friendship) ruptura f, Pol (in party) escisión f; (quarrel) desavenencia f.

rig [rɪg] **I** n **1** Naut aparejo m. **2** (oil) r. (onshore) torre f de perforación, (offshore) plataforma petrolífera. **II** vtr pej amañar. ◆**rig out** vtr fam ataviar. ◆**rig up** vtr improvisar.

rigging [ˈrɪgɪŋ] n aparejo m, jarcia f.

right [raɪt] **I** adj **1** (not left) derecho,-a; the r. hand, la mano derecha. **2** (correct) correcto,-a; (time) exacto,-a.; to be r.; tener razón; all r., de acuerdo; r.?, ¿vale?; that's r., eso es; the r. word, la palabra justa. **3** (true) cierto,-a. **4** (suitable) adecuado,-a; the r. time, el momento oportuno. **5** (proper) apropiado,-a. **6** fam (healthy) bien. **7** fam (complete) auténtico,-a. **8** (in order) en orden. **9** r. angle, ángulo recto.

II n **1** (right side) derecha f. **2** (right hand) mano derecha. **3** Pol the R., la derecha. **4** (lawful claim) derecho m; in one's own r., por derecho propio; r. of way, (across land) derecho de paso; (on roads) prioridad f; civil rights, derechos civiles. **5** r. and wrong, el bien y el mal.

III adv **1** (correctly) bien; it's just r., es justo lo que hacía falta. **2** r. away, (immediately) en seguida. **3** (to the right) a la derecha; r. and left, a diestro y siniestro; to turn r., girar a la derecha. **4** (directly) directamente; to go r. on, sigue recto; r. at the top, en lo alto; r. in the middle, justo en medio; r. to the end, hasta el final.

IV vtr **1** (correct) corregir. **2** (put straight) enderezar.

righteous [ˈraɪtʃəs] adj (upright) recto,-a.

rightful [ˈraɪtfʊl] adj legítimo,-a.

right-hand [ˈraɪthænd] adj derecho,-a; r.-h. drive, conducción f por la derecha; r.-h. side, lado derecho; fam r.-h. man, brazo derecho.

right-handed [raɪtˈhændɪd] adj (person) que usa la mano derecha; (tool) para la mano derecha.

rightly [ˈraɪtlɪ] adv debidamente; and r. so, y con razón.

right-wing [ˈraɪtwɪŋ] adj de derechas, de-

rechista.

right-winger [raɪtˈwɪŋər] n derechista mf.

rigid [ˈrɪdʒɪd] adj rígido,-a, inflexible.

rigidity [rɪˈdʒɪdɪtɪ] n rigidez f, inflexibilidad f.

rigmarole [ˈrɪgmərəʊl] n fam galimatías m inv.

rigorous [ˈrɪgərəs] adj riguroso,-a.

rigour, US **rigor** [ˈrɪgər] n rigor m, severidad f.

rile [raɪl] vtr fam irritar, sacar de quicio.

rim [rɪm] n (edge) borde m; (of wheel) llanta f; (of spectacles) montura f.

rind [raɪnd] n (of fruit, cheese) corteza f.

ring¹ [rɪŋ] **I** n **1** (sound of bell) toque m; (of doorbell, alarm clock) timbre m. **2** Tel llamada f. **II** vtr (pt rang; pp rung) **1** (bell) tocar; fig it rings a bell, me suena. **2** GB Tel llamar por teléfono. **III** vi **1** (bell, phone etc) sonar. **2** my ears are ringing, tengo un pitido en los oídos. **3** Tel llamar. ◆**ring back** vtr GB Tel volver a llamar. ◆**ring off** vi GB Tel colgar. ◆**ring out** vi resonar. ◆**ring up** vtr GB Tel llamar por teléfono a.

ring² [rɪŋ] **I** n **1** (metal hoop) aro m; (curtain r., napkin r.) anilla f; r. binder, carpeta f de anillas. **2** (for finger) anillo m, sortija f; r. finger, dedo m anular. **3** (circle) círculo m; r. road, carretera f de circunvalación. **4** Gymn rings, anillas fpl. **5** (group of people) corro m; (of spies) red f; (of thieves) banda f. **6** (arena) pista f, Box cuadrilátero m; (for bullfights) ruedo m; circus r., pista de circo. **II** vtr **1** (bird, animal) anillar. **2** (surround) rodear.

ringing [ˈrɪŋɪŋ] n (of bell) toque m, repique m; (in ears) zumbido m.

ringleader [ˈrɪŋliːdər] n cabecilla mf.

ringlet [ˈrɪŋlɪt] n tirabuzón m.

rink [rɪŋk] n pista f; ice r., pista de hielo.

rinse [rɪns] **I** n **1** (of clothes, hair) aclarado m; (of dishes) enjuagado m. **2** (tint for hair) reflejo m. **II** vtr **1** aclarar; (the dishes) enjuagar. **2** to r. one's hair, (tint) darse reflejos en el pelo.

Rioja [riːˈɒxə] n Rioja.

riot [ˈraɪət] **I** n **1** disturbio m, motín m; to run r., desmandarse; r. police, policía f antidisturbios. **2** fig (of colour) profusión f. **II** vi amotinarse.

rioter [ˈraɪətər] n amotinado,-a m,f.

riotous [ˈraɪətəs] adj **1** amotinado,-a. **2** (noisy) bullicioso,-a. **3** (unrestrained) desenfrenado,-a.

rip [rɪp] **I** n (tear) rasgón m. **II** vtr rasgar, rajar; to r. one's trousers, rajarse los pantalones. **III** vi rasgarse, rajarse. ◆**rip off** vtr fam to r. sb off, timar a algn. ◆**rip up** vtr hacer pedacitos.

ripcord [ˈrɪpkɔːd] n cuerda f de apertura.

ripe [raɪp] adj **1** maduro,-a. **2** (ready) listo,-a; the time is r., es el momento oportuno.

ripen ['raɪpən] vtr & vi madurar.

rip-off ['rɪpɒf] n fam timo m.

ripple ['rɪpəl] I n 1 (on water, fabric) onda f. 2 (sound) murmullo m. II vtr (water) ondular. III vi 1 (water) ondularse. 2 (applause) extenderse.

rise [raɪz] I n 1 (of slope, hill) cuesta f. 2 (of waters) crecida f. 3 (in status) ascenso m. 4 (in prices, temperature) subida f; (in wages) aumento m. 5 (in sound) aumento m. 6 to give r. to, ocasionar. II vi (pt rose; pp risen ['rɪzən]) 1 (land etc) elevarse. 2 (waters) crecer; (river) nacer; (tide) subir; (wind) levantarse. 3 (sun, moon) salir. 4 (voice) alzarse. 5 (in rank) ascender. 6 (prices, temperature) subir; (wages) aumentar. 7 (curtain) subir. 8 (from bed) levantarse. 9 (land up) levantarse; fig (city, building) erguirse. 10 to r. to a challenge, aceptar un reto; to r. to the occasion, ponerse a la altura de las circunstancias. ◆**rise above** vtr estar por encima de. ◆**rise up** vi (rebel) sublevarse.

rising ['raɪzɪŋ] I adj (sun) naciente; (tide) creciente; (prices) en aumento; r. **damp**, humedad f. II n 1 (of sun) salida f. 2 (rebellion) levantamiento m.

risk [rɪsk] I n riesgo m; at r., en peligro; at your own r., por su cuenta y riesgo; to take risks, arriesgarse. II vtr arriesgar; I'll r. it, correré el riesgo.

risky ['rɪskɪ] adj (riskier, riskiest) arriesgado,-a.

risqué ['rɪskeɪ] adj atrevido,-a; (joke) picante.

rite [raɪt] n rito m; **the last rites**, la extremaunción.

ritual ['rɪtjʊəl] adj & n ritual (m).

rival ['raɪvəl] I adj & n rival (m,f). II vtr rivalizar con.

rivalry ['raɪvəlrɪ] n rivalidad f.

river ['rɪvər] n río m; **down/up r.**, río abajo/arriba.

river-bank ['rɪvəbæŋk] n orilla f, ribera f.

river-bed ['rɪvəbed] n lecho m.

rivet ['rɪvɪt] I n Tech remache m, roblón m. II vtr Tech remachar; fig cautivar.

riveting ['rɪvɪtɪŋ] adj fig fascinante.

road [rəʊd] n 1 carretera f; GB **A/B r.**, carretera nacional/secundaria; **main r.**, carretera principal; (in town) calle f; **r. accident**, accidente m de tráfico; **r. safety**, seguridad f vial; **r. sign**, señal f de tráfico; **r. works**, obras fpl. 2 (street) calle f. 3 (way) camino m.

roadblock ['rəʊdblɒk] n control m policial.

roadhog ['rəʊdhɒg] n fam loco,- a m,f del volante, dominguero,-a m,f.

roadside ['rəʊdsaɪd] n borde m de la carretera; **r. restaurant/café**, restaurante m/cafetería m de carretera.

roadworthy ['rəʊdwɜːðɪ] adj (vehicle) en buen estado.

roam [rəʊm] I vtr vagar por, rondar. II vi vagar.

roar [rɔːr] I n (of lion) rugido m; (of bull, sea, wind) bramido m; (of crowd) clamor m. II vi (lion, crowd) rugir; (bull, sea, wind) bramar; (crowd) clamar; fig to r. **with laughter**, reírse a carcajadas.

roaring ['rɔːrɪŋ] adj fam fig a r. **success**, un éxito clamoroso; to do a r. **trade**, hacer un negocio redondo.

roast [rəʊst] I adj (meat) asado,-a; r. **beef**, rosbif m. II n Culin asado m. III vtr (meat) asar; (coffee, nuts) tostar. IV vi asarse; fam fig I'm **roasting**, me aso de calor.

rob [rɒb] vtr robar; (bank) atracar.

robber ['rɒbər] n ladrón,-a m,f; **bank r.**, atracador,-a m,f.

robbery ['rɒbərɪ] n robo m.

robe [rəʊb] n (ceremonial) toga f; (dressing gown) bata f.

robin ['rɒbɪn] n petirrojo m.

robot ['rəʊbɒt] n robot m.

robust [rəʊˈbʌst] adj (sturdy) robusto,-a.

rock [rɒk] I n 1 roca f; fig to be **on the rocks**, (of marriage) estar a punto de fracasar; fig **whisky on the rocks**, whisky m con hielo. 2 US (stone) piedra f. 3 GB (sweet) stick of r., barra f de caramelo. 4 Mus música f rock; r. **and roll**, rock and roll m. II vtr 1 (chair) mecer; (baby) acunar. 2 (shake) hacer temblar; fig (shock) conmover. III vi 1 (move to and fro) mecerse. 2 (shake) vibrar.

rock-bottom [rɒkˈbɒtəm] adj bajísimo,-a; r.-b. **prices**, precios regalados.

rockery ['rɒkərɪ] n jardín m de rocas.

rocket ['rɒkɪt] I n cohete m; r. **launcher**, lanzacohetes m inv. II vi fam (prices) dispararse.

rocking-chair ['rɒkɪŋtʃeər] n mecedora f.

rocking-horse ['rɒkɪŋhɒs] n caballito m de balancín.

rocky ['rɒkɪ] adj (rockier, rockiest) rocoso,-a; fam fig (unsteady) inseguro,- a; **the R. Mountains**, las Montañas Rocosas.

rod [rɒd] n (of metal) barra f; (stick) vara f; **fishing r.**, caña f de pescar.

rode [rəʊd] pt → ride.

rodent ['rəʊdənt] n roedor m.

roe¹ [rəʊ] n Zool r. (deer), corzo,-a m,f.

roe² [rəʊ] n (fish eggs) hueva f.

rogue [rəʊg] n granuja m.

role n, **rôle** [rəʊl] n papel m; **to play a r.**, desempeñar un papel.

roll [rəʊl] I n 1 rollo m; r. **of banknotes**, fajo m de billetes; fam fig **rolls of fat**, michelines mpl. 2 (**bread**) r., bollo m. 3 (list of names) lista f, nómina f; to call **the r.**, pasar lista. 4 (of ship) balanceo m. 5 (of drum) redoble m; (of thunder) fragor m. II vtr 1 (ball) hacer rodar. 2 (cigarette) liar.

3 (move) mover. 4 (push) empujar. 5 (lawn, road) allanar. III vi 1 (ball) rodar; fam to be rolling in money, estar forrado,-a. 2 (animal) revolcarse. 3 (ship) balancearse. 4 (drum) redoblar; (thunder) retumbar. ◆roll about, roll around vi rodar (de acá para allá). ◆roll by vi (years) pasar. ◆roll in vi fam (arrive) llegar. 2 (money) llegar a raudales. ◆roll over vi dar una vuelta. ◆roll up I vtr enrollar; (blinds) subir; to r. up one's sleeves, (ar)remangarse. II vi fam (arrive) llegar.

roll-call ['rəʊlkɔ:l] n to have a r., pasar lista.

roller ['rəʊlər] n 1 Tech rodillo m; r. coaster, montaña rusa; r. skate, patín m de ruedas. 2 (large wave) ola f grande. 3 usu pl (for hair) rulo m.

rolling ['rəʊlɪŋ] adj 1 Rail r. stock, material m rodante. 2 (countryside) ondulado,-a. II n rodamiento m; (of ground) apisonamiento m; r. pin, rodillo m (de cocina).

ROM [rɒm] Comput abbr of read only memory, memoria f sólo de lectura, ROM f.

Roman ['rəʊmən] adj & n romano,-a (m,f). R. Catholic, católico,-a m,f (romano,-a); R. law, derecho romano; R. numerals, números romanos.

Romance [rəʊˈmæns] adj Ling románico,-a; romance; R. languages, lenguas románicas.

romance [rəʊˈmæns] I n 1 (tale) novela romántica. 2 (love affair) aventura amorosa. 3 (romantic quality) lo romántico. II vi fantasear.

Romania [rəʊˈmeɪnɪə] n → Rumania.

romantic [rəʊˈmæntɪk] adj & n romántico,-a (m,f).

Rome [rəʊm] n Roma f.

romp [rɒmp] I n jugueteo m. II vi juguetear.

rompers ['rɒmpəz] npl pelele m sing.

roof [ru:f] I n (pl roofs [ru:fs, ru:vz]) 1 tejado m; fam fig to go through the r., (of prices) estar por las nubes; (with anger) subirse por las paredes. 2 Aut techo m; r. rack, baca f. 3 (of mouth) cielo m. II vtr techar.

roofing ['ru:fɪŋ] n materiales mpl usados para techar.

rook [rʊk] n 1 Orn grajo m. 2 Chess torre f.

rookie ['rʊkɪ] n US fam (novice) novato,-a m,f.

room [ru:m] n 1 habitación f, cuarto m; single r., habitación individual; r. service, servicio m de habitación. 2 (space) sitio m, espacio m; make r. for me, hazme sitio.

rooming-house ['ru:mɪŋhaʊs] n US pensión f.

roommate ['ru:mmeɪt] n compañero,-a m,f de habitación.

roomy ['ru:mɪ] adj (roomier, roomiest) amplio,-a.

roost [ru:st] I n palo m, percha f; (hen) r., gallinero m; fig to rule the r., llevar la batuta. II vi posarse.

rooster ['ru:stər] n esp US gallo m.

root¹ [ru:t] n 1 raíz f; to take r., echar raíces. II vtr arraigar. III vi arraigar. ◆root out, root up vtr arrancar de raíz.

root² [ru:t] vi (search) buscar; to r. about or around for sth, hurgar en busca de algo.

root³ [ru:t] vi fam to r. for a team, animar a un equipo.

rope [rəʊp] I n 1 (thin) cuerda f; (thick) soga f; Naut cabo m. 2 fig to know the ropes, tener a algn contra las cuerdas; fam fig to know the ropes, estar al tanto. II vtr (package) atar; (climbers) encordar. ◆rope in vtr fam enganchar. ◆rope off vtr acordonar.

rop(e)y ['rəʊpɪ] adj (ropier, ropiest) GB fam chungo,-a.

rosary ['rəʊzərɪ] n rosario m.

rose¹ [rəʊz] pt → rise.

rose² [rəʊz] n 1 Bot rosa f; r. bed, rosaleda f; r. bush, rosal m. 2 (colour) rosa m. 3 (of watering can) alcachofa f.

rosé ['rəʊzeɪ] n (vino m) rosado m.

rosebud ['rəʊzbʌd] n capullo m de rosa.

rosemary ['rəʊzmərɪ] n romero m.

rosette [rəʊˈzet] n (of ribbons) escarapela f.

roster ['rɒstər] n lista f.

rostrum ['rɒstrəm] n tribuna f.

rosy ['rəʊzɪ] adj (rosier, rosiest) 1 (complexion) sonrosado,-a. 2 fig (future) prometedor,-a.

rot [rɒt] I n 1 (decay) putrefacción f; dry r., putrefacción f de la madera. 2 fam (nonsense) tonterías fpl. II vtr pudrir. ◆rot away vi pudrirse.

rota ['rəʊtə] n usu GB lista f.

rotary ['rəʊtərɪ] adj rotatorio,-a, giratorio,-a.

rotate [rəʊˈteɪt] I vt (revolve) hacer girar. 2 (jobs, crops) alternar. II vi (revolve) girar.

rotating [rəʊˈteɪtɪŋ] adj rotativo,-a.

rotation [rəʊˈteɪʃən] n rotación f.

rotten ['rɒtən] adj 1 (decayed) podrido,-a; (tooth) picado,-a. 2 fam (very bad) malísimo,-a; fam I feel r., me encuentro fatal.

rouble ['ru:bəl] n rublo m.

rouge [ru:ʒ] I n colorete m. II vtr poner colorete a.

rough [rʌf] I adj 1 (surface, skin) áspero, -a; (terrain) accidentado,-a; (road) desigual; (sea) agitado,-a; (weather) tempestuoso,-a. 2 (rude) grosero,-a; (violent) violento,-a. 3 (voice) bronco,-a. 4 (wine) áspero,-a. 5 (bad) malo,-a; fam to feel r., encontrarse fatal. 6 (approximate) aproximado,-a. 7 (plan etc) preliminar; r. draft, borrador m; r. sketch, esbozo m. 8 (harsh) severo,-a. II adv duramente; fam fig to sleep r., dormir a la intemperie. III n 1 fam (person) matón m. 2 Golf the r., la hierba alta. IV vtr fam to r. it, vivir sin comodidades. ◆**roughly** adv 1 (crudely) toscamente,-a. 2 (clumsily) torpemente. 3 (not gently) bruscamente. 4 (approximately) aproximadamente.

roughage ['rʌfɪdʒ] n (substance) fibra f.

rough-and-ready [rʌfən'redɪ] adj improvisado,-a.

roughcast ['rʌfkɑːst] n mortero grueso.

roughen ['rʌfən] vtr poner áspero,-a.

roulette [ruː'let] n ruleta f.

Roumania [ruː'meɪnɪə] n → **Rumania**.

round [raʊnd] I adj redondo,-a; in r. figures, en números redondos; r. table, mesa redonda; r. trip, viaje m de ida y vuelta. II n 1 (circle) círculo m. 2 (series) serie f; r. of talks, ronda f de negociaciones. 3 (of ammunition) cartucho m; (salvo) salva f. 4 a r. of toast, unas tostadas. 5 (of drinks) ronda f. 6 the daily r., (routine) la rutina diaria. 7 Golf partido m; Cards partida f. 8 Box round m. 9 (in a competition) eliminatoria f. 10 rounds, (doctor's) visita f sing; (of salesman) recorrido m sing. III adv all year r., durante todo el año; to invite sb r., invitar a algn a casa. IV prep alrededor de; r. here, por aquí; r. the clock, día y noche; r. the corner, a la vuelta de la esquina. V vtr (turn) dar la vuelta a. ◆**round off** vtr acabar, concluir. ◆**round on** vtr (attack) atacar. ◆**round up** vtr (cattle) acorralar, rodear; (people) reunir. ◆**roundly** adv completamente, totalmente.

roundabout ['raʊndəbaʊt] I n 1 (merry-go-round) tiovivo m. 2 GB Aut rotonda f. II adj indirecto,-a.

rounders ['raʊndəz] n GB juego m parecido al béisbol.

round-shouldered [raʊnd'ʃəʊldəd] adj cargado,-a de espaldas.

round-up ['raʊndʌp] n 1 (of cattle) rodeo m; (of suspects) redada f. 2 (summary) resumen m.

rouse [raʊz] vtr despertar; (stir up) suscitar.

rousing ['raʊzɪŋ] adj (cheer) entusiasta; (applause) caluroso,-a; (speech, song) conmovedor,-a.

rout [raʊt] I n aniquilación f. II vtr anquilar.

route [ruːt] I n 1 ruta f; (of bus) línea f; Naut derrota f; fig camino m; r. map, mapa m de carreteras. 2 US R., ≈ carretera f nacional. II vtr encaminar.

routine [ruː'tiːn] I n 1 rutina f. 2 Theat número m. II adj rutinario,-a.

roving ['raʊvɪŋ] adj errante; r. reporter, enviado,-a m,f especial.

row[^1] [rəʊ] n fila f, hilera f; fig three times in a r., tres veces seguidas.

row[^2] [rəʊ] vtr & vi (in a boat) remar.

row[^3] [raʊ] I n 1 (quarrel) pelea f, bronca f. 2 (noise) jaleo m; (protest) escándalo m. II vi pelearse.

rowboat ['rəʊbəʊt] n US bote m de remos.

rowdy ['raʊdɪ] I adj (rowdier, rowdiest) 1 (noisy) ruidoso,-a; (disorderly) alborotador,-a. 2 (quarrelsome) camorrista. II n camorrista mf.

rowing ['rəʊɪŋ] n remo m; r. boat, bote m de remos.

royal ['rɔɪəl] I adj real; r. blue, azul marino; the R. Family, la Familia Real. II npl the Royals, los miembros de la Familia Real. ◆**royally** adv fig magníficamente.

royalty ['rɔɪəltɪ] n 1 (royal persons) miembro(s) m(pl) de la Familia Real. 2 royalties, derechos mpl de autor.

RPI [ɑːpiːaɪ] n abbr of Retail Price Index, IPC.

rpm [ɑːpiːem] abbr revolutions per minute, revoluciones fpl por minuto, r.p.m.

RSPCA [ɑːrespiːsiːeɪ] GB abbr of Royal Society for the Prevention of Cruelty to Animals, ≈ Sociedad f Protectora de Animales, SPA.

RSVP [ɑːresviːtiːpiː] abbr of répondez s'il vous plaît (please reply), se ruega contestación, S.R.C.

Rt Hon GB Pol abbr of (the) Right Honourable, su Señoría.

rub [rʌb] I n to give sth a r., frotar algo. II vtr frotar; (hard) restregar; (massage) friccionar. III vi rozar (against, contra). ◆**rub down** vtr rotar; (horse) almohazar; (surface) raspar. ◆**rub in** vtr 1 (cream etc) frotar con. 2 fam don't r. it in, no me lo refriegues. ◆**rub off** I vtr (erase) borrar. II vi fig to r. off on sb, influir en algn. ◆**rub out** vtr borrar. ◆**rub up** vtr fam fig to r. sb up the wrong way, fastidiar a algn.

rubber[^1] ['rʌbə] n 1 (substance) caucho m, goma f; r. band, goma f; r. plant, gomero m; r. stamp, tampón m. 2 GB (eraser) goma f (de borrar). 3 sl (condom) goma f.

rubber[^2] ['rʌbə] n Bridge rubber m.

rubbery ['rʌbərɪ] adj (elastic) elástico,-a.

rubbish ['rʌbɪʃ] n 1 GB (refuse) basura f; r. bin, cubo m de la basura; r. dump, vertedero m. 2 fam (worthless thing) birria f. 3 fam (nonsense) tonterías fpl.

rubble ['rʌbəl] n escombros mpl.

rubric ['ruːbrɪk] n rúbrica f.

ruby ['ruːbɪ] n rubí m.

rucksack ['rʌksæk] n mochila f.

ructions ['rʌkʃənz] npl fam jaleo m sing.

rudder ['rʌdə'] n timón m.

ruddy ['rʌdɪ] adj (**ruddier**, **ruddiest**) 1 (complexion) rojizo,-a, colorado,-a. 2 GB fam (damned) maldito,-a.

rude [ru:d] adj 1 (impolite) maleducado,-a; (foul-mouthed) grosero,-a; **don't be r. to your mother**, no le faltes al respeto a tu madre. 2 a **r. awakening**, un despertar repentino.

rudimentary [ru:dɪ'mentərɪ] adj rudimentario,-a.

rudiments ['ru:dɪmənts] npl rudimentos mpl.

rue [ru:] vtr arrepentirse de.

rueful ['ru:ful] adj (regretful) arrepentido,-a; (sad) triste.

ruff [rʌf] n 1 (on animal) collarín m. 2 (collar) gorguera f.

ruffian ['rʌfɪən] n canalla m.

ruffle ['rʌfəl] vtr 1 (water) agitar. 2 (feathers) encrespar; (hair) despeinar. 3 fig (annoy) hacer perder la calma.

ruffled ['rʌfəld] adj 1 (hair) alborotado,-a; (clothes) en desorden. 2 (perturbed) perturbado,-a.

rug [rʌg] n alfombra f, alfombrilla f.

rugby ['rʌgbɪ] n rugby m; **r. league**, rugby a trece; **r. union**, rugby a quince.

rugged ['rʌgɪd] adj 1 (terrain) accidentado,-a. 2 (features) marcado,-a. 3 (character) vigoroso,-a.

rugger ['rʌgə'] n fam rugby m.

ruin ['ru:ɪn] I n 1 ruina f. 2 **ruins**, ruinas fpl, restos mpl; **in r.**, en ruinas. II vtr arruinar; (spoil) estropear.

rule [ru:l] I n 1 regla f, norma f; **to work to r.**, hacer una huelga de celo; **as a r.**, por regla general. 2 (government) dominio m; (of monarch) reinado m; **r. of law**, imperio m de la ley. II vtr & vi 1 (govern) gobernar; (of monarch) reinar. 2 (decide) decidir; (decree) decretar. 3 (draw) tirar. ◆**rule out** vtr descartar.

ruled [ru:ld] adj rayado,-a.

ruler ['ru:lə'] n 1 dirigente mf; (monarch) soberano,-a m,f. 2 (for measuring) regla f.

ruling ['ru:lɪŋ] I adj (in charge) dirigente; fig (predominant) predominante; **the r. party**, el partido en el poder. II n Jur fallo m.

rum [rʌm] n ron m.

Rumania [ru:'meɪnɪə] n Rumanía.

Rumanian [ru:'meɪnɪən] I adj rumano,-a. II n (person) rumano,-a m,f; (language) rumano m.

rumble ['rʌmbəl] I n 1 ruido sordo; (of thunder) estruendo m. 2 (of stomach) ruido m. II vi 1 hacer un ruido sordo; (thunder) retumbar. 2 (stomach etc) hacer ruidos.

ruminate ['ru:mɪneɪt] vi (chew, ponder) rumiar.

rummage ['rʌmɪdʒ] vi revolver (**through**, en).

rumour, US **rumor** ['ru:mə'] I n rumor m; **r. has it that ...**, se dice que .... II vtr **it is rumoured that**, se rumorea que.

rump [rʌmp] n (of animal) ancas fpl; fam hum (of person) trasero m; **r. steak**, filete m de lomo.

rumpus ['rʌmpəs] n fam jaleo m.

run [rʌn] I n 1 carrera f; **on the r.**, fugado,-a; **to go for a r.**, hacer footing; **fig in the long r.**, a largo plazo. 2 (trip) paseo m, vuelta f. 3 (sequence) serie f. 4 **ski r.**, pista f de esquí. 5 (demand) gran demanda f; **a r. on**, una gran demanda de. 6 **to give sb the r. of a house**, poner una casa a disposición de algn. 7 Print tirada f. 8 (in stocking) carrera f.
II vtr (pt **ran**; pp **run**) 1 correr; **to r. a race**, correr en una carrera; **to r. errands**, hacer recados. 2 (drive) llevar. 3 (house, business) llevar; (company) dirigir; (organize) organizar. 4 (fingers) pasar. 5 **it's a cheap car to r.**, (operate) es un coche económico; Comput **to r. a program**, pasar un programa. 6 Press publicar.
III vi 1 correr. 2 (colour) desteñirse. 3 (water, river) correr; **to leave the tap running**, dejar el grifo abierto; fam **your nose is running**, se te caen los mocos. 4 (operate) funcionar; **trains r. every two hours**, hay trenes cada dos horas. 5 Naut **to r. aground**, encallar. 6 Pol **to r. for president**, presentarse como candidato a la presidencia. 7 **so the story runs**, según lo que se dice. 8 (range) oscilar (**between**, entre). 9 **we're running low on milk**, nos queda poca leche. 10 **shyness runs in the family**, la timidez le viene de familia. 11 Cin Theat estar en cartel. 12 (last) durar. 13 (stocking) tener una carrera. ◆**run about** vi 'corretear. ◆**run across** vtr (meet) tropezar con. ◆**run away** vi fugarse; (horse) desbocarse. ◆**run down** I vtr 1 (stairs) bajar corriendo. 2 (in car) atropellar. 3 (criticise) criticar. II vi (battery) agotarse; (clock) pararse. ◆**run in** vtr Aut rodar. ◆**run into** vtr 1 (room) entrar corriendo en. 2 (people, problems) tropezar con. 3 (crash into) chocar contra. ◆**run off** I vtr Print (copies) tirar. II vi escaparse. ◆**run on** I vtr Typ enlazar. II vi (function) funcionar con. ◆**run out** vi 1 (exit) salir corriendo. 2 (come to an end) agotarse; (of contract) vencer; **to r. out of**, quedarse sin. ◆**run over** I vtr 1 (in car) atropellar. 2 (rehearse) ensayar. II vi (overflow) rebosar. ◆**run through** vtr 1 (of fear) pasar por. 2 (read quickly) echar un vistazo a. 3 (rehearse) ensayar. ◆**run up** vtr 1 (flag) izar. 2 (debts) acumular. ◆**run up against** vtr tropezar con.

runaway ['rʌnəwet] I n fugitivo,-a m,f. II

adj (person) huido,-a; *(horse)* desbocado, -a; *(vehicle)* incontrolado,-a; *(inflation)* galopante; *(success)* clamoroso,-a.

rundown ['rʌndaʊn] *n fam* to give sb a r., poner a algn al corriente.

run-down [rʌn'daʊn] *adj* 1 *(exhausted)* agotado,-a. 2 *(dilapidated)* ruinoso,-a.

rung¹ [rʌŋ] *pp* → ring.

rung² [rʌŋ] *n (of ladder)* escalón *m*, peldaño *m*.

runner ['rʌnər] *n* 1 corredor,-a *m,f*. 2 *(horse)* caballo *m* de carreras. 3 *(of skate)* cuchilla *f*. 4 *(on table)* tapete *m*. 5 r. bean, judía escarlata.

runner-up [rʌnər'ʌp] *n* subcampeón,-ona *m,f*.

running ['rʌnɪŋ] I *n* 1 he likes running, le gusta correr; *fig* to be in the r. for sth, tener posibilidades de conseguir algo. 2 *(of company)* dirección *f*. 3 *(of machine)* funcionamiento *m*. II *adj* 1 r. commentary, comentario *m* en directo; r. costs, gastos *mpl* de mantenimiento; *Pol* r. mate, candidato *m* a la vicepresidencia; r. water, agua *f* corriente. 2 three weeks r., tres semanas seguidas.

runny ['rʌnɪ] *adj (runnier, runniest)* blando,-a; *(egg)* crudo,-a; *(butter)* derretido,-a; *(nose)* que moquea.

run-of-the-mill [rʌnəvðə'mɪl] *adj* corriente y moliente.

runt [rʌnt] *n fam* enano,-a *m,f*.

run-up ['rʌnʌp] *n (to elections)* preliminares *mpl*.

runway ['rʌnweɪ] *n Av* pista *f* (de aterrizaje y despegue).

rupee [ru:'pi:] *n* rupia *f*.

rupture ['rʌptʃər] I *n* 1 *Med* hernia *f*. 2 *fig* ruptura *f*. II *vtr* 1 to r. oneself, herniarse. 2 *(break)* romper.

rural ['rʊərəl] *adj* rural.

ruse [ru:z] *n* ardid *m*, astucia *f*.

rush¹ [rʌʃ] *n Bot* junco *m*.

rush² [rʌʃ] I *n* 1 *(hurry)* prisa *f*; *(hustle and bustle)* ajetreo *m*; there's no r., no corre prisa; r. hour, hora punta. 2 *(demand)* demanda *f*. 3 *(of wind)* ráfaga *f*. 4 *(of water)* torrente *m*. 5 *Mil* ataque *m*. II *vtr* 1 *(task)* hacer de prisa; *(person)* meter prisa a; to r. sb to hospital, llevar a algn urgentemente al hospital. 2 *(attack)* abalanzarse sobre; *Mil* tomar por asalto. III *vi (go quickly)* precipitarse. ◆**rush about** *vi* correr de un lado a otro. ◆**rush into** *vtr fig* to r. into sth, hacer algo sin pensarlo bien. ◆**rush off** *vi* irse corriendo.

rusk [rʌsk] *n* galleta dura para niños.

Russia ['rʌʃə] *n* Rusia *f*.

Russian ['rʌʃən] I *adj* ruso,-a. II *n* 1 *(person)* ruso,-a *m,f*. 2 *(language)* ruso *m*.

rust [rʌst] I *n* 1 *(substance)* herrumbre *f*. 2 *(colour)* pardo rojizo. II *vtr* oxidar. III *vi* oxidarse.

rustic ['rʌstɪk] *adj* rústico,-a.

rustle ['rʌsəl] I *n* crujido *m*. II *vtr (papers etc)* hacer crujir. III *vi (steal cattle)* robar ganado.

rustproof ['rʌstpru:f] *adj* inoxidable.

rusty ['rʌstɪ] *adj (rustier, rustiest)* oxidado,-a; *fam* my French is a bit r., tengo el francés un poco oxidado.

rut [rʌt] *n* 1 *(furrow)* surco *m*; *(groove)* ranura *f*. 2 *fig* to be in a r., ser esclavo de la rutina. 3 *Zool* celo *m*.

ruthless ['ru:θlɪs] *adj* despiadado,-a.

rye [raɪ] *n* centeno *m*; r. bread, pan *m* de centeno; r. grass, ballica *f*; *US* r. (whiskey), whisky *m* de centeno.

S

S, s [es] *n (the letter)* S, s *f*.

Sabbath ['sæbəθ] *n (Jewish)* sábado *m*; *(Christian)* domingo *m*.

sabbatical [sə'bætɪkəl] *adj* sabático,-a.

sabotage ['sæbətɑ:ʒ] I *n* sabotaje *m*. II *vtr* sabotear.

saccharin ['sækərɪn] *n* sacarina *f*.

sachet ['sæʃeɪ] *n* bolsita *f*, sobrecito *m*.

sack [sæk] I *n* 1 *(bag)* saco *m*. 2 *fam* to get the s., ser despedido,-a; *fam* to give sb the s., despedir a algn. II *vtr* 1 *fam* despedir. 2 *Mil* saquear.

sacking ['sækɪŋ] *n Tex* arpillera *f*.

sacrament ['sækrəmənt] *n* sacramento *m*.

sacred ['seɪkrɪd] *adj* sagrado,-a.

sacrifice ['sækrɪfaɪs] I *n* sacrificio *m*. II *vtr* sacrificar.

sacrificial [sækrɪ'fɪʃəl] *adj* s. lamb, chivo expiatorio.

sacrilege ['sækrɪlɪdʒ] *n* sacrilegio *m*.

sacrosanct ['sækrəʊsæŋkt] *adj* sacrosanto,-a.

sad [sæd] *adj (sadder, saddest)* triste; how s.!, ¡qué pena!

sadden ['sædən] *vtr* entristecer.

saddle ['sædəl] I *n (for horse)* silla *f* (de montar); *(of bicycle etc)* sillín *m*. II *vtr (horse)* ensillar; *fam* to s. sb. with sth, cargarle a algn con algo.

saddlebag ['sædəlbæg] *n* alforja *f*.

sadist ['seɪdɪst] *n* sádico,-a *m,f*.

sadistic [sə'dɪstɪk] *adj* sádico,-a.

sadness ['sædnɪs] *n* tristeza *f*.

sadomasochism [seɪdəʊ'mæsəkɪzm] *n* sadomasoquismo *m*.

sae [eseɪ'i:] *abbr of* stamped addressed envelope, sobre franqueado.

safari [sə'fɑ:rɪ] *n* safari *m*; s. park, reserva f.

safe [seif] **I** adj **1** (unharmed) ileso,-a; (out of danger) a salvo; **s. and sound**, sano,-a y salvo,-a. **2** (not dangerous) inocuo,-a. **3** (secure, sure) seguro,-a; **to be on the s. side**, para mayor seguridad; **s. house**, (for spies etc) piso franco. **4** (driver) prudente. **II** n (for money etc) caja f fuerte. **◆safely** adv **1** con toda seguridad. **2** to arrive s., llegar sin incidentes.

safe-conduct [seif'kɒndʌkt] n salvoconducto m.

safe-deposit [seifdi'pɒzit] n **s.-d. (box)**, cámara blindada.

safeguard ['seifgɑːd] **I** n (protection) salvaguarda f; (guarantee) garantía f. **II** vtr proteger, salvaguardar.

safekeeping [seif'kiːpiŋ] n custodia f.

safety ['seifti] n seguridad f; **s. first!**, ¡la seguridad ante todo!; **s. belt**, cinturón m de seguridad; **s. net**, red f de protección; **s. pin**, imperdible m.

saffron ['sæfrən] n azafrán m.

sag [sæg] vi **1** (roof) hundirse; (wall) pandear; (wood, iron) combarse; (flesh) colgar. **2** fig (spirits) flaquear.

sage[1] [seidʒ] **I** adj (wise) sabio,-a. **II** n (person) sabio,-a m,f.

sage[2] [seidʒ] n salvia f.

Sagittarius [sædʒi'teəriəs] n Sagitario m.

Sahara [sə'hɑːrə] n the S., el Sahara.

Saharan [sə'hɑːrən] adj saharaui, sahariano,-a.

said [sed] adj dicho,-a.

sail [seil] **I** n **1** (canvas) vela f; **to set s.**, zarpar. **2** (trip) paseo m en barco. **II** vtr (ship) gobernar; lit navegar. **III** vi **1** ir en barco. **2** (set sail) zarpar. **◆sail through** vtr fam **he sailed through university**, en la universidad todo le fue sobre ruedas.

sailing ['seiliŋ] n navegación f; (yachting) vela f; fam **it's all plain s.**, es todo coser y cantar; **s. boat** or **ship**, velero m, barco m de vela.

sailor ['seilər] n marinero m.

saint [seint] n santo,-a m,f; (before all masculine names except those beginning Do or To) San; (before feminine names) Santa; **S. Dominic**, Santo Domingo; **S. Helen**, Santa Elena; **S. John**, San Juan; **All Saints' Day**, Día m de Todos los Santos.

saintly ['seintli] adj (saintlier, saintliest) santo,-a.

sake [seik] n **for the s. of**, por (el bien de); **for your own s.**, por tu propio bien.

salad ['sæləd] n ensalada f; **potato s.**, ensaladilla f (rusa); **s. bowl**, ensaladera f; **s. cream**, salsa f tipo mahonesa; **s. dressing**, vinagreta f, aliño m.

salami [sə'lɑːmi] n salchichón m, salami m.

salary ['sæləri] n salario m, sueldo m.

sale [seil] n **1** venta f; **for** or **on s.**, en venta; **sales department**, departamento

m comercial; **sales manager**, jefe,-a m,f de ventas. **2** (at low prices) rebajas fpl.

salesclerk ['seilzklɑːk] n dependiente,-a m,f.

salesman ['seilzmən] n **1** vendedor m; (in shop) dependiente m. **2** (commercial traveller) representante m.

salesroom ['seilzruːm] n sala f de subastas.

saleswoman ['seilzwumən] n **1** vendedora f; (in shop) dependienta f. **2** (commercial traveller) representante f.

salient ['seiliənt] adj fig sobresaliente.

saliva [sə'laivə] n saliva f.

sallow ['sæləʊ] adj cetrino,-a.

salmon ['sæmən] **I** n salmón m. **II** adj (of color) salmón.

salmonella [sælmə'nelə] n Biol Med (bacteria) salmonela f; (food poisoning) salmonelosis f.

salon ['sælɒn] n salón m.

saloon [sə'luːn] n **1** (on ship) cámara f. **2** US (bar) taberna f, bar m; GB **s.** (bar), bar de lujo. **3** (car) turismo m.

salt [sɔːlt] **I** n sal f; fig **to take sth with a pinch of s.**, creer algo con reservas; **bath salts**, sales de baño; **smelling salts**, sales aromáticas. **II** adj salado,-a. **III** vtr **1** (cure) salar. **2** (add salt to) echar sal a.

saltcellar ['sɔːltselə'] n salero m.

saltwater ['sɔːltwɔːtə'] adj de agua salada.

salty ['sɔːlti] adj (saltier, saltiest) salado,-a.

salubrious [sə'luːbriəs] adj salubre, sano,-a.

salutary ['sæljutəri] adj (experience) beneficioso,-a; (warning) útil.

salute [sə'luːt] **I** n (greeting) saludo m. **II** vtr **1** Mil saludar. **2** fig (achievement etc) aplaudir. **III** vi Mil saludar.

salvage ['sælvidʒ] **I** n **1** (of ship etc) salvamento m, rescate m. **2** (objects recovered) objetos recuperados. **3** Jur derecho m de salvamento. **II** vtr (from ship etc) rescatar.

salvation [sæl'veiʃən] n salvación f; **S. Army**, Ejército m de Salvación.

Samaritan [sə'mæritən] n samaritano,-a m,f; **the Samaritans**, ≈ el teléfono de la Esperanza.

same [seim] **I** adj mismo,-a; **at that very s. moment**, en ese mismísimo momento; **at the s. time**, (simultaneously) al mismo tiempo; (however) sin embargo; **in the s. way**, del mismo modo; **the two cars are the s.**, los dos coches son iguales. **II** pron el mismo, la misma, lo mismo; fam **the s. here**, lo mismo digo yo; fam **the s. to you!**, ¡igualmente!. **III** adv del mismo modo, igual; **all the s.**, **just the s.**, sin embargo, aun así; **it's all the s. to me**, (a mí) me da igual or lo mismo.

sample ['sɑːmpəl] **I** n muestra f. **II** vtr (wines) catar; (dish) probar.

sanatorium [sænə'tɔːrɪəm] *n* sanatorio *m*.

sanctimonious [sæŋktɪ'məʊnɪəs] *adj* beato,-a.

sanction ['sæŋkʃən] **I** *n* **1** *(authorization)* permiso *m*. **2** *(penalty)* sanción *f*. **3** *Pol* **sanctions**, sanciones *fpl*. **II** *vtr* sancionar.

sanctity ['sæŋktɪtɪ] *n* *(sacredness)* santidad *f*; *(of marriage)* indisolubilidad *f*.

sanctuary ['sæŋktjʊərɪ] *n* **1** *Rel* santuario *m*. **2** *Pol* asilo *m*. **3** *(for birds, animals)* reserva *f*.

sand [sænd] **I** *n* arena *f*; **s. castle**, castillo *m* de arena; **s. dune**, duna *f*. **II** *vtr* **to s.** *(down)*, lijar.

sandal ['sændəl] *n* sandalia *f*.

sandalwood ['sændəlwʊd] *n* sándalo *m*.

sandbag ['sændbæg] *n* saco terrero.

sandpaper ['sændpeɪpər] *n* papel *m* de lija.

sandpit ['sændpɪt] *n* *(in playground etc)* arenal *m*.

sandstone ['sændstəʊn] *n* arenisca *f*.

sandwich ['sænwɪdʒ, 'sænwɪtʃ] **I** *n* *(bread roll)* bocadillo *m*; *(sliced bread)* sandwich *m*; *Educ* **s. course**, curso teórico-práctico. **II** *vtr* intercalar; **it was sandwiched between two lorries**, quedó encajonado entre dos camiones.

sandy ['sændɪ] *adj* (**sandier, sandiest**) **1** *(earth, beach)* arenoso,-a. **2** *(hair)* rubio rojizo.

sane [seɪn] *adj* *(not mad)* cuerdo,-a; *(sensible)* sensato,-a.

sang [sæŋ] *pt* → **sing**.

sanitarium [sænɪ'teərɪəm] *n US* sanatorio *m*.

sanitary ['sænɪtərɪ] *adj* sanitario,-a; *(hygienic)* higiénico,-a; **s. towel**, *US* **s. napkin**, compresa *f*.

sanitation [sænɪ'teɪʃən] *n* sanidad *f* *(pública)*; *(plumbing)* sistema *m* de saneamiento.

sanity ['sænɪtɪ] *n* cordura *f*, juicio *m*; *(good sense)* sensatez *f*.

sank [sæŋk] *pt* → **sink**.

Santa Claus [sæntə'klɔːz] *n* Papá Noel *m*, San Nicolás *m*.

sap[1] [sæp] *n Bot* savia *f*.

sap[2] [sæp] *vtr* *(undermine)* minar; *fig* agotar.

sapling ['sæplɪŋ] *n Bot* árbol *m* joven.

sapphire ['sæfaɪər] *n* zafiro *m*.

sarcasm ['sɑːkæzəm] *n* sarcasmo *m*.

sarcastic [sɑː'kæstɪk] *adj* sarcástico,-a.

sardine [sɑː'diːn] *n* sardina *f*.

Sardinia [sɑː'dɪnɪə] *n* Cerdeña *f*.

sardonic [sɑː'dɒnɪk] *adj* sardónico,-a.

sash[1] [sæʃ] *n* faja *f*.

sash[2] [sæʃ] *n* **s. window**, ventana *f* de guillotina.

sat [sæt] *pt & pp* → **sit**.

Satan ['seɪtən] *n* Satán *m*, Satanás *m*.

satanic [sə'tænɪk] *adj* satánico,-a.

satchel ['sætʃəl] *n* cartera *f* de colegial.

satellite ['sætəlaɪt] *n* satélite *m*; **s. dish aerial**, antena parabólica.

satin ['sætɪn] *n* satén *m*; **s. finish**, *(acabado m)* satinado *m*.

satire ['sætaɪər] *n* sátira *f*.

satirical [sə'tɪrɪkəl] *adj* satírico,-a.

satisfaction [sætɪs'fækʃən] *n* satisfacción *f*.

satisfactory [sætɪs'fæktərɪ] *adj* satisfactorio,-a.

satisfied ['sætɪsfaɪd] *adj* satisfecho,-a.

satisfy ['sætɪsfaɪ] *vtr* **1** satisfacer. **2** *(fulfil)* cumplir con. **3** *(convince)* convencer.

satisfying ['sætɪsfaɪɪŋ] *adj* satisfactorio,-a; *(pleasing)* agradable; *(meal)* que llena.

saturate ['sætʃəreɪt] *vtr* saturar (**with**, de).

Saturday ['sætədɪ] *n* sábado *m*.

sauce [sɔːs] *n* **1** salsa *f*. **2** *fam (impudence)* descaro *m*.

saucepan ['sɔːspən] *n* cacerola *f*; *(large)* olla *f*.

saucer ['sɔːsər] *n* platillo *m*.

saucy ['sɔːsɪ] *adj* (**saucier, sauciest**) *fam* fresco,-a.

Saudi Arabia [saʊdɪə'reɪbɪə] *n* Arabia *f* Saudita *or* Saudí.

Saudi Arabian [saʊdɪə'reɪbɪən] *adj & n* saudita *(mf)*, saudí *(mf)*.

sauna ['sɔːnə] *n* sauna *f*.

saunter ['sɔːntər] **I** *n* paseo *m*. **II** *vi* pasearse.

sausage ['sɒsɪdʒ] *n* *(frankfurter etc)* salchicha *f*; *(cured)* salchichón *m*; *(spicy)* chorizo *m*; *fam* **s. dog**, perro *m* salchicha; *GB* **s. roll**, empanada *f* de carne.

sauté ['səʊteɪ] **I** *adj* salteado,-a. **II** *vtr* saltear.

savage ['sævɪdʒ] **I** *adj* **1** *(ferocious)* feroz; *(cruel)* cruel; *(violent)* salvaje. **2** *(primitive)* salvaje. **II** *n* salvaje *mf*. **III** *vtr* *(attack)* embestir; *fig (criticize)* criticar despiadadamente.

save [seɪv] **I** *vtr* **1** *(rescue)* salvar, rescatar; *fig* **to s. face**, salvar las apariencias. **2** *(put by)* guardar; *(money, energy, time)* ahorrar; *(food)* almacenar; **it saved him a lot of trouble**, le evitó muchos problemas. **II** *vi* **1** **to s. (up)**, ahorrar. **2** **to s. on paper**, *(economize)* ahorrar papel. **III** *n Ftb* parada *f*. **IV** *prep arch* salvo, excepto.

saving ['seɪvɪŋ] **I** *n* **1** *(of time, money)* ahorro *m*. **2** **savings**, ahorros *mpl*; **s. account**, cuenta *f* de ahorros; **s. bank**, caja *f* de ahorros. **II** *adj* **it's his only s. grace**, es el único mérito que tiene.

saviour, *US* **savior** ['seɪvjər] *n* salvador,-a *m,f*.

savour, *US* **savor** ['seɪvər] **I** *n* sabor *m*, gusto *m*. **II** *vi* saborear.

savoury, *US* **savory** ['seɪvərɪ] *adj (tasty)* sabroso,-a; *(salted)* salado,-a; *(spicy)* picante.

saw[1] [sɔː] **I** *n* *(tool)* sierra *f*. **II** *vtr & vi* *(pt* sawed; *pp* sawed *or* sawn) serrar. ◆**saw up** *vtr* serrar (into, en).

saw² ['sɔː] *pt* → **see¹**.

sawdust ['sɔːdʌst] *n* (a)serrín *m*.

sawmill ['sɔːmɪl] *n* aserradero *m*, serrería *f*.

sawn-off ['sɔːnɒf] *adj* recortado,-a; **s.-o. shotgun**, escopeta *f* de cañones recortados.

saxophone ['sæksəfəʊn] *n* saxofón *m*.

say [seɪ] I *vtr* (*pt & pp* said) 1 decir; **it goes without saying that ...,** huelga decir que ...; **it is said that ...,** se dice que ...; **not to s. ...,** por no decir ...; **that is to s.,** es decir; **to s. yes/no,** decir que sí/no; *fam* **I s.!,** ¡oiga!; **what does the sign s.?,** ¿qué pone en el letrero? 2 (*think*) pensar. 3 **shall we s. Friday then ?,** ¿quedamos el viernes, pues? II *n* I **have no s. in the matter,** no tengo ni voz ni voto en el asunto; **to have one's s.,** dar su opinión.

saying ['seɪɪŋ] *n* refrán *m*, dicho *m*.

scab [skæb] *n* 1 *Med* costra *f*. 2 *fam pej* esquirol *mf*.

scaffold ['skæfəld] *n* (*for execution*) patíbulo *m*.

scaffolding ['skæfəldɪŋ] *n Constr* andamio *n*.

scald [skɔːld] I *n* escaldadura *f*. II *vtr* escaldar.

scale¹ [skeɪl] I *n* (*of fish, on skin*) escama *f*; (*in boiler*) incrustaciones *fpl*.

scale² [skeɪl] I *n* 1 escala *f*; **on a large s.,** a gran escala; **to s.,** a escala; **s. model,** maqueta *f*. 2 (*extent*) alcance *m*. 3 *Mus* escala *f*. II *vtr* (*climb*) escalar. ◆**scale down** *vtr* (*drawing*) reducir a escala; (*production*) reducir.

scales [skeɪlz] *npl* (**pair of**) **s.,** (*shop, kitchen*) balanza *f sing*; (*bathroom*) báscula *f sing*.

scallop ['skɒləp] *n* (*mollusc*) vieira *f*. 2 (*shell*) venera *f*.

scalp [skælp] I *n* cuero cabelludo; (*head*) cabeza *f*. II *vtr* arrancar el cuero cabelludo a.

scalpel ['skælpəl] *n* bisturí *m*.

scamper ['skæmpər] *vi* corretear.

scampi ['skæmpɪ] *n* gambas empanadas.

scan [skæn] I *vtr* 1 (*scrutinize*) escrutar; (*horizon*) otear. 2 (*glance at*) ojear. 3 (*of radar*) explorar. II *n Med* exploración ultrasónica; (*in gynaecology etc*) ecografía *f*.

scandal ['skændəl] *n* 1 escándalo *m*; **what a s.!,** ¡qué vergüenza! 2 (*gossip*) chismes *mpl*.

Scandinavia [skændɪ'neɪvɪə] *n* Escandinavia.

Scandinavian [skændɪ'neɪvɪən] *adj & n* escandinavo,-a (*m,f*).

scanner ['skænər] *n Med* escáner *m*.

scant [skænt] *adj* escaso,-a.

scanty ['skæntɪ] *adj* (**scantier, scantiest**)

escaso,-a; (*meal*) insuficiente; (*clothes*) ligero,-a.

scapegoat ['skeɪpgəʊt] *n* chivo expiatorio.

scar [skɑːr] *n* cicatriz *f*.

scarce [skeəs] *adj* escaso,-a; *fig* **to make oneself s.,** largarse. ◆**scarcely** *adv* apenas.

scarcity ['skeəsɪtɪ] *n* escasez *f*; (*rarity*) rareza *f*.

scare [skeər] I *n* (*fright*) susto *m*; (*widespread alarm*) pánico *m*; **bomb s.,** amenaza *f* de bomba. II *vtr* asustar, espantar; *fam* **to be scared stiff,** estar muerto,-a de miedo. ◆**scare away, scare off** *vtr* ahuyentar.

scarecrow ['skeəkrəʊ] *n* espantapájaros *m inv*.

scarf [skɑːf] *n* (*pl* **scarfs** *or* **scarves** [skɑːvz]) (*long, woollen*) bufanda *f*; (*square*) pañuelo *m*; (*silk*) fular *m*.

scarlet ['skɑːlɪt] I *adj* escarlata. II *n* escarlata *f*; **s. fever,** escarlatina *f*.

scarves [skɑːvz] *npl* → **scarf**.

scathing ['skeɪðɪŋ] *adj* mordaz, cáustico,-a.

scatter ['skætər] I *vtr* 1 (*papers etc*) esparcir, desparramar. 2 (*crowd*) dispersar. II *vi* dispersarse.

scatterbrained ['skætəbreɪnd] *adj fam* ligero,-a de cascos; (*forgetful*) despistado,-a.

scattered ['skætəd] *adj* **s. showers,** chubascos aislados.

scavenger ['skævɪndʒər] *n* 1 (*person*) rebuscador,-a *m,f*, trapero *m*. 2 (*animal*) (*animal m*) carroñero,-a *mf*.

scenario [sɪ'nɑːrɪəʊ] *n Cin* guión *m*.

scene [siːn] *n* 1 *Theat Cin* TV escena *f*; **behind the scenes,** entre bastidores. 2 (*place*) lugar *m*, escenario *m*; **a change of s.,** un cambio de aires. 3 (*view*) panorama *m*. 4 **to make a s.,** (*fuss*) montar un espectáculo.

scenery ['siːnərɪ] *n* 1 (*landscape*) paisaje *m*. 2 *Theat* decorado *m*.

scenic ['siːnɪk] *adj* (*picturesque*) pintoresco,-a.

scent [sent] I *n* 1 (*smell*) olor *m*; (*of food*) aroma *m*. 2 (*perfume*) perfume *m*. 3 (*in hunting*) pista *f*. II *vtr* (*add perfume to*) perfumar; (*smell*) olfatear; *fig* presentir.

sceptic ['skeptɪk] *n* escéptico,-a *m,f*.

sceptical ['skeptɪkəl] *adj* escéptico,-a.

scepticism ['skeptɪsɪzəm] *n* escepticismo *m*.

sceptre ['septər] *n* cetro *m*.

schedule ['ʃedjuːl, *US* 'skedʒʊəl] I *n* 1 (*plan, agenda*) programa *m*; (*timetable*) horario *m*; **on s.,** a la hora (prevista); **to be behind s.,** llevar retraso. 2 (*list*) lista *f*; (*inventory*) inventario *m*. II *vtr* (*plan*) programar, fijar.

scheduled ['ʃedjuːld, *US* 'skedʒʊəld] *adj*

scheme 247 scramble

previsto,-a, fijo,-a; **s. flight,** vuelo regular.

scheme [ski:m] **I** *n* **1** *(plan)* plan *m*; *(project)* proyecto *m*; *(idea)* idea *f*; **colour s.,** combinación *f* de colores. **2** *(plot)* intriga *f*; *(trick)* ardid *m*. **II** *vi* *(plot)* tramar, intrigar.

scheming ['ski:mɪŋ] *adj* intrigante, maquinador,-a.

schism ['sɪzəm] *n* cisma *m*.

schizophrenic [skɪtsəʊ'frenɪk] *adj & n* esquizofrénico,-a *(m,f)*.

scholar ['skɒlə^r] *n* *(learned person)* erudito,-a *m,f*; *(pupil)* alumno,-a *m,f*.

scholarship ['skɒləʃɪp] *n* **1** *(learning)* erudición *f*. **2** *(grant)* beca *f*; **s. holder,** becario,-a *m,f*.

school [sku:l] **I** *n* **1** escuela *f*, colegio *m*; **drama s.,** academia *f* de arte dramático; **of s. age,** en edad escolar; **s. year,** año *m* escolar. **2** *US (university)* universidad *f*. **3** *(university department)* facultad *f*. **4** *(group of artists)* escuela *f*; **s. of thought,** corriente *f* de opinión. **II** *vtr* *(teach)* enseñar; *(train)* formar.

schoolbook ['sku:lbʊk] *n* libro *m* de texto.

schoolboy ['sku:lbɔɪ] *n* alumno *m*.

schoolchild ['sku:ltʃaɪld] *n* alumno,-a *m,f*.

schooldays ['sku:ldeɪz] *npl* años *mpl* de colegio.

schoolgirl ['sku:lgɜːl] *n* alumna *f*.

schooling ['sku:lɪŋ] *n* educación *f*, estudios *mpl*.

schoolmaster ['sku:lmɑːstə^r] *n* profesor *m*; *(primary school)* maestro *m*.

schoolmistress ['sku:lmɪstrɪs] *n* profesora *f*; *(primary school)* maestra *f*.

schoolteacher ['sku:lti:tʃə^r] *n* profesor,-a *m,f*; *(primary school)* maestro,-a *m,f*.

schooner ['sku:nə^r] *n* Naut goleta *f*.

sciatica [saɪ'ætɪkə] *n* ciática *f*.

science ['saɪəns] *n* ciencia *f*; *(school subject)* ciencias; **s. fiction,** ciencia-ficción *f*.

scientific [saɪən'tɪfɪk] *adj* científico,-a.

scientist ['saɪəntɪst] *n* científico,-a *m,f*.

scintillating ['sɪntɪleɪtɪŋ] *adj* brillante.

scissors ['sɪzəz] *npl* tijeras *fpl*; **a pair of s.,** unas tijeras.

scoff¹ [skɒf] *vi* *(mock)* mofarse **(at, de).**

scoff² [skɒf] *vtr* *fam* *(eat)* zamparse.

scold [skəʊld] *vtr* regañar, reñir.

scone [skɒn, skɒn] *n* bollo *m*, pastelito *m*.

scoop [sku:p] *n* **1** *(for flour)* pala *f*; *(for ice cream)* cucharón *m*; *(amount)* palada *f*, cucharada *f*. **2** Press exclusiva *f*. ◆**scoop out** *vtr* *(flour etc)* sacar con pala; *(water)* *(from boat)* achicar. ◆**scoop up** *vtr* recoger.

scooter ['sku:tə^r] *n* *(child's)* patinete *m*; *(adult's)* Vespa® *f*.

scope [skəʊp] *n* **1** *(range)* alcance *m*; *(of*

---

undertaking) ámbito *m*. **2** *(freedom)* libertad *f*.

scorch [skɔːtʃ] *vtr* *(singe)* chamuscar.

scorching ['skɔːtʃɪŋ] *adj* *fam* abrasador, -a.

score [skɔː^r] **I** *n* **1** Sport tanteo *m*; Cards Golf puntuación *f*; *(result)* resultado *m*. **2** *(notch)* muesca *f*. **3** **I have a s.** to **settle with you,** tengo que ajustar las cuentas contigo. **4** **on that s.,** a ese respecto. **5** *(twenty)* veintena *f*. **6** Mus *(of opera)* partitura *f*; *(of film)* música *f*. **II** *vtr* **1** *(goal)* marcar; *(points)* conseguir. **2** *(wood)* hacer una muesca en; *(paper)* rayar. **III** *vi* **1** Sport marcar un tanto; Ftb marcar un gol; *(keep the score)* llevar el marcador. **2** *(have success)* tener éxito **(with, con);** *sl* ligar **(with, con).** ◆**score out** *vtr* *(word etc)* tachar.

scoreboard ['skɔːbɔːd] *n* marcador *m*.

scorer ['skɔːrə^r] *n* **1** *(goal striker)* goleador *m*. **2** *(scorekeeper)* encargado,-a *m,f* del marcador.

scorn [skɔːn] **I** *n* desprecio *m*. **II** *vtr* despreciar.

scornful ['skɔːnfʊl] *adj* desdeñoso,-a.

Scorpio ['skɔːpɪəʊ] *n* Escorpión *m*.

scorpion ['skɔːpɪən] *n* alacrán *m*, escorpión *m*.

Scot [skɒt] *n* escocés,-esa *m,f*.

scotch [skɒtʃ] *vtr* *(plot)* frustrar; *(rumour)* negar, desmentir.

Scotch [skɒtʃ] **I** *adj* escocés,-esa; **S. tape®,** cinta adhesiva, celo® *m*. **II** *n* *(whisky)* whisky *m* escocés.

scot-free [skɒt'friː] *adj* impune.

Scotland ['skɒtlənd] *n* Escocia.

Scots [skɒts] **I** *adj* escocés,-esa. **II** *n* **the S.,** *pl* los escoceses.

Scotsman ['skɒtsmən] *n* escocés *m*.

Scotswoman ['skɒtswʊmən] *n* escocesa *f*.

Scottish ['skɒtɪʃ] *adj* escocés,-esa.

scoundrel ['skaʊndrəl] *n* sinvergüenza *mf*, canalla *m*.

scour¹ [skaʊə^r] *vtr* *(clean)* fregar, restregar.

scour² [skaʊə^r] *vtr* *(search)* *(countryside)* rastrear; *(building)* registrar.

scourge [skɜːdʒ] *fig* *n* azote *m*.

scout [skaʊt] **I** *n* Mil explorador,-a *m,f*; Sport Cin cazatalentos *m inv*; **boy s.,** boy *m* scout. **II** *vi* Mil reconocer el terreno; **to s. around for sth,** andar en busca de algo.

scowl [skaʊl] **I** *vi* fruncir el ceño; **to s. at sb,** mirar a algn con ceño. **II** *n* ceño *m*.

scrabble ['skræbəl] **I** *vi* escarbar; *fig* **to s. around for sth,** revolver todo para encontrar algo. **II** *n* **S.®,** Scrabble® *m*.

scraggy ['skrægɪ] *adj* *(scraggier, scraggiest)* delgado,-a, flacucho,-a.

scramble ['skræmbəl] **I** *vi* trepar; **to s. for,** pelearse por; **to s. up a tree,** trepar a un árbol. **II** *vtr* **1** *Culin* **scrambled eggs,** huevos revueltos. **2** *Rad Tel* (*message*) codificar; (*broadcast*) interferir. **III** *n* (*climb*) subida *f*; *fig* **it's going to be a s.,** (*rush*) va a ser muy apresurado.

scrap¹ [skræp] **I** *n* **1** (*small piece*) pedazo *m*; **there isn't a s. of truth in it,** no tiene ni un ápice de verdad; **s.** (*metal*), chatarra *f*; **s. dealer** *or* **merchant,** chatarrero, -a *m,f*; **s. paper,** papel *m* de borrador; **s. yard,** (*for cars*) cementerio *m* de coches. **2 scraps,** restos *mpl*; (*of food*) sobras *fpl*. **II** *vtr* (*discard*) desechar; *fig* (*idea*) descartar.

scrap² [skræp] *fam* **I** *n* (*fight*) pelea *f*. **II** *vi* **pelearse (with,** con).

scrapbook [ˈskræpbʊk] *n* álbum *m* de recortes.

scrape [skreip] **I** *vtr* (*paint, wood*) raspar; (*knee*) arañarse, hacerse un rasguño en. **II** *vi* (*make noise*) chirriar; (*rub*) rozar. **III** *n fam* (*trouble*) lío *m*. ◆**scrape through** *vi fam* (*exam*) aprobar por los pelos. ◆**scrape together** *vtr* reunir a duras penas.

scraper [ˈskreipəʳ] *n* rasqueta *f*.

scrapheap [ˈskræphiːp] *n* (*dump*) vertedero *m*.

scratch [skrætʃ] **I** *n* **1** (*on skin, paintwork*) arañazo *m*; (*on record*) raya *f*. **2** (*noise*) chirrido *m*. **3** *fig* **to be up to s.,** dar la talla; *fig* **to start from s.,** partir de cero. **II** *adj* **s. team,** equipo improvisado. **III** *vtr* **1** (*with nail, claw*) arañar, rasguñar; (*paintwork*) rayar. **2** (*to relieve itching*) rascarse.

scrawl [skrɔːl] **I** *n* garabatos *mpl*. **II** *vtr* (*message etc*) garabatear. **III** *vi* hacer garabatos.

scrawny [ˈskrɔːni] *adj* (**scrawnier, scrawniest**) flaco,-a.

scream [skriːm] **I** *n* chillido *m*; **screams of laughter,** carcajadas *fpl*. **II** *vtr* (*insults etc*) gritar. **III** *vi* chillar; **to s. at sb,** chillar a algn.

scree [skriː] *n* pedregal *m*.

screech [skriːtʃ] **I** *n* (*of person*) chillido *m*; (*of tyres, brakes*) chirrido *m*. **II** *vi* (*person*) chillar; (*tyres*) chirriar.

screen [skriːn] **I** *n* **1** (*movable partition*) biombo *m*. **2** *fig* cortina *f*. **3** *Cin TV Comput* pantalla *f*; **s. test,** casting *m*. **II** *vtr* **1** (*protect*) proteger; (*conceal*) tapar. **2** (*sieve*) (*coal etc*) tamizar; *fig* (*candidates*) seleccionar. **3** (*show*) (*film*) proyectar; (*for first time*) estrenar. **4** *Med* examinar.

screening [ˈskriːnɪŋ] *n* **1** (*of film*) proyección *f*; (*for first time*) estreno *m*. **2** *Med* exploración *f*.

screenplay [ˈskriːnpleɪ] *n* guión *m*.

screw [skruː] **I** *n* **1** tornillo *m*. **2** (*propeller*) hélice *f*. **II** *vtr* **1** atornillar; **to s. sth down** *or* **in** *or* **on,** fijar algo con tornillos. **2** *vulg* joder. ◆**screw up** *vtr* **1** (*piece of paper*) arrugar; (*one's face*) torcer. **2** *sl*

(*ruin*) joder.

screwdriver [ˈskruːdraɪvəʳ] *n* destornillador *m*.

scribble [ˈskrɪbəl] **I** *n* garabatos *mpl*. **II** *vtr* (*message etc*) garabatear. **III** *vi* hacer garabatos.

script [skrɪpt] *n* **1** (*writing*) escritura *f*; (*handwriting*) letra *f*; *Typ* letra cursiva. **2** (*exam*) escrito *m*. **3** *Cin* guión *m*.

Scripture [ˈskrɪptʃəʳ] *n* **Holy S.,** Sagrada Escritura.

scroll [skrəʊl] *n* rollo *m* de pergamino.

scrounge [skraʊndʒ] *fam* **I** *vi* gorronear; **to s. (around) for,** buscar; **to s. off sb,** vivir a costa de algn. **II** *vtr* (*food etc*) gorronear.

scrounger [ˈskraʊndʒəʳ] *n fam* gorrón, -ona *m,f*.

scrub¹ [skrʌb] *n* (*undergrowth*) maleza *f*.

scrub² [skrʌb] **I** *vtr* **1** frotar. **2** *fam* (*cancel*) borrar. **II** *n* (*cleaning*) fregado *m*.

scruff [skrʌf] *n* pescuezo *m*, cogote *m*.

scruffy [ˈskrʌfi] *adj* (**scruffier, scruffiest**) *fam* desaliñado,-a.

scrum [skrʌm] *n Rugby* melée *f*; **s. half,** medio *m* melée.

scruple [ˈskruːpəl] *n* escrúpulo *m*.

scrupulous [ˈskruːpjʊləs] *adj* escrupuloso,-a. ◆**scrupulously** *adv* **s. honest,** sumamente honrado,-a.

scrutinize [ˈskruːtɪnaɪz] *vtr* escudriñar.

scrutiny [ˈskruːtɪni] *n* escrutinio *m*.

scuff [skʌf] *vtr* (*the floor*) rayar; (*one's feet*) arrastrar.

scuffle [ˈskʌfəl] **I** *n* pelea *f*. **II** *vi* pelearse (**with,** con).

scullery [ˈskʌləri] *n* cuarto *m* de pila.

sculptor [ˈskʌlptəʳ] *n* escultor *m*.

sculpture [ˈskʌlptʃəʳ] *n* escultura *f*.

scum [skʌm] *n* (*on liquid*) espuma *f*. **2** *fig* escoria *f*.

scupper [ˈskʌpəʳ] *vtr GB fam* (*plan etc*) desbaratar.

scurrilous [ˈskʌrɪləs] *adj* (*abusive*) difamatorio,-a.

scurry [ˈskʌri] *vi* (*run*) corretear; (*hurry*) apresurarse; **to s. away** *or* **off,** escabullirse.

scuttle¹ [ˈskʌtəl] *n* cubo *m*; **coal s.,** cubo del carbón.

scuttle² [ˈskʌtəl] *vtr* (*ship*) barrenar.

scuttle³ [ˈskʌtəl] *vi* **to s. away** *or* **off,** escabullirse.

scythe [saɪð] **I** *n* guadaña *f*. **II** *vtr* guadañar.

SDI [esdiːˈaɪ] *abbr of* **Strategic Defence Initiative,** Iniciativa *f* para la Defensa Estratégica.

sea [siː] *n mar mf*; **by the s.,** a orillas del mar; **out at sea,** en alta mar; **to go by s.,** ir en barco; **to put to s.,** zarpar; *fig* **to be all at s.,** estar desorientado,-a; **s. breeze,** brisa marina; *fig* **s. change,** metamorfosis *f*; **s. level,** nivel *m* del mar; **s. lion,** león marino; **s. water,** agua *f* de mar.

seabed ['si:bed] *n* fondo *m* del mar.

seaboard ['si:bɔːd] *n US* costa *f*, litoral *m*.

seafood ['si:fuːd] *n* mariscos *mpl*.

seafront ['si:frʌnt] *n* paseo marítimo.

seagull ['si:gʌl] *n* gaviota *f*.

seal[1] [si:l] *n* Zool foca *f*.

seal[2] [si:l] **I** *n* **1** (*official stamp*) sello *m*. **2** (*airtight closure*) cierre hermético; (*on bottle*) precinto *m*. **II** *vtr* **1** (*with official stamp*) sellar; (*with wax*) lacrar. **2** (*close*) cerrar; (*make airtight*) cerrar herméticamente, **3** (*determine*) this sealed his fate, esto decidió su destino. ◆**seal off** *vtr* (*pipe etc*) cerrar; (*area*) acordonar.

seam [si:m] *n* **1** *Sew* costura *f*; *Tech* juntura *f*; *fam* to be bursting at the seams, (*room*) rebosar de gente. **2** *Geol Min* veta *f*, filón *m*.

seaman ['si:mən] *n* marinero *m*.

seamy ['si:mɪ] *adj* (**seamier, seamiest**) *fig* sórdido,-a.

séance ['seɪɑːns] *n* sesión *f* de espiritismo.

seaplane ['si:pleɪn] *n* hidroavión *m*.

seaport ['si:pɔːt] *n* puerto marítimo.

search [sɜːtʃ] **I** *vtr* buscar en; (*building, suitcase etc*) registrar; (*person*) cachear; (*one's conscience*) examinar. **II** *vi* buscar; **to s. through**, registrar. **III** *n* búsqueda *f*; (*of building etc*) registro *m*; (*of person*) cacheo *m*; **in s. of**, en busca de; **s. party**, equipo *m* de salvamento; **s. warrant**, orden *f* de registro.

searching ['sɜːtʃɪŋ] *adj* (*look*) penetrante; (*question*) indagatorio,-a.

searchlight ['sɜːtʃlaɪt] *n* reflector *m*.

seashell ['si:ʃel] *n* concha marina.

seashore ['si:ʃɔː] *n* (*beach*) playa *f*.

seasick ['si:sɪk] *adj* mareado,-a; **to get s.**, marearse.

seaside ['si:saɪd] *n* playa *f*, costa *f*; **s. resort**, lugar turístico de veraneo; **s. town**, pueblo costero.

season[1] ['si:zən] *n* época *f*; (*of year*) estación *f*; (*for sport etc*) temporada *f*; **the busy s.**, la temporada alta; **the rainy s.**, la estación de lluvias; **in s.**, (*fruit*) en sazón; (*animal*) en celo; *GB* **s. ticket**, abono *m*.

season[2] ['si:zən] *vtr Culin* sazonar.

seasonal ['si:zənəl] *adj* estacional.

seasoned ['si:zənd] *adj* **1** *Culin* sazonado,-a. **2** *fig* (*campaigner*) curtido,-a, avezado,-a.

seasoning ['si:zənɪŋ] *n* condimento *m*, aderezo *m*.

seat [si:t] **I** *n* **1** asiento *m*; (*place*) plaza *f*; *Cin Theat* localidad *f*; **to take a s.**, sentarse; *Aut* **s. belt**, cinturón *m* de seguridad. **2** (*of cycle*) sillín *m*; *fam* (*buttocks*) trasero *m*. **3** (*of power, learning*) sede *f*. **4** *Parl* escaño *m*. **II** *vtr* **1** (*guests etc*) sentar. **2** (*accommodate*) tener cabida

para.

seating ['si:tɪŋ] *n* asientos *mpl*; **s. capacity**, cabida *f*, aforo *m*.

seaweed ['si:wiːd] *n* alga *f* (marina).

seaworthy ['si:wɜːðɪ] *adj* en condiciones de navegar.

sec [sek] *n fam* (*abbr of* **second**) segundo *m*.

secede [sɪ'si:d] *vi* separarse (**from**, de).

secluded [sɪ'klu:dɪd] *adj* retirado,-a, apartado,-a.

second[1] ['sekənd] **I** *adj* segundo,-a; **every s. day**, cada dos días; **it's the s. highest mountain**, es la segunda montaña más alta; **on s. thought(s)** ..., pensándolo bien ...; **to have s. thoughts about sth**, dudar de algo; **to settle for s. best**, conformarse con lo que hay. **II** *n* **1** (*in series*) segundo,-a *m,f*; **Charles the S.**, Carlos Segundo; **the s. of October**, el dos de octubre. **2** *Aut* (*gear*) segunda *f*. **3** *Com* **seconds**, artículos defectuosos. **III** *vtr* (*motion*) apoyar. **IV** *adv* to come s., terminar en segundo lugar. ◆**secondly** *adv* en segundo lugar.

second[2] ['sekənd] *n* (*time*) segundo *m*; *fam* **in a s.**, enseguida; **just a s.!**, ¡un momento!; **s. hand**, (*of watch, clock*) segundero *m*.

secondary ['sekəndərɪ] *adj* secundario,-a; *GB* **s. school**, escuela secundaria.

second-class [sekənd'klɑːs] **I** *adj* de segunda clase. **II** *adv* to travel s.-c., viajar en segunda.

second-hand [sekənd'hænd] *adj & adv* de segunda mano.

secondment [sɪ'kɒndmənt] *n GB* traslado *m* temporal.

second-rate [sekənd'reɪt] *adj* de segunda categoría.

secrecy ['si:krəsɪ] *n* secreto *m*; **in s.**, en secreto.

secret ['si:krɪt] **I** *adj* secreto,-a; **to keep sth s.**, mantener algo en secreto; **s. ballot**, votación secreta. **II** *n* secreto *m*; *fig* clave *f*; **in s.**, en secreto; **to keep a s.**, guardar un secreto. ◆**secretly** *adv* en secreto.

secretarial [sekrɪ'teərɪəl] *adj* de secretario,-a.

secretary ['sekrətrɪ] *n* secretario,-a *m,f*; **S. of State**, *GB* ministro,-a *m,f* con cartera; *US* ministro,-a *m,f* de Asuntos Exteriores.

secretion [sɪ'kri:ʃən] *n* secreción *f*.

secretive ['si:krɪtɪv] *adj* reservado,-a.

sect [sekt] *n* secta *f*.

sectarian [sek'teərɪən] *adj & n* sectario,-a (*m,f*).

section ['sekʃən] *n* **1** (*part*) sección *f*, parte *f*; (*of law*) artículo *m*; (*of community*) sector *m*; (*of orchestra, department*) sección *f*. **2** (*cut*) corte *m*.

sector ['sektə] *n* sector *m*.

secular ['sɛkjʊlər] adj (school, teaching) laico,-a; (music, art) profano,-a; (priest) seglar, secular.

secure [sɪ'kjʊər] I adj seguro,-a; (window, door) bien cerrado,-a; (ladder etc) firme. II vtr 1 (make safe) asegurar. 2 (fix) (rope, knot) sujetar, fijar; (object to floor) afianzar; (window, door) cerrar bien. 3 (obtain) conseguir, obtener. 4 Fin (guarantee) avalar.

security [sɪ'kjʊərɪtɪ] n 1 seguridad f; national s., seguridad nacional; S. Council, (of United Nations) Consejo m de Seguridad. 2 Fin (guarantee) fianza f; (guarantor) fiador,-a m,f. 3 Fin securities, valores mpl.

sedan [sɪ'dæn] n 1 (also s. chair) silla f de manos. 2 US Aut turismo m.

sedate [sɪ'deɪt] I adj sosegado,-a. II vtr sedar.

sedation [sɪ'deɪʃən] n sedación f.

sedative ['sɛdətɪv] adj & n sedante (m).

sediment ['sɛdɪmənt] n sedimento m; (of wine) poso m.

seduce [sɪ'djuːs] vtr seducir.

seduction [sɪ'dʌkʃən] n seducción f.

seductive [sɪ'dʌktɪv] adj seductor,-a.

see¹ [siː] vtr & vi (pt saw; pp seen) 1 ver; I'll s. what can be done, veré lo que se puede hacer; let's s., a ver; that remains to be seen, eso queda por ver; s. page 10, véase la página 10; s. you (later)/soon!, ¡hasta luego/pronto! 2 (meet with) ver, tener cita con; they are seeing each other, (of couple) salen juntos. 3 (visit) ver; to s. the world, recorrer el mundo. 4 (understand) entender; as far as I can s., por lo visto; I s., ya veo; you s., he hasn't got a car, es que no tiene coche, ¿sabes? 5 he sees himself as a second Caruso, se cree otro Caruso. 6 (ensure) asegurarse de. 7 to s. sb home, acompañar a algn a casa. ◆see about vtr (deal with) ocuparse de. ◆see off vtr (say goodbye to) despedirse de. ◆see out vtr 1 (show out) acompañar hasta la puerta. 2 (survive) sobrevivir. ◆see through vtr 1 fam to s. through sb, verle el plumero a algn. 2 (help) I'll s. you through, puedes contar con mi ayuda; £20 should s. me through, con 20 libras me las apaño. 3 to s. sth through, (carry out) llevar algo a cabo. ◆see to vtr (deal with) ocuparse de.

see² [siː] n Rel sede f; the Holy S., la Santa Sede.

seed [siːd] n 1 Bot semilla f; (of fruit) pepita f; to go to s., (of plant) granar; fig (of person) descuidarse. 2 Ten (player) cabeza mf de serie. II vtr 1 (sow with seed) sembrar. 2 (grapes) despepitar. 3 Ten preseleccionar.

seedling ['siːdlɪŋ] n plantón m.

seedy ['siːdɪ] adj (seedier, seediest) fam

(bar etc) sórdido,-a; (clothes) raído,-a; (appearance) desaseado,-a.

seeing ['siːɪŋ] conj s. that, visto que, dado que.

seek [siːk] I vtr (pt & pp sought) 1 (look for) buscar. 2 (advice, help) solicitar. II vtr buscar; to s. to do sth, procurar hacer algo. ◆seek after vtr buscar; much sought after, (person) muy solicitado,-a; (thing) muy cotizado,-a.

seem [siːm] vi parecer; I s. to remember his name was Colin, creo recordar que su nombre era Colin; it seems to me that, me parece que; so it seems, eso parece.

seeming ['siːmɪŋ] adj aparente. ◆seemingly adv aparentemente, según parece.

seen [siːn] pp → see¹.

seep [siːp] vi to s. through/into/out, filtrarse por/en/de.

seesaw ['siːsɔː] I n balancín m, subibaja m. II vi 1 columpiarse, balancearse. 2 fig vacilar, oscilar.

seethe [siːð] vi bullir, hervir; fig to s. with anger, rabiar; to s. with people, rebosar de gente.

see-through ['siːθruː] adj transparente.

segment ['sɛgmənt] n segmento m; (of orange) gajo m.

segregate ['sɛgrɪgeɪt] vtr segregar (from, de).

segregation [sɛgrɪ'geɪʃən] n segregación f.

seize [siːz] vtr (grab) agarrar, asir; Jur (property, drugs) incautar; (assets) secuestrar; (territory) tomar; (arrest) detener; to s. an opportunity, aprovechar una ocasión; to s. power, hacerse con el poder. ◆seize on vtr (chance) agarrar; (idea) aferrarse a. ◆seize up vi agarrotarse.

seizure ['siːʒər] n 1 Jur (of property, drugs) incautación f; (of newspaper) secuestro m; (arrest) detención f. 2 Med ataque m (de apoplejía).

seldom ['sɛldəm] adv rara vez, raramente.

select [sɪ'lɛkt] I vtr (thing) escoger, elegir; (team) seleccionar. II adj selecto,-a.

selected [sɪ'lɛktɪd] adj selecto,-a, escogido,-a; (team, player) seleccionado, -a; Lit s. works, obras escogidas.

selection [sɪ'lɛkʃən] n (choosing) elección f; (people or things chosen) selección f; (range) surtido m.

selective [sɪ'lɛktɪv] adj selectivo,-a.

self [sɛlf] n (pl selves [sɛlvz]) uno,-a mismo,-a, sí mismo,-a; Psych the s., el yo.

self- [sɛlf] pref auto-.

self-adhesive [sɛlfəd'hiːsɪv] adj autoadhesivo,-a.

self-assured [sɛlfə'ʃʊəd] adj seguro,-a de sí mismo,-a.

self-catering [self'keɪtərɪŋ] adj sin servicio de comida.

self-centred, US **self-centered** [self'sentəd] adj egocéntrico,-a.

self-confessed [selfkən'fest] adj confeso,-a.

self-confidence [self'kɒnfɪdəns] n confianza f en sí mismo,-a.

self-confident [self'kɒnfɪdənt] adj seguro,-a de sí mismo,-a.

self-conscious [self'kɒnʃəs] adj cohibido,-a.

self-contained [selfkən'teɪnd] adj (flat) con entrada propia; (person) independiente.

self-control [selfkən'trəul] n autocontrol m.

self-defence, US **self-defense** [selfdɪ'fens] n autodefensa f.

self-discipline [self'dɪsɪplɪn] n autodisciplina f.

self-employed [selfɪm'plɔɪd] adj (worker) autónomo,-a.

self-esteem [selfɪ'stiːm] n amor propio, autoestima f.

self-evident [self'evɪdənt] adj evidente, patente.

self-governing [self'gʌvənɪŋ] adj autónomo,-a.

self-important [selfɪm'pɔːtənt] adj engreído,-a, presumido,-a.

self-indulgent [selfɪn'dʌldʒənt] adj inmoderado,-a.

self-interest [self'ɪntrɪst] n egoísmo m.

selfish [selfɪʃ] adj egoísta.

selfishness [selfɪʃnɪs] n egoísmo m.

selfless [selflɪs] adj desinteresado,-a.

self-made [self'meɪd] adj **s.-m. man,** hombre m que se ha hecho a sí mismo.

self-pity [self'pɪtɪ] n lástima f de sí mismo,-a, autocompasión f.

self-portrait [self'pɔːtreɪt] n autorretrato m.

self-possessed [selfpə'zest] adj sereno, -a, dueño,-a de sí mismo,-a.

self-preservation [selfprezə'veɪʃən] n (instinct of) s.-p., instinto m de conservación.

self-raising [self'reɪzɪŋ] adj GB **s.-r.** flour, harina f con levadura.

self-reliant [selfrɪ'laɪənt] adj autosuficiente.

self-respect [selfrɪ'spekt] n amor m propio, dignidad f.

self-righteous [self'raɪtʃəs] adj santurrón,-ona.

self-satisfied [self'sætɪsfaɪd] adj satisfecho,-a de sí mismo,-a.

self-service [self'sɜːvɪs] n I n (in shop etc) autoservicio m. II adj de autoservicio.

self-sufficient [selfsə'fɪʃənt] adj autosuficiente.

self-taught [self'tɔːt] adj autodidacta.

sell [sel] I vtr (pt & pp sold) vender. II vi

venderse; **this record is selling well,** este disco se vende bien. III n **hard/soft s.,** (in advertising) publicidad agresiva/discreta. ◆**sell off** vtr vender; (goods) liquidar. ◆**sell out** I vi to s. out to the enemy, claudicar ante el enemigo. II vtr Com we're sold out of sugar, se nos ha agotado el azúcar; Theat 'sold out', 'agotadas las localidades'.

seller [selər] n vendedor,-a m,f.

selling [selɪŋ] n venta f; **s. point,** atractivo m comercial; **s. price,** precio m de venta.

sellotape® [seləteɪp] n celo® m, cinta adhesiva. II vtr pegar or fijar con celo®.

sell-out [selaut] n 1 Theat éxito m de taquilla. 2 (act of disloyalty) claudicación f.

semaphore [seməfɔː] n semáforo m.

semblance [sembləns] n apariencia f; there was some s. of truth in it, había algo de verdad en ello.

semen [siːmen] n semen m.

semester [sɪ'mestər] n semestre m.

semi- [semɪ] pref semi-.

semicircle [semɪsɜːkəl] n semicírculo m.

semicolon [semɪ'kəulən] n punto y coma m.

semiconductor [semɪkən'dʌktər] n semiconductor m.

semidetached [semɪdɪ'tætʃt] GB I adj adosado,-a. II n chalé adosado, casa adosada.

semifinal [semɪ'faɪnəl] n semifinal f.

seminar [semɪnɑːr] n seminario m.

seminary [semɪnərɪ] n seminario m.

semolina [semə'liːnə] n sémola f.

senate [senɪt] n 1 Pol senado m. 2 Univ claustro m.

senator [senətər] n senador,-a m,f.

send [send] I vtr (pt & pp sent) 1 (letter) enviar, mandar; (radio signal) transmitir; (rocket, ball) lanzar; **he was sent to prison,** lo mandaron a la cárcel; to s. sth flying, tirar algo. 2 to s. sb mad, (cause to become) volver loco,-a a algn. II vi to s. for sb, mandar llamar a algn; to s. for sth, encargar algo. ◆**send away** I vtr (dismiss) despedir. II vi to s. away for sth, escribir pidiendo algo. ◆**send back** vtr (goods etc) devolver; (person) hacer volver. ◆**send in** vtr (application etc) mandar; (troops) enviar. ◆**send off** vtr I (letter etc) enviar; (goods) despachar. 2 Ftb (player) expulsar. ◆**send on** vtr (luggage) (ahead) facturar; (later) mandar (más tarde). ◆**send up** vtr I hacer subir; (rocket) lanzar; (smoke) echar. 2 GB fam (make fun of) (person) burlarse de; (book etc) satirizar.

sender [sendər] n remitente mf.

sendoff [sendɒf] n fam despedida f.

senile [siːnaɪl] adj senil.

senior ['siːnjəʳ] I *adj* 1 *(in age)* mayor; **William Armstrong S., William Armstrong padre**; s. **citizen**, jubilado,-a *m,f*. 2 *(in rank)* superior; *(with longer service)* más antiguo,-a; *Mil* s. **officer**, oficial *mf* de alta graduación. II *n* 1 **she's three years my s.**, *(in age)* me lleva tres años. 2 *GB Educ* mayor *mf*; *US Educ* estudiante *mf* del último curso.

seniority [siːnɪˈɒrɪtɪ] *n* antigüedad *f*.

sensation [senˈseɪʃən] *n* sensación *f*; **to be a s.**, ser un éxito; **to cause a s.**, causar sensación.

sensational [senˈseɪʃənəl] *adj* 1 *(marvellous)* sensacional; *(exaggerated)* sensacionalista.

sense [sens] I *n* 1 *(faculty)* sentido *m*; *(feeling)* sensación *f*; s. **of direction/humour**, sentido *m* de la orientación/del humor. 2 *(wisdom)* sentido *m* común, juicio *m*; **common** s., sentido común. 3 *(meaning)* sentido *m*; *(of word)* significado *m*; **in a s.**, en cierto sentido; **it doesn't make s.**, no tiene sentido. 4 **to come to one's senses**, recobrar el juicio. II *vtr* sentir, percatarse de.

senseless ['senslɪs] *adj* 1 *(absurd)* insensato,-a, absurdo,-a. 2 *(unconscious)* sin conocimiento.

sensibility [sensɪˈbɪlɪtɪ] *n* 1 *(sensitivity)* sensibilidad *f*. 2 **sensibilities**, susceptibilidad *f sing*.

sensible ['sensɪbəl] *adj* 1 *(wise)* sensato,-a. 2 *(choice)* acertado,-a. 3 *(clothes, shoes)* práctico,-a, cómodo,-a. 4 *fml (difference)* apreciable.

sensitive ['sensɪtɪv] *adj* 1 *(person)* sensible; *(touchy)* susceptible. 2 *(skin)* delicado,-a; *(document)* confidencial.

sensor ['sensəʳ] *n* sensor *m*.

sensual ['sensjʊəl] *adj* sensual.

sensuous ['sensjʊəs] *adj* sensual.

sent [sent] *pt & pp* → **send**.

sentence ['sentəns] I *n* 1 frase *f*; *Ling* oración *f*. 2 *Jur* sentencia *f*; **to pass s. on sb**, imponer una pena a algn; **life s.**, cadena perpetua. II *vtr Jur* condenar.

sentiment ['sentɪmənt] *n* 1 *(sentimentality)* sensiblería *f*. 2 *(feeling)* sentimiento *m*. 3 *(opinion)* opinión *f*.

sentimental [sentɪˈmentəl] *adj* sentimental.

sentry ['sentrɪ] *n* centinela *m*.

separate ['sepəreɪt] I *vtr* separar *(from*, de); *(divide)* dividir *(into*, en); *(distinguish)* distinguir. II *vi* separarse. III ['sepərɪt] *adj* separado,-a; *(different)* distinto,-a; *(entrance)* particular. IV *npl* **separates**, *(clothes)* piezas *fpl*. ◆**separately** *adv* por separado.

separation [sepəˈreɪʃən] *n* separación *f*.

separatist ['sepərətɪst] *n* separatista *mf*.

September [sepˈtembəʳ] *n* se(p)tiembre *m*.

septic ['septɪk] *adj* séptico,-a; **to become s.**, *(of wound)* infectarse; s. **tank**, fosa séptica.

sequel ['siːkwəl] *n* 1 secuela *f*. 2 *(of film etc)* continuación *f*.

sequence ['siːkwəns] *n* 1 *(order)* secuencia *f*, orden *m*. 2 *(series)* serie *f*, sucesión *f*; *Cin* **film** s., secuencia *f*.

serenade [serɪˈneɪd] *n* serenata *f*.

serene [sɪˈriːn] *adj* sereno,-a, tranquilo,-a.

sergeant ['sɑːdʒənt] *n Mil* sargento *m*; *(of police)* cabo *m*; s. **major**, sargento mayor, brigada *m*.

serial ['sɪərɪəl] *n* 1 *Rad TV* serial *m*; *(soap opera)* radionovela *f*, telenovela *f*. 2 s. **number**, número *m* de serie.

series ['sɪəriːz] *n inv* serie *f*; *(of books)* colección *f*; *(of concerts, lectures)* ciclo *m*.

serious ['sɪərɪəs] *adj* 1 *(solemn, earnest)* serio,-a; **I am s.**, hablo en serio. 2 *(causing concern)* grave. ◆**seriously** *adv* 1 *(in earnest)* en serio. 2 *(dangerously, severely)* gravemente.

seriousness ['sɪərɪəsnɪs] *n* gravedad *f*, seriedad *f*; **in all s.**, hablando en serio.

sermon ['sɜːmən] *n* sermón *m*.

serpent ['sɜːpənt] *n* serpiente *f*.

serrated [sɪˈreɪtɪd] *adj* dentado,-a.

serum ['sɪərəm] *n* suero *m*.

servant ['sɜːvənt] *n* *(domestic)* criado,-a *m,f*; *(of state)* servidor,-a *m,f*.

serve [sɜːv] I *vtr* 1 servir. 2 *(customer)* atender a. 3 *Ten* servir. 4 **if my memory serves me right**, si mal no recuerdo; **it serves him right**, bien merecido lo tiene. 5 *fam* **to s. time**, cumplir una condena; **to s. one's apprenticeship**, hacer el aprendizaje. II *vi* 1 servir; **to s. on a committee**, ser miembro de una comisión. 2 *Ten* servir. 3 *(be useful)* servir *(as*, de). III *n Ten* servicio *m*. ◆**serve out**, **serve up** *vtr* servir.

service ['sɜːvɪs] I *n* 1 servicio *m*; **at your s.!**, ¡a sus órdenes!; **how can I be of s. to you?**, ¿en qué puedo servirle?; s. *(charge)* **included**, servicio incluido; s. **area**, área *m* de servicio; s. **industry**, sector *m* de servicios; s. **station**, estación *f* de servicio. 2 **medical** s., servicios médicos; *Mil* **the Services**, las Fuerzas Armadas; **the train s. to Bristol**, la línea de trenes a Bristol. 3 *(maintenance)* mantenimiento *m*. 4 *Rel* oficio *m*; *(mass)* misa *f*. 5 *Ten* servicio *m*; s. **line**, línea *f* de saque. 6 *(set of dishes)* juego *m*. II *vtr (car, machine)* revisar.

serviceable ['sɜːvɪsəbəl] *adj* 1 *(fit for use)* útil, servible. 2 *(practical)* práctico,-a.

serviceman ['sɜːvɪsmən] *n* militar *m*.

serviette [sɜːvɪˈet] *n GB* servilleta *f*.

sesame ['sesəmɪ] *n* sésamo *m*.

session ['seʃən] *n* 1 sesión *f*; **to be in s.**, estar reunido,-a; *(of Parliament, court)* celebrar una sesión. 2 *Educ (academic year)* año académico.

set¹ [set] **I** vtr (pt & pp set) **1** (put, place) poner, colocar; (trap) poner (**for**, para); **the novel is s. in Moscow**, la novela se desarrolla en Moscú; **to s. fire to sth**, prender fuego a algo. **2** (time, price) fijar; (record) establecer; (trend) imponer. **3** (mechanism etc) ajustar; (bone) encajar; **to s. one's watch**, poner el reloj en hora. **4** (arrange) arreglar; **he s. the words to music**, puso música a la letra; **to s. the table**, poner la mesa. **5** (exam, homework) poner; (example) dar; (precedent) sentar. **6** **to s. sail**, zarpar; **to s. sb free**, poner en libertad a algn; **to s. sth going**, poner algo en marcha. **7** (pearl, diamond etc) engastar. **8** Print componer.

II vi **1** (sun, moon) ponerse. **2** (jelly, jam) cuajar; (cement) fraguar; (bone) encajarse. **3** **to s. to**, (begin) ponerse a.

III n **1** shampoo and s., lavar y marcar. **2** (stage) Cin plató m; Theat escenario m; (scenery) decorado m.

IV adj **1** (task, idea) fijo,-a; (date, time) señalado,-a; (opinion) inflexible; (smile) rígido,-a; (gaze) fijo,-a. **s. phrase**, frase hecha; **to be s. on doing sth**, estar empeñado,-a en hacer algo; **s. square**, cartabón m. **2** (ready) listo,-a.

◆**set about** vtr **1** (begin) empezar. **2** (attack) agredir. ◆**set aside** vtr (time, money) reservar; (differences) dejar de lado. ◆**set back** vtr **1** (delay) retrasar; (hinder) entorpecer. **2** fam (cost) costar. ◆**set down** vtr (luggage etc) dejar (en el suelo); GB (passengers) dejar. ◆**set in** vi (winter, rain) comenzar; **panic s. in**, cundió el pánico. ◆**set off** vi (depart) salir. **II** vtr **1** (bomb) hacer estallar; (burglar alarm) hacer sonar; (reaction) desencadenar. **2** (enhance) hacer resaltar. ◆**set out** vi **1** (depart) salir; **to s. out for …**, partir hacia …; **2 to s. out to do sth**, proponerse hacer algo. **II** vtr (arrange) disponer; (present) presentar. ◆**set up** vtr **1** (position) colocar; (statue, camp) levantar; (tent, stall) montar. **2** (business etc) establecer; fam montar; (committee) constituir; fam **we've been s. up!**, ¡te han timado!. **II** vi establecerse.

set² [set] n **1** (series) serie f; (of golf clubs etc) juego m; (of tools) estuche m; (of turbines etc) equipo m; (of books, poems) colección f; (of teeth) dentadura f; chess s., juego de ajedrez; s. of cutlery, cubertería f; s. of kitchen utensils, batería f de cocina. **2** (of people) grupo m; pej (clique) camarilla f. **3** Math conjunto m. **4** Ten set m. **5** TV s., televisor m.

setback ['setbæk] n revés m, contratiempo m.

settee [se'tiː] n sofá m.

setting ['setɪŋ] n **1** (background) marco m; (of novel, film) escenario m. **2** (of jewel)

engaste m.

settle ['setəl] **I** vtr **1** (put in position) colocar. **2** (decide on) acordar; (date, price) fijar; (problem) resolver; (differences) arreglar. **3** (debt) pagar; (account) saldar. **4** (nerves) calmar; (stomach) asentar. **5** fam (put an end to) acabar con. **6** (establish) (person) instalar. **7** (colonize) asentar. **II** vi **1** (bird, insect) posarse; (dust) depositarse; (snow) cuajar; (sediment) precipitarse; (liquid) asentarse; **to s. into an armchair**, acomodarse en un sillón. **2** (put down roots) afincarse; (in a colony) asentarse. **3** (weather) serenarse. **4** (child, nerves) calmarse. **5** (pay) pagar; **to s. out of court**, llegar a un arreglo amistoso.

◆**settle down** vi **1** (put down roots) instalarse; (marry) casarse. **2** **to s. down to work**, ponerse a trabajar. **3** (child) calmarse; (situation) normalizarse. ◆**settle for** vtr conformarse con. ◆**settle in** vi (move in) instalarse; (become adapted) adaptarse. ◆**settle with** vtr (pay debt to) ajustar cuentas con.

settlement ['setəlmənt] n **1** (agreement) acuerdo m. **2** (of debt) pago m; (of account) liquidación f. **3** (dowry) dote m. **4** (colonization) colonización f. **5** (colony) asentamiento m; (village) poblado m.

settler ['setlər] n colono m.

setup ['setʌp] n (system) sistema m; (situation) situación f; el montaje m.

seven ['sevən] adj & n siete (m) inv.

seventeen [sevən'tiːn] adj & n diecisiete (m), diez y siete (m).

seventeenth [sevən'tiːnθ] **I** adj & n decimoséptimo,-a (m,f). **II** n (fraction) decimoséptima parte.

seventh ['sevənθ] **I** adj & n séptimo,-a (m,f). **II** n séptimo m.

seventy ['sevəntɪ] adj & n setenta (m) inv.

sever ['sevər] vtr (cut) cortar; fig (relations) romper.

several ['sevərəl] **I** adj **1** (more than a few) varios,-as. **2** (different) distintos,-as; fml (separate) respectivos,-as. **II** pron algunos,-as.

severance ['sevərəns] n (of relations etc) ruptura f; **s. pay**, indemnización f por despido.

severe [sɪ'vɪər] adj severo,-a; (climate, blow) duro,-a; (illness, loss) grave; (pain) intenso,-a.

severity [sɪ'verɪtɪ] n (of person, criticism, punishment) severidad f; (of climate) rigor m; (of illness) gravedad f; (of pain) intensidad f; (of style) austeridad f.

Seville [sə'vɪl] n Sevilla.

sew [səʊ] vtr & vi (pt sewed; pp sewed or sewn) coser. ◆**sew up** vtr (stitch together) coser; (mend) remendar.

sewage ['suːɪdʒ] n aguas fpl residuales.

sewer ['suːər] n alcantarilla f, cloaca f.

sewerage ['suːərɪdʒ] n alcantarillado m.

sewing ['səʊɪŋ] n costura f; **s. machine**, máquina f de coser.

sewn [səʊn] pp → **sew**.

sex [seks] n sexo m; **s. education**, educación f sexual; **to have s. with sb**, tener relaciones sexuales con algn; **s. appeal**, sex-appeal m.

sexist ['seksɪst] adj & n sexista (mf).

sexual ['seksjʊəl] adj sexual.

sexuality [seksjʊˈælɪtɪ] n sexualidad f.

sexy ['seksɪ] adj (**sexier**, **sexiest**) fam sexi, erótico,-a.

shabby ['ʃæbɪ] adj (**shabbier**, **shabbiest**) 1 (garment) raído,-a; (house) desvencijado,-a; (person) (in rags) harapiento,-a; (unkempt) desaseado,-a. 2 (treatment) mezquino,-a.

shack [ʃæk] n choza f.

shackles ['ʃækəlz] npl grilletes mpl, grillos mpl; fig trabas fpl.

shade [ʃeɪd] I n 1 (shadow) sombra f; **in the s.**, a la sombra. 2 (eyeshade) visera f; (lampshade) pantalla f; US (blind) persiana f. 3 (of colour) tono m, matiz m; fig (of meaning) matiz m. 4 (small amount) poquito m. 5 fam **shades**, gafas fpl de sol. II vtr (from sun) proteger contra el sol.

shadow ['ʃædəʊ] I n 1 (shade) sombra f; (darkness) oscuridad f; fig **without a s. of a doubt**, sin lugar a dudas. 2 GB the **s. cabinet**, el gabinete de la oposición. II vtr fig seguir la pista a.

shadowy ['ʃædəʊɪ] adj (dark) oscuro,-a; (hazy) vago,-a.

shady ['ʃeɪdɪ] adj (**shadier**, **shadiest**) (place) a la sombra; (suspicious) (person) sospechoso,-a; (deal) turbio,-a.

shaft [ʃɑːft] n 1 (of tool, golf club) mango m; (of lance) asta f; (of arrow) astil m. 2 Tech eje m. 3 (of mine) pozo m; (of lift, elevator) hueco m. 4 (beam of light) rayo m.

shaggy ['ʃægɪ] adj (**shaggier**, **shaggiest**) (hairy) peludo,-a; (long-haired) melenudo,-a; (beard) desgreñado,-a.

shake [ʃeɪk] I n sacudida f. II vtr (pt **shook**; pp **shaken**) (carpet etc) sacudir; (bottle) agitar; (dice) mover; (building) hacer temblar; **the news shook him**, la noticia le conmocionó; **to s. hands with sb**, estrechar la mano a algn; **to s. one's head**, negar con la cabeza. III vi (person, building) temblar; **to s. with cold**, tiritar de frío. ◆**shake off** vtr 1 (dust etc) sacudirse. 2 fig (bad habit) librarse de; (cough, cold) quitarse de encima; (pursuer) dar esquinazo a. ◆**shake up** vtr fig (shock) trastornar; (reorganize) reorganizar.

shake-up ['ʃeɪkʌp] n fig reorganización f.

shaken ['ʃeɪkən] pp → **shake**.

shaky ['ʃeɪkɪ] adj (**shakier**, **shakiest**) (hand, voice) tembloroso,-a; (step)

shall [ʃæl, unstressed ʃəl] v aux 1 (used to form future tense) (first person only) I **s.** (or I'll) **buy it**, lo compraré; I **s. not** (or I **shan't**) **say anything**, no diré nada. 2 (used to form questions) (usu first person) **s. I close the door ?**, ¿cierro la puerta?; **s. I mend it for you?**, ¿quieres que te lo repare?; **s. we go?**, ¿nos vamos? 3 (emphatic, command, threat) (all persons) **we s. overcome**, venceremos; **you s. leave immediately**, te irás enseguida.

shallow ['ʃæləʊ] adj poco profundo,-a; fig superficial.

sham [ʃæm] I adj falso,-a; (illness etc) fingido,-a. II n 1 (pretence) engaño m, farsa f. 2 (person) fantoche m. III vtr fingir, simular. IV vi fingir.

shambles ['ʃæmbəlz] n confusión f; **the performance was a s.**, la función fue un desastre.

shame [ʃeɪm] I n 1 vergüenza f; **to put to s.**, (far outdo) eclipsar, sobrepasar. 2 (pity) pena f, lástima f; **what a s.!**, ¡qué pena!, ¡qué lástima!. II vtr avergonzar; (disgrace) deshonrar.

shamefaced ['ʃeɪmfeɪst] adj avergonzado,-a.

shameful ['ʃeɪmfʊl] adj vergonzoso,-a.

shameless ['ʃeɪmlɪs] adj descarado,-a.

shampoo [ʃæmˈpuː] I n champú m. II vtr lavar con champú; **to s. one's hair**, lavarse el pelo.

shamrock ['ʃæmrɒk] n trébol m.

shandy ['ʃændɪ] n GB clara f, cerveza f con gaseosa.

shantytown ['ʃæntɪtaʊn] n barrio m de chabolas.

shape [ʃeɪp] I n 1 forma f; (shadow) silueta m; **to take s.**, tomar forma. 2 **in good/bad s.**, (condition) en buen/ mal estado; **to be in good s.**, (health) estar en forma. II vtr dar forma a; (clay) modelar; (stone) tallar; (character) formar; (destiny) determinar; **star-shaped**, con forma de estrella. III vi (also **s. up**) tomar forma; **to s. up well**, (events) tomar buen cariz; (person) hacer progresos.

shapeless ['ʃeɪplɪs] adj amorfo,-a, informe.

shapely ['ʃeɪplɪ] adj (**shapelier**, **shapeliest**) escultural.

share [ʃeəʳ] I n 1 (portion) parte f. 2 Fin acción f; **s. index**, índice m de la Bolsa; **s. prices**, cotizaciones fpl. II vtr 1 (divide) dividir. 2 (have in common) compartir. III vi compartir. ◆**share out** vtr repartir.

shareholder ['ʃeəhəʊldəʳ] n accionista mf.

shark [ʃɑːk] n 1 (fish) tiburón m. 2 fam (swindler) estafador,-a m,f; **loan s.**, usurero,-a m,f.

sharp [ʃɑːp] I adj 1 (razor, knife)

afilado,-a; (needle, pencil) puntiagudo,-a. 2 (angle) agudo,-a; (features) anguloso,-a; (bend) cerrado,-a. 3 (outline) definido,-a; (contrast) marcado,-a. 4 (observant) perspicaz; (clever) listo,-a; (quick-witted) avispado,-a; (cunning) astuto,-a. 5 (sudden) brusco,-a. 6 (pain, cry) agudo,-a; (wind) penetrante. 7 (sour) acre. 8 (criticism) mordaz; (temper) arisco,-a; (tone) seco,-a. 9 Mus sostenido,-a; (out of tune) desafinado,-a. II adv at 2 o'clock s., (exactly) a las dos en punto. III n Mus sostenido m. ◆**sharply** adv 1 (abruptly) bruscamente. 2 (clearly) marcadamente.

sharpen ['ʃɑːpən] vtr 1 (knife) afilar; (pencil) sacar punta a. 2 fig (desire, intelligence) agudizar.

sharpener ['ʃɑːpənə'] n (for knife) afilador m; (for pencil) sacapuntas m inv.

sharp-eyed [ʃɑːp'aɪd] adj con ojos de lince.

shatter ['ʃætə'] I vtr hacer añicos; (nerves) destrozar; (hopes) frustrar. II vi hacerse añicos.

shave [ʃeɪv] I n afeitado m; to have a s., afeitarse; fig to have a close s., escaparse por los pelos. II vtr (pt shaved; pp shaved or shaven ['ʃeɪvən]) (person) afeitar; (wood) cepillar. III vi afeitarse.

shaver ['ʃeɪvə'] n (electric) s., máquina f de afeitar.

shaving ['ʃeɪvɪŋ] n 1 (of wood) viruta f. 2 s. brush, brocha f de afeitar; s. cream, crema f de afeitar; s. foam, espuma f de afeitar.

shawl [ʃɔːl] n chal m.

she [ʃiː] pers pron ella.

she- [ʃiː] pref (of animal) hembra; s.-cat, gata f.

sheaf [ʃiːf] n (pl sheaves [ʃiːvz]) Agr gavilla f; (of arrows) haz m; (of papers, banknotes) fajo m.

shear [ʃɪə'] I vtr (pt sheared; pp shorn or sheared) (sheep) esquilar; to s. off, cortar. II vi esquilar ovejas.

shears [ʃɪəz] npl tijeras fpl (grandes).

sheath [ʃiːθ] n 1 (for sword) vaina f; (for knife, scissors) funda f. 2 (contraceptive) preservativo m.

sheaves [ʃiːvz] npl → sheaf.

shed[1] [ʃed] n (in garden) cobertizo m; (workmen's hut) barraca f; (for cattle) establo m; (in factory) nave f.

shed[2] [ʃed] vtr (pt & pp shed) 1 (clothes) despojarse de; (unwanted thing) deshacerse de; the **snake s. its skin**, la serpiente mudó de piel. 2 (blood, tears) derramar.

sheen [ʃiːn] n brillo m.

sheep [ʃiːp] n inv oveja f.

sheepdog ['ʃiːpdɒg] n perro m pastor.

sheepish ['ʃiːpɪʃ] adj avergonzado,-a.

sheepskin ['ʃiːpskɪn] n piel f de carnero.

sheer [ʃɪə'] adj 1 (utter) total, puro,-a. 2

(cliff) escarpado,-a; (drop) vertical. 3 (stockings, cloth) fino,-a.

sheet [ʃiːt] n 1 (on bed) sábana f. 2 (of paper) hoja f; (of tin, glass, plastic) lámina f; (of ice) capa f.

sheik(h) [ʃeɪk] n jeque m.

shelf [ʃelf] n (pl shelves [ʃelvz]) (on bookcase) estante m; (in cupboard) tabla f; **shelves**, estantería f.

shell [ʃel] I n 1 (of egg, nut) cáscara f; (of pea) vaina f; (of tortoise etc) caparazón m; (of snail etc) concha f. 2 (of building) armazón m. 3 (mortar etc) obús m, proyectil m; (cartridge) cartucho m; s. **shock**, neurosis f de guerra. II vtr 1 (peas) desvainar; (nuts) pelar. 2 Mil bombardear.

shellfish ['ʃelfɪʃ] n inv marisco m, mariscos mpl.

shelter ['ʃeltə'] I n 1 (protection) abrigo m, amparo m; to take s., refugiarse (from, de). 2 (place) refugio m; (for homeless) asilo m; bus s., marquesina f. II vtr 1 (protect) abrigar, proteger. 2 (take into one's home) ocultar. III vi refugiarse.

sheltered ['ʃeltəd] adj (place) abrigado,-a; to lead a s. life, vivir apartado,-a del mundo.

shelve [ʃelv] vtr fig (postpone) dar carpetazo a.

shelves [ʃelvz] npl → shelf.

shepherd ['ʃepəd] I n pastor m; s.'s pie, pastel m de carne picada con puré de patatas. II vtr fig to s. sb in, hacer entrar a algn.

sheriff ['ʃerɪf] n GB gobernador m civil; Scot juez m presidente; US sheriff m.

sherry ['ʃerɪ] n jerez m.

Shetland ['ʃetlənd] n the S. Isles, S., las Islas Shetland; S. **wool**, lana f Shetland.

shield [ʃiːld] I n 1 escudo m; (of policeman) placa f. 2 (on machinery) blindaje m. II vtr proteger (from, de).

shift [ʃɪft] I n 1 (change) cambio m; US Aut (gear) s., cambio de velocidades. 2 (period of work, group of workers) turno m; to be on the day s., hacer el turno de día. II vtr (change) cambiar; (move) cambiar de sitio, trasladar. III vi (move) moverse; (change place) cambiar de sitio; (opinion) cambiar; (wind) cambiar de dirección.

shiftless ['ʃɪftlɪs] adj perezoso,-a, vago,-a.

shiftwork ['ʃɪftwɜːk] n trabajo m por turnos.

shifty ['ʃɪftɪ] adj (shiftier, shiftiest) (look) furtivo,-a; (person) sospechoso,-a.

shilling ['ʃɪlɪŋ] n chelín m.

shimmer ['ʃɪmə'] I vi relucir; (shine) brillar. II n luz trémula, reflejo trémulo; (shining) brillo m.

shin [ʃɪn] n espinilla f; s. **pad**, espinillera f.

shine [ʃaɪn] I vi (pt & pp shone) 1 (light) brillar; (metal) relucir. 2 fig (excel) sobresalir (at, en). II vtr 1 (lamp) dirigir. 2 (pt & pp **shined**) (polish) sacar brillo a; (shoes) limpiar. III n brillo m, lustre m.

shingle ['ʃɪŋgəl] n 1 (pebbles) guijarros mpl. 2 (roof tile) tablilla f.

shingles ['ʃɪŋgəlz] npl Med herpes m.

shining ['ʃaɪnɪŋ] adj fig (outstanding) ilustre.

shiny ['ʃaɪnɪ] adj (**shinier, shiniest**) brillante.

ship [ʃɪp] I n barco m, buque m. II vtr 1 (take on board) embarcar. 2 (transport) transportar (en barco); (send) enviar, mandar.

shipbuilding ['ʃɪpbɪldɪŋ] n construcción f naval.

shipment ['ʃɪpmənt] n 1 (act) transporte m. 2 (load) consignación f, envío m.

shipper ['ʃɪpər] n (person) cargador,-a m,f.

shipping ['ʃɪpɪŋ] n 1 (ships) barcos mpl; **s. lane**, vía f de navegación. 2 (loading) embarque m; (transporting) transporte m (en barco); **s. company**, compañía naviera.

shipshape ['ʃɪpʃeɪp] adj & adv en perfecto orden.

shipwreck ['ʃɪprek] I n naufragio m. II vtr to be **shipwrecked**, naufragar.

shipyard ['ʃɪpjɑːd] n astillero m.

shire [ʃaɪər] n GB condado m.

shirk [ʃɜːk] I vtr (duty) faltar a; (problem) eludir. II vi gandulear.

shirt [ʃɜːt] n camisa f; **in s. sleeves**, en mangas de camisa; fam **keep your s. on!**, ¡no te sulfures!

shit [ʃɪt] vulg I n mierda f; **in s. the can**, jodido,-a. II interj ¡mierda!. III vi cagar.

shiver ['ʃɪvər] I vi (with cold) tiritar; (with fear) temblar, estremecerse. II n (with cold, fear) escalofrío m.

shoal [ʃəʊl] n (of fish) banco m.

shock [ʃɒk] I n 1 (jolt) choque m; **s. absorber**, amortiguador m; **s. wave**, onda expansiva. 2 (upset) conmoción f; (scare) susto m. 3 Med shock m. II vtr (upset) conmover; (startle) sobresaltar; (scandalize) escandalizar.

shocking ['ʃɒkɪŋ] adj 1 (causing horror) espantoso,-a; fam (very bad) horroroso,-a. 2 (disgraceful) escandaloso,-a. 3 **s. pink**, rosa chillón.

shod [ʃɒd] pt & pp → **shoe**.

shoddy ['ʃɒdɪ] adj (**shoddier, shoddiest**) (goods) de mala calidad; (work) chapucero,-a.

shoe [ʃuː] I n 1 zapato m; (for horse) herradura f; **brake s.**, zapata f; **s. polish**, betún m; **s. repair (shop)**, remiendo m de zapatos; **s. shop, US s. store**, zapatería f. 2 **shoes**, calzado m sing. II vtr (pt & pp **shod**) herrar.

shoebrush ['ʃuːbrʌʃ] n cepillo m para los zapatos.

shoehorn ['ʃuːhɔːn] n calzador m.

shoelace ['ʃuːleɪs] n cordón m (de zapatos).

shoestring ['ʃuːstrɪŋ] n fig **to do sth on a s.**, hacer algo con poquísimo dinero.

shone [ʃɒn, US ʃəʊn] pt & pp → **shine** I & II.

shoo [ʃuː] I interj ¡fuera!. II vtr to **s. (away)**, espantar.

shook [ʃʊk] pt → **shake**.

shoot [ʃuːt] I n 1 Bot retoño m; (of vine) sarmiento m. II vtr (pt & pp **shot**) 1 pegar un tiro a; (kill) matar; (execute) fusilar; (hunt) cazar; **to s. dead**, matar a tiros. 2 (missile, glance) lanzar; (bullet, ball) disparar. 3 (film) rodar, filmar; Phot fotografiar. 4 **s. (up)**, (heroin etc) chutarse. III vi 1 (with gun) disparar (**at** sb, sobre, a algn); **to s. at a target**, tirar al blanco; Ftb **to s. at the goal**, chutar a puerta. 2 **to s. past or by**, pasar flechado,-a. ◆**shoot down** vtr (aircraft) derribar. ◆**shoot out** vi (person) salir disparado,-a; (water) brotar; (flames) salir. ◆**shoot up** vi (flames) salir; (water) brotar; (prices) dispararse.

shooting ['ʃuːtɪŋ] I n 1 (shots) tiros mpl; (murder) asesinato m; (hunting) caza f; **s. star**, estrella f fugaz. 2 (of film) rodaje m. II adj (pain) punzante.

shoot-out ['ʃuːtaʊt] n tiroteo m.

shop [ʃɒp] I n 1 tienda f; (large store) almacén m; **s. assistant**, dependiente,-a m,f; **s. window**, escaparate m. 2 (workshop) taller m; **s. floor**, (place) planta f; (workers) obreros mpl; GB **s. steward**, enlace m/f sindical. II vi hacer compras; **to go shopping**, ir de compras.

shopkeeper ['ʃɒpkiːpər] n tendero,-a m,f.

shoplifter ['ʃɒplɪftər] n ladrón,-ona m,f (de tiendas).

shopper ['ʃɒpər] n comprador,-a m,f.

shopping ['ʃɒpɪŋ] n (purchases) compras fpl; **s. bag/basket**, bolsa f/cesta f de la compra; **s. centre or precinct**, centro m comercial.

shopsoiled ['ʃɒpsɔɪld], US **shopworn** ['ʃɒpwɔːn] adj deteriorado,-a.

shore[1] [ʃɔːr] n (of sea, lake) orilla f; US (beach) playa f; (coast) costa f; **to go on s.**, desembarcar.

shore[2] [ʃɔːr] vtr to **s. (up)**, apuntalar.

shorn [ʃɔːn] pp → **shear**.

short [ʃɔːt] I adj 1 corto,-a; (not tall) bajo,-a; **in a s. while**, dentro de un rato; **in the s. term**, a corto plazo; **s. circuit**, cortocircuito m; **s. cut**, atajo m; GB **s. list**, lista f de seleccionados; **s. story**, relato corto, cuento m; **s. wave**, onda corta. 2 (brief) corto,-a, breve; '**Bob**' **is s. for** '**Robert**', 'Bob' es el diminutivo de 'Robert'; **for s.**, para abreviar; **in s.**, en pocas palabras. 3 **to be s. of breath**, faltarle a uno la respiración; **to be s. of food**, andar escaso,-a de comida. 4 (curt) brusco,-a, seco,-a. **II** *adv* **1 to pull up s.**, pararse en seco. **2 to cut s.**, *(holiday)* interrumpir; *(meeting)* suspender; **we're running s. of coffee**, se nos está acabando el café. **3 s. of**, *(except)* excepto, menos. **III** *n* **1** *Cin* cortometraje *m*. **2** *fam (drink)* copa *f*. **IV** *vi* **to s. (out)**, tener un cortocircuito. ◆**shortly** *adv (soon)* dentro de poco; **s. after**, poco después.

shortage ['ʃɔːtɪdʒ] *n* escasez *f*.

shortbread ['ʃɔːtbred] *n* mantecado *m*.

short-change ['ʃɔːt'tʃeɪndʒ] *vtr* **to s.-c. sb**, no devolver el cambio completo a algn; *fig* timar a algn.

short-circuit ['ʃɔːt'sɜːkɪt] **I** *vtr* provocar un cortocircuito en. **II** *vi* tener un cortocircuito.

shortcomings ['ʃɔːtkʌmɪŋz] *npl* defectos *mpl*.

shortcrust ['ʃɔːtkrʌst] *n* **s. pastry**, pasta brisa.

shorten ['ʃɔːtən] *vtr (skirt, visit)* acortar; *(word)* abreviar; *(text)* resumir.

shortfall ['ʃɔːtfɔːl] *n* déficit *m*.

shorthand ['ʃɔːthænd] *n* taquigrafía *f*; *GB* **s. typing**, taquimecanografía *f*; *GB* **s. typist**, taquimecanógrafo,-a *m.f.*

short-list ['ʃɔːtlɪst] *vtr* poner en la lista de seleccionados.

short-lived ['ʃɔːt'lɪvd] *adv* efímero,-a.

short-range ['ʃɔːt'reɪndʒ] *adj* de corto alcance.

shorts [ʃɔːts] *npl* **1** pantalones *mpl* cortos; **a pair of s.**, un pantalón corto. **2** *US (underpants)* calzoncillos *mpl*.

short-sighted ['ʃɔːt'saɪtɪd] *adj (person)* miope; *fig (plan etc)* sin visión de futuro.

short-staffed ['ʃɔːt'stɑːft] *adj* escaso,-a de personal.

short-tempered ['ʃɔːt'tempəd] *adj* de mal genio.

short-term ['ʃɔːttɜːm] *adj* a corto plazo.

shot¹ [ʃɒt] *n* **1** *(act, sound)* tiro *m*, disparo *m*. **2** *(projectile)* bala *f*; *(pellets)* perdigones *mpl*; *fig* **he was off like a s.**, salió disparado; *Sport* **s. put**, lanzamiento *m* de peso. **3** *(person)* tirador,-a *m,f*. **4** *Ftb (kick)* tiro *m* (a puerta); *(in billiards, cricket, golf)* golpe *m*. **5** *(attempt)* tentativa *f*; **to have a s. at sth**, intentar hacer algo. **6** *(injection)* inyección *f*; *fam* pinchazo *m*. **7** *(drink)* trago *m*. **8** *Phot* foto *f*; *Cin* toma *f*.

shot² [ʃɒt] *pt & pp* → **shoot**.

shotgun ['ʃɒtgʌn] *n* escopeta *f*.

should [ʃʊd, *unstressed* ʃəd] *v aux* **1** *(duty)* deber; **all employees s. wear helmets**, todos los empleados deben llevar casco; **he s. have been an architect**, debería haber sido arquitecto. **2** *(probability)* deber de; **he s. have finished by now**, ya debe de haber acabado; **this s. be interesting**, esto promete ser interesante. **3** *(conditional use)* **if anything strange s.**

happen, si pasara algo raro. **4 I s. like to ask a question**, quisiera hacer una pregunta.

shoulder ['ʃəʊldə] *n* **1** hombro *m*; **s. blade**, omóplato *m*; **s. strap**, *(of garment)* tirante *m*; *(of bag)* correa *f*; *Aut* **hard s.**, arcén *m*. **2** *Culin* paletilla *f*. **II** *vtr fig (responsibilities)* cargar con.

shout [ʃaʊt] **I** *n* grito *m*. **II** *vtr* gritar. **III** *vi* gritar; **to s. at sb**, gritar a algn. ◆**shout down** *vtr* abuchear.

shouting ['ʃaʊtɪŋ] *n* gritos *mpl*, vocerío *m*.

shove [ʃʌv] **I** *n fam* empujón *m*. **II** *vtr* empujar; **to s. sth into one's pocket**, meterse algo en el bolsillo a empujones. **III** *vi* empujar; *(jostle)* dar empellones. ◆**shove off** *vi fam* largarse. ◆**shove up** *vi fam (move along)* correrse.

shovel ['ʃʌvəl] **I** *n* pala *f*; **mechanical s.**, excavadora *f*. **II** *vtr* mover con pala *or* a paladas.

show [ʃəʊ] **I** *vtr (pt* **showed;** *pp* **shown** *or* **showed)** **1** *(ticket etc)* mostrar; *(painting etc)* exponer; *(film)* poner; *(latest plans etc)* presentar. **2** *(display)* demostrar; **to s. oneself to be**, comportarse como. **3** *(teach)* enseñar; *(explain)* explicar. **4** *(temperature, way etc)* indicar; *(profit etc)* registrar. **5** *(prove)* demostrar. **6** *(conduct)* llevar; **to s. sb in**, hacer pasar a algn; **to s. sb to the door**, acompañar a algn hasta la puerta.

II *vi* **1** *(be visible)* notarse. **2** *fam (turn up)* aparecer. **3** *Cin* **what's showing?**, ¿qué ponen?

III *n* **1** *(display)* demostración *f*. **2** *(outward appearance)* apariencia *f*. **3** *(exhibition)* exposición *f*; **on s.**, expuesto,-a; **boat s.**, salón náutico; **motor s.**, salón del automóvil. **4** *Theat (entertainment)* espectáculo *m*; *(performance)* función *f*; *Rad TV* programa *m*; **s. business**, **s. biz**, el mundo del espectáculo. ◆**show off** **I** *vtr* **1** *(highlight)* hacer resaltar. **2** *fam (flaunt)* hacer alarde de. **II** *vi fam* farolear. ◆**show up** **I** *vtr* **1** *(reveal)* sacar a luz; *(highlight)* hacer resaltar. **2** *fam (embarrass)* dejar en evidencia. **II** *vi* **1** *(stand out)* destacarse. **2** *fam (arrive)* aparecer.

showdown ['ʃəʊdaʊn] *n* enfrentamiento *m*.

shower ['ʃaʊə] **I** *n* **1** *(rain)* chubasco *m*, chaparrón *m*. **2** *fig (of stones, blows etc)* lluvia *f*. **3** *(bath)* ducha *f*; **to have a s.**, ducharse. **II** *vtr* **1** *(spray)* rociar. **2** *fig* **to s. gifts/praise on sb**, colmar a algn de regalos/elogios. **III** *vi* ducharse.

showerproof ['ʃaʊəpruːf] *adj* impermeable.

showing ['ʃəʊɪŋ] *n (of film)* proyección *f*.

showjumping ['ʃəʊdʒʌmpɪŋ] *n* hípica *f*.

shown [ʃəʊn] *pp* → **show**.

show-off ['ʃəʊf] n fam farolero,-a m,f.

showpiece ['ʃəʊpiːs] n (in exhibition etc) obra maestra; fig (at school etc) modelo f.

showroom ['ʃəʊruːm] n Com exposición f; Art galería f.

shrank [ʃræŋk] pt → **shrink**.

shrapnel ['ʃræpnəl] n metralla f.

shred [ʃred] I n triza f; (of cloth) jirón m; (of paper) tira f. II vtr (paper) hacer trizas; (vegetables) rallar.

shredder ['ʃredə'] n (for waste paper) trituradora f; (for vegetables) rallador m.

shrew [ʃruː] n 1 Zool musaraña f. 2 fig (woman) arpía f.

shrewd [ʃruːd] adj astuto,-a; (clear-sighted) perspicaz; (wise) sabio,-a; (decision) acertado,-a.

shriek [ʃriːk] I n chillido m; **shrieks of laughter**, carcajadas fpl. II vi chillar.

shrill [ʃrɪl] adj agudo,-a, estridente.

shrimp [ʃrɪmp] I n camarón m. II vi pescar camarones.

shrine [ʃraɪn] n (tomb) sepulcro m; (relic case) relicario m; (chapel) capilla f; (holy place) lugar sagrado.

shrink [ʃrɪŋk] I vtr (pt **shrank**; pp **shrunk**) encoger. II vi 1 (clothes) encoger(se). 2 (savings) disminuir. **3 to s. (back)**, echarse atrás; **to s. from doing sth**, no tener valor para hacer algo. II n fam (psychiatrist) psiquiatra m,f.

shrinkage ['ʃrɪŋkɪdʒ] n 1 (of cloth) encogimiento m; (of metal) contracción f. 2 (of savings etc) disminución f.

shrink-wrapped ['ʃrɪŋkræpt] adj envuelto,-a en plástico.

shrivel ['ʃrɪvəl] I vtr **to s. (up)**, encoger; (plant) secar; (skin) arrugar. II vi encogerse; (plant) secarse; (skin) arrugarse.

shroud [ʃraʊd] n Rel sudario m. II vtr fig envolver.

Shrove Tuesday [ʃrəʊv'tjuːzdɪ] n martes m de carnaval.

shrub [ʃrʌb] n arbusto m.

shrubbery ['ʃrʌbərɪ] n arbustos mpl.

shrug [ʃrʌg] I vtr **to s. one's shoulders**, encogerse de hombros. II vi encogerse de hombros. III n encogimiento m de hombros. **◆shrug off** vtr no dejarse desanimar por.

shrunk [ʃrʌŋk] pp → **shrink**.

shudder ['ʃʌdə'] I n 1 escalofrío m, estremecimiento m. 2 (of machinery) sacudida f. II vi 1 (person) estremecerse. 2 (machinery) dar sacudidas.

shuffle ['ʃʌfəl] I vtr 1 (feet) arrastrar. 2 (papers etc) revolver; (cards) barajar. II vi 1 (walk) andar arrastrando los pies. 2 Cards barajar.

shun [ʃʌn] vtr (person) esquivar; (responsibility) rehuir.

shunt [ʃʌnt] vtr Rail cambiar de vía; Elec derivar.

shut [ʃʌt] I vtr (pt & pp **shut**) cerrar. II vi cerrarse. III adj cerrado,-a. **◆shut down** I vtr (factory) cerrar. II vi (factory) cerrar. **◆shut off** vtr (gas, water etc) cortar. **◆shut out** vtr 1 (lock out) dejar fuera a. 2 (exclude) excluir. **◆shut up** I vtr 1 (close) cerrar. 2 (imprison) encerrar. 3 fam (silence) callar. II vi fam (keep quiet) callarse.

shutdown ['ʃʌtdaʊn] n cierre m.

shutter ['ʃʌtə'] n 1 (on window) contraventana f, postigo m. 2 Phot obturador m.

shuttle ['ʃʌtəl] I n 1 (in weaving) lanzadera f. 2 Av puente aéreo; **(space)** s., transbordador m espacial. II vi ir y venir.

shuttlecock ['ʃʌtəlkɒk] n volante m.

shy [ʃaɪ] I adj (**shyer**, **shyest** or **shier**, **shiest**) (timid) tímido,-a; (reserved) reservado,-a. II vi (horse) espantarse (at, de); fig **to s. away from doing sth**, negarse a hacer algo.

shyness ['ʃaɪnɪs] n timidez f.

Siberia [saɪ'bɪərɪə] n Siberia.

sibling ['sɪblɪŋ] n fml (brother) hermano m; (sister) hermana f; **siblings**, hermanos.

Sicily ['sɪsɪlɪ] n Sicilia.

sick [sɪk] adj 1 (ill) enfermo,-a; **s. leave**, baja f por enfermedad; **s. pay**, subsidio m de enfermedad. 2 **to feel s.**, (about to vomit) tener ganas de devolver; **to be s.**, devolver. 3 fam (fed up) harto,-a. 4 fam (mind, joke) morboso,-a; **s. humour**, humor negro.

sickbay ['sɪkbeɪ] n enfermería f.

sicken ['sɪkən] I vtr (make ill) poner enfermo; (revolt) dar asco a. II vi (fall ill) enfermar.

sickening ['sɪkənɪŋ] adj nauseabundo,-a; (revolting) repugnante; (horrifying) escalofriante.

sickle ['sɪkəl] n hoz f.

sickly ['sɪklɪ] adj (**sicklier**, **sickliest**) 1 (person) enfermizo,-a. 2 (taste) empalagoso,-a. 3 (smile) forzado,-a.

sickness ['sɪknɪs] n 1 (illness) enfermedad f. 2 (nausea) náuseas fpl.

side [saɪd] I n 1 lado m. 2 (of coin etc) cara f; (of hill) ladera f; **by the s. of**, junto a. 2 (of body) costado m; (of animal) ijar m; **a s. of bacon**, una loncha de tocino; **by my s.**, a mi lado; **s. by s.**, juntos. 3 (edge) borde m; (of lake, river) orilla f. 4 fig (aspect) aspecto m. 5 (team) equipo m; Pol partido m; **she's on our s.**, está de nuestro lado; **to take sides with sb**, ponerse de parte de algn; **s. dish**, guarnición f; **s. effect**, efecto secundario; **s. entrance**, entrada f lateral; **s. street**, calle f lateral. II vi **to s. with sb**, ponerse de parte de algn.

sideboard ['saɪdbɔːd] n aparador m.

sideburns ['saɪdbɜːnz] npl patillas fpl.

sidelight ['saɪdlaɪt] n Aut luz f lateral, piloto m.

sideline ['saɪdlaɪn] n 1 Sport línea f de banda. 2 Com (product) línea suplementaria; (job) empleo suplementario.

sidelong ['saɪdlɒŋ] adj de reojo.

side-saddle ['saɪdsædəl] I n silla f de amazona. II adv to ride s., montar a la inglesa.

sideshow ['saɪdʃəʊ] n atracción secundaria.

sidestep ['saɪdstep] I vtr (issue) esquivar. II vi Box fintar.

sidetrack ['saɪdtræk] vtr fig (person) despistar.

sidewalk ['saɪdwɔːk] n US acera f.

sideways ['saɪdweɪz] I adj (movement) lateral; (look) de reojo. II adv de lado.

siding ['saɪdɪŋ] n Rail apartadero m, vía muerta.

sidle ['saɪdəl] vi to s. up to sb, acercarse furtivamente a algn.

siege [siːdʒ] n sitio m, cerco m; to lay s. to, sitiar.

sieve [sɪv] I n (fine) tamiz m; (coarse) criba f. II vtr (fine) tamizar; (coarse) cribar.

sift [sɪft] vtr (sieve) tamizar; fig to s. through, examinar cuidadosamente.

sigh [saɪ] I vi suspirar. II n suspiro m.

sight [saɪt] I n 1 (faculty) vista f; at first s., a primera vista; to catch s. of, divisar; to know by s., conocer de vista; to lose s. of sth/sb, perder algo/a algn de vista. 2 (range of vision) vista f; within s., a la vista; to come into s., aparecer. 3 (spectacle) espectáculo m. 4 (on gun) mira f; fig to set one's sights on, tener la mira puesta en. 5 sights, monumentos mpl. II vtr ver; (land) divisar.

sightseeing ['saɪtsiːɪŋ] n turismo m; to go s., hacer turismo.

sign [saɪn] I n 1 (symbol) signo m. 2 (gesture) gesto m, seña f; (signal) señal f. 3 (indication) señal f; (trace) rastro m, huella f; as s. of, como muestra de. 4 (notice) anuncio m; (board) letrero m. II vtr 1 (letter etc) firmar. 2 Ftb fichar. III vi firmar. ◆**sign on** I vtr (worker) contratar. II vi (worker) firmar un contrato; GB fam apuntarse al paro; (regularly) firmar el paro. ◆**sign up** I vtr (soldier) reclutar; (worker) contratar. II vi (soldier) alistarse; (worker) firmar un contrato.

signal ['sɪgnəl] I n señal f; Rad TV sintonía f; Rail s. box, garita f de señales. II vtr 1 (message) transmitir por señales. 2 (direction etc) indicar. III vi 1 (with hands) hacer señales; (in car) señalar.

signalman ['sɪgnəlmæn] n guardavía m.

signature ['sɪgnɪtʃər] n (name) firma f; Rad TV s. tune, sintonía f.

signet ['sɪgnɪt] n s. ring, (anillo m de) sello m.

significance [sɪg'nɪfɪkəns] n (meaning) significado m; (importance) importancia f.

significant [sɪg'nɪfɪkənt] adj (meaningful)

significativo,-a; (important) importante. ◆**significantly** adv (markedly) sensiblemente.

signify ['sɪgnɪfaɪ] vtr 1 (mean) significar. 2 (show, make known) indicar.

signpost ['saɪnpəʊst] n poste m indicador.

silence ['saɪləns] I n silencio m. II vtr acallar; (engine) silenciar.

silencer ['saɪlənsər] n silenciador m.

silent ['saɪlənt] adj silencioso,-a; (not talkative) callado,-a; (film) mudo,-a; be s.!, ¡cállate!; to remain s., guardar silencio. ◆**silently** adv silenciosamente.

silhouette [sɪluː'et] n silueta f.

silicon ['sɪlɪkən] n silicio m; s. chip, chip m (de silicio).

silk [sɪlk] I n seda f. II adj de seda.

silky ['sɪlkɪ] adj (silkier, silkiest) (cloth) sedoso,-a; (voice etc) aterciopelado,-a.

sill [sɪl] n (of window) alféizar m.

silly ['sɪlɪ] adj (sillier, silliest) tonto,-a.

silo ['saɪləʊ] n silo m.

silt [sɪlt] n cieno m. ◆**silt up** vi obstruirse con cieno.

silver ['sɪlvər] I n 1 (metal) plata f. 2 (coins) monedas fpl (de plata). 3 (tableware) vajilla f de plata. II adj de plata; s. foil, (tinfoil) papel m de aluminio; s. paper, papel m de plata; s. wedding, bodas fpl de plata.

silver-plated [sɪlvə'pleɪtɪd] adj plateado,-a.

silversmith ['sɪlvəsmɪθ] n platero,-a m,f.

silverware ['sɪlvəweər] n vajilla f de plata.

silvery ['sɪlvərɪ] adj plateado,-a.

similar ['sɪmɪlər] adj parecido,-a, semejante (to, a); to be s., parecerse. ◆**similarly** adv 1 (as well) igualmente. 2 (likewise) del mismo modo, asimismo.

similarity [sɪmɪ'lærɪtɪ] n semejanza f.

simile ['sɪmɪlɪ] n símil m.

simmer ['sɪmər] I vtr cocer a fuego lento. II vi cocerse a fuego lento. ◆**simmer down** vi fam calmarse.

simpering ['sɪmpərɪŋ] adj melindroso,-a.

simple ['sɪmpəl] adj 1 sencillo,-a; s. interest, interés m simple. 2 (natural) natural. 3 (foolish) simple; (naïve) ingenuo,-a; (dim) de pocas luces. ◆**simply** adv 1 (plainly) sencillamente. 2 (only) simplemente, sólo.

simplicity [sɪm'plɪsɪtɪ] n 1 sencillez f. 2 (naïveté) ingenuidad f.

simplify ['sɪmplɪfaɪ] vtr simplificar.

simulate ['sɪmjʊleɪt] vtr simular.

simulator ['sɪmjʊleɪtər] n flight s., simulador de vuelo.

simultaneous [sɪməl'teɪnɪəs] adj simultáneo,-a. ◆**simultaneously** adv simultáneamente.

sin [sɪn] I n pecado m. II vi pecar.

since [sɪns] I adv (ever) s., desde

entonces; **long s.**, hace mucho tiempo; it has s. come out that ..., desde entonces se ha sabido que .... **II** *prep* desde; **she has been living here s.** 1975, vive aquí desde 1975. **III** *conj* **1** (*time*) desde que; **how long is it s. you last saw him?**, ¿cuánto tiempo hace que lo viste por última vez? **2** (*because, as*) ya que, puesto que.

sincere [sɪn'sɪəʳ] *adj* sincero,-a. ◆**sincerely** *adv* sinceramente; **Yours s.**, (*in letter*) (le saluda) atentamente.

sincerity [sɪn'serɪtɪ] *n* sinceridad *f*.

sinew ['sɪnjuː] *n* (*tendon*) tendón *m*; (*in meat*) nervio *m*.

sinful ['sɪnfʊl] *adj* (*person*) pecador,-a; (*act, thought*) pecaminoso,-a; *fig* (*waste etc*) escandaloso,-a.

sing [sɪŋ] **I** *vtr* (*pt* **sang**; *pp* **sung**) cantar. **II** *vi* (*person, bird*) cantar; (*kettle, bullets*) silbar.

singe [sɪndʒ] *vtr* chamuscar.

singer ['sɪŋəʳ] *n* cantante *mf*.

singing ['sɪŋɪŋ] *n* (*art*) canto *m*; (*songs*) canciones *fpl*; (*of kettle*) silbido *m*.

single ['sɪŋgəl] **I** *adj* **1** (*solitary*) solo,-a. **2** (*only one*) único,-a. **3** (*not double*) sencillo,-a; **s. bed/room**, cama *f*/habitación *f* individual. **4** (*unmarried*) soltero,-a. **II** *n* **1** *Rail* billete *m* de ida. **2** (*record*) single *m*. **3** *Sport* **singles**, individuales *mpl*. ◆**single out** *vtr* (*choose*) escoger; (*distinguish*) distinguir. ◆**singly** *adv* (*individually*) por separado; (*one by one*) uno por uno.

single-breasted [sɪŋgəl'brestɪd] *adj* (*suit, jacket*) recto,-a.

single-handed [sɪŋgəl'hændɪd] *adj & adv* sin ayuda.

single-minded [sɪŋgəl'maɪndɪd] *adj* resuelto,-a.

singlet ['sɪŋglɪt] *n GB* camiseta *f*.

singular ['sɪŋgjʊləʳ] **I** *adj* **1** *Ling* singular. **2** *fml* (*outstanding*) excepcional. **3** *fml* (*unique*) único,-a. **II** *n Ling* singular *m*. ◆**singularly** *adv* excepcionalmente.

sinister ['sɪnɪstəʳ] *adj* siniestro,-a.

sink¹ [sɪŋk] *n* (*in kitchen*) fregadero *m*.

sink² [sɪŋk] **I** *vtr* (*pt* **sank**; *pp* **sunk**) **1** (*ship*) hundir, echar a pique; (*hopes*) acabar con. **2** (*hole, well*) cavar; (*post, knife, teeth*) hincar. **II** *vi* **1** (*ship*) hundirse. **2** *fig* **my heart sank**, se me cayó el alma a los pies. **3** (*sun*) ponerse. **4** **to s. to one's knees**, hincarse de rodillas. ◆**sink in** *vi* (*penetrate*) penetrar; *fig* **it hasn't sunk in yet**, todavía no me he/se ha *etc* hecho a la idea.

sinner ['sɪnəʳ] *n* pecador,-a *m,f*.

sinus ['saɪnəs] *n* seno *m*.

sip [sɪp] **I** *n* sorbo *m*. **II** *vtr* sorber, beber a sorbos.

siphon ['saɪfən] *n* sifón *m*. ◆**siphon off** *vtr* (*liquid*) sacar con sifón; *fig* (*funds,*

traffic) desviar.

sir [sɜːʳ] *n fml* señor *m*; **yes, s.**, sí, señor. **2** (*title*) sir; **S. Walter Raleigh**, Sir Walter Raleigh.

siren ['saɪərən] *n* sirena *f*.

sirloin ['sɜːlɔɪn] *n* solomillo *m*.

sissy ['sɪsɪ] *n fam* (*coward*) miedica *mf*.

sister ['sɪstəʳ] *n* **1** (*relation*) hermana *f*. **2** *GB Med* enfermera *f* jefe. **3** *Rel* hermana *f*; (*before name*) sor.

sister-in-law ['sɪstərɪnlɔː] *n* cuñada *f*.

sit [sɪt] **I** *vtr* (*pt & pp* **sat**) **1** (*child etc*) sentar (**in, on,** en). **2** *GB* (*exam*) presentarse a. **II** *vi* **1** (*action*) sentarse. **2** (*be seated*) estar sentado,-a. **3** (*object*) estar; (*be situated*) hallarse; (*person*) quedarse. **4** (*assembly*) reunirse. ◆**sit back** *vi* recostarse. ◆**sit down** *vi* sentarse. ◆**sit in on** *vtr* asistir sin participar a. ◆**sit out** *vtr* aguantar hasta el final. ◆**sit through** *vtr* aguantar. ◆**sit up** *vi* **1** incorporarse. **2** (*stay up late*) quedarse levantado,-a.

site [saɪt] **I** *n* **1** (*area*) lugar *m*; **building s.**, solar *m*; (*under construction*) obra *f*. **2** (*location*) situación *f*; **nuclear testing s.**, zona *f* de pruebas nucleares. **II** *vtr* situar.

sit-in ['sɪtɪn] *n fam* (*demonstration*) sentada *f*; (*strike*) huelga *f* de brazos caídos.

sitting ['sɪtɪŋ] **I** *n* (*of committee*) sesión *f*; (*in canteen*) turno *m*. **II** *adj* **s. room**, sala *f* de estar.

situated ['sɪtjʊeɪtɪd] *adj* situado,-a, ubicado,-a.

situation [sɪtjʊ'eɪʃən] *n* **1** situación *f*. **2** (*job*) puesto *m*; *GB* **'situations vacant'**, (*in newspaper*) 'ofertas de trabajo'.

six [sɪks] *adj & n* seis (*m*) *inv*.

sixteen [sɪks'tiːn] *adj & n* dieciséis (*m*) *inv*, diez y seis (*m*) *inv*.

sixteenth [sɪks'tiːnθ] **I** *adj & n* decimosexto,-a (*m,f*). **II** *n* (*fraction*) dieciseisavo *m*.

sixth [sɪksθ] **I** *adj* sexto,-a; *GB Educ* **s. form**, = COU; **s. former**, = estudiante de COU. **II** *n* (*in series*) sexto,-a *m,f*. **2** (*fraction*) sexta parte *f*.

sixty ['sɪkstɪ] *adj & n* sesenta (*m*) *inv*.

size [saɪz] *n* tamaño *m*; (*of garment*) talla *f*; (*of shoes*) número *m*; (*of person*) estatura *f*; (*scope*) alcance *m*; **what s. do you take?**, (*garment*) ¿qué talla tienes?; (*shoes*) ¿qué número calzas? ◆**size up** *vtr* (*person*) juzgar; (*situation, problem*) evaluar.

siz(e)able ['saɪzəbəl] *adj* (*building etc*) (*bastante*) grande; (*sum*) considerable; (*problem*) importante.

sizzle ['sɪzəl] *vi* chisporrotear.

skate¹ [skeɪt] **I** *n* patín *m*. **II** *vtr* patinar.

skate² [skeɪt] *n* (*fish*) raya *f*.

skateboard ['skeɪtbɔːd] *n* monopatín *m*.

skater ['skeɪtəʳ] *n* patinador,-a *m,f*.

skating ['skeɪtɪŋ] *n* patinaje *m*; **s. rink**,

pista f de patinaje.

skeleton ['skelɪtən] I n 1 esqueleto m. 2 (of building) armazón m. 3 (outline) esquema m. II adj (staff, service) reducido,-a; s. key, llave maestra.

skeptic ['skeptɪk] n US → sceptic.

sketch [sketʃ] I n 1 (preliminary drawing) bosquejo m, esbozo m; (drawing) dibujo m; (outline) esquema m; (rough draft) boceto m. 2 Theat TV sketch m. II vtr (draw) dibujar; (preliminary drawing) bosquejar, esbozar.

sketch-book ['sketʃbuk], **sketch-pad** ['sketʃpæd] n bloc m de dibujo.

sketchy ['sketʃɪ] adj (sketchier, sketchiest) (incomplete) incompleto,-a; (not detailed) vago,-a.

skewer ['skjuːəʳ] n pincho m, broqueta f.

ski [skiː] I n esquí m. II adj de esquí; s. **boots**, botas fpl de esquiar; s. **jump**, (action) salto m con esquís; s. **lift**, telesquí m; (with seats) telesilla f; s. **pants**, pantalón m sing de esquiar; s. **resort**, estación f de esquí; s. **stick** or **pole**, bastón m de esquiar. III vi esquiar; **to go skiing**, ir a esquiar.

skid [skɪd] I n patinazo m. II vi patinar.

skier ['skiːəʳ] n esquiador,-a m,f.

skiing ['skiːɪŋ] n esquí m.

skilful, US **skillful** ['skɪlful] adj hábil, diestro,-a.

skill [skɪl] n 1 (ability) habilidad f, destreza f; (talent) don m. 2 (technique) técnica f.

skilled [skɪld] adj 1 (dextrous) hábil, diestro,-a; (expert) experto,-a. 2 (worker) cualificado,-a.

skim [skɪm] I vtr 1 (milk) desnatar; **skimmed milk**, leche desnatada. 2 (brush against) rozar; **to s. the ground**, (bird, plane) volar a ras de suelo. II vi fig **to s. through a book**, hojear un libro.

skimp [skɪmp] vtr & vi (food, material) escatimar; (work) chapucear.

skimpy ['skɪmpɪ] adj (skimpier, skimpiest) (shorts) muy corto,-a; (meal) escaso,-a.

skin [skɪn] I n 1 piel m; (of face) cutis m; (complexion) tez f; s. **cream**, crema f de belleza. 2 (of fruit) piel f; (of lemon) cáscara f; (peeling) mondadura f. 3 (of sausage) pellejo m. 4 (on milk etc) nata f. II vtr 1 (animal) despellejar. 2 (graze) arañar.

skin-deep [skɪn'diːp] adj superficial.

skin-diving ['skɪndaɪvɪŋ] n buceo m, submarinismo m.

skinhead ['skɪnhed] n fam cabeza mf rapada.

skinny ['skɪnɪ] adj (skinnier, skinniest) fam flaco,-a.

skin-tight ['skɪntaɪt] adj (clothing) muy ajustado,-a.

skip¹ [skɪp] I n (jump) salto m, brinco m.

II vi (jump) saltar, brincar; (with rope) saltar a la comba; **to s. over sth**, saltarse algo. III vtr fig saltarse.

skip² [skɪp] n (container) contenedor m.

skipper ['skɪpəʳ] n Naut Sport fam capitán,-ana m,f.

skipping ['skɪpɪŋ] n comba f; s. **rope**, comba f.

skirmish ['skɜːmɪʃ] n escaramuza f.

skirt [skɜːt] I n falda f. II vtr (town etc) rodear; (coast) bordear; fig (problem) esquivar.

skirting ['skɜːtɪŋ] GB n s. **(board)**, zócalo m.

skit [skɪt] n sátira f, parodia f.

skittle ['skɪtl] n 1 (pin) bolo m. 2 **skittles**, (game) (juego m de los) bolos mpl, boliche m.

skive [skaɪv] vi GB fam escaquearse.

skulk [skʌlk] vi (hide) esconderse; (prowl) merodear; (lie in wait) estar al acecho.

skull [skʌl] n Anat cráneo m; fam calavera f.

skunk [skʌŋk] n mofeta f.

sky [skaɪ] n cielo m; s. **blue**, azul m celeste.

skylight ['skaɪlaɪt] n tragaluz m, claraboya f.

skyline ['skaɪlaɪn] n (of city) perfil m.

skyscraper ['skaɪskreɪpəʳ] n rascacielos m inv.

slab [slæb] n (of stone) losa f; (of chocolate) tableta f; (of cake) trozo m.

slack [slæk] I adj 1 (not taut) flojo,-a. 2 (lax) descuidado,-a; (lazy) vago,-a. 3 (market) flojo,-a; **business is s.**, hay poco negocio. II n (in rope) parte floja.

slacken ['slækən] I vtr 1 (rope) aflojar. 2 (speed) reducir. II vi 1 (rope) aflojarse; (wind) amainar. 2 (trade) aflojar.
◆**slacken off** vi disminuir.

slacks [slæks] npl dated pantalones mpl, pantalón m.

slag [slæg] n 1 Min escoria f; s. **heap**, escorial m. 2 GB sl (woman) puta f.
◆**slag off** vtr GB poner verde a.

slain [sleɪn] npl **the s.**, los caídos.

slam [slæm] I n (of door) portazo m. II vtr (bang) cerrar de golpe; **to s. sth down on the table**, soltar algo sobre la mesa de un palmetazo; **to s. the door**, dar un portazo; **to s. on the brakes**, dar un frenazo. III vi (door) cerrarse de golpe.

slander ['slɑːndəʳ] n difamación f, calumnia f. II vtr difamar, calumniar.

slang [slæŋ] n argot m, jerga f.

slant [slɑːnt] I n 1 inclinación f; (slope) pendiente f. 2 fig (point of view) punto m de vista. II vtr fig (problem etc) enfocar subjetivamente. III vi inclinarse.

slanting ['slɑːntɪŋ] adj inclinado,-a.

slap [slæp] I n palmada f; (in face) bofetada f. II adv fam **he ran s. into the fence**, se dio de lleno contra la valla; **s. in the**

middle of ..., justo en medio de .... III *vtr* pegar con la mano; (*hit in face*) dar una bofetada a; **to s. sb on the back**, dar a algn una palmada en la espalda.

slapdash ['slæp'dæʃ] *adj fam* descuidado,-a; (*work*) chapucero,-a.

slapstick ['slæpstɪk] *n* bufonadas *fpl*, payasadas *fpl*.

slap-up ['slæpʌp] *adj fam* **s.-up meal**, comilona *f*.

slash [slæʃ] I *n Typ fam* barra oblicua. II *vtr* 1 (*with knife*) acuchillar; (*with sword*) dar un tajo a. 2 *fig* (*prices*) rebajar.

slat [slæt] *n* tablilla *f*, listón *m*.

slate [sleɪt] I *n* pizarra *f*; *fig* **to wipe the s. clean**, hacer borrón y cuenta nueva. II *vtr GB fam* criticar duramente.

slaughter ['slɔːtə'] I *n* (*of animals*) matanza *f*; (*of people*) carnicería *f*. II *vtr* (*animals*) matar; (*people*) matar brutalmente; (*in large numbers*) masacrar.

slaughterhouse ['slɔːtəhaus] *n* matadero *m*.

Slav [slɑːv] *adj & n* eslavo,-a (*m,f*).

slave [sleɪv] I *n* esclavo,-a *m,f*; **s. trade**, trata *f* de esclavos. II *vi* **to s. (away)**, dar el callo.

slavery ['sleɪvərɪ] *n* esclavitud *f*.

Slavonic [slə'vɒnɪk] *adj* eslavo,-a.

slay [sleɪ] *vtr* (*pt* **slew**; *pp* **slain**) matar.

sleazy ['sliːzɪ] *adj* (**sleazier**, **sleaziest**) sórdido,-a.

sled [sled] I *n US* trineo *m*. II *vi* ir en trineo.

sledge [sledʒ] *n GB* trineo *m*.

sledgehammer ['sledʒhæmə'] *n* almádena *f*.

sleek [sliːk] *adj* (*hair*) lustroso,-a; (*appearance*) impecable.

sleep [sliːp] I *n* sueño *m*. II *vi* 1 dormir; **to go to s.**, dormirse; *fig* **to send to s.**, (hacer) dormir; *fam* **to s. like a log**, dormir como un lirón. 2 **my foot has gone to s.**, se me ha dormido el pie. ◆**sleep in** *vi GB* (*oversleep*) quedarse dormido,-a; (*have a lie-in*) quedarse en la cama. ◆**sleep with** *vtr fam* **to s. with sb**, acostarse con algn.

sleeper ['sliːpə'] *n* 1 (*person*) durmiente *mf*; **to be a heavy s.**, tener el sueño pesado. 2 *GB Rail* (*on track*) traviesa *f*. 3 *Rail* (*coach*) coche-cama *m*; (*berth*) litera *f*.

sleeping ['sliːpɪŋ] *adj* **s. bag**, saco *m* de dormir; **S. Beauty**, la Bella durmiente; **s. car**, coche-cama *m*; *GB Com* **s. partner**, socio,-a *m,f* comanditario,-a; **s. pill**, somnífero *m*.

sleepless ['sliːpləs] *adj* **to have a s. night**, pasar la noche en blanco.

sleepwalker ['sliːpwɔːkə'] *n* sonámbulo,-a *m,f*.

sleepy ['sliːpɪ] *adj* (**sleepier**, **sleepiest**) soñoliento,-a; **to be** *or* **feel s.**, tener sue-

ño.

sleet [sliːt] I *n* aguanieve *f*. II *vi* **it's sleeting**, cae aguanieve.

sleeve [sliːv] *n* (*of garment*) manga *f*; (*of record*) funda *f*.

sleigh [sleɪ] *n* trineo *m*; **s. bell**, cascabel *m*.

sleight [slaɪt] *n* **s. of hand**, juego *m* de manos.

slender ['slendə'] *adj* 1 (*thin*) delgado,-a. 2 *fig* (*hope, chance*) remoto,-a.

slept [slept] *pt & pp* → **sleep**.

slew [sluː] *pt* → **slay**.

slice [slaɪs] I *n* 1 (*of bread*) rebanada *f*; (*of ham*) loncha *f*; (*of beef etc*) tajada *f*; (*of lemon etc*) rodaja *f*; (*of cake*) trozo *m*. 2 (*utensil*) pala *f*. II *vtr* (*food*) cortar a rebanadas *or* tajos *or* rodajas; (*divide*) partir.

slick [slɪk] I *adj* 1 (*programme, show*) logrado,-a. 2 (*skilful*) hábil, mañoso,-a. II *n* (*oil*) **s.**, marea negra.

slide [slaɪd] I *n* 1 (*act*) resbalón *m*. 2 (*in prices etc*) baja *f*. 3 (*in playground*) tobogán *m*. 4 *Phot* diapositiva *f*; **s.** projector, proyector *m* de diapositivas. 5 **s. rule**, regla *f* de cálculo. 6 *GB* (*for hair*) pasador *m*. II *vtr* (*pt & pp* **slid**) deslizar; (*furniture*) correr. III *vi* (*on purpose*) deslizarse; (*slip*) resbalar.

sliding ['slaɪdɪŋ] *adj* (*door, window*) corredizo,-a; *Fin* **s. scale**, escala *f* móvil.

slight [slaɪt] I *adj* 1 (*small*) pequeño,-a; **not in the slightest**, en absoluto. 2 (*build*) menudo,-a; (*slim*) delgado,-a. 3 (*frail*) delicado,-a. 4 (*trivial*) leve. II *n* (*affront*) desaire *m*. III *vtr* 1 (*scorn*) despreciar. 2 (*snub*) desairar. ◆**slightly** *adv* (*a little*) ligeramente, algo.

slim [slɪm] I *adj* (**slimmer**, **slimmest**) 1 (*person*) delgado,-a. 2 *fig* (*resources*) escaso,-a; (*hope, chance*) remoto,-a. II *vi* adelgazar.

slime [slaɪm] *n* (*mud*) lodo *m*, cieno *m*; (*of snail*) baba *f*.

slimming ['slɪmɪŋ] I *adj* (*diet, pills*) para adelgazar; (*food*) que no engorda. II *n* (*process*) adelgazamiento *m*.

slimy ['slaɪmɪ] *adj* (**slimier**, **slimiest**) 1 (*muddy*) lodoso,-a; (*snail*) baboso,-a. 2 *fig* (*person*) zalamero,-a.

sling [slɪŋ] I *n* 1 (*catapult*) honda *f*; (*child's*) tirador *m*. 2 *Med* cabestrillo *m*. II *vtr* (*pt & pp* **slung**) (*throw*) tirar.

slink [slɪŋk] *vi* (*pt & pp* **slunk**) **to s. off**, escabullirse.

slip [slɪp] I *n* 1 (*slide*) resbalón *m*; *fam fig* **to give sb the s.**, dar esquinazo a algn. 2 (*mistake*) error *m*; (*moral*) desliz *m*; **s. of the tongue**, un lapsus linguae. 3 (*underskirt*) combinación *f*. 4 (*of paper*) trocito *m*. II *vi* 1 (*slide*) resbalar. 2 *Med* dislocarse; **slipped disc**, vértebra dislocada. 3 (*move quickly*) ir de prisa. 4

(standards etc) deteriorarse. **III** *vtr* **1** *(slide)* dar a escondidas. **2** it slipped my memory, se me fue de la cabeza. ◆**slip away** *vi (person)* escabullirse. ◆**slip off** *vtr (clothes)* quitarse rápidamente. ◆**slip on** *vtr (clothes)* ponerse rápidamente. ◆**slip out** *vi (leave)* salir. **2** *fig* the secret slipped out, se le escapó el secreto. ◆**slip up** *vi fam (blunder)* cometer un desliz.

slipper ['slɪpəʳ] *n* zapatilla *f*.

slippery ['slɪpərɪ] *adj* resbaladizo,-a.

slip-road ['slɪpɹəʊd] *n GB* vía *f* de acceso.

slipshod ['slɪpʃɒd] *adj* descuidado,-a; *(work)* chapucero,-a.

slip-up ['slɪpʌp] *n fam (blunder)* desliz *m*.

slipway ['slɪpweɪ] *n* grada *f*.

slit [slɪt] **I** *n (opening)* hendidura *f*; *(cut)* corte *m*, raja *f*. **II** *vtr (pt & pp* slit*)* cortar, rajar.

slither ['slɪðəʳ] *vi* deslizarse.

sliver ['slɪvəʳ] *n (of wood, glass)* astilla *f*; *(of ham)* loncha *f*.

slob [slɒb] *n fam* dejado,-a *m,f*.

slog [slɒg] *fam* **I** *n* it was a hard s., costó un montón. **II** *vi* **1** *fam* to s. away, sudar tinta. **2** *(walk)* caminar trabajosamente. **III** *vtr (hit)* golpear fuerte.

slogan ['sləʊgən] *n* (e)slogan *m*, lema *m*.

slop [slɒp] **I** *vi* to s. (over), derramarse; to s. about, chapotear. **II** *vtr* derramar.

slope [sləʊp] **I** *n (incline)* cuesta *f*, pendiente *f*; *(up)* subida *f*; *(down)* bajada *f*; *(of mountain)* ladera *f*; *(of roof)* vertiente *f*. **II** *vi* inclinarse; to s. up/down, subir/bajar en pendiente. ◆**slope off** *vi fam* largarse.

sloping ['sləʊpɪŋ] *adj* inclinado,-a.

sloppy ['slɒpɪ] *adj (sloppier, sloppiest) fam* descuidado,-a; *(work)* chapucero,-a; *(appearance)* desaliñado,-a.

slot [slɒt] **I** *n (for coin)* ranura *f*; *(opening)* rendija *f*; s. machine, *(for gambling)* (máquina *f*) tragaperras *f inv*; *(vending machine)* distribuidor automático. **2** *Rad TV* espacio *m*. **II** *vtr (place)* meter; *(put in)* introducir. **III** *vi* to s. in or together, encajar.

sloth [sləʊθ] *n fml (laziness)* pereza *f*.

slouch [slaʊtʃ] *vi* andar or sentarse con los hombros caídos.

slovenly ['slʌvənlɪ] *adj* descuidado,-a; *(appearance)* desaliñado,-a; *(work)* chapucero,-a.

slow [sləʊ] **I** *adj* lento,-a; in s. motion, a cámara lenta; to be s. to do sth, tardar en hacer algo. **2** *(clock)* atrasado,-a. **3** *(stupid)* lento,-a, torpe. **II** *adv* despacio, lentamente. **III** *vtr (car)* reducir la marcha de; *(progress)* retrasar. **IV** *vi* to s. down or up, ir más despacio; *(in car)* reducir la velocidad. ◆**slowly** *adv* despacio, lentamente.

sludge [slʌdʒ] *n (mud)* fango *m*, lodo *m*.

slug [slʌg] **I** *n* **1** *Zool* babosa *f*. **2** *US fam (bullet)* posta *f*. **3** *fam (blow)* porrazo *m*. **II** *vtr fam (hit)* aporrear.

sluggish ['slʌgɪʃ] *adj* **1** *(river, engine)* lento,-a; *Com* flojo,-a. **2** *(lazy)* perezoso, -a.

sluice [slu:s] *n (waterway)* canal *m*.

sluicegate ['slu:sgeɪt] *n* esclusa *f*.

slum [slʌm] *n (usu pl)* barrios bajos.

slumber ['slʌmbəʳ] *fml* **I** *n (sleep)* sueño *m*. **II** *vi* dormir.

slump [slʌmp] **I** *n* **1** *(drop in sales etc)* bajón *m*. **2** *(economic depression)* crisis económica. **II** *vi* **1** *(sales etc)* caer de repente; *(prices)* desplomarse; *(the economy)* hundirse; *(the morale)* hundirse. **2** *(fall)* caer.

slung [slʌŋ] *pt & pp* → **sling**.

slur [slɜ:ʳ] **I** *n (stigma)* mancha *f*; *(slanderous remark)* calumnia *f*. **II** *vtr (word)* tragarse.

slush [slʌʃ] *n* **1** *(melting snow)* nieve medio fundida. **2** *fam* sentimentalismo *m*. **3** *US fam* s. fund, fondos *mpl* para sobornos.

slut [slʌt] *n offens (untidy woman)* marrana *f*. **2** *(whore)* fulana *f*.

sly [slaɪ] *adj* **(sly, slyest or slier, sliest) 1** *(cunning)* astuto,-a. **2** *(secretive)* furtivo,-a. **3** *(mischievous)* travieso,-a. **4** *(underhand)* malicioso,-a.

smack¹ [smæk] **I** *n* **1** *(slap)* bofetada *f*. **2** *(sharp sound)* ruido sonoro. **II** *vtr* **1** *(slap)* dar una bofetada a. **2** *(hit)* golpear; *fig* to s. one's lips, relamerse.

smack² [smæk] *vi fig* to s. of, oler a.

small [smɔ:l] **I** *adj* **1** pequeño,-a; a s. table, una mesita; in s. letters, en minúsculas; in the s. hours, a altas horas de la noche; s. ads, anuncios *mpl* por palabras; s. print, letra pequeña. **2** *(in height)* bajo,-a. **3** *(scant)* escaso,-a; s. change, cambio *m*, suelto *m*. **4** *(minor)* insignificante; s. businessmen, pequeños comerciantes; s. talk, charloteo *m*. **5** *(increase)* ligero,-a. **II** *n* **1** s. of the back, región *f* lumbar. **2** *GB fam* smalls, *(underwear)* paños *mpl* menores.

smallholder ['smɔ:lhəʊldəʳ] *n* minifundista *mf*.

smallpox ['smɔ:lpɒks] *n* viruela *f*.

smarmy ['smɑ:mɪ] *adj (smarmier, smarmiest) fam* cobista, zalamero,-a.

smart [smɑ:t] **I** *adj* **1** *(elegant)* elegante. **2** *(clever)* listo,-a, inteligente; *fam* s. alec(k), listillo. **3** *(quick)* rápido,-a; *(pace)* ligero,-a. **II** *vi* **1** *(sting)* picar, escocer. **2** *fig* sufrir.

smarten ['smɑ:tən] *I* *vtr* to s. (up), arreglar. **II** *vi* to s. oneself (up), arreglarse.

smash [smæʃ] **I** *n* **1** *(loud noise)* estrépito *m*; *(collision)* choque violento. **2** *Ten* smash *m*. **II** *vtr* **1** *(break)* romper; *(shatter)* hacer pedazos; (crush) aplastar. 2 (destroy) destrozar; (defeat) aplastar. 3 (record) fulminar. III vi (break) romperse; (shatter) hacerse pedazos; (crash) estrellarse; Ten hacer un mate. ◆**smash up** vtr fam (car) hacer pedazos; (place) destrozar.

smashing ['smæʃɪŋ] adj GB fam estupendo,-a.

smattering ['smætərɪŋ] n he had a s. of French, hablaba un poquito de francés.

smear [smɪə'] I n (smudge) mancha f; s. (test), citología f. 2 fig (defamation) calumnia f. II vtr 1 (butter etc) untar; (grease) embadurnar; (make dirty) manchar. 3 fig (defame) calumniar, difamar.

smell [smel] I n 1 (sense) olfato m. 2 (odour) olor m. II vtr (pt & pp smelled or smelt) oler; fig olfatear. III vi oler (a); it smells good/like lavender, huele bien/a lavanda; he smelt of whisky, olía a whisky.

smelly ['smelɪ] adj (smellier, smelliest) fam maloliente, apestoso,-a.

smelt [smelt] vtr (ore) fundir.

smile [smaɪl] I n sonrisa f. II vi sonreír; to s. at sb, sonreír a algn; to s. at sth, reírse de algo.

smiling ['smaɪlɪŋ] adj sonriente, risueño,-a.

smirk [smɜːk] I n (conceited) sonrisa satisfecha; (foolish) sonrisa f boba. II vi (conceitedly) sonreír con satisfacción; (foolishly) sonreír bobamente.

smith [smɪθ] n herrero m.

smithy ['smɪðɪ] n herrería f.

smitten ['smɪtən] adj fam to be s. with sb, estar enamorado,-a de algn.

smock [smɒk] n (blouse) blusón m; (worn in pregnancy) blusón de premamá; (overall) bata f.

smog [smɒg] n niebla tóxica, smog m.

smoke [sməʊk] I n humo m; s. bomb, bomba f de humo; s. screen, cortina f de humo. II vi fumar; (chimney etc) echar humo. III vtr 1 (tobacco) fumar; to s. a pipe, fumar en pipa. 2 (fish, meat) ahumar.

smoked [sməʊkt] adj ahumado,-a.

smokeless ['sməʊklɪs] adj s. fuel, combustible sin humo; s. zone, zona libre de humos.

smoker ['sməʊkə'] n 1 (person) fumador,-a m,f. 2 Rail vagón m de fumadores.

smoking ['sməʊkɪŋ] n 'no s.', 'prohibido fumar'.

smoky ['sməʊkɪ] adj (smokier, smokiest) 1 (chimney) humeante; (room) lleno,-a de humo; (atmosphere) cargado,-a (de humo); (food) ahumado,-a. 2 (colour) ahumado,-a.

smolder ['sməʊldə'] vi US → smoulder.

smooth [smuːð] I adj 1 (surface) liso,-a; (skin) suave; (road) llano,-a; (sea)

tranquilo,-a. 2 (beer, wine) suave. 3 (flowing) fluido,-a. 4 (flight) tranquilo,-a; (transition) sin problemas. 5 pej (slick) zalamero,-a. II vtr 1 (hair etc) alisar. 2 (plane down) limar. ◆**smooth out** vtr (creases) alisar; fig (difficulties) allanar; (problems) resolver. ◆**smooth over** vtr fig to s. things over, limar asperezas. ◆**smoothly** adv sobre ruedas.

smother ['smʌðə'] vtr 1 (asphyxiate) asfixiar; (suffocate) sofocar. 2 fig (cover) cubrir (with, de).

smoulder ['sməʊldə'] vi (fire) arder sin llama; fig (passions) arder; **smouldering hatred**, odio latente.

smudge [smʌdʒ] I n (stain) mancha f; (of ink) borrón m. II vtr manchar; (piece of writing) emborronar.

smug [smʌg] adj (smugger, smuggest) engreído,-a.

smuggle ['smʌgəl] vtr pasar de contrabando.

smuggler ['smʌgələ'] n contrabandista mf.

smuggling ['smʌgəlɪŋ] n contrabando m.

smutty ['smʌtɪ] adj (smuttier, smuttiest) fam obsceno,-a; (joke) verde; (book, film etc) pornográfico,-a.

snack [snæk] n bocado m; s. bar, cafetería f.

snag [snæg] I n (difficulty) pega f, problemilla m. II vtr (clothing) enganchar.

snail [sneɪl] n caracol m.

snake [sneɪk] n (big) serpiente f; (small) culebra f.

snap [snæp] I n 1 (noise) ruido seco; (of branch, fingers) chasquido m. 2 (bite) mordisco m. 3 Phot (foto f) instantánea f. II adj (sudden) repentino,-a. III vtr 1 (branch etc) partir (en dos). 2 (make noise) hacer un ruido seco; to s. one's fingers, chasquear los dedos; to s. shut, cerrar de golpe. 3 Phot sacar una foto de. IV vi 1 (break) romperse. 2 (whip) chasquear; to s. shut, cerrarse de golpe. 3 (dog) amenazar; fam to s. at sb, regañar a algn. ◆**snap off** I vtr (branch etc) arrancar. II vi (branch etc) separarse. ◆**snap up** vtr fam to s. up a bargain, llevarse una ganga.

snappy ['snæpɪ] adj (snappier, snappiest) fam 1 (quick) rápido,-a; look s.!, make it s.!, ¡date prisa! 2 (stylish) elegante. 3 (short-tempered) irritable.

snapshot ['snæpʃɒt] n (foto f) instantánea f.

snare [sneə'] I n trampa f. II vtr (animal) cazar con trampa; fig (person) hacer caer en la trampa.

snarl¹ [snɑːl] I n gruñido m. II vi gruñir.

snarl² [snɑːl] I n (in wool) maraña f. II vtr to s. (up), (wool) enmarañar; (traffic) atascar; (plans) enredar.

snatch [snætʃ] I n 1 fam (theft) robo m;

bag s., tirón m. 2 *(fragment)* fragmentos mpl. II vtr 1 *(grab)* arrebatar. 2 *fam (steal)* robar; *(kidnap)* secuestrar. III vi to s. at sth, intentar agarrar algo.

sneak [sni:k] I n *fam* chivato,-a m.f. II vtr to s. sth out of a place, sacar algo de un lugar a escondidas. III vi I to s. off, escabullirse; to s. in/out, entrar/salir a hurtadillas. 2 to s. on sb, *(tell tales)* chivarse de algn.

sneakers ['sni:kəz] npl US zapatillas fpl de deporte.

sneaky ['sni:kı] adj *(sneakier, sneakiest)* solapado,-a.

sneer [snıə'] vi to s. at, hacer un gesto de desprecio a.

sneeze [sni:z] I n estornudo m. II vi estornudar.

sniff [snıf] I n *(by person)* aspiración f; *(by dog)* husmeo m. II vtr *(flower etc)* oler; *(suspiciously)* husmear; *(snuff etc)* aspirar; *(glue)* esnifar. III vi aspirar por la nariz.

snigger ['snıgə'] I n risa disimulada. II vi reír disimuladamente; to s. at sth, burlarse de algo.

snip [snıp] I n 1 *(cut)* tijeretada f; *(small piece)* recorte m. 2 GB *fam (bargain)* ganga f. II vtr cortar a tijeretazos.

sniper ['snaıpə'] n francotirador,-a m.f.

snippet ['snıpıt] n *(of cloth, paper)* recorte m; *(of conversation)* fragmento m.

snivel ['snıvəl] vi lloriquear.

snivelling ['snıvəlıŋ] adj llorón,-ona.

snob [snɒb] n (e)snob mf.

snobbery ['snɒbərı] n (e)snobismo m.

snobbish ['snɒbıʃ] adj (e)snob.

snooker ['snu:kə'] n snooker m, billar ruso.

snoop [snu:p] vi fisgar, fisgonear.

snooty ['snu:tı] adj *(snootier, snootiest)* fam (e)snob.

snooze [snu:z] fam I n cabezada f. II vi echar una cabezada.

snore [snɔ:'] I n ronquido m. II vi roncar.

snoring ['snɔ:rıŋ] n ronquidos mpl.

snorkel ['snɔ:kəl] n *(of swimmer)* tubo m de respiración; *(of submarine)* esnórquel m.

snort [snɔ:t] I n resoplido m. II vi resoplar.

snout [snaut] n *(of animal, gun etc)* morro m.

snow [snəu] I n nieve f; s. shower, nevada f. II vi nevar; it's snowing, está nevando. III vtr *fig* to be snowed under with work, estar agobiado,-a de trabajo.

snowball ['snəubɔ:l] I n bola f de nieve. II vi *fig* aumentar rápidamente.

snowbound ['snəubaund] adj aislado,-a por la nieve.

snowdrift ['snəudrıft] n ventisquero m.

snowdrop ['snəudrɒp] n campanilla f de invierno.

snowfall ['snəufɔ:l] n nevada f.

snowflake ['snəufleık] n copo m de nieve.

snowman ['snəumæn] n hombre m de nieve.

snowplough, US **snowplow** ['snəuplau] n quitanieves m inv.

snowshoe ['snəuʃu:] n raqueta f (de nieve).

snowstorm ['snəustɔ:m] n nevasca f.

snowy ['snəuı] adj *(snowier, snowiest)* *(mountain)* nevado,-a; *(climate)* nevoso,-a; *(day)* de nieve.

Snr, snr *esp* US *abbr of* senior.

snub [snʌb] I n *(of person)* desaire m; *(of offer)* rechazo m. II vtr *(person)* desairar; *(offer)* rechazar.

snub-nosed ['snʌbnəuzd] adj de nariz respingona.

snuff [snʌf] n rapé m.

snug [snʌg] adj *(snugger, snuggest)* I *(cosy)* cómodo,-a. 2 *(tightfitting)* ajustado, -a. ◆**snugly** adv to fit s., *(clothes)* quedar ajustado,-a; *(object in box etc)* encajar.

snuggle ['snʌgl] vi to s. down in bed, acurrucarse en la cama; to s. up to sb, arrimarse a algn.

so [səu] I adv 1 *(to such an extent)* tanto; he was so tired that ..., estaba tan cansado que ...; it's so long since ..., hace tanto tiempo que ...; he isn't so nice as his sister, no es tan agradable como su hermana; *fam* so long!, ¡hasta luego! 2 *(degree)* tanto; a week or so, una semana más o menos; twenty or so, una veintena; we loved her so (much), la queríamos tanto; so many books, tantos libros; *fam* he's ever so handsome!, ¡es tan guapo!; *iron* so much for that, ¿qué le vamos a hacer? 3 *(thus, in this way)* así, de esta manera; and so on, and so forth, y así sucesivamente; if so, en este caso; I think/hope so, creo/espero que sí; I told you so, ya te lo dije; it so happens that ..., da la casualidad de que ...; so be it!, ¡así sea!; so far, hasta ahora or allí; so it seems, eso parece; so they say, eso dicen; you're late! - so I am!, ¡llegas tarde! - ¡tienes razón! 4 *(also)* I'm going to Spain - so am I, voy a España - yo también.

II conj 1 *(expresses result)* así que; so you like England, do you?, ¿así que te gusta Inglaterra, pues?; *fam* so what?, ¿y qué? 2 *(expresses purpose)* para que; I'll put the key here so (that) everyone can see it, pongo la llave aquí para que todos la vean.

so-and-so ['səuənsəu] n *fam* Mr So-and-so, Don Fulano (de tal); *pej* an old so-and-so, un viejo imbécil.

soak [səuk] I vtr *(washing, food)* remojar; *(cotton, wool)* empapar (in, en). II vi *(washing, food)* estar en remojo. ◆**soak in** vi penetrar. ◆**soak up** vtr absorber.

soaking ['səukıŋ] adj *(object)* empapado,

-a; *(person)* calado,-a hasta los huesos.

soap [səʊp] I *n* 1 jabón *m*; **s. flakes**, jabón en escamas; **s. powder**, jabón en polvo. 2 *TV* **s. opera**, culebrón *m*. II *vtr* enjabonar.

soapy ['səʊpɪ] *adj* **(soapier, soapiest)** jabonoso,-a; *(hands)* cubierto,-a de jabón.

soar [sɔːʳ] *vi* *(bird, plane)* remontar el vuelo; *fig (skyscraper)* elevarse; *(hopes, prices)* aumentar.

sob [sɒb] I *n* sollozo *m*. II *vi* sollozar.

sober ['səʊbəʳ] *adj* *(not drunk, moderate)* sobrio,-a; *(sensible)* sensato,-a; *(serious)* serio,-a; *(colour)* discreto,-a. **◆sober up** *vi* **he sobered up**, se le pasó la borrachera.

so-called ['səʊkɔːld] *adj* supuesto,-a, llamado,-a.

soccer ['sɒkəʳ] *n* fútbol *m*.

sociable ['səʊʃəbəl] *adj* *(gregarious)* sociable; *(friendly)* amistoso,-a.

social ['səʊʃəl] *adj* social; **s. class**, clase *f* social; **s. climber**, arribista *mf*; **S. Democratic**, socialdemócrata; *US* **s. insurance**, seguro *m* social; **s. security**, seguridad *f* social; **the s. services**, los servicios sociales; **s. welfare**, seguro social; **s. work**, asistencia *f* social; **s. worker**, asistente,-a *m,f* social. **◆socially** *adv* socialmente.

socialist ['səʊʃəlɪst] *adj & n* socialista *(mf)*.

socialite ['səʊʃəlaɪt] *n* vividor,-a *m,f*.

socialize ['səʊʃəlaɪz] I *vi* alternar, mezclarse con la gente. II *vtr* socializar.

society [sə'saɪɪtɪ] I *n* 1 sociedad *f*; **the consumer s.**, la sociedad de consumo; **(high) s.**, la alta sociedad. 2 *(club)* asociación *f*. 3 *(companionship)* compañía *f*. II *adj* de sociedad; **s. column**, ecos *mpl* de sociedad.

sociologist [səʊsɪ'ɒlədʒɪst] *n* sociólogo,-a *m,f*.

sociology [səʊsɪ'ɒlədʒɪ] *n* sociología *f*.

sock [sɒk] *n* calcetín *m*.

socket ['sɒkɪt] *n* 1 *(of eye)* cuenca *f*. 2 *Elec* enchufe *m*.

sod¹ [sɒd] *n fml (piece of turf)* terrón *m*.

sod² [sɒd] *vulg* I *n* 1 *offens (bastard)* cabrón,-ona *m,f*; **the lazy s.**, ¡qué tío más vago! 2 *(wretch)* desgraciado,-a *m,f*; **the poor s.**, el pobrecito. 3 *vulg* I've done s. all today, hoy no he pegado ni golpe. II *vtr* **s. it!**, ¡maldita sea!

soda ['səʊdə] *n* 1 *Chem* sosa *f*; **baking s.**, bicarbonato sódico. 2 **s. water**, soda *f*. 3 *US (fizzy drink)* gaseosa *f*.

sodden ['sɒdən] *adj* empapado,-a.

sodium ['səʊdɪəm] *n* sodio *m*.

sofa ['səʊfə] *n* sofá *m*; **s. bed**, sofá cama.

soft [sɒft] *adj* 1 *(not hard)* blando,-a; **s. toy**, muñeco *m* de peluche. 2 *(skin, colour, hair, light, music)* suave; *(breeze, steps)* ligero,-a. 3 *(lenient)* permisivo,-a;

(voice) bajo,-a. 5 *(foolish)* lelo,-a; **to be a s. touch**, ser fácil de engañar. 6 **to have a s. spot for sb**, tener debilidad por algn. 7 *(easy)* fácil; **s. job**, chollo *m*. 8 *(drink)* no alcohólico,-a; **s. drinks**, refrescos *mpl*. 9 **s. drugs**, drogas blandas; **s. porn**, pornografía blanda. **◆softly** *adv (gently)* suavemente; *(quietly)* silenciosamente.

soften ['sɒfən] I *vtr (leather, heart)* ablandar; *(skin)* suavizar; *fig (blow)* amortiguar. II *vi (leather, heart)* ablandarse; *(skin)* suavizarse.

softness ['sɒftnɪs] *n* 1 blandura *f*. 2 *(of hair, skin)* suavidad *f*. 3 *(foolishness)* estupidez *f*.

software ['sɒftweəʳ] *n Comput* software *m*; **s. package**, paquete *m*.

soggy ['sɒgɪ] *adj* **(soggier, soggiest)** empapado,-a; *(bread)* pastoso,-a.

soil [sɔɪl] I *n (earth)* tierra *f*. II *vtr (dirty)* ensuciar; *fig (reputation)* manchar.

soiled [sɔɪld] *adj* sucio,-a.

solace ['sɒlɪs] *n fml* consuelo *m*.

solar ['səʊləʳ] *adj* solar.

sold [səʊld] *pt & pp* → **sell**.

solder ['sɒldəʳ] I *n* soldadura *f*. II *vtr* soldar.

soldier ['səʊldʒəʳ] *n* soldado *m*; *(military man)* militar *m*; **toy s.**, soldadito *m* de plomo. **◆soldier on** *vi fig* continuar contra viento y marea.

sole¹ [səʊl] *n (of foot)* planta *f*; *(of shoe, sock)* suela *f*.

sole² [səʊl] *n (fish)* lenguado *m*.

sole³ [səʊl] *adj (only)* único,-a.

solemn ['sɒləm] *adj* solemne.

solicit [sə'lɪsɪt] I *vtr (request)* solicitar. II *vi (prostitute)* abordar a las clientes.

solicitor [sə'lɪsɪtəʳ] *n* abogado,-a *m,f*; *(for wills)* notario,-a *m,f*.

solid ['sɒlɪd] I *adj* 1 *(not liquid)* sólido,-a; *(firm)* firme. 2 *(not hollow, pure) (metal)* macizo,-a. 3 *(fog etc)* espeso,-a; *(of strong material)* resistente; **a man of s. build**, un hombre fornido. 4 *(reliable)* formal. 5 *(unanimous)* unánime. II *n* sólido *m*. **◆solidly** *adv* sólidamente; **s. built**, *(house etc)* de construcción sólida; **to work s.**, trabajar sin descanso.

solidarity [sɒlɪ'dærɪtɪ] *n* solidaridad *f*.

solidify [sə'lɪdɪfaɪ] *vi* solidificarse.

soliloquy [sə'lɪləkwɪ] *n* soliloquio *m*.

solitaire ['sɒlɪteəʳ] *n* solitario *m*.

solitary ['sɒlɪtərɪ] *adj* 1 *(alone)* solitario, -a; *(secluded)* apartado,-a. 2 *(only)* solo,-a.

solitude ['sɒlɪtjuːd] *n* soledad *f*.

solo ['səʊləʊ] *n* solo *m*.

soloist ['səʊləʊɪst] *n* solista *mf*.

solstice ['sɒlstɪs] *n* solsticio *m*.

solution [sə'luːʃən] *n* solución *f*.

solve [sɒlv] *vtr* resolver, solucionar.

solvent ['sɒlvənt] *adj & n* solvente *(m)*.

sombre, *US* **somber** ['sɒmbəʳ] *adj (dark)*

sombrío,-a; (gloomy) lúgubre; (pessimistic) pesimista.

some [sʌm] **I** adj 1 (with plural nouns) unos,-as, algunos,-as; (several) varios,-as; (a few) unos,-as cuantos,-as; did she bring s. flowers?, ¿trajo flores?; there were s. roses, había unas rosas; s. more peas, más guisantes 2 (with singular nouns) algún, alguna; (a little) un poco de; if you need s. help, si necesitas ayuda; there's s. wine left, queda un poco de vino; would you like s. coffee?, ¿quiere café? 3 (certain) cierto,-a, alguno,-a; in s. ways, en cierto modo; to s. extent, hasta cierto punto; s. people say that ..., algunas personas dicen que .... 4 (unspecified) algún, alguna; for s. reason or other, por una razón o por otra; in s. book or other, en algún libro que otro; s. day, algún día; s. other time, otro día. 5 (quite a lot of) bastante; it's s. distance away, queda bastante lejos; s. years ago, hace algunos años.
II pron 1 (people) algunos,-as, unos,-as; s. go by bus and s. by train, unos van en autobús y otros en tren. 2 (objects) algunos,-as; (a few) unos,-as cuantos,-as; (a little) algo, un poco; (certain ones) algunos,-as.
III adv s. thirty cars, unos treinta coches.

somebody ['sʌmbədɪ] pron alguien; s. else, otro,-a.

somehow ['sʌmhaʊ] adv 1 (in some way) de alguna forma. 2 (for some reason) por alguna razón.

someone ['sʌmwʌn] pron & n → somebody.

someplace ['sʌmpleɪs] adv US → somewhere.

somersault ['sʌməsɔːlt] **I** n (by acrobat etc) salto m mortal; (by child) voltereta f; (by car) vuelta f de campana. **II** vi (acrobat etc) dar un salto mortal; (child) dar volteretas; (car) dar una vuelta de campana.

something ['sʌmθɪŋ] pron & n algo; s. to eat/drink, algo de comer/beber; are you drunk or s.?, ¿estás borracho o qué?; s. must be done, hay que hacer algo; she has a certain s., tiene un no se qué; is s. the matter?, ¿le pasa algo?; s. else, otra cosa; s. of the kind, algo por el estilo.

sometime ['sʌmtaɪm] adv algún día; s. last week, un día de la semana pasada; s. next year, durante el año que viene.

sometimes ['sʌmtaɪmz] adv a veces, de vez en cuando.

somewhat ['sʌmwɒt] adv fml algo, un tanto.

somewhere ['sʌmweəʳ] adv 1 (in some place) en alguna parte; (to some place) a alguna parte; s. else, (in some other place) en otra parte; (to some other place) a otra

parte; s. or other, no sé dónde. 2 s. in the region of, (approximately) más o menos.

son [sʌn] n hijo m; eldest/youngest s., hijo mayor/menor.

song [sɒŋ] n canción f; (of bird) canto m.

songwriter ['sɒŋraɪtəʳ] n compositor,-a m,f (de canciones).

sonic ['sɒnɪk] adj sónico,-a.

son-in-law ['sʌnɪnlɔː] n yerno m.

sonnet ['sɒnɪt] n soneto m.

sonny ['sʌnɪ] n fam hijo m, hijito m.

soon [suːn] adv 1 (within a short time) pronto, dentro de poco; (quickly) rápidamente; see you s.!, ¡hasta pronto!; s. after midnight, poco después de medianoche; s. afterwards, poco después. 2 as s. as I arrived, en cuanto llegué; as s. as possible, cuanto antes. 3 (early) pronto; fig don't speak too s., no cantes victoria. 4 (preference) I would just as s. stay at home, prefiero quedarme en casa. 5 (indifference) I would (just) as s. read as watch TV, tanto me da leer como ver la tele.

sooner ['suːnəʳ] adv 1 (earlier) más temprano; s. or later, tarde o temprano; the s. the better, cuanto antes mejor. 2 no s. had he finished than he fainted, (immediately after) nada más acabar se desmayó. 3 I would s. do it alone, (rather) prefiero hacerlo yo solo.

soot [sʊt] n hollín m.

soothe [suːð] vtr (calm) tranquilizar; (pain) aliviar.

sop [sɒp] n 1 fig (concession) favor m; (bribe) soborno m. 2 sops, (food) sopa f sing. ◆**sop up** vtr empapar.

sophisticated [sə'fɪstɪkeɪtɪd] adj sofisticado,-a.

soporific [sɒpə'rɪfɪk] adj soporífero,-a.

sopping ['sɒpɪŋ] adj fam s. (wet), como una sopa.

soppy ['sɒpɪ] adj (soppier, soppiest) fam sentimentaloide.

soprano [sə'prɑːnəʊ] n soprano mf.

sorcerer ['sɔːsərəʳ] n brujo m.

sorceress ['sɔːsərɪs] n bruja f.

sordid ['sɔːdɪd] adj sórdido,-a.

sore [sɔːʳ] **I** adj 1 dolorido,-a; to have a s. throat, tener dolor de garganta. 2 fam (angry) enfadado,-a; to feel s. about sth, estar resentido,-a por algo. **II** n llaga f. ◆**sorely** adv (very) muy; (a lot) mucho; (deeply) profundamente.

sorrow ['sɒrəʊ] n pena f, dolor m.

sorrowful ['sɒrəʊful] adj afligido,-a.

sorry ['sɒrɪ] **I** adj (sorrier, sorriest) 1 I feel very s. for her, me da mucha pena. 2 (pitiful) triste. 3 to be s. (about sth), sentir (algo); I'm s. I'm late, siento llegar tarde. **II** interj 1 (apology) ¡perdón! 2 GB (for repetition) ¿cómo?

sort [sɔːt] **I** n 1 (kind) clase f, tipo m;

(brand) marca f; **it's a s.** of teapot, es una especie de tetera. **2 he is a musician of sorts,** tiene algo de músico; **there's an office of sorts,** hay una especie de despacho. **3 s. of,** en cierto modo. II *vtr* (classify) clasificar. ◆**sort out** *vtr* 1 (classify) clasificar; (put in order) ordenar. 2 (problem) arreglar, solucionar.

sorting ['sɔːtɪŋ] *n* **s. office,** sala f de batalla.

SOS [esəʊ'es] *abbr* of save our souls, S.O.S. m.

so-so ['səʊsəʊ] *adv fam* así así, regular.

soufflé ['suːfleɪ] *n* soufflé m, suflé m.

sought [sɔːt] *pt & pp →* seek.

soul [səʊl] *n* **1** alma f. **2 he's a good s.,** (person) es muy buena persona. **3** *Mus* (música f) soul m.

soul-destroying ['səʊldɪstrɔɪɪŋ] *adj* (boring) monótono,-a; (demoralizing) desmoralizador,-a.

soulful ['səʊlfʊl] *adj* conmovedor,-a.

sound[1] [saʊnd] *n* **1** sonido m; (noise) ruido m; *fig* **I don't like the s. of it,** no me gusta nada la idea; **s. barrier,** barrera f del sonido; **s. effects,** efectos sonoros. II *vtr* (bell, trumpet) tocar; **to s. the alarm,** dar la señal de alarma. III *vi* **1** (trumpet, bell, alarm) sonar. **2** (give an impression) parecer; **how does it s. to you?,** ¿qué te parece?; **it sounds interesting,** parece interesante.

sound[2] [saʊnd] **I** *adj* **1** (healthy) sano,-a; (in good condition) en buen estado. **2** (safe, dependable) seguro,-a; (correct) acertado,-a; (logical) lógico,-a. **3** (basis etc) sólido,-a. **4** (defeat etc) rotundo,-a; (examination etc) a fondo. **5** (sleep) profundo,-a. II *adv* **to be s. asleep,** estar profundamente dormido,-a.

sound[3] [saʊnd] *vtr* Naut Med sondar. ◆**sound out** *vtr* sondear.

sound[4] [saʊnd] *n* Geog estrecho m.

sounding ['saʊndɪŋ] *n* Naut sondeo m.

soundproof ['saʊndpruːf] *adj* insonorizado,-a.

soundtrack ['saʊndtræk] *n* banda sonora.

soup [suːp] *n* sopa f; (thin, clear) caldo m; *fam* **in the s.,** en un apuro; **s. dish,** plato hondo; **s. spoon,** cuchara f sopera.

sour [saʊəʳ] *adj* **1** (fruit, wine) agrio,-a; (milk) cortado,-a; **to go s.,** (milk) cortarse; (wine) agriarse; *fig* (situation) empeorar; *fam* **fig s. grapes!,** ¡te aguantas! **2** *fig* (person) amargado,-a.

source [sɔːs] *n* fuente f; (of infection) foco m.

south [saʊθ] **I** *n* sur m; **in the s. of England,** en el sur de Inglaterra; **to the s. of York,** al sur de York. II *adj* del sur; **S. Africa,** Sudáfrica; **S. African,** sudafricano,-a (m,f); **S. Pole,** Polo m Sur. III *adv* (location) al sur; (direction) hacia el sur.

southeast [saʊθ'iːst] **I** *n* sudeste m. II *adv* (location) al sudeste; (direction) hacia el sudeste.

southeasterly [saʊθ'iːstəlɪ] *adj* del sudeste.

southerly ['sʌðəlɪ] *adj* (direction) hacia el sur; (point) al sur; (wind) del sur.

southern ['sʌðən] *adj* del sur, meridional; **S. Europe,** Europa del Sur; **the s. hemisphere,** el hemisferio sur.

southerner ['sʌðənəʳ] *n* sureño,-a m,f.

southward ['saʊθwəd] *adj & adv* hacia el sur.

southwest [saʊθ'west] **I** *n* suroeste m. II *adj* suroeste. III *adv* (location) al suroeste; (direction) hacia el suroeste.

souvenir [suːvə'nɪəʳ] *n* recuerdo m, souvenir m.

sovereign ['sɒvrɪn] **I** *n* **1** (monarch) soberano,-a m,f. **2** *arch* (coin) soberano m. II *adj* soberano,-a.

soviet ['səʊvɪət] **I** *n* **1** (council) soviet m. **2 the Soviets,** los soviéticos. II *adj* soviético,-a; *Hist* **S. Union,** Unión Soviética.

sow[1] [saʊ] *vtr* (pt sowed; pp sowed or sown) sembrar.

sow[2] [saʊ] *n* Zool cerda f.

soy [sɔɪ] *n US* soja f; **s. sauce,** salsa f de soja.

soya ['sɔɪə] *n GB* soja f.

spa [spɑː] *n* balneario m.

space [speɪs] **I** *n* **1** espacio m; **s. age,** era f espacial; **s. shuttle,** transbordador m espacial; **s. station,** estación f espacial. **2** (room) sitio m; **in a confined s.,** en un espacio reducido. II *vtr* (also s. out) espaciar, separar.

spacecraft ['speɪskrɑːft] *n inv* nave f espacial.

spaceman ['speɪsmæn] *n* astronauta m, cosmonauta m.

spacing ['speɪsɪŋ] *n* **double s.,** doble espacio.

spacious ['speɪʃəs] *adj* espacioso,-a, amplio,-a.

spade[1] [speɪd] *n* (for digging) pala f.

spade[2] [speɪd] *n* Cards (international pack) pica f; (Spanish pack) espada f.

spaghetti [spə'getɪ] *n* espaguetis mpl.

Spain [speɪn] *n* España.

span [spæn] **I** *n* (of wing) envergadura f; (of hand) palmo m; (of arch) luz f; (of road) tramo m; (of time) lapso m; **life s.,** vida f. II *vtr* (river etc) extenderse sobre, atravesar; (period of time etc) abarcar.

Spaniard ['spænjəd] *n* español,-a m,f.

spaniel ['spænjəl] *n* perro m de aguas.

Spanish ['spænɪʃ] **I** *adj* español,-a. II *n* **1 the S.,** los españoles. **2** (language) español m, castellano m.

Spanish-speaking ['spænɪʃspiːkɪŋ] *adj* de habla española, hispanohablante.

spank [spæŋk] *vtr* zurrar.

spanner ['spænə^r] n llave f (para tuercas); GB fam **to throw a s. in the works**, estropear los planes.

spar¹ [spɑ:^r] n Naut palo m, verga f.

spar² [spɑ:^r] vi 1 Box entrenarse. 2 (argue) discutir.

spare [speə^r] I vtr 1 (do without) prescindir de; **can you s. me 10?**, ¿me puedes dejar 10?; **I can't s. the time**, no tengo tiempo; **there's none to s.**, no sobra nada. 2 (begrudge) escatimar. 3 (show mercy to) perdonar. 4 **s. me the details**, ahórrate los detalles. II adj 1 (left over) sobrante; (surplus) de sobra, de más; **a s. moment**, un momento libre; **s. part**, (pieza f de) recambio m; **s. room**, cuarto m de los invitados; **s. tyre**, Aut neumático m de recambio; GB fam (on body) michelines mpl; **s. wheel**, rueda f de recambio. 2 (thin) enjuto,-a. III n Aut (pieza f de) recambio m.

sparing ['speərɪŋ] adj **to be s. with praise**, escatimar elogios; **to be s. with words**, ser parco,-a en palabras. ◆**sparingly** adv en poca cantidad.

spark [spɑ:k] I n chispa f; Aut **s. plug**, bujía f. II vi echar chispas. ◆**spark off** vtr desatar.

sparking ['spɑ:kɪŋ] adj **s. plug**, bujía f.

sparkle ['spɑ:kəl] I vi (diamond, glass) centellear, destellar; (eyes) brillar. II n (of diamond, glass) centelleo m, destello m; (of eyes) brillo m.

sparkling ['spɑ:klɪŋ] adj 1 (diamond, glass) centelleante; (eyes) brillante; **s. wine**, vino espumoso. 2 fig (person, conversation) vivaz.

sparrow ['spærəʊ] n gorrión m.

sparse [spɑ:s] adj (thin) escaso,-a; (scattered) esparcido,-a; (hair) ralo,-a.

Spartan ['spɑ:tən] adj & n espartano,-a (m,f).

spasm ['spæzəm] n 1 Med espasmo m; (of coughing) acceso m. 2 (of anger, activity) arrebato m.

spasmodic [spæz'mɒdɪk] adj 1 Med espasmódico,-a. 2 (irregular) irregular.

spastic ['spæstɪk] adj & n Med espástico,-a (m,f).

spat [spæt] pt & pp → **spit¹**.

spate [speɪt] n 1 (of letters) avalancha f; (of words) torrente m; (of accidents) racha f. 2 GB (river) desbordamiento m; **to be in full s.**, estar crecido,-a.

spatter ['spætə^r] vtr salpicar (with, de).

spatula ['spætjʊlə] n espátula f.

spawn [spɔ:n] I n (of fish, frogs) huevas fpl. II vi (fish, frogs) frezar. III vtr fig pej generar.

speak [spi:k] I vtr (pt **spoke**; pp **spoken**) 1 (utter) decir; **to s. the truth**, decir la verdad. 2 (language) hablar. II vi 1 (gen) hablar; **roughly speaking**, a grandes rasgos; **so to s.**, por así decirlo; **speaking of ...**, a propósito de ...; **to s. to sb**, hablar con algn. 2 (make a speech) pronunciar un discurso; (take the floor) tomar la palabra. 3 Tel hablar; **speaking!**, ¡al habla!; **who's speaking, please?**, ¿de parte de quién? ◆**speak for** vtr (person, group) hablar en nombre de; **it speaks for itself**, es evidente. ◆**speak out** vi to **s. out against sth**, denunciar algo. ◆**speak up** vi hablar más fuerte; fig to **s. up for sb**, intervenir a favor de algn.

speaker ['spi:kə^r] n 1 (in dialogue) interlocutor,-a m,f; (lecturer) conferenciante m,f; (public) s., orador,-a m,f. 2 (of language) hablante mf. 3 GB Parl **the S.**, el Presidente de la Cámara de los Comunes; US **the S. of the House**, el Presidente de la Cámara de los Representantes. 4 (loudspeaker) altavoz m.

spear [spɪə^r] n lanza f; (javelin) jabalina f; (harpoon) arpón m.

spearhead ['spɪəhed] vtr encabezar.

spec [spek] n fam **on s.**, sin garantías.

special ['speʃəl] I adj especial; (specific) específico,-a; (exceptional) extraordinario,-a; **s. delivery**, (letter) exprés; (parcel) de entrega inmediata; **s. edition**, número m especial; **s. effects**, efectos mpl especiales. II n Rad TV programa m especial. ◆**specially** adv (specifically) especialmente; (on purpose) a propósito.

specialist ['speʃəlɪst] n especialista mf.

speciality [speʃɪ'ælɪtɪ] n especialidad f.

specialize ['speʃəlaɪz] vi especializarse (in, en).

specialty ['speʃəltɪ] n US → **speciality**.

species ['spi:ʃi:z] n (pl **species**) especie f.

specific [spɪ'sɪfɪk] adj específico,-a; (definite) concreto,-a; (precise) preciso,-a; **to be s.**, concretar. ◆**specifically** adv (exactly) específicamente; (expressly) expresamente; (namely) en concreto.

specification [spesɪfɪ'keɪʃən] n specifications, datos específicos.

specify ['spesɪfaɪ] vtr especificar, precisar.

specimen ['spesɪmɪn] n (sample) muestra f; (example) ejemplar m; **urine/tissue s.**, espécimen de orina/tejido.

speck [spek] n (of dust) mota f; (stain) manchita f; (small trace) pizca f.

speckled ['spekəld] adj moteado,-a.

specs [speks] npl fam abbr of **spectacles**.

spectacle ['spektəkəl] n 1 · (display) espectáculo m. 2 **spectacles**, (glasses) gafas fpl.

spectacular [spek'tækjʊlə^r] I adj espectacular, impresionante. II n Cin TV (gran) espectáculo m.

spectator [spek'teɪtə^r] n espectador,-a m,f.

spectre, US **specter** ['spektə^r] n espectro m, fantasma m.

spectrum ['spektrəm] n espectro m.

speculate ['spekjʊleɪt] *vi* especular.

speculation [spekjʊ'leɪʃən] *n* especulación *f*.

speech [spiːtʃ] *n* 1 (*faculty*) habla *f*; (*pronunciation*) pronunciación *f*; **freedom of s.**, libertad *f* de expresión. 2 (*address*) discurso *m*; **to give a s.**, pronunciar un discurso. 3 *Ling* part of s., parte *f* de la oración.

speechless ['spiːtʃlɪs] *adj* mudo,-a, boquiabierto,-a.

speed [spiːd] **I** *n* 1 velocidad *f*; (*rapidity*) rapidez *f*; **at top s.**, a toda velocidad; **s. limit**, límite *m* de velocidad. **II** *vi* 1 (*go fast*) ir corriendo; (*hurry*) apresurarse; **to s. along**, (*car etc*) ir a toda velocidad; **to s. past**, pasar volando. 2 (*pt & pp* **speeded**) (*exceed speed limit*) conducir con exceso de velocidad. ◆**speed up I** *vtr* (*pt & pp* **speeded up**) acelerar; (*person*) meter prisa a. **II** *vi* (*person*) darse prisa.

speedboat ['spiːdbəʊt] *n* lancha rápida.

speeding ['spiːdɪŋ] *n* exceso *m* de velocidad.

speedometer [spɪ'dɒmɪtə'] *n* velocímetro *m*.

speedway ['spiːdweɪ] *n* 1 (*racing*) carreras *fpl* de motos. 2 (*track*) pista *f* de carreras.

speedy ['spiːdɪ] *adj* (**speedier**, **speediest**) veloz, rápido,-a.

spell¹ [spel] **I** *vtr* (*pt & pp* **spelt** *or* **spelled**) (*letter by letter*) deletrear; *fig* (*denote*) significar; **how do you s. your name?**, ¿cómo se escribe su nombre?. **II** *vi* **she can't s.**, comete faltas de ortografía. ◆**spell out** *vtr fig* explicar con detalle.

spell² [spel] *n* (*magical*) hechizo *m*, encanto *m*.

spell³ [spel] *n* 1 (*period*) período *m*; (*short period*) rato *m*; *Meteor* **cold s.**, ola *f* de frío. 2 (*shift*) turno *m*.

spellbound ['spelbaʊnd] *adj* hechizado,-a, embelesado,-a.

spelling ['spelɪŋ] *n* ortografía *f*.

spend [spend] *vtr* (*pt & pp* **spent**) 1 (*money*) gastar (**on**, en). 2 (*time*) pasar; **to s. time on sth**, dedicar tiempo a algo.

spending ['spendɪŋ] *n* gastos *mpl*; **s. money**, dinero *m* de bolsillo; **s. power**, poder adquisitivo.

spendthrift ['spendθrɪft] *adj & n* derrochador,-a (*m,f*).

spent [spent] *adj* gastado,-a.

sperm [spɜːm] *n* esperma *m*; **s. bank**, banco *m* de esperma; **s. whale**, cachalote *m*.

spew [spjuː] *vtr* **to s. (up)**, vomitar.

sphere [sfɪə'] *n* esfera *f*.

spice [spaɪs] **I** *n* 1 especia *f*. 2 *fig* sal *f*. **II** *vtr* 1 *Culin* sazonar. 2 **to s. (up)**, (*story etc*) salpimentar.

spic(k)-and-span [spɪkən'spæn] *adj* (*very clean*) limpísimo,-a; (*well-groomed*) acicalado,-a.

spicy ['spaɪsɪ] *adj* (**spicier**, **spiciest**) 1 *Culin* sazonado,-a; (*hot*) picante. 2 *fig* (*story etc*) picante.

spider ['spaɪdə'] *n* araña *f*; **s.'s web**, telaraña *f*.

spike¹ [spaɪk] *n* (*sharp point*) punta *f*; (*metal rod*) pincho *m*; (*on railing*) barrote *m*; (*on shoes*) clavo *m*.

spike² [spaɪk] *n Bot* espiga *f*.

spiky ['spaɪkɪ] *adj* (**spikier**, **spikiest**) puntiagudo,-a; (*hairstyle*) de punta.

spill [spɪl] **I** *vtr* (*pt & pp* **spilled** *or* **spilt**) derramar. **II** *vi* (*liquid*) derramarse. ◆**spill over** *vi* desbordarse.

spin [spɪn] **I** *vtr* (*pt & pp* **spun**) 1 (*wheel etc*) hacer girar; (*washing*) centrifugar. 2 (*cotton, wool*) hilar; (*spider's web*) tejer. **II** *vi* (*wheel etc*) girar; *Av* caer en barrena; *Aut* patinar. **III** *n* 1 (*turn*) vuelta *f*, giro *m*. 2 *Sport* efecto *m*. 3 *Av* barrena *f*; *Aut* patinazo *m*. 4 *GB* **to go for a s.**, (*ride*) dar una vuelta.

spinach ['spɪnɪtʃ] *n* espinacas *fpl*.

spinal ['spaɪnəl] *adj* espinal, vertebral; **s. column**, columna *f* vertebral; **s. cord**, médula *f* espinal.

spindly ['spɪndlɪ] *adj* (**spindlier**, **spindliest**) *fam* (*long-bodied*) larguirucho,-a; (*long-legged*) zanquilargo,-a.

spin-dryer [spɪn'draɪə'] *n* secador centrífugo.

spine [spaɪn] *n* 1 *Anat* columna *f* vertebral, espinazo *m*; (*of book*) lomo *m*. 2 *Zool* púa *f*; *Bot* espina *f*.

spineless ['spaɪnlɪs] *adj fig* (*weak*) sin carácter.

spinning ['spɪnɪŋ] *n* 1 (*of cotton etc*) (*act*) hilado *m*; (*art*) hilandería *f*; **s. wheel**, rueca *f*. 2 **s. top**, peonza *f*.

spin-off ['spɪnɒf] *n* (*by-product*) derivado *m*; *fig* efecto secundario.

spinster ['spɪnstə'] *n* soltera *f*.

spiral ['spaɪərəl] **I** *n* espiral *f*. **II** *adj* en espiral; **s. staircase**, escalera *f* de caracol.

spirit¹ ['spɪrɪt] *n* 1 (*soul*) espíritu *m*, alma *f*; (*ghost*) fantasma *m*. 2 (*attitude*) espíritu *m*; (*mood*) humor *m*; **to take sth in the right s.**, tomar algo a bien; **community s.**, civismo *m*. 3 (*courage*) valor *m*; (*liveliness*) ánimo *m*; (*vitality*) vigor *m*; **to break sb's s.**, quebrar la voluntad de algn. 5 **spirits**, (*mood*) humor *m sing*; **to be in good s.**, estar de buen humor; **to be in high/low s.**, estar muy animado/desanimado.

spirit² ['spɪrɪt] *n* 1 *Chem* alcohol *m*; **s. level**, nivel *m* de aire. 2 **spirits**, (*alcoholic drinks*) licores *mpl*.

spirited ['spɪrɪtɪd] *adj* (*person, attempt*) valiente; (*horse*) fogoso,-a; (*attack*) enérgico,-a.

spiritual [ˈspɪrɪtjʊəl] *adj* espiritual.

spit¹ [spɪt] **I** *vtr* (*pt & pp* **spat**) escupir. **II** *vi* escupir; *fam* he's the spitting image of his father, es el vivo retrato de su padre. **III** *n* (*saliva*) saliva *f*.

spit² [spɪt] *n Culin* asador *m*.

spite [spaɪt] **I** *n* 1 (*ill will*) rencor *m*, ojeriza *f*. 2 in s. of, a pesar de, pese a; in s. of the fact that, a pesar de que, pese a que. **II** *vtr* (*annoy*) fastidiar.

spiteful [ˈspaɪtfʊl] *adj* (*person*) rencoroso,-a; (*remark*) malévolo,-a; (*tongue*) viperino,-a.

spittle [ˈspɪtəl] *n* saliva *f*.

splash [splæʃ] **I** *vtr* salpicar. **II** *vi* 1 to s. (about), (*in water*) chapotear. 2 (*water etc*) salpicar. **III** *n* 1 (*noise*) chapoteo *m*. 2 (*spray*) salpicadura *f*; *fig* (*of colour*) mancha *f*. ◆**splash out** *vi fam* tirar la casa por la ventana.

spleen [spliːn] *n Anat* bazo *m*.

splendid [ˈsplendɪd] *adj* espléndido,-a.

splendour, US splendor [ˈsplendər] *n* esplendor *m*.

splint [splɪnt] *n* tablilla *f*.

splinter [ˈsplɪntər] **I** *n* (*wood*) astilla *f*; (*bone, stone*) esquirla *f*; (*glass*) fragmento *m*; **s. group**, grupo *m* disidente. **II** *vi* 1 (*wood etc*) astillarse. 2 *Pol* escindirse.

split [splɪt] **I** *n* 1 (*crack*) grieta *f*, hendidura *f*; (*tear*) desgarrón *m*; *fig* (*division*) cisma *m*; *Pol* escisión *f*. 2 *Gymn* to do the splits, abrir las piernas en cruz. **II** *adj* partido,-a; **in a s. second**, en una fracción de segundo; **s. personality**, desdoblamiento *m* de personalidad. **III** *vtr* (*pt & pp* **split**) 1 (*crack*) agrietar; (*cut*) partir; (*tear*) rajar; (*atom*) desintegrar; *fig* **to s. hairs**, buscarle tres pies al gato. 2 (*divide*) dividir. 3 (*share out*) repartir. 4 *Pol* escindir. **IV** *vi* 1 (*crack*) agrietarse; (*into two parts*) partirse; (*garment*) rajarse. 2 (*divide*) dividirse. 3 *Pol* escindirse. ◆**split up I** *vtr* (*break up*) partir; (*divide up*) dividir; (*share out*) repartir. **II** *vi* (*couple*) separarse.

splutter [ˈsplʌtər] *vi* (*person*) balbucear; (*candle, fat*) chisporrotear; (*engine*) petardear.

spoil [spɔɪl] **I** *vtr* (*pt & pp* **spoiled** or **spoilt**) 1 (*ruin*) estropear, echar a perder. 2 (*child*) mimar a; **to be spoilt for choice**, tener demasiadas cosas para elegir. **II** *vi* (*food*) estropearse.

spoilsport [ˈspɔɪlspɔːt] *n fam* aguafiestas *mf inv*.

spoilt [spɔɪlt] *adj* 1 (*food, merchandise*) estropeado,-a. 2 (*child*) mimado,-a.

spoke¹ [spəʊk] *pt* → **speak**.

spoke² [spəʊk] *n* (*of wheel*) radio *m*, rayo *m*.

spoken [ˈspəʊkən] *pp* → **speak**.

spokesman [ˈspəʊksmən] *n* portavoz *m*.

spokeswoman [ˈspəʊkswʊmən] *n* porta-

voz *f*.

sponge [spʌndʒ] **I** *n* esponja *f*; *fig* **to throw in the sponge**, arrojar la toalla; *GB* **s. cake**, bizcocho *m*. **II** *vtr* (*wash*) lavar con esponja. **III** *vi fam* vivir de gorra. ◆**sponge off, sponge on** *vtr* vivir a costa de.

spongy [ˈspʌndʒɪ] *adj* (**spongier, spongiest**) esponjoso,-a.

sponsor [ˈspɒnsər] **I** *vtr* patrocinar; *Fin* avalar; (*support*) respaldar. **II** *n* patrocinador,-a *m,f*; *Fin* avalador,-a *m,f*.

sponsorship [ˈspɒnsəʃɪp] *n* patrocinio *m*; *Fin* aval *m*; (*support*) respaldo *m*.

spontaneous [spɒnˈteɪnɪəs] *adj* espontáneo,-a.

spoof [spuːf] *n fam* 1 (*parody*) burla *f*. 2 (*hoax*) engaño *m*.

spooky [ˈspuːkɪ] *adj* (**spookier, spookiest**) *fam* espeluznante.

spool [spuːl] *n* bobina *f*, carrete *m*.

spoon [spuːn] **I** *n* cuchara *f*; (*small*) cucharita *f*. **II** *vtr* sacar con cuchara; (*serve*) servir con cuchara.

spoon-feed [ˈspuːnfiːd] *vtr* (*baby*) dar de comer con cuchara a; *fig* (*spoil*) mimar.

spoonful [ˈspuːnfʊl] *n* cucharada *f*.

sporadic [spəˈrædɪk] *adj* esporádico,-a.

sport [spɔːt] **I** *n* 1 deporte *m*. 2 *fam* **he's a good s.**, es buena persona; **be a s.!**, ¡sé amable!. **II** *vtr* (*display*) lucir.

sporting [ˈspɔːtɪŋ] *adj* deportivo,-a.

sports [spɔːts] **I** *npl* deportes *mpl*, deporte *m sing*. **II** *adj* **s. car**, coche deportivo; **s. jacket**, chaqueta *f* (de) sport.

sportsman [ˈspɔːtsmən] *n* deportista *m*.

sportsmanlike [ˈspɔːtsmənlaɪk] *adj* deportivo,-a.

sportsmanship [ˈspɔːtsmənʃɪp] *n* deportividad *f*.

sportswear [ˈspɔːtsweər] *n* (*for sport*) ropa *f* de deporte; (*casual clothes*) ropa *f* de sport.

sportswoman [ˈspɔːtswʊmən] *n* deportista *f*.

sporty [ˈspɔːtɪ] *adj* (**sportier, sportiest**) *fam* deportivo,-a.

spot [spɒt] *n* 1 (*dot*) punto *m*; (*on fabric*) lunar *m*. 2 (*stain*) mancha *f*. 3 (*pimple*) grano *m*. 4 (*place*) sitio *m*, lugar *m*; **on the s.**, (*person*) allí, presente; **to decide sth on the s.**, decidir algo en el acto; **s. check**, chequeo rápido; **s. weak s.**, punto débil; **to be in a tight s.**, estar en un apuro; **to put sb on the s.**, poner a algn en un aprieto. 5 *fam* (*small amount*) poquito *m*; **a s. of bother**, unos problemillas. 6 *Rad TV Theat* (*in show*) espacio *m*; (*advertisement*) spot *m*, anuncio *m*. **II** *vtr* (*notice*) darse cuenta de, notar; (*see*) ver.

spotless [ˈspɒtlɪs] *adj* (*very clean*) impecable; *fig* (*reputation etc*) intachable.

spotlight [ˈspɒtlaɪt] *n* foco *m*; *Aut* faro *m*

auxiliar; *fig* to be in the s., ser objeto de la atención pública.

spot-on [spɒt'ɒn] *adj fam* exacto,-a.

spotted ['spɒtɪd] *adj* (with dots) con puntos; (fabric) con lunares; (speckled) moteado,-a.

spotty ['spɒtɪ] *adj* (spottier, spottiest) *pej* con granos.

spouse [spaʊs] *n* cónyuge *mf*.

spout [spaʊt] **I** *n* (of jug) pico *m*; (of teapot) pitorro *m*. **II** *vtr fam* (nonsense) soltar. **III** *vi* to s. out/up, (liquid) brotar.

sprain [spreɪn] **I** *n* esguince *m*. **II** *vtr* torcer; to s. one's ankle, torcerse el tobillo.

sprang [spræŋ] *pt* → **spring²**.

sprawl [sprɔːl] **I** *vi* 1 (sit, lie) tumbarse. 2 (city, plant) extenderse. **II** *n* (of city) extensión *f*.

spray¹ [spreɪ] *n* 1 (of water) rociada *f*; (from sea) espuma *f*; (from aerosol) pulverización *f*. 2 (aerosol) spray *m*; (for plants) pulverizador *m*; s. can, aerosol *m*. **II** *vtr* (water) rociar; (insecticide, perfume) pulverizar.

spray² [spreɪ] *n* (of flowers) ramita *f*.

spread [spred] **I** *n* 1 extensión *f*; difusión *f*; (of disease, fire) propagación *f*; (of terrorism) generalización *f*. 2 (range) gama *f*. 3 (of wings) envergadura *f*. 4 (for bread) pasta *f*; cheese s., queso para untar. 5 *fam* (large meal) banquetazo *m*. 6 *Press* full-page s., plana entera; two-page s., doble página *f*. **II** *vtr* (*pt & pp* spread) 1 (unfold) desplegar; (lay out) extender; *fig* to s. one's wings, desplegar las alas. 2 (butter etc) untar. 3 (news) difundir; (rumour) hacer correr; (disease, fire) propagar; (panic) sembrar. **III** *vi* 1 (stretch out) extenderse; (unfold) desplegarse. 2 (news) difundirse; (rumour) correr; (disease) propagarse.

spread-eagled [spred'iːɡəld] *adj* despatarrado,-a.

spreadsheet ['spredʃiːt] *n Comput* hoja *f* de cálculo.

spree [spriː] *n* juerga *f*; to go on a s., ir de juerga.

sprig [sprɪɡ] *n* ramita *f*.

sprightly ['spraɪtlɪ] *adj* (sprightlier, sprightliest) (nimble) ágil; (energetic) enérgico,-a; (lively) animado,-a.

spring¹ [sprɪŋ] **I** *n* (season) primavera *f*. **II** *adj* primaveral; s. onion, cebolleta *f*; s. roll, rollo *m* de primavera.

spring² [sprɪŋ] **I** *n* 1 (of water) manantial *m*, fuente *f*. 2 (of watch etc) resorte *m*; (of mattress) muelle *m*; *Aut* ballesta *f*. **II** *vi* (*pt* sprang; *pp* sprung) 1 (jump) saltar; the lid sprang open, la tapa se abrió de golpe. 2 (appear) aparecer (de repente). **III** *vtr* 1 to s. a leak, hacer agua. 2 *fig* (news, surprise) dar de golpe ◆**spring up** *vi* aparecer; (plants) brotar; (buildings)

elevarse; (problems) surgir.

springboard ['sprɪŋbɔːd] *n* trampolín *m*.

spring-clean [sprɪŋ'kliːn] *vtr* limpiar a fondo.

springtime ['sprɪŋtaɪm] *n* primavera *f*.

springy ['sprɪŋɪ] *adj* (springier, springiest) (bouncy) elástico,-a; *fig* (step) saltarín.

sprinkle ['sprɪŋkəl] *vtr* (with water) rociar (with, de); (with sugar) espolvorear (with, de).

sprint [sprɪnt] **I** *n* esprint *m*. **II** *vi* esprintar.

sprinter ['sprɪntər] *n* esprinter *m*, velocista *mf*.

sprout [spraʊt] **I** *vi* (bud) brotar; *fig* crecer rápidamente. **II** *n* (Brussels) sprouts, coles *fpl* de Bruselas.

spruce¹ [spruːs] *n inv Bot* picea *f*.

spruce² [spruːs] *adj* (neat) pulcro,-a; (smart) apuesto,-a. ◆**spruce up** *vtr* acicalar.

sprung [sprʌŋ] *pp* → **spring²**.

spry [spraɪ] *adj* (sprier, spriest) (nimble) ágil; (active) activo,-a; (lively) vivaz.

spun [spʌn] *pt & pp* → **spin**.

spur [spɜːr] **I** *n* 1 espuela *f*. 2 *fig* (stimulus) acicate *m*; on the s. of the moment, sin pensarlo. **II** *vtr* 1 (horse) espolear. 2 *fig* incitar.

spurious ['spjʊərɪəs] *adj* falso,-a, espurio,-a.

spurn [spɜːn] *vtr fml* desdeñar, rechazar.

spurt [spɜːt] **I** *n* 1 (of liquid) racha *f*. 2 *fig* (of activity etc) racha *f*; (effort) esfuerzo *m*. **II** *vi* 1 (liquid) chorrear. 2 (make an effort) hacer un último esfuerzo; (accelerate) acelerar.

spy [spaɪ] **I** *n* espía *mf*. **II** *vtr fml* (see) divisar. **III** *vi* espiar (on, a).

spyhole ['spaɪhəʊl] *n* mirilla *f*.

spying ['spaɪɪŋ] *n* espionaje *m*.

squabble ['skwɒbəl] **I** *n* riña *f*, pelea *f*. **II** *vi* reñir, pelearse (over, about, por).

squad [skwɒd] *n Mil* pelotón *m*; (of police) brigada *f*; *Sport* equipo *m*; drugs s., brigada antidroga.

squadron ['skwɒdrən] *n Mil* escuadrón *m*; *Av* escuadrilla *f*; *Naut* escuadra *f*.

squalid ['skwɒlɪd] *adj* (very dirty) asqueroso,-a; (poor) miserable; (motive) vil.

squall¹ [skwɔːl] *n* (wind) ráfaga *f*.

squall² [skwɔːl] *vi* chillar, berrear.

squalor ['skwɒlər] *n* (dirtiness) mugre *f*; (poverty) miseria *f*.

squander ['skwɒndər] *vtr* (money) derrochar, despilfarrar; (time) desperdiciar.

square [skweər] **I** *n* 1 cuadro *m*; (on chessboard, crossword) casilla *f*; *fig* we're back to s. one!, ¡volvemos a partir desde cero! 2 (in town) plaza *f*. 3 *Math* cuadrado *m*. **II** *adj* 1 (in shape) cuadrado,-a. 2 *Math* cuadrado,-a; s. metre, metro cuadrado

s. root, raíz cuadrada. **3** *fam (fair)* justo,-a; **to be s. with sb,** *(honest)* ser franco,-a con algn. **4** s. **meal,** una buena comida. **5** *(old-fashioned)* carroza; *(conservative)* carca. **III** *vtr* **1** *(make square)* cuadrar; **to s. one's shoulders,** sacar el pecho. **2** *Math* elevar al cuadrado. **3** *(settle)* arreglar. **IV** *vi* **1** *(agree)* cuadrar *(with,* con). ◆**squarely** *adv (directly)* directamente, de lleno.

squash¹ [skwɒʃ] **I** *n GB (drink)* concentrado *m*. **II** *vtr* **1** *(crush)* aplastar. **2** *fig (objection)* echar por tierra. **III** *vi (crush)* aplastarse.

squash² [skwɒʃ] *n Sport* squash *m*.

squat [skwɒt] **I** *adj (person)* rechoncho,-a. **II** *vi* **1** *(crouch)* agacharse, sentarse en cuclillas. **2** *(in building)* ocupar ilegalmente. **III** *n (building)* edificio *m* ocupado ilegalmente.

squatter ['skwɒtər] *n* ocupante *mf* ilegal, okupa *m,f*.

squawk [skwɔːk] **I** *n* graznido *m*. **II** *vi* graznar.

squeak [skwiːk] **I** *n (of mouse)* chillido *m*; *(of hinge, wheel)* chirrido *m*; *(of shoes)* crujido *m*. **II** *vi (mouse)* chillar; *(hinge, wheel)* chirriar, rechinar; *(shoes)* crujir.

squeaky ['skwiːkɪ] *adj (squeakier, squeakiest) (voice)* chillón, -ona; *(shoes)* que crujen.

squeal [skwiːl] **I** *n (of animal, person)* chillido *m*. **II** *vi* **1** *(animal, person)* chillar. **2** *fam (inform)* chivarse.

squeamish ['skwiːmɪʃ] *adj* muy sensible.

squeeze [skwiːz] **I** *vtr* apretar; *(lemon etc)* exprimir; *(sponge)* estrujar; **to s. paste out of a tube,** sacar pasta de un tubo apretado. **II** *vi* **to s. in,** apretujarse. **III** *n* **1** *(pressure)* estrujón *m*; *(of lemon)* unas gotas de limón. **2** *(of hand)* apretón *m*; *(hug)* abrazo *m*; *(crush)* apiñamiento *m*; **credit s.,** reducción *f* de créditos.

squelch [skweltʃ] *vi* chapotear.

squid [skwɪd] *n* calamar *m*; *(small)* chipirón *m*.

squiggle ['skwɪgəl] *n* garabato *m*.

squint [skwɪnt] **I** *n* **1** bizquera *f*; **to have a s.,** ser bizco,-a. **2** *fig (quick look)* vistazo *m*. **II** *vi* ser bizco,-a. **2** **to s. at sth,** *(glance)* echar un vistazo a algo; *(with eyes half-closed)* mirar algo con los ojos entrecerrados.

squirm [skwɜːm] *vi* retorcerse; *fig (feel embarrassed)* sentirse incómodo,-a.

squirrel ['skwɪrəl] *n* ardilla *f*.

squirt [skwɜːt] **I** *n (of liquid)* chorro *m*. **II** *vtr* lanzar a chorro. **III** *vi* **to s. out,** salir a chorros.

Sr *abbr* → **Snr.**

Sri Lanka [sriː'læŋkə] *n* Sri Lanka.

St 1 *abbr of* **Saint,** San, Sto., Sta. **2** *abbr of* **Street,** c/.

st *GB abbr of* **stone,** peso que equivale a

6,350 kilogramos.

stab [stæb] **I** *n (with knife)* puñalada *f*; *(of pain)* punzada *f*; *fam fig* **to have a s. at doing sth,** intentar hacer algo. **II** *vtr* apuñalar.

stabbing ['stæbɪŋ] *adj (pain)* punzante.

stability [stə'bɪlɪtɪ] *n* estabilidad *f*.

stable¹ ['steɪbəl] *adj* estable.

stable² ['steɪbəl] *n* cuadra *f*, caballeriza *f*.

stack [stæk] **I** *n (pile)* montón *m*; *fam* **he's got stacks of money,** está forrado. **II** *vtr (pile up)* amontonar, apilar; **the odds are stacked against us,** todo está en contra nuestra.

stadium ['steɪdɪəm] *n* estadio *m*.

staff [stɑːf] **I** *n* **1** *(personnel)* personal *m*; *Mil* estado *m* mayor; **s. meeting,** claustro *m*; *GB* **s. nurse,** enfermera cualificada. **2** *(stick)* bastón *m*; *fig (of shepherd)* cayado *m*. **II** *vtr* proveer de personal.

staffroom ['stɑːfruːm] *n* sala *f* de profesores.

stag [stæg] *n* ciervo *m*, venado *m*; *fam* **s. party,** despedida *f* de soltero.

stage [steɪdʒ] **I** *n* **1** *(platform)* plataforma *f*. **2** *(in theatre)* escenario *m*; **s. door,** entrada *f* de artistas; **s. fright,** miedo escénico; **s. manager,** director,-a *m,f* de escena. **3** *(phase) (of development, journey, rocket)* etapa *f*; *(of road, pipeline)* tramo *m*; **at this s. of the negotiations,** a estas alturas de las negociaciones; **in stages,** por etapas. **II** *vtr* **1** *(play)* poner en escena, montar. **2** *(arrange)* organizar; *(carry out)* llevar a cabo.

stagecoach ['steɪdʒkəʊtʃ] *n* diligencia *f*.

stagger ['stægər] **I** *vi* tambalearse. **II** *vtr* **1** *(amaze)* asombrar. **2** *(hours, work)* escalonar.

staggering ['stægərɪŋ] *adj* asombroso,-a.

stagnant ['stægnənt] *adj* estancado,-a.

stagnate [stæg'neɪt] *vi* estancarse.

staid [steɪd] *adj (person)* conservador,-a; *(manner, clothes)* serio,-a, formal.

stain [steɪn] **I** *n* **1** mancha *f*; **s. remover,** quitamanchas *m inv*. **2** *(dye)* tinte *m*. **II** *vtr* **1** manchar. **2** *(dye)* teñir. **III** *vi* mancharse.

stained [steɪnd] *adj* **s. glass window,** vidriera *f* de colores.

stainless ['steɪnlɪs] *adj (steel)* inoxidable.

stair [steər] *n* escalón *m*, peldaño *m*; **stairs,** escalera *f sing.*

staircase ['steəkeɪs] *n* escalera *f*.

stake¹ [steɪk] **I** *n (stick)* estaca *f*; *(for plant)* rodrigón *m*; *(post)* poste *m*. **II** *vtr* **to s. (out),** cercar con estacas.

stake² [steɪk] **I** *n* **1** *(bet)* apuesta *f*; **the issue at s.,** el tema en cuestión; **to be at s.,** *(at risk)* estar en juego. **2** *(investment)* interés *m*. **II** *vtr (bet)* apostar; *(invest)* invertir; **to s. a claim to sth,** reivindicar algo.

stale [steɪl] *adj (food)* pasado,-a; *(bread)* duro,-a.

stalemate ['steɪlmeɪt] *n Chess* tablas *fpl; fig* to reach s., llegar a un punto muerto.

stalk[1] [stɔːk] *n (of plant)* tallo *m; (of fruit)* rabo *m.*

stalk[2] [stɔːk] I *vtr (of hunter)* cazar al acecho; *(of animal)* acechar. II *vi* he stalked out, salió airado.

stall[1] [stɔːl] I *n* 1 *(in market)* puesto *m; (at fair)* caseta *f.* 2 *(stable)* establo *m; (stable compartment)* casilla *f* de establo. 3 *Theat* stalls, platea *f sing.* II *vi Aut* calar. III *vi Aut* calarse; *Av* perder velocidad.

stall[2] [stɔːl] *vi* dar largas a un asunto.

stallion ['stæljən] *n* semental *m.*

stalwart ['stɔːlwət] *n* incondicional *m,f.*

stamina ['stæmɪnə] *n* resistencia *f.*

stammer ['stæmə[r]] I *n* tartamudeo *m.* II *vi* tartamudear.

stamp [stæmp] I *n* 1 *(postage stamp)* sello *m;* s. album, álbum *m* de sellos; s. collector, filatelista *mf; GB* s. duty, póliza *f.* 2 *(rubber stamp)* tampón *m; (for metals)* cuño *m.* 3 *(with foot)* patada *f.* II *vtr* 1 *(with postage stamp)* poner el sello a; stamped addressed envelope, sobre franqueado. 2 *(with rubber stamp)* sellar. 3 to s. one's feet, patear; *(in dancing)* zapatear. III *vi* patear. **◆stamp out** *vtr fig (racism etc)* acabar con; *(rebellion)* sofocar.

stampede [stæm'piːd] I *n* estampida *f; fig (rush)* desbandada *f.* II *vi* desbandarse; *fig (rush)* precipitarse.

stance [stæns] *n* postura *f.*

stand [stænd] I *n* 1 *(position)* posición *f,* postura *f;* to make a s., resistir. 2 *(of lamp, sculpture)* pie *m.* 3 *(market stall)* puesto *m; (at fair)* caseta *f; (at exhibition)* stand *m;* newspaper s., quiosco *m.* 4 *(platform)* plataforma *f; (in stadium)* tribuna *f; US (witness box)* estrado *m.*

II *vtr (pt & pp stood)* 1 *(place)* poner, colocar. 2 *(tolerate)* aguantar, soportar. 3 to s. one's ground, mantenerse firme.

III *vi* 1 *(be upright)* estar de pie; *(get up)* levantarse; *(remain upright)* quedarse de pie; s. still!, ¡estáte quieto,-a! 2 *(measure)* medir. 3 *(be situated)* estar, encontrarse. 4 *(remain unchanged)* permanecer. 5 *(remain valid)* seguir vigente. 6 as things s., tal como están las cosas. 7 *Pol* presentarse.

◆stand back *vi (allow sb to pass)* abrir paso. **◆stand by** I *vi* 1 *(do nothing)* quedarse sin hacer nada. 2 *(be ready)* estar listo,-a. II *vtr* 1 *(person)* apoyar a; *(promise)* cumplir con; *(decision)* atenerse a. **◆stand down** *vi fig* retirarse. **◆stand for** *vtr* 1 *(mean)* significar. 2 *(represent)* representar. 3 *(tolerate)* aguantar. **◆stand in** *vi* sustituir *(for, -).* **◆stand out** *vi (mountain etc)* desta-

carse *(against, contra); fig (person)* destacar. **◆stand up** *vi (get up)* ponerse de pie; *(be standing)* estar de pie; *fig* it will s. up to wear and tear, es muy resistente; *fig* to s. up for sb, defender a algn; *fig* to s. up to sb, hacer frente a algn.

standard ['stændəd] I *n* 1 *(level)* nivel *m;* s. of living, nivel de vida. 2 *(criterion)* criterio *m.* 3 *(norm)* norma *f,* estándar *m.* 4 *(flag)* estandarte *m.* II *adj* normal, estándar; s. lamp, lámpara *f* de pie.

standardize ['stændədaɪz] *vtr* normalizar.

standby ['stændbaɪ] *n* 1 *(thing)* recurso *m.* 2 *(person)* suplente *mf;* to be on s., *Mil* estar de retén; *Av* estar en la lista de espera; s. ticket, billete *m* sin reserva.

stand-in ['stændɪn] *n* suplente *mf; Cin* doble *mf.*

standing ['stændɪŋ] I *adj* 1 *(not sitting)* de pie; *(upright)* recto,-a; to give sb a s. ovation, ovacionar a algn de pie; there was s. room only, no quedaban asientos. 2 *(committee)* permanente; *(invitation)* permanente; *GB* s. order, pago fijo. II *n* 1 *(social position)* rango *m.* 2 *(duration)* duración *f; (in job)* antigüedad *f.*

stand-offish [stænd'ɒfɪʃ] *adj fam* distante.

standpoint ['stændpɔɪnt] *n* punto *m* de vista.

standstill ['stændstɪl] *n* at a s., *(car, traffic)* parado,-a; *(industry)* paralizado,-a; to come to a s., *(car, traffic)* pararse; *(industry)* paralizarse.

stank [stæŋk] *pt → stink.*

staple[1] ['steɪpl] I *n (fastener)* grapa *f.* II *vtr* grapar.

staple[2] ['steɪpl] I *adj (food)* básico,-a; *(product)* de primera necesidad. II *n (food)* alimento básico.

stapler ['steɪplə[r]] *n* grapadora *f.*

star [stɑː[r]] I *n* estrella *f.* II *adj* estelar. III *vtr Cin* tener como protagonista a. IV *vi Cin* to s. in a film, protagonizar una película.

starboard ['stɑːbəd] *n* estribor *m.*

starch [stɑːtʃ] I *n* almidón *m.* II *vtr* almidonar.

stardom ['stɑːdəm] *n* estrellato *m.*

stare [steə[r]] I *n* mirada fija. II *vi* mirar fijamente.

starfish ['stɑːfɪʃ] *n* estrella *f* de mar.

stark [stɑːk] *adj (landscape)* desolado,-a; *(décor)* austero,-a; the s. truth, la dura realidad; s. poverty, la miseria.

stark-naked ['stɑːkneɪkɪd] *adj fam* en cueros.

starling ['stɑːlɪŋ] *n* estornino *m.*

starry ['stɑːrɪ] *adj (starrier, starriest)* estrellado,-a.

starry-eyed [stɑːrɪ'aɪd] *adj (idealistic)* idealista; *(in love)* enamorado,-a.

start [stɑːt] I *n* 1 *(beginning)* principio *m,*

comienzo m; (of race) salida f; **at the s.,** al principio; **for a s.,** para empezar; **from the s.,** desde el principio; **to make a fresh s.,** volver a empezar. **2** (advantage) ventaja f. **3** (jump) sobresalto m. II vtr **1** (begin) empezar, comenzar; **to s. doing sth,** empezar a hacer algo. **2** (cause) causar, provocar. **3** (found) fundar; **to s. a business,** montar un negocio. **4** (set in motion) arrancar. III vi **1** (begin) empezar, comenzar; (engine) arrancar; **starting from Monday,** a partir del lunes. **2** (take fright) asustarse, sobresaltarse. ◆**start off vi 1** (begin) empezar, comenzar; **to s. off by/with,** empezar por/con. **2** (leave) salir, ponerse en camino. ◆**start up I** vtr (engine) arrancar. II vi empezar; (car) arrancar.

starter ['stɑːtər] n **1** Sport (official) juez m de salida; (competitor) competidor,-a m,f. **2** Aut motor m de arranque. **3** Culin fam entrada f.

starting ['stɑːtɪŋ] n **s. block,** taco m de salida; **s. point,** punto m de partida; **s. post,** línea f de salida.

startle ['stɑːtəl] vtr asustar.

startling ['stɑːtlɪŋ] adj **1** (frightening) alarmante. **2** (news etc) asombroso,-a; (coincidence) extraordinario,-a.

starvation [stɑːˈveɪʃən] n hambre f.

starve [stɑːv] I vtr privar de comida; fig **he was starved of affection,** fue privado de cariño. II vi pasar hambre; **to s. to death,** morirse de hambre.

starving ['stɑːvɪŋ] adj hambriento,-a; fam **I'm s.,** estoy muerto,-a de hambre.

state [steɪt] I n **1** estado m; **s. of emergency,** estado de emergencia; **s. of mind,** estado de ánimo; **to be in no fit s. to do sth,** no estar en condiciones de hacer algo; **the States,** los Estados Unidos; **US the S. Department,** el Ministerio de Asuntos Exteriores. II adj **1** Pol estatal; **s. education,** enseñanza pública; **s. ownership,** propiedad f del Estado. **2** (ceremonial) de gala; **s. visit,** visita f oficial. III vtr declarar, afirmar; (case) exponer; (problem) plantear.

stated ['steɪtɪd] adj indicado,-a.

stately ['steɪtlɪ] adj (statelier, stateliest) majestuoso,-a; **s. home,** casa solariega.

statement ['steɪtmənt] n **1** declaración f; **official s.,** comunicado m oficial; fur **to make a s.,** prestar declaración. **2** Fin estado m de cuenta; **monthly s.,** balance m mensual.

statesman ['steɪtsmən] n estadista m.

static ['stætɪk] I adj estático,-a. II n Rad ruido.

station ['steɪʃən] I n **1** estación f; **s. wagon,** camioneta f. **2** (position) puesto m. **3** (social standing) rango m. II vtr (place) colocar; Mil apostar.

stationary ['steɪʃənərɪ] adj (not moving)

inmóvil; (unchanging) estacionario,-a.

stationer ['steɪʃənər] n papelero,-a m,f; **s.'s (shop),** papelería f.

stationery ['steɪʃənərɪ] n (paper) papel m de escribir; (pens, ink etc) artículos mpl de escritorio.

stationmaster ['steɪʃənmɑːstər] n jefe m de estación.

statistic [stəˈtɪstɪk] n estadística f.

statistical [stəˈtɪstɪkəl] adj estadístico,-a.

statistics [stəˈtɪstɪks] npl (science) estadística f sing; (data) estadísticas fpl.

statue ['stætjuː] n estatua f.

status ['steɪtəs] n estado m; **social s.,** estatus m; **s. quo,** statu quo m; **s. symbol,** signo m de prestigio; **s. quo,** status quo m.

statute ['stætjuːt] n estatuto m.

statutory ['stætjutərɪ] adj reglamentario, -a; (offence) contemplado,-a por la ley; (right) legal; (holiday) oficial.

staunch [stɔːntʃ] adj incondicional, acérrimo.

stave [steɪv] n Mus pentagrama m. ◆**stave off vtr** (repel) rechazar; (avoid) evitar; (delay) aplazar.

stay¹ [steɪ] I n estancia f. II vi **1** (remain) quedarse, permanecer. **2** (reside temporarily) alojarse; **she's staying with us for a few days,** ha venido a pasar unos días con nosotros. III vtr fig **to s. the course,** aguantar hasta el final; **staying power,** resistencia f. ◆**stay in vi** quedarse en casa. ◆**stay on vi** quedarse. ◆**stay out vi to s. out all night,** no volver a casa en toda la noche. ◆**stay up vi** no acostarse.

stay² [steɪ] n (rope) estay m, viento m.

stead [sted] n **in sb's s.,** en lugar de algn; **to stand sb in good s.,** resultar muy útil a algn.

steadfast ['stedfɑːst, 'stedfæst] adj firme.

steady ['stedɪ] I adj (steadier, steadiest) firme, seguro,-a; (gaze) fijo,-a; (prices) estable; (demand, speed) constante; (pace) regular; (worker) aplicado,-a; **s. job,** empleo fijo. II vtr (table etc) estabilizar; (nerves) calmar. III vi (market) estabilizarse. ◆**steadily adv** (improve) constantemente; (walk) con paso seguro; (gaze) fijamente; (rain, work) sin parar.

steak [steɪk] n bistec m.

steal [stiːl] (pt stole; pp stolen) I vtr robar; **to s. a glance at sth,** echar una mirada furtiva a algo; **to s. the show,** llevarse todos los aplausos. II vi **1** (rob) robar. **2** (move quietly) moverse con sigilo; **to s. away,** escabullirse.

stealth [stelθ] n sigilo m.

stealthy ['stelθɪ] adj (stealthier, stealthiest) sigiloso,-a, furtivo,-a. ◆**stealthily adv** a hurtadillas.

steam [stiːm] n vapor m; fam **to let off s.,** desahogarse; **s. engine,** máquina f de vapor. II vtr Culin cocer al vapor. III vi *(give off steam)* echar vapor; *(bowl of soup etc)* humear. ◆**steam up** *vi (window etc)* empañarse.

steamer ['sti:mə^r] *n Naut* vapor *m*.

steamroller ['sti:mrəʊlə^r] *n* apisonadora *f*.

steamship ['sti:mʃɪp] *n* vapor *m*.

steamy ['sti:mɪ] *adj (steamier, steamiest)* lleno,-a de vapor.

steel [sti:l] **I** *n* acero *m*; **s. industry**, industria siderúrgica. **II** *vtr fig* to s. oneself to do sth, armarse de valor para hacer algo.

steelworks ['sti:lwɜːks] *npl* acería *f sing*.

steep¹ [sti:p] *adj (hill etc)* empinado,-a; *fig (price, increase)* excesivo,-a.

steep² [sti:p] *vtr (washing)* remojar; *(food)* poner en remojo.

steeple ['sti:pəl] *n* aguja *f*.

steeplechase ['sti:pəltʃeɪs] *n* carrera *f* de obstáculos.

steer [stɪə^r] **I** *vtr* dirigir; *(car)* conducir; *(ship)* gobernar. **II** *vi (car)* conducirse; *to* **s. clear of sth**, evitar algo.

steering ['stɪərɪŋ] *n* dirección *f*; **assisted s.**, dirección asistida; **s. wheel**, volante *m*.

stem [stem] **I** *n* **1** *(of plant)* tallo *m*; *(of glass)* pie *m*; *(of pipe)* tubo *m*. **2** *(of word)* raíz *f*. **II** *vi* to **s. from**, derivarse de. **III** *vtr (blood)* restañar; *(flood, attack)* contener.

stench [stentʃ] *n* hedor *m*.

stencil ['stensəl] *n* **1** *(for artwork etc)* plantilla *f*. **2** *(for typing)* cliché *m*.

step [step] **I** *n* **1** paso *m*; *(sound)* paso, pisada *f*; **s. by s.**, poco a poco. **2** *(measure)* medida *f*; **a s. in the right direction**, un paso acertado. **3** *(stair)* peldaño *m*, escalón *m*. **4 steps**, escalera *f*. **II** *vi* dar un paso; **s. this way, please**, haga el favor de pasar por aquí; to **s. aside**, apartarse. ◆**step down** *vi* dimitir. ◆**step forward** *vi (volunteer)* ofrecerse. ◆**step in** *vi* intervenir. ◆**step up** *vtr* aumentar.

stepbrother ['stepbrʌðə^r] *n* hermanastro *m*.

stepchild ['steptʃaɪld] *n* hijastro,-a *m,f*.

stepdaughter ['stepdɔːtə^r] *n* hijastra *f*.

stepfather ['stepfɑːðə^r] *n* padrastro *m*.

stepladder ['steplædə^r] *n* escalera *f* de tijera.

stepmother ['stepmʌðə^r] *n* madrastra *f*.

stepping-stone ['stepɪŋstəʊn] *n* pasadera *f*; *fig* trampolín *m*.

stepsister ['stepsɪstə^r] *n* hermanastra *f*.

stepson ['stepsʌn] *n* hijastro *m*.

stereo ['sterɪəʊ] **I** *n* estéreo *m*. **II** *adj* estéreo(fónico,-a).

stereotype ['sterɪətaɪp] *n* estereotipo *m*.

sterile ['steraɪl] *adj (barren)* estéril.

sterilize ['sterɪlaɪz] *vtr* esterilizar.

sterling ['stɜːlɪŋ] **I** *n* libras *fpl* esterlinas; **s. silver**, plata *f* de ley; **the pound s.**, la

libra esterlina. **II** *adj (person, quality)* excelente.

stern¹ [stɜːn] *adj (severe)* severo,-a.

stern² [stɜːn] *n Naut* popa *f*.

steroid ['sterɔɪd] *n* esteroide *m*.

stethoscope ['steθəskəʊp] *n* estetoscopio *m*.

stew [stjuː] **I** *n* estofado *m*, cocido *m*. **II** *vtr (meat)* guisar, estofar; *(fruit)* cocer.

steward ['stjʊəd] *n (on estate)* administrador *m*; *(on ship)* camarero *m*, *(on plane)* auxiliar *m* de vuelo.

stewardess ['stjʊədɪs] *n (on ship)* camarera *f*; *(on plane)* azafata *f*.

stick¹ [stɪk] *n* **1** palo *m*; *(walking stick)* bastón *m*; *(of dynamite)* cartucho *m*; **fam to give sb s.**, dar caña a algn. **2** *fam* **to live in the sticks**, vivir en el quinto pino.

stick² [stɪk] **I** *vtr (pt & pp stuck)* **1** *(push)* meter; *(knife)* clavar; **he stuck his head out of the window**, asomó la cabeza por la ventana. **2** *fam (put)* meter. **3** *(with glue etc)* pegar. **4** *fam (tolerate)* soportar, aguantar. **II** *vi* **1** *(become attached)* pegarse. **2** *(window, drawer)* atrancarse; *(machine part)* encasquillarse. ◆**stick at** *vtr* perseverar en. ◆**stick by** *vtr (friend)* ser fiel a; *(promise)* cumplir con. ◆**stick out** **I** *vi (project)* sobresalir; *(be noticeable)* resaltar. **II** *vtr (tongue)* sacar; *fig* **to s. one's neck out**, jugarse el tipo. ◆**stick to** *vtr (principles)* atenerse a. ◆**stick up** **I** *vi (project)* sobresalir; *(hair)* ponerse de punta. **II** *vtr* **1** *(poster)* fijar. **2** *fam (hand etc)* levantar. ◆**stick up for** *vtr* defender.

sticker ['stɪkə^r] *n (label)* etiqueta adhesiva; *(with slogan)* pegatina *f*.

stickler ['stɪklə^r] *n* meticuloso,-a; **to be a s. for detail**, ser muy detallista.

stick-up ['stɪkʌp] *n US fam* atraco *m*, asalto *m*.

sticky ['stɪkɪ] *adj (stickier, stickiest)* pegajoso,-a; *(label)* engomado,-a; *(weather)* bochornoso,-a; *fam (situation)* difícil.

stiff [stɪf] **I** *adj* **1** rígido,-a, tieso,-a; *(collar, lock)* duro,-a; *(joint)* entumecido,-a; *(machine part)* atascado,-a; **to have a s. neck**, tener tortícolis. **2** *fig (test)* difícil; *(punishment)* severo,-a; *(price)* excesivo,-a; *(drink)* fuerte; *(person) (unnatural)* estirado,-a. **II** *n fam (corpse)* fiambre *m*.

stiffen ['stɪfən] **I** *vtr (fabric)* reforzar; *(collar)* almidonar; *fig (resistance)* fortalecer. **II** *vi (person)* ponerse tieso,-a; *(joints)* entumecerse; *fig (resistance)* fortalecerse.

stiffness ['stɪfnɪs] *n* rigidez *f*.

stifle ['staɪfəl] **I** *vtr* sofocar; *(yawn)* reprimir. **II** *vi* ahogarse, sofocarse.

stifling ['staɪflɪŋ] *adj* sofocante, agobiante.

stigma ['stɪgmə] *n* estigma *m*.

stile [staɪl] *n* escalones *mpl* para pasar por encima de una valla.

stiletto [stɪ'letəʊ] *n* zapato *m* con tacón

de aguja.

still¹ [stɪl] I adv 1 (up to this time) todavía, aún. 2 (with comp adj & adv) (even) aún; **s. colder,** aún más frío. 3 (nonetheless) no obstante, con todo. 4 (however) sin embargo. 5 (motionless) quieto; **to stand s.,** no moverse. II adj (calm) tranquilo,-a; (peaceful) sosegado,-a; (silent) silencioso,-a; (motionless) inmóvil. III n Cin fotograma m; Art s. life, naturaleza muerta. IV vtr fml (fears etc) calmar.

still² [stɪl] n (apparatus) alambique m.

stillborn ['stɪlbɔːn] adj nacido,-a muerto,-a.

stillness ['stɪlnɪs] n calma f; (silence) silencio m.

stilt [stɪlt] n zanco m.

stilted ['stɪltɪd] adj afectado,-a.

stimulant ['stɪmjʊlənt] n estimulante m.

stimulate ['stɪmjʊleɪt] vtr estimular.

stimulating ['stɪmjʊleɪtɪŋ] adj estimulante.

stimulus ['stɪmjʊləs] n (pl **stimuli** ['stɪmjʊlaɪ]) estímulo m; fig incentivo m.

sting [stɪŋ] I n (part of bee, wasp) aguijón m; (wound) picadura f; (burning) escozor m; fig (of remorse) punzada f; fig (of remark) sarcasmo m. II vtr (pt & pp **stung**) picar; (of conscience) remorder; fig (remark) herir en lo vivo. III vi picar.

stingy ['stɪndʒɪ] adj (stingier, stingiest) fam (person) tacaño,-a; (amount) escaso,-a; **to be s. with,** escatimar.

stink [stɪŋk] I n peste m, hedor m. II vi (pt **stank**; pp **stunk**) apestar, heder (of, a).

stinking ['stɪŋkɪŋ] I adj (smelly) apestoso,-a; fam **to have a s. cold,** tener un catarro bestial. II adv fam **he's s. rich,** está podrido de dinero.

stint [stɪnt] I n (period) período m, temporada f; (shift) turno m; **he did a two-year s. in the navy,** sirvió durante dos años en la Marina. II vtr escatimar.

stipulate ['stɪpjʊleɪt] vtr estipular.

stipulation [stɪpjʊˈleɪʃən] n estipulación f.

stir [stɜːr] I n fig revuelo m. II vtr 1 (liquid) remover. 2 (move) agitar. 3 fig (curiosity, interest) despertar; (anger) provocar. III vi (move) rebullirse. ◆**stir up** vtr fig (memories, curiosity) despertar; (passions) excitar; (anger) provocar; (revolt) fomentar.

stirring ['stɜːrɪŋ] adj conmovedor,-a.

stirrup ['stɪrəp] n estribo m.

stitch [stɪtʃ] I n 1 Sew puntada f; (in knitting) punto m; Med punto (de sutura); fam **we were in stitches,** nos tronchábamos de risa. 2 (pain) punzada f. II vtr Sew coser; Med suturar, dar puntos a.

stoat [stəʊt] n armiño m.

stock [stɒk] I n 1 (supply) reserva f; Com

(goods) existencias fpl, stock m; (selection) surtido m; **out of s.,** agotado,-a; **to have sth in s.,** tener existencias de algo; fig **to take s. of,** evaluar. 2 Fin capital m social; **stocks and shares,** acciones fpl, valores mpl; **S. Exchange,** Bolsa f (de valores); **s. market,** bolsa. 3 Agr ganado m. 4 Culin caldo m; **s. cube,** cubito m de caldo. 5 (descent) estirpe f. II adj 1 (goods) corriente. 2 (excuse, response) de siempre; (phrase) gastado,-a. III vtr 1 (have in stock) tener existencias de. 2 (provide) abastecer, surtir (with, de); (cupboard) llenar (with, de). ◆**stock up** vi abastecerse (on, with, de).

stockbroker ['stɒkbrəʊkər] n corredor,-a m,f de Bolsa.

stockholder ['stɒkhəʊldər] n US accionista mf.

stocking ['stɒkɪŋ] n media f; **a pair of stockings,** unas medias.

stockist ['stɒkɪst] n distribuidor,-a m,f.

stockpile ['stɒkpaɪl] I n reservas fpl. II vtr almacenar; (accumulate) acumular.

stocks [stɒks] npl Hist cepo m sing.

stocktaking ['stɒkteɪkɪŋ] n Com inventario m.

stocky ['stɒkɪ] adj (stockier, stockiest) (squat) rechoncho,-a; (heavily built) fornido,-a.

stodgy ['stɒdʒɪ] adj (stodgier, stodgiest) (food) indigesto,-a; fig (book, person) pesado,-a.

stoical ['stəʊɪkəl] adj estoico,-a.

stoke [stəʊk] vtr (poke) atizar; **to s. (up),** (feed) alimentar.

stole¹ [stəʊl] pt → **steal.**

stole² [stəʊl] n estola f.

stolen ['stəʊlən] pp → **steal.**

stolid ['stɒlɪd] adj impasible.

stomach ['stʌmək] I n estómago m; **s. ache,** dolor m de estómago; **s. upset,** trastorno gástrico. II vtr fig aguantar.

stone [stəʊn] I n 1 piedra f; (on grave) lápida f; fig **at a s.'s throw,** a tiro de piedra. 2 Med cálculo m. 3 (of fruit) hueso m. 4 (weight) aprox 6.348 kg. II adj de piedra; **the S. Age,** la Edad de Piedra. III vtr (kill) lapidar.

stone-cold [stəʊnˈkəʊld] adj helado,-a.

stoned [stəʊnd] adj sl (drugged) colocado,-a; (drunk) como una cuba.

stone-deaf [stəʊnˈdef] adj sordo,-a como una tapia.

stonework ['stəʊnwɜːk] n mampostería f.

stony ['stəʊnɪ] adj (stonier, stoniest) (ground) pedregoso,-a; fig (look, silence) glacial.

stood [stʊd] pt & pp → **stand.**

stool [stuːl] n 1 (seat) taburete m. 2 Med heces fpl.

stoop [stuːp] vi 1 (have a stoop) andar encorvado,-a. 2 (bend) inclinarse, agacharse (**down**, -). **3** *fig* **to s. to**, rebajarse a; **he wouldn't s. so low**, no se rebajaría tanto.

stop [stɒp] **I** *n* **1** (*halt*) parada *f*, alto *m*; **to come to a s.**, pararse; **to put a s. to sth**, poner fin a algo. **2** (*break*) pausa *f*; (*for refuelling etc*) escala *f*. **3** (*for bus, tram*) parada *f*. **4** (*punctuation mark*) punto *m*. **II** *vtr* **1** parar; (*conversation*) interrumpir; (*pain, abuse etc*) poner fin a. **2** (*payments*) suspender; (*cheque*) anular. **3** s. singing, deja de cantar; **s. it!**, ¡basta ya! **4** (*prevent*) evitar; **to s. sb from doing sth**, impedir a algn hacer algo. **5** (*hole*) tapar; (*gap*) rellenar. **III** *vi* **1** (*person, moving vehicle*) pararse, detenerse; **my watch has stopped**, se me ha parado el reloj; **to s. dead**, pararse en seco. **2** (*cease*) acabarse, terminar. **3** *fam* (*stay*) pararse. ◆**stop by** *vi fam* visitar. ◆**stop off** *vi* pararse un rato. ◆**stop over** *vi* (*spend the night*) pasar la noche; (*for refuelling etc*) hacer escala. ◆**stop up** *vtr* (*hole*) tapar.

stopgap ['stɒpgæp] *n* (*thing*) medida *f* provisional; (*person*) sustituto,-a *m,f*.

stopover ['stɒpəʊvər] *n* parada *f*; *Av* escala *f*.

stoppage ['stɒpɪdʒ] *n* **1** (*of game, payments*) suspensión *f*; (*of work*) paro *m*; (*strike*) huelga *f*; (*deduction*) deducción *f*. **2** (*blockage*) obstrucción *f*.

stopper ['stɒpər] *n* tapón *m*.

stop-press [stɒp'pres] *n* noticias *fpl* de última hora.

stopwatch ['stɒpwɒtʃ] *n* cronómetro *m*.

storage ['stɔːrɪdʒ] *n* almacenaje *m*, almacenamiento *m*; **s. battery**, acumulador *m*; **s. heater**, placa acumuladora.

store [stɔːr] **I** *n* **1** (*stock*) provisión *f*; *fig* (*of wisdom*) reserva *f*. **2 stores**, víveres *mpl*. **3** (*warehouse*) almacén *m*. **4** *US* (*shop*) tienda *f*; **department s.**, gran almacén *m*. **II** *vtr* **1** (*furniture, computer data*) almacenar; (*keep*) guardar. **2** **to s.** (**up**), acumular.

storekeeper ['stɔːkiːpər] *n US* tendero,-a *m,f*.

storeroom ['stɔːruːm] *n* despensa *f*.

storey ['stɔːrɪ] *n* piso *m*.

stork [stɔːk] *n* cigüeña *f*.

storm [stɔːm] **I** *n* tormenta *f*; (*with wind*) vendaval *m*; *fig* (*uproar*) revuelo *m*; *fig* **she has taken New York by s.**, ha cautivado a todo Nueva York. **II** *vtr* tomar por asalto. **III** *vi* (*with rage*) echar pestes.

stormy ['stɔːmɪ] *adj* (*stormier*, *stormiest*) (*weather*) tormentoso,-a; *fig* (*discussion*) acalorado,-a; (*relationship*) tempestuoso,-a.

story[1] ['stɔːrɪ] *n* historia *f*; (*tale*, *account*) relato *m*; (*article*) artículo *m*; (*plot*) trama *f*; (*joke*) chiste *m*; (*rumour*) rumor *m*; **it's a long s.**, sería largo de contar; **tall s.**,

cuento chino.

story[2] ['stɔːrɪ] *n US* → **storey**.

storybook ['stɔːrɪbʊk] *n* libro *m* de cuentos.

storyteller ['stɔːrɪtelər] *n* cuentista *mf*.

stout [staʊt] **I** *adj* **1** (*fat*) gordo,-a, corpulento,-a. **2** (*strong*) fuerte. **3** (*brave*) valiente; (*determined*) firme. **II** *n* (*beer*) cerveza negra. ◆**stoutly** *adv* resueltamente.

stove[1] [stəʊv] *n* **1** (*for heating*) estufa *f*. **2** (*cooker*) cocina *f*.

stow [stəʊ] *vtr* **1** (*cargo*) estibar. **2** (*put away*) guardar. ◆**stow away** *vi* (*on ship, plane*) viajar de polizón.

stowaway ['stəʊəweɪ] *n* polizón *mf*.

straddle ['strædəl] *vtr* **1** (*horse etc*) sentarse a horcajadas sobre. **2** *fig* (*embrace*) abarcar.

straggle ['strægəl] *vi* **1** (*lag behind*) rezagarse. **2** (*spread untidily*) desparramarse.

straggler ['stræglər] *n* rezagado,-a *m,f*.

straight [streɪt] **I** *adj* **1** (*not bent*) recto,-a, derecho,-a; (*hair*) liso,-a; **to keep a s. face**, contener la risa. **2 I work eight hours s.**, trabajo ocho horas seguidas. **3** (*honest*) honrado,-a; (*answer*) sincero,-a; (*refusal*) rotundo,-a; **let's get things s.**, pongamos las cosas claras. **4** (*drink*) solo,-a, sin mezcla. **II** *adv* **1** (*in a straight line*) en línea recta. **2** (*directly*) directamente, derecho; **keep s. ahead**, sigue todo recto; **she walked s. in**, entró sin llamar. **3 s. away**, en seguida; **s. off**, en el acto. **4** (*frankly*) francamente. **III** *n GB Sport* **the home s.**, la recta final.

straighten ['streɪtən] *vtr* (*sth bent*) enderezar, poner derecho,-a; (*tie, picture*) poner bien; (*hair*) alisar. ◆**straighten out** *vtr* (*problem*) resolver.

straightforward [streɪt'fɔːwəd] *adj* **1** (*honest*) honrado,-a; (*sincere*) franco,-a. **2** *GB* (*simple*) sencillo,-a.

strain[1] [streɪn] **I** *vtr* **1** (*rope etc*) estirar; *fig* crear tensiones en. **2** *Med* torcer(se); (*eyes, voice*) forzar; (*heart*) cansar. **3** (*liquid*) filtrar; (*vegetables, tea*) colar. **II** *vi* (*pull*) tirar (**at**, de); *fig* **to s. to do sth**, esforzarse por hacer algo. **III** *n* **1** tensión *f*; (*effort*) esfuerzo *m*. **2** (*exhaustion*) agotamiento *m*. **3** *Med* torcedura *f*. **4** *Mus* **strains**, son *m sing*.

strain[2] [streɪn] *n* **1** (*breed*) raza *f*. **2** (*streak*) vena *f*.

strained [streɪnd] **II** *adj* **1** (*muscle*) torcido,-a; (*eyes*) cansado,-a; (*voice*) forzado,-a. **2** (*atmosphere*) tenso,-a.

strainer ['streɪnər] *n* colador *m*.

strait [streɪt] *n* **1** (*usu pl*) *Geog* estrecho *m*. **2** (*usu pl*) (*difficulty*) aprieto *m*; **in dire straits**, en un gran aprieto.

straitjacket ['streɪtdʒækɪt] *n* camisa *f* de fuerza.

strait-laced [streɪt'leɪst] *adj* remilgado,-a.

strand¹ [strænd] *vtr fig (person)* abandonar; **to leave stranded,** dejar plantado,-a.

strand² [strænd] *n (of thread)* hebra *f*; *(of hair)* pelo *m*.

strange [streɪndʒ] *adj* 1 *(unknown)* desconocido,-a; *(unfamiliar)* nuevo,-a. 2 *(odd)* raro,-a, extraño,-a.

stranger [streɪndʒər] *n (unknown person)* desconocido,-a *m,f*; *(outsider)* forastero,-a *m,f*.

strangle ['stræŋgəl] *vtr* estrangular.

stranglehold ['stræŋgəlhəʊld] *n* **to have a s. on sb,** tener a algn agarrado,-a por el cuello.

strangulation [stræŋgjʊ'leɪʃən] *n* estrangulación *f*.

strap [stræp] I *n (of leather)* correa *f*; *(on bag)* bandolera *f*; *(on dress)* tirante *m*. II *vtr* atar con correa.

strapping ['stræpɪŋ] *adj fam* fornido,-a, robusto,-a.

strategic [strə'tiːdʒɪk] *adj* estratégico,-a.

strategy ['strætɪdʒɪ] *n* estrategia *f*.

stratosphere ['strætəsfɪər] *n* estratosfera *f*.

stratum ['strɑːtəm] *n (pl strata)* estrato *m*.

straw [strɔː] *n* 1 paja *f*; *fig* **to clutch at straws,** agarrarse a un clavo ardiente; *fam* **that's the last s.!,** ¡eso ya es el colmo! 2 *(for drinking)* pajita *f*.

strawberry ['strɔːbərɪ] *n* fresa *f*; *(large)* fresón *m*.

stray [streɪ] I *vi (from path)* desviarse; *(get lost)* extraviarse. II *n* animal extraviado. III *adj (bullet)* perdido,-a; *(animal)* callejero,-a.

streak [striːk] I *n* 1 *(line)* raya *f*; **s. of lightning,** rayo *m*. 2 *(in hair)* reflejo *m*. 3 *fig (of genius etc)* vena *f*; *fig (of luck)* racha *f*. II *vtr* rayar **(with,** de). III *vi* **to s. past,** pasar como un rayo.

stream [striːm] I *n* 1 *(brook)* arroyo *m*, riachuelo *m*. 2 *(current)* corriente *f*. 3 *(of water, air)* flujo *m*; *(of tears)* torrente *m*; *(of blood)* chorro *m*; *(of light)* raudal *m*. 4 *fig (of abuse)* sarta *f*; *(of people)* oleada *f*. 3 *GB Educ* clase *f*. II *vtr GB Educ* poner en grupos. III *vi* 1 *(liquid)* correr. 2 *fig* **to s. in/out/past,** *(people etc)* entrar/salir/pasar en tropel. 3 *(hair, banner)* ondear.

streamer ['striːmər] *n (paper ribbon)* serpentina *f*.

streamlined ['striːmlaɪnd] *adj* 1 *(car)* aerodinámico,-a. 2 *(system, method)* racionalizado,-a.

street [striːt] *n* calle *f*; **the man in the s.,** el hombre de la calle; **s. map, s. plan,** *(plano m)* callejero *m*.

streetcar ['striːtkɑːr] *n US* tranvía *m*.

streetlamp ['striːtlæmp] *n* farol *m*.

streetwise ['striːtwaɪz] *adj* espabilado,-a.

strength [streŋθ] *n* 1 fuerza *f*; *(of rope etc)* resistencia *f*; *(of emotion, colour)* intensi-

dad *f*; *(of alcohol)* graduación *f*. 2 *(power)* poder *m*; **on the s. of,** a base de. 3 *(ability)* punto *m* fuerte. 4 **to be at full s./below s.,** tener/no tener completo el cupo.

strengthen ['streŋθən] I *vtr* 1 reforzar; *(character)* fortalecer. 2 *(intensify)* intensificar. II *vi* 1 *(gen)* reforzarse. 2 *(intensify)* intensificarse.

strenuous ['strenjʊəs] *adj* 1 *(denial)* enérgico,-a; *(effort, life)* intenso,-a. 2 *(exhausting)* fatigoso,-a, cansado,-a.

stress [stres] I *n* 1 *Tech* tensión *f*. 2 *Med* estrés *m*. 3 *(emphasis)* hincapié *m*; *(on word)* acento *m*. II *vtr* 1 *(emphasize)* subrayar; *(word)* acentuar.

stretch [stretʃ] I *vtr (elastic)* estirar; *(wings)* desplegar. II *vi (elastic)* estirarse; *fig* **my money won't s. to it,** mi dinero no me llegará para eso. III *n* 1 *(length)* trecho *m*, tramo *m*. 2 *(of land)* extensión *f*; *(of time)* intervalo *m*. ◆**stretch out** I *vtr (arm, hand)* alargar; *(legs)* estirar. II *vi* 1 *(person)* estirarse. 2 *(countryside, years etc)* extenderse.

stretcher ['stretʃər] *n* camilla *f*.

strew [struː] *vtr (pt strewed; pp strewed or strewn* [struːn]*)* esparcir.

stricken ['strɪkən] *adj (with grief)* afligido,-a; *(with illness)* aquejado,-a; *(by disaster etc)* afectado,-a; *(damaged)* dañado,-a.

strict [strɪkt] *adj* 1 estricto,-a. 2 *(absolute)* absoluto,-a. ◆**strictly** *adv* 1 *(categorically)* terminantemente. 2 *(precisely)* estrictamente; **s. speaking,** en sentido estricto.

stride [straɪd] I *n* zancada *f*, tranco *m*; *fig (progress)* progresos *mpl*. II *vi (pt strode; pp stridden* ['strɪdən]*)* **to s. (along),** andar a zancadas.

strident ['straɪdənt] *adj (voice, sound)* estridente; *(protest etc)* enérgico,-a.

strife [straɪf] *n* conflictos *mpl*.

strike [straɪk] I *vtr (pt & pp struck)* 1 *(hit)* pegar, golpear. 2 *(collide with)* chocar contra; *(bullet, lightning)* alcanzar. 3 *(match)* encender. 4 *(pose)* adoptar. 5 *(bargain)* cerrar; *(balance)* encontrar. 6 **the clock struck three,** el reloj dio las tres. 7 *(oil, gold)* descubrir; *fam* **to s. it lucky/rich,** tener suerte/hacerse rico,-a. 8 *(impress)* impresionar; **it strikes me ...,** me parece .... II *vi (pt & pp struck)* 1 *(attack)* atacar; *(disaster)* sobrevenir. 2 *(clock)* dar la hora. 3 *(workers)* declararse en huelga. III *n* 1 *(by workers)* huelga *f*; **on s.,** en huelga; **to call a s.,** convocar una huelga. 2 *(of oil, gold)* descubrimiento *m*. 3 *(blow)* golpe *m*. 4 *Mil* ataque *m*. ◆**strike back** *vi* devolver el golpe. ◆**strike down** *vtr* fulminar, abatir. ◆**strike out** I *vtr (cross out)* tachar. II *vi* **to s. out at sb,** arremeter contra algn.

◆**strike up** *vtr* 1 (*friendship*) trabar; (*conversation*) entablar. 2 (*tune*) empezar a tocar.

striker ['straɪkəʳ] *n* 1 (*worker*) huelguista *mf*. 2 *fam Ftb* marcador,-a *m,f*.

striking ['straɪkɪŋ] *adj* (*eye-catching*) llamativo,-a; (*noticeable*) notable; (*impressive*) impresionante.

string [strɪŋ] I *n* 1 (*cord*) cuerda *f*; *fig* to **pull strings for sb**, enchufar a algn; **s. bean**, judía *f* verde. 2 (*of events*) cadena *f*; (*of lies*) sarta *f*. 3 (*of racket*, *guitar*) cuerda *f*; *Mus* **the strings**, los instrumentos de cuerda. II *vtr* (*pt & pp* **strung**) 1 (*beads*) ensartar. 2 (*racket*) encordar. 3 (*beans*) quitar la hebra a.

stringent ['strɪndʒənt] *adj* severo,-a, estricto,-a.

strip[1] [strɪp] I *vtr* 1 (*person*) desnudar; (*bed*) quitar la ropa de; (*paint*) quitar. 2 *Tech* to **s.** (**down**), desmontar. II *vi* (*undress*) desnudarse; (*perform striptease*) hacer un striptease. ◆**strip off** *vtr* quitar. II *vi* (*undress*) desnudarse.

strip[2] [strɪp] *n* tira *f*; (*of land*) franja *f*; (*of metal*) fleje *m*; **s.** *cartoon*, historieta *f*; **s. lighting**, alumbrado *m* fluorescente; to **tear sb off a s.**, echar una bronca a algn.

stripe [straɪp] *n* raya *f*; *Mil* galón *m*.

striped [straɪpt] *adj* rayado,-a, a rayas.

stripper ['strɪpəʳ] *n* persona *f* que hace striptease.

strive [straɪv] *vi* (*pt* **strove**; *pp* **striven** ['strɪvən]) to **s.** to do sth, esforzarse por hacer algo.

strobe [strəʊb] *n* **s. lighting**, luces estroboscópicas.

strode [strəʊd] *pt* → **stride**.

stroke [strəʊk] I *n* 1 a **s. of luck**, un golpe de suerte. 2 (*in golf*, *cricket*) golpe *m*; (*rowing*) remada *f*; *Swimming* brazada *f*. 3 (*of pen*) trazo *m*; (*of brush*) pincelada *f*. 4 (*caress*) caricia *f*. 5 *Med* apoplejía *f*. II *vtr* acariciar.

stroll [strəʊl] I *vi* dar un paseo. II *n* paseo *m*.

stroller ['strəʊləʳ] *n US* (*for baby*) cochecito *m*.

strong [strɒŋ] I *adj* 1 fuerte. 2 (*durable*) sólido,-a. 3 (*firm*, *resolute*) firme. 4 (*colour*) intenso,-a; (*light*) brillante. 5 (*incontestable*) convincente. **6 to be 20 s.**, contar con 20 miembros. II *adv* fuerte; **to be going s.**, (*business*) ir fuerte; (*elderly person*) conservarse bien. ◆**strongly** *adv* fuertemente.

strongbox ['strɒŋbɒks] *n* caja *f* fuerte.

stronghold ['strɒŋhəʊld] *n Mil* fortaleza *f*; *fig* baluarte *m*.

strongroom ['strɒŋruːm] *n* cámara acorazada.

stroppy ['strɒpɪ] *adj* (**stroppier**, **stroppiest**) *GB fam* de mala uva.

strove [strəʊv] *pt* → **strive**.

struck [strʌk] *pt & pp* → **strike**.

structural ['strʌktʃərəl] *adj* estructural.

structure ['strʌktʃəʳ] *n* estructura *f*; (*constructed thing*) construcción *f*; (*building*) edificio *m*.

struggle ['strʌgəl] I *vi* luchar. II *n* lucha *f*; (*physical fight*) pelea *f*.

strum [strʌm] *vtr* (*guitar*) rasguear.

strung [strʌŋ] *pt & pp* → **string**.

strut [strʌt] *vi* pavonearse.

stub [stʌb] I *n* (*of cigarette*) colilla *f*; (*of pencil*) cabo *m*; (*of cheque*) matriz *f*. II *vtr* 1 (*strike*) golpear. 2 to **s.** (**out**), apagar.

stubble ['stʌbəl] *n* (*in field*) rastrojo *m*; (*on chin*) barba *f* de tres días.

stubborn ['stʌbən] *adj* 1 terco,-a, testarudo,-a. 2 (*stain*) difícil. 3 (*refusal*) rotundo,-a.

stucco ['stʌkəʊ] *n* estuco *m*.

stuck [stʌk] *pt & pp* → **stick**[2].

stuck-up [stʌk'ʌp] *adj fam* creído,-a.

stud[1] [stʌd] I *n* (*on clothing*) tachón *m*; (*on football boots*) taco *m*; (*on shirt*) botonadura *f*. II *vtr* (*decorate*) tachonar (**with**, de); *fig* (*dot*, *cover*) salpicar (**with**, de).

stud[2] [stʌd] *n* (*horse*) semental *m*.

student ['stjuːdənt] *n* estudiante *mf*; **s. teacher**, profesor,-a *m,f* en prácticas.

studio ['stjuːdɪəʊ] *n TV Cin* estudio *m*; (*artist's*) taller *m*; **s. apartment**, **s. flat**, estudio.

studious ['stjuːdɪəs] *adj* estudioso,-a. ◆**studiously** *adv* cuidadosamente.

study ['stʌdɪ] I *vtr* estudiar; (*facts etc*) examinar, investigar; (*behaviour*) observar. II *vi* estudiar; **to s. to be a doctor**, estudiar para médico. III *n* 1 estudio *m*; **s. group**, grupo *m* de trabajo. 2 (*room*) despacho *m*, estudio *m*.

stuff [stʌf] I *vtr* 1 (*container*) llenar (**with**, de); *Culin* rellenar (**with**, con or de); (*animal*) disecar. 2 (*cram*) atiborrar (**with**, de). II *n* 1 *fam* (*material*) material *m*. 2 *fam* (*things*) cosas *fpl*; *fam* trastos *mpl*.

stuffing ['stʌfɪŋ] *n Culin* relleno *m*.

stuffy ['stʌfɪ] *adj* (**stuffier**, **stuffiest**) I (*room*) mal ventilado,-a; (*atmosphere*) cargado,-a. 2 (*pompous*) estirado,-a; (*narrow-minded*) de miras estrechas.

stumble ['stʌmbəl] *vi* tropezar, dar un traspié; *fig* to **s. across** or **on** or **upon**, tropezar or dar con.

stumbling ['stʌmblɪŋ] *n* **s. block**, escollo *m*.

stump [stʌmp] I *n* 1 (*of pencil*) cabo *m*; (*of tree*) tocón *m*; (*of arm*, *leg*) muñón *m*. 2 (*in cricket*) estaca *f*. II *vtr* (*puzzle*) confundir; **to be stumped**, estar perplejo,-a.

stun [stʌn] *vtr* (*of blow*) aturdir; *fig* (*of news etc*) sorprender.

stung [stʌŋ] *pt & pp* → **sting**.

stunk [stʌŋk] *pt & pp* → **stink**.

stunning ['stʌnɪŋ] *adj* (*blow*) duro,-a;

(news) sorprendente; *fam (woman, outfit)* fenomenal.

stunt¹ [stʌnt] *vtr (growth)* atrofiar.

stunt² [stʌnt] *n* **1** *Av* acrobacia *f.* **2** *publicity s.*, truco publicitario. **3** *Cin* escena peligrosa; **s. man**, doble *m.*

stunted [ˈstʌntɪd] *adj* enano,-a, mal desarrollado,-a.

stupefy [ˈstjuːpɪfaɪ] *vtr (alcohol, drugs)* aturdir; *fig (news etc)* dejar pasmado,-a.

stupendous [stjuːˈpendəs] *adj (wonderful)* estupendo,-a.

stupid [ˈstjuːpɪd] *adj* estúpido,-a, imbécil.

stupidity [stjuːˈpɪdɪtɪ] *n* estupidez *f.*

stupor [ˈstjuːpər] *n* estupor *m.*

sturdy [ˈstɜːdɪ] *adj (sturdier, sturdiest)* robusto,-a, fuerte; *(resistance)* enérgico,-a.

stutter [ˈstʌtər] **I** *vi* tartamudear. **II** *n* tartamudeo *m.*

sty [staɪ] *n (pen)* pocilga *f.*

sty(e) [staɪ] *n Med* orzuelo *m.*

style [staɪl] **I** *n* **1** estilo *m*; *(of dress)* modelo *m.* **2** *(fashion)* moda *f.* **3 to live in s.**, *(elegance)* vivir a lo grande. **II** *vtr (hair)* marcar.

stylish [ˈstaɪlɪʃ] *adj* con estilo.

stylist [ˈstaɪlɪst] *n (hairdresser)* peluquero,-a *mf.*

stylus [ˈstaɪləs] *n (of record player)* aguja *f.*

suave [swɑːv] *adj* amable, afable; *pej* zalamero,-a.

sub [sʌb] *n fam* **1** *abbr* of **substitute**. **2** *abbr* of **subscription**.

sub- [sʌb] *pref* sub-.

subconscious [sʌbˈkɒnʃəs] **I** *adj* subconsciente. **II** *n* **the s.**, el subconsciente.

subcontract [sʌbkənˈtrækt] *vtr* subcontratar.

subcontractor [sʌbkənˈtræktər] *n* subcontratista *m.*

subdivide [sʌbdɪˈvaɪd] *vtr* subdividir *(into, en).*

subdue [səbˈdjuː] *vtr* **1** *(nation, people)* sojuzgar. **2** *(feelings)* dominar. **3** *(colour, light)* atenuar.

subdued [səbˈdjuːd] *adj* **1** *(person, emotion)* callado,-a. **2** *(voice, tone)* bajo,-a. **3** *(light)* tenue; *(colour)* apagado,-a.

subject [ˈsʌbdʒɪkt] **I** *n* **1** *(citizen)* súbdito *m.* **2** *(topic)* tema *m*; **s. matter**, materia *f*; *(contents)* contenido *m.* **3** *Educ* asignatura *f.* **4** *Ling* sujeto *m.* **II** *adj* **s. to**, *(law, tax)* sujeto,-a a; *(charge)* expuesto,-a a; *(changes, delays)* susceptible de; *(illness)* propenso,-a a; *(conditional upon)* previo,-a. **III** [səbˈdʒekt] *vtr* someter.

subjective [səbˈdʒektɪv] *adj* subjetivo,-a.

subjunctive [səbˈdʒʌŋktɪv] **I** *adj* subjuntivo,-a. **II** *n* subjuntivo *m.*

sublet [sʌbˈlet] *vtr & vi* subarrendar.

sublime [səˈblaɪm] *adj* sublime.

sub-machine-gun [sʌbməˈʃiːngʌn] *n* ametralladora *f.*

submarine [ˈsʌbməriːn] *n* submarino *m.*

submerge [səbˈmɜːdʒ] *vtr* sumergir; *(flood)* inundar; *fig* **submerged in ...**, sumido,-a en ....

submission [səbˈmɪʃən] *n* **1** *(yielding)* sumisión *f.* **2** *(of documents)* presentación *f.* **3** *(report)* informe *m.*

submissive [səbˈmɪsɪv] *adj* sumiso,-a.

submit [səbˈmɪt] **I** *vtr* **1** *(present)* presentar. **2** *(subject)* someter *(to, a).* **II** *vi (surrender)* rendirse.

subnormal [sʌbˈnɔːməl] *adj* subnormal.

subordinate [səˈbɔːdɪnət] *adj & n* subordinado,-a *(m,f).*

subpoena [səbˈpiːnə] **I** *n* citación *f.* **II** *vtr* citar.

subscribe [səbˈskraɪb] *vi (magazine)* suscribirse *(to, a)*; *(opinion, theory)* adherirse *(to, a).*

subscriber [səbˈskraɪbər] *n* abonado,-a *m,f.*

subscription [səbˈskrɪpʃən] *n (to magazine)* abono *m*; *(to club)* cuota *f.*

subsequent [ˈsʌbsɪkwənt] *adj* subsiguiente. ◆**subsequently** *adv* posteriormente.

subside [səbˈsaɪd] *vi (land)* hundirse; *(floodwater)* bajar; *(wind, anger)* amainar.

subsidence [səbˈsaɪdəns] *n (of land)* hundimiento *m*; *(of floodwater)* bajada *f*; *(of wind)* amaine *m.*

subsidiary [səbˈsɪdɪərɪ] **I** *adj (role)* secundario,-a. **II** *n Com* sucursal *f*, filial *f.*

subsidize [ˈsʌbsɪdaɪz] *vtr* subvencionar.

subsidy [ˈsʌbsɪdɪ] *n* subvención *f.*

subsistence [səbˈsɪstəns] *n* subsistencia *f.*

substance [ˈsʌbstəns] *n* **1** sustancia *f.* **2** *(essence)* esencia *f.* **3 a woman of s.**, *(wealth)* una mujer acaudalada.

substantial [səbˈstænʃəl] *adj* **1** *(solid)* sólido,-a. **2** *(sum, loss)* importante; *(difference, improvement)* notable; *(meal)* abundante.

substantiate [səbˈstænʃɪeɪt] *vtr* respaldar.

substitute [ˈsʌbstɪtjuːt] **I** *vtr* sustituir; **to s. X for Y**, sustituir X por Y. **II** *n (person)* suplente *mf*; *(thing)* sucedáneo *m.*

subtitle [ˈsʌbtaɪtəl] *n* subtítulo *m.*

subtle [ˈsʌtəl] *adj* sutil; *(taste)* delicado,-a; *(remark)* ingenioso,-a; *(irony)* fino,-a.

subtlety [ˈsʌtəltɪ] *n* sutileza *f*; *(of remark)* ingeniosidad *f*; *(of irony, joke)* finura *f.*

subtract [səbˈtrækt] *vtr* restar.

subtraction [səbˈtrækʃən] *n* resta *f.*

suburb [ˈsʌbɜːb] *n* barrio periférico; **the suburbs**, las afueras.

suburban [səˈbɜːbən] *adj* suburbano,-a.

suburbia [səˈbɜːbɪə] *n* barrios residenciales periféricos.

subversive [səbˈvɜːsɪv] *adj & n* subversivo,-a *(m,f).*

subway [ˈsʌbweɪ] *n* **1** *GB (underpass)* paso subterráneo. **2** *US (underground railway)* metro *m.*

succeed [sək'siːd] I vi 1 (person) tener éxito; (plan) salir bien; **to s. in doing sth**, conseguir hacer algo. 2 (follow after) suceder; **to s. to**, (throne) suceder a. II vtr (monarch) suceder a.

succeeding [sək'siːdɪŋ] adj sucesivo,-a.

success [sək'ses] n éxito m.

successful [sək'sesful] adj de éxito, exitoso,-a; (business) próspero,-a; (marriage) feliz; **to be s. in doing sth**, lograr hacer algo. ◆**successfully** adv con éxito.

succession [sək'seʃən] n sucesión f, serie f; **in s.**, sucesivamente.

successive [sək'sesɪv] adj sucesivo,-a, consecutivo,-a.

successor [sək'sesər] n sucesor,-a m,f.

succinct [sək'sɪŋkt] adj sucinto,-a.

succumb [sə'kʌm] vi sucumbir (to, a).

such [sʌtʃ] I adj 1 (of that sort) tal, semejante; **artists s. as Monet**, artistas como Monet; at **s. and s. a time**, a tal hora; **in s. a way that**, de tal manera que. 2 (so much, so great) tanto,-a; **he's always in s. a hurry**, siempre anda con tanta prisa; **she was in s. pain**, sufría tanto; **s. a lot of books**, tantos libros. II adv (so very) tan; **it's s. a long time ago**, hace tanto tiempo; **she's s. a clever woman**, es una mujer tan inteligente; **we had s. good weather**, hizo un tiempo tan bueno.

suchlike ['sʌtʃlaɪk] I adj tal. II n (things) cosas fpl por el estilo; (people) gente f por el estilo.

suck [sʌk] I vtr (by pump) aspirar; (liquid) sorber; (lollipop, blood) chupar. II vi (person) chupar; (baby) mamar. ◆**suck in** vtr (of whirlpool) tragar.

sucker ['sʌkər] n 1 fam primo,-a m,f, bobo,-a m,f. 2 Zool ventosa f; Bot chupón m.

suckle ['sʌkəl] vtr (mother) amamantar.

suction ['sʌkʃən] n succión f.

sudden ['sʌdən] adj 1 (hurried) súbito,-a, repentino,-a. 2 (unexpected) imprevisto,-a. 3 (abrupt) brusco,-a; **all of a s.**, de repente. ◆**suddenly** adv de repente.

suds [sʌdz] npl espuma f de jabón, jabonaduras fpl.

sue [suː, sjuː] I vtr demandar. II vi presentar una demanda; **to s. for divorce**, solicitar el divorcio.

suede [sweɪd] n ante m, gamuza f; (for gloves) cabritilla f.

suet ['suːɪt] n sebo m.

suffer ['sʌfər] I vtr 1 sufrir. 2 (tolerate) aguantar, soportar. II vi sufrir; **to s. from**, sufrir de.

sufferer ['sʌfərər] n Med enfermo,-a m,f.

suffering ['sʌfərɪŋ] n (affliction) sufrimiento m; (pain, torment) dolor m.

suffice [sə'faɪs] vi fml bastar, ser suficiente.

sufficient [sə'fɪʃənt] adj suficiente, bastante. ◆**sufficiently** adv suficientemente, bastante.

suffocate ['sʌfəkeɪt] I vtr asfixiar. II vi asfixiarse.

suffocating ['sʌfəkeɪtɪŋ] adj (heat) agobiante, sofocante.

suffrage ['sʌfrɪdʒ] n sufragio m.

suffuse [sə'fjuːz] vtr lit bañar, cubrir (with, de).

sugar ['ʃugər] I n azúcar m & f; **s. beet**, remolacha f (azucarera); **s. bowl**, azucarero m; **s. cane**, caña f de azúcar. II vtr azucarar, echar azúcar a.

sugary ['ʃugərɪ] adj 1 (like sugar) azucarado,-a. 2 fig (insincere) zalamero,-a; (over-sentimental) sentimentaloide.

suggest [sə'dʒest] vtr 1 (propose) sugerir. 2 (advise) aconsejar. 3 (indicate, imply) indicar.

suggestion [sə'dʒestʃən] n 1 (proposal) sugerencia f. 2 (trace) sombra f; (small amount) toque m.

suggestive [sə'dʒestɪv] adj (remark) indecente.

suicidal [sjuːɪ'saɪdəl] adj suicida.

suicide ['sjuːɪsaɪd] n suicidio m.

suit [suːt, sjuːt] I n 1 traje m de chaqueta. 2 Jur pleito m. 3 Cards palo m; fig **to follow s.**, seguir el ejemplo. II vtr 1 (be convenient to) convenir a, venir bien a. 2 (be right, appropriate for) ir bien a; **red really suits you**, el rojo te favorece mucho; **they are well suited**, están hechos el uno para el otro. 3 (adapt) adaptar a. 4 (please) **s. yourself!**, ¡como quieras!

suitable ['sjuːtəbəl] adj (convenient) conveniente; (appropriate) adecuado,-a; **the most s. woman for the job**, la mujer más indicada para el puesto. ◆**suitably** adv (correctly) correctamente; (properly) adecuadamente.

suitcase ['suːtkeɪs] n maleta f.

suite [swiːt] n 1 (of furniture) juego m. 2 (of hotel rooms, music) suite f.

suitor ['sjuːtər] n Lit (wooer) pretendiente m.

sulfur ['sʌlfər] n US → sulphur.

sulk [sʌlk] vi enfurruñarse.

sulky ['sʌlkɪ] adj (sulkier, sulkiest) malhumorado,-a, enfurruñado,-a.

sullen ['sʌlən] adj hosco,-a; (sky) plomizo,-a.

sulphur ['sʌlfər] n azufre m.

sulphuric [sʌl'fjuərɪk] adj sulfúrico,-a.

sultan ['sʌltən] n sultán m.

sultana [sʌl'tɑːnə] n (raisin) pasa f de Esmirna.

sultry ['sʌltrɪ] adj (sultrier, sultriest) 1 (muggy) bochornoso,-a. 2 (seductive) sensual.

sum [sʌm] n 1 (arithmetic problem, amount) suma f. 2 (total amount) total m; (of money) importe m. ◆**sum up** I vtr resumir. II vi resumir; **to s. up ...**, en resumidas cuentas ....

summarize ['sʌməraɪz] *vtr & vi* resumir.

summary ['sʌmərɪ] I *n* resumen *m*. II *adj* sumario,-a.

summer ['sʌmər] I *n* verano *m*. II *adj* (*holiday etc*) de verano; (*weather*) veraniego,-a; (*resort*) de veraneo.

summerhouse ['sʌməhaʊs] *n* cenador *m*, glorieta *f*.

summertime ['sʌmətaɪm] *n* verano *m*.

summit ['sʌmɪt] *n* 1 (*of mountain*) cima *f*, cumbre *f*. 2 Pol s. (**meeting**), cumbre *f*.

summon ['sʌmən] *vtr* 1 (*meeting, person*) convocar. 2 (*aid*) pedir. 3 *Jur* citar. ◆**summon up** *vtr* (*resources*) reunir; to **s. up one's courage**, armarse de valor.

summons ['sʌmənz] I *n* 1 (*call*) llamada *f*, llamamiento *m*. 2 *Jur* citación *f* judicial. II *vtr Jur* citar.

sumptuous ['sʌmptjʊəs] *adj* suntuoso,-a.

sun [sʌn] I *n* sol *m*. II *vtr* to **s. oneself**, tomar el sol.

sunbathe ['sʌnbeɪð] *vi* tomar el sol.

sunbed ['sʌnbed] *n* (*in garden*) tumbona *f*; (*with sunlamp*) solario *m*.

sunburn ['sʌnbɜːn] *n* (*burn*) quemadura *f* de sol.

sunburnt ['sʌnbɜːnt] *adj* (*burnt*) quemado,-a por el sol; (*tanned*) bronceado,-a.

Sunday ['sʌndɪ] *n* domingo *m inv*; **S. newspaper**, periódico *m* del domingo; **S. school**, catequesis *f*.

sundial ['sʌndaɪəl] *n* reloj *m* de sol.

sundown ['sʌndaʊn] *n US* anochecer *m*.

sundry ['sʌndrɪ] I *adj* diversos,-as, varios,-as; *fam* **all and s.**, todos sin excepción. II *npl Com* **sundries**, artículos *mpl* diversos; (*expenses*) gastos diversos.

sunflower ['sʌnflaʊər] *n* girasol *m*.

sung [sʌŋ] *pp* → **sing**.

sunglasses ['sʌnglɑːsɪz] *npl* gafas *fpl* de sol.

sunk [sʌŋk] *pp* → **sink**.

sunlamp ['sʌnlæmp] *n* lámpara *f* solar.

sunlight ['sʌnlaɪt] *n* sol *m*, luz *f* del sol.

sunlit ['sʌnlɪt] *adj* iluminado,-a por el sol.

sunny ['sʌnɪ] *adj* (**sunnier, sunniest**) 1 (*day*) de sol; (*place*) soleado,-a; **it is s.**, hace sol. 2 *fig* (*smile, disposition*) alegre; (*future*) prometedor,-a.

sunrise ['sʌnraɪz] *n* salida *f* del sol.

sunroof ['sʌnruːf] *n Aut* techo corredizo.

sunset ['sʌnset] *n* puesta *f* del sol.

sunshade ['sʌnʃeɪd] *n* sombrilla *f*.

sunshine ['sʌnʃaɪn] *n* sol *m*, luz *f* del sol.

sunstroke ['sʌnstrəʊk] *n* insolación *f*.

suntan ['sʌntæn] *n* bronceado *m*; **s. oil** or **lotion**, (aceite *m*) bronceador *m*.

super ['suːpər] *adj fam* fenomenal.

super- ['suːpər] *pref* super-, sobre-.

superannuation [suːpərænjʊ'eɪʃən] *n GB* jubilación *f*, pensión *f*.

superb [suː'pɜːb] *adj* espléndido,-a.

supercilious [suːpə'sɪlɪəs] *adj* (*condescending*) altanero,-a; (*disdainful*) desdeñoso,-a.

superficial [suːpə'fɪʃəl] *adj* superficial.

superfluous [suː'pɜːflʊəs] *adj* sobrante, superfluo,-a; **to be s.**, sobrar.

superhuman [suːpə'hjuːmən] *adj* sobrehumano,-a.

superimpose [suːpərɪm'pəʊz] *vtr* sobreponer.

superintendent [suːpərɪn'tendənt] *n* director,-a *m,f*; **police s.**, subjefe,-a *m,f* de policía.

superior [suː'pɪərɪər] I *adj* 1 superior. 2 (*haughty*) altivo,-a. II *n* superior,-a *m,f*.

superiority [suːpɪərɪ'ɒrɪtɪ] *n* superioridad *f*.

superlative [suː'pɜːlətɪv] I *adj* superlativo,-a. II *n Ling* superlativo *m*.

superman ['suːpəmæn] *n* superhombre *m*, superman *m*.

supermarket ['suːpəmɑːkɪt] *n* supermercado *m*.

supernatural [suːpə'nætʃərəl] I *adj* sobrenatural. II *n* the **s.**, lo sobrenatural.

superpower ['suːpəpaʊər] *n Pol* superpotencia *f*.

supersede [suːpə'siːd] *vtr fml* suplantar.

supersonic [suːpə'sɒnɪk] *adj* supersónico,-a.

superstitious [suːpə'stɪʃəs] *adj* supersticioso,-a.

supertanker ['suːpətæŋkər] *n* superpetrolero *m*.

supervise ['suːpəvaɪz] *vtr* supervisar; (*watch over*) vigilar.

supervision [suːpə'vɪʒən] *n* supervisión *f*.

supervisor ['suːpəvaɪzər] *n* supervisor,-a *m,f*.

supper ['sʌpər] *n* cena *f*; **to have s.**, cenar.

supplant [sə'plɑːnt] *vtr* suplantar.

supple ['sʌpəl] *adj* flexible.

supplement ['sʌplɪmənt] I *n* suplemento *m*. II ['sʌplɪment] *vtr* complementar.

supplementary [sʌplɪ'mentərɪ] *adj* adicional.

supplier [sə'plaɪər] *n* suministrador,-a *m,f*; *Com* proveedor,-a *m,f*.

supply [sə'plaɪ] I *n* 1 suministro *m*; *Com* provisión *f*; (*stock*) surtido *m*; **s. and demand**, oferta *f* y demanda. 2 **supplies**, (*food*) víveres *mpl*; *Mil* pertrechos *mpl*; **office supplies**, material *m sing* para oficina. II *vtr* 1 (*provide*) suministrar. 2 (*with provisions*) aprovisionar. 3 (*information*) facilitar. 4 *Com* surtir.

support [sə'pɔːt] I *n* 1 (*moral*) apoyo *m*. 2 (*funding*) ayuda económica. II *vtr* 1 (*weight etc*) sostener. 2 *fig* (*back*) apoyar; (*substantiate*) respaldar. 3 *Sport* ser (hincha) de. 4 (*sustain*) mantener; (*feed*) alimentar.

supporter [sə'pɔːtər] *n Pol* partidario,-a *m,f*; *Sport* hincha *mf*.

suppose [sə'pəʊz] *vtr* suponer; *(presume)* creer; **I s. not/so**, supongo que no/sí; **you're not supposed to smoke in here**, no está permitido fumar aquí dentro; **you're supposed to be in bed**, deberías estar acostado,-a ya.

supposed [sə'pəʊzd] *adj* supuesto,-a. ◆**supposedly** *adv* teóricamente.

suppress [sə'pres] *vtr* suprimir; *(feelings, laugh etc)* contener; *(news, truth)* callar; *(revolt)* sofocar.

supranational [su:prə'næʃənəl] *adj* supranacional.

supremacy [su'preməsɪ] *n* supremacía *f.*

supreme [su'pri:m] *adj* supremo,-a; **with s. indifference**, con total indiferencia. ◆**supremely** *adv* sumamente.

surcharge ['sɜːtʃɑːdʒ] *n* recargo *m.*

sure [ʃʊə'] I *adj* **1** seguro,-a; **I'm s. (that) ...**, estoy seguro,-a de que ...; **make s. that it's ready**, asegúrate de que esté listo; **s. of oneself**, seguro,-a de sí mismo,-a. **2** *US fam* **s. thing!**, ¡claro! II *adv* **1** *(of course)* claro. **2** *(certainly)* seguro. **3** **s. enough**, efectivamente. ◆**surely** *adv (without a doubt)* sin duda; **s. not!**, ¡no puede ser!

surety ['ʃʊərɪtɪ] *n* **1** *(sum)* fianza *f.* **2** *(person)* fiador,-a *m,f;* **to stand s. for sb**, ser fiador de algn.

surf [sɜːf] I *n (waves)* oleaje *m;* *(foam)* espuma *f.* II *vi Sport* hacer surf.

surface ['sɜːfɪs] I *n* superficie *f;* *(of road)* firme *m.* II *adj* superficial; **s. area**, área *f* de la superficie; **by s. mail**, por vía terrestre *or* marítima. III *vtr (road)* revestir. IV *vi (submarine etc)* salir a la superficie; *fam (wake up)* levantarse.

surface-to-air [sɜːfɪstu'eə'] *adj* **s.-to-a. missile**, misil *m* tierra-aire.

surfboard ['sɜːfbɔːd] *n* tabla *f* de surf.

surfeit ['sɜːfɪt] *n fml* exceso *m.*

surfer ['sɜːfə'] *n* surfista *mf.*

surfing ['sɜːfɪŋ] *n* surf *m*, surfing *m.*

surge [sɜːdʒ] I *n* **1** *(growth)* alza *f.* **2** *(of sea, sympathy)* oleada *f; fig (of anger, energy)* arranque *m.* II *vi* **to s. forward**, *(people)* avanzar en tropel.

surgeon ['sɜːdʒən] *n* cirujano,-a *m,f.*

surgery ['sɜːdʒərɪ] *n* **1** *(operation)* cirugía *f.* **2** *GB (consulting room)* consultorio *m;* **s. hours**, horas *fpl* de consulta. **3** *US (operating theatre)* quirófano *m.*

surgical ['sɜːdʒɪkəl] *adj* quirúrgico,-a; **s. spirit**, alcohol *m* de 90°.

surly ['sɜːlɪ] *adj* (**surlier, surliest**) *(bad-tempered)* hosco,-a, malhumorado,-a, *(rude)* maleducado,-a.

surmount [sɜː'maʊnt] *vtr* superar, vencer.

surname ['sɜːneɪm] *n* apellido *m.*

surpass [sɜː'pɑːs] *vtr* superar.

surplus ['sɜːpləs] I *n (of goods)* excedente *m;* *(of budget)* superávit *m.* II *adj* exce-

dente.

surprise [sə'praɪz] I *n* sorpresa *f;* **to take sb by s.**, coger desprevenido,-a a algn. II *adj (visit)* inesperado,-a; **s. attack**, ataque *m* sorpresa. III *vtr* sorprender.

surprising [sə'praɪzɪŋ] *adj* sorprendente. ◆**surprisingly** *adv* sorprendentemente, de modo sorprendente.

surrealist [sə'rɪəlɪst] *adj & n* surrealista *(mf).*

surrender [sə'rendə'] I *n Mil* rendición *f;* *(of weapons)* entrega *f;* *fin* rescate *m.* II *vtr Mil* rendir; *(right)* renunciar a. III *vi (give in)* rendirse.

surreptitious [sʌrəp'tɪʃəs] *adj* subrepticio,-a.

surrogate ['sʌrəgɪt] *n fml* sustituto,-a *m,f;* **s. mother**, madre *f* de alquiler.

surround [sə'raʊnd] I *n* marco *m*, borde *m.* II *vtr* rodear.

surrounding [sə'raʊndɪŋ] I *adj* circundante. II *npl* **surroundings**, *(of place)* alrededores *mpl*, cercanías *fpl.*

surveillance [sɜː'veɪləns] *n* vigilancia *f.*

survey ['sɜːveɪ] I *n* **1** *(of building)* inspección *f;* *(of land)* reconocimiento *m.* **2** *(of trends etc)* encuesta *f.* **3** *(overall view)* panorama *m.* II [sɜː'veɪ] *vtr* **1** *(building)* inspeccionar; *(land)* medir. **2** *(trends etc)* hacer una encuesta sobre. **3** *(look at)* contemplar.

surveyor [sɜː'veɪə'] *n* agrimensor,-a *m,f;* **quantity s.**, aparejador,-a *m,f.*

survival [sə'vaɪvəl] *n* supervivencia *f.*

survive [sə'vaɪv] I *vi* sobrevivir; *(remain)* perdurar. II *vtr* sobrevivir a.

survivor [sə'vaɪvə'] *n* superviviente *mf.*

susceptible [sə'septəbəl] *adj (to attack)* susceptible (**to, a**); *(to illness)* propenso,-a (**to, a**).

suspect ['sʌspekt] I *adj (dubious)* sospechoso,-a. II *n* sospechoso,-a *m,f.* III [sə'spekt] *vtr* **1** *(person)* sospechar (**of, de**); *(plot, motives)* recelar de. **2** *(think likely)* imaginar, creer.

suspend [sə'spend] *vtr* suspender; *(pupil)* expulsar por un tiempo.

suspended [sə'spendɪd] *adj* **1** suspendido,-a; *Jur* **s. sentence**, condena *f* condicional. **2** *Sport* sancionado,-a.

suspender [sə'spendə'] *n* **1** *(for stocking)* liga *f;* **s. belt**, liguero *m.* **2** *US* **suspenders**, tirantes *mpl.*

suspense [sə'spens] *n* incertidumbre *f; Cin Theat* suspense *m;* **to keep sb in s.**, mantener a algn en la incertidumbre.

suspension [sə'spenʃən] *n* **1** suspensión *f.* **2** *Sport* sanción *f.* **3** *(of pupil, employee)* expulsión *f* temporal. **4** **s. bridge**, puente *m* colgante.

suspicion [sə'spɪʃən] *n* **1** sospecha *f; (mistrust)* recelo *m; (doubt)* duda *f.* **2** *(trace)* pizca *f.*

suspicious [sə'spɪʃəs] *adj* **1** *(arousing*

suspicion) sospechoso,-a. **2** (_distrustful_) receloso,-a; **to be s. of sb,** desconfiar de algn.

sustain [sə'steɪn] _vtr_ **1** sostener. **2** (_nourish_) sustentar. **3** _Jur_ (_objection_) admitir. **4** (_injury etc_) sufrir.

sustained [sə'steɪnd] _adj_ sostenido,-a.

sustenance ['sʌstənəns] _n_ sustento m.

swab [swɒb] **I** _n_ (_cotton wool_) algodón m; (_for specimen_) frotis m. **II** _vtr_ (_wound_) limpiar.

swagger ['swægəʳ] **I** _n_ pavoneo m. **II** _vi_ pavonearse.

swallow[1] ['swɒləʊ] **I** _n_ (_of drink, food_) trago m. **II** _vtr_ **1** (_drink, food_) tragar. **2** _fig_ (_believe_) tragarse. **III** _vi_ tragar. ◆**swallow up** _vtr fig_ **1** (_engulf_) tragar. **2** (_eat up_) consumir.

swallow[2] ['swɒləʊ] _n Orn_ golondrina f.

swam [swæm] _pt_ → **swim.**

swamp [swɒmp] **I** _n_ ciénaga f. **II** _vtr_ **1** (_boat_) hundir. **2** _fig_ inundar (**with, by, de**).

swan [swɒn] **I** _n_ cisne m. **II** _vi fam_ **to s. around,** pavonearse; **to s. around doing nothing,** hacer el vago.

swap [swɒp] **I** _n fam_ intercambio m. **II** _vtr_ cambiar. ◆**swap round, swap over** _vtr_ (_switch_) cambiar.

swarm [swɔːm] **I** _n_ enjambre m. **II** _vi_ (_bees_) enjambrar; _fig_ Neath was swarming with tourists, Neath estaba lleno de turistas.

swarthy ['swɔːðɪ] _adj_ (**swarthier, swarthiest**) moreno,-a.

swastika ['swɒstɪkə] _n_ esvástica f, cruz gamada.

swat [swɒt] _vtr_ aplastar.

swathe [sweɪð] _vtr_ (_bind up_) envolver.

sway [sweɪ] **I** _n_ **1** (_movement_) balanceo m. **2 to hold s. over sb,** dominar a algn. **II** _vi_ **1** (_swing_) balancearse, mecerse. **2** (_totter_) tambalearse. **III** _vtr fig_ (_persuade_) convencer.

swear [sweəʳ] **I** _vtr_ (_pt_ **swore;** _pp_ **sworn**) (_vow_) jurar; **to s. an oath,** prestar juramento. **II** _vi_ **1** (_formally_) jurar, prestar juramento. **2** (_curse_) soltar tacos, decir palabrotas; (_blaspheme_) jurar; **to s. at sb,** echar pestes contra algn.

swear-word ['sweəwɜːd] _n_ palabrota f.

sweat [swet] **I** _n_ (_perspiration_) sudor m; _fam_ (_hard work_) trabajo duro. **II** _vi_ (_perspire_) sudar; _fig_ (_work hard_) sudar la gota gorda. **III** _vtr fam_ **to s. it out,** aguantar.

sweater ['swetəʳ] _n_ suéter m.

sweatshirt ['swetʃɜːt] _n_ sudadera f.

sweaty ['swetɪ] _adj_ (**sweatier, sweatiest**) sudoroso,-a.

swede [swiːd] _n Bot_ nabo sueco.

Swede [swiːd] _n_ (_person_) sueco,-a m,f.

Sweden ['swiːdən] _n_ Suecia f.

Swedish ['swiːdɪʃ] **I** _adj_ sueco,-a. **II** _n_ **1** (_language_) sueco m. **2 the S.,** _pl_ los sue-

cos.

sweep [swiːp] **I** _n_ **1** (_with broom_) barrido m; _fig_ **to make a clean s. of things,** hacer tabla rasa. **2** (_of arm_) gesto amplio. **3** (_of river, road_) curva f. **4** (**chimney**) s., deshollinador,-a m,f. **II** _vtr_ (_pt_ & _pp_ **swept**) **1** (_floor etc_) barrer. **2** (_of searchlight_) recorrer; (_minefield_) rastrear. **3** (_spread throughout_) extenderse por. **III** _vi_ **1** (_with broom_) barrer. **2 to s. in/out/past,** entrar/salir/pasar rápidamente. ◆**sweep aside** _vtr_ apartar bruscamente; _fig_ (_objections_) rechazar. ◆**sweep away** _vtr_ **1** (_dust_) barrer. **2** (_of storm_) arrastrar. ◆**sweep up** _vi_ barrer.

sweeper ['swiːpəʳ] _n_ **1** (_machine_) barredora f. **2** _Ftb_ líbero m.

sweeping ['swiːpɪŋ] _adj_ **1** (_broad_) amplio,-a; **a s. statement,** una declaración demasiado general. **2** (_victory_) aplastante. **3** (_reforms, changes etc_) radical.

sweet [swiːt] **I** _adj_ **1** dulce; (_sugary_) azucarado,-a; **to have a s. tooth,** ser goloso,-a; **s. pea,** guisante m de olor; **s. shop,** bombonería f. **2** (_pleasant_) agradable; (_smell_) fragante; (_sound_) melodioso,-a. **3** (_person, animal_) encantador,-a. **II** _n_ **1** _GB_ caramelo m; (_chocolate_) bombón m. **2** (_dessert_) postre m.

sweet-and-sour ['swiːtənsaʊəʳ] _adj_ agridulce.

sweetcorn ['swiːtkɔːn] _n_ maíz tierno.

sweeten ['swiːtən] _vtr_ **1** (_tea etc_) azucarar. **2** _fig_ (_temper_) aplacar; **to s. the pill,** suavizar el golpe.

sweetener ['swiːtənəʳ] _n_ (_for tea, coffee_) edulcorante m.

sweetheart ['swiːthɑːt] _n_ **1** (_boyfriend_) novio m; (_girlfriend_) novia f. **2** (_dear, love_) cariño m, amor m.

sweetness ['swiːtnɪs] _n_ dulzura f; (_of smell_) fragancia f; (_of sound_) suavidad f.

swell [swel] **I** _n_ (_of sea_) marejada f, oleaje m. **II** _adj US fam_ fenomenal. **III** _vi_ (_pt_ **swelled;** _pp_ **swollen**) (_part of body_) hincharse; (_river_) subir. ◆**swell up** _vi_ hincharse.

swelling ['swelɪŋ] _n_ hinchazón f; _Med_ tumefacción f.

sweltering ['sweltərɪŋ] _adj_ agobiante.

swept [swept] _pt_ & _pp_ → **sweep.**

swerve [swɜːv] **I** _n_ **1** (_by car_) viraje m. **2** _Sport_ (_by player_) regate m. **II** _vi_ **1** (_car_) dar un viraje brusco. **2** _Sport_ (_player_) dar un regate.

swift [swɪft] **I** _adj_ rápido,-a, veloz. **II** _n Orn_ vencejo m (común). ◆**swiftly** _adv_ rápidamente.

swig [swɪg] _fam_ **I** _n_ trago m. **II** _vtr_ beber a tragos.

swill [swɪl] **I** _n_ bazofia f. **2** (_rinse_) enjuague m. **II** _vtr_ **1** (_rinse_) enjuagar. **2** _fam_ (_drink_) beber a grandes tragos. ◆**swill out** _vtr_ enjuagar.

swim [swɪm] **I** *vi* (*pt* **swam**; *pp* **swum**) nadar; **to go swimming**, ir a nadar; *fam* **my head is swimming**, la cabeza me da vueltas. **II** *vtr* (*the Channel*) pasar a nado. **III** *n* baño *m*; **to go for a s.**, ir a nadar o bañarse.

swimmer ['swɪmə'] *n* nadador,-a *m,f*.

swimming ['swɪmɪŋ] *n* natación *f*; **s. cap**, gorro *m* de baño; **s. costume**, traje *m* de baño, bañador *m*; **s. pool**, piscina *f*; **s. trunks**, bañador.

swimsuit ['swɪmsuːt] *n* traje *m* de baño, bañador *m*.

swindle ['swɪndəl] **I** *n* estafa *f*. **II** *vtr* estafar.

swindler ['swɪndələ'] *n* estafador,-a *m,f*.

swine [swaɪn] *n* **1** (*pl* **swine**) (*pig*) cerdo *m*, puerco *m*. **2** (*pl* **swines**) *fam* (*person*) canalla *m,f*, cochino,-a *m,f*.

swing [swɪŋ] **I** *n* **1** balanceo *m*, vaivén *m*; *fig* (*in votes etc*) viraje *m*; **s. bridge**, puente giratorio; **s. door**, puerta giratoria. **2** *Box Golf* swing *m*. **3** (*plaything*) columpio *m*. **4** (*rhythm*) ritmo *m*; (*jazz style*) swing *m*; **in full s.**, en plena marcha. **II** *vi* (*pt* & *pp* **swung**) **1** (*move to and fro*) balancearse; (*arms*, *legs*) menearse; (*on swing*) columpiarse; **to s. open/shut**, abrirse/cerrarse de golpe. **2** (*turn*) girar; **he swung round**, dio media vuelta. **III** *vtr* **1** (*cause to move to and fro*) balancear; (*arms*, *legs*) menear; (*on swing*) columpiar. **2** (*turn*) hacer girar; **she swung the sack onto her back**, se echó el saco a los hombros.

swingeing ['swɪndʒɪŋ] *adj* drástico,-a.

swipe [swaɪp] **I** *n* golpe *m*. **II** *vtr* **1** (*hit*) dar un tortazo a. **2** *fam* (*steal*) birlar.

swirl [swɜːl] **I** *n* remolino *m*; (*of cream*, *smoke*) voluta *f*. **II** *vi* arremolinarse.

swish [swɪʃ] **I** *adj fam* (*smart*) elegante. **II** *vtr* (*tail*) menear. **III** *vi* (*whip*) dar un chasquido; (*skirt*) crujir.

Swiss [swɪs] **I** *adj* suizo,-a. **II** *n inv* (*person*) suizo,-a *m,f*; **the S.**, los suizos.

switch [swɪtʃ] **I** *n* **1** *Elec* interruptor *m*. **2** (*changeover*) cambio repentino; (*exchange*) intercambio *m*. **3** (*stick*) vara *f*; (*riding whip*) fusta *f*. **II** *vtr* **1** (*jobs*, *direction*) cambiar de. **2** (*allegiance*) cambiar (**to**, por); (*attention*) desviar (**to**, hacia). ◆**switch off** *vtr* apagar. ◆**switch on** *vtr* encender. ◆**switch over** *vi* cambiar (**to**, a).

switchboard ['swɪtʃbɔːd] *n* centralita *f*.

Switzerland ['swɪtsələnd] *n* Suiza.

swivel ['swɪvəl] **I** *n* **s. chair**, silla giratoria. **II** *vtr* & *vi* girar.

swollen ['swəʊlən] *adj* (*ankle*, *face*) hinchado,-a; (*river*, *lake*) crecido,-a.

swoon [swuːn] *arch* **I** *n* desmayo *m*. **II** *vi* desmayarse.

swoop [swuːp] **I** *n* **1** (*of bird*) calada *f*; (*of*

plane) descenso *m* en picado. **2** (*by police*) redada *f*. **II** *vi* **1 to s. down**, (*bird*) abalanzarse (**on**, sobre); (*plane*) bajar en picado. **2** (*police*) hacer una redada.

swop [swɒp] *vtr* → **swap**.

sword [sɔːd] *n* espada *f*.

swordfish ['sɔːdfɪʃ] *n* pez *m* espada.

swore [swɔː'] *pt* → **swear**.

sworn [swɔːn] *adj* jurado,-a.

swot [swɒt] *fam vi* empollar.

swum [swʌm] *pp* → **swim**.

swung [swʌŋ] *pt* & *pp* **swing**.

sycamore ['sɪkəmɔː'] *n* sicomoro *m*.

syllable ['sɪləbəl] *n* sílaba *f*.

syllabus ['sɪləbəs] *n* programa *m* de estudios.

symbol ['sɪmbəl] *n* símbolo *m*.

symbolic [sɪm'bɒlɪk] *adj* simbólico,-a.

symbolize ['sɪmbəlaɪz] *vtr* simbolizar.

symmetry ['sɪmɪtrɪ] *n* simetría *f*.

sympathetic [sɪmpə'θetɪk] *adj* **1** (*showing pity*) compasivo,-a. **2** (*understanding*) comprensivo,-a; (*kind*) amable.

sympathize ['sɪmpəθaɪz] *vi* **1** (*show pity*) compadecerse (**with**, de). **2** (*understand*) comprender.

sympathizer ['sɪmpəθaɪzə'] *n* simpatizante *mf*.

sympathy ['sɪmpəθɪ] *n* **1** (*pity*) compasión *f*. **2** (*condolences*) pésame *m*; **letter of s.**, pésame; **to express one's s.**, dar el pésame. **3** (*understanding*) comprensión *f*.

symphony ['sɪmfənɪ] *n* sinfonía *f*.

symposium [sɪm'pəʊzɪəm] *n* simposio *m*.

symptom ['sɪmptəm] *n* síntoma *m*.

symptomatic [sɪmptə'mætɪk] *adj* sintomático,-a.

synagogue ['sɪnəgɒg] *n* sinagoga *f*.

synchronize ['sɪŋkrənaɪz] *vtr* sincronizar.

syndicate ['sɪndɪkɪt] *n* corporación *f*; *newspaper s.*, sindicato periodístico.

syndrome ['sɪndrəʊm] *n* síndrome *m*.

synonym ['sɪnənɪm] *n* sinónimo *m*.

synopsis [sɪ'nɒpsɪs] *n* sinopsis *f inv*.

syntax ['sɪntæks] *n* sintaxis *f inv*.

synthesis ['sɪnθɪsɪs] *n* (*pl* **syntheses** ['sɪnθɪsiːz]) síntesis *f inv*.

synthesizer ['sɪnθɪsaɪzə'] *n* sintetizador *m*.

synthetic [sɪn'θetɪk] *adj* sintético,-a.

syphilis ['sɪfɪlɪs] *n* sífilis *f*.

syphon ['saɪfən] *n* → **siphon**.

Syria ['sɪrɪə] *n* Siria.

Syrian ['sɪrɪən] *adj* & *n* sirio,-a (*m,f*).

syringe [sɪ'rɪndʒ] *n* jeringa *f*, jeringuilla *f*.

syrup ['sɪrəp] *n* jarabe *m*, almíbar *m*.

system ['sɪstəm] *n* sistema *m*; *fam* **the s.**, el orden establecido; *Comput* **systems analyst**, analista *mf* de sistemas.

systematic [sɪstɪ'mætɪk] *adj* sistemático,-a.

T

T, t [tiː] *n* (*the letter*) T, t *f*.

t *abbr of* ton(s), tonne(s), t.

ta [taː] *interj GB fam* gracias.

tab [tæb] *n* 1 (*flap*) lengüeta *f*; (*label*) etiqueta *f*; *fam* **to keep tabs on sb**, vigilar a algn. 2 *US fam* (*bill*) cuenta *f*.

tabby ['tæbɪ] *n* t. (cat), gato,-a *m,f* romano,-a.

table ['teɪbəl] I *n* 1 mesa *f*; **to lay** *or* **set the t.**, poner la mesa; **t. lamp**, lámpara *f* de mesa; **t. mat**, salvamanteles *m inv*; **t. tennis**, ping-pong® *m*, tenis *m* de mesa; **t. wine**, vino *m* de mesa. 2 (*of figures*) tabla *f*, cuadro *m*; **t. of contents**, índice *m* de materias. II *vtr* presentar.

tablecloth ['teɪbəlklɒθ] *n* mantel *m*.

tablespoon ['teɪbəlspuːn] *n* cucharón *m*.

tablespoonful ['teɪbəlspuːnful] *n* cucharada *f* grande.

tablet ['tæblɪt] *n* 1 *Med* pastilla *f*. 2 (*of stone*) lápida *f*. 3 (*of soap*) pastilla *f*; (*of chocolate*) tableta *f*. 4 *US* (*of writing paper*) bloc *m*.

tableware ['teɪbəlweə'] *n* vajilla *f*.

tabloid ['tæblɔɪd] *n* periódico *m* de pequeño formato; **t. press**, prensa sensacionalista.

taboo [tə'buː] *adj & n* tabú (*m*).

tabulate ['tæbjʊleɪt] *vtr* disponer en listas.

tacit ['tæsɪt] *adj* tácito,-a.

taciturn ['tæsɪtɜːn] *adj* taciturno,-a.

tack [tæk] *n* 1 (*small nail*) tachuela *f*. 2 *Sew* hilván *m*. 3 *Naut* amura *f*; (*distance*) bordada *f*; *fig* **to change t.**, cambiar de rumbo. II *vtr* 1 **to t. sth down**, clavar algo con tachuelas. 2 *Sew* hilvanar. III *vi Naut* virar de bordo. ◆**tack on** *vtr* (*add*) añadir.

tackle ['tækəl] I *n* 1 (*equipment*) aparejos *mpl*; **fishing t.**, aparejos de pescar. 2 *Sport* placaje *m*; *Ftb* entrada *f*. II *vtr* agarrar; (*task*) emprender; (*problem*) abordar; *Sport* placar; *Ftb* entrar a.

tacky¹ ['tækɪ] *adj* (*tackier, tackiest*) pegajoso,-a.

tacky² ['tækɪ] *adj fam* (*shoddy*) cutre.

tact [tækt] *n* tacto *m*, diplomacia *f*.

tactful ['tæktful] *adj* diplomático,-a.

tactical ['tæktɪkəl] *adj* táctico,-a.

tactic ['tæktɪk] *n* 1 táctica *f*; **tactics**, táctica *f sing*.

tactless ['tæktlɪs] *adj* (*person*) poco diplomático,-a; (*question*) indiscreto,-a.

tadpole ['tædpəʊl] *n* renacuajo *m*.

tag [tæg] *n* 1 (*label*) etiqueta *f*. 2 (*saying*) coletilla *f*. ◆**tag along** *vi fam* pegarse.

◆**tag on** *vtr* (*add to end*) añadir.

tail [teɪl] I *n* 1 cola *f*; **t. end**, cola. 2 (*of shirt*) faldón *m*; **to wear tails**, ir de frac;

t. coat, frac *m*. 3 **tails**, (*of coin*) cruz *f sing*. II *vtr sl* (*follow*) seguir de cerca. ◆**tail away**, **tail off** *vi* desvanecerse.

tailback ['teɪlbæk] *n* caravana *f*.

tail-gate ['teɪlgeɪt] *n Aut* puerta trasera.

tailor ['teɪlə'] I *n* sastre *m*; **t.'s (shop)**, sastrería *f*. II *vtr* (*suit*) confeccionar; *fig* adaptar.

tailor-made [teɪlə'meɪd] *adj* hecho,-a a la medida.

tailwind ['teɪlwɪnd] *n* viento *m* de cola.

taint [teɪnt] *vtr* contaminar; *fig* corromper.

tainted ['teɪntɪd] *adj* contaminado,-a; (*reputation*) manchado,-a.

take [teɪk] I *vtr* (*pt* took; *pp* taken) 1 tomar, coger; **to t. an opportunity**, aprovechar una oportunidad; **to t. hold of sth**, agarrar algo; **to t. sth from one's pocket**, sacarse algo del bolsillo; **t. your time!**, ¡tómate el tiempo que quieras!; **to t. a bath**, bañarse; **to t. care**, cuidar; **his car takes six people**, caben seis personas en su coche; **is this seat taken?**, ¿está ocupado este asiento?; **to t. a decision**, tomar una decisión; **to t. a liking/dislike to sb**, tomar cariño/antipatía a algn; **to t. a photograph**, sacar una fotografía; **t. the first road on the left**, coja la primera a la izquierda; **to t. the train**, coger el tren. 2 (*accept*) aceptar; (*bear*) llevar. 3 (*win*) ganar; (*prize*) llevarse. 4 (*eat, drink*) tomar; **to t. drugs**, drogarse. 5 **she's taking (a degree in) law**, estudia derecho; **to t. an exam** (*in* …), examinarse (de …). 6 (*person to a place*) llevar. 7 (*endure*) aguantar. 8 (*consider*) considerar. 9 **I t. it that …**, supongo que …; **what do you t. me for?**, ¿por quién me tomas? 10 (*require*) requerir; **it takes an hour to get there**, se tarda una hora en llegar hasta allí. 11 **to be taken ill**, enfermar.

II *n Cin* toma *f*.

◆**take after** *vtr* parecerse a. ◆**take apart** *vtr* (*machine*) desmontar. ◆**take away** *vtr* 1 (*carry off*) llevarse. 2 **to t. sth away from sb**, quitarle algo a algn. 3 *Math* restar. ◆**take back** *vtr* 1 (*give back*) devolver; (*receive back*) recuperar. 2 (*withdraw*) retractarse. ◆**take down** *vtr* 1 (*lower*) bajar. 2 (*demolish*) derribar. 3 (*write*) apuntar. ◆**take in** *vtr* 1 (*shelter, lodge*) alojar, acoger. 2 *Sew* meter. 3 (*include*) abarcar. 4 (*understand*) entender. 5 (*deceive*) engañar. ◆**take off** I *vtr* 1 quitar; **he took off his jacket**, se quitó la chaqueta. 2 (*lead or carry away*) llevarse. 3 (*deduct*) descontar. 4 (*imitate*) imitar burlonamente. II *vi Av* despegar.

◆**take on** *vtr* 1 (*undertake*) encargarse de. 2 (*acquire*) tomar. 3 (*employ*) contratar. 4 (*compete with*) competir con.

◆**take out** *vtr* sacar, quitar; **he's taking me out to dinner**, me ha invitado a cenar fuera. ◆**take over** *vtr Com Pol* tomar posesión de; **the rebels took over the country**, los rebeldes se apoderaron del país. II *vi* **t. over from sb**, relevar a algn. ◆**take to** *vi* (*become fond of*) coger cariño a; **to t. to drink**, darse a la bebida. ◆**take up** *vtr* 1 *Sew* acortar. 2 (*accept*) aceptar; (*adopt*) adoptar. 3 **I've taken up the piano/French**, he empezado a tocar el piano/a aprender francés. 4 (*occupy*) ocupar.

takeaway ['teɪkəweɪ] *GB* I *n* (*food*) comida *f* para llevar; (*restaurant*) restaurante *m* que vende comida para llevar. II *adj* (*food*) para llevar.

take-home pay ['teɪkhəʊmpeɪ] *n* sueldo neto.

takeoff ['teɪkɒf] *n* 1 *Av* despegue *m*. 2 (*imitation*) imitación burlona.

takeover ['teɪkəʊvər] *n Com* absorción *f*; **military t.**, golpe *m* de estado; **t. bid**, oferta pública de adquisición, OPA *f*.

takings ['teɪkɪŋz] *npl Com* recaudación *f sing*.

talc [tælk] *n* talco *m*.

talcum powder ['tælkəmpaʊdər] *n* (polvos *mpl* de) talco *m*.

tale [teɪl] *n* cuento *m*; **to tell tales**, contar chismes.

talent ['tælənt] *n* talento *m*.

talented ['tæləntɪd] *adj* dotado,-a.

talk [tɔːk] I *vi* hablar; (*chat*) charlar; (*gossip*) chismorrear; *fam* **now you're talking!**, ¡eso sí que me interesa!. II *vtr* **to t. nonsense**, decir tonterías; **to t. sense**, hablar con sentido común; **to t. shop**, hablar del trabajo. III *n* 1 (*conversation*) conversación *f*. 2 (*words*) palabras *fpl*; **he's all t.**, no hace más que hablar. 3 (*rumour*) rumor *m*; (*gossip*) chismes *mpl*. 4 (*lecture*) charla *f*. ◆**talk into** *vtr* **to t. sb into sth**, convencer a algn para que haga algo. ◆**talk out of** *vtr* **to t. sb out of sth**, disuadir a algn de que haga algo. ◆**talk over** *vtr* discutir.

talkative ['tɔːkətɪv] *adj* hablador,-a.

talking ['tɔːkɪŋ] *n* **no t. please!**, ¡silencio, por favor!; **t. point**, tema *m* de conversación.

talking-to ['tɔːkɪŋtuː] *n fam* bronca *f*.

tall [tɔːl] *adj* alto,-a; **a tree ten metres t.**, un árbol de diez metros (de alto); **how t. are you?**, ¿cuánto mides?; *fig* **that's a t. order**, eso es mucho pedir.

tally ['tælɪ] I *vi* **to t. with sth**, corresponderse con algo. II *n Com* apunte *m*; **to keep a t. of**, llevar la cuenta de.

talon ['tælən] *n* garra *f*.

tambourine [tæmbə'riːn] *n* pandereta *f*.

tame [teɪm] I *adj* 1 (*animal*) domado,-a; (*by nature*) manso,-a; (*person*) dócil. 2 (*style*) soso,-a. II *vtr* domar.

tamper ['tæmpər] *vi* **to t. with**, (*text*) adulterar; (*records, an entry*) falsificar; (*lock*) intentar forzar.

tampon ['tæmpɒn] *n* tampón *m*.

tan [tæn] I *n* (*colour*) marrón rojizo. 2 (*of skin*) bronceado *m*. II *adj* (*colour*) marrón rojizo. III *vtr* 1 (*leather*) curtir. 2 (*skin*) broncear. IV *vi* ponerse moreno,-a.

tang [tæŋ] *n* sabor *m* fuerte.

tangent ['tændʒənt] *n* tangente *f*; *fig* **to go off at a t.**, salirse por la tangente.

tangerine [tændʒə'riːn] *n* clementina *f*.

tangible ['tændʒəbəl] *adj* tangible.

tangle ['tæŋgəl] *n* (*of thread*) maraña *f*; *fig* lío *m*; *fig* **to get into a t.**, hacerse un lío.

tank [tæŋk] *n* 1 (*container*) depósito *m*. 2 *Mil* tanque *m*.

tanker ['tæŋkər] *n Naut* tanque *m*; (*for oil*) petrolero *m*; *Aut* camión *m* cisterna.

Tannoy® ['tænɔɪ] *n* sistema *m* de megafonía.

tantalize ['tæntəlaɪz] *vtr* atormentar.

tantalizing ['tæntəlaɪzɪŋ] *adj* atormentador,-a.

tantamount ['tæntəmaʊnt] *adj* **t. to**, equivalente a.

tantrum ['tæntrəm] *n* rabieta *f*.

tap¹ [tæp] I *vtr* golpear suavemente; (*with hand*) dar una palmadita a. II *vi* **to t. at the door**, llamar suavemente a la puerta. II *n* golpecito *m*; **t. dancing**, claqué *m*.

tap² [tæp] I *n* (*for water*) grifo *m*; *fig* **funds on t.**, fondos *mpl* disponibles. II *vtr* 1 (*tree*) sangrar; *fig* **to t. new markets**, explotar nuevos mercados. 2 (*phone*) pinchar.

tape [teɪp] I *n* 1 cinta *f*; (*sticky*), cinta adhesiva; **t. measure**, cinta métrica. 2 (*for recording*) cinta *f* (magnetofónica); **t. recorder**, magnetófono *m*, cassette *m*; **t. recording**, grabación *f*. II *vtr* 1 pegar (con cinta adhesiva). 2 (*record*) grabar (en cinta).

taper ['teɪpər] I *vi* estrecharse; (*to a point*) afilarse. II *n* (*candle*) vela *f*. ◆**taper off** *vi* ir disminuyendo.

tapestry ['tæpɪstrɪ] *n* tapiz *m*.

tapping ['tæpɪŋ] *n* (*of tree*) sangría *f*; (*of resources*) explotación *f*; *Tel* intervención *f* ilegal de un teléfono.

tar [tɑːr] *n* alquitrán *m*.

target ['tɑːgɪt] *n* 1 (*object aimed at*) blanco *m*; **t. practice**, tiro *m* al blanco. 2 (*purpose*) meta *f*.

tariff ['tærɪf] *n* tarifa *f*, arancel *m*.

tarmac® ['tɑːmæk] I *n* 1 (*substance*) alquitrán *m*. 2 *Av* pista *f* de aterrizaje. II *vtr* alquitranar.

tarnish ['tɑːnɪʃ] *vtr* deslustrar.

tarpaulin [tɑː'pɔːlɪn] *n* lona *f*.

tart¹ [tɑːt] n GB Culin tarta f.

tart² [tɑːt] adj (taste) ácido,-a, agrio,-a.

tart³ [tɑːt] fam I n puta f. II vtr GB to t. oneself up, emperifollarse.

tartan ['tɑːtən] n tartán m.

tartar ['tɑːtəʳ] n 1 Chem tártaro m. 2 Culin t. sauce, salsa tártara.

task [tɑːsk] n tarea f; **to take sb to t.**, reprender a algn; Mil t. force, destacamento m (de fuerzas).

tassel ['tæsəl] n borla f.

taste [teɪst] I n 1 (sense) gusto m; (flavour) sabor m; **it has a burnt t.**, sabe a quemado. 2 (sample) (of food) bocado m; (of drink) trago m; **to give sb a t. of his own medicine**, pagar a algn con la misma moneda. 3 (liking) afición f; **to have a t. for sth**, gustarle a uno algo. 4 in bad t., de mal gusto; **to have (good) t.**, tener (buen) gusto. II vtr (sample) probar. III vi to t. of sth, saber a algo.

tasteful ['teɪstful] adj de buen gusto.

tasteless ['teɪstlɪs] adj 1 (food) soso,-a. 2 (in bad taste) de mal gusto.

tasty ['teɪstɪ] adj (tastier, tastiest) sabroso,-a.

tattered ['tætəd] adj hecho,-a jirones.

tatters ['tætəz] npl en t., hecho,-a jirones.

tattoo¹ [tæ'tuː] n Mil retreta f.

tattoo² [tæ'tuː] II n (mark) tatuaje m.

tatty ['tætɪ] adj (tattier, tattiest) GB en mal estado; (material, clothing) raído,-a; (décor) deslustrado,-a.

taught [tɔːt] pt & pp → teach.

taunt [tɔːnt] I vtr to t. sb with sth, echar algo en cara a algn. II n pulla f.

Taurus [tɔːrəs] n Tauro m.

taut [tɔːt] adj tenso,-a, tirante.

tavern ['tævən] n taberna f.

tawdry ['tɔːdrɪ] adj (tawdrier, tawdriest) hortera.

tawn(e)y ['tɔːnɪ] adj leonado,-a, rojizo,-a.

tax [tæks] I n impuesto m; **t. free**, exento,-a de impuestos; **t. collector**, recaudador,-a m,f (de impuestos); **t. evasion**, evasión f fiscal; **t. return**, declaración f de renta. II vtr 1 gravar. 2 (patience etc) poner a prueba.

taxable ['tæksəbəl] adj imponible.

taxation [tæk'seɪʃən] n impuestos mpl.

taxi ['tæksɪ] I n taxi m; **t. driver**, taxista mf; **t. rank**, parada f de taxis. II vi (aircraft) rodar por la pista.

taxidermy ['tæksɪdɜːmɪ] n taxidermia f.

taxing ['tæksɪŋ] adj exigente.

taxpayer ['tækspeɪəʳ] n contribuyente mf.

TB, tb [tiː'biː] abbr of tuberculosis.

tea [tiː] n 1 té m; **t. bag**, bolsita f de té; **t. break**, descanso m; **t. cosy**, cubretetera f; **t. leaf**, hoja f de té; **t. service** or **set**, juego m de té; **t. towel**, paño m (de cocina). 2 (snack) merienda f; (high) **t.**, merienda-cena f.

teach [tiːtʃ] I vtr (pt & pp taught) enseñar; (subject) dar clases de; **to t. sb (how) to do sth**, enseñar a algn a hacer algo. II vi dar clases, ser profesor,-a.

teacher ['tiːtʃəʳ] n profesor,-a m,f; (in primary school) maestro,-a m,f.

teaching ['tiːtʃɪŋ] n enseñanza f.

teacup ['tiːkʌp] n taza f de té.

teak [tiːk] n teca f.

team [tiːm] n equipo m; (of oxen) yunta f.

team-mate ['tiːmmeɪt] n compañero,-a m,f de equipo.

teamwork ['tiːmwɜːk] n trabajo m en equipo.

teapot ['tiːpɒt] n tetera f.

tear¹ [tɪəʳ] n lágrima f; **to be in tears**, estar llorando; **t. gas**, gas lacrimógeno.

tear² [teəʳ] I vtr (pt tore; pp torn) 1 rajar, desgarrar. 2 **to t. sth out of sb's hands**, arrancarle algo de las manos a algn. II vi 1 (cloth) rajarse. 2 **to t. along**, ir a toda velocidad. III n desgarrón m; (in clothes) rasgón m. ◆**tear down** vtr derribar. ◆**tear off** vtr arrancar. ◆**tear out** vtr arrancar. ◆**tear up** vtr 1 romper, hacer pedazos. 2 (uproot) arrancar de raíz.

tearful ['tɪəful] adj lloroso,-a.

tearoom ['tiːruːm] n GB → teashop.

tease [tiːz] I vtr tomar el pelo a. II n bromista mf.

teashop ['tiːʃɒp] n GB salón m de té.

teaspoon ['tiːspuːn] n cucharilla f.

teaspoonful ['tiːspuːnful] n cucharadita f.

teat [tiːt] n (of animal) teta f; (of bottle) tetina f.

teatime ['tiːtaɪm] n hora f del té.

technical ['teknɪkəl] adj técnico,-a; **t. college**, instituto m de formación profesional. ◆**technically** adv (theoretically) en teoría.

technicality [teknɪ'kælɪtɪ] n detalle técnico.

technician [tek'nɪʃən] n técnico,-a m,f.

technique [tek'niːk] n técnica f.

technological [teknə'lɒdʒɪkəl] adj tecnológico,-a.

technology [tek'nɒlədʒɪ] n tecnología f.

teddy bear ['tedɪbeəʳ] n oso m de felpa.

tedious ['tiːdɪəs] adj tedioso,-a, aburrido,-a.

tee [tiː] n Golf tee m.

teem [tiːm] vi **to t. with**, rebosar de; fam **it was teeming down**, llovía a cántaros.

teenage ['tiːneɪdʒ] adj adolescente.

teenager ['tiːneɪdʒəʳ] n adolescente mf.

teens [tiːnz] npl adolescencia f sing.

tee-shirt ['tiːʃɜːt] n camiseta f.

teeter ['tiːtəʳ] vi balancearse.

teeth [tiːθ] npl → tooth.

teethe [tiːð] vi echar los dientes.

teething ['tiːðɪŋ] n **t. ring**, chupador m; fig **t. troubles**, dificultades fpl iniciales.

teetotaller [tiː'təʊtələʳ] n abstemio,-a

m,f.

telecommunications ['telɪkəmjuːnɪ'keɪʃənz] n telecomunicaciones fpl.

telegram ['telɪgræm] n telegrama m.

telegraph ['telɪgrɑːf, 'telɪgræf] I n telégrafo m; t. pole, poste telegráfico. II vtr & vi telegrafiar.

telepathy [tɪ'lepəθɪ] n telepatía f.

telephone ['telɪfəʊn] I n teléfono m; GB t. booth, t. box, cabina f (telefónica); t. call, llamada telefónica; t. directory, guía telefónica; t. number, número m de teléfono. II vtr telefonear, llamar por teléfono.

telephonist [tɪ'lefənɪst] n GB telefonista mf.

telephoto ['telɪfəʊtəʊ] adj t. lens, teleobjetivo m.

teleprinter ['telɪprɪntər] n teletipo m.

telescope ['telɪskəʊp] I n telescopio m. II vi plegarse (como un catalejo). III vtr plegar.

telescopic [telɪ'skɒptk] adj (umbrella) plegable.

televise ['telɪvaɪz] vtr televisar.

television [telɪ'vɪʒən] n televisión f; t. programme, programa m de televisión; t. (set), televisor m.

telex ['teleks] I n télex m. II vtr enviar por télex.

tell [tel] I vtr (pt & pp told) 1 (say) decir; (relate) contar; (inform) comunicar; to t. lies, mentir; to t. sb about sth, contarle algo a algn; you're telling me!, ¡a mí me lo vas a contar! 2 (order) mandar; to t. sb to do sth, decir a algn que haga algo. 3 (distinguish) distinguir; to know how to t. the time, saber decir la hora. 4 all told, en total. II vi 1 (reveal) reflejar. 2 who can t.?, (know) ¿quién sabe? 3 (have effect) notarse; the pressure is telling on her, está acusando la presión. ◆**tell off** vtr fam regañar, reñir.

teller ['telər] n (in bank etc) cajero,-a m,f.

telling ['telɪŋ] adj (action) eficaz; (blow, argument) contundente.

telltale ['telteɪl] n chivato,-a m,f; t. signs, señales reveladoras.

telly ['telɪ] n GB fam the t., la tele.

temp [temp] n (abbr of temporary) fam trabajador,-a m,f temporal.

temper ['tempər] I n 1 (mood) humor m; to keep one's t., no perder la calma; to lose one's t., perder los estribos. 2 (temperament) to have a bad t., tener (mal) genio. II vtr (in metallurgy) templar; fig suavizar.

temperament ['tempərəmənt] n temperamento m.

temperamental [tempərə'mentəl] adj temperamental.

temperate ['tempərɪt] adj 1 mesurado,-a. 2 (climate) templado,-a.

temperature ['temprɪtʃər] n temperatura f; to have a t., tener fiebre.

tempest ['tempɪst] n tempestad f.

temple¹ ['tempəl] n Archit templo m.

temple² ['tempəl] n Anat sien f.

tempo ['tempəʊ] n tempo m.

temporary ['tempərərɪ] adj provisional; (setback, improvement) momentáneo,-a; (staff) temporal.

tempt [tempt] vtr tentar; to t. providence, tentar la suerte; to t. sb to do sth, incitar a algn a hacer algo.

temptation [temp'teɪʃən] n tentación f.

tempting ['temptɪŋ] adj tentador,-a.

ten [ten] adj & n diez (m) inv.

tenable ['tenəbəl] adj (opinion) sostenible.

tenacious [tɪ'neɪʃəs] adj tenaz.

tenancy ['tenənsɪ] n (of house) alquiler m; (of land) arrendamiento m.

tenant ['tenənt] n (of house) inquilino,-a m,f; (of farm) arrendatario,-a m,f.

tend¹ [tend] vi (be inclined) tender, tener tendencia (to, a).

tend² [tend] vtr (care for) cuidar.

tendency ['tendənsɪ] n tendencia f.

tender¹ ['tendər] adj (affectionate) cariñoso,-a; (compassionate) compasivo,-a; (meat) tierno,-a.

tender² ['tendər] I vtr ofrecer; to t. one's resignation, presentar la dimisión. II vi Com tender. III n 1 Com oferta f. 2 legal t., moneda f de curso legal.

tenderness ['tendənɪs] n ternura f.

tendon ['tendən] n tendón m.

tenement ['tenɪmənt] n casa f de vecindad.

tenet ['tenɪt] n principio m.

tennis ['tenɪs] n tenis m; t. ball, pelota f de tenis; t. court, pista f de tenis; t. player, tenista mf; t. racket raqueta f de tenis; t. shoe, zapatilla f de tenis.

tenor ['tenər] n Mus tenor m.

tense¹ [tens] adj tenso,-a.

tense² [tens] n Gram tiempo m.

tension ['tenʃən] n tensión f.

tent [tent] n tienda f de campaña; t. peg, estaca f.

tentacle ['tentəkəl] n tentáculo m.

tentative ['tentətɪv] adj 1 (not definite) de prueba. 2 (hesitant) indeciso,-a.

tenterhooks ['tentəhʊks] npl fig on t., sobre ascuas.

tenth [tenθ] I adj & n décimo,-a (m,f). II n (fraction) décimo m.

tenuous ['tenjʊəs] adj 1 tenue. 2 (argument) flojo,-a.

tenure ['tenjʊər] n 1 (of office) ocupación f. 2 (of property) arrendamiento m.

tepid ['tepɪd] adj tibio,-a.

term [tɜːm] n 1 (period) período m; Educ trimestre m; t. of office, mandato m, legislatura f; in the long/short t., a largo/corto plazo. 2 (word) término m; fig in

terms of money, en cuanto al dinero. 3 **terms**, *(conditions)* condiciones *fpl*; **to come to terms with**, hacerse a la idea de. 4 **to be on good/bad terms with sb**, tener buenas/malas relaciones con algn. II *vtr* calificar de.

terminal ['tɜːmɪnəl] I *adj* terminal; t. cancer, cáncer incurable. II *n* terminal *f*.

terminate ['tɜːmɪneɪt] I *vtr* terminar; **to t. a pregnancy**, abortar. II *vi* terminarse.

terminology [tɜːmɪ'nɒlədʒɪ] *n* terminología *f*.

terminus ['tɜːmɪnəs] *n (pl* **termini** ['tɜːmɪnaɪ]) terminal *m*.

terrace ['terəs] *n* 1 *Agr* bancal *m*. 2 *GB (of houses)* hilera *f* de casas. 3 *(patio)* terraza *f*. 4 *Ftb* **the terraces**, las gradas.

terraced ['terəst] *adj GB* t. houses, casas *fpl* (de estilo uniforme) en hilera.

terrain [tə'reɪn] *n* terreno *m*.

terrible ['terəbəl] *adj* terrible; *fig* **I feel t.**, *(ill)* me encuentro fatal. ◆**terribly** *adv* terriblemente.

terrier ['terɪər] *n* terrier *m*.

terrific [tə'rɪfɪk] *adj* 1 *fam (excellent)* fenomenal. 2 *(extreme)* tremendo,-a.

terrify ['terɪfaɪ] *vtr* aterrorizar.

terrifying ['terɪfaɪɪŋ] *adj* aterrador,-a.

territory ['terɪtərɪ] *n* territorio *m*.

terror ['terər] *n* terror *m*.

terrorism ['terərɪzəm] *n* terrorismo *m*.

terrorist ['terərɪst] *adj & n* terrorista *(mf)*.

terrorize ['terəraɪz] *vtr* aterrorizar.

terry ['terɪ] *n* t. towel, toalla *f* de rizo.

terse [tɜːs] *adj (curt)* lacónico,-a.

test [test] I *vtr* probar, someter a una prueba; *(analyse)* analizar; *Med* hacer un análisis de. II *n* prueba *f*, examen *m*; **to put to the t.**, poner a prueba; **to stand the t.**, pasar la prueba; **t. match**, partido *m* internacional; **t. pilot**, piloto *m* de pruebas; **t. tube**, probeta *f*; **t.-tube baby**, niño *m* probeta.

testament ['testəmənt] *n* testamento *m*; **Old/New T.**, Antiguo/Nuevo Testamento.

testicle ['testɪkəl] *n* testículo *m*.

testify ['testɪfaɪ] I *vtr* declarar. II *vi* *fig* **to t. to sth**, atestiguar algo.

testimonial [testɪ'məʊnɪəl] *n* recomendación *f*.

testimony ['testɪmənɪ] *n* testimonio *m*, declaración *f*.

tetanus ['tetənəs] *n* tétano(s) *m inv*.

tether ['teðər] I *n* ronzal *m*; *fig* **to be at the end of one's t.**, estar hasta la coronilla. II *vtr (animal)* atar.

Texas ['teksəs] *n* Tejas.

text [tekst] *n* texto *m*.

textbook ['tekstbʊk] *n* libro *m* de texto.

textile ['tekstaɪl] I *n* tejido *m*. II *adj* textil.

texture ['tekstʃər] *n* textura *f*.

Thai [taɪ] *adj & n* tailandés,-esa *(m,f)*.

Thailand ['taɪlænd] *n* Tailandia.

Thames [temz] *n* **the T.**, el Támesis.

than [ðæn, *unstressed* ðən] *conj* que; *(with numbers)* de; **he's older t. me**, es mayor que yo; **I have more/less t. you**, tengo más/menos que tú; **more interesting t. we thought**, más interesante de lo que creíamos; **more t. once**, más de una vez; **more t. ten people**, más de diez personas.

thank [θæŋk] *vtr* agradecer a; **t. you**, gracias.

thankful ['θæŋkfʊl] *adj* agradecido,-a.

thankless ['θæŋklɪs] *adj (task)* ingrato,-a.

thanks [θæŋks] *npl* gracias *fpl*; **no t.**, no gracias; **many t.**, muchas gracias; **t. for phoning**, gracias por llamar; **t. to**, gracias a.

thanksgiving [θæŋks'gɪvɪŋ] *n US* **T. Day**, Día *m* de Acción de Gracias.

that [ðæt, *unstressed* ðət] I *dem pron (pl those)* 1 ése *m*, ésa *f*; *(further away)* aquél *m*, aquélla *f*; **this one is new but t. is old**, éste es nuevo pero ése es viejo. 2 *(indefinite)* eso; *(remote)* aquello; **after t.**, después de eso; **like t.**, así; **t.'s right**, eso es; **t.'s where I live**, allí vivo yo; **what's t.?**, ¿qué es eso?; **who's t.?**, ¿quién es? 3 *(with relative)* el, la; **all those I saw**, todos los que vi.
II *dem adj (pl those) (masculine)* ese; *(feminine)* esa; *(further away) (masculine)* aquel; *(feminine)* aquella; **at t. time**, en aquella época; **t. book**, ese *or* aquel libro; **t. one**, ése, aquél.
III *rel pron* 1 *(subject, direct object)* que; **all (t.) you said**, todo lo que dijiste; **the letter (t.) I sent you**, la carta que te envié. 2 *(governed by preposition)* que, el/la que, los/las que, el/la cual, los/las cuales; **the car (t.) they came in**, el coche en el que vinieron. 3 *(when)* que, en que; **the moment (t.) you arrived**, en el momento en que llegaste.
IV *conj* que; **come here so t. I can see you**, ven aquí (para) que te vea; **he said (t.) he would come**, dijo que vendría.
V *adv* así de, tanto, tan; **cut off t. much**, córteme un trozo así de grande; **I don't think it can be t. old**, no creo que sea tan viejo; **we haven't got t. much money**, no tenemos tanto dinero.

thatched [θætʃt] *adj* cubierto,-a con paja; **t. cottage**, casita *f* con techo de paja; **t. roof**, techo *m* de paja.

thaw [θɔː] I *vtr (snow)* derretir; *(food, freezer)* descongelar. II *vi* descongelarse; *(snow)* derretirse. III *n* deshielo *m*.

the [ðə, *before vowel* ðɪ, *emphatic* ðiː] I *def art* 1 el, la; *pl* los, las; **at** *or* **to t.**, al, a la; *pl* a los, a las; **of** *or* **from t.**, del, de la; *pl* de los, de las; **t. Alps**, los Alpes; **t. right time**, la hora exacta; **t. voice of t. people**, la voz del pueblo. 2 *(omitted)*

George t. Sixth, Jorge Sexto. 3 by t. day, al día; by t. dozen, a docenas. 4 (with adjectives used as nouns) t. elderly, los ancianos. 5 (indicating kind) he's not t. person to do that, no es de los que hacen tales cosas. 6 (enough) he hasn't t. patience to wait, no tiene suficiente paciencia para esperar. II adv t. more t. merrier, cuantos más mejor; t. sooner t. better, cuanto antes mejor.

theatre, US theater ['θɪətər] n teatro m.

theatre-goer, US theater-goer ['θɪətəgəʊər] n aficionado,-a m,f al teatro.

theatrical [θɪ'ætrɪkəl] adj teatral.

theft [θeft] n robo m; petty t., hurto m.

their [ðeər] poss adj (one thing) su; (various things) sus.

theirs [ðeəz] poss pron (el) suyo, (la) suya; pl (los) suyos, (las) suyas.

them [ðem] pers pron pl 1 (direct object) los, las; (indirect object) les; I know t., los or las conozco; I shall tell t. so, se lo diré (a ellos or ellas); it's t.!, ¡son ellos!; speak to t., hábleles. 2 (with preposition) ellos, ellas; walk in front of t., camine delante de ellos; they took the keys away with t., se llevaron las llaves; both of t., the two of t., los dos; neither of t., ninguno de los dos; none of t., ninguno de ellos.

theme [θiːm] n tema m; t. tune, sintonía f.

themselves [ðəm'selvz] pers pron pl (as subject) ellos mismos, ellas mismas; (as direct or indirect object) se; (after a preposition) sí mismos, sí mismas; they did it by t., lo hicieron ellos solos.

then [ðen] adv 1 (at that time) entonces; since t., desde entonces; there and t., en el acto; till t., hasta entonces. 2 (next, afterwards) luego. 3 (anyway) de todas formas. 4 (in that case) entonces; go t., pues vete. II conj entonces. III adj the t. president, el entonces presidente.

theology [θɪ'blədʒɪ] n teología f.

theoretic(al) [θɪə'retɪk(əl)] adj teórico,-a.
◆theoretically adv teóricamente.

theory ['θɪərɪ] n teoría f.

therapist ['θerəpɪst] n terapeuta mf.

therapy ['θerəpɪ] n terapia f.

there [ðeər] adv 1 (indicating place) allí, allá; (nearer speaker) ahí; here and t., acá y allá; in t., ahí dentro; is Peter t.?, ¿está Peter t.? 2 (emphatic) that man t., aquel hombre. 3 (unstressed) t. is..., t. are..., hay...; t. were many cars, había muchos coches; t. were six of us, éramos seis. 4 (in respect) t.'s the difficulty, ahí está la dificultad. II interj so t.!, ¡ea!; t., t., bien, bien.

thereabouts [ðeərə'baʊts], US thereabout ['ðeərəbaʊt] adv in Cambridge or t., en Cambridge o por allí cerca; at four o'clock or t., a las cuatro o así.

thereafter [ðeər'ɑːftər] adv a partir de entonces.

thereby [ðeə'baɪ] adv por eso o ello.

therefore ['ðeəfɔːr] adv por lo tanto, por eso.

thermal ['θɜːməl] adj (spring) termal; Phys térmico,-a. II n Meteor corriente térmica.

thermometer [θə'mɒmɪtər] n termómetro m.

Thermos® ['θɜːməs] n T. (flask), termo m.

thermostat ['θɜːməstæt] n termostato m.

thesaurus [θɪ'sɔːrəs] n diccionario m de sinónimos.

these [ðiːz] I dem adj estos,-as. II dem pron pl éstos,-as; → this.

thesis ['θiːsɪs] n tesis f inv.

they [ðeɪ] pron pl 1 ellos, ellas; t. are dancing, están bailando; t. are rich, son ricos. 2 (stressed) t. alone, ellos solos; t. themselves told me, me lo dijeron ellos mismos. 3 (with relative) los, las. 4 (indefinite) that's what t. say, eso es lo que se dice; t. say that ..., se dice que ...

thick [θɪk] I adj 1 (book etc) grueso,-a; a wall two metres t., un muro de dos metros de espesor. 2 (dense) espeso,-a. 3 fam (stupid) tonto,-a. II adv densamente. III n to be in the t. of it, estar metido,-a de lleno.

thicken ['θɪkən] I vtr espesar. II vi espesarse; fig (plot) complicarse.

thickness ['θɪknɪs] n (of wall etc) espesor m; (of wire, lips) grueso m; (of liquid, woodland) espesura f.

thickset [θɪk'set] adj (person) rechoncho,-a.

thick-skinned [θɪk'skɪnd] adj fig poco sensible.

thief [θiːf] n (pl thieves [θiːvz]) ladrón, -ona m,f.

thigh [θaɪ] n muslo m.

thimble ['θɪmbəl] n dedal m.

thin [θɪn] I adj (thinner, thinnest) 1 delgado,-a; a t. slice, una loncha fina. 2 (hair, vegetation) ralo,-a; (liquid) claro,-a; (population) escaso,-a. 3 fig (voice) débil; a t. excuse, un pobre pretexto. II vtr to t. (down), (paint) diluir. ◆thinly adv poco, ligeramente.

thing [θɪŋ] n 1 cosa f; my things, (clothing) mi ropa f sing; (possessions) mis cosas fpl; for one t., en primer lugar; the t. is ..., resulta que ...; what with one t. and another, entre unas cosas y otras; as things are, tal como están las cosas. 2 poor little t.!, ¡pobrecito,-a!

think [θɪŋk] I vtr (pt & pp thought) 1 (believe) pensar, creer; I t. so/not, creo que sí/no. 2 I thought as much, ya me lo imaginaba. II vi 1 pensar (of, about, en); give me time to t., dame tiempo para reflexionar; to t. ahead, prevenir. 2 (have *as opinion*) opinar, pensar; **to t. highly of sb**, apreciar a algn; **what do you t.?**, ¿a ti qué te parece? **3 just t.!**, ¡imagínate! ◆**think out** *vtr* meditar; **a carefully thought-out answer**, una respuesta razonada. ◆**think over** *vtr* reflexionar; **we'll have to t. it over**, lo tendremos que pensar. ◆**think up** *vtr* imaginar, idear.

thinking ['θɪŋkɪŋ] *adj* racional.

think-tank ['θɪŋktæŋk] *n fam* grupo *m* de expertos.

third [θɜːd] I *adj* tercero,-a; (*before masculine singular noun*) tercer; (**on**) **the t. of March**, el tres de marzo; **the T. World**, el Tercer Mundo; **t. party insurance**, seguro *m* a terceros. II *n* 1 (*in series*) tercero,-a *m,f*. 2 (*fraction*) tercio *m*, tercera parte. ◆**thirdly** *adv* en tercer lugar.

third-rate ['θɜːdreɪt] *adj* de calidad inferior.

thirst [θɜːst] *n* sed *f*.

thirsty ['θɜːstɪ] *adj* (**thirstier, thirstiest**) sediento,-a; **to be t.**, tener sed.

thirteen [θɜː'tiːn] *adj & n* trece (*m*) *inv*.

thirteenth [θɜː'tiːnθ] I *adj & n* decimotercero,-a (*m,f*). II *n* (*fraction*) decimotercera parte.

thirtieth ['θɜːtɪɪθ] I *adj & n* trigésimo,-a (*m,f*). II *n* (*fraction*) trigésima parte.

thirty ['θɜːtɪ] *adj & n* treinta (*m*) *inv*.

this [ðɪs] I *dem adj* (*pl* **these**) (*masculine*) este; (*feminine*) esta; **t. book/these books**, este libro/estos libros; **t. one**, éste, ésta. II (*pl* **these**) *dem pron* 1 (*indefinite*) esto; **it was like t.**, fue así. 2 (*place*) **t. is where we met**, fue aquí donde nos conocimos. 3 (*time*) **it should have come before t.**, debería haber llegado ya. 4 (*specific person or thing*) éste *m*, ésta *f*; **I prefer these to those**, me gustan más éstos que aquéllos; (*introduction*) **t. ...is Mr Alvarez**, le presento al Sr. Alvarez; *Tel* **t. is Julia** (*speaking*), soy Julia. III *adv* **he got t. far**, llegó hasta aquí; **t. small/big**, así de pequeño/grande.

thistle ['θɪsəl] *n* cardo *m*.

thong [θɒŋ] *n* correa *f*.

thorax ['θɔːræks] *n* tórax *m*.

thorn [θɔːn] *n* espina *f*.

thorough ['θʌrə] *adj* (*careful*) minucioso,-a; (*work*) concienzudo,-a; (*knowledge*) profundo,-a; **to carry out a enquiry into a matter**, investigar a fondo un asunto. ◆**thoroughly** *adv* (*carefully*) a fondo; (*wholly*) completamente.

thoroughbred ['θʌrəbred] I *adj* (*horse*) de pura sangre. II *n* (*horse*) pura sangre *mf*.

thoroughfare ['θʌrəfeər] *n* (*road*) carretera *f*; (*street*) calle *f*.

those [ðəʊz] I *dem pron pl* ésos,-as; (*remote*) aquéllos,-as; **t. who**, los que, las que. II *dem adj* esos,-as; (*remote*) aquellos,-as; → **that** I & II.

though [ðəʊ] I *conj* 1 aunque; **strange as**

it may seem, por (muy) extraño que parezca. **2 as t.**, como si; **it looks as t. he's gone**, parece que se ha ido. II *adv* sin embargo.

thought [θɔːt] *n* 1 (*act of thinking*) pensamiento *m*; **what a tempting t.!**, ¡qué idea más tentadora! 2 (*reflection*) reflexión *f*. 3 **it's the t. that counts**, (*intention*) lo que cuenta es la intención.

thoughtful ['θɔːtful] *adj* (*pensive*) pensativo,-a; (*considerate*) atento,-a.

thoughtless ['θɔːtlɪs] *adj* (*person*) desconsiderado,-a; (*action*) irreflexivo,-a.

thousand ['θaʊzənd] *adj & n* mil (*m*) *inv*; **thousands of people**, miles de personas.

thousandth ['θaʊzənθ] I *adj* milésimo,-a. II *n* 1 (*in series*) milésimo,-a *m,f*. 2 (*fraction*) milésima parte.

thrash [θræʃ] I *vtr* dar una paliza a. II *vi* **to t. about** *or* **around**, agitarse. ◆**thrash out** *vtr* discutir a fondo.

thread [θred] I *n* 1 hilo *m*; **length of t.**, hebra *f*. 2 (*of screw*) rosca *f*. II *vtr* (*needle*) enhebrar. II **to t. one's way**, colarse (**through**, por).

threadbare ['θredbeər] *adj* raído,-a.

threat [θret] *n* amenaza *f*.

threaten ['θretən] *vtr* amenazar; **to t. to do sth**, amenazar con hacer algo.

threatening ['θretənɪŋ] *adj* amenazador, -a. ◆**threateningly** *adv* de modo amenazador.

three [θriː] *adj & n* tres (*m*).

three-dimensional [θriːdɪ'menʃənəl] *adj* tridimensional.

threefold ['θriːfəʊld] I *adj* triple. II *adv* tres veces; **to increase t.**, triplicarse.

three-piece ['θriːpiːs] *adj* **t.-p. suit**, traje *m* de tres piezas; **t.-p. suite**, tresillo *m*.

three-ply ['θriːplaɪ] *adj* de tres hebras.

three-wheeler [θriː'wiːlər] *n Aut* coche *m* de tres ruedas; (*tricycle*) triciclo *m*.

thresh [θreʃ] *vtr* trillar.

threshold ['θreʃəʊld] *n* umbral *m*; *fig* **to be on the t. of**, estar a las puertas *o* en los umbrales de.

threw [θruː] *pt* → **throw**.

thrifty ['θrɪftɪ] *adj* (**thriftier, thriftiest**) económico,-a, ahorrador,-a.

thrill [θrɪl] I *n* 1 (*excitement*) emoción *f*. 2 (*quiver*) estremecimiento *m*. II *vtr* (*excite*) emocionar; (*audience*) entusiasmar.

thriller ['θrɪlər] *n* novela *f*/película *f* de suspense.

thrilling ['θrɪlɪŋ] *adj* emocionante.

thrive [θraɪv] *vi* (*pt* **thrived** *or* **throve**; *pp* **thrived** *or* **thriven** ['θrɪvən]) 1 (*person*) rebosar de salud. 2 *fig* (*business*) prosperar; **he thrives on it**, le viene de maravilla.

thriving ['θraɪvɪŋ] *adj fig* próspero,-a.

throat [θrəʊt] *n* garganta *f*.

throb [θrɒb] I *n* (*of heart*) latido *m*; (*of machine*) zumbido *m*. II *vi* (*heart*) latir; (*machine*) zumbar; **my head is throbbing**, me va a estallar la cabeza.

throes [θrəʊz] *npl* to be in one's death t., estar agonizando; *fig* in the t. of ..., en pleno, -a ....

throne [θrəʊn] *n* trono *m*.

throng [θrɒŋ] I *n* multitud *f*, gentío *m*. II *vi* apiñarse. III *vtr* atestar.

throttle ['θrɒtəl] I *n* t. (valve), (*of engine*) válvula reguladora. II *vtr* (*person*) estrangular. ◆**throttle back** *vtr* (*engine*) desacelerar.

through [θruː] I *prep* 1 (*place*) a través de, por; to look t. the window, mirar por la ventana. 2 (*time*) a lo largo de; all t. his life, durante toda su vida. 3 (*by means of*) por, mediante; I learnt of it t. Jack, me enteré por Jack. 4 (*because of*) a *or* por causa de; t. ignorance, por ignorancia. II *adj* a t. train, un tren directo; t. traffic, tránsito *m*. III *adv* 1 (*from one side to the other*) de un lado a otro; to let sb t., dejar pasar a algn; *fig* socialist/ French t. and t., socialista/francés por los cuatro costados. 2 I'm t. with him, he terminado con él. 3 *Tel* to get t. to sb, comunicar con algn; you're t., ¡hablen!

throughout [θruː'aʊt] I *prep* por todo,-a; t. the year, durante todo el año. II *adv* (*place*) en todas partes; (*time*) todo el tiempo.

throve [θrəʊv] *pt* → **thrive**.

throw [θrəʊ] I *vtr* (*pt* **threw**; *pp* **thrown**) 1 tirar, arrojar; (*to the ground*) derribar; (*rider*) desmontar; *fig* he threw a fit, le dio un ataque; *fig* to t. a party, dar una fiesta. 2 (*disconcert*) desconcertar. II *n* tiro *m*, lanzamiento *m*; (*in wrestling*) derribo *m*. ◆**throw away** *vtr* (*rubbish*) tirar; (*money*) malgastar; (*opportunity*) perder. ◆**throw in** *vtr* tirar; *Sport* sacar de banda; *fig* to t. in the towel, arrojar la toalla. 5 (*include*) añadir; (*in deal*) incluir (gratis). ◆**throw off** *vtr* (*person, thing*) deshacerse de; (*clothes*) quitarse. ◆**throw out** *vtr* (*rubbish*) tirar; (*person*) echar. ◆**throw up** *vtr* 1 lanzar al aire. 2 *Constr* construir rápidamente. II *vi fam* vomitar, devolver.

throwaway ['θrəʊəweɪ] *adj* desechable.

throw-in ['θrəʊɪn] *n* *Sport* saque *m* de banda.

thrown [θrəʊn] *pp* → **throw**.

thru [θruː] *prep* *US* → **through**.

thrush [θrʌʃ] *n* *Orn* tordo *m*, zorzal *m*.

thrust [θrʌst] I *vtr* (*pt* & *pp* **thrust**) empujar con fuerza; he t. a letter into my hand, me puso una carta violentamente en la mano. II *n* (*push*) empujón *m*; *Av Phys* empuje *m*.

thud [θʌd] *n* ruido sordo.

thug [θʌg] *n* (*lout*) gamberro *m*; (*criminal*) criminal *m*.

thumb [θʌm] I *n* pulgar *m*. II *vtr* 1 manosear. 2 to t. a lift, hacer autostop.

◆**thumb through** *vtr* (*book*) hojear.

thumbtack ['θʌmtæk] *n* *US* chincheta *f*.

thump [θʌmp] I *n* 1 (*sound*) ruido sordo. 2 (*blow*) golpazo *m*; *fam* torta *f*. II *vtr* golpear. III *vi* 1 to t. on the table, golpear la mesa. 2 (*heart*) latir ruidosamente.

thunder ['θʌndə'] I *n* trueno *m*; t. of applause, estruendo *m* de aplausos. II *vi* tronar.

thunderbolt ['θʌndəbəʊlt] *n* (*lighting*) rayo *m*; *fig* (*news*) bomba *f*.

thunderclap ['θʌndəklæp] *n* trueno *m*.

thunderous ['θʌndərəs] *adj* *fig* ensordecedor,-a.

thunderstorm ['θʌndəstɔːm] *n* tormenta *f*.

thundery ['θʌndərɪ] *adj* (*weather*) tormentoso,-a.

Thursday ['θɜːzdɪ] *n* jueves *m*.

thus [ðʌs] *adv* así, de esta manera; and t. ..., así que ...

thwart [θwɔːt] *vtr* frustrar, desbaratar.

thyme [taɪm] *n* tomillo *m*.

thyroid ['θaɪrɔɪd] *n* tiroides *f inv*.

tiara [tɪ'ɑːrə] *n* diadema *f*; *Rel* tiara *f*.

tic [tɪk] *n* tic *m*.

tick[1] [tɪk] I *n* 1 (*sound*) tic-tac *m*. 2 *GB fam* I'll do it in a t., ahora mismo lo hago. 3 (*mark*) marca *f* de visto bueno. II *vi* hacer tic-tac. III *vtr* marcar. ◆**tick off** *vtr* 1 (*mark*) marcar. 2 *GB fam* (*reprimand*) regañar. ◆**tick over** *vi* *Aut* funcionar al ralentí.

tick[2] [tɪk] *n* *Ent* garrapata *f*.

ticket ['tɪkɪt] *n* 1 (*for bus etc*) billete *m*; *Theat* entrada *f*; (*for lottery*) décimo *m*; t. collector, revisor,-a *m,f*; t. office, taquilla *f*. 2 (*receipt*) recibo *m*. 3 (*label*) etiqueta *f*. 4 *Aut* multa *f*.

tickle ['tɪkəl] I *vtr* hacer cosquillas a. II *vi* hacer cosquillas. III *n* cosquillas *fpl*.

ticklish ['tɪklɪʃ] *adj* to be t., tener cosquillas.

tidal ['taɪdəl] *adj* de la marea; t. wave, ola *f* gigante.

tidbit ['tɪdbɪt] *n* *US* → **titbit**.

tiddlywinks ['tɪdlɪwɪŋks] *n* (*game*) pulga *f*.

tide [taɪd] *n* 1 marea *f*; high/low t., marea alta/baja. 2 *fig* (*of events*) curso *m*; the t. has turned, han cambiado las cosas; to go against the t., ir contra corriente.

tidings ['taɪdɪŋz] *npl fml* noticias *fpl*.

tidy ['taɪdɪ] I *adj* (*tidier, tidiest*) 1 (*room, habits*) ordenado,-a. 2 (*appearance*) arreglado,-a. II *vtr* arreglar; to t. away, poner en su sitio. III *vi* to t. (up), ordenar las cosas.

tie [taɪ] I *vtr* (*shoelaces etc*) atar; to t. a knot, hacer un nudo. II *vi* (*knotted*) empatar (with, con). II *n* 1 (*bond*) lazo *m*, vínculo *m*. 2 *fig* (*hindrance*) atadura *f*. 3 (*clothing*) corbata *f*. 4 *Sport* (*match*) partido *m*;

(draw) empate m. ◆**tie down** vtr sujetar; **fig to be tied down**, estar atado,-a; **fig to t. sb down to a promise**, obligar a algn a cumplir una promesa. ◆**tie up** vtr 1 (parcel, dog) atar. 2 (deal) concluir. 3 (capital) inmovilizar; **fig I'm tied up just now**, de momento estoy muy ocupado,-a.

tiebreaker ['taɪbreɪkə^r] n tie-break m.

tiepin ['taɪpɪn] n alfiler m de corbata.

tier [tɪə^r] n (of seats) fila f; (in stadium) grada f; **four-t. cake**, pastel m de cuatro pisos.

tiger ['taɪgə^r] n tigre m.

tight [taɪt] I adj 1 apretado,-a; (clothing) ajustado,-a; (seal) hermético,-a; **my shoes are too t.**, me aprietan los zapatos; **fig to be in a t. corner**, estar en un apuro. 2 (scarce) escaso,-a; **money's a bit t.**, estamos escasos de dinero. 3 (mean) agarrado,-a. 4 fam (drunk) borracho,-a. II adv estrechamente; (seal) herméticamente; **hold t.**, agárrate fuerte; **shut t.**, bien cerrado,-a; **to sit t.**, no moverse de su sitio.

tighten ['taɪtən] I vtr (screw) apretar, (rope) tensar; **fig to t. (up) restrictions**, intensificar las restricciones. II vi apretarse; (cable) tensarse.

tightfisted [taɪt'fɪstɪd] adj tacaño,-a.

tightrope ['taɪtrəʊp] n cuerda floja; **t. walker**, funámbulo,-a mf.

tights [taɪts] npl (thin) medias fpl, panties mpl; (thick) leotardos mpl; (of dancer) mallas fpl.

tile [taɪl] I n (of roof) teja f; (glazed) azulejo m; (for floor) baldosa f. II vtr (roof) tejar; (wall) azulejar; (floor) embaldosar.

tiled [taɪld] adj (roof) de con tejas; (wall) revestido,-a de azulejos; (floor) embaldosado,-a.

till¹ [tɪl] n (for cash) caja f.

till² [tɪl] vtr (field) labrar, cultivar.

till³ [tɪl] I prep hasta; **from morning t. night**, de la mañana a la noche; **t. then**, hasta entonces. II conj hasta que.

tiller ['tɪlə^r] n Naut caña f del timón.

tilt [tɪlt] I n 1 (angle) inclinación f. 2 (at) **full t.**, (speed) a toda velocidad. II vi **to t. over**, volcarse; **to t. (up)**, inclinarse. III vtr inclinar.

timber ['tɪmbə^r] n (wood) madera f (de construcción); (trees) árboles mpl; **(piece of) t.**, viga f.

time [taɪm] I n 1 tiempo m; **all the t.**, todo el tiempo; **for some t. (past)**, desde hace algún tiempo; **I haven't seen him for a long t.**, hace mucho (tiempo) que no lo veo; **in a short t.**, en poco tiempo; **in no t.**, en un abrir y cerrar de ojos; **in t.**, a tiempo; **in three weeks' t.**, dentro de tres semanas; **to take one's t. over sth.**, hacer algo con calma; **fam to do t.**, cumplir una condena; **t. bomb**, bomba f

de relojería; **t. limit**, límite m de tiempo; **(for payment etc)** plazo m; **t. switch**, interruptor m electrónico automático; **t. zone**, huso horario. 2 (era) época f, tiempos mpl; **a sign of the times**, un signo de los tiempos; **to be behind the times**, tener ideas anticuadas. 3 (point in time) momento m; **(at) any t.** (you like), cuando quiera; **at no t.**, en ningún momento; **at that t.**, (en aquel) entonces; **at the same t.**, al mismo tiempo; **at times**, a veces; **from t. to t.**, de vez en cuando; **he may turn up at any t.**, puede llegar en cualquier momento. 4 (time of day) hora f; **about t. too!**, ¡ya era hora!; **in good t.**, con anticipación; **on t.**, puntualmente; **what's the t.?**, ¿qué hora es? 5 **t. of year**, época f del año. 6 **to have a good/bad t.**, pasarlo bien/mal. 7 (occasion) vez f; **four at a t.**, cuatro a la vez; **next t.**, la próxima vez; **several times over**, varias veces; **three times running**, tres veces seguidas; **t. after t.**, una y otra vez. 8 (in multiplication) **three times four**, tres (multiplicado) por cuatro; **four times as big**, cuatro veces más grande. 9 Mus compás m; **in t.**, al compás.
II vtr 1 (speech) calcular la duración de; Sport (race) cronometrar. 2 (choose the time of) escoger el momento oportuno para.

time-consuming ['taɪmkənsju:mɪŋ] adj que ocupa mucho tiempo.

time-lag ['taɪmlæg] n intervalo m.

timeless ['taɪmlɪs] adj eterno,-a.

timely ['taɪmlɪ] adj (**timelier**, **timeliest**) oportuno,-a.

timer ['taɪmə^r] n (device) temporizador m.

timetable ['taɪmteɪbəl] n horario m.

timid ['tɪmɪd] adj tímido,-a.

timing ['taɪmɪŋ] n 1 (timeliness) oportunidad f; (coordination) coordinación f; **your t. was wrong**, no calculaste bien. 2 Sport cronometraje m.

tin [tɪn] I n 1 (metal) estaño m; **t. plate**, hojalata f. 2 (container) lata f. II vtr (tins) enlatar; **tinned food**, conservas fpl.

tinfoil ['tɪnfɔɪl] n papel m de estaño.

tinge [tɪndʒ] I n tinte m, matiz m. II vtr teñir.

tingle ['tɪŋgəl] vi **my feet are tingling**, siento un hormigueo en los pies.

tinker ['tɪŋkə^r] I n pej calderero,-a mf. II vi **stop tinkering with the radio**, deja de toquetear la radio.

tinkle ['tɪŋkəl] vi tintinear.

tin-opener ['tɪnəʊpənə^r] n abrelatas m inv.

tinsel ['tɪnsəl] n oropel m.

tint [tɪnt] I n tinte m, matiz m. II vtr teñir; **to t. one's hair**, teñirse el pelo.

tiny ['taɪnɪ] adj (**tinier**, **tiniest**) pequeño,-a; **a t. bit**, un poquitín.

tip¹ [tɪp] **I** n (end) punta f; (of cigarette) colilla f; (of cigarette) lo tengo en la punta de la lengua. **II** vtr poner cantera a; **tipped with steel**, con punta de acero.

tip² [tɪp] **I** n 1 (gratuity) propina f. 2 (advice) consejo m. 3 Sport (racing) pronóstico m. **II** vtr 1 dar una propina a. 2 Sport pronosticar. ◆**tip off** vtr (police) dar el chivatazo a.

tip³ [tɪp] **I** n GB rubbish t., vertedero m. **II** vtr inclinar; GB (rubbish) verter. **III** vi to t. (up), ladearse; (cart) bascular. ◆**tip over** I vtr volcar. **II** vi volcarse.

tipple ['tɪpəl] fam **I** vi empinar el codo. **II** n bebida alcohólica; **what's your t.?**, ¿qué te gusta beber?

tipsy ['tɪpsɪ] adj (tipsier, tipsiest) contentillo,-a.

tiptoe ['tɪptəʊ] **I** vi andar de puntillas; to t. in/out, entrar/salir de puntillas. **II** n on t., de puntillas.

tiptop ['tɪptɒp] adj fam de primera.

tire¹ ['taɪə] n US → tyre.

tire² [taɪə] **I** vtr cansar; to t. sb out, agotar a algn. **II** vi cansarse; to t. of doing sth, cansarse de hacer algo.

tired [taɪəd] adj cansado,-a; t. out, rendido,-a; to be t., estar cansado,-a; to be t. of sth, estar harto,-a de algo.

tireless ['taɪəlɪs] adj incansable.

tiresome ['taɪəsəm] adj pesado,-a.

tiring ['taɪərɪŋ] adj agotador,-a.

tissue ['tɪʃuː, 'tɪsjuː] n 1 Biol tejido m. 2 Tex tisú m; t. paper, papel m de seda. 3 (handkerchief) pañuelo m de papel, kleenex® m.

tit¹ [tɪt] n to give t. for tat, devolver la pelota.

tit² [tɪt] n sl (breast) teta f.

titbit ['tɪtbɪt] n golosina f.

titillate ['tɪtɪleɪt] vtr excitar.

tit(i)vate ['tɪtɪveɪt] vtr emperifollar.

title ['taɪtəl] n 1 título m; Cin credit titles, ficha técnica; t. page, portada f; t. role, papel m principal. 2 Jur título m.

titter ['tɪtə] **I** vi reírse nerviosamente; (foolishly) reírse tontamente. **II** n risa ahogada; (foolish) risilla tonta.

titular ['tɪtjʊlə] adj titular.

TM abbr of **trademark**, marca f (de fábrica).

to [tuː, unstressed before vowels tʊ, before consonants tə] **I** prep 1 (with place) a; (expressing direction) hacia; from town to town, de ciudad en ciudad; he went to France/Japan, fue a Francia/Japón; I'm going to Mary's, voy a casa de Mary; it is thirty miles to London, Londres está a treinta millas; the train to Madrid, el tren de Madrid; to the east, hacia el este; to the right, a la derecha; what school do you go to?, ¿a qué escuela vas? 2 (time) a; from day to day, de día

en día; from two to four, de dos a cuatro; ten (minutes) to six, las seis menos diez. 3 (as far as) hasta; accurate to a millimetre, exacto,-a hasta el milímetro. 4 (with indirect object) he gave it to his cousin, se lo dio a su primo; what's that to you?, ¿qué te importa a ti? 5 (towards a person) he was very kind to me, se portó muy bien conmigo. 6 (of) de; heir to an estate, heredero m de una propiedad; adviser to the president, consejero m del presidente. 7 to come to sb's assistance, acudir en ayuda de algn; to everyone's surprise, con sorpresa de todos; to this end, con este fin. 8 to the best of my knowledge, que yo sepa. 9 (compared to) that's nothing to what I've seen, eso no es nada en comparación con lo que he visto yo. 10 (in proportion) one house to the square kilometre, una casa por kilómetro cuadrado; six votes to four, seis votos contra cuatro. 11 (about) what did he say to my suggestion?, ¿qué contestó a mi sugerencia?

II with infin 1 with simple infinitives to is not translated but is shown by the verb endings; to buy, comprar; to come, venir. 2 (in order to) para; (with verbs of motion or purpose) a, por; (with verbs to talk, se detuvo a hablar; he fought to convince them, luchó por convencerlos. 3 various verbs followed by dependent infinitives take particular prepositions (a, de, en, por, con, para etc) and others take no preposition; → the entry of the verb in question. 4 (with adj and infin) a, de; difficult to do, difícil de hacer; ready to listen, dispuesto,-a a escuchar; too hot to drink, demasiado caliente para bebérselo. 5 (with noun and infin) the first to complain, el primero en quejarse; this is the time to do it, éste es el momento de hacerlo; to have a great deal to do, tener mucho que hacer. 6 (expressing following action) he awoke to find the light still on, al despertarse encontró la lámpara todavía encendida. 7 (with verbs of ordering, wishing etc) he asked me to do it, me pidió que lo hiciera. 8 (expressing obligation) fifty employees are to go, cincuenta empleados deben ser despedidos; to have to do sth, tener que hacer algo. 9 (replacing infin) go if you want to, váyase si quiere.

III adv to go to and fro, ir y venir; to push the door to, encajar la puerta.

toad [təʊd] n sapo m.

toadstool ['təʊdstuːl] n hongo m (venenoso).

toast¹ [təʊst] Culin **I** n pan tostado; a slice of t., una tostada. **II** vtr tostar.

toast² [təʊst] **I** n (drink) brindis m inv; to drink a t. to, brindar por. **II** vtr brindar por.

toaster ['təʊstər] *n* tostador *m* (de pan).

tobacco [təˈbækəʊ] *n* tabaco *m*.

tobacconist [təˈbækənɪst] *n* GB estanquero,-a *m,f*; **t.'s (shop)**, estanco *m*.

toboggan [təˈbɒgən] *n* tobogán *m*.

today [təˈdeɪ] I *n* hoy *m*. II *adv* hoy; *(nowadays)* hoy en día; **a week t.**, justo dentro de una semana.

toddler ['tɒdlər] *n* niño,-a *m,f* que empieza a andar; **the toddlers**, los pequeñitos.

toddy ['tɒdɪ] *n* (*drink*) ponche *m*.

to-do [təˈduː] *n* lío *m*, jaleo *m*.

toe [təʊ] I *n* dedo *m* del pie; **big t.**, dedo gordo. II *vtr* **to t. the line**, conformarse.

toenail ['təʊneɪl] *n* uña *f* del dedo del pie.

toffee ['tɒfɪ] *n* caramelo *m*.

together [təˈgeðər] *adv* junto, juntos,-as; **all t.**, todos juntos; **t. with**, junto con; **to bring t.**, reunir.

toil [tɔɪl] I *n* trabajo duro. II *vi* afanarse, trabajar (duro); **to t. up a hill**, subir penosamente una cuesta.

toilet ['tɔɪlɪt] *n* **1** wáter *m*, retrete *m*; (*for public*) servicios *mpl*; **t. paper** *o* **tissue**, papel higiénico; **t. roll**, rollo *m* de papel higiénico. **2** (*washing etc*) aseo *m* (personal); **t. bag**, neceser *m*; **t. soap**, jabón *m* de tocador.

toiletries ['tɔɪlɪtrɪz] *npl* artículos *mpl* de aseo.

token ['təʊkən] I *n* **1** (*sign*) señal *f*; **as a t. of respect**, en señal de respeto. **2** Com vale *m*; **book t.**, vale para comprar libros. II *adj* simbólico,-a.

told [təʊld] *pt & pp → tell*.

tolerable ['tɒlərəbəl] *adj* tolerable.

tolerance ['tɒlərəns] *n* tolerancia *f*.

tolerant ['tɒlərənt] *adj* tolerante.

tolerate ['tɒləreɪt] *vtr* tolerar.

toll¹ [təʊl] I *vtr* tocar. II *vi* doblar.

toll² [təʊl] *n* **1** Aut peaje *m*. **2** (*loss*) pérdidas *fpl*; **the death t.**, el número de víctimas mortales.

tomato [təˈmɑːtəʊ, US təˈmeɪtəʊ] *n* (*pl* **tomatoes**) tomate *m*; **t. sauce**, salsa *f* de tomate.

tomb [tuːm] *n* tumba *f*, sepulcro *m*.

tomboy ['tɒmbɔɪ] *n* marimacho *f*.

tombstone ['tuːmstəʊn] *n* lápida *f* sepulcral.

tomcat ['tɒmkæt] *n* gato *m* (macho).

tomorrow [təˈmɒrəʊ] I *n* mañana *m*; **the day after t.**, pasado mañana; **t. night**, mañana por la noche. II *adv* mañana; **see you t.!**, ¡hasta mañana!; **t. week**, dentro de ocho días a partir de mañana.

ton [tʌn] *n* tonelada *f*; **fam tons of**, montones de.

tone [təʊn] I *n* tono *m*. II *vi* **to t. with sth**, armonizar con algo. ◆**tone down** *vtr* atenuar.

tone-deaf ['təʊndef] *adj* **to be t.-d.**, no

tener oído.

tongs [tɒŋz] *npl* (*for sugar, hair*) tenacillas *fpl*; (*fire*) **t.**, tenazas *fpl*.

tongue [tʌŋ] *n* **1** lengua *f*; *fig* **to say sth t. in cheek**, decir algo con la boca pequeña; *fig* **t. twister**, trabalenguas *m inv*. **2** (*of shoe*) lengüeta *f*; (*of bell*) badajo *m*.

tongue-tied ['tʌŋtaɪd] *adj* mudo,-a (por la timidez).

tonic ['tɒnɪk] I *n* **1** Med tónico *m*. **2** (*drink*) tónica *f*. II *adj* tónico,-a; Mus **t. sol-fa**, solfeo *m*.

tonight [təˈnaɪt] *adv & n* esta noche.

tonnage ['tʌnɪdʒ] *n* (*of ship*) tonelaje *m*.

tonne [tʌn] *n → ton*.

tonsil ['tɒnsəl] *n* amígdala *f*; **to have one's tonsils out**, ser operado,-a de las amígdalas.

tonsillitis [tɒnsɪˈlaɪtɪs] *n* amigdalitis *f*.

too [tuː] *adv* **1** (*besides*) además. **2** (*also*) también. **3** (*excessively*) demasiado; **t. much money**, demasiado dinero; **ten pounds t. much**, diez libras de más; **t. frequently**, con demasiada frecuencia; **t. old**, demasiado viejo.

took [tʊk] *pt → take*.

tool [tuːl] *n* (*utensil*) herramienta *f*.

toolbox ['tuːlbɒks] *n* caja *f* de herramientas.

toot [tuːt] Aut I *vtr* tocar. II *vi* tocar la bocina.

tooth [tuːθ] *n* (*pl* **teeth** [tiːθ]) **1** diente *m*; (*molar*) muela *f*; *fig* **to fight t. and nail**, luchar a brazo partido. **2** (*of saw*) diente *m*; (*of comb*) púa *f*.

toothache ['tuːθeɪk] *n* dolor *m* de muelas.

toothbrush ['tuːθbrʌʃ] *n* cepillo *m* de dientes.

toothpaste ['tuːθpeɪst] *n* pasta dentífrica.

toothpick ['tuːθpɪk] *n* mondadientes *m inv*.

top¹ [tɒp] I *n* **1** (*upper part*) parte *f* de arriba; (*of hill*) cumbre *f*, cima *f*; (*of tree*) copa *f*; **from t. to bottom**, de arriba a abajo; **on t. of**, encima de; *fig* **on t. of it all** ..., para colmo ...; **t. hat**, sombrero *m* de copa. **2** (*surface*) superficie *f*. **3** (*of list etc*) cabeza *f*. **4** (*of bottle etc*) tapa *f*, tapón *m*. **5** (*garment*) camiseta *f*. **6** (*best*) lo mejor. **7** *fig* **at the t. of one's voice**, a voz en grito. II *adj* **1** (*part*) superior, de arriba; **the t. floor**, el último piso; **t. coat**, (*of paint*) última mano. **2** (*highest*) más alto,-a; Aut **t. gear**, directa *f*. **3** (*best*) mejor. III *vtr* **1** (*place on top of*) coronar. **2** Theat **to t. the bill**, encabezar el reparto. ◆**top up** *vtr* llenar hasta el tope; **t. up the petrol tank**, llenar el depósito; *fig* **and to t. it all**, y para colmo.

top² [tɒp] *n* (*toy*) peonza *f*.

topic ['tɒpɪk] *n* tema *m*.

topical ['tɒpɪkəl] *adj* de actualidad.

top-level ['tɒplevəl] *adj* de alto nivel.

topmost ['tɒpməust] *adj* (el) más alto, (la) más alta.

topple ['tɒpəl] I *vi* (building) venirse a-bajo; **to t.** (over), volcarse, II *vtr* volcar; *fig* (government) derrocar.

top-secret [tɒp'siːkrɪt] *adj* de alto secreto.

topsy-turvy [tɒpsɪ'tɜːvɪ] *adj & adv* al revés; (in confusion) en desorden, patas arriba.

torch [tɔːtʃ] *n* (electric) linterna *f*.

tore [tɔːr] *pt* → **tear²**.

torment ['tɔːment] I *vtr* atormentar. II *n* ['tɔːment] tormento *m*, suplicio *m*.

torn [tɔːn] *pp* → **tear²**.

tornado [tɔː'neɪdəu] *n* tornado *m*.

torpedo [tɔː'piːdəu] *n* torpedo *m*.

torrent ['tɒrənt] *n* torrente *m*.

torrential [tɒ'renʃəl] *adj* torrencial.

torrid ['tɒrɪd] *adj* tórrido,-a.

torso ['tɔːsəu] *n* torso *m*.

tortoise ['tɔːtəs] *n* tortuga *f* de tierra.

tortoiseshell ['tɔːtəsʃel] *adj* de carey.

torture ['tɔːtʃər] I *vtr* torturar; *fig* atormentar. II *n* tortura *f*; *fig* tormento *m*.

Tory ['tɔːrɪ] *adj & n* GB Pol conservador,-a (*m,f*).

toss [tɒs] I *vtr* 1 (ball) tirar; **to t. a coin**, echar a cara o cruz. 2 (throw about) sacudir. II *vi* 1 **to t. about**, agitarse; **to t. and turn**, dar vueltas en la cama. 3 *Sport* **to t.** (up), sortear. III *n* 1 (of ball) lanzamiento *m*; (of coin) sorteo *m* (a cara o cruz). 2 (of head) sacudida *f*.

tot¹ [tɒt] *n* 1 (tiny) t., (child) nene,-a *m,f*. 2 (of whisky etc) trago *m*.

tot² [tɒt] GB *vtr* **to t. up**, sumar.

total ['təutəl] I *n* total *m*; (in bill) importe *m*; **grand t.**, suma *f* total. II *adj* total. III *vtr* sumar. IV *vi* **to t. up to**, ascender a. ◆**totally** *adv* totalmente.

totalitarian [təutælɪ'teərɪən] *adj* totalitario,-a.

tote [təut] *n fam* Sport totalizador *m*.

tote bag ['təutbæg] *n* petate *m*.

totem ['təutəm] *n* tótem *m*.

totter ['tɒtər] *vi* tambalearse.

touch [tʌtʃ] I *vtr* 1 tocar; *fig* **to t. on a subject**, tocar un tema. 2 (equal) igualar. 3 (move) conmover. II *vi* tocarse; *fig* **it was t. and go whether we caught the train**, estuvimos a punto de perder el tren. III *n* 1 toque *m*. 2 (sense of touch) tacto *m*. 3 **it was a nice t.** of his, fue un detalle de su parte; **to put the finishing touches to sth**, dar los últimos toques a algo. 4 (ability) habilidad *f*. 5 (contact) contacto *m*; **to be/get/keep in t. with sb**, estar/ponerse/mantenerse en contacto con algn; **to be out of t. with sth**, no estar al tanto de algo. 6 (small amount) pizca *f*. 7 *Sport* **in t.**, fuera de banda. ◆**touch down** *vi* (plane) aterrizar. ◆**touch**

up *vtr* (picture) retocar.

touchdown ['tʌtʃdaun] *n* 1 (of plane) aterrizaje *m*; (of space capsule) amerizaje *m*. 2 Rugby ensayo *m*.

touched [tʌtʃt] *adj* 1 (moved) emocionado,-a. 2 *fam* (crazy) tocado,-a.

touching ['tʌtʃɪŋ] *adj* conmovedor,-a.

touchline ['tʌtʃlaɪn] *n* línea *f* de banda.

touchy ['tʌtʃɪ] *adj* (touchier, touchiest) *fam* (person) susceptible; (subject) delicado,-a.

tough [tʌf] I *adj* (material, competitor etc) fuerte, resistente; (test, criminal, meat) duro,-a; (punishment) severo,-a; (problem) difícil. II *n* (person) matón *m*.

toughen ['tʌfən] *vtr* endurecer.

toupee ['tuːpeɪ] *n* tupé *m*.

tour [tuər] I *n* 1 (journey) viaje *m*; **package t.**, viaje organizado. 2 (of monument etc) visita *f*; (of city) recorrido turístico. 3 *Sport Theat* gira *f*; **on t.**, de gira. II *vtr* 1 (country) viajar por. 2 (building) visitar. 3 *Theat* estar de gira en. III *vi* estar de viaje.

tourism ['tuərɪzəm] *n* turismo *m*.

tourist ['tuərɪst] *n* turista *mf*; **t. centre**, centro *m* de información turística; *Av* **t. class**, clase *f* turista.

tournament ['tuənəmənt] *n* torneo *m*.

tousled ['tauzld] *adj* (hair) despeinado, -a.

tout [taut] I *vtr* Com tratar de vender; (tickets) revender. II *vi* salir a la caza y captura de compradores. III *n* Com gancho *m*; **ticket t.**, revendedor *m* de entradas.

tow [təu] I *n* **to take a car in t.**, remolcar un coche. *vtr* remolcar.

towards [tə'wɔːdz, tɔːdz] *prep* 1 (direction, time) hacia. 2 (with regard to) hacia, (para) con; **our duty t. others**, nuestro deber para con los demás; **what is your attitude t. religion?**, ¿cuál es su actitud respecto a la religión?

towel ['tauəl] I *n* toalla *f*; **hand t.**, toallita *f*; **t. rail**, toallero *m*. II *vtr* **to t. dry**, secar con una toalla.

towelling ['tauəlɪŋ] *n* felpa *f*.

tower ['tauər] I *n* torre *f*. II *vi* **to t. over** or **above sth**, dominar algo.

towering ['tauərɪŋ] *adj* impresionante, enorme.

town [taun] *n* ciudad *f*; (small) pueblo *m*; **to go into t.**, ir al centro; *fam* **to go to t.**, tirar la casa por la ventana; **t. council**, ayuntamiento *m*; **t. councillor**, concejal,-a *m,f*; **t. hall**, ayuntamiento *m*; **t. planning**, urbanismo *m*.

townspeople ['taunzpiːpəl] *npl* ciudadanos *mpl*.

towpath ['təupɑːθ] *n* sendero *m* a lo largo de un canal.

towrope ['təurəup] *n* cable *m* de remolque.

toxic ['tɒksɪk] *adj* tóxico,-a.

toy [tɔɪ] I *n* juguete *m*. II *vi* to t. with an idea, acariciar una idea; to t. with one's food, comer sin gana.

toyshop ['tɔɪʃɒp] *n* juguetería *f*.

trace [treɪs] I *n* 1 (*sign*) indicio *m*, vestigio *m*. 2 (*tracks*) huella(s) *f(pl)*. II *vtr* 1 (*drawing*) calcar. 2 (*plan*) bosquejar. 3 (*locate*) seguir la pista de.

tracing ['treɪsɪŋ] *n* t. paper, papel *m* de calco.

track [træk] I *n* 1 (*trail*) huellas *fpl*, pista *f*; to keep/lose t. of sb, no perder/perder de vista a algn. 2 (*pathway*) camino *m*; to be on the right/wrong t., ir por el buen/mal camino. 3 *Sport* pista *f*; (*for motor racing*) circuito *m*; *fig* t. record, historial *m*. 4 *Rail* vía *f*; *fig* he has a one-t. mind, tiene una única obsesión. 5 (*on record*) canción *f*. II *vtr* seguir la pista de; (*with radar*) seguir la trayectoria de. ◆**track down** *vtr* (*locate*) localizar.

tracksuit ['træksuːt] *n* chandal *m*.

tract¹ [trækt] *n* (*expanse*) extensión *f*.

tract² [trækt] *n* (*treatise*) tratado *m*; (*pamphlet*) folleto *m*.

traction ['trækʃən] *n* tracción *f*.

tractor ['træktər] *n* tractor *m*.

trade [treɪd] I *n* 1 (*profession*) oficio *m*; by t., de oficio. 2 *Com* comercio *m*; it's good for t., es bueno para los negocios; the building t., (la industria de) la construcción; t. name, nombre *m* comercial; t. union, sindicato *m*; t. unionist, sindicalista *mf*. II *vi* comerciar (in, en). III *vtr* to t. sth for sth, trocar algo por algo. ◆**trade in** *vtr* dar como entrada.

trademark ['treɪdmɑːk] *n* marca *f* (de fábrica); registered t., marca registrada.

trader ['treɪdər] *n* comerciante *mf*.

tradesman ['treɪdzmən] *n* (*shopkeeper*) tendero *m*.

trading ['treɪdɪŋ] *n* comercio *m*; *GB* t. estate, polígono *m* industrial.

tradition [trə'dɪʃən] *n* tradición *f*.

traditional [trə'dɪʃənəl] *adj* tradicional.

traffic ['træfɪk] I *n* 1 tráfico *m*, circulación *f*; t. island, isleta *f*; t. jam, atasco *m*; t. lights, semáforo *m sing*; t. warden, ≈ guardia *mf* urbano,-a. 2 (*trade*) tráfico *m*. II *vi* (*pt & pp* trafficked) to t. in drugs, traficar con droga.

trafficker ['træfɪkər] *n* traficante *mf*.

tragedy ['trædʒɪdɪ] *n* tragedia *f*.

tragic ['trædʒɪk] *adj* trágico,-a.

trail [treɪl] I *vtr* 1 (*drag*) arrastrar. 2 (*follow*) rastrear. II *vi* 1 (*drag*) arrastrarse. 2 to t. behind, rezagarse. III *n* 1 (*track*) pista *f*, rastro *m*. 2 (*path*) senda *f*, camino *m*. 3 (*of smoke*) estela *f*.

trailer ['treɪlər] *n* 1 *Aut* remolque *m*. 2 *US Aut* (*caravan*) caravana *f*. 3 *Cin* trailer *m*, avance *m*.

train [treɪn] I *n* 1 *Rail* tren *m*. 2 (*of vehicles*) convoy *m*; (*of followers*) séquito *m*; (*of events*) serie *f*. 3 (*of dress*) cola *f*. II *vtr* 1 (*teach*) formar; *Sport* entrenar; (*animal*) amaestrar; (*voice etc*) educar. 2 (*gun*) apuntar (on, a); (*camera*) enfocar (on, a). III *vi* prepararse; *Sport* entrenarse.

trainee [treɪ'niː] *n* aprendiz,-a *mf*.

trainer ['treɪnər] *n* 1 *Sport* entrenador,-a *m,f*; (*of animals*) amaestrador,-a *m,f*; (*of lions*) domador,-a *m,f*. 2 trainers, (*shoes*) zapatillas *fpl* de deporte.

training ['treɪnɪŋ] *n* (*instruction*) formación *f*; *Sport* entrenamiento *m*; (*of animals*) amaestramiento *m*; (*of lions*) doma *f*; to go into t., empezar el entrenamiento; vocational t., formación profesional.

traipse [treɪps] *vi fam* vagar.

trait [treɪt] *n* rasgo *m*.

traitor ['treɪtər] *n* traidor,-a *m,f*.

trajectory [trə'dʒektərɪ] *n* trayectoria *f*.

tram [træm], **tramcar** ['træmkɑːr] *n GB* tranvía *m*.

tramp [træmp] I *vi* 1 (*travel on foot*) caminar. 2 (*walk heavily*) andar con pasos pesados. II *n* (*person*) vagabundo,-a *m,f*; *pej* she's a t., es una fulana.

trample ['træmpəl] *vtr* to t. down the grass, pistotear la hierba; to t. sth underfoot, pisotear algo.

trampoline ['træmpəliːn] *n* cama elástica *f*.

trance [trɑːns] *n* trance *m*.

tranquil ['træŋkwɪl] *adj* tranquilo,-a.

tranquillity [træŋ'kwɪlɪtɪ] *n* tranquilidad *f*.

tranquillizer ['træŋkwɪlaɪzər] *n* tranquilizante *m*.

transact [træn'zækt] *vtr* negociar.

transaction [træn'zækʃən] *n* (*procedure*) tramitación *f*; (*deal*) transacción *f*.

transatlantic [trænzət'læntɪk] *adj* transatlántico,-a.

transcend [træn'send] *vtr* trascender.

transcribe [træn'skraɪb] *vtr* transcribir.

transcript ['trænskrɪpt] *n* transcripción *f*.

transcription [træn'skrɪpʃən] *n* transcripción *f*.

transfer [træns'fɜːr] I *vtr* trasladar; (*funds*) trasferir; *Jur* ceder; *Ftb* traspasar; *Tel* to t. the charges, hacer una llamada a cobro revertido. II ['trænsfɜːr] *n* 1 traslado *m*; (*of funds*) trasferencia *f*; *Jur* cesión *f*; *Ftb* traspaso *m*. 2 (*picture, design*) calcomanía *f*.

transform [træns'fɔːm] *vtr* trasformar.

transformation [trænsfə'meɪʃən] *n* trasformación *f*.

transfusion [træns'fjuːʒən] *n Med* transfusión *f* (de sangre).

transgress [trænz'gres] *vi fml* transgredir.

transient ['trænzɪənt] *adj* transitorio,-a.

transistor [træn'zɪstər] *n* transistor *m*.

transit ['trænzɪt] *n* tránsito *m*; in t., de

tránsito.

transition [træn'zɪʃən] n transición f.

transitive ['trænzɪtɪv] adj transitivo,-a.

transitory ['trænzɪtərɪ] adj transitorio,-a.

translate [træns'leɪt] vtr traducir.

translation [træns'leɪʃən] n traducción f.

translator [træns'leɪtə'] n traductor,-a m,f.

translucent [trænz'luːsənt] adj translúcido,-a.

transmission [trænz'mɪʃən] n transmisión f.

transmit [trænz'mɪt] vtr transmitir.

transmitter [trænz'mɪtə'] n Rad (set) transmisor m; Rad TV (station) emisora f.

transparency [træns'pærənsɪ] n Phot diapositiva f.

transparent [træns'pærənt] adj transparente.

transpire [træn'spaɪə'] vi (happen) ocurrir; **it transpired that ...,** ocurrió que ....

transplant [træns'plɑːnt] I vtr trasplantar. II ['trænsplɑːnt] n trasplante m.

transport [træns'pɔːt] I vtr transportar. II ['trænspɔːt] n transporte m; t. aircraft/ship, avión m/buque m de transporte; GB t. café, bar m de carretera.

transportation [trænspɔː'teɪʃən] n transporte m.

transvestite [trænz'vestaɪt] n fam travestí mf.

trap [træp] I n trampa f; t. door, trampilla f; Theat escotillón m. II vtr atrapar.

trapeze [trə'piːz] n trapecio m.

trappings ['træpɪŋz] npl parafernalia f sing.

trash [træʃ] n (inferior goods) bazofia f; US (rubbish) basura f; fig to talk a lot of t., decir tonterías; US t. can, cubo m de la basura.

trashy ['træʃɪ] adj (trashier, trashiest) de ínfima calidad.

trauma ['trɔːmə] n trauma m.

traumatic [trɔː'mætɪk] adj traumático,-a.

travel ['trævəl] I vi 1 viajar; to t. through, recorrer. 2 (vehicle, electric current) ir; fig (news) propagarse. II vtr recorrer. III n viajar m; t. agency, agencia f de viajes.

traveller, US **traveler** ['trævələ'] n viajero,-a m,f; t.'s cheque, cheque m de viaje.

travelling, US **traveling** ['trævəlɪŋ] I adj (salesman) ambulante. II n viajes mpl, (el) viajar m; **I'm fond of t.,** me gusta viajar; t. expenses, gastos mpl de viaje.

travel-sick ['trævəlsɪk] adj to be t., estar mareado,-a.

travesty ['trævɪstɪ] n parodia f.

trawler ['trɔːlə'] n barco m de arrastre.

tray [treɪ] n (for food) bandeja f; (for letters) cesta f (para la correspondencia).

treacherous ['tretʃərəs] adj 1 (person) traidor,-a; (action) traicionero,-a. 2

(dangerous) peligroso,-a.

treachery ['tretʃərɪ] n traición f.

treacle ['triːkəl] n GB melaza f.

tread [tred] I vi (pt trod; pp trod or trodden) pisar; to t. on, pisar. II vtr 1 (step on) pisar. 2 to t. water, mantenerse a flote verticalmente. III n 1 (step) paso m; (sound) ruido m de pasos. 2 (of tyre) banda f de rodadura.

treadmill ['tredmɪl] n fig rutina f.

treason ['triːzən] n traición f.

treasure ['treʒə'] I n tesoro m. II vtr (keep) guardar como oro en paño; (value) apreciar muchísimo.

treasurer ['treʒərə'] n tesorero,-a m,f.

treasury ['treʒərɪ] n Pol the T., ≈ Ministerio m de Hacienda; T. bill, bono m del Tesoro.

treat [triːt] I n 1 (present) regalo m. 2 (pleasure) placer m. II vtr 1 tratar; to t. badly, maltratar. 2 (regard) considerar. 3 **he treated them to dinner,** les invitó a cenar.

treatise ['triːtɪz] n tratado m.

treatment ['triːtmənt] n 1 (of person) trato m. 2 (of subject, of patient) tratamiento m.

treaty ['triːtɪ] n tratado m.

treble ['trebəl] I adj 1 (triple) triple; Mus t. clef, clave f de sol; Mus t. voice, voz f tiple. II vtr triplicar. III vi triplicarse.

tree [triː] n árbol m; apple/cherry t., manzano m/cerezo m.

treetop ['triːtɒp] n copa f.

trek [trek] I n (journey) viaje m (largo y difícil); fam (walk) caminata f. II vi (pt & pp trekked) hacer un viaje largo y difícil; fam (walk) ir caminando.

trellis ['trelɪs] n enrejado m.

tremble ['trembəl] vi temblar, estremecerse.

trembling ['tremblɪŋ] adj tembloroso,-a.

tremendous [trɪ'mendəs] adj (huge) enorme; (success) arrollador,-a; (shock etc) tremendo,-a; fam (marvellous) estupendo,-a.

tremor ['tremə'] n temblor m.

trench [trentʃ] n (ditch) zanja f; Mil trinchera f. 2 t. coat, trinchera f.

trend [trend] I n (tendency) tendencia f; (fashion) moda f. II vi tender (to, to-wards, hacia).

trendy ['trendɪ] adj (trendier, trendiest) fam (person) moderno,-a; (clothes) a la última.

trepidation [trepɪ'deɪʃən] n turbación f.

trespass ['trespəs] vi entrar sin autorización.

trespasser ['trespəsə'] n intruso,-a m,f.

trestle ['tresəl] n caballete m.

trial ['traɪəl] n 1 Jur proceso m, juicio m. 2 (test) prueba f; on t., a prueba; by t. and error, a fuerza de equivocarse. 3 trials, (competition) concurso m sing. 4 trials, (suffering) sufrimiento m sing;

and tribulations, tribulaciones *fpl*.
triangle ['traɪæŋgəl] *n* triángulo *m*.
tribe [traɪb] *n* tribu *f*.
tribunal [traɪ'bjuːnəl] *n* tribunal *m*.
tributary ['trɪbjʊtərɪ] *n* (*river*) afluente *m*.
tribute ['trɪbjuːt] *n* 1 (*payment*) tributo *m*.
2 (*mark of respect*) homenaje *m*; **to pay t.**
to, rendir homenaje a.
trice [traɪs] *n fam* **in a t.**, en un abrir y cerrar de ojos.
trick [trɪk] I *n* 1 (*ruse*) ardid *m*; (*dishonest*) engaño *m*; (*in question*) trampa *f*. 2 (*practical joke*) broma *f*; **to play a t. on** sb, gastarle una broma a algn; (*malicious*) jugar una mala pasada a algn. 3 (*of magic, knack*) truco *m*; **that'll do the t.!**, ¡eso es exactamente lo que hace falta! 4 *Cards* baza *f*. II *vtr* engañar; **to t. sb out of sth**, estafar algo a algn.
trickery ['trɪkərɪ] *n* engaños *mpl*, trampas *fpl*.
trickle ['trɪkəl] I *vi* discurrir; (*water*) gotear. II *n* hilo *m*.
tricky ['trɪkɪ] *adj* (**trickier, trickiest**) (*person*) astuto,-a; (*situation, mechanism*) delicado,-a.
tricycle ['traɪsɪkəl] *n* triciclo *m*.
tried [traɪd] *pt & pp* → **try**.
trifle ['traɪfəl] I *n* 1 (*insignificant thing*) bagatela *f*; **he's a t. optimistic**, es ligeramente optimista. 2 *GB Culin* postre *m* (de bizcocho, jerez, gelatina, frutas y nata). II *vi* **to t. with**, tomar a la ligera.
trifling ['traɪflɪŋ] *adj* insignificante, trivial.
trigger ['trɪgə'] I *n* (*of gun*) gatillo *m*; (*of mechanism*) disparador *m*. II *vtr* **to t. (off)**, desencadenar.
trill [trɪl] *n* (*of music, bird*) trino *m*; *Ling* vibración *f*.
trilogy ['trɪlədʒɪ] *n* trilogía *f*.
trim [trɪm] I *adj* (**trimmer, trimmest**) (*neat*) aseado,-a; **to have a t. figure**, tener buen tipo. II *vtr* 1 (*cut*) recortar; *fig* (*expenses*) disminuir. 2 (*decorate*) adornar. III *n* 1 (*condition*) estado *m*; *Naut* asiento *m*. 2 (*cut*) recorte *m*.
trimming ['trɪmɪŋ] *n* 1 (*cut*) recorte *m*. 2 (*on clothes*) adorno *m*. 3 *Culin* **trimmings**, guarnición *f sing*.
trinket ['trɪŋkɪt] *n* baratija *f*.
trio ['triːəʊ] *n* trío *m*.
trip [trɪp] I *n* 1 (*journey*) viaje *m*; (*excursion*) excursión *f*; **to go on a t.**, ir de excursión. 2 *sl* **to be on a t.**, (*on drugs*) estar colocado,-a. II *vi* 1 **to t. (up)**, (*stumble*) tropezar (**over**, con); *fig* (*err*) equivocarse. 2 **to t. along**, ir con paso ligero. III *vtr* **to t. sb (up)**, poner la zancadilla a algn; *fig* coger or pillar a algn.
tripe [traɪp] *n* 1 *Culin* callos *mpl*. 2 *fam* bobadas *fpl*.
triple ['trɪpəl] I *adj* triple. II *vtr* triplicar. III *vi* triplicarse.
triplet ['trɪplɪt] *n* trillizo,-a *m,f*.

triplicate ['trɪplɪkɪt] *adj* **in t.**, por triplicado.
tripod ['traɪpɒd] *n* trípode *f*.
trite [traɪt] *adj* (*sentiment*) banal; (*subject*) trillado,-a.
triumph ['traɪəmf] I *n* triunfo *m*. II *vi* triunfar.
triumphant [traɪ'ʌmfənt] *adj* triunfante.
trivia ['trɪvɪə] *npl* trivialidades *fpl*.
trivial ['trɪvɪəl] *adj* trivial, banal.
trod [trɒd] *pt & pp* → **tread**.
trodden ['trɒdən] *pp* → **tread**.
trolley ['trɒlɪ] *n GB* carro *m*.
trombone [trɒm'bəʊn] *n* trombón *m*.
troop [truːp] I *n* 1 (*of people*) grupo *m*. 2 *Mil* **troops**, tropas *fpl*. II *vi* **to t. in/out/off**, entrar/salir/marcharse en tropel.
trooper ['truːpə'] *n* soldado *m* de caballería.
trooping ['truːpɪŋ] *n GB* **t. the colour**, ceremonia *f* de homenaje a la bandera de un regimiento.
trophy ['trəʊfɪ] *n* trofeo *m*.
tropic ['trɒpɪk] *n* trópico *m*.
tropical ['trɒpɪkəl] *adj* tropical.
trot [trɒt] I *vi* trotar. II *n* trote *m*; **to go at a t.**, ir al trote; *fam* **on the t.**, (*in succession*) seguidos,-as.
trouble ['trʌbəl] I *n* 1 (*misfortune*) desgracia *f*. 2 (*problems*) problemas *mpl*; **to be in t.**, estar en un lío; **to cause sb t.**, ocasionar problemas a algn; **to get sb out of t.**, sacar a algn de un apuro; **the t. is that ...**, lo que pasa es que .... 3 (*effort*) esfuerzo *m*; **it's no t.**, no es ninguna molestia; **it's not worth the t.**, no merece la pena; **to take the t. to do sth**, molestarse en hacer algo. 4 (*conflict*) conflicto *m*. 5 *Med* enfermedad *f*; **to have liver t.**, tener problemas de hígado. II *vtr* 1 (*affect*) afligir; (*worry*) preocupar; **that doesn't t. him at all**, eso le tiene sin cuidado. 2 (*bother*) molestar. III *vi* molestarse.
troubled ['trʌbəld] *adj* agitado,-a.
troublemaker ['trʌbəlmeɪkə'] *n* alborotador,-a *m,f*.
troubleshooter ['trʌbəlʃuːtə'] *n Ind* persona encargada de solucionar problemas.
troublesome ['trʌbəlsəm] *adj* molesto,-a.
trough [trɒf] *n* 1 (*drinking*) **t.**, abrevadero *m*; (*feeding*) **t.**, pesebre *m*. 2 (*of wave*) seno *m*. 3 *Geog Meteor* depresión *f*.
trounce [traʊns] *vtr* dar una paliza a.
troupe [truːp] *n Theat* compañía *f*.
trousers ['traʊzəz] *npl* pantalón *m sing*, pantalones *mpl*.
trousseau ['truːsəʊ] *n* ajuar *m*.
trout [traʊt] *n* trucha *f*.
trowel ['traʊəl] *n* 1 (*builder's*) palustre *m*. 2 (*for gardening*) desplantador *m*.
truant ['truːənt] *n* **to play t.**, hacer novillos.
truce [truːs] *n* tregua *f*.
truck[1] [trʌk] *n* 1 *GB Rail* vagón *m*. 2

US Aut camión *m*; **t. driver,** camionero,-a *m,f*.

truck² [trʌk] *n* 1 **to have no t. with,** no estar dispuesto a toerar. 2 *US* **verduras** *fpl*; **t. farming,** cultivo *m* hortalizas.

truculent [ˈtrʌkjʊlənt] *adj* truculento,-a.

trudge [trʌdʒ] *vi* caminar con dificultad.

true [truː] *adj (truer, truest)* 1 verdadero,-a; **it's t. that ...,** es verdad que ...; **to come t.,** cumplirse, hacerse realidad. 2 *(faithful)* fiel. 3 *(aim)* acertado,-a. ◆**truly** *adv* 1 de verdad; **really and t.?,** ¿de veras? 2 *(faithfully)* fielmente; **yours t.,** atentamente.

truffle [ˈtrʌfəl] *n* trufa *f*.

trump [trʌmp] *Cards* I *n* triunfo *m*. II *vtr* fallar.

trumped-up [ˈtrʌmptʌp] *adj* inventado,-a.

trumpet [ˈtrʌmpɪt] *n* trompeta *f*.

trumpeting [ˈtrʌmpɪtɪŋ] *n (of elephant)* berrido *m*.

truncheon [ˈtrʌntʃən] *n GB* porra *f* (de policía).

trundle [ˈtrʌndəl] *vi* rodar.

trunk [trʌŋk] *n* 1 *(of tree, body)* tronco *m*. 2 *(of elephant)* trompa *f*. 3 *(luggage)* baúl *m*. 4 *GB Tel* **t. call,** conferencia interurbana; *GB* **t. road,** carretera *f* principal.

trunks [trʌŋks] *npl (bathing)* **t.,** bañador *m sing*.

truss [trʌs] I *vtr (tie)* atar. II *n* 1 *Constr* cuchillo *m* de armadura. 2 *Med* braguero *m*.

trust [trʌst] I *n* 1 confianza *f*; **breach of t.,** abuso *m* de confianza. 2 *(responsibility)* responsabilidad *f*; **to be in a position of t.,** ocupar un cargo de responsabilidad. 3 *Fin* trust *m*. II *vtr* 1 *(hope)* esperar. 2 *(rely upon)* fiarse de; **to t. sb with sth,** confiar algo a algn. III *vi* confiar (**in, en**).

trusted [ˈtrʌstɪd] *adj* de fiar.

trustee [trʌˈstiː] *n Jur* fideicomisario,-a *m,f; (in bankruptcy)* síndico *m*.

trustful [ˈtrʌstfʊl], **trusting** [ˈtrʌstɪŋ] *adj* confiado,-a.

trustworthy [ˈtrʌstwɜːðɪ] *adj (person)* de confianza; *(information)* fidedigno,-a.

trusty [ˈtrʌstɪ] *adj (trustier, trustiest)* fiel, leal.

truth [truːθ] *n* verdad *f*; **to tell the t.,** decir la verdad.

truthful [ˈtruːθfʊl] *adj (person)* veraz, sincero,-a; *(testimony)* verídico,-a. ◆**truthfully** *adv* sinceramente.

try [traɪ] I *vtr (pt & pp tried)* 1 *(attempt)* intentar; **to t. do sth,** tratar de or intentar hacer algo. 2 *(test)* probar, ensayar; **to t. sb's patience,** poner a prueba la paciencia de algn. 3 *Jur* juzgar. II *vi* intentar. III *n* 1 *(attempt)* tentativa *f*, intento *m*. 2 *Sport* ensayo *m*. ◆**try on** *vtr (dress)* probarse. ◆**try out** *vtr* probar.

trying [ˈtraɪɪŋ] *adj (person)* molesto,-a, pesado,-a; **to have a t. time,** pasar un mal rato.

tsar [zɑː] *n* zar *m*.

T-shirt [ˈtiːʃɜːt] *n* camiseta *f*.

tub [tʌb] *n* 1 *(container)* tina *f*, cuba *f*. 2 *(bath)* bañera *f*.

tuba [ˈtjuːbə] *n* tuba *f*.

tubby [ˈtʌbɪ] *adj (tubbier, tubbiest)* rechoncho,-a.

tube [tjuːb] *n* 1 tubo *m*; *Anat* conducto *m*; *(of bicycle)* cámara *f* (de aire). 2 *GB fam* **the t.,** *(underground)* el metro.

tuberculosis [tjʊbɜːkjʊˈləʊsɪs] *n* tuberculosis *f*.

tubing [ˈtjuːbɪŋ] *n* tubería *f*; **(piece of) t.,** *(trozo m de)* tubo *m*.

tubular [ˈtjuːbjʊlər] *adj* tubular.

tuck [tʌk] I *vtr* **to t. in the bedclothes,** remeter la ropa de la cama; **to t. sb in,** arropar a algn; **to t. one's shirt into one's trousers,** meterse la camisa por dentro (de los pantalones). II *n Sew* pliegue *m*. ◆**tuck in** *vi fam* devorar.

Tuesday [ˈtjuːzdɪ] *n* martes *m*.

tuft [tʌft] *n (of hair)* mechón *m*.

tug [tʌg] I *vtr (pull at)* tirar de; *(haul along)* arrastrar; *Naut* remolcar. II *n* 1 *(pull)* tirón *m*; **t. of war,** *(game)* lucha *f* de la cuerda; *fig* lucha encarnizada. 2 *Naut* remolcador *m*.

tugboat [ˈtʌgbəʊt] *n* remolcador *m*.

tuition [tjuːˈɪʃən] *n* instrucción *f*; **private t.,** clases *fpl* particulares; **t. fees,** honorarios *mpl*.

tulip [ˈtjuːlɪp] *n* tulipán *m*.

tumble [ˈtʌmbəl] I *vi (person)* caerse; *(acrobat)* dar volteretas; *(building)* venirse abajo. II *vtr* volcar. III *n* 1 caída *f*. 2 **t. dryer,** secadora *f*.

tumbledown [ˈtʌmbəldaʊn] *adj* en ruinas.

tumbler [ˈtʌmblər] *n* vaso *m*.

tummy [ˈtʌmɪ] *n fam* estómago *m*, barriga *f*.

tumour, *US* **tumor** [ˈtjuːmər] *n* tumor *m*.

tumult [ˈtjuːmʌlt] *n* tumulto *m*.

tuna [ˈtjuːnə] *n* atún *m*, bonito *m*.

tune [tjuːn] I *n* 1 *(melody)* melodía *f*; *fig* **to change one's t.,** cambiar de tono. 2 *Mus* tono *m*; **in/out of t.,** afinado/ desafinado; **to sing out of t.,** desafinar. II *vtr Mus* afinar. III *vi Rad TV* **to t. in to a station,** sintonizar una emisora. ◆**tune up** *vi* afinar los instrumentos.

tuneful [ˈtjuːnfʊl] *adj* melodioso,-a.

tuner [ˈtjuːnər] *n (of pianos)* afinador,-a *m,f. 1 Rad TV (knob)* sintonizador *m*.

tunic [ˈtjuːnɪk] *n* túnica *f*.

tuning [ˈtjuːnɪŋ] *n* 1 *Mus* afinación *f*; **t. fork,** diapasón *m*. 2 *Rad TV* **t. in,** sintonización *f*.

Tunisia [tjuːˈnɪzɪə] *n* Túnez *m*.

Tunisian [tjuːˈnɪzɪən] *adj & n* tunecino,-a

(m,f).

tunnel ['tʌnəl] **I** n túnel m; *Min* galería f. **II** vtr **to t. through**, abrir un túnel a través de.

turban ['tɜːbən] n turbante m.

turbine ['tɜːbaɪn] n turbina f.

turbulent ['tɜːbjʊlənt] adj turbulento,-a.

tureen [tə'riːn] n sopera f.

turf [tɜːf] n **1** (grass) césped m; (peat) turba f. **2** GB **t. accountant**, (in horse racing) corredor,-a m,f de apuestas. ◆**turf out** vtr GB fam **to t. sth out**, poner a algn de patitas en la calle.

Turk [tɜːk] n turco,-a m,f.

Turkey ['tɜːkɪ] n Turquía f.

turkey ['tɜːkɪ] n pavo m.

Turkish ['tɜːkɪʃ] **I** adj turco,-a. **II** n (language) turco m.

turmoil ['tɜːmɔɪl] n confusión f.

turn [tɜːn] **I** vtr **1** volver; (rotate) girar, hacer girar; **to t. sth inside out**, volver algo del revés; **to t. a page**, volver una hoja; **to t. one's head/gaze**, volver la cabeza/mirada (**towards**, hacia); **to t. the corner**, doblar la esquina; *fig* **he's turned forty**, ha cumplido los cuarenta. **2** (change) transformar (**into**, en). **3** (on lathe) tornear.

II vi **1** (rotate) girar. **2** (turn round) volverse, dar la vuelta; **to t. to sb**, volverse hacia algn; *fig* (for help) acudir a algn; **to t. upside down**, volcarse; *fig* **to t. on sb**, volverse contra algn. **3** (become) volverse; **the milk has turned sour**, la leche se ha cortado.

III n **1** (of wheel) vuelta f; **meat done to a t.**, carne a su punto. **2** (change of direction) cambio m de dirección; (in road) curva f; **to take a t. for the better**, empezar a mejorar; **left/right t.**, giro m al izquierdo/a la derecha. **3** **to do sb a good t.**, hacer un favor a algn. **4** *Med* ataque m. **5** (in game, queue) turno m, vez f; **it's your t.**, te toca a ti; **to take it in turns to do sth**, turnarse para hacer algo. **6** *Theat* número m. **7** **t. of phrase**, giro m. ◆**turn aside I** vtr desviar. **II** vi desviarse. ◆**turn away I** vtr (person) rechazar. **II** vi volver la cabeza. ◆**turn back I** vtr (person) hacer retroceder; (clock) retrasar. **II** vi volverse. ◆**turn down I** vtr **1** (gas, radio etc) bajar. **2** (refuse) rechazar. **3** (fold) doblar. ◆**turn in** fam **I** vtr (person) entregar a la policía. **II** vi acostarse. ◆**turn off I** vtr (electricity) desconectar; (gas, light) apagar; (water) cerrar. **II** vi desviarse. ◆**turn on I** vtr (electricity) encender; (tap, gas) abrir; (machine) poner en marcha; fam **it turns me on**, me encanta. ◆**turn out I** vtr **1** (extinguish) apagar. **2** (eject) echar; (empty) vaciar. **3** (produce) producir. **II** vi **1** (attend) asistir. **2** **it turns out that ...**, resulta que ...; **things have turned out well**, las cosas han salido bien. ◆**turn over I** vtr (turn upside down) poner al revés; (page) dar la vuelta a. **II** vi volverse. ◆**turn round I** vtr volver. **II** vi (rotate) girar, dar vueltas. ◆**turn up I** vtr **1** (collar) levantar; **to t. up one's shirt sleeves**, arremangarse; **turned-up nose**, nariz respingona. **2** *Rad TV* subir. **II** vi **1** *fig* **something is sure to t. up**, algo saldrá. **2** (arrive) llegar, presentarse; **nobody turned up**, nadie se presentó. **3** (attend) asistir.

turning ['tɜːnɪŋ] n **1** *fig* **t. point**, punto decisivo. **2** (in road) salida f.

turnip ['tɜːnɪp] n nabo m.

turnout ['tɜːnaʊt] n asistencia f.

turnover ['tɜːnəʊvə'] n *Com* (sales) facturación f; (of goods) movimiento m.

turnpike ['tɜːnpaɪk] n *US* autopista f de peaje.

turnstile ['tɜːnstaɪl] n torniquete m.

turntable ['tɜːnteɪbəl] n (for record) plato m (giratorio).

turn-up ['tɜːnʌp] n GB **1** (of trousers) vuelta f. **2** fam fig **what a t.-up for the books!**, ¡vaya sorpresa!

turpentine ['tɜːpəntaɪn] n (esencia f de) trementina f.

turquoise ['tɜːkwɔɪz] **I** n (colour, stone) turquesa f. **II** adj **t.** (blue), azul turquesa.

turret ['tʌrɪt] n torrecilla f.

turtle ['tɜːtəl] n tortuga f.

turtledove ['tɜːtəldʌv] n tórtola f.

turtleneck ['tɜːtəlnek] n **a t. (sweater)**, un jersey de cuello alto.

tusk [tʌsk] n colmillo m.

tussle ['tʌsəl] n pelea f, lucha f.

tutor ['tjuːtə'] n *Univ* tutor,-a m,f; **private t.**, profesor,-a m,f particular.

tutorial [tjuːˈtɔːrɪəl] n *Univ* tutoría f, seminario m.

tuxedo [tʌkˈsiːdəʊ] n *US* smoking m.

TV [tiːˈviː] abbr of **television**, TV.

twang [twæŋ] n **1** (of instrument) sonido m vibrante. **2** nasal t., gangueo m. **II** vtr puntear. **III** vi (string) vibrar.

tweak [twiːk] vtr pellizcar.

tweed [twiːd] n cheviot m.

tweezers ['twiːzəz] npl pinzas fpl.

twelfth [twelfθ] **I** adj & n duodécimo,-a (m,f). **II** n (fraction) duodécimo m.

twelve [twelv] adj & n doce (m) inv.

twentieth ['twentɪθ] **I** adj & n vigésimo,-a (m,f). **II** n (fraction) vigésimo m.

twenty ['twentɪ] adj & n veinte (m) inv.

twice [twaɪs] adv dos veces; **he's t. as old as I am**, tiene el doble de años que yo.

twiddle ['twɪdəl] **I** vtr dar vueltas a; **to t. one's moustache**, mesarse el bigote; **to t. one's thumbs**, estar mano sobre mano. **II** vi **to t. with sth**, juguetear con algo.

twig¹ [twɪg] n ramilla f.

twig² [twɪg] vi GB fam caer en la cuenta.

twilight ['twaɪlaɪt] n crepúsculo m.

twin [twɪn] I n mellizo,-a m,f; identical twins, gemelos (idénticos). t. brother/sister, hermano gemelo/hermana gemela; t. beds, camas fpl gemelas. II vtr hermanar.

twine [twaɪn] I n bramante m. II vtr entretejer. III vi to t. round sth, enroscarse alrededor de algo.

twinge [twɪndʒ] n (of pain) punzada f; fig t. of conscience, remordimiento m.

twinkle ['twɪŋkəl] vi (stars) centellear; (eyes) brillar.

twinkling ['twɪŋklɪŋ] n (of stars) centelleo m; fig in the t. of an eye, en un abrir y cerrar de ojos.

twirl [twɜːl] I vtr girar rápidamente. II vi (spin) girar rápidamente; (dancer) piruetear. III n (movement) giro rápido; fig (of dancer) pirueta f.

twist [twɪst] I vtr torcer; (sense) tergiversar; to t. one's ankle, torcerse el tobillo. II vi (smoke) formar volutas; (path) serpentear. III n 1 (of yarn) torzal m. 2 (movement) torsión f; Med torcedura f; fig to give a new t. to sth, dar un nuevo enfoque a algo. 3 (in road) vuelta f. 4 (dance) twist m.

twit [twɪt] n GB fam jilipollas mf inv.

twitch [twɪtʃ] I vtr dar un tirón a. II vi crisparse; his face twitches, tiene un tic en la cara.

twitter ['twɪtər] I vi gorjear. II n gorjeo m.

two [tuː] I adj dos inv; fig to be in or of t. minds about sth, estar indeciso,-a respecto a algo. II n dos m inv; fig to put t. and t. together, atar cabos.

two-faced ['tuːfeɪst] adj hipócrita.

two-party ['tuːpɑːtɪ] adj t-p. system, bipartidismo m.

twopence ['tʌpəns] n GB dos peniques.

two-piece ['tuːpiːs] I adj de dos piezas. II n (suit) traje m de dos piezas.

two-seater ['tuːsiːtər] adj & n biplaza (f).

twosome ['tuːsəm] n pareja f.

two-time ['tuːtaɪm] vtr fam poner los cuernos a.

two-way ['tuːweɪ] adj 1 (street) de dos direcciones. 2 t.-w. radio, aparato m emisor y receptor.

tycoon [taɪ'kuːn] n magnate m.

type [taɪp] I n 1 (kind) tipo m, clase f; (brand) marca f; (of car) modelo m. 2 Typ carácter m; (print) caracteres mpl. II vtr & vi escribir a máquina.

typecast ['taɪpkɑːst] vtr encasillar.

typescript ['taɪpskrɪpt] n texto m escrito a máquina.

typeset ['taɪpset] vtr componer.

typesetter ['taɪpsetər] n 1 (person) cajista mf. 2 (machine) máquina f para componer tipos.

typewriter ['taɪpraɪtər] n máquina f de escribir.

typewritten ['taɪprɪtən] adj escrito,-a a máquina.

typhoid ['taɪfɔɪd] n t. (fever), fiebre tifoidea.

typhoon [taɪ'fuːn] n tifón m.

typical ['tɪpɪkəl] adj típico,-a.

typify ['tɪpɪfaɪ] vtr tipificar.

typing ['taɪpɪŋ] n mecanografía f.

typist ['taɪpɪst] n mecanógrafo,-a m,f.

tyrannical [tɪ'rænɪkəl] adj tiránico,-a.

tyrannize ['tɪrənaɪz] vtr tiranizar.

tyranny ['tɪrənɪ] n tiranía f.

tyrant ['taɪrənt] n tirano,-a m,f.

tyre [taɪər] n neumático m; t. pressure, presión f de los neumáticos.

U

U, u [juː] n (the letter) U, u f.

ubiquity [juː'bɪkwɪtɪ] n ubicuidad f.

udder ['ʌdər] n ubre f.

UFO, ufo ['juːef'əʊ, 'juːfəʊ] abbr of unidentified flying object, OVNI m, ovni m.

ugh [ʌx, ʊh, ʌh] interj juf!, ¡puf!

ugly ['ʌglɪ] adj (uglier, ugliest) feo,-a; (situation) desagradable; fig u. duckling, patito feo.

UK ['juː'keɪ] abbr of United Kingdom, R.U. m.

Ukraine ['juːkreɪn] n the U., Ucrania.

ulcer ['ʌlsər] n (sore) llaga f; (internal) úlcera f.

ulterior [ʌl'tɪərɪər] adj (motive) oculto,-a.

ultimate ['ʌltɪmɪt] adj 1 (final) último,-a; (aim) final. 2 (basic) esencial.
◆**ultimately** adv 1 (finally) finalmente. 2 (basically) en el fondo.

ultimatum [ʌltɪ'meɪtəm] n ultimátum m.

ultrasound ['ʌltrə'saʊnd] n ultrasonido m.

ultraviolet [ʌltrə'vaɪəlɪt] adj ultravioleta.

umbilical [ʌm'bɪlɪkəl, ʌmbɪ'laɪkəl] adj u. cord, cordón m umbilical.

umbrella [ʌm'brelə] n paraguas m inv.

umpire ['ʌmpaɪər] I n árbitro m. II vtr arbitrar.

umpteen [ʌmp'tiːn] adj fam muchísimos,-as, la tira de.

umpteenth [ʌmp'tiːnθ] adj enésimo,-a.

UN ['juː'en] abbr of United Nations (Organization), ONU f sing.

unabashed [ʌnə'bæʃt] adj 1 (unperturbed) inmutable, imperturbable. 2 (shameless) desvergonzado,-a descarado,-a.

unable [ʌn'eɪbəl] adj incapaz; to be u. to do sth/anything, no poder hacer algo/nada.

unacceptable [ʌnək'septəbəl] *adj* inaceptable.

unaccompanied [ʌnə'kʌmpənid] *adj* solo,-a.

unaccountable [ʌnə'kauntəbəl] *adj* inexplicable.

unaccounted-for [ʌnə'kauntidfɔːr] *adj* to be u.-f., faltar.

unaccustomed [ʌnə'kʌstəmd] *adj* he's u. to this climate, no está muy acostumbrado a este clima.

unaffected [ʌnə'fektid] *adj* 1 no afectado,-a (by, por). 2 *(indifferent)* indiferente (by, a). 3 *(natural) (person)* natural; *(style)* llano,-a.

unaided [ʌn'eidid] *adj* sin ayuda, solo,-a.

unanimous [juː'næniməs] *adj* unánime.

unannounced [ʌnə'naunst] *adj* sin avisar.

unanswered [ʌn'ɑːnsəd] *adj* sin contestar.

unapproachable [ʌnə'prəutʃəbəl] *adj* inabordable, inaccesible.

unarmed [ʌn'ɑːmd] *adj* desarmado,-a.

unashamed [ʌnə'ʃeimd] *adj* desvergonzado,-a.

unasked [ʌn'ɑːskt] *adv* u. (for), *(unrequested)* no solicitado,-a; *(spontaneous)* espontáneo,-a.

unassuming [ʌnə'sjuːmiŋ] *adj* sin pretensiones.

unattached [ʌnə'tætʃt] *adj* 1 *(independent)* libre; *(loose)* suelto,-a. 2 *(person)* soltero,-a y sin compromiso.

unattended [ʌnə'tendid] *adj (counter etc)* desatendido,-a; **to leave a child u.,** dejar a un niño solo.

unauthorized [ʌn'ɔːθəraizd] *adj* 1 *(person)* no autorizado,-a. 2 *(trade etc)* ilícito,-a, ilegal.

unavoidable [ʌnə'vɔidəbəl] *adj* inevitable; *(accident)* imprevisible.

unaware [ʌnə'weər] *adj* to be u. of sth, ignorar algo.

unawares [ʌnə'weəz] *adv* 1 *(unexpectedly)* desprevenido,-a. 2 *(without knowing)* inconscientemente.

unbalanced [ʌn'bælənst] *adj* desequilibrado,-a.

unbearable [ʌn'beərəbəl] *adj* insoportable.

unbeatable [ʌn'biːtəbəl] *adj (team)* invencible; *(price, quality)* inmejorable.

unbelievable [ʌnbɪ'liːvəbəl] *adj* increíble.

unbend [ʌn'bend] *vi fam fig* relajarse.

unbia(s)sed [ʌn'baiəst] *adj* imparcial.

unborn [ʌn'bɔːn] *adj* sin nacer, nonato, -a.

unbreakable [ʌn'breikəbəl] *adj* irrompible; *fig* inquebrantable.

unbroken [ʌn'brəukən] *adj* 1 *(whole)* intacto,-a. 2 *(uninterrupted)* continuo,-a. 3 *(record)* imbatido,-a.

unbutton [ʌn'bʌtən] *vtr* desabrochar.

uncalled-for [ʌn'kɔːldfɔːr] *adj (inappropriate)* insensato,-a; *(unjustified)* inmerecido,-a.

uncanny [ʌn'kæni] *adj* misterioso,-a, extraño,-a.

unceasing [ʌn'siːsiŋ] *adj* incesante.

uncertain [ʌn'sɜːtən] *adj* 1 *(not certain)* incierto,-a; *(doubtful)* dudoso,-a; **in no u. terms,** claramente. 2 *(hesitant)* indeciso, -a.

uncertainty [ʌn'sɜːtənti] *n* incertidumbre *f*.

unchanged [ʌn'tʃeindʒd] *adj* igual.

unchecked [ʌn'tʃekt] *adj* 1 *(unrestrained)* desenfrenado,-a. 2 *(not examined)* no comprobado,-a.

uncivilized [ʌn'sivilaizd] *adj (tribe)* incivilizado,-a, salvaje; *(not cultured)* inculto,-a.

uncle ['ʌŋkəl] *n* tío *m*.

uncomfortable [ʌn'kʌmftəbəl] *adj* incómodo,-a; **to make things u. for,** complicarle la vida a.

uncommon [ʌn'kɒmən] *adj* 1 *(rare)* poco común; *(unusual)* extraordinario,-a. 2 *(excessive)* excesivo,-a. ◆**uncommonly** *adv* not u., con cierta frecuencia.

uncompromising [ʌn'kɒmprəmaiziŋ] *adj* intransigente; **u. honesty,** sinceridad absoluta.

unconcerned [ʌnkən'sɜːnd] *adj* indiferente (about, a).

unconditional [ʌnkən'diʃənəl] *adj* incondicional; **u. refusal,** negativa rotunda.

unconnected [ʌnkə'nektid] *adj* no relacionado,-a.

unconscious [ʌn'kɒnʃəs] I *adj* 1 inconsciente (of, de). 2 *(unintentional)* involuntario,-a. II *n* **the u.,** el inconsciente.

unconsciousness [ʌn'kɒnʃəsnis] *n Med* pérdida *f* del conocimiento.

uncontested [ʌnkən'testid] *adj Pol* u. seat, escaño *m* ganado sin oposición.

uncontrollable [ʌnkən'trəuləbəl] *adj* incontrolable; *(desire)* irresistible.

unconventional [ʌnkən'venʃənəl] *adj* poco convencional, original.

uncooperative [ʌnkəu'ɒpərətiv] *adj* poco cooperativo,-a.

uncouth [ʌn'kuːθ] *adj (rude)* grosero,-a.

uncover [ʌn'kʌvər] *vtr* destapar; *fig* descubrir.

undamaged [ʌn'dæmidʒd] *adj (article etc)* sin desperfectos; *(person)* indemne; *(reputation)* intacto,-a.

undaunted [ʌn'dɔːntid] *adj* firme, impávido,-a.

undecided [ʌndɪ'saidid] *adj* 1 *(person)* indeciso,-a. 2 *(issue)* pendiente; **it's still u.,** está aún por decidir.

undefeated [ʌndɪ'fiːtid] *adj* invicto,-a.

undefined [ʌndɪ'faind] *adj*

indeterminado,-a.

undeniable [ʌndɪ'naɪəbəl] adj innegable.

under ['ʌndəʳ] I prep 1 debajo de; u. the sun, bajo el sol. 2 (less than) menos de; incomes u. £1,000, ingresos inferiores a 1.000 libras; u. age, menor de edad. 3 (of rank) de rango inferior a. 4 u. Caesar, bajo César. 5 (subject to) bajo; u. arrest, detenido,-a; u. cover, a cubierto; u. obligation to, en la obligación de; u. the circumstances, dadas las circunstancias; fig I was u. the impression that ..., tenía la impresión de que .... 6 (according to) según, conforme a. II adv abajo, debajo.

under- ['ʌndəʳ] pref (below) sub-, infra-; (insufficiently) insuficientemente.

underarm ['ʌndərɑːm] I adj u. deodorant, desodorante m para las axilas. II adv Sport por debajo del hombro.

undercarriage [ʌndə'kærɪdʒ] n tren m de aterrizaje.

undercharge [ʌndə'tʃɑːdʒ] vtr cobrar menos de lo debido.

underclothes ['ʌndəkləʊðz] npl ropa f sing interior.

undercoat ['ʌndəkəʊt] n (of paint) primera mano.

undercover [ʌndə'kʌvəʳ] adj secreto,-a.

undercurrent ['ʌndəkʌrənt] n 1 (in sea) corriente submarina. 2 fig sentimiento m latente.

undercut [ʌndə'kʌt] vtr Com vender más barato que.

underdeveloped [ʌndədɪ'veləpt] adj subdesarrollado,-a.

underdog ['ʌndədɒg] n desvalido,-a m,f.

underestimate [ʌndər'estɪmeɪt] vtr infravalorar.

underexposure [ʌndərɪk'spəʊʒəʳ] n Phot subexposición f.

underfed [ʌndə'fed] adj subalimentado,-a.

underfoot [ʌndə'fʊt] adv en el suelo.

undergo [ʌndə'gəʊ] vtr experimentar; (change) sufrir; (test etc) pasar por.

undergraduate [ʌndə'grædjʊət] n estudiante mf universitario,-a.

underground [ʌndə'graʊnd] I adj subterráneo,-a; fig clandestino,-a. II [ʌndə'graʊnd] adv fig to go u., pasar a la clandestinidad. III ['ʌndəgraʊnd] n 1 Pol movimiento clandestino. 2 the u., (subway) el metro.

undergrowth ['ʌndəgrəʊθ] maleza f.

underhand ['ʌndəhænd] I adj (method) ilícito,-a; (person) solapado,-a. II adv bajo cuerda.

underline [ʌndə'laɪn] vtr subrayar.

underling ['ʌndəlɪŋ] n pej mandado,-a m,f.

underlying [ʌndə'laɪɪŋ] adj (basic) fundamental.

undermine [ʌndə'maɪn] vtr socavar, mi-

nar.

underneath [ʌndə'niːθ] I prep debajo de, bajo. II adv abajo, debajo. III adj de abajo. IV n parte f inferior.

undernourished [ʌndə'nʌrɪʃt] adj desnutrido,-a.

underpaid [ʌndə'peɪd] adj mal pagado,-a.

underpass ['ʌndəpɑːs] n paso subterráneo.

underprivileged [ʌndə'prɪvɪlɪdʒd] I adj desfavorecido,-a. II npl the u., los menos favorecidos.

underrate [ʌndə'reɪt] vtr → **undervalue.**

undershirt ['ʌndəʃɜːt] n US camiseta f.

underskirt ['ʌndəskɜːt] n combinación f.

understand [ʌndə'stænd] vtr & vi (pt & pp understood) 1 (comprehend) entender, comprender; fam do I make myself understood?, ¿me explico? 2 (assume, believe) entender; she gave me to u. that ..., me dio a entender que .... 3 (hear) tener entendido. 4 to u. one another, entenderse.

understandable [ʌndə'stændəbəl] adj comprensible.

understanding [ʌndə'stændɪŋ] I n 1 (intellectual grasp) entendimiento m, comprensión f. 2 (interpretation) interpretación f. 3 (agreement) acuerdo m. 4 on the u. that ..., a condición de que .... II adj comprensivo,-a.

understatement [ʌndə'steɪtmənt] n to make an u., minimizar, subestimar; to say that the boy is rather clever is an u., decir que el chico es bastante listo es quedarse corto.

understood [ʌndə'stʊd] adj 1 I wish it to be u. that ..., que conste que .... 2 (agreed on) convenido,-a. 3 (implied) sobreentendido,-a.

understudy ['ʌndəstʌdɪ] n suplente mf.

undertake [ʌndə'teɪk] vtr (pt undertook; pp undertaken [ʌndə'teɪkən]) 1 (responsibility) asumir; (task, job) encargarse de. 2 (promise) comprometerse a.

undertaker ['ʌndəteɪkəʳ] n empresario,-a m,f de pompas fúnebres; u.'s, funeraria f.

undertaking [ʌndə'teɪkɪŋ] n 1 (task) empresa f. 2 (guarantee) garantía f.

undertone ['ʌndətəʊn] n in an u., en voz baja.

underwater [ʌndə'wɔːtəʳ] I adj submarino,-a. II adv bajo el agua.

underwear ['ʌndəweəʳ] n inv ropa f interior.

underworld ['ʌndəwɜːld] n (criminals) hampa f, bajos fondos.

underwrite [ʌndə'raɪt] vtr (pt underwrote; pp underwritten) 1 (guarantee) garantizar, avalar. 2 (insure) asegurar.

underwriter ['ʌndəraɪtəʳ] n 1 Fin suscriptor,-a m,f. 2 (insurer) asegurador,-a m,f.

undesirable \ˌʌndɪˈzaɪrəbəl\ *adj & n* indeseable (*mf*).

undeterred \ˌʌndɪˈtɜːd\ *adj* sin inmutarse; **u. by,** sin arredrarse ante.

undies \ˈʌndɪz\ *npl fam* bragas *fpl*.

undignified \ʌnˈdɪgnɪfaɪd\ *adj* (*attitude etc*) indecoroso,-a.

undisciplined \ʌnˈdɪsɪplɪnd\ *adj* indisciplinado,-a.

undisclosed \ˌʌndɪsˈkləʊzd\ *adj* sin revelar.

undiscovered \ˌʌndɪsˈkʌvəd\ *adj* sin descubrir.

undisguised \ˌʌndɪsˈgaɪzd\ *adj fig* no disimulado,-a.

undisputed \ˌʌndɪsˈpjuːtɪd\ *adj* (*unchallenged*) incontestable; (*unquestionable*) indiscutible.

undivided \ˌʌndɪˈvaɪdɪd\ *adj* **to give one's u. attention,** prestar toda la atención.

undo \ʌnˈduː\ *vtr* (*pt* **undid**; *pp* **undone**) 1 deshacer; (*button*) desabrochar. 2 (*put right*) enmendar.

undone¹ \ʌnˈdʌn\ *adj* (*unfinished*) inacabado,-a.

undone² \ʌnˈdʌn\ *adj* (*knot etc*) deshecho,-a; **to come u.,** (*shoelace*) desatarse; (*button, blouse*) desabrocharse; (*necklace etc*) soltarse.

undoubted \ʌnˈdaʊtɪd\ *adj* indudable.

undress \ʌnˈdres\ I *vtr* desnudar. II *vi* desnudarse.

undressed \ʌnˈdrest\ *adj* (*naked*) desnudo,-a.

undue \ʌnˈdjuː\ 1 *adj* (*excessive*) excesivo,-a. 2 (*improper*) indebido,-a.

undulate \ˈʌndjʊleɪt\ *vi* ondular, ondear.

unearth \ʌnˈɜːθ\ *vtr* desenterrar.

unearthly \ʌnˈɜːθlɪ\ *adj* 1 (*being*) sobrenatural. 2 *fam* (*din*) espantoso,-a; **at an u. hour,** a una hora intempestiva.

uneasy \ʌnˈiːzɪ\ *adj* 1 (*worried*) preocupado,-a. 2 (*disturbing*) inquietante. 2 (*uncomfortable*) incómodo,-a.

uneconomic(al) \ˌʌniːkəˈnɒmɪk(əl)\ *adj* poco económico,-a.

uneducated \ʌnˈedjʊkeɪtɪd\ *adj* inculto,-a.

unemployed \ˌʌnɪmˈplɔɪd\ I *adj* en paro, parado,-a; **to be u.,** estar en paro. II *npl* **the u.,** los parados.

unemployment \ˌʌnɪmˈplɔɪmənt\ *n* paro *m*, desempleo *m*, *US* **u. compensation,** subsidio *m* de desempleo.

unending \ʌnˈendɪŋ\ *adj* interminable.

unenviable \ʌnˈenvɪəbəl\ *adj* poco envidiable.

unequal \ʌnˈiːkwəl\ *adj* desigual.

unequivocal \ˌʌnɪˈkwɪvəkəl\ *adj* inequívoco,-a.

uneven \ʌnˈiːvən\ *adj* 1 (*not level*) desigual; (*bumpy*) accidentado,-a. 2 (*variable*) irregular.

uneventful \ˌʌnɪˈventfʊl\ *adj* sin aconteci-mientos.

unexceptional \ˌʌnɪkˈsepʃənəl\ *adj* ordinario,-a.

unexpected \ˌʌnɪkˈspektɪd\ *adj* (*unhoped for*) inesperado,-a; (*event*) imprevisto,-a.

unfailing \ʌnˈfeɪlɪŋ\ *adj* indefectible; (*incessant*) constante; (*patience*) inagotable.

unfair \ʌnˈfeəʳ\ *adj* injusto,-a; *Sport* sucio,-a.

unfaithful \ʌnˈfeɪθfʊl\ *adj* (*friend*) desleal; (*husband, wife*) infiel.

unfamiliar \ˌʌnfəˈmɪljəʳ\ *adj* (*unknown*) desconocido,-a; (*not conversant*) no familiarizado,-a (**with,** con).

unfashionable \ʌnˈfæʃənəbəl\ *adj* pasado,-a de moda; (*ideas etc*) poco popular.

unfasten \ʌnˈfɑːsən\ *vtr* (*knot*) desatar; (*clothing, belt*) desabrochar.

unfavourable, *US* **unfavorable** \ʌnˈfeɪvərəbəl\ *adj* desfavorable; (*criticism*) adverso,-a; (*winds*) contrario,-a.

unfeeling \ʌnˈfiːlɪŋ\ *adj* insensible.

unfinished \ʌnˈfɪnɪʃt\ *adj* inacabado,-a; **u. business,** un asunto pendiente.

unfit \ʌnˈfɪt\ *adj* 1 (*thing*) inadecuado,-a; (*person*) no apto,-a (**for,** para). 2 (*incompetent*) incompetente. 3 (*physically*) incapacitado,-a; **to be u.,** no estar en forma.

unflinching \ʌnˈflɪntʃɪŋ\ *adj* 1 (*determined*) resuelto,-a. 2 (*fearless*) impávido,-a.

unfold \ʌnˈfəʊld\ I *vtr* 1 (*sheet*) desdoblar; (*newspaper*) abrir. 2 (*plan, secret*) revelar. II *vi* 1 (*open up*) abrirse; (*landscape*) extenderse. 2 (*plot*) desarrollarse. 3 (*secret*) descubrirse.

unforeseen \ˌʌnfɔːˈsiːn\ *adj* imprevisto,-a.

unforgettable \ˌʌnfəˈgetəbəl\ *adj* inolvidable.

unforgivable \ˌʌnfəˈgɪvəbəl\ *adj* imperdonable.

unfortunate \ʌnˈfɔːtʃənɪt\ *adj* (*person, event*) desgraciado,-a; (*remark*) desafortunado,-a; **how u.!,** ¡qué mala suerte! ◆ **unfortunately** *adv* desgraciadamente, por desgracia.

unfounded \ʌnˈfaʊndɪd\ *adj* infundado,-a.

unfriendly \ʌnˈfrendlɪ\ *adj* (*unfriendlier, unfriendliest*) antipático,-a, poco amistoso,-a.

unfurl \ʌnˈfɜːl\ *vi* desplegarse.

unfurnished \ʌnˈfɜːnɪʃt\ *adj* sin amueblar.

ungainly \ʌnˈgeɪnlɪ\ *adj* (*gait*) desgarbado,-a.

ungodly \ʌnˈgɒdlɪ\ *adj* (*ungodlier, ungodliest*) (*behaviour*) impío,-a; *fam fig* **at an u. hour,** a una hora intempestiva.

ungrateful \ʌnˈgreɪtfʊl\ *adj* (*person*) desagradecido,-a; (*task*) ingrato,-a.

unguarded \ʌnˈgɑːdɪd\ *adj* 1 (*unprotected*)

desatendido,-a; *(imprudent)* desprevenido,-a. 2 *(frank)* franco,-a.

unhappiness \ʌnˈhæpɪnɪs\ *n* 1 *(sadness)* tristeza *f*. 2 *(wretchedness)* desdicha *f*.

unhappy \ʌnˈhæpɪ\ *adj* *(unhappier, unhappiest)* 1 *(sad)* triste. 2 *(wretched)* desgraciado,-a, infeliz; *(unfortunate)* desafortunado,-a.

unharmed \ʌnˈhɑːmd\ *adj* ileso,-a, indemne.

unhealthy \ʌnˈhelθɪ\ *adj* *(unhealthier, unhealthiest)* 1 *(ill)* enfermizo,-a. 2 *(unwholesome)* malsano,-a.

unheard \ʌnˈhɜːd\ *adj* 1 her request went u., su petición no fue atendida. 2 u. of, *(outrageous)* inaudito,-a; *(without precedent)* sin precedente.

unhesitating \ʌnˈhezɪteɪtɪŋ\ *adj* resuelto,-a.

unhook \ʌnˈhʊk\ *vtr* *(from hook)* descolgar; *(clothing)* desabrochar.

unhurt \ʌnˈhɜːt\ *adj* ileso,-a, indemne.

unhygienic \ʌnhaɪˈdʒiːnɪk\ *adj* antihigiénico,-a.

unidentified \ʌnaɪˈdentɪfaɪd\ *adj* u. flying object, objeto volador no identificado, ovni *m*.

unification \juːnɪfɪˈkeɪʃən\ *n* unificación *f*.

uniform \ˈjuːnɪfɔːm\ *adj* & *nm* uniforme.

uniformity \juːnɪˈfɔːmɪtɪ\ *n* uniformidad *f*.

unify \ˈjuːnɪfaɪ\ *vtr* unificar.

unilateral \juːnɪˈlætərəl\ *adj* unilateral.

unimportant \ʌnɪmˈpɔːtənt\ *adj* poco importante.

uninformed \ʌnɪnˈfɔːmd\ *adj* *(opinion)* sin fundamento.

uninhabited \ʌnɪnˈhæbɪtɪd\ *adj* deshabitado,-a.

uninhibited \ʌnɪnˈhɪbɪtɪd\ *adj* sin inhibición.

uninspired \ʌnɪnˈspaɪəd\ *adj* *(person)* falto,-a de inspiración; *(performance)* insulso,-a.

uninspiring \ʌnɪnˈspaɪərɪŋ\ *adj* que no inspira.

unintelligible \ʌnɪnˈtelɪdʒəbəl\ *adj* ininteligible, incomprensible.

unintentional \ʌnɪnˈtenʃənəl\ *adj* involuntario,-a. ◆**unintentionally** *adv* sin querer.

uninteresting \ʌnˈɪntrɪstɪŋ\ *adj* poco interesante.

uninterrupted \ʌnɪntəˈrʌptɪd\ *adj* ininterrumpido,-a.

union \ˈjuːnjən\ *n* 1 unión *f*. 2 *(organization)* sindicato *m*. 3 *US* the U., los Estados Unidos; **U. Jack**, bandera *f* del Reino Unido; **U.** *adj* sindical.

unique \juːˈniːk\ *adj* único,-a.

unison \ˈjuːnɪsən\ *n* *Mus* unisonancia *f*; *fig (harmony)* armonía *f*; **in u.**, al unísono.

unit \ˈjuːnɪt\ *n* 1 unidad *f*; monetary u.,

unidad monetaria; *GB Fin* u. trust, sociedad *f* de inversiones. 2 *(piece of furniture)* módulo *m*; **kitchen u.**, mueble *m* de cocina. 3 *Tech* grupo *m*; *Comput* central processing u., procesador *m* central; visual display u., pantalla *f*. 4 *(department)* servicio *m*. 5 *(team)* equipo *m*.

unite \juːˈnaɪt\ I *vtr* unir. II *vi* unirse.

united \juːˈnaɪtɪd\ *adj* unido,-a; **U. Kingdom**, Reino Unido; **U. States (of America)**, Estados Unidos (de América); **U. Nations**, Naciones Unidas.

unity \ˈjuːnɪtɪ\ *n* unidad *f*; *(harmony)* armonía *f*.

universal \juːnɪˈvɜːsəl\ *adj* universal.

universe \ˈjuːnɪvɜːs\ *n* universo *m*.

university \juːnɪˈvɜːsɪtɪ\ I *n* universidad *f*. II *adj* universitario,-a.

unjust \ʌnˈdʒʌst\ *adj* injusto,-a.

unkempt \ʌnˈkempt\ *adj* descuidado,-a; *(hair)* despeinado,-a; *(appearance)* desaliñado,-a.

unkind \ʌnˈkaɪnd\ *adj* *(not nice)* poco amable; *(cruel)* despiadado,-a.

unknown \ʌnˈnəʊn\ I *adj* desconocido,-a; **u. quantity**, incógnita *f*. II *n* the u., lo desconocido.

unlawful \ʌnˈlɔːfʊl\ *adj* *(not legal)* ilegal.

unleash \ʌnˈliːʃ\ *vtr* 1 *(dog)* soltar. 2 *fig (release)* liberar; *(provoke)* desencadenar.

unless \ʌnˈles\ *conj* a menos que, a no ser que.

unlike \ʌnˈlaɪk\ I *adj* diferente, distinto, -a. II *prep* a diferencia de.

unlikely \ʌnˈlaɪklɪ\ *adj* 1 *(improbable)* poco probable. 2 *(unusual)* raro,-a.

unlimited \ʌnˈlɪmɪtɪd\ *adj* ilimitado,-a.

unload \ʌnˈləʊd\ *vtr* & *vi* descargar.

unlock \ʌnˈlɒk\ *vtr* abrir (con llave).

unlucky \ʌnˈlʌkɪ\ *adj* *(unluckier, unluckiest)* *(unfortunate)* desgraciado,-a; **to be u.**, *(person)* tener mala suerte; *(thing)* traer mala suerte. ◆**unluckily** *adv* desafortunadamente, por desgracia.

unmanageable \ʌnˈmænɪdʒəbəl\ *adj* *(people)* ingobernable; *(child, hair)* incontrolable.

unmanned \ʌnˈmænd\ *adj* *(spacecraft etc)* no tripulado,-a.

unmarried \ʌnˈmærɪd\ *adj* soltero,-a.

unmask \ʌnˈmɑːsk\ *vtr* *fig (plot)* descubrir.

unmistak(e)able \ʌnmɪsˈteɪkəbəl\ *adj* inconfundible. ◆**unmistak(e)ably** *adv* sin lugar a dudas.

unmitigated \ʌnˈmɪtɪgeɪtɪd\ *adj* 1 *(absolute)* absoluto,-a; *(liar)* rematado,-a. 2 *(grief)* profundo,-a.

unnamed \ʌnˈneɪmd\ *adj* *(anonymous)* anónimo,-a.

unnatural \ʌnˈnætʃərəl\ *adj* 1 *(against nature)* antinatural; *(abnormal)* anormal. 2 *(affected)* afectado,-a.

unnecessary \ʌnˈnesɪsərɪ\ *adj*

innecesario,-a, inútil; **it's u.** to add that ..., sobra añadir que ....

unnoticed [ʌn'nəʊtɪst] adj desapercibido,-a; **to let sth pass un u.,** pasar algo por alto.

unobserved [ʌnəb'zɜːvd] adj inadvertido,-a.

unobtainable [ʌnəb'teɪnəbəl] adj inasequible, inalcanzable.

unobtrusive [ʌnəb'truːsɪv] adj discreto,-a.

unoccupied [ʌn'ɒkjʊpaɪd] adj (house) desocupado,-a; (seat) libre.

unofficial [ʌnə'fɪʃəl] adj no oficial.

unorthodox [ʌn'ɔːθədɒks] adj 1 (behaviour etc) poco ortodoxo,-a. 2 Rel heterodoxo,-a.

unpack [ʌn'pæk] I vtr (boxes) desembalar; (suitcase) deshacer. II vi deshacer la(s) maleta(s).

unpalatable [ʌn'pælətəbəl] adj desagradable.

unparalleled [ʌn'pærəleld] adj 1 (in quality) incomparable. 2 (without precedent) sin precedente.

unpardonable [ʌn'pɑːdənəbəl] adj imperdonable.

unperturbed [ʌnpə'tɜːbd] adj impasible.

unpleasant [ʌn'plezənt] adj desagradable (to, con).

unpleasantness [ʌn'plezəntnɪs] n disgusto m.

unplug [ʌn'plʌg] vtr desenchufar.

unpopular [ʌn'pɒpjʊlər] adj impopular; **to make oneself u.,** ganarse la antipatía de todos.

unprecedented [ʌn'presɪdentɪd] adj sin precedente.

unpredictable [ʌnprɪ'dɪktəbəl] adj imprevisible.

unprepared [ʌnprɪ'peəd] adj (speech etc) improvisado,-a; (person) desprevenido,-a.

unprincipled [ʌn'prɪnsɪpəld] adj sin escrúpulos.

unprintable [ʌn'prɪntəbəl] adj (word, comment) malsonante.

unproductive [ʌnprə'dʌktɪv] adj (inefficient) improductivo,-a; (fruitless) infructuoso,-a.

unprofessional [ʌnprə'feʃənəl] adj (unethical) poco profesional; (substandard) de aficionado,-a.

unprotected [ʌnprə'tektɪd] adj indefenso,-a.

unprovoked [ʌnprə'vəʊkt] adj gratuito,-a.

unpunished [ʌn'pʌnɪʃt] adj impune.

unqualified [ʌn'kwɒlɪfaɪd] adj 1 (without qualification) sin título; (incompetent) incompetente. 2 (unconditional) incondicional; (denial) rotundo,-a; (endorsement) sin reserva; (success) total.

unquestionable [ʌn'kwestʃənəbəl] adj indiscutible.

unquestioning [ʌn'kwestʃənɪŋ] adj incondicional; (obedience) ciego,-a.

unravel [ʌn'rævəl] I vtr desenmarañar. II vi desenmarañarse.

unreadable [ʌn'riːdəbəl] adj 1 (handwriting) ilegible. 2 (book) imposible de leer.

unreal [ʌn'rɪəl] adj irreal.

unrealistic [ʌnrɪə'lɪstɪk] adj poco realista.

unreasonable [ʌn'riːzənəbəl] adj poco razonable; (demands) desmedido,-a; (prices) exorbitante; (hour) inoportuno,-a.

unrefined [ʌnrɪ'faɪnd] adj 1 (sugar, oil etc) sin refinar. 2 (person) tosco,-a, basto,-a.

unrelated [ʌnrɪ'leɪtɪd] adj (not connected) no relacionado,-a.

unrelenting [ʌnrɪ'lentɪŋ] adj (behaviour) implacable; (struggle) encarnizado,-a.

unreliable [ʌnrɪ'laɪəbəl] adj 1 (person) de poca confianza. 2 (information) que no es de fiar; (machine) poco fiable.

unrelieved [ʌnrɪ'liːvd] adj (boredom) total.

unremitting [ʌnrɪ'mɪtɪŋ] adj 1 (efforts etc) incesante. 2 (person) incansable.

unrepentant [ʌnrɪ'pentənt] adj impenitente.

unreserved [ʌnrɪ'zɜːvd] adj (praise, support) sin reserva. ◆**unreservedly** adv sin reserva.

unrest [ʌn'rest] n (social etc) malestar m; political u., agitación política.

unrivalled, US **unrivaled** [ʌn'raɪvəld] adj sin par, sin rival.

unroll [ʌn'rəʊl] vtr desenrollar.

unruffled [ʌn'rʌfəld] adj fig tranquilo,-a.

unruly [ʌn'ruːlɪ] adj (unrulier, unruliest) 1 (child) revoltoso,-a. 2 (hair) rebelde.

unsafe [ʌn'seɪf] adj (dangerous) peligroso,-a; (risky) inseguro,-a; **to feel u.,** sentirse expuesto,-a.

unsaid [ʌn'sed] adj **it's better left u.,** más vale no decir nada; **much was left u.,** quedó mucho por decir.

unsatisfactory [ʌnsætɪs'fæktərɪ] adj insatisfactorio,-a; **it's most u.,** deja mucho que desear.

unsavoury, US **unsavory** [ʌn'seɪvərɪ] adj desagradable.

unscathed [ʌn'skeɪðd] adj ileso,-a, indemne.

unscrew [ʌn'skruː] vtr destornillar.

unscrupulous [ʌn'skruːpjʊləs] adj sin escrúpulos.

unseemly [ʌn'siːmlɪ] adj impropio,-a.

unseen [ʌn'siːn] I adj invisible; (unnoticed) inadvertido,-a. II n GB Educ texto no trabajado en clase.

unselfish [ʌn'selfɪʃ] adj desinteresado,-a.

unsettle [ʌn'setəl] vtr perturbar.

unsettled [ʌn'setəld] adj 1 (person) nervioso,-a. 2 (situation) inestable. 2 (weather) inestable. 3 (matter, debt) pendiente. 4 (land) sin colonizar.

unshaven [ʌn'ʃeɪvən] adj sin afeitar.

unsightly [ʌn'saɪtlɪ] adj feo,-a, desagradable.

unskilled [ʌn'skɪld] adj (worker) no cualificado,-a; (work) no especializado,-a.

unsociable [ʌn'səʊʃəbəl] adj insociable, huraño,-a.

unsophisticated [ʌnsə'fɪstɪkeɪtɪd] adj 1 (naïve) ingenuo,-a. 2 (simple) poco sofisticado,-a.

unsound [ʌn'saʊnd] adj 1 (unstable) inestable; of u. mind, demente. 2 (fallacious) falso,-a.

unspeakable [ʌn'spiːkəbəl] adj 1 indecible. 2 fig (evil) atroz.

unspoken [ʌn'spəʊkən] adj 1 (tacit) tácito,-a. 2 (feeling) interior, secreto,-a.

unstable [ʌn'steɪbəl] adj inestable.

unsteady [ʌn'stedɪ] adj 1 (not firm) inestable; (table, chair) cojo,-a; (hand, voice) tembloroso,-a.

unstinting [ʌn'stɪntɪŋ] adj pródigo,-a (in, en, de).

unstuck [ʌn'stʌk] adj to come u., despegarse; fig venirse abajo.

unsuccessful [ʌnsək'sesfʊl] adj 1 (fruitless) fracasado,-a; (useless) vano,-a. 2 (businessman etc) fracasado,-a; (candidate) derrotado,-a; to be u. at sth, no tener éxito con algo. ◆unsuccessfully adv sin éxito, en vano.

unsuitable [ʌn'suːtəbəl] adj 1 (person) no apto,-a. 2 (thing) inadecuado,-a; (remark) inoportuno,-a; (time) inconveniente.

unsuited [ʌn'suːtɪd] adj 1 (person) no apto,-a; (thing) impropio,-a (to, para). 2 (incompatible) incompatible.

unsure [ʌn'ʃʊər] adj poco seguro,-a.

unsuspecting [ʌnsə'spektɪŋ] adj confiado,-a; he went in u., entró sin sospechar nada.

unswerving [ʌn'swɜːvɪŋ] adj firme.

unsympathetic [ʌnsɪmpə'θetɪk] adj (unfeeling) impasible; (not understanding) poco comprensivo,-a.

untapped [ʌn'tæpt] adj (mine etc) sin explotar.

untarnished [ʌn'tɑːnɪʃt] adj fig sin mancha.

untenable [ʌn'tenəbəl] adj insostenible.

unthinkable [ʌn'θɪŋkəbəl] adj impensable, inconcebible.

untidy [ʌn'taɪdɪ] adj (untidier, untidiest) (room, person) desordenado,-a; (hair) despeinado,-a; (appearance) desaseado,-a.

untie [ʌn'taɪ] vtr desatar; (free) soltar.

until [ʌn'tɪl] I conj hasta que; she worked u. she collapsed, trabajó hasta desfallecer; u. she gets back, hasta que vuelva. II prep hasta; u. now, hasta ahora; u. ten o'clock, hasta las diez; not u. Monday, hasta el lunes no.

untimely [ʌn'taɪmlɪ] adj 1 (premature) prematuro,-a. 2 (inopportune)

inoportuno,-a; (hour) intempestivo,-a.

untold [ʌn'təʊld] adj 1 (indescribable) indecible. 2 fig (loss, wealth) incalculable. 3 (not told) sin contar.

untouchable [ʌn'tʌtʃəbəl] adj & n intocable (mf).

untoward [ʌntə'wɔːd, ʌn'təʊəd] adj 1 (unfortunate) desafortunado,-a. 2 (adverse) adverso,-a.

untrained [ʌn'treɪnd] adj 1 (unskilled) sin preparación profesional. 2 (inexpert) inexperto,-a.

untrue [ʌn'truː] adj 1 (false) falso,-a. 2 (unfaithful) infiel. 3 (inexact) inexacto,-a.

untrustworthy [ʌn'trʌstwɜːðɪ] adj 1 (person) de poca confianza. 2 (source) no fidedigno,-a.

unused [ʌn'juːzd] adj 1 (car) sin usar; (flat etc) sin estrenar; (stamp) sin matar. 2 (not in use) que no se utiliza. 3 [ʌn'juːst] (unaccustomed) desacostumbrado,-a (to, a).

unusual [ʌn'juːʒʊəl] adj (rare) insólito,-a, poco común; (original) original; (exceptional) excepcional. ◆unusually adv excepcionalmente.

unveil [ʌn'veɪl] vtr descubrir.

unwarranted [ʌn'wɒrəntɪd] adj injustificado,-a; (remark) gratuito,-a.

unwavering [ʌn'weɪvərɪŋ] adj (loyalty) constante, firme; (courage) inquebrantable.

unwelcome [ʌn'welkəm] adj (visitor) molesto,-a; (visit) inoportuno,-a; fig (news etc) desagradable.

unwell [ʌn'wel] adj malo,-a, indispuesto,-a.

unwieldy [ʌn'wiːldɪ] adj (difficult to handle) poco manejable; (clumsy) torpe.

unwilling [ʌn'wɪlɪŋ] adj to be u. to do sth, no estar dispuesto a hacer algo. ◆unwillingly adv de mala gana.

unwind [ʌn'waɪnd] (pt & pp unwound) I vtr desenrollar. II vi 1 desenrollarse. 2 (relax) relajarse.

unwise [ʌn'waɪz] adj imprudente, desaconsejable.

unwitting [ʌn'wɪtɪŋ] adj involuntario,-a.

unworkable [ʌn'wɜːkəbəl] adj (not feasible) impracticable; (suggestion) irrealizable.

unworthy [ʌn'wɜːðɪ] adj indigno,-a.

unwrap [ʌn'ræp] vtr (gift) desenvolver; (package) deshacer.

unwritten [ʌn'rɪtən] adj no escrito,-a; (agreement) verbal.

unyielding [ʌn'jiːldɪŋ] adj inflexible.

up [ʌp] I prep 1 (movement) to climb up the mountain, escalar la montaña; to walk up the street, ir calle arriba. 2 (position) en lo alto de; further up the street, más adelante (en la misma calle); halfway up the ladder, a mitad de la escalera.

II *adv* 1 (*upwards*) arriba, hacia arriba; (*position*) arriba; **from ten pounds up**, de diez libras para arriba; **halfway up**, a medio camino; **right up** (*to the top*), hasta arriba (del todo); **to go** or **come up**, subir; **'this side up'**, 'este lado hacia arriba'. 2 **the moon is up**, ha salido la luna. 3 (*towards*) hacia; **to come** or **go up to sb**, acercarse a algn; **to walk up and down**, ir de un lado a otro. 4 (*in*, *to*) **he's up in Yorkshire**, está en Yorkshire. 5 (*increased*) **bread is up**, el pan ha subido. 6 **it's up for discussion**, se está discutiendo; **up for sale**, en venta. 7 *fam* **something's up**, pasa algo; **what's up** (**with you**)?, ¿qué pasa (contigo)? 8 **to be up against sth**, enfrentarse con algo. 9 **up to**, (*as far as*, *until*) hasta; **I can spend up to £5**, puedo gastar un máximo de cinco libras; **up to here**, hasta aquí; **up to now**, hasta ahora. 10 **to be up to**, (*depend on*) depender de; (*be capable of*) estar a la altura de; **I don't feel up to doing it today**, hoy no me encuentro con fuerzas para hacerlo; **it's not up to much**, no vale gran cosa. 11 **he's up to sth**, está tramando algo.

III *adj* 1 (*out of bed*) levantado,-a. 2 (*finished*) terminado,-a; **time's up**, (ya) es la hora.

IV *tr* *fam* aumentar.

V *n* *fig* **ups and downs**, altibajos *mpl*.

up-and-coming [ˈʌpənˈkʌmɪŋ] *adj* prometedor,-a.

upbringing [ˈʌpbrɪŋɪŋ] *n* educación *f*.

update [ʌpˈdeɪt] *vtr* actualizar, poner al día.

upgrade [ʌpˈgreɪd] *vtr* 1 (*promote*) ascender. 2 (*improve*) mejorar la calidad de.

upheaval [ʌpˈhiːvəl] *n* trastorno *m*.

uphill [ˈʌphɪl] I *adj* ascendente; *fig* arduo,-a. II *adv* cuesta arriba.

uphold [ʌpˈhəʊld] *vtr* (*pt* & *pp* **upheld**) sostener.

upholstery [ʌpˈhəʊlstərɪ] *n* tapizado *m*, tapicería *f*.

upkeep [ˈʌpkiːp] *n* mantenimiento *m*.

up-market [ˈʌpmɑːkɪt] *adj* de categoría.

upon [əˈpɒn] *prep* *fml* en, sobre; **once u. a time ...**, érase una vez ...; **u. my word**, (mi) palabra de honor.

upper [ˈʌpə[r]] I *adj* 1 (*position*) superior; **u. storey**, piso de arriba; *fig* **to have the u. hand**, llevar la delantera. 2 (*in rank*) alto,-a; **the u. class**, la clase alta; **the U. House**, la Cámara Alta. II *n* (*of shoe*) pala *f*.

upper-class [ˈʌpəklɑːs] *adj* de la clase alta.

uppermost [ˈʌpəməʊst] *adj* más alto,-a; *fig* **it was u. in my mind**, era lo que me preocupaba más.

upright [ˈʌpraɪt] I *adj* 1 (*vertical*) vertical.

2 (*honest*) honrado,-a. II *adv* derecho. III *n* *Ftb* (*post*) poste *m*.

uprising [ʌpˈraɪzɪŋ] *n* sublevación *f*.

uproar [ˈʌprɔː[r]] *n* tumulto *m*, alboroto *m*.

uproot [ʌpˈruːt] *vtr* (*plant*) arrancar de raíz.

upset [ʌpˈset] I *vtr* (*pt* & *pp* **upset**) 1 (*overturn*) volcar; (*spill*) derramar. 2 (*shock*) trastornar; (*worry*) preocupar; (*displease*) disgustar. 3 (*spoil*) desbaratar. 4 (*make ill*) sentar mal a. II [ˈʌpset] *n* 1 (*reversal*) revés *m*. 2 *Sport* resultado inesperado. III [ʌpˈset] *adj* (*shocked*) alterado,-a; (*displeased*) disgustado,-a; **to have an u. stomach**, sentirse mal del estómago.

upshot [ˈʌpʃɒt] *n* resultado *m*.

upside [ˈʌpsaɪd] *n* **u. down**, al revés.

upstage [ʌpˈsteɪdʒ] *vtr* *fam* eclipsar.

upstairs [ʌpˈsteəz] I *adv* al piso de arriba; **she lives u.**, vive en el piso de arriba. II *n* piso *m* de arriba.

upstart [ˈʌpstɑːt] *n* advenedizo,-a *m,f*.

upstream [ʌpˈstriːm] *adv* río arriba.

uptake [ˈʌpteɪk] *n* *fam* **to be quick on the u.**, cogerlas al vuelo.

uptight [ʌpˈtaɪt] *adj* *fam* nervioso,-a.

up to date [ʌptəˈdeɪt] *adj* 1 (*current*) al día. 2 (*modern*) moderno,-a.

upturn [ˈʌptɜːn] *n* mejora *f*.

upward [ˈʌpwəd] *adj* ascendente.

upward(s) [ˈʌpwəd(z)] *adv* hacia arriba; **from ten (years) u.**, a partir de los diez años; *fam* **u. of**, algo más de.

uranium [jʊˈreɪnɪəm] *n* uranio *m*.

urban [ˈɜːbən] *adj* urbano,-a.

urbane [ɜːˈbeɪn] *adj* urbano,-a, cortés.

urchin [ˈɜːtʃɪn] *n* 1 (*child*) pilluelo,-a *m,f*. 2 **sea u.**, erizo *m* de mar.

urge [ɜːdʒ] I *vtr* 1 instar; (*plead*) exhortar. 2 (*advocate*) preconizar; **to u. that sth should be done**, insistir en que se haga algo. II *n* impulso *m*. ◆ **urge on** *vtr* animar a.

urgency [ˈɜːdʒənsɪ] *n* urgencia *f*.

urgent [ˈɜːdʒənt] *adj* urgente; (*need*, *tone*) apremiante.

urinal [jʊˈraɪnəl] *n* (*toilet*) urinario *m*; (*bowl*) orinal *m*.

urinate [ˈjʊərɪneɪt] *vi* orinar.

urine [ˈjʊərɪn] *n* orina *f*.

urn [ɜːn] *n* 1 urna *f*. 2 **tea u.**, tetera *f* grande.

Uruguay [ˈjʊərəgwaɪ] *n* Uruguay.

Uruguayan [jʊərəˈgwaɪən] *adj* & *n* uruguayo,-a *(m,f)*.

us [ʌs] *pers pron* 1 (*as object*) nos; **let's forget it**, olvidémoslo. 2 (*after prep*) nosotros,-as; **both of us**, nosotros dos; **he's one of us**, es de los nuestros. 3 (*after v to be*) nosotros,-as; **she wouldn't believe it was us**, no creía que fuéramos nosotros. 4 *fam* me; **give us a kiss!**, ¡dame un beso!

US [juːˈes] *abbr* of **United States**,

EE.UU. *mpl.*
USA [ju:es'er] *abbr* of **United States of America**, EE.UU. *mpl.*

usage ['ju:sɪdʒ] *n* 1 (*habit, custom*) costumbre *f.* 2 *Ling* uso *m.*

use [ju:z] I *vtr* 1 emplear, utilizar; **what is it used for?**, ¿para qué sirve?; **to u. force**, hacer uso de la fuerza. 2 (*consume*) consumir, gastar. 3 (*take unfair advantage of*) aprovecharse de. 4 *fam* **I could u. a drink**, no me vendría mal un trago. II *v aux* (*past tense only*) soler, acostumbrar; **where did you u. to live?**, ¿dónde vivías (antes)? III [ju:s] *n* 1 uso *m*, empleo *m*; (*handling*) manejo *m*; **directions for u.**, modo de empleo; **in u.**, en uso; **'not in u.'**, (*on lift*) 'no funciona'; **ready for u.**, listo para usar; **to make (good) u. of sth**, aprovechar algo; **to put to good u.**, sacar partido de. 2 (*application*) aplicación *f.* 3 (*usefulness*) utilidad *f*; **it's no u.**, es inútil; **what's the u.?**, ¿para qué?; *fam* **it's no u. crying**, no sirve de nada llorar; **of u.**, útil; **to be of u.**, servir. ◆ **use up** *vtr* acabar.

used [ju:zd] *adj* 1 (*second-hand*) usado,-a. 2 [ju:st] **to be u. to**, estar acostumbrado,-a a.

useful ['ju:sful] *adj* útil; (*practical*) práctico,-a; **to come in u.**, venir bien.

usefulness ['ju:sfulnɪs] *n* utilidad *f.*

useless ['ju:slɪs] *adj* inútil.

user ['ju:zər] *n* 1 usuario,-a *m,f.* 2 *fam* (*of drugs*) drogadicto,-a *m,f.*

usher ['ʌʃər] I *n* 1 *Cin Theat* acomodador,-a *m,f.* 2 (*in court etc*) ujier

m. II *vtr* **to u. in**, *Cin Theat* acomodar; (*at home*) hacer pasar; **to u. out**, acompañar hasta la puerta.

USSR [ju:eses'ɑ:r] *Hist abbr* of **Union of Soviet Socialist Republics**, URSS *f.*

usual [ju:ʒʊəl] I *adj* corriente, normal; **as u.**, como siempre; **at the u. hour**, a la hora habitual; **earlier than u.**, más pronto que de costumbre; **the u. problems**, los problemas de siempre. II lo habitual; **out of the u.**, fuera de lo común. ◆ **usually** *adv* normalmente.

usurpation [ju:zɜ:'perʃən] *n* usurpación *f.*

utensil [ju:'tensɪl] *n* utensilio *m*; **kitchen utensils**, batería *f sing* de cocina.

uterus ['ju:tərəs] *n* útero *m.*

utilitarian [ju:tɪlɪ'teərɪən] *adj* 1 (*in philosophy*) utilitarista. 2 (*useful*) utilitario,-a.

utility [ju:'tɪlɪtɪ] *n* 1 utilidad *f*; **u. room**, cuarto *m* de planchar; (*for storage*) trascocina *f.* 2 (*public*) **u.**, empresa *f* de servicio público.

utilize ['ju:tɪlaɪz] *vtr* utilizar.

utmost ['ʌtmoʊst] I *adj* sumo,-a; **of the u. importance**, de suma importancia. II *n* máximo *m*; **to do** *or* **try one's u.**, hacer todo lo posible; **to the u.**, al máximo, a más no poder.

utopian [ju:'toʊpɪən] *adj* utópico,-a.

utter[1] ['ʌtər] *vtr* 1 (*words*) pronunciar; (*sigh*) dar; (*cry, threat*) lanzar.

utter[2] ['ʌtər] *adj* total, completo,-a.

utterance ['ʌtərəns] *n* declaración *f.*

U-turn ['ju:tɜ:n] *n* cambio *m* de sentido; *Pol* giro *m* de 180° grados.

V

V, v [vi:] *n* (*the letter*) V, v *f.*

V *abbr* of **volt(s)**, V.

v 1 *abbr* of **verse**, v. 2 (*also* **vs**) *abbr* of **versus**, contra.

vacancy ['veɪkənsɪ] *n* 1 (*job*) vacante *f.* 2 (*room*) habitación *f* libre; **'no vacancies'**, 'completo'.

vacant ['veɪkənt] *adj* 1 (*empty*) vacío,-a. 2 (*job*) vacante; *GB* **'situations v.'**, 'ofertas de trabajo'. 3 (*free, not in use*) libre.

vacate [və'keɪt] *vtr* (*flat*) desalojar.

vacation [və'keɪʃən] I *n* vacaciones *fpl*; **on v.**, de vacaciones. II *vi* *US* pasar las vacaciones (**in, at, on**).

vacationer [və'keɪʃənər], **vacationist** [və'keɪʃənɪst] *n* *US* **summer v.**, veraneante *mf.*

vaccinate ['væksɪneɪt] *vtr* vacunar.

vaccine ['væksi:n] *n* vacuna *f.*

vacuum ['vækjʊəm] I *n* vacío *m*; **v. cleaner**, aspiradora *f*; **v. flask**, termo *m.* II *vtr* (*carpet, room*) pasar la aspiradora por.

vacuum-packed ['vækjʊəmpækt] *adj*

envasado,-a al vacío.

vagina [və'dʒaɪnə] *n* vagina *f.*

vagrant ['veɪgrənt] *adj & n* vagabundo,-a (*m,f*).

vague [veɪg] *adj* 1 (*imprecise*) vago,-a, impreciso,-a; (*indistinct*) borroso,-a.

vain [veɪn] *adj* 1 (*proud*) vanidoso,-a, presumido,-a. 2 (*hopeless*) vano,-a; **in v.**, en vano.

valentine ['væləntaɪn] *n* 1 (*card*) tarjeta *f* que se manda el Día de los Enamorados. 2 (*sweetheart*) novio,-a *m,f.*

valet ['vælɪt, 'væleɪ] *n* ayuda *m* de cámara.

valiant ['vælɪənt] *adj* valiente.

valid ['vælɪd] *adj* válido,-a; **no longer v.**, caducado,-a.

valley ['vælɪ] *n* valle *m.*

valour, *US* **valor** ['vælər] *n* valor *m*, valentía *f.*

valuable ['væljʊəbəl] I *adj* valioso,-a de valor. II *npl* **valuables**, objetos *mpl* de valor.

valuation [vælju'eɪʃən] n 1 (act) valoración f. 2 (price) valor m.

value ['væljuː] I n valor m; **50 pence is good v.**, 50 peniques es un buen precio; **to get good v. for money**, sacarle jugo al dinero; **v. added tax**, impuesto m sobre el valor añadido. II vtr valorar.

valve [vælv] n 1 Anat Tech válvula f. 2 Rad lámpara f.

vampire ['væmpaɪər] n vampiro m.

van [væn] n GB 1 Aut furgoneta f. 2 Rail furgón m.

vandal ['vændəl] n vándalo,-a m,f.

vandalism ['vændəlɪzəm] n vandalismo m.

vandalize ['vændəlaɪz] vtr destruir, destrozar.

vanguard ['vænɡɑːd] n vanguardia f.

vanilla [və'nɪlə] n vainilla f.

vanish ['vænɪʃ] vi desaparecer.

vanity ['vænɪtɪ] n vanidad f; **v. bag, v. case**, neceser m.

vantage ['vɑːntɪdʒ] n ventaja f; **v. point**, posición estratégica.

vaporizer ['veɪpəraɪzər] n (device) vaporizador m; (spray) pulverizador m.

vapour, US **vapor** ['veɪpər] n vapor m; (on windowpane) vaho m; **v. trail**, estela f de humo.

variable ['veərɪəbəl] adj & n variable (f).

variance ['veərɪəns] n fml **to be at v.**, no concordar; **to be at v. with sb**, estar en desacuerdo con algn.

variation [veərɪ'eɪʃən] n variación f.

varicose ['værɪkəʊs] adj **v. veins**, varices fpl.

varied ['veərɪd] adj variado,-a, diverso,-a.

variety [və'raɪɪtɪ] n 1 (diversity) variedad f; (assortment) surtido m; **for a v. of reasons**, por razones diversas. 2 **v. show**, espectáculo m de variedades.

various ['veərɪəs] adj diversos,-as, varios,-as.

varnish ['vɑːnɪʃ] I n barniz m; GB **nail v.**, esmalte m de uñas. II vtr barnizar; (nails) esmaltar.

vary ['veərɪ] vi variar; **prices v. from £2 to £4**, los precios oscilan entre 2 y 4 libras; **to v. in size**, variar de tamaño.

varying ['veərɪŋ] adj **with v. degrees of success**, con más o menos éxito.

vase [vɑːz] n florero m, jarrón m.

Vaseline® ['væsɪliːn] n vaselina f.

vast [vɑːst] adj vasto,-a; (majority) inmenso,-a.

VAT, Vat [viːeɪ'tiː, væt] abbr of **value added tax**, IVA m.

vat [væt] n cuba f, tina f.

Vatican ['vætɪkən] n **the V.**, el Vaticano.

vault¹ [vɔːlt] n bóveda f; (for wine) bodega f; (tomb) cripta f; (of bank) cámara acorazada.

vault² [vɔːlt] I vtr & vi saltar. II n Gymn salto m.

vaunt [vɔːnt] vtr fml jactarse de, hacer alarde de.

VCR [viːsiː'ɑːr] abbr of **video cassette recorder**, (grabador m de) vídeo m.

VD [viː'diː] abbr of **venereal disease**, enfermedad venérea.

VDU [viːdiː'juː] abbr of **visual display unit**, pantalla f.

veal [viːl] n ternera f.

veer [vɪər] vi (ship) virar; (car) girar.

vegetable ['vedʒtəbəl] n (food) verdura f, hortaliza f; **v. garden**, huerta f, huerto m.

vegetarian [vedʒɪ'teərɪən] adj & n vegetariano,-a (m,f).

vegetation [vedʒɪ'teɪʃən] n vegetación f.

vehement ['viːɪmənt] adj vehemente.

vehicle ['viːɪkəl] n vehículo m.

veil [veɪl] I n velo m. II vtr velar.

vein [veɪn] n vena f.

velocity [vɪ'lɒsɪtɪ] n velocidad f.

velvet ['velvɪt] n terciopelo m.

velvety ['velvɪtɪ] adj aterciopelado,-a.

vendetta [ven'detə] n vendetta f.

vending ['vendɪŋ] n **v. machine**, máquina expendedora.

vendor ['vendɔːr] n vendedor,-a m,f.

veneer [vɪ'nɪər] n 1 (covering) chapa f. 2 fig apariencia f.

venerable ['venərəbəl] adj venerable.

venereal [vɪ'nɪərɪəl] adj venéreo,-a.

Venetian [vɪ'niːʃən] adj & n veneciano,-a (m,f); **v. blind**, persiana f graduable.

Venezuela [venɪ'zweɪlə] n Venezuela f.

Venezuelan [venɪ'zweɪlən] adj & n venezolano,-a (m,f).

vengeance ['vendʒəns] n venganza f; **fam it was raining with a v.**, llovía con ganas.

Venice ['venɪs] n Venecia f.

venison ['venzən, 'venɪsən] n carne f de venado.

venom ['venəm] n veneno m.

venomous ['venəməs] adj venenoso,-a; **fig v. tongue**, lengua víperina.

vent [vent] I n 1 (opening) abertura f, orificio m; (grille) rejilla f de ventilación; **air v.**, respiradero m. 2 (of volcano) chimenea f. II vtr fig (feelings) descargar.

ventilate ['ventɪleɪt] vtr ventilar.

ventilation [ventɪ'leɪʃən] n ventilación f.

ventilator ['ventɪleɪtər] n ventilador m.

ventriloquist [ven'trɪləkwɪst] n ventrílocuo,-a m,f.

venture ['ventʃər] I vtr arriesgar, aventurar; **he didn't v. to ask**, no se atrevió a preguntarle. II vi arriesgarse; **to v. out of doors**, atreverse a salir. III n empresa arriesgada, aventura f; Com **business/ joint v.**, empresa comercial/colectiva.

venue ['venjuː] n 1 (meeting place) lugar m de reunión. 2 (for concert etc) local m.

Venus ['viːnəs] n (goddess) Venus f; (planet) Venus m.

veranda(h) [vəˈrændə] *n* porche *m*, terraza *f*.

verb [vɜːb] *n* verbo *m*.

verbal [ˈvɜːbəl] *adj* verbal.

verbatim [vəˈbeɪtɪm] I *adj* textual. II *adv* textualmente.

verbose [vɜːˈbəʊs] *adj* pródigo,-a en palabras.

verdict [ˈvɜːdɪkt] *n* 1 *Jur* veredicto *m*, fallo *m*. 2 *(opinion)* opinión *f*, juicio *m*.

verge [vɜːdʒ] I *n* 1 *(margin)* borde *m*; *fig* **on the v. of**, al borde de; *fig* **to be on the v. of doing sth**, estar a punto de hacer algo. 2 *GB (of road)* arcén *m*. II *vi* rayar (**on**, en).

verification [verɪfɪˈkeɪʃən] *n* verificación *f*, comprobación *f*.

verify [ˈverɪfaɪ] *vtr* verificar, comprobar.

veritable [ˈverɪtəbəl] *adj* auténtico,-a.

vermicelli [vɜːmɪˈselɪ] *n* fideos *mpl*.

vermin [ˈvɜːmɪn] *npl* 1 *(animals)* bichos *mpl*, sabandijas *fpl*. 2 *fig* gentuza *f sing*.

vermouth [ˈvɜːməθ] *n* vermú *m*, vermut *m*.

verrucca [vəˈruːkə] *n* verruga *f*.

versatile [ˈvɜːsətaɪl] *adj (person)* polifacético,-a; *(object)* versátil.

verse [vɜːs] *n* 1 *(stanza)* estrofa *f*. 2 *(poetry)* versos *mpl*, poesía *f*. 3 *(of song)* copla *f*. 4 *(of Bible)* versículo *m*.

versed [vɜːst] *adj* **to be (well) v. in**, ser (muy) versado en.

version [ˈvɜːʃən, ˈvɜːʒən] *n* 1 versión *f*; **stage v.**, adaptación *f* teatral. 2 *Aut* modelo *m*.

versus [ˈvɜːsəs] *prep* contra.

vertebra [ˈvɜːtɪbrə] *n (pl* **vertebras** *or* **vertebrae** [ˈvɜːtɪbriː]) vértebra *f*.

vertical [ˈvɜːtɪkəl] *adj & n* vertical (*f*).

vertigo [ˈvɜːtɪɡəʊ] *n* vértigo *m*.

verve [vɜːv] *n* vigor *m*, brío *m*.

very [ˈverɪ] I *adv* 1 *(extremely)* muy; **to be hungry**, tener mucha hambre; **v. much**, muchísimo; **v. well**, muy bien. 2 *(emphatic)* **at the v. latest**, como máximo; **at the v. least**, como mínimo; **the v. best**, el mejor de todos; **the v. first/last**, el primero/último de todos; **the v. same day**, el mismo día. II *adj* 1 **at the v. end/beginning**, al final/principio de todo. 2 *(precise)* **at this v. moment**, en este mismo momento; **her v. words**, sus palabras exactas; **in the v. middle**, justo en medio. 3 *(mere)* **the v. thought of it!**, ¡sólo con pensarlo!

vespers [ˈvespəz] *npl* vísperas *fpl*.

vessel [ˈvesəl] *n* 1 *(container)* vasija *f*. 2 *Naut* buque *m*, nave *f*. 3 *Anat Bot* vaso *m*.

vest [vest] I *n* 1 *(undershirt)* camiseta *f* de tirantes. 2 *US* chaleco *m*. II *vtr* **to v. sth in sb**, conferir a algn (**with**, -).

vested [ˈvestɪd] *adj Jur Fin* **v. interests**, derechos adquiridos; *fig* intereses *mpl* personales.

vestibule [ˈvestɪbjuːl] *n* vestíbulo *m*.

vestige [ˈvestɪdʒ] *n* vestigio *m*.

vestry [ˈvestrɪ] *n* sacristía *f*.

vet [vet] I *n fam abbr of* **veterinary surgeon**. II *vtr GB* someter a investigación, examinar.

veteran [ˈvetərən] *n* 1 veterano,-a *m,f*. 2 *US (war)* v., ex combatiente *mf*.

veterinarian [vetərɪˈneərɪən] *n US* veterinario,-a *m,f*.

veterinary [ˈvetərɪnərɪ] *adj* veterinario,-a; **v. medicine**, veterinaria *f*; *GB* **v. surgeon**, veterinario,-a *m,f*.

veto [ˈviːtəʊ] I *n (pl* **vetoes**) veto *m*. II *vtr Pol* vetar; *(suggestion etc)* descartar.

vexed [vekst] *adj* 1 *(annoyed)* disgustado, -a. 2 *(debated)* controvertido, -a.

VHF [viːeɪtʃˈef] *abbr of* **very high frequency**, frecuencia muy alta, VHF.

via [ˈvaɪə] *prep* por, vía.

viable [ˈvaɪəbəl] *adj* viable, factible.

viaduct [ˈvaɪədʌkt] *n* viaducto *m*.

vibrant [ˈvaɪbrənt] *adj* 1 *(sound)* vibrante. 2 *fig (personality)* vital; *(city)* animado,-a.

vibrate [vaɪˈbreɪt] *vi* vibrar (**with**, de).

vibration [vaɪˈbreɪʃən] *n* vibración *f*.

vicar [ˈvɪkə] *n* párroco *m*.

vicarage [ˈvɪkərɪdʒ] *n* casa *f* del párroco.

vicarious [vɪˈkeərɪəs] *adj* experimentado,-a por otro; *(punishment)* sufrido,-a por otro.

vice¹ [vaɪs] *n* vicio *m*.

vice² [vaɪs] *n (tool)* torno *m* de banco.

vice³ [vaɪs] *pref* vice-; **v. chancellor**, rector,-a *m,f*; **v. president**, vicepresidente,-a *m,f*.

vice-chairman [vaɪsˈtʃeəmən] *n* vicepresidente *m*.

vice versa [vaɪsˈvɜːsə] *adv* viceversa.

vicinity [vɪˈsɪnɪtɪ] *n (area)* vecindad *f*; **in the v. of**, *(geographic location)* cerca de, en las inmediaciones de; *(amount)* alrededor de.

vicious [ˈvɪʃəs] *adj (violent)* violento,-a; *(malicious)* malintencionado,-a; *(cruel)* cruel; **v. circle**, círculo vicioso.

victim [ˈvɪktɪm] *n* víctima *f*.

victimize [ˈvɪktɪmaɪz] *vtr* perseguir, tratar injustamente.

victor [ˈvɪktə] *n* vencedor,-a *m,f*.

victorious [vɪkˈtɔːrɪəs] *adj* victorioso,-a.

victory [ˈvɪktərɪ] *n* victoria *f*.

video [ˈvɪdɪəʊ] *n* vídeo *m*; **v. camera**, videocámara *f*; **v. cassette**, videocasete *m*; **v. club**, videoclub *m*; **v. game**, videojuego *m*; **v. (cassette) recorder**, vídeo *m*; **v. tape**, cinta *f* de vídeo.

video-tape [ˈvɪdɪəʊteɪp] *vtr* grabar (en vídeo).

vie [vaɪ] *vi* competir (**against**, **with**, con).

Vienna [vɪˈenə] *n* Viena.

Viennese [vɪəˈniːz] *adj & n* vienés,-esa

(m,f).

Vietnam [vjet'næm] n Vietnam.

view [vjuː] I n 1 (sight) vista f, panorama m; in full v., completamente visible; on v., a la vista; to come into v., aparecer; fig in v. of the fact that ..., dado que .... 2 (opinion) opinión f; point of v., punto m de vista; to take a dim v. of, ver con malos ojos. 3 (aim) fin m; with a v. to, con la intención de. II vtr 1 (look at) mirar; (house etc) visitar. 2 (consider) contemplar; (topic, problem) enfocar.

viewer ['vjuːər] n 1 TV televidente mf. 2 Phot visionador m.

viewfinder ['vjuːfaɪndər] n visor m.

viewpoint ['vjuːpɔɪnt] n punto m de vista.

vigil ['vɪdʒɪl] n vigilia f.

vigilante [vɪdʒɪ'læntɪ] n v. group, patrulla ciudadana.

vigorous ['vɪgərəs] adj vigoroso,-a, enérgico,-a.

vigour, US **vigor** ['vɪgər] n vigor m.

vile [vaɪl] adj 1 (evil) vil, infame. 2 (disgusting) repugnante. 3 fam (awful) horrible.

vilify ['vɪlɪfaɪ] vtr denigrar.

villa ['vɪlə] n 1 (in country) casa f de campo. 2 GB chalet m.

village ['vɪlɪdʒ] n (small) aldea f; (larger) pueblo m.

villager ['vɪlɪdʒər] n aldeano,-a mf.

villain ['vɪlən] n villano,-a mf; Cin Theat malo,-a mf.

vinaigrette [vɪneɪ'gret] n vinagreta f.

vindicate ['vɪndɪkeɪt] vtr justificar, vindicar.

vindictive [vɪn'dɪktɪv] adj vengativo,-a.

vine [vaɪn] n vid f; (climbing) parra f.

vinegar ['vɪnɪgər] n vinagre m.

vineyard ['vɪnjəd] n viña f, viñedo m.

vintage ['vɪntɪdʒ] I n 1 (crop, year) cosecha f. 2 (season) vendimia f. 3 (era) era f. II adj 1 (wine) añejo,-a. 2 (classic) clásico,-a; v. car, coche m de época.

vinyl ['vaɪnɪl] n vinilo m.

viola [vɪ'əʊlə] n viola f.

violate ['vaɪəleɪt] vtr violar.

violence ['vaɪələns] n violencia f.

violent ['vaɪələnt] adj violento,-a. 2 (intense) intenso,-a.

violet ['vaɪələt] I n 1 Bot violeta f. 2 (colour) violeta m. II adj violeta.

violin [vaɪə'lɪn] n violín m.

violinist [vaɪə'lɪnɪst] n violinista mf.

VIP [viːaɪ'piː] fam abbr of **very important person**, personaje m muy importante.

viper ['vaɪpər] n víbora f.

virgin ['vɜːdʒɪn] I n 1 virgen f; the V. Mary, la Virgen María; to be a v., ser virgen. II adj virgen.

virginity [və'dʒɪnɪtɪ] n virginidad f.

Virgo ['vɜːgəʊ] n Virgo m.

virile ['vɪraɪl] adj viril.

virtual ['vɜːtʃʊəl] adj virtual; Comput v. reality, realidad f virtual. ◆**virtually** adv (almost) prácticamente.

virtue ['vɜːtjuː, 'vɜːtʃuː] n virtud f; by v. of, en virtud de.

virtuous ['vɜːtʃʊəs] adj virtuoso,-a.

virulent ['vɪrʊlənt] adj virulento,-a.

virus ['vaɪrəs] n virus m inv.

visa ['viːzə] n visado m, Am visa f.

vis-à-vis [viːzɑː'viː] prep 1 (regarding) respecto a. 2 (opposite) frente a.

viscose ['vɪskəʊs] n viscosa f.

viscount ['vaɪkaʊnt] n vizconde m.

visibility [vɪzɪ'bɪlɪtɪ] n visibilidad f.

visible ['vɪzɪbəl] adj visible.

vision ['vɪʒən] n 1 visión f. 2 (eyesight) vista f.

visit ['vɪzɪt] I vtr 1 (person) visitar, hacer una visita a. 2 (place) visitar, ir a. II n visita f; to pay sb a v., hacerle una visita a algn.

visiting ['vɪzɪtɪŋ] adj GB v. card, tarjeta f de visita; Med v. hours, horas fpl de visita; Sport v. team, equipo m visitante.

visitor ['vɪzɪtər] n 1 (guest) invitado,-a mf; we've got visitors, tenemos visita. 2 (in hotel) cliente,-a mf. 3 (tourist) turista mf.

visor ['vaɪzər] n visera f.

vista ['vɪstə] n vista f, panorama m.

visual ['vɪʒʊəl, 'vɪzjʊəl] adj visual; v. aids, medios mpl visuales.

visualize ['vɪʒʊəlaɪz, 'vɪzjʊəlaɪz] vtr 1 (imagine) imaginar(se). 2 (foresee) prever.

vital ['vaɪtəl] adj 1 (lively) enérgico,-a. 2 (essential) fundamental. 3 (decisive) decisivo,-a; fam v. statistics, medidas fpl del cuerpo de la mujer. 4 Med (function, sign) vital. ◆**vitally** adv it's v. important, es de vital importancia.

vitality [vaɪ'tælɪtɪ] n vitalidad f.

vitamin ['vɪtəmɪn, US 'vaɪtəmɪn] n vitamina f.

viva ['vaɪvə] n (abbr of viva voce) GB examen m oral.

vivacious [vɪ'veɪʃəs] adj vivaz.

vivacity [vɪ'væsɪtɪ] n viveza f, vivacidad f.

vivid ['vɪvɪd] adj 1 (bright, lively) vivo,-a, intenso,-a. 2 (graphic) gráfico,-a.

vixen ['vɪksən] n zorra f.

V-neck(ed) ['viːnek(t)] adj con el cuello en pico.

vocabulary [və'kæbjʊlərɪ] n vocabulario m.

vocal ['vəʊkəl] adj vocal; v. cords, cuerdas fpl vocales.

vocalist ['vəʊkəlɪst] n cantante mf.

vocation [vəʊ'keɪʃən] n vocación f.

vocational [vəʊ'keɪʃənəl] adj profesional; v. training, formación f profesional.

vociferous [vəʊ'sɪfərəs] adj 1 (protest) enérgico,-a. 2 (noisy) clamoroso,-a.

vodka ['vɒdkə] n vodka m & f.

vogue [vəʊg] n boga f, moda f; in v., de

moda.

voice [vɔɪs] I n voz f; to lose one's v., quedarse afónico; fig at the top of one's v., a voz en grito. II vtr 1 (express) manifestar. 2 Ling sonorizar.

void [vɔɪd] I adj 1 v. of, sin. 2 Jur nulo, -a, inválido,-a. II n vacío m.

volatile ['vɒlətaɪl] adj volátil.

volcanic [vɒl'kænɪk] adj volcánico,-a.

volcano [vɒl'keɪnəʊ] n (pl volcanoes) volcán m.

volition [və'lɪʃən] n fml of one's own v., por voluntad propia.

volley ['vɒlɪ] I n 1 (of shots) descarga f. 2 fig (of stones, insults) lluvia f. 3 Ten volea f. II vtr Ten volear.

volleyball ['vɒlɪbɔːl] n voleibol m.

volt [vəʊlt] n voltio m.

voltage ['vəʊltɪdʒ] n voltaje m.

voluble ['vɒljʊbəl] adj locuaz, hablador,-a.

volume ['vɒljuːm] n 1 volumen m. 2 (book) volumen m, tomo m; fig to speak volumes, decirlo todo.

voluntary ['vɒləntərɪ] adj voluntario,-a; v. organization, organización benéfica.

volunteer [vɒlən'tɪər] I n voluntario,-a m,f. II vtr (help etc) ofrecer. III vi 1 ofrecerse (for, para). 2 Mil alistarse como voluntario.

voluptuous [və'lʌptjʊəs] adj

voluptuoso,-a.

vomit ['vɒmɪt] I vtr & vi vomitar. II n vómito m.

voracious [vɒ'reɪʃəs] adj voraz.

vortex ['vɔːteks] n (pl vortices ['vɔːtɪsiːz]) vórtice m; fig vorágine f.

vote [vəʊt] I n voto m; (voting) votación f; v. of confidence, voto de confianza; to take a v. on sth, someter algo a votación; to have the v., tener derecho al voto. II vtr 1 votar. 2 (elect) elegir. 3 fam proponer. III vi votar; to v. for sb, votar a algn.

voter ['vəʊtər] n votante mf.

voting ['vəʊtɪŋ] n votación f.

vouch [vaʊtʃ] vi to v. for sth/sb, responder de algo/por algn.

voucher ['vaʊtʃər] n GB vale m.

vow [vaʊ] I n voto m. II vtr jurar.

vowel ['vaʊəl] n vocal f.

voyage ['vɔɪɪdʒ] n viaje m; (crossing) travesía f; to go on a v., hacer un viaje en (barco).

vulgar ['vʌlgər] adj (coarse) vulgar, ordinario,-a; (in poor taste) de mal gusto.

vulgarity [vʌl'gærɪtɪ] n (coarseness) vulgaridad f, ordinariez f; (poor taste) mal gusto m.

vulnerable ['vʌlnərəbəl] adj vulnerable.

vulture ['vʌltʃər] n buitre m.

vulva ['vʌlvə] n vulva f.

W

W, w ['dʌbljuː] n (the letter) W, w f.

W 1 abbr of West, O. 2 abbr of Watt(s), W.

wad [wɒd] n (of paper) taco m; (of cotton wool) bolita f; (of banknotes) fajo m.

waddle ['wɒdəl] vi andar como los patos.

wade [weɪd] vi caminar por el agua; to w. across a river, vadear un río. ◆wade through vtr hacer con dificultad; I'm wading through the book, me cuesta mucho terminar el libro.

wafer ['weɪfər] n barquillo m; Rel hostia f.

waffle¹ ['wɒfəl] n Culin (tipo m de) barquillo m.

waffle² ['wɒfəl] GB fam I vi meter mucha paja; to w. on, parlotear. II n paja f.

waft [wɑːft, wɒft] I vtr llevar por el aire. II vi flotar (por or en el aire).

wag [wæg] I vtr menear. II vi (tail) menearse.

wage [weɪdʒ] I n (also wages) salario m, sueldo m; w. earner, asalariado,-a m,f. II vtr (campaign) realizar (against, contra); to w. war, hacer la guerra (on, a).

wage-packet ['weɪdʒpækɪt] n sueldo m.

wager ['weɪdʒər] I n apuesta f. II vtr apostar.

waggle ['wægəl] I vtr menear. II vi menearse.

wa(g)gon ['wægən] n (horse-drawn) carro m; GB Rail vagón m.

wail [weɪl] I n lamento m, gemido m. II vi (person) lamentar, gemir.

waist [weɪst] n Anat cintura f; Sew talle m.

waistcoat ['weɪstkəʊt] n GB chaleco m.

waistline ['weɪstlaɪn] n Anat cintura f; Sew talle m.

wait [weɪt] I n espera f; (delay) demora f; to lie in w., estar al acecho. II vi 1 esperar, aguardar; I can't w. to see her, me muero de ganas de verla; while you w., en el acto; to keep sb waiting, hacer esperar a algn. 2 to w. at table, servir la mesa. ◆wait about, wait around vi esperar. ◆wait on vtr servir.

waiter ['weɪtər] n camarero m.

waiting ['weɪtɪŋ] n 'No W.', 'Prohibido Aparcar'; w. list, lista f de espera; w. room, sala f de espera.

waitress ['weɪtrɪs] n camarera f.

waive [weɪv] vtr fml (rule) no aplicar.

wake¹ [weɪk] I vtr (pt woke; pp woken) to w. sb (up), despertar a algn. II vi to w. (up), despertar(se). III n (for dead) velatorio m.

wake² [weɪk] n (in water) estela f; fig **in the w. of,** tras.

waken [ˈweɪkən] vtr lit despertar.

Wales [weɪlz] n (el país de) Gales.

walk [wɔ:k] **I** n **1** (long) caminata m; (short) paseo m; **it's an hour's w.,** está a una hora de camino; **to go for a w.,** dar un paseo; **to take the dog for a w.,** sacar a pasear al perro. **2** (gait) modo m de andar. **3** people from all walks of life, gente f de toda condición. **II** vtr **1** we walked her home, la acompañamos a casa. **2** (dog) pasear. **III** vi **1** andar. **2** (go on foot) ir andando. ◆**walk away** vi alejarse; fig **to w. away with a prize,** llevarse un premio. ◆**walk into** vtr **1** (place) entrar en; fig (trap) caer en. **2** (bump into) chocarse contra. ◆**walk out** vi salir; Ind declararse en huelga; **to w. out on sb,** abandonar a algn. ◆**walk up** vi **to w. up to sb,** abordar a algn.

walkabout [ˈwɔ:kəbaʊt] n (by Queen etc) paseo m informal entre la gente.

walker [ˈwɔ:kər] n paseante mf; Sport marchador,-a m,f.

walkie-talkie [ˈwɔ:kɪ'tɔ:kɪ] n walkie-talkie m.

walking [ˈwɔ:kɪŋ] **I** n andar m; (hiking) excursionismo m. **II** adj **at w. pace,** a paso de marcha; **w. shoes,** zapatos mpl de andar; **w. stick,** bastón m.

Walkman® [ˈwɔ:kmən] n (pl **Walkmans**) walkman® m.

walkout [ˈwɔ:kaʊt] n Ind huelga f.

walkover [ˈwɔ:kəʊvər] n **it was a w.,** fue pan comido.

walkway [ˈwɔ:kweɪ] n esp US paso m de peatones.

wall [wɔ:l] **I** n **1** (freestanding, exterior) muro m; fig **to have one's back to the w.,** estar entre la espada y la pared; **city w.,** muralla f; **garden w.,** tapia f. **2** (interior) pared f; **w. map,** mapa m mural. **3** Ftb barrera f. ◆**wall up** vtr (door, fireplace) tabicar.

walled [wɔ:ld] adj (city) amurallado,-a; (garden) cercado,-a con tapia.

wallet [ˈwɔlɪt] n cartera f.

wallflower [ˈwɔ:lflaʊər] n **1** Bot alhelí m. **2** fam **to be a w.,** ser un convidado de piedra.

wallop [ˈwɒləp] fam **I** n golpazo m. **II** vtr **1** (hit) pegar fuerte. **2** (defeat) dar una paliza a.

wallow [ˈwɒləʊ] vi revolcarse (en, in); fig **to w. in self-pity,** sumirse en la autocompasión.

wallpaper [ˈwɔ:lpeɪpər] **I** n papel pintado. **II** vtr empapelar.

wally [ˈwɒlɪ] n fam idiota mf.

walnut [ˈwɔ:lnʌt] n nuez f; (tree, wood) nogal m.

walrus [ˈwɔ:lrəs] n morsa f.

waltz [wɔ:ls] **I** n vals m. **II** vi bailar un vals.

wan [wɒn] adj (**wanner, wannest**) pálido,-a; (look, smile) apagado,-a.

wand [wɒnd] n (magic) w., varita f (mágica).

wander [ˈwɒndər] **I** vtr **to w. the streets,** vagar por las calles. **II** vi **1** (aimlessly) vagar, errar; **to w. about,** deambular; **to w. in/out,** entrar/salir sin prisas. **2** (stray) desviarse; (mind) divagar; **his glance wandered round the room,** recorrió el cuarto con la mirada.

wandering [ˈwɒndərɪŋ] adj errante; (tribe) nómada; (speech) divagador,-a.

wane [weɪn] vi menguar; (interest) decaer.

wangle [ˈwæŋɡəl] vtr fam agenciarse.

wank [wæŋk] sl Ind n w paja f. **II** vi hacerse una paja.

wanker [ˈwæŋkər] n sl mamón,-ona mf inv.

want [wɒnt] **I** n **1** (lack) falta f; **for w. of,** por falta de. **2** (poverty) miseria f. **II** vtr **1** (desire) querer, desear; **to w. to do sth,** querer hacer algo. **2** fam (need) necesitar; **the grass wants cutting,** hace falta cortar el césped. **3** (seek) buscar; **you're wanted on the phone,** te llaman al teléfono. ◆**want for** vtr carecer de; **to w. for nothing,** tenerlo todo.

wanting [ˈwɒntɪŋ] adj **1** she is w. in tact, le falta tacto. **2** he was found w.,** no daba la talla.

wanton [ˈwɒntən] adj **1** (motiveless) sin motivo; **w. cruelty,** crueldad gratuita. **2** (unrestrained) desenfrenado,-a; (licentious) lascivo,-a.

war [wɔ:r] n guerra f; **to be at w.,** estar en guerra (with, con); fig **to declare/wage w. on,** declarar/hacer la guerra a.

warble [ˈwɔ:bəl] vi gorjear.

ward [wɔ:d] **I** n **1** (of hospital) sala f, **2** ʃur pupilo,-a m,f; **w. of court,** pupilo,-a bajo tutela judicial. **3** GB Pol distrito m electoral. ◆**ward off** vtr (blow) parar, desviar; (attack) rechazar; (danger) evitar; (illness) prevenir.

warden [ˈwɔ:dən] n (of residence) guardián,-ana m,f; (of park), guarda m de coto.

warder [ˈwɔ:dər] n GB carcelero,-a m,f.

wardrobe [ˈwɔ:drəʊb] n **1** armario m, ropero m. **2** (clothes) guardarropa m. **3** Theat vestuario m.

warehouse [ˈweəhaʊs] n almacén m.

wares [weəz] npl mercancías fpl.

warfare [ˈwɔ:feər] n guerra f.

warhead [ˈwɔ:hed] n (nuclear) w., ojiva f nuclear.

warm [wɔ:m] **I** adj **1** (water) tibio,-a; (hands) caliente; (climate) cálido,-a; **a w. day,** un día de calor; **I am w.,** tengo calor; **it is (very) w. today,** hoy hace (mucho) calor; **w. clothing,** ropa f de abrigo.

2 *(welcome, applause)* cálido,-a. II *vtr* calentar; *fig* alegrar. III *vi* calentarse; to w. to sb, cogerle simpatía a algn. ◆**warm up** I *vtr* 1 calentar; *(soup)* (re)calentar. 2 *(audience)* animar. II *vi* 1 calentarse; *(food)* (re)calentarse; *(person)* entrar en calor. 2 *(athlete)* hacer ejercicios de calentamiento. 3 *fig (audience, party)* animarse. ◆**warmly** *adv fig* calurosamente; *(thank)* con efusión.

warm-blooded [wɔːm'blʌdɪd] *adj* de sangre caliente.

warm-hearted [wɔːm'hɑːtɪd] *adj* afectuoso,-a.

warmth [wɔːmθ] *n (heat)* calor *m*; *fig* cordialidad *f*.

warn [wɔːn] *vtr* avisar *(of, de)*, advertir *(about, sobre; against, contra)*; he warned me not to go, me advirtió que no fuera; to w. sb that, advertir a algn que.

warning ['wɔːnɪŋ] I *adj* w. light, piloto *m*; w. sign, señal *f* de aviso. II *n* 1 *(of danger)* advertencia *f*, aviso *m*. 2 *(replacing punishment)* amonestación *f*, aviso *m*. 3 *(notice)* aviso *m*; without w., sin previo aviso.

warp [wɔːp] I *vtr* 1 *(wood)* alabear, combar. 2 *fig (mind)* pervertir. II *vi* alabearse, combarse.

warrant ['wɒrənt] I *n* 1 *Jur* orden *f* judicial; death w., sentencia *f* de muerte. 2 *(authorization note)* cédula *f*; Com bono *m*. II *vtr* 1 *(justify)* justificar. 2 *(guarantee)* garantizar.

warranty ['wɒrəntɪ] *n Com* garantía *f*.

warren ['wɒrən] *n* conejera *f*; *fig* laberinto *m*.

warrior ['wɒrɪə'] *n* guerrero,-a *m,f*.

Warsaw ['wɔːsɔː] *n* Varsovia.

warship ['wɔːʃɪp] *n* buque *m* or barco *m* de guerra.

wart [wɔːt] *n* verruga *f*.

wartime ['wɔːtaɪm] *n* tiempos *mpl* de guerra.

wary ['weərɪ] *adj (warier, wariest)* cauteloso,-a; to be w. of doing sth, dudar en hacer algo; to be w. of sb/sth, recelar de algn/algo.

was [wɒz] *pt* → be.

wash [wɒʃ] I *n* 1 lavado *m*; to have a w., lavarse. 2 *(of ship)* estela *f*; *(sound)* chapoteo *m*. II *vtr* 1 lavar; *(dishes)* fregar; to w. one's hair, lavarse el pelo. 2 *(sea, river)* arrastrar. III *vi* 1 *(person)* lavarse; *(do the laundry)* hacer la colada. 2 *(lap)* batir. ◆**wash away** *vtr (of sea)* llevarse; *(traces)* borrar. ◆**wash off** *vi* quitarse lavando. ◆**wash out** I *vtr* 1 *(stain)* quitar lavando. 2 *(bottle)* enjuagar. II *vi* quitarse lavando. ◆**wash up** I *vtr GB (dishes)* fregar. II *vtr* 1 GB fregar los platos. 2 US lavarse rápidamente.

washable ['wɒʃəbəl] *adj* lavable.

washbasin ['wɒʃbeɪsən], **washbowl**

['wɒʃbəʊl] *n* palangana *f*.

washcloth ['wɒʃklɒθ] *n US* manopla *f*.

washer ['wɒʃə'] *n (on tap)* junta *f*.

washing ['wɒʃɪŋ] *n* 1 *(action)* lavado *m*; *(of clothes)* colada *f*; dirty w., ropa sucia; to do the w., hacer la colada; w. line, tendedero *m*; w. machine, lavadora *f*; w. powder, detergente *m*.

washing-up [wɒʃɪŋ'ʌp] *n GB* 1 *(action)* fregado *m*; w.-up bowl, barreño *m*; w.-up liquid, *(detergent m)* lavavajillas. 2 *(dishes)* platos *mpl* (para fregar).

washout ['wɒʃaʊt] *n fam* fracaso *m*.

washroom ['wɒʃruːm] *n US* servicios *mpl*.

wasp [wɒsp] *n* avispa *f*.

wastage ['weɪstɪdʒ] *n* pérdidas *fpl*.

waste [weɪst] I *adj* 1 *(unwanted)* desechado,-a; w. food, restos *mpl* de comida; w. products, productos *mpl* de desecho. 2 *(ground)* baldío,-a. II *n* 1 *(unnecessary use)* desperdicio *m*; *(of resources, effort, money)* derroche *m*; *(of time)* pérdida *f*; to go to w., echarse a perder. 2 *(left-overs)* desperdicios *mpl*; *(rubbish)* basura *f*; radio-active w., desechos radioactivos; w. disposal unit, trituradora *f* (de desperdicios); w. pipe, tubo *m* de desagüe. III *vtr (squander)* desperdiciar, malgastar; *(resources)* derrochar; *(money)* despilfarrar; *(time)* perder. ◆**waste away** *vi* consumirse.

wasteful ['weɪstfʊl] *adj* derrochador,-a.

wasteland ['weɪstlænd] *n* baldío *m*.

wastepaper ['weɪst'peɪpə'] *n* papeles usados; w. basket, papelera *f*.

watch [wɒtʃ] I *n* 1 *(look-out)* vigilancia *f*; to keep a close w. on sth/sb, vigilar algo/a algn muy atentamente. 2 *Mil (body)* guardia *f*; *(individual)* centinela *m*; to be on w., estar de guardia. 3 *(time-piece)* reloj *m*. II *vtr* 1 *(observe)* mirar, observar. 2 *(keep an eye on)* vigilar; *(with suspicion)* acechar. 3 *(be careful of)* tener cuidado con; *fig* to w. one's step, ir con pies de plomo. III *vi* 1 *(look)* mirar, observar; w. out!, ¡cuidado! ◆**watch out for** *vtr (be careful of)* tener cuidado con.

watchband ['wɒtʃbænd] *n US* → **watchstrap**.

watchdog ['wɒtʃdɒg] *n* perro *m* guardián; *fig* guardián,-ana *m,f*.

watchful ['wɒtʃfʊl] *adj* vigilante.

watchmaker ['wɒtʃmeɪkə'] *n* relojero,-a *m,f*.

watchman ['wɒtʃmən] *n* vigilante *m*; night w., *(of site)* vigilante nocturno.

watchstrap ['wɒtʃstræp] *n* correa *f* (de reloj).

watchtower ['wɒtʃtaʊə'] *n* atalaya *f*.

water ['wɔːtə'] I *n* 1 agua *f*; w. bottle, cantimplora *f*; w. lily, nenúfar *m*; w. main, conducción *f* de aguas; w. polo,

water polo m; **w. sports**, deportes acuáti-
cos; **w. tank**, depósito m de agua; **territorial waters**, aguas jurisdiccionales; *fig*
it's all w. under the bridge, ha llovido
mucho desde entonces. **2 to pass w.**, ori-
nar. **II** *vtr* (*plants*) regar. **III** *vi* **my eyes
are watering**, me lloran los ojos; **my
mouth watered**, se me hizo la boca agua.
◆**water down** (*drink*) aguar.

watercolour, *US* **watercolor**
['wɔːtəkʌlə] n acuarela f.

watercress ['wɔːtəkres] n berro m.

waterfall ['wɔːtəfɔːl] n cascada f; (*very
big*) catarata f.

waterfront ['wɔːtəfrʌnt] n (*shore*) orilla f
del agua; (*harbour*) puerto m.

watering ['wɔːtərɪŋ] n (*of plants*) riego m;
w. can, regadera f; **w. place**, abrevadero
m.

waterline ['wɔːtəlaɪn] n línea f de flota-
ción.

waterlogged ['wɔːtəlɒgd] adj anegado,-a.

watermark ['wɔːtəmɑːk] n filigrana f.

watermelon ['wɔːtəmelən] n sandía f.

waterproof ['wɔːtəpruːf] **I** adj (*material*)
impermeable; (*watch*) sumergible. **II** n
(*coat*) impermeable m.

watershed ['wɔːtəʃed] n *Geog* línea divisoria de aguas; *fig* punto decisivo.

water-skiing ['wɔːtəskiːɪŋ] n esquí acuático.

watertight ['wɔːtətaɪt] adj hermético,-a.

waterway ['wɔːtəweɪ] n vía f fluvial.

waterworks ['wɔːtəwɜːks] npl central f
sing de abastecimiento de agua; *fig* **to
turn on the w.**, empezar a llorar.

watery ['wɔːtərɪ] adj **1** (*soup*) aguado,-a;
(*coffee*) flojo,-a. **2** (*eyes*) lacrimoso,-a. **3**
(*pale*) pálido,-a.

watt [wɒt] n vatio m.

wave [weɪv] **I** n **1** (*at sea*) ola f. **2** (*in
hair*) f *Rad* onda f. **3** *fig* (*of anger, strikes
etc*) oleada f. **4** (*gesture*) saludo m con la
mano. **II** *vtr* **1** agitar; (*brandish*) blandir.
2 (*hair*) ondular. **III** *vi* **1** agitar el brazo;
she waved (**to me**), (*greeting*) me saludó
con la mano; (*goodbye*) se despidió de
mí; con la mano; (*signal*) me hizo señas
con la mano. **2** (*flag*) ondear; (*corn*) ondular.

wavelength ['weɪvleŋθ] n longitud f de
onda.

waver ['weɪvə] vi (*hesitate*) vacilar
(*between*, entre); (*voice*) temblar; (*courage*) flaquear.

wavy ['weɪvɪ] adj (**wavier, waviest**)
ondulado,-a.

wax¹ [wæks] **I** n cera f. **II** vtr encerar.

wax² [wæks] vi **1** (*moon*) crecer. **2 to w.
lyrical**, exaltarse.

waxwork ['wækswɜːk] n **waxworks**, museo m de cera.

way [weɪ] **I** n **1** (*route*) camino m; (*road*)
vía f, camino m; **a letter is on the w.**, una

carta está en camino; **on the w.**, en el camino; **on the w. here**, de camino para
aquí; **out of the w.**, apartado,-a; **to ask
the w.**, preguntar el camino; **to go the
wrong w.**, ir por el camino equivocado;
to lose one's w., perderse; **to make
one's w. through the crowd**, abrirse camino entre la multitud; **which is the w.
to the station?**, ¿por dónde se va a la
estación?; *fig* **she went out of her w. to
help**, se desvivió por ayudar; **w. in**, entrada f; **w. out**, salida f; *fig* **the easy way
out**, la solución fácil; **I can't find my w.
out**, no encuentro la salida; **on the w.
back**, en el viaje de regreso; **on the w.
up/down**, en la subida/bajada; **there's no
w. through**, el paso está cerrado; **you're
in the w.**, estás estorbando; (**get**) **out of
the w.!**, ¡quítate de en medio!; *fig* **to get
sb/sth out of the w.**, desembarazarse de
algn/algo; **I kept out of the w.**, me
mantuve a distancia; *Aut* **right of w.**,
prioridad f; **there's a wall in the w.**, hay
un muro en medio; **to give w.**, ceder;
Aut ceder el paso. **2** (*direction*) dirección
f; **come this w.**, venga por aquí; **which
w. did he go?**, ¿por dónde se fue?; **that
w.**, por allá; **the other w. round**, al revés. **3** (*distance*) distancia f; **a long w.
off**, lejos; **he'll go a long w.**, llegará
lejos; *fig* **we've come a long w.**, hemos
hecho grandes progresos. **4 to get under
w.**, (*travellers, work*) ponerse en marcha;
(*meeting, match*) empezar. **5** (*means,
method*) método m, manera f; **do it any
w. you like**, hazlo como quieras. **do it
my w.**, lo haré a mi manera. **6** (*manner*) modo m, manera f; **in a friendly w.**,
de modo amistoso; **one w. or another**,
de un modo o de otro; **the French w. of
life**, el estilo de vida francés; **the w.
things are going**, tal como van las cosas;
to my w. of thinking, a mi modo de ver;
fam **no w.!**, ¡ni hablar!; **she has a w.
with children**, tiene un don para los niños; **by w. of**, a modo de; **either w.**, en
cualquier caso; **in a w.**, en cierto sentido;
in many ways, desde muchos puntos de
vista; **in some ways**, en algunos aspectos;
in no w., de ninguna manera. **7** (*custom*)
hábito m, costumbre f; **to be set in one's
ways**, tener costumbres arraigadas. **8**
(*state*) estado m; **leave it the w. it is**, déjalo tal como está; **he is in a bad w.**, está
bastante mal. **9 by the w.**, a propósito, **in
the w. of business**, en el curso de los negocios.
II *adv fam* mucho, muy; **it was w. off
target**, estaba muy desviado del blanco; **w.
back in 1940**, allá en 1940.

waylay [weɪ'leɪ] vtr (pt & pp **waylaid**) **1**
(*attack*) atacar por sorpresa. **2** *fig* (*intercept*) salirle al paso a algn.

wayside ['weɪsaɪd] n *fig* **to fall by the w.**,

quedarse en el camino.

wayward ['weɪwəd] *adj* rebelde; *(capricious)* caprichoso,-a.

WC [dʌblju:'si:] *abbr of* water closet, wáter *m*, WC.

we [wi:] *pers pron* nosotros,-as.

weak [wi:k] *adj* débil; *(argument, excuse)* pobre; *(team, piece of work, tea)* flojo,-a.

weaken ['wi:kən] **I** *vtr* debilitar; *(argument)* quitar fuerza a. **II** *vi* **1** debilitarse. **2** *(concede ground)* ceder.

weakling ['wi:klɪŋ] *n* enclenque *mf*.

weakness ['wi:knɪs] *n* debilidad *f*; *(character flaw)* punto flaco.

wealth [welθ] *n* riqueza *f*; *fig* abundancia *f*.

wealthy ['welθɪ] *adj* (**wealthier, wealthiest**) rico,-a.

wean [wi:n] *vtr (child)* destetar; *fig* **to w. sb from the habit,** desacostumbrar (gradualmente) a algn de un hábito.

weapon ['wepən] *n* arma *f*.

wear [weəʳ] **I** *vtr (pt* **wore***; pp* **worn)** **1** *(clothes)* llevar puesto, vestir; *(shoes)* llevar puestos, calzar; **he wears glasses,** lleva gafas; **to w. black,** vestirse de negro. **2** *(erode)* desgastar. **II** *vi* **w. thin/smooth),** desgastarse (con el roce); *fig* **my patience is wearing thin,** se me está acabando la paciencia. **II** *n* **1** ropa *f*; **leisure w.,** ropa de sport. **2** *(use) (clothes)* uso *m*. **3** *(deterioration)* desgaste *m*; **normal w. and tear,** desgaste natural. ◆**wear away** *vtr* erosionar. **II** *vi (stone etc)* erosionarse; *(inscription)* borrarse. ◆**wear down** *vtr (heels)* desgastar; *fig* **to w. sb down,** vencer la resistencia de algn. **II** *vi* desgastarse. ◆**wear off** *vi (effect, pain)* pasar, desaparecer. ◆**wear out** *vtr* gastar; *fig* agotar. **II** *vi* gastarse.

wearisome ['wɪərɪsəm] *adj* fatigoso,-a.

weary ['wɪərɪ] **I** *adj* (**wearier, weariest**) **1** *(tired)* cansado,-a. **2** *(fed up)* harto,-a. **II** *vtr* cansar. **III** *vi* cansarse (**of,** de). ◆**wearily** *adv* con cansancio.

weasel ['wi:zəl] *n* comadreja *f*.

weather ['weðəʳ] **I** *n* tiempo *m*; **the w. is fine,** hace buen tiempo; *fig* **to feel under the w.,** no encontrarse bien; **w. chart,** mapa meteorológico; **w. forecast,** parte meteorológico; **w. vane,** veleta *f*. **II** *vtr fig (crisis)* aguantar; **to w. the storm,** capear el temporal.

weather-beaten ['weðəbi:tən] *adj* curtido,-a.

weathercock ['weðəkɒk] *n* veleta *f*.

weatherman ['weðəmæn] *n* hombre *m* del tiempo.

weave [wi:v] **I** *n* tejido *m*. **II** *vtr (pt* **wove***; pp* **woven)** **1** *Tex* tejer. **2** *(intertwine)* entretejer. **3** *(intrigues)* tramar. **III** *vi (person, road)* zigzaguear.

weaver ['wi:vəʳ] *n* tejedor,-a *m,f*.

web [web] *n* **1** *(of spider)* telaraña *f*. **2** *(of*

lies) sarta *f*.

webbed [webd] *adj Orn* palmeado,-a.

wed [wed] *vtr arch (pt & pp* **wed** *or* **wedded)** casarse con.

wedding ['wedɪŋ] *n* boda *f*, casamiento *m*; **w. cake,** tarta *f* nupcial; **w. day,** día *m* de la boda; **w. dress,** traje *m* de novia; **w. present,** regalo *m* de boda; **w. ring,** alianza *f*.

wedge [wedʒ] **I** *n* **1** cuña *f*; *(for table leg)* calce *m*. **2** *(of cake, cheese)* trozo *m* grande. **II** *vtr* calzar; **to be wedged tight,** *(object)* estar completamente atrancado,-a.

Wednesday ['wenzdɪ] *n* miércoles *m*.

wee¹ [wi:] *adj esp Scot* pequeñito,-a.

wee² [wi:] *fam* **I** *n* pipí *m*. **II** *vi* hacer pipí.

weed [wi:d] **I** *n Bot* mala hierba. **II** *vtr* **1** *(garden)* escardar. **2** *fig* **to w. out,** eliminar. **III** *vi* escardar.

weedkiller ['wi:dkɪləʳ] *n* herbicida *m*.

weedy ['wi:dɪ] *adj* (**weeedier, weediest**) *pej* debilucho,-a.

week [wi:k] *n* semana *f*; **a w. (ago) today/yesterday,** hoy hace/ayer hizo una semana; **a w. today,** justo dentro de una semana; **last/next w.,** la semana pasada/ que viene; **once a w.,** una vez por semana; **w. in, w. out,** semana tras semana.

weekday ['wi:kdeɪ] *n* día *m* laborable.

weekend [wi:k'end] *n* fin *m* de semana.

weekly ['wi:klɪ] **I** *adj* semanal. **II** *adv* semanalmente; **twice a w.,** dos veces por semana. **III** *n Press* semanario *m*.

weep [wi:p] **I** *vi (pt & pp* **wept)** llorar; **to w. for sb,** llorar la muerte de algn. **II** *vtr (tears)* derramar.

weeping ['wi:pɪŋ] *adj* **w. willow,** sauce *m* llorón.

weigh [weɪ] **I** *vtr* **1** pesar. **2** *fig (consider)* ponderar. **3** **to w. anchor,** levar anclas. **II** *vi* **1** pesar. **2** *fig (influence)* influir. ◆**weigh down** *vtr* sobrecargar. ◆**weigh in** *vi* **1** *Sport* pesarse. **2** *fam (join in)* intervenir. ◆**weigh up** *vtr (matter)* evaluar; *(person)* formar una opinión sobre; **to w. up the pros and cons,** sopesar los pros y los contras.

weight [weɪt] **I** *n* peso *m*; **to lose w.,** adelgazar; **to put on w.,** subir de peso; *fam fig* **to pull one's w.,** poner de su parte. **2** *(of clock, scales)* pesa *f*. **3** *fig* **that's a w. off my mind,** eso me quita un peso de encima.

weighting ['weɪtɪŋ] *n GB (on salary)* suplemento *m* de salario.

weightlifter ['weɪtlɪftəʳ] *n* halterófilo,-a *m,f*.

weighty ['weɪtɪ] *adj* (**weightier, weightiest**) pesado,-a; *fig (problem, matter)* importante, grave; *(argument)* de peso.

weir [wɪəʳ] *n* presa *f*.

weird [wɪəd] *adj* raro,-a, extraño,-a.

welcome ['welkəm] **I** *adj (person)*

bienvenido,-a; *(news)* grato,-a; *(change)* oportuno,-a; **to make sb w.,** acoger a algn calurosamente; **you're w.!,** ¡no hay de qué!. II *n (greeting)* bienvenida *f*. III *vtr* acoger; *(more formally)* darle la bienvenida a; *(news)* acoger con agrado; *(decision)* aplaudir.

welcoming ['welkəmɪŋ] *adj (person)* acogedor,-a; *(smile)* de bienvenida.

weld [weld] *vtr* soldar.

welfare ['welfeər] *n* 1 *(well-being)* bienestar *m*; **animal/child w.,** protección *f* de animales/de menores; **w. work,** asistencia *f* social; **w. worker,** asistente *mf* social. 2 *US (social security)* seguridad *f* social.

well¹ [wel] *n* 1 pozo *m*. 2 *(of staircase, lift)* hueco *m*. 3 *(of court, hall)* hemiciclo *m*. ◆**well up** *vi* brotar.

well² [wel] I *adj* 1 *(healthy)* bien; **are you keeping w.?,** ¿estás bien de salud?; **to get w.,** reponerse. 2 *(satisfactory)* bien; **all is w.,** todo va bien; **it's just as w.,** menos mal. 3 **it is as w. to remember that,** conviene recordar que.

II *adv (better, best)* 1 *(properly)* bien; **he has done w. (for himself),** ha prosperado; **the business is doing w.,** el negocio marcha bien; **she did w. in the exam,** el examen le fue bien; **w. done!,** ¡muy bien! **he took it w.,** lo tomó a bien. 2 *(thoroughly)* bien; **I know it only too w.,** lo sé de sobra; *Culin* **w. done,** muy hecho,-a. 3 **he's w. over thirty,** tiene treinta años bien cumplidos; **w. after six o'clock,** mucho después de las seis. 4 *(easily, with good reason)* **he couldn't very w. say no,** difícilmente podía decir que no; **I may w. do that,** puede que haga eso. 5 **as w.,** también; **as w. as,** así como; **children as w. as adults,** tanto niños como adultos.

III *interj* 1 *(surprise)* ¡bueno!, ¡vaya!; **w. I never!,** ¡no me digas! 2 *(agreement, interrogation, resignation)* bueno; **very w.,** bueno; **w.?,** ¿y bien? 3 *(doubt)* pues; **w., I don't know,** pues no sé. 4 *(resumption)* **w., as I was saying,** pues (bien), como iba diciendo.

well-behaved ['welbɪheɪvd] *adj (child)* formal, educado,-a.

well-being ['welbiɪŋ] *n* bienestar *m*.

well-built ['welbɪlt] *adj (building etc)* de construcción sólida; *(person)* fornido,-a.

well-earned ['welз:nd] *adj* merecido,-a.

well-educated [wel'edjukeɪtɪd] *adj* culto,-a.

well-heeled ['welhi:ld] *adj fam* adinerado,-a.

wellingtons ['welɪŋtənz] *npl* botas *fpl* de goma.

well-informed ['welɪnfɔ:md] *adj* bien informado,-a.

well-known ['welnəʊn] *adj* (bien)

conocido,-a.

well-mannered ['welmænəd] *adj* educado,-a.

well-meaning [wel'mi:nɪŋ] *adj* bien intencionado,-a.

well-off [wel'ɒf] *adj (rich)* acomodado,-a.

well-read [wel'red] *adj* culto,-a.

well-spoken [wel'spəʊkən] *adj* con acento culto.

well-to-do [weltə'du:] *adj* acomodado,-a.

well-wisher ['welwɪʃər] *n* admirador,-a *m,f*.

Welsh [welʃ] I *adj* galés,-esa; **W. rarebit,** tostada *f* con queso fundido. II *n* 1 *(language)* galés *m*. 2 **the W.,** *pl* los galeses.

Welshman ['welʃmən] *n* galés *m*.

Welshwoman ['welʃwʊmən] *n* galesa *f*.

welterweight ['weltəweɪt] *n (peso m)* wélter *m*.

wench [wentʃ] *n dated pej* moza *f*.

went [went] *pt* → **go**.

wept [wept] *pt & pp* → **weep**.

were [wз:r, *unstressed* wər] *pt* → **be**.

west [west] I *n* oeste *m*, occidente *m*; **in** or **to the w.,** al oeste; *Pol* **the W.,** los países occidentales. II *adj* del oeste, occidental; **the W. Indies,** las Antillas; **W. Indian,** antillano,-a. III *adv* al oeste, hacia el oeste.

westerly ['westəlɪ] *adj (wind)* del oeste.

western ['westən] I *adj* del oeste, occidental; **W. Europe,** Europa Occidental. II *n Cin* western *m*, película *f* del oeste.

westward ['westwəd] *adj* **in a w. direction,** hacia el oeste.

westwards ['westwədz] *adv* hacia el oeste.

wet [wet] I *adj (wetter, wettest)* 1 mojado,-a; *(slightly)* húmedo,-a; **'w. paint',** 'recién pintado'; **w. through,** *(person)* calado,-a hasta los huesos; *(thing)* empapado,-a; **w. suit,** traje isotérmico. 2 *(rainy)* lluvioso,-a. 3 *(person)* soso,-a; **w. blanket,** aguafiestas *mf inv*. II *n fam* apocado,-a *m,f*. III *vtr (pt & pp* **wet)** mojar; **to w. oneself,** orinarse.

whack [wæk] I *vtr (hit hard)* golpear fuertemente. II *n* 1 *(blow)* porrazo *m*. 2 *fam (share)* paste *f*, porción *f*.

whale [weɪl] *n (pl* whale *or* whales) ballena *f*.

wharf [wɔ:f] *n (pl* wharves [wɔ:vz]) muelle *m*.

what [wɒt, *unstressed* wət] I *adj* -1 *(direct question)* qué; **w. (sort of) bird is that?,** ¿qué tipo de ave es ésa?; **w. good is that?,** ¿para qué sirve eso? 2 *(indirect question)* qué; **ask her w. colour she likes,** pregúntale qué color le gusta.

II *pron* 1 *(direct question)* qué; **w. are you talking about?,** ¿de qué estás hablando?; **w. about your father?,** ¿y tu padre (qué)?; **w. about going tomorrow?,** ¿qué te parece si vamos mañana?; **w. can I do for** you?, ¿en qué puedo servirle?; **w. did it cost?**, ¿cuánto costó?; **w. did you do that for?**, ¿por qué hiciste eso?; **w.** (did you say?), ¿cómo?; **w. does it sound like?**, ¿cómo suena?; **w. is happening?**, ¿qué pasa?; **w. is it?**, (definition) ¿qué es?; (what's the matter) ¿qué pasa?; **w.'s it called?**, ¿cómo se llama?; **w.'s this for?**, ¿para qué sirve esto? 2 (indirect question) qué, lo que; **he asked me w.** I thought, me preguntó lo que pensaba; **I didn't know w. to say**, no sabía qué decir. 3 (and) **w.'s more**, y además; **come w. may**, pase lo que pase; **guess w.!**, ¿sabes qué?; **it's just w. I need**, es exactamente lo que necesito. 4 exclam (surprise, indignation) ¡cómo!; **w., no dessert!**, ¡cómo, no hay postre? III interj **w. a goal!**, ¡qué o vaya golazo!; **w. a lovely picture!**, ¡qué cuadro más bonito!

whatever [wɒtˈevəʳ, unstressed wətˈevəʳ] I adj 1 (any) cualquiera que; **at w. time you like**, a la hora que quieras; **of w. colour**, no importa de qué color. 2 (with negative) **nothing w.**, nada en absoluto; **with no interest w.**, sin interés alguno. II pron 1 (anything, all that) (todo) lo que; **do w. you like**, haz lo que quieras. 2 (no matter what) **don't tell him w. you do**, no se te ocurra decírselo; **w.** (else) **you find**, cualquier (otra) cosa que encuentres; **he goes out w. the weather**, sale haga el tiempo que haga. III interr **w. happened?**, ¿qué pasó?

whatsoever [wɒtsəʊˈevəʳ] adj anything **w.**, cualquier cosa; **nothing w.**, nada en absoluto.

wheat [wiːt] n trigo m; **w. germ**, germen m de trigo.

wheedle [ˈwiːdəl] vtr **to w. sb into doing sth**, engatusar a algn para que haga algo; **to w. sth out of sb**, sonsacar algo a algn halagándole.

wheel [wiːl] I n rueda f. II vtr (bicycle) empujar. III vi 1 (bird) revolotear. 2 **to w. round**, girar sobre los talones.

wheelbarrow [ˈwiːlbærəʊ] n carretilla f.

wheelchair [ˈwiːltʃeəʳ] n silla f de ruedas.

wheeze [wiːz] vi respirar con dificultad, resollar.

when [wen] I adv 1 (direct question) cuándo; **since w.?**, ¿desde cuándo?; **w. did he arrive?**, ¿cuándo llegó? 2 (indirect question) cuándo; **tell me w. to go**, dime cuándo debo ir me. 3 (on which) cuando, en que; **the days w. I work**, los días en que trabajo. II conj 1 cuando; **I'll tell you w. she comes**, se lo diré cuando llegue; **w. he was a boy ...**, de niño ... 2 (whenever) cuando. 3 (given that, if) si. 4 (although) aunque.

whence [wens] adv fml lit (from where) de

dónde.

whenever [wenˈevəʳ] I conj (when) cuando; (every time) siempre que. II adv **w. that might be**, sea cuando sea.

where [weəʳ] adv 1 (direct question) dónde; (direction) adónde; **w. are you going?**, ¿adónde vas?; **w. did we go wrong?**, ¿en qué nos equivocamos?; **w. do you come from?**, ¿de dónde es usted? 2 (indirect question) dónde; (direction) adónde; **tell me w. you went**, dime a dónde fuiste. 3 (at, in which) dónde; (direction) adonde, a donde. 4 (when) cuando.

whereabouts [weərəˈbaʊts] I adv **w. do you live?**, ¿por dónde vives? II [ˈweərəbaʊts] n paradero m.

whereas [weərˈæz] conj 1 (but, while) mientras que. 2 Jur considerando que.

whereby [weəˈbaɪ] adv por el or la or lo cual.

whereupon [weərəˈpɒn] conj fml después de lo cual.

wherever [weərˈevəʳ] I conj dondequiera que; **I'll find him w. he is**, le encontraré dondequiera que esté; **sit w. you like**, siéntate donde quieras. II adv (direct question) adónde.

wherewithal [ˈweəwɪðɔːl] n fam pelas fpl.

whet [wet] vtr **to w. sb's appetite**, abrir el apetito a algn.

whether [ˈweðəʳ] conj 1 (if) si; **I don't know w. it is true**, no sé si es verdad; **I doubt w. he'll win**, dudo que gane. 2 **w. he comes or not**, venga o no.

which [wɪtʃ] I adj 1 (direct question) qué; **w. colour do you prefer?**, ¿qué color prefieres?; **w. one?**, ¿cuál?; **w. way?**, ¿por dónde? 2 (indirect question) qué; **tell me w. dress you prefer**, dime qué vestido te gusta. 3 **in w. case**, en cuyo caso.

II pron 1 (direct question) cuál, cuáles; **of you did it?**, ¿quién de vosotros lo hizo? 2 (indirect question) cuál, cuáles; **I don't know w. I'd rather have**, no sé cuál prefiero. 3 (defining relative) que; (after preposition) que, el or la cual, los or las cuales, el or la que, los or las que; **here are the books** (w.) **I have read**, aquí están los libros que he leído; **the accident** (w.) **I told you about**, el accidente del que te hablé; **the car in w. he was travelling**, el coche en (el) que viajaba; **this is the one** (w.) **I like**, éste es el que me gusta. 4 (non-defining relative) el or la cual, los or las cuales; **I played three sets, all of w. I lost**, jugué tres sets, todos los cuales perdí. 5 (referring to a clause) lo cual, lo que; **he won, w. made me very happy**, ganó, lo cual or lo que me alegró mucho.

whichever [wɪtʃˈevəʳ] I adj el/la que, cualquiera que; **I'll take w. books you**

don't want, tomaré los libros que no quieras; **w. system you choose,** cualquiera que sea el sistema que elijas. II *pron* el que, la que.

whiff [wɪf] *n* 1 *(quick smell)* ráfaga *f; (of air, smoke)* bocanada *f.* 2 *fam (bad smell)* tufo *m.*

while [waɪl] *n* 1 *(length of time)* rato *m,* tiempo *m;* **in a little w.,** dentro de poco; **once in a w.,** de vez en cuando. 2 **it's not worth your w. staying,** no merece la pena que te quedes. II *conj* 1 *(time)* mientras; **he fell asleep w. driving,** se durmió mientras conducía. 2 *(although)* aunque. 3 *(whereas)* mientras que. ◆**while away** *vtr* to w. away the time, pasar el rato.

whilst [waɪlst] *conj* → **while III.**

whim [wɪm] *n* capricho *m,* antojo *m.*

whimper ['wɪmpəʳ] I *n* quejido *m.* II *vi* lloriquear.

whine [waɪn] *vi* 1 *(child)* lloriquear; *(with pain)* dar quejidos. 2 *(complain)* quejarse. 3 *(engine)* chirriar.

whip [wɪp] I *n* 1 *(for punishment)* látigo *m; (for riding)* fusta *f.* 2 *GB Parl* oficial *mf* encargado,-a de la disciplina de un partido. II *vtr* 1 *(as punishment)* azotar; *(horse)* fustigar. 2 *Culin* batir; **whipped cream,** nata montada. 3 *fam (steal)* mangar. ◆**whip away** *vtr* arrebatar. ◆**whip up** *vtr (passions, enthusiasm)* avivar; *(support)* incrementar.

whipping ['wɪpɪŋ] *n fig* w. boy, cabeza *f* de turco.

whip-round ['wɪpraʊnd] *n fam* colecta *f.*

whirl [wɜːl] I *n* giro *m; fig* torbellino *m.* II *vtr* to w. sth round, dar vueltas a *or* hacer girar algo. III *vi* to w. round, girar con rapidez; *(leaves etc)* arremolinarse; **my head's whirling,** me está dando vueltas la cabeza.

whirlpool ['wɜːlpuːl] *n* remolino *m.*

whirlwind ['wɜːlwɪnd] *n* torbellino *m.*

whirr [wɜːʳ] *vi* zumbar, runrunear.

whisk [wɪsk] I *n Culin* batidor *m; (electric)* batidora *f.* II *vtr Culin* batir. ◆**whisk away, whisk off** *vtr* quitar bruscamente; llevarse de repente.

whisker ['wɪskəʳ] *n* whiskers, *(of person)* patillas *fpl; (of cat)* bigotes *mpl.*

whisky, *US* **whiskey** ['wɪskɪ] *n* whisky *m.*

whisper ['wɪspəʳ] I *n* 1 *(sound)* susurro *m.* 2 *(rumour)* rumor *m.* II *vtr* decir en voz baja. III *vi* susurrar.

whistle ['wɪsəl] I *n* 1 *(instrument)* pito *m.* 2 *(sound)* silbido *m,* pitido *m.* II *vtr (tune)* silbar. III *vi* 1 *(person, kettle, wind)* silbar; *(train)* pitar.

white [waɪt] I *adj* blanco,-a; **to go w.,** *(face)* palidecer; *(hair)* encanecer; **w. coffee,** café *m* con leche; **w. hair,** pelo cano; **a w. Christmas,** una Navidad con nieve; *fig* **a w. lie,** una mentira piadosa;

US **the W. House,** la Casa Blanca; *Pol* **w. paper,** libro blanco; **w. sauce,** bechamel *f.* II *n* 1 *(colour, person, of eye)* blanco *m.* 2 *(of egg)* clara *f.* 3 **whites,** ropa *f sing* blanca.

white-collar ['waɪtkɒləʳ] *adj* w.-c. worker, empleado *m* de oficina.

whiteness ['waɪtnɪs] *n* blancura *f.*

whitewash ['waɪtwɒʃ] I *n* 1 cal *f.* 2 *fig (cover-up)* encubrimiento *m.* 3 *fig (defeat)* paliza *f.* II *vtr* 1 *(wall)* enjalbegar, blanquear. 2 *fig* encubrir.

whiting ['waɪtɪŋ] *n inv (fish)* pescadilla *f.*

Whitsun(tide) ['wɪtsən(taɪd)] *n* pentecostés *m.*

whittle ['wɪtəl] *vtr* cortar en pedazos; to w. away at, roer; *fig* to w. down, reducir poco a poco.

whiz(z) [wɪz] *vi* 1 *(sound)* silbar. 2 to w. past, pasar volando; *fam* w. kid, joven *mf* dinámico,-a y emprendedor,-a.

who [huː] *pron* 1 *(direct question)* quién, quiénes; **w. are they?,** ¿quiénes son?; **w. is it?,** ¿quién es? 2 *(indirect question)* quién; **I don't know w. did it,** no sé quién lo hizo. 3 *rel (defining)* que; **those w. don't know,** los que no saben. 4 *rel (nondefining)* quien, quienes, el *or* la cual, los *or* las cuales; **Elena's mother, w. is very rich ...,** la madre de Elena, la cual es muy rica ....

whodun(n)it [huː'dʌnɪt] *n fam* novela *f or* obra *f* de teatro *or* película *f* de suspense.

whoever [huː'evəʳ] *pron* 1 quienquiera que; **give it to w. you like,** dáselo a quien quieras; **w. said that is a fool,** el que dijo eso es un tonto; **w. you are,** quienquiera que seas. 2 *(direct question)* **w. told you that?,** ¿quién te dijo eso?

whole [həʊl] I *adj* 1 *(entire)* entero,-a, íntegro,-a; **a w. week,** una semana entera; **he took the w. lot,** se los llevó todos. 2 *(in one piece)* intacto,-a. II *n* 1 *(single unit)* todo *m,* conjunto *m;* **as a w.,** en su totalidad. 2 *(all)* totalidad *f;* **the w. of London,** todo Londres. 3 **on the w.,** en general.

wholefood ['həʊlfuːd] *n* alimentos *mpl* integrales.

wholehearted [həʊl'hɑːtɪd] *adj (enthusiastic)* entusiasta; *(sincere)* sincero,-a; *(unreserved)* incondicional.

wholemeal ['həʊlmiːl] *adj* integral.

wholesale ['həʊlseɪl] *Com* I *n* venta *f* al por mayor. II *adj* al por mayor; *fig* total. III *adv* al por mayor; *fig* en su totalidad.

wholesaler ['həʊlseɪləʳ] *n* mayorista *mf.*

wholesome ['həʊlsəm] *adj* sano,-a.

wholly ['həʊlɪ] *adv* enteramente, completamente.

whom [huːm] *pron fml* 1 *(direct question) (accusative)* a quién; **w. did you talk to?,** ¿con quién hablaste?; *(after preposition)* **of/from w.?,** ¿de quién?; **to w. are you**

referring?, ¿a quién te refieres? 2 *rel* (*accusative*) que, a quien, a quienes; **those w. I** have seen, aquéllos a quien he visto. 3 *rel* (*after preposition*) quien, quienes, el *or* la cual, los *or* las cuales; **my brothers, both of w.** are miners, mis hermanos, que son mineros los dos.

whooping cough ['hu:piŋkɒf] *n* tos ferina.

whopping ['wɒpiŋ] *adj fam* enorme.

whore [hɔːʳ] *n offens* puta *f*.

whose [hu:z] **I** *pron* **1** (*direct question*) de quién, de quiénes; **w. are these gloves?**, ¿de quién son estos guantes?; **w. is this?**, ¿de quién es esto? 2 (*indirect question*) de quién, de quiénes; **I don't know w. these coats are**, no sé de quién son estos abrigos. 3 *rel* cuyo(s), cuya(s); **the man w. children we saw**, el hombre a cuyos hijos vimos. **II** *adj* **w. car/house is this?**, ¿de quién es este coche/esta casa?.

why [wai] **I** *adv* por qué; (*for what purpose*) para qué; **w. did you do that?**, ¿por qué hiciste eso?; **w. not go to bed?**, ¿por qué no te acuestas?; **I don't know w.** he did it, no sé por qué lo hizo; **that is w.** I don't come, por eso no vine; **there's no reason w.** you shouldn't go, no hay motivo para que no vayas. **II** *interj* **1** (*fancy that!*) ¡toma!, ¡vaya!; **w.**, it's David!, ¡sí es David! 2 (*protest, assertion*) sí, vamos.

wick [wik] *n* mecha *f*.

wicked ['wikid] *adj* **1** malvado,-a. 2 *fam* malísimo,-a; (*temper*) de perros.

wicker ['wikəʳ] **I** *n* mimbre *f*. **II** *adj* de mimbre.

wickerwork ['wikəwɜːk] *n* (*material*) mimbre *m*; (*articles*) artículos *mpl* de mimbre.

wicket ['wikit] *n* Cricket (*stumps*) palos *mpl*.

wide [waid] **I** *adj* **1** (*road, trousers*) ancho,-a; (*gap, interval*) grande; **it is ten metres w.**, tiene diez metros de ancho. 2 (*area, knowledge, support, range*) amplio, -a; **w. interests**, intereses muy diversos. 3 (*off target*) desviado,-a. **II** *adv* **from far and w.**, de todas partes; **to open one's eyes w.**, abrir los ojos de par en par; **w. apart**, muy separados,-as; **w. awake**, completamente despierto,-a; **w. open**, abierto,-a de par en par; **with mouth w. open**, boquiabierto,-a. ◆**widely** *adv* (*travel etc*) extensamente; (*believed*) generalmente; **he is w. known**, es muy conocido.

wide-angle ['waidæŋgl] *adj* Phot **w.-a. lens**, objetivo *m* gran angular.

widen ['waidən] **I** *vtr* ensanchar; (*interests*) ampliar. **II** *vi* ensancharse.

wide-ranging [waid'reindʒiŋ] *adj* (*interests*) muy diversos,-as; (*discussion*) amplio,-a; (*study*) de gran alcance.

widespread ['waidspred] *adj* (*unrest, belief*) general; (*damage*) extenso,-a; **to become w.**, generalizarse.

widow ['widəu] *n* viuda *f*.

widowed ['widəud] *adj* enviudado,-a.

widower ['widəuəʳ] *n* viudo *m*.

width [widθ] *n* **1** anchura *f*. 2 (*of material, swimming pool*) ancho *m*.

wield [wi:ld] *vtr* (*weapon*) blandir; *fig* (*power*) ejercer.

wife [waif] *n* (*pl* **wives**) mujer *f*, esposa *f*.

wig [wig] *n* peluca *f*.

wiggle ['wigl] **I** *vtr* (*finger etc*) menear; **to w. one's hips**, contonearse. **II** *vi* menearse.

Wight [wait] *n* **Isle of W.**, Isla *f* de Wight.

wild [waild] **I** *adj* **1** (*animal, tribe*) salvaje; **w. beast**, fiera *f*; *fig* **w. goose chase**, búsqueda *f* inútil. 2 (*plant*) silvestre. 3 (*landscape*) agreste; **the W. West**, el Salvaje Oeste. 4 (*temperament, behaviour*) alocado,-a; (*appearance*) desordenado,-a; (*passions etc*) desenfrenado,-a; (*laughter, thoughts*) loco,-a; (*applause*) fervoroso,-a; **to make a w. guess**, adivinar al azar; *fam fig* **she is w. about him/about tennis**, está loca por él/por el tenis. 5 *GB fam fig* furioso,-a. **II** *adv fig* **to run w.**, (*children*) desmandarse. **III** *n* **in the w.**, en el estado salvaje; *fig* **to live out in the wilds**, vivir en el quinto pino. ◆**wildly** *adv* **1** (*rush round etc*) como un,-a loco,-a; (*shoot*) sin apuntar; (*hit out*) a tontas y a locas. 2 **w. enthusiastic**, loco,-a de entusiasmo; **w. inaccurate**, totalmente erróneo,-a.

wildcat ['waildkæt] *n* **w. strike**, huelga *f* salvaje.

wilderness ['wildənis] *n* desierto *m*.

wildfire ['waildfaiəʳ] *n* **to spread like w.**, correr como la pólvora.

wildlife ['waildlaif] *n* fauna *f*; **w. park**, parque *m* natural.

wilful, *US* **willful** ['wilful] *adj* **1** (*stubborn*) terco,-a. 2 *Jur* premeditado,-a.

will¹ [wil] **I** *n* **1** voluntad *f*; **good/free w.**, buena/mala voluntad; **of my own free w.**, por mi propia voluntad. 2 *Jur* (*testament*) testamento *m*; **to make one's w.**, hacer testamento. **II** *vtr* **fate willed that ...**, el destino quiso que ....

will² [wil] *v aux* (*pt* **would**) **1** (*future*) (*esp 2nd & 3rd person*) **they'll come**, vendrán; **w. he be there?** - yes, **he w.**, ¿estará allí? - sí, (estará); **you'll tell him, won't you?**, se lo dirás, ¿verdad?; **don't forget, w. you!**, ¡que no se te olvide, vale!; **she won't do it**, no lo hará. 2 (*future perfect*) **you w. be here at eleven!**, ¡debes estar aquí a las once! 3 (*future perfect*) **they'll have finished by tomorrow**, habrán terminado para mañana. 4 (*willingness*) **be quiet, w. you!** - no, **I won't!**, ¿quiere callarse? -

no quiero; **I won't have it!**, ¡no lo permito!; **will you have a drink?** - yes, I w., ¿quiere tomar algo? - sí, por favor; **won't you sit down?**, ¿quiere sentarse? **5** (custom) **accidents w. happen**, siempre habrá accidentes. **6** (persistence) **if you w. go out without a coat ...**, si te empeñas en salir sin abrigo .... **7** (probability) **he'll be on holiday now**, ahora probably de vacaciones. **8** (ability) **the lift w. hold ten people**, en el ascensor caben diez personas.

willing ['wɪlɪŋ] *adj* (obliging) complaciente; **I'm quite w. to do it**, lo haré con mucho gusto; **to be w. to do sth**, estar dispuesto,-a a hacer algo. ◆**willingly** *adv* de buena gana.

willingness ['wɪlɪŋnɪs] *n* buena voluntad.

willow ['wɪləʊ] *n* w. (tree), sauce *m*.

willpower ['wɪlpaʊəʳ] *n* (fuerza *f* de) voluntad *f*.

willy-nilly [wɪlɪ'nɪlɪ] *adv* por gusto o por fuerza.

wilt [wɪlt] *vi* marchitarse.

wily ['waɪlɪ] *adj* (wilier, wiliest) astuto,-a.

win [wɪn] **I** *n* victoria *f*. **II** *vtr* (pt & pp **won**) **1** ganar; (prize) (prize) llevarse; (victory) conseguir. **2** *fig* (sympathy, friendship) ganarse; (praise) cosechar; **to w. sb's love**, conquistar a algn. **III** *vi* ganar. ◆**win back** *vtr* recuperar. ◆**win over** *vtr* (to cause, idea) atraer (to, a hacia); (voters, support) ganarse. ◆**win through** *vi* conseguir triunfar.

wince [wɪns] *vi* tener un rictus de dolor.

winch [wɪntʃ] *n* cigüeña *f*, torno *m*.

wind¹ [wɪnd] **I** *n* **1** viento *m*; *fig* **to get w. of sth**, olerse algo; **w. tunnel**, túnel aerodinámico. **2** (breath) aliento *m*; **to get one's second w.**, recobrar el aliento. **3** *Med* flato *m*, gases *mpl*. **4** w. **instrument**, instrumento *m* de viento. **II** *vtr* **to be winded**, quedarse sin aliento.

wind² [waɪnd] **I** *vtr* (pt & pp **wound**) **1** (onto a reel) enrollar; **to w. a bandage round one's finger**, vendarse el dedo. **2** **to w. on/back**, (film, tape) avanzar/rebobinar. **3** (clock) dar cuerda a. **II** *vi* (road, river) serpentear. ◆**wind down I** *vtr* (window) bajar. **II** *vi fam* (person) relajarse. ◆**wind up I** *vtr* **1** (roll up) enrollar. **2** (business etc) cerrar; (debate) clausurar. **3** (clock) dar cuerda a. **II** *vi* (meeting) terminar.

windfall ['wɪndfɔːl] *n fig* ganancia inesperada.

winding ['waɪndɪŋ] *adj* (road, river) sinuoso,-a; (staircase) de caracol.

windmill ['wɪndmɪl] *n* molino *m* (de viento).

window ['wɪndəʊ] *n* ventana *f*; (of vehicle, ticket office etc) ventanilla *f*; (shop) w., escaparate *m*; **to clean the windows**, limpiar los cristales; **w. box**, jardinera *f*;

w. **cleaner**, limpiacristales *mf inv*.

windowpane ['wɪndəʊpeɪn] *n* cristal *m*.

window-shopping ['wɪndəʊʃɒpɪŋ] *n* **to go w.-s.**, ir a mirar escaparates.

windowsill ['wɪndəʊsɪl] *n* alféizar *m*.

windpipe ['wɪndpaɪp] *n* tráquea *f*.

windscreen ['wɪndskriːn], *US* **windshield** ['wɪndʃiːld] *n* parabrisas *m inv*; **w. washer**, lavaparabrisas *m inv*; **w. wiper**, limpiaparabrisas *m inv*.

windswept ['wɪndswept] *adj* (landscape) expuesto,-a a los vientos; (person, hair) despeinado,-a (por el viento).

windy ['wɪndɪ] *adj* (windier, windiest) (weather) ventoso,-a; (place) desprotegido,-a del viento; **it is very w. today**, hoy hace mucho viento.

wine [waɪn] *n* vino *m*; **w. cellar**, bodega *f*; **w. list**, lista *f* de vinos; **w. merchant**, vinatero,-a *m,f*; **w. tasting**, cata *f* de vinos; **w. vinegar**, vinagre *m* de vino.

wineglass ['waɪnglɑːs] *n* copa *f* (para vino).

wing [wɪŋ] *n* **1** *Orn Av* ala *f*. **2** (of building) ala *f*. **3** *Aut* aleta *f*; **w. mirror**, retrovisor *m* externo. **4** *Theat* **(in the) wings**, (entre) bastidores *mpl*. **5** *Ftb* banda *f*. **6** *Pol* ala *f*; **the left w.**, la izquierda.

winger ['wɪŋəʳ] *n Ftb* extremo *m*.

wink [wɪŋk] **I** *n* guiño *m*; *fam fig* **I didn't get a w. (of sleep)**, no pegué ojo. **II** *vi* **1** (person) guiñar (el ojo). **2** (light) parpadear.

winner ['wɪnəʳ] *n* ganador,-a *m,f*.

winning ['wɪnɪŋ] *adj* (person, team) ganador,-a; (number) premiado,-a; (goal) decisivo,-a; **w. post**, meta *f*.

winnings ['wɪnɪŋz] *npl* ganancias *fpl*.

winter ['wɪntəʳ] **I** *n* invierno *m*. **II** *adj* de invierno; **w. sports**, deportes *mpl* de invierno. **III** *vi* invernar.

wintry ['wɪntrɪ] *adj* (wintrier, wintriest) invernal.

wipe [waɪp] **I** *vtr* limpiar; **to w. one's brow**, enjugarse la frente; **to w. one's feet/nose**, limpiarse los pies/las narices. ◆**wipe away** *vtr* (tear) enjugar. ◆**wipe off** *vtr* quitar frotando; **to w. sth off the blackboard/the tape**, borrar algo de la pizarra/de la cinta. ◆**wipe out** *vtr* **1** (erase) borrar. **2** (army) aniquilar; (species etc) exterminar. ◆**wipe up** *vtr* limpiar.

wire [waɪəʳ] **I** *n* **1** alambre *m*; *Elec* cable *m*; *Tel* hilo; **w. cutters**, cizalla *f sing*. **2** (telegram) telegrama *m*. **II** *vtr* **1** **w. (up)** **a house**, poner la instalación eléctrica de una casa; **to w. (up) an appliance to the mains**, conectar un aparato a la toma eléctrica. **2** (information) enviar por telegrama.

wireless ['waɪəlɪs] *n* radio *f*.

wiring ['waɪərɪŋ] *n* (network) cableado *m*; (action) instalación *f* del cableado.

wiry ['waɪərɪ] *adj* (wirier, wiriest) (hair) estropajoso,-a; (person) nervudo,-a.

wisdom ['wɪzdəm] *n* 1 (learning) sabiduría *f*, saber *m*. 2 (good sense) (of person) cordura *f*; (of action) sensatez *f*. 3 **w. tooth**, muela *f* del juicio.

wise [waɪz] *adj* 1 sabio,-a; **a w. man**, un sabio; **the Three W. Men**, los Reyes Magos. 2 (remark) juicioso,-a; (decision) acertado,-a; **it would be w. to keep quiet**, sería prudente callarse. ◆**wisely** *adv* (with prudence) prudentemente.

wisecrack ['waɪzkræk] *n fam* salida *f*, ocurrencia *f*.

wish [wɪʃ] I *n* 1 (desire) deseo *m* (for, de); **to make a w.**, pedir un deseo. 2 **best wishes**, felicitaciones *fpl*; **give your mother my best wishes**, salude a su madre de mi parte; **with best wishes, Peter**, (at end of letter) saludos cordiales, Peter. II *vtr* 1 (want) querer, desear; **I w. I could stay longer**, me gustaría poder quedarme más tiempo; **I w. you had told me!**, ¡ojalá me lo hubieras dicho!; **to w. to do sth**, querer hacer algo. 2 **to w. sb goodnight**, darle las buenas noches a algn; **to w. sb well**, desearle a algn mucha suerte. III *vi* (want) desear; **as you w.**, como quieras; **do as you w.**, haga lo que quiera; **to w. for sth**, desear algo.

wishful ['wɪʃful] *adj* it's **w. thinking**, es hacerse ilusiones.

wishy-washy ['wɪʃɪwɒʃɪ] *adj fam* (person) soso,-a; (ideas) poco definido,-a.

wisp [wɪsp] *n* (of wool, hair) mechón *m*; (of smoke) voluta *f*.

wistful ['wɪstful] *adj* melancólico,-a.

wit [wɪt] *n* 1 (intelligence) (often *pl*) inteligencia *f*; *fig* **to be at one's wits' end**, estar para volverse loco,-a; *fam fig* **to have one's wits about one**, ser despabilado,-a. 2 (humour) ingenio *m*. 3 (person) ingenioso,-a *mf*.

witch [wɪtʃ] *n* bruja *f*; *fig* **w. hunt**, caza *f* de brujas.

witchcraft ['wɪtʃkrɑːft] *n* brujería *f*.

with [wɪð, wɪθ] *prep* con; **a room w. a bath**, un cuarto con baño; **do you have any money w. you?**, ¿traes dinero?; **the man w. the glasses**, el hombre de las gafas; **he went w. me/you**, fue conmigo/contigo; *fam* **w.** (sugar) **or without** (sugar)?, ¿con o sin azúcar?; **I have six w. this one**, con éste tengo seis; **w. all his faults, I admire him**, le admiro con todos sus defectos; **w. your permission**, con su permiso; **we're all w. you**, (support) todos estamos contigo; **you're not w. me, are you?** (understand) no me entiendes, ¿verdad?; **he's w. Lloyds**, trabaja para Lloyds; **she is popular w. her colleagues**, todos sus colegas la estiman mucho; **to fill a vase w. water**, llenar un jarrón de agua; **it is made w.**

butter, está hecho con mantequilla; **she put on weight w. so much eating**, engordó de tanto comer; **to be paralysed w. fear**, estar paralizado,-a de miedo; **w. experience**, con la experiencia.

withdraw [wɪð'drɔː] I *vtr* (*pt* **withdrew**; *pp* **withdrawn**) 1 retirar, sacar; **to w. money from the bank**, sacar dinero del banco. 2 (go back on) retirar; (statement) retractarse de; (plan, claim) renunciar a. II *vi* 1 retirarse. 2 (drop out) renunciar.

withdrawal [wɪð'drɔːəl] *n* retirada *f*; (of statement) retractación *f*; (of complaint, plan) renuncia *f*; **w. symptoms**, síndrome *m* de abstinencia.

withdrawn [wɪð'drɔːn] *adj* (person) introvertido,-a.

wither ['wɪðər] *vi* marchitarse.

withering ['wɪðərɪŋ] *adj* (look) fulminante; (criticism) mordaz.

withhold [wɪð'həʊld] *vtr* (*pt & pp* **withheld** [wɪð'held]) (money) retener; (decision) aplazar; (consent) negar; (information) ocultar.

within [wɪ'ðɪn] I *prep* 1 (inside) dentro de. 2 (range) **the house is w. walking distance**, se puede ir andando a la casa; **situated w. five kilometres of the town**, situado,-a a menos de cinco kilómetros de la ciudad; **w. sight of the sea**, con vistas al mar; *fig* **w. an inch of death**, a dos dedos de la muerte. 3 (time) **they arrived w. a few days of each other**, llegaron con pocos días de diferencia; **w. the hour**, dentro de una hora; **w. the next five years**, durante los cinco próximos años. II *adv* dentro; **from w.**, desde dentro.

with-it ['wɪðɪt] *adj fam* **she is very w. it**, tiene ideas muy modernas; **to get w. it**, ponerse de moda.

without [wɪ'ðaʊt] *prep* sin; **he did it w. my knowing**, lo hizo sin que lo supiera yo; *fig* **to do** *or* **go w. sth**, (voluntarily) prescindir de algo; (forcibly) pasar(se) sin algo.

withstand [wɪð'stænd] *vtr* (*pt & pp* **withstood**) resistir a; (pain) aguantar.

witness ['wɪtnɪs] I *n* 1 (person) testigo *mf*; **w. box**, *US* **w. stand**, barra *f* de los testigos. 2 (evidence) **to bear w. to sth**, dar fe de algo. II *vtr* 1 (see) presenciar, ser testigo de. 2 *fig* (notice) notar. 3 *Jur* **to w. a document**, firmar un documento como testigo.

witticism ['wɪtɪsɪzəm] *n* ocurrencia *f*, salida *f*.

witty ['wɪtɪ] *adj* (wittier, wittiest) ingenioso,-a, agudo,-a.

wives [waɪvz] *npl* → **wife**.

wizard ['wɪzəd] *n* hechicero *m*, mago *m*.

wizened ['wɪzənd] *adj* (face) arrugado,-a.

wobble ['wɒbəl] *vi* (table, ladder etc) tambalearse; (jelly) temblar.

woe [wəʊ] *n lit* infortunio *m*; **w. betide you if I catch you!**, ¡ay de ti si te cojo!

woeful [ˈwəʊfʊl] *adj* **1** (*person*) afligido,-a. **2** (*sight*) penoso,-a; **w. ignorance**, una ignorancia lamentable.

woke [wəʊk] *pt* → **wake¹**.

woken [ˈwəʊkən] *pp* → **wake¹**.

wolf [wʊlf] *n* (*pl* **wolves**) lobo *m*; **w. in sheep's clothing**, un lobo con piel de cordero.

woman [ˈwʊmən] *n* (*pl* **women**) mujer *f*; **old w.**, vieja *f*; **women's libber**, feminista *mf*; *fam* **women's lib**, movimiento *m* feminista; **women's rights**, derechos *mpl* de la mujer.

womanhood [ˈwʊmənhʊd] *n* (*adult*) edad adulta de la mujer.

womanizer [ˈwʊmənaɪzəʳ] *n* mujeriego *m*.

womanly [ˈwʊmənlɪ] *adj* femenino,-a.

womb [wuːm] *n* matriz *f*, útero *m*.

women [ˈwɪmɪn] *npl* → **woman**.

won [wʌn] *pt* & *pp* → **win**.

wonder [ˈwʌndəʳ] **I** *n* **1** (*miracle*) milagro *m*; **no w. he hasn't come**, no es de extrañar que no haya venido. **2** (*amazement*) admiración *f*, asombro *m*. **II** *vtr* **1** (*be surprised*) sorprenderse. **2** (*ask oneself*) preguntarse; **I w. why**, ¿por qué será? **III** *vi* **1** (*marvel*) maravillarse; **to w. at sth**, admirarse de algo. **2** **it makes you w.**, (*reflect*) te da qué pensar.

wonderful [ˈwʌndəfʊl] *adj* maravilloso,-a.
◆**wonderfully** *adv* maravillosamente.

wont [wəʊnt] *fml* **I** *adj* **to be w. to**, soler. **II** *n* costumbre; **it is his w. to ...**, tiene la costumbre de ....

woo [wuː] *vtr* *lit* (*court*) cortejar; *fig* intentar congraciarse con.

wood [wʊd] *n* **1** (*forest*) bosque *m*. **2** (*material*) madera *f*; (*for fire*) leña *f*; *fam fig* **touch w.!**, ¡toca madera! **3** *Golf* palo *m* de madera. **4** (*bowling*) bola *f*.

woodcarving [ˈwʊdkɑːvɪŋ] *n* **1** (*craft*) tallado *m* en madera. **2** (*object*) talla *f* en madera.

woodcutter [ˈwʊdkʌtəʳ] *n* leñador,-a *m,f*.

wooded [ˈwʊdɪd] *adj* arbolado,-a.

wooden [ˈwʊdən] *adj* **1** de madera; **w. spoon/leg**, cuchara *f*/pata *f* de palo. **2** *fig* rígido,-a; (*acting*) sin expresión.

woodlouse [ˈwʊdlaʊs] *n* cochinilla *f*.

woodpecker [ˈwʊdpekəʳ] *n* pájaro carpintero.

woodwind [ˈwʊdwɪnd] *n* **w.** (*instruments*), instrumentos *mpl* de viento de madera.

woodwork [ˈwʊdwɜːk] *n* **1** (*craft*) carpintería *f*. **2** (*of building*) maderaje *m*.

woodworm [ˈwʊdwɜːm] *n* carcoma *f*.

wool [wʊl] *n* **1** lana *f*; *fig* **to pull the w. over sb's eyes**, dar gato por liebre a algn. **II** *adj* de lana.

woollen, *US* **woolen** [ˈwʊlən] **I** *adj* **1** de lana. **2** (*industry*) lanero,-a. **II** *npl* **woollens**, géneros *mpl* de lana or de punto.

woolly, *US* **wooly** [ˈwʊlɪ] *adj* (**woollier**, **woolliest**, *US* **woolier**, **wooliest**) **1** (*made of wool*) de lana. **2** *fig* (*unclear*) confuso, -a.

word [wɜːd] **I** *n* **1** (*spoken*, *written*) palabra *f*; **in other words ...**, es decir ..., o sea ...; **words failed me**, me quedé sin habla; *fig* **a w. of advice**, un consejo; *fig* **I'd like a w. with you**, quiero hablar contigo un momento; *fig* **she didn't say it in so many words**, no lo dijo de modo tan explícito; **in the words of the poet ...**, como diría el poeta ...; *fig* **w. for w.**, palabra por palabra; **w. processing**, procesamiento *m* de textos; **w. processor**, procesador *m* de textos. **2** *fig* (*message*) mensaje *m*; **by w. of mouth**, de palabra; **is there any w. from him?**, ¿hay noticias de él?; **to send w.**, mandar recado. **3** *fig* (*rumour*) voz *f*, rumor *m*. **4** *fig* (*promise*) palabra *f*; **he's a man of his w.**, es hombre de palabra. **5** *vtr* (*express*) formular; **a badly worded letter**, una carta mal redactada.

wording [ˈwɜːdɪŋ] *n* expresión *f*; **I changed the w. slightly**, cambié algunas palabras.

word-perfect [wɜːdˈpɜːfekt] *adj* **to be w.-p.**, saberse el papel perfectamente.

wore [wɔːʳ] *pt* → **wear**.

work [wɜːk] **I** *n* **1** trabajo *m*; **his w. in the field of physics**, su labor en el campo de la física; **it's hard w.**, cuesta trabajo. **2** (*employment*) trabajo *m*, empleo *m*; **out of w.**, parado,-a. **3** (*action*) obra *f*, acción *f*; **keep up the good w.!**, ¡que siga así! **4** a piece of w., un trabajo; **a w. of art**, una obra de arte. **5** **works**, obras *fpl*; **public works**, obras (públicas). **6** **works**, (*machinery*) mecanismo *m sing*. **7** *GB* **works**, (*factory*) fábrica *f*.

II *vtr* **1** (*drive*) hacer trabajar; **to w. one's way up/down**, subir/bajar a duras penas; *fig* **to w. one's way up in a firm**, trabajarse el ascenso en una empresa. **2** (*machine*) manejar; (*mechanism*) accionar. **3** (*miracles*, *changes*) operar, hacer. **4** (*land*) cultivar; (*mine*) explotar. **5** (*wood*, *metal etc*) trabajar.

III *vi* **1** trabajar (**on**, at, en); **to w. as a gardener**, trabajar de jardinero. **2** (*machine*) funcionar; **it works on gas**, funciona con gas. **3** (*drug*) surtir efecto; (*system*) funcionar bien; (*plan*, *trick*) salir bien. **4** (*operate*) obrar; **to w. loose**, soltarse; **we have no data to w. on**, no tenemos datos en que basarnos.
◆**work off** *vtr* (*fat*) eliminar trabajando; (*anger*) desahogar. ◆**work out I** *vtr* **1** (*plan*) idear; (*itinerary*) planear; (*details*) desarrollar. **2** (*problem*) solucionar; (*solu-*

tion) encontrar; *(amount)* calcular; **I can't w. out how he did it**, no me explico cómo lo hizo. **II** *vi* **1 things didn't w. out for her**, las cosas no le salieron bien. **2 it works out at 5 each**, sale a 5 cada uno. **3** *Sport* hacer ejercicio. ◆**work through** *vi* penetrar (to, hasta). ◆**work up** *vtr* *(excite)* aclarar; **to get worked up**, excitarse; **to w. up enthusiasm**, entusiasmarse (for, con).

workable ['wɜːkəbəl] *adj* factible.

workaholic [wɜːkə'hɒlɪk] *n* *fam* trabajoadicto,-a.

workbench ['wɜːkbentʃ] *n* obrador *m*.

worker ['wɜːkəʳ] *n* trabajador,-a *m,f*; *(manual)* obrero,-a *m,f*.

workforce ['wɜːkfɔːs] *n* mano *f* de obra.

working ['wɜːkɪŋ] **I** *adj* **1** *(population, capital)* activo,-a; **w. class**, clase obrera; **w. man**, obrero *m*. **2** *(clothes, conditions, hours)* de trabajo; **w. day**, día *m* laborable; *(number of hours)* jornada *f* laboral. **3 it is in w. order**, funciona. **4** *(majority)* suficiente; **w. knowledge**, conocimientos básicos. **II** *n* **workings**, *(mechanics)* funcionamiento *m sing*; *Min* explotación *f sing*.

workman ['wɜːkmən] *n* *(manual)* obrero *m*.

workmanship ['wɜːkmənʃɪp] *n* *(appearance)* acabado *m*; *(skill)* habilidad *f*, arte *m* **a fine piece of w.**, un trabajo excelente.

workmate ['wɜːkmeɪt] *n* compañero,-a *m,f* de trabajo.

work-out ['wɜːkaʊt] *n* entrenamiento *m*.

worksheet ['wɜːkʃiːt] *n* plan *m* de trabajo.

workshop ['wɜːkʃɒp] *n* taller *m*.

worktop ['wɜːktɒp] *n* encimera *f*.

work-to-rule [wɜːktə'ruːl] *n* huelga *f* de celo.

world [wɜːld] *n* mundo *m*; **all over the w.**, en todo el mundo; **the best in the w.**, el mejor del mundo; *fig* **there is a w. of difference between A and B**, hay un mundo de diferencia entre A y B; *fig* **to feel on top of the w.**, sentirse fenomenal; *fig* **to think the w. of sb**, adorar a algn; *fam fig* **it is out of this w.**, es una maravilla; **the W. Bank**, el Banco Mundial; *Ftb* **the W. Cup**, los Mundiales; **w. record**, récord *m* mundial; **w. war**, guerra *f* mundial.

world-class ['wɜːldklɑːs] *adj* de categoría mundial.

world-famous ['wɜːldfeɪməs] *adj* de fama mundial.

worldly ['wɜːldlɪ] *adj* mundano,-a.

worldwide ['wɜːldwaɪd] *adj* mundial.

worm [wɜːm] **I** *n* **1** gusano *m*; *(earth)* **w.**, lombriz *f*. **2** *Med* **worms**, lombrices *fpl*. **II** *vtr* **to w. a secret out of sb**, sonsacarle un secreto a algn.

worn [wɔːn] *adj* gastado, -a, usado,-a.

worn-out ['wɔːnaʊt] *adj* *(thing)* gastado, -a; *(person)* rendido,-a, agotado,-a.

worried ['wʌrɪd] *adj* inquieto,-a, preocupado,-a.

worry ['wʌrɪ] **I** *vtr* **1** preocupar, inquietar; **it doesn't w. me**, me trae sin cuidado. **2** *(pester)* molestar. **II** *vi* preocuparse *(about, por)*; **don't w.**, no te preocupes. **III** *n* *(state)* inquietud *f*; *(cause)* preocupación *f*.

worrying ['wʌrɪɪŋ] *adj* inquietante, preocupante.

worse [wɜːs] **I** *adj* *(comp of bad)* peor; **he gets w. and w.**, va de mal en peor; **to get w.**, empeorar; *fam* **w. luck!**, ¡mala suerte! **II** *n* **a change for the w.**, un empeoramiento; *fig* **to take a turn for the w.**, empeorar. **III** *adv* *(comp of badly)* peor; **w. than ever**, peor que nunca.

worship ['wɜːʃɪp] **I** *vtr* adorar. **II** *n* **1** adoración *f*. **2** *(ceremony)* culto *m*. **3** *GB* **his W. the Mayor**, el señor alcalde; *Jur* **your W.**, señoría.

worshipper ['wɜːʃɪpəʳ] *n* devoto,-a *m,f*.

worst [wɜːst] **I** *adj* *(superl of bad)* peor; **the w. part about it is that …**, lo peor es que …. **II** *n* *(person)* el or la peor, los or las peores. **2 the w. of the storm is over**, ya ha pasado lo peor de la tormenta. **III** *adv* *(superl of badly)* peor; *fig* **to come off w.**, salir perdiendo.

worth [wɜːθ] **I** *adj* **1 to be w. £3**, valer 3 libras; **a house w. £50,000**, una casa que vale 50.000 libras. **2** *(deserving of)* merecedor,-a de; **a book w. reading**, un libro que merece la pena leer; **for what it's w.**, por si sirve de algo; **it's w. your while**, it's w. it, vale or merece la pena; **it's w. mentioning**, es digno de mención. **II** *n* **1** *(in money)* valor *m*; **five pounds' w.** of petrol, gasolina por valor de 5 libras. **2** *(of person)* valía *f*.

worthless ['wɜːθlɪs] *adj* sin valor; *(person)* despreciable.

worthwhile [wɜːθ'waɪl] *adj* valioso,-a, que vale la pena.

worthy ['wɜːðɪ] *adj* *(worthier, worthiest)* **1** *(deserving)* digno,-a *(of, de)*; *(winner, cause)* justo,-a. **2** *(citizen)* respetable; *(effort, motives, action)* loable.

would [wʊd, *unstressed* wəd] *v aux* **1** *(conditional)* **I w. go if I had time**, iría si tuviera tiempo; **he w. have won but for that**, habría ganado su no hubiera sido por eso; **we w. if we could**, lo haríamos si pudiéramos; **you would have to choose me!**, ¡tenías que elegirme precisamente a mí! **2** *(reported speech)* **he said that he w. come**, dijo que vendría. **3** *(willingness)* **the car wouldn't start**, el coche no arrancaba; **they asked him to come but he wouldn't**, le invitaron a venir pero no quiso; **w. you do me a fa-**

vour?, ¿quiere hacerme un favor? **4** *(wishing)* **he w. like to know why**, quisiera saber por qué; **I'd rather go home**, preferiría ir a casa; **w. you like a cigarette?**, ¿quiere un cigarrillo? **5** *(custom)* **we go for walks**, solíamos dar un paseo. **6 try as I w.**, por mucho que lo intentara. **7** *(conjecture)* **it w. have been about three weeks ago**, debe haber sido hace unas tres semanas; **w. this be your cousin?**, ¿será éste tu primo? **8** *(expectation)* **so it w. appear**, según parece.

would-be ['wudbi:] *adj* en potencia; a **w.-be politician**, un aspirante a político; *pej* a **w.-be poet**, un supuesto poeta.

wound¹ [waund] *pt & pp* → **wind²**.

wound² [wu:nd] **I** *n* herida *f*. **II** *vtr* herir.

wove [wǝuv] *pt* → **weave**.

woven ['wǝuvǝn] *pp* → **weave**.

wow [wau] *fam* **I** *vtr* encandilar. **II** *interj* ¡caramba!

WP 1 *abbr of* word processing. **2** *abbr of* word processor.

wrangle ['ræŋgǝl] **I** *n* disputa *f*. **II** *vi* disputar (**over**, acerca de, por).

wrap [ræp] **I** *vtr* **1 to w. (up)**, envolver; **he wrapped his arms around her**, la estrechó entre sus brazos; *fam* **we wrapped up the deal**, concluimos el negocio. **II** *vi* *fam* **w. up well**, abrígate. **III** *n* *(shawl)* chal *m*; *(cape)* capa *f*.

wrapper ['ræpǝr] *n* *(of sweet)* envoltorio *m*; *(of book)* sobrecubierta *f*.

wrapping ['ræpɪŋ] *n* **w. paper**, papel *m* de envolver.

wreath [ri:θ] *n* *(pl* **wreaths** [ri:ðz, ri:θs]*)* *(of flowers)* corona *f*; **laurel w.**, corona de laurel.

wreck [rek] **I** *n* **1** *Naut* naufragio *m*; *(ship)* barco naufragado. **2** *(of car, plane)* restos *mpl*; *(of building)* ruinas *fpl*. **3** *fig* *(person)* ruina *f*. **II** *vtr* **1** *(ship)* hacer naufragar. **2** *(car, machine)* destrozar. **3** *fig* *(health, life)* arruinar; *(plans, hopes)* desbaratar; *(chances)* echar a perder.

wreckage ['rekɪdʒ] *n* *(of ship, car, plane)* restos *mpl*; *(of building)* ruinas *fpl*.

wren [ren] *n* chochín *m*.

wrench [rentʃ] **I** *n* **1** *(pull)* tirón *m*. **2** *Med* torcedura *f*. **3** *(tool)* *GB* llave inglesa; *US* llave. **II** *vtr* **to w. oneself free**, soltarse de un tirón; **to w. sth off sb**, arrebatarle algo a algn; **to w. sth off/open**, quitar/abrir algo de un tirón.

wrestle ['resǝl] *vi* luchar.

wrestler ['reslǝr] *n* luchador,-a *m,f*.

wrestling ['reslɪŋ] *n* lucha *f*.

wretch [retʃ] *n* *(poor)* **w.**, desgraciado,-a *m,f*.

wretched ['retʃɪd] *adj* **1** desdichado,-a; *(conditions)* deplorable; *fam* *(bad, poor)* horrible. **2 I feel w.**, *(ill)* me siento fatal. **3** *(contemptible)* despreciable. **4** *fam*

(damned) maldito,-a, condenado,-a.

wriggle ['rɪgǝl] **I** *vtr* menear. **II** *vi* **to w.** *(about)*, *(worm)* serpentear; *(restless child)* moverse nerviosamente; **to w. free**, escapar deslizándose.

wring [rɪŋ] *vtr* *(pt & pp* **wrung**) **1** *(clothes)* escurrir; *(hands)* retorcer. **2** *fig* *(extract)* arrancar, sacar.

wringing ['rɪŋɪŋ] *adj* **to be w. wet**, estar empapado,-a.

wrinkle ['rɪŋkǝl] **I** *n* arruga *f*. **II** *vtr* arrugar. **III** *vi* arrugarse.

wrist [rɪst] *n* muñeca *f*.

wristwatch ['rɪstwɒtʃ] *n* reloj *m* de pulsera.

writ [rɪt] *n* orden *f* judicial.

write [raɪt] **I** *vtr* **1** *(pt* **wrote**; *pp* **written**) escribir; *(article)* redactar; *(cheque)* extender. **II** *vi* escribir *(about, sobre)*; **to w. for a paper**, colaborar en un periódico. ◆**write back** *vi* contestar. ◆**write down** *vtr* poner por escrito; *(note)* apuntar. ◆**write in** *vi* escribir. ◆**write off I** *vtr* *(debt)* condonar; *(car)* destrozar. **II** *vi* **to w. off for sth**, pedir algo por escrito. ◆**write out** *vtr* *(cheque, recipe)* extender. ◆**write up** *vtr* *(notes)* redactar; *(diary, journal)* poner al día.

write-off ['raɪtɒf] *n* **the car's a w.-o.**, el coche está hecho una ruina.

writer ['raɪtǝr] *n* *(by profession)* escritor,-a *m,f*; *(of book, letter)* autor,-a *m,f*.

writhe [raɪð] *vi* retorcerse.

writing ['raɪtɪŋ] *n* **1** *(script)* escritura *f*; *(handwriting)* letra *f*; **in w.**, por escrito. **2** *writings*, escritos *mpl*. **3** *(action)* escritura *f*; **w. desk**, escritorio *m*.

written ['rɪtǝn] *pp* → **write**.

wrong [rɒŋ] **I** *adj* **1** *(person)* equivocado,-a; **I was w. about that boy**, me equivoqué con ese chico; **to be w.**, no tener razón; **you're w. in thinking that ...**, te equivocas si piensas que .... **2** *(answer, way)* incorrecto,-a, equivocado,-a; **my watch is w.**, mi reloj anda mal; **to drive on the w. side of the road**, conducir por el lado contrario de la carretera; **to go the w. way**, equivocarse de camino; *Tel* **I've got the w. number**, me ha confundido de número. **3** *(unsuitable)* impropio,-a inadecuado,-a; *(time)* inoportuno,-a; **to say the w. thing**, decir algo inoportuno. **4** *(immoral etc)* malo,-a; **there's nothing w. in that**, no hay nada malo en ello; **what's w. with smoking?**, ¿qué tiene de malo fumar? **5 is anything w.?**, ¿pasa algo?; **something's w.**, hay algo que no está bien; **what's w.?**, ¿qué pasa?; **what's w. with you?**, ¿qué te pasa?

II *adv* mal, incorrectamente; **to get it w.**, equivocarse; *fam* **to go w.**, *(plan)* fallar, salir mal.

III *n* **1** *(evil, bad action)* mal *m*; **you did w. to hit him**, hiciste mal en pegarle. **2**

(injustice) injusticia *f*; *(offence)* agravio *m*; **the rights and wrongs of a matter,** lo justo y lo injusto de un asunto. **3 to be in the w.,** *(to blame)* tener la culpa. **IV** *vtr (treat unfairly)* ser injusto,-a con; *(offend)* agraviar.
◆**wrongly** *adv* **1** *(incorrectly)* incorrectamente. **2** *(mistakenly)* equivocadamente. **3**

(unjustly) injustamente.
wrongdoing ['rɒŋduːɪŋ] *n* maldad *f*.
wrongful ['rɒŋfʊl] *adj* injusto,-a.
wrote [rəʊt] *pt* → **write**.
wrung [rʌŋ] *pt & pp* → **wring**.
wry [raɪ] *adj (wrier, wriest or wryer, wryest)* sardónico,-a.

X

X, x [eks] *n (the letter)* X, x *f*.
xenophobia [zenəˈfəʊbɪə] *n* xenofobia *f*.
xenophobic [zenəˈfəʊbɪk] *adj* xenófobo, -a.
Xerox® ['zɪərɒks] **I** *n* xerocopia *f*. **II** *vtr* xerocopiar.
Xmas ['eksməs, 'krɪsməs] *n abbr of*

Christmas.
X-ray [eks'reɪ] **I** *n* **1** *(beam)* rayo *m* X; **X-r. therapy,** radioterapia *f*. **2** *(picture)* radiografía *f*; **to have an X-r.,** hacerse una radiografía. **II** *vtr* radiografiar.
xylophone ['zaɪləfəʊn] *n* xilófono *m*.

Y

Y, y [waɪ] *n (the letter)* Y, y *f*.
yacht [jɒt] *n* yate *m*; **y. club,** club náutico.
yachting ['jɒtɪŋ] *n Sport* navegación *f* a vela; *(competition)* regatas *fpl*.
yachtsman ['jɒtsmən] *n* balandrista *m*.
yachtswoman ['jɒtswʊmən] *n* balandrista *f*.
yam [jæm] *n* **1** ñame *m*. **2** *US (sweet potato)* boniato *m*.
yank [jæŋk] *fam vtr* tirar; *(tooth)* arrancar.
Yank [jæŋk] *n GB pej* yanqui *mf*.
Yankee ['jæŋkɪ] *adj & n pej* yanqui *mf*.
yap [jæp] *vi (dog)* aullar; *fam (person)* darle al pico.
yard¹ [jɑːd] *n (measure)* yarda *f (aprox 0.914 metros)*.
yard² [jɑːd] *n* patio *m*; *US* jardín *m*.
yardstick ['jɑːdstɪk] *n fig* criterio *m*, norma *f*.
yarn [jɑːn] *n* **1** *Sew* hilo *m*. **2** *(story)* historia *f*, cuento *m*; **to spin a y.,** *(lie)* inventarse una historia.
yawn [jɔːn] **I** *vi* bostezar. **II** *n* bostezo *m*.
yawning ['jɔːnɪŋ] *adj (gap)* profundo,-a.
yd *(pl yds) abbr of* yard.
yeah [jeə] *adv fam* sí.
year [jɪəʳ] *n* **1** año *m*; **all y. round,** durante todo el año; **last y.,** el año pasado; **next y.,** el año que viene; **y. in, y. out,** año tras año; **I'm ten years old,** tengo diez años. **2** *Educ* curso *m*; **first-y. student,** estudiante *m,f* de primero.
yearly ['jɪəlɪ] **I** *adj* anual. **II** *adv* anualmente, cada año.
yearn [jɜːn] *vi* **to y. for sth,** anhelar algo.
yearning ['jɜːnɪŋ] *n* anhelo *m* (**for,** de).
yeast [jiːst] *n* levadura *f*.
yell [jel] **I** *vi* gritar. **II** *n* grito *m*, alarido

m.
yellow ['jeləʊ] **I** *adj* amarillo,-a; *fam fig (cowardly)* cobarde; *Tel* **y. pages,** páginas amarillas. **II** *n* amarillo *m*.
yelp [jelp] **I** *vi* aullar. **II** *n* aullido *m*.
yen [jen] *n* **1** *(currency)* yen *m*. **2 to have a y. for sth,** tener ganas de algo.
yeoman ['jəʊmən] *n GB* **Y. of the Guard,** alabardero *m* de la Casa Real británica.
yes [jes] **I** *adv* sí; **you said y.,** dijiste que sí. **II** *n* sí *m*.
yesterday ['jestədeɪ] *adv & n* ayer *m*; **the day before y.,** anteayer; **y. morning,** ayer por la mañana.
yet [jet] **I** *adv* **1** *not* **y.,** aún no, todavía no; **as y.,** hasta ahora; **I haven't eaten y.,** no he comido todavía. **2** *(in questions)* ya; **has he arrived y.?,** ¿ha venido ya? **3** *(even)* más; **y. again,** otra vez; **y. more,** todavía más. **4** *(eventually)* todavía, aún; **he'll win y.,** todavía puede ganar. **II** *conj* sin embargo.
yew [juː] *n* tejo *m*.
yield [jiːld] **I** *n* **1** rendimiento *m*. **2** *Agr* cosecha *f*. **3** *Fin* beneficio *m*. **II** *vtr* producir; *Agr* dar; *(money)* producir. **III** *vi* **1** *(surrender, break)* ceder. **2** *Aut* ceder el paso.
YMCA [waɪemsiː'eɪ] *abbr of* Young Men's Christian Association, albergue *m* para hombres jóvenes.
yob(bo) ['jɒb(əʊ)] *n fam* gamberro,-a *m,f*.
yoga ['jəʊgə] *n* yoga *m*.
yog(h)urt ['jɒgət] *n* yogur *m*.
yoke [jəʊk] **I** *n* yugo *m*. **II** *vtr (oxen)* uncir; *fig* unir.
yokel ['jəʊkəl] *n pej* paleto,-a *m,f*.
yolk [jəʊk] *n* yema *f*.

yonder ['jɒndə^r] *adv* más allá.

you [ju:, *unstressed* jʊ] *pers pron* 1 (*subject*) (*familiar use*) (*sing*) tú; (*pl*) vosotros, -as; **how are y.?**, ¿cómo estás? 2 (*subject*) (*polite use*) (*sing*) usted; (*pl*) ustedes; **how are y.?**, ¿cómo están? 3 (*subject*) (*impers use*) y. **never know**, nunca se sabe. 4 (*object*) (*familiar use*) (*sing*) (*before verb*) te; (*after preposition*) ti; (*pl*) (*before verb*) os; (*after preposition*) vosotros, -as; **I saw y.**, te vi, os vi; **it's for y.**, es para ti, es para vosotros, -as; **with you**, contigo, con vosotros, -as. 5 (*object*) (*polite use*) (*sing*) (*before verb*) le; (*after preposition*) usted; (*pl*) (*before verb*) les; (*after preposition*) ustedes; **I saw y.**, le vi, les vi; **it's for y.**, es para usted, es para ustedes; **with you**, con usted, con ustedes. 6 (*object*) (*impers use*) **alcohol makes you drunk**, el alcohol emborracha.

young [jʌŋ] I *adj* (*age*) joven; (*brother etc*) pequeño, -a; **y. lady**, señorita *f*; **y. man**, joven *m*. II *n* 1 (*people*) **the y.**, los jóvenes, la juventud. 2 (*animals*) crías *fpl*.

youngster ['jʌŋstə^r] *n* muchacho, -a *m,f*.

your [jɔ:^r, *unstressed* jə] *poss adj* 1 (*familiar use*) (*sing*) tu, tus; (*pl*) vuestro, -a, vuestros, -as. 2 (*polite use*) (*sing*) su, sus. 3 (*impers use*) **the house is on y. right**, la casa queda a la derecha; **they clean y. shoes for you**, te limpian los zapatos. 4 (*formal address*) Su; **Y. Majesty**, Su Majestad.

yours [jɔ:z] *poss pron* 1 (*familiar use*) (*sing*) la tuya, la tuya, los tuyos, las tuyas; (*pl*) el vuestro, la vuestra, los vuestros, las vuestras; **the house is y.**, la casa es tuya. 2 (*polite use*) (*sing*) el suyo, la suya; (*pl*) los suyos, las suyas; **the house is y.**, la casa es suya. 3 (*in letters*) **y. faithfully**, le(s) saluda atentamente; **y. sincerely**, reciba un cordial saludo de.

yourself [jɔ:'self, *unstressed* jə'self] (*pl* **yourselves** [jɔ:'selvz]) I *pers pron* 1 (*familiar use*) (*sing*) tú mismo, -a; (*pl*) vosotros, -as mismos, -as; **by y.**, (tú) solo; **by yourselves**, vosotros, -as solos, -as. 2 (*polite use*) (*sing*) usted mismo, -a; (*pl*) ustedes mismos, -as; **by y.**, (usted) solo, -a; **by yourselves**, (ustedes) solos, -as. II *reflexive pron* 1 (*familiar use*) (*sing*) te; (*pl*) os; **enjoy y.!**, ¡diviértete!; **enjoy yourselves**, ¡divertíos! 2 (*polite use*) (*sing*) se; **enjoy y.**, ¡diviértase!; **enjoy yourselves**, ¡diviértanse!

youth [ju:θ] *n* 1 juventud *f*. 2 (*young man*) joven *m*; **y. club**, club *m* juvenil; **y. hostel**, albergue *m* juvenil.

youthful ['ju:θful] *adj* juvenil, joven.

Yugoslav ['ju:gəʊslɑ:v] *adj* & *n* (*m,f*).

Yugoslavia [ju:gəʊ'slɑ:vɪə] *n* Yugoslavia.

Yugoslavian [ju:gəʊ'slɑ:vɪən] *adj* & *n* yugoslavo, -a (*m,f*).

YWCA [waɪdʌbəljuː'siː'eɪ] *abbr of* Young Women's Christian Association, albergue *m* para mujeres jóvenes.

Z

Z, z [zed, *US* ziː] *n* (*the letter*) Z, z *f*.

zany ['zeɪnɪ] *adj* (**zanier, zaniest**) *fam* 1 (*mad*) chiflado, -a. 2 (*eccentric*) estrafalario, -a.

zap [zæp] I *interj* ¡zas! II *vtr* *sl* 1 (*hit*) pegar. 2 *fam* (*kill*) cargarse a. III *vi* TV hacer zapping.

zeal [ziːl] *n* (*enthusiasm*) entusiasmo *m*.

zealous ['zeləs] *adj* (*enthusiastic*) entusiasta.

zebra ['ziːbrə, 'zebrə] *n* cebra *f*; *GB* z. **crossing**, paso *m* de cebra.

zenith ['zenɪθ] *n Astron* cenit *m*; *fig* apogeo *m*.

zero ['zɪərəʊ] *n* cero *m*; z. **hour**, hora *f* cero.

zest [zest] *n* (*eagerness*) entusiasmo *m*.

zigzag ['zɪgzæg] I *n* zigzag *m*. II *vi* zigzaguear.

Zimbabwe [zɪm'bɑ:bweɪ] *n* Zimbabue.

zinc [zɪŋk] *n* cinc *m*, zinc *m*.

zip [zɪp] I *n* 1 z. (*fastener*), cremallera *f*. 2 *fam* brío *m*; *US* z. **code**, código *m* postal. II *vi* cerrarse con cremallera. ◆**zip by** *vi* pasar como un rayo. ◆**zip up** *vtr* cerrar con cremallera; **to z. sb up**, cerrar la cremallera a algn.

zipper ['zɪpə^r] *n US* cremallera *f*.

zodiac ['zəʊdɪæk] *n* zodiaco *m*, zodíaco *m*.

zombie ['zɒmbɪ] *n* zombie *mf*.

zone [zəʊn] I *n* zona *f*. II *vtr* dividir en zonas.

zoo [zu:] *n* zoo *m*.

zoological [zəʊə'lɒdʒɪkəl] *adj* zoológico, -a.

zoologist [zəʊ'ɒlədʒɪst] *n* zoólogo, -a *m,f*.

zoology [zəʊ'ɒlədʒɪ] *n* zoología *f*.

zoom [zu:m] I *n* 1 (*buzz*) zumbido *m*. 2 z. **lens**, zoom *m*, teleobjetivo *m*. II *vi* 1 (*buzz*) zumbar. 2 *fam* z. **to z. past**, pasar volando. ◆**zoom in** *vi* (*camera*) acercarse rápidamente.

zucchini [zu:'ki:nɪ] *n US* calabacín *m*.

Zulu ['zu:lu:] *adj* & *n* zulú (*mf*).

Santiago 21/7 22-25

La Coruña ~~22/7~~ ~~22-29~~/7

~~23/7~~

→ San ~~~~/7
Sebastian 26-28

→ Paris 28-29/7

→ Maarn 29/7

25 — 26
16:00 - 9:00